The Rou[illegible]

French Hotels & Restaurants

Editor

Philippe Gloaguen

Translation and revision produced by

First Edition Translations Ltd, Cambridge, England

ROUGH GUIDES

NEW YORK • LONDON • DELHI

www.roughguides.com

Contents

◀◀ Tree-lined road, Provence ◀ Apéritif time, France

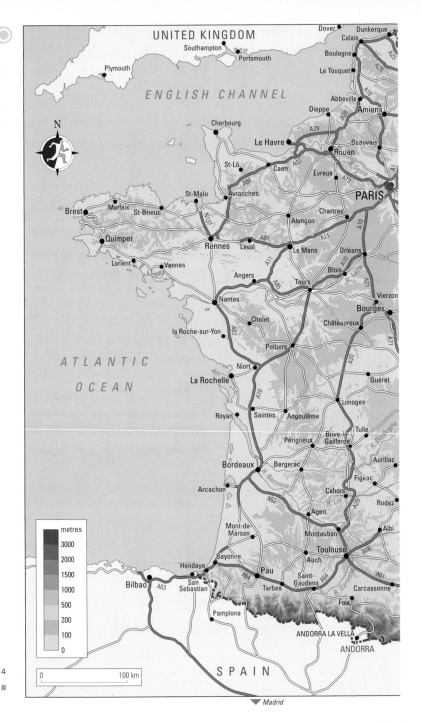

UNITED KINGDOM

Southampton

Plymouth

Portsmouth

Dover

Dunkerque

Calais

Boulogne

Le Touquet

ENGLISH CHANNEL

Abbeville

Dieppe

Amiens

Cherbourg

Le Havre

Beauvais

A29

Rouen

R. Seine

St-Lô

Caen

Évreux

A13

PARIS

Avranches

A84

St-Malo

Chartres

A10

Brest

Morlaix

St-Brieuc

Alençon

N137

Quimper

Rennes

Laval

A81

Le Mans

A11

Orléans

A11

Blois

A71

R. Loire

Lorient

Vannes

Angers

A85

Tours

A83

Vierzon

Nantes

Bourges

Cholet

Châteauroux

la Roche-sur-Yon

A71

Poitiers

ATLANTIC

Niort

OCEAN

La Rochelle

Guéret

A10

Royan

Saintes

Angoulême

Limoges

Périgueux

Brive-la-Gaillarde

Tulle

R. Dordogne

Bordeaux

Bergerac

Aurillac

Arcachon

R. Garonne

Figeac

A62

Cahors

R. Lot

A20

Rodez

Agen

Mont-de-Marsan

Montauban

Albi

Toulouse

A68

Bayonne

Auch

Hendaye

Pau

A61

Bilbao

A63

San Sebastian

A64

Saint-Gaudens

A64

R. Garonne

Carcassonne

Tarbes

Foix

Pamplona

ANDORRA LA VELLA

ANDORRA

SPAIN

Madrid

metres

3000
2000
1500
1000
500
200
100
0

0   100 km

4

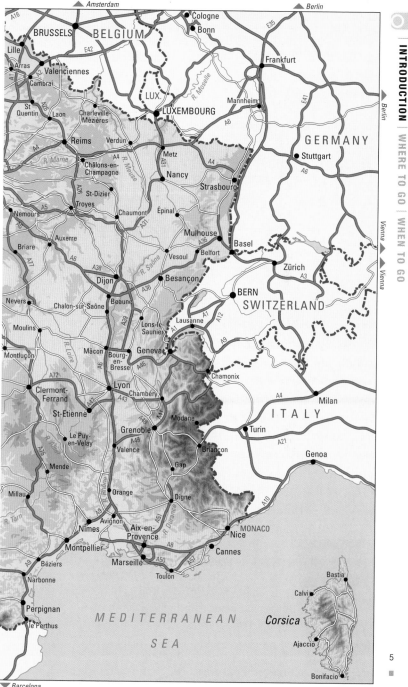

▲ Amsterdam
▲ Berlin

A16
Cologne
BRUSSELS BELGIUM Bonn
Lille E42 Frankfurt
Arras E35
Valenciennes
Cambrai
LUX. Mannheim
St Charleville- LUXEMBOURG
Quentin Laon Mézières A6
Reims Verdun Metz GERMANY
R. Marne A4 Nancy A4 Stuttgart
Châlons-en- Strasbourg A6
Champagne
St-Dizier
Nemours Troyes Chaumont Épinal
Auxerre Mulhouse
Briare A36 Basel
Vesoul Belfort Zürich
Dijon Besançon A3
Nevers Beaune BERN
Chalon-sur-Saône SWITZERLAND
Moulins Lons-le- Lausanne
Saunier
Montluçon Mâcon Geneva
Bourg- A46
en- Chamonix
Bresse
Clermont- Lyon Milan
Ferrand Chambéry A4
St-Etienne Modane ITALY
Le Puy- Grenoble Turin A21
en-Velay Valence Briançon Genoa
Mende Gap
Millau Orange Digne
Avignon MONACO
Nîmes Aix-en- Nice
Béziers Provence Cannes
Montpellier Marseille
Narbonne Toulon
Perpignan Bastia
le Perthus Calvi
MEDITERRANEAN Corsica
SEA Ajaccio
Bonifacio

▲ Berlin
▲ Vienna
▲ Vienna

▼ Barcelona

Introduction to

French Hotels and Restaurants

Now in its eighth edition, the Rough Guide to French Hotels & Restaurants is a translation of the Routard guide, the best-selling French guide to good-value restaurants and accommodation in France. *French Hotels & Restaurants* is up to date, comprehensive and opens up the country in a way that no other guide does. Its listings include everything from simple hostels and family-run bistros to high-comfort rural retreats and city-centre three-stars. All are reviewed by Routard's team of locally based writers, who re-assess the entries for each edition.

The hotels and restaurants selected tend to be small, independent establishments. Many offer local character, distinctive décor, typical regional cuisine or some other special attribute in addition to real value for money. Look out for the Routard stickers on their front doors. Hotels may also display the distinctive yellow-and-green fireplace logo denoting membership of the *Logis de France*. This organization promotes family-run hotels, often in rural locations well away from major towns.

The guide's layout

The Routard/Rough Guide is divided into twenty-two **chapter regions**, each with a regional map. The regions are listed alphabetically and within each chapter the **main towns** (marked by black circles on the maps) are listed in alphabetical order, their names appearing in large type followed by the postcode. **Small towns and villages** within a radius of 30km of a larger town are included after the entries for that town (and marked by white circles on regional maps); these places are listed in the order of their distance from the main town, and their names are displayed in smaller type. Within each town hotels are listed first, followed by restaurants, and both are listed in ascending order of price. Note that stars indicated are the official ratings of the French hotel industry and not of this guide.

The following symbols are used in this guide:

- double room under €35; set menu under €20.
- double room from €35 to €80; set menu from €20 to €35.
- double room over €80; set menu over €35.
- discount
- hotel
- restaurant

After the address of the establishments, tips on **how to get there** are given wherever possible, plus phone number, fax number, web site or email address, closing times and a summary of facilities where relevant.

In addition to regional maps, certain key cities are covered by detailed **city maps**. In these cases, hotels and restaurants are given a two-part map code (eg **Map B2-13**) comprised of a grid reference and the establishment's

▼ Swimming pool at *Hôtel Charembeau*, Forcalquier

7

number in the map key. Where establishments are located outside the area covered by the map, they are listed as **Off map** and marked by an arrow indicating the direction in which you'll find them.

The **discount symbol** (see box overleaf) indicates that an establishment offers some sort of benefit to readers of this guide. In the case of hotels, it's usually a discount (generally 10%) on the room price. You are usually obliged to stay for a minimum of two nights to qualify but sometimes the period or the amount of the discount can

◀ *Hôtel-restaurant Lameloise, Chagny*

be different. The benefit can also be limited to certain periods of the year. Where possible these conditions have been indicated in the text. In some instances, the concession consists of a free breakfast or free garage space; many restaurants in this guide offer a free coffee, house apéritif or house digestif, but you qualify only when you order a complete meal and, more often than not, the choice of drink will not be up to you. All establishments will insist that you are entitled to the benefit only if you are carrying the **current year's edition** of this guidebook. In all cases, show your copy when you check in at the hotel or before you order your meal in a restaurant. Hotels and restaurants are familiar with the French Routard guide, and should you have any difficulties claiming the benefits with this translation, point to the front cover where the Guide du Routard name is clearly displayed.

Hotels

The accommodation reviewed in this Guide ranges from the best of the country's youth hostels (*auberges de jeunesse*) and budget, city-centre hotels to seaside villas, cosy country inns and classy châteaux. The majority are family-run, two- or three-star establishments – all hotels in France are graded from zero to five **stars** by the government. The price more or less corresponds to the number of stars, though the system is a little haphazard, reflecting more on the facilities available, such as room size and whether there's a lift, rather than genuine quality. Some unclassified and single-star hotels can be very good.

Hotels are required by law to display their **prices** (including VAT and any local taxes) outside the hotel and in the rooms. What you get for your money within each category varies enormously. The same applies even within some hotels, so if you're not satisfied with your room, ask to see another. Don't expect much sound-proofing at the cheaper end, especially in older hotels, a few of which still also have communal showers and toilets. **Facilities** at two- and three-star places should include en-suite bathrooms, a TV, phone and perhaps a few extra frills such as a mini-bar and more comfortable furnishings. The majority of hotel rooms are double or twin, with doubles being marginally cheaper. Most also offer family rooms or will add an extra bed at a minimal additional cost. Single rooms are harder to come by and, in any case, aren't that much cheaper than a double. Breakfast is not normally included in the room price and there's no obligation to take it, though some places now offer wonderful spreads including home-made bread, jams and pastries. Hotels with restaurants usually offer half-board rates (*demi-pension*), sometimes only for a minimum stay of three nights. Such deals are often worth considering since the food may be excellent; note, however, that you'll generally be given a set meal with no or only limited choice.

Booking ahead is essential for July and August and strongly recommended during public holidays and the Easter and Christmas school breaks. Most hoteliers and hostel managers speak at least a little English. A growing number offer online booking. Alternatively, you should be able to make a credit-card reservation over the phone. If it's a long time in advance, you may be asked to confirm by letter or fax, and hotels occasionally ask for a deposit (*arrhes* or *acompte*). This should not amount to more than 25–30% of the total. Note that the *arrhes* is fully refundable in the event of a cancellation, as long as you give reasonable notice, while the *acompte* is not.

Many family-run **hotels close** for two or three weeks a year in low season. In rural areas they may also close for one or two nights a week, usually Sunday or Monday. Details are given in the Guide wherever possible, but it's not unusual for smaller places to close for the odd night or two if they have no bookings. The best precaution is to phone ahead.

◄ Sitting room, *Hostellerie Le Vert*, Mauroux

Restaurants

The listings in this Guide cover everything from cheap-and-cheerful pavement cafés to full-blown gastronomic extravaganzas. Between the two lies a vast array of mostly family-run restaurants where you can still find classic French cuisine celebrating local produce. Others, particularly in the cities, specialize in Moroccan, Tunisian, Caribbean (*Antillais*) and Vietnamese fare. Vegetarian restaurants are now reasonably common in urban areas, but hard to come by elsewhere.

In addition to restaurants, you'll find places calling themselves auberges, bistros, brasseries and so forth. The distinctions are not at all clear-cut, but broadly speaking **restaurants** are likely to be more formal and stick to the traditional meal times of noon to 2pm, and 7pm to 9pm or 9.30pm, later in cities and during the summer months. In country areas, restaurants like to adopt the name **auberge** (inn) or **relais** (coaching inn) to give themselves a more rustic air; such places usually offer lodging as well. **Fermes–auberges** are just that: farm restaurants where the majority of ingredients are produced on the farm itself. They are often great places to sample traditional local cuisine.

Like restaurants, **bistros** keep standard hours, but these are very much urban institutions. The archetypal bistro is a small and lively neighbourhood eatery serving a limited range of daily dishes (*plats du jour*) marked up on chalk-boards. **Brasseries** are also more common in towns and cities. They tend to be large and serve a broad range of snacks and sometimes more substantial meals and – importantly – often serve outside normal hours, perhaps to 11pm

▲ Goat's cheese salad

or midnight if you're lucky. Many double as café-bars. Nowadays you will also find a growing number of ultra-chic, city-centre bistros and brasseries. Some are attached to top-end hotels and gourmet restaurants, providing an opportunity to sample culinary genius at an affordable price.

Other eating options include **wine bars** (*bar à vins*), which may serve cheese or cold-meat platters, salads and the like, and **crêperies**, specializing in sweet and savoury pancakes with a choice of toppings. Many **cafés** can

rustle up a sandwich and might even run to a proper meal, especially at lunch time. Cafés come into their own, however, for breakfast, when you can join the locals for the quintessential croissant and a *grand crème* (large, milky coffee).

As with hotels, restaurants must post their **prices** clearly outside. There's normally a choice between one or more *prix fixe menus* – fixed-price menus with a set number of courses and a limited choice, or sometimes no choice at all – and selecting individual dishes from the *carte* (menu). **Prix fixe menus** (generally referred to simply as *menus*) are normally the cheapest option. At the bottom end of the price range, they revolve around standard dishes such as steak and chips (*steak frites*), chicken and chips (*poulet frites*) and the like. But further up the scale, they may run to five or more courses, sometimes with wine and coffee included. If you're on a really tight budget or want to try a top-class restaurant without breaking the bank, it's worth bearing in mind that weekday lunch *menus* are almost always cheaper than those offered at weekends and in the evening. Going **à la carte** offers greater choice and, in the better restaurants, unlimited access to the chef's inventiveness. A **formule** is a shorter version of a *prix fixe menu* usually served at lunchtime. Typical *formules* might consist of a main dish with a choice of either a starter or a dessert, or of a main dish, glass of wine and coffee. When **ordering wine**, the cheapest option will be the house wine, which is usually served in a jug (*pichet*) or carafe; you'll be asked if you want *un quart* (0.25 litre), *un demi* (0.5 litre) or *un litre* (1 litre).

Almost all restaurant prices include a **service charge** of fifteen percent (*service compris* or *prix net*). If you feel the service has been exceptionally

▼ Courtyard, Hôtel Anne D'Anjou, Saumur

good, however, it's customary to leave an additional two-to-three percent cash **tip**. Very occasionally service is not included (*service non compris*), in which case a fifteen percent tip is appropriate.

In popular tourist areas in high season, and for all the more upmarket places, it's wise to make **reservations**. In most cases this is easily done on the same day, though *fermes-auberges* normally require at least a day's notice. **Opening/closing times** are given in the Guide as far as possible, but in country areas it's always wise to phone ahead; places tend to close early if it's a quiet night.

Children are welcome in all but the most upmarket restaurants. Most places provide high chairs and offer a children's menu, though it won't necessarily be very interesting – *steak frites* and ice-cream is all too typical. Alternatively, ask for a starter or a small portion of a main dish from the *carte*.

Bon appétit!

Rough Guide favourites

Our authors have listed below some of their favourite hotels and restaurants, arranged by theme. Whether you're looking for an idyllic rural retreat, gastronomic blow-out meal or somewhere particularly suited to families, our selections below will give you some ideas and pointers. Each category lists the top suggestions arranged in alphabetical order, followed by a page reference to take you straight into the guide where you can find out more; one establishment in each list is illustrated with a photo.

Historic hotels

▶ **Hôtel Arraya, Sare, Aquitaine** ▶ P.96
Hôtel de Bastard, Lectoure, Midi-Pyrénées ▶ P.583
L'Auberge de l'Échauguette, Mont-Dauphin, Provence-Alpes-Côte d'Azur ▶ P.835
Hôtel d'Entraigues, Uzès, Languedoc-Roussillon ▶ P.489
Hôtel-restaurant Vidal, Céret, Languedoc-Roussillon ▶ P.456

Seaside hotels

Hôtel-restaurant Côte du Sud, Pyla-sur-Mer, Aquitaine ▶ P.52
Hôtel-restaurant Kermoor, Concarneau, Bretagne ▶ P.201
◀ **Hôtel-restaurant l'Océan, Bois-Plage-en-Ré, Poitou-Charentes** ▶ P.767
Hôtel de la Pointe du Grouin, Cancale, Bretagne ▶ P.197
Hôtel de la Pointe de Mousterlin, Fouesnant, Bretagne ▶ P.207
Hôtel les Templiers, Collioure, Languedoc-Roussillon ▶ P.456

Family hotels

Hôtel Anne de Bretagne, Blois, Centre ▶ **P.249**

▶ **L'Auberge Campagnarde, Évosges, Rhone-Alpes** ▶ **P.907**

Grand Hôtel des Dunes, Lesconil, Bretagne ▶ **P.211**

La Griyotire, Praz-sur-Arly, Rhône-Alpes ▶ **P.900**

Hôtel Dieu Saint-Nicolas, Noyers-sur-Serein, Bourgogne ▶ **P.176**

Aux Tauzins, Montfort-en-Chalosse, Aquitaine ▶ **P.85**

Romantic breaks

Hôtel de l'Avre, Paris ▶ **P.420**

Auberge des Brizards, Les Brizards, Bourgogne ▶ **P.179**

Le Clos des Iris, Moustiers-Sainte Marie, Provence-Alpes-Côte d'Azur ▶ **P.849**

◀ **Les Lions de Beauclerc, Lyons la Forêt, Haute-Normandie** ▶ **P.690**

Good for outdoor activities

▶ **Domaine de la Rhue, Rocamadour, Midi-Pyrénées** ▶ **P.594**

Domaine de Ramonjuan, Lesponne, Midi-Pyrénées ▶ **P.565**

L'Auberge des Montagnes, Pailherols, Auvergne ▶ **P.132**

Le Moulin du Plain, Goumois, Franche-Comté ▶ **P.346**

Bargain hotels

Le Grand Hôtel, Rochefort-sur-Loire, Pays-de-la-Loire ▶ **P.736**

Hôtel-restaurant de la Grotte, Montignac, Aquitaine ▶ **P.85**

Hôtel de la Paix, Limoges, Limousin ▶ **P.503**

Hôtel de Touraine, Saint-Nazaire, Pays-de-la-Loire ▶ **P.740**

◀ **Hôtel des Voyageurs, Paris** ▶ **P.415**

Country retreats

Hôtel-restaurant Les Bains de Secours, Sévignacq-Meyracq, Aquitaine ▶ **P.81**

▶ **Le Charembeau, Forcalquier, Provence-Alpes-Côte d'Azur** ▶ **P.828**

Auberge de Combreux, Combreux, Centre ▶ **P.262**

Hôtel Au Marais, Coulon, Poitou-Charentes ▶ **P.776**

Le Saut de la Truite, Lepuix, Franche-Comté ▶ **P.347**

Hostellerie Le Vert, Mauroux, Midi-Pyrénées ▶ **P.592**

Regional cuisine

▶ **Hotel-Restaurant Beauséjour, Calvinet, Auvergne** ▶ P.129

Restaurant Mariottat, Agen, Aquitaine ▶ P.50

Les Ménestrels, Saumur, Pays-de-La-Loire ▶ P.742

Auberge la Meunière, Thannenkirch, Alsace ▶ P.33

Le Moulin de Chevillou, Saint-Gence, Limousin ▶ P.506

Auberge Santa Barbara, Sartène, Corsica ▶ P.332

Convivial ambience

Aloha Hostel, Paris ▶ P.419

Hôtel Barbary Lane, Hossegor, Aquitaine ▶ P.79

Hostellerie La Croix Blanche, Fontevraud, Pays-de-la-Loire ▶ P.718

Auberge Le Collet, Saint-Agnan-en-Vercors, Rhône-Alpes ▶ P.943

◀ **Hôtel de Londres, Saumur, Pays-de-la-Loire** ▶ P.742

Hôtel-restaurant Remise, Saint-Urcize, Auvergne ▶ P.141

Contemporary restaurants

L'A Table 77, Strasbourg, Alsace ▶ P.41

▶ **Hôtel-restaurant des Lacs d'Halco, Hagetmau, Aquitaine** ▶ P.78

Le So'Café, La Rivière Thibouville, Haute-Normandie ▶ P.676

Restaurant de la Vallée, Clisson, Pays-de-la-Loire ▶ P.712

Zoko Moko, Saint-Jean de Luz, Aquitaine ▶ P.96

Seafood restaurants

◀ **Hôtel-restaurant Anne de Bretagne, La Plaine-sur-Mer, Pays-de-la-Loire** ▶ P.734

La Bourriche aux Appétits, Saint-Dyé-sur-Loire, Centre ▶ P.255

Le Goéland, Trébeurden, Bretagne ▶ P.235

Restaurant La Pêcherie Ducamp, Capbreton, Aquitaine ▶ P.72

La Poissonnerie, Cassis, Provence-Alpes-Côte d'Azur ▶ P.820

La Poissonnerie du Trégor, Tréguier, Bretagne ▶ P.236

Châteaux

Château de Bazeilles, Bazeilles, Champagne-
Ardennes ▶ **P.315**

Château de Chissay, Chissay en Touraine,
Centre ▶ **P.269**

Château de Creissels, Creissels,
Midi-Pyrénées ▶ **P.586**

▶ **Château de Fourcès, Fourcès,
Midi-Pyrénées ▶ P.589**

Château de Projan, Projan,
Midi-Pyrénées ▶ **P.591**

Hotels with views

Hôtel Anne d'Anjou, Saumur, Pays-de-
la-Loire ▶ **P.742**

Hôtel Belle Vue, Fouesnant, Bretagne ▶
P.207

◀ **Les Chalets de Villard, Saint-
Véran, Provence-Alpes-Côte d'Azur**
▶ **P.864**

Hôtel Cuq-en-Terrasses, Cuq-Toulza,
Midi-Pyrénées ▶ **P.576**

Hôtel du Grand Saint Michel, Chambord,
Centre ▶ **P.255**

La Villa l'Arche, Bidart, Aquitaine ▶
P.61

Gastronomic restaurants

Le Coq d'Or, Chénérailles, Limousin ▶ **P.500**

Lameloise, Chagny, Bourgogne ▶ **P.156**

Le Pont aux Chats, Strasbourg, Alsace ▶ **P.41**

▶ **Le Pressoir, Saint-Avé,
Bretagne ▶ P.238**

Les Saveurs de Saint-Avit,
Saint-Avit, Midi-Pyrénées ▶ **P.576**

La Table Saint-Crescent, Narbonne,
Languedoc-Roussillon ▶ **P.472**

Restaurants for wine-lovers

La Balance, Arbois, Franche-Comté ▶ **P.335**

Le Bistro de la Tour, Quimperlé, Bretagne ▶ **P.226**

Bodega Ibaia, Bayonne, Aquitaine ▶ **P.54**

Le Bouchon Angevin, Angers, Pays-de-la-Loire ▶ **P.706**

L'Envers du Décor, Saint-Émilion, Aquitaine ▶ **P.94**

◀ **Auberge du Vieux Vigneron, Corpeau,
Bourgogne ▶ P.156**

Alsace

Altkirch

68130

⟨ 🎋 🏠 |●| Auberge
Sundgovienne**

1 rte. de Belfort; it's 3km out of town on the
D419 in the direction of Dannemarie.
☎03.89.40.97.18 ⊕03.89.40.67.73
⊛www.auberge.sundgovienne.fr
Closed *23 Dec–23 Jan; a week in July.*
Restaurant closed *Sun evening; Mon; Tues
lunchtime. With booking only Sun and Mon
evenings.* **Disabled access. TV. High chairs
and games available. Pay car park.**

A cross between an American motel (it's
near the road), a Swiss chalet (Switzerland
isn't far) and a traditional Alsatian hotel.
Refurbished double rooms with shower/wc
or bath cost €47–95, are clean and comfortable and some have a balcony. Rooms at
the rear of the hotel or the new suites on
the second floor (slightly more expensive
but worth the extra) are best. The cooking
is a pleasant surprise: it's inspired by the
fresh produce in the market, and the chef
has some interesting ideas. Typical dishes are
sliced duck's liver with caramelized pears,
monkfish steak marinated in pepper, fillet of
pike perch in a Riesling sauce and fresh rhubarb cooked with strawberries and served
with vanilla ice cream. There is a weekday
menu at €11.50 and others at €20–43. The
terrace is a great place to sit over a drink,
admiring the Sundgau countryside. Logis de
France. *10% discount on the room rate offered to
our readers on presentation of this guide.*

Gommersdorf

68210 (12km W)

⟨ 🏠 |●| L'Auberge du Tisserand**

28 rue de Cernay; take the D419. It's on the
D103 as you leave the village.
☎03.89.07.21.80 ⊕03.89.25.11.34
Closed *Mon; Tues; mid-Feb to early March;
20 Dec–1 Jan.* **High chairs available. TV.
Car park.**

This is a typical half-timbered Alsace inn
with a long history, dating from the seventeenth century when it was a weaver's
house. On the first floor the wooden
floor has buckled with age. Good cooking and enormous portions at reasonable
prices. The weekday lunch menu, €8, is
one of the cheapest around; other menus
are €15–30. They offer Alsace specialities
including *choucroute* and grilled ham shank,
bake their own bread in the inn's own
oven and serve flambéed tarts every night.
Charming rooms (nos. 3, 4 and 7 are on
the courtyard side, and are therefore quiet).
We recommend room no. 8 for fans of the
Alsatian illustrator, Hansi.

Barr

67140

⟨ 🏠 |●| Hôtel Maison Rouge**

1 av. de la Gare (South); it's near the post
office.
☎03.88.08.90.40 ⊕03.88.08.90.85
⊛www.maisonrouge-barr.com
Closed *Tues; Wed lunchtime; 5 Jan–15 Feb.*
**High chairs and games available. TV. Car
park.**

Pleasant hotel looking onto a small square
with a superb summer terrace, opposite
the pedestrianized street. The hotel has
been totally refurbished, with a different style for each room (some of which
enjoy views over the Kirschberg vineyard).
There's a dish of the day at €7.50 (weekday

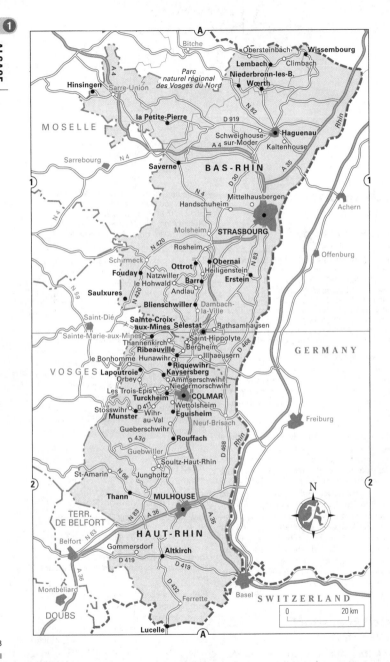

lunchtimes), and menus at €19–35. Alsace specialities include *baeckeoffe*, pike perch with Riesling, flambéed kidneys and tarts. In the bar, there are over sixty kinds of beer, along with cocktails. Friendly, family atmosphere. Double rooms cost €50–60. Logis de France.

Heiligenstein

67140 (1.5km N)

◎ ♠ |●| 🎭 Relais du Klevener**

51 rue Principale; take the D35 in the direction of Ottrott.
☎03.88.08.05.98 ℱ03.88.08.40.83
Closed *1 Jan–12 Feb.* **Restaurant closed** *Mon; Tues lunchtime.* **TV. Car park.**

This inn has wonderful views over the vineyards, the Rhine and Germany beyond. The rooms are simple with no great appeal, but are well maintained and not very expensive. Obviously, it's best to ask for a room with a view. Doubles at €42–55. There's a brasserie and a separate restaurant. Generous set menus €16.50–29 and à la carte. Specialities include homemade foie gras, terrines, *choucroute*, pike perch and *baeckeoffe*. Sit out on the terrace and have a glass of Klevener – it's an old grape variety peculiar to Heiligenstein and pretty rare elsewhere in Alsace. Logis de France. *Apéritif on the house offered to our readers on presentation of this guide.*

Andlau

67140 (4km SW)

◎ 🎭 ♠ Le Zinck Hôtel

13 rue de la Marne; take minor road in the direction of Mittelbergheim, then on to Andlau castle at the bottom of the village.
☎ and ℱ03.88.08.27.30
🌐www.zinckhotel.com
Disabled access. TV. Car park.

Charming hotel in a restored watermill. Eighteen rooms, each with a different theme, but all of them comfortable and decorated with as much humour as taste. We particularly liked the "Vigneron" with its canopied four-poster bed, the "Coloniale" and the "Baroque". Doubles from €59. The hall has been beautifully decorated, and they have preserved the mill wheel. The hotel doesn't have its own restaurant but the owner runs the *Relais de la Poste,* a wine cellar with a good reputation, at 1 rue des Forgerons (closed Mon and Tues).

Hohwald (Le)

67140 (13km W)

◎ ♠ |●| 🎭 Hôtel Marchal**

12 rue Wittertalhof; take the D425 and look for the signs out of the village.
☎03.88.08.31.04 ℱ03.88.08.34.05
Closed *3–27 Nov.* **Restaurant closed** *Sun evening and Mon (except for hotel guests).* **TV. High chairs available. Car park.**

A family hotel set among greenery in this small health and ski resort. The old-style rooms have been freshened up and, although not huge, they are very comfortable and restful. Double rooms at €45. Excellent welcome and a quiet atmosphere. Good, classic, very tasty cooking. Menus €12.20–25.50. Logis de France. *Coffee on the house offered to our readers on presentation of this guide.*

Blienschwiller

67650

◎ ♠ |●| Hôtel Winzenbesg

58 rte. du Vin; on the N422.
☎03.88.92.62.77 ℱ03.88.92.45.22
🌐www.winzenberg.com
Closed *3 Jan–22 Feb.* **Disabled access. TV. Car park.**

The Dreschs believe that it's the division of labour that makes their family tick: the daughter runs the hotel while father and son take charge of the vineyard. The comfortable rooms, with pretty Alsace furniture and brightly coloured curtains, prove good value: doubles cost €41–48. The whole family is very welcoming – they will show you the wine cellar, built in 1508, and invite you to taste the wine. Cheers!

Colmar

68000

◎ ♠ Auberge de Jeunesse

2 rue Pasteur; take the #4 bus to the "Lycée technique" stop; or walk 20 min from the train station (behind the station, cross the bridge in the direction of Ingersheim, following the signposts).
☎03.89.80.57.39 ℱ03.89.80.76.16
Closed *end Dec to mid-Jan.* **High chairs and games available.**

Large, spotless, well-run youth hostel – and quiet, too. New guests are received 7.30–10am and 5pm–midnight. There are eleven rooms with eight beds, one with five, three with four and seven with two. Expect to pay €10 per person in a dormitory and €30 in a double room, including breakfast, plus €4 for sheet hire. No meals. No sporting activities but there's an attractive little park, ideal in fine weather. Very busy from April to June, so it's advisable to book.

✿ 🏠 🏛 Hôtel Colbert**

2 rue des Trois-Épis (West); not far from the station, along the railway line and a stone's throw from the place de Lattre and the historic centre.
☎03.89.41.31.05 📠03.89.23.66.75
TV. Pay garage.

A reliable, functional hotel with no particular charm; the rooms are air-conditioned, comfortable and clean, with double glazing to keep out the noise from the railway. Doubles with bath or shower/wc €44–50. A small detail that will keep beer drinkers happy: there's a bottle-opener on the wall in the bathroom. There's a disco-bar, *The Toucan*, in the hotel basement, but noise levels aren't too bad. *10% discount on a room offered to our readers on presentation of this guide.*

✿ 🏠 🏛 Hôtel Turenne**

10 rte. de Bâle, a few minutes' walk from the centre of town and right next to the romantic district of *Petite Venise* (Little Venice).
☎03.89.21.58.58 📠03.89.41.27.64
🌐www.turenne.com
TV. Pay car park.

A good establishment made up of a collection of buildings hung with geraniums and where the staff welcome you with a smile and are ready to help. The contemporary-looking rooms have been renovated in a functional style, but they're pleasant enough. Air-conditioning throughout. Doubles with bath or shower/wc €59–69; the buffet breakfast is generous. *5% discount on room rate (mid-Nov to mid-March).*

✿ 🏠 🏛 |◉| Hôtel Beauséjour**

25 rue du Ladhof, ten minutes' walk from the centre, to the northeast of the town.
☎03.89.20.66.66 📠03.89.20.66.00
🌐www.beausejour.fr
Closed *Sat lunchtime and Sun out of season.*
Disabled access. TV. High chairs and games available. Pay car park.

Five generations of the Keller family have run this hotel since 1913, although any returning ancestors would quickly get lost: annexes have been added and the rooms tastefully renovated in a contemporary style. Doubles with shower/wc or bath from €50 to €150, depending on the degree of comfort and the season. Menus from €23 to €54, expect €35 à la carte. Weather permitting, customers can relax in the small garden. There is also a sauna, Turkish bath and gym. As for the restaurant, it has an elegant dining room and the new chef (formerly of the renowned *Garbo* restaurant) boldly reworks the classic dishes of the region with his own creative touch. A comfortable and chic establishment that still manages to stay relaxed. Logis de France. *Apéritif (in the restaurant) or one breakfast per room offered on the house to our readers on presentation of this guide.*

✿ 🏛 Hôtel Saint-Martin***

38 Grand-Rue.
☎03.89.24.11.51 📠03.89.23.47.78
🌐www.hotel-saint-martin.com
TV. Disabled access.

It would be hard to be more central. Made up of several buildings of different ages, this hotel offers a whole range of rooms, perfectly fitted out and all equally well maintained; only the size and the décor vary (some having half-timbering, while others have old fabrics, for example). The rooms are arranged around a courtyard: room no. 8, for example, is smaller (and therefore less expensive) and quiet. Each room is different; you choose your room for its colour scheme or its style, and you can ask to see it first. Sadly, breakfast is rather on the expensive side for our liking, even if it is served in a pleasant room. Car park 80m away. Double rooms €69–121, depending on size and facilities. Breakfast €9.50.

✿ 🏛 Grand Hôtel Bristol***

7 pl. de la Gare.
☎03.89.23.59.59 📠03.89.23.92.26
🌐www.grand-hotel-bristol.com
Open *all year.* **TV. Disabled access.**

An attractive establishment opposite the station. Professional welcome, many small services, including a florist, sitting room and bar. Staff here always do their utmost to help. Large, modern and well-kept rooms with fully-fitted bathrooms and spacious beds. Double rooms €90–130, depending on facilities. Twenty percent discount on certain days of the week (contact the hotel for details). Children under 12 free if sharing a room with their parents. Very good and copious buffet breakfast (€11.50) with a selection of sweet and savoury items. In addition, there are two fine restaurants on the ground floor of the hotel: *L'Auberge* if you are looking for a relaxed meal, and *Au Rendez-Vous de Chasse*, for a business or more romantic occasion. Good half board deal at €73 per person per night.

ⓔ |●| Le Caveau Saint-Pierre

24 rue de la Herse.
☎03.89.41.99.33
Closed *Sun evening; Mon; Fri lunchtime; mid-Jan to mid-Feb.* **Disabled access.**

Elegant but affordable, this is undoubtedly the best restaurant in the romantic area known as Petite Venise (Little Venice). It's up against the old town walls and you can only get to it by walking over a wooden footbridge which crosses a charming canal lined with half-timbered houses and beautiful gardens. It's a lovely spot and when it's sunny, tables are set out by the water. The dining room basically tries to be "typically Alsatian" with lots of alcoves, painted furniture and checked tablecloths. Set menus at €13–21.70 or €24 à la carte. Smiling welcome and service. Food produced in the same vein, local and well presented: oxtail with shallots in Pinot Noir, Munster valley pork pie, and, when the chef is in the mood, they offer *baeckeoffe*.

ⓔ |●| Brasserie l'Auberge

7 pl. de la Gare; opposite the station.
☎03.89.23.59.59
Open *all year round.* **Disabled access.**

A good old brasserie very much in "historic monument" mode, including meticulously polished varnished wood-panelling and an old cooking range. Carefully prepared traditional cuisine such as onion tart, gruyère salad, chicken in Riesling and knuckle of ham served on a bed of *choucroute*. Dishes are well presented (they are brought from the kitchens of the *Rendez-vous de Chasse,* one of the town's top restaurants, of which this inn is an annexe). Classic home-made desserts. Pleasing selection of Alsace wines served in stoneware jugs. Lunchtime menu at €14 represents good value for money. Evening menu for €24, or expect to pay €28 à la carte.

ⓔ |●| Chez Hansi

23 rue des Marchands.
☎03.89.41.37.84
Closed *Wed; Thurs.*

Typical Alsace setting, typical Alsace menu, waitresses in typical Alsace costume – you get the feeling you're in a place for tourists. However, this is one of the most reliable restaurants in town and the regulars are locals. All the same, there is a tourist menu priced at €19.

ⓒ |●| Wistub Brenner

1 rue de Turenne; it's just beside Petite Venise.
☎03.89.41.42.33
Closed *Tues; Wed; Feb school holidays; third week in June; third week in Nov.*
High chairs available.

Gilbert Brenner is a real character. He's stocky, rosy-cheeked, loves life – and it shows. He does the cooking and the serving, helped by his wife (who always manages to laugh at his jokes). They keep things simple here, with hearty dishes like salad of *choucroute*, deep-fried Munster cheese, *bibelasskäs*, a local speciality made from soft white cheese, knuckle of ham with potatoes or pig's trotter tournedos. Professional pastrycook, Gilbert keeps back some great surprises for the desserts. Good, convivial, plentiful, but the bill soon adds up in the evening. Count on around €25.

ⓒ |●| Restaurant JY'S-Jean-Yves Schillinger

17 quai de la Poissonnerie; on the banks of the River Lauch.
☎03.89.21.53.60
Closed *Sun and Mon lunchtime. Ten days in Feb.*

This beautiful house with its *trompe l'œil* gable doesn't play any tricks on the stomach, however. The father, Jean, was one of the best chefs in Colmar. The son, Jean-Yves, has carried on the tradition and, much to our delight, has returned to the region after a spell in America. Modern and up-to-the-minute setting for fusion food cuisine that is creative and stylized, sometimes even slightly daring with dishes such as sushi, monkfish tail en croûte, Schillinger tapas or banana crisp. If you can, find a seat on the small terrace behind the house and by the river. Good wine list (about sixty at less than €30, and about twenty available by the glass) complements the dishes. Also pleasant for an evening drink at the bar watching the team working in the kitchen behind the large picture window. Unusually for the area, food is served until 10.30pm. It's advisable to book. Lunchtime menu €28, evening menus €47 (four courses) and €62 (six courses). Expect to pay about €50 à la carte. *Free apéritif offered to our readers on presentation of this guide.*

Wettolsheim

68920 (6km SW)

⟨⟨ ☎ |●| Hôtel au Soleil**

20 rue Sainte-Gertrude; take the D417 or the N83.
☎03.89.80.62.66 ℻03.89.79.84.45
Closed *Thurs; mid-June to early July; 20 Dec–15 Jan.* **TV. High chairs available. Car park.**

In a village on the Alsace Wine Road, but not very touristy. A renovated half-timbered house, run by a young couple, where prices are still reasonable. Rooms are in a very quiet annexe and look out onto a small car park (belonging to the hotel) or onto a few acres of vines. A good option for people wanting to stay in the vineyard area without moving too far from Colmar. Double rooms with shower/wc are at €44. Half board is compulsory June–Sept, at €44 per person. There's a weekday lunch menu at €9, and there's a menu at €16. Logis de France.

Ammerschwihr

68770 (7km NW)

⟨⟨ 🌲 ☎ |●| L'Arbre Vert**

7 rue des Cigognes; take the N415 to the centre of the village.
☎03.89.47.12.23 ℻03.89.78.27.21
ⓦwww.arbre-vert.net
Closed *Mon from Nov to April and Tues (open to welcome hotel guests in season 5.30–7pm); 3 weeks in Feb; last fortnight in Nov.* **High chairs available. TV.**

A very professionally run establishment in a large, pleasant, post-war building. Good gastronomic stopover with a few little surprises such as pig's cheek in Pinot Noir wine sauce, *coq au Riesling* (chicken in Riesling wine sauce), some good cheeses and an unusual sweet potato cake. Set menus for €14 weekdays only, otherwise €20.30–46, including the traditional menu at €33, with a glass of wine with

each course. Impeccable rooms, regularly renovated but slightly lacking in character, cost €37 with basin, €48–60 with shower/wc or bath. Half board from €48 to €60 per person. Note that the rooms in the annexe are slightly more expensive and not necessarily any more attractive. *Free apéritif or coffee offered to our readers on presentation of this guide.*

Niedermorschwihr

68230 (7km W)

⟨⟨ |●| Restaurant Caveau Morakopf

7 rue des Trois-Épis; take the N415 and the D11.
☎03.89.27.05.10
Closed *Sun; Mon lunch; a fortnight in Jan; last week in June and first week in July.* **Disabled access. High chairs available.**

This big pink-and-green house can be found in a charming village tucked away among the vineyards. There is a glorious garden in the summer and a terrace at the back. The restaurant is all wood with comfortable benches and the window panes have been decorated with a "Morakopf" (the same Moorish head that adorns T-shirts in Corsica). The food is meticulously prepared and served in generous portions. Excellent home-made *presskopf* (brawn) and *baeckeoffe* (for four people minimum; order in advance). Also *confit de canard* served on a bed of *choucroute*, munster cheese pie, *schieffala* (smoked pork shoulder), wine grower's fondue and Morakopf cake, all washed down with great little wines. À la carte only. Expect to pay €23–30 excluding wine. Attentive, friendly service. Reservations recommended.

Eguisheim

68420

⟨⟨ |●| Le Caveau d'Eguisheim

3 pl. du Château St. Léon; 7km from Colmar.
☎03.89.41.08.89
Closed *Mon; Tues; Jan; Feb; a week in July.* **High chairs available.**

Jean-Christophe Perrin, who trained at *Trois-Gros* and *Rostang*, cooks local produce with subtlety and originality to create dishes such as eels stewed in Gewürztraminer, carp ravioli, country pork sausage with cinnamon and apple red cabbage and French-toast style *kougloff* cake. In the lovely dining room, the tables are well presented and the service is smiling, professional and discreet. A restaurant to treat yourself to. Menus €28 and €55 in the gourmet restaurant. Business lunch €28, including wine.

Erstein

67150

@ 𝒜 ≜ |●| Hôtel et Estaminet des Bords de l'Ill**

94 rue du Général-de-Gaulle; near the Centre Nautique.
☎03.88.98.03.70 ℻03.88.98.09.49
🖫www.hotel-bordsill.com
Disabled access. TV. High chairs available. Car park.

Small hotel just footsteps from the Ill River. Rooms are decorated in contemporary style; doubles with shower or bath at €52 (prices go down after your third night). The restaurant is across the road and has a terrace by the water. The owners serve carefully cooked Alsace dishes using fresh local produce; there are tartes flambées on offer at the weekend. Set menu €7.50 (lunchtimes only), with others from €18 to €22. Wonderful wine from Alsace and elsewhere. *10% discount on the price of a room offered to our readers on presentation of this guide.*

Fouday

67130

@ ≜ |●| Hôtel Julien**

32 rue Principale.
☎03.88.97.30.09 ℻03.88.97.36.73
🖫www.hoteljulien.com
Closed *Tues; 9–28 Jan.* **Disabled access. TV. Swimming pool. Car park.**

Huge development set alongside the main road, but fortunately, most of the rooms look out over the Bruche and the green slopes of Mont Saint-Jean. There's a whole range of them: the smallest are simple yet comfortable and the largest are a princely 60m square, with wood panelling and ample balconies. Doubles with shower/wc or bath €72–120. Half board €72–92 per person. The Goetz family provides a warm welcome. The interior design is rustic but cosy – wood panelling, flowers and green pot plants everywhere. Seasonal decorations at Easter and Christmas. Staff wear

updated regional costume. The dining rooms are huge, with wooden ceilings, and they're nice and warm. Excellent regional cuisine; weekday lunch menu €13 or others €19–23. The cheapest menu is perfect. The house wines are – unusually – reasonably priced. The terrace is ideal for a drink or meal in the sun. There's a swimming pool, sauna and a fitness room. Booking strongly recommended. Logis de France.

Natzwiller

67130 (10km NE)

@ ≜ |●| Auberge Metzger

55 rue Principale; take the D830 in the direction of Neuviller-la-Roche.
☎03.88.97.02.42 ℻03.88.97.93.59
🖫www.hotel-aubergemetzger.com
Closed *Sun eve and Mon; 5–26 Jan; 23 June–6 July; 22–25 Dec.* **Disabled access. TV. High chairs and games available.**

A pleasant place to stop in this beautiful valley. Mme Metzger takes her guests' comfort very seriously, and the rooms are huge, comfortable, and decorated with a certain style (if not a certain taste). What's more, prices are still quite reasonable. It costs €59–73 for a double room. The cooking at the restaurant is good, lying somewhere between traditional and regional (pigeon with morels or freshwater pike perch in Riesling sauce, for example). Weekday lunchtime menu €13, otherwise €20–55. Reckon on around €25 à la carte. Terrace overlooking valley for fine days. Logis de France.

Haguenau

67500

@ 𝒜 |●| S'Buerehiesel–Chez Monique

13 rue Meyer; it's next to the theatre.
☎03.88.93.30.90
Closed *Sun; Mon; public holidays; last week in May; first fortnight in Sept; Christmas–New Year.*

This *winstub*, a typical Alsatian wine tavern, serving wine from the region (as opposed to a *bierstub*, which serves beer), has a relaxed, cosy feel. Weekday lunch menu €7.50 or around €20–25 à la carte. They concentrate on regional dishes including *choucroute*, of course, *waedele* (hot ham), *quenelles* of liver and so on. Always a pleasant welcome too.

Free coffee offered to our readers on presentation of this guide.

Schweighouse-sur-Moder

67590 (3km W)

@ ⅔ |●| Aux Berges de la Moder

8 rue de la Gare; take the D919, the restaurant is signposted.
☎03.88.72.01.09
Closed *Sun evening; Mon; first fortnight in Nov.* **Disabled access. High chairs and games available.**

The view over the industrial park is hardly idyllic but the two dining rooms are typical Alsace, with a lovely dresser, tiled floor, vermillion walls and decorated beams. The specialities – fish, game and rhubarb strudel – are quite delicious. Weekday lunch menu €7.50, or €18–35. Reckon on €30 à la carte. Cheerful welcome. *Free coffee offered to our readers on presentation of this guide.*

Kaltenhouse

67240 (5km SE)

@ ⅔ ♜ |●| La Crémaillère (Chez Kraemer)

32 rue Principale; very near to Haguenau if you take the D329 in the direction of Bischwiller.
☎03.88.63.23.06 ⊕03.88.63.67.48
Closed *Fri evening; Sat lunchtime; last 3 weeks in Aug.* **TV. High chairs available. Car park.**

In the same family for four generations, this inn is also the village bistro. Locals, pensioners and passing travellers create a convivial atmosphere (there's even dancing on Saturday nights). Home cooking; try the lunchtime dish of the day and the local specialities. Menus €13 (weekdays only) and €20–35. Doubles at €55 have good facilities, though they're slightly gloomy; it's best to avoid the ones overlooking the road. *Free house apéritif to our readers on presentation of this guide.*

Hinsingen

67260

@ |●| La Grange du Paysan

8 rue Principale; about 10km from Sarre-Union.
☎03.88.00.91.83
Closed *Mon; no precise times (best to phone).* **Disabled access. High chairs available. Car park.**

One of the institutions of the "Alsace Bossue" region: large picture window, carved ceiling and as much rustic décor as you could wish for. Excellent welcome. Extremely efficient service, waiters twirling around everywhere. Generous helpings of good, wholesome country cooking. The contented expressions of diners bear witness to the constant quality of the dishes: braised ox cheek, grilled turbot on a bed of fennel, knuckle of ham with a peppery vinaigrette sauce, *baeckeoffe* on Friday and suckling pig roasted over a wood fire at weekends. Weekday menu €10 and a whole range of menus from €17.85 to €50. Expect to pay €17–25 for an à la carte meal.

Kaysersberg

68240

@ |●| Auberge de la Cigogne

73 rte. de Lapoutroie; on leaving the town, take the road in the direction of Lapoutroie.
☎03.89.47.30.33
Closed *Fri; Sun evening; first fortnight in July; between Christmas and New Year.* **Car park.**

A restaurant popular with long-distance lorry drivers and workers from the paper factory next door. This is the type of roadside establishment where you get a good, hearty meal without forking out lots of money. Weekday lunch menu €8.50 and others from €13–27.50. The food ranges from brasserie classics to a few house specialities like fillet of pike perch and *choucroute*, and there's a terrace for outdoor dining.

@ ⅔ |●| Restaurant Saint-Alexis

Lieu-dit Saint-Alexis.
☎03.89.73.90.38
Closed *Fri.* **High chairs available.**

Service noon–8pm. This little gem, hidden away in the forest, is very popular with locals. Inside, there's an appetizing smell of soup and *choucroute*: everyone savours the food with a smile. Three set menus, €11–16, are all very filling: good homemade soup, pies, smoked ham, a generously filled ham omelette and, to round it all off, there's a lovely *tarte alsacienne* (a kind of jam tart). In nice weather you can eat outside. *Free coffee offered to our readers on presentation of this guide.*

Lapoutroie
68650

@ 🎿 🛏 |●| **Hôtel les Alisiers**

5 lieu-dit Faudé; it's 3km out of the village, follow the signs.
☏03.89.47.52.82 ℗03.89.47.22.38
⊛www.alisiers.com
Closed Mon; Tues (except for hotel guests); Wed lunchtime out of season; Jan; a week end June (except the hotel). **TV. High chairs available. Car park.**

Way out in the wilds at an altitude of about 700m, this friendly and unusual little place is classified as a "Hôtel au Naturel" by the National Parks administration. It used to be a farm and the old stone sink and bread oven are still visible. There's a stunning view over the valley and the peaks of the Vosges. The bedrooms and the sitting room, with an open fire where they burn whole logs, are charming and cosy. Double rooms €50–122. Appetizing chef's cuisine, a regular feature for over twenty years, favours a spirited revival of old family recipes such as calves' kidneys steamed with leeks, grandma's *choucroute* and stuffed saddle of rabbit. A really great place. Menus from €15 during the week, to €46. *Free apéritif offered to our readers on presentation of this guide.*

@ 🎿 🛏 |●| **Hôtel-restaurant du Faudé**

28 rue du Général Dufieux.
☏03.89.47.50.35 ℗03.89.47.24.82
⊛www.faude.com
Closed 2–26 Nov; 28 Feb–18 March. **Restaurant closed** Tues; Wed, except for guests on half board and 1 night breaks. **TV. Swimming pool. Car park.**

A traditional hotel that has kept up to date. Besides the extremely comfortable rooms, facilities include a covered and heated swimming pool, Jacuzzi, steam room and gym. Double rooms with shower/wc at €60, with bath €90. The quality extends to the restaurant, where authentic local dishes are served in three different dining rooms. A friendly welcome is assured by waiting staff dressed in local costume. Themed meals and stays are sometimes organized, such as discovering the Pays Welche region of Alsace. Even so, keep an eye on the prices, some of which tend to be on the steep side. Menus start at €20 and go up to €73. Logis de France. *Free coffee offered to our readers on presentation of this guide.*

Orbey
68370 (4km S)

@ 🛏 |●| 🎿 **Hôtel Pairis**

233 lieu-dit Pairis; it's 2km from Orbey on the D48 on the way to Lac Blanc.
☏03.89.70.20.15 ℗03.89.71.39.90
⊛www.hotelpairis.com
Closed Wed; Nov. **High chairs and games available. Car park.**

An excellent little hotel, in a superb 1900 house, run by a delightful German woman. The entrance hall is stylish and minimalist, with designer furniture, attractive contemporary paintings and white everywhere. Lots of natural materials (such as wood, latex and sisal) have been used in the rooms. Doubles with bath at €66. Sumptuous buffet breakfast, with freshly squeezed fruit juices, various types of bread, charcuterie and cheese, is included in the room rate. Half board by arrangement at €15.50 per person (vegetarian menu available). Set menu €18. There's a TV room and a wide choice of books and board games. A favourite with German visitors.

Bonhomme (Le)
68650 (6km NW)

@ 🎿 🛏 |●| **Hôtel de la Poste – Restaurant la Béhine★★**

Take the N415, then the road to the col du Bonhomme; it's next to the post office and opposite the girls' school.
☏03.89.47.51.10 ℗03.89.47.23.85
⊛www.hotel-la-poste.com
Closed Jan and March. **Disabled access. TV. High chairs and games available. Swimming pool. Car park.**

A good village inn, always evolving. Very attractive and well-kept rooms. Not so quiet on the road side, though. An initiative to be welcomed: six rooms have been adapted for disabled use (as have the sauna and the covered swimming pool). Doubles with shower/wc €46–70 depending on the season. The restaurant serves unashamedly regional food such as *magret de canard* with cranberries, *spaetzle* (tiny rolled noodles) and

ALSACE

home-made foie gras. Menus €10–34.
Generous buffet breakfast. The friendly,
professional woman who runs the place
will even let you cancel your skiing holiday if there's no snow. Logis de France.
*Apéritif on the house offered to our readers
on presentation of this guide.*

Lembach

67510

🏠 ▮❚▮ Auberge du Cheval
Blanc et Rossel'Stub

3 rte. de Wissembourg.
☎03.88.94.41.86 ℗03.88.94.20.74
🌐www.au-cheval-blanc.fr
TV. Disabled access.

The size of the buildings on the courtyard
side of this hotel are impressive – that's
the way they are, the Mischler family: they
like space, a certain opulence, but once
you get to know them a little, you will
find they are an Alsace family (almost) like
any other, keen to build up their business.
They offer seven spacious and peaceful
rooms (€110), some with terrace, and a
cosy and charming *winstub*. If you want to
treat yourself to some real luxury, there is
the gourmet restaurant just a stone's throw
away, excellently managed by father-and-
son team Fernand and Franck Mischler.
Their sublime cuisine blends tradition and
innovation, and there's a special children's
menu. À la carte around €20. Logis de
France.

Obersteinbach

67510 (10km NW)

▮❚▮ Hôtel-restaurant Anthon**

40 rue Principale; take the D27 along the
River Sauer, then take the D3 towards
Niedersteinbach.
☎03.88.09.55.01 ℗03.88.09.50.52
🌐www.restaurant-anthon.fr
Closed *Tues; Wed; Jan.*

A great place, with an interesting family
history. Having left to study in Saulieu
and Saint-Tropez, on the death of his
father, Georges Flaig bravely took over
the running of the establishment created
by his great-great-grandfather. Not yet 30
years of age, single-handedly, or practically
single-handedly, he's created a cuisine that
is precise and inventive, reworking original
Alsatian recipes with brio. It's not hard
to see him as a great chef in the making,

having fun with his first menu. The choice
might be somewhat limited, but the dishes
are bursting with flavour – from the carpaccio of goat's milk cheese fresh from
the neighbouring farm, served with a
chiffonade of country ham, to the mini-
Black Forest gateau served with a griottine
cherry sorbet, via traditional savoury ravioli
and *schniderspaetzle* of salmon trout. Other
treats include the "Anthon-noir" egg and
ice creams made from beer brewed by the
Uberach micro-brewery and served with
a malt-iced macaroon. Menus from €24
to €61. Cookery courses available. The
rooms are very simple but pleasant and
most have a view of the castle. Doubles
€48–58, suite €98.

Lucelle

68480

▮❚▮ Hôtel-auberge du Petit
Kohlberg

Locality of Petit Kohlberg; take the D432
as far as Ferrette; then travel 10km south,
through Winkel and taking the Lucelle road;
the hotel is 8km further on: look out for a
minor road on the left.
☎03.89.40.85.30 ℗03.89.07.89.40
🌐www.petitkohlberg.com
Restaurant closed *Mon and Tues, but open
in the evenings on these days in July and
Aug.* **Closed** *a fortnight in Feb and Christmas
week.* **TV. Disabled access.**

Everything here is part of the family
history. The business originally belonged
to the grandfather. His daughter took
it over and now runs it with his granddaughter, Marie-Claude, and they've created a delightful rural retreat. In addition
to its unique setting in the wilds, facing
Switzerland (you can hear the sound of
the bells of the neighbouring cows), the
service is beyond reproach, smiling, attentive, the rooms comfortable and well kept,
each one being different, and the food is
really very good. The restaurant dining
room, bright, made of pine, has a chalet
feel and overlooks a park where stags
wander. As for the food, the dishes served
are specialities of the Sundgau region and
include as much home-made fried carp
as you like, home-produced ham cooked
with *rösti* potatoes, *vacherin*, cherry tart
or a selection of "Routard" desserts. It's
a shame that the hotel lacks charm when
viewed from the outside, but that in no
way detracts from the level of comfort

it offers. And what's more, professional sports people such as F C Sochaux and the Cofidis team know it, and call in once a year to get their strength back. In short, this is a good-value, quality establishment that can't fail to appeal, unless you're averse to being woken by birdsong in the morning. Double rooms €50 and €55. Menus from €15 to €45. Logis de France.

Mulhouse
68100

ⓔ ⌺ ☗ Hôtel Saint-Bernard**

3 rue des Fleurs; five minutes' walk from the town hall square.
☏03.89.45.82.32 ⊕03.89.45.26.32
⊛www.hotel.saint-bernard.com
TV. Pay car park. Cots available.

The *Saint-Bernard* is probably the nicest hotel in Mulhouse. The rooms are all impeccable and have high ceilings; no. 16 has a hundred-year-old fresco depicting the four seasons. Some rooms, such as spacious no. 14, are no smoking. Doubles with shower or bath €35–50, depending on their size and which floor they're on. Guests also have free access to bicycles, an Internet area and a library. Good breakfast and attentive reception staff. *10% discount on a room offered to our readers from the third consecutive night or 50% on the second night (weekends), on presentation of this guide.*

ⓔ ⦿ Le Petit Zinc

15 rue des Bons-Enfants.
☏03.89.46.36.78
Closed Sun; public holidays; first 3 weeks of Aug; Christmas–New Year's Day. Open until 11.15pm.

A chic but cool bar/restaurant that's a gathering place for artists, musicians, writers and their mates, where people like to "read" the menu. There are loads of photos on the wall and a big bar with a huge old calculating machine; it has the feel of an Art Nouveau bar/restaurant, stylish and futuristic. Weekday two-course set lunch for €8; meals à la carte from around €25. Local dishes with unexpected twists such as *choucroute* salad with saveloy or lentil soup and regional dishes such as *haxala* (knuckle of ham) or Alsace ox cheek; great choice of home-made desserts and selection of teas. Suffice it to say that the celebrities that have come here have appreciated this

friendly *Petit Zinc* (Little Bar) and they too have left their photos on the wall. What's more, Myriam, the owner, always has a smile.

ⓔ ⦿ ⌺ Aux Caves du Vieux Couvent

23 rue du Couvent; in the old town centre.
☏03.89.46.28.79
Closed Sun evening and Mon. **Disabled access.**

Large old house with a Maltese cross painted in red on the door in the façade. Warm tavern feel for winter evenings: red and white tablecloths, historical paintings on the walls (old map of the town). Good food, generous portions, Alsace through and through with Sundgau fried carp, kidneys in Pinot Noir wine sauce, home-made tarts and a good selection of wines. Proper welcome and prompt service. Lunchtime *menu du jour* €10, other menus from €15 to €25. *Free coffee or house digestif offered to our readers on presentation of this guide.*

Soultz-Haut-Rhin
68360 (16km NW)

ⓔ ⌺ ⦿ Restaurant Metzgerstuwa

69 rue du Maréchal-de-Lattre-de-Tassigny; take the D429. It's in the main street.
☏03.89.74.89.77
Closed Sat; Sun; a fortnight in June/July; between Christmas and New Year's Day. Open 10am to midnight.

The owner of this little restaurant in a green house on Soultz's main road also runs the butcher's next door. No surprise then that it serves meat, meat and more meat – boned pigs' trotters, skirt with shallots, calves' brains with capers, home-made black pudding and the local delicacy of *rognons blancs à la crème* (bull's testicles in a cream sauce). Big local following, generous portions and good atmosphere. There is a *menu du jour* at €7.50 and others at €16–22.

Jungholtz
68500 (19km NW)

ⓔ ☗ ⦿ Hostellerie Les Violettes***

Thierenbach; take the D429, 3km after Soultz, in the direction of Cernay, then right as you leave the town in the direction of Jungholtz; opposite the basilica, it's signposted on the left.

☎03.89.76.91.19 ⓕ03.89.74.29.12
ⓦwww.les-violettes.com
Restaurant closed Mon. Annual holidays in
Jan. **Disabled access. TV.**

An attractive house built in the pink sandstone typical of the Vosges. Philippe Bosc
and his wife have very successfully restored
this establishment, which had been going
downhill. Good, tasty meals and stylish,
warm rooms, all different and full of character and fine pieces of furniture. True, the
price may deter some, but it's the going
rate for luxury of this sort. As for the food,
M. Bosc teamed up with his childhood
friend, Jean-Yves Schilinger, who divides
his time between here and Colmar, where
he has one of the best restaurants in town.
Typical dishes include asparagus soup, snail
kebab with salad, *cuisse de canard confite* and
his millefeuille of mousseline of artichoke,
steamed monkfish with chicory, rhubarb
and meringue tart and gazpacho. Food is
served either in the pine dining room or
on the veranda with its view over the park
and the valley. Car enthusiasts can ask to
see the collection of ten vintage car models
in the garage. A romantic place, perfect for
a refreshing break in the country. Double
rooms in the "Gentilhommière" annexe
cost €70–110, otherwise from €150 to
€300, depending on facilities. Lunchtime
menus €27 (Wed–Fri), €45 and €60. Half
board from €120 to €160 per person.

Munster

68140

ⓐ ⓘⓞⓘ Hôtel-restaurant La Cigogne***

4 pl. du Marché.
☎03.89.77.32.27 ⓕ03.89.77.54.50
TV.

A large building attractively renovated and
fitted out, opposite the Protestant church.
Tasteful, comfortable and well-equipped
rooms, with coloured walls, modern furnishings and beautiful fabrics. The restaurant dining room is in the same vein: warm
and nicely decorated. There's a pleasant
lounge beyond the large dining room and
also a terrace, though this is a bit noisier.
Tickle your taste buds with delicacies such
as asparagus when in season, *bibelasskäs*, a
local speciality made from soft white cheese,
fleischschnaka (rolled meat) and *quenelles
de foie*. This is followed by the inevitable
portion of munster cheese flavoured with

cumin or caraway, and finally a home-made
dessert to round off your meal. A pleasant
town-centre establishment. Double rooms
€60–99, depending on facilities. Menus
from €18. Expect to pay €23 à la carte.

ⓘⓞⓘ Auberge du Caveau des Marcaires

1 cour de l'Abbaye
☎03.89.77.07.86
Closed Mon, except from June to Sept.

Prices to suit all pockets at this very pleasant little place situated in the former cellar
of the abbey and which serves unusual
mountain and seasonal cuisine. Friendly
proprietors, pleasant, peaceful terrace and
produce suppliers shown on the menus.
Lunchtime menu €7.50 for two courses,
€9 for three. *Choucroute garnie* and dessert €9. Special "cheese" menu €16 and
"mushroom" menu €19.

ⓘⓞⓘ Restaurant à l'Alsacienne

1 rue du Dôme.
☎03.89.77.43.49
Closed Tues lunchtime; Wed; 1–10 March;
1–10 June; 1–10 Sept. **Disabled access.
High chairs and games available.**

Locals and tourists alike enjoy sitting at
the tables on the pavement alongside the
church, or in the rustic dining room. The
décor is typical of the Alsace region, as
is the food. Set menus at €8 (lunchtime
only) and €13–25. Specialities include
choucroute garnie, stuffed pig's trotters, *escalope* of veal with munster cheese or asparagus quiche.

ⓘⓞⓘ À l'Agneau d'Or

2 rue Saint-Grégoire.
☎03.89.77.34.08
Closed Mon; Tues.

The best restaurant in Munster is also a
very welcoming place. Martin Fache and
his wife do their utmost to ensure that
your visit will be "a hugely enjoyable
gourmet stop". Specialities change with
the seasons; the chef uses lots of local
produce and favours fish, as in dishes such
as bouillabaisse terrine and pike perch
served on a bed of *choucroute*, but for all
that, don't shy away from the delicious
pig's cheeks with foie gras or the carpaccio of scallops flavoured with blood
orange. And there's the small wine list of
Alsatian wines to boot. Desserts include

iced beer soufflé and Gewürztraminer. Menus from €25 to €46. Deservedly, the chef has received many accolades from his peers. Reservations highly recommended, especially at the weekend. *Coffee on the house offered to our readers on presentation of this guide.*

Stosswihr

68140 (4km NW)

ⓦ 🎿 🏠 |●| Hôtel-restaurant du Chalet*

Col de la Schlucht; from the centre take the D417 to col de la Schlucht (1139m) on the Alsace-Vosges border.
☎03.89.77.04.06 📠03.89.77.06.11
🌐www.hotel-du-chalet.com
Closed *Wed evening and Thurs outside school holidays; 15 Nov–20 Dec.* **TV. High chairs and games available. Car park.**

The hotel is near one of the busiest passes over the peaks of the Vosges, but being in such a prime location doesn't mean they take their guests for granted. The rooms have been nicely refurbished. Doubles with shower €46. Half board is compulsory during school holidays. In the vast dining room, especially welcoming on cold days, they serve simple but good regional dishes: *choucroute, baeckeoffe* in winter, chicken with bacon, potatoes with munster cheese, *spaetzle*. The lunch menu in the brasserie costs €10.50, and other menus are €14–22.50. Reservations recommended. *Free apéritif offered to our readers on presentation of this guide.*

ⓦ 🎿 |●| Auberge des Cascades

6 chemin de Saegmatt; as you leave the village, take the left turn towards the war memorial.
☎03.89.77.44.74
Closed *Mon; Tues; mid-Jan to mid-Feb; a week in June; a week in October.*

Service until 10pm. A very good inn that hasn't been spoiled by too many tourists (yet). The pretty house is in a flower garden where you can hear the peaceful play of a waterfall nearby. People here live and eat well. There's a hearty weekday lunch menu at €8, and another on Sunday at €23. Expect to pay about €20 for a full à la carte meal. Specialities include flambéed tart of frogs' legs prepared under the attentive gaze of Madame Decker and baked in a wood-fired stove. If you fancy something more classic, there are

traditional flambéed tarts (served at the weekend), trout fillet with sorrel and an awesome *entrecôte* with ceps. Treat yourself to the house Edelzwicker wine, which isn't expensive and is among the best in the region. *Free coffee offered to our readers on presentation of this guide.*

Wihr-au-Val

68239 (7km NE)

ⓦ 🎿 |●| La Nouvelle Auberge

9 rte. Nationale; take the D417 in the direction of Colmar.
☎03.89.71.07.70
Closed *Sun evening to Tues evening; Feb and All Saints' half-terms; first week in July; Christmas period.*

The talented chef has worked in some great kitchens but he hasn't let it go to his head. His roadside restaurant packs them in on weekday lunchtimes on account of the €9.50 menu, which is amazing – you'll be lucky to find a parking space. The other menus, €15–49, list dishes such as cockerel in Riesling and Tricastin lamb with thyme *jus*, and the dishes are remarkable value given the quality of the produce and the chef's skill. Why not try the dish of the day? The simple dining room is very pretty, and the welcome is unaffected and kindly. Here at this inn, they believe in making quality and originality accessible to all. *Free apéritif offered to our readers on presentation of this guide.*

Niederbronn-les-Bains

67110

ⓦ 🏠 |●| Hôtel-restaurant Cully**

33–37 rue de la République; it's near the station.
☎03.88.09.01.42 📠03.88.09.05.80
🌐www.hotel-cully.fr
Closed *7–28 Feb; 22 Dec–5 Jan.* **Restaurant closed** *Sun evening; Mon.* **Disabled access. TV. Car park.**

Doubles €58–62 with shower/wc or bath. Simple and comfortable hotel run by the same family for three generations. Spacious rooms on the whole, all different. Choose one with a balcony, it won't cost you any more. Meticulous cuisine, as they say. Good weekday set menu for €10, another at €20 or around €28 à la carte. Reservations strongly recommended. Logis de France.

ALSACE

❀ 🥢 |●| Restaurant les Acacias**

35 rue des Acacias.
☎03.88.09.00.47
Closed Fri and Sat lunchtimes; second
fortnight in Aug; 27 Dec–15 Jan. **Disabled
access. High chairs and games available.
Car park.**

Quaint, flowery place on the edge of
the forest with a terrace for the summer.
Stylish service. They do a nice set menu
at weekday lunchtimes for €11.50; others
cost €24–42.50. Reckon on €33 à la carte.
Traditional Alsace cooking and dishes such
as pike perch and foie gras parcels and
civet of young wild boar. The view of the
valley is sadly marred by a factory. *Free
coffee offered to our readers on presentation of
this guide.*

Obernai
67210

❀ 🥢 🏠 Hostellerie La Diligence**

23 pl. de la Mairie.
☎03.88.95.55.69 ℗03.88.95.42.46
🖰www.hotel-diligence.com
Open all year round. **Tea room open**
11am–6.30pm, except Tues and Wed. **TV.
Pay car park.**

It would be difficult to find somewhere
more central. Many rooms (and what's
more, these are the most spacious ones)
look out over the town hall square in
the heart of the town, so quiet cannot
therefore always be guaranteed. With such
a great location, you'd think the owners
would just sit back and wait for the customers to roll in. In fact, they go out of
their way to make you feel welcome. The
reception area is designed in contemporary
style, while the rooms are generally more
in the rustic vein and are very comfortable. There is a cosy breakfast room, too.
Double rooms from €47 to €73. Logis
de France. *10% discount on a room after a
minimum of three consecutive nights offered to
our readers on presentation of this guide.*

❀ 🥢 🏠 Hôtel du Gouverneur

13 rue de Sélestat.
☎03.88.95.63.72 ℗03.88.28.74.43
Closed Jan and Feb. **Disabled access. Pay
car park.**

This building dates from 1566 and was the
residence of the town's governor. It's generously proportioned and has an interior
courtyard; one wall forms part of the town
ramparts. There's a gallery and a Louis
XV balustraded staircase. The bright, new
rooms are decorated in contemporary style
and some are very spacious (sleeping three
or four people). Doubles cost €56–70. No
TV for greater peace and quiet. Really
nice welcome. Credit cards not accepted.
*One free breakfast per room offered to our read-
ers on presentation of this guide.*

**❀ |●| Chez Gérard
"O'Baerenhiem"**

46 rue du Général-Gouraud.
☎03.88.95.53.77
Closed Tues eve; Wed. **Disabled access.**

We found it hard to resist the restaurant
of Gérard Eckert, one of the region's great
gourmet chefs. He serves up excellent
dishes of the day, full of regional flavour and
not too heavy. Prices are very reasonable,
too. As the name of the restaurant suggests,
there's a bear theme to the décor.

❀ 🥢 |●| L'Agneau d'Or

99 rue du Général-Gouraud.
☎03.88.95.28.22
Closed Sat lunch; Sun evening; Mon (except
July/Aug); Jan. **High chairs available.**

An authentic *winstub*. The painted ceiling, cuckoo clock, prints and decorated
plates all make for a cosy atmosphere.
Usual regional dishes successfully given a
contemporary twist by a chef who knows
what he's doing. Weekday lunch menu at
€9 and others at €19 and €35. *Free house
digestif offered to our readers on presentation
of this guide.*

Rosheim
67560 (6km NW)

**❀ 🥢 🏠 |●| Hostellerie du
Rosenmeer****

45 av. de la Gare; take the N422 in the direction of Molsheim, then follow the D35.
☎03.88.50.43.29 ℗03.88.49.20.57
🖰www.le-rosenmeer.com
Restaurant closed Sun evening; Mon; early
March; end of July to early Aug.

A modern and comfortable hotel, whose
name ("sea of roses" in Alsatian) recalls a
stream that meanders from the fortified
castle in Guirbaden to Rosheim. People
come here primarily to sample the cooking
of one of Alsace's most brilliant (and unas-

suming) chefs, Hubert Maetz. The weekday lunchtime set menu costs €32, including wine, while gourmet menus range from €44 to €72. Attached to the main house, there is also an authentic *winstub*, which we found irresistible as much for its food as for its traditional atmosphere with wood panelling, heavy faded red curtains, quaint prints and wooden floorboards. The dishes (*plat du jour* from €9) are all served with the house wine, product of the Maetz family's own vineyard. Double rooms €68–90, depending on the season. *Free house apéritif offered to our readers on presentation of this guide.*

Ottrott

67530

@ ⅔ 🏠 |●| À l'Ami Fritz***

8 rue des Châteaux; at the top of the village, on the right after the church.
☎03.88.95.80.81 ☎03.88.95.84.85
@www.amifritz.com
Closed *Wed; fortnight in Jan and first week in Feb.* **Disabled access. TV. High chairs and games available. Car park.**

This seventeenth-century house is impressive both outside and in. It's beautifully decorated and very quiet. Bedrooms are pretty, fresh and colourful; those in the annexe, *Le Chant des Oiseaux*, 600m away, are cheaper but not so nice. The rooms overlooking the street are air-conditioned; the others (nos. 104, 105, 126 and 228) are quiet and attractively decorated. Doubles from €65 to €92. Pleasant dining room with rustic décor and efficient, attentive service. Patrick Fritz, the owner, prepares some cracking regional dishes using fresh produce. Set menus €21–59. Breakfast buffet €11. Lovely terrace on what passes for a village square. Logis de France. *Free coffee offered to our readers on presentation of this guide.*

Petite-Pierre (La)

67290

@ 🏠 |●| Hôtel des Vosges**

30 rue Principale; near the town hall.
☎03.88.70.45.05 ☎03.88.70.41.13
@www.hotel-des-vosges.com
Closed *Tues; mid-Feb to mid-March; end July to early Aug.* **Disabled access. TV. High chairs available. Car park.**

A large place that retains a family atmosphere (we're talking about the third or

fourth generation of Wehrungs here). You're bound to find a room to your taste (whether that's pale modern wood or traditional Alsace). Among the less expensive options (small but comfortable), a few look over the château and the village – gorgeous at sunset. Double rooms €52–76, and some luxury suites from €105 to €155. There's even a gym with Jacuzzi, sauna and sunbed. The focus in the restaurant is strictly regional; *coq* with Riesling is the house speciality. Impressive wine list, too. Beneath the hotel, there is a traditional *winstub*. Menus start at €20.50 (weekdays only), with others at €28–53. Logis de France.

@ ⅔ 🏠 |●| Hôtel-restaurant Au Lion d'Or***

15 rue Principale; opposite the town hall.
☎03.88.01.47.57. ☎03.88.01.47.50
@www.liondor.com
Closed *3 Jan–3 Feb; 27 June–7 July.*
Disabled access. TV. High chairs and games available. Car park.

Good-size, comfortable rooms, nearly all of them having a small balcony. The decoration is somewhere between rustic and 1970s. Good breakfast. Large restaurant dining room slightly lacking in intimacy, terrace on fine days. Brasserie menu offering grills or dishes of greater gourmet pretensions. Covered swimming pool (with spa bath), sauna and Jacuzzi. You have to pay for other activities such as tennis and "Arbrothérapie" treatments (in harmony with nature). Courteous welcome, unrestricted view over the valley and the forest. Double rooms €73–93. Menus from €20 to €65. Logis de France. *Free house apéritif offered to our readers on presentation of this guide.*

Ribeauvillé

68150

@ 🏠 Hôtel Les Vosges***

2 Grand-Rue; opposite the tourist office.
☎03.89.73.61.39 ☎03.89.73.34.21

A pleasant hotel perfectly maintained and presented, with a charming welcome. This period house contains about twenty rooms, some larger than others, with guaranteed comfort and elegant fabrics. What's more, the proprietor is a dynamic lady, always attentive to her guests' needs. Booking advisable. Double rooms €53–68.

⚗ 🏠 Hôtel de la Tour**

1 rue de la Mairie.
☎03.89.73.72.73 📠03.89.73.38.74
🌐www.hotel-la-tour.com
Closed 1 Jan–15 March. **TV. Pay car park.**

An old wine-grower's house in the middle of a little medieval town, offering pleasant rooms for €67–80 with shower or bath. Guests can use the sauna, Turkish baths and Jacuzzi for free. There is no restaurant, but try the local wine and specialities in the typical Alsace *winstub*. Very pleasant, even stylish, place. Logis de France.

⚗ |●| L'Auberge au Zahnacker

8 rue du Général-de-Gaulle.
☎03.89.73.60.77
Closed Thurs; Jan; Feb. **High chairs available. Disabled access.**

Service 9am–10pm. This inn is a little oasis of calm off a main street jammed with tourists. Even though it's grey and next to a roundabout, in summer, when the sweet-smelling wisteria is in full bloom, you can sit out on the terrace and savour a glass of Pinot Blanc while you wait for your classic regional fare: perhaps *presskopf* (brawn) or onion tart. *Menu touristique* €20.50. Reckon on €18 for a main meal and dessert à la carte. Menu offering a wide range of dishes and there is also a blackboard dish of the day. House classic dishes and dishes made from fresh produce from the local market are worth stopping off for. Good little wines from the inn's own cooperative cellar.

Bergheim
68750 (4km NE)

⚗ |●| Auberge des Lavandières

48 Grand'rue; take the D35.
☎03.89.73.69.96
Closed Mon and Tues lunchtimes; Tues evening Oct–May; first fortnight in Jan; first fortnight in Nov. **High chairs available.**

Stroll down the main road and you cannot miss this beautiful, lavender-coloured house with its terrace and stream that brings a refreshingly cool touch. The menu presented by the Ancelot family is quite original: *pastilles* of pigeon, chartreuse with garden snails, Alsace chicken supreme, rhubarb clafoutis or some specialities based on munster cheese. The food stays with the Alsace region, but has a more modern twist than usual. Weekday

lunchtime menu €16, others at €21 and €27 and around €25–30 à la carte.

Saint-Hippolyte
68590 (7km NE)

⚗ 🍴 |●| À La Vignette**

66 rte. du Vin
☎03.89.73.00.17 📠03.89.73.05.69
📧restaurant.la-vignette@wanadoo.fr
Closed Wed; Thurs lunchtime; Christmas to end Jan. **TV. Disabled access.**

Opposite the town hall and the church, this is a large hotel for such a small village. With its attractive, half-timbered façade, you cannot miss it; it's a pity that the rooms do not have the same charm, even if they offer a good level of comfort and some of them have a large terrace (room nos. 22 and 23 have a view over Haut-Kœnigsbourg castle). Rooms on the second floor have balconies. The owners are very obliging and will even offer to put your precious purchases of wine in the cellar on very hot days, or to make you a cold meal on days when the restaurant is closed if you are staying at the hotel. As for the restaurant, although there are no great surprises here, the food is well presented and includes such great Alsace classics as *poulet au Riesling*, *choucroute garnie*, home-made *spaetzle*, or Vosges ice cream sundae. Reasonable prices for the area, warm welcome and away from the tourist hustle and bustle. Double rooms €51–63, depending on facilities (from a simple wash basin to a bath). Menus from €17 to €26. Logis de France. *10% discount on the price of a room (out of season and during the week) offered to our readers on presentation of this guide.*

Illhaeusern
68970 (9km E)

⚗ |●| 🍴 À la Truite

17 rue du 25-Janvier; coming from Ribeauvillé on the D106, it's on the left before the bridge in the centre of the village.
☎03.89.71.88.15
Closed Tues evening; Wed; Thurs lunchtime in season (Thurs evening out of season); mid-Feb to mid-March; a week end of June; a week end of Nov. **Disabled access. High chairs available.**

A nice country inn with a terrace looking onto the river and the weeping willows. The simple, relaxed dining room is full of office and factory workers, farmers, long-distance lorry drivers and many others looking for an inexpensive meal. Here you can eat the best fish stew in all Alsace (you need to order it in advance). Alternatively try the freshly caught trout, fried fillet of carp, smoked meats, trout with almonds or cherry tart. Friendly service and good value for money. Weekday lunch menu €13, others €17.25–38. *Free coffee offered to our readers on presentation of this guide.*

Thannenkirch

68590 (11km NW)

@ 🎿 🏠 |●| Auberge la Meunière**

30 rue Sainte-Anne; to reach this high-up village (510m), take the D35 in the direction of Bergheim, then follow the D42.
☎03.89.73.10.47 ⊕03.89.73.12.31
ⓦwww.aubergelameuniere.com
Closed *Mon; Tues and Wed lunchtimes; 20 Dec–20 March.* **TV. High chairs available. Car park. Disabled access.**

From the road this looks like a classic Alsace inn, festooned with geraniums, small curtains at the windows and curious sunflowers on the shutters. On the valley side, the view is irresistible, especially from the large wooden terrace. The rooms are rustic but contemporary in style, done out in a superb combination of natural materials, with splendid views over the valley. Doubles €45–75 according to the level of comfort. Sauna, Jacuzzi and billiards for guests. The fine, inventive cuisine in the restaurant is reasonably priced and varies depending on what is available at the market. There's a set lunch menu at €17 (except Sunday) and others €22–35: you'll find tasty dishes like *baeckeoffe* of snails in Riesling, munster cheese salad or loin of pork. Perfect welcome and attentive service. A really good place to give yourself a treat. Logis de France. *Free coffee offered to our readers on presentation of this guide.*

Riquewihr

68340

@ 🏠 |●| Hôtel-restaurant Le Dolder

52 rue du Général-de-Gaulle; close to the Dolder gate.
☎03.89.47.92.56 ⊕03.89.47.89.79
ⓦwww.dolder.fr

Closed *Wed evening; Thurs; Jan; a fortnight early Feb; first week in July.* **TV.**

Peaceful, and yet in one of the town's main streets, a sixteenth-century town house, prettily fitted out and well maintained by the Mérius family (now into its fourth generation). Various colourful rooms, cool in summer, some of them half-timbered. Downstairs, an impeccable dining room with snug alcoves. Proper local cuisine. Very reasonable prices in comparison with those in town. Double rooms €36–56, depending on facilities. Menus from €14.50 to €30.

@ 🎿 🏠 Hôtel de la Couronne**

5 rue de la Couronne, just off rue du Général-de-Gaulle.
☎03.89.49.03.03 ⊕03.89.49.01.01
ⓦwww.hoteldelacouronne.com
TV. High chairs and cots available. Car park.

This attractive sixteenth-century hotel is spot-on. Its reception porch reflects the smile of the owners, and there are inviting little wooden benches and tables in the porch where you can enjoy a glass of Gewürztraminer before going off to explore the forests. All the rooms have been tastefully refurbished, some of them having half-timbering with walls decorated in a sober, yet slightly playful fashion: a flower here, a tree there, yet always tastefully done (floral fabrics). Reasonable prices and slightly "medieval" style for some rooms. Doubles €60–68 according to the level of comfort. *Apéritif on the house offered to our readers on presentation of this guide.*

Hunawihr

68150 (4km N)

@ |●| Wistub Suzel

2 rue de l'Église.
☎03.89.73.30.85
Closed *Tues; Jan to end March.* **High chairs available. Disabled access. Car park.**

A very friendly *winstub*, where you will receive a genuine welcome. There's a view of the church tower, and in summer the shady terrace is covered with flowers. The big wooden doors at the back of the restaurant lead to the cellars, where you can sample good Alsatian wine. Simple and subtle food such as onion tart with salad or the "Katel" menu with its stuffed rolled meats and fried potatoes so typical of the region. Menus start at €16 (except Sunday eve) and go up to €23; children's menu €7.50. On Sunday evenings they do flambéed tarts.

Rouffach
68150

@ 🏃 |●| Caveau de l'Haxakessel

7 pl. de la République; it's next to the tourist office and the Tour des Sorcières.
☎03.89.49.76.76
Closed *Tues evening (out of season); Wed (all year round); end of Feb to early March.*

Haxakessel means "the witch's cauldron". Don't panic, though – it's a long time since any sorcery has been practised in Rouffach. For a modest sum you can eat good *chou-croute* – the house version is called the *Witch*, naturally – or the highly prized flambéed tarts. On sunny days you can eat on the ter-race. Set *menu du jour* €8.50, other menus from €16 to €22.20. *Free coffee offered to our readers on presentation of this guide.*

Gueberschwihr
68420 (6km NW)

@ 🏠 |●| Hôtel Le Relais du Vignoble et Restaurant Belle-Vue**

29 rue des Forgerons; take the N83 in the direction of Hattstatt.
☎03.89.49.31.09 ☎03.89.49.27.82
🖰www.chez.com/hotelrelaisduvignoble
Closed *Wed lunchtime; Thurs.* **Disabled access. TV.**

Buffet breakfast with cold meats. Unfortunately the hotel, situated 100m behind the restaurant, is modern in style and not very aesthetically pleasing, but the rooms are comfortable, spacious, clean and, most importantly of all, those that face on to the vineyard have an incredible view over the Alsace plain (more expensive than those at the back and some have a balcony). The restaurant shares the same view from the terraces or from some tables in the main dining room. Quality cuisine, including home-made paté, sliced foie gras and fish *choucroute*. House wine served at the table. The proprietors are also winegrowers, good to know if you're tempted by a wine-tasting session. Double rooms €51–80, depending on facilities.

Half board package per night per person €59. Menus from €15 to €28. Logis de France.

Sainte-Croix-aux-Mines
68150

@ 🏃 🏠 |●| Auberge du Sobach

40 lieu-dit Sobache; 3km from Sainte-Croix on the N2059. Turn right in the centre of the village (signposted); it's right at the end, 1.5km further on in open countryside.
☎03.89.58.83.01 ☎03.89.58.35.20
🖂auberge.sobache@wanadoo.fr
Closed *Wed only in peak season; Tues and Wed out of season. Also from the last weekend in Dec until 1 Jan; 5 weeks after Valentine's Day (mid-Feb).* **Disabled access. TV.**

Seven comfortable, stylish rooms, some with king-size beds, as in room nos. 7 and 8, while room no. 4 offers a pretty view over the Argent valley. Even if you are not staying overnight, you won't regret dining here in between visiting the nearby mine and the saw mill. The smoked shoulder with munster cheese, *choucroute royale* and especially the braised pork will provide you with some excellent memories of your visit, as will the welcome. There's an elegant dining room, floral and all in wood, with a superb view from some tables, and a pleasant, tranquil terrace. A perfect place for families. Double rooms €45. Good half board deal at €38.50 per person for stays of three or more consecutive nights. Menus range from €19 to €45. *10% discount on the price of a room (for three or more consecutive nights) or free house digestif offered to our readers on presentation of this guide.*

Saulxures
67420

@ 🏠 |●| Hôtel-restaurant La Belle Vue***

36 rue Principale.
☎03.88.97.60.23 ☎03.88.47.23.71
🖰www.la-belle-vue.com
Closed *Tues and Wed (except for dinner and breakfast for the hotel); Feb school holidays; 25 Jun–7 Jul and for All Saints.* **TV.**

At the centre of a peaceful little village in the upper Bruche valley. A subtle blend of tradition and modernism, the hotel décor is a great success and rooms are very comfortable. The attractively priced food, friendly welcome and wonderful location explain the success of this charming hotel. Pleasant terrace looking out over the garden for fine days. Double rooms with shower or bath €78; mezzanines and suites €103–113. Weekday menu €19, others using seasonal ingredients at €22–42.

Saverne

67700

ⓔ ⌂ ⅔ Auberge de Jeunesse

Château des Rohan; in the right-hand wing of the splendid Rohan château, above a school.
℡03.88.91.14.84 ℻03.88.71.15.97.
ⓔaj.saverne@wanadoo.fr
Closed 23 Dec–22 Jan.

The interior does not entirely live up to the expectations of the grand exterior, but it is very conveniently situated. New guests are received 8–10am and 5–10pm. €11.80 per night in a dormitory with breakfast (€8.55 without). FUAJ card compulsory (you can buy it on the spot). Ask for a key if you're going to be out after 10pm. *One breakfast per room offered to our readers on presentation of this guide.*

ⓔ ⅔ ⌂ |●| Villa Katz

42 rue du Général Leclerc; it's southwest of the centre in the direction of the campsite.
℡03.88.71.02.02
ⓦwww.tavernekatz.com
Restaurant closed Thurs. **Closed** Tues; 15–30 Jan. **High chairs and games available. TV. Car park.**

An elegant, homely house in Jugendstil (the German version of Art Nouveau), with period furniture, pictures and ornaments, and books in the rooms. The eight rooms are all different but equally charming. Doubles at €55–105 according to the season. The pocket-sized restaurant has the same charm. Weekday menu for €16 or others €24–42. *Free coffee offered to our readers on presentation of this guide.*

ⓔ ⅔ ⌂ Hôtel Europe***

7 rue de la Gare.
℡03.88.71.12.07 ℻03.88.71.11.43
ⓦwww.hotel-europe-fr.com
Disabled access. TV. Pay car park.

This is the best hotel in town. The walls and floors have recently been refurbished

in the rooms, which have good facilities – a number even have whirlpool baths. Doubles with shower/wc €60.50–71 and €85 with bath. The ritzy atmosphere, the first-rate service and the excellent buffet breakfast make sure that guests – including a large number of staff from the European Parliament in Strasbourg – keep coming back. For families there's a flat in an adjoining house. A glass of *Muscat d'Alsace wine on the house offered to our readers on presentation of this guide.*

ⓔ ⅔ |●| Taverne Katz

80 Grand-Rue; it's not far from the château des Rohan, near the town hall.
℡03.88.71.16.56
High chairs and games available.

This beautiful place was built in 1605 for the archbishop's tax collector. Beautiful dining room with wood panelling. The first-rate cooking focuses on traditional dishes and excellent desserts – the dishes rarely change and are totally reliable – and have been for twenty years. Despite such unfailing success, you can still be sure of a warm welcome from Suzie. Lunchtime weekday menus start at €16, and other menus €24–35. The terrace looks out onto the pedestrianized street. *Free coffee offered to our readers on presentation of this guide.*

Sélestat

67600

ⓔ ⅔ ⌂ |●| Auberge des Alliés**

39 rue des Chevaliers.
℡03.88.92.09.34 ℻03.88.92.12.88
ⓦwww.auberge-des-allies.com
Closed Sun evening; Mon; 27 June–11 July; 25 Dec–7 Jan. **TV.**

This place, built in 1372, was a bakery in the first half of the nineteenth century when Louis-Philippe ruled France, and has been a restaurant since 1918. In the middle of the dining room is an impressive old Alsatian stove, and there's also a beautiful fresco showing the place aux Choux in the first half of the nineteenth century. The à la carte menu is typical of this kind of restaurant, with local dishes such as ham hock, *choucroute*, pike perch with Riesling, home-made foie gras and calves' kidneys. Set menus €15–26. Comfortable, modern double rooms with bath €52–60; those at the back are the quietest. *10% discount on a room (from third consecutive night) offered to our readers on presentation of this guide.*

Rathsamhausen
67600 (3km E)

ⓦ 🏠 |●| Hôtel-restaurant à l'Étoile**

Grand-Rue; take the D21 in the direction of Muttersholtz.
☎03.88.92.35.79
@ hoteletoile@evc.net
Closed Mon and Fri lunchtime; early Feb. **TV. Swimming pool.**

This old house has been cleverly modernized by adding an extension with a bright foyer and a stairway in wood and glass. Nice doubles with shower/wc cost €42, rooms for four people €57. Half board €37 per person, available all year. The dining room is warm and inviting. The à la carte menu is limited but lists good dishes, particularly the fried carp or fried small fry. Expect to pay €20 à la carte, or opt for the cheap set menu at €11 (weekday lunchtimes) or others at €14 and €19. In summer the terrace is covered with flowers and there's an open-air pool. A really nice little place.

ⓦ 🌲 🏠 |●| Les Prés d'Ondine

5 rte. de Baldenheim; take the D21, then follow the D209
☎03.88.58.04.60 ☏03.88.58.04.61
ⓦwww.presdondine.com

A small hotel combining the charm of a private house and warmth of a personal welcome with top-of-the-range hotel services (including a sauna, Turkish bath and Jacuzzi area). Twelve rooms, all different, that take their inspiration from extracts from poems by the French poet and author Nerval, or the French philosopher Bachelard. There's nothing of the traditional hotelier about Stéphane Dalibert, he even provides a lounge-cum-bar-cum-library where you can serve yourself, as well as a boat (the property's garden runs down to the River Ill). Evening meal subject to reservation, open to non-residents, and up there with the best of them. Double rooms with shower €71–90 or with bath €78–130. Half board €85 per person. Evening meal €30. *10% discount offered (on arrival) to our readers on presentation of this guide.*

Strasbourg
67000
See map on pp.38–39

ⓦ 🏠 |●| Auberge de Jeunesse René-Cassin

9 rue de l'Auberge-de-Jeunesse La Montagne-Verte; take no. 2 bus from the train station in the direction of Lingolsheim to the "Auberge de Jeunesse" stop. **Off map A4-1**
☎03.88.30.26.46 ☏03.88.30.35.16.
Closed Jan. **Disabled access. Car park.**

Friendly youth hostel occupying a complex of 1970s-style buildings surrounded by geenery (although the railway is nearby). There are 265 beds. Reckon on €15–17 per person (including breakfast) in a room with three to six beds, half board €25.40. You can hire sheets. Fully equipped kitchen available. Bar-café open in the evenings until 1am. Friendly welcome. Booking advisable.

ⓦ 🌲 🏠 Auberge de Jeunesse des 2 Rives

Rue de Cavaliers; 5km from the town centre, near the border, heading in the direction of Kehl. From the station, take bus no. 2 in the direction of Pont-du-Rhin; get off at the "Parc du Rhin" stop 1km from the hostel. **Off map D4–2**
☎03.88.45.54.20 ☏03.88.45.54.21
@ strasbourg.parc-du-rhin@fuaj.org
Reception closed 12.30–2pm **Closed** end of year. **Disabled access. Games available.**

With the FUAJ (French Youth Hostel Association) card (compulsory and on sale at the hostel), €18 per person sleeping in a three- or five-bed dormitory, including breakfast and bed linen. Meals €9. Large modern building a stone's throw from the Rhine. 246 places in three- to five-bed dormitories, most with shower and toilet. Many rooms are adapted for the disabled. Restaurant and bar with disco. *Free coffee offered to our readers on presentation of this guide.*

ⓦ 🏠 Hôtel de l'Ill**

8 rue des Bateliers; a stone's throw from the banks of the river Ill, in a quiet street in the Krutenau district. **Map D3-7**
☎03.88.36.20.01 ☏03.88.35.30.03
Closed 29 Dec–6 Jan. **TV. High chairs available.**

Friendly hotel run with a smile by the Ehrhardt family. Rooms are not very big but they're pleasant and nicely decorated. They're divided between the old building and a new annexe in the courtyard. Some are non-smoking. Doubles €42–44 with shower, €48–50 with shower/wc, €58–65 with bath. There's a lovely sunny terrace on the first floor (from 10am to 7pm). A good, sensibly priced Strasbourg hotel.

ⓒ 🥢 🛏 Hôtel Kyriad-Saint-Christophe**

2 pl. de la Gare. **Map A3-9**
☎03.88.22.30.30 📠03.88.32.17.11
ⓔhotel-kyriad-gare@wanadoo.fr
Disabled access. TV.

In one of the grandest buildings near the station (handy if you are coming by train; otherwise, there is a public car park near by). This well-run hotel offering comfortable, functional rooms (doubles €60–75 depending on season) does not close for staff holidays. The nicest rooms are at the back, despite the double glazing in the rooms overlooking the square. *Apéritif on the house offered to our readers on presentation of this guide.*

ⓒ 🥢 🛏 Hôtel Couvent du Franciscain**

18 rue du Faubourg-de-Pierre; in the road running on from the rue de la Nuée-Bleue, north of the centre, in the place des Halles area. **Map B1-5**
☎03.88.32.93.93 📠03.88.75.68.46
ⓦwww.hotel-franciscain.com
Closed *Christmas to 1 Jan.* **Disabled access. TV. High chairs available. Pay car park.**

Quiet location at the end of a cul-de-sac. It's a classic two-star, and nice and quiet. Doubles cost €64 (€62 in low season). Buffet breakfast is served in the basement, decorated with frescoes depicting some rather merry Franciscan monks. Warm welcome. *10% discount on a room (Jan, Feb, July and Aug, outside parliamentary sessions) offered to our readers on presentation of this guide.*

ⓒ 🛏 Hôtel Suisse**

2–4 rue de la Râpe. **Map D3-3**
☎03.88.35.22.11 📠03.88.25.74.23
ⓦwww.hotel-suisse.com

A hotel with a soul (to call it charm would be far too trite) with two women at reception who know how to welcome guests without overdoing it. A place only

for those who can be bothered to make the effort to go and find it, somewhere that is peaceful day and night, a stone's throw from the cathedral. The rooms with a view of the cathedral are a real delight, while others are smaller. And the breakfast, served in a charming traditional dining room, is one of the most convivial there is. Double rooms €69–89.

ⓒ 🥢 🛏 Le Grand Hôtel***

12 pl. de la Gare. **Map A2-10**
☎03.88.52.84.84 📠03.88.52.84.00.
ⓦwww.le-grand-hotel.com
TV. High chairs available.

This hotel in the square by the train station really is grand. You can't miss the Soviet-looking, concrete, 1950s building, with its stark lines and bulky forms. The enormous reception with a high ceiling is equally imposing, but the striking glass lift (a unique 1950s prototype) whisks you up to comfortable rooms refurbished in modern three-star style, some fitted with air-conditioning. Double rooms start at €70 with shower/wc or €112 with bath. Attentive service. *10% discount on a room (Jan to end of April, July/August and in November) offered to our readers on presentation of this guide.*

ⓒ 🛏 Hôtel Monopole Métropole

16 rue Kuhn. **Map A2-8**
☎03.88.14.39.14 📠03.88.32.82.55
ⓦwww.bw-monopole.com
Pay car park. TV.

A grand hotel, with traditional service, great professionalism at reception and comfortable rooms in all styles, some of which, and these were the ones we liked the most, in a decidedly contemporary vein. Air conditioning is being installed. Good breakfasts are served in the old restaurant dining room, and there's even a fascinating small museum of life in times gone by. Double rooms €75–125.

ⓒ 🥢 🛏 Hôtel du Dragon***

2 rue de l'Écarlate. **Map C4-6**
☎03.88.35.79.80 📠03.88.25.78.95
ⓦwww.dragon.fr
TV. Cots available. Pay car park.

A lovely seventeenth-century building. Some might find the starkly minimalist décor in shades of grey slightly out of keeping, but it's pleasant enough and in a very quiet location. Doubles with shower/

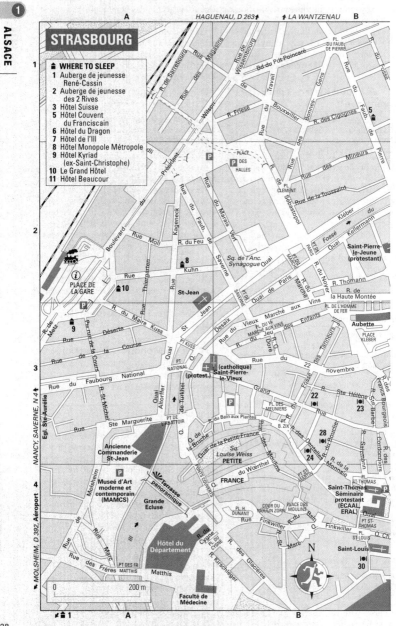

STRASBOURG

WHERE TO SLEEP

1 Auberge de jeunesse
   René-Cassin
2 Auberge de jeunesse
   des 2 Rives
3 Hôtel Suisse
5 Hôtel Couvent
   du Franciscain
6 Hôtel du Dragon
7 Hôtel de l'Ill
8 Hôtel Monopole Métropole
9 Hôtel Kyriad
   (ex-Saint-Christophe)
10 Le Grand Hôtel
11 Hôtel Beaucour

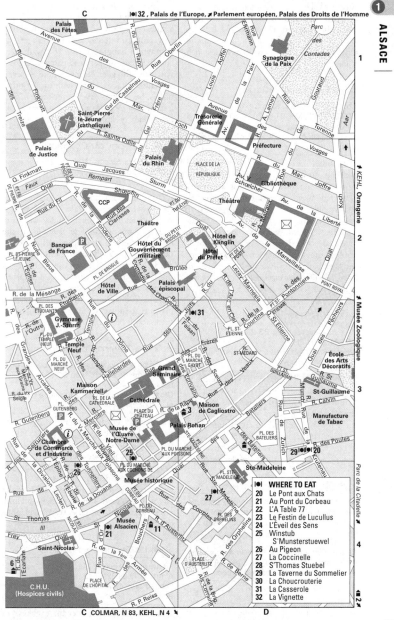

WHERE TO EAT

🅞	
20	Le Pont aux Chats
21	Au Pont du Corbeau
22	L'A Table 77
23	Le Festin de Lucullus
24	L'Éveil des Sens
25	Winstub S'Munsterstuewel
26	Au Pigeon
27	La Coccinelle
28	S'Thomas Stuebel
29	La Taverne du Sommelier
30	La Choucrouterie
31	La Casserole
32	La Vignette

wc or bath €81–112. Generous breakfast – in summer it's served in the paved courtyard. There's a permanent exhibition of work by contemporary artists. Free use of bicycle and motorbike sheds. *10% discount on a room (from Jan to March and in July–Aug) offered to our readers on presentation of this guide.*

⚑ 𝕬 🏠 Hôtel Beaucour***

5 rue des Bouchers. **Map C4-11**
☎03.88.76.72.00 ☎03.88.76.72.60
🖳www.hotel-beaucour.com
Open all year round. **TV. High chairs available.**

This hotel occupies five half-timbered buildings from the eighteenth century. Considerable refurbishment has somewhat detracted from its authenticity, but it's comfortable and has a matchless charm. All the rooms are different (some with attractive sloping ceilings), and each is nicely decorated. Prices €91–128 for a double, the top price ones having bath and spa bath. *Free breakfast per person (in July–Aug) offered to our readers on presentation of this guide.*

⊚ 𝕬 |●| S'Thomas Stuebel

5 rue du Bouclier. **Map B3-28**
☎03.88.22.34.82
Closed Sun; Mon; Easter week; first 3 weeks in Aug; Christmas week.

A pocket-sized *winstub* serving authentic regional specialities. Braised knuckle of pork on a bed of *choucroute*, munster cheese, calves' kidneys in a cream sauce and *bibeleskass* (soft white cheese and sauté potatoes). Lunch menu is €8.30, or expect to pay €15–23 à la carte. *Free coffee offered to our readers on presentation of this guide.*

⊚ 𝕬 |●| La Choucrouterie

20 rue Saint-Louis; cross the river Ill opposite the Protestant seminary. The restaurant is 15m from the church of Saint Louis. **Map B4-30**
☎03.88.36.52.87
Closed Sun evening; 3 weeks in Aug; a week at Christmas. **Open** 7pm–1am, as well as Sat and Sun lunchtimes. **Disabled access.**

Roger Siffer was an Alsatian folk singer before he went into the restaurant business. From time to time he still sings in his restaurant-theatre – either on his own or with his musical pals when they drop by. The building was a post house in the

eighteenth century and was then home to the last *choucroute* makers in Strasbourg – apparently they made the best in town. The cheerfulness, humour, music (it has a fine collection of musical instruments), and eroticism (take a good look at the engravings hanging up on the walls here and there) are all part and parcel of it. And you can still get *choucroute* here – seven varieties, in fact – along with lots of other dishes. Set menus €9–15, reckon on €22 à la carte. *Free coffee offered to our readers on presentation of this guide.*

⊚ |●| Au Pont du Corbeau

21 quai Saint-Nicolas. **Map C4-21**
☎03.88.35.60.68
Closed Sat; Sun lunchtime; first week in Feb; Aug.

The owner here will always give you a warm, friendly welcome, the food is great, and it's one of the few *winstubs* in the town centre near the cathedral that's open on Sunday nights. These little things make all the difference. The house speciality (a must) is grilled ham with sautéed potatoes. Menus at €11 (weekday lunchtimes) or around €23 for a full meal à la carte. This place is a showcase for everything that's great about Alsatian food and drink.

⊚ |●| La Taverne du Sommelier

Ruelle de la Bruche; the alleyway comes out into the rue de Zurich. **Map D3-32**
☎03.88.24.14.10
Closed weekends; a week in Aug; a fortnight at end of the year.

The ruelle de la Bruche is extremely narrow but widens out just by the tavern to make a bit of space. Traditional setting with alcoves and benches. There is typical *winstub* fare on the menu, but the thoughtfully prepared dishes range more widely than the basic regional classics. Dish of the day €10; à la carte around €25. Good little wines, served by the glass. Warm welcome. Simple, smiling service.

⊚ |●| Le Festin de Lucullus

18 rue sainte-Hélène. **Map B3-23**
☎ and ☎03.88.22.40.78
Closed Sun; Mon; 10–31 Aug. **Disabled access.**

Four years' training under the eagle eye of the famous chef Michel Guérard is character-forming to say the least, and the chef here was certainly inspired by his time at

Eugénie-les-Bains – everything from the well-judged cooking times to the use of fresh herbs and seasonings is thoughtful and the results are excellent. The cheerful, friendly welcome, good service and honest prices mean that you'll want to come back, too. Superb weekday lunchtime menu €14. Different evening menu €27 or à la carte around €30. Rather subdued, this very long dining room.

@ 🕏 |●| Au Pigeon

23 rue des Tonneliers. **Map C4-26**
☏03.88.32.31.30
Closed Sun evening; Mon; Tues evening; 3 weeks in Jan; 1 month spread over July and Aug.

Occupying one of the town's oldest buildings – a glorious, half-timbered, gabled residence built in the sixteenth century – this historic *winstub* has been going for years. Above the door are two carved pigeons. The dining room is sober and classic in style, and serves dishes such as *baeckeoffe*, duckling with orange, *choucroute* and knuckle of pork braised in Pinot Noir. Menus €13–23.50. *Free house apéritif offered to our readers on presentation of this guide.*

@ |●| Le Pont aux Chats

42 rue de la Krutenau. **Map D3-20**
☏03.88.24.08.77
Closed Wed; Sat lunchtime.

The event of the year in 2004 in Strasbourg was the arrival of the *Westerman's* former second chef, Valère Diochet, in the kitchen of this eighteenth-century house. This great chef's cuisine, somewhere between traditional and modern, is finally available to a wider clientele at reasonable prices. Behind the stained glass windows, a pleasantly intimate dining room emerges. Its décor, refined in the extreme, is the perfect backdrop to the dishes produced, simply, using really good ingredients, worked with both skill and imagination. With the onset of the hot summer weather, the courtyard terrace becomes a rallying point for Strasbourg's smart set. The welcome is open and warm, the wine list appealing; in short, highly recommended. Lunchtime menu €19; expect to pay about €30 for à la carte.

@ |●| L'A Table 77

77 Grand-Rue. **Map B3-22**
☏03.88.32.23.37

Closed Sun and Mon. **Open** until 10pm.

The dining room is done out in contemporary colours with orange-grey tones, the table decoration is sophisticated and the staff, although initially reserved, are very responsive. The food bears the hallmark of a talented young chef who has returned home having earned his spurs at the *Ledoyen* in Paris. Stéphane Kaiser works as hard on his presentation as he does on the flavour of his dishes, which might include cod served on a bed of smoked aubergine with radish tartare. Remarkable value, especially at lunchtime. Lunchtime menu €22, evening menu €28. *Dégustation* (taster) menu €50, à la carte around €40.

@ 🕏 |●| La Coccinelle

22 rue Sainte-Madeleine; place de l'Étoile. **Map D4-27**
☏03.88.36.19.27
Closed Sat lunchtime; Sun; 18 July–15 Aug.

Two sisters run this place: one does the cooking and the other looks after the dining room. The restaurant is packed with regulars at lunchtime, drawn by the reasonably priced dish of the day (€8). It's less frenetic in the evenings. Good regional specialities include roast knuckle of ham, beef with rock salt and *vigneronne* pie. On Saturday evenings in winter, order the Alsace classic *baeckeoffe*. Reckon on around €22 à la carte. Smiling welcome and service, followed by a "Coccinelle" (ladybird) lucky charm when you leave.

@ |●| L'Éveil des Sens

Rue des Dentelles. **Map B3-24**
☏03.88.32.81.01
Closed Tues; mid-Oct. **Open** until 10.30pm.

One of the wonderful new establishments in the Petite France district of Strasbourg, run by a friendly team and a young chef, Flemish in origin, Gauthier de Baere. Go for a seat on the old-fashioned bench by the window to get the best view of the drama of the kitchen and the dining room décor, or reserve a table on the terrace when the weather is good. With the varied, cosmopolitan menu, you can start with new takes on *crevette croquette* or Basque black pudding before moving on to seasonal dishes prepared with brio, such as the millefeuille of ox cheek and foie gras. Good service. Lunchtime *plat du jour* €14. Good-value set lunch menu

€25 (€29 with a second dish). À la carte around €40.

℗ |◉| La Casserole

24 rue des Juifs. **Map D3-31**
℡03.88.36.49.68
Closed Sat lunchtime; Sun; Mon. **Open** until 10pm.

La Casserole is run by a young couple who trained elsewhere before coming back home and opening this little gem of a place right in the old town centre, popular with diners of all ages, delighted to be able to experience contemporary cuisine at low prices. Éric Girardin, former sommelier at the *Bateau Ivre* in Courcheval, creates wholesome, tasty and colourful dishes, all in keeping with the restaurant's agreeable décor. Booking essential, especially if you want to tuck yourself away in one of the little cubicles at the front. À la carte €27.

℗ |◉| La Vignette

29 rue Mélanie. **Off map D1-32**
℡03.88.31.38.10
Closed Sun; Mon. **Open** until 10pm.

On a fine day, you'd be hard pushed to find anywhere better than this restaurant with outdoor tables set under a large chestnut tree, opposite a Virginia creeper-clad wall. Dishes chalked up on the blackboard might include ham-on-the-bone *presskopf* brawn, chicken vol-au-vent, risotto or a good and simple steak tartare. Inside, the floors creak, nostalgia rules with check tablecloths and old postcards. A stone's throw from the European institutions, here's a place that is never empty, winter and summer alike. Serge Knapp has made a successful return to this region, having worked as a highly respected chef in the most prestigious hotels and restaurants: now he can do exactly as he pleases, backed up in the dining room by Danie Douadic, a woman who knows everyone in Strasbourg, which also goes some way to explaining the restaurant's success. Expect to pay €30–40 à la carte.

℗ |◉| Winstub S'Munsterstuewel

8 pl. du Marché-aux-Cochons-de-Lait. **Map C3-25**
℡03.88.32.17.63
Closed Sun; Mon; early March; mid-Aug to early Sept.

The décor is grander and prices are slightly higher – €30 for a set menu, €38 à la carte – than in a traditional *winstub*, but the quality is undeniable. Home-made whole boned pig's trotter in *baeckeoffe* stuffed with a trio of meats, pig's cheek served on a bed of *choucroute* and potatoes are typical of the hearty fare on offer. Good selection of wines and spirits. Terrace on the square, everyone rushes to grab a seat at the first hint of sunshine.

Mittelhausbergen

67206 (6km NW)

℗ ⌂ |◉| Au Tilleul

5 rue de Strasbourg; take the D31.
℡03.88.56.18.31 ℗03.88.56.07.23
🌐www.autilleul.com
Restaurant closed Tues and Wed. **TV.**

A fine establishment founded in 1888 by Jacques Lorentz's great-great-grandfather, hence the name given to the *winstub* by this enterprising young chef. Though it's a little way out of the way, it's well worth seeking out for its excellent, reasonably priced meals using seasonal ingredients and produce fresh from the market, as well as its great wine list. Service is very nice, too. Double rooms €50–60. Menus €31 and €36 (with three courses). Menus from €9 in the *"1888" winstub*. Logis de France.

Handschuheim

67117 (13km W)

℗ |◉| L'Auberge à l'Espérance

5 rue Principale; take the N4 towards Wasselonne.
℡03.88.69.00.52
Closed lunchtimes; Mon; Tues; a week in March; second fortnight in Sept. **High chairs available.**

Welcoming restaurant in an attractive half-timbered house. You go up the stairs and there's a choice of five pretty dining rooms. *Flammenkéche* (flambéed tart) is a particular speciality, cooked here in the old-fashioned way on wood cinders – which gives it its unique flavour and lightness. The ham is great, too. The place appeals to families and groups of friends, so the atmosphere is warm and friendly. They have some good wines, and they don't push the local vintages too hard. Menus start at €7.20. Expect to pay €18 à la carte.

Thann

68800

@ ⅔ 🏠 |●| Hôtel-restaurant Kléber**

39 rue Kléber.
☎03.89.37.13.66 🅕03.89.37.39.67
Closed *3 weeks in Feb.* **Restaurant closed** *Sat and Sun.* **TV. High chairs available. Disabled access. Car park.**

This hotel-restaurant is in a residential area away from the hustle and bustle of town (five minutes' walk to the centre). It's quite stylish, with fair prices. Rooms 24 and 26 in the annexe are really quiet, with flower-festooned balconies overlooking orchards. Doubles €37.50 with basin, up to €53 with bath. The rooms, although clean, would benefit from a lick of paint; as for the rest, it is well kept. The restaurant, which has a good reputation, offers a weekday lunch menu at €12 and others at €18.80 and €32, with dishes like beef with morels, game in season, munster with pear, home-made clafoutis. Dishes beautifully presented. Courteous service. *10% discount on a room (except in July–August) offered to our readers on presentation of this guide.*

@ 🏠 |●| Hôtel-restaurant Aux Sapins**

3 rue Jeanne-d'Arc
☎03.89.37.10.96 🅕03.89.37.23.83
🖥www.auxsapinshotel.fr
Restaurant closed *Sat.* **TV. Disabled access.**

Don't be put off by the uninspiring modern exterior, this place is actually very nice. The well-kept, colourful, simple rooms are decorated in good taste and are peaceful. Rooms on the second floor are smaller. And, with its prices to suit all pockets, the restaurant is a little gem: pâté en croûte, sides of meat, wonderful salads, whether in the large dining room or on the shady terrace. A popular place and a pleasant surprise. Double rooms €45–49. Weekday lunchtime menu €9, otherwise €17–30. Logis de France.

Saint-Amarin

68550 (11km NW)

@ 🏠 |●| Auberge du Mehrbächel

Route de Geishouse. Leave the N66 at Saint-Amarin signposted to Geishouse; about 4km along the main road, before the village, turn off left and keep going (where all the pine

trees are) until you come to the inn.
☎03.89.82.60.68 🅕03.89.82.66.05
🖂sarl.kornacke@wanadoo.fr
Closed *Mon and Thurs evenings; Fri; All Saints' school holiday.* **TV. Car park. High chairs available.**

This chalet, with woods on one side and pastures on the other, is set on the side of the mountain dominating the Thur valley. The views of the valley from the bedrooms – which are in a modern annexe – are splendid. Doubles with shower/wc or bath €50–55. The restaurant is well worth the effort of getting here. Cooking is traditional, but the chef has added his own touches. Specialities include munster cheese in breadcrumbs, winegrower's salad, *nougat de foie gras, surlawerla* (sliced liver in a red wine sauce), raspberry charlotte. Menus from €16 (except on Sun) to €34. The generous breakfast buffet features smoked bacon, ham, cereal, yoghurt and more. Small, tranquil terrace. Logis de France.

Turckheim

68230

@ ⅔ 🏠 |●| Auberge du Brand**

8 Grand-Rue.
☎03.89.27.06.10 🅕03.89.27.55.51
🖥www.aubergedubrand.com
Closed *first week in July; Nov; ring for details in Jan.* **Restaurant closed** *Wed; open evenings only.* **TV.**

This is a superb, traditional half-timbered Alsace building. The forest, so bounteous in the autumn, has won over the chef, who concocts tasty panfuls of mushrooms and game in a Pinot Noir wine sauce. Also a delicious foie gras flavoured with quince schnapps. The warm décor of the dining room really complements the food. Set menus €25–45. Nine pretty rooms. Doubles €42–100 depending on the level of comfort. Logis de France. *Free coffee offered to our readers on presentation of this guide.*

@ ⅔ 🏠 Hôtel des Deux Clefs***

3 rue du Conseil; in place de l'Hôtel-de-Ville.
☎03.89.27.06.01 🅕03.89.27.18.07
🖥www.2clefs.com
Disabled access. TV. High chairs and cots available. Pay car park.

Here's a hotel that plays on the romantic atmosphere of the place with its own unique setting: a beautiful terrace and half-timbered house dating from the sixteenth century.

The great and the good have stayed here, from General de Gaulle to Dr. Schweizer (a friend of the family), James Stewart and French film star Charlotte de Turckheim. Wood panelling and traditional carpets, mysterious colours and a light that is reminiscent of Rembrandt's paintings. Bedrooms not quite as luxurious as you might think, but comfortable all the same. The attic bedrooms are the cheapest and look out over the town hall square. Room nos. 1, 3, 8, 11 and 12 are the most attractive, spacious and romantic. No credit cards. Logis de France. *10% discount on the price of a room (weekdays only) or 50% discount on buffet breakfast offered to our readers on presentation of this guide.*

⍟ |O| Au Turenne

14 rue Grenouillère;in the passage behind the church on the right, a short distance from the tourist area.
☎03.89.27.25.81
Closed *Mon; Tues.*

A beautiful old house, with its peaceful, flower-decked terrace, a perfect place to enjoy lunch or even just a drink. Service in the large dining room, a former fifteenth-century cellar where an old wine press still holds centre stage. Not much choice on the *menu du jour*, but cooked well and elegantly served: fish terrine, farmhouse *magret de canard*, peach melba, *tarte tatin* and some home-made Alsace classics. And some dishes are served under a domed lid (a rarity nowadays). Attentive service. *Menu du jour* €12, other menus €22–35.

Trois Épis (Les)
68410 (9km NW)

⍟ 🎋 ♨ |O| Hôtel-Restaurant Villa Rosa**

4 rue Thierry-Schoéré; take the D10 in the direction of Zimmerbach, then follow the D11, it's about 400m from the village.
☎03.89.49.81.19 ℱ03.89.78.90.45
🌐www.villarosa.fr
Closed *mid-Jan to mid-Feb.* **Restaurant closed** *lunchtimes; Thurs; Sun (out of season).* **High chairs available. Swimming pool.**

Pretty house with green shutters run by Anne-Rose (a fated name!) who gives her (non-smoking) guests a humorous and spontaneous welcome. Lovely rooms, our favourite ones looking out over the garden, where there is a swimming pool, sauna and Jacuzzi. The renovated attic rooms are spacious. With regard to the

food, the ingredients could not be fresher, as the vegetables come from the kitchen garden, wild garlic from the surrounding countryside, all cooked with both personal flair and enthusiasm. Themed days (varying with the season) and training days include discovering traditional roses or wild vegetables, or cooking with edible flowers (see their website). A wonderful place to relax. Double rooms €52–62, depending on the season. Menus, evenings only (except Sun), from €20 to €25. *10% discount on the price of a room (minimum three nights, weekdays only, outside school holidays) or an apéritif on the house offered to our readers on presentation of this guide.*

Wissembourg
67160

⍟ 🎋 ♨ |O| Hôtel-restaurant Walk**

2 rue de la Walk; take boulevard Clemenceau, which runs along the ramparts, as far as the public swimming pool; then go in the direction of the hospital centre.
☎03.88.94.06.44 ℱ03.88.54.38.03
🌐www.moulin-walk.com
Restaurant closed *Fri lunchtime; Sun evening; Mon; 3–25 Jan; 20 June–5 July.* **Disabled access. TV. High chairs available. Car park.**

This place, outside the town's fortifications and surrounded by lots of greenery and the vestiges of an ancient mill, has a relaxing atmosphere. Comfortable rooms in the small annexe are decorated in a contemporary style. They go for €50–60. In the oldest building, wood is revered and tradition respected. In the restaurant, richly rustic setting, food not badly done, but relatively expensive. Menus at €29 and €37. Logis de France. *Apéritif on the house offered to our readers on presentation of this guide.*

Climbach
67510 (9km SW)

⍟ |O| Restaurant au Col de Pfaffenschlick

Col du Pfaffenschlick. Climbach is on the D3; turn left up to the pass (373m).
☎03.88.54.28.84
Closed *Mon; Tues; 15 Jan–15 Feb.* **Disabled access. High chairs available. Car park.**

The Séraphin family will give you a genuinely warm welcome to their little inn in the heart of the forest. The dining room, with its hefty beams and wood panelling, has a friendly atmosphere, and there's a terrace for summer. For a snack, there are ham or cheese platters, cutlets au gratin, salads, quiches or onion pies, as well as stuffed country chicken à l'ancienne, wild boar casserole or *baeckeoffe* made to order. Weekday lunch menus start at €8.50 and then go up to €17.50–32; or pay about €25 à la carte. A good place, and only a few kilometres from Four à Chaux, an important sector of the Maginot Line.

Woerth

67630

⊛ 🛠 |●| **Restaurant sans Alcool et sans Fumée**

11 rue de la Pépinière; it's at the entrance to the town.

☎ 03.88.09.30.79
Closed *Mon; evenings; Feb school holidays.* **Disabled access.**

This place dates back to 1944, when the owner at the time, under heavy bombardment, swore that if she ever got out alive she would open an alcohol-free inn. She kept her word but had to cope with the most challenging of times: her traditional customers left in droves and it took a while to build up a new clientele – but the quality of the cuisine ensured that she did. Today, even though the inn has moved from its pretty old building in the centre of town to more modern premises on the outskirts, people come from far and wide (especially on Sun) for the marvellous regional cooking. Weekday lunchtime menu €7.60, other menus €15–22. *Free coffee offered to our readers on presentation of this guide.*

Aquitaine

Agen

47000

⟨ 🛉 Hôtel des Ambans*

59 rue des Ambans.
☎ 05.53.66.28.60 ℱ 05.53.87.94.01
Closed *Christmas and New Year; Ascension weekend.* **TV.**

A well-run, clean and simple little hotel on a quiet street in the old part of town. Eight of the rooms are a little shabby (except for one on the ground floor – the first fruit of a scheduled refurbishment), although they're attractively priced: doubles €27 and €30 with shower and €32 with shower/wc. The owner is genuinely friendly and will greet you like a long-lost friend. Note that the hotel reception is closed on Sunday from 11am to 7pm, and after 11pm during the week.

⟨ 🛉 Hôtel des Iles

25 rue Baudin.
☎ 05.53.47.11.33
ℱ 05.53.66.19.25
🕸 www.ot-agen.org
TV.

Behind the white stone façade, this lovely hotel is arranged around a central light well. There's every chance the owner himself will check you in, his cheroot clamped in the corner of his mouth. The laid-back feel is deceptive as it's actually a well-organized place. The ten rooms are clean and nicely maintained and you'll have peace and quiet in this residential area; doubles €32 with shower/wc or bath. It doesn't have an official star rating but it carries on regardless, unaffected by passing fads or displays of style.

⟨ 🎋 🛉 Atlantic Hôtel**

133 av. Jean-Jaurès; 1.2 km from the centre of town, on the N113 towards Toulouse and Montauban. It's set back from the road, behind a petrol station.
☎ 05.53.96.16.56 ℱ 05.53.98.34.80
🖂 atlantic.hotel@wanadoo.fr
Closed *24 Dec–4 Jan.* **Disabled access. TV. High chairs available. Swimming pool. Car park. Basement garage.**

Neither the surroundings nor the 1970s architecture of this building are particularly attractive, but it's welcoming and the rooms are spacious and quiet, and there's a swimming pool. Six rooms overlook the garden and doubles with shower/wc or bath go for €49. *10% discount on the price of a room offered to our readers on presentation of this guide.*

⟨ 🎋 ⏸ Les Mignardises

40 rue Camille-Desmoulins.
☎ 05.53.47.18.62
Closed *Sun lunchtime; Mon; a fortnight in Aug.*

Though it has no pretensions to being gourmet cuisine, the food here is good value. They do four menus that include soup, starter, main dish and dessert, starting at €11 (served on Tues and Wed evenings, and Thurs to Sat lunchtimes) and going up to €24.40. Settle down on one of the plum-coloured benches and get stuck into beef's tongue with a spicy sauce, while enjoying the mouth-watering aromas emerging from the kitchen. The place is always packed at lunchtime. *Free house apéritif offered to our readers on presentation of this guide.*

⟨ 🎋 ⏸ Las Aucos

12 rue de Tonneins.

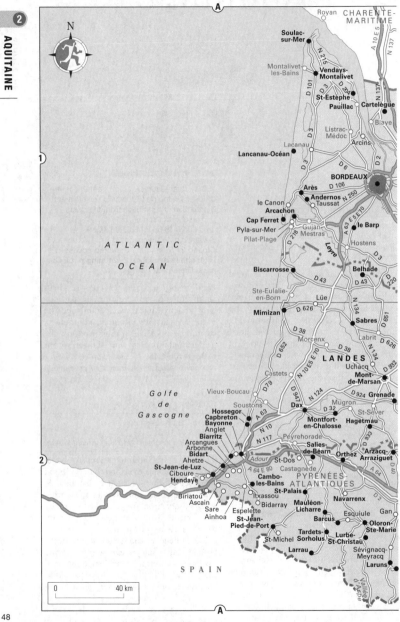

Royan CHARENTE-MARITIME

Soulac-sur-Mer

Montalivet-les-Bains
Vendays-Montalivet
St-Estèphe
Pauillac Cartelègue
Blaye
Listrac-Médoc
Arcins
Lacanau
Lancanau-Océan
BORDEAUX
Arès D 106
Andernos
le Canon Taussat
Arcachon
Cap Ferret le Barp
Pyla-sur-Mer Gujan-Mestras
Pilat-Plage Hostens

ATLANTIC
OCEAN

Biscarrosse Belhade
Ste-Eulalie-en-Born
Lüe
Mimizan Sabres
Morcenx
LANDES
Uchacq
Castets Mont-de-Marsan
Vieux-Boucau Mugron Grenade
Golfe
de
Gascogne Soustons St-Sever
Hossegor Dax
Capbreton Montfort-en-Chalosse Hagetmau
Bayonne
Anglet
Biarritz Peyrehorade
Arcangues Salies-de-Béarn Arzacq-
Arbonne Orthez Arraziguet
Bidart St-Dos
St-Jean-de-Luz Castagnède
Ciboure Cambo- PYRÉNÉES-
Hendaye les-Bains ATLANTIQUES
St-Palais
Biriatou Itxassou Navarrenx
Ascain Bidarray
Sare Mauléon- Gan
Ainhoa Espelette Licharre Esquiule
Barcus Oloron-
St-Jean- Tardets- Lurbé- Ste-Marie
Pied-de-Port Sorholus St-Christau
St-Michel Sévignacq-
Larrau Meyracq
Laruns

SPAIN

0 40 km

48

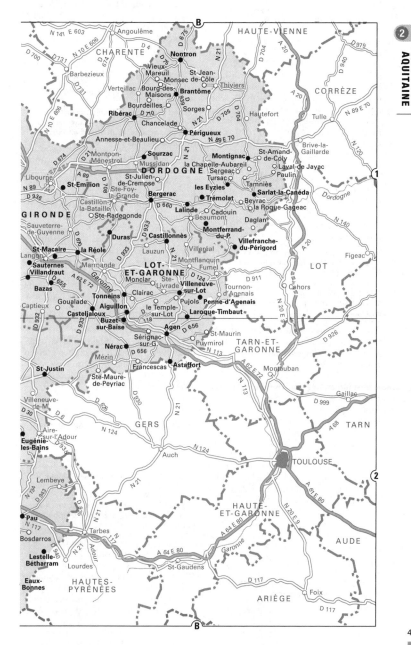

ⓣ and ⓕ 05.53.79.22.52
Closed *Wed; a fortnight in Jan.*

Set in a building typical of the region, close to the famous Abbaye des Automates, this friendly, welcoming restaurant specializes in dishes featuring goose (*aucos* in Provençal). Lunch is a speedy affair, but at dinner you have time to savour the local gastronomic delicacies – stuffed goose neck with herbs, goose and ham fillets, cutlets and so on – in carefully crafted dishes; lunch menu at €14 (except weekends), then others €20, €33 and €39. There's also a wide and interesting selection of wines and a delightful terrace, set between an authentic tobacco drying shed and the farm. *Free house liqueur offered to our readers on presentation of this guide.*

ⓒ 🍴 |●| **Restaurant Le Nostradamus**

40 rue des Nitiobriges; it's on the outskirts, on the way to Colayrac; take the road to Foulayronnes and turn right after the traffic lights – then follow the signs.
ⓣ 05.53.47.01.02
Closed *Sun evening; Mon.* **High chairs available.**

The famous medieval soothsayer supposedly lived here with his first wife (a local girl) – hence this restaurant's name. This all-wooden house is on the edge of town and you feel as if you're in the country – in summer you can have a meal on the terrace in the dappled shade of the trees. Inside, the décor is a successful balance between rustic and modern, and the staff are young and friendly. The chef makes extensive use of herbs and spices in both meat and fish dishes and the wide-ranging menu varies constantly, according to the seasonal ingredients available; weekday menu €15 and another at €20.50, or reckon on around €30–35 à la carte. *Free coffee offered to our readers on presentation of this guide.*

ⓒ 🍴 |●| **L'Atelier**

14 rue du Jeu-de-Paume.
ⓣ 05.53.87.89.22
Closed *Sat; Sun; first week of Jan.* **High chairs and games available.**

Everyone comes to this sparky place in the centre of town, run by a couple of live wires. Monsieur is very skilled in choosing his wines, while Madame is very attentive to her guests. There are

quite a lot of fish dishes on the menu – lunch menus €16–25, evening menus €23 and €29 – and the local speciality, duck, also features strongly. *Free house aperitif offered to our readers on presentation of this guide.*

ⓒ 🍴 |●| **Restaurant Mariottat**

25 rue Louis-Vivent; in the town centre.
ⓣ 05.53.77.99.77
Closed *Sun evening; Mon; Sat lunchtime; Feb school holidays; Christmas week.*
Disabled access. High chairs and games available. Car park.

Éric and Christiane Mariottat run a good restaurant in a fine mansion surrounded by parkland – just a stone's throw from the Jacobin monastery. The house has a warm atmosphere and a cosy décor with ceiling mouldings, splendid parquet and impressive chandeliers. Duck is the speciality of the region and the chef makes full use of it – his duck pâté *en croûte* is a real treat. Every morning he reinvents his dishes depending on what he's bought fresh at the market that day. Everything is wonderful, from the potato *millefeuille* with warm foie gras and truffle gravy to the suckling lamb medley with basil. There's a lunchtime menu for €20, except Sunday and public holidays, other menus €31–55, and a children's menu €13. In addition, there are over sixty items on the excellent wine list. *Free coffee offered to our readers on presentation of this guide.*

Sérignac-sur-Garonne
47310 (8km W)

ⓒ 🍴 🏠 |●| **Hôtel Le Prince Noir***

It's on the D199 in the direction of Mont-de-Marsan, after the bridge over the Garonne.
ⓣ 05.53.68.74.30 ⓕ 05.53.68.71.93
Closed *Fri evening.* **Disabled access. TV. High chairs available. Swimming pool. Car park.**

A wonderful place in a seventeenth-century convent. The Black Prince of the hotel's name was the son of Edward III, the Lieutenant-General of Aquitaine who laid waste to the southwest during the Hundred Years' War. You get to the courtyard through a turreted porch. With high ceilings and period furniture, the rooms at ground level and upstairs are all comfortable; doubles €56 with shower/wc or bath. Choose one of the menus

(€17.50–34), or you can eat carefully prepared regional dishes à la carte. It's worth booking because they often host business seminars, as well as providing accommodation for the Agen rugby team. Logis de France. *Free coffee offered to our readers on presentation of this guide.*

Aiguillon
47190

◎ ⚔ 🏠 |●| Hôtel-restaurant La Terrasse de l'Étoile**

8 cours Alsace-Lorraine.
☎05.53.79.64.64 📠05.53.79.46.48
Disabled access. TV. High chairs available. Swimming pool.

A superb little hotel built in white stone. There are eighteen rooms (€50 for a double) – all different but equally charming – and they're decorated in a vaguely Provençal style (iron bedsteads and country furniture). Particularly striking are the four rooms on the second floor, set in an old loft, with the brick walls exposed to view. Three separate dining rooms (all with plastic chairs, unfortunately) and a terrace overlooking the swimming pool. The menus start at €12 (except Sunday and public holidays) with others at €16–25, and change with the seasons. There's also a children's menu for €7; à la carte, reckon on around €20. They offer traditional fare such as fillets of mullet in cider (simply delicious), duck foie gras au torchon with prunes and ray's fin with grain mustard. Very good local wines, including a fairly dry, syrupy white Tariquet. Logis de France. *10% discount on the price of a room (Dec–Feb) or free coffee offered to our readers on presentation of this guide.*

Clairac
47320 (8km NE)

◎ ⚔ |●| L'Écuelle d'Or

22 rue Porte-Pinte; near the museums.
☎05.53.88.19.78 📠05.53.88.90.77
@écuelle.or@wanadoo.fr
Closed *Sat lunchtime; Sun evening; Mon; a week in Feb; Easter.*

A typical village house in rough brick with oak beams. The two dining rooms are relaxing and there's an inviting open log fire in the oldest one. Fresh produce

appears in imaginative dishes, for example salmon steak and asparagus from Fargues-sur-Ourboise, in springtime. They make everything in their own kitchens, including the bread, and also do more traditional fare such as duck *confit*. The weekday lunch menu is priced at €14 (two courses), with others €17–47; count on €48 à la carte with a plate of fine cheese. *Free house apéritif offered to our readers on presentation of this guide.*

Andernos-les-Bains
33510

◎ 🏠 Hôtel de la Côte d'Argent

180 bd. de la République; 300m from both the town centre and the beach.
☎05.56.03.98.58 📠05.56.03.98.68
Closed *Sun evening.* **Disabled access. TV.**

This newly redecorated roadside hotel, with ten well-equipped rooms, each decorated in one of the colours of the rainbow, offers the best value in the area; doubles with shower/wc or bath €42–65 (depending on the degree of comfort). There's a small flowery patio with a small fountain – the two rooms at garden level have the view. Breakfast includes fresh fruit and real orange juice. Credit cards not accepted.

Taussat
33148 (3km SE)

◎ ⚔ |●| Restaurant Les Fontaines

Port de plaisance de Taussat; take the D3.
☎05.56.82.13.86 📠05.57.70.23.43
Closed *Sun evening and Mon (out of season); a week in Feb; 3 weeks in Nov.* **High chairs available. Car park.**

This modern building near the marina doesn't exactly ooze charm, but it has a pleasant terrace on the edge of a pond where you can sit on a warm evening and enjoy the inspired cooking of chef Jean-Pascal Paubert. Try the scallops with Serraut or the roast langoustines in an aubergine marinade, followed by warm apple tart; menus €22–41 or reckon on €36 à la carte. Good wine list – not surprisingly, as the owner is chairman of the local cellarmasters' association. *Free house apéritif offered to our readers on presentation of this guide.*

Arcachon

33120

ⓒ 🎿 ♨ Hôtel Les Mimosas**

77 [bis] av. de la République; it's near Place de Verdun.
☎05.56.83.45.86 ℗05.56.22.53.40
🌐www.mimosas-hotel.com
Closed mid-Nov to Jan. **TV. Car park.**

This hotel is in a fine, large Arcachon house 500m from the ocean. Warm welcome and clean, neat rooms, with less expensive ones in a motel-like annexe; a few of them have recently been spruced up and doubles go for €40–75, depending on the season. *One free breakfast per room after the third consecutive night (except Nov–May) offered to our readers on presentation of this guide.*

ⓒ 🎿 |●| Le Pavillon d'Arguin

63 bd. du Général-Leclerc.
☎05.56.83.46.96
Closed Sun evening, Mon and Thurs (out of season); Mon (in season). **Disabled access. High chairs available.**

A young team (even the chef is only 26) goes to great lengths to offer both fast service and light, inventive dishes in the large blue-and-white dining room, with a special emphasis on seafood (although the grilled meat is also excellent). Menus at €16.50 and €32, not forgetting the copious spread at €59, which includes two starters, two main courses, cheese, dessert, wine and a liqueur. A safe bet in Arcachon. *Free coffee offered to our readers on presentation of this guide.*

Pyla-sur-Mer

33115 (5km S)

ⓒ ♨ Hôtel Maminotte**

3 Allée des Acacias; from Arcachon take the D217 or the D218 and it's 200m from the beach.
☎05.57.72.05.05 ℗05.57.72.06.06
TV.

This small, twelve-room hotel looks just like all the other houses in this peaceful part of town, lost among the pine trees and 100m from the ocean. Fresh, comfortable and pleasant rooms; doubles with shower/wc or bath at €46–90, depending on the season and degree of comfort – pricey but not atypical for this chic resort. The rooms on the first floor, all

with little balconies, are the most attractive – but also the most expensive. This is a friendly, welcoming hotel with a family atmosphere.

ⓒ ♨ |●| Hôtel-restaurant Côte du Sud**

4 av. du Figuier.
☎05.56.83.25.00 (restaurant) or
05.56.22.59.16 (hotel) ℗05.56.83.24.13
🌐www.cote-du-sud.fr
Closed Dec; Jan. **TV.**

This unpretentious, single-storey, blue-and-yellow hotel faces south (as you might guess) and is right by the sea. Eight comfortable, superbly decorated, themed rooms (Moroccan, Asian, etc) with shower/wc or bath are €59–115, depending on facilities and the season. All but one have a sea view and the Asian room, spread over 30 square metres, is particularly luxurious (and, obviously, the most expensive). The nice restaurant offers friendly service and is renowned for its speciality, mussels *Côte du Sud*, prepared Spanish-style. Set menus are €21.50–28, or it'll cost around €40 à la carte.

Arès

33740

ⓒ 🎿 ♨ |●| Le Saint-Éloi

11 bd. de l'Aérium; 10 min from the town centre on foot.
☎05.56.60.20.46 ℗05.56.60.10.37
www.le-saint-eloi.com
Closed Mon and Sun evening (out of season); Mon lunch (summer); 3 weeks in Jan. **TV.**

An attractively refurbished little hotel situated among the pines 500m from the beach. The clean, spacious double rooms are all named after exotic locations (Borneo, Bangkok, Zanzibar, etc) and decorated with sober elegance and refinement; €50–85, depending on the comfort and the season. Half board, at €127 per person, is compulsory in July and August. The pretty restaurant bedecked with plants has a particularly good reputation on account of its perfectly prepared dishes, good wines and competent service. Try the trio of duck liver or lamprey *à la Bordelaise*; lunchtime menu €14 (except Sun) and €24–39. *10% discount on the price of a room (except July–Aug) or free coffee offered to our readers on presentation of this guide.*

Arzacq-Arraziguet

64410

La Vieille Auberge

Place du Marcadieu; it's in the centre of the town.
☎05.59.04.51.31
Closed *New Year*. **High chairs available.**

A friendly old house with an old-style dining room and a village bistro with formica tables and a TV beaming the world in. The new chef is full of youthful energy and an equal measure of creativity. Try his stuffed, filleted sardines or his pan-fried mussels – tasty, generously served and inexpensive; menus start from €10 (including wine), others €14–25 and fantastic fry-ups for €13–25. An excellent place, and ideal stopover after a visit to the Maison du Jambon in Bayonne, as ham features heavily on the menu. *Free house apéritif or coffee offered to our readers on presentation of this guide.*

Astaffort

47220

Michel Latrille***

5–7 pl. de la Craste; in the direction of Auch.
☎05.53.47.20.40 ☎05.53.47.10.38
ⓦ www.latrille.com
Hotel closed *Sun evening (except July–Aug)*. **Restaurant closed** *Sun evening; Mon; Tues lunchtime*. **Closed** *a week in May; 3 weeks in Nov*. **Disabled access. TV. Pay car park.**

Michel Latrille is passionate about using high-quality produce for his dishes and experiments with different flavours. The results are excellent: langoustine ravioli with truffles, duck *confit* pie with thyme sauce and his famous *moelleux au chocolat* dessert. Menus start at €22 (except Sunday and public holidays), others at €35 or €55, with a children's menu at €12; à la carte, reckon on €52. There are also fourteen very comfortable rooms (€62–122 for a double), individually decorated in bright but subtly harmonious Provençal colours by the owner's wife. No. 6, which has a private balcony, costs €110 and breakfast is €10. *Free coffee offered to our readers on presentation of this guide.*

Barcus

64130

Chilo***

Centre.
☎05.59.28.90.79
ⓦ www.hotel.chilo.com
Closed *Sun evening, Mon and Tues morning (1 Nov–15 March); 3 weeks in Jan*. **Disabled access. TV. Swimming pool. Car park.**

A popular place on the borders of the Béarn and Basque country. It has been extended but hasn't lost its soul, and it's still family-run with attractive, nicely appointed rooms at €51–85 with shower/wc or bath (less expensive out of season). Menus, priced at €28–62, feature unusual, original cooking: fillet of Soule beef with hot foie gras and traditional lamb sweetbreads with white *piperade*; or reckon on €50 à la carte. Keep a space for the speciality desserts, *macaron à l'Izarra* and a *charlotte* made with ewe's milk.

Restaurant Chez Sylvain

Place du Fronton; take the D24.
☎05.59.28.92.11
Closed *Thurs; first fortnight in May.*

You'll get a charming welcome in this family-run restaurant, which has been going for nearly twenty years and is worth going out of your way for. It's like a country inn, and has a mainly local clientele. The country-style cooking is prepared with a great deal of care and taste. Menus €11, €15 and €20 feature dishes including roast lamb, lamb sweetbreads with parsley, delicious omelettes and an excellent home-made *garbure* (Béarnaise vegetable broth). Credit cards not accepted. *Free coffee offered to our readers on presentation of this guide.*

Barp (Le)

33114

Le Résinier**

Route de Bayonne; 36km to the south of Bordeaux.
☎05.56.88.60.07 ☎05.56.88.67.37
Closed *Sun evening, except July–Aug; New Year holiday*. **TV.**

Located in the heart of the village, this small hotel-restaurant has recently been nicely refurbished. There are some ten rooms (€46 for a double with shower or bath) with a colour scheme that manages to be sweet and tart at the same time. The double glazing proves a blessing in the rooms overlooking the N10. In the restaurant, the food is resolutely regional, and none the worse for it, with menus at €14 (weekdays), and €19–45; you can eat on the terrace or in a charmingly old-fashioned dining room. Good taste is the watchword here, and, to top it all, the service is charming as well. All in all, a heartwarming place. Logis de France. *10% discount on the price of a room offered to our readers on presentation of this guide.*

Bayonne
64100

@ ☎ Hôtel des Arceaux

26 rue du Port-Neuf; in the old town.
☎05.59.25.15.53 ℗05.59.25.64.75
ⓦwww.hotel-arceaux.com
Closed *Sun.*

This simple, but attractive, hotel avoids uniformity in its pretty new rooms by decorating them blue, yellow or green, and in some cases incorporating a theme. They are not big but are expertly designed, with doubles priced at €39–51. The enormous lounge has a homely feel, with its glossy red and orangey-yellow walls, old furniture and black Persian cat. You'll get an effusive welcome from Frédéric and Sébastien and there are bicycles available for rent.

@ ☎ |●| Adour Hôtel

13 pl. Sainte-Ursule.
☎05.59.55.11.31 ℗05.59.55.86.40.
TV. Pay car park.

The nearest to a boarding house that you'll find in Bayonne; it is small, with just twelve rooms (although the biggest ones can sleep four people), at €50–80, depending on the size; half board €23 per person. It has recently been taken over by a new young owner, a former fashion stylist, who has redecorated everything in local style and in vivid colours and created a friendly atmosphere in this doll's house setting. At night he also cooks up dinner for the hotel's guests (menu €18) – he only likes cooking for small numbers. In other words, he comes from the mould of the old-style hotelier, eager to make his guests feel at home, so booking is essential.

@ 🎜 ☎ |●| Hôtel Loustau***

1 pl. de la République; it's near pont Saint-Esprit on the river bank.
☎05.59.55.08.08 ℗05.59.55.69.36
ⓦwww.hotel-loustau.com
Restaurant closed *Sat and Sun (15 Oct–30 March).* **Hotel/restaurant closed** *Jan.*
Disabled access. TV. High chairs available.

On the River Adour, with an uninterrupted view of old Bayonne and the Pyrenees, this 200-year-old hotel offers clean, well-sound-proofed, excellent-value rooms at €77–105 for a double with bath or shower; breakfast €8. The restaurant offers specialities such as *piperade* with dried duck breast and Serrano ham, *carpaccio* of beef or duck, scallop stew, roast suckling lamb and Spanish-style cod on set menus (€16–24), or reckon on €35 à la carte. *10% discount on the price of a room (Oct–May) offered to our readers on presentation of this guide.*

@ |●| Bodega Ibaia

49 quai Jauréguiberry; in the old town.
Closed *Sun (except bullfight days and high season); Mon.* **Open** *until late (11pm or later).*

Locals of all ages can be found here, enjoying unpretentious regional food both on the terrace and in the dining room. It gets particularly lively at night, with the arrival of the loyal regular customers. Start with a few of the tasty and original tapas at the bar, washed down with a good rosé, then go on to something more substantial (providing the food has not run out – everything is bought on a day-to-day basis here). Reckon on €7–9 per dish and there's a fine selection of wines, particularly Spanish ones.

@ 🎜 |●| Le Chistera

42 rue Port-Neuf.
☎ and ℗05.59.59.25.93
Closed *Mon, Tues and Wed evenings out of season; a fortnight in May.*

Jean-Pierre manages to combine being a restaurateur and a professional *pelota* player. The food in this local canteen-style place is typical of Bayonne, with fabulous tripe and fish, and daily specials chalked up on the blackboard. If you see pig's trotters, *louvines* (wild bream) or Basque-style tripe, order them at once. Prices are reasonable – there's a €14.50 menu or you'll spend around €24 à la carte – and service is friendly. *Free house liqueur offered to our readers on presentation of this guide.*

⬢ |●| Le Bayonnais

38 av. quai des Corsaires.
☎05.59.25.61.19 📠05.59.59.00.64
Closed *Mon; Sun evening out of season; second fortnight in June; 3 weeks in Dec.* **TV. Pay car park. Disabled access.**

Fresh, tasty food, perfectly produced; portions that make "generous" sound mean; quantity that equals quality. Try roast milk-fed lamb, lamb pie or prawns with the perfect amount of garlic. The weekday €15 menu is a filling three courses (but no wine) and you should pay about €30 per person for a meal à la carte. The wine list has a selection from different regions with bottles for €15. It's a friendly neighbourhood favourite, with a pleasant, rustic dining room and a waterside terrace.

⬢ ⅍ |●| Restaurant El Asador

Place Montaut; it's near the cathedral.
☎05.59.59.08.57
Closed *Sun evening (except when there's a bullfight); Mon; 20 Dec–6 Jan; 13 June–4 July.*

Set on the Montaut square, this ten-table restaurant specializes in grills over the open fire – *asador* is the Spanish word for a grill chef, and the man in question is Maria-Jésus. The line-caught fish is splendid, particularly the cod with garlic and the sea bream *à l'espagnole*. For starters, ask for a *para-pica*, a selection of tasty morsels. There's a weekday menu €19.10, or you'll pay about €35 à la carte. *Free house apéritif offered to our readers on presentation of this guide.*

⬢ |●| Auberge du Cheval Blanc

68 rue Bourg-Neuf; it's near the Bannat and Basque museums.
☎05.59.59.01.33 📠05.59.59.52.26
Closed *Sat lunch; Sun evening; Mon (open Mon evening in Aug); Feb school holiday; first week in July; first week in Aug.* **Disabled access.**

Rather than following the menus, you'll have a much more interesting meal if you allow the chef to guide your gastronomic journey and choose his daily or seasonal dishes; you might be tempted by the cream of chestnut and cep soup with *xingar*, or the *louvine* (wild bream) with salt. He also cooks "peasant" dishes such as ham bone *xamango* served with wholesome mashed potatoes and glamorized with truffle *jus*. Desserts are sublime, in particular his grapefruit and grape soup with figs, and

what's more, the setting is cosy and there's a family atmosphere. With a weekday menu at €25, another at €34, or around €55 à la carte, it's worth putting aside part of your holiday budget to eat here.

Bazas

33430

⬢ |●| Restaurant des Remparts

Espace Mauvezin; near the cathedral.
☎ and 📠05.56.25.95.24
Closed *Sun evening; Mon.* **Disabled access. High chairs available.**

Park near the cathedral and walk down the alleyway running off the square to reach this restaurant. It's superbly situated next to the Mairie, on the *brèche de Bazas*, overlooking the Sultan's garden. You can enjoy these quite exceptional surroundings from the terrace when the weather is fine. The very classic décor is understated, and the cuisine is inspired, using quality produce like Bazas beef or Grignol capon. Set menus, €14 (weekday lunchtimes) and €18–29, feature semi-cooked foie gras, grilled rib-eye steak, cabbage stuffed with duck and prune and Armagnac mousse. À la carte – reckon on around €35 – there is always pig's trotter, prepared in a variety of ways.

Goualade

33840 (16.5km SE)

⬢ ⅍ |●| L'Auberge Gasconne

From Bazas take the D12: it's on the high street, opposite the church.
☎05.56.65.81.77 **Closed** *Mon; Sun evening; 16 Aug–5 Sept.*

This inn is in the middle of nowhere, deep in the woods across the road from an old village church. Inside, though, it is unexpectedly smart and comfortable, and air-conditioned too. A group of regulars, including lorry drivers and electricity-board employees, flock here for good cooking and low prices. No one would dream of "reinventing" local dishes here. The simple country food comes from good old recipes and is substantial, filling and unpretentious. Large slices of Bayonne ham, wood-pigeon stew, pressed foie gras with leeks, *confit* of turkey, duck, pork and wild boar casserole. Set menu €10 (including wine and coffee) and around €18 à la carte.

Belhade

40410

◎ 🌿 |●| L'Auberge du Chêne-
Pascal (Restaurant Euloge)

☎ 05.58.07.72.01
Closed Sun evening; Mon; Tues evening.
High chairs available.

A charming little inn with friendly staff,
situated oppposite an equally charming
church. The quality of the tasty meat
and fish dishes on the weekday lunchtime menu (€16) makes it worth the
detour, the full flavours of the ingredients
brought out in the cooking process; other
menus €24–38. One of the best restaurants in the Haut-Pays Landais. *Free house
apéritif offered to our readers on presentation
of this guide.*

Bergerac

24100

◎ 🌿 🏠 Hôtel de France**

18 pl. Gambetta
☎ 05.53.57.11.61 ℗ 05.53.61.25.70
🌐 www.hoteldefrance-bergerac.com
Closed Jan. **TV. Swimming pool.**

This recently reopened hotel, with parking spaces opposite, offers a very friendly
welcome. The large, comfortable rooms
(€41–55 for a double) have been charmingly refurbished and are fully equipped
(satellite TV, mini-bar, hair-dryer, etc). The
ones overlooking the street are soundproofed and air-conditioned (there is a
small supplement). *One free breakfast per
room offered to our readers on presentation of
this guide.*

◎ 🌿 🏠 |●| Hôtel-restaurant La
Flambée***

153 av. Pasteur; it's 2km north of Bergerac on
the N21, in the direction of Périgueux.
☎ 05.53.57.52.33 ℗ 05.53.61.07.57
🌐 www.laflambee.com
Restaurant closed Sun evening, Mon and
Sat lunchtime out of season. **TV. High chairs
available. Swimming pool. Car park.**

This hotel is on the edge of the
Pecharmant hills set in substantial gardens screened by trees with a tennis
court and a swimming pool – so it's
as quiet as anything. The twenty or so
individualized rooms are split between a
large Périgord residence and a summer

house; each has a small terrace and are
priced €55–85 for a double depending on the season. The restaurant is the
place to be seen on the Bergerac circuit,
thanks to its opulent décor and the finely
cooked local dishes on the set menus,
€16–31, so it's best to book. À la carte
dishes include grilled duck foie gras and
beef-fillet pastry with foie gras. There's a
pleasant terrace near the swimming pool
for when the weather is fine and themed
evenings in summer. *10% discount on the
price of a room offered to our readers on presentation of this guide.*

◎ 🌿 |●| Restaurant La Sauvagine

18–20 rue Eugène-Leroy.
☎ 05.53.57.06.97
Closed Sun evening; Mon; Wed evening; end
of June. **High chairs available.**

Modern air-conditioned restaurant that
serves traditional, well-prepared cuisine
at honest prices; weekday lunchtime
menu at €12.20, then others at €20–45.
Go for fish such as lamprey from the
Bordeaux region, seafood or game in
season, and make room for the delicious
desserts. The clientele is classy but the
welcome is friendly and genuine. *Free
house apéritif offered to our readers on presentation of this guide.*

◎ |●| Restaurant L'Enfance de
Lard

Rue Pélissière.
☎ 05.53.57.52.88 ℗ 05.53.57.52.88
📧 lenfancedelard@yahoo.com
Closed lunchtime; Tues evening (except in
summer); late Sept–early Oct.

A charming restaurant on the first floor
of a twelfth-century house on one of
Bergerac's finest squares. It's small and soon
fills up, so it's essential to book. It
has a warm, intimate atmosphere, a fantastic view of the medieval church and
classical music playing in the background.
The remarkable regional cuisine from
the southwest includes quality meats
grilled over vines in the superb fireplace,
Sarlat-style potatoes which melt in the
mouth, rack of lamb with mint, ceps in
parsley vinaigrette, grilled sirloin of steak
pricked with cloves of garlic and foie
gras served with peaches in the summer
or lentils in winter. Helpings are generous on the menu (€25) and à la carte
(around €35) – not cheap, but worth

every centime, and the kitchen is open from 7pm until late.

Saint-Julien-de-Crempse

24140 (12km N)

⊛ 🚲 🏠 |O| **Le Manoir du Grand Vignoble*****

From Bergerac take the N21 then the D107.
☎05.53.24.23.18
ⓦwww.manoirdugrandvignoble.com
Closed 15 Nov–31 March. **TV. High chairs available. Swimming pool. Car park.**

A very fine seventeenth-century manor house – also an equestrian centre – in beautiful countryside. It's a luxury establishment, with enormous, charming rooms, costing €58–110, depending on the size and the season. The rooms vary in size but all are very well equipped. Facilities include tennis courts, heated swimming pool and fitness centre. The restaurant offers set menus for €23–45; reckon on €38 à la carte. Try dishes such as terrine of foie gras with dried fruit, pan-fried veal served with baby vegetables and chocolate soufflé. *10% discount on the room rate offered to our readers on presentation of this guide.*

Port-Sainte-Foy

33220 (24km W)

⊛ 🏠 |O| **L'Escapade**

Route des Chaumes, La Grâce; take the D936 to Sainte-Foy-la-Grande, then go 2km north on the D708; or take the D32. Just after the blue bridge, take the first left, then follow the signposts.
☎05.53.24.22.79 ⓕ05.53.57.45.05
ⓦwww.escapade-dordogne.com
Closed end of Oct to end of Jan. **Restaurant open** only for dinner (except Sun evening out of season) and Sunday lunch. **Swimming pool. Car park.**

The approach through the ugly shopping precinct is unpromising, but this comfortable little hotel-restaurant in a seventeenth-century house is an oasis of calm in unspoilt surroundings. A dozen delightful rooms priced at €48–52, depending on the season, some set in the attic with exposed beams and stone walls. Beautiful rustic dining room serving menus at €18–28.50. Good service, and value for money unbettered in the region, which has made it very popular with British and Dutch

tourists – so booking is essential. Logis de France.

Biarritz

64200

⊛ 🏠 **Hôtel Palym***

7 rue du Port-Vieux; it's 100m from the sea.
☎05.59.24.16.56 ⓕ05.59.24.96.12
ⓦwww.le-palmarium.com
TV.

A well-maintained old hotel with a décor that strikes a nice balance between past and present, cosy and modern. A little winding staircase leads to the neat and tidy rooms, some of which have been modernized; doubles are €42–55 with shower/wc or bath, depending on season. The rooms at the rear are quieter than those overlooking the nice (but noisy) rue du Port-Vieux. There are also some rooms sleeping three or four. Half board is available; you eat at the *Palmarium*, next door, which is run by the brother of the *patron*.

⊛ 🚲 🏠 **Hôtel Le Saint-Charles****

21 av. Reine-Victoria; 350m from the beach and 500m from the city centre.
☎05.59.24.10.54 ⓕ05.59.24.56.74
ⓦwww.hotelstcharles.com
Closed 15 Nov–15 Dec. **TV. Pay car park.**

A haven just outside the centre of town, very prettily done out in pink. If you like peace and quiet, greenery and flowers, you'll find it hard to leave – especially after breakfast in the lovely garden. Thirteen freshly refurbished rooms with period furniture; doubles are €50–70 with shower/wc and €65–100 with bath/wc. Some single rooms at €43–52 and quadruples €80–110. Well worth going out of your way for, although the welcome could be warmer. *One free breakfast per person after the third consecutive night, offered to our readers on presentation of this guide.*

⊛ 🚲 🏠 **Hôtel Maïtagaria****

34 av. Carnot; it's 500m from the sea.
☎05.59.24.26.65 ⓕ05.59.24.27.37
ⓦwww.hotel-maitagaria.com
TV.

You'd do well to book at this place, which attracts a host of regulars. It's a charming town house, opposite the public gardens, offering quiet, comfortable rooms with great bathrooms and a very pleasant flower-filled garden. Everything is beautifully decorated, and all rooms have a view; doubles with shower/wc or bath for €53–60. This could well be the best place in Biarritz, especially if you get room 16, which has its own terrace. *One free breakfast per person (except in summer) offered to our readers on presentation of this guide.*

◎ ⚶ ⚘ Hôtel La Romance**

6 allée des Acacias; from the centre, take avenue du Maréchal-Foch, then avenue Kennedy. It's near the racecourse.
℡05.59.41.25.65 ℻05.59.41.25.83
℮hotel.la.romance@wanadoo.fr
Closed *15 Jan–1 March.* **TV.**

A perfect romantic hideaway a little off the beaten track in a residential area. The ten rooms of this huge house are attractively decorated with a floral theme and feature painted wood and thick duvets. Half of them look straight out onto the garden. Doubles with shower/wc or bath cost €56–105, including breakfast. *Free coffee offered to our readers on presentation of this guide.*

◎ ⚶ ⚘ Hôtel Montpensier

36 rue Montpensier
℡05.59.27.42.72 ℻05.59.27.70.95
Car park.

This small, slightly quirky hotel, set apart from the bustle of the city centre, is in the process of being very skilfully restored, taking on new life through the application of colour and light, as well as a greater degree of comfort. Doubles (with pretty bathrooms) cost €65–74, buffet breakfast €7. Service is extremely friendly and there are free parking spaces available in the courtyard. *10% discount on the price of a room (at weekends) offered to our readers on presentation of this guide.*

◎ ⚘ Inter-Hôtel de Gramont***

3 pl. Gramont
℡05.59.27.84.04 ℻05.59.27.62.23
℮www.hotelgramont.fr
Closed *a fortnight at Christmas.* **TV. Car park.**

Despite its somewhat forbidding façade, this is one of the few really inviting, highly professional, three-star hotels in Pau, set in an old staging post with a superb view of the town. The recently renovated rooms are comfortable, well equipped and sound-proofed; some of them have air conditioning and are €66–84 for a double.

◎ ⚘ Le Château du Clair de Lune***

48 av. Alan-Seeger; it's near the train station on the Arbonne road.
℡05.59.41.53.20 ℻05.59.41.53.29
℮www.chateauduclairdelune.com
TV. Car park.

A secluded early-twentieth-century residence, splendidly decorated in Art Deco style and set in wonderful flower-filled grounds with landscaped gardens. The enormous rooms are stylishly decorated, painted in muted tones and furnished with antiques. Doubles in the château cost €70–145, depending on the season; there are other rooms in the hunting lodge and one room sleeping four at €120. A dream of a place where you can relax away from the hectic life on the coast so reservations are advisable.

◎ ⚘ Maison Garnier***

29 rue Gambetta.
℡05.59.01.60.70 ℻05.59.07.60.80
℮www.hotel-biarritz.com
Closed *5–20 Jan; 10–20 Dec.* **TV.**

The only three-star hotel in the town centre near all the sights. This is where the owner decided to settle after a ten-year odyssey around the world. There are only seven rooms and they've all been smartly decorated and well updated. Go for no.5 if you want a romantic little nook up in the roof, from where you can see the solid metal column that supports the whole house. No. 3, on the other hand, has heaps of space. Rooms range from €80 to €120, depending on the size and season, and breakfast costs €9. It's a popular place and essential to book.

◎ |◉| Les Terrasses Beaumont

Place Beaumont; right at the end of the boulevard des Pyrénées, at the entrance to the park.
℡05.59.11.21.07
Open *every day, for lunch and dinner.*

This terrace in front of the Beaumont Palace is a favourite meeting place for the locals in fine weather (almost all year round, here). The brilliant young chef from *Chez Ruffet*, Stéphane Carrade, was responsible for devising the enticing repertoire of dishes. It's the ideal place for a quick lunch, with the set menu at €9.50 and another menu at €15; à la carte, the dishes cost €15–20.

© |●| Le Pas Sage

30 av. Édouard-VII
☎05.59.22.59.55
Closed Sun; Mon evening; Tues evening out of season.

The downstairs shop-cum-café glows with bright colours, ideally suited to a breakfast or teabreak, while upstairs, the lights are dimmed and the tables set for a simple but modern and aromatic meal. Don't miss the "Ballade des gens heureux", a dessert created in honour of Gérard Lenormain, the brother of one of the two owners and presiding spirit of this restaurant. There's a weekday lunchtime menu at €12.50 and a summer menu €18. Sunday brunch is served 4–7pm and tables d'hôtes (available dinnertime only) cost €28.

© ⚘ |●| Le Crabe-Tambour

49 rue d'Espagne.
☎05.59.23.24.53
Closed Mon; mid-Oct to mid-Nov.

The chef was formerly responsible for the cuisine on board the *Jaureguibery*, a cruiser that featured in a successful French film starring Jean Rochefort. His voyages have left him with a taste for subtle culinary combinations, such as free-range Landes chicken accompanied by grilled Laotian mango, while Spanish influences are discernible in the fish dishes; menus €15–23 or about €28 à la carte. A restrained use of spices, a love of simplicity and a crew of beaming waitresses are the final touches that make everything shipshape. Booking is essential. *Free house apéritif offered to our readers on presentation of this guide.*

© ⚘ |●| Le Saint Amour

26 rue Gambetta.
☎05.59.24.19.64
Closed Sun; Mon out of season; second fortnight in Feb; June; Nov.

A Lyonnais bistro in exile – this place is a real find. Besides which, they serve lots of wines from small Lyonnais vineyards. The *andouille* and sausage come from the town too but there are also inventive Basque specialities on the menu: sautéed scallops with red peppers and bacon, fresh cod with creamed lentils, *andouillette à la ficelle*

with creamed potatoes. The *moelleux au chocolat* is a very special dessert. There are weekday lunchtime menus at €16–18, or à la carte you'll pay about €32. It's frequented by lots of people who know a good thing when they eat it. *Free house liqueur offered to our readers on presentation of this guide.*

© |●| Restaurant Henri IV

18 rue Henri-IV
☎05.59.27.54.43
Closed Wed lunch; Sat lunch; Sun evening; a week mid-Sept; Christmas school holiday.

The latest haute-cuisine arrival in the old city centre, run by a couple with a gift for reviving culinary traditions. Patrice Schildowski, who served his apprenticeship with Bocuse and other top chefs, works with only the freshest ingredients and takes his time in preparing his dishes. This meticulousness is obviously reflected in the prices, if you succumb to the temptations offered à la carte, but there are also reasonably priced menus at €19 and €26. Eat on the charming little terrace in summer, or by the cosy stone fireplace in winter.

©© |●| Le Sissinou

5 av. du Maréchal-Foch
☎05.59.22.51.50
Closed: Sun; Mon; Feb school holiday; Nov school holiday; a week in early July.

Vaguely Zen-style décor, best appreciated at night, but this is more than just a trendy showcase. Its success is based on solid achievements, and before too long the chef, Michel Cassou-Debat, may be obliged to find larger premises. He has little assistance in the kitchen, and not much more in the dining room, but still manages to produce adventurous dishes such as shellfish capuccino with egg *brouillarde* and marbled cake of leek, foie gras and oxtail, and offers a single menu at €38. It is advisable to book in advance for dinner or any weekend meal.

Anglet
64600 (3km E)

© 🏠 |●| ⚘ Auberge de Jeunesse Gazte Etxea

19 rte. des Vignes, Chiberta area (northeast). Take the blue line no. 9 bus outside Biarritz station; it stops right outside.

☎05.59.58.70.00 ⊜05.59.58.70.07
⊛www.fuaj.org
Closed Nov to end Feb. **Reception open**
8.30am–12.30pm and 6–10pm. **TV. Car park.**

A large, friendly and comfortable youth hostel, just ten minutes' walk from the sea. Spotless dormitories with four, five or six beds from €16 per person, including breakfast. Booking (by post) is only accepted for full-board stays of at least a week. You can cook your own food in the evening (except May–Oct), the cafeteria is open 7–9.30pm in the high season, and there's no curfew. The hostel organizes a variety of sporting and cultural activities, particularly watersports. It organizes week-long courses of surfing and free-surf, and there are also facilities nearby for rafting, diving, golf, tennis, rollerskating, horse riding, *fronton* and *pelota* – as well as a Scottish pub with live music at night.

Arcangues
64200 (4km SE)

☜ ⅍ |●| Auberge du Trinquet

It's in the village.
☎05.59.43.09.64 ⊜05.59.43.15.10
Closed Mon; Tues out of season; Feb; March.

Healthy and solid cuisine using fresh local produce. The dining room, set in a modern building, looks over the *trinquet*, the playing area, where the players test their skills; it's fun to watch them expending so many calories while you enjoy from the copious €24 menu terrine of foie gras, broiled mussels, stuffed crab, *croustillant* of boned pig's trotter or calf's head. Individual dishes are priced around €12. There's a magnificent shady terrace and in the evening, the bar is abuzz with local players. *Free house liqueur offered to our readers on presentation of this guide.*

Arbonne
64210 (5km SE)

☜ ⅍ 🏠 |●| Eskualduna**

Take the D255 from Biarritz.
☎05.59.41.95.41 ⊜05.59.41.88.16
Closed Sun evening. **TV. Car park.**

Jolly place with a lively bar where customers, most of them factory workers, are welcomed into the big dining room. Jacky, the owner, keeps the conversation going between courses, commenting on the

latest rugby match or chatting away while cooking up the sauces. He's as robust as the regional cuisine on his set menus (€11–22). The place also has double rooms with shower or bath for €36–45. *10% discount on the price of a room offered to our readers on presentation of this guide.*

☜ ⅍ 🏠 |●| Laminak***

Route de Saint-Pée.
☎05.59.41.95.40
⊛www.hotel-laminak.com
Disabled access. TV. High chairs available. Car park.

A nice quiet spot which isn't miles away from everywhere, offering clean rooms, fresh décor and good facilities. It's comfortably located in a thoroughly renovated Basque house with a terrace and surrounded by a garden. The owner moved here from a health spa, so he's expert at looking after the inner you. Doubles cost €64–96; those at €64 are on the small side, while nos. 10, 11 and 12 have a private terrace giving onto the garden. Breakfast is served on the veranda or in the garden facing the mountains – sheer heaven. If you fancy a round of golf, the hotel has an arrangement with the local links which offer discounts to guests. A charming place only minutes from the sea. *10% discount on the price of a room (except during school holidays) offered to our readers on presentation of this guide.*

Ahetze
64210 (8km S)

☜ |●| Hiriartia

8 pl. du Fronton; take the D255 in the direction of Arbonne, then turn right onto the D655.
☎ and ⊜05.59.41.95.22
Closed Mon in season; Wed out of season; mid-Dec to mid-Jan.

A beautiful inn offering a warm welcome and pleasant service. You go through a bar which can't have changed for sixty years: dark beams, antique wood and patronized by practically the whole village. The dining room lies beyond and leads through to the terrace and the garden. Typical cuisine without frills – menus €16 and €23, or around €25 à la carte – and generous (very generous) portions: peppers stuffed with cod and crab, monkfish kebabs with *beurre blanc* and omelettes with ceps.

Bidart

64210

ஊ ⚲ ൝ La Villa L'Arche***

Chemin Camboenea; 200m from the town centre.
℡ 05.59.51.65.95 ℻ 05.59.51.65.99.
ⓦ www.villalarche.com
Closed *mid-Nov to mid-Feb.* **TV. High chairs available. Car park.**

A pretty Basque-style house converted into a three-star hotel. The eight rooms (six with large bay windows opening onto the sea) are tastefully decorated and boast large bathrooms; doubles cost €90–260, depending on the season. Continental breakfast is extra (€12–20), and there is an additional charge for a pet (€12 per day). The hotel gardens, complete with teak furniture, lead directly down to the beach; there is also a terrace, with deckchairs offering a fine view of the surfers in the ocean. In bad weather, you can still while away the time in comfort, nestled in a sofa beside the log fire on the veranda. Booking highly recommended.

Biscarrosse

40600

ஊ ⚲ Hôtel Le Saint Hubert**

588 av. Latecoere; it's 500m from the centre of the village, near the lake.
℡ 05.58.78.09.99 ℻ 05.58.78.79.37
ⓦ www.biscarrosse.com/saint-hubert
Disabled access. TV. High chairs available. Car park.

It's just outside the village, but you feel as if you're way out in the country – the summer hordes simply don't come here. You can stretch out with a book in the garden, brimming with scented flowers. They put out tables for tea or breakfast. Double rooms cost €40–64 with bath or shower, according to season. You can order simple food in advance for around €8. The most attractive feature, however, is the owner's expansive welcome, and he'll give you good tips for your meals or on places to see – and, if you've got a bike, the best paths to follow.

ஊ ൝ ⚲ |●| Hôtel La Caravelle**

5314 rte. des Lacs, quartier ISPE, lac Nord. On the bank of Lac Cazaux on the way to the golf course.

℡ 05.58.09.82.67 ℻ 05.58.09.82.18
ⓦ www.lacaravelle.fr
Closed *Mon lunchtime (except in July and Aug); Tues lunchtime; 1 Nov to 14 Feb.* **TV. High chairs available. Car park.**

A fine, large building in a pleasant setting on the banks of the lake with a small beach. The whole place is painted white, and all the rooms have a little balcony or terrace looking out onto the water; doubles €60–80 with shower/wc or bath, half board €50–55. There's also a villa to rent in summer, which sleeps four. A lovely restful place – though the frogs may disturb some guests on spring nights. The restaurant serves good local food on menus €15–37, with dishes such as veal sweetbreads in Jurançon wine, leg of duck with pepper sauce, eel *fricassée* and prawns in Caravelle sauce. Logis de France. *10% discount on the price of a room (except weekends and public holidays from 15 June to 15 Sept) or free house apéritif offered to our readers on presentation of this guide.*

ஊ |●| Restaurant Chez Camette

532 av. Latécoère. 500m from the town centre, going towards the Hydro-aviation Museum.
℡ 05.58.78.12.78 ℻ 05.58.78.12.78
Closed *Fri evening and Sat out of season; Christmas to 1 Jan.* **High chairs available.**

A popular, welcoming and quaint little inn with white walls and red shutters. The food is simple, generously served, and unpretentious: set menus €10 (except Sun), and then €16 and €23. Dishes include thick soup, mussels in white wine and *escalope* in cream sauce. Don't miss out on the house speciality – duck breast grilled over the open fire. Credit cards are not accepted.

Bordeaux

33000
See map on pp.62–63

ஊ ⚲ Hôtel Bristol

4 rue Bouffard. **Map B2-3**
℡ 05.56.81.85.01 ℻ 05.56.81.24.72
ⓦ www.hotel-bordeaux.com

TV. Pay car park.

This is part of a hotel group comprising the *Hôtel de Lyon*, the *Hôtel d'Amboise* and the *Hôtel La Boétie*, each of them in quiet, centrally located streets in a pedestrian

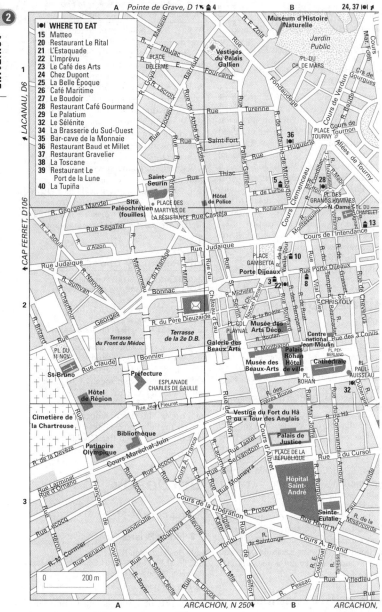

❷

⦿ WHERE TO EAT
15 Matteo
20 Restaurant Le Rital
21 L'Estaquade
22 L'Imprévu
23 Le Café des Arts
24 Chez Dupont
25 La Belle Époque
26 Café Maritime
27 Le Boudoir
28 Restaurant Café Gourmand
29 Le Palatium
32 Le Sélénite
34 La Brasserie du Sud-Ouest
35 Bar-cave de la Monnaie
36 Restaurant Baud et Millet
37 Restaurant Gravelier
38 La Toscane
39 Restaurant Le
    Port de la Lune
40 La Tupiña

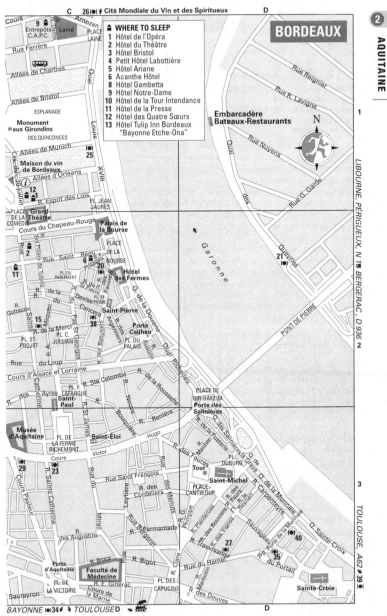

BORDEAUX

26 |●| ✦ Cité Mondiale du Vin et des Spiritueux

🛏 **WHERE TO SLEEP**
1 Hôtel de l'Opéra
2 Hôtel du Théâtre
3 Hôtel Bristol
4 Petit Hôtel Labottière
5 Hôtel Ariane
6 Acanthe Hôtel
8 Hôtel Gambetta
9 Hôtel Notre-Dame
10 Hôtel de la Tour Intendance
11 Hôtel de la Presse
12 Hôtel des Quatre Sœurs
13 Hôtel Tulip Inn Bordeaux
   "Bayonne Etche-Ona"

LIBOURNE, PÉRIGUEUX, N 89 BERGERAC, D 936

TOULOUSE, A62 ⬈ 39 |●|

BAYONNE |●|34 ✦ 🚍 TOULOUSE D ⬊ 🚢

63

zone. Rooms cost €24–46 depending on the hotel and the size of the room. They are all clean and well maintained, each with a shower, toilet and television. It's advisable to book because this is the best value in town and attracts a lot of regulars.

⊛ 🏃 🛗 Hôtel Notre-Dame**

36 rue Notre-Dame; near the Saint-Louis church. **Off map C1-9**
ⓣ05.56.52.88.24 ⓕ05.56.79.12.67
ⓦwww.hotelnotredame.free.fr
TV. Pay car park.

At the heart of Les Chartrons district, which used to be full of wine merchants, this stone-fronted nineteenth-century house has been beautifully restored. It's overlooked by the monumental Cité Mondiale du Vin – where you can find anything and everything related to wine. In contrast to the modern and somewhat neutral décor of the rooms priced at €44.60 for a double with shower/wc, or €48.60 with bath, the rue Notre-Dame overflows with antique dealers and bric-à-brac shops. There's a pay car park nearby. *10% discount on the price of a room (20% in Aug) offered to our readers on presentation of this guide.*

⊛ 🛗 Hôtel Ariane**

5 rue de Lurbe; take the no. 7 or 8 bus from the train station to the Gambetta stop. It's close to place Gambetta. **Map B1-5**
ⓣ05.56.52.27.72 ⓕ05.56.48.07.17
ⓦwww.perso.wanadoo.fr/hotel-ariane
Open *all year round.* **TV.**

Set in a quiet street, a simple but clean and well-run hotel, refurbished in 2002, with welcoming and attentive staff and a charming (albeit tiny) patio swathed in greenery. Most of the rooms overlook the patio and cost €45–50 for a double with shower or bath. There's also a mini-suite at €70 that can sleep four, and a pretty room is set aside for breakfast (€5).

⊛ 🛗 Acanthe Hôtel

12–14 rue Saint-Rémi; tram stop Place-de-la-Bourse (line C).
Map C2-6
ⓣ05.56.81.66.58 ⓕ05.56.44.74.41
ⓦwww.acanthe-hotel-bordeaux.com
Closed *Christmas holidays.* **TV.**

Just twenty metres from the superb place de la Bourse and the riverside, in the picturesque Saint-Pierre area. It's in a quiet street, and there's double glazing. Tasteful, personalized rooms and good facilities with doubles costing €46–62 with shower/wc or bath, and breakfast €5.50. The owner greets you warmly and knows the region well. Parking is difficult around here, though.

⊛ 🛗 Hôtel de l'Opéra**

35 rue Esprit-des-Lois. **Map C1-1**
ⓣ05.56.81.41.27 ⓕ05.56.51.78.80
ⓔhotel-opera.bx@wanadoo.fr
Closed *first fortnight in Aug.* **TV.**

An elegant eighteenth-century house next to the Grand Théâtre offering a warm and friendly welcome. The splendid stone staircase is original, as is the magnificent stained-glass lift, while the rooms have been decorated in bland modern style – doubles €49–54 with shower/wc or bath. The drawback is the noisy location – it's right on one of the busiest streets in the centre of town, although it has benefitted in this respect from the opening of the tram line, as the traffic has been reduced.

⊛ 🛗 Hôtel du Théâtre**

10 rue Maison-Daurade; this pedestrian street is perpendicular to the rue Sainte-Catherine, close to the Grand Théâtre. **Map C2-2**
ⓣ05.56.79.05.26 ⓕ05.56.81.75.06
Open *all year round.* **TV.**

In a pedestrianized street right in the centre of town, this old mansion has rooms in two wings and offers a warm and friendly welcome. The rooms are rather ordinary but they have good facilities and are kept beautifully clean – doubles with shower/wc or bath are €50–58; triples or quadruples (2 adults and 2 children) €63. The hotel can only be reached on foot as a result of the reorganization of the neighbourhood. It is possible to park in the nearby Tourny car park, or in the Grands-Hommes car park.

⊛ 🏃 🛗 Hôtel Gambetta**

66 rue de la Porte-Dijeaux. **Map B2-8**
ⓣ05.56.51.21.83 ⓕ05.56.81.00.40
ⓦwww.gambettahotel.com
TV.

This hotel is a good base, located in a lively part of the town centre, and the owner is pleasant. It's decent value for money given the location and the facilities – there are TVs and mini-bars in the bright and clean rooms and doubles with shower/wc or bath cost €53. *One free breakfast per room offered to our readers on presentation of this guide.*

⍟ ⍟ ⍟ Hôtel des Quatre Sœurs***

6 cours du 30-Juillet; near the Grand Théâtre. **Map C1-12**
☎05.57.81.19.20 ℻05.56.01.04.28
TV. Cots available.

Built in the eighteenth century, between allées de Tourny, the Grand Théâtre and place des Quinconces, this hotel is steeped in history. The composer Wagner stayed here in 1850 when he was having an adulterous affair with a local woman. The staff are really relaxed and there are attractive, freshly decorated, classy rooms. The ones overlooking the cours de Tourny or allées de Tourny are more expensive because they are bigger – they include some family rooms with two double beds – than the quieter rooms above the inner courtyard, and all are air-conditioned. Doubles with shower/wc or bath are €70–75 depending on the season. Special weekends are organized for wine lovers, with a tour of châteaux and tasting of different Bordeaux. *Free bottle of Bordeaux offered to our readers on presentation of this guide.*

⍟ ⍟ ⍟ Hôtel de la Tour Intendance**

16 rue de la Vieille-Tour; near the place Gametta. **Map B2-10**
☎05.56.81.46.27 ℻05.56.81.60.90
TV. Cots and high chairs available. Pay car park open 7.30pm–9am only (€8).

Two sisters take turns on reception in this charming establishment, which was completely refurbished in 2004, and guests always encounter the same friendly and obliging service. Here the welcome includes numerous thoughtful touches like freshly squeezed orange juice served at breakfast. Everything is efficient and well organized. In the cellar, you can see a few vestiges of the third-century tower of the hotel's name. The rooms on the pedestrianized street can be noisy in summer owing to the chatter of passers-by – but it's completely quiet at the rear where the cheapest rooms (singles) have a nice view over the rooftops. The rooms aren't large but they've done their best with the

décor and doubles with shower/wc cost from €76.

⍟ ⍟ ⍟ Hôtel de la Presse***

6 rue de la Porte-Dijeaux; near the junction of two major pedestrian streets. **Map C2-11**
☎05.56.48.53.88 ℻05.56.01.05.82
🌐www.hoteldelapresse.com
Closed 24 Dec–2 Jan. **TV.**

This place is close to the junction of rue Sainte-Catherine and rue Porte-Dijeaux in a central area which is pedestrianized during the day; some cars are permitted in the evening. The comfortable rooms are soundproofed and air-conditioned. If you really can't stand any noise at all, those on the courtyard side are the quietest. This place offers modest luxury at a reasonable price with doubles with shower/wc at €77, with bath €86. *One free breakfast per room offered to our readers on presentation of this guide.*

⍟ ⍟ ⍟ Hôtel Tulip Inn Bordeaux "Bayonne Etche-Ona"***

15 cours de l'Intendance; close to the Grand Théâtre; entrances on 4 rue Martignac and 11 rue Mautrec. **Map C2-13**
☎05.56.48.00.88 ℻05.56.48.41.60
🌐www.bordeaux-hotel.com
Closed 22 Dec–3 Jan. **TV.**

A 63-room hotel, part of which is housed in an eighteenth-century building, very much in keeping with this affluent area, with courteous staff and an attractive 1930s-style lounge. On the upper floors the rooms have been completely refurbished in an impersonal, contemporary style and doubles with bath are €114–132. If you can, choose a room in the Etche-Ona building, which is quieter and more comfortable. A public car park (with charges) is 50m away. *20% discount on the price of a room offered to our readers on presentation of this guide.*

⍟ ⍟ ⍟ Petit Hôtel Labottière

14 rue Francis Martin. **Off map B1-4**
☎05.56.48.44.10 ℻05.56.48.44.14
TV. Pay car park.

The "must-stay" hotel in Bordeaux, an eighteenth-century private mansion and listed building with a small interior courtyard. It's right in the centre of town, close to some public gardens, and it has been restored to perfection, with stucco-work, wainscoting and period furniture. This jewel has just two double rooms costing €180, breakfast (actually, it's more of a brunch) included. Needless to say, the welcome is unbeatable and reservations are essential. No pets are allowed – not with all those deep-pile rugs and silk-covered armchairs. *Free house apéritif or bottle of Bordeaux offered to our readers on presentation of this guide.*

@ ⅔ |●| Restaurant Le Rital

3 rue des Faussets; near place Saint-Pierre. **Map C2-20**
☎05.56.48.16.69
Closed *Sat; Sun; mid-Aug to early Sept.*

In a part of the city where restaurants come and go every few months, this little Italian place has been around for 21 years. The food is very good and you get a warm welcome. Tables are in a series of linked rooms, each of which gives a view of the kitchen. The house specialities include marinated aubergines and fresh pasta with seafood or pesto, but they also serve old favourites like *osso buco* and good home-made desserts with a lunchtime menu at €9.50, and others at €11–18. *Free house apéritif offered to our readers on presentation of this guide.*

@ 🛉 Matteo

9 rue de La Merci. **Map C2-35**
☎05.56.48.10.98
Closed *evenings: all day Sun; 1–15 Jan.*

This restaurant is bang in the city centre, between place Saint-Projet and place Camille-Jullian. The prices are low but the dishes are inventive: *magret* with baked aubergines and *confit* of pears (€8.95), wonderfully fresh salads and lovingly prepared pasta, dish of the day at €7.70; set menu with dessert €9.90. Bright dining room, charming service and, unsurprisingly, a host of regular customers. It's a shame that it does not open at night (although it can be booked for a private party).

@ |●| Le Boudoir

7 rue Traversanne; **Map D3-27**
☎05.56.94.20.45
Closed *Mon evening; Sat lunch; Sun; 15 July–25 Aug.*

This tiny place advertises itself as a "café-cantine" and shrugs off its unmatching crockery and the outlandish but comfortable furniture seemingly put together at random in its two dining rooms. The clientele is suitably arty, albeit middle-class, and revels in the tasty home cooking of Fabienne and Karim, prepared with fresh seasonal ingredients and accompanied by excellent bread; lunchtime menu €10 with a glass of wine; dinner menu €14. In winter, the soups and meat stews are very welcome; in summer they give way to dishes with a touch of the Mediterranean, from Provence to Greece. In the daytime, you can enjoy a cup of tea and leaf through the books stacked on the shelves.

@ |●| Le Palatium

164 cours Victor-Hugo; **Map C3-29**
☎05.56.91.47.47
Closed *Sun; 3 weeks in July.*

A long-established bistro that seems to have set the standard for all other bistros. No menus here; reckon on around €10 à la carte. The dining room is lively, the clientele extremely mixed and the waiters seem to run a marathon every day. The cooking is beyond reproach and the prices are highly attractive: the *andouillette* with mustard sauce (€7.20) will satisfy even the fussiest connoisseur, the chips are delicious (how often can this be said?), the beef tartare (€9.50) is exquisite and the highly prized parsleyed sweetbreads have recently made a welcome comeback to the array of dishes on offer. The quality of the food is vouched for by the loyalty of the local customers, young and not so young.

@ |●| Bar-cave de la Monnaie

34 rue Porte-de-la-Monnaie; behind the train station. **Map D3-35**
☎05.56.31.12.33
Closed *Sun; 1 Jan.*

This is the best-known low-budget restaurant in the Saint-Croix neighbourhood, not to mention the cosiest, with just twenty places in a space measuring a mere 20 square metres. Offerings include a selection of pork products, eggs with lentils or *à la piperade*, stews, oysters, parsleyed calf's head and soup with sausage (plates €9–17, bowls €9–11.50), as well as traditional snacks (from €3). Lunchtime three-course menu for €11. Wine is served by the glass, bottle or in bulk, to take away or drink at the counter or table, or on the terrace, at very affordable prices. This restaurant was created by the owner of the nearby *Tupiña*, and it proves an ideal place for a quick meal or drink.

Le Café des Arts

138 cours Victor-Hugo. **Map C3-23**
℡05.56.91.78.46
High chairs available.

A really popular brasserie in a busy, buzzing part of town, open all year round from 8am to 2am. The terrace is quite wide and the dining room is like an old-style bistro with simple chairs and moleskin benches. Honest, traditional dishes in good-sized portions: herrings in oil, *andouillette*, scallops with ceps, and that rarity, real *frites*. There's a lunch menu for €10.50; or reckon on €22 à la carte. This place has been going for years and is a real favourite with the younger crowd.

La Brasserie du Sud-Ouest

275 cours de la Somme; place Nantousy, to one side of the Capucins, by the Yser. **Off map C3-34**
℡05.56.92.03.06
Closed *Sun; Mon evening; Sat lunch; first 3 weeks in Aug.*

One of the finest restaurants in the Nansouty neighbourhood, with a strong, local following. The dining room, with carvings on the high ceiling dating from 1900, is beautiful and bright, thanks to its large mirrors and two façades of old stained-glass bay windows. The food more than lives up to these surroundings and is based on typical local elements: oysters, eels, entrecôte, wild mushrooms, *tricandilles*, fried foie gras, grilled magret and even superb shad with green sauce in season (€11). For dessert, the goat's curds with honey are recommended. The lunchtime menu at €11 includes starter, main course, dessert and coffee, or opt for the daily specials at €7–15. The dinner menus (€16 and €25) are copious and offer a wide choice.

L'Imprévu

11 rue des Remparts. **Map B2-22**
℡05.56.48.55.43
Closed *Sun; Mon; second fortnight in Feb; 3 weeks in Aug.*

A few bistro tables are set out on the terrace in this pedestrianized street, with a couple of attractive dining rooms inside – one a vaulted cellar decorated with dried flowers and willow baskets – and lots of regulars chatting with the affable owner. Good, quick service and healthy cooking using fresh, market produce: *pot-au-feu*,

beef skirt, pork fillet in mustard and home-made *clafoutis*, and splendid sweet crêpes for dessert; menus at €12.50 (weekday lunch), €14.50 (dinner) and €21. It's a good idea to book and credit cards are not accepted. *Free house apéritif offered to our readers on presentation of this guide.*

La Belle Époque

Quai Louis XVIII or 2 allée d'Orléans. **Map C1-25**
℡05.56.79.14.58
Closed *Mon; Sun evening (Sun lunch and evening July–Aug); 2 weeks in Aug; some long weekends.* **Disabled access. High chairs available.**

New management has brought a breath of fresh air (literally – it's installed air-conditioning) to Bordeaux's most attractive brasserie. It has also changed the furniture and opened a terrace on the quay. The young owner has come up with a simple, short menu (€13) based around meat and traditional dishes such as veal chump and roast chicken, dish of the day €9; other menus from €15 (weekday lunch) to €28. The substantial portions and swift service contribute to its renewed popularity; the gorgeous tiling doesn't hurt, either. *Free coffee offered to our readers on presentation of this guide.*

Chez Dupont

45 rue Notre-Dame. **Off map C1-24**
℡05.56.81.49.59 ℡05.56.51.39.19
Closed *Sun and Mon (except private parties).* **Disabled access.**

About the best value for money you'll get in Les Chartrons district, and the staff provide a cheery welcome. Attractive bistro-style surroundings, good-humoured atmosphere and traditional dishes like *pot-au-feu* chalked up on the blackboard; menu €14.50 or around €30 à la carte. In addition, there's occasional live jazz in the evenings. *Free house apéritif or liqueur offered to our readers on presentation of this guide.*

Restaurant Café Gourmand

3 rue Buffon; near place des Grands-Hommes. **Map B1-28**
℡05.56.56.79.23.85
Closed *Sun and Mon lunchtimes; New Year holiday.*

In sunny weather, nab one of the tables outside this elegant restaurant and admire the covered market. Bruno Olivier comes from a well-known family of chefs, and photos of them adorn the walls. He produces sound, well-judged dishes – using southwestern and Spanish produce – at bistro prices, with a lunch menu at €14.50. Expect to pay €35 for a dinner à la carte with wine. *Free house apéritif or coffee offered to our readers on presentation of this guide.*

ⓔ |●| L'Estaquade

Quai de Queyries; on the right bank. **Map D2-21**
☎05.57.54.02.50

Whoever invested in this place must have made a packet. It's on the river bank, right across from the stock exchange, and it offers a wonderful night-time panorama of the illuminated town. The décor and the lighting are low-key – not surprisingly it's popular with couples looking for a romantic night out. Seasonal produce and perfectly judged cooking make for delicious dishes, such as the flash-fried squid and other seafood delicacies; weekday lunch menu for €15, or reckon on €42 à la carte. It's essential to book for dinner.

ⓔ |●| La Tupiña

6–8 rue Porte-de-la-Monnaie. **Map D3-40**
☎05.56.91.56.37
Disabled access. Pay car park.

An unmissable place serving gastronomic Bordelais dishes that sometimes attracts coachloads of Japanese tourists. It's one of those rare restaurants serving genuine dishes from the southwest, using the finest produce. The décor is attractive, rustic-chic, and the dining room centres on a large fireplace where they roast free-range meats. The prices reflect the quality of the cooking, with a €16 lunchtime set menu and other menus at €32 and €48; reckon on €46 à la carte.

ⓔ |●| Le Sélénite

6 pl. Paul-Avisseau. **Map B2-32**
☎05.56.51.05.64
Closed *Sat lunchtime; Sun; Aug.*

It is stating the obvious to declare that Patrick Gibault's talent is out of the ordinary. His cooking is like nobody else's, but his achievements can be sampled at very reasonable prices. He combines meat, poultry and fish with all kinds of fruit, vegetables and spices, successfully plays with hot-cold effects, such as pepper sorbet served with grilled red tuna, samphire and mashed potatoes. Such experiments are invariably undertaken with great precision, and the exquisite results linger on the tongue. The dining room is simple but extremely modern, and the neighbourhood resembles London's Canary Wharf in its sophisticated trendiness. The lunchtime menus are unbeatable value for money: €16 and €20. The dinner menu costs €26; reckon on €37 à la carte. There's an extensive wine list, with the cheapest bottles at €13.20, so all in all, one of our best restaurants.

ⓔ |●| Café Maritime

Quai Armand Lalande; in the Bacalan neighbourhood. **Map C1-26**
☎05.57.10.20.40
Closed *Mon evening; Sat lunchtime; Sun.*
Disabled access.

This huge, fashionable restaurant, in a reclaimed warehouse, seats 450. In spite of the vast space, the lighting creates an intimate ambience, enhanced by the teak and bottle-green décor and you get a lovely view of the harbour from the mezzanine tables. Dishes are fresh and delicate; the chef reinterprets Japanese and Thai cooking, giving it a Bordeaux twist. The specialities include *sushi*, Spanish-style sea bream and cod *tajine* with cumin. There's a weekday lunch menu for €18 (including wine and coffee) or expect to pay around €30 à la carte.

ⓔ |●| Restaurant Le Port de la Lune

59 quai de Paludate; Gare-Saint-Jean tram station; it's on the extension to the quai de la Monnaie. **Off map D4-39**
☎05.56.49.15.55 ☎05.56.49.29.12
Open *daily until 1am.* **Disabled access.**

Opposite the abattoirs, in one of Bordeaux's nightlife areas, this is a great place for jazz fans, with live bands most nights (blues on Tues, jazz on Wed and Thurs). It's an animated, friendly, "lived-in" place, with photos of jazz legends lining the wall. You can eat very well, with bistro dishes – as well chosen as the music – at reasonable prices and affordable wines. Menu ("casse-croûte") €18.20; seasonal à la carte dishes (reckon on €25 or so) include baby eels *à l'espagnole*, shad in green sauce, lamprey and so on. Michel, the boss, creates an easy-going atmosphere with his ready smile and chat.

🍴 Restaurant Baud et Millet

19 rue Huguerie. **Map B1-36**
☎05.56.79.05.77 📠05.56.81.75.48
Closed Sun and public holidays.

A specialist cheese restaurant – very pleasant, air-conditioned and with friendly staff – serving two hundred kinds of cheese, meticulously selected by M. Baud. He has a great passion for his work and applies strict criteria. The cheeses can be sampled from the cheese board, but are also used in numerous dishes, ranging from *mille-feuille*, *raclette* and *tartiflette* to more daring concoctions. The "cheese and dessert" set menu (€18.50) is a surprising but tasty combination of sweet and savoury ingredients; another menu at €23.50. There is an impressive and well-chosen selection of nearly a thousand different wines from all over the world and the restaurant offers uninterrupted service from 10am to midnight. *Free house apéritif offered to our readers on presentation of this guide.*

🍴 La Toscane

6 rue du Cancéra. **Map C2-38**
☎05.56.01.12.18
Closed Sun; Mon.

This outpost of Florentine cuisine has earned Roberto Camaioli considerable prestige in Bordeaux. He served his apprenticeship in his native Tuscany before marrying and settling down in Bordeaux in 1997. Many of his tasty, well-prepared dishes, served in generous portions, are based on extra-virgin olive oil: the octopus salad is a good example of this. He makes all the fresh pasta by hand, while the dried pasta is supplied by Giuseppe Cocco, considered by Camaioli the best in his field in Italy. The charcuterie, such as the "cinta" (black-pig ham), is similarly unbeatable. The small, gleaming dining room has a charm matching that of the food; try the classic weekday menu at €23, Saturday four-course menu €22, or pay about €35 à la carte. Wines range from €21 to €40, and takeaway olive oil, wine and cheese are available.

🍴 Restaurant Gravelier

114 cours de Verdun; in the Chartrons neighbourhood. **Off map C1-37**
☎05.56.48.17.15
Closed Sat; Sun; Feb school holiday; 3 weeks in Aug. **Disabled access.**

Among the new wave of restaurants in Bordeaux, run by the daughter of one of the famous Troisgros brothers. Her husband, Yves Gravelier, is also a creative chef, capable of coming up with a salad of langoustines and sweetbreads with lemon zest. The surroundings are modern without being flashy, and there's a covered terrace. Prices are reasonable, with a lunch menu at €22 and others at €25, €32 and €40. The menus change frequently, but fish, of the highest quality, is a speciality.

Bourg-sur-Gironde
33710

🏨 Hôtel Les Trois Lis

11 pl. de la Libération; some 15km from the south of Blaye on the D669, running alongside the Dordogne.
☎05.57.68.22.85 📠05.57.68.31.10
🌐www.lestroislis.com
TV.

On the main square, in the heart of the village, this delightful, friendly little hotel has been thoroughly overhauled without losing its old-fashioned charm (creaking parquet, curtains and counterpanes in Jouy fabrics). The bright rooms are generally quite large, but the smaller ones are not cramped; doubles €36–45, depending on degree of comfort (shower or bathtub). Booking is advisable, as there are only eleven rooms and they offer good value for money.

Brantome
24310

🏨 Les Frères Charbonnel***

Rue Gambetta.
☎05.53.05.70.15 📠05.53.05.71.85
✉charbonnel.freres@wanadoo.fr
TV.

One of the most attractive (and best situated) hotels in the town centre; it has three stars and offers a cosy atmosphere. The restaurant is pretty expensive, but the extremely comfortable rooms offer very good value for money at €60–70 for a double, according to the degree of comfort and the view.

🍴 Le Jardin de Brantôme

33-37 rue Pierre-de-Moreuil.
☎05.53.05.88.16
Closed Wed and Thurs (only Wed in July–Aug); Feb.

This beautiful restaurant, set slightly away

from the town centre, was recently taken over by a promising young chef and quickly earned the reputation of offering the best value for money in Brantôme. It's a delightful setting with a fireplace, as well as a secluded garden decked with flowers. All the friendly, dedicated staff in the dining room are proud of what is produced in the kitchen, and with reason: *confit* of rabbit with salad, cushion of pig's cheek, pear, lemon and thyme sorbet, with menus starting at €12 (weekday lunchtime), and others at €16 and €25.

⍟ |●| Restaurant Au Fil de l'Eau

21 quai Bertin. By the riverside, near the Périgueux bridge.
☏ 05.53.05.73.65
Closed *Sun evening; Wed; mid-Oct to early May.*

This was once a fishermen's bistro. The pictures of fish are no longer on sale behind the bar, but it is still possible to hear customers boasting about their latest catch, and the sophisticated décor of the small dining room still draws on this passion. There is even a small boat moored beside the pretty little terrace on the edge of the Dronne. Not surprisingly, river fish (trout, perch, etc) feature prominently on the menu, along with local specialities. The cooking is unpretentious but skilled: home-made foie gras, pike-perch in red Bergerac, *matelote* of freshwater fish, fried bleaks. Menus €29–31, with no other dishes served à la carte. The place has quite a reputation, so it is advisable to book. Warm welcome and attentive service. Meat lovers may prefer to opt for *Le Fils du Temps*, on the other side of the bridge (☏ 05.53.05.24.12), with its fine selection of roast meats and charming terrace.

Bourdeilles
24310 (9km SW)

⍟ 🏠 |●| Les Griffons***

In the town; take the D78.
☏ 05.53.45.45.35 📠 05.53.45.45.20
🌐 www.griffons.fr
TV.

This wonderful sixteenth-century building overlooking the Dronne oozes charm – an ideal haunt for lovers. Extremely comfortable rooms (€84–94) complete with niches, stone carvings, a fireplace

and, above all, a spectacular view of the river. Expertly prepared regional dishes on offer in the restaurant, with service on the terrace in fine weather and three menus at €21.50–37. The service is diligent and exceptionally attentive.

Monsec
24340 (12km NW)

⍟ 🏠 |●| Hôtel-restaurant Beauséjour**

Rue Principale; take the D939.
☏ 05.53.60.92.45 📠 05.53.60.72.38
Closed *Fri evenings and Sat (Oct–April); Christmas to New Year.* **TV. High chairs and games available. Car park.**

Really friendly welcome and quality food served in a pleasant restaurant with a panoramic view of the garden. Fine range of set menus celebrating local cuisine: duck sausage, oyster mushroom omelette, foie gras and duck breast kebab. The cheapest menu, €11 (not Sun), includes a delicious buffet and a quarter of a litre of wine, and there are others at €15–25. Simple but impeccable rooms cost €35 with shower/wc; half board available at €38 per person.

Vieux-Mareuil
24340 (13km NW)

⍟ 🎋 🏠 |●| Hostellerie de l'Auberge de l'Étang Bleu***

Take the D93; it's 2km from the hamlet, and well signposted.
☏ 05.53.60.92.63
🌐 www.perigord-hotel.com
Closed *Sun evening and Mon lunch (except public holidays); early Feb to end March (open during Feb school holiday); mid-Nov to mid-Dec.* **TV. High chairs available. Car park.**

In a huge park at the edge of a private lake, with a small beach where you can bathe. The spacious, nicely furnished rooms are as quiet as can be. Those overlooking the lake (nos. 1–6) have a covered balcony; doubles €57–68 with shower/wc or bath, half board, €63–67 per person, is compulsory in July and August. The elegant dining room has a lakeside terrace which is inhabited by noisy ducks, and nice views from the window tables. Good, generously flavoured dishes include salmon with ceps, along with a fine selection of salads with foie gras, scallops, crayfish tails or smoked duck. There's a weekday lunchtime menu for €16.50 and others €22–36; à la carte it'll cost around €44. Logis de France. *10% discount on the price of a room offered to our readers on presentation of this guide.*

Saint-Jean-de-Côle
24800 (20km NE)

@ ⚘ |●| Hôtel Saint-Jean**

Route de Nontron; take the D78.
℡05.53.52.23.20 **Closed** *Sun evening and Mon evening (out of season).* **TV. High chairs available. Car park.**

Charming little place, of the kind that helps to keep up the good image of country hotels, thanks to the efforts of its diligent and professional owners. Pretty garden and traditional-style rooms – €36.80 for a double with shower/wc – that are comfortable and meticulously maintained. High-quality regional cooking: terrine of foie gras made from home-bred duck, scallops with *fricassée* of ceps, duck breast with orange in truffle and parsley sauce. The weekday lunchtime menu costs €11 and there are others at €14–27.50, or reckon on €22 à la carte. *Free house apéritif offered to our readers on presentation of this guide.*

Buzet sur Baïze
47160

@ ⚘ |●| Auberge du Goujon Qui Frétille

Rue Gambetta; it's opposite the church.
℡ and ℗05.53.84.26.51
Closed *Tues; Wed; first fortnight in Jan.* **High chairs and games available.**

The village is quiet and pretty – and so is this inn, literally "The Inn of the Wriggling Gudgeon", which stands opposite the church. You sit down in peaceful surroundings to generous helpings of fine food, much of it Provençal, all of it based entirely on fresh ingredients, such as wild fish and beef and vegetables supplied by small local farmers. The wine list is similarly dominated by treasures from the Buvet region. No menu here (apart from a children's menu at €7.50), so you have to eat à la carte; reckon on €15–45. It's a good idea to reserve. *Free coffee offered to our readers on presentation of this guide.*

Cambo-les-Bains
64250

@ ⚘ |●| L'Auberge de Tante Ursule**

Fronton du Bas-Cambo; next to the *fronton* court.
℡05.59.29.78.23 ℗05.59.29.28.57
Closed *Tues; mid-Feb to mid-March; 5–30 Nov.* **Disabled access. TV. High chairs available. Car park.**

This very old farm building, painted all in white, has an annexe offering decent rooms for €28 with basin and from €44 with shower/wc. Good, home-prepared food, with a range of set menus at €16 (not Sun or hols) and €20.50–35. Look out for specialities such as braised lamb sweetbreads with ceps, salad of home-made black pudding fried with pickled garlic and sautéed cuttlefish. Logis de France.

Espelette
64250 (5km W)

@ ⚘ ⚘ |●| Hôtel-restaurant Euzkadi**

285 Karrika-Nagusia; take the D918 in the direction of Saint-Jean-de-Luz.
℡05.59.93.91.88
@www.hotel-restaurant-euzkadi.com
Closed *Mon; Tues out of season; 2 Nov–20 Dec.* **TV. High chairs available. Swimming pool. Car park.**

This is one of the most popular country hotel-restaurants in the Basque area and it's a good idea to book well in advance. Michèle and André Darraïdou, both completely mad about Basque cooking, search out old recipes and revamp them. In their enormous restaurant on set menus (€17–30) you'll discover dishes you would have very little chance of finding elsewhere: *tripotxa* (black pudding made from veal and served with a tomato and capsicum sauce); *axoa* (cubed veal browned with onions and peppers); *merluza en salsa verde* (poached hake with pea and asparagus sauce); cockles and hard-boiled eggs in a sauce made with Jurançon wine and fish stock; *elzekaria* (vegetable soup). Pretty double rooms at €48–55; half board at €50–55 per person. Now that there's a bypass, there's no noisy through-traffic. In the back there's a pleasant garden, tennis court and swimming pool. Logis de France. *Free sangría offered to our readers on presentation of this guide.*

Itxassou
64250 (5km S)

@ 꽃 🏠 |●| Hôtel-restaurant du
Chêne**

Place de l'Église: take the D918 towards
Saint-Jean-Pied-de-Port, then the D249 to
the Nive valley.
☎05.59.29.75.01 ☎05.59.29.27.39
Closed Mon; Tues out of season; Jan; Feb.
TV. High chairs available. Car park.

This establishment is superbly situated
and they serve unpretentious but delicious
local cuisine. Specialities on the set menus
(€15–38) include a mix of traditional and
Basque dishes: cod fritters with chilli and
garlic in Basque coulis, duck *carpaccio* with
ewe's cheese, chicken with rice and red
peppers, *escalopes* of foie gras with ceps and
pig's feet salad with potatoes and shallots.
Doubles cost €42–44, depending on the
season. Logis de France. *Free sangría on the
house offered to our readers on presentation of
this guide.*

Ainhoa
64250 (12km SW)

@ 🏠 |●| Ithurria***

Rue Principale; it's at the northern edge of
the village; take the D918 to Espelette then
the D20.
☎05.59.29.92.11
@www.ithurria.com
Closed Wed out of season; Thurs lunchtime
out of season; early Nov–Easter. **TV. High
chairs available. Swimming pool. Car park.**

One of the nicest inns you'll find anywhere, this very fine place is set in a large
seventeenth-century house and former
coaching inn on the pilgrim route to
Santiago de Compostela. The gorgeously
furnished rooms go for €115–135. There's
an attractive dining room, with hand-
made floor tiles and a vast fireplace, serving
menus from €29 to €44; or reckon on
€50 à la carte. Dishes include pepper stew,
Basque *cassoulet* with red kidney beans and
roast pigeon with garlic. Facilites include a
fine garden, sauna and swimming pool to
the rear, so reservations are essential.

Capbreton
40130

@ |●| Le Bistro

Place des Basques. 300m south of the town
centre.

☎05.58.72.21.98
Closed Sat lunch; Sun; Tues and Wed eve-
nings (out of season); Oct; Christmas to New
Year. **Disabled access. Car park.**

This does not look very special from
the outside, but it's delightful inside. The
owner, his apron wrapped round his waist,
will take your order and cook your food.
Chalked up on the blackboard are delicious dishes that are carefully prepared
and perfect in their simplicity: *filet mignon
de porc* with honey and cherry plums and
whole duck magret with pepper. Choose
the menu of the day for €10 (weekday
lunchtimes), or reckon on around €30 à
la carte.

@ 꽃 |●| Les Copains d'Abord

Port des Mille-Sabords; in the pleasure port.
☎05.58.72.14.14
High chairs available.

There's a strong holiday feel to the décor:
sea blue, forest green and sunshine gold.
The restaurant has a lovely terrace which
is at its best on summer evenings – it can
get too hot at lunchtime. Menus at €14.50
(weekday lunchtime), then €18–36, feature dishes that use produce straight from
the farm or the ocean: pan-fried mussels,
cuttlefish with garlic. Or you could go à
la carte (reckon on about €32), and try
pig's trotters, a speciality of the house. *A
free bottle of Côtes-de-Gascogne (with the
bill) offered to our readers on presentation of
this guide.*

@ 꽃 |●| Restaurant La Pêcherie
Ducamp

Rue du Port-d'Albret; near the sea.
☎05.58.72.11.33
Closed Mon, Tues and Fri lunchtimes in
season; Mon–Fri and Sun evenings out of
season; fortnight in Feb; end Sept to early
Oct.

Direct from the fishmonger to the con-
sumer – the tables are arranged around the
fish counter, and the waitresses wear boots
and plastic aprons. On the wide range
of seafood menus, €24–37, you'll find
cuisine such as seafood platter and grilled
fish; the house speciality is *parillada*, a dish
containing seven varieties of fish and seafood. Careful, though: the bill can mount
up quickly. A touristy place, but pleasant
nonetheless and booking is advised. *Free
house apéritif offered to our readers on presentation of this guide.*

Cap-Ferret

33970

☺ ♨ 🛏 |●| Hôtel des Pins**

23 rue des Fauvettes.
☎05.56.60.60.11 ℱ05.56.60.67.41
Closed *lunchtimes; mid-Nov to mid-March.*

A delightful early twentieth-century house quietly situated in a flower-filled garden between the bassin d'Arcachon and the ocean. The meticulously planned décor, all classic advertisements and old billiards tables, creates the impression that time has stood still. The spotless double rooms cost €43–72 with shower or bath, though some of them are tiny. The restaurant specializes in seafood; there are menus at €20 and €27, or you can dine à la carte for about €30.

☺ ♨ 🛏 |●| La Maison du Bassin***

5 rue des Pionniers; in the fishermen's neighbourhood.
☎05.56.60.60.63 ℱ05.56.03.71.47
🖰www.lamaisondubassin.com
Closed *lunchtimes; Tues (except July–Aug); Jan; Feb. Summer weekdays only open in the evening.* **Disabled access. TV.**

A superb colonial-style wooden house in a picturesque district. It reserves a warm welcome for its guests and is undoubtedly the smartest place in Cap-Ferret. Each room has a slightly different feel, with maritime details and lots of pitch pine creating a soothing, timeless atmosphere; doubles, including four in an annexe alongside, go for €114–200, depending on the size and the season. There's a restaurant, too, with a menu at €38; expect to pay €40 à la carte.

☺ 🛏 Le Muscaret Chez Yvan

17 rue des Goëlands; it's near the lighthouse.
☎05.56.03.75.74
Closed *Wed; a fortnight in Feb; a fortnight in Oct.* **High chairs available.**

A favourite haunt of locals who couldn't give a fig about the sea view (they see that every day, after all), but who really care about what is served on their plates. Yvan is a great character and his wife, two daughters and son-in-law make up the rest of the team. It's a convivial place, perfect for an evening out with friends, the food is great with huge helpings of seasonal dishes and a single menu at €21.

Canon (Le)

33950 (6km N)

☺ ♨ 🛏 |●| Hôtel-restaurant de la Plage

L'Herbe, 1 rue des Marins; coming from Arles, turn left at the roundabout in L'Herbe, then left again at the end of the road.
☎05.56.60.50.15
Closed *Mon out of season; 31 Dec–10 Feb.* **High chairs available.**

A typical wooden house just by the water's edge, that's thankfully resisted the pressure to modernize. The restaurant is simple and cheap (set menus from €16 to €25), filled, on Sunday especially, with locals and tourists feasting on *moules marinières*, grilled sea bream and the like. Eight modest double rooms with washbasin and a shower on the landing at €42–45; some have sea views.

Cartelegue

33820

☺ 🛏 |●| Chez Olga**

1 Bel Ormau. It's on the main road.
☎05.57.64.71.18
Closed *Sat; a week in April; 2 weeks in Aug.* **TV.**

A typical old-school truckers' restaurant run by Olga's grandson, who's given the place a make-over but kept the *Routiers* atmosphere. It hardly matters that the rooms are simple and the road rumbles close by as a double costs just €34. The restaurant, with its drab décor, is full of nice surprises; lunch menu around €11, and others €13–27. Simple, tasty cooking, which follows the changing seasons – asparagus in spring, ceps in autumn, and game or fried fish from the Garonne. It's a popular stop for local wine-growers.

Casteljaloux

47700

☺ ♨ 🛏 Hôtel des Cordeliers

1 rue des Cordeliers.
☎05.53.93.02.19. ℱ05.53.93.55.48.
🖰www.hotel-cordeliers.fr
Restaurant closed *Sun; Mon lunch; Fri evening Nov–May; 22 Dec–15 Jan.* **TV. High chairs available. Car park.**

The owners, originally from Normandy, do everything possible to make their

②

guests feel at home – some come a long way to stay here, knowing that the service will be exceptional. Very comfortable rooms (most of them renovated and priced €42–48), with an attractive carpet in warm colours (dark blue, scarlet) and décor with a Provençal touch. Half board is also possible. The restaurant which serves a lunchtime weekday menu for €12 and other menus at €16 and €29, offers many local dishes, and displays a similar attention to detail: for example, the croissants and bread at breakfast are served warm. Logis de France. *10% discount on the price of a room (Nov to end of March) or free house apéritif offered to our readers on presentation of this guide.*

@ 🍴 🏠 |●| **La Vieille Auberge**

11 rue Posterne.
☎ 05.53.93.01.36
🖂 www.casteljaloux.com
Closed *lunchtimes; Tues evening and Wed out of season; 21–27 Feb; 27 June–10 July; 21 Nov–11 Dec.*

In one of the oldest streets in town, this inn has a thoroughly local flavour and a pretty yellow dining room with old-fashioned furniture, and offering attentive, if slightly distant, service. Enjoy all the delicacies Gascony has to offer with produce skilfully selected according to season: fried foie gras with seasonal fruit, roast loin of lamb with rosemary, beef fillet à la bordelaise, on set menus €18–32, with one for children at €11. Alternatively, eat à la carte for around €37. *Free coffee offered to our readers on presentation of this guide.*

Castillones
47330

@ 🍴 🏠 |●| **Hôtel-restaurant des Remparts**

26–28 rue de la Paix.
☎ 05.53.49.55.85 📠 05.53.49.55.89
🖂 lesremparts@wanadoo.fr
Closed *4–31 Jan; last fortnight in Nov.*
Restaurant closed *Sun evenings and Mon (except in summer).* **TV. High chairs available.**

A beautiful and sturdy stone house in the middle of the village, sensitively converted into a hotel. The rooms are spacious (nos. 1–4 are the largest) and painted in pale, soothing colours; the ones overlooking the main road are fitted with double glazing. You'll pay €37 for a double with

shower, €44.50–50.50 with shower/wc or bath. The traditional regional dishes in the restaurant are predictable but well prepared: duck breast with foie gras sauce and prunes preserved in Monbazillac wine, red mullet fillet with thyme butter and a platter of duck. The bread is especially good. The lunch menu is €12.20 (not Sun), and other menus from €15.20 to €40; children's menu €8. Expect to pay around €24 à la carte. Logis de France. *Free house apéritif offered to our readers on presentation of this guide.*

Dax
40100

@ 🍴 🏠 |●| **Les Champs de l'Adour****

5 rue Morancy; between the cathedral and the covered market.
☎ 05.58.56.92.81 📠 05.58.56.98.61
🖂 leschampsdel'adour@club-internet.fr
Closed *20 Dec–5 Jan.* **Restaurant closed** *Sun out of season (except for hotel guests); Sun evening in season; Mon–Wed evenings.* **Disabled access (restaurant). TV. High chairs available. Pay car park.**

This little hotel looks more like a private house. The outside walls and the wooden staircase are original, but inside it's been totally rebuilt with seven quiet rooms; doubles €45–50. The restaurant produces tasty dishes prepared with fresh, natural ingredients and including marinated salmon Scandinavian style, seaweed *à la marinière* and beef skirt with pickled shallots with set menus ranging from €8 to €23. The wine list features organic wines. *10% discount on the price of a room (Dec–March) or free house apéritif or coffee offered to our readers on presentation of this guide.*

@ 🍴 🏠 |●| **Hôtel-restaurant Beausoleil****

38 rue du Tuc-d'Eauze.
☎ 05.58.56.76.76 📠 05.58.56.03.81
🖂 www.hotel-beausoleil-dax.fr
Closed *mid-Dec to early March.* **Restaurant closed** *Mon and Thurs evenings.* **Disabled access. TV. Pay car park.**

This is the most charming and friendly hotel in town, quietly situated near the centre. It's a pretty white house with a terrace and 32 comfortable rooms – doubles €47–72 with shower/wc or bath, half board €50–80 per person. The food is conventional but good, all of it prepared with quality produce. Excellent-value menus start at €12 (except Sun), with others €18–36 – make sure you try the foie gras. Your bottle is already set on the table next to your napkin ring. Every three weeks evening entertainment is laid on for guests. *Free house apéritif and, if you stay, one free breakfast per room per night.*

⊚ ⅄ |●| La Guitoune

Place Roger-Ducos; in the covered market.
℡05.58.74.37.46
Closed evenings; Sun; Mon; Feb. **Disabled access. TV. High chairs available.**

Ideal if you don't want to spend too much. It's best to come on a Saturday when all local life is on show; the place teems with stall-holders from the market and it's a rendezvous for lots of Dax inhabitants. On offer are plates of good food like omelette with asparagus tips or mushrooms, squid cooked in their ink or in a stew, *moules marinières* or a dozen fresh oysters with a glass of local white wine, with dishes of the day priced €5–10. *Free sangría offered to our readers on presentation of this guide*

⊚ ⅄ |●| Lou Balubé

63 av. Saint-Vincent-de-Paul.
℡05.58.56.97.92
Closed Wed; Thurs evening; Christmas to New Year.

Lou Balubé is named after the new owners' three children: Baptiste, Lucas and Bérénice. This charming, brightly decorated, friendly little restaurant not only serves good food but also has the virtue of being open on Sunday (unusual in Dax). Basic dishes include hearty slices of meat or tuna steak with vegetables, but there are more imaginative options if you order à la carte. The weekday lunchtime menu at €11, includes wine and coffee, and there are others priced €16–23. *Free house apéritif offered to our readers on presentation of this guide.*

⊚ ⅄ |●| L'Amphitryon

38 cours Galliéni.
℡05.58.74.58.05
Closed Sat lunchtime; Sun evening; Mon; Jan; last fortnight of Aug.

Eric Pujos will delight you with dishes from the Landes and the Basque country in his bright, modern little restaurant, one of the gourmet establishments in the area, offering very reasonable set menus for €20–37. Dishes include prawn salad with foie gras, shepherds' pie with lamb gravy and Eselette chilli and grilled baby squids. The à la carte menu changes every month, service is prompt and pleasant. *Free house apéritif offered to our readers on presentation of this guide.*

⊚ ⅄ |●| El Mesón

18 pl. Camille-Bouvet.
℡05.58.74.64.26 ℗05.58.74.52.89
Closed Sat lunchtime; Sun; first week in May; last fortnight of Aug; Christmas to New Year. **High chairs available.**

You're in Spain here. The décor and the cooking tell you so: pan-fried squid, grilled whole turbot, paella, gazpacho, parsleyed eels and juicy grilled lamb chops. If all you want is a snack, lean against the bar and order from the range of tapas, washing the delicacies down with a strong Spanish wine or the house sangria. The portions are generous, but be sure to watch your budget. Reckon on a minimum of €25 for a complete meal. *Free house apéritif offered to our readers on presentation of this guide.*

Duras

47120

⊚ ⅄ ☎ |●| L'Hostellerie des Ducs**

Boulevard Jean-Brisseau; it's next to the tourist office.
℡05.53.83.74.58 ℗05.53.83.75.03
ⓦwww.hostellerieducs-duras.com
Restaurant closed Mon, Sat lunchtime and Sun evenings (Oct–June); Sat and Mon lunchtimes (July–Sept). **TV. High chairs available. Swimming pool. Car park.**

Originally a convent, these two fine semi-detached buildings now house the region's most prestigious hotel and restaurant. It's quietly situated, with pleasant terraces, lovely swimming pool and flower-filled garden. There's a friendly atmosphere in the restaurant, where the food enjoys an excellent reputation. You can choose from a €15 weekday lunch menu – glass of wine and coffee included – and others at €26–56. Specialities include terrine of duck foie gras with dried tomatoes, sturgeon with two sauces and omelette with locally-grown asparagus. The chef puts regional produce before originality and the result is good, high-quality cooking. The wine list has a fine selection of Duras vintages. In winter, try to book a table near the fireplace. Comfortable rooms start at €51 for a double with shower/wc and €88 with bath (some have air-conditioning and no. 7 has a balcony with a view); half board is available. It's pretty much essential to book in season. Logis de France. *10% discount on the price of a room (except Aug–Sept) offered to our readers on presentation of this guide.*

Eaux-Bonnes (Les)

64440

@ 🏠 |O| 🎿 Hôtel Richelieu**

35 rue Louis-Barthou; close to the spa.
☎05.59.05.34.10 ⊕05.59.05.43.46.
Closed April; 1 Nov–20 Dec. **Disabled access. TV. High chairs available.**

Despite its location on one of the corners of the main square, this is a quiet place, taken over and refurbished by a young couple from the Alps. It's a charming cross between a nineteenth-century spa hotel and a modern establishment, with attentive service, vast lounges with high ceilings and large, bright rooms, some with antique furniture; doubles in high season, with shower/wc or bath, cost €47–49, depending on the view. The restaurant, on the other hand, serves hearty Alpine specialities ideal for hikers, such as tartiflettes and fondues, with a cheap menu at €13 and others €16–29. *10% discount on the price of a room offered to our readers on presentation of this guide.*

Eugénie-les-Bains

40320

@ |O| La Ferme aux Grives

☎05.58.05.05.06
⊛www.michelguerard.com
Closed Tues evening; Wed (open every day in Aug); Jan.

In this restaurant the visual aspects have been considered down to the last detail, from the terrace and furniture right down to the crockery, while the food investigates local traditions in an attempt to recover the pure flavours of fresh ingredients.

Cured hams hang from the ceiling while a suckling pig turns slowly on the spit in the fireplace – you feel good as soon as you sit down. There's a single menu at €40 and the simple but elegant dishes include mussels *brûle-doigts à la crème*, calf's head with *ravigote* and grilled free-range chicken, with curds ice cream, *crème brûlée* with grilled oats or buttered fruit pie for dessert.

Eyzies-de-Tayac (Les)

24620

@ 🏠 |O| Le Moulin de la Beune – Restaurant Le Vieux Moulin**

In the village; coming from Arlat, it's on the right, below the bridge.
☎05.53.06.94.33 ⊕05.53.06.98.06
⊛www.moulindelabeune.com
Closed 1 Nov–1 April. **Restaurant closed** Tues, Wed and Sat lunchtimes. **Disabled access. Car park.**

This place, which used to be a mill, is on the water's edge at the quiet end of the village. The décor of the rooms is understated, a little austere perhaps for some tastes, but they are comfortable, have recently been renovated and offer good value for money with doubles costing €58–67 with shower/wc or bath. Tasty, well-prepared food is served in *Le Vieux Moulin*, which houses the original mill machinery. There are three menus, running from €29 to €50. You'll find dishes like *escalope* of foie gras, squab casserole, scallops with ceps and chocolate soufflé. In summer you eat in the garden on a delightful terrace, lulled by the murmuring river.

@ 🎿 🏠 |O| Hôtel de France – Auberge du Musée**

Rue du Moulin; on the street leading to the Prehistory Museum.
☎05.53.06.97.23 ⊕05.53.06.90.97
⊛www.hoteldefrance-perigord.com
Restaurant closed Mon and Sat lunchtimes except for groups and on public holidays; Nov to Easter. **TV. Swimming pool. Car park.**

Two establishments standing opposite each other at the foot of a cliff. The inn, which serves traditional and regional food, has two dining rooms – or you can eat outside under the wisteria-covered arbour, with set menus starting at €12 (except Sun) up to €30.50. Expect to pay around €20 à la carte. There are a few rooms – doubles with bath €59–84 – in the main building and others in an annexe on the banks of the Vézère, where there is a garden and a swimming pool. Logis de France. *10% discount on the price of a room (except July–Aug) offered to our readers on presentation of this guide.*

⍟ ☎ |●| Hostellerie du Passeur**

It's opposite the museum.
☎05.53.06.97.13 ℗05.53.06.91.63
⊛www.hostellerie-du-passeur.com
Closed Mon and Tues lunchtime (except July–Sept); early Nov to early March. **TV. High chairs available. Car park.**

On a small, peaceful pedestrian square by the river, its white shutters adding a touch of charm to the old ivy-covered walls, this hotel offers very attractively decorated rooms for €62–64. Half board (from €61 per person) is compulsory in Aug and Sept. The beautifully restored rustic restaurant serves well-prepared, reasonably priced traditional dishes. The weekday menu at €18.50, then four more going up to €45, are good value and list dishes such as *galantine* of pigeon, *délice périgourdin* with foie gras and rabbit *confit* on a bed of cep mushrooms in truffle juices. À la carte, try three styles of foie gras or scallops with ceps. Logis de France.

⍟ ☎ |●| Hôtel-restaurant Le Centenaire***

Rocher de la Penne; it's on the main street.
☎05.53.06.68.68 ℗05.53.06.92.41
⊛www.hotelducentenaire.fr
Closed early Nov to early April. **Restaurant closed** Mon–Thurs lunchtimes. **TV. Swimming pool. Car park.**

This exceptional establishment is quite simply the best restaurant in Périgord. Chef Roland Mazère is a culinary artist and his flavours are subtle, intense and original – try salad of asparagus with foie gras, hot wild cep terrine with garlic and parsley, creamy black truffle risotto or fillet of goose "Rossini" (with foie gras) served with macaroni and Cantal cheese gratin. Despite its cachet, the dining room is not in the least stuffy and serves menus starting at €36 (weekday lunchtimes), then others €66–120. Alain Scholly and his wife offer you a genuine welcome and the service is perfect in its discreet and efficient way. The décor is more opulent than charming, but it is free of ostentation, and the rooms are wonderfully furnished, with doubles priced €138–260, depending on the degree of comfort and the season. Breakfast is extra, at €17, and half board (€145–230 per person) is compulsory in July and August. The swimming pool is complemented by a gym.

Tursac
24620 (6km N)

⍟ ⍩ |●| Restaurant La Source

From Eyzies, take the D706.
☎05.53.06.98.00 ℗05.53.35.13.61
℮leolerschen@aol.com
Closed Sat (except July–Aug), evenings out of season (unless you book a table); early Nov to mid-March. **High chairs and games available.**

Decent little village inn run by a friendly young couple. It's a rustic-style restaurant with a discreet and pleasant staff, and when the weather is fine you can eat out on the terrace and admire the spring running through the garden. Modern cuisine with a good selection of local dishes: foie gras, gizzards, *confit*, cep mushroom omelette, cod *au gratin* and rabbit terrine with hazelnuts. Menus, €14–25, include a vegetarian option (with vegetable pie). *Free coffee offered to our readers on presentation of this guide.*

Tamniès
24620 (14km NE)

⍟ ☎ |●| Hôtel-restaurant Laborderie**

From Eyzies take the D47 and the D48 – it's equidistant (14km) between Sarlat and Montignac.
☎05.53.29.68.59 ℗05.53.29.65.31
⊛www.hotel.laborderie.com
Closed Wed lunch (except July–Aug); 1 Nov to Easter. **TV. High chairs available. Swimming pool. Car park.**

Set on a peaceful square in this hillside market town, surrounded by exceptional countryside, *Laborderie* started off as a farm, became a country café and restaurant, and is now a rather chic hotel-restaurant with a terrace. Lovely rooms at reasonable prices; you'll pay €30–78, depending on the degree of comfort. Some rooms are in the turreted main house, which has a great deal of charm, while others are in a garden annexe looking onto open countryside – those on the ground floor face the swimming pool. The large, bright restaurant has become one of the most popular in Périgord, serving menus €19–42; reckon on €30 à la carte. The chef skilfully prepares generous helpings of classics such as Périgord platter, half-cooked foie gras, duck with peaches and iced soufflé with hazelnuts. Logis de France.

Grenade-sur-L'Adour

40270

⚜ 🏠 |O| Pain, Adour et Fantaisie***

14–16 pl. des Tilleuls; take the N124.
☏05.58.45.18.80 ℻05.58.45.16.57
℮pain.adour.fantaisie@wanadoo.fr
Closed Sun evening, Mon and Wed (Mon and Wed lunchtime only in July–Aug). **Disabled access. TV.**

This gorgeous old village dwelling stands between the main square and the Adour River. It has comfortable, tastefully decorated rooms with great views. Doubles €64–134, according to the degree of comfort and season. The food is unforgettable, served in the sophisticated surroundings of the restaurant or on the riverside terrace. Dishes include foie gras marinated in Jurançon wine, risotto with glazed prawns, potatoes stuffed with ribbons of pork, pan-fried red mullet in lavender vinegar, braised rabbit with ceps in chestnut *jus* and milk-fed lamb from the Pyrenees with cashew curry sauce. The service is unobtrusive. Menus at €28 (except on public holidays) and €37–83. Unbeatable charm and value for money.

Hagetmau

40700

⚜ 🏕 🏠 |O| Le Jambon**

27 av. Carnot; in the town centre, opposite the covered market.
☏05.58.79.32.02. ℻05.58.79.34.78
Closed Sun evening; Mon; Jan. **TV. Swimming pool. Car park.**

Behind the freshly painted pink-and-white exterior is a nice little place famous for its good cooking: foie gras with spices, scallop stew with ceps, best lamb with thyme, quail stuffed with foie gras, pigeon and hot Grand Marnier soufflé.

Menus range from €17 up to €36; meal and overnight stay costs €55 per person. The rooms are also recommended; doubles go for €45–48 with shower/wc or bath. *Free house apéritif offered to our readers on presentation of this guide.*

⚜ 🏕 🏠 |O| Hôtel-restaurant des Lacs d'Halco

Route de Cazalis. 2 km after leaving the town; it is marked on the Orthez road.
☏05.58.79.30.79 ℻05.58.79.36.15
⊛www.hotel-des-lacs-dhalco.fr
Open all year round. **Swimming pool (heated, indoor).**

Off the beaten track, but well worth a detour. The building stands slightly apart from the traditional local style, yet it has been built with natural materials from the region, by the architect Eric Raffy, who also has other top-class restaurants to his name. It is startlingly modern, if somewhat austere at first sight, but guests soon become accustomed to it, especially after they've sampled the comfort of the rooms overlooking the lake (€60–100 for a double, depending on the season) and the sophisticated cooking (including one menu based entirely on foie gras) in the Waterlily Room (one glance will explain the name). Menus range from €30 (based on fish) up to €45. Logis de France. *10% discount on the price of a room (except July–Aug) offered to our readers on presentation of this guide.*

Hendaye

64700

⚜ 🏕 🏠 |O| Hôtel-restaurant Bergeret-Sport**

4 rue des Clématites; it's 150m from the sea and 1km from the centre of town.
☏05.59.20.00.78 ℻05.59.20.67.30
⊛www.hotel-bergeret-sport.com
Closed Christmas. **Restaurant open** daily 1 June–30 Sept. **Disabled access (restaurant only). TV. Car park.**

The photos on the walls are pictures of long-term guests, which creates a friendly atmosphere. It's a family-run hotel with comfortable, renovated rooms – €48–65 with shower/wc – that are well maintained by a charming, chatty woman. Half board (€61 per person) is compulsory in July and August. Her chef husband is a real pro – his classic, regional dishes are to be recommended and the portions are substantial on the range of menus (€18–26), and you can eat in the garden under the shade of the plane trees. Credit cards not accepted. *Free house apéritif offered to our readers on presentation of this guide.*

⊚ 🎿 |●| Le Parc à Huîtres

4 rue des Orangers; opposite the fishing port.
☎05.59.20.32.38
Closed Tues.

This is a grocer's shop which also serves a fine array of seafood and salads, tempting desserts and local wines by the glass – a really good place. All the dishes are cold: ultra-fresh oysters are €9–13 for a dozen, snacks with toast or mixed platters €3–7 and there's a variety of salads for €4.60–8. Service is inside or on the terrace; reckon on around €15 for a full meal. *Free coffee offered to our readers on presentation of this guide.*

⊚ 🎿 |●| La Cabane du Pêcheur

Quai de la Floride.
☎05.59.20.38.09
Closed Sun evening and Mon (15 Oct–31 May). **Disabled access. Car park.**

Given its name and location, there are no prizes for guessing that fish is king in this restaurant and you can expect a charming welcome by the owner – who learned his trade with some of the best chefs in the region. You'll find the freshest of fish landed on the quayside opposite and cooked simply: either chargrilled, Spanish-style with pickled garlic or in a Basque-style stew. The large, simple dining room has a view of the boats and serves menus at €14–30.50, seafood platter €23; or reckon on €24 à la carte. Groups of up to ninety are catered for (with prior booking). *Free coffee offered to our readers on presentation of this guide.*

Biriatou

64700 (4km SE)

⊚ 🎿 🏠 |●| Hôtel-restaurant Bakea**

Take the D258 from Hendaye and follow the signs.
Hotel ☎05.59.20.02.01 ☎05.59.20.58.21
Restaurant ☎05.59.20.76.36
ⓦwww.bakea.fr.st
Closed Mon and Tues lunchtimes (April–end of Sept); Mon and Tues 1 Oct–31 March; 20 Jan–15 Feb. **Disabled access. TV. Car park.**

A gorgeous, isolated place where you'll get complete rest and relaxation. Ten clean and

flowery double rooms cost €39–66 – the prettiest have balconies and views over the Bidassoa valley (nos. 7–10) – and there are another 23 in an annexe nearby. Half board is available during July and August (not compulsory) from €128 for two people. Excellent restaurant (☎05.59.20.76.36) with a dreamy terrace, offering elegant and attentive service; generous portions of imaginative dishes; specialities include lobster salad, warm, sweet and sour duck liver, joint of monkfish and fresh anchovy lasagne marinated in basil. Menus start at €31 (except Sun and public holidays), with others at €48 and €58. *10% discount on the price of a room (except Aug) offered to our readers on presentation of this guide.*

Hossegor

40150

⊚ 🎿 🏠 Hôtel Barbary Lane

156 av. de la Côte-d'Argent. Between the beach and the canal.
☎05.58.43.46.00 ☎05.58.43.95.19
ⓦwww.barbary-lane.com
Closed Jan to mid-Feb. **Restaurant open mid-June to mid-Sept. TV. Pool table. High chairs available. Garage for bikes.**

Barbary Lane is the name of the house that provided the setting for Armistead Maupin's *San Francisco Chronicles*. It enjoys a pretty location, with a small swimming pool to the rear and a terrace giving onto a promenade, just ten minutes' walk from the sea, and offers attractive little double rooms €45–109, depending on the degree of comfort and the season. Similar value for money can be found in the restaurant, the service is very friendly and booking is strongly recommended. Great breakfasts, with coconut *crème caramel* and other titbits. Logis de France. *Free house apéritif or liqueur offered to our readers on presentation of this guide.*

⊚ 🎿 🏠 |●| Hôtel-restaurant Les Huîtrières du Lac**

Avenue du Touring-Club. On the edge of the lake, on the Seignosse road.
☎05.58.43.51.48 ☎05.58.41.73.11
ⓔleshuirieresdulac@wanadoo.fr
Closed Mid-Jan to mid-Feb. **Restaurant closed** Sun evening and Mon out of season. **TV. High chairs available. Garden. Car park.**

A well-run family business, well worth a stop for a meal overlooking the promenade and the lake: fresh oysters, seafood platter, sea bass in a salt crust or foie gras pan-fried with grapes, with set menus priced at €18.50 and €33. Doubles go for €57–85, depending on the season – reserve well in advance to be sure of getting a room with a view of the lake. *Free coffee offered to our readers on presentation of this guide.*

Lacanau-Océan
33680

ⓐ |●| Le Bistro des Cochons

1 rue du Docteur-Darrigan
☎05.56.03.15.61
Closed *lunchtimes, Mon and Tues (Oct–April); also closed on Tues in May and Wed in winter; lunchtimes Mon–Fri (June–Sept).* **Disabled access.**

A delightful spot, somewhere between a fisherman's cabin and a neighbourhood bistro with unusual, witty décor, skilfully assembled from recycled objects. The food follows the same lines: dishes based on traditional local produce, imaginatively reworked and carefully prepared – reckon on €25–30 à la carte. All this plus friendly service and reasonable prices – what more could you ask for?

Lalinde-en-Périgord
24150

ⓐ 沙 🏠 |●| Hôtel-restaurant Le Château***

Rue de la Tour; take rue des Martyrs-du-21-Juillet-1944, then turn down rue de la Poste.
☎05.53.61.01.82 ℻05.53.24.74.60
Closed *Mon; Tues lunchtime; Sun evenings, out of season (hotel only); third week in Sept; mid-Nov to mid-Feb.* **TV. High chairs available. Swimming pool.**

This is a real thirteenth-century castle with its corbelled turret, pepper-pot towers and balcony and small swimming pool overlooking the sleepy Dordogne. Guy Gensou, who has redecorated the entire place, is in charge of the kitchen and gives you a very warm welcome. He adds his own touch to local dishes and uses superb fresh produce. The dining rooms are peaceful and the staff pleasant. Good, traditional cuisine on the menus €25–42 (the first menu includes apéritif), or à la carte: pâté with truffle fragments,

stuffed trout in white Bergerac, *millefeuille* with raspberry *coulis*. Comfortable double rooms go for €52–156, according to the degree of comfort; half board, €62–118, is compulsory from May to the end of September. Guy is a motorbike enthusiast and gives his fellow bikers a particularly warm welcome. Credit cards not accepted. Logis de France. *10% discount on the price of a room (5% discount on half board for bikers in July–Aug, after two consecutive nights) offered to our readers on presentation of this guide.*

Laroque-Timbaut
47340

ⓐ |●| Le Roquentin

It's opposite the church.
☎05.53.95.78.78
Closed *Sun evening; Mon; Thurs and Sat lunch; evenings on public holidays.*

Recently built, and cheerfully decorated in the style of a stone Provençal house. The chef has acquired a good reputation for regional cooking, using the finest quality produce and the traditional methods of the southwest. Dishes include caramelized duck's leg and squabs on a bed of ceps. Weekday lunch menus €10 and €15, except for public holidays; other menus €19–34. There's a fine wine list, with a good Cahors Clos La Coutale 1999 and a Buzet Baron d'Ardeuil.

Larrau
64560

ⓐ 🏠 |●| Hôtel-restaurant Etchemaïte**

☎05.59.28.61.45 ℻05.59.28.72.71
🖥www.hotel-etchemaite.fr
Closed *Sun evening and Mon out of season; 5 Jan–2 Feb; 5–14 Dec.* **TV. High chairs available. Car park.**

It's easy to fall in love with this contempla-tive spot, and the welcome and kindness of the Etchemaïte family help to make it a magical experience. Simple, comfortable doubles go for €42 with shower/wc or €49–58 with bath. Chef Pierre's aim is to combine tradition with originality; mainly using lamb, duck and mushrooms as a basis, he conjures up dishes such as duck breast and duck foie gras with apples, *parmentier* of *boudin* with apples, cutlets of suckling lamb, cep terrine with foie gras *jus*, monkfish with chicory and grilled hake fillet with herb butter. The rustic dining room, serving set menus €15 (in the week) to €58 (surprise menu) or à la carte, has a view over the mountains, and the wine list is full of unexpected treats at reasonable prices. Logis de France.

Laruns
64400

ⓔ |⦿| L'Arrégalet

37 rue du Bourguet.
☎05.59.05.35.47
Closed *Sun evening and Mon out of season; Mon and Tues lunchtimes in season; 10–26 May; 5–26 Dec.* **Disabled access.**

A warmly welcoming restaurant in an old street with a small terrace. The Coudouy family cook typical local dishes using the best ingredients the mountain can produce – service can be a little bit slow though. The owner's brother makes the charcuterie and the bread is baked in the kitchens. Their *garbure* and duck foie gras with leek fondue are both special, but *poule-au-pot*, with the chicken served whole in a vegetable broth, is the house speciality and menus start at €11 (weekday lunchtime), with others €13.50–26. *Arrégalet* is the local word for a crust of garlic bread fried in duck fat.

ⓔ ⅔ |⦿| Auberge Bellevue

55 rue Bourguet; 400m from the town centre.
☎05.59.05.31.58 ℗05.59.05.39.08
Closed *Tues evening and Wed (except 10 July–31 Aug); 3 weeks in Jan; fortnight in June.* **Disabled access.**

The chalet is festooned with flowers and there is an uninterrupted view of the mountains. An attractive, friendly place with appetizing menus at €13.60–27.50, plus a set lunch, in season, for €12. Try the cep omelette, *salmis* of pigeon or veal stew *à l'ancienne*, *garburade*, duck *confit* with ceps or chicken *fricassée* with freshwater crayfish. And don't overlook their *crème catalane*. *Free coffee offered to our readers on presentation of this guide.*

Sévignacq-Meyracq
64260 (15km N)

ⓔ 🏠 |⦿| ⅔ Hôtel-restaurant Les Bains de Secours**

Coming into the vallée d'Ossau, on the D935 leading to Laruns, it's signposted after Rébénacq.
☎05.59.05.62.11 ℗05.59.05.76.56
ⓦwww.hotel-bains-secours.com
Closed *Sun evening; Mon; Thurs lunchtime; Jan.* **TV. High chairs available. Car park.**

A scenic road leads to this restored Béarn farm, now a country inn adorned with flower-filled balconies. Just seven well-appointed rooms go from €50 with shower/wc to €60 with bath. Delicious food is served by the open fire in winter and on the terrace in summer, with set menus €13 (weekday lunchtime, but also available for hotel guests in the evenings and at the weekend) and €25 (lunch and dinner, except Sun), featuring such dishes as squids stuffed with foie gras and ceps, as well as *garbure Béarnaise*. There's also a Sunday lunch menu at €26.50. A very good place to eat, close to the old spa. Logis de France. *10% discount on the price of a room (except July–Aug) offered to our readers on presentation of this guide.*

Lestelle-Betharram
64800

ⓔ 🏠 |⦿| Le Vieux Logis***

Route des Grottes; it's on the outskirts of the village, towards the caves.
☎05.59.71.94.87 ℗05.59.71.96.75
ⓦwww.hotel-levieuxlogis.com
Closed *Sun evening and Mon out of season; Mon lunchtime in season; 25 Jan–1 March; a week in early Nov; a week at Christmas.* **Disabled access. TV. High chairs and games available. Swimming pool. Car park.**

Sizeable modern roadside hotel at the foot of the mountains, with a swimming pool and extensive grounds – an ideal place to relax. It's excellent value, with impeccable double rooms (several of them refurbished) for €46–65 with shower/wc or bath; half board €56–66 per person. There are separate wooden chalets in the grounds where the rooms have balconies. The restaurant has been restored to create a delightful setting for the top-quality regional cooking (menus €24–40) – foie gras with fruits, sole with ceps, duck breast – and particularly good desserts. Logis de France.

Lurbe-Saint-Christau
64660

@ 🎿 🏠 |O| Au Bon Coin***

Route d'Arudy; it's about 1km from the village.
☎05.59.34.40.12 ℗05.59.34.46.40
✉thierrylassala@wanadoo.fr
Closed Sun evening, Mon and Tues
(1 Oct–30 April); Christmas. **Disabled
access. TV. Swimming pool. Car park.**

A good, comfortable, modern hotel set in peaceful countryside in the foothills 300m from a spa. The swimming pool is across the (rarely used) road. Quiet double rooms €52–82; the largest have balconies with tables and chairs. Half board, compulsory in July and Aug, costs €110–127 per person. In the restaurant they serve unusual dishes at reasonable prices – menus €25 (weekday lunchtimes) up to €48 – making best use of what is good at the market: cep pie, Pyrenees lamb with thyme flower, to name only a couple.

Mauleon-Licharre
64130

@ 🏠 |O| Hôtel Bidegain**

13 rue de la Navarre, opposite the château.
☎05.59.28.16.05 ℗05.59.19.10.26
✉hotel-bidegain@wanadoo.fr
Closed Sun evening and Mon out of season.
TV. Pay car park.

One of the oldest and most beautiful town-centre hotels, once inhabited by the smart set, has undergone a renaissance. Pierre and Martine Chilo have taken this place in hand and have very quickly turned it into the best gourmet restaurant in town. On the menus, ranging from €11.50 (in the week) to €33, you'll find cod terrine with a spicy pimento paste smeared on good bread, barbecued beef and chocolate soufflé, while the cheaper menus include delicious dishes such as shin of veal and lamb's sweetbreads. Double rooms go for €40–54 with shower/wc or bath, depending on the season.

Mimizan-Plage
40200

@ 🎿 🏠 |O| Hôtel-restaurant
Atlantique

38 av. de la Côte-d'Argent; it's on the north end of the beach, close to the town centre.
☎05.58.09.09.42 ℗05.58.82.42.63
ⓦwww.hotelatlantique.landes.com
Restaurant closed Wed lunch (except in summer); 10–30 Jan; 1–15 Oct (hotel remains open). **Disabled access. TV. High chairs and games available. Pay car park.**

This modest and friendly family establishment stands on the seafront, though enjoys only a limited sea view. The façade of the old wooden building is intact and they've built a thirty-room modern hotel on the back. The best rooms are in the main house, and four of them have a sea view; doubles cost €31–48, according to the degree of comfort and the season. Half board, €28–48, is compulsory in July and August. Simple, nourishing dishes include duck breast with foie gras and balsamic vinegar, scallop salad with mango, grilled fish with garlic butter, and chicken with prawns. Menus start at €9 in the week, then others at €13–25. *Free house apéritif offered to our readers on presentation of this guide.*

@ 🏠 L'Airial

6 rue de la Papeterie. On the southern end of the beach.
☎05.58.09.46.54. ℗05.58.09.32.10
Closed early Nov to end April. **High chairs and games available.**

The building is nothing much to look at on the outside, but the interior is relaxing and quiet (no TV) and the rooms are meticulously kept and tastefully decorated, with doubles priced at €45–50, depending on the season – and you will wake up to the sound of birdsong. Ask for one at the back, with a balcony overlooking the garden. The owner is very friendly and will be more than willing to fill you in with details about the town and the region.

@ 🎿 🏠 |O| Hôtel-restaurant
L'Émeraude des Bois**

66–68 av. du Courant; take the D626, or it's a ten-minute walk from the centre.
☎05.58.09.05.28
ⓦwwwemeraudedesbois.com
Closed Oct to end of March. **Restaurant open** every day in season, dinner only 5 April–30 Sept. **TV. High chairs, games, cots and feeding bottles available. Car park.**

This hotel-restaurant is another good family establishment in a charming house surrounded by large trees and decorated in traditional style (although change is in the air, as it is in the process of being refurbished). Double rooms go for €52–60, depending on the season and the degree of comfort; half board, compulsory in July and August, costs €48–52 per person. Specialities on the excellent menus (€17–29) include home-made foie gras, salmon tartare, cream of courgette soup, fish soup, sea bream soufflé with shellfish *coulis*, monkfish *à la provençale*, duck breast with honey, chocolate mousse and home-made *crème brûlée*. A great deal of care goes into the preparation and cooking. The veranda and terrace provide welcome shade in summer. Logis de France. *Free house apéritif offered to our readers on presentation of this guide*

⊚ ⅔ 🏠 Le Patio

6 av. de la Côte-d'Argent; on the seafront, by the exit to the car park in the town centre.
☎05.58.09.09.10 ℗05.58.09.26.38
🖲www.le-patio.fr
Closed *4 Nov; 20 Dec–20 Jan; open every day from 1 April to 1 Nov, with reservation only the rest of the year.* **TV. High chairs and games available. Swimming pool. Car park.**

It's advisable to book well in advance for this place because the oceanfront location means it gets full. Stunning little rooms, nicely furnished in Provençal style go for €59–90 for a double with shower/wc, depending on the season, or you could choose to stay in the quiet bungalows at the back near the swimming pool. *10% discount on the price of a room (except 15 June–15 Sept) offered to our readers on presentation of this guide.*

⊚ |●| ⅔ L'Île de Malte

5 rue du Casino; next to the Casino.
☎05.58.82.48.15
Closed *Nov.* **Disabled access. High chairs available.**

There has long been a restaurant called *L'Île de Malte* on this spot, but this one is sparkling new and has great potential. Since April 2003 a young team has taken up the challenge of offering sophisticated, creative food all year round. They have attracted an equally young crowd, and the place is very lively at weekends and on fine days. The friendly service, and large terrace (protected from the wind) with trendy furniture, make it ideal for having lunch or simply enjoying a drink. Menus start at

€12.50 (weekday lunchtime), then from €14 to €30. *Free house apéritif offered to our readers on presentation of this guide.*

Lüe
40210 (22km NE)

⊚ |●| Restaurant L'Auberge Landaise

In the village; take the D626.
☎05.58.07.06.13
Closed *Sun evening; Mon; Oct; 3 weeks in Jan.* **Car park.**

A jolly little inn where they serve a string of eight set menus to suit every pocket, from €10 (weekday lunchtimes) and from €18 up to €31. Unless you're a veggie, it's impossible not to find something you fancy: wood-pigeon or game stew, foie gras, duck gizzard salad, duck breast and duck *confit*, baby squid in ink or monkfish *à l'armoricaine*. The quality of Monsieur Barthet's cooking and the range of prices ensure a varied clientele, from VIPs to factory workers, all tucking into the delicious food.

Mont-de-Marsan
40000

⊚ ⅔ 🏠 |●| Hôtel-restaurant des Pyrénées*

4 rue du 34ème R.I.
☎05.58.46.49.49 ℗05-58-06-43-57
🖲hoteldespyrenees@wanadoo.fr
Closed *Sat lunch; Sun; first week in July.* **TV. High chairs available.**

You can't miss this wonderful old pink house. At lunchtimes – when there's a €10.50 menu – it's rather like a canteen for local workers. Other menus, €21–28, list good, simple, tasty dishes such as duck breast, foie gras, scallops and stuffed *aiguillettes*. When it's hot, the dining room's large bay windows are opened onto a terrace surrounded by trees and flowers. The rooms, from €35 with handbasin to €40 with shower/wc or bath, are attractive, particularly those that overlook the garden – the ones on the crossroads side are noisier, so make sure you call to reserve. *Free kir offered to our readers on presentation of this guide.*

⊚ ⅔ 🏠 |●| Hôtel-restaurant Richelieu**

Rue Wlérick; it's behind the theatre.

☏05.58.06.10.20 📠05.58.06.00.68
🌐www.citotel.com/hotels/richelieu.html
Restaurant closed *Sat; Sun evening.*
**Disabled access. TV. High chairs and
games available. Pay car park.**

The only hotel in the town centre with
a touch of style. The good-value doubles
(€45.50–47) with bath are unremarkable
and rather impersonal, but clean and quiet.
There's a charming breakfast room and in
the restaurant you get some of the best
cooking in town with menus starting at
€15.50 (weekdays), €23.50 on Sundays,
then others at €27.50 and €31. They
include tasty traditional dishes like wild
mushroom ravioli, half-cooked duck foie
gras terrine, roast milk-fed lamb, stuffed
ribs of veal with port and iced nougat.
*10% discount on the price of a room (except
July–Aug) offered to our readers on presentation
of this guide.*

◎ |●| ⅍ Chez Despons – Le Plumaçon

20 rue Plumaçon; it's at the foot of the
train station steps, close to the arenas.
☏05.58.06.17.56
Closed *evenings; Sun; 3 weeks in Aug.*
Disabled access. High chairs available.

At weekday lunchtimes, there is a menu at
€7.50, and others from €9.50 to €14; the
latter includes a large buffet of salads and
cooked meats and wine. Good family food
– the kind you dream of finding on your
travels through France. The €10 menu
lists grilled entrecôte steak with house
or green pepper sauce served with green
beans or *frites*, a salad and dessert, while
the cheapest menu includes raw vegetable
salad and charcuterie. Credit cards not
accepted. *Free coffee offered to our readers on
presentation of this guide.*

◎ |●| Le Bistrot de Marcel

1 rue du Pont-de-Commerce.
☏05.58.75.09.71
Closed *Sun; Mon lunchtime; public holidays.*
Children's games available.

Despite the name, this isn't an old-style
bistro but a good restaurant with tasteful,
modern decoration, fine cooking and a
rather wonderful setting – there are two
terraces with views over the Midouze. The
cooking is defiantly representative of the
Landes region and the chef uses excellent
local produce. Try duck breast, foie gras,
confit, mussels and so on. The cheapest
menu (weekday lunchtime) costs €8, then

others for €14–25, including one at €24
specifically devoted to regional specialities.
They've set aside a play area for kids.

Uchacq
40090 (4km NW)

◎ |●| Restaurant Didier Garbage

It's on the RN134, on the way to Sabres-
Bordeaux.
☏05.58.75.33.66
Closed *Sun evening; Mon; Tues evening; first
week in Jan; last fortnight in June.* **Disabled
access. High chairs available. Car park.**

The chef moved to this small village restaurant – and all his customers followed.
The dining room is a pleasant place in
which to sit and enjoy his fine cooking
(don't be put off by the slightly sloppy
presentation). Recommended are pan-
fried foie gras with figs, lamprey with
leeks, duck *confit* and *tournedos* of pig's
trotter with truffle oil. Weekday set menus
in the bistro corner (which has a host of
loyal regulars) at €11.50 and €20, and
others in the restaurant from €25 to €55,
plus a selection of samples at €75. If you
don't fancy these, you can just have a slice
of country ham and a glass of wonderful
local wine.

Montferrand-du-Périgord
24440

◎ 🛏 |●| ⅍ Hôtel-restaurant Lou Peyrol

La Barrière; take the D703, then the D660
in the direction of Beaumont and finally the
D25; it's below Montferrand, on the D26.
☏ and 📠05.53.63.24.45
🌐www.hotel-loupeyrol-dordogne.com
Closed *Wed lunchtime; 1 Oct to Easter.* **High
chairs available. Car park.**

A pretty little country hotel with a restaurant run by Sarah and Thierry, a friendly
Anglo-Corsican couple who also run the
snack bar across the road. It's a good base
for a walking holiday, with stark but clean
double rooms with little spare bedding
(nos. 7 and 8 offer a view of the gorgeous
village of Montferrand, while nos. 5 and
6 are particularly cool, even in summer)
going for €37 with basin and at €44
with shower/wc or bath. Good cooking
(menus €16–27), too: roast Barbary duck,
omelettes with ceps, morels or girolles, a

perfectly cooked magret, chocolate and walnut gâteau. Or you can expect to pay €23 à la carte. Logis de France. *Free house apéritif offered to our readers on presentation of this guide.*

Cadouin
24480 (7km N)

◎ 🎋 🏠 |●| Auberge de Jeunesse

In a section of the abbey.
☎05.53.73.28.78 ⑨05.53.73.28.79
🕸www.fuaj.org
Closed *10 Dec–1 Feb.* **Disabled access. Car park.**

Stunning setting, inside a lovingly restored abbey with an adjoining park. The one- and two-person rooms are the old monks' cells, giving onto the cloister, and the other rooms are just as delightful. Reckon on €16 per person in a single, double or triple room; €13.40 in one with 4–7 beds (including breakfast) – all have their own bathroom. Meals cost €9. This is a very friendly place. *Free house apéritif offered to our readers on presentation of this guide.*

Montfort-en-Chalosse
40380

◎ 🏠 |●| Aux Tauzins**

1km from the village, in the direction of Hagetmau.
☎05.58.98.60.22 ⑨05.58.98.45.79
🕸www.auxtauzins.com
Closed *Sun evening; Mon (except the first fortnight in Aug); Jan; first fortnight in Oct.* **Disabled access. TV. High chairs and games available. Swimming pool. Car park.**

A fine example of a traditional hotel and restaurant, but with some welcome modern facilities – such as the pool. The owners have been hotel-keepers for three generations, so the establishment has a comfortable family feel with old-style bedrooms overlooking the grounds; it's wonderfully peaceful and doubles go for €57–60. The bright restaurant has a view over the valley and serves a range of menus €21–40. Dishes are from the region: *tournedos* Landais with liver and ceps, liver with apples and grapes, *fricassée* of monkfish and scallops with ceps. Logis de France.

Montignac
24290

◎ 🎋 🏠 |●| Hôtel-restaurant de la Grotte**

63 rue du 4-Septembre.
☎05.53.51.80.48 ⑨05.53.51.05.96
🖂hoteldelagrotte@wanadoo.fr
TV. Pay car park.

This old building was once a staging post but became a hotel when the Lascaux caves were discovered. The delightful rooms are all decorated differently; ask for a room overlooking the garden or the Vézère (nos. 6, 7, 8 and 12). The prices are relatively reasonable for the town (the cheapest only have a washbasin); reckon on €27–50 for a double room, according to the degree of comfort. The enchanting restaurant serves dishes such as *millefeuille* of ceps, chanterelles with walnut cream and magret stuffed with homemade sausage, with a weekday lunchtime menu at €11, then others at €18–26. On fine days there are two terraces for eating out; our preference is the garden by the riverside with a newly decorated veranda. *Free house apéritif and garage space (subject to availability) offered to our readers on presentation of this guide.*

◎ 🏠 |●| Hôtel-restaurant Bellevue

Regourdou; it's on the Lascaux road, after the caves at the top of the hill.
☎05.53.51.81.29
🕸www.hotel-bellevue.info
Closed *evenings; Sat; a week in June; a week in Oct; 3 weeks in Dec–Jan.* **Disabled access. Car park.**

Located close to the Lascaux caves, this is a restaurant with just five bedrooms (€34–40); the décor is drab but this is more than compensated for by the superb views from its bay windows and terrace. It serves decent food with a regional bent: chicken *confit* and *enchaud*, baked loin of pork, pig's trotters with garlic and truffles, gizzard salad, cep mushroom omelette. Prices are reasonable – a weekday menu for €10 and others €13–22.50. Reservations recommended on Sundays, and in the high season (its proximity to the caves makes it very popular).

◎ 🏠 |●| Hostellerie La Roseraie***

11 pl. d'Armes.
☎05.53.50.53.92 ⑨05.53.51.02.23

ⓦ www.laroseraie.fr.st
Closed *lunchtime (except weekends in mid-season); 1 Nov to Easter.* **TV. High chairs and cots available. Swimming pool.**

A solid, elegant nineteenth-century town house on the place d'Armes. The staircase is wooden and there are several small sitting rooms. The rooms, costing €80–135, are exquisite; though each is different, all have en-suite bathrooms. It feels more like an old-style guest house or a family *pension* than a stylish three-star establishment – they even cork your unfinished wine and leave it on the table for the next meal. The small, enclosed grounds have high walls so it's easy to imagine you're out of town, and behind the swimming pool you'll find the rose garden the hotel is named after. The restaurant – which has a delightful terrace – serves sophisticated local dishes, adroitly prepared and reasonably priced (set menus €21–41): foie gras with asparagus and vegetables, glazed free-range guinea-fowl in langoustine broth. Half board is compulsory from July until the end of September, as well as at weekends and on public holidays (€75–115 per person).

ⓔ |●| **L'Auberge de l'Oie Gourmande**

La Grande Béchade; take the Lascaux road, turn left after 500m and it's out in the fields.
ⓣ 05.53.51.59.40
Closed *Sun evening and Mon out of season; Jan and Feb.*

This place is somewhat off the tourist track (although coach parties do visit sometimes). The ample dining room has stone walls – they set tables out on the terrace in summer – and serve fine, creative Périgord cuisine that's a lovely combination of tradition and modern invention. Try the *aumônière* made with *cabécou*, a sweet and salty turnover with cheese, and the delicious desserts are to die for. Attentive service and good prices, too: the €14 menu is particularly good value, and there's another at €22.

Saint-Amand-de-Coly
24290 (8km E)

ⓔ 🎋 🛏 |●| **Hôtel-restaurant Le Gardette**★★

In the village.
ⓣ 05.53.51.68.50 ⓕ 05.53.51.04.25
ⓦ www.hotel-gardette.com

Closed *1 Oct–31 March.* **High chairs available. Car park.**

Two pale stone houses overshadowed by a fantastic church. Unpretentious but prettily refurbished rooms at reasonable prices – €30–38 depending on facilities and the season – some have a balcony with a view of the abbey. The restaurant across the lane has a few small tables in one corner – the owner cooks for the local schoolchildren during term time. For taller customers, set menus are €16–25, offering salads and dishes from the southwest including omelette with cep mushrooms or truffles, duck breast and *confit*. In summer, it's advisable to book during the classical music festival. *10% discount on the price of a room (except 15 July–30 Aug) offered to our readers on presentation of this guide.*

Sergeac
24290 (8.5km SW)

ⓔ 🎋 |●| **Restaurant l'Auberge du Peyrol**

It's on the D65, halfway between Montignac and Les Eyzies.
ⓣ 05.53.50.72.91
ⓦ www.dordogne24.com
Closed *Mon (except July–Aug); evenings (except Sat and summertime); Dec–Feb.* **Disabled access. High chairs available. Car park.**

A traditional stone-built inn standing on its own just outside a quaint little village. A large bay window looks out over the lovely Vézère valley. The fine rustic restaurant has a big fireplace where they smoke fillets of duck breast and offer a selection of local country dishes: *enchaud* of pig *confit*, magret with Périgueux sauce, fresh goose liver, truffle omelettes, with a range of menus €12–35. It's best to book. Credit cards not accepted. *Free house apéritif offered to our readers on presentation of this guide.*

Chapelle-Aubareil (La)
24290 (12km S)

ⓔ 🎋 🛏 |●| **Hôtel-restaurant La Table du Terroir**★★

From Montignac take the road to Lascaux II, from where it's signposted.
ⓣ 05.53.50.72.14 ⓕ 05.53.51.16.23
ⓦ www.tableduterroir.com
Closed *evenings Dec to end of April; 20–28*

Dec. **Disabled access. TV. High chairs and games available. Swimming pool. Car park.**

The Gibertie family have developed a tourist complex around their smallholding, deep in the country. The restaurant is on a hill 100m from the hotel; midway between them there's a swimming pool with views over the countryside. The buildings are new, but in traditional Périgord style, and they blend well with their surroundings. Rooms are pleasant, and the rates €47–62.80 with shower/wc or bath (depending on the season) include breakfast. Half board, compulsory from 10 July to 31 August, costs €42–51 per person. Packed lunch is available on request. Set menus, €12–30, list regional cooking, based on farm produce: sliced duck, duck *confit* and so on. You can expect to pay about €22 à la carte. In summer, however, the turnover of customers (as in the nearby caves) is almost excessive, with a constant stream of coach parties. Credit cards not accepted. Logis de France. *Free house apéritif offered to our readers on presentation of this guide.*

Navarrenx

64190

ⓒ 🍴 🏠 |●| **Hôtel-restaurant du Commerce****

Place des Casernes.
☎05.59.66.50.16 🏷05.59.66.52.67
ⓘwww.hotel-du-commerce.fr
Closed *Jan.* **TV. High chairs and games available.**

One of the oldest houses in Navarrenx. They light a fire in the large fireplace in the foyer at the first sign of cold weather. Pleasant rooms – the nicest up in the attic – are €45 with shower/wc or bath. Wonderful Béarn flavours in the restaurant, which has plush surroundings, or there's a large shady terrace for the summer. Menus are very reasonably priced: €10.50 for the weekday lunch one and others at €16–25. Try the foie gras, salmon steak with *piperade*, duck *confit* and chocolate *fondant*. Logis de France. *Free coffee offered to our readers on presentation of this guide.*

Nérac

47600

ⓒ 🍴 |●| **Aux Délices du Roy**

7 rue du Château; off the place de la Mairie.

☎ and 🏷05.53.65.81.12
Closed *Wed.*

A small, nicely decorated dining room provides the setting for inviting food that has earned a loyal following, based on a winning combination of tradition, subtle flavours and high-quality produce served by polite attentive staff. The menus at €23–65 (children's menu at €9.20) include unusual dishes: snails with Vire *andouille* and crisp cabbage, a whole duck's breast with honey and an array of fish and seafood recipes, including a Mediterranean touch, with the Provençal tuna. The wine list features regional wines. *Free house apéritif offered to our readers on presentation of this guide.*

Francescas

46600 (13km SE)

ⓒ 🍴 |●| **Le Relais de la Hire**

From Nérac take the D930 for 10km towards Condom, then turn left on to the D112.
☎05.53.65.41.59
ⓘwww.perso.wanadoo.fr/la.hire
Closed *Sun evening; Mon; Wed lunch; first week in Nov.* **Games available. Disabled access.**

This restaurant, set in a stunning eighteenth-century manor house with a beautiful terrace, has a peaceful atmosphere. After working with Robuchon at the *Ritz* and running the kitchens at the *Carlton*, Jean-Noël Prabonne returned to Gascony. He is fussy about buying from local suppliers when creating his masterful dishes: Albret artichokes with a soufflé of foie gras, pike-perch with a crust of *fines herbes*, roast squab with foie gras, morels with ravioli and *fricassée* of asparagus. There is a range of menus €20–56, a children's menu for €13, or you can expect to pay around €40 à la carte. Games occupy the children allowing their parents to eat in peace. *Free house apéritif offered to our readers on presentation of this guide.*

Saint-Maure-de-Peyriac

47170 (17km SW)

ⓒ 🍴 |●| **Restaurants Les 2 Gourmands**

Rue Principale; from Nérac take the D656 in the direction of Mézin; from there, continue 4km to the west.
☎05.53.65.61.00
Closed *evenings; Sat.*

At lunchtime during the week this place

is like many others, with a clientele of travelling salesmen, local workers and lost tourists – though the food is better than average and dishes are substantial. The all-inclusive menus at €11 (during the week), €25 and €28 include soup, terrine or omelette as typical starters. But Sunday lunch is a different story: the restaurant is a magnet for gourmets so you have to book in advance, especially for Sunday lunch. The chef has worked at the *Ritz* and *Lasserre* (two of the very best restaurants in Paris) and on Sundays he and his associates give flight to their skill and imagination at prices that would be unthinkably cheap in the capital. Dishes change according to the season, but are typical of the best of the southwest.

Nontron
24300

@ 🛏 |O| ⅔ **Hôtel-restaurant Pelisson****

3 pl. Alfred-Agard
☎05.53.56.11.22 ⊕05.53.56.59.94.
@grand-hotel-pelisson@wanadoo.fr
/pelisson
Closed *Sun evening (Oct–May).* **TV. High chairs available. Disabled access. Swimming pool.**

Right in the town centre, this grand-looking hotel, with an elegant if somewhat austere façade, conceals a pretty garden and lovely pool. The old-fashioned rooms are reasonably priced at €45–54 for a double with shower/wc or bath and, round the back at least, very quiet. The hotel offers very friendly service and family atmosphere (it has been in the hands of the Pélissons for several generations) and has a huge opulent, rustic dining room with beautiful crockery (from a nearby factory) and a terrace giving onto the garden. The traditional food has earned a great reputation: baby rabbit salad with slithers of foie gras, sole *cassolette* with ceps, *tête de veau* with vinaigrette, *aiguillettes* of beef with *pécharmant*, all at reasonable prices – menus at €15 (except Sun) then €22.50–48. The wine list is reasonably priced, too. *10% discount on the price of a room (Oct–May, after two consecutive nights) offered to our readers on presentation of this guide.*

Oloron-Sainte-Marie
64400

@ 🛏 **Hôtel de la Paix****

24 av. Sadi-Carnot; it's opposite the train station.
☎05.59.39.02.63 ⊕05.59.39.98.20
@www.hotel-oloron.com
Closed *Sun 15 Sept–30 June; 15 Oct–15 Nov.* **TV. Car park.**

The son of the family that runs this hotel has made visible changes: the rooms have been refurbished and they boast new bedding and double glazing. All the rooms are huge and light and cost €41–49 for a double.

Esquiule
64400 (12km W)

@ ⅔ |O| **Chez Château**

Place du Fronton.
☎05.59.39.23.03 ⊕05.59.39.81.97
Closed *Sun evening; Mon; 15 Feb–15 March.* **Disabled access. TV. High chairs and games available.**

This is a fantastic place and the food is something else. Bernard Houçourigaray's cheapest menu lists *garbure*, trout with parsley, duck *confit*, black-sausage Parmentier and a crusty turnover. Or you can order a *garburade*; as you dig down to the bottom of the dish you uncover duck drumsticks and chunks of ham. If you're in a mind to treat yourself, opt for the marble cake of boiled chicken and liver or one of the latest creations from the endlessly inventive chef. Seasonally changing menus cost €10 (weekday lunchtime) and then €16–48, and there's a superb wine list at more than reasonable prices. The dining room is country-inn in style and the clientele comprises local people (do not be surprised if everybody here is speaking Basque). The owner is young, energetic (like his friendly team), attentive and chatty. Double rooms with shower/wc are €35.10. *Free house apéritif offered to our readers on presentation of this guide.*

Orthez
64300

@ ⅔ 🛏 |O| **Hôtel-restaurant Au Temps de la Reine Jeanne****

44 rue du Bourg-Vieux; it's opposite the tourist office.

☎05.59.67.00.76
Closed *Sun evening (Oct–April); a fortnight in Feb.* **Disabled access. TV. High chairs available.**

A peaceful and quiet hotel with some rooms overlooking the patio and other, more expensive ones (with air-conditioning) in an adjoining building; doubles with shower/wc or bath €45–49. The restaurant is a pleasant surprise: the décor is modest but the cuisine is opulent and modestly priced – fresh liver with figs, foie gras terrine with artichokes, joint of monkfish with bacon, duck cassoulet, Béarn black pudding on split bread, and suckling pig. Delicious weekday lunchtime menu costs €15 and there's another at €26. Service is excellent and there's occasional live jazz. Logis de France. *Liqueur on the house offered to our readers on presentation of this guide.*

Pau
64000

⊚ ⚘ |●| Don Quichotte

30–38 rue Castetnau; in the Triangle neighbourhood.
☎05.59.27.63.08
Closed *Sat lunchtime; Sun; Mon lunchtime.*

One of the cheapest restaurants of quality in Pau, very attractive to local students – you can eat well for €8. They list fifteen dishes (including tapas, paella and zarzuela) for derisory prices and three lunchtime *plats du jour* at €7.80, including wine. In season, there are menus based on pork specialities, including one featuring extremities (tail, feet and ears); other options include *parrillada* of fish or pork, *axoa* of veal and undercut of beef, also takeaway dishes at €6. Credit cards not accepted.

⊚ ⚘ |●| Restaurant La Brochetterie

16 rue Henri-IV; it's near the château, opposite the church.
☎05.59.27.40.33
✉eric.freyer1@lybertysurf.fr
Closed *Sat lunchtime; Mon; 15–30 Sept.* **Open** *till 11pm.*

This long-standing and attractive stone-built restaurant specializes in duck breast and other meat grilled over the fire. The lunchtime clientele consists mainly of people who work nearby. Weekday lunchtime menu at €11.50, then others at €13.50 and €19.50, with a children's

menu for €8. À la carte you'll spend around €16; try grilled hake flambéed with anis, wild boar cutlets, the mixed grill, foie gras and various fresh salads. On Thursday nights don't miss the milk-fed lamb and the pork. A real treat, so it's best to book. *Free house apéritif offered to our readers on presentation of this guide.*

⊚ |●| Le Majestic

9 pl. Royale.
☎05.59.27.56.83
Closed *Sun evening; Mon.* **Disabled access.**

Locally born chef Jean-Marie Larrère has created a restaurant to match his food: the baroque nineteenth-century décor has been overhauled in a minimalist, vaguely Japanese style, only enhanced by the shady terrace on the Place Royale. In any case, Larrère produces remarkable dishes: hot foie gras with caramelized pears, cannelloni of *confit* or duck foie gras, salad of *croustillant* of pig's trotters with fresh morels, pot-roast pigeon with ceps, saddle of monkfish with a chorizo *jus* and mushrooms. Menus range from €18 (weekday lunchtimes) to €34, or reckon on €45 à la carte. Mme Larrère is very welcoming, and runs the dining room to perfection.

⊚ |●| Au Fin Gourmet

24 av. Gaston-Lacoste; it's opposite the station, about five minutes from the centre.
☎05.59.27.47.71 ☎05.59.82.96.77
Closed *Sun evening; Mon; a week in Feb; a fortnight end July to early Aug.* **Disabled access. High chairs and games available.**

This place, a firm favourite with the people of Pau, really lives up to its name. Quality cooking is on all the menus, which start at €19 (weekday lunchtimes), then go from €27 up to €56. Children's menu from €10. Dishes are finely prepared – highlights include the terrine of duck foie gras with Piquillo peppers and roast pigeon breast with five spices, apples cooked in duck fat and small caramelized turnips.

⊚ ⚘ |●| Restaurant La Table d'Hôte

1 rue du Hedas.
☎ and ☎05.59.27.56.06
Closed *Sun; Mon; Christmas.*

In one of the oldest parts of Pau, Fabrice and Martine will welcome you like a regular to their impressive restaurant with stained-glass windows and beams. The richly flavoured cuisine is spot-on, and uses lots of quality produce, with menus €20 (weekdays only) and €26. Choose from the à la carte menu (around €30): pan-fried foie gras with onion jam, duck pie with truffles and Gascon black pork with fresh fruit. *Free house apéritif offered to our readers on presentation of this guide.*

Bosdarros

64290 (8km S)

@ |●| Auberge Labarthe

Rue Pierre-Bideau; take the N134.
☏5.59.21.50.13
Closed Sun evening and Mon; Tues (Sept–June); Jan.

A charming little inn in an equally charming village swathed in flowers – a wonderful stopover in Jurançon wine country. The staff are young and keen, while the chef, who served his apprenticeship in *Chilo*, in Barcus, skilfully balances classicism with modernity. He not only goes to the market himself but also collects mushrooms and herbs in the countryside; his imagination has won over the locals, despite their initial apprehension, and some of his inventions have become accepted as regional classics – the terrine of smoked eel, green apples and foie gras, for instance. Regional menu at €21, then others at €30–56.

Gan

64290 (8km S)

@ 🏠 |●| Hostellerie L'Horizon**

Chemin de Mesplet: in the hills.
☏05.59.21.58.93 ☏05.59.21.71.80
🖰www.hostellerie-horizon.com
Closed Sun evening and Mon out of season; 1 Feb–1 March; 23–25 Dec. **Disabled access (restaurant only). TV. High chairs and games available. Car park.**

A pink house with a garden full of flowers and a peaceful terrace, in extensive grounds. Attractive, well-equipped rooms for €50; half board at €68 per person. Sophisticated cuisine à la carte: duck foie gras, braised sole with foie gras, salmon trout with ceps, lamb sweetbreads with girolles and so on. Also, a range of menus priced €15 (weekday lunchtime) to €45.

Pauillac

33250

@ |●| Le Pauillac

2 quai Albert-de-Pichon.
☏05.56.59.19.20
Closed Sun (out of season).

A restaurant overlooking the river, with bright and elegant nautical décor to match – and this, in its turn, is a faithful reflection of the skilfully prepared, light and sophisticated cooking. The house specialities are based on fish and seafood, but carnivores will be well satisfied by the Pauillac lamb on offer, and there's an excellent wine list. In fact, the food verges on gourmet territory, but the prices remain extremely reasonable, thereby helping to attract loyal local custom – midweek lunchtime menu €14, then others at €17–26. Reckon on just under €30 à la carte.

Arcins

33460 (13km S)

@ |●| Café-restaurant du Lion d'Or

Take the D2 in the direction of Bordeaux.
☏05.56.58.96.79
Closed Sun; Mon; July; New Year holiday period. **Disabled access.**

The owner can be brusque, but the cooking is superb, with game in season and fish from the estuary prepared to local Médoc recipes. The €11 menu (not served Sat night) offers starter, main course, cheese, dessert and a half-litre of country wine. Dishes of the day are good: roast lamb, beef *tournedos*, liver *à l'anglaise*, or a simple omelette. À la carte, expect to pay less than €35.

Penne-d'Agenais

47140

@ 🎋 |●| Restaurant L'Air du Temps

Mounet area.
☏05.53.41.41.34
Closed Sun evening; Mon; a week in Jan; a week in Nov.

While her husband is away working in Paris, Martine Harasymezuk unassumingly but efficiently runs this old farm, brilliantly restored in a neo-rustic style. The delightful restaurant with terrace serves adventurous cooking that marries tradition (duck foie gras) and modern French (bass tartare with pears, sea-trout terrine with spinach). Weekday lunchtime menu (except public holidays) at €12.20 includes a quarter bottle of Buzet; other menus at €21.50 and €33. Friendly welcome, but the service is a little slack. *Free coffee offered to our readers on presentation of this guide.*

Périgueux

24000

@ 🏠 L'Univers**

18 cours Montaigne, and 3 rue Éguillerie.
℗05.53.53.34.79 ℗05.53.06.70.76
Closed *15 Nov–15 Dec.* **TV. Car park.**

This hotel is superbly situated, right in the town centre, on the edge of the historic quarter. The comfortable rooms, €45–59 for a double with shower, have all been refurbished and adorned with typical Breton furniture to add a rustic touch – ask for a room on the quieter pedestrianized street. Good restaurant, with traditional dishes (also from Brittany), but you would do well to have breakfast in town. You will have to pay by day in the car park in front of the hotel, but it is free by night.

@ 🏠 Hôtel Regina**

14 rue Denis-Papin; opposite the train station.
℗05.53.08.40.44 ℗05.53.54.72.44
TV.

A hotel with some forty rooms, a little way from the old town. It is more expensive than the other hotels around the train station, but it does boast a charm and comfort that none of them can match. Behind the spruce façade, dating from the 1930s, the rooms have recently been completely renovated in bright colours with doubles costing €53 in July and August, €51 the rest of the year.

@ 🍴 |●| Les Berges de l'Isle

2 rue Pierre-Magne; at the foot of the bridge, giving on to the cathedral; entrance via the Hôtel des Barris.
℗05.53.09.51.50 ℗05.53.05.19.08
Closed *Sun evening; Mon. For Sat lunchtime, reserve 48hr in advance.* **High chairs and games available. Disabled access.**

This restaurant is in a picturesque spot – on the shore of the island opposite the cathedral – and they have the only waterside terrace in town. The weekday lunchtime menu at €12.50, then others at €14–23, feature unusual cuisine such as *cassoulet* with four different meats and walnut oil, soufflé of foie gras with *vigneronne* sauce and lamprey with Bordelais sauce. Some wines are served by the glass, the atmosphere is friendly and booking is advised. *Free coffee offered to our readers on presentation of this guide.*

@ 🍴 |●| Le Clos Saint-Front

5-7 rue de la Vertu (second entrance off the rue Saint-Front).
℗05.53.45.78.58
Closed *Sun evening; Mon (except in summer).*

This restaurant sports one of the most pleasant terraces in Périgueux (in a quiet little garden), as well as offering what is undoubtedly the best value for money in town. The dining room on the upper level is ideally suited to an intimate tête-à-tête, while the one below is warmed by a log fire in winter. None of this, however, can compare with the delights of the cooking. It is amazing to discover just how much a chef can do with a few top-rate ingredients, a little imagination and plenty of expertise. On our visit, we were bowled over by the house speciality (pig's feet pancake with snails and sweet garlic cream) and the veal ribs with caramelized parsnips. After this veritable banquet, the bill was extremely reasonable – weekday lunchtime menus at €15 and €19, then others at €25 and €45. Not surprisingly, such a classy restaurant is known far and wide, so it is advisable to book. *Free house apéritif offered to our readers on presentation of this guide.*

@ 🍴 |●| Restaurant Le 8

8 rue de la Clarté; it's next to the Saint-Front cathedral.
℗ and ℗05.53.35.15.15
Closed *Sun; Mon; Feb school holiday; last week in June; Nov school holiday.*

Regional and creative dishes served in a sunny dining room – home-made foie gras or *croustillant* of duck are the star turns. The prices are steepish: set menus €15 (weekday lunchtime), then €19–32; reckon on €45 à la carte. The dishes include regional specialities, creatively reinterpreted: *brandade* pancake with walnut oil, Périgourdin carpaccio, calf's head poached in ginger and squid and aubergine pie. There's a small garden to the rear. Reservations recommended; it's a small place with a good reputation – a wonderful stopover on the way to Compostela. *Free coffee offered to our readers on presentation of this guide.*

⑥ 🎿 |●| Restaurant Hercule Poireau

2 rue de la Nation; it's in a small street opposite the main door of the Saint-Front cathedral.
☏ 05.53.08.90.76
Closed *Sat; Sun; 3 weeks in summer; 31 Dec–3 Jan.*

This impressive sixteenth-century vaulted cellar is distinguished by its sophisticated food and attentive service. The young chef has plied his trade all over France and acquired a skill beyond his years. The dining room is small, so it is advisable to book. The emphasis is on local tradition, with special care taken over the garnishing and presentation of the weekday lunchtime menu at €19, and other menus at €24–48; à la carte, reckon on €30. The restaurant has recently been complemented by an equally charming bistro area, open from 9pm to midnight, which serves plates of charcuterie, foie gras and smoked salmon at very reasonable prices. *Free house apéritif offered to our readers on presentation of this guide.*

Chancelade
24650 (3km NW)

⑥ 🏠 |●| Le Pont de la Beauronne**

4 rte. de Ribérac; it's 3km from Périgueux, at the crossroads of the D710 and D39, on the way to Angoulême.
☏ 05.53.08.42.91 ☏ 05.53.03.97.69
Closed *Sun evening; Mon lunchtime; Feb school holiday; 20 Sept–15 Oct.* **Open** *until 9.30pm.* **TV. High chairs available. Car park.**

The crossroads doesn't exactly enhance the charm of the place, but the rooms are reasonable and well kept, and the hotel has a family atmosphere. Doubles with basin or shower are €26, with bath €38 – try to get one at the back, looking onto the garden. In the rustic-style dining room the cooking is straightforward, with an emphasis on the regional – weekday lunchtime menu at €11.50, then others at €15–33. Logis de France.

Annesse-et-Baulieu
24430 (12km SW)

⑥ 🎿 🏠 |●| Château de Lalande – Restaurant Le Tilleul Cendré***

Go towards Gravelle then take the D3 in the direction of Saint-Astier.
☏ 05.53.54.52.30 ☏ 05.53.07.46.67
⊛ www.chateau-lalande-perigord.com
Closed *early Nov to 15 March.* **Restaurant closed** *Wed lunch.* **TV. High chairs and games available. Swimming pool. Car park.**

Situated in a 32-acre park on the banks of the Isle, this is luxury without ostentation, at accessible prices, where you are welcomed with old-fashioned charm. The quiet and cosy rooms are attractively furnished and most have a river view; doubles €54–85 with shower/wc or bath. Half board, compulsory during the high season and over bank-holiday weekends, costs €61–75. The cuisine is resolutely regional and prepared to the most exacting standards on a range of menus (€24–50): pigeon with truffle, liver with hot, spicy bread, lamb's sweetbreads with Marsala. There's a swimming pool down by the river. Logis de France. *10% discount on the price of a room (except 1 May–1 Oct) or free house apéritif offered to our readers on presentation of this guide.*

Sorges
24420 (23km NE)

⑥ 🎿 🏠 |●| Auberge de la Truffe***

In the village; take the N21.
☏ 05.53.05.02.05 ☏ 05.53.05.39.27.
⊛ www.auberge-de-la-truffe.com
Closed *Sun evening in winter; Mon lunchtime (all year round).* **TV. High chairs and games available. Swimming pool. Car park.**

Serving good traditional food in a region famous for truffles, this restaurant is popular with local business people – a recommendation in itself – as well as tourists. It may be fussily decorated and somewhat lacking in charm, and the service may be a little haughty, but the cheap menus – €16 (except Sun) and €21–53 – are enticing and the place is renowned for its "foie gras" and "truffle" menus. Typical dishes include *escalope* of warm foie gras with fruit, *marbré* of veal sweetbreads with truffle vinaigrette and *croustillant* of lamb with truffles. Though the inn is right on the road, the rooms (€48–53) are attractive, particularly nos. 25–29, which are right on the garden, and the breakfast buffet is good; there is also a quiet annexe, L'Hôtel de la Mairie, in the centre of the village, with delightful rooms overlooking the countryside. Logis de France. *10% discount on the price of a room (except in July–Aug) offered to our readers on presentation of this guide.*

Réole (La)

33190

© |●| Aux Fontaines

8 rue de Verdun
☎05.56.61.15.25.
Closed *Sun; Mon (except public holidays); second week of the Feb school holiday; first fortnight in Nov.*

This restaurant set in an attractive old house on a hill is generally considered one of the best in the region. There are two large, light and airy dining rooms, with vaguely Provençal décor. Five menus at €16–43.50, offer excellent value for money and are served every day, including the weekend, apart from public holidays. The *escalope* of foie gras, accompanied by seasonal fruit, and duck, prepared in a variety of ways, are the main specialities, along with the poultry and egg dishes (the *brouillade* is delicious).

Sainte-Radegonde

33350 (26km N)

《© ≙ |●| Château de Sanse***

Go past Sauveterre-de-Guyenne on the D670, then take the D17, followed by the D18 from Pujols.
☎05.57.56.41.10 ©05.57.56.41.29.
ⓦwww.chateaudesanse.com
Closed *Sun evening; Mon; Tues (Oct–April).* **Disabled access. TV. High chairs and games available. Car park.**

A dozen double rooms at €98–204 (depending on the degree of comfort and the season). If this sounds expensive, just consider that you'll be sleeping in a superbly restored eighteenth-century château with magnificent décor (a successful fusion of traditional materials and high-tech facilities), set in an eighteen-acre park complete with a swimming pool – a perfect place for a treat. What is more, you will receive impeccable service and at night you can enjoy delicate cuisine served on the terrace. There's a weekday

lunchtime menu at €15, then another at €26; reckon on €45 à la carte.

Ribérac

24600

© 𝒜 |●| Restaurant Le Chevillard

Gayet.
2km from Ribérac, on the Montpon-Bordeaux road (D708).
☎05.53.91.20.88.
Closed *Mon and Tues (except July to end Sept); Jan.* **Disabled access. Car park.**

Set in an old farmhouse, in the middle of a huge garden, this is a warmly welcoming restaurant decorated in tasteful rustic style and run by an effusive owner (a former travelling salesman). Wide range of dishes, particularly meat (grilled outside on the terrace) but also an array of fish, fresh poultry bred on the farm and a dessert buffet. All the menus (apart from the cheapest one) feature a superb buffet of oysters and a variety of extremely fresh shellfish; weekday lunchtime menu at €12 (including wine and coffee), then others at €16–31, or reckon on €25 à la carte. Credit cards not accepted. *Free house liqueur offered to our readers on presentation of this guide.*

Bourg-des-Maisons

24320 (14km NE)

《© ≙ |●| Le Domaine de Teinteillac

Teinteillac; take the D708 in the direction of Verteillac, then the D106 in the direction of Chamdeil.
☎05.53.91.51.03
ⓦwww.teinteillac.com
Open *all year and (with reservation).* **Car park.**

This is possibly our best find in the heart of Périgord, distinguished by its inexhaustible charm, enthusiasm and authenticity. A couple of country folk bought this château (dating from the fifteenth and eighteenth centuries) to farm the surrounding land, but also to run this country inn (they have come straight from Lozère, where their hotel was already recommended by us). With an admirably enterprising spirit, they have refurbished four subdued but impressive upstairs rooms (one, set in an old chapel, can sleep four people) – expect to pay around €60 for two people, including breakfast. The chateau is surrounded by 375 acres of woods and fields, where they grow organic vegetables and fruit, as well as rearing ducks (for foie gras) and goats (their milk is also used to make cheese). Unsurprisingly, the dishes on offer are excellent, with meals at €18 and €28 (wine not included) – the simple foie gras cannot be bettered. In fact, the food alone is worth a detour.

Sabres

40630

⊚ 🏠 |●| 🍴 L'Auberge des Pins***

Rue de la Piscine; take the road going right in the centre (coming from Bordeaux or Bayonne).
℡05.58.08.30.00 ℗05.58.07.56.74
℮aubergedespins@wanadoo.fr
Closed Sun evening and Mon (out of season); Mon lunch (in season); fortnight in Jan; a week in Nov. **Disabled access. TV. High chairs and games available. Car park.**

Large, traditional Landais house, with wooden walls, a wide roof and balconies laden with flowers. The family that runs it goes out of their way to satisfy their guests, starting with the bedrooms, with their beautiful furniture, charming knick-knacks and comfortable beds; doubles with shower/wc or bath €60–75. The lovingly prepared food lives up to the setting with a similar combination of the rustic and the sophisticated. The lunchtime "Bistrot Gourmand" offers a fast service of simple, regional dishes, but more elaborate dishes are also on offer: croustillant of duck foie gras, stuffed squab roasted with risotto of baby vegetables, langoustine ravioli with ceps, strawberries marinated in orange skin and fromage blanc. Menus start at €19 (except Sun), with others €28–61, and children's menu at €12. *10% discount on the price of a room (Oct–May) or free coffee offered to our readers on presentation of this guide.*

Saint-Émilion

33330

⊚ 🏠 Hôtel Au Logis des Remparts***

Rue Guadet.
℡05.57.24.70.43 ℗05.57.74.47.44
℮logis-des-remparts@saint-emilion.org
Closed mid-Dec to end Jan. **TV. High chairs available. Swimming pool. Pay car park.**

A fine three-star in a very old building

which has kept the original stone staircase to the entrance, the terrace and the garden bordering the ramparts. Doubles with shower/wc or bath cost €70–180, depending on the season; some rooms can sleep five people. When the weather's fine, breakfast (which is substantial but not expensive – be sure to try the cake) is served on the elegantly paved terrace or in the garden. Be sure to book a parking space in the little courtyard to the rear.

⊚ |●| L'Envers du Décor

Rue du Clocher.
℡05.57.74.48.31
Open all year round. **Disabled access.**

In the heart of the village, a wine bar offering wine by the glass run by real connoisseurs, with vintages from all over France, meticulously chosen by Émilien, the wine waiter, who also regularly organizes blind tastings. As a complement, excellent bistro food, with wonderfully fresh salads and superb cheese. The setting is agreeable, though the staff are sometimes flustered by the summer crowds.

Saint-Estèphe

33250

⊚ |●| Le Peyrat

It's in the port.
℡05.56.59.71.43
Closed Sun evening (out of season); second fortnight in Aug; New Year holidays. **Disabled access. High chairs available.**

This restaurant is in the heart of the village. The boss is jovial and the cooking simple – home-made vegetable soup is a speciality – using fresh seasonal produce and eel, sturgeon and shad from the river. Choose the weekday lunchtime menu at €11, or one of the other menus at €16–34. In summer, the terrace is a wonderful spot from which to enjoy the sunset. There's such a convivial atmosphere that you completely lose track of time. The owner runs the Fête de l'Anguille (the eel festival) at the beginning of June, when the village comes into its own.

Saint-Jean-de-Luz

64500

⊚ 🍴 🏠 Le Petit Trianon**

56 bd. Victor-Hugo.

⊕05.59.26.11.90 ⓕ05.59.26.14.10
ⓔlepetittrianon@wanadoo.fr
Closed Jan. **TV. High chairs available. Pay
car park.**

This hotel is charming, simple, clean and
unpretentious, boasts a pretty, private terrace, and what's more, is reasonably priced.
The new owners have retained the family
character of the place, while systematically
refurbishing all the rooms to make them
more comfortable (new bedding, double
glazing in the rooms overlooking the
street); doubles €47–75, depending on
facilities and the season, breakfast at €7.
The third-floor rooms have sloping ceilings, which makes them rather romantic;
nos. 2 and 3 can sleep a large family. *One
free breakfast per room offered to our readers on
presentation of this guide.*

ⒶⒶ 🏠 Hôtel Ohartzia**

28 rue Garat; it's in a little street between the
church and the sea, 40m from the beach.
⊕05.59.26.00.06 ⓕ05.59.26.74.75
ⓦwww.hotel-ohartzia.com
TV.

The façade is appealing with its Spanish
ceramic flowerpots overflowing with
pansies, geraniums and petunias. Inside,
the peaceful garden seems far from the
hubbub of summer crowds and it's perfect for breakfast. Most of the rooms are
tastefully decorated. The ones on the first
floor have rattan twin beds lacquered in
navy blue while those on the third not
only boast a view of the Rhone but have
also been totally renovated. Double rooms
€59–76 with shower/wc and €65–84
with bath, depending on the season; breakfast included in room rate mid-July to
mid-Sept. *One free breakfast per person offered
to our readers on presentation of this guide.*

ⒶⒶⒶ 🏠 Hôtel La Devinière***

5 rue Loquin; it's 100m from the beach.
⊕05.59.26.05.51 ⓕ05.59.51.26.38
ⓦwww.hotel-la-deviniere.com

A family house right in the middle of
the old town. It's a haven of peace which
makes you want to stay a while. There's a
music room, and even the cosily decorated
rooms strike the right note. All the rooms
are different and furnished with antique
furniture, pictures and ornaments; doubles
€110–150 with bath/wc. *Free house apéritif
or coffee or fruit juice or fizzy drink offered to
our readers on presentation of this guide.*

ⒶⒶ I●I La Buvette des Halles

Boulevard Victor-Hugo; it's in the covered
market.
⊕05.59.26.73.59
Closed Sun (in winter).

There's a great atmosphere on market days.
The oldest (more than 70 years) and smallest (three tables plus the terrace on warm
days) restaurant in town. Jean Laborde
prepares a fine plate of mussels, while the
fish soup and grilled sardines (€6) are
delicious, too. Other specialities include
grilled line-caught tuna with *piperade*, *axoa*
of veal, and anchovy salad with garlic.
Reckon on over €12 for most dishes à la
carte. The bar is open in the morning all
year round.

ⒶⒶ I●I Le Petit Grill Basque – Chez Maya

2 rue Saint-Jacques.
⊕05.59.26.80.76
Closed Wed; Thurs (out of season); 18
Dec–18 Jan.

A timeless place immune from the whims
of fashion, run by imposing women. Don't
bother to come without booking beforehand – this is one of the town's hotspots
and the service is slow (but only because
such meticulous care is taken in the preparation of the food). There are two menus
at €18.50 and €26, or reckon on €35–45
à la carte. The air-conditioning (operated
entirely by hand) was installed when the
building was first built and provides a further attraction. *NEW ENTRY.*

ⒶⒶ I●I Pil-Pil Enea

3 rue Sallagoïty; it's near the covered market
and the post office.
⊕05.59.51.20.80
Closed Sun evening (except in summer);
Mon.

The small dining room houses a dozen
tables and a minimalist décor. The chef is
king of line-caught hake – and it's super
fresh because his wife, the only woman
who owns a fishing boat in the port, is
responsible for catching it. Her whole
crew is female and off they sail to bring
the fish back for Monsieur to cook. The
choice of what to eat depends on what she
lands. There's a set menu for €23; as well
as hake, try salt cod or prawns. Reckon on
€25 à la carte. The clientele is local and a
mixture of fishermen and fishmongers and
the chat is mainly about the price of fish.

ⓦ |●| Zoko Moko

6 rue Mazarin; behind place Louis-XIV.
☎05.59.08.01.23

You'll know what to expect as soon as you
see the exposed stone, soft lighting, trendy
seats and comfortable sofas: no fishermen's
gossip is heard round this bar. In fact, the
customers here are dressed up to the nines
at night, casting glances at each other in
the huge mirror at one end of the dining
room. Like the décor, the food stands out
from that of other restaurants in the vicinity. Although it offers local produce, it is
given a new twist, but at reasonable prices;
this approach has proved a recipe for success. Menus are based on a selection from
all the dishes on offer at €28 (lunch) and
€36 (dinner). There's a small terrace.

Ciboure
64500 (1km S)

ⓦ 🏕 |●| Chez Mattin

Place de la Croix-Rouge; in the town; follow
avenue du Docteur-Speraber to the square.
☎05.59.47.19.52 ⓕ05.59.47.05.57
Closed Mon; Sun evening out of season;
8 Jan–20 Feb, approximately. **Open** until
9.30pm out of season and 10.15pm in season.

One of the best-known fish restaurants
in the area. The agreeable dining room is
bright white with a few good pictures of
the region on the wall. The place is famous
for the "ttoro", a fish soup that may seem
expensive but will suffice for a whole meal.
All the fish landed at the quay make an
appearance on the menu, but you may
prefer deep-fried, breadcrumbed tripe or
pig's cheeks with potato terrine. Reckon
on €25–30 for a meal. In summer this
place gets very busy, so it is advisable to
book. *Free house apéritif offered to our readers
on presentation of this guide.*

Ascain
64310 (7km SE)

ⓦ 🏕 🏠 |●| Hôtel Oberena***

Route des Carrières; it's on the edge of the
village, going towards the Saint-Ignace pass.
☎05.59.54.03.60
ⓦwww.oberena.com
Closed 12 Nov–20 Dec; 3 Jan–3 Feb.
**Disabled access. TV. Swimming pool. Car
park.**

The hotel is in huge grounds with views
of the mountains. It has 25 rooms and is

run by an energetic woman who is systematically doing them up. Doubles with
shower/wc or bath cost €52–87 – the
priciest have a balcony – buffet breakfast
costs €6–10. An alternative is to book
one of the chalets for four in the garden
for €78–110, depending on the season
(they comprise two bedrooms, but no
kitchen). There's a heated indoor pool,
another outside, a Jacuzzi, a sauna and an
exercise room. *10% discount on the price of
a room offered to our readers on presentation
of this guide.*

Sare
64310 (13.5km E)

ⓦ 🏕 🏠 |●| Hôtel Pikassaria**

It's just outside Sare in the hamlet of
Lehenbiscay and is well signposted.
☎05.59.54.21.51 ⓕ05.59.54.27.40
ⓦwww.logis-de-france.fr
Closed Wed out of season; 1 Jan–1 April;
11 Nov–31 Dec. **Disabled access. TV. High
chairs and games available. Car park.**

Located in breathtaking countryside, this
place has built quite a reputation for itself.
However, with its success it's lost that
touch of intimacy which is the charm of
country hotels. Big, bright rooms with a
terrace at €43–47. Half board is compulsory from mid-July to mid-September at
€43–46 per person. The local specialities
in the restaurant (menus €20–27) make
the punters come back time after time –
try the cep omelette, salt cod *à l'espagnole*,
pigeon stew, fruit tart or chocolate *fondant*
– and you'll understand why. There's a
terrace for sunny days and reservations are
recommended. Logis de France. *Free house
apéritif offered to our readers on presentation
of this guide.*

ⓦ 🏕 🏠 |●| Hôtel Arraya

It's on the village square.
☎05.59.54.20.46 ⓕ05.59.54.27.04
ⓦwww.arraya.com
Closed Sun evening and Mon lunch
(4 April–28 June/19 Sept–25 Oct), except
public holidays; early Nov to Easter. **TV. High
chairs available. Car park.**

This place was originally an old coaching
inn on the pilgrim route to Santiago de
Compostela, then it became a presbytery
in the nineteenth century before being
bought by the Fagoaga-Arraya family.
Now it's a hotel again and the twenty
rooms – some very spacious – are

decorated very attractively. A few are at garden level, while others have balconies – doubles €69–120; breakfast €8. Superb period furniture and hand-sewn bed linen decorated with the Basque symbol of a flaming torch. The €16 menu (not Sun) is served only in July and August, on the terrace, and there are gastronomic menus at €21–31, served in the dining room. *Free house apéritif offered to our readers on presentation of this guide.*

@ 🎋 |●| **Restaurant Lastiry**

It's on the village square.
☎05.59.54.20.07
Closed *Tues; Mon and Tues out of season; Jan; first week in July; first week in Sept; second week in Nov.* **High chairs available.**

Guillaume Fagoaga is still very young but he has a passion for his craft, his region and its produce. With his brother Jean in charge front-of-house, he opened this restaurant, which in just a few months became the talk of the area – perhaps because both brothers are equally perfectionist in their approach. Guillaume's dishes are prepared with artistry and invention and they change as often as the produce is available, with a weekday menu at €18, and another at €28 – house classics include creamed salt cod, fresh fish, duck foie gras, cep risotto with foie gras and chargrilled squid.

Saint-Jean-Pied-de-Port
64220

@ 🎋 🏠 |●| **Central Hôtel****

1 pl. du Général-de-Gaulle.
☎05.59.37.00.22 ℗05.59.37.27.79
Closed *Tues (out of season); 10 Dec–1 March.* **TV. High chairs available.**

Rooms here are luxurious and impeccably clean; they cost €56 with shower and €64 with bath. Ask for one with a view of the Nive. Similarly high standards are on offer in the restaurant, with set menus at €19–41 and attentive service. The dining room has charm and the cooking is first-rate: salmon, roast milk-fed lamb, lamb sweetbreads with *piquillos*, soufflé with Izarra (a liqueur similar to Chartreuse), home-made Basque gâteau. *Free kir offered to our readers on presentation of this guide.*

@ 🏠 |●| **Les Pyrénées*****

19 pl. du Général-de-Gaulle.
☎05.59.37.01.01 ℗05.59.37.18.97
@hôtelpyrénées@wanadoo.fr
Closed *Mon evening Nov–March; Tues excluding July–Aug; 6–28 Jan; 20 Nov–22 Dec.* **TV. High chairs available. Swimming pool. Pay car park.**

On paper, €95–230 might seem a lot to pay, but this is a high-class hotel, the rooms are impeccable and there's a very pleasant indoor pool. The chic restaurant, which has a well-established reputation throughout the Basque country, offers fine cuisine artistically conjured from local produce – delicious *piperade*, peppers stuffed with cod, foie gras, hot oysters with "caviar" of salmon, mullets grilled with peppers, sweetbreads with leeks and ceps, lamb sweetbreads with ceps and remarkable desserts and sorbets. There are a range of menus €40–88, or expect to pay about €85 à la carte.

Saint-Michel
64220 (4km S)

@ 🏠 |●| 🎋 **Hôtel-restaurant Xoko-Goxoa****

From Saint-Jean-Pied-de-Port, take the D301.
☎05.59.37.06.34 ℗05.59.37.34.63
Closed *Tues out of season; mid-Jan to early March.* **Car park.**

This is a large traditional house surrounded by greenery and with a large terrace with a wonderful panoramic view. Most of the rooms look straight onto the countryside, but they are rather basic and crying out for refurbishment – doubles €35–40 with shower/wc or bath; half board at €38 in July and August. Atmospheric rustic-style dining room serving no-nonsense, good-value cooking. Set menus, €12 (not Sun) to €25, feature specialities such as fish soup with prawns, trout *etxekoa*, parsleyed ceps, salad *gourmande* and so on. The à la carte prices are very reasonable. Logis de France. *Free house apéritif offered to our readers on presentation of this guide.*

Bidarray
64780 (15km NW)

@ 🎋 🏠 |●| **Hôtel-restaurant Barberaenea****

Place de l'Église; take the D918.

☎05.59.37.74.86 ℱ05.59.37.77.55
🌐www.hotel-barberaenea.fr
Closed *15 Nov–15 Dec.* **Disabled access.**
TV. High chairs available. Car park.

A very old country inn belonging to the Elissetche family, which has been beautifully renovated. You can expect a cheery welcome and attractive, charming rooms with white walls, period furniture and shining parquet floors. The rooms – €46–59 for a double with shower/wc – look out onto the square and its twelfth-century church; the newer rooms are clean and comfortable with views of the countryside. In the restaurant you can get appetizing dishes including salad of warm cod with garlic sauce, thick beef stew, and bread-and-butter pudding. Choose the *menu du randonneur* at €17.50, or the *menu du terroir* at €25. *Free house apéritif offered to our readers on presentation of this guide.*

🍴 Auberge d'Iparla

Place du Fronton; take the D918.
☎05.59.37.77.21.
Closed *Wed (except in summer); Jan–Feb.*

Earthquake in Bidarray: the village inn has fallen into the hands of Alain Ducasse, France's most fêted chef. At first sight, it doesn't look like anything's changed: it is still the same village bar, between the church and the town hall, opposite the *fronton* court, with its card and domino games. Still the same big room opening on to the mountain, even though it has been soberly but attractively redecorated; there's still a menu for €22 and individual dishes at €15. As for the food, it's typical village inn fare: pepper omelettes, Basque tripe, *chipirones a la plancha*, flambéed woodpigeon in season. But everything has a touch of Ducasse; for example, he has added a few chickpeas to the tripe to eliminate the acidity; the omelettes are wonderfully moist. As for the blood pudding, it's based on a recipe from his friend Parra, while the ham comes from a little village in Aragon and the trout is purchased in Banka. Needless to say, the venture has proved a great success and it is essential to book.

Saint-Justin
40240

🏠 🍴 Hôtel de France**

Place des Tilleuls; take the D932.

☎05.58.44.83.61 ℱ05.58.44.83.89
Closed *Sun evening; Mon; Thurs evening; a week in mid-April; mid-Oct to mid-Nov.*
TV.

1930s-style décor in this hotel in the middle of a thirteenth-century fortified town. Peace and quiet reigns here, along with a traditional family atmosphere and the lovely rooms are €38 with shower/wc, or €46 with bath. The restaurant is at the back and offers set menus at €12 (except Sun), then others €22–45. The chef comes up with delicious flavours and prepares everything from fresh produce: salad of duck gizzards and hearts, wild mushroom stew with minced ham, escalope of foie gras with fried duck and caramelized fruit with fruit chutney. The house speciality is goose simmered in red wine. Friendly welcome and relaxed atmosphere, although the service is a bit slow and it's packed in summer.

Saint-Macaire
33490

🏠 🍴 L'Abricotier

On the outskirts of Saint-Macaire, near the stretch of the N113, between Langon and La Réole.
☎05.56.76.83.63 ℱ05.56.76.28.51
Closed *Sun (hotel); Mon and Tues evening (restaurant); 12 Nov–15 Dec.* **TV. Swimming pool. Car park.**

This restaurant would be one of the most beautiful in the region were it not on the edge of the N113. At least the little dining room looks out onto the terrace at the back – lovely when the sun is out. The kitchen turns out imaginative dishes including *cassolette* of snails with *confit* of pig's trotters and lamb chops with aioli and offers menus starting at €18 (lunch and dinner), with others €25–35. There's also a very good wine list – exclusively Bordeaux. Double rooms go for €46 and, in addition, there are three magnificent, very quiet rooms with fully equipped kitchen that give onto the garden and swimming pool.

🏠 🍴 Les Feuilles d'Acanthe**

5 rue de l'Église.
☎05.56.62.33.75
🌐www.feuilles-dacanthe.fr
Closed *Jan.* **Disabled access. TV.**

Swimming pool.

A ravishing, hotel offering remarkable value for money and enchanting. It occupies a sixteenth-century building that's been renovated to perfection with rough-hewn stone walls and beams. The twelve rooms (doubles €60–80, depending on the size) have been intelligently decorated and the bathrooms are sparkling – it's best to reserve in advance because they fill up quickly. The restaurant-crêperie provides original, skilfully prepared dishes like lamb cutlets with yoghurt and coriander on its weekday lunchtime menu at €9, and others at €18–29. *Free house apéritif offered to our readers on presentation of this guide.*

Saint-Palais

64120

@ 🏃 🏠 |O| Hôtel-restaurant de la Paix**

33 rue du Jeu-de-Paume; off the town's main square.
☎05.59.65.73.15 ☞05.59.65.63.83
Closed *Fri evening; Sat lunchtime (except July–Aug); Sun evening; first week in July; 27 Dec–27 Jan.* **Disabled access. TV. High chairs available.**

You'd never think from the outside that this hotel has been around for two hundred years – it's been entirely rebuilt and has all mod cons with double rooms at €48, and a pretty terrace in summer. Good regional cooking, with a weekday menu at €11 and others €22–26. Dishes include lamb's sweetbreads with ham and ceps, *ttoro* (fish stew), eel and game in season. *Free house apéritif offered to our readers on presentation of this guide.*

Saint-Dos

64270 (20km N)

@ 🏃 🏠 |O| Auberge du Béarn

Place de l'Église.
☎05.59.38.40.38 ☞05.59.38.44.28
@alain.darc@wanadoo.fr
Closed *Sun evening; Mon.* **TV. High chairs and games available.**

An authentic country inn in a charming little village of a hundred souls, on the pilgrim route to Santiago de Compostela. The bar is quite a meeting place for villagers and others from further afield.

What a pleasure to sleep in proper sheets that have been dried in the fresh open air – doubles cost €27; half board €26 per person. The local cooking isn't expensive, and only fresh ingredients are used by the inn-keeper/chef on the weekday lunch menu €10, or others €15.50–26. Or, opt for à la carte at around €25, and try the salmon or the chicken dishes. *Free house apéritif offered to our readers on presentation of this guide.*

Sarlat-la-Canéda

24200

@ Auberge de Jeunesse et Gîte d'Étape

77 av. de Selves (North). At the entrance to the town.
☎05.53.59.47.59
Closed *Jan.* **Reception open** *6–8pm.*

A windfall just a stone's throw from the town centre. Fifteen beds spread over three dormitories – €10 per person on the first night, €9 on the following ones. It is also possible to put up a tent for €6 on the first night, then €5. Booking is essential as it is often full – backpackers from 24 different countries have passed through here. Fully equipped kitchen available, but guests are responsible for its upkeep. The hostel is open to individual guests from 15 April to 15 Nov, but it turns away anybody who is under age. Credit cards not accepted.

@ 🏠 Hôtel les Récollets**

4 rue Jean-Jacques-Rousseau; it's in the old town.
☎05.53.31.36.00 ☞05.53.30.32.62
@www.hotel-recollets-sarlat.com
TV. Car park.

This place is in a quiet, picturesque lane away from the cars and the tourist crowds. Sarlat is an old town so it's good to stay in a hotel with a bit of history – this used to be the cloisters of a seventeenth-century convent. Today it's managed by a father-and-son team and you get a convivial welcome. The rooms have been tastefully refurbished; doubles cost €42–62, depending on the degree of comfort. A few look out onto a quiet courtyard where you have breakfast. No. 15 is particularly bright and has a lovely view over the tiled rooftops of the old town, while no. 8 has elegant stone archways.

⟪ 🛏 |●| ⅍ Hôtel-restaurant La Maison des Peyrat**

Le Lac de la Plane; a bit out of the way, overlooking the east of the town, but it's well signposted; carry on for about 2km after the gendarmerie.
℡05.53.59.00.32 ℻05.53.28.56.56
ⓦwww.maisondespeyrat.com
Closed 15 Nov–1 April. **Disabled access. TV. High chairs available. Swimming pool. Car park.**

This hermitage has been converted and refurbished to become a charming, welcoming hotel. Most of it was built in the seventeenth century, although one older section (used to house plague victims) dates from the fourteenth century. The décor – modern, but also restrained and respectful – makes the most of the old stonework, and the setting is very peaceful. Bright, spacious rooms with pretty bathrooms go for €47–95, depending on the degree of comfort and the season; half board is also offered. The menu (€19), available evenings only, is exclusively for hotel guests. *Free coffee offered to our readers on presentation of this guide.*

⟪ 🛏 ⅍ Hôtel Le Mas de Castel**

Sudalissant (South); 3km from the town; take the D704 towards Souillac, then go towards La Canéda; it is signposted.
℡05.53.59.02.59 ℻05.53.28.25.62
ⓔcastalian@wanadoo.fr
Closed 11 Nov to early April. **Disabled access. TV. Swimming pool. Car park.**

An ideal base for a trip to the country, very close to Sarlat. Charming hotel at street level surrounded by greenery, built in the local style (pretty white stones, small stone outhouse) but there's no restaurant. Warm welcome and attractive, comfortable rooms, recently refurbished with relaxing, pastel-coloured décor – doubles go for €48–66, depending on the degree of comfort and the season. Nos. 2, 3, 4, 5 and 14 are bigger and have a terrace or give onto a garden.

⟪ 🛏 |●| La Couleuvrine**

1 pl. de la Bouquerie.
℡05.53.59.27.80 ℻05.53.31.26.83
ⓦwww.lacouleuvrine.com
Closed 10 Jan–6 Feb (restaurant only – hotel open all year round). **TV.**

This hotel is set in the last remaining defensive corner tower on the thirteenth-century town walls. The parapet has preserved a strange pre-Romanesque black Virgin that was decapitated by the Huguenots during the Religious Wars. The rooms (€50–52) are set between the machicolations in the top of the Romanesque tower, which has been exquisitely restored. Beautiful dining room with a fifteenth-century stone fireplace, serving excellent food. Logis de France.

⟪ ⅍ 🛏 |●| La Hoirie***

Rue Marcel-Cerdan – La Giragne; take the Souillac road out of Sarlat; it's well signposted.
℡05.53.59.05.62 ℻05.53.31.13.90
ⓦwww.lahoirie.com
Closed lunchtime; Mon out of season; 15 Nov–15 March. **TV. High chairs and games available. Swimming pool. Car park.**

Some parts of the original thirteenth-century house remain, and the brilliance of its pale stone has not dimmed with the passing of the years. There are large grounds with a pool so you can sunbathe and cool down afterwards. The double rooms, costing €52–110, are all spacious and tastefully decorated, down to the last detail; the more expensive ones almost resemble comfortable apartments. The bathrooms are bright and well equipped, the service excellent, but breakfast is disappointing. *Free house apéritif offered to our readers on presentation of this guide.*

⟪ 🛏 Le Renoir – Hôtel Best Western***

2 rue Abbé-Surgier; slightly removed from the town centre.
℡05.53.59.35.98 ℻05.53.31.22.32
ⓦwww.hotel-renoir-sarlat.com
Open all year round. **TV. Swimming pool.**

This venerable three-star establishment has been renovated from top to bottom. The rooms are extremely well equipped; air-conditioning, mini-bar, safe, modem socket; the most expensive are duplexes or even have spa facilities. The décor is sophisticated and meticulously designed, but its opulence is not devoid of charm. Excellent value for money: double rooms at €60–110, depending on the degree of comfort or the season, and breakfast buffet at €9.

⟪ ⅍ 🛏 Hôtel de Compostelle***

64 av. de Selves; 900m from the town centre, on the road to Montignac/Brives.
℡05.53.59.08.53 ℻05.53.30.31.65

ⓦ www.hotelcompostelle-sarlat.com
Closed *Sun lunchtime until 4.30pm; mid-Nov to end of March.* **Disabled access. TV. Pay car park.**

This hotel has deservedly just won itself three stars, after an extensive refurbishment: air-conditioning and mini-bars installed in the rooms, reception and lounge overhauled, cosy breakfast room giving onto the garden. Excellent, large and pleasant rooms; doubles €62–74 with shower/wc or bath. A few have a glassed-in balcony but they look out onto the street. The quieter rooms at the back overlook a tiny garden. Families can go for the small suites with two bedrooms and bath. *Free coffee offered to our readers on presentation of this guide.*

ⓔ |●| La Rapière

Place du Peyrou.
☎ 05.53.59.03.13
Closed *Sun evening (out of season); early Jan to mid-March.* **Disabled access.**

The best value for money in Sarlat, particularly for its menu at €24.50 with *croustillant* of pig's feet, followed by goose pot-au-feu and walnut gateau; other menus from €14.50 (weekday lunchtime) to €31.50. There's also a pretty dining room and small terrace on a pedestrian street. The service is erratic, but it is an excellent place nonetheless.

ⓔ |●| Restaurant Le 4 Saisons

2 côte de Toulouse.
☎ 05.53.29.48.59
Closed *Wed and Thurs lunchtime (out of season).*

Just like the seasons, this restaurant comes and goes, entering and leaving our guide after reports of drastic fluctuations in the level of service. The cooking, however, never disappoints, combining as it does local produce and original ideas and offering set lunchtime menus at €18 and €22, with other menus at €26 and €30. In fact, with a bit more cheerfulness and humility, the place would be perfect. On fine days, you can eat on a pretty terrace, far removed from the tourist trail.

ⓔ |●| Le Présidial

6 rue Landry; it's 80m from place de la Liberté, behind the town hall.
☎ 05.53.28.92.47 ℻ 05.53.59.43.84
Closed *Sun and Mon lunch; 15 Nov–1 April.*

Great gastronomic feats are accomplished in this restaurant, run by a charming couple. This jewel is their new enterprise and already it's become *the* place to eat in Sarlat. The building is classified as a historic monument and is a gorgeous house from 1552, set in a large, quiet garden in the old town. The dining room is very elegant and the terrace is the loveliest around, serving menus for €19 at lunchtime, and then others €25–38, or reckon on around €40 à la carte. The cheapest menu offers great value for money, the others, dishes like perfect duck foie gras, a nest of tagliatelle and lamb's sweetbreads with rosemary and beautifully cooked guineafowl supreme in pastry. There's an extensive wine list with reasonable prices. No reservations 20 July–25 August.

Roque-Gageac (La)
24250 (9km S)

ⓔ 🏠 |●| Hôtel-restaurant La Belle Étoile**

Rue Principale; take the D46.
☎ 05.53.29.51.44 ℻ 05.53.29.45.63
ⓔ hotel.belle-etoile@wanadoo.fr
Restaurant closed *Mon and Wed lunchtimes; Nov to end March.* **TV. High chairs available.**

Charming, stylish hotel in a glorious setting in one of the most beautiful villages in France. The rooms (€50–74) have all been completely refurbished and tastefully furnished, as well as being fitted with double glazing and a bathroom. A few have a great view of the slow-moving Dordogne. The elegant dining room has a vine-smothered terrace overlooking the river, and the food is excellent, even in the cheapest menus (€23–36); it concentrates on the classics but adds unexpected modern touches: *tatin de* foie gras with apples, *tian* of veal with langoustines, Limousin beef, *croustillant* of pig's feet, purée of foie gras in cabbage leaves, Echourgnac cheesecake. With its attentive, friendly service, all in all, one of our best finds in this district. Logis de France.

Beynac-et-Cazenac
24220 (10km SW)

ⓔ |●| La Petite Tonnelle

La Balme (rue principale); take the D57, then the D49.
☎ 05.53.29.95.18

Open *every day in season.*

Our favourite restaurant in Beynac (and round about), located in the heart of the medieval village, at the foot of a splendid château. The Asian chef reinterprets local dishes with gusto and originality, while her husband serves them in the dining room – set lunchtime menu at €12.50, then another at €16. The artistic presentation of the *magret* and the canny use of spices are just two of the many little details that set this restaurant apart. Even the soups and salads are prepared with amazing finesse. According to the season, you can choose between the small dining room with stone walls and a fireplace or the small terrace under an arbour.

Paulin

24590 (24km NE)

@ |●| La Meynardie

From Sarlat, go in the direction of Salignac-Eyvignes, then towards Archignac; it's well signposted, on the Saint-Genie road.
☎05.53.28.85.98 ℗05.53.28.82.79
@la-meynardie@wanadoo.fr
Closed *Tues (except July–Aug); Wed; Dec to mid-Feb.* **Car park.**

An old farmhouse set deep in the country. The dining room, with its paved floor and massive fireplace dating from 1603, has been carefully restored and has a certain appeal. Courteous welcome, though the atmosphere's a little on the chic side. Weekday lunchtime menu at €12.20, then others at €19.10–49, are all based on traditional dishes, but include creative variations like *carpaccio* of duck breast and goose stew with Bergerac wine. Good desserts include an iced nougat with red fruit *coulis*. Sit out on the terrace in summer, or stroll through the chestnut tree forest after your meal. Best to book, especially for Saturday evening and Sunday lunch. Credit cards not accepted.

Laval-de-Jayac

24590 (25km NE)

@ ≜ |●| ♫ Hôtel-restaurant Coulier**

It's in the village; take the D60.
☎05.53.28.86.46 ℗05.53.28.26.33
@www.hotelcoulier.com
Closed *Fri evening and Sat out of season; 15 Nov to end Feb.* **Disabled access. TV. High chairs available. Swimming pool. Car park.**

You'll find this quiet hamlet in an almost

deserted part of darkest Périgord. The pretty converted farm buildings make a U-shape around a courtyard, on a hillock set well away from the road. The fairly small double rooms with shower/wc, scattered around the building, are decorated in a pretty, rustic style; they go for €40–55. Half board is compulsory in July and August: €53 per person. The restaurant serves regional dishes like trout stuffed with walnuts, scrambled eggs with truffle, warm semi-cooked foie gras, veal sweetbreads, scallops with balsamic, breast of duck with violet mustard and iced hazelnut soufflé. There's a range of menus €16–38, or reckon on €30 à la carte. If you don't want to spend all day by the pool, there are several short trails nearby – the owners know the area very well so don't hesitate to ask them for advice. Logis de France. *10% discount on the price of a room (except July–Aug) offered to our readers on presentation of this guide.*

Daglan

24250 (22km S)

@ |●| Le Petit Paris

In the village; take the D46, then the D60.
☎05.53.28.41.10
Closed *Mon.*

The young chef, Sylvain Guilbot (a former pupil of Blanc and Verger), has gone back to his roots, choosing the pretty village of Daglan as his centre of operations. Clear about his priorities, he first set about renovating the kitchen; for the moment, however, the drab décor of the dining room in the village bar-tobacconist's remains untouched – so, take advantage of the excellent food now, before any refurbishment and subsequent increase in prices. Menus around €15 at lunch, €25 at dinner.

Sauternes

33210

@ ♫ |●| Restaurant Le Saprien

11 rue Principale; it's opposite the tourist office.
☎05.56.76.60.87 ℗05.56.76.68.92
Closed *Mon–Thurs evenings (Nov–March); otherwise, Sun evening, Mon and Wed evening; Feb school holiday; Christmas holiday.*

A little house with thick stone walls on the

outskirts of the village. It's ever so slightly chic, and the elegant interior is a successful blend of old and new. It has a delightful reading room and also a huge terrace that opens out onto the vineyard. They grill food over vine shoots and offer Sauternes by the glass. Primarily they offer dishes that reflect the changing seasons and what the market has to offer: terrine of foie gras in Sauternes jelly, local grilled beef. Various menus, at €23–35; reckon on €40–45 à la carte. *Free coffee offered to our readers on presentation of this guide.*

Soulac-sur-Mer

33780

@ 🎿 🛏 **Hôtel Michelet****

1 rue Baguenard; it's on the sea port.
☎05.56.09.82.18 🖷05.56.73.65.25
Closed *Sun and Mon (out of season); mid-Nov to end Jan.* **Disabled access. TV.**

A typical seaside villa, 50m from the main beach. The staff are beyond compare – their thoughtful gestures include giving out little gifts to the kids. The rooms – doubles with bath, €41–72 depending on facilities and season – are comfortable and well maintained (if a little noisy); some have a balcony and four lead out into a sandy garden. Confirm the booking and prices in writing. *10% discount on the price of a room (after two consecutive nights, except in season and at weekends) offered to our readers on presentation of this guide.*

Sourzac

24400

@ 🍽 **La Table d'Eugénie**

Place de l'Église; on the side of the RN89. au bord de la RN 89.
☎05.53.82.45.23
Closed *Sun evening; Mon (except public holidays).*

We are proud to have discovered this gourmet's haunt with ill-assorted decoration. There's a set lunch menu at €11.50, then others at €14–33, and a regional menu at €24, including wine. Not only are the prices attractive, however; the cheapest menu offers cream of chestnut soup, chestnut salad with soft, locally produced pig's lard and walnut cake (or perhaps chestnut cake). Authentic cooking and an effusive welcome guaranteed. A real find.

Tardets-Sorholus

64470

@ 🛏 🍽 **Ühaltia – Hôtel-restaurant du Pont d'Abense***

Abense-de-Haut; it's 1.5km outside the town, on the opposite bank of the Saison.
☎05.59.28.54.60
🖷uhaltia@wanadoo.fr
Closed *Sun evening; Mon; Jan; first fortnight in Dec.* **Car park.**

This riverside hotel is a lovely place to stay, with nice quiet rooms. Doubles go for €45–55 with shower/wc or bath; they prefer you to stay on a half board basis in summer (add €22 to the price of the room). There's a friendly bar where you can sample the local ales and you can eat outside on the terrace. The restaurant has a good reputation and the chef, who's also the owner, loves preparing simple dishes using the freshest ingredients. Orders are taken, after booking a table, noon–1.15pm and 7.45–9pm. Dishes on the menus (€18–30) change often but are in the style of warm cep terrine, pig's trotter and potato pie, stuffed baby pigeon, foie gras, tart of *piperade* and ham, fondue, pan-fried hake, *aiguillettes* of duck with wine, and crêpes as good as any you'll get in Brittany. Reckon on €45 for a meal à la carte.

Tonneins

47400

@ 🍽 🛏 **Côté Garonne**

36 cours de l'Yser.
☎05.53.84.34.34 🖷05.53.84.31.31
🌐www.cotegaronne.com
Closed *1 May.* **Disabled access. TV. Car park.**

The street doesn't look particularly appealing – neither does the town, for that matter – so this beautiful building really stands out. It's like entering a different world when you step inside. After a lean period in the restaurant, Christian Papillon has completely rethought his menu, rejecting any ideas of cordon bleu to come up with simpler, more affordable local dishes. This is a chance to eat in style at a reasonable cost, in a wonderful atmosphere and sample one of the menus from €12 (lunchtime) to €39. Luxurious, extremely comfortable rooms (€80–96), with a stunning view of the river; breakfast €8–13. *10% discount on the price of a room offered to our readers on presentation of this guide.*

Trémolat
24510

@ |●| ⅔ Le Bistrot d'en Face

It's on the square.
☎05.53.22.80.69
Open *all year round.* **High chairs available. Disabled access.**

It's essential to book – even the day before – because this bistro has a very good reputation. It's a favourite with the English ex-pats who inhabit the region. They also owns the *Vieux Logis* opposite – hence the name. Attentively prepared traditional dishes, enlivened with original touches: *grattons* of duck (something like duck scratchings), chicken pâté with hazelnuts, sautéed chicken thigh with garlic and *verjus*, and brilliant house desserts, including an enormous chocolate mousse. Excellent value, with a weekday lunchtime menu at €11.90, others at €18.50 and €25, or about €25 à la carte. *Free liqueur offered to our readers on presentation of this guide.*

Vendays-Montalivet
33930

@ 🏠 |●| Hôtel de France**

Place de l'Église.
☎05.56.41.70.34 ℗05.56.41.74.33
Closed *Sun; Tues evening and Wed (in winter).* **TV. Disabled access.**

This place is principally a restaurant, with a little dining room decorated with images of the sun. The cuisine is light and the talented young chef uses a lot of sweet spices to enhance the flavours of the local produce – cinnamon with partridge, for example. The menu of the day goes for €11, and there are others €19.50–36. Then there are eight rooms with shower (€37–40), decorated by the owner herself (who has great experience in this field). Each room is a work of art in itself. Ask for one to the rear, as they're quieter, but the atmosphere here is peaceful and it's good value for money.

Villandraut
33730

@ 🏠 |●| Auberge de La Crémaillère

8 pl. du Général-de-Gaulle.
☎05.56.25.30.67 ℗05.56.25.83.12
Closed *Tues evening and Wed (out of season); Jan.* **TV. Disabled access.**

On the edge of a quiet little square, shaded by chestnut and linden trees, a spotless, newly opened inn. Sober but tasteful décor in the comfortable, themed rooms, flooded with light and rounded off with a parquet floor; doubles at €40–55, according to the degree of comfort and the season. The restaurant is equally inviting, with regional dishes given an innovative twist. Logis de France.

Villefranche-du-Périgord
24550

@ 🏠 ⅔ |●| La Petite Auberge**

Les Peyrouillères; 800m to the south of the village, well signposted.
☎05.53.29.91.01 ℗05.53.28.88.10
Closed *end Nov to end Feb (or early March).* **TV. Car park. Swimming pool.**

Large house, typical of the region, lost in the countryside offering a haven of tranquillity. There's a huge garden with inviting sunbeds, and attractive terrace, ideal for summer, and tastefully decorated rooms (€43–50); half board available. Local dishes in the restaurant, vary according to the season: Périgord ceps, semi-cooked foie gras, duck breast in walnut liqueur. The weekday lunchtime menu costs €15, then others €18.50–35, or à la carte is another option. *Free coffee offered to our readers on presentation of this guide.*

Villeneuve-sur-Lot
47300

@ ⅔ 🏠 Hôtel La Résidence**

17 av. Lazare-Carnot; it's near the old train station.
☎05.53.40.17.03 ℗05.53.01.57.34
@hotel.laresidence@wanadoo.fr
Closed *fortnight from Christmas to early Jan.* **TV. High chairs available. Pay car park.**

A pretty little hotel with a pink façade,

green shutters and lots of character, in a very quiet neighbourhood near the old station. As soon as you set foot inside you find a church pew and, at the end of the corridor, the garden where you can have breakfast in fine weather. Cool, tastefully decorated rooms go for €25 with wash-basin, €39 with shower/wc and €46 with bath. It's ideal if you like things simple and if you're looking for peace and quiet. *10% discount on the price of a room (for a two-night stay, except July–August) offered to our readers on presentation of this guide.*

⊚ |●| Restaurant Chez Câline

2 rue Notre-Dame.
☎ 05.53.70.42.08
Closed *Sun evening; Tues.*

A two-level restaurant overlooking the Lot river. One floor has a lovely but tiny balcony (two tables), while the other is in an atmospheric cellar. They serve decent local dishes such as duck *confit* with locally grown apples, salmon fillets with sorrel, and cherry soup with mint for dessert and offer set menus €8.50–22.50. It's a small place, so it's best to book.

Pujols
47300 (3km S)

⊚ ⅔ ♠ Hôtel des Chênes★★★

Lieu-dit Bel-Air; opposite the medieval village of Pujols.
☎ 05.53.49.04.55 ☎ 05.53.49.22.74
ⓦ www.hoteldeschenes.com
Closed 27 Dec–5 Jan. **TV. High chairs and cots available. Swimming pool. Car park.**

Look out for the restaurant *La Toque Blanche* – the hotel is next door. They stand on their own on the side of the valley so they're both very quiet. Lovely, well-equipped rooms looking onto the medieval village; they're all decorated differently. Doubles with shower/wc at €60, or with bath €72; those with a private terrace and direct access to the pool cost €10 more. *Free coffee or house apéritif or fruit juice or fizzy drink offered to our readers on presentation of this guide.*

Temple-sur-Lot (Le)
47110 (17km SW)

⊚ ⅔ ♠ |●| Les Rives du Plantié★★★

It's on the D13 between Castelmoron and Le Temple-sur-Lot.

☎ 05.53.79.86.86 ☎ 05.53.79.86.85
ⓦ www.rivesduplantie.com
Restaurant closed *Mon and Sat lunch; Sun evening out of season; early Jan.* **Disabled access. TV. High chairs and games available. Swimming pool. Car park.**

This place was a crumbling wreck before a brave young couple took it on and converted the house and some of the outbuildings into a hotel and restaurant. The grounds are planted with ancient trees and they slope down towards the River Lot, leaving space for the swimming pool. Double rooms cost €65–80, depending on the season; they are spacious and have good facilities, if rather ordinary décor and furniture (although a refurbishment should be complete by the time this book comes out). Happily, the view over the park is splendid. The cooking features local ingredients subjected to outside influences on the weekday lunchtime menu €20, or other menus €32–62. *10% discount on the price of a room (except July–Aug) or free house apéritif or liqueur offered to our readers on presentation of this guide.*

Monclar
47380 (18km NW)

⊚ ⅔ |●| Le Relais

Rue du 11-Novembre; take the D911 to Sainte-Livrade, follow the D667 for 5km, then turn onto the D113.
☎ 05.53.49.44.74
Closed *Sun evening; Mon; second fortnight in Sept.*

Locals crowd in here for lengthy lunches on Sunday and public holidays. Simple dishes and generous portions; the service is attentive. The rustic dining room has a beautiful terrace overlooking the valley (ask for table no.16 if you want a panoramic view). The cooking has a strong regional bias, with an emphasis on fish dishes, such as fillet of pike-perch with dried tomatoes and curried *rouget* fillets. Menus start at €11 (weekday lunchtimes), with a children's menu at €7 and others at €13 and €18 (some dishes have a supplement). *Free coffee offered to our readers on presentation of this guide.*

Auvergne

Allanche

15160

◎ ⚘ |●| Restaurant le Foirail

Maillargues; it's 1km from the centre of
Allanche on the D679.
☎04.71.20.41.15
Closed *evenings; Sun (early Nov to end
Feb); first week in Jan.* **Disabled access.**
Car park.

You'll find this place on a little hill in
the middle of the summer pastures and
near one of the Auvergne's biggest cattle
markets. In this area the tasty local Salers
beef is a speciality although other breeds
are gradually increasing in numbers. It's
a simple place serving flavourful Salers
beef and regional specialities such as *potée
auvergnate*, *truffade* and *pounti* with a *menu
du jour* €12 (weekdays only) and Sunday
menus at €16 and €18. *Free coffee offered to
our readers on presentation of this guide.*

Chalinargues

15170 (9km S)

◎ ⚘ 🛏 |●| Auberge de la Pinatelle

Take the D39 heading for Murat.
☎04.71.20.15.92 ☎04.71.20.17.90
✉sandrine-civiale@wanadoo.fr
Closed *Wed and Sun evenings; 20 Dec–15
March.* **Disabled access (restaurant only).**
TV. Car Park.

A pretty, popular inn offering friendly
service and a good atmosphere. The young
owners have five comfortable and tastefully
decorated rooms; doubles with wc/shower
or bath €37, half board €34 per person. In
the convivial dining room you can choose
from menus between €12 and €31.
They offer Auvergne and Mediterranean

specialities. Besides the inevitable trout
with bacon, home-made *tripoux* and *coq au
vin* (very well prepared), there is excellent
magret de canard and other Périgord specialities. *Free house apéritif offered to our readers
on presentation of this guide.*

Ambert

63600

◎ 🛏 |●| Hôtel-restaurant Les Copains**

42 bd. Henri-IV; it's opposite the town hall.
☎04.73.82.01.02 ☎04.73.82.67.34
⊛www.multimania.com/restolescopains
Closed *Sat; Sun evening; a week in Feb; 10
Sept–10 Oct.* **Open** *noon–1.30pm and 7.30–
8.30pm.* **TV. High chairs available.**

This hotel-restaurant takes its name from
the Yves Robert film *Les Copains*, which
was shot here. Rather gloomy bedrooms
cost €46–48 for a double with shower/
wc or bath. The traditional cuisine, based
largely on local produce, is simple, but
Thierry Chelle, the fourth generation
of his family to be in charge, picked up
some tricks from the time he spent in
the Robuchon kitchens. Thus the menus
– €12 (lunch only) then €21–45 – have
a touch of class: supreme of guinea fowl
with nettle sauce; frog vol-au-vent with
parsley vinaigrette; warm chocolate cake
with a melting centre and orange coulis.
Service is fast but relaxed. You can almost
hear Brassens' famous song being hummed.
Logis de France.

◎ ⚘ 🛏 |●| Hôtel-restaurant La Chaumière**

41 av. Foch; it's near the station.

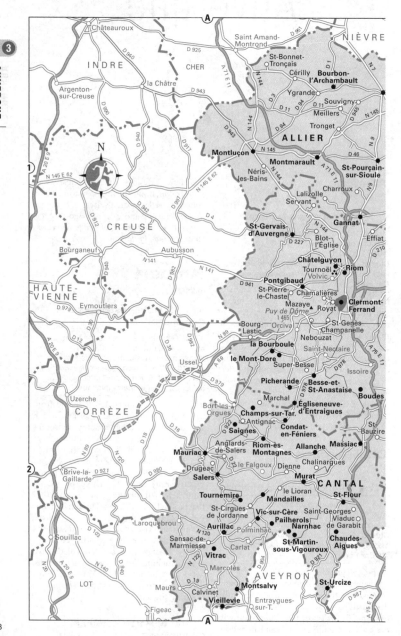

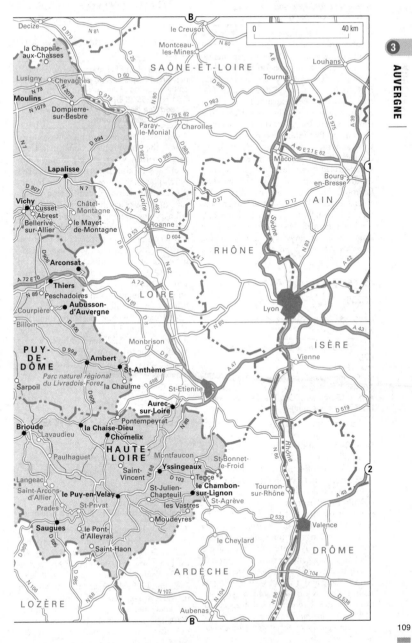

Decize
le Creusot
B
Montceau-
les-Mines
N 81
D 979
D 25
N 80
SAÔNE-ET-LOIRE
la Chapelle-
aux-Chasses
Louhans
A 6
Lusigny
Chevagnes
D 60
Tournus
N 79
N 2079
D 980
D 979
Moulins
N 1079
Dompierre-
sur-Besbre
D 994
N 80
N 79 E 62
D 963
A 39
Paray-
le-Monial
Charolles
D 975
D 982
D 985
D 989
A 40 E 21 E 62
Mâcon
N 7
Bourg-
en-Bresse
1
D 907
Lapalisse
N 7
D 37
D 17
AIN
Vichy
Cusset
Abrest
Châtel-
Montagne
D 482
N 7
Roanne
Saône
Bellerive-
sur-Allier
le Mayet-
de-Montagne
D 53
D 604
RHÔNE
D 906
N 83
D 8
Arconsat
A 72 E 70
A 72
N 82
N 7
A 42
N 89
Thiers
Peschadoires
Aubusson-
d'Auvergne
LOIRE
Lyon
Courpière
Billom
D 906
A 43
Monbrison
ISÈRE
PUY-
DE-
DÔME
D 996
Ambert
D 8
Vienne
St-Anthème
Parc naturel régional
du Livradois-Forez
D 498
A 47
Sarpoil
la Chaulme
St-Etienne
D 906
D 519
Aurec-
sur-Loire
Pontempeyrat
Brioude
Lavaudieu
la Chaise-Dieu
Chomelix
N 88
HAUTE
LOIRE
Montfaucon
St-Bonnet-
le-Froid
N 86
Paulhaguet
Saint-
Vincent
Tence
Yssingeaux
D 103
Langeac
Saint-Arcons-
d'Allier
le Puy-en-Velay
St-Julien-
Chapteuil
le Chambon-
sur-Lignon
St-Agrève
Tournon-
sur-Rhône
A 49
Rhône
Prades
St-Privat
les Vastres
Sauges
le Pont-
d'Alleyras
Moudeyres
D 533
Valence
D 585
Saint-Haon
le Cheylard
DRÔME
LOZÈRE
N 106
D 985
N 88
N 102
N 104
ARDÈCHE
N 86
D 104
D 538
Aubenas
B

0   40 km

℡04.73.82.14.94 ℻04.73.82.33.52
Closed *Sun evening; Fri evening and Sat out of season; end Dec to end Jan.* **Disabled access. TV. Car park.**

A reminder that you can eat well at reasonable prices. Nothing fancy – just good plain cooking and substantial set menus, no frills and no surprises on the bill, with menus at €15 (except public holidays) up to €36, or reckon on €29 à la carte. The restaurant has been expanded and there's a south-facing terrace overlooking the garden, where they do grills at lunchtime in summer. The dining room is in classical style and the cooking similarly sticks to old faithfuls: fresh foie gras, *potée auvergnate*, wood-grilled meats and some dishes based on the local fourme d'Ambert cheese. The bedrooms are clean, modern and comfortable; doubles €49 with shower/wc or bath. Coming soon, Jacuzzi, sauna and hammam. Logis de France. *Free house apéritif, for a maximum of four people, offered to our readers on presentation of this guide.*

Arconsat

63250

🛎 🍴 ⅍ **L'Auberge de Montoncel****

Les Cros d'Arconsat; take the N89 then the D86.
℡04.73.94.20.96 ℻04.73.94.28.33
🖥www.montoncel.com
Closed *Sun evening and Mon except July–Aug; 1-15 Jan; 1–15 Oct.* **Disabled access. High chairs and games available. TV. Car park.**

An old building in the middle of the Bois Noirs, above Chabreloche, with a simple hotel alongside in a recently built annexe, offering refurbished rooms at €32.50. There's a pretty garden and you can expect friendly service. Small, old-fashioned restaurant with a copious menu of the day (€12) and others up to €29. According to the season, the other mouth-watering menus include salmon terrine with Puy lentils, fourme cheese salad au gratin, grilled crayfish and undercut of beef with Bleu d'Auvergne cheese. Just thinking about them is enough to put your tastebuds on alert and make your mouth water. Credit cards not accepted. *10% discount on the room rate (except July–Aug) offered to our readers on presentation of this guide.*

Aubusson-d'Auvergne

63120

🛎 🍴 **Hôtel-restaurant Au Bon Coin**

Le bourg; NB: this is Aubusson-d'Auvergne, between Thiers and Ambert, not Aubusson on the outskirts of Limoges.
℡04.73.53.55.78 ℻04.73.53.56.29
Closed *Sun evening and Mon out of season; 20 Dec–20 Jan.* **Car park.**

A little inn decorated in pleasant country style – the only problem being that it can get a bit noisy when the big dining room is opened up for coach parties (weekdays only). The chef is a member of the Toques d'Auvergne chefs' association and makes sure that the place lives up to Auvergne's culinary reputation. The proprietor-chef uses quality ingredients in his cooking and serves generous portions: try the fresh crayfish in butter and the house speciality: fillet of char with cream and bacon sauce. Or sample the home-made terrines and, for dessert, the superb pears in pastry with egg custard. Don't miss the crayfish season. Set menu at the bar at €12, served weekday lunchtimes; or menus at €19, €29 and €30 or à la carte. Double rooms go for €37 with shower/wc or bath; half board, around €42 per person, is obligatory in July and August. A place where you can feel at ease and get away from things.

Aurec-sur-Loire

43110

🛎 🍴 **Les Cèdres Bleus**

Route de la Rivière; it's 4km from Aurec on the road to Bas-en-Basset.
℡04.77.35.48.48 ℻04.71.77.35.04
Closed *Sun evening; Mon lunch; Jan.* **Disabled access. TV. High chairs available.**

This pink house among the cedar trees is spacious and modern and is set in grounds with a few comfortable guest chalets. All the bedrooms are being refurbished during 2005; doubles €53–55, breakfast €7.50. Well known in the area, with a reputation for quality. Refined local dishes listed on weekday menu at €18 and others up to €70. The large terrace has a good view over the grounds and the service is impeccable. Logis de France.

Aurillac

15000

⊛ 🏠 |●| ⅔ Hôtel-restaurant La Thomasse***

28 rue du Docteur-Mallet.
☎04.71.48.26.47 ℻04.71.48.83.66
ⓦwww.hotel-la-thomasse.com
Closed *22 Dec–10 Jan.* **TV. High chairs and games available. Swimming pool. Car park.**

Not far from the centre, in a residential area. A charming hotel opening onto large gardens with swimming pool and private parking – a comfortable place to stay with a nice provincial feel. Pretty en-suite rooms in rustic style cost €65. Regional dishes and gastronomic cuisine are served in the attractive restaurant with menus priced €25–45. More often than not, the owner will serve you a free glass of champagne as you sit down to eat. He's welcoming and talkative, and the club bar gets lively in the evenings. Logis de France. *Free house apéritif offered to our readers on presentation of this guide.*

⊛ |●| Le Bouchon Fromager

Rue du Buis, pl. des Docks.
☎04.71.48.07.80
Closed *Sun.* **Disabled access. High chairs available.**

A cheese and wine bar where you can grab a delicious plate of cheese with a glass of wine bought direct from the vineyards – Auvergne wines cost from around €2.50 – with a nice terrace for sunny days. Also a number of reasonably priced regional dishes, which are mainly cheese based, including *tartiflette* (potato and cheese baked in wine), raclette and *aligot*. Lunchtime menu is €9.50 and another at €18; reckon on around €15 à la carte for a full meal. Cooked meals are served until 11pm. Good spot too for a drink before eating.

⊛ |●| Café Jean

17 rue des Carmes.
☎04.71.64.96.20
Closed *Sun; first fortnight in July.*

The nicest bistro in town is always packed at lunchtime. In the evening the atmosphere is cosier but just as convivial. It's a bright place, with appealing retro décor and two dining rooms separated by a superb brass bar. The tasty cooking, using fresh produce, is excellent value for money.

You could do worse than follow the lead set by the regulars who invariably plump for the dish of the day and one of the meltingly delicious home-made tarts for dessert. There's a *formule* of the day with main course and pudding for €10, and generous salads for €7. You'll pay about €15 maximum à la carte. And a friendly welcome and efficient service to boot.

⊛ ⅔ |●| L'Arsène

24 rue Arsène-Vermenouze: in the old part of town.
☎04.71.48.48.97
Closed *lunchtime; Sun and Mon; first fortnight in July.*

A warm and cosy dining room, with exposed stonework and modern paintings. It's very popular with many of the town's younger population attracted by the cheap, hearty food. The restaurant specializes in fondue; try also traditional grills, pork fillet with blue cheese or breast of duck with honey (all of which are for two people). They also serve *tartiflette*, raclette and large salads. Generous set menus at €15–19 and reasonably priced wines; house wine costs around €9. At the end of the meal try the "grole de l'amitié" (coffee, cognac and absinthe). *Free coffee offered to our readers on presentation of this guide.*

Sansac de Marmiesse

15130 (11km SW)

⊛ |●| La Belle Époque

Lieu-dit Lasfargues; on the Maurs road (N122); it's well signposted.
☎04.71.62.87.87
Closed *Sun evening and Mon (except July–Aug); early Jan to end Feb.* **Disabled access. High chairs available.**

An old restored farm in the heart of the countryside. You can eat in one of three dining rooms: the Belle Époque (with décor that lives up to the name), the Cantou-style or the rustic – a pleasant change from the usual country style. À la carte, you can try some classic dishes, such as pig's trotters, fried foie gras, *tête de veau* with herbs and, in season, mushroom specialities like cep omelette (the chef is a great mushroom enthusiast), or opt for one of the menus, €19–38. On fine days, you can take advantage of the charming terrace. New bedrooms have recently been added – we hope you will tell us what you think of them.

Besse-et-Saint-Anastaise

63610

☜ ⌂ |●| 🎄 Hôtel-restaurant Le Clos**

It's 400m from the medieval centre in the direction of the route du Mont-Dore. Follow the signs.
☎04.73.79.52.77 ℻04.73.79.56.67
@www.hotel-le-clos.fr
Closed a week in Jan; a week in March; mid-Oct to end Dec. **Restaurant closed** Mon–Fri lunchtimes out of season. **TV. High chairs and games available. Swimming pool. Car park.**

This modern establishment just out of the town centre offers a pleasant, friendly welcome and a wide range of facilities – indoor pool, well-equipped gym, Turkish bath and games room. Bedrooms are pleasant; doubles cost €46–60 with shower/wc or bath, and there are a few family rooms too. Attentive to their customers' needs, the owners can provide suggestions for excursions and walks. The food is decent if nothing out of the ordinary; set menus €15–31. Logis de France. *Free apéritif offered to our readers on presentation of this guide.*

☜ ⌂ |●| Hostellerie du Beffroy**

26 rue de l'Abbé-Blot.
☎04.73.79.50.08 ℻04.73.79.57.87
Closed Mon and Tues (except Feb, July and Aug); early Nov to end Dec. **TV. Pay car park.**

A fifteenth-century building owned and run by Thierry Legros, who has a fine reputation as a chef. The dishes always have a local flavour to which the chef adds an agreeable personal touch. The first menu is at €24 and there are others at €30–55. Rooms are decent and cost €50–80 for a double with shower/wc or bath, but facilities vary. It's a pity the welcome isn't more friendly.

Super-Besse

63610 (7km NW)

☜ |●| Restaurant La Bergerie

Route de Vassivières; take the D149.
☎04.73.79.61.06
Closed from 15 Sept to start of winter season (open on All Saints' Day). **Open**

weekends and public holidays for bookings throughout the year, also for group bookings.

It would be a crime to come here without trying the *truffade*. The young owner serves a hearty portion, with local ham, straight from the frying pan; it's cooked to order and probably the best you'll get in the region, extremely satisfying, well worth the thirty-minute wait. Lots of other local delicacies on menus from €16.50 to €28: pike-perch with a ewe's cheese crust, pig's trotter turnover, fillet of Salers beef with bilberries. You'll really feel at home in this country inn with its delightful décor and atmosphere. It's popular in winter and summer alike – on warm days you can eat on the terrace overlooking the lake.

Boudes

63340

☜ ⌂ |●| 🎄 Le Boudes la Vigne**

Place de la Mairie; take the A75.
☎ and ℻04.73.96.55.66
Closed Sun evening; Mon; a fortnight in Jan. **Disabled access. TV. High chairs available. Car park.**

This popular little hotel-restaurant, in a pleasantly renovated house, is in the centre of a small wine-growing village south of Puy-de-Dôme. The cooking is quite delightful (menus €20–40): foie gras, lobster roasted with seafood butter. For dessert, it's hard to resist the frozen parfait with verbena on crème du Velay. You're right in the midst of the best vineyards of the Auvergne so the wine list is splendid and wine is also served by the glass. The hotel was built only recently and is very quiet. Doubles go for €34 with shower/wc, breakfast €6; also a flat to rent, sleeping four to six people. *10% discount on the room rate (except June, July and Sept) or a free house drink to accompany dessert offered to our readers on presentation of this guide.*

Sarpoil

63500 (17km NE)

☜ 🎄 |●| La Bergerie de Sarpoil

In the direction of Saint-Germain–Lembron; from there take the D34 as far as Auzat, then the D214 going north.
☎04.73.71.02.54
Closed Sun evening and Mon except July–Aug.

The best gastronomic restaurant in the

region. Laurent Jury produces marvels using the finest Auvergne produce: free-range pork, Salers beef, milk-fed lamb with delicate char subtly flavoured with ceps and morels and the fragrance of chestnuts and bilberries ... everything here reveals the magician's flourish. Sample one of the menus (€17–60) – dishes on offer change with the seasons – or reckon on about €45–50 à la carte. The *menu campagnard* lists dishes like mouthwatering *andouille* pancake with onion *confit* and house tripe with thyme. Real food lovers can try the *menu gastronome or the menu dégustation*. On the latter you'll find slightly more elegant dishes like frogs' legs with garlic cream and herb *jus* or roast crayfish. There's a little motto on the menus: "the art of the cook begins where nature's work ceases". So now you know. *Free house apéritif offered to our readers on presentation of this guide.*

Bourbon-l'Archambault

03160

« 𝔄 ☎ |●| Grand Hôtel Montespan-Talleyrand***

2–4 pl. des Thermes; facing the spa.
☎04.70.67.00.24 ℗04.70.67.12.00
ⓦwww.hotel-montespan.com
Closed *end Oct to end March.* **TV. High chairs available. Swimming pool. Car park.**

You could while away the hours speculating about the rather obscure life of the two patrons who in some distant past stayed here and gave their name to this superb hotel with its refined air and old-worldly charm. It's an oasis of peace and quiet, with friendly staff and excellent service – there are reading rooms and card rooms hung with velvet and tapestries, a bright flower-filled dining room and a pool among the greenery of the garden. The same pleasant high standards apply to the bedrooms, some of which are veritable apartments. Bedrooms are tastefully and stylishly decorated; some have been recently refurbished and cost €54–92 for a double depending on the size. The restaurant sticks to old favourites and the cooking is worth the trip. There's a weekday menu at €18.50 and menus up to €45. Logis de France. *Free house apéritif offered to our readers on presentation of this guide.*

Ygrande

03160 (6km SW)

« 𝔄 ☎ |●| Château d'Ygrande***

Le Mont; it's 3km outside the village. Take the D953, then the D94.
☎04.70.66.33.11 ℗04.70.66.33.63
ⓦwww.chateauygrande.fr
Closed *Sun evening and Mon except July–Aug; Jan; Feb.* **TV. High chairs available. Baby changing facilities. Swimming pool. Car park.**

This remarkable place looks out over a copse which you can admire from your candelit dinner table. Classic architecture with superb parquet floors, glorious décor in all the bedrooms, excellent welcome and service, and a quality restaurant to boot. Understandably, it's widely admired, and when the Formula 1 teams race at Magny-Cours or Lurcy-Lévis, they take over the whole château. It's not cheap, yet it's good value for money and well worth making a dent in your holiday budget. Double rooms go for €95–180, depending on the size and the view. There's a lunch menu for €20 and others up to €45. Facilities include a pool, a sauna, a terrace, a billiard room and horse riding. *Free apéritif offered to our readers on presentation of this guide.*

Cérilly

03350 (17km NW)

« ☎ |●| Hôtel-restaurant Chaumat**

Place Péron; on the D953.
☎04.70.67.52.21 ℗04.70.67.35.28
Closed *Mon; Sun evening; a week early July; a week early Sept; a week end Dec.* **TV. High chairs available. Car park.**

Eight well-appointed rooms which have been nicely renovated – doubles €38–56 with shower/wc – but the real attraction here is the quality of the cuisine, as the roomful of regulars attests every lunchtime. The dining room has a rustic, country look. They serve interesting dishes with mixtures of sweet and savoury flavours. Quality fresh produce and generous helpings on the weekday lunch menu (€11) and others up to €30. It's friendly and welcoming and there's air-conditioning throughout. Logis de France.

Tronget
03240 (17km S)

◎ ⅍ ≘ |◉| Hôtel du Commerce**

D945; take the D1 towards Montet.
☎04.70.47.12.95 ℱ04.70.47.32.53
Open *all year round.* **Disabled access. TV.
High chairs available. Car park.**

A hotel that contrasts old and new.
The building is modern, with comfortable bedrooms (€42 with shower/wc),
though they're a bit lacking in character.
Compare that with the traditional cooking of Monsieur Auberger, which is
heavily based on local produce: potato
pâté, lamb chops with thyme and garlic,
Charolais steak with Saint Pourçain wine
or *andouillette* with Charroux mustard.
Range of menus starting at €14 (not
Sun) to €40. Logis de France. *Free house
apéritif offered to our readers on presentation
of this guide.*

Saint-Bonnet-Tronçais
03360 (29km NW)

◎ ⅍ ≘ |◉| Le Tronçais**

Take the N144, then the D978 in the direction
of the forest of Tronçais as far as the Rond
de Tronçais. It's 3km south of Saint-Bonnet-
Tronçais. Take the A71 and the Forêt de
Tronçais exit.
☎04.70.06.11.95 ℱ04.70.06.16.15
Closed *Sun evening; Mon; Tues lunchtime
out of season; mid-Nov to mid-March for the
restaurant; mid-Dec to mid-Jan for the hotel.*
TV. Car park.

A peaceful, very comfortable lakeside
hotel with lots of charm. The forest of
Tronçais, one of the oldest and most
beautiful in France, becomes every shade
of green in spring and every shade
of yellow, red and brown in autumn.
Spacious yet cosy bedrooms €52–68
with shower/wc or bath; avoid the rooms
in the annexe, which overlook the road.
The restaurant is strong on traditional
local dishes with menus at €20–33: snails
with walnuts, eel terrine with blackberries, veal cutlet with ceps. Delightful
service in the two dining rooms which
are very elegantly and tastefully decorated, with great views of the grounds
and surrounding countryside. Logis de
France. *Free coffee offered to our readers on
presentation of this guide.*

Bourboule (La)
63150

◎ ⅍ ≘ |◉| Hôtel Le Charlet**

94 bd. Louis-Chousy; below the town.
☎04.73.81.33.00 ℱ04.73.65.50.82
ⓦwww.lecharlet.com
Closed *mid-Nov to early Dec.* **TV. High
chairs and games available. Swimming
pool. Car park.**

Le Charlet is situated a little below the
town and has an informal atmosphere.
The forty bedrooms are pleasant, with
modern facilities, though the décor is a
little old-fashioned; doubles with shower/
wc or bath go for €40–65 according to
the season. There's a nice pool with a
wave machine, a Turkish bath and a gym.
The cooking is traditional and local, with
dishes like *potée auvergnate, truffade* and *coq
au vin* on the menus (€17–22). The buffet
breakfast offers a wide choice to satisfy
all appetites and includes pastries, cereals,
sausage and red wine. *10% discount on the
room rate (except during school holidays) offered
to our readers on presentation of this guide.*

◎ ⅍ ≘ |◉| Hôtel-restaurant Le Pavillon**

Avenue d'Angleterre.
☎04.73.65.50.18 ℱ04.73.81.00.93
ⓔhotel.lepavillon@wanadoo.fr
Closed *1 Nov–31 March.* **TV. High chairs,
cots and feeding-bottle warmer available.**

In a quiet residential area, this nice little
place has a pretty Art Deco façade. There's
a warm family atmosphere. Rooms are
modern and clean, if a little functional and
cost €45 for a double with shower/wc,
€52 with bath. Simple family cooking
using regional ingredients; menus €15–25.
Logis de France. *Free apéritif offered to our
readers on presentation of this guide.*

Bourg-Lastic
63760 (14km NW)

◎ ≘ |◉| ⅍ La Pomme d'Or

In the town; take the D31 in the direction of
Messeix, then the D987.
☎04.73.21.80.18 ℱ04.73.21.84.15
Closed *Wed; early Nov to Easter.* **Disabled
access. High chairs and games available.
Car park.**

A beautiful, traditional house in a lush setting. On the first floor, seven spotless rooms;
doubles €32–40 with shower/wc, €50–65

with bath, and some family rooms. The cosy, rustic dining room (complete with large fireplace and exposed beams) attracts a loyal following that appreciates fine regional cooking. Many of the local classics are on offer: *tripoux*, pike-perch, duck *confit*, sirloin steak with blue-cheese sauce, all prepared with loving care and the freshest of ingredients. Specialities from other parts of France are also sometimes available: *bœuf bourguignon* or *coq au vin*, for example, on menus (€15–24), or reckon on €20 à la carte. There's also an excellent wine list. On a fine day, you can enjoy the pretty little terrace and garden. *Free coffee offered to our readers on presentation of this guide.*

Brioude

43100

@ 🏕 🏠 |●| **Hôtel de la Poste et Champanne****

1 bd. du Docteur-Devins; RN102 passing through Brioude, near the Maison du Saumon.
℡04.71.50.14.62 📠04.71.50.10.55
Closed *Sun evening; Mon lunch; Feb.* **TV. High chairs available. Car park.**

An old country hotel, updated to suit modern tastes. The bedrooms facing the street are rather noisy, while those in the annexe at the back are very quiet; doubles €30 with shower, €44 with shower/wc or bath. There's a bar on the ground floor; the restaurant on the floor above has long had a reputation for good food and does a number of set menus; weekdays at €14, others up to €37. Traditional, unpretentious food: salmon pie Brivadois style, Salers beef stew, tripe gratin with fourme d'Ambert cheese, Auvergne cheese plate and a fruit basket with delicious desserts (increasingly difficult to find.) All the dishes use regional, seasonal products. The jolly owner serves the food himself. *Free coffee offered to our readers on presentation of this guide.*

@ 🏕 🏠 |●| **La Sapinière****

Avenue Paul-Chambriard; it is signed from the N102, which runs through Brioude.
℡04.71.50.87.30 📠04.71.50.87.39
@hotel.la.sapiniere@wanadoo.fr
Closed *Sun evening; Mon; Feb.* **Restaurant closed** *Easter to All Saints' Day evening.* **Disabled access. TV. Swimming pool. Car park.**

Love at first sight with this hotel – new,

beautiful, welcoming and with air-conditioning. An appealing modern building built from wood, brick and glass, located between two old farm buildings. The fifteen spacious rooms look out over the grounds and are decorated in different styles; doubles with shower/wc €77, with bath €90, breakfast €9.50. They're named rather than numbered – "Vulcania" has a bedhead carved from lava as do "Baldaquin" and "Art Nouveau" which overlook the basilica. There's a lovely indoor swimming pool with Jacuzzi. The restaurant offers fine cuisine using local produce (lentils, cabbage stuffed with foie gras, side of Salers beef, etc) with a range of menus €22 (weekdays only) to €38. *Free coffee offered to our readers on presentation of this guide.*

Saint-Beauzire

43100 (11km SW)

@ 🏕 🏠 |●| **Hôtel Le Baudière – Restaurant Le Vieux Four****

Saint-Beauzire station; from Saint-Beauzire, 2km on the left on the Brioude road and 4km from the A75 interchange.
℡04.71.76.81.70 📠04.71.76.80.66
Closed *end Dec to end Jan.* **Restaurant closed** *Mon.* **Disabled access. TV. High chairs and games available. Swimming pool. Car park.**

A pleasant modern hotel with sauna, indoor and outdoor swimming pools and very comfy bedrooms; doubles with shower or shower/wc €48–50. Rooms 17, 18 and 19 offer views over the countryside. Right next door is the restaurant, which has a handsome stone oven in the main dining room. Set menus €18–43, with a children's menu for €8. The grilled meat is as good as the lentil mousse with morels, or the *crépinette* of pig's trotters and the *crème brûlée*. Good wine list, too. *Free house apéritif offered to our readers on presentation of this guide.*

@ 🏕 |●| **La Marmite**

It's on the way into the village.
℡04.71.76.80.21
Closed *Sun evening; Mon; evenings on public holidays; a week per quarter (to be decided).* **Disabled access. Car park.**

The copper *marmite* (cooking cauldron) is set on the open fireplace in this adorable and lovingly tended family restaurant. Françoise is in charge of the cooking and

Marc takes care of the service – and if you want to know anything about the local area he's your man. Dishes are generously served; try the halibut in pastry or the lamb with tomato. There's a €12 lunch menu or others at €15–26. They don't press you to buy wine you don't want. When the weather is fine you can enjoy the ivy-swathed frontage and large lawn. A really lovely place – it's recently become a three-bedroom hotel. *Free coffee offered to our readers on presentation of this guide.*

Chaise-Dieu (La)
43160

ⓒ ⌂ |O| Hôtel de la Casadeï **

Place de l'Abbaye; it's at the foot of the steps to the abbey.
☎04.71.00.00.58 ℗04.71.00.01.67
ⓦwww.hotel-la-casadei.com
Restaurant closed *Sun evening and Mon except in July–Aug; Nov–April.* **TV. High chairs available.**

You get to the hotel through a flower-filled terrace and an art gallery. The best rooms (which, of course, have all been named after composers) have a view of the abbey but are more expensive than the others; doubles €39–51 with shower/wc. And, as everyone here is a music lover and expert on the Baroque music festival, you will have the opportunity of (re)discovering recordings of all the concerts that have taken place at the nearby abbey. The photos you'll see everywhere are of artists who've stayed at the hotel during the town's sacred music festival. In the restaurant they serve set menus (€15–25) with regional specialities and *coq au vin* cooked in spiced Hypocras wine. There's a little terrace at the back. Logis de France.

ⓒ ⌂ |O| Hôtel de l'Écho et Restaurant de l'Abbaye**

Place de l'Écho; in the centre behind the abbey.
☎04.71.00.00.45 ℗04.71.00.00.22
Closed *Wed lunch except mid-June to mid-Sept; Jan to end March.* **TV. High chairs available. Car park.**

This delightful inn with a large terrace is fully booked during the festival – all the big names have stayed here. The handsome dining room with its antiques and Louis XIII décor is housed in the former monastery kitchens and offers menus at

€16.50–60, with a children's menu at €11. You'll find tasty, regional dishes: crispy snail and cream of watercress, pan-fried *escalope* of foie gras and mushrooms and a trolley of fresh desserts. The wine list is excellent and you can expect an impeccable welcome and elegant table settings. Eleven bedrooms are available; doubles go for €49–60 with shower/wc or bath, breakfast €8.50. Nos. 7 and 15 have wonderful views of the abbey. *10% discount on a room offered to our readers on presentation of this guide.*

Chambon-sur-Lignon (Le)
43290

ⓒ ⌂ ⌂ Hôtel Beau-Rivage*

19 rue de la Grande-Fontaine; it's 200m from the centre. Follow the signs.
☎04.71.65.82.77
Closed *mid-Sept to mid-April.* **Car park.**

With a name that suggests a seaside resort and an atmosphere more like that of a mountain resort, this hotel offers a pleasant welcome and doubles with shower/wc at €38. There isn't a beach here, but it's very peaceful with no disturbance from residents and short-stay guests. Although a bit old-fashioned, it's a very nice place with genuine people. *10% discount on the room rate (in May, June and Sept) offered to our readers on presentation of this guide.*

Tence
43190 (9km N)

ⓒ ⌂ |O| ⌂ Café-restaurant Brolles

Mas-de-Tence; 5km east of Tence, near the village of Mazeaux.
☎04.71.65.42.91
Restaurant open *weekends and weekdays (bookings only).*

An authentic country inn run by friendly people. The restaurant has been tastefully decorated and the stone floor makes the place feel nice and cool. Sit at the table beside the fireplace and enjoy home-made *saucisson* or omelette made from eggs laid by the owner's hens. All the dishes are good and tasty, from the *potée auvergnate* to the salt pork to the cabbage soup, with set menus €13–30; children's menu €6.50. People come from far away to sample the oven-cooked dishes and ewe's milk cheese, eaten warm. Simple but clean rooms with basin at €22 (shower and wc on the landing); breakfast costs €4. It's a small place, so it's best to book. Credit cards not accepted. *Free house apéritif offered to our readers on presentation of this guide.*

Vastres (Les)
43430 (11km SW)

@ 🏠 |●| 🎋 Auberge du Laboureur

It's opposite the village church, 2km beyond Fay-sur-Lignon.
℡04.71.59.57.11 ℻04.71.59.55.23
Open *all year.* **Disabled access. High chairs and baby changing facilities.**

In a village set away from the main roads, this old bakery (with its oven) has been turned into a country inn. It has been very thoughtfully and tastefully decorated, with quiet, elegant rooms that have a separate entrance; doubles €30, breakfast €6. The large dining room has lots of style and there's a terrace, too. Delicious local dishes and desserts (iced soufflé with verbena) are prepared by the owner, and even the rye bread is home-made. There's a menu at €11 (not Sun) and others up to €18. *10% discount on the room rate (except July–Aug) offered to our readers on presentation of this guide.*

Champs-sur-Tarentaine
15270

@ 🎋 🏠 |●| L'Auberge du Vieux Chêne**

34 rte. des Lacs.
℡04.71.78.71.64 ℻04.71.78.70.88
🖥www.advc.free.fr
Closed *lunchtime; Sun evening and Mon in low season; Nov–March.* **TV. Car park.**

A renovated old farm in northern Cantal that's a haven of calm and comfort. Bedrooms have been nicely done up in bright, cheerful colours and all have bathrooms; doubles cost €52–80, according to the season. There's an enormous fireplace on the back wall of the restaurant, and though the dining room is large it's laid out in such a way that it actually feels quite intimate. On offer are regional specialities alongside classic dishes with two menus at €22 and €30, and a children's menu at €10. Try the excellent snails in cream,

the calf sweetbreads with morels and the duck *confit* with ceps. There's a pretty terrace where you can dine or take breakfast. *10% discount on the room rate (except July–Aug) offered to our readers on presentation of this guide.*

Marchal
15270 (8km NE)

@ 🏠 |●| 🎋 L'Auberge de l'Eau Verte

Take the D679 then the D22; on a small hill beside the church.
℡04.71.78.71.48
Closed *Wed out of season.* **High chairs available. Car park.**

A traditional little inn on a small hill beside the church near Champs – a good place to appreciate traditional Auvergne cuisine. Super-friendly welcome in the restaurant, where you'll find special "taste of Auvergne" menus. These have to be ordered in advance and offer a delicious plate of cold meat, *truffade*, salad, cheese and dessert. Servings are generous and well-prepared, and menus range from €11 (weekdays only) up to €21. Double bedrooms with basin (bathroom on the landing) go for €35 – ask for room 5 with its view of the Massif du Sancy, recently refurbished with shower and wc. Half board is available at €33 per person. *Free apéritif offered to our readers on presentation of this guide.*

Châtelguyon
63140

@ 🏠 |●| 🎋 Hôtel-restaurant Castel Régina**

3 av. de Brocqueville; in the spa gardens.
℡04.73.86.00.15 ℻04.73.86.19.44
Closed *Oct–April.* **TV. Car park.**

A stylish spa hotel. The Belle Époque décor gives it a delightful, old-fashioned charm, and the atmosphere is relaxed, if staid – you're hardly going to come to Châtelguyon for the nightlife. Clean, well-kept bedrooms are €31 with wc, €38 with shower/wc or bath. The €13 *menu du jour* (weekdays only) and others at €15–25 are more substantial than you'd expect for a rest cure. Credit cards not accepted. *Free coffee offered to our readers on presentation of this guide.*

◎ ⅔ ⬧ Les Chênes**

15 rue Guy-de-Maupassant.
☎04.73.86.02.88
⊛pageperso.aol.fr/LesChenes63/Index1.htm
Open *all year round.* **TV. Games available.**
Car park.

You can't miss this superb octagonal building. The rooms are quiet and pleasant and are named after friends. Nos. 2 and 7 have balconies with views over the countryside. Doubles are €45 with enormous breakfast of orange juice, yoghurt, ham, cheese and pancakes. On the ground floor there is a leisure room and a dining room. The owner and her daughter, and sometimes her son, offer guests a hearty welcome. An interesting idea here is the special stay option inspired by different cuisines. Credit cards not accepted. *5% discount on the room rate (after two consecutive nights) offered to our readers on presentation of this guide.*

◎ ⬧ |●| Hôtel Bellevue – Restaurant le Cèdre Bleu**

4 rue Punett.
☎04.73.86.07.62 ⊕04.73.86.02.56
⊛www.hotel-bellevue-chatelguyon.com
Closed *Oct–April.* **TV. High chairs available.**

This hotel offers quiet rooms with excellent facilities and above all perfect soundproofing guaranteeing complete peace and quiet. Some of the rooms have just been refurbished; doubles with shower/wc or bath €48–65. They serve local seasonal dishes in the restaurant: fillet of pike-perch, *truffade* with Cantal cheese, pavé of cod in a spicebread crust and frozen nougat with walnuts. There's a menu of the day at €18, regional menu at €20 and menu *Cèdre Bleu* at €32. Logis de France.

◎ ⅔ |●| Restaurant La Potée

34 av. Baraduc.
☎04.73.86.06.60
Closed *Mon; Nov.* **Disabled access.**

The façade of this restaurant is beautifully timbered, and the dining room is pretty with a few tables and an old counter that stands imposingly opposite the door. The owner likes to play Brassens' music, which is very much in keeping with the cosy, genuine atmosphere of the place. Hearty local dishes and generous portions: *potée*, *tripoux*, *truffade*, trout. Stays open at night later than most (service until 10pm), just the thing to give the hungry backpacker a lift. No menus; expect to pay around €18 à la carte. *Free house liqueur offered to our readers on presentation of this guide.*

Chaudes-Aigues

15110

◎ ⬧ |●| ⅔ Au Rendez-vous des Pêcheurs

Ventuéjol, Pont-de-Lanau; take the D921.
☎04.71.23.51.68
Disabled access. Car park.

A little inn at the side of the road which has been modernized. The owner's son is carrying on the long tradition of friendly and unpretentious service. Menus from €12.50 (weekdays) up to €15.50 (Sundays) include starter, main meal (trout with bacon, rabbit stew with ceps, *potée*, *tripoux*, perch *à la meunière*), cheese and dessert. The home-made ice creams and sorbets are the house speciality. There's a terrace open in the afternoons. A few basic but clean double rooms with handbasin go for €28; triple rooms go for €35. Half-board costs €34 per person, full board €42 per person. No credit cards. *Free coffee offered to our readers on presentation of this guide.*

Chomelix

43500

◎ ⅔ ⬧ |●| Auberge de l'Arzon**

Place de la Fontaine; in the centre of the village.
☎04.71.03.62.35 ⊕04.71.03.61.62
Closed *Mon and Tues lunchtimes during July–Aug; Mon, Tues and Sun evening the rest of the year; All Saints' Day to Easter.*
Disabled access. TV. Car park.

This is a good village inn and the restaurant is extremely popular. It's best to book in summer, especially during the music festival in nearby La Chaise. The bedrooms are impeccable and situated in a quiet modern annexe overlooking a pretty little garden; doubles €45–58. The restaurant uses fresh local produce: foie gras, salmon with lentils, and mouthwatering home-made desserts. Set menus €21 (not Sun) and up to €42; also home-made preserves available. A walk down through the village as far as the Gorges de l'Arzon is just the thing to help the food go down. Ask the owner, he was born here. *10% discount on the room rate for more than two nights (July–Aug) offered to our readers on presentation of this guide.*

Pontempeyrat
43500 (13km NE)

≪≋ ≜ |●| Hôtel-restaurant Mistou***

Take the D498, 50km from Craponne-sur-Arzon.
☎04.77.50.62.46 ℗04.77.50.66.70
⊛www.mistou.fr
Closed *early Nov to end April.* **Restaurant closed** *lunchtime (except Sun, public holidays and Aug).* **TV. Car park.**

Unbeatable bucolic setting at the bottom of the beautiful Ance valley: the river laps the fir trees and irrigates the delightful garden with a swimming pool. An old water mill, built around 1730, used to stand here, but now a recycled turbine provides the electricity required by this three-star hotel with sauna and Jacuzzi (at extra charge). All the comfortable and extremely quiet rooms are tastefully decorated, and the biggest ones give on to the garden. Doubles with shower/wc or bath €95–130; breakfast €12. Half board is compulsory in high season and during the Craponne and La Chaise-Dieu festivals. In the kitchen, Bernard Roux, one of the country's great advocates of regional cooking, creates succulent seasonal dishes set off by spices from his native Provence, with several menus from €32–58. The platter of four foies gras and the snails with fat ham were absolute magic – not to mention the touch of vanilla in the butter. Logis de France.

Clermont-Ferrand
63000

See map on pp.120–121

⊚ ⋔ ≜ Hôtel Cartier

19 rue de l'Industrie; 10min walk from the station in the quartier Desaix. **Map D1-9**
☎ and ℗04.73.92.02.14
TV. Cots available.

An unpretentious little hotel in a quiet street in the commercial district, offering very competitive prices. Don't expect luxury, however – for €15.30 for a double room with basin, €20.60 with shower, you get saggy beds, stark décor and a shower on the second floor. If you want

a TV, the owner, who has a room on the first floor, will bring one to your room for €2. Avoid room no. 5, which is noisy. The clientele includes white-collar workers and young people on a budget. *10% on the room rate offered to our readers on presentation of this guide.*

⊚ ≜ Hôtel Foch*

32 rue du Maréchal-Foch; near Place Jaude, so very central. **Map B3-8**
☎04.73.93.48.40 ℗04.73.35.47.41
TV. Pay car park.

The entrance is easy to miss in spite of the sugar-coloured frontage. Reception is on the first floor but the rooms here are best avoided; opt for the ones on the upper floors, even though they're quite small – rooms with basin €34, or €44–51 with shower/wc. An added bonus is the pleasant glass roof in the breakfast room and you can expect a courteous welcome from either the father or son. Remember to ask for the keys if you go out in the evening.

≪≋ ≜ Hôtel Ravel**

8 rue de Maringues. **Map D2-7**
☎04.73.91.51.33 ℗04.73.92.28.48
⊛www.hotelravel63@wanadoo.fr
Closed *23 Dec–2 Jan.* **TV.**

This little family-run hotel is in a quiet neighbourhood tucked away between the station and the town centre. It has a captivating mosaic façade and the proprietress will give you a warm welcome. She runs the place virtually single-handed. The sassy Gisèle may ask you to pay up front for the room but she'll also stay up until you get back at night. During the day she takes bookings, makes breakfast and sees to the rooms. Gisèle is like a tornado, cleaning everything from top to bottom. Just a step away is the Saint-Joseph market (good farm-produced food on Friday mornings) and a laundrette. And just a little further, the town centre beckons. The décor in the bedrooms is simple and charming and they're good value at €44 with shower/wc or bath. Breakfast costs €5.80.

≪≋ ⋔ ≜ Hôtel Albert-Élisabeth**

37 av. Albert-Élisabeth; 100m from the station. **Map D2-5**
☎04.73.92.47.41 ℗04.73.90.78.32
⊛www.hotel-albertelisabeth.com

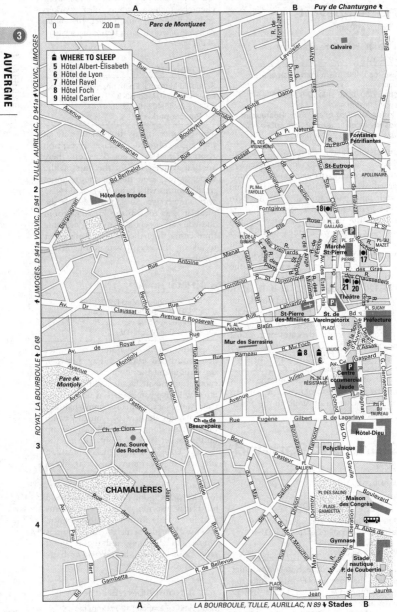

Parc de Montjuzet

WHERE TO SLEEP
5 Hôtel Albert-Élisabeth
6 Hôtel de Lyon
7 Hôtel Ravel
8 Hôtel Foch
9 Hôtel Cartier

0   200 m

Calvaire

Fontaines
Pétrifiantes

St-Eutrope

Hôtel des Impôts

Fontgiève

18

Marché
St-Pierre

17

21 20

Théâtre

St-Pierre
des-Minimes

St. de
Vercingétorix

Préfecture

Mur des Sarrasins

8

6

Centre
commercial
Jaude

Parc de
Montjoly

Ch. de
Beaurepaire

Anc. Source
des Roches

Hôtel-Dieu

CHAMALIÈRES

Polyclinique

Maison
des Congrès

Gymnase

Stade
nautique
P. de Coubertin

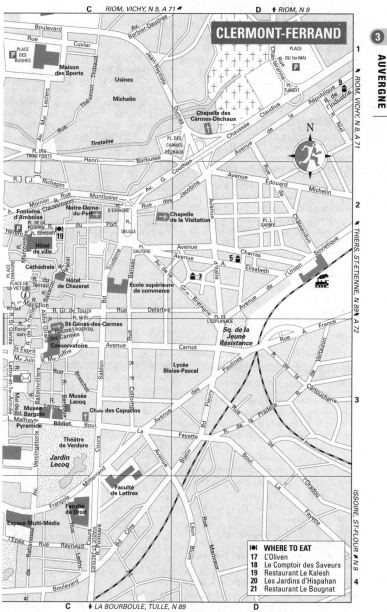

CLERMONT-FERRAND

	WHERE TO EAT
17	L'Oliven
18	Le Comptoir des Saveurs
19	Restaurant Le Kalesh
20	Les Jardins d'Hispahan
21	Restaurant Le Bougnat

TV. High chairs available. Pay car park.

This place is marked by a big red neon sign – you won't miss it. Well-soundproofed rooms, some have just been refurbished, though on the whole they lack character; doubles €46.50–50.50 with shower/wc or bath, breakfast €7.90. Nos. 7 and 15 have a fold-out bed for children. Lock-up garage available. *10% discount on the room rate at the weekend except July–Aug is offered to our readers on presentation of this guide.*

☺ ⅍ 🏠 |●| Hôtel de Lyon***

16 pl. Jaude. **Map B3-6**
☏ 04.73.17.60.80 ☏ 04.73.17.60.81
@ hotel.de.lyon@wanadoo.fr
TV. High chairs available. Pay car park.

You can't get more central than place Jaude – this functional and well-maintained hotel is in the very heart of town. Comfortable if conventional rooms with good facilities, double glazing and air-conditioning; doubles with shower/wc or bath at €76. Weekday lunch menu at €11; reckon on €18 for a meal à la carte. Breakfast (€8) is served as a buffet in the pub downstairs or can be brought to your room. *Free use of garage offered to our readers on presentation of this guide.*

☺ |●| ⅍ Restaurant Le Kalash

8–10 rue du Port; in the pedestrian precinct near the cathedral. **Map C2-19**
☏ 04.73.90.19.22
Closed *Sun.* **Open** *until 10.30pm.*

This Indo-Pakistani restaurant offers typical fare of high quality served in an attractive setting by friendly, if not very talkative, staff. The long list of dishes from different Pakistani ethnic groups is mouth-watering. There's a lunchtime weekday menu at €8.50 and others at €13.50-21. *Free house apéritif offered to our readers on presentation of this guide.*

☺ |●| ⅍ L'Oliven

5 rue de la Boucherie. **Map B2-17**
☏ 04.73.90.38.94
Closed *Sat lunchtime; Sun; Mon.* **Disabled access.**

This place has pretty décor in orange hues and is run by a bright, friendly team. They offer a fresh look at Provençal and Mediterranean cooking and dishes are light and tasty (with produce bought fresh every morning). Didier, the chef,

will take time to present his dishes to you. The restaurant offers a very good value set menu at noon and in the evening the choices are written up on slate. Specialities include terrine of foie gras with fresh figs and spicy preserved tomatoes with clementine basil and cinnamon crème glacée. The set menus and à la carte (around €18) options change every five weeks; menus at €9 (weekday lunch) and €11.50 and *menus-cartes* at €18 and €24. In winter foie gras is a speciality. Fresh, inspired food that is both light and tasty – and done with panache. You guessed it, *L'Oliven* is the place to be. *Free coffee offered to our readers on presentation of this guide.*

☺ |●| ⅍ Restaurant Le Bougnat

29 rue des Chaussetiers. **Map B2-21**
☏ 04.73.36.36.98
Closed *Sun; Mon lunchtime, Wed lunchtime and Fri lunchtime; early July to early Aug.*

Set not far from the cathedral, in the pedestrian zone, this place might sound like a tourist trap, but it's not. The restaurant has a rustic feel, friendly atmosphere and offers a wonderful selection of well-prepared regional dishes – mutton tripe, *pounti*, pigs' trotters and *potée auvergnate*, the thick local soup which is becoming harder and harder to find in Clermont. There's a splendid wood-burning stove in the foyer, which the chef uses to prepare Auvergne pancakes. The €12.50 set menu is very decent, or you can eat à la carte for around €18, and there are good wines from the Auvergne. If you're on your own, try to get one of the stools at the counter where the regulars sit. *Free coffee offered to our readers on presentation of this guide.*

☺ |●| ⅍ Les Jardins d'Hispahan

11 ter rue des Chaussetiers. **Map B2-20**
☏ 04.73.90.23.07
Closed *Sun, Mon and public holidays; first fortnight in Aug.*

You're immediately transported – to Iran, the Iran of fine cuisine. Persian cooking with subtle, flowery, aromatic flavours rather than heavily spiced dishes. Those who like their food strongly flavoured should look elsewhere. The décor's not particularly exciting, which makes it easier to concentrate on the food. The kebab *barque*, made with grilled veal marinated in lemon, is perfect, as is anything cooked with a sauce. And if you think you don't like rice, the way they cook basmati here will change your mind forever. It's a genuine delight to dive into some of the thousand and one recipes of this Middle Eastern cuisine. Menus range from €15.50 up to €25, with a children's menu at €10; around €18 à la carte. *Free house apéritif offered to our readers on presentation of this guide.*

ⓔ |●| Le Comptoir des Saveurs

5 rue Saint-Claire. **Map B2-18**
ⓣ and ⓕ 04.73.37.10.31
Closed *evenings; Sun; Mon; Feb school holiday; Aug.* **Open** *noon–6pm.* **High chairs and games available.**

Slightly out of place, the *Comptoir des Saveurs* has come to rest in a simple, quiet street like some UFO that has landed in a working class part of town. A typical Clermont restaurant with retro-chic décor and welcoming staff who readily offer information about the food or advice about the wines. It's not the cheapest place in town (menus €20–35), but the dishes are tasty and imaginatively prepared. The delights in store include: spiced brochette of calf sweetbread and pigeon; and risotto of squid. The food is prepared with genuine creativity but great precision. Good cheeses and delicious, original desserts, too (try the apple crumble with mustard). And to top it all, it was a culinary adventure that left us with no feeling of heaviness and a spring in our step. They also offer gourmet meals to take away.

Chamalières
63400 (2km W)

ⓔ 🏠 |●| Hôtel Radio★★★

43 av. Pierre-et-Marie-Curie.
ⓣ 04.73.30.87.83 ⓕ 04.73.36.42.44
ⓦ www.hotel-radio.fr
Restaurant closed *Sat lunchtime; Sun; Mon lunchtime; 2–23 Jan; 1–8 May; 31 Oct–6 Nov.* **TV. Car park.**

Built as a radio station in the 1930s, this hotel-restaurant was owned by Michel Mioche for many happy years. Now it's run by his daughter, who gave up her career as a journalist in Paris to do so; she and her young team have maintained the high standards set by her father. Only top-quality produce is used and dishes are as skilfully prepared as they are imaginative with four menus on offer at €33–85.

Good choices include Breton lobster with truffle *jus*, casserole-roast pigeon and hot Caribbean chocolate soufflé. Beautiful bedrooms with lots of Art Deco style; doubles €84–91 with shower/wc and €94–130 with bath.

Royat
63130 (2km SW)

ⓔ 🏠 |●| La Pépinière Chalut

11 av. Pasteur.
ⓣ 04.73.35.81.19 ⓕ 04.73.35.94.23
Closed *Sun evening and Mon; 2–8 Jan; during Feb school holiday; 15–31 Aug.* **TV. High chairs available. Car park.**

You are warmly welcomed by Madame Chalut when you arrive at her charming inn. Her husband's cuisine is appetizing and imaginative, concentrating on fresh regional produce used in old family recipes, such as potato sausage and boned pig's trotters. But his palette is not limited to traditional Auvergnat cuisine – he also handles fish with great skill; try pike-perch *à la pissaladière* or ravioli langoustines with herb sauce. There's a weekday lunch menu at €12, then others €22–50. Four completely refurbished double rooms for €42 with shower/wc.

Saint-Genès-Champanelle
63122 (6km SW)

ⓔ |●| 🍴 Auberge de la Moréno

Col de la Moréno; between Puy de Dôme and Puy de Laschamps, on the D941A.
ⓣ 04.73.87.16.46
Closed *Mon (summer); Mon and Tues (winter); second fortnight in March; second fortnight in Nov.* **Disabled access. High chairs available. Car park.**

Recently acquired by new management, this inn has an interesting history, for the area was once patrolled by Morlac, a legendary (but all too real) highway robber. Little is known about him – hardly surprising, as apparently nobody who fell into his clutches lived to tell the tale. Old locals, with a tear in their eye, sometimes talk about the inn when it was run by Maria. Now guests receive a warm welcome that dispels all thoughts of such horrors, and the inn has retained its period charm, untainted by any touristy additions: large fireplace, dining table and stone floor worn down with age. The food lives up to these surroundings with menus €13 (weekday lunchtime) to €26: the famous *truffades*, *pounti*, stuffed pig's trotter and mountain char with green lentils. You can eat à la carte for around €25. Try washing your meal down with a fine Gamay rosé, for example, and finish off with a *tarte tatin* (unusually, made with pears). Away from the usual tourist bustle – it's worth booking, as the inn has earned a well-deserved success. It's also possible to spend the night here. *10% discount on the room rate (1 Oct–31 March) offered to our readers on presentation of this guide.*

Nebouzat
63210 (11km SW)

◎ 🎎 |●| Auberge de la Fourniale

It's at Récoléine in the Volcans regional park; from the col de la Ventouse, take the N89 in the direction of Nebouzat-Tulle. After Randanne turn right towards Récoléine and it's 4km further.
☎04.73.87.16.63
Closed *Mon; evenings (except Sat) out of season; 3 weeks in Sept.* **Disabled access. High chairs available.**

The Gauthiers gave up the family charcuterie and renovated this old shepherd's house and shed, keeping many of the original features. The chef loves tinkering, so there's an extraordinary décor hung with bells and baskets and a cheese service ingeniously made from horse shoes. Only fresh produce is used in the cooking which majors in traditional, substantial dishes like *pounti* and *truffade*. Be sure to try the *tarte tatin* with whipped cream. The weekday lunch menu (€10) includes charcuterie, *truffade* and dessert, or there's another for €12.50, and a Sunday menu for €17; also a snack *formule* of a plate of Auvergne ham and sausage. *Free liqueur offered to our readers on presentation of this guide.*

Condat-en-Féniers
15190

◎ 🎎 🏠 |●| Hôtel-restaurant Ché Marissou

Le Veysset; it's 3km from Condat on the D62, and well-signposted.
☎04.71.78.55.45
ⓦwww.marissou.com

Open *weekends only from early April to end of Sept, and school holidays during this period.*

This hotel, surely the smallest in the world, was born out of the genuine passion of a Laval industrialist – a local boy made good – and helped along by an elaborate marketing campaign. Transformed from a holiday home into an inn, it has a lot of charm. You'll be welcomed by the owner himself in a dining room that looks as much like a living museum as it does a restaurant. Marissou's job is to send you away full, no matter how hungry you were when you arrived. Special one-day package for two people (full board at €240, half board at €190), with free champagne thrown in. The price of your meal depends on your age: children under 7 eat free; €11 for ages 7–10; €22 for 10–65; €20 for over-65s, and free again for guests aged 100 or over. You can help yourself as often as you like to traditional cold meat and *crudités*. That will be followed by the day's special – *potée*, the thick local soup, perhaps, or mutton tripe – then you serve yourself from a table bearing a selection of perfectly matured regional cheeses and dessert. With the cheese you'll get a chance to sample (on the house) a glass of rare wine made from late-harvested local grapes. The one and only bedroom is traditionally decorated. Perfect for a special night away.

Égliseneuve-d'Entraigues
63850

◎ 🏠 |●| Hôtel du Nord*

Rue Principale.
☎04.73.71.90.28
Closed *Sun evening; Mon; evenings by reservation only out of season; a fortnight in Sept.*

After a day's walking in the Cézallier, this pretty little country inn is a lovely place to stop for a fortifying meal. Menus €10–20, or, if you call in advance, you can choose from menus up to €30. It's local cooking, classic and reliable: frogs' legs with garlic cream, crayfish soup, *andouillette* with bleu d'Auvergne cheese, stuffed cabbage, *truffade* (served in the pan by the chef), pigs' trotters, home-made liver terrine, pear mousse and chocolate tart. Doubles are €25 with bathrooms on the landing. Credit cards not accepted.

Gannat

03800

⚐ 🏠 Hôtel du Château**

9 pl. Rantian; it's opposite the château.
☏04.70.90.00.88 ℻04.70.90.30.79
🌐www.hotel-du-chateau.fr
Closed *Sat out of season.* **TV. Car park.**

This hotel is charming in a way that only nineteenth-century buildings in provincial towns can be. When you go in, the old men playing cards in the middle of the afternoon give the impression that they haven't moved in ages. Clean simple bedrooms €38–49 with shower/wc or bath.

Charroux

03140 (7km N)

⚐ |❷| La Ferme Saint-Sébastien

Chemin de Bourion; take the N9, then the D42 towards Chantelle.
☏04.70.56.88.83
Closed *Mon July–Aug; Mon and Tues Sept-June; Jan; last week in June; last week in Sept.* **Disabled access. Car park.**

This delightful restaurant, in one of the region's most beautiful villages, has quickly become a local favourite. The renovated farmhouse offers an intimate atmosphere in which to enjoy Valérie Saignie's fresh, creative cooking. Excellent interpretations of Bourbonnais cooking on menus priced at €22–60: courgette fritters with cream of chives; three foie gras platter; chicken with Charroux mustard and Jerusalem artichokes with bacon; regional cheeses (Lavort and smoked Lavort); and a fine selection of desserts to finish. They also have an excellent cellar. It's very popular, so you'll definitely need to book.

Effiat

63260 (11km SE)

⚐ |❷| 🎋 Le Cinq Mars

16 rue Cinq-Mars; take the D132 to Château de Villemont; then the D438 to Saint-Genès and after that the D93.
☏04.73.63.64.16
Closed *evenings Sun–Fri; Sat lunchtime; fortnight during Feb school holiday; fortnight end of Aug.* **High chairs available.**

The village and restaurant could not look more ordinary, but the welcome is delightful and the food very good. The chef, who used to preside over much more prestigious venues, abandoned his star rating to move to the area where his wife was born and take over his mother-in-law's restaurant. The food is excellent, plentiful and slow-cooked, or lighter according to the dish and the season: crayfish, *coq au vin*, salmon tartare. Modestly priced dishes of charcuterie are served with Auvergne wine and menus range from €10 to €15 (weekday lunch-times) and €17 to €23 at weekends; children's menu €7. It's best to book. *Free coffee offered to our readers on presentation of this guide.*

Lalizolle

03450 (20km NW)

⚐ 🏠 |❷| Hôtel La Croix des Bois**

Via the D998 heading for Ébreuil then Échassières.
☏ and ℻04.70.90.41.55
🌐www.lacroixdesbois.com
Car park.

A peaceful hotel-restaurant in the heart of the forest, with lovely views from the dining room. Simple but clean rooms cost €35–40 for a double with shower/wc. There's a weekday menu €10, then others €14–21.

Lapalisse

03120

⚐ 🏠 |❷| Hôtel-restaurant Galland**

20 pl. de la République.
☏04.70.99.07.21 ℻04.70.99.34.64
Closed *Sun evenings out of season; Mon; end Jan to Feb; last week in Nov and first week in Dec.* **Disabled access. TV. High chairs available. Car park.**

A real find, even in a region which is known for its excellent food. And that's putting it mildly. What a pleasure to come here and try a mixed green salad with poultry livers, roast langoustines or pan-fried escalope of foie gras with figs in a gingerbread crust. The food is freshly prepared, full of subtle flavours that are released in original dishes – all produced with talent. What else is there to say to tempt the traveller here? The owner is a delightful, jolly woman and her good humour combines well with her classy style. The service is precise and attentive and lives up to the rest. You feel quite at ease in the rather chic and modern décor. Menus start at €24 (not Sun lunch-time) up to €48, or you'll pay around €50 à la carte. The pleasant bedrooms cost €48–53 for a double with shower/wc or €50 with bath. Ask for one overlooking the interior courtyard as they're quieter. Logis de France.

Mandailles-Saint-Julien

15590

@ 🏠 |●| ⅔ Auberge Au Bout du Monde

Nathalie and Laurent Delteil, le bourg.
℡04.71.47.92.47 ℻04.71.47.95.95
🌐www.auberge-auboutdumonde.com
Closed *Wed afternoons and Sat out of season; 15 Nov–26 Dec.*

A nice place in the Jordanne valley, a starting point for hillwalkers going up the Puy-Mary. The hotel is quiet, simple and well run; doubles €34 with wc/shower. The restaurant, with its traditional *cantou* (inglenook fireplace) and gleaming copperware, is as cosy as you could wish. The cooking will satisfy even the hungriest hiker. Menus ranging from €11 to €15, with a regional menu at €19, offer char-cuterie and regional specialities like *truffade*, tripe, *pounti* and *potée* (the substantial local soup). There's a waterside terrace, and it's friendly and welcoming, even at the busiest times of day. *10% discount on a room (except school holidays) offered to our readers on presentation of this guide.*

@ ⅔ 🏠 |●| Hôtel-restaurant Aux Genêts d'Or*

In the centre of the village, a small hotel and restaurant with bakery, set back from the road, 50m down a cul-de-sac.
℡04.71.47.94.65 ℻04.71.47.93.45
Open *all year.* **TV.**

A small hotel, set back from the road down a quiet cul-de-sac. Comfortable doubles costing €34.50 with shower/wc, plus a few duplexes with kitchenette. Breakfast costs €6 and half board is available. Range of set menus, €11–21.30, listing speci-alities such as *tournedos* with gentian sauce, *entrecôte au bleu*, pan-fried escalope of foie gras and a millefeuille pastry with a "global reputation in Mandailles". *Free house apéritif before a meal offered to our readers on presentation of this guide.*

Saint-Cirgues-de-Jordanne

15590 (8km SW)

@ ⅔ 🏠 |●| Hôtel-restaurant Les Tilleuls**

Take the D17.
℡04.71.47.92.19 ℻04.71.47.91.06
🌐www.hotellestilleuls.com
Restaurant closed *Sun evening Nov–April.* **Hotel closed** *mid-Nov to end of March.* **High chairs and games available. TV. Swimming pool. Car park.**

A beautiful building overlooking the road and the Jordanne valley. You can relax in the garden, swimming pool or hot tub when you come back from a walk on the Puy-Mary. The quiet, pleasant bedrooms go for €40–43; half board costs €39–42 per person (obligatory in Aug). The dining room is equally pleasant and the open fire is welcome in winter. Cooking is refined and generous with menus €11–31.50: pork chop with Cantal cheese and morels, duck breast with dandelion honey, *pounti* baked with raisins. Logis de France. *Free breakfast per room per night (except Aug) offered to our readers on presentation of this guide.*

Massiac

15500

@ ⅔ 🏠 |●| Grand Hôtel de la Poste**

26 av. du Général-de-Gaulle.
℡04.71.23.02.01 ℻04.71.23.09.23
🌐www.hotel-massiac.com
Closed *10 days end Nov and 10 days early Dec.* **High chairs and games available. Disabled access. TV. Swimming pools. Car park.**

No shortage of facilities here: indoor and outdoor pools, Jacuzzi, steam bath, squash courts, gym. That's about it – apart from the collection of keyrings and dolls in the reception area which are entertaining if you're tired of the swimming pool or on your way out of the gym. Doubles with all mod cons weigh in at €40–51 with shower/wc or bath. There's a pleasant res-taurant at the back; it offers a set menu at €13 (not served on Sunday or public holi-days), and others €18.50–30. Specialities include *tripoux* with Cantal cheese, potato pâté and grilled pig's trotter with lentils. *10% discount on a room (1 Oct–1 June) offered to our readers on presentation of this guide.*

Mauriac

15200

⊛ 🏛 |O| Hôtel des Voyageurs – La Bonne Auberge**

Place de la Poste.
☎ 04.71.68.01.01 ℱ 04.71.68.01.56
ⓦ www.auberge-des-voyageurs.com
Closed *Sat and Sun evenings Nov–April; a week in June.* **TV. High chairs available.**

The nicest hotel in Mauriac, offering a pleasant welcome, with twenty pretty rooms redecorated in smart, modern colours, lovely bathrooms too; doubles €30 with shower (wc on the landing), €35 with shower/wc, and €41 with bath. Menus, €11–30, feature regional specialities and traditional dishes. Logis de France. *10% discount on the room rate (except July–Aug) offered to our readers on presentation of this guide.*

Anglards-de-Salers

15380 (9km E)

⊛ 🏛 |O| Ferme-auberge Les Sorbiers

It's in the village on the D22.
☎ 04.71.40.02.87
Closed *early Oct to early April except during All Saints' Day holiday.* **Games available. Car park.**

A beautiful old stone building that's attractively arranged, with a warm atmosphere, pleasant dining room with big wooden tables, a huge open fireplace and a very friendly welcome from the Ribes family. Spotless, comfortable rooms with private en-suite bathrooms – two are family rooms and some have garden views, so they're quiet. Doubles go for €39 including breakfast; half board (if you stay three nights or more) at €58 for two. *Table d'hôte* €15, but it's best to book, or there's a set menu priced at €16. An ideal place if you want to enjoy the Cantal area. Credit cards are not accepted.

Drugeac

15140 (12km SE)

⊛ |O| L'Auberge des Saveurs

☎ 04.71.69.15.50.
ⓦ www.chez.com/dessaveurs
Closed *Wed; during Feb holiday.* **Disabled access. High chairs and games available.**

Follow your nose and the delicious smells will lead you to this little village

(or country) inn and its simple, uncluttered dining room. There to greet us is David, whose face and roguish manner remind us of Fred Chichin from the Rita Mitsouko band. But this restaurant is in a classier, more sophisticated league. Nicole Bataille has spent time working in restaurants on the Côte, but doesn't make a big deal about it – or only through her dishes. While her husband charms customers in the dining room, Nicole does battle in the kitchen to bring us some of her specialities: Auvergne ravioli, smoked salmon, *gratinée* of snails, among other dishes, with a weekday lunch menu (€10), and others €17–26. To finish there's a cheese board with home-made bread. The dishes change with the seasons and what's good in the market, but fish remains Nicole's favourite. The "chef's surprise" dessert sums up this faultless little establishment. The food is great and so is the dining room. A warm welcome and a delightful, sunny terrace to enjoy.

Mont-Dore (Le)

63240

⊛ 🏛 |O| 🕮 Auberge de Jeunesse Le Grand Volcan

Route du Sancy; by bus, winter and summer, Le Mont-Dore–Sancy link. 3km to the south of the town.
☎ 04.73.65.03.53 ℱ 04.73.65.26.39
ⓦ www.auberge-mont-dore.com
Closed *10–25 Nov.* **Open** *8am–noon (2pm in season) and 6–8pm (9pm in season).* **Games available.**

A large, wooden chalet on the edge of the forest and the Dordogne with rooms for two to six people (some with mezzanines), of which ten have just been refurbished; €12.80 per person per night, breakfast included. Full-board is compulsory in February. FUAJ membership card is compulsory (you can buy it on site). There's a single menu at €9 – a kitchen is available between June and September. Facilities include bar, pool, table football and TV room. *Free coffee offered to our readers on presentation of this guide.*

⊛ 🕮 🏛 |O| Hôtel de la Paix**

8 rue Rigny.
☎ 04.73.65.00.17 ℱ 04.73.65.00.31
ⓦ www.hotel-de-la-paix.info

Closed *fortnight end March; 15 Nov–25 Dec.*
TV.

Built in 1880, this hotel has a lovely old-fashioned décor. In the semi-pedestrianized quarter, very close to the craftworkers and shops. Simple, functional rooms go for €40 with shower/wc or bath, which is not expensive for le Mont-Dore. Superb Belle Époque dining room serving a range of menus at €19–49, and with a charming sitting room. Logis de France. *Free apéritif offered to our readers on presentation of this guide.*

Hôtel Le Castelet**

Avenue Michel-Bertrand; it's near the town centre.
04.73.65.05.29 04.73.65.27.95
castelet@compuserve.com
Closed *end March to 15 May and 1 Oct–20 Dec.* **TV. High chairs and games available. Swimming pool. Car park.**

There's not as much emphasis on spa cures here as in the other hotels in town. This is one of the most stylish, both in terms of the welcome given by the charming owner and its setting. It's a friendly place, with a swimming pool, garden and terrace. There are some thirty double-glazed rooms, some with rather thin partition walls, with en-suite doubles at €56. Good local cuisine in the restaurant which offers menus from €17 up to €27: fisherman's platter with gentian, salt pork with Puy lentitls, calf sweetbread *fricassée* with chanterelles. Logis de France. *Free house aperitif offered to our readers on presentation of this guide.*

Montluçon
03100

Hôtel des Bourbons – Restaurant aux Ducs de Bourbon**

47 av. Marx-Dormoy; it's near the station.
04.70.05.28.93 04.70.05.16.92
Restaurant 04.70.05.22.79
Restaurant closed *Sun evening and Mon.*
TV. Cots available.

This beautiful eighteenth-century townhouse has been stylishly renovated and offers comfortable, bright bedrooms; doubles €47 with shower/wc or bath. The restaurant has a great reputation, serving serious, not very original but beautifully executed cuisine; the menus, €14–34,

offer dishes such as *pavé* of Charolais beef, *onglets* with shallots and skate with butter. There's a pub, which lets you eat the same standard of food in more casual surroundings. A high-quality stopping point.

La Vie en Rose

7 rue de la Fontaine; it's beside Notre-Dame church.
04.70.03.88.79
Closed *Sun lunchtime.*

If you find yourself in the old part of Montluçon, unwind in this relaxed, cosy place. It all comes together here. First a friendly welcome from a pretty cool owner. The walls are hung with old photos of the town and adverts from the 1950s and 1960s. The ambient music is chosen with care. No elevator music here but a compilation of the best in French music. The cooking is great – the meats (*onglet*, pork chop, *entrecôte* flavoured with local wine) are thick and tasty and the salads generous and fresh. Excellent potato pie in particular. Menus are €8.30 (weekday lunchtimes) and €15; expect to pay €18 à la carte.

Le Safran d'Or

12 pl. des Toiles; it's in the pedestrian zone of the medieval town.
04.70.05.09.18
Closed *Sun evening; Mon; Tues evening; 15 Aug–15 Sept.*

Behind its yellow marbled façade, this place has the ambience of a Parisian brasserie, a pleasant, unhurried atmosphere, and the cooking is of the kind you'd get in a high-class bistro. You'll receive a warm welcome from the owner. The service is quick and efficient but you won't feel rushed, and the excellent cooking (simple, traditional dishes) is prepared using the freshest ingredients of the season; set menus €19 (weekdays only) to €26. *Free coffee offered to our readers on presentation of this guide.*

Néris-les-Bains
03310 (8km SE)

Hôtel-restaurant Le Garden

12 av. Marx-Dormoy; by the N144.
04.70.03.21.16 04.70.03.10.67
monsite.wanadoo.fr/hotellegarden
Restaurant closed *Sun evening and Mon*

(1 Nov–31 March); 24 Jan–5 March. **TV. High chairs and games available. Pay car park.**

The façade of this attractive house is hung with geraniums and inside there's a very lovely wooden staircase which creaks just enough to give added charm. The more than acceptable rooms – €41.70–53 for a double, depending on size – open onto the grounds. Classic yet innovative cuisine with lots of seafood, foie gras, offal and perfectly deglazed sauces; weekday menu €13, others up to €33 (three courses). You'll need a detox to get over all this. *10% discount on the room rate (1 Nov–31 March) offered to our readers on presentation of this guide.*

Montmarault

03390

◉ ⅔ 🏠 |◉| Hôtel de France**

1 rue Marx-Dormoy.
☎04.70.07.60.26 ℗04.70.07.68.45
Closed *Sun evening; Mon; a week in spring; 3 weeks from Nov.* **TV. High chairs available. Car park.**

Not a place you'd stop at if you hadn't heard about Patrick Omont's cooking but it's well worth the trip. Range of menus for €16.50–43.50; try the snails with walnuts, foie gras marbré and caramelized pears, or skate wing with Charroux mustard in a dining room decorated in sunshine colours – and with air conditioning, which makes it very pleasant in summer. Sheer delight. There are rooms, too, at €41.50–46.50 for a double with shower/wc or bath. *Free coffee offered to our readers on presentation of this guide.*

Montsalvy

15120

◉ ⅔ 🏠 |◉| L'Auberge Fleurie**

Place du Barry.
☎04.71.49.20.02 ℗04.71.49.29.65
ⓦwww.auberge-fleurie.com
Restaurant closed *Sun evening; Mon at All Saints' Day and Easter; 1 Jan–13 Feb (restaurant only).* **High chairs available. TV. Car park.**

Gorgeous place in the Châtaigneraie with ivy clambering up the front wall, a fireplace, exposed beams and ancient doors. The cosy restaurant offers delicious menus that change with the seasons and a number

of reasonably priced wines. The lunch menu, €12, and others (€20–35), are good value. The hotel has been completely renovated and offers spacious, comfortable and nicely decorated rooms with shower/wc or bath €39–51; half board is €45.50–47.50 per person. An altogether charming, welcoming spot to stay or eat. Logis de France. *Free house apéritif offered to our readers on presentation of this guide.*

◉ ⅔ 🏠 |◉| Inter-Hôtel du Nord**

☎04.71.49.20.03 ℗04.71.49.29.00
ⓦwww.hotel-du-nord.com
Closed *1 Jan to Easter.* **TV. High chairs and games available. Car park.**

Situated in the heart of the Châtaigneraie, this quiet, plush restaurant has an excellent reputation for its traditional local dishes. A random selection from the à la carte menu: duck foie gras prepared with Sauternes, Salers beef, Cantal veal, iced gentian mousse with blackberry coulis. The menus at €15 (weekdays only) up to €40, with a regional menu at €22, feature "classics" such as *aligot*, *magret* and *confit*. Comfortable double rooms go for €48–52 with shower/wc or bath. There is a lounge, bar and garden. *10% discount on the room rate (except Aug) or a free coffee offered to our readers on presentation of this guide.*

Calvinet

15340 (17.5km W)

◉ ⅔ 🏠 |◉| Hôtel-restaurant Beauséjour**

Route de Maurs; take the D19 towards Maurs.
☎04.71.49.91.68 ℗04.71.49.98.63
ⓦwww.cantal-restaurant-puech.com
Closed *Mon and Tues lunchtime in season; Sun evening, Mon and Tues out of season; Jan.* **TV. Car park.**

Michelin has awarded the restaurant a coveted star – it's the only place in Cantal to have one – and it's won regional awards, too. There's a cheery atmosphere and lots of regulars – from notaries and sales reps to peasant families having a day out. People come from far afield to sample Louis-Bernard Puech's tasty, local dishes. Superb, seasonally changing menus (€25–55) feature dishes such as black-pudding and duck-liver pie, locally produced pork chop cooked under the rind, potatoes stuffed with pig's trotters. À la carte: duck-liver waffle, caramel with gentian and a delicious chestnut shortbread. Good wines, too, at reasonable prices. The comfortable double rooms have just been refurbished and cost from €58; there's also an apartment for four people at €140. Logis de France. *Free house apéritif or coffee offered to our readers on presentation of this guide.*

Moulins
03000

⊚ ⚸ 🏠 |●| Le Parc**

31 av. du Général-Leclerc; it's near the train station.
℡04.70.44.12.25 ℗04.70.46.79.35
Restaurant closed Sat and Sun evening.
Closed 8–24 July; 23 Dec–6 Jan. **TV. Car park.**

The Barret family have been running this hotel since 1956 and they offer a kindly welcome. It's a beautiful building and classic in style. The bright dining room is relaxing, and the furniture, fabrics and colours are simple and harmonious. The restaurant serves traditional and local dishes with no surprises and no nasty shocks: Charolais fillet with fourme d'Ambert cheese, medallion of burbot with shellfish coulis. Set menus range from €19 (not Sun) up to €40. Rooms are well soundproofed; doubles with shower/wc or bath cost €37–61. Some of the rooms are in an annexe. *Free apéritif offered to our readers on presentation of this guide.*

⊚ ⚸ 🏠 |●| Hôtel de Paris-Jacquemart***

21 rue de Paris.
℡04.70.44.00.58 ℗04.70.34.05.39
⊚hotel-de-paris-moulins@wanadoo.fr
Closed 2 weeks in Jan; 3 weeks in Aug.
Restaurant closed Sat lunch except on public holidays; Sun evening; Mon. **Disabled access. TV. High chairs available. Car park.**

The chic-est establishment in Moulins. Elegant décor, refined furnishings and courteous welcome – everything to please. And the prices are more than reasonable for the quality, with doubles at €54 with shower/wc and €69 with bath. The chef specializes in high-quality classic cuisine with a creative twist – weekday menu €25, including coffee, or others up to €52 – and the service is faultless. *Free house apéritif offered to our readers on presentation of this guide.*

⊚ ⚸ |●| Restaurant La Petite Auberge

7 rue des Bouchers; it's near the main post office.
℡04.70.44.11.68 ℗04.70.44.82.04
Closed Sun (except public holidays); Mon evening; 7–28 Aug. **Disabled access.**

You feel right at ease in this dining room decorated throughout in a very local style, providing the perfect setting for good, traditional cooking which is rich in flavour and makes use of good produce and expertise. Safe, classic dishes such as scallop *fricassée* with salad, Charolais steak with Auvergne blue cheese and Saint-Pourçain *andouillette*. There's a quick set menu at €10, including wine, in the brasserie. At greater leisure, in the restaurant, weekday menu at €15, then others at €22 and €30. Delightful welcome which bodes well for the place as a whole. *Free house apéritif or coffee offered to our readers on presentation of this guide.*

⊚ ⚸ |●| Le Grand Café

49 pl. d'Allier.
℡04.70.44.00.05
Closed Sun in winter. **Open** until 11pm. **Car park. Disabled access.**

This superb 1900s brasserie is a listed building, and it's the most popular place in the area – people come for the atmosphere as much as the food. Past regulars have included a youthful Coco Chanel. A single menu for €16 with popular choices including grilled pig's trotters, and oxtail or *andouillette* salad which are the best options for a light meal. *Free coffee offered to our readers on presentation of this guide.*

Souvigny
03210 (7km SW)

⊚ ⚸ |●| Auberge Les Tilleuls

Place Saint-Éloi.
℡04.70.43.60.70
Closed Sun evening; Mon; Tues evening.
High chairs and games available.

In a charming Bourbonnais village with a magnificent basilica church dating from the tenth to fifteenth centuries, this inn is welcoming with its smart, fresh décor, where folk art on the walls portrays village scenes from the 1940s and 1950s. There's a €11.50 weekday lunch menu and others €15–39. Specialities include *marbré* of quail with fois gras and pig's cheek and trotter galette. Choice of superb regional cheeses, too. *Free house apéritif offered to our readers on presentation of this guide.*

Meillers

03210 (14km SW)

◎ |◯| 𝒜 Au Bon Vieux Temps**

It's in the village; take the D945 as far as Souvigny, then the D73.
☎04.70.47.33.36
Closed *Tues; Wed; Mon, Thurs and Fri lunchtimes.* **Disabled access. High chairs available.**

Raymond Tixier is a great chef who has won prizes for his desserts. One day, however, he woke up and realized that chasing Michelin stars was no longer for him. So he left the fancy restaurants behind and re-opened this country inn, opting for a menu of quality and carefully prepared traditional dishes. The rustic décor includes an old oven where he cooks his bread and stews his casseroles. The sauces are unbelievable − try the West Indian colombos − and, of course, desserts are perfect. The menu goes for €26; reckon on €30 for a complete meal à la carte. It's essential to book because the dining room is so small. *Free coffee offered to our readers on presentation of this guide.*

Chapelle-aux-Chasses (La)

03230 (15km NE)

◎ |◯| L'Auberge de la Chapelle-aux-Chasses

6km to the north of Chevagnes; take the D31.
☎04.70.43.44.71
Closed *Tues; Wed; fortnight during Feb; fortnight during All Saints' Day holiday.*

Right next to the church, there is nothing to distinguish this house from the others, except perhaps a certain charm. It looks like a house drawn by a child, a picture postcard house in fact. You cross the garden to go into the tiny dining room, where only the chiming of the bells in the nearby church will remind you of the passing of time. The dishes, which are based on local produce, are just as original. There's a choice of exquisite home-made desserts chalked on a blackboard. The menu changes often; weekday lunchtime menu at €12.50, then others at €19−37.

Dompierre-sur-Besbre

03290 (25km E)

◎ 𝒜 🏠 |◯| Auberge de l'Olive**

129 av. de la Gare; take the D12.
☎04.70.34.51.87 📠04.70.34.61.68
🖥www.auberge-olive.fr
Closed *Fri (except July–Aug); Sun evening in winter; a week at the end of Sept.* **Disabled access. TV. High chairs and games available.**

A handsome, well-maintained building covered in Virginia creeper. Care is taken with the cooking and the service is faultless − advanced booking is essential. Set menus range from €17 (weekdays only) to €50. A free gift is offered to children. Really peaceful, comfortable rooms, particularly the ten rooms at the back of the building; doubles with shower/wc or bath go for €44–47. Logis de France. *Free coffee offered to our readers on presentation of this guide.*

Murat

15300

◎ 🏠 Aux Globe-Trotters**

22 av. du Docteur-Mallet, opposite the train station.
☎04.71.20.07.22 📠04.71.20.16.88
Closed *Sun out of season; first week in July.* **TV.**

It's called *Aux Globe-Trotters* but it could just as well have been called *Aux Routards*. The clean, modern rooms here cost €29–38 − nicest, and most peaceful, are those overlooking the garden. The attic rooms are delightful, too, though watch your head if you're tall. It's run by young owners who are rather casual but friendly, and the atmosphere in the downstairs bar restaurant is very laid-back.

◎ 🏠 Hôtel Les Breuils**

Avenue du Docteur-Mallet; take the D39.
☎04.71.20.01.25 📠04.71.20.33.20
🖥www.cantal-hotel.com/murat/hotelles-breuils.
Closed *mid-Nov to end April; call to check opening periods outside school holidays.* **TV. Swimming pool. Pay car park.**

A substantial nineteenth-century private house which has been turned into a hotel. Decorated with antiques and works of art, it has an old-fashioned, aristocratic charm that's a world away from the sterility of some modern establishments. Peace and quiet are guaranteed as it's surrounded by a garden, and there's a nice heated indoor pool. The owner is a delightful hostess. Ten cosy, comfortable rooms, stylishly redecorated cost €63–76 for a double.

Dienne
15300 (11km NW)

@ |●| Restaurant du Lac Sauvage

Take the D680.
☎04.71.20.82.65
Closed Oct–June. **Open** noon–7pm. **Disabled access. High chairs and games available.**

Paradise for fishermen and walkers on the banks of a private lake 1200m up, offering a friendly welcome and magnificent setting. The kitchen uses local produce to prepare tasty regional specialities, served up in generous portions: especially good are trout with bacon, *truffade* and *pounti*. The set menu costs €13, or reckon on around €16 for a full meal à la carte. In summer, you can even catch your own trout – no permit needed and there's equipment for rent.

Lioran (Le)
15300 (12km SW)

@ 🎋 🏠 |●| Hôtel-restaurant Le Rocher du Cerf**

Take the N122.
☎04.71.49.50.14 ℗04.71.49.54.07
Closed 1 April–1 July and 10 Sept–22 Dec. **TV. High chairs and games available. Car park.**

A typical family hotel in a ski resort offering attentive service with a smile. Located near the slopes, this is the nicest place in the area, a perfect base for skiing in winter and hiking in summer. Bedrooms are simple and well kept; choose one with a view of the mountains. Double rooms with shower or bath go for €34–40. The restaurant has the same kind of homely atmosphere and the guest menus (€12–18) have been planned on fortnightly cycles. Specialities include stuffed cabbage, trout with bacon, truffade, *pounti*, steak or trout with bleu d'Auvergne (a local blue cheese). And recently a gym has been installed in the basement. *10% discount on the room rate (during the summer season) offered to our readers on presentation of this guide.*

Narnhac
15230

@ 🎋 🏠 |●| L'Auberge de Pont-la-Vieille**

Pont-la-Vieille; take the D990.
☎ and ℗04.71.73.42.60
Closed Nov. **TV. Games available. Car park.**

This is a welcoming and relaxing little hotel with a nice terrace on the riverbank. Quiet and pleasant double rooms with shower/wc or bath are €38–40; half board €35 per person. Set menus, €10 (weekdays only), and others €14–25, feature regional specialities – choose from dishes like trout with bacon, *à l'ancienne*, guinea fowl with ceps, *rissole Saint-Flour* (a sort of fritter with a cabbage and bacon filling) and truffade. Logis de France. *10% discount on the room rate (in May, June and Sept) offered to our readers on presentation of this guide.*

Pailherols
15800

@ 🎋 🏠 |●| L'Auberge des Montagnes**

It's southeast of Vic-sur-Cère on the D54.
☎04.71.47.57.01 ℗04.71.49.63.83
🌐www.auberge-des-montagnes.com
Closed 8 Oct–20 Dec. **Restaurant closed** Tues out of season **Disabled access. TV. High chairs and games available. Swimming pool. Car park.**

A pretty little winding road from Vic-sur-Cère will lead you up to this excellent family hotel on the outskirts of the village. It's been thoughtfully renovated and there's a new building constructed in the traditional style with a beautiful turret. The pond and the wonderful view complete the setting. There's a terrace, indoor and outdoor swimming pools, a climbing wall and a games room in the old barn across the road – it also offers horse-drawn carriage rides. The bedrooms, including two completely new ones, are cosy and well decorated; doubles €42–50 with wc/shower or bath, according to the season. Half board is a possible option at €42–49.50 per person. There are two very bright dining rooms, one with the traditional *cantou* (inglenook) fireplace. The set menus offer exceptional value. The €13 *menu du jour*, and others €17–22, list local dishes such as *pounti* with prunes, along with pavé of Salers beef with mushrooms and salmon trout in puff pastry. This place is well known so it's a good idea to book. Logis de France. *10% discount on a room (except weekends and school holidays) offered to our readers on presentation of this guide.*

Picherande

63113

@ 🐾 🏠 |O| Auberge du Tarafet

Lieu-dit Chareire; it's 3km from Picherande on the D149 to Super-Besse.
🕾 and ℻04.73.22.31.17
Closed *Sun evening except July and Aug.* **High chairs available. Car park.**

Christian is a big, friendly soul who has run this gîte-bar-restaurant for the last twenty years. He can tell you everything you need to know about the GR30 walking trail that goes through the area as well as the GR3 and the cross-country ski trails. His gîte is ideally located and very well maintained. You can sleep on one of thirty mattresses laid out on the ground floor, with separate kitchen and dining room on the first. You'll need to bring your own sleeping bag and food. In addition, there are three rooms with double-beds and bunks for practically the same price as the gîte – €28 for a double. Christian also runs a large, rustic inn where he serves regional specialities and sandwiches; allow €13 for a full meal with specialities served only to order. Children's menu available at €6. It's popular with locals who take a glass or two at the bar or at tables with their friends. What more could you ask for? *Free house apéritif offered to our readers on presentation of this guide.*

Pontgibaud

63230

@ 🐾 🏠 |O| Hôtel de la Poste**

Place de la République.
🕾04.73.88.70.02 ℻04.73.88.79.74
Closed *Sun evening; Mon and Tues mornings (except June–Sept); Jan; first fortnight in Oct.* **High chairs available. TV. Car park.**

A traditional hotel-restaurant with appealing, old-fashioned rooms. The locals do their shopping in the square opposite. Doubles go for €38 with shower/wc or bath; half board available for a minimum of three nights at €40 per person. The dining room exudes its share of mouthwatering smells and offers a range of menus, €14–44. The chef uses traditional produce to prepare dishes in a strongly bourgeois register but always adding his own touch. Sated and delighted are the two words that spring to mind at the end of the meal. Trout with bacon and red wine butter, crunchy hot foie gras with apples … Logis de France. *Welcoming glass of Kir offered to our readers on presentation of this guide.*

Saint-Pierre-Le-Chastel

63230 (4km S)

@ 🐾 🏠 |O| Les Genêts Fleuris

Follow the signs from Pontgibaud and it's in the hamlet of Bonnabaud.
🕾04.73.88.75.81
@perso.wanadoo.fr/genets-fleuris
Closed *second fortnight in Oct.* **High chairs and games available. Car park.**

Away from the tourist circuit, out in the country on the edge of the parc des Volcans and the Combrailles, this renovated farmhouse has a very pleasing view of the chain of the Puys. The young couple who own the place are full of information and can advise you on good rambles nearby. The guest rooms have all facilities and they're well maintained with doubles priced at €42, inclusive of breakfast. Joël is a trained chef and cooks traditional fare such as *potée* (local soup) and *truffade* with menus from €14. An ideal spot for its peace and quiet, its location and the warm welcome. *Free house apéritif and coffee offered to our readers on presentation of this guide.*

Mazaye

63230 (5km S)

@ 🐾 🏠 |O| Auberge de Mazaye**

Take the D62, then the D52.
🕾04.73.88.93.30 ℻04.73.88.93.80
@www.restolit-auvergne.com
Closed *Mon (1 Oct–31 March); Tues all year round; 15 Dec–25 Jan.* **Disabled access. TV. Car park.**

Located at the end of a winding road, this former stable has been fabulously converted into a charming and stylish inn, preserving its authentic rustic air (stone walls, big bunches of fresh flowers, a beautiful fireplace, kitchen opening onto the courtyard in fine weather) and its

③

own "genuine" donkey in the cattle shed opposite. It's the perfect place for a peaceful retreat in the country, and you can watch the sun set while sipping an apéritif from the pleasant terrace. What's more, the owner has had the good taste and intelligence to keep the stone channel from the old cattle shed (but watch where you step). The weekday menu (€15.50), and others €20–35, feature proper regional dishes, with an excellent *potée auvergnate* and tasty stuffed pig's trotters leading the way. The attractive rooms cost €56–65 with shower/wc, and breakfast costs €8. Half board, obligatory at weekends and from 1 May to 30 September, costs €53–56 per person. You'll get a warm welcome – in fact an altogether delightful spot. *Free house apéritif offered to our readers on presentation of this guide.*

Puy-en-Velay (Le)
43000

⟨⟨ 🏠 **Dyke Hôtel****

37 bd. Maréchal-Fayolle; at the bottom of the old town.
☎04.71.09.05.30 ℗04.71.02.58.66
Closed *Christmas to 1 Jan.* **TV. Pay car park.**

All the advantages of a chain hotel, plus a central location. Everything's clean and new, the décor is low-key and the service is efficient. Bedrooms – €43–50 with shower/wc or bath – are decorated in a similar, vaguely Japanese style, though they vary in size; no. 20 has a fine, huge mirror, while no. 31 located on the corner of the street, has a double window. Breakfast is served in the bar, the *Birdie*, on the ground floor. "Dyke" refers to the local sugarloaf rock formations which give the area its character, and you'll notice in the corridor that the owner has been awarded a certificate – in Latin – acknowledging his pilgrimage to Santiago de Compostela. NB: make sure to confirm your reservation before arriving; some of our readers have been disappointed.

⟨⟨ 𝄞 |●| 🏠 **Hôtel-restaurant Le Val Vert****

6 av. Baptiste-Marcet; it's around 1.5km from the centre, south of town on the way to Aubenas-Mende.
☎04.71.09.09.30 ℗04.71.09.36.49
⟲www.hotelvalvert.com

Restaurant closed *Sat lunchtime; 20 Dec–5 Jan.* **Disabled access. TV. High chairs, changing table and feeding-bottle warmer available. Car park.**

Though it looks rather like a chain establishment from the outside, inside you'll find a friendly, homely atmosphere and pleasant welcome. Very comfortable rooms, well equipped and well maintained, thoughtfully decorated with large cushions and very quiet thanks to the efficient double glazing, cost €47–50 with wc/shower or bath. The restaurant serves carefully prepared regional dishes with a weekday lunch menu at €12, and others up to €38. The generous buffet breakfast includes home-made pastries and biscuits. Logis de France. *Free coffee offered to our readers on presentation of this guide.*

⟨⟨ 🏠 |●| **Hôtel du Parc – Restaurant François Gagnaire**

4 av. Clément-Charbonnier; behind the place du Breuil, alongside the Henri-Vinay garden.
☎04.71.02.40.40 ℗ 04.71.02.18.72
⟲francoisgagnaire@wanadoo.fr
Closed *first week in Jan (hotel and restaurant); a week end June; ten days after All Saints' Day (restaurant only).* **Restaurant** *closed* (☎04.71.02.75.55) *Sun, Mon and Tues lunchtime (July–Aug); Sun evening, Mon and Tues lunchtime the rest of the year.* **Disabled access. TV. High chairs available. Pay car park.**

This unassuming hotel near the historic quarter is being transformed: the foyer and lounges, decorated with a superb collection of labels from cigar boxes, have been tastefully refurbished. The bedrooms have yet to match this refinement, but they are comfortable, spacious and reasonably priced at €51–69 for a double; breakfast €6.50. The restaurant has won over gourmets through the sophistication of the dining room (with a bay window overlooking the park), the attentive service, the originality of the dishes (using only regional produce) and the unerring elegance of their presentation: fillet of Vourzac trout with Puy lentils, *dodine* of duck foie gras, *millefeuille* of nougatine with pistachio cream. Choose from a range of menus from €28 (weekdays only) to €75. To top it all, a fine wine list, an impressive cheeseboard and excellent home-made bread rolls, including one variety made with lentils. The owner is Lyonnaise and the chef from Le Puy so high standards in the restaurant were to be expected. It is advisable to book and turn up smartly dressed. A good place to sample "nouvelle cuisine", where creativity counts for more than quantity.

@ 🎋 🏠 |●| Hôtel Le Régina***

34 bd. Maréchal-Fayolle; right in the centre, at the bottom of the old town.
℡04.71.09.14.71 🖷04.71.09.18.57
🌐www.hotelrestregina.com
Disabled access. TV. Pay car park.

This hotel, in a beautiful old building right in the centre of town, is something of an institution, offering a friendly welcome in a Polish accent from the pleasant hostess. Prices are very reasonable for a three-star, especially considering the high standard of the facilities and service: doubles with shower/wc or bath €57–78. The rooms – which have been tastefully refurbished – look onto the street or the back (which is quieter). Two of them (nos. 209 and 403) are equipped with a Jacuzzi. On the ground floor the restaurant, which has nothing more to prove in terms of reputation, offers its clientele stylish regional dishes with an original touch in a refined and spacious setting. Famous for its fish specialities (grilled line-caught bass…) and a regularly revised seasonal menu. Dish of the day costs €9 and menus range from €15.50 up to €36.50. *Free house apéritif offered to our readers on presentation of this guide.*

@ 🎋 |●| La Parenthèse

8 av. de la Cathédrale; at the foot of the avenue leading up to the cathedral.
℡04.71.02.83.00
Closed *weekends; a week in June; a week in Sept; between Christmas and New Year.*

In a quiet, cobbled street, offering a warm welcome in a "rustic" setting (check out the collection of coffee pots!), this restaurant is the brainchild of Michèle and Jacques. The menus, €17–23, include regional dishes featuring salmon tartare with green Puy lentils, veal medallion with purple Brive mustard, *aligot* and *truffade*, all accompanied by a glass of Boudes wine from the Auvergne. Desserts include *crème brûlée* with chestnut honey. This is our sort of place – reservations are recommended. *Free house apéritif offered to our readers on presentation of this guide.*

@ 🎋 |●| Restaurant L'Olympe

8 rue du Collège; a 2 minute walk from the town hall.

℡ 04.71.05.90.59
Closed *Sat lunchtime except July–Aug; Sun evening and Mon; a fortnight around Easter; Nov.* **Disabled access.**

A delightful restaurant in a cobbled alleyway in the town's conservation area. Inside, pastel colours and a warm and good-humoured welcome. The young chef sticks resolutely to local specialities but interprets them in his own, sometimes exotic, way; lentils, bilberries, trout and verbena play star roles. In just a few years he's made this one of the best eating places in Le Puy. Menus €20–50, in various formats: "Traditional", "Pleasure" and "Discovery", and a children's menu at €13. *Free coffee offered to our readers on presentation of this guide.*

@ |●| Restaurant Tournayre

12 rue Chênebouterie; it's behind the town hall.
℡04.71.09.58.94
Closed *Sun and Wed evenings; Mon; Jan; first week in Sept.* **Disabled access. High chairs available.**

A delightful place in the old town and with an interesting setting: a turret, a courtyard and a vaulted sixteenth-century dining room decorated with wall paintings. Eric Tournayre is a first-rate chef who creates imaginative dishes of a very high order at what seem fair prices; menus at €20–65. These dishes look to the Auvergne for their inspiration: red mullet and pan-fried foie gras on a bed of green lentils – Puy lentils of course; "Haute-Loire" fillet of beef Rossini; even the delicious home-made desserts. It's best to book in summer.

Saint-Vincent
43800 (14km N)

@ 🎋 |●| Restaurant La Renouée

Cheyrac; take the D103 that follows the gorges of the Loire, and it's signed on the left coming from Puy.
℡04.71.08.55.94
Closed *Sun evening and Mon all year round; Tues, Wed and Thurs evenings in March and from mid-Nov to end Dec; Jan–Feb; a week around All Saints' Day.* **Disabled access. High chairs available.**

This restaurant is named after snakeweed, a local plant the leaves of which are eaten like spinach. It's a charming inn with fresh flowers on the tables. Go through the very pretty little garden, push open the door of the old house and sit down by the fireplace. You will be greeted by a friendly woman who looks after the guests. Dishes with appealing names appear from the kitchen, accompanied by good rye bread: pike perch *en habit vert*, a subtle marinade of mussels, morels "pantoufle" style with a fine duck fois gras stuffing, goat with powdered verbena leaves … Set menus go for €18–36 and children's menu €11. *Free house apéritif offered to our readers on presentation of this guide.*

Saint-Julien-Chapteuil
43260 15km E)

◎ 𝒫 |●| Le Cantamerlou

Place Saint-Robert; in the town centre, opposite the tourist office.
☎04.71.08.46.83
Closed *Wed evening; Sat lunchtime.*
Disabled access. High chairs and games available.

The restaurant, which opened in 2001, looks like a museum of local arts and folklore. The dining room is decorated with various articles foraged from local junk yards; with its wooden tables and open fire, it has a wonderfully nostalgic atmosphere. The owner is a keen collector and has a story to tell about every item. The cuisine is generously served and the weekday menu (€11.50) and others (€16–24) feature big salads and pastry cases stuffed with bleu d'Auvergne cheese. A genuine village inn with a good helping of style and a very peaceful terrace. *Free coffee offered to our readers on presentation of this guide.*

◎ |●| Restaurant Vidal

Place du Marché; take the D15.
☎04.71.08.70.50
⊛www.restaurant-vidal.com
Closed *Sun and Mon evenings, and Tues (except July–Aug); mid-Jan to end Feb.*
Disabled access. High chairs available. Children's room with TV and Play Station. Car park.

Though he modestly describes himself as "a country cook", Jean-Pierre Vidal, formerly at the *Troisgros*, is a brilliant and creative chef and one of the most important in the Haute-Loire. Each menu – they start at €20 (weekdays only) up to €60 – has a different name, such as "Jules Romains" (Giulio Romano to you and me). Specialities include: black Velay lamb

en croûte, langoustine ravioli and clams *gratin* with morels. You'll pay about €40 à la carte. The quiet, pleasant dining room offers courteous, attentive service.

Saint-Haon
43340 (18km SW)

◎ 𝒫 🏠 |●| Auberge de la Vallée**

Take the N88 in the direction of Pradelles/Langogne, travel 7km on the D33 to Cayres and then take the D31.
☎04.71.08.20.73 ⊜04.71.08.29.21
⊛www.auberge-de-la-vallee.fr
Closed *Sun evening and Mon (Oct–May); early Jan to mid-March.* **TV. Car park.**

The village is out in the wilds at 970m and just 3km away the Allier cascades down the rocks of a deep gorge. This rustic, welcoming inn stands in a square dominated by a church with an unusual tower. Its ten comfortable rooms, furnished with solid old furniture, afford a peaceful night's sleep; they're €37–40 for a double with shower/wc or bath, breakfast €6.50. In the restaurant they serve a series of menus, €14.50–33, featuring the chef's specialities which include veal with mushrooms or trout and smoked bacon with Puy lentils. A good staging post between Le Puy and Langogne in Lozère. *10% discount on a room (except July–Aug) offered to our readers on presentation of this guide.*

Moudeyres
43150 (20km SE)

◎◎ 🏠 |●| 𝒫 Le Pré Bossu***

It's as you enter the village on the D361.
☎04.71.05.10.70 ⊜04.71.05.10.21
⊛www.leprebossu.fr.fm
Closed *Nov to Easter.* **Open** *evenings only.*
Car park.

A cosy, characterful cottage in the middle of a field; the air is clean and it's very quiet. Smart, comfortable rooms, with bath/wc cost €90, suites with a view €120–140; half board, at €105–130 per person, is recommended, and the copious breakfast costs €12. Marlène – the charming owner – offers one room and five comfortable suites, decorated with an assured taste. Some (our favourites) look onto the famous "pré bossu" (hunchback meadow) where adorable lambs start to gambol as soon as the sun comes up. Other rooms look onto the vegetable garden from which Carlos Grootaert – a chef well known in Haute-Loire – sources the subtle flavours of his locally inspired cuisine. A roguish, moustachioed character, he creates new tastes, revives old ones and concocts exquisitely refined dishes on a range of menus priced at €38–58. Stuffed leg of rabbit, asparagus tagliatelli, morels, Jerusalem artichokes, *jus* with mace, dodine of rabbit with foie gras, chabrot of river salmon with a verbena infusion, red fruit soup, coconut ice cream – just a few examples from this symphony of flavours, matched in refinement by the excellent vegetable menu which includes "a stroll round the priest's garden". Service is quick and efficient – home-made verbena tea can be sampled on the terrace, which is very pleasant in summer. And as the saying goes, "Traveller touch the *Pré Bossu*, it will bring you good luck". *10% discount on a room (April, May, June, Sept and Oct) offered to our readers on presentation of this guide.*

Pont-d'Alleyras
43580 (25km SW)

◎ ⅔ 🏠 |●| Hôtel-restaurant du Haut-Allier***

Le pont d'Alleyras; take the N88 in the direction of Pradelles as far as Montagnac, then the D33.
☎04.71.57.57.63 ℗04.71.57.57.99
Closed Sun evening, Mon and Tues lunch-time, except high season and public holidays; mid-Nov to mid-March. **Disabled access. TV. High chairs available.**

This delightful hotel-restaurant, tucked away in a little village in the Haut-Allier valley, has been run by the same family for three generations. The building was renovated recently and the large restaurant has a classical décor. Philippe Brun, a big name in the area, creates succulent, colourful dishes that will delight both your eyes and your tastebuds. Try the crayfish gazpacho and poultry wings, the supreme of young pigeon deglazed with honey vinegar, the milk-fed lamb, the black Velay lamb and a whole range of different leaves, freshly picked by an expert friend of the chef. And enjoy all this, plus attentive service in a freshly refurbished setting. There's a well-stocked cellar and a wide choice on the set menus, which range from €25–85; allow €45–50 for a meal à la carte. Comfortable, well-maintained and peaceful doubles with an unrestricted view over the valley, from €48 with shower/wc or bath; suites with Jacuzzi and balcony start

at €95 up to €110. Half board is recommended. *10% discount on the room rate (except in July–Aug) offered to our readers on presentation of this guide.*

Riom
63200

◎ ⅔ |●| Restaurant L'Âne Gris

13 rue Gomot.
☎04.73.38.25.10
Closed Sun; Mon; second fortnight in Aug.

Whether you think this place is insane, ghastly or heaven on earth will depend on how you feel about the owner, Casimir. He's slightly mad but ever so nice – forever making jokes at his customers' expense. He used to just call his chef "baboon" but now he uses the nickname for his favourite customers, too. When you go in you will hear a voice bellow out: "What do you want?" Quite refreshing really. You are invited to join in the fun, to try and find a subtle reply, or else… Casimir has a slogan: people get so bored that they come here for a tongue-lashing, it's better than the cinema. Some days you may end up doing the honours yourself because he's not in the mood. To hear him talk, you might think the food wasn't up to much, but the kitchen produces good traditional dishes: *truffade* with ham, *aligot*, saucisse, *patranque* (an old Cantal recipe with bread and cheese) and salt pork with lentils. Excellent grills are always available. Brilliant list of local wines which Casimir chooses with a genuine passion and he will be delighted to help you discover them. No set menus; you'll pay around €11 for an Auvergne speciality. Personally, we adore it here and are coming back. We suggest you try it yourself. Credit cards not accepted. *Free apéritif offered to our readers on presentation of this guide.*

Tournoël
63530 (4km W)

◎ ⅔ 🏠 Hôtel-restaurant La Chatellenie

It's on the D986.
☎04.73.33.63.23
Closed early Dec to end March. Car park.

Located on the road going up to Tournoël, this hotel is peaceful, service is friendly, and the rooms overlook the valley. Simple, spacious doubles (all recently refurbished) with shower/wc or bath €38–41. *Free house apéritif offered to our readers on presentation of this guide.*

Riom-ès-Montagnes

15400

◎ 🎿 🛏 |●| Hôtel-restaurant Le Saint-Georges**

5 rue du Capitaine Chevalier; opposite the church of Saint-Georges.
☎04.71.78.00.15 ℻04.71.78.24.37
🌐www.hotel-saint-georges.com
Restaurant closed *Sun evening and 3 weeks in Nov.* **Disabled access. TV. High chairs and baby changing facilities available.**

This large house with plain stone walls has been well restored and is right in the middle of the town. Modern doubles with shower and good facilities go for €42–48, according to the season. The restaurant menus – menu of the day €11.50 and other menus (regional and "discovery") €19–27 – boast good regional produce and quality "peasant" dishes: *panachée* of pork with green lentils, *confit* of rabbit with prunes and Auvergne wine, fine apple tart with honey caramel … Logis de France. *Free house apéritif (with the regional and "discovery" menus) offered to our readers on presentation of this guide.*

Saignes

15240

◎ 🎿 🛏 |●| Hôtel Relais Arverne*

Take the D22.
☎04.71.40.62.64 ℻04.71.40.61.14
🌐www.hotel-relais-arverne.com
Closed *winter school holidays and two weeks in Oct.* **Restaurant closed** *Fri and Sun evenings out of season.* **TV. Car park.**

This stone building has a huge corner watchtower, where everything seems a bit home built but well thought out and the tables on the terrace are made from ancient stone wheels. The bedrooms are comfortable and accessed via the terrace, so you can come and go as you please; doubles €38–42.70 with shower/wc or bath, breakfast €4.50. The hotel is full of interesting nooks and crannies – in some rooms the toilet is concealed behind an old cupboard door. The dining

room, where they serve dishes from the Dordogne and elsewhere with menus €12 (weekdays only) and €15–34, has a big clock and a huge fireplace. Specialities include Provençal *fricassée* of frogs' legs, Arctic char with vanilla sauce, sweetbread pastry with morels, etc. Logis de France. *Free house apéritif offered to our readers on presentation of this guide.*

Antignac

15240 (5km NE)

◎ 🛏 |●| Auberge de la Sumène

Take the D236 and it's in the village.
☎04.71.40.25.87

You can enjoy this traditional inn, with its shady terrace at the back, whether you're staying overnight or just eating. The rooms have limited facilities – doubles with basin €18, with bathroom €22 – but they're well maintained. The restaurant is popular with fishermen and locals for the huge portions of sturdy, regional dishes; *Menu ouvrier* with starter, main course, cheese and dessert €10; other menus at €12 and €16 (four courses). You have two options for enjoying the charms of this place: the bistro, with its simple, no frills service and a good workmanlike set menu; or the restaurant which offers traditional dishes.

Saint-Anthème

63660

◎ 🎿 🛏 |●| Hôtel-restaurant Au Pont de Raffiny**

It's 4km along the Saint-Romain road.
☎04.73.95.49.10 ℻04.73.95.80.21
🌐www.hotel-pont-raffiny.com
Closed *Sun evening and Mon out of season; early Jan to mid-Feb; weekdays in March.* **Disabled access. TV. High chairs available. Games room and table football available. Car park.**

If you're looking for a gourmet meal, head for this place, located on the banks of a little river near Saint-Anthème. It has a good reputation for game. The food is light in summer, sauce-based in autumn and varied in spring; €15 weekday menu and others up to €32. The main attraction is Alain Beaudoux's light, creative cooking, typified by *andouillette* of fish or young rabbit *en crépine*. There's an amazing parfait with verbena from Velay. Excellent, reasonably priced wine list. The hotel is quiet and comfortable, offering rooms with shower/wc or bath for €38–41; some have a terrace. There are also a few chalets sleeping four to six, which are available by the week or weekend for €280–420. *10% reduction on the room rate (except July–Aug) or free coffee offered to our readers on presentation of this guide.*

Chaulme (La)

63660 (9km SE)

◎ 🏠 |●| 🎄 Auberge du Creux de l'Oulette

Take the D67 then the D258.
☎04.73.95.41.16 ℱ04.73.95.80.83
⊛www.auberge-creux-oulette.com
Closed *Wed (except June–Sept); 15 Nov to early March.* **Disabled access. High chairs and games available. Swimming pool. Car park.**

This all-round good value village hotel, recently built, is an ideal spot if you want to go hiking in the region – the owners are a dynamic pair who have organized discovery trails for you to follow. Double rooms with shower/wc and telephone go for €39; half board €40 per person. The chef is passionate about cooking and his wholesome family dishes have a good reputation locally. Choose from five menus, €10–29.50, featuring copious salads, snail stew with mushrooms, fish fillet with fourme cheese sauce or calves' sweetbreads with mushrooms… There's a swimming pool and a terrace for use in the summer and a very pretty waterfall on the way out of the village. Logis de France. *10% discount on a room or free coffee offered to our readers on presentation of this guide.*

Saint-Flour

15100

◎ 🏠 |●| Hôtel-restaurant des Roches**

8 place d'Armes; near the cathedral, opposite the museum.
☎04.71.60.09.70. ℱ04.71.60.45.21
⊕info@hotel-des-roches.com
Closed *Sun; Mon evening.* **TV. High chairs available.**

This hotel enjoys an excellent location and offers bright, pleasant bedrooms with shower/wc or bath priced at €38–42. Classic and regional styles dominate in the first-floor restaurant, which has a pretty terrace where you can take an apéritif. Choose from fillet of beef with blue Auvergne cheese, mutton tripe, *potée auvergnate, truffade, aligot* and so on. Dish of the day with dessert costs €7.35 (weekday lunchtimes only), first menu costs €10; other menus €14–20. You'll get a very friendly welcome from the young owners and it's worth noting that meal serving times are not as strict here as elsewhere in the area.

◎ 🎄 🏠 |●| Auberge de la Providence**

1 rue du Château-d'Alleuze; in the lower part of town.
☎04.71.60.12.05 ℱ04.71.60.33.94
⊛www.auberge-de-la-providence.fr
Closed *Mon; Fri evening and Sun evening out of season; 15 Nov–15 Dec.* **Restaurant open** *evenings only.* **Disabled access. TV. Car park.**

This old inn has been completely refurbished. The décor is generally low key and the ten rooms are decorated in pastel shades of pink, blue, green and yellow; all have good bathrooms and cost €45–60 for a double with shower/wc or bath. The set menu at €20 offers some of the best value in town: pastry of meadow mushrooms, beef vigneron, leg of duck in Auvergne wine, morels in season. There's a parking area for motorbikes. Logis de France. *Free house apéritif offered to our readers on presentation of this guide.*

Saint-Georges

15100 (4km SE)

◎ 🏠 |●| Hôtel-restaurant Le Bout du Monde**

Take the D250.
☎04.71.60.15.84 ℱ04.71.60.72.90
⊛www.hotel-leboutdumonde.com
Closed *Sun evening out of season.* **Disabled access. TV. High chairs and games available. Swimming pool. Car park.**

As its name says, this place is indeed at the end of the world, deep in a valley in the countryside outside Saint-Flour – ideal for anglers and walkers. It's also got a heated swimming pool in a lovely natural setting and offers a warm friendly welcome. The restaurant serves a range of delicious regional specialities. Menus, €10 (weekdays only) up to €26.50, feature *pounti, coq au vin, truffade* and *aligot.* Simple, well-maintained rooms cost €43–50 with shower/wc or bath.

Garabit
63520 (12km SE)

@ 🎿 🔔 |●| **Hôtel-restaurant Beau Site****

☎04.71.23.41.46 ℻04.71.23.46.34
ⓦwww.beau-site-hotel.com
Closed 4 Nov to early April. **Disabled access. TV. High chairs and games available. Swimming pool. Pay car park.**

The hotel looks down on Eiffel's viaduct (he of tower fame), and you get wonderful views of the lake. It's a huge building with bright, roomy doubles for €40–57 with shower/wc or bath. Half board, compulsory in July and August, is €40–58 per person. Excellent facilities include a heated swimming pool and tennis courts: it makes a good base for fishing, windsurfing and long walks. The restaurant serves classic French dishes and gourmet cuisine. Set menus at €10 and €14 (weekdays) and €21–37, list specialities such as tartlet with Cantal cheese, clam and burbot brochette, salt pork with green Puy lentils. Logis de France. *10% discount on the room rate (except July–Aug) or a free house apéritif or coffee offered to our readers on presentation of this guide.*

Saint-Gervais-d'Auvergne
63390

@ 🔔 |●| **Le relais d'Auvergne****

Route de Châteauneuf-les-Bains.
☎04.73.85.70.10 ℻04.73.85.85.66
ⓦwww.relais-auvergne.com
Closed 25 Dec–1 March. **Disabled access. TV. Car park.**

A good place in the middle of the village run by an energetic and friendly young couple. Bedrooms are decorated in slightly flashy colours, but they're fresh and modern, with lovely feather eiderdowns; doubles €40 with good facilities including en-suite bath, and half board is the same price per person. The furniture and ornaments have been hunted down at antique fairs by the young owners. The dining room is cosy and there's a huge chimney piece where they light an open fire on chilly evenings. You can even buy some of the antique furnishings. Honest, traditional food: mutton tripe, stuffed cabbage, pork knuckle with lentils, not-to-be-missed truffade, Combrailles basket, chicken *aiguillette* with fourme cheese. Menus, €13 (weekdays lunchtime) rising to €28, are good value. Logis de France.

@ 🔔 |●| **Hôtel-restaurant Castel Hôtel 1904****

Rue du Castel.
☎04.73.85.70.42 ℻04.73.85.84.39
ⓔcastel-hotel-1904@wanadoo.fr
Closed 12 Nov–15 March. **TV. Car park.**

This former residence of M. de Maintenon and later of Cluny nuns has been handed down from generation to generation since 1904, and if you have a taste for the simple pleasures of days gone by, you'll enjoy the genuine atmosphere here. There are two restaurants: the tiny *Comptoir à Moustaches* serves traditional cuisine based on local produce, with menus from €15. The second serves gourmet cuisine delicately prepared by Jean-Luc Mouty, who trained with Robuchon; here menus start from €35. It's cooking from a lost age: *pavé* of pike perch with sherry, cromesquis of calf sweetbread or creamy spider crab tart. The hotel is spacious and very quiet, and the well-equipped rustic rooms are affordable at €65–99 for a double with shower/wc or bath. What's more, each room is named after a member of this illustrious family. Logis de France.

Blot-L'Église
63440 (17 km NE)

@ 🎿 |●| **Auberge Les Peytoux**

Lieu-dit Les Peytoux; take the D227 in the direction of Châteauneuf, then the D122. It's in an isolated valley by the River Morge.
☎04.73.97.44.17
Closed Mon–Thurs, Fri lunch and Sun evening *(except public holidays and the night before them); Christmas and New Year.* **Car park.**

You will not be the only one to decide that this inn is worth a detour. Despite a total lack of advertising, word of mouth has made it necessary to book almost one month in advance. Ingrid is in charge in the kitchen and only fresh farm produce is used. Menus, €10–22, everything included, feature exceptional goat's cheese, wonderful salads and superb poultry – a real treat. *Free coffee or liqueur offered to our readers on presentation of this guide.*

Servant
63560 (20km NE)

@ 犬 🏠 |●| Hôtel-restaurant Le Beau Site*

Gorges de la Sioule; take the D987 and then the N144 as far as Menat; from there continue along the D18 for 5.5km in the direction of "Gorges de Chouvigny".
℡04.73.85.50.65
@www.le-beau-site.com
Closed Feb. **Restaurant closed** out of season; Wed and Thurs (except in July–Aug). **High chairs and games available. Car park.**

Here's a place that really deserves its name. It's in a really wonderful setting, which you reach on the road that follows the Sioule, and offers a perfect base for exploring the area and doing a bit of fishing. Six pleasant double rooms cost €35–43. In summer you can have a meal or a drink on the terrace overlooking the river. Choice of menus from €14.80 (weekdays only) and €19.80–45.20 – one of them lists only house specialities: Roquefort terrine with chestnuts, salad with walnut oil and farm-reared chicken with crayfish, home-made nougat ice cream with Auvergne honey, among others. In fact, there's something for even the heartiest appetite, served in a truly delightful setting which has also recently been refurbished. *Free apéritif offered to our readers on presentation of this guide.*

Saint-Martin-sous-Vigouroux
15230

@ 犬 🏠 |●| Le Relais de la Forge*

℡04.71.23.36.90 @04.71.23.92.48
Closed Wed afternoon out of season and during school holidays. **High chairs and games available. Car park.**

A simple, welcoming country hotel. There's the option of eating in the down-to-earth dining room or the bar offers a very substantial *menu du jour* for €11. The restaurant is very "provincial", the second set menu (€13) is also very generous and includes a selection of charcuterie and dishes such as trout with bacon, *pavé* of beef with morels, *aligot*, salad, cheese and dessert; other menus up to €20. There are ten renovated rooms, available at €30.50 with shower/wc or bath. Half board costs €32 per person and is compulsory in high

season. *Free house apéritif offered to our readers on presentation of this guide.*

Saint-Pourçain-sur-Sioule
03500

@ 🏠 |●| Hôtel-restaurant Le Chêne Vert**

35 bd. Ledru-Rollin.
℡04.70.47.77.00 @04.70.47.77.39
@www.hotel-chenevert.com
Closed Jan (first fortnight for the hotel, whole month for the restaurant). **Restaurant closed** Fri lunch and Sun evening out of season; Mon. **TV. Pay car park.**

A classic, conventional establishment with excellent facilities at decent prices. Pleasant rooms with fresh décor cost from €45.50 up to €54 for a double with shower/wc or bath. (Light sleepers should note that the church bells toll throughout the night.) Good traditional cooking and generous portions, with lots of game in season; menus €17 (weekdays) to €42 (three courses). Logis de France.

Saint-Urcize
15110

@ 犬 🏠 |●| Hôtel-restaurant Remise

At the top of the village.
℡ and @04.71.23.20.02
Closed Mon evening; Dec (except public holidays) and Jan. **Disabled access. Car park.**

No, the name of this place has nothing to do with old sheds! It's named after the owner, Fred Remise, a really friendly chap, and his charming wife. A marvellous country inn that's very popular with anglers, hunters, hikers and cyclists. The menus (€13–20) feature wonderful home cooking with dishes such as *aligot*, nettle soup or trout – it all depends on what's good in the market … Since so many anglers stay here, they make up picnic baskets to see you through a day's fishing. The owner can tell you anything you want to know about the region, from local history to the best walks and places to visit. Friendly, easy-going atmosphere. Doubles go for €42 with shower/wc or bath; half board (€43 per person) is compulsory in July and August. They also have rooms for ten people in a wooden lodge at €35 per person half board. *Free house apéritif offered to our readers on presentation of this guide.*

Salers
15140

ⓔ 🛏 |●| 🍴 Hôtel des Remparts**

Esplanade de Barrouze.
☎04.71.40.70.33 ℻04.71.40.75.32
🖥www.salers-hotel-remparts.com
Closed 15 Oct–20 Dec. **Disabled access. TV. High chairs available.**

Well located, slightly off the tourist trail, with a superb view of the Cantal mountains from some rooms and a delightful, panoramic terrace. Double rooms €45.50–52.50, depending on the season; some have exposed beams and half-timbering. Half board costs €45.50–52.50 and is compulsory between 14 July and 31 August. It's a well-run place serving menus priced at €12–32. Logis de France. *Free coffee offered to our readers on presentation of this guide.*

ⓔ |●| Restaurant La Poterne

Rue Notre-Dame.
☎04.71.40.75.11
Closed Sat (out of season); Tues evening (May, June and Sept); Jan.

A cosy setting (exposed stone and beams, old fireplace) for regional specialities, carefully prepared with high-quality, fresh ingredients. The traditional dishes on offer include *truffade*, *pounti*, stuffed cabbage, *bourriols* (type of crêpe filled with Auvergne blue cheese) and a delicious bilberry pie. Service is friendly and it's good value for money; menu of the day €13.70 and regional menus €16–24. Expect to pay around €15 à la carte.

Saugues
43170

ⓔ 🍴 🛏 |●| La Terrasse**

Cours Gervais; it's in the centre.
☎04.71.77.83.10 ℻04.71.77.63.79
Closed Sun evening and Mon out of season; end Nov to end Feb. **TV.**

This is a lovely area to explore with its many chapels scattered around the countryside. The owner and his wife – keen readers of the *Guide du Routard* when

abroad – are friendly and particularly attentive to their guests. The twelve rooms are comfortable and well kept; doubles go for €50–57 with shower/wc or bath. The ones at the back are particularly quiet and have an uninterrupted view of the Tour des Anglais. There's also a restaurant serving local dishes – which enjoys a good reputation in the region – and is amazing value for money. Impressive service and meticulously prepared family recipes (lost in the cauldron in 1795) such as *tarte tatin* foie gras with potatoes or calf sweetbreads with set menus at €28 and €55. Logis de France. *Free house apéritif offered to our readers on presentation of this guide.*

Thiers
63300

ⓔ 🍴 🛏 Hôtel de la Gare

30 av. de la Gare; it's opposite the train station.
☎ and ℻04.73.80.01.41
Closed Sat and Sun afternoons; in Aug and early Sept.

The cheapest and friendliest hotel in town, completely hidden under a covering of wisteria. Simple, clean rooms €17 with basin and €22 with shower (wc on the landing); no. 7 is the quietest. Friendly, attentive welcome and relaxed atmosphere, and a small bar which is quite cool but can get noisy. The owner knows everyone, or nearly everyone – and vice versa … as you might expect from a former restaurateur. *10% discount on a room (from the fourth consecutive night) or free apéritif or liqueur offered to our readers on presentation of this guide.*

ⓔ 🛏 |●| Hôtel-restaurant Chez La Mère Dépalle**

Pont-de-Dore; take the N89, and it's 2km from the town centre.
☎04.73.80.10.05 ℻04.73.80.52.22
🖥www.chezlameredepalle.com
Closed Sun evening, Fri evening and Sat (Sun only during July–Aug); school holiday in Feb, at All Saints and at Christmas. **TV. High chairs and games available. Car park.**

Though its roadside location is a slight minus, this establishment is a model of hotel and restaurant-keeping, and the owners are unfailingly courteous and helpful. Double rooms with shower/wc or bath go for €51–65; half board costs €48 per person. The large dining room soon fills up at lunchtime with travellers and regulars dropping in for the only thing that really matters: a good meal. And you won't be disappointed. The weekday lunch menu, €15, and others up to €36, list such dishes as a delicious smoked salmon with whisky, Salers fillet with morels, or an aristocratic medallion of fallow deer. The cheese trolley is superb, too, and includes a soft goat's cheese with a remarkable depth of flavour. And to finish off, the *crème brûlée* with kumquats is delightful. In fact we set off again with a happy heart. Logis de France.

⊚ ⚟ |●| Restaurant Le Coutelier

4 pl. du Palais.
☎ and ⊕ 04.73.80.79.59
Closed *Mon evening out of season; Tues; first 3 weeks in June; a fortnight in Oct.*

Thiers is the centre of France's cutlery industry, and this restaurant is in a converted cutler's workshop. What with the collection of old implements and knives displayed on the walls it's almost a museum and restaurant in one. Menus (€13.60–19) list classic dishes like *aligot* with sausage and cabbage, *coq au vin, tripoux*. *Free house apéritif offered to our readers on presentation of this guide.*

Peschadoires
63920 (9km SW)

⊚ |●| La Ferme des Trois Canards

Lieu-dit Biton; take the N89 then the D212, follow the Maringues road; turn left at the sign; the restaurant is 300m further along.
⊕ 04.73.51.06.70
Closed *Sun and Tues evenings; Wed; fortnight in Jan.* **Car park.**

The most delightful place in the area, offering pleasant, refined service. It's a beautifully renovated farmhouse in the heart of the countryside but not far from the motorway exit, and with a terrace in summer. Dishes on the set menus, €22–47, are perfectly cooked and presented: foie gras with an onion *compote*, roast pigeon with spice-flavoured gravy. There's also an impressive cheese board. This is a place to waken the tastebuds.

Tournemire
15310

⊚ ⬚ |●| Auberge de Tournemire

Rue Principale.

⊕ 04.71.47.61.28 ⊕ 04.71.47.68.76
ⓦ www.aubergedetournemire.com
Closed *10 Jan–4 Feb.* **TV. High chairs available. Swimming pool. Car park.**

In one of Cantal's prettiest villages, you'll find this delightful inn with relaxing spa set on the side of a hill; the views of the valley are gorgeous, especially at sunset. The seven simple bedrooms are well maintained and one or two have lovely sloping ceilings; doubles €40–60 with shower/wc or bath; half board from €40 per person. There's a *formule brasserie* at €12, otherwise menus at €15–26 – all reserved for hotel guests in the evening. Good cooking in the restaurant with Auvergnat dishes such as *pounti* and black pudding with a fondue of onions. The *menu gastronomique* offers foie gras, lobster with vanilla and such like. You'll need to call to reserve if you want to eat at the restaurant outside the tourist season; it's also wise to reserve rooms at the hotel.

Vichy
03200

⊚ ⚟ ⬚ Hôtel du Rhône**

8 rue de Paris; look for the station, then take the only one way street to the right; it's the last hotel 300m on the left.
⊕ 04.70.97.73.00 ⊕ 04.70.97.48.25
ⓔ hoteldurhone@hotmail.com
Open *all year round.* **Disabled access. TV. High chairs and games available. Pay car park.**

The rooms are clean and simple. Those in the pretty pavilion at the bottom of the flower garden are particularly nice. Doubles cost from €25 to €49 according to the season and level of comfort. *Free coffee offered to our readers on presentation of this guide.*

⊚ ⚟ ⬚ À l'Hôtel de Naples**

22 rue de Paris; it's opposite the station.
⊕ 04.70.97.91.33 ⊕ 04.70.97.91.28
Open *all year round.* **TV.**

The hotel, located in the most famous (and busiest) street in town, isn't luxurious, but it does have modern facilities. Cosy, well-equipped, refurbished doubles go for €28–35, triples for €39–42. Ask for a room overlooking the pretty garden, which is full of flowers in summer. *10% discount on a room (except summer) offered to our readers on presentation of this guide.*

✆ ⚘ 🛏 |●| Le Pavillon d'Enghien***

32 rue Callou; it's in the spa area of the town.
☎04.70.98.33.30 ℗04.70.31.67.82
🖳www.pavillondenghien.com
Restaurant closed Sun evening and Mon
(except for guests). **Hotel closed** 22 Dec–1
Feb. **High chairs available. TV. Swimming
pool.**

This hotel-restaurant offers some of the
best value for money in town. The spacious double rooms, at €49–75 according
to the level of comfort, are individualized,
in particular nos. 17, 18, 29 and 33. The
best ones overlook the small garden. Food
is good and fresh and features seasonal
produce such as foie gras with figs, tagines;
they offer a weekday lunch menu at €12,
with others from €18 up to €27. Pretty
swimming pool for when the sun shines.
Logis de France. *Free house apéritif offered to
our readers on presentation of this guide.*

✆ |●| ⚘ La Brasserie du Casino

4 rue du Casino.
☎04.70.98.23.06
Closed Tues and Wed; second fortnight in
Feb; Nov. **Disabled access.**

This restaurant has got more character
than any other in Vichy. Big prewar brasseries have a certain something, and this
one, built in 1920, is no exception. The
walls are covered in photos of stars who
used to dine here after performing at
the opera house. Typical bourgeois brasserie fare, with a rich, traditional menu.
The weekday lunch menu costs €15
and there's another at €25. *Free house
apéritif offered to our readers on presentation
of this guide.*

✆ |●| ⚘ La Table d'Antoine

8 rue Bournol.
☎04.70.98.99.71
Closed Sun evening; Mon, except public
holidays and the eve of public holidays; a
fortnight in Feb; a week in June; a fortnight
at the end of Oct. **Disabled access. High
chairs and games available.**

This is one of the nicest restaurants
in Vichy, with décor reminiscent of a
winter garden of the Second Empire.
The dining room is small, the welcome
perfect – quiet and smiling and genuinely disappointed if they can't find you
a table. There's also a terrace on the
pedestrianized street. And the way they
cook the perfectly chosen produce is

superb. There's a *menu du marché* for €20
(weekdays) and others €25–45; children's
menu costs €12. Fish is line-caught, the
Charolais beef is melting, the desserts are
perfectly sweetened and the portions are
generous. Specialities include roast tail of
burbot with chorizo and *magret de canard*
with spicy apricots. And Antoine is really
nice too ... This place is a real find. *Free
coffee or liqueur offered to our readers on presentation of this guide.*

Abrest

03700 (3km SE)

✆ ⚘ |●| La Colombière

Route de Thiers; take the D906, it's 2km
beyond Abrest.
☎04.70.98.69.15 ℗04.70.31.50.89
🖳lacolombiere@wanadoo.fr
Closed Sun evening; Mon; mid-Jan to mid-
Feb; a week in Oct. **Disabled access. TV.
High chairs, booster seats, changing table,
feeding-bottle warmer and games available. Car park.**

An old dovecote converted into a restaurant and set high above the valley
with a superb view over the mountains
of Auvergne and the Allier river. Menus
€17 (weekdays only) to €53, range from
the simple to the refined. The cuisine is
imaginative and dishes change with the
seasons, mixing tradition and new ideas.
Delightful home-made desserts and the
bread, which is also excellent, is made on
site too and accompanies a magnificent
cheese board. Four huge, bright, charming
bedrooms (two with double glazing) are
€49.50 with shower/wc and €57 with
bath. The "yellow" room and the "green"
room have lovely views of the Allier. Logis
de France.

Bellerive-sur-Allier

03700 (3km SW)

✆ ⚘ La Rigon**

Route de Serbannes.
☎04.70.59.86.86 ℗04.70.59.94.77
🖳www.hotel-chateau-la-rigon.com
Closed Sun evening out of season; 1 Oct–31
March. **Disabled access. TV. Swimming
pool. Car park.**

You'll get the best of both worlds here
– the excellent service and kindly welcome you'd expect from a hotel and the
intimacy of a good-quality guesthouse.
It's a beautiful building set in its own

extensive grounds, with a brilliant swimming pool in a large 1900s glasshouse. The bedrooms, decorated in subtle tones, are all lovely; doubles with shower/wc or bath €54 in the low season, €64 in summer.

Cusset
03300 (3km E)

◎ 🎋 |O| Le Brayaud

64 av. de Vichy; it's as you approach Cusset coming from Vichy.
☎04.70.98.52.43
Closed *lunchtime; Tues; Wed; 10 days in April; end of Aug to early Sept. Open 8pm–2am (last orders).*

This is where you come if you want to stay out late in Vichy, but more importantly it's the best place to eat around here. Steaks are exceptional – the *entrecôte* of Charolais beef weighs close on 400g and the *bavette* not less than 300g. The menu also offers other choice cuts such as flank and fillet. The price of the meat varies according to how it's prepared. A €16 menu is served until 10.30pm, offering a good variety of salads, meat, cheese and dessert. There's enough to satisfy even the biggest appetites, and there's a friendly family atmosphere. *Free apéritif offered to our readers on presentation of this guide.*

Mayet-de-Montagne (Le)
03250 (20km SE)

◎ |O| 🎋 La Vieille Auberge

6 rue de l'Église; take the D62. It's behind the church.
☎04.70.59.34.01
Closed *Mon evening in season; Tues evening (Nov–Dec); Wed out of season; 3 weeks in Jan; last fortnight in Sept.* **High chairs and colouring books available.**

Time seems to have stood still in this old inn, in a wonderful little village deep in the Bourbonnais mountains. Décor of stone and wood brightened up by posters. The shortish menu lists traditional dishes, made with fresh local ingredients; *menu campagnard* at €8.70 (excluding Sun lunch) with a selection of charcuterie; others from €10.40 (Mon to Fri) to €21.40. À la carte also available. Credit cards not accepted. *Free coffee offered to our readers on presentation of this guide.*

Vic-sur-Cère
15800

◎ 🎋 🏠 |O| Hôtel-restaurant Bel Horizon**

Rue Paul-Doumer.
☎04.71.47.50.06 ☎04.71.49.63.81
⊛www.hotel-bel-horizon.com
Closed *end Nov to end Dec.* **TV. High chairs and games available. Swimming pool. Car park.**

A pleasant place on the edge of town. It attracts crowds at the weekends for the fine traditional regional cooking – and the huge servings. Menus, €14–35, list such dishes as stuffed cabbage, *pounti*, *tête de veau* with *gribiche* sauce. The homemade ice creams and desserts are delicious. The dining room has a big bay window. Rooms are comfortable and well maintained, and cost €42–52 with shower/wc or bath. Logis de France. *Free house apéritif and 10% discount on the room rate offered to our readers on presentation of this guide.*

Vieillevie
15120

◎ 🎋 🏠 |O| Hôtel La Terrasse**

Rue Principale.
☎04.71.49.94.00 ☎04.71.49.92.23
⊛www.hotel-terrasse.com
Closed *Mon in May, Sept and Oct; Sun evening; 11 Nov–31 Dec.* **Disabled access. High chairs available. Swimming pool. Car park.**

At 200m, this hotel is apparently at a lower altitude than any other in Cantal. Comfortable rooms priced at €44–52, according to the season, for a double with shower/wc or bath. Good outdoor facilities: shaded terrace, beautiful swimming pool, garden and tennis courts. You'll enjoy the cooking on the menus, €17 (weekdays only) and up to €32: specialities include pig's trotters and calf sweetbreads crépinette, skin-roasted fillet of Arctic char with Fel wine, magret with green pepper, and *feuillantine* of caramelized pears. An excellent venue, and if you're interested, they have the key to the château. Logis de France. *Free house apéritif offered to our readers on presentation of this guide.*

Vitrac

15220

⊛ 🏠 |○| L'Auberge de la Tomette**

It's off the D66, a few km northwest of
Marcolès.
℡04.71.64.70.94 🖷04.71.64.77.11
🖳www.auberge-la-tomette.com
Closed 15 Nov–1 April. **Disabled access.**
TV. High chairs and games available.
Swimming pool. Car park.

This charming inn is in the heart of
the Châtaigneraie. A relaxation area has
recently been installed (with sauna, spa,
hammam, and jet shower) and a large,
heated indoor swimming pool. The inn
stands in the middle of a magnificent
garden looking out over the countryside
and offers very comfortable double rooms
with shower/wc or bath for €63–81. Half
board costs €55–71 per person and there
are some duplex rooms for families available. The rustic, convivial dining room
serves hearty dishes on a range of menus,
€25–39. Chef's specialities include calf
sweetbreads with morels and crépinette
of pig's trotter with chanterelles. Logis
de France.

Yssingeaux

43200

⊛ 🎋 🏠 |○| 🎋 Auberge Au Creux des Pierres

It's in Fougères; 5km south of the town on
the D152 in the direction of Queyrière.
℡ and 🖷04.71.59.06.81
🖂christian.sqperissen@free.fr
Closed Feb and Dec. **Restaurant closed**
Mon. **Disabled access. High chairs and
games available.**

More like a bed and breakfast or farm-
inn than a hotel-restaurant. A charming
inn in a superbly renovated property

that's surrounded by a lovely garden.
They offer well-appointed rooms with
views of the countryside and, in the
distance, the Vivarais mountains. There's
a twelve-person dormitory which works
out at €12 a night, four-person rooms
with shower/wc at €55 and doubles for
€37. The restaurant offers excellent food,
simple and homely with Auvergne and
Alsace specialities: fresh starters, *choucroute*,
local cheeses and moist home-made tarts.
Menus start at €13 (weekdays), with
others €16–20. It's a favourite with walkers, cyclists and horse riders; half-board
is available from the first day. *Free house
apéritif offered to our readers on presentation
of this guide.*

⊛ 🏠 |○| Le Bourbon**

5 pl. de la Victoire.
℡04.71.59.06.54 🖷04.71.59.00.70
🖳www.le-bourbon.com
Restaurant closed Sun evening; Mon; Sat
lunchtime; Tues lunchtime (July–Aug); Jan.
TV. High chairs available. Car park.

Attractive, welcoming and agreeable hotel
with comfortable rooms each named after
a flower – a really creative venue. Doubles
with bath or shower/wc go for €60 and
€70; excellent breakfast (€10), using only
local produce. The handsome dining room,
decorated in English-garden style, serves
a lighter version of the regional cuisine.
Set menus from €19 to €43; like the à
la carte menu, they change every three
months. You'll find a list of local suppliers
beside the dishes. This is a really good idea
as it reminds you that the whole area has
its part to play in the food that reaches
your plate. Another good idea: on the
third Saturday of each month a taxi will
bring you and pick you up leaving you to
enjoy a fine meal and have a few drinks.
(Booking required, €5 in a 30km radius.)
Logis de France.

Bourgogne

Ancy-le-Franc

89160

@ 🏠 |●| **Hostellerie du Centre****

Place du Château; 100m from the château.
☎03.86.75.15.11 ℻03.86.75.14.13
🌐www.diaphora.com/hostellerieducentre
Closed 18 Nov–18 March. **Disabled access.
TV. High chairs and games available.
Swimming pool. Car park.**

This old, much refurbished hotel in the main street looks quite classy, but the atmosphere is easy-going. Cosy, restful bedrooms decorated in pastel tones cost €48–60, with either shower/wc or bath en suite. The restaurant consists of two dining rooms, the larger of which is the prettier, and offers traditional local dishes including snails or ham in a Chablis sauce. Set menus are as varied as the portions are generous. The cheapest is €16, with others €21–44. The terrace is opened in fine weather and there's a heated indoor swimming pool. Logis de France.

Pacy-sur-Armançon

89160 (6km SW)

@ 🎋 🏠 |●| **Hôtel-restaurant au Petit Câlin**

4 Grande-Rue. 6 km to the northeast of Ancy-le-Franc via the D905 (in the direction of Lézinnes), then a side road to the left; signposted in the village.
☎ and ℻03.86.75.51.17
📧aupetitcalin@wanadoo.fr
Closed Mon (out of season). **Disabled access. TV. High chairs available. Car park.**

A few no-frills, but huge and comfortable bedrooms (including one suitable for a whole family) have been installed in the old farmhouse, with prices starting at €48. The food is similarly unpretentious but satisfying; it is served in a dining room with small partitions or on the flower-filled terrace. The place settings are delightfully old-fashioned and the service friendly. Highlights include *bougnettes*, home-made potato pancakes, accompanied by a Chablis *andouillette* or a typical local fondue. There are interesting fish dishes as well. There's a weekday lunchtime menu at €15 (except Sun) with others €24–38. Other options are a generous platter or single course for around €13. *Free house apéritif offered to our readers on presentation of this guide.*

Arnay-le-Duc

21230

@ 🎋 🏠 |●| **Chez Camille*****

1 pl. Édouard-Herriot.
☎03.80.90.01.38 ℻03.80.90.04.64
🌐www.chez-camille.fr
Disabled access. TV. High chairs available. Car park.

Nestled at the foot of the old town, this traditional-style, old-fashioned inn with blue shutters could have come straight out of an operetta. Waitresses in flowery dresses serve apéritifs with cheesy choux pastries and home-made ham in the lounge, before conducting you through to the old conservatory that is now the dining room. Here you can sit as though in a theatre and watch the ballet of sous-chefs and kitchen staff being performed on a kind of stage raised up behind a large window – on one side you've got the pastry kitchen, on the other an awning. The whole scene is enacted beneath a glass roof in a room full

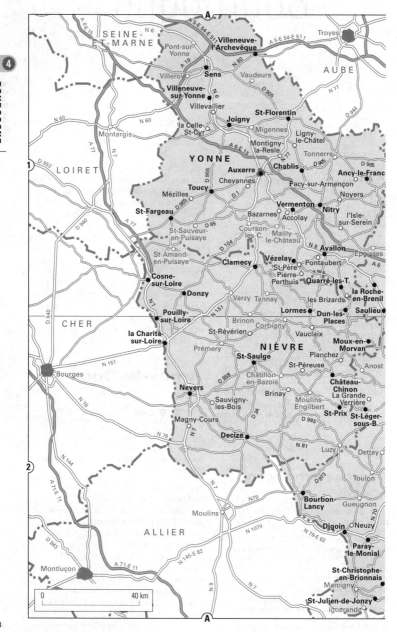

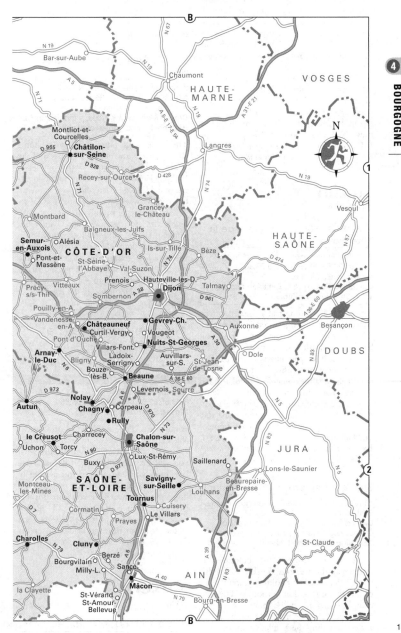

of pot plants and wicker armchairs. The cheapest menu at €19 offers remarkable value for money, providing traditional, refined cuisine: satisfying dishes like pan-fried duck foie gras, Burgundy snails in their shells, fillet of Charolais beef and *bœuf bourguignon*. You can also try speciali-ties such as parsleyed ham. Other menus to €80; children under 11 eat free. The wine list is terrific and the cellar defi-nitely worth a visit. There are a few plush bedrooms, too: doubles with bath at €75 (again, no charge for children under 11 if they share your room); €104 per person half board. *Free house apéritif offered to our readers on presentation of this guide.*

Autun

71400

@ 🏠 |❶| ⚒ Hôtel-restaurant de la Tête Noire**

3 rue de l'Arquebuse.
☎03.85.86.59.99 ℻03.85.86.33.90
🌐www.hoteltetenoire.fr
Closed *15 Dec–31 Jan.* **Disabled access. TV. High chairs available.**

This friendly, comfortable hotel offers charming, recently renovated rooms priced €55–65 for doubles with shower/wc or bath. Several menus, ranging from €13 to €45, feature the hearty, local cuisine that has been delighting customers for a decade. Specialities include Charolais fillet of beef, snail soup and French toast with apples, and wine is available by the glass or pitcher. Air-conditioning in restaurant and some of the bedrooms. Logis de France. *10% discount on the price of a room (from 1 Oct to 30 March) or free coffee offered to our readers on presentation of this guide.*

@ ⚒ |❶| Restaurant Chateaubriant

14 rue Jeannin; behind the municipal theatre.
☎03.85.52.21.58 ℻03.85.52.04.54
Closed *Sun evening; Mon; Wed evening (except Aug); a fortnight in Feb; 3 weeks in July.* **High chairs available.**

Centrally positioned just behind the municipal theatre, this reliable establish-ment offers quality cooking year in, year out, with a classic dining room and decent reception. Set menus €13.50 (on week-days) and €14–36 list good meat speci-alities including beef fillet with Époisse cheese sauce, rack of lamb, *andouillette*, frogs' legs Provençal and fresh foie gras

salad. The *oeufs en meurette* are good too, and there are some nice fish and seafood dishes, such as fillet of pike perch *en meurette*. *Free coffee offered to our readers on presentation of this guide.*

@ ⚒ |❶| Restaurant Le Chalet Bleu

3 rue Jeannin; beside the town hall.
☎03.85.86.27.30 ℻03.85.52.74.56
@le-chalet-bleu@wanadoo.fr
Closed *Mon evening; Tues; a fortnight in Feb.* **High chairs and games available.**

The exterior is nothing to write home about – in no way does it look like a chalet – but you can eat here with confidence. Philippe Bouché, who trained in the kitch-ens of the Elysée Palace, offers five set menus from €15 (weekdays only), then €23–45. The cooking is gloriously imaginative: pike perch with green asparagus and chanterelles; smoked salmon and scallop ravioli with fennel emulsion; chicken supreme; fried kebab of foie gras; marbled foie gras; *aiguil-lette* of duck in an infusion of figs and ratafia, wonderful dessert menu – and the helpings are generous. *Free house apéritif offered to our readers on presentation of this guide.*

Grande-Verrière (La)

71990 (14km W)

@ ⚒ 🏠 |❶| Hôtel de la Poste – Chez Cécile

Take the D3.
☎03.85.82.52.41 ℻03.85.82.55.86
Closed *Sun evening in winter; 21 Dec–4 Jan.*

A stay with "Pépète Cécile" is an unmiss-able experience – there are seven charming rooms from €24 to €44. She decides what you will eat, she tells you off if you arrive late, hugs you and adopts you as one of her own – and, above all, she prepares you huge meals, more than you can possibly eat, with a range of menus, €11–22. Try to leave some space for the desserts, such as the delicious fromage blanc and crème fraîche. *Free house liqueur offered to our readers on presentation of this guide.*

Auxerre

89000

@ ⚒ 🏠 Hôtel Normandie**

41 bd. Vauban; on the promenade round the town centre.

150

☎03.86.52.57.80
🌐www.acom.fr/normandie
Disabled access. TV. High chairs available. Pay car park.

This is a large, bourgeois house, surrounded by a small garden and dating from the late nineteenth century. Named after a famous French liner, this elegant, slightly dated hotel (complete with uniformed night porter) has an atmosphere that is indeed reminiscent of a luxury, transatlantic cruise ship. The stylishly furnished rooms are very comfortable with air-conditioning and extremely well cared for. Prices range from €58 to €80 for a double room with shower/wc or bath. A gym, sauna and billiard room are also at your disposal. There's a lock-up garage for cars and bikes. *10% discount on the price of a room (for 2 consecutive nights) offered to our readers on presentation of this guide.*

≪ |●| Le Jardin Gourmand

56 bd. Vauban; it's on the pedestrian precinct near the town centre, 50m from the Carrefour de Paris.
☎03.86.51.53.52 📠03.86.52.33.82
✉le.jardin.gourmand.auxerre@wanadoo.fr
Closed *15 Feb–2 March; 14–29 June; 8–23 Nov.* **Disabled access. High chairs and games available.**

The chef here is an artist and frequently makes sketches of his dishes. His cooking is very inventive, too, and the service is perfection itself – the staff will guide you expertly through an à la carte menu that changes according to the whims of the chef and the produce from his kitchen garden. The cheapest menu costs €35 (weekday lunchtimes) and others are €45–78, all offering an ideal introduction to what is truly imaginative cooking. Here's a taster: terrine of duck foie gras with spiced bread, salted pigeon in pastry, baked turbot with pears. Also, a fine selection of wines on offer, the dining room is cosy and there's a pleasant terrace for good weather. Reservations highly recommended.

Chevannes
89240 (8km SW)

≪ 🏠 |●| La Chamaille***

La Barbotière – 4 rte de Boiloup. From Auxerre, take the Nevers-Bourgnes road then the D1; once in the village, second street on the left.
☎03.86.41.24.80

✉la-chamaille@wanadoo.fr
Closed *Feb school holiday.* **TV. High chairs available. Car park.**

This old, turreted farm smells reassuringly of polish and is an excellent place to stay – doubles cost €50–75 – located in the middle of wonderful scenery within minutes of Auxerre. It has recently changed hands, and the new owners, Florence and Hervé, offer a sophisticated fusion of traditional cooking and creative invention. There's a choice of menus, €35–70, and you can eat in a bay window overlooking the beautiful countryside (complete with a little stream) or on the terrace.

Montigny-la-Resle
89230 (12km NE)

≪ 🍴 🏠 |●| Hôtel-restaurant Le Soleil d'Or**

From Auxerre, take the N77.
☎ and 📠03.86.41.81.21
✉le-soleil-dor@wanadoo.fr
Disabled access. TV. High chairs available. Car park.

The hotel and restaurant are housed in old farmhouses that have been completely renovated. The pretty bedrooms with shower/wc or bath cost €53. The kitchen turns out classic dishes that are consistent in quality with an occasional touch of imagination. The weekday lunch menus, €12 and €18, include a quarter litre of wine; various others €25–65. Try the pan-fried foie gras with runny caramel, pigeon with sweet cider, roast lamb cutlet with foie gras and artichoke *millefeuille* or crayfish tails with mandarin. Wine by the glass is rather expensive and it's essential to book in the hotel. Logis de France. *A glass of Kir offered to our readers on presentation of this guide.*

Avallon
89200

≪ 🏠 |●| Hôtel-restaurant des Capucins**

6 av. Paul-Doumer; the road leads to the station.
☎03.86.34.06.52 📠03.86.34.58.47
Closed *Tues; Wed; 8 Dec–9 Jan; last week in June.* **TV. Car park.**

The bright dining room is a nice place to enjoy remarkable cooking prepared by a chef who's a real pro. He makes everything himself – try the foie gras – and gets his ingredients and produce from local suppliers. There's a weekday lunchtime menu at €21 with others from €27 to €38. Wines are served by the glass. Although the seven bedrooms (doubles €51) are somewhat nondescript, they're quiet – even those overlooking the road. Logis de France.

◎ 🎴 🍴 Relais des Gourmets

47 rue de Paris; it's 200m from the main square.
℡03.86.34.18.90 ℗03.86.31.60.21
ℯrelais-des-gourmets@wanadoo.fr
Closed Sun evening and Mon from 1 Sept to 30 June; Jan. **Disabled access. High chairs available. Car park.**

This used to be the *Hôtel de Paris* in the days when Avallon was still a staging post and – unlike its contemporaries, which have long since disappeared – it's found a new lease of life. It's no longer a hotel but you can have a good meal in a pleasant atmosphere – weekday lunchtime menu €16.50, then others €25–66. The chef prepares fish (lemon sole with scallops in herb butter) with as much skill as he does the meat from neighbouring Charolais herds, along with dishes such as roast pigeon with hazelnut oil. There's a covered terrace that shelters not only tables but also centuries-old olive trees. It's a popular spot, so it's advisable to book. *Free house apéritif offered to our readers on presentation of this guide.*

Pontaubert
89200 (4km SW)

◎ 🏠 Le Moulin des Templiers**

Vallée du Cousin; take the D957 in the direction of Vézelay, turn right as soon as you cross the bridge and follow the arrows.
℡03.86.34.10.80
ⓦwww.hotel-moulin-des-templiers.com
Closed end-Dec to end-Jan. **Car park.**

This large, ochre-coloured house, covered with Virginia creeper, is located in the Cousin valley. A twelfth-century mill that's been wonderfully restored, it is now a charming waterside hotel with oodles of charm and a friendly welcome. There are sitting rooms for intimate conversations and a flowery waterside terrace for when the sun shines, with lovely walks and mountain-bike rides in the surrounding woods. Comfortable double

rooms cost €42 with shower and €59 with shower/wc or bath, depending on the size. Breakfast can be taken on the terrace beside the river.

◎ 🎴 🏠 🍴 Les Fleurs**

69 rte. de Vézelay; take the D957 in the direction of Vézelay.
℡03.86.34.13.81 ℗03.86.34.23.32
Closed Wed and Thurs 15 Sept–15 June; Wed only, 16 June–14 Sept; Jan; Nov school holiday; Christmas. **TV. High chairs available. Car park.**

This beautiful hotel is surrounded by a delightful flower garden and has been tastefully decorated by the owners, with lovely wood panelling in the dining room. The bedrooms are pretty and comfortable, costing €45 with shower/wc and €50 with bath. The restaurant gets things just right and the prices are reasonable – the cheapest set menu is €15 (weekdays), with others €22–37 – and there's a wealth of fish specialities like trout terrine with basil sauce, smoked salmon maison, fillet of beef Morvandiau and *pavé de Pontaubert*. There's a pleasant terrace and good choice of wines to accompany the dishes. Logis de France. *Free house apéritif offered to our readers on presentation of this guide.*

Isle-sur-Serein (L')
89440 (15km NE)

◎ 🎴 🏠 🍴 Auberge du Pot d'Étain

24 rue Bouchardat; take the D557 then the D86; it's near the edge of the village.
℡03.86.33.88.10 ℗03.86.33.90.93
ⓦwww.potdetain.com
Closed Sun evening. Mon and Tues lunchtime (Mon only in July and Aug); Feb; third week in Oct. **TV. High chairs available. Pay car park.**

This charming and tiny country inn is one of the best places to eat in the entire region. The cooking is a mixture of the traditional and the modern with a range of menus €23–49. Try *andouillette* of snails, flan of foie gras and asparagus tips, langoustines poached with artichokes and citrus fruit, or potato pie with tripe sausage. They have the most fantastic cellar – the spectacular wine list features over a thousand vintages. Nine pleasant rooms, three of them recently renovated, go for €56–75 for a double. The charming ones at the back of the flower-filled courtyard are quieter. Logis de France. *Free coffee offered to our readers on presentation of this guide.*

Beaune

21200

@ 🎿 🛏 **Hôtel Grillon*****

21 rte. de Seurre; follow the directions to
Seurre-Dôle on the boulevard on the outskirts
of town.
☎03.80.22.44.25 📠03.80.24.94.89
🌐www.hotel-grillon.fr
Closed *Feb.* **TV. High chairs and games
available. Swimming pool. Car park.**

It's difficult to see why people make do
with chain hotels when, in a charming
place like this, you can fall into bed after
a visit to the vineyards and wake up to
the sound of chirping birds. The cosy,
air-conditioned rooms in this old family
house have style, all are decorated with
a modern touch and cost €52–65 for a
double with shower or bath; it's a pity that
you can hear the traffic. In the summer
you can eat breakfast in the garden or on
the terrace. Dine at *Le Verger*, in the park
opposite. Logis de France. *10% discount on
a room (1 Dec–15 March) offered to our readers
on presentation of this guide.*

@ 🎿 🛏 **Le Home****

138 rte. de Dijon; take the A31 south of
Beaune in the direction of Dijon, leave at
exit 24.
☎03.80.22.16.43 📠03.80.24.90.74
🌐www.lehome.fr
**Disabled access. TV. High chairs and
games available. Car park.**

It's quite difficult to spot this old Burgundian
house, nestling in lush greenery – it's tucked
away behind a wall on the way into the
town. It makes a very pleasant place to stop,
and an ideal spot in which to relax. The
décor, not surprisingly, is English in style and
the welcome is as charming as the location.
Some of the rooms overlook the garden
and hopefully those on the road will benefit
from soundproofing in a promised refurbishment. €54–65 for a double with shower/wc
or bath; excellent breakfast. *10% discount on
a room (end Nov to end March) offered to our
readers on presentation of this guide.*

@ 🍽 **Restaurant Le P'tit Paradis**

25 rue Paradis; opposite the entrance to the
Wine Museum.
☎03.80.24.91.00

Closed *Mon; Tues; 9–23 March; 10–19 Aug;
16 Nov–3 Dec.* **Disabled access.**

Beaune's road to paradise was gastronomic
purgatory until this restaurant opened
opposite the Musée du Vin. It's painted in
colours as fresh as the cooking, which is
very reasonably priced and includes such
dishes as stewed rabbit with herbs and salad
of fried scallops with pistachio oil. Weekday
lunch menu costs €12.50 and other menus
at €17 and €28. Reckon on €35 à la carte.
In summer you can eat on the terrace.

@ 🍽 **Restaurant La Ciboulette**

69 rue de Lorraine; it's in the old part of town,
opposite the theatre.
☎03.80.24.70.72 📠03.80.22.79.77
Closed *Mon; Tues; last 3 weeks in Feb;
second and third weeks in Aug.*

The renovated premises are small and the
décor is restrained but the atmosphere is
friendly. Two well-priced set menus (€19
and €25) bring in tourists and locals alike,
which is reassuring. An ideal spot to gather
your strength for a tour of the hospices or
the city's numerous wine cellars.

@ 🎿 🍽 **Le Benaton**

25 rue du Faubourg Bretonnière; it's five minutes from the town centre, heading towards
Autun.
☎03.80.22.00.26 📠03.80.22.51.95
✉le.benaton@liberty.surf.fr
Closed *Wed and Thurs lunchtime in season;
Wed and Thurs out of season.* **Disabled
access.**

Though it's not ideally located, this restaurant is worth seeking out. The cooking
is of the traditional, local variety with
modern touches: pan-fried snails, courgette caviar served on a reduced tomato
sauce and custard cream. The €20 weekday lunchtime menu is a model of its type
(served at weekends and evenings too
Nov–Feb), and there are others at €35 and
€48. One way to ensure quality at a reasonable price is by ordering a combination
of the cheapest menu with wine chosen à
la carte. *Free glass of Kir offered to our readers
on presentation of this guide.*

Levernois

21200 (4km SE)

@ 🛏 **Le Parc****

13 rue de Golf: take the D970 in the direction
of Verdun-sur-le-Doubs then turn left.

☎03.80.24.63.00 ℗03.80.24.21.19
ⓦwww.hotelleparc.fr
Closed 1–20 Jan; 25 Nov–31 Dec. **Disabled
access. TV. Car park.**

An old house, now a charming hotel. The
trees in the grounds are a hundred years
old and full of birds. The bedrooms are full
of character and all different; doubles €40
with handbasin, €50 with shower/wc
and €58–89 with bath. A friendly, relaxed
place – it's best to book.

Bouze-lès-Beaune

21200 (7km NW)

☺ ⅍ |❍| La Bouzerotte

It's by the side of the D970, going towards
Bligny-sur-Ouche.
☎03.80.26.01.37 ℗03.80.26.09.37
ⓦperso.wanadoo.fr/la.bouzerotte
Closed Mon; Tues; also Sun evening 1 Dec–30
March; 11–19 Sept; 22 Dec–2 Jan. **Car park.**

A real country inn, ten minutes from the
centre of Beaune, with real Burgundians
and real Burgundy cooking. Real flowers
(so unusual nowadays you have to mention
the fact) decorate the old wooden tables;
there's an old-fashioned sideboard and
a fireplace where a fire crackles in cold
weather. More to the point, there are also
good wines, from small local vineyards,
which Christine, who used to be a wine
waitress, can recommend. The freshest
produce of the highest quality is used in
the dishes and the presentation is wonderful – try ravioli of snails and calf's trotters
with garlic. The cheap menu costs €11.50
(weekdays only), with other menus €15–
38; children's menu €9. *Free coffee offered to
our readers on presentation of this guide.*

Ladoix-Serrigny

21550 (7km NE)

☺ ⅍ |❍| Auberge de la Miotte

4 rue de la Miotte; take the N74 in the direction of Nuits-Saint-Georges; from Ladoix,
follow the road to Corgolain and look out for
the signposts.
☎03.80.26.40.75
Closed Sun, Mon evenings; Tues evenings
in summer; 24 Dec to first week in Jan; first
fortnight in Aug.

An old hunting lodge on the edge of the
forest that calls to mind the set of a swash-
buckling film: enormous wooden tables on
a worn stone floor, with sturdy beams and
metal chandeliers in the ceiling. There's

also a pretty terrace shaded by trees. The
low prices also seem to belong to another
era: weekday lunchtime menu €12, with
others €14–23. Home cooking with fresh,
seasonal ingredients, and an exceptional
(and very cheap) wine list, with several
vintages provided by the owner's friends
from nearby vineyards. Service is cheerful
and unpretentious. *Free house apéritif offered
to our readers on presentation of this guide.*

☺ ⅍ |❍| Les Coquines

N74 – Buisson; 10 minutes from Beaune;
take the N74, in the direction of Dijon.
☎03.80.26.43.58 ℗03.80.26.49.59
Closed Wed; Thurs; 23 Dec–3 Jan; 2–21 Feb;
19 Aug. **High chairs available. Car park.**

A charming old house with views of the
surrounding countryside. You can choose
a table under the glass roof or in the cellar,
depending on how much privacy you
want. Selection of menus in the great gastronomic tradition ranging from €29 to
€39. *Free house apéritif offered to our readers
on presentation of this guide.*

Bourbon-Lancy

71140

☺ ⅍ 🏠 |❍| Le Grand Hôtel★★★

Parc Thermal, in the direction of Dijon.
☎03.85.89.08.87 ℗03.85.89.32.23
ⓦwww.grand-hotel-thermal.com
Closed end Oct to end March. Restaurant
closed Nov–Jan. Open daily April–Oct, weekends only Dec, Feb, March. **TV. Car park.**

Perfect for lovers of charming, old-fashioned
spas. Set in a former Visitandine convent, the
cloister of which remains intact, the hotel
itself is outsize without being overblown.
Clean rooms, several of them recently renovated, with enormous bathrooms at reasonable prices: doubles with washbasin €28.70;
shower/wc or bath €57.20–60.10. The
austerity of the spa does not extend to the
classic cuisine on offer in the *Restaurant du
Cloître* which offers a menu at €10 during
the week for both lunch and dinner, then
others €15–31. Dishes include fried duck
foie gras, scallops in raspberry vinegar, pike
perch *en croûte* with parsley and chive sauce,
pears poached in spices and pink sorbet.
Meals are served on the terrace under the
cloister in fine weather. There's an extensive
wine list and a tea room also available. *10%
discount on the price of a room or free coffee offered
to our readers on presentation of this guide.*

@ 🜨 🏠 Hôtel La Tourelle du Beffroi

17 pl. de la Mairie; at the entrance to the old town, beside the belfry.
☎03.85.89.39.20 ℻03.85.89.39.29
🖥www.latourelle.net **Disabled access. TV.**

A delightful little hotel in the medieval quarter. Only eight rooms, all different and pretty, and with poetic names; three of them look onto the garden. Doubles with shower/wc or bath from €53 to €71; breakfast buffet (€8), with typical local fare, served on the veranda or the terrace, with its fine view of the belfry. For other meals, just follow the owner to her former restaurant *La Grignotte du Vieux Bourbon* (see below), which is close by. *One free breakfast per room offered to our readers on presentation of this guide.*

@ 🜨 |●| La Grignotte du Vieux Bourbon

12 rue de l'Horloge; in the heart of the old town.
☎03.85.89.06.53
Closed *Christmas and New Year.* **High chairs available.**

A heart-warming stopover, on account of both the food and the atmosphere. An authentic bistro with lively regulars and a young owner (commonly known as Hervé de la Grignotte), who is kept busy serving the tasty *entrecôtes* and other dishes of the day. The rustic menu, €11.50, is served in winter, and there's another menu at €12.60; reckon on €17 à la carte. Sale and sampling of wines is available in the shop alongside, *La Cav'atout*. *Free house apéritif offered to our readers on presentation of this guide.*

Chablis
89800

@ 🜨 🏠 Au Relais de la Belle Étoile-Bergerand's

4 rue des Moulins
☎03.86.18.96.08 ℻03.86.18.96.09
📧bergerand-belleetoile@wanadoo.fr
Closed *Tues out of season; 24 Dec–4 Jan.*
Disabled access. TV. Pay car park.

The new owner, nicknamed "the American", has transformed these premises in the town centre into a charming, highly presentable hotel with bright, colourful rooms; these vary in size and cost €45–75 according to the degree of comfort offered.

Bed and breakfast also available. It is advisable to book. *10% discount on the price of a room (1 Sept–30 April) offered to our readers on presentation of this guide.*

@ 🜨 🏠 |●| Hostellerie des Clos***

Rue Jules-Rathier.
☎03.86.42.10.63 ℻03.86.42.17.11
🖥www.hostellerie-des-clos.fr
Closed *20 Dec–17 Jan.* **Disabled access. TV. Car park.**

In this hostelry, housed in a former hospital and chapel, the waiters wear tails, the tinkling chandeliers gleam luxuriously, the illuminated gardens are delightful and Madame sports elaborate jewellery. Despite all this, the waiters don't take themselves too seriously and Madame's laugh makes you feel welcome. Her husband uses only the finest ingredients and his best-known dishes are subtly flavoured with Chablis, so take your credit card – menus start at €35 (every day), with others at €50 and €70. If you're eating à la carte, choose just a main course and a dessert and they won't object. Specialities include *fricassée* of snails with a simple herb *coulis*, roast pike perch or boned ham, and fruit desserts. Pretty double rooms with bath cost €58–125 and the four duplex apartments are €185 each. Logis de France. *Free coffee offered to our readers on presentation of this guide.*

@ |●| Le Vieux Moulin de Chablis

18 rue des Moulins.
☎03.86.42.47.30 ℻03.86.42.84.44
🖥www.vieux-moulin-chablis.com
Closed *Christmas holidays.* **High chairs available. Car park.**

A lot of water from the River Serein has flowed under the bridge since this restaurant started up in a house that used to belong to a wine-growing family. The large dining room has walls of local stone, the regional cuisine is well up to standard and the prices are fair. Best dishes on the four menus (€17–40) are the beef fillet in Pinot Noir, *andouillette* and pike perch in Chablis.

Ligny-le-Châtel
89144 (15km NW)

@ 🜨 🏠 |●| Relais Saint-Vincent**

14 Grande-Rue; take the D91 from Chablis.
☎03.86.47.53.38
📧relais.saint.vincent@libertysurf.fr

Closed 21 Dec–6 Jan. **Disabled access. TV. High chairs available. Car park.**

The village and the street are from another age, and the half-timbered house dates back to the seventeenth century. It has been tastefully converted by the welcoming owner and the rooms have all mod cons; doubles €42–68.50 with shower/ wc or bath. Sit out in the quiet, flowery courtyard and sample the excellent, authentic local cuisine (kidneys flambéed with Marc brandy), with cheapest menu at €13 (served every day, dinner and lunch), others at €16–26, and there's a remarkable cheeseboard, including a local Époisse. Logis de France. *Free house apéritif offered to our readers on presentation of this guide.*

ⓐ |●| Auberge du Bief

2 av. de Chablis; it's next to the church; take the D91.
☏03.86.47.43.42 ⓕ03.86.47.48.14
Closed *Sun evening; Mon; Tues evening in season; Wed–Fri evenings out of season; Christmas school holiday; last week in Aug.* **High chairs available. Car park.**

Very popular locally for lunch on Sunday, and you'll get a charming, smiling welcome. There aren't many tables so it's advisable to arrive early or book – otherwise you might find a small space on the terrace. Well-presented dishes and refined cooking: gâteau of artichokes with lemon and herb butter, crayfish in Chablis *court-bouillon*, Burgundy snails and Bavarois with Chablis on three *coulis*. Good value for money with the cheapest menu at €14 (during the week) and others at €17–45.

Chagny
71150

ⓐ 𝒴 🏠 Hôtel de la Ferté**

11 bd. de la Liberté.
☏03.85.87.07.47
🌐www.hotelferte.com
Closed *1–14 Jan.* **TV. Car park.**

This substantial house has been attractively refurbished and turned into a welcoming hotel – one of the best in this price range in the area. There are thirteen rooms with fireplaces, flowery wallpaper and antique furniture. And, without detracting from the period style, all the bathrooms are modern. The rooms are also efficiently soundproofed; doubles €38–50 with shower/wc or bath. A country breakfast is served in a room overlooking the garden, or outside in good weather. *10% discount on the price of a room (from Oct to April except weekends and public holidays) offered to our readers on presentation of this guide.*

ⓐ 🏠 |●| 𝒴 Lameloise****

36 pl. d'Armes.
☏03.85.87.65.65 ⓕ03.85.87.03.57
🌐www.lameloise.fr
Restaurant closed *Tues lunchtime; Wed; Thurs lunchtime; 1–27 Jan; 21–31 Dec.*
Disabled access. TV. Car park.

The third generation of the Lameloise family runs this establishment, which attracts a varied clientele from local businessmen and committed foodies to well-heeled couples. The decoration in the five small dining rooms is stylish – stone walls, sturdy beams, comfortable chairs, fresh flowers and still-life paintings. The service is unobtrusive, meticulous and perfect; no smoking is permitted. The cooking is based on local produce: snail ravioli in sweet garlic broth, pigeon crumble with truffles. In between each course, delicious morsels, both savoury and sweet, appear out of nowhere. There's a choice of menus priced at €85–120 (selection of sample dishes), and the desserts are served in gargantuan portions. In the hotel, doubles are €125–280.

Corpeau
21190 (8km E)

ⓐ 𝒴 |●| L'Auberge du Vieux Vigneron

Route de Beaune; take the N6 then the D23 in the direction of Meursault; it's opposite the town hall.
☏03.80.21.39.00 ⓕ03.80.21.38.81
Closed *Mon; Tues; a week in Jan; Feb school holiday; 10–25 Aug.* **High chairs available. Car park.**

This village wouldn't merit a special trip were it not for the inn. In the dining room, the atmosphere calls to mind harvest supper: old tables, old furniture and a wide fireplace where lamb cutlets and *andouillettes* are cooked. Two menus, at €15 and €20, also list other dishes such as chicken escalopes and frogs' legs. House wines include a Chassagne-Montrachet and a Puligny, both affordable; try a few other vintages grown by the owner from the newly refurbished cellar. It's a simple place and a good one. *Free house apéritif offered to our readers on presentation of this guide.*

Charrecey

71510 (13 km SW)

☺ |●| ⚲ Le Petit Blanc

Le Pont-Pilley; signposted from the D978.
☏ 03.85.45.15.43
Closed *Sun evening; Mon; Thurs evening and Sun lunch (in winter); a week at Easter; fortnight in late Aug; fortnight at Christmas. High chairs available.*

A country inn with chequered tablecloths, slates, enamelled plaques on the walls and, above all, authentic, traditional dishes, as promised in the menu: home-made *terrine maison* with fried frogs' legs, cockscombs with chicken's kidneys and calf's head *en cocotte*. The lively dining room is always packed – weekday lunchtime menu at €13.50, then others €19.50–28.50 – and customers often spill out on the terrace. Attentive service, friendly welcome and a wine list with a wide range of Mercurey (a bit on the pricey side, however). *Free house liqueur offered to our readers on presentation of this guide.*

Chalon-sur-Saône

71100

☺ ⚑ Hôtel Saint-Jean**

24 quai Gambetta.
☏ 03.85.48.45.65
Disabled access. TV. Pay car park.

If you have to spend a night in Chalon, the *Saint-Jean* is the only hotel on the Saône riverbank and it's away from the traffic – so booking is advisable. The mansion has been tastefully decorated by a former restaurateur who gave up cooking in favour of hotel keeping, and the staff are friendly and professional. A quiet, clean and welcoming establishment with magnificent views, where everything is pleasing and the prices are reasonable; large double rooms decorated in fresh colours are €50. You feel there should be some sort of preservation order on the handsome imitation marble staircase, which dates from the late nineteenth century.

☺ ⚲ ⚑ Hôtel Kyriad**

35 pl. de Beaune.

☏ 03.85.90.08.00 ☏ 03.85.90.08.01
✉ kyriad.chalon@wanadoo.fr
TV. Pay car park.

Small hotel in a renovated old house. Accommodation is in the main building or in two annexes, the more recent of which overlooks an inner courtyard and is quieter. Some rooms have parquet floors, open fireplaces and old furniture; many have been entirely renovated. Doubles with shower/wc or bath €53–63. Facilities include a sauna, a solarium and a gym. *10% discount on the price of a room (1 Jan–31 March; 1–31 Aug; 1 Oct–31 Dec) offered to our readers on presentation of this guide.*

☺ ⚑ |●| ⚲ Le Saint-Georges***

32 av. Jean-Jaurès; it's opposite the station.
☏ 03.85.90.80.50 ☏ 03.85.90.80.55
www.lesaintgeorges.fr
Restaurant closed *Sat lunchtime; Sun evening; 1–22 Aug.* **TV. High chairs available. Pay car park.**

A classic station hotel. All the rooms have been refurbished with good facilities – the armchairs will appeal to fans of modern design. All in all, it's value for money with double rooms for €70–125. The gastronomic restaurant may beckon but if you're looking to spend less try your luck at the friendly bistro *Le Comptoir d'à Côté* instead, where you can have a meal of Burgundian specialities – parsleyed ham with Aligoté, foie gras *escalope* with spiced bread – for around €16. Weekday lunchtime menu in the fine restaurant at €18, with others at €29–43; specialities include such dishes as Bresse chicken terrine with foie gras. *Free house apéritif offered to our readers on presentation of this guide.*

☺ ⚲ |●| Restaurant Ripert

31 rue Saint-Georges; between the sous-préfecture and the Grande-Rue.
☏ 03.85.48.89.20
Closed *Sun; Mon; a week early Jan; a week early May; 3 weeks end Aug.*

Over the last twenty years, Alain Ripert has created something of an institution. The dining room is small with a few touches reminiscent of a 1950s bistro (adverts, enamel signs and so on) and fills up rapidly with locals. Dishes change daily with the fresh produce in the market and set menus cost €14–30. Typical offerings might include *escalope* of veal sweetbreads with spices and honey, monkfish stew with saffron, *croustillant* of oxtail and timbale of lobster tail. Save room for a dessert. Unusually for this part of the world, they serve some good wines in carafes as well as bottles. *Free coffee offered to our readers on presentation of this guide.*

⊚ |O| L'Air du Temps

7 rue de Strasbourg; on the île Saint-Laurent.
☎03.85.93.39.01
Closed *Sun; Mon.* **Disabled access. High chairs and games available.**

Sample the cooking of a great chef at extremely accessible prices: incredible lunch menu at €15; other menus at €20 and €25.50. Cyril Bouchet acquired an impeccable technique working alongside some of France's greatest chefs (Meneau, Jung, Troigros, Robuchon) before branching out on his own in modest surroundings and building up a loyal following. The budgetary limitations are evident in the somewhat neutral setting with sparse decorations, but the dishes provide a subtle, precise splash of colour and tastes, with fresh ingredients and just the right amount of spices to catch you off guard for a moment. What's more, the service is cheerful and attentive.

⊚ 🎋 |O| Le Gourmand

13 rue de Strasbourg; on the île Saint-Laurent.
☎03.85.93.64.61
Closed *Mon; Tues; 1 week in April; 3 weeks in Aug; last week in Dec.*

The ever-smiling, ever-helpful owner sets the tone for this chic but down-to-earth restaurant that has built up a loyal following. The food is sophisticated and exquisitely presented, featuring particularly outstanding sauces with generous quantities of herbs. Specialities on the menus (€15.50–30) include baked turbot on a bed of ratatouille, roast pigeon or *tournedos* of pig's trotters with foie gras, etc. *Free glass of Kir offered to our readers on presentation of this guide.*

⊚ |O| Restaurant Chez Jules

11 rue de Strasbourg; it's on île Saint-Laurent.
☎03.85.48.08.34 ☎03.85.48.55.48
Closed *Sat lunchtime; Sun; a fortnight in Feb; first 3 weeks in Aug.*

This small restaurant, located in a quiet neighbourhood, is popular with the locals, its salmon-pink walls, sturdy beams, copper pots, paintings and old sideboard all adding to the cosy atmosphere. The cooking is inventive, playing with the colours and tastes

of the classic local dishes, with a *menu du jour* at €15.50; others at €23–30. Good wine list available by the glass, bottle and carafe. After all that, a post-prandial stroll along the embankment might well be called for.

Lux-Saint-Rémy
71100 (4km S)

⊚ 🏠 |O| 🎋 Ma Campagne

Quai Bellevue; take the N6 in the direction of Sennecey-le-Grand.
☎03.85.48.33.80 ☎03.85.93.33.72
Closed *Sun evening; Mon evening (and Mon lunch out of season); mid-Jan to mid-March.*
Disabled access. TV. High chairs available. Car park.

This huge country house, set in splendid isolation in the middle of trees on the banks of the Saône, is a bucolic delight with birdsong and walks by the river. While the hotel is undergoing renovation, rooms (€50–70) above the restaurant provide temporary accommodation. Highly accomplished, classic cooking, with an emphasis on fish with a range of menus, €17.30–34. On a fine day you can eat on a large terrace shaded by an awning. *Free house apéritif offered to our readers on presentation of this guide.*

Buxy
71390 (15km SW)

⊚ 🏠 Hôtel Fontaine de Baranges

Rue de la Fontaine-de-Baranges; take the D977.
☎03.85.94.10.70 ☎03.85.94.10.79
🌐www.hotelfb.com
Closed *Jan.* **Disabled access. TV. Car park.**

A substantial, early nineteenth-century residence in grounds planted with shady trees, right next to a pretty old stone washhouse. The whole place has been completely restored and the attractive rooms are spacious and peaceful; some have private terraces overlooking the garden and cost €65–135 for a double, depending on size. No restaurant but there is a charming bar. Breakfast is served in the cellar or the terrace.

Charité-sur-Loire (La)
58400

⊚ 🏠 Hôtel Le Bon Laboureur**

Quai Romain-Mollot; it's on the île de Loire, 500m from the town centre.

☎03.86.70.22.85 ⓕ03.86.70.23.64
ⓦwww.lebonlaboureur.com
TV.

An ancient building, each room of which is a different size and has different facilities – the best rooms overlook an interior garden or the Loire. They've all been refurbished; doubles are reasonably priced at €40–50; some can sleep three or four people, at €8 per extra person. You can expect a warm welcome here.

@ ⅔ |●| L'Auberge de Seyr

4 Grande-Rue.
☎ and ⓕ03.86.70.03.51
Closed *Sun lunch; Mon; 1 week in Feb; 3 weeks end Aug to early Sept.* **High chairs available.**

A simple, unpretentious restaurant serving cuisine with character. Dishes change daily but the fresh fish and home-made pastries are always good. The weekday *menu du jour* at €12 includes a starter – various salads or home-made terrine – and a main dish of meat or fish followed by cheese or dessert (with a wide choice available); other menus €18–28. *Free coffee offered to our readers on presentation of this guide.*

Charolles

71120

@ ⅔ ⚐ |●| Hôtel-restaurant Le Lion d'Or**

6 rue de Champagny.
☎03.85.24.08.28
Closed *Sun evening and Mon except mid-July to mid-Aug.* **TV. Swimming pool. Car park.**

This seventeenth-century coaching inn is on the banks of a small river. Large double rooms with shower cost €45–54. Those overlooking the river are particularly attractive. The top-notch restaurant serves good regional cooking with exceptional meat dishes, as you would expect in Charolais country; set menu €15 (except Sun), with others €26 and €34. *Free coffee offered to our readers on presentation of this guide.*

@ ⚐ |●| Hôtel-restaurant de la Poste***

2 av. de la Libération.
☎03.85.24.11.32 ⓕ03.85.24.05.74
ⓦwww.la-poste-hotel.com

Closed *Sun evening; Mon.* **TV. Pay car park.**

This is a very important establishment in the Charolais – it's run by Daniel Doucet, the ambassador of Burgundy gastronomy, and his cooking is as fresh and tasty as ever. The dining room is richly decorated and the service is faultless and attentive, but this place is definitely not affected. You'll get great advice on wine to suit your taste and an excellent choice of dishes – don't miss the Charolais rib steak with Guérande salt, or the magnificent cheese platter and desserts. There's a set menu at €23 during the week, others at €33–70. Eat out under the maple trees in the interior garden on fine days. Comfy bedrooms cost €48; the recently opened new annexe offers air-conditioned rooms overlooking the garden by the riverside.

Château-Chinon

58120

@ ⅔ ⚐ |●| Hôtel du Parc – Le Relais Gourmand**

Nevers road; on the left of the Nevers road, just before leaving the town.
☎03.86.79.44.94. ⓕ03.86.79.41.10.
Closed *Feb; restaurant closed Sun evening (15 Nov–15 March).* **TV. Disabled access.**

Despite its name, this modern, functional hotel with comfortable, air-conditioned rooms for €41, is not surrounded by a park, although it does fall within the Morvan Region Natural Park. It's a good place to eat, too; the €12 menu is particularly good value (though it's not available on Sundays or public holidays). The food is not only cheap – other menus at €15–38 – but also well prepared (with foie gras the house speciality), and to top it all there's a very friendly atmosphere. *Free coffee offered to our readers on presentation of this guide.*

Planchez

58230 (16km NE)

@ ⚐ |●| ⅔ Le Relais des Lacs

Avenue François-Mitterrand; take the D37.
☎03.86.78.49.00
ⓕ03.86.78.49.09
ⓦwww.morvan.gourmand.fr
Closed *Sun evening and Mon (except 15 June–15 Sept); 5 Jan–end March; 15 Nov–15 Dec.* **High chairs and games available.**

Presentable double rooms, some recently renovated, with shower/wc or bath for

€42–46. Friendly service, splendid dining room with a terrace, and good cooking to match, with a range of menus, €15–36, and a fine wine list. The chef is very fussy about the quality of his ingredients, and all the beef and game comes from the immediate area. The trout with Pouilly is delicious, but the *grapiaud de forment* (a local speciality) is disappointing. Other alternatives include baked turbot with shallots and foie gras. Don't miss the local apéritif, Morvandiau. The chef is a multi-faceted character; he is the mayor of the village and a mine of information about the region. Logis de France. *10% discount on the price of a room or house apéritif offered to our readers on presentation of this guide.*

Saint-Péreuse

58110 (17km W)

⊛ |●| Auberge de la Madonnette

In the town centre; take the D978, then the D231.
☏03.86.84.45.37
Closed *Tues and Wed evening (except July–Aug); 15 Dec–5 Feb.*

Magnificent terraced garden with an unbeatable view of the château nearby; the food holds its own in such a splendid setting by drawing heavily on regional traditions. Just next door, the owner's son has opened an old-style biscuit shop, with extremely tempting tidbits on display. The weekday menu, €11, and others, €16–43, feature tasty country cooking: traditional-style veal's head, lamb fried with parsley, snail pie.

Châteauneuf

21320

⊛ 🏠 |●| Hostellerie du Château**

Rue de Centre. Take the Pouilly-en-Auxois exit off the A6.
☏03.80.49.22.00 ☏03.80.49.21.27
🌐hostellerie-chateauneuf.com
Closed *Mon and Tues except July–Aug; Dec; Jan.* **Disabled access. High chairs and games available.**

Despite the fact that it looks as if it hasn't changed for years, nearly all the twelfth- and fourteenth-century houses in this picturesque hilltop village have been bought by outsiders. Similarly misleading is the medieval exterior of this hotel, which stands in the shadow of a twelfth-century castle – inside it's modern and comfortable. The cheapest menu at €23 (daily, lunch and dinner) and others at €45–70 list traditional local dishes such as Charolais beef and snails. Doubles with shower or bath, €45–70; some have countryside views.

Châtillon-sur-Seine

21400

⊛ 🎋 🏠 Sylvia Hôtel**

9 av. de la Gare; it's on the outskirts of town, in the direction of Troyes.
☏03.80.91.02.44 ☏03.80.91.47.77
🌐www.sylvia-hotel.fr
Disabled access. TV. Car park.

The previous owners transformed this enormous old family home, set in parkland, into a delightful hotel and named it after their daughter. Then Sylvia grew up and the family moved on. The present owners decided to keep the name, however, and do their utmost to help you enjoy your stay, offering simple, cosy rooms for €33 with basin and €40–44 with bath/wc, and wonderful breakfasts (€5.50) that are eaten round a large communal table. *10% discount on the price of a room (Oct–April) offered to our readers on presentation of this guide.*

⊛ |●| 🎋 Le Bourg-à-Mont "Chez Julie"

27 rue du Bourg-à-Mont; in the old town, opposite the old law court, near the Archeological Museum.
☏03.80.91.04.33
Closed *Mon, Wed evening, Sun evening (out of season);high season closures unavailable; Feb and Nov school holidays.* **High chairs available. Disabled access.**

A pleasant surprise in this sleepy town, famous for its Vix vase: a house from another era, replete with gaudy old posters and paintings, that is nevertheless particularly popular with young people. In winter, there is a blazing log fire; in summer, the big windows are thrown open onto the courtyard bedecked with lilacs where you can eat your meal (provided you book on time, as the places are limited). The dishes, which reflect the old-fashioned atmosphere, include Châtillonnais trout terrine, Bourg-à-Mont beef (a spicy, easily digestible version of the famous *bœuf bourguignon* accompanied by blackcurrant cream) and almond tart with chocolate and custard. Menus cost €15–35 and take-away dishes are available. *Free jar of home-made jam offered to our readers on presentation of this guide.*

Montliot-et-Courcelles
21400 (4km NW)

⊚ |●| Chez Florentin

On the N71, at the entrance to the village.
☎03.80.91.09.70.
Closed *Sun evening.* **Disabled access.**

Friendly service and unbeatable prices – lorry drivers' menu at €11 served from Tuesday lunch to Friday dinner: timbale of mushroom with cream, *blanquette* of veal and mouth-watering pies. Other menus range up to €44. You can eat in the bar with the lorry drivers; the large dining room is reserved for banquets and baptisms and is often occupied. At night the customers are usually local, whereas at lunch they are mainly just passing through.

Clamecy
58500

⊚ 🎋 🛏 |●| Hostellerie de la Poste**

9 pl. Émile-Zola.
☎03.86.27.01.55 ⊕03.86.27.05.99
✉hotelposteclamecy@wanadoo.fr
TV. High chairs available.

A substantial building in the centre that looks the part – like a post-house that has been there forever. The rooms (€54) are clean and comfortable and it's obvious that the hotel is seriously well run. The *menu du jour* (not Sun) costs €20, with others at €25 and €31 (gourmet's menu) and a children's menu at €15. The beef is local Charolais and there are fresh river fish too, as well as snails with potatoes and soufflé with locally made Marc brandy. Logis de France. *Free coffee offered to our readers on presentation of this guide.*

⊚ 🎋 |●| La crêperie du Vieux Canal

18 av. de la République; it's opposite the museum.
☎03.86.24.47.93
Closed *Sun (out of season); Mon; first fortnight in Feb; 3 weeks in Sept.* **Disabled access.**

One of Clamecy's friendliest spots to eat, a place where you can have a good,

quick lunch. The décor is Breton and they serve savoury and sweet pancakes (also to take away) – try the Savoyarde, or the Normande – as well as pasta dishes and bruschetta. Menus from €15 (on weekdays) to €27; a pancake costs €6 and €10 will buy you a basic meal. *Free coffee offered to our readers on presentation of this guide.*

⊚ |●| L'Angélus

11 pl. Saint-Jean; opposite the collegiate church.
☎03.86.27.33.98
Closed *Sun evening; Tues evening (out of season); Wed; Feb; 1 week at New Year.* **Disabled access.**

Most locals agree that this Nivernais restaurant is the best in Clamecy with its sophisticated presentation and efficient service. It's a lovely building with wooden sides and is set right in the heart of the old town, close to the town hall that nestles under the beautiful Saint-Martin collegiate church. In fine weather you can eat on the terrace; menus €15 (weekdays only) to €27. The wines are generally a little expensive, but the Irancy from Auxerre, one of the cheapest vintages listed, is good value for money.

Cluny
71250

⊚ 🎋 🛏 Hôtel du Commerce*

8 pl. du Commerce.
☎03.85.59.03.09 ⊕03.85.59.00.87
Closed *first week in Dec.* **TV.**

In this expensive town, this is a small, well-maintained and central hotel that offers basic, clean accommodation at reasonable prices – €24–39 for a double, breakfast €5 – and a wonderfully friendly reception to boot. Some of the €24 rooms have just been renovated. *Discount on the price of breakfast offered to our readers on presentation of this guide.*

⊚ 🎋 |●| La Pierre Sauvage

Col des Enceints. From Cluny take the D980 in the direction of Mazille, then the D22.
☎03.85.35.70.03 ⊕03.85.35.74.71
Closed *From Easter to 30 Sept: Tues; 1 Oct to Easter: Mon–Thurs; 8 Jan–10 Feb.* **Open** *until 9.30pm (10pm in summer).* **Disabled access. High chairs available. Car park.**

This place is on a hilltop 529m high. Some fifteen years ago, it was a ruin that has since been beautifully restored and is now an appealing place to stop. Start off with a hunk of bread and strong cheese or house terrine before getting stuck into the main courses. Specialities include *cassolette* of snails *forestière*, guineafowl with vanilla and fresh figs, chicken with seasonal fruits and pigeon with *pêche de vigne*. They also do good vegetarian platters and terrines with a range of menus starting at €18.50, including a glass of Mâcon, to €28.50. The terrace is superb in summer and it's a good idea to book. *Free house liqueur offered to our readers on presentation of this guide.*

Berzé-la-Ville

71960 (10km SE)

ⓐ 🏃 🏠 |◉| Relais du Mâconnais**

La Croix-Blanche; from Cluny, take the D980 in the direction of Mazille, then follow the D17.
☎03.85.36.60.72 ℗03.85.36.65.47
ⓦwww.lannuel.com
Closed *Sun evening and Mon in low season; Mon lunch July–Sept; 6 Jan–6 Feb.* **TV. High chairs available. Car park.**

The quiet atmosphere here will be to many people's liking and the well-spaced tables mean that you won't overhear your neighbours. Fittingly, Christian Lannuel's cooking has a very personal touch. The appetizers (foie gras confit with red Mâcon, strawberry and rhubarb chutney) are so original that they deserve to be upgraded to the status of starters, and there's a good dessert trolley. Other dishes, based on local produce, are finely flavoured: try *escalope* of foie gras with raspberry vinegar, milk-fed veal cutlets with vegetables *au gratin* or roast pigeon with garlic purée and sautéed mushrooms. The cheapest menu at €24 is served every day; other menus at €34–79, with a children's menu at €11. Ten or so comfy double rooms with shower or bath are €59–69; half board costs €63–67 per person. *Free coffee offered to our readers on presentation of this guide.*

Milly-Lamartine

71960 (16km SE)

ⓐ 🏃 |◉| Chez Jack

Place de l'Église; take the D980 in the direction of Mazille, then follow the D17.
☎03.85.36.63.72
Closed *Mon; Tues evening; Sun evening; all weekday evenings in low season; a week during Feb school holiday; end Aug to early Sept; a week at the end of the year.* **Disabled access.**

A lovely little village restaurant in the shadow of a beautiful church and Lamartine's house, boasting good Beaujolais cooking. Dishes include calf's foot *remoulade*, veal kidneys in cream, *andouillette* with mustard sauce, *entrecôte* steak, hot sausage with Beaujolais and *tablier de sapeur* (a slab of ox tripe egged, crumbed and fried). There's a weekday lunch menu €11; dinner menu €16.50; Sunday and public holidays, menus at €18.50 and €21.50. À la carte, a meal will cost €18.30–22 on average. Tables are set outside on fine days and there's a good wine selection by the jug or the bottle: Mâcon rouge, Régnié, Pouilly-Fuissé and so on. *Free coffee offered to our readers on presentation of this guide.*

Cosne-sur-Loire

58200

ⓐ 🏃 🏠 |◉| Hôtel-restaurant Le Saint-Christophe**

Place de la Gare; it's opposite the train station (500m).
☎03.86.28.02.01 ℗03.86.26.94.28
Closed *Sun evening; Fri; 24 July–22 Aug; 25 Dec–2 Jan.* **TV.**

Comfortable rooms with shower/wc or bath are €38.50–43.50. The smiling owner seems to be doing things right in the newly renovated restaurant too, which serves straightforward, robust cooking and is popular with locals. The weekday set lunchtime menu of main course with a choice of starter or dessert costs €14, with other menus €20–37 and options à la carte. *10% discount on the room rate (weekends) offered to our readers on presentation of this guide.*

ⓐ 🏃 🏠 |◉| Le Vieux Relais***

11 rue Saint-Agnan; in the town centre, near the Eden Cinema.
☎03.86.28.20.21
ⓦwww.le-vieux-relais.fr
Closed *Fri evening, Sat lunch and Sun evening from Sept–May; 25 Dec–10 Jan.* **TV. Pay car park.**

A coaching inn straight out of the nineteenth century. The double rooms are cosy and spacious, as you would expect for the price range (€85–90); half-board €70 per person, compulsory for a stay of 3 nights or more. The cooking is one of the establishment's great strengths. Father and son team up in the kitchen, while mother and daughter-in-law run the dining room. It's a popular place. Specialities include Charolais beef or pike-perch; the cheapest menu is €18 (weekdays only), with others ranging from €25 to €35, and a children's menu at €12 which includes fish, vegetables and chocolate mousse – not just the usual *steak frites*. There's a dream of a courtyard with a balcony overgrown with Virginia creeper and a puzzle of higgledy-piggledy roofs. Logis de France. *Free house apéritif offered to our readers on presentation of this guide.*

Creusot (Le)

71200

ⓔ |●| Le Restaurant

Rue des Abattoirs; coming from Marteau-Pilon, to the south, turn right into rue des Abattoirs; after 500m it's indicated on the left; it's at the end of a cul-de-sac.
☎03.85.56.32.33
Closed *Sun; Mon evening; 1–20 Aug.*
Disabled access.

In a rather unlikely location near the abattoirs, an area that's pretty deserted at night, this culinary beacon is well worth seeking out and it's advisable to book for dinner. You'll find a friendly welcome and a convivial atmosphere in the bright, vividly coloured dining room topped with a mezzanine. The decoration is elegant and uncluttered, with some interesting paintings, and the old zinc bar provides a traditional touch. Inspired cooking based on exhaustive research and a balance between the natural taste of fresh, seasonal ingredients and a skilful use of herbs: eel with onion *confit* sprinkled with parsley, braised red mullet with fennel, veal kidneys with liquorice gravy, rabbit with gingerbread, farm-reared lamb with mint. Menus start at €14, on request at dinner, and then €18–32; reckon on around €25 à la carte. Wonderful selection of wines at a wide range of prices, including some that can be taken away by the bottle. Credit cards not accepted.

Torcy

71210 (3km SE)

ⓔ |●| ⚶ Le Vieux Saule

Route du Creusot; take the D28.

☎03.85.55.09.53
Closed *Sun evening; Mon.* **High chairs available.**

A beautiful setting – an old country inn at the entrance to Creusot – a cheerful atmosphere and some of the tastiest cooking in the region. On weekdays, the cheapest menu costs €15.50, but for a little more the one at €17 is excellent value; after that, there are others in the range €25–64. Dishes include: pastry with frogs' legs and herbs, lobster and scallop casserole, pheasant pie with leeks and foie gras. The desserts are similarly imaginative and there's a good wine list. *Marc du Bourgogne liqueur offered to our readers on presentation of this guide.*

Uchon

71190 (16km W)

ⓔ ⚶ 🏠 |●| Auberge La Croix Messire Jean

La Croix Messire Jean; 1km from Uchon; head for Montcenis, then take the D228.
☎03.85.54.42.06
Closed *Tues evening; Wed; Christmas to New Year.* **High chairs and games available. Car park.**

Ideal base for walkers and bikers planning to tackle the splendid routes up one of the highest mountains (684m) in the *département*. This is a friendly inn and one of only three that have been classified as *Bistrot Accueil du Parc du Morvan*, all offering authentic dishes using local ingredients. The rooms have tasteful, rustic décor and prices to suit all pockets, with doubles at €21. There's a half board option for €39. It's best to book in high season. There's a large, shaded terrace where you can enjoy the exceptionally reasonable set menus, which start at €10.50 and then range from €14 to €21. Mountain bikes are available for rent. *Free coffee or 10% discount on the price of a room (minimum stay of three days) or free use of a mountain bike (with full board only) offered to our readers on presentation of this guide.*

Decize

58300

ⓔ |●| Auberge des Feuillats

116 rte. des Feuillats; take boulevard Voltaire from the tourist office. Cross the bridge of the

152ᵉ-R-I and then take the Moulins road; the inn is 1km away, on the left.
☎03.86.25.05.19.
Closed *Mon and Tues in winter.*

The terrace to the rear, on the edge of a canal leading off the Loire, provides a good view of the pleasure boats going to and fro, setting the tone for the holiday atmosphere inside. You can choose the lunchtime menu for €10 (with full board only) and others at €13–24. This is the place to enjoy Charolais steak, but the service can be slightly sloppy.

◎ 🎋 |●| Restaurant La Grignotte

57 av. du 14-Juillet.
☎03.86.25.26.20
Closed *Sun; Mon evening; a week in March; first fortnight in Aug; last week in Dec.* **High chairs available.**

An unpretentious restaurant unfortunately situated on a busy road. The floral dining room is lovely. You can eat decently and cheaply: the lunch menu (not Sunday) costs €10.50 with others in the range €11.50–35. Fondues are the house speciality, but also of interest are the pies, shellfish and large selection of salads. *Free house apéritif offered to our readers (with a menu at €19.50 or more) on presentation of this guide.*

◎ |●| Le Charolais

33 bis rte. de Moulins.
☎03.86.25.22.27 ☎03.86.25.52.52
🌐www.decize.net/charolais
Closed *Sun evening and Mon (except public holidays); first week in Jan; a week in Feb.* **Disabled access.**

An attractive dining room with quiet service, refined cuisine and a covered terrace at the back. The cheapest menu, at €15.50, will allow you to judge, or there's a dish of the day for €13; other menus €24.50–51.

Digoin

71160

◎ 🎋 🏠 |●| Les Diligences**

14 rue Nationale; it's on a pedestrian street in the town centre.
☎03.85.53.06.31 ☎03.85.88.92.43
🌐www.les-diligences.com
Closed *Mon evening and Tues except July–Aug; Dec.* **TV. High chairs available. Car park.**

In the seventeenth century, travellers arriving in the town by mail coach or boat stayed at this inn. It has recently been restored and the exposed stonework, beams, polished furniture and gleaming coppers make it look very smart. But that doesn't mean the prices in the restaurant are insane: set menus start at €17 (every day, for lunch and dinner), with other menus at €24 and €37. Dining à la carte, you'll find lobster and crayfish tail salad with raspberry vinegar, Charolais fillet steak with five peppers, *fricassée* of ceps Bordeaux-style and John Dory fillet with watercress sauce – all are a bit pricey. Six tastefully decorated and fully refurbished rooms, €45–50 with shower or bath, overlook the quiet banks of the Loire; nos. 6, 8 and 11 are particularly recommended, as they are spacious and have stunning views of the river. If you need even more space, there's also a duplex, a veritable apartment, with a private spa in its huge bathroom. Logis de France. *Free coffee offered to our readers on presentation of this guide.*

Neuzy

71160 (3km NE)

◎ 🎋 🏠 |●| Le Merle Blanc***

36 rte. de Gueugnon-Autun; take the D994 going towards Autun.
☎03.85.53.17.13 ☎03.85.88.91.71
🌐perso.wanadoo.fr/lemerleblanc
Closed *Sun evening; Mon lunchtime.* **Disabled access. TV. Car park.**

The hotel is set back from the road and offers double rooms at €33–46. The substantial set menu at €14.50 (not Sun) and others at €19–38.50 list dishes such as pan-fried duck foie gras terrine with grapes, scallops with Noilly-Prat, Charolais sirloin and fried langoustines with artichokes. Logis de France. *Free house apéritif offered to our readers on presentation of this guide.*

Dijon

21000

See map on pp.166–167.

◎ 🎋 🏠 Hôtel du Palais**

23 rue du Palais; follow the signs to the "Palais des Ducs de Bourgogne" until you arrive in front of another palace (the Palais de Justice). **Map B2-2**
☎03.80.67.16.26

℗03.80.65.12.16
✉hoteldupalais-dijon@wanadoo.fr
TV.

A superb location in the (surprisingly quiet) old city centre, opposite the municipal library (worth a visit, even if you don't intend to read the books) and the Palace of Justice. Most of the rooms – simple but clean and cheerful – have been refurbished and soundproofed; doubles with washbasin go for €20, and with shower/wc or bath €34–50. There's also a beautiful breakfast room with an impressive old ceiling. *10% discount on the price of a room (early Nov to end Feb) offered to our readers on presentation of this guide.*

🛏 Hôtel Le Jacquemart**

32 rue Verrerie; in the heart of the old city, in the antique dealers' neighbourhood, between the Palais des Ducs de Bourgogne and the Préfecture. **Map B1-3**
℗03.80.60.09.60 ℗03.80.60.09.69
🌐www.hotel-lejacquemart.fr
TV.

A huge, old, eighteenth-century house with dauntingly steep stairs and creaky corridors offers rooms with varying degrees of comfort at a range of prices: doubles with washbasin €30, shower/wc or bath €46–48. The rooms are quiet and comfortable and some have recently been renovated. A hotel with old-fashioned charm and friendly service that is ideal for a well-earned rest after a day spent exploring old Dijon; it is also popular with actors on tour and travelling sales agents. *10% discount on the room rate (Dec–March inclusive) offered to our readers on presentation of this guide.*

🛏 Hôtel Le Chambellan**

92 rue Vannerie; close to the Palais des Ducs de Bourgogne and the Saint-Michel church. **Map C2-1**
℗03.80.67.12.67 ℗03.80.38.00.39
✉hotelchambellan@aol.com
TV.

This is the place if you're after the splendours of yesteryear combined with the convenience of mod cons. It's an old building and a delightfully old-fashioned establishment with regularly renovated rooms at extremely reasonable prices; doubles with shower €31; €42–48 with shower/wc or bath. They've all got character, but go for one overlooking the seventeenth-century courtyard. *10% discount*

on the price of a room offered to our readers on presentation of this guide.

🛏 Hôtel Victor Hugo**

23 rue des Fleurs; 5 minutes on foot from the place Darcy. **Map A1-5**
℗03.80.43.63.45 ℗03.80.42.13.01
TV. Pay car park.

Located in Dijon's sedate, middle-class neighbourhood, this isn't the place to let your hair down: it's quiet, spotless and has an atmosphere that is ever so slightly staid. There are twenty or so comfortable, welcoming rooms; doubles €32.50 with washbasin, €37.50 with shower/wc and €46 with bath. *Free parking in the garage offered to our readers on presentation of this guide.*

🛏 Hôtel des Allées**

27 cours du Général-de-Gaulle. **Off map C3-6**
℗03.80.66.57.50
℗03.80.36.24.81
🌐www.hotelallees.com
TV. High chairs available. Car park.

Set in an old villa once used as a maternity hospital, opposite the paths (*allées*) in the park that were traditionally used for strolling but have now been invaded by rollerbladers. The building has a certain charm and the rooms have recently been refurbished; doubles with shower/wc or bath €48–59. There's a pretty garden full of birds. Reception is closed on Sunday and on public holidays from noon to 5pm. The hotel itself closes at 11pm, so you have to ask for the code to get back in.

🍴 Au Goût du Jour

24 rue Chaudronnerie. **Map B2-14**
℗03.80.67.47.99
Closed Sun (except third Sun of month, day of flea market); Mon–Wed evenings; last week of July and first fortnight in Aug. **Disabled access.**

The chef finds reliable suppliers at the market (no mean feat) and keeps his lunch prices down. His regular lunchtime clientele comes back in the evening to enjoy a drink on the terrace with a good sandwich of Comté cheese or mountain ham, pike soufflé with crayfish bisque or duck *aiguillettes* with Cassis. There's a lunch *menu du marché* for €11.70, with other menus €17.50 and 23.10. The service is good humoured and efficient, and the terrace is

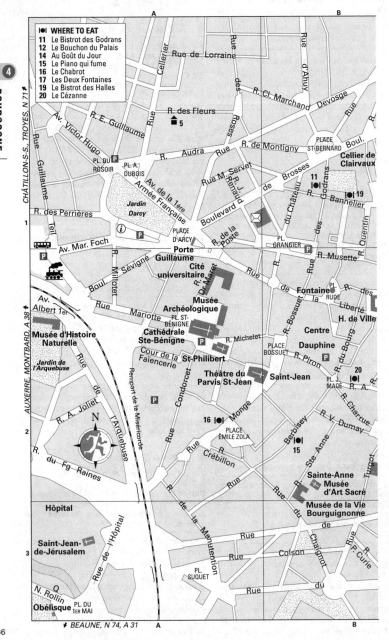

|●| WHERE TO EAT
11 Le Bistrot des Godrans
12 Le Bouchon du Palais
14 Au Goût du Jour
15 Le Piano qui fume
16 Le Chabrot
17 Les Deux Fontaines
19 Le Bistrot des Halles
20 Le Cézanne

CHÂTILLON-S.-S. TROYES, N 71

Rue de Lorraine

Rue d'Anhuy

R. Cl. Marchand

Devosge

Rue

R. des Fleurs
■ 5

R. E. Guillaume

Rue des Roses

R. de Montigny

PLACE ST-BERNARD

Boul.

Cellier de Clairvaux

Av. Victor Hugo

R. Guillaume

PL. DU ROSOIR

PL. A. DUBOIS

R. Audra

Rue M. Servet

R. J. Renard

de Brosses

11
|●|
Godrans

|●| 19
Bannelier

Av. de la 1ère Armée Française

Jardin Darcy

Boulevard

R. de la Poste

du Château

R. Quentin

R. des Perrières

Teil

Av. Mar. Foch

ⓘ

PLACE D'ARCY

PL. GRANGIER

R. Musette

Boul. Militot

R. Sévigné

Porte Guillaume

Cité universitaire

R. D. Maret

Rue

de

Fontaine
PL. RUDE

R. des

Liberté

Av. Albert 1er

Rue Mariotte

Musée Archéologique

PL. ST-BÉNIGNE

R. Michelet

R. de Bossuet

H. de Ville

Musée d'Histoire Naturelle

Cathédrale Ste-Bénigne

Cour de la Faïencerie

St-Philibert

PLACE BOSSUET

R. Piron

Centre Dauphine

du Bourg

AUXERRE, MONTBARD, A 38

Jardin de l'Arquebuse

Rue de l'Arquebuse

R. A. Joliet

Condorcet

Rempart de la Miséricorde

Théâtre du Parvis St-Jean

Saint-Jean

20
|●|
PL. J. MACÉ

R. A.

R. Charrue

N

16 |●|

Monge

R. V. Dumay

R. du Fg Raines

PLACE ÉMILE ZOLA

Rue Crébillon

Berbisey

|●|
15

Ste-Anne

Hurgot

Sainte-Anne Musée d'Art Sacré

Hôpital

Rue de la Menutention

Rue

Musée de la Vie Bourguignonne

de

R. P. Curie

Saint-Jean-de-Jérusalem

Rue de l'Hôpital

PL. SUQUET

Rue

Colson

Chaignot

N. Rollin

Obélisque

PL. DU 1ER MAI

Rue

du

BEAUNE, N 74, A 31

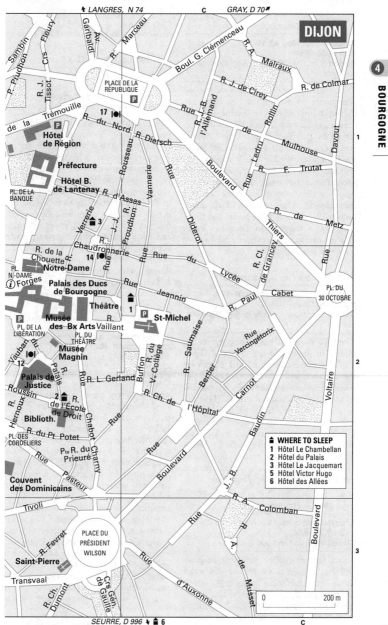

LANGRES, N 74   C   GRAY, D 70

DIJON

Garibaldi
Av.
R. Marceau
Boul. G. Clémenceau
R. A. Malraux
R. de Colmar
Crs Fleury
Sambin
P. Prudhon
R. J. Tissot
R. J. de Cirey
Rotlin
Davout

PLACE DE LA RÉPUBLIQUE

de la Trémouille
17
R. du Nord
R. Diersch
Rousseau
Rue   L.-B.
l'Allemand
de
Mulhouse
Ledru
F. Trutat

Hôtel de Région

Préfecture

Hôtel B. de Lantenay
R. d'Assas
Vannerie
Rue
Boulevard
R.
R. de Metz
Thiers

PL. DE LA BANQUE

Verrerie
3
J.-J. Proudhon
Diderot
R. Cl. de Grancey

R. de la Chouette
Chaudronnerie
R.
14
Rue
Rue   du
Lycée
Rue

PL. N.-DAME
Forges
Notre-Dame

Palais des Ducs de Bourgogne
Rue
Jeannin
R. Paul
Cabet

PL. DU 30 OCTOBRE

Théâtre
1
St-Michel

Musée des Bx Arts
Vaillant
Saumaise
Rue
Vercingétorix

PL. DE LA LIBÉRATION
PL. DU THÉÂTRE

Vauban
12
Musée Magnin

Palais de Justice
R. du Palais
R. L. Gerland
Buffon
R. du V.-Collège
R.
Berbier
Carnot
Voltaire

Roussin
2
R. de l'École de Droit
R. Ch. de l'Hôpital
Baudin

Hernoux
Biblioth.
R. Chabot Charny
Rue

PL. DES CORDELIERS
R. du Pt Potet
Rue

P.te R. du Prieuré

Couvent des Dominicains
Rue
Pasteur
Boulevard

Tivoli
Colomban
J.-B.
R. A.

PLACE DU PRÉSIDENT WILSON
Rue
A. de Musset
Boulevard

R. Fevret
Saint-Pierre

Transvaal
R. Ch. Dumont
Crs Gén de Gaulle
Rue
d'Auxonne

⌂ WHERE TO SLEEP	
1	Hôtel Le Chambellan
2	Hôtel du Palais
3	Hôtel Le Jacquemart
5	Hôtel Victor Hugo
6	Hôtel des Allées

0   200 m

very pleasant. *Free coffee offered to our readers on presentation of this guide.*

@ 🕏 |●| **Le Chabrot**

36 rue Monge. **Map A2-16**
☎ 03.80.30.69.61
Closed Sun; first fortnight in Aug. Open until 10.30pm.

Enter through the wine cellar (choose your bottle on the way) and go on to eat in the bistro or the restaurant upstairs; there's even a tiny terrace. Wines are also served by the glass: Coteaux de l'Auxois and Epineuil red for example. The cooking is emphatically local with a few twists: try the parsleyed ham, *coq au vin*, the pressed goat and smoked salmon, or the signature dish, salmon *unilatérale* (cooked on one side). The weekday lunch menu costs €12, others at €21–30.50, and there are plates of Burgundian specialities available all day long. *Free coffee offered to our readers on presentation of this guide.*

@ 🕏 |●| **Les Deux Fontaines**

16 pl. de la République. **Map B1-17**
☎ 03.80.60.86.45
Closed Sun; Mon; fortnight in Aug. **Disabled access.**

The *Two Fountains* has sprung up in the middle of the square, the centre of Dijon life. This restaurant has a quiet corner by the entrance and a bar at the top of the stairs where you can take in the décor with its watering cans and flowerpots. There are benches and bistro tables, pleasant service and nice wines from small vineyards. Cooking is traditional and rustic, and prices are gentle on the pocket – lunch *formules* €13 or €14; reckon on around €26 à la carte. *Free house apéritif offered to our readers on presentation of this guide.*

@ 🕏 |●| **Le Bouchon du Palais**

4 rue Bouhier; in the city centre. **Map B2-12**
☎ 03.80.30.19.98
Closed Wed; Sat and Sun lunchtimes.

An old favourite offering efficient, attentive and kindly service. Guests are still asked to decorate the paper tablecloths, which are then put up on the walls. The cooking remains straightforward and consistent in quality, and the helpings are ample: gratinéed marrow bone, *andouillette* terrine, calf's head or "*joyeuses*" (white kidneys) of lamb. There's a lunchtime set menu based

around the dish of the day for €14, and other menus at €17 and €20. When the chef is off duty, he is more than likely to offer you a drink at the bar. *Free coffee offered to our readers on presentation of this guide.*

@ 🕏 |●| **Le Piano Qui Fume**

36 rue Berbisey. Map B2-15
☎ 03.80.30.35.45
Closed Wed; Sat lunch; Sun evening; first fortnight in Jan; first 3 weeks in Aug .

The *Smoking Piano* consistently offers seasonal dishes that bring out the taste of the ingredients without any elaborate trickery. The chef returned to his home town after spells working with some of France's most prestigious chefs (Veyrat, Thorel, Tarridec) and seven years of critical acclaim in charge of the *Pot d'Étain* in L'Isle-sur-Serein. There is only a narrow range of dishes on offer, but they are all excellent, reasonably priced and remarkable for their simplicity, professionalism and refusal to bow to passing fads; cheapest weekday menu €15 (lunch and dinner), with others at €25 and €28, or reckon on €45 à la carte. *Free coffee offered to our readers on presentation of this guide.*

@ |●| 🕏 **Le Bistrot des Halles**

10 rue Bannelier; opposite the renovated covered market. **Map B1–19**
☎ 03.80.49.94.15
Closed Sun; Mon.

One of *the* places to eat in the Burgundy region. A lively, old-style bistro (large mirrors, chequered tablecloths) run by one of Burgundy's greatest chefs, Jean-Pierre Billoux, with an attractive terrace giving onto the market. It must be said though that the bistro (an annexe to Billoux's pricier restaurant in place de la Libération) has as many fervent admirers as vociferous detractors who curse the setting, the atmosphere and the noise. The food and the remarkably low prices – lunchtime menu at €16, or reckon on around €20 à la carte – brook no argument, however: old-fashioned *pâté en croûte*, ham terrine with parsley, or dishes of the day. In addition, there are superb local specialities and grilled dishes, along with some fine, reasonably priced wines. *Free house apéritif offered to our readers on presentation of this guide.*

@ 🕏 |●| **Le Cézanne**

40 rue Amiral-Roussin; in a pedestrian street; leave your car in the Sainte-Anne car park.

Map B2-20
☎03.80.58.91.92 ℻03.80.49.86.80
🌐www.bienpublic.com
Closed *Sun; Mon lunchtime; 18 Aug–1 Sept;
22–30 Dec.* **High chairs available.**

Located in an old, pedestrianized street,
the restaurant has vintage stonework and
beams and an intimate atmosphere brightened up by the Provençal décor. The
chef's cooking has become a gastronomic
yardstick in the town. You won't be disappointed by the quality, even of the cheapest menu chalked up on the blackboard
at €10.90 (except Sat evenings). Other
menus are €27–40, and you'll pay about
€40 à la carte. Pleasant little terrace in
summer and very attentive service. *Free
coffee offered to our readers on presentation of
this guide.*

ⓒ 🍴 |●| Le Bistrot des Godrans

28 rue des Godrans. **Map B1-11**
☎03.80.30.46.07
Closed *Sun.*

This old friend has had a youthful re-
think. Out go the drinkers who propped
up the bar, in come stylish waitresses and
dishes of the day that aren't swamped with
unnecessary garnishes. But they've kept
the old chairs, so this is less a revolution
than an evolution. As well as steak *tartare*,
the chef's speciality, dishes include black
pudding with apples (only in winter),
and plates of sausage and ham. You'll pay
around €20–25 à la carte. *Free coffee offered
to our readers on presentation of this guide.*

Hauteville-lès-Dijon
21121 (4km NW)

ⓒ 🍴 🏠 |●| La Musarde**

7 rue des Riottes; 5 min from Dijon, on the
N71 road to Troyes.
☎03.80.56.22.82 ℻03.80.56.64.40
📧hotel.rest.lamusarde@wanadoo.fr
Closed *Tues; Sun evening; 19 Dec–11Jan.*
**Disabled access (restaurant only). TV. High
chairs and games available. Car park.**

Nowadays it's also a restaurant, with a nice
terrace, and it's best to book, especially at
the weekends, to be sure of a table. The
informal, relaxed atmosphere is at the
same time sophisticated and professional.
It's run by Marc Ogé, a true Breton with
his feet planted firmly on the ground.
His dishes include foie gras cooked in a
cloth; pigeon *tajine*; and scallops and pike
perch with saffron. Set menus €22–44,

with weekday menu (lunch and dinner) at
€17 including wine and coffee. Attractive
bedrooms go for €56–64. Credit cards
not accepted. Logis de France. *Free house
apéritif offered to our readers on presentation
of this guide.*

Prenois
21370 (9km NW)

ⓒ 🍴 |●| Auberge de la Charme

Take the N7 in the direction of Val-Suzon,
then the D104.
☎03.80.35.32.84
📧davidlacharme@aol.com
Closed *Sun evening; Mon and Tues lunchtimes; Feb school holiday; 1–15 Aug.*
Disabled access.

Even though the chef's reputation has
grown considerably, the prices remain
very attractive. He uses good-quality, local
produce from which he concocts interesting dishes, seasoned and presented with a
rare attention to detail. There's a set menu
€18 weekday lunchtimes, with four more
menus priced €23–70. This is the best
establishment in these parts and not to be
missed. *Free coffee offered to our readers on
presentation of this guide.*

Donzy
58220

ⓒ 🍴 🏠 |●| Le Grand Monarque**

10 rue de l'Étape; it's near the church (the
bells chime at 8am and 9pm).
☎03.86.39.35.44
🌐www.multimania.com/grandmonarque/
Closed *Sun evening and Mon out of season;
Jan.* **TV. Disabled access. Car park.**

This is a delightful village with a number
of fifteenth-century, half-timbered buildings. The hotel is the old stone house
practically next door to the Romanesque
church, but don't worry – the bells don't
ring between 9pm and 8am. It offers
rustic charm with all mod cons and
a warm, tastefully decorated interior.
Spacious doubles – some have brand-new
bathrooms, and two have been entirely
refurbished – with shower/wc or bath
are €54–56. Good-quality regional cooking with a number of fish dishes on the
set menus: €14 (weekday lunchtimes)
and €23–39. Logis de France. *Free house
apéritif offered to our readers on presentation
of this guide.*

Dun-les-Places

58230

@ 犬 🏠 |❍| **L'Auberge Ensoleillée**

It's on the D6 Lormes to Saulieu road.
☏ 03.86.84.62.76 ℗ 03.86.84.64.57
Closed Christmas; evenings out of season.
Car park.

A typical Morvan inn run by three women – one at the bar, one in the restaurant and one in the kitchen – offering a warm welcome and traditional, local recipes so it's best to book. The substantial weekday menu costs €14.50 and there are others priced €21.50–38. Simple rooms cost €22.50–43 for a double with shower or bath. *Free coffee offered to our readers on presentation of this guide.*

Gevrey-Chambertin

21220

@ 犬 🏠 |❍| **Aux Vendanges de Bourgogne**

47 rte. de Beaune; on the outskirts of town, on the main road.
☏ 03.80.34.30.24 ℗ 03.80.58.55.44
ⓦ www.hotel-bourgogne.com
Closed Sun and Mon; fortnight around Christmas. **TV. Car park.**

Among the gourmet restaurants, world-renowned cellars and inflated prices of the area is this old-fashioned hotel-restaurant. It has a warm Art Deco décor with a stencilled ceiling and stained glass lampshades and there's an interior terrace. Good local dishes in hearty portions at reasonable prices, all charmingly served. Menus change according to the season and what's good at the market; menus €21.50–39. The arrival of the owner's son in the kitchen has steered the menu towards new horizons. Local wines that are usually impossible to find unless you know the grower come at very reasonable prices. Despite being in the epicentre of great Burgundies, they even serve wine by the glass. Double rooms with shower/wc or bath cost €48–54. *Free coffee offered to our readers on presentation of this guide.*

@ 犬 |❍| **Chez Guy**

3 pl. de l'Hôtel-de-Ville.
☏ 03.80.58.51.51 ℗ 03.80.58.50.39
ⓦ www.hotel-bourgogne.com

Closed Wed.

The attempt to be "chic" (and the prices that go with it) are let down by the rather plain décor in the large dining room (choose the terrace in summer), but the service is friendly though rather laid-back. Traditional Burgundy dishes with innovative touches that win over tourists and locals alike with a range of menus priced €21.50–28.50; children's menu €10. An attractive choice of Gevrey wines (but not necesssarily cheap). Reservation is strongly recommended. *Free coffee offered to our readers on presentation of this guide.*

Joigny

89300

@ 犬 🏠 |❍| **Le Paris-Nice****

Rond-point de la Résistance.
☏ 03.86.62.06.72 ℗ 03.86.62.56.99
Closed Sun evening and Mon; 3 weeks in Jan–Feb; fortnight in early Sept . **TV. Car park.**

The N6 from Paris to Nice used to be known as the "Route des Anglais" before the motorway to the Côte d'Azur was built. Those were the glory days of this establishment, though it's recently been done up by its new owners and there's a fine, shady terrace. There are ten simple rooms, all with double-glazing; they're yours for €43 with shower or bath. Good restaurant serving traditional fare and regional dishes: roast pork with honey, salmon with frogs' legs, *île flottante* with spiced bread. Menus go for €10.50 and €13.50 on weekdays only, then €18.50 and €25. Logis de France. *Free house apéritif offered to our readers on presentation of this guide.*

@ 犬 🏠 |❍| **Le Rive Gauche*****

Chemin du Port-au-Bois (Sud-Ouest); it's on the banks of the Yonne, very close to the old town.
☏ 03.86.91.46.66 ℗ 03.86.91.46.93
ⓔ lorain@dial.oleane.com
Closed Sun evening; early Nov to mid-March.
Disabled access. TV. High chairs available. Car park.

The Lorains realized that things were changing – so they constructed a modern building looking just like a chain hotel opposite their famous *Côte Saint-Jacques* (ⓦ www.cotesaintjacques.com) and left it in the capable hands of their daughter. The new establishment is welcoming, with attractive, fully equipped rooms – doubles €60–107. There is a tennis court and also a flower garden. You can eat outside on the terraces, overlooking the Yonne, or in the bright, air-conditioned dining room, where the décor and the food both reflect modern tastes. The cooking is traditional bistro style, with set menus €18 (weekday lunchtimes) and others €27–35. Try lobster and basil ravioli or buckwheat pancakes with snails. Friendly service, and an additional bonus: guests can use the swimming pool in the *Relais & Château* on the other side of the river. If you fancy a dip, feel free to ask. *10% discount on the price of a room (except June–Aug) offered to our readers on presentation of this guide.*

Celle-Saint-Cyr (La)

89116 (8km W)

◎ ⅍ 🛏 |●| Auberge de la Fontaine aux Muses**

Take the D943 in the direction of the A6 motorway, then the D194 in the direction of Vaugenets.
℡03.86.73.40.22 🅕03.86.73.48.66
🅦www.fontaine-aux-muses.fr
Closed *Mon–Thurs, Oct–April (except public holidays); first fortnight in Jan.* **Disabled access. TV. Swimming pool. Car park.**

Hidden away in the Burgundy hills, this country house inn with tennis court and heated swimming pool is covered in Virginia creeper and has wonderfully rustic rooms: doubles with shower or bath for €58–96. The cooking is passionately Burgundian: *escalope* of foie gras with blueberries, duck breast with honey, hot oysters with caramelized endive, Burgundy beef and local wines. Set weekday menu €28 (apart from public holidays), or reckon on €37 à la carte; children's menu €9 (up to age 10). The Langevin family are musicians (father Claude composed the European anthem, no less), so their friends often turn up at weekends and a jam session frequently results – in front of a log fire in winter or in the garden in summer. They also have their own vineyard, the Fontaine aux Muses, which produces white (Chardonnay) and red (Pinot Noir) wines. *10% discount on the price of a room (1 Oct–31 March) offered to our readers on presentation of this guide.*

Villevallier

89330 (9km NW)

◎ 🛏 |●| ⅍ Le Pavillon Bleu**

31 rue de la République; take the N6, to the south of Villeneuve-sur-Yonne.
℡03.86.91.12.17 🅕03.86.91.17.74
Closed *Fri evening; Sun evening; 20 Dec–5 Jan; first fortnight in Aug.* **TV. Car park.**

With its friendly welcome and big blue shutters, this hotel is worth a detour and, furthermore, it is among the most reasonably priced in the area. Admittedly, the rooms are not very big, but they are delightful all the same and cost €35 for a double with washbasin, €40–45 with shower/wc or bath. Copious portions of home cooking on the cheapest menu at €16 (not Sun): snail salad, *œufs meurette*, beef fillet *au gratin* with local Époisse cheese; other menus €25–40. Logis de France. *Free house apéritif offered to our readers on presentation of this guide.*

Lormes

58140

◎ 🛏 |●| ⅍ Hôtel Perreau**

8 rte. d'Avallon; cross the town via the D944 main road from Avallon to Château-Chinon.
℡03.86.22.53.21 🅕03.86.22.82.15
Closed *Sun evening and Mon (early Oct to end May); 6 Jan–15 Feb.* **TV. Car park.**

The village hotel is an imposing and thoroughly restored old house with a large capacity. Spacious double rooms go for €47–60 with shower/wc or bath. The restaurant is pretty, in a rustic style with a large fireplace, and the food is sophisticated, with a particularly good menu of regional specialities; cheapest menu at €11, then others €20–28. Logis de France. *10% discount on a room offered to our readers on presentation of this guide.*

Vauclaix

58140 (8km S)

◎ 🛏 |●| Hôtel de la Poste**

From Lormes take the D944.
℡03.86.22.71.38 🅕03.86.22.76.00
🅦www.hotel-vauclaix.com
Closed *Feb school holiday.* **Disabled access. TV. High chairs and games available. Swimming pool. Car park.**

Located in deepest, darkest Morvan, this is a popular and friendly hotel. Five generations of Desbruères have run the place, and they're constantly doing it up and introducing new ideas – there's a swimming pool in the garden, a giant chess game and ping-pong. The rooms are big but cosy and cost €55 with shower/wc or bath; there are also suites available for €70. You can opt for half board: €54 per person for the rooms, €64 for the suites. It's worth the trip here for the cooking alone. The two-page menu changes regularly according to the season and offers traditional dishes on its €10 weekday menu; others €17–40. You can eat on the terrace, weather permitting. Logis de France.

Mâcon
71000

◎ 犬 ☎ Hôtel d'Europe et d'Angleterre**

92 quai Jean-Jaurès.
℡ 03.85.38.27.94
ⓦ www.hotel-europeangleterre-macon.com
TV. High chairs available. Pay car park.

This eighteenth-century building has character and, with its original staircase and large public rooms, offers the charm of a bygone era. The hotel has been tastefully renovated and is well located on the riverside; although it's right on the N6, the rooms – €45–65 for a double with shower/wc or bath – are soundproofed, and some of them have river views. Nos. 1, 6 and 9 are particularly attractive. *Free parking (except July and Aug) offered to our readers on presentation of this guide.*

◎ 犬 ☎ |●| Charm'hôtel Terminus

91 rue Victor-Hugo.
℡ 03.85.39.17.11 ℗ 03.85.38.02.75
ⓦ www.charmehotel.com
TV. Pay car park.

Astonishing hotel on the doorstep of the train station that hides a highly original interior design behind an old-fashioned façade – it also boasts a charming breakfast room, decorated in warm colours, and a garden with swimming pool. Some rooms (€62–70) retain their classical style, but most have been attractively refurbished along the lines of the murals at the head of each bed, painted by a member of the owner's family. As the mural is reflected in a large mirror, the effect is doubly striking.

Meals are also available every day; menus €18.50–23. Logis de France. *10% discount on the price of a room offered to our readers on presentation of this guide.*

◎ 犬 ☎ |●| Inter Hôtel de Bourgogne**

6 rue Victor-Hugo; follow the signposts to "La Poste"; it's close to the central pedestrian precinct.
℡ 03.85.38.36.57 ℗ 03.85.38.65.92
ⓔ hotel-de-bourgogne@wanadoo.fr
Restaurant closed *Sun; Mon; lunchtime every day (but opens exceptionally for 20 people); first 3 weeks in Jan.* **TV. Pay car park.**

Lovely hotel on a shady, flower-filled square just a step away from the pedestrian area. The interior is delightful with a foyer that's straight out of a Chabrol film, and lots of twists and turns, half-landings, nooks and crannies. Air-conditioned double rooms, painted in pastel shades, cost €63–80 with shower/wc or bath. Meals can be had in the hotel restaurant (€18–32), if you don't feel like venturing out in the evening. Logis de France. *10% discount on the price of a room offered to our readers on presentation of this guide.*

◎ |●| L'Amandier

74 rue Dufour; it's in the town centre, on a pedestrian street near the tourist office.
℡ 03.85.39.82.00 ℗ 03.85.39.82.21
Closed *Sun evening; Mon.* **High chairs available.**

Salad of pig's trotters *gribiche* is the house speciality, but Florent Segain often rejigs his menus to use what's best in the market. It's easy enough to find the restaurant since it's painted blue – the flowers and the plates are the same colour, complemented by the yellow fabrics in the cosy, comfortable dining room, and the terrace is adorned with flowers. Menus (served every day) in the range €19.50–48 include specialities such as *andouillette gratin* with steamed potatoes and roast herb-crusted lamb. Dish of the day (except Sat evening and Sun lunch) costs €12.

◎ |●| Le Poisson d'Or

Port de Plaisance; take the N6 towards Tournus, and it's 1km from the town centre on the banks of the Saône.
℡ 03.85.38.00.88
Closed *Tues evening; Wed; Sun out of season; fortnight end of March; fortnight end*

of Oct. **Disabled access. High chairs available. Car park.**

Contemplate the glinting lights in the water and the shady riverbanks from the picture windows of this plush but informal establishment, which also has a large, shaded terrace. It's a refined place, with tables covered in thick white cloths and enormous vases of flowers everywhere, matched by cooking that enlivens local traditions (pies with Époisse cheese matured in Marc brandy) and offering attentive service. The cheapest menu, €20, is served weekdays only; others €24.50–55.

Sancé

71000 (3km N)

✆ 🏠 |○| La Vieille Ferme**

Bd. du Général-de-Gaulle (Nord); take the N6, the Mâcon Nord exit.
☎03.85.21.95.15 📠03.85.21.95.16
🖥www.hotel-restaurant-lavieilleferme.com
Closed end Dec to early Jan.
Disabled access. TV. Swimming pool. Car park.

An old farm that has been tastefully restored and turned into a small hotel complex with a beautiful swimming pool in summer. It is particularly well positioned on the banks of the Saône, surrounded by real cornfields and real cows, patient anglers, and peaceful cyclists riding along the towpath. The modern part is built like a motel and most of the bedrooms, €47 with bathrooms, overlook the Saône or the countryside. They are spacious and pleasant and you hardly notice the high-speed train hurtling past. The lovely dining room has rustic décor and old-fashioned furniture but, on fine days, the terrace is everyone's favourite place to be. The classic dishes (baby-rabbit *compote*, sweetbreads with blueberries, parsleyed frogs' legs) are executed with care and are perfectly affordable (set menus €12–28); there's a generous lunchtime buffet.

Saint-Vérand

71570 (13km SW)

✆ 🎿 🏠 |○| L'Auberge de Saint-Vérand**

Lieu-dit La Roche; leave the A6 at exit 29 (in the direction of Vinzelles, Juliénas, Saint-Vérand).
☎03.85.23.90.90 📠03.85.23.90.91
🖥www.auberge-saint-veran.com

Closed *Mon and Tues (out of season).*
Disabled access. TV. High chairs and games available. Car park.

A beautiful stone house in a traditional village, with a terrace and garden, a stream nearby, and vineyards and rolling hills all around. A simple hotel, but it is clean and comfortable and the rooms, €56–66 with shower/wc, have been completely renovated. It's worth asking about the half board option. Menus featuring regional cooking cost €21–58.50, and there's an interesting list of local wines. Logis de France. *3% discount on the price of a room (half board only) or free bed for a half aged under two years or free glass of local Kir offered to our readers on presentation of this guide.*

Saint-Amour-Bellevue

71570 (14km SW)

✆ |○| L'Auberge du Paradis

Lieu-dit Le Plâtre-Durand; take the N6 in the direction of Romanèche; a small road in the village of Crêches-sur-Saône leads to Saint-Amour.
☎03.85.37.10.26
Closed *Mon; Tues; Jan.* **Disabled access. High chairs available.**

Pretty dining room decorated with pale colours and plenty of flowers, with some tables adapted from old sewing machines. The real spectacle, however, lies on the plates. The menu changes every two months, according to the availability of ingredients and the whim of the chef, a globetrotting gourmet, who acquired a love of spices and daring sweet/savoury mixtures in Turkey and Morocco. After spells with some of France's greatest chefs (Blanc, Chibois), he now works entirely alone to concoct his mouth-watering dishes and offers a small weekday lunchtime menu at €20, and more extensive ones at €30, €34 and €40 (selection of sample dishes). The service is friendly and the wine list remarkably cheap for the area. Seven delightful bedrooms are due to open this year.

Moux-en-Morvan

58230

✆ 🎿 🏠 |○| Hôtel-restaurant Beau Site*

Bellevue-Moux-en-Morvan: it's on the D121, 7km from the Settons lake.

☎03.86.76.11.75 ☎03.86.76.15.84
Closed *Sun evening and Mon 11 Nov–15
March; Dec and Jan.* **High chairs available.
Car park.**

An ordinary-looking place but the
name's appropriate – it's in a fantastic
setting. Sound home cooking at good
prices, specializing in traditional dishes
with lots of sauce. The menu at €11.80
(except Sun lunchtime) is very respectable; others are €15.50–32. Favourites
include snails with creamed garlic and
chicken terrine. In the hotel, a five-
minute walk away, there are cheap, simple
and spacious rooms; doubles with basin
€27.50 and up to €42 with bath. *Free
house apéritif offered to our readers on presentation of this guide.*

Nevers

58000

� **Hôtel Beauséjour****

5 bis rue Saint-Gildard; it's opposite the
shrine of Ste Bernadette, between the train
station and the town centre.
☎03.86.61.20.84 ☎03.86.59.15.37
Closed *Fri out of season; fortnight in
Aug; Christmas school holiday.* **TV. Pay car
park.**

Cheap, simple, functional rooms that are
kept spotlessly clean. Just out of the town
centre in a busy street, but everything is
well soundproofed and the garden rooms
are very quiet. Doubles with washbasin
go for €27; €33–45 with shower/wc
and a garden view. The welcome is really
charming and breakfast is available on the
veranda from a self-service buffet.

☼ ☆ ☎ **Hôtel de Clèves****

8 rue Saint-Didier; in a quiet street in the
town centre, not far from the train station.
☎03.86.61.15.87 ☎03.86.57.13.80
Closed *a week in Aug; 26 Dec–5 Jan.* **TV.
Pay car park.**

Well placed, not far from the station in
a quiet street in the town centre, this
small establishment is very well run by
an affable woman who's happy to chat
while you have breakfast. The rooms
have been updated with quality bedding;
doubles with shower €42, or €49 with
bath. There's a small, pleasant corner of
a garden. *10% discount on the room rate
offered to our readers on presentation of this
guide.*

☼ ☎ |●| **Hôtel Molière**

25 rue Molière. Take the boulevard du
Maréchal-Juin (ex-RN 7); when you get to the
BP petrol station, turn right into the rue de
Vauzelles and follow the signs.
☎03.86.57.29.96 ☎03.86.36.00.13
Closed *Fri evenings from Dec to Feb; 31
Jul–23 Aug; 16 Dec–9 Jan.* **TV. High chairs
available. Car park.**

A small hotel in a quiet spot near the town
centre run by a kindly, welcoming woman.
The rooms have excellent beds and are
bright and cheerful – half of them have
views over the garden. Doubles go for
€45 with shower/wc and €47 with bath,
although prices can vary on special occasions. There are some non-smoking rooms.
There's a big, enclosed (and free) car park
across the road. *One free breakfast per room
per night (early Nov to end Feb) offered to our
readers on presentation of this guide.*

☼ ☆ ☎ |●| **Hôtel-restaurant La
Folie**

Route des Saulaies; off the quai des
Mariniers.
☎03.86.57.05.31 ☎03.86.57.66.69
🖑www.hotel-lafolie.com
Restaurant closed *Fri and Sun evening
Sept–May; Fri lunchtime, June–Aug.* **Disabled
access. TV. High chairs, cots and games
available. Swimming pool. Car park.**

It's well worth choosing this place – its
park, tennis court and swimming pools
give it the atmosphere of a holiday club.
Bedrooms, very comfortable and contemporary in design, cost €50–52 with shower
or bath – no charge for children under 2
and cots are available. Two bedrooms are
set on the ground floor and are especially
well equipped for disabled guests. You
eat either in the dining room or on the
terrace, which has a distant view of the
Loire; cheapest menu at €13.50 (weekday
lunch only) and others €16.50–26.50. The
house specialities are calf's head and duck
breast. It's advisable to book. Credit cards
not accepted. *Free coffee offered to our readers
on presentation of this guide.*

☼ |●| ☆ **Le Goémon – Crêperie
Bretonne**

9 rue du 14-Juillet.
☎03.86.59.54.99
Closed *Sun; Mon; a week in March; end Aug
to mid-Sept.*

The setting is nothing special but the
service is friendly and the crêpes are good,

whether sweet or savoury (the crêpe with Guéméné *andouillette* is exquisite). Weekday lunchtime menu with starter, pancake and dessert costs €9.20; reckon on €14 à la carte.

ⓒ |●| Restaurant Aux Chœurs de Bacchus

25 av. du Général-de-Gaulle; near the train station.
ⓣ and ⓕ03.86.36.72.70
Closed *Mon and Sat lunch; Sun; a week in April; first 3 weeks in Aug; 23 Dec–3 Jan.*

Excellent little restaurant where the service is slick, fast and friendly. The cuisine has been honed and improved over the years; it's self-confident and delicious, and the dishes strictly follow the seasons. Specialities include the beef and the iced nougat. Enjoy wine carefully chosen to complement each dish, turning your meal into a feast fit for a king – at affordable prices. A €14.50 menu is served in the evenings as well as at lunchtime, and there are others at €19.80 and €31, with a children's menu at €7.70.

ⓒ |●| La Cour Saint-Étienne

33 rue Saint-Étienne; it's behind the church of Saint-Étienne.
ⓣ03.86.36.74.57 ⓕ03.86.61.14.95
Closed *Sun; Mon; 1–6 Jan; 6–15 Feb; 1–23 Aug.* **Disabled access.**

The talented chef concocts pleasing dishes using seasonal ingredients, with the high standard of presentation expected around these parts; menus €16 (not Sat evening) and others at €20 and €30. The only drawbacks are that the portions are slightly small and the service is off-hand. The bells of the nearby church of Saint-Étienne were evoked in *Hiroshima Mon Amour* by Marguerite Duras as ringing out the liberation of Nevers.

ⓒ |●| Restaurant Jean-Michel Couron

21 rue Saint-Étienne; follow the signs to "Centre-ville and parking Saint-Pierre"; the latter is 2 min away.
ⓣ03.86.61.19.28 ⓕ03.86.36.02.96
Closed *Mon; Tues; Sun evening; 2–19 Jan; 10 July–1 Aug.* **High chairs available.**

A Michelin star for the star restaurant of Nevers with three small, elegant rooms, one in a particularly charming Gothic style. Fine, well-balanced cuisine at good

prices: menus start at €20 (weekdays only; includes cheese or dessert), with others €28–45. Particularly recommended are the tomato tart, the Charolais beef and the stewed plaice fillet with a red pepper and sage *compote*. For dessert, the warm spiced chocolate soup is a delight. Booking is advisable.

Savigny-les-Bois

58160 (9km SE)

ⓒ 𝕬 |●| Restaurant Le Moulin de l'Étang

64 rte. de l'Étang; from Nevers, take the D978 towards Château–Chinon then turn right on to the D18. It's just outside the village, on the D209.
ⓣ03.86.37.10.17 ⓕ03.86.37.12.06
Closed *Mon; Wed evening; Sun evening; several weeks in winter.* **High chairs available. Car park.**

One of the area's best restaurants. The €17 menu lists a tasty *mignon* of pork in game marinade and excellent brawn, served with all its fat and a "slimline" *sauce gribiche*; you could try the beef in red wine or, for lighter eaters, a foie-gras salad with oyster mushrooms. Other menus go for €25–45 (selection of sample dishes). The desserts are a little disappointing – the *crème brûlée* is heavy and too sweet – but these are quibbles. The large, provincial-feeling dining room offers attentive, friendly service. *Free coffee, fruit juice or soft drink offered to our readers on presentation of this guide.*

Magny-Cours

58470 (12km S)

ⓒⓒⓒ 𝕬 ⓐ |●| Hôtel-restaurant La Renaissance****

2 rue de Paris. It's in the village; take the N7.
ⓣ03.86.58.10.40 ⓕ03.86.21.22.60
ⓦwww.hotel-la-renaissance.fr
Closed *Sat lunch; Sun evening; Mon; 3 weeks in Feb/March; a fortnight in Aug.* **TV. Car park.**

A smart hotel-restaurant with a good local reputation for its cooking. It's about 3km from Magny-Cours car-racing circuit and full of guys from the pits who enjoy the chef's tasty meals. He uses the freshest produce to create dishes like pan-fried frogs' legs in herb butter with vegetables; braised turbot with pink grapefruit and white port; roast duck breast with pepper. Good Loire wines at affordable prices, served in a pleasant dining room with attentive service. The menus range in price from €40 to €60. Bedrooms have good facilities and cost from €84 to €92 for a double with shower/wc or bath and €107–153 for one of the three luxurious suites. *Free house apéritif offered to our readers on presentation of this guide.*

Nitry
89310

@ 🏠 |❋| Auberge La Beursaudière

Chemin de Ronde; it's on the Sacy road.
℡03.86.33.69.69 📠03.86.33.69.60
🌐www.beursaudiere.com
Closed *Mon evening Nov–March; second and third week in Jan.* **TV. High chairs available. Car park.**

A superb Morvan building with a medieval dovecote. There's an emphasis on "local" character here: waitresses in regional costume, quaint menu titles and the like, but the terrace is great – it really sizzles in summer. Sturdy local dishes built for robust appetites: mosaic of crayfish and scallops, knuckle of ham with *andouillette* terrine, ravioli with Époisse cheese and bacon and *Bersaudes*, the house speciality. In the week, there's an €11.50 *formule* of starter and a main course; the first real menu, served every day, costs €17, with others at €34 and €45; children's menu €8. Eleven hotel rooms, brand new and very comfortable but old-fashioned in style, with shower/wc or bath, cost €65–105.

Noyers-sur-Serein
89310 (10km NE)

@ 🎋 Hôtel Dieu Saint-Nicolas

22 rue de la République; take the D49; it's 300m from the exit to the village, going in the direction of Montbard.
℡03.86.75.97.36 📠03.86.82.65.13
✉maloszek@wanadoo.fr
Closed *12 Nov–1 April.* **Disabled access. High chairs and games available.**

A pleasant surprise close to the historic centre of Noyers, this old farm with a keep has been intelligently overhauled in a tasteful, modern style, and offers modernity in the old style, with high quality and accessibility. Bedecked with flowers and covered in contemporary paintings, it exudes tranquillity, with the courtyard turned into a terrace garden, clean, breezy rooms, beautiful furniture and a range of magazines at hand. Doubles with a view of the washhouse or garden are €61–68, including breakfast, and there's a suite for more than two people also available. The enormous breakfast is served in a lovely rustic room. The friendly owners will welcome you effusively and even lend you bikes to explore the region. *20% discount on the price of a third night in a room (except July–Aug and weekends) offered to our readers on presentation of this guide.*

Nolay
21340

@ 🎋 |❋| Restaurant Le Burgonde

35 rue de la République; on the Beaune-Autun axis; in the town centre, 200m from the town hall.
℡03.80.21.71.25
🌐www.nolay.net/restaurant.htm
Closed *Tues; Wed; Feb school holiday.* **High chairs available.**

Unusual dining room set in an old department store, with old windows, the original floor and a certain crazy charm. The tables are even decorated with brightly coloured (and roughly made) artworks. The chef will come out in his full regalia to explain the dishes on his menu. Selection of menus from €18.20 (except public holidays) to €52 – if you can't make your mind up, there's a regional menu with produce sourced by the chef from neighbouring farms and local producers. You'll pay around €40 à la carte, and wine prices are reasonable. *Free coffee offered to our readers on presentation of this guide.*

Nuits-Saint-Georges
21700

@ 🏠 |❋| Hôtel-bar de l'Étoile*

5 pl. de la Libération.
℡03.81.61.04.68
Closed *Wed.*

This small, family hotel may have only one star but it's certainly well deserved for its genuinely warm welcome alone. The simple, clean rooms have been refurbished, and those at the back are extremely quiet; doubles with washbasin €25 and with shower/wc €32–35. Small restaurant serving regional food: daily dish €8.50; menus

€14.70 and €16.70, wine by the glass and a good selection of real ale. The bar is an ideal place to catch up on local gossip. The kitchen is open from noon to 2.30pm and from 5 to 10pm, but the menu is shorter in the evening.

Villars-Fontaine
21220 (5km W)

◎ |O| Auberge du Coteau

Take the D25, then the D35.
☎03.80.61.10.50 ℻03.80.61.30.32
Closed *Tues evening; Wed; a fortnight in Feb; 15 Aug–5 Sept.* **Car park.**

This is a real country inn, serving home-made terrine, *coq au vin*, snails, beef and lots of other lovely local dishes – not for those on a diet. They'll satisfy your hunger after a walk through the vineyards and your thirst will be more than slaked by the local wines from the Hautes Côtes. There's an open fire, checked tablecloths and old-fashioned prices – the weekday lunch menu costs €10, with others at €14–22.

Vougeot
21640 (10km N)

◎ ⅍ 🏠 Hôtel de Vougeot

18 rue du Vieux-Château; take the N74 in the direction of Beaune.
☎03.80.62.01.15
🌐www.hotel-vougeot.com
Closed *Mon and Tues (Dec–March); 15 Jan–15 March.* **TV. Car park.**

Vougeot is world-famous for the wine festivals organized by the Confrérie du Clos Vougeot, founded to maintain the quality of Burgundy's wines and to promote them across the globe. This odd hotel, with its dreary façade, is not what you'd expect to find here, but the lovely courtyard and the peace and tranquillity make up for that. Double rooms, several with a view of the château and its vineyard, cost €49–85. It has a bar where they serve local wine. Everyone is treated well. *10% discount on the room rate (1 Nov–31 March) offered to our readers on presentation of this guide.*

Curtil-Vergy
21220 (18km NW)

◎ 🏠 Hôtel Le Manasses

Rue Guillaume-de-Tavanes; take the D25 then the D35 in the direction of Messanges.

☎03.80.61.43.81 ℻03.80.61.42.79
🌐www.ifrance.com/hotelmanasses
Closed *Dec–Feb.* **TV. Car park.**

There's a splendid view over the vineyards and a remarkable silence to this place. The Chaleys and other winegrowers in the area have built up the reputation of the wines from the Hautes Côtes. In his younger days, grandfather used to deliver his wines himself on foot; his son does the deliveries today, but at least he has a car. They have constructed this charming little hotel – very comfortable doubles €75–100, complete with marbled bathrooms – and turned a barn into a wine museum where you can sample the goods, with epic wine tasting sessions every evening from 6pm. Breakfast is served Burgundy-style. *Free house apéritif offered to our readers on presentation of this guide.*

Auvillars-sur-Saône
21250 (13km SE)

◎ ⅍ |O| Auberge de l'Abbaye

Route de Seurre; take the D35 then the D20.
☎03.80.26.97.37 ℻03.80.26.92.25
✉auberge-abbaye@wanadoo.fr
Closed *Sun evening; Tues evening; Wed.* **Car park.**

You simply have to stop here, before or after visiting the Citeaux Abbey, only 1km away. And the restaurant offers enough reasons of its own: succulent dishes – langoustine salad with hazelnuts and spice bread and pan-fried foie gras with fruits of the season – at reasonable prices. You can also eat in the delightful bistro corner and opt for the menu of the day, which costs €26 (weekday lunchtimes only); other menus €21.05–45. There's a picturesque terrace, too. *Free coffee offered to our readers on presentation of this guide.*

Paray-le-Monial
71600

◎ ⅍ 🏠 |O| Grand Hôtel de la Basilique**

18 rue de la Visitation; it's 100m from the basilica, opposite the chapel of the Visitation (where the Sacred Heart appeared to Sainte Marguerite).
☎03.85.81.11.13 ℻03.85.88.83.70
🌐www.hotelbasilique.com
Closed *1 Nov–20 March.* **TV. Pay car park.**

Delightful hotel, founded in 1904, but best behaviour is required – it's a favourite of visiting pilgrims. Double rooms, some of them recently renovated, cost €40–57 with shower/wc or bath; half board around €43 per person. Regional dishes are served in the restaurant – menus €12–38. Of the specialities, try the turbot, the Charolais beef steak *label rouge* (which means its origins can be traced) and *œufs en meurette. 10% discount on the price of a room (except 1 July–20 Aug) offered to our readers on presentation of this guide.*

Pouilly-sur-Loire
58150

@ ᘏ ᠍ |●| Le Relais de 200 Bornes

1 av. de la Tuilerie; at the entrance to Pouilly via the A7 (signposted).
☎03.86.39.10.01 ☎03.86.39.18.55
Closed *Weekends (restaurant); Aug; Christmas to New Year.* **TV.**

The last survivor of the petrol station-transport cafés that used to dot the N7 every 100 kilometres or so. The owners have a wealth of anecdotes about the holiday route that used to pass by their doorsteps, before the coming of the motorway. Not exactly thrilling stuff it has to be said, but the fine food is far from humdrum; menus at €10.50 and €15. Double rooms with washbasin go for €36, with shower/wc at €43. *Free house apéritif in the restaurant or 10% discount on the price of a room in the hotel offered to our readers on presentation of this guide.*

@ ᘏ ᠍ |●| Le Relais Fleuri – Coq Hardi***

42 av. de la Tuilerie; it's 1km southeast of the centre, opposite the wine cellars.
☎03.86.39.12.99 ☎03.86.39.14.15
@www.le-relais-fleuri.fr
Closed *Tues; Wed (except July-Aug); mid-Dec to mid-Jan; a week in Feb.* **Disabled access. TV. Games available. Car park.**

Typical Logis de France hotel, with rustic furniture and flowers everywhere – a pleasant, reliable establishment. The rooms are good, particularly those with a view over the Loire (some have a small balcony); doubles with shower/wc or bath €45–80. The restaurant serves regional cooking worth its salt: smoked salmon pancake with vine stems and Nivernais pigeon roast with fresh herbs. Bistro menu available at €15.50; otherwise, there is a

weekday menu at €25, then others at €36 and €55. Good, if a little pricey, wine list. Logis de France. *Free glass of wine (with dessert) offered to our readers on presentation of this guide.*

Quarré-les-Tombes
89630

@ ᠍ |●| Hôtel-restaurant Le Morvan

6 rue des Écoles.
☎03.86.32.29.29
☎03.86.32.29.28
Closed *Mon and Tues (out of season); early Dec to end Feb.*

Despite a forbidding exterior, this is one of those hotels that makes you feel immediately at home, thanks to an inexpensive detail that is all too often overlooked: a smile – the staff here really know how to look after their guests. The rooms (from €47 for a double; half-board per night per person at €52) are all personalized and the delicious, beautifully presented local dishes vary according to the availability of fresh ingredients. The weekday lunchtime menu (beware, it is not always advertised) costs €13, others €19–45, and there's a children's menu (which steers away from the obvious) at €10.50.

@ ᠍ |●| ᘏ Auberge de l'Atre***

Les Lavaults; take the N6, then the D10 in the direction of Lac des Settons.
☎03.86.32.20.79 ☎ 03.86.32.28.25
@www.auberge-de-latre.com
Closed *Tues evening and Wed (out of season); 1–28 Feb; second fortnight in June.* **TV. Disabled access. Car park.**

Isolated in the heart of Morvan, this inn is a haven for any traveller who has gone astray, especially on cold or foggy nights. A few pleasant bedrooms have been installed for guests, doubles with bath costing €69–84, but the main attraction is the outstanding and reasonably priced food. The smaller dining room recalls an old-style bistro, while the main dining room is decorated in a warm, rustic fashion. The chef, Francis Salamolard, loves experimenting with herbs and Morvan mushrooms in the dishes he creates; weekday menu at €28.50; others at €39.50 and €49.50. Logis de France. *Free house apéritif or coffee offered to our readers on presentation of this guide.*

Brizards (Les)
89630 (6km SE)

⋘ ☎ |●| ⅔ **Auberge des Brizards****

Take the D55; follow the signposts.
☎03.86.32.20.12 ℗03.86.32.27.40
ⓦwww.aubergedesbrizards.com
Closed *Mon and Tues (except July–Aug); early Jan to mid-Feb.* **TV. High chairs available. Car park.**

What could be more romantic than this delightful inn, which is lost in the midst of the Morvan forest and seems to have come out of a fairy tale? Facilities include a tennis court and a pond for fishing, and double rooms go for €39–115 with shower or bath, depending on the level of comfort. In the restaurant, cheerful service in a bright, spacious dining room, a world away from the time when grandmother Odette received her customers surrounded by terrines and pickle jars. Outstanding dishes on the weekday menu at €23, including wine, and others €28–46, include *matelote* of pike perch in red wine, pork pie, black pudding with home-grown potatoes and *oeufs en meurette* with snails. *10% discount on a room (15 Oct–15 March, except weekends and public holidays) or free house apéritif offered to our readers on presentation of this guide.*

Roche-en-Brenil (La)
21530

⋐ ⅔ |●| **Aux Portes du Morvan**

It's on the edge of the village, coming from Saulieu.
☎03.80.64.75.28 ℗03.80.64.75.28
Closed *Tues evening; Wed; Jan; second fortnight in June.* **Disabled access.**

Tasty, healthy food that won't turn your stomach when you see the bill; menus at €11, €17 and €22. The chef's specialities include ham with cream, eggs in wine sauce, *filet mignon* with port, and Morvan tarts at the weekend. Omelettes are available all day. Get into the swing before your meal by having a drink at the bar, which is full of local regulars. *Free coffee offered to our readers on presentation of this guide.*

Rully
71150

⋘ ☎ |●| **Le Vendangerot****

Place Sainte-Marie; leave the N6 after Arnay-le-Duc in the direction of Châlon-sur-Saône, taking the D981 then the D978 in the direction of Rully.
☎03.85.87.20.09 ℗03.85.91.27.18
Closed *Tues and Wed lunchtime (July–Sept); 1–15 Jan; 15 Feb–10 March.* **TV. High chairs available. Car park.**

A large house bedecked with flowers and surrounded by greenery, overlooking the square of this picturesque, wine-producing village. It is well kept and fully deserves its two-star classification. The restaurant is a safe bet with menus at €15 (except Sun), then €22–39: foie gras, pig's trotter and oxtail steak, pike perch fillet with Aligoté, snail pastry, squab stuffed with truffles. Neat, spacious doubles go for €47–50. Logis de France.

Saint-Christophe-en-Brionnais
71800

⋐ ⅔ |●| **Bar-restaurant du Midi**

Grand-Rue; either on the D34 from Paray-le-Monial or from Clayette on the D989.
☎03.85.25.87.06
Closed *Mon–Wed evenings; Jan.*

Thursday is market day and for a good number of years Marielle and Dominique Lauvernier have opened at 6am to feed and water the horse-dealers and traders. They all pile into the big dining room-cum-canteen beyond the bar and the kitchen; the dishes, served in copious portions, include calf's head, sirloin steak and *entrecôte* – and the meat is of the highest quality. There's a set lunch menu at €7, a *menu du jour* €10 (weekday lunchtimes) and others €13–20. Decent wines on offer include Côtes-du-Rhône, Mâcon Village and Saint-Véran. If you don't fancy the bustle, it's quieter the rest of the week. *Free coffee offered to our readers on presentation of this guide.*

Saint-Fargeau
89170

⋐ |●| **L'Auberge Les Perriaux**

La Gare; take the Auxerre road going out of the town.

☎ 03.86.74.16.45
Closed *Sat and Sun, weekday lunchtime (Sept–June).* **Disabled access. High chairs available.**

Charming décor in an old railway station converted into a friendly restaurant. You will be greeted by the saying for the day written on a blackboard, before proceeding to the cool, white dining room with old-fashioned decorations or to the terrace lawn to eat under the linden trees and enjoy the fast efficient service. Many of the ingredients, such as the duck and the *confit*, are supplied by six local farms; the cooking is good, if somewhat erratic and there's an irresistible dessert platter (which spares you the dilemma of what to order). Weekday lunchtime menus start at €15, with others at €19 (in summer, on nights when there's a performance in the château), €28 and €34. For lunch you need to make sure you arrive no later than 1pm.

Saint-Florentin

89600

☞ ⚘ 🏠 |●| Les Tilleuls**

3 rue Decourtive.
☎ 03.86.35.09.09
ⓦ www.hotel-les-tilleuls.com
Closed *Sun and Mon (Sept–May).* **TV. Car park.**

In a quiet side street just outside the centre, this building once comprised the residential quarters of a Capuchin monastery, founded in 1635. You can have a peaceful lunch under the lime trees here, on a pretty terrace surrounded by an equally pretty garden and far from the stress of daily life. Set menus start at €16 (weekday lunchtime) and then go from €18 up to €45; reckon on €52 à la carte. Dishes include terrine of foie gras, fillet of beef with Soumaintrain cheese. Comfortable rooms with good facilities cost €49–60 with shower/wc or bath. Logis de France. *Free coffee offered to our readers on presentation of this guide.*

Saint-Julien-de-Jonzy

71110

☞ 🏠 |●| ⚘ Hôtel-restaurant-boucherie Pont Bernard**

It's 8km south of Saint-Christophe-en-Brionnais – from Paray-le-Monial, take the

D34 and then the D20.
☎ 03.85.84.01.95
Closed *Sun and Mon evenings; a fortnight in Feb; a week at the beginning of July.* **TV. High chairs available. Swimming pool. Car park.**

This is Charolais country, 30km north of Roanne, and they don't do things by halves. Monsieur Pont is both butcher and cook so the meat is of superb quality, cooked up in generous portions; this is simple, tasty home cooking. Dishes include *coq au vin*, Charolais steak, fillet of sea bream with champagne sauce, home-made foie gras, *tournedos* and farm-raised veal *escalope* in cream sauce. Excellent desserts. There's a weekday lunch menu at €13.60 and others priced €19–29. Double rooms weigh in at €37.

Saint-Léger-sous-Beuvray

71990

☞ 🏠 |●| ⚘ Hôtel du Morvan*

In the town; take the D3 from Autun.
☎ 03.85.82.51.06 ☏ 03.85.82.45.07
ⓦ www.hoteldumorvan71.com
Closed *Mon and Tues (out of season); 25 Dec–31 Jan.* **High chairs available.**

A village hotel that has enhanced its comfort and created a warm atmosphere while keeping prices within reasonable bounds. There are seven rooms with rural charm; doubles €42-50. Fine regional cooking: weekday lunchtime menu €10.80; others €15.50–24.40, including an amusing Gallic-Roman menu at €19.50 (the major Gallic site of Bibracte is nearby). Logis de France. *5% discount on a room (except 15 July–15 Sept, weekends and public holidays), or free house apéritif or coffee offered to our readers on presentation of this guide.*

Saint-Prix

71990

☞ |●| Chez Franck et Francine

☎ 03.85.82.45.12
Closed *Sun evening; Mon; first 10 days in Jan.* **Disabled access.**

Cooking worthy of the great chefs of Burgundy: fried snails, pig's trotter pancake, pike perch steak cooked with celery cream and sorrel under the skin. Book at least two days in advance to ensure a friendly welcome from Francine who, although still a young woman, is already a firmly established local character. The chef works alone in the kitchen, using only the freshest of ingredients. The market menu (2 dishes) costs €26, *plaisir* menu €32, prestige menu (3 dishes) €40, *dégustation* menu (8 dishes) €55 and children's menu €11. All these menus include cheese and dessert.

Saint-Saulge

58330

ⓔ |●| Le Restaurant des Légendes

6 rue du Commerce; 15km to the southwest of Châtillon-en-Bazois.
☎03.86.58.27.67 ☎03.85.84.01.95
Closed *Sun evening; Mon.*

A huge, bright and cheery dining room crammed with curios: a spyglass, pot-pourri, paintings, hats, tools, etc. The show continues on the table, thanks to a master chef from Niverne: many a local has been startled to find his strawberry soup swimming in a strange blue liquid. More traditional dishes like foie gras are also available; the cheapest menu costs €16.20 then others €23.20–36. Nothing is surprising, however, in Saint-Saulge, the stuff of legends, where, so the story goes, a cow was once hauled up on top of the church roof to graze the village's last blades of grass. Logis de France.

Saint-Révérien

58420 (13km N)

ⓔ |●| Le Chali

Chez Philippe Chanut; take the D34; it's in the centre of the village.
☎03.86.29.08.10
Closed *Mon and Tues (July–Aug); Mon evening to Wed the rest of the year.*

The pride and joy of Saint-Révérien. A beautiful dining room with a striking ceiling, and a tank with a few fish awaiting the intervention of the chef, whose star turn is undoubtedly Nivernais duck breast soaked in Sezchuan sauce. Audacity in the kitchen is combined with great charm at the table; the cheapest menu costs €18, others at €26–34.

Brinay

58110 (11km W)

ⓔ 🎿 |●| L'Ancien Café

Take the D132 for 4.5km, then take the D38.
☎03.86.84.90.79
Closed *Sun evening.* **High chairs and games available.**

A modest bar-cum-grocery-cum-bread-store-cum-garage with a real restaurant attached. It's run by the owners and their daughter and has a shaded terrace. Tasty dishes, generously served: Morvan ham, calf's head, fresh fish, Charolais steaks and house terrine. There's a *formule* (main course and dessert) for €10 and menus €12–23, with a children's menu at €8.50. *Free coffee offered to our readers on presentation of this guide.*

Saulieu

21210

ⓔ 🎿 🏠 |●| La Vieille Auberge

15 rue Grillot.
☎03.80.64.13.74 ☎03.80.64.13.74
Closed *Tues evening and Wed (except July–Aug); 15 Jan–12 Feb; first week in July.* **Disabled access. Car park.**

Everyone who drove south on the N6 to the coast knew Saulieu well, but when the motorway opened the old town fell on leaner times. A new generation of restaurateurs have put Saulieu back on the gastronomic and tourist map, however, and two of them took over this inn. Having said that, you could drive past without even noticing; it's tucked away behind a bend in the road but it boasts an absolutely delightful dining room and an attractive hidden terrace. The cooking is well worth seeking out (menus €12–30): try the brilliant terrine of Charolais beef, *marbré* of rabbit or roast pike perch with red wine. And, there's a fine selection of local cheeses on offer. Rooms with shower/wc or bath go for €33; half board, compulsory in July and August, costs €42–55. *10% discount on the price of a room (after two consecutive nights) offered to our readers on presentation of this guide.*

ⓔ 🎿 🏠 |●| La Borne Impériale**

14–16 rue d'Argentine; on the N6.
☎03.80.64.19.76
🌐www.borne-imperiale.com

Closed *Tues evening; Wed (except in July–Aug); 5 Jan–5 Feb.* **TV. Car park.**

Near Pompom's famous sculpture of a bull – a Saulieu landmark – you'll find *La Borne Impériale*, a gastronomic landmark and one of the last old-fashioned inns in Burgundy. It has seven rooms with shower/wc or bath at €50, some of which could do with updating. Ask for the one with a view of the attractive garden. The beautiful dining room has a terrace for fine days. There's a weekday menu at €18 (lunch and dinner) and others at €22 and €27, listing good, regional cooking: *oeufs cocotte*, snails, *aiguillettes Charolais*, vanilla crunch. *Free coffee offered to our readers on presentation of this guide.*

Savigny-sur-Seille
71440

☜ |●| 🍴 Auberge La Rivière

Tiellay; 11km west of Louhans.
☏ 03.85.74.99.03
Closed *Tues evening and Wed (16 Sept–14 June); Wed (15 June–15 Sept).* **Disabled access. High chairs available.**

Enchanting inn in a natural setting on the banks of the Seille, formerly the home of a ferryman. The charming interior has a slight slope, and you'll get a friendly welcome. Regional cooking: *oeuf cocotte* with snails, ham braised with morels, Bresse chicken with morels or crayfish, poultry-liver cake, crayfish supreme and fish that couldn't be fresher – the owner is a keen fisherman and catches them in the river himself. You may be lucky enough to find silurid (a giant freshwater fish) available. The excellent desserts include raspberries with vanilla ice cream. Cheapest menu at €15, served every day at lunch and dinner, then three others €18.50–28.20. On fine days you can eat on the idyllic terrace, with a lawn stretching down to the water. *Free coffee offered to our readers on presentation of this guide.*

Saillenard
71580 (28km NE)

☜ 🏠 |●| 🍴 Auberge Le Moulin de Sauvagette

Saillenard; pass through Louhans, then take the N78 to Beaurepaire-en-Bresse, then the D87 to Saillenard; from there, follow the directions to Bletterans, 3km away; it's well signposted.

☏ and ☏ 03.85.74.17.58
Closed *Sun evening, Mon and Tues (except for staying guests); end Jan; 2 weeks in Oct.*

An old mill lost in the countryside, attractively fitted out and decorated – the ideal place to get away from it all in a bucolic backwater in the heart of Bresse, so booking is essential. Pretty rooms with old-fashioned furniture go for €40–44 for a double. Cheerful service and excellent regional cooking, served in a beautiful, rustic dining room; regional platter €12, menu €20. Credit cards not accepted. *Free house apéritif or coffee offered to our readers on presentation of this guide.*

Semur-en-Auxois
21140

☜ 🏠 Hôtel des Cymaises**

7 rue du Renaudot; in the town centre, behind the pedestrian precinct.
☏ 03.80.97.21.44 ☏ 03.80.97.18.23
🌐 www.hotelcymais.com
Closed *Feb; 3 Nov–7 Dec.* **Disabled access. TV. High chairs available. Car park.**

In the heart of the medieval city, just behind Porte Sauvigny, there's a beautiful, eighteenth-century building that has adapted extremely well to life as a twenty-first-century hotel. It's cool, clean and comfortable, with a small, flower-filled garden, and you can come and go as you please. Breakfast is served under the pergola. Nicely furnished double rooms with shower/wc or bath are €55–59.

☜ 🍴 |●| Restaurant des Minimes

39 rue Vaux; it's 500m from the town centre.
☏ 03.80.97.26.86
Closed *Sun evening; Mon; Christmas to New Year's Eve.* **Disabled access. Car park.**

This "local" bistro below the ramparts has become an absolute must for tourists in search of the soul and the cooking of Semur. There's a pastoral feel to the décor and an informal atmosphere; on offer are a €16 menu and a *menu-carte* at €26. The owners appreciate fine wine and a good chat. *Free house liqueur offered to our readers on presentation of this guide.*

☜ |●| Le Calibressan

16 rue Feveret.
☏ 03.80.97.32.40
✉ le.calibressan@wanadoo.fr

Closed *Sat lunchtime; Sun evening; Mon; Jan; first week in July.*

A twist of California in this Bresse kitchen – thus the name. An attractive little restaurant combining authentic rustic décor – beams, unadorned brick walls, flowers and pretty curtains – with the vitality and exoticism of America, well-represented by Madame at reception. You'll also detect flavours of the New World in certain dishes à la carte. Try the roast kangaroo fillet with Grand Veneur sauce, the Hawaiian pork salad or the house chilli con carne. Regional dishes are also on offer, including snails and chocolate pudding with a weekday lunch menu at €18 and others €21.50–33.50.

Pont-et-Massene

21140 (3km SE)

⊚ 🎋 🏠 |●| Hôtel du Lac**

10 rue du Lac; follow the signs to Lac de Pont.
℡03.80.97.11.11
⊛www.hoteldulacdepont.com
Closed *Sun evening and Mon out of season; Mon and Tues lunchtime (July–Aug); 28 Nov–6 Jan.* **TV. Car park.**

Just below the lake, this huge building reeks of the 1950s. Some pleasant rooms but others are fairly dreary; doubles with shower/wc or bath at €46–70. There's a family atmosphere in the restaurant and the kind of regional cooking you'd eat during a traditional Sunday lunch: dishes like *jambon persillé* made with local ham, chicken *fricassée* with mushrooms, snails, *coq au vin* and calf's head *ravigote*. A set menu at €12.50 is served every day except Sun; others €14.70–27. Try the local *blanc de l'Auxois*, which is very drinkable and deserves to be more widely known. There's a terrace with a canopy for fine summer days. Logis de France. *Free glass of Kir offered to our readers on presentation of this guide.*

Alésia

21150 (20km NE)

⊚ |●| L'Auberge du Cheval Blanc

Rue du Miroir; take the D954 in the direction of Venarey, then the D6.
℡ and ℡03.80.96.01.55
Closed *Mon; Tues; 1 Jan–15 Feb.* **Disabled access. Car park.**

Repair here after a morning reviewing the excavations at Alésia, where Vercingetorix and the Gauls fought their last battle against the armies of Julius Caesar. The brasserie menu lists parsleyed ham with salad and other simple dishes, and good regional cooking is served in the bigger dining room; weekday lunch menu €17; others €27 and €40. The chef uses vegetables from the garden and the market. Try local snails, fish stew, chicken *fricassée*, scallops, grilled Charolais steak with cream and mushrooms or pineapple *millefeuille*. The place has lots of energy with a team of young serving staff. Have a glass of local Chardonnay or Pinot Noir.

Sens

89100

⊚ 🎋 |●| Restaurant Le Soleil Levant

51 rue Émile-Zola; it's close to the train station.
℡ and ℡03.86.65.71.82
Closed *Sun evening; Wed; Aug.* **Disabled access. High chairs available.**

A restaurant, very classical in both décor and cuisine, which is well known for its fish – particularly the signature dish of salmon with sorrel and the fish *bouillabaisse*. They also do good meat dishes such as house duck foie gras and calf's head *gribiche*, along with some heavenly desserts including chocolate charlotte. The cheapest menu costs €14 (weekday lunchtimes); others are €22 and €33 or you'll pay around €40 à la carte. *Free coffee offered to our readers on presentation of this guide.*

⊚ |●| Au Crieur de Vins

1 rue Alsace-Lorraine.
℡03.86.65.92.80
Closed *Sun; Mon; Tues lunch.* **Disabled access.**

An annexe to a large house (*La Madeleine*). The space is limited but skilfully laid out (you don't have to put your elbow in your neighbour's plate), and the dishes are very good (although a little expensive à la carte): tripe with garlic and parsley, haddock fillets poached with chives and *merleur* with violet mustard, all served by the attentive owner, Guy. Menus at €22.50 and €40; reckon on €35 à la carte. There's also an impeccable selection of wines straight from the growers, but pay attention to the prices before getting carried away. Ask about the suggestions of the day, as these alone are often worth the trip. Booking essential.

Toucy
89130

ⓔ 🏠 |●| 🎋 Le Lion d'Or

37 rue Lucile-Cormier.
☏03.86.44.00.76
Closed *Sun evening; Mon.* **TV. Car park.**

Old hotel with a magnificent wooden staircase. The rooms are modest but cosy and spotless, with a lingering scent of beeswax polish; doubles €35 with washbasin and €55 with shower/wc or bath. The restaurant is charming, as is its manager, and offers a menu at €12 served every day, then others at €16–26, with regional specialities such as fish *en croûte*, snails with croûtons, *steak au poivre*, Dijon-style veal kidneys. Credit cards not accepted. *10% discount on the price of a room offered to our readers on presentation of this guide.*

Mézilles
89130 (10km SW)

ⓔ |●| La Mare aux Fées

Le Vieux-Pont; take the D965.
☏03.86.45.40.43
Closed *Mon evening; Tues evening; Wed; Feb.*

An enchanting restaurant at one end of an old bridge over the River Branlin – a relaxing, bucolic setting with service that pays attention to detail (and genuine respect to non-smokers). The cooking is classic but subtle with menus (€17–22) which feature dishes such as authentic *œufs en meurette*, kidneys with Banyuls, tender undercut with shallots, *andouillette* with white wine and home-made Paris-Brest that melts in the mouth. There's also a fine selection of wines. It is advisable to book.

Tournus
71700

ⓔ 🎋 🏠 |●| Hôtel-restaurant aux Terrasses**

18 av. du 23-Janvier.
☏03.85.51.01.74
Closed *Sun evening (except July–Aug); Mon; Tues lunchtime.* **TV. Car park.**

This place is known primarily for the

quality of the cooking in the restaurant – it's one of the best in town. It's set in an enormous, roadside establishment, probably a former coaching inn. The lounge separates two large, richly decorated dining rooms. Reception's a bit on the smart side but not overly so, and service is attentive. Set menus start at a good-value weekday lunch menu for €20, with others at €26 and €58. À la carte lists a variety of dishes: pike perch with Morvan ham, Bresse chicken with morels, parsleyed ham, *escalope* with blackcurrants, and *millefeuille* with pears and gingerbread ice cream. Comfortable double rooms with bath go for €56–68. Logis de France. *Free coffee offered to our readers on presentation of this guide.*

Villars (Le)
71700 (3km S)

ⓔ |●| 🎋 L'Auberge des Gourmets

Place de l'Église; on the Mâcon road.
☏03.85.32.58.80
Closed *Sun evening; Tues evening; Wed; a week in Feb school holiday; 2 weeks in summer; 23 Dec–2 Jan.* **Disabled access.**

Daniel Rogié, formerly the chef in *Le Rempart* in Tournus, has created this beautiful restaurant in a pretty village overlooking the Saône. It's impossible to miss as it's opposite the double-nave Roman church. The large trees in the square provide shade for the terrace, while the interior is cool and restful. Menus start at €18 in the week, then others from €26 to €42. Booking is essential if you want to have a chance of experiencing seasonal cooking that has managed to renew a tradition, served in a very convivial atmosphere. *Free coffee offered to our readers on presentation of this guide.*

Vermenton
89270

ⓔ 🎋 |●| Auberge L'Espérance

3 rue du Général-de-Gaulle; take the N6.
☏03.86.81.50.42
Closed *Mon; Tues evening; Sun evening; first 4 weeks of Jan; a few days at the end of Sept.* **Disabled access. High chairs, baby changing table and games available.**

However glum you're feeling, the mere mention of this inn's name (*espérance* means "hope") should perk you up.

You'll get a delightful welcome, and the kitchen turns out wonderful dishes that change with the seasons – try the house duck foie gras, Burgundy-style prawns or frogs' legs with garlic cream, all of which are regulars. Set menus are available for €15.50–30, including one grill menu; children's menu costs €8. They've provided a play area for the kids. Everyone will find the air-conditioning a blessed relief in summer. Credit cards not accepted. *Free coffee offered to our readers on presentation of this guide.*

Accolay
89460 (3km W)

⬅ 🎿 ⌂ |●| Hostellerie de la Fontaine**

16 rue de Reigny; take the D39.
☎03.86.81.54.02 ℗03.86.81.52.78
@hostellerie.fontaine@wanadoo.fr
Restaurant closed *Mon–Fri lunchtimes; mid-Nov to 31 March.* **Car park.**

A traditional Burgundy house in a lovely little village in the Cure valley. On fine evenings you can relax in the garden while feasting on salad of snails with mustard dressing, red mullet fillet with cucumber cream or *entrecôte* steak with soft creamy Chaource cheese sauce. There are a range of menus at €23–45, and double rooms go for €48–49. Logis de France. *10% discount on the room rate offered to our readers on presentation of this guide.*

Bazarnes
89460 (6km W)

⬅ 🎿 |●| Restaurant La Griotte

3 av. de la Gare; it's opposite the Cravant-Bazarnes train station; to the west of Vermenton via the N6; going towards Cravant, on the left from the D139.
☎03.86.42.39.38
Closed *Mon–Wed; 24 Dec–15 Feb.*

A nice little restaurant with a great chef who's an expert in seeking out fantastic local suppliers and delightful service. With this fresh produce, his imagination takes him to culinary heights. The dishes really taste of the country – you just have to try the pork *andouille* to know what we mean. The cheapest menu is €13.50, followed by the "market menu" at €22. *Free house apéritif offered to our readers on presentation of this guide.*

Vézelay
89450

⬅ ⌂ Le Compostelle**

Place du Champ-de-Foire.
☎03.86.33.28.63 ℗03.86.33.34.34
@le.compostelle@wanadoo.fr
Closed *3 Jan–15 Feb; 30 Nov–17 Dec.*
Disabled access. TV.

Vézelay was one of the assembly points for pilgrimages to Santiago de Compostela in northwestern Spain. That fact is commemorated by the name of this pretty house, which has reverted to being an inn – as it was at the beginning of the twentieth century. The service is first-rate and the modern, well-equipped bedrooms have views of the countryside or the garden; doubles €47–58. Ask for nos. 2, 5 or 12, as they've recently been completely refurbished. It's best to reserve.

⬅ ⌂ Hôtel La Maison des Glycines

Rue Saint-Pierre; 100m from the basilica.
☎ and ℗03.86.32.35.30
Closed *Thurs.* **Disabled access.**

In summer it is easy see why this hotel is called the "House of Wisterias", as the patio and terrace are swathed in wisteria, and you can have breakfast or afternoon tea in their midst. The rooms, all with names like Marie-Madeleine or Saint-Bernard, are sophisticated with shiny colours, old floor-tiles and, in those highest up, a view of the Basilica. Double rooms go for €54–66, according to the comfort level, and there's a limited choice of food available if required.

⬅ |●| Restaurant Le Bougainville

26 rue Saint-Étienne; on the high street.
☎03.86.33.27.57 ℗03.86.33.35.12
Closed *Tues; Wed; Mon (out of season); mid-Nov to mid-Jan.* **High chairs and games available.**

This restaurant, in a beautiful old building overflowing with flowers, is very good value for money – cheapest menu €15 (served every day), others €19–39 – a pleasant surprise in a town where low prices are a rarity. Traditional local dishes include terrine of Époisse cheese with artichokes and, *andouillette*. The dining room, with its magnificent old fireplace, is extremely attractive and has recently been refurbished.

Saint-Père-sous-Vézelay

89450 (2km SE)

◎ 🏛 🏨 À la Renommée**

19–20 Grande Rue; it's on the D957, at the foot of Vézelay hill.
☎ 03.86.33.21.34 ℱ 03.86.33.34.17
ⓦ www.avallonnais-tourisme.com/renommee
Closed Mon evening and Tues (1 Nov–24 Dec); 25 Dec–1 March. **Disabled access. TV. Car park.**

This hotel is also a newsagent's and a tobacconist's so there's a relaxed atmosphere. The more expensive rooms are spacious and have a small terrace with views over the countryside and the Saint-Pierre church. Some newer rooms are set in the annexe opposite the main building; doubles from €32 with basin, up to €54 with bath.

◎ |●| L'Entre-Vignes

Route de Vézelay; take the D57.
☎ 03.86.33.33.33
Closed Mon; Tues lunchtime; Sun evening; Jan–Feb. **Disabled access. Car park.**

When speaking of Saint-Père, it is impossible not to mention the great chef Marc Meneau. His brand-new "annexe" is still searching for its identity. The formula is simple but a little more choice would not go amiss, and the menu, although very fine, still lacks a touch of the creativity that is so dear to the great chef. The plastic furniture on the large terrace compares badly with the more elegant interior dining room. The single menu (€28) is served at lunchtime only; reckon on €35 à la carte. The service is immaculate, and the whole setting is adorned with flowers. For those whose budgets can stand it, L'Espérance, Marc Meneau's Relais & Château restaurant, is on the other side of the street.

Pierre-Perthuis

89450 (6km SE)

◎ 🏛 |●| Restaurant Les Deux Ponts

It's signposted from Saint-Père-sous-Vézelay.
☎ 03.86.32.31.31 ℱ 03.86.32.35.80
Closed Tues in season; Tues and Wed out of season. **Disabled access.**

Philippe is responsible for reopening this old inn near the two bridges over the Cure. This injection of new blood, combined with high-quality cooking based on fresh ingredients, has brought it into the modern age without sacrificing its charm. In summer, you can while away the time under the chestnut tree on the terrace, eating a snack, a salad or a full meal, centred on local produce such as Charolais fillet of beef or fish from the river; menus €22–52. The atmosphere is equally cosy at night, particularly when the log fire is lit in cooler weather. Double rooms with shower/wc or bath go for €50. Canoes, horses and bikes are all available for hire; if you prefer to stay on foot, there is a wealth of pleasant strolls on offer, with lovely views of Vézelay from the top of the town.

Villeneuve-l'Archevêque

89190

◎ 🏛 |●| 🍴 Les Vieux Moulins Banaux

18 rte. des Moulins-Banaux; on the Arcès-Dilo road out of the town; take exit 19 from the A5.
☎ 03.86.86.72.55. ℱ 03.86.86.78.94
ⓦ www.bourgognehotels.fr
Closed Jan. **Disabled access. TV. High chairs and games available.**

This old mill by the banks of the River Vanne used to belong to the village squire, who rented out its facilities to anybody who wanted to grind their grain. (This practice was known as "banality".) In 1801 it was turned into a paper factory, before becoming a hotel in 1966. It has lost none of its class since it was taken over two years ago by a cosmopolitan team (English and French chefs, a Dutchwoman serving at the tables and a German woman on reception). The setting has been intelligently conceived, with a terrace by the waterside, a quiet garden for apéritifs and a spacious, wood-panelled dining room that displays the mechanism of the mill that once operated here. The dishes are sophisticated and creative, with touches of the Far East – weekday menu €15.75, others at €23.50 and €26.50 – and an impressive selection of wines from all over the world. The rooms, (ask for one to the rear) €39 with shower, €48 with bath, have all mod cons. Booking is highly advisable, as the value for money here is exceptional. Logis de France. *10% discount on the price of a room (Feb–April and Oct–Dec) or free house apéritif offered to our readers on presentation of this guide.*

Villeneuve-sur-Yonne

89500

⟪ 🏠 |●| **La Lucarne aux Chouettes**

7 quai Bretoche.
☎03.86.87.19.26 ℻03.86.87.22.63
🌐www.lesliecaron-auberge.com
Closed *Sun evening; Mon; mid-Nov to mid-Dec.*

Four old houses on a picturesque quay by the River Yonne, transformed into a charming hotel by the actress Leslie Caron. The rooms, €95–140 for a double with shower/wc or bath, and decorated in an old-fashioned style, all overlook the river. The dining room has an almost Zen-like rusticity and the cooking combines local ingredients with a touch of invention. There's a weekday lunchtime menu at €19 and another at €36. At the very least, it is worth dropping into the bar for a drink, even though the service is a bit aloof.

Bretagne

Arzon

56640

@ |●| **Crêperie La Sorcière**

59 rue des Fontaines; take the Arzon turn-off at the Crouesty roundabout, then continue straight on to the sea; it's on the right, in front of a small car park.
℡02.97.53.87.25
Closed *Mon; Nov–Jan*. **High chairs available.**

You'll be bewitched by this pretty stone house, where they conjure up devilishly delicious recipes. All the crêpes have names: la Pensardine, la Vendéenne, la Périgourdine, l'Irlandaise. You'll get a friendly welcome and very good food – quality produce and ingredients are used, such as the black wheat. A meal of good crêpes with interesting fillings costs around €11 (drinks not included) – à la carte menu only. There's a terrace with a view of the old port of Morbihan.

Audierne

29770

@ 🏄 🏠 |●| **Hôtel de la Plage***

21 bd. Emmanuel-Brusq; 2km towards the quay for the île de Sein.
℡02.98.70.01.07 ℗02.98.75.04.69
Closed *Oct–April*. **TV. Car park.**

A hotel on the sea front that helps its guests get into a holiday mood with its cheerful décor of nautical references in the lounge and the bedrooms: treasure chests, white walls and blue curtains and models of tall ships. Bright, attractive rooms, with high-quality bedding – almost all overlooking the beach – go for €45–58 for a double, depending on the season; half

board, around €56, is compulsory in the summer. This restaurant is the perfect place to enjoy fish and seafood on the single menu (€25), fishermen's stuffed crab being a speciality. It has a certain charm and represents good value for money for the area. Logis de France. *One free breakfast per stay offered free to our readers on presentation of this guide.*

Auray

56400

@ 🏠 **Hôtel Le Marin**

1 pl. du Roland Saint-Goustan.
℡02.97.24.14.58 ℗02.97.24.39.59
🌐www.saint-goustan.net/hotel-le-marin.com
Closed *mid-Jan to mid-Feb*. **TV.**

Very close to the port (although it's out of sight). Pretty, comfortable double rooms €57–72 with shower/wc or bath/wc; one room for a family of four, with terrace, at €80. Some rooms overlook the river and all have beautiful bathrooms. On the ground floor, a lounge replaces the old bar-restaurant that was once open to hotel guests. There's also a charming terrace.

@ |●| 🏄 **La Belle Bio**

4 rue Philippe-Vannier.
℡02.97.24.26.75
Games available.

A fine organic crêperie hidden away in an unremarkable street offering friendly service in a warm dining room (log fire in winter) and a beautiful terrace. Exhibitions of original artworks adorn the old walls – all very authentic, just like the smiles of its young owners. The

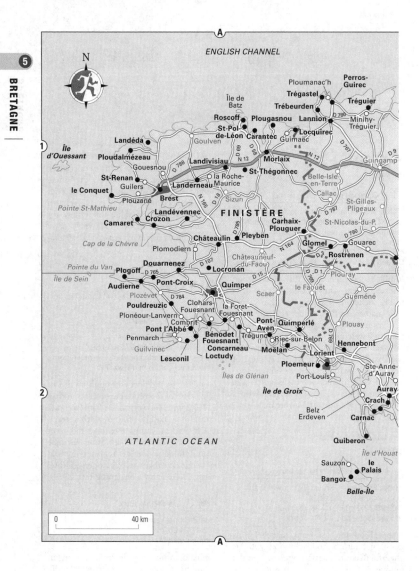

ENGLISH CHANNEL

N

Ploumanac'h Perros-Guirec
Trégastel
Trébeurden Tréguier
Roscoff Plougasnou Lannion Minihy-Tréguier
St-Pol-de-Léon Carantec Locquirec
Île de Batz Guimaëc Guingamp
Landéda
Ploudalmézeau Landivisiau Morlaix Belle-Isle-en-Terre
Île d'Ouessant Gouesnou St-Thégonnec Callac
St-Renan la Roche-Maurice St-Gilles-Pligeaux
Guilers Landerneau
le Conquet Plouzané Brest Sizun St-Nicolas-du-P.
Pointe St-Mathieu Landévennec FINISTÈRE
Crozon Carhaix-Plouguer
Camaret Châteaulin Pleyben Glomel Gouarec
Cap de la Chèvre Plomodiern Châteauneuf-du-Faou Rostrenen
Pointe du Van Douarnenez Locronan Plouray
Plogoff le Faouët
Île de Sein Audierne Pont-Croix Quimper Scaer Guéméné
Plozévet Clohars-Fouesnant la Forêt-Fouesnant
Pouldreuzic Plouay
Plonéour-Lanvern Combrit Pont-Aven Quimperlé
Pont l'Abbé Bénodet Trégunc Riec-sur-Belon Hennebont
Penmarch Fouesnant Moëlan Lorient
Guilvinec Concarneau Ste-Anne-d'Auray
Lesconil Loctudy Ploemeur
Port-Louis Auray
Îles de Glénan Crach
Île de Groix Belz Carnac
Erdeven
ATLANTIC OCEAN Quiberon
Île d'Houat
Sauzon le Palais
Bangor
Belle-Île

0 40 km

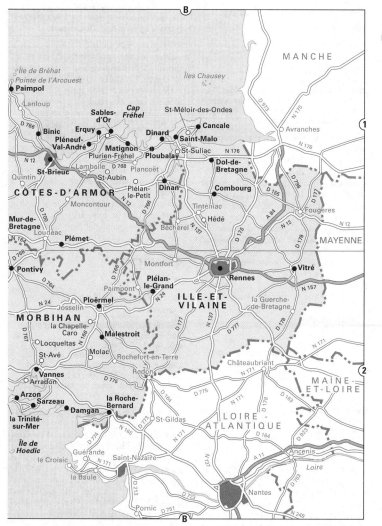

B

MANCHE

Île de Bréhat
Pointe de l'Arcouest
Paimpol

Îles Chausey

Lanloup

N 175

D 973

Avranches

1

N 176

Sables-
d'Or
*Cap
Fréhel*

St-Méloir-des-Ondes

Cancale

N 175

N 176

D 786

Binic
Erquy
Dinard
Saint-Malo

Pléneuf-
Val-André
Matignon
Ploubalay
St-Suliac
N 176

Plurien-Fréhel

N 12
Lamballe
D 768
Plancoët
Dol-de-
Bretagne

St-Brieuc
St-Aubin
Plélan-
le-Petit
Dinan
Combourg
D 155
D 798
D 177

Quintin

CÔTES-D'ARMOR
Moncontour
Tinténiac
Fougères

A 84
N 12
N 12

Mur-de-
Bretagne
Loudéac
Béchérel
Hédé
N 131
D 175
N 178

MAYENNE

N 164
Plémet

D 768
Montfort
Rennes
Vitré

Pontivy
D 766
Plélan-
le-Grand
N 157

D 764
Paimpont
N 24

N 24
Ploërmel
ILLE-ET-
VILAINE

Josselin
la Guerche-
de-Bretagne

MORBIHAN
la Chapelle-
Caro
Malestroit
D 177
N 137
D 777
N 171

D 767
N 166
Locqueltas
Molac
Rochefort-en-Terre
Châteaubriant

St-Avé
Redon
N 171

Vannes
D 775
MAINE-
ET-LOIRE
2

Arradon
D 164
D 775
N 171
D 178
D 163

Arzon
Sárzeau
la Roche-
Bernard
D 923

Damgan
D 773
St-Gildas
LOIRE-
ATLANTIQUE

la Trinité-
sur-Mer
N 166
N 171
D 164

*Île de
Hoedic*
Guérande
Saint-Nazaire
Ancenis

le Croisic
N 171
Loire

A 11

la Baule
N 137
D 763

D 213
Nantes

Pornic
D 751
D 723
N 249

B

food is also excellent – for around €9–15 you can enjoy Roquefort pancake, crêpe with milk jam and organic cider. *Free coffee offered to our readers on presentation of this guide.*

Sainte-Anne-d'Auray
56400 (6km N)

⚫ 🏠 |●| L'Auberge

56 rte. de Vannes.
☎02.97.57.61.55 ℗02.97.57.69.10
🌐www.auberge-larvoir.com
Closed *Mon and Tues lunchtime; Wed; Tues and Wed in July–Aug; winter school holidays; 12 Nov–9 Dec.* **Disabled access. TV. High chairs available. Car park.**

One of the best restaurants in the locality; John-Paul II dined here when he visited the region in 1996. You can savour the delicacy of Jean-Luc Larvoir's culinary approach on all the menus, from the cheapest at €21 (not served Sat evening, Sun lunchtime or public holidays) to those at €26–68: try crab *tartare*, home-smoked salmon, chopped oysters, sea bass with Guéméné *andouille*, truffle *coulis* and the like. The extensive wine list proves excellent value for money. Rooms go for €40–52; half board €57–63 per person. A place of pilgrimage in more ways than one, as people come from afar to eat here.

Erdeven
56410 (15km W)

⚫ |●| La Crêperie du Manoir de Kercadio

Lieu-dit Kercadio; from Auray, take the road to Ploërmel then Erdeven.
☎02.97.55.64.67
Open *daily in July–Aug; weekends from Easter to end June, public holidays and school holidays.*

The setting is elegant, with wood-panelled walls, original fireplace and wide hearth – and the bread oven in the kitchen is the real thing. But costs are actually very reasonable with a first menu at €8, others €9.20–9.80; try the simple crêpe with butter or one stuffed with mushrooms or scallops *à l'armoricaine*. They also offer salads, omelettes and so on. On nice days tables are set in the garden, under the shadow of a large magnolia tree. You can rent a bike or set out from here along the hiking paths.

Belz
56550 (16km W)

⚫ 🎋 🏠 |●| Le Relais de Kergou**

It's on the road from Auray, just before Belz.
☎02.97.55.35.61 ℗02.97.55.27.69
📧jean.francois.lorvellec@wanadoo.fr
Closed *Sun evening and Mon (lunchtime only in July–Aug); end Nov.* **TV. Car park.**

This place was built as a farm with a smithy in the nineteenth century. It's thoroughly charming and is remarkably furnished. Doubles with shower/wc or bath go for €42–54 – three rooms look directly over the road so they're noisier than the others – the ones at the back are quieter. The bathrooms vary in size, also, and some are a real squeeze. The garden is lovely and the beaches are only 4km away. Good cooking is served in the imposing dining room with its majestic proportions and large bay window and menus, €11 (not Sun) and €24, feature lots of fish dishes. *10% discount on the half board rate (except July–Aug) offered to our readers on presentation of this guide.*

Bangor
56360

⚫ 🏠 |●| Hôtel-Village La Désirade***

Le Petit Cosquet; it's outside Bangor on the Port-Colon road.
☎02.97.31.70.70 ℗02.97.31.89.63
🌐www.hotel-la-desirade.com
Closed *Nov to Easter.* **Restaurant closed** *Sun evening and Mon from Oct.* **Disabled access. TV. High chairs available. Heated swimming pool. Car park.**

A charming hotel with architecture typical of Belle-Île: a series of low buildings with painted walls and shutters. Twenty-six thoughtfully decorated and spacious rooms €98.70–122.85; half board is compulsory in high season and holiday weekends at €81.40–110.25 per person. Family rooms for four with half board cost €320.15–381.15. The owner-chef offers delicate dishes – there's a single menu at €30.48; allow €46 for a meal à la carte. They have a lot of regulars in high season and since they've enlarged the restaurant it's also open to non-residents, so it's best to book. You can rent a bike.

Bénodet
29950

🏊 🏠 |O| **Hôtel Kastel**

Corniche de la Plage; opposite the sea, next
to the seawater therapy centre.
☎02.98.57.05.01 📠02.98.57.29.99
🌐www.hotel-kastel.com
Open *all year.* **Closed** *12–25 Dec.* **TV. High
chairs available. Car park.**

A modern and well situated hotel offering attentive service. The twenty-three
bright, spacious and extremely comfortable rooms (€68–116) are complemented
by lovely bathrooms; half board €65–89
per person. Special rates are on offer for
a six-day treatment. Attractive, airy dining
room where you can eat fine local cooking, with fish taking pride of place, in a
contemporary setting; menus from €13
(weekday lunchtime) up to €30. They
serve a hearty breakfast buffet, too. *Free
coffee offered to our readers on presentation of
this guide.*

|O| 🏊 **Restaurant L'Alhambra**

Corniche de l'Estuaire.
☎02.98.57.16.00
Closed *Mon–Thurs, except school holidays
(Oct–March); Jan–March* **Open** *daily 11am–
1am (April–Sept).* **High chairs available.**

At the foot of a lush garden that is only
separated from the beach by a small road,
this bar-restaurant is a friendly, fashionable spot with Moorish décor, with
mosaics and a fountain. You can eat fish
dishes, seafood platters and oysters at any
time of day. First menu weighs in at €18
(lunchtime only), others €20–30; reckon
on around €25 for a full meal à la carte.
You can also enjoy a cocktail on the
terrace, with its stunning view of the Odet
estuary. *Free coffee offered to our readers on
presentation of this guide.*

🏊 |O| **Le Transat**

Quai l'Herminier; in the old port.
☎02.98.66.29.29
Closed *5 Jan–5 Feb.* **Open** *daily 9.30am–
1am.*

The dining room, decorated in a nautical
style, is presided over by the cup won by
the famous steamship *Normandie* – also a
huge, tiered terrace overlooking the port.
Good local cooking and attentive service,
with dishes of the day incorporating
produce coming straight from the sea.

There's a *formule* menu at €18.50, others
€21.50–28.50; reckon on around €32
à la carte. The proprietors rent out six
apartments on the upper floors, with the
option of rental on a nightly basis. *Free
coffee offered to our readers on presentation of
this guide.*

Clohars-Fouesnant
29950 (3km NE)

🏊 |O| **Restaurant La Forge
d'Antan**

---

31 rte. de Nors-Vraz; take the D34, then
follow the signposts.
☎02.98.54.84.00
Closed *Sun evening; Mon; Tues (out of
season); Mon, Tues and Wed lunchtime (July–
Aug).* **Disabled access. Car park.**

Way out in the country, this friendly,
welcoming establishment boasts a superb
rustic décor, with a stylish atmosphere
and clientele to match. The imaginative seasonal cuisine on menus (€20–58)
includes dishes such as lobster and tarragon pancake and farmhouse pigeon with
sesame seeds. Children's menu costs €12;
for à la carte reckon on around €45. *Free
coffee offered to our readers on presentation of
this guide.*

Combrit
29121 (5.5km NW)

🏊 🏠 |O| **Hôtel-restaurant Sainte-
Marine***

---

19 rue Bac; it's in the little port of Sainte-
Marine; opposite Bénodet.
☎02.98.56.34.79 📠02.98.51.94.09
🌐www.hotelsaintemarine.com
Closed *Sun evening and Mon, except school
holidays; Nov.* **TV.**

The wonderful dining room is decorated in a nautical style and has a magnificent view of the River Odet and Pont
de Cornouaille; there's also a terrace.
Inventive cuisine that takes into consid-
eration both the flavour of the produce
and the habits of the clientele is served on
menus from €16.50 (weekday lunchtime)
up to €47. Specialities include fish *carpaccio*
with spices and coriander and grilled fish
with *purée maison*. If you want to prolong
the pleasure, there are a few quirky rooms
also decorated in a nautical style – doubles
with shower/wc or bath €60–85; half
board, compulsory in July and August,
costs €70–80 per person.

Plonéour-Lanvern

29720 (18 km NW)

✆ 🕸 🏠 |O| Hôtel-restaurant des Voyageurs**

1 rue Jean-Jaurès; take the D2 from Pont-l'Abbé; it's behind the church.
☎02.98.87.61.35 ☎02.98.82.67.05
✉hotelvoyageurs@aol.com
Closed *Fri evening and Sat lunch (Sept–Oct); weekends (Nov–Easter); 1–15 Nov; Christmas and New Year.* **TV. High chairs available. Car park.**

Typical, friendly village hotel offering an effusive welcome, excellent cooking and reasonable prices. Attractive rooms, although the ones looking out on the street can be a little noisy, cost €36–52 for a double with shower/wc or bath; half board, compulsory in July and August, €42–54.50 per person. Weekday lunchtime menu at €13, with others up to €33, feature dishes including home-made fish soup and chef's terrine with port. Logis de France. *Free house apéritif offered to our readers on presentation of this guide.*

Penmarch

29760 (25km W)

✆ 🏠 |O| Le Doris

Port de Kerity, pointe de Penmarch; take the D785 in the direction of Pont-l'Abbé then pointe de Penmarch; it's on the port.
☎02.98.58.60.92 ☎02.98.58.58.16
Closed *All Saints' Day to Easter.*

Right on the harbour of this little port, this place is something of an institution, with a reputation for serving good seafood and fresh fish. It's run by a fishing family so the fish are freshly caught and served in traditional ways, with menus at €11 (weekday lunchtime) and others €15.20–61: seafood platters (incidentally, the restaurant holds the Breton regional "*Authentique plateau de fruits de mer*" [Authentic seafood platter] quality label), poached turbot with *beurre blanc* and monkfish with *lardons*. There are also a few simple, spacious and clean bed-and-breakfast rooms for €31 with shower or bath; shared wc; but, as the rooms are above a lively bar, they're not ideal for light sleepers. The bar is open all year.

Binic

22520

✆ 🕸 🏠 |O| Hôtel Benhuyc***

1 quai Jean-Bart; right on the port.
☎02.96.73.39.00 ☎02.96.73.77.04
🕸www.benhuyc.com
Closed *15 Dec–5 Jan.* **Restaurant closed** *Sun evening; Mon lunchtime.* **Disabled access. TV.**

Overlooking the boats moored in the pleasure port, this modern hotel is easy to recommend. The bright, comfortable rooms are well maintained, and most have a view of the harbour or the Banche beach. Doubles with shower or bath/wc go for €52–68 in low season and €81–101 in high season (buffet breakfast included in high season); the smaller ones are the cheapest but they're still pleasant. *10% discount on the room rate (except July–Aug) offered to our readers on presentation of this guide.*

Brest

29200

✆ 🕸 🏠 Hôtel Astoria**

9 rue Traverse; close to the rue de Siam, the quay to the isles and the station.
☎02.98.80.19.10 ☎02.98.80.52.41
🕸www.hotel-brest-astoria.com
Closed *20 Dec–4 Jan.* **TV. Cots available. Pay car park.**

A hotel that looks like so many other buildings in Brest, but offers good value considering its excellent position. Bright, cheerful rooms, some with balconies overlooking the quiet street, cost €26 for a double with basin and €41–50 with shower/wc or bath; breakfast €6. Some rooms have just been renovated. In July and August the Brest *jeudis* are just seven minutes' walk away. The car park costs €6 per day or €31.50 for a week. What's more, you can take advantage of discounts from partner hotels such as *Océanopolis* and *Compagnie maritime Pen-Ar-Bed*. *10% discount on the room rate (except in July–Aug) or 20% discount during the weekends (except in July–Aug) offered to our readers on presentation of this guide.*

✆ 🕸 🏠 Hotel Abalys**

7 av. Georges-Clemenceau: it's 100m from the tourist office.

☎02.98.44.21.86 ⓕ02.98.43.68.32
ⓦwww.abalys.com
Disabled access. TV. Car park.

Very central, with double rooms from
€30 with handbasin, and €46–77 with
shower/wc or bath. They all have double
glazing, though they're a bit small; some
have a sea view. Reception is open round
the clock. Credit cards not accepted. *Free
house apéritif offered to our readers on presentation of this guide.*

ⓔ ☗ Hôtel le Pasteur*

29 rue Louis-Pasteur; it's between the rue de
Siam and the covered market.
☎02.98.46.08.73 ⓕ02.98.43.46.80
TV.

An establishment that holds its own in
its category. It's clean and pleasant with
doubles at €30 with shower/wc, and
though the soundproofing between rooms
is not great, the beds are good and at least
the windows are double-glazed. It's just
a shame the welcome isn't as warm as it
could be.

ⓒ ☗ Citôtel de la Gare**

4 av. Gambetta; it's opposite the station.
☎02.98.44.47.01 ⓕ02.98.43.34.07
ⓦwww.hotelgare.com
**Disabled access. TV. High chairs available.
Pay car park.**

Practically sited and more appealing than
many station hotels, this friendly place
offers some lovely views of the harbour
from the third floor and above. Doubles
cost €42 with shower or €48–60 with
shower/wc or bath. There's a panoramic
view from the room on the fifth floor, and
reception is open around the clock.

ⓒ ☘ ☗ Mercure – Les Voyageurs***

2 rue Yves-Collet; it's on the corner of av.
Clemenceau and rue Yves-Collet.
☎ and ⓕ02.98.80.31.80
ⓦwww.mercure.com
Closed *20 Dec–3 Jan.* **TV.**

It's rare for a chain hotel to fight its way
into this guidebook, but this brilliant
three-star is one of the best of its category
in town. The hotel has retained its superb
1940s entrance hall. The well-equipped
bedrooms have bathrooms with character;
doubles €89–105 with shower/wc or
bath. Reception is open around the clock.

*One free breakfast per room offered to our
readers on presentation of this guide.*

ⓔ |●| Restaurant La Pensée Sauvage

13 rue d'Aboville (and rue de Gasté); behind
Saint-Michel church.
☎02.98.46.36.65
Closed *Sat lunchtime; Sun; Mon; mid-July to
end Aug.* **Disabled access.**

You have to hunt a little for this restaurant – it's way off the beaten track. But
it has two simple little dining rooms
that generate a great atmosphere so it's
worth the effort. The cooking is tasty
and comes in generous servings: try the
home-made *cassoulet*, duck *confit* or the
goat's cheese or fig *gratin*. It's excellent
value, with a lunchtime weekday *plat du
jour* for €8, or you can eat for about €16
à la carte. Portions are huge and they'll
give you a doggy bag if you can't finish
all the *cassoulet*. Getting a table here can
be a challenge.

ⓒ ☘ |●| Restaurant Le Marrakech

44 rue Traverse.
☎02.98.46.45.14
Closed *Wed lunch; Sun lunch; mid-July to
mid-Aug.* **Open** *noon–2.30pm and 7–11pm.*
High chairs available.

Attractive, restrained décor and good-
quality cooking make this an excellent
place. The delicate and aromatic dishes
are expertly spiced according to secret
recipes that have been passed down
from mother to daughter for generations;
lunch menu €8.99, another at €9.80,
and around €15–20 à la carte. *Free house
apéritif offered to our readers on presentation
of this guide.*

ⓒ ☘ |●| Amour de Pomme de Terre

23 rue des Halles-Saint-Louis; it's behind the
Saint-Louis covered market.
☎02.98.43.48.51
Open *lunchtime and evening till 11pm
(10.30pm Sun and Mon).* **Disabled access.
High chairs available. Pay car park.**

This restaurant is devoted to potatoes, and
just the "samba" and "amandine" varieties,
which were developed for their baking
qualities. A multitude of preparations: with
parsley, stuffed with different cheeses or
served with grilled meats, fish and shellfish. There's a menu for €9.50 (weekday

lunchtimes) and à la carte €20–25. The lunchtime dishes of the day change daily with one of the excellent (potato-free) desserts. The walls and the menus give you glimpses of the owner's sense of humour. The setting is pretty nice, sort of revisited rustic. And since the tables are rather tightly packed, you may well make new friends. *Free house apéritif offered to our readers on presentation of this guide.*

⊚ 🏖 |●| Crêperie Moderne

34 rue d'Algésiras.
☎02.98.44.44.36
Closed Sun lunchtime. **Open** 11.30am–2.30pm and 6–10pm. **Disabled access. High chairs available. Car park.**

Behind its dazzling façade lies an extremely classical dining room in the outmoded brasserie style. The crêpes are delicious, however, whether served simply with butter or more elaborately with scallops in vermouth. À la carte costs €10. This establishment has been going since 1922, so they know what they're about. Takeaway option for those who would like to indulge in the sin of gluttony for a little longer. *Free Kir Breton offered to our readers on presentation of this guide.*

Guilers
29820 (5km NW)

⊚ |●| Crêperie Blé Noir

Bois du Keroual. From Brest, follow directions towards Parc de Penfeld. It's near the Exhibition Centre.
☎02.98.07.57.40
Open daily 11.30am–9.30pm. **High chairs available.**

Almost hidden by trees and bushes next to a small lake and located in an ancient mill, this crêperie is a dream of a place. Friendly service, delicious crêpes and plenty of opportunity for wonderful country walks after the meal. There's a single menu at €10.30; reckon on around €10–15 à la carte. Specialities include buckwheat pancakes with medallions of monkfish, with scallops or smoked salmon.

Gouesnou
29850 (10km N)

⊚ |●| Crêperie La Finette

Rue du Bois-Kerallenoc; from Gouesnou follow the road to Kerallenoc for 1km. It's signposted.

☎02.98.07.86.68
Closed Mon and Tues lunchtime out of season; Mon lunchtime July–Aug; a week mid-Sept; a week mid-Nov. **High chairs available.**

Lydie and Jean-Yves Pirou chose this lovely old house with a beautiful garden to prepare their very tasty, traditional crêpes. The interior is old stone with a huge fireplace; you get a real sense of Brittany and the sea. A meal costs about €10 and it's best to book.

Plouzané
29280 (10km W)

⊚ |●| Les Mille et Une Lunes

Plage du Minou; more or less mid-way between Plougonvelin and Brest; well signposted from the D789.
☎02.98.48.41.81
Closed weekday evenings; school holidays (except July–Aug). **Car park.**

Restaurant owned by a scientist from Ilfremer, the French marine research centre, with his students waiting on the tables. He seeks out top-quality ingredients with an appropriately scientific meticulousness (superb local cheeses and tasty organic produce), as well as growing no fewer than 35 different varieties of tomatoes. Dish of the day and *assiette osée* (home-made terrines and charcuterie), served in generous portions, around €11; there's also a menu at €15. Lively wines and aromatic coffees round off the fine meals. There's a small terrace with the sea in the background.

Camaret
29570

⊚ 🏠 |●| Hôtel-Restaurant du Styvel**

Quai du Styvel; one of the last restaurants at the end of the quay.
☎02.98.27.92.74 ☎02.98.27.88.37
✉hotelstyvel@wanadoo.fr
Closed Jan. **TV. High chairs available. Car park.**

The thirteen well-kept rooms are small but generally comfortable and those overlooking the harbour have been redecorated; doubles €36–46 with shower/wc. The cooking is reasonable and, as you'd imagine, revolves around the fish landed in the harbour, with menus at €15–36.

Brasserie Côté Mer

12 quai Toudouze; in the port.
☎02.98.27.93.79
Closed *Tues and Wed in Feb, March and Oct; Thurs in April–June; Nov–Jan.* **Disabled access.**

A beautiful brasserie painted yellow, with pretty lamps creating a very pleasant atmosphere. The various menus offer something for every taste. Set menus chalked up on the blackboard start at €13 (weekday lunchtimes) and €14.50 (not Sat evening, Sun). Other menus at €25 and €38 (the latter is based on lobster). Food is served throughout the day in July and August, but the range of food on offer is more limited. Specialities include seafood stew and *cassolette de Jacques*. The view from the covered and heated terrace looks straight out over the port and the Vauban Tower.

Les Frères de la Côte

11 quai Toudouze.
☎02.98.27.95.42
Closed *Mon–Fri (April to end June); Wed–Thurs (Sept).* **Open** *daily in July–Aug.*

The two brothers of Breton origin who own this restaurant came back to their roots after running another establishment in Guadeloupe, and they use the spices they discovered in the Caribbean to flavour Breton produce in a genuine gastronomic adventure: fish are cooked with cider and mango, spicy caramel, Indian Marsala or pistil of saffron. Other dishes listed on the single menu (€25) include ray salad with passion-fruit vinegar, bass with fennel *confit* and baked lobster with vanilla and pineapple; reckon on €30 à la carte. *Free house apéritif offered to our readers on presentation of this guide.*

Cancale
35260

Le Querrien**

7 quai Duguay-Trouin; it's in the port.
☎02.99.89.64.56 ℱ02.99.89.79.35
🖳www.le-querrien.com
TV. High chairs available.

You'll find some of the loveliest rooms in Cancale at this place. They're all brand new, huge, bright and equipped with good bathrooms; doubles with shower/wc or bath €80–110. The restaurant is decorated like a smart brasserie with wood panelling, copper pans on the walls and a large fish tank. Menus at €15 (not Sun), €23 and €39.50 dish up good cooking; a meal à la carte will cost around €38. They take their work seriously here and offer highly competent service.

Hôtel de la Pointe du Grouin**

Follow the signs to Pointe du Grouin, and it's about 3km from the centre of town.
☎02.99.89.60.55 ℱ02.99.89.92.22
🖳www.hotelpointedugrouin.com
Closed *10 Nov–31 March.* **Restaurant closed** *Tues and Thurs lunchtimes out of season.* **TV. Car park.**

A solidly constructed building out on the Pointe du Grouin, facing the sea. The site is exceptional and the smart hotel is built of local stone and has a cosy interior; quiet is guaranteed. The small, simple rooms have been smartened up – four of them have a private terrace and they all have sea views. Doubles cost €84–98 with shower/wc or bath; half board, at €79 per person, is compulsory from June to September. The dining room has a panoramic view of the bay of Mont-Saint-Michel and serves traditional cuisine on its menus, €19.50–61. It's a good starting-point for walks in the wild countryside hereabouts. Logis de France.

La Cancalaise

3 rue de la Vallée-Porcon; it's 2 min from the Musée des Arts et Traditions Populaires, in the centre.
☎02.99.89.71.22
Closed *Mon and Tues out of season; Mon only during July–Aug and school holidays.* **Disabled access. High chairs available. Car park.**

A place frequented by locals and tourists alike. The walls are made from dressed stone and adorned with old photographs, and the tables are nicely set. At the back of the dining room there's a long range with a double line of hot plates to cook the crêpes – all the dishes are made to order. The crêpes and galettes are crispy and delicate. There's nothing revolutionary here but everything is very tasty. Good range of Breton ciders; try the Ker Avel. About €13 for a meal; they also do a takeaway service. *Free Kir Breton offered to our readers on presentation of this guide.*

✆ |●| Le Surcouf

7 quai Gambetta, in the port.
☎02.99.89.61.75
Closed *Wed and Thurs except July–Aug; 3
weeks in Jan; 15 Nov–15 Dec.*

This gourmet restaurant stands out from
the rest of the establishments along the
port. The produce used is not only wonderful but the ingredients are deftly and
creatively prepared and cooked. The setting is carefully designed in quiet good
taste. Menus cost from €18 (not served
on Sat or Sun) to €60. Not cheap, but
definitely worth the extra.

✆ |●| Au Pied d'Cheval

10 quai Gambetta.
☎02.99.89.76.95
Closed *15 Nov to Palm Sunday.*
Open *9am–9pm (10pm in summer).*
Disabled access.

"Unbeatable oysters" says the slogan, and
the oyster-farming family who run this
place are not wrong. The seafood and
cooked dishes (not available Nov–April)
are great too – the ingredients are ultra-
fresh. Try the *écuelle du Père Dédé*, a mixture
of shellfish in a creamy lemony sauce,
the mussels, or the *patouillou* (whelks) *à
l'armoricaine*. The tables and stools on the
ground floor are rustic but the upstairs
dining room is more comfortable. You'll
pay around €18.50 à la carte and the wines
are good.

✆ |●| Restaurant Le Saint-Cast

Route de la Corniche; it's a 5-min walk from
the centre.
☎02.99.89.66.08
Closed *Wed; Tues and Sun out of season;
mid-Nov to mid-Dec and during the Feb
school holiday.*

A delicious restaurant in all senses of
the word. It's just outside the town in
an elegant building overlooking the sea
– with Mont-Saint-Michel away in the
distance – and an ideal place to spend
a delightful evening dining on fresh
seafood expertly but simply cooked. The
€20 menu served at lunch and dinner
during the week is remarkable for quality and balance. Other menus up to €40
feature specialities prepared in the same
vein, such as lobster tagine with fresh
pasta or *effeuillade* of salt cod and cockles;
€50–60 for à la carte. Reservations recommended.

Saint-Méloir-des-Ondes
35350 (5km SW)

✆✆ 🏠 |●| Restaurant Le Coquillage, Bistrot Marin

Maison Richeux.
☎02.99.89.25.25 ☎02.99.89.88.47
🌐www.maisons-de-bricourt.com
Closed *Mon; Tues and Thurs lunchtimes;
plus Fri lunchtime in winter.* **TV. Car park.**

A ravishing 1920s manor house looking
down over the Mont-Saint-Michel bay.
The prices in the restaurant are fair when
all is said and done, and the wines are
affordable, but the lovely bedrooms are very
expensive indeed – €160–310 depending
on the season. The whole place shows great
refinement and good taste, with a country
interior with checked and plaid fabrics,
leather chairs, a bar and a wide fireplace.
The sea views are breathtaking. There
are no à la carte options; menus €25–47,
with a children's menu for €15.30; *formule
grignotage* for two €57 including three cold
and three hot dishes. Olivier Roellinger,
the darling of Breton cuisine, produces the
best dishes from what the sea has to offer.
Breakfast is costly (€16) but fabulous and
based on traditional Breton produce. Good
news for guests: from the beginning of
May to the end of September, the landlord
courteously invites them on board the
Étoile de Bricourt, an old rig he bought as a
treat to himself.

Carantec
29660

✆ ⛵ |●| La Cambuse et Le Cabestan

7 rue du Port.
☎02.98.67.08.92
Closed *Mon except July–Aug; Tues;
5 Nov–15 Dec.* **Disabled access. High
chairs available.**

Two restaurants in one here: *La Cambuse*
and *Le Cabestan*. Choose the one that suits
your mood; the chef is the same for both
but the serving staff and atmospheres are
very different. *La Cambuse* is a mixture of
a brasserie, a bar and an inn. Generous portions of filling brasserie food and Breton
specialities are served at reasonable prices.
Next door at *Le Cabestan* the mood is
quieter, even hushed. With its smart décor
and softly spoken diners, this is the place
for a romantic dinner. The cuisine is more

refined, too, featuring pan-fried scallops and prawns with thyme. À la carte you will pay about €20 at *La Cambuse*, and €30–40 at *Le Cabestan*. *Free house apéritif offered to our readers on presentation of this guide.*

Carhaix-Plouguer
29270

⊚ ⚹ |●| Créperie Les Salines

23 rue Brizeux; it's near the tourist office.
☎02.98.99.11.32
Closed *Tues–Thurs evenings; Sun out of season and during holidays; June to early July.* **High chairs available.**

They've created a maritime feel in the dining room. The tasty crêpes are made from Breton organic flour and stuffed with unusual fillings. Various weekday lunch *formules* for €7.50 except public holidays, and other menus up to €14.50 list good choices including salmon in seaweed preserve and a Breton crêpe with apple flambéed in Calvados and cream. À la carte, go for the *fleur grand cru* with Guéméné *andouille* and cider preserve. This is a quality place for all budgets. *Free coffee offered to our readers on presentation of this guide.*

Carnac
56340

⊛ ⌂ |●| Hôtel Le Râtelier**

4 chemin Douët; tucked away in an alleyway in the town centre, 200m to the right of the church.
☎02.97.52.05.04 ☎02.97.52.76.11
⊛www.le-ratelier.com
Closed *Tues and Wed (Oct–March); Jan.* **TV. Car park.**

A charming little hotel in an attractive house weighed down by ivy, tucked away down an alley in the town centre. Well-kept rooms for €38–55; most have shower/wc but a few have washing facilities only. Half board, from €55 per person, is compulsory for two people staying in July and August. Dishes change every three months, but they specialize in seafood and fish often served with complicated but delicious sauces. First menu costs €17 (not Sat evenings or public holidays) and others €26–40 – one menu offers nothing but lobster in all shapes, sizes and styles. The welcome that we received was a little on the cold side.

⊛ |●| Restaurant La Côte

Kermario. Take the Auray road and turn right at the first lights; it's 800m further, near the standing stones of Kermario.
☎02.97.52.02.80
Closed *Sat lunch, Sun evening and Mon out of season; Mon and Tues lunchtime (July–Aug); 5 Jan–10 Feb; first week in March; first week in Oct; third week in Nov.* **Car park.**

Pierre Michaud has transformed the family restaurant into the best restaurant in the district, and the staff is extremely pleasant. You will taste dishes of rare subtlety here; a concentration of tastes and colours that will transport you for a couple of hours, with dishes such as terrine of foie gras and young rabbit or Breton lobster *gratin* with slightly salted butter. There's a menu at €22 (not served Sun) and €32–52; the menus change every three months. You will pay around €45 à la carte.

Châteaulin
29150

⊚ ⚹ |●| Créperie Marc Philippe

29 quai Cosmao; it's very close to the tourist office.
☎02.98.86.38.00
Closed *Mon out of season; April–Sept.* **High chairs available.**

A very small, central crêperie. The crêpes are fairly priced and taste great. A meal will cost around €11 à la carte only. It's a cheerful place where they use quality local produce, including Fouesnant cider and local beer; all the grain is grown in Brittany. *Free coffee offered to our readers on presentation of this guide.*

Plomodiern
29550 (15km W)

⊛ |●| Auberge des Glazics

Rue de la Plage; take the D887, then the D47.
☎02.98.81.52.32
Closed *Mon; Tues; Wed except school holidays; a week in March; Oct.*

In the early nineteenth-century, these premises were used as a blacksmith's foundry. As so many customers came, the blacksmith's wife decided to offer them soup, and her grandchildren have continued this culinary tradition, although in less modest style: Olivier Bellin has been declared the best young chef in

Brittany. He has set out to prove that Breton cooking means not only the fine, fresh produce provided by nature but also a creative approach to it; his imagination seems to know no bounds, and his desserts, in particular, are a veritable symphony of tastes and colours. There are a range of menus (€38–96) and excellent wines on offer. The service and atmosphere could be improved by setting a more relaxed tone, but booking is essential.

Combourg

35270

ⓦ ☎ |●| Hôtel du Lac**

2 pl. Chateaubriand; it's on the Rennes road, just outside Combourg.
☎02.99.73.05.65 ℻02.99.73.23.34
ⓦwww.hotel-restaurant-du-lac.com
Closed Fri and Sun evening out of season; Feb; March. **TV. High chairs and games available. Car park.**

This place has a tranquil charm, and it's just a little old-fashioned. On one side there is the château and on the other the lake which was so dear to the writer Chateaubriand. Rooms for €52–82 depending on the facilities; they're fine, though the décor is dated. Ask for a room with a view – it's worth paying extra. Good, traditional dishes in the restaurant with a weekday lunchtime set menu at €17, others up to €40; à la carte about €36. "Regional restaurant" quality label as part of the campaign to promote Breton regional cuisine. Logis de France.

ⓦ |●| Restaurant L'Écrivain

Place Saint-Gilduin; it's opposite the church.
☎02.99.73.01.61
Closed Wed evening; Thurs; Sun evening; Thurs only mid-July to mid-Aug; Feb holiday; All Saints' holiday. **Disabled access. High chairs available. Car park.**

This restaurant has a good reputation, built up over a number of years. The prices are low considering the inventive flavours presented to you, and though there's a limited choice à la carte, that's because the chef uses only the freshest produce: try the home-smoked fish, cod with shellfish jus, or millefeuille of house foie gras and artichokes. Set menus start at €14.60 (weekday lunchtimes) then €21 and €35, with à la carte costing about €30. The restaurant

name means "The Writer", and they sell illustrated books here too.

Hédé

35630 (15km SW)

ⓦ ⅍ |●| Restaurant Le Genty Home

Vallée de Hédé; it's on the N137 in the direction of Tinténiac, 500m outside Hédé.
☎02.99.45.46.07
Closed Tues evening; Wed; Sun evening out of season; 3 weeks end Feb/March; fortnight in Oct. **Disabled access.**

It's hard not to fall for this charming, flower-bedecked hostelry with natural stone walls and a huge fireplace. It's run by a highly talented young chef who has already attracted a following of food lovers. His cooking is excellent and even the most demanding of foodies will be intrigued by the selection of dishes he puts on his menus. Delicious weekday lunch menu at €11.80 and four others €22–36 Specialities include leg of a special breed of chicken, known locally as the Rennes cuckoo, stuffed with foie gras, the recipe for which won him the regional competition. *Free coffee offered to our readers on presentation of this guide.*

Concarneau

29900

ⓦ ☎ ⅍ Hôtel des Halles

Place de l'Hôtel-de-Ville; in the town centre, near the enclosed town.
☎02.98.97.11.41 ℻02.98.50.58.54
ⓦwww.hoteldeshalles.com
High chairs and games available.

Small, modern hotel that is constantly being made more comfortable. Although it is right in the town centre, it is a quiet spot. All the rooms are different, but they are equally attractive and regularly refurbished; doubles €35 with shower, €49–58 with shower/wc or bath, and breakfast €7. Two single rooms are also available. The hotel has come to an agreement with the restaurant and brasserie L'Amiral so that its guests can take advantage of special half board rates. The owner is a friendly man who'll happily ply you with information about the region. *10% discount on a room (1 Oct–30 April) offered to our readers on presentation of this guide.*

⚫ 🏠 Citôtel de France et d'Europe**

9 av. de la Gare; road leads directly to the port.
☎02.98.97.00.64
🌐www.groupecitotel.com/hotels/fraeur.html
Closed *Sat evening (15 Nov–15 March); Christmas to New Year.* **Disabled access. TV. Pay car park (high season only).**

Well-positioned in the centre of town, this hotel offers the kind of pleasant, comfortable rooms – with telephones, alarm clocks, and efficient double-glazing – that you would expect from a modern hotel. Double rooms cost €50 with shower/wc or €58 with bath. Enjoy a drink in the bar or on the sheltered terrace.

⚫ 🏠 Hôtel Kermoor**

Les Sables Blancs; near the beach of Les Sables Blancs.
☎02.98.97.02.96 📠02.98.97.84.04
TV.

The *Kermor* is a characterful turn-of-the-(twentieth)-century hotel right on the beach. The interior bears a strong resemblance to that of a boat. Rooms – €80–90 for a double with shower/wc or bath – are bright and fresh, with wood panelling and, to complete the illusion, some have portholes for windows. Each one has a sea view, and the most expensive have huge bay windows and wooden balconies. Half board is compulsory from mid-July to mid-September. The splendid breakfast room, where breakfast is served until 11.30am, also has a fantastic view of the sea and the dining room has a panoramic view. The chef knows how to create good, tasty and generous snacks and offers menus €16–60. The à la carte menu changes twice a year, but the lobster in cider stew and the famous *kouign aman* are permanent fixtures.

⚫ 🍴 🥞 Crêperie Aux Remparts

31 rue Théophile-Louarn; in a slightly out-of-the-way little road.
☎02.98.50.65.66
Closed *Mon; Nov to Easter, except during winter school holidays.* **High chairs available.**

Outside, a stone façade with carvings in floral designs and a quiet terrace; inside, a rustic setting complete with fireplace. Effusive welcome and fine, professional cooking, with plenty of seafood on the single menu (€12). This is our first recommendation in the enclosed town. *Free coffee offered to our readers on presentation of this guide.*

⚫ 🍴 L'Amiral

1 av. Pierre-Guéguin; in the town centre, opposite the enclosed town and the port.
☎02.98.60.55.23
Closed *Mon (July–Aug); Sun evening and Mon (other months); 3 weeks end Jan to early Feb; fortnight in Sept.* **Disabled access. High chairs available.**

The façade of this old building hides a beautiful modern, dining room, with decoration on a nautical theme centred on brown wood panelling, blue benches and elegant lamps. The young chef, Arnaud Lebossé, served his apprenticeship in some of France's top restaurants (*Le Récamier, Troisgros, La Pérouse*), and the fruits of this experience are plain to see in his inventive cooking that varies according to the availability of fresh ingredients. The menu changes every day, but some of his dishes have already become classics: John Dory with herbs, *cassolette* of squid, lobster pancakes with shellfish *coulis*, pan-fried kidneys with cognac, etc. The bread rolls, foie gras and ice creams are all made on the premises. The menus offer excellent value for money at €17 to €25 (excellent "Simenon" menu), with a children's menu €7; expect to pay €40 à la carte. Alongside the restaurant, there's a brasserie with a menu at €11. In summer, you can buy home-made ice creams and sorbets to take away.

Conquet (Le)
29217

⚫ 🥞 🏠 🍴 Le Relais du Vieux Port

1 quai du Drellac'h; in the port.
☎02.98.89.15.91
Closed *Jan.* **Disabled access. High chairs available.**

In times gone by this old harbour inn provided simple rooms and a restaurant. But after substantial alterations it has been upgraded to the standards of a modern hotel. It's a friendly place, run by a family who know how to make you feel welcome. Stripped wooden floors and white walls are gently brightened up with blue stencilling. Five rooms with a view of the estuary go for €40–58 with shower/wc – really excellent prices for the quality but the cheapest room only has a shower. The dining room is a relatively new addition to the building and they've put in an open fireplace – there's a good choice of crêpes, seafood and good quality fish dishes. There's only one menu at €25; a meal à la carte will cost around €20. Live music is played on Wednesday evenings in summer. *Free Kir Breton offered to our readers on presentation of this guide.*

ⓔ ⚐ 🏠 ⦿ La Ferme de Keringar

It's in the village.
☎02.98.89.09.59 ⓕ02.98.89.04.39
ⓦwww.keringar.com
Restaurant closed *lunchtimes out of season.* **High chairs available.**

The farm is sheltered from the wild sea storms between Le Conquet and the Pointe de Saint-Mathieu and has been in the same family for over two hundred years. The current owner used to teach primary school kids and is a passionate advocate of organic farming: he's turned the farm into a teaching centre and it also provides a welcome stopping place for walkers. Half board only: stay in one of the eight attractively arranged rooms with shower/wc for €42–45 per person per night. In the restaurant there's a massive granite fireplace and wooden tables and benches. The cuisine is a mixture of fish and meat and offers good value for money (menus €16–40): *cotriade, kig ha farz*, Molène sausage smoked over seaweed. Bread is baked on site, and there's a shop selling their produce. Entertainment programme includes Breton *fest-noz*, special evenings and storytelling. To summarize, a sort of mini-cultural centre out in the countryside. *Free house apéritif offered to our readers on presentation of this guide.*

Crach
56400

ⓔ ⦿ Restaurant Crêperie L'Hermine

12 rue d'Aboville; from Auray, follow directions towards La Trinité-sur-Mer; it's on the way.
☎02.97.30.01.17
Closed *Mon–Wed out of season; Tues evening and Wed (April–June and Sept); end Nov to early Dec.* **Disabled access. High chairs and games available.**

You can't miss this lovely house, festooned with flowers. The dining room is bright

and pleasant, and there is also a lovely veranda opening onto the rock garden. There's no set menu but a wide choice of galettes, and fish and seafood dishes. Anyone with a sweet tooth will be spoilt for choice between the tempting desserts. A meal will cost around €12.

Crozon
29160

ⓔ ⚐ 🏠 ⦿ Hôtel de la Presqu'île – Restaurant Le Mutin Gourmand

1 rue Graveran; it's on the church square.
☎02.98.27.29.29 ⓕ02.98.26.11.97
ⓦwww.chez.com/mutingourmand
Closed *Sun evening, Mon and Tues lunchtime out of season; Mon lunchtime in season; mid-Jan to Feb.* **Disabled access. TV.**

A charming hotel that radiates the true style of Brittany. The décor is inspired by the yellow and ochre of local costumes, Breton pottery and the sea. Double rooms go for €44–66 in low season, €44–73 in high season; half board €103–133 for two people. There are several dining rooms decorated in the same style serving menus at €16 (not public holidays) and €24–49. Very good cuisine using fresh market produce: egg *chaud-froid* and sea-urchin coral, fillet of yellow pollack with black wheat pancake and very good desserts. Everything from the bread to the foie gras is prepared in their kitchens. Logis de France. *10% discount on the room rate (except school holidays and long weekends) offered to our readers on presentation of this guide.*

Damgan
56750

ⓔ ⦿ ⚐ Crêperie L'Écurie

31 Grande-Rue à Kervoyal.
☎02.97.41.03.29
Closed *Tues out of season; 11 Nov to Feb half-term.* **Disabled access.**

L'Écurie is a local institution that was founded in 1967 and recently changed hands. Reckon on around €15 for a full meal. The crêpes (€5.40–8.40) are original and delicious, crispy on top and moist inside, as well as being superbly presented. Highlights include the Kerjeannette, with its mustard cream, or for dessert you could try the Arthurette, with vanilla ice cream, caramel, almonds and Chantilly. Gigantic salads are also available. You can eat under the pergola overrun with vines and ivy or in the cosy wood-panelled dining room; either way, a good time is guaranteed. *Free coffee offered to our readers on presentation of this guide.*

Dinan

22100

@ 🏠 Auberge de jeunesse Moulin du Méen

Vallée de la Fontaine-des-Eaux; 600m from the port; from the end of the port, take the Plouer road and then another little one on the left (it's signposted); 2km from the train station: cross the track, then turn right and follow the signposts.
☏ 02.96.39.10.83 ⓕ 02.96.39.10.62
ⓔ dinan@fuaj.org
Closed *22 Dec–31 Jan.* **Games available.**

Old windmill in a charming, wooded valley. With an FUAJ card (compulsory, but available on site), it costs €9.60 per night; half board (with reservation only) €21.20. Breakfast is extra at €3.30 and the menu costs €8.60. Accommodation is in dormitories (75 beds), rooms with one to eight beds and a few doubles with shower/wc at the same rate. There are also eight beds in a large tent (€5.30 per night), and you can camp in your own tent. Facilites include a fully equipped kitchen and a sitting room with fireplace, with piano and guitar available. Trekking in the surrounding countryside and photography courses are two options available to guests.

@ 🏋 🏠 |●| Hôtel Les Alleux**

Route de Ploubalay, Tanen; take the D2 in the direction of Ploubalay
☏ 02.96.85.16.10 ⓕ 02.96.85.11.40
ⓦ www.hotellesalleux.com
Restaurant closed *Sun evening out of season; Nov to end-Feb.* **Disabled access. TV. High chairs available. Car park.**

A modern hotel surrounded by greenery with comfortable rooms at €45–56, breakfast €7; split-level apartment for 4 people €73. In the restaurant on weekdays there's a lunchtime *formule* at €11 and menus for €16.50 (not Sun) and €28. It's popular with groups.

@ 🏋 🏠 Interhôtel Les Grandes Tours**

6 rue du Château; it's opposite the château.

☏ 02.96.85.16.20 ⓕ 02.96.85.16.04
ⓦ www.dinanhotel.com
Closed *mid-Dec to Feb.* **TV. High chairs available. Pay car park.**

Victor Hugo and Juliette Drouet stayed here on 25 June 1836 while they were on a five-week tour of the west of France. "They dined, spent a pleasant night and dined there again the following evening. They found the hotel to their taste." The recommendation still holds good, especially considering the recent updating that's been done – the refurbished rooms on the second floor are more pleasant and it's a quiet place. Doubles with shower/wc or bath go for €45–50, family rooms for up to four people €69. Half board is available for a minimum stay of three nights. The car park is in the courtyard, though there's a charge in summer. *One free breakfast per room offered to our readers on presentation of this guide.*

@ 🏋 🏠 |●| Hôtel Le Challonge**

29 pl. Du-Guesclin.
☏ 02.96.87.16.30 ⓕ 02.96.87.16.31
ⓦ www.lechallonge.fr.st
Disabled access. TV. High chairs available.

Eleven of the twenty rooms look over the square but don't worry about noise – the double glazing is efficient. Doubles cost €67–79 with shower/wc or bath; breakfast, €7.50. There are some family rooms, with a connecting room with two single beds. There's also a room especially adapted for disabled visitors. All the bathrooms have heated towel rails and the rooms have good bed linen. Brasserie-restaurant *(Le Longueville)* on the ground floor serves a weekday lunch menu for €12 and others €15–29. *One breakfast per room offered free to our readers on presentation of this guide.*

@ 🏠 🏋 Hôtel d'Avaugour***

1 pl. du Champ.
☏ 02.96.39.07.49 ⓕ 02.96.85.43.04
ⓦ www.avaugourhotel.com
Closed *11 Nov to mid-Feb.* **Disabled access. TV. High chairs available.**

Cosy hotel in the centre of Dinan. Very comfortable, recently refurbished rooms; some (principally nos. 19, 28 and 38) overlook the garden and the town's ramparts. Doubles go for €70–160, depending on the season and the exhibition, breakfast €11; also a few suites at €130. *Free house apéritif offered to our readers on presentation of this guide.*

⊚ |●| Crêperie des Artisans

6 rue du Petit-Fort; right by the Jerzual gate.
☎02.96.39.44.10
Closed *Mon; Oct to end–March.*

A beautiful building in a charming street in the old town. It's an ancient residence with a rustic setting, bare stone walls and wooden tables. The relaxed atmosphere is enlivened by the really friendly owners. There are four menus from €8.60 (lunchtime) to €14, featuring excellent traditional crêpes and galettes and cider from the barrel. They play nice music and, in summer, set up a large wooden table in the street.

⊚ |●| Le Léonie

17 rue Rolland.
☎02.96.85.47.47
Closed *Sun and Mon in July–Aug; rest of year, Sun evening, Mon and Thurs evening; a week in Feb; a week in May; last week of Aug; first fortnight in Sept.* **Disabled access.**

In a good spot in the centre but away from the tourist hordes. This is the first establishment run by a young pair who have built up a faithful, local clientele. The dining room isn't that big but you don't get distracted by the proximity of your neighbours because your attention is focused on what's on your plate. The young chef produces creative but in no way pretentious dishes using quality, seasonal produce. Just try to resist the dark chocolate *pavé*. At lunchtimes from Tuesday to Saturday, they serve a dish of the day with a coffee for €7.80; add a dessert and it costs €9. Opt for a starter/main course or main course/ dessert menu and it will cost €13; it's €16 for starter/main course/dessert. All in all, a really nice place.

⊚ 🎋 |●| Restaurant La Courtine

6 rue de la Croix.
☎02.96.39.74.41
Closed *Wed evening and Sun evening; a weekend of June; fortnight in Nov.*

A warm and cosy dining room in a quiet side street. The fresh, friendly decoration provides a nice setting for the cuisine. Everything comes straight from the market and the fish and seafood are skilfully prepared, with weekday lunchtime *formules* at €11.50 and €13.80; then menus €16–26.

Free coffee offered to our readers on presentation of this guide.

⊚ |●| Le Bistrot du Viaduc

22 rue du Lion-d'Or, Lanvallay; take the road to Rennes, and you'll see the restaurant on the left at the bend, just beyond the viaduct.
☎02.96.85.95.00 ⊕02.96.85.95.05
Closed *Mon; Sat lunch; Sun evening; second fortnight in June; mid-Dec to mid-Jan.*
Disabled access.

Incredible views of the Rance valley from this restaurant, which is in a splendid setting and has a pleasant interior with pastel colours and a stove in the dining room. They serve delicious local cuisine, including *croustillant* of pig's trotters, and cod with a chicory fondue. There's a short weekday lunch menu for €17.50 and others €29.50 and €38.50; à la carte you'll pay somewhere in the region of €45–60. They offer a range of affordable wines. Booking is essential.

Plélan-Le-Petit
22980 (13km W)

⊚ |●| Le Relais de la Blanche-Hermine

Lieu-dit Lourmel; take the N176 towards Jugon-les-Lacs. At the Plélan-le-Petit roundabout take the old road signposted for the zone artisanal. The restaurant is 800m on the left.
☎02.96.27.62.19
Closed *Sun evening; Wed; Feb school holiday; last week of June.*

This restaurant has a good reputation in the region and is housed in a long stone building by the road. Classy cooking, with menus €18–37, is served in the spacious, lively dining room. Specialities include roast suckling pig on the spit (first and third Thurs of every month). Seafood or shellfish must be ordered in advance.

Dinard
35800

⊚ 🎋 🏠 Hôtel Les Mouettes

64 av. George-V; it's very close to the Yacht Club.
☎02.99.46.10.64 ⊕02.99.16.02.49
🌐www.hotel-les-mouettes.com
Closed *Jan.* **TV.**

A pleasant family hotel with ten charming, cosy rooms which are freshly decorated with a hint of the sea – they're €26–38, depending on facilities and season. It's friendly, simple and inexpensive, a rarity in Dinard. Ask at reception for information about parking. *10% discount on the room rate (in low season) offered to our readers on presentation of this guide.*

ⓔ |◉| Restaurant L'Escale à Corto

12 av. George-V.
☎02.99.46.78.57
Closed *lunchtimes.* **Open** *until midnight.*

A lively little restaurant, popular with young locals. It is also known as *Restaurant des Marins*. Dod is the barman, while Marie runs the kitchen, producing seafood salad, oysters, salmon *tartare* and various other fish dishes. There are no set menus, but you can enjoy a good, healthy meal for around €18. This restaurant is only open in the evening, as Corto likes to take a nap on the beach in the afternoon.

ⓔ |◉| Didier Méril

6 rue Yves-Verney.
☎02.99.46.95.74

Didier Méril has created one of the best restaurants in Dinard yet he's barely 30 years old. He's full of passion and creativity and has recruited a dynamic young team – the welcome comes with a smile and good humour. The setting is a tad minimalistic but not unappealing. The presentation on the plates is original and meticulous and matches the inventive and delicious cuisine; weekday lunch menu €20 and others €27–37. Seafood dishes predominate à la carte and they change frequently. One of the great temptations is the home-made bread – there are eight different types of rolls so go easy because the desserts are too good to miss.

Dol-de-Bretagne
35120

ⓔ 🎄 🏠 Grand Hôtel de la Gare**

21 av. Aristide-Briand; 500m from the centre.
☎02.99.48.00.44 ⓕ02.99.48.13.10
Closed *a week in Feb; second fortnight in Oct.* **TV.**

A small, plain and unpretentious hotel with good value double rooms at €27–42 depending on facilities and season. The new owners have refurbished throughout

and the rooms are bright and fresh. *Free house apéritif offered to our readers on presentation of this guide.*

Douarnenez
29100

ⓔ 🏠 |◉| Le Keriolet

29 rue Croas-Talud; this is the prolongation of rue Jean Jaurès.
☎02.98.92.16.89 ⓕ02.98.92.62.94
Closed *Mon lunchtime (out of season); Feb half-term (zone A).* **High chairs available.**

This slightly eccentric but friendly hotel close to the Plomatc'h footpath has recently been redecorated. Eight comfortable rooms, four of which (the most expensive) over-look the bay; €42–52 for a double with shower/wc; half board €48 per person. The restaurant serves menus from €12.50 (weekday only) up to €35 featuring tasty, traditional dishes prepared with a dash of creativity: flambée of langoustines with pastis, mussels in cider, ray with warm raspberry vinaigrette. Logis de France.

ⓔ 🎄 🏠 |◉| Hostellerie Le Clos de Vallombreuse***

7 rue Estienne-d'Orves; it's near the Sacré-Cœur church.
☎02.98.92.63.64 ⓕ02.98.92.84.98
ⓦwww.closvallombreuse.com
Disabled access. TV. High chairs available. Swimming pool. Car park.

An elegant, early twentieth-century build-ing very close to the church and over-looking the sea – beautifully decorated inside and very welcoming. The rooms are charming and bright, some with a sea view; they go for €56–120. One of the good restaurants in town, offering speci-alities such as grilled lobster sea bass with oyster vinaigrette on menus, €18–54. *10% discount on the price of a room (excluding July and Aug) offered to our readers on presentation of this guide.*

ⓔ 🎄 |◉| Crêperie Au Goûter Breton

36 rue Jean-Jaurès.
☎02.98.92.02.74
Closed *Sun and Mon in winter except during school holidays; fortnight end of June; fort-night end of Nov.* **Disabled access.**

Lots of character here: the proprietor gets around on a Harley-Davidson or in a Cadillac, and inside the décor is very Breton with a soundtrack of Breton bagpipe music mixed with plenty of jazz and rock. Crêpe menus go for €8–14 and a children's menu for €7.30. It's no surprise to find an American hamburger among the list of crêpes, and there's a flower-filled terrace to the rear. *Free house apéritif offered to our readers on presentation of this guide.*

ⓔ 🏠 |●| Le Saint-Pierre

5 rte. des Roches-Blanches à Tréboul.
℡02.98.74.03.33
Closed *Wed; 5 Jan–10 Feb.*

Didier and Antoinette will welcome you into their little hotel on the Sables-Blancs beach with a panoramic view of the bay. Three double rooms cost around €38; breakfast €6. Good traditional cooking, with specialities like fried scallops, flambéed langoustines, lobster salad with garden herbs, fish couscous, locally made *tuiles*. You can sample these delicacies on the lovely terrace but be warned, dinner is served very early (7–7.30pm). Menus start at €10 (weekday lunchtimes only) and go up to €38; reckon on €35 à la carte. *Free Kir Breton offered to our readers on presentation of this guide.*

ⓔ |●| L'Athanor

1 rue Henri-Barbusse.
℡02.98.92.88.97
Closed *Tues (except July–Aug); 3 weeks in March; 3 weeks in Oct.* **Disabled access. High chairs available.**

The tiled décor evokes Spain, and the food on offer will confirm your first impressions: tapas, grilled peppers, Spanish rice dishes (including paella, a meal in itself with different variations, at €16–30). Breton dishes are also served, however. Dish of the day costs €10.60, lunch menu €14.60, except Sunday and public holidays, other menus €19.30–48.60, including a Spanish menu at €27.60. There's also a children's menu for €7.80, and a splendid, extensive wine list with vintages from Portugal, Argentina, Chile, Brazil, Mexico, Uruguay and even Bordelais.

Erquy

22430

ⓔ 🏠 |●| Hôtel Beauséjour**

21 rue de la Corniche.

℡02.96.72.30.39 ℻02.96.72.16.30
🌐www.beausejourquy.com
Restaurant closed *Sun evening and Mon (Oct–June); during Christmas school holidays.* **Disabled access. TV. High chairs available. Car park.**

Only 100m from the port lies this small, traditional holiday hotel. Well-maintained, light and airy doubles with shower/wc €48–63 (nos. 5 and 14 have view over the port). Moderately priced restaurant with generously served set menus at €18–33: specialities include seafood *choucroute* and scallop kebabs with crab *coulis*. Half board (compulsory 10 July–31 Aug) is good value at €51–63 per person. Logis de France.

ⓔ 🏠 |●| La Cassolette

6 rue de la Saline; 50m from the beach.
℡02.96.72.13.08
Closed *Tues lunchtime; Thurs and Fri lunchtime out of season; 15 Nov–15 Feb.* **High chairs available.**

The locals are lucky enough to have two excellent restaurants in town (the other is *L'Escurial*). This one is run by a nice woman who was smart enough to hire a young chef who trained in some excellent kitchens. He uses the best seafood straight from the sea: scallop ravioli, langoustines with orange sauce, semi-cooked foie gras with cider, *cassolette* of crayfish with orange and, for dessert, try the raspberry shortbread served with a lychee ice cream or the caramel *charlotte* made with pancakes and salted butter. Prices are reasonable – there's a weekday lunch *formule* at €12, a weekday lunch menu at €15, and menus for €23–42 or €42 à la carte. Eat in the cosy little dining room, with its large chimney, or out in the garden-terrace on sunny days. *Free liqueur offered to our readers on presentation of this guide.*

Saint-Aubin

22430 (20km S)

ⓔ |●| Restaurant Le Relais Saint-Aubin

At the Super U roundabout, direction St-Aubin.
℡02.96.72.13.22
Closed *Mon (July and Aug); Mon and Tues (mid-season); Mon, Tues and Wed (15 Nov–15 March); Feb school holiday.* **Disabled access. Games available. Car park.**

Situated in a small hamlet, this peaceful, characterful seventeenth-century priory has its own garden. There's a ravishing dining room with ancient beams, antique furniture and a monumental granite fireplace. In summer you can eat on the terrace. A variety of set menus: one at weekday lunchtimes for €13 and others €20–50. Specialities include scallops à la Erquy and there's also a dish of the day written up on the slate; expect to pay about €38 à la carte. A good selection of wines is available, including white or red Menetou Salon. It's best to book in season and at the weekend.

Fouesnant

29170

⑳ 🎋 🏠 Hôtel a l'Orée du Bois**

4 rue de Kergoadig.
☎02.98.56.00.06 ℗02.98.56.14.17
ⓦwww.hotel-oree-du-bois.fr.st
TV. Pay car park.

Small, classic family hotel that's been completely renovated. Good rooms at good prices: €34 with basin/wc, €46–55 with shower/wc and bath. Some have a sea view of the Cap-Coz or of the forest of Fouesnant. Walking trails start just nearby and the beach is three minutes away by car. *10% discount on the room rate for two consecutive nights (out of season) offered to our readers on presentation of this guide.*

⑳ 🏠 |❶| Hôtel Belle Vue**

30 descente Bellevue, Cap-Coz; 3km from the town.
☎02.98.56.00.33 ℗02.98.51.60.85
ⓦwwwhotel-belle-vue.com
Closed *Nov–Feb.* **Restaurant closed** *Mon (except for hotel guests).* **High chairs available.**

A quiet spot just a stone's throw from the sea. This hotel has stayed in the same family since 1919 but it still retains some of the atmosphere of its previous incarnation as a grocer's shop-cum-café. The rooms have a quaint charm, with flowery but discreet wallpaper and old furniture (although the ones overlooking the garden are more modern). Doubles with shower/wc or bath are €55–68; half board (compulsory in July–Aug) costs €51–59. The restaurant, with menus €20–33, is also old, but the chef is young and extremely talented. His fresh duck foie gras is delicious. Booking is essential in season. Logis de France.

⑳ 🏠 |❶| Hôtel de la Pointe de Mousterlin***

108 rte. de la Pointe-Mousterlin; 6.5km from the town.
☎02.98.56.04.12 ℗02.98.56.61.02
ⓦwww.mousterlinhotel.com
Restaurant closed *Sun evening; Mon; Tues lunch; 23 Jan–1 March.* **TV. High chairs and games available.**

This 44-room hotel has been in the same family for four generations, and this experience is reflected in the thoughtfulness of the service and the range of facilities: heated swimming pool, sauna, Jacuzzi, weights room, tennis courts, library and daily programme of activities and excursions. Double rooms are €58–100; half board €61.50–87 per person. The restaurant offers excellent, reasonably priced seafood (menus €18–33), such as trio of crab, *ragoût de langoustines* with ginger or fillet of John Dory with a lobster medallion, all served in a beautiful setting. Just below the hotel, the sand dunes invite guests to explore a natural setting that has remained largely untouched – an ideal place to spend a weekend. Logis de France.

⑳ 🏠 |❶| Hôtel de La Pointe du Cap Coz

153 av. de la Pointe-du-Cap-Coz; 3 km from the town.
☎02.98.56.01.63 ℗02.98.51.53.20
ⓦwww.hotel-capcoz.com
Closed *31 Dec to Feb half-term.* **Restaurant closed** *(out of season) Sun evening, Mon lunchtime and Wed.* **TV. High chairs and games available.**

The rooms are gradually being refurbished, with no.10 particularly outstanding, both for its décor and its view. Doubles go for €59–86; half board €65–78 per person. The restaurant has a deservedly high reputation in the area, so it is advisable to book. There are two dining rooms; one, reserved for hotel guests, looks out on the cove of Penfoulic. The dishes change every four months with a range of menus, €20–40; children's menu €14. Another excellent establishment that will not let you down. Logis de France.

Forêt-Fouesnant (La)

29940 (4km NE)

|❶| Auberge du Saint-Laurent

6 rte. de Beg-Menez; on the tourist road from La Fôret-Fouesnant to Concarneau.

☎02.98.56.98.07
Closed *Tues evening; Wed; Mon evening (winter only).* **Disabled access. High chairs and games available.**

This beautiful inn provides exceptional value for money, matched by attentive service from the couple who run it. The setting is rustic but sophisticated, and in summer the French windows are thrown open so that guests can take full advantage of the garden and terrace. The food is a combination of traditional recipes and imaginative, seasonal cooking. Menus from €15 (weekday lunchtime) to €35; the cheapest dinner menu is €19. Highly recommended, but it is advisable to book.

Glomel

22110

@ 🏠 |O| **La Cascade**

5 Grande-Rue; it's on the main street.
☎02.96.29.60.44.
TV. Disabled access.

A pleasant little country hotel with pretty clean rooms in the main building and more in a brand new extension; some overlook the garden and are very quiet. They are very reasonablly priced at €28 with basin, €34 with shower/wc; half board €32 per person from three consecutive nights. They serve a menu at lunchtime available to hotel guests only at €10. Pets not accepted.

Groux (Île de)

56590

@ 🏠 **Auberge de jeunesse du Fort du Méné**

Fort du Méné; 1.3km from the port and town; take the coastal footpath to La Croix headland; by road, turn to the left of Ty-Mad and follow the signs.
☎02.97.86.81.38 ℗02.97.86.52.43
Closed *15 Oct–31 March.* **Reception open** 8.30am–noon and 6–9pm (6–10pm in July–Aug).** Car park.**

The rooms with three to ten beds are a series of converted bunkers, now covered with murals painted by a German university professor, depicting characters like Asterix and the Little Prince. What a good idea to convert all this ill-advised concrete into a seaside youth hostel.

Altogether, nearly 80 people can be accommodated here; two of the dormitories sleep nineteen people each, and the conditions are very basic but the toilets are clean. €7.70 per person, €6.80 in a twelve-bed tent and €5.30 if you're camping under your own devices. A small studio is also available and breakfast costs €3.30. There's a covered dining room and several kitchens that can be used by guests. This youth hostel has preserved the original spirit of the movement. Credit cards not accepted.

@ 🏠 **Hôtel de la Jetée****

It's in the port.
☎02.97.86.80.82 ℗02.97.86.56.11
Closed *5 Jan–5 March.*

The very last house on the right before you reach the sea, this is a picture-postcard of a place, fronted by a jetty with a lighthouse at the end, with anchored boats bobbing, gulls wheeling and squealing and the sea practically licking the hotel walls. The décor inside is somewhat outdated. Doubles with shower/wc are €53, and up to €79 with bath and a nice view of the coast. There's a first floor lounge with TV.

Hennebont

56700

@ 🏂 🏠 |O| **Hôtel-restaurant du Centre**

44 rue du Maréchal-Joffre.
☎02.97.36.21.44 ℗02.97.36.44.77
Closed *Sun evening and Mon except July–Aug; Feb and All Saints' school holidays.* **TV.**

A likeable young couple have taken over this grand old hotel and brought it up to date without sacrificing its simple provincial appeal. You will appreciate the *patronne*'s charm and the excellent value; doubles €26 with shower (wc on the landing) and others €32–36. Half board, compulsory in July and August, costs €35. Above all, though, this place is a very good restaurant, one of the best in town. Set menus – €14.50 in the week and others €20–39.50 – list good, honest dishes, particularly fish and seafood: grilled crayfish with cream. *Free coffee offered to our readers on presentation of this guide.*

Hoëdic (Île de)
56170

ⓒ |●| Les Cardinaux

☏02.97.52.37.27 ℻02.97.52.41.26
Closed *a week in Jan; a week in Feb; 3 weeks in Oct; Sun evening and Mon out of season.* **Disabled access.**

The three most attractive rooms look on to the garden, a further six are on the first floor; all have shower/wc and cost €51–85 for a double. Half board is recommended (€48–68 per person). There's an intimate, old-fashioned, purple lounge, a pretty breakfast room, a bar in the front, and a restaurant tucked away to the rear. The house speciality is seafood sauerkraut and menus cost €22–35. Booking absolutely essential: it is not only a delightful place, it's also the only hotel on the island. At the height of summer, however, the service loses a bit of its relaxed friendliness.

Landéda
29870

ⓒ 🏠 🍴 Hôtel La Baie des Anges***

350 rte. des Anges; it's on Aber-Wrac'h port.
☏02.98.04.90.04 ℻02.98.04.92.27
🖥www.baie-des-anges.com
Closed *Jan.* **Disabled access. TV. Car park.**

Gorgeous hotel in a lovely, stylish house, dating from the early 1900s, set just across from the beach and overlooking the ocean. The views and sunsets are breathtaking. The place is full of light and has an Art Deco feel. Spotless, attractively decorated rooms, some with sitting rooms go for €68–106 with shower/wc or bath. Breakfast €12 comes with a choice of coffees, home-made jams, and bread and pastries from the local baker – delicious. There's a terrace and a lovely lounge with huge comfy armchairs and plenty of board games. *Fourth night free after three consecutive nights (Feb–March and Oct–Dec, except for the last week of Dec) offered to our readers on presentation of this guide.*

Landerneau
29800

ⓒ 🏠 |●| L'Amandier**

55 rue de Brest; coming down from the station, turn right at the first set of traffic lights, 500m from the town centre.

☏02.98.85.10.89
Restaurant closed *Sun evening and Mon.* **TV.**

This hotel with its very elegant interior, attractive paintings and refined furniture offers remarkable value. The rooms (€48) are particularly pleasant and have superior facilities. Logis de France.

ⓒ 🍴 |●| Resto de la Mairie

9 rue de la Tour-d'Auvergne; it's on the quay opposite the town hall.
☏08.98.85.01.83
🖥www.restaurantdelamairie.com
Closed *Tues evening.* **Disabled access. High chairs and games available. Car park.**

A long, thin, friendly bar-restaurant with plush décor: stained glass, red carpet and lush plants. The patronne has been running the place for thirty years with infectious *bonhomie*. For the kids, there's a tortoise called Nono which hides in the patio. Among the specialities try the *marmite* Neptune, a seriously good fish stew (you'll have to wait thirty minutes for this, because it's prepared to order). Otherwise, depending on the season, try the *gratin* of scallops, or the salmon in *papillote*. Very good value for money: weekday lunchtime menu €9, and other menus up to €29; reckon on around €20 à la carte. *A free Breton Kir offered to our readers on presentation of this guide.*

Roche-Maurice (La)
29220 (4km NE)

ⓒ |●| Auberge du Vieux Château

4 Grand-Place; take the D764 to Kernévez and it's just a few metres further on, on the left.
☏02.98.20.40.52
🖥www.amatable.fr
Closed *evenings during the week.* **Disabled access. High chairs available. Car park.**

A fine inn set in a peaceful village square near a lovely Breton church and in the shadow of a ruined eleventh-century château. It undoubtedly offers the best value for money in the Landerneau region. The first menu, €12.50, served on weekday lunchtimes, attracts crowds of people from all walks of life who know a good place to eat when they find one. There are others from €15.50–32.

Landévennec

29560

© 🕿 🏠 |●| Saint-Patrick

Rue Saint-Guénolé; it's next to the church.
☎02.98.27.70.83
Closed *mid-Oct to mid-March*. **Restaurant closed** *Tues evening and Wed out of season.*

The welcome is friendly and relaxed at this charming little hotel in a peaceful village on the Crozon peninsula, with an unspoilt bistro where old wooden chairs scrape noisily on the tiled floor. There's a parade of aged Irish whiskeys on the shelf behind the cramped bar. Good home cooking in the restaurant with a lot of fish dishes and a weekday menu at €15. The lovely rooms – doubles with basin €33–39 (shared toilets and showers) – are just like you'd find in a private home: marble fireplaces and scattered ornaments. Rooms 1, 4 and 7 have windows overlooking the Rade de Brest. *Free Kir Breton offered to our readers on presentation of this guide.*

Landivisiau

29400

© 🏠 |●| Restaurant Le Terminus

94 av. Foch; take the Landivisiau east exit in the direction of the town centre.
☎02.98.68.02.00
Closed *Fri evening; Sat lunch; Sun evening.* **TV. High chairs available. Car park.**

One of the best transport cafés in Finistère. The number of lorries parked outside vouches for its success and unbeatable value for money. The weekday menu (€10) comprises two starters (including seafood), main course with vegetables of choice, salad, cheese, dessert and coffee – plus some house wine to wash it down; other menus €12.50–22. There's also a restaurant alongside, with more traditional menus and a seafood platter, and some double rooms priced €33.

Lannion

22300

© 🏠 |●| 🕿 Auberge de jeunesse Les Korrigans

6 rue du 73^e-Territorial; 200m from the train station and 300m from the town centre.
☎02.96.37.91.28 ☎02.96.37.02.06

@www.fuaj.org
Disabled access. High chairs available.

This friendly, welcoming youth hostel has recently been done up in pretty colours and offers rooms with two and four beds, a fully-equipped kitchen and no curfew. With a FUAJ card (compulsory, but can be bought on site) you'll pay €13.85–15.20 per person in a four-bed room with shower/wc. There's also the possibility of half board. The hostel organizes a host of artistic and sporting activities – bird-spotting hikes, a boomerang club, Breton dances, archery, acrobatic kite-flying, etc – as well as supplying detailed information about what's going on in the area. *Le Pixie* bar-restaurant hosts concerts, exhibitions, story-telling and theatre. One of the most dynamic youth hostels around. Credit cards not accepted. *10% discount on the room rate offered to our readers on presentation of this guide.*

© 🕿 |●| Le Tire-Bouchon

8 rue de Keriavily
☎02.96.37.10.43
Closed *Sat lunch; Sun; Mon lunch; Christmas week.* **Disabled access.**

A restaurant with a warm, relaxed atmosphere that is noticeable as soon as you open the door. The menu proudly proclaims "No chips, no ketchup" and indeed the food is fresh, traditional – and very good, with set menus €10–13 (weekday lunchtime), then €20–30. A board hanging on the wall announces several dishes of the day. It is often full (a good sign), so don't arrive too late. *Free house apéritif offered to our readers on presentation of this guide.*

© |●| La Ville Blanche

It's 5km along on the Tréguier road, by Rospez.
☎02.96.37.04.28
Closed *Mon; Wed and Sun evening out of season; a weekend of June to early July; 22 Dec–30 Jan.* **Disabled access. High chairs available.**

Great cooking prepared by a pair of brothers who have gone back to their roots. If they offer to show you their aromatic herb garden, don't refuse. Their specialities are seasonal – scallops from October to March, Breton lobster from April to October. Try the pork knuckle pâté with foie gras, the sweet potatoes with walnut oil, the roast brie with rhubarb or the *millefeuille* with caramelized apples. There's a weekday menu at €28 and others €42–70, or reckon on around €58 à la carte. You can also buy good wines by the glass, which is rare in a place of this quality.

Lesconil
29730

@ 🎋 🛏 |●| **Grand Hôtel des Dunes***

17 rue Laennec.
☎02.98.87.83.03 📠02.98.82.23.44
@grand.hoteldesdunes@wanadoo.fr
Closed *mid-Oct to Easter.* **TV. High chairs available. Car park.**

This huge establishment is in a fabulous location: one side looks out over a sand dune which falls away to the sea 100m beyond. There's a lovely walk from the hotel along the shore. The rooms have been refurbished; doubles from €60–80 depending on facilities and season. They're spacious and well appointed – obviously the ones with sea view are the best. The food is pretty good value, and even on the half board menu there's lots of choice: menus at €19.50 (not served Sun lunch) and €29–59.60. Logis de France. *10% discount on the room rate (except July–Aug) or coffee offered to our readers on presentation of this guide.*

Locquirec
29241

@ 🛏 |●| **Hôtel Les Sables Blancs**

15 rue des Sables-Blancs; towards Morlaix.
☎02.98.67.42.07 📠02.98.79.33.25
Closed *Tues; Wed in mid season; Jan–Feb.*
Car park.

Small, chic, welcoming hotel and crêperie, tucked away in the dunes in a wild, magnificent setting facing Lannion Bay. It has recently taken on a new look; its handful of bedrooms – €48–55 for a double with shower/wc – has been renovated and a cosy, little lounge added to its cheery dining room. Crêperie and salad menu can be enjoyed on a veranda looking out over the sea.

Guimaëc
29620 (3km W)

@ |●| **Le Caplan and Co**

Lieu-dit Poul-Rodou; from Guimaëc, take the Plouganou road and turn right at the third crossroads.
☎02.98.67.58.98
Open *daily noon–midnight in summer; out of season, Sat 3–9pm, Sun and public holidays, noon–9pm.*

Right at the end of a track, at the mercy of the howling winds, *Le Caplan* stands defiantly against the elements. Push open the door and you'll find a warm, friendly café-bookshop that is almost unique in France – a brilliantly successful combination of reading room and bar. Piles of books are strewn here and there on the tables, selected by Lan and Caprini, where fishermen and book-lovers can while away the hours over a drink or a book – or both. The menu is even more of a surprise in Brittany – it features a platter of Greek specialities at €10, served with Greek wine.

Locronan
29180

@ |●| **Crêperie Le Temps Passé**

Rue du Four; close to the tourist office.
☎02.98.91.87.29
Closed *Mon and Tues (except school holidays); fortnight in Jan; 3 weeks in October.*
High chairs available.

A beautiful building, with one room with a fireplace below and another upstairs. The menu lists 58 types of pancakes, ranging in price from €2.60–8; if this is not enough for you, you can always fall back on the salads and omelettes. The service here is excellent.

Loctudy
29750

@ 🎋 🛏 **Hôtel de Bretagne***

19 rue du Port; very close to the port.
☎02.98.87.40.21 📠02.98.66.52.71
@hoteldebretagne@msn.com
Disabled access. TV. Car park.

The renovation work they've done on this old building is exquisite – the two owners have added excellent facilities (including sauna and Jacuzzi) yet retained the building's character and charm. Lavishly decorated rooms, all with shower/wc and telephone, cost €40–45. Walkers and cyclists are especially welcome. *Free spa and sauna offered to our readers on presentation of this guide.*

◎ |●| Relais de Lodonnec

3 rue des Tulipes, plage de Lodonnec; it's 2km south of Loctudy.
℗02.98.87.55.34
Closed *Mon (July–Aug); Tues evening and Wed, out of season; 15 Jan–15 Feb.*

This old granite fisherman's house, with pleasant ambience, blond wood and exposed beams, located just 20m from the beach, is home to one of the region's up-and-coming restaurants. Depending on the menu – they're €12 (weekday lunch) and €19.80–42 – you get platters of oysters or seafood and gratinéed sea trout or red mullet fillets in a sea urchin sauce. Specialities include scallops *rosace* with two sauces, foie gras in puff pastry, and grilled bass with basil. The wine list has affordable bottles to satisfy most tastes. Booking is advised at weekends.

Lorient

56100

◎ ☎ |●| Auberge de jeunesse

41 rue Victor-Schœlcher; take no. 2 bus from the town centre, to the "Auberge de Jeunesse" stop; by car, take the Lamor-Plage road and follow the signs.
℗02.97.37.11.65 ℗02.97.87.95.49
ⓔlorient@fuaj.org
Closed *Christmas to New Year holiday.*
Disabled access.

Fairly new youth hostel with some degree of comfort (kitchen, small bar, TV room, table football, table tennis, etc). Accommodation in rooms with four or five beds and washbasins (be sure to book your bed in summer) costs €9.30 per person, breakfast €3.30. Lunch and dinner (€8.60) are available, but you must book first. Superb place, with clean toilets and internet connection (at extra charge), albeit a little far from the town centre.

◎ ⅔ ☎ Hôtel les Pêcheurs*

7 rue Jean-Lagarde.

℗02.97.21.19.24 ℗02.97.21.13.19
Closed *Sun and bank holidays (brasserie only).* **TV. Car park.**

The rooms here are simple but impeccably clean. The cheapest ones don't have private facilities and there are communal ones along the corridor; doubles €23 with basin, €34 with shower/wc – excellent value for money for this town-centre establishment. On the ground floor, there's a brasserie-bar with a very welcoming owner. *Free house apéritif offered to our readers on presentation of this guide.*

◎ ⅔ ☎ |●| Hôtel-restaurant Victor Hugo**

36 rue Lazare-Carnot; it's near the ferry terminal for Île de Groix, 5 min walk from the centre of town.
℗02.97.21.16.24 ℗02.97.84.95.13
ⓔhotelvictorhugo.lorient@wanadoo.fr
TV. Pay car park.

Warm welcome from the cheery patronne and clean doubles with basin for €27 up to €62 with bath/wc, depending on the season; buffet breakfast €6. The rooms overlooking the street are well soundproofed. Dishes include house foie gras and fresh fish. *One free breakfast out of two offered to our readers on presentation of this guide.*

◎ ⅔ ☎ |●| Hôtel-restaurant Gabriel**

45 av. de la Perrière; it's on the main road in the port (towards Keroman).
℗02.97.37.60.76 ℗02.97.37.50.45
ⓦwww.hôtel-le-gabriel.com
Restaurant closed *weekends.* **TV.**

Small, unfussy hotel with an inexpensive, friendly restaurant. Modern, very clean doubles with shower/wc and telephone cost from €30.50; half board around €42. Room no. 304, on the corner of the top floor, overlooks the entrance to the harbours and the citadel of Port-Louis. The set menu costs €10 including wine (not served Sat night or Sun); you will pay around €15 for a meal à la carte. There's a nice atmosphere and warm welcome from the owner. *10% discount on the room rate (outside the festival period and bank holidays) offered to our readers on presentation of this guide.*

◎ ⅔ |●| Tavarn ar Roue Morvan

17 rue Poissonnière; close to the marina, Gabriel Gate, quai des Indes and quai du Péristyle.

☎02.97.21.67.47
Closed *Sun.* **Open** *11am–1am.*

A genuine Celtic establishment with a typical décor and serving dishes of the day for lunch and dinner – one meat, one fish – priced €6 and €9.90. Reckon on €10.20 for a meal à la carte. It's tasty food, particularly the scallops with saffron, Breton soup with cabbage and sausage and the Irish mutton stew. They have a good range of red, white and rosé wines with dry cider as an alternative. There's lots of noisy music, creating a young, energetic atmosphere. They hold regular folk concerts and on Monday evenings there are classes in the Breton language. *Free house apéritif offered to our readers on presentation of this guide.*

◎ |●| Restaurant Le Pic

2 bd. du Maréchal-Franchet-d'Esperey; it's near the post office and the *médiathèque*.
☎02.97.21.18.29
Closed *Sat lunchtime; Sun.* **Disabled access.**

A pleasant spot with Parisian bistro décor and a terrace for sunny days. Simple, tasty cooking on the menus, €15 and €19 (except Sunday evening) up to €29–40, including roast noisette of lamb with rosemary and cod with aïoli. The restaurant has just been included in the Qualité de France list, and the owner, Pierre Le Bourhis, is a wine connoisseur who was voted Brittany's best wine waiter in 1986. Have a good look in the cellar.

◎ |●| Restaurant Le Jardin Gourmand

46 rue Jules-Simon; it's near the train station.
☎02.97.64.17.24
Closed *Sun and Mon; Feb school holiday; 3 weeks Aug–Sept.* **Disabled access. High chairs available.**

Delicious dishes concocted from the freshest local produce are served outside under a pergola and in the airy, elegant dining room. Courteous service from the host and skilful, creative cooking by his wife, who uses fresh market produce. There's a weekday lunch menu at €17, with other menus at €21 and €32 at lunch and €18–48 in the evening; they all change daily. You'll spend €32 à la carte for an excellent meal including wine. There's a selection of coffees or teas on a special menu. This is one of the best restaurants in Lorient so it's best to book.

Port-Louis
56290 (20km S)

◎ |●| La Grève de Locmalo

18 bis, rue Locmalo.
☎ and ☎02.97.82.48.41
Closed *Wed 3pm to Fri 7pm (except July–Aug); All Saints' Day to end Feb school holiday.* **Disabled access. High chairs available.**

The recipe they use for the crêpe batter must have something unusual in it to produce such a light yet firm texture. They also do fish and seafood dishes that change daily depending on the catches landed – you'll pay around €20 à la carte. The place is a charming stone building located on a charming little harbour with bobbing boats.

Malestroit
56140

◎ |●| Restaurant Le Canotier

Place du Docteur-Queinnec.
☎02.97.75.08.69
Closed *Sun evening; Mon; first week Sept.*

You can choose to eat in a romantic dining room divided off by climbing vines or a lush terrace. Copious, fairly complicated dishes revolve around pike perch fillets, scallops, a wide selection of seafood (all the year round) and specialities from Lanvaux. The weekday lunchtime menu costs €10.50, then four others €13.50–28. Parking space is usually available in the place du Marché. The *Bar du Canotier* is next door.

Chapelle-Caro (La)
56460 (12km N)

◎ 🎜 🏠 |●| Le Petit Keriquel**

1 pl. de l'Église.
☎02.97.74.82.44 and ☎02.97.74.88.55
🖳www.lekeriquel.com
Closed *Sun evening out of season; Wed lunchtime July–Aug; Feb school holiday.* **TV. High chairs and games available. Car park.**

This pretty Logis de France hotel has seven decent, inexpensive rooms mostly facing the church; doubles €41 with basin, shower/wc or bath. In the restaurant, classic dishes are made from fresh ingredients and are generously served with menus at €11.50 (not served Sun) and €16–30.

Dishes include salad of artichoke hearts with foie gras, *andouille de Guéméné*, and roast belly of pork stuffed with foie gras. Logis de France. *Free house apéritif offered to our readers on presentation of this guide.*

Molac
56230 (13km SW)

@ ⅔ 🏠 |●| **Hôtel-restaurant À la Bonne Table**

Place de l'Église; take the D166, then the D149.
☎02.97.45.71.88 🖷02.97.45.75.26
Closed *Sun evening; Fri evening out of season; during Christmas school holiday.* **TV.**

The old coaching house standing on the church square dates back to 1683. It offers clean and simple rooms with good beds above the restaurant for €26 with washing facilities only. The annexe, 100m from the restaurant, provides rooms with shower/wc, common entrance hall but private doors and a small sitting room; these are €31. Weekday lunch menu costs €9.20 (served in the evenings to guests only) and others €18–26. Welcoming, busy atmosphere with well-served traditional dishes and attractively laid tables. *Free coffee offered to our readers on presentation of this guide.*

Matignon
22550

@ ⅔ 🏠 |●| **Hôtel de la Poste****

11 pl. Gouyon; next to the station overlooking the railway tracks.
☎ and 🖷02.96.41.02.20
ⓦwww.hoteldelaposte.paysdematignon.net
Closed *Sun evening and Mon, except July–Aug; 3 weeks in Jan; a fortnight in Oct.*
Disabled access. TV. High chairs available.

This establishment is an ideal spot for exploring the whole region and a nice, quiet place to come back to in the evening for a good meal in comfortable surroundings. There are attractively priced bed-and-breakfast or half-board options. There's a family atmosphere and the welcome is kindly. Rooms are classic but pleasant and quiet; doubles with basin €32 or €45–48 with shower/wc or bath. The cuisine served in the restaurant is traditional, but shows dashes of real creativity. Weekday menu €13 and other menus €17–26 list specialities including seafood *pot-au-feu*, fish *au gratin* and duck magret with honey.

Logis de France. *Free coffee offered to our readers on presentation of this guide.*

@ ⅔ |●| **Crêperie de Saint-Germain**

Saint-Germain-de-la-Mer, on the village square; from Matignon, drive 1km on the D786 in the direction of Fréhel, turn right for Saint-Germain and continue 1km.
☎02.96.41.08.33
Closed *1 Oct to Easter; school holidays.*
High chairs available.

It's worth making the trip to this seaside village for the best pancakes in the area. They're made using local black wheat flour and while the fillings are not unusual, Mme Eudes uses top-quality ingredients. And it's not pricey – expect to pay €10 or so for a meal. The old house is lovely and so is the garden terrace in summer. *Free coffee offered to our readers on presentation of this guide.*

Moëlan-sur-Mer
29350

《 ⅔ 🏠 **Manoir de Kertalg******

Route de Riec; from Moëlan take the D24 towards Riec, and after 2km fork off to the right.
☎02.98.39.77.77
ⓦwww.manoirdekertalg.com
Closed *mid-Nov to mid-April.* **TV. Car park.**

An impressive building of hewn stone, smothered in ivy and set in grounds in the forest. The rooms are vast and individually decorated; doubles and duplex rooms €90–180. You can eat breakfast till 10.30am (€12) on the magnificent terrace, which has a panoramic view over the countryside. They hold exhibitions in the tearoom. *10% discount on the room rate (April, June, Sept and Oct) offered to our readers on presentation of this guide.*

Morlaix
29600

《 🏠 **Hôtel du Port****

3 quai de Léon; it's 400m from the viaduct on the quayside.
☎02.98.88.07.54 🖷02.98.88.43.80
ⓦwww.1hotelduport.com
Closed *Christmas to New Year.* **TV. High chairs available.**

With its harbour view, pleasant welcome and reasonable prices, this little hotel offers value for money. Fresh, pleasant rooms with shower/wc or bath go for €50–70, breakfast €7.

⊛ 🎎 |O| Le Bains-Douches

45 allée du Poan-Ben; it's opposite the Palais de Justice.
☎ 02.98.63.83.83
Closed *Sat lunchtime; Sun; Mon evening.*
Disabled access. High chairs available.

One of the most original restaurants in town. They've kept the turn-of-the-century feel, with the railings, tiles and etched glass from the old public baths. Decent bistro food is on offer at very reasonable prices; weekday lunch menu €11 and others €14–24. Specialities include a good range of seafood and the desserts are good. You could start with the *galette* of roast goat's cheese followed by peppered duck steak or *fricassée* of rabbit in cider with gingerbread. The more adventurous can choose the kangaroo or ostrich. *Free Kir offered to our readers on presentation of this guide.*

⊛ |O| La Marée Bleue

3 rampe Saint-Mélaine.
☎ 02.98.63.24.21
Closed *Sun evening and Mon out of season; 3 weeks in Oct.* **High chairs available.**

A good fish and seafood restaurant in elegant and intimate surroundings on two levels, with lots of wood and stone. Dishes are seasonal – the menus change every three months – and they're carefully prepared using very fresh ingredients. Set menus start at €14.50 up to €36.50, or around €25 à la carte.

Mur-de-Bretagne
22530

⊛ 🎎 🏠 |O| Auberge Grand-Maison★★★

1 rue Léon-le-Cerf; it's near the church.
☎ 02.96.28.51.10 ℻ 02.96.28.52.30
✉ grandmaison@armornet.tm.fr
Closed *Sun evening and Mon out of season; Mon lunchtime July–Aug; fortnight during Feb school holiday; fortnight in Oct.* **TV. High chairs available.**

A smart place that will set you back a bit. Jacques Guillo is one of the best respected chefs in the *département*. Just read his menus: *escalopes* of marinated

turbot, aubergine cannelloni with lamb *confit*, foie gras profiteroles with a truffle *coulis*, lobster *fricassée* with crisp vegetables, *tournedos* of pigs' trotters, potato pancakes with *andouille* and hot mandarin crêpes or honey ice cream. This is a serious gastronomic experience, as demonstrated by the prices: weekday lunch menu €30, with others €40–75. The nine magnificent rooms have been nicely redecorated and they're worth the price: doubles €62 with washbasin or shower, €80–115 with bath. Breakfast, €12, is a meal in itself. This is an exceptional place, and it's well worth considering half board at €120–160 per person. *10% discount on the room rate except July–Aug (or 15% if guests dine in, except July–Aug) or free coffee offered to our readers on presentation of this guide.*

Gouarec
22570 (17km W)

⊛ 🎎 🏠 |O| Hôtel du Blavet★★

It's on the N164.
☎ 02.96.24.90.03 ℻ 02.96.24.84.85
🌐 www.perso.wanadoo.fr/louis-leloir/
Closed *a week at Christmas; fortnight in Feb.*
Restaurant closed *Sun evening and Mon out of season.* **TV. High chairs available. Car park.**

A sturdy, stone-built house on the banks of the River Blavet with the relaxed atmosphere you find in remote Brittany. Nice, comfortable rooms for €30 with basin/wc, €36–60 with shower/wc or bath. Room no.6 has a four-poster bed and overlooks the river. There's a pleasant dining room with big mahogany cupboards and a lovely view of the River Blavet. The restaurant offers an interesting range of six menus; weekday lunch menu for €14 and others €25–50. (The last is a *menu gastronomique*.) Traditional dishes are well worked by the owner-chef. Specialities include lobster casserole, fish platter and beef fillet with foie gras ravioli. Logis de France. *10% discount on the price of a room (1 Jan–31 May and from 1 Sept–31 Dec) offered to our readers on presentation of this guide.*

Ouessant (Île d')
29242

⊛ |O| Crêperie Ti à Dreuz

It's in the village.
☎ 02.98.48.83.01

Closed *Oct–April, except for school holidays.*

Ti à Dreuz means "crooked house", and the leaning stone façade looks as if it was built in a force ten gale. Inside it's painted blue and white. There's a huge choice of delicious crêpes. Crêpes are individually priced and you'll pay €8–16 for a meal à la carte.

Paimpol
22500

⑧ 🏠 |●| Le Repaire de Kerroc'h***

29 quai Morand; it's on the marina.
☏ 02.96.20.50.13 ℻ 02.96.22.07.46
🌐 www.chatotel.com
Restaurant closed *Mon lunchtime out of season; Tues; Wed lunchtime; 3 weeks in Jan.* **Disabled access. TV. High chairs available.**

Dating back to 1793, this house, in a style originating in St Malo, was built by a privateer who pillaged the seas for Napoleon. Its thirteen stylish, scrupulously clean and spacious rooms cost €44–114; half board €60–95 per person. Some of them have port views. In the elegant dining room, done out in shades of green, the chef offers menus €15–50.

⑧ 🏠 |●| Hôtel K'Loys***

21 quai Morano; it's on the harbour.
☏ 02.96.20.40.01 ℻ 02.96.20.72.68
✉ anne.conan@wanadoo.fr
Disabled access. TV.

The *Hôtel K'Loys* is in the nineteenth-century shipfitter's house, now an elegant hotel with an intimate atmosphere. The seventeen rooms, €65–120, have been tastefully furnished in keeping with the period; some look over the harbour and one has a sitting room with a bow window. The only concession to modernity is the lift, put in to assist disabled access.

⑧ |●| Crêperie-restaurant Morel

11 pl. du Martray.
☏ 02.96.20.86.34
Closed *Sun; Tues evening out of season; 10 days during Feb school holiday; a weekend of June; 3 weeks in Nov.* **High chairs available.**

A genuine traditional Breton crêperie in a welcoming room that is always bustling with a lively crowd of regulars. It serves delicious crêpes, such as *à l'andouille de Guéméné* (a type of sausage) and excellent cider; count on around €12 à la carte. For an apéritif, try the *pommeau des Menhirs*.

⑧ |●| Restaurant de l'Hôtel de la Marne**

30 rte. de la Marne; 300m from the train station.
☏ 02.96. 20.82.16 ℻ 02.96.20.92.07
✉ restaurant.hotel.marne@wanadoo.fr
Closed *Sun evening and Mon; Feb school holiday.* **Disabled access. TV. High chairs available. Car park.**

This restaurant is in the hotel itself, which looks rather like an ordinary provincial establishment. But there's a good reason why it is a favourite with the locals. The chef is inventive: Breton lobster poached in chicken stock, roast sea bream, fresh foie gras marinated in *verjus* and fresh herbs and some delicious desserts. Menus cost €25 (not Sun) and €30–51; drinks are included in the more expensive ones. There's an impressive wine list, with at least 360 different wines. You can also buy some of their specialities to take away (salmon, house foie gras, terrines and so on).

Palais (Le)
56360

⑧ 🏠 |●| Auberge de jeunesse

Haute-Boulogne; behind the citadelle du Palais, 15 min from the landing stage.
☏ 02.97.31.81.33 ℻ 02.97.31.58.38
✉ belle-ile@fuaj.org
Restaurant closed *early Oct to end of March*; **hostel closed** *1 Oct–2 Nov and 24 Dec–3 Jan.* **Disabled access. Car park.**

Loïc, the owner, is totally dedicated to his youth hostel, and it shows. It is particularly well known for its hiking courses, with a fascinating tour of the island on a coastal footpath in five to six days (packed lunch, back to the hostel by van at night, then back to the same point the following morning). Accommodation comprises a hundred beds, including bunks, in rooms for two people at €9 per person, breakfast €3.50. Half board is available at €21.80, and the menu costs €8.80. Facilities include a reading room, TV lounge, café, communal dining or use of kitchen. Highly popular, especially in summer, so it's best to book.

⊚ 🏠 Hôtel La Frégate

Quai de l'Acadie; it's opposite the ferry terminal.
☎02.97.31.54.16
Closed *mid-Nov to end March.*

Nice, cosy little hotel that's pleasantly furnished and excellent value for money. Most of the rooms look out onto the harbour. They cost €22 with basin or €29–39 with shower/wc. The pleasant salon-bar, furnished with family antiques, also has a great view, and there's a big terrace from where you can watch the arrival of the ferries.

⊚ 🍴 🍽 Crêperie La Chaloupe

10 av. Carnot; it's near the market place.
☎02.97.31.88.27
🌐www.lachaloupe.com
Closed *Jan; mid-Nov to mid-Dec.* **Disabled access. High chairs available.**

Excellent crêpes served in an appealing setting. The batter is made using organic milk, eggs and flour – the pancakes come out light and crispy. They also do fish soup, big salads and good ice cream. A meal costs about €15, and there's a children's menu. *Free house apéritif offered to our readers on presentation of this guide.*

Sauzon
56360 (8km NW)

⊚ 🍴 🍽 Le Petit Baigneur

Rampe des Glycines.
☎02.97.31.67.74
Closed *Mon (outside school holidays); Jan–Feb.*

There are nice photographs on the walls of the pleasant dining room, and the dishes of the day are inscribed on the blackboard. The cuisine is tasty, well executed and combines lovely flavours using only fresh produce. The tuna mousse with lemon and oregano is light, the marinated anchovies and sardines are tasty, then there's clam *fricassée*, haddock stew, stir-fried prawns with aubergines and grilled lamb chops. There are also more substantial dishes such as veal *escalope* and sea bream with crayfish bisque. Keep some room for a home-made dessert – crêpe with apple charlotte and *caramel maison*. Lunch menu €16; children eat half-price. In summer they put a few tables outside. *Free house apéritif offered to our readers on presentation of this guide.*

⊚ 🍽 Le Roz-Avel

Rue du Lieutenant-Riou.
☎02.97.31.61.48
Closed *Wed; Jan–Feb.* **High chairs available.**

An elegant venue that is without doubt the best restaurant on the island. There's a single menu for €24, which is very good value, but à la carte can get pricey – you need to allow around €35–40. The food is sophisticated, though: pig's trotter in oyster marinade, lamb *de l'île*, skate with lemon verbena, monkfish *osso buco* with spices and lobster (to order). The setting and service match the excellence of the food.

⊛ 🍴 🍽 La Maison

In the town; take a sharp left when you enter Sauzon.
☎02.97.31.69.07
Closed *lunchtime; Mon except school holidays and bank holidays.* **Open** *daily until 11pm.* **High chairs available.**

Three distinct sections here: the bistro, popular with Sauzon's last surviving fishermen; the restaurant inside; and the completely separate heated terrace. Some of the best cooking going in these parts, thanks to a highly creative chef who has held court in the kitchen for some twenty years. His specialities include an extraordinarily tender lamb *en croûte*, grilled peppers, tortellini with crab flesh and, above all, wonderful desserts (don't miss the fennel *confit* pie). Reckon on €40 à la carte. Reservations are highly recommended. *Free house apéritif offered to our readers on presentation of this guide.*

Perros-Guirec
22700

⊚ 🍴 🏠 🍽 Hôtel-restaurant La Bonne Auberge

Place de la Chapelle; it's in the hamlet of La Clarté, 3km from Perros-Guirec on the road to Plonmanach.
☎02.96.91.46.05 ☎02.96.91.62.88
✉gouriou.m@wanadoo.fr
Restaurant closed *Sat lunchtime; last 3 weeks in Nov and first week in Dec.* **TV. High chairs available.**

There's a huge wood fire, a piano and sofas that you won't want to get up from, and they serve very more-ish little canapés. Rooms, €26–35.50, are small and simple. Nos. 1, 2 and 3 have a (distant) sea view. Half board, €33.50–39.50 per person, is compulsory 15 June–15 Sept, for long weekends and on public holiday weekends. The food is interesting, and with a modern edge, and the first menu especially proves good value; lunchtime menu €13 during the week, then €19–31. Dishes are based around the best and freshest seafood (the proprietor is also a fisherman). You'll get a warm welcome at this charming place. *10% discount on the room rate 1 Oct–14 June (outside school holidays and holiday weekends) for a stay of at least two consecutive nights or on a half board basis offered to our readers on presentation of this guide.*

◎ 🏠 |◎| Le Gulf Stream

26 rue des Sept-Îles; it's at the start of the road that leads to Trestraou beach; 300m from the centre.
☎02.96.23.21.86 ⓕ02.96.49.06.61
ⓦwww.gulf-stream-hotel-bretagne.com
Closed *Mon lunch and Thurs (July–Aug); Mon lunch, Wed and Thursday (Sept–June).* **TV.**

There is a pleasant turn-of-the-last-century feel to this charming establishment, perched on a hillside above the sea. A few of the simple, pretty and well-maintained rooms have splendid views of the ocean and cost €40–45 with basin, €50–68 with shower/wc or bath. Bikers and hikers welcome, and there's a garage for bikes. In the restaurant there's the same atmosphere. The well-spaced tables are attractively laid and the dining room is brightened up with green plants. The views from here are also spectacular. Fish and seafood are the dishes of choice, and the menus change regularly; €16 (not Sun or public holidays) and €25–45. The cooking holds some pleasant surprises. The local wines are well chosen, too.

◎ |◎| Crêperie Hamon

36 rue de la Salle; it's in a steep little street opposite the marina.
☎02.96.23.28.82
Closed *lunchtime.* **Disabled access. High chairs available.**

This place has been a local institution since 1960. It would be a secret little hideaway if its reputation didn't go before it – Hamon is known for miles around as much for its rustic setting and good atmosphere as for the spectaclular way

the host tosses the crêpes to the waitress to catch. A meal costs about €12 and booking is essential. Credit cards not accepted.

Ploumanac'h
22700 (7km NW)

🏠 |◎| 🍴 Hôtel Le Parc Resto La Cotriade**

Place Saint-Guirec; by the Ploumanac'h car park, 100m from the beach and the customs officers' footpath.
☎02.96.91.40.80 ⓕ02.96.91.60.48
ⓔhotel.duparc@libertysurf.fr
Closed *Sun evening and Mon (plus Tues lunch Oct–Nov); 11 Nov–30 March.* **TV. High chairs and games available.**

All right, it has to be admitted that it's next to a car park, but the attractively decorated modern rooms are impeccable and it's very quiet round the back; double rooms with shower/wc or bath €42–48. Half board, compulsory in July and August, costs €47.50–51 per person. The restaurant, in a classical style with inevitable nautical touches, provides good service and excellent food on menus starting at €13 (except Sun lunch) and €15.50–33.50: tagliatelle with seafood, *cotriade* and fresh foie gras with langoustines. Logis de France. *Free Kir offered to our readers who stay in the hotel on presentation of this guide.*

Plélan-le-Grand
35380

◎ 🍴 |◎| Auberge des Forges

Les Forges; take the D724 to the Forges lake in the middle of the Brocèlioande forest.
☎02.99.06.81.07
Closed *Mon evening; Feb school holiday.* **High chairs available.**

A really pretty country inn – it's been run by the same family since 1850. The traditional cuisine makes the best of the quality of local produce. They place a substantial terrine on the table or you could opt for a "lighter" pan-fried *andouille* with potatoes. The fish, game, meat and poultry cater for all tastes and budgets. There's pretty amazing value for money on the menus €11 (not weekends) and €32. *Free house apéritif offered to our readers on presentation of this guide.*

Plémet

22210

🖉 ☕ |●| Le Saint-Antoine

8 pl. Charles-de-Gaulle; 14km to the east
of Loudéac via the N164, in the direction of
Rennes.
☎02.96.25.61.62
Closed Sun evening; Mon. **Disabled access.**

It is hard to enthuse too much over the
cold, unimaginative, modern setting, but
the meals make up for it with their sophistication and creativity, and the service is
extremely friendly. The excellent bread
and charcuterie are home-made. Menus
start at €10 (weekday lunchtime), then
€18.80–58. This is undoubtedly one of
the best restaurants in the area. *Free house
apéritif offered to our readers on presentation
of this guide.*

Pléneuf-Val-
André

22370

🖉 ☕ |●| Auberge du Poirier

Rond-point du Poirier at Saint-Alban; it's next
to the petrol station.
☎02.96.32.96.21
Closed Sun evening, Mon and Wed out of
season; late Feb to early March; June; Oct.
Disabled access. High chairs available.

Olivier Termet has made such a success of
his restaurant that he's had to build a new
dining room. The chef trained in some of
the most famous kitchens before bringing
his talent home. The first menu at €15
(weekdays only) includes a main course,
dessert, wine and coffee. There are more
original dishes on the menus at €18–35,
which change with each season. Each
dish is prepared with meticulous care. You
would do well to reserve. *Free coffee offered
to our readers on presentation of this guide.*

🖉 |●| Au Biniou

121 rue Clemenceau; it's near Val-André
beach.
☎02.96.72.24.35
Closed Tues evening and Wed out of season;
Feb.

This has long been a favourite locally. It's
a traditional, elegant restaurant with excellent cuisine prepared by the owner-chef.
Specialities include fish and meat dishes
such as John Dory marinated in tandoori

spiced oil and then steamed, and *piperade
à l'andouille et beurre blanc*. Menus start at
€15.50 (weekday lunchtimes), with others
at €23.50, €28.50 and €42.50, or around
€46 à la carte. You can walk it all off
with a bracing stroll on the wind-blown
Val André beach or along the customs
officers' tracks.

Pleyben

29190

🖉 🛏 |●| ☕ Auberge du Poisson
Blanc

Towards Pont-Coblant, at 4.5km on the old
Quimper road in the direction of Briec.
☎02.98.73.34.76 ☎02.98.73.31.21
Closed Mon evening. **High chairs available.**

On the shores of the Nantes-Brest canal,
this inn, affiliated to the *Logis de France*,
serves fresh, hearty dishes like *andouille*
salad with Puy lentils, *cassolette* of scallops
with lambic, mustard *andouillette* and roast
free-range chicken. It has several dining
rooms, one at the water's edge, offering
a range of menus, €12.50–29.60. There's
also a regional menu at €24 that will give
complete satisfaction to the fussier guests,
and a children's menu for €7.50. Expect to
pay around €20 à la carte. Double rooms
go for €48, breakfast €6. *Free liqueur offered
to our readers on presentation of this guide.*

🖉 ☕ |●| Crêperie de L'Enclos

51 pl. du Général-de-Gaulle: opposite the
parish compound.
☎02.98.26.38.68
Closed fortnight in March; fortnight in June;
fortnight Sept–Oct; fortnight Nov–Dec. **Open**
daily for lunch; Fri, Sat and Sun evenings;
during the school holidays, open daily lunch
and evening, except Mon evening. **High
chairs available.**

This crêperie is a gourmet's delight. Just
reading the menu (all twenty pages of it)
is an adventure in itself: 250 varieties of
crêpes, made with wheat or buckwheat,
served in a pretty blue and yellow setting.
Reckon on €12 for a complete meal.
The menu is not restricted to crêpes,
however. Every autumn the owners travel
to the South of France in search of new
flavours and authentic farmhouse produce and they invariably come back with
some veritable treasures. (This explains
the presence of specialities from Gascony
and Provence.) Excellent cider, made by

traditional methods (the same type is served in the presidential palace in Paris, no less). *Free coffee offered to our readers on presentation of this guide.*

Ploemeur

56270

@ 🛏 |●| 𝒜 Le Vivier**

Port de Lomener; 4km from the centre, on the coast road.
☎02.97.82.99.60 ⓕ02.97.82.88.89
✉levivier.lomener@wanadoo.fr
Closed *Christmas to 10 Jan; restaurant closed Sun evening (except July–Aug).*
Disabled access. TV. High chairs available.

The double rooms (€70–80) all boast a bay window with a splendid view of the island of Groix. The restaurant, one of the best in the area, also enjoys a stunning view of the sea and Groix. Seafood is obviously much in evidence; langoustines, oysters, salmon charlotte with crab, *fricassée* of squids with cider, bass fillet grilled with fennel, etc. Good value – menus at €22 (except weekends and public holidays), then €29–43 – and attentive, friendly service, without being overbearing. It's advisable to book. *10% discount on a room (Fri, Sat and Sun, Oct–March) offered to our readers on presentation of this guide.*

@ 𝒜 |●| Crêperie le Grazu

Port de Lomener.
☎02.97.82.83.47
Closed *Tues; Wed in winter except during school holidays; Nov.* **Disabled access. High chairs available.**

The young owners are making a real success of this place. They have sorted out a network of local suppliers for their crêpes, so they use buckwheat as well as ordinary wheat, and the fillings are fresh and very interesting. They do huge salads as well. Weekday menu costs €8.50 and there's another at €10.50. *Free coffee offered to our readers on presentation of this guide.*

Ploërmel

56800

@ 𝒜 🛏 |●| Hôtel-restaurant Saint-Marc**

1 pl. Saint-Marc, near the old station.
☎02.97.74.00.01 ⓕ02.97.73.36.81

Closed *Sun evening.* **TV. High chairs available.**

Trains rarely call at the neighbouring station so it's quiet here. The well-maintained rooms cost €33–40 depending on facilities. The bar is a popular local watering-hole, while the restaurant is generally regarded as the best in Ploërmel with menus €13 in the week then €16–31. *10% discount on the room rate (1 Sept–30 June) offered to our readers on presentation of this guide.*

@ 𝒜 🛏 Le Thy**

19 rue de la Gare.
☎02.97.74.05.21 ⓕ02.97.74.02.97
ⓦwww.lethy.com
TV. Car park.

Each of the seven rooms is dedicated to a painter and decorated in the style of the artist: Klimt is spacious and sensual while Pratt has a travel theme complete with globe and packed trunk. Atelier is bright with light streaming through the windows and sketches on the wall – it's as if the painter has just left. Other rooms are named after Tàpies and van Gogh. Each room is large and the bathrooms are superb; doubles €50–60. On the ground floor, there's a bar and a concert room that looks like a chapel; the apse is flanked by books and hung with purple curtains. The pub is open from Wednesday to Friday – concerts are held here. *Free house apéritif offered to our readers on presentation of this guide.*

@ 𝒜 🛏 |●| Hôtel Le Cobh**

10 rue des Forges; in the city-centre.
☎02.97.74.00.49 ⓕ02.97.74.07.36
ⓦwww.au.cobh.com
Closed *Wed lunch and Sun.* **Disabled access. TV. High chairs and games available. Car park.**

The reputation of this hotel, with its brilliant yellow façade, is totally justified – you'll appreciate the convivial and comfortable atmosphere, the effusive welcome and very cheerful service, and there are lovely furnishings in the spacious rooms (€55–75). Half board costs €50–57.50 per person. The meal they bring to your room on a tray is excellent, so you won't have to dress for dinner. In the park, there's a pavilion for two to six people. The restaurant serves good, unpretentious but wholesome food; the cheapest menu costs €15, a traditional menu €22.50, then other menus up to €32. This hotel has been transformed into one of the most astonishing hotels in the whole of Morbihan. It has been completely redecorated by the Celtia design team, a local company that specializes in giving hotels a new look. Here, the chosen theme is the legends and fairy tales of Brocéliande (somewhat akin to our Arthurian legends). Three types of rooms have been created: the first focus on writing and the sacred (blue background); the second on the forest (green background); and the third on opalescence (red background). This may sound rather daunting but the results are soothing and gently usher guests into the world of dreams. The exterior and the surrounding land are the next areas that will be subject to a major overhaul. Logis de France. *10% discount on meals, drinks included, offered to our readers on presentation of this guide.*

Plogoff

29770

⚓ 🛏 |●| Hôtel de la Baie des Trépassés**

On the seafront; it's 3km from pointe du Raz and pointe du Van.
☎ 02.98.70.61.34 ℻ 02.98.70.35.20
🌐 www.baiedestrepasses.com
Closed *Mon, except school holidays and bank holidays; 15 Nov–15 Feb.* **TV. High chairs available. Car park.**

This large, prosperous hotel stands in splendid isolation in front of a magnificent surfing beach in an exceptionally wild situation. Doubles €32–57; half board, compulsory in August, is €48–63. Menus in the restaurant cost €19.50–53 and feature lots of fish dishes. Logis de France. *Free coffee offered to our readers on presentation of this guide.*

Ploubalay

22650

⊚ ⚓ |●| Restaurant de la Gare

4 rue des Ormelets; the Lancieux road.
☎ 02.96.27.25.16
Closed *30 Sept–30 June, Mon and Tues evenings and Wed; July–Aug, Mon and Tues lunch and Wed; second fortnight Jan; second fortnight June; 10–25 Oct.* **Disabled access. High chairs available.**

They closed the station long since as well as the ragged bar that used to be here.

The three dining rooms are attractively decorated with floral designs. The menu is like some public declaration of intent with the chef explaining his involvement in no uncertain terms: "the scallops are fished locally and placed in the marinade instantly". This is excellent cuisine using fresh Breton produce, prepared with a personal touch, and includes specialities such as Modeste's black pudding and *tête de veau en tortue* and wonderful seafood dishes such as pan-fried langoustines or hot oysters. Menus start at €20 (not Sun), then others €30–40; reckon on around €30–50 à la carte. Reservations are essential for dinner. *Free Kir offered to our readers on presentation of this guide.*

Ploudalmézeau

29830

⊚ ⚓ |●| La Salamandre

Place du Général-de-Gaulle.
☎ 02.98.48.14.00
Closed *Tues evening and Wed out of season; weekdays from Oct to Easter except during the school holidays; mid-Nov to mid-Dec.* **High chairs and changing mats available.**

Grandma opened this pleasant and bright crêperie and grandson is the present owner. The crêpes are tasty – try the one with scallops and baby vegetables, the *bigoudène* (stuffed with *andouille*, fried potatoes and cream), the *forestière* (mushrooms, ham, cream) or the *paysanne* (bacon, potatoes, cheese and cream). For dessert there's the decadent *lichouze* (butter caramel, ice cream and Chantilly cream). Weekday lunch menu costs €10 or around €14 à la carte. Children are very welcome. *Free house apéritif offered to our readers on presentation of this guide.*

Plougasnou

29630

⊚ ⚓ 🛏 |●| Hôtel Roc'h Velen**

Saint-Samson; 6km from the village on a road that leads down to the sea.
☎ 02.98.72.30.58 ℻ 02.98.72.44.57
✉ roch.velen@wanadoo.fr
Closed *Sun evening out of season; Jan.* **TV. High chairs available.**

This hotel is a small place located on the sea road with ten pretty rooms decorated in a maritime style at €35–48.50 for a double with shower/wc or bath, depending on the season. Each has the name of an island from the area; "Molène", "Les Glénans", "Hoedic" and "Sein" look out onto the sea. The restaurant offers lots of seafood and fish dishes cooked by the owner's wife. Menus range from €13 (weekday lunchtime) to €23.50. *10% discount on the room rate on the first night (except July–Aug) or free coffee offered to our readers on presentation of this guide.*

Pont-Aven
29930

☞ 🛏 |⦿| Hôtel Les Ajoncs d'Or

1 pl. de l'Hôtel-de-Ville.
☎02.98.06.02.06 ☏02.98.06.18.91
✉ajoncsdor@aol.com
Closed *Sun evening and Mon out of season; Jan; fortnight in Oct.* **High chairs available.**

A breath of fresh air has swept through this old building since Gauguin stayed here on his last trip to Pont-Aven in 1894. The comfortable, refurbished double rooms with shower or bath go for €50–54, and you'll be sure of a friendly welcome. The old dining room has also been overhauled to serve fine dishes with a maritime touch, such as farandole of stuffed shellfish and bass *en croûte* with cream of hazelnut and cream of chives. There's a range of menus €19–40, and a children's menu €8.

☞ 🍴 |⦿| Crêperie Le Talisman

4 rue Paul-Sérusier; at the entrance to the town, on the Riec road.
☎02.98.06.02.58
Closed *Mon; Sun lunch out of season.*

This crêperie has a beautiful terrace overlooking the garden. The crêpes, and the little dishes that accompany them, are all excellent. Reckon on around €10 à la carte for a meal (three crêpes). Some specialities: the "Talisman" and "seafood" crêpes, and the pancake with flambéed apples. *Free house apéritif offered to our readers on presentation of this guide.*

☞ 🍴 |⦿| Restaurant le Tahiti

21 rue Belle-Angèle; it's on the Bannalec road.
☎02.98.06.15.93
Closed *Mon; Tues; Wed except during school holidays; fortnight in Feb; second fortnight in Nov.* **Disabled access. High chairs available.**

This is run by a local man and his Tahitian wife. The restaurant has been prettily decorated, and the cooking is exotic because

Madame is in the kitchen – Tahitian chow mein with chicken, yellow noodles, black mushrooms and vegetables, Tahitian fish marinated in lemon and blanched with onion. Divine desserts start with the *po'e maïa*, a *compote* of banana with vanilla pod cream. There's a weekday lunch menu at €12, and you'll pay about €19 for a full meal à la carte. They also do a take-away service. The table staff is friendly if sometimes a little too laid-back. *Free liqueur offered to our readers on presentation of this guide.*

Riec-sur-Belon
29340 (4.5km SE)

☞ 🍴 🛏 |⦿| Domaine de Kerstinec et restaurant Le Kerland

☎02.98.06.42.98 ☏02.98.06.45.38
✉restaurant.kerland@wanadoo.fr
Closed *Sun evening in low season; a week before Christmas.* **Disabled access.**

Beautiful rooms looking onto the garden and overlooking the Belon, with smaller ones upstairs. Doubles go for €59–100, depending on the category and season. The restaurant has built up a great reputation in the region, thanks to the talent of the young chef, Yannick Chatelain, the owners' son. The cooking is subtle and, unsurprisingly, based on seafood, with delicious specialities like scallops with five spices, thin buckwheat pancakes with smoked salmon and mango cream, asparagus flan with langoustines and melon *coulis*. The dining room, decorated in a rosewood colour, has a panoramic view of the river and serves menus from €22 (weekday lunchtimes) to €68. All in all, a beautiful place. *Free house apéritif offered to our readers on presentation of this guide.*

Trégunc
29910 (9km W)

☞ 🍴 🛏 |⦿| Les Grandes Roches

Well signposted from the town.
☎02.98.50.10.72 ☏02.98.97.62.97
🌐www.hotel-lesgrandesroches.com
Closed *20 Dec–1 Feb.* **Restaurant closed** *Tues and Wed.* **Disabled access. Swimming pool. Car park.**

Maud and Nicolas Raday welcome you to this magnificent complex made up of several old, restored buildings and two idyllic cottages, in the middle of a flowery five-hectare park complete with rocks and a menhir classified as a historical monument. Double rooms go for €75–130; breakfast €12. Inventive cooking in the restaurant: baked green asparagus and crusty bacon, loin of lamb *en croûte* and its Provençal tian, stuffed courgette with veal sweetbreads and kidneys and tarragon, baked turbot with croustillant of vegetables with aniseed and sea-urchin sauce. Menu at €41, or around €50–65 à la carte, served in two beautiful dining rooms with a fireplace. Facilities include a lovely swimming pool and billiards room – peace and quiet are guaranteed in this distinctive setting. *Free coffee offered to our readers on presentation of this guide.*

Pont-Croix
29790

@ 🍴 🏠 |●| Hôtel-restaurant Ty-Evan**

18 rue du Docteur-Neis; next to the town hall.
☏02.98.70.58.58 🖷02.98.70.53.38
✉tyeva@club-internet.fr
Closed Sat lunchtime and Sun evening out of season; Jan to mid-March. **Disabled access.**

Pont-Croix is a delightful, characterful town, definitely worth visiting for its magnificent cathedral portal. If the crashing waves have got too much for you, this is an ideal place to come for some gentle charm. Good double rooms for €44–51; half board is obligatory in August. Warm welcome and honest food with set menus at €10 (weekday lunchtimes) and €15–44. *10% discount on the room rate (from 2 consecutive nights except in July–Aug) offered to our readers on presentation of this guide.*

Pontivy
56300

@ |●| Crêperie La Campagnarde

14 rue de Lattre-de-Tassigny; it's on the Vannes road on the edge of town.
☏02.97.25.23.07
Closed Tues and Wed. **Disabled access. Car park.**

This country restaurant is decorated like a farm with old farm implements, cartwheels, forks and threshers that the owners have gleaned from here and there. Good crêpes made from Breton black wheat, stuffed with everything from cheese and seafood to apples and pears. All the

cooking methods are respectful of the quality of the produce used. A good meal will cost about €12.

Pont-L'Abbé
29120

@ 🍴 🏠 |●| Hôtel La Tour d'Auvergne

22 pl. Gambetta.
☏02.98.87.00.47 🖷02.98.82.33.78
Closed Sun and Mon; a fortnight end Feb to early March; a week early June; second fortnight Oct.

These premises have recently been taken over by a young couple, who have opened a highly successful gourmet bistro on the ground floor, with cosy décor dominated by wood. In the kitchens, the chef Franck Evin and his colleague Ronan O'Raw, an Irish food journalist enamoured of Brittany, dream up dishes according to the fresh ingredients available – and their own fancy. Their cuisine is based on associations of flavours. No tired routine here; every fortnight or so a new dish is chalked up on the blackboard, and even then it evolves constantly. These dishes of the day are cheap, surprising and available at any time: Morteau-sausage salad, mayonnaise with orange, pears poached in wine with Roquefort and walnuts. There is also a lunch menu at €16 or, à la carte, reckon on €32. The wine list ranges from carefully chosen local wines, available by the glass, to the most prestigious vintages. Well worth the detour for both the quality of the food and the atmosphere. As for the rooms (doubles €43–49; breakfast €6), they are a bit old-fashioned but are due to be refurbished next year. *Free coffee offered to our readers on presentation of this guide.*

Pouldreuzic
29710

@ 🏠 |●| Hôtel-restaurant Breiz-Armor**

It's on the beach of Penhors.
☏02.98.51.52.53 🖷02.98.51.52.30
🌐perso.wanadoo.fr/breiz-armor.fr
Closed Mon; Mon lunchtime in July and Aug; Jan–Feb; Nov school holiday. **Disabled access. TV. Car park.**

A beautifully located hotel right on the sea shore which, over the years, has spread

– it's built of concrete but in the Breton style. It's easy to put up with the building, in any case, because the location and the cuisine make all the difference. You'll find traditional dishes with an oriental streak on menus €13.50 (lunch in the week) and €18.30–46.20. Lovely rooms, some with fabulous views of the sea, go for €58–74; breakfast €6.90. Half board is compulsory in July and August for €63.50–71 per person. Logis de France. *Free house apéritif or coffee offered to our readers on presentation of this guide.*

Quiberon

56170

ⓐ ▲ |O| Parc Tehuen*

1 rue des Tamaris; it's 500m from the town centre.
☎02.97.50.10.26
ⓦwww.a-parc-tehuen.com
Closed *Oct–April (during the closure period, ring to reserve ☎02.97.64.53.70).* **Disabled access. TV. Car park.**

A really nice family *pension*, with a huge, shady garden and only 400m from the beach. Half board costs €47 per person for a room with basin or shower in high season; less if it's a room with shower on the landing. Also has furnished apartments elsewhere in the town for rent by the week.

ⓐ ♣ ▲ |O| Hôtel-restaurant Bellevue***

Rue de Tiviec; it's set back from the beach, by the casino.
☎02.97.50.16.28 ☎02.97.30.44.34
ⓦwww.bellevuequiberon.com
Closed *Oct to end March.* **Disabled access. TV. Cots and high chairs available. Swimming pool. Car park.**

This is a big, angular 1970s block which, while not having the appeal of a more traditional building, is quiet, comfortable and boasts lots of facilities – heated swimming pool, solarium and gardens. First-rate doubles start at €59 for a room with shower overlooking the swimming pool, up to €117 for a large double with bath and a sea view. In the height of summer, half board is compulsory and the price of the room becomes more or less the rate per person. Menus in the restaurant are €16.60–23, with a selection of local and other dishes: the lemon sole fillet with

cockle cream is particularly good. Logis de France. *10% discount on the room rate (April–June) offered to our readers on presentation of this guide.*

ⓐ ♣ |O| Crêperie-restaurant du Vieux Port

42–44 rue Surcouf; the street is above the old port of Port-Haliguen.
☎02.97.50.01.56
Closed *15 Nov–1 Feb.* **Disabled access. High chairs available.**

In a street overlooking the harbour this crêperie is a tad more expensive than others around but in a lovely spot and well worth the money. Non-stop crêpes are available from noon to 10pm, and from noon to 3pm and after 7pm in the restaurant. An all-inclusive menu of crêpes and cider at €13 will limit your cash outlay; you'll spend around €14–18 for a meal à la carte. Their speciality crêpe is served with salt butter and caramel, but they also do great fish and seafood choices. There's a small but very pretty garden; the service is attentive and efficient. *Free coffee offered to our readers on presentation of this guide.*

ⓐ |O| La Chaumine

36 pl. du Manémeur; it's in the village of Manémeur.
☎02.97.50.17.67
Closed *Sun evening except July–Aug; Mon; 3 weeks in March; 1 Nov–16 Dec.* **Disabled access. High chairs available.**

The restaurant is in an adorable spot, surrounded by fishermen's cottages. Arrive in time for an apéritif at the bar and join the fishermen and locals sipping Muscadet – it's a million miles from the stress and traffic jams of city life. The set menus have no frills, just good, honest ingredients – mussels, prawns, fish – while specialities include sole with *girolle jus* and turbot poached in milk. The menu at €13 is served at lunchtime, though not on Sunday, and there are others €24–45.

ⓐ |O| Restaurant La Criée

11 quai de l'Océan; it's on the port Maria.
☎02.97.30.53.09 ☎02.97.50.42.35
Closed *Sun evening and Mon; Mon lunchtime only (July–Aug); 1–15 Dec; Jan.*

One of the best seafood and fish specialists of the peninsula – La Criée means "fish market" and it's the restaurant belonging to the Lucas smokehouse. Not surprisingly, the shellfish and seafood are of the freshest. There are dishes of the day on the €16 menu and they do shellfish platters, fish couscous and fish *choucroute*, along with *sole meunière*, grilled fish and house smoked fish; expect to pay €35 or so à la carte. It offers good value for money and fast service with a smile.

Quimper
29000

BRETAGNE

ⓔ 🎿 🏠 Hôtel Gradlon***

30 rue de Brest.
☎02.98.95.04.39 ℗02.98.95.61.25
🌐www.hotel-gradlon.com
Closed *20 Dec–20 Jan*. **TV. Pay car park.**

Well situated, close to the town centre. Prettily decorated rooms (€69–15) of a good size, some of which have been completely refurbished; excellent breakfast €10.50. Most of the rooms look onto the charming, quiet inner garden; the cheapest rooms, on the street, are soundproofed. We liked the bar with its snug complete with fine fireplace and the veranda leading to the patio. There's a locked garage subject to reservation at a cost of €8. Peace and quiet are guaranteed along with a good welcome from the delightful owner. *One free breakfast per room (from 1 Oct to 31 April) offered to our readers on presentation of this guide.*

ⓔ 🍴 Le Cosy

2 rue du Sallé.
☎02.98.95.23.65
Closed *Sun; Mon; 2 or 3 weeks in May or June; a week at Christmas*. **Disabled access.**

The owner will be offended if you expect chips or crêpes, but she will happily serve you some fine *tartines*, savoury pies, toasted country bread, salmon, smoked duck, well-prepared dishes of the day and excellent desserts; everything is homemade. Many dishes are based on fruit, ably combining sweet and savoury flavours: duck *confit* with dates and cumin, free-range chicken with honey and star anis. The building is equally striking, and the three upstairs dining rooms are very attractive. Reckon on €10–15 for a *tartine* meal with dessert and €20 for

a full meal with one of the dishes of the day. This gourmet bistro really lives up to its name.

ⓔ 🍴 Crêperie Au Vieux Quimper

20 rue Verdelet.
☎02.98.95.31.34
Closed *Sun lunchtime; Mon evening and Tues out of season; first fortnight in June.*

The little dining room has bare stone walls and Breton furniture and it quickly gets full. There's a friendly family atmosphere and everyone tucks into the delicate and crispy crêpes, swigging down tumblers of cider and milk ribot. You'll pay around €11 for a meal, drinks included. It's an excellent place so it's good to book. Credit cards not accepted.

ⓔ 🎿 🍴 Le Steinway

20 rue des Gentilshommes; it's in the centre of the old town.
☎02.98.95.53.70
Closed *Sun and Mon; Sun lunch (July–Aug).*

The décor hails from the 1950s, with local ornaments and memorabilia; there's also an old petrol pump, a trombone, lots of old radios and plenty of telephones. The whole place feels warm and welcoming. They do an excellent slab of steak or simple salmon with fresh basil, and servings are ample. Normally they produce good peasant food but occasionally they'll spice it up with Mexican or American dishes. The weekday lunch menu goes for €13, with others €19.50–26.50 or around €30 à la carte. *Second coffee offered to our readers on presentation of this guide.*

ⓔ 🎿 🍴 Jardin de l'Odet

39 bd. de Kerguelen.
☎02.98.95.76.76
Closed *Sun; Mon; end Aug to mid- Sept.* **Open** *12.15–1.30pm and 7–9.30pm.*

This restaurant, well situated between the Odet and the Évêché garden, is set in a stunning 1930s building and also boasts a lovely garden looking onto the ramparts. You can eat a very reasonably priced dish of the day in the shade of an olive tree. Menus cost €19 (lunch), €27 and €35; you can combine dishes from these menus if you eat à la carte. *Free house apéritif offered to our readers on presentation of this guide.*

⊜ |●| La Fleur de Sel

1 quai Neuf; on the right bank of the Odet.
☎02.98.55.04.71
Closed Sat lunch; Sun; 24 Dec–3 Jan.
Disabled access. High chairs and games available.

Smokers, be warned: tobacco is not permitted in this restaurant. Cosy little dining room, ideal for a sophisticated get together – business meetings are the rule at lunchtime – plus a couple of tables on a terrace, with a glimpse of the river. Menus (€20–35) feature local cooking with a dash of invention; the house speciality is salmon marinated with *fleur de sel*. The service is slow but charming.

⊜ |●| ♫ L'Ambroisie

49 rue Élie-Fréron.
☎02.98.95.00.02
Closed Mon and Sun evening (except summer); end June to early July.

The young chef concocts sophisticated dishes with a touch of daring, without ever straying too far from local tradition: Parmentier d'*andouille* with cider, sautéed langoustines in shellfish broth, etc. The dining room is solidly impressive, and the food it serves is undoubtedly some of the best on offer in the whole town, with menus €22 (weekdays) and then €31–64. Reckon on around €65 à la carte. *Free coffee offered to our readers on presentation of this guide.*

Quimperlé

29300

⊜ 🏠 Le Vintage Hôtel

20 rue de Brémond-d'Ars; in the lower town, next to La Bobine cinema.
☎02.98.35.09.10 ☎02.98.35.09.29
✉bistrotdelatour@wanadoo.fr
TV. Disabled access.

This former savings bank is famous locally for inspiring the hotel in Breton writer Bernard Cariou's *Bistro de la Tour*. Cariou's son is now in charge, and he has successfully introduced original, contemporary design. The ten rooms (€77) are all decorated differently, with highly evocative frescoes on the walls.

⊜ |●| La Cigale Égarée

La Villeneuve Braouïc, Trevoazec; at the entrance to the town coming from Lorient.

☎02.98.39.15.53
Closed Sun and Mon evening; All Saints' Day.
Disabled access. High chairs available.

At the time of going to press, this restaurant had just moved. It's up to you to let us know your impressions regarding its new location. As for the rest, nothing else has changed and you can still expect the same relaxed and charming service. You can savour fine cuisine made from produce fresh from the market, inventive without ever being showy. Despite a certain Mediterranean influence, it is nevertheless firmly anchored in the Breton region, as testified by its carpaccio of salmon with Breton honey or there again a *fricassée* of scallops with mead or grilled bacon with basil and garlic. The desserts are all just as appetizing. There's a *formule* at €18 (lunchtime); other menus €26 and €50. Booking is advisable.

⊜ |●| Le Bistro de la Tour***

2 rue Dom-Morice; it's in the ville basse, by the covered market, opposite Sainte-Croix church.
☎02.98.39.29.58
Closed Sat lunchtime; Sun evening; Mon.
Disabled access.

A choice of settings to suit different occasions with a 1930s bistro on the ground floor and another dining room upstairs with the feel of the old-fashioned family Sunday lunch, complete with everything you need in the way of table mats, old-fashioned centre lights and traditional furniture to make you feel at ease. Here they do their utmost to ensure that the wines complement the dishes. As for the food, seafood takes centre stage, but the Breton *cassoulet à l'andouille de Baye* comes a close second, as does the smoked wild boar ham. The first menu starts at €19 (not Sat evening or Sun), with others up to €39 and a children's menu at €13; à la carte around €38. Jérôme, the young proprietor-cum-sommelier, will recommend you one of his discoveries to suit your pocket. More than eight hundred wines await you in the cellar (along with four hundred whiskies), some absolute gems among them. It's worth knowing that on the first Friday of the month (except July and Aug), there is a *dîner-dégustation* evening with a wine grower (get there early, the place soon fills up). You can buy the wines sampled at competitive prices.

Rennes

35000

See map on p.228.

◎ ♨ Hôtel de la Tour d'Auvergne

20 bd. de la Tour-d'Auvergne; near the law courts. **Map A2-8**
℡02.99.30.84.16 ℻02.23.42.10.01
TV.

On the upper floor of the nice brasserie *Le Serment de Vin*. Plain but spotless rooms go for €26 with basin, up to €38 with shower/wc – a bargain. Ideal family hotel for limited budgets, run by a very kindly woman. She'll bring your breakfast to your room as there's no breakfast room. A great place.

◎ ⚞ ♨ Hotel Garden**

3 rue Duhamel; between the station and the old town. **Map B2-4**
℡02.99.65.45.06 ℻02.99.65.02.62
ⓦwww.logis-de-france.fr
TV. High chairs available. Pay car park.

Charming, tasteful hotel, set between the station and the old town. There's a café decorated in apple-green and a small quiet internal garden. Very nice, individualized rooms in fresh colours go for €45 with washbasin only, €60 with shower/wc or bath. We particularly liked those on the garden level; those on the street side are not so quiet. A point worth noting is that some rooms sleep four. The nearby streets contain many buildings by Odorico, the famous Art Deco mosaicist, with the most famous one adjoining the hotel. *10% discount on the room rate (in July–Aug and at weekends) offered to our readers on presentation of this guide.*

◎ ⚞ ♨ Hôtel Astrid**

32 av. Louis Barthou; opposite the train station. **Off map B3-11**
℡02.99.30.82.38 ℻02.99.31.85.55
ⓦwww.hotelastrid.fr
Closed *24 Dec–2 Jan.* **Disabled access. TV.**

Well-located near the station and only a ten-minute walk from the town centre. A pretty, chic hotel where you'll get a friendly welcome. It's spotless and the rooms – modern, large, quiet and well equipped – cost €50–63 with shower/wc or bath. The breakfast room looks out onto a small garden. *10% discount on the room rate (weekdays out of season) offered to our readers on presentation of this guide.*

◎ ⚞ ♨ Hôtel Lanjuinais**

11 rue Lanjuinais; in a small street leading to quai Lamennais, between the place de Bretagne and the Post Office. **Map A2-6**
℡02.99.79.02.03 ℻02.99.79.03.97
ⓦwww.hotel-lanjuinais.com
TV.

A quiet, well-maintained hotel in a small street leading towards the quai Lamennais. Most rooms look over the street but some look into the (rather dark) courtyard. They have reasonable facilities and cost €51 with shower/wc or €54 with bath. *10% discount on the room rate (weekends only) offered to our readers on presentation of this guide.*

◎ ♨ Hôtel des Lices**

7 pl. des Lices; in the city-centre. **Map A1-7**
℡02.99.79.14.81 ℻02.99.79.35.44
ⓦwww.hotel-des-lices.com
Disabled access. TV. High chairs available. Pay car park.

Reliable establishment on one of the most beautiful squares in the old town offering a very friendly and dynamic welcome. They've completely modernized this hotel, which is full of light and well appointed. The very pleasant rooms have balconies and the ones on the upper floors have good views over the rooftops and the old town. Doubles cost €56 with shower/wc or €58 with bath.

◎ ⚞ |◉| Un Amour de Pomme de Terre

14 place Rallier-de-Baty; very close to place des Lices and place Saint-Michel. **Map A1-21**
℡02.99.79.04.91 ℻02.99.79.06.15
Disabled access. Car park.

The noble tuber stars in all dishes, accompanied by salads, smothered in melted cheese, or served with seaweed-smoked Molène sausage, smoked Camaret trout, and foie gras. The choice seems endless. Portions are mountainous on the lunchtime menu €9.50, or around €20 à la carte, but a shot of vodka or lambig helps the food slip down just so you can make room for a pud. There are several floors and the decoration is really nice. But the dining room on the ground floor, where you can eat by the open fire, is probably the most appealing. It's best of all on a Thursday which is when they serve *kig ha farz*. *Free house apéritif offered to our readers on presentation of this guide*

BRETAGNE

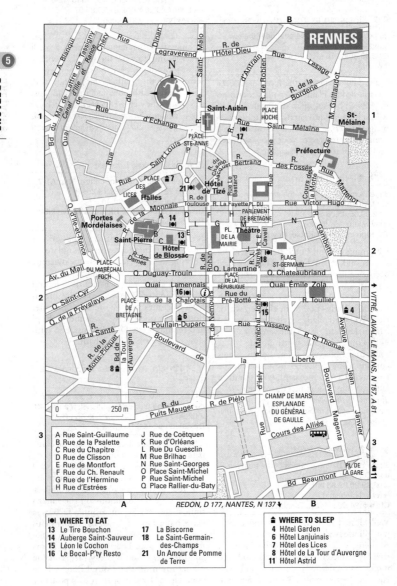

RENNES

A	Rue Saint-Guillaume
B	Rue de la Psalette
C	Rue du Chapitre
D	Rue de Clisson
E	Rue de Montfort
F	Rue du Ch. Renault
G	Rue de l'Hermine
H	Rue d'Estrées
J	Rue de Coëtquen
K	Rue d'Orléans
L	Rue Du Guesclin
M	Rue Brilhac
N	Rue Saint-Georges
O	Place Saint-Michel
P	Rue Saint-Michel
Q	Place Rallier-du-Baty

REDON, D 177, NANTES, N 137 ↓

|O| WHERE TO EAT

13 Le Tire Bouchon
14 Auberge Saint-Sauveur
15 Léon le Cochon
16 Le Bocal-P'ty Resto
17 La Biscorne
18 Le Saint-Germain-des-Champs
21 Un Amour de Pomme de Terre

≜ WHERE TO SLEEP

4 Hôtel Garden
6 Hôtel Lanjuinais
7 Hôtel des Lices
8 Hôtel de La Tour d'Auvergne
11 Hôtel Astrid

ⓔ |●| Le Bocal-P'ty Resto

6 rue d'Argentré, near quai Lamennais. **Map A2-16**
☏ 02.99.78.34.10
Closed *Sat lunch; Sun; Mon; first fortnight in Jan; first fortnight in May; Aug.*

This friendly restaurant is trendy, young and appealing – overflowing with creative ideas. The décor is lovely: glass jars are filled with all sorts of strange things collected here and there and the seals have been used to decorate the walls and even the doors in the toilet. The dishes of the day – for example a huge muffin with chicken, bacon and black pepper – are scrawled up on a blackboard, with menus €10–14. You'll pay about €18 for three courses à la carte. There's a well-chosen, reasonably priced wine list; all wines are served by the glass.

ⓔ ⚵ |●| La Biscorne

8 rue Saint-Mélaine. **Map B1-17**
☏ 02.99.38.79.77
Closed *Sun; Mon; 3 weeks in August.* **Disabled access.**

Warm, rustic charm, harmonizing well with the traditional cuisine. There's lots of wood and an enormous fireplace where the young chef displays his awards. They offer à la carte and a range of set menus at €11.95 (weekday lunchtimes) and €17–28. The nicely realized dishes change every four months, and are always good and fresh. Fish is on the menu of course.

ⓔ ⚵ |●| Le Saint-Germain-des-Champs

12 rue Vau-Saint-Germain; opposite the Saint-Germain church. **Map B2-18**
☏ 02.99.79.25.52
Closed *Sun; Mon; Aug.* **Open** *lunchtime daily, plus Fri and Sat evenings.* **Disabled access. High chairs available.**

When the cows went mad, chickens were steeped in dioxin and vegetables were genetically modified, this had to be the place to come. A genuine organic vegetarian restaurant – delightfully welcoming – where you can have a good meal without eating bits of animal. Interesting ingredients like sprouting grains and seaweed in dishes that are full of colour and generously served. Expect to pay around €12 (weekday lunchtime) and up to €17 for a meal à la carte. Even the wines and fruit juices are organic. One dining room

has a plate-glass window onto the street while the second looks onto the courtyard, and there's a reading and information area. *Free house apéritif offered to our readers on presentation of this guide.*

ⓔ ⚵ |●| Léon Le Cochon

1 rue du Maréchal-Joffre; next to the main post office. **Map B2-15**
☏ 02.99.79.37.54
Closed *Sun (July–Aug).* **TV.**

A lot of thinking has gone into creating this restaurant, which is at once modern, refined and authentic – not an easy achievement. Dried flowers, walls hung with chilli peppers and windows full of leaves are the backdrop for unpretentiously prepared local cooking. There's a weekday lunchtime menu for €11.50; à la carte reckon on around €25. It's best to book. *Free house apéritif offered to our readers on presentation of this guide.*

ⓔ ⚵ |●| Auberge Saint-Sauveur

6 rue Saint-Sauveur; behind the cathedral Saint-Pierre. **Map A2-14**
☏ 02.99.79.32.56
Closed *Sat lunchtime; Sun; Mon lunchtime; 3 weeks from mid-Aug.*

In a lovely sixteenth-century canon's house behind St-Pierre cathedral, this restaurant has a warm, intimate, sophisticated atmosphere. Good-value weekday lunch *formule* costs €12 and menus €18–46, or you'll pay around €30 à la carte. Excellent set lunchtime menu if you want to enjoy the setting without breaking the bank. Good place to treat your partner or an old chum. *Free coffee offered to our readers on presentation of this guide.*

ⓔ |●| Le Tire Bouchon

2 rue du Châpitre. **Map A2-13**
☏ 02.99.79.43.43
Closed *Sat; Sun and public holidays; Feb school holiday; third week in Aug.* **Disabled access.**

A new approach to the wine bar. You sit side by side at the big counter or at one of the small wooden tables. There's a choice of only three or four dishes of the day – the kind that are slowly and carefully cooked. Alternatively, opt for a plate of charcuterie or farmhouse cheese, or for a tartine – toasted sandwich – with cheese, fruit or charcuterie. The prices are modest – around €20 for a meal – and the ingredients of very good quality. The wine list is thoughtfully chosen and includes some unusual vintages from overseas; they're sold by the glass. Super décor, lovely welcome – it's very popular, and so it's best to book.

Roche-Bernard (La)

56130

ⓒ 🛏 |❂| Les Deux Magots**

3 pl. du Bouffay.
℡02.99.90.60.75 ℻02.99.90.87.87
ⓔaubergelesdeuxmagots.
rochebernard@wanadoo.fr
Restaurant closed Sun evening and Mon out of season; Mon and Tues lunchtime in high season; 20 Dec–15 Jan; a weekend of June; a week mid-Oct. **TV.**

This comfortable, welcoming hotel has a lovely façade with arched windows and fifteen pleasantly furnished rooms; doubles €43–55 with shower/wc or bath. Seafood dishes predominate – roast langoustine tails, warm crayfish salad, braised sea bream with baby vegetables, roast turbot served with seasonal mushrooms – though the sweetbreads with morels and home-made foie gras are worth trying, too. Menus start at €13 (before 8.30pm, not weekends), then there are others €23–54. There's a lengthy wine list and the bar has an impressive collection of miniature bottles of apéritifs, cognac, whisky and so on. Credit cards not accepted.

Roscoff

29680

ⓒ 🛏 |❂| 🌿 Les Chardons Bleus**

4 rue Amiral-Réveillère; on the way to the church from the port.
℡02.98.69.72.03 ℻02.98.61.27.86
Closed Thurs and Sun evenings, except July–Aug; mid-Feb to mid-March. **TV. High chairs available.**

Ten rooms with fairly unremarkable contemporary decoration but a good degree of comfort (high-quality bedding, efficient double glazing on the street), the liveliest in the town centre. Doubles with shower/wc or bath go for €55–65. Weekday lunchtime menu €12, then

others €18–42, featuring tasty, traditional food; children's menu €8. *Free house apéritif offered to our readers on presentation of this guide.*

ⓒ |❂| L'Écume des Jours

Quai d'Auxerre.
℡02.98.61.22.83
Closed Tues and Wed out of season; Dec; Jan. **Disabled access. High chairs available.**

A granite mansion house that formerly belonged to a shipbuilder, with a comfortable, intimate interior and a big fireplace. Menus (€20–46) list sophisticated and meticulously conceived dishes that skilfully combine local produce from both the sea and the countryside, such as queen scallops or smoked *magret de canard*. There's also a children's menu €10, and the terrace looks out over the sea.

Batz (Île de)

29253 (5km N)

ⓒ 🛏 |❂| Auberge de jeunesse

Creach-ar-Bolloch; take one of the launches that leaves Creach-ar-Bolloch every half-hour for Roscoff (last departure 8pm).
℡02.98.61.77.69 ℻02.98.61.78.85
ⓦwww.auberges-de-jeunesse.com
Closed 30 Sept to Easter.

The fixtures and fittings in this youth hostel may be the worse for wear, but its location is stunning, right by the sea; its small buildings house dormitories that resemble the cabins of boats. Accommodation is €8.10 a night, breakfast €3.40 and meals €8.30. Youth hostel card is compulsory (LFAJ-FUAJ-IYFH), new sanitary blocks have just been built and there's a kitchen available. Credit cards not accepted.

Rostrenen

22110

ⓒ |❂| Coeur de Breizh

14 rue Abbé-Gibert, in the village.
℡02.96.29.18.33
Closed Wed out of season; 20 Dec–7 Jan. **Open** until 9.45pm (10.30pm weekends). **Disabled access.**

Situated in the middle of the hamlet, in a substantial yellow house. The owners raised the money to get started through the support of friends and clients who had been trying to persuade them to transform their bar into a restaurant; and it worked. The setting is totally seductive – stone walls and a Breton décor. Roger is a natural front-of-house and Anne-Laure is a self-taught chef with talent. She cooks local dishes using fresh, good-quality produce – organic for the most part – which she sources through local farmers and producers. Weekday lunch menu at €11 and menus €18–26 feature delicious main courses and an array of seductive sweets; à la carte, prices are fair. They host occasional exhibitions and concerts with apéritifs.

Sables-d'Or-les-Pins
22240

⚉ 🛏 |●| 𝒜 Hôtel des Pins**

Allée des Acacias; it's 400m from the beach.
☎02.96.41.42.20 ℻02.96.41.59.02
Closed 1 Oct–26 March.

A holiday hotel with the kind of charm that suits the slightly old-fashioned feel of the resort. Doubles go for €38–40 with shower and €50–55 with shower/wc; half board is obligatory in July and August. Menus, €15.50–34.50, feature lots of good seafood and fresh fish. Facilities include mini-golf and a garden. *10% discount on the room rate (out of season) offered to our readers on presentation of this guide.*

Plurien-Fréhel
22240 (2km S)

⚉ 𝒜 🛏 Manoir de la Salle**

Rue du Lac; it's 500m from Sables-d'Or-les-Pins, just before you get to Fréhel.
☎02.96.72.38.29 ℻02.96.72.00.57
🌐www.manoir-de-la-salle.com
Closed 30 Sept–24 March. **Disabled access.**
TV. High chairs available. Car park.

A stone-built, sixteenth-century manor house which you enter through a beautiful gothic portal built a century earlier. Bright, comfortable rooms furnished with modern pieces; doubles with shower/wc or bath for €47–55 depending on the season. They've converted another old building to make a couple of apartments with kitchens sleeping four to six at

€88–109. The hotel is set in two hectares of grounds, and there are lots of things to keep you amused – such as the solarium and ping-pong, along with a golf course nearby – not to mention the beach. They can arrange sea trips for residents, and there are even stalls for horses and ponies if you're on a riding holiday. It's an excellent place. *10% discount on the room rate (except July–Aug) offered to our readers on presentation of this guide.*

Saint-Brieuc
22000

⚉ 🛏 Auberge de jeunesse-Manoir de la Ville-Guyomard

Les Villages; 3km from the town centre, near the *Géant* shopping centre (well signposted from the train station).
☎ and ℻02.96.78.70.70
🌐www.fuaj.org
Open all year round. **Disabled access.**

Youth hostel situated in a wonderful fifteenth-century manor house. Accommodation, €13.25 per night including breakfast, is in rooms with one to four beds. Meals are only served to groups. You can rent mountain bikes. Booking is highly advisable.

⚉ 𝒜 🛏 |●| Hôtel-restaurant Du Guesclin**

2 pl. du-Guesclin; it's in the pedestrian area.
☎02.96.33.11.58 ℻02.96.52.01.18
🌐hotelduguesclin.com
TV. High chairs available.

Centrally located and completely refurbished with comfortable rooms which, though they are nothing to shout about, are reliable. Doubles with shower/wc or bath are €44–46; half board €42 per person. There's a bar-brasserie on the ground floor and an elegant dining room serving menus at €9.90 (weekday lunchtime) and €15–24; specialities include bream with fennel, home-smoked fish and scallops with *andouille*. *10% discount on the room rate (Fri, Sat and Sun) offered to our readers on presentation of this guide.*

⚉ 𝒜 🛏 Hôtel du Champ de Mars**

13 rue du Général-Leclerc; close to place du Champs-de-Mars.

☎02.96.33.60.99 ⓕ02.96.33.60.05
ⓔhoteldemars@wanadoo.fr
Closed *during Christmas/New Year holidays.*
Disabled access. TV. High chairs and cots available.

Well situated, on the edge of the centre and right next to the large Champs-de-Mars car park (free except from 9am to 12pm and 2pm to 6pm). This well-run, pleasant establishment with all the facilities you expect of a two-star hotel has the merit of being reasonably priced: €44–50 for a double. Friendly owners who enjoy what they do. *10% discount on the price of a room (for a stay of over 2 nights, excluding July and Aug) offered to our readers on presentation of this guide.*

ⓒ ✕ |●| Restaurant Le Sympatic

9 bd. Carnot; it's behind the train station; take boulevard Clemenceau and turn right after the railway line.
☎02.96.94.04.76
Closed *Sun; Mon; public holidays; fortnight in Aug.* **Open** *until 10pm.* **Disabled access.**

A happy combination of a good atmosphere and good food grilled over vines. The ambience is warm with lots of wood and bare stone. The service is friendly and efficient; dishes using quality ingredients are served on huge plates with a side vegetable, and they're inexpensive. Set menus cost €14–40, or around €35 à la carte. *Free house apéritif offered to our readers on presentation of this guide.*

ⓒ ✕ |●| Au Petit Bouchon Briochin

10 rue Jules-Ferry; it's behind the train station.
☎02.96.94.05.34
Closed *Sat lunchtime; Sun; fortnight end-Feb to early March; fortnight in Aug.* **Disabled access.**

The cuisine is faithful to the region with a few modern takes on traditional recipes from old-hand local chefs. The set lunch offers dish of the day or a plate of organic hams followed by dessert, and a choice of a glass of wine or a coffee, for €10.60. Menus go for €15–25; coffee and drinks are included in the most expensive one. There's also a menu-carte with starter, a selection of main courses and dessert for the same price. A different glass of wine is offered with each dish. Less impressive is the décor in the dining room – the sepia photographs and old farm implements on the wall clash somewhat with

the 1980s monochrome. But that's just quibbling when the service and welcome are a cut above the ordinary. *Free coffee offered to our readers on presentation of this guide.*

ⓒ ✕ |●| Aux Pesked

59 rue du Légué; it's 1km north of the town centre.
☎02.96.33.34.65 ⓕ02.96.33.65.38
ⓦwww.pesked.fr
Closed *Sat lunchtime; Sun evening; Mon; 1–15 Jan; 1–8 May; 1–8 Sept.* **High chairs available. Car park.**

The gastronomic reputation of this restaurant is highly regarded in Saint-Brieuc. It's got lots going for it – a sober, elegant, modern setting and a terrace which gives superb views of the Légué valley. Delightful light, mouth-watering dishes, with a €20 weekday lunch menu and others at €33–85. Some days they offer a seven-course *menu dégustation*. The extensive cellar contains an impressive collection of 15,000 bottles. Some are rare and expensive, lots are Loire wines, but many are less prestigious and more affordable. *Free house apéritif offered to our readers on presentation of this guide.*

Saint-Malo
35400

ⓒ ✕ 🏠 |●| Hôtel de l'Univers**

Place Châteaubriand.
☎02.99.40.89.52 ⓕ02.99.40.07.27
ⓦwww.hotel-univers-saintmalo.com
Restaurant closed *Wed.* **TV. High chairs available.**

This establishment is right next to the legendary *Bar de l'Univers*, and the hotel stands as testimony to a splendid past. It's one of those local places with style, *je ne sais quoi*, and refined charm. The reception is spacious, the corridors and sitting rooms well proportioned. The atmosphere in the huge bedrooms is lovely – some can sleep three or four. Doubles go for €60–84 depending on the view, facilities and the season. In the restaurant there are menus at €13–35. The management have undertaken work to restore the rooms and the stucco in the dining room to their former glory. *10% discount on the room rate (except July–Aug, New Year, Whit Sun) offered to our readers on presentation of this guide.*

◉ |●| La Touline

6 pl.de la Poissonnerie.
☎02.99.40.10.98
Closed *Mon and Tues out of season; Mon mid-July to end Aug; 3 weeks in March; 3 weeks Nov–Dec.* **High chairs available.**

One of the best crêperies in Saint-Malo. The ideas for the delicious crêpes are original and well executed, and the fillings, such as sausage and *andouille*, are of the highest quality. There are also fresh, tasty salads on offer. Reckon on around €8–12 for a full meal, otherwise you can choose the menu at €11. You can eat out on the attractive terrace on the pretty little place de la Poissonnerie. The service could not be friendlier.

◉ |●| Le P'tit Crêpier

6 rue Sainte Barbe.
☎02.99.40.93.19
Closed *Tues and Wed, except July–Aug; winter except school holidays.*

The pancakes and girdle cakes here are as good as they are surprising, and the service is diligent and attentive. Cosy, enticing nautical-style dining room, or a lovely terrace in fine weather. A good crêperie, thanks to its subtle flavours, excellent ingredients and astonishing but never reckless combinations; you'll pay around €14 for a meal.

◉ |●| La Corderie

Saint-Servan, chemin de la Corderie; not far from the Alet camping site, just behind the World War II memorial.
☎02.99.81.62.38
Closed *Mon.* **High chairs available.**

La Corderie is off the tourist track and wonderfully lacking in traffic noise. It's an old family house filled with old furniture, books and paintings. From the terrace and dining room, there is a beautiful view of the sea, the Solidor tower, La Rance and Dinard beyond. They serve light, well-presented dishes at reasonable prices, and they change practically every day – you can usually count on seeing a good Greek salad and grilled fish. Menu at €16; à la carte a meal will cost around €30–35.

◉ |●| Restaurant Chez Gilles

2 rue de la Pie-qui-Boit.
☎02.99.40.97.25
Closed *Wed; Thurs; 1 Nov–1 April; 18 Nov–14 Dec.* **High chairs available.**

The gloriously fresh seafood here is cooked with enthusiasm and served in a cosy, comfy, bourgeois dining room with intimate corners. There's a €18.70 lunch *formule* and menus at €22.80 and €32; a meal à la carte will cost you €40. The owner/chef cooks fish to perfection in delicate, aromatic sauces: slivers of John Dory with hot oysters and bacon pieces, brill in a chicken stock and foie gras. You get the same quality of cooking on all the set menus.

◉ |●| Fleurs de Sel

93 bd. de Rochebonne Paramé.
☎02.99.40.09.93
Closed *Sat lunchtime; Sun evening and Mon; a fortnight mid-March; second fortnight in Oct.* **Disabled access. High chairs available.**

A fine restaurant, just ten minutes from the beach of Rochebonne. The walls are decorated with murals depicting the exploits of the yachtsman Eric Tabarly and his various *Pen-Duick* boats. The food is tasty and meticulously prepared, as well as being exquisitely presented on beautifully laid tables, with menus €22, €28 and €33; reckon on around €32 à la carte. Not surprisingly, it is always full, so it's advisable to book.

Saint-Suliac

35430 (10km S)

◉ ⌂ |●| Le Galichon

5 La Grande-Cohue; it's on the N17.
☎02.99.58.49.49
Closed *mid-Jan to mid-Feb.* **Open** *daily 11am–9pm (June–Sept); out of season, open for lunch and dinner, Fri, Sat and Sun plus evenings during school holidays.* **TV. High chairs available.**

A really nice place, this. A handful of the rustic, a shake of refinement and a pinch of nostalgia combine to make a delicious venue where they serve good pancakes and dishes using old recipes cooked over the fire. It works a treat. No set menu; dishes around €8 and desserts for €3 or so. In fine weather you can eat in the small courtyard. It's best to book as it's very popular.

Saint-Pol-de-Léon
29250

@ 🏠 |●| **Le Passiflore**

28 rue Penn-Ar-Pont; not far from the station.
☎ and ℻02.98.69.00.52
Closed Sun evening; 24 Dec–2 Jan. **High
chairs available. TV.**

A small, unpretentious hotel, where guests
are given a warm welcome and offered
attractive rooms at very reasonable prices:
€35–40 for a double. Its restaurant, *Les
Routiers*, is also good value; it has two
rooms: one is a little "cantine" that is
packed with locals at lunchtime, the other
serves more elaborate meals based on fish
and seafood. There's a weekday lunchtime
menu €9.50–18; others at €20–32.

Saint-Renan
29290

@ 🎋 |●| **La Maison d'Autrefois**

7 rue de l'Église.
☎02.98.84.22.67
Closed Sun lunch; Mon out of season; 15–25
Jan. **High chairs available.**

Superbly attractive, half-timbered house.
Inside, the natural stone walls are decorated with old farm implements and beautiful furniture. Good, traditional crêpes
– the Bretonne is stuffed with scallops,
chopped leeks and cream and flambéed
with Calvados, while the Sauvage drips
with wine caramel and honey ice cream.
Weekday lunch menu costs €7.20 and a
children's menu for €5.50; expect to pay
€11 to eat à la carte. *Free Kir Breton offered
to our readers on presentation of this guide.*

Saint-Thégonnec
29410

@ 🏠 |●| **Auberge de Saint-
Thégonnec***

6 pl. de la Mairie.
☎02.98.79.61.18 ℻02.98.62.71.10
🌐www.auberge.saint.thegonnec.com
Closed Sat lunchtime; Sun (evening only in
season); Mon lunchtime; 20 Dec–10 Jan. **TV.
Disabled access. High chairs available.
Car park.**

Not only one of the best hotel-restaurants
on the "circuit des Enclos", also one of

the best in the whole of Finistère. It lies
just opposite one of the most beautiful
enclosures in the region (although the
church has been partially destroyed by a
fire). The setting is elegant and refined,
but without being overwhelming, and the
seasonal food is excellent. The bill climbs
up steeply if you eat à la carte (reckon on
around €40), but the chef was shrewd
enough to balance it with more accessible menus (the cheapest is at €25). The
bedrooms are attractive and extremely
comfortable: doubles with shower/wc or
bath €80–120. Breakfast is served in a
charming lounge. Logis de France.

@ |●| **Restaurant du Commerce**

1 rue de Paris; it's in the centre of the village.
☎02.98.79.61.07
Closed evenings; Sat and Sun; 3 weeks in
Aug. **Disabled access.**

A roadside restaurant of the Routier variety offering a friendly welcome, good
cooking, huge portions and cheap prices.
In the pleasant dining room with stone
walls, for €10.50 you get soup, starter, dish
of the day, cheese and dessert – the menu
states that a drink is included for "workers" but not for people "passing through";
children's menu €7.80. They also have
a few specialities like *pot-au-feu*, a broth
with large chunks of meat and vegetables,
choucroute, *kig-ha-farz* and couscous. It's a
lively place.

@ |●| **Crêperie Steredenn**

6 rue de la Gare.
☎02.98.79.43.34
Closed Mon and Tues (except in July and
Aug); mid-Nov to 30 Jan. **Disabled access.
High chairs available.**

Christine and Alain offer a friendly greeting and an open fire. A huge choice of
delicious, cheap crêpes: the Picardie, with
creamed leeks and the sweet Druidique,
with marmalade, almonds and Grand
Marnier. Reckon on between €12 and
€15 à la carte. Wash it down with cider
brewed on the premises.

Sarzeau
56370

@ 🎋 |●| **Auberge de Kerstéphanie**

Route du Roaliguen; at the Sarzeau roundabout take the Roaliguen exit and it is on the

right at the end of a cul-de-sac.
☎02.97.41.72.41
Closed *Mon and Wed lunchtimes; Tues evening, Wed and Sun evening out of season; Christmas and Feb holidays.* **Disabled access. High chairs and games available. Car park.**

One of the very best restaurants in Morbihan, in a gorgeous room with elegant, unfussy service. Jean-Paul Jego is a virtuoso chef, ably helped by his wife. Fabulous food on offer at excellent prices: there's a €15 lunch menu, for example, and others at €23–38, all change with the seasons. Thanks to the spit, there's a different rôtisserie dish each day, perhaps lamb shank or farm-reared rabbit with mustard. The lobster is grilled fresh from the fish tank. *Free coffee offered to our readers on presentation of this guide.*

🍴 |●| Restaurant L'Hortensia

La Grée-Penvins, around 7km from Sarzeau itself.
☎02.97.67.42.15
Closed *Mon and Tues except Aug; fortnight in March; fortnight in Nov.*

The restaurant is in an old house where you go through one dining room to get to the next. They're all painted hydrangea-blue, contrasting attractively with the starkness of the granite walls. A good range of seafood, shellfish and meat is available on the lunch menu for €20, others at €27–65 (including a lobster one for €57). With regard to the food, special mention should be made of the "flowers" (in other words, fish dishes) and the "blossoms" (meat dishes), with dishes such as smoked salmon cannelloni, crab meat and haricot beans in coconut milk or boned pigeon and celery purée served with *jus* from the liver.

Trébeurden

22560

🏠 Auberge de jeunesse

60 la Corniche Goas-Trez, lieu-dit Toëno; 2km to the north of the town, on the hills by the sea.
☎02.96.23.52.22 ☎02.96.15.44.34
🌐www.fuaj.org
Closed *Dec–Feb.* **Car park.**

A modern building that clashes slightly with the landscape – but what a landscape! It has one of the best locations of any youth hostel in Brittany; right by the

sea, with a diving club next door and a botanical trail nearby. FUAJ card is compulsory (you can buy it on site): €8.90 a night in a dormitory with four to twelve beds, breakfast €3.30. Camping is possible and there's no curfew. Credit cards not accepted.

🍴 🏠 |●| Hôtel-restaurant Ker An Nod**

Rue de Pors-Termen; it's opposite île Millau.
☎02.96.23.50.21 ☎02.96.23.63.30
🌐www.kerannod.com
Closed *Mon, Tues and Thurs lunchtimes (except July–Aug and public holidays); 1 Jan–31 March.* **TV. High chairs and games available.**

Peaceful beachside hotel run by a nice couple. Of the twenty rooms, fourteen look out to sea and cost €45–66 for a double with shower/wc depending on the season and view. Half board is compulsory in high season at €51.50–60 per person. They're comfortable and bright with great picture windows. The dining room is equally pleasant and serves menus €16.50–32; you dine here on fresh fish, seafood and local dishes – gratinéed oysters with Muscadet butter, fisherman's soup, Trégor chicken with crayfish, caramelized apples with vanilla ice. Logis de France. *Free house liqueur offered to our readers on presentation of this guide.*

🍴 |●| La Tourelle

45 rue du Trozoul; it overlooks the port.
☎02.96.23.62.73
Closed *Tues evening and Wed (except mid-July to end Aug); weekdays from end Nov; Jan; Feb school holiday; a fortnight mid-Nov.*

The huge, pleasant dining room has wide bay windows with a view over the port. Good, inventive, modern cuisine with an emphasis on fish or seafood, and lots of nice little attentions to detail. Menus €18–55; the most expensive is a lobster menu. Very friendly welcome and service are on offer. *Free coffee offered to our readers on presentation of this guide.*

🍴 |●| Le Goéland

14 rue de Trozoul.
☎02.96.23.53.78
Open *daily (1 July–14 Sept); Thurs lunchtime to Sun evening, 15 Sept–14 June.* **Closed** *mid-Jan to mid-Feb; second fortnight in June.*

According to some people in Trébeurden this is a friendly bistro where fishermen come early in the morning to prop up the bar and to put the world to rights, while other people rate it the trendiest restaurant of the moment, where in the evening you can treat yourself to delicious dishes like grandma used to make and good fish in its stock served with fresh vegetables. Who is right? Both of them. After spending several decades working in the great hotels and restaurants, Louis Le Roy, one of the best restaurateurs on the Côtes-d'Armor, has done out this bar in his own style with real linen, a ship's ladder and furnishings and school benches. This son and grandson of a fisherman, he continues to treat his guests well, serving up 15kg abalone with *cocos de Paimpol* haricot beans over a single weekend, or lobster seaweed parcels with "grandma's pancakes". Weekday lunchtime menu weighs in at €20, otherwise €25–35 (€38 on Sun). *Free house apéritif offered to our readers on presentation of this guide.*

Trégastel
22730

@ 🎿 ♨ |●| Hôtel-restaurant de la Corniche**

38 rue Charles-Le-Goffic; it's in the town centre, not far from the beaches.
☎02.96.23.88.15 ℻02.96.23.47.89
ⓦwww.hoteldelacorniche.fr
Closed *Jan.* **Restaurant closed** *lunchtimes.* **Open** *until 11pm.* **TV. Car park.**

It may not exactly be by the sea (in fact, it faces a roundabout), but this is a bright place where rooms have a range of facilities. They're €39 with shower/wc and up to €58 with bath, depending on the season. The menu at €16 is for hotel guests only. The restored rooms are more attractive, with warm colours and flowery fabrics. *Third consecutive night (except July–Aug and public holidays) offered to our readers on presentation of this guide.*

@ |●| Auberge de la Vieille Église

Place de l'Église; it's in the old town.
☎02.96.23.88.31
Closed *Sun evening; Mon; Tues evening out of season; Mon only July–Aug; March.* **High chairs available.**

This used to do it all: canteen for local workers, butcher's, fruit and veg shop, mini-market – the lot. But it's been completely transformed since

the owner and his family bought the place in 1962. They've turned it into an unmissable restaurant and you won't miss it – the outside is decked in flowers. There's a weekday lunch menu at €15 and others at €22 and €32; à la carte you'll spend about €35. Tagliatelle with scallops, brill, and John Dory roast with bacon are house specialities, along with a good foie gras. Exceptionally high-quality cuisine, served by attentive staff in delightful surroundings. It's best to book in the evening during the season and at weekends.

Tréguier
22220

@ 🎿 ♨ |●| Hôtel Aigue Marine et Restaurant des 3 Rivières***

It's on the marina.
☎02.96.92.97.00 ℻02.96.92.44.48
ⓦwww.aiguemarine.fr
Closed *Sat lunchtime, Sun evening and Mon out of season; lunchtimes (except Sun) July–Aug; early Jan to end Feb.* **Disabled access. TV. High chairs available. Swimming pool. Car park.**

A recently built establishment on the harbour but also overlooking the car park, with 48 very comfortable rooms for €69–91 depending on the season; half board €68–96 per person. There's a heated swimming pool and a garden, and they've built a sauna and Jacuzzi. The owners have passed on responsibility in the restaurant to a talented young chef who shows his skill with local dishes on menus at €27.50 (not Sun) and €31–41. The prices are good for such high-quality cuisine. *10% discount on the room rate except in July and Aug offered to our readers on presentation of this guide.*

@ |●| La Poissonnerie du Trégor

2 rue Renan.
☎02.96.92.30.27
Tasting rooms open *daily July–Sept.*

A warm, unusual establishment which has been run by Mme Moulinet for the last thirty or so years. Her son, Jean-Pierre, runs a fishmonger's (open year round) where you can buy fish to cook – or you can try fabulously fresh fish, seafood and shellfish dishes in the tasting rooms upstairs. Crab mayonnaise €8.50, *moules marinières* €5.50, and platters of shellfish

€18.50 (€27.50 for two people). Marine frescoes line the walls, and the overall atmosphere is such that you could almost imagine you were at sea – minus the seasickness, naturally. They don't do desserts.

Minihy-Tréguier
22220 (1.5km S)

✆ 🏠 |●| Kastell Dinech'h**

Take the N786 towards Lannion.
☎02.96.92.49.39 ℗02.96.92.34.03
Closed *Tues evening and Wed out of season; mid-Nov to end April.* **Restaurant closed** *lunchtimes.* **Disabled access. TV. Swimming pool. Car park.**

An elegant Breton manor house that's been turned into a hotel with a restaurant. They've kept all the period furniture and preserved its intimate atmosphere. The rooms are extremely pleasant; doubles with shower/wc or bath €76–85; some rooms sleep three or four. It's highly advisable to opt for half board, and it's obligatory between 14 July and 20 August: €82–85 per person. Excellent cuisine and attentive service with set evening menus at €30 and €38. The newly created "*jardin des simples*" garden of medicinal herbs is a perfect place to soak up the sun.

Vannes
56000

✆ 🏠 Hôtel Le Bretagne**

36 rue du Mené; it's 50m from the Prison gateway.
☎02.97.47.20.21 ℗02.97.47.90.78
✉hotel.le.bretagne@wanadoo.fr
Closed *Sun afternoon; first week in Oct.* **TV.**

This welcoming place has an old-fashioned charm and is often full. The quiet, smallish rooms, some overlooking the town walls, are all well maintained and represent good value at €35–40 for a double with shower/wc or bath. It's very often fully booked.

✆ 🍴 🏠 Hôtel Le Marina**

Place Gambetta.
☎02.97.47.22.81 ℗02.97.47.00.34
✉lemarinahotel@aol.com
Open *7am–1am.* **TV.**

This hotel is above *L'Océan* bar, one of the drinking holes around the square; it's ideal if you like to be where the action is. Pretty

rooms with double glazing have views of the harbour and town walls, and good facilities. Doubles at €38–58 offer good value for money in the heart of the old town. *Free coffee or Kir offered to our readers on presentation of this guide.*

✆ 🏠 Hôtel Le Richemont**

26 pl. de la Gare.
☎02.97.47.17.24 ℗02.97.54.27.37
🌐www.hotel-richemont-vannes.com
Closed *Sun, noon–6pm; 1–21 Jan.* **TV. Pay car park.**

A station hotel that has found a new lease of life, largely thanks to the bright colours and very professional, friendly service; considering that it is so close to the railway lines, it is surprisingly easy to shut out the outside world and it's remarkably quiet at night. Double rooms cost €52 and the excellent breakfast is served in a room with decoration that recalls the hotel's glory days.

✆ 🏠 🍴 Hôtel La Marébaudière

4 rue Aristide-Briand.
☎02.97.47.34.29 ℗02.97.54.14.11
🌐www.marebaudiere.com
TV. High chairs available. Car park.

A stone's throw from the town's historic centre, huge rooms with all the mod cons and, for those on the ground floor, a small terrace as well. Double rooms go for €69–88; breakfast buffet €8. The enclosed private car park is another bonus. *10% discount on a room (15 Oct–15 March) offered to our readers on presentation of this guide.*

✆ |●| Le Rive Gauche

5 pl. Gambetta; in the port, on the corner of place Gambetta.
☎02.97.47.02.40
Closed *Sun; Mon lunchtime; Sat lunchtime.*

As it was a coastal stopover, Vannes used to import anything from wood to Libourne wine. By opening this pretty, little wine bar-bistro, Nathalie and Stéphane Berrigaud have unknowingly revived an old tradition. Fine choice of Bordeaux wines and some small dishes, such as the mackerel pie with tapenade and fillet of John Dory with aromatic spices, and menus €13 (lunch), €20 (dinner).

✆ |●| Le Carré Blanc

28 rue du Port.

☎02.97.47.48.34
Closed *Sun; Mon lunchtime; first three weeks of Jan.* **Disabled access.**

A restaurant in tune with the times, dreamed up by two friends who had worked sufficiently in big establishments to realize that Vannes lacked a really modern eatery. Minimalist décor, trendy colour scheme, dishes mixing traditional ingredients with unusual spices: young and old enjoy the mackerel menhir aux fines herbes, the Szechuan style *croustillant* of pollack and gingerbread with savoury caramel ice cream. You can eat for €20–25 à la carte, or opt for the weekly lunch menu €15, or the other menu €20.

ⓔ |●| Restaurant de Roscanvec

17 rue des Halles.
☎02.97.47.15.96.
Closed *Mon, except July–Sept; Sun evening; 23 Dec–1 Jan.* **High chairs available.**

This cosy, traditional restaurant occupies two floors of a characterful fourteenth-century house. The owner-chef is full of talent and ambition and he has succeeded in attracting a clientele of informed gourmets. Things get serious from the first menu at €17 (served at lunch and up till 8.15pm, but not on Sun) right up to the lobster menu at €74; try the turbot in honey crust or the *hochepot de bœuf* (boned oxtail). Reckon on around €40 à la carte. Dishes change regularly to reflect what's good in the market, and there's a first-rate wine list.

ⓔ |●| L'Eau à la Bouche

Rue Larmor-Gwened; near the Kerino bridge.
☎02.97.69.02.02

An evocative name (mouth-watering) sets the tone for this intimate setting at the water's edge, with sophisticated decoration and an elegantly dressed clientele. Fashionable cooking that is basically Provençal but also takes advantage of the fresh fish from the nearby Gulf of Morbihan: baked bass with anchovy sauce, mullet with vierge sauce. Dishes cost around €20; desserts €6. The pretty terrace is surrounded by poplars (best appreciated at high tide).

Saint-Avé
56890 (5km N)

ⓔ 🎋 |●| Le Pressoir

7 rue de l'Hôpital; it's 1km out of Saint-Avé.

☎ and 🖷02.97.60.87.63
Closed *Sun evening; Mon; Tues; 1–8 Jan; 1–15 March; 1–10 July; 1–20 Oct.* **Disabled access. Car park.**

Exceptional surroundings and facilities, a warm welcome and gastronomic delights in an attractive house just outside town. It's quite simply the best restaurant in these parts, serving great fresh fish and specialities like galette of red mullet with potato and rosemary, foie gras ravioli with wild mushroom broth, and baked Granny Smith apples. The cheapest set menu at €30 is served only on weekday lunchtimes, but it's worth going out of your way to try it. There's a range of other menus at €43–85. *Free coffee offered to our readers on presentation of this guide.*

Arradon
56610 (8km SW)

ⓔ 🎋 🛏 |●| Hôtel-restaurant Le Stivell***

15 rue Plessis-d'Arradon; take the D101.
☎02.97.44.03.15 🖷02.97.44.78.90
Closed *15 Nov–15 Dec.* **Restaurant closed** *Sun evening and Mon lunchtime out of season.* **TV. High chairs available. Car park.**

An extremely well-run Logis de France with friendly staff in one of the most beautiful parts of the Gulf of Morbihan. Ideal if you want to enjoy the peacefulness of the sea without straying too far from Vannes. Double rooms are €52–67, with a tempting offer of half board at €50–56, depending on the season. The chef, inspired by the ocean, uses the fresh ingredients it provides: seafood sauerkraut, warm oysters with champagne, etc. They serve magnificent seafood platters (order 48hrs in advance), gastronomic menu at €41, and an astonishing gastronomic menu for children, with the dishes on the menu in half portions. Logis de France. *Free house apéritif or coffee offered to our readers on presentation of this guide.*

ⓔ 🛏 Le Logis du Parc Er Gréo

9 rue Mane-Guen, lieu-dit Le Gréo, near Moustoir.
☎02.97.44.73.03 🖷02.97.44.80.48
🖳www.parcergreo.com
Closed *14 Nov–17 March.* **Disabled access. TV. Car park.**

A hotel best described as intimate, with charming, attentive service and impressive furniture. Delightful south-facing rooms, all different, cost €72–124 for a double, depending on the degree of comfort and the season. Breakfast (€11) is served in a room lined with pictures painted by the owner's father (if you want to see more, he's also got a gallery close by). Pretty garden and heated swimming pool, in use from Easter to early November.

Locqueltas
56390 (15km N)

@ 🍴 🏠 |O| **Hôtel La Voltige****

8 rte. de Vannes; from Vannes, take the D767 for Pontivy and Locminé; take the D778 towards Saint-Jean-Brevelay for 1.5km.
☎02.97.60.72.06 🖷02.97.44.63.01
🌐 www.la-voltige.fr
Restaurant closed Sun evening and Mon out of season; Mon in season (except for hotel guests); a fortnight in March; second fortnight in Oct. **TV. High chairs and games available. Car park.**

Located north of Vannes, a dozen impeccable rooms – €37–55 with shower/wc or bath – check out the great split-level rooms for three or four people. Some overlook the road and can be a bit noisy, despite the double-glazing. From 1–25 August they prefer you to stay on a half board basis at €37.50–50. It's an attractive option because of the rather good traditional food that's offered on even the cheapest menu (€14 – not served weekends or public holidays); other menus €21–42. Try the Breton seafood platter or the navarin of sole and cod with spices. There's a garden with an area set aside for games. Logis de France. *10% discount on the room rate (1 Oct–15 March) offered to our readers on presentation of this guide.*

Vitré
35500

@ 🍴 🏠 **Hôtel Le Minotel****

47 rue Poterie; 200m from the train station, right in the city-centre.
☎02.99.75.11.11 🖷02.99.75.81.26
🌐 www.ot-vitre.fr
TV.

Really pretty hotel in the old town; they've virtually rebuilt the house but have respected the local style while providing modern facilities. Perhaps, if you're being very picky, the result is rather unimaginative. The green and tartan décor makes the place look a bit like a golf clubhouse – and aptly enough they've done a deal with the local golf club and offer packages if you want to play a round or two. Doubles cost €49 with bath, twin room €56, and there are family rooms for four people. You can eat at the crêperie-pizzeria adjoining the hotel. *10% discount offered to our readers on presentation of this guide.*

@ 🍴 |O| **La Gavotte**

7 rue des Augustins.
☎02.99.74.47.74
Closed Mon; Tues, except July–Aug; first fortnight in March; first fortnight in Sept.

This restaurant fits in well with the surroundings in this charming village. It's a crêperie with a large pink and green dining room. They serve excellent girdle cakes and pancakes with fillings from the traditional to the unusual: Darley cheese (a Breton variety), *andouille*, various sausages and an apple preparation which is somewhere between purée and chutney. The delicious dishes are accompanied by cider and local beverages. There's a lunchtime *formule* at €9.50 and a menu at €12; à la carte you'll pay around €14 for a complete meal. *Free house apéritif offered to our readers on presentation of this guide.*

@ |O| **Auberge Saint-Louis**

31 rue Notre-Dame, next to Notre-Dame cathedral.
☎02.99.75.28.28
Closed Sun evening; Mon; Tues; a week in Feb; a fortnight in Sept. **Disabled access.**

An elegant fifteenth-century house which has built up a solid reputation. The wood panelling in the dining room creates a warm, sophisticated yet family-style atmosphere. The young patronne will bring you a small plate of appetizers to nibble while you select your meal. You're in for a feast in a cosy setting. *Formule* at €11.80 or menus €13.50–26; à la carte you'll spend around €29. There's a good selection of grilled meats and superb fish, accompanied by flavoursome sauces.

Centre

Amboise

37400

© ⅔ 🏠 Auberge de jeunesse de l'Île d'Or

Centre Charles-Péguy Entrepont.
☎02.47.30.60.90 ℗02.47.30.60.91
ⓦwww.ucrif.asso.fr
Open *all year round*. **Disabled access. Car park.**

A lush setting for one of the very few youth hostels that boast a better view than any of the nearby hotels – in this case of the Amboise château. So, if possible, book a room overlooking it (nos. 2, 3, 4, 10, 12, 13 and 14). Accommodation costs €6.80–8.80 a night, depending on the season, breakfast €2.80; half board is €16.50–18.50 per person, depending on the season, and meals are around €6.90. The place has recently been renovated, and M. Thierry and his team will give you an effusive welcome. *10% discount on a room (in high season) offered to our readers on presentation of this guide.*

© ⅔ 🏠 |◎| Hôtel du Lion d'Or

17 quai Charles-Guinot; at the foot of the château, near the bridge, facing the Loire.
☎02.47.57.00.23 ℗02.47.23.22.49
Closed *Sun evening and Mon out of season; Dec; Jan.* **Pay car park.**

A charming, old-fashioned place with an enormous reception and a restaurant seemingly intent on emulating the nearby châteaux in its décor. It serves excellent regional dishes, very promptly delivered, with several menus ranging from €18.20 to €36.90. Upstairs, the hotel section is in need of refurbishment – the rooms are old and bare, albeit well-kept. The ones

overlooking the quay – some with a balcony – are slightly noisier but they receive more sunlight and go for €41.60 for a double with shower, €55.12 with shower/wc or bath. One particularly spacious room is designed to accommodate five people. Logis de France. *Free coffee offered to our readers on presentation of this guide.*

© 🏠 Le Clos d'Amboise

27 rue Rabelais.
☎02.47.30.10.20 ℗02.47.57.33.43
ⓦwww.leclosdamboise.com
Swimming pool.

Slightly off the tourist trail, tucked away in a quiet corner, an elegant mansion, built by an ecclesiastic from the Court in the seventeenth century and modified in the following century, offering a sophisticated but relaxed atmosphere. The rooms – €65–150, according to the size and season – are decorated in a variety of pastel colours and fitted with all the latest mod cons, including broadband Internet connection. Breakfast is served in an enchanting room with beautiful wood panelling. There's a garden with a 200-year-old cedar and unusual plants and, at the far end, near the heated pool, the peaceful "priest's garden", an ideal spot for reading or just whiling away the time. There's also a sauna and gym.

© |◎| Restaurant L'Épicerie

46 pl. Michel-Debré; between the castle's two towers.
☎02.47.57.08.94
Closed *Mon and Tues out of season; Nov to mid-Dec.*

A splendid old façade with olive-green half-timbering; behind the curtains, out

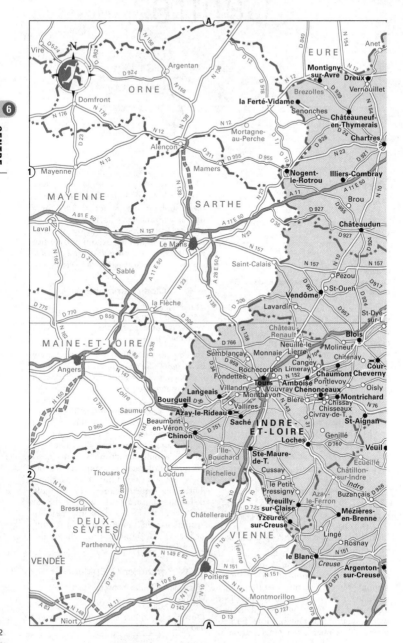

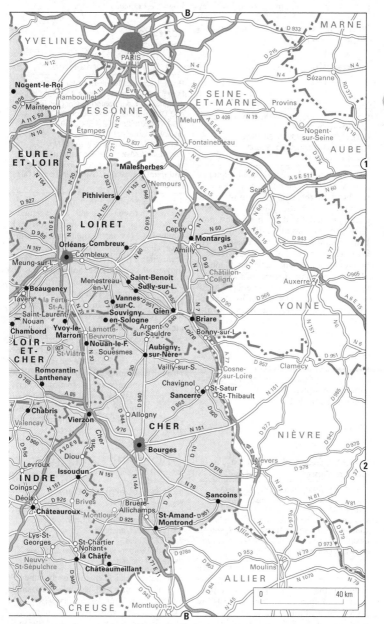

MARNE

YVELINES

D 933

D 215

N 4

PARIS

Sézanne

N 4

N 12

Nogent-le-Roi

Evry

SEINE-

Provins

RD 373

N 19

Maintenon

Rambouillet

ET-MARNE

D 906

A 10

ESSONNE

Melun

D 406

N 19

A 5 E 54

Nogent-sur-Seine

A 11 E 50

N 20

AUBE

N 10

Étampes

D 837

Fontainebleau

A 6 E 15

D 721

N 6

D 374

EURE-

A 10

Malesherbes

A 5 E 511

1

ET-LOIR

Nemours

A 6 E 15

N 154

D 921

N 152

Sens

N 60

Pithiviers

D 948

LOIRET

N 152

D 927

N 20

D 975

N 7

Cepoy

N 60

D 943

N 77

D 955

Orléans Combreux

Montargis

A 6 E 15

N 157

A 10 E 5

Combleux

Amilly

D 943

D 16

N 60

D 965

Meung-sur-L.

N 20

D 93

Châtillon-Coligny

Auxerre

Beaugency

Menestreau-en-V.

Saint-Benoît

Sully-sur-L.

D 965

Tavers

la Ferté-St-A.

D 1

Vannes-sur-C.

D 951

YONNE

Saint-Laurent-Nouan

Souvigny-en-Sologne

Gien

D 952

N 7

D 30

N 6

Chambord

Yvoy-le-Marron

Lamotte-Beuvron

Argent-sur-Sauldre

D 940

Briare

N 151

LOIR-ET-CHER

Nouan-le-F.

Souesmes

Bonny-sur-L.

N 20

St-Viâtre

Aubigny-sur-Nère

A 71

D 951

D 923

Romorantin-Lanthenay

Vailly-sur-S.

Cosne-sur-Loire

D 957

Clamecy

D 765

A 85

D 30

Chavignol

St-Satur

N 151

D 985

Châbris

D 940

Sancerre

St-Thibault

NIÈVRE

Valençay

Vierzon

D 944

Allogny

D 955

D 920

D 960

Cher

85 CD

CHER

N 151

D 917

D 943

D 978

D 556

A 20 E 9

Levroux

Diou

Bourges

D 10

D 976

Nevers

D 978

N 37

2

Issoudun

N 151

N 144

N 76

N 81

INDRE

D 9

Coings

N 151

D 10

D 925

Déols

Brives

Sancoins

D 79a

D 979

Châteauroux

Bruère-Allichamps

St-Amand-Montrond

D 951

Montlouis

D 925

Allier

N 7

D 973

Lys-St-Georges

St-Chartier

Nohant

D 978a

D 953

Moulins

N 79

N 1079

Neuvy-St-Sépulchre

la Châtre

D 940

Châteaumeillant

A 71 E 11

D 94

ALLIER

N 79

D 943

D 145

CREUSE

Montluçon

B

| 0 | | 40 km |

243

of sight of the hordes of tourists, you can enjoy some fine food made with local products in a rustic dining room. Weekday lunch menu goes for €10.50, then several other menus €18.50–35.50. The service is efficient but relaxed.

Limeray
37530 (8km NE)

@ ☎ |●| **Auberge de Launay**

9 rue de la Rivière; next to the Limeray campsite, below the N152.
℡02.47.30.16.82 ℻02.47.30.15.16
✉auberge.de.launay@wanadoo.fr
Disabled access.

A small, simple but comfortable country inn, swathed in Virginia creeper. Set in the heart of the country – most of the rooms overlook the garden – it offers excellent food based on fresh, local produce and the inventiveness of the chef, Laurent Conraux (definitely a major asset). Daily classic or regional dish at weekday lunchtimes, at around €10; set menu of main course plus dessert or starter plus main course at €15; other menus €20–30 and an attractive selection of local wines. On fine days, you can eat outside in the shady garden. The friendly young owners, François and Hélène Thévard, obviously love their work, as their thoughtfulness goes beyond the call of duty; for example, new guests find a welcoming message in their bedroom (€53–75), along with a bottle of water. All in all, a charming stopover. Logis de France.

Bléré
37150 (10km S)

@ ☎ |●| **Hôtel-restaurant Le Cheval Blanc**

5 pl. Charles-Bidault; take the D31; main entrance in the church square.
℡02.47.30.30.14
⊛www.lechevalblancblere.com
Closed 2 Jan–13 Feb. **Restaurant closed** Fri lunch; Sun eve and Mon out of season; Mon in July–Aug. **Swimming pool.**

Set in the church's old convent, which explains the layout of the buildings surrounding the charming garden (complete with swimming pool) where meals are served in summer; weekday menu at €18, then others €20–60. Michel Blériot's cooking is of unimpeachable quality: *gratin* of warm oysters with slithers of leek, veal

medallion with blueberry and tomato preserve. Double rooms go for €57–60. Logis de France.

Cangey
37530 (12km NE)

@ 🎿 ☎ |●| **Le Fleuray Hotel*****

Route Dame-Marie-les-Bois; from Amboise, take the N152 towards Blois, then turn left onto the D74 signposted to Cangey, Fleuray and Dame-Marie, or exit 18 on the A10.
℡02.47.56.09.25 ℻02.47.56.93.97
⊛www.lefleurayhotel.com
Closed a week in Jan; a week in Nov; Christmas to New Year. **Restaurant closed** lunchtime. **Disabled access. High chairs and games available. Swimming pool. Car park.**

This nineteenth-century manor house is a cross between a hotel and a guesthouse. Hazel and Peter Newington and family have decorated their fifteen rooms very elegantly and named each one of them after a flower; doubles €76–88 with shower/wc or bath, according to season. Half board is available from €76–82 per person. Gourmet cooking, with set menus €28–38, is served in a pleasant dining room or out on the terrace. Specialities include pan-fried langoustines with garlic butter, chicken with Creole curry sauce, lamb cutlets with red fruits and Loire wine, pears stuffed with goat's cheese. Heated swimming pool in summer, welcome, and a very international clientele, but you must book. *10% discount on a room (4 Jan–28 Feb and 4 Nov–22 Dec) offered to our readers on presentation of this guide.*

Chisseaux
37150 (17km SE)

@ 🎿 |●| **Auberge du Cheval Rouge**

30 rue Nationale; towards Chenonceaux, on the road to Montrichard.
℡02.47.23.86.67
Closed Tues only in spring; Mon and Tues the rest of the year.

A few steps lead from this lovely auberge into a charming and tastefully decorated dining room. Mme Feron serves her husband's cooking with great kindness. The chef devotes a lot of care to his food, particularly to his creamy sauces that often accompany the fish. This is a place where cooking is taken very seriously; menus €17 (not served Sun lunch) up to €32, or à la carte around €38. You will enjoy Father Paul's lovely garden and terrace. *Free coffee offered to our readers on presentation of this guide.*

Argenton-sur-Creuse

36200

@ 🎿 🛏 |●| Hôtel-restaurant Le Cheval Noir**

27 rue Auclert-Descottes; on the road to Gargilesse-Dampierre.
☎02.54.24.00.06 ℻02.54.24.11.22
Closed *Sun evening out of season.* **TV. High chairs available. Car park.**

The restoration work done on this nineteenth-century posthouse has been particularly well executed. The rooms are quiet and comfortable; doubles €52–60 with shower/wc or bath. The elegant, subtle cuisine is prepared by chef Christophe Jeannot, whose specialities include *millefeuille* of crab served with artichokes and *croustillant* of pig's trotters. Weekday lunch menu at €10 and other set menus at €16–24. Logis de France. *Free apéritif offered to our readers on presentation of this guide.*

Aubigny-sur-Nère

18700

@ 🛏 |●| Hôtel-restaurant La Chaumière**

1 av. du Parc-des-Sports.
☎02.48.58.04.01 ℻02.48.58.10.31
🖝www.hotel-restaurant-la-chaumiere.com
Closed *Feb half-term; a week after 15 Aug; Sun evening (except July–Aug).* **Restaurant closed** *Sun evening; Mon (lunchtime only in Aug).* **TV. Car park.**

An extremely comfortable cottage on the Jacques-Cœur road. The nineteen rooms are of the highest quality (as is the service). Some of the rooms overlooking the garden are currently being updated; €60 for a double with shower/wc or bath. In the restaurant, the cheapest menu, with traditional dishes, goes for €18 (except Sun and public holidays), others €26–40. This Berry region is famous for its witches. If you want to find out more about them, there's a witchcraft museum in Blancafort, a few kilometres from Aubigny-sur-Nère.

Argent-sur-Sauldre

18410 (10km N)

@ 🛏 |●| 🎿 Le Relais du Cor d'Argent**

39 rue Nationale; off the D940.
☎02.48.73.63.49 ℻02.48.73.37.55
🖃cordargent@wanadoo.fr
Closed *Tues and Wed (except July–Aug for the hotel); 15 Feb–15 March; first week of July; a week in Oct or Nov.* **TV. High chairs available.**

This place is worth a stopover in one of the seventy finely refurbished rooms, with old-fashioned wax-polished furniture and comfortable modern beds; doubles €38–42 with shower/wc or bath. The rustic-chic tone continues in the restaurant, with copper pans and hunting trophies hanging on the walls (plus the odd pheasant or partridge) and wild flowers on the tables. The cooking is much appreciated all over Berry: game in season, *fricassée* of lobster with Noilly and leek *confit*, fried scallops and langoustines with chicory. Menus start at €15 (except Sun lunch and public holiday lunchtimes) and go up to €52. Small garden. *Free apéritif or fruit juice or soda offered to our readers on presentation of this guide.*

Vailly-sur-Sauldre

18260 (17km E)

@ |●| Le Lièvre Gourmand

14 Grand-Rue; take the D923 in the direction of Sancerre.
☎02.48.73.80.23 ℻02.48.73.86.13
🖃lelievregourmand@wanadoo.fr
Closed *Sun evening; Mon; Tues; 3-28 Jan; 27 June–5 July; 29 Aug–6 Sept.* **Disabled access.**

Australian William Page shows off his culinary art in these two old village houses. His cooking is exceptional and makes inspired use of spices – *roulade* of semi-cooked foie gras and fig *compote*, sea bream with lemon zest. The menu changes with the seasons but the inventiveness is constant. Set menus, €26–49. And there are even a few good Australian vintages that remind you of the owner's origins. Give it a whirl – it's one of a kind.

Azay-le-Rideau
37190

ⓔ 🕏 🏛 Hôtel de Biencourt

7 rue Balzac; on the pedestrian street leading
to the château.
☏02.47.45.20.75 ⓕ02.47.45.91.73
ⓦwww.hotelbiencourt.com
Disabled access. TV.

A quiet place with unassuming service.
Some of the comfortable rooms look out
onto the small patio decked with flowers
in this typical eighteenth-century house,
formerly a school. Good value for money:
doubles at €35 with washbasin or shower,
at €47 with shower/wc and at €52 with
bath. Logis de France. *One free breakfast per
room offered to our readers on presentation of
this guide.*

ⓔ 🕏 🏛 Hôtel Val de Loire

50-52 rue Nationale
☏02.47.45.28.29 ⓕ02.47.45.91.19
ⓦwww.hotel-val-de-loire.com
Closed *10 Nov–15 March.*

A modern, functional Best Western hotel
offering excellent service and a peaceful atmosphere. Beautifully equipped and
maintained rooms go for €54–75 for a
double, according to the season. No restaurant, but a copious and varied breakfast
buffet in a delightful dining room. *10%
discount on the price of a room offered to our
readers on presentation of this guide.*

ⓔ 🕏 |●| Restaurant L'Aigle d'Or

10 av. Adélaïde-Richer; head towards
Langeais.
☏02.47.45.24.58
ⓔaigle.d'or@wanadoo.fr
Closed *Sun evening; Wed; Tues evening
except July–Aug; Mon evening Dec to
end March; Feb; second fortnight in Nov.*
Disabled access. Games available.

One of the best gastronomic restaurants
in Touraine with a welcoming and refined
setting, attentive service and reasonable
prices. There's a weekday lunch menu at
€19, then others €27–60 including wines;
meals are served in the garden in summer.
The à la carte menu changes frequently,
but retains a few classics: langoustine salad
with foie gras, fillet of beef *à la chinon* and
the chocolate *griottine*. The wine list is
most instructive, with maps showing the
provenance of numerous wines. *Free glass
of sparkling wine with your dessert (1 Nov–31*

*March) offered to our readers on presentation
of this guide.*

ⓔ |●| Les Grottes

23 ter, rue de Pineau; turn left on the
roundabout on the road to Artannes.
☏02.47.45.21.04
Closed *Wed and Thurs; Thurs only in July–
Aug; 3 weeks in Oct; 22 Dec to end of Feb.*

The food here is good, if nothing special
(with menus from €21). The main attraction is the setting: the two inviting dining
rooms are carved out of a troglodyte cave,
and there's also a sheltered terrace, which
comes into its own in fine weather. A
quieter or more discreet restaurant would
be hard to find.

Vallères
37190 (7km N)

ⓔ |●| La Doulce Terrasse "Le Bistrot du Jardin"

Take the D39; it's in the gardens of the château.
☏02.47.50.02.10
Open *daily 9am–7pm, uninterrupted service.*

The idea behind this restaurant – and a
very good one too – is to offer food based
on vegetables from its kitchen garden,
depending on seasonal availability. These
ingredients are skilfully prepared with
spices and herbs (also from the garden) and
are strikingly presented in attractive dishes.
There's a single menu at €15, snacks are
also available, and there's a good selection
of Loire wines, too. In short, a delightful
and unusual place.

ⓔ |●| Le Fournil

22 rue du Val-de-Loire; leave Azay in the
direction of Tours; at the large roundabout,
take the direction of Vallères (the restaurant
is signposted).
☏02.47.45.43.06
Closed *Sun eve; Wed.*

In this old bar-restaurant once devoted to
the traditional local game of *boule de fort*,
the welcoming dining room has preserved
its beautiful fireplace and terracotta decoration. To the rear, a garden shaded by catal-
pas is enlivened by the birdsong from two
large aviaries. The stage is set for enjoying
the excellent cooking: the foie gras stuffed
with pear is particularly delicious. The set
lunchtime menu (Mon–Fri) costs €15, and
there are others at €21–35. The owner and

his Portuguese wife are avid backpackers and know the importance of offering travellers value for money.

Villandry
37510 (10km NE)

ⓐ |●| L'Étape Gourmande – La Giraudière

From the D39, take the direction towards Vallères.
☎02.47.50.08.60 📠02.47.50.06.60
ⓦwww.etapegourmande.com
Open daily noon–5pm and 7.30–9pm. **Closed** 15 Jul–15 March. **Disabled access. High chairs available. Car park.**

This is a splendid seventeenth-century farm, easy to find. The superb dining room has a huge fireplace and you can also eat outside on the terrace. The chef gave up a career as a diplomat to start the place – expect a courteous welcome and punctillious service. They serve their own goat's cheese and other farm produce, accompanied by local wines. Range of set menus at €14.30–28 or à la carte about €23; one of the restaurant's specialities is suckling pig. On the first Saturday of the summer they give concerts with singers and storytellers (reservations necessary). You can buy goat's cheeses and fruits preserved in wine, and they will even show you the goats and take you round the dairy.

Beaugency
45190

ⓐ 🏠 Auberge de jeunesse

152 rue de Châteaudun lieu-dit Vernon; on the D925 (in the direction of Cravant-Châteaudun); no bus from train station, you must take a taxi.
☎02.38.44.61.31 📠02.38.44.14.73
ⓦwww.fuaj.org
Closed Jan. **Disabled access. Car park.**

This youth hostel, set in the old school of a quiet little village, exudes an irresistible charm, with its courtyard with linden trees and gravel that crunches underfoot, reminiscent of the photos of Robert Doisneau. Guests sleep in the old classrooms or in the more recent annexes, which blend in well with the older buildings, in dormitories with five, six and eight beds, with a total capacity of 120 people. There are also five double rooms with toilets and ten studios with bunks to accommodate

families. You can also pitch a tent outside. Accommodation is €9.30 per person per night (FUAJ card compulsory), €3.30 for breakfast, €8.60 for meals. A kitchen is also available.

ⓐ 🏠 🏃 Hôtel de la Sologne**

6 pl. Saint-Firmin; in the old historic centre.
☎02.38.44.50.27 📠02.38.44.90.19
ⓦwww.hoteldelasologne.com
Closed 3 weeks during Dec and Jan. **TV. High chairs available. Car park.**

The medieval rue de l'Evêché leads to a delightful little flower-filled square dominated by a statue of Joan of Arc. This is a wonderfully peaceful setting, and the hotel fits in perfectly. The lovely old rooms – doubles from €45–65 with shower/wc or €63 with bath – are tastefully decorated and two have been recently completely updated. There's a patio where you can eat breakfast on fine days. Reservations are advised for this charming place. *15% discount on the room rate (15 Oct–30 March) offered to our readers on presentation of this guide.*

ⓐ 🏠 |●| Hostellerie de l'Écu de Bretagne**

5 rue de la Maille d'Or; on the main square.
☎02.38.44.67.60 📠02.38.44.68.07
ⓦwww.ecudebretagne.fr
Restaurant closed Sun evening; Mon from Nov to Easter. **TV. High chairs available. Car park.**

There are heraldic shields on the wall and an atmosphere reminiscent of a Chabrol film, but no visible connection with Brittany – in fact, this old staging post gets its name from the Breton family which has owned the place since the fifteenth century. Rooms, most of them refurbished, vary in size, but all are comfortable; double rooms cost €48–65 with shower and €55–78 with bath. The renovated restaurant is pricey but the quality is superb. Menus start from €12 (lunchtime Mon–Fri only) up to €30 (the last one has a few supplements). Logis de France.

Tavers
45190 (3km SW)

ⓐ 🏃 🏠 |●| La Tonnellerie****

12 rue des Eaux Bleues; on the road towards Blois.

☎02.38.44.68.15 ℗02.38.44.10.01
✉tonelri@club-internet.fr
Closed *lunchtimes, except Fri and Sun; Jan–Feb.* **TV. High chairs available. Swimming pool. Car park.**

A rather austere-looking building in the centre of the village – but inside it's a different story. By general consent, this is the best place in Beaugency: very chic, with relaxing, comfortable décor. It's so quiet that you can hear the birdsong and the chimes of the church bell, and you can stroll through the grounds, which are full of chestnut trees (and even have a heated swimming pool). The cooking is luxurious and fragrant, with menus €29–49, putting new spins on old classics: try, for example, the lobster couscous. The super-comfortable doubles and suites cost €126–232 depending on facilities and the season. *10% discount on the price of a room (March, April, Nov and Dec) or a free apéritif offered to our readers on presentation of this guide.*

Saint-Laurent-Nouan
41220 (9km S)

✿ 🛉 🏠 Hôtel Le Verger

14 rue du Port-Pichard
☎02.54.87.22.22 ℗02.54.87.22.82
🌐www.hotel-le-verger.com
Open *all year.*

This hotel at the entrance to La Sologne occupies a nineteenth-century bourgeois house complete with grounds – and all the charm that this implies. It lies close to two golf courses, and its owner, Cédric Beutter, gives a particularly warm welcome to fellow golfing enthusiasts. There are fourteen rooms, €57 for a double with bath/wc, and eight fully equipped studios; breakfast €7. *10% discount on the price of a room and breakfast offered to our readers on presentation of this guide.*

Blanc (Le)
36300

✿ 🛉 🏠 ❙❙ Domaine de l'Étape***

Route de Bélâbre; drive 5km along the D10 in the direction of Bélâbre.
☎02.54.37.18.02 ℗02.54.37.75.59
🌐www.domaineetape.com
Disabled access. TV. Car park.

This magnificent nineteenth-century estate is a magical place. It's set in huge

grounds, with a lake, woods and fields, and the thirty-five rooms (€38–110 for a double with shower/wc or bath) are spread between the château itself, the modern lodge and the rustic farm by the stables. The most splendid are on the first floor in the château: they're immense and beautifully furnished – ideal for a honeymoon or an intimate weekend *à deux*. The rooms in the farm buildings are rustic but charming. There are set menus from €20–54 or you can dine à la carte. The cooking is in keeping with the wonderful surroundings. *Free apéritif offered to our readers on presentation of this guide.*

✿ ❙❙ Le Cygne

8 av. Gambetta; north of the big square.
☎02.54.28.71.63 ℗02.54.28.72.13
Closed *Mon; Tues; Sun evening except July–Aug; first fortnight in Jan; second fortnight in June; few days in Aug.* **Disabled access. High chairs available.**

On the ground floor the décor is fresh, with pinkish walls, while on the first floor the dining room is more rustic, with big beams and walls painted straw-yellow. There's also an intimate salon which is perfect for groups of four to nine. The chef comes out of the kitchen to chat to his clients. Menus go for €15.40–45; specialities include calf's head, pan-fried foie gras and kidneys cooked whole and flambéed in marc. Good food and good value.

Rosnay
36300 (15km NE)

✿ 🛉 ❙❙ Le Cendrille

1 pl. de la Mairie; on the D15.
☎02.54.28.64.94 ℗02.54.28.64.93
Closed *Tues; Wed; 15 Dec–15 Jan.* **Disabled access. High chairs available.**

This delightful restaurant, in the middle of a village in the Brenne, has been stylishly done up by Florence and Luke Jeanneau with the aid of a grant from the town hall. They have chosen strong yellows and blues and created a warm atmosphere; they'll welcome you warmly, too. The cooking is simple, tasty and traditional. Menus start at €10 (weekday lunchtimes), then go up from €15.50 to €23.50. *Free Kir offered to our readers on presentation of this guide.*

Lingé
36220 (16km NE)

◎ 🛏 |◎| 🎄 Auberge de la Gabrière**

La Gabrière; from Le Blanc, take the D975 in the direction of Azay-le-Ferron, then the D6; at Lingé follow the signs for La Gabrière.
℡02.54.37.80.97 ℻02.54.37.70.66
Restaurant closed *Tues evening and Wed, except July–Aug; Mon during July–Aug.*
Disabled access. TV. High chairs and games available.

The inn is beautifully situated on Lake Gabrière. The restaurant is crowded all year because the cuisine is good and you can enjoy the view while you eat. Menus range from €10.90, served on weekdays, to €25.20. They specialize in Brenne produce: fillet of carp *paysanne*, oak-smoked pike perch. The inn has a number of rather ordinary, but clean rooms, some with a lake view; doubles with shower/wc or bath €35. Logis de France. *Free coffee offered to our readers on presentation of this guide.*

Blois
41000

◎ 🎄 🛏 Auberge de jeunesse

18 rue de l'Hôtel-Pasquier; take the #4 bus, in the direction of Les Grouëts, to the "Église" or "Auberge-de-Jeunesse" stop.
℡ and ℻02.54.78.27.21
🖳www.fuaj.org
Closed *mid-Nov to 1 March; 10am–6pm.*
Car park.

Total of 48 beds (one dormitory for men and one for women); reckon on €7.50 per night and €3.30 for breakfast. You can cook your own meals in the fully fitted kitchen. *One free night (for seven paid for) offered to our readers on presentation of this guide.*

◎ 🎄 🛏 Hôtel Saint-Jacques*

7 rue Ducoux; it's opposite the train station.
℡02.54.78.04.15 ℻02.54.78.33.05
🖳www.hotelsaintjacquesblois.com
Closed *24 Dec–5 Jan.* **TV.**

Small, simple, friendly place with well-maintained rooms. Doubles range from €39 for a big room with shower/wc down to €27 for a simpler, smaller room with handbasin. *Discount on breakfast (€4 instead of €6) offered to our readers on presentation of this guide.*

◎ 🎄 🛏 Hôtel Le Savoie**

6 rue Ducoux; it's opposite the train station.
℡02.54.74.32.21 ℻02.54.74.29.58
🖳hotel.le.savoie@wanadoo.fr
Closed Christmas to New Year. **TV. High chairs available.**

This is a nice little hotel, reminiscent of a guesthouse, away from the hustle and bustle of the tourist area. Rooms (€42–50) are clean and bright; breakfast buffet €6. You'll get a very nice welcome and it's best to book. *10% discount on a room (Sept-June for two consecutive nights) offered to our readers on presentation of this guide.*

◎ 🛏 Hôtel de France et de Guise**

3 rue Gallois; it's in front of the castle.
℡02.54.78.00.53 ℻02.54.78.29.45
Closed *Nov–Feb.* **TV.**

Very, very *Vieille France*, from the welcome to the atmosphere. Fortunately, the entrance has been recently updated and the rooms (€48–72) are generally bright and nicely decorated. Some are particularly attractive, with plaster mouldings and big fireplaces, and a few have a view of the château. All are well maintained.

◎ 🎄 🛏 Hôtel Anne de Bretagne**

31 av. Jean-Laigret; it's 300m from the castle and the city centre, near the tourist office.
℡02.54.78.05.38 ℻02.54.74.37.79
🖳annedebretagne@free.fr
Closed *2 Jan–4 Feb.* **TV. High chairs available. Car park.**

A family hotel, stylishly provincial and situated in the middle of town. The rooms at the rear of the building have double-glazing; those at the front have a nice view of the square and the bar terrace, which is set back from the road. All the rooms are pleasant and cost €52–58. *Free coffee offered to our readers on presentation of this guide.*

◎ |◎| Au Bouchon Lyonnais

25 rue des Violettes; head for place Louis-XII.
℡02.54.74.12.87
Closed *Sun and Mon except in summer and on public holidays; 21 Dec–20 Jan.* **High chairs available.**

A genuine traditional Lyon-style bistro serving authentic Lyon-style specialities: calf's liver in cider vinegar, calf's head *ravigote* and *quenelle* of pike *à la Lyonnaise*. The prices – set menus €19–26 – are really very reasonable given quality and quantity. The setting is a superb Louis XII house and there's a terrace for sunny days.

ⓦ |❂| Au Rendez-vous des Pêcheurs

27 rue Foix.
☏02.54.74.67.48
Closed *Sun and Mon lunchtime except bank holidays; first 2 weeks in Jan; 3 weeks in Aug.*

It must be said that this is not only the most pleasant place to eat in the town, but maybe also in the entire region: relaxed bistro atmosphere, cheerful, keenly attentive service and very good value for money with an enticing market menu at €26 (not available Sat evening and Sun), and another menu at €74. Also, they have superb Loire wines. The chef, Christophe Cosme, is young but has already made a name for himself, and his inspired, personal cooking and frequent appearances in the dining room have attracted an equally young crowd. Booking is essential.

Molineuf

41190 (9km W)

ⓦ ⚶ |❂| Restaurant de la Poste

11 av. de Blois; take the D766 in the direction of Angers; it's in the outskirts of Molineuf.
☏02.54.70.03.25 ☏02.54.70.12.46
ⓦwww.poidras.com
Closed *Tues evening out of season; Wed and Sun evenings; 3 weeks from 15 Nov; 3 weeks in Feb.* **High chairs available.**

This little restaurant on the outskirts of Molineuf is a good place to stop and treat yourself to some of the delicious creations of chef Thierry Poidras. An extremely good restaurant, decorated in bright citrus colours, with menus at €16.90 (weekdays only) to €30; the menu changes regularly. *Free coffee offered to our readers on presentation of this guide.*

Chitenay

41120 (15km S)

ⓦ ⚶ 🏠 |❂| L'Auberge du Centre**

Place de l'Église; take the D956 as far as Cellettes and then the D38.
☏02.54.70.42.11 ☏02.54.70.35.03
ⓦwww.auberge-du-centre.com
Closed *Mon, Tues lunchtime and Sun evening in low season; Mon and Tues lunchtime in high season; Feb.* **Disabled access.**

High chairs and games available. TV. Car park.

The classical frontage doesn't really give any clue to the handsome interior of this hotel and its delightfully peaceful garden. It's a great place to park the car or the bike for a day or two and simply relax. Some of the rooms have been recently updated; doubles €57–68. Half board, preferred May to September, costs €55–63. Excellent cuisine, bringing out the full flavour of all the ingredients, is served in a friendly atmosphere – the clientele is really mixed. On the menu: suprême of chicken cooked in cider, pâté of semi-cooked foie gras, plaice with shellfish served with wheat cooked with mushrooms and parmesan. There's a good *menu du marché* (not served at weekends or public holidays) for €20, other menus €26–42, and a good wine list. Logis de France. *Free Kir offered to our readers on presentation of this guide.*

Bourges

18000

See map on pp.252–253.

ⓦ 🏠 ⚶ Hôtel Le Christina**

5 rue de la Halle. **Map A2-4**
☏02.48.70.56.50 ☏02.48.70.58.13
ⓦwww.le-christina.com
TV. Pay car park.

Well-located on the edge of the historic town, near the pedestrianized area, this hotel has recently been entirely renovated and offers good facilities and a pleasant welcome. All rooms (€46–75) have effective soundproofing and air-conditioning; some have attractive rustic furniture and a toilet separate from the bathroom. *10% discount on the room rate (1 Nov–31 March) offered to our readers on presentation of this guide.*

ⓦ 🏠 ⚶ Relais de l'Agriculture**

18 bd. de Juranville; from boulevard de Juranville (car park) or from rue du Prinal near the city-centre, opposite the stadium of *Île d'Or*. **Map A2-3**
☏02.48.70.40.84 ☏02.48.65.50.58
TV. Car park.

You'll get a very warm welcome from Madame Maigret, who likes to talk delightedly about how she realized her dream of having a farm in the Sologne. If you arrive by car, use the door opposite the car park on boulevard de Juranville. Rooms are pretty as well as quiet, and cost €54 for a double with kitchenette. Some are air-conditioned and have exposed beams, but they're on the top floor. *10% discount on the room rate (1 Nov–31 March) offered to our readers on presentation of this guide.*

ⓐ 🕂 🏠 Inter Hôtel Les Tilleuls**

7 pl. de la Pyrotechnie; take rue Jean-Baffier and follow directions towards Moulin; it's on the left after avenue Carnot. **Off map C3-2**
☏02.48.20.49.04 ℗02.48.50.61.73
ⓦwww.les-tilleuls.com
Disabled access. TV. Games available. Swimming pool. Car park.

This hotel is on a little square just out of the centre; you'll need a car. Doubles with shower/wc or bath go for €55–63 according to the season. The annexe rooms, with air-conditioning and nice bathrooms, lead to the flower-filled garden; those in the old building have been recently renovated and are now very comfortable and air-conditioned. There's a gym and a heated pool. Meals can be brought to your room on a tray. *10% discount on the room rate offered to our readers on presentation of this guide.*

ⓐ ❙●❙ Les 3 P'tits Cochons

27 bis av. Jean-Jaurès. **Map B1-16**
☏02.48.65.64.96
Open *until 2am*. **Restaurant closed** *Sat lunchtime; Sun.*

A switched-on place with a young, local crowd. Join the line at the lengthy bar for a drink or take over the benches for a meal. The cuisine, with a lunch menu at €10.10 or around €20 à la carte, combines local and far-away flavours: *andouillette*, *filet mignon* with morels or goat terrine with beetroot. Attractive décor – soft lights, ochre walls decorated with maps, old sewing tables and a lovely spiral staircase. They also host raucous concerts and DJ nights.

ⓐ 🕂 ❙●❙ Le Guillotin

15 rue Jean-Girard. **Map B2-17**
☏02.48.65.43.66
Closed *Sun and Mon lunchtime; in May after the Printemps de Bourges.*

The walls of this large, friendly restaurant are smothered with posters of the Printemps de Bourges festival and pictures of the artists who appear in the small café-theatre upstairs (*La Soupe aux Choux*). Gilles Brico feeds the whole person – the heart, the stomach and the spirit – and the meat grilled over the open fire is said to be the best in Bourges. There's a lunch *formule* for €11 or around €16 for dinner à la carte. Concerts are staged every week from September to April. *Free house apéritif offered to our readers on presentation of this guide.*

ⓐ ❙●❙ Le Comptoir de Paris

Place Gordaine. **Map B2-15**
☏02.48.24.17.16 ℗02.48.24.68.90
Closed *Sun.* **Open** *10.30pm.* **Car park.**

This place is painted bright red so it stands out from the wonderful houses in the prettiest square in Bourges. Inside the décor is wood, so it's a bit more subdued. There's a friendly atmosphere and lots of animated conversation; this is where the lively and creative people of Bourges congregate. The speciality is *andouillette à l'ancienne*. Good simple meals from €15; also a *formule* at €9 with main meal and either a starter or a dessert. The downstairs dining room is cosier than the one upstairs.

ⓐ 🕂 ❙●❙ Restaurant Le Jardin Gourmand

15 bis av. Ernest-Renan; follow directions towards Nevers until you reach the Malus crossroads. **Off map C3-20**
☏02.48.21.35.91 ℗02.48.20.59.75
ⓦjardingourmand.com
Closed *Sun evening; Mon; Tues lunchtime; 20 Dec–20 Jan.* **Disabled access. High chairs available. Car park.**

This is a very pleasant restaurant, much appreciated by local *gourmands* who enjoy a good meal in delightful surroundings. Handsome building with panelling and beams; the dining room is decorated with flowers and watercolours on the walls. Staff are pleasant, the service is unobtrusive and the cooking shows the same refinement as the décor. Specialities on the set menus – good value for money at €15 and €23–38 – include fish *pot-au-feu* and *fondant* with arabica extracts. From June to September there's also a lobster menu at €49. You can eat in the garden, weather permitting. *Free liqueur offered to our readers on presentation of this guide.*

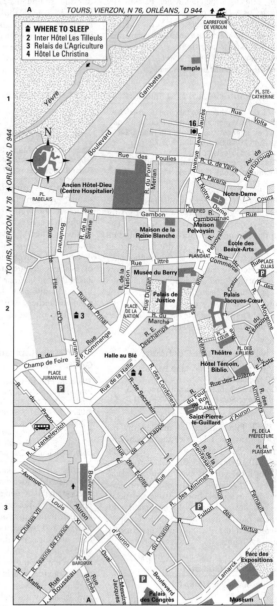

TOURS, VIERZON, N 76, ORLÉANS, D 944

CARREFOUR DE VERDUN

WHERE TO SLEEP
2 Inter Hôtel Les Tilleuls
3 Relais de L'Agriculture
4 Hôtel Le Christina

Temple

PL. STE-CATHERINE

Yèvre

Gambetta

Boulevard

Rue Volta

16

Rue des Poulies

Avenue Jean Jaurès

R. G. de Varye

Av. de Peterborough

Rue de la Sirène

R. du Pont Merian

R. Parerie

Ancien Hôtel-Dieu
(Centre Hospitalier)

PL. RABELAIS

Notre-Dame

Rue

Cours

Rue Gambon

PL. MIREPIED

Cambournac
Maison
Pelvoysin

Maison de la
Reine Blanche

PL. PLANCHAT

École des
Beaux-Arts

Rue du Commerce

PLACE CUJAS

Rue Littré

Musée du Berry

Palais de
Justice

Palais
Jacques-Cœur

PLACE
DE LA
NATION

R. du
Marché

R. E. Deschamps

Théâtre

PL. DES
4 PILIERS

R. de Turmenine

R. Zola

Rue des Linières

Hôtel Témoin,
Biblio.

Halle au Blé

Rue de la Halle

R. des Cordeliers

R. de Sécretain

R. du Four
Rol

PL. CLAMECY

Saint-Pierre-
le-Guillard

d'Auron

PL. DE LA
PRÉFECTURE

PL. M.
PLAISANT

R. V. Jankelevitch

Rue de la Chappe

Rue des Flores

R. de la Bienfaisance

R. des Minimes

Avenue Louis XI

Auron

Boulevard

R. Charles VII

Rue Jeanne de France

d'Auron

R. du Chariot

R. Fulton

P

des

Fernault

Vertus

Parc des
Expositions

PL. A.
BARDOUX

Quai

Rue J. Rousseau

D. Mestre
Jacques

Rue Barbès

R.-L. Mallet

Boulevard

Lamarck

P

Palais
des Congrès

Museum

A
A 71, N 151 CHÂTEAUROUX ↓ MONTLUÇON, LA CHÂTRE ↓

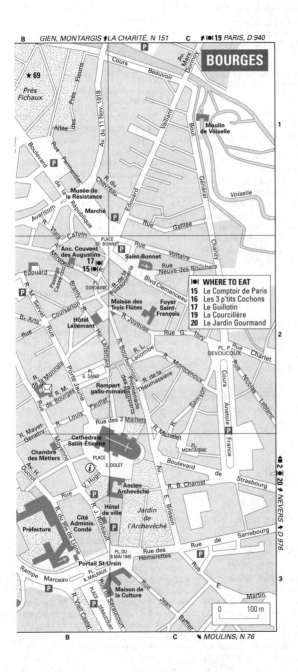

BOURGES

★ 69

Prés
Fichaux

Allée

Boulevard

de la République

Musée de
la Résistance

Marché

Avaricum

Vrais   Calvin

Anc. Couvent
des Augustins
17 |●|
15 |●|

Saint-Bonnet

Edouard

Maison des
Trois Flûtes

Foyer
Saint-
François

Hôtel
Lallemant

Rempart
gallo-romain

Rue des 3 Maillets

Cathédrale
Saint-Etienne

Chambre
des Métiers

PLACE
E. DOLET

Ancien
Archevêché

Hôtel
de ville

Cité
Adminis.
Condé

Préfecture

Jardin
de
l'Archevêché

Portail St-Ursin

Maison de
la Culture

Cours   Beauvoir

Moulin
de Voiselle

Voiselle

Rue   Galilée

PLACE
ST-BONNET

Rue   Voltaire

Rue
Neuve-des-Bouchers

Blvd Clemenceau

Rue   G.   Tory

PL. P.
DEVOUCOUX

Rue   Charlet

Boulevard   de   Strasbourg

R. B. Charost

Rue   de   Sarrebourg

Martin

|●| WHERE TO EAT
15 Le Comptoir de Paris
16 Les 3 p'tits Cochons
17 Le Guillotin
19 La Courcillère
20 Le Jardin Gourmand

0   100 m

6

CENTRE

⊚ ♉ |●| Restaurant La Courcillière

Rue de Babylone; head for avenue Marx-Dormoy and look for a narrow street off to the right, just after the Hôtel Saint-Jean. **Off map C1-19**
℡02.48.24.41.91
Closed *Tues evening; Wed; Sun evening out of season.* **Disabled access. Car park.**

In the heart of the magical marshlands on the banks of the River Yèvre – you can admire the view either from huge bay windows in the cosy dining room or from a waterside terrace. Denis Julien serves lovingly prepared regional cuisine on the weekday menu at €17, and others at €22 and €28. The terrines are made on site, and among the specialities you should look out for the famous *couilles d'âne* (eggs in wine sauce) and calf's head sauce *ravigote*. Everything is authentic here, from the smile of the *patronne* to the local accent of the gardeners. *Free apéritif offered to our readers on presentation of this guide.*

Allogny

18110 (18km NW)

⊚ |●| Restaurant Le Chabur

Route de Mehun-sur-Yèvre; take the D944 in the direction of Neuvy-sur-Barangeon.
℡02.48.64.00.41 ℡02.48.64.04.87
Closed *Mon.* **Disabled access. Car park.**

The infamous witches of Berry supposedly gathered in the forest near here. Maryse and Bruno serve classic dishes – calf's head, *coq au vin* and so on – to a crowd of locals. Lunchtime menus €10–22; à la carte only in the evening.

Bourgueil

37140

⊚ ♠ Le Thouarsais

10 pl. Hublin.
℡02.47.97.72.05
Closed *Sun evening Oct to Easter; first 2 weeks in Oct.* **TV.**

A simple, well-maintained hotel in a quiet, centrally located square. The rooms in the annexe are more comfortable and some of them look out over a garden; doubles go for €25–33 with basin and €35–48 with shower or bath and wc. Cheaper rates are offered for a stay of three or more consecutive nights. When the weather is warm, breakfast (€5) is

served outside in the flower garden. Pets are not allowed.

⊚ |●| Auberge La Lande

Take the D35 in the direction of the "Cave touristique".
℡02.47.97.92.41
Closed *Sun evening; Mon; Tues evening in winter.* **Car park.**

In an old residential building in the middle of vineyards. No-nonsense, carefully prepared, regional cooking is served here according to the season and in a refined décor. Meals can be eaten on the terrace; menus from €13.95 (weekdays) up to €26. It's best to book.

Briare

45250

⊚ |●| Restaurant Le Bord'Eau

19 rue de la Liberté; it's on the main street.
℡02.38.31.22.29
Closed *Wed and Thurs; Jan.* **High chairs and games available.**

With a name like this, you'd be forgiven for expecting a lovely waterside terrace. However, the cuisine (menus €15 to €26) and the maritime décor will soon help you swallow any disappointment about the surroundings. The restaurant's name is more to do with the fresh fish that they serve here, and the food is very good: fillet of pike perch with *beurre blanc* and calf's head with *gribiche* sauce.

Bonny-sur-Loire

45420 (10km SE)

⊚ ♠ |●| Les Voyageurs

10 Grande-Rue; from Briare take the N7 and then the A77.
℡02.38.27.01.45 ℡02.38.27.01.46
Closed *Sun evening; 2–11 Jan; 7–22 Feb; 22 Aug–6 Sept.* **Restaurant closed** *Sun evening; Mon; Tues lunchtime.* **TV. Car park.**

Given the prices – menus are listed at €16.50 (weekdays) and €25–40 – you might not realize that this is one of the best gourmet restaurants in the area. Philippe Lechauve is a local, but he was the chief *saucier* for the renowned Troisgros brothers for years; the prices are even more unbelievable given his pedigree. He manages to provide such interesting dishes by simplifying the ingredients and relying on his talent to produce something wonderful. The menus change every three months, but you can count on the delicious *chocolat fondant* – the chocolate oozes over the pistachio sauce and *crème anglaise* as you cut the cake – on the second menu. There are also some decent wines. Double rooms with shower/wc go for €34–37. Logis de France.

Chabris

36210

@ ▲ |●| ⅔ Hôtel de la Plage**

42 rue du Pont; 25km east of Saint-Agnan, via the D17 then the D35.
℡02.54.40.02.24 ℻02.54.40.08.59
✉hoteldelaplage@wanadoo.fr
Closed *Sun evening; Mon (open Mon evening mid-July to end Aug); 1 Jan to mid-Feb.* **Car park. TV.**

On the road from Valençay to Romorantin, going to Sologne, an ideal stopover for a meal or a night's rest. Comfortable rooms, but choose one that overlooks the garden, as those on the first floor are bigger, and those on the second have been modernized, at €40 for a double with shower/wc or bath. In the kitchen, Madame d'Agostino prepares traditional food, and her husband proudly serves it in the dining room or, on fine days, in the garden which has a refreshing fountain. Her specialities are duck foie gras and veal kidneys sautéed with port. The menu changes every three months, and the fish varies according to availability; menus from €16 (weekdays) to €32. Logis de France. *Free house apéritif or coffee offered to our readers on presentation of this guide.*

Chambord

41250

@ ⅔ ▲ |●| Hôtel du Grand Saint-Michel**

Château de Chambord.
℡02.54.20.31.31 ℻02.54.20.36.40
Closed *Sun evening 1 Jan–1 April; Mon; Tues lunchtime; 15 Nov–20 Dec.* **TV. Car park. High chairs available.**

This hotel is in an exceptional location opposite the château, and it boasts spacious, comfortable and pleasant rooms (even without the view) at €52–79 for a double with shower or bath. The dining

room is traditionally decorated, providing an appropriate setting for the cuisine, which includes *millefeuille* of crab with artichokes and *croustillant* of pigs' trotters on menus, €19 and €25. Considerate, attentive service and a friendly welcome – not at all the mechanical toil you might expect in such a touristy place. In summer you can eat on the terrace with the château right in front of you – very romantic. You'll need to book well in advance. Logis de France. *10% discount on the room rate (1 Oct–1 April) offered to our readers on presentation of this guide.*

Saint-Dyé-sur-Loire

41500 (5km NW)

@ ⅔ ▲ |●| Le Manoir de Bel-Air**

1 rte. d'Orléans.
℡02.54.81.60.10 ℻02.54.81.65.34
🌐www.manoirdebelair.com
Closed *mid-Jan to mid-Feb.* **Disabled access. TV. High chairs and games available. Car park.**

This old ivy-smothered building is on the banks of the Loire. It has a delightfully provincial feel and there's a lovely smell of beeswax polish. Rooms are reasonably priced given the facilities and cleanliness: doubles with shower or bath go for €54–89. (The ones with a view of the river are the best.) The dining room, which also has the view, is bright and spacious. Set menus, €22–43, list very good regional cooking. There's a track along the riverbank if you fancy a post-prandial walk. *10% discount on the room rate (15 Nov–15 March) offered to our readers on presentation of this guide.*

@ |●| La Bourriche aux Appétits

65 rue nationale.
℡02.54.81.65.25
Closed *Mon–Thurs, except public holidays; fortnight in Jan.* **Shop open** *Tues–Sat 10am–noon and 4–7pm.*

Take a stroll along the banks of the Loire at Saint-Dyé, where the sailing barges that brought the hewn stone for Chambord used to tie up. Then make your way to the restaurant run by Gilles Quesneau, an epicurean who has opened a shop selling home-made dishes alongside. The décor is as tasty as the food, with menus at €23 and €28; specialities include river fish, *gratin* of crayfish tails, Loire eel kebab and fish couscous. You can stock up with terrines or pâtés in jars to take home.

An exceptional place, with old-fashioned cooking at its best and a warm welcome for guests.

Chartres
28000

A practical place to stay, given its excellent location. The hotel has been recently entirely renovated and even if it's not exactly a bundle of laughs, you'll be given a nice welcome. Quiet, clean and comfortable rooms with shower/wc or bath/wc from €52 to €65; some have a lovely view of the cathedral. The buffet breakfast, €8, is generous. Brasserie style menus are served for €15–25. *Free house apéritif, coffee or a breakfast per room and per night (Nov–March) offered to our readers on presentation of this guide.*

Just twenty metres from the forecourt, this restaurant is not called "the pike" for nothing: the fish appears in various guises on the no-frills menus (€11 and €14), often in combination with wine. Other dishes include the standard fair of the region: calf's head *ravigote, confit* of duck, chicken *au pot Henri-IV* and the mysteriously named hen's milk with fruit as dessert.

There's a 1930s atmosphere in this brasserie with its classic zinc-topped bar, bistro tables, benches covered in red velvet and retro posters covering the walls. Traditional food cooked using exclusively fresh produce, speedy yet relaxed service and a pleasant and enthusiastic welcome. There's

an outdoor terrace in the pedestrian area. There's an €11.90 *formule*, or you can eat à la carte for around €22.

Don't even think of visiting Chartres without eating in this delightful little restaurant (which has just ten tables). Everything is of a piece: the welcome, the service, the cooking and the décor. Benoît Pasquier's family have been in the Beauce for five generations and he makes a point of showing off local produce to its best advantage. The first menu starts at €15 (weekdays only), and there are others at €23.30 and €38. The dishes change with the seasons, though favourites such as *petit-gris* snails with a *fondue* of tomato, pan-fried foie gras with lentils, veal sweetbreads cooked in a haybox, *crème brûlée* and regional cheeses are available all year.

Arguably the most attractive summer table in Chartres. It's in a romantic, charming situation on an arm of the river, just behind the cathedral. There's a covered terrace at the waterside and another summer terrace made from an old wash-house – once numerous in these parts. They serve attentively and laboriously produced dishes that may seem a bit pricey – menus €20 (weekday lunchtimes) and €24–41 – but the setting adds considerably to the pleasure. Specialities include terrine of foie gras, prawns *royales* and white chocolate ice cream. *Free house apéritif offered to our readers on presentation of this guide.*

Maintenon
28130 (18km NE)

☎02.37.23.06.67
Closed *Sun; Mon; 15 July–15 Aug.*

A little restaurant in a rustic style – evidenced by the old iron cooking pot in the entrance. It's one of the best in Maintenon for both its welcome and the family dishes the boss prepares. He's particularly famous for his calf's head *ravigote* and classic sauces. There's a lunch menu at €11.50; others €15.50–25. Booking is essential. *Free coffee offered to our readers on presentation of this guide.*

Châteaudun

28200

◎ 斗 🛊 |O| **Le Saint-Louis****

41 rue de la République.
☎02.37.45.00.01 ℗02.37.45.16.09
Ⓦwww.lesaintlouishotel.fr
Restaurant closed *Sun.* **TV. Car park.**

Ben Maamar pulled off quite a stunt in a very few years, first by turning a ruin into a decent, comfortable hotel and then by adding a restaurant and a lively brasserie next door. This is the place to eat in Châteaudun, especially in summer when the piano bar gets going outdoors – a real success. It's got the loveliest terrace in town. Mussels, salads, grills – dishes to satisfy all tastes and pockets, with menus for €12–15 and pizzas €5.50. And the hotel rooms are priced at €45 for doubles with shower/wc or bath. *Free liqueur offered to our readers on presentation of this guide.*

◎ |O| **La Licorne**

6 pl. du 18-Octobre; it's on the main square.
☎02.37.45.32.32
Closed *Tues evening; Wed; 20 Dec–15 Jan.*

The dining room is long and narrow and decorated in salmon pink. You'll find solid cooking in big portions on the set weekday menu for €11, others €15–28; dishes include oysters and leeks *au gratin* (in winter), breast of duck with orange and honey and cake *grand-mère*. Service, usually very pleasant, can get a bit rushed when they're busy. There's a nice terrace on sunny days.

◎ 斗 |O| **Aux Trois Pastoureaux**

31 rue André-Gillet; it's between place du 18-Octobre and espace Malraux.
☎02.37.45.74.40 ℗02.37.66.00.32
Ⓦwww.aux-trois-pastoureaux.fr
Closed *Sun evening; Mon; Wed lunchtime;*

a fortnight in Jan; a fortnight in July–Aug. **Open** *noon–1.45pm and 7.15–9pm.* **Disabled access. High chairs and games available.**

This is the oldest inn in Châteaudun and there's a calm atmosphere and pleasant welcome – choose between the simply set tables in the green dining room and a seat in the sun on the terrace. There's a wide variety of dishes on offer here, including some very unusual taste combinations, such as chicken kebabs with liquorice *jus*, veal kidneys *au coteaux-du-layon*, escalope of bass with its orange caramel sauce – this is sophisticated cooking with a range of menus, €19.80–65. *Free house apéritif offered to our readers on presentation of this guide.*

Châteaumeillant

18370

◎ 🛊 |O| **Hôtel-restaurant Le Piet à Terre****

21 rue du Château.
☎02.48.61.41.74 ℗02.48.61.41.88
Ⓔle.piet.a.terre.free.fr
Closed *Sun evening; Mon; Tues except July–Aug; 12 Nov–28 Feb.* **TV. High chairs available.**

A two-star hotel with a three-star restaurant. The dining room has blue shutters and a fine chimney place for open fires in winter, and there's a new veranda too. Thierry Finet is passionate about cooking and he makes the bread and breakfast rolls on the premises. Menus €34.50–88; the cuisine revolves around fresh produce from the market and reflects the mood of the chef. The vegetables and herbs come from grandfather Piet's garden and the jardin des Aydes. The newly renovated bedrooms are named after flowers and go for €46–70 with shower/wc or bath. No dogs admitted.

Châteauneuf-en-Thymerais

28170

◎ 🛊 |O| **L'Écritoire****

43 rue Émile-Vivier; take the Dreux road.
☎02.37.51.85.80 ℗02.37.51.86.87
Restaurant closed *Mon; Wed; Sun evening; Feb half-term; early Nov.* **Car park.**

This old sixteenth-century staging post has been a restaurant ever since 1743 and is recognized as one of the best in Eure-et-Loir, offering impeccably attentive service. The chef, Luc Pasquier, is a veteran of gastronomic adventures in Asia and Africa, but he has come back to his roots to create classical dishes inspired by the produce of the region. You must try the lamb; it's so tender you could eat it with a spoon... Overall, excellent menus, at very reasonable prices, considering the quality: €23 (weekday lunch) to €57. There are also a few simple but clean and comfortable rooms, at €45 for a double with shower/wc or bath, giving onto a little courtyard with balconies bedecked with flowers.

Senonches

28250 (13km W)

@ ⅔ ☗ |●| Auberge La Pomme de Pin**

15 rue Michel Cauty; take the D928 to Digny then the D24.
℡02.37.37.76.62 ℗02.37.37.86.61
⊛www.restaurant-pommedepin.com
Closed *Sun evening; Mon; Tues lunchtime or Fri evening in winter; 2–31 Jan; a week during Oct.* **TV. High chairs and games available. Pay car park.**

A half-timbered inn which used to be a posthouse on the edge of the Zandere area. Ten comfortable rooms, two of which have been completely renovated, from €50 with shower/wc, €63 with bath/wc. Half board, €47 per person, is compulsory for a stay of more than three nights. They serve good quality, wholesome food with an emphasis on local specialities: dishes include carp with crayfish, Chartres pâté, oxtail with foie gras or game and wild mushrooms in season. Set menus start at €15 (weekday lunchtimes), then €22.50–40. Logis de France. *10% discount on the room rate (1 Nov–28 Feb) offered to our readers on presentation of this guide.*

Châteauroux

36000

@ ☗ Hôtel Le Boischaut**

135 av. de la Châtre; 900m from the train station towards the stadium.
℡02.54.22.22.34 ℗02.54.22.64.89
⊛www.citotel.com
Closed *Christmas holidays.* **Disabled access. TV. Car park.**

This recently built hotel has large, comfortable double rooms at €39.50–48 with

shower/wc or bath. Ask for one overlooking the garden. No restaurant – but there is a bar, and they can provide a meal on a tray for €12 with a hot main dish, cheese and dessert, except at weekends. There's free lock-up parking available for two-wheelers.

@ ⅔ ☗ Élysée Hôtel***

2 rue de la République; it's practically opposite the Équinoxe cultural centre.
℡02.54.22.33.66 ℗02.54.07.34.34
ℯelysee36@aol.com
Closed *25 Dec–1 Jan.* **Disabled access. TV. High chairs and other children's accessories available. Car park.**

An excellent little hotel run by a Norman couple who used to run a newsagent's. It's in the centre of town, with spotless, pleasant rooms which have been recently renovated; doubles €47–60.50, breakfast €8. There's a salon-bar filled with old Routard guides; you can indulge in a little wine-tasting here or in your room. Though there's no dining room they have a deal with a nearby restaurant and can offer a meal on a tray until 11pm. *10% discount on the room rate (weekends and 14 July–25 Aug) offered to our readers on presentation of this guide.*

@ |●| ⅔ Le P'tit Bouchon

64 Rue-Grande.
℡02.54.61.50.40
Closed *Sun; Mon; public holidays.*

The old-fashioned green façade, the little tables inside, the blackboard menu, the old bar jammed with bottles and the waiters in long aprons – all these are redolent of a Lyonnais *bouchon* (bistro). The owner gave up being an insurance salesman; his good humour is as choice as the tasty cuisine which tends more towards the Berry region than to Lyon. Very good value for money with menus at €12–16: smoked carp salad, warm goat's cheese with acacia honey, larded scallop kebab, tied *andouille* with Beaujolais. There's also a wine bar offering at least a hundred different wines by the glass. Cheese lovers can indulge themselves further in the owners' cheese shop. *Free house apéritif offered to our readers on presentation of this guide.*

@ ⅔ |●| Le Bistrot Gourmand

10 rue du Marché; 20m from rue Grande, right in the city-centre.

ⓣ and ⓕ02.54.07.86.98
Closed *Sun; Mon lunchtime; public holidays;
fortnight around the end of Feb to early
March; 3 weeks from mid-Aug to early Sept.*

Cheerful dining room decorated bright
yellow and soft green. A huge blackboard
displays the dishes of the day. They use
only the freshest produce: try the beef
Limousin. There's a menu at lunchtime
for €12.50, and another €16.50, or
you'll pay around €15–23 à la carte. *Free
house apéritif or coffee offered to our readers on
presentation of this guide.*

ⓖ 🌿 |●| **Restaurant La Ciboulette**

42 Rue-Grande; near the museum.
ⓣ02.54.27.66.28
Closed *Sun; Mon; bank holidays; Aug; fortnight during the Christmas/New Year holiday.*
High chairs and games available.

This is Châteauroux's gourmet restaurant
– everybody dines here. It has pleasant
décor and friendly service, and the menus
have been thoughtfully put together.
There's a weekday menu at €14 and
others up to €40; they include such
local specialities as *couilles d'âne* (eggs
poached in red wine and shallot sauce),
foie gras and lentil terrine, roast pigeon
with balsamic vinegar and vanilla Bavarois.
Around fifteen wines are sold by the glass.
Foie gras and truffles can be bought from
the restaurant for private use. *20% discount
on the price of a meal when you show your
guide in advance.*

Déols
36130 (2km N)

ⓖ |●| **L'Escale Village**

Take the N20 towards Paris. It's 5km north of
the city, very close to the entrance to the airport zone (in the direction of the airport).
ⓣ02.54.22.03.77 ⓕ02.54.22.56.70
Open *noon–2.30pm and 7pm–midnight.*
Disabled access. High chairs available.

This restaurant attracts people of all ages
from across the region – whole families
crowd into this lively, vibrant place. Good
traditional dishes include seafood platter, sole *meunières*, beef with shallots and
moules marinières. Menus start at €10.70,
then go up to €25.50; reckon on around
€25 à la carte. Long-distance lorry drivers prefer the brasserie where they can
watch TV while they eat. It's open round
the clock – you never know who you'll
bump into.

Coings
36130 (8km N)

ⓖ 🏠 |●| **Le Relais Saint-
Jacques*****

Take exit 12 off the A20 going in the direction
of the airport, then Coings. Turn left before
Céré.
ⓣ02.54.60.44.44 ⓕ02.54.60.44.00
ⓦwww.relais.st.jacques.com
Restaurant closed *Sun evening.* **Disabled
access. TV. Car park. High chairs available.**

Don't let the dreary setting near the airport
put you off: this modern hotel is pleasant,
comfortable and quiet. Each of the rooms
is decorated differently and looks onto
the garden or over the countryside at the
rear; doubles start at €57.50 with basin,
and go up to €63. But the establishment
is best known for the excellent cuisine of
the chef/proprietor, Pierre Jeanrot, and
offers menus at €20, €30 and €46.50.
The dishes change frequently, but specialities include pan-fried scallops. In good
weather, there's a less expensive brasserie
service available on the terrace.

Levroux
36110 (21km N)

ⓖ 🌿 |●| **Restaurant Relais Saint-
Jean**

34 rue Nationale; it's near place de la
Collégiale-de-Saint-Sylvain.
ⓣ02.54.35.81.56 ⓕ02.54.35.36.09
ⓦwww.relais.saint.jean.fr
Closed *Sun evening; Tues evening Oct-May;
Wed; last week in Aug; during winter school
holidays.* **High chairs available.**

The chef who owns this old coaching inn
has made this one of the best restaurants
in the Indre region. His skilful use of
first-rate ingredients, and the charming
welcome you get from his wife, make for
a winning combination. The dining room
is pleasant, and in summer you can admire
the sunsets over the Saint-Sylvain collegiate church from the terrace. There's a
menu at €15 (not served on Sat night, Sun
or public holidays), and others at €22–38
with an impressive children's menu at €11
including fruit juice. Specialities include
lobster tails with herbs and fillet of beef
with a succulent duck foie gras. The cooking is judged to perfection and practically
sings with flavour. Take-away meals are
also available. *Free coffee offered to our readers
on presentation of this guide.*

Buzançais

36500 (25km NW)

@ 🎿 🏠 |●| **Hôtel-restaurant**
L'Hermitage**

1 chemin de Villaine, route d'Argy-Écueille;
take the N143 then follow the signs for Argy.
☎02.54.84.03.90 ℱ02.54.02.13.19
Closed *Sun evening and Mon except July–*
Aug for the hotel; 3–25 Jan; 26 Sept–4 Oct.
Disabled access. TV. Car park.

It really is as peaceful as a hermitage. The
hotel is covered in Virginia creeper and
overlooks a broad expanse of greenery on
the banks of the Indre. There's a big kitchen
garden and a really nice terrace. Comfortable
double rooms are €48–52 with shower or
bath; rooms in the main building have
been carefully decorated and have a view
of the grounds. The ones in the annexe are
slightly less attractive, but they too have been
redecorated and overlook the courtyard. Set
menus are €16 (weekday lunchtimes), €26
and €49. Logis de France. *10% discount on*
the half-board rate (1 Nov–30 March) offered to
our readers on presentation of this guide.

Châtre (La)

36400

@ 🎿 🏠 **Hôtel Notre-Dame****

4 pl. Notre-Dame.
☎02.54.48.01.14 ℱ02.54.48.31.14
@hotelnotredame@club-internet.fr
Disabled access. TV. High chairs available.
Car park.

A nice place to stay, in a fifteenth-century
building with a flower-filled balcony. It
overlooks a quiet little square that echoes
with birdsong. Bedrooms are spacious and
nicely furnished, perfectly in keeping with
the style of this pretty town. Some are particularly big and well laid-out, overlooking
the square, and cost €36.10 for a double
with washbasin only, €39 with shower/wc,
€42–47 with bath. There's a private garden
with a terrace. Hotels like this are rare. *10%*
discount on the room rate (Jan–Feb) offered to
our readers on presentation of this guide.

Nohant-Vic

36400 (6km N)

@ 🏠 |●| **L'Auberge de la Petite**
Fadette***

Place du Château; it's on the D943.
☎02.54.31.01.48 ℱ02.54.31.10.19
@www.auberge-petite-fadette.com

Disabled access. TV. High chairs available.
Car park.

This beautiful building, covered in Virginia
creeper, is totally in keeping with the
world of novelist George Sand, who spent
the greater part of her life in Nohant.
The bedrooms – €58 for a double with
shower/wc, and €100–130 with bath – are
very prettily decorated in assorted shades
of blue. The dining room features marvellous nineteenth-century wood panelling
and serves menus (€18–48) with tasty,
classic dishes. Logis de France.

Saint-Chartier

36400 (6km N)

@ 🎿 🏠 |●| **Hôtel-restaurant La**
Vallée Bleue***

Route de Verneuil. Take the D943 then the
D918; it's at the end of the village, towards
Verneuil.
☎02.54.31.01.91 ℱ02.54.34.04.48
@www.chateauvalleebleue.com
Closed *Sun evening and Mon in March, Oct*
and Nov. **Restaurant closed** *lunchtimes*
except Sun and public holidays, Nov to end
March; Sun evening and Mon in March, Oct
and Nov. **TV. High chairs and games avail-**
able. Swimming pool, children's pool and
sandpit. Car park.

This building, once owned by George
Sand's doctor, has been wonderfully converted into a hotel, retaining many original features. Everything is in keeping – the
dining rooms, the lounge and the bedrooms. You'll have a pleasurable stay here
and the restaurant, which serves set menus
at €29 (not public holidays), another at
€39, and a children's menu at €12, is
pretty good, too. À la carte lists specialities
such as fillet of pike perch with a cream
of crayfish, salad of Puy lentils and duck
foie gras with blackcurrant vinegar. There
are two terraces and a swimming pool in
four hectares of grounds. Very comfortable
rooms go for €95–220 with shower/wc
or bath; half board, at €85–120 per person,
is preferred for a stay of more than two
consecutive nights. *Free house apéritif offered*
to our readers on presentation of this guide.

Lys-Saint-Georges

36230 (23km NW)

@ 🎿 |●| **La Forge**

Take the D927 in the direction of Neuvy-Saint-
Sépulcre and then the D74. It's opposite the
castle.

☎02.54.30.81.68 ☎02.54.30.94.96
✉restaurantforgelys@club-internet.fr
Closed *Sun evening, Mon and Tues (Sept–June); Mon (July–Aug); 3 weeks in Jan; a fortnight in Sept.* **Disabled access. High chairs and games available.**

This rather good inn has handsome beams, an open fire in winter and a terrace in summer where you can enjoy the peace and quiet of the Noire valley. The *patronne* is friendly and very witty, and her husband, the chef, prepares tasty classic dishes with strong flavours. Menus, €16–40, change regularly with the seasons – though you may well see specialities such as guinea fowl with apple *jus*. The €23 menu is especially popular with locals on Sunday and reservations are advised. *Free house apéritif offered to our readers on presentation of this guide prior to ordering.*

Chaumont-sur-Loire
41150

⌨ |●| **Restaurant Le Grand Velum**

Entrance via the car park, on the flat area near the farm.
☎02.54.20.99.22
Closed *20 Oct–15 May.*

Make your way across the château car park to this restaurant. François-Zavier Bogard's cooking is enjoyed by horticulturalists and gourmets alike. At the brasserie-style *Comptoir Méditérranéen*, you will enjoy fresh pasta cooked in front of you and seasoned with fresh herbs from the garden. Menus range from €14.90 to €35. It's probably best to plan a meal here in good weather because they haven't yet installed heaters to cope with cooler days. But overall, the experience is extraordinary.

Chenonceaux
37150

⌨ 🎋 🏠 **Hôtel du Bon Laboureur et du Château**

6 rue du Docteur-Bretonneau
☎02.47.23.90.02 ☎02.47.23.82.01
🌐www.bonlaboureur.com
Closed *Wed evening and Thurs, Nov–Easter; 7 Jan–7 Feb; 11 Nov–20 Dec.* **Open** *every day in season.* **Swimming pool.**

Five generations of the Jeudi family have run this old staging post covered with

Virginia creeper. The air-conditioned rooms are all different, but all equally pretty, with good bathrooms, a writing desk, etc. Doubles cost €65–120, depending on the degree of comfort and the season. The food on offer in the restaurant is typically French, with a motley range of sauces; menus at €29, €46 and €69. In fine weather, meals are served on the patio decked with flowers. There's also a swimming pool. *10% discount on the price of a room offered to our readers on presentation of this guide.*

Civray-de-Touraine
37150 (1km N)

⌨ 🎋 🏠 |●| **L'Hostellerie du Château de l'Isle****

Take the D176; on the banks of the Cher
☎02.47.23.63.60 ☎02.47.23.63.62
🌐www.chateaudelisle.en-france.com
Closed *5 Jan–12 Feb.* **Restaurant closed** *lunchtime (except for groups).* **TV. High chairs and games available.**

A beautiful eighteenth-century building in the midst of a huge park on the banks of the Cher. Comfortable rooms, all different, go for €53–84 for a double with shower/wc or bath. The attractive dining room overlooks the pond, although on fine days you can eat on the terrace, before strolling in the park among centuries-old trees. There's a single menu at €25; the excellent food is prepared with fresh local produce. Boat trips on the Cher are also on offer. *10% discount on the price of a room (except July–Aug) offered to our readers on presentation of this guide.*

Chinon
37500

⌨ 🎋 🏠 |●| **Restaurant de l'Hôtel de la Treille**

4 pl. Jeanne-d'Arc.
☎02.47.93.07.71
Closed *Wed and Thurs evening.*

Simple, clean double rooms at €28 with toilet, €36 with shower; the bathrooms are on the landing. Dining room with beautiful worn floor tiles; the delicious and highly original food is based on plants and flowers with menus from €11.50 (weekday lunchtimes) to €24. You'll get very friendly service here. *Free house apéritif offered to our readers on presentation of this guide.*

@ ╦ Hôtel Agnès Sorel

4 quai Pasteur.
☎02.47.93.04.37 ℻02.47.93.06.37
🕸www.agnes-sorel.com

A friendly, energetic couple will welcome you as if you were their house guests. Some rooms overlook the river, and another has a charming window directly above the bathtub. Double rooms go for €46–57 with shower/wc or bath, as well as suites with a terrace at €95; copious and varied breakfast at €8. Bikes are available for rent, along with picnic baskets (book in advance).

@ 🍴 ╦ Hôtel Diderot**

4 rue Buffon; it's away from the centre, 100m from place Jeanne-d'Arc.
☎02.47.93.18.87 ℻02.47.93.37.10
🕸www.hoteldiderot.com
Disabled access. TV. Car park.

Through the big gateway at the end of the courtyard you'll see a very handsome eighteenth-century house covered in Virginia creeper. Inside there's a fifteenth-century fireplace, an eighteenth-century staircase and beams everywhere. It's all very lovely and the greeting is professional and welcoming. The twenty-eight cosy rooms are all decorated differently, and range in price from €50 to €71 with shower or bath/wc. Breakfast, €6.10, comes with wonderful preserves and is served on the terrace on sunny days and by the fire in winter. *20% discount (1 Nov–31 March) offered to our readers on presentation of this guide.*

@ 🍴 ╦ |●| Hôtel de France – Restaurant au Chapeau Rouge***

47–49 place du Général-de-Gaulle; right in the city-centre.
hotel: ☎02.47.93.33.91 restaurant:
☎02.47.98.08.08 ℻02.47.98.37.03
🕸www.chinon-hoteldefrance-restaurant.com
Closed a fortnight in Feb; 3 weeks in Nov.
Restaurant closed Sun evening (Oct–March).
TV. Pay car park.

This beautiful sixteenth-century building has been pleasantly renovated and is now a *Best Western* hotel. The rooms are comfortable and cost €67–96 for a double with shower or bath (breakfast

€8) – some have views of the château and the Fountain Square, a pedestrianized medieval street. The public spaces are pleasant, with little seating areas here and there. Banana, orange, lemon and bay trees grow in the Mediterranean garden in the inner courtyard. Traditional dishes predominate in the restaurant, with specialities such as pike perch with *beurre blanc*, duck terrine with foie gras, braised lamb's sweetbreads with white truffle and pears with Chinon wine preserve. Menus go for €25–36, gourmet menu €54; cheaper menus served, October to March. *10% discount on the room rate (Oct–March) or free apéritif offered to our readers on presentation of this guide.*

Beaumont-en-Véron
37420 (5km NW)

@ 🍴 ╦ |●| Manoir La Giraudière – Restaurant Le Petit Pigeonnier**

Beaumont-en-Véron; take the D749 towards Beaumont for about 4km; when you reach the Château de Coulaine, turn towards Savigny-en-Vecon (it's a small road); turn left at Domaine de la Giraudière; the restaurant is 800m further on.
☎02.47.58.40.36 ℻02.47.58.46.06
🕸www.hotels-france.com/giraudiere
Disabled access. TV. High chairs available. Baby-changing facilities. Baby-bottle warmer. Car park.

This delightful country seat of some seventeenth-century gentleman has been made into an incredibly peaceful hotel; the sixteenth-century dovecote has been turned into a sitting room and library with a piano. Twenty-five rooms with shower/wc or bath go for €40–115, breakfast €6.50; half-board from €45 per person. Good gourmet cooking at affordable prices (menus €20–35) is served in the restaurant; they prepare foie gras in a different way according to the season. Logis de France. *Free coffee offered to our readers on presentation of this guide.*

Combreux
45530

@ 🍴 ╦ |●| L'Auberge de Combreux**

35 rte. du Gâtinais; take the D10, then the D9. It's on the outskirts of the village.
☎02.38.46.89.89 ℻02.38.59.36.19
🕸www.auberge-de-combreux.fr

Closed *20 Dec–25 Jan.* **TV. High chairs available. Swimming pool. Car park.**

This magnificent nineteenth-century coaching inn, swathed in ivy and Virginia creeper, has been thoughtfully refurbished. There's a cosy little sitting room with an open fire and a rustic dining room with a veranda overlooking the flower garden. In fine weather you can sit under the trees. Elaborate and traditional cooking on the weekday menu €19 and others €29–36; well-prepared dishes include *escalope* of hot foie gras and game in season. The bedrooms – €60 with shower/wc to €63–75 with bath and €79 with Jacuzzi – are in the main building or in one of the little annexes hidden among the trees. They're delightful, with flower-sprigged wallpaper, beams and large wardrobes. Half board, requested at weekends in July and August, costs €64–74 per person. You can rent a bike to explore the Orléans forest nearby and there's a tennis court and a heated swimming pool. It's one of the best hotels around. Logis de France. *10% discount on the room rate (except at the weekend and in July–Aug) offered to our readers on presentation of this guide.*

Cour-Cheverny
41700

⌂ ⚞ ⌘ |❂| Hôtel-restaurant des Trois Marchands**

Place de l'Église; next to the church, in the main street.
☎02.54.79.96.44 ⨁02.54.79.25.60
🌐www.hoteldes3marchands.com
Closed *Mon; mid-Feb to mid-March.* **TV. High chairs available. Car park.**

This half-timbered village inn has a lot of charm. There are 36 rooms priced at €43–56, some overlooking the garden; half board €47–53. Avoid the ones in the annexe across the way if you can. The cooking has earned the place a good reputation, especially for frogs' legs with garlic and herbs. There are two dining areas: an upmarket gourmet restaurant and a smaller, rustic-style brasserie. The brasserie serves *formules* at €16 and €20, and the restaurant offers a first menu €22 (weekdays); other menus €30–35. *10% discount on the room rate offered to our readers on presentation of this guide.*

Dreux
28100

⌂ ⚞ Hôtel Le Beffroi**

12 pl. Métézeau; opposite the cathedral and right next to the belfry.
☎02.37.50.02.03
Closed *Sun noon–5.30pm; 1–15 Aug.* **TV.**

This is a good place to spend the night when you're just passing through, with its pleasant welcome and bright, quiet, comfortable rooms overlooking the river or the square. Doubles with shower/wc are €62, not including breakfast; some rooms sleep three. Prices have gone up but are still good value for money.

⌂ ⚞ |❂| Aux Quatre Vents

18 pl. Métézeau; right in the city-centre.
☎02.37.50.03.24
Closed *evenings; end of Aug.* **High chairs available.**

They've given this bistro a good retro look. Range of menus (€16–24) includes a buffet option where you help yourself to as many hors d'œuvres from the buffet as you like: choose from salmon, shellfish, excellent charcuterie and *crudités*. Follow that with a main course like kidneys in mustard sauce, veal in cream sauce or roast chicken, then finish with dessert. Make the most of the terrace when the weather's good – it faces the belfry. *Free house apéritif offered to our readers on presentation of this guide.*

Vernouillet
28500 (3km S)

⌂ ⚞ ⌘ |❂| Auberge de la Vallée Verte**

6 rue Lucien-Dupuis; near the church.
☎02.37.46.04.04 ⨁02.37.42.91.17
Closed *Sun; Mon; 1–26 Aug; 22 Dec–7 Jan.*
TV. Car park.

This recently refurbished hotel offers cosy rooms – some of them have been recently added – with shower/wc for €65-90, breakfast €6.10. But the big draw is the cooking: there's a brigade of professionals in the kitchen and they produce classic cuisine using locally farmed produce (veal, lamb and game according to season) and fresh seasonal fish. Cheapest menu at €25 and a fish menu, wine included, for €45. You can dine either in the pretty rustic dining room or under the eaves on the mezzanine. There's an intimate atmosphere and a convivial, smiling welcome. It's best to book at weekends. Logis de France. *Free house apéritif offered to our readers on presentation of this guide.*

Ferté-Vidame (La)

⊚ |●| La Trigalle*

Just on the ouskirts of the village; from Verneuil, turn right at the crossroads.
☎06.12.97.82.00 ℻02.37.37.51.75
⊛www.cc-la-ferte-vidame.fr
Closed *Mon and Tues, except on public holidays.* **Open** *Fri evening, Sat and Sun only, between All Saints' Day and Easter.*
Disabled access. Car park.

This restaurant is a real pleasure: classical music plays in the background but Emmanuel's cooking is far from classical. He invents delicious concoctions, changing the specialities on a regular basis: typical choices include scallops with oysters, pan-fried rump steak, fillets of red mullet with preserved lemon and basil oil, chestnut *truffade* with Armagnac, steamed turbot steak with *andouille de Vire*, bacon and truffles, honey ice cream with almond crackling, Bavarois with sweet wine and raspberry and basil *coulis*. Evening menus, €19–23, are good and generously served. The wine list is exceptional and, if you're feeling flush, there are a number of bottles with three-figure prices. Saint-Simon, the famous eighteenth-century diarist who chronicled events at the court of Louis XIV, had a château here. It's in ruins now but it's worth a visit – the grounds are enormous. NB: for dinner, you must book before 3pm.

Gien

45500

⊚ 🏃 🛏 |●| La Bodega

17 rue Bernard-Palissy.
☎02.38.67.29.01 ℻02.38.67.98.47
Closed *Sun except by reservation; Aug.* **Car park.**

Odd to find such a traditional French hotel with such a Spanish name. Whatever the nomenclature, this is a straight-down-the-line establishment for travellers on a

tight budget. It's a small hotel with pretty, old-style rooms that have all been made over with shower rooms added (the wc is still on the landing) and are excellent value for money at €29–36 for a double. It has to be said, however, that the two rooms in the courtyard are not well soundproofed on the road side. The restaurant doesn't go in for complicated cooking, but it's good nourishing fare and the little dining room is pleasant. There's a lunch *formule* for €7 (as much hors d'œuvre and pizza as you can eat), along with grills and simple salads, menus at €8 and €11, or dinner à la carte for around €20. Weekday lunchtime, you can enjoy free hors d'oeuvre from the buffet with any grilled meat. They welcome you very naturally, almost as if you were part of the family. *Free Kir offered to our readers on presentation of this guide.*

⊚ |●| Restaurant Le Régency

6 quai Lenoir; it faces the Loire, near the bridge.
☎02.38.67.04.96
Closed *Sun evening; Wed; 1–15 July; a week between Christmas and New Year.*

The restaurant specializes in freshwater fish from the Loire, as well as local dishes cooked simply and with care. Prices are reasonable with menus at €16 (not weekends or holidays), €20 and €22. À la carte options include *croustade* of snails, fillet of pike perch with lemon butter, chilled nougat. It's a tiny place, so think about reserving.

Illiers-Combray

28120

⊚ |●| Le Florent

13 pl. du Marché; it's opposite the church.
☎02.37.24.10.43 ℻02.37.24.11.78
℮leflorent@aol.com
Closed *Sun evening to Wed evening except on public holidays.* **Disabled access. High chairs available.**

An elegant, unpretentious restaurant – they don't flog the Proust connection to death. The little dining rooms are delightful, and Hervé Priolet is an excellent and imaginative chef. There are tempting set menus at €19 (weekdays, except public holidays) and ranging up to €42 – and, yes, one is named after Proust. There's also a good choice of à la carte dishes, from around €12–21, and wines are sold by the glass. The house specialities include *tournedos*, veal sweetbreads and stuffed brocket breast. Note that service can be a bit slow and finishes quite early – reservations are advised.

Brou

28160 (13km SW)

⟨⟨ ♣ |●| Le Plat d'Étain**

15 pl. des Halles; on the main square.
℗02.37.96.05.65 ℗02.37.96.09.29
🖦www.leplatdetain.com
TV.

A spotless setting with a thick carpet, staff members dressed up to the nines and reasonable prices. Spruce double rooms €50–55. The quality extends to the kitchen, even though the chef does not take many risks; the menus revolve around standard but well-prepared dishes like fried foie gras and stuffed rabbit with spring vegetables: €14 (weekdays), then €16–40. Logis de France.

Issoudun

36100

⟨⟨ ♣ |●| ⅄ Hôtel-restaurant La Cognette***

2 bd. Stalingrad; take the N151, go into the town centre. It's near the big marketplace.
℗02.54.03.59.59 ℗02.54.03.13.03
🖦www.la-gognette.com
Closed *Sun evening; Mon and Tues lunch-time except 1 June–30 Sept; Jan.* **Disabled access. TV. High chairs available. Car park.**

Balzac gives a very vivid description of this hotel in *La Rabouilleuse*. Then, it was run by a pair called Cognet and a widow from Houssaye who had a reputation as a fine cook. Nowadays the kitchens are in the hands of Alain Nonnet and his son-in-law, Jean-Jacques Daumy, who prepare delicious food that is some of the best in the region on a range of menus, €22–67. The hotel is perfect; rooms with bath (€66–110) are comfortable and the well-equipped bathrooms are supplied with robes and hairdryers. Some have terraces where you can have breakfast in fine weather and enjoy the scent of roses. It thoroughly deserves its three stars. *Free house apéritif offered to our readers on presentation of this guide.*

⟨⟨ ⅄ |●| Pile ou Face

11 rue Danielle-Casanova; in the pedestrian street between Place de la Poterie and Place du 10-juin (belfry).
℗02.54.03.14.91
Closed *Sun evening; Mon; Thurs evening in winter; fortnight in May; fortnight in Nov.*

Whether you choose to eat in the conventional dining room or out on the more pleasant covered terrace, the menus are the same: weekday lunch menu €13, then €20–30, children's menu €7. Specialities include *cassolette berrichonne* and calf kidneys. *Free coffee offered to our readers on presentation of this guide.*

Diou

36260 (12km N)

⟨⟨ |●| ⅄ L'Aubergeade

Route d'Issoudun; from Issoudun take the D918, heading for Vierzon.
℗ and ℗02.54.49.22.28
Closed *Wed and Sun evenings.* **Disabled access. High chairs available. Car park.**

A warm welcome, a pretty terrace, a pleasant, comfortable dining room and careful, varied and inventive cooking. Menus (€16–33) feature specialities such as roast loin of lamb with herbs, polenta croquette with Parmesan cheese, scallops fried in poppy-seed oil. *Free coffee offered to our readers on presentation of this guide.*

Langeais

37130

⟨⟨ ♣ |●| Hôtel-Restaurant Errard-Hosten

2 rue Gambetta.
℗02.47.96.82.12 ℗02.47.96.56.72
🖦www.errard.com
Closed *Sun evening Oct–April; Mon; Tues lunchtime except public holidays; Dec–Jan.* **TV. Pay car park.**

An old inn right in the centre of the town with ten cosy, comfortable rooms; doubles with shower/wc are €49, or €65–75 with bath. The ones overlooking the courtyard are the quietest. There's a warm dining room on the ground floor with a small bar just off it. Reliable, high-quality gastronomic cooking with dishes precisely cooked and seasonings finely judged: typical choices on the menus (€28–47) include pigeon with honey and ginger or the classic pike perch with *beurre blanc*. It's all delicious, the service and welcome are exemplary. Logis de France.

Loches

37600

ⓒ 🏨 |●| Hôtel La Fontaine - Restaurant Le Chenin

Rue des Buissons; going towards Tours, it's about 500m after the roundabout, on the left (look out for the signposts).
☏02.47.91.47.47 ⓕ02.47.91.68.88
ⓦwww.hotellafontaine.com
Closed *22 Feb–7 March*. **Restaurant closed** *Sun evening; Monday; Christmas*. **Disabled access.**

Hotel set in a former clinic, on a hill overlooking the Indre valley. It belongs to an association for young and adult disabled people, some of whom work here. It must be said that the concrete building is lacking in charm, but the surroundings are lush and peaceful, the rooms are very comfortable, with simple but cosy decoration; they sleep two to four guests and cost €39–42 for a double. Facilities on offer include a gym and Internet connection. In *Le Chenin* restaurant, the food is excellent, starting from the cheapest menu – the "Express du Formule" lunchtime set menu (main dish and dessert) for €10; other menus are €16–35. The large dining room is divided into alcoves by flower-filled urns, and the tablecloths and curtains are in matching shades of orange, yellow and white. The locals flock here to eat (always a good sign) and the service is attentive and diligent. It is also possible to just have a drink on the large terrace. All in all, exceptional value for money for a place of this quality.

ⓒ 🏨 |●| Hôtel-restaurant George-Sand

39 rue Quintefol; on the banks of the Indre, in an old fifteenth-century staging post, below the château.
☏02.47.59.39.74 ⓕ02.47.91.55.75
ⓦwww.hotelrestaurant-georgesand.com
Closed *a week in Feb*. **Disabled access**.

Opt for one of the rooms overlooking the river, as these are bigger and more attractive (some even have fireplaces) but are also more expensive than the rest; doubles €49–110. The ones overlooking the street are dull and small. Range of

menus (€17–63) on offer in the dining room, which has a veranda over the water, adding to the pleasure of the fine food, coupled with friendly and efficient service. Logis de France.

ⓒ 🏨 |●| Hôtel-restaurant de France**

6 rue Picois.
☏02.47.59.00.32 ⓕ02.47.59.28.66
Closed *Sun evening; Mon; Jan*. **TV. Pay car park.**

This is an old posthouse with a wide courtyard and flower garden where you can have lunch in the summer, offering lovely rooms priced €50–63 with shower/wc or bath. Some are split-level, and they're all very cosily furnished; half-board €61–76 per person. In the classical dining room they serve menus at €15 (not served Sun) and €21–43, featuring good regional cooking such as *géline* (local chicken) and stewed eel. The desserts are prepared on the premises. Apparently Lodovico Sforza, the duke of Milan, was imprisoned in the dungeons in Loches and had his meals brought in from this hotel – if the quality was anything like this, it can't have been much of a hardship. Logis de France.

ⓒ |●| La Gerbe d'Or

22 rue Balzac.
☏02.47.91.67.63
Closed *Sun evening; Wed evening; Thurs*.

Austere but warm rustic dining room, and a charming terrace for fine weather. Set lunchtime menu, with wine or mineral water included (Mon–Fri, except public holidays) costs €10.50, then another menu at €23, with interesting propositions from the chef, Didier Marque, such as *rillons* of young rabbit with Sauvignon and onion *confit*, crusty cod with *confit* of vegetables with lemon butter, goat's cheese with salad and pears poached in wine with cinnamon. These were all on offer during our visit, but the menu changes frequently.

Genillé

37460 (10km NE)

ⓒ 🛋 🏨 |●| Auberge Agnès Sorel

6 pl. Agnès-Sorel (or pl. de l'Église); take the D764 in the direction of the Montpoupon Château.
☏02.47.59.50.17 ⓕ02.47.59.59.50
ⓔagnessorel@wanadoo.fr

Closed *Wed (July–Aug); Sun evening, Monday and Tues lunchtime (early Sept to end of June); a week mid-March; a week early Oct.*

The charmingly old-fashioned façade overlooks the church, and the three bedrooms inside evoke all the magic of a rural house. Doubles with shower or bath go for €38–49; one of them gives onto the garden, but it is no. 2 that is particularly appealing, with its tufa walls, its (disused) fireplace and its terracotta floor. The food prepared by Fabrice Menant is highly appreciated by the locals and has been warmly recommended to us. There are menus at €19, €27 and €43; reckon on €40–43 à la carte. Logis de France. *Free coffee offered to our readers on presentation of this guide.*

Malesherbes
45330

⊛ 🏠 |●| L'Écu de France**

10 pl. du Martroy.
☎02.38.34.87.25 ⊕02.38.34.68.99
Closed *6–19 Aug.* **Restaurant closed** *Thurs and Sun evenings.* **TV. High chairs available. Car park.**

Housed in a seventeenth-century staging post. The courtyard, where the stagecoaches used to turn in, has been transformed into the reception hall. Comfortable, well-maintained double rooms (some of them are new) for €50–62 with shower/wc or bath. The restaurant won't blow you away, but the *formule brasserie* served in the bistro is tasty and eating here can prove good value with menus at €20 (not served on Sun) and €32. Their specialities include calf's head and warm foie gras with fruit and a particularly good dessert with cream and cream cheese beaten together – it's even better with strawberries. A good place to stop if you're driving on the A13, which is just 13km away, and Fontainebleau is also nearby. Logis de France.

Mézières-en-Brenne
36290

⊛ 🏠 |●| Hôtel-restaurant Au Bœuf Couronné**

9 pl. Charles-de-Gaulle (Centre); 20km south of Châtillon-sur-Indre via the D43 and around

40km west of Châteauroux.
☎02.54.38.04.39 ⊕02.54.38.02.84
Closed *Sun evening and Mon (except public holidays); 15 Nov–31 Jan.* **TV. High chairs available.**

In the heart of Brenne's lake country, this former staging post, with a front porch dating from the mid-sixteenth century, has established a reputation that has spread far beyond the region. It offers very friendly and attentive service and an enticing mixture of warmth and elegance, with a decidedly rural touch. The bedrooms are small but perfectly adequate and cost €40 for a double with shower/wc; the ones overlooking the inner courtyard are the quietest. Menus at €14 (weekdays), then €20–40.50 offer subtle and inventive cooking, prepared and served with loving care. Credit cards not accepted. Logis de France.

Montargis
45200

⊛ 🏠 Hôtel Le Bon Gîte*

21 bd. du Chinchon.
☎02.38.85.31.01 ⊕02.38.93.28.06
Disabled access. TV. Car park.

Good place for a decent night's sleep at a reasonable price. It's not much to look at from the outside, but inside it's clean and quiet. Simple rooms, some of which look over the inner courtyard – in summer you could almost imagine you were somewhere in the Mediterranean. Doubles cost €28 with shower/wc and go up to €37 with bath. The very nice owners have been here for more than forty years.

⊛ |●| Restaurant Les Petits Oignons

81 bis av. du Général-de-Gaulle; it's near the train station.
☎02.38.93.97.49
Closed *Sun evening; Mon; Feb school holiday; first 3 weeks in Aug.* **Disabled access. High chairs available.**

They've got an effective "two-in-one" formula here. On one side is the bistro with its typical cooking (herring and potatoes in oil, skate wing and so on), while on the other, is the gastronomic restaurant, with its bright, uncluttered and rather modern décor and more elaborate dishes, such as pike perch with saffron and *cendré de Pannes* (goat's cheese coated in grey ash, produced less than 30km away). Menus are realistically priced at €12.50–32. In the summer you can also dine out in the garden and terrace. Wherever you eat, you can be sure of refined cuisine using only the freshest produce, a cordial welcome and impeccable service.

Amilly
45200 (2km SE)

◎ 🎋 |●| L'Auberge de l'Écluse

741 rue des Ponts; from the main street, follow directions towards Mormant.
℗02.38.85.44.24
Closed Sun evening; Mon; Tues.

From the dining room you can watch while the keeper opens the lock on the nearby canal; there's also a terrace on the waterside. Inside, the classic décor contrasts with the modern and inventive cooking; weekly menu €23, others €27–32. They specialize in fish – pike perch, red mullet – and use whatever the day's catch yields. Even if sometimes a bit pricey, the dishes are in no way disappointing. You should reserve on sunny days. *Free coffee offered to our readers on presentation of this guide.*

Cepoy
45120 (6km N)

◎ 🏠 |●| 🎋 Auberge de jeunesse

25 quai du Port; take the no. 2 bus via the N7 to the "Église de Saint-Loup" stop; from there, it's a 200-metre walk to the hostel.
℗02.38.93.25.45 ℗02.38.93.19.25
ⓔajcepoy@aol.com
Closed 20 Dec–1 Feb. **New arrivals** 8am–noon and 6–10pm. **Games available.**

Ideally situated on the banks of the Loing canal, in a charming seventh-century château on the outskirts of the town. Twenty-seven rooms with two to eight beds; doubles with washbasin or shower cost €24. FUAJ card is compulsory (you can buy it on the spot). You can also put up your own tent – there's certainly enough space, as the huge garden stretches over 4000 square metres and includes a volleyball court and ping-pong tables. Mainly group bookings, but there's usually room for individual travellers too. Meals cost €10, but a kitchen is also available. There's also a garage for bikes, with the possibility of renting a mountain bike. *Free coffee offered to our readers on presentation of this guide.*

Montbazon
37250

◎ 🏠 |●| 🎋 Le Moulin Fleuri

Route du Ripault; in the Veigné district, but closer to the centre of Montbazon; around 3km to the west of Montbazon. Leave via the N10 in the direction of Tours; after about 1km, at Gués-de-Veigné (traffic lights), turn left down the D287 towards Ballan-Miré, then take the D87, following the signs.
℗02.47.26.01.12 ℗02.47.34.04.71
ⓔlemoulinfleuri@wanadoo.fr
Closed Mon and Thurs lunchtime (1 April–11 Nov); Sun evening and Mon the rest of the year; 1 Feb–8 March. **Open** Evenings at 9pm (8.30pm Sun).

Sixteenth-century mill, rebuilt three hundred years later and superbly restored since, with its base lapped by water, surrounded by an idyllic seven-acre park awash with flowers. Comfortable double rooms with shower/wc go for €61.40; half board, available (and encouraged) from early April to late October, costs around €67.70. The restaurant is excellent: the chef (and owner) Alain Chaplin can always be relied on to produce an enticing meal inspired by whatever takes his fancy in the market that day. Menus €28.40–49, with a particularly extensive one at €39, feature seasonal specialities including cream of Jerusalem artichokes with fried duck foie gras, Lochois grouse roasted with cider and baked Granny Smith apples. They also offer an impressive selection of wines from the Loire valley. Logis de France. *10% discount on the price of a room (early Nov to end of March) offered to our readers on presentation of this guide (mention it on arrival).*

◎ 🎋 |●| La Chancelière – Le Jeu de Cartes

1 pl. des Marronniers; in the centre, on the road from Monts to Azay-le-Rideau.
℗02.47.26.00.67
Closed Sun and Mon (except public holidays); 15 Feb–2 March; 16–26 Aug.

This is a bistro-style restaurant, although the setting is exceptionally elegant and the food is exquisite: *croustillant* of langoustine tails with mixed salad and seafood butter, *cotriade* of white fish and shellfish with spices and chives (depending on seasonal availability). "Au jeu de cartes" and "Nostalgie" menus at €29 and €37, respectively. Lunch is served from 12.15pm and dinner from 8pm. A fine selection of local wines is on offer. *Free coffee offered to our readers on presentation of this guide.*

Montigny-sur-Avre

28270

🌊 ⚭ ⛟ |●| Hôtel-restaurant Moulin des Planches

☏02.37.48.25.97 📠02.37.48.35.63
🌐www.moulin-des-planches.fr
Closed *Sun evening; Mon; Jan.* **Disabled access. TV. High chairs available. Car park.**

This breathtaking windmill on the Avre is set deep in the country, surrounded by woods. It has been restored by a couple of former farmers who, in this restful and strangely luminous spot, perpetuate the tradition of the boarding house (there is no greater compliment for a hotel). Delightful, comfortable rooms cost €49 for a double with shower/wc, up to €63 with bath; they have a terrace too. There's a range of menus at €26–55. Logis de France. *Free house apéritif offered to our readers on presentation of this guide.*

Montrichard

41400

🌊 ⚭ ⛟ Hôtel de la Croix-Blanche**

64 rue Nationale, right next to the dungeons.
☏02.54.32.30.87 📠02.54.32.91.00
🌐www.hotel-lacroix-blanche.com
Closed *2 Nov–15 March.* **TV. High chairs available.**

This hotel has been completely renovated and is wonderfully clean. It started life as a coaching inn in the sixteenth century and it's right next to the dungeons. The rooms are well appointed, some with a view over the River Cher, and have en-suite bathrooms and phones; doubles €55–60. Half board is available at €49 per person per night. There's an attractive patio where they serve breakfast. *10% discount on the room rate (except public holidays weekends and July–Aug) offered to our readers on presentation of this guide.*

Chissay-en-Touraine

41400 (4km W)

🌊 ⚭ |●| 🌊 Château de Chissay

It's on the right bank of the Cher. From Montrichard, take the D176 in the direction of Tours.
☏02.54.32.32.01 📠02.54.32.43.70
🌐www.chateaudechissay.com
Closed *mid-Nov to mid-March.* **TV. High chairs available. Swimming pool. Car park.**

Historic château built by Charles VIII. It's a wonderful, meticulously restored building, located in the heart of the Cher valley. The terrace is under the arcades, while the splendid dining room is luxuriously decorated with period furniture and offers a weekday *formule* at €18 and menus €33–52. Double rooms cost €100–185 (the most expensive are in effect small apartments). *Free house apéritif offered to our readers on presentation of this guide.*

Pontlevoy

41400 (7km NE)

🌊 ⚭ |●| Hôtel-restaurant de l'École**

12 rte. de Montrichard; it's on the main road coming from Montrichard.
☏02.54.32.50.30 📠02.54.32.33.58
Closed *Sun evening and Mon except public holidays; 15 Nov–15 Dec; 16 Feb–17 March.* **TV. High chairs available. Car park.**

This is a charming little hotel with eleven comfortable rooms with shower/wc at €44 or €49.50–52.50 with bath. The cooking is very traditional but sophisticated and nicely presented. They do several set menus starting at €17 and going up to €46.50. Try their calf's head sauce *gribiche*, the pike balls with crayfish tails, game (in season) and fillet of pike perch *au beurre blanc*. In fine weather, you can eat under the pergola in the garden. Logis de France

Oisly

41700 (16km NE)

🌊 🌊 |●| Restaurant Le Saint-Vincent

From Montrichard take the D764 as far as Pontlevoy then turn right onto the D30.
☏ and 📠02.54.79.50.04
Closed *Tues; Wed; Mon evening 15 Sept–15 June; mid-Dec to end Jan.*

This is quite an exceptional restaurant. It doesn't look like much – the sign is very ordinary and you might mistake it for just another restaurant in just another village square. But step inside and notice the attention to detail: the décor is fresh, there's a decent amount of space between the tables, and the linen and cutlery have been chosen to match the rustic ambience. The menu is varied and full of tempting and original dishes: lobster *boudin* with Thai green curry, lamb braised with chickpeas and lemon *confit*, John Dory in its broth (with added vitamins). The creative chef will probably have invented even more culinary delights by the time you read this. Set menus go for €25 (not public holidays) up to €53. *Free coffee offered to our readers on presentation of this guide.*

Nogent-le-Roi
28210

ⓔ ⚶ |●| Le Capucin Gourmand

1 rue de la Volaille; near the church.
☎02.37.51.96.00
Closed *Thurs and Sun evening; Mon; Mon and Tues lunchtime in July–Aug; end of August to early Sept.*
High chairs available.

In this prettily decorated fifteenth-century house with half-timbering, the chef concocts highly attractive dishes infused with Mediterranean flavours, such as grilled swordfish with tapenade and turbot supreme. Before that, though, whet your appetite with the house apéritif, a skilful mixture of champagne and Grand Marnier. In the air-conditioned dining room they serve a weekday lunchtime menu at €15, then others €25–40. A warm welcome is guaranteed. *Free coffee offered to our readers on presentation of this guide.*

Nogent-le-Rotrou
28400

ⓔ ⚶ 🛏 Inter Hôtel Sully***

12 rue des Viennes; 200m from the city-centre.
☎02.37.52.15.14 ℻02.37.52.15.20
✉hotel.sully@wanadoo.fr
Closed *23 Dec–4 Jan.* **Disabled access. TV. High chairs available. Pay car park.**

Sure, it's a chain hotel but you get a genuine, smiling welcome that inspires confidence. The prices are affordable for a three-star; doubles with en-suite bathrooms start at €57. Breakfast costs €6.60. It's quietly located just away from the centre of town in an area that's recently been developed. *Free house apéritif offered to our readers on presentation of this guide.*

ⓔ ⚶ |●| La Papotière

3 rue Bourg-le-Comte.
☎02.37.52.18.41
Closed *Sun lunchtime; Mon.*

A strange name (it means "the gossiping woman") for this superb early-sixteenth-century stone house with mullioned windows and gargoyles. The snug interior is equally enchanting and the service is friendly, so guests quickly feel at ease. Delicious bistro-style menu €12.50 served every day at lunch and dinner, with other menus at €26–35, features traditional bourgeois cooking: veal sweetbreads with morels, *noisette* of lamb. As for dessert, you must try the house speciality of chocolate *kanougat*. *Free house apéritif offered to our readers on presentation of this guide.*

Nouan-le-Fuzelier
41600

ⓔ 🛏 Hôtel Les Charmilles

19 rte. de Pierrefitte-sur-Sauldre; by the exit to the town, on the D122.
☎02.54.88.73.55 ℻02.54.88.74.55
Closed *Feb.* **Disabled access.**

On the edge of a fairly quiet road, a small, modest but charming hotel in a woody park with a little pond, run by a young man with the help of his father. Fifteen very well-kept rooms (€45–62) with shower or bath; nos. 12 and 14 are on the ground floor overlooking the garden. The reception area and corridors have just been updated. There is no restaurant, but the father used to be a baker and now provides excellent brioches and croissants for breakfast (€7).

ⓔ |●| Le Raboliot

1 av. de la Mairie; in the main square; the town is between Salbris and Lamotte-Beuvron, a little way off the RN20 and 5 min from the motorway.
☎02.54.94.40.00
Closed *Feb; Sun evening; Mon.* **Disabled access. Car park.**

Philippe Henry, the owner of this restaurant near the woods and lakes of Malvaux is a local character renowned for his enthusiasm and good humour. His personality has left its mark on this excellent, warm-hearted and reasonably priced restaurant. The menu varies constantly, according to seasonal availability: snail ravioli, pike perch in Belle-de-Fontenay shells and a wide range of game, at the appropriate time of the year. The desserts are just as mouth-watering, there's a superb wine list and impeccable service is guaranteed. Set menus start from €15 (except weekends); à la carte you'll pay around €40. Regulars know that the owner also serves simpler, but equally exceptional, dishes from the bar at lunchtime: Orléanais free-range chicken with sage, *gratin* of potatoes with Sauvignon. Booking is compulsory.

⸪ |●| Le Dahu

14 rue Henri-Chapron; take the N20 in the direction of Ferté-Saint-Aubin.
℡ 02.54.88.72.88
Closed *Tues; Wed; 2 Jan–13 Feb.* **Disabled access. Car park.**

One of the outstanding restaurants in the region. Marie-Thérèse and Jean-Luc Germain have created an extraordinary garden for *Le Dahu*. Tucked away in an unattractive housing estate, this Solognote farmhouse has shrouded itself in greenery, echoed by the centuries-old beams and posts in the cosy, rustic but chic interior. The food also matches its surroundings admirably: fillet of bass with grapefruit, red mullet and risotto with black olives, Oriental-style guinea fowl stewed with white peaches, game in season. This is one of the best restaurants in the region, with menus at €21 (weekdays), then €29–49; reckon on €55 à la carte. Do not feel obliged to finish off your bottle of wine, you can take what's left away with you (along with fresh foie gras).

Souesmes
41300 (16km SE)

⸪ 🍴 |●| 🪑 Hôtel-restaurant La Croix Verte

Place de l'Église. Take the D122 in the direction of Pierrefitte-sur-Sauldre, then the D126.
℡ 02.54.98.93.70 ℻ 02.54.98.88.71
Closed *Sun, Mon and Tues evening; Wed; 2 weeks in summer; 3 weeks in winter.* **High chairs available.**

Just simple, traditional, seasonal food, but the chef's artistry on menus (€21.50–27) has begun to earn it a very high reputation: *croustillant* of goat's cheese with bacon, *fricassée* of calf kidneys with bacon and mustard, lightly salted caramelized apple tart.

A few modest but well-kept rooms are available at €25 for a double (washbasin only) to €40 with shower or bath, to enable you to explore the area more fully. To top it all, art lovers can buy the prints hanging on the walls. *Free coffee offered to our readers on presentation of this guide.*

Orléans
45000

See map on pp.272–273.

⸪ 🏠 Auberge de jeunesse

1 bd. de la Motte-Sanguin; to the east of the town centre (barely 10 min on foot); from the train station, take buses no. 4 or 8 to the "Pont-Bourgogne" stop. **Map D3-4**
℡ 02.38.53.60.06 ℻ 02.38.52.96.39
✉ asse.crjs@libertysurf.fr
Open *all year round 8am–7pm (8pm in summer).* **TV. Disabled access. Car park.**

This youth hostel is in a listed building in the heart of a woody park stretching along the quays of the Loire. Accommodation is €8.80 per person per night, hire of sheets €3.20, breakfast €3.50. There are sixty beds in all, so groups can be accommodated (and they can also buy cooked meals, unlike individual visitors). A kitchen, TV room, ping-pong table and laundry are also available. FUAJ membership card is required (on sale on site).

⸪ 🪑 🏠 Hôtel de l'Abeille**

64 rue d'Alsace-Lorraine; at the corner of rue de la Republique and rue Alsace-Lorraine. **Map C1-3**
℡ 02.38.53.54.87 ℻ 02.38.62.65.84
✉ hoteldelabeille@wanadoo.fr
TV. High chairs available.

There's something very special about this hotel. It was opened way back in 1903 and has been run by the same family since 1919, which makes it one of the oldest hotels in town. They've put green shrubs and flowers out all over the pavement, and the reception area is wonderfully nostalgic, complete with its own statue. The old wooden staircase gleams from years of polishing and the rooms – all decorated differently – have a quiet, antiquated charm. Prices are fair: €37–42 for a room with shower, €47–72 for a room with shower/wc or bath. *10% discount on the room rate offered to our readers on presentation of this guide.*

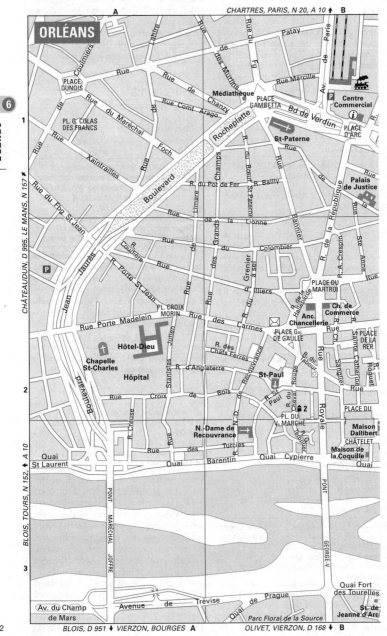

ORLÉANS

PLACE DUNOIS

PL. G. COLAS DES FRANCS

Coulmiers

Rue

Lahitte

Rue du Fg des Murlins

Rue du

Patay

Rue Marcille

Médiathèque

PLACE GAMBETTA

Bd de Verdun

Centre Commercial

PLACE D'ARC

Av. de Paris

de

Rue

de

Rue Comt Arago

Rue du Maréchal

Rue

de Chanzy

Rocheplatte

St-Paterne

Rue

bd

Foch

Xaintrailles

Champs

R. du Breul

R. Bailly

Rue

de

Palais de Justice

Boulevard

R. du Pot de Fer

R. Ste-Paterne

Bannier

R. de la République

R. A. Crespin

Ste Anne

Rue

Rue du Fbg St-Jean

Rue

de

la

Lionne

des Grands

du

Colombier

Grenier à Sel

PLACE DU MARTROI

Ch. de Commerce

Jean

Jaurès

R. Porte St-Jean

R. Coudière

Rue

d'Illiers

Rue

des

Carmes

R. de la Halle

Anc. Chancellerie

Rue

Rue

PLACE Gal DE GAULLE

Rue Ste Catherine

PLACE DE LA RÉR

PL. CROIX MORIN

Rue Porte Madelein

Hôtel-Dieu

Chapelle St-Charles

Hôpital

R. des Chats Ferrés

R. d'Angleterre

Stanislas

Julien

R. de la Recouvrance

N.-D.

St-Paul

R. St Paul

R. du Cheval Rouge

R. du Tabour

Rue Royale

Sanglier

Roquet

Rue

PLACE DU

Rue

Croix

de

Bois

PL. DU V. MARCHÉ

2

Maison Dallibert

CHÂTELET

R. Creusa

R.

Rue

des

Turcies

N.-Dame de Recouvrance

Quai Barentin

Quai Cypierre

Maison de la Coquille

Quai

Quai St Laurent

PONT MARÉCHAL JOFFRE

PONT GEORGE V

Quai Fort des Tourelles

St. de Jeanne d'Arc

Av. du Champ de Mars

Avenue

de

Trévise

Quai

de Prague

Parc Floral de la Source

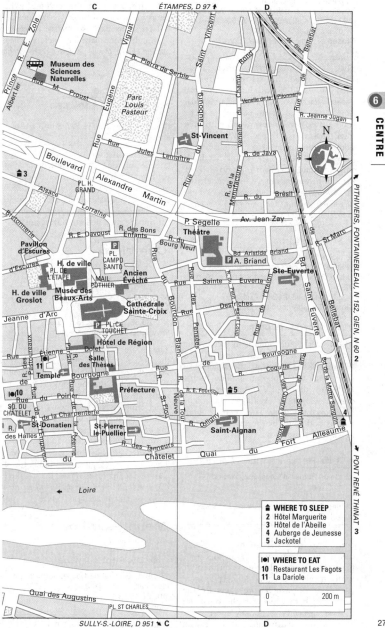

ÉTAMPES, D 97 ↑

C   D

Museum des Sciences Naturelles

R. E. Zola

Prince

Albert Ier

Rue M. Proust

Rue Eugène

Vignat

R. Pierre de Serbie

Saint Vincent

Parc Louis Pasteur

Rue Jules Lemaître

du Faubourg

St-Vincent

du Champ

Rond

Venelle de Gien

Bellebat

R. Jeanne Jugan   **1**

Venelle de la Pitonnerie

R. de Java

R. de la Manufacture

R. du   Brésil

N

🏛 3

Boulevard

PL. H. GRAND

Alexandre   Martin

Alsace

Lorraine

Bretonnerie

d'Escures

R. E. Davoust

R. des Bons Enfants

R. du Bourg Neuf

P. Segelle

Théâtre

Av. Jean Zay

Bd Aristide Briand

P A. Briand

R. de St-Marc

PITHIVIERS, FONTAINEBLEAU, N 152, GIEN, N 60

Pavillon d'Escures

H. de ville

PL. DE L'ÉTAPE

PL. CAMPO SANTO

MAIL POTHIER

Ancien Évêché

Ste-Euverte

Rue   Sainte   Euverte

H. de ville Groslot

Musée des Beaux-Arts

Cathédrale Sainte-Croix

Rue   des

Desfriches

Rue   Bourdon

Jeanne   d'Arc

PL. DU TOUCHET

Hôtel de Région

Blanc

Pensées

Bourgogne

2

Bd St-Euverte

Rue des

Étienne

Dolet

Salle des Thèses

Rue   Bourgogne

de

R.

Coquille

Bd de la Motte Sanguin

Rue   des

Pastoureaux

11

Temple

⬛10

Rue   du   Poirier

SQ. DU CHÂTELET

R. de la Charpenterie

Préfecture

St-Flou

de la Tour

Neuve

R. E. Fournier

🏛 5

R. Olligny

Rue   des   Quatre   Fils   Aymon

Saterno

4

🏛

R. des Halles

St-Donatien

R. Poterne

St-Pierre-le-Puellier

R. des Tanneurs

Saint-Aignan

Fort

Alleaume

PONT RENÉ THINAT

du   Châtelet

Quai

du

N

3

Loire

◀

🛏 **WHERE TO SLEEP**
2 Hôtel Marguerite
3 Hôtel de l'Abeille
4 Auberge de Jeunesse
5 Jackotel

🍴 **WHERE TO EAT**
10 Restaurant Les Fagots
11 La Dariole

0 ———————— 200 m

Quai des Augustins

PL. ST CHARLES

☞ 🏠 ♃ Hôtel Marguerite**

14 place du Vieux-Marché; it's 50m from rue Royale, near the main post office. **Map B2-2**
☎02.38.53.74.32 📠02.38.53.31.56
📧hotel.marguerite@wanadoo.fr
Closed *Sat and Sun noon–4.30pm.*
TV.

Nice hotel with a pretty brick façade. Prices are good, the welcome is friendly, and you could almost believe this was a three-star. Two types of accommodation – renovated rooms painted in pastel tones, and older, spotless rooms with their own charm. You'll pay €47–57 for a double with shower/wc or bath. Breakfast includes as much coffee as you can drink, fruit juice and honey for only €5 – they'll bring it to your room for no extra charge. *20% discount on the room rate (Fri–Sun and July–Aug) offered to our readers on presentation of this guide.*

☞ 🏠 Jackotel**

18 cloître Saint-Aignan; follow quai du Châtelet in the direction of Montargis and turn left before you get to the bridge. **Map D2-5**
☎02.38.54.48.48 📠02.38.77.17.59
Closed *Sun afternoon and public holidays 1–6pm.*
Disabled access. TV. Car park.

This recently built hotel is in a charming location, in a flower-filled courtyard near a lovely little square in the shadow of the church of Saint-Aignan. The rooms, €51–56 with bath, TV and phone, though comfortable, aren't exciting – you come here for the setting. They're mad about parrots, and you'll be greeted by a display of carved parrots in reception.

☞ ♃ |●| Restaurant Les Fagots

32 rue du Poirier; it's near the covered market. **Map C2-6**
☎02.38.62.22.79
Closed *Sun; Mon; first week in Jan; 3 weeks in Aug.* **Disabled access.**

You'll see all types here, from romantic couples to convivial groups and chatty locals. The dining room has a huge fireplace, and features old posters on the wall, with enamel and china coffee pots here and there. But you'll come here for the grills, which they do over the open fire – their speciality is donkey meat steak, though you have to order this a day in advance. The friendly welcome and service are also an attraction. The lunchtime set menu costs €10.90, there's another at €14.20, and à la carte you'll pay around €22. It's better in the evening (when reservations are strongly recommended) but on sunny days, the terrace makes it a thoroughly nice place for lunch. *Free house apéritif offered to our readers on presentation of this guide.*

☞ |●| La Dariole

26 rue Étienne-Dolet. **Map C2-9**
☎02.38.77.26.67
Closed *Wed lunchtime; Sat; Sun; 3 weeks in Aug.*

Wood panelling, old-rose tones and refined cuisine in this lovely restaurant with its friendly but formal welcome. Nice menu at €19.50, then others at €25.50 and €32; specialities change frequently according to the seasons. In summer you eat outside on a pedestrianized square.

Combleux
45800 (5km E)

☞ ♃ |●| Auberge-Restaurant La Marine

Take the N460.
☎02.38.55.12.69 📠02.38.52.03.65
🌐www.residence-la-marine.com

The house is smothered in wisteria and there's a terrace on the canal bank. The Loire flows through the village, revealing sandy beaches on the banks. The specialities are freshwater fish from the Loire – eel, lamprey and pike perch – in dishes that complement each other expertly, and the desserts are divine. The superb dining room is built from stone and pale wood and offers menus for €21 and €27. They also have a gîte and studios to rent – around €185 for two people for a three-day weekend. *Free house apéritif offered to our readers on presentation of this guide.*

Meung-sur-Loire
45130 (20km SW)

☞ |●| Dix Sept sur Vins

17 rue du Général-de-Gaulle; opposite the town hall, on the N152.
☎02.38.45.13.41
Closed *Mon.*

Even though it is on a main road, this restaurant is a real gem. The noise of traffic recedes as soon as you enter the simple but cheerful little dining room. The traditional cooking is unfailingly wholesome, always managing to find the right note, without the fussy pretensions so often found elsewhere. Depending on what's on the menu at the time, you could try, for example, *croustillant* of salmon, *magret* with *cassis*, foie gras, sea bream in a salt crust or kidneys in red wine. There's a lunchtime menu of the day (except Sun) at €14, other menus €19–25. The name of the restaurant is a play on words that makes clear, however, the owner's knowledge of wines – and it must be added that his father has a restaurant in Paris that is also unmissable.

Pithiviers

45300

@ 🎋 ♠ |●| Le Relais de la Poste**

10 Mail-Ouest; it's opposite the tourist office.
℡ 02.38.30.40.30. ⓕ 02.38.30.47.79
ⓦ www.relais-de-la-poste45.com
Restaurant closed *Sun evening.* **TV. High chairs and cots available. Car park.**

Despite its crumbling façade, this provincial hotel dominating the square is a good place to stop. Don't hesitate to enter; you'll be greeted warmly by the Polish-born patron. Some rooms – €49 with shower/wc or bath – have been entirely renovated, others only partially. Most of them have wooden wainscoting and the ones up in the eaves boast beamed ceilings. The dining room, recently redecorated, is nicely soundproofed. The first menu is well worth a look at €17 (other menus up to €30); you may also want to order the famous local delicacy, Pithiviers with puff pastry and almond paste, for dessert. Logis de France. *10% discount on the room rate or free house apéritif offered to our readers on presentation of this guide.*

Preuilly-sur-Claise

37290

@ ♠ |●| Auberge Saint-Nicolas**

4-6 Grande-Rue; very close to the Abbey of Saint-Pierre.
℡ 02.47.94.50.80 ⓕ 02.47.94.41.77
Closed *Sun evening; Mon; 15 Sept–15 Oct.* **TV. Car park.**

This hotel offers nine rooms painted in warm colours and fitted with all the necessary conveniences at a rate of €37–43

for a double with shower/wc or bath. The array of staircases, so typical of old houses, recalls the gangways of a ship. The dining room, brightly coloured and air-conditioned, serves a weekday lunchtime menu at €10.50, then others going up to €34.50, featuring regional dishes. It offers friendly service and good value for money. Logis de France.

Petit-Pressigny (Le)

37350 (9km N)

@ |●| Restaurant La Promenade

11 rue du Savoureulx; take the D41 in the direction of Loches, then the D50.
℡ 02.47.94.93.52 ⓕ 02.47.91.06.03
Closed *Sun evening, Mon and Tues except in July and Aug; Jan; 19 Sept–4 Oct.*

Some of the most ordinary-looking villages hide real treasures – this is one. Jacky Dallais was a pupil of Robuchon, and he's converted his father's old smithy into a splendid restaurant with two pretty, contemporary-looking dining rooms. He's a chef with integrity and imagination and creates dishes of great distinction – the choice changes constantly. Set menus, €37–73, are generous; the €70 menu includes four dishes, cheese and dessert; reckon on €60 à la carte. Specialities include free-range pork chop with beans and black pudding with mashed potatoes. Don't miss the home-made bread. The wine list is sumptuous and there's efficient service.

Romorantin-Lanthenay

41200

@ ♠ |●| Hôtel-restaurant Le Colombier**

18 pl. du Vieux-Marché; it's 150m from the town hall.
℡ 02.54.76.12.76 ⓕ 02.54.76.39.40
Closed *Sun evening; Mon; Sat lunchtime; Feb.* **TV. Car park.**

Rooms (€37) are comfortable, though nothing more; those overlooking the courtyard are quieter. The cosy restaurant serves menus at €18.50–35 specializing in cooking from the Sologne, and the carefully prepared dishes change with the seasons, using fresh regional produce. The specialities are the *suprême* of pike perch with crayfish and the raspberry shortbread.

The hotel has a pleasant garden and enjoys a good reputation.

Saché

37190

◎ |●| Auberge du XIIᵉ Siècle

Rue principale, opposite the main square.
℡02.47.26.88.77 ℻02.47.26.88.21
Closed *Sun evening; Mon; Tues lunchtime; a fortnight in Jan; a week in June; Sept; Nov.*

This village is enough to make many a restaurateur green with envy. It's a place of pilgrimage for devotees of Balzac, and the splendid restaurant is one of the best in the region – the old beams and wide fireplace can't have changed in centuries. Xavier Aubrun and Thierry Jimenez, the two excellent chefs, reinvent the region's traditional dishes on the basis of local ingredients, such as grouse, and fish from the Loire, according to seasonal availability. Set menus are priced at €29–63 and offer a great gastronomic experience.

Saint-Aignan

41110

◎ ⅍ 🏠 |●| Grand Hôtel Saint-Aignan**

79 quai J. J. Delorme.
℡02.54.75.18.04 ℻02.54.75.12.59
Closed *Sun evening; Mon and Tues lunchtime Nov to end March; second fortnight in Feb; first week in March; second fortnight in Nov.* **Disabled access. TV. High chairs and games available. Pay car park.**

An old coaching inn covered in ivy, standing on the banks of the Cher. Warm greeting, friendly setting and chic atmosphere – the walls are hung with medieval tapestries. Pretty rooms €25–54; some have a view of the river. Specialities in the restaurant include smoked salmon with onion rings, braised ox kidneys with ceps and *assiette de trois provinces* – all delicious, but portions are a little small. Menus go for €16 (weekdays only), and €24–35. Logis de France. *10% discount on the room rate offered to our readers on presentation of this guide.*

◎ |●| Restaurant Chez Constant

17 pl. de la Paix.
℡02.54.75.10.75
Closed *Mon and Tues out of season except*

public holidays; Mon only in July–Aug; during Feb and Nov school holidays.

This somewhat surprising restaurant, in the centre of town, pulls a cosmopolitan crowd. The specialities are the *andouillette* turnover with goat's cheese and the roast pike perch fillet on *andouillette* mash. Menus start at €11 (weekday lunch), followed by the set menu for €16; or around €23 à la carte. The charming owner, Chantal Ragot, has drawn together a list of fairly priced local wines.

Saint-Amand-Montrond

18200

◎ ⅍ 🏠 |●| Hôtel-Restaurant de la Croix d'Or

28 rue du 14-juillet; in the city-centre.
℡02.48.96.09.41 ℻02.48.96.72.89
Closed *Fri and Sat lunchtimes Nov–March except public holidays.*

The rooms are a bit dreary and ramshackle – doubles €40–53 – but the restaurant is a different story. It's been run for the last thirty years by the twin Moranges brothers, who have created a cuisine in perfect keeping with the small dining room – classic and bourgeois. Traditional dishes include hot foie gras with spiced caramel with a menu at €20 (not weekends or public holidays), or others at €30–48. *A free glass of Berrichon offered as apéritif to our readers on presentation of this guide.*

◎ ⅍ 🏠 |●| Le Noirlac

It's on the N144 towards Bourges, about 5km from the A71 motorway exit.
℡02.48.82.22.00 ℻02.48.82.22.01
🌐www.lenorliac.fr
Closed *19 Dec–1 Jan.* **Restaurant closed** *Fri evening, Sat lunchtime and Sun evening Nov–April.* **Disabled access. TV. High chairs and games available. Swimming pool.**

Situated near the hypermarket in an unprepossessing district on the outskirts of town, this establishment is of most use to travellers with a car. It's an ultra-modern place with good facilities including a pool, tennis court, golf course and also a lake and park. Rooms (€65) are comfortable and functional, and some of them have nice views of the countryside; buffet breakfast €5.95. The first menu (€13), served daily, is generous; others up to €25.50. Specialities include *charlottine* of red mullet with langoustine tails, *noisette* of beef fillet with shavings of Roquefort. *Free house apéritif offered to our readers on presentation of this guide.*

ⓐ |○| ⅍ Restaurant Le Saint-Jean

1 rue de l'Hôtel-Dieu; it's in the old town near the church.
☎02.48.96.39.82 ⓕ02.48.96.46.80
ⓔlesaintjean@wanadoo.fr
Closed Sun, Tues and Wed evenings; Mon; a week during winter school holidays; last week of Sept; first week in Oct.

Great restaurant with a rustic dining room complete with flowers, beams and a wonderful old parquet floor. Chef Philippe Perrichon prepares a quite incredible set menu for €17, with others at €20 and €26. Specialities include home-smoked pike perch with blinis and seaweed, salmon stuffed with green Berry lentils, and iced nougat. It's brilliant value and booking is essential at weekends. *Free coffee offered to our readers on presentation of this guide.*

Bruère-Allichamps
18200 (9km NW)

ⓐ |○| Auberge de l'Abbaye de Noirlac

2km up the N144 in the direction of Bourges and 5km up the A71 toll road.
☎02.48.96.22.58 ⓕ02.48.96.86.63
Closed Tues evening and Wed Sept–March; 15 Nov–20 Feb. **Disabled access.**

One of the old abbey chapels has been transformed into a restaurant with a bistro where, in summer, you can get cheap snacks – sandwiches, an omelette or a plate of charcuterie at reasonable prices. The restaurant proper, which serves more serious food, has red quarry-tiles on the floor, beams and exposed stonework. Chef Pascal Verdier cooks meat and fish with equal skill; try his fresh salmon with a fish purée, the Charolais steak, the goat's cheese terrine or the flambéed pineapple with chocolate. Prices are good – menus €17–28. The cheapest menu is not available during bank holidays.

Saint-Benoît-sur-Loire
45730

ⓐ ⅍ ⋔ Hôtel du Labrador**

7 pl. de l'Abbaye; it's opposite the basilica.

☎02.38.35.74.38 ⓕ02.38.35.72.99
ⓦwww.hoteldulabrador.fr
Hotel closed 26 Dec–20 Jan. **Restaurant closed** Sat lunchtime; Sun evening; Mon; 26 Dec–10 Jan. **Disabled access. TV. Car park. High chairs available.**

The hotel is in a little square which is wonderfully peaceful; it's a charming place. The rooms in the main building are a little cheaper than the others, and a couple of them have partial views of the abbey; doubles €50–65 with shower/wc or bath. Those in the newer annexe are more comfortable, though they lack the charm of the others. There's no restaurant but half board (€56 per person per night) can be arranged in conjunction with the Grand Saint-Benoît (see below), which is 200m away. *Free coffee offered to our readers on presentation of this guide.*

ⓐ ⅍ |○| Le Grand Saint-Benoît

7 pl. Saint-André.
☎02.38.35.11.92 ⓕ02.38.35.13.79
ⓦwww.hoteldulabrador.fr
Closed Sat lunchtime; Sun evening; Mon; 21 Aug–7 Sept; 18 Dec–11 Jan. **Disabled access. High chairs available.**

This establishment is one of the best tables in the region – but it's not one of the most expensive. The heavenly cuisine is simple, unusual and stamped with the personality of the chef. The weekday menu, €16, is perfectly adequate, but the €22.20 menu is splendid (other menus up to €45): snail pancake, roast pike perch with Chinon wine, and a hot savarin with chocolate and vanilla ice cream. There's a nice terrace on a pedestrian street. It's best to book. *Free coffee offered to our readers on presentation of this guide.*

Sainte-Maure-de-Touraine
37800

ⓐ ⋔ |○| ⅍ Hôtel-restaurant Le Cheval Blanc

55 av. du Général-de-Gaulle N10.
☎02.47.65.40.27 ⓕ02.47.65.58.90
ⓔgauvin.claude@wanadoo.fr
Closed Thurs evening and Fri lunchtime (in season); Fri all day and Sun evening (out of season); first fortnight in March; first fortnight in Dec. **Car park.**

This old staging post offers rooms with varying degrees of comfort, although they are all extremely well kept; the reserved but friendly owners, M. and Mme. Gavin, run their establishment with thorough diligence. Double rooms with shower/wc or bath go for €42–45. M. Gavin is an excellent cook who serves classic dishes with striking attention to detail on menus from €13. Logis de France. *Free house apéritif offered to our readers on presentation of this guide.*

ⓔ 🎄 |●| La Ciboulette

78 rte. de Chinon; 2km from the centre of Sainte-Maure, opposite the interchange of the A10 motorway, exit no. 25.
☏02.47.65.84.64
Closed *Mon evening, Tues evening and Sun evening from 10 Jan to 30 March, except in school time and for groups.* **Disabled access. Car park.**

Contemporary restaurant in a lush, flowery setting offering fast, friendly service. Huge dining room flooded with light, looking out onto the countryside, or a terrace under a pergola in fine weather. Pascal Daguet, the chef, is equally adept in the garden as in the kitchen; everything is home-made (even the bread), except the *andouillettte*. His cheapest menu, with an appetizer thrown in at the beginning, is very good value for money at €13, ideal for a quick meal, comprising starter plus main course or main course plus dessert or cheese; then three-course menus at €15.50–34.30. *Free house apéritif or coffee offered to our readers on presentation of this guide.*

Cussay
37240 (16km SE)

ⓔ |●| Auberge du Pont-Neuf

Take the D59 to Sepmes, then the D99.
☏02.47.59.66.37
Closed *Tues evening; Wed; 3 weeks in Feb; 2 weeks in early Nov.*

William Gellot, a chef renowned for his sauces, gave us a special treat with his cheapest menu (€17, including a dainty appetizer before the meal proper): beef pastry with vegetables to start, followed by exquisitely fresh cod with seafood, rounded off by a mouth-watering chocolate fondant. The sauces are extremely light, the presentation is delectable and the dining room is extremely elegant. The menu obviously changes with the season and the availability of ingredients, but the regulars who recommendeded this inn

have yet to be disappointed. It is worth noting the special coffee menu, with details of the beans' origin and characteristics. Logis de France.

Sancerre
18300

ⓔ |●| Auberge La Pomme d'Or

1 rue Panneterie. It's in the old town, towards the town hall.
☏02.48.54.13.30 ☏02.48.54.19.22
Closed *Tues and Wed; winter and All Saints' school holiday.* **Disabled access.**

An elegant restaurant in a narrow street in the old part of town. The dining room is cosy and attractive, while the cooking uses fresh, seasonal produce. It's traditional without being too heavy, with a few rustic touches: try the hot goat's cheese wrapped in sheets of brick pasta. The €17 menu (not Sat evening or Sun lunch) is excellent value and there are others at €25–42. The proprietor, Didier Turpin, is the master of his cellar and offers a wonderful selection of wines at very attractive prices. Reservations essential.

Saint-Satur
18300 (3km NE)

ⓔ 🎄 🏠 |●| Hôtel-restaurant Le Laurier**

29 rue du Commerce; take the D955 and the D4.
☏02.48.54.17.20 ☏02.48.54.04.54
🌐www.tablegourmandeduberry.com
Closed *Sun evening; Mon; Thurs except July–Aug; 3 weeks in March; 3 weeks in Nov.* **TV. High chairs and games available. Car park.**

You'll find this place swathed in Virginia creeper and a stone's throw from a handsome abbey. The dining room, with its copperware, exposed beams and old wooden furniture, has clearly been decorated by someone with a taste for authenticity. There are six newly refurbished double rooms with bath costing €45 – prices are truly reasonable for this very touristy area. The restaurant offers good regional cooking with set menus at €15–40. Its specialities are poached eggs in wine *à l'ancienne* and calf's kidneys with mustard seeds. Logis de France. *Free coffee offered to our readers on presentation of this guide.*

Saint-Thibault

18300 (3km E)

☜ ☎ ⚓ Hôtel de la Loire***

2 quai de la Loire in Saint-Thibault, 3km from
Sancerre on the road to Cosne.
☎02.48.78.22.22 ☎02.48.78.22.29
www.hotel-de-la-loire.com
Closed 18 Dec–8 Jan. **Disabled access.**

This charming hotel, on the roadside
but overlooking the Loire, is well worth
the room rate. The comfortable rooms
(€65–85) are each decorated on a different theme – you wouldn't be surprised to
see them in a modish interiors mag. Their
names give you a clue as to their look;
Georges Simenon (he wrote two of his
novels here), African Queen, Louis XIV,
Provençal, Colonial, Indian and so on. *Free
coffee offered to our readers on presentation of
this guide.*

Chavignol

18300 (5km W)

☜ ❙●❙ Restaurant des Monts Damnés

☎02.48.54.01.72 ☎02.48.54.14.24
Closed Sun evening; Tues evening; Wed;
Feb. **High chairs and baby changing tables
available. Disabled access.**

The "damned mountains" give their
name both to a highly reputed vineyard
in Sancerre and to this inn, a rustic place
with beams, patterned curtains and a
cosy atmosphere. Local produce plays the
central role in robust dishes with a very
distinct character on menus €26–46.
The wine list is full of bargains from
all parts of France. There's a pergola for
sunny days.

Sancoins

18600

☜ ☎ Hôtel du Parc**

8 rue Marguerite-Audoux.
☎02.48.74.56.60 ☎02.48.74.61.30
www.hotel-du-parc-sancoins.com
Closed sometimes on Sun noon–6pm. **TV.
Car park.**

This classy place looks like a château and
is set in extensive grounds. The rooms are
lovely and quiet; very good-value doubles
with shower or bath €44, or €54 for
rooms sleeping up to four.

Souvigny-en-Sologne

41600

☜ ❙●❙ ⚓ La Perdrix Rouge

22 rue du Gâtinais.
☎02.54.88.41.05
Closed Mon; Tues; 17 Feb–3 March; 1–9
July; 27 Aug–4 Sept. **Disabled access.
Games available.**

Lovely dining room, both rustic and sophisticated, with an impressive fireplace, shrewdly
chosen furniture and prettily laid tables. You
will receive a warm welcome, elegant but
discreet service and food that is a delight
to behold – traditional dishes injected with
new life and prepared with only the best
and freshest ingredients. First there are some
delicious appetizers before the starter itself,
then comes the main course – light, savoury
and aromatic: *fricassée* of blue lobster with
herbs and farm-raised squab with cabbage.
Good value for money: menus €15 (weekdays), then others €25–50 (from €30 on
Sunday). *Free liqueur offered to our readers on
presentation of this guide.*

Sully-sur-Loire

45600

☜ ⚓ ☎ ❙●❙ Hôtel-restaurant de la Poste**

11 rue du Faubourg-Saint-Germain.
☎02.38.36.26.22 ☎02.38.36.39.35
TV. Car park.

This place is an old staging post, and
despite its slightly forbidding exterior it's
something of a local institution – the large
cage full of parrots is equally renowned.
Some of the rooms in the annexe have
a limited view of the Loire; in the main
building, you'll have to make do with the
TV. Doubles cost from €40 with washing
facilities to €46 with shower/wc or bath.
A few have been set aside for non-smokers. Menus, €15–40, feature lots of local
dishes and fish specialities. *Free coffee offered
to our readers on presentation of this guide.*

Tours

37000
See map overleaf

☜ ☎ Auberge de jeunesse

5 rue Bretonneau; close to the old Tours city-
centre and the Loire. **Map A1-1**

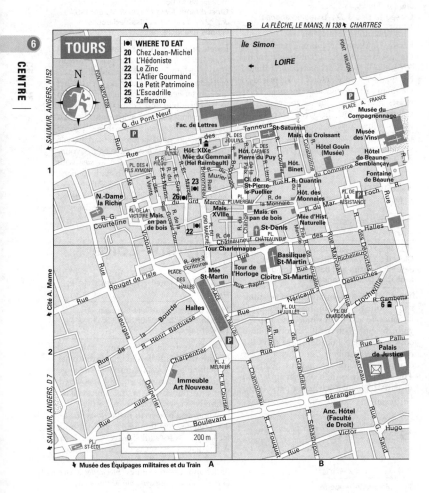

TOURS

|●| WHERE TO EAT
20 Chez Jean-Michel
21 L'Hédoniste
22 Le Zinc
23 L'Atlier Gourmand
24 Le Petit Patrimoine
25 L'Escadrille
26 Zafferano

A
B   *LA FLÈCHE, LE MANS, N 138* ↖ *CHARTRES*

Île Simon

LOIRE

PONT WILSON

PLACE   A. FRANCE

Musée du
Compagnonnage

SAUMUR, ANGERS, N152

PONT NAPOLÉON

N

Q. du Pont Neuf

Fac. de Lettres

Tanneurs   St-Saturnin

Mais. du Croissant

Musée
des Vins

Rue

Rue

des

PL. DES
JOULINS

PL. DES
CARMES

Constantine

Hôtel Gouïn
(Musée)

Hôtel
de Beaune-
Semblançay

Hôt. XIXe

PL. J.
DUVAL

PL. R.
PIGOU

Mée du Gemmail
(Hel Raimbault)

Hôt.
Pierre du Puy

du Commerce

PL. DES 4
FILS AYMONT

R. du
Péronneau

Rue

Marcel

du Murier

R. des
4 Vents

Paix

Cl. de
St-Pierre-
le-Puellier

R. R. Quantin

Hôt.
Binet

Fontaine
de Beaune

1

N.-Dame
la Riche

R. G.
Courteline

PL. DE LA
VICTOIRE

Mais.
en pan
de bois

23

26

Grd

Marché PLUMEREAU

Mais.
XVIIIe

R. de
la Monnaie

Rue de

Hôt. des
Monnaies

R. du Mar.

PL. DE
LA
RÉSISTANCE

Foch

R.

22

R. de la
Grosse Tour

R. du
GRD MARCHÉ

R. du
Change

PL.
CHÂTEAUNEUF

Mais. en
pan de bois

St-Denis

Mée d'Hist.
Naturelle

Prés
Mervin

Rue Marceau

Halles

des

Rue des Déportés

Rue de Châteauneuf

Tour Charlemagne

Rue

R. des 3
Écritoires

Cité A. Mame

Rue

Rue

Rouget de l'Isle

PLACE
DES
HALLES

Mée
St-Martin

Tour de
l'Horloge

Rue Rapin

Basilique
St-Martin

Cloître St-Martin

Rigoleux

Richelieu

Destouches

R. Gambetta

6

Clocheville

Georges

la

Bourde

R. Henri Barbusse

Halles

PLACE

G. Paillou

Rue

Néricault

PL. DU
14 JUILLET

PL. DU
CHARDONNET

Rue

de

Rue E. Pallu

Palais
de Justice

SAUMUR, ANGERS, D 7

2

Rue

de

Charpentier

PL. J.
MEUNIER

R. la Coursat

Rue

Rue

Chamonaliau

R. de Vinci

la Grandière

Rue

Béranger

Marceau

Immeuble
Art Nouveau

Jules

Delpetier

Rue

Boulevard

R. J. Fouquet

R. Sébastopol

Anc. Hôtel
(Faculté
de Droit)

Rue

Victor

R. G. Hugo

R. Sand

PL.
ST-ÉLOI

0   200 m

↓ Musée des Équipages militaires et du Train   A
B

6

CENTRE

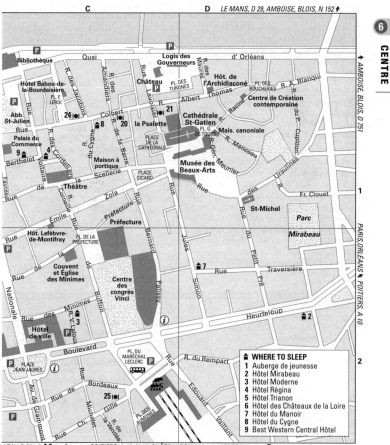

C   D   LE MANS, D 29, AMBOISE, BLOIS, N 152 ↑

AMBOISE, BLOIS, D 751 →

PARIS, ORLÉANS ↘ POITIERS, A 10

WHERE TO SLEEP
1 Auberge de jeunesse
2 Hôtel Mirabeau
3 Hôtel Moderne
4 Hôtel Régina
5 Hôtel Trianon
6 Hôtel des Châteaux de la Loire
7 Hôtel du Manoir
8 Hôtel du Cygne
9 Best Western Central Hôtel

AZAY, D 751 ↓ ♜ 5, St-Étienne, POITIERS, A 10, N 10, CHÂTEAUROUX, N 143, VIERZON, N 76   D

℗02.47.37.81.58 ℗02.47.37.96.11
Open 8am-noon and 6-10pm.

Impressive, brand-new youth hostel in a functional, modern building. It sleeps 146 people, spread out in rooms with two to six beds, and in some cases with showers/wc (otherwise they're on the landing), for €17 the first night (including sheets and breakfast), €14 the following ones. One section houses rooms intended for families, and a kitchen is available for use by guests. There's a garage for bikes and motorbikes; cars can be parked by the quay on the Loire.

◎ ☖ Hôtel Régina*

2 rue Pimbert; behind the Grand Théâtre.
Map C1-4
℗02.47.05.25.36 ℗02.47.66.08.72
Closed Christmas school holiday. **Open** until 1am.

A cheap, cheerful, simple and clean hotel with window boxes full of flowers. It's excellent value for money, really pretty and you quickly feel at home. The soundproofing is good and the cleanliness is evidenced by the nice smell of polish. The rooms are fresh looking and all different; a double room with hand basin is €24, €28 with shower, €32 with shower/wc. There's a free garage for motorcycles and bikes.

◎ ☖ Hôtel Mirabeau

89 bis bd. Heurteloup. **Map D2-2**
℗02.47.05.24.60 ℗02.47.05.31.09
ⓦwww.hotel-mirabeau.fr
Closed 24 Dec–2 Jan. **Car park.**

In this long-standing, efficiently run family hotel, the rooms are attractively decorated and furnished in an old-fashioned style, complemented by modern conveniences (those overlooking the boulevard are soundproofed), and a lift has been installed. Doubles go for €35–50, according to the size and the season, with shower/wc or bath. Breakfast is served in the pretty dining room or, in summer, in the garden.

◎ ☖ |◉| ⅔ Hôtel-restaurant Moderne**

1–3 rue Victor-Laloux; parallel to rue Buffon, close to the train station and the town hall.
Map C2-3
℗02.47.05.32.81
ⓔhotel.moderne37@wanadoo.fr

Restaurant closed evenings (open for hotel guests only). **TV.**

This hotel, a fine building in traditional Touraine style, is on a corner in a quiet neighbourhood. There are twenty-three rooms in all (€37 with shower/wc, €55.50 with bath); the ones in the attic are cosy and have sloping ceilings, others have mezzanines. Set menus featuring superb rustic family cooking, €12.50 and €15.50, are served weekday evenings for hotel guests only. Logis de France. 10% discount on the room rate (Nov to end Feb) or free apéritif offered to our readers on presentation of this guide.

◎ ⅔ ☖ Hôtel des Châteaux de la Loire

12 rue Gambetta. **Map B2-6**
℗02.47.05.10.05 ℗02.47.20.20.14
ⓔhoteldeschateaux.tours@wanadoo.fr
Closed Early Dec to end Feb. **Pay car park.**

The rooms here (doubles at €39.50–55, with shower/wc or bath) are spacious and comfortable, and most have been completely renovated. There's a beautiful reception flooded with light and a lift going up to the upper floors, and also a pretty breakfast room. This reliable hotel offers attentive and friendly service. 10% discount on the price of a room offered to our readers on presentation of this guide.

◎ ☖ Hôtel Trianon

57 av. Grammont from pl. Jean-Jaurès, go down avenue Grammont; the hotel is situated after the fourth turning, on the left. **Off map C2-5**
℗02.47.05.35.27 ℗02.47.64.22.45

The rooms here (€40–55) are all different, with cosy decoration, cane furniture and pretty fabrics. Recommended.

◎ ⅔ ☖ Hôtel du Manoir

2 rue Traversière; in a quiet street near the train station. **Map D2-7**
℗02.47.05.37.37 ℗02.47.05.16.00
Closed a week in Feb.

A family hotel in the fashionable part of Tours dating from the nineteenth century (although the rooms have been tastefully refurbished). Some rooms are charming garrets, while others have communicating doors, making them ideal for families. All have been decorated with pastel colours and English-style furniture and cost €46–52 for a double, with shower/wc or bath. Breakfast is served in a delightfully refurbished vaulted cellar. Friendly welcome and tranquillity are guaranteed. *Free parking offered to our readers on presentation of this guide.*

ⓔ ⓐ Hôtel du Cygne

6 rue du Cygne. **Map C1-8**
ⓣ02.47.66.66.41 ⓕ02.47.66.05.13
ⓦperso.wanadoo.fr/hotelcygne.tours
Pay car park.

One of Tour's oldest hotels, right in the city centre. Behind the white façade, the interior has been totally refurbished. Doubles cost €48–62, depending on the size and which floor they are on (no lift). The spacious rooms with high ceilings on the first floor are all different and especially attractive (particularly nos. 4, 5, 6 and 8); those on the higher floors are smaller but less expensive. For breakfast, there are several fine cafés on the nearby rue Colbert.

ⓔ 🎴 ⓐ Best Western Central Hôtel

21 rue Berthelot; in a quiet street behind the theatre. **Map C1-9**
ⓣ02.47.05.46.44 ⓕ02.47.66.10.26
ⓦwww.tours-online.com/central-hotel
Closed 26 Dec–4 Jan. **Pay car park.**

Beautiful four-storey building, overlooking a pretty garden on one side, and an immense courtyard on the other (part of which has been equipped to serve breakfast on fine days – although the room used in winter is also pleasant). Spacious and functional rooms with high ceilings and decoration in pastel colours go for €91–113, with shower or bath, double bed or twin beds. You'll get highly professional service, as to be expected in a hotel of this category. *Free house apéritif offered to our readers on presentation of this guide.*

ⓔ ⏣ Chez Jean-Michel

123 rue Colbert. **Map C1-20**
ⓣ02.47.20.80.20
Closed Sat, Sun and public holidays; 25 Dec–4 Jan; 1–10 May; 1–20 Aug.

A good spot for lovers of meat (*croustillant* of pigeon, grouse with foie gras) and fine wines, particularly as the owner was formerly a wine waiter in several prestigious restaurants. He is always on hand to provide a personal touch in this relaxed, bistro-style setting. There are menus for

€10 and €13 (lunchtime only), then €26. It is advisable to book.

ⓔ ⏣ Le Zinc

27 pl. du Grand-Marché. **Map A1-22**
ⓣ02.47.20.29.00
Closed Sun.

Excellent little, family-run restaurant, with food that fuses innovation and tradition – with particular emphasis on the latter in winter: *pot-au-feu* and calf's head. In summer, the dishes are lighter and more adventurous – the exquisite honey-roasted Camembert, for example. Pretty dining room with small zinc tables and exposed beams, serving a lunchtime menu at €10.50, dinner menus at €18.50 or €23.50. The selection of wines is resolutely local; wine can be ordered by the glass.

ⓔ 🎴 ⏣ L'Hédoniste

16 rue Lavoisier. **Map C1-21**
ⓣ02.47.05.20.40
Closed Sun; Mon.

A few bistro-style tables, exposed stone on the walls, a lacquered red ceiling, a cosy little nook by the fireplace (not used, unfortunately). The young owner and his father (retired researcher in molecular biology and wine lover, with an extraordinary gift of the gab) have only recently flung themselves into the adventure of running a restaurant, treating both regulars from the clinic opposite and first-timers with the same amiability and respect. The set menus are well balanced, and even the cheapest (€11) is highly satisfying (choice of at least two starters and main courses, plus coffee or a glass of wine); other menus €22 and €29. You can wash them down with a choice of a dozen wines sold by the glass. Dishes include delicacies such as farmhouse *andouillette* and fillet of pike perch with pickled shallots and red wine – and, unusually, the desserts maintain the same high standard. All in all, an unpretentious but excellent restaurant, often enlivened by a soundtrack of jazz. *Free Touraine sloe apéritif offered to our readers on presentation of this guide.*

ⓔ ⏣ Le Petit Patrimoine

58 rue Colbert; in the old town, near the Loire and the castle. **Map C1-24**
ⓣ02.47.66.05.81
Closed Sun lunchtime.

A regional restaurant of quality. The

owner has a real interest in preserving the cuisine of the Touraine, though he's always looking for ways to take it gently forward; menus €12–26. If you've got room for dessert, try the pears in wine or the *pruneaux* in Vouvray. Very long dining room painted salmon-pink, with old photos of the region on the wall. AmEx not accepted. It's best to book.

@ ⅓ |●| Zafferano

7–9 rue de la Grosse Tour; in the old town, near Place Plumereau. **Map A1-26**
☎02.47.38.90.77
Closed *Sun; Mon; a week in the winter school holidays; 3 weeks in Aug.*

This is no ordinary pizzeria. They serve an array of Italian dishes from different regions and the pasta is fresh and homemade. Forget about turgid tomato sauce and let them surprise you with dishes like pasta zafferano (fresh home-made ribbons of pasta with smoked bacon and saffron cream sauce), rigatoni alla bolognese (winter only), or fettuccine with saffron cream. And their meat dishes are amazing – the saltimbocca, the veal escalope with lemon, the lamb noisettes with herb marinade and the osso buco are prepared with precision; killer desserts, too, especially their ultra-light tiramisù. Pasta dish of the day costs €9, menus at €15 and €25. You'll find the same quality on the mainly Italian wine list, and there's a small grocery counter selling Italian specialities and a bookshop selling titles on cookery, wine, and the regions and music of Italy. Several dining rooms with simple, elegant décor dominated by bright yellows. A few tables are put out on the little square next door in fine weather. All this, plus a fantastic atmosphere means that reservations are advised. Credit cards accepted for bills of more than €15. *Free digestif offered to our readers on presentation of this guide.*

@ ⅓ |●| L'Atelier Gourmand

37 rue Étienne-Marcel; in the old Tours city-centre. **Map A1-23**
☎02.47.38.59.87
Closed *Mon lunchtime; Sat lunchtime; Sun; 15 Dec–15 Jan.* **Open** *noon–2pm and 7.30–10.30pm.*

In the heart of old Tours, locals flock assiduously to the culinary laboratory of Fabrice Bironneau, formerly of *Chez Bardet*. A long room decorated in rustic bistro style, with reassuringly solid-look-

ing beams and walls painted in warm colours, covered in posters announcing major cultural events from the past and a few paintings produced by friends. There's a friendly atmosphere and the food is equally heartwarming and colourful, demonstrating invention, precision and quality. The essence of the ingredients is respected and they are cooked meticulously, enriched by carefully chosen herbs and spices – and the result is succulent delicacies like pork cheek with honey and rosemary. Or, what can be more refreshing than a spicy curried courgette gazpacho or a tomato and melon soup with Sichuan pepper when there's a sweltering heat outside? Such dishes are simple and tasty but light (like the bill). The set lunchtime menu of main course, salad and dessert costs €8.50; there's another menu at €18, or à la carte. *Free glass of sparkling Vouvray offered to our readers on presentation of this guide.*

@ ⅓ |●| L'Escadrille

30 rue Charles-Gille; 100m from the train station. **Map C2-25**
☎02.47.20.94.94
Closed *Sun; 15–20 Aug.* **Open** *noon–2.30pm, 6.45–10.30pm.*

This *Escadrille* (squadron) is well worth an inspection. In a delightful, air-conditioned wooden setting, reminiscent of a flying club, under a sky painted with a constellation of aeroplanes, "passengers" are served extremely fresh food, in a style somewhere between bistro and *cordon bleu*, prepared, in full view, by a graduate from *Chez Bardet*. It is famous for its crunchy pig's trotters and also offers a fine selection of fish on menus at €18 (lunchtime only), €23 and €30. The owner is charming. *Free coffee offered to our readers on presentation of this guide.*

Rochecorbon
37210 (3km NE)

@ ⅓ 🏠 Hôtel Les Fontaines**

6 quai de la Loire; on the RN52, towards Blois.
☎02.47.52.52.86 ℻02.47.52.85.05
🌐www.tours-online.com/lesfontaines
TV. Car park.

A charming, professionally run hotel; it's a pity it's so close to the main road, although the big trees in the shady park form a relatively effective sound barrier. The bedrooms, spread over three floors, are all different but equally large, comfortable and prettily furnished. The double rooms in the manor house, with shower/wc or bath, go for €39–57 according to the season; those in the old gardener's lodge are simpler, ideal for families (bunks for children) or limited budgets (€39). There's a delightful breakfast room and the service is faultless. *10% discount on the room rate (Oct–March) offered to our readers on presentation of this guide.*

◎ |●| KAuberge des Belles Rives

Lieu-dit Vauvert; at the Rochecorbon exit going towards Vouvray, on the N152.
☎02.47.52.52.97

In a dining room with a view of the Loire, or in the garden on fine days, Yannick Bruneau prepares delicious, healthy food based on fresh ingredients. Particularly outstanding on our visit were the langoustine gazpacho and thin strips of lamb with tarragon pistou available on the cheapest menu (€21, others up to €40). Efficient and friendly service is provided by the owner and her team.

Fondettes
37230 (5km W)

◎ |●| Auberge de Porc-Vallières

Vallières; take the N152 in the direction of Langeais-Saumur.
☎02.47.42.24.04 ☎02.47.49.98.83
Closed *Mon and Tues evenings; Wed; winter school holidays; last 3 weeks in Aug.*

Because the inn is right on the edge of the N152, you might hesitate to stop. But it's worth it. There are armfuls of wild flowers from the fields in huge vases and a relaxed, pleasant atmosphere; you hardly hear the traffic at all. The welcome and service are friendly and straightforward and the inventive cuisine brilliantly judged. There's a €20 menu in the week or reckon on €38 à la carte. They list original dishes and various specialities subtly prepared by one of the owners, such as authentic fried fish from the Loire and pig's trotters "Mary-Magdalene". The first dining room (near the road) is reserved for groups, who usually manage to drown out the noise of the traffic with their festivities. The other room, situated in the back (and therefore quieter), is austere but pretty, with walls painted and decorated by an artist friend of the owners.

Vouvray
37210 (8km E)

◎ ☗ |●| ♨ Le Grand Vatel

8 rue Léon Brulé.
☎02.47.52.70.32
Closed *Sun evening; Mon; a week over Christmas/New Year; second fortnight in March.* **Car park.**

The main reason for coming here is the high-quality food prepared by Frédéric Scicluma, based on fresh ingredients. It is served in a large, opulent dining room with a high ceiling or, weather permitting, on the terrace (due to be enlarged to escape from the noise of the road); Scicluma's jovial wife will give you sound advice when you choose your meal. One particularly striking dish is the *beuchelle tourangelle*, an original reinterpretation of a regional classic; the desserts are no less enticing: try the delicious egg *brouillade* with red fruit. Menus range from €18.50 (except public holidays) to €40, and there are impressive lists of Vouvray wines, served by the glass. There are a few simple, slightly run-down rooms upstairs: doubles with shower/wc or bath €36–39. *Free house apéritif offered to our readers on presentation of this guide.*

◎ |●| Les Chalands, Au Virage Gastronomique

Off the N152, at the traffic lights, at the entrance to Vouvray.
☎02.47.52.70.02
Closed *Mon evening and Tues (except July–Aug).*

An excellent restaurant as regards the prices, the quality of the food and its presentation, and the genuinely friendly welcome of the owners (all qualities that are becoming increasingly rare in the region). There's a bistro-style mid-week lunchtime menu (starter plus main course or main course plus dessert) at €12; a copious tasting menu at €14; and menus at €15, €18.50 and €25. Some of the produce on offer is from Hardouin, the famous charcuterie next door (*rillettes de Tours, andouillette au Vouvray*).

Semblançay
37360 (12km NW)

◎ ♨ ☗ |●| Hostellerie de la Mère Hamard**

Place de l'Église; take the N138 in the direction of Le Mans.

☎02.47.56.62.04 ℗02.47.56.61.67
✉merehamard@wanadoo.fr
Closed *Sun evening; Mon; Tues lunchtime in high season; Feb.* **TV. High chairs available. Car park.**

You'll dine on delicious regional dishes and gourmet cuisine. The dining room is comfortable and welcoming with menus €16 (not Sun) up to €45. Specialities include duck foie gras with morels, pigeon with truffle jus and potato cakes with foie gras. There are ten lovely double rooms in a delightful annexe at €61 with shower/wc or bath; half board around €77 per person. Logis de France. *Free coffee offered to our readers on presentation of this guide.*

Monnaie
37380 (14km NE)

⌨ ⚞ |●| Restaurant Au Soleil Levant

53 rue Nationale; it's on the N10.
☎02.47.56.10.34 ℗02.47.56.45.22
Closed *Sun and Thurs evenings; Mon; 1–15 Jan; 1–21 Aug.* **High chairs available.**

This is among the best gourmet restaurants in the area, with a stylish interior decorated in bright, luminous colours. Jean-Pierre Kahlem produces exceptional dishes imaginatively combining the best ingredients of the season. There's a *formule* at €13 and menus at €18 (except Sun) and €27–37. Good dishes include calf kidneys with mustard. *Free coffee offered to our readers on presentation of this guide.*

Neuillé-le-Lierre
37380 (15km NE)

⌨ ☎ |●| ⚞ Auberge de la Brenne

19 rue de la République; 10 min northwest of Vouvray.
☎02.47.52.95.05 ℗02.47.52.29.43
Closed *Tues evening; Wed; Sun evening (Oct–May); 26 Jan–2 March.* **Disabled access.**

This village inn set amidst bucolic scenery offers traditional food at its most rustic. Do not expect anything too subtle or light here on the menus, €19 (except weekends and public holidays), and €23–45. The owner, Ghislaine Sallé, is so devoted to time-honoured practices that she even makes her own rillettes (potted meat) and jams – for sale in the reception area. Her pride and joy, however, is her "île flottante" (the "real" version, accord-

ing to her). Double rooms go for €57–74 with shower or bath. Expect unbeatable cooking, charming décor and genuine atmosphere. Logis de France. *Free Kir or home-made produce (for guests taking at least one meal a day at the hotel) offered to our readers on presentation of this guide.*

Vannes-sur-Cosson
45510

⌨ |●| Restaurant Le Vieux Relais

2 rte. d'Isdes; 25km east of La Ferté-Saint-Aubin.
☎02.38.58.04.14
Closed *Sun evening; Mon; Tues; first fortnight in Aug; mid-Dec to mid-Jan.* **Car park.**

It's obvious that this superb Solognote manor house is pretty old – but you probably wouldn't guess that the original buildings go back to 1462 and that the beams come from a building in the 800s. It's been an inn since 1515 and is one of the six oldest in France. It's an absolutely sumptuous place and the cooking doesn't let the surroundings down, so it's essential to book. You should certainly go for the chef's foie gras if it's on the menu. He uses seasonal produce for all his dishes so it's hard to list his specialities but the game is superb, as are the langoustine tails – and don't miss out on the *crème brûlée* either. Menus start at €16 (not served on public holidays), then €23.50 and €31. Credit cards not accepted.

Ménestreau-en-Villette
45240 (18km E)

⌨ |●| ⚞ Le Relais de Sologne

63 pl. du 8-Mai. Take the D120 to Sennely, then the D17.
☎02.38.76.97.40
Closed *Sun evening; Tues evening; Wed; several weeks in Feb.*

This restaurant-caterers is run by the chef Thierry Roger, a virtuoso of French cuisine. The inviting dining room is decorated in the purest local style: red bricks and half-timbering, warm, diffuse lighting, an abundance of fresh flowers and green plants, all in a rich harmony of colours. It is hard to imagine a more pleasant setting for enjoying the sophisticated traditional cooking. The menu changes regularly according to the seasonal produce available: weekday lunchtime menu €16, other menus €26–46.50. The speciality is the pan-fried veal sweetbreads with ceps. The desserts are exquisite, and you can wash the whole meal down with some splendid wines. All in all, a visit to *Le Relais* is an essential stopover for visitors to the beautiful Sologne countryside. *Free coffee offered to our readers on presentation of this guide.*

Vendôme
41100

@ 🛍 |O| 🎋 Hôtel-restaurant
L'Auberge de la Madeleine**

Place de la Madeleine; head in the direction of Blois.
☎02.54.77.20.79 ℻02.54.80.00.02
Closed *Feb.* **Restaurant closed** *Wed.* **TV.**

An unpretentious, welcoming and friendly place with attractive rooms; nos. 7 and 8 are the largest. Doubles are €34.50 with shower/wc and €38.50 with bath. Good plain cooking with set menus €15–36.30. Specialities include calf's head, pike perch with vanilla and *tournedos* with morels. You can eat out in the garden. *Free coffee offered to our readers on presentation of this guide.*

@ 🎋 |O| Restaurant Le Paris

1 rue Darreau; from the city-centre, take faubourg Chartrain towards the SNCF train station and turn left after the railway track.
☎02.54.77.02.71 ℻02.54.73.17.71
Closed *Mon; Tues; Aug.*

An excellent gourmet restaurant. It's run by a charming woman, the service is faultless and the chef – who has a particular talent for sauces and for meat and fish dishes – is inspired. The specialities include the semi-cooked foie gras *pain d'épices*, or the *ravioles* of duck or prawns with set menus €14–29.50. Try a good local wine like the Bourgueil Domaine Lalande. *Free coffee offered to our readers on presentation of this guide.*

Saint-Ouen
41100 (2km N)

@ |O| La Vallée

34 rue Barré-de-Saint-Venant; from Vendôme, take the D92 and head for Paris and the centre of Saint-Ouen.

☎02.54.77.29.93 ℻02.54.73.16.96
Closed *Mon; Tues; Sun evening Nov to Easter; a week in Jan; fortnight early March; last fortnight in Sept.* **Disabled access. High chairs, games and swings available.**

Don't let the uninspiring exterior put you off – go straight in and take a look at the menus. You won't regret it: even the cheapest at €17 (not served Sat or Sun) boasts a selection of delights; other menus €24–32. The specialities change with the seasons, the cooking is sophisticated and the dishes are beautifully presented. Note that they stop serving at 8.45pm.

Pezou
41100 (15km NE)

@ |O| Auberge de la Sellerie

Fontaine; it's off the RN10 between Chartres and Vendôme.
☎02.54.23.41.43 ℻02.54.23.48.00
Closed *Sun evening; Mon; Wed evening; Jan.* **Open** *noon–1.45pm and 7.30–9pm.* **High chairs available.**

It's a good inn, with rustic but chic décor, set back from the main road from Chartres to Vendôme. There's an appetizing menu at €14.20, which changes nearly every day and includes half a bottle of wine and coffee; other menus up to €44. The cuisine is rich, inventive and of good quality. The specialities include *flambées* prawns and roasted lobster.

Lavardin
41800 (18km SW)

@ |O| Le Relais d'Antan

6 pl. du Capitaine du Vignau; take the D917, when you get to Saint-Rimay, turn left on the road to Montoire.
☎02.54.86.61.33 ℻02.54.85.06.46
Closed *Mon; Tues; Sun evening Oct–April; fortnight in Feb; 3 weeks in Oct.* **Disabled access. High chairs available.**

You're in for a real feast – and at a reasonable price. The choice is deliberately limited so the chef can ensure only the freshest ingredients are used to create his refined, inventive dishes: the menu changes monthly. Two menus at €26 and €35; the last includes a fish and a meat course. Service is friendly and the dining room is pretty; they only have a few tables so you need to book.

Veuil

36600

@ |●| **Auberge Saint-Fiacre****

5 rue de la Fontaine; take the D15. It's 6km
from Valençay.
☎02.54.40.32.78
Closed *Sun evening and Mon except public
holidays; Tues and Wed in low season (prior
booking only); 3 weeks in Jan; a fortnight
early Sept.*

A seventeenth-century inn in a flower-
filled village with a stream running
through it. In summer you dine under
the ancient chestnut trees to the accom-
paniment of the trickling fountain, and in
winter around the giant fireplace. The chef
changes his menus frequently, inspired by
fresh seasonal produce and what is good at
the market. Menus range from €20 (not
Sun) to €44.

Vierzon

18100

@ |●| ⚒ **La Maison de Célestin**

20 av. Pierre Sémard; it's opposite the station.
☎02.48.83.01.63
Closed *Sun evening; Mon; Sat lunch; 1–20
Jan; 1–23 Aug.* **Disabled access. High
chairs available.**

A modern, stylish restaurant in a semi-
circular veranda overlooking a garden and
some quite lovely old industrial buildings.
Pascal Chaupitre is a young chef who's
going places. He uses fresh produce combining inventivenes and convention; he
has a talent for putting surprising flavours
together but is respectful of Berry traditions as well. The dishes on the cheapest
menu (€22) are really excellent, which
is unusual, and there are other menus up
to €58. *Free coffee offered to our readers on
presentation of this guide.*

Yvoy-le-Marron

41600

@ 🏠 |●| **Auberge du Cheval
Blanc**

1 pl. du Cheval-Blanc; it's 4.5 km to the
northwest of Chaumont-sur-Tharonne via
the D35.

☎02.54.94.00.00 ☎02.54.94.00.01
✉www.aubergeduchevalblanc.com
Closed *2–7 Jan; 7–23 March; 29 Aug–6 Sept.*
Restaurant closed *Mon–Thurs lunchtimes (1
Jan–30 April); Mon and Tues lunchtimes
(1 May-31 Dec).* **Disabled access. TV.**

This hotel-restaurant in the heart of the
Sologne has a decidedly Parisian feel –
unsurprising perhaps, as all the rooms have
been superbly refurbished and redecorated
by an interior designer from the capital.
The result is a chic, tasteful setting, with
thick carpets, warm colours and impeccable bedding that even the most coddled
city slicker will find comfortable. Doubles
go for €75–85. There's a weekday lunchtime menu for €20, others €28–35. You
can expect discreet but friendly service.

Yzeures-sur-
Creuse

37290

@ 🏠 |●| **Hôtel-restaurant La
Promenade*****

1 pl. du 11-Novembre; take the D104
towards Yzeures-sur-Creuse. It's just opposite the church.
☎02.47.91.49.00 ☎02.47.94.46.12
Closed *Mon and Tues (except guests on half-
board); 15 Jan–13 Feb.* **Open** *noon–2pm and
7.30–8.45pm.* **TV. Car park.**

This hotel is in a handsome eighteenth-century building which used to
be a coaching inn. The fifteen rooms are
decorated in restrained rustic style, some
with beams and others with fireplaces;
doubles with bath/wc €47-53. Half
board is available at €49 per person.
There's a small sitting room with a piano
on the mezzanine. Mme Bussereau creates delicious dishes that bear her own
inventive imprint from the best produce
she can find in the market – game in
season, free-range poultry and excellent
fish. She also makes the house terrines
and bakes the bread. Set menus are €20
(except for public holidays) and €47.

Champagne

Arcis-sur-Aube
10700

ⓔ |●| Le Saint-Hubert

2 rue de la Marine; it's signposted from the centre.
☎03.25.37.86.93
Closed Sat; Fri and Sun evenings; last week in Dec; first week in Jan; last week in July and first fortnight in Aug. **High chairs available.**

You'll go a long way to find an owner who puts her guests so quickly at ease and, in the midst of the service, even finds time to set the world to rights. The dining room has a certain elegance, and the traditional cuisine is well prepared and astonishingly good value. The lunch menu costs €13, with others €15–27. The lovely terrace looks over the river.

Bar-sur-Aube
10200

ⓔ 🏃 🏠 Hôtel Bar à Vins Saint-Pierre

5 rue Saint-Pierre; opposite the Saint-Pierre church.
☎03.25.27.13.58 ⊕03.25.27.24.35
Closed Sun and Mon. **Car park.**

A simple, well-run small hotel just opposite the twelfth-century Saint-Pierre church, a nice place offering very reasonable prices. Rooms 1, 8, 9 and 10 have a view of the church but be warned: the bells start ringing at 7am. Doubles with basin €27, or €33 with shower/wc. There's no restaurant, but there is a lively bar where you can eat breakfast (€4; not available Sun and public holidays). There is also a menu at

€14. *Free house apéritif offered to our readers on presentation of this guide.*

ⓔ 🏃 🏠 Hôtel Le Saint-Nicholas***

2 rue du Général-de-Gaulle.
☎03.25.27.08.65 ⊕03.25.27.60.31
TV. High chairs available. Swimming pool.

A short distance from the centre. This old bourgeois house is on the corner of two streets and has a garden with a swimming pool behind it. All the rooms are sound-proofed and air-conditioned and have shower/wc or bath – €60 for a double; €85 for a suite with Jacuzzi. The décor is contemporary but has a charm dictated by the lovely old building. There's also a sauna. *10% discount on the room rate offered to our readers on presentation of this guide.*

ⓔ |●| Un P'tit Creux

Place du Corps-de-Garde; entrance 24 rue Nationale.
☎03.25.27.37.75
Closed Sun and Mon (except Whitsun); March; Oct.

This bright, friendly little restaurant is in a modern shopping centre in the old centre of Bar. Traditional, unpretentious cuisine, with crêpes and pizzas listed on menus €11–16.50. It's great in summer, when you can sit outside on the terrace.

ⓔ 🏃 |●| Le Cellier aux Moines

Rue du Général-Vouillemont; it's behind St-Pierre church.
☎03.25.27.08.01
Closed Fri and Sat evenings; Tues lunchtime.

This twelfth-century cellar is remarkable in more than one way. It's the site where

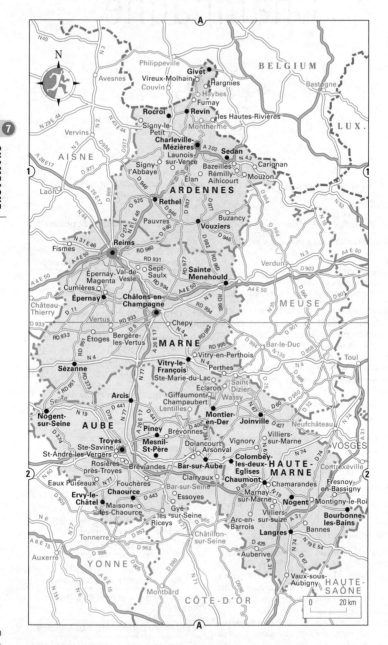

N

BELGIUM

LUX.

Philippeville
Avesnes
Vireux-Molhain
Givet
Hargnies
Couvin
Haybes
Fumay
Rocroi
Revin
les Hautes-Rivières
Signy-le-Petit
Monthermé
Vervins
Charleville-Mézières
Sedan
Launois-sur-Vence
Carignan
AISNE
Signy-l'Abbaye
Bazeilles
Rémilly-Aihicourt
Mouzon
Laon
Élan
ARDENNES
Fismes
Rethel
Buzancy
Pauvres
Vouziers
Verdun
Reims
MEUSE
Épernay
Magenta
Val-de-Vesle
Sept-Saulx
Sainte-Menehould
Cumières
Château-Thierry
Épernay
Châlons-en-Champagne
Vertus
Chepy
Étoges
Bergère-les-Vertus
MARNE
Bar-le-Duc
Toul
Sézanne
Vitry-le-François
Vitry-en-Perthois
Perthes
Ste-Marie-du-Lac
Saint-Dizier
Arcis
Éclaron
Giffaumont
Champaubert
Wassy
Nogent-sur-Seine
Lentilles
Montier-en-Der
Joinville
AUBE
Piney
Brévonnes
Vignory
Villiers-sur-Marne
VOSGES
Troyes
Mesnil-St-Père
Dolancourt
Arsonval
Neufchâteau
Ste-Savine
St-André-les-Vergers
Rosières-près-Troyes
Bréviandes
Bar-sur-Aube
Colombey-les-deux-Églises
HAUTE-MARNE
Contrexéville
Eaux Puiseaux
Fouchères
Bar-sur-Seine
Chaumont
Chamarandes
Fresnoy-en-Bassigny
Ervy-le-Châtel
Chaource
Essoyes
Marnay-sur-Marne
Nogent
Montigny-le-Roi
Maisons-lès-Chaource
Gyé-sur-Seine
Arc-en-Barrois
Villiers-sur-suize
Bourbonne-les-Bains
les Riceys
Langres
Bannes
Tonnerre
Châtillon-sur-Seine
Auxerre
Auberive
YONNE
Vaux-sous-Aubigny
HAUTE-SAÔNE
Montbard
CÔTE-D'OR

0   20 km

local winegrowers chose to meet when the local sparkling wine lost the right to be called "champagne" in 1912; scrawled inscriptions on the walls recount the suffering of the villages. After a struggle, the wine was reclassified – you'll find it on the pricey end of the wine list. The confident cooking is traditional and unpretentious, and can be sampled on menus costing €12 (weekdays) and €19–30. The décor is a bit spartan, though the candles on the tables soften the general appearance. *Free coffee offered to our readers on presentation of this guide.*

ⓔ ✗ |●| La Toque Baralbine

18 rue Nationale; on the RN19.
ⓣ and ⓕ 03.25.27.20.34
Closed *Sun evening and Mon except public holidays; 10 days in March; 10 days in Nov.*
Disabled access. High chairs available.

After years working in different establishments on the Côte d'Azur, the owner returned to his roots and opened his own gourmet restaurant – and won a loyal local following within months of opening. Sophisticated cooking (lobster ravioli, squab off the bone, warm prune soufflé with Ratafia liqueur) in very pleasant surroundings: it's a nice rustic dining room with a small terrace. Menus start at €17 (weekdays), then €20 (weekends) and €25–50. *Free coffee offered to our readers on presentation of this guide.*

Arsonval
10200 (6km NW)

ⓔ 🏠 |●| Hostellerie La Chaumière**

Take the N19 in the direction of Troyes and it's on the left as you're leaving Arsonval.
ⓣ 03.25.27.91.02 ⓕ 03.25.27.90.26
ⓦ www.pem.net/lachaumiere.fr
Closed *Sun evening and Mon except in summer and public holidays; 10 Dec–20 Jan.*
Disabled access. TV. High chairs available. Car park.

This old village inn, run by an Anglo-French couple who extend a very friendly welcome to guests, has an old red English telephone box to add a bit of *couleur locale.* There are two refurbished rooms in the main building, and others in a modern structure which is somewhat out of keeping with the old half-timbered house – but they're equipped with all mod cons and have views of the grounds and the

river; doubles with shower/wc or bath go for €53–56. Carefully prepared meals are generously served in a lovely dining room with wooden beams, and in fine weather you can eat on the terrace; menus are €20–50. Logis de France.

Dolancourt
10200 (9km NW)

ⓔ 🏠 |●| Le Moulin du Landion***

5 rue Saint-Léger; from Bar drive towards Troyes on the N19, then take the left fork 2km after Arsonval and follow the signs in the village.
ⓣ 03.25.27.92.17 ⓕ 03.25.27.94.44
ⓦ www.moulindulandion.com
TV. High chairs and games available. Swimming pool. Car park.

This place is ultra-classy and it has recently been completely refurbished. The shady garden has a swimming pool and inside the décor is smart. The bright, spacious rooms have small balconies and they are modern in contrast to the rustic dining room in the old mill. The restaurant overlooks the river, while the bay windows open onto the working millwheel; tables are also set at the waterside. Prices reflect the quality of the surroundings: double rooms range from €68 to €82. The cheapest set menu at €21 is not served at the weekend; others are €27–52. The food is light and tasty, and the restaurant serves regional specialities such as fondue made with the local Chaource cheese and served on a bed of mixed green salad. The fish are smoked at the mill, the trout's breeding grounds lie before your very eyes. This tranquil spot, offering a warm, friendly welcome, is not far from the mad world of the Nigoland amusement park. Logis de France.

Clairvaux-sur-Aube
10310 (14km SE)

ⓔ ✗ 🏠 |●| Hôtel-restaurant de l'Abbaye*

18–19 rte. de Dijon; where the D12 and D396 cross.
ⓣ 03.25.27.80.12 ⓕ 03.25.27.75.79
Closed *Sun evening; Mon; 20 Dec–10 Jan.*
TV. Car park.

Saint Bernard of Clairvaux founded the first Cistercian abbey in these very woods in the twelfth century; the same building is now a prison, with high walls and watchtowers. If you really want to enjoy your freedom, take room 17, which looks directly onto it. The double rooms, at €20–30 with basin, and €28–38 with shower/wc, could do with updating, but are comfortable nonetheless. It's very quiet at night, despite the hotel's position on a crossroads. Honest cooking served in the restaurant, with a weekday menu at €10, then others at €15 and €20. *Free coffee at the restaurant or 10% discount on the room rate offered to our readers on presentation of this guide.*

Essoyes
10360 (28km SW)

◎ ☃ 📦 |●| Hôtel-restaurant des Canotiers

Lieu-dit Les Crépadots; take the D4, followed by the D79; it's in the Essoyes hills, in the direction of Bar-sur-Seine.
☎03.25.38.61.08 🖷03.25.38.61.09
ⓦwwwinfo@hoteldescanotiers.com
TV. Swimming pool. Car park.

A brand-new hotel comprising fourteen rooms with all mod cons; double rooms with bath cost €65–70. It has views over the village of Essoyes and its vineyards, and the slope of the hotel's hillside setting frames this modern building, which extends over three storeys, with lifts. The top floor is home to the restaurant and bar, while below there is a large terrace with a heated open-air swimming pool. Situated about a hundred metres from one of the four footpaths marked with reproductions of paintings by Renoir, the hotel also pays homage to the painter in its own way, decorating its walls with reproductions of his paintings, calling its rooms by the first names of the painter's models, and serving in its restaurant dishes such as *Poulet Renoir*, made to recipes devised by Renoir's wife. Regional produce is also to the fore, most notably with tripe sausage in crispy pastry with Chaource cheese or Ratafia roast cod. Weekday lunchtime menu is €12.50, and others are €15–38. The welcome is as warm as the hotel is inside. Logis de France. *NEW ENTRY.*

Bourbonne-les-Bains
52400

◎ ☃ ☃ |●| Hôtel des Sources**

Place des Bains; it's next to the baths.
☎03.25.87.86.00 🖷03.25.87.86.33
ⓦwww.bourbonne-thermes.fr/hotel des sources
Closed *Wed evening; 30 Nov–1 April.*
Disabled access. TV. Pay car park.

A dynamic young couple run this establishment and offer modern, functional and pleasant rooms. Ask to see a selection, because their size varies considerably – no. 34 is big and has a corner sitting room and a garden view. All rooms have en-suite facilities and some have a separate wc; doubles with shower/wc and corner kitchen are €48–58. The dining room, which serves a range of menus for €12–25, opens out onto a lovely patio and attractive kitchen, in the contemporary style, with no concession to the "spa town" aspect. Guests are entitled to free entry to the *Hôtel d'Orfeuil* swimming pool. Logis de France. *Free house apéritif offered to our readers on presentation of this guide.*

◎ ☃ ☃ |●| Hôtel d'Orfeuil**

29 rue d'Orfeuil; 80m from the spa.
☎03.25.90.05.71 🖷03.25.84.46.25
ⓦwww.bourbonne-thermes.fr/orfeuil
Closed *Mon; 25 Oct–1 April.* **Disabled access. TV. High chairs available. Swimming pool. Pay car park.**

This lovely eighteenth-century house has aged beautifully – inside it's very tasteful, with antique family furniture, rugs and fireplaces. Set on a hillside, it's surrounded by a leafy garden in which they've built a very pleasant pool. It's a welcoming place where you get good value for money: €49–51 for a double with shower/wc in the new annexe — the old part is reserved for people taking the waters. Ask for a room with a balcony and a view over the park. Very classical restaurant with set menus €10–20; try salmon *sauce orfeuil* or the langoustine salad. Logis de France. *Free house apéritif offered to our readers on presentation of this guide.*

◎ ☃ ☃ |●| Les Armoises (Hôtel Le Jeanne d'Arc)***

12 rue de l'Amiral-Pierre; in the main street.
☎03.25.90.46.00 🖷03.25.88.78.71
ⓦwww.hotel-jda.com
Closed *Sun evening; 25 Oct–25 March.* **TV. High chairs available. Swimming pool. Pay car park.**

Not surprisingly, this is the only gourmet restaurant in this health-obsessed spa town. The standard is good: snail jelly with small chanterelles, supreme of chicken with *vin jaune* and morels, foie gras soufflé, and for dessert chocolate marquise. Set menus range from €18 to €35. There's service in the garden in fine weather. The nicest rooms, on the garden side of the building, have been renovated: doubles with shower cost €50-58 or €60-68 with bath. Most people come to the town to take the waters so it's quiet in the evenings; last orders here are at 9pm. Logis de France. *Free house apéritif or coffee offered to our readers on presentation of this guide.*

Fresnoy-en-Bassigny
52400 (12.5km NW)

@ 🕱 |●| Restaurant du Lac de Morimond

From Bourbonne take the D139; 2.5km beyond Fresnoy-en-Bassigny, take the little road on the right towards Lac du Morimond and follow the signs.
☏03.25.90.80.86
Closed *Mon; Tues and Wed evenings; Oct–March*. **Disabled access. Car park.**

In the depths of the country close to the ruined Cistercian abbey, there's a little lake encircled by a forest, where anglers come to tickle carp in the dark of the night. It's the ideal spot to enjoy freshly caught fish or a nice fillet steak with wild girolle mushrooms, which you eat on the terrace overlooking the water. The dining room is also lovely, with an attractive, welcoming fireplace. You get a good selection of traditional dishes such as fillet of pike perch *meunière* or whitebait. Menus, €20–22, are served on Sundays only, or reckon on €12–20 à la carte. It's best to book in advance. *Free house apéritif or coffee offered to our readers on presentation of this guide.*

Châlons-en-Champagne
51000

@ 🕇 Auberge de jeunesse

Rue Kellermann; in the town centre, 1.8km from the train station. Take bus no. 1, 4, 5 or 7 to place Tissier, then no. 3 to Vallée Saint-Pierre; or walk (10 min).
☏03.26.68.13.56
Open *check-in 6.30–10.30pm (9.30pm in winter)*. **Car park.**

An old-fashioned youth hostel near a large, shady square, with forty beds spread over two dormitories. Reminiscent of a dingy boarding house, but the atmosphere is friendly (although the toilets are a bit primitive). Rooms are €7.80 per person, and breakfast (July–Aug) €3.35; hire of sheets €2.80.

@ 🕱 🕇 Hôtel de la Cité**

12 rue de la Charrière; 800m from the place de la République. From the centre of town, take the sign for Cité administrative; it leads you straight to the hotel.
☏03.26.64.31.20 ☎03.26.70.96.22
Disabled access. TV.

This is a peaceful, provincial place, very much like a family guesthouse, with a regular clientele of businessmen, sales reps and students. Everyone is warmly greeted by the owners, who spare no effort in keeping their hotel nice – it's not high luxury, bit it's very well kept. A few rooms look onto the garden where you can enjoy breakfast (€5) in fine weather or just relax with a book. They cost €27 for a room with basin, €37 with shower, €40 with shower/wc and €43 with bath. *Free coffee, fruit juice or soda offered to our readers on presentation of this guide.*

@ 🕇 Hôtel Pasteur**

46 rue Pasteur; it's about 500m from the place de la République.
☏03.26.68.10.00 ☎03.26.21.51.09
Closed *after Christmas and over the New Year*. **Disabled access. TV. Car park.**

Part of this hotel used to be a convent which explains the superb, grand staircase. It offers a friendly welcome and the rooms are simply decorated but comfortable and well-kept; those over the quiet courtyard at the back get the sun. Doubles go for €28 with shower, €40 with shower/wc and telephone or €47 with bath; breakfast €5.

@ 🕱 🕇 |●| Restaurant Jean-Paul Souply

8 faubourg Saint-Antoine; it's 800m from the town centre opposite the young workers' hostel, direction Saint-Martin-sur-le-Pré.
☏03.26.68.18.91 ☎03.26.68.97.69
🌐www.souply.fr.st
Closed *Fri evening; Sun except certain holidays; first three weeks in Aug*. **TV. High chairs available. Car park.**

A family affair which involves members of three generations. Grandmother runs the bar – she's been in the business more than 65 years – the daughter-in-law manages the restaurant and the son is the owner and chef, who carefully prepares dishes using fresh market produce. He specializes in traditional dishes served in portions that would satisfy a famished giant. Menus are €12.50–28.50 and there's a weekday *formule* at €10.50. They have a few modest rooms for €35, or you can stay half board for €42 or €49 per person. *Free house apéritif offered to our readers on presentation of this guide.*

7

⊚ 🎿 🏠 Hôtel du Pot d'Étain**

18 pl. de la République; right in the city-centre.
☎03.26.68.09.09 🖨03.26.68.58.18
🌐www.hotel-lepotdetain.com
TV. Pay car park.

This impressive fifteenth-century house has been beautifully renovated by the family that owns it. There are 27 rooms, quite a few of which can accommodate three or four people; doubles with shower/wc or bath and phone €63–75. Many have been recently refurbished and are lovely and light. Those on the third floor (no lift) have gorgeous views over the square and the rooftops. Monsieur Georges, who used to be a baker, prepares the croissants for breakfast and all the tarts and puddings – he'll bake different things as the mood takes him. You can leave your car parked outside the hotel and explore Châlons on foot. *Free house apéritif or coffee offered to our readers on presentation of this guide.*

⊚ |●| Chez Justin

2 bis rue de l'Abbé-Lambert; next to the place de la République.
☎03.26.68.20.05

This restaurant, accommodated in a huge nineteenth-century residence and offering an attentive welcome, is the new meeting place for local high society. There is something seductive about the setting, with its magnificent Belle Époque glass roof and garden terrace that seem from a slightly different age. The inspired and meticulous cuisine lives up to the setting, with a weekday lunchtime menu for €15.50, and other menus ranging from €25.50 to €35.50. As for the wine cellar, it's a minor miracle concealing real gems at reasonable prices.

⊚ |●| Le Petit Pasteur

42 rue Pasteur; 500m from the place de la République.
☎03.26.68.24.78
Closed *Mon; Sat lunchtime; Sun evening; first week in Jan; last 3 weeks in Aug.*

In a long dining room, the friendly staff offer you a series of sophisticated traditional dishes prepared with care, such as *tournedos* of roast monkfish with bacon or fresh duck foie gras with Ratafia liqueur. Menus, at €16–39, vary depending on what has come back from the market; you can expect to pay €40 à la carte. In brief, this is a delightful little restaurant which is well worth trying out, especially when the weather is fine and the terrace is open.

Chepy
51240 (7km SE)

⊚ 🎿 |●| Comme Chez Soi

49 rte. Nationale; from Châlons, take the N44 in the direction of Vitry-le-François.
☎03.26.67.50.21
Closed *Sun and Mon evenings; Tues; a fortnight in Jan; a week in Aug.* **High chairs available.**

Provincial setting, friendly welcome, and good, classic cooking. Choices on the weekday menu at €11 and others €26–31.50 range from a simple *steak-frites* to more elaborate options such as parsleyed scallops with apples and regional specialities including snails with Chaource cheese and panfried foie gras with Ratafia liqueur. *Free house apéritif offered to our readers on presentation of this guide.*

Chaource
10210

⊚ 🎿 |●| Hôtel-restaurant Les Fontaines

1 rue des Fontaines; take the D 443.
☎03.25.40.00.85
Closed *Sun and Mon evenings; Tues; 2–23 Jan; last week in July to first week in Aug.*

Chaource is located where Champagne borders Burgundy, and the classy restaurant serves authentic regional dishes from both *départements*. There's a very cheap *formule* at €8 with a salad, plus a main course. Menus range from €12 weekdays (€15 weekends), up to €25. The cheapest menu is exemplary; it's a shame about the supplements on the others. *Free coffee offered to our readers on presentation of this guide.*

Maisons-lès-Chaource

10210 (6km S)

⬅ 🏠 🍴 **Hôtel-restaurant Aux Maisons***

Take the D34; it's in the village.
☎03.25.70.07.19 ℻03.25.70.07.75
🖳www.logis-aux-maisons.com
Closed *Sun evening 15 Nov-15 March.*
Disabled access. Swimming pool. Car park.

An old farm, onto which modern annexes have been grafted, located at the heart of a charming little village. The impeccable bedrooms, some contemporary and functional, others more rustic, are all quiet and cost €53–68 for a double with shower/wc or bath. Some rooms (nos. 4, 5, 6 and 7) really do have all mod cons, such as air-conditioning and a mini-bar. The elegant dining room is furnished with large round tables and comfortable armchairs. Here you will find regional and traditional cuisine full of character, with menus €15–38. There is a swimming pool, and nearby you can visit an amazing museum of old dolls in a cheese dairy. Logis de France.

Riceys (Les)

10340 (22km SE)

⬅ 🏠 🍴 **Hôtel-restaurant Le Magny***

Route de Tonnerre; take the D17; at the Ricey-Haut exit on the D453 (route de Tonnerre).
☎03.25.29.38.39 ℻03.25.29.11.72
🖳lemagny@wanadoo.fr
Closed *Tues evening; Wed; Jan; Feb; last week in Aug.* **Disabled access. TV. Swimming pool. Car park.**

Les Riceys is not content with having three churches. It's also the only village in France to produce three AOC wines – one of them a famous rosé that was one of Louis XIV's favourite tipples. The chef uses the wine in a number of dishes, including Chaource cheese pastries or Troyes tripe sausage with mustard, with set menus at €12–40. The rooms are peaceful; doubles with shower/wc or bath are €48–64, depending on the season. The most expensive rooms look out over the

garden. There's a heated swimming pool in summer. Logis de France.

Gyé-sur-Seine

10250 (28km E)

⬅ 🏠 🍴 💺 **Hôtel Les Voyageurs – Le Relais**

It's on the old route nationale; take the D70, and it's on the far edge of the village on the left.
☎03.25.38.20.09 ℻03.25.38.25.37
Closed *Wed; Sun evening; the Feb school holiday; a week in Aug.* **Disabled access (restaurant). TV. High chairs and games available. Car park.**

In a village of no little charm, this pretty inn with its friendly family atmosphere has been revitalized by a nice young couple. Tiny renovated doubles with shower/wc cost €45–47, depending on the season. Menus €13–32.50 feature good cuisine, simple and generous. Logis de France. *10% discount on the room rate offered to our readers on presentation of this guide.*

Charleville-Mézières

08000

⬅ 🏠 **Hôtel Le Pélican***

42 av. du Maréchal-Leclerc; near the train station.
☎03.24.56.42.73 ℻03.24.59.26.16
TV. Car park.

The charming proprietor will welcome you with a broad smile and will do her utmost to ensure you have a pleasant stay in one of the elegant and completely renovated rooms; doubles with shower/wc or bath €42–45. If you are concerned about noise from the street, choose a room at the rear of this yellow sandstone- and brick-fronted building.

⬅ 💺 🏠 **Hôtel de Paris***

24 av. Georges-Corneau; it's opposite the station.
☎03.24.33.34.38 ℻03.24.59.11.21
🖳hoteldeparis08.fr
Closed *23 Dec–2 Jan; 7–21 Aug.* **TV.**

Rimbaud was born here, and although he cursed the arrival of the railway, his statue stands proudly in the station square. The hotel owner and her cat provide a friendly welcome, and the rooms are classically decorated; doubles with shower/wc or bath €49.50. The ones on the street side are soundproofed, while those overlooking the inner courtyard couldn't be quieter. *Free fruit juice or soda offered to our readers on presentation of this guide.*

☎ |●| Restaurant Le Damier

7 rue Bayard; enter Mézières from Charleville by the avenue d'Arches and take the second on the right after the bridge over the Meuse.
☎03.24.37.76.89
Closed *Mon–Fri evenings; Sun evening.*

This is a unique restaurant run by an association set up to give young and disadvantaged people training and experience, so be patient if the service is sometimes a bit below par. It's nice and bright with a chequered floor, the food is simple but tasty, and eating here is good value for money. Menus are €9 (weekday lunch only) and €10.50–17.60; dish of the day is €6.50. Prices go up a notch on Saturday evening, when the cooking is slightly more sophisticated.

Launois-sur-Vence
08430 (20km S)

☎ 🏠 |●| Hôtel-restaurant Le Val de Vence

Rue Cécilia-Gazanière; take the A34, exit 13, then take the D35 or D3.
☎03.24.35.02.93 ℱ03.24.35.59.25
Closed *Sun evening.* **Disabled access. Car park.**

This large house in the heart of the Thiérache region of the Ardennes is a real favourite. Built in local Dom-le-Mesnil yellow stone, it stands opposite the old seventeenth-century Launois coaching house. Under the management of its young proprietors, the children's holiday camp has become a fine new establishment of considerable charm where guests are treated to an enthusiastic welcome. The rooms are simple, smart and peaceful (even more so on the courtyard side). Double rooms range from €36 (no TV) to €43 (with TV). There are also family suites (2 separate rooms) €60–70, and half board is available at €80 for two people. The large dining room is extended by a beautiful terrace looking out over the countryside. The lady of the house serves Ardennes specialities with a pleasing new twist; dishes include *salade aux deux boudins blancs ardennais* and *ballottine*

of guinea-fowl stuffed with foie gras. Weekday lunchtime *menu du jour* is at €11 including a 250ml drink; other menus €15–35. Logis de France.

Chaumont
52000

☎ 🍴 🏠 |●| Grand-Hôtel Terminus Reine***

Place Charles-de-Gaulle; it's opposite the train station.
☎03.25.03.66.66 ℱ03.25.03.28.95
✉relais.sud.terminus@wanadoo.fr
Closed *Sun evening.* **Disabled access. TV. High chairs available. Pay car park.**

The former residence of the Counts of Champagne. It was rebuilt in the middle of the twentieth century and its turreted, yellow façade and blue shutters give it a modern air. You get all the facilities you'd expect in a three-star hotel along with extremely professional welcome and service. Nearly all the 63 rooms have been refurbished; they're spruce and spacious with modern bathrooms. Doubles with basin go for €37, with shower €55, and with bath €74–105. The restaurant serves classic dishes at quite high prices; menus range from €13 (lunchtime only) to €38. As for the food, again there is a choice between traditional classical cuisine and dishes served in a pizzeria with a more relaxed atmosphere. *Free house apéritif offered to our readers on presentation of this guide.*

☎ 🍴 🏠 |●| Hôtel-restaurant Le Relais

20 faubourg de la Maladière; it's 1km from the centre of Chaumont, on the N74 to Nancy, just after the Marne–Saône canal, known locally as *Port de Chaumont* or Chaumont Harbour.
☎03.25.03.02.84
Closed *Sun evening; Mon; a fortnight in Jan; a fortnight end July to early Aug.* **Disabled access. High chairs and games available. TV. Car park.**

A former coaching inn on the outskirts of Chaumont, this is an unpretentious but friendly and welcoming place set between the roadside and the banks of the canal linking the Marne and the Saône. There are seven fairly peaceful rooms which have been renovated – nos. 6 and 7 are particularly quiet – and prices are reasonable: €42 for a double with bath. Carefully prepared, sophisticated cuisine using the freshest seafood and seasonal produce. Try the warm chicken salad, the calf's head *ravigote* and the house terrine. There's a *formule* for €13 and one at €14; set menus at €14–24. You'll pay around €26 à la carte. Credit cards not accepted. *Free house apéritif offered to our readers (May–Oct) on presentation of this guide.*

◎ 🎿 🛏 |●| Hôtel-restaurant des Remparts***

72 rue de Verdun; it's very close to the town walls, and a minute's walk from the railway station.
☎03.25.32.64.40 ℗03.25.32.51.70
✆www.hotel-des-remparts.fr
Closed *Sun evening 1 Nov to Easter.*
Restaurant closed *Sun evening (1 Nov–Easter); Mon (except public holidays); New Year's Day evening and Christmas Day evening.* **Disabled access. TV. High chairs available.**

This place offers the best value for money in Chaumont. The rooms, decorated with posters from the Chaumont Arts Festival, are clean and efficiently soundproofed, and there are newer, more spacious ones in the annexe; doubles with shower/wc or bath €61–76. Classic setting in the classy restaurant and first-rate, imaginative cooking; set menus go for €24–46. The *1-2-3* provides a more relaxed atmosphere and brasserie dishes at modest prices. *Free house apéritif offered to our readers on presentation of this guide.*

Chamarandes
52000 (2km SE)

◎ 🎿 🛏 |●| Au Rendez-Vous des Amis**

4 place du Tilleul. From Chaumont, head towards Langres then Chamarandes on the D162.
☎03.25.32.20.20 ℗03.25.02.60.90
✆www.au-rendezvous-des-amis.com
Restaurant closed *Fri evening; Sat; Sun evening; first week in May; 1–20 Aug; 22 Dec–2 Jan.* **TV. High chairs available. Car park.**

The River Marne runs through this unspoilt little village where the old church and school stand near the shady banks. You can glimpse the manor house through the trees of the estate. This is a genuine, quiet country inn with charm, and you get a friendly welcome – all in all, a great

place to stop. Rooms have been tastefully renovated and doubles cost €44 with basin/shower or €57–63 with shower/wc or bath. The restaurant is full of hunters, fishermen, businessmen and people travelling through. Weekday menu €19 and others from €27–46 offer creative gourmet cooking, and in summer they serve outside on a lovely terrace shaded by an ancient lime tree. The wine list has 320 different vintages. Logis de France. *10% discount on the room rate (Fri–Sun) offered to our readers on presentation of this guide.*

Marnay-sur-Marne
52000 (18km SE)

◎ 🎿 🛏 |●| Hôtel-restaurant La Vallée

It's on the N19, in the direction of Langres.
☎03.25.31.10.11 ℗03.25.03.83.86
✆www.hotel-de-la-vallee.fr
Closed *Sun evening; Mon; a fortnight in Oct; 10 days in March; 23 Dec–2 Jan.* **TV. High chairs available. Car park.**

Monsieur Farina produces such good food that it's easy to forget the noise of the main road outside. His place has a great reputation, and rightly so, because his local dishes are skilfully prepared. The small, rustic dining rooms are crammed with diners – the overflow goes onto the terrace when the weather is good. Menus start at €12 (weekdays), with others €17–38.50. The half-dozen bedrooms (€40–45 with shower/wc), decorated in provincial style, are pleasant but quite noisy because of the main road; some of them would need to be redecorated. Really warm welcome and a family atmosphere. *Free house apéritif offered to our readers on presentation of this guide.*

Vignory
52320 (20km N)

◎ 🛏 |●| Le Relais Verdoyant**

Rue de la Gare. From Chaumont take the N67 in the direction of Saint-Dizier then follow signs to Vignory gare.
☎03.25.02.44.49 ℗03.25.01.96.89
✉le-relais-verdoyant@wanadoo.fr
Closed *Sun evening; Mon lunchtime; Mon evening Oct–April; 1 Nov; 20 Dec–15 March; All Saints' school holiday.* **Disabled access. High chairs available. TV. Car park.**

This house was built in the early 1900s to provide accommodation for travellers getting off the train at Vignory station. There aren't so many trains nowadays, but the hotel and garden are as elegant as ever. The small, stylish rooms are named after flowers and cost €41 for a double with shower/wc. They're as charming now as they look in the sepia photos of the hotel in the reception area. The restaurant serves traditional dishes such as duck breast with shallots, chicken liver terrine with port, and iced nougat with a fruit *coulis* on set menus €14–26. Logis de France.

Villiers-sur-Suze

52210 (20km S)

⟨ ⟩ 𝄯 🏠 ❚❘❙ Auberge de la Fontaine**

2 pl. de la Fontaine; from Chaumont take the N19 in the direction of Langres, then the D143 to Villiers-sur-Suze.
☎03.25.31.22.22 🖷03.25.03.15.76
🖳www.aubergedelafontaine.fr
Closed *a fortnight in March; a fortnight in Sept.* **Restaurant closed** *Mon, Tues and Wed.* **Disabled access. TV. High chairs available.**

A nice little inn with red shutters smothered in ivy, set in a village surrounded by woods and fields. It's a lovely place to stop for a drink, buy your papers or have a bite to eat. Do as the locals do and settle down in the bar with its shiny ceiling, in the corner sitting room in front of the open fire, in the restaurant with its ancient stone walls, or, in sunny weather, on the terrace. Set menus €11 (weekday lunchtimes) and €16–30 with good, simple, flavoursome dishes that change frequently. Seven or so newly decorated, comfortable rooms in a separate building are just a step away. They're €43 for a double with shower/wc or €48 with bath. And if you've forgotten your toothpaste, no worries – the village grocery is in the hotel. A genuine, warm welcome extended by the young owner: this place has brought life back to the village. Logis de France. *Free house apéritif offered to our readers on presentation of this guide.*

Arc-en-Barrois

52210 (25km SW)

⟨ 🏠 ❚❘❙ 𝄯 Hôtel du Parc**

1 pl. Moreau; take the D10.
☎03.25.02.53.07 🖷03,25,02,42,84
🖳www.relais-sud-champagne.com

Closed *Tues evening and Wed (15 Sept–29 Feb); Mon and Sun evening (April to mid-June); March.* **TV. High chairs available.**

An unassuming but highly reputed inn with friendly service. Set in a tiny village, opposite a château, it once served as a hunter's lodge, and it is surrounded by woods with abundant game. The rooms are quiet and comfortable – they were all refurbished in 1998 to accommodate the Jamaican football team during the World Cup and cost €47–60 for a double, with shower/wc or bath. Menus €17–40, with two lunch *formules* at €8 and €14, feature typical local food served in generous portions – roe deer and wild boar in season. In fine weather you can eat on the terrace. You can also go hunting or fishing, play golf or hire a mountain bike. Logis de France. *Free house apéritif or coffee offered to our readers on presentation of this guide.*

Colombey-les-deux-Églises

52330

⟨ 🏠 ❚❘❙ L'Auberge de la Montagne**

17 rue de la Montagne.
☎03.25.01.51.69 🖷03.25.01.53.20
Closed *Mon; Tues; first fortnight in Jan; second week of March; second week of Sept.* **TV. High chairs available. Car park.**

In 2005, this inn plans to leave its mountain setting for another location in this small village known for its great man (De Gaulle, for those who didn't know). We won't therefore go on at length with regard to the setting. On the other hand, however, it is impossible not to devote a few lines to its cuisine, which, if truth be told, is not really "inn food". From the very first mouthful, you would put it more in the category of the "greats". The young chef has clearly travelled and learned his trade in other restaurants. The result on his return to the family kitchen is a very modern cuisine, creating extremely personal and sometimes, adventurous dishes that combine regional produce with flavours from beyond (take the Chinese cabbage served with the local Chaource cheese, for example). There are extensive menus at €26 (weekdays only), and €40–85. Rooms are available at €50–55 for a double with shower/wc or bath. A future star, at prices that it is hoped will remain unchanged despite the move. Logis de France.

Épernay

51200

ⓒ ☗ Hôtel de Saint-Pierre*

14 av. Paul-Chandon; south of the place de la République; follow the sign towards the "Palais des Fêtes – Piscines".
☎03.26.54.40.80 ℻03.26.57.88.68
TV. Car park.

The hotel is in a small, quiet street, just away from the city centre (in the direction of the Palais des Fêtes and the swimming pool). It looks like a pleasant family pension and the Jeannels are very welcoming. The rooms are simple yet spacious and very clean; doubles with basin €24, €31 with shower and €36 with shower/wc.

ⓒ ☗ |●| Hôtel-Restaurant de la Cloche**

5 pl. Mendès-France; it's next to Notre-Dame cathedral.
☎03.26.55.15.15 ℻03.26.55.64.88
TV. Disabled access.

A nineteenth-century posthouse right in the centre of town. It's recently been updated to suit modern tastes. The rooms (€40–45) are not huge but they're comfortable, attractive and well maintained; buffet breakfast at €6. The dining room has an appealing Belle Époque ambiance and the cooking is fresh and prepared with care, with dishes such as Champagne zabaglione or Provençal legs. Set menus start at €18 and there's a lunch *formule* at €12. The nice welcome completes the picture.

ⓒ ☗ |●| Hôtel-Restaurant Les Berceaux***

13 rue des Berceaux; it's near the place de la République.
☎03.26.55.28.84 ℻03.26.55.10.36
ⓔles.berceaux@wanadoo.fr
Closed *3 weeks in Feb; second fortnight in Aug.* **Restaurant closed** *Mon; Tues.* **Wine bar closed** *Sat; Sun.*

An old hotel built in 1889 on the site of the old city walls. Comfortable and very pleasant rooms - each has a different style. Doubles with shower or bath cost €66–75, buffet breakfast €11 – some of the rooms have just been updated. On the ground floor, our readers can have

the great good fortune to eat their fill in an excellent restaurant, *Les Berceaux*. The restaurant serves a weekday menu for €27, then others €45–59; or opt for the *menu-carte* in the wine bar at €26.

ⓒ 🍴 ☗ Hôtel de Champagne***

30 rue Eugène-Mercier.
☎03.26.53.10.60 ℻03.26.51.94.63
ⓦwww.bw-hotel-champagne.com
Closed *during Christmas holidays.* **TV. Car park.**

The best hotel in the town centre – it's modern and comfortable, and has double glazing. Room prices depend on facilities: €75 with shower/wc and up to €115 with bath. Some of the rooms have now been fitted with air-conditioning and there's an all-you-can-eat buffet breakfast at €9.50. *10% discount on the room rate (Nov–March) offered to our readers on presentation of this guide.*

Épernay-Magenta

51530 (1km N)

ⓒ |●| Chez Max

13 av. A.-Thevenet; it's 1km from the town centre on the Magenta road.
☎03.26.55.23.59
Closed *Sun and Wed evenings; Mon; a fortnight in Feb; first 3 weeks in Aug.*
High chairs available.

This popular restaurant has been going since 1946 and has kept up its good reputation and wonderful welcome. Dishes change frequently, because they are all cooked using fresh seasonal produce. Weekday set menus cost €12.50 with a choice of four starters, three main courses then salads or cheese and dessert; other menus at €16.50–35. In addition, there is an à la carte menu that many diners treat themselves to at the weekend.

Cumières

51480 (6km NW)

ⓒ 🍴 |●| Le Caveau

44 rue de la Coopérative; take the N51 in the direction of Reims, turn on to the D301 and then the D1; it's opposite the wine cooperative.
☎03.26.54.83.23
Closed *Sun and Tues evenings; Wed; Feb school holiday.* **High chairs available.**

The restaurant is in vaulted cellars hewn

out of chalk. It's a typical Champagne setting, decorated with tools used in vineyards and cellars, and the young staff is dressed in local costume. The local theme continues with the cuisine; the chef has real talent and offers a weekday lunch menu at €16, then others €23–50. There is a fine wine list which gives pride of place to the Cumières nectars that have had a fine reputation since the sixteenth century. *Free house apéritif offered to our readers on presentation of this guide.*

Bergères-les-Vertus
51130 (24km SE)

@ 🏂 🛏 |●| Hostellerie du Mont-Aimé***

4 rue de Vertus; take the D3 in the direction of Châlons-en-Champagne then the D9 in the direction of Vertus.
☎03.26.55.23.59 ℻03.26.52.21.39
ⓦwww.hostellerie-mont-aime.com
Closed Sun evening; Feb school holiday. **Disabled access. TV. Swimming pool. Car park.**

Not far from the hotel is the famous Mont Aimé, a hill 240m high which dominates the Champagne plain, and the Côte des Blancs – there's an orientation table, which is a big help. In the hotel, the pleasant air-conditioned rooms (€75–110) look onto the garden or the swimming pool. Lovely, bourgeois cooking is served in the restaurant and the seasonal produce is efficiently prepared with precision and style. There is a weekday menu at €23 and others range from €35 to €70. *Free house apéritif offered to our readers on presentation of this guide.*

Étoges
51270 (24km S)

@@ 🏂 🛏 |●| Château d'Étoges***

4 rue Richebourg; take the D51 from Épernay to Montmort-Lucy then turn onto the D18.
☎03.26.59.30.08 ℻03.26.59.35.57
ⓦwww.etoges.com
Closed noon Mon–Fri; end Jan to mid-Feb. **TV. High chairs and games available. Car park.**

The Château d'Étoges, once a stopping place for the kings of France on their way east, was built in the seventeenth century and is now a classified Ancient Monument. A favourite with British travellers, it well deserves all its accolades. There are twenty refined rooms, each

different and furnished with antiques. Doubles are €110; suites are more expensive. Breakfast is €12. In high season, half board, €110–120 per person, is compulsory. The extensive parkland offers wonderful romantic walks, and there's a billiard room to play a frame or two before dinner. Service in the elegant dining room is as refined as you would expect. There are four menus available for €30, €40, €50 and €60. Reservations only from November to April, and it's advisable to book the rest of the year as well. *10% discount on the room rate (except Sat and eve of public holidays) offered to our readers on presentation of this guide.*

Ervy-le-Chatel
10130

@ |●| Auberge de la Vallée de l'Armance

25 av. de la Gare; from the centre of Ervy, take the D374 in the direction of Aix-en-Othe. It's on the outskirts of the village, on the left.
☎03.25.70.66.36
Closed Sun, Mon and Wed evenings. **Car park.**

An old-style bistro serving good menus. The dining room, behind the pretty garden, has been converted from an old cowshed: part of an old wooden manger has been left in its place and it's decorated with old implements – hay forks and wooden bread paddles hang on the wall. Good regional food includes tripe sausage *gratin* with local cheese, or the champagne delight with Ratafia liqueur. The weekday menu is at €10.50, with others €20–38.

Givet
08600

@ 🛏 |●| Hôtel-restaurant Le Nord*

27 rue Thiers.
☎ and ℻03.24.42.01.78
Restaurant closed Mon lunchtime; Sun evening. **Disabled access. TV. Car park.**

A small place that won't break the bank. Located in the town centre, but in a fairly quiet road, it offers a friendly and attentive welcome. The unpretentious bedrooms are above the restaurant, the ones with bath are in the annexe opposite. Double rooms range from €22.90 with wash basin/wc to €33.60 with shower/wc or bath. The bar-restaurant has a bygone-age feel and offers classical cuisine with a small grill menu.

◎ 🏠 Hôtel les Reflets Jaunes***

2-4 rue du Général-de-Gaulle.
☎03.24.42.85.85 🖷03.24.42.85.86
🖳www.les-reflets-jaunes.com
Disabled access. TV.

A yellow (and blue) box in the centre of this border town, this new air-conditioned hotel combines affordable luxury, peace and quiet and a sense of well-being. The opulent rooms (some with Jacuzzi) are decorated in coordinated fabrics, and there are attic rooms with a small sitting room. The bathrooms are superbly equipped. Double rooms with shower/wc or bath are €43–95 (the latter being suites). It's worth noting the very original, extremely generous, varied and fortifying buffet breakfast, which is just €7.50. The welcome ranges from polite to devoted. Logis de France.

◎ 🎋 🏠 |◎| Hôtel Le Val Saint-Hilaire**

7 quai des Fours; coming from Charleville, it's on the left as you enter the town.
☎03.24.42.38.50 🖷03.24.42.07.36
🖳www.chez.com/valsthilaire
Closed Sun evening; Mon lunch; 20 Dec–5 Jan. **Disabled access. TV. High chairs available. Car park.**

The area is famous for its blue stone – back in the eighteenth century it was used in the construction of this old printer's. The bedrooms are pleasant and subtly decorated in contemporary style; doubles with shower/wc or bath are €54.50. The ones overlooking the road and the River Meuse have double glazing (triple glazing on the ground floor) but if you're very sensitive to noise, ask for a room overlooking the courtyard. The restaurant specializes in local dishes such as red turkey, white meat sausage *feuilleté* and trout *à l'ardennaise*. There's a weekday menu at €16 (dish of the day €10); other menus are at €19.50 and €30, and expect to pay €30 for à la carte. The bar has a terrace on the waterside where the pleasure boats are moored. You get the best welcome in town and the owners are very informative about local walks. Logis de France. *Free house apéritif offered to our readers on presentation of this guide.*

Vireux-Molhain
08320 (10km S)

◎ |◎| Sul' Pouce – Le restaurant d'Adrienne

23 av. Roger-Posty; it's on the N51, opposite the bridge.
☎03.24.41.75.62
Open *lunchtime daily; Fri and Sat evenings.*

Winner of the Ardennes Gastronomy Academy first prize, Adrienne Lair is a name and a cuisine that will stand the test of time. Passionate about food, she banks on the freshness of the regional produce (some of which comes from her own garden). People don't come here for the simple décor (or the very fine ceramics from Heiress Castle). Those who have sampled her dishes come back for more, but not because they are hungry. Dishes of the day, salads and terrines, the famous (and substantial) *gratin de salmon*, Ardennes pigeon, stews or seasonal game, are all presented with enthusiasm and a smile. The *menu du jour* is at €12.50 (individual dishes €7.50), with other menus at €19.50 and €27.50. Expect to pay €30 for an à la carte meal.

Fumay
08170 (20km S)

◎ |◎| Hostellerie de la Vallée

146 pl. Aristide-Briand; it's on the N51.
☎03.24.41.15.61
🖳www.hostelleriedelavallee.com
Closed *Sun evening; Mon; Wed evening; Feb school holiday; last week of Aug.* **Disabled access. High chairs available.**

This is the country inn you were looking for. The owner is in charge of the dining room and serves varied local dishes in substantial portions: Ardennes charcuterie, stone-grilled *pierrades* and Ardennes knuckle of ham. Weekday lunch menu costs €10 and others from €16–26.

Hargnies
08170 (20km S)

◎ |◎| La Table du Pays

Rue des Gros-Chênes; N51 and D989; on leaving the village, go towards Fumay.
☎03.24.40.42.46
Closed *Wed; Sun evening; a week in March; a week end of Aug; a week early Sept; open*

Tues evening for bookings only. **Disabled access. Games available.**

This restaurant offers relaxed, friendly service and Ardennes cooking based on local produce from this tiny village full of charcuteries (there are four of them). There is a small stone dining room, or you can dine on the terrace in summer. The regional dishes are simple but (extremely) substantial, including black pudding, ham, game terrines, and bacon, potatoes stuffed with minced meat and pork brawn. The *menu du jour* is at €10 (lunchtime and evenings) and other menus range from €15 to €20. An à la carte menu is available at weekends (expect to pay between €20 and €25). There is a wide selection of keenly priced wines available by the half bottle. *NEW ENTRY.*

Joinville

52300

◎ ☎ |●| **Le Soleil d'Or*****

9 rue des Capucins; it's beside Notre-Dame church.
℡03.25.94.15.66 ℻03.25.94.39.02
🌐www.hotelsoleildor.com
Closed *Sun evening; Mon; Tues lunch; 1–15 Feb; 1–8 Aug.* **TV. Pay car park.**

A rather chic restaurant in the town set in a substantial house dating from the end of the seventeenth century, where the décor, with its old stones and wooden beams, combines memories of the past and more contemporary glass structures. Fine contemporary and original cuisine is served on the weekday menu for €20, and a gastronomic menu at €40, and you'll spend around €57 à la carte. The hotel rooms are both charming and cosy; doubles cost €40–85 with shower/wc or €55–95 with bath. An attentive welcome is assured.

◎ 🎄 ☎ |●| **Hôtel-restaurant de la Poste****

Place de la Grève; it's at the edge of town on the St-Dizier road.
℡03.25.94.12.63 ℻03.25.94.36.23
Closed *Sun evening; 10–27 Jan.* **TV.**

Small family hotel which, to be honest, isn't much to look at. But that won't stop people from staying here (unless the chef and proprietor has retired, as he plans to do) for its substantial traditional cuisine is reflected in menus that represent good

value for money; weekday set menu for €12.20, other menus €21–33. A few bedrooms, renovated, but not particularly attractive, are good for an overnight stopover. They cost €43 for a double with double glazing and bath/wc. Logis de France. *Free coffee offered to our readers on presentation of this guide.*

Villiers-sur-Marne

52320 (17km S)

◎ 🎄 |●| **La Source Bleue**

Take the N67 in the direction of Chauon. At Villiers, take the Doulaincourt road and follow the signs.
℡03.25.94.70.35
Closed *Sun evening; Mon; Tues.* **Disabled access. High chairs available. Car park.**

An ideal country retreat in an old mill by a river way out in the country. A succession of small, cosy rooms in an eighteenth-century water mill. There's a view over the sturdy paddle wheel and the spring (*source* in French, and blue of course) that gushes from the bottom of a trout pond. In the restaurant it's fish (and trout caught in said pond) that take centre stage in the short menu, and rightly so. Also included are other small dishes that are simply but attractively presented. There's a short weekday lunch menu at €14, others €20–42, or around €20 à la carte. Relaxed welcome in the style of the young couple who run the place. There's a terrace in the garden and by the pond in summer. *Free house apéritif offered to our readers on presentation of this guide.*

Langres

52200

◎ 🎄 ☎ |●| **L'Auberge des Voiliers****

Lac de la Liez; it's 4km from Langres, on Vesoul road.
℡03.25.87.05.74 ℻03.25.87.24.22
🌐www.hotel-voiliers.com
Closed *Sun evening out of season; Mon July-Aug; 1 Jan–1 March; Dec.* **TV. High chairs and games available.**

This hotel has about the best location in Langres, close to a peaceful lake. The small, air-conditioned bedrooms are decorated in blue tints, wood panelling and porthole windows to look like ship's cabins. Doubles are €50–60 with shower/wc and telephone or €60–70 with bath. Rooms 4, 5, 6 and 8 have views over the lake. The air-conditioned dining room has specialities on offer such as fillet of pike with nettles, frogs' legs *millefeuille*, and foie gras served on a bed of rhubarb. There is a menu at €16 (weekday lunch only), with others ranging from €26 to €40. You can also eat on the veranda and terrace, which open onto the lake. Logis de France. *Free digestif or miniature bottle of locally made schnapps per room (for a one night stay with meal) offered to our readers on presentation of this guide.*

℮ 𝒜 🏨 |●| Grand Hôtel de l'Europe**

23–25 rue Diderot.
☎03.25.87.10.88 ℗03.25.87.60.67
℮ hoteleurope.langres@wanadoo.fr
Closed *Sun evening in winter.* **TV. High chairs available. Pay car park.**

A historic place (the former coaching inn is over two centuries old) at the heart of the ramparts. A wide wooden staircase rises to the first floor bedrooms, completely renovated, but still charming with their high ceilings, Liberty-style prints and creaking floorboards; doubles go for €58 with shower/wc and €75 with bath. On the second floor, the rooms, mainly yellow and blue, are functional but not quite so charming – ask for a room on the courtyard side if you want a peaceful night's sleep. Further rooms in the old style are available in the annexe. Elegant dining room surrounded by seventeenth-century wood panelling offers good traditional cuisine, with a weekday set menu at €15.50 and others up to €45. Logis de France. *Free house apéritif offered to our readers on presentation of this guide.*

℮ 🏨 |●| Le Cheval Blanc**

4 rue de l'Estres; road at right angles to rue Diderot.
☎03.25.87.07.00 ℗03.25.87.23.13
℮ www.hotel-langres.com
Restaurant closed *Wed lunch except July–Aug; 10–30 Nov.* **Disabled access. TV. High chairs available. Pay car park.**

The *Cheval Blanc* is a converted medieval abbey and has gothic arches in some rooms (nos. 4, 7, 8, 21 and 22), a terrace overlooking the medieval church, rough-hewn stone walls and exposed beams on every floor. The décor is simple

yet refined: all the rooms have been refurbished and they are as quiet as monks' cells. The new rooms in the *Pavillon Diderot*, opposite, are equally well equipped but don't have the same charm. Doubles with shower or bath range from €65 to €85; half board (compulsory 1 June–30 Sept) costs €80–95 per person. The fine, inventive cuisine uses market produce; weekday lunch menu is €19, other menus €25–70. Logis de France.

℮ 𝒜 |●| Bananas

52 rue Diderot; in the main street.
☎and ℗03.25.87.42.96
Closed *Sun Sept–June; Sun lunchtime July–Aug; a fortnight in Jan.* **High chairs available.**

A TexMex restaurant, whose rather sparse décor (a few photos and a bison's head) makes no attempt whatsoever in leading us to believe we have been transported to the Mexican frontier. They leave that to the classical and rather successful dishes such as tacos, enchiladas, chilli con carne, fajitas, guacamole, burgers and steaks. On the whole there's a good atmosphere. There's a lunch *formule* €11.80, and a menu at €13.70 (served Sunday lunch in summer); à la carte you'll spend about €13. *Free coffee offered to our readers on presentation of this guide.*

Bannes

52360 (8km NE)

℮ 🏨 |●| Chez Françoise*

6 route de Langres; take the D74.
☎03.25.84.31.20 ℗03.25.84.47.78
Closed *Sat lunchtime and Sun evening out of season.*

Françoise, after whom the restaurant is named, has not retained the petrol pumps from the country establishment that used to be run by her mother (who still works on reception). On the other hand, the little lunchtime *menu ouvrier* or workers' menu is still there, as is the family atmosphere of the place. As for the rest, everything has been thoroughly refurbished. The bedrooms are pleasant (double rooms cost €42–46). The cooking is quite simply good, with menus from €11 (weekday lunchtimes) to €28, and there is a very pleasant, huge shady terrace that runs into a bit of lawn where the children can play. Logis de France.

Vaux-sous-Aubigny

52190 (25km S)

✉ ☎ |○| Auberge des Trois Provinces

Rue de Verdun; it's on the N74 towards Dijon.
☎03.25.88.31.98 ⓕ03.25.84.25.61
Closed *Sun evening; Mon; 12 Jan–3 Feb.*
Car park.

The wonderful paved stone floor and impressive fireplace are from another era. This décor goes well with the food, which makes good use of local produce with a glimmer of originality. It's not long since the chef was running the kitchen of a top restaurant in Saint-Maxime and it shows. Good set menus go for €16 and €25, and the wine list contains one or two curiosities from the little-known neighbouring vineyard in Montseaugeon. A stone's throw away, there are a few elegant modern rooms in a pretty stone house: double rooms with shower/wc at €49. This is a good village location to make an overnight stop.

Auberive

52160 (27km SW)

✉ ☎ |○| Hôtel-restaurant du Lion d'Or

From Langres take the Dijon Road then the D428 to Auberive; from the A5, exit Langres Sud.
☎03.25.84.82.49 ⓕ03.42.79.80.92
✉liondor@mscacommunication.com
Closed *Tues; 1 Nov to end April.* **Disabled access. Car park.**

A former country holiday home, now a charming seasonal hotel. There are only about ten rooms (€58), which with simple yet inspired décor, are all different. A handful of tables are arranged around an old-fashioned fireplace for cooking dishes that change with the seasons; set menu €16, or reckon on €28 for a complete meal à la carte (drinks not included). A pleasant chance to make an overnight stop in this peaceful and wooded little village, where visitors will discover a twelfth-century Cistercian abbey.

Mesnil-Saint-Père

10140

✉ ☎ |○| Auberge du Lac – Le Vieux Pressoir***

5 rue du 28-Août; it's at the start of the village as you come from Troyes on the N19.

☎03.25.41.27.16 ⓕ03.25.41.57.59
ⓦwww.auberge-du-lac.fr
Closed *Sun evening; Mon lunchtime (1 Oct–31 March).* **Disabled access. TV. Car park.**

This is a stylish timber-framed house near the lake in the Orient forest – the ideal place for a romantic weekend. Quiet, air-conditioned doubles with shower or bath are €67–115. The rooms in the annexe are even nicer. The rustic-chic restaurant is a great place to eat refined cuisine with a selection of classic regional dishes and modern interpretations. Menus start at €22 (weekday lunchtimes), with others €32–72. You'll get an excellent welcome. Logis de France.

Montier-en-Der

52220

✉ ⅔ ☎ |○| Auberge de Puisie

22 pl. de l'Hôtel-de-Ville.
☎03.25.94.22.94
Restaurant closed *Tues.* **TV. High chairs available. Pay car park.**

There's a twelfth-century abbey in this town, just five minutes from the Lac de Der. This simple hotel, which is a nice place to stop, offers prices that are far from ruinous: doubles €32 with shower/wc. The six rooms are not very big but they're pretty enough and have good facilities; nos. 1 and 2 look over the quiet courtyard. A range of good sweet and savoury crêpes are served in the yellow and blue dining room or out on the shaded terrace; menus €10–22. *Free coffee offered to our readers on presentation of this guide.*

✉ |○| Au Joli Bois

Route de Saint-Dizier; it's 1km out of the village; on the right coming from Saint-Dizier.
☎and ⓕ03.25.04.63.15
Closed *Mon–Fri evenings Oct–June; 1–15 Jan; first fortnight of Sept.* **High chairs available. Car park.**

This big building is easy to miss even though it's by the road – it's slightly set back and hidden by a tall hedge. Keep your eyes peeled, because it's worth finding. The dining room is rustic-modern and the terrace on the edge of the wood is very pretty. Fresh produce, meticulously prepared cuisine (to use the set expression) where they take real care with presentation. The €10.30 weekday lunch menu is good value. Other menus are €17.90 and

€25.10 or you'll pay around €25 à la carte. Unusually, they have a list of thirty beers.

Éclaron

52290 (15km NE)

ⓐ 𝒜 🏠 |●| L'Hôtellerie du Moulin**

3 rue du Moulin; take the D384 in the direction of the Lac de Der-Chantecoq; it's just after the lake.
☎03.25.04.17.76 ⊕03.25.55.67.01
🌐hotellerie.moulin.free.fr
Closed Sat lunch; Sun evening; Mon; 13–29 April; 5–14 July; 13–29 Dec. **TV. High chairs available. Car park.**

At the canal side, the building, which is very much of the local colour with its wood façade, presents an illusion. Contrary to appearances, it is not the old mill, which was destroyed by a fire at the beginning of the 1970s. The rooms are on the small side, but quiet and pretty; doubles are €60-80 with shower/wc or bath. Menus, €18–54, feature cuisine that is tasty but somewhat sophisticated and expensive, especially for the region. Logis de France. *Free house apéritif offered to our readers on presentation of this guide.*

Perthes

52100 (25km N)

ⓐ 𝒜 |●| Auberge Paris-Strasbourg

6 rue de l'Europe; take the D384 as far as Éclaron, then go in the direction of Ambrières. Perthes is 2.5km from Ambrières; alternatively, take the D384 as far as Saint-Dizier, and it's the first restaurant on the right after you leave the RN4.
☎ and ⊕03.25.56.40.64
Closed Sun evening; Mon; last week in June; second fortnight in Aug.

A must for gourmets with prices to suit all pockets. Very cosily decorated with faultless welcome and service. The dining room is full of businessmen in the week, and tourists and local residents at the weekend. Menus, €15–40, include a few Alsace-inspired dishes to ensure that it lives up to its name. *Free coffee offered to our readers on presentation of this guide.*

Nogent

52800

ⓐ 𝒜 🏠 |●| Hôtel du Commerce**

Place Charles-de-Gaulle, opposite the town hall.

☎03.25.31.81.14 ⊕03.25.31.74.00
🌐www.relais-sud-champagne.com
Restaurant closed Sun (Sept—June); Christmas to New Year. **TV. High chairs available. Pay car park.**

The entrance hall of this hotel is huge and ever so slightly kitsch, as is the restaurant with its exposed beams and eighteenth-century-style décor. Well-kept and pleasant single rooms go for €32 with basin/wc; doubles go for €55–63 with shower/wc or bath (nos. 25, 26 and 27 have their own balconies). Set menus are generous and well thought out; there's a weekday lunch menu at €10 (except bank holidays), and others are €17–27. With its very friendly welcome, this is the ideal place to stay if you're visiting the cutlery museum. *Free house apéritif offered to our readers on presentation of this guide.*

Montigny-Le-Roi

52140 (15km SE)

ⓐ 🏠 |●| Hôtel Moderne – Restaurant l'Arcombelle**

25, av. de Lierneux.
☎03.25.90.30.18 ⊕03.25.90.71.80
Disabled access. TV. Car park.

A huge edifice on the edge of the village, the rooms (and sign) of this hotel are decorated in a modern style that is reminiscent of the 1980s. There are all mod cons, including good soundproofing, which is important given its location close to a crossroads; double rooms with shower/wc or bath cost €50–68. The restaurant dining room, in the same style, with numerous house plants, serves decidedly traditional food. There's a good lunchtime menu in the bar: weekday at €10.70; other menus from €15.50 to €39.50. In terms of atmosphere, the place comes somewhere between a family establishment and a hotel chain. Logis de France.

Nogent-sur-Seine

10400

ⓐ 🏠 |●| Hôtel-restaurant Beau Rivage**

20 rue Villiers-aux-Choux; from the city-centre, follow directions towards the swimming pool and the campsite; it's about 1km from place de l'Église.
☎03.25.39.84.22 ⊕03.25.39.18.32

ⓔ aubeaurivage@wanadoo.fr
Closed Sun evening; Mon; Feb school holiday; mid-Aug to early Sept. **TV.**

A newish place in a peaceful, almost bucolic environment. There's a large flowery, shaded garden (with a nice terrace in summer) gently sloping towards the river. Ask for one of the rooms with a view (nos. 1, 2, 4, 5, 9 or 10). Doubles with shower/wc or bath go for €58. The cuisine, using seasonal produce and seasoned with herbs picked by the patron, is excellent. The cheapest set menu is €20 (except public holidays) and others are €29 and €38. Logis de France.

Piney
10220

ⓔ 🏃 🏠 |◎| **Le Tadorne****

1 pl. de la Halle; from Troyes, take the D960 in the direction of Nancy and Brienne-le-Château.
☎03.25.46.30.35 ⓕ03.25.46.36.49
ⓦ www.le-tadorne.com
Closed Sun evening 1 Oct–1 April; 24 Dec–23 Jan; the Feb school holiday. **Disabled access. TV. Swimming pool. Car park.**

Nice old half-timbered building facing the old market. The hotel has been extended and now has 27 bedrooms, nine of which have air-conditioning, with sitting room and mezzanine; doubles €45 with shower/wc, and €63 with bath/wc. Regional cuisine in the restaurant, where they serve a weekday lunchtime menu for €10, and others €16.80–43. There's also a lovely, private swimming pool. *Free house apéritif offered to our readers on presentation of this guide.*

Brévonnes
10220 (5km E)

ⓔ 🏃 🏠 |◎| **Au Vieux Logis**

1 rue de Piney; it's on the D11.
☎03.25.46.30.17 ⓕ03.25.46.37.20
ⓦ www.auvieuxlogis.com
Closed Sun evening; Mon; 21 Feb–16 March; 5–13 Dec. **TV. High chairs and games available. Car park.**

This old Champenois house, with nice shaded garden, has kept its style – exposed beams, antique furniture, a large ceramic cauldron hanging in the fireplace. They serve traditional dishes prepared with great care: snails with garlic cream and Chaource cheese, tripe sausage, rabbit. The service is

wonderfully efficient. The €15 menu (not served Sat evening or Sun) is good value, and there are a couple of others for €25 and €36. The rooms are warm and cosy – doubles €40–45 with shower/wc or bath. Half board at €49–52 per person is usually required. Logis de France. *10% discount on the room rate offered to our readers on presentation of this guide.*

Reims
51100

See map on pp.308–309

ⓔ 🏠 |◎| 🏃 **Centre International de Reims**

Parc Léo-Lagrange, chaussée Bocquaine; take bus B or N (Colin stop) or H (Charles-de-Gaulle stop). **Map A2-2**
☎03.26.40.52.60 ⓕ03.26.47.35.70
ⓦ www.cis-reims.com
Open round the clock, but check in before 6pm. **Disabled access. Car park.**

A wonderful youth hostel close to the city centre (but quiet, as it's in the middle of a park), with a total of 140 beds spread over rooms with one to five beds. The recently refurbished rooms are modern, attractive and comfortable. They cost €11 per person with washbasin, and €18 with shower/wc. Self-service restaurant offers menus €5.50–10.50; there's a fully equipped kitchen also available. Facilities include leisure areas with Internet, pool, table football, TV. *10% discount on the room rate offered to our readers on presentation of this guide.*

ⓔ 🏠 **Ardenn' Hôtel****

6 rue Caqué; not far from the train station; take boulevard du Général-Leclerc. Rue Caqué is at the top of the Cirque. **Map A2-4**
☎03.26.47.42.38 ⓕ03.26.09.48.56
ⓦ www.ardennhotel.fr
Closed Sun (reservations only); 20 Dec–7 Jan. **TV. Pay car park.**

Nice little hotel, with a warm, friendly atmosphere, in a quiet road in the centre of town. Rooms aren't that big or prettily decorated, but they're clean and well-kept; doubles with shower cost €31, and €47–49 with shower/wc or bath. Nos. 1, 2, 5 and 6 overlook the garden.

ⓔ 🏃 🏠 **Hôtel Azur****

9 rue des Écrevées; 200m from the town hall. **Map B1-6**

☎03.26.47.43.39 📠03.26.88.57.19
🌐www.hotelcrystal.fr
Closed *first fortnight in Jan.* **TV. Cots available. Pay car park.**

Just ten minutes by foot from the lively Place d'Erlon and five minutes from the train station, this charming little hotel is in a quiet area. Rooms are nice and spacious, and much of the place has been renovated and tastefully redecorated by the young owners. It feels a bit more like a bed and breakfast than a run-of-the-mill two-star. Doubles cost €46 with shower/wc and €57 with bath. *Fourth breakfast offered free to our readers on presentation of this guide.*

⊚ 🎿 🛏 Hôtel Crystal**

86 pl. Drouet-d'Erlon; 150m from the train station, at the entrance to place Drouet-d'Erlon. **Map A1-5**
☎03.26.88.44.44 📠03.26.47.49.28
🌐www.hotelcrystal.fr
Closed *Christmas to New Year.* **TV.**

There are two good reasons to stay here: its location in a tranquil spot near the liveliest square in Reims, and its wonderful old antique interior with a beautiful old lift and a glorious *vieille France* dining room. The comfortable and quiet rooms have been renovated and boast good, modern bathrooms; they're €52–66 for a double with shower/wc or bath. There's also a pretty little courtyard where breakfast is served in warm weather. *10% reduction on the room rate (for two or more consecutive nights Nov to end Feb) offered to our readers on presentation of this guide.*

⊚ 🛏 Hôtel de la Cathédrale**

20 rue Libergier; 200m from the cathedral. **Map B2-1**
☎03.26.47.28.46 📠03.26.88.65.81
TV.

A friendly, welcoming family establishment that's trim and maintained with care. In spite of its location on the main road leading to the cathedral, every step has been taken to ensure a quiet stay: double glazing and insulated doors guarantee peaceful nights. Pretty and comfortable rooms with refined décor, and shower/wc go for €52.50 or up to €62 with bath.

⊚ |●| Le Chamois

45 rue des Capucins. **Map B2-16**
☎03.26.88.69.75

Closed *Wed; Sun lunchtime; a week in May; 3 weeks in Aug.*

This intimate, relaxing restaurant draws its inspiration from the mountains, with a menu of *fondues savoyardes* and *raclette valaisanne* or *vaudoise.* If you don't like cheese, go for the great salads or the *fondue bourguignonne.* Short lunch menus at €8.60 and €13.50 (weekdays only); in the evening, reckon on spending around €20 à la carte.

⊚ 🎿 |●| Chez Anita

37 rue Ernest-Renan; in a road rather on the outskirts, behind the train station. **Off map A1-18**
☎03.26.40.16.20
Closed *Wed evening; Sat lunchtime; Sun; a week in late April; first 3 weeks in Aug; a week at Christmas.* **Disabled access.**

If you like authentic Italian food, *Chez Anita* is for you. Come here for brilliant oven-baked pizza with a choice of toppings and pasta galore. It's a really popular place with a good local reputation. The portions are generous and very filling – so go easy ordering lunch if you want to stay awake to explore the town in the afternoon. Lunch *formule* €10.60, lunch menu €14.80; in the evening you'll pay about €20 for a meal à la carte. *Free coffee offered to our readers on presentation of this guide.*

⊚ |●| Brasserie du Boulingrin

48 rue de Mars; close to the town hall and the Boulingrin market. **Map B1-21**
☎03.26.40.96.22
Closed *Sun.*

A genuine brasserie that has been running since 1925 – it does credit to its kind. The lunchtime din echoes in the vast Art Deco dining room but in the evening it's warm and convivial. The walls are painted with murals and there's an army of uniformed waiters. The excellent €16 weekday *formule* offers a choice of three starters, three main courses, cheese or dessert with a half-litre of wine and coffee included. There's also a menu at €23.

⊚ |●| Restaurant Chèvre et Menthe

63 rue du Barbâtre; between the basilica of Saint Rémi and the cathedral. **Map C2-19**
☎03.26.05.17.03

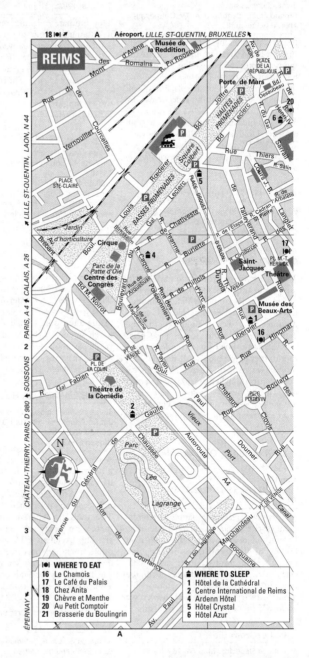

REIMS

Aéroport, LILLE, ST-QUENTIN, BRUXELLES

Musée de la Reddition

Porte de Mars

Musée des Beaux-Arts

Saint-Jacques

Cirque

Parc de la Patte d'Oie

Centre des Congrès

Théâtre de la Comédie

Jardin d'horticulture

PLACE STE-CLAIRE

PLACE DE LA RÉPUBLIQUE

PL. M-T HERRICK

PL. DE LA COLIN

PL. G. POLITEVIN

CHÂTEAU-THIERRY, PARIS, D 980, SOISSONS, PARIS, A 4, CALAIS, A 26, LILLE, ST-QUENTIN, LAON, N 44

ÉPERNAY

|◯| WHERE TO EAT
16 Le Chamois
17 Le Café du Palais
18 Chez Anita
19 Chèvre et Menthe
20 Au Petit Comptoir
21 Brasserie du Boulingrin

♠ WHERE TO SLEEP
1 Hôtel de la Cathédral
2 Centre International de Reims
4 Ardenn Hôtel
5 Hôtel Crystal
6 Hôtel Azur

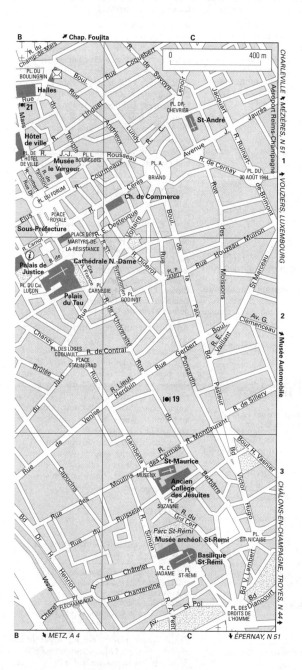

B ↗ Chap. Foujita C

0   400 m

R. du Champ-de-Mars
PL. DU BOULINGRIN
Boul.
Rue
Coquebert
de Savoye
Lenoir
Jacquart

Halles
Rue
21
du Mars
Rue
Linguet
Andrieux
Lundy
R.
C.
PL. DR-CHEVRIER
Jaurès
St-André
R. Ruinart
Avenue

Hôtel de ville
PL. DE L'HÔTEL DE VILLE
R. de l'Arbalète
Rue Danton
J.-J.
PL. L.
BOURGEOIS
Rousseau
Courmeaux
Cérès
PL. A. BRIAND
R. de Cernay
PL. DU 30 AOÛT 1944
de Brimont

Musée le Vergeur
PL. DU FORUM
R.
Ch. de Commerce
Rue
de
des
Houzeau
Mutron

Éus
PLACE ROYALE
Sous-Préfecture
R. Carnot
E. Desteuque
Voltaire
PLACE DES MARTYRS-DE-LA-RÉSISTANCE

(i)
Palais de Justice
PL. DU CAL LUÇON
Cathédrale N.-Dame
C. A. France
PL. CARNEGIE
Palais du Tau
PL. GODINOT
R. Diderot
Symphorien
PL. P. JAMOT
la
Rue
Rue
de
St-Marceau
Moissons
Marceau

de l'Université
PL. P. JAMOT
Paix
Av. G. Clemenceau
Boul.
R. E. Vaillant
Boul. H. Vasnier

Chanzy
PL. DES LOGES COQUAULT
R. de Contrai
PLACE STALINGRAD
Rue
Rue
Gerbert
Pont-sardin
Bd
Pasteur
R. de Sillery
Victor

Brûlée
Jard
du
Rue
R. Lieut. Herduin
19
Venise
du

Rue
de
Gambetta
R. des Carmes
St-Maurice
R. Montlaurent
Bd
Barbâtre
Hugo

Capucins
des
Moulins
MUSEUX
Ancien Collège des Jésuites
PL. SUZANNE
R. du Grd Cerf
Bd
PL. ST-NICAISE

Bd
Dr H.
Rue
du
Ruisselet
R.
Simon
Parc St-Rémi
Musée archéol. St-Remi
Basilique St-Rémi
PL. C. JADAME
PL ST-RÉMI
V. Lambert
Bd
Diancourt

Henriot
Vesle
Châtel
FLÉCHAMBAULT
du Châtelet
Rue Chantereine
R.
St-Pol
AV.
Petit
PL. DES DROITS DE L'HOMME

B ↘ METZ, A 4 C ↓ ÉPERNAY, N 51

Closed *Sun; Mon; a week at Easter; 3 weeks in Aug; a week between Christmas and New Year.*

This friendly, welcoming place has had an excellent reputation for years, so you won't be disappointed. The food sounds modest enough but is actually very impressive, and proves good value: try the house tart of goat's cheese with mint or the Jura turkey escalope. A meal à la carte will cost around €18, drinks not included; there are no set menus.

⑦

ⓒ |●| **Restaurant Au Petit Comptoir**

17 rue de Mars. **Map B1-20**
☎03.26.40.58.58
Closed *Sun; Mon; first week in March; first fortnight in Aug; 24 Dec–6 Jan.*

Fabrice Maillot has worked with famous chefs in the past and is enjoying great success with this bistro. He's a clever, creative chef who produces first-rate cooking that looks simple, but is finely and precisely judged. The place appeals to people who appreciate good food, and the quality of the cuisine is often amazing. The desserts are equally delicious. The menus, €15 (lunchtime only), €22 and €33, change with the seasons, and the impressive wine list features a good selection from the Rhône valley. Expect to pay around €45 à la carte. There's also a terrace.

ⓒ |●| ⅍ **Le Café du Palais**

14 pl. Myron-Herrick. **Map B2-17**
☎03.26.47.52.54
Closed *Sun lunch; Wed; a week in June; 3 weeks in Aug.* **Open** *11am to 3pm.*

This remarkable bistro, founded in 1930, is frequented by the local great and good, including a number of magistrates and lawyers. The superb rococo décor, Art Deco stained-glass dome, photos and decorations on the wall, and the background music, all conspire to create an elegant, relaxed atmosphere. Add to that a genuinely courteous welcome and lively brasserie cuisine that's lovingly prepared. The menu is short but well judged and the desserts are delicious; you'll pay €25 for a meal. There's a nice terrace. *Free house apéritif offered to our readers on presentation of this guide.*

Val-de-Vesle
51360 (18km SE)

ⓒ |●| **L'Étrier**

Take the N44 in the direction of Châlons and then the D8.

☎03.26.03.92.12 ⓕ03.26.03.29.72
Closed *Sun–Fri evenings; Sat lunch.*

Run by a family who make a delightful team. During the week there are two menus: the workers' favourite at €11 includes a starter and charcuterie, dish of the day, cheese, dessert and wine. The €19.30 menu has house terrine, escargots de Bourgogne, smoked salmon or calf's head, cheese and dessert. And the weekend menu (€24) is a real feast: savoury petits fours followed by foie gras of duck with toast or a terrine, then a choice of fish, a choice of meat, finishing with salad, cheese and dessert.

Sept-Saulx
51400 (20km SE)

ⓒ ⅍ ≜ |●| **Le Cheval-Blanc*****

Rue du Moulin; take the N44 in the direction of Châlons-en-Champagne then turn left on the D37.
☎03.26.03.90.27 ⓕ03.26.03.97.09
ⓦwww.chevalblanc-sept-saulx.com
Closed *Tues; Wed lunch; Feb; 1 Oct–1 April.* **Disabled access. TV. High chairs and games available. Car park.**

An old coaching inn with a flower-filled courtyard, set in a large park with the Vesle running through it. The comfortable rooms look onto the courtyard and are peaceful and relaxing; doubles with shower €64, €77 with bath and up to €155 for a suite, breakfast €9. There's a tennis court, volley ball court, mini-golf and some swings for the children. Or you could do nothing at all and simply enjoy the beauty of the surroundings. The restaurant is quite pricey: weekday lunch menu €25 and seven others €29–86. *Free house apéritif offered to our readers on presentation of this guide.*

Fismes
51170 (23km W)

ⓒ ⅍ ≜ |●| **Hôtel-Restaurant La Boule d'Or****

11 rue Lefèvre; follow directions to Laon.
☎03.26.48.11.24 ⓕ03.26.48.17.08
ⓦwww.boule-or.com
Closed *Sun evening; Mon; Tues lunch; last week in Jan and first week in Feb.* **TV. Car park.**

Small family place offering sweet little well-kept rooms. Double rooms cost €49–55; the nicest rooms are nos. 4, 5 and 8, at the back. The restaurant is a well-known gourmet stop in the region but it's exceptional value for money, with a weekday menu at €11, and others ranging from €15.90 up to €45. Huge care is taken over the cooking and the welcome is very pleasant. Logis de France. *Free digestif offered to our readers on presentation of this guide.*

Rethel

08300

⊚ 🏠 |●| Hôtel-restaurant La Champagne**

Boulevard de la 2e-D-I; it's opposite the Aisne, near the bridge.
℡03.24.38.03.28 ℗03.24.38.37.70
ℯyves.grustiniam@wanadoo.fr
Restaurant closed Sun evening. **Disabled access. TV. Car park.**

Originally built as a block of flats surmounting a parade of shops, this place got turned into a hotel. Not exactly what you'd call charming, but the rooms are nice and clean and it's good value: from €30 for a double with shower/wc, €36 with bath; half board is €44. There are two restaurants: a cafeteria where you come for the prices rather than the surroundings, and a more attractive dining room with good traditional cuisine. Set menus are €13 at weekday lunchtimes, and €17–25 at other times.

⊚ 🏠 |●| Hôtel-restaurant Le Moderne**

Place de la Gare.
℡03.24.38.44.54 ℗03.24.38.37.84
ℯhotel.le.moderne@wanadoo.fr
TV. Pay car park.

For over forty years, this place – situated across from the station – has been a favourite with travellers; there aren't many trains now so the rooms are nice and quiet. Despite being renovated they've kept some of their old style, which fits in with the overall look of the solid brick-and-stone building. Well-equipped doubles cost €37 with shower/wc and €42 with bath. In the restaurant, decent menus are €18 and €26 with a dish of the day around €10; à la carte you'll get modern classics such as *cassolette* of *boudin* served with nettle cream sauce, roast monkfish with smoked bacon and *tête de veau* with a vinaigrette sauce with chopped boiled eggs, gherkins, capers and herbs. Logis de France.

Pauvres

08310 (15km SE)

⊚ 🎋 |●| Restaurant Au Cheval Blanc

Route de Juinville. Take the D946 and it's at the start of the village.
℡03.24.30.38.95
Closed Mon evening; first week in Jan; last week in Aug. **Disabled access.**

Pauvres may man "poor", but this town is the richer for this gem of a place. There's a sign outside saying they welcome people on foot or on horseback – today you're more likely to see vans and commercial vehicles at lunchtime, when it's full of people who work locally. They generally opt for the €10 *menu du jour*, which includes a litre of red wine, and is served in the evenings (though not at the weekend). The good, hearty portions of family cooking are served with a smile, though the desserts are a little uninspired. At the weekend families flock here for the regional set menus: first menu (weekday lunch only) is €10.50, then €19 (gastronomic menu), and three menus at €26-38. *Free coffee offered to our readers on presentation of this guide.*

Signy-l'Abbaye

08460 (23km N)

⊚ 🎋 🏠 |●| Auberge de l'Abbaye**

Place Aristide-Briand; take the D985.
℡03.24.52.81.27 ℗03.24.53.71.72
Restaurant closed Wed lunch; mid-Jan to end Feb. **TV. High chairs available. Car park.**

This lovely inn has been in the same family since the Revolution. It's in the middle of a small picturesque market town on the edge of a huge forest. You'll get a warm welcome and there's a nice family atmosphere. The stylish rooms, all of them different, are regularly smartened up; room 9 has its own little sitting room. Doubles with basin/wc cost €38–56, with shower €32, with shower/wc or bath €50. In winter they light a fire in the dining room. The Lefebvres are still farmers and you'll find plenty of local produce in the home cooking: the excellent beef comes from their own herd, while the rhubarb for the rhubarb tart is grown in their garden. Menus at €13–35 list local specialities; try parsleyed lamb. It's rare to find this sort of place anywhere, let alone in such a wonderful spot. Logis de France. *Free house apéritif offered to our readers on presentation of this guide.*

Revin
08500

ⓐ ⚲ ☗ |●| Auberge du Malgré-Tout

Chemin des Balivaux; from Revin, take the D1 and follow directions towards Givet-Monthermé and the Hautes-Buttes for 6km, it's signposted thereafter.
℡03.24.40.11.20 ⑤03.24.40.18.90
Closed *Sun evening; 3 weeks in Aug.* **Games available. Car park.**

The *ferme-auberge* (a farm offering food and lodging) of your dreams, way out in the forest. There are sturdy, wooden tables and a stone fireplace. They serve terrine, house foie gras, charcuterie and game – and in generous quantities, too. Menus are €17.60 and €24.40. The rooms are extremely quiet, as you'd expect, and cost €38.11 with shower/wc. It's essential to book. *Free coffee offered to our readers on presentation of this guide.*

Hautes-Rivières (Les)
08800 (30km E)

ⓐ ☗ |●| Auberge en Ardenne

15 rue de l'Hôtel-de-Ville; D1 via Monthermé and D31.
℡03.24.53.41.93 ⑤03.24.53.60.10
ⓦwww.aubergeenardenne.com
Restaurant closed *Sat lunchtime and Sun evening out of season; end Dec and first fortnight in Jan.* **TV.**

The long tradition of family hotels continues on the banks of the River Semoy, in the country of legends. There is a little bit of heaven here for nature lovers. The quiet annexe has ten smart bedrooms, and there are a further four bedrooms in the Lallouette's house, provided guests stay in in the evening. Doubles cost €47 with bath; the two rooms that look onto the river are clear favourites. The tradition continues at the table too, where there are generous portions of gourmet meals such as *sauté de sanglier* (wild boar) *au miel*, sausage of white meat salad, wild boar ham and game. Meals are served in the two dining rooms or on the terrace that runs along the Semoy. The weekday lunchtime *menu du jour* is at €11.50, and others are

€16–30 (Ardennes menu €22). There are also three chalets available for rent in the next village (Tournavaux), with a catering service and delivery of tray meals in the forest for walkers. There are maps available. Logis de France.

Rocroi
08230

ⓐ ☗ |●| Le Commerce

4 place d'Armes.
℡03.24.54.11.15.⑤03.24.54.95.31
Restaurant closed *Sun evening (Sept to end April); a week early Jan.* **TV. High chairs available.**

Right in the centre of the village, this is a typical country hotel, a bit on the old side but well kept. The rooms (€40) are small and unremarkable but spotless. There is a wide choice of resolutely regional dishes, including the famous "cacasse à cul-nu" (potatoes and lard), slices of Ardennes red turkey in oyster-mushroom sauce and calf's head in gribiche sauce; menus at €10 (weekday lunchtime), and then €14–37. Do not miss the perfectly preserved star-shape fortifications in the village. Logis de France.

Signy-Le-Petit
08380 (20km W)

ⓐ ☗ |●| Hôtel-restaurant La Hulotte au Lion d'Or***

Place de l'Église; no D877 towards Mon Idée; N43 and D34 to Targny.
℡03.24.53.51.76. ⑤03.24.53.36.96
ⓦwww.le-lion-d-or.org
Closed *Sun evening; Tues lunchtime; Wed lunchtime; first fortnight in July; last fortnight in Dec and first week in Jan.* **Disabled access. TV.**

The *Hulotte* (tawny owl) watches over you at night at the base of the fortified church in Thiérache. And the comfort of this fine Belgian-owned establishment, with its huge, yet cosy, impeccable rooms helps ensure a good night's sleep. Double rooms, with bath range from €59 to €61. Room no. 1 is extremely spacious and overlooks the square. The proprietor also keeps an eye on your gourmet platter, ensuring that the produce used is absolutely fresh with dishes such as frogs' legs and snails *au pistou*, trout with bacon and nettle juice, freshwater pike-perch with chanterelle mushroom cream sauce or *magret* and pan-fried peaches in lavender. Menus range from €19 (market day produce) to €55 (the eponymous "*Hulotte*", including drinks from apéritif right through to coffee). A substantial and varied breakfast buffet with charcuterie and cheese is served in the old vaulted cellar. You'll get impeccable service and welcome, full of *joie de vivre*. Logis de France.

Sainte-Ménehould

51800

◖ ✿ |●| ♫ Hôtel-restaurant de la Poste**

54 av. Victor-Hugo; as though leaving the town, go in the direction of Verdun-Metz, not far from the train station.
℡03.26.60.80.16 ℻03.26.60.97.37
Closed *Fri evening; Sun evening; 15 Dec–15 Jan.* **TV. High chairs available. Pay car park.**

An unassuming place, not far from the station, run by friendly owners. The rooms aren't very big, but they've been recently refurbished and are comfortable: doubles with shower/wc and telephone range from €36.60 to €41.50. Nos. 7, 8 and 9 are quietest and no. 9 can sleep up to four people. Menus are €11–20; try the local speciality, pig's trotters *à la Sainte-Ménehould. Free house apéritif or coffee offered to our readers on presentation of this guide.*

◖ ✿ |●| Hôtel-restaurant Le Cheval Rouge**

1 rue Chanzy.
℡03.26.60.81.04 ℻03.26.60.93.11
⊛www.lechevalrouge.com
Closed *21 Dec–11 Jan.* **TV.**

The fabulous €11 weekday (except holidays) brasserie menu is reason enough to stay at this place. No boring old *steak-frites* and *crème caramel* here. The restaurant menus, €16–55, are equally imaginative. À la carte you'll find the local speciality: pig's trotters, which according to those in the know are really quite something, given a twist by being served in *galettes* with truffle *jus*. Comfortable double rooms go for €40–45 with shower or bath. Logis de France.

Sedan

08200

◖ ✿ |●| Le Relais**

Rue Gaston-Sauvage; at the Sedan exit, go in the direction of Charleville-Mézières; turn left onto the D6 after the railway.
℡03.24.27.04.41 ℻03.24.29.71.16
⊛l.lamboley@wanadoo.fr
Restaurant closed *Sun evening.* **TV. Car park.**

A huge brick pile of a building with quite a lot of character. It used to be a soap factory, but is now our favourite hotel in Sedan. The hotel is still in the town, but already has the feel of the countryside. The welcome is warm and friendly, and the rooms are peaceful and quiet, representing good value for money. Double rooms range from €43 to €47; room nos. 31 and 32 look out over the garden. The huge restaurant dining room serves traditional cuisine on menus at €12–30 with a few regional options, such as Ardennes ham crispy pancake and melon sorbet or gizzard salad with minced Ardennes ham. Logis de France.

◖ ♫ ✿ |●| Le Saint-Michel*

3 rue Saint-Michel.
℡03.24.29.04.61 ℻03.24.29.32.67
⊛www.le-saint-michel.fr
Restaurant closed *Sun evening.* **TV. High chairs available.**

This is in an ideal spot in a quiet little street beside the high castle walls – the castle is said to be the largest in Europe, and the town is no less than a thousand years old. Double rooms are available at €65 with shower/wc. The restaurant is fairly traditional in its approach, with one menu at €12 (not Sun), and others €17–33. They do a few local specialities, like sautéed wild boar, seafood platters and fish dishes. *5% discount on the room rate or free coffee offered to our readers on presentation of this guide.*

◖ ✿ |●| Hôtellerie du Château Fort***

Porte des Princes.
℡03.24.26.11.00 ℻03.24.27.19.00
⊛www.hotelfp-sedan.com
Open *noon–2.30pm and 7.30–10.30pm (bar open till midnight).* **Disabled access. TV. High chairs and games available. Car park.**

Listed as a *Ville d'Art et d'Histoire* (Town of Art and History), Sedan has a fortified castle dating from the fifteenth century. This is a restored historic monument converted in part to form a hotel complex. Double rooms with shower/wc or bath range from €85 to €150. To experience life in the castle and even the fortress, there are four types of bedroom (graded) fitted with all mod cons and decorated with taste and luxurious restraint: "Histoire" (History) (€85 – baths on the first two floors and showers on the third and fourth floors, with lift), "Tradition" (€100) or "Grande Tradition" (€135 – old fireplace, kitchenette, private access with terrace over the ramparts), and "Suites" (2 at €150). Beyond a shadow of a doubt, our favourites are the duplexes with small garden and fireplace in this unique complex. The restaurant dining rooms bear names related to the history of the castle. The hotel is run by France Patrimoine (as is the restaurant in Chambord Castle). Fine local gourmet food is served in surroundings decorated in keeping with the period.

⊚ 🍴 |O| Le Médiéval

51 rue de l'Horloge.
☎03.24.29.16.95
Closed *Sun evening; Tues evening.* **Disabled access.**

At the heart of the old town, close to the castle, nestles this charming little restaurant with its rustic bistro-style dining room complete with fireplace, beams and stone walls – it's a real favourite. The food represents incredible value for money with menus from €11.50 (weekday lunchtimes) to €23. Regulars know what they are doing when they choose to dine here on the specialities created by a friendly, jovial chef. The medieval *hippocras* drink served for the apéritif is followed by a salad of calves' trotters, *escalope* of salmon *au lard*, *biscuit* of pike and scallop petal or *tête de veau* with two sauces. *Free glass of champagne offered to our readers on presentation of this guide.*

⊚ 🍴 |O| Restaurant La Déesse

35 avenue du Général-Margueritte; go towards Saint-Menges-Floing; it's about 200m after the Dijonval museum of bygone industries, on the right.
☎03.24.29.11.52
Closed *Sat (except banquets); a week in Feb; Aug.* **High chairs available.**

This little bar-restaurant is always full of regulars so you have to grab a table when you get the chance. The atmosphere is warm, friendly and definitely informal. They use only fresh ingredients, even in the desserts – and there's not a microwave in sight. They do game in season. It's authentic, simple and classy. There's a good weekday lunch set menu at €12, and the Sunday (and public holiday) menu, at €19, is popular with families. The service is relaxed but efficient, and the owner goes round to make sure everyone's all right. *Free coffee offered to our readers on presentation of this guide.*

⊚ |O| La Ferme du Landi

Carrefour de Bellevue.
☎03.24.22.22.22
Closed *Mon; Wed evening; Sun evening.* **Disabled access.**

La Ferme du Landi in the sunshine is an experience you will never forget, especially if you sit on the panoramic terrace overlooking the meadows and the River Meuse. Crossing the threshold is a bit like entering a gourmet "religion", and the regional gourmets have made their choice. The dining rooms are rustic but intimate, and the menus favour fine cuisine based on freshness and quality produce expertly worked to make generous platters. Specialities include Ardennes and fish, or alternatively frogs' legs *mousseline*, veal rice in a hazelnut breadcrumb coating or thyme infused lamb. Weekday lunchtime menu at €14; "express" menu €15 with one drink and one coffee; "Ardennes" menu €21 with one apéritif, a half-bottle of Meuse wine and one coffee; other menus €21–32.

Bazeilles

08140 (4km SE)

⊚ 🍴 🏠 |O| Auberge du Port**

Route de Rémilly; from Bazeilles take the D129 towards Rémilly for about 1km.
☎03.24.27.13.89 ☎03.24.29.35.58
🌐www.auberge-du-port.fr
Closed *Fri and Sat lunchtimes (open Fri evening May–Oct); Sun evening; last 3 weeks in Aug; 15 Dec to early Jan.* **TV. High chairs and games available. Car park.**

This pretty white house stands at the end of a little mooring berth on the River Meuse. There's a rather polite atmosphere to the place, and the garden and surrounding meadows make it really charming; there's also a shaded terrace for the summer months. The characterful bedrooms are in a separate building; those looking out over the river are brighter. They cost €58 for a double with shower or bath. There's an excellent menu at €16 (not Sun), and others are from €22.50 to €39.50. The food is beautifully presented and imaginative with lots of fish dishes. *10% discount on the room rate offered to our readers on presentation of this guide.*

☞ 🏠 |O| Château de Bazeilles et Restaurant l'Orangerie

It's on the D764, on the edge of the village; exit no. 3 from the N43 Sedan bypass.
☎03.24.27.09.68 ℗03.24.27.64.20
🌐www.chateaubazeilles.com
Restaurant closed *Sun evening; Mon lunch; 2 weeks in Feb; a week in Aug.* **Disabled access. TV. Car park.**

Within the precincts of the château, this lovely establishment offers quiet, spacious rooms with modern décor and great views. There's a special one, no. 201, in a huge separate pavilion with its own open fireplace. They're excellent value at €88 with shower/wc or bath. The restaurant is of superb quality and is situated in the old orangery in the middle of the grounds. It offers inventive cooking with constantly changing menus costing €26–52, served on the terrace in the summer.

Rémilly-Aillicourt
08450 (6km SE)

☞ 🎿 🏠 |O| Hôtel-restaurant La Sapinière**

1 rue de Sedan. From Sedan take the D6 towards Raucourt-Mouzon.
☎03.24.26.75.22 ℗03.24.26.75.19
🌐www.lasapiniere08.com
Closed *15 Jan–15 Feb; second fortnight in Aug.* **Restaurant closed** *Sun evening; Mon.* **Disabled access. TV. Car park.**

This is a traditional country hotel-restaurant which used to be a coaching inn. The rooms are clean and smart with good facilities, and because they look out onto the garden, they're quiet too; doubles €50 with shower/wc, €52 with bath. The restaurant has a large dining room which is often used for wedding parties and the like. First menu starts at €15, except Sundays and holidays, then others at €22–38. Cuisine is traditional and uses a lot of local produce, sometimes with a nice original touch: dish of snails with champagne and herbs, pan-fried home-made foie gras and

a generous gourmet "butcher's platter". Game is served in season, as are large summer salads. There's a pleasant terrace. *Free house apéritif or 10% discount on the room rate offered to our readers on presentation of this guide.*

Élan
08160 (18km SW)

☞ |O| Aux Plaisirs Gourmands

Site de la Manse Abbatiale; D764 towards Flize; then D133 towards Élan.
☎03.24.37.84.09
Open *Tues–Sun in July–Aug; at other times by reservation only.*

In the distant past, the abbey church of Our Lady of Élan was built amongst the greenery and springs of Val de Bar country. The church has survived, as has the castle (visits by appointment: contact Eugène Classine on ☎03.24.54.02.72). The tourist office and a small restaurant have been set up in the former manse of the abbey church. Specialities using local produce are served, and newly discovered dishes such as Ardennes nettle tart, as well as market day dishes are served in the small dining room with its beamed ceiling. Expect to pay €15–20 for a meal from the à la carte specialities menu. The fine terrace, heated in the evening, looks out over the Cistercian site. It's a good starting point for superb walks, perhaps the best one being towards the chapel of Saint Roger (tourist office website: 🌐www.paysdes sources.com).

Mouzon
08210 (18km SE)

☞ |O| Les Échevins

33 rue Charles-de-Gaulle; from Sedan take the D6, the D4 and then the D27. It's near the church.
☎03.24.26.10.90 ℗03.24.29.05.95
Closed *Mon; Sat lunchtime; Sun evening; 3–20 Jan; 1–25 Aug.*

The dining room is on the first floor of a glorious seventeenth-century Spanish house. The excellent cuisine combines traditional style with a modern approach and the dishes are meticulously prepared. While you order, a profusion of *amuse-bouches* and other delicacies are served with a smile by the professional waiting staff. There's a weekday lunch *formule* at €16.50 that includes dish of the day and dessert. The first menu at €23 and others from €35–50 change every couple of months; these may list dishes such as asparagus and leeks with *ravigote* sauce and fish *paupiettes*. This is one of the best restaurants in the area.

Carignan
08110 (20km SE)

ⓒ |●| Restaurant La Gourmandière

19 av. de Blagny; take the N43 and it's 300m from the centre, direction Montmédy-Longwy.
ⓣ and ⓕ 03.24.22.20.99
ⓔ la-gourmandiere2@wanadoo.fr
Closed *Mon except bank holidays.* **Disabled access. High chairs and games available. Car park.**

The rather fancy dining room is in keeping with the style of this elegant bourgeois residence, and there's still a very homely atmosphere about the place. The talented and daring chef mixes local produce with foreign spices: try the lobster charlotte and the trio of foie gras. Weekday menu at €15, others €24–50, and there's a great choice of wines. For sunny days, there's a lovely terrace in the garden.

Sézanne
51120

ⓒ ⬢ |●| Hôtel-restaurant Le Relais Champenois**

157 rue Notre-Dame; it's on the Troyes road, at the Sézanne exit, 500m from the church.
ⓣ 03.26.80.58.03 ⓕ 03.26.81.35.32
ⓦ www.relaischampenois.com
Closed *Sun evenings; Christmas to New Year.* **Disabled access. TV. High chairs available. Car park.**

As you come into the village you enter real Champagne country. This is a friendly old inn with ancient walls. The lovely rooms have been delightfully renovated and cost from €42 with shower/wc to €63 with bath. Monsieur Fourmi is the chef here, and he prepares superb food inspired by local produce: scallop salad in Reims vinegar, medallion of monkfish with wild nettles and veal. There are set weekday menus for €15.50, with others up to €44. There's also a gastronomic menu at €139. Over more than twenty years, Monsieur and Madame Fourmi have built up a well-

deserved reputation for offering quality service and a great welcome. Ask to try a glass of Ratafia de Champagne – it's delicious. Logis de France.

ⓒ ⬢ |●| Hôtel-restaurant de la Croix d'Or**

53 rue Notre-Dame; a stone's throw from the centre, on the Troyes road.
ⓣ 03.26.80.61.10 ⓕ 03.26.80.65.20
ⓦ www.hotel-lacroixdor.fr
Closed *Tues.* **Disabled access. TV.**

This pleasant house is totally covered in ivy and flowers, and has all the usual facilities. The bedrooms, which are quite small, are decorated in a sophisticated and personal style, which gives them a rather warm feel. Double rooms go from €45 to €54. The friendly ambiance extends to the restaurant, where there are menus from €11 (except Sun) to €35.

Troyes
10000

ⓒ ⌖ ⬢ Hôtel des Comtes de Champagne**

54–56 rue de la Monnaie; it's in an old street between the town hall and the station, 300m from Saint-Jean church.
ⓣ 03.25.73.11.70 ⓕ 03.25.73.06.02
ⓦ www.comtesdechampagne.com
Disabled access. TV. High chairs available. Pay car park.

A twelfth-century building, which was originally the bank of the counts of Champagne. The walls are thick and the wood panelling from the time of Louis XIV creates an authentic feeling of the past. There's also a small, quiet conservatory. Good prices for a two-star hotel: doubles €35 with shower/wc or €42-65 with bath. Some rooms are particularly spacious. *10% discount on the room rate for a stay of two nights or longer offered to our readers on presentation of this guide.*

ⓒ ⌖ ⬢ Hôtel Arlequin**

50 rue de Turenne; it's near the church of Saint-Pantaléon.
ⓣ 03.25.83.12.70 ⓕ 03.25.83.12.99
ⓦ www.hotelarlequin.com
Closed *Sun and public holidays 12.30–6pm; 23 Dec–2 Jan.* **TV. Motorbike garage.**

The *Arlequin* is a brightly coloured hotel where friendliness seems to be the byword.

The staff takes real pride in looking after guests. They have about twenty bright, spacious rooms at reasonable prices: doubles with shower €39, €52.50–57 with shower/wc or bath. They also have a number of family rooms that can sleep three to five people. *10% discount on the room rate offered to our readers on presentation of this guide.*

⭐ 🎿 🏨 Hôtel de Troyes**

168 av. du Général-Leclerc; from the train station, follow the signs for "Paris, Provins, Soissons"; the hotel is 1.5km from the station.
☎03.25.71.23.45 ☎03.25.79.12.14
🖥 www.hoteldetroyes.fr
Disabled access. TV. Cots available. Car park.

This is for those who prefer somewhere quiet outside the town centre. The immaculate rooms, €47.50 with shower/wc, are decorated in a contemporary style; buffet breakfast at €6.50. There's no restaurant but the owners will gladly guide you to good places to eat nearby. You'll get a charming welcome. *10% discount on the room rate offered to our readers on presentation of this guide.*

⭐ 🏨 Hôtel Le Champ des Oiseaux****

20 rue Linard-Gonthier; it's near the Saint-Pierre cathedral and the modern art museum.
☎03.25.80.58.50 ☎03.25.80.98.34
🖥 www.champdesoiseaux.com
Disabled access. TV. High chairs available. Pay car park.

In a cobbled street with half-timbered houses, this four-star hotel occupies two fifteenth-century houses. There are twelve rooms and a private courtyard, which is a lovely spot to eat breakfast in the summer. Most of the rooms range between €98 and €210 for a double (breakfast is extra at €15), but if you want the very best, the two enormous suites will set you back an extra €20 or so. They're both gorgeous, with exposed beams, armchairs, period furniture and so on. A delightful place, ideal for a special occasion or a romantic break – it's worth a splurge, if you can afford it.

⭐ 🏨 La Maison de Rhodes****

18 rue Linard-Gonthier; near Saint Peter's Cathedral and the Museum of Modern Art.
☎03.25.43.11.11 ☎03.25.43.10.43

🖥 www.maisonderhodes.com

You'll find here the same spirit and liveliness as in the *Champ des Oiseaux* hotel next door, and there's nothing remarkable about that, because the proprietors are from the same family. The bedrooms combine traditional materials and contemporary lines; double rooms €98–198. A sophisticated atmosphere, with a welcome to match, this place is just as enchanting as the house next door. The restaurant is for hotel guests only.

⭐ 🍴 Le Laganum

34 rue Viardin.
☎03.25.73.91.34
Closed *Sun; Mon lunchtime.*

Bernardo, a local character, is the boss in this sixteenth-century half-timbered house. The period dining room has ancient stone walls, beams and a wide chimney – a nice, relaxed place to eat tasty Italian dishes. The pasta is exceptional and the sauces aren't bad either. Expect to pay €15–20 à la carte.

⭐ 🍴 Au Jardin Gourmand

31 rue Paillot-de-Montabert; it's near the town hall.
☎03.25.73.36.13
Closed *Sun; Mon lunchtime; second and third weeks in Jan and Sept.*

This stylish and intimate little restaurant is right in the old part of Troyes. It has a pretty courtyard, which is heated and sheltered in winter and which looks out onto a sixteenth-century timbered wall that the owner restored himself. There's a menu for €16.50; à la carte costs around €30. But what really makes this place stand out is its speciality: home-made tripe sausage cooked ten different ways. All their other dishes use only fresh ingredients, and wine is sold by the glass.

⭐ 🍴 Restaurant Le Bistroquet

10 rue Louis-Ulbach; at the heart of the commercial centre. It's around the corner from rue Émile-Zola, opposite place Langevin.
☎03.25.73.65.65
Closed *Sun evening.*

In the purest style of a 1900s brasserie, this eatery has an impressive menu full of regional specialities, including the succulent home-made *andouillette*, an absolute must, and the market dish of the day.

ⓔ |●| Restaurant Le Valentino

35 rue Paillot-de-Montabert; in the old town centre.
☎03.25.73.14.14
Closed *Sun evening; Mon; Sat lunchtime.*

An extremely pleasant setting (terrace on fine days) for equally pleasant food, this sixteenth-century half-timbered house looks out onto a charming and peaceful little flower-decked courtyard, and accommodates one of the best restaurants in town. There's a perfectly harmonious balance of flavours, spices and herbs in the dishes. The successful partnership of hot and cold create a light and inventive cuisine designed to inspire the maximum pleasure in serious gourmets. The lunchtime menu is at €18, with others at €27 and €44. Diners often return to sample the menu that changes with the season; you are therefore urged to book.

ⓔ |●| Aux Crieurs de Vin

4–6 pl. Jean-Jaurès.
☎03.25.40.01.01
Closed *Sun; Mon; public holidays; a week in March; a fortnight in Aug.*

An old bakery turned into a wine bar, with fashionable décor and a friendly atmosphere. You can sit at wooden tables to enjoy a plate of excellent charcuterie or unfussy bistro dishes, washing them down with a glass of wine from a list that has some interesting finds. Reckon on €20 for a meal, not including drinks.

ⓔ |●| Restaurant Le Café de Paris

63 rue du Général-de-Gaulle; it's next to the church of la Madeleine.
☎03.25.73.08.30
Closed *Sun evening; Tues; a week from mid-Feb; 3 weeks end July to mid-Aug.*

One of the best restaurants in town, with generous servings of good food dished up in a cosy dining room; set menus €21.50–40. Try hot foie gras with apples, Bourgogne snail stew, or Troyes tripe sausage with Chaource cheese. Although it's essentially a lunch spot, it's also a warm and friendly choice for a candlelit dinner.

Sainte-Savine

10300 (2.5km W)

ⓔ ⌂ |●| Motel Savinien**

87 rue La Fontaine; from Troyes take the N60, the "Paris par Sens" road, then turn right less than 2km further on.
☎03.25.79.24.90 ℻03.25.78.04.61
🌐www.motelsavinien.com
Restaurant closed *Sun evening; Mon lunchtime.*
Disabled access. TV. Swimming pool. Car park.

Numerous signposts ensure that this hotel is not hard to find. Though it looks as if it could be part of a chain, it isn't; it is, however, popular with people on the road for business. Facilities include an indoor pool, sauna, tennis, and a gym. The rooms are pretty standard, but prices are attractive considering the quality of service: €45.15–50.40 for doubles with shower/wc or bath. Menus start at €11.70 (weekdays) and up to €30.49. Logis de France.

Bréviandes

10450 (5km SE)

ⓔ ⌂ |●| Hôtel-restaurant Le Pan de Bois**

35 av. du Général-Leclerc; coming from the centre of Troyes, in the direction of Dijon, it's west of the N71 before the intersection on the southbound bypass.
☎03.25.75.02.31 ℻03.25.49.67.84
🌐www.hoteldupandebois.fr
Hotel closed *Sun evening out of season.*
Restaurant closed *Sun evening; Mon lunch; 22 Dec–3 Jan.* **Disabled access. TV. Car park.**

A fairly new, well-designed establishment with all the facilities you'd expect from a chain. The building is designed to suit the local style. The rooms at the back, looking out onto a row of trees, are the most peaceful. Doubles with bath are €50. The restaurant is just next door in a similar building; menus at €16 and €17 (not served on public holidays), and there's another menu at €29. They specialize in house terrines and meats and steaks chargrilled over the open fire, and they serve good local wines. The terrace is especially pleasant in summer. Logis de France.

Saint-André-les-Vergers

10120 (5km SW)

ⓔ ⍤ ⌂ Citotel les Épingliers**

180 rte. d'Auxerre; take the N77 in the direction of Auxerre, and it's less than 1km after the Saint-André roundabout.
☎03.25.75.05.99 ℻03.25.75.32.22

Closed *Christmas school holiday.* **Disabled access. TV. High chairs and cots available. Car park.**

A long seven minutes from the centre, in an unprepossessing commercial zone intersected by the main road. But this little modern house is covered in flowers, the rooms prettily renovated and well-equipped cost €48 for a double (buffet breakfast €8), and they look out onto a bit of the flower garden. All in all, it's a good place. *Free fruit juice or soda offered to our readers on presentation of this guide.*

🄴 ⅀ |❶| La Gentilhommière

180 route d'Auxerre; right next door to the hotel mentioned above.
🕾03.25.49.35.64 📠03.25.75.13.55
🄴 gentilhommière@wanadoo.fr
Closed *Sun and Tues evenings; Wed; last 3 weeks in Aug.* **High chairs available. Car park.**

Next to the *Citotel les Épingliers*, this restaurant suffers from the same unappealing surroundings, and is in a modern building; inside, however, you have a rather chic establishment. The atmosphere, service and food are refined: blinis of crab and lobster, slivers of veal sweetbreads with a concentrate of *Vin de Paille*, and French toast with seasonal fruits. Set menus start at €18 (not Sun), with others €25–53. *Free house apéritif offered to our readers on presentation of this guide.*

Rosières-près-Troyes
10430 (7km S)

🄴 ⅀ ➤ |❶| Auberge de jeunesse

Chemin de Sainte-Scholastique; take bus #6 or 8 from the place des Halles (behind the town hall) right to the terminus.
🕾03.25.82.00.65 📠03.25.72.93.78
🄦 www.fuaj.org
Car park.

Located on the site of a twelfth-century priory, of which a chapel and a parlour surrounded by a moat remain; the youth hostel's premises are modern, but they do not spoil the charm and, what is more, they are surrounded by a large wooded park, a huge garden and a screen of trees. The hubbub of the town seems a world away. There are 104 beds, with six in each room, and bathrooms that are each shared by two rooms; €11.70 including sheets, but you must have an FUAJ (French Youth Hostel

Association) card (sold on site). Meals, which need to be booked, cost are at €8.60; there's a kitchen available. *Free coffee offered to our readers on presentation of this guide.*

Fouchères
10260 (23km SE)

🄴 ⅀ |❶| L'Auberge de la Seine

1 faubourg de Bourgogne; it's on the N71 between Troyes and Bar-sur-Seine.
🕾 and 📠03.25.40.71.11
🄴 cyrillemicard@net-up.com
Closed *Wed; 4 weeks between Jan and Feb; last week in Nov.* **Disabled access. Car park.**

A charming restaurant on the banks of the Seine that looks as if it could be straight out of a de Maupassant story. The dining room has been carefully arranged: the bay windows open onto the river so you can enjoy the cool view, and quacking ducks will serenade you as you dine. The cuisine is delicate and inventive with dishes changing with the seasons. There's a weekday lunch menu for €18, another for €28 or around €35 à la carte. This is a stylish place where you will be warmly welcomed. *Free house apéritif offered to our readers on presentation of this guide.*

Eaux-Puiseaux
10130 (30km SW)

🄴 🏠 |❶| Hôtel L'Étape du P'tit Sim – Restaurant La Ferme du Clocher

5 Grande-Rue.
🕾03.25.42.02.21 📠03.25.42.03.30
Restaurant closed *during Christmas school holiday.* **TV. Car park.**

From a family of champions, the youngest brother, Simon, became part of the history of the 2001 Tour de France when he was the winner of the *maillot jaune* (yellow jersey) for five days. He has now retired from sport to the heart of the region where he was born and in 2004, opposite *La Ferme du Clocher* restaurant, he opened a nineteen-bed hotel, to which he gave his cycling nickname, "p'tit Sim". For all that, he has not forgotten the cycling world, and throughout the hotel photographs recall the Tour de France and some famous stages. In a relaxing orchard setting, the bedrooms are spacious and comfortable; double rooms cost €49. The restaurant is set within a superbly restored old farm.

The dining room is elegantly rustic, with exposed beams and a huge fireplace. You can eat on the veranda and terrace in summer. The cuisine is regional, tasty, comes in generous helpings and changes with the season. Meals range from €16 to €29. The team that greets you on arrival is young, friendly and dynamic. Logis de France.

Vitry-le-François
51300

◎ 🏠 |●| Hôtel-restaurant de la Poste***

Place Royer-Collard; it's behind the Notre-Dame cathedral.
☎03.26.74.02.65 ℗03.26.74.54.71
🌐www.hotellaposte.com
Closed *Sun; 3 weeks in Aug; a fortnight at Christmas.* **Disabled access. TV. Pay car park.**

This comfortable, friendly hotel, on a quiet street, is somewhat better value for money than the pricey restaurant which specializes in fish. Menus go for €24, €38 and €75 or you can choose à la carte. You'll pay €49 for a double room with shower/wc and telephone, and €53 and €74 for a double with bath; breakfast at €8. Nine rooms have Jacuzzis and parking is easy. Logis de France.

◎ 🍴 🏠 |●| Hôtel-restaurant de la Cloche**

34 rue Aristide-Briand; a stone's throw from the place d'Armes.
☎03.26.74.03.84 ℗03.26.74.15.52
✉chef.sautetdomicile@wanadoo.fr
Closed *Sat lunchtime; Sun evening out of season; last fortnight in Dec.* **High chairs available. TV. Pay car park.**

A peaceful provincial town which was much damaged during World War II – as a consequence, it's not exactly an architectural jewel today. However, Mme Sautet will make you feel welcome in her establishment and everything is impeccable, be it the napkins in the restaurant, the sheets, the bedspreads or the bathroom towels. The windows have been double glazed so nothing will disturb your sleep. A double room with shower/wc or bath costs €55–58 a night. Jacques Sautet, the chef, was classically trained and certainly knows his stuff – so much so that he's won three stars for the restaurant. He specializes in good traditional French food and has a talent for pâtisseries. He has given a more contemporary twist to the famous recipe for *matelote* sauce and other dishes, including trout soufflé with a champagne sauce and ox cheek braised in beer; menus at €21–43. Next door to the hotel, the *Brelest* charcuterie is recommended for its excellent *boudins* and tripe sausage (perfect for barbecues), garlic sausage and pork brawn (great for sandwiches). Logis de France. *Free house apéritif offered to our readers on presentation of this guide.*

◎ 🍴 |●| La Pizza chez Didier

17 Grande-Rue-de-Vaux.
☎03.26.74.17.63
Closed *Sat and Sun lunchtimes; Mon; Sept.*

The pizzas come in a range of sizes to suit all appetites, and with original, tasty toppings. They also offer a nice selection of dishes such as fresh pasta with lobsters' tails. There's a special night-time cinema deal (one dish of your choice = a discount on a cinema ticket). Reckon on around €7–12 à la carte. The menus and the décor change often. *10% discount on the bill offered to our readers on presentation of this guide.*

◎ 🍴 |●| Restaurant du Marché

5 rue des Sœurs; a stone's throw from the place d'Armes.
☎03.26.73.21.98
Closed *Mon.*

Without question, the best value for money in town. The setting and the cooking are unfussy, and the only aim is to feed you decently without ruining you. And that's not a bad ambition. The dishes are simple and very traditional – prepared with fresh produce and generously served. The menus range from €11.90 to €21.50, and it's a big favourite with the locals who crowd the place. *Free coffee offered to our readers on presentation of this guide.*

Vitry-en-Perthois
51300 (4km NE)

◎ |●| Auberge la Pavoise

26 rue de la Trinité; take the D982 in the direction of Sainte-Ménehould and the D995 towards Bar-le-Duc.
☎03.26.74.59.00

Closed Open *every day except Sun, subject to reservation; 31 Dec–15 Jan; 15–31 Aug.* **High chairs available.**

A converted cowshed, formerly part of the working farm, decorated in a rustic style. Menus vary according to the seasons and are prepared with fresh local produce; reckon on €22–38 à la carte. Try chicken with Champagne or duck fillet with Ratafia liqueur. Desserts are a hit with everyone, and good wines are sold at reasonable prices. They don't accept credit cards.

Sainte-Marie-du-Lac

51290 (20km SE)

ⓦ 🏠 🍴 La Bocagère

Les Grandes-Côtes; take the D13 as far as Larzicourt, then take the D57 to Blaize, followed by the D60.
☎03.26.72.37.40.
🖥free.bocagere.fr.
Closed *Dec–Jan.* **Restaurant closed** *lunchtimes and Sun.*

A charming farm converted into a simple but pleasant inn offering double rooms at €42. Nestled in a peaceful hamlet on the edge of the Lac du Der, it is the perfect base from which to explore Europe's largest artificial lake (11,861 acres). The manager, a Parisian convert, also serves some simple but wholesome dishes. There is just one menu at €20 (it is advisable to book in advance).

ⓦ 🍴 Le Cycloder

Les Grandes Côtes. Take the D13 to Larzicourt, then the D57 to Blaize, then the D60.
☎03.26.72.37.05
Closed *1 Dec–28 Feb.* **Disabled access.**

A lovely *crêperie* where you can get quality *galettes* for €2–5.10 and crêpes at €1.60–4.10 – not to mention a friendly welcome. They rent out bikes, which are perfect for exploring the banks of the Lac du Der nearby. Credit cards not accepted.

Giffaumont-Champaubert

51290 (26km SE)

ⓦ 🏠 🍴 Hôtel-restaurant Le Cheval Blanc***

21 rue du Lac; take the D13.
☎03.26.72.62.65 🖨03.26.73.96.97
📧lechevalblanc6@aol.com
Restaurant closed *Sun eve; Mon; Tues lunchtime; 2 weeks in Jan; 2 weeks in Sept.* **TV. Disabled access. High chairs available. Car park.**

Set in an adorable village full of half-timbered houses near the Lac du Der, the largest artificial lake in Europe and also a bird reserve. Thierry Gérardin, the young owner, was spurred into rapid action when he took over: all the bathrooms have been renovated and there's a new reception and sitting room. You'll get a wonderful welcome, and the modern rooms cost €65 for a double with shower/wc or bath. They serve meals in the open air in spring and summer or on the flower-ornamented terrace. The cheapest set menu, €21, is simple and generous. Other menus cost up to €41. Logis de France.

Vouziers

08400

ⓦ 🏠 🍴 Argonne Hôtel**

Route de Reims; it's on the way out of town on the Châlons-Retel road, by the first roundabout.
☎03.24.71.42.14 🖨03.24.71.83.69
📧argonnehotel@wanadoo.fr
Restaurant closed *Sun evening.* **TV. High chairs available. Car park.**

This modern building in the commercial park is neither characterful nor charming, though the welcoming owners certainly are. It's an ideal place for an overnight stop. The rooms are attractively decorated and good value: €43 for a double with shower/wc or bath. Menus €10.50 (not Sun) and €14.50–23 list classic cuisine with occasional exotic touches — try terrine of foie gras with Armagnac or the duck breast with gingerbread.

Buzancy

08240 (22km NE)

ⓦ 🌲 🏠 🍴 Hôtel du Saumon**

Place Chanzy; from Vouziers take the D947.
☎03.24.30.00.42 🖨03.25.30.27.47
🖥www.hoteldusaumon.com
Restaurant closed *Sat lunchtime.* **High chairs available. TV.**

A charming hotel that it would be easy to fall in love with, right in the middle of the small town and offering a particularly friendly welcome. The house has been totally refurbished – each of the nine rooms is decorated differently but with the same good taste throughout, and though the rooms vary in size they all have the same facilities. Doubles cost €50–60 with shower/wc or bath; some have a garden view. There are two dining rooms, one of them a very pleasant bistro offering a *menu-carte* assembled from the fresh produce bought at market. Menus start at €11 (except Sundays), then €17 and €25. *Free coffee offered to our readers on presentation of this guide.*

Corsica

Ajaccio
20000

ⓒ ⅔ 🏠 Hôtel Marengo**

2 rue Marengo, BP244; it's near the casino and the beaches, on the road going to the Îles Sanguinaires.
☎04.95.21.43.66 ⓕ04.95.21.51.26
Closed *mid-Nov to early April.* **TV.**

This is a lovely and very reliable little place at the end of a quiet cul-de-sac. One of our most long-standing recommendations in Ajaccio, and also one of the most trustworthy. Double rooms with shower or bath cost €45–64, according to the season; some rooms look out onto a peaceful courtyard with flowers everywhere. It's basic but well run, offers a warm welcome and has good facilities, including air-conditioning and double glazing. *10% discount on the room rate (1 Oct–30 July) offered to our readers on presentation of this guide.*

ⓒ ⅔ 🏠 Hôtel Fesch***

7 rue Fesch.
☎04.95.51.62.62 ⓕ04.95.21.83.36
ⓦwww.hotel-fesch.com
Closed *15 Dec–15 Jan.* **TV.**

The *Fesch* is a very well-kept hotel in a pedestrian street, superbly located in the centre of town. The rooms are generally comfortable and renovated, with chestnut furniture, a minibar and air-conditioning. The price of a room depends on the facilities and the season: doubles are €60–85 with shower/wc or bath, breakfast €7. If you want a top-floor room with a balcony, it'll cost a bit more. *One free breakfast per room (except 15 July–15 Sept; maximum of*

two people per room) offered to our readers on presentation of this guide.

ⓒ ⅔ 🏠 |●| Hôtel Imperial***

6 bd. Albert-1er.
☎04.95.21.50.62 ⓕ04.95.21.15.20
Closed *Nov–March.* **TV.**

A three-star hotel with a lovely Second Empire-style entrance. Take a look at the poster for Abel Gance's film epic *Napoléon* in reception. The large rooms are comfortable and well maintained and cost €65–87, depending on facilities and the season. Rooms in the more modern annexe are smaller and cheaper, but they don't have air-conditioning. There's a private beach just across the way. They like you to stay half board (€54–68 per person) in July and August. *Free house apéritif offered to our readers on presentation of this guide.*

ⓒ ⅔ |●| A Casa

21 av. Noël-Franchini; it's 2km north – go along the coast road towards the airport and turn left at the traffic lights at the end of boulevard. Charles-Bonaparte.
☎04.95.22.34.78
Closed *Sun; 10 Dec–10 Feb.*

This restaurant is outside the centre, but the originality of the place draws a lot of local people. They've squeezed about ten tables onto the patio/balcony, which is surrounded by plants, flowers and parasols. The cooking is uncomplicated but good: the *menu Corse* is particularly tasty. The weekday menu is €12.20, with others at €19.82 and €32.78. There's a single menu for €30 on magic nights and a children's menu at €15.24 or €18.29, depending on

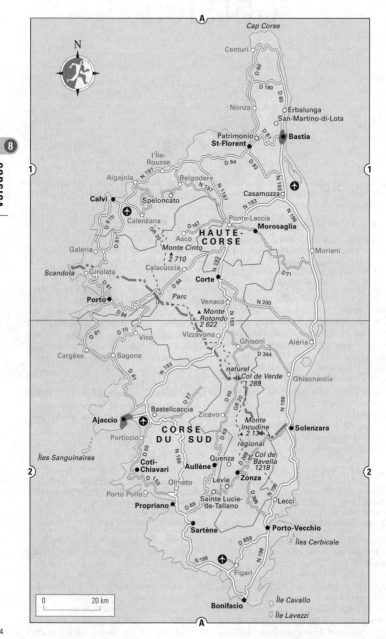

their age; also, excellent Sartène or Muscat wine. The real attraction is on a Friday or Saturday night when Frank, the boss (also a professional magician), puts on a show with an astonishing succession of conjuring tricks. Be sure to book for the show – you won't be disappointed. *Free coffee offered to our readers on presentation of this guide.*

Le 20123

2 rue du Roi-de-Rome; it's in the old town.
☎04.95.21.50.05
Closed *lunchtimes; Mon; mid-Jan to mid-Feb.*

This restaurant, which opened in 1987, used to be in Pila Canale, up in the mountains behind Ajaccio. They moved into a pedestrian street in the old town and set up with the same décor as before. Inside it's almost like a Corsican village with cottages, lanterns and a fountain; there's even an old Vespa parked on the small terrace outside. The single menu, €27, lists serious Corsican charcuterie, *brocciu* tart made with sheep's-milk cheese, and a variety of meats – pork, veal, lamb and boar – which are grilled or served as stews. Finish with some genuine local cheese and a simple dessert like flan made with ground chestnuts. Credit cards not accepted. *Free liqueur offered to our readers on presentation of this guide.*

Bastelicaccia

20129 (13km NE)

Môtel l'Orangeraie**

It's on the way out of the village towards Porticcio, on the left.
☎04.95.20.00.09 Ⓕ04.95.20.09.24
TV. Swimming pool. Car park.

The garden, which is filled with palms, arbutus and orange trees, is one of the most amazing in Corsica and it's maintained with passionate care by Monsieur Grisoni. The bungalows are hidden away in glorious Mediterranean vegetation. The setting is wonderful and you'll get a warm welcome. You can rent studios for one to three people or two rooms for two to five people, on a daily or weekly basis; they cost €35–65/€58–88 depending on the season. They're not brand new but they're well equipped, with good bedding, heating, TV, hair-dryers, kitchen, terrace and barbecue. There's a small swimming pool. Remember to book early, as it's often full. Credit cards not accepted.

Aullène

20116

Hôtel-restaurant de la Poste*

Rue Principale.
☎04.95.78.61.21 Ⓕ04.95.78.61.21
Closed *1 Oct–30 April.*

This attractive stone inn with a lovely view of the mountains was built when people were travelling around in carriages; it's one of the oldest hotels in Corsica, dating back to 1880. The rooms are clean, simple but comfortable, with toilets upstairs. Double rooms with shower are €40; half board, €50 per person. The cooking in the restaurant is simple, but the house charcuterie is excellent; menus €15.50 and €21. It is worth trying – in season – the wild boar or sautéed veal with olives. The owner, Jeannot Benedetti, a larger than life character and great promoter of the region, has compiled a small guide of southern Corsica, which he lends out to guests.

Quenza

20122 (8km E)

Auberge Sole e Monti**

Take the D420.
☎04.95.78.62.53 Ⓕ04.95.78.63.88
Ⓦwww.solemonti.com
Closed *1 Oct–30 April.* **Restaurant closed** *Mon; Tues lunchtime.* **TV.**

Félicien Balesi, a bon vivant who knows how to make his guests feel at home, has run this friendly inn since 1968. The relatively new building has a loggia that would be lovelier still with a sea view; at any rate, it's the perfect spot to admire the beauty of the Corsican mountains, although a bit pricey. There's a huge garden on the other side of the road available for the guests to enjoy. When the weather is inclement regulars gather around the open fire in a cosy salon. The menu changes daily because only fresh produce is used and the delicious dishes are inspired by old Corsican recipes; set menu €28 (not Sun), or reckon on €40-45 à la carte. Rooms are pleasant and well equipped. They prefer people to stay half board; the cost per person, sharing a double room with shower/wc or bath, is €70–90. Logis de France. *Free coffee offered to our readers on presentation of this guide.*

Bastia

20200

◉ 🎋 🏛 Hôtel Cyrnéa**

Route du Cap; 2km from the centre of Bastia, on the right as you enter Pietranera.
☎04.95.31.41.71 📠04.95.31.72.65
Closed *15 Dec–15 Jan.* **Disabled access. TV. Pay car park.**

A long 1970s building, very well maintained, with air-conditioned rooms and fans. Behind, the big garden slopes down to a small pebbly beach 30m from the hotel. Depending on the season and whether you have a view of the road or the sea, doubles with shower/wc cost €46–83, including breakfast. The sea-view rooms all have a balcony – ideal for watching the sun rise over Elba and Monte Cristo at breakfast. *Free coffee, and free use of the garage (except 1 Oct–31 May), offered to our readers on presentation of this guide.*

◉ 🏛 L'Alivi***

Route du Cap; it's 1km from the marina on the right.
☎04.95.55.00.00 📠04.95.31.03.95
🖳 www.hotel-alivi.com
Closed *Dec.* **Disabled access. TV. Swimming pool. Car park.**

Seen from the sea, this long oblong structure, three storeys high, doesn't do the coastline any favours. But inside, you really appreciate the comfort of the rooms and direct access to the pebble beach as well as the very professional service. All rooms have a sea view, a balcony and all the facilities you'd expect from a three-star hotel. A double room with shower or bath costs €95–165, depending on the season.

◉ ❘◉❘ Restaurant a Casarella

6 rue Sainte-Croix; it's in the citadel.
☎04.95.32.02.32
Closed *Sat lunchtime; Sun; Nov.* **Disabled access.**

You have to climb up to the citadel, near the Palais of the Genoese governors, to find this place. The long terrace has a few tables with a view of the port (booking advisable). The inventive chef prepares

good authentic Corsican dishes scented with herbs from the maquis that are worth going miles for. Try the *casgiate*, a fromage frais fritter baked in the oven, the (absolutely delicious) rolled veal with herbs, or the stuffed baby crabs. Desserts include the curious *strozzapreti*, a stodgy cake that the people here used to bake for the parish priest on Sundays, and the wonderful *fiadone*, a cheese and orange flan. There is a lunchtime "discovery" platter at €15 and a menu at €28 in the evening; expect to pay around €28 à la carte. It's highly recommended.

San-Martino-Di-Lota

20200 (5km NW)

◉ 🎋 🏛 ❘◉❘ Hôtel-restaurant de la Corniche;

Take the D131 to Castagnetu.
☎04.95.31.40.98 📠04.95.32.37.69
🖳 www.hotel-lacorniche.com
Closed *Sun evening; Mon and Tues lunchtimes; Jan.* **Open** *noon–2pm; 7.30–10pm.* **TV. Swimming pool. Car park.**

The first impression of this place evokes an eagle's nest – the terrace shaded by plane trees offers a stunning view of a natural amphitheatre of mountains plunging down to the sea. The comfortable rooms are reasonably priced with doubles from €49 to €89, depending on the season; half board is €50–75 per person. The restaurant is very popular with local people. Although the talented and enthusiastic chef is adept at tastefully revising his menu according to the season (menus €25–45), it is the classic Corsican recipes of Madame Anziani that take pride of place. It is advisable to book. *10% discount on the room rate (1 Nov–30 April) offered to our readers on presentation of this guide.*

Erbalunga

20222 (8km N)

◉ 🏛 Hôtel Castel Brando***

Along the coast via the D80.
☎04.95.30.10.30 📠04.95.33.98.18
🖳 www.castelbrando.com
Closed *1 Nov–13 March.* **Disabled access. TV. Swimming pool. Car park.**

This hotel is in a nineteenth-century Corsican mansion (a *palazzu*) and has great character and charm. It has been tastefully restored and furnished with antiques. The walls are colour-washed in strong pigments and there's an impressive monumental staircase; it all feels slightly Latin American. The garden is planted with palm trees. Near the heated swimming pool, the pretty rooms in the annexe are quieter than those in the main building (where the rooms overlooking the road are to be avoided). All rooms have air-conditioning, shower or bath, and telephone, and the service is excellent. Doubles go for €69–134 depending on facilities and season.

Casamozza

20200 (20km S)

⊛ 🕭 🛎 |●| Chez Walter***

It's on the N193, about 4km beyond the airport crossroads.
☏ 04.95.36.00.09 ℗ 04.95.36.18.92
🖳 www.chez-walter.com
Closed 15 Dec–10 Jan **Restaurant open** noon–2.30pm and 7.30–10.30pm.
Restaurant closed Sun in season; New Year.
Disabled access. TV. High chairs available. Swimming pool. Car park.

A fine, comfortable, professionally run and reliable establishment on the Bastia road, just to the south of the town. Air-conditioned doubles with shower or bath are €80–100 depending on the season; breakfast costs €8. There's a pool, tennis court and a lovely garden. It's a place used by ship crews stopping over, and by visiting football teams who come to play Bastia. The restaurant has a good reputation with tasty fish dishes (sea bream, crayfish and other seafood) and a single menu at €20. *Free coffee offered to our readers on presentation of this guide.*

Bonifacio

20169

⊛ 🕭 🛎 |●| Domaine de Licetto

Route du Phare-de-Pertusato; 2km from the port.
Hotel ☏ and ℗ 04.95.73.03.59
Restaurant ☏ 04.95.73.19.48
Restaurant open April–Oct **Restaurant closed** lunchtimes; Sun. **Disabled access. Car park.**

There's an unusual view of both the upper and lower towns from the grounds here. The *Domaine* is right in the maquis and the modern hotel is in a separate building 50m from the restaurant. The fifteen or so rooms are smart and good-value for Bonifacio; doubles €36–67 with shower/

wc or €45–77 with bath, depending on the season. The restaurant, one of the best in Bonifacio, serves traditional Corsican cooking with a single set menu at €31; dining is from 8pm. Note that booking is essential and credit cards are not accepted. *Free house apéritif or liqueur (for a stay of one week in high season) offered to our readers on presentation of this guide.*

⊛ 🕭 🛎 Hôtel des Étrangers*

Avenue Sylvère-Bohn; it's 300m from the port, hidden beneath a cliff, on the right of the road from Ajaccio.
☏ 04.95.73.01.09 ℗ 04.95.73.16.97
Closed 1 Nov–31 March. **Disabled access. TV. Car park.**

Pretty close to the road but the soundproofing is efficient. The most expensive rooms have TV and air-conditioning, but they are all very clean. Room prices – €42–74 for a double, depending on the season – include breakfast. This is good value for Bonifacio. There's a lock-up for motorbikes. *10% discount (in April) on the room rate offered to our readers on presentation of this guide.*

⊛ 🕭 🛎 |●| A Trama

Cartarana, route de Santa-Marza; it's 1.5km from the town centre.
☏ 04.95.73.17.17 ℗ 04.95.73.17.79
🖳 www.a-trama.com
Restaurant closed 15 Nov–31 March.
Disabled access. TV. Swimming pool. Car park.

In a peaceful setting surrounded by greenery, this new complex has been handsomely built and is well maintained. There are 25 rooms at garden level, each with a private terrace facing the swimming pool – perfect for breakfast. All rooms have modern facilities such as TV, mini-bar and air-conditioning, and the beds are "dorsopedic", apparently. Doubles go for €83–150, depending on the season. It's a nice place, the welcome is courteous and professional, but it is a little pricey. The restaurant, *Le Clos Vatel*, has a good reputation. There's a single menu at €29 or à la carte. *Free house apéritif or digestif offered to our readers on presentation of this guide.*

⊛ 🕭 🛎 |●| Hôtel-restaurant du Centre Nautique***

It's on the north side of the marina across from the quai Jérôme-Comparetti, next to the harbour master's office.

☎04.95.73.02.11 ⓕ04.95.73.17.47
ⓦwww.centre-nautique.com
Closed Mon (Oct–March). **Restaurant open**
noon–3pm and 7–10pm. **TV. High chairs**
available. Car park.

This grand and beautiful building stands on
its own quay, which is quiet compared to the
one opposite. It has ten spacious and classy
duplex rooms, with contemporary interiors
and plenty of facilities such as mini-bars and
air-conditioning. There are sofa beds in the
ground-floor sitting rooms; bedroom and
shower are upstairs. A duplex with sea view
costs €85 (Oct–March), €140 (April–June
and Sept), or €190 (July–Aug). The garden-
view rooms are cheaper. Add €34 per
person for half board. There's also a restaurant, à la carte only, serving excellent and
huge plates of fresh pasta; reckon on around
€40 for a meal. *Free house liqueur offered to our*
readers on presentation of this guide.

Calvi

20260

◎ 🏠 Hôtel les Arbousiers**

Route de Pietra-Maggiore; from the centre,
take the road towards Bastia and L'Île
Rousse; after 800m turn right at the start of
the pine forest running along the Calvi beach,
and follow the signs.
☎04.95.65.04.47 ⓕ04.95.65.26.14
Closed end Sept to 1 May. **TV. Car park.**

It can be best to stay just outside Calvi,
simply because you get more space. This
hotel is in an attractive big house with
pink walls and an old wooden staircase
leading up to the bedrooms. The décor
isn't spectacular, but the rooms are spick
and span, quiet and sunny (especially on
the south side). Pretty little balconies overlook the courtyard. Ask for a south-facing
room to maximize the sun. The prices are
reasonable: doubles with bath €38–54.
The beach is just five minutes' walk away.

◎ 🍴 🏠 ▮◐▮ Hôtel-restaurant Casa-vecchia

Route de Santore; it's 500m from the town
centre and 200m from the beach and pine
woods.
☎04.95.65.09.33 ⓕ04.95.65.37.93
Hotel open all year. **Restaurant open** evenings only early May to mid-Sept. **Disabled**
access. TV. Car park.

The accommodation is in ten quiet, clean
rooms in a garden full of flowers. The hotel

has been refurbished and the bungalows
have given way to entirely new rooms,
including two rooms especially fitted out
for disabled guests, studios, duplexes, a
small cottage and guest rooms in a villa.
Double rooms are €44–55 with shower/
wc, €55–60 for extra-large ones; breakfast
is served in an arbour. Half board (compulsory during July–Aug) costs €85–110
for two people. The owner and her daughters will welcome you warmly; they offer
good, generously served family cooking
on two menus, €15 and €17. *Free house*
liqueur (1 Oct–31 May) offered to our readers
on presentation of this guide.

◎ 🍴 🏠 Résidence Les Aloès**

Quartier Donatéo; from the centre of town,
take the road to Île Rousse and go straight
on towards the stadium. It's signposted.
☎04.95.65.01.46 ⓕ04.95.65.01.67
ⓦwww.hotel-les-aloes.com
Closed 20 Oct–15 April. **Disabled access. TV.**
High chairs and cots available. Car park.

This hotel was built in the 1960s on a
fabulous site above Calvi – you get a
panoramic view of the bay, the citadel
and the wild countryside towards Monte
Cinto. The surroundings are peaceful and
there are flowers everywhere. The décor
combines designer furniture with more
old-fashioned pieces, and the refurbished
rooms have telephone, air-conditioning
and balcony. Prices are €46–58 (high
season €56–68) for a double, depending
on the view (garden or sea). *10% discount*
for a minimum three-night stay (15 April–30
May and 15 Sept–20 Oct) offered to our read-
ers on presentation of this guide.

◎ 🏠 Le Grand Hôtel***

3 bd. Wilson.
☎04.95.65.09.74 ⓕ04.95.65.25.18
ⓦwww.grand-hotel-calvi.com
Closed 31 Oct–1 April. **TV. High chairs**
available.

They don't build places like this early-
twentieth-century grand hotel any more:
corridors as wide as rooms, a smoking
room as large as a ballroom and bedrooms
as big as – well, big bedrooms. The TV
room looks a bit dated, and the armchairs need to be re-covered, but they're
comfortable; the rooms themselves have
been given a lick of paint and have tasteful furnishings as well as air-conditioning.
Doubles cost €86–95, depending on the
season and facilities. Nice welcome, a good

atmosphere and a spectacular view from the breakfast room: it's high up, so you look down on the rooftops of Calvi to the sea beyond. Somewhere out of the ordinary.

◎ 🎿 |●| L'Abri Côtier

Quai Landry; it's by the harbour.
☏04.95.65.12.76
Open *noon–2pm and 7–10pm (10.30pm at weekends) out of season, until 10.30pm (11pm at weekends) in high season.* **Closed** *end Nov to early March.* **Disabled access. High chairs available.**

The restaurant is on the first floor, above a bar and tearoom. There's a big dining room overlooking the terrace and the marina serving menus €12.50 (lunch) and others €20–35. The cooking zings with fresh flavours – try their fish grilled with a drizzle of olive oil, starters of fruit and vegetables or their dishes using *brocciu* (mild sheep's milk cheese) – an unusual, fresh and enticing touch. Pleasant, efficient service; this is one of the most reliable places in Calvi. *Free coffee offered to our readers on presentation of this guide.*

Speloncato

20226 (34km E)

◎ 🎿 🏠 A Spelunca**

Place de l'Église; take the N197 heading towards l'Île Rousse, then the D71.
☏04.95.61.50.38 ☏04.95.61.53.14
Closed *1 Nov–31 March.*

An attractive, privately owned hotel close to the church offering a particularly courteous and friendly welcome. This pink house with a little turret and a lovely terrace was built as the summer residence of Cardinal Savelli, the Secretary of State to Pope Pius IX, and you can see his portrait in the grand drawing room. The rooms, some of them with views of the valley, lead off from a superb staircase. Doubles cost €50–70 with shower or bath, depending on the season. It cannot be bettered for value for money, or for authentic Corsican atmosphere. *One free breakfast per room offered to our readers on presentation of this guide.*

Corte

20250

◎ 🏠 Hôtel de la Poste

2 pl. du Duc-de-Padoue; in the lower town.

☏04.95.46.01.37
Open *all year.* **Disabled access.**

An old hotel on a shady square, with a dozen totally refurbished and reasonably priced rooms, looking onto the *place* or out over the back (these are quieter). Doubles are €36 with shower, or €45 with shower/wc – good if you're on a budget and want somewhere central. They don't take credit cards, though.

◎ 🎿 |●| L'Oliveraie

Lieu-dit Perru; from the centre head for the university, and when you come to the junction with the main road, take the road to Erbagolo. It's 150m further on the left.
☏04.95.46.06.32
Closed *Mon evening in winter; 1 Nov–15 Dec.*

This very good restaurant, on the outskirts of town, is in a large stone house with a covered terrace dominated by an imposing olive tree and a garden full of fruit trees. Mme Mattei uses Corsican produce to prepare tasty dishes such as *buglidicce* (fromage frais fritters), herb tart, squid stuffed with *brocciu* (mild sheep's-milk cheese), and for dessert, hazelnut and ground chestnut tart – the house speciality. Delicious Set menus, €10–24, with generous helpings – it's popular with students and staff from the nearby campus. *Free liqueur offered to our readers on presentation of this guide.*

◎ |●| U Museu

Rampe Ribanelle; at the foot of the citadel, pl. des Armes.
☏04.95.61.08.36
Closed *8 Nov–2 April.* **Open** *10am–2pm and 5–10pm.*

A charming restaurant with a pretty terrace in the shadow of two round canopies that create the effect of an arbour. The excellent dishes are served in generous proportions and there's lots of choice. Expect to pay €13 for a main course plus dessert, or €15 for the menu. The cuisine – including dishes such as herb tart, wild boar stew and *délice* of chestnuts – is truly delicious. If you're on a budget you can't go wrong with the salad of two different kinds of goat's cheese, almonds, bacon and potatoes. The jugs of AOC wine go down a treat.

Coti-Chiavari

20138

@ ☎ |●| Hôtel-restaurant le Belvédère

Take the D55 from Porticcio towards the village of Coti-Chiavari; it's on the left of the Acqua Doria road before you get to the village.
℡04.95.27.10.32 ℻04.95.27.12.99
Hotel closed *11 Nov–15 Feb.* **Restaurant closed** *lunchtimes June–Oct.* **Disabled access. Car park.**

A long, low and fairly modern building on its own overlooking the bay of Ajaccio. From the arc of the circular terrace, you get one of the best views of the island. On some nights the sea is covered by a layer of clouds, and guests can feel as if they're on top of the world, looking down from afar. Caroline, the patronne, really takes care of her guests. Good, generous Corsican family cooking is served in the restaurant with set menus at €20 (weekdays) and €25. The rooms are simple, very clean and have balconies: €50–66 for a double with shower/wc or bath, breakfast €5. Half board, €90–106 for two, is obligatory in summer. This place is reliable and offers good service – nothing like the rip-off joints you'll find on the coast – but they don't accept credit cards. And it's a good idea to phone before coming, for the hotel as well as the restaurant.

Morosaglia

20218

@ |●| Osteria di u Cunventu

Santa Croce; take the D71; it is near the old convent, in the town.
℡04.95.47.11.79
Open *noon–2pm and 8–10.30pm.* **Closed** *Mon (15 April-30 Sept); Mon to Fri lunchtimes (winter); last fortnight in Feb; last fortnight in Oct.*

A new arrival on the scene that has quickly earned a reputation for the quality of its cuisine. There is a short menu that changes with the seasons – the meat *confits* are particularly delicious, and the homemade desserts are also outstanding – otherwise it's à la carte only: expect to pay €21–35 per meal. There are only a few tables, so it's advisable to book. Credit cards not accepted.

Porto

20150

@ ☎ Hôtel le Colombo**

Porto village; on the right, just by the entrance to the village on the Calvi road.
℡04.95.26.10.14 ℻04.95.26.19.90
@www.porto-tourisme.com
Closed *11 Nov to Easter.* **High chairs and games available.**

If the owners continue to overhaul this once-classic little hotel as they are doing, it will soon merit the label of a "designer hotel". The whole place is lined with wood and the walls have been painted blue with a sponge. The little garden is equally splendid. Double rooms cost €59–120, according to the season and the position, with an excellent breakfast included. Rooms are also available for three or four people. All are decorated according to a different theme, and most of them offer a stunning view (in some cases, from their balcony) of the Gulf of Porto and the mountain. The service is very attentive.

Porto-Vecchio

20137

@ 🎿 |●| Le Tourisme

12 cours Napoléon; it's in the upper town near the church.
℡04.95.70.06.45
Closed *Sun lunchtime.*

This restaurant in the upper town has been given a breath of fresh air by the new chef, who offers tasty, inventive recipes inspired by the fresh produce available in the region. There are several set menus ranging from €18 to €36, plus a large selection of dishes à la carte; attractive dining room and pretty terrace dominated by various shades of blue. *Free house apéritif offered to our readers on presentation of this guide.*

Lecci-de-Porto-Vecchio

20137 (9km N)

@ ☎ Hôtel et Résidence Caranella Village

Route de Cala-Rossa; 3km along then N198, at La Trinité turn right at the Cala-Rossa signpost, turn left at the next roundabout and head straight on for 4km.

☎04.95.71.60.94 ⓕ04.95.71.60.80
🌐www.caranella-village.com
Closed *Jan.* **Disabled access. TV. Swimming pool. Car park.**

Set in flower-filled grounds just 300m from the Cala Rossa beach. About forty self-catering studios, villas and apartments (some with oven, microwave, telephone and dishwasher), either at ground level or upstairs. Most have a terrace and are set around the heated swimming pool. Facilities include bike rental, a bar, restaurant, linen hire (at an extra cost), a cleaning service and a washing room. Given the prices in Porto-Vecchio and taking into account the level of comfort and position, the *Caranella Village* is really unbeatable value. Standard rooms cost €56–126, depending on the season; studios with shower and corner kitchen cost €560 per week in the high season; you pay more for a bathroom. There are also villas and apartments of varying degrees of comfort for 4 to 6 people. Friendly welcome and easygoing atmosphere are assured; reservations are recommended.

Propriano
20110

ⓒ 🛏 Loft Hôtel**

3 rue Jean-Paul-Pandolfi; in a residential block by the port.
☎04.95.76.17.48 ⓕ04.95.76.22.04
Closed *1 Nov–14 April.* **Disabled access. TV. Car park.**

This hotel, a converted old wine warehouse huddled among a group of houses, lives up to its name. As you might expect, its clean rooms have a modern minimalist look, with pale-coloured tiles and wood. Doubles are €46–65 depending on the season; the cheaper rooms are on the ground floor. There's a nice welcome on offer, too.

ⓒ 🛏 Motel Aria Marina**

Lieu-dit la Cuparchiata; it's in the hills above Propriano. From the centre, take the road to Sartène then turn left towards Viggianello; left again and follow the signs to the motel.
☎04.95.76.04.32 ⓕ04.95.76.25.01
Closed *15 Oct–2 April.* **TV. Swimming pool. Car park.**

This is a good motel, some distance from the brouhaha in Propriano and, better still,

with a great view of the Gulf of Valinco. Double rooms cost €60–81, depending on the season. The studios, two- and three-roomed apartments are spacious and have good facilities. In July and August they rent the studios by the week only at €572–628; the two- and three-roomed apartments cost more so you'll need to check. Nice staff, and the pool is lovely, too.

ⓒ |●| Terra Cotta

29 av. Napoléon; in the port.
☎04.95.74.23.80

This is *the* place to eat in Propriano. You can dine in a small, tastefully decorated dining room or over the road on a pretty, intimate terrace overlooking the port. The food is distinctive, with fresh meat, fish, seafood and vegetables combined to create inventive, subtle flavours, aptly complemented by the fine wines on offer. Reckon on €40 for a full meal à la carte. The sophistication and colour of the presentation provide a feast for the eyes and make the mouth water. Altogether outstanding – only the most voracious customers will manage to finish the gargantuan helpings.

Saint-Florent
20217

ⓒ 🛏 Hôtel Maxime**

Route de la Cathédrale; small quiet street off place des Portes.
☎04.95.37.05.30 ⓕ04.95.37.13.07
Disabled access. TV. Car park.

A fairly new and very clean hotel, good value for the resort. Each room has a mini-bar and balcony; some of them overlook the River Poggio, where you can arrange to moor your (small) boat. Doubles €48–70; prices vary with the season. There's a lock-up for motorbikes. Pets are not allowed.

Patrimonio
20253 (5km NE)

ⓒ 🍴 🛏 Hôtel U Casone

Coming from Saint-Florent, climb to the centre of Patrimonio, but don't take the left turn towards the church; continue 250m on the D81, then take the right hairpin and you'll see the sign.
☎04.95.37.14.46 ⓕ04.95.37.17.15

Closed *1 Nov–1 April.* **Car park.**

Located in the upper village, this is a large house faced with grey rough-cast. There is a large terrace with lawns and cherry trees, where you can have breakfast or enjoy the sun. The simple, well-kept rooms, with a view of the mountains or the distant sea, come in a range of sizes, and the prices vary accordingly. Doubles are €35–80, depending on facilities and the season. There's a family atmosphere to this unpretentious place. Make sure you try a bottle or two of the Clos Montemagni – the vineyard isn't far. There's a lock-up for motorbikes and the beaches are about 3km away. Credit cards not accepted.

Sartène
20100

@ 🏠 **Hôtel Villa Piana*****

Route de Propriano; it's 1km before Sartène.
☎04.95.77.07.04 ℗04.95.73.45.65
🖰www.lavillapiana.com
Closed *early Nov to end March.* **TV. Swimming pool. Car park.**

A pretty, ochre-coloured house amid trees and flowers. The rooms have been carefully decorated, and most have a view over Sartène. Avoid the ones overlooking the back because they're not great, particularly those on the ground floor. Doubles cost €57–95, breakfast €8. Facilities include tennis court, bar and a pool with a superb panoramic view. There's also a lock-up for motorbikes. Recommended.

@ |●| **Auberge Santa Barbara**

In Santa Barbara, on the Propiano road; 2km from Sartène, via the Propriano road.
☎04.95.77.09.06
Open *noon–1.45pm and 7.30–10pm.* **Closed** *Mon in low season, Mon lunchtime from 1 July to 15 Sept; end Oct to end March.*

The very good food has earned this restaurant a reputation even outside Corsica. The owner, Gisèle Lovichi, knows, like few others, how to bring out the best of her island's culinary traditions. There's a menu at €27, or expect to pay €35–40 à la carte. Booking is essential.

Saint-Lucie-de-Tallano
20112 (19km NE)

@ 🎋 |●| **La Santa Lucia**

Place du monument aux morts.

☎04.95.78.81.28
Closed *Sun out of season; Jan.* **Car park.**

There's a pleasant terrace with a view of the fountain. The owner greets his guests with a warm, natural smile and serves excellent Corsican food. The cheaper menu at €15.30 is decent enough – if rather ordinary – but the €21.30 one really showcases the talents of the chefs. The dishes are very attractively presented, the food is tasty and the cooking judged to perfection: the wild boar and rabbit with myrtle are both superb. *Free coffee offered to our readers on presentation of this guide.*

Solenzara
20145

@ 🎋 🏠 **Hôtel la Solenzara****

It's on the Bastia road as you leave town.
☎04.95.57.42.18 ℗04.95.57.46.84
🖰www.lasolenzara.com
Closed *mid-Nov to mid-March.* **Disabled access. TV. Swimming pool. Car park.**

Built two hundred years ago by the Squire of Solenzara, this building has been simply and tastefully redecorated and is now a charming hotel with direct access to the beach or the port. Tall palm trees sway in the garden, and there's a magnificent swimming pool. The old rooms are vast and have newly equipped bathrooms; the high ceilings mean that they're cool in summer, too. If you don't fancy these, there are a few more conventional rooms available in a new annexe. Prices are reasonable for a place of such character: doubles in the main building or annexe €60–93 according to the season. *Seventh night free on a week's stay (15 March–15 May and 11 Sept–15 Nov) offered to our readers on presentation of this guide.*

Zonza
20124

@ 🏠 |●| **Hôtel-restaurant la Terrasse***

In the centre of the village, but set back from the main road; it's on the right as you come from the Ospédale.
☎04.95.78.67.69 ℗04.95.78.73.50
Open *11.30am–2.30pm and 7–9.30pm.*
Closed *31 Oct–1 April.* **Car park.**

The best thing about this place is the terrace – and, even better, you can eat on it. It's the best-positioned place in the village and boasts a view over the roofs of the town and the impressive mountains, so it's fantastic at sunset. Good Corsican food, too, on a range of menus at €15.50–28.50: the house charcuterie is particularly tasty and their regional dishes are the genuine article, served in generous helpings. Highlights include wild boar with noodles, cannelloni and chestnut desserts. The owners, the Mondolini-Pietris, welcome you with warmth and good humour. The renovated rooms are simple and well maintained; some have a terrace over the valley. There isn't a half-board requirement but they do like you to have lunch or dinner. Since the cooking is good and prices are fair, that's not much of a bind. Double rooms go for €48.90–60.90 with basin, shower/wc or bath, depending on the season; half board €48.80–53.30 per person. Credit cards not accepted.

Levie

20170 (12km SW)

@ 🏕 🛏 🍽 **Ferme-auberge A Pignata**

Route du Pianu; from Levie, drive 3km along the Sainte-Lucie road, then turn right as you approach Cucuruzzu; 1.5km further on, take a winding track to the left after a small hill, then turn left through the second gate.
℡04.95.78.41.90 ℻04.95.78.46.03
Closed *Nov.* **High chairs and games available. Car park.**

A very secretive place: you have to be in the know to find it. No signposts, no arrows, no board – nothing. When you get there, though, the hospitality is tremendous. There are only a few rooms but they're clean and spacious and have nice linen. Only half board stays are available, at €63–69 per person. The restaurant is by prior reservation only. You can eat either in the large dining room with a fireplace or on the shady terrace. According to the locals the authentic Corsican specialities you get here are the best in the region. These include cannelloni with *brocciu* (a mild sheep's milk cheese), stuffed aubergines and *daube farcie*. There's just the one menu for €33, but it's excellent and the portions are large. Wines are extra; there's a good house wine. A great place, which also offers horseback excursions (by reservation). Credit cards not accepted. *Free liqueur offered to our readers on presentation of this guide.*

Franche-Comté

Arbois

39600

◎ 🎿 🏠 **Hôtel des Messageries****

2 rue de Courcelles.
☎03.84.66.15.45 ℗03.84.37.41.09
✉hotel.lesmessageries@wanadoo.fr
Closed Wed 11am–5pm out of season; Dec; Jan. **TV. High chairs and games available.**

Old post house with a nice stone exterior behind the ivy – all the atmosphere of the old days, and all mod cons. Rooms are comfy, and those that have recently been renovated are particularly lovely; €30 with basin, or €54 with shower/wc or bath. There's no restaurant, but there is a peaceful bar with a pretty tree-shaded terrace. It's a popular stopping point for foreign travellers passing through, so there's an international feel. Logis de France. *10% discount on the room rate (in Feb, Oct and Nov) offered to our readers on presentation of this guide.*

◎ 🎿 |◉| **La Balance – Mets et Vins**

47 rue de Courcelles.
☎03.84.37.45.00
Closed Sun evening; Tues evening; Wed (except for public holidays); Mon only during July–Aug; 27 June–4 July; 28 Nov–2 Feb. **Disabled access. High chairs available.**

The talented chef at this famed restaurant is onto a winner – the atmosphere is young, lively and genuinely friendly, the staff is efficient and professional, and there's a lovely terrace. Menus are varied, dishes local with a modern touch and prices modest. The weekday lunch *formule*, €14.20, includes dish of the day, dessert, a glass of wine and coffee; there are other

menus at €19.80 (vegetarian menu) up to €36.80. Many dishes use Jura wines to very good effect; it's worth knowing that the restaurant has a link with its wine-growing neighbours and that you can buy the wines you have sampled with your meal by the box at cost price. Reservations highly recommended. *Free liqueur offered to our readers on presentation of this guide.*

Baume-Les-Dames

25110

◎ 🎿 🏠 |◉| **Hostellerie du Château d'As*****

24 rue du Château-Gaillard.
☎03.81.84.00.66 ℗03.81.84.59.67
🌐www.chateau-das.fr
Closed Sun evening and Mon; last week of Jan; first week of Feb; last fortnight in Nov; first fortnight in Dec. **TV. Car park.**

This hotel/restaurant is in an odd-looking building perched high above the town and resembles something between a haunted house from a horror movie and a seaside villa on the Normandy coast. A pair of brothers, both gifted cooks, set up this place – two stars whose fame is spreading across the region. The dining room is big and round and somewhat sombre in atmosphere. The weekday lunch menu (€19) offers lots of choice. There are others (€29–68) featuring local dishes with a smattering of individuality; good wine list, too. Doubles go for €59 with shower/wc or bath, and the breakfast is generous. There's also a sauna. *10% discount on the room rate (1 Oct–30 March) offered to our readers on presentation of this guide.*

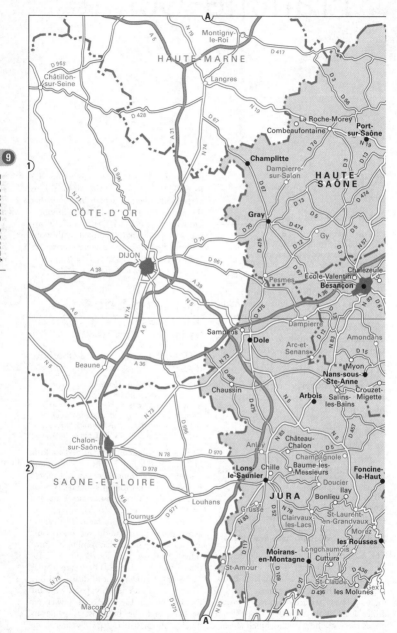

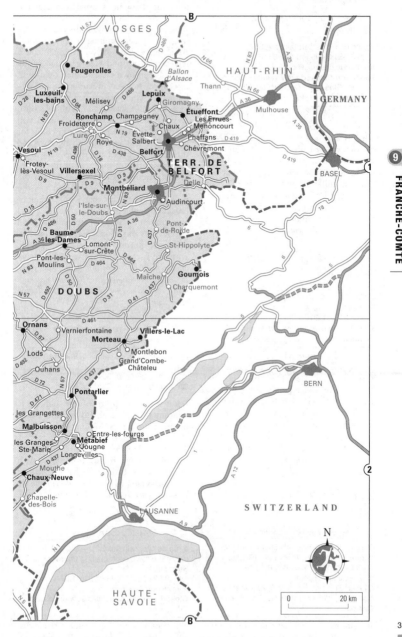

Pont-les-Moulins

25110 (5km S)

⚐ ≜ |●| ⚎ L'Auberge des Moulins**

Route de Pontarlier; take the D50.
☎03.81.84.09.99 ⓕ03.81.84.04.44
✉auberge.desmoulins@wanadoo.fr
Restaurant closed *Fri; Sat lunch; Sun out of season.* **Closed** *22 Dec–28 Jan.* **High chairs available. Car park.**

A cosy spot in the Cusancin valley. Attractive, very comfortable rooms in various sizes and styles; doubles €50 with shower/wc or bath. There's also an apartment for four people at €70. In the restaurant, a very reasonable menu at €16 (except Sun), then others up to €25. The chef is fond of using fish, especially trout from farm ponds. Logis de France. *One free breakfast per room offered to our readers on presentation of this guide.*

Lomont-sur-Crête

25110 (9km SE)

⚐ ⚎ |●| Chez La Marthe

23 Grande-Rue.
☎03.81.84.01.50
Closed *Sun evening; end of Aug.* **Disabled access.**

A friendly, simple village café-restaurant where you'll get a pleasant welcome – a surprise of a place. The cheapest menu (€12) features nice family dishes prepared using good produce. If you want fish, whitebait or trout, you have to order them beforehand because the cook uses only fresh fish. They also serve frogs' legs and game in season. *Free coffee offered to our readers on presentation of this guide.*

Belfort

90000

⚐ ≜ ⚎ Au Relais d'Alsace**

5 av. de la Laurencie; it's 500m from the centre, north of the town walls (Brisach gate).
☎03.84.22.15.55 ⓕ03.84.28.70.48
ⓦwww.arahotel.com
Closed *Sun evening from 9pm (except for bookings), all day at the end of season.* **TV. Car park.**

It's almost a social fairy tale: once upon a time there was a dynamic and adorable Franco-Algerian couple who were looking for work. They decided to take on an abandoned hotel, left to the state for want of any heirs, situated outside the walled town (but less than five minutes' walk away), to renovate it throughout and to get it up and running again as a hotel. After many years of toil, laughter and a few tears, Kim and Georges successfully created their own place in their own style, in other words very warm and as colourful as you could wish for. The bedrooms have a certain charm, and, with television and a good bed, what more could you want? It's the type of place you come for one night and end up staying two and then three, because, and this is what matters most of all in this case, of the quality of the welcome. All the good tips on the town and the region displayed on the walls and on top of that Kim's delicious breakfast (including real orange juice and hot croissants) and her infectious good cheer. This small independent hotel is our favourite by a long chalk for people with the backpacking spirit. *10% discount on the room rate for a minimum stay of two consecutive nights, or free fruit juice or soft drink, offered to our readers on presentation of this guide.*

⚐ ≜ ⚎ Hôtel-restaurant Le Saint-Christophe**

Place d'Armes; you can walk from the château.
☎03.84.55.88.88 ⓕ03.84.54.08.77
Closed *last week in Dec.* **TV.**

Located in the heart of the old town, opposite the cathedral, this dynamic establishment is always looking to improve itself. Décor evokes the Alsace region. The main building has comfortable and spacious double rooms from €62 with shower/wc or bath; some have a view of the town's famous lion. *10% discount on the room rate offered to our readers on presentation of this guide.*

⚐ ≜ Hôtel Vauban**

4 rue du Magasin; take the A36; slightly out of the town centre, along the river Savoureuse.
☎03.84.21.59.37 ⓕ03.84.21.41.67
ⓦwww.hotel-vauban.com
Closed *Feb and Christmas school holidays.* **TV.**

The hotel is in a peaceful district just a few minutes' walk from the old town and offers a pleasant welcome. The owner has covered the walls with his paintings, adding freshness and a party atmosphere to the place. Pleasant bedrooms, some opening onto the lovely garden; doubles with shower or bath start at €63. On fine days, you can breakfast (€7) beside the lily pond and enjoy the birdsong. No pets. Pleasant welcome.

◀ 🏠 |●| 🦃 Grand Hôtel du Tonneau d'Or***

1 rue Reiset; take the A36.
☎03.84.58.57.56 ℻03.84.58.57.50
🖳www.tonneaudor.fr
Closed Sat; Sun (except first in month); Aug.
Disabled access. TV. High chairs available. Car park.

The foyer is like the hall of a palace, with an elaborately decorated ceiling, grand staircase and all the atmosphere and charm of the 1900s. There's a lovely Art Nouveau rotunda and domed drawing room – as you'll gather, this small luxury establishment is full of character. Spacious and comfortable rooms are €98 with bath; they're decorated in a modern and tasteful style. There's a well-run restaurant serving reliable, traditional cuisine (andouillette, confit), with a weekday lunch menu at €13.50 and others up to €22.50. *One free breakfast per person offered to our readers on presentation of this guide.*

◉ |●| 🦃 L'Ambroisie

2 pl. de la Grande Fontaine; in the heart of the old town.
☎03.84.28.67.00
Closed Tues lunchtime; Wed.

A hushed little restaurant in the centre of town offering a successful new view of traditional cuisine. Nothing is left to chance and the careful presentation only serves to enhance the flavours of the house specialities; tasty morel-filled pastry cases, moist pike soufflé and blueberry *sabayon*. There are several menus ranging from €11.95 (weekday lunchtime) up to €30, to choose from. Quality wines, but they're pricey. *Free coffee offered to our readers on presentation of this guide.*

◉ |●| L'Auberge des Trois Chênes

29 rue de Soissons; from the town centre take the Vesoul road (boulevard Kennedy), then follow the signs to the Alstom factory and Cravanche. The restaurant is opposite the factory.

☎03.84.22.19.45
Closed Mon; Tues evening; Wed evening; Sun evening; Aug. **Disabled access. Car park.**

This comfortable, cosy inn, just outside town, specializes in modern cuisine which is anchored in tradition. There's a decent lunch menu for €13 on weekdays with three others from €26 to €35, listing super-fresh dishes; many of the veggies come from the garden. Menus are changed four times per year and reasonably priced wines are sold.

◉ |●| Le Molière

6 rue de l'Étuve.
☎03.84.21.86.38
Closed Tues evening; Wed. **Disabled access.**

This establishment is in an attractive tree-lined square, surrounded by smart buildings fronted with local sandstone. Only fresh produce is used here and the owner makes a trip to Mulhouse every morning to get his fish. The à la carte choice is almost too extensive, and there are lunch and dinner *formules* at €25 and €30, plus a selection of menus to suit all pockets at €39–55. Here's a taster: trout fillet on a bed of black pudding and buttered potatoes or knuckle of lamb with herbs and garlic cream and so on (yes, it made our mouths water, too, as soon as we re-read the text). Desserts are delicious and the wine list impressive (but check what you are being served and the price). The custom of drinking a *digestif* at the end of the meal may be going out of fashion, but here there's a large selection of liqueurs.

Chèvremont

90340 (4km E)

◉ |●| 🦃 Les Amis de Georges

14 bis rue du Texas; take the D28.
☎03.84.27.50.55
Closed Sun evening; Mon; Sat lunchtime; first fortnight in Jan; first fortnight in Sept. **Disabled access. High chairs available.**

The building has the appealing look of a chalet, and the fortifying cooking features *fondues* and *raclette* with a weekday lunch menu at €13 and others up to €23. What really gets you going, though, is the music. Jean-Luc plays French *chansons* all night long featuring all the great Georges – Moustaki, Brassens – and his enthusiastic guests sing along. It's essential to book. *Free coffee offered to our readers on presentation of this guide.*

Évette-Salbert
90350 (7km NW)

@ 🏠 |●| 🍴 Gîte de séjour Le Malsaucy

Le Malsaucy; leaving Belfort, go through Valdoie, then take the D24 (follow the direction of "Lac de Malsaucy").
☏03.84.29.21.84 🖶03.84.29.14.71
🖥www.malsaucy.org
Open *all year round.* **Car park.**

This is something like a huge youth hostel, with austere but very pleasant rooms and impeccable toilets on the landing. It is open to all comers, but it often has school parties staying so it's best to check availability beforehand. Rooms with two to four beds cost €10 per night per person (based on two people sharing); single menu €9 (prior reservation only). Water sports and open-air activities are available (special rates for our readers on presentation of this guide). Credit cards not accepted.

Phaffans
90150 (7km NE)

@ |●| 🍴 L'Auberge de Phaffans

10 rue de la Mairie. Take the N83, then turn right onto the D46 in the direction of Denney.
☏03.84.29.80.97
Closed *Sat lunchtime; Sun; Mon; 22 June–15 July; 20–31 Dec.* **Car park.**

The influence of nearby Alsace is evident in this quaint little village inn. They serve traditional dishes and their speciality is frogs' legs, guaranteed fresh year-round thanks to regular arrivals from the Vendée. The same goes for the farmed eels, served from April to December. They also offer unmissable morel mushrooms *en croûte*, pigeon *paysanne* with prunes, quails with red and white grapes and Arbois wine, marinade of haunch of venison with cranberries (when in season), as well as young wild boar *jambon cru*. Dish of the day costs €11 during the week; menus €18.50–22.50. *Free house apéritif offered to our readers on presentation of this guide.*

Chaux
90330 (10km N)

@ |●| 🍴 Restaurant L'Auberge de la Vaivre

36 Grande-Rue; on the road between Belfort and Giromagny (D465).
☏03.84.27.10.61
Closed *Sat; mid-July to mid-Aug.* **Open** *lunchtime only.* **Car park.**

This inn on the Vosges road is run by a mother and daughter who have decorated it most attractively; they really make you feel welcome. It's an old barn with a mezzanine. A lot of care goes into preparing traditional dishes such as terrines, freshly caught trout, calf's kidneys, duck *confit* with cider, and thinly sliced liver with *knoepfle*. They also offer delicious homemade puddings including fresh fruit tarts, *biscuit* with chocolate, and hazelnut dessert. There's a lunch menu at €15, with two others at €23 and €33, and a nicely presented wine list, served by the glass or jug. *Free coffee offered to our readers on presentation of this guide.*

Besançon
25000

See map opposite

@ 🏠 |●| Auberge de la Malate**

Chemin de la Malate. It's 4km out of the centre in the direction of Lausanne; after the Porte Taillée, take the Calèze-Arcier road. **Off map B2-1**
☏03.81.82.15.16
Restaurant closed *Mon lunchtime in season; in Jan and Feb.* **TV. Car park.**

A picturesque country inn just out of town in the forest facing the Doubs – peace and quiet are assured (the small road it's on has little traffic). Fairly comfortable rooms go for €33 or €37 for a double. The restaurant is lovely in summer, when you can sit in the shade on the terrace near the water's edge. Menus €13 (weekday lunchtimes) and €22–26, feature regional dishes with fish as the speciality – small fry or fillets of perch, or pike perch with morels.

@ 🍴 🏠 Hôtel du Nord**

8–10 rue Moncey. **Map B1-2**
☏03.81.81.34.56 🖶03.81.81.85.96
🖥www.hotel-du-nord-besancon.com

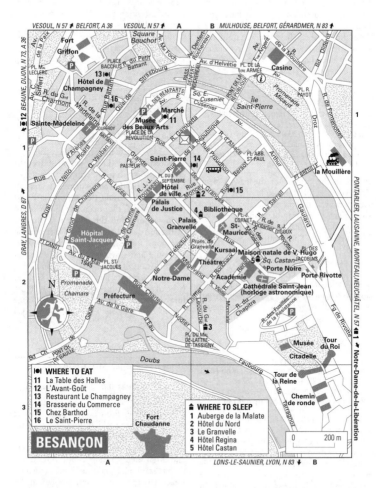

BESANÇON

WHERE TO EAT
11 La Table des Halles
12 L'Avant-Goût
13 Restaurant Le Champagney
14 Brasserie du Commerce
15 Chez Barthod
16 Le Saint-Pierre

WHERE TO SLEEP
1 Auberge de la Malate
2 Hôtel du Nord
3 Le Granvelle
4 Hôtel Regina
5 Hôtel Castan

FRANCHE-COMTÉ

9

341

Open *all year.* **Disabled access. TV. Pay car park** (€6.10).

A pleasant city-centre hotel run by real professionals who are always ready to be of service. Some 44 functional but comfortable and impeccably maintained rooms with good facilities, offering good value for money; doubles with shower/wc or bath €38–54. Several of the rooms have two double beds, and they all have good bedding, double glazing and room service. The public areas have been completely refurbished. *10% discount on the room rate (in July and Aug) offered to our readers on presentation of this guide.*

⊚ 🎄 🛏 Hôtel Regina**

91 Grande-Rue; in the direction of the town centre. **Map B2-4**
℡03.81.81.50.22 📠03.81.81.60.20
✉regina.hotel@wanadoo.fr
Closed *2–10 Aug; 23 Dec–2 Jan.* **TV. Car park.**

Right in the middle of the town's main drag, you'd be hard put to be more central. And yet, hidden away at the end of one of the inner courtyards of which Besançon has so many, this little welcoming hotel is a haven of peace. The rooms are well maintained, and some have balconies or terraces hung with wisteria; doubles €45–50 with shower/wc or bath. There's also a small studio to rent. Nice welcome. *10% discount on the room rate for a two-night stay (Nov–March) offered to our readers on presentation of this guide.*

⊚ 🎄 🛏 Le Granvelle**

13 rue du Général-Lecourbe; next to the police station, beneath the citadel. **Map B2-3**
℡03.81.81.33.92 📠03.81.81.31.77
🌐www.hotel-granvelle.fr
TV. High chairs available. Pay car park.

An elegant stone building that is very much in keeping with this district of old town houses. Despite being just a stone's throw from the centre, this area is still quiet. Rooms with shower/wc cost €45–59; they are sparse in terms of décor, but very comfortable and some are suitable for families. Credit cards not accepted. *10% discount on the room rate offered to our readers on presentation of this guide.*

⊚ 🎄 🛏 Hôtel Castan***

6 square Castan. **Map B2-5**
℡03.81.65.02.00 📠03.81.83.01.02

🌐www.hotelcastan.fr
Closed *1–20 Aug; 24 Dec–3 Jan.* **Disabled access. TV. Car park.**

Chic and charming hotel in a private mansion dating back to the seventeenth and eighteenth centuries – wide fireplaces, wood panelling, period furniture and a luxurious atmosphere. You can choose your room – Versailles, Pompadour, Pompeii (which has a Roman-style bathroom and Jacuzzi), Trianon, Regency and so on. Doubles are €95–170 – not surprising given the facilities. Breakfast is €11. *Free welcome drink offered to our readers on presentation of this guide.*

⊚ 🎄 🍴 Restaurant Le Champagney

37 rue Battant. **Map A1-13**
℡03.81.81.05.71
Closed *Sun.* **Disabled access.**

This restaurant is in a splendid sixteenth-century town house – in summer they make use of the old courtyard and set tables outside. Inside, the old fireplace and the beams of the original ceiling have been retained and the décor is a mixture of modern and baroque with lots of style but no stuffiness. Simple, straightforward welcome and service, and the cuisine is a combination of classic favourites and contemporary inspiration. Menus are €12.20 (weekday lunchtimes) and €15.20–30.50; Jura wines are sold by the glass. *Free house apéritif offered to our readers on presentation of this guide.*

⊚ 🍴 Brasserie du Commerce

31 rue des Granges. **Map B1-14**
℡03.81.81.33.11
Closed *Christmas and New Year.* **Open** *daily from 8am (9am Sun) to 1am.*

This brasserie, founded in 1873, is not only one of the oldest in the town, it's also the most beautiful: huge mirrors and stucco "pâtisseries" in pure Art-Deco style (although there's a more modern room on the mezzanine). Its famous regulars include Colette, who always stopped by when she was staying in the region. Today's clientele still manages to live up to the elegance of its surroundings. Since you can also eat here, and eat well at that, we see no reason why anyone would deny themselves such a treat. À la carte, reckon on €15; dish of the day €8. Open on Sunday, which is something of a miracle in Besançon.

⊚ 🏃 |◉| La Table des Halles

22 rue Gustave-Courbet; very close to the covered market. **Map A1-11**
🕾 03.81.50.62.74
Closed Sun; Mon.

An old Carmelite convent that became first a scooter shop then a rubber factory before being transformed into this New York-style loft by the interior designer Daniel Humair: contemporary lamps and pictures, spotlights on the ceiling and on rails and comfortable, modern furniture contrasting with the beautiful vaults and imposing pillars. This trendy setting is matched by tasty experiments with traditional ingredients by the fine Burgundy chef Jean-Pierre Billoux: Morteau sausage with *court-bouillon*, snails with absinthe, chicken with Savagnin. The cooking focuses on the essential, both in its presentation and in the choice of flavours' with a lunchtime menu at €15 and evening menu at €20. There is also a pretty inner courtyard. A real feast for both the eyes and the palate. *Free house apéritif offered to our readers on presentation of this guide.*

⊚ |◉| L'Avant-Goût

4 rue Richebourg; beside the train station. **Off map A1-12**
🕾 03.81.81.48.86
Closed Sat lunch; Sun; Mon; a week in May; 4 weeks in July/Aug; 4 days between Christmas and the New Year.

A pleasant surprise, three minutes from the centre of Besançon. Don't be put off by the unappealing exterior, for inside there is a small, friendly bar and a dining room that gets packed with lunchtime regulars who know that they will always find exemplary value for money. After a few years learning with great masters like Girardet in Switzerland, the chef, Thierry Perrod, branched out on his own and treats lovers of fine produce, conjuring up unfussy but visually elegant dishes entirely on his own. He excels with fish, and his past experience as a pâtissier is put to good use in the desserts. Two lunch menus are on offer at €15 and €28, and two dinner menus at €30 and €45, and a fine wine list with plenty of foreign vintages. There's a small terrace for summer evenings.

⊚ |◉| Chez Barthod

22 rue Bersot. **Map B1-15**

🕾 03.81.82.27.14
Closed Sun; Mon; a fortnight during Feb school holiday.

This is first and foremost a wine bar where people always meet up on evenings of existential doubt, but first you come across a shop with many regional products. Then you can relax by a table at the back of the courtyard (but it's advisable to book the table first) and sample a menu (€25 and €50) featuring gourmet dishes, not only from eastern France but also from the Southwest. Whatever their provenance, they are best washed down by a good wine – some forty different wines are available by the glass. You'll enjoy the friendly welcome and pleasant terrace.

⊚ 🏃 |◉| Le Saint-Pierre

104 rue Battant; in the town centre, Battant quarter. **Map A1-16**
🕾 03.81.81.20.20.99 🕾 03.81.81.97.33
Closed Sat lunchtime; Sun; fortnight at Easter; Aug; fortnight at Christmas.

The setting is elegant – ancient beams, bare stone walls and contemporary pictures. Very good and sensitively prepared dishes, featuring lots of fish. First menu at €35 includes wine and coffee; other menus at €40–55. All are satisfying in every respect and the home-made bread is excellent. The atmosphere is welcoming and very relaxed even though this is one of the smarter places in town and there's a nice terrace in warm weather. *Free house apéritif offered to our readers on presentation of this guide.*

Chalezeule
25220 (6km NE)

⊚ 🏠 Hôtel des Trois Îles**

1 rue des Vergers; take the N83 in the direction of Baume-les-Dames.
🕾 03.81.61.00.66 🕾 03.81.61.73.09
🕸 www.hoteldes3iles.com
Closed 21 Dec–6 Jan. **TV. High chairs available. Car park.**

Amazing to find such a quiet village only a few minutes' drive from the town centre. It's a recently built hotel in a lovely garden enclosed by high walls; the garden and sitting room are for guests' use. It's part of the *Relais du Silence* group so the peace and quiet come as standard. Double rooms go for €48–65 according to facilities and the season. They serve evening meals with a menu at €16, which changes daily.

École-Valentin

25480 (6km NW)

⊛ |●| 🌿 Le Valentin

Espace Valentin, Vert Bois Vallon; take the N57
in the direction of Châtillon-le-Duc.
☎03.81.80.03.90
Closed *Sun evening; Mon; Feb school holi-*
day; first 3 weeks in Aug. **Disabled access.**
High chairs available.

Close to Besançon, a good spot to enjoy
superbly fresh produce prepared with a
sure touch and an exquisite balancing of
flavours. Not much to look at, though,
with Peynet décor. The dishes are also
beautifully presented, in a classical style.
Outstanding dishes on the menus (€31–
71) include ragoût of snails au Vieux
Pontarlier or duck breast with Morello
cherries. *Free coffee offered to our readers on*
presentation of this guide.

Champlitte

70600

⊛ 🌿 🏠 |●| Hôtel-restaurant du Donjon**

46 rue de la République.
☎03.84.67.66.95 ℻03.84.67.81.06
✉hotel.du.donjon@wanadoo.fr
Restaurant closed *Fri evening and Sat*
lunchtime from end Sept to mid-June;
Sun evening from mid-Nov to mid-April;
Mon from mid-June to end Sept; between
Christmas and New Year. **TV. High chairs**
available.

The only remaining medieval element in
this old house is the vaulted cellar which
is used as the dining room. The cuisine is
traditional (trout fillet with Caucoillotte
cheese sauce); menus start at €11 (weekdays only), with others €17.50–33. Clean,
light rooms are €37.50 for a double with
shower/wc or bath; no special charm, but
comfortable and completely refurbished.
There's a garage for motorbikes and bicycles. Logis de France. *Free coffee offered to our*
readers on presentation of this guide.

Chaux-Neuve

25240

⊛ 🌿 🏠 |●| Auberge du Grand-Gît**

8 rue des Chaumelles.
☎03.81.69.25.75 ℻03.81.69.15.44
🌐www.aubergedugrandgit.com

Closed *Sun evening and Mon except public*
holidays; end March to 6 May; 16 Oct–20
Dec. **Disabled access. Car park.**

Quiet place on the outskirts of the village. It's fairly new, but in keeping with
local architecture with a sloping roof and
wooden façade. Only eight bedrooms,
but they're wood-panelled and cosy –
€41–47 for a double. Nos. 5 and 6 have
a mezzanine and can sleep five. There are
also two large rooms with four and six
beds for hikers. Classic regional dishes
predominate in the restaurant; menus
€13 (Mon–Fri except public holidays),
and €16–€21. The owner is a skiing
instructor and uplands guide so he knows
all the local long-distance footpaths and
cross-country skiing routes intimately
– it's the ideal place for sporty types
and nature lovers, and gets lively in the
evening. Credit cards not accepted. Logis
de France. *Free house apéritif offered to our*
readers on presentation of this guide.

Dole

39100

⊛ 🏠 |●| La Chaumière

346 av. du Maréchal-Juin.
☎03.84.70.72.40 ℻03.84.79.25.60
✉lachaumiere@wanadoo.aol.com
Closed *Mon lunch; Sat lunch; Sun.* **Disabled**
access. TV. Swimming pool. Car park.

A huge *faux* cottage by the roadside, hidden
behind Virginia creeper and boasting a
sweet garden and pretty swimming pool.
It's cosy and bourgeois, and the rooms
are particularly comfortable, if a little old-
fashioned, and maybe slightly overpriced
– €63–77 for a double with shower/wc or
bath. It owes its reputation with locals and
passing tourists to the quality of the cooking in the restaurant. Carrying on a long
family and culinary tradition, the young
chef treated us to his menus, extremely
reasonably priced given the quality, but not
the place for people with large appetites.
And, for once, the first menu, €19 (lunchtime), is especially interesting (it is also the
most generous). Everyone will be able to
find what they want in the à la carte menu,
which changes regularly.

⊛ 🏠 Hôtel de la Cloche***

1 pl. Grévy.
☎03.84.82.06.06 ℻03.84.72.73.82
🌐www.lacloche.fr

Closed *23 Dec–3 Jan*. **TV. High chairs available. Car park.**

A provincial hotel that started life as a coaching inn. It's conventional, with classical and rather bland décor. Nonetheless the rooms are clean and well maintained, the façade is pretty, there's a sauna upstairs, and it's in the middle of town – a big plus in a place where central hotels are a rare commodity. Inevitably, it's often full. Doubles with shower/wc or bath go for €70–80. Logis de France.

|●| Le Bec Fin

67 rue Pasteur; marina in summer, or alternatively rue Pasteur; the restaurant overlooks the very romantic canal des Tanneurs (tanners' canal).
☎03.84.82.43.43
Closed *Tues and Wed (except July–Aug); 1–15 Jan.* **High chairs available.**

Light, nicely decorated restaurant with a delightful terrace beside the canal for sunny days. The delicious seasonal cuisine is prepared by a chef who has just been declared the best worker in France; menus €15 (weekday lunchtimes) and €24–54.

Sampans
39100 (4km NW)

🏠 |●| Le Chalet du Mont-Roland**

Take the N5 and before Monnières turn right towards Mont Roland.
☎03.84.72.04.55 ☎03.84.82.14.97
🌐www.chalet-montroland.com
Disabled access. TV. High chairs available. Car park.

This chalet is on the road to Notre-Dame-du-Mont-Roland, an important pilgrimage site. Some of the rooms (nos. 5, 6, 9, 14 and 16) have a superb view over Chaux Forest. It's definitely the place to spend a relaxing Sunday in the country, with its chic but bustling atmosphere; there's even a dance floor. Double rooms with shower/wc or bath cost €46. Classical cuisine, but that's what everybody likes. Logis de France.

Chaussin
39120 (14km SW)

🏠 |●| Hôtel-restaurant Chez Bach**

4 pl. de l'Ancienne-Gare; take the N73, then turn onto the D468 at La Borde.

☎03.84.81.80.38 ☎03.84.81.83.80
🌐www.hotel-bach.com
Closed *Sun evening; Mon lunchtime; 26 Dec–6 Jan.* **Disabled access. TV. High chairs and games available. Car park.**

Make a little detour to enjoy the gastronomic cuisine here. The large building doesn't look promising from the outside but its reputation has been established since the 1930s. The grandson is now at the helm in the kitchen. Weekday menu at €17 and others €22–52; they all list fine regional specialities: escalope of foie gras with cep mushrooms, lobster *au vin jaune*, *parfait* of crayfish tails and fillet steak with red berries. The rooms are comfortable and all have direct Internet access; it'll cost €54–64 for a double with shower/wc or bath. Half board, compulsory in July and August, costs €58 per person. Logis de France.

Étueffont
90170

🏠 |●| Auberge Aux Trois Bonheurs

34 Grande-Rue; north of Belfort, take the D23 from Valdoie.
☎03.84.54.71.31
Closed *Sun and Tues evenings; Mon; evenings (Sun–Thurs) in winter.*
Disabled access. High chairs available. Car park.

If this elegant town-house is the *Inn of the Three Happinesses*, then the fourth is the journey through flower-filled villages to get there. It's built in brick and natural stone and occupies a delightful rustic setting. The restaurant is very popular because of the hearty, tasty cooking served in generous portions – it's a place for family gatherings and groups out on a spree. They come for fantastic home-made brawn, fried carp or pike perch (kept warm), parsleyed frogs' legs, girolle mushrooms, the special *planchette des Trois Bonheurs, tartiflette,* etc. Weekday lunch menu starts at €8.70, or €18.50 at other times. There's seafood *pot-au-feu* available à la carte; reckon on around €18. The welcome may be slightly gruff, but service is efficient. *Free coffee offered to our readers on presentation of this guide.*

Errues-Menoncourt (Les)

90150 (6km SE)

@ ≜ |O| La Pomme d'Argent

13 rue de la Noye; take the N83; locality 3km from Menoncourt.
℡03.84.27.63.69
Closed *Mon; Tues evening; Sun evening.*
Disabled access. High chairs available. Car park.

This lovely place, well off the beaten track (but still only 12km from Belfort), is a real find. There's a good choice of menus starting at €15 (weekdays only) and then €20–40. The new proprietors have retained the style that gained the restaurant its reputation, while on the food front fish is to the fore.

Foncine-le-Haut

39460

@ ⅍ ≜ |O| Auberge Le Jardin de la Rivière**

Take the D437.
℡03.84.51.90.59 ℻03.84.51.94.69
℮eve5@club-internet.fr
Closed *Sun evening and Mon out of season; in Oct.* **TV. High chairs and games available. Swimming pool. Car park.**

A young couple have taken over this place – the atmosphere is peaceful and you'll get an excellent, really attentive, welcome. The rooms are very classic in style, but they're comfortable and cost €47.50–61 for a double with shower/wc or bath. The food served in the restaurant is nicely presented and enlivened by an idea or two; weekday lunch menu €11.50, then others at €16.50–28.50. In the summer you can enjoy the outdoor swimming pool in the garden flanking the river bank. Logis de France. *Free coffee offered to our readers on presentation of this guide.*

Fougerolles

70220

@ ⅍ |O| Restaurant Le Père Rota

8 Grande-Rue.
℡03.84.49.12.11
Closed *Sun evening; Mon; Tues evening; Jan.*
Disabled access. High chairs available. Car park.

Jean-Pierre Kuentz is a fantastic advocate

of the cuisine of the Haute-Saône. He uses local produce of the highest quality to prepare regional dishes with a modern twist: duck terrine with sour cherries, escalope of pike perch with *jambon cru de Luseuil*, fillet of beef with red Jura wine sauce. Weekday menu starts at €17.50, then others €23–59. The service is thoughtful and the table settings and modern, bright décor have been put together with care. *Miniature bottle offered to our readers on presentation of this guide.*

Goumois

25470

@ ⅍ ≜ |O| Auberge Le Moulin du Plain**

Follow the small road which runs alongside the Doubs (it's signsposted).
℡03.81.44.41.99 ℻03.81.44.45.70
℗www.moulinduplain.com
Closed *1 Nov to end Feb.* **TV. High chairs available. Car park.**

This house is on the banks of the Doubs, which cuts through a fabulous wild valley. Pleasant and comfortable double rooms – all with shower/wc or bath – are €52.70–59.30; some have balconies. A place that does brisk business thanks to fishermen (the neighbouring watercourse is famous), who feel at home here, especially in the restaurant (fish features strongly on the menu and in the conversation). There's a weekday menu for €15 and others €19–32. *10% discount on the room rate (March, April and Oct) or a free house apéritif offered to our readers on presentation of this guide.*

@ ≜ |O| Hôtel-restaurant Taillard

3 rte. de la Corniche; at the top of the village of Goumois.
℡03.81.44.20.75 ℻03.81.44.26.15
℗www.hoteltaillard.com
Restaurant closed *Mon lunch; Wed lunch (except July–Aug)* **Closed** *Nov–March.*
Disabled access. TV. Swimming pool.

Genuine charm and a serene setting have made this establishment one of the most pleasant stopovers in this watch-making region for over a century. It seems to have everything: rooms (€57–85) with beautiful views, a sunny terrace where you can have breakfast reading the latest world news, a good restaurant that also makes the most of authentic fresh produce. Menus start at €21 (lunch) and go up to €70. There's an outdoor pool and even a gym and sauna.

FRANCHE-COMTÉ

9

Gray

70100

@ 🏠 Auberge de jeunesse Le Foyer

2 rue André-Maginot; road at right angles to avenue de Verdun.
☎03.84.64.99.20 ℗03.84.64.99.29
🌐www.foyer-gray.asso.fr
Car park.

Attractively renovated modern building with a number of services, such as laundry. It is essentially a hostel for workers, but some rooms are reserved for FUAJ card-holders. Accommodation costs €24 per person in a single or double room with shower/wc; €27 with breakfast; self-service menu at €7.60. In July and August sports activities such as go-karts, archery, volleyball and fencing are organized (on a daily or weekly basis).

@ |●| Relais de la Prévôté

6 rue du Marché.
☎03.84.65.10.08
Closed Sun; Mon; 27 Dec–8 Jan. **Disabled access.**

The hushed atmosphere, the elegant room and almost intimidating size of the huge fireplace give you a real sense of privilege. So, when the waitress gracefully places the first dish before you, you say to yourself that you have been truly lucky to have found such good value for money. *Menu du jour* starts at €14; other menus at €19 and €35.

Lepuix

90200

@ 🎋 🏠 |●| Le Saut de la Truite

23 rte. du Ballon d'Alsace; take the D465.
☎03.84.29.32.64 ℗03.84.29.57.42
Closed Fri; first fortnight in Jan. **TV. High chairs available. Car park.**

This place is a mountain refuge that's been open since 1902 and run by the same family for forty years. It's in a superb setting in a sharp bend in the road that climbs to the Ballon d'Alsace in a forest clearing, facing the waterfall Saut de la Truite. There are some rooms but it's best as a place to eat – the trout freshly caught from the pond make the journey there worthwhile – here they serve mainly

fario trout, a succulent mountain trout, the skin of which is speckled with distinctive red dots. There's a fine selection of regional specialities such as cockerel in Riesling and bilberry tart; game in season. Weekday menu costs €16 and others €23–33. Logis de France. *Free house apéritif offered to our readers on presentation of this guide.*

Lons-le-Saunier

39000

@ 🎋 🏠 Hôtel-Restaurant Terminus**

37 av. Aristide-Briand; opposite the station.
☎03.84.24.41.83 ℗03.84.26.68.07
🌐www.hotel-terminus-lons.com
Closed 20 Dec–6 Jan. **TV. Pay car park.**

A solid establishment that was gradually fading as the years passed in much the same way as the rail traffic from the neighbouring station. Luckily a massive renovation programme has put a stop to the process of decay, without losing too much of the charm of the old building: the relatively large rooms have all been modernized and painted white so they look a lot brighter. Doubles with shower/wc go for €40–46, with bath €60. Conceived primarily to be functional, they would benefit from being a little smarter (the décor on the whole is frugal), but that being said you still get a perfectly good night's sleep; the ones at the back are quieter. Logis de France. *Free house apéritif or coffee offered to our readers on presentation of this guide.*

@ |●| Le Bamboche

23 rue Perrin.
☎03.84.86.21.25
Closed Sun; Mon.

Young, friendly atmosphere and good, original cooking. No less than five types of *carpaccio* available: not only beef, but also veal, goose and rabbit. There are excellent grills (ham shank, knuckle of lamb, whole chicken), which you can watch gently cooking on the huge old-fashioned spit – it's worth the visit just to see this. If you don't like meat, there's a good selection of filling salads. There's a weekday lunch *formule* for €10.50 and a menu at €17.50; you'll spend around €22 à la carte. This is the best place in town.

⊚ |●| La Comédie

Place de la Comédie.
☎03.84.24.20.66
Closed Sun; Mon; a fortnight at Easter; 3
weeks in Aug. **Disabled access.**

This stylish restaurant, with a lovely internal flowery terrace, is the swankiest in town. The cooking steers a course between modern and traditional, with a preference for fish caught fresh that day (such as ling in a basil crust or salmon tartare), and the service is very much that of the "grand restaurant". The cheapest menu at €18 is available at lunchtime and dinner, and there's another menu at €28; it's around €50 à la carte.

Chille
39570 (2km NE)

⊚ 🛪 🏠 |●| Hôtel-restaurant Parenthèse***

186 chemin du Pin; head for Besançon on
the D70, then go 1km on the D157 and look
for the signs.
☎03.84.47.55.44 ☎03.84.24.92.13
ⓦwww.hotelparenthese.com
Restaurant closed Sat lunchtime, Sun evening and Mon lunchtime, unless you book
first. **Disabled access. TV. High chairs and
games available. Swimming pool. Car park.**

Set in a peaceful little village, this beautiful eighteenth-century residence has been converted into a comfortable hotel and restaurant, with wooded grounds and a superb swimming pool. The rooms deserve their three stars (those with whirlpool baths deserve four) and are decorated in tasteful modern style; €78–138. The restaurant offers a good classic cuisine: *pressé de foie gras de canard pomme fruit* and Bresse chicken supreme with morels infused in *vin jaune*. There's a weekday menu at €19 and others €25–47. *One free breakfast per room per night offered to our readers on presentation of this guide.*

Château-Chalon
39210 (11km NE)

⊚ |●| 🛪 La Taverne du Roc

Rue de la Roche; take the D5.
☎03.84.85.24.17
Closed Mon evening and Tues in season; 15
Dec–15 March.

A restaurant comprising two small rooms with stone walls in a timeless house, right in the middle of Château-Chalon. The chef has been concocting delicious dishes for years – try her Bresse chicken with *vin jaune* and morels, which is the best for miles around. Any of her Jura dishes are also worth a try and, for the greedy, one of the menus (€24 and €30) offers both trout and chicken. *Free coffee offered to our readers on presentation of this guide.*

Baume-les-Messieurs
39210 (14km NE)

⊚ 🛪 |●| Restaurant des Grottes

Lieu-dit des Grottes; take the D471 to
Roches-de-Beaume, then the D70.
☎03.84.48.23.15 ☎03.84.44.61.59
Closed evenings (except Fri and Sat in July
and Aug); Mon except in July and Aug; 15
Dec–10 March. **Disabled access. Car park.**

The restaurant is in a little 1900 house opposite a marvellous foaming waterfall cascading down from the high rocks of the Baume-les-Messieurs amphitheatre. Menus start at €14 (weekday lunchtime), with others €20–34, and list mainly Franche-Comté specialities. The terrace is open in summer where you can enjoy platters of charcuterie or cheese washed down with a glass of Jura wine. *Free coffee offered to our readers on presentation of this guide.*

Luxeuil-les-Bains
70300

⊚ 🏠 |●| Hôtel-restaurant Le Rallye

49 rue Edouart-Herriot.
☎03.84.40.04.92
ⓔrallye70.ifrance.fr
Closed Sun evening; Fri evening; Sat lunchtime. **High chairs available.**

Some names are misleading, and this is one of them. Because, a far cry from the screeching of a car rally, the only noise here comes more from the chicken browning under the Comté cheese alongside a helping of *gratin dauphinois* potatoes, as crisp as you could wish for. Warm welcome, bedrooms rather on the old-fashioned side, but pleasant tables complete with pepper mill. The dishes are tasty and well presented; *menu du jour* at €9.90, and others ranging from €11.40 up to the gastronomic 'Rolls' menu at €30. Despite being on the main road, this place is a favourite spot for family Sunday lunches. The hotel rooms are simple and clean, with doubles from €24.50. It's a really good discovery and booking is advisable.

◎ 👫 🛏 |◉| Hôtel-restaurant Beau Site***

18 rue Georges-Moulimard; it's close to the spa.
☎03.84.40.14.67 ℻03.84.40.50.25
Closed Fri evening; Sat lunchtime and Sun evening (mid-Nov to mid-March). **TV. High chairs and games available. Swimming pool. Car park.**

Near the casino and the spa you find this large, very pleasing establishment surrounded by a green park with a swimming pool. Dominating the town, this complex is considered as a definite asset in Luxeuil, a good place in terms of its setting and unobtrusive welcome. Doubles with shower/wc or bath go for €70. Things have slipped a little at the restaurant, however. There's a weekday menu for €13 and others €22–40. Logis de France. *Free coffee offered to our readers on presentation of this guide.*

Malbuisson
25160

◎ 🛏 |◉| 👫 Hôtel-restaurant Le Lac et Hôtel Beau Site***

31 Grande-Rue.
☎03.81.69.34.80 ℻03.81.69.35.44
🌐www.lelac-hotel.com
Closed mid-Nov to mid-Dec (except weekends). **High chairs and games available. Swimming pool. Car park.**

An institution in the area, in an elegant, imposing 1930s building that you would swear comes straight from a Fitzgerald novel, with an annexe for guests on a tight budget. The amazing kitsch decoration is a little overpowering and the service slightly offhand, but there's a charming bar and the rooms have been attractively refurbished (ask for one with a balcony and a view of the lake). Doubles go for €32–107, depending on the degree of comfort; half board €37–74.50. You quickly get used to the incredible theatrical décor which comes to life at meal times. Classic cuisine with menus at €17–41 (snails, *Comté* trout, fillet of beef with morels, duck with cherries) and a fine dessert trolley, with tempting pâtisserie. The pool is in the

big garden that slopes gently down to the lake. *Free coffee offered to our readers on presentation of this guide.*

◎ 🛏 |◉| Le Bon Accueil***

32 Grand-Rue; it's in the centre of the village.
☎03.81.69.30.58 ℻03.81.69.37.60
Closed Sun evening; Mon; Tues lunchtime; a week in end April; a week around All Saints'; mid-Dec to mid-Jan. **TV. Car park.**

The restaurant offers traditional cooking with a modern touch; the chef-owner, Marc Faivre, is committed to using only fresh, quality, local produce, "creating fresh cuisine using authentic products for the good and the beautiful". A few specialities: fine tart with Morteau sausage, braised leeks with poached egg, tomatoes stuffed with snails and herbs with a parsley sauce and, for dessert, a gentian sorbet or *macaronade* with grapefruit. It's excellent, characterful cuisine. There's a *formule* (main dish, dessert, glass of wine, coffee) for €22 and menus €26–45. Double rooms with shower/wc and bath cost €44–70.

Granges-Sainte-Marie (Les)
25160 (3km SW)

◎ 👫 🛏 |◉| Hôtel-restaurant du Coude**

☎03.81.69.31.57 ℻03.81.69.33.90
Closed Sun evening and Wed (except school holidays); mid-Nov to mid-Dec. **Disabled access.**

This restaurant has earned a good reputation in the region for its perch fillets, frogs' legs and other delicacies with menus at €16–45. The atmosphere is informal but the tables are laid out so that you have space to eat in comfort (not always the case in establishments of this kind). Double rooms are €45 and €50. Logis de France. *Free house apéritif offered to our readers on presentation of this guide.*

Métabief
25370

◎ 👫 🛏 |◉| Hôtel-restaurant L'Étoile des Neiges**

4 rue du Village.
☎03.81.49.11.21 ℻03.81.49.26.91
🌐wwwhoteletoiledesneiges.com

TV. Disabled access. High chairs available. Car park.

A modern building a little way (600m) from the ski resort and above a small river. The fourteen renovated rooms (four of which are duplexes) are cosy and comfortable; all have balconies with exceptional views of the Mont d'Or or the countryside and cost €49. In the restaurant there's a welcoming family atmosphere. They serve local specialities using the freshest produce: morels and Comté cheese pasty, salmon with sorrel. Weekday lunch *formule* starts at €10, with menus €18–25. There's a private lock-up garage available. *Free coffee offered to our readers on presentation of this guide.*

Longevilles-Mont-d'Or (Les)
25370 (4km SW)

@ 🎿 🏠 |●| **Hôtel-Restaurant Les Sapins***

58 rue des Bief-Blanc; take the D45.
℡03.81.49.90.90 ℗03.81.49.94.43
Closed *April; 1 Oct–15 Dec*. **Car park.**

This place is situated in the centre of a little village which hasn't lost any of its character – despite being part of the Métabief resort. The pleasant rooms are the best value for money in the area at €33 for a double with shower/wc and bath; half board €35 per person. Worthwhile weekday menu at €11, and another at €15, feature homemade regional cooking: *franc-comtoise* salad, cheese flan, *entrecôte* of beef and *gratin dauphinois*. The welcome here is really genuine. Logis de France. *Free coffee offered to our readers on presentation of this guide.*

Jougne
25370 (8km E)

@ 🎿 🏠 |●| **Hôtel-restaurant de la Couronne***

Place de l'Église; take the D9 and the N57, then head for the Swiss border (D423).
℡03.81.49.10.50 ℗03.81.49.19.77
Closed *Mon evenings (except school holidays); Sun evening; Nov*. **Disabled access. TV. High chairs available. Car park.**

Set on a proper village square with a church and fountain, this small country hotel is far enough away from the main road to be nice and quiet, and it's very welcoming too. Pleasant, refurbished rooms go

for €43–55; reckon on €49–53 per person for half board. Nos. 11, 12 and 14 have a nice view over the lovely Jougnenaz valley. Classic cuisine with lots of Franche-Comté dishes: duck fillet with wild mushrooms, morels and *petit-gris* snails in flaky pastry, trout fillet in Savagnin. The cheapest menu is €15.50 (not Sun), and there are others at €24–40. *Free house apéritif offered to our readers on presentation of this guide.*

Entre-les-Fourgs
25370 (10km NE)

@ 🎿 🏠 |●| **Auberge les Petits Gris**

3 pl. des Cloutiers; take the D45 then the N57 to Jougne, then take the D423.
℡03.81.49.12.93 ℗03.81.49.13.93
@www.hotel-les-petits-gris.com
Restaurant closed *Wed*. **Closed** *20 Sept–20 Oct.*

A well-run little inn with comfortable rooms (€36–44) in a quiet, isolated village at the foot of the ski runs (downhill and cross-country) – the road goes no further. You'll get a friendly welcome and there are plenty of beautiful walks round these parts. The restaurant serves unpretentious but well prepared local dishes; cheapest menu is €14.50, then others €17.50–27.50. Logis de France. *Free coffee offered to our readers on presentation of this guide.*

Moirans-en-Montagne
39260

@ 🎿 |●| **Le Regardoir**

45 av. de Franche-Comté; it's at the Belvédère. Take the D470 northwest of town.
℡03.84.42.01.15
Closed *Mon, Tues and Wed evenings (except 15 June–30 Aug); 17 Dec–15 March.* **High chairs and games available.**

Stop for a snack here just so you can take a seat on the terrace and enjoy the panoramic view over the Lac de Vouglans way below. There's something special about the light at sunset – it's a moment to linger over with an apéritif. Nice, smiling welcome and a straightforward menu, though the cook is serious about his work; weekday menu €11.50 (wine included) and others €13 and €16. It's always busy at lunchtime and in the evening so booking is highly recommended. *Free glass of*

Kir *offered to our readers on presentation of this guide.*

Cuttura
39170 (18km E)

🅰 🍴 L'Auberge du Vieux Moulin

Restaurant du Lac; take the D470 (between Moirans and St-Claude), then at Lavans take the D118.
☎03.84.42.84.28
Closed *Sat lunchtime; evenings (except bookings and during school holidays); Christmas school holiday.* **Car park.**

A very simple looking house, with a small menu that attracts all the traveling salesmen, and you can see why. This is a lovely old water mill and you eat down by the water accompanied by ducks and moorhens. The cooking is the second surprise, being regional, served in generous portions and attractively presented: pan-fried escalope of foie gras with Fougerolles griottine cherries, fillet of pikeperch, crayfish tail *gratin* in *vin jaune* sauce with morels. The weekday lunch menu costs €12 and other menus €16.50–29. *Free coffee offered to our readers on presentation of this guide.*

Molunes (Les)
39310 (30km SE)

🍴 Le Collège

Take the D470 then the D436 to Saint-Claude then Septmoncel, then the D25 in the direction of Moussières; it's in the middle of the village.
☎03.84.41.61.09
Closed *Mon evening; Tues; 21 June–2 July; 27 Nov–25 Dec.* **High chairs available.**

Established on the site of a former bakers-cum-grocers in a hamlet 1250m up and so small it doesn't even have a church, this restaurant has a reputation that's spread through the Haut-Jura – it can seat 64 but there's often a fight to get in at the weekend. And you can see why as soon as the first course arrives – very good traditional cooking, no fancy bluffing, but full of flavour. The cheapest menu (not Sat evening) costs €11.50, several others at €14.50–25, and an attractively priced wine list. The dining room is decorated nicely enough in rustic style (but the room that you go through when you come in, where the locals eat, is decidedly less pleasant).

Montbéliard
25200

🅰 🛏 🍴 Hôtel de la Balance★★★

40 rue de Belfort; it's in the old town.
☎03.81.96.77.41 ℻03.81.91.47.16
🌐www.hotel-la-balance.com
Closed *Christmas.* **Restaurant closed** *Sat; Sun.* **Disabled access. TV. High chairs, feeding-bottle warmer, baby changing facilities and games available. Pay car park.**

Like a lot of the other buildings in the old town, the façade of this sixteenth-century house has been painted yellow. Inside, the elegant yellow-ochre dining room, the antique furniture and a solid wooden staircase add to the charm of the place – which definitely belies the rather sad image people tend to have of the town. The rooms are stylish, all with bath, and cost €75–100; buffet breakfast €9. If you're interested in history, ask for the room where Field Marshal Lattre de Tassigny stayed in 1944. Classic and regional dishes are listed on the weekday menu at €14, and on the others at €18–22. Logis de France. *Free coffee offered to our readers on presentation of this guide.*

🍴 Chez Cass'Graine

4 rue du Général-Leclerc
☎03.81.91.09.97
Closed *Sat; Sun; public holidays; 3 weeks in Aug.*

It is hard to imagine a more delightful little family restaurant: a mother and daughter team produce all the superb seasonal food and complement it with fine wines and a warm welcome. The décor is highly original and, what is more, it's spruced up several times a year; the overall effect is like a picture from a design magazine, with wonderful tastes and aromas on top. This place has many loyal regulars, and it's easy to see why. Reckon on €25 à la carte.

Audincourt
25400 (5km S)

🛏 Hôtel des Tilleuls★★

51 av. Foch; it's on the D126.
☎03.81.30.77.00 ℻03.81.30.57.20
Disabled access. TV. Swimming pool. Car park.

In a quiet street – be sure to go to the *avenue*, not the *rue* Foch. The rooms are very well equipped with air-conditioning, fridge, power shower and hairdryer, and the décor is modern but warm. Doubles go for €48–57; suites €57–62. They're dotted about the main building or in annexes around the garden where there's also a lovely heated swimming pool. There's no restaurant but they'll get meals brought in for you in the evening.

Morteau

25500

⊛ ▲ Hôtel des Montagnards**

7 bis pl. Carnot.
℡03.81.67.08.86 ℻03.81.67.14.57
Closed *23–27 Dec.* **Disabled access. TV. Pay car park.**

This is a small, friendly hotel in the centre of the village. It offers attractive panelled rooms for €56, some of which have been redecorated in pastel shades.

⊛ ⩍ |●| Restaurant L'Époque

18 rue de la Louhière; it's on the Besançon road just outside the centre.
℡03.81.67.33.44
Closed *Mon evening, Wed evening and Sun (except public holidays); 20 July–20 Aug.* **Car park.**

They know what they're about in this restaurant – the welcome is natural and the service friendly. There are a couple of bistro-like dining rooms where you feel instantly at home. The tasty food is inventive without ignoring its regional origins: Morteau sausage *à l'arboisienne*, Bresse chicken with *vin jaune* sauce and morels, wild mushroom and bacon in a pastry case. Set menus start at €13 (weekday lunchtimes), then others €16–32. There's an impressive selection of whiskies (450 different ones listed), as impressive as the moustache sported by the owner, a local man who has also created a club for whisky lovers. *Free house apéritif offered to our readers on presentation of this guide.*

Grand'Combe Châteleu

25500 (4km SW)

⊛ |●| Restaurant Faivre

Rue Principale; take the D437, then the D47.
℡03.81.68.84.63
Closed *Aug.*

A huge chalet with a cosy and very pleasant dining room. The classic, regional

dishes betray little in the way of inventiveness but are decent and carefully prepared: trout, fillet of beef with morels and so on. There's a lunch menu at €18 and others €23–60. A good place to stop where you are placed under no pressure to eat.

Nans-sous-Sainte-Anne

25330

⊛ ▲ |●| ⩍ Hôtel de la Poste**

11 Grande-Rue.
℡03.81.86.62.57 ℻03.81.86.55.32
⊛hoteldelaposte@aol.com
Closed *Tues evening and Wed out of season; 20 Dec–31 Jan.*

A practical base for exploring the stunning but largely unknown Lison valley. A typical, no-frills, family-run hotel-restaurant: ivy on the front, a bar-tobacconist's that is the village meeting point, wholesome local dishes at reasonable prices and simple but comfortable rooms with good bedding – not forgetting the terrace for fine days. Doubles with shower/wc go for €37; menus €13–19.

Crouzet-Migette

25270 (3km SE)

⊛ |●| Auberge du Pont du Diable

In the direction of the source of the Lison river.
℡03.81.49.54.28
Closed *weekdays except school holidays and bookings; a week in Jan; during Nov; Christmas and New Year (but it's best to phone).* **High chairs and games available.**

Set in an old farm, with large, shared tables for enjoying cheap, filling and convivial meals. The fine local dishes are available (at around €10) throughout the day at the weekend; other menus €13 and €17.50. Snacks are also on offer: cabbage soup or ham on the bone, the local "Niaud" omelette. The friendly owner, Bobo, will enthusiastically guide you through the interesting selection of wines from the Jura. In the evening, Marie and her band of helpers welcome you. There's a log fire and sometimes a singer-guitarist performing in the background. You can take horse rides from the village next door (reckon on €13 per person, further information at the inn).

Salins-les-Bains
39110 (13km SW)

◎ 🎿 ♟ |●| Le Relais de Pont-d'héry

Route de Champignole, Chaux-Champagny; take the D492.
☎03.84.73.06.54 ⓕ03.84.73.19.00
Closed *Mon evening and Tues (Sept–May); Mon only (June, July and Aug); Feb school holiday (zone B); Nov school holiday plus an extra week.* **TV. High chairs and games available. Swimming pool. Car park.**

A nice little place inside a dreary-looking house on the edge of the road. The dining room is pretty and the terrace in the garden lovely in summer, with the added attraction of the pool. There are just two rooms with bath, priced at €50, but they're spacious and comfortable. The cuisine is bang up to date and full of fanciful ideas and flavours. Perfect menus (from the starters to the desserts that follow the impeccable cheese board). Very professional, yet relaxed, service (yes, it does exist). Weekday lunch menu for €12 then others at €16–35; they all include cheese and dessert. *A glass of Coupe de Crémant sparkling wine (taken with dessert) offered to our readers on presentation of this guide.*

Myon
25440 (15km NW)

◎ 🎿 |●| ♟ Auberge Marle

Take the D492, then turn left on the D15.
☎03.81.63.78.47
Closed *Sun evening; fortnight end of Sept.* **Disabled access. Car park.**

Charming country inn that is one of the last of a dying breed. Refurbished double rooms go for €30 with basin and €36 with bath; half board €39 per person. Generous and unchanging house specialities predominate on the menus at €20–30: *croûte forestière*, fillet of pike perch with hazelnuts, pike sorbet with Savagnin. There's a lovely terrace and small old-fashioned garden, with traditional elements that only add to the charm: pergola, rose garden at the foot of the church. *Free house apéritif offered to our readers on presentation of this guide.*

Ornans
25290

◎ ♟ |●| Hôtel de France***

51 rue Pierre-Vernier; opposite the Grand Pont.
☎03.81.62.24.44 ⓕ03.81.62.12.03
✉hoteldefrance@europost.org
Closed *Mon lunchtime; 8–22 Nov; 20 Dec–11 Feb.* **TV. High chairs available. Pay car park.**

Traditional hotel, very *Vieille France*, friendly and cosy. You can enjoy a lunchtime *formule* at the bar. As for the restaurant (pleasant décor, in extremely traditional classical style), good attempt at reworking regional dishes (foie gras with Morello cherries, trout fillets in *vin jaune* sauce with morels). Lovely market day menu costs €23; two other menus €34 and €43. The rooms (€70–80) are comfortable and old-fashioned; some look out onto the famous Grand Pont, but the road is a bit noisy. You'll get peace and quiet in the rooms at the back, which overlook the courtyard. There's a big terrace and a garden behind the hotel, and a wonderful art shop just over the road. Private fishing is available.

◎ |●| Restaurant Le Courbet

34 rue Pierre-Vernier.
☎03.81.62.10.15
Closed *Sun evening; Mon; Tues lunchtime; during July/Aug closed Mon only; mid-Feb to mid-March.* **High chairs available.**

Choose your meal from a menu illustrated with a Courbet painting (although the painter himself would have felt out of place in such a quiet, reflective place). The view over the Loue from the two terraces is magnificent, while the cooking is a gourmet's delight, as the masterly chef plays with different tastes and colours to bring out the qualities of the meticulously chosen fresh ingredients. There's a range of menus at €16.50–30.50 (with two or three courses). Welcome and service are in keeping with the rest of the picture.

Lods
25930 (12km SE)

◎ ♟ |●| 🎿 Hôtel-restaurant La Truite d'Or**

40 rue du Moulin-Neuf; take the D67.
☎03.81.60.95.48 ⓕ03.81.60.95.73

la-truite-dor@wanadoo.fr
Closed *Sun evening and Mon out of season;* *15 Dec–25 Jan.* **TV. High chairs available. Car park.**

An old stone windmill that, despite appearances, is only half sleeping and which conceals a good regional restaurant serving a range of menus €15.70–42. You need go no further to sample the regional speciality of trout in wine stuffed with salmon and chopped morels. Comfortable rooms go for €43; half board €47 per person. Logis de France. *Free house apéritif offered to our readers on presentation of this guide.*

Vernierfontaine
25580 (17km E)

≈ ♪ ≙ |●| L'Auberge Paysanne

18 rue du Stade; take the D492 in the direction of Saules, then the D392 to Guyans-Durnes then Vernierfontaine.
☏ and ℻ 03.81.60.05.21
Closed *Tues evening to Thurs between early Nov and early March; 10 days end June to early July; Dec; Jan.* **Car park.**

An old farmhouse in a remote village way out in the country. The décor is cluttered but the cuisine is traditional and full of flavour, utilizing a panoply of wonderful local produce: flaky pastry cases with morels in rich sauce, country pan-fry, Morteau sausage, *roësti* (grated potatoes fried in a heavy pan), fondues. First menu starts at €11.50 and others €14–23. There are four rooms with wood panelling at €39 for a double; breakfast is gigantic. Credit cards not accepted. *10% discount on the room rate (Oct–March) or free coffee offered to our readers on presentation of this guide.*

Pontarlier
25300

≈ ♪ ≙ |●| Hôtel-Restaurant le Saint-Pierre*

3 pl. Saint-Pierre.
☏ 03.81.46.50.80 ℻ 03.81.46.87.80
TV. High chairs available.

This place sits on a square in an area that feels rather quiet and villagey. Nearly all the rooms look out onto the porte Saint-Pierre, the rather elaborate triumphal arch that has become the symbol of the town. The double rooms with shower/wc aren't exactly huge, but they are stylish as well as good value with prices at €40–48

according to level of comfort. The restaurant serves decent traditional food; menus €12 (weekday lunchtimes), and others €15–20. They have the sunniest terrace in town – a great place to linger over an apéritif. *10% discount on the room rate for a minimum of two consecutive nights (outside July/Aug) and free coffee offered to our readers on presentation of this guide.*

Grangettes (Les)
25160 (12km SW)

≈ ≙ |●| Hôtel-restaurant Bon Repos**

It's on the lac de Saint-Point; follow the D437 then, after Oye-et-Pallet take the D129.
☏ 03.81.69.62.95 ℻ 03.81.69.61.61
🖥 www.hotelbonrepos.com
Closed *Sun evening and Mon out of season;* *17 Oct–21 Dec.* **TV. High chairs available. Car park.**

On the edge of a little village by the lake. An old-fashioned inn – the tablecloths are white and the welcome is inviting. Numerous menus, €14.75–31.20, feature substantial platters of home-made charcuterie and fine fish specialities. Comfortable, well-maintained rooms, all recently renovated, go for €43.70 for a double with shower/wc or bath.

Ouhans
25520 (16km NW)

≈ ♪ ≙ |●| Hôtel-restaurant des Sources de la Loue**

13 Grande-Rue; take the N57, and at Saint-Gorgon-Main turn left onto the D41.
☏ 03.81.69.90.06 ℻ 03.81.69.93.17
🖥 www.hotel-sources-de-la-loue.com
Closed *Fri evening out of season; Mon; 20 Dec–1 Feb.* **TV. High chairs available. Car park.**

A lovely country inn in an unspoilt village amidst wonderful countryside and offering a pleasant welcome. The cooking concentrates on local dishes, as you would expect – they specialize in house smoked meats, bacon and mushrooms in a pastry case, home-made foie gras. Weekday lunch menu starts at €11.50 and others €15–33. Pleasant, simple rooms (some in the roof), which at €45–50 are reasonably priced for the area. A good base from which to explore this splendid region. Logis de France. *Free coffee offered to our readers on presentation of this guide.*

Port-sur-Saône
70170

ⓔ ♨ |◉| Hôtel-restaurant de la Paix

3 rue Jean-Bogé; it's opposite the church.
☏03.84.91.52.80 ℻03.84.91.61.21
Closed *Sun evening; Jan.*

Modest little hotel located in a sixteenth-century priory. Nicely renovated doubles €26 with basin, €34 with shower/wc; they're all quiet, as it's on a pedestrianized street. Bikers' bistro, and honest traditional cooking in the restaurant: scrambled eggs with the local cancoillotte cheese, morels in a pastry case, deep-fried smelt, stew of pike perch and salmon, etc. The cheapest menu starts at €9 (weekdays) and there are others €15–26. There's a pretty, shaded terrace.

ⓔ |◉| Restaurant La Pomme d'Or

1 rue Saint-Valère; at the traffic lights, on the N19.
☏03.84.91.52.66
Closed *Sun evening; Mon; Thurs evening; 3 weeks from the end of Aug to early Sept.* **Disabled access. High chairs and games available.**

You eat in a smart little dining room right on the banks of the Saône. The cuisine is good and dishes change with the seasons: pan-fried snails and wild mushrooms in vermouth, fish or meat terrine, freshwater pike perch in *beurre blanc* sauce, hot duck pie. There's a weekday menu at €9.50 and others up to €26. In summer, you might find a table on the tiny terrace overlooking the water; private function room available for family reunions or banquets.

Combeaufontaine
70120 (14km NW)

ⓔ ♨ |◉| Hôtel-restaurant Le Balcon**

Take the N19.
☏03.84.92.11.13 ℻03.84.92.15.89
Closed *Sun evening; Mon; Tues lunchtime; 28 June–7 July; 26 Dec–12 Jan.* **TV. High chairs available. Car park.**

Just where you would expect the typical stopover hotel, in a village situated on a major road, instead you find a really good place. Admittedly, behind the small, flower-filled garden and the ivy-bedecked façade, the rooms are simple (but well kept) and,

given the situation, quieter than at the front. But the food, from the first menu, makes all the difference. Whether they are regional dishes such as chicken in *vin jaune* sauce with morels, Montbéliard sausage with lentils or more innovative ones: the chef comes up with the goods; €11.50 weekday lunch menu and others €24–56. Double rooms are €42 with shower/wc or bath. Logis de France.

Roche-Morey (La)
70120 (18km NW)

ⓔ ⅋ |◉| Le Point de Vue

La Roche-Morey; take the N19 then, near Cintrey, the D1; from the village of the Morey, take the little road to the peak of La Roche-Morey, passing through Saint-Julien.
☏03.84.91.02.14
Closed *Sun evening and Mon out of season; Dec and Jan (except groups).* **Open** *every day in June.* **Disabled access. High chairs and games available.**

The top of the hill has been invaded by a small amusement park (mini-golf, Indian village, little merry-go-round), with this family restaurant in the middle, with a stunning panoramic view. Excellent, copious, meticulously prepared meals at very reasonable prices, with friendly and diligent service. The house speciality is *feuilleté* with onions or fresh asparagus; menus €11–37. *Free house apéritif offered to our readers on presentation of this guide.*

Ronchamp
70250

ⓔ ♨ |◉| ⅋ Hôtel-restaurant Le Rhien Carrer**

Le Rhien; it's 3km from the centre of Ronchamp on the N19 (in the direction of Belfort).
☏03.84.20.62.32 ℻03.84.63.57.08
🌐www.ronchamp.com
Closed *Sun evenings in winter.* **Disabled access. TV. High chairs and games available. Car park.**

Nice country inn in a quiet hamlet in a green valley. The family cooking is very orthodox and they use the best quality fresh produce. The results are delicious and the restaurant is very popular with the locals: pan-fried *escalope* of foie gras with sour cherries, trout or pike perch in *vin jaune*, fried carp and game in season, with a weekday lunch menu at €11 and others

€19–40; "four seasons" menus at €15 and €21. Rooms are simple, comfortable and have been refurbished: doubles at €42 with shower/wc or bath. To aid the digestion, why not go for a post-prandial stroll or bike ride in the forest close to the Mont de Vannes? Logis de France. *Free house apéritif offered to our readers on presentation of this guide.*

Champagney
70290 (4km NE)

ⓒ ♨ |●| 𝄞 Le Pré Serroux***

4 av. du Général-Brosset. Take the N19 then the D4 in the direction of Giromagny.
☎03.84.23.13.24 ⓕ03.84.23.24.33
ⓦwww.lepreserroux.com
Restaurant closed *Sun evening Oct–March.*
Closed *31 July–14 Aug; 19 Dec–9 Jan.* **TV.**
Disabled access. High chairs and games available. Swimming pool. Car park.

This old house has been entirely transformed, but the family that owns it has taken care to retain its original character. There are four dining rooms, each one different: one has a wide fireplace where they serve country dishes, another is more like a sitting room-cum-library. The rooms are either starkly modern or have period furniture; doubles with shower/wc or bath €50. Some things haven't changed, though – the waitresses still wear white aprons and the chef is still committed to preparing sound regional and traditional dishes including *marbré de lapereau, céleri et foie gras*, scallops in grapefruit butter or Champlitte glazed pork. The weekday menu starts at €12, with a range of others €18–62. There's a fitness room, a sauna and a Turkish bath. Logis de France. *Free liqueur offered to our readers on presentation of this guide.*

Mélisey
70220 (11km NW)

ⓒ |●| 𝄞 Restaurant La Bergeraine

27 rte. des Vosges; take the N19 towards Lure then the D73.
☎03.84.20.82.52
Closed *Tues evening and Wed (except public holidays and on the day before a public holiday).* **Disabled access. Car park.**

The chef has created a place which brings people out into the country to eat – but it's so small here that, unless you want to go away hungry, it's advisable to book.

He serves appetizing, classic dishes prepared with individualistic flair. Favourites include house-smoked salmon, mixed seasonal salad with crayfish, game, and morels in a pastry case with *vin jaune* sauce. The weekday lunch menu at €15, with others €20–65, change with the seasons. *Free coffee offered to our readers on presentation of this guide.*

Roye
70200 (11km SW)

ⓒ |●| Le Saisonnier

56 rue de la Verrerie; on the N19, in the direction of Lure, then turn left at La Verrerie.
☎03.84.30.46.00
Closed *Sun evening; Mon evening; Wed; around 6–26 Aug.* **Disabled access. High chairs and games available.**

You can stumble on some quite surprising places in the Haute-Saône – and this is one. It used to be a farm, as evidenced by its low ceilings (if you're tall, mind your head) and thick stone walls, which keep it warm in winter and cool in summer. Rather sober décor but pleasant nonetheless, and there's friendly service. Excellent seasonal cooking with a lot of up-to-date dishes offering good value for money (menus €18–46): saddle of rabbit conserved in fat with chicken livers, pork fillet stuffed with Comté and Jura morbier cheeses and coated in bacon, butter roast cod. There's a quiet terrace at the back.

Froideterre
70200 (13km W)

ⓒ 𝄞 |●| Hostellerie des Sources

4 rue du Grand-Bois; take the N19 in the direction of Lure and when you get to La Verrerie, take the road that goes north.
☎03.84.30.34.72
Closed *Sun evening; Mon and Tues (except public holidays); a fortnight in Jan.*

From the moment you see the blue and golden awning that creates an attractive extension to the entrance, it is clear that this is no ordinary country inn. The décor is very plush, almost luxurious, and perhaps seems like too much of a contrast with the classic farm inn exterior. The main event is the cuisine, however, which is creative and intelligently conceived and which stimulates all the senses; menus €35–90. Impossible to resist the *foie gras de canard* marinated in Jurançon wine, the braised loin of lamb with parsley or the crayfish flambéed in Cognac (when in season). And impossible to resist the *crème brûlée* with vanilla Bourbon. The wine list holds its own too. Reservations are highly recommended. *Free coffee offered to our readers on presentation of this guide.*

Rousses (Les)
39220

◎ 🏠 Hôtel du Village**

344 rue Pasteur.
☎03.84.34.12.75 ℗03.84.34.12.76
Closed *Sun evening out of season; 1–15 June; 1–15 Dec.* **TV. Pay car park.**

This ten-room hotel in the middle of the resort has been renovated from top to bottom, with taste and imagination. The double rooms, all with shower/wc or bath, are decorated slightly differently – some are bright, others more sober – and go for €47–58. Pleasant welcome, and there's a lock-up garage available.

◎ 🎿 🏠 |◎| Hôtel Arbez France-Suisse**

La Cure; it's 2km out of town on the D5.
☎03.84.60.02.20 ℗03.84.60.08.59
🌐www.hotelarbez.fr.st
Closed *Mon evening; Tues out of season; Nov.* **TV. High chairs available.**

With one foot in France and another over the Swiss border, this is an odd place – depending on your room number, you could be sleeping either in France or Switzerland. We leave it to you to imagine all the anecdotes that this situation has produced. The border runs right through the middle of room nos. 2, 6, 9 and 12. All the rooms are nevertheless cosy and comfortable; doubles €54–59 with shower/wc or bath. Half board, requested during the February school holiday, costs around €53–55 per person. They offer two ways to dine: a brasserie (with filling portions) and a gourmet restaurant. They serve a €13 menu in the brasserie at lunchtime, and in the restaurant there's a range of menus at €26–33. This is a really good place and the welcome is charming. Logis de France. *10% discount on the room rate (except in Feb and 20 Dec–4 Jan) offered to our readers on presentation of this guide.*

◎ 🎿 🏠 |◎| Le Lodge**

309 rue Pasteur.
☎03.84.50.50.64 ℗03.84.50.04.58
🌐www.hotellodge.com
Closed *Sun evening, Mon and Tues out of season; 1–30 June; first 3 weeks in Nov.* **Disabled access. TV.**

It's rare to find such a charming place in Megève these days, and the Jura is the only place you will. The building is made of stone and wood, with tiled floors and stuffed toy bears hanging from the country-style wardrobes. All the rooms are different, of course, and all are extremely comfortable; doubles with shower/wc cost €60–90 according to the season. Excellent welcome, not at all stiff, as can sometimes be the case in this sort of place. There's also a restaurant. *Free coffee offered to our readers on presentation of this guide.*

Ilay
39150 (31km NW)

◎ 🎿 🏠 |◎| L'Auberge du Hérisson*

5 rte. des Lacs; take the N5 and the N78; it's 3km after Bonlieu.
☎03.84.25.58.18 ℗03.84.25.51.11
🌐www.herisson.com
Closed *Mon; Tues in Oct; early Nov to end Jan.* **Open** *noon–2pm; 7–8.30pm.* **TV. High chairs available. Car park.**

A good base for local excursions and visits to the nearby waterfalls. Refurbished rooms are cosy and comfortable; doubles cost €40–55 with shower/wc or bath. In the restaurant, they serve a range of menus at €15–40; the ingredients are fresh and the results are good: snails with morels, *boudin* of pink trout. The cheese selection is exceptional (offered on an eat-as-much-as-you-like basis with salad and dessert in one of the menus). There are also a few Jura specialities and fondues, and an interesting children's menu. Logis de France. *Free house apéritif offered to our readers on presentation of this guide.*

Bonlieu
39130 (34km NW)

◎ 🎿 🏠 |◎| La Poutre**

25 Grande-Rue; take the N5 as far as Saint-Laurent-en-Grandvaux, then the N78 after the Pic de l'Aigle.
☎03.84.25.57.77 ℗03.84.25.51.61

Closed *Mon; Tues; I Nov–5 May.* **TV. Car park.**

Large house in the heart of the village in this lake-filled region (it is not too taxing a problem to work out why the restaurant has chosen its name, which means "beam" in French). It's a local institution, run by a new generation, who have added personality and warmth to the enterprise. The dining room has gained in character, the welcome in warmth. Lovely creative cooking, using regional specialities, is featured on menus €15–62, and served by an attentive staff. Double rooms go for €46–57 depending on facilities and the season. *Free house apéritif offered to our readers on presentation of this guide.*

Vesoul
70000

@ ﾠ ﾠ Hôtel du Lion**

4 pl. de la République.
☏03.84.76.54.44 ℻03.84.75.23.31
✉hoteldulion@wanadoo.fr
Closed *Sat evening in Jan and Feb; 1–16 Aug; 26 Dec–9 Jan.* **TV. Car park.**

Family-run, very traditional hotel in the centre of town – the staff is welcoming and knows what good service is. The comfortable rooms have modern furnishings and are spacious; doubles with shower/wc or bath cost €45. *10% discount on the room rate (in July–Aug) offered to our readers on presentation of this guide.*

Frotey-lès-Vesoul
70000 (3km E)

@ ﾠ |O| ﾠ Eurotel – restaurant Le Saint Jacques***

Route de Luxeuil; on the way out of Vesoul heading east on the D13.
☏03.84.75.49.49 ℻03.84.75.55.78
⊛www.eurotel.fr
Closed *Sun evening.* **TV. High chairs available. Car park.**

The outside is very off-putting – it looks exactly like lots of chains throughout France – and the roundabout is hardly the most attractive view, but you leave all that behind once inside. The rooms are pleasant and contemporary; doubles with bath €55. The bar and dining room are modern, too, as well as being truly elegant. The restaurant offers very good food pre-

pared from seasonal produce with menus €18–50. The staff offers a warm, professional welcome. *Free house apéritif offered to our readers on presentation of this guide.*

Villersexel
70110

@ ﾠ |O| Hôtel-restaurant du Commerce**

1 pl. du 13-Septembre; it's near the château museum.
☏03.84.20.50.50 ℻03.84.20.59.57
⊛www.hotelcommerce-villersexel.fr
Closed *Sun evening (except 15 June–15 Aug); 20 Dec–10 Jan.* **TV. High chairs and games available. Car park.**

Classic provincial inn with simple, clean and reasonably priced rooms; doubles €40 with shower/wc or bath. The owner prepares good regional dishes: ham on the bone cooked in a hay box, home-produced smoked and braised ham, terrines and hot *cancoillotte* cheese, fried carp. Set menus start at €11 (except Sat evening and Sun) and €19–36. Logis de France.

@ ﾠ |O| Hôtel de la Terrasse**

Route de Lure.
☏03.84.20.52.11 ℻03.84.20.56.90
Closed *Sun evening; Fri evening out of season; 15 Dec–2 Jan.* **TV. High chairs available. Car park.**

This hotel beside the river is quiet, cosy and very relaxing, and the rooms are prettily and tastefully furnished. Doubles go for €40–49 with shower/wc or bath. The rustic-style restaurant is warmed by an open fire in winter; in summer you can eat on the terrace surrounded by greenery. Regional dishes are served and include casserole of morels, pike perch in *vin jaune*, Montbéliard sausage, leek fondue and poached egg. Weekday lunch menu starts at €11.50, then others €14–23. Logis de France.

Villers-le-Lac
25130

@ ﾠ ﾠ |O| Hôtel-restaurant Le France

8 pl. Cupillard.
☏03.81.68.00.06 ℻03.81.68.09.22
⊛www.hotel-restaurant.lefrance.com

Closed *Sun evening out of season; Mon;*
Tues lunchtime; Jan; a week in Nov. **TV. High**
chairs and games available. Pay car park.

The best addresss in this corner of France,
thanks to its dynamic chef. Hugues Droz
has a reputation for his subtle, inventive
cuisine. He has his own herb garden and
a pungent collection of spices brought
back from his travels. Tastes and textures
contrast beautifully; the food is inventive
and simple at the same time. There's a
lunch menu at €19, and others at €25
and €65; also an interesting wine list.
Restaurant dining room is very pleasant,
as is the service. Attractively decorated
doubles with shower/wc or bath go for
€55–100. Don't miss the little museum of
gastronomy upstairs. Babysitting is available on Thursday and Friday evenings.
Logis de France. *10% discount on the room*
rate (except July–Aug) offered to our readers on
presentation of this guide.

☜ |●| L'Absinthe-restaurant du Saut du Doubs

6km from the town centre, 200m from the
waterfall; you can also go by boat.

☎03.81.68.14.15
Closed *early Nov to Easter (except for*
bookings). **Open** *10am–7pm in July–Aug.*
Disabled access.

Located 200m from the waterfall, this
building on the river bank, with *tavillons*
(small wooden planks) on the façade,
typical of the Haut-Doubs, is set off by
beautiful stone terraces surrounded by
absinthe plants and blessed with a fine
view of the Doubs lakes. The cooking is
simple but excellent based on regional
cheeses and salted meat and fish. A platter of local dishes costs €7.50; menus of
the day are €10 and €12. You can learn
all about the drink that gives the place its
name by merely crossing the threshold
of the lovely dining room, with its décor
from the turn of the twentieth century,
as you will be shown posters and utensils
associated with the ritual of its consump-
tion. Try to come before it fills up, so
that you have time to savour a glass of
absinthe.

Île-de-France

Angerville
91670

⋘ 🍴 🏠 |●| Hôtel de France***

2 pl. du Marché; take the N20 in the direction of Orléans, exit Angerville.
☎01.69.95.11.30 ☎01.64.95.39.59
🌐www.hotelfrance3.com
Hotel closed *Sun evening.* **Restaurant closed** *Sun evening; Mon evening.* **TV. High chairs available. Car park.**

This beautiful old inn, built in 1715, has been restored a number of times without losing its elegance or character – the old beams, fireplace, conservatory and drawing room exude an air of gracious living. There's a sitting room where you can relax over an apéritif before proceeding to the dining room. The cuisine is reassuringly traditional and reliable: terrine with watercress (this is the region for watercress) and *salade mérévilloise*. On fine days you can eat outside in the beautiful interior courtyard. Set menu costs €29 or expect to pay around €43 à la carte. Double rooms with shower/wc or bath go for €90–130, including a pair of ravishing rooms with canopied beds – they are much in demand with honeymoon couples. *Free coffee offered to our readers on presentation of this guide.*

Asnières
92600

⋘ |●| Le Petit Vatel

30 bd. Voltaire; M° Asnières-Gabriel-Péri.
☎01.47.91.13.30
Closed *evenings; weekends; Aug.*

This very ordinary-looking, Formica-table lunch place doesn't seem worth a second glance, but the welcome here is genuinely warm and the food is very good – and, what's more, you almost get more than you can eat. They take care in preparing traditional family dishes like ham hock or *provençal* beef stew, and the salads are huge. Weekday lunch menu at €12; you'll spend around €18 à la carte. Reasonably priced wine.

⋘ |●| La Petite Auberge

118 rue de Colombes; take the overground train from Saint-Lazare to Asnières or Bois-Colombes.
☎01.47.93.33.94
Closed *Sun and Wed evenings; Mon; 3 weeks in Aug.* **Open** *12.15–2pm and 7.30–9pm.*

The décor is completely over the top, like the set of a Grande Époque operetta – wood panelling and pictures everywhere. You're scooped up by the *patronne* or her daughter and conducted to your table; Dad, in the kitchen, produces wonderful food. There's a *menu-carte* for €27.75 which provides a superb meal, with dishes that change with the seasons. Typical offerings include *croustillant* of pig's trotters with salad or rump steak with truffle sauce. The fish is as fresh as can be – try the bass flambéed in pastis butter – and desserts are great. Wines are in the region of €21–64. You should definitely call to book a table.

Aubervilliers
93300

⋘ |●| 🍴 L'Isola

33 bd. Édouard-Vaillant; M°Fort-d'Auberviliers. It's in the north of the town, opposite the municipal greenhouses.
☎01.48.34.88.76

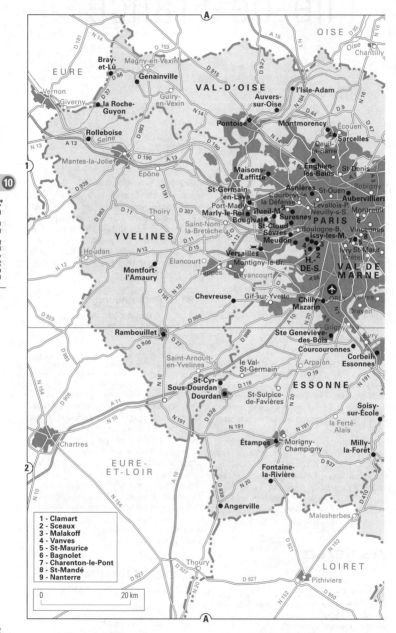

OISE

EURE

Bray-
et-Lû

Magny-en-Vexin

Genainville

la Roche-
Guyon

Vernon

Giverny

Guiry-
en-Vexin

VAL-D'OISE

Auvers-
sur-Oise

l'Isle-Adam

Chantilly

Oise

Rolleboise

Seine

Pontoise

Montmorency

Écouen

Sarcelles

Deuil-
la-Barre

Mantes-la-Jolie

Épône

Maisons-
Laffitte

Enghien-
les-Bains

St-Denis

Bobigny

Thoiry

St-Germain-
en-Laye

Port-Marly

Asnières

St-Ouen

Aubervilliers

Montreuil

YVELINES

Saint-Nom-
la-Bretèche

Marly-le-Roi

Bougival

Courbevoie
la Défense

Levallois-P.
Neuilly-s.-S.

Rueil-M.

Suresnes

PARIS

Houdan

Élancourt

Trappes

St-Cloud
Sèvres
Meudon

Boulogne-B.
4
1 3
H.-
2
DE-S.

Issy-les-M.

Vincennes

Ivry St-Maur
Créteil

VAL DE
MARNE

Versailles

Montigny-la-Br.

Guyancourt

Montfort-
l'Amaury

Chevreuse

Gif-sur-Yvette

Chilly-
Mazarin

Yerres

Draveil

Rambouillet

Ste Geneviève-
des-Bois

Évry

Saint-Arnoult-
en-Yvelines

le Val-
St-Germain

Courcouronnes

Arpajon

Corbeil-
Essonnes

St-Cyr-
Sous-Dourdan

Dourdan

St-Sulpice-
de-Favières

ESSONNE

Soisy-
sur-École

Chartres

Étampes

Morigny-
Champigny

la Ferté-
Alais

Milly-
la-Forêt

EURE-
ET-LOIR

Fontaine-
la-Rivière

Angerville

Malesherbes

1 - Clamart
2 - Sceaux
3 - Malakoff
4 - Vanves
5 - St-Maurice
6 - Bagnolet
7 - Charenton-le-Pont
8 - St-Mandé
9 - Nanterre

Thoury

LOIRET

Pithiviers

0   20 km

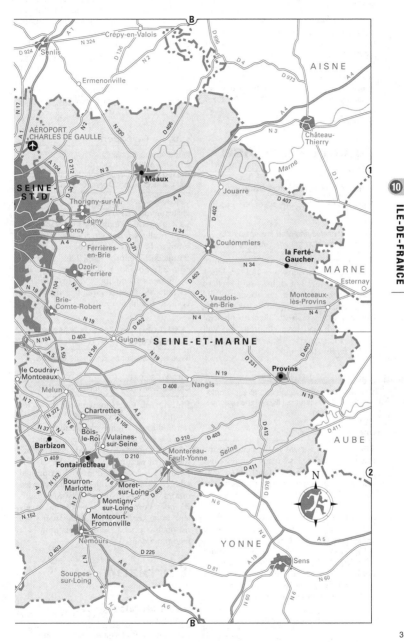

Closed *Sun; Mon–Wed evenings; Aug.* **Car park.**

This is a genuine Italian restaurant run by a pair of charming sisters who are kindness itself. The décor is pleasant but not ostentatious and dishes are cooked using fresh produce from the market: fresh pasta, veal *escalope*, *osso buco*, ricotta ravioli, lasagne and a delicious Sardinian dish called *coulourgionisi*. Reckon on €25–30 for a meal. *Free house apéritif offered to our readers on presentation of this guide.*

Auvers-sur-Oise
95430

10

ⓔ |●| Les Roses Écossaises

3 [bis] rue de Paris; in the street going up to the church.
☏01.30.36.14.15
Closed *evenings and Mon (except public holidays); mid-Aug to early Sept.*

This pretty restaurant offers a selection of salads, quiches, savoury pies and omelettes, as well as a few hot dishes and excellent cakes (there is also a tea room on the premises). The dish of the day costs €10, the set lunches €16–25. Reckon on €23 à la carte. If you have children, you will be able to arrange a special deal for them, with a large selection of dishes.

ⓔ |●| Le Cordeville

18 rue du Rajon; leave the A15 at exit 7 onto the N184, then take the N322 in the direction of Méry-sur-Oise.
☏01.30.36.81.66
Open *daily 11.30am–2pm.*

This restaurant is right in the centre of the town that attracted so many Impressionist painters. They serve traditional family cuisine and don't stint on the portions. The *patronne* is very sweet and sets the pot on the table for you to help yourself, just like at home. It appeals to a range of people, from local workers to holidaymakers, and has a brigade of regulars. The cheapest menu is €13.50 (weekday lunch) and there's another at €20 which includes apéritif, wine (a bottle for four people) and coffee. There's a limited choice of wines available and booking is essential. No credit cards.

ⓔ 🎋 |●| Au Verre Placide

20 rue du Général-de-Gaulle; opposite the train station at Auver-sur-Oise.
☏01.34.48.02.11

Closed *Mon; Wed and Sun evenings; Aug.*

One of the oldest restaurants in Auvers, with a spacious and bright dining room. There's a weekday menu (€15) and other menus for €20–34, or it's around €31 à la carte. Try the salad of quail *confit*, turbot with a fennel *compote*, or lamb in a pastry case. Wines start at €13 per bottle and service is very polite. It's advisable to book at the weekend. *Free coffee offered to our readers on presentation of this guide.*

ⓔ |●| La Guinguette

In the Auvers château.
☏01.34.48.43.29
Closed *evenings; Mon except public holidays; first 3 weeks in Jan.* **Open** *noon–2.30pm.*

Once you have finished your tour of the château, you can have a drink or meal in La Guingette, whose wooden tables are strategically set on a terrace off the last room to be visited (as well as in a vaulted seventeenth-century hall). The set menus cost €15.50 and €19.50; there is a also a children's menu for €9. The service is friendly and attentive, and it is advisable to book in the high season.

ⓔ |●| Auberge Ravoux – Maison de Van Gogh

8 rue de la Sansonne; it's on the town hall square.
☏01.30.36.60.60
Closed *evenings; Mon; Tues; 1 Nov–1 March.*

Vincent van Gogh lived in this hotel for a while, and died here in 1890 – it's been restored to its original glory and the décor is just as it would have been in the painter's day. The cooking is good, and helpings are substantial with menus at €28–35. Choose from old-fashioned dishes such as pressed rabbit on a bed of lentils and pickled onions and "seven-hour" slow-roast lamb. It's not cheap but it's nevertheless excellent value for money and the wines are reasonably priced, too. Reservations are recommended.

Barbizon
77630

ⓔ 🎋 🏠 |●| Auberge Les Alouettes**

4 rue Antoine-Barye; at the tobacconist's on the corner of Grande-Rue turn up the street and it's 500m along.

☎01.60.66.41.98 ℻01.60.66.20.69
🌐www.barbizon.net
Open *12.15–2pm and 7.30–9.15pm.*
Restaurant closed *Sun evening; Mon.* **TV.**
High chairs and games available. Car park.

This rather chic nineteenth-century house, set in its own substantial grounds (two hectares) with a garden and trees, has been turned into an inn. It's the only hotel in the town that's away from the main street and peace and quiet are guaranteed. Doubles start at €43 with shower to €59 with bath – there are also two apartments which sleep four people. In the restaurant they serve a range of menus at €28–33. *Free house apéritif offered to our readers on presentation of this guide.*

Bougival
78380

⊚ |●| Chez Clément

It's on the N13 about 1km outside the town.
☎01.30.78.20.00 ℻01.30.78.20.09
🌐www.chezclement.com
Open *daily until 1am.* **Disabled access. Car park.**

You come here as much for the décor – a lovely dining room with fireplaces and an interior waterfall – as the food; simple cooking using fresh, seasonal produce. All of this in spacious grounds where you can dine on sunny days. The rotisserie *formule* at €15.90 (with starter, main meal and dessert) includes salad with mixed fresh herbs and purée with home-made butter; there's also a menu at €21, otherwise a meal will cost you around €30 à la carte. This is a very pleasant place, a haven of peace off the main road with private parking.

⊛ |●| Le Camélia

7 quai Georges-Clemenceau; it's off the A86.
☎01.39.18.36.06
Closed *Sat; Sun; a week in Feb; last week in July and first 3 weeks in Aug.* **Open** *noon–2.30pm and 7.30–10.30pm.* **High chairs available. TV.**

A welcoming, refined setting where you can enjoy swift, efficient service. The cuisine is prettily prepared and manages to be both solid and delicate. All the produce used is fresh and the cooking shows off the flavours extremely well; menus €38 and €68.

Bray-et-Lû
95710

⊚ 🏠 |●| Le Faisan Doré

12 rte. de Vernon.
☎ and ℻01.34.67.71.68
Closed *Sun evening; Mon.* **TV.**

The balconies here are festooned with an abundance of geraniums and petunias and there's a family atmosphere. In the summer, it's pleasant to sit on the terrace under the flowery parasols. The set weekday menu is €12; others, €17–26, include starter, main course, cheese and dessert. Specialities include scallops and duck with olives. À la carte, try the veal chops Normandy-style. It's good value for money, with attentive service. The rooms are plain; doubles with basin €23–28. Half board costs €42 per person.

Charenton-le-Pont
94220

⊚ |●| La Bolée d'Arvor

38 rue de Paris.
☎01.43.76.85.77
Closed *Sun; Mon.*

In the town's prettiest neighbourhood (pedestrian only at weekends), this restaurant offers some thirty copious and generous dishes in a restaurant run by Bretons for the past fifteen years: Tuareg pancake (€5.50), Aubrac pancake (€6.30) and seafood (€7.50). There's a terrace in summer.

Chevreuse
78460

⊚ |●| 🍴 Auberge La Brunoise

2 rue de la Division-Leclerc.
☎01.30.52.15.75
Open *noon–2pm and 7.30–9.45pm.* **Closed** *Mon and Tues evenings; Wed; a week in Feb; a week during the Easter holidays; 3 weeks end July to early Aug.* **High chairs available. Disabled access.**

The village is charming and the walk over the bridges of the Yvette River and the canal is incredibly picturesque. Unpretentious cuisine is on offer here (seafood is the speciality including *bouillabaisse*) – honest and good dishes feature on all the menus, which start at €11.30 (weekday lunch), then €15.50 (weekdays only) rising to €23.50 and €31. Natural, friendly service; the young owners' eagerness to keep the clients satisfied has earned them a good number of regulars. The dining room has a rustic aspect, though the glorious terrace looks onto the main road. *Free coffee offered to our readers on presentation of this guide.*

Chilly-Mazarin
91380

@ 🎋 |●| **Thym et Basilic**

97 rue de Gravigny; take the Longjumeau exit off the A6 and continue along the right of the motorway.
☎01.69.10.92.75
Closed *Sat lunchtime; Sun evening; Mon; last week in July and first 3 weeks in Aug.* **Disabled access.**

There's a hint of Provence in the yellow and blue dining room, and a taste of the same in the dishes: *bouillabaisse* (to order), prawns with pastis, scallop *provençale*, langoustines and lobster. The €13.50 lunch *formule* offers a dish of the day plus starter or dessert. Menus start at €16.50 (not Sun or public holidays), €22.60 and €32. The welcome and service are very pleasant. *Free digestif offered to our readers on presentation of this guide.*

Clamart
92140

@ 🎋 |●| **Restaurant La Cosse des Petits Pois**

158 av. Victor-Hugo; it's outside the centre of town, 300m from the Clamart train station.
☎01.46.38.97.60 ☎01.46.38.08.75
Closed *Sat lunchtime; Sun; Mon; in Aug.*

This restaurant is situated halfway between the centre of town and the station. The chef creates simple, generous food here, and attracts a good crowd of enthusiastic regulars. The set menu, €28, lists traditional dishes that change regularly with the season. Duck *foie gras*, however, is always on offer – enjoy it with a glass of Coteaux-du-layon (small supplement payable). *Free house apéritif offered to our readers on presentation of this guide.*

Corbeil-Essonnes
91100

@ |●| **Aux Armes de France**

1 bd. Jean-Jaurès; it's on the N7.
☎01.64.96.24.04 ☎01.60.88.04.00
🖳www.auxarmesdefrance.com
Closed *Sat lunch and Sun, except during public holidays.* **High chairs available. Car park.**

Friendly, unobtrusive service, winning cuisine and dishes that change according to the seasons and what's good at the market: soft-boiled egg baked in a crust of ceps, macaronade of creamy baked langoustines, pan-fried foie gras, fresh fish of the day brought straight from the market, soufflés of pike perch *quenelles*. They serve menus at €33.55–75.50 with wine, €51.10 without wine. *Free coffee offered to our readers on presentation of this guide.*

Coudray-Montceaux (Le)
91830 (3km S)

@ 🎋 |●| **Restaurant La Renommée**

110 berges de la Seine; take exit 11 off the A6, signposted Le Coudray-Montceaux; or take the N7 in the direction of Saint-Fargeau, then golf de Coudray, towards the station.
☎01.64.93.81.09
Closed *Tues evening; Wed; Sun evening; Feb school holiday.* **Car park.**

A pleasurable place whatever the weather. In summer or winter, you'll feel tranquil on the large veranda, watching the fishermen glide along the Seine. This is a great setting in which to enjoy salmon tartare, *millefeuille* of beef fillet and foie gras, scallop kebabs with exotic fruit. There is a weekday menu at €16, then others at €26 and €36. It's a good idea to reserve at the weekend. *A free glass of wine champenoise offered to our readers on presentation of this guide.*

Courcouronnes
91080

@ 🎋 |●| **Le Canal**

31 rue du Pont-Amar; it's in the Quartier du Canal, near the Courcouronnes hospital.
☎01.60.78.34.72

Open *noon–4pm and 7pm–midnight.* **Closed** *Sat; Sun; Aug.* **Disabled access.**

Courcouronnes is a concrete city and this restaurant is a spark of life in an otherwise desolate wasteland. It's a nice place with an attractive bar and friendly service, serving local produce. The owner cooks robust, colourful dishes as good as you'd get from many of the great-name chefs. There's a new speciality every day: duo of bream and salmon with chives, say, or pig's trotters. First menu costs €14.95 with others up to €29. Credit cards not accepted. *Free house apéritif offered to our readers on presentation of this guide.*

Dourdan
91410

⊚ |●| L'Auberge de l'Angelus

4 pl. du Chariot; it's 300m from the church, near the library on the banks of the Orge.
℡01.64.59.83.72
Closed *Mon and Tues evenings; Wed; Feb school holiday; first 3 weeks in Aug.* **Open** *noon–1.30pm and 7–9pm.* **Disabled access.**

In warm weather, you can eat in the flower garden of this old post house in a relaxed, summery atmosphere. Inside the décor is classic, with beige furnishings and tartan fabric stretched across the walls. Music gently playing in the background accompanies the delicious cuisine: bass steak with mango and spicy butter, duo of sole with a champagne sauce. Menus start at €22 (weekdays) up to €38; reckon on around €50 à la carte. You'll get a pleasant welcome and the service is efficient and attentive.

Enghien-les-Bains
95880

⊚ 🎿 🏠 |●| Villa Marie-Louise**

49 rue de Malleville; it's behind the spa, near the lake.
℡01.39.64.82.21 ℡01.39.34.87.76
📧www.hotel-marie-louise.com
Restaurant closed *Fri; Sat; Sun.* **Open** *noon–10pm.* **TV.**

This is a fine turn-of-the-(nineteenth)-century house with a big garden in the centre of town near the lake. The 22 simply furnished, comfortable rooms have been nicely decorated; ask for one with a garden view. Doubles €43–50 with shower/wc or bath (breakfast €5) – it's probably the cheapest hotel in town. If you're looking for a meal, you have a choice of simple, tasty dishes. There's a €10 menu (not Sun); otherwise it costs around €12 for a meal à la carte. The atmosphere is very relaxed and the food is good – you can eat outside in fine weather. *Free coffee offered to our readers on presentation of this guide.*

⊚ |●| Le Chalet

6 pl. du Cardinal-Mercier; next to the Saint-Joseph church.
℡01.34.28.09.95
Closed *Sun evening; Mon; fortnight in mid-Aug.*

The wood panelling, exposed beams, false stone and terracotta set a sober note, but this restaurant offers original, high-quality dishes, superbly executed. Some of the house specialities, such as the raclette and the fondue bourguignonne, have won this restaurant many loyal customers. There are set lunchtime menus at €12.50 (starter plus main course or main course plus dessert, with coffee) and €15.50 (three courses); for dinner, there is just one menu (€28), or you can eat à la carte. Watch out for supplements that may be added to the bill.

⊚ |●| Le Pavillon du Lac

66 rue du Général-de-Gaulle.
℡01.34.12.11.22
High chairs available.

This beautiful metal-and-glass rotunda, in a stunning location on the shores of Lake Enghien, is a delight for children, on account of the trees growing inside and the amazing metal sculpture. There is a special kids' menu at €14, a midweek set lunch at €22 and another menu at €35 (including a drink). Reckon on €4 for a tea. This restaurant does not offer *haute cuisine*, but its dishes are well prepared and attractively presented. Special emphasis is placed on meat, with an assortment of grills or the *assiette du petit rotisseur* – the choice of a piece of beef, poultry or leg of lamb. Unfortunately, the service is rather slow.

Deuil-la-Barre
95170 (1km NE)

⊚ 🎿 |●| Verre chez Moi

75 av. de la Division-Leclerc.
℡01.39.64.04.34

Closed *Sun; Mon; Aug; a week after Christmas.*

This restaurant feels like a Lyonnais tavern and occupies the ground floor of a villa which has been converted into flats. They serve good, well-prepared traditional dishes. There are no set menus, only a daily list on which you'll find *coq au vin, miroton* of beef – a typical Lyonnais dish with slices of boiled beef in a rich sauce with onions – or top-quality *andouillette*. Simple starters include herrings and warm steamed potatoes or charcuterie, and they offer a limited range of cheeses (the farmhouse Camembert is excellent) as well as basic but brilliant desserts like *crème brûlée*. The place is lovely and cosy, with a friendly feel and very fair prices: you should pay €19–23 for a meal with a jug of wine. *Free digestif offered to our readers on presentation of this guide.*

Étampes
91150

⊚ 🏠 Hôtel de l'Europe à l'Escargot

71 rue Saint-Jacques. Heading towards the station, go along the road parallel to the rail track for 200m, then turn left then left again; the entrance is down a narrow road.
☎01.64.94.02.96
Closed *July.* **TV. Car park.**

A small, very well-run hotel offering a smiling welcome, comfortable rooms and good value for money for Étampes. It's in the middle of town yet quiet. Doubles are €27 with shower, with shower/wc or bath €30–39. Room no. 1 is spacious and light, and particularly nice. The new owners are undertaking a complete refurbishment of the hotel during 2005.

⊚ |●| Le Saint-Christophe

28 rue de la République; it's next to the church Notre-Dame-du-Fort.
☎01.64.94.69.99
Closed *Sun evening.*

The speciality of this Portuguese restaurant is, and always has been, cod. It's the national dish, after all, and they're not going to change a winning formula. It's a nice place, attracting a host of regulars who appreciate the simple, tasty cooking. You can eat well for less than €20. There's a weekday menu for €10.

⊚ 🎋 |●| Restaurant Les Piliers

2 pl. Saint-Gilles.
☎01.64.94.04.52
Closed *Sun evening; Mon; Tues evening; in Aug.*

The restaurant is in the oldest house in town, and it dates from the twelfth century – go through the paved arcade to find the entrance. Good home cooking with a fair dash of creativity: sole fillet, duck breast, house *confit* and the like. The €17 *formule* gives you a couple of courses, while the one at €28 gives three. A few *appellation* wines at good prices, which is unusual in a place this classy. *Free coffee offered to our readers on presentation of this guide.*

Morigny-Champigny
91150 (5km N)

⊚ |●| 🏠 🎋 Hostellerie de Villemartin

21 allée des Marronniers; it's on the D17.
☎01.64.94.63.54
ⓦwww.hostellerie-villemartin.fr
Restaurant closed *last week in Feb; a week at Christmas.* **Open** *all year round.* **Car park.**

An impressive manor house in the middle of a huge estate next to a fortified farmhouse. You'll get a simple, attentive welcome with a family atmosphere that puts you at your ease. Both the hotel and the restaurant offer excellent value for money. The food is a happy surprise; fresh, creative cooking offering a wide choice. The €27 menu and the à la carte choices change with the seasons. Double rooms with shower/wc or bath go for €55–75. *10% discount on the room rate (from the third consecutive night) or free house apéritif offered to our readers on presentation of this guide.*

Saint-Sulpice-de-Favières
91910 (8km N)

⊚ 🎋 |●| Auberge de Campagne La Ferronnière

10 pl. de l'Église; take the N20 towards Arpajon.
☎01.64.58.42.07
Closed *Sat; first fortnight in Aug.*

A jewel of a village with a country inn that looks like a Wild West saloon. It must have been an old coaching inn originally, with the smithy next door. You won't find a better welcome or service; there's even a shower available for use by walkers. Huge plates of wonderful traditional food with a few authentic regional dishes besides: house terrine, snails, duck breast, rack of lamb, steak with shallots. Weekday lunch menu at €12 and another at €22. There's a terrace in summer. This place is not to be missed (it's the only one in the village). *Free house apéritif offered to our readers on presentation of this guide*

Val-Saint-Germain (Le)
91530 (18km NE)

☞ |●| ⚘ Auberge du Marais

1 rte. de Vaugrigneux. Drive towards Dourdan, and it's near the château du Marais. From Dourdan, take the D116 in the direction of Saint-Chéron, turn left at Sermaise along the winding road through the forest.
☎01.64.58.82.97
Closed *Sun evening; Mon; Christmas.* **Disabled access.**

A large rustic house on the edge of the forest, with a terrace that's open in summer. Traditional dishes made with fresh, quality produce; the terrines and the foie gras are particularly fine, as is the game in season, and it's worth following the chef's suggestions. He's a cheery man; if you ask nicely, perhaps he'll give you his recipes for pan-fried foie gras with potato *fondant* or duck stuffed with mushrooms with foie gras and grape sauce. Weekday lunch menu €12, then others €19–29, with a children's menu for €10. The first menu is particularly good, including a starter, dish of the day, cheese plate, salad or dessert, and coffee. Reservations are recommended for Sunday lunch. *Free house apéritif offered to our readers on presentation of this guide.*

Ferté-Gaucher (La)
77320

☞ ⚘ 🏠 |●| Hôtel du Sauvage**

27 rue de Paris.
☎01.64.04.00.19 ℗01.64.04.02.50
🖳www.hotel-du-sauvage.com
Restaurant closed *Mon lunch; Fri evening; Sun evening.* **Disabled access. TV. High chairs and games available. Swimming pool. Pay car park.**

This sixteenth-century inn was once a brothel, and its name is said to come

from the wild game once abundant in the marshland that used to surround it. The Teinturier family have been innkeepers here for six generations. They've had the courage to refurbish the place, providing attractively modern and comfortable rooms while keeping its all-important character. Doubles with shower/wc are €49–55, or €60–65 with bath/wc. Delicious regional dishes made with local produce are offered on set menus at €18–38. Try poached eggs with Brie, fillet of beef or ham on the bone. Perfect service and smiling welcome make this a very special place. Logis de France. *Free house apéritif or 10% discount on the room rate offered to our readers on presentation of this guide.*

Fontainebleau
77300

☞ ⚘ 🏠 Hôtel Victoria**

112 rue de France.
☎01.60.74.90.00 ℗01.60.74.90.10
🖳www.hotel.victoria.fr
TV. Disabled access. High chairs and games available. Pay car park.

George Sand and Alfred de Musset frequented this place in the 1830s. Here and there you'll discern the vestiges of the original master-craftsman's house, even though all nineteen rooms have been renovated. They're clean and pleasant, particularly the ones overlooking the large garden, and it's a real pleasure to be woken by the cooing of the birds. Paul and Isabelle will welcome you like old friends and with great kindness. Double rooms with bath cost €58–73; breakfast €7. A piano and billiard table are available to guests. *10% discount on the room rate (1 Nov–31 March) offered to our readers on presentation of this guide.*

☞ |●| ⚘ La Petite Alsace

26 rue de Ferrare; next to the Caveau des Ducs.
☎01.64.23.45.45
Open *daily noon–2pm (2.30pm on Sun) and 7–10.30pm.*

Pretty décor and setting (complete with storks). Fine Alsatian specialities and succulent onion pies; weekday lunchtime menu at €15, then at €25 and €30. Eat on the small pavement terrace in fine weather. *Free house apéritif offered to our readers on presentation of this guide.*

Restaurant Chez Arrighi

53 rue de France.
☎01.64.22.29.43
Closed *Mon.* **Open** *noon–2pm and 7–10pm.*

This place has got an old-fashioned feel about it, with its sturdy, stone façade and luxurious curtains. The two Art Deco dining rooms have been decorated in refined old rose tones, and soft music plays in the background. Menus at €16.50 (not served Sun), with others €23.50 and €32, include dishes like home-made duck foie gras, frogs' legs in parsley, boned quail in flaky pastry stuffed with foie gras, and crêpes suzette. They're all well prepared and will delight any fan of good traditional cooking. The first menu offers excellent value for money. *Free house apéritif offered to our readers on presentation of this guide.*

Le Caveau des Ducs

24 rue de Ferrare; it's near the château.
☎01.64.22.05.05
Open *daily for lunch and dinner.* **Disabled access. High chairs available.**

You'll know you're in Fontainebleau in this seventeenth-century vaulted cellar with its period décor and chandeliers. Classical cooking, faultlessly served. Set menus at €22.30 and €39; midday *formule* at €19 includes starter plus main meal, main meal plus dessert, or large salad plus a glass of wine. The chef uses excellent ingredients to produce great food; the generous desserts are excellent and there's an impressive wine list. The bread is a bit of a let-down, though. *Free house apéritif offered to our readers on presentation of this guide.*

Bois-le-Roi

77590 (4km NE)

Le Pavillon Royal***

40 av. du Général-Galliéni; it's near the train station.
☎01.64.10.41.00 ☎01.64.10.41.10
Disabled access. TV. Swimming pool. Car park.

A new building in neoclassical style, plain and aesthetically pleasing. Quiet, spacious and impeccably clean rooms are €55 with shower/wc or €60 with bath, each with a mini bar. Lovely swimming pool and relaxation centre. *10% discount on the room rate (except June, July, Aug and Sept) offered to our readers on presentation of this guide.*

Vulaines-sur-Seine

77870 (5km E)

L'Île aux Truites

Promenade Stéphane Mallarmé; take the D210 out of Fontainebleau, cross the Valvins bridge then head left. It's about 1km further on, on the banks of the Seine.
☎06.85.07.01.35
Closed *Wed; Thurs lunchtime; 21 Dec–25 Jan.* **Open** *noon–2pm and 7–10pm.* **Disabled access.**

You're right on the Seine here, in a thatched cottage surrounded by huge willow trees and trout ponds where the children can fish for their lunch – and, as the tables are right by the water's edge, you can keep an eye on them at the same time. Alternatively, in winter you can cosy up by the huge fireplace. Very decent cuisine and perfect service make this restaurant one of the most attractive in the region. They specialize in grilled fish served with baked potatoes. Or try the *assiette de l'Île aux truites* which includes smoked trout, marinated fillet of trout and fish terrine. In summer they offer nice tarts made with raspberries from the garden. Menus €22 and €30; reckon on €32 for a meal à la carte. You must reserve in summer to have any hope of getting a table. Trout fishing is offered for children. *Free house apéritif offered to our readers on presentation of this guide.*

Bourron-Marlotte

77780 (8km S)

Restaurant Les Prémices

12 bis rue Blaise-de-Montesquiou; take the N7 in the direction of Nemours-Montargis, and at the Bourron-Marlotte ZI exit, follow the signs to the village.
☎01.64.78.33.00
Closed *Sun evening; Mon; Tues; a week in the Feb school holiday; 1–15 Aug; a week at Christmas.* **TV. Car park.**

The restaurant is in the outbuildings of the superb château Bourron-Marlotte, and they've built a conservatory so you can appreciate the glory of the countryside. Menus €35 and €60 (gourmet): pan-fried foie gras with apricots, Kobé beef with apples, camembert in Calvados with a spicy cider caramel. The wine list is unusually good. Reserve well in advance.

Montigny-sur-Loing

77690 (10km S)

≪≫ |●| Restaurant de la Vanne Rouge

Rue de l'Abreuvoir; take the D148 along the banks of the Loing river.
☎01.64.78.52.30
Closed *Sun evening; Mon; Tues in winter; 4 weeks spread throughout the year.* **TV. Car park.**

Charming, super-quiet restaurant with a large sunny terrace where you're lulled by the sound of the waterfalls and you can practically trail your feet in the water while you eat. Chef Serge Granger's speciality is fish (*menu-carte* €33.54). There's an exceptional wine list. This is one of the best places in the are so it's wise to book. *Free house apéritif offered to our readers on presentation of this guide.*

Moret-sur-Loing

77250 (10km SE)

≪ |●| La Poterne

1 rue du Pont-du-Loing; take the N6.
☎01.64.31.19.89
Closed *Mon (April–Oct); Mon and Tues (Nov–March).* **Open** *public holidays; uninterrupted service all day Sat and Sun.*

This restaurant is in the shortest street in France – it is one building, the gate in the town walls where the restaurant is housed. It's a fine historic dwelling with an alleyway that looks over the Loing. Inventive, local dishes that the manager, Michelle, ferrets out of old recipe books: try that sixteenth-century delight, the *ouin*, sautéed veal like grandma used to make, and *casse-museau* (the favourite dessert of Louis XIII). They also do traditional Moroccan food (couscous, tajines and so on) in summer, along with vegetarian food and salads. There's no set menu but a large number of dishes priced around €10. Dine by candlelight on Saturday evenings and watch the *son et lumière* show on the river (no extra cost). For those who wish to spend the night, there's now one room "La Maison des Peintres" with shower/wc and terrace on the ramparts (€65 per night for two people, €90 on show nights).

Chartrettes

77590 (11km N)

≪ 🎋 |●| Restaurant Le Chalet

37 rue Foch; take the D39 and it's the last

village on the Seine before you reach Melun. Cross the Seine and the restaurant is on the right, near the marina in a little residential street.
☎01.60.69.65.34
Closed *Sun and Mon evenings; Wed.* **Open** *12.15–2pm and 7.30–10pm.* **High chairs available. Car park.**

This place buzzes with energy and laughter. Barely noticeable from the outside, it's a friendly, popular restaurant in a private mansion that fits in well with the rest in the street. The large rustic dining room decorated in Louis XIII style extends onto an elevated terrace with a pergola, and the cuisine consists of traditional dishes with good sauces: calf's head vinaigrette, duck *confit*, home-made goat's cheese tart. A substantial set menu is priced at €13 (not served Sat, Sun or public holidays), then others €21 and €28. *Free coffee offered to our readers on presentation of this guide.*

Moncour-Fromonville

77140 (13km S)

≪ |●| 🎋 Le Chaland qui passe

10 rue du Loing. Take the N7 to Montigny-sur-Loing, then the D40. It's on the banks of the Loing, opposite Grez-sur-Loing.
☎01.64.29.12.95
📧chaland.qui.passe@wanadoo.fr
Closed *Sun evening; Mon; during the Nov half term.*

A nice inn on the banks of the canal near the Loing river; the shady terrace gives you a good view of the pleasure boats sliding quietly by. The dining room has a country décor with a wide chimney. The first menu, €13, is great, and there are others up to €25. These feature dishes such as lamb's kidneys, skate wings and duck *confit*. Easy-going family atmosphere and perfect service with a smile. *Free house digestif offered to our readers on presentation of this guide.*

Fontaine-la-Rivière

91690

≪ 🏠 |●| Auberge de Courpain

It's 8km from Étampes heading towards Pithiviers.
☎01.64.95.67.04 ☎01.60.80.99.02
🌐www.auberge-de-courpain.com

10

Closed *1–15 Aug; 25–28 Dec.* **Disabled access. TV. High chairs and games available. Swimming pool. Car park.**

An old post house offering eighteen rooms (of which four are suites) with good facilities, each with en-suite bathrooms. The décor is charmingly rustic. Doubles are €70 and suites €115 for four people. There's a flower garden with a pleasant terrace for summer lunch, with tables made from old cart wheels and shaded by white parasols. Delicate dishes are flavoured with subtle mixtures of spices: sea bream with aniseed, monkfish and salmon steaks with vanilla, roasted rack of lamb with a herb crust and melon and lime soup for dessert. À la carte, starters go for around €13, main courses €20, and desserts €9; menu of the day costs €15. The menus change regularly and the service is attentive. Logis de France.

Genainville
95420

@ 𝒜 |●| **La Table Verte**

10 pl. de l'Église.
☏01.34.67.05.00
Closed *Tues; 3 weeks in Aug; a week at Christmas.* **Open** *lunchtimes; Fri and Sat evenings.* **High chairs available.**

Here, you can eat in the garden in summer, while in winter you can revel in the warmth of a log fire in this delightful restaurant run by a friendly female chef. The quality of the food – a mixture of local ingredients and exotic spices – and the extremely reasonable prices have won *La Table Verte* a loyal throng of regular customers – some even have a special chair with their name on it. The dish of the day costs €8.50. There is a weekday lunchtime menu at €14.50 (starter plus main course or main course plus dessert), plus another menu at €18 (weekdays) or €22 (weekend). It is essential to book. *Free Kir or orange juice offered to our readers on presentation of this guide.*

Isle-Adam (L')
95290

@ 𝒜 ☗ |●| **Le Cabouillet****

5 quai de l'Oise; it's after Cabouillet bridge, on the Oise.
☏01.34.69.00.90

Closed *Sun evening; Mon; Feb school holiday.* **Disabled access. High chairs available.**

This big, beautiful bourgeois country house is covered with ivy. Inside, Old Masters hang on the walls and there's a beautiful, polished wooden staircase – the prettily decorated rooms go for €70 with shower, €75 with bath; breakfast €9. The restaurant is the best in L'Isle-Adam; it offers a Logis-de-France menu for €30 and *menu carte* for €45. The cooking is refined and tasty and the dishes change with the seasons: calf's liver with onion chutney, curried monkfish with aubergine caviar, pear fritters with chocolate sauce. From some tables and from the terrace you get a view of the Oise River. Logis de France. *Free house digestif offered to our readers on presentation of this guide.*

@ |●| **Restaurant de la Plage**

On the beach site.
☏01.34.69.33.29
Open *lunchtimes, Fri and Sat evening during June and July.* **Disabled access.**

This is a traditional restaurant with a large Norman-style dining room and a terrace, on the banks of the Oise and not far from the beach. The food revolves around tried and tested classics like Norman-style chicken, spaghetti bolognaise and kidneys *grand-mère*, but some delicious exotic dishes also make an appearance from time to time. There are also other dishes especially designed for children. The cheapest menu costs €13, then there are others at €23 and €39 (including wine), and a children's menu at €9 (starter, main course plus drink).

@ |●| **Au Relais Fleuri**

61 rue Saint-Lazare; it's 300m from St Martin's church.
☏01.34.69.01.85
Open *noon–2pm and 7–9.15pm.* **Closed** *Sun evening; Mon evening; Tues; Wed evenings; first 3 weeks in Aug.* **Disabled access.**

The décor is absolutely classic, with blue fabric stretched across the walls and matching curtains. The Roland brothers will give you a courteous welcome and their delicate, sophisticated cooking offers good value for this town. Dishes change with the seasons. There's a weekday lunch menu for €19, set menu €26 with starter, main dish, cheese, salad and dessert; or reckon on around €45 à la carte: snail casserole with garlic butter, *fricassée* of lobster with Sauternes and basil, *bouillabaisse*. There's an enormous shady terrace where you can enjoy a meal when the weather permits.

Issy-les-Moulineaux

92130

« |●| Issy-Guinguette

113 [bis] av. de Verdun; M° Mairie-d'Issy, then by bus 123 to the Chemin des Vignes stop; RER C, Issy.
℡ 01.46.62.04.27
Closed *Sun; Mon evening; Sat (lunchtime only in summer); Aug; a week at Christmas.*

Yves Legrand, the boss of this place, is the driving force behind the resuscitation of the vineyard in Issy. On sunny days, sit out on the terrace among the vines with a view of lovely old houses – it's hard to believe you're in the suburbs of the capital, and if it gets too hot Yves puts up the parasols. Bistro dishes are carefully cooked and served in generous portions. There's not an extensive choice but the options change all the time: salmon *unilatérale* (cooked on one side), rolled lamb with fresh herbs, pork with cabbage, roast rabbit fillet with sage, stuffed breast of veal, cod with cream sauce, duck *fricassée* and pineapple preserved in red wine and ginger. There's an excellent wine list, as you might expect given the owner's enthusiasm. The service is perfect and the atmosphere relaxed and often quite festive; lunchtime sees lots of businessmen from the area. In winter, they serve in the bright dining room where they light a fire in the hearth. There's a menu for €24 or you'll pay around €31 à la carte. You are strongly advised to book.

« |●| La Manufacture

20 esplanade de la Manufacture; M° Corentin-Celton.
℡ 01.40.93.08.98 ℻ 01.40.93.57.22
🖰 www.restaurantmanufacture.com
Closed *Sat lunchtime; Sun; fortnight in Aug.* **Disabled access.**

The restaurant takes up the ground floor of an old tobacco factory. It's a huge room with a high ceiling painted cream and beige, and it's brightened up with a few modern pictures and green plants. At lunchtime it's full of media execs and exhibitors from the exhibition centre – the huge space makes this a perfect place

for private conversations or tricky negotations because you can hear each other without being overheard. The cooking is particularly fine, revelling in subtle flavours. Try the lamb shank braised in cider, which literally melts in the mouth. It's the best kind of home cooking rethought and served to suit modern styles and tastes. The menu changes frequently, but there are some staples including delicious crunchy pigs' ears, and beef cheek braised in Graves wine with a pea purée. Desserts are excellent, and the bill won't be a shock – especially if you go for one of the *formules* at €25 and €30. Reservations are essential (at least the day before).

« |●| Les Quartauts

19 rue Georges-Marie; M° Porte-de-Versailles or Corentin-Celton.
℡ 01.46.42.29.38
Closed *weekends; evenings except Thurs; Aug.*

It's hard to believe that you could find such a good establishment in a place like this: the street's so quiet that this award-winning bistro can only have made its reputation by word-of-mouth. Simplicity and quality are the watchwords here, with a welcoming warmth generated by the owners, Régine and Christophe. Succulent home cooking is served in substantial helpings, and they do superb meat dishes. There's a good choice of wines from small vineyards at very reasonable prices. The cheese selection is impressive and the desserts are all made on the premises. Dishes of the day cost €10; you'll pay about €27 à la carte.

Maisons-Lafitte

78600

« 🎿 🏠 |●| Hôtel-Restaurant au Pur-Sang*

2 av. de la Pelouse; RER A to Maisons-Laffitte or N° 12 bus to the place Montaigne. Go over the Maisons-Lafitte bridge, turn right, and skirt the racecourse until the roundabout, then turn right into avenue de la Pelouse.
℡ 01.39.62.03.21 ℻ 01.34.93.48.69
Closed *Sat evening; Sun; 3 weeks in Aug; Christmas holidays.* **TV. High chairs and games available. Car park.**

Just by the entrance to the racecourse you'll find this thoroughly provincial-looking hotel-restaurant offering rooms with shower/wc for €40. This place is hugely popular with anyone to do with the racecourse, all of whom enjoy the simple but carefully prepared cooking. Take a seat in the rustic dining room or on the large sunny terrace, and opt for the €12.50 set menu – it will offer something along the lines of egg mayonnaise or beef salad with tomatoes, followed by roast beef with cauliflower cheese or calves' sweetbreads with morels, and finishing with a classic dessert like *crème caramel*. À la carte will set you back around €24. *Free house apéritif or coffee offered to our readers on presentation of this guide.*

✍ |●| La Vieille Fontaine

8 av. Grétry.
☎01.39.62.01.78 ℗01.39.62.13.43
Closed *Sun evening; Mon; a week from 15 Aug.*

The building is a fine example of Second Empire architecture and it's situated in the grounds of the château. There's been a restaurant here since 1926, and over the years it's built up a solid reputation. The dining room and interior decoration are very attractive and there's a lovely terrace in the garden. Tasty dishes are produced with great skill: terrine of foie gras, calves' kidneys with *pommes boulangères*. The service is beyond reproach. The *menu-carte* at €34 (children's menu €12) means you can get a good meal for a fair price, and there are affordable wines too. The place has a certain atmosphere: it has hosted scores of film stars (Catherine Deneuve, Rita Hayworth, Cocteau, Depardieu), was used as a set for a couple of (forgettable) movies – and was also the haunt of some of the Nazi high command during the Occupation.

Malakoff
92240

✍ ✂ ⚑ Hôtel des Amis

17 rue Savier; accessible by train, bus, metro or car. It's in a small street opposite Notre-Dame church.
☎ and ℗01.42.53.57.63
ⓦwww.hoteldesamis.com
Closed *Sat evening; Sun evening (except reservations); a fortnight in July.*

It would be impossible to find a quieter place – the owner even says the district is too quiet. And you can't miss it – the roof

is outlined in blue neon. The rooms are regularly refurbished and the whole place is spotless. There's a small bar on the ground floor. Doubles are €31–40 with wash basin or shower, and €50 with shower/wc; breakfast €6.20. Parking is a nightmare, however. It's advisable to book at least a week in advance. *10% discount on the room rate (for stays of upwards of one week) or free house apéritif, coffee, fruit juice or soft drink offered to our readers on presentation of this guide.*

Marly-le-Roi
78160

✍ ✂ ⚑ |●| Les Chevaux de Marly – Restaurant La Tempête***

Place de l'Abreuvoir.
☎01.39.58.47.61 ℗01.39.16.65.56
Disabled access. TV. High chairs available. Swimming pool. Car park.

Ten faultlessly presented rooms at €80 for a double with bath – good value for a three-star hotel in this area. Some of them have a view over the imposing Abreuvoir (the drinking fountain for horses). There's a very high standard in the restaurant, which is presided over by the *sommelier*, the master pastry chef, and the chef, who has won a string of medals. You'll understand why with the excellent fish specialities and dishes such as lobster stew, turbot *hollandaise* and foie gras. There are two menus at €24 and €34, but watch out if you order à la carte because many dishes attract supplements. *Free house digestif or coffee offered to our readers on presentation of this guide.*

Port-Marly
78560 (2km NE)

✍ ✂ ⚑ L'Auberge du Relais Breton

27 rue de Paris.
☎01.39.58.64.33
Closed *Sun evening; Mon.*

The cuisine is deliciously prepared and served in substantial portions: try the stuffed sole or the chocolate tart to get the picture. Menus €19–38; the most expensive one includes apéritif, wine and coffee. Reckon on €38–45 à la carte. Nice terrace and garden for the summer. It's a shame it's a bit pricey but the service is good. *Free house apéritif or coffee offered to our readers on presentation of this guide.*

ℰ 𝒜 🏠 L'Auberge du Relais de Marly

13 rue de Paris.
☎ and 📠 01.39.58.44.54
Closed *Sun and Tues evenings; Wed; Aug.*

The fact that the owners have been successfully running this charming country inn for more than a quarter of a century suggests they're doing something right. Madame produces delicious Normandy dishes but adds a few from other regions as well. Monsieur is debonair and smiling. Most people opt for a dish of the day – around €12 each – or for the menu at €24.50. You'll spend around €35 à la carte. In winter you can cosy up by the fire; in summer the garden is gorgeous. If you fancy fishing, simply wander across the road and drop your line in the Seine. *Free coffee offered to our readers on presentation of this guide.*

Meaux

77100

ℰ 🏠 𝒜 Acostel**

336 av. de la Victoire. Take the N3 in the direction of Châlons-sur-Marne, and it's on the right just after the Total garage; if you get to Trilport, you've gone too far.
☎ 01.64.33.28.58 📠 01.64.33.28.25
🌐 www.acostel.fr
Reception open *from 7am to midnight.*
TV. High chairs and games available.
Swimming pool. Car park.

This unadorned concrete building is forbidding, but don't let that put you off – it's the back of the hotel. The front is much more appealing, with a lawn leading from the front door to the banks of the Marne, which is quite beautiful here. The hotel is set in large grounds with games for the children and a swimming pool. Clean rooms at garden level are €54 with shower/wc or €56 with bath; breakfast €7.50. *10% discount on the room rate (except Easter weekend and New Year's Day) offered to our readers on presentation of this guide.*

ℰ 𝒜 |●| La Marée-Bleue

8 rue Jean-Jaurès; in the historic centre.
☎ 01.64.34.08.16
Open *11.30am–3pm and 6.30–11pm.*

This inn, surrounded by a lovely garden, has huge, rustic dining rooms, and offers a warm welcome and efficient service. The specialities are seafood, fish and Alsatian cooking like *baeckoffe*, fish *aïoli* and fish *choucroute* – their star dish. Menus €15, €21.70 and €26.25 (the last is a gourmet menu). There's a reading corner adorned with works of art, where they hold exhibitions of paintings and sculpture. *Free house apéritif offered to our readers on presentation of this guide.*

Meudon

92190

ℰ 𝒜 |●| Restaurant La Mare aux Canards

Carrefour de la Mare-Adam; at the Meudon-Chaville exit on the N118, take the first left at the radio mast then head in the direction of Mare Adam.
☎ 01.46.32.07.16
Closed *Sun; Mon; fortnight in Aug.* **Open** *noon–2.30pm and 8–11pm.*

This restaurant, miles from anywhere, is the perfect place for lunch after a long walk in the Meudon woods. The big family dining room is convivial: they roast chicken, duck and pigeon on a spit in the handsome fireplace, and you're made to feel welcome. The service is fast, and the terrace pleasant in fine weather. There's a €12.50 *formule* of starter plus a quarter of chicken, and another at €17.30; à la carte you'll spend about €27 a head including wine. *Free house apéritif offered to our readers on presentation of this guide.*

ℰ 𝒜 |●| Le Brimborion

8 rue de Vélizy; it's next to Bellevue station.
☎ 01.45.34.12.03
Closed *Sat lunch; Sun evening.* **Open** *noon–1.45pm and 7.45–10pm.*

This is not a modern house – witness the faded sign of the old hotel-restaurant Billard where the railway workers on the Versailles line used to come for a glass or two. Nowadays it's the place to lunch in Meudon. The dining rooms, one of them reserved for non-smokers, both have a certain style, and the family cooking is creative and delicious. They offer a classic tomato, Cantal cheese and mustard tart, salad of *andouille* with apples, saddle of rabbit or scallops with finely sliced chicory. Whatever you do, leave space for the crumble. *Formules* at €19 and €26; menu at €32 includes starter, main meal, dessert, wine and coffee. The owner, who thinks of everything, has put together a comprehensive and original wine list including wines from overseas and wines available by the jug. There's the tiniest irritation about the service – the staff start packing up as soon as they stop taking orders – but you can still enjoy the terrace. *Free coffee offered to our readers on presentation of this guide.*

ⓐ ⓘⓞⓘ Chez Pierrot

26 rue Marcel-Allégot.
☎01.46.26.15.83
Closed *Sat evening; Sun; fortnight in Aug.*
Disabled access. High chairs available.

Whether you've got a raging hunger or a small appetite, you'll find just what you want here. Try a few Cancale oysters at the bar with a glass or two of Pouilly or sit down in the very pleasant dining room for *coq au vin*. The aim of the owners is to send their customers away with a smile on their faces – and there are two arrivals of fresh fish each day. Starters vary in price from €8 to €13 (semi-cooked foie gras), main meals €13–26, and dishes of the day range from €8.50 to €22.

Milly-la-Forêt
91490

ⓐ ⓐ ⓐ Hôtel-restaurant Au Colombier

26 av. de Gamay; it's in the centre of Milly, 200m from the market place.
☎01.64.98.80.74
Closed *Fri evening (May–Sept); Sat (Oct–April).* **High chairs available.**

Several completely refurbished rooms for €27.50 with wash basin, €35.10 with shower or bath (wc on the landing). Breakfast is served from 9am onwards. All the rooms have double glazing – they're not very big, but the decoration and colours are light and modern. This is a convenient address (located on the edge of the village near a car park) and it's not expensive. *Free apéritif offered to our readers on presentation of this guide.*

Montfort-L'Amaury
78490

ⓐ ⓘⓞⓘ ⓐ L'Hostellerie des Tours

Place de l'Église.

☎01.34.86.00.43
Closed *Tues evening; Wed; 5–9 Feb; 14 July–8 Aug.*

They hold the market on the pretty church square near to where this restaurant serves sound, traditional cuisine as it has for decades. The regulars come here because they know the dishes are well prepared. Four menus from €21 to €30 (with a *menu provençale* for €23). The dining room is large and light, and there's a vaulted dining area in the basement. *Free coffee offered to our readers on presentation of this guide.*

ⓐ ⓘⓞⓘ Chez Nous

22 rue de Paris.
☎01.34.86.01.62
Closed *Sun evening and Mon (except public holidays); during Nov school holidays.* **Open** *noon–2pm and 7.30–9.30pm.*

The best place to eat in town. The dining room is long and decorated in bourgeois style and warm colours. The cooking is good value but sophisticated – marinated raw salmon, duck foie gras, a selection of fried fish and *aiguillettes* of duck with soft fruit sauce. Monsieur plays the piano, while Madame organizes the service: it's a successful family affair which attracts gourmands in the know. Menus €22 and €28; à la carte reckon on around €46 including drinks. Service is a little slow when the place is full.

Montmorency
95160

ⓐ ⓐ ⓘⓞⓘ La Paimpolaise

30 rue Galliéni; it's on the hill on the way to Champeaux, and signposted off to the left.
☎01.34.28.12.05
Closed *Sun; Mon; Aug; a week at Christmas.* **Open** *lunchtimes only.* **Disabled access.**

It's like being in Brittany but without the sea – Breton pictures, Breton furniture and Breton cuisine produced by a woman from Paimpol. Her *galettes* are the genuine article. There's a lunch menu at €8 (green salad, *galette* and dessert) and a more extensive menu at €20. Try the good *trégoroise* (*andouillette* and mustard), a fantastic *galette* with Maroilles cheese, and the creamy flan with pears and whipped cream. Good dry cider, too. There's a quiet terrace for when the sun shines. *Free house apéritif offered to our readers on presentation of this guide.*

◉ |◉| Au Cœur de la Forêt

Avenue du Repos-de-Diane; on the top of
the plateau via the Domont road; follow the
signs.
℡01.39.64.99.19
Closed Mon; Thurs evening; Sun evening;
during the Feb school holidays; in Aug.

You reach this restaurant lost in the middle
of trees via a forest track full of potholes.
So, if you're thinking of going at night,
be warned. Sophisticated décor with pale
wood, two cosy fireplaces that are kept
alight throughout the winter, a pretty
terrace for the summer – and cooking
that more than justifies the detour, with
unbeatable ingredients: beef from Aubrac,
fish from Brittany and foie gras from
Périgord. Everything is home-made –
from the bread to the *pâtisserie* – and it's all
delicious. Menus are €24.50 (weekdays)
and €32; reckon on at least €45 à la carte.
The wines are searched out by the owner
from the Loire and Rhône regions so they
are therefore not too pricey. It's advisable
to book, especially on Sundays.

Paris

75000

See map overleaf

1st arrondissement

◉ ♠ BVJ Centre International

20 rue Jean-Jacques-Rousseau; M° Louvre-
Rivoli or Palais-Royal-Musée-du-Louvre.
℡01.53.00.90.90 ℻01.53.00.90.91
⊛www.bvjhotel.com

This is a kind of youth hostel, with two
hundred beds in rooms for two–six people,
but you don't have to be a member of
any organization to sleep here. It is open
round the clock, but arrive or telephone
from 9 to 9.30am to find out about availability, otherwise book two–three days
in advance. (If it's full, you can go to a
similar hotel in the Quartier Latin, with
the same management.) If you want to
book as a group, say so when you book
and the necessary arrangements will be
made. Check-out at 10am, although there
are some small luggage lockers (€2). A
bed for one person costs €25–27, including breakfast, sheets and blankets, sharing
in a room for over two people, or €28
per person in a double room. The place is
well kept and the communal showers have

recently been refurbished. If you want to
stay together as part of a group, mention
this when booking, and they will do their
best to accommodate your wishes.

◉ ♠ ⚘ Hôtel de Lille**

8 rue du Pélican; M° Palais-Royal, Louvre or
Pyramides.
℡01.42.33.33.42

This hotel is in a quiet street with a notorious past. In the fourteenth century it was
called "rue du Poil-au-Con" because of
the brothels situated nearby, but the more
respectable residents elected to rename it
"rue du Pélican", which caused much less
of a sensation on their address cards. It's
small, with just fourteen rooms (romantic
and slightly old-fashioned), but it's well
looked after by a nice family, welcoming
and good value for small budgets. Doubles
are €40–55 depending on the level of
comfort; breakfast €6. There's a machine
that dispenses both hot and cold drinks.
*10% discount on the room rate (in Jan) offered
to our readers on presentation of this guide.*

◉ ♠ Hôtel Londres Saint-Honoré**

13 rue Saint-Roch; M° Tuileries or Pyramides.
℡01.42.60.15.62 ℻01.42.60.16.00
⊛hotel.londres.st.honore@gofornet.com
TV.

Here's a charming hotel with a warm
family atmosphere in an area that is not
exactly alluring. It's in an old bourgeois
house, facing the church of St Roch. The
rooms are spacious and comfortable with
double glazing, satellite TV and mini-bar;
some are air-conditioned. Doubles are
€90–107 according to facilities, and for a
fee of €15 per day your dog can stay, too.
There are a number of pay car parks round
about the hotel.

◉ |◉| Foujita 1

41 rue Saint-Roch; M° Pyramides or Tuileries.
℡01.42.61.42.93
Closed Sun. **Open** noon–2.15pm and in the
evening until 10.15pm.

One of the best sushi bars in Paris, with
reasonable prices (though it's more expensive in the evening) and a generous lunchtime menu at €11. There's *sushi, sashimi*
and *natto*, a bowl of rice topped with raw
fish. It's a small place, often full, so try to
get there early. There's also a *Foujita 2* at 7

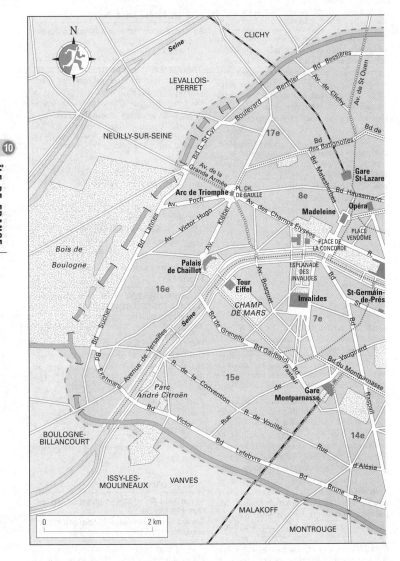

N

CLICHY

Seine

LEVALLOIS-
PERRET

NEUILLY-SUR-SEINE

Bd Bessières

Av. de Clichy

Av. de St Ouen

Boulevard

Berthier

Bd de

17e

Bd
des Batignolles

Bd Malesherbes

Bd-Malesherbes

Gare
St-Lazare

Bd G. St-Cyr

Av. de la
Grande Armée

PL. CH.
DE GAULLE

8e

Bd Haussmann

Arc de Triomphe

Av.   Foch

Av. des Champs Élysées

Madeleine

Opéra

Bd   Lannes

Av.   Victor Hugo

Kléber

PLACE
VENDÔME

R.

Bois de
Boulogne

Palais
de Chaillot

Av.   Bosquet

PLACE DE
LA CONCORDE

ESPLANADE
DES
INVALIDES

Tour
Eiffel

16e

CHAMP
DE MARS

Invalides

Bd

St-Germain-
de-Prés

Bd

Bd Suchet

Seine

Bd de Grenelle

Bd Garibaldi

7e

Bd

Bd du Montparnasse

Raspail

Vaugirard

Avenue de Versailles

R. de la Convention

Bd Exelmans

15e

Bd Pasteur

Gare
Montparnasse

Parc
André Citroën

de

14e

Bd

Victor

Rue

R. de Vouillé

Rue

d'Alésia

BOULOGNE-
BILLANCOURT

Bd   Lefebvre

Bd

Brune   Bd

ISSY-LES-
MOULINEAUX

VANVES

MALAKOFF

0   2 km

MONTROUGE

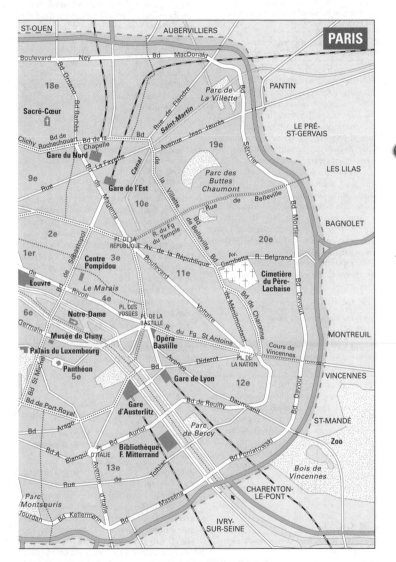

PARIS

ST-OUEN
AUBERVILLIERS

Boulevard Ney Bd MacDonald

18e
Parc de
La Villette
PANTIN

Sacré-Cœur

Bd de Rochechouart Bd de la Chapelle Bd
Clichy
Rue de Flandre
Saint-Martin
Avenue Jean Jaurès
LE PRÉ-
ST-GERVAIS

Gare du Nord
Canal
Bd La Fayette
19e
LES LILAS

9e
Rue
Gare de l'Est
Parc des
Buttes
Chaumont
Sérurier
Rue de Belleville
BAGNOLET

Bd de Magenta
10e
de
Villette

2e
PL. DE LA
RÉPUBLIQUE
R. du Fg
du Temple
Bd de Belleville
20e
Bd Mortier

Bd Sébastopol
Av. de la République
Av. Gambetta R. Belgrand

1er
Centre
Pompidou
3e
Boulevard
11e
Cimetière
du Père-
Lachaise
Bd Davout

de
Louvre
Rue de Rivoli
Le Marais
4e
Voltaire
Bd de Charonne

6e
Notre-Dame
PL. DES
VOSGES
PL. DE LA
BASTILLE
R. du Fg St Antoine
de Ménilmontant
MONTREUIL

Germain
Musée de Cluny
Opéra
Bastille
PL. DE
LA NATION
Cours de
Vincennes
VINCENNES

Palais du Luxembourg
Avenue Diderot
Bd

Bd St Michel
Panthéon
5e
Bd
Gare de Lyon
12e
ST-MANDÉ

Bd de Port-Royal
Arago
Gare
d'Austerlitz
Bd de Reuilly
Daumesnil
Zoo

Bd A. Blanqui
PL. D'ITALIE
Bd Auriol
Bibliothèque
F. Mitterrand
Parc
de Bercy
Bd Poniatowski
Bois de
Vincennes

Rue
Avenue d'Italie
de
Tolbiac
13e

Parc
Montsouris
Bd Kellermann
Bd
Masséna
CHARENTON-
LE-PONT

Jourdan
IVRY-
SUR-SEINE

ÎLE-DE-FRANCE
10

rue du 29-Juillet, 75001. It's much bigger but not as nice as *Foujita 1*.

⊚ 🎄 |●| La Fresque

100 rue Rambuteau; Mº Étienne-Marcel or Les Halles.
☎01.42.33.17.56
Closed *Sun lunch; a fortnight in mid-Aug.*
Open *noon–3.30pm and 7pm–midnight.*

This is a friendly little restaurant in a shop that used to sell snails. The interior is lovely, with very old white tiles on the walls, brilliantly coloured frescoes and long wooden tables. It's very friendly, relaxed and cosmopolitan – you're jammed right up against your neighbour. The lunchtime rapid *formule* offers starter, carefully prepared main course, and wine for €12.50. There's no evening menu. Every day there are good starters, five or six traditional main course dishes, each with an original touch, and a vegetarian dish. About €22 à la carte; options vary a little at lunch and dinner. It's a lively place, everyone knows each other, and the staff rush around doing their best, but when it's very busy, you may be disappointed. *Free house apéritif offered to our readers on presentation of this guide.*

⊚ |●| Le Rubis

10 rue du Marché-Saint-Honoré; Mº Pyramides.
☎01.42.61.03.34
Closed *Sun; public holidays; 3 weeks in Aug; 10 days over Christmas.* **Open** *until 10pm (3pm on Sat).*

The kind of typical Parisian bistro/wine bar that's on the verge of extinction – great little dishes and wines direct from producers in Beaujolais. You can have a sandwich at the bar with a glass of red. Wines are served by the glass at really decent prices. They do excellent charcuterie and dishes of the day at around €10. In summer, they set up a couple of barrels on the pavement where you can prop yourself up and enjoy a cool glass of wine.

⊚ |●| Ca d'Oro

54 rue de l'Arbre-Sec; Mº Louvre-Rivoli.
☎01.40.20.97.79
Closed *Sun; Mon evening; first fortnight Aug.*
Open *noon–2.30pm and 7–11pm.* **Disabled access.**

This welcoming, unobtrusive little Italian restaurant sticks to what it does best. Go through a tiny room and down a narrow corridor and you'll come to another room where the decoration is gently evocative of Venice, the chef's home town. Before moving on to the pasta, treat yourself to grilled peppers with basil or some bruschetta – a slice of toast fried in olive oil and rubbed with garlic, basil and tomato. Main dishes include pasta or, for two, an excellent risotto with ceps, seafood or cuttlefish. You can round off the meal with a hot mousse with marsala. There's a lunchtime menu, €14.50; reckon on €26 à la carte, not including wine. The cooking is authentic and generous.

⊚ 🎄 |●| Juvéniles

47 rue de Richelieu; Mº Palais-Royal/Musée-du-Louvre or Bourse.
☎01.42.97.46.49
Closed *Sun.* **Open** *noon–11pm.*

This is a very Parisian wine bar run by a lively Scot with a wonderful sense of humour and a good knowledge of wines. The place is frequented by groups who come to share a bottle of wine and tapas or eat a meal rounded off with a great tiramisu. Lunchtime *formule* at €14.50 and others at €17 and €23; à la carte you'll pay around €28. It's a bit crowded but the warm atmosphere encourages conversation. They sell a good selection of wines and sherries by the glass, and an impressive array of malt whiskies. Service is friendly and attentive. *Free house apéritif offered to our readers on presentation of this guide.*

⊚ |●| Chez Elle

7 rue des Prouvaires; Mº Châtelet-Les Halles.
☎01.45.08.04.10
Open *noon–2.30pm and 7–10.30pm (11pm Thurs–Sat).* **Closed** *at weekends.* **Disabled access.**

Atmospheric place, with a bright dining room decorated with a collection of pin-up photos from the Belle Époque and the 1930s. Terrace, covered by a pretty green awning on sunny days. Well-balanced bistro menu with suggestions on the blackboard that may include steak *tartare*, whole kidneys, *osso buco* or pork brawn. The portions are so huge that they're hard to finish, and classic desserts. Several menus of two–four dishes at €18.50–26. The *Elle* in the name is Cécile, who enjoys herself every Thursday night by singing typically Parisian songs – part raunchy, part nostalgic – with a trio *musette*. Musical evenings take place every Thursday and Saturday.

|●| Saudade

34 rue des Bourdonnais; M° Châtelet.
℡01.42.36.03.65
Closed *Sun.* **Open** *noon–2pm and 7.30–11pm.*

This sophisticated institution is a veritable ambassador for top-quality Portuguese cooking. Mirrors on the ceiling, tiles on the walls, the sounds of Madredeus or Cesaria Evora in the background (or live *fado* on the first Tuesday of every month). *Pasteis de bacalhau* or *escabeche de sardina* are followed by *carnes* (meat) or *peixes* (fish), with cod being the favourite: it comes in eight different preparations (fried, *gratiné*, grilled, with breadcrumbs, etc). For dessert, try the delicious *arroz doce*, a kind of rice pudding with cinnamon and a *Vinho verde*, or a more full-bodied red wine to wash it down, plus a vintage port to round off. Lunch menu €20; reckon on around €30 à la carte.

|●| Lescure

7 rue de Mondovi; M° Concorde.
℡01.42.60.18.91
Closed *weekends; in Aug; a week at Christmas.* **Open** *noon–2.15pm and 7–10.15pm.*

A very good restaurant which is often full with Members of the National Assembly who've popped across the river for lunch. They've been feeding people here since 1919. The cooking is bourgeois, and the prices are popular; you eat squashed up against your neighbour. On the €21 menu you get a starter (the mackerel is delicious), a generously portioned main dish (beef bourguignon, maybe, or poached haddock), cheese, dessert and wine. The desserts are delicious. À la carte, one of the best combinations to go for is hot pâté *en croûte* with stuffed *poule-au-pot* – yours for around €8. All in all you'll pay around €30 à la carte. In the evening, they sit people at the big communal table at the back of the room, creating a relaxed atmosphere. In summer people jostle for tables on the terrace.

|●| Macéo

15 rue des Petits-Champs; M° Pyramides, Bourse or Palais Royal.
℡01.42.97.53.85

Closed *Sat lunchtime; Sun; fortnight in Aug.* **Open** *noon–2.30pm and 7–11pm.*

The mere sight of Thierry Bouronnais' menu, which changes every day, will make your mouth water, because the dishes evoke the seasonal flavours of Provence, with tantalizing combinations of sweet and sour. Vegetarians can be reassured that they too can fully participate in these delights. The décor has been modernized but a period feel has been preserved. This is an achievement in itself, because it is only too easy to fall into kitsch vulgarity or cold iconoclasm when refurbishing an establishment as old as this one. Exactly the right balance has been found here, and the results are both comfortable and colourful. Lunch menu costs €27, other menus €30 and €35; or you can expect to pay around €40–50 for a meal à la carte. It has to be admitted that the prices are high, but the Macéo's popularity attests to its quality and impeccable service.

|●| L'Ardoise

28 rue du Mont-Thabor; M° Tuileries.
℡01.42.96.28.18
Closed *Aug; Christmas to New Year.* **Open** *noon–2.30pm and 6.30–11pm.*

The décor resembles a cantine with tightly packed tables, but the food is prepared with intelligence and a hint of inventiveness, and it's beautifully presented. The chef's most interesting ideas have made their way onto the €30 menu (which includes starter, main meal and dessert): fillet of beef with love apples, duck foie gras. The wines are really well priced, too. It's popular with locals and tourists; occasionally groups of tourists can be quite noisy.

|●| À La Tour de Montlhéry, Chez Denise

5 rue des Prouvaires; M° Louvre-Rivoli, Châtelet or Les Halles.
℡01.42.36.21.82
Closed *weekends; 14 July–15 Aug.* **Open** *24 hours.*

This is one of the oldest all-night restaurants in Paris. It's kept the atmosphere of an old Halles bistro, but the prices have definitely gone up since those days. The welcome is off-hand but the place is lively. There are moleskin benches, checked tablecloths and hams hanging from the ceiling. Big-hearted cooking includes *andouillette*, tripe, roast lamb with beans, beef *gros sel*, calf's head and other such traditional fare. No set menu; dishes cost between €16 and €26; reckon on a minimum of €35 a head with wine.

2nd arrondissement

⊚ ⅍ ⌂ Hôtel Sainte-Marie*

6 rue de la Ville-Neuve; M° Bonne-Nouvelle.
☎01.42.33.21.61 ℗01.42.33.29.24
ⓔ ste.marie.hotel@ifrance.com
Open *24 hours.* **TV. Cots available. Car park.**

This is a pretty little hotel in a quiet street, very close to the shopping area of the Grands Boulevards. It has about twenty rooms, all well equipped. Some have beamed ceilings, but if you're tall and have a room in the attic mind your head because the ceilings slope. They're quite pleasant and even quite bright. Doubles with basin €30–38, with shower/wc €46–54, according to the season; communal showers on the ground floor. It's popular with visitors from overseas. *One free breakfast per room offered to our readers on presentation of this guide.*

⊚ ⌂ Tiquetonne Hôtel*

6 rue Tiquetonne; M° Étienne-Marcel or Réaumur-Sébastopol.
☎01.42.36.94.58 ℗01.42.36.02.94
Closed *Aug and one week between Christmas and New Year.* **Open** *7.30am–midnight.*

The pedestrianized streets leading to this one-star hotel are calm and beautiful. It's located near Les Halles and the Pompidou Centre and is a very peaceful and welcoming place. The rooms, which vary in size, are very well maintained, though the décor is faintly old-fashioned and the bathrooms pretty ordinary. Doubles with shower/wc are €56, nearly all of them have double glazing. Take the time to admire the work of the artist who painted the false marble in the stair well.

⊚ ⌂ Hôtel Bonne Nouvelle**

17 rue Beauregard; M° Bonne Nouvelle, Sentier or Strasbourg-Saint-Denis.
☎01.45.08.42.42 ℗01.40.26.05.81
ⓦ www.hotel-bonne-nouvelle.com
TV. Pay car park.

Doubles €59–72 with shower/wc or bath; triple or quadruple rooms €85–115. They're equipped with cable TV, modem

connection, direct phone and hairdryer. They're an intriguing blend of old-fashioned and modern. The recent refurbishment has not detracted from the hotel's charm but it's a pity that some of the rooms are rather small. Exceptionally warm welcome is on offer.

⊚ ⌂ Hôtel Vivienne**

40 rue Vivienne; M° Rue-Montmartre, Richelieu-Drouot or Bourse.
☎01.42.33.13.26 ℗01.40.41.98.19.
ⓔ paris@hotel-vivienne.com
Open *all year round.* **TV.**

This hotel is in a neighbourhood with lots of tiny streets and lanes filled with shops specializing in coins and medals. It's very close to the *Hard Rock Café*, the Musée Grévin, the wax museum and the Théâtre des Variétés. The welcome is young, warm and informal. The rooms are bright, clean, comfortable and quiet. No. 14 is particularly attractive, and there's a communicating door through to no. 15, which makes it good for families. On the fifth and sixth floors you get a lovely view of Paris, and a few rooms have balconies. You can also take breakfast in your room for no extra charge. Doubles are €72 with shower, €84 with shower/wc or €87 with bath, and family rooms are €119–122.

⊚ ⌂ Hôtel France d'Antin***

22 rue d'Antin; M° Quatre-Septembre or Opéra.
☎01.47.42.19.12 ℗01.47.42.11.55
ⓔ carlotta.hotels@wanadoo.fr
TV. Car park.

This pleasant three-star hotel is just 100m from the Opéra Garnier and the Louvre. It is classy yet congenial, and has been completely overhauled and redecorated. Many of the public rooms have exposed stonework and vaulted ceilings. The thirty pretty rooms all have mini-bar and safe, and they're air-conditioned to give you respite from the Paris summer heat. Doubles with shower/wc are priced from €160; breakfast €7.

⊚ ⏐⚬⏐ La Souris Verte

52 rue Saint-Anne; M° Quatre-Septembre.
☎01.40.20.03.70
Closed *Sun.* **Open** *lunch and dinner (from 7pm, last orders 11.15pm).*

A warm, friendly restaurant which looks like a small nineteenth-century house with its beams and red fabric stretched on the walls, and the vases of fresh flowers on every table. The cuisine is very French; freshly cooked, refined dishes that are excellent value for money. Menu (lunch and dinner) with starter, main course and dessert for €14, €20 including drinks. À la carte a meal costs about €15. A friendly, intimate atmosphere; the regulars add to the spirit of the place. It's best to book.

◎ ⅍ |●| L'Escalier

80 rue Montmartre; M° Bourse.
☏01.42.36.95.49
Closed *Sat lunch; Sun.* **Open** *noon–3pm and 7.30–11pm.*

A tiny restaurant with a modern, warm décor. It attracts a thirty-something, intellectual, hyperactive crowd – this is where they come to relax over lunch with a few mates or co-workers. There's a chattering, laughing atmosphere. The cuisine is cutting-edge and incredibly fine – unusual for the price. The dishes on the lunch *formules* (€14.50 and €20.50) change every day: *croustillant* of goat's cheese with pears on a salad with balsamic vinegar, chicken in a paprika sauce served with rice. Otherwise it's à la carte only; a meal costs around €15–20. They show regular exhibitions of work by young artists. *Free house apéritif offered to our readers on presentation of this guide.*

◎ |●| Le Tambour

41 rue Montmartre; M° Châtelet, Les Halles or Sentier.
☏01.42.33.06.90
Open *daily 6pm–6.30am (service from 7.30pm–4am).*

The owner, André Camboulas, will immediately make you feel welcome; having built up a group of authentic Parisian bistros similar to this one, he's had plenty of practice. The dining room is decorated with urban detritus – cobblestones, drain covers and road signs. The cooking is very French. Expect to pay at least €23 for dinner à la carte including drinks. When it's full inside, you can eat outside on a covered, heated terrace.

◎ |●| Il Buco

18 rue Léopold-Bellan; M° Sentier.
☏01.45.08.50.10

Closed *Sat lunch; Sun.* **Open** *noon–2.30pm and 8–11pm.*

A long, narrow restaurant lined with tables, with ochre walls and the menu written on mirrors. It's very convivial but hardly intimate. Reckon on around €25 à la carte. Pasta, salads, *antipasti,* ham and fresh figs. Wine by the glass is priced from €2.30. Nice touches on the tables include three kinds of bread, fresh flowers, flute glasses and candles.

◎ |●| La Grille Montorgueil

50 rue Montorgueil; M° Les Halles or Étienne-Marcel.
☏01.42.33.21.21
Open *noon–3pm and 7.30pm–midnight; continuous service on weekends.*

This establishment, which has been around a good hundred years, has been attractively renovated – as has the pedestrianized street it stands on. The menu is full of traditional Parisian bistro fare: hot goat's cheese *amandine,* duck thigh *confit, andouillette,* grills and fish dishes and chocolate *fondant.* Straightforward, honest cooking with no frills. There are no set menus but you choose from dishes written up on the board which always include one or two reasonably priced suggestions. A meal will probably set you back about €30; dishes of the day cost €12 or so. There's a terrace in summer.

3rd arrondissement

◎◎ ⅍ ♙ Hôtel du Vieux Saule***

6 rue de Picardie; M° République or Filles du Calvaire.
☏01.42.72.01.14 ☏01.40.27.88.21
ⓦwww.hotelvieuxsaule.com
TV. Pay car park.

The window boxes and tiny flower garden brighten up the exterior of this lovely hotel; inside, the "high-tech" décor is beginning to date. Modern, comfortable rooms go for €91–106 with shower/wc or €106–121 with bath/wc, according to the season; prices increase during trade fairs. On the fourth floor there are more luxurious rooms with wood flooring and wood panelling on the walls for €136–166. Some rooms are small, but all are comfortable, air-conditioned and equipped with hairdryer, trouser press, iron, telephone, safe and cable TV (thirty channels), and there's free use of the sauna and Internet access. Two floors are reserved for non-smokers. Buffet breakfast, €10, is served in a sixteenth-century vaulted cellar. *One free breakfast per person per stay offered to our readers on presentation of this guide.*

⍟ |❶| Le Sablier

4 rue Dupetit-Thouars; M° République or Temple.
☏ 01.48.87.38.45
Closed *Aug; Christmas; New Year's Day; long weekends with public holidays.* **Disabled access.**

A small, spruce little dining room with wood panels and pink-dyed half-timbering and Sophie, the beaming owner, to greet you. She and her husband Jean have been running this romantic, slightly kitsch place in a quiet backstreet opposite the Carreau du Temple for years. Jean sometimes pops his head out of the kitchen to greet regular customers. His cooking adroitly mixes sweet and savoury elements: calf's liver with sour cherries. Old but comfortable Métro benches serve as seats and a collection of hourglasses is displayed in one corner. Lunchtime menu is €12.50; in the evening you have to eat à la carte (around €30 for a full meal without wine). It's best to book.

⍟ |❶| 🍴 La Mule du Pape

8 rue du Pas-de-la-Mule; M° Bastille or Chemin-Vert.
☏ 01.42.74.55.80
Open *noon–4pm and 7–11pm.* **Closed** *Tues and Sun evenings; 3 weeks in Aug.*

You could write off this bourgeois-looking restaurant as being prissy and probably bad news for your wallet. But appearances can be deceptive; in fact, the setting is bright and comfortable, and they welcome you with a simple kindness that immediately puts you at your ease. The menu offers dishes to satisfy anyone, whether they're on a zero-calorie diet or looking to pig out: *œufs de la Mule* will do for the slimmers and *assiettes de la Mule* for the hungry; the *plats de la Mule* fit somewhere in between. Desserts are great. There's a menu with main meal and either a starter or dessert for €15; a meal à la carte will cost about €21. At the weekend they serve brunch and the place also doubles as a salon de thé. *Free house apéritif or coffee offered to our readers on presentation of this guide.*

⍟ |❶| Le Progrès

1 rue de Bretagne; M° Saint-Sébastien-Froissart.
☏ 01.42.72.37.00
Closed *Sun; a week in Feb; a week end of July and first 3 weeks in Aug.* **Open** *noon–3.30 pm.* **High chairs available.**

Just what you expect a Parisian bistro to be: set on the street corner, with old chairs, cheerful service, regular customers from the neighbourhood, a Seventies look, an antique clock and metal Banania tins. Make sure you order as soon as you arrive, as the service is slow; consult the blackboard to find out about the two dishes of the day. Generous portions of seasonal food, sometimes including oysters; the preparation of meat is particularly superb. Dishes are around €15, with good homemade desserts, and a varied and reasonably priced wine list. There's a dining room upstairs, and a terrace for fine days.

⍟ |❶| Au Vieux Molière

12 passage Molière; M° Rambuteau.
☏ 01.42.78.37.87
Open *10am–2am (service noon–2pm and 7.30–11pm).*

This is an attractive gourmet restaurant. It's located in an untouched part of Paris in the Beaubourg area, and is surrounded by galleries and bookshops. The atmosphere is equally charming inside: there are portraits and photographs on the wall. The menu offers appetizing, traditional cuisine: eggs *cocotte* with foie gras, calf's liver with balsamic vinegar and good sauces. Fine ingredients and well-judged cooking. Weekday lunch *formules* for €17 and €23, or reckon on paying around €35–40 à la carte in the evening.

⍟ |❶| Chez Nénesse

17 rue de Saintonge; M° Filles-du-Calvaire.
☏ 01.42.78.46.49
Closed *weekends; public holidays; Aug; Christmas to New Year.* **Open** *noon–2.30pm and 7.45–10.30pm.*

The allure of old Paris is everywhere in this typical, traditional place with tiles on the floor and a lovely Formica bar. Good general atmosphere and a disarmingly smiling welcome. Good, classic well-prepared French cooking with substantial portions to make up for the lack of creative flair. This is a fine example of a successful family business – at lunchtime there's hardly any elbow-room, it's so packed. There are always two or three appetizing dishes of the day for around €10–12. In the evening, the cooking is more elaborate but still in the same spirit: quenelles of pike, calf's kidneys with shallots. A meal à la carte will cost around €30–38.

◉ |◉| Chez Omar

47 rue de Bretagne; M° Temple.
☎01.42.72.36.26
Closed *Sun lunchtime.* **Open** *daily until around 11.30pm.*

Omar has been here for a good twenty years, and he serves an eclectic mix of locals and visitors from all over the world in a restaurant where Paris meets North Africa. The ceilings are high, the mirrors have bevelled edges, there's a superb bar counter and the tables are snugly spaced. Waiting staff are smiling and attentive. The couscous is excellent, as are the pastries, but their meat dishes are particularly tender and worthy of note. Expect to pay €25 à la carte: starters €5, couscous from €9 (vegetarian) to €20, dishes of the day €11–18. Credit cards are not accepted.

◉ |◉| Le Pamphlet

38 rue Debelleyme; M° Filles-du-Calvaire or Saint Sébastien-Froissart.
☎01.42.72.39.24
Closed *Sat lunch; Sun; Mon lunch; first fortnight in Jan; fortnight in Aug.* **Open** *noon–2pm and 7.30–11pm.*

An elegant, wood-panelled setting with comfortable seats and a restful atmosphere. The menus (at €30 and €45, lunch and dinner) change constantly. There are four original, mouth-watering choices per course: *aiguillette* of John Dory with purée of *andouillette*, prime cut of beef with tagliatelle and Fourme d'Ambert, and a subtle banana *clafoutis* for dessert. Apéritifs are accompanied by tasty dry Laguiole sausage. Good choice of wines to complement the dishes.

4th arrondissement

◉ 🏠 |◉| ⚘ Hôtel MIJE Maubuisson

12, rue des Barres; M° Saint-Paul-le-Marais or Pont-Marie.
☎01.42.74.23.45 ☎01.40.27.81.64

ⓦ www.mije.com
Closed *Aug.* **Restaurant closed** *Sat and Sun lunch.*

Set in a wonderful medieval house with oriel windows, half-timbering and saw-tooth gables, in a pedestrianized area of the Marais that is dotted with café terraces in summer. Tastefully decorated interior, Gothic-style doors, old furniture made of solid wood. View of the neighbouring roofs and the stained-glass windows of the Saint-Gervais church. Reckon on paying €29 per person in a room for four, €30 in a triple room, upwards of €34 in a double, €44 in a single, breakfast included. Half board is compulsory for groups. Set menu with dish of the day €8.50. Credit cards not accepted. Annual membership costs €2.50 *Free annual membership offered to our readers on presentation of this guide.*

◉ 🏠 |◉| ⚘ Hôtel MIJE Fourcy

6 rue de Fourcy; M° Saint-Paul-le-Marais or Pont-Marie.
☎01.42.74.23.45 ☎01.40.27.81.64
ⓦ www.mije.com
Closed *Aug.* **Restaurant closed** *Sat; Sun lunch.* **Open** *11am–2pm and 5–10pm.*

This veritable palace opposite the Maison Européene de la Photographie was originally a seventeenth-century mansion before becoming one of the city's most famous brothels (this episode was concluded in 1946 by a law banning brothels). Now superbly renovated, it is divided into two wings connected by elegant corridors lined with wood. Small garden on the corner of rue Charlemagne. Rooms with one to eight beds, complete with mezzanine, washbasin and shower; toilets are on the landing. Reckon on paying €29 per person in a room for four, €30 in a triple room, upwards of €34 in a double (or €68 for two people), €44 in a single, breakfast included. Half board is compulsory for groups. Restaurant in the stunning dining room with vaults and exposed stone; it is shared by the other two MIJE hotels in the neighbourhood. Set meal with dish of the day costs €9. Credit cards not accepted. Annual membership is €2.50. *Free annual membership offered to our readers on presentation of this guide.*

◉ 🏠 |◉| ⚘ Hôtel MIJE Le Fauconnier

11 rue Fauconnier; M° Saint-Paul-le-Marais or Pont-Marie.

☎01.42.74.23.45 ℻01.40.27.81.64
🖳www.mije.com
Closed *Aug.* **Restaurant closed** *weekend lunchtimes.*

Magnificently restored seventeenth-century mansion with an imposing front door embellished with wood carvings. Inside, huge old wardrobes, massive chests, long, rustic tables and a splendid wrought-iron staircase with a ramp. All the rooms (one–eight beds) have been refurbished and complemented by excellent little bathrooms with shower and wash basin. The toilets are in the corridor. It costs €29 per person in a room for four, €30 in a triple room, upwards of €34 in a double, €44 in a single, breakfast included. Half board is compulsory for groups. In summer you can have breakfast in the paved courtyard. Set menu with dish of the day costs €9. Credit cards not accepted. Annual membership is €2.50. *Free annual membership offered to our readers on presentation of this guide.*

⊛ ⚲ 🛏 Grand Hôtel du Loiret*

8 rue des Mauvais-Garçons; M° Hôtel-de-Ville.
☎01.48.87.77.00 ℻01.48.04.96.56
🖂hotelloiret@hotmail.com
TV.

Rooms are redecorated here every two years. Some are available with handbasin only for €45; those from the first to the fourth floors are in warm colours and have en-suite shower/wc (€60) or bath (€80). There is one room sleeping four on the seventh floor which has a panoramic view over the Panthéon and the Sacré Coeur – there's a lift. Nos. 727 and 728 have just been refurbished. *One free breakfast per person (in Jan and Feb) offered to our readers on presentation of this guide.*

⊛ ⚲ 🛏 Hôtel du 7e Art**

20 rue Saint-Paul; M° Saint-Paul or Sully-Morland.
☎01.44.54.85.00 ℻01.42.77.69.10
🖂hotel7art@wanadoo.fr
TV.

A fairly friendly hotel which is well managed and original. The staircase is black, the walls white, and the rooms are decorated with photomontages and posters of films from the 1940s, 1950s and 1960s. Rooms cost €75–130 depending on the size and level of comfort. The top prices are for suites in the attic, which have sloping ceilings

and whose TV sets can receive several French and foreign television channels. There's a bar on the ground floor, and an unusual display case with plaster figures of Ray Charles, Mickey Mouse, Donald Duck and Laurel and Hardy. Cheques are not accepted. *Free house apéritif or coffee offered to our readers on presentation of this guide.*

⊛ 🛏 Hôtel Jeanne d'Arc**

3 rue de Jarente; M° Saint-Paul, Chemin-Vert or Bastille; RER Châtelet.
☎01.48.87.62.11 ℻01.48.87.37.31
TV.

You couldn't find a better location than this quiet neighbourhood near place Sainte-Catherine. The hotel is classy and well run, and it's been stylishly decorated – there's an enormous mirror in the foyer made by a local artist. All of the rooms have been refurbished and have shower/wc or bath, phone and cable TV. Doubles are €80–95; family rooms cost €112–140. It's essential to book.

⊛ 🛏 Hôtel de Nice**

42 bis rue de Rivoli; M° Hôtel-de-Ville.
☎01.42.78.55.29 ℻01.42.78.36.07
TV.

A very elegant and refined hotel with a small entrance and a multilingual welcome at reception. The owners used to run an antique business – they've kept a large number of attractive pieces to furnish the hotel. Breakfast is served in the television lounge, which has soft-coloured furnishings, eighteenth-century engravings and a portrait of an elegant woman surrounded by her pets. The soundproofed rooms are decorated with sumptuous wallpaper and have good bathrooms. Doubles with bath or shower (and hairdryer) cost €105 (breakfast €7), which isn't bad value for money; in summer the rooms overlooking place du Bourg-Tibourg are particularly good – some have balconies.

⊛ ⚲ 🛏 Hôtel de la Place des Vosges**

12 rue de Birague; M° Saint-Paul or Bastille.
☎01.42.72.60.46 ℻01.42.72.02.64
🖂hotel.place.des.vosges@gofornet.com
TV.

This hotel is in a grand street leading from place des Vosges to the Pavillon du Roi. The entrance is delightful. There are sixteen rooms which, though they're not spacious and have pretty ordinary furniture, are quiet, comfortable and impeccably clean. Doubles cost €120 with bath; double rooms with shower/wc have just been refurbished and cost €140. There's also a suite with Jacuzzi, plasma screen TV, marble, wooden floor and beams at €205. *One free breakfast per person offered to our readers on presentation of this guide.*

ⓔ |●| Aux Vins des Pyrénées

25 rue Beautreillis; M° Bastille or Sully-Morland.
☏01.42.72.64.94
Closed *Sat lunchtime; fortnight mid-Aug.*
Open *for lunch and dinner (service until 11.30pm).*

A friendly cellar-bar-restaurant with a crowd of regulars – though new faces are warmly welcomed. The place is a nice mix of formal city and easy-going provincial, and it's reassuring that a place like this has managed to survive. The recipe is simple: select excellent quality meat and fish, grill it and serve with good side dishes and a decent glass of wine in a wood-panelled dining room with engraved mirrors and moleskin chairs. Finish by issuing a reasonable bill – lunch menu for €12.50 or around €23 for a full meal without wine (€17 at luchtime). One of our favourite restaurants.

ⓔ |●| L'Enoteca

25 rue Charles-V; M° Saint-Paul.
☏01.42.78.91.44
Closed *lunchtimes in Aug; a week in mid-Aug; 1 or 2 days at Easter; a week around mid-Aug; a few days at Christmas; New Year's Day.* **Open** *daily noon–1am (service until 11.30pm).*

This wine bar, which specializes in Italian wines, is a must. The décor is typical of the Marais, with exposed beams and old stonework. It gets really full and appeals to a very Parisian clientele – it's not unusual to spot the odd TV star. The famous, the not-so-famous and the downright obscure jostle to sample some of the 450 different Italian wines – the ones available by the glass change every week. You can travel north to south, tasting the whites of Trentino and Sicily or giving the reds of Piedmont and Basilicata a go. Accompany them with a few *antipasti misti*, slices of warm aubergine with fresh goat's cheese, *crostini* with Parma ham and mozzarella,

fresh pasta with beef stew or chicken livers and tomatoes. The desserts are pretty good, too. Reckon on paying €10 for a dish of the day, or there's a €13 weekday lunch *formule* which includes a drink. À la carte a meal will cost around €30.

ⓔ |●| Le Temps des Cerises

31 rue de la Cerisaie; M° Bastille or Sully-Morland.
☏01.42.72.08.63
Closed *evenings (but you can get a drink until early evening); weekends; public holidays; Aug.*

This picturesque low-ceilinged eighteenth-century building used to house the office of the Celestine convent's bursar, but it's been a bistro since 1900. The décor looks immediately familiar – zinc-topped bar where you can have a drink, marble-topped tables, leather benches – and the day's menu is written up on a blackboard. These, in addition to the photos of old Paris, the cheerful atmosphere and the good-natured customers, are reminders of what a Paris bistro used to be like. You'll find cooking to match: fricassée of frogs' legs, mutton tripe Aveyron. There's a menu at €13.50, and à la carte dishes from €11. It's essential to arrive before noon to get a table. There's an eclectic selection of wines. Credit cards are not accepted.

ⓔ 🎋 |●| La Belle Histoire

6 pl. du Marché-Sainte-Catherine; M° Saint-Paul-le-Marais.
☏01.42.74.04.85
Closed *Mon and Tues lunchtimes (Nov–March); first fortnight in Jan.* **Open** *noon–3pm and 7–11.30pm (midnight from Fri to Sun).*

The restaurants on the small square of the Marché-Sainte-Catherine are much of a muchness – not that it matters, as they're all acceptable and all packed in summer – but we particularly like this one, with its tiny dining room and equally tiny terrace, somewhat set apart. The menu is simple but inventive, with an Italian touch (the pasta is delicious). Other possibilities are loin of lamb, fish salad and ostrich steak. The service is friendly, and the prices very reasonable for the location. Individual dishes cost around €10, but there is also a lunchtime menu for €14 and others for €18, €21 and €26. *Free house apéritif offered to our readers on presentation of this guide.*

ÎLE-DE-FRANCE

⊚ |●| 🎢 Le Coude Fou

12 rue du Bourg-Tibourg; M° Hôtel-de-Ville.
⊕01.42.77.15.16
Closed evenings 24–31 Dec. **Open** noon–
2.45pm and 7.30pm–midnight.

An extremely successful wine bar-
restaurant with a convivial atmosphere
that attracts both true connoisseurs
and curious beginners. The owner has
assembled a highly original wine list,
with many vintages from lesser-known
vineyards. The slightly tatty walls in the
two dining rooms are embellished with
pretty, naive murals, and the tables are
covered with old wine-bottle crates.
Set lunch of starter plus first course or
main course plus dessert, both with a
glass of wine, at €16; set dinners €19
and €23. Reckon on around €30 à la
carte, without drink. Small, traditional
dishes, as well as more innovative dishes
like ostrich steak with foie gras sauce or
monkfish with saffron. The cooking is
finely judged and the welcome warm.
*Free house apéritif offered to our readers on
presentation of this guide.*

⊚ 🎢 |●| Le Dôme du Marais

53 bis rue des Francs-Bourgeois; M° Hôtel-
de-Ville.
⊕01.42.74.54.17
Closed 15 Aug–10 Sept. **Open** Tues–Sat,
noon–2.30pm and 7.30–11pm. **High chairs
available.**

All traces of hardship have been banished
from this former sale room for the state
pawnbroker's, now a chic, refurbished restaurant. Dine under an eighteenth-century
frosted-glass dome, surrounded by gold-
leaf decorations on the burgundy walls.
The chef served his apprenticeship abroad,
and he has brought from this experience
a subtle understanding of unusual spices,
seen to good effect in his baked sea bream
and haunch of venison. Cheapest menu
€17 and another €23 (both served lunchtime only), evening menu at €29; reckon
on €40 à la carte. Friendly, painstaking
service and an excellent wine list. If you
want a quiet meal, avoid weekends, as
it will be crowded and noisy. *Free house
apéritif offered to our readers on presentation
of this guide.*

⊚ |●| 🎢 L'Endroit

24 rue des Tournelles; M° Bastille.
⊕01.42.72.03.07

Open noon–2pm and 7–10.30pm (midnight
Fri and Sat). **Closed** Sun; Mon.

Small restaurant with tasteful decoration
that combines the warmth of wood with
light sophistication, and white plumes
with a *Routard* statuette. The cooking
is simple but has some equally original
touches: knuckle of lamb caramelized with
rosemary: *carpaccio* of scallop with pistachio
oil and *tatin* with tomato *confit* (delicious).
Set menus at €17 and €29. Good wine list
and cheerful, efficient service. *Free sweets
after the meal offered to our readers on presentation of this guide.*

⊚ 🎢 |●| Le Café de la Poste

13 rue Castex; M° Bastille.
⊕01.42.72.95.35
Closed Sun; public holidays. **Open** 10am–
2pm (from 7pm on Sat).

This café is opposite the post office, a brick
building from the 1930s. It's a stylish place,
with mosaic walls, wide benches, a huge
mirror and a splendid wooden bar. Dishes
change every day but there's always a pasta
dish on the blackboard and a few meat
and fish dishes as well – beef Stroganoff or
sausage *fricassée*. Expect to pay around €19
for a meal; dishes cost €8.50–15; starters
and desserts around €5. *Free coffee offered to
our readers on presentation of this guide.*

⊛ |●| Brasserie Bofinger

5-7 rue de la Bastille; M° Bastille.
⊕01.42.72.87.82
Open noon–3pm and 6.30pm–1am (weekend
non-stop noon–1am).

This famous brasserie, created in 1864 and
transformed in 1919, sports a décor much
appreciated by the tourists who flock here
to eat – although Parisians prove to be
equally impressed by the beautiful stained
glass and the upstairs room decorated
by Hansi. Whether you eat here or stay
downstairs, do not miss the house specialities of *choucroute* and seafood, especially the
"*choucroute paysanne*" and the "*Spéciale*", as
well as the "*Mareyeur*" and the "*Royal*" seafood platters. Weekday lunchtime *formule*
€22.50, with another menu at €32.90;
choucroutes from €16.50 and seafood platters at €39.50 and €53, or €96 for two.

⊛ |●| À l'Escale

1 rue des Deux-Ponts; M° Pont-Marie.
⊕01.40.46.89.96

Closed *evenings; Sun; Aug; between Christmas and New Year.* **Open** *7.30am–9pm (food is served noon–3pm only).*

This pleasant restaurant gets the sun and overlooks the Seine. It's a perfect place to restore your spirits after you've trailed round Notre-Dame or the Île Saint-Louis. There's no set menu, so opt for the dish of the day at €10–11.45 (ox tongue is good); salads are €6.90–9.20; savoury tarts and toasted sandwiches €8.80 (including salad). The wine list includes some intelligent choices. You'll pay about €23 for a full meal without a drink.

⟪ |◉| Bel Canto

72 quai de l'Hôtel-de-Ville; M° Hôtel-de-Ville.
℡01.42.78.30.18
Closed *Aug.* **Open** *daily 8–10pm.*

You don't have to sing for your supper here, as the waiters and waitresses will do it for you, bursting into song and metamorphosing into Carmen or Don Giovanni right by your table! The whole team is vivacious and superbly trained for this new style of dinner-performance. The show's the thing here, but the food is appealing too, with all the Italian standards on the menu, from carpaccio to tiramisu and, from prosciutto to Lambrusco; "Lyric" menu €60, excluding drinks. It's a no-smoking restaurant and the combination of light opera and classical Italian cuisine has become so successful that the management has opened a similarly musical annexe in the 14th *arrondissement* (88, rue de la Tombe-Issoire ℡01.43.22.96.15). Booking essential.

5th arrondissement

⟪ ♠ Young and Happy Hostel

80 rue Mouffetard; M° Monge.
℡01.47.07.47.07 ⓕ01.47.07.22.24
ⓦwww.youngandhappy.fr
Closed *11am–4pm and after 2am.*

Basic but clean hostel, undoubtedly the cheapest in this throbbing part of the city centre (the street outside is pretty noisy). It sleeps 55 people, with showers and toilets on the landing. Depending on the season, reckon on €21–23 per person in a dormitory, €24–26 in a double room, with breakfast included. You can cook in the communal kitchen or eat in the nearby university canteen. Facilities include telephone in the hall, soft-drinks machine, Internet area, TV and young,

friendly staff. The hostel has been thriving for nearly twenty years, and has become particularly popular with English-speaking travellers. You can book in writing with a night's deposit, or try your luck by turning up between 8am and 11am – but you'll be lucky to get in at the weekend without booking first. Credit cards not accepted.

⟪ ♠ Port-Royal Hôtel

8 bd. du Port-Royal; M° Gobelins.
℡01.43.31.70.06 ⓕ01.43.31.33.67
ⓦwww.portroyalhotel.fr.st

This pretty little hotel, run by the same family for nearly seventy years, offers the advantage of a central location and reasonable prices. There is also a discreet charm in the subdued, floral decorations in the bedrooms and the patio where you can have breakfast on a sunny day. Double rooms up to €48–51 with washbasin, €73–82 with shower/wc, €82–87 with bath/wc. The owners go to great lengths to make their guests' stay enjoyable. They even give them a little guide to the area when they arrive, with information about taxis, buses, the Métro, museums, walks, restaurants, etc. It is advisable to book. Credit cards not accepted.

⟪ ♱ ♠ Hôtel Marignan*

13 rue du Sommerard; M° Maubert-Mutualité.
℡01.43.54.63.81
ⓦwww.hotel-marignan.com

Located in a quiet stret, this hotel has been a landing point for travellers for more than three decades. There are lots of common facilities: a dining room for picnics, a microwave, fridges, washing and drying machines, an iron and ironing board. Doubles with shower/wc €70–80, according to the season; also a few family rooms at €90 and €120 with shower/wc, breakfast and taxes included. Out of season, rates go down after three nights. Credit cards not accepted. *A free trip on a bateau-mouche offered to families on presentation of this guide.*

⟪ ♠ Hôtel Esmeralda*

4 rue Saint-Julien-le-Pauvre; M° Saint-Michel.
℡01.43.54.19.20 ⓕ01.40.51.00.68

This small seventeenth-century hotel is a listed monument with a listed staircase. The nineteen rooms (€80–85 with bath/wc) are fussily decorated with lots of attention to detail but you should probably ignore the furniture, which is a bit dated. The whole place is really due a redecoration, but because of its location it's always full – some rooms offer a glimpse of Notre-Dame or Square Viviani. Don't miss the church of Saint-Julien-le-Pauvre which is just across from the hotel. It's one of the oldest and most charming churches in Paris.

✍ 🕏 🛏 Familia Hôtel

11 rue des Écoles; M° Jussieu or Cardinal-Lemoine.
℡01.43.54.55.27 ℻01.43.29.61.77
ⓦwww.hotel-paris-familia.com
TV. Disabled access. Pay car park.

A comfortable hotel run by the welcoming Gaucheron family, who'll go out of their way to help you. Décor is sophisticated and classic, with medieval-style tapestries and an old library. Well-equipped doubles go for €84–113 with shower/wc or bath; breakfast €6. Some rooms have four posters and frescoes; those on the fifth or sixth floors – some have been recently renovated – have views of Notre-Dame and the Paris rooftops. It's essential to reserve in advance if you wish to stay in this friendly, tasteful hotel right in the heart of the Latin Quarter. *10% discount on the room rate (4 Jan–27 Feb, 1–31 Aug, and 25 Nov–25 Dec) offered to our readers on presentation of this guide.*

✍ 🛏 Hôtel de la Sorbonne**

6 rue Victor-Cousin; M° Cluny-Sorbonne or RER B Luxembourg.
℡01.43.54.58.08 ℻01.40.51.05.18
ⓔreservation@hotelsorbonne.com
TV.

This charming little hotel is just opposite the venerable Sorbonne and is thus right in the heart of the student district. It has recently been completely refurbished; doubles with shower/wc or bath are €100–120, which is very reasonable considering that the place is so well run and friendly. Breakfast costs €10. The décor is a warm and colourful mixture of the contemporary and the retro, with a vaguely nineteenth-century feel to bring out the cosy atmosphere of the building. To make the pretty lounge even snugger, a log fire is lit as soon as winter starts to set in.

✍ 🛏 Hôtel des Grandes Écoles***

75 rue du Cardinal-Lemoine; M° Cardinal-Lemoine or Monge.
℡01.43.26.79.23 ℻01.43.25.28.15
ⓦwww.hotel-grandes-ecoles.com
Disabled access. Pay car park.

The hotel is in a private lane just round the corner from place de la Contrescarpe. It's a house of some charm and character, with a small paved courtyard and a leafy garden. The owner and her daughter have long welcomed tourists from around the world and, since this is a favourite with Americans in Paris, it's worth booking well in advance. Rooms are on either side of the lane, and they're carefully maintained and tastefully arranged. They have shower/wc or bath and cost €105–130; breakfast €8. In fine weather you can take tea in the garden – even if you're not staying here. Television addicts should not come here as peace and quiet reign.

ⓔ 🕏 |❍| Rotiss'bar

57 rue Galande; M° Saint-Michel or Maubert-Mutualité.
℡01.46.34.70.96
Closed *Mon lunchtime.* **Open** *daily noon–2.30pm and 7pm–1am (last orders 11pm).*

The rue Galande follows a route laid down in the thirteenth century and even in those days there was a roasting house barbecuing geese and suckling pig to calm the raging hunger of pilgrims and journeymen. The tradition has been stoutly maintained in this place where the menu lists mouthwatering dishes; you can even watch the gently turning hunks of golden meat basting in their juices before they make their way onto your plate. There are two lunch *formules* at €8 and €11 (starter, main course and dessert). Platters of barbecued meats cost from €9.30 to €37 (shoulder of lamb for three people). *Free house apéritif offered to our readers on presentation of this guide.*

ⓔ |❍| Foyer du Vietnam

80 rue Monge; M° Monge.
℡01.45.35.32.54
Closed *Sun.* **Open** *noon–2.30pm and 7–10.30pm.*

This restaurant is very plain indeed but it is worth a visit. The genuine Vietnamese cooking makes no concessions to Western taste and remains resolutely authentic. They do an excellent pork soup (which, despite its small serving, is very substantial) and delicious steamed dumplings. The other dishes – pork kebabs, Hanoi soup – are of the same calibre. There are a few interesting specialities at the weekend, such as rice soup with tripe (alternating with duck soup) and grilled prawns with vermicelli. Menus €8.20 and €12.20 are served both for lunch and dinner, with a student menu at €7; à la carte you'll pay around €15.

ⓔ 🎋 |●| Tashi-Delek

4 rue des Fossés-Saint-Jacques; M° Monge or RER B Luxembourg.
☎01.43.26.55.55
Closed Sun; 15–27 Aug.**Open** noon–2.30pm and 7–11pm.

This was the first Tibetan restaurant in Paris, run by people who fled their country after the Chinese invasion. The big eye-catching Mandala in the entrance serves as a declaration of national pride, but the rest of the restaurant is more soberly decorated. Lunchtime menu €9, then other menus €10–19; if you do not opt for the menu, which offers the traditional *momoks* (steamed meat turnovers), take the opportunity of ordering several dishes to familiarize yourself with this remote culinary tradition: *sharil gobetsu* (meat balls with garlic, ginger and tomato sauce), the Tibetan dessert *baktsa markou* (balls of pasta with melted butter and goat's cheese) and then, for the brave of heart, tea with salted butter. NB: there is an extra charge for the accompaniments. It is essential to book at night, as this place is well-known and justifiably popular. *Free house apéritif offered to our readers on presentation of this guide.*

ⓔ |●| Au Bon Coin

21 rue de la Collégiale; M° Gobelins or Censier-Daubenton.
☎01.43.31.55.57
Closed Sun; first 3 weeks in Aug. **Open** noon–2.30pm and 7–11pm (11.30pm Fri and Sat).

Generous, hearty French cooking at very reasonable prices, in a classic setting (checked tableclothes): lunch menu €11.20 (except Sat and public holidays), dinner €13.50, and another at €18.50 (starter, main meal and home-made dessert). House specialities include herring fillets with apple, fried *escalope* of foie gras, *croustillant* of bass and *cassoulet* – and an enticing dessert buffet to round it off.

Arrive early in summer if you want to eat on the terrace – it fills up quickly. This restaurant offers excellent value for money, a good atmosphere and cheerful service – you're advised to book. Credit cards not accepted.

ⓔ |●| Au Coin des Gourmets

5 rue Dante; Maubert-Mutualité or Saint-Michel.
☎01.43.26.12.92
Closed Mon lunch. **Open** noon–2.30pm and 7–10.30pm.

This very popular restaurant offers "Indochinese specialities" and lives up to its promise by serving delicious dishes from all over the region, with greater subtlety than many Asian restaurants in Paris. The extensive menu includes grated green-papaya salad, *tea khtoeun* (braised duck stuffed with mushrooms – must be ordered 48hrs in advance), *bank xeo* (Vietnamese pancake) and Cambodian *amok*. There's a weekday lunchtime menu at €11.50, otherwise reckon on around €25 à la carte. Special *soirées* are organized every three months, with a chance to try three or four dishes, each with a different glass of wine (with reservation only); around €45. Booking is essential.

ⓔ |●| Le Buisson Ardent

25 rue de Jussieu; M° Jussieu.
☎01.43.54.93.02
Closed Sat lunch; Sun; Aug; Christmas.
Open lunch and dinner until 10pm.

This is a very French place, the kind of restaurant you'd miss if ever it closed. The décor is as comforting as the cooking, but while they use a lot of good regional produce, the approach is modern and the results tasty and full of colour. Dishes change frequently in response to the fresh market produce available. They do lunch menus for €15 and €29; a full meal à la carte will be about €35.

ⓔ |●| Le Reminet

3 rue des Grands-Degrés; M° Maubert-Mutualité.
☎01.44.07.04.24
Closed Tues; Wed; 3 weeks in Aug. **Open** noon–2.15pm and 7.30–11pm in the week, later at the weekend.

A restaurant which is situated in this quiet and charming *arrondissement* yet close to the hustling superficiality of Saint-Séverin.

The cuisine is refined and the Norman chef prepares many of his region's dishes with certainty and simplicity: mussels, cockles, plaice – heaven for lovers of fresh fish and seafood. There's also rabbit and salt-flat lamb on offer, and the desserts are sublime. Weekday lunch menu €13, two more at €17 (weekdays) and €50; à la carte expect to pay around €35. The dining room is elegant and the service is attentive but relaxed. It's best to book.

⊚ 🎿 |●| Pema Thang

13 rue de la Montagne-Sainte-Geneviève; M° Maubert-Mutualité.
☎01.43.54.34.34
Closed *Sun; Mon lunchtime; Sept.***Open** *noon–2.30pm and 7–10.30pm.*

The Latin Quarter is still a magnet for the various ethnic groups in the French capital. Take this restaurant, for example, which feels rather like an inn on the high plateaux of Tibet. The cooking, which involves a lot of steaming, is full of delicate, subtle flavours and deserves to be more widely known. While the dishes are pure Tibetan, the flavours might remind you of India, China or Japan – and the cuisine is just as good as any of those. The lunch-time crowd consists of students from the Sorbonne and white-collar workers; they come here to savour *sha momok* (rather like *dim sum*), *then thouk* (home-made noodles in clear soup) and *pemathang* (meat balls in a sweet-and-sour sauce with sautéed vegetables). Menus €13–17; one is vegetarian, another offers Tibetan specialities. Reckon on around €17 à la carte, with a range of dishes €9.50–12.20. Wines are reasonably priced and the desserts are surprisingly good. *Free coffee offered to our readers on presentation of this guide.*

⊚ |●| 🎿 ChantAirelle

17 rue Laplace; M° Cardinal-Lemoine or Maubert-Mutualité; RER B Luxembourg.
☎01.46.33.18.59
Closed *Sat lunch; Sun; a week around 15 Aug.* **Open** *noon–2pm and 7–10pm.*

An embassy from Auvergne run by a radical proselyte for the produce of his homeland (which you can also buy to take away). Copious portions of heart-warming rural specialities, including stuffed cabbage and *pounti auvergnat*, excellent bread and good wine from small vineyards (belying the general belief that Auvergne has nothing to drink except water – although

there are some fine mineral waters, such as the *Chateldon*). The attempt to re-create Auvergne even extends to a soundtrack with birdsong and the croaking of frogs. Lunchtime menu €14 (starter, main course and dessert); dinner menus €18 and €25. Lovely, relaxing garden terrace; you'll need to reserve to be sure of a table. Unfortunately, the service is sometimes a bit sloppy. *A platter with samples of Auvergne farmyard cheeses offered to our readers who eat à la carte, on presentation of this guide.*

⊚ |●| Le Languedoc

64 bd. de Port-Royal; M° Gobelins; RER Port-Royal.
☎01.47.07.24.47
Closed *Tues; Wed; 14 July–15 Aug; 20 Dec– 6 Jan.* **Open** *noon–2pm and 7–10pm.*

They specialize in dishes of the southwest here, and the cooking is excellent. The service is reminiscent of the kind you'd get in a country restaurant. The duck *confit* with garlic potatoes (for two people) and the *cassoulet* of goose are the star turns, but the meat dishes are well worth a try and the Rouergue wine washes it all down superbly. The poached haddock is also recommended. The white and red Gaillac from the proprietor's own vineyard aren't bad either. They do a set menu for €19 (lunch and dinner), or you can expect to pay around €24 à la carte. This place never changes, which is all for the good.

⊚ |●| Le Vin Sobre

25 rue des Feuillantines; M° Monge; RER B: Port-Royal or Luxembourg.
☎01.43.29.00.23
Open *daily lunchtimes and evenings until 10.30pm.*

This bistro is a real find. Its name refers to a village in the Côtes-du-Rhône and, not surprisingly, wine is given great prominence. It is sold, at very reasonable prices, by the glass, the pitcher (in around fifteen cases) or the bottle. Furthermore, the food is superb, with top-quality, extremely fresh ingredients, prepared without pretensions but with great skill. Shrimp and whelk tartare with avocado pear, figs baked in red wine, accompanied by a sorbet and rib of Limousin veal with seasonal mushrooms – these are just some of the specialities to be found chalked up on the blackboard: starters €7; dishes of the day €10–12 at lunch, €15 at dinner; desserts €5.50. The culinary excellence is only enhanced by the extremely convenient opening hours, the simple but cosy setting, with a sheltered terrace close to the Val-de-Grâce, and the friendly and efficient service. Wine, charcuterie and cheese are served until 1.30am.

⟨⟨ |●| ⅔ L'Équitable

47 bis rue Poliveau; M° Censier-Daubenton or Saint-Marcel.
℗01.43.31.69.20
Closed Mon; 2–15 Aug. **Open** noon–2.30pm and 7.30–10.30pm. **Pay car park.**

The setting recalls a slightly rundown, provincial inn, but the cooking is inventive (the young chef served his apprenticeship with some great masters) and has attracted a well-heeled following. Traditional dishes are revitalized by exotic touches (vanilla in the Emperor fish, served on a banana leaf, or celery chips as a garnish for a tasty meat dish) and the desserts are full of surprises. The lunchtime menu is €21; other menus €26 and €32. *Free house apéritif or coffee offered to our readers on presentation of this guide.*

⟨⟨ |●| ⅔ Le Mauzac

7 rue de l'Abbé-de-l'Épée; RER B Luxembourg.
℗01.46.33.75.22
Closed Sun; week of 15 Aug. **Open** 8am–midnight; service noon–2.30pm and 8–11.30pm.

Charming 1950s décor, a terrace that can be heated on fine days and hearty food. The menu rarely changes: *andouillette*, prime cut of beef, *blanquette*, a few less imaginative dishes of the day. Starters are €4.75; platters of Auvergne charcuterie €5–10; main courses €11–13; desserts €4.55. The menu-carte, however, changes daily and may include spicey roast duck or pan-fried scallops and chicory with caramelized orange. A broad selection of wines at reasonable prices, with a particularly outstanding white Mauzac, are sold by the glass, or in a carafe or bottle. *Free coffee offered to our readers on presentation of this guide.*

⟨⟨ ⅔ |●| L'Atlas

10–12 bd. Saint-Germain; M° Maubert-Mutualité.
℗01.46.33.86.98
Closed Mon. **Open** noon–2.30pm and 7.30–11pm. **Disabled access.**

If you've been nosing round the Institut du Monde Arabe nearby, you can prolong the experience by eating here. Benjamin El-Jaziri, who has worked with some of the really big names, has remained faithful to the cooking of his native Morocco but goes easier on the fat and sugar. Try his incredibly light couscous served with meat and vegetables (it's beyond reproach), or one of sixteen superb *tajines*. As well as these classics, you can feast on grilled gambas, large prawns with paprika, lamb with mallow leaves, seafood *pastilla* or, in season, partridge with sweet chestnuts. À la carte only; count on €30 without a drink. *Free digestif offered to our readers on presentation of this guide.*

⟨⟨ |●| Le Balzar

49 rue des Écoles; M° Cluny-la-Sorbonne or Odéon.
℗01.43.54.13.67
Open 8am–midnight (continuous service from noon).

This fairly plush brasserie has been taken over by the Flo group. It's a pleasant place for supper after the theatre or the cinema, with artificial leather benches, large mirrors and waiters in white aprons. There's an amazing long aquarium and in winter you can people-watch in the warmth. House specialities include poached eggs in jelly, sole *meunière*, skate in melted butter and *choucroute*: average food of the classic variety, rather expensive but the main thing is to be there. A meal à la carte will set you back about €32.

⟨⟨ |●| Le Petit Pontoise

9 rue de Pontoise; M° Maubert-Mutualité.
℗01.43.29.25.20
Open noon–2.30pm and 7.30–10.30pm.

The friendly owner worked in some famous French restaurants and obviously learned a thing or two, to judge by the inventive baked goat's cheese on gingerbread, or the more traditional but equally impressive dishes like duck *parmentier* with foie gras. The desserts draw their inspiration from Italy, although the results are *île flottante* with pink praline. Reckon on paying €35 à la carte for a full meal including starter, main course and dessert. A small, bistro-style dining room with plenty of regular customers. The owner also has a take-away outlet nearby (*Le Canard des Pharaons*, 7 rue de Pontoise, ℗01.43.25.35.93), with a couple of tables too. The dishes are mainly Italian, and some customers say they're even better than those of the main restaurant. You'll need to book.

6th arrondissement

◀◀ 🏊 🛏 Hôtel des Académies*

15 rue de la Grande-Chaumière; M° Vavin; RER B Port-Royal.
☎01.43.26.66.44 ℻01.43.26.03.72

Small family hotel in a quiet street. It has been going since the 1920s, but the atmosphere is more reminiscent of the 1950s. Some twenty doubles, equipped with TV and double glazing, range from €50–56 with shower to €60–68 with shower/wc. You'll need to book in advance, and they'll ask for a deposit of at least the cost of one night (depending on the length of your stay). The more expensive rooms (with wc) are slightly overpriced. *One free breakfast per room per night on presentation of this guide.*

◀◀ 🛏 Hôtel de Nesle

7 rue de Nesle; M° Odéon or Pont-Neuf.
☎ and ℻01.43.54.62.41
🌐www.hoteldenesle.com
Open *8am until midnight.* **Car park.**

This hotel, located in a quiet street close to the Pont-Neuf and the *Samaritaine*, is full of history. Anglo-Saxon and American accents mingle with Madame's North African one. She and her son shower affection on her guests and reign over their little kingdom with infinite good humour. There's a small interior garden where you can have a quiet read, and when it's not open there's a pretty terrace overlooking the garden. The twenty rooms are simple, clean, well maintained and individually decorated; some look onto the street, others look over the small interior garden and terrace. Doubles range from €75 with basin or shower to €100 with bath and wc; there's no breakfast. Each room has its own personality: the shower is rather awe-inspiring and there's even a little *hammam*, or steam bath, in "Sahara". You'll need to reserve at least a week in advance, if you can get through to them by phone (or by e-mail). Booking can be problematic.

◀◀ 🛏 Grand Hôtel des Balcons**

3 rue Casimir-Delavigne; M° Odéon; RER B Luxembourg.

☎01.46.34.78.50 ℻01.46.34.06.27
🌐www.balcons.com
TV. Pay car park.

You'd be hard-pressed to find another place in the Latin Quarter, just 100m from the Odéon theatre, offering such value for money: spacious doubles range from €80 (recently refurbished attic rooms) up to €150 depending on the season. There's an all-you-can-eat buffet breakfast for €10. The reception and public areas of the hotel are Art Deco style, though the rooms are merely functional but some are quite spacious. Everyone gets a polite if somewhat business-like welcome.

◀◀ 🛏 Hôtel Saint-André-des-Arts*

66 rue Saint-André-des-Arts; M° Odéon.
☎01.43.26.96.16 ℻01.43.29.73.34
✉hsainand@wanadoo.fr

Superb location in the heart of Saint-Germain, opposite the famous passage Saint-André-des-Arts. There's nothing very luxurious (it has only one star) but it has a certain charm and offers very friendly service. The rooms are well kept, the bathrooms are spotless and the ceilings are adorned with pretty half-timbering. Double rooms with shower/wc or bath €83–88, including breakfast; reckon on €104 for three people and €115 for four, including breakfast. No TV, but the local cinemas present eclectic, high-quality programmes day and night.

◀◀ 🏊 🛏 Hôtel des Canettes**

17 rue des Canettes; M° Saint-Germain-des-Prés or Mabillon.
☎01.46.33.12.67 ℻01.44.07.07.37
TV.

This establishment, hidden away in a very busy street full of pubs and chain stores, looks old, but inside the décor is rather modern. It was done up in 2001, and the twenty rooms are colourful and clean, with bright bathrooms, though on the whole they are rather small. At the weekend, ask to stay in a room above the second floor so as to avoid the noise of the musical evenings emanating from the bars in the street. Doubles with shower/wc €105, €119 with bath/wc; family rooms are €155–204. *10% discount on the room rate offered to our readers on presentation of this guide.*

ⓌⒶ Hôtel du Lys**

23 rue Serpente; M° Saint-Michel or Odéon.
☎01.43.26.97.57 ℗01.44.07.34.90
Ⓦwww.hoteldulys.co
TV.

A pleasant hotel in a seventeenth-century house on a quiet street – a really cosy place for lovers. Brightly decorated in pink or blue, with roses or check, some large and some small, the rooms are all different, though they all have super bathrooms; some have a small balcony and some have just been refurbished. Doubles with shower/wc or bath go for €115–120 including breakfast; €135 for three people. Reservations are advised.

ⒺⓘⓄⓘ Indonesia

12 rue de Vaugirard; M° Odéon; RER B Luxembourg.
☎01.43.25.70.22
Closed Sat lunchtime; lunchtimes in Aug.
Open noon–2.30pm and 7–10.30pm (11pm Fri and Sat).

This is the only Indonesian restaurant in Paris to be set up as a workers' cooperative. The food is good and service comes with a smile. They serve a series of dishes from Java, Sumatra, Bali and Celebes; fish in coconut milk, *nasi goreng* (fried rice), *rendang* (meat in coconut milk with spices), *balado ikan* (fish in spicy tomato sauce), and satay (kebabs in peanut sauce). There's a weekday lunch *formule* for €9, then menus at €17–23 or around €20 à la carte. Indonesian restaurants are rare in Paris, more's the pity. It's best to book for dinner.

ⒺⓘⓄⓘ L'Assignat

7 rue Guénégaud; M° Odéon.
☎01.43.54.87.68
Closed Sun; July. **Restaurant open** noon–3pm.

Who would have thought you'd find a little neighbourhood restaurant in this crowded narrow street? It's popular with local art dealers (fed-up with coughing up €30 for lunch), people who work at the Mint and art students – many regulars grab what they want, write down what they've had and settle up at the end of the month. You'll enjoy good, simple food in a lively atmosphere, elbow to elbow with the other diners. Dish of the day costs €6.50; set lunch menu €11 or around the same à la carte. Credit cards are not accepted.

ⒺⓘⓄⓘ Le Petit Vatel

5 rue Lobineau; M° Mabillon.
☎01.43.54.28.49
Closed Sun; second fortnight in Feb.
Open noon–2.30pm and 7–10.30pm.

This tiny little place has been revamped by its new owners but has kept its reasonable prices. There's an €12 lunch *formule*; if you opt for individual dishes, a meal will cost no more than €20, with a glass of wine of the month for €2.50. Try the home-made terrine or, if you feel like something more elaborate, kidneys in white wine, sautéed lamb or beef *miroton*. The wines complement the cooking perfectly; they offer quite a few by the glass. This is a non-smoking restaurant. Credit cards are not accepted.

ⒺⓘⓄⓘ La Bauta

129 bd. du Montparnasse; M° Vavin.
☎01.43.22.52.35
Closed Sat lunchtime; Sun. **Open** noon–2pm and 7.30–11pm.

The décor is inspired by Venice and there's a superb collection of masks on the walls. The beautiful people who eat here are on to a good thing: everything is remarkably fresh and cooked with finesse. The pasta will satisfy everyone, and the chef cooks it perfectly *al dente* with all manner of sauces and accompaniments like squid ink and clams; some fish and meat dishes are also available. There are lunchtime menus for €16.90 and €23.20; an evening menu for €24.90, or you'll pay around €40 for a meal à la carte. The service is great.

Ⓔ♨ⓘⓄⓘ La Rôtisserie d'En Face

2 rue Christine; M° Odéon.
☎01.43.26.40.98
Closed Sat lunchtime; Sun. **Open** noon–2pm and 7–11pm.

Top chef Jacques Cagna, whose flagship restaurant is just across the way, has every reason to be pleased. He's made this enterprise one of the Left Bank's institutions. Try his guineafowl *en pastilla*, with onion preserve in honey and aubergines, and you'll understand why. There are lots of things cooked on the *rotisserie*, all served with old-fashioned mashed potatoes. The food is definitely the high-point. The wine list isn't very tempting, and it can get noisy. Menus €17, €24 and €27 are served at lunchtime, as well as a *menu-carte* for €39; reckon on €53 or so à la carte. *Free house*

ÎLE-DE-FRANCE

apéritif offered to our readers on presentation of this guide.

ⓐ |●| L'Épi Dupin

11 rue Dupin; M° Sèvres-Babylone.
☏01.42.22.64.56
Closed *Sat; Sun; Mon lunch; first 3 weeks in Aug.* **Open** *noon–2.30pm and 7–10.30pm.*

François Pasteau, who trained under Kérever and Faugeron, is a happy man, as you can tell from his beaming smile – his restaurant is full at lunchtime and his customers leave nothing on their plates but the pattern. You'll also get pretty good value for money: there's a lunchtime *formule* for €20 and a children's menu with starter, main course and dessert for the same price; you'll spend around €30 à la carte. Dishes change according to what's good at the market. You get a daily choice of six starters, six main courses and six desserts; these might include chicory with caramelized goat's cheese, scallops with lemon and green pepper in flaky pastry, warm apples with a mascarpone sorbet. This is all good value for money and a sheer delight from start to finish. You need to reserve a week in advance for first sitting at dinner.

ⓐ |●| Le Machon d'Henri

8 rue Guisarde; M° Mabillon or Saint-Germain-des-Prés.
☏01.43.29.08.70
Open *noon–2.30pm and 7–11.30pm.*

This is a good wine bar with stone walls and hefty beams. They serve a rich selection of carefully prepared classic dishes: slow-roast lamb cooked for seven hours, courgette terrine with tomato *coulis*, crunchy fruit tart. Dishes of the day cost around €12; you'll spend €24 or thereabouts for a full meal. Reservations are strongly advised.

ⓐ 🎋 |●| Le Procope

13 rue de l'Ancienne-Comédie; M° Odéon.
☏01.40.46.79.00
Open *noon–1am.* **Disabled access.**

This is the oldest café in Paris. In 1686, an Italian called Francesco Procopio dei Cotelli came to the city and opened a café serving a then-unknown drink called coffee. His establishment, close to the *Comédie Française*, soon gathered a clientele of writers and artists. In the eighteenth century it was a meeting place for

Enlightenment philosophers – the idea for Diderot's famous *Encyclopedia* was spawned here during a conversation between him and d'Alembert. During the French Revolution, Danton, Marat and Camille Desmoulins met here, and it was also a haunt of Musset, Sand, Balzac, Huysmans, Verlaine and many others. It's still a haunt for intellectuals and, incredibly, its prices are still reasonable. The cooking is unabashedly French with meat and fish dishes swathed in sauce, platters of seafood, *coq au vin*, home-made sorbets and ice creams – you haven't been to Paris if you haven't eaten at *Procope*. The set menu "Procope", served noon–7pm, costs €24 and the "Privilège" is €30; otherwise about €45 à la carte. *Free house apéritif offered to our readers on presentation of this guide.*

ⓐ 🎋 |●| La Méditerranée

2 pl. de l'Odéon; M° Odéon or RER B Luxembourg.
☏01.43.26.02.30
Open *noon–2.30pm and 7.30–11pm.*

Time was when the stars of the silver screen and other notables would congregate here. Everyone had their own table – from Orson Welles to Aragon, Picasso to Chagall, Man Ray to Jean-Louis Barrault. It has been delicately renovated to reveal its former glory. À la carte there's a good number of fish dishes and a handful of starters, main courses and desserts: red tuna *tartare*, house *bouillabaisse*. There's a *formule* of main course with a choice of starter or dessert for €25, a menu for €29 and à la carte expect to pay around €45. A doorman will park the car for you if you have had the misguided idea to come here by car. *Free house apéritif offered to our readers on presentation of this guide.*

7th arrondissement

ⓐ 🏠 Hôtel du Champ-de-Mars**

7 rue du Champ-de-Mars; M° École-Militaire; RER C Pont-de-l'Alma or Invalides.
☏01.45.51.52.30 ☏01.45.51.64.36
🌐www.hotel-du-champ-de-mars.com
TV. Car park (Place-Joffre).

This charming hotel offers excellent value for money, and its location, not far from the Eiffel Tower and the gardens of the Champs-de-Mars, as well as the lively neighbourhood market on rue Cler, provides an added bonus. It is spotless and extremely well kept, with exemplary service. The quiet double rooms with bathrooms (€76–80) overlook either the street or the pretty courtyard. Smartly decorated in yellow or blue, they all have a distinctive, personalized touch and are each named after a flower (Buttercup, Poppy, Sunflower, etc), with slightly old-fashioned floral engravings to emphasize this bucolic theme.

⍟ 🍴 🛆 Hôtel du Palais Bourbon**

49 rue de Bourgogne; M° Varenne or RER C Invalides.
☎01.44.11.30.70 ℻01.45.55.20.21
ⓦwww.hotel-palais-bourbon.com
TV.

Run by the same family for more than thirty years, this hotel has a pleasant reception with lofty beamed ceilings. Some of the rooms are vast – one of the benefits of being in an old building – and all have double glazing, mini-bar, TV, renovated bathrooms and sockets for connnecting a fax or modem. Air-conditioned doubles are €78–125, breakfast included – good prices for the district. *10% discount on the room rate (15 July–31 Aug) offered to our readers on presentation of this guide.*

⍟ 🍴 🛆 Grand Hôtel Lévêque*

29 rue Cler; M° École-Militaire or Latour-Maubourg.
☎01.47.05.49.15 ℻01.45.50.49.36
ⓦwww.hotel-leveque.com
TV.

The Eiffel Tower is very close by but you may find the picturesque street market in rue Cler even more appealing – rooms over the street get snapped up first. This is an authentic part of the district and the hotel with its fifty renovated rooms is reasonably priced; doubles €87–110 with shower/wc. The décor doesn't leave a lasting impression but the rooms are clean and they have safes (€5 per stay) and hairdryers. The beds and carpets are new. Downstairs you'll find a gallery of the hotel's most favourable press cuttings (under glass) and a wonderful team (including Christophe and Pascale). It's a well-known place, so you may have to book. *One free breakfast per person offered to our readers on presentation of this guide.*

⍟ 🛆 Hôtel Muguet**

11 rue Chevert; M° École Militaire or Latour-Maubourg.

☎01.47.05.05.93 ℻01.45.50.25.37
ⓦwww.hotelmuguet.com
Disabled access. TV. Pay car park.

This hotel stands out in this quiet little road, away from the traffic noise, with a small plant-filled patio where it's very pleasant to sit out in fine weather. The rooms are mainly on the small side but they're impeccably clean and have been refurbished; doubles with shower or bath €100–107. Ask for a room on the sixth floor with a view of the Eiffel Tower or Les Invalides. It's a good idea to reserve.

⍟ 🍴 🛆 Hôtel Bersoly's Saint-Germain***

28 rue de Lille; M° Rue-du-Bac or Saint-Germain-des-Prés.
☎01.42.60.73.79 ℻01.49.27.05.55
ⓦwww.bersolyshotel.com
Closed Aug. **Disabled access. TV. Pay car park.**

Gorgeous hotel in a proud mansion built in the eighteenth century, in the middle of this historic part of Paris near the musée d'Orsay. The sixteen rooms may be small, but they're absolutely lovely and perfectly clean. Each bears the name of a painter, and there's a reproduction of one of the artist's pictures on the wall; "Gauguin" and "Turner" are particularly attractive. The hushed atmosphere, period furniture and exposed beams create a nostalgic ambience – but the telephones have Internet points. Rooms cost €125–135 with shower or bath; breakfast €10. There are lots of little extras: newspapers, electric kettle in the room, restaurant and theatre guides at reception. *Free fruit juice or soft drink offered to our readers on presentation of this guide.*

⍟ 🛆 Hôtel d'Orsay**

93 rue de Lille; M° Solférino or Assemblée Nationale, RER Musée d'Orsay.
☎01.47.05.85.54 ℻01.45.55.51.16
ⓔhotel.orsay@esprit-de-france.com
Disabled access. TV. High chairs available.

A quiet, comfortable and classy hotel very near the museum in the buildings of the old *Hotel Solférino* and the *Résidence d'Orsay*. It's been completely refurbished and fully air-conditioned: attractive reception, automatic lights in the corridors, double washbasins in the rooms and wc separate from the bathroom. Double rooms are €140–160, which is the going rate in this district.

ⓔ |●| Chez Germaine

30 rue Pierre-Leroux; M° Duroc and Vanneau.
ⓣ01.42.73.28.34
Closed *Sat evening; Sun; Aug.* **Open** *noon–2.30pm and 7–9.30pm.*

A simple, clean little dining room with a slightly provincial feel and a truly warm welcome. It appeals to everyone: workers, young lovers, retired people. They do a menu for €13; or reckon on €19 for a meal à la carte. Dishes might include creamed salt cod or braised beef with carrots; it's good value for money for the left bank.

ⓔ |●| L'Auvergne Gourmande

127 rue Saint-Dominique; M° École-Militaire or RER C Pont-de-l'Alma.
ⓣ01.47.05.60.79
Closed *Sun; Aug.* **Open** *noon–3pm and 7.30–11pm.*

Two large communal tables take up all the space in what used to be a handkerchief-sized butcher's shop. It's a no-smoking room and as soon as the weather permits, they put out a couple of small tables on the pavement. You'll enjoy a nice, convivial atmosphere and excellent, mouth-watering bistro dishes with a strong Auvergnat accent. Virtually all the produce is trucked up from the region. Dish of the day costs €11.50, starters and desserts €6. It's best to book. Credit cards are not accepted.

ⓔ 🍴 |●| Le Roupeyrac

62 rue de Bellechasse; M° Solférino.
ⓣ01.45.51.33.42
Closed *Sat; Sun; 3 weeks in Aug.* **Open** *noon–3pm (for brunch, 9–11.30am).*

This is the kind of neighbourhood restaurant you used to find everywhere in Paris; there's none of the flim-flam or the fancy décor that you'll find in lesser (but commoner) places. Wonderful country home cooking, with three or four fresh dishes every day and menus at €19 and €23. It offers excellent value for money for the area. *Free apéritif offered to our readers on presentation of this guide.*

ⓔ |●| Au Babylone

13 rue de Babylone; M° Sèvres-Babylone.
ⓣ01.45.48.72.13
Closed *Sun; some public holidays; Aug.* **Open** *lunchtime only.*

The large dining room is delightfully old-fashioned; the pictures on the walls have yellowed with age and the imitation leather benches are comfortable. The cooking is good, too, with a €19.50 lunch menu that includes starter, main meal, cheese or dessert, and a drink; dishes of the day cost around €11. This is the kind of restaurant you always enjoy coming to and which never seems to change. Credit cards are not accepted.

ⓔ |●| 🍴 L'Œillade

10 rue Saint-Simon; M° Rue-du-Bac.
ⓣ01.42.22.01.60
Closed *Sat lunch; Sun; 15–31 Aug.* **Open** *12.30–2pm and 7.30–10pm.*

The two rooms in this restaurant run by Pascal Molto are usually full, with a mixture of locals and tourists. He likes to serve his customers as if they were his house guests, and offers hearty dishes that satisfy even the most voracious appetite. À la carte costs from €25. Wines are reasonably priced and service comes with a smile. *Free house apéritif offered to our readers on presentation of this guide.*

ⓔ |●| Le Clos des Gourmets

16 av. Rapp; M° Alma-Marceau or RER C Pont-de-l'Alma.
01.45.51.75.61
Closed *Sun; Mon; Aug.* **Open** *12.15–2pm and 7.15–11pm.* **Disabled access.**

This restaurant, five minutes away from the Eiffel Tower, is not particularly inviting from the outside but it is worth a detour to discover the cooking of Arnaud Pitrois. Like many young chefs, Pitrois (who studied with some great masters) has opted for a single menu that changes with the seasons, although there are a few permanent fixtures that set the tone: warm oysters with *ravigote* sauce, fennel *confit* with spices and lemon sorbet. The prices are not over the top for gourmet food. At lunchtime during the week you can choose a *formule* for €25, €29 or €35; at dinner, you can eat a full meal, without wine, for €32. The lunchtime *formule* that offers a choice of two dishes from the menu, is a good option to go for.

ⓔ |●| L'Ami Jean

27 rue Malar; M° La Tour-Maubourg or École-Militaire.
ⓣ01.47.05.86.89
Closed *Sun; Mon; 3 weeks in Aug.*

The décor is old-provincial with a touch of Parisian humour. The young chef, who worked as Camderborde's second in command at the *Régalade*, is going places and producing a cuisine which loudly proclaims its Basque origins. Here is a recipe for success: since Stéphane's arrival in the kitchen, the dining room has been packed out. The word has spread so quickly that it is almost essential to book (admittedly the place was already firmly established as a local institution for several decades). Very convivial surroundings, ideal for dining amongst friends, but a little less so if you want to enjoy an intimate meal. There's a menu for €28, or reckon on around €30–35 à la carte. All the classic Basque specialities are to be found chalked up on the board: cold meats, cod, cuttlefish, black pudding – all prepared according to the chef's whim. First-rate desserts, pleasant wines from the southwest, all in all, a gourmet bistro for food lovers.

« |●| Le Basilic

2 rue Casimir-Périer; M° Solferino.
℗01.44.18.94.64
Open *noon–2.30pm and 7.30–10.30pm.*

Everyone in the 7th *arrondissement* comes to this chintzy, comfortable brasserie with its welcoming terrace facing the Sainte-Clothilde church. The menu changes with the season but some favourites are always on offer. Try the roast lamb in salt, terrine of aubergines with tomato *coulis*, the sole *meunière* or any of the other classics. A complete meal will amount to €30–40. A very relaxing place to go to after a long walk around the streets in the neighbourhood.

« |●| Le Poch'tron

25 rue de Bellechasse; M° Solférino.
℗01.45.51.27.11
Closed *Sat; Sun.* **Open** *noon–2.30pm and 8–10.30pm.* **Disabled access.**

The restaurant has an outlandish name but the welcoming *patronne* has a popular touch and her husband prepares the dishes with great care. You'll find calf's head with *sauce gribiche*, *andouillette* with Vouvray, terrines, grilled rib steak and all the traditional fare you'd expect in a good bistro. You'll spend about €30 à la carte, not including wine – if you're just after a toasted sandwich it will set you back around €10.50–12. They won the Bouteille d'Or "best bistro" award in 1996, so you can rely on the wine list

– it has particularly good bottles from Alsace.

8th arrondissement

« ♠ Hôtel Bellevue

46 rue Pasquier; M° Saint-Lazare ("Rue de Rome" exit).
℗01.43.87.50.68 ℗01.44.70.01.47
TV.

This hotel's proximity to Saint-Lazare station may serve you in good stead if you arrive in the city late at night, as well as providing a good base for exploring the neighbourhoods of the Opera, La Madeleine and the Grands Boulevards. The rooms overlooking the courtyard are darker but also quieter (although all the rooms are fitted with double glazing). They also all have a direct telephone line. Prices vary (doubles €53–77), according to whether they have a washbasin, shower or bathroom; in the latter two cases, air-conditioning is also available. The hotel is extremely well kept and the service is attentive; the degree of comfort is highly acceptable, without being exceptional, and the prices reflect this very fairly.

« ♠ Timhotel Opéra-Saint-Lazare

9 rue de Constantinople; M° Europe.
℗01.40.08.00.14 ℗01.40.08.01.44
⊛www.timhotel.fr

This hotel is spread over three buildings, linked by a maze of corridors. If possible, opt for a room on rue d'Édimbourg, as those on rue de Constantinople are noisier. Double rooms cost €90–165.

« ♠ New Orient Hôtel

16 rue de Constantinople; M° Villiers, Europe or Rome.
℗01.45.22.21.64 ℗01.42.93.83.23
⊛www.hotel-paris-orient.com
TV.

This is the kind of cosy, well-kept hotel that feels like a home from home, making it tempting to stay inside in winter. The rooms, many with a balcony, are all decorated with furniture picked up from country auction rooms and then restored by the delightful family that runs the place. The prices are very reasonable for the quality on offer: doubles cost €95–130. There is a car park close by.

⊛ |●| Chez Léon

5 rue de l'Isly; M° Saint-Lazare or Havre-Caumartin.
℡01.43.87.42.77
Closed *Sun; Aug.*

There's a "Relais Routier" sign outside – curious, because this place, right in the centre of town, is near a station, not a main road. But it is the real thing: waitresses in white aprons, transparent plastic table covers to protect the tablecloths, hole-in-the-ground loos and huge 1950s fridges in black and canary yellow. On the food front there are main courses like cottage pie with green salad, cod provençale and beef stew. The wine comes in quarter litre jugs. Starters cost around €4, main dishes €10; expect to pay €15. In case you're still puzzled, the only *Routier* in Paris earned its sign because the Federation of Road Hauliers is across the street.

⊛ |●| Le Bœuf sur le Toit

34 rue du Colisée; M° Franklin-D.-Roosevelt or Saint-Philippe-du-Roule.
℡01.53.93.65.55
Open *daily noon–3pm and 7pm–1am (midnight in July and Aug).*

It's not the best of the Flo brasseries, neither is it the cheapest, but its nostalgic air will seduce any Art Deco admirer. It's an age since Cocteau, Picasso, Poulenc, Milhaud and friends gathered in the *Bœuf*. This isn't the original 1940s establishment but it's been rebuilt a few streets away and pays creditable homage to the great inter-war brasserie. The engravings, drawings and sculptures hung on the wall also bear witness to the Années Folles. Typical – even predictable – brasserie menu with a few additions; seafood platters are the speciality. Lunch *formule* €23.50 and a set menu for €33. À la carte is pricey.

⊛ 🍴 |●| Le Boucléon

10 rue de Constantinople; M° Europe.
℡01.42.93.73.33
Closed *Sat; Sun; 3 weeks in Aug.* **Open** *noon–2.30pm and 7.30–10.15pm.*

An easy-going local restaurant named after one of the gates of Constantinople that offers a cuisine from the southwest. The décor is simple but colourful, conjuring up vague images of a mixture of rugby, Basque *pelota* and the bullfight. This complements perfectly the simple but tasty dishes on offer – *parmentier* of

black pudding, tender roast pork in beer – accompanied by a large choice of wines by the glass (€4–5). Starters cost €8–12; main meals €16–20; desserts around €8. Starters and desserts are all simple but good and well presented. Service is attentive and the fifteen tables are frequently all taken, sometimes by mysterious characters carrying violin cases. It's not the Cosa Nostra but more likely that these are people who frequent the many music workshops which abound in this area of the Paris Conservatoire. Opposite, at the *P'tit Bouco*, salads, sandwiches, *tapas* and toasted sandwiches. *Free coffee offered to our readers on presentation of this guide.*

⊛ |●| La Ferme des Mathurins

17 rue Vignon; M° Madeleine.
℡01.42.66.46.39
Closed *Sat; Sun; public holidays; Aug; 10 days at Christmas.* **Open** *lunch and dinner until 10pm.* **Disabled access.**

Georges Simenon, the creator of the fictional French detective Maigret, used to be a regular here in the 1930s – as the plaque tells you. The cooking is straight out of the Lyonnais area; *andouillette* with mustard, wine sausage, ham with cream sauce, salmon fillet with sorrel, succulent chunks of Charolais steak. Set menus €29 or €39; around €45 à la carte not including wine. They have a good selection of Burgundies – try the Irancy. The boss runs the kitchen and his wife is on duty in the dining room. Easy going welcome; most clients are, like Simenon, long-term regulars.

⊛ |●| Spoon, Food and Wine

14 rue de Marignan; M° Franklin-D.-Roosevelt.
℡01.40.76.34.44
Closed *Sat; Sun; end July to end Aug; Christmas to the New Year.* **Open** *noon–2pm and 7–11pm.*

The minimalist, sober interior creates a peaceful atmosphere; nothing is allowed to interrupt your studious enjoyment of the flavours produced by Alain Ducasse, one of the high priests of modern cooking. It's new-concept world cuisine: a fusion of flavours, spices and fragrances without a hint of fat. Diners can catch glimpses of the kitchen from the dining room, adding to the enjoyment and the spectacle, and the "classic" dishes which emerge have American, Thai and Italian influences – sea bream *ceviche à la grenobloise*. Expect to pay around €50 at lunch and €70 for dinner (not including wine). There's a selection of wines which is unique in Paris (just a shame they are quite so expensive). And don't forget the cheesecake for dessert.

9th arrondissement

ⓦ 𝕏 ⌂ Woodstock Hostel

48 rue Rodier; M° Anvers.
℡01.48.78.87.76 ℻01.48.78.01.63
ⓦwww.woodstock.fr
Open 8am–2am.

A cheap hotel for students, similar to a youth hostel. No frills but friendly. You'll pay €17–20 per person in a dormitory, €20–23 in a double room, including breakfast. The charming inner patio is a big bonus in summer, but it is closed at 9.45pm (the neighbours complained about the partying). Several (clean) showers can be found on the landing on each floor. The décor is dotted with rock references, and the reception is presided over by a masked cow called Lily. *10% discount on the room rate (in low season) offered to our readers on presentation of this guide.*

ⓦ 𝕏 ⌂ Hôtel Chopin**

46 passage Jouffroy; M° Grands Boulevards or Bourse.
℡01.47.70.58.10 ℻01.42.47.00.70
TV.

This jewel of a nineteenth-century town house is in a picturesque setting at the end of a narrow street – a quiet backwater round the corner from the Grands Boulevards. The handsome façade dates from 1850 and features elegant old woodwork. The rooms are quite pretty and the vista over the rooftops is reminiscent of an Impressionist painting – particularly if you're lucky enough to have a view of the setting sun. See if you can get a room on the fourth floor, as these are the brightest. It's best to avoid the ones looking onto the courtyard – all you'll see from these is a massive wall. Doubles with shower/wc or bath go for €74–86. The welcome is perfect and you'll need to reserve well in advance. *One free breakfast per room offered to our readers on presentation of this guide.*

ⓦ ⌂ Hôtel des Arts**

7 cité Bergère; M° Grands-Boulevards or Cadet.
℡01.42.46.73.30 ℻01.48.00.94.42

Disabled access. TV. Car park.

A two-star hotel with a pretty, pastel-pink façade in a lovely passageway. There's a confusing array of hotels to choose from around here – this one is the cheapest. It's far enough from the noise to be peaceful, and the rooms, which have been refurbished recently, are clean. Doubles are €82 with shower/wc or bath; breakfast €6. The stairway is decorated with old showbills – it is the *Hôtel des Arts*, after all. Why not engage the handsome grey parrot in the lobby in conversation? He talks and sings the *Marseillaise*.

ⓦ ⌂ Hôtel Langlois-Hôtel des Croisés**

63 rue Saint-Lazare; M° Trinité.
℡01.48.74.78.24 ℻01.49.95.04.43
ⓦwww.hotel-langlois.com
TV.

This fantastic two-star attracts a host of regulars, so you will have to book to have a chance of getting a room. It's in a marvellous location and looks wonderful: the superb reception area has old wood panelling and you just sink into the carpet. The wood-panelled lift with wrought iron gates takes you up to rooms which are sheer magic. They're absolutely huge and each has an individual style with period furniture and marble fireplaces; some have Art Deco wood panelling. Ask for one of the rooms on the fifth or sixth floor with an alcove which doubles as a little sitting room; some of the bathrooms are enormous. Doubles with shower/wc or bath €94–104, depending on the season and the facilities; breakfast costs €8.60. It's a super place with lots of charm, and offers exceptional value for money.

ⓦ 𝕏 ⌂ Hôtel de la Tour d'Auvergne***

10 rue de la Tour d'Auvergne; M° Cadet.
℡01.48.78.61.60 ℻01.49.95.99.00
ⓦwwwhoteltourdauvergne.com
TV.

A pretty three-star in a quiet street near the Sacré-Cœur. The spacious, elegantly decorated rooms are doubles with bath €100–145 for a double with bath; breakfast, €10, is very good. Ask to see more than one room as they do vary. There's a bar and 24-hour room service. The fifth floor is exclusively for non-smokers. *10% discount on the room rate offered to our readers on presentation of this guide.*

⊛ |●| ⅔ L'Auberge du Clou

30 av. Trudaine (on the corner of rue des Martyrs); M° Pigalle or Anvers.
℡01.48.78.22.48
Closed Mon. **Open** until 11.30pm.

You will be welcomed effusively in this charming rustic setting that recalls Normandy and its half-timbering. French classics reinterpreted by a chef with a passion for spices: artichoke hearts with warm foie gras; followed by a *magret* with Jakarta spices, rounded off by the Iranian dessert of saffron ice cream with pistachio pancake and orange supreme. Everything is prepared with finesse and subtlety, with a total respect for the ingredients. Two-dish lunchtime menu costs €15, dinner *formule* €18.50 and menu €24; or expect to pay a minimum of €30 à la carte. Excellent wine list, although a bit expensive for an average budget (although you do not have to drink a whole bottle). On Sundays you can bring your own bottle of wine. There's a terrace for dining outside on fine days. Credit cards not accepted. *Free house apéritif offered to our readers on presentation of this guide.*

⊛ |●| Chartier

7 rue du Faubourg-Montmartre; M° Grands-Boulevards.
℡01.47.70.86.29
Open 11.30am–3pm and 6–10pm.

You come in through a huge revolving door and find yourself in an immense turn-of-the-nineteenth-century restaurant with its original décor completely intact – in fact they've made it a listed building. Get there quickly before someone has the bright idea to refurbish it; there are only two or three places like this left and they're not half as wonderful as this one. It's always packed with regulars, local pensioners, students, poverty-stricken artists and tourists: there are 325 covers, 16 waiters and 1500 meals served a day. Expect to pay under €15 for a meal à la carte: starters €1.70, main dishes from €8, desserts from €2.10. The food is passable, though not always as hot as it could be.

⊛ ⅔ |●| Au Petit Riche

25 rue Le Peletier; M° Richelieu-Drouot.
℡01.47.70.68.68
Closed weekends (15 July–31 Aug). **Open** noon–2.15pm and 7pm–12.15am.

The restaurant was founded in 1854 – and with its labyrinth of intimate salons and Belle Époque décor, you might as well be dining in an Impressionist painting. They serve dishes like salad of Berry lentils, black pudding *parmentier*, rack of lamb, calf's head *en cocotte*. There's also a strong emphasis on seafood; the Oléron mussels are worth a particular mention. The cooking in this restaurant highlights the qualities of fine old recipes, and long may it continue; menus €22.50–28.50, excluding drinks; à la carte around €35. There are some private rooms on the first floor. The restaurant buzzes with atmosphere and is frequented by theatre-goers and businessmen and women. *Free house apéritif offered to our readers on presentation of this guide.*

⊛ |●| Velly

52 rue Lamartine; M° Cadet.
01.48.78.60.05
Closed weekends; 3 weeks in Aug. **Open** noon–2pm and 7.30–11pm (last orders 10.45pm).

A shoebox on two floors, with bistro décor and a kitchen open to view. Well-balanced menu that is being permanently renewed, according to what fresh fish is available and what is good at the market; it contains traditional dishes, but with occasional daring additions. Menus are €23 (lunchtime) and €31 (with starter, main course and dessert), and the wines from small vineyards priced from €16 are also served by the glass. Highly attentive service; it's often full, so book in good time.

⊛ |●| Restaurant Pétrelle

34 rue Pétrelle; M° Anvers or Poissonnière.
℡01.42.82.11.02
Closed Mon; Sat lunch; Sun; Aug; a week at Christmas. **Open** noon–1.30pm and 8–9.30pm.

Snug dining room with ten tables, with a maximum of six people each. Customers are treated with the utmost respect; once they're ensconced in their seats, nobody will try to rush them to finish quickly as there's only one serving per session. Similarly, only the freshest ingredients are used for the dishes. Set menu €25, without a drink; reckon on €45–50 à la carte. It's advisable to book. The owners have just opened a shop at no. 28, *Les Vivres,* which also serves *table d'hôte* lunches (around €15) and sells products selected or prepared by the chef. Here also, quality is the watchword.

◉ |◉| La Petite Sirène de Copenhague

47 rue Notre-Dame-de-Lorette; M° Saint-Georges.
☎01.45.26.66.66
Closed *Sat lunch; 3 weeks in Aug; Christmas to New Year.* **Open** *(Tues–Sat) noon–2.30pm and 7.30–11pm.*

This Danish restaurant offers specialities somewhat modified to appeal to Gallic gourmands, all served in a bright and pleasant bistro. It's worth making the effort to come because the food is delicious and the prices are appealing. Fish and smoked salmon are regulars on the menus, flavoured with anything from juniper to curry – known to the Danish since the seventeenth century; try the spiced herring. Menu of the day, chalked on the slate, is €26; there's a dinner version, including cheese, for €31; à la carte reckon on around €47. The young owner, Peter, will advise you on which wine to choose – he is also liable to offer you a shot of *aquavit*.

10th arrondissement

◉ 🛏 Hôtel Vicq d'Azir

21 rue Vicq d'Azir; M° Colonel-Fabien.
☎01.42.08.06.70 ☎01.42.08.06.80
✉vicqazir@club-internet.fr
Open *8am–10pm.*

A simple hotel with low-priced rooms which look out onto a charming interior courtyard planted with bushes. You have to pay when you check in: doubles €22–34 depending on facilities. Most of the rooms have been renovated, but due to space restrictions some have wc and shower (€2) down the hall. At these prices you can't expect luxury, but it's good value.

◉ 🛏 Hôtel Marclau

78 rue du Faubourg-Poissonnière; M° Poissonnière or Bonne-Nouvelle.
☎1.47.70.73.50 ☎01.44.83.95.89
Closed *Jan.*

Strategically situated close to the gares du Nord and de l'Est and the Grands Boulevards, this charming hotel is run by a delightful old couple, who until recently owned a tobacconist's-newspaper shop. The service is so attentive that you will feel as if you are visiting your grandparents; you will even find your pyjamas or nightdress neatly folded under your pillow when you return in the evening. Double

rooms cost €33 with wc, €36 with shower and €39 with shower/wc.

◉ 🛏 Hôtel du Nord – Le Pari Vélo

47 rue Albert-Thomas; M° République.
☎01.42.01.66.00 ☎01.42.01.92.10
🌐www.hoteldunordparisvelo.com
TV.

A wonderful little hotel nestling between the place de la République and the canal Saint-Martin. Twenty-odd rooms that all differ in size, colour scheme and inspiration. They are meticulously decorated and create a welcoming atmosphere, with red floor tiles and exposed beams and stonework, plus china knick-knacks, bright colours and house plants that thrive in the overhead light: the effect is one of a guest house rather than a traditional hotel. It is also good value for money: doubles €60–71 and family rooms €91. Breakfast (with home-made jam) is served in the basement, in a vaulted cellar. You can choose between a romantic table for two or a large, communal table – less intimate but more convivial. The owners are avid cycling enthusiasts and they have made bikes available to their guests so that they can explore Paris from a different viewpoint.

◉ 🚴 🛏 New Hôtel**

40 rue Saint-Quentin; M° Gare-du-Nord.
☎01.48.78.04.83 ☎01.40.82.91.22
🌐www.newhotelparis.com
TV. Pay car park.

Areas around train stations are notoriously grim, and it would be wrong to pretend that this place is anything other than a cheap hotel – but it does have the advantage of being quiet. The rooms are functional, and most of them have the facilities you'd expect from a two-star: multi-channel TV, hairdryer, air-conditioning and some have a balcony. The vaulted basement has been transformed into a cellar with three dining rooms, each decorated in medieval style with rough stone walls; here you can have a generous breakfast, €5. If you turn right when you leave the hotel, you'll come to a terrace at the end of a short street affording a rare view over Paris. Double rooms €70–98 with shower or bath. Internet access is available to guests. *One free breakfast per person offered to our readers on presentation of this guide.*

❀ ⌂ ☎ Nord-Est Hôtel**

12 rue des Petits-Hôtels; M° Gare-du-Nord or
Gare-de-l'Est.
☎01.47.70.07.18 🖷01.42.46.73.50
✉hotel.nord.est@wanadoo.fr
TV. Pay car park.

Well situated in a quiet street between the
gare du Nord and the gare de l'Est, near
the Saint-Quentin market, this hotel has
a delightful provincial charm – fitting in a
street with such a name. It's actually in a
little garden where you can relax in good
weather. There's a good deal of oak in the
sitting room, dining room and reception.
Small, clean, functional rooms that have
recently been refurbished; doubles €73
with shower/wc or bath. Book well in
advance. *10% reduction on the room rate (for
a minimum two-night stay Nov–Feb, except
during trade fairs and festivals) offered to our
readers on presentation of this guide.*

❀ |●| Restaurant de Bourgogne – Chez Maurice

26 rue des Vinaigriers; M° Jacques-
Bonsergent or Gare-de-l'Est.
☎01.46.07.07.91
Closed *Sat evening (except by prior booking);
Sun; public holidays.* **Open** *noon–2.15pm and
7–11.15pm.*

This little neighbourhood restaurant, not
far from the *Hôtel du Nord* and the romantic
Saint-Martin canal with its Venetian bridge,
hasn't changed for years; it's got a provincial
feel and still serves local people. Maurice,
the *patron* and a good friend of ours, and
his daughter, Céline, take great care of their
customers. Very inexpensive set menus at
€8 and €12 for lunch (€1 supplement in
the evening); dishes include beef *bourguignon*, steak with shallots and salmon *carpaccio*.
Round this off with a Côtes du Rhône (€3
for a quarter-litre) or a Cheverny.

❀ |●| Fils du Soleil

5 rue René-Boulanger (opposite no. 70); M°
République or Strasbourg-Saint-Denis.
☎01.44.52.01.21
Closed *Sat lunch; Sun; Mon; first 3 weeks in
Aug.* **Open** *noon–2pm and 7–11.15pm.*

Formerly a Mexican restaurant, now more
Colombian, like its friendly owner. It lives
up to its name's promise of sunny cooking.
The main courses (traditional chilli dishes
or delicious Colombian risotto) and exotic
desserts (delicious milk jam with figs in
syrup) are real talking points. The tequila

is also guaranteed to loosen tongues.
Lunchtime menu is €10.50; reckon on
around €23 à la carte. *Free digestif offered to
our readers on presentation of this guide.*

❀ |●| SAS Le Chansonnier

14 rue Eugène-Varlin; M° Château-Landon.
☎01.42.09.40.58
Closed *Sat lunchtime; Sun; during the week
of 15 Aug.* **Open** *noon–3pm and 7–11pm.*

The bistro is on the corner of rue Pierre-
Dupont, the songster in question, who
wrote a famous drinking song to toast the
world. Jean-Claude Lamouroux provides
the atmosphere for a truly enjoyable meal;
it's warm, the setting is well preserved, the
service efficient and the dishes traditional
– roast free-range chicken, *confit* of pork
cheek, fillet of fish roasted with Provençal
herbs. All perfectly prepared and served
with jugs of Bergerac. There's a lunch
formule at €10.50, and menus at €22 and
€23.50. Enough to get you up on the
table to raise your glass for a toast. This is a
really good place.

❀ |●| ❀ La Marine

55 bis quai de Valmy; M° Jacques-
Bonsergent or République.
☎01.42.39.69.81
Closed *Sun; 1 Jan.* **Open** *8.30am–2am.*
Service *noon–3pm and 8–11.45pm.*

This restaurant, which is run by three brothers, has a wonderful atmosphere, like a kind
of East Parisian *Flore* with an extra dash of
cocky humour. It is often packed, and its
popularity can be gauged by the tables and
chairs – somewhat the worse for wear – and
the mouldings on the ceiling – blackened
by cigarette smoke. Enticing bistro cooking:
millefeuille of mullet, rolled larded salmon
with lentils. Lunchtime menu €11; reckon
on around €27 for dinner, excluding drinks.
They offer a limited selection of good wines
in carafes and some home-made desserts to
round off the meal. Friendly and efficient
service. *Free coffee offered to our readers on
presentation of this guide.*

❀ |●| La Vigne Saint-Laurent

2 rue Saint-Laurent; M° Gare-de-l'Est.
☎01.42.05.98.20
Closed *Sat; Sun; 3 weeks in Aug; Christmas
to New Year.* **Open** *noon–2.30pm and
7–10.30pm.*

If you've got a train to catch or you're
seeing someone off, don't just dive into the

nearest brasserie – take a couple of minutes to find this pleasant wine bar instead. Inside there's a long, narrow room with a beautiful spiral staircase. At the far end, the pair of polite chaps with fine moustaches who run the place prepare delicious dishes (a different region of France is represented each day) with great care: rabbit with house *tapenade*, calf's head *sauce ravigote*, beef stewed in red wine. The *menu-assiette*, €13.50, gets you a platter of two types of sausage, a green salad, two cheeses and a glass of wine; a meal will cost about €20 à la carte. If you just want a snack, try a plate of charcuterie or some perfectly ripened cheeses (both €9.50). They offer a good selection of wines by the glass, jug or bottle (about €16.50) – Saint-Nicolas-de-Bourgueil, Madiran. And to follow up, what could be better than a home-made dessert. If you want a liqueur, you could try the *mirabelle de Lorraine* or a glass of Savoie Marc brandy.

⊚ |●| Le Parmentier

12 rue Arthur-Groussier; M° Goncourt.
☎01.42.40.74.75
Open for lunch and dinner until 11pm.
Closed Sat lunch; Sun; Aug.

A modest but highly successful restaurant a stone's throw from the Sainte-Marthe neighbourhood. Its blue façade and colourful mosaics, its small dining room with shiny yellow walls, its cheerful, attentive service and its fresh gourmet food add up to a winning combination. The menus are chalked up on the blackboard: *hachis parmentier* (home-made, appropriately enough), poached salmon with Maussane olive oil (cooked just as it should be, a little pink in the centre), an orange crêpe for dessert. Weekday lunchtime *formule* €15; dinner menu €25 and another menu €28, including wine and coffee. If you are not very hungry, you can pick isolated dishes from the menu on an à la carte basis.

⊚ |●| 🍴 Le Réveil du Xe

35 rue du Château-d'Eau; M° Château-d'Eau or République.
☎01.42.41.77.59
Closed Sun; public holidays; Sat in Aug.
Open 7.15am–9pm (service noon–3pm, plus Thurs evening 7–9.30pm).

Simple but pleasant and authentic bistro run by wine connoisseurs who will give you a warm welcome and some tasty traditional food: tripoux, *pounti*, ox cheek *à l'auvergnate* with steamed potatoes, *aligot-sausage* (lunch on the first Tues and dinner on first Thurs of each month), succulent charcuterie and creamy cheeses from Auvergne. Lunchtime dishes of the day cost around €9–13; à la carte €18–20. Only snacks in the evening (except Thurs) and a wonderful selection of reasonably priced wines. *Free house apéritif or coffee offered to our readers on presentation of this guide.*

⊚ |●| 🍴 Café Panique

12 rue des Messageries; M° Poissonnière.
☎01.47.70.06.84
Closed weekends; public holidays; Aug.
Open noon–2.30pm and 7.30–10pm.

A sober, restful setting with walls decorated with contemporary paintings that are regularly changed. The food combines fresh ingredients and subtle, delicious flavours, so just follow your fancy when you order: baked tail of monkfish with artichokes, caramelized sweet and sour veal breast and grapefruit mousse with chocolate. There is one set menu for dinner (starter, main course and dessert, €29) and a lighter version at lunchtime (main course, glass of wine and coffee, €19); reckon on €31 à la carte. As for the wine, follow the owner's advice, as she is certain to make a good choice. *Free house apéritif offered to our readers on presentation of this guide.*

⊚ 🍴 |●| Flo

7 cour des Petites-Écuries; M° Château-d'Eau.
☎01.47.70.13.59
Open daily noon–3pm and 7pm–1am. **High chairs available.**

This is the place to go for *choucroute*. Herr Floederer's old brasserie dates from 1886 and is sparkling. Sarah Bernhardt used to have her meals delivered from here when she was at the Renaissance – others followed suit. Superb décor with stained-glass windows separating the rooms, richly decorated ceilings, leather benches, brass hatstands and period lighting. As well as the *choucroute*, you can enjoy platters of shellfish and seafood, warm foie gras with cherries. Given the wonderful surroundings, prices are reasonable: menus from €22.90 to €32.90; dish of the day €15, or around €40 à la carte. The place is always buzzing with people, young and not-so-young. *Free house apéritif, fruit juice or soft drink offered to our readers on presentation of this guide.*

≪ |●| Julien

16 rue du Faubourg-Saint-Denis; M°
Strasbourg-Saint-Denis.
℡01.47.70.12.06
Open *noon–3pm and 7pm–1am.* **Disabled access. High chairs and games available.**

Another restaurant – one of the oldest in Paris – which has been given a makeover by the talented Monsieur Bücher. The same ingredients continue to work their magic: dazzling Art Nouveau interior, efficient service and a reasonable bill. There's also a menu at €23 (served at lunchtime and after 10pm, but not Sun) and another, served in the evening, at €33. You can expect to pay around €40 for a meal à la carte. It's very popular with tourists.

≪ |●| Chez Michel

10 rue de Belzunce; M° Gare-du-Nord.
℡01.44.53.06.20
Closed *Mon lunchtime; weekends; Aug.*
Open *noon–2pm and 7pm–midnight.*
Disabled access.

The countless people who choose to stay in one of the many hotels near the station will be delighted to know that they can now eat in the area as well. The supreme skill of the Breton chef draws attention to this place, which is in a part of the city where greasy spoons abound. The terrine of *andouille* with peppercorns and short-bread biscuits is out of this world, while the guineafowl ravioli with a sauce of ceps and crushed walnuts is so incredibly good that you'll have to loosen your belt to make room for *kig ha farz* (pig's cheeks with country bacon) or Breton lobster with a little sprinkling of parmesan cheese. Great desserts include warm *kouign aman* (traditional Breton yeast cake) – worth every calorie. Reckon on paying in the region of €30 à la carte.

11th arrondissement

≪ 🛏 Hôtel Notre-Dame**

51 rue de Malte; M° République or
Oberkampf.
℡01.47.00.78.76 ℻01.43.55.32.31
✉hotel-notredame@wanadoo.com
TV.

A well-run two-star hotel in a good location. Everything is grey, down to the business cards and the cat. The tastefully redecorated rooms have direct-dial phones, clock-radios and colour TV. The ones on the street are brighter. Doubles are €37–66.50, according to season and facilities. It's best to book. Cheques are not accepted.

≪ 🍴 🛏 Hôtel Mondia**

22 rue du Grand-Prieuré; M° République or
Oberkampf.
℡01.47.00.93.44 ℻01.43.38.66.14
🖥www.hotel-mondia.com
TV.

This well-run hotel in a quiet little street is a good base if you're doing the sights on foot. The welcome is as pleasant as the décor: mouldings on the ceilings, stained-glass effects especially in the break-fast room. The comfortable rooms have shower or bath, hairdryer, safe and direct telephone – some even have marble fire-places and the three on the top floor have sloping ceilings. Doubles cost €56–67, according to season; prices may be nego-tiable if you're planning a long stay, except during trade fairs and festivals. Breakfast €5. *10% discount on the room rate (excluding trade fairs and festivals) offered to our readers on presentation of this guide.*

≪ 🍴 🛏 Hôtel Beauséjour**

71 av. Parmentier; M° Parmentier or
Oberkampf.
℡01.47.00.38.16 ℻01.43.55.47.89
TV. Disabled access.

A hotel with 31 rooms on six floors – with a lift. They are small, but well equipped with bath or shower, double glazing, TV and direct telephone, and cost €60–78, some sleeping three or four. Breakfast costs €5. The little bar in the reception area is open 24 hours a day, and they offer room service. The welcome is not always up to scratch. *10% discount on the room rate offered to our readers on presentation of this guide.*

≪ 🍴 🛏 Hôtel Daval**

21 rue Daval; M° Bastille.
℡01.47.00.51.23 ℻01.40.21.80.26
✉hoteldaval@wanadoo.fr
TV.

A nice two-star in the heart of the lively Bastille neighbourhood, near the bars of rue de Lappe and rue de la Roquette. It has modern décor and facilities – TV, double glazing, air-conditioning and mini-safe. The rooms and the bathrooms are on the small side; ask for one overlooking the courtyard or on the upper floors to avoid the racket that goes on in this area during the weekend. Doubles with shower are €69; better than average breakfast €8. *One free breakfast per room offered to our readers on presentation of this guide.*

⟪⟪ 🏠 Hôtel Beaumarchais***

3 rue Oberkampf; M° Filles du Calvaire or Oberkampf.
☎01.53.36.86.86 ☎01.43.38.32.86
🌐www.hotelbeaumarchais.com
TV.

An ideal situation in a lively street full of bars, close to the Bastille, the République and the Marais. It's a modern hotel, decorated in bright sunshine colours and with slicked-up bathrooms. Very comfortable, spacious double rooms cost €110 with en-suite shower/wc or bath.

ⓔ 🎋 |●| Au P'tit Cahoua

24 rue des Taillandiers; M° Bastille.
☎01.43.00.20.42
Closed *24 and 25 Dec.* **Open** *noon–3.30pm and 7.30–11pm (11.30pm at weekends).*

Philippe Journoud has created a corner of France which is forever Morocco: ceramic tables, wrought iron, pottery, Berber hangings from the ceiling and on the walls, Arab rhythms in the background. Food-wise you'll find tangy *tajines* and fluffy, spicy couscous; make sure you try the *kemias*, a selection of starters or main dishes, or the *pastilla*. In the week, there's a lunch formule for €10; à la carte a meal will cost about €23. The welcome is warm and relaxed – very Mediterranean. There's another restaurant at 39, bd. Saint-Marcel, in the 13th *arrondissement*, ☎01.47.07.24.42; M° Gobelins or Saint-Marcel. *Free house apéritif offered to our readers on presentation of this guide.*

ⓔ |●| Paris Main d'Or

133 rue du Faubourg-Saint-Antoine; M° Ledru-Rollin.
☎01.44.68.04.68
Closed *Sun.* **Open** *noon–2.30pm and 3–7.30pm.*

This pleasant, recently expanded restaurant, attractively designed by an Argentinian architect-decorator, probably serves the most authentic Corsican food in Paris: *brocciu* omelette, roast kid and cod with chard and raisins, as well as carefully selected charcuterie, cheese and wine brought directly from the island. All this comes out only at night, however – at lunch, it's packed with customers eating mainland fare (although there are some Corsican snacks available). Lunchtime menu €11; reckon on €25–30 for dinner.

ⓔ |●| Au Vieux Chêne

7 rue du Dahomey; M° Faidherbe-Chaligny.
☎01.43.73.23.89
Closed *Sat lunch; Sun.* **Open** *for lunch and dinner until 10pm (11pm Sat).*

This little side-street almost passes unnoticed, but it hides this charming bistro, which is a relic from the days when carpentry was the lifeblood of this area. Amusing advertising signs and toys from the 1950s liven up the well-worn dining room (which even boasts three cast-iron pillars that are classified as a historic monument). The excellent cooking uses seasonal produce and is accompanied by good wines: there's a lunchtime menu for €13, or reckon on €30 for a meal à la carte. Fine cuisine, warm atmosphere and attentive welcome all combine to make this a good place. It's advisable to book in advance for the evening.

ⓔ |●| Chez Ramulaud

269 rue du Faubourg-Saint-Antoine; M° Faidherbe-Chaligny or Nation.
☎01.43.72.23.29
Closed *Sat lunch; a week in spring; a week at Christmas.* **Open** *noon–2.30pm and 8–11pm; Sunday brunch noon–6pm.*

Hearty, copious and often innovative meals in a pretty, gleaming bistro setting (with a terrace for fine days). Classic dishes such as terrine and grilled *andouillette* are complemented by *ballotin* of smoked trout, haddock *mousse* and spicy loin of lamb *en croûte*. Lunchtime dish of the day is €9.50, *formules* €13 and €15, depending on the number of dishes; dinner menu €28; Sunday brunch €19. Reckon on €35 per person à la carte (but be careful, your bill can easily get out of hand, although you're bound to get your money's worth). This is first and foremost a bistro, however, so wine takes pride of place, with an emphasis on value for money (bottles from €18–25). So, Bordeaux are out of the question and there are only a few Burgundies, but plenty of little-known wines from Languedoc, Southwest France, the Rhône and the Loire. No half-bottles, but wine is sold by the glass. Booking is highly advisable; it fills up even on Mondays.

ÎLE-DE-FRANCE

⑨ |●| ⅍ Les Domaines qui montent

136 bd. Voltaire; M° Voltaire.
℗01.43.56.89.15
Closed *Sun; 7–22 Aug.* **Open** *noon–2pm.*

You think you're entering a wine cellar until, among the racks of bottles, you notice a few tables with reserved signs on them and a few more out on the terrace. The smiling owners, who are wine experts, have transformed this old hardware shop into one of the few *tables d'hôte* in the capital. They get deliveries of fresh produce daily and your meal will be accompanied by a bottle from the choice of 300 different wines or a glass from one of the eleven wine fountains. The huge choice of dishes ranges from a plate of sausage to accompany your *apéritif* to savoury tarts, big salads, soups, dishes of the day, farmhouse cheeses and simple, tasty desserts. There's a *formule* at €13. There are a few surprises, too, like the kiwi juice made in Brittany, the organic beer, or the *bernache* from Touraine. The latter, a sugary drink that's somewhere between cider and wine, is perfect with the homemade *tapenade*. It's best to book, especially on Saturdays. There's another restaurant in the 17th *arrondissement. Free house apéritif or coffee offered to our readers on presentation of this guide.*

⑨ |●| La Vache Acrobate

77 rue Amelot; M° Saint-Sébastien-Froissart or Chemin-Vert.
℗01.47.00.49.42
Closed *Sat lunch; Sun.* **Open** *noon–3pm and 7–11pm.*

A lively little café where the regulars know they'll enjoy warm, inventive cooking: salad of spinach and marinated chicken with raisins, grilled pork in honey and rosemary, steak tartare. Lunch *formule* costs €13.50; à la carte expect to pay €20 for a main meal and dessert. Elegant, hearty dishes – a starter here is equivalent to a main meal. It's just a shame that the surroundings don't quite match the quality of the cooking (small tables jammed in close together); fine for two or three but not for a bigger party. There's a good wine list with particular emphasis on wines from vineyards in the Southwest. They're all the same price: by the glass, quarter litre or by the bottle. And the welcome is very friendly, too.

⑨ ⅍ |●| Cefalù

43 av. Philippe-August; 10 min from Père-Lachaise and 5 min from place de la Nation; M° Nation.
℗01.43.71.29.34
Closed *Sat lunchtime; Sun; 4 weeks in Aug.* **Open** *noon–2pm and 7.30–10pm.*

Mr Cala comes from Mussomeli, famous for its impregnable fortress. His skill does his homeland proud, and his Sicilian restaurant is one of the best places to eat Italian food in Paris: Sicilian antipasti, sole with aubergine caviar, swordfish carpaccio, *spaghetti à l'orange.* Try the *cannolo,* a Sicilian dessert traditionally served on Sunday, something like a brandy snap filled with fresh ricotta, candied fruit and chocolate; it's usually accompanied by a glass of Marsala. There's a €14.50 *formule* at weekday lunchtimes and a *menu dégustation* offering three courses and dessert for €30; reckon on around €33.50 for a meal à la carte. Reservations are advised for the evenings (even during the week). *Free digestif offered to our readers on presentation of this guide.*

⑨ ⅍ |●| L'Ami Pierre

5 rue de la Main-d'Or; M° Ledru-Rollin.
℗01.47.00.17.35
Closed *Sun; Mon; 19 July–19 Aug.* **Open** *until 2am (last orders midnight).* **Disabled access.**

Marie-Jo's been in the Bastille area for years; she's very easy-going and treats her clients like friends. The atmosphere can get a bit heated some evenings if the rugby fans tangle with the regulars – arty types like film-makers and designers. You can have a glass or two of Pouilly, Cahors or Quincy – you only pay for what you drink. Dish of the day might be *magret de canard* or *andouillette.* Portions are substantial – the speedy service is ideal for a quick lunch. There's no set menu; a meal will cost you around €15 à la carte without drinks. *Free digestif after a meal offered to our readers on presentation of this guide.*

⑨ |●| Le Villaret

13 rue Ternaux; M° Parmentier.
℗01.43.57.89.76
Closed *Sun; 10 days in April; Aug; 10 days at Christmas/New Year.* **Open** *noon–2pm and 7.30–11.30pm (1am Fri and Sat).*

Joël and the young chef Olivier Gaslain are in charge. Olivier goes to Rungis market for the produce and devises his menus according to what he selects. The prices haven't changed much over the years and the wide-ranging wine list has great vintages (from all over the world) at reasonable rates. Starters include dishes such as red mullet bisque or scallops and thyme *en papillote* (baked in a paper sack); for a main course try calf's liver in Banyuls vinegar. Food is served on beautiful square plates – a bell rings to announce that a dish is ready – in simple surroundings with wooden beams and stone walls. This is one of the best restaurants in Paris for a business meal or supper between friends. Lunch menus at €20 and €25, include main meal and either starter or dessert. In the evening there's a *menu dégustation* for €46.

◎ ❙◉❙ L'Homme Bleu

55 bis rue Jean-Pierre-Timbaud; M°
Couronnes or Parmentier.
℡ 01.48.07.05.63
Closed *Sun; Aug.* **Open** *5pm–2am (last orders 1am).*

Set apart from the thronging couscous joints of the Bastille, Ali and his team have been delighting their guests for over sixteen years in a replica of a Tuareg tent pitched in the desert. The food on offer comprises not only couscous but also *kefta*, delicious tajines and stuffed *brik* pastries, all prepared in front of your eyes at the fireplace in the corner. You can only eat à la carte – reckon on around €23 for a meal.

◎ ❙◉❙ ⅄ Les Amognes

243 rue du Faubourg-Saint-Antoine; M°
Faidherbe-Chaligny.
℡ 01.43.72.73.05
Closed *Sat lunchtime; Sun; Mon lunchtime (open Mon evening by prior booking); a fortnight in Feb; 3 weeks in Aug.* **Open** *noon–2pm and 8–11pm.* **Disabled access.**

The new owner, Jean Louis Thuillier, who has learnt his trade at *Robuchon,* offers seasonal dishes cooked for just the right amount of time, and accompanied by daring sauces: roast monkfish with vanilla and rice flavoured with turmeric, cod steak roast on a banana leaf with coconut milk. There's a *menu-carte* at €33; at lunchtime you can choose a dish from the menu for €19. The wine list offers some great finds – both for the palate and the pocket. Word of mouth means that this is fast becoming a restaurant not to be missed in the 11th

arrondissement. *Free coffee offered to our readers on presentation of this guide.*

12th arrondissement

◎ ❢ Hôtel des Trois Gares**

1 rue Jules-César; M° Gare-de-Lyon or
Bastille.
℡ 01.43.43.01.70 ℻ 01.43.41.36.58
✉ h3g@tiscali.fr
TV.

This is a well-located two-star in a quiet street between the Gare de Lyon, the Gare d'Austerlitz and Bastille-Plaisance. The façade is smart and the reception is decidedly modern, as are the functional rooms. Doubles cost €55 with shower, €64–68 with shower/wc or bath, TV and direct dial telephone. This welcoming hotel is popular with businessmen.

◎ ❢ Nouvel Hôtel**

24 av. du Bel Air; right next to the place de la
Nation; M° and RER A Nation.
℡ 01.43.43.01.81 ℻ 01.43.44.64.13
🌐 www.nouvel-hotel-paris.com
TV.

This establishment is a stone's throw from place de la Nation where you can hook up with any number of buses, the Métro or the RER. The street couldn't be quieter and all the rooms have double glazing and are decorated in Laura Ashley style. It's as clean as a whistle, and most rooms overlook a delightful garden where you can sit and relax in the shade of a tree; doubles with shower €73, €83 with bath. Room no. 109 looks directly over the garden and is especially nice. The delightful welcome and service only add to the attraction of this hotel which is one of our favourites in Paris. You might also be interested to know that grapes from the vines in the garden are harvested and produce a few bottles of wine, thus keeping alive an old tradition.

◎ ❢ ⅄ Hôtel Claret***

44 bd. de Bercy; M° Bercy.
℡ 01.46.28.41.31
℻ 01.49.28.09.29
🌐 www.hotel-claret.com
TV. Pay car park.

This unusual but elegant building, formerly a post house, stands out from its concrete surroundings. Now transformed into a charming three-star hotel, it reconciles modern comfort and traditional trappings.

The 52 cosy rooms are decorated with painted furniture, thick gingham bedspreads and stained half-timbering to create a vaguely rural feel (evoking the neighbourhood's past as an agricultural and wine-growing area). Rooms on the fourth floor have air-conditioning. If you want some real greenery, the Bercy gardens are close by, while the no. 14 bus will take you to Châtelet in four minutes and the Opéra in eight minutes – so you are in a central location. Double rooms are €77–135, according to the degree of luxury. Logis de France. *10% discount on the price of a room (subject to availability) offered to our readers on presentation of this guide.*

ⓐ ♨ Hôtel Marceau**

13 rue Jules-César; M° Gare-de-Lyon or Bastille.
☎01.43.43.11.65 ⓕ01.43.41.67.70
ⓦwww.hotel-marceau.com
TV. Pay car park.

It's anyone's guess as to whether General Marceau really slept here. He led the troops in who in 1793 put down the insurrections in the Vendée against the revolutionary government. But the fact that the hotel and the general share a name gives the proprietor a good excuse to display in reception a page in the general's handwriting that he bought at auction. The rooms aren't bad, and some are quite nicely decorated with coordinating fabric, wall lights and wood panelling; those overlooking the road are more spacious. Doubles cost €80–95 with shower or bath; breakfast €8. This is a charming hotel with old faded wallpaper and wonderful old lift.

ⓐ ♨ 🍴 Le Relais de Paris Lyon Bastille**

35 rue de Cîteaux; M° Faidherbe-Chaligny or Reuilly-Diderot.
☎01.43.07.77.28 ⓕ01.43.46.67.45
ⓔLyon.Bastille@Lesrelaisdeparis.fr
Open *all year round.* **TV.**

A two-star hotel near the Faubourg Saint-Antoine that is a awash with colours. Choose between pink, blue, green or beige for your room; whatever the colour, it will be modern and comfortable, with a mini-bar and a direct phone line. Basically, it's run on classic lines, however, and it is popular with sales reps who are passing through for a trade fair. Double rooms go for €82–93, with shower or bath and wc;

rooms for families €112–132 (extremely good value). Breakfast buffet €7.50, is served in a superb vaulted cellar. *10% discount on a room offered to our readers on presentation of this guide.*

ⓐ 🍴 🍴 Au Pays de Vannes

34 bis rue de Wattignies; M° Michel-Bizot.
☎01.43.07.87.42
Closed *evenings; Sun; public holidays; Aug.*
Open *11.45am–2.45pm.*

A good local eatery with a large Breton flag on the wall – the proprietors are proud of their roots. With the €10.30 menu (big choice of dishes and wine included) you'll get a good simple traditional French meal and the best value for money in the *arrondissement*. There's another menu at €13.80, also including wine. Whole families turn up on Saturday lunchtime (from Sept to March) for a feast of seafood (oysters, grey and pink shrimps and half a crab) – €19.50 for a platter, including a quarter litre of Valencay white wine. All this, plus warm welcome and good service.

ⓐ 🍴 Comme Cochons

135 rue de Charenton; M° Reuilly-Diderot.
☎01.43.42.43.36
Closed *Sun; Mon.* **Open** *lunch and dinner until 11pm.*

A newish place that will blow you away first with its look – a modern bistro with a series of interesting paintings on the wall and topiary out front. There's also the remarkably priced lunch *formule* which, for €13, lists starter, main course, dessert and drink. There's also another menu for €15. The bill doubles in the evening but at no detriment to the pleasure; it's à la carte only and a meal will cost €23–28. Classic and traditional dishes chalked on the board are prepared with the freshest seasonal ingredients: veal *piccata*, rumpsteak with chestnut purée, fillet of pike perch with stewed aubergines. Everything is tasty, generously served and attractively presented. They also offer a good wine list so it's no surprise that it's always full. It's first-come first-served at lunchtime, but you'd do well to book in the evening.

ⓐ 🍴 L'Alchimiste

181 rue de Charenton; M° Montgallet.
☎01.43.47.10.38
Service *noon–2pm and 7.30–10pm Mon–Sat.*

This neighbourhood bistro surrounded by computer wholesalers is one of a dying breed. Its old-fashioned façade heralds the treats in store within: meticulously maintained décor with exquisite details, retro lamps, wooden chairs – and classic dishes, originally reinterpreted with a Mediterranean touch. There's a weekday lunchtime menu for €13; dinner à la carte, for around €30, excluding drinks. Depending on the season, you can expect to find veal *piccata*, rump steak and chestnut purée (authentic and home-made, with pieces of chestnut in it) or fillet of pike perch and *compotée* of aubergines. The appeal of the cooking is enhanced by the garnishes and astute combinations of ingredients, as well as the thoughtfully compiled wine list. The crowning glory is the impeccable and cheerful service. Booking is advisable.

◎ |●| Si Señor!

9 rue Antoine-Vollon; M° Ledru-Rollin.
☏01.43.47.18.01
Bar closed in the afternoon. **Closed** *Sun; Mon; Aug.* **Open** *noon–2.30pm and 7.30–11pm.*

This Spanish restaurant, run by a group of French and Spanish friends, has nothing to do with those Parisian tapas bars – not least because it isn't a bar. This is honest, robust cooking that is very delicious: great Spanish omelettes and *gambas* grilled *a la plancha* and astonishingly light deep-fried *calamares*. Different specialities from remote regions appear on the menus on a regular basis and there are good desserts. Menus €13.90 at lunchtime, and €23 in the evening; reckon on €26 à la carte. They have a few tables on the terrace.

◎ ⚔ |●| Cappadoce

12 rue de Capri; M° Michel-Bizot or Daumesnil.
☏01.43.46.17.20
Closed *Sat lunchtime; Sun; Aug.* **Open** *noon–2.30pm and 7–11.30pm.*

Turkish hospitality and kindness are the hallmarks of this establishment and, together with the elaborate cooking, they have helped spread its reputation far beyond the neighbourhood. Small (but not cramped), intricate dining room with soft lighting. The cheese roll and the aubergine caviar are exquisite, while the *pides* (Turkish pizzas), the grilled chicken with aubergines and yoghurt, the stuffed leg of lamb with mushrooms and spices and the grills and kebabs will give your tastebuds a real treat. It's obvious why the restaurant is a success and it's best to book for dinner. They serve three well-thought-out menus (one vegetarian, one diet, and one gourmet) in the range €14–23. Don't turn down the home-made desserts – the pumpkin in syrup is extraordinary, a bit like quince paste. Delightful, attentive service. *Free digestif offered to our readers on presentation of this guide.*

◎ ⚔ |●| Les Zygomates

7 rue de Capri; M° Michel-Bizot or Daumesnil.
☏01.40.19.93.04
Closed *Sun; Mon; Aug.* **Open** *noon–2pm and 7.30–10.45pm.*

Virtually nothing has changed here since the turn of the twentieth century – the *trompe l'œil* décor, the varnished wood and the marble were all here when this was a butcher's shop. Best of all, the prices are still reasonable – there's a set lunch menu for €14, and others at €22 and €27 (with starter and main course, or main course and dessert). Quite complex dishes include salad of foie gras with pinenuts, pig's tail stuffed with morels, bitter chocolate fondant with a sorbet. It's best to book as it's well known. *Free coffee offered to our readers on presentation of this guide.*

◎ |●| Square Trousseau

1 rue Antoine-Vollon; M° Ledru-Rollin.
☏01.43.43.06.00
Closed *Sun; Mon.* **Open** *lunch and dinner until 11.30pm.*

Two layers of curtains – lace and red velvet – shield you from prying eyes as you dine. In style and atmosphere the restaurant resembles an elegant 1900s bistro: there's a superb antique bar, a mosaic tiled floor, red leather benches and mouldings on the ceiling. The day's specials are chalked up on big blackboards and the €19 *formule* comprises starter and main course, or main course and dessert. There's also a menu at €20 (served lunchtimes only). The à la carte dishes change weekly; reckon on paying around €35, without drinks. Presentation is pretty and the wine list has been well researched. A very good restaurant with lots of regulars, though it's not exactly cheap; reservations are highly recommended. In summer the terrace is very popular. They've opened a shop next door selling a selection of home-made produce.

◉ |◉| ⅔ À La Biche au Bois

45 av. Ledru-Rollin; M° Gare-de-Lyon.
☎01.43.43.34.38
Closed *weekends; Mon lunch; 25 July–25 Aug; 23 Dec–2 Jan.* **Open** *noon–2.30pm and 7–11pm.* **Disabled access.**

Situated close to the gare de Lyon, this restaurant is a favourite with travellers. The décor and tightly packed tables might not appeal to lovers, but the menu is a pure delight. It gives good value on its €22.30 set menu, which lists dishes such as wild duck with fruits of the forest, pheasant casserole with *foie gras*, not forgetting the *coq au vin* with its delicious sauce that is served all year round. The home-made pastries, selection of mature cheeses, and reasonably priced wines are a bonus. All in all, this is an excellent restaurant where you can eat well for under €26. It's a good idea to reserve. *Free coffee offered to our readers on presentation of this guide.*

13th arrondissement

◉ ⬛ Hôtel Tolbiac

122 rue Tolbiac; M° Tolbiac or Place-d'Italie.
☎01.44.24.25.54 ☎01.45.85.43.47
🌐www.hotel-tolbiac.com
TV.

An enormous hotel with 47 rooms just five minutes from place d'Italie – it's welcoming and good news for those on a small budget. There's a pleasant reception and the rooms are clean; nos. 19, 29, 39 and 49 are the largest and sunniest. Doubles with basin are €32, €39 with shower/wc. In good weather, breakfast (€6) is served in a small, flower-filled courtyard. Rue de Tolbiac is quite noisy but a number of the rooms are fitted with double glazing. Free Internet access is available to guests in the afternoon. Credit cards are not accepted.

◉ ⬛ Hôtel Coypel**

2 rue Coypel; M° Place-d'Italie.
☎01.43.31.18.08 ☎01.47.07.27.45
Open *all year round.* **TV.**

The *Coypel*, conveniently situated close to place d'Italie, is the kind of hotel that's

becoming increasingly hard to find. The rooms may lack imagination but they are well kept and offer all the necessary comfort, including double glazing. All the (recently refurbished) bathrooms are impeccable. Choose a room on the top floor, to take advantage of the view. Double rooms with shower/wc €50–60 depending on the size. Breakfast costs €5 (it's best to have it in your room as the breakfast room is minute).

◉ ⅔ ⬛ Résidence Les Gobelins**

9 rue des Gobelins; M° Gobelins; buses 27, 47, 83, 91.
☎01.47.07.26.90 ☎01.43.31.44.05
🌐www.hotelgobelins.com
Open *all year round.* **TV.**

The rue des Gobelins follows the same route it did in the Middle Ages. The château that belonged to Blanche of Castile, wife of Louis VIII and mother of Louis IX, is just round the corner. The hotel is peaceful and great value for money. Lovely double rooms €75 with shower/wc or bath; breakfast €7. The bathrooms are impeccably clean. Ask for room no. 32, 42, 52 or 62 – they all enjoy a lovely view of the *château de la Reine Blanche*. You can sit outside in the little garden on warm evenings. *10% discount on the room rate for a minimum stay of two nights offered to our readers on presentation of this guide.*

◉ ⅔ ⬛ Résidence Hôtelière Le Vert Galant***

41–43 rue Croulebarbe; M° Gobelins or Corvisart.
☎01.44.08.83.50 ☎01.44.08.83.69
Restaurant closed *Sun; Mon.* **Disabled access. TV. Pay car park.**

A corner of the Basque country in the middle of the 13th *arrondissement*, just across from the Gobelins gardens. It's next to the Auberge Etchegorry restaurant, and belongs to the same people. It's set back from the road with a garden and lawn so it's quiet and has a certain charm. Superb, comfortable rooms – doubles €87 with shower, €90 with bath, and studios with kitchenette for €100. Delightful buffet breakfast (€7) served in a room overlooking the garden; private parking is available to guests for a charge of €10. *Free breakfast (for stays of more than three consecutive nights) offered to our readers on presentation of this guide.*

◄◄ ⅔ ♜ Hôtel La Manufacture**

8 rue Philippe-de-Champaigne; M° Pl. d'Italie.
☎01.43.35.45.25 ⊕01.43.35.45.40
⊛www.hotel-la-manufacture.com
TV. Cots available.

A new and elegant, three-star hotel, just next to the local town hall and the old Gobelins tapestry workshop. It's managed by a trio of women who run things like clockwork. The décor is in browns and beiges with splashes of red. The beautiful entrance hall has a wooden floor and a corner bar where you can have a drink next to the open fire in winter. Rooms are not huge but they're air-conditioned and go for €99–139 for a double with shower/wc or bath, according to which floor they are on and the season. It's popular with businessmen and women, of course, but they're not alone in wanting to stay here. Delicious French breakfast (€10) will set you up for the day. *One free breakfast per person offered to our readers on presentation of this guide.*

◉ |◉| Virgule

9 rue Véronèse; M° Place-d'Italie.
☎01.43.37.01.14
Closed *Wed; Aug.* **Open** *noon–2pm and 7–11pm (last orders).*

The owners of this restaurant, situated just a stone's throw from the place d'Italie, originate from Cambodia. The first menu offers good value for money and offers enough choices to suit everyone. At lunch time you can choose a main meal and coffee for €8.40, or a menu for €10; otherwise, two *formules* at €18.60 and €24.20, and evening menus €12–18. Space is a bit cramped and it can get noisy, but the food is served very generously and, on top of all that, the owners are charming.

◉ ⅔ |◉| La Touraine

39 rue Croulebarbe; M° Corvisart or Gobelins.
☎01.47.07.69.35
Closed *Sun.* **Open** *daily till 10.30pm.* **High chairs available.**

If you want a table on the terrace, you have to book, but in the evenings there's not such a crush. There are two dining rooms, both decorated in subtle rustic style. The cuisine is filling and tasty and the dishes are what you'd expect to find in provincial France: lamb's sweetbreads with morels, *tournedos Rossini* and a *panaché* of lamb with pickled garlic. There is a selection of

filling menus to choose from: first menu €11, others €20.50–29.90, or à la carte around €30. They also have a pretty garden on the other side of the street. *Free house apéritif offered to our readers on presentation of this guide.*

◉ |◉| L'Avant Goût

26 rue Bobillot; M° Place-d'Italie.
☎01.53.80.24.00
Closed *Sat; Sun; Mon; first week in Jan; first week in May; last fortnight in Aug and first week in Sept.* **Open** *noon–2pm and 7.30–11pm.* **Disabled access.**

Christophe Beaufront has spent a lot of thought and energy on this place, from the dishes on the menus to the vintages on the wine list. He offers a triumphant combination of peasant food and elegant preparation. Try the fantastic pork *pot-au-feu*, for instance. Dishes on the lunchtime *menu du marché* at €12 change regularly. Another option is the *menu-carte* at €26, which changes every fortnight but lists a choice of five starters, six main dishes and five desserts. On Thursday evening there's a single menu, according to the chef's whim, for €36–40. À la carte, a complete meal will cost about €28. The wine list includes a sparkling Vouvray from Champalou, a Gamay D. Richou, or a Côtes-du-Rhône – not forgetting the wine of the month.

◉ |◉| Tricotin 1

15 av. de Choisy; M° Porte-de-Choisy.
☎01.45.85.51.52
Open *daily 9am–11pm.* **Disabled access.**

One of the longest-serving establishments in the district and a veritable institution – at the weekend there's a queue to get in. The big dining room is pretty noisy with efficient waiters, a menu as long as your arm and your neighbour's elbow in your ribs. It's worth it for the *dim sum* – probably the finest and most varied in town – you could easily make a whole meal of it. À la carte only – you'll pay €12–22 or so. Opposite there's another smaller dining room (closed Tuesdays; open 11am–3.30pm) in the same canteen style, always packed out. In here Thai dishes are the speciality.

◉ ⅔ |◉| Etchegorry

41 rue Croulebarbel; M° Corvisart or Gobelins.

☎01.44.08.83.51
Closed *Sun; fortnight in Aug.* **Open**
noon–2.30pm and 7.30–10.30pm.

On the façade of this building you can still make out the old inscription "Cabaret de Madame Grégoire". Some two hundred years ago, Victor Hugo, Châteaubriand and various poets wined and dined here. The old charm still remains; the décor is rustic and warm and the windows look onto the square. The local clientele enjoy authentic Basque and Béarnaise cuisine: *piperade*, stuffed squid and cod with red peppers, duck and pork *confit* with garlic potatoes, sheep's cheeses and delicious desserts. Lunch menu €19.50 and others €25–31.50; everything is cooked fresh on the premises, even the bread. Reservations are recommended. *Free digestif offered to our readers on presentation of this guide.*

ⓐ |●| L'Ourcine

92 rue Broca; M° Gobelins.
☎01.47.07.13.65
Closed *Sun; Mon; a fortnight end July to early Aug.*

The chef, Sylvain Danière, served his apprenticeship in *La Régalade* (under Camdeborde); armed with that experience, he is now forging his own personality. The inscription on the glass front represents his declaration of intent: "cooking from a cook, wine from a wine grower". Danière's pretty little restaurant is skilfully decorated in a bistro style: note the cupboard with a hole knocked out, allowing it to serve as an improvised serving hatch. The food is based on the fresh ingredients available in the market; the menu changes every day, but it may include such delicacies as suckling pig, ox tongue, pork *carpaccio*, fresh citrus fruit with Campari and coconut blancmange. Lunchtime menu at €19, and another three-course one at €28.

ⓐ |●| Anacréon

53 bd. Saint-Marcel; M° Gobelins.
☎01.43.31.71.18
Closed *Sun; Mon; Wed lunch; Aug.* **Open**
noon–2.30pm and 7.30–11pm.

Situated in a rather dreary street, this restaurant offers gourmet food. Try the splendid €32 *menu-carte*, which lists well-devised, well-prepared dishes using country produce: rabbit terrine with foie gras and vegetables, *fricassée* of snails with tomatoes, veal kidneys in a mustard sauce,

plum clafoutis with Armagnac. There's also a set lunch menu for €20. Extremely good service and a wine list that matches the cooking.

ⓐ |●| 🎄 Le Petit Marguery

9 bd. de Port-Royal; M° Gobelins.
☎01.43.31.58.59
Closed *Sun; Mon; Aug; a week at Christmas.*
Open *noon–2pm and 7.30–10.15pm.*

It was a tall order taking over from the Cousin brothers who ran this establishment for two decades: during the season they prepared grouse, pheasant and wildboar to the great delight of their wealthy, joyful guests. The nineteenth-century décor has not changed, and the Parisian brasserie tradition lives on here. There's a lunch menu for €22.20 and others at €25.20, €28.60 and €33.60. The menu lists the same specialities: saddle of scorpion fish with *tapenade* and kidneys with mustard seed still live up to expectations. Film lovers – if they don't happen to bump into Claude Chabrol in the restaurant – can always pop into the *Escurial*, one of the favourite Parisian cinemas. *Free coffee offered to our readers on presentation of this guide.*

ⓐ 🎄 |●| Chez Trassoudaine

3 pl. Nationale; M° Nationale.
☎01.45.83.06.45
Closed *Sun; Sat lunchtime (except for reservations); Aug.* **Open** *10am until 10pm.*
Disabled access.

Pop Robert and Mom Astrig have run the kitchen for years. A quick look at the menu betrays their Armenian origins. Their sons, Araket and Haigo, and their Dutch and Mexican wives, are also part of the team in this unusual restaurant. Dishes include Limousin beef with white pepper, veal chop with sorrel, grilled bass, scallops with garlic or cream sauce, and plump, pink Senegal prawns with garlic and Cayenne pepper. There are no menus; expect to pay around €14 for a meat main course, or upwards of €9 for fish and seafood; starters between €5 and €10. There are also some classic French dishes; herring fillets, egg mayonnaise and so on. Produce used is always of the highest quality and the welcome is kindly. *Free house apéritif offered to our readers on presentation of this guide.*

ⓦ ⚮ |●| Chez Paul

22 rue de la Butte-aux-Cailles; M° Place-d'Italie or Corvisart.
☎01.45.89.22.11
Closed 24 Dec–2 Jan. **Open** daily noon–2.30pm (3pm Sun) and 7.30pm–midnight.

Pleasant, low-key bistro decorated with plenty of plants and offering excellent cooking. The menu is quite extensive, with dishes such as oxtail terrine and roast suckling pig with sage. There are always one or two dishes of the day on the slate and the desserts are delicious; expect to pay around €35. Wine is reasonably priced with some served by the jug. *Free house apéritif offered to our readers on presentation of this guide.*

14th arrondissement

ⓦ ⚑ ⚮ FIAP Jean Monnet

30 rue Cabanis; M° Glacière.
☎01.43.13.17.17 ☎01.45.81.63.91
ⓦwww.fiap.asso.fr

This hostel was co-founded by Jean Monnet (one of the fathers of the European Union) for European students participating in cultural exchanges. It provides beautiful rooms for individual guests (subject to availability) but it gives priority to groups (with compulsory half board). All the rooms (200 in all, with 500 beds) have a shower and toilets (towels provided): €23 per person in a six-bed dorm, €29.90 in four-bed room, €33 in a double room and €51 in a single, breakfast included. There's no age limit; Internet area, tourist information centre and luggage lockers are available. Doors close at 2am. *Free coffee offered to our readers on presentation of this guide.*

ⓦ ⚑ ⚮ Hôtel des Voyageurs

22 rue Boulard; M° and RER Denfert-Rochereau.
☎01.43.21.08.20 ☎01.43.21.08.21
ⓦwww.hoteldesvoyageursparis.com
Open all year round. **TV. Disabled access.**

An enchanting hotel very close to the lively rue Daguerre, one of the best in this price range. The young owner greets his guests warmly, and livens up the ground floor with regular exhibitions of paintings. The furniture in the 26 rooms is basic but they are cool, colourful and spotless; doubles with shower/wc are €50, breakfast €5. There's a large garden and free

Internet access. Be sure to book. *Free coffee or fruit juice, or free breakfast (on Mon morning for guests who arrived Sun evening) offered to our readers on presentation of this guide.*

ⓦ ⚑ ⚮ Cecil Hôtel**

47 rue Beaunier; M° Porte-d'Orléans.
☎01.45.40.93.53 ☎01.45.40.43.26
ⓦwww.cecilhotel.net
Open all year round. **TV.**

Sophie (who comes from the 14th *arrondissement*), Francois (a Savoyard) and Peachy, the labrador, have got the right idea in focusing on the quality of the welcome. Their good taste is evident in the furnishings of the rooms which have been redecorated recently, each with its own theme: "Marrakesh", "Île de Ré", "violet", "romantic" – the choice is yours. Double rooms cost €69 with shower, and €74 with bath. Numerous small attentions to detail make all the difference – the hearty breakfast, €6.50, is served until 2pm, a spray of lily-of-the-valley is given on 1 May (and chocolates at Easter), a house guidebook detailing everything to be seen and done in the area (including restaurants, walks etc). They even reserve parking spaces in the street for their guests. In the morning the newspapers will be waiting for you on the peaceful, sunny terrace. A wonderful place whose reputation is spreading by word-of-mouth – be sure to book in advance. Please note that the hotel is non-smoking. *One free breakfast per room (at weekends) and 10% discount on the room rate (15 July–15 Aug) offered to our readers on presentation of this guide.*

ⓦ ⚮ ⚑ Hôtel du Parc Montsouris**

4 rue du Parc-Montsouris; M° Porte-d'Orléans; RER B Cité-Universitaire.
☎01.45.89.09.72 ☎01.45.80.92.72
ⓦwww.hotel-parc-montsouris.com
TV. Disabled access.

Great location if you like an early jog – Parc Montsouris is nearby. Everyone can appreciate the peace and quiet of this delightful street, and parking does not present a problem. The hotel is resolutely modern and functional; all the rooms have Internet access. Doubles cost €71 with bath/wc; twin rooms cost €80 and apartments €98. All the rooms and bathrooms have been refurbished from top to bottom.

Reserve well in advance. *5% discount on the room rate offered to our readers on presentation of this guide.*

◎ ⅔ 🏠 Hôtel Virginia**

66 rue du Père-Corentin; Porte-d'Orléans.
☎01.45.40.70.90 ℗01.45.40.95.21
🌐www.123.france.com
TV. High chairs and cots available. Pay car park (€10).

This hotel has successfully introduced contemporary design (dark wood, colour scheme of plum, ivory and ochre) into a classical structure (charming wooden lift and Art-Deco stained glass). It is clear from the outset that comfort is one of the main priorities. Double rooms are €75–85, depending on the size; there is a €7 supplement when a trade fair is on. Breakfast buffet is served in an attractive room. The only drawback is that it is a long way from the city centre but you will quickly feel at ease here. *Free parking (except during trade fairs) offered to our readers on presentation of this guide.*

◎ ⅔ 🏠 Hôtel des Bains*

33 rue Delambre; M° Vavin or Edgar-Quinet.
☎01.43.20.85.27 ℗01.42.79.82.78
www.hotel-des-bains-montparnasse.com
Open *all year round.* **TV. Pay car park.**

This one-star hotel has real character and an elegantly restrained façade. The rooms, overlooking the road or the courtyard, have been tastefully decorated and even the bedspreads and lampshades have been carefully chosen to complement the colour scheme. They're very quiet and comfortable and so are the suites, especially those located in a separate building at the bottom of the courtyard, which are very popular with families. Doubles with shower/wc or bath €76–80; suites sleeping two to four people €95–141. Breakfast costs €7.50 and the charge of the car park is around €11. It's really not expensive considering what you get, and it's one of our favourites in the category. *10% discount on the room rate (Sat and Sun during July–Aug) offered to our readers on presentation of this guide.*

◎ ⅔ 🏠 Hôtel Delambre***

35 rue Delambre; M° Edgar-Quinet or Vavin.
☎01.43.20.66.31 ℗01.45.38.91.76
🌐www.hoteldelambre.com

Open *all year round.* **Disabled access. TV.**

This peaceful, efficient hotel has changed a good deal since André Breton, Paul Gauguin and other leading lights of the Surrealist movement stayed here. Very reasonable prices for a hotel in this category: air-conditioned doubles with shower/wc or bath €80–95, depending on size of room and whether it looks onto the courtyard or the road; pleasant buffet breakfast for €8. No. 7, which has a large terrace, is particularly recommended for lovers looking for peace and quiet. *One free breakfast per room offered to our readers on presentation of this guide.*

◎ ⅔ 🏠 Hôtel Daguerre***

94 rue Daguerre; M° Gaité or Denfert-Rochereau.
☎01.43.22.43.54 ℗01.43.20.66.84
🌐www.france-hotel-guide.com
Open *all year round.* **Disabled access. TV.**

If you have a taste for luxury but not the means, this place is for you. It's treated itself to a facelift of the kind usually reserved for great hotels: the marble, the statues, the *trompe l'oeil* painting, the co-ordinated fabrics and the exposed beams in the dining room all combine to create the illusion of a much more glamorous era. And all the rooms have been done up, too: everything is clean and shiny, and they've got safes, mini-bars and cable TV. There are even one or two equipped for disabled visitors. And talking of money, the rates really are reasonable considering the level of service; doubles with shower or bath €85–95, buffet breakfast €11. *10% discount on the room rate (in Jan, Feb and Aug) offered to our readers on presentation of this guide.*

◎ 🍴 Aux Produits du Sud-Ouest

21–23 rue d'Odessa; M° Edgar-Quinet.
☎01.43.20.34.07
Closed *Sun; Mon; public holidays; mid-July to end Aug.* **Open** *noon–2pm and 7–11pm (last orders).*

This restaurant-cum-shop sells home-made preserves and conserves from the Southwest and the prices are unbeatable. It's not gourmet cooking but decent country fare like platters of charcuterie, terrine of rabbit or wild boar, *cassoulet* with goose *confit*, pigeon in a red wine sauce, duck *confit*, goose and duck foie gras. They also do great sandwiches to take away at €3–4.50, and salads for €2.30–9. The lunch *formule* at €6.50 includes dish of the day and a coffee or glass of wine; you'll pay around €12–25 à la carte. There's also a children's menu for €6.

ⓔ |○| Les Tontons

38 rue Raymond-Losserand; M° Gaîté ou Pernety.
☎01.43.21.69.45
Open *daily noon–2.30pm and 7.45–11pm.*

At lunchtime, you will think you're entering a genuine bistro from the 1920s, where you can choose from the blackboard dishes such as *blanquette* or rib of beef with Guérande salt, from the €12 set menu. At dinner time, the atmosphere changes. The bar is just as full of regulars having a drink before a table becomes free, but the lighting is softer, the conversation is more subdued, and you find yourself noticing the beautiful mosaic made of molten glass, or maybe casting a glance at your neighbour's tartare before deciding which of the dozen dishes to choose à la carte (€12–15 per dish, €22–30 for a full meal). Other options include veal *escalope* with leek fondue or *filet mignon* with honey – not for nothing did the chef (one of the four "tontons" who have just revitalized this corner bistro) serve his apprenticeship as the sauce chef in *Robuchon*, and he loves improvising with fresh ingredients according to his fancy. *Free house liqueur offered to our readers on presentation of this guide.*

ⓔ |○| 🍴 La Coupole

102 bd. du Montparnasse; M° Vavin.
☎01.43.20.14.20
Open *breakfast served 8–10.30am (8.30am weekends); brasserie service from 11.30am (last orders at 1am, Sun–Thurs, and 1.30am, Fri and Sat).*

La Coupole, one of Montparnasse's last surviving dinosaurs, is the largest restaurant in the whole of France. It was founded in 1927 in a wood and coal depot by the former managers of the nearby Dôme, who had just been sacked. To get their own back, they decided to go into competition against their former employers. Right from the start, it proved popular with artists – in fact, Cocteau and Man Ray were thrown out of the opening by the police! – and it is impossible to compile a definitive list of its famous customers. They include Chagall, Man Ray, Soutine, Josephine Baker and her lion cub,

Hemingway, Lawrence Durrell, Henry Miller, Buñuel, Dalí, Picasso, Artaud, Colette, Simone de Beauvoir, Mayakovsky – not to mention a young Simenon, even then rarely seen without a pipe, whose hero Maigret sometimes ate in *La Coupole*. It was spruced up for its seventieth anniversary, with its famous 33 pillars recovering their original green colour, and the paintings were restored to their former glory. The frescoes on the ceiling and the Cubist floor tiles were retained, along with the dance floor, and the bar was returned to its original central position. In 1998, this legendary brasserie was taken over by the Flo group. It operates as a nightclub at weekends and on Tuesdays (salsa night). As for the food, the innovations of the Flo group have been skilfully tempered by a sense of continuity, so *La Coupole*'s famous curry is still on the menu, along with its now less famous hot almond fudge and ice cream. Menus start at €17.50, served lunchtimes only, with others at €22.90 and €32.90; à la carte reckon on around €38, excluding drinks.

ⓔ |○| L'Auberge de Venise

10 rue Delambre; M° Vavin.
☎01.43.35.54.09
Closed *Sun.* **Open** *noon–3pm and 7–11pm.*

Montparnasse may no longer have the mystique it once had, but the remaining cinemas and a handful of good restaurants still give an illusion of old Montparnasse. This is one of them – an Italian inn run by Enzo, a jovial host who has the gift of putting you instantly at your ease, and not forgetting his son, Massimo. You might be surprised to find just the classic dishes of mainland Italy, but even though the menu holds no surprises, everything is masterfully prepared and well balanced. Menu at €18, served at lunch and dinner, or expect to pay €35 à la carte. Enzo's clientele is a mixture of writers and show performers, and he reserves the same smiling welcome and service for everyone.

ⓔ |○| L'O à la Bouche

124 bd. du Montparnasse; M° Vavin or RER B Port-Royal.
☎01.56.54.01.55
Closed *Sun; Mon; first week in Jan; second week in April; first 3 weeks in Aug.* **Open** *noon–2.30pm and 7–11pm.* **Disabled access.**

Franck Paquier – young and talented yet tried and tested after his time with

Troisgros and Guy Savoy – creates new dishes daily. All the ingredients are fresh and expertly cooked, and the ideas are creative: pan-fried duck foie gras with fruits of the forest, fillets of duckling with figs and raisins. The wines are reasonably priced and the desserts – honey crumble with blackcurrants, sweet chestnut flavoured ice cream and liquorice *sabayon* – are fabulous. There's a lunch menu for €19, and a *menu dégustation* at €48; à la carte, reckon on around €40.

◎ |●| 🎿 Natacha

17 bis rue Campagne-Première; M° Raspail.
☏01.43.20.79.27
Closed *a week in Aug.* **Open** *noon–2.30pm and 8–11.30pm (except Sun and Mon).*

A comfortable, relaxing setting that blends red velvet seats with modern paintings. At lunch it attracts mainly businessmen, stylists and publishers, while the evening crowd is more hip. Lunchtime menus go for €19 and €26, with a half-bottle of good red wine at a very reasonable price; or expect to pay €40 à la carte. Be sure to book, as the word is already out that a masterly young chef has taken over the reins in this venerable establishment. His cooking is basically classical, but the recipes are modernized and reinterpreted with gusto: succulent *pressé* of snails with a fragrant side-salad, the humble *hachis parmentier* turned into an aristocratic splendour, or cold cucumber soup in summer. *Free coffee offered to our readers on presentation of this guide.*

◎ |●| L'Amuse-Bouche

186 rue du Château; M° Mouton-Duvernet.
☏01.43.35.31.61
Closed *Sun and Mon; Aug.* **Open** *noon–2pm and 7.30–10.15pm.* **Disabled access.**

Gilles Lambert, formerly of *Cagna* and *Miravile* fame, is a consummate artist in the kitchen. If you want proof, try his *menu-carte*. Starters might be langoustine ravioli with tarragon, while for a main course you can choose pig's cheeks with ginger and lemon, and for dessert iced nougatine with walnuts and plums. Menu, served at lunch and dinner, costs €25; also a *menu-carte* at €27, and another at €31.

◎ |●| Le Vin des Rues

21 rue Boulard; M° Denfert-Rochereau or Mouton-Duvernet.

☏01.43.22.19.78
Closed *Sun lunch; a week from 15 Aug.*
Open *noon–3pm and 7.30–11pm.*

This is one of those places where you're not sure who's running the show, the owner or the customers. The Lyonnaise cuisine is consistent and well constructed, with, in pride of place, classic *andouillette* dishes and Salers *entrecôte* steak with *fourme* d'Ambert. On Thursday evening, it's the big spectacle. With his accordion before him, Danny enters the room escorted by Nini or Jean, or possibly both, to give a colourful recital reminiscent of Boudard. The bench seats are crammed to overflowing and the assembled crowd join in with the old refrains. Monsieur Henri invites you to join as he leads the dance, there's a portraitist whose sketches adorn the walls, and the usual regulars propping up the bar. Excellent Lyon-style cooking, with two or three very substantial dishes that change every day. Wines and the day's menu are chalked up on a blackboard – which also tells you what saint's day it is. À la carte only; dishes cost around €15–19, plate of cooked meats €10 or plate of cheese €12, and you'll spend something like €25 for a meal, without drinks.

◎ |●| La Régalade

49 av. Jean-Moulin; M° Alésia or Porte-d'Orléans.
☏01.45.45.68.58
Closed *Sat, Sun and Mon lunchtimes; Aug; a week at Christmas.* **Open** *noon–2pm and 7–11pm.*

This is a gem of a place, with a décor that's both low-key and refined and a chef who is inspired. There's just the one *menu-carte* at €30 offering fresh, inspired cuisine using authentic local produce. And so far, success hasn't changed this very special restaurant which has recently been taken over by a new young chef. You have to book ahead, especially for a Saturday night.

◎ |●| Monsieur Lapin

11 rue Raymond-Losserand; M° Gaîté, Pernety or Montparnasse.
☏01.43.20.21.39
Open *noon–2pm and 7.30–10pm.* **Closed** *Mon; Tues lunch; Aug.*

The setting is attractive with a lot of warm, faded pink, and, surprise surprise, lots of little rabbits used in the decoration.

Service is perfection and complements the refined cuisine. The *menu-carte* for €30 and the *menu-dégustation* for €47 give free rein to the chef's imagination. There's plenty of rabbit on the menu: *émincé* of rabbit with tarragon, sautéed rabbit with preserved lemons, rabbit *croustillant,* etc, but also roast rack of lamb or fillet of beef with foie gras *escalope*, and three or four fish dishes. Tasty starters show off interesting combinations of flavours and ingredients; try the small dish of oysters in champagne. Desserts are lovely, too, with an *île flottante* that's as light as a cloud. And there's a particularly good selection of wines.

15th arrondissement

℮ ⌂ Aloha Hostel

1 rue Borromée (opposite no. 243 rue de Vaugirard); M° Volontaires.
℡ 01.42.73.03.03 ℻ 01.42.73.14.14
⊛ www.aloha.fr
TV.

Regular visitors to this hostel have been astonished by its recent transformation. Absolutely everything has been done up, redecorated and adapted to modern tastes: diffused lighting, wooden shutters and upbeat colours. As there's no point in changing a winning formula, however, the prices are still appealing and the atmosphere is still friendly. The US flag and the clocks showing the time in Paris, New York and Sydney reflect the high proportion of English-speaking travellers among the guests. Dormitories with four to six beds or double rooms with exposed beams. Depending on the season, reckon on €18–22 per person in a dormitory, €22–25 in a double room, including breakfast; hire of sheets (€3) and towels (€1). There are two small showers/wc on each floor and a kitchen in a pretty vaulted cellar is available for use. You must be out of your room between 11am and 5pm, and the doors are closed at 2am. Internet access is available. Charge cards not accepted.

℮ ⌂ 3 Ducks Hôtel

6 pl. Étienne-Pernet; M° Félix-Faurre.
℡ 01.48.42.04.05 ℻ 01.48.42.99.99
⊛ www.3ducks.fr

No access to rooms 11am to 5pm. Curfew at 2am. It's like a youth hostel but privately run and jammed with Brits. It's all pretty out-dated – just so you know – but the accommodation is some of the cheapest in the *arrondissement*; €22.50–24.50 per person in winter and €17–21 per person in summer, including breakfast. Sheets for hire at €3.50. Rooms have bunk beds or there are dormitories with four or six beds. Bathrooms and loos are on the landing. There's a good atmosphere, and a pub. They put a few tables out in the internal courtyard.

℮ ⌂ Le Nainville Hôtel

53 rue de l'Église; M° Félix-Faure or Charles-Michels.
℡ 01.45.57.35.80 ℻ 01.45.54.83.00
Closed *6 weeks starting from the Fri before 14 July.* **TV.**

An unobtrusive little hotel with a retro café on the ground floor, a genial proprietor and bedrooms that are old-fashioned in the nicest possible sense. It's incredible to find a place like this in a neighbourhood where they're throwing up blocks of flats everywhere. Clean and cheerful inside; go for a room which has a view over square Violet. Doubles with basin go for €39 (showers €4), €57 with shower, €67 with shower/wc; breakfast costs €6.50. All the rooms have double glazing so you can be sure of a peaceful night. Credit cards not accepted.

℮ ⚲ ⌂ Hôtel Amiral

90 rue de l'Amiral-Roussin; M° Vaugirard.
℡ 01.48.28.53.89 ℻ 01.45.33.26.94
⊛ www.france-hotel-guide.com/h75015amiral. htm
Open *all year round.* **TV. Disabled access.**

This small, discreet hotel is at the back of the area's town hall but has much to recommend it, not least the decent rooms and honest prices. Nos. 7, 25, 26, 31 and 32 all have a balcony and a very Parisian view of the Eiffel Tower in the distance and all have been redecorated in a nautical theme. Doubles with basin cost €45, with shower/wc or bath €75–78; breakfast €7. For those attending a trade fair, the porte de Versailles is only a fifteen-minute walk away. *10% discount on the room rate (15 July–31 Aug) offered to our readers on presentation of this guide.*

℮ ⌂ Hôtel de la Paix***

43 rue Duranton; M° Boucicaut or Convention.
℡ 01.45.57.14.70 ℻ 01.45.57.09.50

www.hotelpaixparis.com
Open *all year round.* **TV. Disabled access.**

Very comfortable, three-star family hotel in a quiet street. The cosy rooms are attractively decorated in vivid, warm colours and they all have air-conditioning. The bathrooms are splendid, with all mod cons (hairdryer, etc) and marble fittings. Double rooms €66–166 with shower/wc or bath, depending on the season; breakfast at €7 (free for children under ten), is served 6am–noon in a room with wrought-iron tables and a fountain. The reception is equipped with a fireplace. Friendly atmosphere and excellent value for money.

Hôtel Lilas Blanc Grenelle

5 rue de l'Avre; M° La Motte-Piquet-Grenelle.
℡01.45.75.30.07 ℻01.45.78.66.65
@hotellilasblanc@minitel.net
Closed *Aug; a week at Christmas.* **TV. Cots available.**

This hotel, very close to Motte-Piquet-Grenelle, is one of the hidden jewels of the neighbourhood. The service is highly professional and the bedrooms and bathrooms are very comfortable (hair dryer, safe). Go for the ones in series 3, as they're bigger. Doubles at €67–75 with shower or bath offer good value for money; breakfast €6. Don't miss the fresco painted on the lounge wall. There's a small patio and the welcome is very courteous. American Express cards not accepted. *€3 discount on the room rate offered to our readers on presentation of this guide.*

Hôtel Le Fondary**

30 rue Fondary; M° Émile-Zola.
℡01.45.75.14.75 ℻01.45.75.84.42
www.hotelfondary.com
Open *all year round.* **TV. Disabled access.**

Good location in a quiet street in one of the liveliest parts of the 15th *arrondissement.* Modern décor and pretty patio with a well where you can take breakfast, €6.50. Prices are reasonable considering the quality of the service – doubles with direct phone, cable TV and mini-bar cost €72 with shower or €76 with bath. Be sure to book in advance as the hotel has its regulars. The welcome is variable. *10% discount on the room rate (July–Aug) offered to our readers on presentation of this guide.*

Hôtel de l'Avre**

21 rue de l'Avre; M° La Motte-Piquet-Grenelle.
℡01.45.75.31.03 ℻01.45.75.63.26
www.hoteldelavre.com
Disabled access. TV.

The hotel is located in a quiet and narrow street, 150m away from the noisy Motte-Picquet-Grenelle crossroads. In summer the amiable owner sets out deckchairs in the pleasant garden where breakfast is served. He warmly welcomes all his guests in an atmosphere akin to a country hotel. The prices are fairly reasonable for Paris, with doubles at €73–83 with shower/wc or bath; breakfast €7.50. The tastefully renovated rooms are decorated in blue or yellow; the ones overlooking the garden have large bathrooms and are particularly pleasant. There's also an attractive family room for four people. It's difficult to park in the street but there are two car parks just minutes away. *10% discount on the room rate (at weekends) offered to our readers on presentation of this guide.*

Carladez Cambronne**

3 pl. du Général-Beuret; M° Vaugirard.
℡01.47.34.07.12 ℻01.40.65.95.68
www.hotelcarladez.com
Open *all year.* **TV.**

Carladez is a region in Auvergne where the original owners came from. This is a charming hotel in a little square with a pretty fountain. All the rooms are soundproofed and well-equipped; ask for room no. 3 which looks over the patio. Doubles with shower cost €73.50, €80 with bath, family suite for four €128; breakfast €7.50. *10% discount on the room rate (during school holidays and at weekends, except during trade fairs), offered to our readers on presentation of this guide.*

Hôtel du Parc Saint-Charles

243 rue Saint-Charles (on the corner of rue Leblanc); M° Balard or RER C Boulevard-Victor.
℡01.45.57.83.86 ℻01.45.53.60.68
www.hotelduparcstcharles.com
TV.

Professionalism and friendliness are the mottos of this hotel, recently taken over by its young owner. It has been spruced up while awaiting a major overhaul to turn it into a three-star establishment. This is a good time to take advantage of it, therefore, as it is already fully equipped and the bedding is all brand new. The rooms are very quiet and cost €117–147. A note of warning, however: during some trade fairs the prices go up by €20. The crowning glory is the apartment on the top floor: it sleeps four people, has exposed beams and is fully equipped (kitchen, music centre, pretty bathroom); you can really make yourself "at home". Excellent breakfast and light meals on a tray available (produce and wines from Southwest France) until 10.15pm, and it's also possible to share a half-board arrangement with the *Bistrot d'André* (see right), which is just opposite. *One free breakfast per room offered to our readers on presentation of this guide.*

Ⓔ |●| Aux Artistes

63 rue Falguière; M° Falguière or Pasteur.
℡01.43.22.05.39
Closed Sat lunchtime; Sun; Aug; Christmas and New Year. **Open** noon–2.30pm and 7.30pm–midnight.

This restaurant is really something. The price of the set menu has hardly increased in years, and the atmosphere and the décor haven't changed much either. The customers are a mixed bunch – students, teenagers from nearby housing estates, professionals, a few artists (Modigliani came here in his time) – who all enjoy their meals in a noisy, lively atmosphere. You'll have to wait for a table on weekend evenings, but the bar serves a mean Kir. Two-course lunch *formule* €10 (starter, main course with chips and salad, or main course and dessert), and a menu, €13, served all day. Hors d'œuvres are substantial, and they can prepare you a steak in many different ways. The surprise of the house is a dessert poetically entitled "young girl's dream". Credit cards not accepted.

Ⓔ 🍴 |●| Banani

148 rue de la Croix-Nivert; M° Félix-Faure.
℡01.48.28.73.92
Open noon–2.30pm and 7.30–11pm. **Closed** Sun lunchtime.

The dining room here is so large that it's divided into two by a low wall and has tables hidden away in bays. A gold statue of Ganesh adorns the entrance; inside there's a wall painting of a Hindu temple, warm wood panelling and low lighting. The Indian dishes come from different corners of the continent and the spicing is skilfully judged: fresh tender tandoori dishes, authentic *birianis* and excellent *massalas*. The *naan* breads come fresh and hot, and you can have your *lassi* salty or sweet. Portions are generous and the Indian lager is well worth trying. Lunchtime menus cost €10 and €16, and there's a substantial evening set dinner at €26; expect to pay around €20–25 à la carte, without drinks. *Free house apéritif offered to our readers on presentation of this guide.*

Ⓔ 🍴 |●| Le Bistrot d'André

232 rue Saint-Charles (on the corner of the rue Leblanc); M° Balard.
℡01.45.57.89.14
Closed Sun; Christmas; New Year's Day.
Open noon–2.30pm and 8–10.30pm.
Disabled access.

This is one of the few survivors from the (André) Citroën era. It's been updated to cater for today's tastes by the people from the Perraudin (in the 5th *arrondissement*) and given a shot in the arm. "Pre-war" prices for appealing family dishes such as pan-fried duck breast with honey sauce, veal kidneys with wild mushrooms and turbot with sorrel sauce. Set menu €12.50 served on weekday lunchtimes. It's à la carte in the evening, when you should reckon on a bit more: €22, with dishes of the day priced €12–15. Wine-lovers take note: there's a tasting of wines from very small vineyards every month. "Wines of the month" are selected because of their superb quality and value for money. It's great to discover such a decent restaurant in an area where there's little else to see. *Free house apéritif offered to our readers on presentation of this guide.*

Ⓔ 🍴 |●| Le Garibaldi

58 bd. Garibaldi; M° Sèvres-Lecourbe.
℡01.45.67.15.61
Closed evenings; Sat; Sun; Aug.

This used to be a working-man's café, though nowadays white collars are much more in evidence. It's almost compulsory to have the *museau* vinaigrette or *crudités* as a starter. The €13.50 three-course set menu features sautéed lamb with flageolet beans or beef *bourguignon*, and includes wine and service. Expect to pay around €15 à la carte. Service is friendly and there are still traces of the old décor – such as the beautiful counter at the door and a 1900 ceiling in an otherwise plain dining room. It's best to book at lunchtime as it's so busy, and there are a few tables outside on the terrace. *Free coffee offered to our readers on presentation of this guide.*

ⓔ |●| Beurre Noisette

68 rue Vasco-de-Gama; M° Lourmel, Balard or Porte-de-Versailles.
☏01.48.56.82.49
Closed *Sun; Mon; 3 weeks in Aug.* **Open** *noon–2.30pm and 7.15–11pm.*

This restaurant in a slightly out-of-the-way little street illustrates how this neighbourhood is acquiring more and more innovative places to eat. In this case, it is thanks to a young chef who skilfully approaches traditional specialities (blood pudding, free-range chicken and braised cabbage, for example) with an inventive touch. As for the desserts, the exquisite chocolate *quenelles* with honey *madeleines* have helped put this new arrival firmly on the map. There are two immaculate dining rooms to choose from; lunch menu is €20, dinner €29, or reckon on €30 à la carte.

ⓔ |●| Le Troquet

21 rue François-Bonvin; M° Sèvres-Lecourbe or Cambronne.
☏01.45.66.89.00
Closed *Sun; Mon; a week in May; 3 weeks in Aug; a week at Christmas.* **Open** *noon–2pm and 7.30–11.30pm.*

Hidden in a back street, a huge dining room dotted with white tablecloths and Basque waiters bearing dishes with enticing aromas passing between the tables. Their taste lives up to this first impression, as the food is delicious and imaginative. Lunchtime menus are €22 and €26 (starter, main course and dessert); these are superb, but fade in comparison with the dinner menus (€30 and €37), comprising four or five dishes (which you can't select – the only blemish – as you have to pay a hefty supplement for any alternatives). Wines start at €15. The quality of the produce and the convivial atmosphere make this a great success, so booking is recommended.

ⓔ |●| Je Thé...me

4 rue d'Alleray; M° Vaugiraud.
☏01.48.42.48.30
Closed *Sun; Mon; Aug; 23 Dec–3 Jan.* **Open** *noon–3pm and 7.15–10.30pm.*

It is a pleasure merely to enter this old late-nineteenth-century grocery; it is like

walking into a doll's house, complete with period tiles and a wonderful array of odds and ends. This intimate setting is ideal for a romantic rendezvous, as the tables are sufficiently far apart to prevent neighbours from overhearing any passionate declarations. There's a lunchtime menu for €23 and a *menu-carte* in the evening for €33. The menu, chalked on a blackboard, is particularly strong on fresh seafood, but there are also well-judged variations on traditional meat dishes, such as kidneys in cognac and calf's sweetbreads. The desserts include a tasty rum baba, or a red fruits crumble. The service is warm and attentive.

ⓔ |●| Restaurant Stéphane Martin

67 rue des Entrepreneurs; M° Félix-Faure, Charles-Michels or Commerce.
☏01.45.79.03.31
Closed *Sun; Mon; a week in Feb; 3 weeks in Aug; Christmas.* **Open** *noon–2pm and 7.30–11pm.*

There are some suburban restaurants that are OK for filling you up on a Sunday night if you happen to be in the area, and there are others that are worth crossing the city for. This is in the latter category. Its lunch menu (€25) is particularly competitive (three courses, wine and coffee included); another menu with a wider choice at €32. The subtle, creative cooking reflects the availability of fresh seasonal ingredients, but there are some dishes that are served all year round: sliced duck foie gras with herbs, braised pork knuckle with spicy honey and buttered red cabbage, *moelleux* of chocolate *fondant* and caramelized orange. All are accompanied by a selection of home-made breads (with thyme, sesame, etc) that you can eat at will. A classy setting in warm colours, with courteous if slightly slow service, but at these prices we would go again tomorrow.

ⓔ |●| De la Garde

83 av. de Ségur; M° Ségur or Cambronne.
☏01.40.65.99.10
Closed *Sun; Mon; public holidays; first 3 weeks in Aug; 25 Dec–2 Jan.* **Open** *noon–2.30pm and 8–10.30pm.*

It takes courage to open a restaurant in such a quiet area, but Yohann Marracini, a chef from Alain Passard's stable, is clearly up to the challenge. He has attracted an elegant crowd eager to try cooking that boldly strays from the beaten track. His dishes may sometimes lack polish but he is bursting with ideas: *croustillant* of haddock with turmeric, kidneys with Beaumes-de-Venise and ricotta *gnocchi*, pollack with smoked ham flanked by (slightly overcooked) sweet-onion risotto, and rum baba with passion fruit. Two-course lunch menu €25, full menu €29; at night, a three-course menu at €35. Expect to pay around €35 à la carte. Unfortunately, the atmosphere is often a bit starchy – can't the waiters unwind a little bit?

⟪ |●| ⅔ L'Épopée

89 av. Émile-Zola; Mᵒ Charles-Michels.
℡01.45.77.71.37
Closed *Sat lunch; Sun; 28 July–28 Aug.*
Open *noon–1.45pm and 8–10pm.*

The 15th *arrondissement* may have a host of restaurants, but there are very few where you can dine with any intimacy. This is one of them, as some of its round tables are set slightly apart. The décor is sophisticated but somewhat conventional, but what does it matter if the food is so mouth-wateringly delicious? The menu varies according to the availability of the ingredients; specialities include truly exquisite langoustine ravioli with *saté* and steamed bass with mashed potatoes and olive oil, but all the dishes are of irreproachable quality and extremely well presented. There's a menu at €32, and a *formule* of main course with either a starter or dessert for €27. *Free digestif offered to our readers on presentation of this guide.*

⟪ |●| L'Os–Moelle

3 rue de Vasco-de-Gama: Mᵒ Lourmel.
℡01.45.57.27.27
Closed *Sun; Mon; a month in summer; a week in winter.* **Open** *until 11.30pm (midnight Fri and Sat).*

Thierry Faucher, formerly of the *Crillon,* skilfully produces bistro food in the style of a great chef. According to what he finds in Rungis market, you may be able to try cream of langoustine with chorizo or fried calf's liver with Banyuls vinegar. Lunchtime menu costs €32, and the dinner menu (samples of four dishes) €38. Well-chosen wine list, with prices that won't overload your bill.

16th arrondissement

⟪ ☎ Hôtel Le Hameau de Passy**

48 rue de Passy; Mᵒ Passy, La Muette or RER C Muette-Boulainvilliers.
℡01.42.88.47.55 ⊕01.42.30.83.72
ⓦwww.hameaudepassy.com
Disabled access. TV.

The entrance is in a small passageway between a leather shop and an estate agent. You come out into a small courtyard full of flowers and ringing with birdsong – a far cry from the luxury designer shops nearby. The hotel is run by an energetic team. Doubles with shower/wc or bath are €113–125, breakfast included; family rooms €155. There's a room for three people and one for four, and some of the double rooms have communicating doors.

⟪ ⅔ ☎ Au Palais de Chaillot**

35 av. Raymond-Poincaré; Mᵒ Trocadéro or Victor-Hugo.
℡01.53.70.09.09 ⊕01.53.70.09.08
ⓦwww.palaisdechaillot-hotel.com
TV. High chairs available. Pay car park.

This is a delightful hotel which is fresh and clean-looking. The rooms, all equipped with safe and hairdryer, are decorated in yellow with curtains in red or blue; doubles go for €120–140 according to level of comfort and the season. Continental breakfast is served in a bright little room on the ground floor or they'll bring it to your room. A two-star hotel that easily deserves three – book well ahead. *15% discount on the room rate offered to our readers on presentation of this guide.*

⟪ ☎ Hôtel Passy Eiffel

10 rue de Passy; Mᵒ Passy.
℡01.45.25.55.66 ⊕01.42.88.89.88
ⓦwww.passyeiffel.com
TV.

A stone's throw from the Trocadéro, in what is primarily a residential area, this luxurious, well-run hotel boasts a stunning patio flooded with light and lined with teak tables. The lounge is decorated with exquisite taste, in a modern, designer style. The rooms, which overlook either the street or the patio, are bright, spotless and spacious, although the functional, standardized décor is disappointing for the price: doubles cost €130 or €140 and suites €215 (not including breakfast).

Suite no. 51 offers an unbeatable view of the Eiffel Tower. Parking is available at 19, rue de Passy.

⊚ 🎋 |●| Le Mozart

12 av. Mozart; M° La Muette.
☎01.45.27.62.45
Closed *Sun.* **Open** *noon–3pm and 7pm–10pm.*

The best *andouillette* from Duval, meat and mushrooms shipped in from Lozère, ice cream from Berthillon, bread from the ovens of Michel Moizant and home-made pastries. This kind of quality is coordinated by a man who loves to root out the best produce and good wines. It's hardly surprising that you have to wait for a table – but the Kir they provide you with at the bar while you wait soothes your impatience. Lunch or dinner *formules* are €12 (including a platter of foie gras and salad); à la carte you'll pay around €25. *Free house apéritif offered to our readers on presentation of this guide.*

⊚ |●| 🎋 Restaurant GR5

19 rue Gustave-Courbet; M° Rue-de-la-Pompe, Trocadéro or Victor Hugo.
☎01.47.27.09.84
Closed *Sun.* **Open** *until 11pm.* **Disabled access.**

A hiker with a fondness for the GR5 route from Holland to the South of France hung up his boots to open this modest restaurant right on his doorstep. It is packed for both lunch and dinner but it is worth trying to get in. The little dining room is decorated in a mountain style, with check, red gingham tableclothes, and the menu revolves around a winning trio: *tartiflette* with Reblochon, *fondue* and a superb *raclette savoyarde*. Menus cost €14 (lunch) and €19.50 (dinner); reckon on around €20 à la carte. Great care is put into the choice of wines, with a wine of the month on offer by the bottle or carafe (large or small) and several fine vintages from the Lyon region. *Free house apéritif offered to our readers on presentation of this guide.*

⊚ |●| 🎋 Le Petit Rétro

5 rue Mesnil; M° Victor-Hugo.
☎01.44.05.06.05
Closed *Sat lunch; Sun; Aug; a week between Christmas and New Year.*

The flowery tiles on the walls, beautiful mirrors, round lamps, old-style zinc counter and a practical, long coat rack (reminiscent of a school) all add up to create the illusion that time has stood still. They provide a feast for the eye to prepare the way for the delicacies to come. Typical bistro dishes, given a new twist and varied according to the seasons, to maintain a constant quality and freshness: poached egg with cream of chorizo, oxtail terrine, *croustillant* of black pudding, *papillote* of *andouillette*; the great speciality of the house, however, is *blanquette à l'ancienne*. Lunchtime menus €19 (main course with starter or dessert) and €24 (starter, main course and dessert); reckon on €32 for a full meal à la carte. They do a good selection of wines (some served by the glass), with a wine of the month on special offer, and the welcome is very friendly. *Free house apéritif offered to our readers on presentation of this guide.*

⊚ |●| 🎋 Mathusalem

5 bis bd. Exelmans; M° Exelmans.
☎01.42.88.10.73
Closed *Sat; Sun; public holidays.* **Open** *noon–2.30pm and 8–10.30pm.*

Customers come from far and wide to this spot on the outskirts of Paris, and that is a recommendation in itself. The neighbourhood is a bit rundown, but the road leading to *Mathusalem* has been well trod for a long time. The well-established reputation of this restaurant with décor from the 1920s guarantees a packed house every day of the week and, despite the somewhat noisy dining room, its success is fully deserved. The menu is relatively limited and the portions are not over-generous, but the ingredients are fresh and the traditional dishes are tasty, including the enticing desserts. The *formule* includes a main course with a choice of either a starter or dessert for €20; or you can expect to pay around €26 à la carte. There's a terrace for sunny days. *Free house apéritif offered to our readers on presentation of this guide.*

⊚ 🎋 |●| Restaurant du musée du Vin, Le Caveau des Échansons

5–7 square Charles-Dickens-rue des Eaux; M° Passy.
☎01.45.25.63.26
Closed *Mon; 24 Dec–1 Jan.* **Open** *noon–3pm.* **Disabled access.**

The restaurant is in the wine museum and the dining room is in a fifteenth-century vaulted cellar dug out of the Chaillot clay by the monks who used to cultivate the vines. Even if the restaurant is really just a pretext for drinking and talking wine with one's neighbours, it's nevertheless a superb place with good food. The wine list is twelve pages long and lists 200–250 vintages all the way up to a Château d'Yquem 1908 at €1980 a bottle. Along the way you'll come across *grand crus* from Bordeaux, Burgundy, Alsace and Jura as well as wines from lesser regions in France. Every day there's a selection of fifteen sold by the glass. A glass of wine is offered after a visit to the museum or as an apéritif before a meal. Dishes cost around €12; range of menus at €20–50. *A free glass of wine offered to our readers on presentation of this guide.*

◎ |●| La Marmite

10 rue Géricault; M° Michel-Ange-Auteuil.
℡01.42.15.03.09
Closed *Sat lunch; Sun; Aug.* **Open** *lunch and dinner.*

A modest restaurant in a nondescript neighbourhood, with equally unremarkable décor inside; not very promising, maybe, but the place comes into its own with the delicious old-fashioned cooking. The dinner menu at €25 is particularly recommended; it's astonishingly good value for money, and whatever you choose, be it calf's liver, scallops or anything else, it will always be of unbeatable quality, as is the service. Reckon on around €27 à la carte. Booking is essential.

17th arrondissement

◎ ⚘ 🏠 Hôtel Champerret-Heliopolis**

13 rue d'Heliopolis; M° Porte de Champerret.
℡01.47.64.92.56 ℗01.47.64.50.44
ⓦwww.champeret-heliopolis-paris-hotel.com
Disabled access. TV. Cots available.

A very quiet hotel with pretty wooden balconies situated close to Porte Maillot and the Arc de Triomphe. Most rooms overlook a delightful patio where you can have breakfast (served 7am–noon) when the weather's nice. The place was beginning to look a little rundown; however it's now under new management and refurbishment is underway, so things are looking up. Doubles with bath or shower are €85–93; to date the bedding has been replaced. *One free breakfast per room or 10% discount on the room rate (15 July–31 Aug)*

offered to our readers on presentation of this guide.

◎ 🏠 Hôtel de Prony***

103 bis av. de Villiers; close to the place Pereire and 10 min from porte Maillot; M° Pereire.
℡01.42.27.55.55 ℗01.43.80.06.97
ⓦwww.hoteldeprony.com
TV.

An excellent hotel close to place Pereire and five minutes from Porte Maillot. The place has undergone a complete refurbishment – absolutely necessary in order to justify the prices. The rooms are double glazed and vary in size but are mostly very pleasant, if a little impersonal. Doubles cost €90–130 with bath or shower, depending on the facilities and the season. Room no. 32 is huge, and ideal for families of three to four people.

◎ ⚘ 🏠 Hôtel Palma**

46 rue Brunel; M° Porte-Maillot or Argentine.
℡01.45.74.74.51 ℗01.45.74.40.90
ⓦwww.hotelpalma-paris.com
Open *all year.* **TV.**

This 37-room hotel is a stone's throw from the Arc de Triomphe, the convention centre and the Air France terminal. It has an attractive frontage and foyer, and offers a degree of comfort at reasonable prices. Service is variable but efficient. The rooms (€85 with shower/wc, €95–110 with shower/wc or bath and all mod cons) have been redecorated in Provençal style, and have a warm, bright feel. Breakfast can be served in your room. The sixth-floor rooms are extremely popular, so it's best to book. *One free breakfast per person offered to our readers on presentation of this guide.*

◎ ⚘ |●| La Loggia

41 rue Legendre; M° Villiers.
℡01.44.40.47.30
Closed *Sun lunchtime; Mon; Aug.* **Open** *noon–2pm and 7–11pm.*

This Italian restaurant is as much about fast cars as good food – there's a Ferrari here, another there, and a mural of magnificent machines along the wall. Even the waitresses' T-shirts are emblazoned with that famous rearing horse. The owner-chef produces tasty food: marinated fresh sardine fillets, rigatoni with prawn cream sauce. The dish of the day when we were there – *ravioli au sugo di noce* – deserves a round of applause. And let's hear it for the tiramisù. An enjoyable meal won't cost you a bomb, either – there's a lunch menu for €12, and you'll pay around €28 à la carte. Reservations are highly recommended. *Free house apéritif offered to our readers on presentation of this guide.*

ⓔ |O| Le Petit Villiers

75 av. de Villiers; M° Wagram.
℡01.48.88.96.59
Open *noon–2.30pm and 7–11pm.* **Closed** *New Year holiday.*

At night this is a beacon that shines in an otherwise deserted street. What is the secret of its success, in such inhospitable surroundings? It is a combination of rural warmth, a convivial and relaxed atmosphere, impressive waxed table linen, romantic candles on the tables, a terrace for sunny days and, last but not least, superb cooking at prices that cannot be matched in the neighbourhood. Foie gras, for example, can be found on the €18 weekday lunchtime menu. There is another lunch menu at €13, which is a combination of starter with main course or main course with dessert (there are plenty to choose from – about a dozen items for each course). Excellent salads and lovingly prepared traditional dishes (calves' kidneys, trout *meunière*, duck breast with green peppercorns, etc), all served in generous portions. There's also a *formule* at €10.90 including a main course plus either starter or dessert.

ⓔ |O| Le Verre Bouteille

85 av. des Ternes; M° Porte-Maillot.
℡01.45.74.01.02
Closed *at Christmas.* **Open** *noon–3pm and 7pm–4am.*

Excellent wine bar where night owls can fill up on robust main dishes like steak *tartare* made with chopped – not minced – steak, or very, very large salads. There's one called *nain jaune*, "the yellow dwarf" (also the name of an old card game), which includes Comté cheese, chicken, raisins and curry sauce. Wines come from around the world and about thirty are available by the glass. Things can get lively on weekends by the time 4am rolls around. Three *formules* at €14.50 (lunch only), €20 (main course with either starter or dessert) and €28.50 (three courses). You'll pay around €30–35 for a full meal à la carte. There's a second

Verre Bouteille at 5 bd. Gouvion-Saint-Cyr (M° Porte-de-Champerret) in the 17th *arrondissement*, ℡01.47.63.39.99 – but that one closes at midnight.

ⓔ ⅔ |O| L'Impatient

14 passage Geoffroy-Didelot; M° Villiers.
℡01.43.87.28.10
Closed *Sat lunchtime; Sun; Mon; a fortnight in Aug.*

The entrance is between 92 bd. de Batignolles and 117 rue des Dames. The décor in this restaurant is refined – beautifully laid tables, old posters on the walls, elegant dishes. It's surprising to find such a difference in quality between the menus and à la carte – the former lacks originality, but the latter boasts carefully prepared dishes using the finest ingredients which explains the high prices. The menus cost €17 at lunchtime, €23 in the evening – a meal à la carte will cost around €30 not including drink. Dishes include pan-fried *escalope* of foie gras and *axao* of veal or duck. Reservations strongly recommended at the end of the week. *Free house apéritif offered to our readers on presentation of this guide.*

ⓔ |O| ⅔ Le Petit Champerret

30 rue Vernier; M° Porte-de-Champerret.
℡01.43.80.01.39
Open *12.30–2pm and 7.30–10.30pm.* **Closed** *Sat lunch; Sun; Mon evening.*

The couple who have taken over these premises have transformed what was once a humble café into what they call a "gourmet bistro". The old mirror and zinc counter are still there, but the wood panelling has been tinted a raspberry colour and the walls painted cream (a delicious combination). The cornerstones of the new gastronomic adventure are several starters of the day, all supremely fresh; fish and meat dishes cooked to perfection, and a dazzlingly long list of desserts. Lunch and dinner *formule* costs €18 (starter with main course or main course with dessert); reckon on around €30 for a full meal à la carte. Wines are sold by the glass or carafe, and the service is efficient and friendly. It's advisable to book, especially for lunch. *Free coffee offered to our readers on presentation of this guide.*

ⓔ |O| Le Café d'Angel

16 rue Brey; M° Charles-de-Gaulle-Étoile.
℡01.47.54.03.33

10

Closed *Sat; Sun; public holidays; first 3 weeks in Aug; New Year's holiday.* **Open** *noon–2pm and 7.30–10pm.*

In the shadow of the Arc de Triomphe, in a stolidly middle-class street in the 17th arrondissement, this bistro packs them in. Its attractions include an inviting dining room with the kitchen open to view in the back, behind the bar; dashing, thirty-something customers from the many nearby offices, who seem to have taken the place to their heart; and finally, attractive cooking that reinterprets tradition in the style of today's great masters (the chef, Jean-Marc Gorsy, served his apprenticeship in the *Jules Verne*), with a touch of fantasy that is all its own. *Croustillant* of pig's foot, calves' kidneys, fish of the day and, to finish, home-made chocolate gâteau or orange mousse. The menus are remarkably good value: lunch €19 and €22, dinner €38. Reckon on around €40 à la carte, excluding drinks.

✀ ✶ |●| Graindorge

15 rue de l'Arc-de-Triomphe; M° Charles-de-Gaulle-Étoile.
℡ 01.47.54.00.28
Closed *Sat lunch; Sun.* **Open** *noon–2pm and 7–10.30pm.*

Bernard Broux is an inspired chef who uses his expertise to the greater glory of his native Flanders, reinterpreting his culinary heritage: *escalope* of warm foie gras à la kriek, *salmi* of guinea-fowl, fish *waterzoï* with shrimps, and for dessert, dark chocolate *fondant* with *speculoos* and café *liégeois*. All the produce is fresh, and dishes are cooked to order. Forget the wine list and stick to beer – any one of the many varieties goes perfectly with the food. Lunch menus at €24 and €28; €32 and €59 in the evening. You'll pay around €45 à la carte, not including drinks. Best to book at the weekend. *Free liqueur offered to our readers on presentation of this guide.*

18th arrondissement

✀ ✶ Hôtel Bouquet de Montmartre**

1 rue Durantin; M° Abbesses.
℡ 01.46.06.87.54 ℻ 01.46.06.09.09
ⓦ www.bouquet-de-montmartre.com

A conventional hotel run by a young couple and completely refurbished in an unusual but not unpleasant style. There's no lift and the stairs are rather steep. The

rooms are decent if small, and they are all different. Doubles, €66, all have double glazing, their own wc and a choice of shower or bath. Excellent location, good reception, great value for money and a wonderful view over Paris from room 43.

✀ ✶ Hôtel Prima Lepic**

29 rue Lepic; M° Blanche.
℡ 01.46.06.44.64 ℻ 01.46.06.66.11
ⓦ www.hotel-paris-lepic.com
TV. High chairs available. Pay car park.

This is the ideal place to set off for a stroll through the neighbourhood. The impasse Marie-Blanche is close by, and definitely worth a look. The reception is bright and fresh and there's a *trompe l'oeil* of an English garden, a theme which they've developed by choosing garden furniture. Rooms, which look like something out of a magazine, are well maintained. Doubles €96–110 with shower/wc or bath look onto the road or the courtyard.

✀ ✀ ✶ Timhôtel Montmartre**

11 rue Ravignan (place Émile-Goudeau); M° Abbesses, Blanche or Pigalle.
℡ 01.42.55.74.79 ℻ 01.42.55.71.01
ⓦ www.timhotel.com
TV.

This beautiful hotel is located in a wonderfully pretty square. Doubles with shower or bath €115–130 (ground floor to the third floor), and €130–160 for the rooms on the fourth and fifth floors which have recently been refurbished and have air-conditioning. Each floor is dedicated to a painter: you have a choice of Toulouse-Lautrec, Utrillo, Dalí, Picasso, Renoir or Matisse. All have direct-dial phone and TV, and those on the fourth floor and above have a view of the square or the city; nos. 417 and 517 are especially nice as they have a view of the Sacré-Cœur. It's a great place for a romantic weekend which won't break the bank. *One free breakfast per person offered to our readers on presentation of this guide.*

✀ |●| Sonia

8 rue Letort; M° Jules-Joffrin, Simplon and Porte de Clignancourt.
℡ 01.42.57.23.17
Closed *Sun lunchtime, except in summer.* **Open** *noon–2.30pm and 6.30–11.30pm (last orders).*

A small Indian restaurant with a pink and purple dining room seating only 26

ÎLE-DE-FRANCE

people (it's often full). Menus are €7.50 and €13 at lunchtime, €16 in the evening. Everything is delicately spiced, beautifully presented and cooked to perfection – from the *naan* to the chicken *Madras* and *vindaloo*, not to mention the lamb *korma* and the aubergine *bhartha*.

⊚ |●| L'Étoile de Montmartre

26 rue Duhesme; M° Lamarck-Caulaincourt.
☎01.46.06.11.65
Closed *Tues.* **Open** *noon–2.20pm only.*
Children's games available.

In the shadow of the Butte, a little café that evokes a bygone era. High dining room with walls yellowed by age but set off by delightful friezes, a mosaic embedded in the floor and a bar with a Formica counter. This old-fashioned charm attracts regular customers every lunchtime: young and old, office workers in ties and labourers in overalls rub shoulders to enjoy the cheap, unpretentious home cooking – dish of the day €10 and full meal €11. The authenticity of the atmosphere and the conviviality are the responsibility of the Giordano family, which has been running the place for over three decades. Credit cards not accepted.

⊚ |●| Le Rendez-Vous des Chauffeurs

11 rue des Portes-Blanches; M° Marcadet-Poissoniers.
☎01.42.64.04.17
Closed *Wed; Aug.* **Open** *noon–2.30pm (3pm on Sun) and evenings until 11pm.*

This place has a long history, and when Jeannot took it over he was wise enough to change things as little as possible: the old wood counter and mirrors are still there, the tightly packed tables are covered by glazed cotton checked tablecloths and the benches are leather – he's even kept the brownish paint so typical of old restaurants. The menu hasn't changed much either – cottage pie, calves' kidneys. The wines are good and guaranteed to loosen the tongues of both the regulars and passing customers. There are weekday menus at €10 and €14, and a meal à la carte will cost you €25.

⊚ |●| 🍴 Chez Pradel

168 rue Ordener; M° Guy-Môquet or Jules-Joffrin.
☎01.46.06.75.48

Closed *Sun; fortnight in Aug.* **Open** *noon–3.30pm (Mon–Sat) and 7.30–10pm (Thurs and Fri evenings).*

This restaurant with décor from the 1920s is extremely popular with the locals of this lively neighbourhood. The owner and his wife prepare classic dishes with no frills but plenty of loving care. Some specialities from the southwest of France are available à la carte, and classic dishes on the menus include beef steak with morels, *andouillette de Vouvray*. Other options are mackerel in white wine, poached eggs with chives and *blanquette* of veal. Dish of the day costs €9.50, sandwiches €2.44–3.80, salads €7, and there's a menu for €11. Reckon on around €20 à la carte, excluding wine. Wide choice of wines served by the glass or in a carafe or bottle, at extremely reasonable prices. *Free house apéritif offered to our readers on presentation of this guide.*

⊚ 🍴 |●| La Casserole

17 rue Boinod; M° Marcadet-Poissoniers or Simplon.
☎01.42.54.50.97
Closed *Sun; Mon and Sat lunchtimes; public holidays; 15 July–24 Aug.* **Open** *noon–2pm and 7.30–10pm.*

The atmosphere, the service and the cuisine are all so good that it's worth making an effort to go to this restaurant. There's a jovial welcome and smiling service and the chef often chats to you when you've finished your meal. The décor includes postcards, posters and souvenirs brought back by regular customers over the past 40 years. Their traditional cuisine respects the changing seasons and the fresh produce from the markets may include quail or venison. Menu €12.50 (served Tues–Fri lunchtimes only), or à la carte reckon on around €30 with wine on top. They won't let you use the loos unless you're over 18. *Free digestif offered to our readers on presentation of this guide.*

⊚ |●| 🍴 La Preuve par 9

5 rue Damrémont; M° Lamarck-Caulaincourt or Place-de-Clichy.
☎01.42.62.64.69
Closed *24, 25 and 31 Dec; 1 Jan.* **Open** *daily noon–3.30pm and 7–11.30pm.* **Disabled access.**

According to one of the blackboards in this restaurant, it is open nine days out of nine. This theme is continued in the menu, where there is a choice of nine starters, nine main courses and nine desserts that all change constantly. The setting has the air of a classroom, and here you can learn about original recipes like shark steak with vanilla or *sautéed* bison with red fruits. Lunchtime menus €14 and €18; dinner €24. Even though it's more expensive at night, you must book to be sure of a table. *Free house apéritif offered to our readers on presentation of this guide.*

© |●| Taka

1 rue Véron; M° Pigalle or Abbesses.
☎01.42.23.74.16
Closed *Sun; Mon; public holidays; 14–31 July; 15–31 Aug.* **Open** *7.30–10pm.*

Tiny little Japanese restaurant in a narrow, dingy street at the foot of the Butte. It's often absolutely crammed so it's best to book. Mr Taka is a lovely man and attentive to your needs. Typically Japanese décor and ambiance right down to the abacus used by Mr Taka to calculate the bill. Authentic Japanese cooking, perfectly executed: the quality never wavers. You'll find all the Japanese classics – *sushi, sashimi, miso* soup and so on. Try the *shabu-shabu* (finely sliced beef and vegetables cooked in a seaweed broth), *sukiyaki* (a sort of beef and vegetable *fondue* served in a casserole dish), or the *maku no uchi* (house menu with tasty starters, raw and fried fish, cooked lotus roots) presented in a typically Japanese box. Save room for dessert: warm sweet red beans with green tea flavoured ice cream. Reckon on about €30 a head à la carte, including a bottle of hot *saké*. It's essential to book one day in advance.

© 🕏 |●| Le Bouclard

1 rue Cavalotti; M° Place-de-Clichy.
☎01.45.22.60.01
Closed *14–28 Aug.* **Open** *7pm–midnight.*

The nicely thought-out rustic setting creates the right atmosphere for traditional, regional cooking and a selection of carefully chosen wines you can drink at the bar. Michel Bonnemort's formula has been running successfully for the last ten years. The boss is a real *bon vivant*, enthusiastic about the simple dishes he creates from quality ingredients: gratin of crayfish tails, cabbage stuffed with pike perch, *fricassée* of black pudding and apples with Calvados with mash... all of it is delicious. The lunch menu, which includes a glass of wine

and coffee, is excellent value for money but it's expensive in the evening. Expect to pay around €40 à la carte. *Free house apéritif offered to our readers on presentation of this guide.*

19th arrondissement

© 🕏 🏠 Hôtel Crimée**

188 rue de Crimée; M° Crimée.
☎01.40.36.75.29 ☎01.40.36.29.57
🌐www.hotelcrimee.com
TV. Pay car park.

A simple, comfortable hotel not far from the canal de l'Ourcq and the Parc de la Villet. There's air-conditioning and sound-proofing in the rooms, as well as good bathrooms and hairdryers. Doubles with shower/wc or bath are €63–€67; triples cost €77. Some rooms for three or four. There's a pay car park nearby (€10 for 24 hrs). *5% discount on the room rate (on Sun and during July–Aug) offered to our readers on presentation of this guide.*

© 🕏 |●| Cok Ming

39 rue de Belleville; M° Belleville or Pyrénées.
☎01.42.08.75.92
Open *11am–1.30am.* **High chairs available.**

This place is run by Cambodian staff, who fly and swerve round the tables providing super-efficient service. It's been going for a good 20 years. You can make up your own menu from a selection of seafood for two, arrange a *fondue* or a hot pot for a group of mates, throw back a bowl of soup or take your time over some of their excellent roasts and barbecued meats and all for very fair prices. The menu is massive and includes a number of Thai dishes. The weekday menu includes starter, main course and dessert for €7.50; the vegetarian menu costs €11 and the *Cok Ming* €13.50. You'll pay around €15–18 for a meal à la carte. There's also a good choice of teas, wines and beers. *Free house apéritif offered to our readers on presentation of this guide.*

© |●| Aux Arts et Sciences Réunis

161 av. Jean-Jaurès; M° Ourcq.
☎01.42.40.53.18
Closed *Sun; public holidays.* **Open** *noon–2.30pm and 7–10pm.* **Disabled access.**

You'll see compasses and a set square on the façade of this "canteen" for people who work at the headquarters of the carpenters' guild. Go past the bar to an extremely attractive dining room with a parquet floor, ceiling mouldings and lots of photos of guild members on the walls. The food, like the atmosphere, is provincial in style. The weekday lunch menu (€9.70) is good value, with generous helpings and wine included; there's also a *menu campagnard* at €19 and a gourmet menu at €24.50.

◎ |◎| 🎎 Au Rendez-Vous de la Marine

14 quai de la Loire; M° Jaurès.
℡01.42.49.33.40
Closed *Sun; Mon; a week at Christmas.*
Open *noon–2pm and 8–10pm.*

A delightful bistro with flowers on the tables, nautical souvenirs scattered around and photos of film stars. It's the place to come and it's noisy, especially at lunchtime and on every other Saturday evening in the winter when a talented female singer out-Piafs Piaf. In summer, tables are set on the terrace and you have a view of the canal. Food is reasonably priced and helpings are generous, though the cooking, really, is pretty ordinary. Regular dishes include calf's head and scallops *à la grecque*. Dish of the day costs €11.60, or expect to pay around €26 à la carte. It's a good idea to book. *Free Kir or coffee offered to our readers on presentation of this guide.*

◎ |◎| La Cave Gourmande

10 rue du Général-Brunet; M° Botzaris.
℡01.40.40.03.30
Closed *Sat; Sun; a week in Feb; 3 weeks in Aug.* **Open** *12.15–2.30pm and 7.30–10.30pm.*

The previous owner, Éric Frechon, has left this restaurant in the extremely capable hands of Mark and Dominique Singer. Dishes on the lunchtime menu, €28, and seasonal menu, €32, may include *croustillant* of pike perch with chorizo, *tatin* of sirloin steak with shallots and *aumônière* of oxtail, quail in "*demi-deuil*" (half-mourning) with white summer truffles – all highly original dishes, served with brio in a chic, wine-cellar setting. Even when it is full, there is plenty of space for everybody to enjoy their meal at leisure.

◎ |◎| Le Pavillon Puebla

Parc des Buttes-Chaumont; on the junction of rue Botzaris and av. Simon-Bolivar; M°

Buttes-Chaumont.
℡01.42.08.92.62
Closed *Sun; Mon; public holidays.* **Open** *noon–1.30pm and 7.30–10.30pm.*

Standing in the middle of the city's most beautiful park, this restaurant has a refined setting with fresh flowers everywhere. The terrace is out of this world. You'll be received with style, but there's no bowing or scraping. The cooking is first-rate and chef Christian Verges changes his dishes regularly so they reflect the seasons: squid *à la catalane*, lobster stew with Banyuls wine, *pinata* (braised fish), and oyster ravioli with a curry sauce. And the desserts are to die for. It's expensive – in fact it's very expensive if you go à la carte and have wine too (reckon on at least €65) – but the €33 Catalan menu lists Serrano ham and bread dipped in oil, *calamari* with saffron, grilled black pudding with potato and cabbage *galette* or cod steak *à la tapenade*. It's absolutely terrific and comes complete with canapés, home-made rolls and so on. There's another menu at €48.

20th arrondissement

◎ 🏨 Tamaris Hôtel*

14 rue des Maraîchers; M° Porte-de-Vincennes or RER A, Nation.
℡01.43.72.85.48 ℻01.43.56.81.75
🌐www.tamaris-hotel.fr
TV.

Reservations are advisable at this extremely well-run little hotel which has prices you might expect in the depths of the country. The rooms are small and pretty and have flowery wallpaper. Doubles with basin €35, with shower €42, with shower/wc €48; the rooms are not very big but they are clean and some have been refurbished. *Free coffee, fruit juice or soft drink offered to our readers on presentation of this guide.*

◎ 🎎 🏨 Hôtel Paris Gambetta**

12 av. du Père-Lachaise; M° Gambetta.
℡01.47.97.76.57 ℻01.47.97.17.61
🌐www.parisgambetta.com
TV. Cots available.

A pleasant, welcoming two-star in a quiet street near Père-Lachaise cemetery. The completely refurbished rooms are perfectly adequate, with large beds pushed into alcoves, and all have TV and mini-bar. Doubles with shower/wc or bath cost €75–80, depending on the size and outlook. It's a good place; quiet and cosy, and in a non-touristy neighbourhood that's worth discovering. The new owner has got everything in hand and is particular about cleanliness. *One free breakfast per room or 10% discount on the room rate offered to our readers on presentation of this guide.*

ⓔ |●| La Boulangerie

15 rue des Panoyaux; M° Ménilmontant.
☎01.43.58.45.45
Closed *Sat lunch; Sun.*

A delightful place. This is an offshoot of *Lou Pascalou*, the café over the road, as the premises have been bought by its owner's son, Momo, and turned into a restaurant serving traditional dishes livened up by local herbs: roast rack of lamb with lime and lavender, cod poached with balsamic vinegar and pecans, red-tuna *tartare* with lemon grass, and mosaic of grilled vegetables. Dish of the day costs €7.50; lunchtime menus €10.50 and 12.50; dinner menu (with starter, main course and dessert) €18.50. Reckon on around €25 à la carte. The wonderful food is matched by impeccable service.

ⓔ ⅍ |●| Aristote

4 rue de la Réunion; M° Maraîchers or Buzenval.
☎01.43.70.42.91
Closed *a fortnight in Aug.* **Open** *lunch and dinner until 11.30pm (last orders).* **Disabled access.**

This little restaurant, simple but welcoming, may not be much to look at, but you won't have to go to the cashpoint before eating here. It offers generous helpings of Greek and Turkish specialities with lots of kebabs and grills. Try the *hunkar beyendi* (rack of lamb with puréed aubergines), *pacha kebab* (leg of lamb with aubergines and potatoes in a sauce), the *guvec* (veal with vegetables in sauce) or the yoghurt dishes with minced steak or lamb. There are also good fish dishes for non-carnivores. The weekday lunch menu is €8.50; in the evening, à la carte costs €18; wines are around €10 a bottle. Local clientele, background music, pleasant setting and a good atmosphere. *Free digestif offered to our readers on presentation of this guide.*

ⓔ ⅍ |●| Pascaline

49 rue Pixérécourt; M° Pl.-des-Fêtes.
☎01.44.62.22.80

Closed *Sat lunchtime; Sun; Mon evening; Aug; Christmas to New Year.* **Open** *11am–3pm and 6–11.30pm.* **Disabled access.**

This is not the type of Paris restaurant that you'd hunt high and low for, but it's perfectly adequate when you're in the area. Generous portions of good regional dishes: duck *confit*, tripe, *andouillette*, are chalked up on the board and served at the table in sizzling earthenware dishes. To round off the meal, try a tart of clafoutis with fruits of the season. Vegetarians, or anyone on a diet, should give it a miss. Lunch *formule* costs €9; menu €16; à la carte about €20. Interesting wines, especially from the Loire region, start at €15. *Free house apéritif or coffee or digestif offered to our readers on presentation of this guide.*

ⓔ ⅍ |●| Au Rendez-Vous des Amis

10 av. du Père-Lachaise; M° Gambetta.
☎01.47.97.72.16
Closed *Sun; Mon; 20 July–20 Aug.* **Open** *noon–3pm.*

There's a good atmosphere in this friendly restaurant situated near the Père-Lachaise cemetery. Robust dishes: *escalope* of foie gras with apples and sirloin with blue cheese sauces – it's satisfyingly old-fashioned cooking. The €11.30 menu gives you a starter and main course, there's a *formule* for €10.20 and à la carte will set you back between €22 and €25. *Free house apéritif or coffee offered to our readers on presentation of this guide.*

ⓔ |●| Café Noir

15 rue Saint-Blaise; M° Porte-de-Bagnolet or Alexandre-Dumas.
☎01.40.09.75.80
Closed *20 Dec–2 Jan.* **Open** *7pm–midnight.*

This was a dispensary at the beginning of the twentieth century, but there's little sign of its medical past – the owners collect coffee pots, hats, enamel signs and posters rather than medicine bottles. They serve generous portions of good food: dishes such as fillet of pike perch with lemon and liquorice and fillet of beef with foie gras and spiced bread. And you can indulge in a cigar afterwards – the bar sells single Havanas. You'll pay about €25 for a meal, not including a drink.

ⓔ |●| Chez Ramona

17 rue Ramponeau; M° Belleville or Couronnes.

☎01.46.36.83.55
Closed *lunchtimes; Mon.* **Open** *7–11pm.*

This little grocer's is always crowded but the restaurant is on the first floor up a steep, narrow staircase. The dining room is astonishing – crammed with Spanish souvenirs, velvet bulls' heads, *banderillas* in cellophane, artificial flowers, photos and posters of flamenco dancers – kitsch city. Paella, which you need to order in advance, costs €36.60 for two; though it lacks subtlety the helpings are huge. Otherwise you can choose from a variety of traditional, peasant-style dishes – deep-fried squid rings, mussels, Galicia-style hake – all of them taste good. Reckon on about €23 à la carte.

Neuilly-sur-Seine
92200 (0.5km NW)

ⓦ 🎍 |●| Le Chalet

14 rue du Commandant-Pilot; M° les Sablons; it's near the market square.
☎01.46.24.03.11
Closed *Sun in July/Aug.* **Open** *noon–2.30pm and 7.30–11pm.* **High chairs available.**

A Swiss chalet for those who didn't get away on a skiing holiday last year. There are snowscape photos on the wall to help the illusion and bits of equipment scattered around. At lunchtime there's a *formule express* at €12.50 which helps to fill the restaurant with customers, and the evening menus "Mont Blanc" and "savoyard" at €26 and €28, draw the regulars in. Specialities include *fondue savoyarde*, *raclette* and *tartiflette*. It's a great place and very welcoming. *Free house apéritif offered to our readers on presentation of this guide.*

ⓦ 🎍 |●| Restaurant Foc Ly

79 av. Charles-de-Gaulle; M° Les Sablons.
☎01.46.24.43.36
Closed *a fortnight in Aug.* **Disabled access. Pay car park.**

You can't miss this place – it's got a pyramid roof and a pair of lions guarding the entrance. If you cast your eye over the long menu to the right of the front door, you'll also see numerous rave reviews from such figures as Jacques Chirac, Inès de la Fressange and Claude Chabrol. You might find better in Peking, Taiwan or Hong Kong, but this is undoubtedly one of the best Chinese restaurants in Neuilly, with a very refined and varied style of cooking.

Weekday lunchtime *formule* costs €16, menu €18.60, or about €30 à la carte. There's also a children's menu at €12.20 including a drink. *Free house apéritif offered to our readers on presentation of this guide.*

ⓦ 🎍 |●| Les Pieds dans l'Eau

39 bd. du Parc; it's on the Île de Jatte. M° Pont de Neuilly, then 10 minutes' walk.
☎01.47.47.64.07
Closed *Sat lunchtime and Sun.*

There's a feeling of times past in this riverside restaurant – an atmosphere of fishing parties and languid summer picnics. The furniture is English-style and there are old engravings on the wall, creating a sort of club-house ambience. The terraces run right down to the edge of the River Seine, under the poplars, fig trees and weeping willows. The chef landed in town from elsewhere and provides flavours from those far-off parts – grilled fish and meats, trout or perch *carpaccio*, tuna *aumônière*, chicken breasts with figs. Set menus €21, €23 and €29, or around €40 à la carte. *Free digestif offered to our readers on presentation of this guide.*

Bagnolet
93170 (1km E)

ⓦ 🎍 |●| Indigo Square

7 rue Marceau; M° Gallieni.
☎01.43.63.26.95
Closed *Sat lunch; Sun; Mon; 22 Dec–3 Jan.*

Close to the town hall and opposite the covered market (which isn't an elegant one), this jewel of a restaurant combines French taste and flavours from further afield. You sit on benches with acid-coloured cushions or 1950s chairs. Dishes are delicately prepared – you might see Munster cheese *croustillant* with cumin, or turkey kebab with Jerusalem artichoke flan served with soya sauce – and desserts are fine and original. The €12 *formule* offers a starter/main course or main course/dessert, and there's a dinner *formule* at €20. It's a deservedly popular place. *Free Kir offered to our readers on presentation of this guide.*

Boulogne-Billancourt
92100 (1km SW)

ⓦ 🎍 🏠 Le Quercy

251 bd. Jean-Jaurès; M° Marcel-Sembat.

☎01.46.21.33.46 ⊕01.46.21.72.21
⊛www.hotel-le-quercy.com
TV.

This hotel has been refashioned, and now has a proper reception with a waiting area, and a security guard at night. The décor is still a bit old-fashioned, but who cares, given that this is one of the least expensive places in town and the welcome comes with a smile. Doubles €48–65 depending on facilities; breakfast €5. *One free breakfast per room offered to our readers on presentation of this guide.*

ⓔ |●| Chez Michel

4 rue Henri-Martin; M° Porte-de-Saint-Cloud.
☎01.46.09.08.10
Closed *Sat lunchtime; Sun; Aug.*

At lunchtime this place has the atmosphere of a noisy canteen. But in the evening, when friends come and talk more intimately, the noise levels drop. The dishes are chalked up on a blackboard so you can choose your own menu. Try terrine of red mullet with peppers and aubergine or terrine of foie gras with spiced bread. There's a weekday lunch menu for €13, or reckon on spending around €30 à la carte.

Ivry-sur-Seine
94200 (1km SE)

ⓔ |●| L'Europe

92 bd. Paul-Vaillant-Couturier; M°Mairie-d'Ivry.
☎01.46.72.04.64
Open *daily for lunch and dinner.*

At lunchtime, the two large dining rooms are full of noise and overflow with customers. They dish up copious portions of excellent couscous, €8–11, and also do good grills with cheap wines. The welcome is warm, the service efficient and there's a lively atmosphere – particularly at the bar.

Levallois-Perret
92300 (1km NW)

ⓔ |●| Au Petit Sud-Ouest

4 rue de Baudin; M° Pont de Levallois.
☎01.47.59.03.74
Closed *Sat evening and Sun (May–Sept); 5 July–1 Sept.* **Open** *to 10pm.*

This is a shop as well as a restaurant that features food from the southwest. The window has a display of sheep's cheeses and country ham. On the menu,

scrambled eggs with ceps, raw foie gras with sea salt, *cassoulet* with *confit* of duck, beef in Madiran wine, *garbure* – Gascony by the Seine. Salads are sold for around €8, dishes €10–22. There's a relaxing terrace in a paved courtyard.

ⓔ |●| Le Petit Poucet

4 rond-point Claude-Monet; it's at the eastern end of the île de la Jatte. M° Pont-de-Levallois.
☎01.47.38.61.85
Open *daily until 10.30pm (11pm at weekends).*

There's been a restaurant here for almost a century. Back in the 1900s, it was a country tavern where working-class men used to bring their sweethearts. In the 1980s it became terribly fashionable, before being transformed ten years ago into a cosy place with lots of wood panelling and a warm atmosphere. It has three lovely terraces, one on the bank of the Seine, where elegant women and fashionable young men come to relax as soon as the sun comes out. Good, classic French cooking with a weekday lunchtime *formule* for €19 (main course with either a starter or a dessert) and a weekend evening menu at €27; expect to pay around €42 for a meal à la carte. Fast, efficient service and it's best to book, especially when the sun is out.

Montreuil
93100 (1km E)

ⓔ ⚘ |●| La Grosse Mignonne

56 rue Carnot; coming from the Croix-de-Chaveaux, it's on a little street off rue Gabriel-Péri, to the right.
☎01.42.87.54.51
Closed *Sun; in Aug.* **Children's games available.**

This restaurant's name refers to a variety of peach that was once the pride and joy of Montreuil; it is hardly seen in town these days, but it has not been forgotten by this charming restaurant. It is one of our favourite places, recommended to young and old alike. The décor is highly colourful, with a motley collection of fabrics and patchworks, naive paintings on the walls and unmatching chairs. The cosmopolitan cuisine follows suit, with Senegalese-style chicken, couscous, sparerib of honeyed pork and Provençal-style bass. One can hardly ask for more variety. On Saturday, when families gather, tables are invariably put together to make way for pushchairs, while older children go and play in the corner especially reserved for them, while waiting for their (scrumptious) chocolate mousse. Meanwhile, their parents have an opportunity to chat and sip their drinks at leisure. There are no specific children's menus, but every effort is made to come to a satisfactory arrangement for them. There is a weekday lunchtime menu at €10, then others at €11 and €20; reckon on €16–27 for a complete meal. *Free house apéritif offered to our readers on presentation of this guide.*

⟨⟨ |●| Le Gaillard

71 rue Hoche; M° Mairie-de-Montreuil.
☎01.48.58.17.37
Closed *Sun evening; Mon lunch; 3 weeks in Aug.*

It's worth braving the boulevard Périphérique to get here. Atop the Guillands hill, in the middle of nowhere, this old residence is a haven of culinary taste and *savoir-vivre*. The starters are delicate and the mains have *panache* – whole calves' kidneys, pan-fried foie gras, duck *parmentier* with salad – while desserts are simple but delicious. Menus €26.70 and €35.80, but à la carte the bill can shoot up – not least because the wines are expensive. There's an appealing open fire in winter and an amazing garden/terrace that comes into its own in the summer (it's best to reserve if you want to sit outside).

Nanterre
92000 (1km NW)

⟨⟨ 🏠 Hôtel Saint-Jean

24-26-33 av. de Rueil; RER A, Nanterre-Ville.
☎01.47.24.19.20 ☎01.47.24.17.65
✉hotel.stjean@wanadoo.fr

This hotel, 500m from the centre of town in a quiet neighbourhood, has been in the same family for three generations. Each room is different, but they're all clean and well maintained; doubles from €27 with basin, €34 with shower or €39 and €40 with shower/wc. Some of them look over the pretty garden. You'll get a very pleasant welcome.

Saint-Mandé
94160 (1km E)

⟨⟨ |●| Le Bistrot Lucas

8 rue Jeanne d'Arc; M° Saint-Mandé Tourelle.
☎01.48.08.74.81

Closed *Sun; Mon; 3 weeks in Aug.*

This lyonnais-style bistro, on the outskirts of Paris, is within striking distance of the Vincennes woods. They treat you very well amid the wooden tables, simple décor and postcards on the walls. Attractive dishes are all perfect, from the lentil *rémoulade* with hot Lyon sausage to the calf's head *ravigote*. There's a lunch menu at €20.50 and another menu at €26.50.

Saint-Ouen
93400 (1km N)

⟨⟨ |●| Le Soleil

109 av. Michelet; it's opposite the Biron market; M° Porte-de-Clignancourt.
☎01.40.10.08.08
Open *lunchtimes; evenings, Thurs–Sat.*

This restaurant attracts a crowd of regulars, and the owner scurries between the tables hailing his well-heeled guests. The décor is appealingly elegant – there's a huge sun in the centre of the ceiling and unusual blinds at the windows. The tables are well dressed, with *fleur de sel* (salt) from the Île de Ré, Saint-Lô butter pats and free-flowing olive oil from the Italian Riviera. Starters €10–16: marinated herring fillets, Andalusian mountain ham, smoked salmon marinated in dill. Main courses €17–22: royal sea bass, steak with red wine sauce. Excellent desserts include a huge rum baba, *crème catalan* with Bourbon vanilla, and apple tart. There's a good wine list, too; some are served by the jug, for around €12. All this adds up to a substantial bill but, given the quality, that's fair enough. A very, very good place.

Vincennes
94300 (2km SE)

⟨⟨ 🍴 |●| Ristorante Alessandro

51 rue de Fontenay; M° Château-de-Vincennes; RER A, Vincennes; it's beside the town hall.
☎01.49.57.05.30
Closed *Sun; 3 weeks in Aug.* **Disabled access.**

It's a pity that the décor of this pizzeria is quite so ordinary, as the food itself certainly isn't. Italian specialities include aubergine parmigiana, spaghetti with king prawns, tagliatelle with scallops and *saltimbocca alla romana* (a wonderful combination of veal, Parma ham and sage). The *antipasti*

− artichokes, olives, sun-dried tomatoes, pickled onions and charcuterie − are fantastic. And the pasta dishes and pizzas − delicious crispy bases and generous, classic toppings − are the real thing. Set weekday lunch menu costs €11, then others at €23 and €30.50 served in the evening; reckon on around €30 for a meal à la carte. *Free house apéritif offered to our readers on presentation of this guide.*

Courbevoie-La-Défense
92400 (3km NW)

⬢ 𝒜 🏠 Hôtel George-Sand

18 av. Marceau; M° Esplanade-de-La Défense; it's 50m from Courbevoie station.
☎01.43.33.57.04 ℗01.47.88.59.38
🖥www.hotel-paris-georgesand.com
Open *all year.* **TV. Pay car park.**

Ask for one of the renovated rooms but, before mounting the stairs, take a look at the collection of George Sand memorabilia on the ground floor: busts, letters, souvenirs. The décor has echoes of the period she lived in. Each room is personalized and furnished by the owner who picks things up at auctions and junk shops. His family have run the place for a couple of generations. It's a quiet hotel that offers good value for money given you're not far from the Défense. Fully-equipped doubles with en-suite bathrooms go for €130; buffet breakfast €10. They even provide decent room service; meals on trays, dry-cleaning etc. *10% discount on the room rate offered to our readers on presentation of this guide.*

⬢ |●| 𝒜 Chez Natale, Pasta, Amore e Fantasia

80 av. Marceau; train from Saint-Lazare to Courbevoie station (direction Versailles-Saint-Nom-la-Bretèche or Houilles) or RER line A, La Défense.
☎01.43.33.68.30
Closed *Sun; Mon evening; Aug.*

You'll be blown away here by the exuberant colours of Naples − they've even strung washing on a line across the room. The dining room is vast but manages to feel intimate. The cuisine is equally exuberant and colourful: delicious *antipasti*, a huge choice of pizzas, *osso buco à la piémontaise*, Sicilian ravioli, *piccata parmigiana* and so on. Weekday lunch menu at €20, then others €30 and €42, or around €25 à la carte. There's live music on Friday and Saturday

nights. It's a good idea to book, whenever you come. *Free house apéritif, coffee or digestif offered to our readers on presentation of this guide.*

Saint-Denis
93200 (10km N)

⬢ |●| 𝒜 Les Verdiots

26 bd. Marcel-Sembat; 200m from M° Porte-de-Paris and 400m from the Stade de France.
☎01.42.43.24.33
Closed *Sun; Mon; Aug; a week around Christmas and the New Year.* **Open** *noon–2.30pm and 7.30–9.30pm.*

Patrick Perney specializes in confident, tasty dishes originating from les Landes on the Atlantic coast − ham from the Aldudes, chicken with foie gras, spicey roast cod, scallops with leeks. The service is friendly and charming, the dining room classic and clean, and the prices honest. There's a substantial weekday lunch menu at €11.40 (starter, main course and dessert) and another menu at €18.50; otherwise it's about €40 à la carte. A good place with good wines − not too expensive if you stick to the wine of the month. *Free house apéritif offered to our readers on presentation of this guide.*

⬢ 𝒜 |●| Le Wagon

15 bis av. Jean-Moulin; M° Porte de Paris; it's near the Baleine swimming pool.
☎01.48.23.23.41
Closed *July–Aug.* **Open** *Tues, Thurs and Fri lunchtimes only.*

This is an amazing restaurant, housed in a railway carriage. It's run by a restaurant school, so the waiters and kitchen staff apply themselves to their tasks with great concentration. You eat cheaply but well; à la carte, reckon on around €14 (there's a children's menu for €5). They specialize in fish and seafood; good dishes include red mullet with vanilla, duck breast with orange, pan-fried scallops, and excellent house desserts. It's well worth booking. *Free apéritif or coffee offered to our readers on presentation of this guide.*

Saint-Maur-des-Fossés
94100 (16km E)

⬢ |●| Le Bistrot de la Mer

59 bis av. du Bac; from Paris, it's a turning off the A4 autoroute.

☎01.48.83.01.11
ⓦwww.le-bistrot-de-la-mer.com
Closed *Sun evening.* **Open** *until 11pm.*

The dining room is decorated in blue and white, creating just the right atmosphere for a seafood restaurant, and dishes are prepared with style. There's lots of originality and skill in the cooking and the quality is reliable so the place has earned itself a regular following. There's a weekday lunch *formule* at €12, menus €16 (weekday lunchtimes only) and €26 (children's menu €8); à la carte reckon on around €35. The lunch *formules* offer excellent value for money. Specialities include scallops, smoked salmon and a superb fish soup. They even do seafood to take away and cocktails are available at the bar in the evenings. The welcome and service are superb.

⊜ |●| ⅔ **Le Gourmet**

150 bd. du Général-Giraud.
☎01.48.86.86.96
Closed *Sun evening; Mon; 20 Aug–10 Sept.*
Disabled access.

There are decent places to eat and there are good restaurants – and then there's *Le Gourmet*, which offers high-class cuisine at its best. The setting is wonderfully done: the dining room is elegant Art Deco with armfuls of flowers in big vases, and there's a wide bay window looking out onto a lovely terraced garden where you dine in the summer. And that's not all: the proprietor learned his profession in some of the greatest kitchens in the capital and is on absolutely top form. The food is succulent, delicious and prepared with meticulous care – flavours are delicately balanced and each dish is cooked to perfection. The speciality of the chef, Dominique, is duck breast stuffed with lobster, but he also offers more classical dishes – it's even possible to buy meals to take away. There's a lunch *formule* at €15 (not served Sunday or public holidays) including drink and coffee. Menus go for €25, €30 and €40 (with a half bottle of wine and coffee included) not served on public holidays. This is a really great place. *Free house digestif offered to our readers on presentation of this guide.*

⊜ ⅔ |●| **Chez Nous Comme Chez Vous**

110 av. du Mesnil; take the A4 from Paris.
☎01.48.85.41.61
ⓦcheznouscommechezvous.com

Closed *Sun evening; Mon and Tues lunchtimes (plus 1 Tues evening per week); a week early May; Aug.*

There's an old provincial feel about this place. They've got a battery of copper pots on the walls and it would take an earthquake to disrupt the solid traditions in the kitchen, which are rooted deeply in regional cuisine. You're in the hands of real professionals who focus on providing quality rather than originality. Madame has been running front-of-house for a good quarter of a century and the service is first rate; her husband, the chef, keeps his standards similarly high. Dishes of the day (around €13) might include paella or beef. There's a weekday lunch *formule* at €18, and menus ranging from €27 up to €57. You will be asked whether you are enjoying your meal and any crumbs are swept away before dessert. *Free coffee offered to our readers on presentation of this guide.*

Pontoise
95300

⊜ ⅔ |●| **Au Pavé de la Roche**

30 rue de la Roche; it's a turning off the place de l'Hôtel-de-Ville (free parking noon–2pm).
☎01.34.43.14.05
Closed *Sat lunchtime; Sun evening; Mon; 3 weeks in Aug; a week at Christmas.*

You'll find this establishment on a bend of a road climbing above the Oise. Try the €12.50 weekday lunch menu, with wine included: you start by choosing from the *crudités* buffet, which has at least twenty dishes, and follow with a good main dish and home-made dessert. They also offer a menu at €28, and à la carte you can expect to pay around €35. Specialities include rabbit *à la provençale*, *velouté* of melon with cardamom, fruit coucous with rum flambé and pan-fried scallops with caramelized butter. The owners will welcome you with a warm smile, there's a terrace for fine weather, and a peaceful courtyard. *Free coffee offered to our readers on presentation of this guide.*

Provins
77160

⊜ ☗ ⅔ |●| **Hostellerie Aux Vieux Remparts**

3 rue Couverte; in the heart of the medieval city.

☎01.64.08.94.00 📠01.60.67.77.22
🌐www.auxvieuxremparts.com
Closed 20 Dec–2 Jan. **Open** daily noon–
2.30pm and 7.30–9.30pm. **Disabled access.**
TV. High chairs available. Car park.

This hotel, set in a beautiful medieval
house with a garden ablaze with flowers,
has earned an excellent reputation, but
it is expensive: 32 rooms at €65–140,
according to the degree of comfort;
breakfast €12. These rooms are extremely
classy, however: mini-bar, telephone with
a direct outside line, luxurious bathroom
and any number of mod cons. The restaurant, which has a beautiful shady terrace,
offers specialities in the great French
tradition, although the chef Lionel Sarre
adds modern touches, combining fresh
ingredients, interesting combinations and
striking presentation. The result is the
most sophisticated restaurant in the prov-
ince par excellence. Suggestions menu €26
(weekday), pleasure menu €37 and gourmet menu €56. 10% discount on the room
rate (15 Nov–15 March) or free coffee offered
to our readers on presentation of this guide.

Rambouillet
78120

@ 🎋 |●| **Restaurant La Poste**

101 rue du Général-de-Gaulle.
☎01.34.83.03.01
Closed Sun evening; Mon; Thurs evening;
second fortnight in June.

If you want to eat here, one of the best
restaurants in town, it's best to book. The
two dining rooms are extremely pretty, and
service is efficient and friendly. Cooking is
light and refined, with dishes like house
foie gras, lamb noisette, chicken fricassée
with crayfish, and house raspberry soufflé. Set menus €21.50 (not served during
public holidays) and €28.20–33. Free Kir
Normand offered to our readers on presentation of this guide

Roche-Guyon (La)
95780

@ 🏠 |●| 🎋 **Hôtel-Restaurant Les
Bords de Seine**★★

21 rue du Docteur-Duval; it's near the tourist
office on the banks of the Seine.
☎01.39.98.32.52

Open daily lunch and dinner.

As its name suggests, you can watch the
Seine flowing by from this restaurant. The
formule at €15 is served at weekday lunchtime, and there's a menu for €21. The food
is well-cooked, served attractively and you
won't go hungry. They serve a wine of
the month by the glass. The dining room
is decorated in blue and white, and, like
the service, is both elegant and informal.
There's a lovely terrace with parasols for
the summer and heaters in winter. The
hotel is well run, and although the rooms
are small they all have en-suite bathrooms
and phones. Doubles €45–64 with shower
or bath/wc; some have that river view. It's
a good idea to reserve. Logis de France.
Free house apéritif offered to our readers on
presentation of this guide.

@ |●| **La Cancalaise**

18 rue du Général-Leclerc; it's on the main
street.
☎01.34.79.74.48
Closed Mon; Tues; mid-Dec to mid-Jan.
Disabled access. High chairs available.

This place may be aimed at tourists, but
its rustic charm will make you feel at ease
and the freshly made crêpes are reasonably
priced. There are menus at €11 (including
a drink) and €13 (including a drink and
a Kir), as well as an afternoon tea option
at €5.50. The terrace gives on to the main
street of La Roche-Guyon. It is advisable
to book.

Rolleboise
78270

@ 🎋 🏠 |●| **Le Château de la
Corniche**

5 rte. de la Corniche; from Paris take the A13
towards Rouen, leaving by exit 13 direction
of Rosny-sur-Seine or Vernon; from Rouen
take the A13 towards Paris, leaving by exit 15
direction of Bonnières-sur-Seine or Mantes-
la-Jolie.
☎01.30.93.20.00 📠01.30.42.27.44
🌐www.chateaudelacorniche.com
Closed Sun evening and Mon lunch, early
Sept to end April; a fortnight end of Dec to
early Jan. **TV. Car park.**

The rooms in this nineteenth-century
folly have every modern comfort; doubles
from €60 to €168 with bath/wc. The
restaurant is elegant and there's a panoramic view from the terrace. Refined and

innovative gourmet cuisine. Lunch menu €18, served Tuesday to Friday; others €29, €46 and €55 – it may not be cheap but it's definitely good value in this category. There are lots of country walks around and it's a good base from which to visit Monet's house at Giverny. *One free breakfast per room or free coffee offered to our readers on presentation of this guide.*

Rueil-Malmaison

92500

@ ☕ |●| Le Jardin Clos

17 rue Eugène-Labiche; RER A Rueil-Malmaison.
☎01.47.08.03.11
Closed *Sun; Mon; first 3 weeks in Aug.* **Open** *noon–2pm and 8–10pm.*

This restaurant is situated close to the capital but it's already the countryside. The bland exterior doesn't really give you a clue about what you'll find inside: there's a peaceful garden with a well, and you can eat on the terrace. The cooking is seriously tasty and generously served, and you'll get a good-natured welcome. The good-value €22 lunch menu includes a self-service buffet of hors d'œuvres; other menus, €28 and €37, are served both for lunch and dinner. Specialities include *fricassée* of scallops and prawns in balsamic vinegar, duo of scallops and king prawns and fillet of beef Rossini. Main dishes are often accompanied by rissoled potatoes. Booking is recommended. *Free Kir offered to our readers on presentation of this guide.*

Saint-Cloud

92210

@ |●| Le Garde Manger

21 rue d'Orléans; go up the hill leading from the Saint-Cloud bridge to the A13 and keep going straight ahead.
☎01.46.02.03.66
Closed *Sun.*

Bottle-green front and cosy little dining room with young, extremely friendly staff. Traditional food from Southwest France: fried squids with Espelette peppers, *féroce* of chicken breast and the classic duck *magret*. Weekday lunchtime menus cost €13 (main course with either starter or dessert) and €16. On the blackboard, eight starters and eight main courses, along with some suggestions of the day.

Saint-Cyr-sous-Dourdan

91410

@ |●| ☕ La Ferme des Tourelles

2 rue de l'Église.
☎01.64.59.15.29
Closed *Mon evening; Tues.* **Open** *noon–2pm and 7–9.30pm.* **High chairs available.**

The quality of the cooking and the kindness add to your appreciation of this beautiful place. It's one of the most beautiful fortified farms in the Hurepoix. The sixteenth- and seventeenth-century buildings surround a huge, square central courtyard. There are small turrets at each corner (hence the name of the place), with a well in the middle. You can eat in the courtyard where they set tables with red and white checked cloths; from here you glimpse the village church. There's a wide choice of dishes chalked up on a blackboard and it's delicious, traditional food; rabbit *à l'ancienne*, camembert salad, supreme of guinea-fowl with pan-fried foie gras, monk fish with mushrooms and shellfish. Try the coffee and walnut or chocolate and hazelnut desserts. Dishes on the single set menu, €16, change regularly. *Free coffee offered to our readers on presentation of this guide.*

Saint-Germain-en-Laye

78100

@ ☕ ☗ Havre Hôtel*

92 rue Léon-Désoyer; it's on the old road to Chambourcy.
☎ and ☎01.34.51.41.05
Closed *Sun afternoon; first 3 weeks in Aug.* **TV.**

Clean, well-run little hotel in the middle of town where a double with shower/wc or bath will cost €47. Some overlook the cemetery, so there are no extraneous noises to wake you, and all are double-glazed and quiet, even the ones overlooking the road. A good place where you can be sure of a pleasant, friendly welcome. *10% discount on the room rate offered to our readers on presentation of this guide.*

⚲ 🎿 🏠 |●| L'Ermitage des Loges – Le Saint-Exupéry***

11 av. des Loges.
☎01.39.21.50.90 ⊛01.39.21.50.91
🌐www.ermitage-des-loges.com
Disabled access. TV. High chairs available. Car park.

This place is really smart, and there's a wide view of the avenues of trees leading through the forest to the château. Refurbished rooms are extremely comfortable and service is faultless; doubles from €107 (low season) up to €138 in high season. Fine, classic cuisine is served in the Art Deco dining room. The lunchtime *menu du jour* is excellent value for money at €21 and includes a small bottle of mineral water and coffee; there's another evening menu at €31. Specialities include duck foie gras with apples and pinenuts, *confit* of pork, and orange soufflé with Grand Marnier. *Free house apéritif offered to our readers on presentation of this guide.*

⚲ |●| Restaurant La Feuillantine

10 rue des Louviers.
☎01.34.51.04.24 ⊛01.34.51.41.03
Closed *Sun and public holidays.*

Speedy service in a tasteful dining room – you eat very well here. Dishes listed on the lunch *formules*, €19–28, and menu, €30, include excellent foie gras and omelette with smoked salmon.

Saint-Maurice
94410

⚲ |●| La Pibale

11 rue Paul-Verlaine; RER Joinville-le-Pont.
☎01.42.83.62.35
Closed *Sat lunch; Sun; Mon evening; a week at Easter; a week in Aug.* **Pay car park.**

There's something typically Spanish-Basque here – it's not the paintings – but rather the ropes of Espelette peppers, the tables with *azulejos*, and the kitchen open to the dining room. It's also in the way they prepare the food: marinated sardines, anchovy purée with leeks, *axoa* (veal, ham and *piperade*), *pimientos del piquillo* (peppers stuffed with cod)... and what of their eels? Elvers (available in winter only) are highly prized but too expensive (€60 per 80g). In March they serve lamprey cooked in white wine. For dessert there's *gateau basque* and *tourtière*

Marie. Lunch *formule* of main meal with either starter or dessert costs €20, and the *menu-carte* goes for €28. Eating here is expensive but it's really excellent, so much so that you will need to book in advance at weekends.

Sainte-Geneviève-des-Bois
91700

⚲ |●| La Table d'Antan

38 av. de la Grande-Charmille-du-Parc; 200m from the town hall, at the roundabout, it's the first road on the right.
☎01.60.15.71.53
Closed *Mon; Sun, Tues and Wed evenings; Aug.* **Open** *noon–1.15pm and 7.30–9pm.*

This place is in a quiet part of the town in a neat, refurbished house. The chef specializes in duck dishes – duck foie gras in particular, cooked in several different ways – but menus also include tasty fish and meat. All the dishes on the *menu tradition*, €26, and the other menu, €46, are expertly prepared using the freshest of ingredients. The mistress of the house extends a charming welcome and it's essential to book.

Sarcelles
95200

⚲ 🎿 |●| Le Chanteclerc

3 pl. du Souvenir-Français - 144, rue Pierre-Brossolette; near the church, in the upper part of the old village, behind the cemetery; take the Chantilly road (N16), in the direction of Écouens.
☎01.39.90.0087
Closed *Mon; in Aug.* **High chairs available.**

This restaurant is a highly reputed local institution, run by Jean Claude Impens with warmth and efficiency for many years. The large dining room can seat 100 people – and that's without mentioning the terrace. The cooking is based on fresh produce: casserole of scallops, fish *choucroute* and fillet of beef with mustard sauce. The prices have gone up considerably since our last visit – does this have anything to do with its increasing popularity among local celebrities? The menus cost €26 and €37 and the excellent "autumn salads" €12–29; reckon on around €40 à la carte. It is advisable to book at the weekend. *Free glass of champagne offered to our readers on presentation of this guide.*

Sceaux
92330

⊚ 🎋 |❶| L'Auberge du Parc

6 av. du Président-Franklin-Roosevelt; RER B Bourg-la-Reine, then bus #192.
☏01.43.50.35.15
Closed *in Aug.* **Open** *evenings until 11pm.*

A nice detached house opposite the entrance to the Lycée Lakanal, with a small, sunny terrace at the front. Unsurprisingly, it attracts a regular crowd of students during the week. The dining room has provincial charm and looks down on the garden. The *formules* are of the speedy, efficient type; there's one for students at €5. They offer a selection of reasonably priced Iberian specialities including cod with a range of sauces; certain dishes have to be reserved in advance and are for a minimum of seven people. Weekday lunch menu, €9, includes starter, main course and cheese or dessert and 25cl of wine; expect to pay around €20 à la carte. An ideal stop if you're on a Sunday walk. *Free coffee offered to our readers on presentation of this guide.*

Sèvres
92360

⊚ 🎋 |❶| La Salle à Manger

12 av. de la Division-Leclerc.
☏01.46.26.66.64
Closed *Sat lunchtime; Sun; Mon; Aug.*

The décor is bright and fresh and you immediately feel you're in the country. On the menu you'll find *œufs en meurette* (in red wine sauce), tomato tart with Cantal cheese and mustard, *fricassée* of rabbit with herbs, calf's cheek with orange and cumin and duck breast in honey – a cornucopia of flavours. The place is a hive of activity and the service is quiet, quick and efficient; take your time to enjoy it. It's often full because it's such good value: menus €17–29.50. *Free house apéritif offered to our readers on presentation of this guide.*

Soisy-sur-École
91840

⊚ 🎋 |❶| Le Saut du Postillon

On the D948, north of Courances near the fork for Soisy-sur-École.
☏01.64.98.08.12
Closed *Sun and Wed evenings; Mon; Aug; Christmas and New Year holidays.* **Open** *noon–2pm and 7–9pm.* **High chairs available.**

Leaded lights, a broad fire place and copper pots on the walls give this inn its authentic rustic look. It's a historic place – good King Henri went to call on his lady friend, Juliette d'Antraygues, in Malesherbes, when a rut in the road caused a carriage wheel to come off. He ordered the *postillon* to jump down to fix it, and that's where the restaurant gets its name, so it's said. The road's in better shape today and there's a car park for your carriage. Excellent classic dishes served with friendliness and efficiency. The plates are hot, the dishes tasty and well presented. Just what you want. Weekday menu served until 9pm for €12.20, standard menu for €22.50 or gourmet menu at €29.50. *Free coffee offered to our readers on presentation of this guide.*

Suresnes
92150

⊚ 🎋 |❶| La Cave Gourmande

20 rue des Bourets.
☏01.42.04.13.67
Closed *Sat lunch; Sun; Mon lunch; Aug.*

This stylish restaurant, right in the centre of Suresnes, has nothing to do with a cellar. So don't panic if you're claustrophobic; the dining room is actually at street level. It's a good place for foodies, serving nicely composed dishes: minced scallops marinated in dill, medallions of monkfish, sautéed crayfish with champagne, panfried foie gras. There's a weekday lunch menu at €20, then other menus €24 and €35; expect to pay around €39 à la carte. *Free house apéritif offered to our readers on presentation of this guide.*

⊚ 🎋 |❶| Les Jardins de Camille

70 av. Franklin Roosevelt; take bus #244 to the Pont de Suresnes stop or take the train to the Suresnes-Mont-Valérien station.

☎01.45.06.22.66
Closed *Sun evening.* **Disabled access.**

This big house stands on the hillside of the Suresnes vineyards, way up high with a fabulous view of Paris below. They serve Burgundy wine here, and the cuisine is good – country dishes like foie gras terrine, poached half lobster with langoustines, Bresse chicken with foie gras. You'll find food like this on their *menu-cartes* at €32.50 and €55. The Poinsots know what they're about, greet you well and really take care of you. *Free digestif offered to our readers on presentation of this guide.*

Vanves
92170

⟨ |●| Aux Sportifs

51 rue Sadi-Carnot; it's near the cemetery.
☎01.46.42.12.63
Closed *Sat; Sun; Aug.* **Open** *up to 9pm.*

This is a popular bistro-restaurant serving a regular blue- and white-collar clientele. It's as if a bell rings at noon and they all flood in. You could be forgiven for thinking the décor hasn't changed since the 1960s – and that's sort of a compliment. The lovely woman who owns the place puts her heart and soul into the traditional home cooking; it's simple and good. There's only one set menu, which will set you back €11.50 for starter, main course and dessert; otherwise you'll pay around €8.80 for a main course.

Versailles
78000

⟨ 🏠 Home Saint-Louis**

28 rue Saint-Louis.
☎01.39.50.23.55 ☎01.30.21.62.45
TV.

This is a quiet, comfortable, well-looked-after hotel in the heart of the pretty Saint-Louis neighbourhood. Very clean doubles with shower €48, €60 with shower/wc or bath – all have double glazing, TV and hair dryers, and are redecorated regularly, but the bathrooms are a bit small. It's very good value for money.

⟨ ⅍ 🏠 Hôtel Richaud***

16 rue Richaud.
☎01.39.50.10.42 ☎01.39.53.43.36

TV. Car park.

This must be the most central and yet the most peaceful hotel in town. It has forty very clean rooms with TV and direct-dial telephone – ask for one looking over the buildings of the Hôpital Richaud opposite. The furnishings and decoration are very 1970s – they certainly didn't stint on the carpeting – and make sure you see the bar, which is a monument to kitsch. It doesn't really deserve three stars but it has two-star prices, so that's OK: doubles €51–61 with shower/wc or bath. *One free breakfast per room offered to our readers on presentation of this guide.*

⟨ 🏠 ⅍ Hôtel du Cheval Rouge**   ⑩

18 rue André-Chénier; it's on the market square.
☎01.39.50.03.03 ☎01.39.50.61.27
TV. Cots available. Car park.

This well-located, comfortable hotel – with the atmosphere of a small motel – also has a pretty tearoom (where you take breakfast). Doubles €68 with shower/wc and €82 with bath/wc – not bad for a town where prices are sky-high, especially near the château. The car park is a definite plus. *10% discount on the room rate offered to our readers on presentation of this guide.*

⟨ ⅍ 🏠 Paris Hôtel**

14 av. de Paris; RER Versailles-rive-gauche.
It's 400m from the pl. d'Armes.
☎01.39.50.56.00 ☎01.39.50.21.83
🌐www.paris-hotel.fr
Disabled access. TV. High chairs available.

You will get a very warm welcome in this newly refurbished hotel and the proprietor will give you a friendly handshake when you come down for breakfast. Spacious, clean rooms, the nicest overlooking the courtyard; doubles €72 with shower/wc and €100 with bath. The rooms overlooking the avenue are double glazed. *One free breakfast per room offered to our readers on presentation of this guide.*

⟨ |●| ⅍ Sister's Café

15 rue des Réservoirs; not far from the château, on the street running along the Neptune pond and the north side of the park.
☎01.30.21.21.22
Open *daily noon–3pm and 7–11pm.*

Long, American-style bar restaurant with brash decoration, popular with a young, local crowd for their American or Tex-Mex dishes (chicken wings, *quesadillas*). They put a few tables on the terrace in fine weather. Menus go for €13.50–18.50; brunch served at the weekend for €18. *Free Kir offered to our readers on presentation of this guide.*

◎ 𝔸 |●| La Cuisine Bourgeoise

10 bd. du Roi.
☎01.39.53.11.38
Closed *3 weeks in Aug.* **Open** *evenings (Mon–Sat).* **Disabled access. Car park.**

This very cosy dining room, decorated in shades of green, is a little more gourmet than bourgeois. You'll see asparagus, foie gras and morels in light, flavoursome dishes. The €21.50 lunch menu is chalked up on the blackboard and there's another at €29.50; menus €39 (two-course) and €46 (full) in the evening. À la carte you'll pay about €55. There's an excellent list of vintages by the glass. *Free digestif offered to our readers on presentation of this guide.*

◎ 𝔸 |●| La Flottille

☎01.39.51.41.58
Brasserie open *daily 8am–5.30pm (9pm in summer).* **Restaurant open** *lunchtimes only until 3.30pm.* **Disabled access.**

The restaurant is located immediately opposite the landing stage where, on a fine day, small boats can be hired. Undeniably the most agreeable place imaginable: in summer, the terrace flows down to the water's edge. There are two dining rooms and two styles of dining: the brasserie, and the slightly more expensive restaurant. On the whole the cooking is as it should be, and in the brasserie, the dishes and salads are nicely presented. Pancakes and pastries are also on offer. There's a *formule* at €23, or you'll pay around €35 à la carte excluding drinks. Otherwise, in the brasserie (serving all day) dishes of the day cost around €10.50. A word of warning – you'll be charged an entry fee of €4.50 to come here by car. *Free coffee offered to our readers on presentation of this guide.*

Montigny-le-Bretonneux
78180 (10km SW)

◎ 𝔸 🏠 |●| L'Auberge du Manet***

61 av. du Manet; coming from Paris on the A13 then the A12 (towards Saint-Quentin), take the Montigny exit; follow the signs to Ferme du Manet.

☎01.30.64.89.00 ☎01.30.64.55.10
🌐www.aubergedumanet.com
Open *noon–2pm and 7–10pm.* **Disabled access. TV. High chairs and games available. Car park.**

The huge farm used to be part of the domaine of the Abbaye de Port-Royal-des-Champs which is about 2km away. They've converted it into a hotel-restaurant in a perfect pastoral setting and they've done it very well. Attractive dining room with a large terrace overlooking a pretty pond. The rooms are faultless and definitely worth the price (€120); all have mini-bar, satellite TV and en-suite bathroom with bath or shower/wc, and they're cheaper at the weekend (€85). In the restaurant the cooking is deftly prepared and reasonably priced, starting with the weekday menu at €30, then the weekend menu at €37; there's also a vegetarian menu at €30, a children's menu at €10, and a few light dishes for €8–14. Menus change three times a year. Classic dishes cooked with confidence; specialities include foie gras *à la tapenade* and home-made brioche, *bouillabaisse*, semi-bitter chocolate soufflé. *10% discount on the room rate or free house apéritif offered to our readers on presentation of this guide.*

Gif-sur-Yvette
91190 (18km S)

◎ 𝔸 |●| Le Bœuf à Six Pattes

D128 Chemin du Moulon; take the Centre universitaire exit 9 off the N118.
☎01.60.19.29.60
Open *11.30am–2.30pm and 7–10pm. (10.30pm Fri and Sat).* **Disabled access. High chairs, crayons and games available. Car park.**

You could well get a crick in the neck as you crane round to look at the cow Slavik has hung up in this restaurant. Unsurprisingly, he specializes in meat dishes, which are first-rate and served with wonderful chips. They also do *confit* of duck thigh and grilled salmon steak, and for dessert they offer a great caramelized rice pudding. *Formule* at €10.60 with salad and a beef dish; menus, €14 and €18, and another at €22.50 which includes *apéritif*, starter, main meal, dessert, drink and coffee. Reckon on €20–22 à la carte. Children's menu (under 12 years) €6.50 – children eat for free at lunchtime on Saturdays and Sundays. There's a terrace for summer and the dining room is strictly non-smoking. *Free house apéritif offered to our readers on presentation of this guide.*

Languedoc-Roussillon

Agde

34300

⚌ 🏠 Hôtel Le Donjon**

Place Jean-Jaurès.
☏04.67.94.12.32 ☏04.67.94.34.54
🌐www.hotelledonjon.com
Closed *2 Dec–4 Jan.* **TV. Pay car park.**

An old stone building practically next door to the ancient cathedral of Saint-Étienne on a pleasant square that buzzes with life in summer. The fresh-looking rooms are comfy, exceptionally well maintained and good value in the range €49–76 for a double with shower/wc or bath. There's a nice atmosphere and good prices (given the location).

⚌ |●| Numéro Vin

2 pl. de la Marine; at the bottom end of the town, very close to the Hérault river and the town.
☏04.67.00.20.20
Closed *Sat and Sun lunchtimes; Mon.*

A great find and a great asset for Agde, a town located on a volcano. Lionel Albano and his team will give you a friendly welcome to the restaurant. The courtyard has been kept traditional despite a definitive new look for the restaurant, which has been decorated on a budget but to great effect. An original and tasteful menu, with a touch of gastronomic interest, offering dishes that smack of the sea and the garrigue: weekday lunch menu at €15; à la carte for about €22. Generous selection of good quality local wines is on offer ranging from €17 to €115, with an appealing range of wines by the glass, too.

⚌ |●| Le Calamar

La Tamarissière,
33 quai Cornu; on the right bank of the Hérault
☏04.67.94.05.06
Closed *Tues and Wed in low season; Sat and Mon lunchtimes in the summer; mid-Nov to mid-Feb.*

Friendly seaside décor for this former fishermen's café that has been transformed into a genuine regional bistro. Enjoy the simply grilled fish or the *parrillada*, while watching the boats or the cars go by, depending on where you're sitting and the time of day. There's a range of menus €20–32; à la carte around €30.

Marseillan

34340 (7km NE)

⚌ |●| Le Jardin du Naris

24 bd. Pasteur; take the D51.
☏04.67.77.30.07
Closed *Mon evening and Tues out of season; Tues lunchtime in summer; Feb.*

The walled garden allows you to dine among the flowers and the trees. Simple traditional dishes using seasonal market produce include poached egg with *foie gras* and oysters *au gratin* served with leeks. The crayons on the tables are used to calculate your bill – weekday lunch menu €10 and others €17–33 – and you can even scribble on the paper tablecloths between courses: the efforts of previous diners are pinned on the walls.

⚌ |●| Côté Sud

18 quai Antonin-Gros. On the port on the left bank of the river.

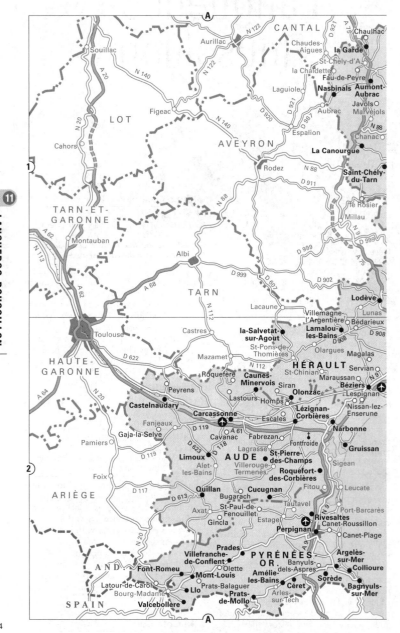

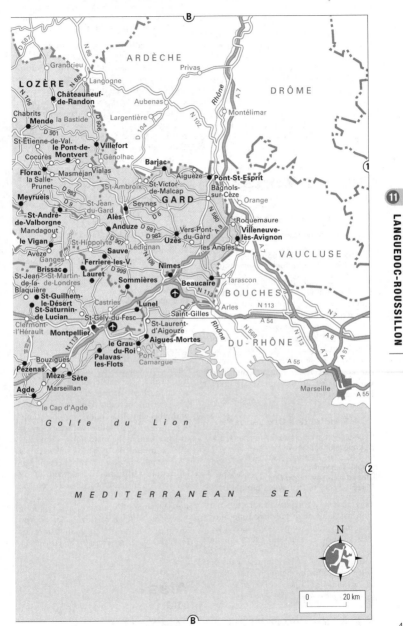

ARDÈCHE

Privas

DRÔME

LOZÈRE

Grandrieu

Langogne

Rhône

Montélimar

Châteauneuf-
de-Randon

Aubenas

Chabrits

Mende

la Bastide

Largentière

St-Étienne-de-Val.

le Pont-de-
Montvert

Villefort

Cocurès

Génolhac

Barjac

Florac

Masméjan

Vialas

Aiguèze

Pont-St-Esprit

la Salle-
Prunet

St-Victor-
de-Malcap

Bagnols-
sur-Cèze

Meyrueis

St-Ambroix

GARD

Orange

St-André-
de-Valborgne

St-Jean-
du-Gard

Seynes

Roquemaure

Mandagout

Alès

Anduze

Vers-Pont-
du-Gard

Villeneuve-
lès-Avignon

le Vigan

St-Hippolyte

Uzès

les Angles

VAUCLUSE

Avèze

Ganges

Lédignan

Sauve

Ferriere-les-V.

Nîmes

Brissac

Lauret

Sommières

Beaucaire

Tarascon

St-Jean-
de-la-
Blaquière

St-Martin-
de-Londres

BOUCHES

St-Guilhem-
le-Désert

Castries

St-Saturnin-
de Lucian

St-Gély-du-Fesc

Lunel

Saint-Gilles

Arles

N 113

Clermont-
el'Hérault

Montpellier

le Grau-
du-Roi

St-Laurent-
d'Aigouze

Aigues-Mortes

DU-RHÔNE

Bouzigues

Palavas-
les-Flots

Port-
Camargue

Pézenas

Mèze

Sète

Rhône

Marseille

Agde

Marseillan

le Cap d'Agde

Golfe du Lion

MEDITERRANEAN SEA

N

0   20 km

☎04.67.01.72.42
Closed *Thurs out of season; Weds and Thurs lunchtimes in high season; Nov–March.*

A friendly little place in the port, providing good, simple fresh dishes cooked using seasonal market produce and at reasonable prices: weekday lunchtime menu including dish of the day and dessert €13.50; other menu at €22. Warm salad of scallops and prawns, grilled fish, *bourride de lotte* and *aioli* are among the appetizing dishes of the day you will find written on a large blackboard – you might well be tempted by a seafood platter. Good view from the terrace.

Aigues-Mortes
30220

✆ 🏠 |●| Hôtel-restaurant L'Escale*

3 av. de la Tour-de-Constance. Opposite the ramparts.
☎04.66.53.71.14 ☏04.66.53.76.74.
Closed *Sun evenings from the beginning of Nov until Feb.*

A hotel-restaurant with a friendly atmosphere situated opposite the ramparts. The regulars linger over a pastis or lunch, which costs from €10 to €18; make sure you try the cuttlefish *à l'aigues-mortaise*. Simple but spotless rooms from €29 with basin to €36 with bath. The ones over the bar are a bit noisy but air-conditioned, while the ones in the annexe are quieter. Relaxed welcome.

✆ 🍴 🏠 Hôtel des Croisades**

2 rue du Port; it's outside the ramparts, but just opposite and above the canal.
☎04.66.53.67.85 ☏04.66.53.72.95
✉hotel@lescroisades.fr
Closed *mid-Nov to mid-Dec.*
Disabled access. TV. Pay car park.

This fairly new hotel has an attractive, tranquil atmosphere and the added appeal of a delightful garden. Some rooms have a view over the town walls and the Constance Tower: air-conditioned doubles at €53 with shower/wc or bath represent the best value for money in the town. *10% discount on the room rate (15 Jan–15 Feb) offered to our readers on presentation of this guide.*

✆ 🏠 |●| Hôtel-restaurant Les Arcades***

23 bd. Gambetta.

☎04.66.53.18.13 ☏04.66.53.75.46
🌐www.les-arcades.fr
Closed *Mon all day, Tues and Thurs lunchtimes; fortnight in March and fortnight in Oct.*
TV. Swimming pool. Car park.

A charming hotel with a gastronomic restaurant. This is an ancient, noble building with thick walls and spacious, beautiful rooms: doubles with shower/wc or bath cost €90–110. The dining room is elegant and features a small, secluded terrace under some arcades – hence its name. The classic, regional cuisine is nicely prepared and perfectly served with menus at €34 and €45: warm oysters, *pavé* of beef served with a juniper berry sauce.

Saint-Laurent-d'Aigouze
30220 (7km N)

✆ 🍴 🏠 Hôtel Lou Garbin**

30 av. des Jardins; the village is on the Nîmes road from Aigues-Mortes and the hotel is on the right.
☎04.66.88.12.74 ☏04.66.88.91.12
🌐www.lougarbin.com
Restaurant closed *lunchtimes 1 July–31 Aug; 15 October–1 March. Reservations only outside July and Aug.* **Disabled access. TV. High chairs and games available. Swimming pool. Car park.**

A really pleasant place to stop between Nîmes and Aigues-Mortes in a typical village of this little corner of the Camargue. It's at the heart of the village, surrounded by a string of cafés with terraces and with the church at one side. The rooms – €50–60 for a double with shower/wc or bath – are in the main house or in bungalows around the pool, or rather pools, as a second one has recently been added. Dishes are reassuringly local with lots of beef on the menu. Unfortunately, you can see and hear the main road about 200m away, but pretty soon the bushes will have grown big enough to form a screen. You can play boules, and they do barbecues. *Free coffee offered to our readers on presentation of this guide.*

Alès
30100

✆ 🏠 Hôtel Orly**

10 rue d'Avéjan.
☎04.66.91.30.00 ☏04.66.91.30.30

TV.

A very central hotel run by a pair of friendly young people who have lots of ideas. The façade dates back to the 1970s but the interior has been completely renovated and styled with taste. No. 108 has two windows, no. 106 is the biggest and no. 109 is rather *zen* in style. There's also a studio with a corner kitchen and an apartment for four people. It's excellent value for money, given the location, with doubles in the range €32–53.

ⓐ ⅔ ♨ |●| Hôtel-restaurant Le Riche**

42 pl. Pierre-Sémard; it's opposite the train station.
℡ 04.66.86.00.33 ⓕ 04.66.30.02.63
Ⓦ www.leriche.fr
Closed *Aug.* **TV. Pay car park. High chairs available.**

This is one of the best restaurants in town and something of an institution, with menus €17–48. The Belle Époque dining room is a great place to eat creatively prepared dishes in classic style: shellfish salad with fresh basil, fillet of sea bass with a delicate shrimp bisque, good Saint-Nectaire cheese, apricot tart. The hotel is run with great professionalism and has all the comforts you need. Compared to the dining room, the rooms are modern and rather uninteresting, but they have good facilities: doubles with bath cost €50. *10% discount on the room rate on presentation of this guide.*

ⓐ ⅔ |●| Le Mandajors

17 rue Mandajors.
℡ 04.66.52.62.98
ⓔ frederic-beguin@wanadoo.fr
Closed *Sat lunchtime and Sun; first fortnight in Aug and a week around Christmas.* **Open** *noon–1.30pm and 7.30–9pm.*

The décor doesn't seem to have changed since World War II – when the owner helped members of the Resistance disappear out of the back door. The place is now in the hands of a young man, whose wife helps at lunchtime. In the evening, he's on his own in the kitchen and dining room. To make it work, he keeps strict opening hours. It's worth it as you'll find delectable, appetizing old-style cuisine at more than reasonable prices; menus €10–25. Credit and debit cards not accepted. *Free liqueur offered to our readers on presentation of this guide.*

ⓐ ⅔ |●| Le Jardin d'Alès

92 av. d'Alsace; it's on the Aubenas road.
℡ 04.66.86.38.82 ⓕ 04.66.86.21.74
ⓔ lejardinales.resto@libertysurf.fr
Closed *Sun evening; Mon; first fortnight in Jan; first fortnight in July.* **Disabled access. Car park.**

This place is located outside the centre on the edge of an area with a number of looming high-rises – the terrace is almost too close to the roundabout for comfort. But you will receive a warm welcome from the owners, who have also decorated the dining room with great taste. Weekday lunch menu costs €11.50, otherwise €16.50 and €26.50; menus change with the seasons. *Free coffee offered to our readers on presentation of this guide.*

Seynes
30580 (18km E)

ⓐ ♨ |●| La Farigoulette**

It's in the centre of the village. Take the D6 from Alès.
℡ 04.66.83.70.56 ⓕ 04.66.83.72.80
Ⓦ www.lafarigoulette.com
Closed *Sun evening in Jan–Feb.* **TV. Swimming pool.**

A lovely, unfussy country establishment with a garden and swimming pool. Customers from far afield come to enjoy the powerfully flavoured homemade dishes, featuring delicious pâtés, terrines, sausage, casseroles and *confits* prepared by the owner and his family, who run the local charcuterie. Prices are reasonable – set menus from €13, except at weekends and public holidays, others €17–30. Service is in the beautifully simple, rustic dining room. Ten decent double rooms with shower/wc go for €45 (ask for room no. 4, 6 or 10, with a panoramic view or a view over the pool). Logis de France.

Saint-Victor-de-Macalp
30500 (23km NE)

ⓐ ⅔ ♨ |●| La Bastide des Senteurs***

It's in the centre of the village; from Alès, take the D904 then the D51 to Saint-Victor.
℡ 04.66.60.24.45 ⓕ 04.66.60.26.10
Ⓦ www.bastide-senteurs.com
Closed *early Nov until late March.*
Restaurant closed *lunchtimes in July and Aug, except Sun and public holidays; out of*

⑪

LANGUEDOC-ROUSSILLON

season. **Disabled access. TV. High chairs available. Swimming pool. Car park.**

In a hill village set in beautiful countryside right on the edge of the Cévennes, this hotel spreads across a collection of houses that have been soberly and tastefully renovated. Pretty rooms, decorated in the local style with bare, stone walls, cost €72–75 with bath, depending on the season. Outside there's a glorious swimming pool overlooking the Cèze valley. The superb restaurant is named after the chef, Franck Subileau, who produces dishes of wonderful invention; menus €25–73. Credit cards not accepted. *10% reduction on the room rate in October on presentation of this guide.*

Amélie-les-Bains
66110

ⓦ 🏠 |●| 🎋 Le Castel-Émeraude**

Route de la Corniche; 1km from the centre; go through the town and over the bridge following signs for the "Centre sportif".
☎04.68.39.02.83 ⒻAX04.68.39.03.09
ⓦwww.lecastelemeraude.com
Closed *mid-Nov to end of March.* **Disabled access. TV. High chairs and cots available. Car park.**

A quiet, tranquil inn on the banks of the river and surrounded by greenery. It's a big white building with two turrets that would resemble a castle if it weren't for the modern façade with lots of balconies. Inside the décor is modern and nearly all the rooms have been refurbished. Some fifty double rooms priced at €48–66; the four rooms between the turrets are particularly pleasant, and two of them have a terrace. The rooms that have not yet been renovated are best avoided. In the restaurant, menus €16–35 feature flavoursome traditional cuisine served by attentive staff. Nice welcome is offered by a friendly team led by a gentle, pétanque-loving patron. Logis de France. *Free local apéritif offered to our readers on presentation of this guide.*

Anduze
30140

ⓦ 🏠 |●| La Porte des Cévennes**

Route de Saint-Jean-du-Gard; take the D907 in the direcion of Saint-Jean-du-Gard; the hotel is on the right about 3km after the Anduze exit.

☎04.66.61.99.44 ⒻAX04.66.61.73.65
ⓦwww.porte-cevennes.com
Restaurant closed *lunchtimes, open for lunch and dinner for group bookings only; annual holiday: from 15 Oct to 1 April.* **TV. Highchairs and games available. Swimming pool. Car park.**

Located just outside the village of Anduze, past the bamboo fields, this modern hotel has spacious, clean and comfortable rooms. Doubles with shower/wc or bath are €60–69; half board is available for a minimum of three days (€55–58 per person per day). The rather grand swimming pool is covered and heated and is used as a restaurant in the evenings. It serves traditional dishes with a choice of menus at €18–30. This is a reliable place. Logis de France.

ⓦ 🏠 |●| Le Moulin de Corbès

Corbès; take the rte. de Saint-Jean du Gard.
☎04.66.61.61.83 ⒻAX04.66.61.68.06
Closed *Mon and Tues out of season. Annual holiday: from mid-Nov to mid-Jan.* **Disabled access. Car park.**

This isn't just any old restaurant – the crunch of gravel underfoot as you approach and the grand staircase inside help to create a special atmosphere. The dining room is painted yellow and flooded with sunlight, and the flower arrangements on the tables add a touch of class. Dishes change with the season but they're always simple and full of cleverly combined, delicate flavours – you can count on the pan-fried liver and liver terrine (set menus €35–60). Three double rooms with shower/wc or bath at €70, breakfast included.

Argelès-sur-Mer
66700

ⓦ |●| Le Cayrou

18 rue du 14-Juillet.
☎04.68.81.34.08
Closed *Wed.*

Charming, efficient service in this restaurant which offers generous helpings of fresh traditional cuisine with a regional touch, in a small, well-decorated rustic dining room; weekday lunchtime menu €10.50, otherwise €12.20 and €24. Local clientele at lunchtime, replaced on holiday season evenings by tourists (not many foreigners), who have spread the word. A warm, unassuming place that is a change from cheap and cheerful holiday cafés.

Aumont-Aubrac

48130

☜ 🏠 |O| 🎿 Chez Camillou

10 av. du Languedoc.
☎04.66.42.80.22 ℗04.66.42.86.14
Restaurant closed *Sun evening and Mon
(except July and Aug); early Nov to early
April.* **TV. High chairs available. Swimming
pool. Car park.**

Impressive place being run by the fourth,
or maybe the fifth generation. Rooms
are well appointed but rather charmless
(doubles €46–130), the décor in the
restaurant is stunning, and the service
friendly, and there's a heart-shaped swimming pool. The main attraction, however,
is Cyril Attrazic's cooking – perfectly
calibrated preparations, wonderful flavours and tons of creativity on menus
€16–60. Follow Madame's advice and
let yourself be tempted. The desserts are
just divine. Logis de France. *Free coffee
offered to our readers on presentation of this
guide.*

☜ 🎿 🏠 |O| Grand Hôtel
Prouhèze***

2 rte. du Languedoc; it's opposite the train
station, 300m from the town centre.
☎04.66.42.80.07 ℗04.66.42.87.78
🌐www.prouheze.com
Gourmet restaurant closed *Tues lunch
(except July and Aug), Dec and Jan.* **Le
Compostelle restaurant open** *every day
except Dec and Jan.* **TV. High chairs available. Secure garage (fee payable).**

Pierre Roudgé joined the restaurant
early in 2004. Like his predecessor, he
offers top-of-the-range cuisine, served
in the enormous, warm dining room
decorated in charming taste. Weekday
lunch menus served in the restaurant at
€33 and €58; bistro menus (served in Le
Compostelle) at €18 and €27. Comfy,
attractive rooms of varying sizes: the
bigger ones have the better facilities, the
smaller ones are quiet, stylish and comfortable. Doubles go for €67–90 with
bath, and one with shower/wc is €50.
*Free house apéritif offered to our readers on
presentation of this guide.*

Javols

48130 (7km SE)

☜ 🏠 |O| Auberge Le Régimbal

Take the D50.

☎04.66.42.89.87 ℗04.66.42.65.53.
TV.
Closed *in winter.* **High chairs and games
available.**

A newly built inn belonging to the
Mazets. It overlooks Gévaudan, which
was the ancient Gallo-Roman capital
for eight centuries. It's an exceptional
archeological site and important excavations have been undertaken (exhibition at
the museum in summer). There are eight
peaceful rooms (€47) with good facilities
and views of the village and the surrounding hills; half board €45 per person.
Local cuisine is served in the dining room
where there's a granite fireplace. *Plat du
jour* is €11.50; lunchtime menu €16,
evening menu €18.

Fau-de-Peyre

48130 (10km NW)

☜ 🏠 |O| Hôtel-restaurant
Boucharinc-Tichit, Del Faou**

Take the D50 from Aumont-Aubrac.
☎04.66.31.11.00 ℗04.66.31.30.00
Closed *Sun evening out of season; 20 Dec–6
Jan.* **TV. Car park.**

In the local dialect of this old Aubrac village, *faou* means "beech tree". And indeed
there are some around this inn, which
serves generous helpings of excellent
family food at low prices, with a choice
of three very generous menus ranging in
price from €10 to €20. And in this neck
of the woods, people literally jostle past
each other, so keen are they to sample
the frogs' legs or *manouls* (tripe and
lamb's stomach parcels). Nearby, a fairly
new building accommodates impeccable
rooms (€40) with all mod cons; half
board €39 per person. Guests receive
a natural and warm welcome from the
ladies who run the place. A cure guaranteed to produce a sense of well-being in
one of the best places in this guide for the
Aubrac region.

Banyuls-sur-Mer

66650

☜ 🎿 🏠 Villa Miramar**

Rue Lacaze-Outhiens; on the hillside just outside the village. It's 200m from the beach and
500m from the centre.
☎04.68.88.33.85 ℗04.68.66.88.63
🌐www.villa-miramar@fr.st

Closed mid–Oct to end of April. **Disabled access. TV. Swimming pool. Car park.**

This hotel with its exotic charm is surrounded by a shaded garden full of flowers, with hammocks in a corner. It's a peaceful place, packed with Far Eastern souvenirs, many from Thailand. The rooms are comfortable with modern facilities – mini-bar, telephone, air-conditioning, TV – and cost €52–67 for a double with shower/wc or bath, depending on the season. There are also two more basic bungalows in the grounds at €43 or €49. A place to go for a really welcome change of scene at a reasonable price, even if you take the suite, with its huge balcony, Jacuzzi and king-size bed for €150. *10% discount in April offered to our readers on presentation of this guide.*

Barjac

30430

@ 🏠 |●| 🎿 **Hôtel-restaurant Le Mas du Terme*****

Route de Bagnols-sur-Cèze; it's 3km from the village, out in the vineyards.
☎04.66.24.56.31 ℗04.66.24.58.54
ⓦwww.mas-du-terme.com
Closed early Nov to mid-March. **Restaurant closed** out of season – phone to check. **Disabled access. TV. High chairs and games available. Swimming pool. Car park.**

This eighteenth-century silkworm-breeding house has been tastefully converted in the local style by the owners. There's a vaulted sitting room and dining room and a pretty courtyard. The hotel has quiet, attractive rooms with modern facilities, including air-conditioning; they're €60–110 with shower/wc or bath, depending on the season. The restaurant is not bad at all: the price of a menu (if you're staying half board) is €29. The local specialities – *escabèche* of red mullet fillets with garlic, cod steaks with black olive paste, stuffed rack of lamb with sea salt and so on – are carefully prepared. Logis de France. *10% discount on the room rate offered to our readers on presentation of this guide except for July and August.*

Beaucaire

30300

@ 🏠 |●| 🎿 **Hôtel-restaurant Le Robinson****

Route de Remoulins; it's signposted on the road to Remoulins.

☎04.66.59.21.32 ℗04.66.59.00.03
ⓔcontact@hotel-robinson.fr
Closed Feb. **Disabled access. TV. High chairs and games available. Swimming pool. Car park.**

A good place just on the edge of Beaucaire offering a smiling welcome and family atmosphere. On the *menu du terroir* you'll find beef *gardiane*, the local speciality – here they make it like nobody else and serve it up with locally grown rice. It goes well with a wine like a Costières-de-Nîmes. Menus €14–38; try donkey and pork sausage as a starter, and a *crème catalane* to finish. The bright dining room has huge bay windows overlooking the trees in the garden, and it's run by diligent waiting staff. Rooms are pretty, comfortable and air-conditioned; doubles €64–80 with shower/wc or bath. They have tennis courts as well as a pool. Logis de France *A free Kir offered to our readers on presentation of this guide.*

@ |●| 🎿 **L'Ail Heurre**

Place du Château (Centre).
☎04.66.59.29.13
Closed Sat lunch; Sun evening; January.

This stylish little dining room is decorated with taste, with wrought iron tables and chairs and pictures and works of art on the walls. The chef is jovial and very gifted – he has worked in some great kitchens but decided to come home. Exquisite and creative cuisine, attentively served, with lunch menus €15–47; expect to pay around €50 for a meal à la carte. It's good value for money. *Free coffee offered to our readers on presentation of this guide.*

Béziers

34500

@ 🏠 **Le Champ-de-Mars****

17 rue de Metz; it's near the pl. du 14-Juillet.
☎04.67.28.35.53
TV. Pay car park.

This little hotel in a quiet side street has had its façade thoroughly renovated and it's smothered in geraniums. The meticulous rooms overlook the garden. Double rooms €33.50–46 with shower/wc or bath (cheaper in low season) – it's the best value for money in Béziers. The cheerful owner can tell you anything you need to know about the town.

Le Patio

21 rue Française; you get there via the rue de la République.
☎04.67.49.09.45 ⓕ04.67.49.20.84
Closed *Sun; Mon; 21 Dec–5 Jan.*

The name tells you what to expect: they do good, tasty grills of meat and fish. The restaurant, in a cool and charming courtyard with an olive tree in the middle, offers a choice of menus €11–23.50. Nice furniture made from wrought iron outside, while in the dining room the setting is warm and welcoming.

La Raffinerie

14 av. Joseph-Lazare; follow the canal, just outside Béziers, direction Stade de Sauclières.
☎04.67.76.07.12
Closed *Sat lunchtime; Sun; Mon.* **Disabled access.**

The former sulphur factory, essential to wine-making (we are right in the middle of the old wine merchants' neighbourhood), has been turned into a contemporary restaurant. In the summer, a terrace near the water allows you to enjoy *alfresco* a refined Mediterranean cuisine; menus €17–22. Many inventive dishes at reasonable prices: tajine of cockerel with Morello cherries, squid *a la plancha* served with a black risotto, not forgetting the exquisite *pot au chocolat* for dessert.

L'Ambassade

22 bd. de Verdun; it's opposite the station.
☎04.67.76.06.24 ⓕ04.67.76.74.05
Closed *Sun; Mon; end of May to mid-June.*

Patrick Olry is a fine chef with a sure touch; he uses fresh produce and his menus list dishes that change with the seasons – the food is colourful, full of aromas and robustly flavoured. The cheese is out of this world and so are the desserts; the weekday menu costs €26 and others are €34–70. Food is served in a vast dining room with a modern look. The waiters dress smartly but are informal in their approach and are eager to advise – even the bill is a pleasant surprise.

Maraussan

34370 (7.5km NW)

Parfum de Garrigues

37 av. de la Poste.

☎04.67.90.33.76
Closed *Tues and Wed; end Feb to mid-March; mid to end August; All Saints' Day.*
Disabled access. High chairs available.

Jean-Luc Santuré came here from Béziers and turned this place into the best restaurant in the area. You'll notice the easy-going atmosphere as soon as you arrive, and the cooking is smart and subtle and full of flavour (menus from €25–55) – a real tour de force, with dishes such as *marbré de foie gras de canard aux figues et note de miel* and farmhouse pigeon with thyme. There isn't a garden as such, but you can stroll around the heath. *Free glass of dessert wine offered to our readers on presentation of this guide.*

Lespignan

34710 (10 km SW)

Hostellerie du Château

4 rue des Figuiers.
☎04.67.37.67.71
Closed *Tues and Sun evenings out of season. 2nd and 3rd weeks of Jan; Wed.*
Disabled access.

In the evening, the regulars come back especially from the coast to enjoy a good meal here. At lunch you will enjoy a quiet meal in the coolness of this beautiful old house built with the stones from the old feudal castle of Lord Lespignan that used to overlook the whole countryside. Frank Le Maner is more modest though. After having worked with the best (*Rostang, Le Jardin des Sens*), he now works with his wife, cooks the best ingredients in his own way, puts the finishing touches to his dishes and checks his sauces with the utmost attention. Prices are very reasonable with menus ranging from €19 to €55. There's an impressive selection of dishes and a judicious choice of wines, too. *Free coffee offered to our readers on presentation of this guide.*

Nissan-lez-Enserune

34440 (11km SW)

Hôtel Résidence**

35 av. de la Cave; take the N9.
☎04.67.37.00.63 ⓕ04.67.37.68.63
ⓦwww.hotel-residence.com
Closed *Jan.* **TV. High chairs available. Pay car park.**

A beautiful provincial building with bags of charm. There's a relaxed, informal, peaceful atmosphere with flowers everywhere, and several rooms have recently been added – you'll find them in the garden annexe. The owners have retained its charm while using slightly off-beat décor. Doubles go for €52–72 depending on facilities and season; half board €54–62. The oppidum and the Midi canal are only a few kilometres away. Logis de France. *Free house apéritif offered to our readers on presentation of this guide.*

Magalas
34480 (22km N)

ⓒ |●| The Boucherie of Magalas

Place de l'Église. Take the D909 towards Bédarieux.
☎04.67.36.20.82
✉theboucherie@aol.com
Closed *Sun (lunchtime only in summer); Mon; Feb; All Saints' Day.* **Disabled access.**

This butcher's shop doubles as a restaurant, and a good one at that. It has two dining rooms, both decorated with odds and ends that look like they were bought in a charity shop, and there's an attractive terrace that leads out onto the village square. Menus €16–22 feature fresh tapas, a selection of cold sausage, stews, steak tartare made in front of you and delicious *carpaccio*. If you like tripe, you'll love the way they do it here. Jazz plays gently in the background and, to cap it all, there are some good wines. It's advisable to book.

Brissac
34190

ⓒ |●| Le Jardin aux Sources

30 av. du Parc.
☎04.67.73.31.16
Closed *Mon; Wed lunchtime and Sun evening in low season only; fortnight in Jan and last fortnight in Nov.*

This restaurant offers the most creative cuisine north of the Hérault river, though the décor does not match (yet) its prices. Weekday lunchtime set menu €19 includes starter and main course or main course and dessert, and there's also a €26 menu (weekdays), others at €28–64; à la carte around €50. Well-travelled chef Jérôme Billod-Morel has found inspiration in many a place and his dishes are far from being commonplace. Each dish is a real work of art in itself, and this kind of perfection takes time; quite surprising desserts, too.

Know-how and friendliness make up for a relatively slow service. You'll spend a very agreeable time on the terrace facing the garden, or in the small dining room next to the kitchens. Highly recommended if you like good-quality products cooked with passion and originality by a local lad. And recently the owners have added three large rooms, a lounge and a swimming pool.

Canorgue (La)
48500

ⓒ ⊜ |●| Le Portalou

Place du Portalou; 20km southwest of Marvejols.
☎04.66.32.83.55 ☞04.66.32.92.54
ⓦwww.hotelleportalou.com
Closed *Jan.*

A large bourgeois house with spacious and quiet rooms (€35–46 depending on facilities and the season) with creaking parquet flooring – quite charming. There's a beautiful garden and terrace beneath the wisteria. Simple fast food is on offer, with menus from €11, except Sun, to €18.50. On request, the proprietor will arrange short trips for anyone that is interested. Logis de France.

Carcassonne
11000

ⓒ ⊜ Auberge de jeunesse

Rue du Vicomte-Trencavel; in the medieval city.
☎04.68.25.23.16 ☞04.68.71.14.84
ⓦwww.fuaj.org
Closed *15 Dec–15 Jan.*

This is a beautiful hostel, well-kept, in the very heart of the historic city of Carcassonne offering 120 beds. Each room accommodates four to six people; all the rooms have been recently updated. Accommodation costs €13.25 per night, breakfast and sheets included, and a youth hostel card is required. Meals are available at the bar in the summer; menu at €8.60. Facilities include a foyer with fireplace, private kitchen, bar, TV room, courtyard, Internet, laundry and bike stands. Advance booking is recommended.

ⓒ ⋇ ⊜ Hôtel du Pont-Vieux

32 rue Trivalle; near the medieval city.

☎04.68.25.24.99 ℻04.68.47.62.71
✉hoteldupontvieux@minitel.net
Pay car park. TV. High chairs available.

Located in a quiet street, a few strides away from the main entrance into the medieval city centre. Simple but comfortable rooms, recently redecorated, go for €48–74, according to season and facilities. The buffet breakfast (€7) is served until 10am, and there's a terrace with a view over the town. *10% discount on the room rate (1 Nov–31 March) offered to our readers on presentation of this guide.*

✎ 🏛 ⬤ Hôtel du Donjon – Les Remparts***

2 rue du Comte-Roger; it's in the heart of the medieval city.
☎04.68.71.08.80 ℻04.68.25.06.60
🖥www.hotel-donjon.fr
Closed *Sun evening from early Nov to end March.* **TV. High chairs available. Pay car park.**

This place has everything: it's a medieval building with magnificent beams and an unusual staircase, but it also offers modern facilities such as double glazing, air-conditioning, a bar, lounges and a very nice garden. There's good reason for the staff to be proud of the establishment and it's very popular with American visitors. Doubles with shower/wc or bath are €80–160 (breakfast buffet €10); some are in an annexe and two new bedrooms have just been created. You can also stay in the *Maison du Donjon* (refurbished rooms) or the *Maison des Remparts*, two medieval gems attached to the *Château Comtal*. The restaurant offers a good range of local specialities with menus €14.50–26.50. The garage allows you to bring your car right into the middle of the town. *Free garage (except July-Aug) offered to our readers on presentation of this guide.*

⬤ ✎ Le Petit Couvert

18 rue de l'Aigle-d'Or.
☎04.68.71.00.20
Closed *Sun; Mon.* **Disabled access.**

A very simple place, with Provençal décor and a few tables out on a terrace on a pedestrian street, run by two lively and friendly young women. Good cheap menus that are very satisfactory (a quarter litre jug of wine included) – lunch menu €11 weekdays; others €14–18 – feature large plates of charcuterie, cheese and salad. For those who are weight-conscious, a light menu is also on offer, still good value for money, with steamed vegetables, etc. Otherwise, the chef's specialities are the *cassoulet* and the *confit*. No credit cards. *Free house apéritif offered to our readers on presentation of this guide.*

⬤ Chez Saskia

Place de l'Église.
☎04.68.71.98.71
Closed *Dec–Jan.*

If the *Barbacane* is full (or perhaps beyond your means as their menus start at €60), then come to *Chez Saskia*, the brasserie annexe of Franck Putelat's restaurant. A more subdued décor, but you will still be eating surrounded by pictures of movie stars. The first menu (€19) is amusing (it follows for example in the summer an "all tomato" theme), but only the dessert (a strawberry and tomato gazpacho served with rice pudding) is really unusual; other menus up to €35. If you really want to spoil yourself though, try the menu at €31 or choose à la carte. The tiger prawn salad served with a mango chutney is worth a try. The service is impeccable and friendly, and they have a good selection of wines at reasonable prices.

⬤ Le Jardin de la Tour

11 porte d'Aude; in the heart of the medieval city.
☎04.68.25.71.24
Closed *lunchtimes.*
High chairs available.

This restaurant has become a real favourite in the whole town and beyond – a family affair that works. Not surprising: a friendly convivial atmosphere inside, and outside dinner among the trees. In the summer a Berber tent is raised underneath the arbour and you are entertained with live music and tapas. Nice-looking dishes and exquisite cooking predominate on menus (€20–28); trendy waiters and good music, too. What more could you ask for? Advance booking highly recommended, as it's full every night.

✎ ⬤ ✎ Le Comte Roger

14 rue Saint-Louis; in the medieval city.
☎04.68.11.93.40
Closed *Sun and Mon out of season and public holidays; 15 Feb to 15 March.*

High chairs available.

Pierre Mesa, who had a fine reputation at the Château, took over this restaurant formerly run by his father. Although he changed premises he brought his team and style of cooking with him. The warmth and sincerity of the welcome hasn't changed either. The menus focus on local recipes and local wines. Uncomplicated, flavoursome, well-seasoned dishes are listed on good-value menus from €22 (weekday lunchtimes), otherwise €28 and €38; à la carte menu up to €50. Specialities include *cassoulet* with two *confits* and creamed salt cod with parsley. The setting is modern and really pleasant. In summer, head for the terrace. *Free Carcassonnais wine offered to our readers on presentation of this guide.*

Cavanac
11570 (4km S)

@ 🎋 🏠 |●| **Château de Cavanac*****

Take the D104 in the direction of St Hilaire.
☎04.68.79.61.04 ⊕04.68.79.79.67
Closed *Jan; Feb.* **Restaurant closed** *Sun evening, except June–Sept; Mon; lunchtimes; Jan; Feb.* **Disabled access. TV. High Chairs available. Swimming pool. Car park.**

An overgrown farmhouse with a very pretty garden in a quiet village. Exquisite rooms with period furniture, lustrous fabrics, canopied beds and elegantly contemporary décor go for €65–150, depending on the size and facilities. The restaurant, in a converted stable, is the bigger draw. There's a genuine country feel – they've kept the mangers and hung some old implements on the walls. Ask to be placed in the room with a fireplace, the most pleasant one. There's a single menu, €36, of delicious local dishes which change regularly: snails *à la carcassonnaise*, foie gras or suckling pig with honey. Apéritif, bread and wine are included. Hotel guests can also choose à la carte. There's a tennis court, a swimming pool, a fitness centre and a sauna – it's a great place. *Free house apéritif or coffee on presentation of this guide.*

Lastours
11600 (12km N)

@ 🎋 |●| **Le Puits du Trésor**

Route des 4-Châteaux.
☎04.68.77.50.24
Brasserie closed *evenings (Oct–May).*
Restaurant closed *lunchtimes (except Sun);*

Sun, Mon and Tues evenings. **Closed** *last week Feb to mid-March.*

The brasserie offers good fresh dishes made with products from the market; weekday lunchtime brasserie menu €15, others €18–25. The seasonal restaurant menu (€51) includes artichoke with rosemary and fried foie gras with cardamom; reckon on about €60 à la carte. There are two separate entrances: a street entrance for the gastronomic restaurant, where Jean-Marc Boyer works, and a courtyard entrance for its brasserie. *Free house apéritif offered to our readers on presentation of this guide.*

Roquefère
11380 (22km N)

@ |●| **Le Sire de Cabaret**

Take the Mazamet road, turn onto the Conques road, then right onto the D101 to Roquefère.
☎04.68.26.91.90
Closed *Wed and Sun evenings, except July–Aug; week nights, Nov to Easter; 10 Jan–10 Feb.* **High chairs available.**

A magnificent house in an attractive village in the middle of the Montagne Noire and the Cabardès. There's an imposing fireplace in the dining room, but it's not just a picturesque feature – it's used to chargrill meat. A choice of menus, €18–31, is served, and also a children's menu at €10. When you order charcuterie, a huge platter appears laden with sausage, terrines and hams, and you can help yourself to more. They also plonk down a bottle of wine. And why not finish the meal with a liquorice-flavoured *crème brûlée*? It's all handsomely served.

Castelnaudary
11400

@ 🎋 🏠 **Hôtel du Canal****

2 ter av. Arnant-Vidal; 500m from the city centre, opposite the Gendarmerie.
☎04.68.94.05.05 ⊕04.68.94.05.06
Disabled access. TV. High chairs available. Car park.

A recently built hotel on the edge of the Canal du Midi offering a smiling welcome. There's a towpath you can walk along nearby. The rooms, modern, spacious and well looked-after, cost €43–53 for a double with shower/wc or bath. *Internet access or one free breakfast per night (in low*

11

season) offered to our readers on presentation of this guide.

◉ 🏛 |◉| Hôtel du Centre et du Lauragais**

31 cours de la République.
☎04.68.23.25.95 ℗04.68.94.01.66
Closed *Jan; first week in July.* **TV.**

A huge house on the main square in the town. The rooms are well maintained and comfortable; €43 with shower/wc and €48 with bath/wc. The plush restaurant serves what is probably the best cuisine in town, with menus €18.51. It's famous for its *cassoulet*, but also serves local specialities and dishes like tripe and pigeon with ceps. Slightly impersonal welcome, but the service is faultless.

Peyrens
11400 (4km N)

◉ 🎋 |◉| Auberge La Calèche

On the D624 towards Ravel, in the village.
☎04.68.60.40.13
Closed *Tues evening; Wed; Feb school holiday and 1–15 Nov.*
High chairs available.

The first menu (€15.50) is excellent and very hearty, especially if you choose the *cassoulet* as the main course; other menus up to €28.50. It is so generously served that you could order just that. It is definitely one of the best *cassoulets* in the area, so much so that regulars come all the way from Toulouse to sample it, along with the very friendly welcome and pleasant rural location. *Free sparkling white wine cocktail offered to our readers on presentation of this guide.*

Gaja-la-Selve
11270 (18km S)

◉ 🎋 🏛 |◉| Auberge du Puget

16km from Foueaux, on the D102 towards Belpech.
☎and ℗04.68.60.51.76
🖥www.aubergedupuget.com
Restaurant closed *Sun evening; Mon.*
High chairs and games available.

Located in the middle of an agricultural farm, the inn offers very nice rooms (€56) that bear exotic names such as Kuala Lumpur, Santiago or Bangkok… Beautiful old farm furniture and comfortable beds. It also has a nice big swimming

pool in the garden with even a few hammocks at your disposal. The cuisine on the menus, €29–41, is traditional, authentic and refined. It uses local produce from nearby smallholdings and farms; also local wines and apéritifs are served. You have to book. *Free liqueur offered to our readers on presentation of this guide.*

Caunes-Minervois
11160

◉ 🎋 🏛 |◉| Hôtel-restaurant d'Alibert**

Place de la Mairie; take the D11 for 6km then turn right for Cannes onto the D620 and it's 2.5km further on.
☎04.68.78.00.54 ℮frederic.dalibert @wanadoo.fr
Closed *Sun evening; Mon and Tues lunchtimes; mid-Nov to mid-March.* **Car park.**

This house, thoroughly lost in the narrow lanes of this Minervois village, looks as if it's suddenly appeared from the sixteenth century. The owners, Monsieur and Madame Guiraud, have run it for years. There are only eight rooms – €50–70 for a double depending on facilities and season – but they're spacious, well maintained and pleasant. The elegant country-manor style restaurant is totally in keeping with the rest of the place, and the open fire adds to the warmth of the atmosphere in cold weather. Single menu €20 with good, authentic local dishes like *cassoulet*, calves' heads, and stews produced with great skill. The owner will give you advice about the wines – he's a connoisseur of the local *crus* and his enthusiasm is infectious. *Free house apéritif offered to our readers on presentation of this guide.*

Céret
66400

◉ 🏛 Hôtel des Arcades**

1 pl. Picasso.
☎04.68.87.12.30 ℗04.68.87.49.44
🖥www.hotel-arcades-ceret.com

Behind a modern-looking façade that is not really anything to look at, the thirty or so rooms came as a pleasant surprise. Huge and comfortable, they have been smartened up and given modern furnishings. Double rooms with shower and wc go for €40–49, with bath €44–54. With their photographs and reproductions, the hall and the breakfast room pay homage to the artists that put Céret on the map. What's more, some of these artists used to visit the *Le Pablo* bar beneath the hotel (so it's perhaps better to avoid the rooms situated directly above). There are also some rooms in an annexe behind the hotel, but these do not have TV. The whole complex exudes a sense of peace and quiet and of being extremely well maintained.

Ⓒ 🏠 |◯| Hôtel-restaurant Vidal

4 pl. Soutine; it's in the centre between the town hall and pl. Picasso.
Ⓣ04.68.87.00.85 Ⓕ04.68.87.62.33
Ⓦwww.hotelvidal.com
Closed *Tues and Wed in winter; Nov.* **TV.**

The old bishop's palace dates back to 1735 and is a classified historic monument, with a wonderful sculpted façade. Fairly spacious, clean rooms, almost all of them tastefully refurbished, with good facilities cost €40 for a double. The young owners come from the village so, if you want any hints about where to go and what to see, just ask. On the ground floor, they also run a Catalan bistrot with dishes starting at €3.50; for the genuine article, head for the Catalan restaurant (although it's rather more expensive in relation to the room rates; menus €23–33), where you can dine either in the bishop's dining room with its gleaming red floor tiles or on the terrace.

Châteauneuf-de-Randon
48170

Ⓒ 🌿 🏠 |◯| Hôtel de la Poste**

L'Habitarelle: take the N88 and it's beside the Mausolée du Guesclin.
Ⓣ04.66.47.90.05 Ⓕ04.66.47.91.41
Ⓦwww.hoteldelaposte48.com
Closed *Fri lunchtime; Sat and Sun evening (except in July and Aug); autumn school holiday; Christmas to end Jan; 4–9 July.*
Disabled access. TV. High chairs available. Car park.

Though this establishment is on the main road the traffic noise won't bother you – most rooms overlook the countryside. They've been modernized and are absolutely spotless; doubles cost €43.50 and €46.50. The large restaurant is in a converted barn which has lost none of

its rustic charm. José Laurens prepares tasty traditional dishes with set menus €14.50–30, and an attractively priced wine list. Logis de France. *10% discount on the room rate for a stay of at least two nights (except in July and August) on presentation of this guide.*

Collioure
66190

Ⓒ 🏠 Les Caranques**

Route de Port-Vendres; it's 300m from the town centre and the beach.
Ⓣ04.68.82.06.68 Ⓕ04.68.82.00.92
Ⓦwww.les-caranques.com
Closed *mid-Oct to end April.* **Car park.**

Nestling beneath the cliffs, this welcoming family-run hotel is right on the sea and has the most wonderful view of Collioure and the port of Avall. The hotel has about twenty peaceful rooms, all of which come with a sea view and (nearly all) have a small balcony. Doubles with basin cost €40, €60–74 with shower/wc or bath; breakfast is €7. No beach, but a terrace where you can sunbathe and have private access to the rocks. And how nice it is to have breakfast while admiring the castle.

Ⓒ 🏠 |◯| Hôtellerie des Templiers**

Quai de l'Amirauté; opposite the castle.
Ⓣ04.68.82.98.31 Ⓕ04.68.98.01.24
Ⓦwww.hotel-templiers.com
Closed *Mon evening and Tues (Oct–May); 5 weeks from the first Sun in Jan.* **Restaurant closed** *usually from end Oct to mid-Feb, except over New Year; Mon–Fri, from mid-Feb; January to end April.* **TV.**

The owner's grandfather, René Pous, used to give painters and sculptors board and lodging in return for works of art. Sounds fair enough, especially when you consider that Matisse, Maillol, Dalí, Picasso and Dufy were among them. René's son, another lover, carried on the tradition, so that there are now two thousand original works of art on display all over the hotel, including in the bedrooms – but potential burglars needn't get any ideas, as the most valuable paintings are no longer kept here. The rooms (which have air-conditioning) are nice, with painted wooden beds, quirky chairs and, of course, the paintings; doubles with shower/wc or bath cost €46–75 depending on the season and the facilities. Those at the front do not have double glazing and can therefore be noisy; the rooms at the rear are more modern in style. The welcome is sometimes rather excitable, especially at mealtimes. The restaurant has a menu at €19 or you can dine à la carte for around €27. You can eat out on the terrace overlooking the port or in the dining room covered with abstract paintings. The hotel is in a pedestrianized road, so cannot be reached by car. The hotel also has three annexes in Collioure, less comfortable but also less expensive and definitely worth a look.

◎ 🏠 |◉| 🦌 Le Mas des Citronniers**

22 av. de la République.
☎04.68.04.82 ℻04.68.82.52.10
🌐www.hotel-mas-des-citronniers.com
Closed *21 Nov–5 Feb.* **Restaurant open** *7.15–9.15pm.* **TV.**

A generously proportioned 1930s villa with an Art Deco staircase. Well-maintained rooms with good facilities, bathrooms and air-conditioning go for €51–84, depending on the season. There are some triple and family rooms. Those in the annexe, the most recent ones, have either a balcony overlooking the garden or a private terrace leading onto the garden. Half board is available in summer at €50–66 per person. They serve two set menus for €21 and €24. Logis de France. *10% discount on the room rate (Feb–April and Oct–Nov, except for bank holidays) on presentation of this guide.*

◎ 🏠 |◉| 🦌 L'Arpède – Restaurant La Farigole

Route de Port-Vendres; it's 2km from the centre of town.
☎04.68.98.09.59 ℻04.68.98.30.90
🌐www.arapede.com
Closed *Dec–Jan.* **Restaurant closed** *lunchtimes (Mon–Fri except public holidays).* **Disabled access. TV. High chairs available. Swimming pool. Car park.**

This place is sturdily built on the rocks above the Mediterranean – the view is wonderful. It's quite near the road, though, and a bit of a trek into town, but benefiting from peace and quiet. Attractive rooms (air-conditioned) decorated in warm colours; most of them have terraces overlooking the sea. Doubles with bath go for €60–105, depending on the season; half board €62–84.50 per person. There are menus at €19 (weekdays only) and €46.

You walk down the hill to a lovely swimming pool. *Free coffee offered to our readers on presentation of this guide.*

◎ 🦌 🏠 Hôtel Casa Païral***

Impasse des Palmiers; it's beside pl. du 8 Mai-1945.
☎04.68.82.05.81 ℻04.68.82.52.10
🌐www.hotel-casa-pairal.com
Closed *Nov to Easter.* **Disabled access. TV. Swimming pool. Car park.**

A dream of a place, with a fountain on a patio surrounded by masses of greenery (majestic magnolias), a Hollywood-style swimming pool, a cosy lounge and absolute peace and quiet: luxury indeed. Comfy, spacious rooms with period furniture; doubles are €73–80 with shower/wc or €95–138 with bath; suites €154–170. It's a reliable establishment run by professional staff. Reservations are taken well in advance, especially for summer holidays. *10% discount (March, April and Oct, except public holidays) offered to our readers on presentation of this guide.*

◎ 🦌 |◉| Le Trémail

1 rue Arago; it's in the old town.
☎04.68.82.16.10
Closed *Mon and Tues out of season; Jan.*

Located in a lively area, with a few tables on a streetside terrace and more in the warmly decorated dining room, this is one of the nicest restaurants in the old town. Here, it's the women who serve at table, while the men slave over a hot stove. The restaurant serves Catalan and seafood specialities such as grilled fish and shellfish stew, with menus at €22–34. À la carte expect to pay €30. Wine is by the bottle only – a bit of a pity when there are so many good local vintages to try. It's best to book. *Free glass of Banyuls wine or coffee on presentation of this guide.*

Cucugnan

11350

◎ 🏠 |◉| Auberge de Cucugnan

2 pl. de la Fontaine.
☎04.68.45.40.84 ℻04.68.45.01.52
Closed *Wed; 31 Dec–15 March.* **High chairs available.**

The first menu (€16) fulfils all its promises with a generous platter of charcuterie and fantastic rabbit; other menus up to about €40. Doubles go for €43–56; if the hotel is full, you may be offered a *chambre d'hôte* or a self-catering flat, very convenient for a large family. There's a friendly welcome and convivial atmosphere; also a small terrace in summer. Logis de France.

⟪ 🛏 |●| L'Auberge du Vigneron**

2 rue Achille-Mir; it's opposite the theatre.
☎04.68.45.03.00 ℻04.68.45.03.08
🌐www.auberge-vigneron.com
Closed *Sun evening and Mon; 12 Nov–15 Feb.* **TV.**

The inn offers a lovely overnight stop and rustic rooms with rough-hewn stone walls; doubles with shower/wc €43–65. Make your way down to the old wine store – it's been turned into a lovely restaurant serving menus at €19 and €35, and a children's menu at €12. They've decorated it using hogsheads and there's an open fire as well as a terrace. You'll find regional dishes such as crayfish *fricassée*, guinea-fowl with morels and a delicious apple omelette. Logis de France.

Bugarach
11190 (27km W)

⟪ 🎋 |●| L'Oustal d'Al Pech

It's on the superb D14, 19km from the château de Peyrepertuse. Allow 40 min travel time.
☎ and ℻04.68.69.87.59
📧oustalddalpech@wanadoo.fr
Closed *Wed and Sun evening (except public holidays), evenings Nov–March; Jan.* **Disabled access.**

An isolated country inn in a totally unspoilt village. The rustic décor creates a lovely setting for a gourmet meal. Classic, flavoursome dishes using good local produce – foie gras, goose gizzard *confits*, free-range chicken served with a crayfish sauce, wild boar stew and iced nougat with caramel. Everything is made on the premises and the young team running the place are to be congratulated, even if service was on the slow side. They offer a range of menus €16–25, and a children's menu €8.50. It's essential to book for Sunday lunch and in winter. Please keep your dog on its lead. *Free coffee offered to our readers on presentation of this guide.*

Ferrières-les-Verreries
34190

⟪ 🛏 |●| Hôtel Mas de Baumes – Restaurant La Cour

266 av. Louis-Cancel.
☎04.66.80.88.80 ℻04.66.80.88.82
🌐www.oustaldebaumes.com
Closed *2 Jan–2 Feb.* **Disabled access. High chairs available. Car park.**

Having spent ten years in Mexico, Éric Tapié returned to France with a new family and longing for the sunny food and flavours of the New World. An admirer of the Aubrac restaurateur, Michel Bras, and a great fan of fine produce, Tapié has given Mediterranean cuisine a new lease of life. There's a weekday lunchtime menu for €16, otherwise €40–84. Treat yourself, for example, to baby vegetables fresh from the market, marinated in olive oil and coriander and served with a roast tail of monkfish and grilled Ratte potatoes with a drizzle of *aïoli*. For dessert, a future classic: warm pan-fried white peaches with vanilla and lavender flowers served with an iced zabaglione flavoured with dry Pic-Saint-Loup wine. As for the rooms (€95–102 for a double with shower), they are very fresh and new; so it's up to you to update us about them.

Florac
48400

⟪ 🛏 |●| Hôtel des Gorges du Tarn – Restaurant l'Adonis

48 rue du Pêcheur.
☎04.66.45.00.63 ℻04.66.45.10.56
🌐www.lozere.net/gorges-du-tarn.htm
Closed *Wed (except July–Aug); All Saints' Day to Easter.* **TV. Highchairs available. Car park.**

The name of the restaurant might send your imagination into flights of fancy – but don't be misled. However, if you want a place to rest and a good meal then you won't go far wrong choosing this perfectly run establishment. The quality of the produce on the menus (€17–37) and the skill of the chef ensure your complete satisfaction. Rooms (€36–52) are in the same vein. Logis de France.

Salle-Prunet (La)

48400 (2km SE)

🏚 ♿ |●| L'Auberge Cévenole-Chez Annie et Serge

Take the Alès road.
☎04.66.45.11.80
Closed Sun evening and Mon out of season, except public holidays and July–Aug; mid-Nov to mid-Feb. **TV.**

An old building faced in local stone, with a summer terrace, deep in the Mimente valley. You feel as if you're eating in the family dining room. Set menu €15 showcases good local charcuterie, *noisette* of veal with a cep sauce. Double rooms to tide you over for €31–39.

Cocurès

48400 (5km NE)

🏚 ♿ |●| La Lozerette**

Take the D998.
☎04.66.45.06.04 ☎04.66.45.12.93
@lalozerette@wanadoo.fr
Closed Tues (lunchtime only July–Aug); Wed lunchtime; 1 Nov to Easter. **Restaurant closed** Mon (except for guests). **Disabled access. High chairs and games available. TV. Car park.**

This establishment, set in a quiet little village on the picturesque road up to Mont Lozère, is a family affair. Granny Eugénie once owned an inn herself, but nowadays Pierrette Agulhon's in charge. There's a first menu at €15 (except Sunday lunch) and another at €21. Overall the cuisine exhibits a successful combination of imagination, good taste and magnificent flavours, and the wines are carefully chosen. The guest rooms are as stylish as the dining room – floral, pastel-painted and decorated with a keen eye for detail; expect to pay €51–64 for doubles. Breakfast is good.

Font-Romeu

66120

🏚 ♿ |●| Hôtel Carlit
– Restaurant La Cerdagne
– Restaurant El Foc***

Rue du Docteur-Capelle. In the centre of the resort.
☎04.68.30.80.30 ☎04.68.30.80.68
@www.carlit-hotel.fr
Closed mid-Oct to mid-Dec. **Grillroom open** lunchtimes. **TV. High chairs and cots available. Swimming pool.**

Though the modern building looks boring, this three-star place is more than adequate and prices are fair. Reception is professional and the rooms have good facilities and are clean, but rather old-looking, the decoration is perhaps over-bright and in the style of the 1970s and 1980s. Double rooms with shower/wc go for €56–82. There are two restaurants: chic La Cerdagne, which has a €32 menu and à la carte, as well as a good mushroom menu, and El Foc, with its cheaper grill *formules* from €12 to €19.50. If you're planning to stay a day or two, half board is reasonably priced at €55–75 per person, compulsory during February school holidays. *10% discount (except February and summer school holidays) on the room rate offered to our readers on presentation of this guide.*

Latour-de-Carol

66760 (17km SW)

🏚 ♿ |●| L'Auberge Catalane

10 av. de Puymorens. Take the D618, then the N20.
☎04.68.94.80.66 ☎04.68.04.95.25
@www.auberge-catalane.fr
Closed Mon; Sun evening except in school holidays; a fortnight in May; mid-Nov to Christmas. **TV. High chairs available. Car park.**

A good place to stop on the road up to the Puymorens pass. When the inn was taken over by the present owners they did up all the rooms, decorating them in attractive warm colours and fitting good soundproofing. They cost €48 and €52 with shower/wc, depending on the season; some have balconies and TV. There's a little shady terrace and a dining room where they serve menus (€14.50–31.40) featuring honest traditional dishes: grilled black pudding with apple, chicken *à la catalane* and *crème catalane*. Logis de France. *Free regional apéritif offered to our readers on presentation of this guide.*

Garde (La)

48200

🏚 ♿ |●| Le Rocher Blanc**

It's 1km from exit 32 on the A75.
☎04.66.31.90.09 ☎04.66.31.93.67

Closed *1 Nov to Easter.* **Restaurant closed** *Sun evening and Mon outside school holidays.* **TV. High chairs and games available. Swimming pool. Car park.**

Margeride is a wild and beautiful part of the country and the hotel is just 3km from France's smallest museum at Albaret-Sainte-Marie – a good place to stop over. The warm welcome and the swimming pool and tennis courts go a long way towards compensating for the hotel's lack of charm. The rooms here are fairly spacious and they're clean and quiet. Doubles with shower/wc or bath go for €40–50; half board, compulsory 15 July–20 August, is €43–52 per person. Set menus cost €17 (not served Sun) and up to €45. Credit cards not accepted. Logis de France. *Free house apéritif offered to our readers on presentation of this guide.*

Chaulhac

48140 (10km N)

⊚ 🎋 |●| La Maison d'Elisa

Take the D8.
℡04.66.31.93.32
Closed *Mon (except July–Aug).*

This isolated village, with flowers blooming everywhere, is absolutely idyllic. Originally from Lille, the owners now run a cosy and unassuming inn. They offer decent, nicely presented menus which change daily. The one at €14 includes wine and coffee, and there are others up to €23. Madame exhibits her skill in the kitchen and Monsieur serves with a smile. *Truffade* and *aligot* are made to order. Credit cards not accepted. *Free coffee offered to our readers on presentation of this guide.*

Grau-du-Roi (Le)

30240

⊚ 🛉 Hôtel Bellevue et d'Angleterre**

9 Quai Colbert.
℡04.66.51.40.75 ℻04.66.51.43.78
Closed *Christmas school holiday.* **TV.**

There are a good number of rooms in this hotel blessed with a grandstand view over Grau-du-Roi. All the rooms are pretty, well maintained and air-conditioned, and prices are competitive: doubles €35–50 out of season, €45–69 in the summer. Breakfast is included in the summer.

⊚ |●| Le Gafétou

6 bis rue Frédéric Mistral, rive gauche, promenade de la plage.
℡04.66.51.60.99 ℻04.66.51.56.54
Closed *Sun evening, Mon; early Nov to end Feb.*

Fronted by an awning, the large dining room is decorated in aquatic shades – setting the scene for the fish, seafood and shellfish you'll enjoy here. The menus from €13 (weekdays lunchtime only) to €39.50 offer good value, and the fish is as fresh as can be. You'll find a friendly welcome and perfect service in this ideal seaside location.

Gruissan

11430

⊚ |●| Le Lamparo

14 rue Amiral-Courbet; it's in the village beside the pond.
℡04.66.49.93.65
Closed *Mon and Tues, except from mid-June to mid-Sept, when open Tues lunchtime; mid-Dec to end Jan.*

This is a good restaurant specializing in fish and seafood at reasonable prices. The dining room is spruce and the tables are laid with salmon-pink cloths; there are more tables on the terrace, which has a view of the pond (and the car park). Excellent menus €20–35 listing dishes such as roast oysters with duck breast, fillet of sea bream with olive paste, cheese and double chocolate truffle.

Lamalou-les-Bains

34240

⊚ 🎋 🛉 |●| Hôtel-restaurant Belleville**

1 av. Charcot. Take the A9, exit Béziers est.
℡04.67.95.57.00
ⓦwww.hotel-belleville.com
Disabled access. TV. Car park.

Typical of a spa town, this is a substantial provincial hotel which has been owned by the same family since 1900. The house has character and has been entirely refurbished. It's spacious and boasts good facilities – doubles with shower/wc or bath €30–50 (many overlooking the garden, the more expensive ones air-conditioned). The restaurant is decorated in Belle-Époque style, and they serve a series of set menus at €14.50–34, specializing in local dishes. If you're in a hurry, go for the *menu express*, served on the veranda. Specialities include fish stew, duck with figs and Banyuls wine, and *fondant* with almonds. And a dish has been created especially for the backpackers among you. *10% discount on the room rate from the second consecutive night or a free apéritif offered on presentation of this guide.*

ⓔ 🎋 |●| Les Marronniers

8 av. de Capus; it's on the way out of town before the town hall.
☎04.67.95.76.00
Closed *Sat lunchtime; Sun evening; Mon; 2–24 Jan.*

A small and rather insignificant house above the town – but the restaurant is currently one of the very best in town. The chef Gilles Aubert approaches local dishes from a fresh perspective and produces seriously good cooking: his roulade of beef oxtail with foie gras is a treat. The market menu starts at €14 (weekdays only) with *menu-cartes* for €17–40. Service is efficient and they do good seasonal wine by the glass. There's a terrace under an awning. *Free coffee offered to our readers on presentation of this guide.*

Villemagne-l'Argentière
34600 (7km NE)

ⓔ |●| L'Auberge de l'Abbaye

Place du Couvent. Take the D908 and follow the signs.
☎04.67.95.34.84
Closed *Mon; Tues lunchtime; Wed (Nov–May); 31 Oct–4 Feb.* **Car park. High chairs available.**

Set in the middle of a charming village, this picturesque place has old stone walls and a terrace at the foot of an old tower. It's a very pleasing setting in which to sample authentic local cooking, carefully prepared. Specialities include fish platter with spiced caramel, and foie gras *tournedos* with truffle *jus*. Menus €25–52.

Bédarieux
34600 (8km NE)

ⓔ 🏠 🎋 Hôtel Delta

1 rue de Clairac; it's on the street that runs at right angles to av. Jean-Jaurès.

☎and ☎04.67.23.21.19
TV.

A friendly and unconventional couple have converted this small clinic into a hotel. It may have no stars, but the rooms are clean and spacious. Fresh, unusual décor, with Egyptian symbols and Chinese fans here and there. Double rooms with shower go for €26 or with shower/wc and TV €32. *10% discount on the room rate for two consecutive nights on presentation of this guide (except July and August).*

Lauret
34270

ⓔ 🎋 🏠 |●| L'Auberge du Cèdre

Domaine de Cazeneuve; it's 1km from the village.
☎04.67.59.02.02 ☎04.67.59.03.44
🖰www.auberge-du-cedre.com
Closed *early Dec to mid-March.* **Restaurant closed** *Mon–Thurs and Fri lunch (but open for hotel guests).* **High chairs, baby changing mats and games available. Swimming pool.**

This old house in an ancient wine area has been converted into a very attractive hotel and restaurant with a swimming pool. Simple but adequate rooms are yours for €28–42; some sleep three or four, with the newest one being rather spacious at 60 square metres. Half board costs €32–38 per person. Weekend menus are €26–33; also a children's menu available. Look out for the hiker's platter – sausage, terrine with juniper berries, Serrano ham and other good traditional terroir dishes. There's a wide range of good Mediterranean wines, many of which are available by the glass. *Free house apéritif offered to our readers on presentation of this guide.*

Lézignan-Corbières
11200

ⓔ 🎋 🏠 |●| Hôtel Le Tassigny – Restaurant Le Tournedos**

Rond-point de-Lattre-de-Tassigny; from the centre, take av. des Corbières towards the A9.
☎04.68.27.11.51 ☎04.68.27.67.31
🖂tournedos@wanadoo.fr

Closed *Sun evening; last week in Jan; a week in March; 1–15 Oct.* **Restaurant closed** *Sun evening;* **Mon. Disabled access. TV. High chairs available. Car park.**

A great place for an overnight stay if you don't want to spend a fortune. The place is freshly refurbished and modernized, with doubles at €40–43 with shower/wc or bath; the cheaper ones are also the noisiest. The restaurant is popular locally; set lunchtime *formule* at €14, menus €17–36. Hearty specialities cooked by chef, Pierre, include *cassoulet, tournedos* with morels, meats and fish grilled over a wood fire. Logis de France. *Free coffee offered to our readers on presentation of this guide.*

Escales

11200 (7km NW)

⊛ |O| Les Dinedourelles

Impasse des Pins; from Lézignan, take the Olonzac road, the D611, for 2km, then turn left onto the D127.
☎04.68.27.68.33
Closed *evenings (except Mon–Wed during March–June and Sept–Oct).* **Disabled access.**

A good atmosphere and a pleasant, unusual setting – unusual because you get to eat inside a variety of barrels, including a 10,000-litre one seating six. If that doesn't appeal there's always the lovely terrace under the pine trees with a panoramic view of the Montagne Noire. The cuisine is generously flavoured and original: pan-fried *escalope* of foie gras, celery ravioli stuffed with goat's cheese and black olive *coulis*. Menus range from €19 to €35; à la carte you'll spend around €26. Out of season on two or three Friday nights a month, they feature entertainment such as French song, jazz, storytelling and even short plays. A very comfortable *chambre d'hôte* and two *gîtes* that can accommodate up to six people have recently been opened.

Fabrezan

11200 (9km SW)

⊛ 🌴 🏠 |O| Le Clos des Souquets

Av. de Lagrasse; take the D611 towards Lagrasse.
☎04.68.43.52.61
✉clossouquets@infonie.fr
Closed *Sun; 1 Nov–1 April.* **TV. High chairs available. Swimming pool. Car park.**

This is a jewel of a place on the route to the Cathar châteaux and the Corbières caves. It only has five rooms; doubles with bath €50–75. Half board from €85 per person is compulsory in summer. The Julien family spend the winter in the Caribbean, as you'll notice from the exotic touches in the rooms and the cuisine. Simple tasty food served around the pool with a choice of menus €19–32 – the first menu lists salad *méridionale, moules gratinées* and soft cheese with honey. Choose the second menu if you want to sample the grilled fish of the day, which is always superb. Or go for a *carpaccio* of meat or fish. Logis de France. *Free house apéritif on presentation of this guide.*

Homps

11200 (10km N)

⊛ 🏠 |O| Auberge de l'Arbousier

Route de Carcassonne. Take the D611 towards Olonzac.
☎04.68.91.11.24 📠04.68.91.12.61
Closed *Mon all day and Tues lunchtime; Sun evening Sept–June; 15 Feb–15 March; Nov.* **TV. High chairs and games available. Bicycle racks. Car park.**

The Canal du Midi flows alongside this inn, where old stonework and exposed beams contrast well with the modern art on the walls. It's a nice place, with a shaded terrace in summer and quiet, comfortable rooms; doubles €43–75 with shower/wc or bath. You could almost imagine you were staying in a bed and breakfast. The kitchen prepares classic but refined dishes: red mullet, rabbit and purple artichokes salad, fig tart (only when in season). Set weekday lunchtime menu costs €15, otherwise €21–36. Logis de France.

⊛ |O| Restaurant Les Tonneliers

Port du Canal du Midi.
☎04.68.91.14.04
Closed *mid-Dec to mid-Feb.* **Disabled access.**

The Canal du Midi runs through the village and only a few metres away from it you'll find this place. It offers good food in rustic surroundings. There's a *formule* for €13 and menus €15–31, listing specialities like *cassoulet* with *confit* of duck, marinated salmon in two kinds of lemon and *tarte tatin.* Tourists come to see the canal in the evening. In summer, sit

⑪

in the attractive garden or on the shaded terrace.

Limoux

11300

ⓦ 🎋 🛏 |●| Grand Hôtel Moderne et Pigeon***

Place du Général-Leclerc; it's by the post office.
☎04.68.31.00.25 ℻04.68.31.12.43
🖰www.grandhotelmodernepigeon.fr
Restaurant closed Mon, Sat lunch and Sun evening (except July–Aug); 15 Dec–15 Jan. **TV. High chairs available. Pay car park.**

This magnificent building had many lives before being converted into a hotel in the early 1900s. Originally a convent, it became a grand town house and later a bank; make sure you take a good look at the seventeenth-century frescoes on the wall above the splendid staircase. As a hotel it's comfy and well run without being too formal. Lovely doubles (nearly all with air-conditioning) with shower/wc or with bath go for €70–130, depending on size and comfort. The dining room has sophisticated décor and a quiet atmosphere with set menus €29.50–55. Logis de France. *Second breakfast free (except in July and Aug) offered to our readers on presentation of this guide.*

Llo

66800

ⓦ 🎋 🛏 |●| Auberge Atalaya***

Llo-Haut.
☎04.68.04.70.04 ℻04.68.04.01.29
🖂 atalaya66@aol.com
Closed 2 Nov–20 Dec; 15 Jan–Easter. **Restaurant closed** Mon–Thurs out of season. **TV. Car park.**

A charming stone house with a courtyard overlooking the village – the walls are covered in vines and there's a small garden. Doubles go for €90–118; a flat and a large bedroom with a terrace are also available for €140. The restaurant offers seasonal dishes, which vary according to the whim of the chef. The menu costs €30, à la carte menu is also available. This is a really charming, welcoming place. *Free house apéritif or coffee offered to our readers on presentation of this guide.*

Lodève

34700

ⓦ 🎋 🛏 |●| La Croix Blanche**

6 av. de Funel.
☎04.67.44.10.87
🖰www.hotelcroixblanche.com
Restaurant closed Fri lunchtime; 1 Dec–1 April. **TV. High chairs available. Pay car park.**

An impressive collection of copper pots, pans and basins decorate this place and create a welcoming atmosphere. Generations of sales reps and businessmen have stopped by to enjoy the local hospitality and simple accommodation – doubles €36–42. Unfussy cooking and generous portions in the dining room on set menus €13–30, with specialities such as snails à *la lodevoise* and home-made tripes. *Free coffee offered to our readers on presentation of this guide.*

ⓦ 🛏 |●| Hôtel-restaurant de la Paix**

11 bd. Montalanque.
☎04.67.44.07.46 ℻04.67.44.30.47
🖰www.hotel-dela-paix.com
Closed Sun evening and Mon (except 1 May–1 Oct); 1 Feb–8 March. **TV. High chairs available. Swimming pool. Pay car park.**

The same family has been running this place since 1876. It's clean and comfortable and has views of the mountains and the Lergue River. Doubles with bath/wc go for €57; half board, €54 per person, is available for stays of three days or more. The hearty cooking specializes in regional dishes and uses fresh produce, with set menus €20 and €30, or à la carte. House dishes include Labeil trout with almonds. In summer, you can eat outside on the terrace around the swimming pool.

ⓦ |●| Le Petit Sommelier

3 pl. de la République; it's beside the tourist office.
☎and ℻04.67.44.05.39
Closed Sun evening; Mon; Wed evening in low season; autumn school holiday. **Disabled access.**

An informal, unpretentious little place with simple bistro décor. Set menus €14–32 feature tasty cooking with dishes like trout with Chardonnay, roast lamb, breast of duck with apples and honey and warm mussels in a cream sauce with Banyuls wine. You'll get a warm, friendly welcome, and there's a pleasant terrace.

Lunel
34400

@ 🏡 |O| Auberge des Halles

26 cours Gabriel-Péri; it's next to the covered market.
☏04.67.83.85.80
Closed *Sun evening and Mon (except public holidays); Feb.*

A well-known restaurant serving honest, traditional cuisine which follows the changing seasons and whims of the owner. You must try the pan-fried foie gras with the local Muscat. Weekday lunch menu costs €11, others €20–35. There are tables on the terrace outside and the service is friendly. *A free glass of Muscat de Lunel offered to our readers on presentation of this guide.*

Mende
48000

@ 🏡 🏢 |O| Hôtel Le Lion d'Or

12–14 bd. Britexte.
☏04.66.49.16.46 ☏04.66.49.23.31
🖥www.liondor-mende.com
Disabled access. TV. Swimming pool. Car park.

If you're looking for comfortable, quiet rooms in the centre of town, look no further. Doubles are €54–76 depending on the season. It's quite luxurious and there's even a swimming pool for you to splash around in. You can dine here, too, if you can't face struggling out. If you do, try the pigs' trotters *à la gabale*. Menus are €18–30, and they have a fine wine list. *Free coffee offered to our readers on presentation of this guide.*

@ 🏡 🏢 |O| Hôtel-restaurant du Pont-Roupt***

2 av. du 11-Novembre.
☏04.66.65.01.43 ☏04.66.65.22.96
🖥www.hotel-pont-roupt.com
Closed *15 Feb–15 March.* **Restaurant closed** *weekends out of season.* **TV. High chairs and games available. Swimming pool. Car park.**

A nice hotel in a large house on the banks of the Lot on the edge of town. The décor is contemporary and plain but the rooms

– €60–69 for a double with shower/wc or bath – are comfortable, and there's an indoor swimming pool. Gastronomic weekend deals are available. The chef draws on a long tradition of cuisine while also creating some modern dishes; menus €23–51. If you've got to spend the night in Mende, this is fine. But if you're after a romantic weekend, perhaps look elsewhere. Logis de France. *10% discount on the room rate on presentation of this guide.*

@ |O| Le Mazel

25 rue du Collège.
☏and ☏04.66.65.05.33
Closed *Mon evening; Tues; 15 Nov–15 March.*

This is one of the few modern buildings in the town centre. Jean-Paul Brun uses first-rate ingredients to create fine, flavoursome dishes such as tripoux with white wine, truffle omelette and duck with wild mushrooms; menus €14–27. It's a popular place for business lunches and the best value for money in town. The decoration is simple and straightforward, and so is the welcome.

@ 🏡 |O| La Safranière

Hameau de Chabrits, it's 3.5km northwest of Mende. Take the N88, cross the Roupt bridge, then straight ahead on the D42.
☏04.66.49.31.54
Closed *Sun evening; Mon; March; a week in Sept.* **High chairs available.**

This is where to come if you're in Mende or the surrounding area and want a gourmet experience. The dining room is bright and elegant, and it's in a very old building which has been attractively refurbished. Sebastien Navetch's light, delicate cooking makes clever use of herbs, spices and seasonings like basil, tarragon, cumin, saffron and coconut; try roast pigeon breast with caramelized spices. The cheapest menu at €20 is served on weekdays (except Friday evening), others €27–44. Reservations are recommended. *Free coffee offered to our readers on presentation of this guide.*

Meyrueis
48150

@ 🏢 |O| Hôtel de La Jonte**

Aux Douzes; follow the D996 and the gorges of La Jonte.

☎05.65.62.60.52 🖷05.65.62.61.62
Closed *mid-Nov to early March.* **Disabled access. TV. Swimming pool. Car park.**

A large establishment by the road which is well known for its good cooking and the warmth of its welcome – and it's cheap too. There are two dining rooms: opt for the one used by workers and travelling salesmen because the cooking is better and the prices are more reasonable, with set menus at €11–24. The rooms are very well maintained and are above the restaurant or in an annexe overlooking the gorge of the River Jonte. Doubles with shower/wc or bath cost €33–35; half board €37 per person. The rooms with a view of the river are the most expensive.

☜ 🎿 🏠 |●| Hôtel Family**

Rue de la Barrière.
☎04.66.45.60.02 🖷04.66.45.66.54
🖂hotel.family@wanadoo.fr
Closed *5 Nov to Palm Sunday.* **Disabled access. TV. High chairs and baby-changing facilities available. Swimming pool. Car park.**

A large building standing by the fast-flowing stream that runs through the village. Well-maintained and redecorated rooms go for €36–46 for a double with shower/wc or bath. Those on the top floor are the best. The cuisine focuses on local dishes and menus are fairly priced at €12 (weekday lunchtimes only) up to €30. There's a pleasant garden with a swimming pool opposite the hotel which you reach by crossing a little wooden bridge. *10% discount on the room rate (in April, May and October) or free house apéritif offered to our readers on presentation of this guide.*

☜ 🏠 |●| Hôtel du Mont Aigoual**

34 quai de la Barrière.
☎04.66.45.65.61 🖷04.66.45.64.25
🖳www.hotel-mont-aigoual.com
Closed *Tues lunchtime in April and Oct; Nov to end March.* **TV. Swimming pool. High chairs available. Car park.**

From the outside this place looks ordinary enough, but appearances are deceptive. Stella Robert is energetic and lively and she'll give you a charming welcome. There's a beautiful swimming pool at the back of the hotel in an enormous garden. The rooms are spacious and quiet; they're priced at €44–73 with bath. Half board is compulsory in July and August, and costs €45–57 per person. The restaurant

is one of the best in the area, offering consistent quality at reasonable prices. Daniel Lagrange uses authentic, tasty local produce to create appetizing local dishes: pan-fried foie gras with creamed lentils, say, or roast saddle of lamb. The local menu costs €18, and the *menus gourmands* are €27 and €38. Logis de France.

Mèze
34140

☜ 🎿 |●| Le Pescadou

33 bd. du Port; go towards the harbour.
☎04.67.43.81.72
Closed *Tues and Wed in winter; Mon and Tues July–Aug; a week in Jan; a week in June; a fortnight in Oct.* **Disabled access.**

Le Pescadou has a pretty terrace on the harbour and a spacious dining room attractively decorated with engravings of ships and lots of green plants. It's a fresh, relaxing place, very popular with the locals. First menu at €14 (not served Sun lunch) with others €19.90–30 – all the fresh fish is good, along with the mussels and oysters. Advance booking is recommended. *Free Kir offered to our readers on presentation of this guide.*

Mont-Louis
66210

☜ 🎿 🏠 |●| Hôtel-restaurant Lou Rouballou

Rue des Écoles-Laïques; it's on the ramparts, opposite the local primary school.
☎04.68.04.23.26 🖷04.68.04.14.09
Closed *May; Oct–Nov.* **Restaurant closed** *Wed out of season; lunchtimes in season.* **TV. Car park.**

A family guesthouse with lots of rustic character; it's comfy, delightful and full of charm. You'll be greeted warmly by Christiane Duval, who is Catalan – you can practically feel the sun in her voice when she talks about the Pyrenees. You'll feel perfectly at home in one of the attractive rooms, which go for €40–58.50 according to the facilities; half board (compulsory from mid-June to end of September) is €50 per person. The restaurant is tastefully decorated and fresh, authentic cooking is offered on the single menu, €25. House specialities include game with hand-picked mushrooms, wild boar stew, duck breast with fruit and honey, and Catalan meatballs. In winter, don't miss the *ollada*, a rustic soup from Cerdagne. Year round there are delicious mushrooms – including the roubaillou, which grows locally. *Free house apéritif and digestif offered to our readers on presentation of this guide.*

Prats-Balaguer

66360 (1km SE)

⊛ 🎢 🏠 |●| Auberge de la Carança

Take the N116 to Fontépouse, then follow directions to Prats-Balaguer.
☎04.68.97.10.84
Closed *mid-Nov to 20 Dec.*

A little inn at the end of a village, at the end of a lane. There's nothing beyond but the mountain. It's full of walkers who come to restore their strength with the tasty cooking. Specialities including rare Pyrenean veal and omelettes, and lots of mushrooms predominate on the menus €12.20–18.30. Simple, clean doubles €30–34, or €14 for a night in a dormitory. It's essential to book a bed and to order your meal – the nearest baker is an hour away. They can advise you on walks in the area. Three gîtes are being constructed near the inn. *Discount at the hot baths at Saint-Thomas-les-Bains offered to our readers on presentation of this guide.*

Montpellier

34000

See map on pp.468–469

⊛ 🏠 Auberge de jeunesse

Rue des Écoles-Laïques; entrance by La Petite-Corraterie; from the station, take the tramway to Mosson, stop "Louis-Blanc".
Map B1-1
☎04.67.60.32.22 ☎04.67.60.32.30
@montpellier@fuaj.org
Closed *14 Dec–11 Jan.* **Reception open** *7am–noon and 1pm–2am.*

Nineteen rooms, generally well kept, with 89 dormitory beds; each room sleeping two to ten people. One night costs €12.30 (breakfast included). In the summer, there's a nice shaded terrace, and the bar is open from 6pm until midnight. Left-luggage facilities are available, as well as table football and snooker.

⊛ 🏠 Hôtel Les Fauvettes*

8 rue Bonnard; it's on the no. 7 bus route, tramway also available. Behind the Jardin des Plantes. **Map A1-2**
☎04.67.63.17.60 ☎04.67.64.09.09
Closed *Christmas to 7 Jan.*

It's a small establishment in a quiet street, run by a friendly lady, and probably the cheapest hotel in Montpellier. The rooms may be basic but they're quiet and clean; most of them look onto the interior courtyard; only two out of eighteen look onto the street. Doubles with basin are €30, with shower €33, with shower/wc or bath €39. They serve breakfast on the veranda, which is popular in summer.

⊛ 🏠 Hôtel Floride**

1 rue François-Perrier. **Map D3-5**
☎04.67.65.73.30 ☎04.67.22.10.83
@hotel.floride@gofornet.com
TV.

Situated in a quiet street near the place de la Comédie and the Antigone district. You'll receive a warm welcome. Twenty-five air-conditioned doubles €43–57 depending on the season and facilities; the best ones overlook the terrace, which is a riot of flowers. Good breakfast at €6.

⊛ 🏠 🎢 Hôtel des Arts

6 bd. Victor-Hugo; 50m from pl. de la Comédie, near the station. **Map B3-6**
☎04.67.58.69.20 ☎04.67.58.85.82
@www.hotel-des-arts.fr

A very convenient place to stay offering a friendly welcome and colourful décor. The twenty rooms have all been recently refurbished; doubles with shower or bath €47–49. *Free coffee offered to our readers on presentation of this guide.*

⊛ 🏠 Hôtel Du Parc**

8 rue Achille-Bège; it's on the other side of Verdanson, 300m from the cathedral. **Off map B1-10**
☎04.67.41.16.49 ☎04.67.54.10.0
@www.hotelduparc-montpellier.com
Disabled access. TV. Car park.

This is a typical eighteenth-century Languedoc building offering twenty air-conditioned rooms. They give you a friendly welcome and there's a quiet, attractive garden with pots of flowers on the terrace. The rooms leading onto the terrace have small balconies. The rooms are all clean and comfy; doubles €48 with shower, €63–72 with shower/wc or bath, mini-bar, telephone and TV.

⧉ 🏛 Hôtel de la Comédie**

1 bis rue Baudin. **Map C2–8**
☎04.67.58.43.64
TV.

You'd be hard pushed to find a more central hotel. It's good, quiet and friendly. The rooms have been redecorated in light colours, and cost €52–69 depending on size and time of year. They're simple but clean and welcoming. All the windows are double-glazed.

⧉ 🏊 🏛 Hôtel Les Arceaux**

33–35 bd. des Arceaux; it's behind promenade du Peyrou. **Off map A2-7**
☎04.67.92.03.03 ⓕ04.67.92.05.09
TV. Car park.

This is an attractive two-storey house, swathed in greenery, with a view on one side of the seventeenth-century aqueduct. The garden is south-facing, so it's perfect for relaxing. Homely atmosphere and comfortable rooms painted in fresh, pretty colours. Ask for one which has been recently refurbished, as the young owners are still in the process of updating the rooms. Some of the bathrooms have retained their trendy Seventies tiling. Doubles go for €52–72 with shower/wc or bath; some have a private balcony and others can sleep three. No. 302 has its own little terrace. Opt for the first-floor rooms with high ceilings. The breakfast room is very Mediterranean in style with its wrought-iron tables and sisal chairs. *10% discount on the room rate (15 Sept–15 June) offered to our readers on presentation of this guide.*

⧉ 🏛 Hôtel du Palais**

3 rue du Palais-des-Guilhem. **Map A2-12.**
☎04.67.60.47.38 ⓕ04.67.60.40.23
TV.

This handsome nineteenth-century building with its splendid marble entrance is near a quiet little square just five minutes from the centre. The bright rooms are furnished with copies of famous paintings, creating a cosy country atmosphere. They're all air-conditioned and have double glazing; doubles €61–73 with shower/wc or bath, and the generous breakfast costs €12. You'll get a friendly welcome.

⧉ 🏊 🏛 Citadines Antigone***

588 bd. d'Antigone (and pl. du Millénaire); close to pl. de la Comédie. **Map D2-9**
☎04.99.52.37.50 ⓕ04.67.64.54.64
ⓦwww.citadines.com
Reception open *7.30am–8pm (Mon–Fri); 8am–noon and 3–8pm (weekends and public holidays).* **Disabled access. TV. Pay car park.**

Situated in the neighbourhood designed by the modern architect Bofill, the studios are plain but modern and functional, just like the area they're in. Spacious and clean studios offering a range of hotel services (fresh linen, cleaning, breakfast, etc); €71–85 for two with bath and sofa-bed. Discounts are available after the first week. Each has a fully equipped kitchen which will ease the strain on your restaurant bill. There's an entry-phone system and direct-dial telephones. *10% discount on the room rate (except June–Sept) offered to our readers on presentation of this guide.*

⧉ 🏛 |●| 🏊 La Maison Blanche***

1796 av. de la Pompignane; it's on the corner of 46 rue des Salaisons, on the road to Castelnau. **Off map D1-14**
☎04.99.58.20.70 ⓕ04.67.79.53.39
ⓦwww.hotel-maison-blanche.com
Restaurant closed *Sat lunchtime; Sun; Christmas holidays.* **Disabled access. TV. Swimming pool. Car park.**

This very quiet establishment is located in a small park filled with ancient (and now officially protected) trees. The building itself looks somewhat like a mansion from the American Deep South, with spacious light rooms elegantly decorated with wood panelling. There's a poster at the reception signed by Alain Delon (he came here in 1991 to film *Casanova*) that shows how popular this hotel used to be with movie stars a few years back. The hotel's exterior is today in need of a makeover to restore its former glory. It is of a good size though, with 38 rooms available, so very popular with groups, and there's a small swimming pool. You'll pay €81–91 a night for a double room; breakfast €8. In the restaurant, menus start at €22 (weekdays) up to €36. *One free breakfast per room on presentation of this guide.*

⧉ |●| L'Actuel

4 rue Bourrely; in a side street off the av. Georges-Clemenceau, level with the local technical secondary school. **Off map A3-24**

LANGUEDOC-ROUSSILLON

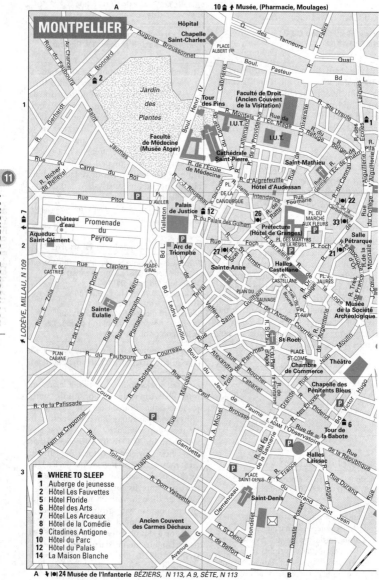

MONTPELLIER

LANGUEDOC-ROUSSILLON

♨ **WHERE TO SLEEP**
1 Auberge de jeunesse
2 Hôtel Les Fauvettes
5 Hôtel Floride
6 Hôtel des Arts
7 Hôtel Les Arceaux
8 Hôtel de la Comédie
9 Citadines Antigone
10 Hôtel du Parc
12 Hôtel du Palais
14 La Maison Blanche

↓ LODÈVE, MILLAU, N 109

A ↓ ⬤ 24 Musée de l'Infanterie *BÉZIERS*, N 113, A 9, *SÈTE*, N 113 B

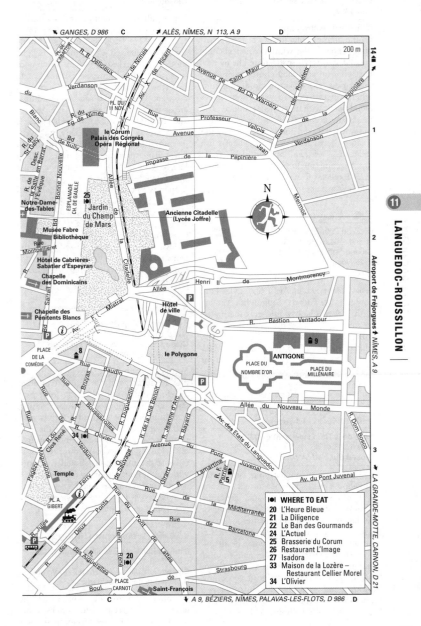

GANGES, D 986   C   ALÈS, NÎMES, N 113, A 9   D

0   200 m

14

1

2

Aéroport de Fréjorgues ➤ NÎMES, A 9

3

LA GRANDE-MOTTE, CARNON, D 21

Av. de Nîmes

R. de Ricard

Avenue de Saint Maur

Bd Ch. Warnery

R. des Rondelets

Pépinière

R. Delicieux

R. B.

R. de Maroton

Verdanson

du

Blanc

R. du Fg de Nîmes

PL. DU 11 NOV.

Av. X.

Rue

du

Professeur

Vallois

de

la

rue

R. du St Gely

Desc. en Barrat

R. de la Salle l'Évêque

Bonne Nouvelle

Bd de Sully

le Corum
Palais des Congrès
Opéra Régional

Avenue

Jean

Verdanson

Impasse

de

la

Pépinière

Mermoz

Notre-Dame-des-Tables

ESPLANADE
CH. DE GAULLE

25

Jardin
du Champ
de Mars

Allée

de

la

Citadelle

Ancienne Citadelle
(Lycée Joffre)

N

Musée Fabre
Bibliothèque

Rue
Montpellieret

R. Sarrail

Bd

Hôtel de Cabrières-
Sabatier d'Espeyran

Chapelle
des Dominicains

Allée

Henri II

de

Montmorency

Chapelle des
Pénitents Blancs

F. Mistral

Hôtel
de ville

Av.

i

R. Bastion Ventadour

P

PLACE
DE LA
COMÉDIE

i

8

Rue

Baudin

le Polygone

ANTIGONE

9

PLACE DU
NOMBRE D'OR

PLACE DU
MILLÉNAIRE

Rue

Rue

Rue

Bruys

Boussairolles

R. Duguesclin

Allée

du

Nouveau

Monde

R. Dom Bosco

R. du Clos René

34

A. Olivier

R. de la Cité Benoît

R. Jeanne d'Arc

R. Bayard

Avenue

du

Pont

Juvenal

Av. du Pont Juvenal

Pagézy

R. Jules

Maguelone

O. Sauvage

Temple

i

PL. A.
GIBERT

Ferry

Pons

Rue

du

R.

Girard

Lamartine

R. F.
Perrier

5

Avenue

de

la

Méditerranée

P

R. des Aiguerelles

René

R. des Deux

Pont de Lattes

R.

20

Rue

de

Barcelone

Strasbourg

PLACE
CARNOT

Boul.

Saint-François

	WHERE TO EAT
20	L'Heure Bleue
21	La Diligence
22	Le Ban des Gourmands
24	L'Actuel
25	Brasserie du Corum
26	Restaurant L'Image
27	Isadora
33	Maison de la Lozère – Restaurant Cellier Morel
34	L'Olivier

C   A 9, BÉZIERS, NÎMES, PALAVAS-LES-FLOTS, D 986   D

☎04.67.58.37.87
Closed *lunchtimes Sat-Sun; evenings Sun–Wed.*

This small gastronomic restaurant located on the premises of a former bar (darkened glass panels in the windows, general outdated décor) is worth a detour. The owners have concentrated their efforts on producing varied and inventive home cooking, where sauces flavoured with exotic spices blend well with the local produce. The lunchtime menus (€10 and €12) are the most delicious and good value with a good balance between meat (roast beef), fish (fillet of *sébaste*), and seafood dishes (scallops); evening menu €21, à la carte around €25. Expect a friendly welcome. Advance booking is recommended in the evening.

© |●| 🎿 **Isadora**

6 rue du Petit-Scel. **Map B2-27**
☎ and ☎04.67.66.25.23
Closed *Sat lunchtime; Sun; Mon lunchtime; 1–15 Nov.*

A wonderful thirteenth-century vaulted cellar decorated in Art Deco style. Fine cooking by Gilbert Saugo: hot oysters with braised chicory, foie gras marinated in muscat. A wonderful place to escape from the crushing heat of the summer. Lunch menu at €13, with others at €23 and €28 and a gastronomic menu at €43 represent good value for money; the service is very friendly. *Free coffee offered to our readers on presentation of this guide.*

© |●| **L'Heure Bleue**

1 rue de la Carbonnerie. **Map C3-20**
☎04.67.66.41.05
Closed *Sun and Mon.*

It is situated in a charming city-centre townhouse with a rather oriental décor and offers refined teas and delicious savoury and sweet platters for all budgets. At lunchtime, a savoury platter will cost you €10. If you fancy any of the items on display in the lounge, don't be disappointed as Pierre, the owner and a proud antiques collector, is keen to sell them. All in all, a nice place to go if you enjoy antiques and good food. It's also a library/tea room and you can even buy tea and coffee there to take home with you.

© 🎿 |●| **Brasserie du Corum**

Esplanade Charles-de-Gaulle. **Map C1-25.**

☎04.67.02.03.04
Closed *evenings; Sun.*

Three different functions for one building: art gallery, wine bar and gastronomic restaurant. The latter isn't such good value for money though. The wine bar is light, modern and relaxed, with a view both over the rather futuristic esplanade and over the archeological garden – quite a contrast. Comfortable and quiet dining areas with teak chairs for the terrace and brightly coloured moulded plastic chairs inside. Mouth-watering and well-garnished bruschettas with swordfish and citrus fruit marinated in ginger, chicken kebab with grilled aubergines or thinly sliced beef… not to mention the one topped with the local cheese (*Pérail Saint-pargoire*). Several menus are on offer: bruschetta with salad and dessert of the day €12.50, bruschetta alone €9. As for desserts, the fresh fruit compote (the yogurt mousse to be enjoyed mixed with the fruit) is a winner – neither too sour nor too sweet. *Free coffee offered to our readers on presentation of this guide.*

© 🎿 |●| **Le Ban des Gourmands**

5 pl. Carnot. **Map B2-22**
☎and ☎04.67.65.00.85
Closed *Sat lunchtime; Sun; Mon; Feb; 3 weeks in Aug; Christmas.*

You get a warm, natural welcome in this fine restaurant, not to mention creative, delicious dishes cooked using fresh produce and served in an intimate setting. Lunchtime *formule* is priced at €13 (starter, dish of the day and coffee) and there's a menu at €25, or an à la carte menu around €35. Dishes change according to what's good at the market: try shoulder of pork with figs. It's not a touristy place – more a haven for gourmands and even gourmets. *Free house apéritif offered to our readers on presentation of this guide.*

© 🎿 |●| **Restaurant L'Image**

6 rue du Puits-des-Esquilles. **Map B2-26**
☎04.67.60.47.79
Closed *Sun; July–Aug.* **Open** *7–10pm only.*
Disabled access. Car park.

If you're claustrophobic, head for the dining room upstairs. The simple dishes are suffused with Mediterranean flavours and the portions are generous. Set menus €14–22 include a few specialities like the *croustillant* of duck with honey and pears.

Free house digestif offered to our readers on presentation of this guide.

⊚ 🎄 |●| La Diligence

2 pl. Pétrarque. **Map B2-21**
☎04.67.66.12.21
🖥www.la-diligence.com
Closed *Sat and Mon lunchtimes; Sun; Aug.*

The restaurant has a splendid dining room with stone walls and a vaulted ceiling – it feels gloriously old. There's also a patio at the back. A traditional cuisine with an Asian and Mediterranean twist: sushi of foie gras with a *carpaccio* of aubergines, beef fillet served with calvados, or whisky straight from the owner's astonishing cellar. Lunch menu at €18 and others at €33 and €59; the food is good but challenging and requires a certain open-mindedness. It's best to book at the weekend. *Free house apéritif offered to our readers on presentation of this guide.*

⊚ 🎄 |●| Maison de la Lozère – Restaurant Cellier Morel

27 rue de l'Aiguillerie. **Map B2-33**
☎04.67.66.46.36
Closed *Sun; Mon and Wed lunchtimes; a week in Jan; a fortnight in Aug.*

This restaurant and its little sister in Paris are both showcases for Lozère specialities. Éric Cellier's top-of-the-range cooking is served in the superb vaulted dining room down in the basement. On fine days you can eat outside in the courtyard. Dishes on the €28 lunchtime menu change constantly; other menus €32–58, à la carte menu around €65. Good choice of thoughtfully selected local wines by Pierre Morel. *Free house apéritif offered to our readers on presentation of this guide.*

⊚ 🎄 |●| L'Olivier

12 rue Aristide-Ollivier. **Map C3-34**
☎04.67.92.86.28
Closed *Sun; Mon; July–Aug.*

Modern décor and fine cooking, both popular with local gourmands. The fish is prepared as skilfully as the meat: try the Dover sole and lobster with morels or the lamb *en croute*. Delicate sauces, good presentation and efficient service are the order of the day. Menus go for €30 (weekday lunchtimes) and €45 (evenings and lunchtimes), or around €55 à la carte. *Free*

house apéritif offered to our readers on presentation of this guide.

Saint-Gély-du-Fesc

34980 (6km NW)

⊚ |●| Le Clos de l'Olivier

53 rue de l'Aven.
☎04.67.84.36.36
Closed *Sun evening; Mon evening.* **Disabled access.**

Only ten minutes away from Montpellier, you will be surprised to find a quiet terrace here where you will enjoy imaginative and well-prepared dishes in the company of local businesspeople; weekday lunchtime menu at €17.90, others at €25 and €35. In the evening, as the guests are generally a bit younger, the atmosphere is generally more lively. The cuisine is also more adventurous, with local aromas mixing with more exotic flavours. Service is very friendly.

Narbonne

11100

⊚ 🏠 🎄 Will's Hôtel**

23 av. Pierre-Sémard; it's in the avenue opposite the station.
☎04.68.90.44.50 📠04.68.32.26.28
TV. Pay car park.

There's something solidly reassuring about the beautiful façade of this bourgeois house, an impression reinforced by the owner's friendly reception. The rooms are clean and they've been decorated in pastel shades. Doubles at reasonable prices: €33–43 with shower/wc or bath. *10% discount on the room rate (except for July and Aug) offered to our readers on presentation of this guide.*

⊚ 🎄 🏠 |●| Le Grand Hôtel du Languedoc

22 bd. Gambetta, halfway between the train station and the city-centre.
☎04.68.65.14.74 📠04.68.65.81.48
🖥www.hoteldulanguedoc.com
Restaurant closed *Sun; Mon.* **TV. High chairs available. Pay car park.**

A turn-of-the-century mansion with a certain something. It's extremely well maintained, though the corridors are a little dark and gloomy (they are due to be redecorated soon). The rooms, meanwhile, have recently been refurbished and are bright, with excellent beds and double glazing; some have a view of the cathedral. Doubles with shower/wc or bath go for €49–66.50. In the restaurant, they specialize in seafood; there's a weekday lunch menu at €14, and another at €32. *Free fruit juice or soda offered to our readers on presentation of this guide.*

◎ ⅔ |◉| L'Estagnol

5 bis cours Mirabeau.
℡04.68.65.09.27 ✉lestagnol@net-up.com
Closed *Sun; Mon evening; 15–31 Jan.*
Disabled access. High chairs available.

A friendly brasserie with a Parisian atmosphere but local cuisine. Prices are reasonable: weekday set lunch €9.50, and menus €16 and €20; children's menu at €6.50. Good choices include grilled cod or *fricassée* of prawns with oyster mushrooms. The terrace – open to the sunshine in summer, closed and heated in winter – overlooks the cathedral and the canal. It's a place to eat quickly and simply, and is popular as an after-show hang-out for actors and performers. In addition to the brasserie, the owners have just opened a restaurant (specializing in simple, home cooking) across the way, on the quay. *Free coffee offered to our readers on presentation of this guide.*

◎ |◉| Le Petit Comptoir

4 bd. du Maréchal-Joffre.
℡04.68.42.30.35.
Closed *Sun; Mon.*

It's best to book as this little bar-restaurant has become very popular thanks to its pleasant location and its cheerful owner who's well-known for choosing the best produce available. Try the scallop casserole, lobster coulis, duckling with foie gras and Banyuls sauce and soufflé lemon pancake. The menus change often according to the whims of the chef and what's available at the market; lunchtime menu €15, others €23 and €29; à la carte around €35. It's a good little place to go.

◎ |◉| La Table Saint-Crescent

Av. du Général-Leclerc; it's on the Perpignan road.
℡04.68.41.37.37
Closed *Sat lunchtime; 1–15 Sept; 1–15 March.*

The Palais du Vin was set up to help market local wines and is ideally located

just off the motorway. But it also serves a second purpose as the site for this gourmet restaurant. The décor is extraordinary – a mixture of ancient, rough-hewn stone and modern metal sheeting – and the dining room is in an ancient chapel, adding to the feeling of displacement as it is situated in an industrial area. The chef, Claude Giraud, brings you back to this world with his thoughtful cuisine. The lunchtime menu (€17) includes savouries, dish of the day, cheese, dessert, a glass of wine and coffee; other menus at €30 and €48. The quality of the produce is shown to best advantage in all his dishes, and the astonishing menu "saveurs et terroirs" always changes according to the season and to what's available at the market, although the emphasis is usually on Mediterranean cuisine.

Nasbinals
48260

◎ 🏠 |◉| ⅔ Hôtel-restaurant La Route d'Argent**

Route d'Argent; it's the big building beside the church and the village car park.
℡04.66.32.50.03 ℡04.66.32.56.77
🌐www.nasbinals.com
Disabled access. TV.

Pierre Bastide's place is something of an institution – everybody in Nasbinals drops in. Guests always get a warm and friendly welcome in the restaurant, and the chef's portions are some of the most generous you'll see. He does cep omelette, duck *confit*, stuffed cabbage, *truffade* and, of course, *aligot* made to Bastide's special recipe. Set menus are €11 (except Sunday) and €13–22. Doubles with shower/wc go for €41 and breakfast is served at the lively bar. The family has also opened two other hotels: *Le Bastide,* a three-star just outside the town, and *La Randonnée,* a two-star. *Free house apéritif offered to our readers on presentation of this guide.*

Nîmes
30000

See map on pp.474–475

◎ 🏠 |◉| Auberge de jeunesse***

257 chemin de l'Auberge-de-Jeunesse (off map A2-1); 2km from the city-centre.

Signposted from the Jardin de la Fontaine.
Bus 2 towards Alès from the train station.
Minibus available from the station after 8pm.
☎04.66.68.03.20 ⓕ04.66.31.37.00
ⓦwww.fuaj.org/aj/nimes
Disabled access. Games available. Car park.

In the heart of a wooded park, this well-maintained youth hostel has recently been entirely refurbished. The dormitories, in the main building or in the small units scattered around the park, sleep two, four, six or eight people. It is equipped with a kitchen, launderette, bike park, mountain bikes (for rent), Internet and a *pétanque* area. One night costs around €9.70. The reception is open to newcomers from 7.30am to 11pm. Be sure to book in advance in summer.

ⓒ ♠ Cat Hôtel**

22 bd. Amiral-Courbet. **Map D2-3**
☎04.66.67.22.85 ⓕ04.66.21.57.51
ⓔcat.hotel@free.fr
TV. Pay car park.

The owners arrived from the cold, wet north determined to open a hotel in warmer climes, and they've made quite a success of it: the *Cat* is both pleasant and cheap. They've done everything up, installing double glazing, good ventilation and satellite TV. Everything is just right. Double rooms with shower/wc or bath go for €34 and 37; with shower/wc on the landing, €27. Breakfast is €4.

ⓒ ♠ Hôtel de l'Amphithéatre**

4 rue des Arènes; 30m from the arenas. **Map C3-7**
☎04.66.67.28.51 ⓕ04.66.67.07.79
ⓦwww.perso.wanadoo.fr/hotel.amphitheatre
Closed *Jan.* **TV. High chairs available.**

This is a quiet hotel in a generously proportioned eighteenth-century house. The décor has been spruced up, the place is clean and the beds are comfortable; doubles with shower/wc or bath are €43–65. There's a good breakfast buffet.

ⓒ ♠ Hôtel Kyriad-Plazza**

10 rue Roussy; on boulevard A.-Courbet, before the pharmacy, 2 min from the museums and historic centre. **Map D3-5**
☎04.66.76.16.20 ⓕ04.66.67.65.99
ⓦwww.hotel-kyriad-nimes.com
TV. Pay car park.

This place is part of a hotel chain, but you wouldn't think so from its appear-ance – it's charming old Nîmes house in a quiet street. Its air-conditioned rooms have shower or bath and telephone and cost €59–66. Each floor has a different colour scheme and the corridors are decorated with posters advertising bullfights and opera performances. Rooms on the fourth floor have very attractive little terraces and a view of the old tiled rooftops – they cost €75. *10% discount on the room rate (except during Easter, Whitsun and public holidays) offered to our readers on presentation of this guide.*

ⓒ ♣ ♠ |○| Hôtel Royal***

3 bd. Alphonse-Daudet. **Map B2-4**
☎04.66.67.28.36 ⓕ04.66.58.28.28
Restaurant closed *Sun; Mon.* **TV.**

Most rooms look towards the fountain on the quiet pedestrian place d'Assas. The hotel is popular with actors and artists passing through, and the welcome is hospitable. The rooms are individually decorated and are attractive and charming; they don't all have the same facilities but prices are fair for this town: doubles €60 with shower or €70–85 with bath. *La Bodeguita*, the restaurant, serves tapas and Mediterranean specialities (dish of the day €12); the terrace is lively in summer (some rooms overlook the terrace and can be a bit noisy when the weather's warm). Concerts are organized twice a month. *Free house apéritif offered to our readers on presentation of this guide.*

ⓒ ♠ |○| ♣ L'Orangerie***

755 Tour l'Évêque. **Off map A4-9.** From the city centre, take the A9 towards the airport, then turn left at the Kurokawa roundabout on to the N86; it's 10 min from the centre on foot.
☎04.66.84.50.57 ⓕ04.66.29.44.55
ⓦwww.orangerie.fr
Closed *23–28 Dec.* **Disabled access. TV. High chairs and games available. Swimming pool. Car park.**

An unusually attractive modern hotel in a big garden with a swimming pool – though the surrounds of the commercial district and the noise from the traffic don't immediately draw you to the area. Professional staff at reception and reasonably priced, well-maintained rooms at €66–115 for a double with shower/wc or bath; the nicest have access to a terrace or garden. The restaurant has already established a decent reputation, with a nice

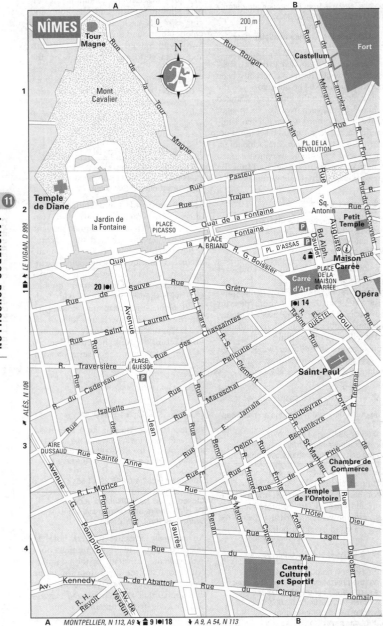

NÎMES

0   200 m

N

Tour
Magne

Mont
Cavalier

Fort

Castellum

PL. DE LA
RÉVOLUTION

Temple
de Diane

Jardin de
la Fontaine

PLACE
PICASSO

Rue Pasteur

Rue Trajan

Quai de la Fontaine

Sq.
Antonin

Petit
Temple

PLACE
A. BRIAND

Fontaine

PL. D'ASSAS

R. G. Boissier

Bd Alph. Daudet

4

Maison
Carrée

PLACE
DE LA
MAISON
CARRÉE

Carré
d'Art

Opéra

20

Quai de la

Rue de Sauve

Rue

Grétry

14

PL.
QUESTEL

Avenue Saint Laurent

Rue des Chassaintes

R. B. Lazare

Racine

Boul.

Rue Traversière

Rue du Cadereau

PLACE
J. GUESDE

Rue

R.-S. Clement

Pelloutier

F.

Mareschal

E. Jamais

Soubeyran

Bécdelièvre

St-Mathieu

Saint-Paul

Porte

R. Tédenat

AIRE
DUSSAUD

Rue Sainte Anne

Isabelle

des

Jean

Rue

Rue

Benoit

Delon

Rue

Rue

Émile

de la Pitié

R.

Chambre de
Commerce

Avenue G. Pompidou

R. L. Morice

Florian

Tilleuls

Rue de Mahon

Hugues

Rue

Émile

Zola

Temple
de l'Oratoire

l'Hôtel

Dieu

Rue

Jaurès

Benan

Rue Caper

Louis

Laget

Dagobert

Av. Kennedy

R. H. Revoit

Av. de Verdun

R. de l'Abattoir

Rue du

Mail

Cirque

Centre
Culturel
et Sportif

Romain

A   MONTPELLIER, N 113, A9   9   18   A 9, A 54, N 113   B

LE VIGAN, D 999   ALÈS, N 106

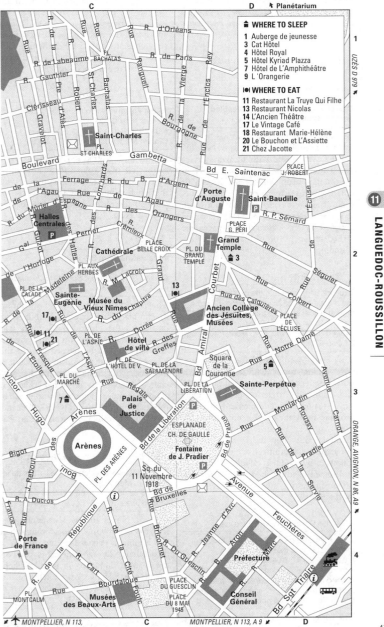

C   D   ⇖ Planétarium

🛏 WHERE TO SLEEP

1 Auberge de jeunesse
3 Cat Hôtel
4 Hôtel Royal
5 Hôtel Kyriad Plazza
7 Hôtel de L'Amphithéâtre
9 L 'Orangerie

🍽 WHERE TO EAT

11 Restaurant La Truye Qui Filhe
13 Restaurant Nicolas
14 L'Ancien Théâtre
17 Le Vintage Café
18 Restaurant Marie-Hélène
20 Le Bouchon Et L'Assiette
21 Chez Jacotte

🔟 LANGUEDOC-ROUSSILLON

R. d'Orléans
R. de Labeaume
PL. BACHALAS
Rue de Paris
R. de Paris
Rangueil
Gauthier
St-Charles
R. de la Vierge
Enclos Rey
R. de Bourgogne

Pre des Arts
Clérisseau
Robert
Gravelot

Saint-Charles
PL. ST CHARLES

Boulevard   Gambetta

Bd E. Saintenac
PLACE J. ROBERT

Ferrage
R. du B.
d'Argent
Porte
d'Auguste
Saint-Baudille

de la
l'Agau
Rue
de
l'Agau
R. des
Orangers

R. du Mûrier d'Espagne
Perrier
R. Crémieux
Halles
Centrales

PLACE G. PÉRI
R. P. Sémard

Gal Guizot
des Halles
PLACE BELLE CROIX
PL. DU GRAND TEMPLE
Grand
Temple
🛏 3

de l'Horloge
Cathédrale
Courbet
Rue
Séguier

PL. DE LA CALADE
Sainte-
Eugénie
PL. AUX HERBES
R. M. Lacroix
Rue des Calquières
Colbert

Madeleine
R. du Chapître
Grand
13
🍽

R. de
Musée du
Vieux Nîmes
Dorée
Ancien Collège
des Jésuites,
Musées
PLACE DE L'ÉCLUSE

17 🍽 11
🍽 21
PL. DE L'ASPIC
Hôtel
de ville
R. des
Greffes
Amira
Rue
Notre Dame

de l'Étoile
Square
de la
Couronne
5 🛏

Victor
PL. DE L'HÔTEL DE V.
PL. DE LA SALAMANDRE

PL. DU MARCHÉ
Rue
Régale
PL. DE LA LIBÉRATION
Sainte-Perpétue
Montjardin
Roussy

7 🛏
Arènes
Palais
de
Justice
P
Bd de la Libération
Carnot

Hugo
des
ESPLANADE
CH. DE GAULLE
Rue
de
Pradier

Bigot
Arènes
Fontaine
de J. Pradier
P

R. A. Ducros
Boul
PL. DES ARÈNES
Sq. du
11 Novembre
1918
Bd de
Bruxelles
Avenue
Servie

France
Rue
de la
République
Bd de Praio

Porte
de France
R. Cart
R. Du Guesclin
Jeanne d'Arc
Feuchères

PL. MONTCALM
R.
Bourdatoue
Foulc
PLACE DU GUESCLIN
Préfecture
Marc

Musées
des Beaux-Arts
PLACE DU 8 MAI 1945
Conseil
Général
Bd Sgt Triaire

ℹ

🚌

↙ ⬆ MONTPELLIER, N 113,

C   MONTPELLIER, N 113, A 9 ↙   D

dining room and stylish food. There is a weekday lunchtime menu from €19, then others going up to €29. *One free breakfast per person offered to our readers on presentation of this guide.*

ⓒ |●| Restaurant La Truye Qui Filhe

9 rue Fresque. **Map C2-11**
℡04.66.21.76.33
Closed *evenings; Sun; Aug.* **Disabled access. High chairs available.**

The oldest restaurant in town has been an inn since the fourteenth century. Now it's a self-service place with pleasant service and a lovely patio. There's a set lunch at €7.90 (hot main course and dessert) or €8.70 (with starter as well). Local dishes such as *rouille du pêcheur* (fish soup with a spicy mayonnaise), *brandade* (creamed salt cod in flaky pastry) and paella are dished up on plastic plates in lovely surroundings.

ⓒ |●| Le Vintage Café

7 rue de Bernis; right in the centre, between the arenas and the Maison Carrée; near the market place, in the historic city. **Map C2-17**
℡04.66.21.04.45
Closed *Sat lunchtime; Sun; Mon; 15–31 Aug; 24 Dec–2 Jan.*

Tiny place based around a vintage bistro-style dining room with a fountain. It hosts frequent exhibitions of photographs and paintings. Attractive cooking, delicately seasoned to complement the fresh produce from the market; lunchtime set menu at €12.35, or a more extensive menu at €25. The dishes change daily, but expect something like Serrano ham, followed by sautéed ravioli with pesto and mixed salad, washed down with one of the interesting southern wines served by the glass.

ⓒ 🍴 |●| Restaurant Nicolas

1 rue Poise. **Map C2-13.** In old Nîmes, near the archeological museum.
℡04.66.67.50.47 ℗04.66.76.06.33
✉martin-pascal@wanadoo.fr
Closed *Sat lunchtime; Sun evening; Mon except public holidays; 1st fortnight in July; end of Dec.* **Disabled access.**

The large stone-walled dining room here has been tastefully decorated; inside it you'll be served uncomplicated and reliable home cooking. The menus rarely change because that's how the regulars like it: *anchoïade provençale*, monkfish *bourride* (a fish stew with saffron and garlic), creamed salt cod, beef *gardiane*, and house desserts such as *clafoutis*. Three set menus at €13–25; all of them include a dish of the day. *Free coffee offered to our readers on presentation of this guide.*

ⓒ |●| Chez Jacotte

15 rue Fresque; 2 min from the foot of the arenas. **Map C3-21**
℡04.66.21.64.59
Closed *Sun;15–22 Aug.*

Inventive, well-prepared Nîmeois specialities, full of flavour and totally satisfying. Good wines and attentive service; the lunch menu costs €15, or reckon on €25–30 à la carte. There are three or four tables outside.

ⓒ |●| L'Ancien Théâtre

4 rue Racine. **Map B2-14**
℡04.66.21.30.75
Closed *Sat lunchtime; Sun; 1–15 Jan; last week July; 1–15 Aug.*

They say that there used to be a theatre on the place du Carré nearby, but it was burned to the ground by a singer who went crazy when her son wasn't engaged as a singer. You'll be pleased to hear that you won't find that kind of behaviour in this place: the hospitality and the well-crafted Mediterranean dishes create an altogether more tranquil atmosphere. The reasonably priced menus (€15–20) change every two months; reckon on around €26 à la carte.

ⓒ |●| Le Bouchon et L'Assiette

5 rue de Sauve; it's close to the jardins de la Fontaine. **Map A2-20**
℡04.66.62.02.93 ℗04.66.62.03.57
Closed *Tues; Wed; 2–17 Jan; 1–22 Aug.*

One of Nîmes' nicest restaurants, in a red and blue house. The cooking here has as much personality and finesse as that offered by far fancier places, and the beamed dining room is full of light. Menus cost €15 (weekday lunchtime) and €20–41. *Free coffee offered to our readers on presentation of this guide.*

ⓒ |●| 🍴 Restaurant Marie-Hélène

733 av. Maréchal-Juin; it's next to the Chambre de Métiers, on the Montpellier road.

Off map A4-18
☎04.66.84.13.02
Closed *Sat lunchtime; Sun; evenings Mon–Wed; 3 weeks in Aug.* **Disabled access.**

This little restaurant is a real Provençal treasure through and through, from its warm and lively colours, its flower displays and table arrangements to the cuisine itself with its grilled meats cooked on open fires in front of you. There's a choice of menus at €15.50–26.50. *Free house apéritif, fruit juice or coffee offered to our readers on presentation of this guide.*

Saint-Gilles
30800 (19km SE)

◎ 🎋 🏠 |●| **Le Cours****

10 av. François-Griffeuille; take the D42.
☎04.66.87.31.93 ☎04.66.87.31.83
🌐www.hotel-le-cours.com
Closed *10 Dec–10 March.* **Disabled access. TV. High chairs available. Car park.**

This white house, shaded by an avenue of tall plane trees, has 33 rooms, most of them air-conditioned but all of them with restrained, contemporary décor. They cost €47–67 with shower/wc or bath. The restaurant offers good-value traditional cooking. The set menus from €11.50 (weekdays) to €29.50 list tempting dishes like scallop terrine and warm seafood salad. Logis de France. *5% discount on the half board rate (except long weekends and 14 July–15 Aug) offered to our readers on presentation of this guide.*

◎ 🎋 🏠 **Hôtel Héraclée*****

Quai du Canal; take the D42.
☎04.66.87.44.10 ☎04.66.87.13.65
🌐www.hotel-heraclee.com
Closed *first fortnight in Jan.* **Disabled access. TV.**

This Greek name graces a friendly, pretty hotel housed in a bright building. It looks onto the canal so you can watch the launches, the horse-drawn barges and the houseboats gliding by – though the view is somewhat marred by a metal monstrosity on the other bank. There are 21 tastefully decorated rooms; some have a terrace, and all of them are nice and quiet. At €50–60, they're worth it. *10% discount on the room rate (except in July–Aug and during ferias) offered to our readers on presentation of this guide.*

Olonzac
34210

◎ |●| **Restaurant du Minervois "Bel"**

Avenue d'Homps.
☎04.64.91.20.73
Closed *Sat and Sun evening (except July–Aug); evenings mid-Oct to mid-April.*

The first set menu at €11 (weekday lunchtimes) is quite delicious with its house terrine and a perfect omelette aux fines herbes. Other menus cost €20–50, the last of which is spectacular. Specialities include duck foie gras with Muscat and crêpes with vanilla ice. The wine list has a particularly rich choice of regional vintages at good prices. A consistently good restaurant that deserves its popularity, perfect to get some strength back before tackling the climb towards Minerve and the Hauts Cantons, or the walk back towards the Canal du Midi.

Siran
34210 (10km NW)

◎ 🎋 🏠 |●| **La Villa d'Éléis*****

Avenue du Château; take the D52 in the direction of Pépieux, then turn right on to the D56; in the village, follow the signs to "château de Siran".
☎04.68.91.55.98 ☎04.68.91.48.34
🌐www.villadeleis.com
Closed *Tues and Wed (Oct–April); Feb.* **Disabled access. TV. High chairs available. Car park.**

An old country house which has been carefully restored. The twelve stylish rooms are quiet and spacious; doubles are €66–160 with shower/wc or bath. Marie-Hélène will greet you warmly and the cooking is full of southern sunshine. Bernard Lafuente is a talented young chef who has won critical acclaim. The set menus range from €22.50 (weekday lunchtimes) to €69.50 (a series of samples, with wine included). The owners organize musical evenings in summer, including piano and flute recitals, and lead walks to help you learn about the wildlife and history of the area. *10% discount on the price of a room (1 Oct–31 March) offered to our readers on presentation of this guide.*

11

LANGUEDOC-ROUSSILLON

Palavas-les-Flots
34250

ⓒ 🏖 🛏 |●| Hôtel du Midi**

191 av. Saint-Maurice; it's on the left bank.
ⓣ04.67.68.00.53 ⓕ04.67.68.53.97
ⓦwww.hotel-palavas.com
Closed 15 Nov–31 March. **Disabled access.
TV. High chairs available. Car park.**

Not the height of luxury, but the rooms
are clean, comfortable and they've just
been refurbished. And with a bit of luck
you might get a room with a sea view or
overlooking the lagoon. Doubles go for
€41–77; half board, compulsory in August,
costs €47–66 per person. The restaurant is
a pleasant surprise, with inventive, clean
cuisine that's very affordable; menus €12
and €18. Credit cards not accepted. *10%
discount on the price of a room (out of season) or
free Kir before a meal in the restaurant offered to
our readers on presentation of this guide.*

ⓒ 🛏 Les Alizés

6 bd. Joffre; on the left bank.
ⓣ04.67.68.01.80 ⓕ04.67.50.36.19
TV.

A charming and entirely refurbished hotel
with a seaside décor right in the middle
of town. The rooms are light, air-conditioned, soundproofed and comfortable.
The bathrooms are nicely equipped and
decorated. The double rooms overlooking
the lighthouse or the sea cost €85–100;
the smaller ones without a view of the sea
cost €65–80, breakfast €5.

ⓒ |●| Le Petit Lézard

63 av. de l'Etang-du-Grec; very close to the
embankments.
ⓣ04.67.50.55.55
Closed Mon and Tues (lunchtime only in the
summer).

This restaurant has recently been completely refurbished, adding to its already
substantial attractions. This is an ideal
place for those who like grilled fish *a la
plancha*, even though it also has a pizzeria.
Lots of different dishes on the menu; the
fish of the day is always very fresh and the
vegetables cooked in olive oil just delicious. There are two weekday lunchtime
menus at €10 and €12, then another at
€17. As for deciding between the dining
room, the conservatory or the terrace, it's
down to you and the time of day. *Free
coffee offered to our readers on presentation of
this guide.*

ⓒ |●| Au 10, place du Marché

Rue Saint-Roch.
ⓣ04.67.68.57.41
Closed Mon and Tues out of season; 15
Oct–15 Jan.

Real mussels and chips with a Belgian
proprietor (hence the convincing beer
list), who fell in love with the accent and
vintages of the Hérault, hence a list of
regional wines that is not at all bad, with
humorous notes. Menus range from €11
to €23. It's a place with a warm atmosphere, to sit out on the terrace under the
plane tree. On Wednesday morning, the
market still takes place in the street, lend-
ing it even greater charm.

ⓒ 🏖 |●| La Rotisserie Palavasienne

Rue de l'Église.
ⓣ04.67.68.52.12
Closed lunchtimes; Sun; Mon out of season;
Jan.

A place that made its reputation by word
of mouth; the restaurant was the brainchild
of a local man who wanted to provide cuisine that was typical of his area. The dishes
are different each day because he uses only
fresh produce; the fish cooked in salt water
is particularly good. The menu goes for
€19, or expect to pay around €23 à la
carte. *Free house apéritif offered to our readers
on presentation of this guide.*

Perpignan
66000

ⓒ 🛏 Auberge de jeunesse**

Allée Marc-Pierre parc de la Pépinière; halfway beween the train station and the coach
station, behind the police station.
ⓣ04.68.34.63.32 ⓕ04.68.51.16.02
ⓦwww.fuaj.org
Closed 20 Dec–20 Jan. **Reception open**
7.30–11am and 5–11pm.

Set in a big traditional house swathed
with a luxurious bougainvillea on its
front, it is one of the oldest youth hostels
in France. A night in the dormitories
with four to eight bunk beds costs
€12.40 (breakfast included); youth hostel
card compulsory. The downside is that
there are only 49 places available, but

it's very clean and there's a kitchen and linen available. A shame the *voie rapide* is at the back.

ⓔ 🏠 Avenir Hôtel*

11 rue de l'Avenir; near the train station.
ⓣ04.68.34.20.30 ⓕ04.68.34.15.63
ⓦ www.avenirhotel.com
Closed *Sun and public holidays, 11am–6pm.*
Pay car park.

A pleasing hotel in a quiet street not far from the station. The rooms are simple but well maintained and nicely decorated. Prices are reasonable: double rooms cost €17.65–33.60, according to the season and degree of comfort. A few very big rooms for families (for up to four people) are also available at €40, and no. 18 has a pretty terrace. Vacationing American students sometimes stay here, as do trainees on work placements. It has a homely atmosphere and there's a sunny terrace on the first floor where you eat breakfast. It's a place to enjoy the sun and the peace and quiet.

ⓔ 🏠 Hôtel Mondial

Near the coach station.
40 bd, Clemenceau.
ⓣ04.68.34.23.45 ⓕ04.68.34.55.07
ⓦ www.hotel-mondial-perpignan.com
TV.

The *Mondial* is a favourite with touring performers – apart from big stars, who go to the *Villa Duflot* – clearly delighted with the amazing rooms, done out by the owner, a keen interior decorator, in either Indonesian, jazzy, Egyptian or Chinese style. She still has about ten rooms to redecorate, which explains the differences in price: double rooms €35–46 with shower/wc, €46–72 with bath. A word of warning: the rooms do not have air-conditioning – and it is hot on the fifth floor in summer – and despite the double glazing, we would recommend the rooms looking out onto the back, where you can open the windows without being disturbed by noise. There is also a pleasant little terrace on the fifth floor, ideal for sunbathing. The service is excellent.

ⓔ 🏠 |●| Park Hôtel-restaurant Le Chapon Fin***

18 bd. Jean-Bourrat; it's 2 min from the tourist office and 5 min from the city centre,

opposite place Bir-Hakeim, on the large boulevard leading to the Canet-Plage road.
ⓣ04.68.35.14.14. ⓕ04.68.35.48.18
ⓦ www.parkhotel-fr.com
Restaurant closed *Sun; first fortnight in Jan; last fortnight in Aug.* **Disabled access. TV. Pay car park.**

The amazing luxury, impeccable service and reasonable prices on offer belie this hotel's dull modern frontage. The rooms are decorated in Spanish Renaissance style and have numerous mod cons, including air-conditioning and soundproofing. Double rooms cost €70 with shower and €80–100 with bath, according to the size. The restaurant is one of the best in town; weekday lunch menu €25, then others at €50 (including wine) to €100. À la carte, dishes are pricey but perfect. The chef, Pascal Bofrell, is one of the rising stars of French cuisine. The portions are truly huge (one may be enough for two people), and there's a good selection of wines and vintage liqueurs.

ⓒ 🏠 |●| Hôtel-restaurant Villa Duflot****

Rond-point Albert-Donnezan. It's two minutes from the Perpignan toll booth, going towards Argelès.
ⓣ04.68.56.67.67 ⓕ04.68.56.54.05
ⓦ www.villaduflot.com
Disabled access. TV. High chairs available. Swimming pool. Car park.

If you're planning to stay in Perpignan itself there are better options (the surroundings here aren't very attractive), but if all you want is a night of luxury on the way to Spain, it's well worth stopping, as this is the only four-star hotel in Perpignan. (It's barely signposted from the city centre, however.) The rooms (€120–160) have been furnished with enchanting taste – ask for one overlooking the swimming pool rather than the dreary shopping area. The restaurant tends towards modern cooking but also has traditional Catalan dishes, based on fresh seasonal produce; weekday business menu at €31 including wine, weekend gastronomic menu also at €31 including wine. À la carte you'll pay around €39. There's a nice selection of Roussillon wines.

ⓔ |●| 🍴 Casa Sansa

3 rue Fabrique-Couverte.
ⓣ04.68.34.21.84

@ www.casasansa.com

This local institution has been recently taken over by a young, energetic woman, who seems to have put it back in order after a period of decline. Students, travellers and intellectuals hang out here in the large dining room, decorated with bright paintings, old photos and posters of the corrida. The cooking is Catalan, generous and simple with a few original touches, and succeeds in packing the place at the weekend. Lunchtime menu is €9 and tapas menu €26. *Free house apéritif offered to our readers on presentation of this guide.*

@ 🎋 |◉| Al Très

3 rue de la Poissonnerie.
Ⓣand Ⓕ04.68.34.88.39
Closed *Sun; Mon (open Mon evening in summer); 1 to 2 weeks end of Feb; 1 week in Sept.*

The décor in the dining room has a fresh new look but there's still plenty of old Provence and Catalonia in the sun-drenched cuisine. Good value generally, with a €11 weekday lunch menu and another menu for €30; you'll pay around €32 à la carte. Good Catalan specialities and excellent desserts. The wine list features 150 wines from the region. There's a small terrace in the summer. This place is always buzzing with people. This is a safe bet in Perpignan, even though the prices have gone up steeply. *Free coffee offered to our readers on presentation of this guide.*

@ 🎋 |◉| Bistrot Le Saint-Jean

1 cité Bartissol.
Ⓣ04.68.51.22.25
Closed *Sun and Mon evening out of season; 20 Dec–17 Jan.*

The speciality here is substantial filled sandwiches on country bread. Plus good local cuisine at reasonable prices: *excalivades*, *esqueizada* of cod, broad beans in Catalan style and so on. Dish of the day costs €9, set lunch €12 and there's another menu for €19 in season, €17 out of season. The dishes are accompanied by glasses of delicious wine chosen by the boss – he's a bit of an expert. Out of season, they hold wine tasting evenings. In summer there's a superb terrace flanked by the cathedral and the church. *Free apéritif offered to our readers on presentation of this guide.*

@ |◉| L'Ail y Oli

Allée des Chênes; 5km west of the town centre by the N116 in the direction of Prades (turn left at the *Total* garage).
Ⓣ04.68.55.58.75
Closed *Sun and Mon, June–Sept.*

This typical Catalan inn boasts a fine rustic (and air-conditioned) dining room with exposed beams and a large fireplace complete with copper hood. The lunchtime menu costs €18.50; expect to pay €35 for the evening à la carte menu. It might seem a tourist trap, with its wrought-iron adornments and hams, loaves and strings of garlic hanging from the ceiling, but it is slightly off the beaten track, a little way from the town centre. The fact that many of the traders from the nearby Saint-Charles market (Perpignan's major wholesale market) meet up here for lunch vouches for its authenticity. The staff, dressed in Catalan costume, serve authentic regional cuisine, including grilled dishes prepared before your very eyes: *parillade* (grilled seafood served with a mixture of sauces) and *cargolade* (a dish of snails, lamb, local sausages and *boudin* all grilled over a fire of vine branches). All in all, it provides a striking setting for discovering genuine Catalan cooking.

@ |◉| 🎋 Le Sud

12 rue Louis-Bausil; take rue Élie-Delcros from the Palais des Congrès then turn left into the rue Rabelais. Rue Louis-Bausil is a continuation of that street.
Ⓣand Ⓕ04.68.34.55.71
Closed *lunchtime; Mon; Tues; Wed; Jan and Feb.* **Disabled access.**

This place, in Perpignan's Romany quarter, has a patio planted with scented bushes and jasmine flowers. The food is fragrant, too, with cumin, mint, coriander . . . and the delicacies on offer are a delight, combining the best from Provence, the Orient, Mexico, Greece and Catalonia. À la carte only – you'll pay around €30. Some evenings the local guitarists gather here to play flamenco music. *Free house apéritif offered to our readers on presentation of this guide.*

Canet-en-Roussillon
66140 (11km E)

@ |◉| La Vigatanne

2 rue des Remparts.

☎04.68.73.16.30
Closed *Mon in winter; lunchtime in season.*

An old farm building with thick stone walls and a large terrace, it's near the château and well away from the bucket-and-spade crowds. The décor is madly exuberant, with a miniature yellow train that chugs around the ceiling. The food is of high quality and astonishingly fresh – grills are prepared before your eyes on the open fire next to where the old-fashioned fresh loaves are piled up. Taken together these elements create something very special – a kind of gastronomic theatre. There is a set menu at €13, otherwise you should expect to spend around €30 on dinner à la carte. It's best to book, especially in winter. *Free house apéritif offered to our readers on presentation of this guide.*

Canet-Plage
66140 (12km E)

@ 🏠 |●| 🍴 **Le Clos des Pins – Le Bistro Fleuri*****

34 av. du Roussillon.
☎04.68.80.32.63 ☎04.68.80.49.19
🌐www.closdespins.com
Closed *Nov to mid-March.* **Restaurant closed** *lunchtime (except Sun).* **TV. Swimming pool. Car park.**

This is an old but attractive restaurant, slightly set back from the road, with a pretty garden that is ideal for eating in romantic surroundings. There's just one menu at €25; reckon on around €40 à la carte. There are also some appealing rooms priced at €110–140 with shower/wc or bath, some with their own terrace. *10% discount on the price of a room (April, May and Oct) or free house apéritif offered to our readers on presentation of this guide.*

@ |●| **La Rascasse**

38 bd. Tixador; it's parallel to the seafront.
☎04.68.80.20.79
Closed *Mon (April, June and Sept); lunchtime July–Aug (except Sun); 30 Sept–1 April.*

This is a very well-known fish restaurant as well as a wonderful and untouched example of Vieille France. All the fish, shellfish and seafood are gloriously fresh and the dishes are delicately prepared. Try the *crème catalane* for dessert. Reasonably priced menus are €20–31, and affordable wines. Service is friendly and efficient.

Banyuls-dels-Aspres
66300 (15km S)

@ |●| 🍴 **Domaine de Nidolières**

It's 4km before Le Boulou, on the N9; just after the intersection with the D40A, go in the direction of Banyuls-dels-Aspres, then take the side road on the left, before crossing the railway line; from there, it's 200m away.
☎04.68.83.04.23
Closed *Mon and Tues lunchtime (in season); Mon–Wed (out of season); 30 Sept–1 April.* **Disabled access.**

A lovely little inn among the vineyards, run by wine-makers. There is a wonderful large terrace endowed with cane chairs and a stunning view of the vineyards and the Albères massif. The cooking and the wine are equally superb; local speciality menu at €25 and a selection of samples at €40. Try, for example, the roast rabbit with their own red wine. And the helpings are huge. *Free house apéritif offered to our readers on presentation of this guide.*

Saint-Paul-de-Fenouillet
66220 (33km NW)

@ |●| **Relais des Corbières**

10 av. Jean Moulin. Take the D117.
☎04.68.89.23.89 ☎04.68.59.03.04
Closed *Sun evening and Mon, except July/ August.* **High chairs and games available.**

What a wonderful place – despite its location, right next to the road and the level crossing (there's only one train a day, however – at 8.30am). The rooms are big and well maintained; doubles go for €37–50 depending on facilities. The restaurant serves tasty regional dishes on menus €16–41, lovingly served in a traditional dining room or pretty covered terrace by the genuinely friendly owner. (And that in itself makes up for the location.) In the evening, indulge yourself with a glass of Maury on the terrace and enjoy the play of the fountains. Logis de France.

Pézenas
34120

@ |●| **La Pomme d'Amour**

2 bis rue Albert-Paul-Allies; it's near the tourist office.
☎04.67.98.08.40
Closed *Mon and Tues evening except in summer; Jan–Feb.*

This is a pleasant little restaurant in an old

stone building in the picturesque old part of town. Good, simple cooking and traditional local dishes. Weekday lunch menu at €8, and others at €15.50 and €21 list a few specialities such as mussels in garlic cream sauce and salmon with sorrel. You'll get a friendly welcome.

@ 🕏 |●| Les Marronniers

6 av. de Verdun; from Agde or Béziers, on the outskirts.
☎04.67.90.13.80
Closed Sun and Mon; Jan. **Disabled access. High chairs available.**

Popular restaurant with a pretty décor and a friendly service; the clientele is mostly local. The cooking is good and hearty: saucisson or more refined tapas (at night). Relaxed atmosphere in the dining room or on the terrace outside under the chestnut trees. It's generally good value; à la carte €20–22, and good local wines priced €12–30. *Free coffee offered to our readers on presentation of this guide.*

Pont-de-Montvert (Le)
48220

@ 🕏 🏠 |●| La Truite Enchantée

On the main road that goes through the village.
☎04.66.45.80.03
Closed 11 Nov–15 March (hotel); mid-Dec to mid-March (restaurant). **Car park.**

The hotel, run by Corinne and Edgard, has eight basic double rooms which are bright, clean and spacious – they cost €25 with shower (wc on the landing); half board €32.50 per person. Choose those overlooking the River Tarn or the garden. Good, hearty, regional cooking is served in the dining room next to the kitchen. Set menus €14–24: typical dishes include salmon with sorrel or rabbit *à la royale.* Booking is advised for both hotel and restaurant. *Free liqueur offered to our readers on presentation of this guide.*

Masméjean
48220 (7km E)

@ 🕏 |●| Chez Dedet

Take the D998 Pont de Montvert–Saint-Maurice-de-Ventalon road, then turn left after 5km, just before the bridge, then follow directions to Masméjean.

☎04.66.45.81.51 ☎04.66.45.80.91
Closed Wed and evenings out of season; last 10 days June; last 10 days in Nov.

The food here is out of this world. It's a real country restaurant in an old farm building with enormous beams, walls made out of great slabs of stone and a hearth you could roast an ox in. They use pigs, sheep and poultry from the family farm and get their snails, trout and mushrooms from local suppliers; in season, the wild boar and hares are also sourced from the area. Set menus are €12 (weekday lunchtimes only) and up to €45. The service is perfect. Credit cards aren't accepted and booking is advisable, especially on Sunday and in winter. *Free coffee offered to our readers on presentation of this guide.*

Vialas
48220 (18km E)

@ 🏠 |●| 🕏 Hostellerie Chantoiseau★★★

Take the D998.
☎04.66.41.00.02 ☎04.66.41.04.34
@patrick.pages48@wanadoo.fr
Closed Tues evening; Wed; Oct–30 April. **TV. Swimming pool.**

A pleasant combination of smart and rustic décor in this former coaching inn which offers authentic local cuisine of high quality. Patrick Pagès knows and loves this part of the world, its wild valleys, mushrooms, chestnut trees, its fish and its game. The gourmet restaurant is a must (menus €22–79), and it has one of the region's best wine cellars. Try the *moche* (pork sausage with cabbage, potatoes and prunes), the saucisse d'herbes, the *pompétou* of trout or the *coupétade.* Double rooms with shower/wc are €46, or €89 with bath; you'll feel almost as if you are staying in someone's home. Credit cards not accepted. *10% discount on the price of a room (out of season) or free house apéritif offered to our readers on presentation of this guide.*

St-Étienne-du-Valdonnez
48000 (27km NW)

@ 🕏 🏠 |●| Auberge des Laubies

Take the N106; from the col du Montmirat, take the D35 for 9km in the direction of Pont-de-Montvert.
☎04.66.48.01.25

Hotel closed *Nov–May.* **Restaurant closed** *evenings Easter to 1 May and Nov to mid-Dec; mid-Dec to Easter.*

A lovely inn, run by a local family, located in an isolated hamlet on the plateau of Mont Lozère, which is magnificent and totally tree-less. Copious helpings of local dishes (eg, potatoes with bacon), that are cheap as anything; menus €13–19 (€21 on Sundays). Double rooms cost €26 with basin; half board is €29 per person. It's an amazing place to talk, meditate or just dream. You can also fish or go on walks. *Free house apéritif offered to our readers (hotel guests only) on presentation of this guide.*

Pont-Saint-Esprit

30130

◎ ☎ |◎| Auberge Provençale**

Take the N86 as you leave the village.
℡04.66.39.08.79 ℻04.66.39.14.28
Closed *Sun evening Oct–March; 24 Dec–1 Jan.* **Disabled access. High chairs available. Car park.**

This inn looks far better inside than out. The same family has run it for more than forty years, cheerfully welcoming travellers, long-distance lorry drivers, families and local worthies alike. They serve large portions of honest traditional food in the two large and air-conditioned dining rooms. The cheapest set menu (€9.50) sets the tone: charcuterie, *crudités*, a dish of the day, seasonal vegetables, cheese platter and fresh fruit or ice cream; other menus up to €19. Gigondas and Tavel are served by the glass and reasonably priced. Rooms with shower/wc or bath cost €29; the ones that overlook the courtyard are more peaceful. Logis de France.

◎ ⅔ |◎| Lou Récati

6 rue Jean-Jacques; in a side street perpendicular to the allées F.-Mistral (opposite the fontaine au Coq).
℡04.66.90.73.01
Closed *Mon; Tues.* **Disabled access.**

"Lou Récati" is a local term to describe those little mounds of furniture or clothing thrown together to save them from the floodwaters of the Rhône. It's a rather wonderful name for a restaurant run by a talented young chef who produces delicate, skilfully cooked dishes.

The prices are fair considering his professionalism: weekday lunch menu €12 and others at €21 and €31. They list such dishes as snail ravioli, duck with pan-fried artichokes and peas and, for dessert, an unrivalled *crème brûlée* scented with lavender. It's a real treat to dine here. *Free coffee offered to our readers on presentation of this guide.*

Aiguèze

30760 (10km NW)

◎ ☎ ⅔ Résidence Le Castelas**

From Pont-Saint-Esprit, take the N86 for Montélimar then turn left onto the D901, in the direction of Aigueze.
℡04.66.82.18.76 ℻04.66.82.14.98
ⓦwww.residencelecastelas.com
Closed *Jan–Feb.* **High chairs available. Swimming pool. Car park.**

Le Castelas enjoys a wonderful location in a hillside village overlooking the Ardèche. It also has some remarkable qualities of its own: the rooms are all within the ancient castle walls, and are charmingly decorated and fitted with small corner kitchens. You can stay in the main building near the first swimming pool where the rooms have terraces and views over the gorges of the Ardèche; the annexe, just two streets away, has another pool. The owner is polite and attentive. Double rooms with shower/wc or bath go for €63–80 depending on the season; studios and flats are available for rent. They serve a good, generous buffet breakfast. They'll lend you a bicycle and tell you where to go, or advise on hiring a canoe. *Free house apéritif offered to our readers on presentation of this guide.*

Bagnols-sur-Cèze

30200 (15km S)

◎ ☎ ⅔ Hôtel Bar des Sports**

3 pl. Jean-Jaurès; take the N86 from Pont-Saint-Esprit in the direction of Nîmes.
℡04.68.89.61.68 ℻04.66.89.92.97
TV. Pay car park.

This is a serious place which deserves its two stars: it offers delightful, clean, comfortable double rooms with shower/wc or bath and double glazing for €44. The owner is very kind, and it's quiet at night, even when the bar is open. *Free car park at the weekend (out of season)* offered to our readers on presentation of this guide.

Prades
66500

⑪

@ 🎋 |●| Le Jardin d'Aymeric

3 av. du Général-de-Gaulle; it's opposite the coach station, set slightly apart from the town centre.
☎04.68.96.53.38 ℗04.68.96.08.72
Closed *Sun evening; Mon; Wed (in winter); Feb school holiday; last week in June; first week in July.* **Disabled access.**

A small restaurant with a warm dining room where excellent cuisine is served speedily and with energy by smiling, chatty waiting staff. It's often full, so consider booking. The generously flavoured regional cooking uses fresh produce (saddle of lamb with thyme, Serdinya kid), and the menus change regularly. Dish of the day is €9.50 (weekday lunchtimes) and menus €17–29. They serve regional wines – and the house wine is as good as some on the wine list. For an apéritif, try a glass of Muscat-de-Rivesaltes – an exquisite rarity. *Free Kir offered to our readers on presentation of this guide.*

Prats-de-Mollo
66230

@ 🎋 🏠 |●| Hôtel des Touristes**

Avenue du Haut-Vallespir; it's on the right as you arrive in the village on the road from Arles-sur-Teche.
☎04.68.39.72.12 ℗04.68.39.79.22
ⓦwww.hotel.lestouristes.free.fr
Closed *31 Oct–1 April.* **Disabled access. TV. High chairs available. Car park.**

This solidly built stone hotel is an ideal spot from which to explore the wild, mountainous Vallespir region. The rooms are well maintained; doubles cost €25–33 with basin/wc or €45–48.50 with shower/wc or bath. Some have balconies, others little terraces, and the ones at the back have a view of the river. In the huge dining room they serve traditional family-style dishes (pig's foot with snails, gournard casserole with potato ragout) on menus €16–32; à la carte is also available and breakfast costs €9–12. Logis de France. *One free breakfast per room or free house apéritif offered to our readers on presentation of this guide.*

Quillan
11500

@ 🏠 |●| Hôtel-restaurant Cartier

31 bd. Charles-de-Gaulle (Centre).
☎04.68.20.05.14 ℗04.68.20.22.57
ⓦwww.hotelcartier.com
Closed *Sat lunch (April–June and Oct–Dec); 15 Dec–25 March (restaurant).* **TV. High chairs available. Pay car park.**

Comfortable rooms €32–56, depending on the degree of comfort; those overlooking the street are soundproofed. Very good local cuisine right through from the starters to the desserts with menus €15–26; children's menu €8.50. Try especially the regional soup *à la rouzole*, made with vegetables, eggs and meatballs. Complete the meal with the mouth-watering chocolate and citrus fruit fudge cake. The service is friendly, too. Logis de France.

Gincla
11140 (27 km SE)

@ 🏠 |●| Hostellerie du Grand Duc

2 rue de Boucheville; 5km from the Puilaurens château; take the D117 towards Axat and Puilaurens; turn right onto the D22 towards Gincla.
☎04.68.20.55.02 ℗04.68.20.61.22
ⓦwww.host.du.grandduc.com
Closed *Wed lunchtime (except July–Aug); 3 Nov–1 April.* **High chairs available.**

Beautiful mansion set in a lovely garden with a pond. The rooms (€60–67) are decorated in a country style with a comfortable, bourgeois feel. Good traditional cuisine: duck, pears with cinnamon and good local wines too. Menus are €28–58, à la carte around €38. Logis de France.

Rivesaltes
66600

@ 🏠 |●| Hôtel-restaurant La Tour de l'Horloge

11 rue Armand-Barbès.
☎04.68.64.05.88 ℗04.68.64.66.67
ⓦwww.hotel-la-tour-horloge.com
TV. Pay car park.

This historic hotel was recently taken over by an enterprising and very charming couple. Its small, quiet rooms are extremely well kept and most have been attractively refurbished (some have air-conditioning).

Double rooms with shower cost €40–45, those with bath €45–50, depending on the season. The new owners have managed to persuade the town hall not to ring the bells at night for the comfort of their guests (much to the displeasure of some of the older locals). The restaurant, with its two facing rows of tables, is also appealing; it is distinguished by generous portions, attentive service and a delightfully provincial atmosphere. The weekday menu costs €13, with others at €18, €26 and €49. Logis de France. *Free glass of Muscat-de-Rivesaltes offered to our readers on presentation of this guide.*

Roquefort-des-Corbières
11540

@ 𝒴 |●| Le Lézard Bleu

Rue de l'Église; near the town centre.
☎04.68.48.51.11
Closed *1 Oct–30 June.* **Disabled access.**

The lizard signs outside direct you to this restaurant with the blue door. Inside, the walls are white and hung with modern paintings. The food is lovingly prepared by the owner, a friendly woman who's full of life; menus from €17.50 to €40. It's best to book. *Free coffee offered to our readers on presentation of this guide.*

Saint-André-de-Valborgne
30940

@ 𝒴 🏠 |●| Hôtel-restaurant Bourgade**

Place de l'Église.
☎04.66.60.30.72 ☎04.66.60.31.25
@henribourgade@aol.com
Closed *Mon–Thurs (Sept–June); Jan–Feb.* **TV.**

This place started as a posthouse in the seventeenth century and has been in the family for generations. The latest lot have shaken out all the cobwebs and offer an enthusiastic welcome. Simple, charming rooms overlook the church square or the stream; doubles with shower/wc or bath €40–50. Flavourful and inspirational cuisine is prepared by a chef who did part of his apprenticeship with the great chef Alain Ducasse. He makes lots of regional dishes using fresh produce, and

has kept his grandmother's famous crayfish dish on the menu; weekday lunchtime menu €22. *Free liqueur offered to our readers on presentation of this guide.*

Saint-Chély-du-Tarn
48210

@ 🏠 |●| L'Auberge de la Cascade*

In the gorges of the Tarn, in the direction of Millau; is the restaurant, separate from the inn, just on the left as you come into the village.
☎04.66.48.52.82 ☎04.66.48.52.45
@www.aubergecascade.com
Closed *end-Oct to end-March.* **Disabled access. TV. Swimming pool.**

This inn provides good value for money, with comfortable, brand-new rooms in an annexe in the village and a swimming pool on the terrace alongside the River Tarn. Double rooms with shower/wc cost €41, those with bath €54; half board is compulsory in July and Aug (€39–46 per person). It is advisable to book in advance: even though the service is a little rushed and the food is of no special interest, the stunning scenery constitutes a great attraction in itself. The cheapest menu costs €14.50 (weekdays). Credit cards not accepted. Logis de France.

Saint-Guilhem-le-Désert
34150

@|●| L'Auberge sur Le Chemin

38 rue Font-du-Portal, in the heart of the village.
☎04.67.57.75.05
Closed *Wed out of season.* **High chairs available.**

Olivier Crossay has come a long way before opening this village restaurant and he has created a real surprise. The décor of the dining room is imposing, with its eleventh and twelfth century vaults. A few touches of colour and a few modern paintings here and there bring it into the twenty-first century. Formerly trained with Bocuse, Olivier now works almost on his own in the kitchens, but the results are very impressive. Menus €23–70; try the truffle soup and the cockerel in a puff pastry crust. Good choice of coffees too. This restaurant only opens for advance bookings.

Saint-Pierre-des-Champs

11220

🅰 ☖ |○| Hôtel-restaurant La Fargo

☏04.68.43.12.78 ℗04.68.43.29.20
🖰www.chez.com/lafargo
Closed *Mon-Thurs out of season.* **Disabled access. Car park.**

This former Catalan forge, entirely reno-vated, enjoys delightful views over moun-tains, orchards and lavender bushes. Only six rooms at €59–72; they are elegantly decorated and furnished with a mixture of Indonesian and family pieces, and on the beds are displayed beautiful batiks from the Asian island of Sonde. Each room is named after a tree in honour of Mother Nature. The cooking has subtle Mediterranean flavours and changes according to season; menus €20–27. No pets.

Saint-Saturnin-de-Lucian

34725

🅰 ☖ |○| Ostalaria Cardabela

10 pl. de la Fontaine; take the D130 and it's in the centre of the village.
☏04.67.88.62.62 ℗04.67.88.62.82
🖂ostalaria.cardabela@wanadoo.fr
Closed *Mon; lunchtimes (except Sun); Sun evening (except July–Aug); 1 Nov–10 March.* **TV.**

A lovely place if you like your creature comforts – enjoy the gorgeous, cosy rooms and big beds with Egyptian cotton sheets. Great care is taken over everything, starting with the welcome. Rooms go for €65–90; breakfast €9.50. The restaurant is called *Le Mimosa*, and it's to be found in Saint-Giraud 2km away. It's an equally stylish place in a charming old house; only one menu (with six courses) at €52, or at €78 with six dif-ferent glasses of wine. Reckon on €55–85 à la carte. The cuisine is flavoursome and full of creativity; there is also a wide range of wine on offer (from €6 a glass).

🅰 |○| 🍴 Le Pressoir de Saint-Saturnin

17 pl. de la Fontaine.
☏04.67.88.67.89
Closed *Mon evening; Tues evening; Wed evening; Sat lunchtime; 2 Jan–13 Feb.*

It would be easy to fall in love with this authentic Languedoc inn, which has a great atmosphere in the dining room and on the terrace. You'll find some dishes prepared to very old recipes like the *escoubille* stew simmered in local red wine. Make sure you try the melting cheese croquettes and the free-range lamb or beef grilled over the wood fire. Dish of the day costs €9; oth-erwise menus at €16.80–28.60. There's a good selection of regional wines. *Free house apéritif offered to our readers on presentation of this guide.*

Saint-Jean-de-la-Blaquière

34700 (7km E)

🅰 ☖ |○| Hôtel-restaurant Le Sanglier

Domaine de Cambourras.
☏04.67.44.70.51℗04.67.44.72.33.
🖰www.logassist.frsanglier
Closed *20 Oct–25 March.* **TV.**

Handsome hotel situated in the middle of the heathland. Ten quiet and comfortable rooms (€67–84, breakfast €8.80) on the first and top floors exude a warm, rustic charm. The dining room is a former sheep pen (quite common around here). Tasty dishes served in the garden or on the ter-race in the summer with a range of menus €18–38. Wild boar dishes are plentiful on the menu, but there are also several fish dishes on offer; also an impressive choice of wines. There are lots of walks to do in the area, starting with a walk along the red canyon right next to the hotel. Logis de France. *Free coffee offered to our readers on presentation of this guide.*

Salvetat-sur-Agout (La)

34330

🅰 ☖ |○| Hôtel-restaurant La Plage

Les Bouldouires; on the banks of Lac de la Raviège. Au bord du lac de la Raviège.
☏04.67.97.69.87 ℗04.67.97.51.98
Closed *Fri evening and Sun out of season.* **TV. High chairs available. Car park.**

A newcomer here in the *Hauts Cantons* region that already has an old, established feel, which is rather a good sign. Rooms (€40–45) are of no particular distinction other than a rather attractive view over the lake, and peaceful and quiet, especially out of season, of course. Everything runs smoothly at this inn, so people come from far and wide to savour the pork salad or the fried egg and bacon delicacies of the Salvetois region. There's a *menu du jour* for €11, except Sun, other menus €17–35, and good wines served by the glass. Jean-René Pons is of that tradition, as is the dining room. It's best to book to be sure of a place. Logis de France.

Sauve

30610

ⓒ 🍴 |●| Chez La Marthe

20 rue Mazan; it's near the town hall.
☎04.66.77.06.72
🌐www.vallee-vidourle.com/heberge/marthe-htm
Closed *Sun evening; Mon; first week in June; Nov.* **High chairs available.**

Marthe was a woman who ran the local grocery more than two decades ago and the restaurant named after her has been delightfully decorated in local style. Weekday lunch menu €12.50, with others at €20 and €25, lists dishes such as *pieds-paquets* (lamb tripe and trotters) and Cévenole salad. They have a habit of closing unexpectedly in winter, so check in advance. In summer you should call in order to guarantee a table. *Free coffee offered to our readers on presentation of this guide.*

Sète

34200

ⓒ 🏠 |●| Le P'tit Mousse*

Rue de Provence; it's in the Corniche area.
☎04.67.53.10.66
Closed *Oct–March.* **High chairs available.**

A bright ochre building in a quiet little street off the Corniche, very close to the sea. The rooms are clean and good value at €30–33.50 for a double with shower/wc; breakfast €4.70. Half board is compulsory in July and August, and costs around €30 per person per night. Simple cooking and homely atmosphere are on offer in the restaurant, with set menus at €13–22.

ⓒ 🏠 Hôtel Venezia

Les Jardins de la Mer, La Corniche; 50m from place Édouard-Herriot.
☎04.67.51.39.38 ⊕04.67.74.15.05

🌐www.hotel-sete.com
Closed *20 Nov–1 March.* **Disabled access. TV. Car park.**

A good family hotel with eighteen quiet and well-equipped rooms that have all been refurbished (all with terrace and television); doubles cost €40–52 depending on the season. Car park available for each room, which is quite unusual in the area. There's no restaurant, but you'll get a friendly welcome. And the beach is only 50m away.

ⓒ 🏠 Le Grand Hôtel***

17 quai de Lattre-de-Tassigny.
☎04.67.74.71.77
🌐www.hotel-sete.com
Closed *23 Dec–2 Jan.* **TV. Pay car park.**

This magnificent hotel was built in the 1880s, and it hasn't lost a trace of character. It's spacious and filled with period furniture, and there's a striking patio with a glass roof – a great place to eat breakfast. Rooms with shower/wc go for €65–130, or with bath €85–120. Service is faultless, as befits a grand hotel. Its restaurant, *La Rotonde*, is the finest in town and is just around the corner.

ⓒ 🍴 🏠 |●| Les Terrasses du Lido***

Rond-point de l'Europe-La Corniche; follow the signs to "La Corniche".
☎04.67.51.39.60 ⊕04.67.51.28.90
Closed *Sun evening and Mon out of season.* **Disabled access. TV. High chairs available. Swimming pool. Car park.**

Everything's just right in this hotel, from the décor of the rooms to the friendly welcome and the creative cooking. There are only nine rooms painted in a relaxing pale blue colour, so it's advisable to book well in advance; doubles with bath €68–125. Half board is compulsory in July and Aug at €73–80 per person. You will enjoy the terrace by the pool and the hotel is only 300m away from the beach. The gourmet cooking is original and includes local specialities as well as creations from the new chef Philippe Mouls, who only uses fresh seasonal ingredients, so the menus change often. Philippe is particularly renowned for his flavoursome and tasty fish and seafood dishes. Try the delicious lasagne of oysters with tomato and basil or the monkish fillets with squid served with a black ink parmesan risotto. Midweek lunchtime menu (July–Aug) goes for €16, then others at €28 and

€52. Service is faultless too and advance booking is advised. Logis de France. *10% discount on the price of a room (out of season) or free coffee offered to our readers on presentation of this guide.*

Ⓔ |●| L'Oranger

5 pl. de la Mairie.
☎04.67.51.96.12
Closed *Mon and Tues except public holidays; Jan.* **Disabled access. High chairs available.**

Near place du Pouffre in the centre, with a refined country décor, this restaurant is owned by a couple who know their trade well. While he serves in the dining room in a relaxed and competent manner, she prepares delicious and well-presented octopus bruschettas with aïoli, warm Camembert with pepper caramel and *bourride de baudrole.* Menus cost €14–26 and they offer a good selection of apéritifs and local wines. Advance booking is advised.

Ⓔ |●| Le Marie-Jean

26 quai Général Durand; it's near the canal.
☎04.67.46.02.01
Closed *Mon lunchtime; Mon out of season; Feb.*

A really good restaurant which suggests that this quayside, once the pride of the town, might have an interesting future – if only it were possible to get rid of the tourist traps lining the front. Gourmet specialities here on the weekday menu €17 and others €24–40: *bouillabaisse,* tuna *carpaccio,* sardine tartare, stuffed squid Sétoise, fresh fish grilled over the coals. The décor is quite smart, the service stylish.

Bouzigues

34140 (15km N)

Ⓔ |●| Chez la Tchèpe

Avenue Louis-Tudesq; opposite the Thau pond.
☎and ☎04.67.78.33.19
Closed *Wed; Jan.* **Disabled access.**

This little terrace catches the eye; apart from anything else, it's often chock-a-block. There are lots of places in this area where everything comes straight from the sea to the table, but this one offers the best value for money. You can get two dozen oysters, a dozen mussels, one violet (a small sea creature native to the Mediterranean and eaten raw), two warm tielles (a small squid soufflé with tomato sauce) for €22, with a

bottle of wine. There are no menus – you just choose what you want from the display. Eat in or take away, with service all through the day. Credit cards not accepted.

Sommières

30250

Ⓔ 🏠 Le Relais de l'Estelou**

Route d'Aubais. By the entrance to the town, in the old train station; 5 min from the town centre on foot.
☎04.66.77.71.08 ☎04.66.77.08.88
ⓦhoteldelestelou.free.fr
Disabled access. TV. Car park.

This hotel's bright rooms (€46.50–60) have been decorated and furnished with great care (reed matting on the floors, strikingly attractive bathroom doors). They look onto the garden at the back or onto the (quiet) courtyard in front of the hotel. Other rooms are situated in an annexe by the garden. The large veranda has been fitted out with an inviting bar, also decorated with great care and originality. Very good service and it's excellent value for money.

Ⓔ 🎎 |●| L'Olivette

11 rue Abbé-Fabre.
☎04.66.80.97.71 ☎04.66.80.39.28
Closed *Tues in season; Tues evening and Wed out of season; Jan.*

They certainly know how to make you feel welcome here. The dining room is wonderful, with stone walls and wooden beams and it's air-conditioned. There's a lunch *formule* at €12.50 (starter plus main course or main course plus dessert), and menus €16.50–29.50. Much of the cuisine is local – snails, salt cod with tapenade – with a few flavours from further afield. *Free sample of tapenade (home-made olive paste) offered to our readers on presentation of this guide.*

Sorède

66690

Ⓔ |●| La Salamandre

3 rte. de Larroque.
☎and ☎04.68.89.26.67
Closed *Wed (out of season).*

This place has recently been take over by a couple of restaurateurs recently returned from Canada. The dining room is on the small side but is prettily decorated, although it lacks intimacy and is disturbed by noise from the street. The cooking is worth a detour, however, as it abounds in originality, combining regional tradition with recipes from elsewhere. The results are delicate and tasty – and good value, too, with a lunchtime menu at €16, then another at €23, and good local wines sold by the glass.

Uzès

30700

⊚ 🎿 🏠 Hôtel Saint-Géniès**

Quartier Saint-Géniès; it's 1.5km from the town centre in the direction of Saint-Ambroix.
☎04.66.22.29.99 ℗04.66.03.14.89
🖲www.hotel-saintgenies.com
Closed Dec–Jan. **High chairs and games available. Swimming pool. Car park.**

New hotel in a quiet residential district offering twenty tastefully decorated rooms, some with TV; doubles go for €46–52 with shower/wc or bath. Nos. 9, 10 and 11, set in the roof, have sloping ceilings, which makes them feel more intimate. *Free coffee offered to our readers on presentation of this guide.*

⊚ 🏠 |⊙| Hôtel-restaurant La Taverne**

4–9 rue Xavier-Sigalon; it's in the same street as the cinema.
☎04.66.22.13.10 ℗04.66.22.47.08
🖲lataverne.uzes@wanadoo.fr
Closed last fortnight in Nov. **TV. High chairs available.**

The pleasant garden in the small court-yard provides a quiet setting for your meal, though sometimes it's overrun by groups. The owner knows the town like the back of his hand, so he's a good source of information. Good tasty cook-ing is served on menus €17–30. They do bull fillet with olive *velouté*, *brandade de Nîmes* and excellent scrambled eggs with truffles. The hotel is a few metres further on and provides rooms that are comfortable, air-conditioned and quiet (particularly at the back). They're all dif-ferent and some have beamed ceilings and stone walls from the original house; €52–59 for doubles with shower/wc or bath, depending on the season. Logis de France.

⊚ 🏠 |⊙| Hôtel d'Entraigues – Restaurants Les Jardins de Castille et Le Bain-Douche***

Place de l'Évêché; it's opposite the Bishop's palace and the cathedral of Saint-Théodorit.
☎04.66.22.14.48 ℗04.66.22.57.01
🖲www.lcm.fr/savry/
Disabled access. TV. High chairs available. Swimming pool. Car park.

This stylish, charming establishment is spread across a group of town houses from the fifteenth, seventeenth and eighteenth centuries. The thirty air-conditioned rooms and apartments are furnished in classic style, and some have a private ter-race; doubles €55–152, depending on the season and facilities. Half board is com-pulsory in July and August. The restaurant *Les Jardins de Castille* has a panoramic terrace and an elegant dining room; since 2004, this has been complemented by another (gourmet) restaurant. The menus start at €22.

⊚ |⊙| Terroirs

5 pl. aux Herbes.
☎04.66.03.41.90
Closed Feb; 11–30 Nov.

This restaurant is on the loveliest square in town. It's the extension of a food and wine shop selling local specialities (oil, tapenade, herbs, honey). Dominique Becasse, the owner, travelled widely before settling in Uzès, his adoptive home. He serves only quality produce that's meticulously chosen, yet his prices are fair. This is the best of southern cooking, natural and healthy: pesto, Pélardon and delicious platters. There are no menus; reckon on around €12–20 per meal.

⊚ |⊙| Le Bistrot du Grézac

Place Belle-Croix, at the foot of the Saint-Étienne church.
☎04.66.03.42.09 ℗04.66.03.62.45
Closed Mon.

Just next to the Saint-Étienne church, this brand-new, old-style bistro has been brilliantly done up – when it's aged a little it will be perfect. The simple, deli-cious cuisine is Provençal in style; menus from €15.24 (weekday lunchtimes) to €20. Easy-going, efficient service, but sadly, the terrace is just too close to the road for comfort.

Vers-Pont-du-Gard

30210 (10km SE)

⊚ ⅄ ᚦ |●| La Bégude Saint-Pierre

Les Coudoulières; take the D981; it's just before the Gard bridge.
☎04.66.63.63.63 ℻04.66.22.73.73
🖳www.hotel-saintpierre.fr
Closed *Sun evening and Mon (Nov–30 March).* **Disabled access. TV. High chairs available. Swimming pool. Car park.**

"Bégude" is the Provençal word for a farm that doubled as a posthouse way back when letters were carried on horseback. Times may have changed but fortunately the road that goes past isn't busy. The beautiful seventeenth-century building has been carefully restored and decorated with Provençal prints. The rooms look onto the coachyard or the swimming pool; they're air-conditioned and individually decorated. Doubles or suites with bath are €54–120 depending on the season. The chic restaurant serves cuisine of Provençal pedigree and has menus from €29. *10% discount on the price of a room (except public holidays) offered to our readers on presentation of this guide.*

Valcebollière

66340

⊚ ᚦ |●| Auberge Les Écureuils***

Take the N116 and the D30 from Bourg-Madame.
☎04.68.04.52.03 ℻04.68.04.52.34
📧auberge-ecureuils@wanadoo.fr
Closed *8–18 May; 1 Nov–20 Dec.* **TV. High chairs available. Swimming pool. Car park.**

This cosy inn, built of solid wood and stone, lies deep in the heart of Cerdagne near the Spanish border. Étienne Laffitte's creativity blossoms in the kitchen, where he conjures up hearty dishes based on local produce. Dishes include hot duck foie gras, *noisette* of lamb and trout braised with saffron. The setting is as traditional as the food – but all this comes at a price: the set menus cost from €25 to €48. Comfortable rooms with shower/wc or bath go for €70–108; breakfast €9–11. There's a small gym, sauna and pool table. You can go on beautiful walks up the mountain, which is 2500m high and towers over the hotel. In the winter, it offers a chance to do downhill skiing. Logis de France.

Vigan (Le)

30120

⊚ ᚦ Hôtel du Commerce*

26 rue des Barris; it's next to the police station.
☎04.67.81.03.28 ℻04.67.81.43.20
Car park.

This quiet, cheap hotel is just away from the middle of the village and it's a great base from which to explore the area. Bright, simple, spacious and super-clean doubles cost €23 with basin, €30 with shower/wc or bath. There's a small garden.

Avèze

30120 (2km S)

⊚ ᚦ |●| ⅄ L'Auberge Cocagne**

Place du Château; it's on the road from the Navacelles Circus.
☎04.67.81.02.70 ℻04.67.81.07.67
Closed *Dec; Jan.* **Disabled access. High chairs available. Car park.**

In the south of France "cocagne" means "luck", and this typical country inn, shielded by a clump of trees, couldn't be more aptly named. It's a 400-year-old building with massive stone walls, red shutters and simple yet comfortable rooms; doubles €28.50 with basin, €41–45 with shower/wc or bath. Half board is compulsory mid-July to mid-August and over long weekends and costs €35.50–44.50 per person. You get a warm welcome as well as cool jazz in the dining room. The place has personality and so has the home cooking which, typical for the Mediterranean, is drenched in olive oil and strewn with spices: terrine with sweet onion chutney, lamb from the Causse and vegetarian dishes. The vegetables are organic and the cheeses bought direct from the farmer. There's a choice of set menus €13.55–23. The wines and apéritifs come from local winegrowers. Logis de France. *Free coffee or herb tea offered to our readers on presentation of this guide.*

Mandagout

30120 (10km N)

⊚ ᚦ |●| Auberge de la Borie*

Take the D170; 9km along, turn right towards Mandagout, past the village, continue towards Saint-André-de-Majencoules, then follow a sloping road on the left for 250m.
☎and ℻04.67.81.06.03

Closed *Wed out of season; Jan; Feb; Dec.*
Disabled access. TV. High chairs and games available. Swimming pool.

An old Cévennes *mas* on a sunny mountainside, with a swimming pool and breathtaking views over the mountains, the chestnut forests and the fig groves. There are ten nicely appointed rooms with old stone walls; doubles with basin are €29, those with shower/wc or bath €51. Half board is compulsory in season and over long weekends. Nos. 8, 9 and 10 (with wc only), down in the ancient vaulted cellars, are wonderfully cool in summer. In the restaurant they serve home cooking based exclusively on local produce – specialities include foie gras with fig jam, frogs' legs with *persillade*, and set menus start from €14.

Villefort
48800

⟪ 🕇 ♨ |●| Hôtel-restaurant du Lac**

Lac de Villefort; take the D906 for 1.5km and it's an isolated white building on the left, by the lake.
☎04.66.46.81.20 ℗04.66.46.90.95
Closed *Tues evening and Wed except in July–Aug; Jan.* **TV. High chairs available.**

The rooms all have a view of the lake, where you can swim in summer: doubles with shower/wc go for €43 or €58 with bath; half board €44 per person. In the restaurant you'll find regional specialities on the menus (€14.50–23) like cep omelette, trout *meunière*, veal *blanquette* and chestnut gâteau. It's very popular in high season, so it can get noisy. *Free coffee offered to our readers on presentation of this guide.*

⟪ 🕇 🕇 |●| Hôtel-restaurant Balme**

Place du Portalet; take the A75 and A6; it's in the centre of the village.
☎04.66.46.80.14 ℗04.66.46.85.26
🖱www.hotelbalme.free.fr
Closed *Sun evening and Mon out of season; 15 Nov–15 Feb.* **TV. High chairs available. Car park.**

A well-known place which has aged elegantly. It's somewhat reminiscent of a spa hotel – same type of comfort, same English atmosphere. The cuisine is excellent, combining local dishes and specialities from the East, especially Thailand. Menus €21–34; the meals are the best value for money

in the region. Good choices include hot foie gras coated with poppy seeds, terrine of calf's head with cep oil or Thai curry with scented rice. The kitchen opens onto the dining room so you can follow what's going on, and since Micheline is a qualified sommelier, they've got a magnificent cellar. In the hotel, doubles go for €46 with shower/wc and €54 with bath. Logis de France. *10% discount on the price of a room (except July–Aug) offered to our readers on presentation of this guide.*

Villefranche-de-Conflent
66500

⟪ |●| Auberge Saint-Paul ⑪

7 pl. de l'Église.
☎and ℗04.68.96.30.95
🖱www.auberge.stpaul.free.fr
Closed *Mon (Easter–Oct); Sun evening, Mon and Tues (Oct to Easter); 3 weeks in Jan; third week in June; last week in Nov.*

Patricia Gomez has a remarkable culinary imagination: she combines unexpected flavours with top-quality ingredients and produces unforgettable dishes. Set menus €27–85; you'll pay around €50 à la carte. Brilliant wines selected by Charly Gomez. One of the best restaurants in the district, with a beautiful terrace to boot.

Olette
66360 (10km SW)

⟪ 🕇 |●| ♨ Hôtel-Restaurant La Fontaine

5 rue de la Fusterie; on a small square slightly set back from the main road.
☎04.68.97.03.67 ℗04.68.97.09.18
Closed *Tues evening; Wed; Jan.* **TV. High chairs available. Car park.**

A substantial building painted a brilliant salmon-pink. The rooms are attractive and have good facilities – good-value doubles with shower/wc €39–56. There's a terrace with three or four tables and a pretty dining room on the first floor where you can eat well-executed, authentic local dishes. There's a set lunch at €11, then menus from €13.50 (except Sun) to €38. There's a friendly family atmosphere. The kitchen stays open until 8.45pm. *Free coffee offered to our readers on presentation of this guide.*

Villeneuve-lès-Avignon

30400

⊚ ☎ |●| Centre de Rencontres International YMCA

7 bis chemin de la Justice; from Avignon, take the av. Général-Leclerc towards Bellevue-aux-Angles at the Royaume bridge, turn left into Chemin de la Justice after about 300m.
℡04.90.25.46.20 🖷04.90.25.30.64
🖳www.ymca-avignon.com
Closed *Christmas week*. **Disabled access. Car park.**

Set in completely renovated old buildings, the centre contains around 100 beds in rooms of three with wc. Doubles go for €22–28 with basin, €34–42 with shower/wc, depending on the season; half board compulsory in July. There's a menu at €12. The swimming pool, bar and the breathtaking views over Avignon, the Rhône, Mount Ventoux and Philippe-le-Bel tower make it a worth-while place to stay. The atmosphere is pretty wild during the festival season.

⊚ ☎ 🍴 Hôtel de l'Atelier**

5 rue de la Foire.
℡04.90.25.01.84 🖷04.90.25.80.06
🖳www.hoteldelatelier.com
Closed *3 Jan–18 Feb.* **TV. High chairs and games available. Car park.**

This is a quite delightful sixteenth-century building with 23 rooms, all of them different, furnished with antiques. Doubles with shower are €46–61 or €61–91 with bath. Breakfast (€8) is served in the dining room or on the patio, where plants and flowers proliferate, and there's a rooftop terrace and tea room. It's good value for money – you'd be wise to book in season. *One breakfast per room (out of season) offered to our readers on presentation of this guide.*

⊚ |●| Restaurant La Maison

1 rue Montée-du-Fort-Saint-André; it's behind the town hall, overlooking pl. Jean-Jaurès.
℡04.90.25.20.81
Closed *Tues evening; Wed; Sat lunchtime; Aug.*

This restaurant is attractive to look at, with lace curtains, ceiling fans and a good-looking pottery collection. Simple cooking is served in generous portions: you get a good meal on the €20 menu. The service is absolutely delightful.

Angles (Les)

30133 (4km S)

⊚ ☎ |●| Le Petit Manoir**

15 av. Jules-Ferry; it's on the Nîmes road.
℡04.90.25.03.36 🖷04.90.25.49.13
🖳www.hotel-lepetitmanoir.com
Closed *end Jan to early Feb.* **Disabled access. TV. High chairs available. Swimming pool. Car park.**

This group of modern buildings set around a swimming pool is hardly what most people would call a manor, but the place is not without character or comfort – and most of the quiet, clean rooms have a private terrace; doubles €43–58 with shower/wc or bath. The restaurant serves traditional, regional cuisine using fresh seasonal produce; menus €16–50. Logis de France.

Roquemaure

30150 (11km N)

⊚ 🍴 ☎ |●| Le Clément V**

6 rue Pierre-Semard; take the D980.
℡04.66.82.67.58 🖷04.66.82.84.66
🖳www.hotel-clementv.fr.st
Closed *5–30 Jan.* **TV. High chairs and games available. Swimming pool. Pay car park.**

A very nice place in a medieval village in the Côtes du Rhône which has so far eluded the tourists. It's in a 1970s-style house in a residential area; the rooms are conventional but they've been renovated with a touch of Provence and cost €60–65 with shower/wc, including breakfast. The ones overlooking the swimming pool have balconies but those at the back are larger and quieter. Half board, €46–48.50, is obligatory in summer. Menus (€18–23), featuring typical, simple local dishes, are available to hotel residents only. Bikes are available for rent. Logis de France. *Free house apéritif or 5% discount on the price of a room (for a stay of more than four nights) offered to our readers on presentation of this guide.*

LANGUEDOC-ROUSSILLON

Limousin

Argentat

19400

@ ⚘ 🏠 |O| **Hôtel-Restaurant Fouillade****

11 pl. Gambetta.
☎05.55.28.10.17 ℗05.55.28.90.52
Closed 13 Nov–16 Dec. **Restaurant closed Mon. Disabled access. TV. High chairs and cots available.**

A beautiful house that's been running as a hotel-restaurant for two centuries. Menus, €12 (weekdays) up to €31, list scrumptious dishes such as *confit* with chestnuts, ceps with sorrel butter, and calf sweetbreads Limousin style. All the bedrooms have been renovated and are comfortable and tastefully decorated. Doubles with shower/wc or bath go for €41–45; half board €40 per person. *Free house apéritif offered to our readers on presentation of this guide.*

Saint Julien-aux-Bois

(14km NE)

@ ⚘ 🏠 |O| **Auberge de St Julien-aux-Bois**

Take the D980.
☎05.55.24.41.94 ℗05.55.28.37.85
🖥www.auberge-saint-julien.com
Closed Tues evening and Wed out of season; Wed lunch in July and Aug; mid-Feb to mid-March. **TV. High chairs and games available. Play area.**

This lost village on the edge of La Xaintrie and the Dordogne valley offers an unexpectedly pleasant surprise. Neither the village nor the restaurant look that appealing and even the décor in the dining room is ordinary – but it's the food that makes the place different. It's run by a German couple who fell in love with the area and decided to open a restaurant. Madame is the chef, and many of her delicious Limousin specialities have a touch of German cuisine about them. There are lots of rarely used cereals, herbs and vegetables and most of the ingredients are organic; the choice of cheeses is amazing. There are also some vegetarian dishes, and hearty German desserts. The menus offer excellent value for money: €13, then €16–40. Doubles with shower/wc or bath are €40–53, a few cheaper doubles with basin are due for refurbishment; half board costs €38–46 per person. A perfect spot for lunch before or after visiting the Tours de Merle. Logis de France. *Free house apéritif offered to our readers on presentation of this guide.*

Arnac-Pompadour

19230

@ 🏠 |O| **Auberge de la Mandrie****

Route de Périgueux; 5km from Pompadour on the D7 going towards Payzac and Périgueux.
☎05.55.73.37.14 ℗05.55.73.67.13
🖥www.la-mandrie.com
Closed Sun evening (1 Nov–31 March). **TV. Games available. Swimming pool. Car park.**

This place, near the Cité du Cheval and the medieval village of Ségur-le-Château, looks like a holiday club with its little chalets dotted around in a park. There is a fabulous heated pool and a play area for children. The bedrooms are all at ground level and have a tiny terrace and either a shower or bath and telephone; doubles €42 including buffet breakfast. Half board, €37–52 per person, is compulsory

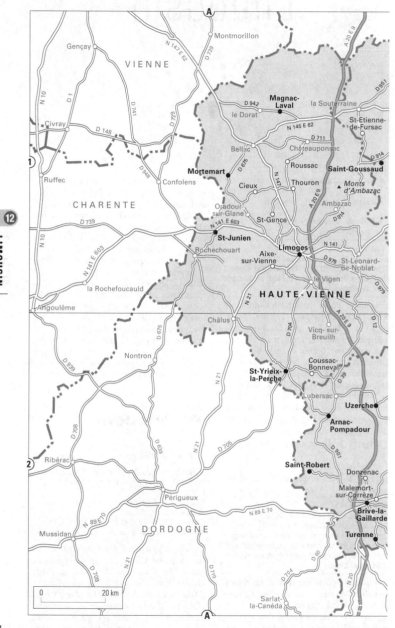

A

Montmorillon

Gençay

VIENNE

N 147 E 62

D 729

N 10

D 1

D 741

D 729

Civray

D 148

Magnac-
Laval

D 942

le Dorat

la Souterraine

St-Etienne-
de-Fursac

D 951

N 145 E 62

D 711

Châteauponsac

D 914

Ruffec

D 948

Confolens

Bellac

Roussac

Saint-Goussaud

Mortemart

D 675

N 147

Cieux

Thouron

Monts
d'Ambazac

CHARENTE

D 739

Oradour-
sur-Glane

A 20 E 9

Ambazac

D 914

St-Gence

N 141 E 603

N 10

N 141 E 603

St-Junien

Limoges

N 141

Rochechouart

Aixe-
sur-Vienne

D 979

St-Léonard-
de-Noblat

la Rochefoucauld

le Vigen

D 979

Angoulême

N 21

HAUTE-VIENNE

A 20 E 9

D 12

Châlus

D 675

Vicq-
sur-
Breuilh

D 704

Nontron

D 939

N 21

Coussac-
Bonneval

Uzerche

St-Yrieix-
la-Perche

D 39

Lubersac

D 708

D 639

N 21

D 705

Arnac-
Pompadour

D 901

Ribérac

Saint-Robert

Donzenac

Malemort-
sur-Corrèze

Périgueux

N 89 E 70

N 89 E 70

Brive-la-
Gaillarde

Mussidan

N 89 E 10

DORDOGNE

Turenne

N 21

D 709

D 710

D 704

D 80

D 20

Sarlat-
la-Canéda

0   20 km

A

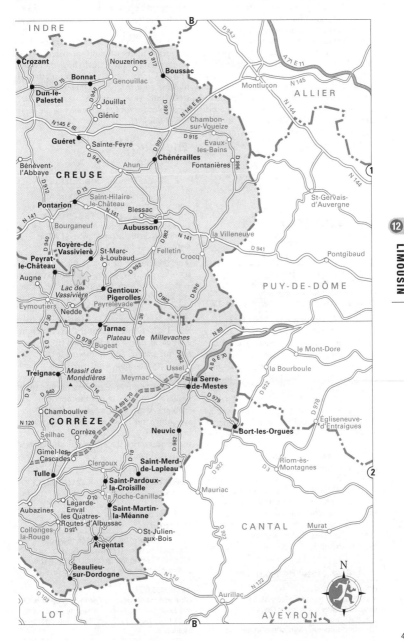

INDRE

Crozant

Nouzerines

Boussac

D 943

A 71 E 11

Bonnat

Genouillac

Montluçon

N 145

ALLIER

Dun-le-Palestel

D 15

D 940

Jouillat

N 145 E 62

Glénic

D 997

Chambon-sur-Voueize

N 145 E 62

D 144

Guéret

Sainte-Feyre

D 915

Evaux-les-Bains

D 917

N 144

Bénévent-l'Abbaye

D 942

Ahun

Chénérailles

Fontanières

D 996

St-Gervais-d'Auvergne

CREUSE

Saint-Hilaire-le-Château

D 73

Blessac

N 144

Pontarion

N 141

N 141

Aubusson

la Villeneuve

Bourganeuf

D 982

Royère-de-Vassivière

St-Marc-à-Loubaud

N 141

D 941

Pontgibaud

Peyrat-le-Château

D 940

Felletin

Crocq

Augne

D 992

Lac de Vassivière

Gentioux-Pigerolles

D 996

PUY-DE-DÔME

Eymoutiers

Peyrelevade

D 982

Nedde

Tarnac

D 36

N 89

D 3

D 979

Plateau de Millevaches

Bugeat

D 982

Treignac

Massif des Monédières

Meymac

Ussel

A 89 E 70

la Bourboule

le Mont-Dore

D 3

D 940

D 16

la Serre-de-Mestes

D 922

D 978

Chamboulive

D 979

Éqliseneuve-d'Entraigues

N 120

CORRÈZE

Corrèze

Neuvic

Bort-les-Orgues

Seilhac

A 89 E 70

D 982

Gimel-les-Cascades

D 18

Clergoux

Saint-Merd-de-Lapleau

Riom-ès-Montagnes

Tulle

D 922

D 3

Saint-Pardoux-la-Croisille

la Roche-Canillac

Mauriac

Aubazines

Lagarde-Enval

D 10

Saint-Martin-la-Méanne

Collonges-la-Rouge

les Quatres-Routes-d'Albussac

D 921

St-Julien-aux-Bois

CANTAL

Murat

Argentat

D 922

Beaulieu-sur-Dordogne

N 120

N

D 103

N 122

Aurillac

LOT

AVEYRON

mid-June to mid-September. There is a refurbishment programme; some rooms are already finished, while the rest are being done at the moment. The results are generally attractive (although one could quibble about some of the decorative details) and the rooms are certainly value for money. The owners take pride in their work, and you'll get a warm welcome. The regional dishes are particularly tasty and are often prepared with an individual touch; menus €11.50–25. The food is basic regional, but it is sometimes set off by unusual complements: black sausage with apples, Correzian pot roast (fillet of pork *confit*) and Vacherin cheese with walnuts. You can eat in the dining room or on the enormous terrace. Logis de France.

Aubusson

23200

@ ☎ |●| Le Lion d'Or**

11 pl. du Général-d'Espagne.
℡05.55.66.65.71 ℗05.55.66.71.97
ⓦwww.liondor-aubusson.com
Closed *Sun and Mon; a fortnight in Jan.* **TV.**

Completely refurbished in 2004 by Hélène and Patrick, who hail from Aubusson, *Le Lion d'Or* is enjoying a new lease of life. The rooms don't yet have all the style one might hope for but the new owners are working on it. They are clean and comfortable though (no. 5 is also spacious) and cost €45 for a double. There is a brasserie area with an attractive yellow décor and some old pieces of advertizing, as well as a smart, bright restaurant section with nice round tables and an impressive collection of fans hanging on the walls. Menus, €8–14, served in the brasserie and, €23–60, in the restaurant feature high-class, local cooking: Limousin beef, Creuse fondue, river fish in season, Creuse gâteau with chestnut ice cream … And don't be surprised if you bump into film actress Nathalie Baye; she often spends time in the area.

@ ⚘ ☎ |●| Hôtel de France**

6 rue des Déportés.
℡05.55.66.10.22 ℗05.55.66.88.64
Closed *Sun evening (early Dec to mid-April).*
Open *all year round.*
Disabled access. High chairs available. TV.

An establishment in the best tradition of provincial hotel-keeping, with exposed

stone and wall hangings. Comfortable and spacious refurbished doubles go for €59–92. In the restaurant there are menus at €16 (not Sun) up to €38; weekday brasserie menus go for €10 and €11.50. The restaurant offers carefully prepared dishes using local produce, including the well-known Creuse fondue. There's a pretty old interior courtyard. An eighteenth-century style hotel that is not to be missed. *Free house apéritif offered to our readers on presentation of this guide.*

Blessac

23200 (4km NW)

@ ☎ |●| Le Relais des Forêts*

41 rte. d'Aubusson. Take D941 towards Pontarion, then right towards Blessac.
℡05.55.66.15.10 ℗05.55.83.87.91
Closed *Fri evening; Sun evening. 3 weeks in Feb; All Saints' school holiday.* **TV. Car park.**

The building itself looks a bit austere but it's a simple, easy-going and honest place – if you like generous portions of home cooking, this is where to come. Menus start at €10.50 (weekdays only), then others at €14 and €33. They offer a balanced selection of regional dishes, such as *entrecôte marchand de vin,* stuffed trout, crayfish in season, and home-made pastries. Some rooms look a bit tired but others have been refurbished; they're all clean and quiet and cost €26 for a double with basin/wc (shower along the corridor), or €38–65 with shower/wc or bath. Nice welcome, and it enjoys a good reputation in the area. There's a pleasant walk from the restaurant to the château in the village. Logis de France.

Saint-Marc-à-Loubaud

23460 (24km SW)

@ ⚘ |●| Restaurant Les Mille Sources

It's in the centre; take the N141 towards Limoges, then the D7 towards Royère, turn left at Vallières in the direction of Saint-Yrieix and follow the signs for Saint-Marc-à-Loubaud.
℡05.55.66.03.69
Closed *Sun evening and Mon outside school holidays; out of season it's best to telephone and check opening times; Jan.* **High chairs available.**

The *Mille Sources* is the restaurant of choice for well-known personalities who spend time in the area, like actress Nathalie Baye. Located way up in the north of the Millevaches plateau, this place is very popular, so it's advisable to book. The quality of the cooking is quite astonishing and although the prices are a little high (set menus €28 and €44), it shouldn't be missed. Philippe Coutisson is a great chef, as his duck *à la ficelle* will attest, and his specialities – duck and leg of lamb chargrilled over the open fire – also hit the spot. The décor is delightful and the lovingly tended garden is always full of flowers. *Free house apéritif offered to our readers on presentation of this guide.*

Beaulieu-sur-Dordogne
19120

ⓔ 🏠 Auberge de jeunesse La Riviera Limousine

Place du Monturuc; by the Dordogne.
☏05.55.91.13.82 ℗05.55.91.26.06
ⓦwww.fuaj.org
Closed 5 Nov–1 April. **Car park.**

This large, charming building by the Dordogne, opposite the Pénitents chapel, is exceptionally luxurious for a youth hostel, and the setting is worthy of a postcard. There are some thirty beds spread over rooms with four beds each. It costs €9.25 a night per person, breakfast €3.30; meals are €8.60 (by request only, for a minimum of ten people). There's a friendly atmosphere and cosy fireplace. Credit cards not accepted.

ⓔ 🎋 🏠 |●| Auberge Les Charmilles

20, bd. Rodolphe-de-Turenne.
☏05.55.91.29.29 ℗05.55.91.29.30
ⓦwww.auberge-charmilles.com
Closed Wed (except June–Sept).

Away from the throng of the tourists who invade Beaulieu in summer, this pale-stone inn exudes an unusual feeling of calm and serenity. The tone is set on arrival by the tree-lined terrace. The same high standard applies to the rooms (€52 with bath), which are charmingly decorated in the English style, and to the restaurant (menus €17–38) which offers terrine of foie gras with Sauternes, noisette of lamb in tapenade... All of which suggests a blend of Correzian and Provençal cuisine – a combination we found really worked. *A*

free house apéritif is offered to our readers on presentation of this guide.

Bonnat
23220

ⓔ 🏠 |●| L'Orangerie

3 bis rue de la Paix; opposite the church.
☏05.55.62.86.86 ℗05.55.62.86.87
ⓦwww.hotel-lorangerie.fr
Closed Sun evening; Mon out of season; Feb. **Disabled access. TV. Swimming pool. Car park.**

A handsome, substantial building in the old style, but new. An accessible stylishness, with attentive service; beautiful, large, quiet, clean rooms tastefully decorated with fine fabrics cost €73–106 for a double, depending on the standard. Good half board options are available. You can eat in the dining room or on the terrace, choosing from a creative cuisine that draws on local produce; €17 menu served weekday lunchtimes, then a range of menus at €29–54. The clientele includes company managers and visitors who enjoy a refined ambience. Facilities include a lovely swimming pool, billiard room, reading room and library. Logis de France.

Bort-les-Orgues
19110

ⓔ 🏠 |●| Central Hôtel

65 av. de la Gare.
☏05.55.96.81.05 ℗05.55.96.71.86
ⓦwww.centralhotelbort.fr
Closed Fri and Sun evenings in low season; every weekend from mid-Feb to mid-March. **Disabled access. TV.**

A good, solid, traditional hotel situated on the banks of a pretty river with a split personality: calm and peaceful most of the time but becomes a raging torrent when the floodgates at the dam are opened. Rooms (€34–43) are in the old style, mainly renovated but only moderately soundproof. Nos. 31 and 32 have balconies overlooking the river. When the weather's good you can eat out on the large terrace, which is very pleasant for an apéritif. The cheapest menu at €11 is served at lunchtime, and there's another at €21; the food is unsurprising but you'll get a warm welcome from the dynamic owner. Logis de France.

Boussac

23600

☞ |●| ♨ Café de la Place

4 pl. de l'Hôtel-de-Ville.
℡ 05.55.65.02.70
Closed *Sun in June.*

Patronne Paulette Roger is a warm and welcoming figure. A typical meal might consist of melon, shellfish, meat *en paupiette* and potatoes, with pear tart to finish. The weekday menu is €11 and on Sundays it's €12.50; the menu changes daily. It's a simple, original formula, which does the trick. It's good value, but they don't accept credit cards. *Free coffee offered to our readers on presentation of this guide.*

☞ |●| Le Relais Creusois

40 La Maison Dieu. Route de la Châtre; after the traffic lights, downhill on the left, look out for the modern frontage with its mauve columns.
℡ 05.55.65.02.20
Closed *Wed, Fri and Sat evenings; in winter the other evenings by reservation only; Jan; Feb; a week in June.*

The cooking is good and the chef prepares lots of local dishes, but he also dreams up his own specialities, such as glazed leg of duckling with semolina and spicy whipped cream. The Tulleau family likes things done properly, which justifies the prices; menus €25–58. Go through to the table at the back with its view over the Petite Creuse valley.

Nouzerines

23600 (13km NW)

☞ ♠ |●| La Bonne Auberge

1 rue des Lilas; in the village, opposite the church.
℡ 05.55.82.01.18
🌐 www.labonneauberge-boussac.com
Closed *Sun evening; Mon; a fortnight in Jan; a fortnight in Oct.* **Open** *bookings preferred in the evenings.*

In a small, isolated village, a pleasant spot well managed by a young, local couple who love their region and who give their guests a warm welcome. This carries over into the food on offer in the attractive dining room: cep rissoles, foie gras combo, stuffed hare, roast figs with quince … A special bistro menu (€9.50) is served at lunchtimes, and there's a range of other menus at €15–39. The rooms are nice and clean, quiet and with no (nasty) surprises. Doubles go for €23–35, according to standard (with or without TV).

Brive-la-Gaillarde

19100

☞ ♠ ♨ Auberge de jeunesse

56 av. du Maréchal-Bugeaud, parc Monjauze; beside the municipal swimming pool.
℡ 05.55.24.34.00 📠 05.55.84.82.80
✉ aj.brive@wanadoo.fr
Closed *15 Dec–15 Jan (except for group bookings).* **Reception open** *8am–noon and 2–10pm (6–9pm Nov–March).* **Disabled access. Car park.**

Only five minutes from the town centre. The reception building also contains some bedrooms and two dining rooms (meals €8.60, with booking only). Otherwise rooms with two, three or four beds are in a long, recently built annexe. Some have the addition of a small balcony and all are clean and well kept, just like the communal shower area. Current membership card compulsory, but you can buy it on arrival. It costs €9.60 a night per person; breakfast €3.25. Hostel guests get a discount in the swimming pool next door; guests have at their disposal: a ping-pong table, a TV room, Internet access, a kitchen and a garage for bikes. *10% discount on the price of a room (Sept–March) offered to our readers on presentation of this guide.*

☞ ♠ Hôtel L'Andréa

39 av. Jean-Jaurès; near the station.
℡ 05.55.74.11.84 📠 05.55.17.25.73
TV.

This is an old-fashioned-style hotel offering a friendly welcome and good, local atmosphere, particularly in the bar, where breakfast is served. All nine rooms have been completely refurbished and cost €38 for a double with shower/wc. It's not expensive and shows good taste, although the soundproofing is not the best. Meals are also served (the dishes are Italian, like the owner, or there's paella).

☞ ♠ Hôtel Le Coq d'Or

16-18 bd Jules-Ferry.
℡ 05.55.17.12.92 📠 05.55.88.39.90
TV.

Ask at *Le Conti* bar next door. Located in

the town's big, main square, this attractive building has eight refurbished rooms. The pleasant owner has had the good sense to make the most of the stonework and to decorate the rooms in traditional toile de Jouy fabrics with old-style furniture that his wife's hunted down in antique shops. The result is excellent. All rooms have a telephone and air-conditioning and cost €48.50 for a double. Family rooms (€70) have a shower and bathroom. The bar next door serves light lunches.

ⓔ |●| Bistrot de Brune

13 av. de Paris.
℡05.55.24.00.91
Closed Sun in summer; Sat evening and Sun in winter; a week during each of the school holidays. **Disabled access. High chairs available.**

A new-look brasserie opposite the market square in Brive, offering tempting, cheap dishes: magret with honey, duck *andouillette* with Brive mustard, calf's head with *sauce gribiche* and quality Limousin beef. There's a range of menus at €13–25 or expect to pay around €25 à la carte. The chatty owner has a good selection of local wines and some fine vintages besides. This is a place that achieves that rare combination of relaxed atmosphere and really excellent food; not always easy to find in Brive.

ⓔ |●| Chez Francis

61 av. de Paris.
℡05.55.74.41.72
Closed Sun; Mon; some public holidays; 10 days in Feb; a fortnight in early Aug.

The flattering comments scribbled on the walls of this delightful place add up to one thing – it's successful and popular, so much so that you have to book. And the welcome suffers a little from the highs and lows that go with very busy establishments. The cooking is well thought out and they produce wonderfully executed dishes, prettily presented; dish of the day €9 and menus €14–21. All the meats come from the Limousin and they're very tasty.

ⓔ |●| La Table d'Olivier

3 rue Saint-Ambroise.
℡05.55.18.95.95
Closed Sun evening; Mon.

After a successful spell in Beaulieu-sur-Dordogne in the Turenne area, Pascal Cavé and his wife have set up on their own in a quiet, little street in the centre of town. You'll need to book if you want to enjoy this little dining room with its warm tones and exposed stone walls because its reputation has quickly spread. Madame Cavé welcomes you with a smile, while her husband prepares hearty yet refined dishes based on what's good in the market; special lunchtime menu €14 and full menus €19–30. Depending on the season, there's oxtail and foie gras terrine, a creamy risotto or calf sweetbreads with fondant carrots. And it's going from strength to strength.

Malemort-sur-Corrèze
19360 (3km NE)

ⓔ 🎿 🛏 |●| Auberge des Vieux Chênes**

31 av. Honoré-de-Balzac.
℡05.55.24.13.55 ⓕ05.55.24.56.82
Closed Sun; public holidays. **TV. High chairs available. Car park.**

This establishment isn't much to look at from the outside, but take a glance at the menus. They range from €12 (except Sat) up to €30, and list inventive country-style cooking such as *escalope* of foie gras pan-fried with soft fruits. The rooms lack character. They've been done up and have modern facilities; they're similar to the ones you'd find in a chain hotel but cheaper at €42–52 for a double with shower or bath/wc. Half board costs €40 per person. *10% discount on the room rate offered to our readers on presentation of this guide.*

Aubazines
19190 (11km E)

ⓔ 🛏 |●| Hôtel-café-restaurant de la Tour (Chez Lachaud)

Place de l'Église; par la N 89.
℡05.55.25.71.17 ⓕ05.55.84.61.83
Closed Mon lunchtime and Sun evening in winter; Jan. **Disabled access.**

In the heart of the village, opposite the venerable old abbey church, the *Hôtel de la Tour* has more than one trick up its sleeve. You may be lucky enough to enjoy the duplex suite in the tower with its circular room and terrace overlooking the abbey. Doubles are priced €46–48; the best rooms are in the main building, which is the most appealing part of the hotel, rather than the annexe, although the décor is rather ordinary. The chef has spent time in some of the major Paris establishments and produces healthy, honest, no-frills dishes that are always excellent, with a special weekday menu at €9 and full menus €18–37. Try, for example, the filet mignon of veal with violet mustard. And enjoy the atmosphere of the two dining rooms with their magnificent fireplaces. There's a friendly welcome from the Lachaud family. Logis de France.

Chénérailles

23130

@ 🎋 🛏 |●| **Le Coq d'Or**

7 pl. du Champ de Foire; opposite the place du Champ-de-Foire.
☎and 📠05.55.62.30.83
Closed Sun evening; Mon; Wed evening; 3 weeks in Jan; 10 days in June; a week at the end of Sept. **TV. High chairs available. Pay car park.**

Not far from the Château Villemonteix, this place has a reputation for quality cuisine. Everything is clean and thoughtfully executed – from the handful of rooms to the service, not forgetting the delicious, carefully prepared food. Perhaps this is because the Ruillère family are related to the late master chef Bernard Loiseau. In any case the tradition of quality endures. The décor is interesting … with cockerels on everything from the crockery to the napkins – but not on the menu. The chef updates local dishes for today's tastes starting with the weekday lunch menu €11, others €17–37 – go for the potato tart with fromage frais, the fillet of trout with blackwheat spaghetti, or the crunchy goat's cheese bake with apples. They have a few double rooms which are currently being refurbished (prices not fixed yet). *Free house apéritif offered to our readers on presentation of this guide.*

Crozant

23160

@ 🛏 |●| **Restaurant du Lac**

Pont de Crozant; it's on the banks of the Creuse, leaving the town on the road to Saint-Plantaire.
☎05.55.89.81.96
Closed Mon; Wed evening; Sun evening; Feb; a week in early March.

Don't miss this place. It has an exceptional location on the water's edge, with a splendid view of the cathedral and the bridge that links two départements – and though it's on the Indre bank of the river, it's actually in Creuse. Well-executed, often inventive cooking, which frequently includes fish, predominates on the menus, €17.50–37. It's built a solid reputation so it's best to book. The rooms on offer are a bit tired and not up to the standard of the cooking, but some (nos. 2 and 7) have a magnificent view. Doubles with shower cost €32–46.

@ |●| **Auberge de la Vallée**

Rue principale; it's in the town.
☎05.55.89.80.03
Closed Mon evening; Tues.

This classic inn has everything you could ask for with the added bonus of the staff wearing traditional marchois costume, which is a nice touch. A flowery décor and well-prepared recipes make this place rather special. Dishes on the menus, €16–35, include leg of guinea-fowl, crunchy calf sweetbreads, chocolate dessert, home-made ice cream, to mention but a few. There's also a children's menu at €9.

Dun-le-Palestel

23800

@ 🛏 |●| **Hôtel Joly – Restaurant La Table Dunoise****

Rue Bazennerie; opposite the church.
☎05.55.89.00.23 📠05.55.89.15.89
@wwwhoteljoly@wanadoo.fr
Closed Sun evening; Mon lunchtime. **TV.**

A good restaurant offering quality food – just what you need in a stopover town like this. It has recently changed hands and there's been a significant transformation in terms of style and professionalism. The food is pleasant, if unsurprising, and is based on local produce (sirloin steak Limousin style, medallion of young rabbit…). There's a special €13 weekday menu and other menus at €18.60–33; you can sense the desire to make this a good restaurant. The rooms are clean and simple and cost €31.50–42; some are situated in a modern building further down the street. Half board is available at €50 per person. There's a pleasant terrace at the rear and mountain bikes for hire. Logis de France.

Évaux-les-Bains

23110

@ 🏨 |●| **Hôtel-restaurant La Fontaine**

From the town follow the route to the spa centre; near the thermal baths, after the Parc au Daims, opposite the car park.
☎05.55.65.51.36
Open all year round. **Disabled access. TV.**

A friendly welcome, honest food, a convivial atmosphere and reasonable prices. The rooms are in the process of being given a makeover and are really quiet and good value at €43–55 for a double, or €49 per person for half board; some look onto the forest. Meals are served in the dining room or on the terrace and include butcher's specials, fish in sauce and home-made terrine. There's a weekday lunchtime menu at €11, other menus at €20–28; also a very practical self-service buffet option for starters and desserts. In addition, this is one of the few restaurants in the area to offer seafood platters (seafood is freshly delivered every two days).

Fontanières

23110 (8km S)

@ |●| **Le Damier**

On the main road, on the left-hand side.
☎05.55.82.35.91
Closed Mon; Tues; Feb; Sept. **Disabled access.**

This is a lovely country inn hidden inside an adorable little stone-built house. It has a quiet, stylish atmosphere and offers quality regional cuisine. Weekday lunch menu €10.50 and others €16–31, list house terrine of duck with foie gras and slabs of beef cooked in different ways according to the season. It's a very pleasant place, with a terrace where you can eat snacks in summer. It's best to book.

Gentioux-Pigerolles

23340

@ 🎿 🏨 |●| **La Ferme de Nautas**

Pigerolles; it's 5km from Gentioux, towards La Courtine. Take the D982, the D35 and then the D26.
☎05.55.67.90.68 ℱ05.55.67.93.12
⊛www.perso.wanadoo.fr/les.nautas

Closed Tues; mid-Dec to mid-Jan. **Open** for B&B all year round; the inn is only open weekends out of season but every day in July, Aug and Sept.

This place, a working farm run by the hospitable François Chatoux, is a winner. He used to be an engineer but took up farming instead, and he runs an original place brimming with warmth and hospitality. Genuine local cuisine, using first-rate ingredients and serving generous helpings of tasty regional dishes – potato pie, cep tarts and superb meat. There's a menu at €17 for hotel residents only and then €21 (with coffee and wine) but you have to book it in advance. The double rooms cost €45 with shower/wc, breakfast included. There's also the B&B option in comfortable rooms decorated in yellow in the Provençal style. *Free coffee offered to our readers on presentation of this guide.*

Guéret

23000

@ 🎿 🏨 |●| **Hôtel de Pommeil**

75 rue de Pommeil.
☎and ℱ05.55.52.38.54
Closed Sat evening (Nov–March), Sun; mid-June to mid-July. **TV. Games available. Car park.**

A very simple, clean and welcoming hotel with a friendly atmosphere and good prices. Ask to see the rooms first as some have been refurbished. There are just nine rooms, so it's best to book; doubles €28–35 with shower. They have a menu at €10.60 (two courses) and another at €12.40 (all inclusive). Dishes on offer include home-made paté, veal *escalope* with a mushroom and cream sauce and the hazelnut cake. The dining room is a bit bar-restaurant and boasts an impressive collection of miniature bottles. There's a small veranda with a view over the town and countryside. *10% discount on the room rate for a two-night stay (Sept–June) offered to our readers on presentation of this guide.*

@ 🎿 |●| **Le Pub Rochefort**

6 pl. Rochefort; it's in a pedestrianized street.
☎05.55.52.61.02
Closed Sun; Mon; end Aug to early Sept. **Open** until 11pm.

This place is right in the heart of the town and has an intimate, warm setting with old stone walls and ancestral beams. The food won't get Michelin stars, but it's honest and good value, and service comes with a smile. Weekday lunch menu at €11 and others €15–23; reckon on €16 à la carte. There's a nice covered terrace in the interior courtyard that gets full very quickly. *Free house apéritif offered to our readers on presentation of this guide.*

⊚ |O| Le Coq en Pâte

2 rue de Pommeil.
☎05.55.41.43.43.
Closed *Mon.* **Disabled access.**

This place provides the touch of class the town needed. Jean-François Rodallec was already running a successful establishment with a good reputation when he decided to come to Guéret and to put all his know-how and knowledge of regional produce to good effect at *Le Coq en Pâte*. The result is a refined cuisine with good Limousin meat, *dodine* of guinea-fowl, potato pâté, gâteau creusois and sorbet for dessert. There's a weekday menu at €14 and also a range of menus €25–50. Once the house of a notary, this place retains a little starchiness but is very well presented and overall has a family feel. There's a terrace onto the garden where a fountain plays in good weather.

Sainte-Feyre

23000 (5km SE)

⊚ 🎿 |O| Restaurant Les Touristes

1 pl. de la Mairie; take the D942, towards Aubusson. It's in the village.
☎05.55.80.00.07
Closed *Sun evening; Mon; Wed evening; Jan.* **Disabled access. High chairs available.**

Tasty, classic local cooking prepared by Michel Roux and served in generous portions. There's a quiet atmosphere and the surroundings are lovely. You will get the measure of the excellent cooking from the menus: €17.50 (not Sun) and €26–45.50. The chef's specialities include fresh duck foie gras poached in spicy wine, fried Rossini-style sweetbreads, good local meat and skilfully prepared fish. A pleasant welcome but watch out for the upwardly revised prices! *Free coffee offered to our readers on presentation of this guide.*

Glénic

23380 (8km NE)

⊚ 🏠 |O| Le Moulin Noyé

Route de La Châtre, D 940; in the direction of La Châtre; on the left, 3km after the viaduct.
☎05.55.52.81.44 ℻05.55.52.81.94
🖥www.moulin-noye.com
Closed *Sun evening out of season.* **TV. High chairs available. Swimming pool. Car park.**

An excellent special menu option at €60 for two persons. We received lots of letters recommending this place. And our readers are right, the *Moulin Noyé* is certainly worth a visit. Dominique and his wife offer a warm welcome to their large dining room overlooking the Creuse gorge. It's a stunning sight. The rooms – €48.50–53.50, depending on standard and view – are bright and clean and named after artists; we preferred Bizet and Debussy. Half board is available for stays of three nights upwards: room and evening meal €59. Set menus (weekday lunchtimes) €14, and €24–55, feature local cuisine with handsome slices of meat, foie gras specialities, excellent salads and giant *crèmes brûlées*. Make sure you ask for a table with a view. There's also a terrace, a swimming pool, mountain bikes for rent and even a boat if you fancy a romantic trip on the river. As the name "Noyé" suggests, you're completely submerged out here but in a good way – deep in the countryside and spoilt for choice.

Jouillat

23220 (14km NE)

⊚ |O| L'Auberge du Château

9 pl. de l'Église; follow route de la Châtre, turn right when you get to Villevaleix and it's beside the church.
☎05.55.41.88.43
Closed *Sun evening; Mon.* **Disabled access.**

Don't expect one of those touristy olde-worlde inns that you often find in the neighbourhood of a château. *L'Auberge du Château* fulfils an important role in holding the local community together. There's a rustic dining room and a terrific paved garden at the back. Fresh, local produce predominates on the weekday lunchtime menu at €16, and on the single menu served on Sunday at €23. A la carte will cost about €20. When we stopped off there was *coq au vin* with oyster mushroom pastries and home-made dessert. And think about booking in advance because it's very popular locally.

Limoges

87000

See map overleaf

◎ ♨ Hôtel de Paris

5 cours Vergniaud. **Map C1-4**
☏05.55.77.56.96 ℗05.55.77.02.91
Open all year round. **TV.**

This old private residence has recently been given an excellent makeover transforming most of the rooms (they're not all finished yet so ask for one that is) into comfy, spacious accommodation. Double rooms are €28 with toilet, then €40–47; some have a balcony with a view over the Champ de Juillet and the station in the distance. There are some lovely, large, bright bathrooms, nos. 16 and 17 for example. A nice surprise, even though the welcome from the owner can leave something to be desired.

◎ 🍴 ♨ Hôtel de la Paix**

25 pl. Jourdan. **Map C2-2**
☏05.55.34.36.00 ℗05.55.32.37.06
Open all year round. **TV. Pay car park.**

Well located in the corner of a quiet square – and it's central. Between the entrance and the breakfast room there's a small museum displaying the owner's impressive collection of phonographs and mechanical music. The rooms are huge; they're well maintained, regularly redecorated and variously furnished – one has a fireplace, another a big bathroom. You couldn't call it luxury but there's an appealing retro style. It's reliable and offers good value for money: doubles €36–50 according to the facilities. *10% discount on the room rate offered to our readers on presentation of this guide.*

◎ 🍴 ♨ Hôtel Familia

18 rue du Gal-du-Bessol; take rue Théodore-Bac; it's in a quiet street near the station.
Map C1-1
☏05.55.77.51.40 ℗05.55.10.27.69
Open all year round. **TV.**

A pleasant spot just a short ten-minute walk away from the centre in a quiet street. Though the district has no great appeal, this modest establishment is a find. You get to the rooms across a pretty, shaded courtyard. They are simple, spacious, perfectly maintained and fairly priced: doubles with shower/wc €40. *One free breakfast per*

room or 10% discount on the room rate at the weekend offered to our readers on presentation of this guide.

◈ 🍴 ♨ Le Richelieu***

40 av. Baudin; near the town hall. **Map B3-3**
☏05.55.34.22.82 ℗05.55.34.35.36
🌐www.hotel-richelieu.com
Disabled access. TV. High chairs available. Pay car park.

A quiet three-star where there's a deep understanding of professionalism – matchless welcome, service and cleanliness. The rooms have everything you need, though the junior suites are a tad tight for space. The facilities are better than you might expect in a hotel such as this. There's an attractive breakfast room with a *trompe l'œil* painting. €85–95 for a double with shower/wc or bath is a tad expensive, however. Not the most economic of places but good of its type. *Free parking space offered to our readers on presentation of this guide.*

◎ ❙●❙ Le Pont Saint-Étienne

8 pl. de Compostelle. **Off map D3-16**
☏05.55.30.52.54
Open all year round.

Beautifully situated on the banks of the Vienne, with a terrace below the old part of town. The *Pont Saint-Étienne* offers a generous, inventive cuisine driven by a young team. Whether it's country cooking, something exotic or a light meal, there's something for everyone on their truly mouthwatering menus. Specialities include the "Admiral" (grilled fillet of mullet on a bed of small vegetables with Thai sauce), the "Porcenet" (sliced shoulder of pork *confit* and vegetable crumble) and the "Orchards of Camelas" (baked apricots with rosemary and almond-milk ice cream). Lunchtime menu costs €13.50 (except Sun) and other menus €14.50–33.30 (evenings and Sun). Wine is a bit pricey. This place can get very busy and the service can sometimes suffer. Make sure you book ahead (in fine weather ask for a table on the terrace).

◎ 🍴 ❙●❙ Les Petits Ventres

20 rue de la Boucherie. **Map B3-11**
☏05.55.34.22.90
Closed Sun; Mon; 1–15 May; 10–25 Sept.
High chairs and games available.

An attractive, half-timbered house with one of the best restaurants to be found in the old district of the town. Although *Petits Ventres*

12

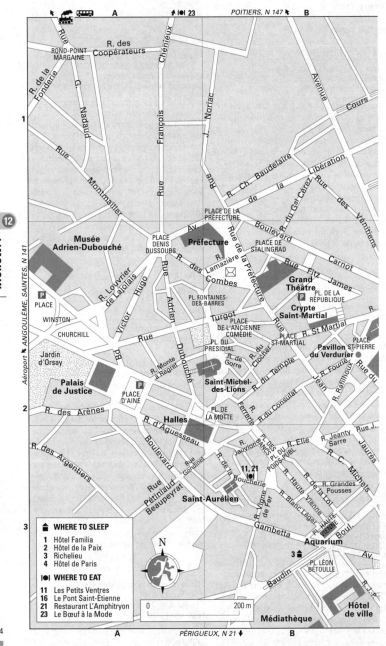

WHERE TO SLEEP

1. Hôtel Familia
2. Hôtel de la Paix
3. Richelieu
4. Hôtel de Paris

WHERE TO EAT

11. Les Petits Ventres
16. Le Pont Saint-Étienne
21. Restaurant L'Amphitryon
23. Le Bœuf à la Mode

0   200 m

POITIERS, N 147

PÉRIGUEUX, N 21

Aéroport, ANGOULÊME, SAINTES, N 141

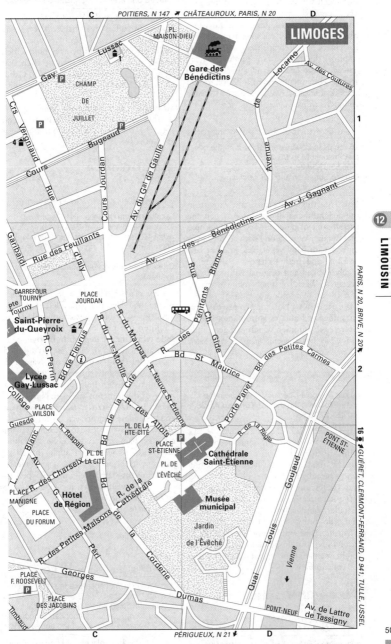

LIMOGES

PL. MAISON-DIEU

Lussac

Gare des Bénédictins

Gay

CHAMP

DE

JUILLET

Bugeaud

Cours

Rue

Crs. Vergniaud

Garibaldi

Cours Jourdan

Pisly

Rue des Feuillants

Av. du Gal de Gaulle

Av. des Bénédictins

Av. J. Gagnant

Lecarne

Av. des Coutures

de

Avenue

CARREFOUR TOURNY

Pte Tourny

PLACE JOURDAN

Saint-Pierre-du-Queyroix

R. G. Perrin

Bd de Fleurs

Lycée Gay-Lussac

Collège

Guesde

Blanc

R. du 71e Mobile

R. du Maupas

R. des Cités

R. Neuve St-Étienne

Bd de la Cité

R. des Allois

R. des Pénitents Blancs

Ch. Gide

Bd St Maurice

R. Porte Panet

Bd des Petites Carmes

PLACE WILSON

R. Raspail

PL. DE LA HTE-CITÉ

PLACE ST-ETIENNE

PL. DE LA CITÉ

R. des Charseix

PLACE MANIGNE

PLACE DU FORUM

G. Hôtel de Région

Bd

R. des Petites Maisons

Péri

R. de la Cathédrale

de la Corderie

PLACE ST-ETIENNE

PLACE DE L'ÉVÊCHÉ

Cathédrale Saint-Étienne

R. de la Règle

Musée municipal

Jardin de l'Évêché

Vienne

Gouyaud

Quai Louis

PONT ST-ÉTIENNE

PLACE F. ROOSEVELT

PLACE DES JACOBINS

Timbaud

Georges

Dumas

PONT-NEUF

Av. de Lattre de Tassigny

12

LIMOUSIN

PARIS, N 20, BRIVE, N 20 ↗

16 ⚒ ↗ GUÉRET, CLERMONT-FERRAND, D 941, TULLE, USSEL

means "little stomachs", you can forget the diet when you eat here: pan-fried foie gras, black sausage with mash, *andouillette* and tripe. If you like offal, this place is for you – one dish is a feast of calf's head, tongue and mesentery (a membrane that keeps the guts in place); the quality of the produce is guaranteed. Great desserts and attractive rustic setting, with menus at €17–32, or reckon on €25 à la carte. *Free house apéritif offered to our readers on presentation of this guide.*

⊚ 🏠 |●| Restaurant L'Amphitryon

26 rue de la Boucherie; not far from the covered market. **Map B3-21**
☎05.55.33.36.39
Closed *Sun; Mon and Sat lunchtimes; second fortnight in Aug.*

You'll find this quality restaurant across from the delightful chapel of Saint-Aurélien, the patron saint of butchers. Try the duck foie gras, tajine of pigeon with dates, roast pigeon with baby vegetables, roulé of langoustine and fresh tomatoes – they're all nicely cooked and original without being eccentric. Weekday lunch menu is priced at €18–22, then others at €26–35 or €40 à la carte – not a bad price to pay to eat in an authentic Limoges atmosphere. There's a terrace in summer, which can get a little noisy. *Free house apéritif offered to our readers on presentation of this guide.*

⊚ |●| Le Bœuf à la Mode

60 rue François-Chénieux; 150m from the centre, towards the theatre. **Off map A1-23**
☎05.55.77.73.95
Closed *Sat lunchtime; Sun; Aug.*

A restaurant with pleasant décor and white linen napkins, in a butcher's shop run by master butcher Claude Lebraud, who's proud of his trade. He's a real pro and knows how to choose his meat and serve it perfectly prepared: sirloin of beef in cider, *épigramme* of lamb (cooked on one side only) with honey and spices, Chateaubriand with bone marrow. À la carte only; you'll spend around €26. It might seem expensive but you get value for your money.

Aixe-sur-Vienne
87700 (13km SW)

⊚ |●| Auberge des Deux Ponts

Avenue du Général-de-Gaulle; on the N21; on the left before crossing the river.

☎05.55.70.10.22
Closed *Sun evening; Mon.* **Disabled access.**

On the banks of the Vienne, this pleasant restaurant offers reasonable prices. The décor is quite rustic and dominated by yellow, by flowers and by navy blue which suggests… the sea. No surprise then that there is plenty of seafood on offer. Other than that, there's a nice grill-bar with good meat cooked over wood, *magret* with a Roquefort sauce and grilled bream. There's a special weekday lunchtime menu for €10, then a choice of four menus at €14.50–30.

Saint-Gence
87510 (13km NW)

⊚ 🏠 |●| Le Moulin de Chevillou

Take the Route de Bellac (N147), turn left towards Nieul and Saint-Gence is only 3km away. Go through the village and turn right 300m further on. It's signposted.
☎05.55.75.86.13
Closed *Mon–Thurs (Oct–March).* **High chairs available.**

Lovely place hidden in a secluded valley beside the Glane, in a park filled with donkeys, goats, ponies, pheasants and doves. Children can play on the swings and the slide while their parents fish. Enjoy a pancake and a flagon of cider as you're lulled by the splashing sound of the watermill. In the restaurant, there's an impressive first menu at €15 (not served Sun) and a range of other menus €20–36. The second menu includes starter, fish course, main course, cheese and dessert; go for timbale of fresh goat with leek fondue, trout with country ham and ceps, saddle of rabbit with girolles, *douillon* of apple (baked in pastry) with blackberry jam. Service is efficient and the staff is delightful. It's best to book as it's well known locally. *Free house apéritif offered to our readers on presentation of this guide.*

Thouron
87140 (22km N)

⊚ 🏠 🏠 |●| La Pomme de Pin

Hameau de la Tricherie; take the N147, then turn right onto the D7.
☎ and ☎05.55.53.43.43
Closed *Mon; Tues lunchtime; Feb school holiday; 3 weeks in Sept.* **Disabled access. TV.**

One of the best places in Haute-Vienne, in an old mill in the forest near a small lake. Appealing dishes and delicious charcoal grills are cooked over the fire in a handsome dining room with stone walls. Weekday lunch menu goes for €16 with others €24–37. There's a remarkable list of excellent wines. On fine days you can eat outside on the terrace. The rooms are comfortable and very clean with views of the river; doubles with shower/wc €55, and with bath €65. *Free house apéritif offered to our readers on presentation of this guide.*

Magnac-Laval
87190

☕ 🎿 |●| La Ferme du Logis

Drive as far as Magnac-Laval, and in the centre turn right in the direction of Bellac; the restaurant is 2km along on the left-hand side, on the D7.
☎05.55.68.57.23
Closed *Sun evening except June–Oct; Mon lunchtime; early Jan to mid-Feb.* **Disabled access. High chairs and games available. Car park.**

A pleasant rustic setting with flowers in the dining room and a flower-filled terrace which is lovely in fine weather. Generous portions of tasty local dishes are served by accommodating staff; they specialize in beef and venison in season or *escalope* of foie gras with apples. Appetizing and satisfying menus range from €15.50 to €32. The wines are fairly priced, too. There's a pond nearby (free fishing for guests). There's space for ten in their luxury camping ground and mobile homes for hire. *Free house apéritif offered to our readers if you show this guide before your meal.*

Mortemart
87330

☕ 🏠 |●| Hôtel Le Relais*

☎and ☎05.55.68.12.09
Closed *Tues (except mid-July to end Aug); Wed; Feb.* **High chairs available.**

A pleasant and very attractive country hostelry in a beautiful village. There are a few pretty rooms; doubles €46 with shower/wc, and a stylish stone-walled dining room. Attentive service and plenty of flavour in dishes such as pan-fried foie gras with morel turnovers, duck breast with caramelized pears, roast lamb, etc,

with set menus €16.60 (except Sun) and €23–38.80. Logis de France.

Cieux
87520 (13km SE)

☕ 🎿 🏠 |●| Auberge La Source**

Avenue du Lac; take the D3 as far as Blond, then turn right for Cieux. It's in the village.
☎05.55.03.33.23 ☎05.55.03.26.88
📧awaldbauer@aol.com
Closed *Sun evening; Mon; Tues lunch; 20 Jan–11 Feb; 10 days in early Nov.* **Disabled access. TV. High chairs available. Car park.**

This old staging post stands at the entrance to this pretty little village. The charming owners are highly experienced and make you feel totally welcome. The restaurant is light and airy and the cuisine, which is classic in style, is confidently and meticulously cooked. There's a weekday lunch menu at €15 and others from €21–56. The fish is startlingly fresh and if you ask for your meat to be done in a particular way it will be cooked to perfection. The décor in the rooms doesn't have the same charm, though, and the bathrooms are rather impersonal. Even so there's lots of space and they're well maintained; doubles €56 with shower/wc and €70 bath. And, of course, there's that wonderful view. *Free house apéritif offered to our readers on presentation of this guide.*

Roussac
87140 (20km E)

☕ |●| La Fontaine Saint-Martial

12 rue de la Fontaine. Take the D5 to Berneuil, then towards Châteauponsac. It's in the village.
☎05.55.60.27.42
Closed *Wed evening.* **Disabled access. High chairs available.**

A very attractive bar-restaurant which also serves as a grocer's and tobacconist's. Marc Foussat, the modest young proprietor-chef, does a marvellous job. You can enjoy classic cooking and friendly professional service in the spick-and-span dining room or on the terrace. There are several menus, €10 (with wine and coffee) up to €18. Everything is good – from the simplest dish, the pavé of young stag Rossini, the carp mousse with sorrel, and including the home-made pastries. You'll find decent and inexpensive bottles on the short wine list. The bar is the meeting place for local football fans, so things really heat up on match nights. It's a convivial, relaxed place.

Neuvic

19160

⊛ 🏠 |●| 🌳 Château Le Mialaret**

It's 4km west of Neuvic, on the D991 in the direction of Égletons.
☎05.55.46.02.50 ℗05.55.46.02.65
ⓦ www.lemialaret.com
TV. Swimming pool. Car park.

This nineteenth-century château, set in a gorgeous park, has been turned into a modestly luxurious hotel with many of its original features. Some bedrooms are in the towers; the largest ones, which are superb, have monumental fireplaces. If you have the choice, pick no. 1, 2 ,4, 8 or 9. Their conference centre (built in the grounds and rather a blot on the landscape) brings in the bulk of the income, so they can charge modest prices: doubles €52–71.50 with full en-suite facilities. The dining room is impressive and the cooking is elegant, with menus €19.50–45. Hotel guests can use the tennis court. It's worth noting that the château also has a lovely tiled, spiral swimming pool – one of the most attractive in the area. There is also the possibility of camping and there are some chalets to rent. *Free house apéritif offered to our readers on presentation of this guide.*

Peyrat-le-Château

87470

⊛ 🌳 🏠 |●| Auberge du Bois de l'Étang**

38 av. de la Tour; take the D940 in the direction of Bourganeuf.
☎05.55.69.40.19 ℗05.55.69.42.93
ⓦ www.boisdeletang.com
Closed Sun evening and Mon (1 Oct–30 April); 20 Dec–31 Jan. **TV. Car park.**

An imposing building with an ivy-clad façade. The rooms are decent but the standard and situation are variable (those in the motel are best as they're quieter and have been refurbished); double rooms €46–54 depending on standard. There's a warm welcome from Serge who also mans the kitchen, producing good, local dishes: crayfish in pastry, fillet of young pigeon in garlic. The à la carte option is a bit expensive – we went for the menu at €23. Otherwise,

there's a cheap menu at €14, except Sunday lunchtime, then others €18–35. *10% on the room rate or free coffee offered to our readers on presentation of this guide.*

Nedde

87120 (10km SE)

⊛ 🏠 |●| Auberge Le Verrou

Le Bourg-Nedde.
☎05.55.69.98.04
ⓔ Brigitte.marvier@wanadoo.fr
Open *daily lunchtimes and evenings in summer; by reservation only out of season.*

A warm, atmospheric establishment with several dining rooms. One has a beautiful old counter where you can prop yourself up while you have an apéritif; another has a pancake corner, and in summer they open up a charming little terrace. It's very popular locally. The short menu offers dishes cooked with fresh market produce, good Limousin meat, a choice of salads and sweet or savoury pancakes. Expect to pay €20–25 for a meal à la carte according to what is available. There are a few pleasant rooms with shower/wc at €36–40. Breakfast, with home-made jam and pastries, costs €6. The owner has adapted this sturdy building to provide comfortable accommodation where you're assured of a good night's sleep. As in the restaurant, she's spared no expense on the decoration and there's a lot of attention to detail that makes all the difference: old furniture, old-fashioned, quality sheets, etc, etc. And needless to say, there's a friendly welcome. Credit cards not accepted.

Augne

87120 (12km SW)

⊛ 🏠 |●| Le Ranch des Lacs

Take the D14 towards Bujaleuf and go through Chassat. At the next junction go left towards Négrignas; just before the small group of houses take the little road to the left to Verville.
☎05.55.69.15.66 ℗05.55.69.59.52
Open *all year but telephone out of season.*
High chairs and games available.

An attractive establishment run by a Belgian couple. It used to be a riding school, and the walls and beams are decorated with old saddles. Nowadays it's a cross between a hotel and a hostel, with a bar-restaurant offering a €12 lunchtime *formule*, and menus from €16–32. They serve a big choice of

Belgian beers and a selection of national dishes such as *coffret du boulanger* (a loaf filled with scrambled eggs flavoured with herbs), *coucou de Malines* (chicken breast stuffed with chicory) and, if you order in advance, as many helpings of mussels and chips as you like. There are also some African specialities on offer as the owners once lived in the Congo. From the veranda you'll get a view of the unspoiled Vienne valley. If you want accommodation, they have a couple of doubles with bath from €34 and basic hostel rooms with three or four beds in each and communal washing facilities (€12.50 a head). Children, who are particularly welcome, have a special games area, with Playmobil and Lego, all to themselves.

Pontarion

23250

@ 🏠 |●| **Air du Temps**

2 rue du Thaurion (N 141); it's in the village. There's parking at the château (behind the restaurant).
☎05.55.64.98.78 📠05.55.64.98.77
Closed *Mon; Sun evening from early Sept to end of June.*

People really come here for the food, which is delicious and diverse: *quenelles* of pike, *émincé* (thin slivers) of pork, potato blinis, potted beef, crusty lamb, etc. Real food lovers should try the "Potence" (potatoes and beef), which is the house speciality and better discovered in the eating than the description. The cheapest menu (which includes a quarter litre of wine, and coffee) is €11, except Sundays and public holidays; other menus €16–23. The desserts are also excellent: terrine of Morello cherries, red fruit soup, chestnut pastry. No doubt about it – you can have a real feast here. And to help the food go down there's a pleasant walk along the River Thaurion below the château to a spot where you can fish or simply enjoy nature. The rooms, priced from €27, are nice and clean, but ask for one on the garden side.

Royère-de-Vassivière

23460

@ |●| **Les Saveurs Buissonnières**

Les Bordes; 6km from Royère, in the direction of Peyrat-le-Château; after 4km turn off to Les Bordes on the right; signposted in the hamlet.
☎05.55.64.93.17
Closed *Jan; Feb.* **Open** *daily except Mon and Tues from April to Sept (open Tues in summer); Fri evening to Sun evening in March, Nov and Dec.*

Agnès and Dominique take a simple approach: be natural, welcoming and provide quality. The beautiful old dining room only seats twenty (so it's essential to book). There are two set menus only, €13 weekday lunchtimes, or €18, plus a children's menu for €6.50. The weekly menu is set in advance, but is creative, subtle and carefully prepared using aromatic and wild plants from the garden, which you are also able to visit. All the food is pleasantly different: there's carrot tart, *borribout* (leg of duck with flageolet beans) and cabbage purée, accompanied by home-made organic bread. It's a genuine pleasure to eat here. Charge cards not accepted.

Saint-Goussaud

23430

@ |●| **Le Relais de Saint-Goussaud**

13km to the south of Bénévent-l'Abbaye via some small but pretty roads; go to Marsac and then Saint-Goussaud; it's opposite the church.
☎05.55.64.32.71
Closed *Sun evening and Mon in mid-season.* **Open** *daily in summer; Fri and Sat evenings only in winter.* **Disabled access. Swimming pool.**

It's not the easiest place to get to but it's certainly worth the trouble. It's hard to believe that such a small village in the middle of nowhere boasts one of the best restaurants in the region. It has everything: fast, friendly service, a view over the countryside (as far as Mont Dore in fine weather) from the dining room or the terrace, bonsai trees on the tables, little local sausages with your apéritif, a small garden with playthings for children and the impeccable and creative cuisine of Philippe Laboure: Limousin *cassoulet*, *pressé* of mussels with chorizo, ox cheek and home-made purée, foie gras with Rivesaltes wine, and home-made millefeuille pastry or a fine chocolate cream with pistachio for dessert. Menus start at €10 (weekday lunchtime), including a quarter litre of wine; then others at €15, €25 and €30 on Sundays, including apéritif, wine and coffee. There's also a children's menu for €7.50. This place is a real little gastronomic paradise so it's best to book in advance. The only downside is the radio playing in the background.

Saint-Junien

87200

@ 🎿 🏠 |O| Le Rendez-Vous des Chasseurs**

Lieu-dit Pont-à-la-Planche; on the way out of Saint-Junien on the Bellac road.
☎05.55.02.19.73 📠05.55.02.06.98
Restaurant closed *Fri; Sun evening.* **Closed** *a fortnight in Jan.* **Disabled access. TV. High chairs available. Car park.**

This place is renowned for its gourmet menu – but it's not as pricey as you might expect. There's a menu at €12 (not served on Sunday), a *menu terroir* at €17, and others up to €37. The dining room has all the charm of Vieille France and there's a terrace in summer. Well-maintained, newly refurbished doubles go for €32.50; half board €42.50 per person. Logis de France. *Free house apéritif offered to our readers on presentation of this guide.*

@ 🎿 🏠 |O| Le Relais de Comodoliac**

22 av. Sadi-Carnot.
☎05.55.02.27.26 📠05.55.02.68.79
🌐www.comodoliac.com
Restaurant closed *Sun evening from Nov to end Feb.* **Disabled access. TV. High chairs available. Car park.**

The building is modern but they've created a very pleasant feel to it. The rooms, €52-62 with shower or bath, are huge and well maintained; those at the back are quietest. The restaurant looks onto a little corner of greenery. The cooking is well prepared using the freshest ingredients, and the dishes change with the seasons: baked cod, poached eggs in jelly with tomato, Limousin *tournedos* and home-made desserts. Prices are fair and the quality above average for the region. There's a lunchtime *formule* at €10 and menus at €13.50-34.50. Ask for a table on the terrace. Logis de France. *Free house apéritif offered to our readers on presentation of this guide.*

@ 🎿 |O| Le Landais

6 bd. de la République.

☎05.55.02.12.07
Closed *Tues; 15–30 Sept.* **Disabled access.**

As soon as you cross the threshold, you sense you're going to be looked after. As you might expect from the name, Suzy, the owner, has created a little corner of the Landes in this part of Haute-Vienne. The restaurant adjoins the bar and it's easy to get comfortable. Honestly prepared dishes include a Landais *cassoulet*, scallops with ceps, *escalope* of duck liver with apples. A real treat for the wallet and the stomach; choice of menus €16–36, tasty salads around €10. A reliable place with quality service that has not disappointed our readers. *Free coffee offered to our readers on presentation of this guide.*

Saint-Léonard-de-Noblat

87400

@ 🎿 |O| Les Moulins de Noblat – L'Auberge de Mattre-Pierre

In the lower part of the town, in the direction of Limoges.
☎05.55.56.29.73

There are several water-mills, most of which date from the twelfth century. They make a harmonious group and have been restored in order to serve as gallery spaces for local art and crafts; one has been turned into an inn with a terrace on the bank of the Vienne. It's particularly lovely in fine weather, though the noise of the road is hard to ignore. Menus €14–38 feature fine, traditional cuisine with some good grills. It's also a hotel, and from June to September they organize giant barbecues. *Free house apéritif offered to our readers on presentation of this guide.*

Saint-Martin-la-Méanne

19320

@ 🎿 🏠 |O| Hôtel Les Voyageurs**

Place de la Mairie.
☎05.55.29.11.53 📠05.55.29.27.70
Closed *Sun evening and Mon out of season; from All Saints' Day to end Feb.* **TV. High chairs available.**

This typical Corrèze village house,

12

LIMOUSIN

surrounded by a small garden, has been turned into a family inn with lots of character and is a welcome surprise for passing visitors. You'll be hooked straight away by the delightful owner who offers you a table or a room as if you were part of the family. She's the fifth generation of hers to run this place. Local produce is much in evidence in the cooking, which includes such dishes as *magret de canard* with bilberries, Limousin veal, pike perch, trout, *fricassée* of frogs' legs and snails with parsley, and crêpe soufflé with orange for dessert. There are four set menus at €15–33. The rooms aren't particularly attractive but they're well maintained and well appointed; doubles with shower cost €39–50 depending on the facilities. *Free coffee offered to our readers on presentation of this guide.*

Saint-Merd-de-Lapleau

19320

@ 祎 🏠 |●| **Hôtel-restaurant Fabry****

Pont du Chambon; take the D13.
☎05.55.27.88.39
⊛www.rest-fabry.com
Closed *Sun evening and Mon out of season; mid-Nov to mid-Feb.* **TV. High chairs available. Car park.**

A substantial building in a magnificent setting on the banks of the Dordogne – a paradise for anglers and anyone who appreciates a view of the river from their bedroom window. Lots of sea- and freshwater fish on the menus (€16–36) including trout, char and pike perch. The eight rooms (doubles €38 to €40) are smart and prettily decorated; five have a river view. Half board is compulsory in high season at €41 per person. The family welcome and the magnificent setting is enough to keep you here. You can go for a trip on a *gabare* – the flat-bottomed boats that used to navigate the Dordogne. It's like being in the classic French film *La Rivière Espérance*. On a sadder note, you can walk to the Grotte des Maquisards where members of the Resistance were attacked and killed by the Vichy police during the World War II. *Free coffee offered to our readers on presentation of this guide.*

Saint-Pardoux-la-Croisille

19320

@ 祎 🏠 |●| **Hôtel-restaurant Beau Site*****

Take the D131.
☎05.55.27.79.44 ⓕ05.55.27.69.52
⊛www.hotel-lebeausite-correze.com
Restaurant closed *Tues and Wed lunchtimes (except for guests on half board).* **Closed** *1 Jan–25 April; 15 Oct–31 Dec.* **TV. High chairs, games and children's books available. Swimming pool. Car park.**

Hotel and leisure complex with a large garden, fishing pond, swimming pool, tennis courts and mountain bikes for hire – a place for people who like sporty holidays, good food and quiet comfortable surroundings. Doubles with shower/wc cost €59, or €63 with bath; the rooms lack soul but they're well maintained. Half board costs €49–65 per person. The country cooking in the restaurant is fine, for example, *parmentier* of house duck *confit*. Menus go for €14.50 (weekday lunchtimes) up to €43. If you like peace and quiet, check whether the hotel has any group bookings before you make yours. Logis de France. *Free house liqueur offered to our readers on presentation of this guide.*

Saint-Robert

19310

@ 祎 🏠 |●| **Le Saint-Robert**

Route d'Ayen.
☎05.55.25.58.09 ⓕ05.55.25.55.13
Closed *Sun evening and Mon out of season; Oct–March.* **TV. Games available. Swimming pool. Car park.**

A charming place that's as appealing for a family stay as it is for a romantic break. This lovely residence was built on a hillside on the border between Limousin and Périgord by a rich banker in the nineteenth century and boasts breath-taking views over the valley – enjoy them from the terrace, whilst eating breakfast or a meal, or from the swimming pool. The rooms have retained all their charm and style; doubles with shower/wc or bath €46–65, according to the level of comfort and season. The restaurant offers dishes using local produce

LIMOUSIN

and succulent meat with menus starting at €13 (weekday lunchtimes) up to €30. The whole place smells of polished wood and happy holidays. There are also two rooms with hydromassage. *10% discount per room for the first night (except 14 July– 25 Aug) offered to our readers on presentation of this guide.*

Saint-Yrieix-la-Perche
87500

◎ ☆ |●| Hostel de la Tour Blanche**

74 bd. de l'Hôtel-de-Ville.
☎05.55.75.18.17 ☎05.55.08.23.11
🅦www.resto-latourblanche.fr
Closed *Sat lunchtime; Sun evening; a fort-night in Feb.* **TV. Car park.**

The bedrooms are nice enough, and although those in the rafters are a bit cramped they're comfortable; doubles €42–50. You won't be disappointed by the restaurant. The first of the two dining rooms is the more traditional, serving terrine of fresh foie gras, good local meat, or snails stuffed with lardons of goose (menus €20–31.50). Lunchtime dish of the day is served from Monday to Friday at €9. The other is more like a snack bar: the cooking is simpler but still pleasant and you get big helpings. They do great salads and a dish of the day with vegetables.

◎ |●| ☆ Restaurant Le Plan d'Eau

Plan d'eau-d'Arfeuille; it's on the outskirts of town, head for the campsite.
☎05.55.75.96.84
Closed *Tues evening; Wed; from Christmas to end of Jan; a week around All Saints' Day.* **Disabled access. Car park.**

This is a very nice restaurant with a view of Lake Arfeuille. Proprietor Jean Maitraud always has time for a chat with his guests and prepares special menus for important dates. There's a lunchtime weekday menu at €8 and other menus €11–24. On Sunday it's à la carte only; reckon on €22. Traditional home cooking and local dishes including Limousin beef and veal, fillet of perch and *tarte tatin*. There's also the bistro option: a refreshing place to spend a hot afternoon with supervised swimming in summer. *Free soup offered to our readers on presentation of this guide.*

◎ |●| À La Bonne Cave

7 pl. de la Pierre-de-l'Homme; it's near the church.
☎05.55.75.02.12
Closed *Mon; Tues evening; a fortnight in Sept; a week in Oct.*

A pleasant restaurant in an old white stone buildling with a pleasant, flowery dining room decorated in pastel tones. The cooking is simple and good and has a few surprises (such as pig's ear cake), prices are reasonable and service comes with a smile. Weekday lunch *formule* costs €10, others €12–25 and a healthy eating option is also available; à la carte on Sundays. Dishes include snail profiteroles, veal *tourtière* with ceps and apple *croustade* with caramel sauce. They have some good bottles of wine, too. There's a pleasant little terrace.

Coussac-Bonneval
87500 (11km E)

◎ ☆ ☆ |●| Les Voyageurs **

21 av. du 11 Novembre; in the village, near the château, on the D901.
☎05.55.75.20.24 ☎05.55.75.28.90
Closed *Sun evening (except in summer); Wed; last fortnight in Jan; last fortnight in Nov.* **TV. High chairs available.**

This place has recently changed hands and has been given a fresher, younger feel. The new owners have decided to get things moving and to enhance the village's reputation by offering quality service: a friendly welcome, bright, refurbished rooms (€41–46 with bath), some with a view of the château and the little garden (ask for no. 8). Excellent cuisine using local produce is served in a beautiful, well-kept dining room. Menus start at €12.50 weekdays, then €20–37; set menu deal, including entry to the château, is €20 and €11 for children. There's a delicious Limousin salad, a "Cul-noir" dish using pork from the region's "black-bottomed" pigs, side of beef with a wine sauce and crunchy baked local potatoes – a real treat. *Free liqueur offered to our readers on presentation of this guide.*

Serre-de-Mestes (La)
19200

◎ |●| Bar-restaurant La Crémaillère

Take the D982.

☎05.55.72.34.74
Closed *evenings; Mon; last fortnight in June; first fortnight in Sept.* **Car park.**

Go through the bar to get to the restaurant, where you'll be welcomed by the friendly smile of the owner. The dining room is simply dinky with its red check tablecloths and wood panelling. It's the sort of place they just don't make any more – worth preserving and worth spreading the word. So that's what we're doing. The cooking is simple and generously served, with regional specialities such as foie gras, the excellent local meat, and terrific home-made fruit tarts for dessert. Weekday lunch menu is €11 and there's another for €22.10. This is a simple-looking place from the outside, but you'll certainly get your money's worth and excellent service.

Souterraine (La)
23300

@ 🏠 |●| **Hôtel-restaurant Jinjaud**

4 rue de Limoges.
☎ and ☎05.55.63.02.53
Closed *last week in Dec.*

A fine, well-kept hotel (the beautifully cared for parquet flooring says it all) which has just undergone some redevelopment (the lobby and small terrace in the courtyard). Rooms, €25–31 with or without bath, are decorated with flowers in pastel tones, which gives them a homely feel. The owner bends over backwards to make you happy so it's no surprise that the hotel also boasts the most pleasant restaurant in the area. Sample quality home cooking based on fresh produce on the set menu at €10, another at €12. There's an excellent potato pâté (order it the day before), Limousin faux filet and Creuse gâteau.

Saint-Étienne-de-Fursac
23290 (12km S)

@ 🏠 |●| **Hôtel Nougier★★**

2 pl. de l'Église. Take the D1 in the direction of Fursac. It's in the village.
☎05.55.63.60.56 ☎05.55.63.65.47
Closed *Sun evening, Mon and Tues lunchtime out of season and on public holidays; Mon and Tues lunchtimes in high season; Dec to mid-March.* **TV. High chairs available.**

Swimming pool. Car park.

A very appealing, typically Limousin country inn with twelve bedrooms, some looking onto the garden. Doubles go for €55–65; half board €50–58 per person. The elegant dining room serves local dishes updated for modern tastes: typical dishes include terrine of crayfish tails, duck thighs in mushroom sauce, and *croustillant* of pig's trotters. The prices seem a little high for what you get, though; menus €18 and €30, or reckon on €35 à la carte. There's a pretty terrace, swimming pool and table tennis table. Logis de France.

Bénévent l'Abbaye
23210 (20km SE)

@ 🍴 🏠 |●| **Hôtel du Cèdre★★**

Rue l'Oiseau. Take the D10. It's in the village on the road to Fursac.
☎05.55.81.59.99 ☎05.55.81.59.98
Closed *Fri, Sat lunchtime and Sun evening from March to May and end-Sept to end-Dec; Feb.* **Disabled access. TV. High chairs available. Swimming pool. Car park.**

A magnificent eighteenth-century building which has been carefully restored. The bright rooms are all different and have been decorated with great taste; the nicest have a view of the grounds, an ancient majestic cedar tree and the heated swimming pool. Doubles are €46–100, depending on the facilities, size and aspect; half board costs €66 per person. In summer the attractive terrace serves as the setting for the gourmet restaurant; menus €23–55. It's one of the most appealing places in the region. Logis de France. *Free coffee offered to our readers on presentation of this guide.*

Tarnac
19170

@ 🍴 🏠 |●| **Hôtel des Voyageurs★★**

☎05.55.95.53.12 ☎05.55.95.40.07
@www.hotel-voyageurs-correze.com
Closed *Sun evening and Mon (except July/Aug); Feb.* **TV. High chairs available.**

A huge stone house in the heart of the village near the church and the two commemorative oak trees planted by Sully. It's wonderfully maintained by the Deschamps: Madame runs the restaurant with an easy charm while her husband practises his culinary arts in the kitchen. He produces local dishes with a deep knowledge of the region and uses only the freshest produce – fish, Limousin beef, mushrooms in season. Try the calf's feet with ceps, the fillet of char with chive butter or the veal with girolles. Set menus start at €14 (not served Sun lunchtime) up to €27, and very reasonably priced à la carte dishes are on offer. The large, bright bedrooms upstairs are very pleasant and cost €43 with shower/wc or bath; half board costs €47.50 per person. This place, off the beaten track on the Millevaches plateau, offers excellent value for money in the restaurant and for accommodation. Logis de France. *Free coffee offered to our readers on presentation of this guide.*

Treignac
19260

◎ |●| La Flambée

At the top of the village, next to the *Intermarché* on the D16.
☎ 05.55.98.13.08
Closed *Wed and Thurs evenings.* **Open** *until 8.30pm.*

A small restaurant that was rather difficult to find, but it probably offers the best food in the village. And, with menus at €11–21, it's not expensive either, even à la carte. The rather rustic décor is enjoyed by regulars and the welcome is in keeping, but not stand-offish. The menus offer classic, well prepared dishes such as *confit*, trout with almonds and a recipe from the Sologne area: *andouillette au cul de Breuil.* Fish and meat are included on the second menu, and everything is bought fresh daily. Excellent desserts too. The kind of value for money we'd like to see more often.

Tulle
19000

◎ 🕅 🏠 |●| Hôtel du Bon Accueil*

8–10 rue Canton.
☎ and ℻ 05.55.26.70.57
Closed *Sat evening and Sun (except July/Aug); 22 Dec–12 Jan.* **TV.**

A welcoming hotel-restaurant in a quiet street that you probably wouldn't find

unless you knew about it. It's like a hotel in some novel or where Claude Chabrol could have shot a film. Behind the façade and the old arched windows there are several dining rooms, all packed out at lunchtime, where you can eat excellent duck or chicken *confits*, potato pies and, in season, cep omelettes. Set menus €12–22.50; the menu with two starters should satisfy even the most demanding appetites. The bedrooms are a bit dated but they're very clean – this place deserves its one star. Doubles cost €30–35 according to the facilities. *Free house apéritif offered to our readers on presentation of this guide.*

◎ 🏠 |●| La Toque Blanche**

28 rue Jean-Jaurès, pl. Martial-Brigouleix.
☎ 05.55.26.75.41 ℻ 05.55.20.93.95
Closed *Sun evening; Mon; 10 days end Feb to early March; a week end July to early Aug.* **TV.**

The welcome here is much more informal and relaxed than the smart dining room might lead you to expect. The food is excellent but you'd better be prepared to dig deep in your pocket to pay for it. You'll find classic cuisine which is wonderfully executed, generously served and attractively presented: boned pig's trotter, home-made foie gras and calf's head. Menus €21–54. For a decent price – €40 for a double – you can spend the night here in one of the rustic, old rooms with concealed bathroom; half board is €55 per person.

◎ 🕅 🏠 |●| Hôtel-restaurant de la Gare**

25 av. Winston-Churchill; it's opposite the station.
☎ 05.55.20.04.04 ℻ 05.55.20.15.87
✉ hotel.de.la.gare.tulle@wanadoo.fr
Closed *Sun evening in winter; 1–15 Sept.* **TV.**

A classic station hotel with a restaurant that's popular with the locals. The kitchen has a good reputation: the crayfish salad and duck fillet stuffed with morels are recommended. The cheapest menu costs €12 (not served Sun), with others €19.28–23.52. The rooms are comfortable and well soundproofed, though the decoration may not be to everyone's taste; doubles €48.79–51.30 with shower/wc or bath. *Free coffee offered to our readers on presentation of this guide.*

Lagarde-Enval

19150 (11km S)

⊛ ☎ |●| Le Central**

It's opposite the church.
Ⓣ05.55.27.16.12 ⒻN 05.55.27.13.79
Closed *Sat; Sun; first 3 weeks in Sept.* **TV.**

This large house, smothered in Virginia creeper, has been in the same family for four generations. It's across from the church and the pretty manor. Regional and gourmet dishes – cep omelette, Limousin *escalope* and duck *confit* – listed on the generous menus (€12 at lunch, except on Sun, and others at €16–23). You'd better go hungry before eating here, however, as it's really filling. Very clean, comfortable rooms go for €35. It's a pleasant establishment and the staff make sure you enjoy your stay. There are quite a few activities available in the surrounding area.

Gimel-les-Cascades

19800 (12km NE)

⊛ ☎ |●| L'Hostellerie de la Vallée**

ⓉN05.55.21.40.60 ⒻN05.55.21.38.74
Closed *20 Dec–20 Jan.* **TV. High chairs available.**

Crowds of people come to see the Gimel waterfalls, and since the sunny dining room in this charming hotel has a fine view of them and the terrace is idyllic for dining in warm weather, you'll need to book in summer. On the accommodation side, the beds are comfy, although the (refurbished) rooms can be a little cramped. Doubles go for €45–54 according to the facilities; some rooms (nos. 5, 6 and 7) have views of the valley. Good cuisine in the restaurant, with lots of local produce: meat from the Limousin and veal with morels. Menus range from €21 to €30; à la carte you'll spend around €25.

Quatre-Routes-d'Albussac (Les)

19380 (16km S)

⊛ 🎣 ☎ |●| Hôtel Roche de Vic**

Les Quatre-Routes; it's at the junction of the N921 and the D940.
ⓉN05.55.28.15.87 ⒻN 05.55.28.01.09
✉roche.voc@wanadoo.fr
Closed *Sun evening (Oct-Dec); Mon (except public holidays and in summer); early Jan to*

mid-March; a week in Oct. **Disabled access. TV. High chairs and games available. Swimming pool. Car park.**

This double hotel-restaurant is located at a crossroads in this amusingly named village, which is the crossing point for a number of roads. The large stone building is a 1950s-style manor with towers. Most of the bedrooms are at the back, overlooking the extensive grounds, the play area and the swimming pool and don't suffer too much from their roadside location. Doubles €36 with shower/wc and €45 with bath – most have been renovated and have telephones. Some still have a certain old-worldly charm – be sure to ask for one of these. Even on the cheapest menus the restaurant offers a large choice of regional dishes; weekday lunchtime *formule* for €12 and menus €15–35. Logis de France. *Free house apéritif (hotel guests only) offered to our readers on presentation of this guide.*

Corrèze

19800 (22km NE)

⊛ |●| 🎣 Le Pêcheur de Lune

Place de la Mairie; in the direction of Égletons; at Corrèze station take the D26 for 5km direction Égletons.
ⓉN05.55.21.44.93
Closed *Mon except in July and Aug; evenings during winter (except bookings).*

An atypical restaurant, where local dishes are served with a twist – the duck thigh is cooked with bilberries. The little set menu has made this place popular and the veal's head *à l'ancienne* and the *escalope* of milk veal with chanterelles are particularly delicious. There's a weekday *menu du jour* at €12 and others €21–30. *Free coffee offered to our readers on presentation of this guide.*

Chamboulive

19450 (24km N)

⊛ 🎣 ☎ |●| L'Auberge de la Vézère

Pont de Vernéjoux; take the D26 or the A20 exit 44 to Uzerche from Limoges or exit 45 from Brive.
ⓉN05.55.73.06.94 ⒻN05.55.73.07.05
Car park.

A charming riverside inn popular with local anglers. It's a good idea to book whatever the season as there are only seven charming bedrooms under the eaves; they cost €32 for a double with shower/wc. Half board costs €38 per person. On the ground floor there's a friendly, dimly lit bar with a *cantou* (inglenook fireplace) as its focal point, and also a bright, sunny dining room overlooking the river. Duck features prominently on the menus (as *civet, confit* and foie gras) but there's also good Limousin meat and trout. There's a €10 weekday lunch menu and two others at €15 and €22. You'll get a cheery welcome from the proprietress, and after your meal you can go for a quiet stroll along the banks of the beautiful River Vézère. *Free house apéritif offered to our readers on presentation of this guide.*

Turenne
19500

@ 🏠 |●| La Maison des Chanoines

Rue de l'Église; take the D38 then the D150.
☏ and ℻05.55.85.93.43
ⓦwww.maison-des-chanoines.com
Closed *Sun lunchtime; Mon; public holidays; mid-Oct to Easter.* **Open** *every evening except Wed during June.*

Turenne is a beautiful old town and this hotel, with its friendly, refined welcome, is quite delightful. You'll find it at the start of the lane that leads up to the church and the château built by the Knights Templar. The dining room has a vaulted ceiling, or you can eat under the awning on the lovely terrace. Imaginative cooking and nicely presented dishes:

escalope of foie gras marinated in truffle vinegar served with home-made walnut bread, milk veal "under the mother" with morels and lots of desserts with walnuts. *Menu-cartes* go for €30–36, and there's a truffle menu (to order). There are six comfortable, stylish bedrooms for €60–85; you'll need to book as they are quickly snapped up.

Uzerche
19140

@ |●| Chez Denise

8 rue Gabriel-Furnestin; via Place Marie-Collein (Barachaude gate); in a small street in the old part of town.
☏05.55.73.22.12
Closed *evenings out of season; 4 weeks in Jan–Feb.*

This bistro is run by Denise, with the help of the irreplaceable Francine, and they will welcome you in a friendly, genuine manner. It's not much to look at but the view from the narrow balcony overlooking the Vézère is truly lovely. And the food is excellent, from the cheapest menu upwards. Home cooking with several different menu options (€9–25) offering dishes such as Limousin platter, *confit*, meat of the day, etc. Or try the simple but delicious cep omelette (on the à la carte menu) accompanied by salad. With its view of the setting sun, it's also a great spot for an apéritif.

Lorraine

Abreschviller

57560

⊛ ⬆ |●| La Roche du Diable

182 route du Donon.
☎03.87.07.06.85 ✆03.87.07.06.92
Closed *Mon evening; Tues evening.*

Facing the forest, this large, ochre-coloured house is awash with flowers in the
spring and summer. Sandrine Stemart has
six stylish, comfortable rooms for guests at
€40, including breakfast, either overlooking the valley (nicer) or the forest. The
food is generous and locally inspired and
as warm and welcoming as the large oven
in the dining room where *andouillettes* and
other homely dishes are cooked. There's
a weekday lunchtime menu for €10; or
choose from the selection of dishes on
the board. Specialities include *piquade* and
berthelon. A real find, with a very friendly
welcome and attentive service.

Saint-Quirin

57560 (5km SW)

⊛ ⬆ |●| L'Hostellerie du Prieuré**

163 rue du Général-de-Gaulle; take the D96.
☎03.87.08.66.52 ✆03.87.08.66.49
Closed *Tues evening; Wed; Sat lunch; Feb
school holiday; All Saints' school holiday.*
**Disabled access. High chairs available. TV.
Car park.**

In the eighteenth century, the Church did
not have a reputation for modesty – witness the imposing sandstone priory which
now houses this restaurant. The cooking
is rich and inventive and has won the restaurant a "*Moselle Gourmande*" award – try
baeckeoffe of snails in white wine sauce,

fish *pot-au-feu*, roast squab, fresh cod with
tomato butter sauce and lime, grilled *escalope* of foie gras with Guignolet cherries.
There's a weekday lunch menu for €10.70,
with others at €20–52. A chef's menu for
€60 is served Sunday lunchtimes, booking required (two people minimum). You
could do worse than stay the night here,
too. The new rooms, in an annexe, have
modern bathrooms but lack the charm of
the restaurant. You'll pay €44 for doubles
with shower/wc or bath; half board €52.
No. 5 is very spacious and has a pretty balcony where you can eat breakfast.

Lutzelbourg

57820 (22km NE)

⊛ 🏊 ⬆ |●| Les Vosges**

149 rue Ackermann; take the RN4, the A4
and then the CD38.
☎03.87.25.30.09 ✆03.87.25.42.22
🌐www.hotelvosges.com
Restaurant closed *Wed; Sun evening.* **TV.
Pay car park.**

In a delightful village in the crook of the
pretty Zorn valley, this hotel is on the
bank of a small canal. The long-established family hotel has lost none of its
charm over the years. All the bedrooms
are furnished with antiques, and the
beds have lace eiderdowns. Doubles with
shower/wc go for €48; with bath €55.
The traditional dining room suits the
classic cooking; menus €18.50–29.50,
with a day menu at €10.20. During the
hunting season, try *sautéed* deer with
prunes, pheasant with a truffle *jus*, or
noisettes of wild boar with Pinot Noir.
Logis de France. Open terrace. *Free house
apéritif on presentation of this guide.*

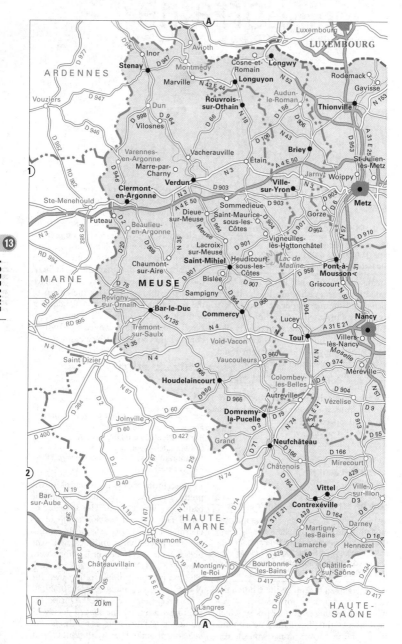

ARDENNES

Luxembourg
LUXEMBOURG

Inor
Avioth
Stenay
D 977
D 947
Montmédy
Cosne-et-Romain
Longwy
Marville
D 947
N 43 E 44
Longuyon
Rodemack
Vouziers
D 947
N 52
Gavisse
N 153
Dun
Rouvrois-sur-Othain
Audun-le-Roman
Thionville
D 998
D 964
N 18
D 156
D 506
A 31 E 25
Vilosnes
D 946
D 66
D 106
N 43
D 953
Varennes-en-Argonne
Vacherauville
Briey
St-Julien-lès-Metz
Marre-par-Charny
Étain
A 4 E 50
Jarny
Woippy
Verdun
N 3
Ville-sur-Yron
N 3
1
D 946
D 903
D 903
Clermont-en-Argonne
N 3
Sommedieue
D 903
Gorze
D 6
Metz
Ste-Menehould
A 4 E 50
Saint-Maurice-sous-les-Côtes
D 904
D 952
D 907
D 910
Futeau
Dieue-sur-Meuse
D 964
N 57
N 3
D 2
Beaulieu-en-Argonne
Vigneulles-lès-Hattonchâtel
Lacroix-sur-Meuse
RD 982
D 988
N 35
D 901
Lac de Madine
Pont-à-Mousson
RD 994
Chaumont-sur-Aire
Saint-Mihiel
Heudicourt-sous-les-Côtes
D 958
MARNE
MEUSE
Bislée
D 907
Griscourt
N 51
D 75
Sampigny
D 964
D 958
D 904
Revigny-sur-Ornain
Bar-le-Duc
Commercy
Lucey
Nancy
RD 982
N 135
D 904
A 31 E 21
Trémont-sur-Saulx
N 4
N 4
Toul
Villers-lès-Nancy
RD 995
N 35
Void-Vacon
N 74
Moselle
Saint Dizier
N 4
D 960
D 974
Méréville
Vaucouleurs
N 57
D 966
Colombey-les-Belles
D 4
D 904
Houdelaincourt
Autreville
Vézelise
D 9
N 67
D 960
D 966
Domremy-la-Pucelle
D 19
N 74
A 31 E 21
D 913
Joinville
D 384
D 2
D 60
D 3
D 55
D 400
D 427
Grand
D 71
Neufchâtel
D 166
2
D 2
D 25
Châtenois
Mirecourt
N 74
D 164
D 429
Bar-sur-Aube
N 19
N 40
N 74
Vittel
Ville-sur-Illon
D 396
N 19
D 74
Contrexéville
D 3
N 19
N 67
A 31 E 21
D 429
D 164
Darney
Chaumont
D 417
Martigny-les-Bains
D 164
Châteauvillain
N 19
D 429
D 460
Lamarche
Hennezel
D 434
D 85
Montigny-le-Roi
Bourbonne-les-Bains
Châtillon-sur-Saône
D 417
D 460
D 417
A 5 E 17
Langres
HAUTE-SAÔNE
HAUTE-MARNE

0   20 km

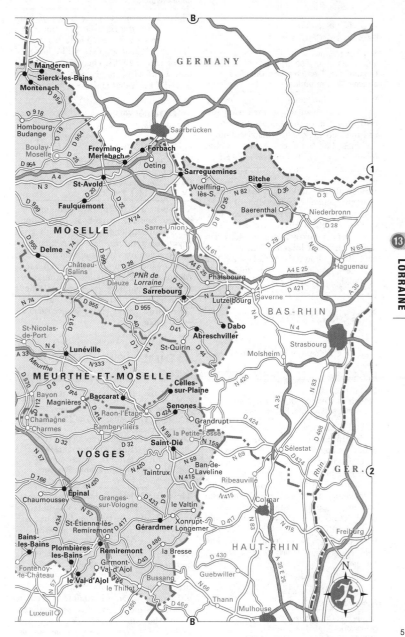

Phaskbourg

57370 (28km NE)

⬟ 🏠 |⦿| Hôtel-restaurant Erckmann-Chatrian***

14 place d'Armes.
☎03.87.24.31.33 ℻03.87.24.27.81
Closed Mon; Tues lunchtime. **Disabled access. TV. Car park.**

Restrained but opulent luxury in the heart of the town where Erckmann was born (one half of the nineteenth-century writing duo Erckmann-Chatrian known for their books on old Alsace). Stylish furniture and stylish food served by attentive, discreet and efficient staff. Charming rooms (nos. 16, 29 and 30 are more spacious with a small lounge area and view over the square) go for €53–61 for a double with bath/wc. Fine produce used to tasty, excellent effect in classic dishes (rich hors d'œuvre Erckmann-Chatrian style with a half lobster), with menus at €11.50–42; allow €50 for à la carte. The only low note is the rather austere €8 breakfast.

Baccarat

54120

⬟ 🎋 🏠 |⦿| Hôtel-restaurant de l'Agriculture

54 rue des Trois-Frères-Clément.
☎03.83.75.10.44
Closed Fri evening; Sat lunch; Sun evening. **High chairs available. Pay car park.**

Colourful window boxes and bright flowers adorn the façade of this irresistible country hotel. It's just outside the centre, with its famous glass museum, and is a perfect place to stop on a long hike through the Santois or the Mortagne valley. Simple rooms go for €32 with basin shower (wc on the landing). The convivial family atmosphere in the restaurant and menus, €13.50 (weekday lunchtimes) to €22, attracts a lot of local custom. *Free coffee offered to our readers on presentation of this guide.*

⬟ 🏠 |⦿| Hôtel-restaurant La Renaissance**

31 rue des Cristalleries; it's opposite the glassworks.
☎03.83.75.11.31 ℻03.83.75.21.09
ⓦwww.hotel-la-renaissance.com

Closed Fri and Sun evenings. **TV. High chairs available.**

This is a convenient place to stay if you want to visit the Baccarat glass museum. The rooms have been simply but tastefully refurbished; doubles with shower/wc or bath €49–61. The classic cooking uses fresh farm produce, with menus €16–37. Logis de France.

Magnières

54129 (15km W)

⬟ 🎋 |⦿| Le Wagon du Pré Fleury

Old station: take the D47 from Baccarat.
☎03.83.72.32.58
Closed Sun evening; Mon; 3 weeks Jan/Feb. **TV.**

This restaurant occupies a genuine old railway carriage, parked at the station of Magnières. The station is also the departure point for *fraisines*, which are like pedalos on rails, and which go for trips up and down the local branch lines. Menus €14–29.30; cooking is a mixture of French and foreign styles, and they sometimes host theme evenings. *Free coffee offered to our readers on presentation of this guide.*

Bains-les-Bains

88240

⬟ 🎋 🏠 |⦿| Hôtel de la Poste**

11 rue de Verdun; it's next to the spa.
☎03.29.36.31.01 ℻03.29.30.44.22
ⓦwww.hpost.com
Closed a week at the end of Oct; 15 Oct–1 April; 15 Dec–15 Jan. **Restaurant closed** evenings 15 Oct–1 April, except Mon and Sat. **TV. High chairs available. Pay car park.**

This establishment has a somewhat forbidding façade, but it's undoubtedly the best place in the area. There are fourteen attractive rooms at €38.30 with shower/wc or €41.80 with bath. The hotel has fifteen nicely refurbished bedrooms in a style both rustic and modern. A few of the rooms overlook the flower garden. The cuisine is traditional and can't be faulted. There's a €13.80 menu (weekday lunchtimes only); the other is €16.30. Logis de France. *10% discount on the room rate on presentation of this guide.*

Bar-le-Duc
55000

⊛ ⌂ |●|* Hôtel-restaurant Bertrand*

19 rue de l'Étoile; it's behind the train station, near the park of Marbeaumont.
☎03.29.79.02.97 🖷03.29.79.06.98
🕸www.hotel-bertrand.com
Restaurant closed Sun evening; Sat evening and Sun 14 July–15 Aug. **Disabled access. TV. Car park.**

A friendly, warm, no-frills one-star with a family atmosphere. There's a day menu at €9.50, but it's à la carte only on Saturday and Sunday. The rooms are ordinary but well maintained – those in the annexe opposite are more welcoming; doubles with shower/wc €40, with bath €43. Some rooms have a balcony over the garden. The gorgeous Parc Marbeaumont is just a couple of minutes away.

⊛ |●| Patati et Patata

9 rue Ernest Bradfer.
☎03.29.45.48.03
Closed Sun; bank holidays lunchtimes; Christmas school holiday.

Take a table in the superb, fresh, green terrace-garden on the banks of the Ornain. Lots of garnished and gratinéed dishes, many of them potato-based (hence the name of the restaurant), and salads served in this young, cool place where you can eat quickly, cheaply and late into the night. Weekday lunch menu is €10, except in high season; à la carte €15–20.

⊛ 🎄 |●| Grill-restaurant de la Tour

15 rue du Baile; from the Avenue du Château, in the upper town.
☎03.29.76.14.08
Closed Sat lunchtime; Sun; public holidays.

This sixteenth-century building is quite magnificent. You eat in a tiny room where they grill great andouillettes and black puddings over the open fire. The cooking, like the setting, is simple and authentic; weekday lunch menu €12, with another at €16.80, omelettes from €4.08. Specialities include house duck terrine, grilled meats, and tarte tatin. Dinner is served only until 8pm. *Free house apéritif offered to our readers on presentation of this guide.*

⊛ |●| À La Meuse Gourmande

1 rue François-de-Guise; in the upper part of town, at the foot of the clock tower.

☎03.29.79.28.40
Closed Sun evening; Wed; 15 Feb–15 March; 10 days at the end of Aug; mid-Feb to mid-March and ten days at the end of Aug.

At the end of the little garden, behind the gate, stands this superb Renaissance building with a light-filled dining room and refined kitchen overlooking the town. Dishes reflect the Meuse's culinary reputation in a register of subtle flavours: terrine of duck foie gras and Morello cherry chutney, fillet of roast bass with lovage sauce, *persillé* of pullet and preserved vegetables in mustard cream sauce – a symphony of food from the chef and a friendly, welcoming smile. Weekday business lunches go for €14; then there's a "Gourmand" menu €24, "Symphonie" menu €46 (€37 with two dishes less). Allow €40 for à la carte. It's a highly regarded restaurant, so best to book in advance.

Chaumont-sur-Aire
55260 (20km N)

⊛ ⌂ |●| Auberge du Moulin Haut

Take the N35 then the D902.
☎03.29.70.66.46 🖷03.29.70.60.75
🕸www.moulinhaut.fr
Closed Sun evening; Mon; first fortnight in March. **Disabled access. TV. High chairs available. Car park.**

The wheel of this eighteenth-century mill turns gently to supply electricity to the restaurant, and the noise is masked by the tinkling of a 1910 pianola. It's a peaceful and delightful place, run by a welcoming couple who have travelled widely in Africa, and the cuisine is balanced and full of flavour. The weekday lunch menu costs €15 and there are six others from €25 to €90, variously featuring duck specialities, regional dishes and, at the top of the scale, a gastronomic menu. Keep some space for dessert, especially the *croustillant flambé* of mirabelle plums. There are two simple but comfortable double rooms in a charming annexe, costing €45 with shower/wc or bath. Breakfast is €6; half board €67 for one person, €103 for two.

Bitche
57230

⊛ ⌂ |●| Hôtel-Pension de la Gare

2 av. Trumelet-Faber; it's near the station, 800m from the centre.

☎and 🖷03.87.96.00.14
Closed *Sat; Sun; a fortnight in Aug; last 2 weeks in Dec; first week in Jan.* **Car park.**

This is the only cheap hotel in town, and though the rooms (€25 with shower) are modest they're very clean. The *patronne* is so kind that you won't notice the slightly fading décor; sometimes the guests even lend a hand behind the bar. You'll eat unpretentious country cooking with a weekday set menu at €8.50; half board is €24 per person. It's advisable to book early.

☜ 🍴 |●| L'Auberge de la Tour

3 rue de la Gare; it's close to the Vauban citadel, near the station.
☎03.87.96.29.25
Closed *Mon; Tues evening; Feb school holiday.* **High chairs available. Car park.**

Atmospheric and cosy with its Belle Époque décor, this place has a popular brasserie atmosphere; the local paper, the *Républicain Lorrain*, lies about on the tables, and locals talk politics while they drink and eat. There's a weekday menu for €11.50, and others from €18–51; reckon €20–30 à la carte. Interesting food combinations include tomato and mozzarella tart with *pistou* and pike perch. Try the home-made sorbets for dessert. *Free coffee offered to our readers on presentation of this guide.*

Baerenthal
57230 (20km SE)

☜ 🍴 🏠 Le Kirchberg**

8 rue de la Fôret; take the N62 and when you get to Bannstein take the little road on the right.
☎03.87.98.97.70 🖷03.87.98.97.91
🖳www.le-kirchberg.com
Closed *Jan.* **Disabled access. TV. High chairs available. Car park.**

This unpretentious hotel is in a modern, very quiet building where it's easy to get a good night's sleep. Double rooms go for €50–58 with shower or €62 with bath; even the smallest are spacious and comfortable. They have family rooms with two communicating rooms at €75. They also have studios sleeping two or four that they rent by the week or weekend. To eat, try *Le Raisin*, 50m down the road. *5% discount on a stay of three consecutive nights on presentation of this guide.*

Briey
54150

☜ 🏠 |●| 🍴 Hôtel Ancona**

63 rue de Metz; in Briey-Bas near the bridge.
☎03.82.46.21.00 🖷03.82.20.29.85
TV. High chairs available.

Benefiting from its efficient double glazing, which effectively blocks out the passing traffic noise, this place offers comfortable rooms that are modestly priced at €43–59 with shower/wc or bath. The very friendly welcome makes it a pleasure to stay here. Decent, traditional food is served in the restaurant; menus €12 (weekday lunchtimes) up to €31. *Free house apéritif offered to our readers on presentation of this guide.*

☜ 🍴 🏠 |●| Hôtel Aster**

Rue de l'Europe; take the A4 Jarny exit, then the N103 as far as Briey-Bas; by Sangsue lake.
☎03.82.46.66.94 🖷03.82.20.91.76
🖂spitoni@wanadoo.fr
Disabled access. TV. High chairs available. Car park.

A large, modern block that bears no resemblance to that charming inn you could be looking for. But the modern and comfortable rooms, at €57 with shower or shower/wc, are bright and sunny and the surrounding greenery is appealing. The remains of the old town walls are just opposite. There are menus for €12 (weekday lunchtimes) and €22–31; try the steak tartare. *Free house apéritif offered to our readers on presentation of this guide.*

Celles-sur-Plaine
88110

☜ 🍴 🏠 |●| Hôtel des Lacs**

2 place de l'Église; it's opposite the campsite.
☎03.29.41.17.06 🖷03.29.41.18.21
🖂hotel-des-lacs@netcourier.com
Closed *Tues Oct–May; Sun evening except July–Aug; 23 Dec–26 Jan.* **Disabled access. TV. High chairs available.**

A good old-fashioned country hotel, entirely refurbished but still full of character, with a warm family atmosphere and friendly welcome. In the entrance, the piano and old furnishings immediately create a homely atmosphere. None of the fifteen rooms has a view over the lake but they are nonetheless really nice and comfortable, and cost €45 with shower/wc or bath. Good cooking in the restaurant, where choices change frequently, and prices are reasonable; menus €16–35. The dining room has kept its 1940s feel. Try the snails in flaky pastry with ceps if they're listed. Logis de France. *Free coffee offered to our readers on presentation of this guide.*

Clermont-en-Argonne

55120

@ 🎋 ♨ |●| Hôtel-restaurant Bellevue**

14 rue de la Libération; N3, A4 motorway.
☎03.29.87.41.02 ℻03.29.88.46.01
✉hotel.bellevue.jpc@wanadoo.fr
Closed *Sun evening and Wed; 23 Dec–6 Jan.*
TV. High chairs available. Car park.

Guest rooms are functional and anonymous but the façade and the dining room are ravishing. The dining room, which retains all its original Art Deco features from 1923, leads onto a balcony overlooking the garden and the countryside. The cooking is simple, and portions are generous: in season they offer game dishes such as navarin of wild boar with *fricassée* of wild mushrooms. Other specialities include salad of rabbit liver, crayfish tails with whisky and calves' kidneys with violet mustard. The €14 menu is served daily except for Sunday, and there are others at €24 and €36. There are seven rooms, ranging from €48 with shower/wc to €52 with bath. Peace and quiet are guaranteed, especially in the rooms at the back. Logis de France. *Free house apéritif offered to our readers on presentation of this guide.*

Futeau

55120 (10km SW)

@ ♨ |●| Hôtel-restaurant L'Orée du Bois***

Take the N3; at Islettes, turn left (south) onto the D2 and it's on the left, 500m beyond Futeau.
☎03.29.88.28.41 ℻03.29.88.24.52
✉www.aloreedubois.fr
Closed *Mon and Tues lunchtimes in season; Mon and Tues (Nov–March); from last week in Nov to end of Jan.* **Disabled access. TV. High chairs available. Car park.**

This place, with its friendly and enthusiastic staff, is set on the edge of a wood,

so you'll sleep well. The fifteen large bedrooms all have en-suite bathrooms and are all nicely decorated; doubles go for €75–120; half board €83–110 per person. Some rooms even have a Jacuzzi and the newest ones, in the old barn, are even more of a treat. They serve a weekday menu at €20 and others from €25–65. The local pigeon is particularly good, so are the foie gras, game and wild mushrooms. The *patronne* has two passions – cheese and wine – and there's a good selection of fine cheeses and vintages to choose from. Logis de France.

Commercy

55200

@ ♨ |●| Hôtel-restaurant Côté Jardin***

40 rue de Saint-Mihiel; take the D964 in the direction of Verdun.
☎03.29.92.09.09 ℻03.29.92.09.10
✉www.hotelcommercy.com
Closed *Fri and Sun evenings.* **Open** *(booking required) 7.30pm–8.30pm and Sun lunch.*
Disabled access. TV. High chairs and games available. Car park.

An elegant establishment on the outskirts of town, restrained luxury aimed at comfort, tranquillity (you forget how close you are to the street) and customer service. A plush, modern décor with charming, air-conditioned rooms and Internet access; double rooms with shower/wc or bath are €62–80. Some rooms have massage baths and some on the garden side have a balcony; half board €87–108. An airy restaurant rotunda offering tasty, inventive dishes; "hotel" menu €18–20 and another menu €40. Reckon on €55 for à la carte. The Mirabelle menu focuses on fruit from apéritif to dessert. Other specialities to delight the region's food-lovers include foie gras and pike perch with brie de Meuse.

Sampigny

55300 (12kmSE)

@ |●| L'Atelier

13 rue Raymond-Poincaré; take the D964, turn right at the entrance to the village.
☎03.29.90.75.15
Closed *Mon.*

A bar-cum-restaurant-cum-exhibition space-cum-music venue-cum-antique and curiosity shop. And all this in the former stables of the château of Henriette of Lorraine. The friendly restaurant if full of antiques, enamel plaques, old crockery, with music and a bar offering foreign beers (the Belgian beers are best). A nice off-the-wall, switched-on place for a drink on the terrace, for antique-hunting or sampling their speciality: frog pie with morels (legs de-boned); in fact Sampigny is the only village where hunting for frogs all year round is legally allowed. Dish of the day is €8; menu €12; excellent salads €6–8.

Contrexéville

88140

@ ⅗ 🏠 |●| Hôtel de Lorraine*

122 av. du Roi-Stanislas; it's near the train station.
☏03.29.08.04.24 ⓕ03.29.08.09.63
Closed *13 Oct–31 March.* **High chairs and games available.**

A big, pleasant old place with some style. The cooking is traditional, though special diets can be catered for. Set menus start at €12 (except Sun lunch) and rise to €16 and €22 – the last features Lorraine specialities. Try for example the frogs' legs and snails in pastry. Simple but well-maintained rooms go for €30 with washing facilities and €35 with shower/wc or bath. The hotel has an authentic spa town atmosphere and offers a really friendly welcome. *Free coffee offered to our readers on presentation of this guide.*

@ ⅗ 🏠 |●| Hôtel des Sources**

Rue Ziwer-Pacha; it's opposite the town hall.
☏03.29.08.04.48 ⓕ03.29.08.63.01
ⓔschbach@wanadoo.fr
Closed *10 Oct–15 March.* **Disabled access. TV. High chairs and cots available. Pay car park.**

An elegant building very close to the esplanade with its colourful fountains. The atmosphere is just what you'd expect in a spa, with guests playing Scrabble or cards. The rooms are comfortable and have been decorated with care. On the third floor they've got a few attic rooms with basin for €35–41 depending on the season; otherwise doubles with shower/wc or bath cost €45-55. The restaurant isn't bad at all, with set menus at €12 (not Sun) and €16–25. Special diets can

be catered for. Specialities include snail flan and fillet of pike perch with morels and a watercress *coulis*. Logis de France. *7% discount on the final bill on presentation of this guide.*

@ ⅗ 🏠 |●| Villa Beauséjour**

204 rue Ziwer-Pacha.
☏03.29.08.04.89 ⓕ03.29.08.62.28
ⓦwww.villa-beausejour.com
Closed *mid-Oct to Easter.* **TV. Games available.**

A charming hotel with a cosy salon and reception area offering a very friendly welcome and rooms that are individually decorated and furnished with period pieces and old mirrors. Those at the back or looking over the tranquil garden are the nicest; doubles with basin/wc €41, with shower/wc €45–49. The restaurant provides good food, diet or not, with a range of menus €19–35. *Free digestif offered to our readers on presentation of this guide.*

@ 🏠 Hôtel de la Souveraine***

Parc thermal.
☏03.29.08.09.59 ⓕ03.29.08.16.39
ⓦwww.souveraine-hotel.com
Car park. TV.

This elegant building, which used to be the residence of the Duchess Wladimir, aunt of Nicolas II, the last Russian tsar, looks onto the spa's park. Beautifully renovated rooms, though they've kept most of the old panelling, wooden floor and antique furniture. The prices are reasonable with rooms around €67 with shower/wc or bath. There's no restaurant.

Dabo

57850

@ |●| Restaurant Zollstock

11 route Zollstock, La Hoube; it's 6km from Dabo on the D45.
☏03.87.08.80.65
Closed *Mon; Thurs evening; end June to early July; Christmas to New Year.* **High chairs available. Disabled access.**

Looking across a forested valley, this peaceful restaurant doesn't get much passing trade, and most of the customers are regulars. There's a weekday menu for €9 and three others from €14.80 to €19.50, listing simple but tasty specialities. Plump for venison haunch and fresh charcuterie in season or salmon in champagne sauce and, for dinner, frogs' legs, and *mignon* of veal with morels. It's small and extremely pleasant with an appealing family atmosphere, and is especially popular for Sunday lunch.

Delme

57590

@ 🍴 🏠 |●| Hôtel-restaurant à la XIIe Borne**

6 place de la République.
☎03.87.01.30.18 ℗03.87.01.38.39
Ⓦwww.12eme-borne.com
Disabled access. TV. High chairs available. Pay car park.

Delme was once a Roman encampment at the twelfth marker or *borne* on the road from Metz to Strasbourg – hence the establishment's name. The hotel has been refurbished and rooms cost €47-66 with shower/wc or bath. There's also a sauna, free for all guests. Menus go for €12 (weekday lunchtimes) and €18–40; choose from dishes such as calf kidneys in pepper crust and its own gravy, calf sweetbread pastry with young morels, gilthead bream in a salt crust flavoured with rosemary, and bergamot orange ice soufflé. There's a good list of local wines. You will find a shop where you can buy local produce and for those who like to soak up the local atmosphere, a bistro open in the evenings with its own little terrace. Logis de France. *Free house apéritif offered to our readers on presentation of this guide.*

Domrémy-la-Pucelle

88630

@ 🏠 Hôtel Jeanne d'Arc

1 rue Principale; it's next to the church.
☎03.29.06.96.06
Closed 15 Nov–1 April. **Car park.**

A welcoming little hotel with seven rooms, very near St Joan's house. Little has changed over the years, and that includes the prices: you'll pay €25 for a quiet, plain but clean double with shower/wc. Breakfast, €4, is brought to your room. Credit cards not accepted, and pets are not allowed.

Autreville

88300 (14km NE)

@ 🍴 🏠 |●| Hôtel Relais Rose**

24 rue de Neufchâteau; take the D19 then the N74.
☎03.83.52.04.98 ℗03.83.52.06.03
Ⓔcatherine.loeffler@wanadoo.fr
Disabled access. TV. Car park. High chairs available.

The hotel, right on the main road, is not an obvious place to stop, but it's worth it. Over the last two generations, it's been a favourite stop for many holiday-makers on their way south. Inside it's a charming old family house with lovely rooms; some (like "Pivoine" or "Dahlia") have balconies or views over the garden and the countryside beyond. With bath or shower they go for €43–69. The weekday lunch menu costs €11.50 and there are others at €22–29. *10% discount on the room rate for a minimum stay of two consecutive nights or free house apéritif on presentation of this guide.*

Épinal

88000

@ 🍴 🏠 Hôtel Kyriad**

12 avenue du Général-de-Gaulle; it's opposite the train station.
☎03.29.82.10.74 ℗03.29.35.35.14
Ⓔhotel-kyriad-epinal@wanadoo.fr
Closed 23 Dec–1 Jan. **TV. Pay car park.**

The hotel is part of a chain and is located in a dull neighbourhood, but it has the charm of a family-run station hotel where they make you feel very welcome. They've put in soundproofing, which is essential to block out the noise of the road and passing trains, and there's a bar. Doubles with shower/wc or with bath are good value for money at €59; there are also three air-conditioned suites for €80. *10% discount on the room rate (Fri, Sat and Sun) offered to our readers on presentation of this guide.*

@ |●| 🍴 Restaurant Le Pinaudré

10 av. du Général-de-Gaulle; it's opposite the train station.
☎03.29.82.45.29
Closed Sat lunchtime; Sun; a fortnight in Aug; a week at Christmas.

Good welcome and good service at this discreet restaurant that's easy to miss. The large, attractive dining room has been done up to look like a modern bistro, and the cooking is traditional with a few modern touches. There's an excellent weekday lunchtime menu at €12, and others at €15–27. Fish and seafood predominate, both on the menus and à la carte, but you'll find a few local dishes too on the menu. *Free coffee offered to our readers on presentation of this guide.*

◎ 🎴 |◉| Restaurant Les Fines Herbes

15 rue La Maix; it's near place des Vosges.
☎03.29.31.46.70
Closed *Sun evenings; Mon; first fortnight in Sept.* **Open** *until 10pm.*

The décor is streamlined and modern while managing to feel intimate, and the refined cooking is served with care and attention in a modern dining room. Menus change every month and are reasonably priced; the lunchtime menu costs €13, with others €18–28. There are a lot of fish dishes on the menus and à la carte. *Free house apéritif offered to our readers on presentation of this guide.*

◎ |◉| Le Petit Robinson

24 rue Raymond-Poincaré.
☎03.29.34.23.51
Closed *Sat lunch; Sun; mid-July to mid-August; 24 Dec–2 Jan.*

A classic restaurant, with a friendly welcome, offering traditional French cuisine on menus at €19–35. The classic décor – all wood panelling and light colours – is warm and welcoming.

Chaumousey
88390 (10km W)

🎴 |◉| Le Calmosien

37 rue d'Épinal; take the N460 in the direction of Darney.
☎03.29.66.80.77
🌐www.vosgeshotels.com/calmsien
Closed *Sun evening; Mon; last 2 weeks in July.* **High chairs available. Car park.**

From the outside you might mistake this place for a country station, but inside the dining room is elegant and contemporary. In the summer they set a few tables out in the garden. The imaginative chef comes up with classic cuisine and a few local dishes that change regularly; menus €19–49. There's a great wine list, with a

few pleasant surprises. Since it has such an excellent reputation locally it's best to book. *Free house apéritif offered to our readers on presentation of this guide.*

Faulquemont
57380

◎ 🏨 Hôtel Le Châtelain**

1 place Monroë.
☎03.87.90.70.80 ☎03.87.90.74.78
🌐www.hotel-lechatelain.com
Disabled access. TV. Car park.

There were still cows here in 1980… The old farmhouse with its austere exterior now offers 25 modern, comfortable rooms at €52 with shower/wc or bath. Rooms in the old loft overlook the peaceful village square or are arranged on a two-floor mezzanine around the old poultry house, now a light well and winter garden filled with plants. Decorated in blue or pink (those on the second floor are smaller), the rooms are spacious and impeccably clean and fresh. No restaurant, but the hotel has arrangements with three local establishments.

Forbach
57600

◎ 🏨 Hôtel Le Pigeon Blanc

42 rue Nationale.
☎and ☎03.87.85.23.05
Closed *Sun.* **Disabled access. TV. Car park.**

This establishment is one of the best unstarred hotels in the area – the rooms in the annexe, which are very spacious and quiet, are particularly good. Doubles range from €16 with basin to €19 with shower/wc and €30 with shower/wc; TV available in the annexe bedrooms only. There's no restaurant.

◎ 🎴 🏨 Hôtel de la Poste**

57 rue Nationale.
☎03.87.85.08.80 ☎03.87.85.91.91
TV. Car park.

This is the oldest hotel in Forbach and it's been providing decent accommodation for a hundred years. Rooms have been fully renovated and decorated in blue, yellow or pink depending which floor they're on; doubles with basin €28, with shower/wc or bath €43. It's set back from the street so you won't be disturbed by noise. *10% discount on the room rate in July and August or one free breakfast per room on presentation of this guide.*

Oeting
57600 (2km S)

⊚ 🅐 |○| **Restaurant À l'Étang**

386 rue de Forbach; at Oeting church, sign-posted as far as the no through road.
☏03.87.87.33.85
Closed *Sun evening; Tues evening; Wed; mid-Aug.* **High chairs available.**

A restaurant in a big, pleasant house with country-style décor and a little pond. The weekday lunch menu, €10, and others, from €20–42, change according to the seasons. Specialities include fish – cod in sweet paprika crust and skin-on mullet. There's a shady terrace by the pond. *Free coffee offered to our readers on presentation of this guide.*

Freyming-Merlebach
57800

⊚ |○| **Sainte-Barbe**

25 rue de Metz; it's on the edge of town on the way to Metz, opposite the unmissable Houillères du Bassin Lorrain building.
☏03.87.81.24.24
Closed *Sat and Sun evenings; 15–30 June.*
Disabled access.

A good local restaurant that's ideal if you want a quick midday meal. Business workers pile into the big, old-fashioned – not to say kitsch – dining room at lunchtime, when they can enjoy huge helpings of hearty family cuisine; menus €10–22. Service is cheery.

Gérardmer
88400

⊚ 🅐 🏠 |○| **Aux P'tits Boulas***

4 place du Tilleul.
☏03.29.27.10.06 ℗03.29.27.11.91
🌐www.auxptitsboulas.wml.fr
Closed *Wed evenings; Thurs; fortnight in March; 3 weeks during the autumn school holiday.* **TV. High chairs available.**

A charming family hotel with four bright, nicely refurbished and well-maintained

but small double rooms at €30 with basin, €44 with shower/wc; half board €37 per person. Only three bedrooms (including our favourite no. 5) have a shower. Menus, €11 (except Sun) and €14, served in the restaurant provide good local dishes including sirloin steak with Munster cheese sauce, trout in Riesling, flambéed mirabelle plums and so on. *Free house apéritif offered to our readers on presentation of this guide.*

⊚ 🅐 🏠 **Hôtel de Paris****

13 rue François-Mitterrand.
☏03.29.63.10.66 ℗03.29.63.16.47
Closed *first week of March; first week of Nov.*
TV. Games available. Car park.

A very simple little hotel located in the ski resort's busiest street. It's not a luxurious place, but the rooms are reasonably priced; doubles go from €32 with basin, €41 with shower/wc or bath/wc. The ones overlooking the interior courtyard are the quietest. The hotel fills up at the weekend so you should secure your room by sending a deposit. There's a separate brasserie on the ground floor, and a lively bar with a large selection of beers. *10% discount on the room rate on presentation of this guide.*

⊚ 🅐 🏠 |○| **Hôtel Viry – Restaurant L'Aubergade**

Place des Déportés; 200m from the lake and the city-centre.
☏03.29.63.02.41 ℗03.29.63.14.03
🌐www.gerardmer.net/hotel-viry
Restaurant closed *Fri evening out of season.*
TV. High chairs available. Car park.

The hotel has been around for a good forty years, so it's almost an institution in its own right. The rooms which have been recently refurbished are small but nice; they cost €40–44 for a double with basin, €49–60 with shower/wc or bath and satellite TV. Half board, recommended in high season and on holiday weekends, costs €50–55 per person. The rustic-looking dining room offers particularly good value, and in summer you can eat on a covered terrace on the square. They serve sound regional cuisine with a decent *menu du marché* at €12.50 and others up to €39. The friendly welcome and courteous service are the order of the day. *Free house apéritif offered to our readers on presentation of this guide.*

ⓦ 🎿 🏠 Hôtel Gérard d'Alsace**

14 rue du 152e R.I.
☎ 03.29.63.02.38 📠 03.29.60.85.21
📧 gerard.dalsace.hotel@libertysurf.fr
Closed *15 Nov–1 Dec.* **TV. High chairs available. Swimming pool.**

This substantial Vosges house, just 150m from the lake on a small track, is a peaceful place. It's got a retro feel – the hotel opened in the early 1950s – but it's not unattractive, and it does have a heated swimming pool. The rooms have been refurbished quite nicely; most of them have double glazing, and all of them overlook the garden. You'll pay €50–65 for a double with shower/wc or bath/wc. Four rooms accommodating up to four persons are also available, all with bath/wc. *10% discount on the room rate (except in Feb, July, Aug and Christmas holidays) on presentation of this guide (breakfast must be taken at the hotel).*

ⓦ 🏠 🍽 Hôtel-restaurant Chalet du Lac**

97 chemin de la Droite-du-Lac; it's beside the lake, 1km from the town centre on the D147 in the direction of Épinal.
☎ 03.29.63.38.76 📠 03.29.60.91.63
Closed *Oct.* **TV. High chairs available.**

Historic wooden chalet with a lovely garden and overlooking the lake and the road, which is far enough away not to be distracting. Though the rooms have been renovated, they've kept their antique furniture and have a really nice, old-fashioned feel. All of them have shower/wc and a balcony for those overlooking the lake, and they each cost €55. There's an annexe in another chalet a few metres away on the edge of the forest. As for the restaurant, the food is traditional with regional influences; menus around €20–40, à la carte €31. Logis de France.

ⓦ 🎿 🏠 Le Grand Hôtel***

17–19 rue Charles-de-Gaulle, place du Tilleul.
☎ 03.29.63.06.31 📠 03.29.63.46.81
🌐 www.grandhotel.gerardmer.com
Disabled access. TV. High chairs and games available. Swimming pool. Car park.

A grand hotel in the old style that has seen many famous guests passing through its doors since its opening in 1870: from Napoleon III who came to open the route over the Schlucht pass to the movie stars of the Fantastic Movie Festival. From its glorious past remain the cosy Louis XIII bar, the huge hall and a large oak staircase. The

spacious rooms are however modern and attractively decorated, some on a mountain theme, others with romanticism in mind. Some have balconies or a large terrace where you can have breakfast in summer. Doubles with bath go for €92–130, and they have a few suites, too; half board, compulsory during school holidays and weekends, costs €71–91. There are two restaurants and two swimming pools – the heated indoor one has a wave machine and a Jacuzzi, with a fitness room and beauty salon. *Free house apéritif offered to our readers on presentation of this guide.*

ⓦ 🎿 🍽 Le Bistrot de la Perle

32 rue Charles-de-Gaulle.
☎ 03.29.60.86.24
Closed *Tues evening and Wed out of season; first week in March; 1–22 Oct.* **High chairs and games available.**

This place, which used to be a butcher's shop, retains its original picturesque façade. The light, pleasant dining room offers a friendly service and eclectic dishes, from fried mussels and *choucroute* to snail clafoutis. Choose the €10 *formule* for good, freshly cooked dishes; there are also menus at €15 and €21.50. There's a patio planted with flowers at the back. *Free house apéritif offered to our readers on presentation of this guide.*

ⓦ 🎿 🍽 L'Assiette du Coq à l'Âne

Place du Tilleul.
☎ 03.29.63.06.31
🌐 www.grandhotel.gerardmer.com
High chairs and games available.

This recently built hotel has successfully re-created the appearance of an old local country house. The floor tiles, high beamed ceiling and fireplace are all pleasantly rustic, and the local cuisine though not worth a detour is good. Menus start at €16 (weekday lunch), with others at €21 and €25. The service is professional and efficient (this is an annexe of the *Grand Hôtel*). *Free coffee offered to our readers on presentation of this guide.*

Xonrupt-Longemer

88400 (7km NE)

ⓦ 🎿 🏠 🍽 Hôtel Le Collet – Restaurant Lapôtre***

9937 route de Colmar; it's beyond Xonrupt on the D417 in the direction of Col de la Schlucht Munster.

☎ 03.29.60.09.57 ⓕ 03.29.60.08.77
✉ www.chalethotel.le.collet.com
Closed *10-24 April; 12 Nov–12 Dec.*
Restaurant closed *Wed outside school holidays; Thurs lunchtimes.* **TV. High chairs available. Car park.**

This is a big traditional chalet, set at 1100m in the heart of the Vosges nature reserve; it's near the cross-country ski trails and the ski lifts. The welcome is simple yet special and there's a luxurious feel to the place. Pretty double rooms with shower/wc or bath go for €69; the nicest ones have a balcony with a view of the forest. The very good regional cuisine has been revamped by a young chef bursting with ideas and enthusiasm. Menus start at €15 (weekday lunchtimes), then €22 and €26. The wine list features many Alsace wines along with a few gems from other regions. Logis de France. *10% discount on the room rate on presentation of this guide.*

Bresse (La)
88250 (13km S)

✎ ♨ |●| Hôtel-restaurant Les Vallées

31 rue Paul-Claudel.
☎ 03.29.25.41.39 ⓕ 03.29.25.64.38
✉ hotel.lesvallees@remy-loisirs.com
TV. High chairs and games available. Indoor swimming pool. Tennis courts. Car park.

This hotel complex is definitely very contemporary, the rooms are nice and the bathrooms spacious. Doubles with bath go for €55–81, depending on the season, and the breakfast (€9.50) is really good and the helpings generous. A few fully equipped flats with kitchenette are also available. The dining room is very big, hence a bit noisy, but it opens up onto a nice garden. Good traditional cuisine predominates on the weekly lunchtime menu €16.50, and other menus €21–44. Logis de France.

✎ |●| ⚘ Le Clos des Hortensias

51 route de Cornimont; just outside Bresse on the road to Remiremont.
☎ 03.29.25.41.08
Closed *Sun evening; Mon; 3-12 Jan; 29 March–6 April; 27 June–6 July.*
High chairs available.

Elegant dining room in an old country house offering a friendly welcome.

Refined but simple regional cuisine (the *andouillette* from Val-d'Ajol is really delicious) features on the weekly menu at €14.50; other menus €20–36. The chef is particularly renowned for his fish specialities, such as *rillettes* of salmon or fisherman's pot. *Free coffee offered to our readers on presentation of this guide.*

Valtin (Le)
88230 (13km NE)

✎ ♨ |●| Auberge du Val Joli**

12 bis Le village; from Gérardmer follow the signs to Saint-Dié, turn right onto the D23 in the direction of Colmar, then left at Xonrupt over the mountain road to Le Valtin.
☎ 03.29.60.91.37 ⓕ 03.29.60.81.73
✉ www.levaljoli.com
Closed *Sun and Mon evenings and Tues lunch (except school holidays); Mon lunchtime all year (except public holidays); 14–22 March; 13 Nov–3 Dec.* **Disabled access. TV. High chairs and games available. Car park.**

A superb place in one of the region's prettiest villages, set near pine forests and mountains. This is a real old-fashioned inn, with a warm and friendly atmosphere. Doubles go for €75–80 with shower/wc; with spa bath €125–155. Half board, at €50–105 per person, is compulsory during the school holidays. The dining rooms are wonderfully rustic with superb old beams on the ceiling and a tiled floor. There is also a conservatory overlooking the mountains. The cooking is good and traditional. There's a weekday menu at €18, with others for €21–60, listing dishes such as pâté lorrain (traditional pure pork meat pie), smoked trout, *blanc de sautret* (Vosges chicken in cream and Riesling sauce) and bilberry tart. Logis de France.

Houdelaincourt
55130

✎ ⚘ ♨ |●| L'Auberge du Père Louis**

8 rue Alainville.
☎ 03.29.89.64.14 ⓕ 03.89.78.84
✉ www.aubergedupercelouis.fr
Closed *Sun evening; Mon; Sept.* **TV.**

For anyone who likes good food, this is one of the places to eat in the region. The cooking is innovative and exciting, and though the menus change with the seasons you may well see dishes like langoustines, foie gras, sweetbreads casserole with truffle and flower and herb sorbet. Menus start at €18 (weekdays), then two others at €27 and €70. There are six quiet, pleasant rooms with shower/wc, which go for €38. *10% discount on the room rate on presentation of this guide.*

Longuyon

54260

⊚ 𝒜 🏠 |●| **Hôtel de la Gare – Restaurant La Table de Napo***

2 rue de la Gare; it's next to the train station.
☎03.82.26.50.85 ℗03.82.39.21.33
Closed *Fri and Sun evenings (except July– Aug); a fortnight in March; a fortnight in Sept.* **High chairs available. Car park.**

The good-natured owner creates a family atmosphere in her establishment. It feels like an old guesthouse with pretty pieces of furniture and bright, comfortable rooms; a double will cost €35 with shower, €50 with shower/wc. The entrance to the hotel is on the station platform, and some rooms look over the tracks – sadly, the double glazing doesn't cut out all the noise. If you're worried about not sleeping well, ask for a room looking onto the street. The three-star restaurant serves superb dishes cooked with fresh market produce, listed on five menus from €13 to €48. Logis de France. *Free coffee offered to our readers on presentation of this guide.*

⊚ 🏠 |●| **Hôtel de Lorraine – Restaurant Le Mas*****

65 rue Augistrou.
☎03.82.26.50.07 ℗03.82.39.26.09
ⓦwww.lorraineetmas.com
Closed *Mon except public holidays; Jan.* **TV. Pay car park.**

This Belle Époque hotel has an attractive façade and a lovely lounge sporting old beams and ceiling mouldings. The rooms, however, are completely different – though bright, they lack the style of the common areas. Doubles with shower/wc or bath cost €55. In the winter there's a blaze in the open fireplace and in summer they open up the terrace and plant troughs of flowers. The restaurant, with menus at €19 (weekdays) and €38.50, has a good reputation. Logis de France.

Longwy

54400

⊚ 🏠 |●| 𝒜 **Hôtel du Nord****

Place Darche; it's right in the middle of the upper town, on the handsome Place d'Armes.
☎03.82.23.40.81 ℗03.82.23.17.73
Closed *last three weeks in Aug.* **Restaurant closed** *Mon evening; Sat lunchtime; Sun; public holidays.* **TV. Car park.**

Many towns in France have a bar-hotel like this, but this one has particular charm because of its unique location on the impressive square. The modern rooms are clean and quiet; they cost €45 with shower/wc or bath. The brasserie offers traditional dishes; reckon on spending €19; dish of the day will cost around €9.50. *Free house apéritif offered to our readers on presentation of this guide.*

Cosnes et Romain

54400 (5km W)

⊚ |●| **Le Train Bleu**

Rue Béarn; from Longwy-Haut, take the N18 in the direction of Longuyon for 4km, turn right at the sign towards Cosnes-et-Romain.
☎03.82.23.98.09
Closed *Mon; Sat lunchtime.*

They've joined two railway carriages together to create this attractive dining room, and you have to push a button to open the door. Inside, the décor is plush and the cooking is great. Menus offer something for every budget, starting with the weekday menu at €12 and ranging up to €36. It's particularly popular at weekends.

Lunéville

54300

⊚ 🏠 |●| **Hôtel des Pages- Restaurant le Petit Comptoir*****

5 quai des Petits-Bosquets; it's across the river from the castle.
☎03.83.74.11.42 ℗03.83.73.46.63
Disabled access. TV. Car park.

Small, new buildings grouped around a car park; a bit American-motel-looking from the outside. Inside it's a completely different story. Extremely pretty rooms decked out with all the style you find in glossy magazines for €50–95 with shower/wc or bath; half board €58 per person. Originality (even in the bathrooms), contemporary charm and warm, welcoming design ideas. The restaurant is neo-bistro style, with an equally delightful décor and offers traditional dishes and menus at €16 and €22. Just across the river lies the château known as the "Versailles of Lorraine" (which is being restored after a serious fire) and its superb gardens. Logis de France.

ⓒ |●| Marie Leszczynska

30 rue de Lorraine; in a street running parallel to the right wing of the château.
℡03.83.73.11.85
Closed *Sun evening; Mon; Tues evening; end Aug to early Sept; end Dec to early Jan.*

This restaurant, named after the wife of King Louis XV, offers a friendly welcome and elegant cuisine with menus in the range €13.50–36. The pretty dining room is refined and understated, with an intimate setting, and there's a pleasant terrace in a pedestrianized street.

Manderen
57480

ⓒ 🏠 |●| ⅍ Le Relais du Château Mensberg**

15 rue du Château; it's on the D64.
℡03.82.83.73.16 ℻03.82.83.23.37
ⓦwww.aurelaismensberg@aol.com
Closed *3 weeks in Jan.* **Restaurant closed** *Tues.* **Disabled access. TV. Games available. Car park.**

The château of Mensberg – known as the "Château de Malbrouck" – was built in the seventh century and, according to legend, rebuilt in the fifteenth with the help of the devil. Today the impressive building, which dominates the village, offers fifteen comfortable, pretty double rooms for €60; half board €55 per person. It's excellent value for money. There's an extremely handsome dining room where you can enjoy a number of carefully prepared Lorraine specialities that change with the seasons (piglet marinaded in beer, trout from their own ponds); menus €18–50. A warm welcome makes you feel even more like staying by the large fireplace or out on the summer terrace – if only to sample a fine bottle of wine from across the Rhine or enjoy a generous breakfast. Logis de France. *10% discount on the room rate for a*

minimum stay of over three consecutive nights (15% during Nov–March) on presentation of this guide.

Metz
57000

See map overleaf

ⓒ ⅍ 🏠 Hôtel Moderne**

1 rue Lafayette; opposite the station, 15min on foot from the pedestrian zone. **Off map B3-4.**
℡03.87.66.57.33 ℻03.87.55.98.59
ⓦwww.hotel-moderne-metz.com
TV. Pay car park.

A classic station hotel with a predominantly business clientèle. Rooms are modern and functional but not impersonal; the ones at the back are the quietest, while those with two double beds, like nos. 19, 22, 23, 30 and 44, are terrific value. You'll pay €34–56 for a room with shower/wc or bath; half board from €61 per person. *20% discount on the room rate (Fri, Sat, Sun and public holidays) on presentation of this guide.*

ⓒ ⅍ 🏠 Hôtel La Pergola**

13 route de Plappeville; Bus 5 or 25, Tignomont stop. 3km from the centre; Devant-les-Pons district; cross the Île de Saulcy and continue in the direction of Plappeville. **Off map A1-2**
℡03.87.32.52.94 ℻03.87.31.41.60
ⓦwww.hotel-la-pergola.com
TV. Car park.

The hotel, with a 1950s-look façade, is 3km from the centre and its sign is not very obvious. It's worth the effort of getting there, though; rooms (€45–48), which are all furnished differently, feature brass beds and period furniture, and you are woken by the birds singing in the wonderful garden, where afternoon tea is served under the trees. Rooms up in the eaves have sloping ceilings, and some of the bathrooms are as big as the rooms themselves. Dogs accepted (€4.50 per night). *10% discount on the room rate offered to our readers on presentation of this guide.*

ⓒ ⅍ 🏠 Hôtel du Centre**

14 rue du Pont-des-Loges. **Map B2-8**
℡03.87.36.06.93 ℻03.87.75.60.66
ⓦwww.perso.wanadoo.fr/hotelducentre-metz

⑬

LORRAINE

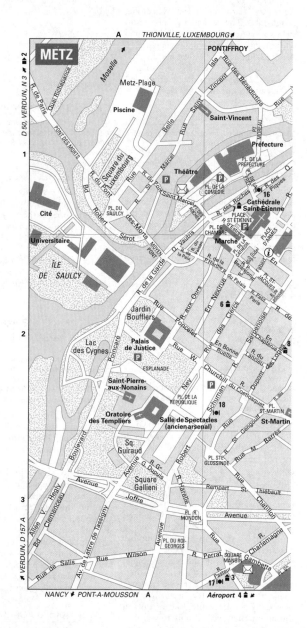

LORRAINE

13

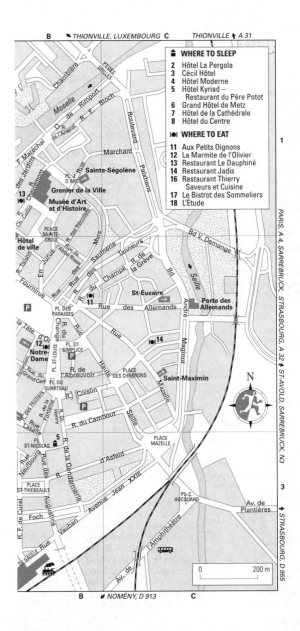

WHERE TO SLEEP

2 Hôtel La Pergola
3 Cécil Hôtel
4 Hôtel Moderne
5 Hôtel Kyriad –
   Restaurant du Père Potot
6 Grand Hôtel de Metz
7 Hôtel de la Cathédrale
8 Hôtel du Centre

WHERE TO EAT

11 Aux Petits Oignons
12 La Marmite de l'Olivier
13 Restaurant Le Dauphiné
14 Restaurant Jadis
16 Restaurant Thierry
    Saveurs et Cuisine
17 Le Bistrot des Sommeliers
18 L'Étude

PARIS, A 4, SARREBRUCK, STRASBOURG, A 32 ↑ ST-AVOLD, SARREBRUCK, N3

STRASBOURG, D 955

LORRAINE

13

0   200 m

Closed *25 Dec–2 Jan; 31 July–22 Aug.* **TV. Pay car park.**

Ideally located on a pedestrianized street and – hardly surprisingly, given the name – in the centre of the town. An old wooden staircase (no lift) takes you to the attractively arranged, charming rooms; those on the top floor, under the roof, have nice sloping ceilings. Doubles with shower/wc cost €47; baby cots are available (€7 per night). Breakfast includes home-baked breads and pastries cooked on the premises. *One free breakfast per room per night on presentation of this guide.*

◎ ☆ ☎ Cécil Hôtel**

14 rue Pasteur; near the train station. **Map B3-3**
℡03.87.66.66.13 ℻03.87.56.96.02
ⓦwww.cecilhotel-metz.com
Closed *26 Dec–3 Jan.* **TV. High chairs available. Billard tables. Pay car park.**

The hotel is in a handsome early twentieth-century building between the station and the centre. Prices for the refurbished, modern and well-equipped rooms, decorated in a 1970s style, range from €54 for a double with shower/wc to €57 with bath. Ask for one on the first floor in the annexe, or one of the larger ones. *Free use of garage offered to our readers on presentation of this guide.*

◎ ☎ ☆ Grand Hôtel de Metz**

3 rue des Clercs. **Map B2-6**
℡03.87.36.16.33 ℻03.87.74.17.04
ⓦwww.hotel-metz.com.
TV. High chairs available. Pay car park.

This hotel, in a pedestrianized street in the old part of town, boasts an ultra-modern entrance with a superb staircase. The clean, comfortable rooms are decorated in pastels and flower-patterned fabrics, and overlook the inner courtyard; doubles €59–70 with shower/wc or bath. Half board is available for an extra €14 per person. *10% discount on the room rate (Fri–Sun) offered to our readers on presentation of this guide.*

◎ ☆ ☎ |◎| Hôtel Kyriad – Restaurant du Père Potot**

8 rue du Père-Potot. **Map B3-5**
℡03.87.36.55.56 ℻03.87.36.39.80
ⓦwww.kyriad.fr
Disabled access. TV. Pay car park.

Centrally located but looking a bit out of place in this particular neighbourhood,

this hotel offers refurbished rooms. They're all alike but not unpleasant; doubles with shower/wc go for €59.50; half board €43–69. Note that the odd-numbered ones look onto the courtyard of an old abbey. The restaurant is good, too, with a weekday menu for €12 and others at €15, €18 and €23. *Free house apéritif or 10% discount on the room rate offered to our readers on presentation of this guide.*

◎ ☎ ☆ Hôtel de la Cathédrale***

25 place de la Chambre; next to the cathedral. **Map B1-7**
℡03.87.30.27.25 ℻03.87.75.40.75
ⓦwww.hotelcathedrale-metz.fr
Disabled access. TV.

Chateaubriand and Madame de Staël stayed in this coaching inn, which was built in 1627, and various other famous people have slept here since. Monsieur Hocine restored the building himself and Madame undertook to decorate it – they've done it beautifully, and the period beams, iron work, casements and interior courtyard are all amazing. The rooms, too, are full of character and charm; each is decorated differently, but they're all bright with elegant fittings, and some have a view of the cathedral (nos. 103 and 104). Doubles go for €68–75 with shower/wc or €73–115 with bath. Booking is strongly advised. *10% discount on the room rate (except for the cheapest) on presentation of this guide.*

◎ ☆ |◎| Aux Petits Oignons

5 rue du Champé. **Map B2-11**
℡03.87.18.91.33
Closed *Sat lunch; Sun; Mon lunch; 2–3 weeks in July–Aug.*

Welcome to Provence – in this small, out-of-the-way street. Only the regulars know how to find this delightful, cosy little dining room which offers an original apéritif idea: small shots of different brands of pastis. Well turned out Provençal dishes: mozzarella fritters with anchovy sauce, cold soup with olives and fresh anchovies, bream stuffed with ricotta, beef in a tapenade crust and fine desserts – try the home-made apple, honey and rosemary tart. Good value menus and generous, original salads (to put together yourself), all beautifully presented; set menu €10.75, "Lavandou" lunch menu €14.90, and other suggestions on the board. However, the à la carte option remains a bit pricey: reckon on €25–30 without the drinks.

LORRAINE ⑬

Free liqueur offered to readers on presentation of this guide.

⊚ ⚇ |●| Restaurant Le Dauphiné

8 rue du Chanoine-Collin; opposite the administrative centre, in a street looking onto the north of the Place d'Armes, next to the cathedral. **Map B1-13**
☎ 03.87.36.03.04
Closed *evenings except Fri and Sat; Sun by reservation only; Aug.*

An unpretentious restaurant and tearoom with exposed beams. There's a €13 menu (not Sun), and others at €18 and €21. Regulars enjoy value-for-money lunchtime menus: specials €6.60–7.50 and set menus €9.50–10.50. Unbeatable value and simple cooking but generous helpings: calf's head with *sauce gribiche*, duck breast with honey and fillet of pike perch with basil. *Free coffee offered to our readers on presentation of this guide.*

⊚ ⚇ |●| Restaurant Thierry Saveurs et Cuisine

5 rue des Piques. **Map B1-16**
☎ 03.87.74.01.23
Closed *Sun; Wed evening; first 3 weeks in Aug.* **Disabled access.**

One of our long-time favourites has been transformed into a nice bistro, the *Saveurs et Cuisine*, with a friendly atmosphere, serving authentic cuisine from sunny climes. Typical dishes include scampi with tandoori spices, crunchy black sausage with preserved lemon, *magret* braised in pineapple juice, pan-fried scallops on a bed of sauerkraut with ginger sauce, green cabbage stuffed with crabmeat, and some scrumptious delicacies for dessert. Enjoy very reasonable prices on the menus at €13.50 and €19.50 (weekdays) and from €27.50 (from Fri evening). *Free house apéritif offered to our readers on presentation of this guide.*

⊚ |●| L'Étude

11 avenue Robert-Schuman. **Map B2-18**
☎ 03.87.35.36.32
Closed *Sun; Mon (July–Aug); first fortnight in Aug.* **High chairs available.**

One of the most fashionable restaurants in Metz offering excellent service. The astonishing décor evokes the library of an old English university: the walls are covered with shelves holding some 5,000 books (customers are welcome to sit in one of the cosy armchairs in the lounge area and read to their hearts' content). The food is equally striking; it is basically traditional but infused with new ideas (mullet salad with herbs, scorpion fish with thyme and preserved vegetables, spiced duck with cocoa). There's a weekday lunchtime menu for €14, then others at €19.80–24.60. On Fridays and Saturdays dinner is accompanied by live music (jazz, chanson, blues) with menus €22.60–26.30; the programme is available on the website. Reckon on €13.40 à la carte.

⊚ |●| Le Bistrot des Sommeliers

10 rue Pasteur; near the train station. **Map B3-17**
☎ 03.87.63.40.20
Closed *Sat lunchtime; Sun; Christmas to New Year; bank holidays.*

Youthful, good-value place with leatherette-covered benches and wine-bottle candlesticks, and a terrace in summer. There's an interesting selection of wines to drink, too, by the glass or the jug, and traditional dishes that are as simple as they are tasty; dish of the day around €8.50. The single menu at €14 is good value for money, while if you eat à la carte you'll spend about €20–25.

⊚ |●| ⚇ La Marmite de l'Olivier

9 place Saint-Louis. **Map B2-12**
☎ 03.87.37.05.82
Closed *Mon; Thurs and Sun evenings; fortnight end Aug to early Sept.*

This strategically situated restaurant has three dining rooms (one in a listed wine cellar), as well as an enormous terrace under the arches. Highly convincing renditions of regional specialities are the order of the day: snail *cassolette*, home-made foie gras and terrines, veal sweetbreads, calf's head, suckling pig with mirabelle plums, fillet of pike perch with Toul broth and various home-made terrines. Menus range from €14.90 (weekdays) to €22. *Free house apéritif offered to our readers on presentation of this guide.*

⊚ |●| Restaurant Jadis

1–3 rue du Grand-Wad. **Map C2-14**
☎ 03.87.74.10.38
Closed *Sat lunchtime; Sun; 3 weeks in Aug.*

A simple, friendly, old-fashioned setting: candles, an old organ, an old mirror and

⑬

LORRAINE

outmoded wooden tables. Very generous helpings and carefully blended flavours predominate on the menus (€17.50 and €23); weekday lunchtime special €9.50, including a glass of wine. Reckon on €30–35 for à la carte. The chef trained under French and foreign master chefs – if everyone's talking about this place it's with good reason as it's remarkable value for money. Specialities include baby tomatoes in the old style, *cassolette* of snails with mushrooms, crunchy pig's trotter, *entrecôte* with Guérande salt. What's more you'll get a friendly welcome and convivial service. A good wine list is on offer, with wines not just from the southwest – which is where the owner hails from.

Saint-Julien-lès-Metz
57070 (3km NE)

⊚ |O| Restaurant du Fort Saint-Julien

Route de Thionville; it's in the restored part of the fort right in the middle of the wood.
☎03.87.75.71.16
Closed *Wed; Sun evening; 1–10 Jan, last fortnight in July; first week in Aug.* **Car park.**

A good-natured place for a blow-out with friends in an impressive cellar setting. They serve substantial dishes like sauerkraut, *baeckeoffe* of salmon, quiche lorraine, roast suckling pig or game in season. Menus start at €13 (weekday lunch), up to €20.60, or around €25 à la carte. A terrace is available in summer.

Woippy
57140 (4km N)

⊚ 🎋 |O| L'Auberge Belles Fontaines

51 route de Thionville; take the Woippy-La-Maxe exit on the A31.
☎03.87.31.99.46
Closed *evenings; Sat lunch; 26 July–19 Aug.* **Disabled access. High chairs available.**

A restful inn just minutes from the centre of Metz. It's decorated in classical fashion in the same shades of green as the trees in the park, and there's a terrace. Customers are mainly regulars. Five substantial menus are offered in the range €19–49.50. *Free coffee offered to our readers on presentation of this guide.*

Gorze
57680 (20km SW)

⊚ 🎋 🏠 |O| Hostellerie du Lion d'Or**

105 rue du Commerce; take the Fey exit on the A31.
☎03.87.52.00.90 ☏03.87.52.09.62
Closed *Sun evening; Mon.* **Disabled access. High chairs and games available. TV.**

You'll find this establishment in the narrow main road of this sleepy town. Once a post house, it still has character and charm, with hand-made floor tiles, timbered walls, a small interior pond, and a huge bay window that lets lots of light into the restaurant. All in all, it's an appropriate setting for the traditional cuisine; weekday lunch menu at €18 (and evenings for hotel guests only); others at €25–63 list such dishes as calf's head, trout *au bleu*, and house foie gras. Reckon on around €40 à la carte. It's silver service, but you don't need to dress formally. You can stay here too, in renovated rooms; the soundproofing does a pretty good job of cutting down the noise from low-flying jets. Doubles with shower/wc go for €48, or €55 with bath; half board €63 per person. Logis de France. *Free house apéritif offered to our readers on presentation of this guide.*

Montenach
57480

⊚ 🎋 🏠 |O| Hôtel-restaurant Au Val Sierckois

3 place de la Mairie.
☎03.82.83.85.20 ☏03.82.83.61.91
Closed *Mon evening; Tues; last fortnight in July; first week in Aug.* **High chairs available.**

Among the valleys and woods of northern Moselle, where France meets Luxembourg and Germany, this delightful, friendly inn is the ideal place to recharge your batteries. You'll be woken by birdsong and you can go for long walks in the forest. The cooking is unpretentious with menus of Lorraine specialities for €14.50–30. This is hunting country, so try the haunch of venison *Grand Veneur*. They have seven pretty rooms, €31 with shower or €49 with bath; half board €49 per person. They are currently refurbishing all the rooms. *Free liqueur offered to our readers on presentation of this guide.*

⊚ |◉| L'Auberge de la Klauss

1 rue de Kirschnaumen; take the D956.
☎03.82.83.72.38
Closed *Mon; 24 Dec–8 Jan.* **Disabled access.**

This is a friendly, welcoming place serving quality cooking prepared on the spot using fresh ingredients. You can eat substantial menus (€14–48) in one of four dining rooms; one is decorated with clocks and old time pieces and another looks like a hunting lodge. The owner raises pigs and ducks – you can visit his farm and buy home-made treats – and the game comes from the nearby forest. Specialities include charcuterie (try especially the delicious old-fashioned smoked wild boar and pork hams) and fresh pan-fried duck foie gras with hot caramelized apples.

Nancy

54000

See map overleaf

⊚ ♦ Hôtel Carnot**

2 cours Léopold; 5 min from the station; from Avenue Foch take Rue Serre and go round Place Carnot. **Map A2-2**
☎03.83.36.59.58 ℗03.83.37.00.19
TV. Pay car park.

The façade of this hotel had to be rebuilt after the war and is somewhat charmless, but the rooms are decent and the prices attractive; doubles with shower €28 and €33 with shower/wc or €45 with bath. Nos. 16, 24, 25 and 34 are the best: quiet, with nice views of the old town. In April, when there is a country fair in the square, make sure to ask for a room at the back.

⊛ ⅔ ♦ Hôtel Le Jean-Jaurès**

14 bd. Jean-Jaurès; 10 min on foot from the train station. **Off map A3-4**
☎03.83.27.74.14 ℗03.83.90.20.94
ⓦ www.hotel-jeanjaures.fr
TV. Pay car park.

This place was built as a craftsman's house and has retained a pleasant old-fashioned atmosphere enhanced by the mouldings and tapestries. The rooms over the street have been soundproofed, but you may still prefer the quieter ones over the garden; doubles with shower/wc €45. The young owner is genuinely welcoming and pays great attention to the comfort of his

guests. *10% discount on the room rate at weekends on presentation of this guide.*

⊛ ♦ Hôtel Albert 1er-Astoria**

5 rue de l'Armée-Patton; in the station district. **Off map A3-3**
☎03.83.40.31.24 ℗03.83.28.47.78
ⓦ www.albert1-astoria.com
Pay car park. TV.

A recently built, large-capacity hotel (which also takes parties). Rooms are modern, well-equipped and comfortable but lack real charm; doubles with shower/wc or bath €49–69. On the plus side: all or nearly all the rooms are laid out around a large, plant-filled patio where you can eat breakfast when the weather is fine. Offers real peace and quiet in what is a rather noisy area.

⊛ ♦ Hôtel de Guise**

18 rue de Guise. **Map A1-5**
☎03.83.32.24.68 ℗03.83.35.75.63
ⓦ www.hoteldeguise.com
Disabled access. TV.

A handsome private residence dating from the seventeenth and eighteenth centuries, converted into a hotel in the 1930s, located in a peaceful little street in the heart of the old part of town. It has masses of character: a majestic stone and wrought-iron staircase, fleur-de-lys panelling and a huge fireplace in the breakfast room. Not all the rooms are done out in the same style (some are more modern), but the most expensive (nos. 1 or 41, for example) have the same classy touches: Versailles-style wooden flooring, fireplace, Louis XV or Art Deco furniture… Double rooms with shower/wc or bath go for €56–60; suites €69–90. Overall, despite some renovation, this place still has an old-fashioned feel, which explains the reasonable prices.

⊛ ♦ Hôtel La Résidence***

30 boulevard Jean-Jaurès. **Off map A3-8**
☎03.83.40.33.56 ℗03.83.90.16.28
ⓦ www.hotel-laresidence-nancy.fr
TV. Pay car park.

From the moment you enter you can tell this is a civilized place to stay. The charming, attentive welcome must have something to do with it. Even though the building has been substantially renovated, the general atmosphere remains that of a family home: a cosy, little lounge with knick-knacks and engravings. Rooms are

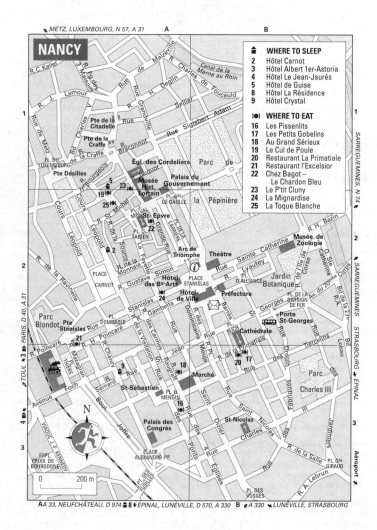

NANCY

METZ, LUXEMBOURG, N 57, A 31

WHERE TO SLEEP

2 Hôtel Carnot
3 Hôtel Albert 1er-Astoria
4 Hôtel Le Jean-Jaurès
5 Hôtel de Guise
8 Hôtel La Résidence
9 Hôtel Crystal

WHERE TO EAT

16 Les Pissenlits
17 Les Petits Gobelins
18 Au Grand Sérieux
19 Le Cul de Poule
20 Restaurant La Primatiale
21 Restaurant l'Excelsior
22 Chez Bagot –
   Le Chardon Bleu
23 Le P'tit Cluny
24 La Mignardise
25 La Toque Blanche

A A 33, NEUFCHÂTEAU, D 974 ⛴ 8 ↓ ÉPINAL, LUNÉVILLE, D 570, A 330   B ↙ A 330 ↘ LUNÉVILLE, STRASBOURG

LORRAINE

⑬

in keeping, but each one is different, warm and welcoming and pleasantly comfortable; doubles with shower/wc or bath are €58–66. Good soundproofing on the street side but even quieter on the garden side with the bonus of a view over some of the local houses, including excellent examples of the Nancy school of architecture. Logis de France.

⟪⟪ ⌂ ♨ Hôtel Crystal

5 rue Chanzy; very close to the train station. **Map A3-9**
☎03.83.17.54.00 ℻03.83.17.54.30
✉hotelcrystal.nancy@wanadoo.fr
Closed 24 Dec–2 Jan. **TV. High chairs available. Pay car park.**

Conveniently located near the station with small, cosy rooms that are very comfortable and tastefully decorated. The quality beds and linen will ensure you have a good night's sleep. Doubles with shower/wc or bath go for €81–97; suites available at €112. *One free breakfast per person offered to our readers on presentation of this guide.*

ⓔ |●| ♨ La Mignardise

28 rue Stanislas; a few steps away from Place Stanislas. **Map A2-24**
☎03.83.32.20.22
ⓦwww.lamignardise.com
Closed Sun evening; 5–18 July. **Disabled access. High chairs available.**

This salmon-coloured restaurant has just a few tables but offers efficient, unobtrusive service. The menus, €14–22 at lunchtime, and €29–40, list refined dishes such as pike perch with snails and frogs' legs; dishes change with the season. Desserts are always good. There's a shady terrace for sunny days. *Free coffee offered to our readers on presentation of this guide.*

ⓔ |●| Les Petits Gobelins

18 rue de la Primatiale; just behind the cathedral, in a pedestrianized street. **Map B3-17**
☎03.83.35.49.03
Closed Sun; Mon.

A limited number of tables (so booking advisable) in this Lilliputian eatery installed in an old town-centre house. There's an assortment of furniture and collectables about the place and paintings and photos by local artists on the walls. At weekday lunchtimes there's a €14 market menu offering good traditional cuisine;

others range from €18.50–60. The welcome and service are a little diffident.

ⓔ |●| Au Grand Sérieux

27 rue Raugraff. **Map A3-18**
☎03.83.36.68.87
Closed weekends; evenings.
Open lunchtimes only, plus Fri evening.

A genuinely typical French bar-café with a counter where the regulars are on first-name terms, faded red imitation leather benches along the walls, tables squeezed together, dishes written up on the board and hurried service, so expect to sit where there's a space. The day's special at around €8 (or €15 for à la carte) serves up very good food decided by what's available in the market that day and a notch above what you normally find in a place like this. And the name can be taken with a pinch of salt – at least once you've also sampled the owner's humour.

ⓔ |●| Chez Bagot – Le Chardon Bleu

45 Grande-Rue. **Map A2-22**
☎03.83.37.42.43
Closed Sun evening; Mon; Tues lunchtime; 3 weeks in Aug.

Wood panelling and engravings in a rather conventional dining room in a house in the old part of town. It's a fair way from the shores of Brittany to the streets of Nancy, but that doesn't deter Breton Patrick Bagot from offering his customers authentic fish and shellfish from back home. Weekday lunch menu at €14.50 and others up to €31.50; you'll spend around €35 à la carte, which is a bit expensive. The wine list is superb, but again the prices are quite high.

ⓔ ♨ |●| La Toque Blanche

1 rue Monseigneur-Trouillet; just a few steps from the ducal palace. **Map A2-25**
☎03.83.30.17.20
Closed Sun evening; Mon; Sat from March onwards; first week of the Easter school holiday; first week of the Feb school holiday; last week in July; first week in Aug.

A refined place with a fresh feeling. Though the dining room is not desperately original, this restaurant offers some of the best cooking in town. It's popular locally for the interesting, good-value lunch menu at €16; they also have others from €22–65. The excellent wine list offers a

LORRAINE

carefully chosen selection at fair prices. This is just the place for a celebration. *Free coffee offered to our readers on presentation of this guide.*

⊚ |●| 🎄 Restaurant La Primatiale

14 rue de la Primatiale; 2 min from "Stan" square; from Rue Saint-Jean go round the cathedral. **Map B3-20**
☎03.83.30.44.03
Closed *Tues evening; Sat lunchtime; Sun.*

On a pedestrianized street and opposite *L'Échanson*, a wine bar where you can stop for an apéritif, this is a friendly, appealing restaurant. The cooking is original, light and delicate, and they've designed a really attractive wine list with a huge selection by the glass. The choice of menus starts at €16 up to €33, or reckon on around €37 à la carte. There's an agreeable terrace on the street. *Free house apéritif offered to our readers on presentation of this guide.*

⊚ |●| 🎄 Les Pissenlits

25 bis rue des Ponts; on the market square. **Map A3-16**
☎03.83.37.43.97
Closed *Sun; Mon; 1–15 Aug.* **Disabled access.**

Les Pissenlits is the younger sibling of *La Table des Mengi* next door and the cooking is just as good. It's a good-looking place, with marble tables in the large dining room and a handsome dresser showing off a collection of Longwy porcelain. The food is café-bar-brasserie style (*tête de veau*, for example) or old-fashioned home-cooking (rabbit *fricassée* in wine, dandelion salad). The dish of the day costs €8.60 (to book ahead), while menus range from €17.90–22.20. Danièle Mengin, one of France's best wine waiters, is responsible for the quite exceptional cellar and there is always a specially chosen selection of splendid wines available by the glass. It's extremely popular and often full. *Free house apéritif offered to our readers on presentation of this guide.*

⊚ |●| Le Cul de Poule

22 place de l'Arsenal. **Map A2-19**
☎03.83.32.11.01
Closed Sun and Mon (except public holidays).

Quite a trendy place to eat, hectic in the evenings, quieter at lunchtime, offering friendly, pleasant service. Attractive period-style dining room housed in an old workshop serves à la carte meals for around €20–35. Displayed on the board are dishes, decided by what's good in the market and cooked with respect for the produce, simply prepared but flavoursome.

⊚ 🎄 |●| Restaurant L'Excelsior

50 rue Henri-Poincaré; close to the train station. **Map A2-21**
☎03.83.35.24.57
Closed *Christmas Eve dinner.* **Open** *8am–12.30am (11pm on Sun).*

An institution in Nancy, known as the "*Excel*", this is something of a historic monument with its Art Nouveau décor; all the greatest names of the Nancy School are represented, with mahogany furniture by Majorelle and stained glass by Gruber. The cooking and service are in the best brasserie style, with menus from €20.90–29.90. Don't miss the fresh oysters, Strasbourg sauerkraut or the pike perch with snails. *Free coffee offered to our readers on presentation of this guide.*

⊚ 🎄 |●| Le P'tit Cluny**

95 Grande Rue; opposite Musée Lorrain. **Map A1-23**
☎03.83.32.85.94
Closed *Sun; Mon; Aug.* **High chairs available.**

A typical rustic Alsace wine cellar with walls of rough-hewn stone and tankards and other drinking utensils suspended from the ceiling. Among the local specialities you should try the tasty *flammenküche* – which are enough to satisfy a big appetite. Standards are high, as you will find if you order the *choucroute*, the barbecued suckling pig or the calf's head. À la carte, you'll spend from €23. *Free liqueur offered to our readers on presentation of this guide.*

Villers-lès-Nancy

54600 (4km SW)

⊚ 🎄 🏠 Auberge de jeunesse – Château de Rémicourt-Nancy

149 rue de Vandœuvre; from the A33 or N74, take the exit "Nancy-Sud-Ouest-Brabois" (av. de la Forêt-de-Haye, av. Paul-Muller); from the city centre, follow the signs to "Brabois-Rémicourt".
☎03.83.27.73.67 ☎03.83.41.41.35
✉aubergeremicourt@mairie-nancy.fr

Closed *between Christmas and New Year.* **Open** *for new arrivals 8.30am–9pm; accommodation from 5.30pm.* **Disabled access. Car park.**

In the middle of a huge nine-hectare park, this château is a youth hostel with more than a touch of class. It is ideal for nature-lovers with a limited budget who want to stay clear of big towns. It costs €13.50 per person per night staying in a dormitory for three to ten people and €15.50 sleeping in a double room. Stopover menu at €6, then weekday menus €8.50–16.50, for a minimum of six people; you must book for these, but you can share your order with other visitors to the hostel. It's the perfect base for visiting the very close-by Nancy's National Botanic Conservatory. More than 10,000 species of plants are on display there. *Free coffee or fruit juice offered to our readers on presentation of this guide.*

Méréville
54850 (16kmS)

@ 🏠 |❤| Maison Carrée

12 rue du Bac.
☎03.83.47.09.23 ☏03.83.47.50.75
🌐www.maisoncarree.com
Hotel closed *Sun evening (Dec–Feb).* **TV. Swimming pool. Car park.**

A small, peaceful 1960s building set among large, pleasant gardens. Rooms are not huge and the décor is a bit dated, but they're comfortable and cost €72–82 with bath. The best rooms have balconies overlooking the Moselle. There's a restaurant 100m away in a funny little house right by the river, under the chestnut trees, in a really delightful setting. Conventional dining rooms open onto the river bank, offering good, traditional, regional dishes with a menu at €18 (except weekends and public holidays), and another at €38. The very professional welcome, pleasant, heated pool and bike rental give this place a real holiday feel. Logis de France.

Neufchâteau
88300

@ 🎿 🏠 |❤| Le Rialto**

67 rue de France.
☎03.29.06.09.40 ☏03.29.94.39.51
🌐www.rialto.vosges.com

Closed *Sun (except July–Aug); 21 Dec–6 Jan.* **TV. Car park.**

You'll get a pleasant welcome from the young proprietors of this long-standing hotel on the edge of the historic old town. Clean doubles cost €43 with shower/wc or bath; those overlooking the river are particularly nice. Good, traditional cooking in the restaurant – nothing fancy – with a €9 weekday lunch menu and others at €15 and €25. There's a nice terrace open on sunny days. *Free house apéritif offered to our readers on presentation of this guide.*

@ 🎿 🏠 |❤| Le Saint-Christophe**

1 av. de la Grande-Fontaine.
☎03.29.94.68.71 ☏03.29.06.02.09
🌐www.relais-sud.champagne.com
Disabled access. TV. High chairs available. Pay car park.

Rooms here are on the small side but comfortable nonetheless; doubles range from €45–65 with shower/wc or bath. Go for one that overlooks the River Mouzon or the Saint Christophe church, which is illuminated at night. The breakfast is very good and there's lots of it. Along with a brasserie, there's a classic restaurant with wood panelling typical of this leafy region. Friendly welcome and very decent cooking; menus are €10–34. Logis de France. *10% discount on the room rate offered to our readers on presentation of this guide.*

@ 🎿 |❤| Restaurant Le Romain

74 av. Kennedy; it's on the Chaumont road, as you leave town.
☎03.29.06.18.80
Closed *Sun evening; Mon; winter holidays; 18 Aug–1 Sept.* **Disabled access. High chairs available. Car park.**

It's the décor rather than the food here that recalls ancient Rome. The chef shows considerable flair in his approach to traditional dishes. Cooking times are judged perfectly and he has an intuition for balancing flavours – you'll feel that you're tasting standard dishes for the first time. There's a weekday lunch menu for €12.50 and others from €20–32. You can eat on the terrace in summer but it's a bit too close to the road despite a good thick hedge. Good cheeses and desserts, and a great wine list with a few wines by the glass. *Free coffee offered to our readers on presentation of this guide.*

Plombières-les-Bains
88370

‹‹ ☎ |O| 𝒜 **Hôtel de la Fontaine Stanislas****

Fontaine Stanislas, Granges-de-Plombières – it's 4km from Plombières on the road to Épinal via Xertigny.
☎ 03.29.66.01.53 ℱ 03.29.30.04.31
📠 www.fontaine.stanislas.com
Closed *15 Oct–1 April.* **Disabled access (restaurant). TV. High chairs available. Car park.**

The same family has owned this hotel for four generations. It's miles out in the forest overlooking the valley, with a lovely terraced garden and footpaths through the woods, and you'll get an extremely friendly welcome. Bedrooms are regularly decorated and have an old-style charm; doubles go for €38 with shower/wc and €49–53 with bath; half board from €46. Nos. 2, 3 and 11 have their own terrace while 18 and 19 have a corner sitting area. There's a fantastic view from the restaurant, where they're strong on traditional cuisine and regional dishes (menus €17–39): *andouille* from Val d'Ajol, duck leg with mirabelle sauce and home-made ice creams. Logis de France. *10% discount on the room rate (except July/Aug) on presentation of this guide.*

Pont-à-Mousson
54700

‹‹ ☎ **Hôtel Bagatelle*****

47–49 rue Gambetta; exit 26 from the A31.
☎ 03.83.81.03.64 ℱ 03.83.81.12.63
📠 www.bagatelle.hotel.fr
Closed *Christmas to New Year.* **TV. Pay car park.**

This modern hotel is brilliantly located near the abbey and the banks of the Moselle. The rooms are outdated but functional – fortunately they are in the process of being redecorated (second floor only so far); a double with en-suite bathroom will cost €52–57.

‹‹ |O| **Pierre Bonaventure**

18 place Durol.
☎ 03.83.81.23.54

Tucked beneath the superb Renaissance arcades of this large square sits this friendly, new-bistro style eatery with a long dining room and a good-humoured atmosphere. This place is a temple to meat: *onglet*, veal chops, pig's trotters, *andouillette*, sweetbreads – prime cuts, offal and other charcuterie direct from the producer, carefully prepared in a wood-fired oven. There's a lunchtime special for €11.50, or reckon on €25 for à la carte. Wine by the glass and some light dishes (Italian-style pasta, for example) are also available.

Griscourt
54380 (12km S)

‹‹ ☎ |O| **Winstub-Auberge de la Petite Suisse Lorraine**

4 place de la Belle-Croix.
☎ and ℱ 03.83.23.66.70
Closed *Tues; Sept.* **TV.**

A typical country inn with beams, large fireplace and rustic-kitsch dining room located in a peaceful village at the entrance to a delightful, little valley in the heart of the Lorraine national park. It doesn't take long to work out that the charming couple who run the place are from Alsace (their accent gives them away), and the atmosphere here reflects their region with its village *winstubs* and farmhouse inns among the peaks of the Vosges mountains. Three quiet and comfortable, bedrooms only, in an appealing, rustic style, go for €50 with shower/wc. Special menu at weekday lunchtimes (dish of the day plus starter or dessert) costs €10.70, otherwise a menu at €23; reckon on €20–25 for à la carte. There is good-humoured service, music on the accordion and hearty, flavoursome home-cooking with a regional touch. Logis de France.

Remiremont
88200

‹‹ 𝒜 ☎ **Hôtel du Cheval de Bronze****

59 rue Charles-de-Gaulle; entrance below the arcade in the town centre.
☎ 03.29.62.52.24 ℱ 03.29.62.34.90
Closed *Nov.* **TV. Pay car park.**

Once a coaching inn, this old hotel has retained a lot of its charm. Clean, quiet rooms go for €35 for a double with shower, €42–54 with shower/wc or bath; the ones overlooking the road have all been soundproofed. Others look over the flowery courtyard. *Free parking offered to our readers on presentation of this guide.*

@ |●| Restaurant Le Clos Heurtebise

13 chemin des Capucins; from the town centre go down rue Charles-de-Gaulle; after the big crossroads turn right and follow the signs.
☎03.29.62.08.04
Closed *Sun evening; Mon; Tues; 13–27 Jan.* **Disabled access. Car park.**

This rather stylish restaurant stands at the edge of a wood in the hills that circle the town. The décor is chic and classically provincial and the service is impeccable. You'll eat excellent cuisine using fresh ingredients; try house specialities such as pan-fried foie gras with blueberries, *croustillant* of crayfish, twice-cooked bream and frogs' legs in season. There's a trolley of wicked desserts, too. The €16.60 menu is served during the week and on Saturday lunchtimes; others range from €25 to €43. The wine list will delight connoisseurs. In summer you can eat outdoors.

St-Étienne-lès-Remiremont
88200 (2km NE)

@ 🎿 🏠 |●| Le Chalet Blanc**

34 rue des Pêcheurs; from Remiremont, take the road in the direction of Bresse; it's next to the Centre Leclerc.
☎03.29.26.11.80 ☎03.29.26.11.81
🖳www.lechaletblanc.com
Closed *Sat lunchtime; Sun evening; Mon; Feb school holiday; 10–25 Aug.* **Disabled access. TV. Car park.**

Despite its uninviting surroundings, in a shopping centre and a main road in full view, the restaurant serves finely prepared food à la carte and excellent-value menus at €20 (not Sun) and €29–65. The décor inside transports you into the Alps – exactly what you need to forget the grim surroundings outside. Good value for money and very good lunch menu; the cuisine is contemporary and innovative: salad of langoustine and orange with blue poppy, dover sole with hazelnuts, rhubarb and herb butter. If you don't want to face the motorway to get back into town after a good dinner, they have a few comfortable and contemporary rooms for €66–75 with bath. *Free coffee offered to our readers on presentation of this guide.*

Girmont-Val-d'Ajol
88340 (10km S)

@ 🎿 🏠 |●| Auberge de la Vigotte**

1 la Vigotte; take the D57 (follow the signs).
☎03.29.61.06.32 ☎03.29.61.07.07
🖳www.lavigotte.com
Closed *Tues; Wed; 15 Oct–20 Dec.* **TV. High chairs available.**

This old Vosges farmhouse, built in 1750, stands in isolated splendour on one side of a valley but, against all expectations, the interior resembles a modern establishment that would not be out of place in any capital city, without a traditional art or craft in sight. All the rooms are different but all are equally enchanting; doubles with shower/wc or bath from €43–64. The whole place has an extremely relaxed atmosphere. The dishes on the menus – €14 (weekdays), €21 and €35 – are in keeping with the times (a mixture of traditional fare and elements from all over the world). *10% discount on the room rate on presentation of this guide.*

Rouvrois-sur-Othain
55230

@ |●| La Marmite

It's on the N18; out in the country, in the direction of Verdun.
☎03.28.85.90.79
Closed *Sun evening; Mon; Tues in winter; a week after New year; a week after 18 Aug.* **Disabled access.**

This bourgeois gastronomic restaurant is typical of its type; quality ingredients are cooked to perfection and servings are very generous. There's an excellent welcome and you get great value for money with menus at €20–48, and dish of the day €12. Good dishes to try include pig's trotter vinaigrette, oven-cooked *andouillette* and *tête de veau* with a mustard and herb dressing.

Saint-Avold

57500

◎ ⅔ ☎ |◎| Hôtel-restaurant de Paris**

45 rue Hirschauer.
☎03.87.92.19.52 ℗03.87.92.94.32
Closed Sat and Sun evenings. **High chairs available. TV.**

In the sixteenth century, this building belonged to the counts of Créhange, who were Protestants. They built a small chapel at the back of the inner courtyard where they could practise their religion without hindrance. That courtyard is now the dining room and the chapel, now an art gallery, retains its sculpted keystones and a fine vaulted ceiling. The restaurant's not that great (menus €13.50–40), but the rooms are decent and freshly refurbished. Doubles with bath go for €60; half board €75. Logis de France. *Free coffee offered to our readers on presentation of this guide.*

Saint-Dié-des-Vosges

88100

◎ ⅔ ☎ Hôtel des Vosges**

57 rue Thiers; it's near the cathedral.
☎03.29.56.16.21 ℗03.29.55.48.71
Disabled access. TV. Car park and pay garage.

A welcoming, well-managed hotel. Doubles with shower go for €38.10, the ones overlooking the courtyard are quieter and more spacious. It's open 24 hours – they have a night porter – which is convenient for late arrivals but there's no restaurant. *10% discount on the room rate for a stay of at least two consecutive nights.*

◎ ⅔ ☎ Hôtel de France**

1 rue Dauphine; it's next to the post office.
☎03.29.56.32.61 ℗03.29.56.01.09
Closed Sun afternoon. **TV. Cots available.**

A well-located hotel with a courtyard. The rooms that look out onto it – nos. 3, 6, 9 and 10 – are particularly quiet and also have a view of the cathedral. Don't be put off by the wallpaper in the staircase; most of the rooms have been renovated. They go for €39 with shower/wc or bath; breakfast €5. *10% discount on the room rate offered to our readers on presentation of this guide.*

◎ ⅔ |◎| Restaurant des Voyageurs

22 rue d'Hellieule.
☎03.29.56.21.56
Closed Sun evening; Mon; 15 July–1 Aug.
Disabled access.

Air-conditioned dining room, classical in style but with a distinctive veranda, from which, if you choose your table right, you can enjoy a view of the Tower of Liberty. Good food that stays strictly within the French tradition and offers probably the best value for money in town with a choice of menus €17–26; reckon on €25 à la carte. *Free coffee offered to our readers on presentation of this guide.*

Taintrux

88100 (6km SW)

◎ ⅔ ☎ |◎| Le Haut-Fer**

230 chemin du Port-Rougiville; take the N420 in the direction of Épinal, then turn left on the D31 towards Taintrux.
☎03.29.55.03.48 ℗03.29.55.23.40
ⓦwww.lehautfer.fr
Closed Sun evening and Mon (except July–Aug and public holidays); a week early Jan. **TV. Games available. Swimming pool. Tennis court. Car park.**

A highly attractive, tranquil spot, set in an old sawmill (hence the name: the *haut-fer* was the biggest blade used to cut up wood). There is little danger of getting bored here, as there's a garden, a swimming pool, and some tennis courts. The rooms are conventional but comfortable, and some of them have a balcony overlooking the surrounding fields. Doubles with bath go for €48–50. Even if you don't stay the night, the restaurant is highly recommended, as it's one of the most outstanding in the region, and the prices are very reasonable too, with menus €10 (weekdays), then €16–33. The cheerful owner goes to great lengths to make her customers feel at ease. Logis de France. *Free coffee offered to our readers on presentation of this guide.*

Ban-de-la-Veline

88520 (15km SE)

◎ ⅔ ☎ |◎| Auberge Lorraine

5 rue du 8-Mai; take the N59 in the direction of Sainte-Marie-aux-Mines.
03.29.51.78.17. ℗03.29.51.71.72.
ⓦwww.auberge-lorraine.com

Closed *Sun evening; Mon; a week end March; a week early July.* **Disabled access. TV. High chairs and games available. Pay car park.**

A small bistro with old-fashioned floor tiles and a wooden bar that is, in time-honoured fashion, the meeting point for the whole village. Behind this rural *façade*, however, lie brand new bedrooms with contemporary floral decoration and a high degree of comfort. Doubles with wash-basin go for €37, with shower/wc or bath €48–50. The restaurant is imbued with the same spirit; the food draws purpose-fully on local tradition but adds some new twists. The weekday lunchtime menu starts at €12, then other menus €17–35. Note the relaxed atmosphere in which guests are received with unforced friendliness. Logis de France. *Free house apéritif offered to our readers on presentation of this guide.*

Saint-Mihiel
55300

⟨⟨ 🍴 🏠 |●| Hôtel-restaurant Rive Gauche**

Place de la Gare; it's near the old station bridge.
☎03.29.89.15.83 ⨍03.29.89.15.35
⟨⟩www.rive-gauche.fr
Disabled access. TV. High chairs and games available. Car park.

They've done a wonderful job of restoring the old station house. The en-suite doubles have shower/wc or bath, cable TV and phone; they go for €40, which is fair given the facilities and the atmosphere; half board €47.50. You'll get good traditional cooking in the restaurant, and fairly generous portions; the €11.50 menu is served daily except Sunday lunch, and others €17–25. *Free house apéritif offered to our readers on presentation of this guide.*

⟨⟨ |●| Resto-Première

8 place des Alliés; near the post office.
☎03.29.89.13.55
Closed *Sun evening; Tues evening; Sat lunchtime; fortnight between Christmas and early Jan.* **Disabled access.**

Friendly welcome and a bonus smile when you sit down to share a table with the regulars from the centre of town. There is a light, airy dining room (or a terrace to share with passing pedestrians) where you can sample the generous set menu or

simply enjoy a large salad (or a smaller one for smaller appetites). Simple, good-quality food, inexpensive and excellent travellers' fare with a regional touch: bone-in knuckle of ham and Charolais beef tartare are among the specialities. Dish of the day is €6, menus €10 weekday lunchtimes; reckon on €20–25 for à la carte. Or there are more sophisticated menus available evenings and weekends.

Bislée
55300 (5km SW)

⟨⟨ 🏠 |●| La Table des Bons Pères – relais de Romainville**

Chemin de Pichaumé; on the D964; don't go into Bislée
☎03.29.89.09.90 ⨍03.29.89.10.01
Closed *Sun evening; Mon lunch; 3 weeks in winter; a week in Sept.* **Disabled access. TV. High chairs and games available. Car park.**

This restaurant, in a restored farmhouse by the River Meuse, is on the side of a road that is not too busy in summer. You dine in a bright airy room overlooking the meandering river, or on a delightful terrace on the bank. The cheery, traditional food includes some fine specialities (terrine of foie gras, thinly sliced *magret, tête de veau* with a herb, caper and egg sauce, apple tart) among its seasonal menus. The weekday lunchtime menu, €10, is served in the bar (wine included); other menus, €15–27. The cooking uses plenty of seasonal produce including wild mushrooms. Eight refurbished doubles go for €43–54 with bath.

Lacroix-sur-Meuse
55300 (10km N)

⟨⟨ 🍴 🏠 |●| Auberge de la Pêche à la Truite

Route de Seuzey; take the D964 then the D109 after Lacroix.
☎03.29.90.15.18 ⨍03.29.90.16.88
⟨⟩www.aubergedelapechealatruite.com
Closed *Fri out of season; 10 Jan–10 Feb.* **Disabled access. Games available. Car park.**

This is more than a hotel-restaurant – it's a concept. You come here to catch the trout and ling that they let out of the fishponds at 9am and 2pm daily – rods are available for hire. There are lots of facilities, including outdoor games for the children, so it's a good spot for families.

The restaurant itself is a converted paper mill, and they've built a terrace with an arbour. Naturally, they serve a lot of fish dishes (menus €16–29): char, trout, carpaccio, and excellent home-made potted trout with hazelnut. Seven immaculate, freshly decorated rooms (all with bath, wc and hairdryer) where you'll be lulled to sleep by the sound of the water. They go for €40–46 depending on the facilities. There is even an outlet selling regional produce, and the welcome is warm and genuine. Logis de France. *Free house apéritif offered to our readers on presentation of this guide.*

Heudicourt-sous-les-Côtes

55210 (16km NE)

◎ ☎ |◉| **Hôtel-restaurant du Lac de Madine***

22 rue Charles-de-Gaulle; take the D901, then the D133 to Chaillon; next to the church.
☏03.29.89.34.80 ℗03.29.89.39.20
🖥www.hotel-lac-madine.com
Restaurant closed *Sat evening; 15 Oct–15 April; Mon (except July–Aug); mid-Dec to early March (except New Year and St Valentine's Day).* **Disabled access. TV. Car park.**

Beside the church in this little village huddled among the mirabelle orchards and 1km from the lake. This place has a quiet charm, very comfortable rooms (in the annexe too, where they're even quieter), some with the added luxury of a massage bath. Double rooms with shower/wc or bath go for €48–85 (top end with massage bath). The restaurant has its regulars and offers regional produce prepared by the chef and served in a tranquil setting with weekday menus at €14; otherwise €22–65. Dishes include: foie gras (excellent selection), tourte Lorraine, quail (boned), pigeon, turbot fillet in a potato crust. Attentive service from the Herbin-Drapier family provides the finishing touch. Logis de France.

Vigneulles-lès-Hattonchâtel

55210 (17km NE)

◎ ⚒ ☎ |◉| **L'Auberge Lorraine**

50 rue Poincaré; take the D901; in the Lorraine regional park, to the north of Lac de Madine.

☏and ℗03.29.89.58.00
Closed *Mon; Sun evening; fortnight in Dec.* **Disabled access.**

A quiet restaurant in a peaceful village in the Lorraine regional park, north of the Lac de Madiane. Simple local fare is listed on the weekday lunch menu (€10) and on others from €13.50 to €25. Some of the appetizing dishes on the menu are crayfish *cassolette*, duck *magret* or pink trout fillet with *flambée* mirabelles. In the evening you can also get pizza, pasta and various cheese-topped dishes. Simple rooms with basin or shower cost €28; half board €34 per person. *Free coffee offered to our readers on presentation of this guide.*

Saint-Maurice-sous-les-Côtes

55210 (22km NE)

◎ ☎ |◉| **Hôtel-restaurant des Côtes de Meuse***

Avenue du Général-Lelorrain; take the D901, then left at the Vigneulles-lès-Hattonchâtel exit, to the D908.
☏03.29.89.35.61 ℗03.29.89.55.50
Closed *Sun evening; Mon; last fortnight in Oct and first week in Nov.* **Disabled access. TV. High chairs and games available. Car park.**

Situated in one of the villages that produces the refreshing Côtes de Meuse wine with its flinty flavour, and also a fresh, fruity sparkling wine, this establishment lacks a little charm despite the terrace that opens onto the garden. The rooms are well kept and well fitted but rather ordinary. Fortunately, they are very quiet and cost €34–43 for a double with shower/wc or bath; half board €45 per person. The restaurant serves regional dishes including items from small, local producers (such as foie gras and rillettes) and well-prepared fish dishes on menus €10.50 (weekdays) and €15–32. You could end the meal with a game of billiards in the bar. Logis de France.

Sarrebourg

57400

◎ ☎ |◉| **Hôtel-restaurant Les Cèdres***

Zone de Loisirs-chemin d'Imling; from the N4 take the exit to Terrasses de la Sarre, then

follow the signs to Zone de loisirs; the hotel is right in the middle.
ⓦwww.hotel-lescedres.fr
☎03.87.03.55.55 ⓕ03.87.03.66.33
Closed 24 Dec–1 Jan. **Restaurant closed** Sat lunchtime; Sun evening. **Disabled access. TV. High chairs and games available. Car park.**

The architecture looks good in this rural setting and the spacious dining rooms are bright and peaceful. There's a piano with a see-through lid for the guests to play after a game of snooker. Chef Monsieur Morin cooks good food: calf's head, fillet of pike perch on a bed of *choucroute* and iced *bergamot soufflée*. They do a weekday lunch menu for €11.60, and others €19.40–34.10; around €41 à la carte. Expect to pay €59.90 for a double room with a bath or shower, or €50.20 per night at the weekends.

ⓔ 🍴 |●| L'Auberge Maître Pierre

24 rue Saint-Martin; cross the railway bridge at the Sarrebourg exit towards Morhange, then follow the arrows.
☎03.87.03.10.16
Closed Mon; Tues. **High chairs available.**

Good, family-style Lorraine cooking, with tasty specialities; a past owner, Marguerite Pierre, invented *flammenküche*, an open bacon and cream tart, which is still on the menu along with flambéed tarts and meats grilled on the open fire; menus €17.50–27.50. Also a Tex-Mex menu on Friday, Saturday and Sunday evenings served at the lower level. There's a convivial atmosphere and late on it can get riotous. *Free coffee or house apéritif offered to our readers on presentation of this guide.*

Sarreguemines
57200

ⓔ 🍴 🏠 Hôtel Aux Deux Étoiles**

4 rue des Généraux-Crémer.
☎03.87.98.46.32 ⓕ03.87.02.93.09
ⓦauxdeuxetoiles.free.fr
Closed Sun and public holidays 10am–6pm. **Disabled access. TV.**

A simple, friendly welcome from Esther and Émile, in keeping with this smart and colourful hotel situated right in the centre of town. If you consider the reasonable prices, the space in the larger corner rooms (the rooms with private wc or one of the nine non-smoking rooms are best) and the

(relative) peace and quiet of this shopping area at night, you'll find this place offers excellent value for money. Double rooms with shower are €34–40, with bath and wc €42–48. *One free breakfast per room or 10% discount on the price of the room offered to our readers on presentation of this guide.*

ⓔ 🏠 |●| Hôtel-restaurant L'Union**

28 rue Alexandre-de-Geiger; from the city-centre, cross the River Sarre, then take rue du Maréchal-Foch and take the second on the left.
☎03.87.95.28.42 ⓕ03.87.98.25.21
ⓔhotelunion@free.fr
Closed Sat; Sun; second and third week in Aug; 23 Dec–1 Jan **TV. Car park.**

A classic hotel set slightly away from the centre. The decoration in the rooms is nothing to shout about, but the facilities are good. You'll pay €51–61 for a comfortable room with shower/wc or bath; half board €56 per person. The restaurant has some style, with a display of minerals in the window and Sarreguemines plates on the walls. Food is regional and perfectly judged, with menus €13–29. Logis de France.

ⓔ 🍴 🏠 Amadeus Hôtel **

7 avenue de la Gare.
☎03.87.98.55.46 ⓕ03.87.98.66.92
ⓦwww.amadeus-hotel.fr
Closed Sun noon–6pm; Christmas to New Year. **Disabled access. TV. Games available.**

As the station hotel this place was getting very down at heel, but since its face-lift it's looking a lot better. The façade has a vaguely Art Deco appearance, and the rooms are beyond reproach – contemporary and attractive with good facilities including hairdryers. Doubles with shower/wc or bath go for €57; triples are €65. *A free breakfast per room offered to our readers on presentation of this guide.*

ⓔ |●| Restaurant La Bonne Source

24 av. de la Gare; in the centre.
☎03.87.98.03.79
Closed Sat lunchtime; Sun evening; Mon; 14 July–15 Aug.

A traditional-looking restaurant with wood panelling and a display of Sarreguemines china, proper tablecloths and cloth napkins. You'll be offered good Alsace and

Lorraine specialities here – *flammenküche* (bacon, cream and onion flan), *lever knepfle* (liverballs with bacon and cream), home-made charcuterie, terrines, *choucroute* and spare ribs. For dessert try the bread and butter pudding made with mirabelle plums. They serve a good-value lunch menu for €11.50 on weekdays and three others at €12.50–20.

@ ⚞ |●| Restaurant Laroche

3 place de la Gare; opposite the train station.
☎03.87.98.03.23
Closed *Fri evening; Sat; 6–28 Aug; 24 Dec–7 Jan.* **Disabled access. High chairs available.**

There are two dining rooms, one of which offers a speedier service than the other. The décor is rustic and a little old-fashioned, but it's as clean as can be. Dishes are nicely presented and good value; there's a weekday menu at €11.50 and set menus €15–22. Good choices include home-made terrine, pike perch Lorraine-style and tripe in Riesling wine. *Free coffee offered to our readers on presentation of this guide.*

@ |●| Le Casino des Sommeliers

4 rue du Colonel-Cazal; opposite the town hall, just under the casino.
☎03.87.02.90.41
Closed *Sun evening; Mon; fortnight in Aug; Christmas to New Year.*

Located in the middle of a small park inside the town's old casino, an unusual building from the late nineteenth century, this classy bistro is decorated with wood panelling and porcelain. In summer there's a lovely terrace under the arcade looking towards the river. As for the food, it's tasty and well priced; €11 menu, dish of the day €8.50 and à la carte (reckon on €25–30). There's an attractively priced wine list, too, with a good number of wines by the glass.

Woelfing-lès-Sarreguemines

57200 (12km SE)

@ |●| Pascal Dimofski

113 rte. de Bitche; it's on the N62 going in the direction of Bitche.
☎03.87.02.38.21
Closed *Mon; Tues; Fri evening; a fortnight in Feb; 3 weeks in Aug.* **High chairs available.**

This may look like an ordinary roadside restaurant from the outside, but owner Pascal Dimofski has turned a simply run family establishment into a gastronomic restaurant that's been rated by the "Moselle Gourmande". The dining room has a refined, quiet atmosphere and it's full of business people and regulars. Weekday lunch menus €20–25; others €35-65: choose dishes such as duck foie gras in roast black pepper and flower of salt terrine, finely seasoned roast blue lobster and golden calf sweetbreads. If you're lucky with the weather, eat in the garden.

Senones

88210

@ ⚞ ♨ |●| Hôtel-restaurant au Bon Gîte**

3 place Vaultrin.
☎03.29.57.92.46 ☎03.29.57.93.92
Closed *Sun evening; Mon; winter school holiday.* **TV. Car park.**

This lovely old house has been renovated inside and out and the resolutely modern décor complements the texture of the old walls. Monsieur and Madame Thomas, the owners, are very welcoming. There are about ten attractive rooms which are most comfortable; doubles go for €40 with shower or €45 with bath. Half board is €54 per person. Nos. 2, 5, 6, and 7 are the quietest. In the dining room you'll eat reliable regional cooking with lots of imagination. There's a weekday lunch menu at €11, then others from €17–30. It gets busy at weekends, and reservations are recommended. *Free coffee offered to our readers on presentation of this guide.*

@ ⚞ |●| La Salle des Gardes

7 place Clémenceau; next to the town hall.
☎03.29.57.60.06
Closed *evenings (except Fri–Sun); 1–15 Jan; 3 weeks in June.* **Disabled access. Car park.**

A simple, attractive brasserie run by a friendly woman with a light culinary touch. Prices are reasonable; menus €9.70–20. She specializes in meats grilled over the open fire. It's a favourite with young people from all around the area. *Free coffee offered to our readers on presentation of this guide.*

Grandrupt

88210 (8km SE)

⊚ 🎿 🏠 |●| Hôtel-restaurant La Roseraie**

3 rue de la Mairie. From Senones, take the D24 then the D45.
☎03.29.41.04.16 ℗03.29.41.04.74
✉laroseraie88@wanadoo.fr
Closed *Tues evening; Wed; 2–24 Jan; autumn school holiday.* **TV. High chairs and games available. Car park.**

The perfect place if you're looking for tranquillity and mountain walks in the forest. Simple but comfortable rooms go for €36–48; they also have a bungalow. The pretty dining room is the ideal setting for their tasty traditional food; menus €10.50 (weekday lunchtimes only) and €16–26. You get a nice welcome, not least from the resident Saint Bernard. There's a terrace. Logis de France. *Free coffee offered to our readers on presentation of this guide.*

Sierck-les-Bains

57480

⊚ 🎿 |●| Restaurant La Vieille Porte

8 place Jean-de-Morbach.
☎03.82.83.22.61
Closed *Tues; Wed; fortnight in Feb; last fortnight in Aug; Christmas-New Year.* **High chairs available.**

Sierck was a refuge for Cistercian monks during the religious wars, and there's an underground tunnel leading from the château to the eleventh-century tower. You reach the restaurant courtyard through an old gate dating from 1604. As for the food, you'll be offered confident dishes from chef Jean-Pierre Mercier who has a good reputation in these parts and further afield (potted clams and frogs' legs, fillet of Charolais beef in pepper and flambéed in cognac, tomatoes stuffed with snails, lamb chops en croûte with mirabelle liqueur). Menus start at €13 (weekdays), with others €24–57; also a regional menu for two, including drinks and coffee at €65 and a "Prestige" menu at €90 can be ordered 48 hours in advance. *Free house apéritif offered to our readers on presentation of this guide.*

Gavisse

57570 (9km W)

⊚ 🎿 |●| Restaurant Le Megacéros

19 place Jeanne-d'Arc; it's on the D64.
☎03.82.55.45.87
Closed *Mon; Tues; 26 Dec–6 Jan.* **Disabled access. High chairs available.**

The *megacéros* is an extinct ancestor of the deer, but there's nothing prehistoric about this restaurant. The cuisine is innovative and the chef creates subtle combinations with local ingredients on menus €16–62 – try the duck foie gras with cocoa beans, the boned pig's trotter with snails and the frozen mirabelle parfait; reckon on €30-35 à la carte. *Free house apéritif offered to our readers on presentation of this guide.*

Rodemack

57570 (13km W)

⊚ |●| Restaurant La Maison des Baillis

46 place des Baillis; take the D64 then the D62; in the centre of the village.
☎03.82.51.24.25
Closed *Mon; Tues; last fortnight in Feb; a fortnight in Nov.* **High chairs and games available. Car park.**

The first lords of Rodemack settled in this handsome village in the twelfth century, and at the end of the fifteenth century the Austrians confiscated the estate. In the sixteenth century, the new owner, bored with being so far from the Viennese court, went home and left a bailiff in the house to manage the place. The restaurant is in this magnificent building. They serve good food in the glorious dining rooms. The menus, €16–30, are built around a robust, local dish such as ham cooked in a hay box with two different sauces. You'll spend about €25 à la carte.

Stenay

55700

⊚ 🏠 |●| 🎿 Hôtel-restaurant Le Commerce**

9 porte de France.
☎03.29.80.30.62 ℗03.29.80.61.77

13

Closed *Fri evening; Sat and Sun lunchtimes; first 3 weeks in Jan.* **TV. High chairs and games available.**

Comfortable, spacious rooms with mini-bar and good bathrooms priced at €40–65 with shower or bath/wc. The dining room serves simple, generous dishes and an array of starters; there's a weekday menu at €12 and others €13–50. À la carte there are a few specialities cooked with beer. Another local delicacy not to be missed are the "crottes du diable": sponge cakes and biscuits from the neighbouring confectioner. Logis de France. *Free house apéritif offered to our readers on presentation of this guide.*

Inor

55700 (7km N)

@ 🏛 |●| Auberge Le Faisan Doré**

Rue de l'Écluse; take the D964.
☎03.29.80.35.45 ℗03.29.80.37.92
ⓦwww.aubergedufaisandore.com
Closed *Fri.* **TV. High chairs available. Car park.**

This place, by the river in a village in the Meuse forest, is popular with hunters. You will eat well – try sweetbread terrine, duck *confit* with mirabelle plums, monkfish with *girolles*, sirloin with local morels or trout *à la lorraine*. The weekday menu costs €11, and there are themed menus, focusing on Lorraine specialities or traditional dishes, from €20 to €40. There's a bar, too. The hotel is decent, though the timbers are fake. Doubles cost €40 with bath; half board €45. Logis de France. *Free house apéritif offered to our readers on presentation of this guide.*

Marville

55600 (16kmE)

@ 🏛 |●| Auberge de Marville

1 Grand-Place; take the D69 as far as Jametz, then the D905 in the direction of Longuyon.
☎03.29.88.10.10 ℗03.29.88.14.60
ⓦwww.AubergeMarville.aol.com
Disabled access. TV. High chairs available.

Behind the old walls of this small, historical village, beside the church, this charming inn is housed in an old, restored barn. A real find that successfully combines old and new – both in the comfortable rooms (some with sloping ceilings and a small lounge area and others looking out over the countryside) which have been personalized with the names of places in the village, and also in the delightfully airy dining room. Double rooms with wc and bath/shower go for €41–54. Quick, friendly service adds to the warmth of this place and there is even a fire in the big fireplace. The Lorraine cuisine is to die for: thinly sliced cured ham and Marville saucisson, fillet of pike perch with red Meuse wine, *cassolette* of frogs' legs with *vin gris de Toul*. Menus start at €10.50 (weekdays), with others €19–39 (evenings and weekends). Allow an average of €30 for a meal à la carte. Not forgetting the impressive breakfast (only €8) with cheese, cold meats, fruit, and a lot more besides. This is an excellent choice in the Meuse region. *A 10% discount on the dinner/room option is offered to readers on presentation of this guide.*

Vilosnes

55100 (20km S)

@ 🏛 |●| Hôtel-restaurant du Vieux Moulin

Rue des Petits-Ponts; take the D964; right in the centre of the village.
☎03.29.85.81.52 ℗03.29.85.88.19
Closed *Wed lunchtimes out of season; 15 Jan–15 Feb.* **TV. High chairs and games available. Car park.**

This Logis de France hotel is in the very heart of this quietest of quiet villages. The mill wheel stopped turning years ago but you can watch the Meuse flow peacefully by from the lovely terrace and from some of the guest rooms. Rooms with shower or bath go for €50–51. They are all renovated, simple and charming, though some of the beams are fake. They serve wholesome family cooking in the restaurant, with good regional dishes listed on menus from €12 to €35. Specialities include roast duck with mirabelle plums, frogs' leg tart and pike cooked in white wine. Logis de France.

Thionville

57100

@ 🏛 |●| Hôtel-restaurant des Amis**

40 av. de-Bertier; leave the motorway at exit 40 and turn right at the fifth set of lights.
☎03.82.53.22.18 ℗03.82.54.32.40

Restaurant closed *Sun; fortnight in Aug; 23 Dec–2 Jan* **TV. High chairs available. Car park.**

For generations, a charming, unpretentious little hotel has hidden behind this vine- and geranium-covered façade. The son of the family has embarked on a complete renovation of the place and work still remains to be done on what has for many years been our favourite spot in town. The rooms have had a makeover but remain simple, despite the floral fabrics, and are all equipped with shower and wc (if sometimes a little narrow). Doubles with shower/wc or bath go for €40–46. The rustic cooking is locally based and it's the Lorraine menu that makes it such a success; menus €11.50–22. The young owner (and his son, Laurent) are so pleasant and helpful that this makes up for any small shortcomings elsewhere.

◎ ▲ Hôtel des Oliviers

1 rue du Four-Banal.
☎03.82.53.70.27 ℱ03.82.53.33.34
ⓦwww.hoteldesoliviers.com
TV.

This town centre hotel is unlikely to appeal to you for its outward appearance but the hugely friendly welcome by its young owner will. As will the light, airy, pastel-coloured rooms, all identical and quiet (even on the pedestrianized street side) and the little terrace where you can enjoy a refreshing breakfast in summer. Double rooms with shower/wc or bath go for €50–52; family rooms (two linking rooms) are €73. Completely refurbished, this is an ideal spot. The only low note is the distance from the parking area.

◎ ▲ |◎| Hôtel L'Horizon***

50 rte. du Crève-Coeur; take exit 40 on the A31 onto the Thionville ring-road then straight on towards Bel Air hospital.
☎03.82.88.53.65 ℱ03.82.34.55.84
ⓦwww.lhorizon.fr
Restaurant closed *Sat and Mon lunchtimes; Jan.* **TV. Car park.**

The striking façade of this luxurious hotel marks the building out from others nearby. In the restaurant, the dishes are finely prepared with a sure hand on menus €38.50 and €53; à la carte around €55–65. Specialities include foie gras with apple chutney and *gigotine* of burbot with saffron. The real luxury is in the rooms. The fine-wood furniture, the little

bedside lamps and the large armchairs will make you – almost – feel at home. In the bathroom you are spoilt with perfumes, soaps, shampoos and other extras. Doubles with shower/wc go for €100, €120–140 with bath.

◎ |◎| Les Sommeliers

23 place de la République.
☎03.82.53.32.20
Closed *Sat lunchtimes; Sun; Christmas to New Year; public holidays.* **High chairs available.**

This reasonably priced restaurant has filled a gap in the market. The frontage is impressive (the building used to be a bank) and the dining room is a lovely space, decorated in brasserie style. They offer really tasty little dishes – depending on the season, what's good at the market, and the inspiration of the chef – and a skilfully selected choice of wines, including some served by the glass. The menu is €14, or around €25 à la carte. It's simple and good, and the service is just as it should be.

Hombourg-Budange
57920 (15km SE)

◎ |◎| L'Auberge du Roi Arthur

48 rue Principale; it's on the D918 to Bouzonville.
☎03.82.83.97.15
Closed *Sun–Tues evenings; early July or after 15 Aug.* **High chairs, games and books available.**

Nothing to do with the legend of King Arthur, but worth a trip anyway. It's a popular place, with lots of regular customers. They have a series of portraits on the walls from the château, and display a splendid porcelain dish made in Sarreguemines. Good country cooking is listed on menus at €11 and €25: try the *croustade* of snails with Moselle wine and mushrooms or the fillet of beef with Roquefort.

Toul
54200

◎ 🍴 ▲ La Villa Lorraine**

15 rue Gambetta.
☎03.83.43.08.95 ℱ03.83.64.63.64
TV. Pay car park.

The style of this building was influenced by the École de Nancy. It's central, clean, charming in an old-fashioned way, and inexpensive. Really nice doubles go for €36–48 with shower/wc or bath. *One free breakfast per room per night or 10 % discount on the room rate (1 Oct–30 April) on presentation of this guide.*

ⓒ ☎ Hôtel de l'Europe**

373 av. Victor-Hugo; it's near the station.
℡03.83.43.00.10 ℻03.83.63.27.67
Closed *a week in mid-Aug; Christmas and New Year.* **TV. Pay Car park.**

This place is paradise for fans of 1930s style; almost everything dates from that period, including the doors, carpets, furniture and the bathrooms. Some rooms have been redecorated, but what they may have lost in authenticity they have maintained in charm. No. 35 is particularly splendid. Doubles with shower or bath/wc cost €44–47.

ⓒ 🍴 |●| Pizza Remi

10 avenue Victor-Hugo; it's opposite the station.
℡03.83.6318.18
Closed *Sat lunchtime; Sun; fortnight in Aug.* **High chairs available.**

A friendly and unaffected restaurant looking onto a little garden where you can eat breakfast in summer. The team of young cooks produce really tasty Italian food including home-made pasta and a wide variety of inexpensive pizzas and meat dishes. A quality place offering menus €8.50 (lunchtimes), with others €15 and €20. The wines aren't pricey either. *Free house apéritif offered to our readers on presentation of this guide.*

Lucey
54200 (9km NW)

ⓒ |●| L'Auberge du Pressoir

Rue des Pachenottes; it's on the D908 (known as the Route des Vins et de la Mirabelle).
℡03.83.63.81.91
Closed *Wed and Sun evenings; Mon; 16 Aug–3 Sept.* **Disabled access.**

It's essential to book at this popular place at the weekend and in summer – not least because of its beautiful countryside setting. It's in what used to be the village station, and there's a genuine antique winepress in the courtyard. The cooking is regional and eclectic; weekday lunch menu €12.70,

then others €16.60–26.80. The wine list features a good variety, including a Côtes de Toul, and you can pick up a few bottles at the wine merchant's next door.

Val-d'Ajol (Le)
88340

ⓒ 🍴 ☎ |●| Hôtel-restaurant La Résidence***

5 rue des Mousses; at the church take the D20 signposted to Hamanxard.
℡03.29.30.68.52 ℻03.29.66.53.00
ⓦwww.la-residence.com
Closed *Sun evening and Mon, 1 Oct–30 April (except during the school holidays); 26 Nov–26 Dec.* **Disabled access (restaurant). TV. High chairs and games available. Swimming pool. Car park.**

Handsome nineteenth-century master craftsman's house set in a spectacular two-hectare park. The rooms are pretty, cosy and very quiet. In addition to the main building there are two modern annexes in the park where you'll also find the pool and the tennis court. Double rooms with shower/wc or bath cost €58–85. The cooking is equally good, with menus from €16.50, €23 and €38.50. You should definitely try the famous Val d'Ajol *andouille*, which is served in its own dish, the pig's trotters stuffed with *andouillette*, and the flambéed chicken flan with morello cherries. Service is impeccable and you're strongly advised to book. Logis de France. *10% discount on the room rate (not available on half board) on presentation of this guide.*

Verdun
55100

ⓒ ☎ Hôtel Les Colombes*

9 av. Garibaldi.
℡03.29.86.05.46 ℻03.29.83.75.25
ⓦwww.hotel-les-colombes.com
Closed *last fortnight in Dec; first fortnight in Jan.* **Open** *daily.* **TV. Pay car park (€5.34).**

The ideal location, close to the centre, with a private (paying) garage, and clean, airy rooms make this hotel a first-class "low-budget" choice. Some rooms (we liked nos. 29, 31, 33 and 35 best) even have a small terrace looking onto the garden; doubles with shower/wc or bath €34–60. Others opening onto the courtyard are a little gloomy. The really friendly welcome adds to the attraction of this simple but recently renovated hotel.

⟪ 🛏 |●| Hostellerie du Coq Hardi***

8 av. de la Victoire.
☎03.29.86.36.36 📠03.29.86.09.21
🌐www.coq-hardi.com
Restaurant closed Sun evening and Fri (bistro open daily). **Disabled access. TV. High chairs available. Pay car park.**

The style and good taste, the prestige of a fine restaurant, the opulent but discreet charm of a "Château-Hôtel de France" and the cosy comfort of the rooms give a sense of character to this hotel in the heart of town, in the pedestrianized area on the banks of the Meuse. You simply can't invent a place like this. Only genuine food lovers need apply – though this luxury does come at a (certain) price. Double rooms, with every convenience, go for €87–135. The "Tradition" rooms offer a very high standard but our preference is for the "Privilège" rooms. The welcome and service are thoughtful and attentive, ensuring an exceptional stay with exceptional eating. The fine, high-quality food is inventive, offering a perfect blend of flavours (eel *marbré* with white leeks, pullet in aspic with a pepper infusion). There's a set menu for €22.50, other menus €32–83; for à la carte allow €75–80. This place has been a hotel for almost two hundred years and the restaurant boasts an excellent chef. On days when the restaurant is closed the more democratic bistro stays open.

ⓔ |●| Le Forum

35 rue des Gros-Degrés.
☎03.29.86.46.88
Closed Wed evening; Sun; last week of July; first week of Aug. **Disabled access.**

Good value, and with a strong local following, this restaurant has a lovely dining room tastefully decorated with subtle watercolours – the vaulted basement, however, is best avoided if you're claustrophobic. Cooking is simple but fresh and light, adapting traditional regional recipes with a modern twist. There's a lunch menu at €8 during the week, with others from €10–25. Good choices à la carte include *pavé* of lamb with goat's cheese and *aumônière* of clams. There's also a small terrace.

ⓔ |●| Le Poste de Garde

47 rue Saint-Victor.
☎03.29.86.38.49
Closed Mon–Fri evenings; Sat; Sun; Aug.
Disabled access. High chairs available.

This establishment was set up to employ young disadvantaged people – ironically, it's in an old guard room. It has been brightly restored in pastel shades with green shutters, and the atmosphere is excellent; the guests all seem to be satisfied. Simple, straightforward cooking, which doesn't attempt to be subtle, is served in large portions that will satisfy your appetite; menus €9–€17.70, and various options à la carte.

ⓔ |●| Restaurant Le Picotin

38 avenue Joffre; direction Étain-Longwy.
☎03.29.84.53.45
Closed Sun evening.

If you prefer to eat in peace, opt for the dining room, as the terrace can get fairly noisy. Inside, the décor is cheery, very "Montmartre", with a fireplace for when it gets cold. Wherever you eat, you'll get good-quality, inventive cooking. The weekday lunch menu costs €10, and there are others at €17 and €26. Try the excellent *tournedos 1900* or one of their big and delicious salads. This place is popular with theatre folk and night-owls, because it stays open late. The owner has also opened the nearby *Chez Mamie* restaurant which offers good, home cooking (52, av. de la 42ᵉ Division – closed Mon and Tues evening ☎03.29.86.45.50 – menu €10).

Vacherauville

55100 (8.5km N)

⟪ 🛏 |●| Hôtel-restaurant Le Relais

Rue du Colonel-Driant; take the D964 in the direction of Stenay; at the exit from the village.
☎03.29.84.51.74 📠03.29.85.17.30
Restaurant closed Sat. **TV. Car park.**

After operating for 23 years, the restaurant is now joined by a thirteen-bedroom hotel, each room (doubles €54–61) decorated differently, immaculate and completely new. This is an ideal staging post, particularly as the hotel is accessible all hours thanks to the automatic barrier system, no reservation necessary (subject to availability, of course). A large car park separates the hotel from the restaurant where you can help yourself from a varied buffet at lunchtime (choice of nine hors d'œuvres, nine main courses and nine desserts). Menus start at €13.50 (weekdays), then other menus €20 and €30. Traditional dishes are served in the evenings and at weekends.

Dieue-sur-Meuse

55320 (12km S)

◉ 🌲 🏠 |●| Château des Monthairons****

Les Monthairons; take the D34.
☎ and ℻03.29.87.78.55
🌐www.chateaudemonthairons.fr
Closed 1 Jan–10 Feb. **Restaurant closed** Mon and Tues lunchtimes (1 April–14 Nov); Sun evening to Tues lunchtime (15 Nov–31 March). **Hotel closed** Sun and Mon. **Disabled access. TV. High chairs available.**

A nineteenth-century château in a walled park with the Meuse meandering gently through it, this hotel is a member of the classy *Châteaux Hôtels et Indépendants* group. It's undeniably stunning to look at, and the comfortable rooms are furnished with antiques. Some are prettier than others, but for €85–155 for a double room you will spend the night in a lovely place where you get lots of little extras such as dressing gowns and luxury toiletries. Half board is compulsory from June to September at €125–195 per person. The restaurant has a good reputation, and attracts people from all over the département; you'll pay €22 for the weekday lunchtime menu and €32–78 for other set menus. Specialities include foie gras and truffles. *Free house apéritif or coffee offered to our readers on presentation of this guide.*

Marre-par-Charny

55100 (12km NW)

◉ 🏠 |●| Le Village Gaulois**

11 rue du Parge; take the D 964 towards Senay; at Bras take the D38 towards Charny and Marre.
☎03.29.85.03.45 ℻03.29.85.00.09
🌐www.villagegaulois.com
Closed early Jan to mid-Feb. **Disabled access. High chairs available. Mini-golf.**

Stone by stone, beam by beam, Lucien and Jean-Marie Hergott built the cosy

central room which serves as a restaurant and created this hotel, using traditional village masonry but with taste and originality. A haven of peace in the shade of old oaks, it offers nine immaculate, stylish rooms with coordinating fabrics; doubles with shower/wc or bath €50. Half board costs from €50 per person. The family rooms with mezzanine and the balcony rooms are delightful. The traditional-style restaurant offers hearty, original dishes you can sample on the shady terrace or in the dining room with its horns, animal skins and rustic furniture carved by the owner. The cheapest menu, served weekday lunchtimes, is €14, and there's another menu at €23; reckon on €40 for à la carte. Try the *chaudée* of pig's ear, the lentil salad with preserved quail, the *pavé* of young stag or the kangaroo with frogs' legs with a nice Meuse wine. You'll get a very friendly welcome. Note that there is a special area set aside for camper vans staying overnight. Logis de France.

Sommedieue

55320 (15.5km SE)

◉ 🏠 |●| Le Relais des Épichées

7 rue du Grand-Pont; take the D 964 as far as Dieue, then left on the D159; not far from the war memorial.
☎03.29.87.61.36 ℻03.29.85.76.38
Closed Fri; Sat lunchtime. **TV. Car park.**

The bar has its regulars who come to sip an apéritif and play snooker; the restaurant attracts a clientele who appreciate the inventive, local cuisine that relies on what's good in the market; weekday menus €11 and €16; market specials €25–30. The terrine of Meuse snails in parsley vinaigrette and preserved garlic, the crunchy pike perch in basil, the Meuse duck stew and the duck saucisson are enough to make you forget the false beams on the ceiling. The hotel offers a warm, sincere welcome, and simple, clean rooms (€34–37 for a double with shower/wc or bath) overlook the Dieue stream and a pretty little washplace.

Étain

55400 (20km NE)

◉ 🌲 🏠 |●| Hôtel-restaurant La Sirène**

22 rue Prud'homme-Navette; take the N3.
☎03.29.87.10.32 ℻03.29.87.17.65

@hotel.sirene@free.fr
Closed *Sun evening; Mon out of season; Jan.*
TV. High chairs available. Car park.

Apparently, Napoleon III dined in this handsome house after the battle of Gravelotte in 1870. The interior is very rustic in style and it's filled with antiques. You'll get a pleasant welcome, the atmosphere is hushed and the customers are well-to-do. Rooms are quite comfortable, all of them double-glazed; doubles go for €42–59 with shower/wc or bath. Choose one at the back for the view. The cheapest menu, €12, is served daily except Sunday, and there are others up to €39. Good, conventional cooking that often relies on the combination of sweet and savoury (roast veal with mirabelle plums, ham braised with peaches). Try out the new conservatory that lightens up the dining room and opens onto the terrace. There are two tennis courts to try out too. Logis de France. *Free coffee offered to our readers on presentation of this guide.*

Ville-sur-Yron
54800

@ 🎏 |●| La Toque Lorraine

1 rue de l'Yron; 25km from Metz via the D903 and 13km from the A4 motorway (exit 33). Take the D952 through Jarny in the direction of Mars-la-Bur, then the D132 as far as the village.
℡03.82.83.98.13
Closed *evenings except Fri and Sat; July.*
Disabled access.

This village, which is typical of the region, has been transformed into an eco-museum. You can take a stroll around and see an old mill, the wash-house, the Romanesque church and some pretty, traditional Lorraine houses, like the one housing this restaurant. It has several dining rooms, one of which has a proud fireplace. It's got a farmhouse atmosphere, refined but formal, with stone walls beautifully shown off by discreet lighting. There's a weekday lunch menu at €12, evening menus €19.80–41.50. The cooking is full of flavour, and will set you up for a good walk round the village. *Free coffee offered to our readers on presentation of this guide.*

Vittel
88800

@ 🎏 🛏 |●| Hôtel-restaurant La Chaumière

196 rue Jeanne-d'Arc.
℡03.29.08.02.87
Closed *Sun in winter.* **Car park.**

A tiny hotel with a bar and restaurant. It's not much to look at, but the proprietress is delightful, and the chef cares about what he's doing. They give the impression that they are enjoying themselves, which makes a nice change from the health farm-style strictness that pervades the rest of the town. Rooms, €28 a night, are simple and clean, with washing facilities only. Menus €10.50–15, list a selection of local, regional or international dishes. *Free coffee offered to our readers on presentation of this guide.*

@ 🎏 🛏 |●| Hôtel de l'Orée du Bois**

1 lieu-dit L'Orée-du-Bois; take the D18 out of town in the direction of Contrexéville, it's 4km north on the D18 opposite the race course.
℡03.29.08.88.88 ℻03.29.08.01.61
@www.loreeduboisvittel.fr
Closed *Sun evenings from Nov to end Feb.*
Disabled access. TV. High chairs and games available. Swimming pool. Car park.

A modern hotel and conference centre in a quiet spot. They specialize in getting guests back into shape; sports facilities include a gym, tennis courts, indoor heated swimming pool with sauna and Jacuzzi. The rooms are comfortable; reckon on paying €56–75 for a double with shower/wc or bath. The décor of the rooms varies: some are rustic while others are contemporary. The owners have recently refurbished a few rooms using environmentally friendly materials. The restaurant serves menus from €11.80 to €33. The cuisine is traditional and the menu changes regularly. Logis de France. *Free coffee offered to our readers on presentation of this guide.*

@ 🛏 |●| Hôtel-Restaurant d'Angleterre***

162 rue de Charmey.
℡03.29.08.08.42 ℻03.29.08.07.48
@www.abc-gesthotel.com

Classic, imposing spa hotel with a pink frontage and an all-pervading air of faded grandeur. In general, and particularly in the rooms, everything has been done up. To guarantee peace and quiet, take a room at the back – the railway isn't that far. Doubles with shower/wc or bath start at €84; €180 for the two suites with a spa bath. The restaurant provides traditional, sometimes regional, dishes on menus between €17 and €40. There's a garden. Logis de France.

Ⓔ |●| Le Rétro

158 rue Jeanne d'Arc.
☎03.29.08.05.28

Tasty southern dishes served all year round in this easy-going, rustic dining room with stone walls, flowery tablecloths and a rustic fireplace: frogs' legs *à la provençale* or *à l'andalouse*. Note though that if you want to try the frogs' legs you need to order before 11am for lunch and before 6pm for dinner. And in case you don't fancy the frogs' legs there's *tête de veau*, coq au vin and dishes grilled over a wood fire. Menus start at €11.50 (weekdays only), and there are others at €15–32. There's a small outdoor terrace in the summer, a friendly welcome and diligent service. American Express cards not accepted.

13

LORRAINE

Midi-Pyrénées

Aignan

32290

@ 犬 ♠ |●| **Le Vieux Logis**

Rue des Arts; it's behind the town hall.
☎ 05.62.09.23.55
Closed *Sun evening.* **TV.**

An unobtrusive establishment near the town square offering doubles with shower/wc or bath at €40. The welcome might be a little forced but the bright curtains, period furniture and beautiful flowers are inviting. Good food on €10–21 menus which offer soups, cep omelette, shrimps *à la provençale*, lamb kebabs and desserts. The specialities, produced only when the ingredients are available at market, include such things as fresh duck foie gras with peaches, pike perch with *beurre blanc* and prawns flambéed with Armagnac. There's a terrace for dining in fine weather. *Free coffee offered to our readers on presentation of this guide.*

Alban

81250

@ 犬 |●| **Restaurant du Midi★★**

9 pl. des Tilleuls.
☎ 05.63.55.82.24
Closed *Mon and Tues evenings; last week in Dec.*

This unassuming but very welcoming little restaurant on the village square serves high-quality food – the chef trained in some of the great local kitchens before taking over his grandmother's bistro. There's a set menu at €11.50 (starter, main meal, cheese, and dessert, drinks extra), which is probably the best in the *département* in this price range, and others possible by reservation and consultation with the chef. Only quality ingredients and the freshest produce go into the tasty dishes. *Free house apéritif offered to our readers on presentation of this guide.*

Albi

81000

@ ♠ **Hôtel GeorgeV★★**

29 av. du Maréchal-Joffre; it's 150m from the train station.
☎ 05.63.54.24.16 ⊕ 05.63.49.50.78
⊛ www.hotelgeorgev.com
TV.

This is a simple but pleasant place that is easy on the wallet – more of a quiet, friendly family *pension* than a hotel, with around ten fairly spacious rooms. Double rooms cost €33–44, according to the degree of comfort (slight discount possible in low season), with toilets on the landing for the cheapest ones. On fine days, breakfast is served on the terrace.

@ ♠ **Hôtel Saint-Clair★★**

8 rue Saint-Clair; it's near the cathedral.
☎ 05.63.54.25.66 ⊕ 05.63.47.27.58
⊛ www.andrieu.michele.free.fr
TV. Pay car park.

A small two-star hotel in the old part of town with two different types of room at €38–60, depending on facilities. The least expensive rooms are very simple and have retained the old-fashioned charm of the 1960s (although some of the bathrooms have also retained the slightly less appealing plumbing installations of the period). In

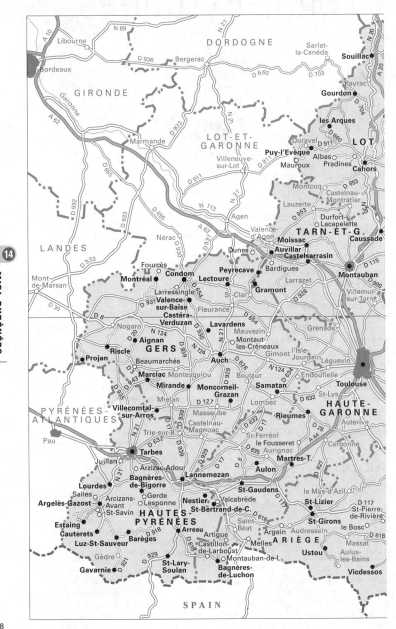

Libourne
N 89
DORDOGNE
Sarlat-
la-Canéda
Souillac
D 936
Bergerac
N 21
Bordeaux
A 10
D 6 60
D 703
A 20
Payrac
GIRONDE
Garonne
Gourdon
D 704
les Arques
Marmande
D 933
LOT-ET-
GARONNE
Duravel
D 911
D 660
LOT
Puy-l'Evêque
Albas
Pradines
Cahors
A 62
Villeneuve-
sur-Lot
D 911
Mauroux
Montcuq
D 653
Castelnau-
Montratier
N 20
D 665
Garonne
N 113
D 911
Agen
Lauzerte
D 953
Durfort-
Lacapelette
Nérac
A 62
D 931
Valence-
d'Agen
TARN-ET-G.
Caussade
D 932
Dunes
Moissac
Auvillar
Castelsarrasin
Montauban
D 115
LANDES
D 333
D 30
Fourcès
D 665
Condom
Lectoure
Peyrecave
Bardigues
Larrazet
Villemur-
sur-Tarn
D 999
Mont-
de-Marsan
D 933
Montréal
Larressingle
Valence-
sur-Baïse
D 654
St-Clar
Gramont
D 928
D 931
Fleurance
D 6
Castéra-
Verduzan
Lavardens
D 654
Grenade
Nogaro
D 930
N 21
Mauvezin
Montaut-
les-Créneaux
l'Isle-
Jourdain
D 220
Aignan
N 124
GERS
Auch
D 626
Gimont
N 124
Léguevin
Toulouse
Riscle
N 124
Beaumarchés
D 929
Bouleur
Endoufielle
Projan
D 843
Marciac
Montesquiou
Moncorneil-
Grazan
Samatan
St-Lys
HAUTE-
GARONNE
D 935
Mirande
Mielan
D 127
Lombez
Rieumes
D 632
Auterive
PYRÉNÉES-
ATLANTIQUES
Villecomtal-
sur-Arros
Masseube
Castelnau-
Magnoac
D 632
D 17
D 28
A 64
Carbonne
Pau
D 939
Trie-sur-B.
St-Ferréol
le Fousseret
Martres-T.
D 627
Tarbes
D 632
D 929
D 17
Aurignac
D 635
Aulon
Jujllan
N 21
Arzizac-Adour
Lannemezan
Lourdes
Bagnères-
de-Bigorre
Gerde
Lesponne
Nestier
Valcabrède
St-Gaudens
le Mas-d'Azil
Salles
Arcizans-
Avant
St-Savin
St-Bertrand-de-C.
D 117
St-Lizier
St-Pierre-
de-Rivière
D 117
Argelès-Gazost
HAUTES-
PYRÉNÉES
Saint-
Béat
D 618
St-Girons
le Bosc
Estaing
Cauterets
Arreau
Artigue
Argein
Audressein
D 618
Luz-St-Sauveur
Barèges
Castillon-
de-Larboust
Melles
ARIÈGE
Massat
Gèdre
D 918
D 921
D 929
St-Lary-
Soulan
Montauban-de-L.
Ustou
Aulus-
les-Bains
Gavarnie
Bagnères-
de-Luchon
Vicdessos

SPAIN

CANTAL

Saint-Flour

Martel
Tauriac
D 703
Carennac
Meyronne St-Céré Sousceyrac
Autoire Latouille-
Rocamadour Lentillac
N 140
Gramat Leyme
Lacapelle-Marival
Assier
Labastide- Cardaillac
Murat Figeac
D 19
Decazeville
Tour-
de-Faure Cajarc
St-Cirq-Lapopie
D 1
Limogne-en-
D 19 Rignac
Villefranche- Belcastel
de-Rouergue D 911
Monteils
Caylus
D 926 Najac
Monteils D 922
St-Antonin-
Noble-Val
Montricoux Monestiés
Cordes
Brousses N 88
Larroque Cahuzac-
sur-Vère Castelnau-
Puyceloi de-Lévis
Castelnau- Gaillac Albi
de-Montmiral
D 68
Rabastens TARN
St-Sulpice Giroussens Lasgraïsses
Réalmont
St-Lieux- D 631 Graulhet
lès-Lavaur Lavaur
Roquecourbe
Cuq-Toulza Puylaurens
Castres
N 126 St-Avit St-Salvy-
St-Julia Revel de-la-Balme
St-Félix- Dourgne N 112
Lauragais Soréze
Saint-Ferréol Mazamet
Villefranche-
de-Lauragais
Nailloux N 113
A 61
Carcassonne
D 623
D 119 AUDE
Limoux
Foix
Montgaillard
Nalzen Lavelanet
Tarascon- Montségur
sur-Ariège
N 20 E 9
Ax-les-
Thermes
N 116
PYRÉNÉES-ORIENTALES
AND

Aurillac
D 922
D 920
Thérondels
N 122
Cassuéjouls
Grand- Entraygues-
Vabre sur-T. Laguiole
D 963 le Fel
D 920 D 921
Conques
N 140 Estaing Espalion
Marcillac Mandailles
Ste-Eulalie-
Salles- Bozouls d'Olt St-Géniez-
la-Source D 988 Gabriac d'Olt
Rodez N 88
Ste Radegonde Sévérac-
le-Château
D 911
N 88 Salmiech
D 902
AVEYRON
Faussergues
Carmaux
Millau
D 902 Creissels
Villeneuve- St-Jean-
sur-Tarn du-Bruel
Plaisance D 999 Nant
D 989 Saint-Affrique
D 999
Alban D 607

A 75
Mende
N 88
LOZÈRE
A 75
Florac
N 106
D 907
Meyrueis
le Vigan
GARD

Lacaune
Lodève A 75
Lacrouzette
Burlats D 922
D 622

HÉRAULT
N 9
A 9
Béziers
N 112
Narbonne
N 9

MEDITERRANEAN
SEA

N

0   20 km

Perpignan

contrast, the four most expensive rooms (in the annexe) have been prettily restored and modernized (air-conditioning, pale colours and parquet floors).

◎ 🏠 |O| Hôtel-restaurant du Vieil-Alby**

25 rue Henri-de-Toulouse-Lautrec; it's 200m from the cathedral in the heart of the old town.
℡05.63.54.14.69 ℻05.63.54.96.75
℮le-vieil-alby.sicard@wanadoo.fr
Closed Sun evening; Mon; Feb school holiday; first week in July. **Restaurant closed** Sun evening; Mon lunchtime; Sat lunchtime. **TV. High chairs available. Pay car park.**

This simple, well-run hotel is one of the most reasonably priced in this part of town: spacious double rooms with shower/wc go for €46, or €53 with bath. The owner is very congenial, but he doesn't allow smoking anywhere in the hotel, nor does he accept pets. The cooking offers excellent local cuisine on menus starting at €13 (weekday lunch), then €17.50–45, with house specialities such as tripe, radish with salty pig's liver and *melsat*. The food has deservedly won a great reputation and attracts a loyal following. Logis de France.

◎ 🍴 🏠 |O| Hôtel Mercure Albi Bastides***

41 rue Porta; it's on the left after the bridge over the Tarn in the direction of Paris-Carmaux.
℡05.63.47.66.66 ℻05.63.46.18.40
🕸www.accorhotels.com
Restaurant closed Fri evening to Sun afternoon (Nov–Feb); Sat and Sun lunchtime (March–Oct); 20 Dec–3 Jan. **Disabled access. TV. High chairs available. Car park.**

This luxury hotel in a redbrick, eighteenth-century mill stands proudly opposite the cathedral, overlooking the lush banks of the Tarn. It has now been restored, with its monumental porch and façade kept intact, and work to create a new section especially for business guests is currently underway. For a hotel of this category, it can be recommended, but you pay for the comfort of course – well-equipped, air-conditioned rooms go for €80–92 with bath – but there is the added bonus of the view, which is probably the finest in Albi. The cooking is wonderful, and if you eat on the terrace you get views of the river and the old town. Set menus range from

€17 to €40, and you'll pay around €35 à la carte. Specialities include *marbré* of foie gras with duck *aiguillette*, house *cassoulet* and fillet of pike perch. There's a wonderful wine list at rock-bottom prices – try the restaurant's own Mercure. The service is amiable and efficient. *Free coffee offered to our readers on presentation of this guide.*

◎ 🍴 |O| Le Lautrec

13 rue Henri-de-Toulouse-Lautrec.
℡and ℻05.63.54.86.55
Closed Sun evening; Mon; first week in Feb; fortnight in Nov. **High chairs and games available.**

This restaurant, located in the most touristy part of town, is sited in converted stables that belonged to the painter Henri de Toulouse-Lautrec. The décor skilfully combines brickwork and soft colours. There is a quiet, intimate patio, ideal for the summer. The regional food on the weekday lunch menu (€11) is cooked exceedingly well; other menus €14–34. Try any of the excellent meat or fish dishes: scallop with Lautrec pink garlic, lamb sweetbreads with a walnut wine sauce. *Free apéritif offered to our readers on presentation of this guide.*

◎ |O| Le Tournesol

Rue de l'Ort-en-Salvy; it's in a side street leading to place du Vigan.
℡05.63.38.38.14
Closed 1–15 May; 15–31 Aug. Open lunchtime only Tues–Sat. **Disabled access.**

This is the best vegetarian restaurant in the Tarn region, serving good food at realistic prices. The airy dining room is simply decorated and air-conditioned, and in summer you can eat on the terrace. The cooking is uncomplicated and very tasty; a meal costs about €13. They serve organic apple juice and beer.

Castelnau-de-Lévis
81150 (8km W)

◎ |O| La Taverne

Rue Abijoux, Castelnau-de-Lévis; from Cordes, take the D600, after 4km turn left onto the D1 and Castelnau is 3km further on.
℡05.63.60.90.16
Closed Mon; Tues; Feb and All Saints' school holidays.

Heaven on earth for lovers of good food and definitely worth the trip. The "chef's suggestions" include *émincé* of veal with wild mushroom *compote*, superlative roast duckling stuffed with raspberries and grilled lobster. The desserts are out of this world, and the extensive wine list includes a terrific Buzet. You eat either in the dining room, with its country-style décor, or on the covered terrace. The service is as good as the food. The excellent menus range from €23 to €60; expect to pay around €50 à la carte. In short, it's one of the best restaurants in the region.

Argelès-Gazost

65400

◎ 🏠 Hôtel Beau Site**

10 rue du Capitaine-Digoy.
☎05.62.97.08.63 ℻05.62.97.06.01
🖳 www.hotel-beausite-argeles.com
Closed *5 Nov–15 Dec.* **TV. High chairs available.**

A characterful hotel with a stone wall façade brightened up with flowers. Genuine welcome, cosy atmosphere and period furniture, though the look is outdated. The rooms are all different and the ones overlooking the huge and luxuriant garden are particularly appealing; doubles cost €39–40 with shower/wc or bath. Half board is available at €40–41 and the menu offers two starters, main course, cheese and dessert. You can enjoy your meal seated on the terrace, which has a splendid view of the gorgeous garden. Logis de France.

◎ 🏠 |●| Le Miramont***

44 av. des Pyrénées; at the first roundabout, take the road to Cauterets and it's opposite the spa.
☎05.62.97.01.26 ℻05.62.97.56.67
🖳 www.hotelmiramont.com
Closed *Sun evening and Wed (Jan–June and Oct–Dec); a fortnight in Jan; 15 Nov–15 Dec.* **Disabled access. TV. High chairs available. Car park.**

A fine Art Deco hotel set in a park planted with rose gardens and hydrangeas. The rooms are spacious, elegant and calming, with up-to-date facilities (new mattresses, hair dryers, en-suite bathrooms) and balconies with views of the old town or over the Pyrenees. Rooms 114, 121 and 122 are larger than standard; doubles with shower/wc or bath cost €41–70 depending on the season. The restaurant deserves

a mention in its own right, and has won a loyal local following. The chef, Pierre, is the owner's son, and his wife runs the dining room. Dishes, which change with the seasons, include good fish specialities and light versions of regional dishes, along with superb desserts. The cheapest menu at €20 (not available for Sun lunch and public holidays) is fine and generous; the second menu at €34 is very elaborate, with *amuse-bouches* and cheese. The service is ultra-professional but never stuffy, and the clientele is made up mainly of regulars who come again and again.

Saint-Savin

65400 (3km S)

◎ 🌂 🏠 |●| Le Viscos***

☎05.62.97.02.28 ℻05.62.97.04.95
🖳 www.hotel-leviscos.com
Closed *Sun evening and Mon (except school holidays); Mon lunchtime (July–Aug); a week in Jan; a week in Dec.* **Disabled access. TV. Car park.**

A lovely hotel with recently refurbished rooms. Doubles go for €46–76 with shower/wc or bath, and half board is also available at €52–79 per person, depending on the season. The chef has come up with an original idea: he structures his menus around different themes. The creative cooking is based on fresh local produce: great seafood dishes, such as stuffed squid and prawns, as well as pigeon *craquelin* with foie gras and ceps. There's a set lunch for €16 (Tues–Sat), and other menus at €22–52; the cheapest menu includes cheese and dessert. You should allow about €50 for a meal à la carte. This restaurant justifies its good reputation. *10% discount on the room rate (except during school holidays) offered to our readers on presentation of this guide.*

Arcizans-Avant

65400 (4km S)

◎ 🏠 |●| Auberge Le Cabaliros**

16 rue de l'Église; take the D921, then the D13.
☎05.62.97.04.31 ℻05.62.97.91.48
Closed *Tues evening and Wed out of season; early Nov to end of Jan.* **TV. Car park.**

This attractive inn, where you'll get a good-hearted welcome, has a terrace with views over the valley. There are ten doubles with shower/wc or bath at €50–56;

some of the rooms are under the eaves and are lovely but others are not that attractive, though they do have decent facilities. The traditional regional cooking, with menus at €16–36, can be enjoyed under the arbour in fine weather. The à la carte menu includes an authentic *garbure*, a broth with pickled goose and stuffed neck of duck (Fri evenings or by reservation only) as well as pigeon in choux pastry with foie gras. The staff are pleasant. Logis de France.

Salles
65400 (4km N)

◎ 🧖 🛏 |●| La Châtaigneraie

It's in the centre of the village. Take the D102.
☎05.62.97.17.84
Closed *Mon; Jan; open only for bookings on Sun, public holidays and in the summer.* **TV. High chairs available. Car park.**

A very beautiful dining room in a renovated farm. Grills are a speciality, and they are prepared in front of you: try the *magrets* or the grilled Pyrenean lamb with beans. Also good are the scallops on a bed of leeks, pan-fried foie gras with grapes and the bilberry tart. Menus cost €23–45, and in the summer you can eat on a lovely terrace. The staff are smiling and the service is faultless so it's essential to book. There are rooms available in the gîte – €40 for a double or €45 per person half board. A studio is also available for rent at €280 per week, with a special offer for visitors to the local spa of €550 for three weeks' rental in May, June, Sept and Oct. *10% discount on the room rate or free coffee offered to our readers on presentation of this guide.*

Arques (Les)
46250

◎ |●| La Récréation

☎05.65.22.88.08
Closed *Wed; Thurs; early Dec to end Feb.* **Open** *weekends only in low season.*

The village is marvellously situated, perched overlooking a valley surrounded by copses and oak forests; the restaurant is in the refurbished village school, strategically located for the famous church and a museum housing the work of the artist, Zadkine. In good weather aim for a table on the little shaded terrace, otherwise you will eat in an old classroom. The cuisine is a delight: lobster ravioli with coral sauce, excellent meat dishes and lots of fish too. There's a single menu at €26; in July and August there's another menu for €18 served for lunch on weekdays.

Arreau
65240

◎ 🧖 🛏 |●| Hôtel d'Angleterre**

18 rte. de Luchon; take the D618 (route des Cols).
☎05.62.98.63.30 ℱ05.62.98.69.66
ⓦwww.hotel-angleterre-arreau.com
Closed *Easter to Pentecost; 1 Oct to Christmas.* **TV. Disabled access. High chairs and games available. Swimming pool. Car park.**

A seventeenth-century coaching inn which has been tastefully restored to create a warm, comfortable hotel with quality furnishings and service, though it's a bit pricey. Doubles with shower/wc cost €50–72, and half board (€58–63 per person) is compulsory from mid-July to mid-September. There's a pretty garden and a pool behind the hotel. On offer in the restaurant is good regional cooking supervised by the chef from *La Grange*, in Saint-Lary. Menus at €18–38 include the specialities: foie gras *au torchon*, beef cuts with subtle woody flavours and country custard with raspberries. *Free house apéritif offered to our readers on presentation of this guide.*

Auch
32000

◎ 🧖 🛏 |●| Hotel de France Le Jardin des Saveurs***

2 pl. de la Libération.
☎05.62.61.71.99 ℱ05.62.61.71.81
TV. High chairs available. Pay car park.

This old staging post in the town centre has all the standard facilities of a modest hotel; doubles cost around €63 – the price varies according to the degree of comfort – with a supplement of €16 for children aged under ten and an optional buffet breakfast at €10. It is in the restaurant that the place comes into its own, however, as it is one of the most highly rated not only in the town but also in the *département* (not that there's much competition). There are four menus ranging in price from €25 to €62. We chose the cheapest one: *pressé de foie gras*, salmon and cod with crispy vegetables and apple-and-grape *clafoutis*, ice cream with spiced bread. It could be said that the prices are slightly excessive and the atmosphere a little stuffy, but the customers – mainly local worthies and English-speaking tourists – don't seem to mind. Experienced gourmets might expect something a little more special for their money, but it's a good place nonetheless. *Free coffee offered to our readers on presentation of this guide.*

⊛ |●| La Table d'Hôte

7 rue Lamartine.
☎05.62.05.55.62
Closed *Sun; Wed; first week in March; first week in July; 24–31 Dec.*

A discreet little place between Sainte-Marie Cathedral and the Jacobean Museum, with space for only twenty in the cosy rustic dining room. The *menu du jour* at €16 is particularly good value, and it's best to book if you're determined to taste their famous speciality – Gascon "Hamburgers" (duck and foie gras). There's another menu at €22. Terrific welcome is given by the young owners.

Montaut-les-Créneaux
32810 (10km NE)

⊛ ⚘ |●| Le Papillon

It's on the N21, 6km from the centre of town, in the direction of Agen.
☎05.62.65.51.29
⊛lepapillon@wanadoo.fr
Closed *Sun evening; Mon; a fortnight in Feb; a fortnight Aug–Sept.* **Disabled access. Games available.**

Good restaurant in a modern building where the chef cooks meat in a traditional style with painstaking precision. He is also one of the few local chefs with an interest in seafood (particularly fish) and is an expert in its preparation. Both traditionalists and more adventurous spirits can find satisfaction here. Try the sole stuffed with foie gras, the swordfish *croustade*, the *cassoulet* with Gascon beans, *millefeuille* of monkfish with asparagus tips or the tenderloin with cranberries. There's a weekday lunchtime menu at €13.50, and four others at €15.50–40; the mid-range ones are particularly good value. In fine weather you can dine out-

side on the terrace. *Free glass of dessert wine offered to our readers on presentation of this guide.*

Aulon
65240

⊛ |●| Auberge des Aryelets

Take the D929 from Arreau as far as Guchen (in the direction of Saint-Lary), then turn right on the D30.
☎05.62.39.95.59
Closed *Sun evening–Tues (out of season); 15–30 June; mid-Nov to mid-Dec.*

A typical mountain dining room with timbers and beams, a mezzanine floor and a fireplace flanked by a pair of old-fashioned skis. The décor has been brightened by Provençal tablecloths and napkins and a few watercolours. The cuisine (menus €18.50–29.50) is rooted firmly in the local tradition: *garbure* (broth with pickled goose), snail stew, *magret* of duck with bilberries, duck's liver fried with walnuts, pineapple and lychees with spicy syrup and upside-down tomato tart. In fine weather they put a few tables on the terrace. The place is impeccably clean and the service is friendly and swift. It's best to book in advance.

Auvillar
82340

⊛ ⚘ ⚐ |●| Hôtel-restaurant L'Horloge**

Place de l'Horloge.
☎05.63.39.91.61 ☎05.63.39.75.20
Closed *Fri and Sat lunchtimes (15 Oct–15 April); 7 Dec–8 Jan.* **TV.**

The restaurant caters for all appetites and pockets. It's a charming place and has a superb terrace under the shady plane trees. Lunchtime menus range from €15 to €20. The cheapest and fastest of the lunchtime menus is the "*bouchon*" set menu, which is very satisfying and very popular. The food at dinner is more sophisticated (menus €24–65) allowing the promising chef to show off his expertise. The atmosphere is friendly and informal; the place is well equipped to receive tourists and it's an ideal spot to stay, with very clean doubles at €42 and €50. *Free house apéritif offered to our readers on presentation of this guide.*

Bardigues

82340 (4km S)

◉ |●| Auberge de Bardigues

Take the D11.
☎05.63.39.05.58
Closed Mon; 3 weeks in Jan. **High chairs
available.**

A very nice restaurant in a charming village, run by a young couple called Camille
and Cyril. The dining room on the first
floor has contemporary décor with splendid stone walls, and there's a beautiful
shady terrace opening onto the village and
the surrounding countryside. The cuisine
is intelligently prepared; light, tasty and
fresh, and dishes change with the seasons:
millefeuille of salmon and artichoke, veal
blanquette. The weekday lunch *menu du jour*
for €12 includes wine and there's another
menu at €25; the wine isn't too expensive.
Long may it thrive.

Dunes

82340 (12.5km W)

◉ |●| Restaurant Les Templiers

1 pl. des Martyrs; take the D12 towards
Donzac then the D30 on the left. It's under
the arcades.
☎05.63.39.86.21 ☎05.63.39.56.21
Closed Sun evening; Mon; Tues evening; Sat
lunchtime; All Saints' Day holiday. **Disabled
access. High chairs available.**

A nice local restaurant, with a bright, cosy
dining room, prettily set on a lovely village
square. The €20 lunch menu (not served
weekends and public holidays) offers
refined local dishes based on seasonal produce and recipes at very affordable prices;
other menus go up to €44. The wine
menu includes cheap local wines.

Ax-les-Thermes

09110

◉ 𝕏 🛏 |●| Le Châlet**

Avenue Turrel; it's opposite the thermal baths
of Le Teich.
☎05.61.64.24.31 ☎05.61.03.55.50
🌐www.le-chalet.fr
Restaurant closed Sun evening; Mon; mid-
Nov to mid-Dec. **TV. High chairs available.**

A really nice young couple run this
appealing hotel. All the rooms (€42 for a
double) have either recently been updated
or are brand new. They are bright and

clean and some look over the Oriège
that runs alongside the thermal spa of
Le Teich. The beautiful restaurant is one
of Ariège's gourmet establishments and
serves a weekday lunch menu at €16;
other menus €20–40. Logis de France.
*Free house apéritif offered to our readers on
presentation of this guide.*

◉ 𝕏 🛏 |●| L'Orry Le Saquet**

It's 2km from Ax-les-Thermes going towards
Andorra.
☎05.61.64.31.30 ☎05.61.64.00.31
🌐www.auberge-lorry.com
Closed Tues evening; Wed; autumn school
holiday. **TV. High chairs available. Car
park.**

This is one of the best restaurants in
Ariège, run by Marc Heinrich, an excellent chef from Alsace. There is a lunchtime
menu at €16, with others going up to
€46. They all offer exceptional value for
money; for €21, for example, you can
savour duck and ceps ravioli and mouthwatering poultry *jambonette* stuffed with
Rouzolle and stewed in sauce. As for the
hotel, the smart, new rooms are perfectly
equipped; one suite (€145 for two people)
even offers a hydromassage bathtub. Other
doubles with bath cost €55. *Free house
apéritif offered to our readers on presentation
of this guide.*

Bagnères-de-Bigorre

65200

◉ 𝕏 🛏 |●| Hôtel de la Paix**

9 rue de la République.
☎05.62.95.20.60 ☎05.62.91.09.88
🌐www.hotel-delapaix.com
Closed 25 Dec–30 Jan. **TV.**

With sparkling white and pink fabrics
in the hall, this hotel's décor is as kitsch
as you'd like, but the facilities are very
good and the welcome cannot be faulted.
The rooms are all different (ask to see
more than one) and offer good value for
money. They're set around a sunny patio
or look onto the garden and cost €20
with basin, up to €45 with bath. There are
three dining rooms serving reassuringly
traditional dishes that change with the
seasons; the cheapest menu (€13) is available every day for lunch and dinner; you
can expect to pay around €25 à la carte.
Typical dishes on offer include trout fillet

with chanterelles, *pavé* of beef with morels and *magret* of duck with fruit sauce. *Free apéritif offered to our readers on presentation of this guide.*

@ ☕ ☎ Hôtel d'Albret**

26 rue de l'Horloge; it's on the corner of place Jeanne-d'Albret.
☎05.62.95.00.90 ℗05.62.91.19.13
✉eric-coel@wanadoo.fr
Closed *early Oct to early Feb.*

The hotel has a pretty Art Deco façade with balconies, a glass porch and stained glass on the staircase. The old-style rooms are quite large and are painted in fresh colours; the bathrooms have old-fashioned shoe-box baths. Rooms with washing facilities cost €22 (shower along the landing at a charge of €1.50), or €33 with bath; breakfast is €5. There's no double glazing but the hotel is situated on the corner of a quiet square. Good value for money. *10% discount on the room rate (from the second consecutive night) offered to our readers on presentation of this guide.*

@ ☕ |●| Le Bigourdan

14 rue Victor-Hugo.
☎05.62.95.20.20
Closed *Sun evening; Mon; a fortnight in spring; a fortnight in Nov.* **Disabled access. High chairs available.**

This place is on the first floor of an old traditional house in a pedestrianized street, so it's not noisy. Hefty beams, rough-cast walls, floral fabrics and still lifes on the walls. Good regional specialities are cooked using fresh produce – and the menu's as long as your arm. Menus start with a weekday lunch menu at €10, with others up to €50. Dishes include foie gras, scallops and meat. Children can enjoy pizzas while their parents treat themselves to a gourmet meal. *Free house apéritif offered to our readers on presentation of this guide.*

Gerde
65200 (1km SE)

@ |●| L'Auberge Gourmande

4 pl. du 14-Juillet.
☎05.62.95.52.01
Closed *Mon; Tues; Nov.* **Children's games available.**

A calculated reworking of the traditional bistro format, with soothing yellow walls,

charming floor tiles and a few tables on the terrace next to the village hall. The seasonal dishes are concocted by Gilles Béal, who invites his customers to take a stroll in the kitchen garden complete with aromatic herbs. Specialities include rabbit with sage and sweetbreads with ceps and Banyuls gravy. The ingredients are fresh and tasty and, unlike some chefs, Béal seems to have applied his imagination more to preparing the food than dreaming up fancy names for it. Menus are at €18.30 ("*gourmet*"), €23 ("*gourmand*" or greedy!) and €46 (samples of a variety of dishes). A few wines with AOC (classification of origin), such as Madiran and Buzet rosé, are available at reasonable prices. Service at the tables is provided by Vincent, in his immaculately white apron. The attention to detail extends to the little basket of games given to children, allowing their parents to eat in peace.

Lesponne
65710 (10km S)

@ ☕ ☎ |●| Domaine de Ramonjuan**

Take the D935 to Baudéan and turn right onto the D29; leaving Lesponne in the direction of Chiroulet, it's on the right.
☎05.62.91.75.75 ℗05.62.91.74.54
🌐www.ramonjuan.com
Restaurant closed *Sun evening; Mon; Easter and All Saints' Day.* **Disabled access. TV. High chairs and games available. Swimming pool. Car park.**

This farm, at a height of 800m, has been turned into a nice hotel without losing its homely feeling. The pleasant rooms are named after flowers and are furnished with pine; doubles with shower/wc cost €45–58, and half board (compulsory in the summer) is €45–55 per person. There are also some holiday apartments for rent. They offer a host of facilities including tennis, a sauna, a whirlpool bath, a gym, table tennis, a swimming pool, a pool hall and table football (in the old farm). Nearby you can also try rafting, go-carts, paragliding and mountain biking in the park beside the Adour. The restaurant serves a lunch menu at €12 and others €15–23. They hold a good number of conferences so it's advisable to book. *Free house apéritif offered to our readers on presentation of this guide.*

Bagnères-de-Luchon

31110

@ 🎋 ♿ |●| L'Auberge de Castel-Vielh

Route de Superbagnères; 3km from Bagnères-de-Luchon, take the road on your left towards Superbagnères.
☎and ℱ05.61.79.36.79
Closed *Wed (except during school holidays).* **Open** *noon–2pm and 8–10pm.* **Disabled access. TV. High chairs and games available. Car park.**

A nice house in the local style, situated on a hilltop, with a big garden and pretty terrace, a children's play area, and spacious doubles with shower/wc (€38.15–45.75) overlooking the mountains. The restaurant is famous for its cooking. There are set menus at €19–37, and the à la carte menu includes *pétéram luchonnais*, prawns with meadow mushrooms, trout in matelote sauce, and *pan cremat* (burnt bread in Catalan), a foie-gras speciality. There are lots of lovely walks in the area. *Free house apéritif offered to our readers on presentation of this guide.*

Montauban-de-Luchon

31110 (2km E)

@ 🎋 ♿ |●| Le Jardin des Cascades**

Follow the signs for the Herran forest road and head for the hillside church of Montauban; from there, you will have to climb 150m on foot (if you call in advance, staff will come to collect your luggage).
☎05.61.79.83.09 ℱ05.61.79.79.16
Closed *Oct–April.* **TV.**

It's advisable to book at this exceptional establishment. The house is a listed building and it's in a wonderful, peaceful location, clinging on to the mountainside in the middle of an enormous park just 50m from a gushing waterfall. In summer you eat outside and enjoy the superb views over the valley; otherwise, it's the elegant, black-and-blue dining room, with its cosy fireplace. The weekday lunchtime menu, at €19, offers superb traditional cooking with dishes such as *pétéram* (stew of sheep's trotters and tripe) and *pistache* (braised leg of mutton with haricot beans); other menus are available at €26–32. There are a few double rooms; €35 with basin and €40 with shower/wc; half board is

available from the third night at €46 per person. *Free house apéritif offered to our readers on presentation of this guide.*

Castillion de Larboust

31110 (6km W)

@ ♿ |●| Hôtel L'Esquérade**

Take the D618, the road to the Payresourde pass. Approximately 1km after Saint-Aventin, the hotel is at the bottom of the road.
☎05.61.79.19.64 ℱ05.61.79.26.29
🖰www.esquerade.com
Closed *Mon, Tues and Wed lunchtimes (except June–Sept); 1–15 April; 6 Nov–16 Dec.* **TV. High chairs available. Car park.**

The village is 954m up in gorgeous green countryside. The hotel itself is comfortable, and the building typical of the locality – it's built of stone with wooden balconies. Most of the rooms (€44–60 for a double) overlook the valley. A young and gifted chef recently took the place over and he produces excellent regional dishes served in a warm and welcoming atmosphere. The menus, starting at €23 and going up to €90 for the *menu dégustation*, change with each season, because he uses only fresh local produce: *pétéram luchonnais*, *zarzuella* or frogs' legs. There's also an excellent wine list. Logis de France.

Artigue

31110 (11km NE)

@ 🎋 |●| Les Hauts Pâturages

It's in the village; take the roads to Juzet, Sode and Artigue.
☎05.61.79.10.47
Closed *Mon (except public holidays); Oct–March.* **High chairs available.**

This little restaurant perched on a mountain slope makes no effort to draw attention to itself, so we are thrilled to have discovered it. The location is stunning, with an unbeatable view of the Pyrenees (when there are no clouds); the food is solid, country fare guaranteed to satisfy even the most voracious of appetites and is served with loving care in a convivial, welcoming atmosphere. The prices are extremely reasonable: there are no less than eight menus ranging from €8.50 to €27. It is advisable to book, to make sure that you can enjoy the pleasures of this exceptional spot. *Free house apéritif offered to our readers on presentation of this guide.*

Melles

31440 (30km NE)

⚮ 🏠 |●| Auberge du Crabère

Take the D618 then the N230.
☏05.61.79.21.99 ℻05.61.79.74.71
Closed Tues evening and Wed (Sept–June);
end Nov to mid-Dec. **Open** noon–1.30pm
and 7–8.30pm.

The imposing house is right in the middle of the village, on the route of the GR10 walking trail. There are a few spacious, country-style rooms, with half board compulsory all year round at €31 per person. Patrick Beauchet toiled long and hard as a chef on transatlantic cruise liners before going for this post. He's made the mountains his home and his cuisine is bursting with local goodies such as wild mushrooms, crayfish, and game in season. He's become so expert that he's even written two recipe books: *Mes Recettes de Comminges et des Pyrénées Centrales* and *La Vanille: 10 façons de la préparer.* There's also a short *menu randonneur* for €12 (not served on Sun) – specially designed for hikers – or you can choose one of the other menus €23.90–27.45. To best appreciate the delights on offer, it is worth taking the plunge into the more expensive menus.

Barèges

65120

⚮ 🍴 |●| Le Rozell

39 rue Ramond; go up the main street towards the tourist office.
☏05.62.92.67.61

Small restaurant with space for just thirty people in a basement with pinewood panelling, roughcast walls and rustic tables. It opts for efficient service and for quality at a reasonable price (menus €19 and €27) that is all too rare in ski resorts. Diligently prepared fish, meat and *fondues* provide a tour of France's traditional dishes: *magret fondue,* salad of fried shrimps and queen scallops tossed in Jurançon wine, scallops with morels, grilled swordfish, without forgetting the generously proportioned crêpes (€3–8 according to the number of ingredients). The restaurant's name even refers to the crêpes – a *rozell* is a wooden implement used to spread out pancake dough. *Free coffee offered to our readers on presentation of this guide.*

⚮ 🍴 |●| Auberge du Lienz, Chez Louisette

It's 3km from Barèges; travel in the direction of Tourmalet, then turn onto the road to the Plateau de Lienz.
☏05.62.92.67.17
Closed 2 weeks end April to early May; Nov. **High chairs and games available.**

One of the nicest spots in the valley; it's surrounded by trees and is to be found at the beginning of the route around lakes Glère and Néouvielle. In winter, this is where the ski runs finish. It's a bit like a country inn you might find near a big town, not least because of its glorious summer terrace. The *menu garbure* for two at €30 includes ham *garbure* (stew with ham, cabbage and bacon), honeyed loin of Bigorre black pig and stuffed trout with ceps. There's a second menu at €30; à la carte will cost around €30, or try the good regional menu, based on a sample of dishes featuring Barèges-Gavarnie mutton. Desserts are on the pricey side. This auberge has become a real institution in the region, but it has now lost some of its original authenticity. *Free house apéritif offered to our readers on presentation of this guide.*

Belcastel

12390

⚮ 🏠 |●| Hôtel-restaurant du Vieux Pont***

It's opposite the bridge.
☏05.65.64.52.29 ℻05.65.64.44.32
🖥www.hotelbelcastel.com
Closed Sun evening; Mon; Tues lunchtime; 1 Jan–15 March. **TV. Car park.**

Sisters Michèle and Nicole Fagegaltier have turned their beloved childhood home into a much-admired hotel that is a faithful reflection of Belcastel itself – perfect from every viewpoint. The restaurant serves some of the best food in the area, based on old family recipes. Top-quality local produce is given a feminine touch that makes all the difference. Some dishes are pricey but there's a range of menus from €26 (weekdays) up to €75. Situated on the other side of the river and reached by the little fifteenth-century bridge, the accommodation is as good as the cooking. Rooms are comfortable, bright, well maintained and full of little extras that show great attention to detail. Doubles cost €73–80; half board is available at €88–95 per person. The service is exceptional. It is essential to book.

Bozouls

12340

ⓒ 🏠 |●| Hôtel à la Route d'Argent**

La Rotonde, route d'Espalion.
☎05.65.44.92.27 ℗05.65.48.81.40
Closed *Sun evening and Mon (out of season); Jan and Feb.*

This hotel provides an excellent stopover on the l'Aubrac road. Double rooms are available at €40–56. The restaurant offers fresh produce straight from the market in Rodez, prepared with real skill and professionalism to bring out all its flavour. Outstanding dishes, all served in extremely generous portions, include fried pigeon breast with figs, l'Aubrac beef with truffle gravy and lamb's brains with parsley and herb pancake. Most desserts are prepared to order, and the ice creams are homemade. Menus range in price from €16 to €42; the one at €24 offers particularly good value for money. The wines (Gaillac and Marcillac) start at €12. The inviting dining room is lined with portraits, and on Sundays it is more or less essential to book, because it is popular for family get-togethers. The service is efficient and friendly.

Cahors

46000

ⓒ 🏠 Auberge de jeunesse

20 rue Frédéric-Suisse.
☎05.65.53.97.02 ℗05.65.35.95.92
🌐www.fuaj.org
Restaurant closed *Sat evening; Sun.*

A charming, friendly youth hostel that shares an atmospheric seventeenth-century monastery with a hostel for young workers. The imposing façade is bordered by a small garden, while the interior is dominated by a splendid staircase and long corridors paved with worn flagstones. Guests are accommodated in rooms for two to ten people at €9.50 a night, and meals are available a €8.60. It's compulsory to have a FUAJ card, and Internet connections and laundry

are both available. Credit cards are not accepted.

ⓒ 🍴 🏠 Hôtel de France***

252 av. Jean-Jaurès; it's in the avenue leading to the station.
☎05.65.35.16.76 ℗05.65.22.01.08
🌐www.hoteldefrance-cahors.fr
Closed *3 weeks Dec to early Jan.* **Disabled access. TV. Car park.**

Modern, functional architecture in this eighty-room hotel, with large, spotless doubles priced at €44–62. Rooms are all very well-equipped and some have air-conditioning too; the ones overlooking the courtyard are quieter. The setting is as charmless as any hotel from a chain but nobody comes here for a long stay. The service is courteous and unobtrusive. *10% discount on the room rate (15 Oct–15 April) offered to our readers on presentation of this guide.*

ⓒ 🍴 🏠 Hôtel À l'Escargot**

5 bd. Gambetta.
☎05.65.35.07.66 ℗05.65.53.92.38
Closed *Sun evening out of season; fortnight in Feb; fortnight at the end of the year.* **TV.**

The attractive, south-facing façade of this hotel overlooks the boulevard, but the modern bedrooms inside are situated to the rear and are therefore peaceful. Some are set in a medieval tower and so have a special character. Friendly service is guaranteed. *10% discount on the room rate for a minimum stay of two nights (except July–Aug) offered to our readers on presentation of this guide.*

ⓒ 🏠 |●| Le Grand Hôtel Terminus – Le Balandre***

5 av. Charles-Freycinet; it's 50m from the train station.
☎05.65.53.32.00 ℗05.65.53.32.26
🌐www.balandre.com
Restaurant closed *Sun; Mon; fortnight end of Nov.* **Disabled access. TV. High chairs available. Pay car park.**

The charm of this spruce, comfortable hotel evokes the early twentieth century. In fact, for almost a century it has been in the hands of the same family, intent on preserving a traditional approach to running a hotel. The large, pleasant rooms – €57–95 with bath/wc, all with air-conditioning and some with a terrace – allow guests to forget the somewhat dreary surroundings and the nearby train station. The decoration is strictly classical, with heavy curtains, pedestal tables, snug armchairs and even a pretty desk for writing letters. There's an award-winning restaurant, highly reputed throughout the region, with menus at €31 and €40 (weekdays), €55 and €90, and a weekday set lunch for €16, served in the bar.

ⓔ |●| Restaurant Le Lamparo

76 rue Clemenceau (place de la Halle).
☎05.65.35.25.93
Closed Sun; first week in June. **Open** 10am–3pm and 7pm to midnight. **Disabled access. High chairs available.**

This restaurant, right by the market, is pleasant in all seasons. You can enjoy anything from a home-made pizza to *magret* with foie gras. The two dining rooms are always full and the place appeals to all ages because of the range of menus, speed of service and good atmosphere. There's a weekday menu at €11.20, with others €14.90–21. The charming owner, Lola Lestrade, had the inspired idea of turning the rooms in the old hotel into three appealing mini-apartments. Priced at €46–62 and each with its own entrance, these are warmly furnished with bright colours and are spotlessly clean.

ⓔ |●| Bateau-restaurant Au Fil des Douceurs

90 quai de la Verrerie; it's next to the Cabessut bridge.
☎05.65.22.13.04
Closed Sun; Mon (except holidays); 3 weeks early Jan; a fortnight end June to early July.

This restaurant is set in a delightful little barge firmly anchored amidst the ever-changing colours of the Lot, opposite the old town of Cahors. Unfortunately, the decoration is somewhat tatty and the food rudimentary (albeit well prepared), but its sleepy charm is irresistible. There's a set lunch menu at €12.50 with others €18.50–43.

ⓔ |●| Auberge des Gabares

24 pl. Champollion.
☎05.65.53.91.47
Closed Sun; Mon evening.

In this small family restaurant, you can eat under a pergola on the terrace overlooking

the Lot, or in the pretty, rustic dining room. The food is not particularly sophisticated but it is reliable and comes in huge portions. Every table is set with a bottle of mineral water and another of chilled red wine. The owners serve their guests themselves, with unfailing and much-appreciated cheerfulness. There is just one menu, at €13 (everything included). Credit cards not accepted.

Pradines
46090 (3km NW)

ⓔ ▲ |●| Le Clos Grand**

Laberaudi; take the D8 in the direction of Pradines Luzech.
☎05.65.35.04.39 ℱ05.65.22.56.69
Closed Sat lunch; Sun evening; Mon (except July–Aug); ten days end June; during Christmas holiday. **TV. High chairs available. Swimming pool. Car park.**

A good provincial inn with a lush garden and a lovely swimming pool, offering very pleasant and comfortable rooms; a double costs €36–57 depending on the level of comfort and the season. The rooms are plainly decorated but they are clean and pleasant. Ask for a room in the annexe as they have views over the countryside. You can eat in the pretty, rustic dining room or, in sunny weather, on the shady terrace in the garden. The restaurant has a very good reputation; specialities include the fisherman's grilled fish and *tournedos Rossini*. The cheapest set menu costs €16.50 (weekdays), and others are €24.50–36. Logis de France.

Albas
46140 (25km W)

ⓔ |●| Auberge d'Imhotep

Rivière Haute; between Luzech and Albas, via the D8, it's on the lefthand side of the road.
☎05.65.30.70.91
Closed Sun evening; Mon. **Disabled access. High chairs available.**

This small restaurant boasts food as original and colourful as its décor. Local produce is served almost raw, with duck being the star turn. There are also exotic and vegetarian influences, all contributing to the personal touch. Menus range from €13 to €39. You are guaranteed a very warm welcome here, but you are highly advised to book beforehand.

Cahuzac-sur-Vere
81140

ⓔ |●| La Falaise

Route de Cordes; it's 15km north of Gaillac, on the D922.
☎05.63.33.96.31
ⓔguillaume.salvan@wanadoo.fr
Closed Sun evening, Mon and Wed lunchtime. **Disabled access. High chairs available.**

One of the most popular restaurants in the area where you will find refined cuisine from Guillaume Salvan, who has a real talent for introducing new, unexpected flavours into traditional regional dishes. Dishes change with the seasons: succulent roast shin of veal with ceps, warm *croustade* with apples and plums. There is a lunch menu at €20 (except Sun), with others €29–40. The interesting wine list features good local Plageoles, and the staff give well-judged advice about the wine, always bearing in mind the accompanying dishes. The colourful dining room is delightful, with pale-wood furniture, and the terrace is almost a match for it. You are strongly advised to book – in fact it's essential.

Cajarc
46160

ⓔ ⅔ ♠ |●| Hôtel-restaurant La Ségalière

Route de Cadrieu.
☎05.65.40.65.35 ℗05.65.40.74.92
ⓦpro.wanadoo.fr/hotelsegaliere
Closed lunchtimes (except Sat and Sun and during July–Aug); 1 Nov–1 March. **Disabled access. TV. Swimming pool. Car park.**

In this region of old stone houses, here is a modern hotel that merits an extended stay (it's certainly our best find in the vicinity). Its lush surroundings are enhanced by the beautiful big swimming pool, and the functional bedrooms are complemented by a terrace. Doubles are €60–80, depending on the season. The restaurant sticks to tradition (but not slavishly so) and the dishes are prepared with a skilled hand by an experienced chef: trout sautéed with almonds and honey, foie gras – either half-cooked with saffron or flambéed in vintage plum brandy. There's also a fine choice of wines to wash all this down. There is a weekday lunchtime menu at €14, then others at €19–48. Logis de France. *10% discount on the price of a room (except summer) or free house apéritif offered to our readers on presentation of this guide.*

Carennac
46110

ⓔ ⅔ ♠ |●| Hostellerie Fénelon**

Rue Principale.
☎05.65.10.96.46 ℗05.65.10.94.86
ⓦwww.hotel-fenelon.com
Closed Mon lunchtime; Fri and Sat lunchtimes out of season; 6 Jan–15 March; 17 Nov–Dec. **TV. High chairs available. Swimming pool. Car park.**

A conventional hotel with very decent, cosy rooms furnished in country style, with the prettiest ones overlooking the Dordogne. Doubles with shower are priced at €49.50–60, half board (compulsory July/Aug) €52–61. The cooking is good and does not take excessive liberties with either the flavours or the presentation; the set lunch menu at €13 is served on weekdays and there are several other menus at €19–37. The dining room looks over the garden and swimming pool and some tables have views of the river; there's also a nice fireplace. You can eat on the terrace in fine weather. Logis de France. *Free coffee offered to our readers on presentation of this guide.*

ⓔ ♠ |●| Auberge du Vieux Quercy**

☎05.65.10.96.59 ℗05.65.10.94.05
ⓦwww.vieuxquercy.com
Closed Sun evening and Mon out of season; 15 Dec–15 March. **TV. High chairs available. Swimming pool. Car park.**

This distinctive old staging post offers pleasant rooms, completely refurbished by the new owner and endowed with a view of the garden and surrounding cluster of shiny roofs; double rooms cost €65–72, depending on the season. There are also a few bungalows around the swimming pool. Traditional dishes and excellent service are the order of the day in the restaurant, where menus range from €20 to €35.

Tauriac
46130 (4km E)

ⓔ |●| Côté Jardin

Take the D43, then the D20 and D3 in the direction of Castelnau.

☎05.65.38.49.51
Closed *Sun evening; Mon; Sat lunchtime.*

People come from far and wide to savour the deliciously fresh food of the chef and Ghislaine Forges, who use only the very best local produce. Specialities on the menus (€12–23) include duck (in countless presentations), Quercy lamb and *croustade* of sweetbreads. In summer, these can be enjoyed amidst the flowers in the large garden. The service is enchanting.

Carmaux
81400

◎ 𝒳 |●| **Restaurant La Mouette**

4 pl. Jean-Jaurès.
☎05.63.36.79.90
Closed *Sun (except July–Aug); Mon; ten days in Oct.*

This is without doubt the best gastronomic restaurant in Carmaux. In an original, modern setting, Monsieur Régis has devised a series of interesting menus (including a *"Jauressien"* menu written in Occitan). The weekday lunch menu is at €12.50, with others at €16–43. Specialities include meats grilled over an open fire, ravioli stuffed with smoked duck breast, and *millefeuille* of spiced-bread ice cream. Practically everything is prepared on the premises. *Free house apéritif offered to our readers on presentation of this guide.*

Faussergues
81340 (25km E)

◎ |●| **Le Moulin de Faussergues**

Take the D91, then the D74 to Valence-d'Alibigeois; there is a signpost on the right, before reaching Faussergues.
☎05.63.53.49.11
Open *Wed evening to Sun; public holidays. May be open at other times during summer.*
Closed *Nov–March.*

This restaurant is set in a wonderful little millhouse tucked in the bottom of an unspoilt valley. There are only set menus here (€19, €28 and €34), so you don't have to waste time choosing from a vast list of dishes and can make the most of your apéritif on the terrace. The second menu features grilled lobster (with supplement) and truffle *brouillade*. Excellent service but, be warned, the clientele is fairly

posh (even the Préfet comes here to eat). *Free coffee offered to our readers on presentation of this guide.*

Castelnau-de-Montmiral
81140

◎ 𝒳 🏠 |●| **Auberge des Arcades**

It's on the place des Arcades, the main square.
☎05.63.33.20.88
🖥www.castelnaudemontmiral.com
Closed *15 Jan–1 Feb.* **Open** *until 9pm.* **High chairs available.**

Decent, very simple rooms under the eaves, with shower or bath (wc on the landing) for €30–34; some overlook the beautiful village square. The communal areas, in contrast, are fairly dowdy. In the restaurant the cheapest weekday no-frills lunchtime *menu du jour*, at €10, includes cheese, wine and dessert; there's a second lunch menu for €10 and other menus range from €15 to €33. The house specialities include wild boar stew and duck *confit*. The bar is an important meeting place for locals. *10% discount on the room rate (except July–Aug) or free house apéritif offered to our readers on presentation of this guide.*

Castelsarrasin
82100

◎ 𝒳 🏠 **Hôtel Marceillac★★**

54 rue de l'Égalité; it's in a road off the place de la Liberté.
☎05.63.32.30.10 📠05.62.32.39.52
🖥www.hotelmarceillac.com
Closed *5–12 Jan.* **TV. Pay car park.**

There's a surprise when you walk into this seemingly ordinary hotel, built in the early twentieth century and run by five generations of the same family. Away from the noise of the road, the rooms overlook a small interior courtyard with a glass roof and the reception area is in a kind of glass cage; the whole place is light and airy, making it look like a hotel typical of a spa town. The rooms, with their antique furniture, are equally delightful: €39–52 for a double with shower/wc or bath. To top it all, the service is charming. *10% discount on the room rate (except July–Aug) offered to our readers on presentation of this guide.*

MIDI-PYRÉNÉES

Castera-Verduzan

32410

@ 🎄 |●| Le Florida

Rue du Lac.
☎05.62.68.13.22
Closed *Sun evening and Mon (except public holidays); Feb school holiday.* **Disabled access.**

This is a long-established restaurant renowned for its food. It is run today by Bernard Ramouneda under the watchful eye of his grandmother, Angèle, who ran it herself in her younger days. Distinguished by delicious, seasonal local produce, dishes are cooked with respect and precision, and are served with attentiveness and efficiency. Typical offerings on the excellent weekday lunch menu (€15) include salad of warm *boudin* with apples, fig tart with foie gras, *poule au pot* and *croustillant* of pig's feet; other menus are €22.50–50. For dessert, there's the prune soufflé. Angèle can rest assured that her legacy is in good hands. *Free coffee offered to our readers on presentation of this guide.*

Castres

81100

@ 🏠 Hôtel Rivière**

10 quai Tourcaudière; it's on the banks of the Agout, opposite the old tanners' houses.
☎05.63.59.04.53 ℻05.63.59.61.97
⊛perso.wanadoo.fr/hotelriviere
TV. Pay car park.

The attractive décor – reproductions of Impressionist paintings – and the congenial staff make this a pleasant hotel. The pretty rooms smell fresh and clean. You'll pay €26 for a double with wc, or €45–48 for a double with bath (1 or 2 beds). The rooms overlooking the embankment can be noisy even though they have double glazing.

@ 🎄 |●| Resto des Halles

Place de l'Albinque.
☎05.63.62.70.70
Closed *Sun evening; Mon; first fortnight in Aug.*

A good brasserie specializing in meat that is carefully chosen and tastefully prepared. Menus are at €11 for a weekday lunch, and €15 (quarter litre of wine and coffee included in both); expect to pay around €22 à la carte. The salads are guaranteed to be fresh, as all the ingredients come from the market downstairs. Good value for money that also extends to the wines. You will be gracefully received even if you turn up a little late. *Free house apéritif offered to our readers on presentation of this guide.*

@ 🎄 |●| Le Pescadou

20 rue des Trois-Rois.
☎05.63.72.32.22
Closed *Sun; Mon; public holidays; first week in Jan; fortnight in Aug.*

When there's no space left in this little restaurant they set extra tables in the fish shop – the owner is a fishmonger and opens his shop very early every morning to receive the daily catch. Though some dishes are always on the menu – *bouillabaisse* – what you'll be offered depends on the catch of the day. There are no menus but expect to pay around €25 à la carte. Everything is good, fresh and served generously with good humour – which explains why the place is always so full. In summer you can dine outside on the terrace. This is indeed fortunate, as the restaurant is tiny. *Free house apéritif offered to our readers on presentation of this guide.*

Burlats

81100 (10km NE)

@ 🏠 Le Castel de Burlats

8 pl. du 8-Mai-1945; take the D89 or the D4 then follow the signs to Burlats.
☎05.63.35.29.20 ℻05.63.51.14.69
⊛le.castel.de-burlats@wanadoo.fr
Closed *Feb school holiday; a weekend Aug to early Sept.* **Disabled access. TV. Games, high chairs and other baby equipment available. Car park.**

This splendid château, built between the fourteenth and sixteenth centuries, stands opposite the Romanic collegiate church. The owners have retained the natural charm of the building and the interior, and the extensive gardens are attractive. The ten or so lovely rooms are very large; some have fireplaces or floors laid with hand-made tiles. They're non-smoking and priced €61–75 for a double with shower/wc or bath; dogs are permitted at €8 per night. The huge, beautifully furnished salon is the perfect place for curling up with a good book, and other facilities include a handsome billiard room, and a tea room open to non-guests. There's just one menu (€20), which is available for hotel guests only.

Roquecourbe

81210 (10km N)

⍟ ⍟ |●| La Chaumière

14 allée du Général-de-Gaulle; take the D89 from Castres, follow directions to Vabre, turn right at the square with a fountain.
☎05.63.75.60.88
Closed Sun evening; Mon; 3 weeks Jan; last week in June; first fortnight in July. **Disabled access. High chairs available.**

A friendly, welcoming, recently refurbished restaurant with a family atmosphere and a huge, peaceful dining room to the rear. The excellent food is strongly rooted in local tradition. The menus cost €16.50–38 and specialities include duck foie gras with apples, and pike perch with shallot butter. If you want to reproduce this regional food back home, the owner will happily pass on the secrets of her *melsa* and *bougnette* – as well as many useful tips. *Free house apéritif offered to our readers on presentation of this guide.*

Saint-Salvy-de-la-Balme

81490 (16km E)

⍟ ⍟ |●| Le Clos du Roc

Take the D622 in the direction of Brassac for 15km then turn right into the lane to Saint-Salvy.
☎05.63.50.57.23
Closed Mon evening; Wed evening; Sun evening; Christmas to New Year.
Disabled access. High chairs and games available.

A reliable restaurant in a solid granite house – it's popular locally, so it may be best to book. The spacious dining room is in a converted barn with enormous beams and the décor is stylish and charming. The tasty, regional cuisine has a good reputation and prices are affordable; they do a weekday lunch menu for €11, which includes cheese, dessert and wine, and others at €17–34. *Free house*

apéritif offered to our readers on presentation of this guide.

Caussade

82300

⍟ ⍟ 🏠 |●| Hôtel Larroque**

Avenue de la Gare; it's opposite the train station.
☎05.63.65.11.77 ℗05.63.65.12.04
Restaurant closed Sat lunchtime and Sun evening out of season; mid-Dec to mid-Jan.
Disabled access. TV. High chairs and games available. Swimming pool. Car park.

A family business that goes back five generations and has a solid reputation. Guests and atmosphere are both rather elegant and the décor is plush; there's a very pleasant swimming pool and a solarium. Double rooms go for €46–48 with bath – no. 6 has a small terrace opening onto the swimming pool. The restaurant offers imaginatively reinterpreted regional cuisine, with menus from €11.50 (weekday lunch) up to €30. There is a dining area near the swimming pool. Logis de France. *Free house apéritif offered to our readers on presentation of this guide.*

Monteils

02300 (2km NE)

⍟ |●| Le Clos de Monteils

Take the D17.
☎05.63.93.03.51
Closed Sat lunchtime; Sun evening; Mon; Tues (Nov–May); mid-Jan to mid-Feb.

Just minutes from the motorway, this gourmet restaurant is well worth the detour; it is not the place for anybody in a hurry, however: good food requires time and patience. It's run by chef Bernard Bordaries, who has worked in some of the greatest restaurants before settling in this lovely priory, swathed in Virginia creeper. He and his delightful wife have created a place of refined charm. Dishes change with the seasons but may include charlotte with goat's cheese and artichokes, chestnut *velouté* with walnut oil, duo of pork with red cabbage, and luscious desserts. There are two weekday lunch menus at €16 and €23, and evening menus at €25–43 (also Sun lunchtime). The terrace is ideal for outdoor dining in fine weather. Credit cards not accepted.

Cauterets

65110

⊚ ≜ |●| Le Sacca**

11 bd. Latapie-Flurin.
☎05.62.92.50.02 ℗05.62.92.64.63
℮hotel.le.sacca@wanadoo.fr
Closed *mid-Oct to mid-Dec.* **Disabled access. TV.**

The recently refurbished décor is modern and provides the perfect setting for the chef, Jean-Marc, to create his excellent food – the best in Cauterets. He's refined the regional recipes and given pride of place to vegetables – a pretty rare occurrence. His dishes are exquisitely presented on warmed plates with consummate professionalism. The selection changes according to his fancy, but could include squab with foie gras, sea bream with garlic petals or Espelette peppers. The menus range in price from €13.50 (weekday lunch) to €42, with *amuse-bouches* thrown in before the meal proper. The rooms have shower/wc or bath and cost €41–66 for a double; some have balconies with a view of the mountains.

⊚ 🎋 ≜ |●| Hôtel du Lion d'Or**

12 rue Richelieu.
☎05.62.92.52.87 ℗05.62.92.03.67
ⓦwww.cauterets.com/hotel-liondor
Closed *1 Oct–20 Dec.* **High chairs available. TV.**

The *Lion d'Or*, run by sisters Bernadette and Rose-Marie, is the oldest hotel in this spa town – the ancient yellow-and-white façade is a bit of a clue. Nothing here has been left to chance: the lift hidden by a wooden door, the magnificent coffee machine in the bar and the very cosy bedrooms – all different, all renovated, with elegant wall lamps and old-fashioned beds and (fully working) telephones. As the two sisters are sticklers for detail, they are now going to gradually replace the carpets with oak floor boards and add mouldings to the ceiling. Doubles with shower/wc or bath are €41–85; buffet breakfast is at €8.50, or you can go half board from €37 per person. Good home cooking is served in the dining room, which has been prettily redecorated in blue without detracting from the original style. The menus, at €18 and €24, are for hotel guests only. Logis de France. *10% discount on the room rate (except during school holidays and weekends) offered to our readers on presentation of this guide.*

⊚ 🎋 |●| La Ferme Basque

It's on the road to Le Cambasque, 2km from Cauterets on the road to Lac d'Ilhéou and the ski resort.
☎05.62.92.54.32
Open *daily in season; by reservation only out of season.* **Closed** *Nov.*

Lots of crêpes and sandwiches are served in this old farm, which has been going since 1928. Some more elaborate dishes have been added to the menus (€15 and €19): *garbure* with wild spinach, black pudding with onions, *piperade*, *blanquette* of lamb. In season meals are served on the huge terrace, which has a fabulous view down to Cauterets. Farm produce is on sale, along with specially prepared regional specialities (if you order in advance). Léon is a shepherd and he likes to talk about his work; Chantal spent twenty years abroad and speaks lots of languages. She's brilliant at managing even the most difficult guests without losing her sense of humour. *Free coffee offered to our readers on presentation of this guide.*

Caylus

82160

⊚ ≜ |●| 🎋 Hôtel Renaissance**

Avenue du Père-Huc.
☎05.63.67.06.26 ℗05.63.24.03.57
Closed *Sun evening; Mon; a fortnight in Feb; a week in June; a fortnight in Oct.* **TV. Pay car park.**

The rooms are modern and comfortable; doubles cost €38 with shower/wc or €41 with bath. The restaurant is also commendable, with interesting menus and a wide selection à la carte. There's a weekday lunch menu at €11, with others €18.50–32. Logis de France. *Free coffee offered to our readers on presentation of this guide.*

Condom

32100

⊚ 🎋 ≜ Hôtel Continental**

20 av. du Maréchal-Foch; it's on the quay, opposite the Baïse.
☎05.62.68.37.00 ℗05.62.68.23.71
℮lecontinental@lecontinental.net

14

MIDI-PYRÉNÉES

Closed *Sun evening and Mon (except 15 July–31 Aug).* **TV. Disabled access. Pay car park.**

Charm and comfort are the twin mottos of this hotel, built in the nineteenth century but now completely renovated. The décor is warm and tasteful, with the emphasis on pale wood and madras fabrics, and there's a pretty little interior garden. The double rooms are air-conditioned and go for €40–64, according to the level of comfort and season; there's also a lovely suite with a terrace at €122. The rooms with showers are markedly less expensive, but they are no less attractive, only slightly smaller. The restaurant is also starting to make a name for itself. Preferential rates in the nearby gym are offered to guests. *One free session in the gym (with at least one night spent in the hotel) offered to our readers on presentation of this guide.*

Larressingle

32100 (3km SW)

⊛ 🎋 🛏 |O| L'Auberge de Larressingle**

Take the D15.
☎05.62.28.29.67 ℻05.62.68.33.14
⊛www.auberge-de-larressingle.fr
Closed *Sun evening and Mon out of season.* **Disabled access. TV. Car park.**

Beautiful restaurant with stone walls, its own vegetable garden and a lovely terrace with a view of the château. The regional cooking is nothing special, although it does occasionally attempt to stray from the beaten path. The Gers poultry, Gascon *cul-noir* pork and pike perch in Madiran wine are all tasty, eye-catching alternatives to the usual *magret* of duck. The weekday lunchtime menu is at €14 (with a main course like a *garbure* or a stew, wine included); other menus are at €20 and €25. The rooms in the grounds of this old building also impress with their great comfort, although they fail to live up to the charm of their surroundings. Double rooms cost €44–50. *Free coffee offered to our readers on presentation of this guide.*

Conques

12320

⊛ 🛏 |O| Le Domaine de Cambelong***

It's at the bottom of the village next to the Dourdou.

☎05.65.72.84.77 ℻05.65.72.83.91
⊛www.moulindecambelong.com
Closed *lunchtimes (except Sun and public holidays); 5 Nov–5 Feb.* **Disabled access. TV. Swimming pool. Car park.**

One of the few remaining water-mills on the Dourdou. The setting is superb, and the extremely comfortable rooms – some with balconies or private terraces overlooking the river – do it justice, as they should do for the price: doubles cost €100–170. Half board is compulsory in high season and costs €105 per person. The two menus (both at €40) illustrate the chef's pride and enthusiasm for "*Allaiton Triple-A*" lamb and *tournedos* of duck seasoned with local spices.

Grand-Vabre

12320 (5.5km N)

⊛ |O| Chez Marie

Take the D901.
☎05.65.69.84.55
Closed *Mon–Thurs evenings, mid-Sept to mid-May; mid-Dec to mid-Feb.* **Car park.**

Marie, the owner, is the niece of the village grocer and knows how to concoct unpretentious local dishes at unbeatable prices. The restaurant is decorated simply, with a covered terrace that allows you to eat amidst lush greenery. Quality produce and traditional dishes are on offer: lamb sweetbreads with cep sauce, *aligot* to order, *estofinado* in season, home made cakes. There are three menus, €12.50–22, and there's an *aligot* menu on Friday nights for €12. You can try a glass of Saint-Hervé, a local apéritif made with elder flowers. The staff are amiable and the service is attentive. All in all, a good village restaurant with fast service, but it's advisable to book.

Cordes-sur-Ciel

81170

⊛ 🎋 🛏 |O| Hostellerie du Parc**

Les Cabannes; it's on the edge of Les Cabannes, 1km downhill from Cordes.
☎05.63.56.02.59 ℻05.63.56.18.03
⊛www.hostellerie-du-parc.fr
Closed *Sun evening and Mon out of season; mid-Nov to mid-Dec.* **Disabled access. TV. High chairs available. Swimming pool. Car park.**

This substantial stone country house, which overlooks an old park and garden, has a large rustic dining room. Chef Claude Izard is a force to be reckoned with; his cooking, based on local tradition (rabbit with cabbage, calf's feet with morels), revels in spontaneity, so it is quite acceptable to ask him what fresh ingredients he has in his larder and then marvel at the dishes he conjures up with them. Menus are at €20 (except Sun) and €28–55. It's also a hotel, with slightly tatty rooms, admittedly, although some have recently been spruced up; doubles go for €55–70 with shower/wc or bath. Logis de France. *Free house apéritif offered to our readers on presentation of this guide.*

@ ☎ Hôtel de la Cité**

19 rue Raymond-VIII; it's in the upper town.
☎05.63.56.03.53 ℗05.63.56.03.53
ⓦwww.thuries.fr
Closed *15 Oct–30 April.* **TV.**

Eight charming and characterful rooms in this complex of medieval buildings with high ceilings and stout beams. Some have fantastic views over the countryside, and all have modern facilities. Prices are very affordable for a tourist town – €59–64 for a double with bath according to the size of the room and the view. You can enjoy breakfast on the attractive patio.

@ ☎ |●| Les Ormeaux

3 rue Saint-Michel; it's in the heart of the old town.
☎and ℗05.63.56.19.50
ⓦwww.lesormeaux.com
Closed *Tues; Jan.* **TV. Car park.**

This restaurant may be expensive (menus are €22–61), but you do not have to indulge in the most expensive menus to appreciate the talent of the young chef, who is also a professional photographer and a painter-sculptor in his spare time. His cooking is based on regional ingredients but it abounds in innovative touches and meticulous attention to detail. Similar concern is shown with the personalized and discreet service. The double rooms, available for €61, are pretty, but it's a shame that the music from the patio climbs the stairs so readily in summer.

Cuq-Toulza
81470

@ ☎ |●| Hôtel Cuq-en-Terrasses

Cuq-le-Château; it's on the N126, 10km to the west of Puylaurens.

☎05.63.82.54.00 ℗05.63.82.54.11
ⓦwww.cuqenterrasses.com
Closed *Dec–Feb.* **Swimming pool.**

This charming place, somewhere between a hotel and a boarding house, in the tiny hilltop village of Cuq-le-Château, really does the Cocagne region proud. We were bowled over by the unassuming and sincere welcome from the owner, Adonis. The eight rooms are all different but equally superb and inviting: doubles cost €90–120. The typical local dishes are embellished with Mediterranean (particularly Greek) nuances and the results are mouthwatering. Dinner is served to hotel guests only for €30. To top it all, there is a swimming pool with a stunning view of the surrounding landscape.

Dourgne
81110

@ ⚄ ☎ |●| Restaurant de la Montagne Noire**

15 pl. des Promenades.
☎05.63.50.31.12 ℗05.63.50.13.55
ⓦwww.montagnenoire.net
Closed *Sun evening; Mon; a fortnight in Feb; a fortnight in Nov.*
Disabled access. TV.

Take a seat on the pleasant terrace overlooking the long village square and enjoy the wonderfully creative and skilfull reinterpretation of local dishes, served in generous portions. Do not miss the salad of pig's trotters (completely off the bone) with shallot *confit* or the quail supreme baked in a potato crust. The desserts are equally enticing. Menus are at €14 (lunchtimes except Sun) and €20–33. Double rooms cost €40–45. *10% discount on the room rate (Sept–June) offered to our readers on presentation of this guide.*

Saint-Avit
81110 (5km NW)

@ |●| Les Saveurs de Saint-Avit

La barraque; it's on the D14 between Soval and Massaguel.
☎05.63.50.11.45
ⓔmh_scott@hotmail.com
Closed *Sun evening; Mon; Sat lunchtime; Jan.* **Disabled access.**

This old farmhouse, with its modern, rustic interior (plus a few Oriental touches) and pretty terrace on the veranda, has earned a reputation as one of the top restaurants in the Tarn area. The chef, Simon, was voted Britain's best young chef in 1991 and has worked in both the Ritz and the Savoy. He loves going to the local markets, choosing his own ingredients and giving full rein to his creativity. For cooking of this quality, the prices are very reasonable: weekday lunch menus are at €17 and €23 (coffee and glass of wine for a supplement of €3) and €34–73; expect to pay around €50 à la carte.

Entraygues-sur-Truyère
12140

◎ 🏠 |●| Hôtel du Lion d'Or**

Tour de Ville; it's in the main street.
℡ 05.65.44.50.01 🅟 05.65.44.53.43
🖳 www.hotel-lion-or.com
Closed Mon out of season; Jan. **Disabled access. TV. Swimming pool. Car park.**

Large, solid, stone-built hotel with doubles and studios at €44–70. The décor is a little kitsch for some tastes, but the facilities are pretty good: indoor pool, tennis and crazy golf. There's also a gym, Jacuzzi and sauna. The restaurant is separate from the hotel and is nothing out of the ordinary. It offers good traditional dishes such as mullet stuffed with *confit* of baby onions and pigeon pie *en feuilleté* with morel cream. The menus range from €15 up to €32.

Fel (Le)
12140 (7km W)

◎ 🏠 |●| Auberge du Fel

It's in the centre of the village; take the D107 then turn right after the Roussy chapel.
℡ 05.65.44.52.30 🅟 05.65.48.64.96
Open every day from early April to 2 Nov.
Closed lunchtimes (except weekends, school holidays and 15 June–15 Sept); 3 Nov–31 March. **Disabled access. TV. High chairs available. Car park.**

A totally charming mountain inn, off the beaten track, with peace and quiet guaranteed, and the extra bonus of high-quality service. The pretty rooms – €49–58 with shower/wc or bath – have recently been updated, painted in light colours and arranged with taste. Some have balconies and views of the valley. Half board costs €43–53 per person depending on the season. Recent alterations

have opened up the building to the surrounding countryside. The family cooking has a good reputation, using recipes passed down from mother to daughter, with menus €18–38. Specialities include *pounti*, *truffade*, *farçous* and stuffed cabbage in the style of *mémé Lucienne*. It is strongly recommended to book. Logis de France.

Espalion
12500

◎ 🎋 |●| L'Eau Vive

27 bd. de Guizard.
℡ 05.65.44.05.11
Closed Sun evening and Mon (except July and Aug); first fortnight in Jan; early Nov to early Dec. **Disabled access. High chairs available.**

This place is easy to spot with its ochre, half-timbered walls. It offers delicious food in a friendly atmosphere. Jérome is an enthusiastic fisherman, as you might guess from the décor. Fish dishes have pride of place on the menus that range from €12 (weekdays) up to €45. Try the *papillotte* of pike perch with foie gras accompanied by fresh vegetables, or roast pigeon breast brushed with local honey. *Free apéritif, fruit juice or soft drink offered to our readers on presentation of this guide.*

Gabriac
12500 (8km S)

◎ 🏠 |●| Hôtel-restaurant Bouloc

Take the road to Bozouls, after 5km turn left to Gabriac and it's as you come into the village.
℡ 05.65.44.92.89 🅟 05.65.48.86.74
🖂 franckbouloc@wanadoo.fr
Closed Tues evening and Wed (except July and Aug); a fortnight in March; a week in June; 3 weeks in Oct. **TV. Swimming pool.**

This was the big surprise of our last research trip. The rooms, which overlook the garden and the swimming pool, are comfortable enough and cost €38–44 for a double; half board is €43–44 per person. The elegant dining room is charming, with fresh flowers on the tables. This hotel has been family-run since 1848, and the founders would surely be proud of Franck, the latest in the line, and his *fricandeau* flavoured with mustard seeds and his chocolate

Charlotte. The splendid wine list is not overly long. The weekday menu is at €16, with others at €20 and €32. The service is efficient. It's best to book in advance. Logis de France.

Mandailles

12500 (10km E)

◎ ⅔ |●| Auberge du Lac

It's opposite the church.
℗05.65.48.90.27
Open *every day (lunch only in May, June, Sept and Oct).* **Closed** *1 May; 1 Nov.*

If you have time to linger, enjoy a drink on the terrace and take in the view over the lake. They serve quality, country cooking: *gratin* of mullet and prawns, loin of lamb with garlic cream, stuffed cabbage and various salads. Menus are €12–26, or around €20 à la carte. The kindly service creates a good atmosphere.

Estaing

12190

◎ 盦 |●| Auberge Saint-Fleuret**

Rue François-d'Estaing.
℗05.65.44.01.44 ℗05.65.44.72.19
ⓦperso.wanadoo.fr/auberge.st.fleuret
Closed *Sun evening and Mon out of season; mid-Nov to mid-March.* **TV. High chairs available. Car park.**

This inn may not look much from the outside, but this is because it guards its treasures out of view. Rooms cost €41–47 and are regularly redecorated; the ones overlooking the garden are particularly pleasant. To the rear lies a big garden with a brand-new swimming pool. The cosy dining room swathed in flowers offers superb, resolutely traditional dishes. The chef, a pupil of Michel Truchon (from the Sénéchal), creates small but impressive dishes with great flair: grilled lamb sweetbreads with curry sauce, whole pig's foot cooked in Estaing white wine and wild bass with sesame seeds. The desserts are equally excellent and the price fair with menus €17–45.

◎ 盦 |●| Hôtel-restaurant Aux Armes d'Estaing**

1 quai du Lot.
℗05.65.44.70.02 ℗05.65.44.74.54
ⓔremi.catusse@estaing.net

Closed *Mon out of season; Sun evening; mid-Nov to mid-March.* **TV. Car park.**

A traditional hotel with provincial charm. The rooms in the main building have been renovated, and some have views of the Lot; doubles cost €44–68 with shower or bath, and half board (compulsory in Aug) is €36.50–43 per person. There is an annexe reserved for hikers, but this does not imply any second-class treatment, as the twenty rooms here are spotless and most have been refurbished. The pretty restaurant offers outstanding dishes on menus that change with the seasons. Specialities include monkfish baked with vanilla and star anis, fillet of pike perch with Estaing wine and beef with fried foie gras. Set menus range from €13.50 to €43.

Figeac

46100

◎ ⅔ 盦 Hôtel Champollion**

3 pl. Champollion; it's in the heart of the old town.
℗05.65.34.04.37 ℗05.65.34.61.69
TV.

Ideally located right in the middle of town, this place offers a bit of a change from traditional establishments. We like it a lot, it's good value for money and you are guaranteed a warm welcome. The rooms are bright, spacious and attractive, with high-quality beds and linen and tastefully decorated bathrooms; well-equipped doubles go for €47. Overall, the hotel's décor, dominated by pale wood and black lacquer, is outstanding, and it's superbly set off by the beautiful staircase in a small atrium, the friendly bar and the pretty terrace. *10% discount on the room rate offered to our readers on presentation of this guide.*

◎ ⅔ |●| Restaurant La Cuisine du Marché

15 rue Clermont.
℗and ℗05.65.50.18.55
Closed *Sun.* **Disabled access.**

The open-plan kitchen lets you watch the chefs preparing tasty dishes that are much lighter and more refined than most of the local specialities. The colours, flavours and smells really show off the fresh market produce. There are menus to suit most budgets or appetites, and they change regularly: weekday lunchtime menu at

€18, others €27–36. There is a small terrace on the pedestrian street. *Free house apéritif offered to our readers on presentation of this guide.*

Foix
09000

@ 🛉 🏠 Hôtel Pyrène***

"Le Vignoble", rue Serge-Denis; it's about 2km from the centre of town on the Soula-Roquefixade road, going towards Spain.
☎05.61.65.48.66 ℗05.61.65.46.69
🌐hotel.pyrène.com
Closed *Sun (1 Oct–1 March); 20 Dec–1 Feb.* **Disabled access. TV. High chairs and games available. Swimming pool. Car park.**

This gloriously peaceful hotel is modern compared to others in town, and it is perfectly placed to catch tourists as they head south towards the Spanish border. Take a dip in the pool in the garden and you'll forget all about the journey. Doubles with shower/wc or bath cost €49–53. *Free house apéritif or coffee offered to our readers on presentation of this guide.*

@ 🛉 🏠 |●| Hôtel Lons***

6 pl. G.-Duthil; it's in the old town near Pont-Vieux.
☎05.61.65.52.44 ℗05.61.02.68.18
🌐www.hotel-lons-foix.com
Closed *1–5 Jan; 20–31 Dec.* **Restaurant closed** *Fri evening; Sat lunchtime.* **Disabled access. TV.**

This place has all the discreet charm and friendly welcome of a classic, provincial hotel and is ideal for a stopover. The double rooms, €50, with shower/wc or bath, are comfortable and the restaurant, with bay windows overlooking the Ariège, serves traditional fare: foie gras, *magret* of duck, *cassoulet au confit*, trout. The menus range in price from €14 (with buffet and *cassoulet ariégeois*) to €25. Logis de France. *8% discount on the room rate (1 Nov–31 March) offered to our readers on presentation of this guide.*

Montgailhard
09330 (1km S)

@ |●| Le Poëlon

14 av. de Paris.
☎05.61.03.54.24

Closed *Sun evening; Mon; Wed evening; 1–15 Jan; 1–15 July.*

This restaurant, close to the Pyrène ironworks, is always packed because of the quality of the tasty cuisine – the fish and meat are excellent. With menus at €11 (weekday lunchtimes), €16.50 and €23, it offers good value for money that's not to be missed.

Saint-Pierre-de-Rivière
09000 (5km W)

@ 🛉 🏠 |●| Hôtel-restaurant La Barguillère**

Take the D17.
☎05.61.65.14.02 ℗05.61.02.62.16
Closed *Tues evening and Wed out of season (except for group bookings); Wed in season; mid-Jan to early Feb; mid-Nov to mid-Dec; call to reserve.* **High chairs available.**

Pleasant little village hotel with a nice garden. Double rooms go for €36 with bidet, and €42 with shower/wc or bath. Half board, at €42 per person, is compulsory in July and August. The €12.50 set menu includes cheese, dessert, wine and coffee. There are other menus at €21–35 including a regional menu, a fish menu, country menu and classic menu. An all-inclusive menu is served at the bar for €10.90, ideal for tight budgets. Specialities include pink trout with crayfish and chives sauce, fresh foie gras with creamed apples flambéed in Hypocras and kid *fricassée* with morels. Logis de France. *Free coffee offered to our readers on presentation of this guide.*

Bosc (Le)
09000 (12km W)

@ 🛉 🏠 |●| Auberge les Myrtilles**

Col des Marrous; take the D17 from Foix.
☎ and ℗05.61.65.16.46
🌐wwwperso.wanadoo.fr/auberge.les.myrtilles
Closed *Mon, Tues and Wed lunchtimes (except school holidays); Nov to end Jan.* **TV. High chairs available. Swimming pool.**

A lovely chalet 1000m up and just 4km from the ski runs at the Tour Laffont. In summer it's wonderful for walkers – and year round it's good for people who enjoy their food. The seven bedrooms all look out on the natural scenery, with doubles with shower/wc or bath at €50–60 depending on the season; half board, €50.50–58 per person, is compulsory in high and mid season. In the dining room you'll find delicious dishes, including *azinat* (hotpot with cabbage), *magret* with morels, *cassoulet* and bilberry pie. Menus range from €16 to €24.50. There's an indoor pool, a sauna and Jacuzzi. *Free apéritif offered to our readers on presentation of this guide.*

Nalzen
09300 (17km SE)

@ 🥄 |O| **Les Sapins**

Route de Foix; take the D117 towards Lavelanet.
☎05.61.03.03.85
Closed *Mon; Wed and Sun evenings.* **Disabled access. High chairs and baby changing table available.**

A pretty, excellent family-run restaurant offering gourmet cuisine. Fresh, local dishes such as pigeon with morels are always presented with exquisite taste. Menus are €13 (weekday lunchtimes) and €22–42. *Free coffee offered to our readers on presentation of this guide.*

Gaillac
81600

@ 🥄 🛏 |O| **La Verrerie****

1 rue de l'Égalité; it's on the road to Montauban and well signposted.
☎05.63.57.32.77 ☎05.63.57.32.27
ⓦwww.la-verrerie.com
Restaurant closed *Sat lunchtime and Sun evening (mid-Oct to mid-April).* **Disabled access. TV. High chairs and games available. Swimming pool. Car park.**

Gaillac can now boast a top-class hotel. This is a newish place, but it's housed in a splendid nineteenth-century building which used to be a glass factory. The interior design is remarkably tasteful, retaining the original character while establishing a warm modern style. All the rooms are really pleasant and comfortable and have a personal feel; some have a view over a huge park. Doubles cost €50 with shower/wc or €65 with bath. You'll find the best in local cooking in the restaurant and prices are very reasonable: there's a *formule* for €13 (weekdays only) and menus at €25–35. Logis de France. *Free apéritif offered to our readers on presentation of this guide.*

@ |O| **Les Sarments**

27 rue Cabrol; it's near the tourist office.

☎05.61.57.62.61
Closed *Sun evening; Mon; Wed evening; mid-Feb to mid-March; mid-Dec to mid-Jan.* **Disabled access.**

Located in a narrow medieval street in the old quarter, this restaurant has built a reputation by word of mouth. The setting is splendid – it's an old cellar with four-teenth- and sixteenth-century vaulting which has retained its original character and style, with no thoughtless refurbishment. The tables are well spaced and the food is good, taking its inspiration from local produce and combining tastes and flavours in intriguing ways. The dishes vary according to seasonal availability, but there is always plenty of choice: fried duck foie gras, *fondant* apple pie. Menus are at €23 (weekdays only) and €28–46. The bottles of Sarment on display are not yet ready to be opened. It is a pity that the service is slightly aloof.

Lasgraïsses
81300 (17km SE)

@ 🥄 |O| **Chez Pascale**

It's on the D84, in the direction of Albi.
☎05.63.33.00.78
Closed *Sun–Thurs evenings; Mon (it's best to phone as this is liable to change); last fort-night in Aug.*

This classic village bistro, with its old photographs on the walls and trophies in the cabinet, is invariably enlivened by the locals' philosophical-political discussions or exchanges of gossip. It is one of the last of its kind in this impoverished region. There is a wealth of menus: the cheapest one at €12 and served weekdays only, allows your own choice of starters from the buffet (including smoked country ham), followed by well-prepared local dishes such as stuffed chicken (served on certain days only); other menus go up to €29.50. There's a good cheese board, but leave some space for the house flan. *Free coffee offered to our readers on presentation of this guide.*

Gavarnie
65120

@ 🛏 **Compostelle Hôtel****

Rue de l'Église.
☎05.62.92.49.43
ⓦwww.compostellehotel.com

Closed *30 Sept–26 Dec.* **Disabled access. Car park.**

Sylvie, a keen hiker and Velvet Underground fan, travelled a fair bit before taking over this pleasant little family hotel. Rooms are named after mountain flowers; you get the best view from the one called "*Lys*", which has a balcony. Those on the second floor have skylights. Doubles cost €34 with shower, €35–46 with shower/wc or €44–45 with bath – unfortunately the soundproofing isn't great, even in the section of the hotel that's been renovated, but it's still a lovely place. Breakfast is at €6.

Gourdon
46300

@ ☎ |●| **Le Domaine de Berthiol**

Route de Cahors, D704.
℡05.65.41.33.33 ℻05.65.41.14.52
@www.hotelperigord.com
Restaurant closed *Sun evening and Mon out of season; I Jan–31 March.* **Disabled access. Swimming pool. Car park.**

This hotel in a 1960s-style manor house would be worth mentioning just for the effusive welcome and exceptionally attentive service afforded to its guests. To add to that, it is set in glorious isolation, in the middle of a large park. The rooms have been decorated with lavish care (verging on kitsch). Doubles cost €63–93, depending on the degree of comfort and the season. You will eat splendidly here. The regional menu is excellent with dishes such as home-made terrine, pike perch or *confit* and red-fruit soup with almond milk. The young chef adds occasional Asian touches that are surprising but never overwhelming. There is a lunchtime menu at €17, then others at €24–48. In summer, the terrace provides panoramic views of the garden and surrounding countryside.

Gramat
46500

@ 🍴 ☎ |●| **Le Relais des Gourmands****

2 av. de la Gare; it's opposite the station.
℡05.65.38.83.92 ℻05.65.38.70.99
@www.relais-des-gourmands.fr
Closed *Sun evening and Mon lunchtime*

(except July and Aug); Feb holiday. **TV. High chairs and games available. Swimming pool.**

An enormous house with a swimming pool, an outside bar and a flower garden. All credit goes to Suzy Curtet for her great accessibility and kindness, as well as the diligent attention with which she has made this hotel even more charming than before. Large, well-kept modern rooms with bathrooms go for €50–59. The restaurant has a good reputation for light, inventive cooking based on regional produce such as veal's head and tongue with home-made *gribiche* sauce and salad of lamb sweetbreads with sweet and sour sauce. They also serve good cheeses, fine desserts and a choice of inexpensive local wines. The weekday menu is priced at €15.50, with other menus €17.50–37. *10% discount on the room rate (early Sept to end April) offered to our readers on presentation of this guide.*

@ ☎ |●| **Le Lion d'Or*****

8 pl. de la République.
℡05.65.38.73.18 ℻05.63.65.38.84.50
@www.liondorhotel.com
Closed *15 Dec–15 Jan.* **TV. Pay car park.**

Excellent reception and service in the best tradition of French hotel-keeping. The setting is ultra-classic and refined, complete with a quiet, lush garden. Rooms cost €55–86, and are comfortable and splendidly maintained; the décor, however, is extremely old-fashioned. The superb chef, René Momméjac, has extensive experience, and offers some of the best food in the region without getting bogged down in an overly rigid format. Menus start from €18 (weekday lunchtimes) and go up to €60. Good-value bottles are available on the marvellous wine list. As M. Momméjac has been running this splendid institution for 50 years, you are guaranteed to find the best food in Le Quercy at any time of the year – but hurry up, he is talking about retiring.

Leyme
46120 (11km E)

@ 🍴 ☎ |●| **Hôtel-restaurant Lescure****

Route de St-Céré.
℡05.65.38.90.07 ℻05.65.11.21.39
Closed *Sat and Sun evening out of season;*

Christmas school holiday. **TV. Swimming pool. High chairs available. Car park.**

This characterful hotel-restaurant, which has been run by the same family for more than fifty years, offers comfy accommodation at reasonable prices: doubles €34–45 depending on the facilities. The large dining room overlooks a pond; you'll find terrific regional dishes and a nice, varied wine list, with a menu at €13 (not Sun), then others at €15–30. The decoration is thoughtful and tasteful, with a genuine Picasso and a number of Matisse reproductions. The owner is a striking character with a great love of modern art. Logis de France. *Free house apéritif offered to our readers on presentation of this guide.*

Gramont
82120

@ 🎋 |●| Le Petit Feuillant

It's next to the château.
☏05.63.94.00.08
Open *for bookings only.* **Closed** *Sun evening; Wed; Mon and Tues in winter; Feb.* **TV.**

The place is wonderfully friendly. No à la carte options, but six menus from €15.50 to €32 (including apéritif, wine and coffee) list the likes of soup, home-made paté, roast pork with prunes, *cassoulet*, stuffed chicken, tart with garlic and cheese, meat stew and duck *confit*. Everyone gets a complimentary apéritif, which they can enjoy on the terrace overlooking the château. The good local cuisine is a big draw in the area, so you must book ahead. *Free liqueur offered to our readers on presentation of this guide.*

Labastide-Murat
46240

@ 🎋 🏠 |●| Hôtel-restaurant La Garissade

It's in the village, a few km from the exit from the A20 motorway, which crosses the Lot from top to bottom.
☏05.65.21.18.80 ℻05.65.21.10.97
🌐www.garissade.com
Closed *20 Dec–20 Jan.* **TV. High chairs available.**

A gem of a place where all the comfortable rooms have been renovated and decorated in an individualistic colour scheme. Double rooms go for €48–66, depending on the season; some overlook the town square at the back. It's the perfect place to stay if you want to explore the limestone plateaux of Le Quercy or La Bouriane. The chef offers tasty, authentic dishes, with a weekday lunch menu for €14 (weekday lunch) and another for €18, and he doesn't cheat on the produce or the flavourings: farm-raised lamb or scrambled eggs with Lalbenque truffles. It's a friendly place and the wines are very fairly priced. Some regulars come from far away to relax and de-stress. *10% discount on the room rate (except in July and Aug) offered to our readers on presentation of this guide.*

Lacrouzette
81210

@ 🎋 🏠 |●| L'Auberge de Crémaussel

From Castres, take the D622 in the direction of Lacaune; go through Lafontasse (5km) and turn left 2km further on, in the direction of Lacrouzette-Rochers du Sidobre; 4km further down the D30, turn left, then right 2km further on, following the directions to Rochers du Sidobre.
☏ and ℻05.63.50.61.33
Closed *Christmas to end of Jan.* **Restaurant closed** *Wed; Sun evening.* **Car park.**

A friendly country restaurant with five simple, spotless rooms with shower/wc at €32; breakfast is at €4. The cosy dining room has stone walls and a fine fireplace, and the cooking has a good reputation. Specialities, including cheese soup in winter and crayfish soup in summer, have to be ordered ahead, but they serve a very good Roquefort salad at any time. Menus go for €15–22; à la carte, prices are fair. Finish with the local pastry known as *croustade*, which is sheer heaven. There are also some beautiful walks available in the vicinity (the rocks of l'Oie and the Trois Fromages are 600m and 900m away, respectively). It is advisable to book. *Free house apéritif offered to our readers on presentation of this guide.*

Laguiole
12210

@ 🏠 Auberge du Combaïre

It's on the D42, in the direction of the Château du Bosquet.

☎05.65.44.33.26 ⓕ05.65.44.37.38

Lost in the countryside, this picturesque old farm-windmill has been attractively restored. Ideal for those seeking simplicity and conviviality, it offers peace (complete with running stream), an inviting lounge and a superb library with regional archives available for guests. The delightful combination of the natural setting and fine service is cheap at the price: double rooms at €32. Booking is essential.

ⓒ 🏠 |●| Grand Hôtel Auguy***

2 allée de l'Amicale.
☎05.65.44.31.11 ⓕ05.65.51.50.81
ⓦwww.chateauxhotels.com/auguy
Closed Sun evening, Mon and Tues lunchtimes (except July and Aug); mid-Nov to early Feb. **Disabled access. TV. High chairs and games available.**

A very good, smart establishment with a solid reputation located in the centre of town. The recently refurbished doubles, which cost €50–90, are pleasant and well-equipped, although some are a bit on the small side. Ask for the "*grand confort*" rooms with wood panelling – they are slightly more expensive but far more attractive. The large dining room is bright – there's also a terrace and garden – and the cooking first-rate. Most dishes, prepared by Isabelle Muylaert, are traditional with a modern twist. There are menus from €29 (not served at weekends) up to €75. Try the side of veal or the pig's trotter pancake with chanterelles.

Lannemezan
65300

ⓒ 🎋 |●| Chez Maurette

10 rue des Pyrénées.
☎05.62.98.06.34
Closed Sun; end Aug to early Sept. **High chairs available. Car park.**

The inauspicious frontage of this restaurant, located in a dreary town, wouldn't make you slam on the brakes to stop – but that would be an error. This is usually full of regular customers – always a sure sign of a popular and satisfying place to eat. The house speciality is the prize-winning tripe, and there's excellent *daube* of beef and calf's head. The weekday menu is at €10 and there's a more gourmet-style menu at €16. The delightful service comes courtesy of the owner and her daughters,

whose family, according to local records, has been in the restaurant trade since 1653. Wednesday is sheep market day, and simply everybody comes in for lunch. *Free coffee offered to our readers on presentation of this guide.*

Lavardens
32360

ⓒ |●| Le Restaurant du Château

It's at the foot of the château.
☎05.62.64.58.90
Closed Sun; Mon (except July–Aug); Oct–April.

A delightful place, both inside and out: the interior of stone and wrought iron is swathed in cotton and linen, while the terrace is dominated by a pergola with vines and Liberty prints. The rural tone is further developed in unpretentious, seasonal dishes such as marinated fish and veal medallions with "grand-mother's sauce". There are set menus at €19–26, or you can go à la carte for around €30. The friendly welcome and service ensure that this is a truly lovely place. Don't miss the opportunity to visit the magnificent Lavardens.

Lectoure
32700

ⓒ 🎋 🏠 |●| Hôtel de Bastard**

Rue Lagrange.
☎05.62.68.82.44 ⓕ05.62.68.76.81
ⓦwww.hotel-de-bastard.com
Closed Sun evening; Mon; Tues lunch; 21 Dec–1 Feb. **TV. High chairs available. Swimming pool. Car park.**

This marvellous hotel is a fine example of eighteenth-century architecture. It's furnished and decorated with taste and is both ideal for a romantic weekend and incredible value for money. Doubles cost €45–68 with shower/wc or bath. The hotel also has one of the most charming restaurants in the area, with a carefully planned repertoire of dishes executed with great finesse. The food is not constrained by local tradition but is enriched by influences from Italy and Provence. Gourmets should not miss the sublime "Liver Variations" menu (wine included), which offers four different varieties of foie gras. Menus range from €15 (weekday lunchtimes) up to €28. In summer they serve meals on the terrace, which has a wonderful view over the rooftops, the swimming pool and the cypresses. *Free coffee offered to our readers on presentation of this guide.*

Lourdes
65100

◎ 🏠 Hôtel Relais des Crêtes**

72 av. Alexandre-Marqui; it's on the right as you come into Lourdes from Tarbes.
℡05.62.42.18.56
Closed 11 Nov–20 March.

The location of this small family guest-house, at the end of a side street behind a pretty hedge, protects it from the noise of the nearby main road. There are eleven tasteful, simple rooms looking out onto the courtyard; they range from €23 to €29 and are all spotlessly clean. Breakfast is at €3.60. Delightful service from the charming owner, who runs her house with dedication and warmth. In warm weather, breakfast is served on the hydrangea-filled terrace, and picnics are also permitted. This place is highly recommended to low-budget travellers.

◎ 🍴 🏠 |◎| Hôtel Majestic**

9 av. Maransin; it's a ten-minute walk from the shrines, at the corner of the avenue and a cul-de-sac where you can park.
℡05.62.94.27.23 ℡05.62.94.64.91
Closed end Nov to Easter. **Disabled access.**

A classy 1925 establishment, with lovely staircase and beautiful wood floors, run by the friendly Cazaux family. The rustic rooms (€30–50) are extremely comfortable with direct-dial phones, TV (on request) and spotless en-suite bathrooms with hairdryers; some have balconies, and the bedding is new in almost all of them. Family cooking is served in the chic dining room dotted with paintings and flowers; the €8 *formule* is served daily (lunch and dinner) and there's a menu at €15. The *patronne* takes a lot of trouble for her guests; the only drawback, in fact, is the traffic noise during the day (although soundproofing work has just been completed: we would be grateful for any information about its effectiveness). *10% discount on the room rate (1 May–1 July) offered to our readers on presentation of this guide.*

◎ 🍴 🏠 |◎| Hôtel Beauséjour***

16 av. de la Gare.
℡05.62.94.38.18 ℡05.62.94.96.20
🌐www.hotel-beausejour.com
Disabled access. TV. High chairs available. Car park.

A reasonably priced three-star hotel, conveniently situated near the station. Classy rooms all have telephones, safes and hair-dryers; they go for €58–75 for a double with shower/wc or bath, depending on the season. The rooms overlooking the station itself are larger but a bit noisier; the ones at the back are smaller but they have a view over the town and towards the distant Pyrenees. In summer you can dine outside in the lovely garden. *10% discount on the room rate (15 Oct–30 March) or free apéritif offered to our readers on presentation of this guide.*

◎ 🍴 |◎| Le Magret

10 rue des 4-Frères-Soulas; behind the tourist office in place Peyramale.
℡05.62.94.20.55
Closed Mon; Jan; last ten days in Aug. **High chairs available.**

Beautiful dining room with old red tiles on the floor and gleaming copper pots and pans hanging from the roughcast white walls, setting off the red-and-white tablecloths and strikingly designed carafes containing the fine local water. Hearty food with an original touch: the cheapest menu at €13 (lunchtimes) features dishes such as *garbure paysanne*, a plate of duck and a platter of cheeses from Ossau. The other menus (€24 and €33) include *magret* with *edelweiss* and medallions of whole foie gras with Jurançon. It is impossible to resist the temptation of enticing desserts like the pear *confit* with Madiran and the excellent prune delight with Armagnac. The staff knows a smattering of several languages and provides diligent but unfussy service. *Free coffee offered to our readers on presentation of this guide.*

Luz-Saint-Sauveur
65120

◎ 🏠 Auberge de jeunesse – Gîte d'étape Les Cascades

17 rue Sainte-Barbe; it's close to the GR10 and 150m from the church.

☎ 05.62.92.94.14
🌐 www.auberges-de-jeunesse.com
Car park.

A first-rate youth hostel run by some particularly dynamic young people – a warm atmosphere is guaranteed. Attractive rooms with two, four, six or eight beds (but you will need a sleeping bag) go for €10 a night. There are also four double rooms at €22 and half board is compulsory in winter at €22 per person. The excellent meals are served in a large, pretty communal dining room. There is a "hiker's menu" at €9 (€10 if you're not staying the night) and thematic dinners revolving around dishes like paella, *garbure* or grilled meat. The staff will also give you all the information you need about hiking in the region.

◉ ⅔ ⓧ Hôtel les Templiers**

Place de la Comporte; opposite the church of Saint-André.
Open *evenings only.* **Closed** *Mon, Tues and Wed (except July–Aug); May; Oct; Nov.* **TV. High chairs available.**

A wooden staircase with a pretty carved ramp leads to rooms that are simple but spacious and not without charm – there's some wonderful, highly polished local furniture. Doubles with shower/wc cost €37; nos. 1 and 2 sleep three people and have shutters opening onto the square and the fortified church. There's a welcoming crêperie at street level. Monday is market day, when the front of the hotel is transformed into a Spanish-style flower stall. *Free house apéritif offered to our readers on presentation of this guide.*

Marciac
32230

◉ ⓧ Les Comtes de Pardiac**

Place de l'Hôtel-de-Ville; it's in the heart of the village.
☎ 05.62.08.20.00 ℗ 05.62.08.28.05
🌐 www.hotel-comtespardiac.fr
TV. Games available. Car park.

The 25 bedrooms all look out on the back, which is good news when the village jazz festival takes place, as it means you can sleep in peace. The décor is unremarkable, but the rooms have been refurbished with modern facilities and you can expect friendly service. Doubles go for €50 with shower/wc and €60 with bath; there is also a suite and two rooms with private gardens that are ideal for families.

Beaumarchés
32160 (11km NW)

◉ ⅔ ⓧ ⎮◉⎮ Le Relais du Bastidou**

Cayron; take the D3 in the direction of Riscle, then follow the signs.
☎ and ℗ 05.62.69.19.94
🌐 www.le-relais-du-bastidou.com
Restaurant closed *Sun evening and Mon (except in summer); 20 Oct–20 Nov.* **TV. Disabled access. Cots, high chairs and games available. Swimming pool. Car park.**

A sophisticated haven of peace and quiet – a wonderful old Gascon farmhouse with a swimming pool, lost in the countryside. The eight rooms have recently been refurbished and are splendid with reasonably priced doubles for €43–61, depending on the size (but reckon on €95 during the Marciac festival); they have not only their own TV but also a VCR. The delicious breakfast is included in the room rate, although there are savoury dishes that cost more. Half board is compulsory (1–15 Aug) and costs €76–98 per person. Three menus are on offer at €15–28; the "*Bastide*", for example, offers Gascon charcuterie based on *cul-noir* pork, duck stew or baby cuttlefish with Côtes de Gascogne wine. The other two list regional and gourmet dishes, respectively. Logis de France. *Free house apéritif offered to our readers on presentation of this guide.*

Martel
46600

◉ ⓧ ⎮◉⎮ Auberge des 7 Tours

Avenue de Turenne; it's 100m from the centre.
☎ 05.65.37.30.16 ℗ 05.65.37.41.69
🌐 www.auberge7tours.com
Closed *Sat evening, Sun evening and Mon (mid-Sept to mid-July).* **Open** *daily mid-July to mid-Sept.* **TV.**

A small hotel, located 100m from the centre of town, with eight renovated rooms (€36.40–42.20) that have personality. The restaurant, set apart from the hotel, is a good new place to eat in the Lot; the couple that runs it has travelled extensively, as far as Australia, and the cooking shows the extent of their adventures – try slivers of duck in honey and thyme or kangaroo Rossini. The female half is in the kitchen, while her husband waits the tables. There are *formules* at €12.20 (weekday lunchtime) and €14.80, and a range of menus €21–50. In summer you can eat outside on the terrace. It is advisable to book.

Martres-Tolosane

31220

⊛ 🏠 |●| **Hôtel-Restaurant Castet***

Avenue de la Gare; it's opposite the station.
℗05.61.98.80.20 ℗05.61.98.61.02
✉hotelcastet@wanadoo.fr
Open *noon–2pm and 8–9.30pm.* **Closed** *Sun evening; Mon.* **TV. High chairs available. Swimming pool.**

A quiet house just opposite the station (only two trains stop here each day), with a swimming pool for hotel guests and offering good value for money. Pleasantly renovated double rooms with shower/wc or bath go for €36–39. In the dining room, classics based on fresh local produce are exquisitely prepared and presented: weekday menu at €15 and other menus €22–45. They do duck specialities and a rib of beef cooked in a salt crust alongside other classic dishes. There's a wonderful shady terrace, but the dining room is less appealing and rather dated.

Fousseret (Le)

31430 (15km NE)

⊛ |●| **Restaurant des Voyageurs**

1 Grande-Rue; take exit 23 off the A64 motorway as far as Fousseret and it's on the road up to the central square.
℗05.61.09.53.06
Closed *Sat; Sun and Mon evenings; Aug; a weekend of Dec.* **Open** *noon–1.30pm and 7.30–9pm.*

The welcome is as charming as the interior. Family-style cooking and dishes influenced by the region: *pot Gascon*, beef fillet, ceps and liver, fresh foie gras with green pepper and foie-gras *raviolides*. The menu at €10 is excellent value and there are others at €22 and €36. In summer you can dine on the terrace behind the house under pretty blue lights. This restaurant has long been a favourite with the locals. Credit cards not accepted.

Millau

12100

⊛ 🏠 **Hôtel Emma Calvé**

28 av. Jean-Jaurès.
℗05.65.60.13.49 ℗05.65.60.93.75
⊛www.emmacalv.ifrance.com
TV.

This hotel is named after a celebrated singer who lived in Millau (in this house) before seeking greater fame and fortune on the other side of the Atlantic. Appropriately enough, Nathalie receives you like a diva in her glorious bourgeois house (ideally located in the centre of Millau), and the reception looks a little like a boudoir. Each of the thirteen rooms is decorated differently; comfortable doubles cost €58–80 including breakfast; €75 for a triple. Those at the back look over the wonderful garden; if you like to sleep with the window open, avoid the rooms which look over the road. We particularly liked the one in the old chapel with stained-glass windows and an old-fashioned bathroom, as well as another with a balcony and veranda.

⊛ |●| **Restaurant Chez Capion**

3 rue J.-F.-Alméras; it's close to the Boulevard de la République and the town hall.
℗05.65.60.00.91
Closed *Tues evening and Wed, out of season and in early July; Feb school holiday.*

It is best to book for lunch, as many local workers come to eat here. The pretty dining room, its tables set well apart, is brightened up by paintings on the wall. Solid regional fare based on good vegetables and fresh produce is served. Excellent blanquette of veal *à l'ancienne*, lacquered chicken fillet with vanilla and foie-gras ravioli with shavings of truffle – as well as a dessert trolley and particularly enticing sorbets. There are five menus, ranging in price from €10.67 to €29.73, an extensive wine list and good service.

Creissels

12100 (2km S)

⊛ 🏠 |●| **Le Château de Creissels**

Route de St-Affrique; it's in the middle of the village opposite the church.
Hotel ℗05.65.60.16.59 ℗05.65.61.24.63
Restaurant ℗05.65.61.24.63
⊛www.chateau-de-creissels.com

Closed *Sun evening and Mon lunchtime (30 Sept–30 April); Jan; Feb.* **TV. High chairs and games available. Car park.**

Here is a chance to enjoy a candlelit dinner under the stone vaults of an authentic château – or, if you book far enough in advance, on its quiet, narrow terrace. You will be offered classic regional dishes, prepared with great expertise and no little imagination. Take the menu "Variations on lamb from the Grandes Causses", for example, with four mouthwatering dishes featuring tender lamb; only the dessert strays from the format (unless the caramel sauce is made with sheep's milk!). The "Gourmet stroll" menu offers a succulent *pressé* with foie gras and artichoke, followed by pike perch baked to perfection. The other menus tend to concentrate on fish. The lunchtime menu costs €23, with others going up to €48. There is a superb wine list, with the emphasis on regional vintages. You can also stay the night here, in charming rooms with antique furniture, at astonishingly reasonable prices: doubles at €49 with shower/wc, or €54–84 with bath.

Saint-Jean-du-Bruel

12230 (35km SE)

◎ ☎ |●| **Hôtel-restaurant du Midi-Papillon****

Take the N9 to La Cavalerie then go to Nant on the D999; Saint-Jean-du-Bruel lies 7km further on.
℗05.65.62.26.04 ℗05.65.62.12.97
Open *daily from Palm Sunday to 11 Nov.*
High chairs available. Swimming pool. Car park.

This exceptional hotel in the depths of Aveyron welcomed its first guests in 1850 and has since been run by successive generations of the Papillon family. It is now in the hands of Jean-Michel, the first man in the dynasty to be in charge of the cooking. The rooms are exceptionally pleasant, particularly those overlooking the Dourbie, they're regularly redecorated and prices are appealing: doubles €31.90–57.50. Nos. 3, 4, 5 and 6 have a terrace overlooking the river, while nos. 18 and 21 are suites. The dining room is decorated with flowers and overlooks the river, and there's a pretty and pleasant terrace that is often full. Jean-Michel uses only the freshest produce – he grows his own fruit and vegetables, rears his own chickens, fattens his own pigs and

gathers his own mushrooms, so the cuisine is full of authentic flavours: sausage dried over the log fire and black pudding flavoured with local thyme. Tradition and creativity are the watchwords here, as evident in the "*Papillon*" tripe, the turbot steak with ratatouille and shrimps, the partridge with carrot cake and the *ragoût* with mushrooms and plums. To top it all, these dishes are presented with exquisite elegance. Choice of menus from €13 (weekday lunchtimes) to €36.20, and there's a large range of wines at moderate prices (75cl of red for €4.30). There is also a cosy lounge that encourages guests to linger and chat. The pleasant staff offers unobtrusively efficient service. Reservations are recommended.

Mirande

32300

◎ ⅍ ☎ |●| **Auberge de la Halle**

Rue des Écoles.
℗05.62.66.76.81
Closed *Fri evening; Sat; mid-Aug to mid-Sept.*

A simple place run by friendly young owners where you feel relaxed right away. Traditional cuisine in handsome portions on a range of appetizing menus from €10 (lunchtime only) to €25. There are also a few rooms in a separate building – some overlooking the road, others the garden. They're modest and clean and cost €25 with basin and €28 with shower/wc. *Free coffee offered to our readers on presentation of this guide.*

Moissac

82200

◎ ⅍ ☎ |●| **Le Pont Napoléon****

2 allée Montebello; take the A62, exit 9, onto the N113 and it's just by the bridge.
℗05.63.04.01.55 ℗05.63.04.34.44
℮dussau.lenapoleon@wanadoo.fr
Closed *Sun evening; Mon; fortnight early Jan; fortnight in March.* **TV. High chairs available. Pay car park.**

The hotel is a dream, with fair prices and amazing bathrooms. Redecorated and soundproofed doubles go for €36–55. For all that, the restaurant is better known. The gastronomic cuisine of Michel Dussau can be sampled on menus starting at €24 (not Sun) up to

€70. Special mention should be made of the truly delicious breakfast, with home-made bread and pastries, fruit salad and chasselas grape juice. *Free house apéritif offered to our readers on presentation of this guide.*

Durfort-Lacapelette
82390 (6km NE)

ⓓⓃ ☑ |●| **Hôtel-restaurant Aube Nouvelle****

In the village, take the D16 in the direction of Cazes-Mondenard or the D2 in the direction of Lauzerte.
℡05.63.04.50.33 ℻05.63.04.57.55
℠www.chez.com/aubenouvelle
Closed Sat lunch (except reservations); 23 Dec–20 Jan. **Disabled access. Car park.**

Owner Marc de Smet's parents moved from Belgium to Quercy in 1955, and he and his wife Claudine took over their business. It's an idyllic spot surrounded by fields, which you can admire from the lovely terrace and garden. The clean, well-maintained rooms have been renovated to a high standard and cost €53 with shower/wc or bath. Half board, €37–56.50 per person, is compulsory from July to September. The cooking is regional in flavour and Belgian in influence: rabbit *à la flamande* with Agen prunes, shellfish *waterzooi* and beef in brown ale sauce Portions are generous – in the words of the owner: "just because you don't pay much, that doesn't mean you won't have enough to eat" – on menus that range from €11.70 (weekday lunchtimes) and €35. *10% discount on the room rate for a minimum stay of three consecutive nights offered to our readers on presentation of this guide.*

Moncorneil-Grazan
32260

ⓓⓃ |●| **Restaurant L'Auberge d'Astarac**

It's between Masseube and Simorre, in the heart of the village.
℡05.62.65.48.81
Closed lunchtimes (except Sun and bank holidays); Mon; 5 Jan–13 Feb; 15 Nov–15 Dec.

This inn has been lovingly restored by two exceptional people who fell in love with the area. There's an old bar, a delightful dining room and a glorious terrace. At the bottom of the flower garden you'll see Christian Termote's kitchen garden, full of vegetables and herbs. He taught himself to cook and uses those herbs with great subtlety. Try the snail and ceps *ragoût*, the leg of lamb with rosemary, the chicken supreme reduced in Madiran and the rhubarb pie. The cooking is inspired, expressive and refreshingly free of pretension. It is also marked by astonishing combinations such as braised sweetbreads and liquorice. The set menu is at €29, or reckon on €40 for a meal à la carte. There's a beautiful wine cellar, specializing in the vintages of southern France. A special mention should be made of Lucie, the unusual hostess, capable of sending guests to look for their own wine in the cellar and praising her husband's cooking to the skies. Such character and spontaneity help make this inn special so booking is essential. *Free coffee offered to our readers on presentation of this guide.*

Montauban
82000

ⓓ ☑ **Hôtel du Commerce****

9 pl. Roosevelt; you can reach it from the place de la Cathédrale.
℡05.63.66.31.32 ℻05.63.66.31.28
℠www.hotel-du-commerce.com
TV. Disabled access.

This hotel, right in the centre of Montauban, is a real boon – you can park just outside. The owners are sure to give you an effusive and generous welcome. They have totally refurbished the rooms, using floor tiles and fabrics in bright and warm Mediterranean colours. The bathrooms are brand new; double rooms with every comfort cost €46–63.

ⓓⓃ ☑ **Hôtel Mercure*****

12 rue Notre-Dame.
℡05.63.63.17.23 ℻05.63.66.43.66
℮mercuremontauban@wanadoo.fr
Disabled access. TV. Pay car park.

Chain hotels don't usually appear in this guide, but this is an exception. The *Mercure* is simply the best hotel in town, very well managed, welcoming and with a restaurant – and it dates back to the eighteenth century. Inevitably, it's also the most expensive – double rooms cost

€98. The décor is bright and warm; the rooms are spacious and decorated in contemporary style, with particularly splendid bathrooms. *Free house apéritif offered to our readers on presentation of this guide.*

@ 2⁄₄ |●| Le Sampa

21 rue des Carmes; it's near the town hall.
☎05.63.20.36.46
Closed *Sun; public holidays; 25 Dec–3 Jan.*

The trendy décor with a rustic twist suits the cooking well: *œuf cocotte*, salads, chicken curry, duck *aiguillette* with acacia honey, Dover sole fillet or shark steak. There's a selection of dishes of the day for €7.50; à la carte you'll pay around €23. The welcome and service are congenial, and in the evenings the warm, friendly atmosphere at the bar extends to the dining room. *Free liqueur offered to our readers on presentation of this guide.*

@ 2⁄₄ |●| Restaurant Le Ventadour

23 quai Villebourbon; it's on the banks of the Tarn, opposite the Ingres museum.
☎05.63.63.34.58
Closed *Sat lunchtime; Sun; Mon; 1–15 Jan; 15–30 Aug.*

This restaurant is extremely popular with the locals, and rightly so: the vaulted brick dining room is worthy of a painting, and it has the advantage of staying cool when it's hot outside. The food is painstakingly prepared and the service is excellent. Prices are reasonable – weekday lunch menu €18.50 with others €24 and €44. *Free liqueur offered to our readers on presentation of this guide.*

Montréal

32500

@ |●| Chez Simone

It's in the village.
☎05.62.29.44.40
Closed *Mon; Tues; Sun evening (except during public holidays).*

There are two entrances – one goes into the designer bistro, the other leads via the terrace to a main dining room that has all the attributes of a modish, gourmet restaurant. In the middle there's a display showing off all the bottles on the wine list and an impressive collection of Armagnac

flagons – more than thirty vintages. There are menus at €15–30 and one at €50 (the "*ronde des tapas*"). The cuisine, using ingredients of impeccable quality, is essentially regional, but it is enriched by unusual sauces; the fish dishes are particularly good. Goose and duck foie gras is sliced in front of you and served without adornment.

Fourcès

32250 (6km N)

@ 🏠 |●| Château de Fourcès***

Take the D29; it's in the village.
☎05.62.29.49.53 ⊕05.62.29.50.59
⊛www.chateau-fources.com
Closed *Wed and Thurs in winter; 3–30 Jan; 1–22 Dec.* **TV. High chairs and games available. Swimming pool. Car park.**

A smart, charming place in a twelfth-century château in the middle of the village. It has been magnificently restored and has all the modern facilities you could wish for. The rooms are in soft colours and elegantly coordinated; doubles cost €80–130, suites are more expensive. Formal, stylish welcome and attentive service, and very good cooking to match, at more affordable prices than the rooms; menus range from €25 up to €49 (gourmet menu). There's a river running through the garden and a swimming pool nearby.

Montségur

09300

@ 🏠 |●| Hôtel-restaurant Costes**

52 rue Principale.
☎05.61.01.10.24 ⊕05.61.03.06.28
⊛www.montsegur.com/costes.ht
Closed *Sun evening and Mon out of season; 1 Jan–1 Feb.* **High chairs available. Car park.**

The building is covered in Virginia creeper, there's a pleasant terrace and garden, and it's a nice place to stop. A dozen simple rooms, fairly priced at €33–47. They serve very good home cooking in the restaurant with menus at €17–30. Dishes include *civet* of game, duck breast with figs, tenderloin of pork with spice bread, salad of gizzards, *confit* with chanterelle mushrooms and local specialities, such as trout with hazelnuts. Logis de France.

MIDI-PYRÉNÉES

Najac

12270

◎ ⅔ 🏠 |●| L'Oustal del Barry**

Place du Bourg; it's on the way into the village.
☎05.65.29.74.32 🖷05.65.29.75.32
🖥www.oustal-del-barry.com
Restaurant closed *Mon (except for residents); Tues in low season; mid-Nov to Easter.* **Disabled access. TV. Pay car park.**

This lovely inn is an appealing place to stop on account of its location, its service and the quality of its food and rooms. The décor is plush and the air-conditioned rooms are very elegant while retaining an authentic rustic feel. Our favourite (no. 23) has a view of the natural surroundings that stretches to the horizon. Doubles with shower/wc or bath go for €51–75; half board €54–75 per person. The thoughtfully designed dining room and the view of the château is matched by the food, based on recipes from Rouergue prepared with fresh, seasonal produce and extremely tender meat. The result is a feast of colours and flavours, such as the half-cooked duck foie gras served with warm walnut brioche or the chef's speciality of *astet najacois* (roast pork stuffed with parsley). You can visit the pretty kitchen garden, and there is also a children's playground outside. There's a good wine list, compiled by Corinne and Rémy Simon, and the desserts are mouthwatering. Logis de France. *Free coffee offered to our readers on presentation of this guide.*

◎ 🏠 |●| Le Belle Rive**

Le Roc du Pont.
☎05.65.29.73.90 🖷05.65.29.76.88
🖃hotel-bellrive.najac@wanadoo.fr
Closed *Mon lunchtime in April, May and Oct; All Saints' Day to early April.* **Disabled access. TV. High chairs available. Swimming pool. Car park.**

A pleasant hotel in restful, leafy surroundings on a bend in the river, ideal for families on account of the swimming pool, tennis court, pool table and crèche. Rooms are bright and pleasant; doubles with shower/wc or bath cost €53. Half board (compulsory in July–Aug) costs €48–55 per person. The cooking is good – house specialities include lightly cooked Aveyronnais sirloin steak, *astet najacois* and *crème brûlée* with vintage plum brandy. Menus are €17–39, à la carte around €40, and you can eat outside in good weather. Logis de France.

◎ |●| La Salamandre

Rue du Barriou; it's at the beginning of the street that leads to the château.
☎05.65.29.74.09
Closed *Tues evening and Wed out of season; mid-Nov to end Jan.*

An unpretentious restaurant offering straightforward, local dishes – sausages, duck breast, salads, mushroom pie and local cheeses – as well as more elaborate dishes such as *clafoutis* with asparagus and orange sauce or pike fillet with carrot cream. There's a lunch menu at €10, with other menus at €16 and €20. There is an impressive view of the château from the terrace at the back. Magical.

Nestier

65150

◎ ⅔ 🏠 |●| Le Relais du Castera**

Centre.
☎05.62.39.77.37 🖷05.62.39.77.29
Closed *Sun evening, Mon and Tues evening (Oct–May); Jan; early June.* **TV.**

The *Relais* looks pretty uninteresting outside but there's nothing remotely dull about the cooking of Serge Latour – he's one of the best chefs in the Hautes-Pyrénées. He assembles and presents dishes with elaborate care. You'll discover all kinds of new flavours at excellent prices: weekday lunch menu €17 and others up to €42. Regional and fish specialities include fresh fish with Jurançon sauce, duck foie gras in many different forms, *cassoulet* with Tarbais beans, crayfish with creamed Tarbais beans, *garbure de Bigorre* prepared *au confit* or *au camou* (in winter), warm *millas* with seasonal fruit and a chocolate dessert platter. Varied wine. Upstairs, there are a few comfortable rooms costing €41–56 with shower/wc; half board €44–56 per person. *Free coffee offered to our readers on presentation of this guide.*

Peyrecave

32340

◎ ⅔ |●| Chez Annie

It's halfway between Lectaure and Castelsarrasin on the Tarn and Garonne border.
☎05.62.28.65.40
Closed *Sat; Sun; second fortnight in Sept.*

Annie runs this stunning little roadside inn and she also does the cooking: try her house *cassoulet, daube* with prunes, *poule-au-pot* (all can be ordered in advance). Menus go for €10–18.50. This is the kind of inn we particularly like; it is off the tourist trail and makes eating out a real pleasure. *Free coffee offered to our readers on presentation of this guide.*

Projan

32400

◄◄ ⅀ ☎ |●| Le Château de Projan**

It's on the road from Saint-Mont to the N134 (towards Pau and Aire-sur-Adour; on the edge of the the Gers, the Landes and the Atlantic Pyrenees).
☎ 05.62.09.46.21 ℗ 05.62.09.44.08
ⓦ www.projan.fr
Closed *Fri evening out of season; Jan.* **Games available. Car park. Swimming pool.**

A genuine château standing alone on a hill. The family who've owned it since 1986 have transformed the place, letting in light and colour and filling it with contemporary art: there's a beautiful mosaic by a Swiss artist right in the entrance. This good taste extends to the reading nook, the dining room, the bar and the pictures on the wall. The salon, which has been decorated in a modern style, looks out over the countryside. Also worthy of mention are the woods surrounding the building (where deer can sometimes be glimpsed in the early morning), the baby grand piano, the huge terrace with views of the Pyreneees and the brand-new swimming pool. Double rooms with shower/wc or bath are €92–120, and there's a suite at €150. It's not a fully-fledged restaurant but they offer *table d'hôte* in the evening if you order in advance, for €24–35. *Free apéritif or 10% discount on the room rate (except July, Aug, Sept and public holidays) offered to our readers on presentation of this guide.*

Puycelci

81140

◄◄ ☎ |●| L'Ancienne Auberge

Place de l' Église.
☎ 05.63.33.65.90 ℗ 05.63.32.21.12
ⓦ www.ancienne-auberge.com
Closed *Sun and Mon (bistro open every day in season); first fortnight in Dec.* **TV.**

This attractive little hotel, expertly run by Dorothée, is set in one of the region's finest country houses, which has been tastefully refurbished. Some of the bright rooms have large bay windows; they vary in price according to the view: doubles €65–120. The lounge with a fireplace boasts a display case with a German suit of armour worthy of any museum, while the pretty terrace lies in the shadow of the clock tower. High-quality food is also on offer, striking a fine balance between tradition and creativity, with good local produce and menus that change every day. Try the game dishes (in season) or the succulent fillet of beef. Menus range in price from €18 to €27; reckon on around €15 for the lunchtime bistro service.

Larroque

81140 (3km NW)

◄ ⅀ |●| Au Val d'Aran

It's on the D964 towards Bruniquel.
☎ 05.63.33.11.15
Open *daily in season, lunch and dinner; out of season, lunch only (Sat lunch and dinner).* **Closed** *Christmas to 30 Jan.*

A typical village inn with a comfortable dining room, terrace or veranda, depending on the season, and very engaging owners. The countryside is close at hand, ideal for a siesta after your meal. The weekday lunch menu, at €12, starts with a lavish plate of charcuterie and is followed by *crudités*, a main course, cheese and dessert – traditional French cooking, in other words. Other menus are available for €20–34. *Free coffee offered to our readers on presentation of this guide.*

Puy l'Evèque

46700

◄◄ ⅀ ☎ |●| Hôtel Bellevue – Restaurant Côté Lot

Place de la Truffière.
☎ 05.65.36.06.60 ℗ 05.65.36.06.61
ⓦ www.lothotel-bellevue.com
Restaurant closed *Sun and Mon; 15 Jan–12 Feb; 15–30 Nov.* **Disabled access. TV.**

The building is completely new, with elegant and tasteful rooms in a contemporary style; it is perfectly integrated into the landscape, with a lovely view over the Lot and the plains. Doubles go for €70–87; the more expensive ones are the most spacious. Delicious cooking, and bang up to date; robust local dishes are interspersed with regional recipes that are light and full of flavour. You'll get the strong flavours of the Mediterranean and the delicacy of Atlantic fish. There's a range of menus at €26.50 (lunch) and €42–60. In a separate building, the popular *L'Aganit* brasserie offers simpler fare with a weekday lunch menu at €12.50, or €24 à la carte. *Free house apéritif offered to our readers on presentation of this guide.*

Mauroux

46700 (10km S)

⚫ 🎿 🏠 |●| Hostellerie Le Vert

It's on the D5.
℡05.65.36.51.36 ℻05.65.36.56.84
ⓦwww.hotellevert.com
Closed *1 Nov–31 March.* **Restaurant** open *evenings (except Thurs); Sun lunch.* **TV. High chairs and games available. Swimming pool.**

A superb, typical Quercy residence way out in the country, surrounded by landscaped grounds and with a heated swimming pool. The orchard and swimming pool offer utter peace. You'll receive a charming welcome, and the staff can give you all sorts of information on local rambles. The seven very comfortable rooms have been decorated in exquisite taste; one has a beautiful vault in bare stone, while another has an open fireplace. Doubles are €55–110, and half board costs €62.50–90. The bright, pleasant restaurant well deserves its fine reputation; dishes change with the seasons and what's good at the market. The single gastronomic menu costs €42. Logis de France. *10% discount on the room rate (except during school holidays) offered to our readers on presentation of this guide.*

Revel

31250

⚫ 🎿 🏠 |●| Hôtel-restaurant du Midi**

34 bd. Gambetta.
℡05.61.83.50.50 ℻05.61.83.34.74
ⓦwww.hoteldumidi.com
Restaurant closed *Sun evening and Mon lunchtime (Nov to Easter); 12 Nov–6 Dec.* **TV. High chairs available. Car park.**

Pleasant country hotel with smart rooms, each one different, for €49–54 with bath. The the most expensive rooms look over

the garden, while the others look over the road but have good double glazing. The décor in the bright dining room is chic and in summer you can eat outside. Weekday lunch menu of the day is €20; others cost €22.50–46 and list many aromatic dishes and the wines are very affordable. Logis de France. *Free apéritif offered to our readers on presentation of this guide.*

⚫ 🏠 |●| Hôtellerie du Lac

Avenue Pierre-Paul-Riquet.
℡05.62.18.70.80 ℻05.62.18.71.13
ⓦwww.hotellerie-du-lac.com
Restaurant closed *Sun evening (Sept—end June); last week in Dec; first fortnight in Jan.* **Disabled access. TV. Swimming pool. Car park.**

Claude Chabrol filmed most of the interior scenes of *Hell* here just before it changed owners, but it is in fact quite heavenly, with comfortable, skilfully decorated rooms (€62 with bath), some with a view of the lake. On the ground floor, the décor in the dining rooms, lounge and bar creates an atmosphere that is both cosy and colourful. The food is excellent, although the first menu (€15, weekday lunchtime) is nothing extraordinary; Chabrol, a notorious gourmet, would undoubtedly have preferred the next menus at €23 and €34. The service is very friendly. There's a heated swimming pool, sauna and a charmingly old-fashioned inner courtyard with a glass canopy, in contrast to the more classical style of the façade and garden.

Rieumes

31370

⚫ 🏠 |●| Hôtel Les Palmiers**

13 pl. du Foirail.
℡05.61.91.81.01 ℻05.61.91.56.36
ⓦwww.auberge-lespalmiers.com
Closed *Sun evening; Mon; last week in Aug; first fortnight in Sept.* **High chairs available.**

Pretty but subdued décor, with African *bogolan* prints alongside modern paintings in the dining room. Very attractive and quiet courtyard with palm trees – an ideal place for relaxing in fine weather. The inviting rooms cost €56–58 and combine the charm of the old with the comfort of the new. The cooking draws its inspiration from regional traditions, with pride of place going to fish dishes, but carnivores are also catered for. There's a weekday lunchtime menu at €13, and others €19–35. After your meal you can always take a dip in the pool. Logis de France.

Riscle
32400

ⓒ |●| Le Pigeonneau

36 av. de l'Adour.
℡05.62.69.85.64
Closed *Sun evening; Mon; Tues evening; a weekend Jan; a week early July.*

A chic place to eat exquisite traditional food that is given a subtle, exotic twist. The chef's English background is apparent in the discreet Asian influences: *croustillant* of gizzards with prunes, squab with sweet spices and Pacherenc wine, *croustade* with apples and an unforgettable cardamom ice cream. The weekday lunch menu costs €16, with two other menus at €25 and €32. Wine is served by the glass or bottle at reasonable prices. This is one of the best (no-smoking) restaurants in the *département* and they prefer you to book in the evening.

Rocamadour
46500

ⓒ ⅋ ⌂ |●| Hôtel-restaurant Le Lion d'Or**

It's in the medieval town.
℡05.65.33.62.04 ℗05.65.33.72.54
ⓦwww.liondor-rocamadour.com
Closed *early Nov to end of March.* **TV. Car park.**

A traditional hotel-restaurant which offers a lovely view of the old town. The clean, comfy bedrooms are reasonable value, and the best ones enjoy a beautiful view, some from a balcony. Doubles cost €36–51.50 depending on the level of comfort. In the restaurant, menus go for €11.90–38.50 and list specialities such as foie gras *tarte tatin* with walnut sauce or truffle and ceps omelette. Brilliant desserts – it's impossible to resist the walnut gâteau with egg custard. Reservations recommended – ask for a table with a view. Logis de France. *10% discount on the room rate (except Aug) on a stay of at least two consecutive nights offered to our readers on presentation of this guide.*

ⓒ ⅋ ⌂ |●| Le Troubadour

Belveyre; it's 800m from L'Hospitalet in the direction of Alvignac.
℡05.65.33.70.27 ℗05.65.33.71.99
ⓔtroubadour@rocamadour.com
Closed *mid-Nov to mid-Feb.* **Restaurant closed** *lunchtimes (meals may not be served between mid-June and mid-Sept).* **Disabled access. TV. High chairs and games available. Swimming pool.**

This large white stone house, set back from the road, is a godsend for anyone who wants to avoid the tourist-tussle that is Rocamadour. It's a quiet place surrounded by greenery, and there's a magnificent view of the limestone plain from the pool. The rooms, decorated with floral wallpaper, are delightfully fresh in summer and cost €44–80 for a double depending on the level of comfort and season. The air-conditioned restaurant serves traditional and regional dishes with menus at €23 and €35. It's best to book. Logis de France. *10% discount on the room rate (15 Feb–15 June) offered to our readers on presentation of this guide.*

ⓒ ⌂ |●| Hôtel-restaurant Beau Site***

It's on the only street in the medieval town, on the right.
℡05.65.33.63.08 ℗05.65.33.65.23
ⓦwww.bw-beausite.com
TV. High chairs available. Car park.

This beautiful hotel-restaurant, in the heart of Rocamadour, has been in the Menot family for five generations, and it is superbly equipped. The reception and lounges boast antique furniture; some of the rooms are furnished with similar stylishness, and all are well maintained, tastefully decorated and endowed with a breathtaking view of the abbey perched on the hill. Some rooms are set under the sloping roof in the attic, while others are fitted with a mezzanine in order to sleep a whole family. Doubles go for €48–95 depending on the level of comfort and the season. The food, delicate and tasty, is served by discreet, competent and cheerful waiters, although the "bistro" area does not meet the same high standards. The ingredients on the menus, €17 to €52, come from strictly local sources; à la carte about €30. The pretty terrace is shaded by lime trees and offers a great view of the château – an excellent establishment in its category.

14

☜ 🚹 |●| Hôtel-restaurant Les Vieilles Tours***

Lieu-dit Lafage; take the D673 in the direction of Payrac, and continue for 2.5km.
☎05.65.33.68.01
🌐www.chateauxhotelsfrance.com/vieilles-tours
Closed *mid-Nov to end March.* **Disabled access. TV. Swimming pool. Car park.**

This charming, cosy hotel, complete with a car park and swimming pool, has been converted from a splendid sixteenth-century manor house. It offers seventeen large, attractive rooms, each furnished differently and spread over various buildings. Doubles go for €60–110; half board is obligatory in July–Aug at €75–100 per person. The food alone is worth a visit, as it is sophisticated, regionally based and delicious with several menus available at €25–61.You can go hiking or ride a horse or mountain bike nearby – and, to make the most of these activities, the hotel offers picnic lunches as well as snacks by the swimming pool.

☜ 🚹 Domaine de la Rhue***

Take the D673 for 6km in the direction of Brive, then the N140, then turn left for 1km.
☎05.65.33.71.50 ⊕05.65.33.72.48
🌐www.domainedelarhue.com
Closed *All Saints' Day to Easter.* **Swimming pool. Car park.**

The old stables of a nineteenth-century manor house, set in the heart of the countryside, have been converted into a rustic but elegant hotel. The results are wonderful: a warm setting dominated by wood and stone; a relaxed atmosphere; good service; fourteen quiet, comfortable rooms with a view, all different, and a superb suite with a small kitchen and terrace (€125). Doubles cost €65–107. No restaurant, but a generous country breakfast is served for €10, and a continental one for €7.50. There is also a swimming pool, and the opportunity to go ballooning, mountain biking and horse riding (€125).

☜ |●| Roc du Berger

Route de Padirac.
☎05.65.33.19.99
Open *daily from the last weekend in March to the last weekend in Oct.*

This large chalet close to Rocamadour is undoubtedly the most attractive hotel in the vicinity. Between the restaurants and the farmhouse-inn, you can sample many local

foodstuffs: Le Quercy lamb, *cabécou* cheese, duck, trout from the Ouyse, foie-gras sausages, charcuterie – all supplied by local producers and friends. Sit on the large terrace amidst the oak trees, and enjoy the expertly prepared grilled dishes. Devoted carnivores will opt straight away for the selection of grilled meats (€29). Superb service.

Meyronne
46200 (14km N)

☜ 🎿 🚹 |●| Hôtel-restaurant La Terrasse**

Take the D673 for 4km then turn left onto the D15.
☎05.65.32.21.60 ⊕05.65.32.26.93
🌐www.hotel-la-terrasse.com
Closed *Tues lunchtime; mid-Nov to end March.* **TV. Swimming pool.**

Meyronne is an adorable little village up in the hills, and this establishment was at one time the summer residence of the bishops of Tulle. The building is full of charm and character: the stone walls are covered in ivy and it has beams and turrets with sloping roofs, as well as classic (and attractive) bourgeois décor from another age. Here you can stay in a château at reasonable prices: doubles in the hotel or the castle proper go for €60–115, depending on the level of comfort and the season. Rooms in the hotel are comfortable; those in the castle are small suites and remain deliciously cool in summer. The terrace is shaded by a pergola and overlooks the valley; the swimming pool has a panoramic view, and the restaurant specializes in copious, regional dishes. There's a *formule* for €18 on weekday lunchtimes, and several menus €25–49. *Free house apéritif offered to our readers on presentation of this guide.*

Rodez
12000

☜ 🎿 🚹 Hôtel de la Tour-Maje***

Boulevard Gally.
☎05.65.68.34.68 ⊕05.65.68.27.56
🌐www.hotel-tour-maje.fr
Closed *Christmas to New Year.* **Disabled access. TV.**

This classic hotel incorporates a fourteenth-century tower, a remnant of the old ramparts. The rooms are pleasant, modern and tastefully decorated – some with view of the cathedral (nos. 1 to 4) – and doubles cost €58–66, depending on facilities. Some lovely rooms sleeping two-to-four are available in the tower for €110. The fifth floor has been completely refurbished. You can expect excellent service, both sophisticated and discreet. *10% discount on the room rate offered to our readers on presentation of this guide.*

ⓔ ⚄ 🏠 Hôtel Biney

7 bd. Gambetta or rue Victoire Massol; it's between the cathedral and the tourist office. There's a sign at the end of the passage.
☎05.65.68.01.24 ⓕ05.65.75.22.98
ⓔhotel.biney@wanadoo.fr
TV. Pay car park.

This quiet little hotel is conveniently located right in the middle of Rodez and has been completely refurbished. The interior design is very tasteful, with warm colours and beautiful fabrics, and there's a peaceful flower garden at the back – some rooms overlook it. There are 29 double rooms with modern bathrooms at €68–105, and there's a steam room and a sauna (€4). The generous buffet breakfast costs €9 and you can order a tasty TV meal to have in your room for €13.

ⓔ |●| Restaurant La Taverne

23 rue de l'Embergue.
☎05.65.42.14.51
Closed *Sat lunchtime; Sun; public holidays; a fortnight early May; a fortnight in Sept.*
Disabled access. High chairs available.

Stained-glass windows on the façade and a beautiful collection of signed drawings of cartoon characters. A vaulted basement dining room where you'll be served traditional and regional food – shin of pork with honey, stuffed cabbage and lots of other delicious choices. Prices are very reasonable: weekday lunch menu €10.50 and an extensive *menu-carte* for €15. There's a large quiet terrace at the back, overlooking the garden.

ⓔ |●| Restaurant Willy's

2 rue de la Viarague; it's in a street leading to pl. de la Madeleine, near the Saint-Amans church.
☎05.65.68.17.34
Closed *Sun; Mon; a week in spring; a week in Sept.*

The building is painted blue and the dining room is in warm, pleasant colours.

It's a friendly restaurant specializing in regional cooking with a touch of originality and exoticism that changes with the seasons and is based on quality produce. Menus cost €13.50 (lunch) and €20. You'll be welcomed without fuss and the atmosphere is young, informal and relaxed. You are advised to book.

ⓔ |●| Les Jardins d'Acropolis

Rue d'Athènes, rond-point de Bourran.
☎05.65.68.40.07
Closed *Sun evening; Mon.*

This restaurant boasts impeccable service and two comfortable, breezy and attractive dining rooms with tables adorned with fresh flowers and set well apart. As for the food, Dominique Panis, formerly of *Bras* and *Gagnaire*, offers inspired, highly personal cooking that spurns outlandish novelty in favour of strong roots in local tradition – albeit reinterpreted and enlivened. Try, for example, the kebab of foie gras and lamb sweetbreads in chestnut broth or the langoustine-tail *nems* with peppered mint. Menus are €15-26; the weekday lunch menu provides surprisingly good value (starter, main course, glass of wine and coffee all included). The wine list, with a particularly wide range of Bordeaux, is also impressive, ranging from a glass of wine at €2.50 to a litre of rosé at €7.50 and a Pauillac Mouton-Rothschild 1994 at €475.

ⓔ |●| Restaurant Goûts et Couleurs

38 rue de Bonald; it's in a pedestrian street in the old town centre.
☎05.65.42.75.10
Closed *Sun; Mon; Jan; 10 days early May; a fortnight in mid-Sept.*

The dining room is decorated in pastel colours, with gastronomically themed paints on the walls, and there's a warm atmosphere – perfect for an intimate dinner. The chef, Jean-Luc Fan, is a culinary artist himself, as is apparent from the wonderful crockery and the menu: leg of rabbit stuffed with cuttlefish cooked in its ink and rice; Gascon black pig's head grilled with herbs; asparagus and Puy lentils with ginger. Jean-Luc is still honing his talent but is a name to watch out for in the future. The weekday lunch menu is at €20, with others €30–65; expect to pay around €45 à la carte. Attentive but relaxed service, and they have a large, attractive terrace to the rear. Booking is advised.

Sainte-Radegonde

12850 (6km SE)

⬤ 🏠 |◉| Saloon Guest Ranch***

Landrevrier-Sainte-Radegonde; in the direction of Sainte-Radegonde, then towards Landrevier/Inières (signposted).
☎05.65.42.47.46 ℗05.65.78.32.36
🌐www.le-saloon.com
Open *evenings by reservation only; Sun lunchtime.* **TV. Swimming pool. Car park.**

A little corner of the American Wild West right in the heart of the Aveyron countryside, complete with horses and saloon. The latter is authentic down to the smallest detail, with mahogany furniture, red wallpaper and lots of photographs. Not surprisingly, meat looms large on the menu, and it's some of the best in the area. The very generous set menus are at €19–28. Rooms are spacious and the décor, of course, is cowboy-style but luxurious; doubles with shower/wc or bath €50–60. The staff are friendly and considerate, and don't forget to book.

Salles-la-Source

12330 (10km NW)

⬤ |◉| Restaurant de la Cascade

Take the D901 and it's next to the museum.
☎ and ℗05.65.67.29.08
Open *lunchtimes except Sat (l Oct–30 April); lunch and dinner except Sat lunch and Sun evening (1 May–30 Sept).* **Closed** *early Dec.* **Disabled access.**

The small dining room is decorated in pinkish tones and has a ravishing view of the surrounding valleys – there's also a shady terrace. Honest cuisine with a weekday lunch menu at €12 and another at €16; the cheaper menu changes every day and offers two starters, main course (perhaps *aligot*, or a seasonal dish), cheese and dessert.

Saint-Affrique

12400

⬤ 🏠 |◉| Hôtel Moderne**

54 rue Alphonse-Pezet; it's next to the train station (now out of service).
☎05.65.49.20.44 ℗05.65.49.36.55
🌐www.lemoderne.com

Closed *mid-Dec to mid-Jan; a week in Oct.* **Disabled access. TV. Pay car park.**

The surroundings may be banal, but the hotel offers thirty or so spotless rooms. Doubles with shower/wc or bath cost €43–58; half board costs €38.11 per person. The restaurant has established a solid reputation in the region, with regular customers who appreciate the effusive welcome from the owner, the nostalgic, typically provincial atmosphere in the large dining room – and, of course, the food. Dishes include leg of baby rabbit, lamb sweetbreads and house specialties with Roquefort (including a platter of ten surprisingly diverse varieties). Excellent desserts are also available. There are several menus ranging in price from €12 to €45. Be sure to take a look at the unusual caricatures by Raoul Cabrol on display in the lounge. Logis de France.

Saint-Antonin-Noble-Val

82140

⬤ 🏠 |◉| Hôtel des Thermes**

1 pl. des Moines; if you're coming from the gorges, it's after the bridge on the left, beside the Aveyron.
☎05.63.25.06.00 ℗05.63.25.06.06
🌐www.nobleval.com
Restaurant closed *Tues evening and Wed (except July–Aug); Jan.* **TV. High chairs available.**

The prices and the waterside location are the best things about this place. Rooms look suspiciously like those you'd find in a chain, but the location and the warmth of the welcome make up for that. Doubles with bath are priced €30–42; some have a view of the river and the Anglars cliff-face. Good little restaurant serving a weekday lunch menu for €10, others €14–20. There's a wonderful waterside terrace and a cybercafé. Logis de France.

Brousses

82140 (9km S)

⬤ |◉| La Corniche

It's in the village; take the coast road (D115 bis).
☎05.63.68.26.95
Closed *Mon and Sun evening (except July–Aug); Oct–Feb.*

The young chef in this little restaurant

tucked away above the Aveyron gorges invites you to a sensual treat. Working alone in his kitchen, he toils away to offer seasonal, traditional food that is really out of the ordinary. Don't be fooled by his shy and modest demeanour – he's a magician, and his best trick is achieving all this with such little expense: weekday lunchtime menu €16, and another at €25.50. There is a terrace with a view of the Capucins rock, which is very popular with rock climbers. It's best to book at the weekend. Credit cards not accepted.

Saint-Bertrand-de-Comminges
31510

◉ 🏠 Hôtel du Comminges**

Place de la Cathédrale; it's opposite the cathedral.
☎05.61.88.31.43 ⓕ05.61.94.98.22
Closed Nov to end March.

This hotel is in a quite delightful old family house opposite the cathedral, swathed in ivy and wisteria with a small internal courtyard – the whole place is utterly charming. Large rooms with period furniture go for €29.50–50; family room for four people at €68. The only reservation is the erratic service. If you stay here, take advantage of the night time and early morning to explore the nearby alleyways when they are relatively free of tourists.

◉ 🎋 🏠 ◉�‖◉ L'Oppidum**

Rue de la Poste; it's near the cathedral on the road down to the post office.
☎05.61.88.33.50 ⓕ05.61.95.94.04
🌐www.hotel-oppidum.com
Closed Sun evening; Mon; 15 Nov–15 Dec.
Open noon–2pm and 7–9.30pm. **Disabled access. TV. High chairs available.**

A small, pretty hotel in an old building. The rooms are comfortable and bright but rather small. Doubles are at €42–48 with shower/wc or bath – one is big enough to be a honeymoon suite and is more expensive. Menus range from €15 (not Sun and public holidays) up to €32. Decent food is on offer, enhanced by irreproachable service. Logis de France. *Free coffee offered to our readers on presentation of this guide.*

Valcabrère
31510 (1.5km E)

◉ ◉�‖◉ Le Lugdunum

After Valcabrère, join the N25, turn right and it's 400m further on.
☎05.61.94.52.05 ⓕ05.61.94.52.06
Closed Sun–Wed evenings out of season. **Disabled access.**

There is nothing in France to match this truly original restaurant that resembles a Roman villa and takes visitors on a culinary trip through time. It has a terrace overlooking the pastures and a fantastic view of Saint-Bertrand. Renzo Pedrazzini, whose family comes from Lombardy, serves traditional local dishes, but the real attraction here is the recipes he has taken from the ancient Romans: sea bream with grapes or lamb with ginger. He mixes honey and vinegar, won't use tomatoes or lemons because they were unknown to the ancients and gets his spices from a local herbalist – he regards himself as an apprentice of Apicius, who wrote a treatise on cooking two thousand years ago. Take his wife's advice and have a spiced wine with your meal and try the rose or violet apéritif. There's a range of menus costing €35–50; you must book ahead for the most expensive menu. À la carte you can expect to pay around €65.

Saint-Cirq-Lapopie
46330

◉ 🎋 🏠 Auberge du Sombral**

Place du Sombral.
☎05.6531.26.08 ⓕ05.65.30.26.37

This charming and reliable inn, recognizable by its high roof with four slopes, is set in the heart of the village. It offers attractively furnished rooms (€65 with shower, €72 with bath), elegantly decorated in soft, warm colours. *Free coffee offered to our readers on presentation of this guide.*

◉ ◉�‖◉ Restaurant L'Atelier

☎and ⓕ05.65.31.22.34
Closed Tues evening and Wed in low season; Jan.

This restaurant, situated on a hairpin bend, is well worth the detour from the main village. It is housed in a picturesque old building with a pretty terrace overlooking Saint-Cirq. At sunset you really have a magical view from the terrace. Inside, you will find a sincerely friendly welcome and copious portions of well-prepared local dishes on menus at €13, €20 and €30. The drawings on the walls, the work of friends passing through, only enhance the delightful atmosphere.

Tour de Faure
46330 (3km E)

⊚ 🏠 Hôtel Les Gabarres**

Take the D662 towards Figeac.
☎05.65.30.24.57 🖷05.65.30.25.85
Closed end of Oct to Easter. **Disabled access. High chairs available. Swimming pool. Car park.**

It isn't the most beautiful building but the excellent reception and the bright, clean, spacious bedrooms more than make up for that. Half the rooms overlook the swimming pool and in some parts of the establishment you get great views of the valley. Rooms range from €48 to €50 (including buffet breakfast) depending on the season. The couple in charge can tell you all about the various walks around the area. "Gabarres", by the way, were boats that once used to sail on the Lot.

Saint-Félix-Lauragais
31540

⊚ 🏠 |●| Auberge du Poids Public***

Faubourg Saint-Roch.
☎05.62.18.85.00 🖷05.62.18.85.05
Closed Sun evening; Jan; a week in Nov. **Open** noon–1.30pm and 7.30–9.30pm. **TV. High chairs available. Car park.**

Delightful rooms, some with views of the Lauragais hills, are €65–75 depending on the size and view. Also available are two luxurious rooms at €95–135. There are several little sitting rooms and a large, rustic dining room with fine exposed stonework and panoramic views. The atmosphere is classy and the terrace extremely pleasant in summer. Set menus (€25–65) include foie gras cooked in a cloth, milk-fed lamb and summer fruit croustillant. There is also the "Dégustation" menu, a selection of five dishes that vary according to the produce available. You'll find comparatively unknown wines as well as great vintages on the wine list, priced from affordable to astronomical. One of the best restaurants in the region.

Saint-Julia
31540 (6km N)

⊚ 🌴 |●| L'Auberge des Remparts

Rue du Vinaigre.
☎05.61.83.04.79
Closed Sun; Mon and Tues evenings. **Open** noon–1.30pm and 7–9pm. **High chairs available.**

A village inn with a growing reputation. The appetizing €11 weekday lunch includes soup, crudités, charcuterie, dish of the day, cheese, dessert, wine and coffee. In the evening (when reservations are advised), the young chef shows his colours with more elaborate, refined cooking on menus at €19 and €25. In good weather they serve meals on the shady terrace. Free apéritif offered to our readers on presentation of this guide.

Saint-Gaudens
31800

⊚ 🌴 |●| Restaurant de l'Abattoir

Boulevard Leconte-de-Lisle; take the boulevard Gambetta to the train station, then go straight on in the direction of the abattoirs; the restaurant is just opposite.
☎05.61.89.70.29
Open noon–1.45pm and 7.45–10pm. **Closed** Sun; Mon–Wed evenings; public holidays; 12–18 Aug.

One of the best restaurants in the region. Nowhere else will you get meat that's as fresh, tender and downright delicious as at Christian Gillet's place. After exploring deserts on a motorbike, he has settled here, as close as possible to the abattoir. He goes there every morning at dawn to choose cuts of meat to feed the dealers who arrive from the country to sell their animals at market. Try the "drunken" pig's trotter, calf's head with ravigote sauce, tartare steak or salted entrecôte, all excellent and all served in copious portions. For all that, the prices are very reasonable: weekday lunch menu €12.20, others €15.50 and €20. The large dining room is bright and pleasant and the atmosphere is matey. Free house apéritif offered to our readers on presentation of this guide.

Saint-Geniez-d'Olt

12130

@ 🏠 |❂| Hôtel de la Poste**

3 pl. du Général-de-Gaulle; it's in the main
street leading away from the Lot.
☎05.65.47.43.30 ℻05.65.47.42.75
🖦www.hoteldelaposte12.com
Closed early Dec to end of March. **Disabled
access. TV. High chairs and games available. Swimming pool. Car park.**

A traditional village inn with an old section and a modern annexe. The former,
furnished with superb antiques, is comfortable and cosy and the rooms, priced at
€35–50, are pleasant and well equipped.
Ask for one of the following rooms: nos.
207, 208 or 311 to 339. The restaurant is
well known for its quality cooking, with
set menus at €16 (weekday lunchtimes) or
€22–48. Dishes include roast pike perch,
ceps pie and parsleyed beef. You can eat
in the dining room, or on the terrace surrounded by greenery.

Sainte-Eulalie-d'Olt

12130 (3km W)

@ 🏠 |❂| Au Moulin d'Alexandre**

☎05.65.47.45.85 ℻05.65.52.73.78
Closed Sun evening in winter; a fortnight in
May and June; a fortnight in Oct. **TV. High
chairs available. Car park.**

A delightful country inn in a renovated
seventeenth-century water mill offering
pretty rooms at €45–50. Half board, costing €45 a head, is compulsory from May
to September. The cooking's good and
prices are reasonable, with a weekday lunch
menu at €11 and others up to €27. The
restaurant specializes in regional dishes
such as monkfish with *homardine* sauce,
feuilleté of lamb sweetbreads with Noilly,
ceps with parsley – all of which you can eat
on the shady terrace. Boats are available for
hire to guests. Credit cards not accepted.

Saint-Girons

09200

@ 🎋 🏠 |❂| Domaine de Beauregard-Hôtel-restaurant La Clairière **

Avenue de la Résistance; it's on the outskirts
of town in the direction of Seix-Massat.

☎05.61.66.66.66 ℻05.34.14.30.30
🖦www.domainedebeauregard.com
Closed Sun evening, Mon, Fri evening and
Sat (early Dec to end of May). **Disabled
access. TV. High chairs available.
Swimming pool. Car park.**

A really wonderful place away from the
traffic, in an eight-acre park with a private
swimming pool and rose garden. Rooms
are available in the small hotel dating
from the nineteenth century, as well as in
a cottage in the grounds. They are bright
and comfortable, with views of the park.
Doubles with shower/wc or bath go for
€48–55; half board, at €48–55, is compulsory in high season. In the pleasant restaurant, the architecture is bright and modern,
with the decoration changing every two
years (alternating between maritime and
mountain atmospheres). Menus cost €19
at weekday lunchtimes and then up to
€65. Charming service; this is our favourite spot in Saint-Girons. *10% discount
on the room rate (except July, Aug and public
holidays) offered to our readers on presentation
of this guide.*

Argein

09800 (17km SW)

@ 🎋 🏠 Hostellerie de la Terrasse**

Take the D618, 3km after Audressein.
☎05.61.96.70.11
Closed early Nov to Easter. **Restaurant
closed** lunchtimes. **TV. High chairs available.**

Charming little mountain hotel on the
Portet-Aspet road. Simple but renovated
rooms (ask for one with a view of the
mountain) from €36–53 with shower/
wc or bath; half board €45 per person.
Excellent service and fine regional cooking; the trout with ceps is particularly
recommended. Credit cards not accepted.
*Free house apéritif offered to our readers on
presentation of this guide.*

Saint-Lary-Soulan

65170

@ 🎋 🏠 |❂| Hôtel-restaurant La Pergola**

25 rue Vincent-Mir.
☎05.62.39.40.46 ℻05.62.40.06.55
🖦www.hotellapergola.fr
Restaurant closed Mon and Tues lunchtimes in winter. **Closed** 10 days in May; Nov.

Disabled access. TV. Car park.

A pleasant establishment dating from 1957 with a pretty garden and a pergola. The spacious rooms are comfortable, with wonderful beds. Doubles with shower/wc or bath go for €52–100; breakfast at €9. The rooms facing southwest have a view of the peak of Tramezaïgues and the peak of Aret. The food is original, very tasty, and makes good use of herbs and spices (pistou, rosemary, basil, etc). Set lunches cost €14 and €20; four other menus €23–45. The service is very professional without being overly formal. All in all, a good hotel that has just acquired its third star. *Free house apéritif or coffee offered to our readers on presentation of this guide.*

Saint-Lizier

09190

⑭

ⓐ ⚄ ⌂ |●| Hôtel de la Tour

Route du Pont; it's at the foot of the old town on the banks of the Salat.
☏05.61.66.38.02 ☏05.61.66.38.01
🕸www.hotel-restaurant.net/hoteldelatour
Closed *Sun evening (except July and Aug).*
TV. High chairs available.

This, the only historic hotel in the capital of the Couserans, has nine lovely rooms with shower/wc or bath for €35–45; some look over the river and others have little balconies. The chef is creative, offering menus from €15 (not Sun) and €20–38; he also does good simple grills. *10% discount on the room rate (Oct–April) offered to our readers on presentation of this guide.*

Saint-Sulpice

81370

ⓐ ⚄ |●| Le Bersy

It's 9km west of Giroussens, on the main square opposite the post office.
☏05.63.40.09.17
Closed *Sun; winter school holidays; 3 weeks in Aug.* **Disabled access.**

An excellent bar-restaurant-pizzeria that's always full. They list dishes of the day on the blackboard, and there's quite a good choice à la carte. The weekday lunch menu costs €10 and there are others up to €20; pizzas cost around €9. Friendly welcome and swift service, but they don't rush you. In summer there's a pleasant terrace for eating outside. *Free house apéritif offered to our readers on presentation of this guide.*

Saint-Lieux-Lès-Lavaur

81500 (8km E)

ⓐ |●| Le Col Vert

In the village; take the D38 in the direction of Giroussens.
☏05.63.41.32.47
Closed *Tues; Sat lunchtime.*

This restaurant is very attractive, both inside with its brick walls and exposed beams, and outside with its terrace shaded by fruit trees and a venerable chestnut tree. Weekday lunchtime menus go for €10 and €13; other menus at €18–32. The menu gives the impression of seasonal, regional cooking in a fairly classical vein, but in fact the dishes reveal originality and flair, as in the *magret* of duck in venison. These surprises are helping the restaurant to forge a well-deserved reputation.

Salmiech

12120

ⓐ ⌂ |●| Hôtel-Restaurant du Céor

☏05.65.74.25.88 ☏05.65.46.70.13
Closed *Mon out of season; early Jan to end of March.* **High chairs available.**

This nineteenth-century coaching inn offers terrific value and a warm welcome from the staff. There are some twenty pleasant rooms costing €27.30–31.70; breakfast €5.50. Half board is €29.10–38.50 per person. Room nos. 1, 2, 4 and 6 are quietest; others look out onto the village. Regional dishes on the menus (€10.50–28) dominate in the pretty, rustic dining room: crayfish, duck breast in vine shoots and *aligot*, just to mention a few. You can sit out on the terrace in good weather and admire the view of the village.

Samatan

32130

ⓐ ⚄ |●| Au Canard Gourmand

La Rente; it's on the road to Lombez/L'Isle-Jourdain.
☏05.62.62.49.81
Closed *Mon evening; Tues; ten days in Jan; a week in June; a fortnight in Oct.* **Disabled access. High chairs available. Car park.**

Ingenious interpretations of local cuisine. Lots of different foie gras dishes: one with dill, another pan-fried with vanilla sauce and an amazing one with liquorice. Dishes change with the seasons and fresh market produce. The cheapest menu at €16 is served weekday lunchtimes, then there are three others at €23–34. The dining room is modern and colourful, and the service is efficient. It's very popular, so best to book one week ahead. If you can't eat here, however, you may at least be able to take advantage of one of the five brand-new bedrooms. *Free house apéritif offered to our readers on presentation of this guide.*

Sauveterre-de-Rouergue
12800

@@ 🏠 |●| Le Sénéchal***

It's north, outside the fortifications.
℡05.65.71.29.00 ℻05.65.71.29.09
🌐www.senechal.net
Closed Sun evening, Mon and Tues lunchtime (except July and Aug); early Jan to mid-March. **Disabled access. TV. Swimming pool. Car park.**

Local boy Michel Truchon loves this region. He also cares about quality produce, and sets about his cooking like an artist, creating wonderful dishes that are sophisticated and subtle. Set menus at €25 (weekdays) and €42–100 (taster menu) include elegant, meticulously prepared dishes such as roast foie gras of duck. Be sure to try the loin of lamb and sweetbreads with fresh herbs. You get a lovely welcome and the rooms (some with their own terrace) are quite magnificent. Doubles are priced at €100–150; half board at €100–120 per person. This fashionable hotel is rounded off by a swimming pool complemented by leisure equipment.

Sévérac-le-Château
12150

@ 🏠 |●| Hôtel-Restaurant des Causses

38 av. Aristide-Briand; take exit 42 off the A75 and it's opposite the train station.
℡05.65.70.23.00 ℻05.65.70.23.04
@les.causses-aveyron@wanadoo.fr
Hotel and restaurant closed Sun evening (Sept–June); 3 weeks in Oct. **Restaurant**

closed Mon lunchtime.

A comfortable hotel with slightly faded yet clean rooms which, given the price (€30–46), are no disappointment; half board €31–41. "Bob, le bon vivant" will certainly give you a charming welcome. Good quality cuisine is served on the terrace or in the rustic dining room, with menus €12–26; the locally produced meat is carefully selected and perfectly cooked to create dishes such as *pascade* with lamb sweetbreads. Try the *flaune*, a local cheesecake, for dessert.

Souillac
46200

@@ 🍴 🏠 |●| Grand Hôtel***

1 allée Verninac.
℡05.65.32.78.30 ℻05.65.32.66.34
🌐www.grandhotel-souillac.com
Closed Nov–April. **TV. Car park.**

This house offers numerous comfortable rooms, all attractively furnished and fairly spacious; some are set around an atrium and the most expensive ones have a private terrace. There is also a beautiful communal terrace on the roof, with a solarium and panoramic view. Double rooms cost €40–80, depending on the degree of comfort. You can eat in the large dining room, with its exquisitely designed décor, or in the equally charming open-air area (with shade on sunny days). Menus €13–25. *10% discount on the price of a room (in April and Oct) offered to our readers on presentation of this guide.*

Sousceyrac
46190

@@ 🏠 |●| Au Déjeuner de Sousceyrac

Place des Condamines; take the D673.
℡05.65.33.00.56 ℻05.65.33.04.37
Closed Sun evening and Mon (except in summer). **TV.**

You will not regret a journey to this out-of-the-way part of Quercy, not least for the beautiful dining room with worn wood panels and flickering log fire. We have particularly fond memories of its chef, who loves his work and takes endless care with even the simplest dish. On our visit, to the delight of his customers, he had prepared his duck necks stuffed with gizzards and walnuts, one of the best *magrets* of duck we've ever tasted, and a simple but exquisite *fromage-blanc* mousse with strawberries – all for €15. Other menus are also available up to €40. Double rooms are priced €38.11–45.73.

Latouille-Lentillac
46400 (11km SW)

◎ 🎿 🏠 |◉| Restaurant Gaillard**

It's 7km out of town, in Latouille-Lentillac.
℗05.65.38.10.25 ℗05.65.38.13.13
🅦www.hotel-gaillard.fr
Closed *a week in June; Nov.* **Disabled access. TV. High chairs and games available. Car park.**

Rooms here are all pleasantly decorated, simple, clean and air-conditioned, and some have a view of the river. Doubles with shower/wc or bath cost €40–50. The restaurant enjoys an excellent reputation and draws in a regular local crowd. Dishes include fresh trout, *confits* and other tasty regional delicacies. The cheap set menu is at €15.50 (not Sun lunch) with others €20–31. Logis de France. *Free coffee offered to our readers on presentation of this guide.*

Autoire
46400 (23km W)

◎ 🏠 |◉| Auberge de la Fontaine**

It's in the village; take the D673, then the D30 and the D38.
℗05.65.10.85.40 ℗05.65.10.12.70
🅦www.auberge-de-la-fontaine.com
Closed *Sun evening and Mon out of season.* **TV.**

This well-run inn offers a friendly welcome and nine comfortable, totally renovated rooms at €38–45 for a double. The satisfying home cooking (*tourin*, homemade *confit*) is served in a rustic dining room or on a terrace in the heart of the village. It is difficult to imagine better value for money: menus €10–25. Logis de France.

Tarbes
65000

◎ 🏠 Auberge de jeunesse

88 av. Alsace-Lorraine; 2km from the station towards Bordeaux; bus no. 1 at 150m from the station towards Bordeaux (terminus FJT).

℗05.62.38.91.20. ℗05.62.37.69.81.
🅦www.fuaj.org
Restaurant closed *Sat evening; Sun.* **Hostel open** *all year round.* **Disabled access. Car park.**

One night in the dormitory will set you back €12.30 including breakfast, and a meal €7.10 (Mon–Sat lunchtime). You will find a lot of young local workers residing here. The view over the Pyrenees is breathtaking and the staff friendly. Garden, sports facilities with climbing wall. Credit cards not accepted.

◎ 🎿 🏠 Hôtel de l'Avenue**

78–80 av. Bertrand Barère; it's 50m from the train station.
℗ and ℗05.62.93.06.36
Disabled access. TV.

This is a quiet little hotel, despite being near the station. The rooms are a bit bland but they're good value for money – doubles with shower/wc or bath €34 – and as clean as can be. The ones overlooking the courtyard are the quietest. There's a family atmosphere and the owner's father, who retired some time ago, still welcomes the guests occasionally, or serves them breakfast in the bar. *10% discount on the room rate (except July–Sept) offered to our readers on presentation of this guide.*

◎ 🏠 L'Isard**

70 av. du Maréchal-Joffre; it's 100m from the station.
℗05.62.93.06.69
Closed *Sun evening.* **TV.**

A tiny, likeable hotel on a main road, with eight pleasant rooms; doubles with shower/wc or bath €30–36. Some overlook the garden and are really quiet – ask for nos. 1 to 4, or risk the noise from traffic and trains. The main selling points are the prices and the effusive welcome of the owner, who is a mine of information on both the town and the region.

◎ 🎿 |◉| Chez Patrick

6 rue Adolphe d'Eichtal; on the corner of rue Saint-Jean.
℗05.62.36.36.82
Closed *evenings; Sun; a week in mid-Aug.*

A wonderful local restaurant just out of the centre, with a clientele of regulars who work round the corner or live nearby. It's run by a big family who keep a cheery atmosphere in the dining room and are not afraid of changing the menu every day. The cooking is generously flavoured and prices are reasonable: the €10 weekday menu includes soup, starter, dish of the day (tripe or stew), wine and dessert. It's best to arrive early as it quickly gets full. *Free coffee offered to our readers on presentation of this guide.*

@ Le Fil à la Patte

30 rue Georges-Lasalle.
☎05.62.93.39.23
Closed *Sat lunchtime; Sun; Mon; 12–18 Jan; 11–31 Aug.*

A tiny and chic little restaurant looking for all the world like a Parisian bistro with its ageing yellow walls. New-style, inventive cuisine with lots of fish and local dishes given fresh interpretations; choices change according to the season and what's good at the market. Prices are reasonable with a weekday menu at €16, and another at €24. The service is extremely polite but a light touch would not go amiss.

Juillan

65290 (5km SW)

@ 🛏 |●| L'Aragon**

2 ter rte. de Lourdes; it's about 5km from the centre, on the D921A.
☎05.62.32.07.07 ⊕05.62.32.92.50
🕸www.hotel-aragon.com
Restaurant and bistro closed *Sun evening.* **Disabled access. TV. Car park.**

It really is well worth coming to this road-side establishment for its very fine cooking. There's a bistro with a modestly priced €17 set lunch, and a rather plush dining room with a terrace where the service is impeccable and menus at €31.45 and €54. The cooking rightly enjoys a high reputation. The cuisine combines French classics, bistro dishes and Basque influences: *gazpacho* with crayfish, scrambled eggs with caviar, duck and goose *confit* with kidney bean stew, a soufflé of pears and fruit brandy. You can stay in double rooms, each decorated in a different theme (maritime, rugby), costing €50–55 with shower/wc or bath and double-glazing. Logis de France.

Arcizac-Adour

65360 (11km S)

@ |●| La Chaudrée

10 rte. des Pyrénées; it's on the D935 in the direction of Bagnères-de-Bigorre.

☎05.62.45.32.00
🕸www.pyrenees.tournalet.com
Closed *Sun evening; Mon; five days in Feb; Aug.*

A classic little establishment that, despite its unassuming appearance, is one of the best places to eat locally. The dining room has a rustic feel with solid beams, a splendid walnut buffet table and lots of pinks and blues (curtains, napkins, tablecloths). There's a lunchtime menu for €11.50 (not served Sun), with others €17–27. Dishes include veal sweetbreads, *magret de la chaudrée*, duck foie gras with apple and bilberry sauce. The cooking is sophisticated, the presentation of the dishes painstaking and the service attentive.

Thérondels

12600

@ 🛏 |●| Hôtel Miguel

12km to the north of Mur-de-Barrez, on the D18, the last village to the north of the Aveyron.
☎05.65.66.02.72 ⊕05.65.66.19.84
🕸www.hotel-miguel.com
Closed *20 Dec–15 Feb.* **Open** *all year round.* **TV. High chairs available. Swimming pool.**

A pleasant place, in the northernmost village in Aveyron, which has been run by the same family for three generations. Rooms are simple, clean and quiet; doubles with shower/wc or bath €40–52. You'll need to call in advance out of season. The dining room has been carefully designed, with lots of green plants, a terrace overlooking the swimming pool, and Sinatra standards playing in the background. Tasty dishes – menus €9.80 (weekdays) and others up to €26 – are generously served: duck *confit* with spinach purée, *persillade* of snails with Auvergne ham, frogs' legs and sweetbreads in a cream sauce, raspberry dessert from a Dax recipe. Good wine list and particularly agreeable welcome.

Toulouse

31000

See map overleaf

@ 🛏 Hôtel Beauséjour*

4 rue Caffarelli; it's close to the station and the Capitole. **Map D1-3**

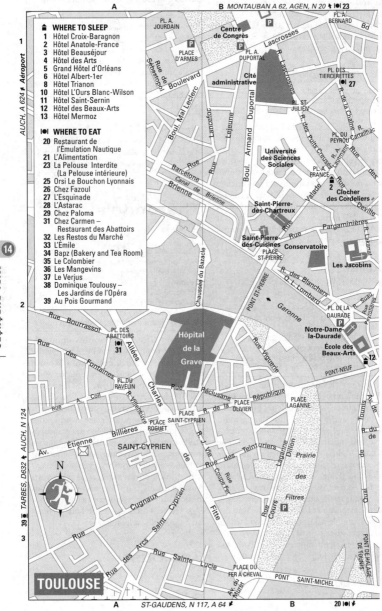

WHERE TO SLEEP
1 Hôtel Croix-Baragnon
2 Hôtel Anatole-France
3 Hôtel Beauséjour
4 Hôtel des Arts
5 Grand Hôtel d'Orléans
6 Hôtel Albert-1er
8 Hôtel Trianon
10 Hôtel L'Ours Blanc-Wilson
11 Hôtel Saint-Sernin
12 Hôtel des Beaux-Arts
13 Hôtel Mermoz

WHERE TO EAT
20 Restaurant de
   l'Émulation Nautique
21 L'Alimentation
23 La Pelouse Interdite
   (La Pelouse intérieure)
25 Orsi Le Bouchon Lyonnais
26 Chez Fazoul
27 L'Esquinade
28 L'Astarac
29 Chez Paloma
31 Chez Carmen –
   Restaurant des Abattoirs
32 Les Restos du Marché
33 L'Émile
34 Bapz (Bakery and Tea Room)
35 Le Colombier
36 Les Mangevins
37 Le Verjus
38 Dominique Toulousy –
   Les Jardins de l'Opéra
39 Au Pois Gourmand

TOULOUSE

MIDI-PYRÉNÉES

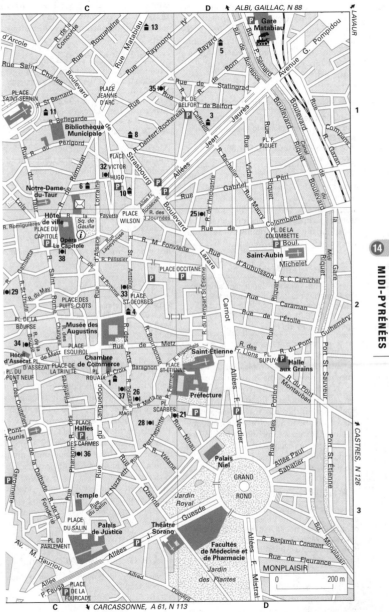

Rue de la Concorde
d'Arcole
Rue Saint Charles
Boulevard
R. St-Bernard
PLACE SAINT-SERNIN
R. de la Concorde
Rue Roquelaine
Rue Matabiau
Rue Raymond IV
Bayard
Bd de Bonrepos
R. Sémard
Avenue G. Pompidou

Gare Matabiau

13
5
Rue de Stalingrad
35
PL DE BELFORT de Belfort
3
Jaurès
Boulevard
Boulevard
Rue Compans
Rue Gazan

11
R. Bellegarde
Bibliothèque Municipale
PLACE JEANNE D'ARC
Rue Denfert-Rochereau
de
Cantalin
Jean
R. Bachelier
PL F. RIQUET
Rue Riquet
Boulevard
de

R. du Périgord
8
Rue de Strasbourg
Allées
Rue de l'Industrie
Rue Vidal
Rue Maury
Gabriel
Péri
Boulevard

Notre-Dame-du-Taur
6
PLACE VICTOR HUGO
32
10
Alfr. Fr.
Roosevelt
R. des Journées
Boulevard
Rue
Colombette
de
PL DE LA COLOMBETTE
Boul.

Hôtel de ville
PLACE DU CAPITOLE
Le Capitole
Opéra
38
Lois
R. Romiguières
R. de la Fayette
Sq. de Gaulle
PLACE WILSON
d'Alsace
Rue Lapeyrouse
25
Lazare
Rue d'Aubuisson
Saint-Aubin
Michelet
R. C. Camichel
Rue Gare
Midi
la

29
R. du May
Rome
Saint
R. M. Fonvielle
R. Pélissier
Antoine
PLACE OCCITANE
Carnot
Caraman
Guilhemery

PL. DE LA BOURSE
PLACE DES PUITS-CLOTS
33
PLACE ST-GEORGES
4
la Pomme
Rue du Rempart-St-Étienne
Rue de l'Étoile
Port St-Sauveur

34
Musée des Augustins
Rue de Metz
R. des Arts
R. Bourbonne
Saint-Étienne
R. des Lions
PL. DUPUY
Halle aux Grains
R. du Pont Montauban

Hôtel d'Assézat
PL. D'ASSÉZAT
PL. DE LA TRINITÉ
Chambre de Commerce
PLACE ROUAIX
R. Croix Baragnon
PLACE ST-ÉTIENNE
Fermat
Préfecture
Allées
F. Verdier
R. des Potiers
Port St-Étienne

PL DU PONT NEUF
R. des Couteliers
Filatiers
1
37
26
R. Tolosane
R. Mage
R. Martiane
PL. SCARBES
Rue Ninau
21
Bd de Montplaisir

Pont Tounis
Languedoc
R. de la Dalbade
Rue du
Halles
DES CARMES
36
28
R. Perchepinte
R. Vélane
Ozenne
Palais Niel
Allée Paul Sabatier
CASTRES, N 126

Temple
R. de la Fonderie
R. du Salin
R. Nazareth
Palais de Justice
PLACE DU SALIN
Théâtre Sorano
J. Guesde
Jardin Royal
GRAND ROND
R. Benjamin Constant

Av. M. Hauriou
PL. DU PARLEMENT
Allée P. Feuga
PLACE DE LA FOURCADE
Allées
Alfred
Duméril
Facultés de Médecine et de Pharmacie
Jardin des Plantes
MONPLAISIR
Rue de Fleurance
0   200 m

14

MIDI-PYRÉNÉES

☏ and 📠 05.61.62.77.59
Open *all year round.*

A nice, quiet little one-star just like they used to be. It's clean and cheap and you get a friendly, family welcome. Prices are low despite the fact that all the rooms have recently been refurbished: doubles with basin €20, with shower/wc €27, extra bed €8.

✉ 🏨 Hôtel Anatole-France*

46 pl. Anatole-France; it's close to the Capitole and even closer to the Saint-Sernin. **Map B1-2**
☏ 05.61.23.19.96 📠 05.61.21.47.66
TV.

Though the façade is nothing to get excited about, you'll get a wonderful welcome in this good-value hotel; reception is on the first floor. All rooms have double-glazing, direct-dial phones and are exceptionally clean; doubles €23 with basin to €34 with shower/wc.

✉ 🏨 Hôtel des Arts*

Rue des Arts, 1 bis rue Cantegril; it's between the Augustins museum and place Saint-Georges. **Map C2-4**
☏ 05.61.23.36.21 📠 05.61.12.22.37
Open *all year round.*

In a picturesque neighbourhood in the middle of town, this hotel has a maze of corridors leading to pleasant, spacious, renovated rooms. Some of them have fireplaces, some overlook the courtyard and all the ones overlooking the street have been double-glazed; they cost €31.50–34.50 with one or two beds. Some of the rooms have en-suite shower/wc, for those that do not, facilities are on each floor. You order your breakfast the night before; it's served in your room because there's no breakfast room.

✉ 🏨 Hôtel Croix-Baragnon*

17 rue Croix-Baragnon; it's right in the city centre, not far from a beautiful thirteenth-century Roman house and the Saint-Étienne cathedral. **Map C2-1**
☏ 05.61.52.60.10 📠 05.61.52.08.60
Open *all year round.* **TV.**

The hotel itself is very charming and has an external staircase entwined with plants. You go up to the first floor to find reception where a warm welcome awaits. The rooms are comfortable rather than amazing – some have windows over the courtyard – but the atmosphere is lovely.

Doubles cost €35 with a street view; €37 for a courtyard view, and there are two family rooms at €43. Several set menus for breakfast (served informally in front of the reception). You need to reserve in advance.

✉ 🍴 🏨 Hôtel Trianon**

7 rue Lafaille; it's between the boulevard de Strasbourg and the rue Denfert-Rochereau. **Map C1-8**
☏ 05.61.62.74.74 📠 05.61.99.15.44
🌐 www.perso.wanadoo.fr/hoteltrianon
Closed *3 weeks in Aug; a fortnight in Dec/Jan.* **TV. Pay car park.**

A delightful little family hotel with pleasant, comfortable rooms that offers friendly service and good value for money. Doubles cost €45–55 with shower/wc or bath. Those with blue-painted brick walls have some charm, but the others are darker and somewhat oppressive. In winter you eat breakfast in the magnificent vaulted wine cellars. *10% discount on the room rate for the first night offered to our readers on presentation of this guide.*

✉ 🍴 🏨 Hôtel Saint-Sernin**

2 rue Saint-Bernard; it's on the corner of place Saint-Sernin, opposite the basilica. **Map C1-11**
☏ 05.61.21.73.08 📠 05.61.22.49.61
TV. Pay car park.

A totally renovated comfortable private hotel, in one of the city's most attractive neighbourhoods and opposite one of its most impressive buildings. It is comfortable, decorated in a tasteful, bourgeois style and the staff will welcome you with a smile. Attractive double rooms with shower/wc or bath go for €50–68.80; triples €80. There are four pink rooms with a stunning view of the basilica. The local flea market is held in the square at the weekend. It's a lovely little place, despite the regular chiming of the church bells. *10% discount on the room rate for two consecutive nights offered to our readers on presentation of this guide.*

✉ 🍴 🏨 Grand Hôtel d'Orléans**

72 rue Bayard; it's 5 min from the train station on foot. **Map D1-5**
☏ 05.61.62.98.47 📠 05.61.62.78.24
🌐 www.grand-hotel-orleans.fr
TV.

This hotel near the train station is excellent. Admittedly, there is something provincial about it, but that is offset by a Mediterranean touch, evident in the covered patio and balconies brimming with plants. There is a family atmosphere, and guests are warmly welcomed; it is spotlessly clean and very well run. Fairly spacious rooms, overlooking either the street or the patio; the latter are smaller, but they are quieter and also air-conditioned, which alleviates the heat in summer. Good value for money: doubles with shower or bath cost €51–61 and triples €61–72.50. *One free breakfast per room offered to our readers on presentation of this guide.*

⟨⟨ 🏠 Hôtel L'Ours Blanc-Wilson✶✶

2 rue Victor-Hugo. **Map C1-10**
☎05.61.21.62.40 ⓕ05.61.23.62.34
ⓦ www.hotel-ours-blanc.fr
Open *all year round.* **TV.**

This district is full of mid-range hotels and this one, in a beautiful 1930s building, has good facilities including TV, telephone and air-conditioning. The rooms are not very big but they have all been renovated and are well equipped: doubles €62–69. The four rooms on the rounded corner have good views of place Wilson. They've modernized the foyer but have kept the very old wooden lift cage. There is an annexe not far away, but the architecture is less attractive.

⟨⟨ 🛎 🏠 Hôtel Albert-1er✶✶

8 rue Rivals; it's near the Capitole. **Map C1-6**
☎05.61.21.17.91 ⓕ05.61.21.09.64
ⓦ www.hotel-albert-1er.com
TV. Games available.

Located in a quiet street in the commercial centre, this is a model of an independently run hotel. Excellent, professional welcome but with a family feel: the owner produces home-made jams for breakfast. The pleasant foyer is decorated with mosaics and pink Toulouse bricks. The rooms are all of a reasonable size, comfortable and most have air-conditioning; some with one or two beds, shower or bath. You'll pay €66–70 for a double room. *10% discount on the room rate for a stay of two consecutive nights (at weekends and during the Toulouse school holidays) on presentation of this guide.*

⟨⟨ 🏠 Hôtel des Beaux-Arts✶✶✶✶

1 pl. du Pont-Neuf. **Map C3-12**
☎05.34.45.42.42 ⓕ05.34.45.42.43

ⓦ www.hoteldesbeauxarts.com
TV.

This classy hotel is a favourite with visiting politicians and actors staying in Toulouse. The façade is eighteenth-century but the décor inside is up to modern standards. Very pretty rooms – the cheaper ones are rather small. Doubles with shower/wc or bath go for €92–195; buffet breakfast at €16. There's a room on the top floor with a terrace and a wonderful view of the Garonne.

⟨⟨ 🛎 🏠 Hôtel Mermoz✶✶✶

50 rue Matabiau; it's not far from the train station, but isolated from the street by an inner courtyard. **Map C1-13**
☎05.61.63.04.04 ⓕ05.61.63.15.34
ⓦ www.hotel-mermoz.com
Disabled access. TV. Pay car park.

This hotel is protected from the noisy street by an interior courtyard. It's a modern, vaguely Neoclassical building with an elegant flight of stairs. The décor makes lots of references to the airmail service which operated from the city, with Art Deco furniture and drawings of aeroplanes on the walls. There are fifty very well-equipped, air-conditioned bedrooms; doubles cost €101, buffet breakfast at €10. Choose the upstairs rooms because they're quieter and have warmer colours. Friendly welcome. *10% discount on the room rate offered to our readers on presentation of this guide.*

⟨ 🍽 L'Esquinade

28 rue de la Chaîne; it's in the Arnaud-Bernard neighbourhood, opposite the pl. des Tiercerettes. **Map B1-27**
☎05.61.12.12.72
Closed *Sat; Sun; Mon; a fortnight in Aug; a fortnight in Dec.*

Vincent runs a friendly, pocket-handkerchief-sized restaurant. Meat and fish are cooked on the open grill and, depending on what day it is, dishes may also include seafood paella, garlicky cod *brandade* with olive oil and so on. Tapas dishes are around €5 each, menus at €9 (weekday lunch) and €12; expect to pay around €15 à la carte. It is advisable to book, as the place is well known in this surprising little Arnaud-Bernard neighbourhood. Credit cards not accepted.

⟨ 🍽 L'Alimentation

6 bis pl. Saintes-Scrabes; it's close to the Saint-Étienne cathedral. **Map C3-21**

⑭

MIDI-PYRÉNÉES

℗05.34.31.61.09
Closed *Sun; Mon evening.* **Open** *noon–2pm and 8–10pm.*

Only a few years ago all you would have found here would have been packets of pasta and rice . . . to cook yourself. But the local food shop has been turned into a warm restaurant garlanded with multicoloured lights, with a quiet terrace to enjoy a drink in summer. They serve daring salads at lunchtime – and nobody cares if the tables are jammed together. Lunch menus are €9.90 and €11.50, and evening menus €17–28. At night the flickering candles and jazz create an intimate atmosphere and the cooking changes tone, too, with regional dishes on the menu. It's run by a friendly, young team.

⊚ 🎋 |●| Chez Paloma

54 rue Peyrollières. **Map C2-29**
℗05.61.21.76.50
Closed *Sat; Sun.* **Disabled access.**

A nice local restaurant that's made its reputation by word of mouth. Excellent value for money if you want a really satisfying lunch; there's a weekday set lunch for €10 with other menus €18 ("country meal"), €21 ("village meal") and €26 ("Gascon feast"). In this backstreet in old Toulouse, discover fine simple food from Gascogny, served with delicate attention. The high dining room is impressive with its exposed beams, long brick wall, cotton tablecloths and napkins, cosy, intimate wall seats and stuffed goose on the bar in the back. Depending on the season, dishes such as duck conserve salad and fish platter are available, as well as selections of foie gras, duck *tournedos* with ceps sauce or grilled Gascogny style. Also, a few wines at moderate prices (Fronton, Côtes-de-Saint-Mont). *Free Armagnac plum brandy offered to our readers on presentation of this guide.*

⊚ 🎋 |●| L'Astarac

21 rue Perchepinte; it's on the corner of rue Mage and Grande-Rue-Nazareth. **Map C3-28**
℗05.61.53.11.15
Open *lunchtimes and dinner until 10pm.*
Closed *Sat lunchtime; Sun; mid-July to mid-Aug.* **Disabled access.**

This excellent restaurant is tucked away in a narrow street in the old town; the tall room has sturdy beams and brick walls.

There are discreet booths with comfy benches where you can have an intimate, cosy dinner. Tremendous Gascon cooking is presented in dishes such as the *manchons de canard* salad or fish platter, etc. Sample the foie gras, duck *tournedos* with ceps sauce or Gascon stew. The weekday lunch menu is €10.70, with others €18–26. Sensibly priced wines like Fronton and Côtes-de-Saint-Mont. *Free Pruneau à l'Armagnac offered to our readers on presentation of this guide.*

⊚ 🎋 |●| Chez Fazoul

2 rue Tolosane; it's on the corner of pl. Mage
Map C2-26
℗05.61.53.72.09
Closed *Sun.* **Open** *noon–2pm and 7.45–10.30pm.* **Disabled access.**

This restaurant has been serving good food for some time in this former seventeenth-century town house. The dining room is elegant with its red brick walls, beautiful old beams and candlelight. The €11.50 lunch menu includes wine, service and a self-service buffet of hors d'œuvres – extremely good value for money. Other menus at €18 and €23 list good regional dishes, particularly rabbit leg with *aïoli*, *cassoulet* and foie gras cooked old-style. *Free house apéritif offered to our readers on presentation of this guide.*

⊚ |●| Les Restos du Marché

Place Victor-Hugo. **Map C1-32**
Open *lunchtime only, noon–2pm (a little later at the end of the week).* **Closed** *Mon.*

A real Toulouse special. On market days at lunchtime, go up to the first floor of this concrete shed. There you'll find an amazingly lively and colourful scene, with half a dozen small restaurants providing plates of wholesome food cooked using the freshest market produce for the cheapest prices – menus around €12–16 including a quarter of a litre of wine. The names give you a clue to the style of cuisine on offer: *Le Méditerranée, Le Magret, Chez Attila* (which specializes in fish and *zarzuela*, a sort of Spanish *bouillabaisse*). *Le Louchébem* offers good meats and a broad bean *cassoulet* on the first weekend in the month, while at *Samaran* you can buy your foie gras fresh or cooked. There are a few tables on the long balcony. It's always full. Come early, come late, or be very patient.

MIDI-PYRÉNÉES

@ ⅍ |●| Restaurant de l'Émulation Nautique

Allée Alfred-Mayssonière. **Off map B3-20**
☎05.61.25.34.95
Closed Sun evening and Mon (May to mid-Sept); every evening during the rest of the year; Christmas to early Jan.

This sailing club, one of the three oldest in France, has a cosy restaurant. It has a beautiful terrace, shaded by plane trees and looking out over the water, and an elegant dining room offering a weekday lunch menu at €16 or à la carte at around €30. The grills are enormous, the fish dishes nice and fresh, and they do tasty salads. Informal service. *Free house apéritif offered to our readers on presentation of this guide.*

@ |●| Bapz (Bakery and Tea Room)

13 rue de la Bourse; it's in the heart of the old town. **Map C2-34**
☎05.61.23.06.63
Closed Sun (except for brunch Oct–April); a fortnight in early Aug. **Open** 11.30am–7pm. **High chairs available.**

The décor of this good lunch spot, with its rugs, willow chairs, pictures and old engravings on the walls, creates a relaxing atmosphere. Come here for savoury tarts, quiches and curried pork, or pastries, scones, bread rolls and other sweet delicacies. The excellent cakes and pastries are displayed on a long wooden table. The set lunch menu, at €9.80, includes main course, dessert and coffee, or you can pay around €7.30 for a dish. Brunch is served daily until 2pm and lunch from noon until 4pm.

@ |●| Les Mangevins

46 rue Pharaon. **Map C3-36**
☎05.61.52.79.16
Closed Sun; Aug. **Open** noon–2pm and 8–11pm.

Gérard and Jean-Claude opened this place mainly to sell and enjoy wines. They're real connoisseurs, and choose excellent dishes, and very good bread, to best complement the taste of the wine. The vast salads, *andouillette*, duck breast, foie gras with sea salt and roast beef are all good. There's a nice cheese selection, too, and some seafood. Count on spending around €15 at lunchtime, or a bit less than €30 in the evening. Reservations are recommended, as it's not a very big place.

@ ⅍ |●| Chez Carmen – Restaurant des Abattoirs

97 allée Charles-de-Fitte. **Map A2-31**
☎05.61.42.04.95
Open noon–2pm and 8–11pm. **Closed** Sun; Mon; public holidays; Aug. **Disabled access.**

A reliable restaurant off the usual tourist circuit, on the left bank of the Garonne. The local abattoirs have gone – they've been turned into a contemporary art centre – but the meat here is as good as ever. The bistro (it's been going forty years) buzzes with life and efficient if brusque service under the watchful eye of the owner. On offer are great plates of grilled meat or local dishes à la carte – beef is king here. Try *onglet* with shallots, steak *tartare*, hearty beef stew, or typical dishes like calf's head and pig's trotters. There's just one menu, served at lunch and dinner, at €17; expect to pay around €26 à la carte. There are a few tables outside in summer. *Free house apéritif offered to our readers on presentation of this guide.*

@ ⅍ |●| Le Colombier

14 rue de Bayard. **Map C1-35**
☎05.61.62.40.05
Closed Sat lunchtime; Sun; Aug; a week at Christmas.

You'll come here for the *cassoulet*, which contains a goose *confit* that's been renowned for several generations – the recipe is top-secret and is in the safe keeping of a notary. It is eaten under the benevolent eye of Rabelais' Gargantua, the main figure on the fresco in this elegant dining room that successfully combines wood and brickwork. As well as *cassoulet* (€21), they offer a lunchtime menu during the week for €17, then others at €19.50–34; more regional specialities are available à la carte. Impeccable service. *Free cocktail offered to our readers on presentation of this guide.*

@ |●| L'Émile

13 pl. Saint-Georges. **Map C2-33**
☎05.61.21.05.56
Closed Sun and Mon (except Mon evening in summer); Aug; a week at Christmas. **High chairs available.**

The out-of-date décor is knowingly ordinary (terrible pictures), but the cooking is generously flavoured, fine and tasty with lots of fish dishes. The cheapest lunch menu (€18) always lists pike perch fillet, *zarzuela,* which is a fish stew, and *rosace* of prawns. There's another lunch menu at €28, with evening menus for €35 and €45. Precise attention is paid to preparation and cooking times. The main ingredient is brought to the fore, enhanced but never obscured. We are impressed by the consistently high quality and the subtle power of the flavours.

@ 𝄞 |●| Orsi Le Bouchon Lyonnais

13 rue de l'Industrie. **Map D2-25**
℗05.61.62.97.43
Open noon–2pm and 7–11pm. **Closed** Sat lunchtime; Sun.

This establishment, with its classy but welcoming Belle Époque dining room and terrace in summer, is run by the younger brother of Orsi, the famous gourmet chef from Lyons. He produces specialities from his adopted region: the first menus list dishes such as grilled pig's trotters and Canut brains. There are four other menus at €19–31. The most expensive menu is dedicated to southwestern cooking and features one of the best *cassoulets* in town which can be ordered as a takeaway. Mention should also be made of the superb, highly informative wine list (wine by the glass, wine of the month). There is a wine-lovers' meal every third Thurs of the month, on a different theme every month, sometimes accompanied by a show. Such events have attracted a devoted middle-class following, attracted by both the excellent food and the diligent waitresses. *Free apéritif offered to our readers on presentation of this guide.*

@ 𝄞 |●| Au Pois Gourmand

3 rue Émile-Heybrard; from pl. Saint-Cyprien, take av. Étienne-Billières, which becomes av. de Grande-Bretagne, then turn right into av. Casselardit; go under the bypass, take the first right, then the second right. **Off map A3-39**
℗05.34.36.42.00
Closed Sat lunchtime; Sun; Mon lunchtime; a week during Feb school holiday; a week at Easter; a fortnight in Aug. **Open** noon–1.30pm and 8–9.30pm. **Disabled access.**

It's not easy to find this place but it's worth the effort. It's a lovely colonial-style house on the banks of the Garonne, built in 1870 as the holiday home of a lacemaker from Toulouse who used to come here in a barouche. Chickens and other poultry still run free in the garden, and it soon

becomes easy to forget the proximity of the bypass. There's a weekday lunch menu at €21 and others €36–60. The cooking certainly deserves its excellent reputation: just try the foie gras with bilberries or the deboned pigeon, stuffed and roasted. The dining room is magnificent, and there are green plants all round the terrace. There are sometimes lapses in the service. *Free house apéritif offered to our readers on presentation of this guide.*

@ 𝄞 |●| La Pelouse Interdite (La Pelouse Intérieure)

72 av. des États-Unis; to the north of the town, going towards the N20; it is distinguished by the façade from its previous existence as "Au Bon Vin". **Off map B1-23**
℗05.61.47.30.40
Closed lunchtimes; Sun; Mon in winter; 3 weeks in Oct.

An unusual place – the extraordinary garden is illuminated by numerous candles, furnished with junk-shop tables, chairs and large armchairs, and even hammocks and beds. Inside (*La Pelouse Intérieure*) there's a brilliantly coloured bar with a DJ who plays soothing music at the weekend. The delicious, inventive cuisine includes such dishes as *magret* of duck with honey and spices, shark sliced Japanese style, ostrich steak with bilberries. There's a single menu for €24. It's essential to book, and, when you get there, ring the bell and wait. Credit cards not accepted. *Free house liqueur offered to our readers on presentation of this guide.*

@ |●| Le Verjus

7 rue Tolosane; it's near the Saint-Étienne cathedral. **Map C2-37**
℗05.61.52.06.93
Closed Sun; Mon; in July and Aug. **Open** until 10.30pm.

This is an unfussy bistro with typical marble tabletops and shrewdly placed pictures on the wall, much appreciated by regulars from the publishing world for its unpretentious elegance. The service is equally charming, while the cooking is inspired and meticulous. Once the owner–waiter has explained the dishes with exactitude and enthusiasm (a spectacle in itself), you can choose interesting propositions like lamb sausages or salmon *carpaccio*. The menu changes constantly according to the whim of the chef. Reckon on €25 for a starter, main course and dessert. This restaurant is one of our strongest recommendations. Credit cards not accepted.

@ 🎿 |●| Dominique Toulousy – Les Jardins de l'Opéra

1 pl. du Capitole. **Map C2-38**
☎05.61.23.07.76
Open *noon–1.30pm and 7.45–9.45pm.*
Closed *Sun; Mon; public holidays; first week in Jan; Aug.* **Disabled access. Games available.**

Not to be confused with the *Brasserie de l'Opéra* (which overlooks the street), *Les Jardins de l'Opéra* is situated some way beyond the entrance to the opera house, on the left, opposite the swimming pool. It serves sophisticated and refined food prepared by one of the city's top chefs, Dominique Toulousy. It is very expensive à la carte, but the constantly changing weekday lunchtime ("*Capitole*") menu is more accessible at €42. The dinner menus cost €68 ("*Opéra*") and €98 ("*dégustation surprise*"). Specialities include foie-gras ravioli with truffle gravy, squab supreme with spices, cep tops and pig's feet *en crépinette* and figs poached in Banyuls and stuffed with vanilla ice cream. Good wines are available à la carte, at reasonable prices, considering the finesse of the food. Even if eating here is out of the question, go to the porch and sneak a look at the luxurious décor inside, which really comes into its own at night. *Free house apéritif offered to our readers on presentation of this guide.*

Ustou
09140

@ 🎿 🏠 |●| Auberge Les Ormeaux

Trein; take the D8, 13km northeast of Aulus-les-Bains.
☎05.61.96.53.22 ☎05.61.66.84.19
ⓦwww.ariege.com/aubergedesormeaux
Closed *Tues evening; Wed (except school holidays).*

An enchanting, atmospheric little hotel in the heart of the Ustou valley with pretty rooms and a lounge-cum-library. The owner creates a lovely atmosphere and welcomes you with genuine friendliness. Double rooms are €44, including breakfast. There's a single menu at €20, served in the evening. *Free coffee offered to our readers on presentation of this guide.*

Valence-sur-Baïse
32310

@ 🏠 |●| La Ferme de Flaran**

Route de Condom; it's on the outskirts of the village on the D930.
☎05.62.28.58.22 ☎05.62.28.56.89
ⓦwww.fermedeflaran.com
Closed *Mon (except July–Aug); Sun evening; Jan; 1–10 Dec.* **TV. High chairs available. Swimming pool. Car park.**

This old farm has been successfully converted into a hotel, with a terrace and swimming pool. The fifteen well-kept rooms are very comfortable and go for €49–59 (depending on the season) for a double with bath. Fresh produce from the markets and local producers are used for good regional specialities. Even the cheapest menu (€18) is appealing, with other menus up to €38, and an affordable wine list. Logis de France.

Vicdessos
09220

@ 🎿 🏠 |●| Hôtel Hivert

2 rte. de Montréal-de-Sos; it's just at the exit from Vicdessos, after the crossroad towards Suc-et-Santenac and Auzat.
☎05.61.64.88.17
ⓦwww.hotelhivert.com
Closed *Oct.* **Car park.**

A peaceful refuge nestling between two valleys. You can bask in the sunshine and revel in a view of the mountains without even getting out of bed. Doubles with shower/wc cost €36. At night, you can dine on the terrace by the sprawling vines, with the murmur of the river below in the background. You will be guided through the dishes on offer: weekday menu €12 (except Sun), and others €13–20. *Free house apéritif offered to our readers on presentation of this guide.*

Villecomtal-sur-Arros
32730

@ |●| Le Rive Droite

1 chemin Saint-Jacques.
☎05.62.64.83.08

Closed *Mon–Wed (except mid-July to mid-Aug); Nov school holiday.*

This restaurant is superbly located in an old nineteenth-century bourgeois house nestling in the back of a park. George Sand was seduced by its charm in her day. The décor is sophisticated, while the atmosphere is intimate and relaxed. The dining room is cosy and comfortable; as for the food, it is inventive without being revolutionary with menus at €32 and €39 (a "*Gourmand*" menu). The mouth-watering specialities include *paupiette de porc cul-noir*, *piquillo* stuffed with *brandade*, duck *parmentier* with ceps and French toast with apples. All the essential ingredients for having a great time are on hand here.

Villefranche-de-Lauragais

31290

@ ☎ |●| Hôtel de France**

106 rue de la République.
☎05.61.81.61.31 ☎05.61.81.66.04
Closed *Sun evening.* **TV. Pay car park.**

Villefranche-de-Lauragais is one of the best places to eat *cassoulet*, the famous local dish made with dried beans and goose and duck *confit*. Unsurprisingly, it's the house speciality, along with egg flan. The décor of the rooms is outdated – with the exception of those that have just been renovated – but a complete refurbishment is under way. Doubles cost €28. The restaurant has got a good local reputation; menus range from €11 (not Sat evening, Sun or public holidays), then €20 (weekends and public holidays) up to €22.

Villefranche-de-Rouergue

12200

@ ☎ |●| Le Relais de Farrou***

Route de Figeac, Farrou. It's 3km from the village, on the Figeac road.
☎05.65.45.18.11 ☎05.65.45.32.59
@www.relaisdefarrou.com
Restaurant closed *Sat lunch, Sun evening and Mon out of season; autumn, winter and Christmas school holidays.* **Disabled access. TV. Swimming pool. Car park.**

A small tourist complex with a park, pool,

Turkish bath and hot tub – there's even a helicopter pad. Alternate your relaxation with the numerous leisure activities on offer: tennis, mini-golf, mountain biking, play area for children. The rooms, all comfortable and air-conditioned, with shower/wc or bath, cost €49.50–80.50; half board €59.50–69.50 per person. The cooking in the restaurant has a good reputation. There's a range of menus: €15.50 at lunch (except Sun) and others €21–40. Logis de France.

@ |●| L'Épicurien

8 bis av. Raymond Saint-Gilles; it's between the station and place de la République.
☎05.65.45.01.12
Closed *Mon and Tues out of season.*
Disabled access.

This restaurant knows how to handle fresh produce, be it fish or beef. Try the scallop *ragoût* with ceps or the *magret* with acacia honey. The attractive décor consists predominantly of wood, set off by the exposed old beams. Elegant crockery is used in both the dining room and on the terrace. Range of menus: €13 (weekday lunch) and others €20.50–31.80. There's a good choice of wines, too.

@ |●| L'Assiette Gourmande

Place A.-Lescure; it's beside the cathedral.
☎05.65.45.25.95
Closed *Tues, Wed and Thurs evenings out of season; Sun; All Saints' Day to Easter; first week in Sept.* **High chairs available. Car park.**

The décor is fairly clichéd, all wooden beams and copper pots, but the cooking is good with set menus €14–32. They grill on an open fireplace fuelled with oak, which gives the dishes a distinctive flavour: crusty lamb sweetbreads with ceps, tripe with saffron, orange cream caramel. In winter it's cosy by the fire and the terrace is nice in summer.

Monteils

12200 (22km SW)

@ 🎋 ☎ |●| Restaurant Le Clos Gourmand

Take the D47 and it's the large house at the entrance to the village.
☎05.65.29.63.15 ☎05.65.29.64.98
Closed *mid- Oct to mid- March.*

This substantial master craftsman's house is

lovely to look at and you'll get a friendly welcome from Anne-Marie Lavergne, who's well known for the excellent regional specialities she serves her guests. Menus cost €12–30 and list regional dishes such as the salad of pan-fried foie gras, pike perch fillet with sorrel and beef with Roquefort. Reservations are essential. She also has a few rooms for €45 with bath/wc; they're large, with fireplaces and pretty views. Half board costs €44 per person. *Free house apéritif offered to our readers on presentation of this guide.*

Villeneuve-sur-Tarn

81250

◎ 🎋 🏠 ◑ Hostellerie des Lauriers**

It's on the D77, 32km east of Albi.
☎05.63.55.84.23 ℗05.63.55.89.20
ⓦwww.leslauriers.net
Closed *Sun evening and Mon out of season;* *end Oct to mid-March.* **Disabled access. Swimming pool. Car park.**

An absolutely delightful village hotel right next to the church (the chimes are silent at night), with a lawn running all the way down to the riverbank. It's brilliantly run by a lovely young couple. Most of the comfortable rooms (the ones on the river) have been refurbished; they cost €44–54 with shower/wc or bath, depending on the season and the view. The food, cooked by Monsieur, is excellent, and it is served in the attractive dining room by Madame. There's a weekday lunch menu at €15, with others €22–40. There is also a bar, which is a good place to meet local people and find out about the walks on offer in the region. A lovely terrace overlooks the grounds, and hotel guests have exclusive use of a heated indoor swimming pool with Jacuzzi. Games for the kids are available. Logis de France. *Free coffee or house liqueur offered to our readers on presentation of this guide.*

Nord-Pas-de-Calais

Arras

62000

ⓔ 🏃 ♿ Auberge de jeunesse (FUAJ)

59 Grand'Place; it's at the very north end of the Grand Place.
☎03.21.22.70.02 ⓕ03.21.07.46.15
🌐www.fuaj.org
Closed I Dec–I Feb. **New arrivals** 7.30am–noon and 5–11pm.

Holders of FUAJ youth hostel cards (strictly compulsory but you can buy one here) have the good fortune of being able to spend the night in the superb Grand'Place d'Arras. There are only two double rooms in the place; all the others have three to eight beds per room (54 in total). A stay here costs €8.90 per night, with about €2.80 to rent sheets; breakfast is €3.30. There are showers and toilets on each floor, and individual wardrobes. Meals are available for groups only, but there is a kitchen. A covered bike park is also available to guests. *One free breakfast per room offered to our readers on presentation of this guide.*

ⓔ ♿ |●| Café-hôtel du Beffroi*

28 pl. de la Vacquerie; it's behind the bell-tower.
☎03.21.23.13.78 ⓕ03.21.23.03.08
Open all year round. **Closed** Sun. **TV.**

The *Beffroi* is located in the corner of this charming square which, though it may not be on the same scale or share the style of Arras's famous squares, is right next door to them. It's a classic bistro at street-level, where you can get good food on the €15 menu or on the "dish of the day" and "*petit menu*". The rooms (€34–45), reached by a

steep staircase, are charming and well maintained, with basin, shower/wc or bath in the rooms or on the landing. No. 10 overlooks the square, so you have a perfect view of the bell-tower. On the ground floor, a bar has opened under the new management of a youthful and dynamic team.

ⓔ ♿ |●| Hôtel-Restaurant aux Grandes Arcades**

8–12 Grand'Place. It's situated at the heart of the city centre.
☎03.21.23.30.89 ⓕ03.21.71.50.94
ⓔaux-grandes-arcades@wanadoo.fr
Open all year. **Disabled access. TV. High chairs available.**

Following a total overhaul, rooms here are comfortable, modern, clean and well soundproofed – and you couldn't possibly be more central. Doubles cost €45–56 with shower/wc or bath; some rooms (the more expensive ones, of course) look onto the Grand' Place. The main dining room is one of the most beautiful in town, in the style of a 1900s brasserie with a lofty ceiling and gleaming dark wood panelling – there's a second room decorated more traditionally. The cheapest menu – served at lunchtime and in the evening (except Sun) – costs €15; allow about €30 for a meal à la carte. The service is traditional, a little starchy but sincere.

ⓔ ♿ 🏃 Hôtel des Trois Luppars**

49 Grand'Place; take the Lille-Paris bypass.
☎00.32.16.02.03 ⓕ03.21.24.24.80
TV. High chairs and cots available.

Located on the edge of the huge paved esplanade of the Grand'Place – surely one of the most beautiful in Northern France

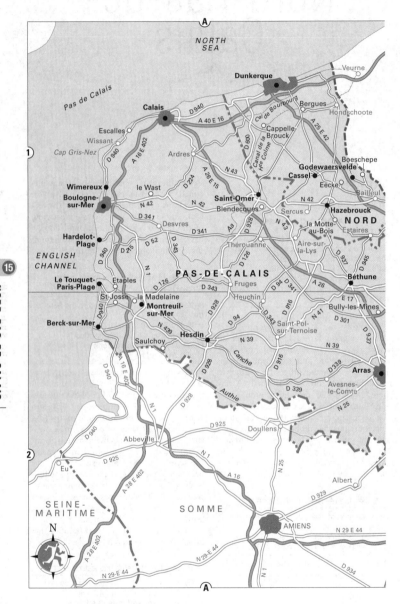

⑮

A

NORTH SEA

Veurne

Dunkerque

Pas de Calais

Calais
D 940

A 40 E 16
Bergues
Hondschoote
Cal de Bourbourg

Escalles
Wissant
Cap Gris-Nez

Cappelle-
Brouck

A 25 E 42
Boeschepe

①
D 940

A 16 E 402

Ardres

D 224
A 26 E 15
N 43

Canal de la Hte Colme
D 600

Godewaersvelde
Cassel

Wimereux
**Boulogne-
sur-Mer**
N 42

le Wast

N 42

Saint-Omer
Blendecques

Eecke
Bailleul

N 42
Sercus
Hazebrouck

N O R D

D 341

Desvres
D 341
Aa
D 928

la Motte-
au-Bois
Estaires

**Hardelot-
Plage**

D 215
D 52
D 343

Thérouanne

D 126

Aire-sur-
la-Lys

N 43

D 937
D 945

*ENGLISH
CHANNEL*

N 1

PAS-DE-CALAIS

D 343
Fruges

D 94
D 341

A 26

Béthune

**Le Touquet-
Paris-Plage**
Etaples
St-Josse
la Madeleine
**Montreuil-
sur-Mer**

D 928

Heuchin

D 916

E 17
Bully-les-Mines
N 41
D 301

D 937

Berck-sur-Mer

N 439
Hesdin
Saulchoy

D 928

D 94
Canche

Saint-Pol-
sur-Ternoise

D 343

D 916

N 39

N 39

D 940

A 16 E 402

N 1

D 928

Authie

D 339

D 339

Arras

Avesnes-
le-Comte

N 25

D 940

D 925

D 925

Abbeville

D 925

Doullens

N 25

② Eu

N 1

A 28 E 402

A 16

Albert

D 929

**SEINE-
MARITIME**

N

SOMME

AMIENS

N 29 E 44

A 28 E 402

N 29-E 44

N 29-E 44

N 1

D 934

A

– this building in a pure Flemish Baroque style and listed as a Historic Monument, now houses a delightful hotel. The contemporary decoration in the bedrooms may clash slightly with the surroundings, but they are very restful and comfortable. Double rooms with shower/wc or bath go for €58–63, and there's an enchanting terrace in the inner courtyard. The owners give their guests a really friendly welcome. *One free breakfast offered per room per night to our readers on presentation of this guide.*

© |O| Le Bouchot

3 rue de Chanzy: it's near the station.
☎03.21.51.67.51
Open *until 11pm Fri–Sat.* **Closed** *Mon lunchtime.*

A bright, freshly decorated canteen-style restaurant with a marine theme – there's a boat in the middle of the dining room – which specializes in huge portions of good mussels prepared in twenty-one different ways. Pleasant service, very generous helpings, good quality mussels and seafood platters. The chips are up to scratch, as they should be, and they also get full marks for their honestly cooked, inexpensive regional dishes: the generous *ficelle picarde* (oven-baked pancakes with savoury fillings) and *potje vleesch* (meat casserole). Menus and *formules* range from €11 to €17.90.

© 🎋 |O| Restaurant La Rapière

44 Grand'Place.
☎03.21.55.09.92
Closed *Sun evening.*

This friendly restaurant is hidden away under the sandstone arcades of one of the 155 houses enclosing the Grand'Place. It has a contemporary décor but serves solid, traditional cuisine on a range of menus, €14.50–27 – *tournedos* Rossini, house foie gras, beef with morels – and local specialities such as Maroilles cheese flan, beef fillet with Maroilles and *andouillette* in pastry. You'll need to be on expenses to dine in the vaulted seventeenth-century cellar, but definitely one of the best restaurants in Arras, with friendly service and relaxed atmosphere. *Free coffee offered to our readers on presentation of this guide.*

© |O| Le Troubadour

43 bd. Carnot; it's opposite the station.
☎03.21.71.34.50

Closed *Sun; Mon evening.*

The *bouchon* (Lyonnais restaurant) atmosphere in this place is very appealing; you feel almost as if you're dining with friends in the country. The warm welcome from the *patronne* has something to do with it, as does the cooking. Choices of the day are scrawled up on a blackboard (three lots of starters, main courses and desserts), with traditional dishes such as calf's head *sauce gribiche* and *pot-au-feu* (boiled beef and veg). The dish of the day, served at lunch and dinner, costs €15; expect to pay €26 for à la carte. The desserts are a bit expensive, as is the wine served by the jug. It's worth booking.

© |O| La Faizanderie

45 Grand'Place.
☎03.21.48.20.76
Closed *Sun evening; Mon; Tues lunchtime; first week in Jan; a week during the Feb school holiday; 3 weeks in Aug.*

La Faizanderie on the Grand' Place is *the* "gastronomic" restaurant of Arras and has the décor you might expect from a seventeenth-century building. Table settings are beautifully laid out amongst sandstone columns under the brick vaults in an ancient cellar. There is a market menu €25 (not Sat night, Sun and public holidays), with other menus €42 and €67. The cuisine is in the grand tradition and very competent with some fine modern touches here and there: roast leg of pigeon with sugared almonds. Friendly, welcoming service of a high standard.

Berck-sur-Mer

62600

© 🎋 🏠 |O| Hôtel-restaurant Le Voltaire

29 av. du Général-de-Gaulle.
☎03.21.84.43.13 ☎03.21.84.61.72
Closed *Feb school holiday.* **Restaurant closed** *Tues in winter (except for guests).* **TV. High chairs available.**

The renovated rooms here are spacious (20 square metres minimum), spotless and efficiently soundproofed, with practical, modern décor. Doubles with shower/wc or bath cost €29–44.20, depending on the season. Apart from some decent local specialities such as the Welsh-style *ficelle picarde* (baked savoury pancakes) or carbonade, the restaurant – which is of the snack bar variety – didn't leave a great impression on us. Menus range from €11.55 to €21.20. *Free coffee offered to our readers on presentation of this guide.*

◎ |●| ♨ L'Auberge du Bois

149 av. Quetier. In the direction of Berck-Ville, turn left at first big roundabout, then right at the traffic light. It's 30m on the left.
℡ 03.21.09.03.43
Closed *Sun evening; Mon out of season; 4 Jan–4 Feb.* **Disabled access.**

Everyone in Berck knows the *Auberge du Bois* but they usually refer to it as "Chez Ben" because the owner makes as much of an impression as the building or the food. This bar-restaurant has a large, simple yet pleasant dining room decorated in warm tones, with menus €14–49. The house speciality, fish *choucroute*, is good and there's plenty of it; if you want one of their impressive seafood platters for two, you'll need to order in advance. Other specialities include the Moroccan style monkfish *tagine* and *bouillabaisse*. The service is very pleasant, making this a delightful little spot, perfect for an evening meal with friends. *Free second apéritif offered to our readers on presentation of this guide.*

◎ ♨ |●| La Verrière

Casino de Berck-sur-Mer, place du 18-Juin.
℡ 03.21.84.27.25
Open *all year round.* **Disabled access. High chairs available. Car park.**

You don't have to go through the gaming room with the jangling slot machines to reach *La Verrière*, Berck-sur-Mer's casino restaurant, which is just as well. You can go straight to the dining room, which is spacious and elegant in a conventional way, though the carpet is rather hard on the eye. The food is very good, undoubtedly the best in town, if not the best on the Opale coast. The chef produces excellent, classic dishes based on what's good at the market and specialises in seafood – all absolutely delicious. Star billing goes to the snails in paper-thin potato slices. Weekday lunchtimes there is a small "*menu affaires*" (business menu), also the "*saveurs du temps*" (special seasonal menu) and the "*dégustation*", all for €20; other menus range from €25 to €50. The service is impeccable; it's dressy but not stuck up and there's a competent sommelier. All in

all, excellent quality at a reasonable price. *Free house apéritif offered to our readers on presentation of this guide.*

Béthune

62400

◎ 🏠 |●| Hôtel du Vieux Beffroi**

48 Grand'Place.
℡ 03.21.68.15.00 ℻ 03.21.56.66.32
Disabled access. TV. Pay car park.

A vast, very well kept hotel with turrets and gables, opposite the fourteenth-century bell-tower. You are woken by the bells in the morning, but thankfully they don't ring at night. You may not get a very personal welcome but some of the old-fashioned rooms have been renovated and they're not short on charm – doubles cost €43–75 with shower/wc or bath. Meals are served in a classic dining room or lively brasserie. In the brasserie, you can choose from a range of *formules* starting from €10.60, and in the restaurant menus are between €18 and €26. Unfortunately, the restaurant and the brasserie lack interest.

◎ |●| La Ripaille

20 Grand'Place.
℡ 03.21.56.22.33
Closed *Sun; Mon evening; 1–15 Aug; Christmas holidays.*

Though there's little to see from the outside – just a narrow, very ordinary frontage – this place is usually crammed with regulars who are very obviously enjoying themselves. The portions are big, the sauces and broths are appetizing and the fish and meat invariably splendid; this is a very good place indeed. Take a seat and choose from the dish of the day at €12 or one of the seasonal specials on the à la carte menu (expect to pay around €25). There are regional specialities, the produce is always first rate and the fish and seafood are worth a special mention. Everything else, right down to the dessert, is equally satisfactory. The owner gives her guests a really friendly welcome and children are well catered for. Note that the restaurant may be moving a few metres down the road during 2005, which will of course affect its opening times, prices, etc. So make sure you phone before turning up.

Bully-les-Mines

62160 (12km SE)

ⓔ 🏠 |●| L'Enfant du Pays

152 rue Roger-Salengro. Follow Lens, after Mazingarbe.
☎03.21.29.12.33 ℗03.21.29.27.55
🌐www.enfantdupays.com
Restaurant closed Sun evening. **TV. Car park.**

The *Enfant du Pays* stands opposite the station, at the back of the old coal tip, and is well known in the area for its generous, unfussy food based on fresh local produce. The pigeon with baby onions, the pork fillet with spice bread and the rabbit cooked in beer should more than satisfy, and the home-matured cheeses would tempt the smallest appetite. The dining room is large, friendly and provincial in atmosphere with uniformed staff. There's a weekday lunchtime menu at €10, with another at €23; reckon on €35 for à la carte. Upstairs the refurbished rooms offer accommodation at knock-down prices: double rooms €17 with washbasin, €26 with shower/wc or bath.

Boulogne-sur-Mer

62200

ⓔ 🏠 Auberge de jeunesse

Place Rouget-de-l'Isle; just opposite the train station.
☎03.21.99.15.30 ℗03.21.99.15.39
🌐www.fuaj.org
Closed weekends 11am–5pm (Sept–March); 22 Dec–31 Jan. **New arrivals** received 7.30am–1pm, then 24hr access code. **Disabled access. High chairs, children's games, babies' changing table and plastic sheets available.**

This dynamic youth hostel is very comfortable – the building was formerly part of a hotel chain – and ideally situated if you're travelling by train. Accommodation is €15.30 a night, including sheets and breakfast (you are obliged to pay for this) in bedrooms with three or four beds and shower/wc. Half board costs €24.50 per person for groups. There is also a bar and cheap restaurant (at €8.40), as well as a fully equipped kitchen, and also an IBN booking service for youth hostels all over the world. The FUAJ card (compulsory, sold on site) gives you the right to several discounts in the town: visits to Nausicaa, bowling, shows, sea sports.

ⓔ 🏠 Hôtel Faidherbe**

12 rue Faidherbe; in the town centre, near the harbour.
☎03.21.31.60.93 ℗03.21.87.01.14
Closed 3 weeks end Dec to early Jan. **TV.**

Well located near the harbour (though the neighbourhood, rebuilt after the War, is without much charm). If the weather's fine, Victor, the resident mynah bird, might decide to say a few words. There's a small, comfy Victorian-style lounge, and individually decorated rooms with good facilities. Most of the rooms have just been refurbished. Doubles with shower/wc or bath cost €50–60, depending on the facilities and season.

ⓔ 🍴 |●| Le Châtillon

6 rue Charles-Tellier; in the port area.
☎03.21.31.43.95
Closed Sat; Sun. **Open** noon–4.15pm.

Nobody can deny that this place has atmosphere: it nestles among huge metal hangars in the heart of the port, opposite a street as wide as a runway where articulated lorries constantly go to and fro. Inside, the downstairs dining room may be noisier than the one on the first floor, but it's the place to see the heart and soul of this city; you can find fishermen and sea captains, sometimes still in their oilskins and boots, huddled round the bar or one of the cramped tables, knocking down drinks and spinning yarns. All this plus fine home cooking, with unerringly fresh fish taking pride of place, with menus at €14 and €16. *Free coffee offered to our readers on presentation of this guide.*

ⓔ |●| Chez Jules

8–10 pl. Dalton; it's in the heart of the town.
☎03.21.31.54.12 ℗03.21.33.85.47
Closed Sun evening (except July–Aug); 1–15 Sept; 23 Dec–15 Jan. **Disabled access.**

Well situated on Place Dalton with a terrace extending out onto the square, this is *the* Boulogne brasserie. It's been around for aeons so the service is efficient and the cooking reliable (although occasional lapses are always possible). They have two rooms, one is a brasserie, the other one is a more traditional restaurant/pizzeria where you'll find businessmen taking their clients out to lunch and students coming for a pizza before going to the cinema. À la carte includes pizza, reasonable fish, decent *moules marinières*, paella, sauerkraut with seafood or – for those who like it – a memorable calf's head in the old style with *ravigote* dressing. The cheapest menu at €13.80 is not served on Sundays or public holidays; other menus go for €22.10–39.60.

Wast (Le)

62142 (15km E)

⊛ 🏝 🏠 🍴 Hostellerie du Château des Tourelles**

Take the N42 towards Saint-Omer then take the D127 to Le Wast. The hotel is in the centre of the village.
☎03.21.33.34.78 🖷03.21.87.59.57
🌐www.hotel-chateau2.com
Disabled access. TV. Car park.

As you enter the village you'll see the hotel, which is housed in a very elegant nineteenth-century mansion, hidden behind the trees in a small park. There's also a modern annexe next to the tennis courts. Ideally, you should stay in the superb rooms of the "château" with their Louis-Philippe furniture and small balconies. If your funds won't stretch to that, go for an attic room. Doubles with shower/wc or bath cost €70–75, and half board, at €50–55 per person per night is compulsory all year round. Tennis, table tennis and billiards are all free for residents. The well-kept restaurant serves menus at €13 (weekday lunchtimes) up to €40 and has a wine list to die for. A delightful welcome is guaranteed. Logis de France. *Free house apéritif offered to our readers on presentation of this guide.*

Calais

62100

⊛ 🏠 Hôtel Pacific**

40 rue du Duc-de-Guise; it's near Notre-Dame cathedral.
☎03.21.34.50.24 🖷03.21.97.58.02
🌐www.cofrase.com/hotel/pacific
Closed *1 or 2 weeks in winter.* **TV. High chairs available. Pay car park.**

A small, friendly hotel that's centrally located but gratifyingly peaceful and has a lounge and retro bar. It proves good value for this part of the world, though some rooms are rather small; doubles for €38 or €48 with shower/wc or bath. They also have family rooms that sleep up to four people, some non-smoking rooms and an accommodating, voluble and welcoming staff.

⊛ 🏟 🏠 Hôtel Richelieu**

17 rue Richelieu; it's opposite Richelieu park.
☎03.21.34.61.60 🖷03.21.85.89.28
🌐www.hotelrichelieu-calais.com
Closed *Christmas school holidays.* **TV. High chairs available. Pay car park.**

Bright, comfortable rooms, some of which have been refurbished, from €46 for a double with shower/wc or bath up to €55. Nine of them have balconies looking over the huge, lush Richelieu park – a soothing contrast to the garish neon signs in the adjacent streets. It's easy to relax here; the street is very quiet and the classical statues on the Musée des Beaux Arts make for peaceful neighbours. There's a lounge and retro bar. *One breakfast per room and per night offered to our readers on presentation of this guide.*

⊛ 🏟 🍴 Histoire Ancienne

20 rue Royale.
☎03.21.34.11.20
Closed *Sun; Mon evening; last week in Feb; first fortnight in Aug.* **High chairs available.**

Something for everybody in this pretty bistro with a marked Art-Deco influence in the décor and highly efficient service. The chef skilfully manages to combine Lyonnais dishes, meat and fish grilled in the hearth, classic brasserie recipes, time-honoured rural fare and a few appetizing side dishes (such as stuffed sole with thyme) with a contemporary touch. Combination of main course plus starter or dessert available during the week for €11 at lunch and at night until 8pm; the menus at €17.50–30 are good value, but eating à la carte here will set you back a bit more. *Free Kir offered to our readers on presentation of this guide.*

⊛ 🍴 La Pléiade

32 rue Jean-Quéhen; in a street to the west of the place d'Armes.
☎03.21.34.03.70
Closed *Sun; Mon; Feb school holiday; last 3 weeks in Aug.* **Disabled access.**

An unassuming restaurant that has nevertheless established itself in just a few years as one of the best (if not *the* best) restaurant in Calais. It offers quality food in a modern setting (but one that doesn't make too many waves – the nearby Channel provides more than enough it seems). Dishes listed on the menus (€22–50) are excellent, modern, with occasional daring strokes of inspiration that produce exciting combinations. The ambience is subdued, perhaps a little too subdued at times, but the welcome is very pleasant.

Escalles
62179 (20km W)

⊚ 🏠 |●| Hôtel-restaurant L'Escale**

4 rue de la Mer; take the D940 towards Wissant.
℡03.21.85.25.00 ℻03.21.35.44.22
⊛www.hotel-lescale.com
Restaurant closed *Wed lunchtime Nov–Dec (except public holidays and school holidays).* **Closed** *2 Jan–10 Feb; 18–28 Dec.* **Disabled access. High chairs, cots (for under twos) and games available. Car park.**

In the annexe – a stone building smothered with ivy – the rooms are tidy, comfortable and quite pretty; other rooms in the main hotel are more modest and noisier due to their proximity to the bar/restaurant. Doubles with basin cost €32.50–39, and doubles with shower/wc or bath €49–65. Menus €14.50–36.50; in the past the restaurant was in a lot better form. The garden has outdoor games for children and loungers for the adults. You can play tennis or you can try your hand at mountain biking. Logis de France.

Cambrai
59400

⊚ 🏠 Hôtel de France*

37 rue de Lille; it's 100m from the train station.
℡03.27.81.38.80 ℻03.27.78.13.88
⊛lacanardiere@free.fr
TV.

A typical station hotel – neat and tidy and quaintly old-fashioned, in particular those rooms that have not yet had a makeover. It's remarkably quiet, even the rooms overlooking the tracks – few trains run at night. Doubles with basin go for €38, with shower/wc or bath €41–45. You'll get a charming welcome from the owner, who's something of a wine buff.

⊚ 🍴 🏠 |●| Le Mouton Blanc***

33 rue d'Alsace-Lorraine; it's about 200m from the train station, in the street opposite.
℡03.27.81.30.16
⊛www.mouton-blanc.com
Restaurant closed *Sun evening; Mon; first week in Aug (restaurant only).* **TV. High chairs available. Car park.**

First of all, the *Mouton Blanc* (White Sheep)

makes a pleasant change from the hundreds of *Lion d'Or* (Gold Lions) you come across on the roads of France. Solidly built nineteenth-century house with a great deal of charm. It may be a three-star establishment but it has successfully maintained a decidedly family ambience. The completely refurbished rooms exude a certain opulence without going over the top, and cost €55 for a double with shower/wc or €62–90 with bath. There is a large, half-timbered dining room serving menus €19.50–42, with staff in formal attire. It's the kind of establishment that smacks of quality accommodation (under constant refurbishment) and good French catering. Logis de France. *10% discount on the room rate offered to our readers on presentation of this guide.*

⊚ 🍴 |●| Le Grill de l'Europe

15 pl. Marcellin-Berthelot; it's in the port district, in the Village-Suisse.
℡03.27.81.66.76
Closed *Sun evening; Fri evening; Sat lunchtime; first 3 weeks Aug.* **Disabled access. High chairs available.**

A little out of the way but easily accessible on foot from the centre of town with a terrace and large garden for the summer. A popular haunt of truck drivers, sailors and fishermen, this is a simple, warm and lively bar where they serve straightforward home cooking. You can't go wrong with the €11.40 menu: steak, dessert and a quarter-litre of wine. There are other menus at €18 and €23, or reckon on €25 à la carte. There's also a self-service hors d'œuvre buffet, dishes of the day and à la carte choices include frogs' legs *provençale*, *fricassée* of sole with port, etc. *Free coffee offered to our readers on presentation of this guide.*

⊚ |●| 🍴 Le Resto du Beffroi

4 rue du 11-Novembre; easy to find, at the foot of the belltower.
℡03.27.81.50.10
Closed *Sat lunchtime; Sun; 1–15 Jan; first 3 weeks in Aug.* **Baby seats available.**

A friendly, if rather unusual, restaurant tucked away in a little street behind the Grand'Place. The décor is a mixture of traditional bistro and night club (mirror fragments stuck on the pink and black walls), and some of the cuisine takes its influence from the southwest, where chef Yves Galan used to breed ducks before becoming a cook (some thirty years ago). Today he prepares good robust food, including duck breast and *cassoulet* with duck *confit*, farm-produced chicken from the Landes with ceps, huge salads. There's a menu at €15.24 or you can eat à la carte. You still feel that you're in Cambrai. To be honest, the food lacks a certain something, but the ambience is friendly and, on another note, the lunchtime special (which could be *coq au vin*, for example) is more than adequate. *Free Kir offered to our readers on presentation of this guide.*

Ligny-en-Cambrésis
59191 (15km SE)

⬚ 🏠 |●| Le Château de Ligny Haucourt****

2 rue Pierre-Curie; from Cambrai, take the N43 in the direction of Cateau-Cambrésis, and in Beauvois turn off to Ligny.
☎03.27.85.25.84 ℻03.27.85.79.79
Closed Mon (except public holidays); a fortnight in Feb. **TV. Car park.**

In the centre of the village, in a little oasis of greenery with does and fawns frolicking about, an elegant little twelfth-century château which still boasts a round tower. The rest, which dates from the fifteenth century is in the Flemish Renaissance style. Inside everything exudes good taste. There are delightful lounges with ornamented ceilings. Each room has its own character and offers good standards of comfort. Double rooms with bath go for €90–200 and there are three suites available at €280. The restaurant enjoys an excellent reputation and is open to non-residents; two menus, €48 and €82, served lunchtimes and evenings. Here too, the ambience is magnificent. The "library room" with its handsome parquet flooring, panelling, wall hangings and superb carved fireplace has a distinguished charm, while the "salle d'armes" (weapons room) lower down, with its white stone walls has a quite different appeal. The service is classy and professional, a touch stiff maybe for such a light, inspired and excellent cuisine.

Cassel
59670

⬚ |●| La Taverne Flamande

34 Grand'Place; it's opposite the town hall.
☎03.28.42.42.59 ℻03.28.40.51.84
Closed Tues evening; Wed. 1–7 Feb; Aug; Oct. **High chairs available.**

If you're in a place called the "Flemish Tavern" (with its giant enthroned at the entrance) and you're in Cassel – where it seems people have not yet entirely digested the Nijmegen treaty which in 1678 marked the final annexation of maritime Flanders to France – it seems obvious that you should try the authentic Flemish menu (€16). The cheapest menu is €11 (except Sunday) then €14–22.50 (Sundays): you can sample Flemish fritters, the terrine of chicken livers with juniper berries, the Ghent-style chicken *waterzoï* (fatted chicken stew accompanied by a home-made sauce), ox tongue in a local sauce, Flemish apple tart with brown sugar and pancakes flambéed in Houlle gin. On Sunday evenings excellent ham platters are served. Sit on the veranda, which is perched on the slopes of Mont Cassel, and enjoy the same panorama that so delighted the Romantic poet Lamartine and Charles X.

⬚ |●| Estaminet't Kasteel Hof

8 rue Saint-Nicolas; it's opposite the mill; city centre.
☎03.28.40.59.29
Closed Mon–Wed; last 3 weeks in Jan; first week in July; 1–15 Oct. **Disabled access. High chairs and games available.**

Reckon on about €16 for a meal but you could just settle for one of the hearty "platters" typical of the area with three pâtés from Houtland (the "wooded country" that overlooks Cassel) or cheeses. This tavern is the highest in French Flanders, standing at 175.90m on the top of Mont Cassel. The dining room is charming: there's a tiny counter, only a handful of tables, wooden chairs that scrape the floor, a fireplace, etc. There's also a fine collection of basins, pitchers and coffee pots hanging from the ceiling. The dining room on the upper floor has a panoramic view. But, as you might have guessed, this tavern is just too typical to be true – it's a recreation with Flemish nationalism taken a little too far. Everything on the menu here, from the starters – endive soup or *cœur casselois* (mince and potato fritter) – to the more well-known dishes such as *waterzoï* stew, and the famous *potje vleesch* (meat stew) that Lamartine so enjoyed, via the duck *confit* with a spicy *speculoos* sauce and cheeses (such as *zermezeelois* or *mont-des-chats*) right through to the beer tart, is one hundred per cent Flemish. Even the mineral water comes from Saint-Amand. Wine is not on the menu as we're in hop-growing country here and the list of locally crafted beers on offer at *T'Kasteel Hof* could serve as a guide. On Saturday evenings and Sunday lunchtimes you can listen to Flemish tales and legends while you dine.

Eecke
59114 (10km SE)

@ 🎋 |●| Brasserie Saint-Georges

5 rue de Castre; take the D933 then the D947 and it's halfway between Cassel and Bailleul.
☎03.28.40.13.71
Open *Fri evening; Sat; Sun; end Aug.*

This bastion of Flemish culture has its own newsletter. The building started out as a farm in the sixteenth century, after which it became a mill, and then a posthouse, and the jumbled architecture and décor combine elements from this varied past (including old brewery tools such as the "tinet" – a wooden support for carrying barrels – and the "fourquet" – a wooden handled spatula). They were brewing beer here until the end of the 1970s and now sell 63 specialist beers – des Chênes, brewed locally, is the most popular. Good traditional Flemish cooking includes rame-kin of *andouillette*, grilled pork chitter-lings with *standevleech* (potatoes cooked in coals), melted Maroilles cheese with cumin, grilled pork fillet and ham *à la Trois-Monts* (ham on the bone marinated in beer with potatoes and Maroilles cheese *au gratin*). They also do various types of meat grilled over a wood fire. Prices are reason-able with a menu at €17, coffee included, or €8.50–19 à la carte. Before you leave don't forget to visit the *Klokhuis*, a three-centuries old wooden church tower stand-ing on its own and the pride of the local area. *Free house apéritif offered to our readers on presentation of this guide.*

Boeschepe
59299 (15km E)

@ 🎋 🏠 |●| Auberge du Vert Mont**

Route du Mont-Noir; take the D948 towards Steenvoorde, then the N348 to the Belgian border, and finally the D10 towards Bailleul; it's signposted from Boeschepe.
☎03.28.49.41.26 ●03.28.49.48.58
Closed *Mon lunchtime out of season. 1–15 Jan.* **TV. High chairs and games available. Car park.**

This small tourist complex, next to a hop field, used to be a farm. It retains a

rural feel, with ducks splashing about in the pond and goats and sheep bleating in the fields. They offer games for children and there are a couple of tennis courts. There's a young, friendly welcome. The rooms are adorable too; they're €58–80 for a double with shower/wc or bath. There are flowers everywhere in the restaurant, which offers a range of tried-and-tested, well-prepared regional dishes: try fish stew, cheese tart, scallops *à la Hoegarden* or the *potjevfleisch* (which came fifth in a competition of fifty-two entries), rabbit in beer, and wash it down with one of their many Belgian and French beers. There's a weekday lunchtime menu for €17, with others up to €35 and you'll pay around €12 à la carte. On the sub-ject of beer, don't miss the field of hops growing next to the inn. The Flanders hills are one of the few places in France where you can still find hopfields. Logis de France. *Third night (room only) offered to our readers on presentation of this guide.*

Douai
59500

@ 🏠 |●| Hôtel Le Chambord**

3509 rte. de Tournai; it's in Frais-Marais, 4km from the centre of Douai on the D917.
☎03.27.97.72.77 ●03.27.99.35.14
Hotel closed *first week in Jan; 3 weeks in Aug.* **Restaurant closed** *Sun evening; Mon.* **TV. Car park.**

Frais-Marais, a suburb of Douai, still feels like a village, though the main road runs past the hotel – don't take a room on that side of the building. The comfort-able, attractive rooms here are reasonably priced for the area – €49 for a double with shower/wc or bath - oddly enough, hotels in Douai cost a lot. The restaurant offers a €12.50 weekday menu (except public holidays) with others for €15–40. There's a special clam and langoustine combo dish.

@ 🏠 |●| Hôtel-Restaurant La Terrasse****

36 terrasse Saint-Pierre.
☎03.27.88.70.04 ●03.27.88.36.05
🌐www.laterrasse.fr
Open *all year round.* **TV. High chairs avail-able. Car park.**

This is a four-star place and a member of the Châteaux et Hôtels Indépendants organization. It's beautifully situated near the collegiate church in a charming old house. Serious and traditional, run by very professional staff, it offers rooms at €62–68 with shower/wc or bath. With its red brick and white stone walls hung with paintings, the dining room evokes traditional France; the ideal setting to enjoy one of the finest menus we've sampled in a long time. Fish, including lobster fresh from the tank, dominates, but they also do game in season and good foie gras dishes – and prices are more than honest with a range of set menus €20.50–66. There's a spectacular wine list of nine hundred different appellations. Logis de France.

ⓒ 🏠 🍽 Hôtel Volubilis***

Boulevard Bauban; coming from Tournai, it's where the road comes to the Pont de Lille. It's 5 min from the station.
☎ 03.27.88.00.11 ℻ 03.27.96.07.41
✉ contact@hotel.volubilis.fr
Restaurant closed Sun evening. **TV. High chairs available. Car park.**

Despite appearances – at first glance it looks like a chain hotel – this is a very pleasant establishment with a fresh, brightly coloured interior and comfortable double rooms with shower/wc or bath for €65–90. We didn't try the restaurant but heard good things about it. There are menus at €16.50–32 (weekdays only), and a special €17 evening menu for hotel guests.

ⓒ 🍽 🎋 Restaurant Au Turbotin

9 rue de la Massue; it's near the Scarpe River, opposite the law courts.
☎ 03.27.87.04.16
Closed Sun evening; Mon; Sat lunchtime; fortnight in Feb; Aug.

With its imposing fish tank, Au Turbotin is primarily a fish and seafood restaurant, though they also offer other regional dishes. Try the turbot with Maroilles cheese, the fish and seafood sauerkraut, the lobster brioche. The weekday menu costs €17, with others at €26.50–43. With chic yet low-key surroundings, courteous and refined service and customers who don't have to watch the pennies, it's one of the town's classiest establishments. It's a place where you feel good and, above all, eat well. *A free glass of champagne offered after a meal to our readers on presentation of this guide.*

Dunkerque
59240

ⓒ 🎋 🏠 Trianon Hôtel**

20 rue de la Colline, Malo-les-Bains; follow the signs for Malo-les-Bains and the hotel is signposted.
☎ 03.28.63.39.15 ℻ 03.28.63.34.57
TV.

The *Trianon* is surrounded by pretty seaside houses dating from the early twentieth century that are typical of this resort created in 1865 by one Gaspard Malo. This is a peaceful place, like its residents taking their afternoon nap behind the bow windows of their "dunroamin" abodes. The hotel is quite charming and the rooms – fairly priced at €42–45 for a double with shower/wc or bath - are pleasant, as is the tiny indoor garden next to the breakfast room. Bicycles are available for hire. *One free breakfast, per room and per night, offered to our readers on presentation of this guide.*

ⓒ 🎋 🏠 🍽 Hôtel-restaurant L'Hirondelle**

46–48 av. Faidherbe; from the centre head towards Malo-les-Bains, where it's signposted.
☎ 03.28.63.17.65 ℻ 03.28.66.15.43
🌐 www.hotelhirondelle.com
Restaurant closed Sun evening; Mon lunch; last 2 weeks in Feb; last 3 weeks in Aug. **Disabled access. TV. High chairs and cots available. Pay car park.**

Right next to a lovely little square – sadly marred by the thunder of the traffic – and not far from the sea, this is a faultless establishment with modern décor. The modern functional rooms are priced from €59 for a double with shower/wc or bath. There has been a recent increase in the number of bedrooms as well as the meeting rooms. The welcome is professional, the restaurant rather ordinary and there's a small bar where you can have a drink. Menus start at €11.50 during the week; you'll spend around €30 à la carte. *Free house apéritif offered to our readers on presentation of this guide.*

ⓒ 🎋 🍽 Au Petit Pierre

4 rue Dampierre.
☎ 03.28.66.28.36 ℻ 03.28.66.28.49
Closed Sat lunchtime; Sun evening. **Disabled access. High chairs available.**

This is one of the town's very few eighteenth-century residences that wasn't shelled in World War II. The owners

15

NORD-PAS-DE-CALAIS

have lovingly renovated it, creating an elegantly sober setting with varnished wooden furniture and salmon-pink walls. The combination of a genial, friendly welcome and one of the best restaurants on the coast are guaranteed to make your evening a memorable one. The cuisine is regional and particularly inspired, full of good ideas and subtle flavour associations with menus €14.98–28. The meat and fish dishes are splendid (saddle of rabbit with a beer and spice bread stuffing, monkfish Dunkirk style) and delicious desserts. As far as we are concerned this is simply the best spot in town. *Free coffee offered to our readers on presentation of this guide.*

@ 🎿 |●| Le Péché Mignon

11 pl. du Casino; across the square from the casino.
☎03.28.66.14.44
Closed *Sat lunchtime; Sun evening; Mon.*
High chairs available.

A cosy little dining room in pastel shades with soft armchairs. If you've lost your shirt in the casino, you will probably still be able to afford the cheapest menu, modestly priced at €15, with others up to €28. Generously flavoured dishes include foie gras specialities such as the *marbré* of smoked *magret de canard*, eels in a wine sauce, fillet of sole with a champagne sauce and regional desserts such as *speculoos mille-feuille* and spiced bread ice cream. When it's sunny, make for the little terrace in the garden – a consolation for the lack of sea view. The welcome is also excellent. *Free house apéritif or coffee offered to our readers on presentation of this guide.*

Bergues
59380 (10km SE)

@ 🎿 🏠 |●| Hôtel-restaurant Au Tonnelier**

4 rue du Mont-de-Piété.
☎03.28.68.70.05 ☎03.28.68.21.87
Restaurant closed *Sun evening; Mon lunchtime; Fri lunchtime.* **Closed** *23 Dec–6 Jan.*
TV. High chairs available. Car park.

An attractive, quiet, ochre-yellow brick inn at the heart of the medieval village, located opposite the Mont-de-Piété, a superb seventeenth-century building which has been converted into a museum. The rooms (€52–58 with shower/wc or bath) looking onto the lovely little paved

courtyard are the quietest, and get the most light – in summer this is where they serve meals. The good, regional cooking seems very in keeping with the opulent surroundings of the dining room. There are a number of regional specialities, including a terrific *potjes vleesch* (unpronounceable but very good: veal, rabbit and chicken in aspic cooked in white wine and vinegar) or the sea perch Armorican style. Menus start at €13 (weekday lunchtimes), with others at €18.50–28 or you'll pay around €30 à la carte. Logis de France. *Free coffee or one free breakfast per room (1 Nov–31 March) offered to our readers on presentation of this guide.*

Cappelle-Brouck
59630 (23km SW)

@ 🎿 |●| Le Campagnard

Les Dondaines; take the N316 then the D600; turn left towards Pont-l'Abesse, then follow the signs.
☎03.28.29.56.09
Closed *evenings (except for groups) except July–Aug; 15 Dec–15 Jan.* **Disabled access.**
Games available.

A nice restaurant housed in a former tavern at the edge of the campsite and run by a young local couple who are passionate about the region but also love to travel. They serve excellent country cooking amid a friendly atmosphere with eclectic music playing in the background in a pretty dining room. In summer there is a terrace alongside the canal where you can watch the barges gliding slowly by. The weekday menu at €15 proves excellent value; dish of the day weekdays and Sunday at €10.60. Credit cards are not accepted. *Free coffee offered to our readers on presentation of this guide.*

Etroeungt
59219

@ |●| Ferme de la Capelette

La Capelette; it's 7km south of Avesnes.
☎03.27.59.28.33
Closed *Wed; weekdays by reservation only.*
Disabled access.

Naf and Dany Delmée converted their farmhouse into a country inn with splendid results. There's a pleasant dining room, and a vast terrace high above the Helpe valley. Best of all is the superb local cuisine, prepared with passion and professionalism. Nothing but fresh produce is used – the delicious oyster mushrooms are grown right here on the farm. The terrines are always good, particularly the one with duck and shiitake mushrooms. Other hits include the suckling pig *civet* prepared with dry cider, duck with sweet and sour sauce and baby onions. Of course Dany makes sure that the menu changes with the seasons but you can sample the incomparable home-made lamb's tongue Lucullus (slivers of tongue with foie gras in aspic) all year round. And if you can still find room there's the apple tart made with crisp pastry and fruit picked from the orchard. There's a weekday lunchtime menu for €14.50, with others €25–30. After eating you can go for a boat ride on the pond or watch the children playing. Groups are welcomed and booking is essential.

Godewaersvelde

59270

⊚ 🏃 |●| Het Blauwershof

9 rue d'Eecke; it's between Steenvoorde and Bailleul on the D18.
℡ 03.28.49.45.11
Closed *Mon; first fortnight in Jan; second fortnight in Aug.*

The most famous tap-room in Flanders, and one of a dying breed, though not if the owner has anything to do with it. He's one of the staunchest supporters of the traditional Flanders tap-room and has worked to ensure the revival of these establishments and their culture. But he's not averse to some Breton music either, where needed to provide the right ambience. The bar and dining room have enormous charm – old furniture, rustic pots and long wooden tables where a happy group of patrons sit round enjoying the convivial atmosphere. There are traditional Flemish bar games (such as "la grenouille" [the frog game], "la toupie" [the spinning top] and "billard Nicolas" [a kind of bar billiards]) as well as brochures on local culture. The atmosphere is heartwarmingly friendly. If you're hungry, there are menus at €11 and €16, and it's well worth ordering here: herring fillets, leek tart, mustard tart, streaky bacon, *potjevleesh* with chips and beef *carbonade* are all good. For pudding, there's *clafoutis* with apples or ice

cream. *Free coffee offered to our readers on presentation of this guide.*

⊚ |●| Le Roi du Potje Vleesch

31 rue du Mont-des-Cats.
℡ 03.28.42.52.56
Closed *Mon; evenings Mon–Thurs; in Jan.*
Disabled access. High chairs available.

First of all, this restaurant is also home to a brilliant shop selling regional products, nearly all of which are home-made, including excellent terrines of *potje vleesch*, of which, as the name suggests, this establishment is the undisputed master. Right next door, the dining room here is warm and welcoming; odd to think that it used to be the family-run abattoir (you can still see the tethering rings on the walls). It's a characterful place, decorated with old domestic objects, plates, tools, photographs, and check tablecloths and the cuisine is resolutely Flemish. There's typical Dunkirk carnival music or music by Raoul de de Try pâté with garlic, *carbonade* or cockerel in beer brewed by the manager Henri le Douanier. You'll eat excellent meals at very modest prices, with menus starting at €15 and going up to €24, or around €25 for a meal à la carte. It's a good idea to reserve at the weekend.

Hardelot-Plage

62152

⊚ 🏠 |●| Le Régina**

185 av. François 1er.
℡ 03.21.83.81.88 ℻ 03.21.87.44.01
⊛ www.lereginahotel.fr
Closed *Sun evening and Mon except Whitsun; Easter; July–Aug; 11 Nov–13 Feb.*
TV. High chairs and games available. Car park.

In the smart resort of Hardelot-Plage, a handsome, two-storey, modern establishment in a quiet residential district with opulent houses discreetly concealed behind flowery hedges and pine trees, surrounded by wooded countryside. It's quiet, and not bad value given the facilities; doubles with shower/wc or bath are €65. The restaurant, *Les Brisants*, has a bright, elegant dining room and offers fresh, assured cooking; good value for money with menus at €21–34. Half board available from the third night is good value. Tennis, golf and stables are all close by, and the beach is 1km away. Logis de France.

Hazebrouck

59190

@ 🎿 🏠 Hôtel Le Gambrinus**

2 rue Nationale; it's between the Grand'Place and the train station.
☎03.28.41.98.79 ℗03.28.43.11.06
Closed *Sun evening; second and third week of Aug.* **TV.**

The interior of this substantial nineteenth-century house, Hazebrouck's only hotel, is bright and well decorated; pleasant doubles with shower/wc cost €50. The owners have gone to a lot of trouble to improve the bedding and the decoration and they really know how to make you feel welcome. *5% discount on the room rate from the third consecutive night offered to our readers on presentation of this guide.*

@ |O| Restaurant-Estaminet La Taverne

61 Grand'Place.
☎03.28.41.63.09
Closed *Sun evening; Mon; a week in Feb; 3 weeks in Aug.* **High chairs available.**

This convivial restaurant has a warm atmosphere, elegant Flanders décor and good, local cooking: Maroilles cheese and leek quiche, tart with brown sugar, with rhubarb or chicory, *potjevfleisch* (a veal, rabbit and chicken *pâté*), veal kidneys flambéed with juniper, *carbonade flamande* (beef braised in Trois-Monts beer), *magret de canard* with Kriek beer and calf kidneys flambéed in gin. You'll get generous portions, dished up by good-natured staff; menus €13.50 (not Sun) and €16, €18 and €25 (the last two are only served on Sundays). They offer occasional specials, too – mussels and chips on Friday, say, or *fondues* in the evening.

Motte-au-Bois (La)

59190 (5km SE)

@ 🏠 |O| Auberge de la Forêt**

It's five minutes from Hazebrouck on the D946 heading towards Merville.
☎03.28.48.08.78 ℗03.28.40.77.76
Closed *Sun evening; Mon; Sat lunchtime (except in season); 17–23 Aug; 26 Dec–20 Jan.* **TV. Car park.**

This 1950s hunting lodge, almost buried under foliage, is situated in the heart of a village deep in the vast Nieppe forest. The panelled rooms are simple but pleasant, particularly those with latticed windows opening onto lovely little gardens. You will pay €39–44 for a double with shower/wc, or €54–60 with bath. The restaurant offers a weekday menu for €23.50 and others up to €48 listing regional specialities along with some exceptionally inventive cooking that justifies the rather high prices. Good options include *fricassée* of veal kidneys with ceps, fillet of turbot with squid, whole baked sole or sole with langoustines, roast duckling, etc. There's a good wine list – the cellar is one of the best in the region. Customers are well-heeled and slightly classy. Logis de France.

Hesdin

62140

@ 🎿 🏠 |O| Hôtel des Flandres**

20–22 rue d'Arras.
☎03.21.86.80.21 ℗03.21.86.28.01
Closed *mid-Dec to early Jan.* **TV. High chairs available. Car park.**

The small town of Hesdin has little worth mentioning (although in the Middle Ages it boasted the much talked about "Merveilles d'Hesdin", a kind of vast amusement park before its time) apart from this hotel. It has a family atmosphere (which has continued since 1920), conventional, comfortable rooms, at €53 for a double with shower or bath, and unchanging local dishes such as chicken terrine, cockerel in beer, *crème brûlée* with foie gras and slow-cooked (for seven hours) lamb shank. Menus start at €14 on weekdays, up to €31. *Free coffee offered to our readers on presentation of this guide.*

Saulchoy

62870 (22.5km SW)

@ 🎿 |O| Le Val d'Authie

60 La Place; take the D928 (chemin des écoliers) towards Abbeville, then turn right onto the D119, which follows the River Authie.
☎03.21.90.30.20
Closed *Thurs out of season; first week in Sept.* **High chairs available.**

In the heart of one of the little villages of the Authie valley "filled with the rustling of leaves and the burbling of flowing water" to quote the French novelist Georges Bernanos, who was born in the area. This is a friendly old country inn with character. You'll get good home cooking here; tried and tested recipes include young

NORD-PAS-DE-CALAIS 15

guinea fowl, *coq au vin*, duck breast and leg of lamb. There's a weekday menu at €13, then others €23–44. In season they serve copious portions of game: hare casserole, wild boar stew, venison in cream sauce, pheasant in port. *Free coffee offered to our readers on presentation of this guide.*

Liessies

59740

ⓒ 🏃 🏠 |●| Le Château de la Motte**

Take the D133 towards the lac du Val-Joly.
☏03.27.61.81.94 ℻03.27.61.83.57
Ⓦwww.chateaudelamotte.fr
Closed Sun evening and Mon lunch out of season; 21 Dec–9 Feb. **TV. High chairs and games available. Car park.**

So you thought the Nord region was flat and gloomy? Here in the Avesnois area the countryside is resplendent, green and hilly. Backing onto the Bois-l'Abbé national forest, this château was built in 1725 as a place of retreat for the monks of Liessies Abbey. It's a good-looking place, made from unusual pink brick and slate reflected in the waters of the nearby pond. The rooms, which offer the peace and silence the monks sought, cost €64 for a double with shower/wc or bath. Specialities include *carré* of lamb, foie gras with Sauternes, and *flamiche* with Maroilles. Menus start at €20 (weekdays only) up to €70, and include a €36 menu served on Sundays and public holidays. Alternatively, you can eat à la carte for around €45. They host gastronomic evenings and weekends. Logis de France. *A free glass of champagne offered to our readers on presentation of this guide.*

ⓒ |●| Le Carillon

It's in the centre of the village, opposite the church.
☏03.27.61.80.21
Closed Sun–Tues evenings; Wed; Thurs evening; 2–23 Feb; 15–30 Nov.

A beautiful Avesnois house located right in the middle of the village and which has been tastefully restored. It's run by a couple of young professionals who have enhanced the gastronomic reputation of this region for the past seventeen years with their simple, skilled cooking. Try the *millefeuille* with Maroilles cheese and herby butter or the pike perch baked in *bière de garde*. All

the dishes change with the seasons and their desserts are spectacular: *fondant* of chocolate flavoured with Earl Grey, *croustillant* with lemon and lemon zest sauce. There's a weekday menu for €16, and others at €21–36. The wine cellar next door sells a selection of *vins de pays* and vintages at all sorts of prices (generally rather prohibitive), as well as a good range of whiskies. They also have a store selling regional produce.

Lille

59000

See map overleaf

ⓒ 🏃 🏠 Hôtel Flandre-Angleterre**

13 pl. de la Gare; facing the train station, city centre. **Map D2-3**
☏03.20.06.04.12 ℻03.20.06.37.76
Ⓦwww.hotel.flandre.angleterre.fr
TV. Pay car park.

Despite being opposite the station, the rooms – €64–74 for a double with shower/wc or bath – are well-soundproofed with nice bathrooms and modern décor. Try to ignore the rather cramped lobby and the not very attractive station environment. It's used mainly by business people. *10% discount on the room rate at the weekend and school holidays offered to our readers on presentation of this guide.*

ⓒ 🏃 🏠 Le Grand Hôtel**

51 rue Faidherbe; midway between the Lille-Flandres train station and the centre. **Map C2-6**
☏03.20.06.31.57 ℻03.20.06.24.44.
Ⓦwww.legrandhotel.com
Closed first 3 weeks in Aug. **TV.**

Typical of the sort of hotels France is famous for, this comfortable establishment near the station has attractive rooms decorated with a feminine touch. The very pleasant female owner and efficient staff are an added bonus. Doubles cost €70–80 with shower/wc or bath, and they also have a few family rooms sleeping three people. *One free breakfast per room per night offered to our readers on presentation of this guide.*

ⓒ 🏃 🏠 Le Brueghel**

5 parvis Saint-Maurice. **Map C2-5**
☏03.20.06.06.69 ℻03.20.63.25.27
Ⓦwww.hotel-brueghel.com
TV. Pay car park.

This hotel, in an enormous brick building

NORD-PAS-DE-CALAIS

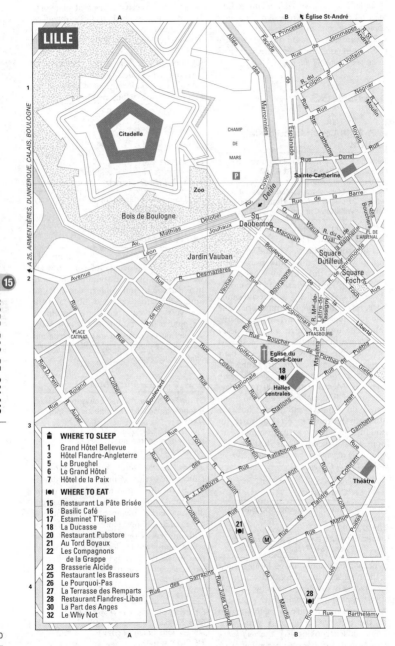

LILLE

♦ Église St-André

Citadelle

CHAMP DE MARS

Zoo

Sainte-Catherine

Bois de Boulogne

Sq. Daubenton

Jardin Vauban

Square Dutilleul

PLACE CATINAT

Square Foch

Église du Sacré-Cœur

Halles centrales

18

Théâtre

PL. DE STRASBOURG

PL. DE L'ARSENAL

21

28

WHERE TO SLEEP

1 Grand Hôtel Bellevue
3 Hôtel Flandre-Angleterre
5 Le Brueghel
6 Le Grand Hôtel
7 Hôtel de la Paix

WHERE TO EAT

15 Restaurant La Pâte Brisée
16 Basilic Café
17 Estaminet T'Rijsel
18 La Ducasse
20 Restaurant Pubstore
21 Au Tord Boyaux
22 Les Compagnons
   de la Grappe
23 Brasserie Alcide
25 Restaurant les Brasseurs
26 Le Pourquoi-Pas
27 La Terrasse des Remparts
28 Restaurant Flandres-Liban
30 La Part des Anges
32 Le Why Not

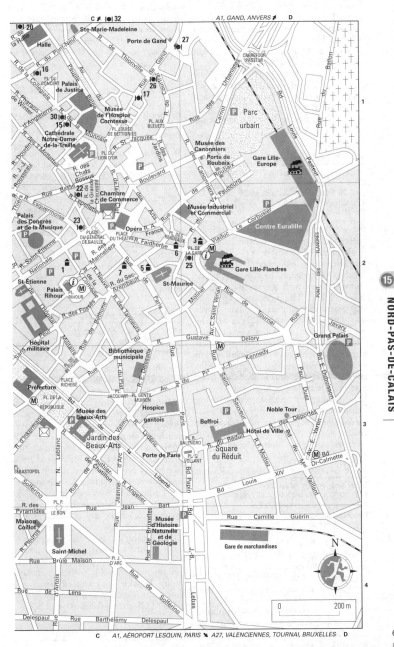

|●| 20
R. de la Halle
Halle
|●| 16
PL. DU CONCERT
R. de la Collégiale
R. du Pont-Neuf
Palais de Justice
Av. du Peuple Belge
Ste-Marie-Madeleine
Porte de Gand 27
R. de Gand
R. de Thionville
R. de Courtrai
|●| 26
17
30 |●|
15 |●|
R. Pharaon de Winter
R. d'Angleterre
R. des 3 Mollettes
Monnaie
Musée de l'Hospice Comtesse
Cathédrale Notre-Dame-de-la-Treille
PL. LOUISE DE BETTIGNIES
PL. AUX BLEUETS
R. St-Jacques
PL. DU LION D'OR
R. des Jardins
Musée des Canonniers
Porte de Roubaix
Gare Lille-Europe
Parc urbain
Bd du Louis
Carnot
Rue des Urbanistes
CARREFOUR PASTEUR
Rue du Ballon
Pasteur
R. Droulin
R. J.-J. Rousseau
R. des Chats Bossus
R. Basse
R. Esquermoise
Thiers
22
R. Lepelletier
Chambre de Commerce
Boulevard
de la Chaussée
R. des Arts
R. du Faubourg
R. des Canonniers
de Roubaix
Musée Industriel et Commercial
Le Corbusier
Centre Euralille
Viaduc
FLANDRES
PONT DES FLANDRES
Palais des Congrès et de la Musique
23 |●|
PLACE DU GÉNÉRAL DE GAULLE
PLACE DU THÉÂTRE
Opéra
R. A. France
R. Faidherbe
R. Neuve
3
PL. DES REIGNAUX
6
PL. DE LA GARE
M
i
Gare Lille-Flandres
R. Nationale
St-Étienne
1
R. des Manneliers
R. St-Étienne
Rue
7
5
25
de la Comédie
R. du Sec Arembault
St-Maurice
Rue de Paris
Av. C. Saint Venant
Rue
Monnet
Rue de Tournai
Rue
Javary
Grand Palais
Palais Rihour
PL. RIHOUR
M
i
R. de l'Hôpital
R. des Fossés
R. des Tanneurs
R. de Béthune
Gustave
Delory
M
Bibliothèque municipale
R. Delezenne
R. du Priez
J.-F. Kennedy
Rue du Pr Saint
R. Sauveur
R. Paul Duez
Bd J.-B. Dubuisson
Hôpital militaire
Sébastopol
R. du Molinel
R. Gentil Muiron
PL. JACQUART
PL. GENTIL MUIRON
Av. du Pr
Paris
Noble Tour
R. des Déportés
Préfecture
PLACE RICHEBÉ
PL. DE LA RÉPUBLIQUE
M
Musée des Beaux-Arts
Valmy
Jardin des Beaux-Arts
R. Gauthier de Châtillon
Lydéric
Hospice gantois
Beffroi
PL. R. SALENGRO
Hôtel de Ville
Square du Réduit
XIV
R. du Réduit
R.F. Mortez
Bd Vaillant
M Bd Dr-Calmette
R. de l'Intermaire
R. N. Leblanc
Rue
d'Arc
Jeanne
R. Angellier
Porte de Paris
PL. S. VOLLANT
Liberté
Bd Papin
Bd Louis
PL. SÉBASTOPOL
Solférino
R. des Pyramides
PL. P. LE BON
Rue
Jean
Bart
Musée d'Histoire Naturelle et de Géologie
Rue
Camille
Guérin
Maison Coilliot
R. Pleurus
Saint-Michel
Rue Brûle Maison
PL. J. D'ARC
Gare de marchandises
N
Rue
de Artois
Lens
Rue
Bart
Rue de Soliférino
Lebas
Delespaul
Rue
Barthélémy
Delespaul
Rue des Bruxelles
J.-B.

0   200 m

15

NORD-PAS-DE-CALAIS

near the St-Maurice church, has personality and – better still – soul. The décor shows excellent taste, with antique furniture everywhere. Even the ancient wooden lift has a certain charm. The rooms, €73–87, are rather small but bright and decorated in warm tones with prints on the walls. The welcome couldn't be better. It's a popular meeting place for actors performing in shows in town and one of our favourites. *One free breakfast per room per stay offered to our readers on presentation of this guide.*

⊚ ⚐ 🏠 Hôtel de la Paix**

46 bis rue de Paris; access city centre. **Map C2-7**
℗03.20.54.63.93 ℗03.20.63.98.97
ⓔhotelpaixlille@aol.com
TV.

Beyond the grand reception of this hotel there's an eighteenth-century staircase that's so superb it's a shame to use the lift. The rooms, equipped with modem sockets, are tastefully furnished and spacious; doubles with shower/wc €72 or €77 with bath. The owner gave up painting when she entered the hotel business, but it has remained a passion. She has also created a small breakfast room with a bar, decorated with Art Nouveau-inspired paintings. She has devoted each room to a different contemporary artist and put reproductions on the walls (how many hoteliers do you know who hang a Magritte on their bedroom walls?) adding a little extra charm to the place. *10% discount on the room rate (weekends excluding the Braderie de Lille weekend) offered to our readers on presentation of this guide.*

⊚⊚ ⚐ 🏠 Grand Hôtel Bellevue

5 rue Jean-Roisin. **Map C2-1**
℗03.20.57.45.64 ℗03.20.40.07.93
ⓦwww.grandhotelbellevue.com
Disabled access. TV.

A handsome eighteenth-century private residence where Mozart himself once stayed as a child, in August 1765. There's an elegant circular entrance with numerous rosettes, gilding and freizes. The rooms are spacious and decorated in the old style (with attractive furniture and old pictures) but the standard of comfort is very much of today (air-conditioning, bathtub, etc). Double rooms with bath go for €90–115, depending on the season; some rooms overlook the Grand-Place and cost

€100–125. This is a stylish hotel offering restrained luxury and keen prices. The professionalism and kindness of the staff, from the chamber maid to the receptionist deserves a special mention. *One breakfast per room, per night offered to our readers on presentation of this guide.*

⊚ |●| Restaurant La Pâte Brisée

65 rue de la Monnaie; close to Hospice-Comtesse museum in the old Lille. **Map C1-15**
℗03.20.74.29.00
Disabled access.

In the face of stiff competition, this restaurant is still the place for sweet and savoury tarts – Roquefort, Maroilles cheese or *tarte tatin* – and regional baked cheese dishes like *tartiflette* with potatoes, diced bacon, braised onion and melted Maroilles cheese. The reasonably priced *formules*, €7.80–15.70, include drinks, and portions are generous. There's a relaxed atmosphere, with a mainly student clientele; it's packed at lunchtime so it's best to arrive early. After 2.15pm, it also doubles as a tearoom.

⊚ |●| Restaurant Les Brasseurs

18 pl. de la Gare. **Map D2-25**
℗03.20.06.46.25
Closed Christmas Day.

If only there were more places like this lively, friendly pub. First of all, there's the well-executed décor and the nice, informal atmosphere. The place is vibrant, boisterous and happy and you feel like you're among friends. You can choose from several brews including amber, Scotch, Lille white and a pale ale, all brewed on the premises using the best barleys and hops. There's an extensive menu, too, from tartine with morels and Flemish carbonade to the home-made *flammenküche* and salads, as well as grills and good brasserie-style dishes. Dish of the day is around €8.50 and there's a lunchtime special at €11.30. There are also plenty of reasonably priced dishes on the à la carte menu. The quality is decent and the portions generous. We bet you won't be able to finish the tasty grilled knuckle with sautéed apples and sauerkraut. If you're famished go for the *formule* "*Choucroute Brasseurs*" with beer.

⊚ ⚐ |●| Estaminet T' Rijsel

25 rue de Gand. **Map C1-17**
℗03.20.15.01.59

The name of this place is pronounced "Reilleseul", which is the Flemish name for Lille. It's an absolute treasure house of old-fashioned tap-room décor; in fact it's hard to believe that all this was only put together recently. There's a small dining room with a cast iron stove and a large fireplace with a heraldic coat of arms. The shelves are edged in lace and there's an abundance of local everyday objects: zinc saucepans and kettles, biscuit tins, religious trinkets, enamelled signs, engravings and bar games. There are small wooden tables, candlesticks and assorted chairs inviting you to sit and sample true Flemish cooking based on true Flemish produce: chicory soup, *flamiche* (vegetable pie), *hochepot* (a stew of assorted meats), black pudding, brown sugar tart, *speculoos* ice cream and *babeluttes* (local sweets) served with coffee. The lunchtime menu costs €11.50, or reckon on about €15 for à la carte. The service is fast and friendly – in fact the whole place is a success. *Free house digestif is offered to readers on presentation of this guide.*

⊚ |●| Basilic Café

10 rue du Pont Neuf. **Map C1-16**
℡03.28.36.91.33
Open *daily for lunch and also as a tearoom until 7pm.*

Just a stone's throw from the famous Rue de la Monnaie, the *Basilic Café* is the trendy spot for light, intelligent cuisine. The special *Must* menu at €12.90, includes one dish, a drink and a coffee, or you can choose a single dish such as the excellent home-made "thousand flavours" terrine, tasty but subtle, from €12. Or, expect to pay about €20 for à la carte. Navigate your way between the re-invented club sandwiches and the "meal in themselves" salads. There's a small selection of fusion food, a mixture of well knitted flavours like the light sauté of grated courgette with saffron and the winter vegetable stew. The clientele is both classy and alternative. This restaurant is a real success.

⊚ |●| Le Why Not

9 rue Maracci. **Off map C1-32**
℡03.20.74.14.14
Closed *Sat lunchtime; Sun (open by reservation only).* **Pay car park (evenings and weekends).**

An extra special little establishment where you can immerse yourself in the typical ambience of the old city of Lille. The affable and attentive welcome is quite in keeping with the authentic, warm décor in this beautiful vaulted cellar. There are small tables for two or big ones for groups, all arranged higgledy-piggledy around a central bar. Dishes are traditional and regional, though inventive enough to satisfy the most exacting of foodies. There's something for all budgets on menus starting with the weekday lunchtime one at €12.90, with starter/dish of the day or dish of the day/dessert; other menus €16.40–32.30. Lots of reasonably priced options are given on the wine list. There's a piano bar ambience every evening.

⊚ 𝕏 |●| Au Tord Boyaux

11 pl. Nouvelle-Aventure; close to the market in Wazemmes. **Map B4-21**
℡03.20.57.73.67
Closed *Sat and Sun evenings.*

In the Wazemmes district, on the famous market place which is the real popular heart of the city. If the owner manages to drag herself away from the stove you'll discover that she's every bit as delightful as her cooking, which is tasty and generous. There's something of the French film star Arletty about this lady – though she may be more amply covered and northern of course – and there's no such thing as a sad Sunday lunch in this little temple of conviviality (it's a good idea to book). The weekday menu, €14, features good family cooking, as you've probably guessed, and done with a lot of heart. A full meal à la carte is around €20. We were lucky enough to be there on the day of the sauerkraut with pheasant, but any dish (according to the season and the market) will satisfy and fill you up. *Free house apéritif offered to our readers on presentation of this guide.*

⊚ |●| Brasserie Alcide

5 rue des Débris-Saint-Étienne; close to the Grande-Place. **Map C2-23**
℡03.20.12.06.95
Closed *Sun evening; 15 July–15 Aug.*

A Flemish-style brasserie, with a completely redesigned décor with a post-modern feel (including Mondrian-style glassware). There are three menus to choose from: the market menu, the regional menu and the "Alcide" menu. There's also the à la carte option, including *flamiche* (pie) with Maroilles cheese, *potje vleesch* (meat stew), mussels in beer, etc.

⊚ |O| La Terrasse des Remparts

Rue de Gand; in the middle of the old town. **Map C1-27**
☏03.20.06.74.74
Open *daily noon–2pm and in the evening up till 11pm (10pm on Sun).*

This place combines a softly lit seating area with red brick walls and a veranda on two levels that opens onto a terrace in good weather. Here you can be sure of a warm welcome and efficient, attentive service. The menus – weekday lunch menu at €15 (except Sun and public holidays), others up to €24–42 – list appetizing dishes which change with the seasons, and the dessert buffet offers a panoply of pastries and delicious home-made sorbets. You'll pay around €30 à la carte. The wine list is a bit limited but the *Terrasse des Remparts* – a bit of an institution in Lille – is really worth a visit.

⊚ 🎢 |O| Restaurant Flandres-Liban

125–127 rue des Postes. 5 min away from place Sébastopol. **Map B4-28**
☏03.20.54.89.92
Closed *Sun evening.* **Disabled access. High chairs available.**

A Lebanese restaurant on the edge of Wazemmes, the last working-class part of Lille. The décor, with its delicate panels of carved wood, fountains and hangings, is a far cry from the usual places around here. They do a very good *mezzé*, and the waiters, whose polite demeanour is impeccable, explain the secrets of the twenty or so specialities and how they should be eaten: hummus, *shwarma, kofte* kebabs, cucumber and yoghurt, chicken kebab with three flavours, *kebbé* (a beef rissole with ground wheat). The menus, €17 and €20, are reasonably priced for what is definitely the best Lebanese restaurant in or around Lille. *Free coffee, fruit juice or fizzy drink offered to our readers on presentation of this guide.*

⊚ 🎢 |O| La Ducasse

95 rue Solférino. **Map B3-18**
☏03.20.57.34.10
Closed *Sat lunchtime; Sun; 3–24 Aug.*

An old–style local restaurant recently taken over by a new team. Wisely, they have left things well alone – the long

carved benches, the traditional tables and a truly lovely counter. In a corner there's a mechanical music player dated 1910 that is activated once in a while, but the huge wooden jukebox seems to be there just for show. There's a really friendly atmosphere here (especially so on the Friday "accordeon" evenings) and authentic bistro cuisine, with some gems of speciality dishes and Flemish draught beers from small local breweries. Dish of the day costs €7.50, or you'll pay around €22 for a menu à la carte without any drinks. *Free house apéritif offered to our readers on presentation of this guide.*

⊚ |O| Le Pourquoi-Pas

62 rue de Gand. **Map C1-26**
☏03.20.06.25.86
Closed *Sat lunchtime; Sun; Mon lunchtime; 3 weeks in Aug.* **Open** *until 11pm weekdays, midnight weekends.*

One of a row of restaurants in an old Lille street, this place is nicely refined, with sponge-painted walls adorned with modern paintings, a wooden floor, well-spaced tables and mood lighting – an ideal spot for a romantic dinner. As the name of the place suggests: "Why not?" You'll receive a very courteous welcome. The food includes some interesting associations, well-prepared sauces and is sufficient to satisfy the largest appetite (bordering on the really hearty). There are a few gems on the menu: the medallion of monkfish with cheddar and honey, the *escalope* of foie gras pan-fried with honey and raspberries and a *pavé* of beef cooked exactly as it should be. All of which you can enjoy against a background of discreet, exotic and well-chosen music (Brazilian, the Peruvian singer Ima Sumac, Jules des Églises, etc). There are menus for €20–30 and reasonably priced wines. You'll need to reserve at the weekend.

⊚ 🎢 |O| Restaurant Pubstore

44 rue de la Halle; in the old town next to the Charles-de-Gaulle museum. **Map C1-20**
☏03.20.55.10.31
Closed *Sun.* **Open** *all year round.*

A busy restaurant on a busy street in the north of the old town – it's even full mid-week. Inside the lights are dimmed, creating a sort of old-fashioned gangster-movie atmosphere, but it's bright enough to read the menus, which list poetically named dishes and their more prosaic explanations. They've been serving the same quality food for the past thirty years: grilled ham with pineapple, grilled steak with vegetables, veal chop with mushrooms and noodles with grated cheese, and a wide range of desserts to finish you off. At lunchtime you can choose a dish of the day for €12–15, or you'll pay around €25 à la carte. As for drinks – the wine list includes some reasonably priced and well chosen Médoc and Saint-Émilion wines, and there's a friendly, genial welcome, as you might expect. *Free house apéritif offered to our readers on presentation of this guide*

ⓒ |●| La Part des Anges

50 rue de la Monnaie; centre of the old city.
Map C1-30
☎03.20.06.44.01
Open *every day.* **Disabled access.**

A noisy Parisian-style wine bar in the busiest street in the middle of the old town. The dining room has a mezzanine, sponge-painted walls and some greenery, and serves very decent bistro-style food; expect to pay €25 for a meal. You'll be greeted by the hubbub associated with the trendy businesspeople, decision-makers of all kinds, yuppies and students from the high-ranking university schools who make up the usual clientele of this place. Transplanting a bit of Paris here has been a real success to judge by the crowd thronging the place at lunchtime and in the evenings. You can nibble something at the bar, sitting on a barrel, or eat in the little dining room behind. The day's specials are written on a blackboard, with two portion choices. The dishes are fresh and well prepared. There are also platters of cold meats or cheeses. Some twenty or so wines selected from the enormous range available (this place is a wine lover's paradise) – professional advice on wine selection is offered. There are also some foreign wines available for those who want to try something different. The service can suffer from the popularity of the place, but it's not hard to forgive.

Villeneuve-d'Ascq
59650 (8km E)

ⓒ |●| Restaurant Les Charmilles

98 av. de Flandre.
☎03.20.72.40.30
Closed *Wed; 6 days in Feb; 3 weeks in Aug.*

Open *lunchtimes; Fri and Sat evenings.* **High chairs available.**

A very spacious dining room, painted pale and olive green, ideal for intimate meals for two. The cooking is creative, with lunchtime menus €12.50–14 (weekdays), in the evening €22–26.50 and Sunday lunch menus €28–32. You'll pay around €22 à la carte. The lunchtime menus are particularly good value for money.

Maroilles
59550

ⓒ ⅔ |●| L'Estaminet

83 Grand'Rue; it's opposite the church.
☎03.27.77.78.80
Closed *Sun evening; Fri evening; Christmas.*
High chairs available.

A typical village restaurant in the town that produces the famous local cheese. Over the years this place has established a solid reputation for good, reliable local and regional dishes; they do a weekday lunchtime menu at €11, and another at €17.35. You might get steak with Maroilles cheese sauce, mushroom tart, *andouillette*, fried Maroilles cheese or a cheese fondue with bilberries, or a good selection of cheeses and *crème brûlée* with vanilla caviar. Wines are reasonably priced. A bonus is the calm and pleasant welcome from the lady in charge and the quiet but good-natured welcome from her husband. This is a place where you can feel really comfortable. When you've finished your meal why not help the food go down with a stroll round the pretty village? It's best to phone for a weekend or evening reservation out of season. *Free liqueur offered to our readers on presentation of this guide.*

Locquignol
59530 (6km NW)

ⓒ ⅔ 🛏 |●| Auberge du Croisil

Route de Maroilles; from Maroilles, follow the D233, and it's well signposted.
☎03.27.34.20.14 🖷03.27.34.20.15
Closed *Sun evening; Mon (except public holidays); Tues evening; 19 Dec–10 Jan.* **High chairs and games available.**

This inn, way out in the Mormal forest, serves splendid traditional dishes in a tranquil atmosphere. It's frequented only by regulars or those who've heard of it by word of mouth and come to enjoy the owner's good country cooking. We liked his friendly talkativeness, sometimes tinged with a hint of melancholy at the future of his profession. The terrines and goose *cassoulet* are winners, not to mention the frogs' legs, scallops *à la provençale*, pigeon *chasseur* and cockerel cooked in beer. The menus, €11.30 weekdays, other menus €18–23.50, change every week; in the hunting season they do a lot of game, including wild boar cutlets with green peppercorns and delicious venison steak with raspberry. They also offer a couple of double rooms, €30 and €35, with shared washing facilities; they're simple but clean. *Free house apéritif offered to our readers on presentation of this guide.*

Maubeuge
59600

@ 𝒜 🏠 |●| **Le Grand Hôtel – Restaurant de Paris****

1 porte de Paris; it's near the station.
☎03.27.64.63.16 🖷03.27.65.05.76
🌐www.grandhotelmaubeuge.fr
Disabled access. TV. High chairs available. Pay car park.

The best restaurant in the area, a place for family celebrations and business lunches. Menus from €18–42 list lots of local produce: smoked lamb's tongue Lucullus, foie gras, calf sweetbreads, fish (including pike perch cutlet in Bouzy wine), seafood and game in season. Renovated rooms go for €42 with basin, or €60 with shower/wc or bath. Logis de France. *20% reduction on the room rate (except Tues and Wed) or free house apéritif offered to our readers on presentation of this guide.*

Montreuil-sur-Mer
62170

@ 🏠 |●| **Le Darnétal**

Place Darnétal; in the old town on a little square.
☎03.21.06.04.87 🖷03.21.86.64.67
Closed *Mon; Tues; end June to early July; end Dec.*

This traditional hotel has been in existence for over a century. The restaurant, which boasts a collection of great antiques, serves lots of delicate, delicious fish dishes: try the poached turbot with hollandaise sauce. There's a weekday menu at €16, and two others at €23 and €30. The four spacious, if rather bare, guest rooms are decorated in late nineteenth-century style and cost €35–50 for a double with shower/wc or bath. Ask to see them before handing over your money, because they're very different and don't have telephone or TV.

@ 𝒜 🏠 |●| **Le Clos des Capucins****

46 pl. du Général-de-Gaulle.
☎03.21.06.08.65 🖷03.21.81.20.45
Closed *Sun evening; Mon; Thurs evening in winter.* **Disabled access. TV. High chairs available.**

A neat, pretty dining room and a lovely welcome – you just know you're going to have a good meal. It's a particular favourite of English foodies who've popped across the channel for a gourmet experience. Good wines at reasonable prices and menus €18–37: options include house smoked salmon followed by a spicy shoulder of pork stew or langoustine grilled with a taste of Provence. They have a choice of good, well-matured cheeses to finish. Saint-Vaast oysters are also a speciality. All in all, a reliable spot for a meal and one familiar to and appreciated by English tourists who enjoy gourmet weekend jaunts across the Channel. Above the restaurant, there are a few rooms for €53 with shower/wc or bath. *Free house apéritif offered to our readers on presentation of this guide.*

Madelaine-sous-Montreuil (La)
62170 (3km W)

@ 𝒜 🏠 |●| **Auberge de la Grenouillère***

It's 2.5km from the centre of the village.
☎03.21.06.07.22 🖷03.21.86.36.36
🌐www.lagrenouillere.fr
Closed *Tues and Wed except July/Aug; in Jan.* **Disabled access. High chairs available. Car park.**

This old coaching inn, down in the Canche valley, has several rooms where you can have a drink and a dining room with real charm – low beams, a fire, copper pots and decorative frogs (have a look at the murals). In summer you dine in a pretty flower garden.

The chef has reinvented local dishes to create delicate, interestingly seasoned food, with menus €30 (not served Sat evening or public holidays), €50 and €70, and affordable wines. There are four perfectly charming rooms for €75–100 with shower/wc or bath, and the service is meticulous. All in all an excellent staging post, not cheap but worth the price. *Free Kir offered to our readers on presentation of this guide.*

Ⓒ |●| Auberge du Vieux Logis

Place de la Mairie; take the D139 or the D917 and it's at the foot of the walls.
℡03.21.06.10.92
Closed *Tues evening; Wed; Sun evening.*

Rustic country inn in one of those peaceful little villages where time seems to have stood still serving traditional dishes which change regularly and use quality produce from the market: house *cassoulet* with goose fat, veal kidneys Vieux Logis, brains with capers and excellent grilled beef. They have four menus called *Solo* (one dish), *Duo*, *Trio* and *Quatuor* (the last consisting of starter, main course, cheese and dessert) for €12–26 or you'll pay around €25–30 for a menu à la carte. The ambience is very rustic and in fine weather you can eat on the terrace. A genuine welcome and thoughtful service are guaranteed.

Saint-Omer

62500

Ⓒ ⚐ ⌂ |●| Hôtel-Restaurant le Vivier

22 rue Louis Martel. Near place Foch and place Victor-Hugo.
℡03.21.95.76.00
ⓦ www.au-vivier-saintomer.com
Closed *Sun evening.* **TV.**

A charming hotel situated in the pedestrianized centre of this attractive town. Good-looking, clean rooms with all facilities; doubles cost €54 with shower/wc or bath, hairdryer and phone. Appetizing dishes and regional specialities are served in the pleasant dining room: try fresh fish or any of the numerous shellfish and seafood platters including grilled lobster or the beer tart. Menus start at €16 (not Sat evening or Sun), then €22 and €34, and the service is friendly and efficient. Logis de France. *10% reduction on the room rate (15 Dec–31 March) or free*

coffee offered to our readers on presentation of this guide.

Ⓒ ⚐ ⌂ |●| Hôtel Saint-Louis – Restaurant Le Flaubert**

25 rue d'Arras.
℡03.21.38.35.21 ⓕ03.21.38.57.26
ⓦ www.hotel-saintlouis.com
Closed *Sat and Sun lunchtimes; 22 Dec–4 Jan.* **Disabled access. TV. High chairs available. Car park.**

The hotel has been around since the 1920s, though it has been attractively renovated since, and offers calm, comfortable rooms from €64 with shower/wc or bath. The restaurant offers an eclectic choice: the *Petit Flo* which has a brasserie-style menu and the *Flaubert* room with more elaborate dishes, though still in the classic style. The weekday menu goes for €13, with others €16–34, and there's a friendly, retro-style bar. Logis de France. *Free house apéritif offered to our readers on presentation of this guide.*

Ⓒ |●| Auberge du Bachelin

12 bd. de Strasbourg.
℡03.21.38.42.77
Closed *Sun evening; Mon; Tues, Wed and Thurs evening (except for reservations for a minimum of 15).*

A friendly restaurant decorated in sunny colours that serves menus for €13–22. The owner mans the stoves while his wife provides a cheery welcome. On Friday they make couscous; other specialities include perch fillet with garlic, fish stew and beef *carbonade* with beer. The service is pleasant and efficient.

Blendecques

62575 (4km SE)

Ⓒ ⚐ ⌂ |●| Le Saint-Sébastien**

2 Grand'Place; take the A26 and exit after 4 or 5km.
℡03.21.38.13.05 ⓕ03.21.39.77.85
ⓔ saint-sebastien@wanadoo.fr
Closed *Sun evening; Mon; evenings on public holidays.* **Disabled access. TV. High chairs available.**

Stone-built inn on a pretty square, with pleasant, comfortable rooms that cost €47 for a double with shower/wc or bath. In the nice rustic restaurant you'll find dishes like offal and other pork-based specialities (including pork tripe in white wine), veal kidneys with Houlle juniper and local ale pie, as well as delicious desserts to end the meal on a high note. The cheapest menu costs €14.50 (weekdays) and there are others up to €33. Good country catering and accommodation. Logis de France. *Free coffee offered to our readers on presentation of this guide.*

Touquet (Le)

62520

☕ ⚘ ♨ |●| Hôtel Blue Cottage**

41 rue Jean-Monnet; it's behind the market place.
☎03.21.05.15.33 ℻03.21.05.41.60
ⓦwww.blue-cottae.com
Closed *Mon from mid-Nov to end March.*
Open *daily for lunch; Fri–Sat evenings.* **TV. High chairs available. Car park.**

Reasonably priced hotel with pretty blue and yellow rooms; doubles cost €40–78 with basin, or €56–85 with shower/wc or bath, depending on the season. They prefer you to stay half board, at €21 per person, in July and August. In the restaurant there are menus at €14 weekdays, and others €20–38. The owners offer a pleasant welcome and there's an English-style bar with a terrace open in the summer. *Free house apéritif offered to our readers on presentation of this guide.*

☕ ⚘ ♨ Hôtel Les Embruns**

89 rue de Paris. Access A16.
☎03.21.05.87.61 ℻03.21.05.85.09
ⓦwww.letouquet-hotel-les-embruns.com
Closed *15 Dec–15 Jan.* **Disabled access. TV.**

In a quiet situation set back from the road and not far from the sea. The renovated, comfortable rooms are clean and attractive; some look onto the garden, others have terraces. Doubles €41–59 with shower/wc or bath; they also have rooms for three or four. The breakfast room is charming and the hotel offers good value for money. You can park bikes or motorbikes in the garden. *10% discount on the room rate offered to our readers on presentation of this guide (for a minimum stay of two nights, except July–Aug).*

☕ ⚘ ♨ Hôtel Le Chalet**

15 rue de la Paix; take the A16. It's 60m from the sea.

☎03.21.05.87.65 ℻03.21.05.47.49
ⓦwww.lechalet.fr
Closed *in Jan.* **TV. Cots available.**

In a quiet, little street near the town centre, the sea and the market, stands this attractive seaside house with something of a Swiss chalet about it (certainly true of the decoration). The hotel offers spick and span rooms at prices that are more than reasonable for Le Touquet. Doubles with shower/wc or bath go for €42–65; some rooms look onto a small patio full of green plants and cacti. You'll pay the top price if you want a view of the sea – it's more of a glimpse than a view. *One free breakfast per room per night (not weekends) offered to our readers on presentation of this guide.*

☕ ♨ Hôtel Le Nouveau Caddy**

130 rue de Metz.
☎03.21.05.83.95 ℻03.21.05.85.23
ⓦwww.lenouveaucaddy.com
Reception closed *1–3.30pm (9pm on Sun); in Jan.* **Disabled access. TV. Pay car park.**

Tastefully decorated, welcoming hotel with four floors (and a lift), each painted a different colour to represent a different season, green for spring, for example. All the rooms are nice and comfortable with en-suite bathrooms; doubles €50–70. Everything is pleasant and charming including the breakfast room and reception area.

☕ |●| Auberge L'Arlequin

91 rue de Paris.
☎03.21.05.39.11
Closed *Wed; Thurs (except school holidays); 20 Dec–25 Jan.* **Disabled access. High chairs available.**

A classic, small restaurant where the owner cooks straightforward dishes: monkfish kebab with cabbage, *coq au vin* and skate with raspberry vinegar. The first menu (not served Sat evening, Sun lunchtime or on public holidays) costs €14, and there are others at €17 and €23.

☕ |●| Restaurant Au Diamant Rose

110 rue de Paris.
☎03.21.05.38.10
Closed *Tues (except July–Aug); Wed; in Jan.* **Disabled access.**

This pastel-pink restaurant attracts a loyal crowd of regulars and quiet holidaymakers who lap up the traditional, honest French cuisine. Typical dishes on the €17 and €23 menus include poached monkfish with sorrel, duck thigh *confit* in goose fat, foie gras and *fruits de mer* – and they've got a good wine list.

ⓒ ⅔ |●| Les Deux Moineaux

12 rue Saint-Jean.
☏03.21.0509.67
Closed *Mon and Tues.*

This brick-walled dining room has a warm, intimate atmosphere, with gentle jazz playing in the background. The owner will welcome you pleasantly and the staff are equally kind. Try the langoustine in filo pastry with two-caramel sauce, the baked fillet of bass in a spicy crust or the calf sweetbreads with morels in cream, finishing with an array of well-matured regional cheeses. Menus start at €22 (except Sun), with others at €35–50; you'll pay around €38 for a full meal à la carte. The wine list has a few reasonably priced bottles. All in all it's a good place for a meal when in Le Touquet, pleasant and reasonable. *Free coffee offered to our readers on presentation of this guide.*

Étaples

62630 (5km E)

ⓒ |●| Aux Pêcheurs d'Étaples

Quai de la Canche (boulevard de l'Impératrice).
☏03.21.94.06.90
Closed *Sun evening (Oct–March); end Dec to end Jan.*

The ground floor is occupied by a fishmonger's run by the maritime cooperative of this lively little fishing port – and it is this fishmonger's that supplies the restaurant upstairs, so the ingredients could not be fresher. There is the inevitable seafood platter, simply prepared, with contents that vary according to the latest catch. The lunchtime *formule* costs €13 and there are menus at €19–35, plus a scallops menu for €36, or you'll pay around €30 for à la carte. It's a bit expensive overall, but the quality cannot be faulted. The dining room is decorated in appropriately nautical blue and white, and there's a pretty view of the Canche if you get the right table. The service is efficient, not to say hyperactive.

Saint-Josse

62170 (7km SE)

ⓒ |●| L'Auberge du Moulinel

116 chaussée de l'Avant Pays, in Moulinel; take the road to Moulinel, go under the motorway and 2km further there's a sign where you turn left.
☏03.21.94.79.03
Closed *Mon; Tues (except for school holidays); Sun evening; 10 days in Jan; last week in June.*

One of the best restaurants along the Opal coast, housed in a restored farmhouse way out in the countryside between Le Touquet and Montreuil-sur-Mer. The chef likes to use strong flavours and unusual but intriguing combinations and offers menus from €25 (weekdays) up to €51, and affordable wines. You're advised to book as there aren't many tables and it's a popular place.

Tourcoing

59200

ⓒ ⅔ |●| Restaurant Le Rustique

206 rue de l'Yser; from the town centre follow rue de Gand for 3km as it leads into rue de l'Yser. It's close to the Belgian border.
☏03.20.94.44.62
Closed *Mon.* **Open** *lunchtimes only; Fri and Sat evenings by reservation.* **High chairs available. Car park.**

The surroundings have a rustic feel – logs burn in the fireplace and copper pans hang from the walls – but the service and food are rather more refined. Dishes include steak with Carré du Vinage cheese, ham on the bone, scallops on the shell, house foie gras, rack of lamb with herbs and tart Jacqueline. This is gourmet food at modest prices: weekday lunch menu €12 (Tues–Fri), with other menus at €24–42, drinks included, or around €32 à la carte. You can eat on the terrace when the weather is fine. There's even a big park nearby so you can walk off your meal. *Free house apéritif offered to our readers on presentation of this guide.*

Trélon

59132

ⓒ ⅔ |●| Le Framboisier

1 rue F-Ansieau; from the main street take the road to the war memorial; it's 300m down in the direction of Val Joly.

⊕03.27.59.73.34
Closed *Sun evening and Mon (except during public holidays); a fortnight end Feb; 3 weeks end of Aug to early Sept.* **Disabled access. High chairs available.**

A rare oasis of quality in a culinary desert, run by a couple who wanted to improve the region's gastronomic reputation. The dining room is fresh and pleasant, with sturdy beams, pink paint, pictures on the walls and classical music playing in the background. Service is quietly efficient. The dishes are full of new flavours and often inspired, changing depending on what's available in the markets. You could try the *escalope* of arctic char with foie gras pan-fried in a caramel sauce, one of the many types of fish available (including pike perch, weever, skate and turbot), or the game in season. The home-made desserts are great too. There are menus from €14 (weekday lunchtimes) up to €43, and "Assiettes de pays" €11–15, drinks included. They host theme evenings twice a month and it's best to book at the weekend. *Free house apéritif offered to our readers on presentation of this guide.*

Valenciennes
59300

⊛ 🏠 **Le Bristol****

2 av. de-Lattre-de-Tassigny; it's near the train station.
⊕03.27.46.58.88 ⊕03.27.29.94.51
Closed *10 to 15 days around mid-Aug.* **TV.**

There's nothing original about this hotel, but it's quiet and clean, the pleasant staff have ready smiles and there's a bar. Some of the light, spacious rooms overlook a courtyard and others the street – fortunately you don't hear the trains. Good-value doubles with basin go for €32, €39 with shower/wc, €49 with bath. It's one of the best hotels in the lower price bracket.

⊛ 🏠 🍴 **Hôtel Le Clemenceau****

39 rue du Rempart; it's 300m from the centre and 200m from the train station.
⊕03.27.30.55.55 ⊕03.27.30.55.56
Disabled access. TV. High chairs available.

Right near the station, this is a solid red-brick hotel with about twenty recently refurbished rooms, all with double glazing, fully equipped bathrooms, hairdryers

and safes. Doubles €45.75–54.90, which is good value for money; breakfast buffet €5.50. *10% discount on the room rate at weekends offered to our readers on presentation of this guide.*

⊛ 🏠 **Hôtel Notre-Dame****

1 pl. de l'Abbé-Thellier-de-Poncheville; it's opposite the basilica of Notre-Dame near the old restored Wantiers district.
⊕03.27.42.30.00 ⊕03.27.45.12.68
ⓦwww.hotelnotredame.fr
Open *all year 24 hr a day.* **TV. Car park.**

This charming little hotel in a converted convent has been completely renovated. The interior decoration is chic but not flashy, and staff pleasant and smiling. Doubles with shower/wc or bath cost €48–62 according to the facilities. No. 36, on the ground floor, looks out onto the indoor garden and is superb.

⊛ 🏠 🍴 **Le Grand Hôtel*****

8 pl. de la Gare.
⊕03.27.46.32.01 ⊕03.27.29.65.57
ⓦwww.grand-hotel.de.valenciennes.fr
TV. High chairs available. Pay car park.

In a superb 1930s building just opposite the station, this thoroughly refurbished hotel boasts an elegant interior and spacious, attractive rooms, charmingly decorated (with floral fabrics in fresh, bright tones, etc). Doubles with shower/wc or bath start at €83 with a supplement of €8 for a third person sharing, and buffet breakfast is extra at €9.50. There's also an excellent restaurant (see *Restaurant du Grand Hôtel* on p.642). *10% discount on the room rate (during the week) offered to our readers on presentation of this guide.*

⊛ 🏠 |🍽| 🍴 **Auberge du Bon Fermier******

64 rue de Famars.
⊕03.27.46.68.25 ⊕03.27.33.75.01
ⓦwww.home-gastronomie.com
Closed *24 Dec.* **TV. High chairs available. Pay car park.**

An old coaching inn in a splendidly preserved listed building. You half expect to find a mail coach and coachman wearing a top hat, frock coat and riding boots. Inside, the corridors are skewed and tilted, and the staircases are narrow; the place resembles a museum, with ornaments and trinkets displayed in the smallest nooks and crannies. Guests on the top floor will be able to admire the stations of the cross recovered from a church destroyed during the war. The rooms are equally charming; €126 for a double with shower/wc or bath. Room A has a strongly medieval feel while others are more classic in style. Room B is also nice, with a high ceiling and square structure. Another room has a Louis XV bed and a mezzanine bathroom. In short, there's something for every taste and excellent standards of comfort. The ground-floor restaurant offers menus from €23 (except Sun) up to €47, and there's a children's menu at €16. *10% discount on the room rate (Fri, Sat and Sun) offered to our readers on presentation of this guide.*

ⓔ ⅍ |●| La Planche à Pain

1 rue d'Oultreman; it's 2 min walking distance to the city centre.
☏03.27.46.18.28
Closed *3–26 Aug.* **High chairs available.**

A solid establishment in a quiet street – the dining room is cosy, and you feel cosseted as soon as you arrive. Everyone comes here for the quality traditional cooking – they prepare dishes from the region and from the Mediterranean, including warm king prawn salad with oyster mushrooms and foie gras, and offer menus at €13 (weekday lunch), €23 and €28. This place is popular with the whole town so don't forget to book. Reservations recommended. *Free house apéritif offered to our readers on presentation of this guide.*

ⓔ |●| Restaurant La Tourtière

32 rue E.-Macarez; it's just out of the town centre, near the tax office. A little way out of the centre, between the shopping area and the allotments; as a guide, Rue Macarez runs in a straight line behind Le Phœnix cultural centre.
☏03.27.29.42.42
Closed *Mon and Wed evenings; Sat lunchtime; 1–31 Aug.*

The outside is dreary, but it's much more friendly inside, with a relaxed, lively atmosphere. There's a *menu du Nord* and a *menu d'Italie* (€15.20 and €18.20), and in general the food is a mixture of regional favourites and Italian specialities – sometimes they're even combined, as in the macaroni with Maroilles cheese. Good bets include Avesnois veal, steak with Maroilles, and *tarte à la cassonade*. À la carte you'll find pizza and pasta, cheese and onion quiches, veal with Maroilles cheese, Nord *entrecôte*

and so on. Everything in this popular restaurant is served in vast portions in a relaxed and lively atmosphere.

ⓔ |●| Le Bistrot d'en Face

5 av. d'Amsterdam.
☏03.27.42.25.25
Closed *Sun evening.*

This is the bistro belonging to the gastronomic restaurant *Rouet* opposite. It's cheaper and more relaxed and the décor is fresh and pleasant. There are menus at €16 and €18 (not served on Sun or public holidays), or reckon on €25 à la carte. They serve wholesome home cooking, and there's a huge choice on the bistro menu: navarin of lamb with spring vegetables, bowls of mussels, frogs' legs, fresh scallops, *blanquette de veau, cassoulet* and oysters.

ⓔ |●| L'Orangerie

128 rue du Quesnoi.
☏03.27.42.70.70
Closed *Sat lunchtime; Sun; Mon evening; in Aug.*

Old local restaurant that's been transformed into a popular, lively, modern place. It has an easy-going, relaxed atmosphere with a warm setting: a brick and wood décor, white stone statues, filtered lighting and a wooden floor. They serve fresh bistro dishes at affordable prices; the all-inclusive menu, €18, lists such dishes as *veal blanquette à l'ancienne*, grilled shoulder of lamb with thyme, salmon *escalope* with leek fondue and various salads and terrines. You'll pay around €20–25 à la carte. On Thursday, Friday and Saturday nights they hold dances after dinner.

ⓔ ⅍ |●| Restaurant du Grand Hôtel

8 pl. de la Gare; 500m from the centre, opposite the station.
☏03.27.46.32.01
High chairs available. Pay car park.

The totally refurbished dining room provides a marvellous setting. It has a high ceiling with Art Deco styling. The Tiffany-style glass, green pillars, panelling, heavy hangings, retro lighting and long, comfortable benches give it an Alsatian feel. Cuisine with an excellent reputation at reasonable prices, which explains the success of this place; menus range from

€20 in the week to €46.50 on Sundays and public holidays. There's a fine selection of regional dishes and traditional home cooking. You can try real, home-made *potje vleesch*, Valenciennes lamb's tongue Lucullus (smoked tongue layered with foie gras), the *bouillabaisse*-style seafood stew with *rouille*, etc. There's also a range of salads and a home-made sweet trolley that includes *mousseline* with rum and chestnut *confit*. In addition, there's a wine list to suit all pockets. *A house apéritif is offered free to our readers on presentation of this guide.*

Wimereux

62930

@ ♜ |●| Hôtel du Centre

78 rue Carnot.
☎03.21.32.41.08 ℱ03.21.33.82.48
@www.hotelducentre-wimereux.com
Closed *20 Dec–20 Jan.* **Restaurant closed** *Mon.* **TV. High chairs and cots available. Pay car park.**

A well-established, Belle Époque, seriously run establishment in the centre of the town where you'll get a first-rate welcome. Recently renovated bedrooms are clean and comfortable; doubles go for €61–80 with shower/wc or bath. The dining room is cheery and traditional; they offer a *formule* with two dishes for €16 and menus at €19 and €29. The superb sea wall (and beach) is just two minutes' walk away.

@ ♜ |●| L'Atlantic***

Digue de Mer. 5 min walking distance to city centre.
☎03.21.32.41.01 ℱ03.21.87.46.17
@www.atlantic-delpierre.com
Closed *in Feb.* **Restaurant closed** *Sun evening; Mon lunchtime.* **TV. Car park.**

An impressive seafront place in one of the prettiest resorts on the Opal coast. There are eighteen spacious, bright rooms, fourteen of which look over the pedestrianized esplanade and the sea; doubles at the back go for €70, or you'll pay €84–117 for a room with a sea view. Just the place for a truly relaxing weekend – but it's best to book. There are two restaurants: one is a brasserie with an airy dining room and a terrace serving good, decent fish dishes like fish soup and seafood platters; the other one, *La Liégeoise,* is the more stylish and enjoys a good reputation. Menus start at €17.50 in the brasserie; in the restaurant they're priced at €33 to €61.

Basse-Normandie

Aigle (L')
61300

ⓐ |●| Toque et Vins

35 rue Pasteur.
☎02.33.24.05.27
Closed *Sun; Mon and Tues evenings.*

Small, two-room wine bar providing an ideal solution for travellers in a hurry, but who enjoy their food. Fresh seasonal produce is used and dishes are full of flavour. Good choices include salad with Camembert fritters, caramelized apples with Calvados, home-made foie gras, *andouillette*, and smoked salmon with egg in aspic and dentelle of orange with chocolate. There's a *formule* – dish of the day with a glass of wine – at €10.80; and menus at €15.80–26.90. A very good spot with, of course, an excellent wine list and really pleasant service. It's a good idea to reserve.

Saint-Michel-Tubeuf
61300 (3km E)

ⓐ |●| ⅋ Auberge Saint-Michel

3km from L'Aigle, on the Dreux road (N26).
☎02.33.24.20.12
Closed *Tues and Wed evenings; Thurs (except for lunch on public holidays); first fortnight in Jan; first 3 weeks in Sept.* **High chairs and games available.**

The charm of this country inn is barely diminished by its proximity to the main road. The tables are spread over several intimate, personalized rooms and the service is diligent and friendly. The hearty food on the menus (€15–31.50) combines tradition with fresh ingredients, so this is a good place for authentic French cooking: poultry liver terrine, excellent veal kidneys with Calvados, crunchy baked apples and a whole ladleful of *fromage blanc* for food lovers who like the authentic touch. *Free Kir offered to our readers on presentation of this guide.*

Chandai
61300 (8.5km E)

ⓐ |●| Auberge L'Écuyer Normand

23 rte. de Verneuil; on the N26, on the road to Verneuil; at the crossroads turn right and park 50m further on.
☎02.33.24.08.54
Closed *Mon; Sun and Wed evenings; out of season (eg, fortnight in March; telephone first to check holiday closures).*

A stone and brick building behind the ivy and window boxes full of geraniums. There's an inviting atmosphere in the hushed dining room with its open fire, beams and whitewashed walls. It's excellent for fish and produce from the Normandy coast; the gifted chef adds a personal, modern touch to good regional dishes such as crab cannelloni, steamed arctic char with seaweed. Home-made bread and ice cream. There's a "one dish and sweet tray" option for €14, and a range of menus €22–35. Very warm welcome and attentive service are guaranteed.

Ferté-Frênel (La)
61550 (14km NW)

ⓐ ⅋ ⌂ |●| Le Paradis**

10 Grande-Rue; on the road to Vimoutiers.
☎02.33.34.81.33 ☎02.33.84.97.52
⊕www.perso.wanadoo.fr/hotel.paradis/

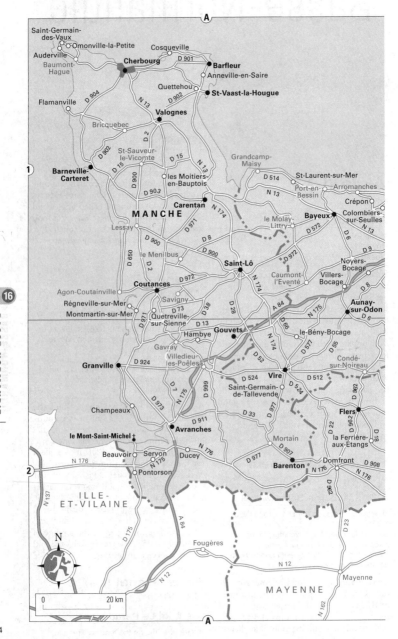

Saint-Germain-
des-Vaux
Omonville-la-Petite
Cosqueville
Auderville
Baumont-
Hague
Cherbourg D 901 **Barfleur**
Anneville-en-Saire
Quettehou D 902 **St-Vaast-la-Hougue**
Flamanville D 904 N 13
Valognes
Bricquebec D 2
D 902 St-Sauveur-
le-Vicomte D 15
D 15 N 13
Barneville-
Carteret D 900 Grandcamp-
Maisy
les Moitiers- D 514 St-Laurent-sur-Mer
en-Bauptois Port-en- Arromanches
D 903 N 13 Bessin
Carentan N 174 Crépon
le Molay- **Bayeux** Colombiers-
Lessay D 971 Littry D 572 sur-Seulles
D 900 D 8 D 6 N 13
D 650 D 900 D 972 Noyers-
le Ménilbus Bocage
D 2 **Saint-Lô** Caumont- Villers- D 9
l'Eventé Bocage D 8
Coutances D 972 N 174 **Aunay-**
Agon-Coutainville Savigny **sur-Odon**
Régneville-sur-Mer D 38 D 28 A 84 N 175 D 6
Montmartin-sur-Mer D 73 Quetreville-
sur-Sienne D 13 D 66 le-Bény-Bocage
Hambye **Gouvets** D 577 D 55
Gavray N 174 Condé-
Villedieu- D 52 sur-Noireau
Granville D 924 les-Poêles **Vire** D 512
D 999 D 524 D 962
D 7 N 175 Saint-Germain- D 524
de-Tallevende **Flers**
D 973 D 22 D 962
Champeaux D 911 D 33 D 977 la Ferrière- D 18
Avranches aux-Étangs
le Mont-Saint-Michel Mortain D 907 Domfront
Beauvoir Servon N 176 D 977 **Barenton** D 908
N 176 N 175 Ducey N 176 N 176
Pontorson D 962
ILLE-
ET-VILAINE N 137
D 175 D 23
A 84
N
Fougères
N 12
0 20 km N 12 Mayenne
MAYENNE N 162

MANCHE

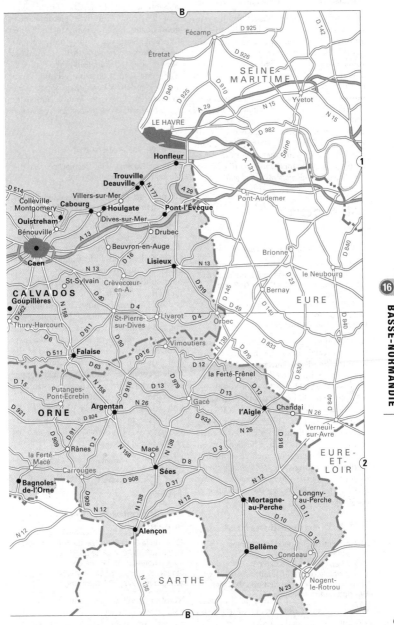

Closed *Mon in season; Sun evening out of season; 3 weeks in Feb; a fortnight in Oct.* **Disabled access. TV. High chairs available.**

This attractive little village inn lives up to its name and has a homely, friendly atmosphere. Doubles are €30 with basin, €40–46 with shower/wc or bath; the most romantic room is nestled under the roof. The restaurant serves generous portions of lovingly prepared, traditional dishes: mussels in cream sauce, young guinea fowl served with apples, *tarte tatin* flambéed in Calvados. There's a €10 weekday menu and others at €13.50–40; a meal à la carte will cost around €25. It's a very pleasant place to spend a summer or autumn evening. Logis de France. *Free apéritif offered to our readers on presentation of this guide.*

Alençon

61000

⊚ ☎ 🍴 Le Chapeau Rouge

3 bd. Duchamp; 3 min from town centre via rue de Bretagne (turn left at the traffic lights), leaving town in the direction of N12 and Saint-Céneri.
☎02.33.26.20.23 ⊛02.33.26.54.05
⊜lechapeaurouge@wanadoo.fr
Open *all year.* **TV. Car park.**

A small, immaculately clean hotel, superbly run by a couple who offer friendly service, attention to detail and reasonable prices. The rooms with shower/wc have just been refurbished; doubles €30 with washbasin, €37–40 with shower, €40–45 with bath/wc. All are decorated in Louis-XV style, with thick carpets, rustic furniture, large mirrors and small painting. The red hat is a reminder of the distinctive headgear worn by the coachmen who used to stop over in this old staging post. *10% discount on a room (not to be taken in conjunction with other offers) offered to our readers on presentation of this guide.*

⊚ 🍴 ☎ 🍴 Le Grand Cerf**

21 rue Saint-Blaise; head towards the "Préfecture".
☎02.33.26.00.51 ⊛02.33.26.63.07
⊛www.hotelgrandcerf-61.com
Closed *Sun; during the New Year holidays.* **TV. High chairs available.**

With its splendid 1843 Neoclassical façade, this hotel has a faded grandeur. The rooms are nevertheless spacious and fairly priced depending on the season, the level of

comfort and the view; they're €47–59 and breakfast costs €6.50. There's a business break available at €62. The cooking is well regarded locally – elegant and of good quality – and is vying to be the best in town. Staff are smiling and welcoming. There's a *formule* with main meal and dessert at €15; the *menu-carte* costs €25. There are several charming dining rooms and a garden where they serve meals in summer. Logis de France. *Free house apéritif offered to our readers on presentation of this guide.*

⊚ 🍴 🍴 Au Petit Vatel

72 pl. du Commandant-Desmeulles: near the Museum of Fine Arts and Lace.
☎02.33.26.23.78
Closed *Wed; Sun evening.* **Disabled access. High chairs and games available.**

One of the best places in town offering diligent service and professional cuisine. The interior is elegant and stylish, with silver cutlery and little bouquets on the table. Set menus start with the weekday lunchtime menu at €15, and go up to €37, including a *Normandie* menu at €29. There is also a *Gourmand* menu at €69. Highlights include delicious nibbles, small apple cocktail, salad with Camembert fritters (a house speciality) and *magret de canard sauce pays d'Ouche*. The crowning glory comes at the end, however, with the traditional dessert trolley, complete with impressive copper bowls, which has sealed the restaurant's reputation. Unfortunately, the place is a little stuffy, but it would probably be an ideal place to celebrate a wedding anniversary. *Free coffee offered to our readers on presentation of this guide.*

Argentan

61200

⊚ ☎ 🍴 Hostellerie de la Renaissance**

20 av. de la 2e-D-B; it's on the road to Flers.
☎02.33.36.14.20 ⊛02.33.36.65.50
⊛www.hotel-larenaissance.com
Closed *Sun evening; Mon; a week in Feb; a fortnight mid-Aug.* **TV. Car park.**

Nothing medieval here, but it's the best place around (hence, no doubt, the rather pretentious name). The local cuisine has been wonderfully reinvented. To tell you what's on the menu would be too cruel.

Just reading it is sin enough. The cheapest menu at €16 is served at lunchtimes during the week, with other menus up to €47. It's often full, so it's a good idea to reserve. The hotel has comfortable, well-soundproofed rooms; doubles are €56–60.

Aunay-sur-Odon
14260

◎ ⅔ ⋒ |●| Hôtel-restaurant Saint-Michel**

6–8 rue de Caen.
℡02.31.77.63.16 ⓕ02.31.77.05.83
Closed *Sun evening and Mon (except July–Aug and public holidays); 15 Jan–15 Feb.*
Disabled access. TV. High chairs available. Car park.

A pleasant country hotel with a modern dining room seving traditional cooking. The chef uses all the good things that Normandy produces on menus €13–38, with a children's menu for €8. There are a few simple but decent, double rooms with shower/wc at €40. Breakfast costs €7 and half board, €42 per person, is compulsory over long weekends. Logis de France. *10% discount on the room rate (from the third consecutive night) offered to our readers on presentation of this guide.*

Avranches
50300

◎ ⅔ ⋒ |●| Hôtel de la Croix d'Or**

83 rue de la Constitution; near the Patton monument.
℡02.33.58.04.88 ⓕ02.33.58.06.95
Closed *Sun evening (mid-Oct to end March); Jan.* **TV. High chairs available. Car park.**

This delightful seventeenth-century coaching inn is the smart address in town. Inside, it's like a museum with its stone walls, beams, enormous fireplace and walls hung with copper, pewter and earthenware pots. Doubles with shower/wc or bath €56 to €70; rooms are faultlessly comfortable and nos. 14–27 and 31 are in pretty, little half-timbered cottages around the edge of a very attractive flower-filled garden. Service in the dining room is impeccable if a little starchy. Try the *millefeuille* of crab with basil and peas, the small lobster casserole with sweetbread ravioli, the *moelleux* of pink trout with bacon or the turbot fillet in a potato crust. The lunch menu is priced

at €15 and they have others €22.50–48. Tables are decorated with flowers in a very attractive dining room, and there's excellent food from a menu that varies day by day. Logis de France. *Free coffee offered to our readers on presentation of this guide.*

◎ |●| Le Bistrot de Pierre

5 rue du Général-de-Gaulle.
℡02.33.58.07.66
Closed *Sun.*

Apart from the chalked-up dishes on the board there is very little of the simple bistro about this place: an attractive, comfortable dining room in a contemporary modern style that looks to Asia for its inspiration, with fast, friendly service. Good food based on what's fresh in the market and prepared with considerable skill, features on the two lunchtime menus, €10.70 and 13.20, and the two evening menus, €12.50 and €15.

Ducey
50220 (10km SE)

◎ ⅔ ⋒ |●| Auberge de la Sélune**

2 rue Saint-Germain; take the Ducey exit off the N176, and you'll find it on the left just before you get to the bridge at Sélune.
℡02.33.48.53.62 ⓕ02.33.48.90.30
ⓦwww.selune.com
Closed *Mon; 1 Oct–31 March; 20 Jan–10 Feb; 10 Nov–10 Dec.* **Disabled access. TV. High chairs available. Car park.**

Originally a hospice, this huge inn is located on the old road to Mont-Saint-Michel. The pleasant rooms, at €54–57 for a double with bath, are attractively decorated and very conventional. A lucky few will get a view of the garden that runs down to the slow-moving Sélune – it's full of fish, so pack your fishing rod. There are also some tables on the garden side, in the elegant dining room. And good food, in the great tradition "prepared with care" (as the expression goes); menus start at €15 (weekdays), then from €23 up to €37. Logis de France. *Free digestif offered to our readers on presentation of this guide.*

Bagnoles-de-l'Orne
61140

◎ ⅔ ⋒ |●| La Potinière du Lac**

Rue des Casinos.

☎02.33.30.65.00 ⓕ02.33.38.49.04
ⓦwww.hoteldelapotiniere.com
Closed *Mon and Tues (1 Nov–31 March);*
7–14 March; 1 Dec–31 Jan. **TV. High chairs**
available.

An ideal spot to enjoy the antiquated
atmosphere of a thermal spa, but without
having to mix with the more serious
souls there to take the waters. It's hard to
miss this place because the façade, with
its turret, is one of the prettiest and most
striking in town. There's a view of the lake
from the dining room and most of the
rooms – the others look onto a main road
which is very quiet at night. This is a nice
place and prices are modest: double rooms
€33–47. The turret room is rather special
with its flowery wallpaper and pretty view.
The home cooking is simple and perfectly prepared, with many light and tasty
Normandy specialities: Camembert tartlet,
pavé of *andouille*, ham in cider. There's a
choice of menus €14.50–28.50, including
a special game menu during the hunting
season. Logis de France. *Free coffee offered to*
our readers on presentation of this guide.

ⓐ 🏕 🛍 🍴 Le Celtic**

14 rue Pierre-Noal; below the château.
☎02.33.37.92.11 ⓕ02.33.38.90.27
ⓦwww.leceltic.fr
Closed *Sun evening and Mon out of season;*
19 Jan–4 March. **Disabled access. TV. High**
chairs and games available.

Érick Alirol inherited the unfortunate
"tobacco-bar" name of this place, which
is rather unfair as it is an attractive venue
built in the typical local style and decorated with flowers. The pleasant rooms,
which have been renovated, all have
telephone and cost €39–43 for a double
with shower/wc or bath. Half board is
available for a minimum stay of three
nights at €74 for two people. Lots of fresh
local ingredients and seasonal produce
are used in the rustic dining room with
menus priced at €15.50–30. There's also
a snooker table and you can be sure of a
friendly welcome. Logis de France. *Free*
house apéritif offered to our readers on presen-
tation of this guide.

ⓐ 🏕 🛍 🍴 Manoir du Lys***

Route de Juvigny-sous-Andaine; take the
D235 and it's 3km from Bagnoles.
☎02.33.37.80.69 ⓕ02.33.30.05.80
ⓦwww.manoir-du-lys.fr
Closed *Sun evening and Mon (1 Nov–31*
March); early Jan to mid-Feb. **Disabled**

access. TV. High chairs and games avail-
able. Swimming pool. Car park.

A delightful manor deep in the Andaines
forest where you'll hear cuckoos in the
springtime and glimpse deer straying into
the orchard in search of fruit. The rooms
are bright, tastefully decorated and very
contemporary; some have balconies overlooking the garden and cost €60–190 for
a double with shower/wc or bath; suites
€190–240. The staff and the cooking are
as wonderful as the setting. The restaurant
uses fresh local produce and revives traditional flavours – *andouille de Vire* in flaky
pastry and crunchy camembert bake with
apples, squab in a garlic cream, cappuccino
of black pudding with truffles, and divine
desserts. The range of menus, €26–65,
includes special weekend menus based
on regional produce such as mushrooms
and fish. A perfect spot for a romantic
weekend. *10% discount on the room rate*
(1 Nov–31 March) offered to our readers on
presentation of this guide.

Domfront

61700 (16km W)

ⓐ 🍴 L'Auberge du Grandgousier

1 pl. de la Liberté; in the heart of the town,
opposite the post office and law courts.
☎02.33.38.97.17
Closed *Mon evening; Wed evening; Thurs;*
Feb; Oct. **Disabled access.**

Rustic touches (some genuine, some con-
trived) in a house built with stone and
half-timbering, and – no surprise here – a
restaurant serving excellent regional produce. Elegant, aromatic Normandy cooking
is based on fresh produce, with several fish
and stuffed shellfish specialities – served
with a smile. Considering the quality, the
prices are remarkably low: menus €15–29.
The attractive dining room is large, remarkably clean and flooded with light.

Rânes

61150 (20km NE)

ⓐ 🏕 🛍 🍴 Hôtel Saint-Pierre**

6 rue de la Libération; take the D916 as far as
La Ferté-Macé, then head towards Argentan.
☎02.33.39.75.14 ⓕ02.33.35.49.23
ⓦwww.hotelsaintpierreranes.com
Restaurant closed *Fri evening.* **TV. High**
chairs and games available. Car park.

This place, housed in a substantial stone
building, has been going strong for some

thirty years. You can relax in their deep sofas and the dining room is decorated in a contemporary style with paintings and display cases. The cooking is excellent and prices are reasonable – the house speciality is tripe, which has won countless prizes and awards (check out the certificates on the walls). Other hits include the roast *vallée d'Auge* chicken, which is perfectly cooked, the *bœuf à la ficelle* (where the meat is tied with string, cooked in stock and served with a Camembert sauce). There's a weekday menu at €13 and others €15–36. The owner is friendly and attentive and the pleasant rooms are in keeping with the rest – some have old Normandy wardrobes with a lovely smell of furniture wax. They cost €43–58 with shower/wc or bath; half board is €50 per person. Ask for one overlooking the courtyard; you'll get absolute peace and quiet. Logis de France. *10% discount on the room rate (1 Nov–1 April) offered to our readers on presentation of this guide.*

Barenton

50720

◎ |●| Restaurant Le Relais du Parc

46 rue Pierre-Crestey; it's on the D907.
☎02.33.59.51.38
Closed *Mon; Christmas to New Year; Feb school holiday.* **Open** *weekday lunchtimes (evenings and weekends by reservation).* **Disabled access.**

If you're here early enough, you'll be able to listen to the *patron* issuing orders in the kitchen in jovial but commanding tones. You're in good hands – he's a member of the Brotherhood of Vikings of the Normandy *Bocage*. He prepares attractive dishes using typical local produce – apples in particular – with imagination, and offers menus €12–30. Enjoy a good meal in a setting that includes a handsome fireplace and a grandmother clock.

Barfleur

50760

◎ 🏠 |●| Le Moderne

1 pl. du Général-de-Gaulle; it's opposite the post office, 50m from the harbour.
☎02.33.23.12.44 ℗02.33.23.91.58

Closed *Tues evening and Wed (except mid-July to mid-Sept); early Jan to mid-Feb.*

A colourful, pretty place with lots of flowers and the indefinable charm that some good old country inns exude; it's the sort of place you'd make the effort to book into to celebrate your grandmother's birthday or your nephew's exam success. The young couple who have recently taken over here have had the good sense not to change any of the delightful ways of this place. In the restaurant they serve simple and very tasty traditional cuisine using the freshest of produce: a weekday lunch option from €17.50 and up to €34. Seafood will cost you €28; lobster €54. The house specialities are fish *choucroute* and seafood platters. The bread is homemade and the desserts will take you back to your childhood. If you can't bear to leave, there are three simple but well-maintained rooms. Doubles with shower and wc go for €40–54 depending on the room size.

◎ 🏠 |●| Le Conquérant**

16–18 rue Saint-Thomas-Becket; it's in the main street, 50m from the port.
☎02.33.54.00.82 ℗02.33.54.65.25
Hotel closed *15 Nov–15 March.* **Restaurant open** *evenings (residents only).* **TV. Pay car park.**

A handsome seventeenth-century building. There's no sea view but there's a sizeable formal garden at the back where you can take breakfast on fine days. The rooms are, on the whole, pleasant and some are furnished in the local style; doubles go for €55–80 with shower/wc or bath. There is an elegant dining room with a crêperie serving buckwheat pancakes prepared in the traditional way and using organic flour; set menus at €14–25.

Anneville-en-Saire

50760 (5km S)

◎ |●| Café du Cadran GPLM

Take the D902 in the direction of Quettehou.
☎02.33.54.61.89
Closed *evenings (except bookings); Sat; Sun; 1–15 June; 20 Aug–20 Sept.* **Disabled access.**

This place is almost hidden by the crowd of tractors and juggernauts on their regular round of delivering and collecting the fruit and veg produced in the Val de Saire. The talk is all of cabbages and cauliflowers, European subsidies, yields and set-asides. If a glass of white wine at 11am is tempting, so is the lunchtime menu of the day: steak and mash, lamb stew – solid classics and cheap as you like. Menu €9, drink included.

Cosqueville
50330 (12km W)

⊚ 🍴 🛏 |◉| Au Bouquet de Cosqueville

Hameau Remoud; it's on the coast road (D116) between Barfleur and Cherbourg.
☎02.33.54.32.81 ℻02.33.54.63.38
🌐www.bouquetdecosqueville.com
Closed *Tues and Wed (Tues only in July); Jan.* **Disabled access. TV. High chairs available.**

A big house in a little hamlet where you'll find one of the best restaurants in the Nord-Cotentin area. The main attraction is the carefully prepared fish and seafood dishes. Stylish, unobtrusive service and menus €19–68; à la carte €50. In the same establishment there's another restaurant, the *Petit Gastro*, which is run by the same team. The atmosphere is less self-important with menus €12.50–16, but the chef takes equal care over the quality of the dishes. Classically comfortable doubles with basin go for €29, and with shower/wc or bath €44–50. *10% discount on the room rate (Oct–March) offered to our readers on presentation of this guide.*

Barneville-Carteret
50270

⊚ 🍴 🛏 |◉| L'Hermitage

4 promenade Abbé-Lebouteiller; it overlooks the port.
☎02.33.04.46.39 ℻02.33.04.88.11
🌐www.hotelrestauranthermitage.com
Closed *Sun evening and Mon in winter; 7–31 Jan, 12 Nov–20 Dec.* **TV. Pay car park.**

A large white house looking over the port. There's a delightful view of the sea and Carteret's little fishing port from the dining room and the terrace. Doubles cost €30–75 with shower/wc or bath and some have a sea view (rooms 1, 2, 3, 5 and 6). The restaurant of course offers the very best and freshest seafood (mussels *au gratin* with baby vegetables, dogfish in a cider

sauce), but also lists other regional classics on menus, €16–30, such as pig's trotter prepared in the old style and home-made tripe. *10% discount on the room rate (5–30 March and 1 Oct–15 Nov) offered to our readers on presentation of this guide.*

⊚ 🛏 |◉| Hôtel de la Marine★★★

11 rue de Paris.
☎02.33.53.83.31 ℻02.33.53.39.60
Closed *Mon and Thurs lunchtimes (April, May, June and Sept); Sun evening and Mon (March, Oct and Nov); 12 Nov–1 March.* **TV. Car park.**

There are breathtaking views from this large white nineteenth-century building overlooking the harbour. Some rooms have a balcony, others a tiny terrace, and the décor throughout is fresh and stylish. The views are delightful and doubles with bath cost €78–138. The good reputation of this establishment is due mostly to its restaurant. If you put to one side a few rather conventional dishes (probably there to keep the regulars of this old family restaurant happy – it's been open since 1876 after all), the set menu and à la carte options reveal a contemporary approach that successfully juggles regional specialities with the spices and flavours of further afield. You can see this in the way the chef prepares his oysters: in an iced gherkin bouillon or in a light soup flavoured with cappuccino with an egg and smoked herring sauce. Menus start at €28 (served everyday except Sat evening and public holidays), and there are others at €41.50–80. The décor reflects the location with its elegantly modern "transatlantic" style dining rooms looking out over the sea. Obviously a place like this doesn't come particularly cheap, so be prepared to pay a little extra.

Bayeux
14400

⊚ 🛏 Hôtel Mogador★★

20 rue Alain-Chartier, place Saint-Patrice; take rue de Saint-Malo (a continuation of Rue Saint-Martin).
📧hotelmogador@wanadoo.fr
☎02.31.92.24.58 ℻02.31.92.24.85
Closed *Feb school holiday; Christmas school holiday.* **TV.**

A discreet hotel with a welcoming, friendly owner, located on the edge of the touristy centre of town. The rooms, some recently refurbished, are elegant and comfortable, and those around the courtyard are very quiet; doubles with shower/wc or bath €41–51. Breakfast costs €6.

◉ ☎ Hôtel d'Argouges**

21 rue Saint-Patrice.
☎02.31.92.88.86 ℻02.31.92.69.16
✉dargouges@aol.com
Closed first fortnight in Jan; 24–25 Dec. **TV. Pay car park.**

A lovely eighteenth-century mansion, right in the centre but in a peaceful location with a large courtyard. The hotel slogan is "old-worldly charm with the comfort of today" – what more is there to say? The dining room is majestic and, behind the house, there's a big tree-filled garden where it's wonderful to have breakfast. Double rooms with shower/wc or bath cost €52–100. This is a delightful place.

◉ |◉| Le Petit Bistrot

2 rue du Bienvenu; it's beside the cathedral.
☎02.31.51.85.40
Closed Sun and Mon; Jan.

This is a genuine little bistro, chic yet very pleasant. You will find the owner on duty behind her rather splendid counter. She's a bit of a character and although she may seem a little brusque at first, once the ice has been broken everything will be fine. Her husband runs the kitchen and he's good at it, preparing fresh, tasty, seasonal food and making the best of local produce with some intelligent recipes. The calf kidneys in a bayleaf sauce are outstanding, as is the three-fish cassolette stew. Set menus cost €19 (up to 9pm) and €31.

Crépon
14480 (13km NE)

◉ ☎ |◉| La Ferme de la Rançonnière**

Route d'Arromanches; take the D12 as far as Sommervieu, then the D112.
☎02.31.22.21.73 ℻02.31.22.98.39
⊕www.ranconniere.com
Restaurant closed Jan. **Disabled access. TV. High chairs available. Car park.**

In a quiet village in the Bessin area, just a short drive from the landing beaches and Bayeux. The oldest parts of this beautiful and imposing fortified farmhouse date

from the thirteenth century. The place is charming and not at all stuffy, offering a friendly, sincere, family welcome. All the rooms are individually decorated and tastefully furnished in traditional style with doubles priced at €45–168 with shower/wc or bath. Breakfast is €11 and half board, compulsory in high season, costs €55–112 per person. The dining room has vaulted ceilings and the cuisine enjoys a good reputation in the area: fish and shellfish stew, duck breast with tarragon, terrine of Isigny beef, and good desserts. Menus €15 (weekdays) up to €25–40; there's a children's menu for €9. Logis de France.

Colombiers-sur-Seulles
14480 (14km E)

◉ 🌴 ☎ |◉| Château du Baffy**

10km from the Normandy landing beaches. Take exit 7 from the Caen ring-road in the direction of Creully; turn right after Pierpont on the D176.
☎02.31.08.04.57 ℻02.31.08.08.29
Closed 1 Nov–15 Feb. **Disabled access. High chairs and games available. Car park.**

A perfectly charming place, ideal for a romantic weekend – there's even a small river in the lovely garden. The rooms are pleasant and comfortable – doubles go for €74–84 including breakfast. In the restaurant there are menus ranging from €24 up to €29. They offer refined, traditional cuisine served in generous portions; try the home-made foie gras or the langoustines croquantes flavoured with vanilla. There's a games room, tennis and mountain biking. *10% discount on the room rate offered to our readers on presentation of this guide.*

Saint-Laurent-sur-Mer
14710 (18km NW)

◉ 🌴 ☎ |◉| Hôtel-restaurant La Sapinière

Le Ruquet; take the D514, then continue in the direction of the beach.
☎02.31.92.71.72 ℻02.31.92.92.12
⊕www.chez.com/lasapiniere
Closed 15 Nov–20 March. **TV. Disabled access. High chairs available. Car park.**

This is an enchanting place right by the beach, with accommodation in little wooden chalets. All the rooms (€60–80) are large and breezy, soberly decorated and all have their own terrace. To top it

BASSE-NORMANDIE

all, the beds are exceptionally comfortable. The restaurant is in a beautiful room with bay windows, and a terrace (heated when necessary) for fine days. Its walls are covered with exuberant paintings by the artist John Pepper (evidently a fan of *Toy Story*). Small menu with simple, brasserie-style dishes like fried mussels or superb salads, as well as interesting suggestions of the day; reckon on around €20 for a meal. The restaurant is used by locals as much as by hotel guests, and take-away sandwiches and waffles (far better than the run of the mill) are also on offer for the bathers on the beach. The owner is extremely friendly and laid-back – he wanders around everywhere in bare feet – and is sure to give you an effusive welcome. You'll need to book for dinner. *Free Kir normand offered to our readers on presentation of this guide.*

Bellême

61130

⑯ 🏠 |●| Domaine du Golf de Bellême

Les Sablons; at the foot of the bourg de Bellême.
☏02.33.85.13.13 ℻02.33.85.13.14
🌐www.belleme.com
Open *until midnight*. **Disabled access. TV. High chairs and games available. Swimming pool with health suite. Car park.**

This restaurant is located in the old convent of the sixteenth-century priory of Saint-Val. Bathed in light and with its magnificent woodwork and old stone walls, it could not be more appealing. The food is good too, though perhaps a little uneven, given the prices. Menus €23–42, with a brasserie menu at €20, are served up to 9.30pm. There are a few comfortable rooms in the outbuildings which have modern facilities: doubles €70–99 with bath. Winter terrace.

Cabourg

14390

⑯ 🏠 Hôtel Le Cottage**

24 av. du Général-Leclerc; it's opposite the church.
☏02.31.91.65.61 ℻02.31.28.78.82
TV. High chairs available. Car park.

It's easy to fall under the spell of this delightful hotel in a charming, traditional

Normandy house with a pretty flower garden. The owner will greet you like an old friend, and the rooms are cosy and charming with their Laura Ashley style floral décor. Room no. 2 has a Jacuzzi, and no. 5, "Citrine", has been refurbished. Doubles with shower or bath will set you back €64–78; with spa bath €86–89 for two people and €100–115 for four people. Although it's beside the road, the double-glazing is good and the rooms are quiet. Facilities include a gym and a sauna.

⑯ 🏠 Hôtel Castel Fleuri**

4 av. Alfred-Piat; in the centre, 200m from the beach.
☏02.31.91.27.57 ℻02.31.91.31.81
🌐www.castel-fleuri.com
Closed *5–24 Jan.* **TV.**

A very pleasant hotel, in what was once a family *pension*, surrounded by a pretty garden. The rooms are comfortable and inviting; doubles €64–80 including breakfast. The decoration is gradually being renewed by the new owner, and the results so far reveal good taste and a sure touch.

Dives-sur-Mer

14160 (2km S)

⑯ 🎋 |●| Restaurant Chez le Bougnat

29 rue Gaston-Manneville; in the centre.
☏02.31.91.06.13
Closed *Sun–Wed evenings out of season; Jan.* **Open** *daily for lunch; daily for lunch and dinner (15 July–31 Aug).*

Filled with trinkets that would turn a junk dealer green with envy, this old place serves excellent food, traditional and simple. Specialities include *pot-au-feu*, calf's head and kidneys, plus home-made ice cream. The weekday menu at €14.90 offers starter, main dish, cheese and dessert – this is the best value for money locally so it's a good idea to book. At weekends there are menus at €19.90 and €24.90. You can also choose à la carte, which will set you back about €26. *Free liqueur offered to our readers on presentation of this guide.*

Beuvron-en-Auge

14430 (14km SE)

⑯ 🎋 |●| Auberge de la Boule d'Or

Place Michel Vermughen; take the D400, then the D49.

T 02.31.79.78.78
Closed *Tues evening and Wed (except July, Aug and Sept); Jan.*

Right in the middle of one of the loveliest villages in the Auge, this superb half-timbered house was built in the eighteenth century. The beautiful façade is such a fine example of local architecture that it was photographed for a publicity shot. On a note of interest: the tiling in the kitchen is the same as that in the kitchen of the Élysée Palace. The dining room is stylishly rustic, intimate yet friendly. They serve good local cooking, with tasty dishes at honest prices; menus €19–26. It's frequently full in summer so it's best to book. *Free coffee offered to our readers on presentation of this guide.*

Caen
14000

See map overleaf

⊚ ♨ 🏠 Hôtel Saint-Étienne*

2 rue de l'Académie. **Map A2-3**
T 02.31.86.35.82 F 02.31.85.57.69
e contact@hotel-saint-etienne.com
Closed *Sun 1–6pm.* **TV.**

Awarded a Normandy Quality Tourism certificate, this is a characterful hotel in a peaceful street. It was built before the Revolution and much of the stonework and wood panelling is original. The rooms are pretty; doubles €25 with basin and €35–40 with shower/wc. No. 8 has a lovely view of the Abbaye aux Hommes. It's the cheapest hotel in Caen, and often full, so reservations are strongly recommended. *10% discount on the room rate (Nov–March) offered to our readers on presentation of this guide.*

⊚ 🏠 ♨ Hôtel des Quatrans**

17 rue Gémare; right in the centre, near the château and the pedestrian area. **Map B2-4**
T 02.31.86.25.57 F 02.31.85.27.80
w www.hotel-des-quatrans.com
TV.

In a neighbourhood that was rebuilt after World War II, the unappealing façade hides quiet, well-equipped, comfortable rooms (€60) decorated in pastel colours. Some of the rooms have recently been constructed. Attentive service. This hotel has been awarded a Normandy Quality

Tourism certificate. *One free breakfast per room offered to our readers on presentation of this guide.*

⊚ ♨ |●| Crêperie Les Canotiers

143 rue Saint-Pierre. **Map B2-14**
T 02.31.50.24.51
Closed *Sun (July–Aug); Mon lunch (in winter); 3 weeks in Sept.* **Open** noon–7pm. **High chairs and baby changing table available.**

A rather "British" feel to this place with a slight Scandinavian touch. The decoration here is as warm as the welcome, with flowery tablecloths and curtains, palewood furniture and ornate trinkets – all rather Laura Ashley. Menus €8.38–9.90; at lunchtime it is packed with locals who appreciate the cosy atmosphere and the fine selection of crêpes, omelettes, salads and crumbles. In the afternoon it becomes a tea room (although it is the exquisite hot chocolate that takes pride of place). *Free coffee offered to our readers on presentation of this guide.*

⊚ |●| Restaurant Maître Corbeau

8 rue Buquet; it's near the castle. **Map B1-11**
T 02.31.93.93.00
Closed *Sun; Mon and Sat lunchtimes; first 3 weeks in Aug.* **High chairs available.**

A restaurant entirely devoted to cheese, with a bizarre, dairy-obsessed décor. Among other tasty dishes they serve fondues using local cheese or goat's cheese and *escalopines* of Roquefort flambéed with Calvados, and also chocolate fondue. The weekday lunch menu goes for €9.60 and there are three others up to €19. Reckon on around €19 à la carte. Informal, enthusiastic welcome and service; the diners are mainly students. It's busy in the evening, so you'd do well to reserve.

⊚ |●| La Petite Auberge

17 rue des Équipes d'Urgence; beside the church of Saint-Jean. **Map C2-17**
T 02.31.86.43.30.
Closed *Sat; 20–31 Dec.* **Disabled access.**

The dining room is small and cosy; it's extended by a glassed-in terrace. The good local dishes change with the seasons and are honestly priced. Highlights include tripe *à la mode de Caen*. There's an impeccable *formule du jour* at €12 and an interesting *menu-carte* for €19. It offers a

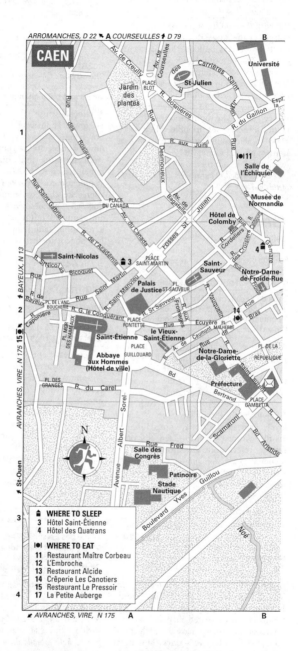

ARROMANCHES, D 22 ↘ A COURSEULLES ↑ D 79   B

CAEN

Université

Av. de Creully

Av. de Courseulles

des Carrières Saint-Julien

PLACE BLOT

St-Julien

Rue des Rosiers

Jardin des plantes

R. Bosnières

R. aux Juifs

Desmoueux

R. du Gaillon

Esplanade

1

Rue Saint-Gabriel

PLACE DU CANADA

Av. de Bagatelle

Av. de Bagatelle Saint-Julien

|●|11
Salle de l'Échiquier

Musée de Normandie

R. de l'Académie

Fossés St.

Hôtel de Colomby

R. des Cordeliers

Gémare

R. des Croisiers Calibourg

Saint-Nicolas

St-Nicolas

Bicoquet

Saint Martin

PLACE SAINT-MARTIN

Saint-Sauveur

4

Notre-Dame-de-Froide-Rue

Rue de Bayeux

Rue

PL DE L'ANC BOUCHERIE

R. de Caponière

R. Saint-Manvieu

Palais de Justice

PL ST-SAUVEUR

R. St-Sauveur

R. aux Fromages

Rue Vauquelin

Rue de Bras

2

R. G. le Conquérant

PLACE FONTETTE

le Vieux-Saint-Étienne

Rue

Ecuyère

PL MALHERBE

R. de Caumont

14
|●|

PL. MGR DES HAMEAUX

Saint-Étienne

PLACE GUILLOUARD

Notre-Dame-de-la-Gloriette

PL DE LA RÉPUBLIQUE

15|●|↖

Abbaye aux Hommes (Hôtel de ville)

A. de Caumont

R. du Carel

Bd Bertrand

Préfecture

Rue Saint-Jean

PLACE GAMBETTA

R. D.

PL. DES GRANGES

Sorel

Albert

Avenue

Rue Fred

Scamaroni

Bd Aristide

N

St-Ouen

Salle des Congrès

Patinoire

Guillou

Stade Nautique

Yves

Boulevard

Noé

3

▲	**WHERE TO SLEEP**
3	Hôtel Saint-Étienne
4	Hôtel des Quatrans

|●|	**WHERE TO EAT**
11	Restaurant Maître Corbeau
12	L'Embroche
13	Restaurant Alcide
14	Crêperie Les Canotiers
15	Restaurant Le Pressoir
17	La Petite Auberge

4

16

BASSE-NORMANDIE

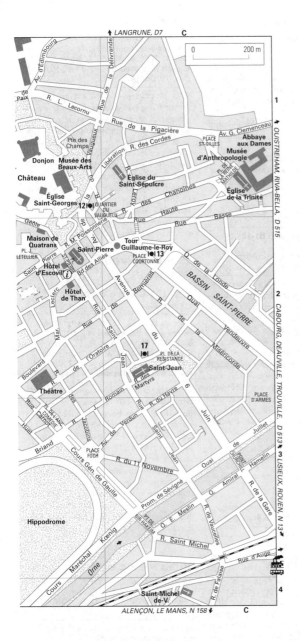

LANGRUNE, D7   C

Av. d'Etambourg

de la Délivrande

de Paix

R. L. Lecornu

Rue de la Pigacière

1

Av. G. Clemenceau

OUISTREHAM, RIVA-BELLA, D 515

Pte des Champs

R. des Cordes

Libération

PLACE ST-GILLES

Abbaye aux Dames

Musée d'Anthropologie

Donjon

Musée des Beaux-Arts

Château

Église du Saint-Sépulcre

R. Leroy

des Chanoines

Église de la Trinité

PL. DE LA REINE MATHILDE

Église Saint-Georges

12

QUARTIER DU VAUGUEUX

Rue Haute

Rue Basse

Géôle

R. M. Poissonnerie

Maison de Quatrans

Tour Guillaume-le-Roy

13

PL. LETELLIER

Saint-Pierre

PLACE COURTONNE

Q. de la Londe

Saint Pierre

Hôtel d'Escoville

Bd des Alliés

Avenue

Bernières

Quai

Vendeuvre

BASSIN SAINT-PIERRE

CABOURG, DEAUVILLE, TROUVILLE, D 513

Hôtel de Than

Leclerc

Rue

de

Saint

du

de la Miséricorde

2

Rue

de l'Oratoire

17

Jean

PL. DE LA RESISTANCE

Saint-Jean

Théâtre

R.

de

Romain

R. des Martyrs

R. du Havre

PLACE D'ARMES

PL. DE LA COMEDIE

Rue

Huet

J.

Jacobins

Rue

Verdun

Av. de

Saint

Jean

Juin

de

Juillet

3

LISIEUX, ROUEN, N 13

Briand

PLACE FOCH

R. du 11 Novembre

Quai

PONT CHURCHILL

Hamelin

R. de la Gare

Cours Gén. de Gaulle

Prom. de Sévigné

PL. DE BIR-HAKEIM

Q. E. Meslin

O. Amiral

R. de Vaucelles

Hippodrome

Maréchal

Kœnig

Orne

R. Saint Michel

Rue d'Auge

Cours

Saint-Michel de-V.

R. de Falaise

4

ALENÇON, LE MANS, N 158   C

16

BASSE-NORMANDIE

low-key welcome, peaceful atmosphere and professional service.

☕ |●| Restaurant Alcide

1 pl. Courtonne. **Map C2-13**
☎02.31.44.18.06
Closed Sat; 20–31 Dec.

Behind the sky-blue façade the décor isn't exactly earth-shattering, but the warm atmosphere makes up for it. This is not the place to come if you're on a diet – they serve honest, robust local cuisine on menus €14.50–22.50, including calf's head and baked sole and tripe *à la mode de Caen* (which is what people come here for). One of the town's classics – it's just a shame that the welcome is not quite of the same standard.

☕ |●| 🍴 L'Embroche

17 rue Porte-au-Berger. **Map B1-12**
☎02.31.93.71.31
Closed Sun; Sat and Mon lunchtimes; 15 Sept–5 Oct; 24 Dec–6 Jan.

In a district that boasts lots of restaurants, this is really very good. Pretty little dining room – where you can see through into the kitchen – and charming, efficient service. Chalked up on the board you'll find local dishes cooked with fresh produce and bags of imagination – fried Camembert in Calvados, rump steak *aiguillette* with caramelized balsamic vinegar. There's a lunch menu for €17, with others up to €21, and all the wines on the short but interesting list are the same price. *Free house liqueur offered to our readers on presentation of this guide.*

☕ |●| Restaurant Le Pressoir

3 av. Henry-Chéron; 2km to the west of the town centre. **Off map A2-15**
☎02.31.73.32.71
Closed Sun evening; Mon; Sat lunchtime; Feb school holiday; 3 weeks in Aug. **High chairs available.**

This may be some way from the centre, in a pretty charmless area, and the atmosphere may be a bit formal, but it's well worth a detour. The cooking is accomplished and precise, never masking the flavour of the products and avoiding any fancy tricks. Fish, meat and game (in season) are all treated with the same respect; menu €27 (Tues–Fri evenings), with other menus €42–62.

Noyers-Bocage
14210 (12km SW)

☕ 🏠 |●| 🍴 Hôtel-restaurant Le Relais Normand**

Take the D675 from the Noyers-Bocage exit.
☎02.31.77.97.37 ☎02.31.77.94.41
Closed Tues; Wed; 25 Jan–8 Feb; 15 Nov–15 Dec. **TV. Car park.**

The proprietor-chef is a Grand Master of the *Confrérie de Fins Goustiers du Pré-Bocage*, an association which defends "real" food and the preparation of local produce. Set menus €16–45 – dishes include warm oysters and duck *à l'orange*. Modern, functional and comfortable doubles with shower/wc or bath go for €42–53; breakfast €8. Very attentive service is guaranteed in this perfect country hotel with plush but rustic dining room. Logis de France. *Free house apéritif offered to our readers on presentation of this guide.*

Saint-Sylvain
14190 (20km SE)

☕ |●| 🍴 Auberge de la Crémaillère

2 rue du 18-Juillet-1944; it's in the town centre – take the N58 then the D132A.
☎02.31.78.11.18
Closed Sun evening; Mon (except public holiday; Wed evening; 25 July–12 Aug. **High chairs available. Disabled access.**

From the outside, this looks like a simple country inn, but appearances can be deceptive. It has been decorated to great effect, with a combination of white and raspberry-red. The food is equally sophisticated and enticing. The desserts are to die for and even the apple pie manages to breathe new life into an old recipe. The menus start at €19.50 (excellent) and go up to €35. A warm welcome and impeccable service are guaranteed in this first-rate place. *Free liqueur offered to our readers on presentation of this guide.*

Villers-Bocage
14310 (26km SW)

☕ 🏠 |●| Restaurant Les Trois Rois**

2 pl. Jeanne-d'Arc; it's on the A84 in the direction of Mont St Michel.
☎02.31.77.00.32 ☎02.31.77.93.25

Closed *Sun evening; Mon; Tues lunchtime; Jan; last week in June.* **TV. High chairs available. Car park.**

This stone inn on the large village square looks like the classic country inn but appearances can be deceptive. The chef has run the kitchens for thirty years – his *tripe à la mode de Caen* has won so many awards that we've lost count. His food is full of joy and inventiveness and he continues to create delightful, market-led recipes dominated by fish, shellfish and tripe with menus at €20 (weekdays, except public holidays), others at €30–50. The rooms in this excellent establishment are well maintained and regularly refurbished. Doubles go for €33 with basin and shower and €48–59 with bath; breakfast costs €8. Logis de France.

Carentan

50500

◎ 🏛 |◉| Hôtel-restaurant
L'Escapade*

34 rue du Docteur-Caillard; it's opposite the train station.
☎02.33.42.02.00 ⊚02.33.42.20.01
Closed *1 Dec–1 March.* **TV. High chairs available. Car park.**

The hotel has a beautiful, ivy-covered façade. The restaurant is attractive too: it's an intimate place with low lighting, a soothing colour scheme, and a polished parquet floor. You'll get very good traditional cooking on the set menus at €14–24. There's a sign encouraging customers to tell the chef what they thought of the food. The rooms – €31–40 with shower/wc or bath – have all been recently renovated and are comfortable and pleasant, despite being huge. You would do well to reserve, as it is very popular with its regular customers.

Moitiers-en-Bauptois (Les)

50360 (20km NW)

◎ |◉| Auberge de l'Ouve

Village Longuérac; take the D903 to Saint-Jores, then the D24 in the direction of Pont-l'Abbé.
☎02.33.21.16.26
Open *April–Sept (reservations only).* **Disabled access.**

This lovely, welcoming inn stands on the banks of the Ouve; it's miles from anywhere, surrounded by a cluster of old farms, with a few horses frolicking about, a line of trees at the water's edge and romantic sunsets. The restaurant has an attractive décor and a warm atmosphere. The cuisine is wonderful and the menus – very cheap at €10–24 – typically feature as much terrine as you can eat, eels *à la Normande* and smoked ham in cider. To work up an appetite or to help the food go down, there are boats for hire, boat trips on the Douve (in the season) and lovely walks in the nearby woods and marshlands.

Cherbourg

50100

◎ 🏛 Auberge de jeunesse

55 rue de l'Abbaye; half-way between the Arsenal and the town centre.
☎02.33.78.15.15 ⊚02.33.78.15.16
📧cherbourg@fuaj.org
Closed *21 Dec–4 Jan.* **Reception open** *9am–1pm and 6–11pm.* **Disabled access. Car park.**

Located in part of the old naval buildings and intelligently refurbished in 1998. The rooms and fittings are impeccable and the furniture modern – nothing has been overlooked. Accommodation costs €14 per night, including breakfast (FUAJ card compulsory), plus €3 for renting sheets. You can have breakfast on the terrace in sunny weather; other meals are available, but you can also use the kitchen yourself. There's the possibility of taking a course in the nearby sailing centre at Cherbourg. You are sure of a friendly, efficient welcome.

◎ 🎿 🏛 Hôtel de la Croix de Malte**

5 rue des Halles; it's near the harbour, the theatre and the casino.
☎02.33.43.19.16 ⊚02.33.43.65.66
📧hotel.croix.malte@wanadoo.fr
Closed *20 Dec–5 Jan.* **Disabled access. TV.**

This small modern hotel has been totally refurbished; its quiet rooms have been spruced up and are extremely comfy. You'll get a very warm welcome from the owners. Doubles with shower/wc are excellent value for money at €26–45, according to the season, and €48 with bath. If you book in advance, ask for room no. 3, 6, 8, 13 or 15 – they're the biggest. *10% discount on the room rate offered to our readers on presentation of this guide.*

Hôtel de la Renaissance**

4 rue de l'Église.
☎02.33.43.23.90 ℱ02.33.43.96.10
TV. Pay car park.

This hotel has a great location in front of the wonderful church of La Trinité – if you're into frothy, frivolous architecture, you'll love the sugar-candy façade. All the comfortable rooms have been recently refurbished and are attractive and pleasant; every one has a view of the port. Doubles go for €45–60 with shower/wc or bath, according to the season. You'll get a pleasant welcome and excellent value for money.

|●| Le Faitout

25 rue Tour-Carrée; it's 100m from the town hall.
☎02.33.04.25.04
Closed Sun; Mon; a week in Feb, fortnight in May; a week over Christmas.

The attractive basement dining room is built of wood and stone and has a relaxed atmosphere. It's the archetype of a small, reliable restaurant that does precisely what it's supposed to – consequently it's often full. Good traditional cooking at prices that won't give you indigestion: the *formule* of the day "Faitout" €19, gives you starter, dish of the day, cheese and dessert. The generous dish of the day on its own costs €9.50. À la carte you can expect to pay €20–25; good choices include supreme of guinea fowl with honey and ginger, *andouillette* with Calvados, local mussels (in season only, of course) and simply grilled fish of the day. There's an agreeable wine list. It's best to book for dinner and at weekends.

Omonville-la-Petite
50440 (20km NW)

☆ La Fossardière**

Hameau de la Fosse; take the D901 or the quieter, coastal, D45.
☎02.33.52.19.83 ℱ02.33.52.73.49
Closed mid-Nov to mid-March. **Disabled access. Car park.**

You'll find this lovely hotel in a hamlet just 500m from the sea, in this wonderful part of Cotentin. First, prepare to be charmed by this adorable little hamlet with its flower-filled streets standing astride a stream in the very heart of nature. Then you'll be treated to a warm, laid-back welcome from the owner of this former village bakery. The rooms with bath are comfortable, extremely peaceful and reasonably priced at €40–63. There's a tiny sauna and whirlpool bath (which costs a little more). Prices are very reasonable and have not been increased recently. *Free breakfast (from the second consecutive night, except in July–Aug) offered to our readers on presentation of this guide.*

Auderville
50440 (28km NW)

|●| L'Auberge de Goury

Port de Goury; it's 1km from Auderville on the D901, at cap de La Hague.
☎02.33.52.77.01
Closed Mon (Easter to Nov); 3 weeks in Jan.
Disabled access. High chairs available. Car park.

The restaurant is located at the very tip of La Hague. With its very colourful owner (just how we like them), this rustic old fishermen's haunt has become a veritable institution in La Hague. There's a wide fireplace in the old dining room, where you'll find the owner; the new one has enormous windows that give you a marvellous vista of the sea (calm or wild depending on the weather). Appreciative comments from movie and theatre stars decorate the visitors' book. The specialities on the menus, €15.50–51, are fish grilled over an open wood fire and lobster.

Flamanville
50340 (28km SW)

☆ Hôtel Bel Air***

Rue du Château. Take the D4 and you'll find it 300m from the château.
☎ and ℱ02.33.04.48.00
🌐 www.hotelbelair.biz
Closed 20 Dec–15 Jan. **Disabled access. TV. Car park.**

An attractive hotel in the countryside near the magnificent Flamanville headland. The friendly welcome and the surroundings will instantly make you feel at home. Rooms – either overlooking the fields or the garden – are comfortable and have a certain charm for €55–90 according to the level of comfort and season. Lovely little rooms, as cosy as you could wish in the annexe or more spacious and modern in the main building; make up your own mind, but it's a great place to stay.

Saint-Germain-des-Vaux

50440 (29km NW)

◎ |●| 2️⃣ **Restaurant le Moulin à Vent**

Hameau de Danneville; take the D901; at the Saint-Germain-des-Vaux exit take the road to Port-Racine.
☎02.33.52.75.20
Closed Sun evening and Mon (except festivals and public holidays). **Disabled access. High chairs available. Car park.**

A gastronomic restaurant high above the bay beside the ruins of an old mill in a large granite house with a façade decorated with lots of old-fashioned signs. The large, pleasant, softly coloured dining room overlooks a little garden full of exotic plants, and beyond to Saint-Martin's cove. Superb cooking using the freshest produce from the market and the sea is featured on the good-value €15 menu, served during the week; other menus €25–45. If you venture into the à la carte menu expect a considerably heftier bill. The chef takes a traditional approach (squid tossed in garlic and parsley, grilled lobster), allowing the food to speak for itself. And it's very, very good. *Free house apéritif is offered to our readers on presentation of this guide.*

Coutances

50200

◎ |●| **Crêperie Le Râtelier**

3 bis rue Georges-Clemenceau; it's near the cathedral.
☎02.33.45.56.52
Closed Sun; Mon out of season; Feb school holiday. **Disabled access. High chairs available.**

A nice little crêperie with a bright and pleasant dining room with a few attractive engravings and decorative plates on the wall and, of course, as the name implies, a rack. There's a choice of at least fifty different pancakes made with black wheat and almost as many made with rye. There's a choice of menus €7.50–16.20; galettes cost €2.30–10.

Montmartin-sur-Mer

50590 (10km SW)

◎ 2️⃣ 🏠 |●| **Hôtellerie du Bon Vieux Temps**★★

7 rue Pierre-des-Touches; it's opposite the post office.

☎02.33.47.54.44 ⊕02.33.46.27.12
Closed Sun evening and Mon (except July and Aug); 10 days end Jan; 10 days end Sept. **TV. Car park**

This inn, just a couple of kilometres from the sea, is appropriately named. There is the large stone house, typical of the area, the little tobacconist's shop on the ground floor, the old-style tiling, the wood panelling … in fact everything needed for this place to live up to its name. But that doesn't mean that it's stuck in the past. The chef works with local produce, mainly fish, but gives it a very modern accent; weekday lunch menu €13.50, and others €22–42. The rooms are pleasant and the most expensive are really spacious; doubles €50–62 with shower/wc or bath. *Free coffee offered to our readers on presentation of this guide.*

Quettreville-sur-Sienne

50660 (10kms)

◎ 🏠 |●| **Au Château de La Tournée**

2 rue de la Libération.
☎02.33.07.82.07 ⊕02.33.07.48.07
Closed Mon; Wed; Sun evening; a fortnight during Feb school holiday; mid-Sept to mid-Oct.

A town house with an attractive façade but not one to be confused with the château whose name it bears. Situated at the side of the road and with very basic rooms, this is perhaps not the ideal spot for an extended stay. So why include it on your route? Quite simply for the food – which is absolutely great, a touch of fusion in the tradition devised by some of the great chefs: saté spiced bread crumble with mullet on a bed of risotto with ceps, supreme of young pigeon in *vin fumé* garnished with *shitake* and walnuts. The lunchtime menu (€14) is more "classic" (but impeccable); other menus cost €35–57. The décor is that of an old-fashioned Normandy inn whose owner has paid a visit to craftsmen in India. But the quality of service (notably lacking the day we were there) doesn't seem to be entirely reliable. Double rooms with shower (wc on the landing) are €30.50.

Regnéville-sur-Mer
50590 (10km SW)

◎ 🏠 |●| Le Jules Gommès

Take the D20 towards Granville, then 7km further turn onto the D49 towards Regnéville.
☎02.33.45.32.04
Closed Mon and Tues (except during school holidays); Nov. **Disabled access. High chairs available.**

Part-restaurant, part-crêperie and part-Irish pub, this is one of the cosiest places in the area and it has magnificent sea views. The first-class décor includes beautiful furniture and walls covered in gorgeous watercolours of the region. It's run by a nice young couple who serve terrific crêpes and *galettes*. Reasonably priced menus range from €11.50 up to €24.50; the pub is convivial. *Free coffee offered to our readers on presentation of this guide.*

Hambye
50450 (20km SE)

◎ 🏠 |●| Auberge de l'Abbaye d'Hambye**

5 route de l'Abbaye; take the D7 in the direction of Villedieu-les-Poêles, then the D27 on the left.
☎02.33.61.42.19 ☎02.33.61.00.85
Closed Sun evening; Mon; Feb school holiday; 1–15 Oct. **TV. High chairs and games available. Car park.**

Inside this large stone building, typical of the region, located in a beautiful country setting, you'll find this quiet little hotel. The decoration in the comfortable rooms (€50 with shower/wc) is vaguely romantic. The place is meticulously run, and the owners welcome you in a friendly, courteous fashion. The menus served in the elegant dining room, ranging from €20 to €54, list appetizing and delicious traditional dishes.

Deauville
14800

◎ 🏠 🏠 Le Patio**

180 av. de la République; it's near the racecourse.
☎02.31.88.25.07 ☎02.31.88.00.81
✉claude.may@wanadoo.fr
Closed Jan. **Disabled access. TV.**

The rooms in this large, white hotel are comfortable and pleasant; some overlook the shaded flower-filled patio. Prices are reasonable for Deauville, with doubles at €35–72 depending on facilities and the season; breakfast €7. There's a gym to help counteract the effects of all that Normandy cream. *10% discount on the room rate (except weekends and school holidays) offered to our readers on presentation of this guide.*

◎ 🏠 Hôtel Le Chantilly**

120 av. de la République; it's 500m from the train station.
☎02.31.88.79.75 ☎02.31.88.41.29
✉hchantilly@aol.com
TV.

This hotel, renovated throughout and with modern facilities, radiates a certain charm. Doubles are €62–90 depending on the season and breakfast costs €8. You'll get a warm welcome and it's advisable to book.

◎ 🏠 🏠 Hôtel de la Côte Fleurie**

55 av. de la République; 500m from the train station, opposite the *Hôtel Le Chantilly*.
☎02.31.98.47.47 ☎02.31.98.47.46
Closed Jan. **TV. High chairs available.**

This hotel has been completely refurbished; its lovely, bright rooms have brand-new bathrooms and a flower on their door. Doubles with shower/wc are €62–75; the most expensive one looks onto a pretty garden – it's exquisite, and well worth the extra cost. There are also some rooms for four people at €91–116. Service is friendly and unfussy. *10% discount on a room (except weekends and school holidays) offered to our readers on presentation of this guide.*

Villers-sur-Mer
14640 (7km W)

◎ 🏠 🏠 Hôtel et Salon de Thé Outre-Mer***

1 rue du Maréchal-Leclerc; right in the town centre, opposite the sea.
☎02.31.87.04.64 ☎02.31.87.48.90
🌐www.hoteloutremer.com
Closed Jan. **TV. High chairs available. Car park.**

This looks like a classical hotel, but open the door and you are greeted by shrill colours (pink, green and orange) and thoughtfully arranged furnishings (wicker chairs, garlands). The explosion of colours continues in the rooms (€92–115), which are all different but all brilliantly executed. There's also a jazz bar and tea room: home-made cakes and an extensive range of teas and coffees. Be warned, however, that if you go into the tea room in the afternoon you're more than likely to end up staying the night, as the place is so enticing that you won't want to leave. Ticks all the boxes – the place to stay in the Calvados area. *One free breakfast per room offered to our readers on presentation of this guide.*

Falaise
14700

◎ 🍴 🏠 |●| Hôtel-restaurant de la Poste**

38 rue Georges-Clemenceau.
☎02.31.90.13.14 ☎02.31.90.01.81
✉hotel.delaposte@wanadoo.fr
Closed *Sun evening; Mon; Fri evening 1 Oct–30 April; Sat lunchtime 1 May–30 Sep; 2–16 Jan; a fortnight in Oct.* **High chairs available. TV. Car park.**

This is a pleasant inn. Nearly all the rooms have been refurbished and cost €48–50 for a double with shower/wc or bath; breakfast €7. Simple, traditional food in the restaurant: try the pan-fried langoustines in cider or the rosette of lamb with goat's cheese. Menus, which range from €15 (not Sun) up to €39, change regularly. Logis de France. *10% reduction on the room rate (early Sept to end of March) offered to our readers on presentation of this guide.*

◎ 🍴 |●| La Fine Fourchette

52 rue Georges-Clemenceau.
☎02.31.90.08.59
Closed *Tues evening out of season; 19 Feb–8 March.* **Disabled access. High chairs available. Car park.**

The shimmering colours in the dining room raise the spirits of the hungry traveller who stops here. The food is of excellent quality and makes constant use of new recipes. Every year the chef goes off to work with great chefs in different parts of the country, so his cooking is always innovative and dynamic. You get a good idea of the cooking even on the €14 menu (excluding public holidays) and there are other menus up to €36 and a children's menu at €8.50. Tasty options include fillet of duckling in spicy honey and leg of duck *confit* with apples. Efficient service is offered by genuinely friendly staff. *Free coffee or liqueur offered to our readers on presentation of this guide.*

Flers
61100

◎ |●| Auberge des Vieilles Pierres

Le Buisson-Corblin; take the Argentan road and it's 3km from the centre.
☎02.33.65.06.96
Closed *Sun evening; Mon; Tues; Feb school holiday; 1–22 Aug.* **Disabled access. High chairs and games available.**

One of the best eating establishments in the Swiss Normandy region with young owners and a young, natural atmosphere. And it's full of surprises, beginning with the attractively refurbished dining room – nothing heavy about the décor. And then there's the sense that there's a genius at work in the kitchen, because the food is superb and intelligently prepared. The chef has a particular way with fish and grilled lobster. There's a brilliant €15 weekday menu and the other menus, €22–37, are equally good. In short, the *Vieilles Pierres* with its talented, promising young owners and fine, modern taste completely won us over.

◎ |●| Restaurant Au Bout de la Rue

60 rue de la Gare; at the end of the road leading from the town centre to the station.
☎02.33.65.31.53
Closed *Wed evening; Sat lunchtime; Sun; public holidays; during Aug.* **Disabled access.**

The jazzy retro décor works well in this excellent place, and the attentive staff make you feel welcome. Menus €19.50–34 feature cooking that is as imaginative as the surroundings, with dishes such as salmon with Camembert cream sauce, salad with warm *andouille* and *pommeau caramel,* fresh pan-fried prawns with star anise, finely chopped beef *tartare* – good enough to make Japanese customers forget their sushi. And good desserts: pistachio macaroon with red fruits, *panna cotta* with *coulis* and exotic fruits, smooth Saint-Dominique chocolate fondant. Good selection of wines at reasonable prices, and interesting coffees from Costa Rica, Ethiopia and Guatemala.

Ferrière-aux-Étangs (La)
61450 (10km S)

◎ |●| Auberge de la Mine

Le Gué-Plat; in a large village halfway

16

between Flers and La Ferté-Macé, on the northwest edge of the Andaines forest; from Flers go to La Ferrière; then take the Domfront road, turning left after about 1.5km; it's well signposted.
℡02.33.66.91.10
Closed *Sun evening; Tues; Wed; first 3 weeks in Jan; 3 weeks end Aug/early Sept.* **Disabled access. High chairs available. Car park.**

Apparently this large ivy-covered brick house was once a miners' canteen – as the nearby slag heaps attest. But times have moved on and this delightful little place with its stylish décor and cheerful, friendly staff is now a chic, intimate restaurant and one of the best in the area. An ideal spot for an evening meal in intimate surroundings where you can enjoy quality, regional produce prepared with delicacy and creativity starting with the weekday menus, €19 and €24, others €27–50. There's also a children's menu for €12. The chef is an artist and his dishes are as beautiful to look at as they are delicious to eat: foie gras with *pommeau*, *crépinette* of *andouille de Vire*, an excellent cheese board, interesting desserts including an almond ice cream with drizzled chocolate.

Goupillères
14210

⊛ |●| **Auberge du Pont de Brie****

La Halte de Grimbosq.
℡02.31.79.37.24
Closed *Mon; Tues; Sun evening (1 Oct–30 March); Mon–Fri during Nov and Dec; 15 Dec–8 Feb.* **High chairs and games available. Car park.**

A restaurant with a classic décor standing all alone in the middle of some beautiful countryside. Menus €17.50–32.50 feature authentic Normandy cuisine, including chicken (thighs) *jambonette* with apple fondue and fillet of bass with cider butter. For dessert we have fond memories of the treble-scented stewed apple. Impeccable service and a very friendly welcome combine to make this a good place to eat and a good starting point for visiting Swiss Normandy, beginning with the Grimbosq forest. It holds the Normandy Quality Tourism certificate.

Gouvets
50420

⊛ 🍴 |●| **Restaurant Les Bruyères**

It's on the RN175 (the main Villedieu-les-Poêles – Caen road); can also be reached without leaving the A84, via the Vallée de la Vire services (access is situated behind the *Shell* service station).
℡02.33.51.69.82
Closed *Sun.* **Open** *lunchtimes and evenings (July–Aug); lunchtimes plus Fri and Sat evenings (Sept–June).* **Disabled access. Car park.**

A fairly new building sitting by the side of the road. It's not especially attractive from the outside, but the welcome, the springtime décor and the value for money make it worth stopping. The chef changes the dishes on the menu every week to take account of the fresh produce or the fish that's been landed. The array of pastries is immensely tempting and wickedly good. The first menu costs €11 and is served weekdays and on Friday evenings; other menus go for €13, €17 and €22. *Free coffee offered to our readers on presentation of this guide.*

Granville
50400

⊛ 🏠 🍴 **Le Michelet****

5 rue Jules-Michelet; it's on the seashore, near the thalassotherapy centre.
℡02.33.50.06.55 ⑫02.33.50.12.25
TV. Car park.

In a fairly elevated position in a quiet street very close to the town centre stands a small, family hotel in an old house with a certain charm. The rooms are simple, bright and pleasantly refurbished; doubles €29–30 with basin, €35–48 with shower/wc or bath. Some of the rooms face the city centre and the sea and have balconies or terraces. *10% discount on the room rate (for a minimum of two consecutive nights, outside school holidays) offered to our readers on presentation of this guide.*

⊛ 🍴 |●| **Restaurant Le Phare**

11 rue du Port; it's on the harbour.
℡02.33.50.12.94
Closed *Tues; Wed out of season; 20 Dec–10 Jan.* **Disabled access. High chairs available.**

The panoramic view from the first-floor dining room of the harbour with its fishing boats and yachts is splendid, and the fish market, just footsteps away, supplies the restaurant with ultra-fresh seafood. Reliable cuisine that goes straight to the heart of local produce: seafood stew, stuffed pollock with lobster butter sauce, excellent seafood platters. The cheapest menu costs €12 (not served weekends): it includes *moules marinières* or nine oysters with a jug of wine. If you're feeling hungry – and flush – go for the huge €59 menu, which includes lobster. Plenty of regulars eat here, the service is friendly (even for non-regulars) and really efficient. *Free Kir offered to our readers on presentation of this guide.*

Champeaux

50530 (15km S)

◎ 🎋 🛎 |◐| Hôtel Les Hermelles – Restaurant Au Marquis de Tombelaine

25 rte. des Falaises; take the D911 that runs along the Channel coast between Carolles and Saint-Jean-le-Thomas.
☎02.33.61.85.94 ℻02.33.61.21.52
⊛www.marquisdetombelaine.com
Closed *Tues evening and Wed (except July–Aug); Jan; 10 days at the end of Nov.* **Disabled access. TV. High chairs available. Car park.**

You'll find this lively hotel atop the Champeaux cliffs and across the bay from Mont-Saint-Michel. Magnificent panoramic view, which, from the windows of room nos. 2, 4 and 5, is enough to forget the rather dated décor of what are nevertheless comfortable rooms – doubles with shower/wc €48–54. The restaurant is across the road and the intimate dining room is a successful combination of stonework, panelling and beams. The chef is a disciple of Auge Escoffier, the classic French cook, so the dishes on the menus (€20–49) are rich: fillet of cod with hot *andouille*, warm oysters cooked in cider, bass *feuillantine* (in a light pastry) and foie gras with apple. *Free house apéritif offered to our readers on presentation of this guide.*

Honfleur

14600

◎ 🛎 🎋 Motel Monet**

Charrière du Puits; on the Côte de Grâce.
☎02.31.89.00.90 ℻02.31.89.97.16
⊛www.motelhotel.fr

Closed *Dec–Feb.* **TV. Disabled access. Cots available. Car park.**

In a lush, romantic setting on the heights of Honfleur, on the Côte de Grâce, this small family hotel offers ten pretty, independent and comfortable rooms. All the bathrooms have been refurbished recently and doubles go for €57–70 with shower/wc or bath; breakfast €6. The owners, who are vintage-car enthusiasts, are sure to give you a warm welcome. Awarded the Normandy Quality Tourism certificate. *One free breakfast (on the third consecutive night) offered to our readers on presentation of this guide.*

◎ 🛎 Hôtel du Dauphin**

10 pl. Pierre-Berthelot; near the Church of Sainte-Catherine.
☎02.31.89.15.53 ℻02.31.89.92.06
⊛www.hotel-du-dauphin.com
Reception open *until 10pm.* **TV. High chairs available.**

A small hotel set in a seventeenth-century house with the half-timbered façade typical of Honfleur. Some rooms (with Jacuzzi) are in the house itself; the rest are in an annexe, offering a pretty view of the church. Doubles with shower or bath and wc cost €61–124; breakfast €6.90.

◎ 🛎 🎋 Hôtel du Cheval Blanc***

2 quai des Passagers; on the old dock.
☎02.31.81.65.00 ℻02.31.89.52.80
⊛www.hotel-honfleur.com
Closed *Jan.* **TV.**

A building dating from the fifteenth century in a wonderful location, extending along the harbour, opposite the Lieutenance. Most of the rooms overlook the port and cost €70–230 for a double with shower/wc or bath; also two suites €300–425, depending on the season. According to the time of year and the availability, it is possible to negotiate the price with the owner and choose your own room – she will happily show them to you. There's a pay car park nearby. Awarded the Normandy Quality Tourism certificate. *One free breakfast per person offered to our readers on presentation of this guide.*

◎ 🛎 Hôtel des Loges***

18 rue Brûlée; close to the Church of Sainte-Catherine.
☎02.31.89.38.26 ℻02.31.89.42.79
⊛www.hoteldesloges.com

Disabled access. TV. High chairs and cots available.

A veritable love nest in a picturesque alley close to the church of Sainte-Catherine. It has recently been refurbished. The owner worked in the cinema as a young woman and has since unleashed her dramatic instincts on the décor, while not neglecting the standards of modern comfort. She is more than willing to share her passion with you, and if you see something you like she will even sell it to you. If it's not available, it will be ordered for you. Rooms with shower/wc or bath go for €10–135, according to size and the season; breakfast €10. A place to remember – awarded the Normandy Quality Tourism certificate and the Tourism and Disability certificate.

⊚ ⅍ |●| La Tortue

36 rue de l'Homme-de-Bois; it's near the church of Sainte-Catherine.
☎02.31.89.04.93
ⓦwww.latortue.net
Closed *Mon evening and Tues out of season.*

This is a friendly place – though when they get busy at the weekend the welcome and the speed of service suffer. Other than that, this is an excellent restaurant offering a range of menus €16–30; also a vegetarian one at €12 and a children's menu at €7. Pretty dining room and traditional cuisine: pan-fried foie gras on a bed of spinach in a cider vinegar *jus*, fillets of seabass in a *tapenade*, slivers of duck in port, apple turnover with caramel sauce. *Free coffee offered to our readers on presentation of this guide.*

⊚ |●| Le Bouillon Normand

7 rue de la Ville; on the place Arthur-Boudin, behind the Saint-Étienne quay.
☎02.31.89.02.41
Closed *Wed; Sun evening; end Dec to end Jan.* **Children's comics and games available.**

This old yellow, wood-lined bistro reflects the traditional food on offer on menus €16–23: foie gras salad with smoked salt, fisherman's pot with cider, Camembert crunch. One small detail: here you add salt and pepper to your own taste. You can eat on the terrace or in the delightful, recently refurbished dining room and enjoy the cheerful, relaxed service.

⊚ |●| Au P'tit Mareyeur

4 rue Haute.
☎02.31.98.84.23

Closed *Mon; Tues; Jan.* **Disabled access.**

Inviting restaurant with stylish, chic décor, without being pompous; the stone, half-timbering, greenery and fabrics combine to perfection. The chef, Julien Domin, already a seasoned professional at the age of 26, regularly changes his menus and creates a culinary festival that is a pleasure to both the eyes and stomach: marinated smoked salmon with lentils, fried mullet fillets with *pistou* sauce and *bouillabaisse honfleuraise*. There's a set menu based on selected à la carte dishes at €20; or reckon on €24 à la carte. If you are not satisfied, don't hesitate to tell the chef, as he will really value your opinion. Fast, cheerful service; consider booking in season, as the dining room is not very big.

Houlgate
14510

⊚ 🏠 ⅍ Santa Cecilia**

25 allées des Alliés; it's 100m from the beach between the rue des Bains and the route des Belges.
☎02.31.28.71.71 ☎02.31.28.51.73
ⓦwww.hotel-santa-cecilia.com
TV. Swing.

On the stairs of this picturesque 1880 seaside house it feels as if you might come across gentlemen wearing stripey bathing suits and handlebar moustaches. The rooms share the same timeless, or even priceless, quality with doubles priced at €55–64 with shower/wc or bath; breakfast €6.70. *Free coffee offered to our readers on presentation of this guide.*

Lisieux
14100

⊚ 🏠 |●| ⅍ La Coupe d'Or**

49 rue Pont-Mortain; near the André Malraux multimedia library.
☎02.31.31.16.84 ☎02.31.31.35.60
ⓦwww.la-coupe-d-or.com
Closed *Fri; Sun evening; Feb school holiday.*
TV. High chairs, cots and changing tables available.

A convivial, well-run hotel in the heart of this often pilgrim-filled town offering a pleasant, friendly welcome. The rooms are clean, simple and comfortable, with classic décor; some have recently been refurbished (with computer sockets) and go for €52–57 for a double with shower/wc. Breakfast costs €6.50; half board is €54–57 per person. The cooking is reliable, with seafood-based dishes such as *andouille* and crayfish in *beurre blanc*, fillet of turbot, and regional specialities including *vallée d'Auge* calves' kidneys and iced soufflé with Calvados. There's a weekday lunch menu for €11 and others up to €32. Logis de France. *Free house apéritif offered to our readers on presentation of this guide.*

⍟ ♨ ᴣᴕ Azur Hôtel***

15 rue au Char.
☎02.31.62.09.14 ⊕02.31.62.16.06
ⓦwww.azur-hotel.com
TV.

A bright, fresh three-star hotel with pleasant, clean, well-equipped rooms; doubles €60–85 with shower/wc or bath. The breakfast room is very pretty; breakfast €8.40. Pleasant welcome. *One free breakfast offered per room to our readers on presentation of this guide.*

⍟ |❶| ᴣᴕ Restaurant Aux Acacias

13 rue de la Résistance.
☎02.31.62.10.95
Closed *Sun evening and Mon (except for public holidays); Thurs out of season; holiday dates still to be fixed.*

An appealing, centrally located restaurant with a cosy décor – spring colours, vases of dried flowers and little ornaments. It's fresh and pleasant, just like the cooking: finely seasoned roast bass, beef fillet pan-fried with truffle *jus*, pan-fried apples in half-salt butter, vanilla ice cream – just a few examples of the tasty, innovative dishes on offer here. Menus range from €15.50 (not served Saturday evening or public holidays) to €45, and the efficient service comes with a smile. The children's menu costs €8.50 and a meal à la carte will set you back about €40. *Free coffee offered to our readers on presentation of this guide.*

Mont-Saint-Michel (Le)

50170

⍟ ♨ |❶| Hôtel Du Guesclin**

Grande-Rue; it's one of the first hotels you come to as you climb the main street.
☎02.33.60.14.10 ⊕02.33.60.45.81
⊛hotelduguesclin@wanadoo.fr
Closed *Tues evening; Wed out of season; early Nov to end March.* **TV. High chairs available.**

A well-maintained hotel offering reasonable value for money when you compare it to the local competition. Comfortable, very clean doubles, some of which have been refurbished, go for €60–85 with shower/wc or bath; rooms 14, 15 and 17 have a sea view. There are two dining rooms; if you want quick service and *formules* for €9.50–11, head for the brasserie downstairs. Upstairs you get a breathtaking view over the bay, and they serve classic regional and fish dishes on set menus €17.50–35. The only drawback is that the service and welcome are sometimes rather slow here, too.

Beauvoir

50170 (4km S)

⍟ ᴣᴕ ♨ Hôtel Le Gué de Beauvoir*

5 rte. de Pontorson.
☎02.33.60.09.23
Closed *1 Oct to Easter.* **Car park.**

This place is in complete contrast to the dull hotels that proliferate around here. A small, one-star hotel in a not unattractive old house set back behind a scrap of garden. A relaxed welcome, a café-style veranda where you can eat breakfast and simple rooms which, like the rest of the house, have a certain old-fashioned charm. Rooms go for €33 with basin and €42–45 with shower/wc or bath. *10% discount on the room rate (Easter to 31 May) offered to our readers on presentation of this guide.*

Pontorson

50170 (9km S)

⍟ ᴣᴕ ♨ |❶| Hôtel-restaurant Le Bretagne**

59 rue Couesnon; it's on the main street, in the centre of town on the D976 heading towards Rennes.
☎02.33.60.10.55 ⊕02.33.58.20.54
ⓦwww.lebretagnepontorson.com
Closed *Sun evening to Tues lunchtime, out of season; 5 Jan–10 Feb.* **Hotel open** *every day during the season.* **Disabled access. TV. High chairs available.**

A lovely eighteenth-century coaching inn where you'll be welcomed warmly. The rooms are all very pleasant, most are spacious and some have traditional furnishings. Doubles cost €39–64 with shower/

wc or bath. In the restaurant the dishes are prepared with care: potted mackerel with cucumber *coulis*, *millefeuille* of *andouille* with two varieties of apple, pear shortbread with Normandy caramel sauce. There's a choice of menus €14.50–38 offering excellent value for money in every respect. *Free house apéritif offered to our readers on presentation of this guide.*

⚓ 🏠 |◉| Hôtel Montgomery**

13 rue Couesnon.
☎02.33.60.00.09 ℻02.33.60.37.66
🕸www.hotel-montgomery.com
Closed one day a week. 13–24 Feb; 14–25 Nov. **Restaurant open** evenings (for hotel guests only). **TV. Pay car park.**

A sober but elegant building dating from 1526, granite-built like so many in this area. This sixteenth-century house was the seat of Gabriel de Montgomery who, in 1559, slayed King Henri II (though not on purpose it seems). The interior has been renovated with some degree of concern for the historical character of the place. The superb sixteenth-century staircase takes you back in time as you ascend to the rooms, which are all different. Doubles with bath or shower/wc go for €60–93 depending on the season; de-luxe rooms with massage bath are €150–250 depending on the season. Some (the best and most expensive) are in keeping with the spirit of the house; these include the Grand Gabriel room with its carved canopy and Renaissance ceilings and the honeymoon suite; others are more modern but all rooms offer every comfort and convenience. There is a pleasant courtyard-garden to the rear. The restaurant is exclusively open to hotel guests and serves dinner only, €15–25.

Servon
50170 (10km SE)

⚓ 🏠 |◉| Auberge du Terroir**

It's on the road from Pontaubault to Pontorson; take the D107.
☎02.33.60.17.92 ℻02.33.60.35.26
✉aubergeduterroir@wanadoo.fr
Closed Wed; Sat lunchtime; Feb school holiday; mid-Nov to early Dec. **Disabled access. TV. High chairs and cots available. Car park.**

A charming hotel with pretty grounds in a tranquil village – the friendly young owners have created a peaceful, tasteful atmosphere. Three rooms in the old presbytery have been attractively refurbished and they're named after famous musicians and composers. The three lovely doubles in the old village school all have shower/wc and are named after flowers; €54–58 with shower/wc or bath. The chef serves wonderful Périgord specialities in the pleasant dining room on menus €18–40: semi-cooked foie gras and breast of duck with honey, along with wild bass with parsley, salmon with green cabbage and monkfish with vanilla. There's a pretty garden and a tennis court. Booking is essential.

Mortagne-au-Perche
61400

⚓ 🎋 🏠 |◉| Hôtel du Tribunal**

4 pl. du Palais.
☎02.33.25.04.77 ℻02.33.83.60.83
Open all year. **TV. Disabled access. High chairs available.**

The oldest parts of this handsome, traditional Percheron house date from the thirteenth century, though most of it is younger than that. The square and the façade have hardly changed since the end of the nineteenth century, when the inn was called "John who laughs, John who weeps", perhaps in reference to the fate of those processed by the law courts which stood next door. Yves Montand stayed here while filming *IP5*. Doubles €48–100, according to the facilities; some rooms have a Jacuzzi, terrace or view of the courtyard garden and the old town of Mortagne. There's a lovely annexe at the back where the rooms are even quieter. The food is very good and menus, €19–35, list dishes such as *croustillant* of black pudding, calf sweetbreads Normandy style, fine apple tart. This is a delightful, quite chic place where the welcome is warm. *Free house apéritif offered to our readers on presentation of this guide.*

Longny-au-Perche
61290 (18km E)

⚓ |◉| 🎋 Le Moulin de la Fenderie

Route de Bizou; from Mortagne, take the D8 through the forest of Rénovaldieu.

☎02.33.83.66.98
Closed *Mon and Tues in summer; Sun evening to Wed lunch from Oct onwards; mid-Jan to mid-Feb.* **Disabled access. Car park.**

A restaurant housed in a superb watermill which has been patiently restored by the two owners. It's a delightful place, and all the more pleasant on fine days when you can eat on the terrace by the water's edge. Menus €26–49 include langoustines, foie gras, monkfish and turbot. It's best to reserve. *Free apéritif offered to our readers on presentation of this guide.*

Ouistreham-Riva-Bella

14150

◉ 🏠 |●| Hôtel-restaurant Le Normandie – Le Chalut**

71 and 100 av. Michel-Cabieu; it's near the harbour.
☎02.31.97.19.57 ☎02.31.97.20.07
🌐www.lenormandie.com
Closed *Sun evening and Mon from Nov to March; 20 Dec–15 Jan.* **TV. Car park.**

Two classic, and slightly old-fashioned, hotels opposite each other. Doubles cost €58–70 with shower/wc or bath according to the season and breakfast is €9; some of the bathrooms could do with updating. You'll find wonderful food on the menus €21–59, such as the *millefeuille* of langoustines with sesame seeds, in the magnificent, yellow and blue dining room. Awarded the Normandy Quality Tourism certificate – the service can be a tad uptight, though.

◉ |●| Restaurant Le Métropolitain

1 rte. de Lion; it's near the post office and the library, heading towards Ouistreham-bourg.
☎02.31.97.18.61
Closed *Mon evening and Tues from Oct to April; a week end Jan; a week end Nov.* **Car park**

Decorated to look like a 1930s Parisian métro station, but the set menus – €10.67 (weekdays) up to €24.50, children's menu €7 – and à la carte dishes soon bring you back to the Normandy coast: grilled turbot with *fleur de sel*, *pavé* of fresh cod with cider, etc.

Bénouville

14970 (5km S)

◉ 🏠 |●| Hôtel-restaurant La Glycine**

11 pl. du Commando no.4.
☎02.31.44.61.94 ☎02.31.43.67.30
Closed *Sun evening out of season; 20 Dec–15 Jan.* **Disabled access. TV. Car park.**

This is a beautiful stone building covered in wisteria. The modern, functional rooms have been refurbished recently; doubles with shower/wc or bath go for €58; breakfast is €7.50. Same style of décor in the restaurant (the round tables are a plus), but forget the "aesthetic" touches, you're here for the food. The young chef is in a class of his own and produces dishes such as lobster in coral sauce, seafood *gratin*, fillet of sole and pan-fried foie gras in balsamic vinegar on menus €24–42. Logis de France.

Colleville-Montgomery

14880 (5km W)

◉ 🎋 |●| Restaurant La Ferme Saint-Hubert

3 rue de la Mer; take the D35A.
☎02.31.96.35.41
Closed *Sun evening and Mon, except in season and on public holidays; 24 Dec–15 Jan.* **Disabled access. High chairs available. Car park.**

A large Normandy house where you can lunch either in the cosy rustic dining room or the bright conservatory. Generous portions of well-executed local food on the weekday lunch menu €17, with others up to €45: duck foie gras or lemon sole with cider. There's also game in season. *Free coffee offered to our readers on presentation of this guide.*

Pont-L'Évêque

14130

◉ 🏠 Hôtel de France

1 rue de Geôle.
☎02.31.64.30.44 ☎02.31.64.98.90
Closed *Sun evening from early Nov to end Jan; Feb; Christmas.* **TV.**

A small hotel in a quiet street close to the town centre. The rooms have all been refurbished, each with its own personality, but retaining their charm and country style; discreetly flowery wallpaper, 1940s furniture. Some even have a view over fields of grazing cows. Doubles with basin go for €30 or up to €45 with shower/wc or bath. No pets.

@ |●| 🍴 Auberge de la Touques

Place de l'Église; it's 1km from the autoroute exit, behind the church, in the town centre.
℡02.31.64.01.69
Closed *Mon lunchtime and Tues (except in Aug); Jan; Dec.* **Car park.**

This is a handsome Normandy building on the bank of the Touques river near the village church. The chef prepares all the Norman classics: veal cutlet *à la normande*, tripe *à la mode de Caen*, caramelized apple mousse. Menus go for €22 and €32.50, and the service is pleasant and attentive. You can expect to pay about €44 à la carte. *Free glass of Calvados offered to our readers on presentation of this guide.*

@ 🍴 |●| Auberge de l'Aigle d'Or

68 rue de Vaucelles.
℡02.31.65.05.25
Closed *Tues evening, Wed and Sun evenings (11 Nov to Easter); Feb school holiday; last week in June.*

A beautiful old staging post dating from 1520, complete with stained-glass windows and half-timbering, so there's no shortage of atmosphere. Highly accomplished, classic Norman bourgeois cooking, with a few dishes that are hard to find these days: fattened, farm-raised chicken cooked in the style of the Auge country, roast pigeon with foie gras and Sauternes sauce. The prices are pretty high, but this is one of the best restaurants in the whole of Normandy; you might even bump into a few film stars on a visit to the sticks, taking a break from their partying in Deauville. Menus start at €26 (not Sat evening) and go up to €47; reckon on €60 à la carte. *Free coffee offered to our readers on presentation of this guide.*

Drubec

14130 (8km SW)

@ |●| La Haie Tondue

Take exit 29A off the A13, then the D58 and it's 2km south of Beaumont-en-Auge at the N175 junction.
℡02.31.64.85.00

Closed *Mon evening except in Aug; Tues; 3 weeks in Jan; a week at end of June; a week in Oct.* **High chairs available. Car park.**

This restaurant, in a beautiful old house covered in vines, offers very good food at reasonable prices. The setting is most agreeable, the service is faultless and there's a good wine list. As for the cuisine, it's perfectly prepared, even on the cheapest of the menus (€21) and offers fish and country style terrines, with other menus up to €38 and a children's menu for €11. Menus change each month but are likely to include snail *gratin* or pan-fried crayfish.

Saint-Lô

50000

@ 🏠 Armoric Hôtel*

15 rue de la Marne; it's two minutes from the centre.
℡02.33.05.61.32 ℡02.33.05.12.68
TV. Car park.

Set away from the traffic in a small, terraced, 1950s building behind a small garden. There's an old-fashioned family boarding house feel to this place and the welcome may seem a little grudging when you first arrive. All the rooms are different, with a slightly retro décor (which in fact is rather charming) and a modern degree of comfort. Doubles are €31 with basin, €38 with shower/wc, and they have two rooms at €49 with spa bath. If you've had a tiring journey, you'll love nos. 16 and 21 which have a whirlpool bath. Even considering the rather frugal breakfast and the fact that some rooms (those on the ground floor in particular) are not very big, it offers very good value for money. Booking is recommended.

@ 🍴 |●| Le Péché Mignon

84 rue du Maréchal-Juin; go towards Bayeux. It's well away from the town centre.
℡02.33.72.23.77 ℡02.33.72.27.58
Closed *Mon; Sat lunchtime; Sun evening; 20 July–10 Aug.* **Disabled access.**

The service in this comfortable restaurant is impeccable and the food is marvellous – top-class gourmet cuisine prepared by a talented young chef. A subdued, contemporary setting that can seem a little gloomy (refurbishment work is planned). You will be overwhelmed by the palate fresheners between dishes (it's enough to make you feel like a VIP). The chef brings an inventive, personal touch to his work, marrying local produce with more contemporary flavours. Why can't life be like this every day? There's a lunchtime *formule* at €14.50 and menus at €21.50 and €28.50. *Free house apéritif offered to our readers on presentation of this guide.*

⊚ |●| Le Bistrot de Paul et Roger

42 rue du Neubourg; it's halfway between the town hall and the church of Sainte-Croix.
☏02.33.57.19.00
Closed Sun. **Disabled access. High chairs available.**

While the checkered tablecloths go out on the terrace at daybreak it would be a pity not to take a peep inside. There you'll find an improbable 1900 décor with enough bric-à-brac to turn an antique dealer green with envy... The atmosphere is very congenial and the kitchen exudes a smell of good, seasonal produce and a love for the art of cooking; menus €11.50 and €12.50, or reckon on €20 for à la carte. There are homely dishes and bistro-style meals including 'catch of the day', as well as superb home-made desserts. Everything is simple but good, with super-fast service (with a smile) and a pleasantly presented bill. All in all – a good place to eat.

Saint-Vaast-la-Hougue
50550

⊚ 🛏 |●| Hôtel de France – Restaurant Les Fuchsias**

20 rue du Maréchal-Foch; it's less than two minutes from the harbour.
☏02.33.54.42.26 ℻02.33.43.46.79
🖷www.france-fuchsias.com
Hotel closed Mon and Tues lunchtime, except in July–Aug; Tues in March; Nov–Dec. **TV. High chairs available.**

Most of the pretty rooms (the most expensive ones) overlook an idyllic little garden. Double rooms are €41 with basin, €51–60 with shower/wc, €72–100 with bath; half board, requested in July and August, costs €51–80 per person. This old staging post has plenty to offer in the way of charm but the atmosphere is rather well-mannered and conventional (hence a welcome that can seem somewhat reserved). The restaurant, which has a veranda also looking out

on to the garden, offers good food in the grand tradition, including excellent seafood. The produce couldn't be fresher – the chef sources it from the family farm, just like in the old days. There's a weekday lunchtime menu at €17.50, and others €25–44. Logis de France.

Quettehou
50630 (3km W)

⊚ |●| Auberge de Ket'Hou

17 rue du Général-de-Gaulle; take the D1.
☏02.33.54.40.23
Closed Sun evening and Mon (except public holidays, in which case closed Tues); generally in Jan.

A small establishment that (given the quality of its food) could justifiably print "gastronomic" on its business cards but prefers to take a more discreet approach. The small, simply decorated dining room offers a very pleasant welcome and service. And excellent food (as we mentioned earlier) based on what's good in the market and prepared with great skill and inventiveness, which is exactly as it should be. There are some interesting variations using local produce (like the snails in a Camembert cream sauce) and an expertise that follows through to the dessert. The cheapest menu, €14, is served on weekday lunchtimes, other menus €17.50–36.50.

Sées
61500

⊚ 🎭 🛏 The Garden Hôtel**

12 bis rue des Ardrillers; it's 400m from the cathedral, hidden behind a courtyard.
☏02.33.27.98.27 ℻02.33.28.90.07
Closed Sun lunchtime to Mon morning in winter. **TV. Cots available. Car park.**

An old favourite for many years and one that still produces the goods. The house with its façade eaten away by ivy has plenty of character. Once an orphanage and then a hotel, it gets its English name from the previous owner who was Australian. It couldn't be more peaceful and there's no danger of the sisters in the adjoining Sainte-Famille convent kicking up a storm. As a mark of respect, none of the rooms looks onto it; they overlook a flower garden instead. The rooms are unpretentious, most of them refurbished and decorated with care, though each in a different style (no. 12A, for example, is more traditional than no. 14 with its mauve décor). This place represents excellent value for money and offers an attentive and pleasant welcome. Doubles go for €26 with basin and wc, and up to €40 with bath; breakfast €5. In keeping with the spiritual atmosphere, there's an amusing collection of religious knick-knacks. Dogs are allowed: €4, all of which is donated to the French RSPCA. *10% discount on the room rate offered to our readers on presentation of this guide.*

Macé
61500 (5km N)

◎ 🎿 🛏 |◎| L'Île de Sées**

Head for Macé; it's well signposted.
☎02.33.27.98.65 ℻02.33.28.41.22
🌐www.ile-sees.fr
Closed *Sun evening; Mon; end Oct to end Feb.* **TV. High chairs available. Car park.**

This hotel and restaurant has been renovated and its original colour and spirit restored: the dining room with its pink and red décor and little bunches of flowers on the tables continues to offer customers a warm welcome. Out in the country, off the beaten track, this hotel was chosen by the *US Postal* cycling team to prepare for the Orne stage of the Tour de France in 2002. Check out the visitors' book – Lance Armstrong was here and ate at the table at the back. The ivy-clad building is impressive with its gardens and terrace. It's a shame some of the rooms at the rear lack old-fashioned charm – but they are still very peaceful. Doubles are €53–62 with shower/wc or bath; breakfast €8. The weekday lunch menu €16, and other menus €23–34, feature good, local cooking: excellent tripe, home-made duck foie gras and side of beef with Camembert … *Free coffee offered to our readers on presentation of this guide.*

Trouville-sur-Mer
14360

◎ 🛏 La Maison Normande**

4 pl. de Lattre de Tassigny; very close to the centre.
☎02.31.88.12.25 ℻02.31.88.78.79
🌐www.maisonnormande.com
TV. Cots available.

In a quiet corner of the centre of town, this

Norman half-timbered house is fronted by carved stone columns. You'll receive a terrific welcome and experience the charm of the place from the lobby itself which was created by combining two small shops. The rooms have been refurbished in keeping with the charming ambience; doubles €36–62 depending upon facilities and the season, breakfast €6.50. They are very British in style, subtly outmoded but very clean and genuinely appealing.

◎ 🛏 Les Sablettes**

15 rue Paul-Besson; it's near the casino and the beach.
☎02.31.88.10.66 ℻02.31.88.59.06
🌐www.trouville-hotel.com
Closed *Jan.* **TV.**

The frontage of this place is perfect and the hotel itself is as pretty as can be. It has a very cosy atmosphere, almost like a guesthouse, with a comfortable lounge and a lovely old wooden staircase. The whole place is sparklingly clean and good value for money for Trouville. Recently renovated doubles go for €40–55 with shower/wc, €50–62 with bath; breakfast €6.

◎ |◎| Le Bistrot sur le Quai

68 bd. Fernand-Moureaux; near the tourist office.
☎02.31.81.28.85
Closed *Wed; 15 Dec–1 Feb.*

This bistro is always full, even out of season – a really convivial place that we recommend without hesitation. For this, all credit is due to the effusive welcome of the Finnish owner and the delicious house specialities: prawns grilled with garlic, flambéed shrimps with aniseed, *court-bouillon* of three fish, etc. There's a choice of menus at €12–27, or you can expect to pay €30 à la carte.

◎ |◎| Restaurant Les Mouettes

11 rue des Bains; close to the fish market.
☎02.31.98.06.97
Disabled access. High chairs available.

This place is a cosier annexe to *Le Central* brasserie and offers a warm welcome. The décor is reminiscent of a Parisian bistro and, for sunny days, there are two pleasant terraces on the pedestrianized street. Menus, €13–25.50, feature lots of seafood and the dishes on the board include salmon with Chavignol cheese and fish (and sauerkraut) stew. There's even a children's menu for €8. The writer Marguerite Duras liked to eat here.

◎ |●| Les Vapeurs

160 bd. Fernand-Moureaux; it's next to the town hall, opposite the fish market.
☎02.31.88.15.24
Open *11am–1pm.* **Disabled access. High chairs available.**

This, the best-known brasserie in Trouville, opened in 1927. All the actors who come to the Deauville film festival eat here, and it's always packed. Try the house specialities – steamed local mussels with cream and freshly cooked prawns. Everything is fresh as can be; after all, the fishing boats land their catch only ten minutes away. The tripe's particularly good, too, especially with a nice glass of Saumur. Expect to pay about €25–35 à la carte. You'll have to book at the weekend unless you get here by 11am and down a few oysters and a glass of Muscadet.

◎ |●| Restaurant La Petite Auberge

7 rue Carnot; it's in a little street off place du Maréchal-Foch, in front of the casino.
☎02.31.88.11.07
Closed *Tues; Wed.* **Open** *every day in Aug.*

Without a doubt this little inn is typically Norman, both in its décor (a lot of copper and plates on the walls in a rather attractive setting) and its cooking. À la carte will set you back about €60, and the reasonably priced menus, €26–44, change frequently with the seasons. They list such dishes as seabass served with langoustines and charlotte of aubergines, foie gras with apple and celeriac in puff pastry. The service is efficient and the welcome is as you would expect of a place like this.

◎ |●| Bistrot Les Quatre Chats

8 rue d'Orléans.
☎02.31.88.94.94
Closed *Mon lunchtime; Tues; Wed; Thurs lunchtime; 15 Nov–15 Dec.* **Open** *noon–1pm and 7.30–9.30pm (11pm at weekends).*

This place may seem a little anachronistic in what is a rather typical part of town. The young owners have played host to a lot of Paris society in this bistro. If you need further convincing just check out the photo of TV presenter Karl Zéro, along with some of his colleagues, on their

business card. It's worth a look. As is the dining room with its faded old rose décor, filled with books, postcards, photos and newspapers. Seated around bistro tables you can enjoy classic dishes to which the chef has added one or two unexpected flavours, lifting them out of the ordinary. Purists will love the slow-cooked lamb or, more inventively, the prawns in soya and ginger. A special touch is the bread which is made on the premises and *grand cru* wine is available by the glass. There's a delightful mezzanine and cocktail bars. Expect to pay €40 for a meal à la carte.

Valognes
50700

◎ |●| ⌂ Grand Hôtel du Louvre**

28 rue des Religieuses.
☎02.33.40.00.07 ☎02.33.40.13.73
📧grand.hotel.du.louvre@wanadoo.fr
Restaurant closed *Sun evening and Mon (Oct–May); 15 Dec–15 Jan.* **TV. Pay car park.**

This hotel stands in the centre of a pleasant town in the Normandy bocage. An old seventeenth-century staging post, it has kept its character. You park in the cobbled courtyard, in the old coach house then climb up to your room by a handsome spiral staircase. Doubles go for €38.50 with washbasin, €44.50–55.50 with shower/wc or bath. Rooms on the first floor are retro, spacious and have a certain crazy charm, ideal for lovers and poets (the nineteenth-century French writer Barbey d'Aurevilly stayed at no. 4). Those on the second floor are more traditional but just as pleasant. There's a delightful little dining room, also in a retro style, serving excellent food with a rather more modern approach. Savour the relaxed and happy "family" ambience of this splendid place. Logis de France.

Vire
14500

◎ ⌂ |●| Hôtel de France**

4 rue d'Aignaux.
☎02.31.68.00.35 ☎02.31.68.22.65
Closed *20 Dec–20 Jan.* **Disabled access. TV. High chairs available. Pay car park**

Each room is differently styled (like it or not) and bright. Only the corridors are a bit gloomy. The hotel is situated at a crossroads and although it has efficient double-glazing it's best to ask for a room at the rear where the view over the little valleys wooded is really lovely. Doubles cost €38–58 with shower/wc or bath; half board, compulsory in high season, costs €42–44 per person and breakfast is €6.50. In the restaurant, which specializes in honest, classic cuisine, try the local *andouille*, which is made in Vire, or the veal cutlet Archiduc. Set menus cost €12–40; à la carte €32. Logis de France.

Saint-Germain-de-Taillevende
14500 (5km S)

|●| L'Auberge Saint-Germain

Place de l'Église; take the D577.
℡02.31.68.24.13 ℻02.31.68.89.57
✉le.castel.Normand@wanadoo.fr
Closed *Sun evening; Mon; end Jan to early Feb; 15–30 Sept.* **Disabled access.**

A pretty granite house, typical of the architectural style of the Virois marshes. The dining room is warm and welcoming with its low-slung beams and open fire and you'll experience smiling, speedy service. The chef puts a lot of local dishes on the menu such as upside-down tart of Vire *andouille* with cider cream. These are artfully prepared and offer good value for money: menus from €15 up to €30; à la carte €35. They open a small terrace out the front in summer.

Bény-Bocage (Le)
14350 (14.5km N)

Le Castel Normand**

Take the D577 Caen road for about 9km, then turn left onto the D56 for 2km. It's opposite the market place.
℡02.31.68.76.03 ℻02.31.68.63.58
🌐www.lecastelnormand.com
Closed *Mon; Tues.* **TV. Car park.**

Refined rustic décor and first-class service in a lovely stone building near the handsome covered market on the town square and the fountain. The cooking on the menus (€21–50) is full of flavour and the chef combines unusual ingredients to produce dishes that are in keeping with the establishment: Chartreuse of *andouille* in a *pommeau* sauce and larded burbot cutlets. If you want to linger, the rooms are as charming as the restaurant: doubles cost €50 with shower/wc or bath, breakfast €6.10. *10% discount on the room rate offered to our readers on presentation of this guide.*

16

BASSE-NORMANDIE

Haute-Normandie

Andelys (Les)

27700

◉ 🏠 |◉| Hôtel de Normandie**

1 rue Grande, Le Petit Andely; beside the Seine.
☎02.32.54.10.52 ℗02.32.54.25.84
🌐www.hotelnormandie-andelys.com
Closed *Wed evening; Thurs; Dec.* **Disabled access. TV. High chairs available. Car park.**

Run by the same family for several decades, this large hotel, in a traditional Normandy building, has a pretty garden on the banks of the Seine. It's a shame that some of the rooms (€55–60) are rather antiquated. On the same note, the soundproofing is not the best. Half board is preferred from March to November. You'll get a warm welcome and enjoy good cooking. There's a set menu in the week at €17.50; other menus €25–46, with dishes such as monkfish stew with Pommeau, calf sweetbreads from the Vallée d'Auge and other regional specialities, with a Calvados sorbet presented as a variation on the *trou normand* (a shot of Calvados served between courses). A well situated establishment with a country atmosphere.

◉ 🎋 🏠 |◉| Hôtel de Paris – Restaurant Le Castelet**

10 av. de la République; from the main square follow the signs to Le Petit Andely.
☎02.32.54.06.33 ℗02.32.54.65.92
🌐www.giverny.org/hotels/deparis/index.htm
Restaurant closed *Wed; Thurs lunchtimes.* **TV. High chairs and games available. Car park.**

A young, dynamic owner has taken over this small castle hotel with pointed roofs. Some evenings he plays his accordion or

hosts poetry readings. The rooms are very comfortable at the *Hôtel de Paris* and cost €58–68 for a double, depending on the level of comfort. Those overlooking the garden are quieter, though even the ones at the front don't get much traffic noise at night. The restaurant, *Le Castelet*, which has a huge terrace in summer, specializes in good regional cuisine with a classical note made with fresh ingredients. Menus start at €15 (weekday lunchtimes), with others €21–41. Ask to see the cells down in the basement where sadly, during the war, this establishment served the Gestapo. Logis de France. *Free house apéritif offered to our readers on presentation of this guide.*

◉ 🎋 🏠 |◉| Hôtel de la Chaîne d'Or***

Place St-Saveur; it's opposite the church on the banks of the Seine.
☎02.32.54.00.31 ℗02.32.54.05.68
🌐www.lachainedor.com
Restaurant closed *in high season, Mon lunchtime and Tues lunchtime; from 1 Nov to Easter, Sun evening to Tues lunchtime.* **Closed** *in Jan.* **TV. Car park.**

This solidly constructed hotel has a quiet riverside location. Built in 1751, it gets its name from the chain that once stretched from the riverbank to the nearby island. Anyone wishing to pass the chain had to pay a toll; it became known as the "Chaîne d'Or" because it made a fortune. The hotel is luxurious but the easy-going staff make you feel welcome. Doubles, €78–130, have all facilities; those overlooking the Seine are tastefully decorated and classically furnished, while others are more modern. You get a view of the barges on the river from the wonderful dining room where a fire is lit when it gets cold.

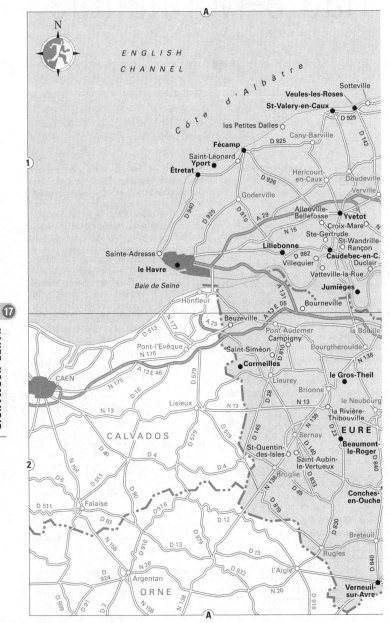

N

A

ENGLISH
CHANNEL

Côte d'Albâtre

Sotteville
Veules-les-Roses
St-Valery-en-Caux
D 925
D 142

les Petites Dalles
Cany-Barville
D 925

Fécamp
Saint-Léonard
Yport
Étretat

Héricourt-
en-Caux
Doudeville
Verville

D 926

Goderville
Allouville-
Bellefosse
Yvetot
D 910
A 29
Croix-Mare
N 15
Ste-Gertrude
St-Wandrille-
Rançon
Lillebonne
D 982
Caudebec-en-C.
Villequier
Duclair
Vatteville-la-Rue
Jumièges

Sainte-Adresse
le Havre
D 940
D 925

Baie de Seine

Honfleur
A 131
A 13 E 05
Bourneville
la Bouille

Beuzeville
Pont-Audemer
Campigny
Bourgtheroulde
N 138

D 513
N 177
A 29
D 810

Pont-l'Evêque
N 175
Saint-Siméon
Corneilles

CAEN
A 13 E 46
N 175
D 579
Lieurey
Brionne
le Gros-Theil
le Neubourg
N 138
la Rivière-
Thibouville
D 23

N 13
D 16
Lisieux
N 13
D 28
N 13
Bernay
E U R E
D 140
**Beaumont-
le-Roger**
D 840

CALVADOS
D 579
D 519
D 145
St-Quentin-
des-Isles
Saint-Aubin-
le-Vertueux
D 833
**Conches-
en-Ouche**

N 158
D 40
D 4
D 4
N 138
Broglie
D 49
D 819
D 830

D 6
D 511
D 90
Falaise
D 916
D 916
D 13
D 979
D 12
D 13
l'Aigle
Breteuil
D 840

D 63
N 158
Rugles

D 909
D 91
D 2
D 924
Argentan
N 138
N 158
N 26
D 932
N 26
D 918
**Verneuil-
sur-Avre**

O R N E

A

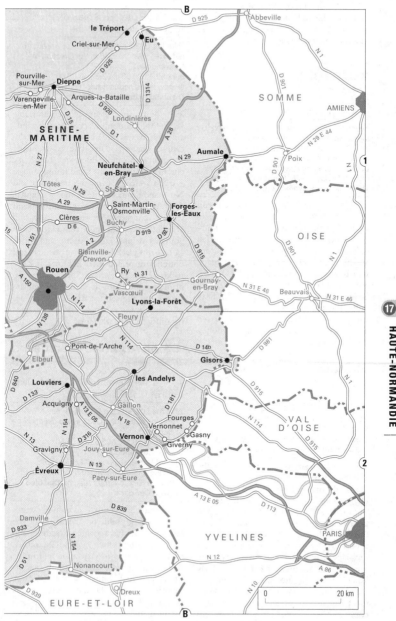

It's one of the best restaurants in this part of the world, serving generous menus at €29–58, featuring traditional and gastronomic cooking. *10% discount on the price of the room (from Nov to Easter) is offered to our readers on presentation of this guide.*

Aumale
76390

@ 🏠 |O| **La Villa des Houx****

Avenue du Général-de-Gaulle; take the N29, the street is opposite the station.
☎02.35.93.93.30 ⊕02.35.93.03.94
⊛www.lavilladeshoux.com
Closed *Sun evening and Mon lunchtime (15 Oct–15 March); 1–28 Jan.* **Disabled access. TV. High chairs available. Car park.**

In an Anglo-Norman house, this well-run three-star hotel has 22 rooms. Doubles €62–75 with bath/wc – one has a four-poster bed and costs a little more. Half board, €65–70 per person, is compulsory at the weekend. The stylish restaurant, which has a good view of the garden, lists attractive dishes on its weekday lunch menu €16; other menus at €23–32. Tasty dishes include duck foie gras with apricots and quail stuffed with foie gras and cooked in a salt crust. It's good value for money. Logis de France.

Beaumont-le-Roger
27170 (17km E)

@ 🎋 |O| **La Calèche**

54 rue Saint-Nicolas; take the D133.
☎02.32.45.25.99
Closed *Tues; Wed; 2 weeks in Jan; 3 weeks in July.* **High chairs available.**

The chef's creativity extends beyond the kitchen – when there's a festival or a holiday, he decorates the front of the building. His cooking revels in a host of influences, and includes dishes such as *andouille* in puff pastry with Livarot cheese sauce, house terrine with onion preserve, and house apple tart. There are a number of fish specialities, and all desserts are cooked on the premises. Menus start at €14 (weekday lunch), then €17 and €27. After the meal the chef invites you to turn the handle on the barrel organ. There's a friendly welcome and a convivial atmosphere at this place – well worth a visit. *Free house apéritif or coffee offered to our readers on presentation of this guide.*

Rivière-Thibouville (La)
27550 (9km NW)

@ 🏠 |O| **Hôtel Le Soleil d'Or et restaurant Le So'Café**

Take the D133 in the direction of Beaumont-le-Roger, then the D46 in the direction of Nassandres.
☎02.32.45.00.08 ⊕02.32.46.89.68
⊛www.domainedusoleildor.com
Disabled access.

The rooms are pleasant and comfortable (€52–90 for a double, according to standard) but it was the restaurant that really caught our eye. The style is decisively modern with simple lines, grey armchairs, curtains in violet velvet and lounge music – quite a change from the traditional old Normandy inn. The food, too, is original, with daring flavour combinations and texture contrasts between melting and crunchy. There are appetizing sandwiches, gourmet drinks, ethnic dishes and more. In fact this place is full of surprises. Menu options are priced €16–20; for à la carte reckon on €25, and on Sundays they do brunch from 11am at €22. The staff are young and the service friendly. There are weekend music events (world music, electro music, blues, jazz, etc).

Saint-Aubin-le-Vertueux
27300 (15km W)

@ 🎋 🏠 |O| **L'Hostellerie du Moulin Fouret**

Take the D25 and the D34 as far as Grandchain, then the D833 in the direction of Bernay.
☎02.32.43.19.95 ⊕02.32.45.55.50
⊛www.moulin-fouret.com
Closed *Sun evening and Mon (except July–Aug and during public holidays); Tues lunchtime (Oct to end of March).* **Disabled access. Car park.**

This sixteenth-century windmill stands in spacious grounds on the banks of the Charentonne. It's a gorgeous setting, and you can go fly-fishing nearby. The outside walls are covered in vegetation and inside there's an inviting dining room, exquisitely decorated, softly lit and with a large fireplace. François Deduit creates imaginative dishes and sauces using fresh local produce and offers very simple choices alongside more elaborate options with menus €30–60. You'll pay around €55 à la carte; specialities include hot *escalopes* of foie gras and hot oysters. The wine cellar is a credit to the owners with wines carefully selected by the chef, and the service is top-class. The rooms are quite simple, not too big and are mainly reserved for the restaurant's customers; double rooms €47 with shower/wc. There's a terrace for when the weather is fine, surrounded by the Charentonne, the park and its sheep. *10% discount on the room rate offered to our readers on presentation of this guide.*

Saint-Quentin-des-Isles
27270 (16km E)

ⓔ 🎿 |●| Restaurant La Pommeraie

It's on the N138 towards Broglie.
☎02.32.45.28.88
Closed *Sun evening; Mon; 10 days in Jan; first week of Aug.* **Disabled access. High chairs available.**

This long, low building, just set back from the road, has a Neoclassical façade and stylish décor throughout. The huge, bright dining room overlooks the pretty garden where you can watch the ducks splashing about in the pond – all very relaxing. Local dishes (pan-fried foie gras with redcurrants and other foie gras dishes), with some exotic accents, predominate on the menus, €14 (weekdays) and €27–46; reckon on about €50 for à la carte. *Free coffee is offered to our readers on presentation of this guide.*

Caudebec-en-Caux
76490

ⓔ 🎿 🏠 |●| Le Cheval Blanc*

4 pl. René-Coty; from the town hall on the banks of the Seine, go towards Saint-Arnoult-Lillebonne; place René-Coty is a few metres further on.
☎02.35.96.21.66 ☞02.35.95.35.40
ⓦwww.le-cheval-blanc.fr
Closed *Christmas to New Year.* **Restaurant closed** *Sun evening, except the day before public holidays.* **Open** *until 9pm.* **TV. Disabled access. High chairs available. Car park.**

Friendly staff, tasty cooking and attractive décor are all part of the attraction. Pretty, comfortable double rooms (three have just been completely refurbished) go from €50 up to €53 with shower/wc or bath. Regional dishes are served in the restaurant where the speciality is tripe

with Calvados. There's a weekday menu at €15 then others €22.50–34. In the week there are huge salads with dessert and coffee for €9–15. Secure parking is available for bikes. Logis de France. *10% discount on the room rate (minimum of two consecutive nights, except in July–Aug) offered to our readers on presentation of this guide.*

Saint-Wandrille-Rançon
76490 (3km E)

ⓔ |●| Restaurant Les Deux Couronnes

Opposite the church.
☎02.35.96.11.44
Closed *Sun evening and Mon (except public holidays).* **Open** *until 9pm.*

A seventeenth-century inn virtually in the precincts of the famous abbey. Tempting dishes include veal *escalope* served with apples or grilled bass served with smoked *andouille*. There's a €15 *formule* served during the week, and menus at €22 (two-course meal) and €26.50 (three-course meal); à la carte you're looking at €40.

Sainte-Gertrude
76490 (3km N)

ⓔ |●| Restaurant Au Rendez-Vous des Chasseurs

1040 rte. de Sainte-Gertrude. It's opposite the church.
☎02.35.96.20.30
Closed *Wed; Sun evening; 15–30 Aug.* **Disabled access. High chairs available.**

This quiet little restaurant nestling between the forest and the small village church serves good regional cooking at prices to suit all pockets. Hunters and travellers have been coming here for more than 150 years. Menus, €15–25, might feature pork cheek salad, calf's head sauce *gribiche*, clams and prawns flambéed in Pastis and red fruit *gratin* with mascarpone, while in winter the chef makes a delicious game stew with pheasant, venison and hare. You can eat out on the terrace in the garden in fine weather.

Villequier
76490 (4.5km SW)

ⓔ 🏠 |●| Hôtel du Grand Sapin

Quai de Seine; it's on the outskirts of Villequier going towards Caudebec.
☎02.35.56.78.73 ☞02.35.95.69.27

Closed *Tues evening and Wed (except July–Aug); Feb school holiday; first fortnight in Nov.* **Disabled access. TV. Car park.**

Magnificent Normandy house on the banks of the Seine, with a lovely flower garden featuring an enormous magnolia – unusual in these parts. Throughout, the place is friendly and cosy, with a terrace for summer. Five double rooms are priced at €42 with bath; all of them overlook the river. In the large rustic dining room menus go for €20–34; there's also a short €11.50 menu served during the week and Saturday lunchtime. Specialities include foie gras, scallops and pike perch with *andouille*. It's essential to call and make a reservation. Very good value for money but the welcome is variable.

Vatteville-la-Rue
76490 (8km S)

◎ |●| Auberge du Moulin

Take the D65 from the bridge over the Brontonne. Don't go into Vatteville, but take the road to Aizier; the hamlet of Quesnay is on the left.
☎02.35.96.10.88
Closed *evenings; Wed; 15 Aug to early Sept.* **Disabled access.**

Other villages still have places like this multi-purpose establishment – restaurant-bar-tobacconist's-grocer's – but they're not usually as nice. The dining room offers a rustic setting with checked tablecloths, hunting trophies and wild boars' heads on the wall, and a wide, open fire. The few tables are usually taken. Food here is just what you might expect from the setting – lots of rugged, hearty, traditional dishes at inexpensive prices: go for calf's head sauce *gribiche*, scallops *à la provençale*. Menus are €11.20 (weekday lunchtimes) and €14–25.

Conches-en-Ouche
27190

◎ 🎿 🏠 |●| Hôtel-restaurant le Cygne**

2 rue Paul-Guilbaud. At the bottom of Rue Sainte-Foy.
☎02.32.30.20.60 ℗02.32.30.45.73
Restaurant closed *Sun evening; Mon; Fri noon; Feb school holiday; Oct.* **Disabled access. TV. High chairs available. Car park.**

This welcoming hotel has a few comfortable rooms that are very simple with classic décor; doubles cost €43–50 depending on facilities. The restaurant, meanwhile, is refined but rustic – the ideal backdrop for traditional, well-flavoured cooking with some touches of originality. The produce is fresh, cooked *al dente* and to order – a sign of real expertise. Dishes change with the seasons and good-value menus range from €15 to the *menu terroir* at €28. *Free Kir normand offered to our readers on presentation of this guide.*

Cormeilles
27260

◎ 🏠 |●| Auberge du Président**

70 rue de l'Abbaye.
☎02.32.57.88.31 ℗02.32.57.88.31
✉aubergeduprésident@wanadoo.fr
Closed *Sun evening; Mon (lunchtime only during summer).* **Disabled access. TV. High chairs and games available. Car park.**

A large, half-timbered house at the entrance to the town, next to the Busnel distillery. This is classic Normandy cooking, though the chef comes from Arras – lots of dishes with cider sauces or Camembert on menus €16 (lunchtime), others €18–32. The rooms, €52–80, are very cute, in soft colours and completely refurbished. Good, solid stuff from this pleasant inn and a welcoming atmosphere, too. Logis de France.

◎ |●| Le Florida

21 rue de l'Abbaye; it's opposite the town hall.
☎02.32.57.80.97
Closed *Mon; second fortnight in June.* **Open** *Tues to Sun lunchtimes and Sat evening (Oct–March); Tues to Sat lunchtime and evening, and Sun lunchtime (April–June and Sept); Tues to Sun lunchtime and evening (July–Aug).*

Nice family atmosphere and high-quality, good-value cuisine is on offer. Weekday lunch menu at €11, and others at €16 and €24, feature specialities such as rabbit in cider. A nice little venue, though you can feel a bit cramped on the ground floor.

Saint-Simeon
27560 (10km NE)

◎ |●| L'Auberge de la Fontaine

Place de l'Église; take the D810 in the direction of Bernay.

⊕02.32.57.29.14
Closed *Mon; Sun evening (Sept–March).*

Philippe Autechaud is a demanding cook who keeps a very close, albeit good-natured, eye on his suppliers because his style of cuisine demands fresh, quality produce. His dishes take their inspiration from good quality, home cooking, but to this he brings his own touch and considerable technical expertise, inventing and reinventing, always trying out daring, new, inspired ideas and working with the seasons. And this is the result; tasty, unusual dishes such as his snail stew with nettle tips or rabbit with a crusty topping and cream cider sauce. Excellent meals are guaranteed at very reasonable prices: menus €16 weekday lunchtimes, then €18–30.

Beuzeville
27210 (12km W)

⊛ 🛏 |◉| Auberge du Cochon d'Or**

Place du Général-de-Gaulle. Take the D139 as far as Épaignes then the D27; it's opposite the town hall.
⊕02.32.57.70.46 ⊕02.32.42.25.70
ⓦwww.le-cochon-dor.fr
Closed *Mon; Sun evening (Oct–March); mid-Dec to mid-Jan.* **TV. Car park.**

This inn owes its continuing reputation to the chef who's been marshalling his forces in the kitchen for four decades. He specializes in Normandy dishes like *pavé* of *andouille* with a Camembert sauce and fillet of bass with citrus fruit, all of which you can enjoy in the large rustic dining room. There's a weekday menu at €14 and others €19 (except Sun lunchtime) up to €40. There's an annexe across the road called the *Petit Castel*; here the quiet and comfortable rooms overlook a garden where you can have breakfast. Doubles go for €39–54 with shower/wc or bath. This is a very well-kept establishment. Logis de France.

⊛ 🍴 🛏 |◉| Le Relais-Hôtel de la Poste**

60 rue Constant-Fouché; it's opposite the town hall.
⊕02.32.20.32.32 ⊕02.32.42.11.01
ⓦwww.le-relais-de-poste.com
Restaurant closed *Sun evening (except July–Aug); Thurs.* **Closed** *mid-Nov to 1 April.* **TV. Car park.**

This authentic coaching inn, which dates back to 1844, has a garden and a terrace at the back. Bedrooms €44–63 according to the level of comfort; if you're there at the weekend or public holidays, half board, €54–65 per person, is compulsory. It's a good deal, with a large choice of menus starting with the weekday lunchtime menu at €18, then others €25–36. The chef cooks a good number of regional specialities, and has a particular weakness for *andouille*, which he prepares in several ways, also foie gras, smoked salmon, smoked duck, and lamb *noisette*. A warm welcome awaits, just fifteen minutes from Honfleur, where hotels have the reputation of being expensive and often full. Logis de France. *10% discount on the room rate for a minimum two-night stay (except weekends and Jul-Aug) offered to our readers on presentation of this guide.*

Campigny
27500 (18km NE)

⊛ 🛏 |◉| 🍴 Restaurant L'Andrien – Hôtel Le Petit Coq aux Champs****

La Pommeraie sud. Take the D29 as far as Épaignes then the D98 followed by the D810 in the direction of Pont-Audemer; Campigny is on the left on the D29.
⊕02.32.41.04.19 ⊕02.32.56.06.25
ⓦwww.lepetit.coqauxchamps.fr
Closed *Sun evening and Mon (Nov–March).* **TV. High chairs available. Heated swimming pool. Car park.**

Beautifully located in glorious Normandy countryside, this welcoming restaurant has a relaxed atmosphere. That said, it's fairly sophisticated, and the food is excellent. Chef Jean-Marie Huard is constantly inventing new dishes that delight both the palate and the eye. His two specialities are home-made foie gras *maison* and a terrific foie gras *pot-au-feu* with crunchy cabbage. They have a choice of different menus, which change with the seasons, €27 weekday lunchtimes, €37–64 at other times. Double rooms with bath cost from €121 up to €141. *10% discount on the room rate (Oct–March) offered to our readers on presentation of this guide.*

Bourneville
27500 (22km NE)

⊛ |◉| Restaurant Risle-Seine

Take the D139.
⊕02.32.42.30.22

Closed *Tues evening; Wed.*

We wanted to stop and eat on our way through this area but didn't know where to go when the pretty, yellow façade of the Risle-Seine caught our eye. In we went… and it was a good choice. The menu boasts "traditional dishes with local Normandy accents, tinged with a touch of originality". And that's what we got. The first menu, served weekday lunchtimes, costs €10.80, then other menus are €16–27. The service is unobtrusive but attentive and booking is advisable at weekends.

Dieppe
76200

⊚ 🏠 Auberge de jeunesse

48 rue Louis-Fromager; a long way out; take the no. 2 bus in the direction of Val Druel to the "Château-Michel" stop.
☏02.35.84.85.73 ℱ02.35.84.89.62
Closed *early Oct to end May.*

The building is a little forbidding – it used to be a school – but the warm welcome dispels all doubts. It sleeps 42 people, spread over dormitories or rooms with four beds for €8 per person; breakfast €3.20. FUAJ card is compulsory. Kitchen and barbecue are available for preparing your own meals.

⊚ 🏠 Hôtel Au Grand Duquesne*

15 pl. Saint-Jacques; it's in the street opposite the church of Saint-Jacques.
☏02.32.14.61.10 ℱ02.35.84.29.83
ⓦwww.augrandduquesne.fr
TV.

This hotel, which has just been decorated in a tasteful, modern style, offers pretty, well-equipped bedrooms. Doubles start at €31 and go up to €43 depending on the facilities. Logis de France.

⊚ 🏠 🎋 Les Arcades de la Bourse**

1–3 arcades de la Bourse; it's on the marina.
☏02.35.84.14.12 ℱ02.35.40.22.29
ⓦwww.lesarcades.fr
TV.

Modern, comfortable rooms – nothing over the top – some of which have wonderful views over the marina. Doubles with shower and wc range from €43 to €75, according to season and view. It also

has a restaurant. Logis de France. *Free house apéritif is offered to our readers on presentation of this guide.*

⊚ |●| Le Bistrot du Pollet

23 rue de Tête de Bœuf; it's on the quai, between Ango bridge and Colbert bridge, opposite the post office.
☏02.35.84.68.57
Closed *Sun; Mon; a fortnight in March; Aug.*

A small, friendly restaurant with a cosy interior – lots of old photographs on the walls and old-fashioned music in the background. It may be wise to book, especially at lunchtime, when it fills up with loyal regulars. Fish is a speciality here – the grilled bass and sea bream are wonderful – along with foie gras *du pêcheur*, a typical Dieppois recipe of marinated, puréed monkfish liver. Prices are more than reasonable, with a lunch menu at €11.43 during the week, or around €22 à la carte.

⊚ 🎋 |●| À la Marmite Dieppoise

8 rue Saint-Jean; it's just by quai Duquesne.
☏02.35.84.24.26 ℱ02.35.84.31.12
Closed *Sun and Mon Nov–March; Sun evening, Mon and Tues evening April–Oct.* **High chairs available.**

A classic Dieppoise restaurant serving fine food. Menus revolve around fish dishes prepared with cream; their superb signature dish is *marmite dieppoise*, a tasty stew of monkfish, brill, sole and scallops, with mussels and crayfish, all cooked together in a pan. The prices are not as easy on the pocket as one might wish but the food is really excellent; menus €18 (weekday lunchtimes), others €29–42. *Free coffee offered to our readers on presentation of this guide.*

Pourville-sur-Mer
76550 (4.5km W)

⊚ |●| L'Huîtrière

Rue du 19-Août; it's 4km west of Dieppe on the seashore.
☏02.35.84.36.20
Open *daily 10am–8pm.* **Car park.**

A seafood restaurant, open all year, above the store where oysters are sold direct from the oyster beds. It specializes in oysters, of course, along with clams, whelks, winkles, cockles and crêpes. The décor is appealing, with sea-blue walls, oyster baskets hung from the ceiling and an ancient diving suit in the corner, and the bay windows open right onto the beach. In summer, they set up a huge terrace. A dozen average size oysters are €13.50, the salmon platter €12; a bottle of Muscadet €13.50. Though the food is good, prices are high for such a simple place. Take away service available all year round. Credit cards not accepted.

Varengeville-sur-Mer

76119 (8km SW)

◉ ☎ |◉| Hôtel-restaurant La Terrasse**

Route de Vasterival. Take the D75.
☎02.35.85.12.54 ℗02.35.85.11.70
@www.hotel-restaurant-la-terrasse.com
Closed 13 Oct—15 March. **High chairs and games available. Car park.**

This cosy family hotel snuggling among the pine trees is a regular favourite with British visitors. It's in a remarkable location on the cliffs, and the terrace is a superb spot to admire the Channel over a drink. The 22 attractive rooms, all with shower/wc or bath, go for €47–52 per person per night. Half board is compulsory. The restaurant serves lots of fish on menus €18–30, however the view seems nicer than the quality of the food. In fine weather, there are always lots of people, so it's best to reserve.

◉ ⅔ |◉| La Buissonnière

Route du Phare-d'Ailly.
☎02.35.83.17.13
Closed Sun evening; Mon; Jan–Feb.

This beautiful private house, flooded with light and bedecked with flowers, is an ideal place for prolonging a visit to the Moutiers wood. The food is a perfect match for the setting; the ingredients, mainly derived from the sea, are superbly fresh and managed with sensual skill. There are two menus at €30 and €44, or you can eat à la carte. *Free coffee offered to our readers on presentation of this guide.*

Arques-la Bataille

76880 (9km SE)

◉ ☎ Le Manoir d'Archelles

It's on the D1, Neuchâtel road, on the edge of town.
☎02.35.85.50.16 ℗02.35.85.47.55

Closed Sat lunchtime; Sun evening; Fri evening in winter; second fortnight in Feb; last week in Aug; Christmas. **TV. Disabled access. Car park.**

This stunning sixteenth-century manor house, built of a mosaic of brick and flint stones, offers doubles for €30 with shower, €40–46 with shower/wc or bath; they also have a suite that sleeps four. The décor is more rustic than chic but that doesn't diminish its charm. The rooms in the fortified gatehouse, reached by a spiral stone staircase, are particularly attractive, giving good views of the château. Have a wander round the orchard and carefully tended vegetable garden.

◉ |◉| L'Auberge d'Archelles

Archelles; it's on the D1, Neuchâtel road, on the edge of town, next to *Le Manoir* (above).
☎02.35.83.40.51
Closed Fri evening; Sat lunchtime; Sun evening; second fortnight in Feb; first week in July; Christmas and New Year holidays. **TV. Car park.**

This good-value restaurant, owned by the same people as *Le Manoir*, is housed in beautifully converted old stables. The cuisine is as attractive as the setting, featuring regional and gastronomic dishes with a nice weekday menu at €13.80 and other menus €18–32.50. Try the Camembert *croquettes*, duck in cider sauce, bass with fennel and home-made pastry.

Étretat

76790

◉ ☎ Hôtel d'Angleterre

35 av. George-V; it's 100m from the sea on the Le Havre road that starts at the tourist office.
☎02.35.28.84.97 ℗02.35.28.05.57
TV.

A clean, welcoming, reasonably priced hotel, well away from the touristy part of town and refurbished – in other words, something of a find. Doubles go for €40 with shower/wc.

◉ ☎ |◉| L'Escale**

Place Foch; it's opposite the old market.
☎02.35.27.03.69 ℗02.35.28.05.86
TV.

This hotel-brasserie is a really nice place. The wood-panelled bedrooms are a bit

HAUTE-NORMANDIE

small but pleasant enough; doubles with shower/wc go for €47. The lively ground-floor restaurant-brasserie serves simple dishes – mussels and chips, omelettes, salads, pizzas and crêpes – along with a few gourmet options. You'll pay about €10 for a main course. Sit on the terrace and watch the world hurry by in the square.

◎ ⅔ |◉| L'Huitrière

Rue Traz-Perrier; it's on the seafront, towards Aval cliffs.
℗02.35.27.02.82

An extraordinary circular dining room with a sensational panoramic view over the beaches and cliffs. They specialize in seafood and fish and take great care over the preparation of each dish. The €20 menu proves very good value and is also served at weekends, other menus go up to €39; you'll spend around €46 for a seafood tray for two people. *Complimentary trou normand – a shot of Calvados – offered to our readers on presentation of this guide.*

◎ ⅔ |◉| Restaurant Le Galion

Boulevard René-Coty.
℗02.35.29.48.74 ℗02.35.29.74.48
ⓦwww.etretat.net
Closed *Tues and Wed out of season (except during school holidays); 15 Dec–15 Jan.* **Disabled access. High chairs available.**

Cosy restaurant with seventeenth-century décor – enormous fireplace, little tinted window panes, old beams – and high-class service. The €23 menu is beautifully balanced and offers excellent value for money, listing velvety smooth fish soup, crunchy cheese bake, fillet of fish (type according to what's available) with beurre blanc, other menus up to €41. *Free coffee offered to our readers on presentation of this guide.*

◎ ⅔ |◉| La Salamandre

4 bd. René-Coty; on the ground floor of the splendid Salamandre manor house.
℗02.35.27.02.87
High chairs available.

This place has really won us over. No need for a sea view here, the food provides sufficient spectacle of its own. The establishment takes pride in offering only ingredients that are organically grown or bred on a farm (apart from the seafood, obviously), not just to show off but because they taste better. Menus €29–38, but you can also

eat economically à la carte, with mussels at €8 and large platters at €16. Whatever you choose, it will be presented elegantly and served gracefully, and you're bound to leave contented. *Free house liqueur offered to our readers on presentation of this guide.*

Eu

76260

◎ |◉| ♙ Centre des Fontaines – Auberge de jeunesse

Rue des Fontaines; in the royal kitchens of the castle.
℗02.35.86.05.03 ℗02.35.86.45.12
ⓔcentre-des-fontaines@wanadoo.fr
Closed *over Christmas and New Year holidays.* **Reception open** *2–9pm (6–9pm Sun and public holidays).*

A bed costs €12.10 a night in rooms with five to thirteen beds and washbasin or shower (wc in the corridor). The bedding has just been renewed and half board is €22.50 per person. Meals are available for groups at 7pm. You can come back any time after 9pm, but you must ask for the key first. A French youth hostel card is obligatory.

◎ ⅔ ♙ |◉| Hôtel-Restaurant Maine**

20 av. de la Gare; 5 minutes from city centre.
℗02.35.86.16.64 ℗02.35.50.86.25
ⓦwww.hotel-maine.com
Restaurant closed *Sun evening; 17 Aug–8 Sept.* **Hotel open** *all year.* **TV. Car park.**

Bright and peaceful establishment in a master-craftsman's house opposite the old station. Though some have been refurbished more recently than others, the bedrooms have all facilities, with en-suite bathrooms, TV and telephones. Doubles with shower/wc cost €48, with bath €56 and €70 with spa bath. Half board is compulsory over public holiday weekends and from Easter to September; the quality of the cuisine is good value. Indeed, it's worth coming just for a meal. The Maine has been serving food since 1867, and the dining room is an exceptional example of Art Nouveau. Dishes are modern yet firmly rooted in local and traditional cuisine, with fish dishes a speciality. There's a weekday menu at €15 (including drinks) and two other menus, the "*boucher*" and "*pêcheur*" at €24. Logis de France. *10% discount on the room rate offered to our readers on presentation of this guide.*

Évreux

27000

@ |●| Restaurant La Croix d'Or

3 rue Joséphine.
☎02.32.33.06.07
Open *daily at lunchtimes and evenings.*
Disabled access. High chairs available.

Fine food intelligently prepared by people who care about what they do. The restaurant is convenient for the administrative quarter, and is often full of local civil servants enjoying a good lunch in a relaxed atmosphere with a bit of a classy setting. They specialize in seafood and fish – particularly *bouillabaisse*, but carnivores aren't forgotten, either. Superb weekday lunch menu at €10.90, with others from €14 to €29; reckon on about €30 for à la carte. This is a really practical choice for Sunday evening when all the other restaurants in town are shut.

@ |●| La Gazette

7 rue Saint-Sauveur.
☎02.32.33.43.40
Closed *Mon; Sat lunchtime; Aug.*

A pleasant, refurbished setting where you can enjoy good food, scrupulously prepared from fresh, local produce with menus at €17–35 – outstanding even in terms of the area's already very high standards. There's originality, a personal touch and a charming welcome – what more could you ask? This is one of the best restaurants Évreux has to offer. Advance booking at weekends is strongly recommended.

Gravigny

27930 (4km N)

@ |●| ⅄ Le Saint-Nicolas

38 av. Aristide-Briand; it's on the D155 towards Louviers, on the right.
☎02.32.38.35.15
Closed *Sun evening.* **Car park.**

This unobtrusive house conceals a number of lovely little dining rooms decorated in a simple style, if a tad kitschy – intimate ones for candlelit dinners, larger ones for lively groups and a terrace for outside dining. The chef, Claude Sauvant, takes pride in

using top quality produce depending on what's in season, such as foie gras and figs in tea and boned pig's trotters with truffles. There are special menus, €15–25, served at lunchtime on weekdays, then others €20–32; also a superb wine list. *Free coffee offered to our readers on presentation of this guide.*

Fécamp

76400

@ 🏠 Hôtel de la Plage**

87 rue de la Plage.
☎02.35.29.76.51 ☎02.35.28.68.30
✉hoteldelaplagefecamp@wanadoo.fr
TV. Cots available. Pay car park.

Charming, well-equipped hotel, a stone's throw from the beach. Most of the rooms are refurbished and quiet, and cost €35–50 for a double, depending on the comfort and the season; some have a sea view. There's a very pretty breakfast room (although you can also have breakfast in bed). Guests are given a really delightful welcome and plenty of tips on how to take full advantage of their stay.

@ 🏠 Hôtel Normandy

2 bis av. Gambetta.
☎02.35.29.55.11 ☎02.35.27.48.74
🌐www.normandy-fecamp.com
TV.

A hotel with an alluring, totally renovated façade with double rooms for €45; some are particularly spacious. A good place to stay in the town centre with a very attractive, old-fashioned restaurant and offering excellent service. Logis de France.

@ |●| Chez Nounoute

3 pl. Nicolas-Selle; in Bout-Menteux, in the port.
Closed *Sun evening; Wed.*

Nounoute is a real character. She greets customers with cheeky, maternal attention and soon makes them feel at ease. The restaurant used to be a fishmonger's, and Nounoute similarly stresses the quality of the local fish by serving marinated mackerel, smoked herring, fresh cod and many more besides. Menus are €14–25, conviviality and good humour included. Many of our readers are already devoted customers, and a visit to *Chez Nounoute* alone will make any trip to Fécamp worthwhile.

17

HAUTE-NORMANDIE

◉ |◉| Le Vicomté

4 rue du Président-Coty; it's 50m from the port, behind the Palais Bénédictine.
℡02.35.28.47.63
Closed *Wed evening; Sun; public holidays; a fortnight end Aug; a fortnight end Dec.*

A very welcoming, and rather unusual, retro bistro with checked tablecloths and posters from the *Petit Journal* adorning the walls. They serve just one set menu at €15.40, but the dishes – regional cooking, based on fresh produce – change every day. They also do a children's menu for €6.50. It's excellent value for money with impeccable service.

Saint-Léonard
76400 (2km S)

◉ ⚜ 🏠 |◉| Auberge de la Rouge**

Route du Havre; on the outskirts of Fécamp.
℡02.35.28.07.59 ℻02.35.28.70.55
🖥www.auberge-rouge.com
Closed *Mon; Sat lunchtime; Sun evening; a fortnight in Feb.* **TV. High chairs available. Car park.**

One of the best restaurants in the *département*. The décor and service obey classical rules, but in contrast the cooking takes some risks. Menus €18 and €28 (except Sun), then €34 and €50; the flavours and cooking techniques are skilfully controlled to bring out the qualities of the high-quality ingredients. Double rooms €60; there are also a few soberly decorated duplex rooms at the end of the garden. Logis de France. *Free house apéritif offered to our readers on presentation of this guide.*

Forges-les-Eaux
76440

◉ 🏠 Le Continental***

110 av. des Sources; it's near the casino, 50m.
℡02.32.89.50.50 ℻02.35.90.26.14
🖥www.casinoforges.com
Disabled access. TV. Car park.

An impressive half-timbered building that's been thoroughly renovated. With its large foyer and balconies, it still has the nicely old-fashioned atmosphere of old casino hotels, and offers well-equipped bedrooms for between €60 and €76. Guests can use the nearby Club Med facilities by arrangement (℡02.32.89.50.40), and the Casino's restaurant is very close.

Saint-Martin-Osmonville
76680 (23km W)

◉ ⚜ |◉| Auberge de la Varenne

2 rte. de la Libération; take the D919 to Buchy, then the D41.
℡02.35.34.13.80
Closed *Sun evening; Mon; Thurs evening.*

They stick firmly to traditional, local cooking in this pleasant roadside inn – the menu changes twice a year, but typical offerings might include *croustillant* of *andouille* with apple and beef cheek with cider. The weekday menu costs €16.05, with others €19.10–33.55. With very attentive service and a warm welcome, it's a good place to eat after visiting the old market in Buchy. There's an open fire in the winter, and a lovely terrace in good weather. *Free house apéritif offered to our readers on presentation of this guide.*

Gisors
27140

◉ |◉| ⚜ Le Cochon Gaulois

8 pl. Blanmont; it's opposite the château.
℡02.32.27.30.33
Closed *Sun.*

They serve mainly pork dishes; charcuterie, pork cheek salad, ham hock terrine, grilled spare ribs and all sorts of grills. They have a weekday lunchtime menu at €11 and another menu for €14.90; evenings there's à la carte, reckon on about €22. But their roast suckling pig is the sensation (€11.90); it's served in its own juice or with any sauce you choose. It's tender, crumbling and delicious. There are also some fish dishes, mussels with chips as well as sandwiches. Friday is karaoke night. *Free coffee offered to our readers on presentation of this guide.*

◉ |◉| Le Cappeville

17 rue Cappeville.
℡02.32.55.11.08
Closed *Wed; Thurs; a fortnight early Jan; a fortnight end Aug.* **Disabled access.**

A good place to pause in this little town where you can get a quality meal that absolutely follows the region's traditions. The chef, Pierre Potel, has worked with some of the greats. Specialities include *millefeuille* of beef with preserved shallots and turbot with mussel stock. Menus start at €18 (except Sun), and from €24 to €41; reckon on about €55 for à la carte.

Gros-Theil (Le)

27370

🏚 |●| Au Vieux Brabant

13km northeast of Brionne via the D83; opposite the church.
☎02.32.35.51.31
Closed Wed; during Feb school holidays.

This is the kind of village you can drive through without really noticing, but our eye was caught by the pleasant-looking façade of the inn; we got out to look at the menu, and there was the chef, as he is every day, busy with his *coq au vin* simmering away, chopping up meat for his pâtés, keeping an eye on his tarte tatin … The heady, subtle odour of his wine sauce tempted us in; the *coq au vin* did not disappoint in the slightest, in fact we remember it still … They do a set menu at €11 and others at €19.90–39. The setting is rustic and in fine weather there are tables in the pleasant, flower-filled garden. There are also two rooms (€36) at the end of the garden if you want to spend the night. *Free house apéritif is offered to our readers on presentation of this guide.*

Havre (Le)

76600

See map overleaf

🏚 Hôtel Séjour Fleuri

71 rue Émile-Zola; 500m from the beach and 500m from the ferries. **Map B3-3**
☎02.35.41.33.81
☏02.35.42.26.44
TV. Car park.

A godsend for travellers on a small budget, although more prosperous visitors can easily find satisfaction here as well. This modest hotel has been totally refurbished, with no little imagination; double rooms are €24–35 according to comfort and the season. The owner is full of ideas for strolls and takes great pains to give her guests fine memories of Le Havre when they leave. It is not for nothing that she has won a Normandy Quality Tourism certificate. So, frankly, why go elsewhere to pay more? *10% discount on the price of the room (excluding long weekends) is offered to our readers on presentation of this guide.*

🏚 Hôtel-Celtic**

106 rue Voltaire; situated in city centre. **Map B3-1**
☎02.35.42.39.77 ☏02.35.21.67.65
✉www.hotel.celtic.com
Closed Christmas school holidays. **TV. Car park.**

Delightfully located hotel with views of the Volcan theatre and the merchant port. The double rooms are brightly painted with all facilities, the price varying according to size and floor level; those with shower go for €32; with shower/wc or with bath they're from €45 to €49. It's excellent value for money. *10% discount on the room rate offered to our readers on presentation of this guide.*

🏚 Le Petit Vatel**

8 rue Louis Brindeau. **Map B2-4**
☎02.35.41.72.07 ☏02.35.21.37.86
✉www.lepetitvatel.com
Closed Sun 2–7pm; during Christmas school holidays. **TV.**

A central hotel where the brightly painted, clean rooms have modern facilities and bathrooms; doubles €40–45 according to comfort. There's nothing special about the view but the hotel offers very good value and has been awarded a Normandy Quality Tourism certificate. *One free breakfast per room offered to our readers on presentation of this guide.*

🏚 Hôtel Vent d'Ouest***

4 rue de Caligny; near Saint-Joseph church. **Map B2-5**
☎02.35.42.50.69 ☏02.35.42.58.00
✉www.ventdouest.fr
TV. High chairs, games and cots available. Pay car park.

The *Hotel Vent d'Ouest* has three floors, each with its own style, and the 35 rooms are individually decorated with a country, seaside or mountain look. The little details and ornaments give the rooms a personal touch. Doubles with shower or bath range in price from €80 up to €105, depending on the size of the room.

|●| Restaurant Le Lyonnais

7 rue de Bretagne; Saint-François area. **Map C3-12**
☎02.35.22.07.31
Closed Sat lunchtime; Sun.

Successfully re-creating the atmosphere of a typical Lyonnais bistro, this place has

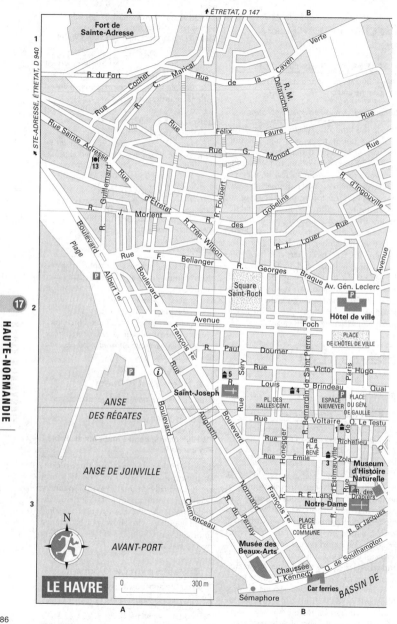

LE HAVRE

HAUTE-NORMANDIE

17

Fort de
Sainte-Adresse

STE-ADRESSE, ÉTRETAT, D 940

ÉTRETAT, D 147

R. du Fort
Cochet
Rue
Marical
Rue
de
la
Caven
Verte
R. M.
Delaroche
Rue
R.
C.

Rue
Rue
Félix
Faure
Rue
Rue Sainte-Adresse
Rue
R. Foubert
G.
Monod
Rue
13
d'Étretat
R. Prés. Wilson
des
Gobelins
R. d'Ingouville

Boulevard
Plage
R.
J.
Morlent
R.
R. J.
Louer
Rue

Rue
F.
Bellanger
R.
Georges
Braque
Avenue

Boulevard
Albert 1er
Square
Saint-Roch
Av. Gén. Leclerc

Hôtel de ville

Avenue
Foch
PLACE
DE L'HÔTEL DE VILLE

R.
Paul
Doumer

Séry
Rue
Victor
Hugo
Paris

François 1er
Rue
5
Louis
4
Brindeau
Quai

Saint-Joseph
PL. DES
HALLES CENT.
ESPACE
NIEMEYER
PLACE
DU GÉN.
DE GAULLE

ANSE
DES RÉGATES
Rue
Voltaire
Q. Le Testu

Boulevard
Augustin
Rue
de
1
de
Richelieu

ANSE DE JOINVILLE
Rue
Honegger
de
PL. A.
RENÉ
Émile
3
Zola
Museum
d'Histoire
Naturelle

François 1er
Normand
R. E. Lang
Rue d'Estimauville
R. des
Drapiers

Clemenceau
R. du Perrey
Notre-Dame
R. St Jacques

N

PLACE
DE LA
COMMUNE
Q. de Southampton

AVANT-PORT
Musée des
Beaux-Arts
Chaussée
J. Kennedy
Car ferries
BASSIN DE

LE HAVRE
0
300 m
Sémaphore

A
B

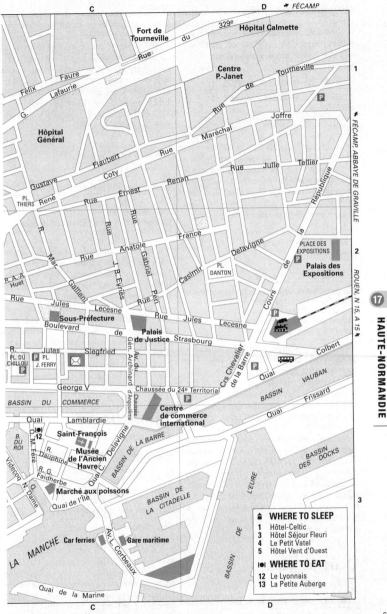

C   D   ↗ FÉCAMP

Fort de Tourneville
Hôpital Calmette
329e
du
Rue

Centre P.-Janet

Félix
Faure
Lafaurie
G.
Rue
de
Tourneville

1

Rue
Joffre

Hôpital Général

Maréchal
Rue

Flaubert
Coty
Renan
Rue
Julte
Tellier

Gustave
René
Rue
Ernest

PL. THIERS
Mar.
Rue
Rue
France
Anatole

R.-A.-A Huet
Galliéni
Gabriel
Péri
Casimir
J.-B.-Eyriès
Delavigne

Rue
Jules
Lecesne
Rue
PL. DANTON

PLACE DES EXPOSITIONS

Palais des Expositions

2

Sous-Préfecture
Boulevard
de
Palais de Justice
Rue
Jules
Lecesne
Strasbourg

Cours

ROUEN, N 15, À 15 ↗

R. PL. DU CHILLOU
Jules
Siegfried
Av. du Gén. Archinard
Crs Chevalier de la Barre
Colbert

PL. J. FERRY

George V
Chaussée du 24e Territorial

BASSIN DU COMMERCE
Quai
Lamblardie
Centre de commerce international

BASSIN VAUBAN
Quai
Frissard

B. DU ROI
Saint-François
R. Dauphine
Musée de l'Ancien Havre
BASSIN DE LA BARRE
Chaussée d'angulème

BASSIN DES DOCKS

R. G. Faidherbe
Marché aux poissons
Quai de l'Île
BASSIN DE LA CITADELLE
L'EURE

3

Videcoq
N.-Dame
Car ferries
Gare maritime
Av. L. Corbeaux
BASSIN DE

LA MANCHE

Quai de la Marine

C   D

⌂ WHERE TO SLEEP
1 Hôtel-Celtic
3 Hôtel Séjour Fleuri
4 Le Petit Vatel
5 Hôtel Vent d'Ouest

|●| WHERE TO EAT
12 Le Lyonnais
13 La Petite Auberge

17

HAUTE-NORMANDIE

a copper chimney breast, checkerboard floor tiles and brick walls. Dishes include fish stew, gâteau of chicken livers, *andouillette* and *saucisson lyonnaise*, and warm upside-down apple tart. The €12.50 menu is served during the week only, but the others, from €15 to €23, are good too, and the €18 menu is worth trying.

@ ⚘ |O| La Petite Auberge

32 rue de Sainte-Adresse. **Map A1-13**
☎02.35.46.27.32
Closed *Sat lunch; Sun evening; Mon.*

One of the safest bets for trying authentic cooking from Le Havre on a choice of menus €19.50–39; it has been delighting gourmets for generations and it is not unusual to see whole families enjoying the exquisite food in this most classical of settings. It is advisable to book. *Free coffee offered to our readers on presentation of this guide.*

Sainte-Adresse
76310 (2km NW)

@ ⚘ |O| Les Trois Pics

Promenade des Régates; it's at the northern-most end of Le Havre beach.
☎02.35.48.20.60
Closed *Sun evening and Mon (Oct–April).*
Open *daily (May–Sept).*

This place, standing on the quay, looks for all the world like a liner in dry dock. The large wooden dining room has a wonderful, panoramic view of the mouth of the Seine, and the maritime décor is imaginative and refined. From the ship's rail you can see Deauville, ten miles off in the distance. Menus served weekday lunchtimes, including a main course with a starter or dessert, are €13 and €17. Other menus are from €23 to €35. Have a drink on the terrace in the summer (or even in the winter as it's a heated terrace) – when dusk falls and the lights are turned on across the bay, you can almost imagine you're out at sea. *Free house apéritif offered to our readers on presentation of this guide.*

Jumièges
76480

@ |O| Auberge des Ruines

Place de la Mairie; it's opposite the monastery.
☎02.35.37.24.05

Closed *Sun and Tues evenings; Wed; Mon and Thurs evenings (1 Nov–15 March); 25 Aug–5 Sept; 20 Dec–10 Jan.* **Disabled access.**

The best restaurant in town where fish takes pride of place. One slight quibble – the "cheap" weekend menu is a bit expensive. If you regard yourself as a foodie, try the chicken *tartare* with peppers and chorizo, pork chop with juniper berries or the chocolate soufflé. The weekday lunch menu goes for €18, with others €33–55. On winter days there's a log fire burning in the hearth.

Duclair
76480 (9km NE)

@ |O| Restaurant Le Parc

Take the D982.
☎02.35.37.50.31
Closed *Wed in winter.* **Disabled access.**

Away from the road, and therefore from the cars, an unbeatably romantic setting with décor that would have appealed to Flaubert or Maupassant. It offers unquestionably the best view of the Seine in these parts, with a magnificent terrace and garden overlooking the water, exquisite, old-fashioned atmosphere, with porcelain tableware in pretty floral designs, lace tablecloths and charming fireplaces. Traditional cooking is served on menus from €15 (weekdays) to €44. The welcome you receive is as enchanting as everything else.

Lillebonne
76170

@ ⚘ 🏠 |O| La P'tite Auberge

20 rue du Havre; it's beside the church.
☎02.35.38.00.59 ☎02.35.38.57.33
@www.la-ptite-auberge.com
Closed *Sat lunchtime; Sun evening; Fri; 2–29 Aug.* **High chairs available. TV.**

This hotel is in a large, half-timbered house. Most of the bright rooms have had new bathrooms fitted; doubles go for €29 with basin (the wc is along the landing) and €43 for shower/wc or bath. The rustic dining room is a good place to eat traditional cuisine, with a weekday lunch menu for €14 and others for €19–27. There's a shady flower-filled terrace open during warm weather. *Free coffee offered to our readers on presentation of this guide.*

Louviers

27400

◎ 弍 |O| Le Jardin de Bigard

39–41 rue du Quai; it's on the corner of rue du Coq.
☎02.32.40.02.45
Closed *Wed and Thurs evenings; Sun.*
Disabled access.

A centrally located, unpretentious restaurant with a bright, airy dining room that's been given a makeover, offering simple but carefully prepared dishes at reasonable prices. The weekday lunch menu costs €10.50, and there are others from €13.80 to €22.50. Specialities include calf's head sauce *gribiche*, and fillet of trout with Camembert. *Free house apéritif offered to our readers on presentation of this guide.*

◎ |O| Le Clos Normand

Rue de la Gare–chaussée du Vexin; cross the Eure by rue des Anciens-Combattants d'AFN and it's right there.
☎02.32.40.03.56
Closed *Mon; mid-Aug to early Sept.*
Disabled access.

Rustic décor, quite smart but warm, and traditional, though imaginative, cooking and attentive service. They do a number of fish specialities and lots of dishes using cream and locally grown produce. Lunch menus are €12–15 during the week, with others €20–35; the €15 menu is really good value.

Acquigny

27400 (5km SE)

◎ 弍 |O| La Chaumière

15 rue Aristide-Briand; it's opposite the town hall.
☎02.32.50.20.54
Closed *Tues; Wed; Feb holiday; a few days around Christmas.* **High chairs available.**

A really nice restaurant with rustic décor and a relaxed atmosphere. The chef produces new dishes every day, but typical offerings might be ceps on toast, veal chops *à la normande*, and game in season. When it's chilly, they grill meat and fish over the fire. No menus, but the à la carte prices are reasonable at €22–50. There's a very good selection of wines available. *Free house digestif offered to our readers on presentation of this guide.*

Pont-de-l'Arche

27340 (11km N)

◎ 🏠 Hôtel de la Tour**

41 quai Foch; take the N15 over the bridge and it's on the left on the Eure riverbank.
☎02.35.23.00.99 ℻02.35.23.46.22
ⓦ www.hoteldelatour.net
TV. Car park.

The old façade is perfectly in keeping with the pretty houses along the quay, but the interior has been expertly refurbished by the charming owners. Everything about it – the colours, the décor, the little details that make for a comfortable stay and the friendly welcome – gives this place a quality not normally found in a hotel in this category. Doubles cost €60, and whether you opt for one overlooking the ramparts and the church of Notre-Dame-des-Arts or one with a view of the lush riverbank, they're all equally quiet and comfortable. There's a small, terraced garden at the rear and an excellent 2km walk along a footpath on the banks of the river Eure, leading to the Lévy-Poses leisure area.

Lyons-la-Forêt

27480

◎ 弍 🏠 |O| Hostellerie du Domaine Saint-Paul**

It's 800m out of the village on the D321.
☎02.32.49.60.57 ℻02.32.49.56.05
ⓦ www.domaine-saint-paul.fr
Closed *1 Nov–1 April.* **TV. High chairs and games available. Swimming pool. Car park.**

A substantial house with various annexes around the main building. It's been in the same family since 1946 and offers complete peace and quiet, and a friendly welcome. The five hectare grounds are quiet, planted with flower beds, and there's a pleasant, open-air swimming pool (charge for use on Sundays, except for residents). Most of the rooms (€49–72) still have their old wallpaper, though others have undergone a well-deserved refurbishment; half board is compulsory at the weekend (May–Sept) for €51–63 per person. The restaurant serves typical regional cooking with a few original touches: Camembert *croquettes*, and duck *fricassée* with cider and Pommeau. There's a weekday lunchtime menu at €20 and others from €24 to €36. Reservations are recommended, especially at the weekend.

Logis de France. *Free house digestif offered to our readers on presentation of this guide.*

✆ 🏨 |O| Les Lions de Beauclerc

7 rue de l'Hôtel-de-Ville.
℡02.32.49.18.90 ⓕ02.32.48.27.80
🖰www.lionsdebeauclerc.com
Restaurant closed Tues. **Tearoom open** weekends and public holidays.

A classy establishment right in the heart of the village. Only five rooms, priced €54–69 with shower or bath, but very comfortable – they captivated us with their stylishness and romanticism so much in keeping with the gentle atmosphere of the pays de Lyons. The chests of drawers, armchairs and paintings in the bedrooms are for sale. In fact the owners have a second passion – antiques. You can eat in the elegant dining room or in the small garden at the rear where they serve Normandy dishes, particularly galettes and crêpes with menus €14–26.

Neufchâtel-en-Bray
76270

✆ 🎎 🏨 |O| Hostellerie du Grand Cerf**

9 Grande-Rue-Fausse-Porte; go down the main street and it's beyond the church.
℡02.35.93.00.02 ⓕ02.35.94.14.92
🖂grand-cerf.hotel@wanadoo.fr
Closed Fri; Sat lunchtime; a fortnight end Dec. **TV. High chairs available. Car park.**

A rustic setting, family atmosphere and very traditional Normandy dishes of a very high standard. There are a variety of menus ranging from €14 on weekdays to €30; children's menu €8.60. The rooms are well maintained, and well sound-proofed with double glazing. Doubles go for €43 with shower/wc; half board from €52 per person. Logis de France. *Free house apéritif and coffee offered to our readers on presentation of this guide.*

Rouen
76000
See map on pp.692–693

✆ 🏨 Hôtel du Palais**

12 rue du Tambour. **Map B2-8**
℡02.35.71.41.40

Closed Sun noon–7pm. **TV.**

In a tiny street between the law courts and the Gros Horloge, right across from the underground station, this hotel has two trump cards – its central location and its modest prices. Don't go expecting any great luxury, but the make-believe courtyard and the slightly random décor will appeal to the young at heart. Double bedrooms are €34–40, with shower/wc for the most expensive ones.

✆ 🎎 🏨 Hôtel Céline**

26 rue de Campulley; near the train station.
Off map B1-1
℡02.35.71.95.23 ⓕ02.35.89.53.71
🖂hotelceline@wanadoo.fr
TV.

A large white building in remarkably peaceful surroundings. The bedrooms in pastel shades are modern and clean; some of those on the top floor are particularly big, but they can get a little too hot in the height of summer. Reasonably priced doubles with shower/wc cost €37–42. *One free breakfast per room offered to our readers on presentation of this guide.*

✆ 🏨 🎎 Hôtel Bristol

45 rue aux Juifs; opposite the law courts.
Map B2-6
℡02.35.71.54.21 ⓕ02.35.52.06.33
Closed Sun; public holidays; second week in April; 3 weeks in Aug. **TV.**

A beautifully restored half-timbered building with nine comfortable, refurbished bedrooms, €38–57 for a double with bath and phone; some have a view of the Palace of Justice. The bedding is not always up to scratch but you can be sure of a fantastic welcome. *5% discount on the price of the room (after two consecutive nights) is offered to our readers on presentation of this guide.*

✆ 🎎 🏨 Hôtel Beauséjour**

9 rue Pouchet. 200m from the train station.
Map B1-2
℡02.35.71.93.47 ⓕ02.35.98.01.24
🖰www.hotelbeausejour76.com
Closed 15–30 July; 24–31 Dec. **TV.**

One of the best places near the station, this quiet hotel has a smart exterior with freshly renovated, well-equipped rooms, a charming garden and a salon-bar. Prices are fair for the category, with doubles at €43. *10% discount on the room rate for a minimum two-night stay at the weekend (except July and Aug) offered to our readers on presentation of this guide.*

⟪ 🏠 Hôtel Andersen*

2 bis and 4 rue Pouchet; near the train station. **Map B1-3**
☎02.35.71.88.51 ☎02.35.07.54.65
🌐www.hotelandersen.com
TV.

An old house that's been turned into a lovely hotel, conveniently located near the station. The bright rooms are delightful, and the décor, which evokes the turn of the eighteenth and nineteenth centuries, has been assembled with taste. All the bathrooms are completely modern and doubles go for €45–55 with shower/wc. There's a pay car park nearby.

⟪ 🍴 🏠 Hôtel des Carmes*

33 pl. des Carmes. **Map C2-5**
☎02.35.71.92.31 ☎02.35.71.76.96
🌐www.hoteldescarmes.fr.st
TV.

A very attractive place on one of the liveliest squares in the middle of town. The décor is bright and new, full of circus imagery, and the young team welcomes you with a smile. Rooms are pleasant, colourful and refurbished. Doubles are €48–60 with shower/wc or bath; six of them have *trompel'œil* ceilings. Breakfast costs €6 – the butter and yoghurt come direct from the farm and the jams (try the apple and Calvados preserve) are made by the best Rouen companies using old methods. It's excellent value for money. *10% discount on the room rate offered (Oct–March) to our readers on presentation of this guide.*

⟪ 🍴 🏠 Hôtel du Vieux Carré**

34 rue Ganterie; on a pedestrianized street in the city centre. **Map C2-10**
☎02.35.71.67.70 ☎02.35.71.19.17
🌐www.vieuxcarre.fr
Disabled access. TV.

There are a few characterful rooms in this pretty, half-timbered house in the centre of the old town. They're inevitably quite small given the size and age of the building, but they're pretty, with soothing décor, and some of them overlook a delightful courtyard ablaze with colourful flowers. Friendly welcome and reasonable prices: doubles with all conveniences go

for €54 and €58 depending on whether they look onto the courtyard or the street. The tearoom offers savoury tarts, salads and cakes, with a brunch menu for €15; in good weather you can take tea out in the courtyard. Friendly welcome. *Free coffee offered to our readers on presentation of this guide.*

⟪ 🍴 🏠 Le Cardinal**

1 pl. de la Cathédrale; city centre. **Map B3-7**
☎02.35.70.24.42 ☎02.35.89.75.14
🌐www.cardinal-hotel.fr
Closed *23 Dec–22 Jan.* **TV. Pay car park.**

This place has got the best location in town. Almost every room overlooks the cathedral – a splendid sight, particularly when floodlit at night – and there's a terrace opposite the hotel, by the cathedral, where they serve breakfast in fine weather. You can also have breakfast on your own little terrace if you ask for room nos. 19, 21 or 22 on the fourth floor. Doubles with shower/wc or bath are from €56 to €68. *10% discount on the room rate (Oct–March) offered to our readers on presentation of this guide.*

⟪ 🏠 Hôtel de la Cathédrale**

12 rue Saint-Romain; near the cathedral. **Map C3-9**
☎02.35.71.57.95 ☎02.35.70.15.54
🌐www.hotel-de-la-cathedrale.fr
TV. High chairs available. Pay car park.

In a good, quiet location, on a pedestrianized street that runs alongside the cathedral, this is a delightful little hotel with an internal courtyard. The rooms range from €62 with shower/wc up to €72 with bath; some have views of the cathedral. There's a tearoom offering a wide choice of unusual teas.

⟪ 🍴 🏠 |❚| Hôtel de Dieppe***

Place Bernard-Tissot; near the train station. **Map C1-4**
☎02.35.71.96.00. ☎02.35.89.65.21
📧hotel.dieppe@wanadoo.fr
TV.

A large hotel run with style by a family who've been in the business longer than anyone else in town. The rooms are comfortable and some (on the third floor) have recently been refurbished. Rooms with spa baths cost €92, or you might enjoy a two-night stay at the weekend for €105. The restaurant is famed for

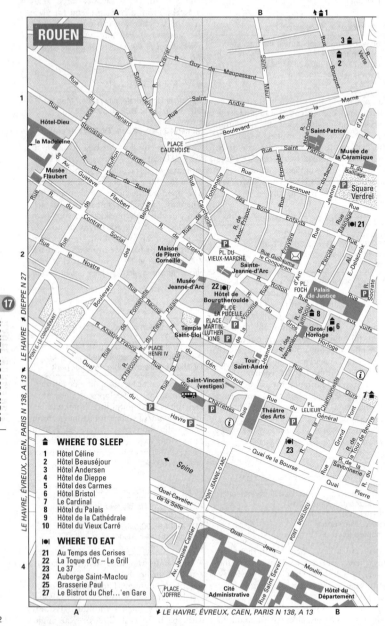

ROUEN

WHERE TO SLEEP

1 Hôtel Céline
2 Hôtel Beauséjour
3 Hôtel Andersen
4 Hôtel de Dieppe
5 Hôtel des Carmes
6 Hôtel Bristol
7 Le Cardinal
8 Hôtel du Palais
9 Hôtel de la Cathédrale
10 Hôtel du Vieux Carré

WHERE TO EAT

21 Au Temps des Cerises
22 La Toque d'Or – Le Grill
23 Le 37
24 Auberge Saint-Maclou
25 Brasserie Paul
27 Le Bistrot du Chef…'en Gare

HAUTE-NORMANDIE

17

LE HAVRE, ÉVREUX, CAEN, PARIS N 138, A 13 ↙ LE HAVRE ↙ DIEPPE N 27

↙ LE HAVRE, ÉVREUX, CAEN, PARIS N 138, A 13

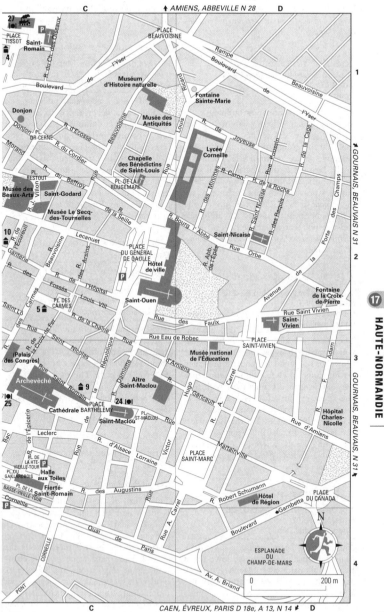

pressed Rouen duck. Menus start at €14 (weekdays), with others from €27 up to €36. If you like to eat late, try the hotel bar, which is open until 1am. *Free house apéritif offered to our readers on presentation of this guide.*

@ 🎝 |●| La Toque d'Or – Le Grill

11 pl. du Vieux-Marché. **Map B2-22**
☏02.35.71.46.29
Open *daily.*

This attractive Normandy building is on the very square where Joan of Arc was burned at the stake. The stylish dining room on the ground floor is dignified and peaceful; menus start from €12. The dishes in the beamed informal grill upstairs are less sophisticated than on the ground floor, but they prove good value for money; try the *formule* at €10. Of course the cuisine is the same in both, it's just the ambience and the bill that are different. *Free house apéritif offered to our readers on presentation of this guide.*

@ 🎝 |●| Au Temps des Cerises

4–6 rue des Basnage. **Map B2-21**
☏02.35.89.98.00
Closed *Sat and Mon lunchtimes; Sun.* **High chairs available.**

The décor – a kitsch dairy theme – tells you immediately what this place is about. No other restaurant in Rouen offers such a wide range of cheese dishes. Don't miss the *truffade*, grilled Camembert with sour cherry preserve or cream cheese ice cream with caramel sauce. Lunch menu for €10.50, others €15–21 – the low prices and good food make this a popular haunt for young locals. There's a nice terrace. *Free house apéritif offered to our readers on presentation of this guide.*

@ 🎝 |●| Brasserie Paul

1 pl. de la Cathédrale. **Map C3-25**
☏02.35.71.86.07
Open *daily until 2am.*

This place has been a brasserie since 1911. Many famous figures have sat down to eat here, Apollonaire and Marcel Duchamp among them. Simone de Beauvoir was a regular, and if today's food is anything to go by, she had good reason. Menus are €10.50 and €17.10: huge salads, sandwiches, small tasty dishes – and the speciality of the house, parcels of Camembert

with apples and cider sauce. It's lovely to dine on the terrace in the evening, facing the illuminated cathedral. *Free house apéritif offered to our readers on presentation of this guide.*

@ 🎝 |●| Auberge Saint-Maclou

224–226 rue Martainville. **Map C3-24**
☏02.35.71.06.67
Closed *Sun and Mon except public holidays.*

Housed in a timber-clad building, with genuine rustic décor, a nice bar and a little terrace open in summer, this restaurant serves comforting food including rabbit terrine, duck with cider or chanterelles, roast potatoes in a frangipane style. Menus go for €14 weekday lunchtimes, with others from €14 except on Saturday evenings and public holidays when the menus costs €24. *Free Kir offered to our readers on presentation of this guide.*

@ 🎝 |●| Le Bistrot du Chef... en Gare

Place Bernard-Tissot. **Map C1-27**
☏02.35.71.41.15 ☏02.35.15.14.43
@media-restauration@wanadoo.fr
Closed *Sat lunchtime; Sun; Mon evening; Aug.* **Disabled access.**

Good station food. On the floor above the buffet, there's a large, hushed dining room that's always full of regulars. There's a tasty menu for €14.50; expect to pay around €25 for à la carte. There's a pianist playing on Friday and Saturday evenings. *Free house apéritif offered to our readers on presentation of this guide.*

@ |●| Le 37

37 rue Saint-Étienne-des-Tonneliers. **Map B3-23**
☏02.35.70.56.65
Closed *Sun; Mon; Aug.*

This bistro is run by Gilles Tournadre, Rouen's best chef, and is an offshoot of his renowned *Gill* restaurant, nearby. The ambience is very Elle Deco, modern, warm, and the food is more exotic than at *Gill*. They have dishes which change throughout the seasons, including pork's head with sweet and sour sauce, cod with onion chutney and caramel tart. The prices aren't at all bad, with a €16.50 *formule* served all day from Tuesday lunchtime to Friday lunchtime. À la carte, reckon on around €33 without wine.

Clères
76690 (18.5km N)

⊚ 𝕏 |◉| **Le Flamant Rose**

Place de la Halle; take the D27 and turn off
onto the D6 at Boulay.
☎02.35.33.22.47
Closed *evenings; Tues; Nov.*

This simple place serves regional dishes
and a few brasserie classics such as terrine
of duck breast with six flavours, *Vallée
d'Auge* veal chops and trout Dieppe style.
There's a lunch menu for €9.80, with
another at €13; and a special menu on
Sunday at €16. *Free coffee offered to our readers on presentation of this guide.*

Ry
76116 (20km E)

⊚ |◉| 𝕏 **Restaurant Le Bovary
– La Table d'Oscar**

Grande-Rue. Take the N31 towards
Martainville, then take the D13.
☎02.35.23.61.46

A venerable establishment that welcomes
travellers who have lost their way… For
a long time the owners ran the restaurant
Casino de Forges, before coming to this
cosy and peaceful place. They offer weekday lunch menus for €9.50 and €12, with
other menus at €16.50, €22 and €30.
Good Normandy specialities are served
in generous portions. *Free house apéritif or
coffee offered to our readers on presentation of
this guide.*

Saint-Valéry-en-
Caux
76460

⊚ 𝕏 🏠 **Hôtel Henri IV****

16 rte. du Havre; from the centre take the
Fécamp–Cany-Barville road; it's several hundred metres along on the left.
☎02.35.97.19.62 🖷02.35.57.10.01
TV. Disabled access.

Owner Michèle loves taking care of her
guests, and she creates a cheerful atmosphere in this large, ivy-covered, brick-
built hotel with patio. Comfortable bedrooms are at €32 and €39 with basin
(these have the best views), and from
€40 up to €49 with shower/wc or
bath; those at the back are the quietest.
Michèle also loves flying; if you'd like

a trip along the coast, she can arrange
it with her friends at the flying club.
There's a nice flowery terrace. *Free house
apéritif offered to our readers on presentation
of this guide.*

⊚ 🏠 |◉| **Hôtel-restaurant La
Marine**

113 rue Saint-Léger; from the bridge go past
the Maison Henri IV, the tourist office; it's on
the first road on the left.
☎ and 🖷02.35.97.05.09
Closed *Tues evening; Wed; 3 weeks in Jan; a
fortnight in March.* **TV. High chairs available.**

You'll be made to feel very welcome in
this quiet family-run hotel and restaurant.
There are no fancy trimmings, but facilities are perfectly adequate. You'll spend
from €36 up to €40 for a room with
shower/wc or with bath. Weekday menu
at €11.50, and other menus €17.50–
29.50, feature specialities such as skate
in cider.

⊚ |◉| **Le Restaurant du Port**

18 quai d'Amont; it's at the entrance to the
port.
☎02.35.97.08.93
Closed *Sun evening; Mon and Thurs evenings (except July–Aug).*

As you can guess from the name, this
seafood restaurant stands right by the harbour. It's the most refined establishment in
town, and the prices reflect that. The €20
menu is simple and classic, while the more
interesting one at €36 features mackerel
tart and grilled turbot. There's also an à
la carte menu for around €48 as well as
some alternative dishes to cater for meat
lovers. Portions are not overly generous.
Ask for a table by the wide window with
a view over the port.

Sotteville-sur-Mer
76740 (10km NE)

⊚ 𝕏 🏠 **Hôtel des Rochers****

Place de l'Église.
☎02.35.97.07.06 🖷02.35.97.71.73
Closed *Jan–Feb.* **Disabled access.**

A big building, which used to be a presbytery, with a delightful walled garden. They
have ten or so quiet, comfortable rooms
with shower/wc or bath for €43–46.
Excellent welcome is guaranteed. *Free
coffee offered to our readers on presentation of
this guide.*

HAUTE-NORMANDIE

◎ |O| Restaurant Les Embruns

Place de l'Église; go towards Dieppe and turn left onto the D68 at Veules-les-Roses.
☎02.35.97.77.99
Closed *Sun evening; Mon; Tues (Oct to end March); 3 weeks end Jan to mid-Feb; a fortnight end Sept to early Oct.* **Disabled access.**

This used to be a bar and tobacconist's, but has since been transformed into a gourmet restaurant. At lunchtime you can choose the *menu-carte* from €12.50, and in the evening there's a choice of menus €23–39. Specialities, drawn from the local region and further afield, include lamb *noisette* in Provençal style and *escalope* of veal with citrus fruits.

Petites-Dalles (Les)
76540 (17km W)

◎ 🛏 |O| Hôtel-restaurant de la Plage

92 rue Joseph-Heuzé; take the D925 towards Fécamp and it's in the main street 50m from the beach.
☎02.35.27.40.77
Closed *Sun and Mon evenings, Wed; Mon only in season; during Feb and Christmas school holidays.*

Monsieur and Madame Pierre will welcome you warmly to this handsome brick establishment with its wooden balconies and delightful turrets. The whole place is very quiet, with cosy, inexpensive rooms; doubles €39 with shower/wc or €42 with bath. It's rare to find such a reasonably priced hotel of such quality on the coast. The little dining room, meanwhile, a mixture of traditional and modern styles, is also a good bet. It's great food, prepared with the best produce; they specialize in seafood, including delicious warm oysters wrapped in lettuce – or try *civet* of winkles and oysters with cider and *coulis* of beetroot with apples. Menus range from €15.80 up to €33.

Tréport (Le)
76470

◎ 🎎 🛏 Hôtel de Calais**

1 rue de Paris; from the quay, head up towards the church.
☎02.27.28.09.09 📠02.27.28.09.00
🌐www.hoteldecalais.com

Open *daily 7.30/8am–9.30/11pm, depending on the season.* **Car park.**

This former coaching inn, perched above the harbour, was built almost two centuries ago. Previous guests have included Victor Hugo as well as American GIs and ordinary folk on their first paid holidays – this place has seen them all. Rooms are nice and bright, and the bathrooms have been refitted. Only some of the rooms overlook the harbour, and they're not all the same size, so it's worth asking for what you want. Doubles cost €42–68 with shower/wc, or €55–65 with bath. They also have apartments. The atmosphere is warm and friendly and you'll receive a very pleasant welcome. *One free breakfast per room per night (except public holidays and July–Aug) offered to our readers on presentation of this guide.*

◎ |O| Mon P'tit Bar

3–5 rue de la Rade; it's in the port.
☎02.35.86.28.78

A nice, authentic, unstuffy little place that's less a conventional restaurant than a bar which serves food, including good seafood platters, all day until late. They have three different menus at €10.80, €12.50 and €15.80. Dishes are cooked using fresh market produce, prices are low and you get a friendly reception.

Criel-sur-Mer
76910 (8.5km SW)

◎ 🎎 🛏 |O| Hostellerie de la Vieille Ferme**

Mesnil-Val-Plage; take the cliff road, and it's in the main street, 300m from the beach.
☎02.35.86.72.18 📠02.35.86.12.67
Closed *Sun evening and Mon, out of season; mid-Dec to mid-Jan.* **TV. Car park.**

An enormous, traditional Normandy building with a terrace, manicured lawn, a large garden with twittering birds and an old cider press. The comfortable, quiet bedrooms which have just been refurbished go for €52–115 with bath. Half board is requested in season. The dining room is decorated in a beautiful, traditional style and the menus cost €14.50 weekday lunchtime, €17–37 at other times. Logis de France. *10% discount on the room rate (15 Sept—15 March) offered to our readers on presentation of this guide.*

Verneuil-sur-Avre

27130

@ 🎋 🏠 |O| Hôtel Le Saumon**

89 pl. de la Madeleine; it's on the church square.
☎02.32.32.02.36 ℱ02.32.37.55.80
🕸www.hoteldusaumon.fr
Closed Sun evening, Nov to Easter; end Dec to early Jan. **Disabled access. TV.**

A good, reliable provincial hotel offering comfortable, impeccably clean rooms in warm tones; doubles are €42–52 with shower/wc or bath. The restaurant is very good, serving dishes typical of this part of Normandy such as salmon, grilled lobster and veal sweetbreads Normandy style. The €11 menu is served on weekdays only, with a range of other menus €15–50. You'll receive a professional welcome. This hotel is perfect for a short stay in Verneuil. Logis de France. *A free coffee is offered to our readers on presentation of this guide.*

Bourth

27580 (10.5km NW)

@ |O| Auberge Chanteclerc

6 pl. de l'Église; to the west of Verneuil-sur-Avre via the N26, in the direction of l'Aigle, then the D54.
☎02.32.32.61.45
Closed Sun evening; Mon; Thurs evening; Aug; a fortnight in Feb.

The pretty façade adorned with geraniums and petunias inspired immediate confidence in the place and we weren't disappointed. The restaurant is good, run by a charming couple and offering well prepared dishes with menus at €15 weekday lunchtimes, and others at €24–42. From the traditional to the inventive – there's something to suit every palate. In summer you can eat on the terrace.

Breteuil-sur-Iton

27160 (11km N)

@ 🎋 |O| Le Grain de Sel

Take the D840.
☎02.32.39.70.61
Closed Sun evening; Mon; Tues evening; first fortnight in Aug.

The dining room is cosy and tastefully decorated and the food is fresh and fruity with a touch of the exotic – the use of spices giving a new take on the traditional local cuisine. The ambience is pleasant and the dishes attractively presented. The standard is reliably good and the prices very accessible with a special menu at €13 (served on Sun too) and other menus at €15–25.50. In fact, this restaurant scores highly on all counts. *Free coffee is offered to our readers on presentation of this guide.*

Vernon

27200

@ 🏠 |O| Hôtel d'Évreux – Restaurant Le Relais Normand***

11 pl. d'Évreux; it's opposite the post office.
☎02.32.21.16.12 ℱ02.32.21.32.73
📧hoteldévreux@libertysurf.fr
Restaurant closed Sun (except Easter and Whitsun). **TV. High chairs available. Car park.**

This is one of those establishments where the rooms exude the antiquated charm of the rather quaint hotels that are both bourgeois and rustic at the same time. Rooms will set you back €33–59 according to comfort and season. The restaurant offers a cosy but smart setting where you can sample excellent, mouthwatering specialities, including foie gras *au torchon* (the foie gras is wrapped in a cloth and simmered in broth) and fillet of beef Rossini. Menus €21 and €27 feature classic, traditional cooking and no unpleasant surprises. In the summer they open the conservatory. Reservations are recommended.

@ |O| La Halle aux Grains

31 rue de Gamilly; it's near the place de la République.
☎02.32.21.31.99
Closed Sun evening; Mon; 1–15 Aug; Christmas school holidays. **Disabled access.**

The welcome at this restaurant is warm, the setting attractive and the service diligent, like a rather smart brasserie – no wonder it's packed year-round. Everything – including the pizza dough – is prepared on the premises from the freshest produce. The puff pastry is delicious (in both starters and desserts), and the grilled meat is first-rate. Dishes of the day average at around €7.50 lunchtimes except weekends and public holidays, and on Sunday you'll pay €23. The wine list is attractively priced and varied.

17

HAUTE-NORMANDIE

Vernonnet

27200 (2km NE)

◎ ⅍ |◉| Le Relais des Tourelles

Rue de la Chaussée; it's opposite Vernon on the other side of the Seine.
☏02.32.51.54.52
Closed *Wed; Sun evening.* **Disabled access. Car park.**

A good spot and just 4km from Giverny – a chance to leave the tourist coaches and Monet's fan club behind. This charming restaurant serves a range of regional specialities along with classic dishes including hot oysters with a leek fondue and John Dory with Nantes butter sauce. Menus start at €12 (weekdays only), with others €21.50–29.50. They host regular jazz evenings. *Free coffee offered to our readers on presentation of this guide.*

Giverny

27620 (5km E)

◎ ⅍ 🛏 |◉| Hôtel La Musardière**

123 rue Claude-Monet; it's 200m beyond the Monet museum.
☏02.32.21.03.18 ☏02.32.21.60.00
@iraymonde@aol.com
Closed *Mon lunchtime; 1 Nov–31 March (restaurant only).* **TV. Car park.**

A large house with a veranda and a huge garden, near Monet's house. The little restaurant, which does good salads, can get very full, so you may have to wait a long time to be served. They also serve crêpes and classic dishes such as grilled *entrecôte*. They have a *formule* at €16, and other menus for €18 and €28, salads are priced €7–10. Spacious double rooms go for €55–74 with shower/wc or bath. *One free breakfast per room is offered to our readers on presentation of this guide.*

Gasny

27620 (10km NE)

◎ |◉| Auberge du Preuré Normand

1 pl. de la République; take the D313 or the D5 via Giverny.
☏02.32.52.10.01
Closed *Tues evening; Wed; first 3 weeks in Aug.* **Disabled access.**

A gourmet stop ideally situated between La Roche-Guyon and Giverny. The cheapest menu is €15 weekday lunchtimes, and others are from €22.50 to €42. There

are different menus to try – the Prieuré, the Tradition, the Découverte and the Dégustation – all of them with a distinctly festive touch. There's a judicious selection of wines at very reasonable prices, and the whole experience proves to be excellent value. One or two gripes: the bread rolls could be better, and although the setting is meticulous it's rather bland. But that won't spoil your enjoyment of the wonderful food.

Fourges

27630 (15km NE)

◎ |◉| Le Moulin de Fourges

38 rue du Moulin; take the D5 towards Magny-en-Vexin and follow the signposts in Fourges.
☏02.32.52.12.12
Closed *Sun evening; Mon; Nov–March.* **Disabled access. High chairs available.**

It's worth coming to this splendid mill on the banks of the fast-flowing Epte for the romantic setting alone. There's a good-value *formule* served on weekday lunchtimes at €24, and a *menu-carte* at €35. You'll find traditional dishes but also some strokes of inspiration from the creative young chef. Unfortunately the welcome and service leave something to be desired. Try to avoid coming at the weekend when the tour buses and cars fight over the parking spaces. From April to October there are concerts some weekends with dinner at €45 (including an apéritif, wine and coffee).

Veules-les-Roses

76980

◎ ⅍ 🛏 Rélais hôtelier Douce France***

13 rue du Docteur Girard.
☏02.35.57.85.30 ☏02.35.57.85.31
⊕www.douce-france.fr
Closed *Tues evening out of season; Jan.* **Disabled access. TV. High chairs and cots available.**

This exceptional place is an absolute winner. It's become a hotel only recently after considerable refurbishment of the original seventeenth-century coaching inn. An immense fortified building built of brick and pale-coloured wood, with the coach yard in the middle, it's a quiet, restful and romantic place. The extremely spacious and comfy rooms, more like mini-suites, go for €90–130; they have five family flats for four to five people at €200. Their *campagnard* breakfast, €10, includes all sorts of charcuterie, breads and sweet buns, and they serve a brunch for €15. If the weather is good, you can eat in the garden, which is delightful. *10% discount on the room rate (except school holidays and weekends) offered to our readers on presentation of this guide.*

Yport
76111

@ 🎋 |○| 🏠 La Sirène**

7 bd. Alexandre-Dumont.
☎02.35.27.31.87 ℗02.35.29.47.37
🌐www.hotel-sirene.com
TV. High chairs and games available.

This charming seaside hotel has recovered from a lean patch, thanks to the efforts of a local who was perturbed to see it deteriorating and decided to take it over herself. She has renovated the place from top to bottom, no mean achievement. Now *La Sirène* can once again stand tall on the seafront with its impressive half-timbered façade and magnificent view of the cliffs. The new décor is in a tasteful nautical style, in both the rooms and the restaurant. Double rooms are €58; also a few triples at €80. You can enjoy a panoramic view as you eat the carefully selected fresh produce and seafood. Menus start at €18 (except Fri, Sat and Sun in July and Aug) with two others at €26 and €31. A platter of local dishes is available all year round. The owner's younger brother has opened a pub on the ground floor. All in all, an ideal spot for a romantic getaway. *Free coffee offered to our readers on presentation of this guide.*

Yvetot
76190

@ |○| La Fontaine Gourmande

70 rue Bellanger.
☎02.35.96.11.01
Closed *Mon; Sat lunch.*

An adorable, convivial little restaurant hidden in a little street behind the town hall. Both the décor and the food are traditional, but with the odd modern touch: pig's-trotter tart, ox-cheek lasagne, *millefeuille* of Livarot cheese. At lunchtime they offer a *formule* at €9 and a menu at €12; other menus €20–30. We think this is the best restaurant in Yvetot, and we are not alone in our opinion – so booking is well advised.

Croix Mare
76190 (5km SE)

@ 🏠 |○| Auberge du Val au Cesne

It's 3km beyond Yvetot, on the D22 towards Fréville, then, at the stop sign, take the D5 towards Val-au-Cesne.
☎02.35.56.63.06 ℗02.35.56.92.78
🌐www.valaucesne.fr
Closed *Mon and Tues; 10–30 Jan; 22 Aug–4 Sept.* **Disabled access. TV. High chairs available. Car park.**

The ducks and beautiful doves outside this cosy old Normandy inn create a perfect pastoral setting. You can eat outside in summer, and the bantams will come and peck up the crumbs. The food is excellent; try the calf sweetbreads in puff pastry, sole stuffed with shellfish mousse, the *escalope* of turkey made to a peasant recipe, or succulent meat dishes. They offer a €25 menu with starter, main course and dessert, another at €45 or you'll pay at least €40 à la carte. The delicious food and the unusual setting make the prices a bit easier to swallow. There are a few rooms with en-suite bathrooms at €80. Logis de France.

@ |○| Auberge de la Forge

It's on the N15 towards Rouen.
☎02.35.91.25.94
Closed *Tues; Wed.* **Disabled access. Car park.**

A discreetly decorated country restaurant serving traditional regional dishes in a friendly and professional manner. There's a lunchtime weekday menu at €13.80; other menus go for €17.50–29. Though menus change according to the seasons, there are always lots of tasty treats on offer: eggs cocotte with cream of courgette, aubergine with tuna, warm terrine of *andouillette* and lentils, *fricassée* of fish with red pepper and anchovy cream, pan-fried veal stuffed with mushrooms and hazelnuts, warm biscuit with *compote* of apples and honey or a Normandy ice dessert.

Allouville-Bellefosse

76190 (6km W)

⊛ |●| Au Vieux Normand

Take the N15 or the D34.
☎02.35.96.00.00
Closed *evenings (except Fri and Sat).*

You'll find this country inn next to a grand old oak tree on the village square and most of the local population sitting at the tables. Owner's reserve wine list – and draught cider; there's a great atmosphere around the fire. They offer a huge choice of dishes which change constantly: terrine, blood sausage cake, seafood platter, *andouillette*, skate in caper sauce (when available), cheese tart and house tripe, which is a must. Substantial menus begin with the €10 weekday lunchtime menu, others €16–20.

HAUTE-NORMANDIE

Pays-de-la-Loire

Angers

49000

See map on pp.704–705

© 🏠 Centre d'accueil International du Lac de Maine

49 av. du Lac-de-Maine, about 2km from the centre; take no. 6 or 16 bus in the direction of Bouchemaine to "Lac de Maine" or "Perussaie" stop. **Off Map B3-1**
☎02.41.22.32.10 📠02.41.22.32.11
🌐www.lacdemaine.fr
Disabled access. Car park.

A lively hostel with nearly 150 beds that is particularly popular with young people in the summer. It is well equipped, spacious, and is surrounded by a park with a lake. Some forty double rooms have recently been refurbished. A stay costs €16.22 per person per night in a room for four, and €33.60 for a double room, breakfast included. You can obtain a self-service cafeteria-style lunch for a minimum of €8.45, with toasted sandwiches, pizzas, etc at night. Facilities include nautical activities (with a charge), visits to the Environment Centre, free use of sports fields, swimming from mid-June to mid-Sept, a TV room and good (and free) Internet access.

◎ 🍴 🏠 Hôtel Iéna**

27 rue Marceau; it's near the train station. **Map B3-2**
☎02.41.87.52.40 📠02.41.86.01.58
✉ienahotel@wanadoo.fr
TV.

A fine provincial hotel, neither too big nor too small, set on the corner of a quiet street not far from the château. The rooms (€44–48) are not very spacious but they are modern and comfortable (with shower or bath), and the owners go to great lengths to make you feel at home. *One free breakfast per room offered to our readers on presentation of this guide.*

◎ 🍴 🏠 Hôtel Continental**

12–14 rue Louis-de-Romain; it's behind the theatre. **Map B2-8**
☎02.41.86.94.94 📠02.41.86.96.60
🌐www.hotellecontinental.com
Closed *Sun 12.30–5pm.* **Disabled access. TV. Cots available.**

The pretty frontage has an old-style sign outside. The communal areas are warm and bright, and the whole place has been refurbished; there's a pleasant little lounge and breakfast room. Comfortable rooms, with broadband Internet connection, cost €46–60 with shower/wc or bath. There's a friendly welcome from the owners, who are justifiably proud of their hotel. Reservations are recommended. *10% discount on the room rate (Fri–Sun) for two consecutive nights offered to our readers on presentation of this guide.*

◎ 🍴 🏠 Hôtel Le Progrès**

26 av. Denis-Papin; it's opposite the train station. **Map B3-10**
☎02.41.88.10.14 📠02.41.87.82.93
🌐www.hotelleprogres.com
Closed *a week in mid-Aug; Christmas Day and New Year's Day.* **TV.**

This comfy hotel offers good value for money in a district which is a bit dreary but handy for the train station. The rooms are decorated in tones of blue with identical furnishings, though they're of

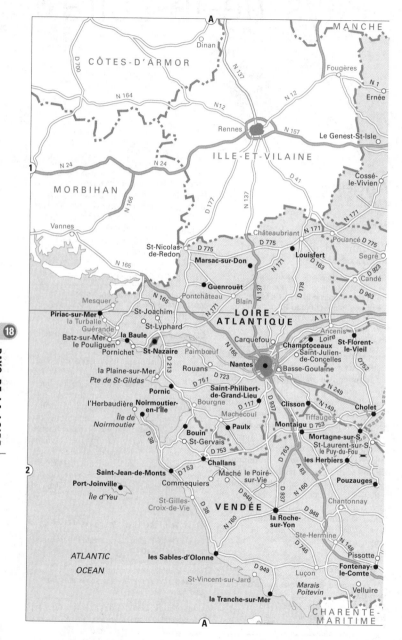

A

MANCHE

CÔTES-D'ARMOR

Dinan

D 700

Fougères

N 164

N 137

N 1

Ernée

N 12

N 12

Rennes

N 157

Le Genest-St-Isle

ILLE-ET-VILAINE

N 24

N 24

D 41

Cossé-
le-Vivien

MORBIHAN

N 166

D 177

N 137

N 171

Vannes

Châteaubriant

N 171

Pouancé D 775

St-Nicolas-
de-Redon

D 775

D 775

Segré

N 165

D 775

Marsac-sur-Don

N 171

Louisfert

D 163

D 823

Candé

Mesquer

N 165

Guenrouët

Pontchâteau

Blain

D 178

D 963

Piriac-sur-Mer

St-Joachim

N 171

LOIRE-
ATLANTIQUE

A 11

la Turballe

Guérande

St-Lyphard

Carquefou

Ancenis

Loire

St-Florent-
le-Vieil

Batz-sur-Mer

le Pouliguen

la Baule

Champtoceaux

Pornichet

St-Nazaire

Paimbœuf

N 165

Saint-Julien-
de-Concelles

D 752

la Plaine-sur-Mer

D 213

Rouans

Nantes

Basse-Goulaine

Pte de St-Gildas

D 751

D 723

Pornic

Saint-Philibert-
de-Grand-Lieu

N 249

l'Herbaudière

Noirmoutier-
en-l'Île

Bourgne

D 117

D 937

Clisson

N 149

Cholet

Île de
Noirmoutier

Machécoul

Montaigu

D 753

Tiffauges

D 38

Bouin

Paulx

St-Gervais

D 753

Mortagne-sur-S.

St-Laurent-sur-S.
le Puy-du-Fou

Challans

D 753

les Herbiers

Saint-Jean-de-Monts

D 153

Maché

le Poiré-
sur-Vie

A 83

Port-Joinville

Commequiers

Pouzauges

Île d'Yeu

St-Gilles-
Croix-de-Vie

D 38

VENDÉE

D 948

D 937

N 160

Chantonnay

ATLANTIC
OCEAN

N 160

la Roche-
sur-Yon

D 948

Ste-Hermine

N 148

les Sables-d'Olonne

D 949

D 746

Pissotte

St-Vincent-sur-Jard

Luçon

Fontenay-
le-Comte

Marais
Poitevin

Velluire

la Tranche-sur-Mer

CHARENTE-
MARITIME

A

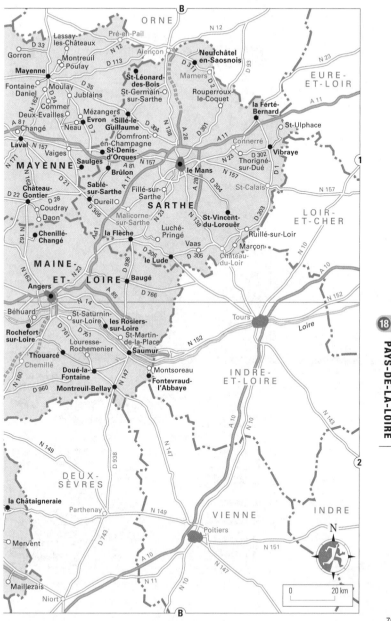

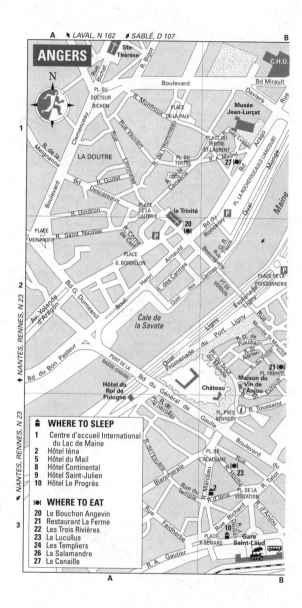

ANGERS

N

↖ *LAVAL, N 162*   ↗ *SABLÉ, D 107*

C.H.U.

Bd Mirault

R. Daviers

Boulevard

PL. DU DOCTEUR BICHON

R. Montroux

PLACE DE LA PAIX

Musée Jean-Lurçat

Rue Bichat

R. Bigot

Ste-Thérèse

R. de la Meignanne

Clemenceau

Rue Vauvert

R. de l'Hommeau

LA DOUTRE

Bd

R. Guitet

Descazeaux

R. Dindron

PLACE MONPROFIT

R. Saint Nicolas

L'Homaige

R. de la Censerie

PL. DU TERTRE

PLACE DE LA LAITERIE

la Trinité

20 |○|

R. du Cornet de Cerf

PLACE G. BORDILLON

PLACE DU TERTRE ST-LAURENT

R. A. Michel

27 |○|

R. Ger-Lurçat

Arago

Bd

PL. LA ROCHEFOUCAULD LIANCOURT

Monge

Rue

Maine

Bd du Roncelay

P

Quai

P

PLACE DE LA POISSONNERIE

Arnauld

Henri

R. des Carmes

Quai   des

PL. DE VERDUN

Carmes

Esplanade Ligny

Rue

Av. Yolande d'Aragon

Bd G. Dumesnil

Boul.

Cale de la Savate

Ligny

Ligny

du Port

R. D. de Puy-charic

R. St Aignan

R. du Voltier

Bd du Bon Pasteur

PONT DE LA BASSE-CHAINE

Bd de la

Quai Promenade

R.-le-bout du Monde

Monte St-Maurice

21 |○|

PL. FREPPEL

Maison du Vin de l'Anjou

Hôtel du Roi de Pologne

Bd du Général de

R. de Pig nerolles

Château

PL. PRÉS KENNEDY

R. Toussaint

Evriou

Gaulle

PL. DE L'ACADÉMIE

Rue

Boulevard

du

R. Talot

R. Hoche

|○|

23

PL. DE LA VISITATION

R. Lenepveu

R. de l'Esvière

Blancherie

Rue du Temple

R. Marceau

▲ 2
R. d'Iéna

R. Richard

R. d'Anjou

R. Faidherbe

PLACE P. SEMARD

10

Gare Saint-Laud

R. A. Gautier

NANTES, RENNES, N 23

18

PAYS-DE-LA-LOIRE

🛏 **WHERE TO SLEEP**
1 Centre d'accueil International du Lac de Maine
2 Hôtel Iéna
5 Hôtel du Mail
8 Hôtel Continental
9 Hôtel Saint-Julien
10 Hôtel Le Progrès

|○| **WHERE TO EAT**
20 Le Bouchon Angevin
21 Restaurant La Ferme
22 Les Trois Rivières
23 Le Lucullus
24 Les Templiers
26 La Salamandre
27 La Canaille

A   B

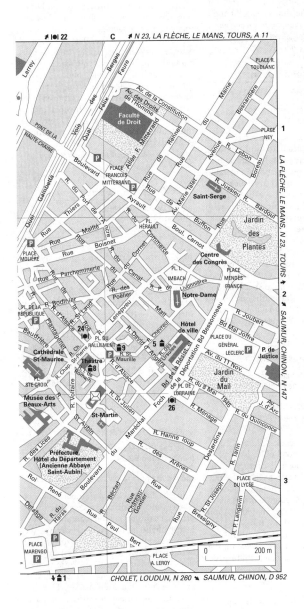

varying size; doubles are between €51 and €53 with telephone, shower/wc or bath. Excellent facilities and very friendly reception; only the district is a bit uninspiring. *10% discount on the room rate at weekends (July–Aug) offered to our readers on presentation of this guide.*

◎ ⅔ � Hôtel Saint-Julien**

9 pl. du Ralliement; it's on the main square.
Map C2-9
☎02.41.88.41.62 ⓕ02.41.20.95.19
ⓔs.julien@wanadoo.fr
TV.

You'd be hard pushed to find anything more central, and you'll get a nice welcome here. The thirty comfortable, air-conditioned rooms are pleasantly decorated – and most have been nicely refurbished. Doubles cost €51–58 with shower/wc or bath; the rooms overlooking the square are the most expensive. The small interior courtyard is ideal for breakfast on a fine day. When you book, you could ask them to reserve a table at the *Provence Café* next door (☎02.41.87.44.15), which specializes in tasty cooking from the south, but fills up days in advance. *10% discount on the room rate offered to our readers on presentation of this guide.*

◎ ☱ Hôtel du Mail**

8 rue des Ursules; it's near place du Ralliement and place de l'Hôtel-de-Ville. **Map C2-5**
☎02.41.88.56.22 ⓕ02.41.86.91.20
ⓦwww.destination-anjou.com/mail
Closed *Sun noon–6.30pm; public holidays.*
TV. Pay car park.

There isn't another hotel quite like this in Angers – it's a seventeenth-century townhouse in a very quiet street with a definite touch of Vieille France. The atmosphere is sophisticated and pleasingly conventional. Bedrooms are decorated tastefully, and go for €51–63 with shower/wc or bath. Some have just been refurbished. In fine weather, a buffet breakfast is served on the terrace in the shade of an ancient lime tree. It's essential to book.

◎ ⅔ |●| La Canaille

8 bd. Arago; it's in the Doutre neighbourhood, beside the Jean-Lurçat museum. **Map B1-27**
☎02.41.88.56.11
Closed *Sat lunchtime; Sun; Mon evening; public holidays; first 3 weeks in Aug.*
Disabled access. High chairs available.

This run-down district is undergoing regeneration, and the young owners opened this restaurant to add some sun and life to the scene. The cooking is simple, tasty and appealing: steak kebabs and other red meat cooked in the fireplace, simple grilled fish, and puddings with playful names. The cheapest menu is €10, there are several set lunches from €14 to €26 during the week, with other menus at €17 (weekday dinner), €20 and €27 (both lunch and dinner); you'll pay around €25 à la carte. *Free glass of Crémant de Loire after your meal offered to our readers on presentation of this guide.*

◎ ⅔ |●| Le Bouchon Angevin

44 rue Beaurepaire. **Map A2-20**
☎02.41.24.77.97
Closed *Sun; Mon; first week in Aug.*

A wine cellar with a restaurant at the back in the heart of the Doutre district. There are two small dining rooms full of character, and a big fireplace. The principle of the house is that there's only ever one menu to choose from: the weekday lunch menu is at €10.50; weekday dinner €15; Friday and Saturday dinner €17. There's an interesting selection of dishes à la carte, including salad with hot *rillauds* and a selection of home-made pastries; you'll pay around €20 à la carte. You can choose from an excellent selection of 500 or so wines. *Free apéritif offered to our readers on presentation of this guide.*

◎ ⅔ |●| Les Templiers

5 rue des Deux-Haies; it's on the pedestrian precinct. **Map B2-24**
☎02.41.88.33.11
Closed *Sun; Mon lunchtime; 3 weeks in July.*

A bright dining room with medieval décor – lances, old swords, tapestries and pennants ornament the walls, which are illuminated by torchlight. It's best to book, because the tasty, traditional cooking has a lot of local fans. The dishes, generally served in copious portions, are based on classic recipes, and they are well prepared using fresh produce from the daily market. There's a weekday lunch menu at €10.50, a *menu du Templier* at €18 and a *menu du Roy* at €25. There's not a dress code exactly, but they're not keen on jeans. *Free Kir offered to our readers on presentation of this guide.*

ⓔ 🎍 |●| Restaurant La Ferme

2–4 pl. Freppel. **Map B2-21**
☎02.41.87.09.90
Closed *Sun evening; Wed; 22 Dec–10 Jan;*
20 July–12 Aug. **Disabled access.**

One of the most popular restaurants in town, with a terrace in the quiet shadow of the cathedral and a stunning dining room. It's stayed successful over the years by offering reliable cooking and generously flavoured dishes – but when it's crowded the service can get slapdash. There's a weekday lunch menu at €11.50, then others €15.50–30. They specialize in poultry: *poule-au-pot* and the warm *rillauds d'Anjou*. *Free coffee offered to our readers on presentation of this guide.*

ⓔ |●| Restaurant Les Trois Rivières

62 promenade de Reculée; it's on the shores of the Maine, next to the hospital. **Off map B1-22**
☎02.41.73.31.88
Car park.

This famous riverside fish restaurant with its panoramic dining room is always full, even on weekdays, so it's best to book. They specialize in fish and the cooking is excellent; try the platter of the three rivers, or the pike perch with *beurre blanc*. Menus start from €13 (weekday lunch), going up to €35. Lots of good dry white wines – try the Domaine de Brizé – alternatively, follow the advice of your hosts. The welcome and service are efficient but not formal.

ⓔ |●| Le Lucullus

5 rue Hoche; it's near the château and the train station. **Map B3-23**
☎02.41.87.00.44
Closed *Sun and Mon (except Mother's Day and Christmas); Feb; last week in July; first 3 weeks in Aug.* **Disabled access. High chairs available.**

A very good restaurant in fifteenth-century cellars. Faultless service and carefully prepared dishes; the weekday set lunch (€14) is a good way of investigating the region's specialities and the dishes are accompanied by local wines. Other menus range from €20 to €54 (wine is included with the €54 menu).

ⓔ |●| La Salamandre

1 bd. du Maréchal Foch; it's near the garden of Mail. **Map C3-26**

☎02.41.88.99.55
Closed *Sun; Mon.*

This restaurant, on the premises of the *Hôtel d'Anjou*, has a reputation for consistently good cuisine, excellent wine list, smart clientele and perfect service. The well-proportioned dining room has an elegant, classic décor, with a portrait of François I on a wooden medallion. The dishes speak for themselves: langoustines fried in olive oil and cream of velvet swimming crab for starters, followed by John Dory; game is served in season. There are two lunch menus, one for €24 and one at €44, as well as a menu offering a selection of dishes for €74.

Saint-Saturnin-sur-Loire

49320 (17km SE)

ⓔ |●| 🎍 Auberge de la Caillotte

2 rue de la Loire; take the D751. It's in the village, well signposted.
☎02.41.54.63.74
Closed *Mon and Tues in winter; Sun evening; Mon only in summer; Nov.* **Disabled access. High chairs available. Car park.**

In autumn and winter you eat in the ravishing rustic dining room; for summer there's a spacious, shady terrace (think of reserving before eating here). Best of all, though, are the cooking and the appealing wine list. Menus, €22–32, list an ever-changing selection of dishes and include a regional dessert, *crème d'Anjou*. À la carte you'll pay €26 – and it's worth it. Hospitable welcome with a touch of humour; you'll feel very relaxed here. *Free house apéritif offered to our readers on presentation of this guide.*

Béhuard

49170 (18km SW)

ⓔ |●| Restaurant Les Tonnelles

Rue Principale; it's opposite Savennières, on the left bank of the Loire.
☎02.41.72.21.50
Closed *Mon and Sun evenings; Wed evening in low season; 23 Dec–31 Dec.*

The terrace is delightful in summer when you sit under the arbour and enjoy the wonderful food. The repertoire varies regularly but the specialities are principally fish dishes from the Loire, as well as rabbit and pigeon recipes. There's a weekday set

18

PAYS-DE-LA-LOIRE

lunch for €23, with other menus €33–76. Very tasty.

Baugé
49150

@ ⚑ 🏠 |O| **Hostellerie de la Boule d'Or****

4 rue du Cygne.
☎02.41.89.82.12 📠02.41.89.06.07
Restaurant closed Sun evening; Mon; **Hotel closed** around the New Year. **Disabled access. TV. Car park.**

A friendly little hotel with ten attractively decorated rooms overlooking an internal courtyard. Doubles with shower/wc or bath go for €54–65. The restaurant specializes in good regional cooking; menus at €19–33. It's best to book. Logis de France. *Free coffee offered to our readers on presentation of this guide.*

Baule (La)
44500

@ ⚑ 🏠 **Hôtel Marini****

22 av. Clémenceau; it's between the tourist office and the railway station.
☎02.40.60.23.29 📠02.40.11.16.98
Ⓦwww.lemarinihotel.com
TV. High chairs available. Swimming pool. Pay car park.

Pleasantly fresh, youthful hotel with an indoor heated swimming pool. The comfortable, tastefully furnished rooms are particularly good value: doubles with shower/wc or bath cost €52–96 depending on the season. The restaurant is for residents only in the evening. The swimming pool is covered and heated. *10% discount on the room rate after two consecutive nights (excluding July–Aug and weekend holidays) offered to our readers on presentation of this guide.*

@ ⚑ 🏠 |O| **Hôtel Lutétia et Restaurant Le Rossini**

13 av. des Evens; it's near the town hall.
☎02.40.60.25.81 📠02.40.42.73.52
Ⓦwww.lutecia-rossini.com
Closed Sun evening; Tues lunchtime; Mon out of season; Jan. **High chairs available. TV. Car park.**

This is a fairly sophisticated hotel, with clean, refurbished rooms with the smell of newness. Double rooms range from €55

to €100 according to level of comfort. The elegant restaurant has become a classic in only a few years, and the new owner has succeeded in preserving this reputation by serving fresh, carefully prepared, heartwarming food in the cosy, well-maintained dining room. Try the fillet of beef Rossini, or the fish of the day, which is invariably satisfying. Tasty desserts are also on offer. There's a €22 weekday menu; others from €28 up to €44. Logis de France. *Free house apéritif offered to our readers on presentation of this guide.*

@ ⚑ |O| 🏠 **Hostellerie du Bois****

65 av. Lajarrige.
☎02.40.60.24.78 📠02.40.42.05.88
Ⓦwww.hostellerie-du-bois.com
Restaurant closed lunchtime; Sat. **Hotel closed** 15 Nov–15 March. **TV. Pay car park.**

Set back from a lively street, this hotel is shaded by pine trees and has a flower garden. Bedrooms go for €60–70 with shower/wc or bath, depending on the season; half board is compulsory in July and August. It's a delightful and pleasantly cool place filled with souvenirs of travels. The new owners are running their business with meticulous care and attentiveness. *One free breakfast per room, or 10% discount on room rate (not including July–Aug), offered to our readers on presentation of this guide.*

Pouliguen (Le)
44510 (3km W)

@ |O| **Restaurant L'Opéra de la Mer**

Promenade du Port.
☎02.40.62.31.03
Closed Wed (lunchtimes only July–Aug); fortnight end Nov. **Disabled access. High chairs available.**

The stage for the *Opéra de la Mer* (Sea Opera) comprises a touristy but nevertheless attractive terrace, with a good atmosphere guaranteed. Here, you can enjoy a fisherman's salad, a seafood *gratin*, a platter of oysters or a mussel casserole. Menus range from €18.50 to €25.50.

Pornichet
44380 (6km E)

@ ⚑ 🏠 |O| **Villa Flornoy**

7 av. Flornoy; it's near the town hall.

☎ 02.40.11.60.00 ℱ 02.40.61.86.47
🌐 www.villa-flornoy.com
Closed *Nov–Feb.* **Disabled access. TV. High chairs available.**

A charming hotel in a quiet street just 300m from the beach. It feels like a family home and has been decorated with taste. The pleasant and comfortable sitting room is attractively furnished with period furniture, and there's a lovely garden where you can relax with a book. Doubles with shower/wc or bath go for €68–88. There is also a restaurant serving locally produced meat, vegetable pie or a seafood platter. Menus are available from €20. *Free house apéritif offered to our readers on presentation of this guide.*

✆ 🕅 ♿ |●| Hôtel-restaurant Le Régent**

150 bd. des Océanides; it's on the seafront.
☎ 02.40.61.05.68 ℱ 02.40.61.25.53
🌐 www.le-regent.fr
Restaurant closed *Fri out of season; mid-Nov to mid-Feb.* **Hotel closed** *mid-Dec to mid-Feb.* **Disabled access. TV. High chairs and games available. Car park.**

A family hotel facing the sea on the edge of La Baule. The decoration in the rooms follow an aquatic theme: portholes in the bathrooms, wooden walls and small fountains, etc. It's bright and colourful, and doubles go for €72–90 with bath/wc depending on the season. There are also seven new rooms in an old building. The restaurant specializes in inventive fish and seafood, with a surprising variety and turnover of dishes. On fine days you can eat on the terrace overlooking the sea. Menus start from €19 (weekday lunchtimes) up to €32. *Logis de France. Free house apéritif offered to our readers on presentation of this guide.*

Batz-sur-Mer
44740 (8km W)

✆ 🕅 |●| Restaurant Le Derwin

Route du Dervin, côte Sauvage; it's on the coastal road between Batz and Le Pouliguen.
Closed *Tues; Wed; and Thurs (except school holidays); Oct–March.* **Car park.**

This place is popular with the sailing fraternity and is ideal for a plate of mussels, seafood and crêpes while you gaze out to sea; expect to pay €18 per person. Reservations are not possible; credit cards and other electronic methods of payment are not accepted. *Free coffee offered to our readers on presentation of this guide.*

Saint-Lyphard
44110 (16km NE)

✆ 🕅 ♿ |●| Auberge de Kerhinet

Take the D92 to Guérande, then the D51.
☎ 02.40.61.91.46 ℱ 02.40.61.97.57
Restaurant closed *Tues and Wed (except school holidays); mid-Dec to mid-Jan.* **Games available. Car park.**

One of the nicest places in the area, charming and simple, with rooms (€50) in little cottages reminiscent of *Snow White and the Seven Dwarfs.* The décor is chic but country-style and there's a beautiful collection of old photographs. The restaurant serves solid, authentic cooking with a light refinement about it, with a choice of menus €21–38. Specialities include eel, frogs' legs, duck and game. In summer, wooden tables are set out in the courtyard, in the middle of the village. They put a whole dish of terrine down on the table for you to help yourself. *Free house apéritif offered to our readers on presentation of this guide.*

Bouin
85230

✆ 🕅 ♿ |●| Hôtel Le Martinet**

1 pl. de la Croix-Blanche; it's beside the church.
☎ 02.51.49.08.94 ℱ 02.51.49.83.08
🌐 www.lemartinet.com
Disabled access. TV. High chairs and games available. Swimming pool. Car park.

This large and beautiful eighteenth-century house offers a choice of bedrooms – old-fashioned ones overlooking the square or newer rooms at ground level that give direct access to the garden and swimming pool. Doubles cost €53–63 with shower/wc or bath. A duplex, ideally suited to families, is also available. Françoise has redecorated the place and takes care of reception. Her sons also have a role: Emmanuel looks after the kitchen garden and does the cooking while Jean-François supplies the fish and seafood. Meals, including breakfast, are served in the old dining room, which smells delightfully of beeswax, or on the veranda overlooking the swimming pool;

menus are €21–25. Logis de France. *Free sauna session (hotel guests only) or house apéritif offered to our readers on presentation of this guide.*

◎ ⚘ |●| Restaurant Le Courlis

15 rue du Pays-de-Monts; it's on the edge of town.
☎02.51.68.64.65
Closed *Mon and Wed evening out of season.* **Games available. Car park.**

A white, rather squat building that is typical of the area. The gleaming, turquoise dining room contrasts with the predominantly rustic atmosphere, however, and is a nice place to enjoy the mouthwatering cuisine. Specialities change with the seasons and according to whichever fresh fish has been landed: scallops fried in celery salts with five spices, *escalope* of duck foie gras with wine caramel. There's a weekday lunch menu at €12, with others €18–28. *Free coffee or house apéritif offered to our readers on presentation of this guide.*

Challans
85300

◎ ⚘ 🏠 Hôtel de l'Antiquité

14 rue Gallieni.
☎02.51.68.02.84 ☎02.51.35.55.74
ⓦwww.hotelantiquite.com
Closed *a week at Christmas.* **Disabled access. TV. Swimming pool. Car park.**

This hotel is very ordinary from the outside but inside it's charming, with refined period furniture displayed to its best advantage. The rooms are spacious and most of them have been tastefully renovated. The double rooms – €50–56 according to the season – are all set around the swimming pool, which is where you have breakfast. It's a blissful place, run by a nice, energetic couple. *10% discount on the room rate (except July–Aug, weekends and public holidays) offered to our readers on presentation of this guide.*

Commequiers
85220 (12km SE)

◎ ⚘ 🏠 |●| Hôtel de la Gare

66 rue de la Morinière; take the D32, then the D82.
☎02.51.54.80.38 ☎02.28.10.41.47

Closed *1 Oct–31 May.* **Restaurant closed Mon. Disabled access. High chairs and games available. Swimming pool.**

In the early twentieth century, when the railway network extended into the remotest parts of France, this substantial Victorian house was built. No trains now – but at least the nights are quiet. The rooms here are inviting, pleasant and attractively decorated. Doubles range from €34 to €40; the least expensive have washbasin and shower. The dining room is fresh and bright, with lots of green, and a railway theme – old photographs, station lanterns, ticket punchers. Good, original dishes are served in ample portions: seafood, fish, scallops with saffron, veal's liver in port. Menus start at €11.50 (not Sun), then €17.50 and €25. There's a shady garden where you can relax after a swim. *Free house apéritif offered to our readers on presentation of this guide.*

Saint-Gervais
85230 (12km NW)

◎ ⚘ |●| Restaurant La Pitchounette

48 rue Bonne-Brise; it's on the D948 in the direction of Beauvoir and Noirmoutier.
☎02.51.68.68.88
Closed *Mon and Tues (except July–Aug); a week in June; a week in Jan; a fortnight Sept–Oct.* **Open** *noon–1.30pm and 7.30–9.30pm.*

A really welcoming and pretty house with flowers everywhere – but Gérard Thoumoux's cooking outshines the décor. There are many tempting specialities, including duck foie gras with a warm *brioche*, loin of lamb with garlic cream, freshwater eels, fish of the day (depending on the catch!). The weekday lunch menu is €9.50, with others €15.25–32.10. Seafood must be ordered 48 hours in advance (freshness guaranteed). Weather permitting, you can sit on the terrace amidst the garden blooms. *Free coffee offered to our readers on presentation of this guide.*

Champtoceaux
49270

◎ 🏠 |●| ⚘ Hôtel-restaurant Le Champalud**

Promenade du Champalud; it's in the centre of town.
☎02.40.83.50.09 ☎02.40.83.53.81

ⓦ www.lechampalud.fr.st
Restaurant closed *Sun evening 1 Oct–30 March.* **Disabled access. TV. High chairs available.**

This hotel is in a charming village on the banks of the Loire and offers twelve comfortable rooms for €49–65 with shower/wc or bath. The restaurant has a good reputation; the *étape* menu (€12) includes wine, and there are others at €15.50–39. À la carte features regional specialities. There's also a brasserie that serves a worldwide selection of beers and cheaper menu options. They offer various facilities – tennis courts nearby, a sitting room filled with board games and a gym. This place has a friendly, very energetic owner and is good value for money. Logis de France. *10% discount on the room rate (1 Oct–31 March) offered to our readers on presentation of this guide.*

Châtaigneraie (La)
85120

ⓦ ⅍ 🏠 |●| L'Auberge de la Terrasse**

7 rue de Beauregard.
☎02.51.69.68.68 ℻02.51.52.67.96
Closed *Fri evening, Sat lunchtime and Sun evening (15 Sept–31 May); autumn school holiday.* **Disabled access. TV. High chairs available.**

This hotel, which occupies a well-restored, substantial house in a quiet road, has a family atmosphere and a quality restaurant. Double rooms, comfortable and recently renovated, are €59 with shower/wc. The owner provides a culinary voyage through the Vendée marshes and across the sea with a range of menus €12–32 – specialities include eel with butter and bacon, snails prepared in many different ways, and French-toast *brioche*. There's a shady square opposite with a lovely view. Logis de France. *Free digestif offered to our readers on presentation of this guide.*

Château-Gontier
53200

ⓦ ⅍ 🏠 Le Parc Hôtel***

46 av. Joffre; it's at the entrance to Château-Gontier, coming from Angers.

☎02.43.07.28.41 ℻02.43.07.63.79
ℯ contact@parchotel.fr
Closed *Feb school holiday.* **Disabled access. TV. High chairs available. Swimming pool. Car park.**

A wonderful place to get away from it all: a beautiful nineteenth-century mansion house in a wooded park complete with a tennis court and swimming pool. The rooms (€56–71) are bright, colourful and thoughtfully furnished; they are all different, and each is designed around a foreign country; for example, there is a red-and-green Chinese room. The service is as hospitable as the setting. *Free apéritif offered to our readers on presentation of this guide.*

ⓦ ⅍ |●| Restaurant L'Aquarelle

2 rue Félix-Marchand, in Pendu-en-Saint-Fort. It's 400m from the centre; follow the road that runs along the north bank of the Mayenne towards Sablé, and at the roundabout take the Ménil road.
☎02.43.70.15.44
Closed *Wed (May–Sept); Sun and Mon evenings (Oct–April); early March.* **High chairs available. Car park.**

Situated outside town on the banks of the Mayenne, this place will set you dreaming. The terrace is beautiful on summer days, and the panoramic dining room, air-conditioned in summer, offers a magnificent view of the river. The light, creative cooking includes dishes like red mullet terrine with *confit* of tomatoes, crab in a saffron cream sauce or fillet of bass with a Parmesan biscuit. A menu *formule* is available for €10, as well as a weekday lunchtime menu for €14; other menus €21–35. *Free coffee offered to our readers on presentation of this guide.*

Coudray
53200 (7km SE)

ⓦ |●| Restaurant L'Amphitryon

2 rue de Daon; take the D22 and it's opposite the church.
☎02.43.70.46.46
Closed *Tues evening; Wed; Sun evening; Feb school holiday; 1 May; first fortnight in July; a week at All Saints'; 23–25 Dec.* **Disabled access. High chairs available. Car park.**

This place might look like any other inn, but it's gained a reputation as one of the most delightful places in the *département*. There's something invigorating about both the cooking and the décor. Dishes are light and colourful: calf's head and tongue in cider-flavoured *bouillon*, *vieux-pané* turnover, apple tart (made with locally grown fruit). Set menus are at €16 and €25; expect to pay around €35 à la carte. There's a pleasant terrace and a garden.

Chenillé-Changé
49220

⊚ ⛺ |●| Auberge La Table du Meunier

Le Moulin, 31km north of Angers. Take the N162 north from Lion-d'Angers, then the D78.
☎02.41.95.10.98
Closed *Sun evening, Mon, Tues and Wed (March and Nov–Dec); Mon evening, Tues and Wed (April–June and Sept–Oct); 1 Jan–11 Feb.* **Open** *every day (July–Aug).* **Disabled access. Car park.**

Situated in a village full of flowers with a gentle river running nearby and a restored oil mill, this dreamy place offers guaranteed peace and quiet. There are five charmingly decorated dining rooms and a huge panoramic terrace. Menus from €17.30 (except Sun and public holidays) going up to €33.50, reflect the really tasty local cuisine that has gained a good reputation. Dishes include home-made terrine of duck foie gras, fillet of pike perch with *beurre blanc* and iced nougat and red-fruit *coulis*. They have a few rooms on a boat nearby, where you'll be lulled to sleep by the sound of the flowing water; cruises are also available. *Free house apéritif offered to our readers on presentation of this guide.*

Cholet
49300

⊚ |●| Restaurant Le Croquignolet

13 rue de la Vendée; it's just outside the centre, to the northwest.
☎02.41.58.77.00
Closed *Sun and Mon evenings.* **High chairs available.**

A traditional restaurant with rustic décor. The food has character; seafood, snails and locally grown asparagus are just some of the options. The weekday lunch menu is at €10.50, with other menus from €13.50 to €20.50; the cheap menu is sufficient for most appetites, as the portions are gargantuan. There are round tables, which make

for a more convivial atmosphere, and the service is charming.

Clisson
44190

⊚ |●| Restaurant de la Vallée

1 rue de la Vallée
☎02.40.54.36.23
Open *Tues–Sun lunchtimes and Tues, Wed, Fri and Sat dinner (Mon only in July–Aug).* **Closed** *Feb; Nov and Feb school holidays.* **Disabled access.**

This restaurant serves good regional food, enlivened here and there with exotic, spicy touches: bass fillet with champagne sauce, beef with Saint-Émilion gravy and shortbread with cinnamon coulis. The weekday lunchtime menu costs €18, with others at €21.50–31. The excellence of the food is matched by the service and, above all, by the magnificent terrace nestling above the Sèvre, with a stunning view of the château and the town.

Doué-la-Fontaine
49700

⊚ |●| Restaurant-bar La Halte

108 rue de Cholet; it's opposite the zoo.
☎02.41.59.14.16
Closed *Tues, Wed and Thurs evenings (except July–Aug); a fortnight* around *New Year.* **Car park.**

This restaurant is by the side of the road; it's nondescript inside but the cooking is sophisticated and uses the finest local ingredients, such as mushrooms and fish from the Loire. Menus range from €12 to €33; there's even a pink *crème brûlée* – made without any artificial colourings. If you notice any strange noises, they are probably not being made by fellow customers with poor table manners but by the guests of the zoo over the road.

⊚ |●| Le Caveau

4 bis pl. du Champ-de-Foire; it's signposted from the town centre.
☎02.41.59.38.28
Open *daily lunchtime and evening, Easter to Oct; Fri evening to Sun lunchtime, out of season.* **Closed** *early Jan.* **High chairs available.**

A warm, welcoming place in the heart of the village, which started life as a medieval cellar before becoming a famous dance hall. People head here for the *fouaces*, or hearth-cakes – a sort of unleavened bread traditionally cooked in cinders. Try the *fouaces* with *rillettes*, goat's cheese or smothered with local butter. Several *formules* are on offer (generously served and easy on the pocket), as well as a €13 "Express" weekday lunch menu, another evening menu at €20 in high season, and a children's menu at €9.50. The team will fill you in on all manner of activities in the region, and service with a smile is guaranteed; once in a while they have a theatrical evening.

Louresse-Rochemenier
49700 (6km NW)

◎ |●| Les Caves de la Génévraie

13 rue du Musée-Rochemenier; take the D761 or the D69 north from Doué-la-Fontaine.
☎02.41.59.34.22
Closed *Mon (Sept–June); 24 Dec–15 Jan.* **Open** *daily (July–Aug).* **Disabled access. High chairs available. Car park.**

This gallery, hewn out of the rock, was used as a hiding place during the Wars of Religion. Nowadays there are several small dining rooms and, when it's hot outside, the stone keeps them cool. They offer the local speciality *fouaces* (wheat cakes cooked in cinders), which they stuff with *rillettes,* beans, *rillauds* (small pieces of pork), mushrooms and goat's cheese. Dishes are served with hors d'œuvres and Layon wines; there's one menu only, at €20, which includes wine and coffee. It's reservations only – and smoking is not permitted. Before leaving, be sure to visit the delightful cave behind the restaurant, with its light shafts, stained-glass windows and baker's oven. *L' Ammonite* nearby (an annexe) offers the same menus.

Évron
53600

◎ 🎋 🏠 |●| Hôtel-restaurant Brasserie de la Gare**

13 rue de la Paix; it's opposite the station.
☎02.43.01.60.29 📠02.43.01.58.28
🌐www.hotelevron.com
Restaurant closed *Sat evening*; *Sun; public holidays.* **TV.**

This *Logis de France* establishment looks like something out of another era and

you'd probably hesitate before deciding to give it a go. It's a good place, however, and offers quiet, comfortable bedrooms with shower/wc at €38, or €43 with bath. They serve generous portions of good regional cooking in the restaurant with dishes such as house terrine and rib steak *façon vallée de l'Erve*. The brasserie menu costs €11 (Mon–Sat only) and there are others at €15–18. *Free coffee offered to our readers on presenation of this guide.*

Mezangers
53600 (3km NW)

◎ 🎋 🏠 |●| Relais du Gué de Selle***

Route de Mayenne; it's on the D7.
☎02.43.91.20.00 📠02.43.91.20.10
🌐www.relais-du-gue-de-selle.com
Closed *Fri and Sun evenings, and Mon (1 Oct–31 May); Mon lunchtime (1 June–1 Oct); 1 May; winter and Christmas school holidays.* **Disabled access. TV. High chairs available. Swimming pool. Car park.**

Though this farmhouse, which is located in the middle of the country with the forest at its back and a pond at the front, has lost nearly everything of its original atmosphere, it's been restored and converted into a welcoming inn. It offers great menus from €21 (weekdays only); others €25–46. Try the Mayenne specialities such as the *blanquette* of lobster with baby vegetables and local poultry with bilberries. You'll get absolute peace and quiet in the pleasant, comfortable bedrooms (€66–112), which overlook either the garden, the swimming pool or the countryside. Logis de France. *10% discount on the room rate offered to our readers on presentation of this guide.*

Neau
53150 (6km W)

◎ 🏠 |●| Hôtel-restaurant La Croix Verte**

2 rue d'Évron; in Évron; take the D32 in the direction of Laval.
☎02.43.98.23.41 📠02.43.98.25.39
🌐www.croixverte.com
Restaurant closed *Fri evening (Oct–Easter); Sun evening; winter school holidays.* **TV.**

Your heart might sink when you catch sight of this place – it's set on an unattractive junction and sports a dreary façade.

But you'll be pleasantly surprised when you step inside, and might even be tempted to stay longer than you planned. Superbly refurbished bedrooms with shower/wc or bath are €41, and there's a nice bar. The à la carte menu is full of tasty specialities – delicious foie gras steak with candied ginger chestnuts. Or you can choose the weekday menu at €12.50, or one of the other menus €19–32. Logis de France.

Deux-Évailles
53150 (12km NW)

⊛ |●| La Fenderie

Site de la Fenderie; it's on the D129 between Jublains and Montsurs, at the edge of the village.
☎02.43.90.00.95
Closed Mon; autumn school holiday. **Open evenings by prior booking only. Disabled access. High chairs and games available.**

This place stands in forty acres of grounds; normally the birds have the place to themselves but at the weekends picnickers crowd in – so avoid the scrum by relaxing on the terrace opposite the pond. They serve local dishes that change daily, with weekly lunch menus at €11, and others €17.70–33. Good bets include fillet of beef with morels, duck breast with Pommeau, scallops in cider with caramelized apples, warm apple tart flambéed with Calvados and numerous other mouthwatering dishes. When skies are grey, enjoy the dining room with its fireplace and exposed beams; in good weather you can gaze out of the bay windows at the surrounding countryside.

Jublains
53160 (17km NW)

⊛ |●| Crêperie-grill l'Orgétorix

9 rue Henri-Barbe; take the D7.
☎02.43.04.31.64
Closed evenings out of season (except by reservation). **Disabled access. Car park.**

Monsieur takes command of the stove here, while Madame oversees the dining room. They're obviously doing something right – after 12.30pm there's hardly a seat left. The menus are delicious and very cheap: two-course *formule* for €5.90, three-course menu at €9.20 including drink. À la carte, the *galettes* and crêpes are good. Follow your meal with a stroll around this old Gallic village.

Ferté-Bernard (La)
72400

⊛ 🎿 🏠 |●| Hôtel-restaurant La Perdrix**

2 rue de Paris.
☎02.43.93.00.44 ℗02.43.93.74.95
✉restaurantlaperdrix@hotmail.com
Closed Mon evening; Tues; Feb. **TV. Pay car park.**

At the tender age of 6, Serge Thibaut declared that he wanted to be a chef when he grew up. He learned his trade first in Loué and then in Paris, and went on to open his own restaurant. For some time now he has been delighting customers with his talent and generosity, as well as his ceaseless ability to surprise – as in his turbot fillet *meunière* with emulsified butter and Curaçao. Menus are at €18 (except Sat evening and bank holidays), then at €26 and €38. The wine cellar boasts almost four hundred vintages. The rooms are nothing special, but the breakfast is excellent, with good coffee and home-made bread. Doubles cost €47–52, and there's a duplex that sleeps five. The talent here goes hand in hand with great modesty and hospitality. Logis de France. *Free coffee offered to our readers on presentation of this guide.*

⊛ 🎿 |●| Le Bocage Fleuri

14 pl. Carnot; it's near the Notre-Dame church and the fountain.
☎02.43.71.24.04
Closed Sun; Tues evening; Wed evening; 3 weeks in Aug.

A little place in the middle of town, much praised by the locals. The terrace is ideal when the weather's fine. Very professional cuisine and they don't stint on the helpings. The weekday lunchtime menu costs €8, with others up to €22. There's a lovely interior garden. *Free coffee offered to our readers on presentation of this guide.*

⊛ |●| Le Dauphin

3 rue d'Huisne; it's in a pedestrianized street.
☎02.43.93.00.39
Closed Sun evening; Mon; a week in March; a fortnight in Aug. **Disabled access. High chairs available.**

This delightful, quiet restaurant is located in a historic building near the port, Saint-Julien, and is popular with couples and gourmets alike. Menus start at €15 (except Sat evening, Sun and public holidays), with others €23.50–38.50. The menu is changed twice a year, although other variations may be introduced to take into account seasonal availability and the whims of the chef.

Rouperroux-Le-Coquet
72110 (13km SE)

◉ ⚶ |◉| Le Petit Campagnard

It's on the D301; take the D7 to Bonnétable, then the D301 in the direction of Saint-Cosme-en-Vairais.
☎02.43.29.79.74
Closed *Mon; Tues, Wed and Thurs evenings; 3 weeks in Aug.* **Disabled access. Car park.**

A pretty little place, especially popular on Sundays, offering good regional dishes. The cheapest ("*Sarthois*") menu, at €9,50, is unbeatable, and the next menu, at €17.10, is not bad either; expect to pay around €23 à la carte. *Free coffee offered to our readers on presentation of this guide.*

Saint-Ulphace
72320 (14km SE)

◉ ⚶ 🏠 |◉| Le Grand Monarque

5 pl. du Grand-Monarque; take the D7, it's right in the heart of the village.
☎02.43.93.27.07 ☎02.43.71.13.18
Closed *Tues; Wed.* **Disabled access. TV.**

This restaurant is a hit with the locals – who enjoy long, convivial Sunday lunches here. Menus are priced from €9.50 for a weekday lunch, with others €13–30, and offer good solid cuisine. There's a covered terrace in summer and in winter they have themed evenings based around dishes such as paella, *choucroute*, seafood and so on. They also have a few furnished double rooms, priced at €30–45 depending on facilities, in a house near the restaurant. *Free coffee offered to our readers on presentation of this guide.*

Flèche (La)
72200

◉ ⚶ 🏠 |◉| Relais Henri IV

Route du Mans; it's 2km northeast of town, towards Paris-Le Mans.
☎02.43.94.07.10 ☎02.43.94.68.49
🌐www.logis-de-france.fr

Closed *Sun evening; Mon; Feb school holiday; first week in Nov.* **TV. High chairs and games available. Lock-up car park.**

The inn is on the edge of the town and set back from the road. The recently renovated rooms are bright, cheerful and soundproofed; doubles go for €42–45. The food is good: since the chef is really passionate about chocolate, make sure you try his *millefeuille*. To keep with the chocolate theme, the walls in the dining room are plastered with 200 chocolate moulds and figurines. Menus range from €13.50 to €31; it's excellent value and you can be sure of a warm welcome. Logis de France. *Free house speciality offered to our readers on presentation of this guide.*

◉ ⚶ 🏠 Relais Cicero★★★

18 bd. d'Alger; it's near place Thiers, close to the Prytanée.
☎02.43.94.14.14 ☎02.43.45.98.96
🌐www.cicero.fr
Closed *Sun; 1–15 Aug; 20 Dec–21 Jan.* **TV. Car park.**

A beautiful residence in a sixteenth-century building (modified in the eighteenth century), well away from the crowds and noise of the town. There's an English bar, a reading room, a comfortable breakfast room and an open fire. Bedrooms in the main house are so stylish and comfortable that they're well worth splashing out on, but the hotel proper is actually on the other side of the garden, which remains pretty all year round. There you get cosy doubles with shower or bath for €69–109; breakfast at €9. This place oozes charm. Reservations are recommended during the week of the 24-hour Le Mans circuit. *10% discount on the room rate (Jan–Feb and Oct–Nov) offered to our readers on presentation of this guide.*

◉ |◉| Restaurant La Fesse d'Ange

Place du 8-Mai-1945; it's next to the theatre.
☎02.43.94.73.60
Closed *Mon; Tues lunchtime; Sun evening; a fortnight in Feb; first week in Aug.*

The young chef, Sébastien Gasnier, has not taken long to establish this restaurant, resolutely modern and sophisticated in both food and décor, as one of the best in the area. He juggles with flavours and spices while also taking great pains over the visual impact of both the dishes and the setting (even the paintings on the walls are all his own work). The terrines are particularly delicious. There are menus at €19 (except weekends and public holidays), €29 and €38.

⊚ 𝒜 |○| Le Moulin des Quatre Saisons

Rue Gallieni; it's opposite the town hall, on the N23.
☎02.43.45.12.12
Closed Sun and Wed evenings; Mon; a fortnight in Jan; a week in March; autumn school holiday. **Disabled access. High chairs available.**

This restaurant has a great riverside location opposite the Château des Carmes, and with the country inn décor and the syrupy background music you could almost imagine yourself on the banks of the Danube. There's a wonderful terrace, too. The food is tasty and good value on menus costing €20.10 (except Sat evening) and €25–29. Camille Constantin's cooking is full of vitality and her menu changes with every season – hence the name of the restaurant. *Free coffee offered to our readers on presentation of this guide.*

Luché-Pringé
72800 (13km E)

⊚ 🏠 |○| Auberge du Port-des-Roches**

Le Port-des-Roches.
☎02.43.45.44.48 ☎02.43.45.39.61
Closed Sun; Mon; Tues out of season; 26 Jan–9 March. **TV. Car park.**

This charming inn is situated in an idyllic setting on the banks of the Loir. Brightly coloured bedrooms cost €42–52 for a double. In the cosy dining room they serve skilfully prepared dishes at good country prices – set menus are €20–42. The superb flowery terrace under the 200-year-old yew tree overlooks the river, as do some of the bedrooms. Logis de France.

Fontenay-Le-Comte
85200

⊚ 𝒜 🏠 |○| Hôtel Fontarabie – Restaurant La Glycine**

57 rue de la République.
☎02.51.69.17.24 ☎02.51.51.02.73
ⓦwww.hotel-fontarabie.com

Closed Christmas period. **Disabled access. TV. High chairs and games available. Car park.**

A long time ago, it was traditional for Basque merchants to travel to Fontenay to trade horses during the Feast of St John. They stayed in this very coaching inn – though the handsome white stone building with its slate roof has been restored somewhat since then. The new contemporary décor is tasteful, the staff is young and cheerful, while the bedrooms are comfortable with adequate facilities; doubles €47–55 with shower/wc or bath. The restaurant, which is named after the wonderful wisteria over the front door, offers good regional cooking and generous portions, and there's a new terrace. Menus range from €7.90 to €24.80. Logis de France. *Free house apéritif offered to our readers on presentation of this guide.*

⊚ 𝒜 |○| Aux Chouans Gourmets

6 rue des Halles; it's next to the town hall.
☎02.51.69.55.92
Closed Sun evening; Mon and Tues lunchtimes (July–Aug); Mon and Tues (Sept–June); first week in Jan; a fortnight in March; a fortnight Aug–Sept.

A solidly built house with a noble façade; the dining room has splendid rough-hewn stone walls and there's a covered terrace overlooking the Vendée. You'll find traditional and gourmet cuisine that uses fresh ingredients bought from the market, which is literally on the doorstep. There are lots of local specialities on the menus €14–34.50: *farci poitevin,* Vendée ham and roast farm-raised pigeon with *confit.* The service is irreproachable. *Free coffee offered to our readers on presentation of this guide.*

Pissotte
85200 (4km N)

⊚ 𝒜 |○| Crêperie Le Pommier

9 rue des Gélinières; take the D938.
☎02.51.69.08.06
Closed Mon and Tues (Mon only in July); 15–30 Sept. **Disabled access. Car park.**

This serene old building is next to an ancient wine cellar. It has a garden and a conservatory, and is covered in wisteria and Virginia creeper. They do crêpes served with a generous side dish – try the "Bretonne" with *andouillette,* apples and salad, the "Blanchette" (goat, bacon, *crème fraîche* and green salad) or the "Syracuse" with smoked breast of duck, pan-fried apples and orange sauce. Wash it all down with a nice bottle of local wine. There's a weekday lunch menu at €7.60, with another at €11. *Free house apéritif offered to our readers on presentation of this guide.*

Mervent
85200 (11km NE)

@ ⚘ |●| Crêperie du Château de la Citardière

Les Ouillères; take the D938, then the D99; from Mervent, take the D99 in the direction of Les Ouillères, then follow the signs.
☎02.51.00.27.04
Closed *Dec–Jan.* **Open** *daily (July to mid-Sept); weekends only (mid-Sept to end June).* **High chairs available.**

A pretty place in a rather strange seventeenth-century castle. Parts of it have been converted in order to welcome walkers. There's a gorgeous rustic dining room, which smells of wood smoke and pancake batter, or you can enjoy the fresh air out on the terrace in summer. They serve the most wonderful crêpes including a sweet one with flambéed apples. Expect to pay about €13 for a complete meal. There's a cellar where they hold exhibitions and musical evenings. *Free coffee offered to our readers on presentation of this guide.*

Velluire
85770 (11km SW)

@ ⚘ ♠ |●| L'Auberge de la Rivière**

Take the D938 as far as Nizeau, then the D68.
☎02.51.52.32.15 ℗02.51.52.37.42
Closed *Mon and Sun evening out of season; Mon lunchtime in season; 20 Dec–2 March.* **Disabled access. TV. Car park.**

This place is ideal if you're after quiet, luxury and fine cooking. The attractive dining room, all yellow tablecloths, beams, pot plants and tapestries, makes a great setting to eat hot oysters, bass with artichokes, crayfish in flaky pastry or young pigeon with morels; menus range from €36 to €48. The charming country-style bedrooms cost €75–94 with bath; no. 10 is the only one without a river view. You can rent bicycles. Credit cards are not accepted. Logis de France. *One free breakfast per room for a stay of at least two consecutive nights (excluding high season and weekends) offered to our readers on presentation of this guide.*

Maillezais
85420 (15km SE)

@ ⚘ ♠ Hôtel Saint-Nicolas**

24 rue du Docteur-Daroux.
☎02.51.00.74.45 ℗02.51.87.29.10.
Open *April–Oct.* **TV. Lock-up garage.**

The young owner of this friendly little hotel looks after everything – from the rooms, €38–55 with shower or bath, to the terrace with its tiny gardens. The rooms are rather old-fashioned but comfortable and they are arranged in terraces, almost on the same level as the sloping inner courtyard-garden. The owner knows the area like the back of his hand and will show you his own walks through the Poitou marshlands; it's an excellent base from which to explore the area. Logis de France. *10% discount on the room rate (except during school holidays and on long weekends) offered to our readers on presentation of this guide.*

@ ⚘ |●| Le Collibert

Rue Principale.
☎02.51.87.25.07
Closed *Sun evening; Mon.*

The rustic setting and hearty food make this an ideal refuge from the rigours of winter, but any time of year is suitable for appreciating the fine dishes created by the chef from Poitou, who is clearly enamoured of his region and its culinary traditions. (The owner, on the other hand, is a mine of information about the cooking of Vendée.) Menus €11.50–34; the regional menu at €22 is particularly worthy of note, with *farci poitevin*, frogs' legs with eels, Mizotte (a local cheese) and gâteau with angelica. À la carte, you can find ham with *mojhettes* (dwarf runner beans), *lumas* (snails) and crayfish. You are guaranteed a meal as steeped in local knowledge as it is in flavour. *Free coffee offered to our readers on presentation of this guide.*

@ |●| La Grande aux Roseaux

Le Grand-Port; it's by the waterside, at the foot of the abbey.
☎02.51.00.77.54
Open *daily April to end Sept.* **Disabled access. High chairs available.**

A romantic setting with a bower outside that attracts both tourists and locals (a recommendation in itself). Good *farci poitevin*, eels and snails from the vicinity. The menus, ranging from €12.60 to €21.50, are served by friendly staff.

Fontevraud-L'Abbaye
49590

⚇ ⚇ ⬛ |●| Hostellerie La Croix Blanche**

7 pl. des Plantagenêts; it's beside the abbey.
℡02.41.51.71.11 ℻02.41.38.15.38
🌐www.fontevraud.net
Closed *Sun evening and Monday out of season; Jan; 17–27 Nov.* **TV. High chairs available. Swimming pool. Car park.**

A delightful hotel in an elegant building, right next to the abbey of Fontevraud, with 25 bedrooms set around a quiet, flower-filled courtyard. Everything here has recently been refurbished to great effect, although the prices obviously reflect all the work involved: doubles with shower/wc or bath cost €63–90. The restaurant, well known for its good cooking, offers menus from €18 (vegetarian) up to €52. Dishes might include foie gras and salad of black pudding. You can choose the type of meal you want by selecting between the brasserie, crêperie and more traditional restaurant. There is also a swimming pool, a pub and a pool hall. Nice welcome, too. Logis de France. *10% discount on the room rate (Nov–March) offered to our readers on presentation of this guide.*

Guenrouet
44530

⚇ ⚇ |●| Le Jardin de l'Isac

31 rue de l'Isac; it's on the Plessé road, on the way out of the town.
℡02.40.87.66.11
Closed *Sun and Mon (Sept–June); Jan.* **Disabled access. High chairs available.**

Sitting below a gastronomic restaurant run by the same people, this cheaper place offers professional service and unbeatable prices. Inside, opt for the dining room on the edge of the garden. In summer, you can eat on the flower-filled terrace in the shade of a magnificent wisteria. Menus, €11 (weekday lunchtimes) and €16, include a buffet of starters and desserts. Tuck into the hors-d'œuvre buffet, which offers a wide selection including

fish terrine, charcuterie and a selection of *crudités*. Then, for a main course, opt for grilled meat or the dish of the day and then head straight back to the buffet for dessert. *Free coffee offered to our readers on presentation of this guide.*

Guérande
44350

⚇ |●| Le Parc du Careil

Careil; it's 2km away on the road to La Baule.
℡02.40.24.20.65
Closed *Mon; Sun out of season.*

This big roadside restaurant is the favourite haunt of the local gourmets. It looks like a transport café but it has recently been taken over by a young couple and has been completely transformed. Both the décor and the food reflect a multicultural mix: there is a pretty Asian garden, and the typical local dishes are served with spicy, sweet-and-sour sauces – with highly satisfactory results. The menus cost €18–60.

Herbiers (Les)
85500

⚇ ⬛ |●| Hôtel-restaurant Le Relais – La Cotriade**

18 rue de Saumur.
℡02.51.91.01.64 ℻02.51.67.36.50
🌐www.hotellerelais.com
Closed *Sun evening; Mon lunchtime.*
Disabled access. High chairs available. TV.

This good hotel, with its beautiful, well-renovated façade, offers 26 luxurious bedrooms; doubles cost from €49 to €52 according to the season. Although it's by the roadside, the double glazing is effective. There's a brasserie, which offers traditional dishes, and a swanky dining room, *La Cotriade*, where you can enjoy gourmet cuisine in extremely generous portions on a range of menus €19–52: medallion of young venison sautéed in thyme butter and liquorice, Saint-Paul snails with foie gras, braised sweetbreads with chicory and Ambert Fourme cheese.

⚇ ⬛ |●| Hôtel-restaurant du Centre**

6 rue de l'Église.
℡02.51.67.01.75 ℻02.51.66.82.24
Restaurant closed *Fri evening and Sat*

(out of season); Sun (in summer); 1–10 Aug; Christmas school holiday. **TV.**

This place is located in the middle of the town, but it's quiet enough and warmly welcoming – ideal as a base from which to explore the region. Doubles go for €45–53 with shower/wc or bath; half board is compulsory from June to mid-September and over the weekend. This is no hardship because the owner is a good chef, creating dishes based on fresh produce, particularly fish, with steaming as a favourite method of cooking. There's a choice of menus at €12–26. Logis de France.

Saint-Laurent-sur-Sèvre
85290 (20km NE)

ⓔ 🍴 🏠 |●| Hôtel-restaurant L'Hermitage**

2 rue de la Jouvence; take the D752 and it's on the River Sèvre, by the bridge opposite the basilica.
℡ 02.51.67.83.03 ℻ 02.51.67.84.11
Closed *Sun evening; Sat lunchtime (mid-Oct to April); Nov.* **High chairs available. TV. Car park.**

A nice family inn with a terrace overlooking the river. Half board isn't compulsory even during the Puy-du-Fou film festival. The menus, €13–25, list good traditional dishes, and you'll get generous portions. The dining room has been refreshingly refurbished and the bedrooms are comfortable; the nicest ones look over the River Sèvre. Doubles with shower/wc or bath cost €35–40. *Free coffee offered to our readers on presentation of this guide.*

Laval
53000

ⓔ 🍴 🏠 Marin Hôtel**

102 av. Robert-Buron; it's opposite the train station.
℡ 02.43.53.09.68 ℻ 02.43.56.95.35
Disabled access. TV. Pay car park.

This establishment, which belongs to the Inter-Hôtel chain, is modern, functional, well soundproofed, and an ideal place to stop if you've just got off the TGV. Doubles cost €45–52 with shower/wc or bath and the service is excellent. There are lots of restaurants in the area. *10% discount*

on the room rate (Fri and Sat) offered to our readers on presentation of this guide.

ⓔ 🍴 |●| L'Avenio

38 quai de Bootz; it's alongside the Mayenne, to the north of the Béatrix-de-Gavre quay.
℡ 02.43.56.87.51
Closed *Sat; Sun.*

This is a haunt of local fishermen, decorated with old fishing lines, reels and hooks, often buzzing with conversations revolving around the ones that got away. You get good home cooking here, including suckling pig grilled to a traditional recipe every first Saturday of the month (served to ten people or more, booked in advance); everything is delicious and served in gargantuan portions. The set lunch at €11 includes a drink; mussels and chips are also available at €8. There's a covered terrace. *Free house apéritif offered to our readers on presentation of this guide.*

ⓔ 🍴 |●| L'Antiquaire

5 rue des Béliers; it's behind the cathedral.
℡ 02.43.53.66.76
Closed *Wed; Sat lunchtime; a week in the Feb school holiday; 15 July–6 Aug.* **High chairs available.**

The food here is simply magnificent. The cheapest menu is a bargain at €16 and there are others from €17.50 up to €35.50. They list dishes like foie gras terrine with apple and cider preserve, *escalope* of pike perch with cider butter, pork steak with Camembert *au gratin*, and iced *marquise* with green apple custard. *Free coffee offered to our readers on presentation of this guide.*

ⓔ |●| La Braise

4 rue de la Trinité; it's in the old town, near the cathedral.
℡ 02.43.53.21.87
Closed *Sat lunchtime; Sun; Mon; a week at Easter; a week around 15 Aug.*

You will be impressed immediately by the homely atmosphere created by the fireplace nooks, old pots, beautiful furniture, exposed beams on the ceiling and hexagonal floor-tiles. The simple, authentic dishes are skilfully cooked, many of them over charcoal, and, as you would expect, grilled fish and meat are the specialities with menus from €20 – try the monkfish kebab, seafood, beef and other meat. If it's sunny, sit on the terrace. You receive a wonderful welcome.

ⓒ |●| Restaurant Le Bistro de Paris

67 rue du Val-de-Mayenne; it's on the banks of the Mayenne.
☎02.43.56.98.29
Closed *Sat lunchtime; Sun evening; Mon; 5–26 Aug.* **Disabled access.**

This is the best restaurant in town and can be the most expensive (menus €23–42) unless you choose the *menu-carte*. Lots of wonderful dishes are served: mushroom pie, bass with parsley and pepper, orange crumble. Guy Lemercier comes up with creative ideas to delight his regulars, who get a good-natured but not overly effusive welcome. Old-fashioned brasserie décor with rows and rows of mirrors, good service and fine wines.

Changé
53810 (4km N)

ⓒ |●| La Table Ronde

Place de la Mairie; it's near the church.
☎02.43.53.43.33
Closed *Sun, Tues, Wed and Thurs evenings; Mon; last fortnight in Aug.* **Disabled access.**

The upstairs restaurant is impressive and expensive; downstairs, there's an attractive bistro with Art-Nouveau décor. At the weekend, you will probably have little option but to choose the restaurant, as the bistro is usually reserved for groups. There's a weekday menu for €16 and others go up to €39. Dishes include guinea-fowl supreme with rhubarb, backed *vivaneau* (type of mullet) with Sichuan pepper – but, as the menu changes regularly, you may discover a brand-new creation. Everything is skilfully prepared, rich in flavour (but not necessarily in calories) and colourful – it's well worth leaving Laval to get here. On a fine day you can sit on the terrace, which faces the town on one side and the park on the other.

Genest-Saint-Isle (Le)
53940 (12km NW)

ⓒ |●| Restaurant Le Salvert

Route d'Olivet.
☎02.43.37.14.37
Closed *Sun evening; Mon; first 3 weeks in Jan.* **Disabled access. High chairs available. Car park.**

Just ten minutes from Laval on the Olivet lake, this restaurant has a terrace open in summer and an open fire when the weather is cooler. It's classy, too – this isn't a place to come to wearing shorts or hiking boots. The food is marked by influences from the Toulouse area. Menus, €17 (weekdays) and €21.50–33, change three times a year. Their bread is home-made, just like everything else.

Cossé-Le-Vivien
53230 (18km SW)

ⓒ ♜ |●| Hôtel-restaurant L'Étoile**

2 rue de Nantes; take the N171.
☎02.43.98.81.31 ⊕02.43.98.96.64
Closed *Sun evening; Mon; a week in Feb; a fortnight in Aug.* **Open** *Fri evening by reservation only.* **TV. Car park.**

The seven bedrooms here are pretty and bright; doubles go for €28 with shower/wc or bath. The restaurant serves good traditional cooking, with a weekday menu at €8.40 and three others €12.20–22.11; reckon on €12 à la carte (weekdays only). The house specialities are oxtail *fondant* and *aiguillettes* of guinea-fowl with Morello cherries. It's best to book at weekends.

Vaiges
53480 (22km E)

ⓒ ♜ |●| Hôtel du Commerce***

Rue du Fief-aux-Moines; take exit 2 off the A81.
☎02.43.90.50.07 ⊕02.43.90.57.40
🖳www.hotelcommerce.fr
Closed *Fri and Sun evenings (Oct to end of April); 1 May; 26 Dec–19 Jan.* **Disabled access. High chairs available. TV. Swimming pool. Car park.**

Ever since 1882, when the Oger family first started running this successful hotel, the only concern of the owners has been to ensure that their guests sleep soundly and eat well. You can quite happily spend a night or two in one of their quiet bedrooms (two of which are specially equipped for disabled guests) – €54–95 with shower/wc or bath – and dine in the conservatory where they serve good food based on local produce: fresh duck foie gras, fried beef fillet with conserve of shallot *confit*, and hot Grand Marnier soufflé. Menus are priced at €17 (weekday lunchtimes) and €27–47.50. To top it all, there's a garden and swimming pool. Logis de France.

Ernée

53500 (30km NW)

@ ⅍ 🏠 |●| Le Grand Cerf**

17–19 rue Aristide-Briand; it's on the N12 in the direction of Mayenne.
☎02.43.05.13.09 🖷02.43.05.02.90
🖳www.perso.wandadoo.fr/hotel-restaurant
-le-grand-cerf
Closed Sun evening and Mon (out of season); 15–31 Jan. **Disabled access. TV. High chairs available. Car park.**

The establishment is known for its facilities and good food. The dishes are intelligently planned around seasonal produce and are offered on various menus. The weekday lunch *formule* (starter, dish of the day, dessert) is €15, with others €22–30. Beautiful renovated bedrooms, several suitable for an entire family and one equipped for disabled guests, with all comforts cost €45 with bath/wc. Credit cards are not accepted. Logis de France. *Free house apéritif offered to our readers on presentation of this guide.*

@ ⅍ |●| La Table Normande

3 av. Aristide-Briand; it's on the N12 in the direction of Mayenne.
☎02.43.05.16.93
Closed Sun; a fortnight in Feb; 1–15 Aug. **High chairs available.**

The owners are deeply committed to what they do, and their restaurant has a nice atmosphere. Serving delicious home-made dishes, it's popular with local workers and tourists alike; the first menu (served during the week) is good value at €9.50; others cost €12.50–18.50. *Free house apéritif offered to our readers on presentation of this guide.*

Louisfert

44110

@ ⅍ 🏠 |●| Les Pierres Bleues

4 pl. de l'Église.
☎02.40.81.23.71
🖂fabrice.suzenet@tiscali.fr
Closed Mon; Sun evening; booking required for dinner on Tues, Wed and Thurs.

This attractively decorated inn offers charming rooms (doubles €34–39) and skilfully reworked local dishes in a genuine village setting. There are mid-week lunchtime menus at €9.15 and

€12.50, and there's a weekend one at €16; reckon on around €27 à la carte. *10% discount on the room rate or free coffee offered to our readers on presentation of this guide.*

Lude (Le)

72800

@ ⅍ 🏠 |●| La Renaissance**

2 av. de la Libération; take the Grande-Rue behind the *Crédit Agricole*.
☎02.43.94.63.10 🖷02.43.94.21.05
🖳www.renaissancelelude.com
Closed Sun evening; Mon; Feb holiday; All Saints' holiday. **TV. High chairs available. Car park.**

Though this is a pretty grand place, the atmosphere is in no way formal and men don't even have to wear ties. The chef uses the freshest produce and monitors the cooking of each dish meticulously; week-day menu at €10 and others €13.50–35.50. Double rooms cost €45–50 with shower/wc or bath. Logis de France. *Free house apéritif offered to our readers on presentation of this guide.*

Vaas

72420 (13km E)

@ ⅍ 🏠 |●| Hôtel-restaurant Le Védaquais**

Place de la Liberté; take the D305, in the direction of Château-du-Loir.
☎02.43.46.01.41 🖷02.43.46.37.60
🖂vedaquais@aol.com
Closed Fri and Sun evenings; Mon; Feb and Christmas school holidays. **Disabled access. High chairs and games available. TV. Car park.**

This old-fashioned village hotel occupies the old schoolhouse. Daniel Beauvais is an excellent chef who doesn't talk much, while his wife, Sylvie, is a very good hostess who chats away quite happily. The food here is a real treat – fresh-tasting, straightforward and brimming with creativity. They offer a weekday *"menu du marché"* for €10, and others at €21–44 or à la carte. The €21-menu includes two glasses of wine (from the Loire region, naturally). The rooms – €42 with shower/wc or €55 with bath – are every bit as pleasant. Logis de France. *Free apéritif offered to our readers on presentation of this guide.*

Mans (Le)

72000

⊛ 🏠 ⅍ Auberge de jeunesse Le Flore

23 rue Maupertuis; take the no. 12 bus in the direction of Californie to the "Erpell" stop; or no. 4, in the direction of Gazonfier, to the same stop.
℡02.43.81.27.55 ℗02.43.81.06.10
ⓦwww.mapage.noos.fr/florefjt
Closed *Christmas school holiday.* **Disabled access. TV.**

A youth hostel with 22 beds (40 in July–Aug); there are several rooms with two or three beds, one with four and a flat that sleeps seven. Accommodation here costs €12.50 per night, including breakfast; meals €4.97–6.20. Half board (€18.25) is compulsory for a stay of more than three nights. FUAJ card is required. Bikes and motor bikes can be parked free of charge inside the hostel. Credit cards not accepted. *Free Internet connection for our readers on presentation of this guide.*

⊛ ⅍ 🏠 |O| Hôtel Green 7**

447 av. Georges-Durand; it's in the south of the town on the road to Tours.
℡02.43.40.30.30 ℗02.43.40.30.00
ⓦwww.hotelgreen7.com
Disabled access. TV. Car park.

A pleasant hotel less than 2km from the 24-hour Le Mans circuit offering friendly service. Comfortable, well-decorated rooms with shower or bath cost €49. Though the restaurant is not brilliant, it produces more than adequate traditional dishes using fresh produce, and its breakfasts and buffet lunches are reliable. Menus range from €15 (weekdays) to €32. *10% discount on the room rate (July–Aug) offered to our readers on presentation of this guide.*

⊛ ⅍ 🏠 Anjou Hôtel**

27 bd. de la Gare; it's opposite the train station.
℡02.43.24.90.45 ℗02.43.24.82.38
TV. Pay car park (except weekends).

A well-located hotel opposite the station, with double glazing (and even two full-length windows) in the rooms overlooking the boulevard. The whole place is gradually being refurbished, but there is an adequate level of comfort throughout. Doubles go for €50 with shower/wc or bath. *One free breakfast per room (weekends only) offered to our readers on presentation of this guide.*

⊛ ⅍ 🏠 Hôtel Chantecler***

50 rue de la Pelouse; it's between the train station and the conference centre.
℡02.43.14.40.00 ℗02.43.77.16.28
ⓦwww.hotelchantecler.fr
TV. High chairs available. Car park.

Just a short distance from the station, this hotel offers peace and comfort within easy reach of the old part of Le Mans. Decent doubles with shower/wc or bath go for €65–110. The welcome is sincere, the parking easy and the breakfast, which is served in the conservatory, rather good. *10% discount on the room rate at weekends (July–Aug) offered to our readers on presentation of this guide.*

⊛ ⅍ 🏠 |O| Hôtel Concorde

16 rue du Général-Leclerc.
℡ and ℗02.43.24.12.30
ⓦwww.concordelemans.com
Car park.

This has long been the most chic hotel in Le Mans, with extremely stylish and comfortable rooms that are no match for its competitors. They do not come cheap, however: doubles cost €110 upwards, with a breakfast buffet at €12. The dining room in the *Amphitryon* restaurant has recently been refurbished with an elegance that does not preclude cosiness; the food is similarly sophisticated, although it is rooted in local tradition. There are weekday lunchtime menus from €19 to €27, then an "*Amphitryon*" menu at €37 and a "*Prestige*" menu at €47. The service is very friendly. *10% discount on the room rate offered to our readers on presentation of this guide.*

⊛ ⅍ |O| L'Atlas

80 bd. de la Petite Vitesse.
℡02.43.61.03.16
Closed *Mon and Sat lunchtimes; Aug.* **Open** *until 11.30pm.* **Disabled access.**

Close to the station, in an area otherwise lacking in good restaurants, this Moroccan restaurant is a real find. The proprietor has done his country proud with both the opulent décor and the cuisine – try the excellent *tajines*, couscous, and fresh Moroccan pastries; menus at €11.50 and €23.90. There's live music at weekends. *Free house apéritif offered to our readers on presentation of this guide.*

⊚ 🎿 |●| Auberge des 7 Plats

79 Grande-Rue; it's in the old town.
☎02.43.24.57.77
Closed *Sun; Mon.*

The large half-timbered house has real style – there are several in the street but this is one of the best you'll find in the old part of Le Mans. Their gimmick, as you'll guess from the name, is that they offer seven hot dishes on the same menu, including an excellent *pavé* of beef, served in thin slices. Everything is fresh, home-made with meticulous care and good value for money: €11.80 for a main course and a dessert, and another menu at €14.50. The youthful, relaxed welcome adds considerably to the appeal. It's advisable to book. *Free digestif offered to our readers on presentation of this guide.*

⊚ 🎿 |●| Le Nez Rouge

107 Grande-Rue; it's in the centre of the old town.
☎02.43.24.27.26
Closed *Sun; Mon; a week in Feb; mid-Aug to 5 Sept.*

This old-town gourmet restaurant is the place to come for *montgolfière* of mussels, *fricassée* of langoustines with red butter, *escalope* of foie gras with warm balsamic cabbage and seafood platter (for two, with advance reservation only). The weekday menu costs €18.50, with others €26–38. It is advisable to book for dinner. *Free coffee offered to our readers on presentation of this guide.*

⊚ 🎿 |●| Le Flambadou

14 bis rue Saint-Flaceau; it's near the town hall.
☎02.43.24.88.38
Closed *Sat lunchtime; Sun; fortnight around Easter; second fortnight in Aug.*

The owner, a native of Mimizan, has not only retained the reference to traditional cooking methods in the restaurant's name (a *flambadou* was a kind of ladle that was heated up over the fireplace and used to pour fat over meat), but has also gone back in time with the food: gizzard *confit* salad with fresh grapes, rabbit legs with red onions and *cassoulet Flambadou*. Allow around €28 à la carte. You can dine in the attractive little dining room, or, in summer, on the pretty terrace on the Gallo-Romanic ramparts. The wine list comes in the form of a photo album with

explanatory captions. *Free house apéritif offered to our readers on presentation of this guide.*

⊚ |●| La Ciboulette

16 rue de la Vieille-Porte; it's in the old town, near place de l'Éperon.
☎02.43.24.65.67
Closed *Sun; Mon lunchtime; Sat lunchtime; a week in Jan; 1–9 May; 3 weeks in Aug.*

This is a fine restaurant with tasty food (menu €31.70) and an elegant little dining room decked with flowers. The emphasis is on fish dishes, but meat eaters are catered for as well, thanks to excellent dishes such as veal kidneys and pig's trotters. The atmosphere is sophisticated without being stuffy, and the service is friendly.

Yvré-L'Évêque

72530 (5km E)

⊚ 🎿 🏠 Hôtel-Motel Papea**

Bener; leave Le Mans on the N23 and follow signs to Papea.
☎02.43.89.64.09 ☎02.43.89.49.81
🌐 www.hotelpapea.com
Closed *Sun evening (Oct–Feb); Christmas to New Year.* **TV. Car park.**

This motel is set in lovely grounds near the abbey of Epau. Some twenty comfortable chalets for two to five people, separated from each other by bushes and trees, cost €30–44 with bath/wc. Ideal if you want to stay in the country but also be very close to the city. *One free breakfast per room offered to our readers on presentation of this guide.*

Fillé-sur-Sarthe

72210 (15.5km SW)

⊚ 🎿 |●| Restaurant Le Barrage

Rue du Passeur; it's the last house past the church.
☎02.43.87.14.40
Closed *Sun evening; Mon; All Saint's school holiday.*

This restaurant is very popular locally, so if you want a table on the terrace looking directly onto the towpath and the Sarthe river, you should reserve, especially on a Sunday. It's a serene, rural setting, and a perfect place to enjoy the good food – foie gras flan with port sauce, grilled *filet mignon* with rosemary, fillet of duck with oyster mushrooms. Menus range from €16 to €27. *Free coffee offered to our readers on presentation of this guide.*

Domfront-en-Champagne
72240 (18km NW)

◎ |●| Restaurant du Midi

33 rue du Mans; it's on the D304, towards Mayenne.
☎02.43.20.52.04
Closed *Mon; Tues, Wed and Thurs evenings, Sun evening; 15 Feb–15 March.* **Disabled access. High chairs available.**

This reliable restaurant offers a fine week-day lunchtime menu (€12.90) with a spicy piece of beef or stuffed duck leg roasted in its gravy; the other menus cost €18.30–35. À la carte, the selection includes excellent foie-gras ravioli with a touch of bilberries. The prices are very reasonable considering the quality of the food and service.

Thorigné-sur-Dué
72160 (28km NE)

◎ 𝒜 🏠 |●| Hôtel-restaurant Saint-Jacques***

Place du Monument; take the N23 and D302.
☎02.43.89.95.50 ☎02.43.76.58.42
🌐www.logis-de-france.fr
Closed *Sun evening; Mon; Jan; last fortnight in June.* **Disabled access. High chairs available. TV. Car park.**

This family hotel celebrated its 150th anniversary – in the same family – in 2000, and the comfort, courtesy and good food it offers are an excellent example of traditional hotel-keeping. The rooms have been refurbished since the original openings – such a venerable institution and pioneer of tourism in Sarthe has to set an example – and doubles with shower/wc or bath cost €56–72. In the restaurant, menus are €16–40. Specialities include steamed veal kidneys. Logis de France. *10% discount on the room rate (Oct–May) offered to our readers on presentation of this guide.*

Saint-Germain-sur-Sarthe
72130 (35km N)

◎ 𝒜 |●| Restaurant Le Saint-Germain

La Hutte; take the N138. It's at the crossroads.

☎02.43.97.53.06
Closed *Mon, Tues and Wed evenings; winter school holidays; 3 weeks in Aug.* **Disabled access.**

This restaurant may not look much from the outside, but the drivers on the main road between Le Mans and Alençon do not know what they are missing when they whizz past disdainfully; it is one of a kind. Madame makes sure there are fresh flowers in the dining room and Monsieur keeps up the high standards of French sauce-making in the kitchen. Try the rabbit terrine, served as an entrée. The dish of the day costs €10, with menus at €12 (weekday lunchtime) and €17–36. *Free house apéritif offered to our readers on presentation of this guide.*

Marsac-sur-Don
44170

◎ 𝒜 🏠 |●| Hôtel-restaurant du Don

16 rue du Général-de-Gaulle.
☎02.40.87.54.55 ☎02.40.87.52.66
Closed *Mon evening; Sun evening; first week in Jan; first 3 weeks in Aug.*

The charm of the small bedrooms (€40–45 with bath) is matched by that of the delicious dishes prepared in the restaurant by Thérèse (the third generation of female chefs in her family). She concentrates on regional specialities according to the availability of the fresh ingredients. The week-day lunchtime menu is at €10, then others at €15–38. The service is cheerful and attentive. Logis de France. *Free coffee offered to our readers on presentation of this guide.*

Mayenne
53100

◎ 𝒜 🏠 Hôtel La Tour des Anglais**

13 bis pl. Juhel.
☎02.43.04.34.56 ☎02.43.32.13.84
🌐www.latourdesanglais.com
Disabled access. TV. Car park.

Very close to Château de Mayenne, this hotel has one wonderful room in a fortified tower with a dramatic view of the Mayenne River. The other rooms are comfortable but more modern; they're €46–55. There's an English-style bar with a billiard table and impressive wooden beams. *10% discount on the room rate (for stays of at least ten days) offered to our readers on presentation of this guide.*

◎ 🎇 🏠 |●| Le Grand Hôtel**

2 rue Ambroise-de-Loré; it faces the Mayenne river.
☎02.43.00.96.00 ℻02.43.00.69.20
🌐www.grandhotelmayenne.com
Restaurant closed *Sat lunchtime and Sat and Sun evenings (Nov–April).* **Hotel closed** *Sat (Nov to mid-April); a fortnight at New Year, a fortnight in Aug.* **TV. High chairs and games available. Car park.**

If only the rest of the town could be renovated and maintained as well as this hotel. Tourists arriving by car, bike and even boat are greeted with a cheery smile. Well-appointed rooms, the oldest of which have just been redorated, cost €71–85 depending on facilities. In the restaurant you get Breton or Norman cuisine in a quaint ambience, with menus at €15.50–33; lunchtime salad menu at €11, including dessert and coffee. Round off the evening with a good whisky in the bar. Logis de France. *10% discount on the room rate offered to our readers on presentation of this guide.*

Fontaine-Daniel
53100 (4km SW)

◎ 🎇 |●| Restaurant La Forge

La Place; it's in the middle of the village.
☎02.43.00.34.85
Closed *Mon; Wed evening; Sun evening.* **Disabled access. High chairs available.**

This lovely restaurant on the main square of the pretty village boasts a very nice terrace where you can enjoy excellent cuisine. Dishes change according to the season but typical offerings include snails in onion shells on a bed of couscous, ice cream *beignet* with strawberries and apple crumble with caramel sauce. Menus start at €14 (weekday lunch), with others €18–32. It's best to book. *Free coffee offered to our readers on presentation of this guide.*

Moulay
53100 (4km S)

◎ 🎇 🏠 |●| La Marjolaine**

Le Bas-Mont; it's on the way out of Moulay heading towards Laval.
☎02.43.00.48.42 ℻02.43.08.10.58
📧lamarjolaine@wanadoo.fr

Closed *Sun evening, Mon lunchtime; Fri evening (15 Oct–15 April); first week in Jan; a fortnight in Feb; first week in Aug.* **Disabled access. TV. Car park.**

A hotel with eighteen very comfortable and elegant rooms (although the owners have just bought the château opposite with the intention of creating new rooms there). Doubles go for €49–75 with shower/wc or bath. In the restaurant, the quality of the cuisine and freshness of the ingredients is exemplary; go for the fish of the day and the chef's suggestions. The first menu, €18.50, is served on weekdays (but not Fri evening) and there are other menus up to €49. Logis de France. *10% discount on the room rate offered to our readers on presentation of this guide.*

◎ 🎇 🏠 |●| Hôtel-restaurant Beau Rivage

Route de Saint-Baudelle; it's on the N162 between Mayenne and Moulay.
☎02.43.00.49.13 ℻02.43.00.49.26
📧fbeaurivage@9online.fr
Closed *Sun evening; Mon.* **TV. High chairs available. Car park.**

This lovely hotel-restaurant, set on the bank of the Mayenne River, is quite a sight. The dining room and the terrace (which stretches right down to the water) are often full, so make sure you reserve a table. The €15 menu (not served Sun) and others (€24–30) list such dishes as calf's head *ravigote* served with a spicy vinaigrette, spit-roasted duckling, fillet of pike perch with sorrel and seafood *pot-au-feu* with herbs. Spit-roasted fish and meat dishes are prepared in front of you. There are eight cosy rooms with all facilities, costing €56. Logis de France. *Free house apéritif offered to our readers on presentation of this guide.*

Commer
53470 (9km S)

◎ 🎇 🏠 Chambre d'Hôte La Chevrie***

It's 5km south of Mayenne on the N162 towards Laval; follow the signposts to La Mayenne.
☎02.43.00.44.30
📧agdlt@aol.com
TV. Games available. Car park.

This farmhouse is at least a hundred years old. You'll receive a natural, kind welcome. There are two rooms only, at €35 with breakfast. There's a wonderful view over the countryside and a neighbouring organic dairy farm. The towpath is close by and a good place for an outing on foot, bike or horseback. Horse-riders are very welcome, and the overnight accomodation for the horse is free. Credit cards not accepted. *Free jar of honey (after two nights) offered to our readers on presentation of this guide.*

Montreuil-Poulay
53640 (12km NE)

@ |O| L'Auberge Campagnarde

Le Presbytère; take the N12, then the D34.
☎02.43.32.07.11
Closed *Sun evening; Mon; a week in March; a week in Oct.* **Disabled access. Games available. Car park.**

You'll get a kind welcome in this restaurant, and the service is friendly without being over-familiar. They serve *apéritifs* and coffee on the terrace even when the weather isn't quite fine enough to eat a full meal outside. You'll find a tasty selection of traditional, local dishes on the weekday lunch menu at €10.50 (also available on Sun if you ask for it), with other menus €19–30. There is also a small park with animals, much appreciated by children.

Gorron
53120 (25km NW)

@ 🏠 |O| Hôtel-restaurant Le Bretagne**

41 rue de Bretagne; take the D12 to Saint-Georges-Buttavent and then the D5.
☎02.43.08.63.67 ☎02.43.08.01.15
@phbto@aol.com
Closed *Sun evening; Mon.* **TV. Car park.**

A good village restaurant where you can get a hearty meal and gourmet cooking. The menus, €13–25, change with the seasons. The décor is spruce in pastel colours, and the dining room looks over the River Colmont. After your meal, you can enjoy a stroll around the adjoining park and pond. Double rooms with shower/wc or bath cost €42. Logis de France.

Montaigu
85600

@ 🏠 |O| Hôtel-restaurant Les Voyageurs**

9 av. Villebois-Mareuil.

☎02.51.94.00.71 ☎02.51.94.07.78
@www.hotel-restaurant-les-voyageurs.fr
TV. Swimming pool. Car park.

A flag flies over this long, pink hotel made up of three buildings constructed around a swimming pool. Each facing wall is painted in a different colour and there's definitely a Mediterranean feel. The rooms are comfortable and of varying sizes; doubles €42–62. Choose to have a bath rather than a shower as the rooms with bath are bigger and more modern. The dining room is on the ground floor and looks over the swimming pool; it's huge and bright and the cooking is very tasty. Menus start at €10.90 (lunchtime only) going up to €46. In the basement there's a fitness room. Friendly staff.

@ 🎝 |O| Le Cathelineau

3 bis pl. du Champ-de-Foire.
☎ and ☎02.51.94.26.40
Closed *Sun evening; Mon; first week in March; 1–24 Aug.* **Disabled access. High chairs available.**

Michel Piveteau's cooking is original, combining unusual flavours, and his menus change every three weeks. The weekday menu costs €14 (except public holidays), with others €18–55; expect dishes like warm oysters with liquorice, fillet of pike perch with cider and turmeric and chocolate charlotte. *Free coffee offered to our readers on presentation of this guide.*

Montreuil-Bellay
49260

@ 🎝 🏠 |O| Splendid'Hôtel**

139 rue du Docteur-Gaudrez; it's near the château.
☎02.41.53.10.00 ☎02.41.52.45.17
@www.splendid-hotel.fr
Closed *Sun evening out of season.* **Disabled access. TV. Swimming pool. Car park.**

This convivial establishment has everything you could ask for. The beautiful building comprises adjoining fifteenth- and seventeenth-century wings with a wide range of conventional, clean rooms (some recently renovated); doubles with shower/wc or bath cost €47–52. In the mornings the only sound you'll hear is the fountain (unless there is a wedding or party – check first). There's a pleasant dining room where they serve freshly prepared dishes in copious portions and a range of menus €13–35. There's a big choice of fish dishes; the house speciality is pike black pudding. Logis de France. *10% discount on the room rate offered to our readers on presentation of this guide.*

⊛ ⚲ ⌂ Hôtel-relais du Bellay**

96 Rue Nationale; it's opposite the château.
☎02.41.53.10.10 ⊕02.41.38.70.61
⊛www.splendid-hotel.fr
Closed *Sun evening (Oct–Easter).* **Disabled access. TV. Swimming pool. Car park.**

This hotel has the same owners as the *Splendid'Hôtel;* it is slightly more expensive (but also quieter) and offers relaxed, friendly service. There are two buildings: the cheapest is the town's former girl's school, a big, old Angevin-style house, with a certain charm, while the new building is more expensive (and also more comfortable). The comfortable and spacious rooms go for €48–70 with shower/wc or bath. Some look out onto the château and the fortifications. There's no restaurant – residents can dine at the *Splendid* – but a buffet breakfast costs €8. There's a large, pleasant garden with a swimming pool (covered and heated in winter), as well as a fitness room, sauna, Turkish bath and Jacuzzi. *10% discount on the room rate (Oct–April) offered to our readers on presentation of this guide.*

Mortagne-sur-Sèvre
85290

⊛ ⌂ |⊙| Hôtel-restaurant de France et La Taverne**

4 pl. du Docteur-Pichat; it's at the crossroads of the Nantes-Poitiers/Paris-Les Sables roads.
☎02.51.65.03.37 ⊕02.51.65.27.83
Closed *Sat lunchtime and Sun evening (1 Oct–1 June).* **TV. Swimming pool.**

The *Hôtel de France*, built in 1604, was renovated in 1968, and since then, nothing has changed. You can't miss this beautiful and noble building as you arrive in the main square – it's smothered in ivy. Inside, endless corridors and odd little corners lead to plush, comfortable rooms; doubles go for €45–54. *La Taverne* has a sumptuous medieval-style dining room with period-looking furniture and collections of copper pans around the fireplace. The food is a festival of delicate, surprising flavours: crayfish in *verjus*, beef fillet in a salt crust, bass with fennel. Menus start from €13 for a weekday lunch, with others €17–44.50. During the week, the *Petite Auberge* next door offers three affordable lunch menus. There's a heated swimming pool in the old curé's garden and the service is impeccable.

Nantes
44000

See map overleaf.

⊛ ⌂ Hôtel Saint-Daniel*

4 rue du Bouffay; it's on the old town's pedestrian precinct, in the heart of the Bouffay neighbourhood. **Map C2-2**
☎02.40.47.41.25 ⊕02.51.72.03.99
⊛hotel.st.daniel@wanadoo.fr
Closed *Sun noon–8pm.* **TV. Pay car park.**

The functional double rooms are €32 with shower/wc or bath; family rooms with two double beds cost €42. Some rooms face the pedestrianized street; quieter rooms look onto the garden and the charming Sainte-Croix church. The prices attract younger travellers especially, so it's essential to book. Be warned: there are four floors and no lift.

⊛ ⚲ ⌂ Hôtel Fourcroy*

11 rue Fourcroy; it's near place Graslin and the cours Cambronne. **Map B2-3**
☎02.40.44.68.00 ⊕02.40.44.68.21
Closed *23 Dec–8 Jan.* **TV. Car park.**

Plain but quiet and central, this simple one-star offers very good value for money. Doubles cost €34 with shower/wc; the larger rooms look onto a private courtyard. You may receive a somewhat reserved welcome but will ultimately find the service friendly. Credit cards not accepted. *10% discount on the room rate for a stay of more than one night (15 July–15 Aug) offered to our readers on presentation of this guide.*

⊛ ⌂ Hôtel Pommeraye**

2 rue Boileau; it's near place Graslin. **Map B2-5**
☎02.40.48.78.79 ⊕02.40.47.63.75
⊛info@hotel-pommeraye.com
TV.

This hotel is set in a beautiful nineteenth-century building that has preserved its original entrance hall. The rest of the building has recently been refurbished: the

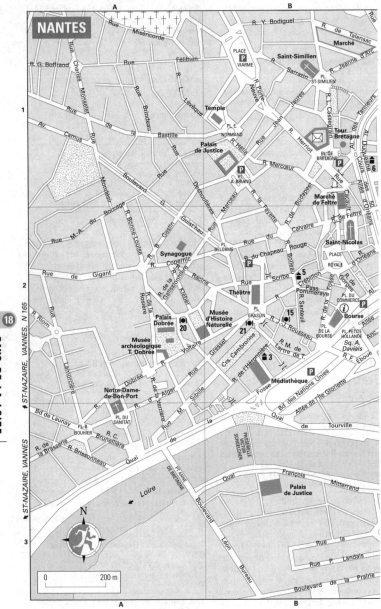

NANTES

PAYS-DE-LA-LOIRE

18

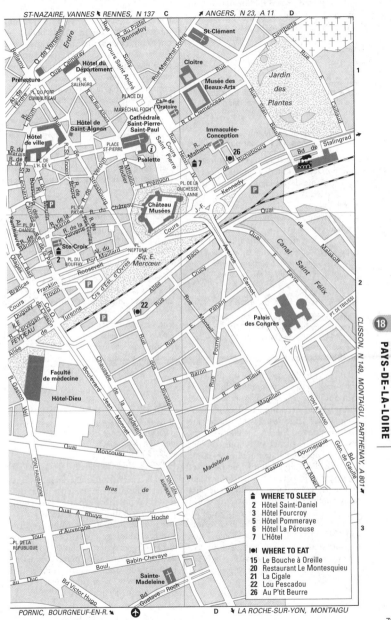

ST-NAZAIRE, VANNES ➘ RENNES, N 137   C   ✈ ANGERS, N 23, A 11   D

18

PAYS-DE-LA-LOIRE

CLISSON, N 149, MONTAIGU, PARTHENAY, A 801 ➘

St-Clément

Hôtel du
Département

Préfecture

PL. R.
SALENGRO

Cloître

Musée des
Beaux-Arts

Jardin
des
Plantes

PLACE DU
MARÉCHAL FOCH

Ch.lle de
l'Oratoire

Hôtel de
Saint-Aignan

Cathédrale
Saint-Pierre-
Saint-Paul

Immaculée-
Conception

Stalingrad

Hôtel
de ville

PLACE
ST-PIERRE

Psalette

26

7

Bd de

PL. DE L'
H. DE V.

PL. DE LA
DUCHESSE
ANNE

Kennedy

P

Château
Musées

Ste-Croix

2

PL.
NEPTUNE

Sq. E.
Mercœur

Cours

Quai

P

22

Palais
des Congrès

Canal Saint Félix

P

Faculté
de médecine

Hôtel-Dieu

Quai

Moncousu

la   Madeleine

Bras   de

Quai A. Rhuys

Quai Hoche

d'Auvergne

Sainte-
Madeleine

Babin-Chevaye

PORNIC, BOURGNEUF-EN-R. ➘   ✈   D   ➘ LA ROCHE-SUR-YON, MONTAIGU

🛏 **WHERE TO SLEEP**
2 Hôtel Saint-Daniel
3 Hôtel Fourcroy
5 Hôtel Pommeraye
6 Hôtel La Pérouse
7 L'Hôtel

🍴 **WHERE TO EAT**
15 Le Bouche à Oreille
20 Restaurant Le Montesquieu
21 La Cigale
22 Lou Pescadou
26 Au P'tit Beurre

comfortable rooms have been painted in restful colours and equipped with modern, elegant furniture, and the functional bathrooms have been fitted out in a similar style. Depending on the size, doubles go for €59–74, with shower or bathroom; the weekend rate is €43–55.

◎ ⚒ 🏠 L'Hôtel***

6 rue Henri-IV; it's between the train station, the château and the cathedral. **Map D1-7**
℡02.40.29.30.31 ℻02.40.29.00.95
🖥www.nanteshotel.com
Closed *Christmas and New Year period.*
Disabled access. TV. Pay car park.

A pleasant hotel that's very comfortable and perfectly located opposite the château of Anne de Bretagne. The rooms are soundproofed and attractively furnished. Doubles cost €74 with bath – some have private terraces with views over the garden, others overlook the château. The hotel offers both a car park and an indoor garage. *10% discount on room rate (weekends in high season) or free parking offered to our readers on presentation of this guide.*

◎ ⚒ 🏠 Hôtel La Pérouse***

3 allée Duquesne, cours des 50 Otages; it's in the city-centre. **Map B1-6**
℡02.40.89.75.00 ℻02.40.89.76.00
🖥www.hotel-laperouse.com
Disabled access. TV.

There's no middle ground with this contemporary hotel – you either love it or loathe it. A large block of heavy, compact white granite, echoing a Nantais mansion, it has large windows overlooking the cours des 50 Otages and the rooftops. Inside there is plenty of wood, designer furniture, space and tranquillity – not a place for those nostalgic for the hotels of yesteryear. Everything down to the shape of the lamps, washbasins and chairs has been carefully chosen to evoke the world of the sea. Standard doubles cost €79, with luxury rooms at €94 in low season, and €95–112 in high season. There's free parking between 7pm and 9am in the neighbouring car park. *One free breakfast per room offered to our readers on presentation of this guide.*

◎ 🍴 La Cigale

4 pl. Graslin; it's opposite the Graslin theatre. **Map B2-21**
℡02.51.84.94.94

Open *7.30am–12.30am.* **Disabled access.**

This is the restaurant to be seen in – from tourists and students, to visiting celebrities and high-society types who come for supper after the theatre (which is just opposite). The cuisine isn't bad, but it's the décor of this 1895 brasserie – a perfect example of Art Nouveau, with painted ceilings, wood panelling and coloured ceramics – that is the real pull. Jacques Demy used the place in his classic movie *Lola*, and actor Jean-Louis Trintignant called it the most beautiful brasserie in the world. It's not too expensive to dine – the weekday lunch menu is priced €11.90, with others €15.20–24.80. You can come here for breakfast or tea, too. In the evening, after a show you can order a seafood platter.

◎ 🍴 Le Bouche à Oreille

14 rue Jean-Jacques-Rousseau. **Map B2-15**
℡02.40.73.00.25
Closed *Sat lunch; Sun; public holidays; 3 weeks in Aug.*

Situated very close to the opera house, this is a gathering place for theatre-goers and sports fans alike. It's more of a place to drink than a restaurant, and the cuisine isn't fancy: large *andouillette*, *quenelles*, *tabliers de sapeurs* (grilled ox tripe) and various appetizers. Delicious salads are served in the summer. The set lunch menu costs €12, or expect to pay about €22 à la carte.

◎ 🍴 Restaurant Le Montesquieu

1 rue Montesquieu; it's beyond the Gaslin pedestrian precinct, near the Dobrée museum. **Map A2-20**
℡02.40.73.06.69
Closed *Fri evening; Sat; Sun; public holidays; 20 July–31 Aug.*

A friendly local restaurant in a quiet spot beyond the pedestrianized Graslin area. The dining room walls are decorated with Rouen and Moustier plates and the tables are covered with checked cloths. Specialities include tuna with aïoli, leek terrine with onion marmalade, Dauphinois potatoes and home-made pastries. There's a lunch menu at €12; the evening equivalent is €16.

◎ ⚒ 🍴 Au P'tit Beurre

18 rue de Richebourg; it's near the castle. **Map D1-26**

☎02.40.74.11.61
Closed *Sat lunchtime; Sun evening; Mon; first fortnight in Jan; second fortnight in Aug.* **Disabled access.**

This is a delightful restaurant in an attractive setting, with a shady terrace ideal for fine weather. The food is based on local tradition, with carefully prepared starters, delicious fish specialities and a few classic meat dishes. Wine is sold by the glass, carafe or bottle. There is a weekday lunchtime menu at €13.70, then a three-course "market menu" at €17.20 (including a drink and coffee) and others at €22.10–28.80. *Free house apéritif offered to our readers on presentation of this guide.*

ⓔ |●| Lou Pescadou

8 allée Baco. **Map C2-22**
☎02.40.35.29.50
Closed *Sat lunchtime; Sun; Mon; a fortnight in early Jan; a fortnight in Aug.* **Disabled access. High chairs available.**

It's a good idea to book here, since this is one of the best seafood restaurants around and it gets pretty busy. The chef is a real enthusiast and a Muscadet *aficionado* – anything that he prepares in a white wine and butter sauce (*beurre blanc*) is a surefire winner. The sea bass baked in a salt crust is magnificent, too, as are specialities such as sole *meunière*, wild sea bream in salt and, if you can afford it, lobster and crayfish from the tank. Lunch menus at €14 and €19.50, with others €30–65; the most expensive menu includes drinks.

Basse-Goulaine

44115 (5km SE)

ⓔ 🌴 |●| Villa Mon Rêve

Route des Bords de Loire; it's on the D751 (going in the direction of Saint-Julien), below the road.
☎02.40.03.55.50
Closed *a fortnight in Nov; Feb.* **Disabled access. High chairs and games available. Car park.**

A regional institution that's been run for a number of years by Cécile and Gérard Ryngel. It's pleasantly situated among the trees and has a terrace that's particularly lovely in summer. Menus (€23–40) offer typical Loire produce: sea bass with *girolles*, frogs' legs with Gros Plant wine sauce and meat juices, fish of the day with *beurre blanc* sauce; there's an excellent children's

menu for €11. They have a fine selection of Muscadets and offer good service. *Free coffee offered to our readers on presentation of this guide.*

Saint-Julien-de-Concelles

44450 (6km NE)

ⓔ |●| La Divatte

28 levée de la Divatte "Boire courant".
☎02.40.54.19.66
Closed *Sun evening; Mon and Tues evenings; Wed; Feb school holiday; first fortnight in Aug.*

This is a delightful restaurant, especially in fine weather, when you can have lunch in the garden alongside the river. The inventive food is based on regional produce with a lunchtime menu at €13, and others at €19–46: lamprey (in season: Jan–March), white tuna steak, *crémet nantais*. The service is excellent.

Carquefou

44470 (10km N)

ⓔ |●| L'Auberge du Vieux Gachet – Le Vieux Gachet

Le Gachet; take the D178.
☎02.40.25.10.92
Closed *Sun.*

An attractive country inn with a terrace on the banks of the Erdre. Their inventive, delicious poultry and fish dishes present you with the best of France, and your food is served under a dome cover; weekday lunch menu €17, with others €27–46. To walk here from Nantes, simply follow the path along the Erdre – it'll take about two hours. The *Château de la Gacherie* is just opposite.

Rouans

44640 (22km W)

ⓔ 🌴 |●| Le Tisonnier

It's on the D723 Saint Brévin-Painbœuf road on the way into Messan.
☎02.40.64.29.83
Closed *evenings; 3 weeks in Aug.* **Disabled access.**

Plain restaurant-café (also a tobacconist's and newsagent's) where the cheapest menu at €9.50 gets you a tasty meal including sausage in Muscadet; other menus,

€11.50–38, offer dishes such as frogs' legs or eels with *beurre blanc*. It would be hard to find better value for money and swifter service. *Free house apéritif offered to our readers on presentation of this guide.*

Neufchâtel-en-Saosnois

72600

@ 🎿 🏠 |●| Relais des Étangs de Guibert

It's 10km northwest of Mamers. In the village, turn right by the church into rue Louis-Ragot.
☎02.43.97.15.38 ℻02.43.33.22.99
ⓦwww.saosnois.com.
Closed *Mon; Sun evening; winter school holidays; third week in Nov.* **Disabled access. Car park.**

Set at the edge of the Perseigne forest near the pond, this place comes to life as soon as the sun shows its face. The idyllic setting may explain why it can be difficult to get a room at the weekend. Rooms are decorated with sailing or hunting themes, and cost €55–95 for a double, depending on the facilities. In the restaurant there's a weekday lunch menu for €17 and others up to €32. Beautiful excursions are available on horseback, by boat or simply on foot, to enable you to explore one of the prettiest parts of the Haute-Sarthe. Credit cards not accepted. *Free coffee offered to our readers on presentation of this guide.*

Noirmoutier-en-L'Île

85330

@ 🎿 🏠 Hotel Autre Mer**

32 av. Joseph-Pineau; it's halfway between the town centre and the Bois de la Chaise.
☎02.51.39.11.77 ℻ 02.51.39.11.97
ⓦwww.autremerhotel.fr
Closed *mid-Nov to end March.* **Disabled access. TV. High chairs available. Car park.**

This hotel has been redecorated in an unfussy, modern style, inspired by a nautical theme, to match the façade with its immaculate white walls and sea-green shutters. Doubles go for €51–69 depending on facilities and season. It's good value for money and the service is extremely friendly. *One free breakfast per room offered to our readers on presentation of this guide.*

@ 🏠 |●| Hôtel-restaurant Fleur de Sel***

Rue des Saulniers, BP 207; follow the signs from the château. It's 500m behind the church.
☎02.51.39.09.07 ℻02.51.39.09.76
ⓦwww.fleurdesel.fr
Restaurant closed *Mon and Tues lunchtimes (except weekends and public holidays).* **Closed** *2 Nov–17 March.* **Disabled access. TV. High chairs and cots available. Car park. Swimming pool.**

A magnificent place now classified as a *Châteaux et demeures de tradition* hotel, built some twenty years ago in a style which is typical of the island. It's set apart from the town in the middle of a huge estate with Mediterranean landscapes, and has a lovely swimming pool. All 35 rooms are well equipped; the ones overlooking the pool are cosy and have English pine furniture, while those with private flowery terraces have yew furniture and a maritime feel. Doubles go for €77–150 with bath/wc; half board, at €71–112 per person, is compulsory for a two-night minimum stay in July and August. The restaurant is one of the best on the island, if not in the Vendée. The cuisine mixes ingredients from the land, the offshore waters and the high seas: grilled red tuna, Vendée coconuts with *chorizo*, bass *tartare* with vanilla cream. Weekday menus are €25 (not July–Aug), with others €34–45. The wine list has some reasonably cheap wines. You can rent bikes or go on excursions, play tennis or practise your golf, and there's free broadband Internet connection on offer. All in all, ideal for a relaxing stay.

@ 🎿 🏠 Hôtel du Général-d'Elbée***

Place d'Armes; it's at the foot of the château near the canal port.
☎02.51.39.10.29 ℻02.51.39.08.23
ⓦwww.generaldelbee.com
Closed *Oct to early April.* **Disabled access. Swimming pool.**

A marvellous hotel in a historic eighteenth-century building. VIP-types stay here but it's quite unspoilt and is still affordable to people who prefer refined places with a bit of character. The rooms in the historic part of the building are a bit pricey, but the décor is magnificent, so well worth it; doubles cost €101–152, depending on the season. There's also a cosy bar-sitting room. *Free third night offered to our readers (except weekends and bank holidays, and 20 July–31 Aug) on presentation of this guide.*

ⓒ |●| Le Petit Bouchot

3 rue Saint-Louis
☎02.51.39.32.56
Closed *Tues; Wed; Mon (July–Aug); mid-Dec to mid-Feb.* **Disabled access.**

This small restaurant in the heart of the town reflects Noirmoutier's character, both smart and relaxed at the same time. It attracts a loyal following among the locals, and the extremely friendly owner gives everybody his personal attention. Specialities on the menus, €12, €16 and €23, revolve around fish and seafood, particularly mussels. They set out a few tables in the cool courtyard dotted with flowers.

ⓒ |●| Restaurant Côte Jardin

1 bis rue du Grand-Four; it faces the château at the top of the old town.
☎02.51.39.03.02
Closed *Thurs, Wed and Sun evenings in low season; 15 Nov to early Feb.*

This elegant restaurant is in a splendid building sheathed in Virginia creeper. Menus €16–36; the cooking takes most of its inspiration from the sea and will satisfy even the most demanding gourmet. It offers good local specialities such as white kidney bean *croustillant* or *chaudrée* of potatoes. The cordial welcome only enhances the pleasure derived from the food.

Herbaudière (L')

85330 (2km NW)

ⓒ 🏠 Hôtel Bord à Bord

6 rue de la Linière
☎02.51.39.27.92 ☎02.51.35.74.17
Open *all year round.* **Disabled access. TV. Heated swimming pool. Car park.**

A pretty, modern building with comfortable rooms overlooking the sea, decorated in cheery nautical colours. Some of the rooms are small but they are fitted with big mirrors which make them look more spacious. Double rooms go for €50–70 with shower/wc; there are also two duplex sleeping four to five people at €105. No restaurant, but if you feel like cocooning yourself inside, the rooms are equipped with a kitchen unit for a supplement of €12. The owner is guaranteed to give you a warm welcome.

ⓒ |●| La Marine

In the port.
☎02.51.39.23.09
Closed *Tues evening; Wed; Sun evening; Oct.* **Disabled access. High chairs available.**

This is one of our top spots in the *département*. The nautical-style dining room has a view of the port – and the local priest's garden. The menu varies according to the seasons, and 95 per cent of the produce comes from the island; the suppliers, such as the fish auctioneers and the market gardeners, are even listed. The cheap menu (€15 for a weekday lunch) is superb, but it is in the others (€24–42) that the young chef really excels himself. Specialities include *bar de ligne* (a highly-prized variety of bass) and wild turbot, *remoulade* of beans and Granny Smith with cauliflower cream and crusty beetroot, monkfish tail baked with local ham, risotto of cereals and foam of maize and, for dessert, red-fruit shortbread and rosemary sorbet. All in all, the cooking is eye-catching, inventive and really delicious, with an exquisite array of fragrances, fresh herbs, flowers and spices.

Paulx

44270

ⓒ 🎋 |●| Restaurant Les Voyageurs

1 pl. de l'Église; it's opposite the church.
☎02.40.26.02.76
Open *Wed–Sun lunchtimes; Fri and Sat evenings.* **Closed** *Mon; Tues; first fortnight in March; 3 weeks in Sept.* **Disabled access. High chairs available. Car park**

This restaurant is quiet but nevertheless buzzes with creativity – and the chef has an armful of diplomas to prove it. He follows his whims to create tasty dishes with seasonal ingredients, such as Vendée ham with samphire and mixed green salad with shellfish and sherry. The weekday menu starts at €15.50, with others €25.50–34.50. There is a wine list devoted entirely to Muscadet. All in all, it makes a good stopover. *Free coffee offered to our readers on presentation of this guide.*

Piriac-sur-Mer

44420

@ 🎋 |◉| Crêperie Lacomère

18 rue de Kéroman.
☎ 02.40.23.53.63
Open *weekends only in March, Sept and Oct; during winter and autumn school holidays.*
Closed *Tues lunchtime only (July–Aug); Mon and Tues, in mid-season; Nov to mid-Feb.*

This restaurant is a little more inventive than the standard crêperie, with a menu inspired by the owner's travels around the world. There's a weekday lunch menu at €11.50, or expect to pay around €18 à la carte; try the fish *tajine*, the red mullet *escabèche* or the fish *choucroute*. There are only ten tables, and it's popular with those in the know, so best to book in advance. *Free house apéritif offered to our readers on presentation of this guide.*

Pornic

44210

@ 🏠 |◉| Auberge La Fontaine aux Bretons

Rue des Noëlls, Fontaine aux Bretons; it's 2km along the road to La Bernerie (sign-posted).
☎ 02.51.77.07.07 ☎ 02.51.74.15.15
🌐 www.auberge-la-fontaine.com
Restaurant closed *Sun and Mon evenings (Nov–March except during school holidays).*
Disabled access. TV. High chairs available. Swimming pool. Car park.

This beautiful inn is the result of a conversion of an old farm once run by La Salle friars. The buildings have been thoroughly overhauled, with exquisite taste. Doubles are €80–110, depending on the season; most of them have a view of the sea or the magnificent kitchen garden (open to visitors) and small park-farm or the heated swimming pool. The restaurant has a similar charm, enhanced by the speedy, friendly service and appetizing menu. Menus, €18 (weekday lunch), and others €25 and €30, feature delicious roast meat (supplied by local farmers), vegetables from the kitchen garden in season and good desserts. In addition, the bread is home-made and there's a fine wine list. It is worth booking in advance, as this inn has a high reputation – a slightly exaggerated one, in fact, although it provides an agreeable stopover nonetheless.

@ |◉| Restaurant L'Estaminet

8 rue du Maréchal-Foch.
☎ 02.40.82.35.99
Closed *Sun evening; Mon; first fortnight in Oct; 20 Dec–20 Jan.*

This restaurant in a busy street doesn't look out of the ordinary, but once you step inside you cannot fail to be impressed by the décor (based on the theme of wine) in the intimate dining room (complete with a beautiful collection of petrol lamps at one end) and Madame's warm welcome – not to mention the enticing cooking of Monsieur: delicious grilled bass and fennel, ray with samphire and buttered vegetables and, for dessert, home-made Vienna bread with chocolate. The weekday menu costs €14, with others €16–27. It's best to book.

@ |◉| Restaurant Beau Rivage

Plage de la Birochère; take the road going up to the train station, then follow the signs.
☎ 02.40.82.03.08
Closed *Mon and Wed evenings; Sun evening (out of season); 15 Dec–31 Jan.*

A restaurant with carefully designed nautical décor in a beautiful spot looking right over the beach. Seafood is the speciality here, and the chef thoughtfully crafts excellent dishes from fresh ingredients: Atlantic *bouillabaisse*, sea bream grilled in its skin with olive oil, duckling in Muscadet gravy and ivory mousse with rice pudding. Set lunches from €16 to €21 are served in the bistro (with no view of the sea), other menus €25–66; there is also a "Taste Discovery" menu for children aged under 12. The wine list is excellent. To top it all, it will be hard to resist a pleasant stroll along the shore after your meal.

Plaine-sur-Mer (La)

44770 (9km NW)

@ 🏠 |◉| Hôtel-Restaurant Anne de Bretagne***

Port de la Gravette, 163 bd. de la Tara; take the D13.
☎ 02.40.21.54.72 ☎ 02.40.21.02.33
🌐 www.annedebretagne.com
Restaurant closed *Mon and Tues lunchtimes and Sun evening (mid-Sept to mid-March).*
Closed *Mon; Tues (open Tues lunchtime in summer); early Jan to mid-Feb.* **Disabled access. TV. Swimming pool. Car park.**

A charming, tastefully decorated hotel with lovely rooms that have garden or sea views. The location is splendid and it's very quiet. Doubles with shower/wc or bath go for €66–138 depending on view and season; breakfast buffet €13. The bright, attractive dining room has been decorated in a resolutely contemporary style and has a magnificent bay window overlooking both the sea and the Saint-Nazaire bridge. The specialities on offer include baked monkfish with red Anjou, small sole cooked in its skin and bass in a crust of caramelized algae. You'll experience a large selection of menus based on seasonal ingredients; the weekday lunchtime menu (main course and dessert) is €19, with other menus from €24 (except Sun) to €75. Superb cellar with 20,000 bottles (the owner is a wine connoisseur).

Port-Joinville (Île d'Yeu)

85350

ⓒ ♠ Hôtel L'Escale**

Rue de la Croix-du-Port.
℡02.51.58.50.28 ℻02.51.59.33.55
ⓦ www.site.voila.fr/yeu_escale
Closed 15 Nov–15 Dec. **Disabled access. TV. Car park.**

Painted white with yellow shutters, this is the prettiest place on the Île d'Yeu. Despite having thirty rooms, it retains a guesthouse atmosphere, with cool marine décor; doubles cost €32–65 depending on facilities and season. The bedrooms in the new part of the building are air-conditioned and well equipped; they lead onto the garden, either at ground level (the ones we prefer) or from upstairs. Breakfast is served around the old well in the middle of the bright dining room – you can see the garden through French windows. The owner gives good advice about where to visit and what to see in the area.

ⓒ 🍴 ♠ Atlantic Hôtel***

3 quai Carnot; it's in the port, 50m from the landing stage.
℡02.51.58.38.80 ℻02.51.58.35.92
ⓦ www.hotel-yeu.com
Closed 3 weeks in Jan. **TV.**

This hotel has eighteen comfortable, air-conditioned rooms (six of them are brand new). You'll pay €42–70 for doubles; the most expensive ones have a view of the port, the focus of local activity, while the others, set to the rear, overlook the village and are slightly quieter. There's a buffet breakfast at €7 and the service is good. *10% discount on the room rate (except July–Aug and school holidays) offered to our readers on presentation of this guide.*

ⓒ 🍴 ♠ |●| Flux Hôtel – Restaurant La Marée**

27 rue Pierre-Henry; it's 100m from the harbour station.
℡02.51.58.36.25 ℻02.51.59.44.57
Closed Sun evening; Fri evening and Sat lunchtime out of season; mid-Nov to mid-Jan. **Disabled access. High chairs available. TV. Car park.**

Away from the bustle of Port-Joinville, this hotel's peaceful grounds, bordering the seashore, give it a delightful aspect. Well-kept double rooms overlooking the garden cost €49–62; room no. 15, set away from the main hotel, is especially spacious and has a fireplace. The restaurant, *La Marée*, is in an enormous dining room with a huge fireplace for winter evenings and a lovely terrace for dining out beneath the shade of the trees in summer. It serves traditional food based on fish, with the constant presence on the menu of the house speciality *patagos à la crème* (typical of the island) and mussels sauce *poulette*. There's a set lunch at €13 and other menus €16–37. *10% discount on the room rate (Sept–June, excluding springtime public holidays) offered to our readers on presentation of this guide.*

ⓒ 🍴 |●| Restaurant du Père Raballand – L'Étape Maritime

6 pl. de la Norvège; it's on the harbour.
℡02.51.26.02.77
Closed Mon; 1 Dec–28 Feb. **Disabled access.**

A bar-brasserie decorated to look like the inside of a boat. The cuisine is refined, and they serve seafood accompanied by wines bought direct from the vineyards. If you want more intimacy, go for the "gastronomic" dining room upstairs, but the food is the same, and extremely good value for money. The menus start from €20.80, and there's also a cheaper set lunch at €11.80. Père Raballand is well known in town and the atmosphere in his restaurant in summer or at the weekend is unmatched. He has also opened a bistro slightly further along the port, serving tuna and mussel specialities. *Free coffee offered to our readers on presentation of this guide.*

◎ ⅍ |●| Les Bafouettes

8 rue Gabriel Guist'hau; it's 100m from the port, past the tourist office.
☏02.51.59.38.38
Closed *Sun evening; Mon; 3 weeks Jan; fortnight end Sept to early Oct.* **Disabled access. High chairs available.**

The dining room is freshly decorated with pictures by local artists, and the cuisine is delicious and served by enthusiastic staff. Menus start at €14 (weekday lunch) with others €18.50–47. Dishes include fish soups with a variety of optional garnishes and pan-fried crayfish with curry. *Free coffee offered to our readers on presentation of this guide.*

Rochefort-sur-Loire
49190

◎ ⅍ ♙ |●| Le Grand Hôtel – Restaurant La Grand'Prée**

30 rue René-Gasnier; it's in the main street.
☏02.41.78.80.46 ☏02.41.78.83.25
🖳www.le-grand-hotel.net
Restaurant closed *Sun evening; Mon; Wed evening out of season; 20 Dec–20 Jan.*

A nice old house with a garden, located in the main street and ideal as a base for exploring the Layon area. The ground-floor dining room is decorated in shades of yellow and green. Carefully prepared dishes feature lots of local specialities with dishes changing regularly; menus €17–38. The *patronne* is a passionate wine-lover which explains the well-researched wine list. The rooms are fairly big but quite simple and cost €31–37; the nicest are on the first floor overlooking the garden. *Free coffee offered to our readers on presentation of this guide.*

Roche-sur-Yon (La)
85000

◎ ♙ |●| Marie Stuart Hôtel**

86 bd. Louis-Blanc; it's opposite the station.
☏02.51.37.02.24 ☏02.51.37.86.37

🖳www.mariestuarthotel.com
Restaurant closed *Sat lunchtime and Sun.* **TV.**

This hotel overflows with Scottish trappings, including tartans, coats of arms and a portrait of Mary, Queen of Scots. The spacious rooms are each decorated differently; doubles cost €57 with bath/wc. The restaurant serves good, simple food with some quasi-Scottish specialities: Highland steak, Scotch eggs and dumplings but also fisherman's stew. Menus are €18 at the bar (starter and main course), €23 and €25; expect to pay around €19 à la carte. They have a good selection of malts and the service is excellent.

◎ |●| Le Clémenceau

40 rue Georges-Clémenceau; it's in the centre of town.
☏02.51.37.10.20
🖳www.brasserie-le-clemenceau.fr
Closed *1 May; 25 Dec; 1 Jan.* **Disabled access. High chairs available.**

This is a genuine brasserie with an attractive terrace. It's well known for the freshness of its shellfish, seafood and fish – the names of the suppliers are even inscribed on the menu. Range of menus €13.50–27; there is a very tasty fish soup and a generous seafood platter, as well as a foie gras speciality. If you want a closer look at the workings of the kitchen, a special table for six is placed right inside it. The atmosphere and the staff are both extremely pleasant.

◎ |●| Saint Charles Restaurant

38 rue du Général-de-Gaulle; it's 200m from pl. Napoléon, in the direction of Cholet.
☏02.51.47.71.37
🖳www.restaurant-stcharles.com
Closed *Sat lunchtime; Sun; 2 or 3 weeks in Aug.*

Photos of jazz musicians and instruments adorn the walls, jazz plays softly in the background and even the menu features jazz references. In this relaxed atmosphere the chef produces seafood dishes. The menus, at €16 (weekday lunch) and €20.50–34, offer good value for money.

◎ ⅍ |●| Le Rivoli

31 bd. Aristide-Briand
☏02.51.37.43.41

Closed *Sat lunch; Sun; Mon; 3 weeks in Aug.*
Games available.

It certainly cannot be said that this charmingly refurbished bistro lacks colour or a sense of humour: it is decorated in a combination of zebra stripes, leopard spots and apple green. The food is a light blend of local cooking and Mediterranean touches; menus range from €18 to €35. The service is friendly enough, but rather impersonal. *Free house apéritif offered to our readers on presentation of this guide.*

Poiré-sur-Vie (Le)

85170 (13.5km NW)

Hôtel-restaurant Le Centre**

19 pl. du Marché; take the D6, it's in the centre of the village.
℡02.51.31.81.20 ℻02.51.31.88.21
🖳www.hotelducentre-vendee.com
Closed *Mon–Fri; Sun evening out of season.*
Disabled access. TV. High chairs and games available. Swimming pool. Car park.

This welcoming hotel, right in the middle of the village, has clean, comfortable rooms at €37 with basin, €59 with bath. The restaurant offers simple authentic regional dishes at reasonable prices, including sliced monkfish with Noilly, locally produced ham with Muscatel, home-made foie gras. Menus start from €10.70 up to €34. Logis de France. *Free house apéritif offered to our readers on presentation of this guide.*

Maché

85190 (22km NW)

Auberge du Fougerais

Take the D948; after Aizenay turn left beyond the River Vie bridge and follow the signposts.
℡02.51.55.75.44
Closed *Mon, Tues and Wed evenings (except July–Aug).* **Disabled access. High chairs available. Car park.**

A lovely converted barn covered in ivy and with a shady terrace. It's a peaceful place, where unfussy, tasty food is served at simple tables. The chef adds a few vine stems to the open fire when he grills eel, rib of beef or quail. The menus (€18.50–37) offer good value for money. *Free house apéritif offered to our readers on presentation of this guide.*

Rosiers-sur-Loire (Les)

49350

La Toque Blanche

2 rue Quarte; it's on the way out of the village on the Angers road, after the bridge.
℡02.41.51.80.75
Closed *Tues and Sun evenings; Wed; end Jan; end Nov.* **High chairs available. Car park.**

It is becoming increasingly necessary to book a table at this up-and-coming restaurant – and it's absolutely essential for Sunday lunch. Inventive cuisine is served in an elegant, air-conditioned dining room. The menus (€19–42) include wine, and the €42 menu includes a fish and a meat dish. Dishes are cooked using fresh produce chosen from the market. Specialities include hot oysters, Loire fish with *beurre blanc* and casserole of calf sweetbreads. You can be sure of a friendly welcome here. *Free coffee offered to our readers on presentation of this guide.*

Saint-Martin-de-la-Place

49610 (7 km SE)

Domaine de la Blairie

5 rue de la Mairie; it's 7km away from Rosiers, towards Saumur, along the Loire valley.
℡02.41.38.42.98 ℻02.41.38.41.20
🖳www.lablairie.com
Closed *mid-Nov to mid-Feb.* **Disabled access. Swimming pool. Car park.**

This eighteenth century building was once a convent and an old people's home, but the conversion has been pretty successful and this hotel offers a good retreat for families. Doubles cost €45–49 and the welcome is friendly and relaxed. It has a lovely park, a swimming pool and a good restaurant. *Free house apéritif offered to our readers on presentation of this guide.*

Sables-d'Olonne (Les)

85100

Hôtel Les Embruns**

33 rue du Lieutenant-Anger; take the ferry or go by road.
℡02.51.95.25.99 ℻02.51.95.84.48

Ⓦ www.hotel-lesembruns.com
Closed *Sun evening (Oct–May); Nov; Dec.*
TV. Pay car park.

You can spot the yellow frontage of this building with its green shutters from the other side of the harbour. The rooms are very pretty and painted in attractive colours, and they're brilliantly maintained by the welcoming young pair who run the place. Some of the rooms overlook the port, while the ones looking onto a small side street are cooler in summer; doubles cost €39–57 according to view and season. Dogs not allowed. *10% discount on room rate (Sept–June, except at weekends and public holidays) offered to our readers on presentation of this guide.*

ⓦ ⅔ ☆ Hôtel de la Tour**

46 rue du Docteur-Canteteau; take the ferry or go by road. It's above the hotel *Les Embruns*.
Ⓣ 02.51.95.38.48 Ⓕ 02.51.95.89.84
Ⓦ www.hotel-lessablesdolonne.com
Closed *Feb school holiday; Christmas.* **TV.**

This nice little place is in a typical street in the Chaume district, and it's run by a couple who make guests feel like friends. Madame has decorated each room in a different theme, with colours inspired by the sea. Doubles are very good value for money at €40–60, depending on the facilities and season; some rooms have a view of the port. There's also an interior garden full of flowers where you can have breakfast, or you can eat in the pretty dining room next to the wood stove. A TV room has recently been installed. Credit cards not accepted. *10% discount on the room rate (except school summer holidays and weekends) offered to our readers on presentation of this guide.*

ⓦ ☆ Hôtel Antoine**

60 rue Napoléon; it's in the centre of town, between the port and the beach.
Ⓣ 02.51.95.08.36 Ⓕ 02.51.23.92.78
Ⓦ www.antoinehotel.com
Restaurant open *evenings (residents only).*
Closed *mid-Oct to mid-March.* **TV. Pay car park.**

A delightful haven right in the centre of town. The quiet rooms refurbished in warm, cheerful colours (some of them looking over the garden) are divided between an annexe and the main hotel and cost €45–60. Prices are a little lower out of season. Half board, compulsory in

July and August, is €45–52 per person. The food is abundant, excellent and prepared from the freshest market produce.

ⓦ ⅔ ☆ Hôtel Les Hirondelles**

44 rue des Corderies; it's 50m from the beach.
Ⓣ 02.51.95.10.50 Ⓕ 02.51.32.31.01
Ⓦ www.perso.wanadoo.fr/leshirondelles
Closed *lunchtime.* **Disabled access. High chairs and cots available. TV. Pay car park.**

This hotel doesn't look particularly attractive from the outside but the rooms have a fresh, modern décor, and the atmosphere is warm and friendly. Some rooms have balconies which are ideal for breakfast and others lead onto a pretty white patio planted with exotic, perfumed plants. Doubles cost €55.50–63 according to the season. There's a lift. Logis de France. *Free coffee offered to our readers on presentation of this guide.*

ⓦ ⅔ |●| L'Affiche

21 quai Guiné; it's near the port, opposite the dock for the boats for the Île d'Yeu.
Ⓣ 02.51.95.34.74
Closed *Mon; Sun and Thurs evenings (out of season); Wed (in season); 12 Dec–20 Jan.*

The outside is painted yellow and beckons you in. The chef uses fresh local produce and the dishes are deliciously exotic and flavoursome. Menus, €11.80–27, offer good value for money. *Free house apéritif offered to our readers on presentation of this guide.*

ⓦ ⅔ |●| Restaurant George V

20 rue George-V; it's on the extension to the port, on the left.
Ⓣ 02.51.95.11.52
Closed *Sun evening; Mon (out of season); Jan; Nov.* **High chairs available.**

There are two dining rooms here, one at ground level and one on the first floor, both looking out onto the harbour entrance. The setting is bright, fairly sophisticated and charmingly decorated. Chef Olivier Burban cooks excellent food – not surprisingly, fish is the main ingredient, but it's imaginatively prepared. Unexpected flavours pop up in dishes such as gateau of crayfish or oysters with foie gras sauce. Menus range from €13 to €30. *Free coffee offered to our readers on presentation of this guide.*

Sablé-sur-Sarthe

72300

⊚ |●| L'Hostellerie Saint-Martin

3 rue Haute-Saint-Martin; it's in a small street
leading off the town hall square towards the
château.
☏02.43.95.00.03
Closed *Mon; Sun and Wed evenings.*
Disabled access.

This restaurant seems to be in a clement microclimate – or so the palm tree
across the street would suggest. The high-
ceilinged dining room has an antiquated
charm and traditional décor, with a dresser,
Normandy clock, heavy red velvet curtains, copper pots and pans and fresh flowers on every table; the parquet floor creaks
underfoot. You'll find good local food on
menus from €15 to €32. You can also eat
on the attractive, flower-filled terrace.

⊚ 🌿 |●| Les Palmiers

54 Grande-Rue.
☏02.43.95.03.82
Closed *Tues; Sat lunchtime.* **Disabled
access. High chairs and baby changing
tables available.**

The exceptionally warm Moroccan hospitality and North African food you'll
encounter here offers quite an antidote
to the *rillette* and fish stew that otherwise
abounds in these parts. Abdou mans the
kitchens while his French wife greets the
guests. There is little passing trade in this
run-down street in the old part of town, so
the owners depend on the restaurant's reputation for its survival. Fortunately, this seems
to be working. The two large dining rooms
are smart and very well decorated, offering
comfortable surroundings in which to enjoy
the best of Moroccan cuisine. They offer
large helpings of aromatic stews, vegetables
and excellent meat: superb *tajines*, couscous
with a selection of meats, as well as delicious
home-made pastries. You'll pay €18–20 for
a meal à la carte. *Free coffee or mint tea offered
to our readers on presentation of this guide.*

Saint-Denis-
d'Orques

72350

⊚ 🌿 |●| L'Auberge de la Grande
Charnie

Rue Principale; it's on the N157, halfway

between Laval and Le Mans.
☏02.43.88.43.12
Closed *Mon.* **Open** *lunchtimes only; Sat
evening.* **Disabled access.**

An exquisite dining room and excellent
local cuisine at prices that won't break
the bank. They offer a dish of the day but
always take the advice of the *patronne* who
will tell you what's best. There's a menu
at €15 (weekday lunch), with others
€25–57. You can also eat on the covered
terrace. *Free coffee offered to our readers on
presentation of this guide.*

Saint-Florent-le-
Vieil

49410

⊚ 🏠 |●| L'Hostellerie de la
Gabelle**

12 quai de la Loire.
☏02.41.72.50.19 ☏02.41.72.54.38
✉la-gabelle@wanadoo.fr
Closed *Mon lunchtime; Sun evening
(Oct–June); 23 Dec–1 Jan.* **High chairs available. TV.**

A traditional provincial hotel, well located
on the banks of the Loire – it's a good spot
to stop if you're travelling between Nantes
and Angers. The twenty or so rooms
have been decorated on various different
themes: stars, games, lace. Doubles cost
€40–43 depending on facilities; breakfast
at €6.10. Weekday menus are at €13, with
others €20–38. Logis de France.

Saint-Jean-de-
Monts

85160

⊚ 🌿 🏠 |●| Hôtel-restaurant Le
Robinson**

28 bd. Leclerc.
☏02.51.59.20.20 ☏02.51.58.88.03
🌐www.hotel-le-robinson.com
Closed *Dec–Jan.* **Disabled access. TV. High
chairs available. Swimming pool. Car park.**

This family business has become a substantial tourist complex over the years. The
original hotel has changed considerably
with many extensions and additions, but
the quality has been maintained (in fact,
one annexe with six rooms has just been
refurbished and fitted with air-conditioning). There are several types of room, all

comfortable – some overlook the leafy avenues, others have a view of the road; doubles €41–68. The cuisine is traditional, pleasant and carefully prepared: scallop kebabs and other seafood dishes, duck breast, fillet of beef. There's a €13.50 menu (not Sun or public holidays) and others at €21–39.50. A €5 supplement is payable for dogs. Logis de France. *Free coffee offered to our readers on presentation of this guide.*

Saint-Léonard-des-Bois

72590

ⓒ 🏂 🏠 |❍| Touring Hôtel***

Follow the Alpes Mancelles route.
☏02.43.31.44.44 ℗02.43.31.44.49
ⓦwww.letouring.com
Closed 20 Dec–30 Jan. Disabled access. TV. Swimming pool. Car park.

A good place to stay, near the Sarthe river in the heart of the hills known as les Alpes Mancelles. Although the building is constructed from concrete, the atmosphere, hospitality, cuisine and swimming pool soon make you forget the dull architecture – it's the only outpost of the English Forestdale chain in France. Quiet, well-appointed rooms with shower/wc or bath cost €90–121. Menus range from €21 to €38. *10% discount on the room rate offered to our readers on presentation of this guide.*

Saint-Nazaire

44600

ⓒ 🏂 🏠 Hôtel de Touraine*

4 av. de la République; it's near the town hall.
☏02.40.22.47.56 ℗02.40.22.55.05
ⓔhoteltouraine@free.fr
Closed 19 Dec–5 Jan. TV. High chairs available. Pay car park.

It's hard enough to find a reasonably priced and pleasant hotel in Saint-Nazaire – let alone one that offers a substantial breakfast (served in the garden in good weather) and a free ironing service to boot. Doubles are good value for money at €26–40, depending on facilities; service is excellent. *10% discount on the room rate (1 Oct–31 March) offered to our readers on presentation of this guide.*

ⓒ 🏂 🏠 Korali Hôtel**

Place de la Gare; it's near the train station.
☏02.40.01.89.89 ℗02.40.66.47.96
ⓦwww.hotelkorali.fr
Disabled access. TV.

This hotel offers a practical location close to the train station, as well as modern architecture set off by floral decoration, comfortable rooms (€50–81), Internet connection and friendly service. *10% discount on the room rate offered to our readers on presentation of this guide.*

ⓒ |❍| Le Sabayon

7 rue de la Paix.
☏02.40.01.88.21
Closed Sun.

This small restaurant (eight tables only) is like the town itself – unassuming but surprising. Its nautical décor heralds the skilfully prepared fish specialities, such as cod baked with *beurre blanc*, although meat-lovers can tuck into the gizzard salad or duck leg with cream of cider. The desserts prepared with Valrhona chocolate are irresistible. Whatever you choose, rest assured that it will be distinguished by its sophisticated creativity and perfect judgement of cooking times. Menus cost €15–52; those between €26 and €40 achieve a perfect balance. The service is similarly professional. It is advisable to book – and if your party has more than six people, you can ask for a separate room.

Saint-Joachim

44720 (10km N)

ⓒ 🏂 🏠 |❍| La Mare aux Oiseaux

162 île de Fédrun; take the D50 through the Brière Park.
☏02.40.88.53.01 ℗02.40.91.67.44
ⓦwwwauberge-du-parc.com
Closed Mon lunchtime. High chairs available. Car park.

The inhabitants of Île de Fédrun have adopted Éric Guérin – an alumnus of the famous *Tour d'Argent* in Paris – as their favourite chef. He's full of ideas and produces inspired dishes: small stuffed eels with "a thousand scents of Brière" and a *croquant* of frogs legs with Breton algae; menus are €35–70. In keeping with the local Brièronne atmosphere, a few rooms with bath/wc are set under the reed-thatched roof in an annexe raised on piles at the end of the garden; doubles cost €80–150. *Free coffee offered to our readers on presentation of this guide.*

Saint-Philbert-de-Grand-Lieu

44310

ⓒ 🏠 |●| **Hôtel-restaurant La Bosselle**

8 rue du Port.
☎02.40.78.73.47
Open *every day.* **Disabled access. TV.**

The welcome in the restaurant may be a little offhand, but the large dining room, adorned with fishing gear, and its rear terrace-garden are delightful – as are the skilfully prepared regional dishes on offer. Fish is the order of the day, whether from the sea or the river (but always fresh): eel, trout, pike, mussels. If these don't appeal, crêpes provide an alternative option; whatever you choose, you can wash it down with a good Muscadet. The prices are reasonable (so it's advisable to book): there are some ten menus ranging from €17.50 to €28.50. There is also a modern annexe with well-kept hotel rooms: doubles are at €48, one night with dinner at €58. Logis de France.

Saint-Vincent-du-Lorouër

72150

ⓒ |●| **L'Auberge de l'Hermitière**

Sources de l'Hermitière; it's 4.5km south of Saint-Vincent-du-Lorouër.
☎02.43.44.84.45
Closed *Mon evening; Tues and Wed (Oct–April); Mon and Tues (May–Sept); 20 Jan–2 March.* **Disabled access.**

The setting of this house is splendid: it's in a wood, just by the river, and there's a terrace under the trees. Guy Podevin has created wonders here and has endowed the restaurant with great elegance. It's one of the finest in the Sarthe, yet it still serves a weekday menu for €17 – others are €24–48. Specialities include *blinis* with pig's-head *andouille;* some dishes are a little expensive but they are all magnificent.

Marçon

72340 (8.5km NE)

ⓒ ⅔ |●| **Restaurant du Bœuf**

21 pl. de l'Église; take the D304 to La-Chartre-sur-le-Loir, then the D305.
☎02.43.44.13.12
Closed *Sun evening and Mon; Mon lunchtime (July–Aug); 21 Jan–7 March.*

Creole dishes take pride of place on the menus (€10–35) of this popular restaurant. Dishes include chicken with crayfish, stuffed crab and lamb colombo, as well as duck breast with raspberry vinegar. Have some punch and a few fritters to start with and round things off with a house liqueur. *Free coffee offered to our readers on presentation of this guide.*

Ruillé-sur-Loir

72340 (17km SE)

ⓒ ⅔ 🏠 |●| **Hôtel-restaurant Saint Pierre**

42 rue Nationale; take the D304 to La-Chartre-sur-le-Loir, then the D305.
☎02.43.44.44.36
Restaurant closed *Sat and Sun evenings (except for guests); Dec school holiday.*

This appealing little village hotel, with an unassuming façade and a cosy, friendly atmosphere, is one of a dying breed. The proprietress fusses over all her customers and nobody around these parts can rival her "*menu ouvrier*" – the dozens of plates of hors-d'œuvres are even served out ahead of time to deal with the rush. A bottle of red wine is included in the price. Other menus are at €9.50 (served weekdays for hotel guests only), €14 and €20. On Sunday there is a choice of leg of lamb, fillet of beef or duck with pepper, with salad, cheese platter and dessert. They offer a few simple double rooms with basin for €26.70. *Free coffee offered to our readers on presentation of this guide.*

Saulges

53340

ⓒ ⅔ 🏠 |●| **Hôtel-restaurant L'Ermitage***

Place Saint-Pierre; 34km southeast of Laval. Take the N157 and the D24, turn left in Chémeré-le-Roi, it's opposite the church.
☎02.43.64.66.00 📠02.43.64.66.20
🖰www.hotel-ermitage.fr

Closed *Fri evening; Sun; Mon evening (Oct to mid-April); Mon and Fri lunchtimes (April—Sept); Feb; autumn school holiday.* **Disabled access. TV. Swimming pool. Pay car park.**

A modern hotel with bright, spacious, comfortable rooms overlooking the park, swimming pool and countryside. Doubles cost €53–89 with shower/wc or bath; the most expensive ones have just been refurbished. The restaurant serves traditional dishes with a modern twist: red mullet roasted on the fire with warm balsamic vinaigrette, home-smoked meat with green lentils, lobster stew, foie gras. There's a wide selection of menus at €23–50. After your meal, you can take advantage of one of the pleasant walks on offer in the vicinity. Logis de France. *Free house apéritif offered to our readers on presentation of this guide.*

Saumur

49400

ⓔ 🍴 🏨 Hôtel de Londres**

48 rue d'Orléans.
☏02.41.51.23.98 ℗02.41.51.12.63
ⓦwww.lelondres.com
TV. Pay car park.

Friendly hotel in a busy location, but the soundproofing cuts out the noise of the street, and there's a lift. It's been redecorated in a charming English style and is well maintained. Doubles cost €35–54 with shower/wc or bath; there are a few family rooms. Copious buffet breakfast costs €6. *One free breakfast per room offered to our readers on presentation of this guide.*

ⓦ 🍴 🏨 Central Kyriad**

23 rue Daillé; from quai Carnot take rue Fidélité and it's the first on the left after rue Saint-Nicolas.
☏02.41.51.05.78 ℗02.41.67.82.35
ⓦwww.multi.micro.com/kyriad.saumur
TV. High chairs available. Pay car park.

This modern building, in a quiet street, offers pleasant, rather refined décor with exposed beams and an affable welcome from the host. The 27 rooms are spacious and some surprise with their flights of stairs, sloping ceilings and stylish furniture; there are some family rooms with large bathrooms. Doubles cost €45–75 according to facilities and the season; buffet breakfast €7. *10% discount on the room rate in low season offered to our readers on presentation of this guide.*

ⓦ 🍴 🏨 Hôtel Anne d'Anjou***

32–33 quai Mayaud; it's below the château, beside the Loire.
☏02.41.67.30.30 ℗02.41.67.51.00
ⓦwww.hotel-anneanjou.com
Disabled access. TV. High chairs available. Pay car park.

An elegant and charming eighteenth-century building with a flower-filled internal courtyard and a superb (listed) staircase. Comfortable doubles with antique furniture go for €85 with shower/wc or €130 with bath; breakfast is €10. Some rooms are under the eaves; there's also an opulent, Empire-style bedroom ideal for a special treat or a honeymoon. Menus range from €19 to €48. *10% discount on the room rate (1 Nov–31 March) offered to our readers on presentation of this guide.*

ⓔ 🍽 🍴 La Pierre Chaude

41 av. du Général-de-Gaulle; on the island of Offard, between the two bridges. Cross the Loire in the direction of the train station; it's on the left, behind the trees.
☏02.41.67.18.83
Closed *Tues evening (in winter); Wed evening; Sat lunch; Sun evening; first fortnight in Aug; a week at Christmas.*

The house speciality, "*the hot butcher's stone*", is extremely filling: a mixture of meat and poultry (pork, duck, etc) cooked on a stone and accompanied by delicious sauces. Other traditional dishes are also on offer on various menus: weekday lunchtime menu at €10, "*saloon*" menu at €13.90 and "*diligence*" (stagecoach) menu at €19.10. You'll find the service charming. *Free house apéritif offered to our readers on presentation of this guide.*

ⓔ 🍽 Les Ménestrels

11–13 rue Raspail; it's in the gardens of the *Hôtel Anne d'Anjou*, at the bottom of the castle.
☏02.41.67.71.10
Closed *Sun; Mon lunchtime; a week at Christmas.* **High chairs available.**

Without doubt the best restaurant in Saumur, boasting a rustic setting, original beams and exposed stonework. As for the food, the set menus from €19.50 (lunchtimes Mon–Fri) to €52 offer fine combinations of complex flavours. Specialities change frequently, but expect a lot of chicken dishes and local produce.

Montsoreau

49730 (11km SE)

⊚ 🎄 |O| Restaurant le Saut-aux-loups

Route de Saumur; coming from Saumur on the D947, it's on the edge of the village.
☎02.41.51.70.30
Closed *Mon (July–Aug); mid-Dec to mid-Jan.* **Open** *lunchtimes only; weekends; public holidays; Sat evening (July–Aug); weekends only (15 Nov–28 Feb)* **Disabled access. High chairs available.**

This was the first restaurant in the region to relaunch an almost-forgotten local speciality called the *galipette*. It's made by stuffing three big mushrooms with *rillette* or *andouillette* and *crème fraîche*, snails or goat's cheese. Then they're browned gently in a bread oven fuelled by vine cuttings and served with a light, fruity Gamay. Reckon on €20 for a meal à la carte (wine and coffee included), with individual dishes starting at €7.90. Excellent welcome delivered by the young owner; in summer he puts tables outside. Credit cards not accepted. *Free coffee offered to our readers on presentation of this guide.*

Sillé-le-Guillaume

72140

⊚ 🎄 🏠 |O| Le Bretagne**

1 pl. de la Croix d'Or; it's near the station.
☎02.43.20.10.10 ℗02.43.20.03.96
ⓦwwwlebretagne.ifrance.com
Closed *Fri and Sun evenings, and Sat lunchtime (Oct–March); 20 July–10 Aug.* **TV. Car park.**

Inside this newly renovated family hotel, there's a superb restaurant offering fresh-tasting and exciting dishes that change with the seasons: leek terrine, hot foie gras with fruit chutney, lightly smoked salmon, green lentils, *fondant* of oxtail, scorpion fish with lemongrass, and a delicious Paris-Brest filled with butter icing. The weekday menu is €15, with others €25–49. Double rooms cost €48–59 with shower or bath. Logis de France. *10% discount on the room rate (except in the week of the 24-hour race and the French motorcycling Grand Prix) offered to our readers on presentation of this guide.*

Thouarcé

49380

⊚ |O| Le Relais de Bonnezeaux

Take the D24 for about 2km from Thouarcé heading towards Angers; it's in the old train station.
☎02.41.54.08.33
Closed *Sun and Tues evenings; Mon; 3 weeks in Jan.* **Disabled access. High chairs available. Car park.**

Though this restaurant is housed in a nineteenth-century station, there's little of the old atmosphere left. Nevertheless, the dining room, with its panoramic view, is an elegant setting for the refined cuisine. There's a "*Queniau*" menu at €10, then a €17 menu (not served Sat evening and Sun) and others at €26–43. They specialize in delicious, original fish dishes. Some of the menus offer a different wine with each course; the wine list includes some amazing old vintages. There's a shady terrace and a children's playground.

Tranche-sur-Mer (La)

85360

⊚ |O| Restaurant Le Nautile

103 rue du Phare.
☎02.51.30.32.18
Closed *Sun evening and Mon out of season; Feb.* **Disabled access. High chairs available.**

Anonymous-looking restaurant with a terrace, hidden away in the residential part of La Tranche. The setting may lack character, but this is one of the region's most fashionable venues. Cyril Godard's fine, flavoursome cuisine makes it worth a visit – as do the grounds and the veranda. Menus €16–40; try the mussels, the langoustines flambéed with Pineau or the fisherman's casserole.

Vibraye

72320

⊚ 🎄 🏠 |O| Hôtel-restaurant Le Chapeau Rouge**

Place de l'Hôtel-de-Ville; it's opposite the town hall.
☎02.43.93.60.02 ℗02.43.71.52.18
ⓦwww.le-chapeau-rouge.com

Closed *Fri and Sun evenings; 1–15 Jan; last week in Nov.* **Disabled access. TV. High chairs available. Car park.**

This old staging post covered in Virginia creeper is well situated to enjoy the jovial atmosphere of market days. In the old dining room lined with hunting trophies, you can enjoy superb meat, fish (including smoked salmon) and farmhouse cheese, all served with great pride. Everything they serve is made in their own kitchens – from the bread to the desserts. Menus range in price from €16.50 up to €39.50. The sixteen large bedrooms are very quiet and cost €46–54, according to the season. *Three nights for the price of two (weekends only) offered to our readers on presentation of this guide.*

L'Auberge de la Forêt**

Rue Gabriel Goussault.
☎ 02.43.93.60.07 ℻ 02.43.71.20.36
🌐 www.auberge-de-la-foret.fr
Closed *Sun evening; Mon; 15 Jan–15 Feb.* **TV. Car park.**

Peaceful, central hotel with comfortable rooms (if on the small side) costing around €55 with shower/wc or bath. In the restaurant you can take your time over good, tasty food: there's a *menu du terroir* for €16.50 and others up to €45. They list mainly regional dishes, based on locally produced poultry, fish and meats. There's a pleasant terrace. Logis de France. *Free house apéritif offered to our readers on presentation of this guide.*

Picardie

Albert

80300

⊚ 🏠 |●| Hôtel de la Paix**

43 rue Victor-Hugo; it's near the basilica, take the road directly opposite, turn left at the end, then go straight on.
☎03.22.75.01.64 ⊕03.22.75.44.17
Closed *Sun evening; Feb school holiday.* **TV. High chairs available. Car park.**

A small hotel dating from 1925 that has retained the character of the period with wood-panelling and a lovely little bistro. The rooms have been prettily refurbished and are comfortable; doubles with basin €40, or €58–62 with shower/wc or bath. The dining room is pleasant and simple, with appealing family cooking on menus €15–28: potatoes with snails and Camembert cream sauce, calf's head *sauce gribiche*, steak with shallots. Very good welcome from the proprietor; it's a good stopping-off point en route. Logis de France.

⊚ 🕺 🏠 |●| Hôtel de la Basilique**

3–5 rue Gambetta.
☎03.22.75.04.71 ⊕03.22.75.10.47
ⓦwww.hoteldelabasilique.fr
Closed *Sun evening; Mon; 3 weeks in Aug; Christmas school holiday.* **TV. High chairs available.**

With its red brick, its *Virgin with Child* and its stained glass windows, the basilica in Albert is well worth the detour. This fairly conventional hotel near the basilica is also worth a visit on account of the friendly welcome, comfortable rooms – €53 for a double with shower/wc or bath – and good regional cooking. There's a weekday *formule* for €11.50 or menus €13.50–26; try the home-made duck pâté and the

rabbit with prunes. *Free coffee offered to our readers on presentation of this guide.*

Amiens

80000

See map on p.748

⊚ 🏠 Hôtel Victor Hugo**

2 rue de l'Oratoire. **Map C2-1**
☎03.22.91.57.91 ⊕03.22.92.74.02
TV.

This very old establishment, in a lovely quarter of town, has retained some of its original charm and its natural wood staircase. There are ten or so rooms priced at €39–44 with shower/wc or bath. Each one is different – including a few attic rooms at the same rate – and some of them are more comfortable than others. The owner will give you a good welcome and you'd be wise to book.

⊚ 🏠 Hôtel de Normandie

1 bis rue Lamartine; a stone's throw from the station. **Map C2-2**
☎03.22.91.74.99 ⊕03.22.92.06.56
ⓦwww.hotelnormandie-80.com
TV. Pay car park.

Thirty simple but recently refurbished rooms; doubles with basin, shower/wc or bath €41–51. The 1930s breakfast room has splendid stained glass, and the Parisian couple who own the place are lovely and welcoming.

⊚ 🕺 🏠 Hotel Alsace-Lorraine**

18 rue de la Morlière; between the station and the Somme. **Map C1-3**

19

PICARDIE

745

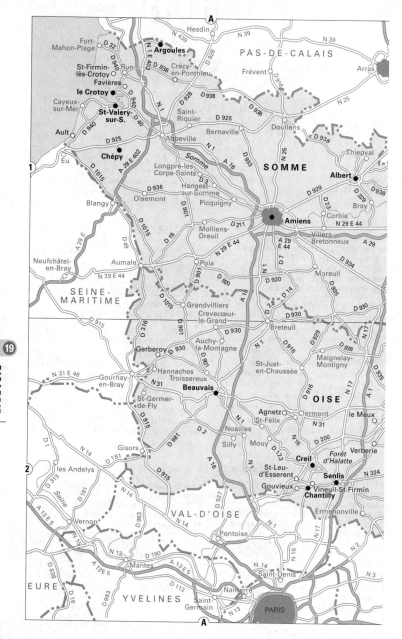

PICARDIE

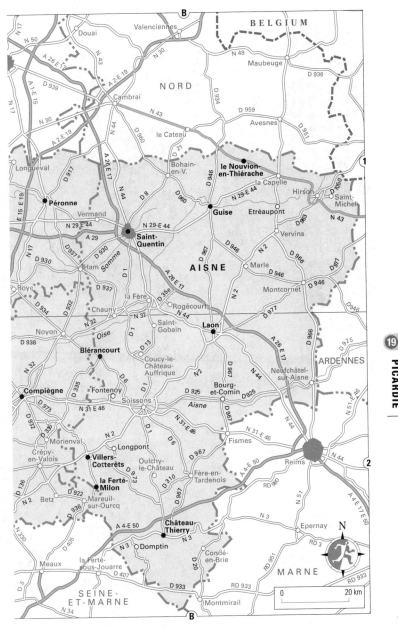

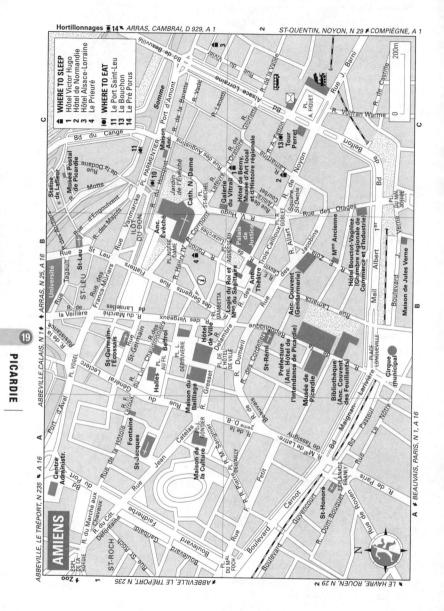

AMIENS

WHERE TO SLEEP
1 Hôtel Victor Hugo
2 Hôtel de Normandie
3 Hôtel Alsace-Lorraine
4 Le Prieuré

WHERE TO EAT
11 Le Port Saint-Leu
13 Le Bouchon
14 Le Pré Porus

PICARDIE 19

748

☎03.22.91.35.71 ℻03.22.80.43.90
🖳www.alsace-lorraine.fr.st
Closed *Sunday afternoon*. **TV.**

Just away from the centre in a quiet area, there's a delightful little hotel behind a lovely blue door. Thirteen rooms painted brilliant white and simply but tastefully decorated; some rooms are accessible from the pleasant interior courtyard. A few of the rooms are singles, with shower/wc on the landing; otherwise, doubles with shower/wc or bath go for €52–65. *One free breakfast per room offered to our readers on presentation of this guide.*

⑳ 🏠 Le Prieuré**

6 and 17 rue Porion; a stone's throw from the cathedral. **Map B1-4**
☎03.22.71.16.71 ℻03.22.92.46.16
Closed *1–21 Nov.* **TV.**

Situated in a quiet, picturesque street, *Le Prieuré* exudes the quaint charm of old residences. All the rooms have been refurbished and each one is different, with carefully chosen furniture and thoughtful decoration; €55–58 with shower/wc or bath. The welcome and the service are variable. Logis de France.

⑳ 🍴 🍽 Le Bouchon

10 rue Alexandre-Fatton. **Map C2-13**
☎03.22.92.14.32
Closed *Sun evening (afternoon and evening during July–Aug); some public holidays.* **Open until 10.30pm (later at weekends).**

Lovely, old-style bistro with round tables, red benches and a zinc-topped bar – it's a stylish little place with an atmosphere and cooking to match. As you might have guessed, it's modelled on a Lyonnais *bouchon*, basically a brasserie, offering such fare as hot sausage and *andouillette à la ficelle*. The weekday lunch menu costs €12, with others €22–42, including a menu where they serve a different wine with each course. You'll probably have to steer away from the wine list, though, because prices are heady. Smiling, easy-going service; separate rooms for smokers and non-smokers. *Free house apéritif offered to our readers on presentation of this guide.*

⑳ 🍽 Le Porc Saint-Leu

45–47 quai Bélu; in the Saint-Leu district. **Map C1-11**
☎03.22.80.00.73

Closed *mid-Dec to 3 Jan.*

We are very pleased to have found this porky base. The dining room is very long and rather cabin-like – low ceilings, soft lights, checked table cloths, a small patio and a terrace for sunny weather. The phrase "everything in the pig is good to eat" is clearly demonstrated in this place. Dishes include grilled suckling pig, pork knuckle with trotter attached, marrow bone or *filet mignon* with mirabelle plums. The side dishes are good: cabbage peasant style or good mashed spuds. There's a *formule* (€12.50) of starter, main meal and coffee, and a choice of menus €18–26; expect to pay €25 à la carte. In brief, good old-fashioned cuisine served with a flair for presentation to boot, all accompanied with a little fashionable, even trendy, touch.

⑳ 🍴 🍽 Restaurant Le Pré Porus

95 rue Voyelle; it's on the edge of Camon just before the bridge, coming from Amiens. **Off map C1-14**
☎03.22.46.25.03
Closed *Mon and Tues evenings; 15 Feb–15 March.* **Disabled access. Car park.**

Everybody agrees that this is one of the finest settings for a picnic on the banks of the Somme. A stone's throw (or a couple of leafy boughs, if you prefer) away from marshland used for vegetable farming. Menus from €16 (weekdays) up to €35 include fish specialities and grills when in season. Quite the fashionable open-air café, but the surcharges are not always justified by the quality of the cuisine. *Free coffee offered to our readers on presentation of this guide.*

Argoules
80120

⑳ 🏠 🍽 Auberge du Gros Tilleul***

Place du Château; it's 2km from the abbey.
☎03.22.29.91.00 ℻03.22.23.91.64
Closed *Mon (Nov–April); Jan.* **Disabled access. TV. Swimming pool. Pay car park.**

This inn is listed in all the guide books, not only for its delightful surroundings, but also due to its history – Sully is said to have planted the lime tree it is named after, and this inn was said to be a Sienese trading post in the service of the kings of France. Rooms go for €58–84 for a double (a word of warning: some problems with reservations; send a written confirmation and make sure it's been received). Half board is compulsory at the weekend and on public holidays, at €58–64. Some rooms look out over a small park, but they are more basic. There are menus at various prices from the weekday *formule* express for €11 to the gourmet menu for €38; the cuisine is rich but not very refined. There's a heated pool, golf driving range and gym.

ⓒ |●| Auberge Le Coq en Pâte

Route de Valloires; it's 500m from the abbey.
☎03.22.29.92.09
Closed Sun evening; Mon; Jan; a fortnight early Sept. **Disabled access.**

They serve excellent local dishes in this pretty establishment even if the à la carte menu is a little pricey – around €30 for a meal. There's only one menu for €19, served on weekdays, but dishes change regularly with the seasons and depending on what's fresh at the market: cod pricked with pink garlic or, in winter, cockerel in beer sauce or a pastry crust – by far the best cooking in the area. What's more, thanks to the proprietor's charming service, you really will be living in clover, as the inn's name suggests in French.

Beauvais
60000

ⓒ 🎢 🏠 Hôtel La Résidence**

24 rue Louis-Borel.
☎03.44.48.30.98 ☎03.44.45.09.42
ⓦwww.hoteldelaresidence.fr
Closed Sun evening, Oct–April (except bookings); 1–23 Aug. **TV. Car park.**

This hotel is on a very quiet street in a residential area twenty minutes' walk from the town centre, where the only thing disturbing the silence is the sound of the odd passing bicycle. You'll get a jokey, good-natured welcome, a modern, well-equipped room and good value for money; doubles with shower €45, or €55 with bath. And that is probably why it is one of our favourite places in Beauvais. *10% discount on the room rate for a stay of at least two consecutive nights offered to our readers on presentation of this guide.*

ⓒ 🎢 |●| Restaurant Le Marignan

1 rue de Malherbe.

☎03.44.48.15.15
Closed Sun evening; Mon (except public holidays); 25 July–20 Aug. **High chairs available.**

On the ground floor there's a typical bar-brasserie where they serve a decent weekday menu. But if you want to get the most out of this place, head instead for the plush first-floor dining room with the added attraction of a representation of the famous battle. Here you can sample well-prepared Picardie specialities, including fish dishes, coddled eggs, veal kidneys, scallop *gratin* or *crème brûlée* with demerara sugar. The first menu at €19.90 is already a very tempting proposition in its own right, while the one at €38 comes with delicious home-made terrine of foie gras and there is a further menu at €58. *Free house apéritif offered to our readers on presentation of this guide.*

Agnetz
60600 (20km SE)

ⓒ |●| Auberge de Gicourt

466 av. de la Forêt-de-Hez, Gicourt; head for Gicourt and take the Gicourt-zone hôtelière exit.
☎03.44.50.00.31
Closed Sun evening; Mon; Wed evening. **Disabled access. High chairs available.**

This pleasant inn is popular with locals and backpackers passing through. They serve a "regional" menu for €18, "gourmet" menu for €26 and a third menu for €45; children's menus are €7 and €15. Reservations are recommended.

Gerberoy
60380 (21km NW)

ⓒ 🎢 |●| L'Ambassade de Montmartre

2 allée du Jeu-de-Tamis; take the D133 in the direction of Abbeville, at the foot of the old ramparts, at the Gerberoy exit coming from Gournay-en-Bray.
☎03.44.82.16.50
Closed Sun evening; Mon; Tues evening; early Dec to mid-Feb.

This place is sited right at the end of this wonderful village – which is listed as one of the most beautiful in France. Both it and the restaurant are worth making the effort to visit. The pretty half-timbered house is owned by Jean-Pierre, the President of the République de Montmartre, and he makes you feel welcome. With tears in his eyes, he will perhaps tell you his memories of the Butte Montmartre cabaret scene. The spacious, rustic dining room has a mezzanine where he holds art exhibitions. Slow and patchy service, but decent regional cuisine is served on the two menus for €17.50 and €24.50. When the weather gets warm you can sit on the terrace out front. *Free house apéritif offered to our readers on presentation of this guide.*

Blérancourt

02300

@ 🏠 |○| Hostellerie Le Griffon

22 pl. du Général-Leclerc.
℡03.23.39.23.39 ℻03.23.39.11.20
✉hostellerie.legriffon@wanadoo.fr

Perfectly placed on the edge of the Blérancourt château estate, *Le Griffon* casually benefits from the advantages of this close proximity. It's worth making a detour for the view from its terrace, and also from some rooms, stretching over the park and the fine seventeenth-century building. Double rooms with shower or bath go for €40–50. The excellent welcome and high quality of the bedding make it a tempting proposition to extend your stay. There's also a good restaurant on site. Logis de France.

Chantilly

60500

@ |○| Restaurant Le Goutillon

61 rue du Connétable.
℡03.44.58.01.00
Open *every day of the year.*

This restaurant has an old-fashioned décor with exposed beams and stone walls covered with vintage advertisements. The waiter brings a blackboard to the table and places it on a chair and you make your choice from the dishes listed on it. But the place also owes its charm to the character of the owner who is actively involved, and to the relaxed (but sometimes erratic) service. There's a lunch *formule* for €11 and a menu for €18; à la carte reckon on €30. A variety of tasty starters, and house specialities include *andouillette*, steak *tartare au poivre*, and calf's kidney flambéed in Cognac.

@ |○| Aux Goûters Champêtres

Hameau du parc du Château; it's inside the grounds of the château where you have to pay to get in.
℡03.44.57.46.21
Closed *evenings; mid-Nov to mid-March.*

A lovely place to eat when it's fine, but at the weekend you have to book to have any hope of getting a table. You eat outside in nicely maintained little gardens, under sun-shades – utterly charming and the welcome and service are friendly. Take a peek at the murals in the Prince de Condé's tea room. First menu at €16.80 offers you one main dish and one dessert, but it is substantial; the next menu, at €27.80, is the most popular and comes with crown of duck breast, *confit de canard* or pork, cheese and dessert (*crème Chantilly* like you've never had before). Alternatively, all year round, but again only at lunchtime, you might prefer the kitchens at the *Capitainerie du Château* (℡03.44.47.15.89) in the castle, the very ones at which the famous seventeenth-century French chef François Vatel officiated. It's a bit more expensive, it's very touristy, but the quality is more than decent and the setting grand.

Vineuil-Saint-Firmin

60500 (4km NE)

@ 🎋 |○| Les Grands Prés

CD 138.
℡03.44.57.71.97
Closed *Sun evening; Mon.*

Very pleasant in fine weather, because you can eat outside, right in the countryside. Menus at €19 (not weekends) and €28 offer straightforward, traditional cuisine with dishes such as marbled foie gras and pan-fried kidneys. *Free coffee offered to our readers on presentation of this guide.*

Gouvieux

60270 (5km W)

@ 🎋 🏠 |○| Hôstellerie du Pavillon Saint-Hubert**

Chemin de Marisy, lieu-dit Toutevoie; take the D909, then, in Gouvieux, follow the sign for "Toutevoie".
℡03.44.57.07.04 ℻03.44.57.75.42
Closed *15 Jan–13 Feb.* **Restaurant closed** *Sun evening and Mon.* **TV. High chairs and games available. Pay car park.**

This old fisherman's house is set in a

charming spot on a bend in the Oise River on the towpath, and it's a lovely place to bring family, friends or a special person. From the terrace you can watch the barges slip by or simply listen to the birds. The cooking is traditional, with a weekday menu at €24.50 (€32 on Sundays and public holidays), listing a choice of six starters and à la carte dishes such as calf's kidneys with mustard sauce and home-made fresh foie gras. Double rooms go for €47–75 according to the facilities and the view. The rooms overlooking the river, despite being the most expensive, are the most popular and they're often taken at the weekend – so do book. The only regret is that you cannot take your breakfast on the terrace – just a minor matter, but irritating all the same in summer. Logis de France. *Free coffee offered to our readers on presentation of this guide.*

Saint-Leu-d'Esserent
60340 (5.5km NW)

 Hôtel de l'Oise*

25 quai d'Amont; take the N16 then follow the D44.
℡03.44.56.60.24 ℻03.44.56.05.11
ⓦwww.hoteldeloise.com
Restaurant closed Sun (open for lunch early April to end Sept); Fri evening; Sat; first 3 weeks in Aug. **TV. High chairs available. Car park.**

Charming little two-star hotel on the banks of the Oise, where, just a stone's throw (or thereabouts) from Paris, tranquillity and hospitality are *de rigueur*. The rooms are very well kept and go for €53 with shower/wc or bath. The restaurant, fully refurbished, offers a full first menu, served weekday lunchtimes, for €13 and other menus €25.50–40; otherwise good speciality dishes are available on the à la carte menu. A great hotel/restaurant with secure parking. *Free coffee offered to our readers on presentation of this guide.*

Château-Thierry
02400

 Hôtel-restaurant Hexagone*

50 av. d'Essômes; take the Paris road from the centre of town then follow the signs for Charly-sur-Marne.
℡03.23.83.69.69 ℻03.23.83.64.17
Closed Sun (except for groups); 21 Dec–4

Jan. **Disabled access. TV. High chairs available. Car park.**

You'll get a warm welcome in this modern hotel, and you will also be well looked-after. Comfortable doubles with shower/wc or bath go for €42; the hearty buffet-style breakfast includes cereals, cheese and charcuterie. The restaurant serves good traditional home cooking, which is very good value for money; the cheapest menu, €13, is perfectly adequate, and there are four others at €16–30. The home-made *tarte Tatin* is also worth a mention. The River Marne flows past the bottom of the garden. *10% discount on the room rate offered to our readers on presentation of this guide.*

Domptin
02310 (12km SW)

 Hôtel-restaurant Le Cygne d'Argent

24 rue de la Fontaine; take the N3 west from Château-Thierry, then the D11 and it's in the main street.
℡03.23.70.79.90 ℻03.23.70.79.99
ⓦwww.otsichateauthierry.com
Closed Mon evening. **Disabled access. TV. Car park.**

Lovely country hotel fringed with hollyhocks on the Champagne wine route. Inside, a very rustic dining room, where they serve fine local cuisine including specialities with Ratafia de Domptin red wine sauces, home-made terrines and wonderful fish (although the menu changes with the seasons), and also home-made sorbets. There's a weekday menu for €13 and others €18–38. There are five comfortable rooms; doubles with bath go for €45. This is a great place. Logis de France. *Free house apéritif offered to our readers on presentation of this guide.*

Chépy
80210

 L'Auberge Picarde*

Place de la Gare; it's opposite Chépy-Valines train station.
℡03.22.26.20.78 ℻03.22.26.33.34
ⓔauberge.picarde@wanadoo.fr
Restaurant closed Sat lunchtime; Sun evening. **Closed** 1–9 Jan; 16 Aug–2 Sept. **Disabled access. TV. Car park.**

The large, modern building is more motel than charming inn, but it has one of the best restaurants in the region. The dining room has ample proportions and is decorated in traditional style. They serve good seafood and local dishes using seasonal market produce based on the local *ficelle picarde* pancake dish, salmon and asparagus tips in vinaigrette, fried fish with seaweed butter. There's a weekday menu at €14.50 and others €20.50–34. The rooms are standard but comfortable; doubles with shower/wc or bath cost €44–47. It's very popular at weekends, so it is probably best to book. Welcome and service would benefit from being a little more personal. Logis de France.

Compiègne
60200

⊚ 🎄 🏛 Hôtel de Flandre**

16 quai de la République; a three-minute walk from the centre.
☎03.44.83.24.40 🖷03.44.90.02.75
🖳www.hoteldeflandre.com
Closed holiday dates to be decided. **TV. Pay car park.**

An enormous classical building on the banks of the Oise. The hotel, which has been completely refurbished in pastel colours, is very comfortable and offers a pleasant range of rooms: €32 for a double with basin, €53–56 with shower/wc or bath. Rooms are spacious and the double glazing guarantees peace and quiet. *10% discount on the room rate for a stay of at least two consecutive nights, on presentation of this guide.*

⊚ 🎄 |●| Restaurant Le Bouchon

4 rue Austerlitz; next to the Vivenel museum.
☎03.44.20.02.03
Closed Sun during winter; Christmas and New Year holidays. **Disabled access.**

With its *formule* you can enjoy just a fine salad or alternatively tuck into a substantial *plat du jour* with a glass of good wine (there are about forty to choose from). The idea, while not original, has been taken further here. Despite its move, *Le Bouchon* has retained its rustic décor in a half-timbered building, its friendly atmosphere (have your leg pulled by the proprietor) and its regional cuisine with dishes such as *saucisson lyonnais, confit de canard* and saffron sea bream. Opt for the lunch *formule* which includes main dish plus starter or dessert for €10.50; oth-

erwise there are two menus at €19 and €25. *Le Bouchon* regularly puts on wine tasting dinners and the opportunity to taste six different wines. The proprietor is not short of ideas – a place where hospitality goes hand in hand with personality. *Free liqueur offered to our readers on presentation of this guide.*

⊚ 🎄 |●| Le Palais Gourmand

8 rue Dahomey.
☎03.44.40.13.13
Closed Sun evening; Mon; 3 weeks in Aug.
High chairs available.

An old baker's transformed into a modern restaurant with lots of corners and little dining rooms. This restaurant could easily be renamed "Le Loft Gourmand" because the elevated light from the glass roof shows off to best advantage the attractive décor, restrained and colourful at one and the same time, with its old floor and wall tiles. The cuisine offers both seasonal dishes and modern interpretations; *formules* and menus €12.50–20.50. Good wines are served by the jug at very reasonable prices. Overall, it's excellent value for money. *Free coffee offered to our readers on presentation of this guide.*

⊚ |●| Le Bistrot des Arts

35 Cours Guynemer; it's on the river, on the left bank.
☎03.44.20.10.10
Closed Sun; Sat lunchtime.

The easy-going, professional service perfectly suits the setting of this bistro, which is where the gourmands in town come to eat. The weekday lunch *formule* costs €18, and the set menu €24; à la carte, a meal costs around €30. Although there is no small menu, the prices are still very reasonable when all's said and done. Sadly there are no wines by the jug so it's hard to keep the price down. But even so, you won't regret this little moment of madness, because the brasserie dishes here take on a festive feel in the capable hands of the young chef, Yves Mejean. The region assumes a subtle originality while we sit back and enjoy. Bon appétit! It's best to book.

Meux (Le)
60880 (10km SW)

⊚ |●| La Maison du Gourmet

1 rue de la République; take the A1.

☎03.44.91.10.10
Closed *Sun evening; Mon; Sat lunchtime; 10 days end Jan to early Feb; 3 weeks end July to early Aug.* **Disabled access. High chairs and games available. Car park.**

The owner-chef isn't new to this game – seven years at *Maxim's* in Paris and at the *Château de Raray*. Today word of mouth has spread his fame, so that you now have to book. That's the price you have to pay for being famous. The €16 menu alone makes it worth a visit; a typical selection might be duck breast with blackcurrants, home-made duck foie gras, *filet mignon* with cider sauce, strawberry crisp and warm soufflé with crystallized orange, although the chef will have many more up his sleeve. There's more choice on the €24 menu and a wide range of dishes à la carte. It's great value, and you'll be greeted and served in a friendly, efficient manner. There's parking available in the courtyard.

Verberie
60410 (15km SW)

ⓔ 🚩 🏠 |●| **Auberge de Normandie**

26 rue de la Pêcherie; take the D200 or the D932A near the Oise River; 2.7km from exit no. 9 on the A1.
☎03.44.40.92.33 ☎03.44.40.50.62
🌐www.auberge-normandie.com
Closed *Sun evening; Mon.* **TV. High chairs available.**

A nice country inn with a classic dining room furnished with imitation rustic furniture and a pleasant terrace festooned with flowers. Half board is compulsory and costs €46 per person sharing a double room. The unexpectedly interesting cuisine on the menus (€20–39) uses quality ingredients and is produced with art and craft. From the meat specialities, try the stuffed shoulder of lamb with rosemary or the stuffed pigs' trotters. The desserts are also delicious. You'll get a warm welcome.

Creil
60100

ⓔ 🏠 |●| **Auberge de jeunesse – Le Centre des Cadres Sportifs**

1 rue du Général-Leclerc; 10 min from town centre by bus. Take the # 1 bus, from the train station, or use the shuttle service.
☎03.44.64.62.20 ☎03.44.64.62.29
🌐www.fuaj.org

TV. Games available. Car park.

A well-equipped youth hostel that offers a host of sporting activities. Accommodation is €16.20 a night per person in a dormitory, including breakfast; FUAJ card compulsory but you can buy it on site. You must book in advance for food: full meal €8.70; one hot dish €4.60; children's menu €6.40. The rooms are in immaculate condition, the atmosphere is relaxed and you can expect an efficient welcome.

Crotoy (Le)
80550

ⓔ 🚩 🏠 |●| **Les Tourelles***

2–4 rue Pierre Guerlain; take the A16.
☎03.22.27.16.33 ☎03.22.27.11.45
🌐www.lestourelles.com
Closed *6–30 Jan.* **Disabled access. High chairs and games available.**

This red-brick turreted building, erected on the Somme estuary, was once the mansion of perfumier Pierre Guerlain. Overlooking the bay of the Somme with the sea at its feet, this restaurant's setting receives unanimous approval. Nothing is left to chance: neither the charming rooms with an open view (our favourites are room no. 33 in the turret and south-facing room no. 14, or there again room nos. 10 and 19), all looking out over the bay, nor the Gustavian-style lounge-bar where you can relax and take your ease, nor the games room intended for children. The rooms (€63–68.25 for a double) are booked up weeks in advance so you'll be lucky to get in. Menus range from €19.80 up to €29. Pets are permitted. *Free house apéritif offered to our readers on presentation of this guide.*

Favières
80120 (4km NE)

ⓔ 🚩 🏠 |●| **Restaurant La Clé des Champs**

Place des Frères-Caudron; take the D940 in the direction of Crotoy, then the D140.
☎03.22.27.88.00
Closed *Mon; Tues; week preceding the return to school in Sept.* **Disabled access. Car park.**

As its name suggests, they really have run off to the country in this famous inn, situated in a village in the midst of salt meadows. Its cuisine specializes in using produce fresh from the market and fish fresh from the small fishing boats. Madame makes you feel very welcome in a refined bourgeois setting. There's a weekday menu for €12 and others €18–38. *Free liqueur offered to our readers on presentation of this guide.*

Saint-Firmin-lès-Crotoy
80550 (7km N)

◎ ⅍ 🏠 |●| Auberge de la Dune**

Rue de la Dune; take the D104 in the direction of Saint-Firmin, at the D204 turn-off take the signs to the Marquenterre bird sanctuary. Exit 24 off the A16 motorway.
☎03.22.25.01.88 📠03.22.25.66.74
Closed *Tues and Wed (outside school holidays); 15 Nov–25 March.* **TV. High chairs and games available. Car park.**

This small farmhouse has been nicely restored and is situated close to the bird sanctuary. The eleven brightly painted bedrooms are cosy as you like and, though they're not big, they're comfortable and cost €57; all come with shower/wc and phone. They serve decent food in the restaurant offering both classical and regional dishes. Picardy specialities are listed on the stopover menu, €17, served at lunchtime from Monday to Saturday, and the other menus €22–42. Pleasant welcome is guaranteed. Logis de France. *Free house apéritif offered to our readers on presentation of this guide.*

Ferté-Milon (La)
02460

◎ ⅍ 🏠 Hôtel Racine**

Place du Port-au-Blé.
☎03.23.96.72.02 📠03.23.96.72.37
✉iap@club-internet.fr
TV. High chairs available. Car park.

This charming former hotel has gone for the bed, breakfast and evening meal option to avoid wrecking its authenticity as it would have to do in order to comply with the drastic hotel-trade norms. As a result this beautiful seventeenth-century house has become more intimate and offers a pleasant welcome. It comes as no surprise that the seventeenth-century French poet and man of letters Jean de La Fontaine, most famous for his *Fables*, came here to celebrate his marriage (yes, it's true!). The eight rooms have been tastefully decorated

and they're reasonably priced: doubles with shower/wc €50, €55 with bath. Outside there's a garden with a paved courtyard and a pretty corner tower overlooking the banks of the Ourcq. The owners organize art courses. *One free breakfast per room or 10% discount on the room rate (early Dec to end of March) offered to our readers on presentation of this guide.*

◎ |●| Restaurant Les Ruines

2 pl. du Vieux-Château.
☎03.23.96.71.56
Closed *Mon; Aug.* **Car park.**

A good inn owned by a former landscape gardener; you dine outside in his lovely garden next to the ruined château. Traditional, good-value cooking features on the €12 *formule rapide*, served during the week, and other menus at €21–32: pan-fried pigeon fillet, monkfish steak with spicy shrimps, game depending on the season. The welcome comes with a smile.

Guise
02120

◎ |●| Restaurant Le Petit Manoir**

83 rue Camille-Des-Moulins.
☎03.23.61.38.24
Closed *Sun evening; Mon; a week in Feb; 10 days in Aug.*

A friendly, courteous little restaurant nestling at the start of the road leading to the castle of the famous duke. Regulars give their wholehearted approval to its cooking, which frequently produces delicious aromas from the region, to be enjoyed around the old wood stove – designed by the nineteenth-century French industrialist and social engineer, Godin, of course. Specialities include *escalope de foie gras au cidre* and *cuisse de canard aux morilles*. There's a weekday *formule* served at lunchtimes for €12.50 and menus for €17.85–23.65.

Laon
02000

◎ 🏠 ⅍ Hôtel Les Chevaliers**

3–5 rue Sérurier; it's in the middle of the medieval town, between the cathedral and the place de la Mairie.

☎03.23.27.17.50 ⊜03.23.79.12.07
⊜hotelchevaliers@aol.com
Closed Sun, Mon and Tues, except on public
holidays and in the tourist season; mid-Jan to
mid-Feb. **TV.**

You'll find this small, friendly hotel in a
stylish old building, just a short walk from
the cathedral. The bedrooms are attractively decorated with low ceilings and
exposed beams; doubles go for €55 with
shower/wc and €60 with bath (including breakfast). Some have an unrestricted
view over the surrounding countryside.
On the ground floor is a café-tea room
(books available and music). *10% discount
on the room rate (except from early Oct to end
of March) offered to our readers on presentation
of this guide.*

⊛ ℀ |●| Bar-Restaurant Le Rétro

18 bd. de Lyon; it's in the main street in the
lower town.
☎03.23.23.04.49
Closed Sun.

Unchanging and with no fuss, this local
brasserie has people queuing at lunchtime to sample its skilfully prepared yet
unpretentious traditional cooking. Marie-
Thérèse, a colourful character, will welcome you as a member of the family into
her slightly kitsch dining room or onto
the terrace where you can sample the set
menu for €12.50, or opt for the à la carte
menu. *Free coffee offered to our readers on
presentation of this guide.*

⊛ |●| Restaurant La Petite Auberge

45 bd. Brossolette; it's near the train station
in the lower town.
☎03.23.23.02.38
Closed Sun except public holidays; Mon
evening; Sat lunchtime; a week in Feb; a
week at Easter; fortnight in Aug. **High chairs
available.**

In a tastefully decorated country inn
complete with Louis XIII furniture, the
cooking is modern and the owner's son,
Willy Marc Zorn, introduces a touch of
originality to tasty dishes such as pan-
fried pigeon fillets and lemon *confit* semolina or roast monkfish in a sesame pastry
case. This is Laon's gourmet restaurant for
a special occasion dinner, but the prices
are quite high: weekday menu €19.90,
and other menus €24.90–40. For those
on more limited budgets, the *Saint-Amour*
(☎03.23.23.31.01) just next door and run

by the same people, offers family food
à la lyonnaise and – yes, you've guessed
it – some excellent Beaujolais wines
in a brasserie setting, with an astonishing fresco on the ceiling in the style of
Michelangelo. Food is served on the terrace if you wish.

Bourg-et-Comin
02160 (22km S)

⊛ ℀ � |●| Auberge de la Vallée**

6 rue d'Oeuilly; take the D967 in the direction
of Fismes. It's in the centre of the village.
☎03.23.25.81.58 ⊜03.23.25.38.10
Closed Tues evening; Wed; 2–22 Jan; 31
March–6 April; 22–27 Sept. **TV. Car park.**

Evelyne is the owner of this small, classic
hotel located in the centre of the village, and she will welcome you warmly.
Rooms are clean and recently redecorated and you'll pay €45–60 for a double
with shower/wc. She provides traditional
cuisine using good local produce with
a weekday lunch menu for €12, then
others €15–38. A good place to stopover
en route; dogs are allowed (€6). Logis de
France. *Free digestif offered to our readers on
presentation of this guide.*

Nouvion-en Thiérache (Le)
02170

⊛ ℀ � |●| Hôtel de la Paix**

37 rue Mont-Vicary.
☎03.23.97.04.55 ⊜03.23.98.98.39
⊛www.hotel-la-paix.fr
Closed Sun evening; Sat lunchtime; Feb
school holiday; last fortnight in Aug. Open
on Mon by reservation only. **TV. High chairs,
baby feeding-bottles and changing table
available. Car park.**

This is a good country hotel with
friendly staff. It's been completely refurbished, the restaurant is a delight and
the cooking out of the ordinary. They
offer regional dishes such as steak with
Maroilles cheese melt, seafood specialities such as home-smoked salmon, and
tasty desserts to satisfy even the most
demanding palate. There's a weekday
menu €17, then two more at €27 and
€37. The large, comfortable bedrooms
cost €47 with shower/wc and €62 with
bath. No. 1 faces south and has a private
terrace. Logis de France. *10% discount*

on the room rate (in July–Aug) or free house apéritif offered to our readers on presentation of this guide.

Étréaupont

02580 (19km SE)

◎ 🏠 |◎| Le Clos du Montvinage et l'Auberge du Val de l'Oise**

8 rue Albert-Ledent; it's on the N2.
☎03.23.97.91.10 ℗03.23.97.48.92
🌐www.clos-du-montvinage.fr
Restaurant closed Sun evening. **Closed** a week in Jan; a week in Aug; a week at Christmas (restaurant only). **Disabled access. TV. Car park.**

A huge nineteenth-century bourgeois residence in relaxing grounds with tennis courts. Staff have had the good sense to keep the welcome charming and simple. The rooms are spacious and comfortable; those on the second floor have exposed beams and go for €61–81 with shower/wc or bath. Half board costs €51–61 per person. In the restaurant, menus €20–37, with a weekday lunchtime *menu express* for €13, list fine fish specialities depending on the catch, veal sweetbreads with *Vieille Prune* plum brandy, Marouilles cheese clafoutis with its *compote* or *vacherin* with red berry fruits. Logis de France.

Péronne

80200

◎ 🎍 🏠 |◎| Hostellerie des Remparts**

23 rue Beaubois; it's 100m off the main street.
☎03.22.84.01.22 ℗03.22.84.31.96
🌐www.logisdefrance.fr
Disabled access. TV. High chairs available. Pay car park.

A country inn with a post-war feel in peaceful grounds on a quiet street. The rooms have all been refurbished and doubles with shower/wc and bath go for €65–70. They serve traditional local dishes with a creative touch in the cosy dining room. There are weekday *formules* (not served on public holidays) at €12 and €16, including drinks, and menus at €20–50. You'd do well to stick to the menus as à la carte is very expensive. Logis de France. *10% discount on the room rate (11 April–5 May) offered to our readers on presentation of this guide.*

Saint-Quentin

02100

◎ 🏠 |◎| Hôtel de la Paix**

3 pl. du 8-Octobre; it's near the train station.
☎03.23.62.77.62 ℗03.23.62.66.03
🌐www.hoteldelapaix.com
Restaurant closed Sun. **TV. Car park.**

An impressive 1914 building which has been pleasantly modernized. A maze of corridors leads to well-kept functional rooms, quiet at the rear of the building, some of which have a really good view. Doubles with shower/wc go for €48 and €52.50 with bath. Friendly welcome; there's a restaurant on the ground floor.

◎ 🎍 🏠 Hôtel des Canonniers***

15 rue des Canonniers; near the town hall.
☎03.23.62.87.87 ℗03.23.62.87.86
🌐www.hotel-canonniers.com
Closed Sun evening, except for reservations; 1–15 Aug, except for reservations. **TV. High chairs available. Car park.**

Originally a private residence with mouldings, fireplaces and beautiful drawing rooms built in the eighteenth and nineteenth centuries, this hotel is located in the quiet central area of Saint-Quentin. The female owner will greet you very kindly. The spacious rooms are extremely comfortable and feature many personal touches; doubles with shower/wc are €60, with bath €75, and suites with kitchen are €105. Breakfast is served in the pretty internal garden. This is one of our best addresses in Saint-Quentin. *10% discount on the room rate at weekends (early Nov to end of March) offered to our readers on presentation of this guide.*

◎ |◎| Le Vert Bouteille

80 rue d'Isle.
☎03.23.05.13.25
Closed Sat lunchtime; Sun.

Le Vert Bouteille has rapidly become popular with the people of Saint-Quentin. The cuisine *à la lyonnaise* with its substantial and generous dishes meets with wholehearted approval, and the good thing about its chic bistro atmosphere is that it is not in the least stiff. What's more, the cartoons displayed on the walls (green… bottle to go with its name) are sure to cheer up anyone who's feeling a little glum. Expect to pay about €30 à la carte.

Saint-Valéry-sur-Somme

80230

◎ 🛏 |●| Hôtel du Port et des Bains***

1 quai Blavet; it's in the lower town, on the mouth of the River Somme.
℡03.22.60.80.09 📠03.22.60.77.90
✉hotel.hpb@wanadoo.fr
Closed 1–15 Jan. **TV.**

A friendly little place with its old-fashioned façade and alleyway. Rooms aren't huge but they're well decorated and painted in bright colours. They all overlook the Somme and cost €60–75 for a double with shower/wc. The restaurant, which has a view, serves classical cuisine and seafood platters, with menus in the region of €15–35. A little on the expensive side, but then it is in Saint-Valéry.

◎ 🛏 |●| Le Relais Guillaume de Normandy**

46 quai Romerel; at the foot of the upper town, along the sea wall promenade, near the Nevers Gate.
℡03.22.60.82.36 📠03.22.60.81.82
🌐www.guillaumedenormandy.com
Closed Tues; 21 Dec–17 Jan. **TV. Car park.**

This tall, narrow manor house, set in a garden by the water's edge, is a bit of an architectural mish-mash. It was built about a hundred years ago by an English lord for his mistress. Quite stylish, but some bedrooms (not those that have been recently refurbished) feel a bit tired – though they're comfortable enough. Doubles are €67–125 with shower/wc or bath, depending on the size and view (sea or grounds); room no. 1 has a delightful little terrace but is more expensive. The beautiful dining room breathes *Vieille France*, and serves appropriately traditional fare which is filling but not hugely exciting. Menus range from €15 (weekdays) up to €35. Logis de France.

◎ 🛏 Hôtel Picardia***

41 quai du Romerel; it's opposite the hotel Relais Guillaume de Normandy.
℡03.22.60.32.30 📠03.22.60.76.69
🌐www.picardia.fr
Closed first fortnight in Jan. **TV.**

This is a place that will appeal to families or those with a bit of cash and it's friendly and welcoming. It's a pretty village house which has been thoroughly refurbished from top to bottom so the rooms are bright with immaculate white walls, furnishings somewhere between designer and traditional, and quite luxurious bathrooms – perhaps a little over-restored for some people's liking. Rooms have all mod cons, including TV and double glazing (useful as the hotel is on a main road); doubles cost €70 and there is an apartment available for families or groups.

Ault

80460 (21km SW)

◎ |●| Restaurant l'Horizon

31 rue de Saint-Valéry; in upper Ault-Onival on top of the cliffs.
℡03.22.60.43.21
Closed Wed evening and Thurs (out of season); Jan.

A little restaurant with a maritime theme and a fabulous view of the beach; be warned, only six tables have a sea view. Other tables have a pleasant enough view, and through the two picture windows, you can see the most beautiful (moving) watercolours in the restaurant. An attractive selection of seafood and platters is on offer, with a choice of menus €12.80–27.90, or à la carte.

Senlis

60300

◎ 🎄 🛏 |●| Hostellerie de la Porte Bellon**

51 rue Bellon; it's just off rue de la République.
℡03.44.53.03.05 📠03.44.53.29.94
🌐www.portebellon.com
Closed a fortnight end Dec to early Jan. **Restaurant closed** Sun evening. **TV. High chairs available.**

A superb old house, with attractive internal decoration, and set back from the road so it's quiet. The eighteen comfortable and spacious double rooms, €58–73, have been refurbished. You can eat in the shady garden in good weather, and there's an eighteenth-century cellar where you can enjoy an apéritif. There's a weekday menu €21 (€23 on Sun) with others €28–39. Logis de France.

Free house apéritif offered to our readers on presentation of this guide.

Villers-Cotterêts

02600

ⓒ ⌂ Hôtel Le Régent***

26 rue du Général-Mangin; in the historic town centre.
☏03.23.96.01.46 ℗03.23.96.37.57
ⓦwww.hotel-leregent.com
Disabled access. TV. Car park.

There's an authentic sixteenth-century coaching inn behind the eighteenth-century façade. Personalized rooms, sometimes having decorative mouldings or beams, some rooms furnished in old-fashioned style, others with a balcony or even a private terrace looking out over a paved inner courtyard. What's more, some rooms are even listed in the Register of Historic Monuments. Doubles in this charming little hotel are priced at €58–74 with shower or bath/wc.

Longpont

02600 (11.5km NE)

ⓒ 🏃 ⌂ |●| Hôtel de l'Abbaye**

Rue des Tourelles; turn off the N2 onto the D2.
☏ and ℗03.23.96.02.44
TV. High chairs available.

Gorgeous ivy-covered inn with its stone chimney in a romantic setting on the edge of the Retz forest. Rooms cost €48–50 for a double with shower/wc or bath; half board €57 per person. No. 111 has a view over the fortified port. Excellent, fresh local produce is served in the restaurant, as well as game in season, and menus range from €19 up to €30. If you are visiting the superb abbey just opposite, it is worth knowing that you can come here for a good pancake in the afternoon. A romantic place for gourmets offering an excellent, obliging and attentive welcome. Logis de France. *Free house apéritif offered to our readers on presentation of this guide.*

19

Poitou-Charentes

Aix (Île de)
17123

⬱ 🏨 |●| **Hôtel-restaurant Le Napoléon et des Bains Réunis****

Rue Gourgaud.
☎05.46.84.66.02 ℗05.46.84.69.70
🌐www.hotelnapoleon-aix.com
Closed *Sun evening and Mon (Oct–March); Nov; Dec.*

This comfortable establishment, which has fifteen attractive rooms, is the only hotel on the island. Doubles go for €58 with washbasin, €68 with shower/wc, and €72 with bath; half board is compulsory in July and August at around €50 per person. Menus (€19–30) list fish dishes such as salmon *tartare* or cod baked in red wine. As the island has no other restaurant open out of season, hotel guests have to eat here. There's a pleasant sitting room where you can have a drink after cycling round the island (cars are out of bounds on Aix). The service is sometimes lacking in quality.

Angles-sur-l'Anglin
86260

⬱ 🎋 🏨 |●| **Le Relais du Lion d'Or*****

4 rue d'Enfer; it's 50m from the town centre.
☎05.49.48.32.53 ℗05.45.84.02.28
🌐www.lyondor.com
Closed *Dec–Feb.* Restaurant closed *weekday lunchtimes; Mon.* **Disabled access. TV. High chairs available. Car park.**

Guillaume and Heather met when he worked as a banker in London; since then they've made their home in this fifteenth-century staging post and restored it with great style. The ten welcoming guest rooms are individually decorated and comfortable, with furniture gleaming with the patina of age, and subtle, pastel colour schemes that are both invigorating and charmingly old-fashioned. Doubles cost €55–80 with shower/wc or bath. Meals are served in the regal surroundings of the restaurant where they range in price from €23 to €29. Specialities include foie gras flan with shellfish *coulis*, duck breast with preserved lemons and garlic and, for dessert, apple *croustillant* or chocolate *fondant*. The wine cellar is stocked by Augé, a highly reputed supplier. They run short courses in interior design. *Free house apéritif offered to our readers on presentation of this guide.*

Angoulême
16000

⬱ 🎋 🏨 |●| **Le Flore****

414 rte. de Bordeaux; it's 1km from the town centre.
☎05.45.25.35.35 ℗05.45.25.34.69
🌐www.leflore-16.com
Closed *Sat; Sun; first 3 weeks in Aug.*
Open *noon–2pm; 7–9.30pm; bar open until 10.30pm.* **TV. High chairs available. Pay car park.**

A short distance from the centre, this totally refurbished hotel offers comfortable rooms for €34 with shower/wc or bath. Half board is also available at €49.90 per person. The restaurant generally offers classical dishes, such as foie gras fried in lard, but there are occasional exotic touches: ostrich steak *grand veneur*, sautéed kangaroo. There's

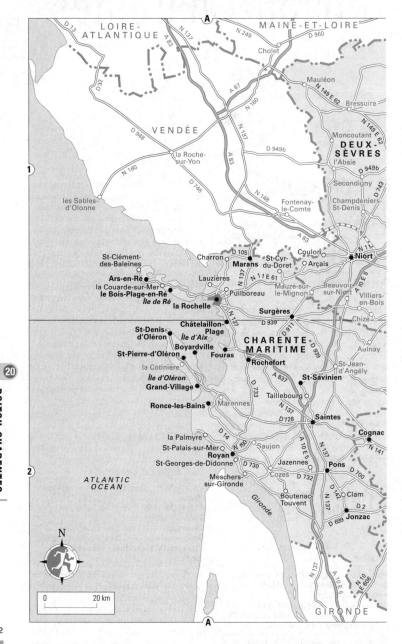

POITOU-CHARENTES

20

a two-course set lunch for €9 and other menus €19–25. You can eat on the terrace in summer. *Free house apéritif offered to our readers on presentation of this guide.*

◎ ⚭ 🏠 |●| Le Saint-Antoine**

31 rue Saint-Antoine. It's near the train station.
☎ 05.45.68.38.21 📠 05.45.69.10.31
🖥 www.hotel-saint-antoine.com
Closed 24 Dec–2 Jan. **Restaurant closed** Sat; Sun. **Disabled access. TV. Car park.**

This is located on the edge of a commercial district – the pleasant terrace looks onto a roundabout – and offers soundproofed bedrooms with shower/wc or bath from €37 to €47. The bedrooms are comfortable and the ones that have recently been renovated have gained in character. It offers impeccable service, and a good restaurant with menus at €13 (not weekends) and €22–29, and a children's menu at €7. *One free breakfast per room or free house apéritif offered to our readers on presentation of this guide.*

◎ ⚭ 🏠 Hôtel du Palais**

4 place Francis-Louvel; it's near the law courts.
☎ 05.45.92.54.11 📠 05.45.92.01.83
Closed last week in Dec. **TV. Pay car park.**

This small, traditional hotel – one of the few to be found in the old town – overlooks a pretty square. Inside, it is a delight, with a wide staircase, wood panelling and a high-ceilinged breakfast room – and old-fashioned courtesy to match. Decent doubles go for €43 with basin and €62 with shower/wc or bath. Some have big balconies with views of the old town. *10% discount on the room rate (June–Sept and weekends Oct–May) offered to our readers on presentation of this guide.*

◎ ⚭ 🏠 |●| Le Palma

4 rampe d'Aguesseau; it's between the train station and the town centre.
☎ 05.45.95.22.89 📠 05.45.94.26.66
🖥 lepalma16@.com
Closed Sat lunchtime; Sun; a fortnight at Christmas. **TV. High chairs available.**

Located on the edge of old Angoulême in a rather ordinary-looking area, this hotel has an attractive frontage, and the classic local food makes it worth seeking out. The restaurant is pleasant, with a corner bodega, and offers good value, too, with

a menu at €13.50 and others at €17.50 and €26.50. The hotel has been totally refurbished, and nine new rooms have been added. All the rooms are attractive, but the best ones are at the back: €45 with shower/wc. *Free coffee offered to our readers on presentation of this guide.*

◎ |●| Chez Paul

8 pl. Francis-Louve; it's opposite the law courts.
☎ 05.45.90.04.61
Open 11am–3pm; 6.30pm–midnight. **Disabled access. High chairs available.**

A large and very long dining room, which has been successfully decorated to keep you cosy even when the weather is bad. On warmer days, you can choose from the veranda, a terrace on the square and a cool garden with a stream. There's a weekday lunch menu for €10.85 and others €18–23. The modest dishes are well prepared, and the service is friendly, youthful and efficient. It's a great spot for a drink.

◎ ⚭ |●| Restaurant La Cité

28 rue Saint-Roch; it's in the Champ de Mars, next to the CGR cinema.
☎ 05.45.92.42.69
Closed Sun; Mon; Feb school holiday; last week in July; first fortnight in Aug. **High chairs available.**

The smiling owner is very efficient, the tables are attractively set and all the fish is exceptionally fresh. Try the seafood platter, shellfish, home-made squid fritters or *brochette la cité* (a kebab of mussels, prawns and scallops). There's a meat menu too. The weekday lunch menu costs €12.70, and there are others at €16.25–26. There is a smartly renovated lounge upstairs, in which smoking is not allowed. *Free coffee offered to our readers on presentation of this guide.*

Gond-Pontouvre (Le)

16160 (2km N)

◎ ⚭ |●| L'Entrecôte

45 rte. de Paris; take the D737 in the direction of Montignac.
☎ 05.45.68.04.52
Open noon–1.30pm; 8–10pm. **Closed** Mon evening; Sun; the week of 15 Aug. **Disabled access. High chairs available.**

This cosy, friendly tavern houses the best meat restaurant in the area, with a wood-fired grill. Ask for the table near the grill so that you can watch the food being prepared. They'll show you your slab of meat before it's cooked, in case you think it's too big, and will prepare it exactly as you request. The mega-rib of beef is a good choice for families. They'll also bring you as many plates as you need if you want to share a dessert – a rare touch, typical of the impeccable service found here. Menus €15–20, and there's also a menu at €30 for two people; expect to pay around €25 à la carte. *Free coffee offered to our readers on presentation of this guide.*

Puymoyen
16400 (7km S)

⊚ ☎ |●| **L'Auberge des Rochers**

6 chemin des Rochers; take the D104. It's opposite the church.
☎ and ℗05.45.61.25.77
Car park.

An enchanting paper mill (the Moulin du Verger) was converted into this modest (but recently refurbished) inn, run by a delightful and attentive family. The rooms are simple and quiet; they cost €28 with washbasin, €32 with shower. Half board is €32.80 per person. The food is equally unpretentious; the menu at €11.50 offers starter, main course, cheese and dessert. Other menus vary according to the season.

Champniers
16430 (9km NE)

⊚ |●| **Restaurant Le Feu de Bois****

Take the N10 in the direction of Poitiers, then the D23.
☎05.45.68.69.96
Closed Sun evening. **Disabled access. High chairs available. Car park.**

Large octagonal dining room where they grill meat and fresh fish over a fire fuelled by vine cuttings. The food incorporates local touches, such as the grilled ham with shallots, regional charcuterie and hors-d'oeuvre buffet. Menus range from €15.50 to €26. Before setting off on the N10, take a detour towards Les Cloux to enjoy the wooded valleys dotted with traditional old houses topped with pretty roof-tiles.

Mouthiers-sur-Boëme
16440 (13km S)

⊚ 🍴 |●| **Café-restaurant de la Gare**

Place de la Gare; take the D674 in the direction of Chalais, then take the D12 from Voril-et-Giget.
☎05.45.67.94.24
Closed Sun and Mon evenings; 25 Dec–5 Jan.

This is the type of easy-going, popular place you might have found here fifty years ago. There's a gravel terrace under the plane trees, an old zinc-topped bar and a beautiful old-school dining room. The food is of a high standard and good value; the menu of the day gets you soup, starter, main course, cheese, dessert, coffee and a quarter litre of wine. The weekday lunch menu is at €11.50, with others €15.60–30. *Free house apéritif offered to our readers on presentation of this guide.*

Vibrac
16120 (22km W)

⊚ 🍴 ☎ |●| **Les Ombrages****

Route Claude-Bonnier; take the N141, and 3.5km from Hiersac, turn left to Malveille, then follow the route Claude-Bonnier.
☎05.45.97.32.33 ℗05.45.97.32.05
ⓦwww.monsite.wanadoo.fr/lesombrages
Closed Sun evening; Mon; Tues lunchtime; 15 Dec–15 Jan. **TV. Disabled access. High chairs and games available. Swimming pool. Car park.**

Though the building itself is pretty charmless, it does boast a fantastic location, with its lush, shady country garden, swimming pool, tennis courts and table tennis facilities. There is also a delightful beach nearby. Rooms, which are quiet and comfortable, cost €49 with shower/wc and €54 with bath; breakfast at €8. The restaurant has become a local institution; it has two dining areas, including one on the veranda overlooking the garden and pool. You can't go wrong with the fish: try monkfish fillet with citrus fruit or scallops with asparagus tips. There's a €13.50 weekday lunch menu, with others €21–48. Logis de France. *Free house apéritif offered to our readers on presentation of this guide.*

POITOU-CHARENTES

Ars-en-Ré

17590

@ 涂 🏠 Hôtel le Sénéchal**

6 rue Gambetta; it's in the town centre by the church.
℡05.46.29.40.42 ℻05.46.29.21.25
🌐www.hotel-le-senechal.com
Closed 5 Jan–15 Feb; 12 Nov–20 Dec. **TV. Games available. Swimming pool. Pay car park.**

The owners, Christophe (an architect) and Marina, have breathed a modern spirit and serene, delicate atmosphere into this hotel. The overall impression is one of warmth, with frequent splashes of colour (both pale and dark). The twenty or so rooms in this welcoming place have been superbly renovated with natural floors, stone walls and wooden ceilings, old furniture and sleek, modern lighting. Depending on the size and season, the rooms range in price from €40 to €170 for a suite with a terrace; some have been completely renovated. There's also a flower-filled patio where you can read in peace, and board games are available in the lounge, which has an open fire. Nothing is wanting outside either, as there is a swimming pool and small garden. Reservations are essential. *10% discount on the room rate (out of season) offered to our readers on presentation of this guide.*

@ |●| Côté Quai

9 quai de la Crée; it's on the port.
℡05.46.29.94.94
Closed Wed out of season except for the school holidays; Jan; mid-Nov to mid-Dec. **Disabled access.**

Well-deserving of its good reputation, this small dining room, with a small terrace overlooking the port, exudes a seaside ambience and is simplicity itself. The menu, unsurprisingly, features a lot of fish dishes, all of which are delicately judged and tasty. The chef's inventions will keep you guessing: which herb does he use in the cuttle fish *fricassée*? How on earth does he make the hot chocolate *fondant* truffles? There's a menu at €25 or main dishes from €15 up to €25.

Saint-Clément-des-Baleines

17590 (4km NW)

@ 🏠 Hôtel Le Chat Botté**

Place de l'Église.

℡05.46.29.21.93 ℻05.46.29.29.97
🌐www.hotelchatbotte.com
Closed early Jan to early Feb; end Nov to 21 Dec. **Disabled access. TV. Car park.**

A quiet, charming hotel on the church square. The bright rooms feature lots of natural wood and some are panelled throughout. Double rooms cost €61–150 with shower/wc or bath. Friendly welcome, and traditional breakfast is served on the flowery patio. There's a health complex, which offers mineral baths and various treatments, a couple of tennis courts and a number of sun-loungers dotted around the vast, beautiful grounds. Bikes are available for rent. You'll need to book in advance.

@ |●| Restaurant Le Chat Botté

20 rue de la Mairie; it's 30m from the church, and the same distance from the hotel of the same name.
℡05.46.29.42.09
Closed Mon out of season; 1 Jan–1 Feb; 1–31 Dec. **Disabled access. High chairs available.**

The dining room is decorated with lots of natural wood, and they light a fire in the open hearth in winter; in summer there's a south-facing terrace to enjoy. As for the food, the quality is good and you're looking at top-notch fresh fish dishes such as *mouclade,* bass *en croûte* with *beurre blanc* or baked turbot *des maraîchers.* The dishes are classical, but prepared with flair. The cheapest menu costs €22, served weekdays (excluding public holidays), and there are others €30.50–60; children's menu at €12.

Aubeterre-sur-Dronne

16390

@ 🏠 |●| Hostellerie du Périgord**

It's in the pleasure port area on the Ribérac road.
℡ and ℻05.45.98.40.46
🌐www.hpmorel.com
Closed Sun evening; Mon (out of season); 2 weeks end Nov to early Dec; 3 weeks in Jan. **Disabled access. TV. Swimming pool. Car park.**

This is an old establishment that was saved from ruin by an Anglo-French couple – take a look at the "before" photographs in reception. The rooms have been very nicely renovated and are as lovely as you could wish for; doubles with shower/wc or bath cost €46–69. There's a quiet sitting room where you can read peacefully, and a pleasant dining room with a veranda opening onto the garden (with a pocket-size pool). The cuisine is modern and bursting with ideas; the weekday lunch menu goes for €16 (not Sun), with others from €25 to €36.

Availles-en-Châtellerault
86530

◖ ♜ Le Pigeonnier du Perron**

About 10km to the south of Châtellerault.
℡05.49.19.76.08 ⊕05.49.19.12.82
ⓦwww.lepigeonnierduperron.com
TV.

This beautifully restored fifteenth-century farmhouse, deep in the countryside, once belonged to René Descartes – a slightly forbidding prospect, but the relaxed and friendly welcome will soon put you at ease. The pretty rooms upstairs in the main building have exposed stone walls, as do the rooms in the annexe, which is reached via an attractive garret. The extremely comfortable double rooms start at €57.

Bois-Plage-en-Ré (Le)
17580

◖ ♜ |●| Hôtel-restaurant L'Océan**

172 rue Saint-Martin; it's 50m from the church.
℡05.46.09.23.07 ⊕05.46.09.05.40
ⓦwww.re-hotel-ocean.com
Restaurant closed Wed lunchtime and evening (lunchtime only during school holidays); 5 Jan–5 Feb. **Disabled access. TV. High chairs available. Swimming pool. Car park.**

This wonderful hotel is in a typical island house, on a quiet street away from passing traffic. There's a string of delightful little sitting rooms furnished with antiques, and the charmingly decorated guest rooms are set round a huge flower-filled patio with an ancient pine tree growing in the middle. A garden ensures the tranquillity of the other small buildings, set at street level, and the scene has recently been completed by a swimming pool. Doubles go for €61–150 with shower/wc or bath, and half board is available from €62 up to €106 per person. The dining room is equally delightful, with a terrace on the patio. Dishes, prepared from fresh market produce, change seasonally. Try the *jonchée charentaise* with fennel conserve, cod with thyme butter or braised fillet of bass with vanilla for their finely balanced flavours. Menus range from €16.50 for a weekday lunch to €32; expect to pay around €30 à la carte. There's also a children's menu at €10. Parking space is available for bikes. Typical welcome on the island – stylish and very relaxed. Logis de France.

◖ ♜ Les Bois Flottais

Chemin des Mouettes; it's perpendicular to the avenue de la Plage.
℡05.46.09.27.00 ⊕05.46.09.28.00
ⓦwww.lesboisflottais.com
Closed 4 Jan to first weekend in March; 15 Nov–15 Dec. **Disabled access. TV. High chairs available. Heated swimming pool. Car park.**

Hidden away in a quiet back street, this unassuming building with green shutters is an outstanding hotel with a pool set off by a wooden terrace. The owners' expansive welcome will put you at ease immediately. Doubles range from €79 to €97; every detail of the ten rooms has been treated with consummate care, from the red, tiled floor to the teak washbasin and ceramic wall tiles in the bathroom. Equal attention goes into the presentation of breakfast. All in all, a fine place for a relaxed, intimate break.

◖ ⚶ |●| La Bouvette Grill de Mer

Le Moulin de Morinand; take the Saint-Martin-de-Ré bypass, then the road to Le Bois-Plage, and it's about 1km further.
℡05.46.09.29.87
Closed Sun evening; Mon and Tues lunchtimes (out of season); 15 Nov–15 Dec. **Disabled access. High chairs available.**

One of the island's most interesting restaurants, partly because it's housed in an old garage in magnificent surroundings (with a terrace and barbecue) but also because the seafood is wonderfully fresh and the atmosphere is enchanting. Suggestions are chalked up on the board – *salade terre-mer*, langoustine *fricassée*, monkfish on skewers, fish *cassoulet*, sardines, sole, salmon, grilled bass and, for dessert, fresh pineapple and meringue. Star choices include the mouth-watering *salade bouvette*, the *éclade* of mussels served on pine needles with a dash of raspberry vinegar, and the glorious stuffed crab. There are two lunchtime *formules* at €13.50 (two dishes) and €19.50 (three dishes), and other menus for €25–40. *La Bouvette* has everything going for it and is extremely popular as a result, so it's best to book several days in advance in season. *Free house apéritif or coffee offered to our readers on presentation of this guide.*

Couarde-sur-Mer (La)

17670 (3km N)

◎ 🎿 🏠 |●| Hôtel-restaurant La Salicorne.

16 rue de l'Olivette.
☎ and ℱ 05.46.29.82.37
Open *daily July–Aug (excluding Thurs lunchtime); Easter holidays; weekends only in mid-season.* **Closed** *early Nov to Easter.*

You can eat either in a charming little dining room (with a permanent exhibition of artworks produced by members of the owner's family) or on the handful of tables on the quiet street outside. The menu, €22, offers just a glimpse of the chef's great talent. To experience the best, order à la carte: the bass steak with foie gras and scallops with Roquefort demonstrate his deft combinations of spices and flavours. You'll end up paying about €44 a head, which isn't all that bad for this pricey island. The rooms have been completely refurbished, but the prices remain very reasonable: €31 for a double with basin. *Free coffee offered to our readers on presentation of this guide.*

◎ 🎿 🏠 |●| Hôtel-restaurant Les Mouettes**

28 Grande-Rue. Opposite the church.
☎ 05.46.29.90.30 ℱ 05.46.29.05.41
Restaurant closed *Sat and Sun from the autumn school holiday to 1 April.* **TV. High chairs available.**

One of the most charming places on the island, yet one of the least expensive. Some ten rooms overlook the interior terrace, with another twelve in an annexe on a very quiet street. Doubles with shower/wc cost €44–64. Book early if you want to stay in summer, as there are regulars who return every year. The ter-

race is open all day, with affordable menus from €15 to €25. Try the bass steak with red-wine sauce or the cod with clams and basil. Logis de France. *10% discount on the room rate (for a minimum two night stay) offered to our readers on presentation of this guide.*

◎ 🎿 🏠 |●| Hôtel Le Vieux Gréement

13 pl. Carnot; it's behind the church.
☎ 05.46.29.82.18 ℱ 05.46.29.50.79
ⓦ www.levieuxgreement.com
Bar closed *Wed (except July–Aug).* **Closed** *mid-Nov to mid-March.* **Hotel open** *all year.* **Disabled access. TV.**

This hotel has been tastefully restored, drawing inspiration from the colours of the sea. The well-appointed rooms with shower/wc or bath go for €60–110, but the ones directly overlooking the square should be avoided – for all their charm, the noise is a bit much to bear. They serve oysters and tasty sandwiches out on the terrace or in the courtyard, which is shaded by a vine-covered arbour; reckon on €15 for a main dish plus dessert. Pleasant service. *Free house apéritif offered to our readers on presentation of this guide.*

◎ |●| Au Jardin du Pélican

35 ter rue de la Raigon; it's at the end of the Grande-Rue de la Raigon, on the corner of the impasse.
☎ 05.46.29.59.26
Open *Thurs–Sun (May and Sept).* **Closed** *Wed lunchtime and public holidays (June–Aug); early Nov to Easter.*

The owner's father is a highly reputed fishmonger, so fish of the highest quality is guaranteed here. His wife will greet you warmly and will offer you oysters, grilled sardines with a pinch of salt or a delicious *mouclade*. Dishes are around €10, and everything is cooked simply to allow the flavours to express themselves freely. The wines, served by the glass, are more than passable. A popular spot with cyclists, as there is a bike trail nearby.

◎ 🎿 |●| Restaurant La Cabine de Bain

33 Grande-Rue; it's at the beginning of the pedestrian street.
☎ 05.46.29.84.26
Closed *Tues lunch (Easter to end Sept); 2 Jan to Easter; 14 Nov–21 Dec.* **Open** *Thurs evening to Sun evening (Oct); daily (autumn*

and Christmas school holidays). **Disabled access.**

Run by a dynamic young couple who focus on the fish from the area and know how to prepare it with an exquisite touch: lightly cooked tuna, squid seasoned with salt and pepper and sautéed in a wok. The set lunch menu is €16, or reckon on around €32 à la carte. Inside they've preserved the original décor and there's an attractive terrace looking onto the pedestrian street. *Free Kir offered to our readers on presentation of this guide.*

Boyardville

17190

@ 🍴 |●| La Roue Tourne

Route de Boyardville; it's on the left of the road from Boyardville to Sauzelle, practically opposite the fishponds of the Surine.
☎05.46.47.21.47
Closed *Oct to end March.*

This is an example of the kind of out-of-the-way restaurant that we love to unearth. A family venture that started on the Boyardville beach has been kept alive for more than 30 years. It's a stone house with beams and a huge open fireplace, and big communal tables with benches (plus cushions). Seafood is the speciality here, along with fish caught directly from the ponds across the road, with good white Bordeaux on hand to wash them down. There is also a delicious *éclade* of mussels. Lunchtime dishes range in price from €7 to €10, while the dinner menus go for €29 (the "*charentais*") and €30. Around 11pm in season, when you've struggled your way through a vast seafood platter, the atmosphere hots up as the owner gets out his guitar and leads the gathering in a chorus of *Viva España* and other cheesy classics, while somebody invariably gets up to dance on the benches. There's no other place like it on the island. You should book for dinner (and even order your menu in advance), but it's not necessary at lunchtime, when the atmosphere is quieter. *Free coffee offered to our readers on presentation of this guide.*

Chalais

16210

@ 🍴 |●| Le Relais du Château

Château Talleyrand.

☎05.45.98.23.58
Closed *Sun evening to Tues lunchtime; Nov.* **Car park.**

The restaurant occupies the old guard room of the enormous fourteenth-century château of the Talleyrands, which dominates the Tude and the Vivonne rivers. You reach it across a working drawbridge. There's a period interior, with a vaulted ceiling that gives the dining room real style. The chef, committed to using only fresh produce, adopts an innovative approach to typical local dishes. Menus are at €17 for a weekday lunch, with others €22–29. *Free house liqueur offered to our readers on presentation of this guide.*

Charroux

86250

@ 🏠 |●| Hostellerie Charlemagne**

7 rue de Rochemeaux; it's next to the ruined abbey, opposite the covered market.
☎05.49.87.50.37
Closed *Sun evening and Mon (except July–Aug).* **TV. Car park.**

The décor of this inn, built with stone from the ruined abbey, takes you back to a romantic past. The charming dining room, heated by a log fire in winter, looks like an illustration for *The Three Musketeers*. Three of the bedrooms are somewhat basic, but the others boast a degree of comfort worthy of a two-star hotel. Room no. 8, with its bathroom of dressed stone, is very special. Doubles go for €35 with shower/wc or bath. The tasty food is based on regional recipes: beef with Pineau, loin of lamb with garlic *en chemise*. Prices are fair, with menus from €16 to €40.

Châtelaillon-Plage

17340

@ 🍴 🏠 Hôtel d'Orbigny**

47 bd. de la République; it's between the town hall and Fort Saint-Jean.
☎05.46.56.24.68 ☎05.46.30.04.82
🌐www.hotel-dorbigny.com
Closed *early Dec to end Feb.* **High chairs available. TV. Swimming pool. Pay car park.**

This reliable hotel began life as a holiday home at the start of the twentieth century. It's a large, typical seaside building just 100m from the beach – and there's a swimming pool so you can take a dip when the tide goes out (it can recede a good kilometre hereabouts). The rooms, decorated simply but attractively, prove fair value – doubles cost €37–60 with shower/wc or bath. Though the rooms over the street have good double glazing, those on the swimming pool side are quietest. Note that there's a charge for the car park during public holiday weekends and in the summer. *One free breakfast per room offered to our readers on presentation of this guide.*

⬩ 🎿 🏠 Hôtel Victoria**

13 av. du Général-Leclerc.
☎05.46.30.01.10 ℱ05.46.56.10.09
✉hotel.victoria@fresbee.fr
Closed *Jan; Dec.* **TV. Pay car park.**

It is not hard to imagine the countless families armed with buckets and spades, rubber rings and shrimp nets that this typical early-twentieth-century seaside building has seen wander past its doors. Inside, the décor exploits this nostalgia to charming effect. The pleasant rooms are fitted out with taste, and bouquets of dried flowers add a delicate fragrance; doubles cost €45–63 with shower/wc or bath, and half board is available from €78 to €99 per person. The station is just across the road but there are very few trains at night and the place is large enough for you to find a quiet room. *Free house apéritif (15 Feb–1 June) offered to our readers on presentation of this guide.*

⬩ 🏠 |●| Les Flots**

52 bd. de la Mer; it's on the seashore.
☎05.46.56.23.42 ℱ05.46.56.99.37
Closed *Tues; Dec–Jan.* **Disabled access. TV. High chairs available. Car park.**

A quietly charming restaurant with a lovely parquet floor and attractive wooden furniture. Savour the aromas of high-class bistro cuisine, with a preponderance of fish dishes and traditional recipes, and try the wonderfully fresh cod with garlic purée or ray's wing with cabbage. Pastries are cooked in-house, and they serve wine by the glass. There's a €24 menu; à la carte you can expect to pay around €44. They also offer double rooms from €60 to €90, with half board at €57–75 per person.

Chauvigny
86300

⬩ 🏠 |●| Hôtel-restaurant Le Lion d'Or**

8 rue du Marché; it's next to the church.
☎05.49.46.30.28 ℱ05.49.47.74.28
Closed *24 Dec–2 Jan.* **Disabled access. TV. Car park.**

A traditional, well-kept hotel in the heart of a charming medieval town. Some of the bedrooms are set in the main building, others in an annexe overlooking the quiet car park at the back, but all are welcoming and comfortable in a classical style; there's one room suitable for a whole family. They charge €42 for doubles with shower/wc or bath. The restaurant, which has acquired a reputation in the region, offers tasty dishes like lamb *noisette* with warm goat's cheese or *gâteau de crêpe soufflé* with raspberry *coulis*. There's a choice of five menus starting from €16.50 up to €34. Logis de France.

⬩ 🏠 |●| Le Chalet Fleuri**

31 av. Aristide-Briand; take the Poitiers road out of Chavigny then first left after the bridge over the Vienne.
☎05.49.46.31.12 ℱ05.49.56.48.31
Restaurant closed *Mon lunchtime (except public holidays).* **TV. High chairs available. Car park.**

This hotel is a fairly modern building on the banks of the River Vienne just outside the village. It has the advantage of being very peaceful. The functional interior is nice and bright. Guest rooms are impeccable, with comfortable beds and views either of the river or of the medieval town. Doubles go for €45 with shower/wc or bath; half board at €40 per person. They serve appealing, traditional cuisine in the large, attractive dining room: try veal *blanquette* or frogs' legs *à la provençale*. There's a weekday menu at €14.50, with others €19.50–36. The service is somewhat erratic.

Cognac
16100

⬩ 🎿 🏠 |●| L'Étape**

2 av. d'Angoulême; it's on the D945 (Châteaubriand), at the entrance to the town, coming from Jarnac.

☎05.45.32.16.15 ⓕ05.45.36.20.03
🖰www.hotel-letape.com
Closed *Sat lunchtime; Sun; 22 Dec–4 Jan.*
TV. Car park.

With its informal welcome and homely atmosphere, this is an ideal base if you want to visit the Hennessy or Martell Cognac houses. Comfy doubles go for €47 with shower/wc or bath. There are two dining rooms here; the one on the ground floor is a brasserie offering a €10.50 *"menu rapide"* (weekdays only), while in the basement a more traditional dining room features a range of sophisticated menus from €12 to €20 featuring local dishes such as chicken *confit* with Pineau or steak with Cognac. *10% discount on the room rate (Sept–June) or free coffee at the end of a meal offered to our readers on presentation of this guide.*

@ 🎋 |O| **Restaurant La Boune Goule**

42 allée de la Corderie.
☎05.45.82.06.37
Closed *Sun; Mon.* **High chairs available.**

Typically Charentes – a quiet cosy atmosphere, characterful country-style décor and good home-made food. The traditional dishes are served in generous portions – try the *cagouilles* (local snails) with Pire sauce, eels, American calamars or *jaud* with Cognac. The cheapest menu costs €11.50 (Mon to Fri lunchtime) with others €15.50–22.90; all menus include a carafe of Bordeaux, while the interesting wine list includes a selection of local wines. Musical evenings take place on Fridays and Saturdays in summer. *Free house apéritif or liqueur offered to our readers on presentation of this guide.*

@ |O| **Le Coq d'Or**

33 pl. François 1er. It's in the town centre.
☎05.45.82.02.56
Open *all year, noon–midnight.* **High chairs available.**

This is a Parisian-style brasserie right in the middle of town. Quick service, friendly welcome, large portions and a good range of prices (menus €12.80–38.30) and lots to choose from à la carte: salads, *choucroute*, shellfish, grills, calf's head, and so on. There are also some delicious specialities such as mussels *marinière* with Pineau and grilled *magret*. Go for the Charentais desserts: *jonchée* (cream cheese, drained on rush mats) or

caillebotte (sour milk served with sugar and a Cognac chaser).

@ |O| **Restaurant La Boîte à Sel**

68 av. Victor-Hugo. Towards Angoulême.
☎05.45.32.07.68
Closed *Mon; 20 Dec–5 Jan.* **Disabled access.**

The chef in this converted grocer's store is committed to promoting regional produce and he changes his menus with the seasons. He's kept the shop's original shelves and windows, using them now to display a range of fine wines and cognacs, many of which can be served by the glass. Excellent cooking: snails, rolled sole fillets stuffed with Dublin Bay prawns, *fondant* with three types of chocolate. There are menus from €14 (weekdays) up to €38; expect to pay around €30 à la carte. The restaurant is air-conditioned.

Segonzac
16130 (14km SE)

@ |O| **La Cagouillarde**

18 rue Gaston-Briande; take the D24 towards Barbezieux. It's close to the town centre, near the place de l'Église.
☎05.45.83.40.51
Closed *Sat lunchtime; Sun evening; Mon.*

This restaurant occupies the site of an old hotel. To judge by the décor the first dining room was probably the old bistro; it has charm, but is perhaps a little too large to achieve any kind of atmosphere. The second, more intimate room has a large fireplace fuelled with vine cuttings for the grills. There's also a terrace for the summer. Food is good – though portions aren't over-generous – with lots of regional specialities like stuffed Cagouille snails (a local variety), ham with shallots and vinegar or grilled lamb cutlets with walnut oil. They also offer a nice selection of Pineau wines. There's a weekday lunch menu at €12.50, with others at €18.50 and €25.50, or you can go à la carte for around €28.

Confolens
16500

@ 🎋 🏠 |O| **La Mère Michelet**★★

19 allée de Blossac; it's on the left bank of the Vienne.

℡05.45.84.04.11 ℗05.45.84.00.92
✉mere-michelet@wanadoo.fr
TV. Car park.

A dynamic family-run business that's become something of a local institution. In the restaurant, try any of the local dishes and the tempting home-made pastries. Menus range from €12 (weekday) to €35. Classic, clean bedrooms go for €29–32 with basin or shower, €40–46 with shower/wc or with bath; half board costs €38.50–44.50 per person. Logis de France. *Free coffee offered to our readers on presentation of this guide.*

Font-d'Usson (La)
86350

◎ ⅔ ≜ |○| Auberge de l'Écurie**

It's on the D727, 3.5km from Usson-du-Poitou.
℡05.49.59.53.84 ℗05.49.58.04.50
Closed *Sun evening except public holidays; a fortnight in Oct.* **Disabled access. TV. Car park.**

In a wonderfully remote rural location, this place is in a beautifully converted stable that's been decorated in rustic style. The simple dishes, cooked using quality ingredients, include lamb noisette with herbs and *civet* of kid with wild garlic. Menus are at €15 (except Sunday), €19 and €26. The rooms are simple and unexceptional, but comfortable nonetheless: €40 with shower/wc. Friendly welcome. Credit cards not accepted. *Free coffee offered to our readers on presentation of this guide.*

Fouras
17450

◎ ≜ Grand Hôtel des Bains**

15 rue du Général-Brüncher; it's 50m from the Vauban fort and the beach.
℡05.46.84.03.44 ℗05.46.84.58.26
⊛www.perso.wanadoo.fr/grand.hotel.des.bains
Closed *1 Nov–15 March.* **TV. Pay car park.**

Attractive old coaching inn right in the middle of Fouras. The classic rooms have some style, and most of them look out onto the pretty garden where you eat breakfast in the summer. Doubles with shower/wc or bath cost €41–65.

◎ ≜ Hôtel La Roseraie**

2 av. du Port-Nord; follow the signs for port de la Fumée.
℡05.46.84.64.89
Open *all year.* **Disabled access. TV.**

Monsieur and Madame Lacroix lavish lots of attention on their little hotel, a detached house with an unlikely-looking entrance hall (somewhere between a zebra and a leopard) done up to look like a 1950s nightclub. Prices are reasonable for the area: bright, clean doubles, all of which overlook the sea or garden, cost €48–58 with shower/wc or bath, depending on facilities and the season. Dogs are accepted. The welcome varies.

Grand-Village-Plage
17370

◎ ⅔ |○| Le Relais des Salines

Port des Salines.
℡05.46.75.82.42
Closed *Sun evening and Mon (out of season); Nov–March.* **Disabled access.**

You'll find this attractive restaurant in one of a cluster of brightly painted wooden huts beside the canals in the marshes. Wherever you dine, be it inside or at one of the tables on a boat moored on the quay, the traditional cuisine is delicious and good value, with superb fish and seafood specialities including warm oysters with fondue of leeks, pan-fried *céteaux* (which resembles sole) or red mullet fillets with Pineau. The short lunch menu (not Sunday) is at €15; à la carte will set you back around €25. The only drawback is that the meticulous preparation of the freshly prepared dishes can result in long waits between courses. *Free coffee offered to our readers on presentation of this guide.*

Jarnac
16200

◎ ⅔ |○| Restaurant du Château

15 pl. du Château.
℡05.45.81.07.17
Closed *Sun, Tues and Wed evenings; Mon; 15–31 Jan; 6–28 Aug.* **Disabled access.**

With a cosy dining room painted yellow and blue, this is the best restaurant in the area, and the cooking is taken very seriously indeed. Dishes change according to the season and what's fresh at the market, but specialities include veal chop garnished with truffles *à la jarcanaise*, veal kidneys baked with tarragon and red butter and iced soufflé with Cognac. They offer a weekday lunchtime menu at €18, with others from €27–40.50; expect to pay €39 à la carte. The wine list is as impressive as the cooking and includes more than one hundred Bordeaux vintages (and nearly as many Cognacs). *Free house apéritif offered to our readers on presentation of this guide.*

Jonzac
17500

◎ 🎋 🏠 |◎| Hôtel Le Club**

8 pl. de l'Église.
℡05.46.48.02.27 ℻05.46.48.17.15
Restaurant closed *evenings; weekends.*
Closed *Dec.* **TV. High chairs available.**

This little hotel, which stands on the church square, offers large, clean, well-equipped bedrooms. Nos. 1, 2, 3 and 4 are the biggest. Rooms prove excellent value for the location: doubles with shower/wc go for €40, or €47 with bath. The dining room serves à la carte only, where you'll pay around €20. Good value for money. *Free coffee offered to our readers on presentation of this guide.*

Clam
17500 (6km N)

◎ 🏠 |◎| Hôtel-restaurant Le Vieux-Logis**

Take the D142 in the direction of Pons.
℡05.46.70.20.13 ℻05.46.70.20.64
✉info@vieuxlogis.com
Closed *Sun evening and Mon lunchtime (early Oct to end March); 5 Jan–5 Feb.*
Disabled access. TV. High chairs available. Swimming pool. Car park.

You'll feel as if you've been invited to a friend's house when you walk into this welcoming country inn. The owner used to be a photographer and his prints decorate the walls. Madame's cooking is first-rate, with lots of traditional family dishes and regional specialities. Try the scallops with oyster mushrooms or duck stew with ceps. They offer a €15 menu (not served Sun), and another at €32. Guest rooms, which all overlook a small garden,

are in a separate, modern-style chalet with private terrace; doubles cost €43–45 with shower/wc and €46–48 with bath. There's a small swimming pool and you can even borrow mountain bikes. Reservations are recommended. Logis de France.

Loudun
86200

◎ 🎋 🏠 |◎| Le Ricordeau

Place de la Boeuffeterie; it's by the church.
℡05.49.22.67.27 ℻05.49.22.53.16
Closed *Sun evening; Sat lunchtime (July and Aug); Mon out of season; Feb school holiday.*
TV. High chairs available.

An enthusiastic young couple own this characterful establishment right in the middle of old Loudun. They offer just three simple but bright and comfortable rooms, each of which is very spacious. Doubles cost €35 with shower/wc or bath and half board is available at €45 per person. The blue, orange and green colour of the bedrooms and dining room breathe new life into the old stonework – this may not be to everybody's taste but it undoubtedly creates an upbeat atmosphere. The large, bright dining room is an attractive setting for a meal, and in summer you can eat on a flowery terrace right next to the Saint-Pierre church. It's very high-class cuisine here, with tasty, subtle dishes like beef cheek *millefeuille* with tomato *confit*, pike-perch fillet with saffron, chocolate *île flottante*. The *"formule express"* and other menus are served every day, lunchtimes and evenings, and range from €13.65 to €31.90. *Free house apéritif offered to our readers on presentation of this guide.*

◎ 🎋 🏠 |◎| Hostellerie de la Roue d'Or**

1 av. d'Anjou.
℡05.49.98.01.23 ℻05.49.22.31.05
Closed *Sat; Sun evening (Oct to Easter).*
Disabled access. TV. High chairs available. Car park.

This cosy former coaching inn stands at a quiet crossroads, its walls swathed in ivy to create a highly relaxing, provincial atmosphere. In the restaurant, really good regional dishes include calf's head in a warm vinaigrette and poultry ravioli with foie gras. There's a €14 menu served during the week, with others €18–35. The bedrooms are in the same provincial vein as the restaurant; all doubles cost €43 with shower/wc or bath, and half board is available at €45 per person. Logis de France. *Free house apéritif offered to our readers on presentation of this guide.*

Marans
17230

《 🏠 |●| **La Porte Verte**

20 quai Foch; take the N137, then the main street and rue de la Maréchaussée.
☎05.46.01.09.45
🌐www.la-porte-verte.com
Closed Wed; Nov to end Feb. **TV.**

This place, in the most attractive part of Marans, has a pocket-handkerchief garden overlooking the Pomère canal – a nice place to dine on a warm evening. It is run by a friendly couple that previously owned a hotel-restaurant in Winston-Salem in North Carolina. Inside, there are two charming, cosy dining rooms; one has a magnificent fireplace with a roaring fire in winter. The cuisine is of a high standard, bringing out all the flavours of the carefully selected ingredients. Menus range from €16 to €32. There's a good wine list, too. The bedrooms are scattered over several buildings; they are all of varying size but all inviting, with their carpets and typical local furniture. Double rooms prove good value starting from €50 and including breakfast. A cottage is also available.

Charron
17230 (11km SW)

《 |●| **Restaurant Theddy-Moules**

72 rue du 14-Juillet; take the D105 in the direction of Anse de l'Aiguillon. It's on the dock road.
☎05.46.01.51.29
Closed Oct–April. **Disabled access.**

People come to Charron for one reason: to eat mussels at *Theddy-Moules*. Theddy, a mussel farmer, came up with the bright idea of arranging a few tables under a big veranda and serving the freshest seafood you can imagine – don't miss the house speciality of mussels with Pineau and cream. The portions are so huge that they pose a challenge to even the heartiest eater. Try also the *moules marinières* at €4.50 or the mussels with cream for €6. They serve fish à la carte, too: sole, perhaps, or sea

bass. A full meal will set you back around €22, depending on the catch. Theddy also proposes a generous seafood platter at €19.50. Reservations are recommended in the evening as Theddy has many faithful regulars.

Saint-Cyr-du-Doret
17170 (14km SE)

《 🌿 |●| **La Pommerie**

Take the D114 to Courçon, then the D116 in the direction of Maillezais; 150m after Margot, you will see a sign on the left.
☎05.46.27.85.59
Closed Feb. **Open** Thurs–Sun lunchtimes; Sat evening. **Disabled access.**

To open a restaurant in the countryside is a real challenge. However, Catherine and Gilles were proved to be right with this peaceful place surrounded by an apple orchard. This nice country restaurant presents a rustic look and offers lovingly prepared local food. Try the house terrine, snail stew, parsleyed eels or pike-perch *paupiettes*. The food on offer is limited to menus with apéritif, wine and coffee at €25 and €35. Portions are massive, the welcome is charming, and it's excellent value for money. *Free house terrine offered to our readers on presentation of this guide.*

Melle
79500

《 🏠 |●| **Hôtel-restaurant Les Glycines****

5 pl. René-Groussard; it's on the square with the covered market.
☎05.49.27.01.11 📠05.49.27.93.45
🌐www.hotel-lesglycines.com
Closed Sun evening and Mon except July–Aug. **TV. High chairs available.**

Housed in an impressive nineteenth-century building, this hotel takes its name from the wisteria that smothers it. Some of its rooms are on the small side – no. 1, for example – but everything has recently been tastefully refurbished, with attractive fabrics, modern shower cubicles and big pillows. Expect to pay €44 for a double with shower/wc or €52 with bath; half board is available at €44.50–50 per person. The kitchen has a great reputation locally, and the warm, traditional dining room is a nice place to sample the regional cuisine, which is more sophisticated than usual:

Poitevin turnover, eels stewed in wine sauce and, to demonstrate the chef's prowess as a dessert specialist, shortbread biscuits with caramelised apples and *confit* of figs. There's a €13.50 menu served during the week only, then others €16.50–38.50. You'll pay around €48.50 for a meal à la carte. The cooking may be refined, but you'll get an informal, relaxed welcome and service. Logis de France.

Celles-sur-Belle
79370 (8km NW)

ⓔ 🛏 |●| Auberge de l'Hostellerie**

1 place des Époux-Laurant; take the D948. It's opposite the church.
☎05.49.32.93.32 ☎05.49.79.72.65
ⓦwww.hotel-restaurant-abbaye.com
Closed *Sun evening (1 Oct–30 April); 15 Feb–3 March.* **Disabled access. TV. High chairs available. Car park.**

Offering good value and attentive service, this inn enjoys a nice setting and a peaceful little terrace from where you can watch your food being prepared in the kitchens. The elegant, original dishes show off fascinating flavours while keeping in the traditional mould; try the salmon with langoustine's tail or the codfish with warm vinegar. Menus start at €9 weekday lunchtimes, then cost €12–40. The cocktails are excellent, too, and they offer a good wine list. Guest rooms are spotless, with a warm, refined décor; they go for €40–60. It's essential to book in advance. Logis de France.

Montmorillon
86500

ⓔ ⅔ 🛏 Hôtel de France**

4 bd. de Strasbourg; it's in the town centre, opposite the Sous-Préfecture.
☎05.49.84.09.09
Closed *12 Nov–6 Dec.* **Disabled access. TV. Pay car park.**

This hotel-restaurant is a good stopover, as it's the only one of this category in Montmorillon. The modern rooms are smart and well equipped. Air-conditioned doubles cost €43 with shower/wc, or €53 with bath; room number 205 is the most spacious one. Logis de France. *Free coffee offered to our readers on presentation of this guide.*

ⓔ ⅔ |●| Le Roman des Saveurs

2 rue Montebello; it's 5 min away from the town centre.
☎05.49.91.52.06
Closed *Sun evening; a week at the end of Dec.* **Disabled access.**

This restaurant is set in a beautiful, totally renovated sixteenth- to eighteenth-century house that has had an eventful history (one part was used as a prison for a while). Different staircases lead to four small dining rooms with venerable wooden beams and tasteful pictures all around the stone walls. There's nothing fussy to distract you from your food, which is simple, fresh and ungimmicky, listed on menus ranging from €13.50 to €25. Ask for a table in the bay window that looks down on the Gartempe. *Free coffee offered to our readers on presentation of this guide.*

Niort
79000

ⓔ ⅔ 🛏 France Hôtel**

8 rue des Cordeliers; it's in the town centre.
☎05.49.24.01.34 ☎05.49.24.24.50
ⓦwwwfrancehotelniort.ht.st
Open *all year.* **Closed** *Sun afternoon.* **TV. Pay car park.**

The rooms are regularly renovated, and the quietest ones overlook the charming interior courtyard. Doubles with shower/wc or bath go for €30–42, with family rooms available for six people. There's a cupboard full of comics in the lobby and you can be sure of friendly, helpful service. The car park is enclosed, and there is also space to park bikes. *10% discount on the room rate offered to our readers on presentation of this guide.*

ⓔ 🛏 Hôtel du Moulin**

27 rue de l'Espingole; it's on the riverbank on the Nantes road.
☎05.49.09.07.07 ☎05.49.09.19.40
Disabled access. TV. Car park.

This recently built hotel, overlooking the River Sèvre, offers comfortable bedrooms and a genuinely cordial welcome. It's good value for money; doubles with shower/wc or bath cost €44 with double bed, or €50 with twin beds. Two of them are designed especially for disabled visitors and nine have a balcony overlooking the neighbouring gardens. This is where the performers stay when they're appearing at the cultural centre across the river; if you want to know if anybody famous has stayed in your room, you can check the list pinned up at reception.

ⓒ 🏠 Hôtel de Paris**

12 av. de Paris.
☎05.49.24.93.78 ℱ05.49.28.27.57
ⓦwww.hotelparis79.com
Closed 24 Dec–2 Jan. **TV. Pay car park.**

This is a welcoming hotel with an attractive façade and foyer, as well as identical, somewhat small, bedrooms which have all been repainted. Doubles go for €48–50 with shower/wc or bath; reductions available for an extended stay. It's near the centre, with lots of restaurants nearby.

ⓒ |●| Restaurant Les Quatre Saisons

247 av. de La Rochelle; it's on the outskirts of the town, towards La Rochelle.
☎05.49.79.41.06
Closed Sun; 1–16 Aug. **Disabled access.**

A family-run restaurant offering sound, traditional, and often regional, cooking in dishes such as stuffed snails, eel stew with wine from the Haut-Poitou, pork *filet mignon* with Pineau des Charentes, goat's cheeses and angelica soufflé. The cheapest menu costs €10 during the week, with others €11–30.

ⓒ |●| La Tartine du Pressoir

2 rue de la Boule d'Or.
☎05.49.28.20.15
Closed Sat lunchtime; Sun.

Just off Niort's noisy main square, this charming place is housed in the old stables of a nineteenth-century coaching inn. Your meal will be excellent from start to finish, with a huge choice of salads, tarts, meat and fish dishes, along with tasty sandwiches made using country bread. Watch out for the desserts, though, as they can be pricey, but otherwise this is a classy, original restaurant that is not overly expensive. Menus start at €12.90 (weekdays only), and then others at €18.90–23.90 – the cheerful head waiter will talk you through them. There's a fine wine list (175 vintages) – hardly surprising, since the restaurant is

next door to the most famous wine merchant in town. If the weather is fine, eat on the pleasant, tastefully furnished terrace. It's safest to book a table. Fish lovers may prefer the owners' other restaurant, the *Mélane*, in the town centre.

ⓒ 🍴 |●| La Table des Saveurs

9 rue Thiers; it's between the covered market and the town hall.
☎05.49.77.44.35
Closed Sun except public holidays. **Disabled access. High chairs available.**

An efficient, refined place in the centre of town, where classic food – lots of fish – is served with good wines. Menus, €15–45, list such dishes as foie gras with nine flavours, chicory tart and pan-fried monkfish. You'll pay around €40 for a meal à la carte. *Free house apéritif offered to our readers on presentation of this guide.*

Coulon
79510 (10km W)

ⓒ 🏠 Hôtel au Marais***

46–48 quai Louis-Tardy; take the D9. It's on the towpath.
☎05.49.35.90.43 ℱ05.49.35.81.98
ⓦwww.hotel-aumarais.com
Closed 15 Dec–31 Jan. **Disabled access. TV.**

A classic riverside hotel where you can really relax. The bright cheerful doubles have river views and go for €65–75 with shower/wc or bath. The owners organize enjoyable walks through this intriguing area of lakes and marshes. Friendly welcome and it's best to book.

ⓒ |●| La Pigouille

52 quai Louis-Tardy; take the D9. It's on the towpath.
☎05.49.35.80.99
Closed Wed (Oct–March); early Dec to end Feb.

Excellent local food (eels, *lumas*, frogs) exquisitely served in three pretty, rustic dining rooms, or on the terrace overlooking the Sèvre. There's a menu of the day at €10.80, with other menus €14.30–24.50. The restaurant's name refers to the pole used to propel flat-bottomed boats; *La Pigouille* owns just such a boat and offers packages that combine a boat trip with a meal for a very reasonable price.

Arçais

79210 (20km SW)

ⓔ 🍴 |●| Auberge de la Venise Verte

14 rte. de Damoix; take the D3 in the direction of Sansais, then take the D115 in the direction of Saint-Georges-de-Rex; Arçais is about 4km away.
☎05.49.35.37.15
Closed *Tues and Sun evenings; Wed except July–Aug; 1 Dec–15 March.* **Disabled access. Car park.**

Nicely renovated restaurant with a family atmosphere and muted décor. They offer a wealth of regional dishes in the dining room or out on the terrace, including good sliced country ham cooked with *mojhettes* (explained in the menu) and eel *millefeuille*, with a range of menus from €16 to €33. They also have a nice (rather pricey) wine list. There's a grassy play area for the kids. Try the house apéritif, the *trousseepinette* – it's delicious. *Free coffee offered to our readers on presentation of this guide.*

Oléron (Île d')

17000

Towns on the Île d'Oléron: Boyardville; Grand Village; Saint-Denis-d'Oléron; Saint-Pierre-d'Oléron.

Parthenay

79200

ⓔ |●| La Truffade

14 pl. du 11 Novembre; it's on the town's main square.
☎05.49.64.02.26
Closed *Tues; Wed; 3 weeks in spring; 3 weeks in autumn.* **Disabled access. Car park.**

This place has a strong taste of the Auvergne, from the décor and the cuisine right down to the cubes of Tome de Laguiole cheese and the apéritif; the chef belongs to the Auvergne association of female restaurateures. There's accordion music in the background and an occasional shout from the boss, all tempered by the good-natured serving staff. You will eat well here, menus range from €13 to €30: the specialities are full of flavour and precisely prepared – try the *truffade*, tripe, *aligot* or cabbage stuffed with duck *confit*,

and round it off with one of the home-made desserts. They have a nice terrace on the square.

Poitiers

86000

See map overleaf

ⓔ 🏠 Auberge de jeunesse

1 allée Roger-Tagault; from the train station, take the # 7 bus in the direction of Pierre-Loti to the "Cap Sud" stop. By car, take the road to Bordeaux and turn right towards Bellejouanne. **Off map A3-1**
☎05.49.30.09.70 ☎05.49.30.09.79
🖳www.fuaj.org
Closed *end Dec–15 Jan.* **Disabled access. Car park.**

As nearly a third of Poitiers' population is made up of students, it is bound to have a youth hostel worthy of the name. This is clean, modern and well designed; it comprises two buildings, flanked by a park – choose the second one, as it is enlivened by frescoes depicting a journey undertaken by students from the Art Faculty. The spruce rooms, decorated in pale colours, have four or six beds each. Accommodation here costs €9.30 a night per person for a room with four beds; all-in package of night's accommodation plus meal: €10.70 for ages under 26 and €15.25 for those over 26. Dish of the day costs €4.90 and hire of sheets at €2.80. A campsite is also available at €5.30 a night per person. The activities available include football, badminton, pool – or chatting over coffee in the large dining room overlooking the park. You can also do your own cooking, as a kitchen complete with crockery is available to guests. The municipal library and swimming pool are close by.

ⓔ 🍴 🏠 |●| Hôtel de Paris*

123 bd. du Grand-Cerf; it's opposite the train station. **Map A2-2**
☎05.49.58.39.37
Restaurant closed *Sat evening and Sun.* **Hotel open** *all year.* **TV.**

This small old-fashioned hotel in the station area has old furniture, faded wallpaper and toilets on the landing (one between three rooms on each floor), but its lack of pretention provides a degree of charm. Choose the rooms to the rear, as the old windows on the boulevard do nothing to muffle the noise. Doubles go for €23 with

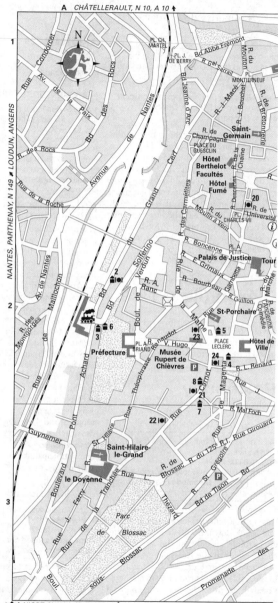

POITOU-CHARENTES

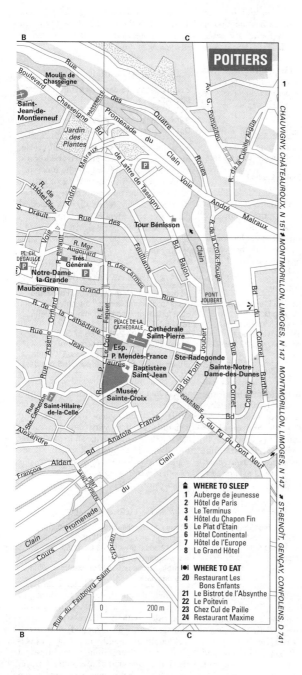

POITIERS

WHERE TO SLEEP
1 Auberge de jeunesse
2 Hôtel de Paris
3 Le Terminus
4 Hôtel du Chapon Fin
5 Le Plat d'Étain
6 Hôtel Continental
7 Hôtel de l'Europe
8 Le Grand Hôtel

WHERE TO EAT
20 Restaurant Les
   Bons Enfants
21 Le Bistrot de l'Absynthe
22 Le Poitevin
23 Chez Cul de Paille
24 Restaurant Maxime

0   200 m

20

POITOU-CHARENTES

basin, or €32 with shower and TV. The food is equally unpretentious and much appreciated by students for its accessible prices: menus €10–25. Try the *fricassée* of small eels caught in the marsh, scallops with leek *effilochée* and the *tartare du boucher*. *10% discount on the room rate or free house apéritif offered to our readers on presentation of this guide.*

◎ 🛏 Le Terminus**

3 bd. Pont-Achard; it's opposite the train station, 10 min on foot from the town centre. **Map A2-3**
☎05.49.62.92.30 ℱ05.49.62.92.40
TV. Pay car park.

This hotel near the train station has no unpleasant surprises: the rooms are conventional but clean, comfortable and suitably shielded from the street by double glazing. Doubles cost €39 with shower/wc or bath. There's a bar for guests.

◎ 🎿 🛏 Hôtel du Chapon Fin**

11 rue Lebascles, place du Maréchal-Leclerc; it's near the town hall. **Map B2-4**
☎05.49.88.02.97 ℱ05.49.88.91.63
℮hotel.chaponfin-poitiers@wanadoo.fr
Closed *Sun afternoon until 7pm; 29 Dec–12 Jan.* **TV. Pay car park.**

This small, well-kept hotel is strategically situated in the town centre; you will receive an effusive welcome from the owners, as well as good advice for exploring the town. The quiet bedrooms are spacious and comfortable, and each one is decorated differently. They cost €44–48 with shower/wc and from €49–53 with bath. *10% discount on the room rate (weekends only 15 Nov–15 March) offered to our readers on presentation of this guide.*

◎ 🎿 🛏 Le Plat d'Étain**

7–9 rue du Plat-d'Étain; it's next to the town hall, behind the theatre. **Map B2-5**
☎05.49.41.04.80 ℱ05.49.52.25.84
ⓦwww.hotelduplatdetain.fr
TV. Pay car park.

A restored coaching inn hidden away in a narrow side street in the centre offering very attentive service. The rooms are comfortable and each one is given a name rather than a number. "*Basilic*", "*Absinthe*" and "*Aneth*" in the eaves have lovely views of the bell tower of Saint-Porchaire, and some look into the interior courtyard; those on the third floor are non-smoking.

Doubles with shower/wc go for €45, and those with bath are €52. *25% discount on the price of breakfast offered to our readers on presentation of this guide.*

◎ 🎿 🛏 Hôtel Continental**

2 bd. Solférino; it's opposite the train station. **Map A2-6**
☎05.49.37.93.93 ℱ05.49.53.01.16
ⓦwww.continental-poitiers.com
Open *all year.* **Disabled access. TV.**

Medium-sized classical hotel with clean, functional and well-planned bedrooms; rooms 204, 209 and 304 are the most spacious. Doubles with shower/wc or bath at €51, depending on season; buffet breakfast €6. There's a lift. All in all, it's a practical place for an extended stay in Poitiers. *10% discount on the room rate (1 Nov–31 March) offered to our readers on presentation of this guide.*

◎ 🎿 🛏 Hôtel de l'Europe**

39 rue Carnot; it's in the centre. Follow the signs to "Parking Carnot"; the hotel is about 50m further on (under a porch, on the left). **Map B2-7**
☎05.49.88.12.00 ℱ05.49.88.97.30
ⓦwww.hoteldeleuropoitiers.com
Open *all year.* **Disabled access. TV. High chairs available. Pay car park (€5 per day).**

This classy hotel is endowed with attractive, individual and well-equipped rooms (eg, hairdryer). Opt for those in the small courtyard, where some look onto a garden. Doubles with shower/wc cost €53, €58 with bath, and the buffet breakfast will set you back €6.70. There's a pleasant welcome. *10% discount on the room rate offered to our readers on presentation of this guide.*

◎ 🎿 🛏 Le Grand Hôtel***

28 rue Carnot; follow the signs to "Parking Carnot". **Map B2-8.**
☎05.49.60.90.60 ℱ05.49.62.81.89
ⓦwww.grandhotelpoitiers.fr
Disabled access. TV. High chairs available. Pay car park.

A quiet, decent hotel in the heart of the city, much appreciated by passing celebrities, with Art Deco-style interior and spacious, well-equipped rooms with air-conditioning and a mini-bar. Doubles go for €74–82 according to facilities, and the buffet breakfast (on a pretty terrace) costs €10. The service is attentive and thoughtful. *One free breakfast per person offered to our readers on presentation of this guide.*

⊚ ⅔ |●| Le Poitevin

76 rue Carnot. **Map A3-22**
☎05.49.88.35.04
Closed *Mon; Sun evening; Easter school holiday; a fortnight in mid-July.* **Disabled access.**

This intimate restaurant has a charming staff, matched by the attractive décor with warm colours and criss-cross beams. It's popular with businesspeople at lunchtime and with couples who want some quiet, intimate time together in the evening. There's a choice of six different dining rooms, all lit by candles. The lunch *formule* at €10 and other menus at €19–28 list classic regional dishes including beef fillet with foie gras or the *bouilleture* (eel cooked with wine, mushrooms, prunes, onions and herbs). *Free tasting of the rabbit compote offered to our readers on presentation of this guide.*

⊚ ⅔ |●| Restaurant Les Bons Enfants

11 bis rue Cloche-Perse; it's near the town centre. **Map B1-20**
☎05.49.41.49.82
Closed *Mon; Sun evening; a week during the Feb school holiday.* **Disabled access. High chairs available.**

This place, in Poitiers' delightful sixteenth-century walled city, is straight out of a fairy tale. The walls are decorated with a large fresco of *Alice in Wonderland*, and there are angel clocks and old photographs of school children dotted around. The food's good too, with a lunchtime menu at €10.50, and others at €18 and €22. Try the house foie gras, fish stew or meat dishes chalked up on the blackboard, before finishing off with a delicious chocolate soufflé. *Free coffee offered to our readers on presentation of this guide.*

⊚ |●| Le Bistro de l'Absynthe

36 rue Carnot; it's next to the Parking Carnot, close to the town hall. **Map B2-21**
☎05.49.37.28.44
Closed *Sat lunchtime; Sun.*

There is something about this bistro's approach to regional dishes that sets them apart and gives them a distinctive touch. The answer may lie in the nationalities of the couple in charge: French and English.

The décor is just what you would expect from a traditional bistro, with period adverts, badges and knick-knacks creating a relaxed atmosphere that encourages customers to chat. The set lunch (starter plus main course or main course plus dessert) costs €16.50, with another menu at €20.

⊚ |●| Restaurant Chez Cul de Paille

3 rue Théophraste-Renaudot. **Map B2-23**
☎05.49.41.07.35
Closed *Sun; public holidays; Aug.*

The walls of this institution, yellowed with age, have scrawled messages from famous people all over them, and there are strings of garlic and chilli peppers hanging from the beams. You sit on straw-seated stools and eat at wooden tables where they serve authentic regional cooking ranging from grilled kidneys *en brochette* to the local *farci poitevin*, a tasty variation of stuffed cabbage. Pork is a speciality. There's a weekday menu at €18.50, or you'll spend around €25 à la carte.

⊚ ⅔ |●| Restaurant Maxime

4 rue Saint-Nicholas; it's beside the Carnot-Préfecture-town hall in the town centre. **Map B2-24**
☎05.49.41.09.55
Closed *Sat lunchtime in winter; Sun; 14 July–20 Aug.*

Serving the best food in Poitiers, this fine restaurant is a gourmet's dream. There's a warmly decorated dining room where you can eat inspired, inventive food prepared with fresh seasonal produce. The *"menu fraîcheur"* goes for €20, while others range from €31 to €50. The convivial atmosphere just goes to show you don't have to lock yourself in an ivory tower to appreciate quality food, while the perfect service manages to be at once attentive and unobtrusive. *Free house apéritif offered to our readers on presentation of this guide.*

Saint-Benoît

86280 (2km S)

⊚ 🏠 |●| Le Chalet de Venise***

6 rue du Square; it's in the centre of Saint-Benoît.
☎05.49.88.45.07 ☎05.49.52.95.44
Restaurant closed *Sun evening; Mon; Tues lunchtime; Feb school holiday; last week*

in Aug. **Disabled access. TV. High chairs available. Car park.**

Tucked away in a quiet area, this cosy village inn hides a pretty, enclosed garden set on an islet surrounded by a tributary of the Clain. The rooms – unfussy but inviting and well equipped – are rounded off on the garden side by balconies with chairs and a table and cost €54–59 with bath. The atmosphere is fairly sophisticated in the bright, pale-coloured dining room with a large bay window, and complemented by a terrace in summer. As for the food, every dish is skilfully prepared by Serge Mautret, a talented chef who's always searching for new flavours and combinations. Depending on the season, try the fine tart of rabbit and foie gras laced with Cognac, the Poitou snail ravioli or sweetbreads of veal. There's a weekday menu for €25, with others €32–45.

Coulombiers

86600 (12km SW)

@ 🏠 |●| Le Centre Poitou**

39 rte. Nationale; take the N11 towards Lusignan.
℡ 05.49.60.90.15 ℻ 05.49.60.53.70
ⓦ www.centrepoitou.com
Restaurant closed *Sun evening and Mon (except July–Aug).* **Hotel open** *daily.* **Closed** *autumn and Feb school holidays.* **Disabled access. TV. High chairs available. Car park.**

This large, charming restaurant is a gourmet's dream, serving subtle, refined cuisine – duckling with spiced caramel, poached chicken, warm foie gras *tartelettes* with sautéed truffles and autumn fruit tart flavoured with vanilla. The menu changes with the seasons, including the set lunch. You can eat under an arbour set back from the road or in the comfortable dinning room (heated by a log fire in winter). The menus, €25–70, are named after queens – "*Clothilde*", "*Diana*" and "*Aliénor*" – and you eat like a king. The hotel lives up to these high standards. The bedrooms have been enlarged and impressively renovated; doubles go for €50–75 with shower/wc or bath depending on the season. Logis de France.

Vivonne

86370 (14km SW)

@ 🍴 🏠 |●| Le Saint-Georges**

12 Grande-Rue; take the N10 in the direction

of Couhé, then take the D4 for 1km. It's beside the church.
℡ 05.49.89.01.89 ℻ 05.49.89.00.22
ⓦ www.hotel-st-georges.com
Open *daily until 10pm.* **Disabled access. TV. High chairs available.**

A very old hotel in the centre of Vivonne that has been entirely refurbished and now has a modern character. In fact, it would be more correct to say two hotels. The extremely friendly mother of the family looks after most of the plain but modern and comfortable rooms; the rest are in an annexe (complete with a lift). These rooms are more expensive but also more spacious, with big beds and air-conditioning. Doubles go for €45–52 with shower/wc, €50–58 with bath. Buffet breakfast costs €6. There are two restaurants: one is a bistro, while the other is intended for gourmets; weekday menu at €10, then others €16–29. It's very near Futuroscope and is good value for money, so if you want a room you should book in advance. Logis de France. *Free house apéritif offered to our readers on presentation of this guide.*

@ 🍴 |●| Restaurant La Treille

10 av. de Bordeaux; take the N10. It's opposite the park de Vonnant.
℡ 05.49.43.41.13
Closed *Wed evening; Feb school holiday.* **Car park.**

Napoleon paused long enough on his long march south to Spain to dine in this inn. Panic broke out as staff tried to prepare a dinner fit for the emperor. They served *farci poitevin*, a local variation on stuffed cabbage, and apparently he loved it. Today the inn is as welcoming as ever and the cooking is invariably good, rich in traditional flavours. Weather permitting, you can eat on the terrace or next to the garden. There's a €13 menu (not served on Sunday); if you want to try the famous *farci poitevin*, you'll have to go for the €22 *saveurs régionales* menu. Those with huge appetites will appreciate the two other menus at €26 and €32. Menus list such dishes as *cassolette* of scallops with cream and chives, and duck *compote* in white sauce with mushrooms. Special menus are created for certain holidays. *Free house apéritif offered to our readers on presentation of this guide.*

Dissay

86130 (15km NE)

☜ ⚐ |●| Hôtel-restaurant Binjamin**

It's on the N10, towards Châtellerault, then D15.
☎05.49.52.42.37 ⓕ05.49.62.59.06
ⓦwww.binjamin.com
Closed *Sat lunchtime; Sun evening; Mon; second week during Feb school holiday.*
Disabled access. TV. High chairs available. Swimming pool. Car park.

The unusual architecture – a slightly strange marriage between a cube and a round building – contains a nice establishment with a pretty dining room where you can enjoy appealing, subtle cuisine. Try the pan-fried foie gras with apples or the pike-perch with potato "scales" and red butter. There's also a good wine list. Menus are at €24–48, with various options à la carte. If you want to stay the night, modern, comfortable doubles with good soundproofing and shower/wc go for €44; some overlook the pool. Half board is available at €64 per person.

☜ 🎄 |●| Restaurant Le Clos Fleuri

474 rue de l'Église; it's on the road to Saint-Cyr.
☎05.49.52.40.27
Closed *Sun evening; Wed.* **Disabled access. Car park.**

Across the road from the fairytale château de Dissay, this restaurant has been run by Jean-Jack Berteau for some three decades. Scouring the region for genuine Poitou produce, he prepares a famously good calf's head with two sauces. There's a weekday set lunch at €18, with others from €23.50 to €28.50. The wine list has a careful selection of local vintages. The dining room overlooks a pretty garden. *Free house apéritif offered to our readers on presentation of this guide.*

Neuville-de-Poitou

86170 (15km NW)

☜ 🎄 ⚐ |●| L'Oasis**

2 rue Daniel-Ouvrard; take the N147 in the direction of Loudun.
☎05.49.54.50.06 ⓕ05.49.51.03.46
ⓔoasis-hotel@wanadoo.fr
Closed *Sun out of season; 15 Dec–15 Jan.*
Disabled access. TV. High chairs available. Pay car park.

A good place, not too far from Futuroscope, with bright, spring-like rooms. Those looking onto the street are soundproofed – in any case, the street is quiet at night – others look onto a small garden. Doubles cost €49 with shower/wc including breakfast; half board is also available at €39 per person. The brightly coloured restaurant offers simple, unpretentious dishes like *colombo* of frogs' legs, *farci poitevin* and steak with foie gras. Menus are €14 (weekdays only), and €18. Logis de France. *10% discount on the room rate (Feb–March) offered to our readers on presentation of this guide.*

Vouillé

86190 (17km NW)

☜ 🎄 ⚐ |●| Hôtel-restaurant Le Cheval Blanc et Le Clovis**

3 rue de la Barre; take the N149 towards Parthenay.
☎05.49.51.81.46 ⓕ05.49.51.96.31
ⓦwww.blondinhotel.fr
Disabled access. TV. High chairs, cots and baby-changing table available.

Two names for one establishment. To clarify, the *Cheval Blanc* is a restaurant and the *Clovis* is a hotel. And as there is only a hundred yards between the two buildings, it is tempting to take a stroll from your room to sample the hearty regional cooking on offer in the attractive dining room. There's a weekday lunch menu at €13.50, and others from €17 to €38. The hotel rooms are well kept and modern: doubles with basin go for €31, with shower/wc €45, with bath/wc €48; half board €44 per person. Logis de France. *10% discount on room rate (1 Oct–30 June) offered to our readers on presentation of this guide.*

Pons

17800

☜ 🎄 ⚐ |●| Hôtel-restaurant de Bordeaux**

1 av. Gambetta; from Saintes, take the N137 in the direction of Bordeaux (coming from Saintes) or exit 36 from the A10, signposted to Pons.
☎05.46.91.31.12 ⓕ05.46.91.22.25
ⓦwww.hotel-de-bordeaux.com
Restaurant closed *Sat lunchtime; Sun evening and Mon (Oct–April).* **Hotel closed** *Sun evening only.* **TV. High chairs available. Pay car park.**

The austere façade may not promise much, but appearances are misleading. It's actually a welcoming place, with a classy dining room and immaculate service. The young owner has returned to his home town after working in some of the great kitchens of France, and the food he prepares is outstanding, using only the freshest ingredients. Menus, €15–42, list a range of fine dishes that change with the seasons; children's menu at €8. The wine waitress recommends good aromatic wines to heighten the flavours of the dishes. There's an English-style bar where you can extend your evening and in good weather you can dine out on the rose-bordered patio. The rooms are simple but elegant, and some look onto the patio; all have air-conditioning and are soundproofed. Doubles with shower/wc or bath go for €47–54. Half board is compulsory in summer at €43–47 per person per night. All in all, you'll get everything you'd expect to find in a luxury establishment – except for the prices. Logis de France. *10% discount on the room rate (1 Oct–31 March) offered to our readers on presentation of this guide.*

Jazennes
17260 (9km W)

◎ 沐 |O| **La Roze**

La Foy; it's on the D732 about 1km from Gemozac.
℡05.46.94.55.90
Closed *Sun evening except July–Aug; Mon evening; a week in February; 10 days during the autumn school holiday.* **Disabled access. High chairs and games available.**

Charming restaurant in a wonderful old Charentais house with a glorious courtyard – a fabulous place to dine in summer, with a play area for the kids. Inside, there's a relaxed family atmosphere, which has proved very popular with English tourists. Good gourmet dishes appear on the menus – mussel soup, for example, and veal sweetbreads with ceps – with a variety of options using fresh, seasonal ingredients. All this at very reasonable prices: weekday lunchtime menu at €10, other menus €13–22. The service is discreet and charming. *Free coffee offered to our readers on presentation of this guide.*

Ré (Île de)
17000

Towns on the Île de Ré: Ars-en-Ré; Le Bois-Plage-en-Ré.

Rochefort
17300

◎ 沐 🏠 **Auberge de jeunesse**

20 rue de la République.
℡ and ℗05.46.99.74.62
ⓦwww.fuaj.org
Closed *a fortnight during Christmas and New Year.* **Open** *9am–noon and 2–5pm (4–8pm July–Aug).*

A small, well-situated youth hostel a stone's throw from the centre but in a quiet street. It is set in an old, narrow building, typical of the neighbourhood, with a small communal dining room and a kitchen available for use. Around fifty places are distributed in rooms with two, four, six or eight beds that share showers and wc. A stay here costs €8.90 a night per person, with hire of sheets at €3.10 and breakfast at €3.30; double rooms €22.20. There is room for three tents in the small courtyard-garden. There is a menu for €9.20, packed lunch €6. Credit cards not accepted. It is advisable to book. *10% discount on the room rate (except July–Aug) offered to our readers on presentation of this guide.*

◎ 🏠 **Hôtel Roca Fortis****

14 rue de la République; it's in the historic centre.
℡05.46.99.26.32 ℗05.46.99.26.62
Closed *20 Dec–15 Jan.* **TV.**

A charming, peaceful place situated on a historic street. Most of the rooms have views of the flower-filled courtyard or an internal garden. The rooms, all renovated, are huge and exude all the quaint charm of an old-fashioned hotel; all of them are comfy, and there's a pretty breakfast room. Doubles cost €44–49 with shower/wc, or €52–59 with bath. Friendly welcome.

◎ 🏠 |O| 沐 **La Belle Poule**

Route de Royan; take the road to the Arsenal industrial estate just after the Charente bridge.
℡05.46.99.71.87 ℗05.46.83.99.77
ⓔbelle-poule@wanadoo.fr
Closed *Fri and Sun evening (out of season); first fortnight in November.* **TV. High chairs available. Car park.**

It may seem strange to recommend a hotel-restaurant on the outskirts of the town; furthermore, the conventional interior is nothing special and the garden by the terrace is unassuming. The food, however, is in a different class, as the chef skilfully juggles aromatic ingredients such as chives, rosemary, ginger, coconut milk, aniseed and fennel to create subtle, delicate dishes; the *jonchée* with almond milk is outstanding. Excellent value for money, with menus from €20 to €36 and a children's menu at €8; expect to pay around €45 à la carte. Double rooms go for €50, and half board is available at €48 per person. The place is run by a family, and the owner's son has proudly put his model boats on display. Logis de France. *Free house apéritif offered to our readers on presentation of this guide.*

◎ 犬 |◎| Le Cap Nell

1 quai Bellot; it overlooks the pleasure port.
℗05.46.87.31.77
Closed *Tues evening and Wed (out of season); 3 weeks in Oct; a week in Feb.* **Open daily (July–Aug). Disabled access. High chairs available.**

A bunch of friends have banded together to open this wine bar-cum-fisherman's tavern, where the decent local cooking – lots of seafood – isn't fettered by finesse. There's a *formule* for €8.60, which includes the dish of the day and dessert of the day, and menus from €14.90 to €21, with a children's menu at €6. If you're after a drink, make for the terrace; it's the perfect place to relax with a glass of something cold. The tavern's mysterious name refers to a legend that's revealed in the pages of the menus. *Free house liqueur offered to our readers on presentation of this guide.*

Rochefoucauld (La)
16110

◎ 犬 🏠 |◎| La Vieille Auberge de la Carpe d'Or***

1 rte. de Vitrac; it's 300m from La Rochefoucauld Château. Watch out for Logis de France signs.
℗05.45.62.02.72 ℗05.45.63.01.88
Disabled access. TV. High chairs, baby-changing tables and baby baths available. Car park.

This quiet old inn is an attractively converted sixteenth-century coaching stop in the centre of town. The bedrooms have been done up without losing the style of the house: doubles with shower/wc or bath are €36–48. In the dining room, which is rustic and cosy with relatively

formal service, you'll eat generous servings of traditional cuisine (although the breakfast is a bit meagre). Menus start at €10 (not on weekends) with others €16–34. Logis de France. *Free house apéritif offered to our readers on presentation of this guide.*

Chasseneuil-sur-Bonnieure
16260 (11km NE)

◎ 犬 🏠 |◎| Hôtel de la Gare*

9 rue de la Gare; take the N141.
℗05.45.39.50.36 ℗05.45.39.64.03
Closed *Mon; Sun evening; 1–20 Jan; 1–21 July.* **TV. High chairs available. Car park.**

A no-nonsense, good-value place. The decoration in the dining room may have passed its sell-by date but the food is fresh: go for the specialities – *noisette* of lamb *à la charentaise* or the trout fillet with Pineau. Menus are €11 (not Sun) and €17–36; there's a very good wine list. The pretty, rustic rooms present an acceptable level of comfort, with nos. 1, 2, 3, 5 and 7 being particularly spacious and bright. If you're staying, reckon on €36 for a double with basin, and €46 with shower/wc or bath. Breakfast at €5. Logis de France. *Free house apéritif offered to our readers on presentation of this guide.*

Rochelle (La)
17000

See map overleaf

◎ 🏠 犬 Auberge de jeunesse

Avenue des Minimes; it's in the port des Minimes, around 20 min from the town centre on foot. **Off map C3-1**
℗05.46.44.43.11 ℗05.46.45.41.48
🌐www.fuaj.org/aj/la-rochelle
Closed *Christmas school holiday.* **Reception open** *8am–noon; 2–10pm.* **Disabled access. TV. High chairs available.**

More than a youth hostel, this is a modern, very large international meeting point – if you want to practise a foreign language, just hang out in the upstairs bar that extends onto the terrace overlooking the pleasure port. The long zinc counter is a perfect place to make friends, and the background music and TV corner only enhance the lively atmosphere. The rooms are simple but adequate, with clean toilets and, in some cases, the recent addition of

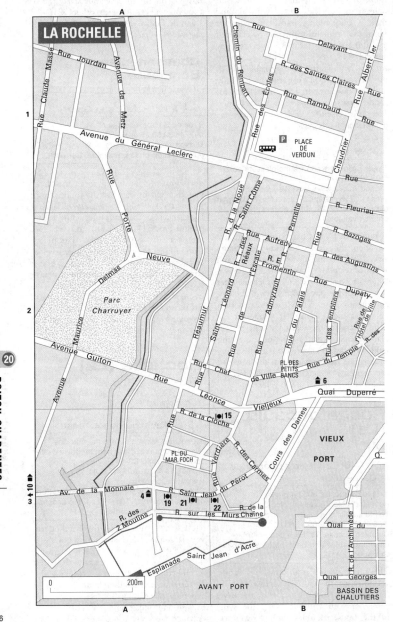

LA ROCHELLE

Rue Delayant

Rue Claude Masse

Rue Jourdan

Avenue de Metz

Chemin du Renard

R. des Saintes Claires

Rue Albert 1er

Rue Rue

Rue des Écoles

Rue Rambaud

Rue

Avenue du Général Leclerc

Rue Porte

P PLACE DE VERDUN

Chaudrier

Rue

R. Fleuriau

R. d la Noue

Saint Côme

Rue Aufredy

Pernelle

R. Bazoges

R. des Augustins

△ Neuve

Delmas

R. T. des Réaux

R. de l'Escale

R. E. Fromentin

Admyrault

Rue du Palais

Dupaty

Maurice

Parc Charruyer

Réaumur

Saint Léonard

Rue de

Rue

Rue des Templiers

Rue de l'Hôtel de Ville

R. des

Avenue Guiton

Rue Chef de Ville

PL DES PETITS BANCS

Rue du Temple

Avenue

Rue Léonce

Vieljeux

Quai Duperré

▲ 6

R. de la Cloche

|●| 15

VIEUX

Verdière

R. des Carmes

Cours des Dames

PORT

Q.

PL DU MAR. FOCH

Avenue du Pérot

Av. de la Monnaie

R. Saint Jean

4 ▲

|●| 19

|●| 21

|●| 22

R. de la Chaîne

Quai du

R. de l'Archimède

R. des 2 Moulins

R. sur les Murs

Esplanade Saint Jean d'Acre

Quai Georges

AVANT PORT

BASSIN DES CHALUTIERS

0   200m

POITOU-CHARENTES

20

◀ 10 ▶

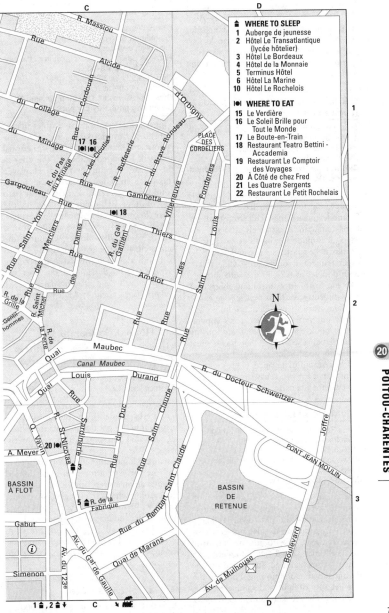

WHERE TO SLEEP
1 Auberge de jeunesse
2 Hôtel Le Transatlantique
   (lycée hôtelier)
3 Hôtel Le Bordeaux
4 Hôtel de la Monnaie
5 Terminus Hôtel
6 Hôtel La Marine
10 Hôtel Le Rochelois

WHERE TO EAT
15 Le Verdière
16 Le Soleil Brille pour
   Tout le Monde
17 Le Boute-en-Train
18 Restaurant Teatro Bettini -
   Accademia
19 Restaurant Le Comptoir
   des Voyages
20 À Côté de chez Fred
21 Les Quatre Sergents
22 Restaurant Le Petit Rochelais

N

a shower. A stay costs €13 or €15.50 per person in a room with six or four beds respectively, including breakfast and sheets. Double rooms with washbasin go for €31.50; half board (compulsory July–Aug) is €22 per person. There's a menu for €8.20, or eat à la carte. Luggage lockers are available. *One free breakfast per person offered to our readers on presentation of this guide.*

⊛ ≜ |◉| Hôtel Le Transatlantique (Lycée Hôtelier)

1 av. des Minimes; it's just opposite the youth hostel. **Off map C3-2**
☏05.46.44.20.60 ⓕ05.46.44.95.43
ⓦwww.lycee-hotelier.com
Closed *weekends; school holidays.* **Disabled access. TV. Car park.**

The district, near Minimes port, is frankly unappealing (unless you have a penchant for modern maritime architecture), but the hotel-restaurant is extremely attractive and beats all competition hands down. Run by La Rochelle's hotel school and staffed by eager trainees, it offers unbeatable prices, with doubles at €24.50–29 with shower/wc and bath (not including breakfast). The students give their best service as the teachers assess them. There are only eight rooms, not very large ones, so it's imperative to book early. The restaurant, on the other hand, seats sixty – but it's so great and such good value that it's booked up nearly a month in advance. There's a lunch menu for €15; you'll pay around €22 in the evening à la carte.

⊛ ⅔ ≜ Hôtel Le Bordeaux**

43 rue Saint-Nicolas; it's near the old port, 500m from the train station. **Map C3-3**
☏05.46.41.31.22 ⓕ05.46.41.24.43
ⓦwww.tourisme-francais.com/hotels/bordeaux
Closed *5 Dec–5 Jan.* **TV.**

This small, pretty hotel, decorated with colourful window boxes, is in the fisherman's district of the old town. It's like a quiet village during the day but gets very lively at night. The rooms are colourful and well maintained, all different, in a variety of sizes, and all fitted with double glazing and air-conditioning. Those in the attic get a lot of light, and some even have a balcony. They're fair value, too: doubles cost, according to the season, €38–49 with basin, €43–59 with shower or €48–68 with shower/wc. *10% discount on the room*

rate (out of season) offered to our readers on presentation of this guide.

⊛ ⅔ ≜ Hôtel Le Rochelois**

66 bd. Winston-Churchill; coming from the old port on the allée du Mail, take the rue Philippe-Vincent in the direction of La Rochelle Casino. It's about 2km from the city centre. **Off map A3-10**
☏05.46.43.34.34 ⓕ05.46.42.10.37
ⓦwww.le-rochelois.fr
Open *all year round.* **Disabled access. TV. Swimming pool. Pay car park.**

This is a modern hotel in a quiet neighbourhood overlooking the sea. The rooms are expensive, albeit functional and well equipped (although the ones in the annexe are a little cramped). However, the price includes access to the tennis court, gym, Jacuzzis, sauna, Turkish bath and outdoor swimming pool, so it's the place for more energetic holidaymakers. Depending on the season, double rooms cost €39–45 with shower/wc but without a view of the sea and €52–77 with bath and view. *One free breakfast per room per night, 10% discount on the room rate (except July, Aug and public holidays) and free parking offered to our readers on presentation of this guide.*

⊛ ≜ Hôtel de la Marine**

30 quai Duperré; it's opposite the port. **Map B2-6**
☏05.46.50.51.63 ⓕ05.46.44.02.69
ⓔhotel.marine@wanadoo.fr
Open *all year.* **TV.**

Squeezed between the terraces of two different establishments, this pleasant hotel is easy to miss. It's got thirteen spruce rooms, all renovated, and some with a really lovely view of the old port and the sea in the distance. Despite the efforts on the décor and the intimate atmosphere, the double glazing doesn't keep out all the noise in the evening when the port gets busy. You'll pay €46–95 for a double with shower/wc or bath, depending on the season and the view. There's no dining room, so breakfast is served in the rooms. Good value for money out of season but expensive in summer.

⊛ ⅔ ≜ Terminus Hôtel

Place du Commandant-de-La-Motte-Rouge. **Map C3-5**
☏05.46.50.69.69 ⓕ05.46.41.73.12
ⓦwww.tourisme-francais.com/hotels/terminus.

20

POITOU-CHARENTES

Disabled access. TV. Games available. Pay car park.

As you might guess, this place is close to the rail station and the aquarium, but it's on the boundary of the Gabut district and the old port. There are small personal touches in the décor here, and furnishings are rustic – there's a pleasant breakfast room with a charming wooden counter. Rooms at the back are simple and quiet while those overlooking the road are bright and spacious but noisier. Prices are more than reasonable, doubles with shower/wc or bath go for €49–67, depending on the season and the size of the room. Pet owners should note that only small dogs are accepted. Friendly service, and there's a family atmosphere. *10% discount on the room rate (1 Oct–31 March) offered to our readers on presentation of this guide.*

☜ ⅔ ≜ Hôtel de la Monnaie***

3 rue de la Monnaie; near the port. **Map A3-4**
℡05.46.50.65.65 ℗05.46.50.53.19
⊛www.hotel-monnaie.com
Open all year. **Disabled access. TV. High chairs and games available. Pay car park.**

This seventeenth-century Mint was saved from ruin in 1988 and converted into a hotel. Facilities – attractive bathrooms, air-conditioning and efficient sound insulation – are top-notch, and the modern-looking rooms are arranged round a lovely paved courtyard with a pocket-size garden. Double rooms cost €95–112 depending on the season. *10% discount on the room rate (early Oct to end March) for a minimum two-night stay offered to our readers on presentation of this guide.*

⊚ |●| Le Soleil Brille pour Tout le Monde

13 rue des Cloutiers; it's near the covered market. **Map C1–16**
℡05.46.41.11.42
Closed Sun; Mon; public holidays; 10 days during Christmas and New year. **Disabled access. High chairs available.**

In addition to the small dining room, which has mosaic-encrusted walls and tables tightly packed around the open kitchen, there's a sunny terrace with two to three tables in summer. Everything is made in-house with fresh, organic ingredients and subtle mixtures of herbs and spices, and portions are more than generous. Delicious desserts are on offer such as *tiramisù* and crumble. The *formule* – starter and dish of the day accompanied by fresh vegetables – is good value at €10.50, while the small à la carte menu offers tasty, well-seasoned dishes, including a few vegetarian options. Reckon on paying €15 à la carte. Credit cards not accepted.

⊚ ⅔ |●| Le Verdière

6 rue de la Cloche; it's close to the port. **Map B3-15**
℗05.46.50.56.75
Closed Mon; Sun evening in winter; a fortnight in March; 8 days in Oct. **Open** noon-2.30pm; 7–11pm. **High chairs available.**

If you happen upon this place, you'll find it hard to drag yourself away. The décor might be tired, but the cooking more than makes up for it; the owner is always on the go and creates invariably fine food that extends to even the cheapest *formules* and menus. Intelligently prepared dishes use only the freshest produce, with lots of fish; a speciality is the foie gras deliciously prepared with fresh fruit. Desserts are no let-down, either. There's a weekday menu at €12 (before 9.30pm), with two others at €23 and €33. *Free house liqueur offered to our readers on presentation of this guide.*

⊚ |●| Les Quatre Sergents

49 rue Saint-Jean-du-Pérot; it's beside the port. **Map A3-21**
℡05.46.41.35.80
Closed Mon. **Disabled access. High chairs available.**

In a nineteenth-century townhouse, this dining room is in a wonderful winter garden with a glass roof. A gallery on the top floor looks down onto green plants and trees in pots. It's a superb setting and the formal service is perfectly in keeping. The chef doesn't limit himself to classic brasserie food, and enjoys adding contemporary twists to some dishes. Try haddock pitta with pepper sorbet, tuna *ceviche* with coriander, shrimps coated with sesame flour. The €14.50 menu is good value, and there are others at €22–36, with a children's menu for €6.90. Expect to pay around €35 à la carte. Wine is served by the glass. Good traditional cuisine with a hint of the sea. Reservations are advised.

⊚ ⅔ |●| Restaurant Teatro Bettini – Accademia

3 rue Thiers; it's beside the covered market.

Map C2–18
☎05.46.41.07.03
Open noon–2pm; 7.30–11pm. **Closed** Sun;
Mon; autumn and Christmas school holidays.
**Disabled access. High chairs and books
available.**

Pizza might not be the first thing that
springs to mind in La Rochelle, but they're
well above average at this popular joint,
cooked in a real wood-fired oven. It's
worth trying the pasta, too, and the *escalope corrado*. Whatever you choose, you'll
want to wash it down with one of the
large selection of Italian wines. You'll pay
around €10 for a pizza, €6 for children's
menu, €18 for a meal à la carte. The
dining room has recently been refurbished.
*Free house apéritif offered to our readers on
presentation of this guide.*

◎ |●| Restaurant Le Petit Rochelais

25 rue Saint-Jean-du-Pérot. **Map B3-22**
☎05.46.41.28.43
Closed Sun except public holidays. **High
chairs available.**

A friendly bistro with waxed cotton tablecloths and good Lyonnais cuisine. The
kitchen produces seasonal dishes using
the freshest local produce. Traditional
dishes, changing regularly, include calf's
head sauce *ravigote* and seven-hour lamb.
Desserts are delightful, featuring such
treats as chocolate soup with banana
and orange. The wine list ranges from
Chopine de Merlot to Saint-Estèphe.
There's a set lunch menu at €19.90, with
another menu at €25; not necessarily
hearty but good value for money. The
friendly welcome is an added bonus.

◎ 🎋 |●| Le Boute-en-Train

7 rue des Bonnes Femmes; it's on the place
du Vieux-Marché. **Map C1-17**
☎05.46.41.73.74
Closed Sun; Mon; 25 Aug–8 Sept; 24 Dec–1
Jan. **Disabled access. Games available.**

A really attractive bistro which, painted in
shades of blue with bronzed, aged wood,
manages to be bright and intimate at the
same time. It's as good for a hasty lunch
as it is for a family supper – they provide
crayons, felt-tips and paper to keep the
children happy and there's a collection
of this infant art on the walls. You'll eat
good hearty home cooking such as mar-
rowbone on toast with salt from the Île
de Ré or *tian* of red mullet. The *menu-*

carte is €22, à la carte around €26, and
there are a variety of house specialities
for around €12.50. *Free coffee offered to our
readers on presentation of this guide.*

◎ |●| Restaurant Le Comptoir des Voyages

22 rue Saint-Jean-du-Pérot; it's in the old
port. **Map A3-19**
☎05.46.50.62.60
Open 12.15–2pm; 7.15–10pm (7pm–12.30am
during July–Sept). **High chairs available.**

The reference to voyages in this unusual
restaurant's name is not amiss; it is fired
by a youthful enthusiasm that takes its
customers on a veritable culinary world
tour, with spicy stopovers such as braised
pork with vegetables cooked in a wok
and tagliatelle with curry sauce. A menu
is available for around €23, and reckon
about the same for à la carte. The atmosphere is chic and laid-back.

◎ 🎋 |●| À Côté de chez Fred

30–34 rue Saint-Nicolas. **Map C3-20**
☎05.46.41.65.76
Closed Sun and Mon lunchtimes (in winter);
Christmas. **High chairs available.**

Fred, a well-known local character, runs
the neighbouring fishmonger's as well
as the restaurant; what's on the menu
depends on what has been landed that day.
It's best to opt for the simplest, seasonal
dishes. There are no set menus, but you can
expect to pay around €25 for a good meal
à la carte. As the years go by the prices have
increased but the formula is as successful as
ever. It gets very full, so reservations are
recommended whether you want to eat
in the simple, unadorned dining room or
the terrace. *Free house liqueur offered to our
readers on presentation of this guide.*

Puilboreau

17138 (5km E)

◎ 🎋 🏠 |●| Auberge de la Belle Étoile

12 rue de la Belle Étoile; take the N11 in the
direction of Niort, take the Chagnolet exit and
follow the signs.
☎05.46.68.01.43 ℻05.46.68.06.10
⊛www.labelleetoile17.free.fr
Closed Sat lunchtime; Sun; lunchtimes (July–
Aug). **Disabled access. TV. Car park.**

A nice family affair installed in delightfully renovated old buildings. The wife

rules the dining room, the children welcome the guests during school holidays and the husband, who used to be a pastry cook, now follows the seasons for his inspiration. Good, simple and traditional food from meat to fish (cheese *tartines*, fried whitebait, grilled dishes). There's a menu at €16 and a children's menu for €6.10; expect to pay around €25 à la carte. The guest rooms vary; some are simple, bright and colourful, while others bask in the muted charm of the old stonewalls. Each of them looks onto the beautifully maintained garden. Doubles with shower/wc or bath cost around €40 out of season; half board (compulsory July–Aug) from €41.50 per person. *Free house apéritif offered to our readers on presentation of this guide.*

Lauzières

17137 (10km N)

◎ 🎿 |◉| **Bar Port Lauzières**

Port du Plomb; it's at the seafront facing the île de Ré.
℗05.46.37.45.44
Closed *Tues (except July–Aug); 1 Oct–15 March*. **Disabled access.**

An old fisherman's hut converted into a shellfish bar. Local oyster farmers gather at the old-fashioned zinc-topped bar; on the other side, the dining room has a sea view and a cosy fireplace ideal for wintry evenings. Choose from fish soup, mussels, langoustines, grilled sardines, flambéed prawns, half a dozen oysters and a seafood platter. Add a splash of wine and you're looking at not much more than €15–20 for a meal; children's menu at €4. *Free house apéritif offered to our readers on presentation of this guide.*

Roche-Posay (La)

86270

◎ 🏠 **Hôtel de l'Europe**

19 av. des Fontaines.
℗05.49.86.21.81 ℗05.49.86.66.28
ⓦwww.hotel-l-europe.fr
Closed *1 Oct–1 April*. **TV. Car park.**

This large hotel with a garden in the back has thirty rooms that are functional and lovingly maintained by the charming couple in charge. Those on the first floor have a balcony. Double rooms cost €33–36 with shower/wc or bath. An unpretentious but pleasant and easily affordable hotel.

Ronce-les-Bains

17390

◎ 🎿 🏠 |◉| **Hôtel Le Grand Chalet – Restaurant Le Brise-Lames****

2 av. de la Cèpe; it's at the end of the Arvert peninsula and the beaches with fine sand that extend to Royan.
℗05.46.36.06.41 ℗05.46.36.38.87
ⓔfrederic.moinardeau@wanadoo.fr
Restaurant closed *Sun evening to Tues (out of season); Mon lunchtime and Tues (mid-season); Tues (in summer); normally mid-Nov to early Feb*. **Disabled access. TV. High chairs available. Car park.**

An attractive, classic seaside hotel on the edge of the ocean, near the fine sandy beaches that run all the way to Royan. The nice rooms lead onto the garden with terrace, or come with balconies with sea views; all of them have bathrooms (with shower/wc or bath) that have recently been refurbished. Rates, depending on the season, range from €39 to €54, facing the village, to €54–69, overlooking the sea. The superb chef adapts the menus according to season and whatever's fresh at the market, but you can count on being offered lots of fish and seafood. The desserts are worthy of note, as are the homemade bread and pastry – not to mention the thoughtfully compiled, but pricey wine list. There's a menu for €22, and others at €32–42; children's menu at €10. The welcome and service are professional. *Free house apéritif offered to our readers on presentation of this guide.*

Royan

17200

◎ 🎿 🏠 **Villa Trident Thyrsé**

66 bd. Frédéric-Garnier; in the direction of Saint-Georges-de-Didonne. It's in the boulevard running along the place de Royan.
℗05.46.05.12.83 ℗05.46.05.69.17
ⓔtrident.thyrse1@wanadoo.fr
Closed *Sun afternoon and evening (out of season)*. **TV. Car park.**

There have been a few alterations since this place was built, but that doesn't stop it looking like something from a time warp. Vivid colours, a set of bongo drums next to the Formica bar and salsa music wafting out onto the terrace that looks out to sea

– blink and you could be in an Art Deco hotel in Miami Beach. All the rooms are simple and pleasant with vintage 1950s décor; you'll pay, according to the season: €35–48 for doubles with basin or €46–74 with shower/wc or bath. They also have a few self-contained studios available for rent by the week or for an out-of-season weekend. The sandy beach is just across the road. *10% discount on the room rate offered to our readers on presentation of this guide.*

☺ ☎ Hôtel Belle-Vue**

122 av. de Pontaillac; it's on the D25 from Saint-Palais.
☎05.46.39.06.75 ℗05.46.39.44.92
ⓔbell-vueroyan@wanadoo.fr
Closed *1 Nov–1 April.* **Disabled access. TV. Car park.**

Starting out as a family guesthouse in the 1950s, this place has grown into a cosy hotel with antiques in the comfortable rooms and, as the name suggests, a lovely view over Pontaillac bay. Some rooms have a balcony, while others look onto the garden. Doubles cost €40–70 with shower/wc or bath, depending on the season, size, comfort and view. Four studios have recently been installed.

☺ ⅔ ☎ |●| Hôtel Abysse – Restaurant l'Anjou**

17–19 rue Font-de-Cherves; it's very close to the centre and the Grande Conche beach.
☎05.46.05.30.79 ℗05.46.05.30.16
ⓔfrancoise.branco@wanadoo.fr
Restaurant closed *Sun evening and Mon (out of season); Mon (in summer).* **Hotel closed** *a fortnight end Jan to early Feb; a week end June; a week end Sept.* **Disabled access. TV.**

The restaurant here serves generous portions of good traditional food, and naturally they do lots of fish. The dining room is decorated rather fussily but the owner welcomes you enthusiastically and the service is efficient and unpretentious. Menus go for €12 (weekday lunchtimes) and €19–41; the children's menu is at €8. The rooms are bright, attractive and prettily coloured in pastel blue, yellow and orange. No. 11 is a suite with a sitting room, while no. 31 has an outdoor terrace. Doubles cost €46–59 with shower/wc or bath; there are also a few apartments, perfect for families. *10% discount on the room rate for a minimum two-night stay offered to our readers on presentation of this guide.*

☺ ⅔ |●| Restaurant Le Chalet de Royan

6 bd. de la Grandière; it's at the eastern end of the seafront opposite the tourist office.
☎05.46.05.04.90
Closed *Tues evening and Wed (except July–Aug); 21 Nov–5 Dec.*

A towny version of a country inn, with rustic décor, local cuisine and slick service. It's built up its reputation over the years with dishes like cod with *mojhettes*, bass *marinière* with herbs and *trilogie de pastilles* with chocolate and red fruit. The expertise with which it has recently been taken over has avoided any drop in standards. The weekday lunch menu at €15 will not disappoint, others are €20–58. *Free glass of champagne offered to our readers on presentation of this guide.*

Saint-Georges-de-Didonne
17110 (4km S)

☺ ⅔ ☎ |●| Hôtel-restaurant Colinette et Costabéla*

16 av. de la Grande-Plage; follow the signs on the seafront when you arrive from Royan.
☎05.46.05.15.75 ℗05.46.06.54.17
ⓦwww.colinette.fr
Restaurant closed *Sun lunchtime (out of season); evenings (except for hotel guests); 1 Dec–1 Feb.* **Disabled access. High chairs and games available. TV.**

Amidst the pines of the Vallières Forest, *Colinette* offers rooms that lack imagination in their unassuming decoration but are nevertheless comfortable and, in some cases, complemented by a balcony. One street away, its annexe, *Costabéla*, provides back-up in the form of ten renovated rooms. Doubles in both buildings cost €46–77 with shower/wc or bath depending on the season; half board is available at €45–61 per person. There's a menu at €11 (weekday lunch), with others €15–25. There's also a children's menu at €7. It's a nice stopping point for peaceful holidays, two strides from the beach. Credit cards not accepted. Logis de France. *10% discount on the room rate (except 15 June–15 Sept and long weekends) offered to our readers on presentation of this guide.*

☺ |●| L'Escapade

7 rue Autrusseau.
☎05.46.06.24.24

Restaurant closed *Mon and Tues (except July and Aug);* mid-Oct to end March. **Disabled access. High chairs available.**

A seafood bistro with really nice décor, a terrace and a sweet little patio with vines climbing over the awning. The quality of the food is well appreciated, however it can sometimes vary slightly in high season. Specialities include fish *choucroute* and beautifully presented seafood platters. Menus range from €17 to €35, with a children's menu at around €9, and a nice wine list.

Saint-Palais-sur-Mer
17420 (6km NW)

ⓒ |●| Le Petit Poucet

La Grande Côte; it's on the coast road to La Palmyre.
℡05.46.23.20.48
Closed *Wed (Oct and Nov); 12 Nov–20 Dec; Jan.* **Disabled access. High chairs available.**

This concrete 1950s block used to be a real eyesore, but it's since been camouflaged by Virginia creeper and ivy, and the trees and shrubs planted around it make it much more attractive. Inside, in the spacious dining room, you get a magnificent view of the Grande Côte beach and the ocean beyond. The decent cooking is good value; it's best to plump for the seafood – Dublin Bay prawns with Pineau, *mouclade, persillade* of scallops. The cheapest menu goes for €15.50 (weekdays only), with other menus at €21–30, and a children's menu at €7. Good value for money.

Meschers-sur-Gironde
17132 (12km SE)

ⓒ 🕏 🏠 |●| Les Grottes de Matata**

Boulevard de la Falaise; take the the D25. It's on the side of the cliff.
℡05.46.02.70.02 ℗05.46.02.78.00
ⓦwww.grottes-de-matata.com
Restaurant closed *Sun evening (out of season);* **Crêperie closed** *Nov–Feb.* **Hotel open** *all year.* **High chairs available.**

Touristy place on the pathway through the Matata grottoes. It's a modern, clifftop building with a few rooms: doubles with shower/wc cost €60, or €65 with bath. The terrace, which affords breathtaking views of the turbulent grey-blue waters

of the Gironde estuary, is a great place for breakfast; you get the same view from the crêperie, which is set up in one of the troglodyte dwellings in the cliffs – check out the walls, made of compacted rock packed full of fossils. There's a menu at €15. *10% discount on the room rate (except July–Aug and long weekends) offered to our readers on presentation of this guide.*

Palmyre (La)
17570 (13km NW)

ⓒ 🕏 🏠 |●| Le Palmyrhotel**

2 allée des Passereaux; take the D25 in the direction of the Pointe de la Courbe. It's 5 min from the town centre and 10 min from the beach.
℡05.46.23.65.65 ℗05.46.22.44.13
ⓦwww.palmyrhotel.com
Closed *Nov to end March.* **Open** *every day in season.* **Disabled access. TV. High chairs and games available. Car park.**

This vast hotel offers good value for money for the region. It's a contemporary, alpine-style building surrounded by a Mediterranean-style garden on the edge of the pine forest and La Palmyre's famous zoo. The rooms are functional and comfortable, some have balconies, others have a terrace or even a garden room (if facing the entrance), all have en-suite shower/wc or bath; doubles cost between €50 and €88 depending on the season. The restaurant offers menus for €22 and €28, and there's a children's menu at €10. *10% discount on the room rate for a stay of at least two consecutive nights offered to our readers on presentation of this guide.*

Boutenac-Touvent
17120 (23km SE)

ⓒ 🕏 🏠 |●| Le Relais de Touvent**

4 rue de Saintonge; it's on the D730, in the direction of Cozes.
℡05.46.94.13.06 ℗05.46.94.10.40
Closed *Sun evening and Mon (except in summer);* Christmas school holiday. **Disabled access. TV. Car park.**

This dreary building, plonked down on a roundabout, doesn't immediately appeal, but it has an absolutely enormous garden and nice, newly decorated rooms. Better still, the prices are attractive for the region. Bedrooms are very clean and comfortable; they're €56.50 for a double with shower/wc or bath. Half board, compulsory in high season, costs €45 per person. They serve good, honest cooking, with plenty of regional dishes; try the *mouclade*, lamprey or oyster *tartare*. The cheapest menu goes for €12, with others at €16–27. Check out the interesting wine list. Friendly welcome is guaranteed. Logis de France. *10% discount on the room rate offered to our readers on presentation of this guide.*

Saint-Denis-d'Oléron

17650

ⓒ 🎿 🏠 |●| Hôtel-restaurant Le Moulin de la Galette**

8 rue Ernest-Morisset; it's on the town square, near the church.
☎05.46.47.88.04 ℻05.46.47.69.05
ⓦwww.oleron.com/loiselay
Closed *Oct to Easter*. **Disabled access. High chairs available.**

You can't miss this florid seaside villa on the town square. It's a genuine family guesthouse with simple but large and comfortable rooms decorated in period style or in a more modern annexe with terrace; doubles are €37–60 with shower/wc, while half board, compulsory in July and August, costs €41–53 per person. You'll find the same old charm in the dining room, where a few tables are laid on the terrace facing the market square. The cheapest menu, served every day (except during July–Aug), is €13.50, there's another menu at €18.60, and a children's menu at €6.40. The exacting owner-chef won't use anything but the freshest ingredients in mainly fish and seafood dishes. Every guest is welcome and treated as an old friend. *10% discount on the room rate (Sept–June) offered to our readers on presentation of this guide.*

Saint-Pierre-d'Oléron

17310

ⓒ 🏠 Le Square**

Place des Anciens-Combattants.
☎05.46.47.00.35 ℻05.46.75.04.90
Closed *5 Jan–5 March; 15 Nov–15 Dec.*
Open *every day*. **TV. High chairs available. Swimming pool. Car park.**

An unpretentious little hotel with a certain style, renovated with all the necessary

comfort. It's far enough away from the centre to be peaceful, and it has some real attractions, among them a pretty courtyard, a swimming pool surrounded by flowers and a sauna. Double rooms go for €45–67 with shower/wc or bath. There is a possibility of half board, organized in conjunction with three local restaurants.

ⓒ |●| Le Petit Coivre

It's on the departmental road 734, opposite the Claircières area (use the famous windmill as a landmark).
☎05.46.47.44.23
Closed *Sun evening; Mon and Tues evenings (except school holidays); Mon lunch during Aug.* **Disabled access.**

This is definitely one of the finest restaurants on the island, although its position on the side of the road, in the heart of a dreary commercial area, is hardly promising. The interior, however, is charming, with a décor dominated by wood (scrubbed parquet, grey and white walls and beams), a warm welcome from the lady of the house and exquisite cooking from her husband, who has notched up experience in some of the finest restaurants in Paris. The cheapest menu is €14.95 (weekday lunch) with a three-course menu from €23 (some dishes carry a supplement), served at lunch and dinner. The menu changes regularly according to seasonal availability and the tides. Unsurprisingly, the ingredients are dominated by seafood. Some of the mouthwatering dishes you may find are a superb *mouclade* with Pineau, langoustine salad, grilled fillets of swordfish with courgette fritters, cabbage stuffed with shellfish, ice creams and other light desserts.

Cotinière (La)

17310 (3km S)

ⓒ 🎿 |●| L'Assiette du Capitaine

It's on the port.
☎05.46.47.38.78
Closed *Mon evening and Tues (out of season); Nov–Jan.* **Disabled access.**

Overlooking the port where fish are sold direct from the boats, and decorated with old sea charts and a lovely collection of mussel baskets, *L'Assiette* serves seafood which is fresh as can be. Dishes are creative, original and change with the seasons: highlights include *mouclade* and shark with banana, swordfish and country-style langoustines. Unusually for a seafood restaurant, the desserts are great. Menus range from €13.50 to €29.50. *Free coffee or house liqueur offered to our readers on presentation of this guide.*

Saint-Savinien

17350

@ 🏃 |●| Auberge du Quai des Fleurs

51 quai des Fleurs; it's the continuation of the main street.
☎05.46.90.12.59
Open *every day June–Sept except Mon in June, Thurs–Sat evenings and Sun.* **Closed** *Jan.* **Disabled access.**

An unexpected establishment in an old riverside house with two terraces. Old pedal sewing machines are used as table bases and hastily knotted sackcloth covers the chairs; meanwhile Billie Holiday croons in the background. It's run by a Swedish woman so most of the mouthwatering dishes hail from her homeland – choose from a weekday lunch menu at €12 or others from €20 to €35. They also host occasional live jazz or blues, two to three times a week in summer and a few Saturdays in winter, and in August there's a week-long festival of eclectic music. *Free coffee offered to our readers on presentation of this guide.*

Saint-Savin-sur-Gartempe

86310

@ 🏃 🏠 |●| Hôtel de France

38 pl. de la République.
☎05.49.48.19.03 ℗05.49.48.97.07
🖥www.hoteldefrance86.fr
Closed *2–28 Jan.* **Restaurant closed** *Sun evening and Fri (except July–Aug).* **Disabled access. TV. High chairs available. Car park.**

A pleasantly traditional hotel behind a welcoming façade, with fifteen good rooms. The three in the eaves are charming and cheaper than the others. Doubles with shower/wc cost €38, and with bath they're €48. Good traditional cuisine is served in the flowery dining room, where you can choose from a variety of traditional dishes on menus at €13 for a weekday lunch, then €18–24; à la carte is also available. Logis de France.

Free house apéritif, fruit juice or children's breakfast offered to our readers on presentation of this guide.

Saintes

17100

@ 🏠 Auberge de jeunesse

2 pl. Geoffroy-Martel; it's beside the Abbaye aux Dames.
☎05.46.92.14.92 ℗05.46.92.97.82
🖥www.fuaj.org/aj/saintes/index.htm
Closed *during Christmas school holiday.* **Disabled access. Car park.**

Ideally situated in the town centre, just five minutes from the train station, this spotless youth hostel can sleep seventy people in simple but comfortable rooms with brick or panelled walls that contain four to six beds. There is one toilet for every two rooms. A stay here costs €12.20 a night, including breakfast; hire of sheets at €3.15. There's a menu at around €8. The only thing that's missing is a dash of imagination in the décor.

@ 🏠 Hôtel de l'Avenue**

114 av. Gambetta; it's near the Abbey aux Dames.
☎05.46.74.05.91 ℗05.46.74.32.16
🖥www.hoteldelavenue.com
Closed *24 Dec–3 Jan.* **TV. Pay car park.**

A friendly, colourful hotel with some fifteen pleasant rooms. They're all different, but none of them looks over the street, so they're all quiet, and there's a peaceful calm in the breakfast room to ease you into the day. Doubles range from €35 with basin to €49–51 with shower/wc or bath – good value for money.

@ |●| Le Pistou

3 pl. du Théâtre; it's near the theatre, on a pedestrian square opposite the law courts.
☎05.46.74.47.53
Closed *Mon; Sun; a week end June; a week mid-Sept; end Dec to early Jan.*

A centrally located Provençal-style restaurant with a terrace laid out on the pedestrian part of the square, where the prices won't break the bank. Some of the dishes have a Mediterranean flavour (mussels with *pistou* – the French version of Italian pesto), while others have their basis in local tradition (shrimps fried in Cognac). There's always a fish dish of the day (bass flambéed with pastis, for example) and lots of salads in summer. The chef gives his students carte blanche to prepare a different dish of the day each week. You'll spend around €20 à la carte and there's a children's menu at €7.

☺ |●| Restaurant La Ciboulette

36 rue Pérat; go down the cours National and cross the Charente, follow avenue Gambetta and, after the bridge, turn left.
☏05.46.74.07.36
Closed Sat lunchtime; Sun. **High chairs available.**

This restaurant, one of the best in town, has a pretty dining room. The chef, who comes from Brest, prepares lots of fish and shellfish – his successes include a tasty John Dory fried in the gravy of roast poultry and beef fillet braised in spicy caramel. He also pays culinary homage to the Charente with dishes such as *jaud* (chicken marinated in Cognac) and *fricassée* of eel *à la charentaise*. Menus vary according to the inspiration of the chef. He makes all the bread and the desserts, too. The €20 menu is served daily except Saturday night and public holidays, and there are others at €26–62, with a children's option at €12; expect to pay around €40 à la carte. There's a reasonably priced wine list with lots of regional choices, or even wine by the glass for the ascetics.

Taillebourg
17350 (12km N)

☺ |●| Auberge des Glycines

Quai des Gabariers; take the D114 in the direction of Saint-Savinien.
☏05.46.91.81.40
Open every day (15 May–15 Sept). **Closed** Tues evening and Wed (out of season); a fortnight in Feb; Nov.

Located in an absolutely delightful riverside town, this inn stands on the banks of the Charente and is well known. On warm days you eat in the old flower garden or on the shady first-floor terrace, which is especially nice in springtime. Menus range from €18 to €23.50; expect to pay around €35 à la carte, and there's a children's menu at €11. The atmosphere is friendly and the welcome comes with a smile. Reservations are recommended at the weekend.

Soudan
79800

☺ ⌂ |●| L'Orangerie

It's on the N11; take the A10 from exit 31, it's 5 min away.
☏05.49.06.56.06 ℗05.49.06.56.10
Closed Sun evening and Wed (1 Oct–31 March); Feb school holiday. **Disabled access (restaurant). TV. Car park.**

Tasty and refined regional cooking at really affordable prices (menus €18–40). Choices change according to the seasons, but don't miss the delicious home-made desserts. There's an original vegetarian weekday menu for €15. The dining room is cosy, bright and spacious, with windows opening onto a small garden, and service is swift, attentive and friendly. Should you need to stay, their double rooms are not at all bad for €43 with bath. Logis de France.

Mothe-Saint-Héray (La)
79800 (5km S)

☺ ⌂ |●| Hôtel-restaurant Le Corneille**

13 rue du Maréchal-Joffre; take the N11 in the direction of Lusignan, then the D5. It's on the main street.
☏05.49.05.17.08 ℗05.49.05.19.56
🖥www.perso.wanadoo.fr/lecorneille
Hotel closed 20 Dec–10 Jan. **Restaurant closed** Fri and Sun evenings (and Sat out of season). **High chairs available. TV. Car park.**

Based in the home of Dr Pierre Corneille, who was the last descendant of the famous seventeenth-century tragedian, this charming old family hotel provides a pleasing rustic setting for a series of small dining rooms. Quality local dishes are listed on all the menus – €10.50 weekdays, then €12.80–28 – which you can enjoy inside or out in the garden. Comfortable doubles cost €43–46 with shower/wc or bath, and there's half board at €35–40 per person. Don't miss breakfast – it's unusually delicious (*fromage-frais* spongecake and home-made jam).

Surgères
17700

☺ ⚒ ⌂ |●| Hôtel-restaurant Gambetta*

49 rue Gambetta; it's on the Niort road.

☎ 05.46.07.03.64 📠 05.46.07.37.32
Closed *Sun lunchtime (July–Aug); Sat evening and Sun (Sept–June); 22 Dec–2 Jan.* **TV. Car park.**

This place, popular with sales reps and travelling businesspeople, offers clean and well-maintained, standard doubles for €37 with basin and €42 with shower/wc; half board at €39 per person is obligatory in July and August. The rooms on the garden side are quietest. There is a simple menu at €13 and others at €16–23. À la carte choices include Burgundy specialities as well as local dishes. The proprietress comes from Beaujolais country and the wine list features good wines from her region, all at very decent prices. *Free house apéritif offered to our readers on presentation of this guide.*

Thouars
79100

⊚ |●| Au Trésor Belge

1 rue Saugé, place Saint-Médart.
☎ 05.49.67.85.74
Closed *Wed; 9–16 June; 3–30 Nov.* **Open** *lunchtimes and evenings until 11pm.*

Jean Cocteau would have loved the fairy-tale atmosphere of this simple but refined restaurant, where the bar is decorated like a theatre, complete with red curtain. Two Belgian chefs, Marc de Cock and André Willemsen, produce specialities from their home country like chicken *waterzoöï*, mussels in Hommel beer, beef stew with Tierenteyn mustard, marinated beef in a brown abbey beer and eels in frothy lambic beer. If you are still not convinced that this place is out of the ordinary, how about trying the strawberry soup with tarragon. There's a lunchtime menu at €9.90, then others from €15.50; à la carte, it's a little pricey – reckon on around €30, excluding beer.

⊚ |●| Restaurant du Logis de Pompois

Sainte-Verge; on leaving Thouars, go in the direction of Argenton-Château, then turn right in the direction of Saumur; take the first road on the right after the *Hotel-restaurant l'Acacia*, then follow the signs.
☎ 05.49.96.27.84
Closed *Sun evening; Mon; Tues; first week in Jan.* **Disabled access.**

A remarkable restaurant set in a magnificent old wine house. You dine in a huge room with beams and unadorned stone. The cuisine is top of the range and the welcome is outstanding. There's a weekday lunch menu at €17.50, and others go for €24–44 – try the mousse of foie gras with chicken *compote* or the *croustillant* of farmyard duckling with cider vinegar.

Saint-Jean-de-Thouars
79102 (1km S)

⊚ 🏠 |●| Hôtellerie Saint-Jean

25 route de Parthenay; it's on the way out of the town, on the Parthenay road.
☎ 05.49.96.12.60 📠 05.49.96.34.02
🌐 www.hotellerie-st-jean.fr
Closed *Sun evening and public holidays; Feb school holiday; a fortnight in Aug.* **TV. Car park.**

This high-quality hotel with impeccable service has deservedly won itself a high reputation. Its charming rooms have recently been refurbished and painted a pretty, bright yellow: doubles go for €36–43. The food is standard local fare – foie gras, kid with green garlic – but the prices are exceptionally reasonable with menus at €14–30.50.

Verteuil-sur-Charente
16510

⊚ 🏠 |●| La Paloma**

14 rue de la Fontaine; it's 500m from the town centre.
☎ 05.45.29.04.49 📠 05.45.29.51.31
Closed *Sun evening and Mon (out of season); 1–15 March; 15 Oct–5 Nov.* **TV. High chairs and games available. Car park.**

There's a goat and some Vietnamese pigs roaming around the garden here. The rooms have been pleasantly and sensitively renovated by the young couple who own this place; doubles with shower go for €32, or €42–48 with bath/wc. The cooking is tasty, too; menus prove good value at €14 and €23, served every day. The old film stills on the walls are the pretext for a quiz (with the prize of a free liqueur), but we are not going to give away the answers.

Vigeant (Le)
86150

⊚ 🏠 Hôtel Val de Vienne***

Port de Salles; it's 5km south on the D110.

☎ 05.49.48.27.27 🖷 05.49.48.47.47
🌐 www.hotel-valdevienne.com
Closed 20 Dec–9 Jan. **Disabled access.**
High chairs and games available. TV.
Swimming pool. Car park.

In the hollow of a green valley, on the banks of the Vienne, this hotel stands in over seven acres of grounds and provides twenty functional rooms. The modern architecture gives it the look of a stylish motel, which works well, and there's a private terrace opening onto a heated swimming pool. The setting is enchanting and quiet as can be – it's been awarded a Relais du Silence badge. Doubles with bath range from €65 in low season, to €75 between June and September. Logis de France.

Villebois-Lavalette
16320

🔲 🎿 🏠 ◉◉ **Hôtel-restaurant du Commerce**

It's in the village. Take the D16.

☎ 05.45.64.90.30
Closed Wed afternoon and Sun (in winter).
High chairs available. Car park.

An attractive old hotel in a nice hillside village, run by a hard-working couple. Rooms are very simple but well maintained (if a little noisy), costing from €30 with washbasin to €40 with shower/wc. The menus are straightforward, too: you'll get for the menu of the day a starter, main course, cheese, dessert, coffee and a quarter litre of wine. Menus are at €12 (not served Sun), €20 and €30. There's a nice enclosed terrace, with lots of greenery and flowers. *Free house apéritif offered to our readers on presentation of this guide.*

Provence-Alpes-Côte d'Azur

Aix-en-Provence

13100

See map on p.802

ⓔ 🏠 Auberge de jeunesse – CIRS

3 av. Marcel-Pagnol, Le Jas-de-Bouffan; 2km from the city centre, near the Vasarely Foundation; from Aix, take the N7 in the direction of Le Jas-de-Bouffan; via the A7, A8 or A51, take Aix-Ouest or Le Jas-de-Bouffan exit and follow signs to youth hostel. **Off map A2-1**
☎04.42.20.15.99 ℗04.42.59.36.12
ⓦwww.fuaj.org
Closed *20 Dec–8 Feb.* **Reception open** *7am–1pm* **TV. Games available.**

This international meeting place is made up of a set of modern buildings surrounded by green spaces (although it's maybe slightly too close to the bypass). It has been completely refurbished, so it is now very comfortable and functional. The TV and games room provides an ideal forum for guests of different nationalities to mix. FUAJ card is compulsory but you can buy it on site; accommodation costs €16 a night, including breakfast. They do a set menu for €9, and also packed lunches for €6.

ⓔ 🍴 🏠 Hôtel Le Prieuré**

It's on the N96 in the direction of Manosque-Sisteron, exit 12. **Off map B1-5**
☎04.42.21.05.23 ℗04.42.21.60.56
Open *all year.* **Car park.**

Madame Le Hir will welcome you with a smile to this former seventeenth-century priory. All of the cosy rooms (€56–72 with bath depending on the size) look out onto the ornate Pavillon Lanfant park – a fabulous view but it's not open to visitors. In fine weather you can sit on the small terrace at the front and enjoy a coffee or simply take the air.

ⓔ 🏠 🍴 Hôtel Cardinal**

24 rue du Cardinal. **Map B2-7**
☎04.42.38.32.30 ℗04.42.26.39.05
TV.

There's an appealing atmosphere in this quiet, comfortable hotel, and a relaxed, friendly welcome. Doubles are €65 with bath; most of the rooms have been refurbished – people who know the place opt for the bigger ones in the annexe. *10% discount on the room rate (Dec–March) offered to our readers on presentation of this guide.*

ⓔ 🏠 Les Quatre Dauphins**

54 rue Roux-Alphéran. **Map B2-6**
☎04.42.38.16.39 ℗04.42.38.60.19
TV.

A quiet, charming hotel named after the nearby fountain with its four amazing dolphins, covered in scales. You will need to reserve well in advance if you want to have the pleasure of staying in one of the small, tastefully furnished rooms, located across three floors. Doubles are priced at €65–78 with shower/wc or bath; triples €100. There's no lift but the new owners have installed air-conditioning.

ⓔ 🏠 🍴 La Bastide du Roy René

31 av. des Infirmières, 2km from the city centre. **Off map B2-4**

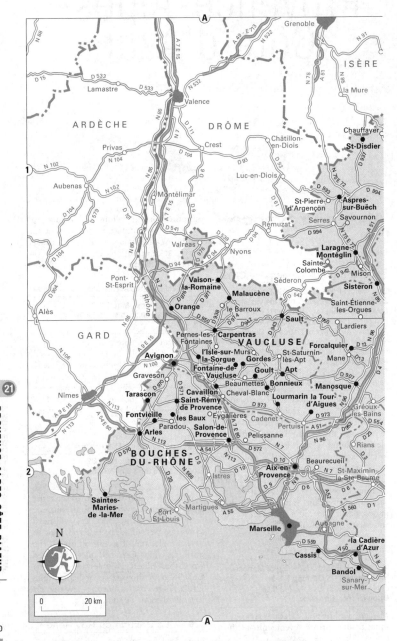

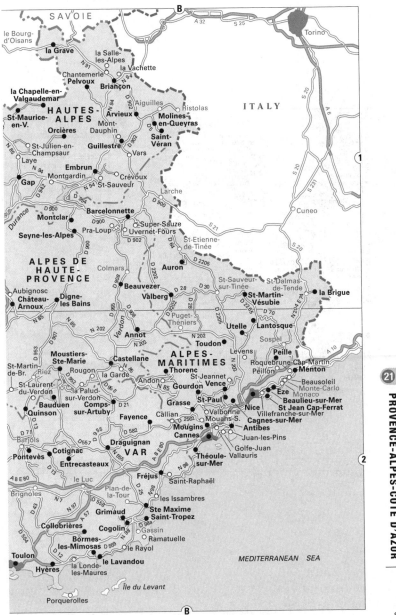

PROVENCE-ALPES-CÔTE D'AZUR

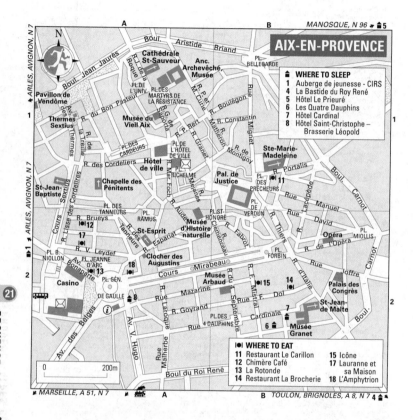

AIX-EN-PROVENCE

MANOSQUE, N 96

WHERE TO SLEEP
1 Auberge de jeunesse - CIRS
4 La Bastide du Roy René
5 Hôtel Le Prieuré
6 Les Quatre Dauphins
7 Hôtel Cardinal
8 Hôtel Saint-Christophe –
   Brasserie Léopold

WHERE TO EAT
11 Restaurant Le Carillon
12 Chimère Café
13 La Rotonde
14 Restaurant La Brocherie
15 Icône
17 Lauranne et sa Maison
18 L'Amphytrion

MARSEILLE, A 51, N 7

TOULON, BRIGNOLES, A 8, N 7

☎ 04.42.37.83.00 📠 04.42.27.54.40.
🌐 www.bastideduroyrene.com
Open all year. **TV. Disabled access.**

This *bastide* (country house) was originally built in the fifteenth century for King René; it later became the property of the canons of Aix cathedral, before being used as a hospice for victims of epidemics in the seventeenth century. It has now been superbly restored and converted into a charming hotel-residence. Splendid, comfortable rooms decorated in a modern Provençal style, go for €68–75 with bath, according to the season; also studios and apartments. An ideal way to enjoy the country whilst remaining in close contact with the city. *10% discount on the room rate offered to our readers on presentation of this guide.*

⑥ 🏠 |●| 🥢 Hôtel Saint-Christophe – Brasserie Léopold**

2 av. Victor Hugo; next to the tourist information centre. **Map A2-8**
☎ 04.42.26.01.24 📠 04.42.38.53.17
🌐 www.francemarket.com/stchristophe
Disabled access. TV. Pay car park.

Slap-bang in the centre of town, this is one of *the* places in Aix because of its Art Deco design. Doubles, €77.20–87, are air-conditioned and have en-suite bathrooms; some even have small terraces. The trump card is the brasserie on the ground floor – a real institution crammed with tables and with waiters in long aprons. The weekday lunchtime menu is €17 and there's another menu at €26. *Free house apéritif offered to our readers on presentation of this guide.*

⑥ |●| Restaurant Le Carillon

10 rue Portalis; near the Law Courts and the church of the Madeleine. **Map B1-11**
Closed Sat evening; Sun; Aug. **Disabled access.**

You have to turn up early at this restaurant which has been in the same family since 1952 and take a seat with the regulars, many of them pensioners, who appreciate the home cooking. A completely unpretentious place which is ideal for lunch or dinner; menus are €10 and €13. Credit cards not accepted.

⑥ 🥢 |●| Restaurant La Brocherie

5 rue Fernand-Dol; in the Mazarin quarter. **Map B2-14**

☎ 04.42.38.33.21
🌐 www.brochaix.com
Closed Sat; Sun; Aug.

Pleasant, rustic atmosphere, with a huge Renaissance fireplace where they cook whole chickens on the spit. Lunchtime *formule* at €13.50 includes a self-service hors d'œuvre buffet and dish of the day; there's also a tasty dinner menu for €15. Grilled meat and fish take pride of place on the menu and the patio is very pleasant in summer. *Free house digestif offered to our readers on presentation of this guide.*

⑥ |●| 🥢 Lauranne et sa Maison

16 rue Victor-Leydef. **Map A2-17**
☎ 04.42.93.02.03
Closed Sun; Mon; 15–30 Jan; 15–30 Sept.
High chairs available.

As the name suggests, this is a real house, with real inventive, Mediterranean-style home cooking – not to mention the washing hanging out to dry, the old cans of cleaning products and the step ladder. Weekday lunchtime menu is priced at €14 and another at €32. *Free house liqueur offered to our readers on presentation of this guide.*

⑥ |●| Icône

3 rue Frédéric-Mistral. **Map B2-15**
☎ 04.42.27.59.82.

Mahogany furniture, a fibre-optic bar and cooking that is open to a host of influences (although the basis is Italian); all this adds up to a supremely trendy restaurant that's very popular with the "in crowd" of Aix. It's fairly quiet at lunch, but at night the lighting changes and the conversations become more animated – and the prices soar. Lunchtime dish of the day costs around €14, and there's a lunch menu for €17.

⑥ |●| La Rotonde

13 place Jeanne-d'Arc; beside the Rotonde. **Map A2-13**
☎ 04.42.91.61.70.
Open 8am–2am.

This restaurant-café-lounge has reconciled a *clientele nostalgique* for the city's good old days with this fast-changing neighbourhood, while also attracting a crowd that no longer knew where to go to make an impression on the local scene. It would be hard to find a more beautiful setting for a rendezvous than the terrace under the shade of plane trees. The interior, decorated by Gilles Dez, is no less striking. The food is just as chic; try the risotto or the prawns cooked in a wok. Lunchtime dish of the day costs around €14 and there are two menus at €18 or €23; reckon on €37–42 in the evening.

⊚ ⅍ |●| L'Amphytrion

2 rue Paul Doumer. Map A2-18
☎04.42.26.54.10
Closed *Sun; Mon lunchtime; second fortnight in Aug.*

The chef, Bruno Ungar, loves Provençal cuisine – and you certainly experience it in his cooking, which features local colourful, richly flavoured dishes on menus €17 (weekday lunchtimes) and €29–45. There's plenty of space to be comfortable on the terrace and the *menu du marché* is an ideal option for lunch. *Free house apéritif offered to our readers on presentation of this guide.*

⊚ |●| Chimère Café

15 rue Bruyès. Map A2-12
☎04.42.38.30.00.
Closed *Sun.*

A theatrical setting for gourmets: this old nightclub has retained its décor and seems to be inviting customers to take part in a play among the stucco cherubs. Despite appearances, however, this is not a Parisian cabaret, and the real star of the show is the food. The single set menu (€22.50) features highly accomplished seasonal cooking that brings out the flavour of its ingredients without any fancy tricks; also good, relatively inexpensive wines. Booking essential; wearing a suit and tie or a piercing is not essential, but neither would go amiss here.

Beaurecueil
13100 (10km E)

⊚ ⅍ 🏠 |●| Relais Sainte-Victoire***

☎04.42.66.94.98 ℗04.42.66.85.96
🖳www.relais-sainte-victoire.com
Closed *Mon; Fri lunchtime (Fri evening in winter); Sun evening; 1–8 Jan; Feb and All Saints' school holidays.* **Disabled access. TV. High chairs available. Swimming pool. Car park.**

This hotel, isolated in the countryside with Sainte-Victoire as a backdrop,

has been run by the same family for fifty years. The rooms, all different, are equipped with air-conditioning (except one) and, in the most expensive cases, a Jacuzzi. Doubles with shower/wc or bath go for €61–122. The restaurant, one of the best in the region, serves inventive food (menus €34–61) in the image of the ebullient owner/chef, René Berges – you are guaranteed an effusive welcome here. The décor is original, too, with pride of place going to a unique pottery collection. There's a superb covered veranda. *Free house apéritif offered to our readers on presentation of this guide.*

Annot
04240

⊚ ⅍ 🏠 |●| Hôtel de l'Avenue

Avenue de la Gare; it's in the centre of town.
☎04.92.83.22.07 ℗04.92.83.33.13
Closed *1 Nov–1 April.* **Restaurant closed** *Wed and Fri lunchtimes.* **TV.**

Here, Provence meets the Alps. The hotel building was constructed to withstand the rigours of winter but the cooking is decidedly from sunny Provence. You are welcomed with a smile, front of house, and fresh flowers adorn the tables. The decoration in the pleasant, modern doubles – €53 with shower/wc or bath – has a hint of Provence. The dining room is elegant and so is the cooking with menus priced at €16 (weekdays) and €25. Try the fine tart of red mullet or the lamb steak cooked with herbs and served with potatoes in olive oil. *Free house apéritif offered to our readers on presentation of this guide.*

Antibes
06600

⊚ ⅍ 🏠 Hôtel de l'Étoile**

2 av. Gambetta; it's 5 min from the station.
☎04.93.34.26.30 ℗04.93.34.41.48
🖳www.hoteletoile.com
TV. Pay car park.

The only hotel of this category in the centre of Antibes. Although modern and comfortable, it's better for an overnight stop than as a place to spend a holiday. Spacious rooms with good sound insulation; doubles with shower/wc or bath €54–58 depending on the season. Reservations recommended. *10% discount* on the room rate for two consecutive nights (except July–Sept) on presentation of this guide.

««« 🏊 🏠 |●| Le Mas Djoliba***

29 av. de Provence.
☎04.93.34.02.48 ☏04.93.34.05.81
🕸www.hotel.djoliba.com
Closed 4 Nov–4 Feb. **TV. Swimming pool. Car park.**

A pretty Provençal house surrounded by greenery where the welcome is pleasant and professional. The delightful rooms, decorated in the local style, go for €82–122; half board, compulsory between 1 May and 30 September, costs €78–96 per person. There's a relaxing swimming pool so you don't have to fight your way to the crowded beach. *Free house apéritif offered to our readers on presentation of this guide.*

⊚ 🏊 |●| Le Bastion Caffé

1 av. du Général-Mazière; in the old town, at the end of the ramparts.
☎04.93.34.59.86
Closed weekday lunchtimes; Sun evening and Mon (out of season). **High chairs available.**

When a restaurant is recommended by the butcher, by the bistro next door and by the antique dealer nearby, then you know you're on to a good thing. The menu varies according to seasonal availability but the original, meticulously prepared dishes always offer a blend of Provençal and Italian influences. There's a set menu at €20 or reckon on €25 à la carte. Friendly service; you can eat on a delightful terrace with flowers, a well and an old fig tree. *Free house apéritif offered to our readers on presentation of this guide.*

Cap d'Antibes
06160 (1km W)

««« 🏠 La Jabotte*

13 av. Max-Maurey: it's off bd. James-Wyllie which borders Cap d'Antibes.
☎04.93.61.45.89 ☏04.93.61.07.04
🕸www.jabotte.com
Closed Sun afternoon; 5–30 Nov; a week at Christmas. **Disabled access. Car park.**

This hotel offers good value for money: spotless rooms with basin €46–66, €54–80 with shower or bath. The bungalows looking onto the terrace are particularly nice. Friendly welcome, but you should

avoid arriving between 1pm and 6pm on a Sunday, when they take a break. Relaxing atmosphere and a gentle pace.

Juan-les-Pins
06160 (1km SW)

««« 🏊 🏠 |●| Hôtel Sainte-Valérie***

Rue de l'Oratoire.
☎04.93.61.07.15 ☏04.93.61.47.52
🕸ww.juanlespins.net
Closed 30 Sept–15 April. **TV. Swimming pool. Pay car park.**

A stylish – rather pricey – hotel, ideal for a romantic holiday; you'll need to book well in advance. Set in a quiet part of Juan-les-Pins just a short distance from the Gould pine woods and the sea, it has a pool and a pretty, shady garden where you can take refuge from the heat. Meals are served in the garden, under the magnolia tree or beside the pool – there's one menu at €32. Modern, tastefully decorated double rooms go for €125–230, depending on the season and the facilities. *10% discount on the room rate (in low season) on presentation of this guide.*

Apt
84400

⊚ 🏠 |●| 🏊 Hôtel Le Ventoux**

785 av. Victor Hugo; it's opposite the station, roughly 1km from the centre of the road to Cavaillon.
☎and ☏04.90.04.74.60
TV. High chairs available. Car park.

This small hotel, recently taken over by new owners, offers excellent, prettily decorated (albeit small) rooms that are bright, quiet and comfortable. Ask for one to the rear, with a view of the valley; doubles €40–44. The *Pétunia* restaurant on the ground floor offers light, Italian-Provençal meals. *Free breakfast (on arrival) offered to our readers on presentation of this guide.*

⊚ |●| Thym Te Voilà

59 pl. Saint-Martin.
☎04.90.74.28.25
Open 11.30am–6pm (Tues–Sat).

The name suggests a tearoom, but in fact it is a restaurant – albeit one given to daintiness, in both the food and the décor. On our visit, pink was the order of the day – on the walls, curtains and tablecloths,

PROVENCE-ALPES-CÔTE D'AZUR

while the tables themselves are made from the bases of old sewing machines. From the dining room, you can see straight into the small kitchen and watch the preparation of slightly exotic dishes like seafood *caplana* and duck *clafoutis* (a kind of pie).

◉ 𝒜 |●| Le Goût des Choses

17 pl. du Septier.
☎04.90.74.27.97
Closed Sun; Mon and Tues out of season.

This is a cosy place, somewhere between a tearoom and a bistro, where you can try a couple of savoury pies or merely enjoy a good cup of tea. The tiny dining room, painted in white and ochre, has only six or seven tables, but there is also a terrace overlooking one of the town's most peaceful and enchanting squares, distinguished by its fountain and huge plane tree. You can get snacks for around €10 or pay €11–14 for a meal. *Free coffee offered to our readers on presentation of this guide.*

Saint-Saturnin-lès Apt

84490 (9km N)

◉ |●| 𝒜 L'Hôtel des Voyageurs

2 pl. Gambetta; it's on the D943.
☎04.30.75.42.08
Closed Wed; Thurs lunchtime; end Jan to early March; end Oct to early Nov. **High chairs available.**

This "hotel" is actually a restaurant. The setting is hardly mind-blowingly original – a few tables on a terrace and a country-ish dining room with whitewashed walls – and it certainly doesn't prepare you for the quality of the cooking. The simple dishes are prepared with extraordinary skill and intriguing use of herbs and spices that flatter the palate. Menus €16–28; there's also a lunch menu in the summer at €13. It's not a place to come if you're in a hurry; service is relaxed ... Logis de France. *Free coffee offered to our readers on presentation of this guide.*

Arles

13200

◉ 🏠 Auberge de jeunesse

20 av. Foch; 5 min from the centre; by bus from the train station via the Starlette line (to the Clemenceau stop in the town centre), then take bus # 4 to the Fournier stop.

☎04.90.96.18.25 📠04.90.96.31.26
🌐www.fuaj.org
Closed 15 Dec–7 Feb.

This building near the stadium is by no means new but it is well kept, sleeping a hundred people in dormitories of eight beds. FUAJ card is compulsory but you can buy it on site. Accommodation is €15.50 a night, including sheets and breakfast. Meals are available (only in season and at night for individuals) for €8.60. Facilities include luggage lockers, Internet connection and mountain bikes for hire.

◉ 🏠 Hôtel Le Cloître**

16 rue du Cloître; it's between the amphitheatre and Saint-Trophime.
☎04.90.96.29.50 📠04.90.96.02.88
✉hotel_cloitre@hotmail.com
Closed 1 Nov–15 March. **TV. High chairs and games available. Car park.**

A charming, really tranquil hotel which is supported by thirteenth-century vaulted arcades. The largest rooms, which date from the thirteenth and seventeenth centuries, have big beams and have been completely refurbished by the owner and decorated with gleaming tiles. Doubles go for €40 with shower, €45–60 with shower/wc or bath. You can expect an outstanding welcome and to be treated with great kindness in this tranquil spot.

◉ 🏠 |●| 𝒜 Hôtel Calendal**

5 rue Porte de Laure; between the arenas and the ancient theatre.
☎04.90.96.11.89 📠04.90.96.05.84
🌐www.lecalendal.com
Closed 5–25 Jan. **Disabled access. TV. High chairs and games available. Pay car park.**

This hotel, situated in the middle of the town, is decorated with local fabrics and dotted with huge vases of stunningly coloured flowers. Arles is famous for photography and the stairwell is hung with lots of unusual photographs. There's a cool patio where you can shelter from the sun. Small, air-conditioned rooms are €45–64 with shower/wc and €74–99 with bath. By way of food, they offer a buffet *formule* for €14 (lunchtime only in season, dinner out of season), snacks and home-made pastries are served in the garden, and there's a tearoom. If you want a parking space it's essential to book. *10% discount on the room rate (Nov–March) offered to our readers on presentation of this guide.*

⊚ 🛉 🏛 Hôtel de l'Amphithéâtre**

5 rue Diderot.
☎04.90.96.10.30 📠04.90.93.98.69
🌐www.hotelamphitheatre.fr
TV.

Renovated hotel, full of charm, near the Roman theatre. All the bedrooms have been decorated in Provençal style; they're not huge, but they are bathed in light and cost €45–79 for a double with bath or shower/wc according to the season. Each one has air-conditioning, safe, hair-dryer and Internet access. The charming owner will greet you warmly. *10% discount (16 Oct–31 March) offered to our readers on presentation of this guide.*

⊚ 🛉 🏛 Hôtel Saint-Trophime

16 rue de la Calade.
☎04.90.96.88.38 📠04.90.96.92.19
TV. Pay car park (€8).

This building was once a clinic for mental patients, but its sad history has been totally dispelled by the striking sculpture in the entrance and the colourful décor reflecting the surrounding landscape: lavender, olive green and raspberry. Double rooms go for €50–55, with lounge €65–70. The place is a delightful cocoon where you can sleep undisturbed, even overlooking the courtyard (the only noise comes from the clock nearby chiming the hours). *10% discount (1 Nov–15 March) offered to our readers on presentation of this guide.*

⊚ 🏛 |●| 🛉 Hôtel Mireille***

2 pl. Saint-Pierre; it's the other side of the Rhône in the Trinquetaille district.
☎04.90.93.70.74 📠04.90.93.87.28
🌐www.hotel-mireille.com
Closed Nov–March. **TV. High chairs available. Swimming pool. Car park.**

A curtain of trees screens off the swimming pool, which is presided over by a watchful old statue. Doubles overlooking the garden and pool cost €82–120; nos. 32, 35, 38 and 40 are quiet and sunny. Half board is compulsory during the *feria* at Easter. The huge, pleasant dining room serves lovely seafood (including *bouillabaisse provençale*) and quality meat dishes on menus €22–30. Free car park and a pay lock-up garage are available. *10% discount on the room rate (for one week at half board March–Oct) or free house apéritif or coffee on presentation of this guide.*

⊚ |●| Le Jardin de Manon

14 av. des Alyscamps; it's a little way from the town centre, at the bottom end of boulevard des Lices, beyond the police station.
☎04.90.93.38.68
Closed Wed; autumn and winter school holidays.

A friendly restaurant with a small garden at the back. Excellent, creative regional cuisine. There's a €14 lunch menu and others €19–40; they all change with the seasons. The extensive wine list offers good value for money.

⊚ 🛉 |●| La Charcuterie Arlésienne

51 rue des Arènes.
☎04.90.96.56.96
Closed Sun and Mon (except public holidays); 20 July–20 Aug.

A genuine Lyon-style bistro right in the centre of Arles. The owner drives all the way to Lyon to supply the kitchen with authentic produce like the *andouillette de Bobosse* – a must. His restaurant is on the premises of an old charcuterie dating back to the 1940s (note the butchers' hooks), and Regouya cooks very tasty dishes in front of you on an old marble counter. The *patron* is also a painter: his canvases cover the walls. In summer, the menu lists salads, grills and tapas and there's a welcoming terrace seating about ten or so customers. Menu €15; à la carte reckon on €25. *Free house digestif offered to our readers on presentation of this guide.*

⊚ |●| La Paillotte

28 rue du Docteur-Fanton.
☎04.90.96.33.15
Closed Wed and Thurs lunchtimes; 12 Jan–2 Feb; 30 Nov–7 Dec.

This local institution has been taken over by a young chef, Stéphane Bognier, who, working almost alone in the kitchen, produces a variety of dishes to cater for different tastes. Menus €16–26; a selection of fresh, tasty starters (aubergine *papeton*, vegetable *tian*) precede more traditional main courses like blanquette of veal with chanterelle mushrooms. In hot weather sit on the pleasant shady terrace and enjoy the fish casserole.

⊚ 🛉 |●| Au Brin de Thym

22 rue du Docteur-Fanton.
☎04.90.49.95.96

Closed *Tues; Wed lunchtime.*

A small restaurant where nothing escapes the attention of the owner, a real character who fusses over her guests. Authentic, sensual traditional cooking in a warm setting. Opt for the menu at €17 or expect to pay €29 for a full meal; otherwise, you can have just a main course for €13, such as grilled tuna with pepper sauce, or a starter for €8 and/or a dessert for €8. If you like the food, drop into the shop next door on the way out (open 10am–11pm). It is highly original, with exclusive creations like the extremely kitsch *Cakes de Bertrand*. *Free house apéritif offered to our readers on presentation of this guide.*

Arvieux

05350

@ 🏠 |●| La Ferme d'Izoard***

Hameau de la Chalp; it's 30km northwest of Saint-Véran in the direction of Brançion over the col de l'Izoard or via Guillestre in winter when the col is closed.
☏04.92.46.89.00 📠04.92.46.82.37
🌐www.laferme.fr
Closed *lunchtimes in May (except weekends and public holidays); 20 Sept–15 Dec.* **Disabled access. TV. High chairs and games available. Swimming pool. Car park.**

A family-run establishment with good facilities including a heated pool. The building is rustic, but the décor is elegant and stylish. Prices are fair considering the high standards: they go for €54–74 for a double with shower/wc, €68–140 for a double with bath, and some well-equipped studios; half board €53–98. Simple but tasty cooking, with lots of regional dishes and grills on the open fire; first menu starts at €14 (lunchtimes), with others €17–51 or expect to pay around €20 for a meal à la carte. There's also a tearoom serving less expensive crêpes, and there's a garage for use by guests (charge payable). It's a lovely place to relax in superb countryside.

Aspres-sur-Buëch

05140

@ 🎋 🏠 |●| Hôtel du Parc**

Route de Grenoble; between Grenoble and Sisteron, on the N75.
☏04.92.58.60.01 📠04.92.58.67.84

🌐www.hotel-buech.com
Closed *Sun and Wed out of season; public holidays; 6 Dec–6 Jan.* **TV. High chairs available. Car park.**

It's very pleasant to lunch on the terrace near the rose garden or the patio – in spite of the main road that passes in front. Specialities on the menus, €20–37, include regional lamb, pork and salads, *pieds-paquets* and pear cake with caramel sauce. All the rooms have recently been updated; doubles with basin €32, €42–47 with shower/wc or bath. They are clean, comfortable and have good facilities including double glazing. *10% discount on the room rate (from the third consecutive night on full board) offered to our readers on presentation of this guide.*

Saint-Pierre-d'Argençon

05140 (5km SW)

@ 🎋 |●| Auberge de la Tour

Near the entrance to the village.
☏04.92.58.71.08
Closed *Mon–Thurs (apart from school holidays); Nov.* **High chairs and games available. Disabled access.**

An outstanding place, set back from the road in this charming, peaceful village, whose heart and soul is provided by the owners of this old staging post. They organize a host of activities (concerts, storytelling, weekend hikes, self-catering accommodation and camping) and effectively constitute an unofficial tourist office. It is here that the locals come to meet, chat and eat (very well too). Menus €14–25 feature fresh seasonal products (trout in *feuilleté* with tarragon), sweet-and-savoury mixtures (goat with honey) and house specialities (order the "*frout-frout*", a cake with a secret recipe). The atmosphere is warm, jovial and full of *joie de vivre*, and the décor is colourful, imaginative and elegant. Eat on the terrace or in the dining room; there is even a special little table for children. *Free house apéritif offered to our readers on presentation of this guide.*

Auron

06660

@ 🎋 🏠 |●| Hôtel Las Donnas**

Grande-Place; it's 7km south of Saint-Étienne-de-Tinée, and next to the ice-rink.

☎04.93.23.00.03 ⓕ04.93.23.07.37
Closed *1 April–20 July; 1 Sept–19 Dec.* **TV.**
High chairs available.

A pleasant, peaceful hotel with some forty sunny rooms, €35–110, half of which have balconies overlooking the ski runs. Half board, compulsory during the school holidays, costs €48–80. In winter the restaurant serves good wholesome food – menus, €20–25, offer beef fondue and *raclette*, *mousseline* of fish, *rillettes* of young rabbit and so on. There's also a lovely glassed-in terrace. *Free house apéritif offered to our readers on presentation of this guide.*

Avignon
84000

See map overleaf

◎ 𝕬 🏠 **Hôtel Mignon***

12 rue Joseph-Vernet. **Map A2-4**
☎04.90.82.17.30 ⓕ04.90.85.78.46
ⓦwww.hotel-mignon.com
TV.

Though the décor in this well-kept and welcoming place is a little busy, it's not unattractive. The rooms have double glazing; doubles €39 with shower/wc, breakfast €5. Each room has a telephone, cable TV and a whole host of services you wouldn't expect in a one-star hotel. Nos. 2, 6 and 8 are particularly nice. *10% discount on the room rate (1 Nov–28 Feb) offered to our readers on presentation of this guide.*

◎ 𝕬 🏠 **Hôtel Le Splendid***

17 rue Agricol Perdiguier. **Map A3-5**
☎04.90.86.14.46 ⓕ04.90.85.78.46
ⓦwww.avignon-splendid-hotel.com
Closed *mid-Nov to mid-Dec.* **TV.**

A small family hotel with very pleasant rooms that are bright, well appointed and painted yellow and red. They are excellent value for money at €50–54 with shower/wc. *10% discount on the room rate (Nov–March) offered to our readers on presentation of this guide.*

◎ 🏠 𝕬 **Hôtel Bristol***

44 cours Jean-Jaurès. **Map A3-7**
☎04.90.16.48.48 ⓕ04.90.86.22.72
ⓔbristol.avignon@wanadoo.fr
Disabled access. TV. Pay car park.

A modern, rather stylish and welcoming hotel. All 67 rooms have air-condition-

ing, mini-bar and efficient double glazing. Doubles with shower or bath go for €51–55, according to the season and type of room; buffet breakfast €10. *10% discount on the room rate (except in July) offered to our readers on presentation of this guide.*

◎ 🏠 **Hôtel de Blauvac***

11 rue de la Bancasse. **Map A2-8**
☎04.90.86.34.11 ⓕ04.90.86.27.41
ⓦwww.blauvac-hotel.com
Closed *a fortnight in Jan; a week in Nov; a week in Dec.* **TV.**

A good hotel in an elegant seventeenth-century mansion, ideally located in a narrow street in the historic centre close to place de l'Horloge. It's retained some of the original features of the house, which was the residence of the Marquis de Blauvac – the elegant wrought-iron staircase and some of the arched stone doorways. Well-appointed doubles, all of them different, cost €55–70 with shower/wc or bath; breakfast €7. The décor is a happy combination of old stone and modern design. Attentive service is guaranteed. *10% discount on the room rate (out of season) offered to our readers on presentation of this guide.*

◎ 𝕬 🏠 **Citôtel de Garlande***

20 rue Galante. **Map A2-9**
☎04.90.85.08.85 ⓕ04.90.27.16.58
ⓦwww.avignon-et-provence.com/hotel-garlande
Closed *Sun out of season.* **TV.**

An old house, beautifully situated near the Saint-Didier bell tower. It's a comfortable and welcoming place with eleven rooms priced at €62–113 with shower/wc or bath; they vary widely in size and style, so do try to have a look at a few if possible. Nos. 3 and 9, along with "Tulip" and "Anemone", are recommended. *10% discount on the room rate (after two nights, except during the festival) offered to our readers on presentation of this guide.*

◎ ▮●▮ **Le Mesclun**

46 rue de la Balance. **Map A1-21**
☎04.90.85.24.83
Closed *Sun and Mon (except during July).*

This is the bistro offshoot of the neighbouring *Mesclun*, run by Robert Brunel, the leading light of Avignon's *haute cuisine*. The dishes include summer salads and pasta with an aroma of olive oil and herb,

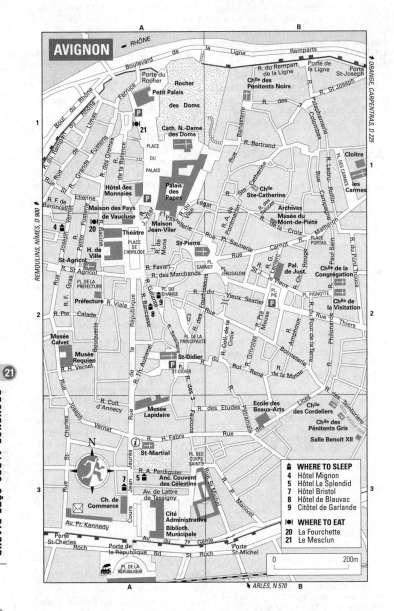

AVIGNON

← RHÔNE

A

B

Boulevard de la Ligne — Remparts

R. du Rempart de la Ligne

Porte de la Ligne

Porte St-Joseph

ORANGE, CARPENTRAS, D 225

Porte du Rocher

Rocher

Ch⁽ˡˡᵉ⁾ des Pénitents Noirs

R. St-Joseph

R. des

Petit Palais

des Doms

Boul. du Rhône

1

P

21

Cath. N.-Dame des Doms

R. Bertrand

R. Banasterie

Ste. Catherine

Ch⁽ˡˡᵉ⁾ Ste-Catherine

PL. DES CARMES

Cloître

1

les Carmes

R. Ledru-Rollin

R. des Grottes

R. Ferruce

PLACE DU PALAIS

Hôtel des Monnaies

P

Palais des Papes

R. de la Balance

R. de Mons

R. Grande Fusterie

R. Limas

R. du Rempart de la Ligne

Rue St-Pierre

R. A. de Pontmartin

R. des Chauves

Musée du Mont-de-Piété

R. de la Croix

R. Campana

Archives

R. F. de Baroncelli

REMOULINS, NÎMES, D 900

Maison des Pays de Vaucluse

R. Étienne

Fusterie

Théâtre

Maison Jean-Vilar

PL. Saunerie

R. Carnot

PLACE PORTAIL

R. Matheron

4

20

Bancasse

PLACE DE L'HORLOGE

St-Pierre

PL. CARNOT

R. G. Leclerc

R. du Chapeau Rouge

R. du Pont Trouca

St-Agricol

H. de Ville

R. Favart

R. des Marchands

PL. JÉRUSALEM

R. St-J.

Pal. de Just.

Ch⁽ˡˡᵉ⁾ de la Congrégation

R. St Agricol

PL. DU CHANGE

9

PL. PIE

Rue Vieux

PL. PIGNOTTE

Ch⁽ˡˡᵉ⁾ de la Visitation

PL. DE LA PRÉFECTURE

R. Viala

8

R. des Teinturiers

R. du Vieux Sextier

P

Rue Philonarde

R. Thiers

2

Préfecture

R. Pte Calade

R. F. Gras

Rue de la République

R. Bancasse

R. Galante

R. du Bourg neuf

Vieux-Sextier

R. Prés Meuse

R. Amphoux

R. du Four de la Terre

2

Musée Calvet

Bouquerie

PL. DE LA PRINCIPAUTÉ

R. Grivolas

R. Bonneterie

R. H. Vernet

Musée Requien

R. d'Aubanel

R. Coll. de la Croix

R. René

R. de la Masse

R. Coll. d'Annecy

Musée Lapidaire

Saraillerie

R. des 3 Pilats

R. des Études

Ecole des Beaux-Arts

Licés

Ch⁽ˡˡᵉ⁾ des Cordeliers

R. des Teinturiers

Vernet

R. H. Fabre

R. des Lices

Rue

Ch⁽ˡˡᵉ⁾ des Pénitents Gris

Salle Benoît XII

N

St-Martial

Jaurès

St-Charles

R. A. Perdiguier

PL. DES CORPS SAINTS

Rue St-Michel

3

7

5

Anc. Couvent des Célestins

Av. de Lattre de Tassigny

R. Manivet

3

Rue Jean

Ch. de Commerce

Cours

Av. Pr. Kennedy

Cité Administrative

Biblioth. Municipale

R. Maréchal

WHERE TO SLEEP
4 Hôtel Mignon
5 Hôtel Le Splendid
7 Hôtel Bristol
8 Hôtel de Blauvac
9 Citôtel de Garlande

Porte St-Charles

Porte de la République

Av. du 7e Génie

Bd

St Roch

Roch

Porte St-Michel

WHERE TO EAT
20 La Fourchette
21 Le Mesclun

PL. DE LA RÉPUBLIQUE

0   200m

A

↓ ARLES, N 570

B

PROVENCE-ALPES-CÔTE D'AZUR

as well as extremely fresh fish and meat. This may not sound particularly special, but in the hands of this pioneering chef, dishes that would be run-of-the-mill elsewhere are transformed into original creations through their unusual combination of ingredients and their fine-tuned precision. The weekday lunchtime menu costs €18; reckon on €25 à la carte. You can eat on the terrace on sunny days and watch the world go by.

ⓒ |●| La Fourchette

17 rue Racine. **Map A2-20**
☎ 04.90.85.20.93
Closed Sat; Sun; Feb school holiday; 15 Aug–10 Sept.

This gastronomic restaurant is fast becoming an institution. Good prices, an elegant setting and, above all, well-worked dishes: sardines marinated in coriander, *daube à l'avignonnaise*, meringue with hazelnuts. Lunch menu starts at €23, with other menus €25–28 in the evening and reasonably priced wines, particularly those served by the carafe. It's essential to book.

Bandol

83150

ⓒ 🛪 🏠 |●| Hôtel Bel Ombra**

32 rue de la Fontaine; between the port and Renecros beach (it's signposted).
☎ 04.94.29.40.90 ℗ 04.94.25.01.11
ⓔ bel.ombra@wanadoo.fr
Closed 15 Oct–30 March.

This spotless little hotel with smartly decorated rooms (some with a balcony) is set in a very quiet residential area, a little way from the town centre. It has all the atmosphere and effusive welcome of a family boarding house. Double rooms cost €49–66, depending on the season; half-board is compulsory mid-June to early Sept (€54–59 per person). A dinner menu is offered to hotel guests at €18.80. There is room outside to sit in the sun or, if you prefer, under a bower. *One breakfast per room offered to our readers on presentation of this guide.*

ⓒ 🛪 🏠 |●| Hôtel-restaurant L'Oasis**

15 rue des Écoles; take rue Gabriel-Péri up from the pleasure port; it's the 3rd street from the left.

☎ 04.94.29.41.69 ℗ 04.94.29.44.80
Closed Sun evening out of season; Dec.
Disabled access. TV. Pay car park.

This small hotel-restaurant, close to the port and the beach, is simple but clean and attractive – what is more, the owner is a real charmer. There are only a dozen rooms, so it's worth booking in advance, but avoid nos. 1 and 4, as they overlook the street. No. 14, in contrast, is slightly set apart, at the foot of the garden, with its own small terrace (although all the guests can enjoy the shady garden and another terrace). Double rooms with shower/wc or bath go for €59–71; half board, compulsory between 15 June and 15 September, costs €58 per person. All the rooms have their own bar and telephone. They offer a choice of menus from €22 to €49. *10% discount on the price of a room (1 Jan–31 March and 15 Sept–30 Nov) offered to our readers on presentation of this guide.*

ⓒ 🛪 |●| L'Oulivo

19 rue des Tonneliers; it's 100m from the port beside the church.
☎ 04.94.29.81.79
Closed Sun evening (out of season); Mon; Tues; lunchtimes and all day Mon (in summer); a fortnight in Dec.

Very simple, very good restaurant, where a wonderfully kind *patronne* serves fresh, authentic Provençal cuisine. They offer a weekday lunch menu at €12.80 and another at €24.50. There's a pleasant terrace, which is heated in winter. *Free coffee offered to our readers on presentation of this guide.*

Barcelonnette

04400

ⓒ 🏠 Aztéca Hôtel***

3 rue François-Arnaud.
☎ 04.92.81.46.36 ℗ 04.92.81.43.92
ⓦ www.hotel-azteca.fr.st
Closed Nov. **Disabled access. TV. Car park.**

This beautiful hotel may look modern but it is in fact built around a nineteenth-century "Mexican villa". It is only two minutes from the town centre on foot, but it is surrounded by a garden and is very quiet. The rooms – €49–95 for a double with shower/wc or bath depending on the season – are attractively decorated, and the cheapest ones offer the best value for money in town. The prettiest and most spacious (and therefore the most expensive) are fitted out in an exuberant Mexican style, along with the communal areas. The theme is continued in the hotel bar, where tapas are served every night. You can eat breakfast in the garden in summer.

◎ ☎ |●| Hôtel du Cheval Blanc**

12 rue Grenette.
☏04.92.81.00.19 ℱ04.92.81.15.39
℮gbarneaud@free.fr
Restaurant closed *lunchtimes; Oct to end Dec.* **TV. High chairs available. Car park.**

This hotel-restaurant has been in the Barneaud family for four generations. Double rooms with shower/wc go for €50. People come here nowadays more for the food than the rooms, though the dining room is for guests only and offers menus at €13–20. The traditional cooking is generously served and features game, fresh noodles and spinach pie. It's popular with cycle tourists; you can store bikes in the stables, and they prepare special "sporty" breakfasts and packed lunches on request.

Uvernet-Fours
04400 (4.5km SW)

◎ ⅔ |●| Le Passe Montagne

Take the D902 towards Pra-Loup, and turn before the junction for col d'Allos.
☏04.92.81.08.58
Closed *Tues and Wed (except during school holidays); last fortnight in June; mid-Nov to mid-Dec.* **Car park.**

This place has the warm atmosphere of a wooden chalet, and you can admire the peaks of Pain de Sucre and Chapeau de Gendarme from the terrace. It's a relaxed place with a peaceful atmosphere heightened in winter when they light a roaring fire in the huge fireplace. The chef has rediscovered traditional Provençal cooking and used his talent to adapt it to the present day with a range of set menus €18–25 – dishes include gratin of cabbage rissoles with Tomme cheese from Ubaye and absinthe. *Free coffee offered to our readers on presentation of this guide.*

Super-Sauze
04400 (5km SE)

◎ ⅔ ☎ Le Pyjama**

It's at the foot of the ski runs.
☏04.92.81.12.00 ℱ04.92.81.03.16
Closed *15 April–25 June; Sept to mid-Dec.*

Disabled access. TV. Car park.

The rooms are furnished with old pieces of furniture and ornaments, and they look out onto a peaceful panorama of larches. All have wide terraces, and some have mezzanines; doubles €46–78 according to the facilities and the season. Also some studios with kitchens are available. There are places where you can curl up with a book in winter and tables outside where you can have a cool drink in summer. Pets very welcome. *Free house apéritif offered to our readers on presentation of this guide.*

Pra-Loup
04400 (6km SW)

◎ ⅔ ☎ |●| Le Prieuré***

Les Molanes; take the D109 and it's at the foot of the ski runs.
☏04.92.84.11.43 ℱ04.92.84.01.88
℮www.hotel.leprieure.fr
Closed *May; mid-Sept to mid-Dec.* **TV. High chairs available. Swimming pool.**

An eighteenth-century priory which has been converted into a very warm, rustic hotel with breathtaking views of the Pain de Sucre and Chapeau de Gendarme mountains. Doubles with shower/wc or bath go for €60–95. Menus, €16.50 at lunchtime (in summer), then €19–45, feature appetizing cooking; dishes include *charbonnade* or rack of lamb with Génépy butter. *Free fruit juice or soft drink offered to our readers on presentation of this guide.*

◎ ⅔ ☎ |●| Auberge du Clos Sorel**

Les Molanes; it's next to the train station entrance.
☏04.92.84.10.74 ℱ04.92.84.09.14
℮www.clos-sorel.com
Closed *early April to mid-June; early Sept to mid-Dec.* **Restaurant closed** *lunchtimes in winter except during school holidays.* **TV. Swimming pool.**

A charming mountainside inn in a very old farmhouse offering a friendly welcome. It's very close to the ski slopes and there's a lovely pool. Cosy rooms with beams and stone walls are priced at €64–140 according to the facilities; half board, €61–97, is requested during school holidays. You can have tea by the fireside, and they serve honest dishes in the candlelit restaurant, where there's a *menu-carte* for €26; dishes change every day. *Free house apéritif offered to our readers on presentation of this guide.*

Bauduen

83630

@ 2ª ☎ |●| L'Auberge du Lac**

Rue Grande.
☎04.94.70.08.04 ℻04.94.84.39.41
ⓔauberge.lac@wanadoo.fr
Closed *mid-Nov to mid-March.*

This rustic inn is located in a charming little village on the banks of lake Sainte-Croix. The owner has been pampering his guests here for more than forty years. The rooms are attractive and pleasant, particularly those which look onto the lake; they cost €72 with bath. Half board, €67 per person, is preferred during the school holidays. In summer, you can eat on a little terrace wreathed with vines, while in the winter the warm dining room is very welcoming. Good local cuisine features on the menus, €20–55, with game in season, fish and local wine. *Free coffee offered to our readers on presentation of this guide.*

Baux-de-Provence (Les)

13520

@ ☎ |●| 2ª Hostellerie de la Reine-Jeanne**

☎04.90.54.32.06 ℻04.90.54.32.33
ⓦwww.la-reinejeanne.com
Closed *Jan; 15 Nov–20 Dec.* **TV.**

When the main street is heaving with tourists in the summer, all you want to do is get out of town – but this is a charming refuge. The old house has been lovingly and astutely renovated. The rooms are pleasant and individual. Doubles €48–65 with shower, shower/wc or bath; the most expensive one is like an apartment with an amazing view and incredible terrace at €92. In the restaurant they serve quality local dishes. Menus, which start at €16 (weekday lunch) with others €22–30, list quality local cuisine. *Free coffee offered to our readers on presentation of this guide.*

Paradou (Le)

13520 (4km S)

@ ☎ |●| 2ª Du Côté des Olivades

Lieu-dit de Bourgeac; outside the village.
☎04.90.54.56.78 ℻04.90.54.56.79
ⓦwww.ducotedesolivades.com

Closed *Mon (Nov to mid-March).* **TV. Disabled access. High chairs available. Swimming pool. Car park.**

This is owned by a Belgian, André Bourguignon, who, having had enormous success with a brasserie in Brussels, decided to change the northern fogs for the sunshine of the Alpine foothills. He came here with his wife and small daughter to create the hotel of his dreams in the midst of an olive grove. He now has an international clientele, some of whom come back year after year to this idyllic landscape in order to relax in his old farmhouse. Ten cosy rooms complete with beautiful terraces and top-rate cooking, courtesy of his wife, that brings out the best of the local produce without any fancy pretensions. Double rooms with shower/wc go for €95–172, including breakfast. Good, simple dishes of exemplary freshness and precision are served on a range of menus from €30 to €45.

Beaulieu-sur-Mer

06310

@ ☎ Hôtel Riviera*

6 rue Paul-Doumer; between the town centre and the port; 150m from the sea.
☎04.93.01.04.92 ℻04.93.01.19.31
ⓦwww.hotel-riviera.fr
Closed *All Saints' to Christmas.*

Small hotel in a quiet street, with a typically spruce Provençal façade set off by wrought-iron balconies. The interior has been refurbished but retains a certain old-world charm. The redecoration of the rooms is stunning, and the prices are a bargain for this area: doubles with shower/wc or bath €46–62, depending on the season. Some of the rooms give onto the shady patio where breakfast is served in the morning. The welcome is so warm that you won't want to leave. This is maybe our best hotel in Beaulieu. *5% discount on the room rate (out of season) offered to our readers on presentation of this guide.*

@ 2ª ☎ Hôtel Le Havre Bleu**

29 bd. du Maréchal-Joffre; 3 min from the beach and 400m from the railway station.
☎04.93.01.01.40 ℻04.93.01.29.92
ⓦwww.hotel-lehavrebleu.fr
Closed *a fortnight in Nov.* **TV. Car park.**

A nineteenth-century hotel with a quiet family atmosphere. The clean, simple

PROVENCE-ALPES-CÔTE D'AZUR

décor, white paintwork and blue shutters are very Mediterranean. Doubles €49–70 (breakfast included) depending on facilities and season; some have a sunny balcony or terrace. The rooms at the back are quieter. *10% discount on the room rate out of season offered to our readers on presentation of this guide.*

⬱ 𝒴 🏠 Hôtel Comté de Nice***

25 bd. Marinoni; on the main artery, next to the main square.
☎04.93.01.19.70 ℱ04.93.01.23.09
🖱www.hotel-comtedenice.com
Open *all year.* **TV. Pay car park.**

You immediately feel good when you walk into this hotel, five minutes from the beach and the harbour. The façade is very 1950s or 1960s, but the rooms are well appointed, with air-conditioning, telephone, mini-safe and hairdryer. Most of them have sea views but it's a shame the railway line is on that side too. Doubles with shower/wc or bath go for €130, depending on the season. Good breakfasts for €8.50, and you pay €8.50 for a space in the garage too. There's also a sauna and fitness centre. *10% discount on the room rate (except July–Sept, Grand Prix, Easter and Christmas) offered to our readers on presentation of this guide.*

Beauvezer
04370

⬱ 𝒴 🏠 |●| Hôtel Le Bellevue**

Place du Village; 13km south of Allos.
☎04.92.83.51.60 ℱ04.92.83.51.60
🖱www.hotelbellevue.org
Closed *Wed until 5pm; mid-Oct to April.* **TV.**

A charming place to stop between Provence and the Alps – a haven of peace and tranquillity behind an ochre façade. The comfortable double rooms, tastefully decorated in warm colours and Provençal prints, go for €42–49 with shower or bath, depending on the season; no. 3 has a lovely balcony with a view of the square. You eat heartily in the restaurant (for hotel guests only) though the cuisine is nothing to write home about – lunch menu €13.50, with another menu at €25. There's a pretty, shady terrace. It's best to book. Logis de France. *Free house apéritif offered to our readers on presentation of this guide.*

Bonnieux
84480

⬱ |●| Le Fournil

5 pl. Carnot.
☎04.90.75.83.62
Closed *Mon; Tues lunchtime (all day Tues out of season); Jan; Dec.*

This establishment has a terrace on the pretty square, with its fountain, and an intriguing stone-built interior. It also has a solid reputation, so you might need to book. Good-value traditional cooking features on the lunchtime menu at €25 and the dinner menu at €36: minestrone with prawns, roast piglet.

Bormes-les-Mimosas
83230

⬱ 🏠 Le Grand Hôtel***

167 route du Baguier.
☎04.94.71.23.72 ℱ04.94.71.51.20
🖱www.augrandhotel.com
Closed *Nov–Feb.* **Car park.**

This hotel, one of the least expensive three-star hotels on this coast (but not, admittedly, one of the most luxurious), is superbly located above the village, in the midst of palms and pines. The rooms come in a variety of shapes and sizes, some in the attic (those with no view are the cheapest of all), others on the ground floor or with a balcony; doubles with shower or bath cost €32–52 in low season and €54–62 in high season. Weather permitting, you can have breakfast in the garden. All in all, the atmosphere is reminiscent of an early-twentieth-century spa, but none the worse for that. No pets allowed.

⬱ 🏠 Hôtel le Paradis**

62 impasse de Castellan, domaine du Mont des Roses; going down to the village, it's on the right.
☎04.94.01.32.62 ℱ04.94.01.32.60
🖱www.hotelparadis.fr
TV. Car park.

This old-style holiday hotel, perched halfway between the old and new villages, has been taken over by a charming couple; they have completely refurbished it, with glossy paint and attractive friezes on the walls. The rooms are all different: they vary in size, some have a balcony, some overlook the garden, others the village, etc. They all have in common, however, a TV set, telephone and bathroom (or shower). There is a beautiful terrace in the middle of a garden blessed with flowers and rare plants, as well as a view of the village – what better place to have breakfast? Double rooms cost €40–70, according to the degree of comfort and the season; there is also a small, two-bedroom house for rent (€80–120 per day).

⊛ |●| Lou Cantoun de Mireio

4 pl. Gambetta; opposite the tourist office in the old village.
℡04.94.71.27.80
Closed *evenings out of season; mid-Oct to end of Jan.*

Eating out in Bormes is generally a bit pricey, but this is an exception, with authentic local dishes (such as the excellent *ratatouille provençale*), as well as crêpes. There are no set menus, but you can eat for around €20 à la carte, and even less if you stick to the crêpes. The fine food is complemented by friendly service, an attractive little dining room and a terrace.

⊛ |●| Lou Poulid Cantoun

6 pl. Lou Poulid Cantoun.
℡04.94.71.15.59
Closed *lunchtimes (July–Aug); Sun evening and Mon (out of season); Nov–March.*

It's not everyone that has the luck of running a restaurant on the most photographed square in Bormes. In summer there are tables on the terrace and at dusk the place is illuminated by twinkly lights, creating an intimate, relaxed atmosphere. Refined, honest cuisine with Provençal flavours – balsamic vinegar, basil and fennel. Leave room for dessert. There's a single menu for €34, or expect to pay €40 à la carte. It's best to book.

Briançon

05100

⊛ ♒ 🏠 |●| L'Auberge de l'Impossible**

43 av. de Savoie; in the direction of Grenoble.
℡04.92.21.02.98 ℻04.92.21.13.75
ⓔ auberge.impossible@wanadoo.fr
Closed *lunchtimes in winter; Wed (out of*

season except by prior booking). **TV. High chairs and games available. Car park.**

An unpretentious hotel-restaurant with thirty or so decent rooms. Doubles go for €47 with shower/wc or bath – reasonable prices for the area. Simple, nourishing family cooking is served in the restaurant with a single menu at €23: barbecue (in season), *fondue* with morels and ceps, *tartiflette*. In summer you dine on the terrace. There's a good atmosphere in the evenings, and in the winter they host occasional crêpe parties or karaoke evenings for the residents. They also offer half board, weekly rates and ski packages. *Free house apéritif offered to our readers on presentation of this guide.*

⊛ ♒ 🏠 Hôtel Edelweiss**

32 av. de la République; near the Vauban city, opposite the cultural centre and the congress hall.
℡04.92.21.02.94 ℻04.92.21.22.55
ⓔ hotel.edelweiss.brianon@wanadoo.fr
Closed *15–30 April; 15 Nov–15 Dec.* **TV. High chairs and games available. Car park.**

A small non-smoking hotel, located very near Vauban's magnificent fortress, opposite the cultural centre and the conference centre. The east-facing rooms have a lovely view of the local woods; those facing west overlook the town. It's clean and quiet and doubles go for €55–60 with shower/wc or bath. *10% discount on the room rate (except school holidays) offered to our readers on presentation of this guide.*

⊛ |●| Le Péché Gourmand

2 rte. de Gap.
℡04.92.21.33.21
Closed *Mon.* **Disabled access. Car park.**

Though it's set on a corner of a huge junction, this restaurant has a shaded terrace well away from the streams of cars, and two elegant dining rooms. The excellent menus list such delicious things as *marbré* of young rabbit with sage and tomato *confit*, and lobster lasagna. There's a respectable selection of cheeses and good desserts. Weekday lunch menu €16, then others €23–43; the most expensive menu includes both fish and meat. Service is a little stiff but pleasant enough – it's just a shame that the dining room is so impersonal.

⊛ |●| Le Pied de la Gargouille

64 Grande-Rue; it's in the old town opposite the municipal library.

☎04.92.20.12.95
Open *Fri–Sun evenings (out of season); evenings daily (in season).*

This non-smoking restaurant centres on an open fire where the host keeps an expert eye on the delicious grilled dishes. The walls are adorned with antique skis and snowshoes. Excellent sweet and savoury *tourtons*; other specialities include mountain dishes and steak grilled over the embers. Two menus for €16 and €18; à la carte you'll pay around €21, which is very reasonable. You can be sure of an enthusiastic welcome.

☜ ⚘ |●| Restaurant Le Rustique

Rue du Pont-d'Asfeld; coming down from the Grande Gargouille take the first left after the fountain and it's 300m further on.
☎04.92.21.00.10 ☎04.92.21.40.06
Closed *Mon and Tues (except public holidays); second fortnight in June; second fortnight in Nov.* **Open** *until 10pm.* **High chairs available. Disabled access.**

Country décor, good quality cooking and a warm welcome. The speciality is fresh trout served with all manner of sauces – try it with apples flambéed in Calvados, leek coulis, garlic and cream, orange or Roquefort cheese. The generous salads are good, too, and they do a tasty *fondue savoyarde* with morels. Menus are €22–29, and à la carte will set you back around €32. *Free house apéritif offered to our readers on presentation of this guide.*

Vachette (La)
05100 (4km NE)

☜ |●| Le Nano

Route d'Italie, Val des Prés; take the N94, in the direction of Montgenèvre and Italy, then head towards La Vachette-Névach on the D944. The restaurant is 1km further on on the left.
☎04.92.21.06.09
Closed *Sun and Mon (out of season); Tues in July–Aug; a few days in May; in Nov around All Saints' Day.*

The warm, pleasant setting, the quietly efficient service and above all the quality of the cooking make this one of the best places to eat in the area. The fine, classical dishes are skilfully seasoned and of the highest quality – duck foie gras with spices, *roulade* of rabbit with basil, boned cockerel with spiced sauce, fine orange tart with caramel – and there are very

good desserts. There's a single menu for €23, or expect to pay around €45 for a meal à la carte. Their wine list is expertly chosen with quality vintages. It's a good idea to book, and not turn up too late.

Chantemerle
05330 (7km NW)

☜ ⌂ |●| La Boule de Neige**

15 rue du Centre; it's on the road to Grenoble. Turn left in the village of Chantemerle, then left again.
☎04.92.24.00.16 ☎04.92.24.00.25
Closed *end April to end June; end Aug to mid-Dec.* **TV. High chairs and games available.**

Prices aren't the cheapest, but this is a wonderfully comfortable establishment and you won't want to leave. Doubles with shower/wc or bath go for €78–122; half board (compulsory during school holidays) costs €57–79. The restaurant is very pleasant, the *patronne* is discreet and welcoming, and the cooking is delicate; menu €25. The ski-lift for the Serre-Chevalier slopes is 100m away.

Salle-lès-Alpes (La)
05240 (8km NW)

☜ |●| La Marotte

36 rue de la Guisane; take the road to Grenoble, and turn right at the La Salle roundabout towards the old town.
☎04.92.24.77.23
✉ pierreaubert@wanadoo.fr
Closed *lunchtimes; Sun; May–June; Oct–Nov.*

A really nice restaurant which has been here for years. The boss prepares delicious dishes; there's a menu at €17, or à la carte expect a bill of around €25. Try the terrines, which are the house speciality, made from vegetables, meat or fish. The herring and shallot bread and the apple *tarte tatin* also deserve a mention. Credit cards not accepted. It's best to book.

Brigue (La)
06430 (3km E)

☜ |●| La Cassolette

20 rue du Général-de-Gaulle; it's 3km east of Saint-Dalmas-de-Tende, between place Saint-Martin and place de Nice.
☎04.93.04.63.82

Closed *Sun evening and Mon; evenings (Oct–April); end of March/early April.*

This tiny, pretty, family-run restaurant serves good home cooking. The dining room is full of models and trinkets of chickens in all shapes and sizes. If they run out of things, the boss will go next door to the butcher to fetch an extra *tournedos* or breast of duck. Menus range from €15 to €27; reckon on around €30 à la carte.

Cadière d'Azur (La)
83740

⊚ |●| Le Regain

39 rue Marx Dormoy; 10km from Bandol.
☎04.94.98.32.68
Closed *Tues and Sat lunchtimes in high season; Tues, Wed and Sun evenings out of season.*

Set apart from the restaurants in the upper village, this place is appealing for the views from its tiny terrace, shaded by a plane tree, its cheerful service and, last but not least, its food (which can also be enjoyed in the pretty pastel-yellow dining room). There are no set menus; reckon on around €30 à la carte. Dishes include stuffed vegetables in season, home-made foie gras and other regional specialities. The deliciously tender knuckle of lamb convinced us that we had found a good restaurant with reasonable prices for the area.

Cagnes-sur-Mer
06800

⊚ 🛏 Le Mas d'Azur

42 av. de Nice, Cros-de-Cagnes; 400m from the town centre.
☎04.93.20.19.19
TV. Car park.

At first sight, this hotel, set on the edge of the main road, doesn't look very promising. But inside you travel back in time. It's a charming old Provençal house with a courtyard and an appealing garden, and you're warmly welcomed by the kindly owners. Quiet doubles with shower/wc go for €44–56.

⊚ 🛏 Le Val Duchesse**

11 rue de Paris; it's 50m from the beach.

☎04.92.13.40.00 ☎04.92.13.40.29
Closed *25 Nov–15 Dec.* **TV. Swimming pool. Car park.**

Set in a quiet street, away from the traffic and the impersonal high-rises down by the sea, this place has a pretty garden planted with palm trees, a swimming pool, a ping-pong table and games for the children. The décor is full of southern colour. You can rent studios from €51–70 and apartments from €69–95.

⊚ 🎄 |●| Le Renoir

23 pl. Sainte-Luce; it's opposite les Halles.
☎04.93.22.59.58
Closed *Sun and Thurs evenings; Mon; mid-Dec to end of Jan.*

This is a warm, appealing place serving good, flavoursome food with a choice of menus €17–27: pike-perch ravioli, sautéed pork and *fricassée* of fish. The *patronne*, who is wonderfully kind, will help you choose. *Free coffee offered to our readers on presentation of this guide.*

⊚ |●| Fleur de Sel

86 montée de la Bourgade.
☎04.93.20.33.33
Closed *Wed; Thurs lunchtime; fortnight early Jan; first week in June; fortnight during autumn school holiday.*

Pretty little restaurant with typical Provençal stone walls. Philippe Loose had worked for lots of other restaurants until he and his wife decided to give others pleasure by working for themselves. Their guests are glad of it. *Menu saveur* €21 (€29 with wine and coffee) and other menus €30–52 feature authentic, well-presented local dishes that are simply served.

Cannes
06400

⊚ 🛏 🎄 Hôtel Chanteclair

12 rue Forville; it's near the Palais des Festivals and the Midi beach.
☎and ☎04.93.39.68.80
Closed *Nov; Dec.*

Despite its central location (100m from the liveliest part of town), this hotel is nonetheless perfectly quiet. Functional rooms with white walls and simple pine furniture cost €40–42. There's a charming patio where you can have breakfast. You'll get a warm welcome from the chatty host, who will tell you where you can park for free nearby. Credit cards not accepted. *Free breakfast for children under eight years' old or free coffee or fruit juice offered to our readers on presentation of this guide.*

◉ ⅍ 🏠 Hôtel de France***

85 rue d'Antibes; near the palais des Festivals.
☎04.93.06.54.54 ⓕ04.93.68.53.43
🌐www.h-de-france.com
TV. Closed *22 Nov–26 Dec.*

This place has been completely refurbished without losing its Art Deco style. It's in the busiest part of town, right on the main thoroughfare, and has thirty rooms with modern facilities – air-conditioning, safe, hairdryer and the rest – go for €70–106 depending on the season. Rooms 501–508 have a view of the sea. *10% discount on the room rate (except in Aug) offered to our readers on presentation of this guide.*

◉ ⅍ 🏠 Hôtel Molière**

5–7 rue Molière; it's 100m from La Croisette.
☎04.93.38.16.16 ⓕ04.93.68.29.57
🌐www.hotel-moliere.com
Closed *17 Nov–25 Dec.* **Disabled access. TV.**

This friendly nineteenth-century hotel with a pretty façade is furnished in the appropriate style. Lovely rooms are priced at €70–110, breakfast included. Although the hotel is very close to the town centre, the location is quiet and there is a large garden in which to enjoy breakfast. *10% discount on the room rate for a stay of at least two consecutive nights (except in July/Aug) on presentation of this guide.*

◉◉ ⅍ 🏠 Le Splendid***

4–6 rue Félix Faure; in the centre facing the sea and the port.
☎04.97.06.22.22 ⓕ04.93.99.55.02
🌐www.splendid-hotel-cannes.fr
Disabled access. TV. High chairs available.

It's not a palace such as you find on La Croisette but it's pretty close. Behind the majestic turn-of-the-century façade, there's one of the town's loveliest hotels, wonderfully run by Annick Cagnat and her family. The beautiful rooms have antique furniture and great bathrooms, which have all been refurbished, along with some of the rooms. If you reserve in advance they provide a welcoming fruit basket, and a half bottle of champagne for

anyone celebrating a birthday or wedding anniversary. Some of the rooms have a balcony and a big terrace overlooking the sea. The prices – €90–215 for a double, depending on the season – are fair. *Free breakfast per person per night offered to our readers on presentation of this guide.*

◉ |◉| Le Bouchon d'Objectif

10 rue Constantine.
☎04.93.99.21.76
Closed *Sun evening and Mon out of season (Mon only in season); 20 Nov–15 Dec.*

Each month this friendly restaurant stages an exhibition of a different photographer's work. The simple, original food on the two menus, €16 and €26, includes crab and salmon *tartare*, duck breast with sour cherries and piglet with a soya caramel sauce. There's a pretty terrace facing a modern pedestrianized area.

◉ |◉| Restaurant Aux Bons Enfants

80 rue Meynadier; it's opposite Forville market.
Closed *Sat evening (except in season); Sun; August; 15 Nov–1 Dec.*

There's no telephone, so regulars pop in during the morning to reserve a table while the staff are still peeling the vegetables bought in the Forville market. Home cooking and regional dishes feature on the single menu (€18) terrine of roast artichoke with cheese and pancetta, *estouffade* of lamb, goat's cheese terrine with a *coulis* of tomatoes, rabbit with rosemary, aubergine and sardine fritters, *aïoli*, tarts and home-made iced nougat.

◉ ⅍ |◉| Restaurant Au Bec Fin

12 rue du 24-Août; it's between the train station and the rue d'Antibes.
☎04.93.38.35.86
Closed *Sat evening and Sun (out of season); Sun and Mon lunch (in summer); a week in July; a fortnight in Nov.* **Disabled access.**

This restaurant gets very full, so it's best not to arrive too late. The menus, €19 and €23, offer a staggering choice with nearly twenty starters and almost as many mains. Mostly local cuisine: *daube provençale* (a slowly braised beef stew), vegetable soup, scorpion fish *à la pêcheur*. Good daily specials, too – you won't even notice the bland décor. *Free house apéritif offered to our readers on presentation of this guide.*

Le Comptoir des Vins

13 bd. de la République; close to the rue
d'Antibes.
⊕04.93.68.13.26
Closed *Mon–Wed evenings; Sun; Feb.*

You enter via the cellar, selecting your wine
first, then choose food to suit. It took the
owner some time to get the local Cannois
used to the idea of a bistro-cellar, but he
succeeded. It's busy and buzzy, especially
in the evening. Good, wholesome dishes
on the menu (€22.50): sausage with pis-
tachios, *tartiflette*, and a range of Savoyard
specialities. Wine, served by the glass or by
the bottle, is good value starting at €8.50
per bottle. *Free coffee offered to our readers on
presentation of this guide.*

Golfe-Juan

06220 (4km NE)

Hôtel California*

222 av. de la Liberté; it's on the N7, 800m
from the station, close to the seashore.
⊕and ⊕04.93.63.78.63
⊛www.californiagolfe.fr.st
Closed *Nov school holiday.* **TV. Games
available. Car park.**

This 1920s house, set back from the main
road, has been converted into a hotel with
pretty double rooms available for €23.50–
43 with basin or €34–50 with shower/wc;
depending on the season. There's a nice
old garden. Cards not accepted. *One free
week for every two consecutive weeks (1 Oct–1
April) or 10% discount on the room rate for a
stay of at least two nights (1 Oct–1 June) on
presentation of this guide.*

Vallauris

06220 (6km NE)

Le Manuscrit

224 chemin Lintier; it's in the centre of town
off the boulevard du Tapis-Vert.
⊕04.93.64.56.56
Closed *Mon (in season); Sun evening; Mon
and Tues evening (out of season); 18 Nov–4
Dec.*

The interior of this fine stone building,
which used to be a perfume factory, is
exceptional, and the food is pretty good,
too. You can eat in the dining room (where
there's a wonderful display of prints and
canvases), in the conservatory (full of
subtropical flowers) or on the terrace
beneath the hundred-year-old chestnut

tree. Menus, at €18–32, offer a nice range
of fish and meat dishes; also a selection of
affordable wines.

Carpentras

84200

Le Comtadin***

65 bd. Albin-Durand
⊕04.90.67.75.00 ⊕04.90.67.75.01
⊛www.le-comtadin.com
Closed *mid-Dec to end of Feb (except
Christmas and New Year holidays).* **TV. Pay
car park.**

This hotel's unassuming nineteenth-century façade hides extremely comfortable
rooms boasting air-conditioning, double
glazing, a mini-bar, safe and even a modem
connection. Reckon on €69–78 for two,
depending on the room and the season,
or half board at €63–68 per person.
Other assets include friendly service, a
pleasant breakfast room, pretty patio and
L'Aromate, a restaurant recently opened
on the ground floor, with contemporary
décor and food to match. Menus range
from €12 (weekday lunchtimes) to €30.
*Free house apéritif offered to our readers on
presentation of this guide.*

Chez Serge

90 rue Cottier.
⊕04.90.63.21.24
Closed *Sun.* **Disabled access. High chairs
and games available.**

A very lovely restaurant with a modern
décor that really works – New York loft
meets timeless Provence. They serve very
good pizzas, along with dishes such as
fricassée of scallops with truffles, farm-
raised chicken breast, Armenian platters
(Thurs) and delicious desserts. Weekday
lunch menu costs €13, with others up to
€25; children's menu €7. *Free house apéritif
on presentation of this guide.*

Le Comptoir du Sud

80 bd. du Nord.
⊕04.90.67.93.55
Open *Tues–Sat (in summer); Tues to Sun
lunchtime (out of season).*

This small air-conditioned restaurant
close to the old town centre is ideal for
gourmets in search of fresh ingredients
cooked without any fancy pretensions:
spicy foie gras cooked in a cloth with its

21

PROVENCE-ALPES-CÔTE D'AZUR

jelly flavoured with Muscat-de-Beaumes-de-Venise, iced nougat with lemon and honey and fresh fish prepared in typical Provençal style. Menus are €18 (lunch), €23 (dinner), and the wine list offers a fine selection of local wines. Another plus is the friendly service.

Pernes-les-Fontaines
84210 (6km S)

◎ 🎋 |●| Dame l'Oie

56 rue Troubadour; it's on the D938.
℡04.90.61.62.43
Closed Mon; Tues lunch (also Tues evening out of season); autumn and winter school holidays. **High chairs available.**

There's a fountain in the middle of the dining room, where the décor is English country style and very Beatrix Potter. The cuisine, however, is typically southern – simple but nicely prepared, with stunning flavours and delicious desserts. It's good value, with a weekday lunch menu at €15 and two other menus for €23 and €29; children's menu €11. *Free coffee offered to our readers on presentation of this guide.*

Cassis
13260

◎ 🛏 Auberge de jeunesse

La Fontasse; by road from Marseille, turn right after about 15km towards Col de la Gardiole (3km of good road, then 2km of stony road); on foot, climb up from Cassis, taking the avenue de l'Amiral-Ganteaume, then the avenue des Calanques until you reach the calanque (creek) of Port-Miou and then start climbing (around 1hr).
℡04.42.01.02.72
ⓦwww.fuaj.org
Closed 6 Jan–14 March. **New arrivals 8–10am and 5–9pm. Car park.**

The only lodging available on the massif des Calanques. A very pretty Provençal house in what is obviously an exceptional setting. You really get back to nature here: there's a tank to collect the rain water (and pools for washing yourself), and solar panels and windmills for electricity. The hostel sleeps 60, in shared rooms with ten beds at €9.30 per night (FUAJ card compulsory, but you can buy it on site). There's a kitchen available but you'll need to bring your own provisions. The manager is very friendly and knows the area backwards. Guests can indulge in a host of activities:

hikes (the GR 98 passes alongside), climbing, swimming, botanical observation (450 varieties of plants), *pétanque*, etc. Come early in the morning in July and August, as otherwise you may find it full (although walkers and cyclists are never turned away). Children are accepted from the age of seven, but there are no bedrooms specifically for families. Credit cards not accepted.

◎ 🎋 🛏 |●| Le Clos des Arômes**

10 rue Paul-Mouton; it's a two-minute walk from the town centre.
℡04.42.01.71.84 ℡04.42.01.31.76
Closed 5 Jan–20 Feb. **Restaurant closed** Mon; Tues and Wed lunchtimes (except public holidays). **TV.**

Old village house prettily renovated in a peaceful street. The dining room is cute, with a fireplace and there's a shady, flower-filled courtyard for when the sun shines. Menus at €25 and €35 list refined local cuisine. Charming rooms with subtle Provençal décor; doubles €63–73 with shower/wc or bath. *Free house apéritif offered to our readers on presentation of this guide.*

◎ 🛏 |●| Le Jardin d'Emile

Plage du Bestouan.
℡04.42.01.80.55 ℡04.42.01.80.70
ⓦwww.lejardindemile.fr
Closed lunchtimes (except Sun lunch); Sun evening; mid-Nov to mid-Dec. **TV. Car park.**

A charming, enjoyable place with a great view. Seven ravishing rooms – including a honeymoon suite and two attic rooms – go for €80–130 with shower/wc or bath. The chic but relaxed restaurant serves creative Mediterranean cooking. There's a weekday lunch menu at €25 and another at €45. Dine in the garden if at all possible, under ancient pines, olives trees, fig trees and cypresses.

◎ |●| La Poissonnerie

6 quai Barthélemy.
℡04.42.01.71.56
Closed Mon; evenings (Nov to late March).

You are among genuine fishing folk here. The eldest son, Laurent, a boatman and fisherman, gets up at 6am. While his mother takes charge of the fishmonger's, the rest of the family makes sure that everything is shipshape in this house that has now been home to five generations of fishermen. Beware of Éric, Laurent's brother, who will shut the restaurant at the first sight of tourists in flip-flops… The *formule* costs €12.90, then there's a fisherman's menu at €19.90, or reckon on €35 for a meal à la carte. On Tuesday, there's *aïoli*, on Wednesday *bourride*, on Thursday cod, served in the Christmas Eve style (*raïto*), and on Friday and Saturday there's fish couscous. If you want something else, just point it out in the fishmonger's. There are also snacks (€13) of fresh baby cuttlefish or sardines with a glass of wine.

✿ |●| Fleurs de Thym

5 rue Lamartine.
☎04.42.01.23.03
Open *every evening, all year round.*

An unusual but really appealing little restaurant. Here also, you have to show your credentials, and do not even consider wearing shorts. Once you pass the initial test, however, it's a relaxed place where you'll be treated like royalty. The décor aspires to sophistication but cannot take itself seriuosly enough to really bring it off. The mother of the family works in the kitchen, producing tasty dishes of remarkable precision: various small *farcis*, *pressé* of sardines, aubergine and tomato with basil, fillet of bass with ceps risotto. Dishes on the menus, €26.50 and €41, vary according to the season, and the whims of the chef. In fine weather you can also eat on the terrace. Credit cards not accepted.

Castellane

04120

✿ 🏠 |●| Nouvel Hôtel du Commerce***

Place Centrale.
☎04.92.83.61.00 ℗04.92.83.72.82
⊛www.hotel-fradet.com
Closed *Tues; Wed lunchtime; Nov–Feb.* **TV. Disabled access. Car park.**

This large house by the post office and town hall is decorated like a Provençal family home. It is much appreciated by tourists passing through the town. Spacious, comfortable double rooms with shower/wc or bath from €57–65, depending on the season. You can choose between a view of the town square or one of a 184-metre-high cliff. The food on the

menus, €18–40, is meticulously prepared with fresh ingredients: a feast of wonderful flavours in a friendly if rather stuffy atmosphere. A pleasant terrace, very polite service and warm welcome are guaranteed.

Garde (La)
04120 (3km SE)

✿ 🌳 🏠 |●| Auberge du Teillon**

Route Napoléon; it's on the N85 towards Grasse.
☎04.92.83.60.88 ℗04.92.83.74.08
⊛aubergeteillon@club-internet.fr
Closed *Sun evening and Mon (out of season); Tues lunch (July–Aug); mid-Nov to early March.* **TV. High chairs available. Car park.**

People come here from all along the coast at the weekend. You feel cocooned in the rustic little dining room, where chef Yves Lépine uses Provençal ingredients to produce flavoursome dishes on menus at €20–45: smoked lamb, calves' kidneys with morels and such like. Prolong the pleasure by staying the night; doubles cost €40–45 with basin, €50–55 with shower/wc depending on the season. Half board is requested in summer and at the weekends, at a cost of €50–55 per person. Rooms facing the main road can be noisy, so ask for ones at the back if you want a lie-in. *10% discount on the room rate offered to our readers on presentation of this guide.*

Rougon
04120 (17km SW)

✿ 🌳 🏠 |●| Auberge du Point-Sublime**

It's on the D952 at the entrance to the Verdon Gorges.
☎04.92.83.60.35 ℗04.92.83.74.31
⊛ point.sublime@wanadoo.fr
Closed *Wed and Thurs lunch (except public holidays and July–Aug); mid-Oct to early April.* **TV. High chairs and games available. Car park.**

There are two small dining rooms here, one of them non-smoking. Whichever you choose, you've got quite a treat in store: traditional and local dishes are listed on the menus €20.50–40. Décor is pleasant, with checked tablecloths, tiled floors, green plants and photographs of Verdon around the rooms. Recently refurbished doubles, €49 with basin, and €52.50 with shower/wc, are blissfully peaceful; nos. 10, 12, 14 and 16 have a wonderful view of the Point-Sublime. Half board, €52.50, is compulsory at weekends, on public holidays and during the school holidays. You'll need to book during July and August. Logis de France. *Free house apéritif offered to our readers on presentation of this guide.*

Palud-sur-Verdon (La)
04120 (25km SW)

◎ ♠ |◎| 朱 Hôtel-restaurant Le Provence**

Route La Maline; take the D23, it's 50m from the village.
℡04.92.77.38.88 ℗04.92.77.31.05
℮hotelleprovence@aol.com
Closed *Nov to end March.* **Restaurant closed** *lunchtimes.* **Disabled access. TV. High chairs and games available. Car park.**

This hotel has wide views of the route des Crêtes. Simple rooms, clean and recently refurbished: doubles with shower/wc or bath go for €41–55. Half board is requested in July and Aug. In the restaurant, specialities include duckling in honey, rabbit *à la provençale*, and salmon with sorrel. Menus €17–30. There's a relaxing lounge, or you can sip a cool drink on the terrace and savour the peace and quiet. *Free house apéritif offered to our readers on presentation of this guide.*

◎ 朱 ♠ |◎| Hôtel des Gorges du Verdon***

Take the D952, the road north of the gorges.
℡04.92.77.38.26 ℗04.92.77.35.00
ⓦwww.hotel-des-gorges-du-verdon.fr
Closed *All Saints' to Easter.* **Open** *7.30–9pm only.* **Disabled access. High chairs and games available. TV. Swimming pool. Car park.**

This hotel is in the heart of the Verdon Gorges, on a hillside facing the village and the surrounding countryside. The spectacular scenery helps you forget the hotel's rather brutal architecture. The rooms are similarly modern, but they're well equipped, clean and comfortable and decorated in Provençal style. Doubles with shower/wc or bath go for €93–150, suites for two to six people are €190–450. Half board is recommended in season. They serve very decent food, mostly traditional Provençal dishes, with a single menu at €30. There's a swimming pool and tennis courts. *Free house apéritif offered to our readers on presentation of this guide.*

Cavaillon
84300

◎ ♠ Hôtel du Parc**

183 pl. François-Tourel; in the centre of town.
℡04.90.71.57.78 ℗04.90.76.10.35
ⓦwww.hotelduparccavaillon.com
TV. High chairs and games available. Pay car park.

A huge nineteenth-century house opposite the Roman arch. Good hospitality and family atmosphere, with nice communal spaces (especially the patio). The rooms are classically decorated and fit in well with the architecture; doubles with shower/wc or bath will set you back €56–66, depending on the season.

◎ |◎| 朱 La Cuisine du Marché

Place Gambetta; in the centre of town.
℡04.90.71.56.00
Closed *Wed and Sun lunchtimes (July–Aug); Sun evening; Mon and Wed evenings (out of season).* **High chairs and games available.**

Climb the stairs to the first floor and you'll find an attractive, unfussy dining room (recently redecorated) with a view over the main square. Excellent fresh dishes with a strong Provençal accent: Provence-style stuffed squid, *pavé* of bull with beef marrow. Weekday lunch menu starts at €13.50, then others €17–25.50; children's menu €8.50. *Free house apéritif offered to our readers on presentation of this guide.*

◎ |◎| Restaurant Pantagruel

5 pl. Philippe-de-Cabassole.
℡04.90.76.11.98
Closed *Sun; Mon lunchtime.*

This reasonably priced restaurant seems dauntingly austere at first sight, with its sign at the entrance reading "To avoid arguments, it is forbidden to chat at the table", but it soon warms up with the smile of Christel Tanneau and the arrival of the dishes prepared by Yann, her husband. They run the place entirely on their own. The beautiful building has previously served as both a bishop's palace and a brothel; its array of green plants shields the interior from the street, while the large fireplace provides a cosy touch in winter. The tables are set well apart from each other, so there is no danger of your conversation being overheard by the neighbours. The food comprises simple aromatic local dishes, with no great sophistication but an original modern twist. The lunchtime menu of the day costs €14, while the others range from €20 to €40.

ⓔ |O| La Régalade

28 rue Poissonnerie.
☎04.90.76.15.71
Closed Sun; Tues.

This restaurant-*épicerie*-wine cellar seems to have been transported straight from the 1960s, with its collection of arm-chairs, posters, advertising signs and vinyl records that give this hideaway a special atmosphere, making it seem sunny on even a cloudy day. The dishes of the day (€10–12), prepared by the owner, are similarly imbued with character. You can enjoy lasagne with ceps or an olive *confit*, with an old record playing in the back-ground, either in the offbeat bar lined with regular customers or the attractive second room, decorated with Chinese lanterns, as if every day were Bastille Day. There is also a small terrace, guaranteed to enliven this part of old Cavaillon in summer.

Cheval-Blanc
84460 (5km SE)

ⓔ |O| L'Auberge de Cheval-Blanc

On the D973, going in the direction of Pertuis.
☎04.32.50.18.55
Closed Mon evening; Tues; Wed lunchtime.

This restaurant is unexceptional on the outside, but the quality of the cook-ing and fresh ingredients found inside is talked about far and wide. Its tables, covered with long orange tablecloths, are set out both in a simple dining room with colourful fabrics on the wall and on a terrace to the rear. The food on offer is mainly Provençal but not exclusively so, as the chef, Hervé Perrasse, has plenty of experience of other climes, includ-ing a ten-year spell with *Yvan* in Paris, and can endow even the humblest dish with an invigoratingly original touch. For an astonishing mixture of flavours and aromas, try his pork couscous or roasted cinnamon with honey and spices (to name just two examples). The week-day lunchtime menu costs €20, with a choice of other menus at €23–45.

Chapelle-en-Valgaudemar (La)
05800

ⓔ 🏠 |O| Hôtel-restaurant du Mont-Olan**

It's right in the centre of town.
☎04.92.55.23.03 🖷04.92.55.34.58
Closed 1 May–4 Oct. **TV. Car park.**

Chalet-style hotel where all the rooms look out towards the soaring peaks that dominate the village. Monsieur and Mme Voltan's large dining room has a panoramic view of the fast-flowing Navette River. You'll consume huge quantities of robust food – potato pie, ravioli with honey, etc – perfect to build up your strength for an assault on the mountains. Menus go for €11.50–24; à la carte around €23. Comfortable doubles go for €43–45 with shower/wc or bath. Credit cards not accepted.

Chauffayer
05800 (22km SW)

ⓔ 🎿 🏠 |O| Le Bercail**

It's on the N85, the route de Napoléon, on the right on the road to Gap.
☎04.92.55.22.21 🖷04.92.55.31.55
Closed Sun evening; 1 Nov–1 Dec. **TV. Car park.**

This hotel-restaurant offers good value for money, with prettily decorated, com-fortable rooms – doubles €40–50 with shower/wc or bath. The large dining room has a lovely Provençal feel and there's a shaded terrace filled with glorious gera-niums. The cuisine is regional and clas-sic, with menus at €17–32; scallops and balsamic vinegar, pan-fried lamb, duck terrine with green pepper, trout *meunière* and ravioli are the specialities. There's also a *menu terroir* at €22. *Free coffee offered to our readers on presentation of this guide.*

ⓔ 🎿 🏠 |O| Le Château des Herbeys***

Head towards Saint-Firmin, then take the route de Gap and you'll see the sign on the left.
☎04.92.55.26.83 🖷04.92.55.29.66
Closed Tues except in school holidays; mid-Nov to mid-April. **TV. High chairs available. Swimming pool. Car park.**

Looking out over the route that Napoleon took on his return from Elba, stands this noble and beautiful residence surrounded by substantial grounds. The rooms are high-ceilinged and luxurious, with parquet floors, plush and tasteful fabrics and splendid bathrooms. The "Roy" room is a truly royal suite with a canopied bed, sitting room and Jacuzzi; it's also the most expensive. Doubles with bath will set you back €61–115; half board from €60–90. In the park there is a tennis court, mini-golf, fountain, giant chess set, swimming pool and a terrace looking out over the valley. The restaurant offers a range of menus €19.50–38 listing such dishes as foie gras with figs in port, snails, lamb roasted with garlic, local cheeses and home-made desserts. You would do well to reserve. *Free coffee or digestif offered to our readers on presentation of this guide.*

Château-Arnoux
04160

@ |●| L'Oustaou de la Foun

It's 2km from the centre of town on the N85, on the route de Sisteron.
℡04.92.62.65.30
Closed *Sun evening; Mon; a week in Jan; June; All Saints'.* **Disabled access.**

This restaurant, which occupies a Provençal hacienda, manages to be chic yet relaxed. The young chef, who comes from a family of farmers and *charcutiers*, really knows his stuff, and he organizes cookery courses. Menus €20–49; his dishes balance fine ingredients and create delightful flavour combinations. The side dishes are unusual while remaining simple.

Aubignosc
04200 (3km NW)

@ ☎ |●| La Magnanerie

Les Fillières; it's on the N85, 3km from Château-Arnoux.
℡04.92.62.60.11 ℗04.92.62.63.05
Closed *Sun evening; Mon; Thurs evening; Jan; a week in early Sept; 22–30 Dec.*
Disabled access. TV. High chairs available. Car park.

An old silk house has been turned into a quality hotel-restaurant by the Paroche family. There are eight quiet and elegant rooms named after flowers of the region; doubles with shower/wc or bath €43–58. The rooms at the back are so pleasant and

quiet that you completely forget about the main road at the front of the hotel. Original dishes with flavoursome ingredients are on offer in the elegant dining room; menus start at €18 (weekday lunchtime), with others €27–40. The warm atmosphere and genuine concern of the owners for the welfare of their guests are what make this place special.

Cogolin
83310

@ 🎿 ☎ |●| Coq'Hôtel

Place de la Mairie.
℡04.94.54.13.71 ℗04.94.54.03.06
ⓦwww.coqhotel.com
Restaurant closed *Fri.* **Closed** *Jan.* **Car park.**

This family hotel is not only pleasant but also relatively easy on the pocket; doubles go for €48–68 depending on the facilities and season. It also has a highly appropriate name, given its splendid array of depictions of cockerels in all shapes and sizes. The bedrooms, some with their own terrace, have been renovated in typical Provençal style; the ones overlooking the terrace are a bit noisy, although they are air-conditioned and soundproofed. No. 12 is particularly appealing. Breakfast is served in a pretty garden, and they serve a choice of menus €16–26. *10% discount on the price of a room (1 Oct–30 March) offered to our readers on presentation of this guide.*

@ |●| L'Olivier sur le Port

Quai La Galiote, Marines de Cogolin.
℡04.94.56.19.27
Closed *lunchtimes in July/Aug; Mon and Tues lunchtimes (out of season); mid-Nov to mid-Feb.* **Disabled access.**

This delightful restaurant undoubtedly offers the best value for money in the vicinity, which has made it extremely popular – so booking is essential (ask for a table on the pretty terrace). Its menus cost €18, €23 and €39, and even the cheapest (also served in the evening) is much more than mere bait for tourists; the tuna *tartare* and mullet with baby vegetables are excellent – so just imagine what the more expensive menus are like. And there's an extra bonus of olives picked from the tree that gives the restaurant its name. All this, plus charming service.

Collobrières

83610

⊛ ⅔ 🛏 |O| **Hôtel-restaurant des Maures**

19 bd. Lazare-Carnot.
☏04.94.48.07.10

A genuine family restaurant that's popular with the locals – everyone crowds in to watch the football on weekday evenings. The simple rooms cost €20 with shower (toilets on the landing) – at that price you can't argue. Nicely cooked Provençal cuisine is served in gargantuan portions on a range of menus €10–39. There's a charming terrace by the river. *Free coffee offered to our readers on presentation of this guide.*

⊛ ⅔ |O| **La Petite Fontaine**

Place de la République.
☏04.94.48.00.12
Closed *Sun evening; Mon; winter school holidays; 15–30 Sept.* **High chairs available.**

One of the best places for miles around, in a peaceful village in the Maures mountains. This rustic restaurant is decorated with old farming implements and the cooking is delicious: *fricassée* of chicken with garlic, rabbit in white wine, beef *daube à la provençale*, duck breast with ceps. Weekday menu costs €23, with another menu at €26. They serve wine from the local cooperative by the glass. It's so popular that reservations are absolutely essential. *Free digestif offered to our readers on presentation of this guide.*

Comps-sur-Artuby

83840

⊛ 🛏 |O| ⅔ **Grand Hôtel Bain**✶✶

It's between Draguignan and Castellane.
☏04.94.76.90.06 ⊕04.94.76.92.24
ⓦwww.grand-hotel-bain.fr
Closed *mid-Nov to Christmas.* **TV. High chairs available. Car park.**

The Bain family has owned this hotel since 1737. Today it's frequented by local hunters, who relish the hearty local dishes offered on the menus, €13–35: truffle pâté, omelettes with truffles (in season), trout with basil in pastry, rabbit with tarragon, *daube à la provençale*, roast rack of lamb and goat's cheese. Pleasant rooms cost €48–52

with shower/wc or with bath; half board €48 per person. *Free coffee offered to our readers on presentation of this guide.*

Cotignac

83570

⊛ |O| **La Table de la Fontaine**

27 cours Gambetta.
☏04.94.04.79.13
Closed *Mon.*

This beautiful terrace under the plane tree on the village's main square guarantees a fine meal. At lunchtime, you can have a set menu (€13.50) comprising a starter and main course, although the copious salad on offer with fish or meat (€11) may well prove sufficient. At dinner, the three-course menus (€28 and €36) provide excellent value for money, with interesting dishes like aubergine biscuits, home-made *anchoïade*, mullet and sweetbreads. The terrace is tastefully arranged, the service is attentive and the food refreshingly light.

Digne-les-Bains

04000

⊛ 🛏 |O| ⅔ **L'Origan**

6 rue Pied-de-Ville; in the pedestrianized area.
☏and ⊕04.92.31.62.13
ⓦwww.hotel-restaurant.net/origan
Closed *Mon; last fortnight in Feb; at Christmas.*

A restaurant in the heart of the old quarter of the spa town. Delicious Provençal food is served on the weekday lunch menu €11 and other menus up to €30. They have some simple, well-kept rooms with basin or shower (wc on the landing) for a very reasonable rate of €25–30. *Free house apéritif offered to our readers on presentation of this guide.*

⊛ ⅔ 🛏 |O| **Hôtel and Pension Villa Gaïa**✶✶✶

Route de Nice; it's 3km from the centre on the Nice road.
☏04.92.31.21.60 ⊕04.92.31.20.12
ⓦwww.hotelvillagaia.fr
Closed *Sun evening (except in July and Aug); early Nov to mid-April.* **Open** *evenings only from 8pm.* **Disabled access. Car park.**

This quiet hotel, an impressive building set in shady, green grounds, was converted from an old convalescent home and still keeps to some of the old rules. Dinner is served at the same time every night, and there's a single menu (€26; reservations preferred) featuring superb regional dishes based on seasonal ingredients – and they make their own bread. You dine on the terrace, in the library or the salon. Breakfast is magnificent, served with green tomato jam and the newspapers – you can choose where you wish to eat it. Rooms are €65–95 with shower or bath; half board, which is recommended in summer, costs €152 per person for three days. *Free upgrade (according to availability), or free house apéritif or coffee offered to our readers on presentation of this guide.*

ⓔ ♠ |●| Hôtel du Grand Paris****

19 bd. Thiers.
ⓣ04.92.31.11.15 ⓕ04.92.32.32.82
ⓦwww.chateauxhotels.com/grandparis
Closed *Mon and Tues lunchtimes (out of season); 1 Dec–1 March.* **TV. Pay car park.**

Stylish hotel that has been converted from a seventeenth-century convent. The welcome is slightly formal but the place oozes discreet charm. The chef prepares classic dishes using good ingredients: try the pigeon, the *brandade* of peppers or the delicious *mignonette* of lamb. Menus €23–64 or around €41 à la carte. Lovely, comfortable double rooms with shower/wc or bath go for €80–145. The decoration in no. 2 is particularly nice – it's all in yellow, and there's a terrace and a TV cleverly hidden in an old piece of furniture.

Draguignan
83300

ⓔ |●| Le Domino

28 av. Carnot; it's on the main street.
ⓣ04.94.67.15.33
Closed *Sat lunch; Sun; Mon; a fortnight around Easter; early May; first fortnight in Nov.*

This building has a lot of character and so does the stylish Tex-Mex restaurant inside. À la carte you'll pay around €20–25 per person for salads, spiced-up meat dishes and Mexican specialities such as chicken and beef fajitas and spare ribs. Dish of the day costs €10. You can dine on the veranda or out under the palm trees. Customers are greeted with kindness and can look forward to attentive service.

Embrun
05200

ⓔ ⌖ ♠ |●| Hôtel de la Mairie**

Place de la Mairie or place Barthelon.
ⓣ04.92.43.20.65
ⓦwww.hoteldelamairie.com
Closed *Sun evening and Mon (in winter); 1–20 May; Oct; Nov.* **Disabled access. TV. High chairs available. Pay car park.**

This hotel is a model of its type, with a convivial brasserie, high-quality food and competent, charming staff. It's a favourite with locals for an evening drink or Sunday lunch. Menus €16–23; specialities include ravioli with morel sauce, fillet of pike-perch with red butter and an excellent duck *confit*. Clean, bright rooms are €47–50 for a double with shower/wc or bath; choose nos. 20, 28 or 35 as they are bigger and quieter (they do not look out onto the square). *Free coffee offered to our readers on presentation of this guide.*

ⓔ |●| Restaurant Pascal

Hameau de Caléyère; from Embrun take the pretty road to Caléyère and it's in a road to the right.
ⓣ04.92.43.00.69
Closed *Sat lunch (outside school holidays); Sept.*

It's not the place for a romantic *tête-à-tête*, but the family atmosphere is convivial and infectious – you'll leave in a good mood. The *patronne* greets all her customers by shaking their hand. There's only one menu, at €11, and it's substantial. The vegetables, eggs and meats all come from local farms. The local *digestif* is called *vipérine* – it bites like a snake. Credit cards not accepted.

Saint-Sauveur
05200 (10km SE)

ⓔ |●| Restaurant Les Manins

Les Manins; take the road to Les Orres and it's sign-posted off to the left – don't take the ones for St-Sauveur.
ⓣ04.92.43.09.27
Open *noon–3pm and 6–9pm from early July to mid-Sept; the rest of the year by reservation only.* **Closed** *end of May/early June; mid-Sept to mid-Oct.* **High chairs and books available.**

Fantastic restaurant with breathtaking views from the terrace looking down at Lac de Serre-Ponçon and Embrun. Architect Eric Boissel built this elegant wooden structure with his own hands, and designed all the furniture including the chairs, on which guests sit and enjoy Nicole's cooking. Try *grand mézé*, a complete Middle Eastern meal with individual dishes of red peppers, tzatziki, hummus, köfte, feta cheese, fresh onions, tapenade and the like. They also do mixed salads, substantial pizzas and good crêpes, and there's a splendid crumble for dessert. Pizzas are about €9; expect to pay €22 à la carte. Credit cards not accepted.

Crévoux
05200 (15km E)

@ ⦁ |⦿| **L'Auberge**

Le Chef-lieu; it's at the top of the village opposite the teleski.
☎ 04.92.43.18.18
@ auberge.crevoux@wanadoo.fr
Closed Oct. **Restaurant closed** *Wed and Thurs during April–June (except public holidays); Sept; Nov; Dec.* **Car park.**

An excellent spot at the foot of the ski runs run by two young local brothers. The clean rooms are freshly decorated and warm, though they're not all huge; €22.50 per person bed and breakfast, €33 per person half board or €41.50 full board. Special rates are available for children. The dining room is very spacious and the dishes are typical of the area with menus €14–25: egg fondue with blue cheese sauce, cheese turnovers, trout with creamed peppers, pork *filet mignon* with blue cheese crust. If you want information about the walking trails, don't hesitate to ask the owners who know the area well.

Entrecasteaux
83570

@ 🎋 |⦿| **La Fourchette**

Le Courtil; it's next to the church in the old town.
☎ 04.94.04.42.78
Closed *Mon; Tues; Dec–Feb.* **High chairs available.**

In the shadow of the famous château, this place attracts gourmet travellers who enjoy delicious food while admiring the wonderful view from the terrace. Chef Pierre Nicolas runs the kitchens while his American wife greets you. Simple, quality cooking and honest

prices: menus are €17 (weekday lunch-times) and €26, or €35 à la carte. Dishes include foie gras cannelloni and sautéed king scallops with truffles. *Free coffee offered to our readers on presentation of this guide.*

Èze
06360

@ 🎋 ⦁ |⦿| **Hermitage du Col d'Èze★★**

Grande Corniche; from Èze, take the D46 and then the Grande Corniche; it's 500m on the left.
☎ 04.93.41.00.68 ℗ 04.93.41.24.05
ⓦ www.eze.riviera.com
Closed *early Dec to end of Jan.* **Open** *7.30–8.30pm for residents only.* **TV. High chairs and games available. Swimming pool. Car park.**

A place in which to relax in peace and quiet. The swimming pool will ease your aching limbs after a mountain walk – the location is at the start of a lot of trails. There is a splendid view of the southern Alps and the cooler air at this altitude provides relief from the heat of the coast. Doubles cost €35–89 with shower/wc or bath; half board is €47.50–69 per person. Choose one of the newly renovated rooms. They serve a weekday lunch menu for €15 and another menu for €25. *Free house apéritif offered to our readers on presentation of this guide.*

Fayence
83440

@ 🎋 ⦁ **Hôtel La Sousto**

4 rue du Paty.
☎ 04.94.76.02.16
@ hotel.sousto@wanadoo.fr
Closed *a week in June; Nov school holiday.*

You get the best of Provence in this attractive little hotel in the centre of an old village above the valley. The simply furnished rooms have a hotplate, fridge and basin; some also have a shower. Each room has personality – no. 5 has a sunny little terrace overlooking the valley. Doubles with shower/wc are priced at €44. *10% discount on the room rate for a stay of at least two consecutive nights (except July/Aug) offered to our readers on presentation of this guide.*

Callian

83440 (8km E)

🅰 ♨ 🏠 |●| Auberge des Mourgues**

17 chemin des Mourgues; take the D19, then the D56; it's below the village.
☎04.94.76.53.99 ☏04.94.39.11.32
🌐www.aubergedesmourgues.com
Restaurant closed Mon. **Closed** end of the year (telephone for details). **TV. Swimming pool.**

This is a pretty, quiet country inn, complete with a swimming pool and grounds, run by a delightful man from La Réunion with a mischievous sense of humour. The rooms have all been tastefully renovated. Double rooms cost €45–69, depending on the season and degree of comfort. The food is simple but satisfying, with special emphasis on fish dishes. *Free house apéritif offered to our readers on presentation of this guide.*

Fontaine-de-Vaucluse

84800

🅰 ♨ 🏠 Hôtel du Poète***

☎04.90.20.34.05 ☏04.90.20.34.08
🌐www.hoteldupoete.com
Closed Jan. **TV. Swimming pool. Pay car park.**

As its name suggests, this quiet hotel is unashamedly romantic, in keeping with its setting surrounded on all sides by the waters of the river. Poeticism is not allowed to exclude comfort, however, and the thoughtfully conceived rooms are all equipped with air-conditioning, good bedding, a mini-bar and a splendid bathroom. Reckon on €90–115 for a double room. There is also an impressive room for the superb breakfast buffet based on local produce (€16), with a terrace on the river bank. *10% discount on the price of a room offered to our readers on presentation of this guide.*

Fontvieille

13990

🅰 ♨ 🏠 Hôtel Le Daudet***

7 av. de Montmajour; it's on the way out of the village on the road to Arles.

☎04.90.54.76.06 ☏04.90.54.76.95
Closed 1 Oct–1 April. **Swimming pool.** Car park.

This new hotel is built around a patio and offers straightforward rooms with terrace; doubles €57–65 with shower/wc or bath. There's a swimming pool among the pine trees. *Free house apéritif or coffee offered to our readers on presentation of this guide.*

🅰 🏠 |●| 🅰 La Peiriero

34 av. des Baux.
☎04.90.54.76.10 ☏04.90.54.62.60
🌐www.hotel-peiriero.com
Closed Easter; early Nov. **TV. Disabled access. High chairs and games available. Swimming pool. Car park.**

This hotel has a forbiddlingly austere façade but inside it's exceptionally welcoming. It has recently been superbly refurbished and redecorated in pure Provençal style and has a lovely pool. Double rooms with bathroom go for €84–118. There's a great atmosphere (both laid-back and chic) and it's good value for money, including the single menu for €24. You can also order refreshing snacks when you are lounging outside under a parasol. The free car park has a security system. *Free Kir offered to our readers on presentation of this guide.*

🅰 🅰 |●| La Cuisine au Planet

144 Grand'Rue; it's in the old village.
☎and ☏04.90.54.63.97
Closed Mon lunchtime (and evening in winter); Feb; Nov.

This charming, creeper-covered restaurant is run by a couple who are crazy about the area and prepare local cuisine with a light touch all their own. Menus, at €25 and €31, list superb dishes. There's also a lunch menu at €15 in the summer. Impressive wine list. *Free house aperitif, coffee or liqueur offered to our readers on presentation of this guide.*

Forcalquier

04300

🅰 🏠 🅰 Auberge Charembeau**

Route de Niozelles; it's 3.5km out of town on the N100 in the direction of Niozelles.
☎04.92.70.91.70 ☏04.92.70.81.83
🌐www.charembeau.com

Closed *mid-Nov to mid-Feb.* **Disabled access. TV. High chairs and games available. Swimming pool. Car park.**

This hotel occupies a converted eighteenth-century farm in the middle of a seven-hectare expanse of hills and meadows. It's a lovely place to stay, looking down over the valley with a swimming pool and bike rental. Ten freshly decorated, attractive rooms: some have balconies, others wide terraces and all have good facilities. One room has been converted for disabled visitors. Doubles go for €54–57 with shower/wc, or €79–87 with bath, depending on the season. Self-catering apartments (with bedroom and kitchenette) for two to five people cost €460–790. On fine days, breakfast is served in the park under the trees. *Free half-day rental of two bikes offered to our readers on presentation of this guide.*

Mane
04300 (5km SW)

⚛ ⬆ Le Mas du Pont Roman**

Campagne la Laye, chemin de Châteauneuf; on the outskirts of the town, on the N100.
☎04.92.75.49.46 ℱ04.92.75.36.73
ⓦwww.ifrance.com/pontroman/
Disabled access. Swimming pool. Car park.

This hotel is set in the heart of the countryside, sufficiently far from the road to fully enjoy the tranquillity of this charming, intelligently restored seventeenth-century house. It has a mere ten roooms (€70), all different but meticulously decorated, with either a shower/wc or bath. There are two swimming pools – one in the garden, the other inside the house, with a sauna and other spa facilities. The service is as appealing as the prices.

Lardiers
04230 (18km NW)

⚛ |●| Le Café de la Lavande

Take the D950 towards Banon, and at Notre Dame turn right onto the D12 towards Saumane.
☎04.92.73.31.52
Closed *Tues evening; Wed; Feb school holiday; 15 Nov–10 Dec.*

Old-fashioned country café in a village that looks out to the Lure mountains. Regulars drop in for a morning glass of white wine or a pastis in the evening, but it's worth taking the time for a meal (menu

€21). It's simple food, all fresh and good: duck with cherries, lamb stew, creamed salt cod. Space is limited so reservations are essential. Credit cards not accepted.

Saint-Étienne-Les-Orgues
04230 (21km N)

⚛ |●| Au Coquelicot

Place des Ormeaux; take the D12.
☎04.92.73.15.41
Closed *Mon, from mid-June to mid-Sept; Tues, the rest of the year.* **Disabled access.**

This small restaurant with a minimalist design is resolutely trendy, even down to the background music. Some may find this out of place on such a typically Provençal square, but they should be quickly reassured by the selection of small, well-conceived fresh dishes on the (short) menus (which change every month), as well as by the cheerful young owner. The weekday lunchtime menu costs €16, and there are others at €23–25.

Fréjus
83600

⚛ ⬆ Auberge de jeunesse

627 chemin du Counillier; 2km from the old town; by train, get off at Saint-Raphaël station, then go to the bus station, from where a bus will take you to the hostel from platform no. 7 at 6pm. There's also a bus leaving in the morning but it drops you off 800m from the hostel.
☎04.94.53.18.75 ℱ 04.94.53.25.86
ⓦwww.fuaj.org
Closed *11 Nov to 31 Jan.* **Open** *8–11am and 7.30–8.30pm.*

A very pleasant hostel, situated in a seven-hectare park. It's 4.5km from the beach but only a few minutes from old Fréjus; there's a bus every morning to take you to either the train station or the beach. A night in a four- or five-bed dormitory (men and women separate) costs €13 or €15, including breakfast. FUAJ card is compulsory (you can buy it on site). Unfortunately, there's a strict curfew at 10.30pm. Buses leave each morning for the station or the beach.

⚛ ⬆ Hôtel Oasis**

Impasse J.B. Charcot, Fréjus Plage; 1.5km from the centre of town.

PROVENCE-ALPES-CÔTE D'AZUR

☎04.94.51.50.44 ⒻAX04.94.53.01.04
🌐www.hotel-oasis.net
Closed *11 Nov–31 Jan.* **TV. Car park.**

A small, quiet 1950s building in a cul-de-sac five minutes from the beach. It's run by a young couple who welcome you like family friends. The rooms are varied – old-fashioned wallpaper in some, pretty Provençal décor in others – and though not big, they're more than adequate and have recently been equipped with air-conditioning. Doubles cost €39–64 depending on the level of comfort and the season. Breakfast is served on the terrace under an awning.

@ 🛉 🏠 |●| Hôtel Arena***

139 rue du Général-de-Gaulle; it's next to place Agricola.
☎04.94.17.09.40 ⒻAX04.94.52.01.52
🌐www.arena-hotel.com
Restaurant closed *Mon (1 Nov–15 March).*
Disabled access. TV. High chairs available.
Swimming pool. Pay car park.

A lovely place if you're not on a tight budget. It's an old establishment that's been attractively and tastefully renovated, and the décor is pure Provence: warm colours on the walls, mosaic floors and painted furniture. The rooms (€80–160 with shower/wc or bath) aren't huge but they're very pretty, air-conditioned and soundproofed. There's a lush garden and a swimming pool. The flavoursome cuisine consists of mainly Mediterranean dishes with a dash of individuality. Menus start at €25 (weekday lunchtimes), and there are others at €35–58. *Free coffee offered to our readers on presentation of this guide.*

Saint-Raphaël
83700 (3km E)

@ 🛉 🏠 Le Thimothée**

375 bd. Christian-Lafon; it's 1.5km from the centre in the Plaines district.
☎04.94.40.49.49 ⒻAX04.94.19.41.92
🌐www.thimothee.com
Closed *Jan.* **TV. Car park.**

A nineteenth-century bourgeois villa in a quiet, residential district that's several minutes from the sea. This charming hotel is surrounded by grounds with lots of ancient trees. All rooms have TV and mini-bar and some have air-conditioning; doubles €35–75 according to the season. Rooms 22 and 21 have balconies and views over the sea. *10% discount on the*

room rate (out of season) offered to our readers on presentation of this guide.

@ |●| Côté Jardin

Rue du 11-Novembre-1943; in Agay, some 10km from Saint-Raphaël via the N98 in the direction of Cannes.
☎04.94.82.79.98
Closed *early Nov to early Feb.*

It is easy to see that in this restaurant things are done thoroughly, from the delightfully inviting little Provençal-style dining room to the glorious garden, which has been selected as the best flower garden in the whole town. What about the cooking? It's a feast for the eyes, firstly, and then proves to be delicious, creative and prepared with love, or even passion. Weekday lunchtime menu €15, then others from €26 to €55; there's a huge choice, so there is bound to be something for every taste. This restaurant with its charming welcome has earned a great reputation, and it is fully justified. It's advisable to book.

Gap
05000

@ 🛉 Hôtel Porte-Colombe**

4 pl. Frédéric-Euzières; near the pedestrian area.
☎04.92.51.04.13 ⒻAX04.92.52.42.50
Closed *2–18 Jan; 30 April–23 May.* **Hotel open** *all year.* **Restaurant open** *evenings (Mon–Thurs).* **TV. High chairs available. Pay car park.**

Don't let the electric shutters and cable TV distract you from the beautiful view of Gap and its cathedral. This hotel is in a modern, unappealing building but the rooms are individualized and comfortable with double-glazing – most have been refurbished and go for €46–49 for a double with shower/wc or bath. The welcome is a bit lacking in warmth. *10% discount (Oct–June) offered to our readers on presentation of this guide.*

@ 🛉 |●| Le Tourton des Alpes

1 rue des Cordiers.
☎04.92.53.90.91
Closed *Sun; Mon; a weekend June to early July.* **High chairs available.**

A well-established, successful restaurant that does the region's best *tourtons*

– potato fritters, served here with green salad and raw ham. They're included in the menus at €16.70–22.50, or available to order à la carte – portions are generous, service fast and you can eat as many as you want. The setting is a large, vaulted dining room with bare stone walls. The simple décor is freshened by a fountain and enlivened by the smiles of the waiting staff. If you're tempted, there's a shop where they sell local specialities. *Free coffee offered to our readers on presentation of this guide.*

@ |●| Les Olivades

Malcombe on the Veynes road. Take the Veynes/Valence road; at the second roundabout, look for the signs to Les Olivades on the right.
☏04.92.52.66.80
Closed Sun evening; Mon. **Disabled access. High chairs available.**

This place overlooks Gap and the neighbouring mountains. It has a huge terrace in dark brown wood, and the tall trees provide shade. If the weather gets bad, you can take refuge in the old sheep shelter with its vaulted ceilings. The regional dishes are deliciously prepared and infused with Provençal flavours: fillet of beef in pastry with morels, cheese-filled ravioli with honey butter, roast *noisette* of lamb. Simple, elegant fare which isn't too rich or too heavy – just delicious. The young owners provide friendly, diligent service and the menus, €17–26, offer good value for money.

@ |●| La Musardière

3 pl. du Revelly.
☏04.92.51.56.15
Closed Tues; Wed; 20–30 June; 2–10 Nov.

Many of the dishes at this spruce, pretty restaurant are traditional Alsatian specialities – the owners come from that part of the world. The substantial *menu Alsacien* includes knuckle of pork braised in beer, fish *choucroute* and fillet of beef with morels. Courteous service from Madame and menus priced at €19.50–27.

@ |●| Restaurant Le Pasturier

18 rue Pérolière.
☏04.92.53.69.29
Closed Sun and Mon (except public holidays); first fortnight in July; second week Sept.

The elegant, intimate atmosphere at this restaurant makes it ideal for a romantic dinner. The owners are lively and welcoming, and chef Pascal Dorche changes his menus frequently, sometimes producing unusual dishes. His honest cooking is more than satisfying with menus €25–62 – duck foie gras, rack of lamb, wild boar ham; à la carte around €51. There's a small terrace open in summer.

Laye

05500 (11.5km N)

@ 🎿 |●| Le Petit Renard

It's in the ski resort.
☏04.92.50.06.20
Closed Wed, from spring to autumn; 15 Nov–15 Dec. **Disabled access. High chairs and games available.**

The locals flood in to this restaurant which offers the best value for money in town as well as speedy, friendly service. Classic regional dishes including *tourtons*, ravioli and fish *choucroute*, along with roast pigeon and house foie gras. The raclettes and fondues are good – the Savoyard cheese variety includes ceps. The cheapest menu at €14 is served at lunchtime during the week, with other menus €18.50–36. The large dining room has a lovely atmosphere: it's like a room in a spacious chalet and it has a mezzanine. In summer, the terrace offers a ravishing view and there's a children's games corner. *Free Kir royal offered to our readers on presentation of this guide.*

@ |●| Restaurant La Laiterie du Col Bayard

Take the N85 from Gap to Grenoble and follow the signs. It's 11km along on the left.
☏04.92.50.50.06
Closed Mon; Tues, Wed and Thurs evenings (except school holidays and public holidays); 11 Nov–20 Dec. **Disabled access. High chairs and games available.**

The farmer, the farmer's son and the farmer's grandson run this place – and they've been running it since 1935. They serve platters of charcuterie, salads with blue cheese sauce, cheese kebabs, the *plateau Champsaurin* (which offers a selection of ten different cheeses) and a variety of generous salads. There's a weekday lunch *formule* at €12, and a choice of menus at €16–35.

Montgardin

05230 (12km E)

✉ 🏠 |◉| L'Auberge du Moulin

Take the N94 in the direction of Embrun and it's on the right in the village.
☎04.92.50.32.98
Closed *Sun evening and Mon; reservations only.* **TV.**

Known locally as the Three Sisters, this place is run by three women who are wonderful cooks. Many of the superb local dishes feature duck or goose. The single menu at €23 is satisfying and skilfully prepared; it lists such dishes as gâteau of spleen and duck liver, *fricassée* of whole duckling cooked *coq au vin* style, fresh cheese with honey and a good *bavarois*. Two self-catering studios are available at €45 per person (maximum four persons). There's a family atmosphere in the pretty rustic dining room and not many tables (just fifteen covers). Credit cards not accepted.

Saint-Julien-en-Champsaur

05500 (20km NE)

✉ 🎋 🏠 |◉| Les Chênets

Take the Grenoble road to Fare, then turn right towards Saint-Bonnet and Saint-Julien.
☎04.92.50.03.15 ☎04.92.50.73.06
Closed *Wed and Sun evening (out of season); April; 12 Nov–27 Dec.* **High chairs available.**

A mountain chalet with a warm family feeling. Simple double rooms with shower/wc or bath go for €35.50–41.50. The cuisine is better than good and focuses on regional dishes. Try the *tourtons* (potato fritters with ham and salad), goat's cheese ravioli and *crème brûlée* for dessert. They also do a mean upside-down tart of hot foie gras. Perfectly ripened cheeses, excellent home-made desserts and a good wine list. Weekday menu costs €17, with other menus at €25 and €34. Credit cards not accepted. *Free house apéritif offered to our readers on presentation of this guide.*

Gordes

84220

✉ 🏠 |◉| Auberge de Carcarille**

Les Gervais; it's 2km below Gordes on the D2 in the direction of Joucas.

☎04.90.72.02.63 ☎04.90.72.05.74
🌐www.auberge-carcarille.com
Closed *Fri (lunchtime only April–Sept); Dec; Jan.* **Disabled access. TV. High chairs and games available. Swimming pool. Car park.**

A welcoming inn located at the foot of the village. The dining room is quite elegant and the cuisine is fine with menus €18–40: saddle of rabbit with sage, tripe and so on. Very appealing rooms with terrace or balcony; doubles €60–80 with bathroom. Half board, compulsory between April and September, is €68–78 per person. It's good value for this part of the world.

✉ 🏠 Hôtel Le Mas de la Sénancole***

Imberts; 5km outside Gordes on the D2.
☎04.90.76.76.55 ☎04.90.76.70.44
🌐www.mas-de-la-senancole.com
Disabled access. TV. High chairs available. Swimming pool. Car park.

Exceptionally comfortable doubles, decorated with splashes of local colour, go for €79–135 with shower/wc or bath depending on the season; half board, compulsory in July and August, costs €147 per person. There are also family rooms with small terrace, a restaurant, nice garden and a swimming pool surrounded by greenery.

✉ 🎋 🏠 Le Mas des Romarins

Route de Sénanque, lieu-dit l'Enclos.
☎04.90.72.12.13
🌐www.hoteldesromarins.com
Closed *mid-Nov to mid-March (except during Christmas and New Year holidays).*

This hotel is essentially modest, making no effort to match plusher establishments at their own game, but it is none the worse for that and has many charming assets that are all its own. Most of the rooms offer a spectacular view, as does the terrace, where guests can enjoy a simple but tasty candle-lit dinner several nights a week (for €26). Double rooms cost €92–120. *10% discount on the price of a room offered to our readers on presentation of this guide.*

✉ |◉| L'Estellan

Hameau des Imberts, route des Gordes.
☎04.90.72.04.90
Closed *Wed in Oct–Feb; Jan.*

This is a sophisticated bistro with original décor based on contemporary materials and colour schemes. It is best appreciated at night or out of season, as the set lunchtime menu (main course plus dessert for €19) is not the best showcase for the talents of a chef devoted to combining the tastes and aromas of exquisitely fresh local ingredients. There is another, more complete menu costing €34. On fine days, you can eat alongside the back garden on a terrace decorated in typical local style, with charming terracotta flowerpots and cruets (also on sale in a shop in the village run by the owner). The service from the young staff is a bit offhand.

Murs
84220 (8.5km NE)

ⓒ 🏠 |●| Le Crillon

Take the D15 and it's in the middle of the village.
☏04.90.72.60.31 🖷04.90.72.63.12
🌐www.lecrillon.com
Closed *Thurs (lunchtime in season); 5 Jan–8 March.* **TV. High chairs available. Car park.**

Sweet doubles, nicely painted and furnished with tasteful pieces, cost €50–65 with shower/wc or bath; breakfast at €7. The pleasant dining room offers a weekday lunch menu for €14, then others €22–35. There are some lovely country-style dishes which are made using wild mushrooms, truffles or game in season: *tournedos* with morels, cod with truffles – for lovers of country fare.

Goult
84220

ⓒ |●| Auberge Le Fiacre

Quartier Pied-Rousset; it's 3.5km out of the village on the N100 in the direction of Apt.
☏04.90.72.26.31
Closed *Wed; Thurs (in season); Sun evening (out of season); 11 Nov–15 Dec.* **Car park.**

An excellent restaurant serving light, inventive Provençal cooking using local produce. The crayfish ravioli, rack of lamb, salt cod *tian* and pan-fried duck foie gras are fabulous; they also do game in autumn. In summer you can dine outside under the lime trees, where you're serenaded by a chorus of cicadas. Menus – €17 (weekday lunchtimes), or €28 and €33 at dinner, and children's menu €10 – offer good value for money. This is a super place.

ⓒ |●| La Terrasse

Rue de la République.
☏04.90.72.20.20
Closed *Tues; 1 Nov–28 Feb.*

The terrace is on the first floor and overlooks the square car park. World décor with Indian and Thai fabrics on the walls, hammocks swinging from the ceiling, and Indonesian fans; it works really well, as does the fine, carefully prepared cooking. There are no set menus but individual dishes cost €9–15 and you can reckon on around €24 for a full meal. Unsurprisingly, there are lots of tourists.

Beaumettes
84220 (3km W)

ⓒ 🍴 |●| Restaurant La Remise

Take the N100 and it's in the middle of the village.
☏04.90.72.23.05
Closed *Tues evening (out of season); Wed; 20 Dec–20 Feb.* **Disabled access.**

A nice, unpretentious country restaurant with a number of specialities including *pieds-paquets à la marseillaise* and monkfish fillet with tarragon. Menus are €15–35, children's menu €9.20; individual dishes are served at lunchtime for €11. *Free coffee offered to our readers on presentation of this guide.*

Gourdon
06620

ⓒ |●| Au Vieux Four

Rue Basse; it's a turning off to the left as you come into the village.
☏04.93.09.68.60
Closed *evenings; Mon; mid-Nov to mid-Dec.*

A pleasant, welcoming place for a spot of lunch after a hike through the gorges du Loup. Try the rabbit with thyme, squid with aniseed or meat grilled over the coals, and finish off with *clafoutis.* They do a set menu for €19.50, or you'll spend around €20–23 à la carte.

Grasse
06130

ⓒ |●| 🍴 Le Café des Musées

1 rue Jean Ossola.

☎04.92.60.99.00
Closed *Sun (Oct–March).* **Open** *daily 8.30am–6.30pm (April–Sept).*

This café, in the historic centre, has a surprisingly ultra-modern décor. It's not far from the Musée Provençal du Costume et du Bijou. The very Mediterranean cooking is warm and strongly flavoured, involving light, tasty salads, fresh savoury tarts and home-made pastries. Expect to pay between €11 and €15 for a meal à la carte. *Free coffee offered to our readers on presentation of this guide.*

Mouans-Sartoux
06370 (6km SE)

⊛ |●| ⚒ **Le Relais de la Pinède**

Route de La Roquette, the D409.
☎04.93.75.28.29
Closed *Mon and Tues evenings; Wed and Sun evenings (out of season); 5–10 Feb.*

Surprising to find a Canadian cabin in the land of the cicadas. Lavish decoration, professional service, and dishes for every pocket and to meet all tastes; the weekday menu costs €18 and there's another menu for €26. There's a lovely terrace under the pines. *Free coffee offered to our readers on presentation of this guide.*

Valbonne
06560 (9km E)

⊛ ⚒ |●| **La Fontaine aux Vins**

3 Rue-Grande; it's in the old town.
☎04.93.12.93.20
Closed *Sun and Mon (out of season); Mon only (in season).*

Predominantly a wine bar, this place also serves "Provençal tapas" – little dishes of tasty morsels – along with original sandwiches and attentively prepared dishes. Expect to pay around €18 à la carte. Wines are carefully selected and affordable, and you can also buy them in the adjoining a shop. *Free coffee offered to our readers on presentation of this guide.*

⊛ |●| **L'Auberge Fleurie**

1016 rte. de Cannes; it's 1km outside the centre of Valbonne, coming from Grasse, set back slightly from the road.
☎04.93.12.02.80
Closed *Mon; Tues; Dec.* **Disabled access.**

A very good restaurant in a pretty, wisteria-covered building with huge mirrors in the dining rooms. Inventive, sunny dishes are made from the best ingredients with the simplest flavours; menus €24–45. All this plus a smiling welcome attract lots of regular patrons to the restaurant.

Grave (La)
05320

⊛ ⚒ 🏠 |●| **L'Edelweiss****

On the right, as you enter the town coming from Briançon.
☎04.76.79.90.93 ☏04.76.79.92.64
⊛www.hotel-edelweiss.com
Closed *lunchtimes in winter (restaurant); 5 May–5 June; 1 Oct–10 Dec.* **TV. Games available. Car park.**

This enjoyable hotel is owned by the organizers of the world-famous annual Mieje ski race. The modern hotel stands well away from the noise of the road. The clientele is international and sporty and there's always a riotous atmosphere late into the evening. You can relax on the terrace and gaze upon the summits of the 4000m Écrins, or enjoy the sauna and Jacuzzi. Rooms are on the small side; they start at €59 for a double with shower/wc or bath. Half board, compulsory in winter, costs €51 per person; range of menus €17–29. *Free house apéritif offered to our readers on presentation of this guide.*

Grimaud
83310

⊛ ⚒ 🏠 **Hôtel La Pierrerie*****

Quartier du Grand Pont; it's 2km from Port-Grimaud on the D61.
☎04.94.43.24.60 ☏04.94.43.24.78
⊛www.lapierrerie.com
Closed *mid-Nov to 1 April.* **TV. Swimming pool. Games available. Car park.**

An attractive little hotel way out in the countryside above the gulf of Saint-Tropez. It's built like a typical Provençal *mas*, with lots of small stone buildings in the greenery and among the flowers, set around a swimming pool where everyone congregates on sunny days. Rooms with shower/wc or bath go for €75–105. It's wonderfully quiet – just a shame that the internal decorations are less appealing. *Seventh consecutive night free (except July–Aug) offered to our readers on presentation of this guide.*

Guillestre

05600

⟨ 🏠 ❙●❙ Le Chalet Alpin**

Route du Queyras; as you leave Guillestre,
turn left onto the Queyras road.
☎04.92.45.00.35 ℗04.92.45.43.41
Closed *Sun evening and Mon (outside the
school holidays); 26 May–10 June; mid-Nov
to mid-Dec.* **High chairs and games available. Car park.**

A family-run establishment with decent
rooms at honest prices: doubles €36–45
with shower/wc or bath. It's best to avoid
the ones that look out over the road
even though they have the best view.
Traditional, well-prepared cooking in
the restaurant, on menus at €16.50–33:
scallops with fresh fruit, terrine of duck
foie gras, *crépinettes* of salmon with a
saffron infusion, duck breast with sour
cherries and Génépi wine. Doubles go
for €36–44 with shower or bath/wc;
half board available from €45 per person
and is compulsory from 15 July to 31
August.

Mont-Dauphin

05600 (4km N)

⟨ 🎋 🏠 ❙●❙ L'Auberge de l'Echauguette**

Rue Catinat; it's on the main street.
☎04.92.45.07.13 ℗04.92.45.14.22
🌐www.echauguette.com
Restaurant closed *Mon (out of season); 10–
30 April; 30 Sept–15 Dec.* **Open** *daily during
the school holidays.* **TV.**

The building used to be the school
for the children of the soldiers sta-
tioned here. The place was restored two
years ago and has been impressively
done. The welcome is very warm and
at the weekend the staff wear local
costume. There's a tavern, a restful
garden at the back where you can eat or
have a drink and an elegantly decorated
dining room. They offer a single menu
for €16 (weekdays only), otherwise
expect to pay €22 à la carte. The spacious rooms all have en-suite bathrooms
and they've been charmingly decorated
and named after flowers of the region;
doubles €43–50, half board €42–46
per person. Those with a bit more cash
can stay in the "Vauban" suite. *Free coffee
offered to our readers on presentation of
this guide.*

Vars

05560 (13km SE)

⟨ ❙●❙ La Montagne

Résidence Le Grizzli.
Espace Rodde; it's on the right when you
come into the resort, opposite the tourist
office.
☎04.92.46.58.53
Closed *May–June; Sept–Nov.* **Open**
*evenings only (in season) and during school
holidays.*

Emilie and Jacquot put the world to
rights with their customers over the bar
while Luc, who's a ski instructor during
the day, gets busy in the kitchen. His specialities are big salads, fondues, *tartiflette*
and grills. À la carte only; a meal costs
around €24. There's a great atmosphere
in the dining room with its fireplace
and charming, smiling service; the bay
windows give views of the town and the
mountain.

Hyères

83400

⟨ 🎋 🏠 Hôtel du Soleil**

Rue du Rempart; in the centre of town, not
far from the place Clemenceau.
☎04.94.65.16.26 ℗04.94.35.46.00
🌐www.hotel-du-soleil.fr
TV.

A hotel absolutely engulfed by ivy in a
very peaceful spot next to the medieval
town. The rooms of this old building are
haphazardly furnished and smell of lavender. Try to get one on the top floor; they
have a view of the sea in the distance.
Doubles go for €40–80 with shower/wc,
including breakfast in high season, and
€44–84 with bath. *10% discount on the
room rate for a minimum two-night stay
offered to our readers on presentation of this
guide.*

⟨ ❙●❙ Le Jardin

19 av. Joseph Clotis.
☎04.94.35.24.12
Open *noon–midnight.*

All the tables are set out in the lovely,
shady garden. The setting is elegant and
relaxed, and the cuisine is varied and
sometimes a little exotic. Fair prices with
dishes at €12–15; a full meal will cost
around €25.

Porquerolles

83400 (2km SE)

≪ 🛖 |●| Les Glycines**

Place d'Armes.
☎04.94.58.30.36 ℱ04.94.58.35.22
ⓦwww.aubergedesglycines.net
Closed *lunch on 1 May.* **TV. High chairs and cots available.**

A charming hotel which has been renovated in the spirit of Provence. The time to come is in March when the "glycines" (wisteria) are in bloom, or in autumn; avoid it in high summer if you want to be pampered. Double rooms with shower/wc or bath go for €99–269; they only do their cosy rooms on a half board basis – €109–169 per person depending on the season. The patio is the best place to eat and the cuisine leans heavily in the direction of fish and seafood with a choice of menus priced €16.90–39.

Lalonde-les-Maures

83250 (8km E)

🍴 |●| Le Jardin Provençal

15–18 av. Georges-Clemenceau.
☎04.94.66.57.34
Closed *Mon; Tues lunchtime; 15 Dec–20 Jan.* **Disabled access. High chairs available.**

The dining room has a stylish Provençal décor – with a fireplace and a pleasant terrace in the garden. Charming welcome with equally good service and local dishes: *tartines*, mussels with garlic cream, free-range cockerel gently stewed in local wine. The weekday lunch *formule* costs €16, or there's a range of menus €28–40. *Free house apéritif offered to our readers on presentation of this guide.*

Isle-sur-la-Sorgue (L')

84800

≪ 🛖 |●| L'Étape

136 route de Carpentras
☎04.90.38.07.64 ℱ04.90.38.60.85
Restaurant closed *Mon and Tues evening (in summer).* **Open** *weekends only (out of season).*

This small hotel seems to belong to another age, with just a few rooms, with no soundproofing but cheery and comfortable nonetheless, and above all spotlessly clean, under the watchful eye of the owner (an enchanting character). The rooms cost €50–70. The restaurant abounds in local colour, with fervent discussions at the bar and simple grilled food at the table, both hearty and wholesome. There's a barbecue at the weekend in summer, under the plane trees on the terrace; in winter, this is replaced by spit-roasted meat indoors. There is a modest midweek lunchtime menu at €11 (including wine), and others at €18–22.

≪ |●| Le Jardin du Quai

91 av. Julien-Guigne.
☎04.90.20.14.98
Closed *Tues; Wed.*

Beside the train station, near the antique shops, stands the vicinity's latest gastronomic beacon. Daniel Hébet, the former chef of *La Mirande* in Avignon and other fine restaurants, has perhaps found here the spot best suited to his temperament. At lunchtime, you can savour the master's cooking at an accessible price (single menu €25) under the chestnut trees in the slightly unkempt garden. The ingredients are bought fresh from the market and turned into simple but classy dishes, created with a precision which ensures that their flavours linger in the mouth. The dinner menu is more expensive (€35) and is served in the more refined setting of the dining room. The service is not perfect, but nobody's complaining.

Lantosque

06450

≪ 🍴 🛖 |●| L'Auberge du Bon Puits**

Le Suquet de Lantosque; it's 5km south of Lantosque.
☎04.93.03.17.65 ℱ04.93.03.10.48
Closed *Tues (except July–Aug); 1 Dec–20 April.* **TV. High chairs and games available. Car park.**

Though all the rooms are soundproofed, it's still best to ask for a room with a garden view. Renovated doubles, all of them different, are available for €60–65. The restaurant serves substantial, tasty, family-style dishes prepared with care with a range of menus €20–32: *confit* of goose, grilled Barbary duckling, home-made ice creams. There's a terrace which provides welcome shade in the heat of summer.

Across the road there's a large play area for children: ping-pong, slides and so on. Credit cards not accepted. *Free coffee offered to our readers on presentation of this guide.*

Laragne-Montéglin

05300

@ 🏊 🏠 **Hôtel Chrisma****

25 rte. de Grenoble; it's 300m from the town centre on the Serres road.
☎04.92.65.09.36 🖷04.92.65.08.12
🖳www.hotelchrisma.multimania.com
Closed *10 Dec.* **TV. Swimming pool. Car park.**

More than just somewhere to stop for the night, this is a good place where you'll get a warm welcome and honest prices. Neat rooms with shower/wc or bath go for €42–50. Some of the rooms have been refurbished but the ones overlooking the garden – where they do frequent barbecues – are lovely and quiet. The swimming pool is worth a visit with its magnificent view of the mountains. *Free coffee offered to our readers on presentation of this guide.*

@ 🏊 |❶| **L'Araignée Gourmande**

8 rue de la Paix.
☎04.92.65.13.39
Closed *Tues evening; Wed; Feb; Oct.*
Disabled access.

Located in the centre of the town, this unpretentious place is pleasant and clean. Attentive service by Madame, good traditional cooking and a range of set menus: weekday lunch €12 and others at €20 and €29. Dishes include chicken with pastis, terrine with juniper, fillet of red mullet on leek fondue, cheese steeped in pear brandy, and home-made desserts. *Free coffee offered to our readers on presentation of this guide.*

Sainte-Colombe

05700 (17km SW)

@ 🏠 |❶| 🏊 **Le Céans****

Les Bégües; take the N75 in the direction of Serres, then the D30 towards Orpierre, then take the Laborel road out of the village to Bégües.
☎04.92.66.24.22 🖷04.92.66.28.29
🖳www.leceans.fr.st/
Closed *Wed (15 March–15 April and in Oct); Nov to mid-March.* **Disabled access.**

TV. High chairs and games available. Swimming pool. Car park.

A family-run establishment halfway up the mountains in the Buech area, surrounded by orchards and lavender fields. The cheapest menu is €15, with others €20–33. Specialities include *fricassée* of chicken with morels, duck with thyme and honey, fillet of trout and iced nougat with raspberry *coulis*. The rooms are small but quiet; doubles with shower/wc or bath €40–65. Ask for no. 2, 3 or 4 – they've been refurbished, are quite spacious and have a view over the park. Garden, swimming pool (adored by the children), sauna, Jacuzzi – there's everything for a pleasant stay. *Free coffee offered to our readers on presentation of this guide.*

Savournon

05700 (18km NW)

@ 🏠 |❶| **L'Auberge des Rastel****

Take the N75 in the direction of Laragne-Montéglin, then left on the D21 towards col de Laye. You'll see the sign for the inn just before the village of Savournon.
☎and 🖷04.92.67.13.05
@ auberge.lesrastel@wanadoo.fr
Closed *Wed (out of season); school holiday at Christmas.* **Car park.**

A cheap, friendly inn away from it all in a village midway up the mountains. It's a perfect spot for walkers wishing to explore the area. Simple, functional double rooms go for €30 with shower/wc – there are bunk beds for children. The young owner-chef prepares delicious, no-frills dishes using only the freshest local produce (portions could be bigger, though); lunchtime menu €13 (also Sun in July–Aug), with another menu at €16 and others on request. There's a terrace and a bright, large dining room. Credit cards are not accepted.

Lavandou (Le)

83980

@ 🏊 🏠 **Hôtel California****

Avenue de Provence.
☎04.94.01.59.99 🖷04.94.01.59.28
🖳www.hotelcalifornia.com
TV.

The young couple who own the hotel – just eight minutes from the beach – have completely refurbished it. The husband is an architect who has put his talents to good use, while the wife is wonderfully welcoming. You'll feel immediately at ease, and you can spend hours gazing out at the bay and the islands. The rooms aren't huge, but they have been thoughtfully arranged. Doubles with shower/wc €39–65; the cheaper rooms look over the garden. *One free breakfast per room (for the first night during low season) offered to our readers on presentation of this guide.*

◉ ▦ Hôtel Le Rabelais**

2 rue Rabelais; it's opposite the old port.
℡04.94.71.00.56 ℻04.94.71.82.55
@www.le-rabelais.fr
Closed *Dec–Jan.* **Disabled access. TV. Car park.**

A small hotel close to the centre and not far from the beaches either. Fully refurbished, comfortable, pretty rooms with shower/wc go for €40–85 depending on the season. On warm days breakfast is taken on the terrace overlooking the fishing harbour.

◉ ⅍ ▦ |◉| Hôtel-restaurant Beau Soleil**

Aiguebelle-plage; it's 5km from the centre on the St-Tropez road.
℡04.94.05.84.55 ℻04.94.05.70.89
@www.beausoleil-alcyons.com
Closed *Oct to Easter.* **TV. Disabled access.**

A quiet little hotel, which on summer nights makes a peaceful respite from the cacophony in Lavandou. The dynamic young owners offer a kind and considerate welcome to tourists. Simple but pleasant rooms, all with sea view and air-conditioning; they go for €50–85. Half board, compulsory in high season, is €140 for two people. Menus, from €23 to €29, list a wide choice of local specialities, including lobster, *bouillabaisse* and fish stew. There's also a shady terrace. *10% discount on the room rate offered to our readers on presentation of this guide.*

◉ ⅍ ▦ Azur Hôtel

Domaine de l'Araguil at Cavalière.
℡04.94.01.54.54 ℻04.94.01.54.55
@www.lelavandou.com/azur-hotel
Closed *early Nov to early Feb.* **TV. Games available. Swimming pool. Car park.**

The 23 rooms are situated in several separate buildings. Each has a terrace with sensational views from the heights down to the sea. In the distance you can see the Îles d'Hyères – quite magnificient. If you can't be doing with the stress of the beach, just climb up to the top of the little hill and crash out by the pool in complete silence, broken only by the cicadas. Doubles go for €52–80 depending on the season, and some of the rooms have TV and fridge. Breakfast is served in the shade of the eucalyptus. You can be sure of a real family welcome in this little corner of paradise. *One free night (for a minimum stay of seven nights in low season) offered to our readers on presentation of this guide.*

◉ ⅍ |◉| Le Relais du Vieux Sauvaire

Route des Crêtes. A wonderful spot, 1500ft up, opposite the Islands of the Levant. From Le Lavandou, go to Bormes, and from there climb the Cagoven hill, before turning to the right; after some 10km of the pretty Route des Crêtes, with its stunning views, you will reach this forty-year old *relais*, overlooking Lavandou (although technically part of it).
℡04.94.05.84.22
Open *end May to end Sept.* **High chairs and games available. Swimming pool.**

This four-hundred-year-old coaching inn is on a pretty road up to the mountain peaks and there's a lovely view over Le Lavandou below. You can have a dip in the pool, between 11am and 6.30pm, before heading to your table. The dishes are typical of the region – fresh tomato pizza, fish in salt crust and so on – with a range of menus (€18.50–34) to satisfy all tastes and all pockets. *Free house apéritif offered to our readers on presentation of this guide.*

Rayol-Canadel
83820 (13km NE)

◉ ⅍ |◉| Maurin des Maures

Avenue du Touring-Club; it's on the main street in the centre of the village.
℡04.94.05.60.11
Open *lunchtimes (mid-Nov to mid-Dec).* **High chairs and games available.**

The owner, Dédé Del Monte, paces up and down behind his bar while the locals, perched on their stools, exchange gossip over a pastis (drunk undiluted in these parts). Dishes in the restaurant include *bouillabaisse*, *millefeuille* of aubergines, a trio of grilled vegetables, mixed grills and grilled fish. The weekday lunch menu starts at €13.50, with others at €20.80

and €25.80. Reserve a table by the window so that you can admire the view of the bay. *Free house apéritif offered to our readers on presentation of this guide.*

Île du Levant
83400 (20km SE)

«« 🏠 |●| ⚓ **Hôtel Le Ponant**

It's on the island that's 30 min by boat off Le Lavandou.
☎04.94.05.90.41 ℱ04.94.05.93.41
🌐www.ponant.fr
Closed *21 Sept–1 June.*

It's a thirty-minute crossing to get to the island from here – for information call ☎04.94.71.01.02. The 1950s building stands out like the prow of a ship on a crest of coastal cliffs. There are balconies or huge, wide terraces leading out from the rooms; each is personally decorated by Frets, the unusual boss of this unusual place. They're all different – a chunk of rock emerges in one bathroom while another is done entirely in wood. Rooms have shower/wc; they are available on half board basis only at €90 per person. This is a good spot for naturists. *Free house apéritif offered to our readers on presentation of this guide.*

Lourmarin
84160

«« |●| **Le Bistrot d'Édouard**

Rue du Temple.
☎04.90.68.06.69
Closed *mid-Jan to mid-Feb.*

In the shadow of the old village mill (now one of the area's most fashionable hotel-restaurants) stands one of this year's great finds, on a small square near a pretty moss-covered fountain. The mill's chef, Édouard Loubet, has branched out to make his cuisine more accessible and the result is this excellent little bistro, which will surely set the pace for other competitors in this field. Lunch is served on the terrace in the summer, under white parasols; the dishes of the day bear the distinctive Loubet touch, with a pervasive presence of herbs and flowers, even in the ice cream, evoking the rusticism of days gone by. Attention to detail is meticulous: the coffee, and even the petits fours, are presented on a tray made from a log. The service is similarly classy, without being starchy. On colder days, operations decamp into the building opposite, with its warm, intimate little dining room. Dishes cost €8–12; reckon on €25–30 for a meal, and €3 upwards for a glass of wine.

Malaucène
84380

« |●| **La Chevalerie**

Place de l'Église.
☎04.90.65.11.19
Closed *Mon lunchtime; Thurs lunchtime; Jan.*

Philippe Galas has taken over this old hotel-restaurant with its beautiful, lush garden and focused his energy on creating a repertoire of seasonal dishes, largely based on local produce. As he has a restless spirit, the menu changes frequently, but even so some of his dishes have almost become classics, such as the prawn pie with shavings of Parmesan or foie gras with figs. In summer, a midweek lunchtime menu is on offer for €10.50; there are other menus from €17 to €35, the latter based on a single product (such as Caromb figs). In summertime, when guests can eat in the garden, the place sometimes stays open well into the night – basically because nobody is in a hurry to leave. The atmosphere is convivial and the service delightful.

Barroux (Le)
84330 (6km S)

«« 🏠 |●| **Hôtel-restaurant Les Géraniums**★★

Place de la Croix; take the D938 in the direction of Carpentras, and it's in the centre of town.
☎04.90.62.41.08 ℱ04.90.62.56.48
Closed *5 Jan–5 March.* **Disabled access. High chairs available. Car park.**

A village hotel in a handsome white stone building which has been beautifully renovated. Some rooms have sweeping views of the plains; it's a quiet spot where only the cicadas disturb the silence. Doubles go for €55–60 with shower/wc or bath; breakfast €10. Menus, €20 (weekdays only) and €25–46, list traditional Provençal cooking with innovative twists. It's a pleasure to dine on the flower-filled terrace.

Manosque

04100

ⓒ ⓔ Hôtel du Terreau**

21 pl. du Terreau.
☎04.92.72.15.50 ⓕ04.92.72.80.42
ⓦwww.hotelduterreau.fr
Closed *Christmas and New Year holidays.* **TV.
Car park.**

This small hotel on the edge of the old
town centre is extremely pleasant, not
only because of its pretty, comfortable little
rooms, tastefully renovated in regional
style, but also because of its relaxed, permanently cheerful service. There is a large
car park opposite (free for hotel guests).
Double rooms with washbasin or shower
go for €38 with shower/wc, or €44–
53 with bath. Remember to reserve in
advance.

ⓒ ⓘⓞⓘ Restaurant Le Luberon

21 bis pl. Terreau; follow the one-way system
round the town centre to the square.
☎04.92.72.03.09
Closed *Sun evening and Mon (except mid-
July to end Aug); Sept.* **High chairs available.**

The intense flavours of Provence are found
in the food here – even though the chef
comes from the north of France. He's got a
creative imagination and offers dishes such
as grilled pigeon with rosemary and lamb
daube, and uses lots of olive oil and basil.
Weekday lunch menu, €13, includes main
meal and dessert, with others €18–33.50.
In the restaurant the décor is tasteful and
rustic, and outside there's a terrace with
a pergola.

ⓒ ⓚ ⓘⓞⓘ Restaurant Dominique Bucaille

43 bd. des Tilleuls.
☎04.92.72.32.28
ⓔ dombucaille@aol.com
Closed *Wed evening (except public holidays);
Sun; a week in Feb; mid-July to mid-Aug.*
Disabled access.

This is the outstanding restaurant in
Manosque, set under the vaults of an old
spinning mill, elegantly refurbished in a
bright, modern Provençal style. The cooking is incredibly inventive, bringing out
the full flavour and aroma of the regional
ingredients by judging the cooking times
with absolute precision. There's a weekday
lunchtime menu at €25, and others at

€43–75 (including an astonishing one
revolving around the Mona Lisa, a local
variety of apple). *Free coffee offered to our
readers on presentation of this guide.*

St-Martin-de-Brômes

04800 (10km SE)

ⓒ ⓔ ⓘⓞⓘ Hôtel-restaurant La Fontaine

It's on the D952.
☎04.92.78.02.05 ⓕ04.92.78.02.21.
ⓔhotel-rest-lafontaine@wanadoo.fr
Closed *Jan; Feb.* **Open** *daily.* **TV. High chairs
available. Car park.**

The only establishment in this charming
village. The ten rooms are simple and well
maintained; doubles €32–37 with basin,
€41–43 with shower/wc or bath. When
you arrive in the restaurant, you will be
welcomed by the smiling couple who
seat you and immediately offer you *tapenade* (olive paste) with toast. From there
you can choose from lots of local dishes
including home-made black pudding with
ratatouille, snails, a fine cheese platter and
lots of desserts including rhubarb *clafoutis*
and pineapple tart. Menus are attractively
priced at €14–20. The house apéritif is
made from lemon, vanilla and cinnamon
and is very tasty. The small terrace is near
the cool of the fountain and looks over the
village. It's best to book in high season.

Marseille

13000

See map on pp.842–843.

1st arrondissement

ⓒ ⓔ Hôtel Beaulieu-Glaris*

1 & 3 pl. des Marseillaises; M° St-Charles.
Map D1-15
☎04.91.90.70.59 ⓕ04.91.56.14.04
ⓦwww.hotel-beaulieu-marseille.com
Closed *between Christmas and New Year.*
TV.

A stone's throw from the monumental
steps of Saint-Charles station, where you
get a breath-taking view of the city. The
hotel is handy if you're travelling by train
and while it's not the height of luxury, it's
clean and well maintained. The rooms at
the back are huge and quiet, and get lots
of sun; those at the front are really very
noisy. Doubles go for €27–54 depending
on the facilities.

⊚ 🏊 🏠 Hôtel Béarn

65 rue Sylvabelle; M° Préfecture. **Map C3-3**
☏04.91.37.75.83 📠04.91.81.54.98
🌐www.hotel-bearn.com
Closed Jan.

A family hotel in an old apartment building that's been renovated by the new owner. The rooms are €30–42, depending on the level of comfort. There are also two rooms that sleep four; rooms with a garden view are quieter. They organize scuba training and dives for trained divers. *10% discount on the room rate offered to our readers on presentation of this guide.*

⊚ 🏊 🏠 Hôtel Azur**

24 cours Franklin-Roosevelt; M° Réformés-Canebière. **Off map D1-2**
☏04.91.42.74.38 📠04.91.47.27.91
🌐www.azur-hotel.fr
TV.

A pleasant hotel with friendly owners on a steep, quiet street lined with handsome buildings. The rooms have been renovated and have air-conditioning; doubles cost €50–57, depending on the level of comfort and the season. The nicest look out onto little gardens at the back. They do a lovely breakfast with home-made pastries. *Free coffee, fruit juice or soft drink offered to our readers on presentation of this guide.*

⊚ 🏠 🏊 Hôtel Saint-Ferréol ***

19 rue Pisançon; M° Vieux-Port. It's on the corner of the pedestrianized rue Saint-Ferréol. **Map C2-5**
☏04.91.33.12.21 📠04.91.54.29.97
🌐www.hotel.stferreol.com
TV.

This hotel is in a good location, close to the old port. The glitzy rooms are named after famous painters – Van Gogh, Picasso, Monet, Cézanne. Comfortable rooms with good soundproofing and double-glazing go for €75–100 with bath; breakfast €9. The new owners are carrying out regular refurbishment of the hotel. *10% discount on the room rate (Nov–March and at weekends throughout the year) offered to our readers on presentation of this guide.*

⊚ 🏊 🍴 La Part des Anges

33 rue Sainte; M° Vieux-Port. **Map C3-40**
☏04.91.33.55.70

Closed 1–6pm (Sun and public holidays). **Open** noon–2.30pm and 7pm–midnight.

A friendly restaurant-wine bar where you come to buy your table wine from the barrel (€2–7 for a glass) or a good bottle as a treat (from €10). There's a little dining room at the back where you can eat salads, meat kebabs or dish of the day. A full meal costs around €7–12. Lovely atmosphere and you can also buy to take away (same opening hours). *Free house apéritif offered to our readers on presentation of this guide.*

⊚ 🍴 Les Colonies

26 rue Lulli; M° Vieux-Port. **Map C2-41**
☏04.91.54.11.17
Closed public holidays; Aug. **Open** 9am–7pm, Mon–Sat.

A warm, welcoming, original place where they don't allow smoking because it's too small. This is where you buy tea, chocolates and biscuits baked by "*Le Petit Duc*" from Saint-Rémy. It occupies an old bank building which has been decorated to within an inch of its life – voluminous curtains, elaborate chandeliers. Good for lunch: cannelloni with *brousse* (a local cheese), tarts, or cream cheese with honey and spiced bread. Tart with salad costs €8.40; in winter, there's *tartiflette* for €13. Credit cards not accepted.

⊚ 🍴 Pizzeria Au Feu de Bois

10 rue d'Aubagne; M° Noailles. **Map C2-33**
☏04.91.54.33.96
Closed Sun; Mon; fortnight in March; 3 weeks in Aug. **Open** until 10pm.

This place is well known for its outstanding pizzas cooked in a wood-fired oven. They're coated with a range of toppings including *royale* (mushrooms, garlic, sausage and cheese) and *orientale* (meat, cream cheese, egg and tomatoes). À la carte you can get *pieds-paquets* (mutton tripe cooked with sheep's trotters) and home-made lasagne; around €8.50 for a meal. An excellent place, offering kind, attentive service – you can also buy to take away.

⊚ 🏊 🍴 Les Menus Plaisirs

1 rue Haxo; M° Vieux-Port or Hôtel-de-Ville. **Map C2-32**
☏04.91.54.94.38
Closed weekends. **Open** lunchtimes only.

A nice little place with lots of old clocks on the wall. The boss is a proud

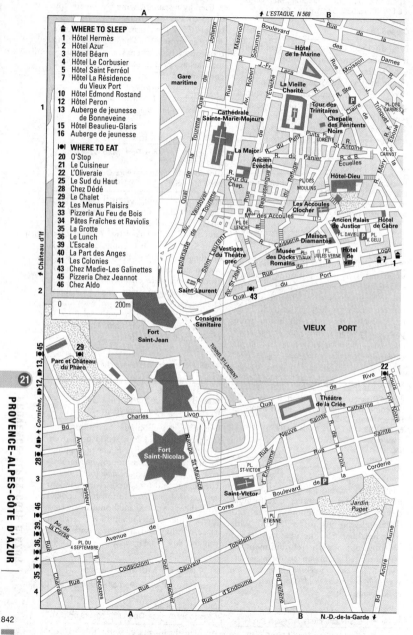

WHERE TO SLEEP

1 Hôtel Hermès
2 Hôtel Azur
3 Hôtel Béarn
4 Hôtel Le Corbusier
5 Hôtel Saint Ferréol
7 Hôtel La Résidence
   du Vieux Port
10 Hôtel Edmond Rostand
12 Hôtel Peron
13 Auberge de jeunesse
   de Bonneveine
15 Hôtel Beaulieu-Glaris
16 Auberge de jeunesse

WHERE TO EAT

20 O'Stop
21 Le Cuisineur
22 L'Oliveraie
25 Le Sud du Haut
28 Chez Dédé
29 Le Chalet
32 Les Menus Plaisirs
33 Pizzeria Au Feu de Bois
34 Pâtes Fraîches et Raviolis
35 La Grotte
36 Le Lunch
39 L'Escale
40 La Part des Anges
41 Les Colonies
43 Chez Madie-Les Galinettes
45 Pizzeria Chez Jeannot
46 Chez Aldo

0   200m

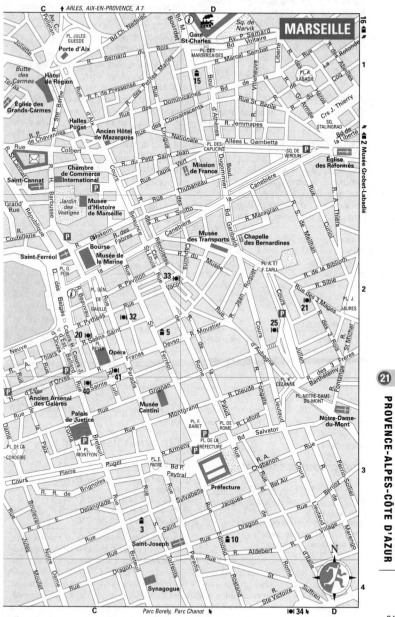

MARSEILLE

PROVENCE-ALPES-CÔTE D'AZUR

21

843

Marseillais who champions his town while taking orders and serving dishes. A really warm atmosphere reigns here, attracting hordes of customers who appreciate good value. The menu changes daily and dishes are appetizing; menus from €12. Credit cards not accepted. *Free house apéritif offered to our readers on presentation of this guide.*

◎ |❂| O'Stop

16 rue Saint-Saens; M° Vieux-Port. **Map C2-20**
☏04.91.33.85.34
Open *8am–7am (23 hours out of 24), except Christmas Day.*

The snack bar opposite the opera is an institution; it attracts everyone from the well-dressed gentleman to local shopkeepers, and it's not uncommon to bump into an opera singer or stagehand. The house specialities – *alouettes* (or meatballs), rabbit with mustard sauce and *daube à la provençale* – are very decent and a meal will cost you about €14 à la carte. The sandwiches have good fillings and should not be ignored. There's a great atmosphere in the early hours, but only six tables.

◎ 🕮 |❂| L'Oliveraie

10 pl. aux Huiles; M° Vieux-Port. **Map B2-22**
☏04.91.33.34.41
Closed *Sat lunchtime; Sun; Jan.* **Pay car park.**

A typical local bistro with a welcoming owner, good service and superb Provençal cooking. The lunch menu is priced at €17, with others at €24–30 for dinner. *Free coffee offered to our readers on presentation of this guide.*

2nd arrondissement

◎ 🕮 🛏 Hôtel Hermès**

2 rue Bonneterie; M° Vieux-Port–Hôtel-de-Ville. **Map B2-1**
☏04.96.11.63.63 ☏04.96.11.63.64
🖰www.hotelmarseille.com
TV. High chairs available.

A small, renovated hotel superbly located near the Old Port. Well-equipped rooms (with shower/wc or bath) are air-conditioned and soundproofed; doubles €69. "*La Nuptiale*" has a terrace with a fantastic view of the port. *10% discount on the room rate offered to our readers on presentation of this guide.*

◎ 🕮 🛏 Hôtel La Résidence du Vieux Port***

18 quai du Port; M° Vieux-Port or Hôtel-de-Ville. **Map B2-7**
☏04.91.91.91.22 ☏04.91.56.60.88
🖰www.hotelmarseille.com
Disabled access. TV.

This great family hotel, on the town hall side of the Vieux Port, has a good view of Notre-Dame. Rooms are large, light, air-conditioned and pleasantly furnished, as you would expect from a three-star hotel. You can sit on your balcony and watch the boats chug past. Doubles €118.50. Good breakfast and the welcome is friendly. *10% discount on the room rate offered to our readers on presentation of this guide.*

◎ 🕮 |❂| Chez Madie – Les Galinettes

138 quai du Port; M° Vieux-Port–Hôtel-de-Ville. **Map B2-43**
☏04.91.90.40.87
Closed *Sun; Sat (June–Sept).*

You'll find this restaurant on the quay – it's a great place to come for robust, authentic Provençal cooking. It's now run by Madie's granddaughter and, although she still serves the excellent chicken *meunière*, her real speciality is meat (her father was a wholesale butcher) – authentic *pieds et paquets* (lamb tripe and trotters). The clams with thyme are also good. There's a lunch menu for €17 and other menus up to €27. *Free house apéritif offered to our readers on presentation of this guide.*

6th arrondissement

◎ 🛏 Hôtel Edmond-Rostand**

31 rue Dragon; M° Estrangin-Préfecture. **Map D3-10**
☏04.91.37.74.95 ☏04.91.57.19.04
🖰www.hoteledmondrostand.com
Closed *24 Dec–10 Jan.* **TV.**

A well-kept family hotel in a quiet street run by France-Rodolphe and Tamara de Wurstemberger. It is named after the dramatist who wrote *Cyrano de Bergerac* – he was born in a house close by. The bright, modern rooms (€56) all have soundproofing and bathrooms; some rooms have a view of the garden, which is pretty and quiet. It's good value and attracts a wide clientele.

@ 🎋 |●| **Le Sud du Haut**

80 cours Julien; M° Noailles. **Map D2-25**
℡04.91.92.66.64
Closed Sun–Tues evening; 15 Aug–6 Sept.
Disabled access.

The setting is like a bric-à-brac shop with its assorted holiday souvenirs. Outside, there's a terrace where you can admire the wonderful fountain in *cours Julien*, and the good atmosphere is enhanced by the Afro-Cuban-Caribbean music that plays in the background. Old recipes are revamped here, and a touch of finesse added to dishes – stuffed vegetables, chicken with basil, duck *confit* with a walnut crust, rack of lamb with herbs. Prices are reasonable: between €14 at lunchtime and €27–30 in the evening. *Free house apéritif offered to our readers on presentation of this guide.*

@ |●| **Le Cuisineur**

2 rue des Trois-Rois; M° Notre-Dame-du-Mont. **Map D2-21**
℡04.96.12.63.85
Closed Wed. **Open** evenings only.

One of our favourite places in Marseille. Two intimate little dining rooms separated by an arch, decorated in a mixture of Baroque and garish colours. The atmosphere is genuinely friendly, as is the jovial young owner; sometimes his mother lends a hand waiting at the tables – in short, this is a family affair. There's a menu for €20, or reckon on around €30 for a meal. It is popular with small groups who come to enjoy the good meat and *clafoutis* with fruits of the season. The short wine list is dominated by vintages from the Rhône. On fine evenings, you can dine on the cool terrace. Credit cards not accepted.

7th arrondissement

@ 🎋 🏠 **Hôtel Peron****

119 corniche Kennedy; take bus # 83 from the Vieux Port and get off at the Corniche-Frégier stop. It's 2km south of the Vieux Port. **Off map A3-12**
℡04.91.31.01.41 ℡04.91.59.42.01
🖢www.bestofprovence.com
TV. Car park.

Irresistibly kitsch 1960s hotel, where each room is decorated in the style of a different French region with moulded plaster murals and dolls in traditional dress. The bathrooms teem with ceramic fish and sea creatures. Doubles with shower or basin are €64–75, or with bath €72.50–79.80;

nos. 15, 25 and 35 are the most spacious. As it's right beside the sea, you get a nice view from the balconies at the front and the rooms are soundproofed – which keeps out some of the traffic flashing past on the Corniche. Rooms at the back, though lacking the view, are quieter. *10% discount on the room rate offered to our readers on presentation of this guide.*

@ 🎋 |●| **Le Chalet**

Jardin Émile-Duclaux (palais du Pharo); from the garden, the entrance is in boulevard Charles-Livon. **Map A2-29**
℡04.91.52.80.11
Closed Oct–March. **Open** noon–3pm (April–Sept).

Outdoor café in the gardens of the palace built by Napoléon III for the Empress Eugénie. You'll pay around €20–30 for a complete meal. In summer, when the centre of town can be unbearably hot, the shaded terrace gets a light, refreshing sea breeze. A lovely place for a quiet afternoon drink, with a very beautiful view of the old port. *Free coffee offered to our readers on presentation of this guide.*

@ 🎋 |●| **Pizzeria Chez Jeannot**

Vallon des Auffes; at the bottom of the Vallon des Auffes. **Off map A3-45**
℡04.91.52.11.28
Open in summer, daily except Mon (also Sun evening in winter).

Nestling in the bottom of the Vallon des Auffes, this big pizzeria has a significant reputation. As well as succulent pizza and pasta they serve the best of Marseillaise and Provençal cooking: mussels, sea urchins, clams, periwinkles. Everything is incredibly fresh and it'll cost you around €25–30 a head. *Free coffee offered to our readers on presentation of this guide.*

8th arrondissement

@ 🏠 **Auberge de jeunesse de Bonneveine**

Impasse du Docteur-Bonfils; M° Rond-Point-du-Prado, then bus 44 to "Place Bonnefon" stop; opposite 47 av. J.-Vidal. **Off map A3-13**
℡04.91.17.63.30
🖢www.fuaj.org/aj/marseille/
Open 5pm–1am. **TV. Car park.**

A modern and fairly charmless hostel, but it's not far from the beach and the neighbourhood is quiet (but there's a night watchman, just in case). 150 beds in dormitories sleeping five people; reckon on around €15 per person in a dormitory, €17.60 in a double room with washbasin, including sheets and breakfast. Membership card is compulsory. Luggage lockers are available, and there are also snacks if you're feeling peckish.

⌜ 犮 ♨ Hôtel Le Corbusier

280 bd. Michelet; M° Rond-Point-du-Prado. **Off map A3-4**
☏04.91.16.78.00 ⓕ04.91.16.78.28
🖥www.hotellecorbusier.com
TV.

The largest rooms look out towards the sea in the distance and the smallest (€45) look over the garden. Doubles with bath go for €80, buffet breakfast €8 – the new owners are carrying out refurbishment in all the rooms. The suite has a kitchen and large terrace with view over the bay. There's a small snack bar near reception and they do Sunday brunch. The area is quiet except on match nights in the Vélodrome stadium nearby. *Free coffee offered to our readers on presentation of this guide.*

⌜ |●| Pâtes Fraîches et Raviolis

150 rue Jean-Mermoz, on the corner of rue Émile Sicard; M° Rond-Point-du-Prado. **Off map D4-34**
☏04.91.76.18.85
Open *lunchtimes; Thurs, Fri and Sat evenings; in season open daily 11am–midnight.* **Closed** *Sun on public holidays (out of season); 3 weeks in Aug.*

You have to go through the kitchens of this Italian deli to get to the veranda, where all the windows open out onto a gravel courtyard. Marcel Pagnol, Raimu and Fernandel used to love eating here. Start with San Daniele ham or a mozzarella kebab before devouring one of the great pasta or ravioli dishes. Expect to pay around €15–18 for a meal. It's in a very quiet, middle-class area.

⌜ |●| Chez Dédé

32 bd. Bonne Brise. Follow the coast road to La Madrague, after Pointe-Rouge; signposted from the main road, it is on a sandy beach lined with typical chalets. **Off map A3-28**
☏04.91.73.01.03
Closed *Christmas holidays.* **Open** *daily (April–Sept); Thurs–Sat and Sun lunch (Oct–March).*

The terrace juts out over the water, while the dining room is decorated with model

boats. You'll eat simple food here: oven-baked pizzas, pasta, mussel kebabs and grilled fish. It's one of the few places to offer grilled sardines – truly delicious. There's no menu; expect to pay around €25–30 à la carte.

⌜ 犮 |●| Chez Aldo – La Madrague de Montredon

28 rue Audemar-Tibido; head towards port de la Madrague de Montredon. **Off map A3-46**
☏04.91.73.31.55
Closed *Sun evening; Mon; mid-Feb to mid-March; Christmas holidays.*

An insignificant-looking place, you might think, but it's packed day and night. The pizza and the fresh fish should explain why. The grilled fish is brilliant, or try fresh prawns, mussels and squid cooked over the embers. There's no set menu; expect to pay around €30 à la carte. Friendly welcome and the lovely terrace affords a gorgeous view over the bay. *Free house apéritif offered to our readers on presentation of this guide.*

⌜ |●| La Grotte

Calanque de Callelongue; M° Castellane. Take a no. 19 bus to La Madrague, and from there a no. 20 bus to Callelongue, the starting point for the Cassis–Calanques walk. **Off map A3-35**
☏04.91.73.17.79
Disabled access.

Installed in a nineteenth-century factory, this lovely restaurant has a décor fully in keeping with its history. The terrace, shaded by an awning, is much beloved by locals at lunchtime; in the evening they prefer to book a table on the superb interior patio. Excellent pizza and very tasty grilled fish; you will pay between €30 and €35 for a meal à la carte.

⌜ |●| L'Escale

2 bd. Alexandre Delabre – Les Goudes. **Off map A3-39**
☏04.91.73.16.78
Closed *Mon and Tues (in low season); mid-Jan to mid-Feb.* **Disabled access.**

This restaurant is on the edge of the fishing village. It's run by a man who used to be a fishmonger, so the quality and freshness of the fish can't be bettered; you will pay around €40–60 for a meal à la carte. The setting is lovely, with a big terrace overlooking the sea and the delightful fishing port, and a beautiful dining room with a big wooden bar. They offer generous portions of excellent *bouillabaisse* and seafood paella, as well as grilled fish. Service is just a little bit slow.

9th arrondissement

ⓒ ⵣ |●| Le Lunch

Calanque de Sormiou; M° Rond-Point-du-Prado. At the métro stop take a no. 23 bus to La Cayolle. **Off map A3-36**
☏04.91.25.05.37
Open *lunch and dinner until 10pm (mid-March to end Oct).*

In summer, when the road is closed to cars and motorbikes, you have to phone the day before to sort out your pass (€3 for parking). Going down towards the creek you get a magnificent view of the blue sea dotted with little spots of turquoise. All you have to do then is to sit on the terrace with a glass of chilled local Cassis and order a plate of sea bream or red mullet. Fish is sold by weight, which is worth bearing in mind or the bill could be hefty; expect to pay about €35–50 for a meal without wine. Credit cards not accepted. *Free Kir or pastis offered to our readers on presentation of this guide.*

12th arrondissement

ⓒ ♙ Auberge de jeunesse

Château de Bois-Luzy, allée des Primevères; around 5km from the centre, but with a (distant) view of the sea. Take bus no. 6 via the Montolivet neighbourhood to the "Marius-Richard" stop: take the métro from Saint-Charles station in the direction of La Rose (line 1) and get off at the "Réformés-Canebière" stop; from there, take bus no. 6 to the "Marius-Richard" stop. **Off map D1-16**
☏and ☏04.91.49.06.18
ⓦwww.fuaj.org
Closed *noon–5pm; 20 Dec–6 Jan.* **Open** *until 10.30pm (11.30pm in summer).* **Car park.**

Situated in a magnificent bastide (country house) built in 1850, with an impressive hall dominated by two gangways. Ninety beds in dormitories with four to six beds; reckon on €12 per person in a dorm, €13 in a double room, including sheets and breakfast. Meals can be bought for around €8, and there's also a kitchen available.

Menton
06500

ⓒ ⵣ ♙ Auberge de jeunesse

Plateau Saint-Michel; from the town hall, follow the signs to *Camping Saint-Michel*

on the Ciappes and Castellar roads. Cross the campsite, the hostel is on the left. You can also go on foot, but it's a steep climb; better to choose the shuttle from the bus station.
☏04.93.35.93.14 ☏04.93.35.93.07
ⓦwww.fuaj.org
Reservation *exclusively on the Internet:* ⓦwww.hihostels.com.
Closed *10am (noon in summer) to 5pm; Nov–Dec.*

The owner, a pioneer of youth hostels, is an important figure in the local community; he also runs his hostel brilliantly, and makes sure that it's absolutely spotless. Dormitories with eight beds; reckon on €10.70 (under 26) or €15.25 per person with breakfast and shower; FUAJ card is compulsory. Half board costs €24.50, meals €8.60. Dinner is served in a refectory with bay windows that offer a stunning view of Menton and the surrounding areas. As you can't book by phone, make sure you arrive early in the morning. *Free house apéritif or coffee offered to our readers on presentation of this guide.*

ⓒ ♙ ⵣ Hôtel Beauregard*

10 rue Albert 1er; it's west of the city centre, about 300m from the train station.
☏04.93.28.63.363 ☏04.93.28.63.79
ⓦwww.hotelmenton.com/hotel-beauregard
TV. High chairs available.

The garden surrounding the hotel is planted with palms, lemon trees and bougainvillea; the building has charm and character and is over a hundred years old. It's a remarkable place well away from the bustle of the town. The refurbished rooms are fresh and quiet and offer good facilities; doubles with shower/wc €34–39 depending on the season. The jovial, friendly owner will give you a warm welcome. *Free house apéritif, coffee, fruit juice or soft drink offered to our readers on presentation of this guide.*

ⓒ ♙ ⵣ Hôtel Chambord***

6 av. Boyer; it's next to the tourist office and the casino.
☏04.93.35.94.19 ☏04.93.35.30.55
ⓦwww.hotel-chambord.com
Closed *4 Nov–6 Dec.* **TV. Pay car park.**

A friendly family hotel on the main street in the centre of Menton. Spacious, really comfortable rooms with bath go for €74–98. The doubles are at the rear of the building; twin rooms have a view of the gardens. It's all just a stone's throw from the sea and the tennis club. *10% discount on the room rate (except Aug, and depending on availability at busy periods) offered to our readers on presentation of this guide.*

⟨⟨ 🎋 |○| A Braïjade Méridiounale

66 rue Longue; in the old town.
☎04.93.35.65.65
Closed *3 weeks around mid-Nov.* **Open** *evenings only (July–Aug); lunch and dinner, the rest of the year (except Tues and Wed).* **High chairs available.**

The rustic dining room has exposed stonework and behind the bar there's a big wood-fired oven that gives a good flavour to the meat dishes. You know exactly what you're getting here – there's a wide range of menus from €26 (weekday lunchtimes) up to €45. Lots of marinated and grilled meats feature along with Provençal favourites such as fish *aïoli* and flambéed kebabs. Everything is served in generous portions by nice, friendly staff. *Free house digestif offered to our readers on presentation of this guide.*

Roquebrune-Cap-Martin
06190 (3km S)

⟨⟨ 🏠 |○| Les Deux Frères

Place des Deux Frères.
☎04.93.28.99.00 ℻04.93.28.99.10
ⓦwww.lesdeuxfreres.com
Restaurant closed *Mon and Tues (in season); Sun evening and Mon (out of season).* **Closed** *second week in March; 15 Nov–15 Dec.* **Disabled access. TV. High chairs and games available.**

This special place, which stands on the outskirts of the old village, is housed in a belvedere that gives a marvellous view of the whole area. The young Dutch owner has restored and redecorated the house charmingly; you'll pay €110 for an air-conditioned double with sea or mountain view, and €9 for breakfast. The lovely dining room is the perfect setting to savour dishes that are full of flavour and prepared with imagination from high-quality produce. There's a lunch menu for €20 and other menus up to €45. Credit cards not accepted.

Beausoleil
06240 (8km SW)

⟨⟨ 🎋 🏠 Hôtel Diana**

17 bd. du Général-Leclerc.
☎04.93.78.47.58 ℻04.93.41.88.94
ⓦwww.monte-carlo.c/hotel-diana-beausoleil
TV. Pay car park.

This hotel has an amazing green Belle Époque façade, and is less expensive than a hotel on the other side of the street – this side is France, the other is Monte Carlo. You get to the rooms using an old lift; they're all air-conditioned and cost €51–53 for a double with shower/wc, or €56–62 with bath. Good welcome is guaranteed. *10% discount on the room rate (for a minimum of two consecutive nights) offered to our readers on presentation of this guide.*

Molines-en-Queyras
05350

⟨⟨ 🎋 🏠 |○| La Maison Gaudissard**

Gaudissard. As you come into town, turn left after the post office; the hotel is 600m further on.
☎04.92.45.83.29 ℻04.92.45.80.57
ⓦwww.gaudissard.queyras.com
Closed *5 April–15 June; 15 Sept–20 Dec.* **Open** *daily during summer and winter seasons.* **High chairs and games available. Car park.**

This establishment has been a tourist centre since 1969 when Bernard Gentil transformed his home into France's first cross-country ski centre. He's constantly introducing new services and facilities. In winter, they offer courses in cross-country skiing and other ski-related activities, including treks through the mountains; in summer, hiking and paragliding bring the crowds in. After your exertions, relax on the terrace high above the village, where you get a wonderful view of the mountains. There's also a sitting room and a Finnish sauna. Doubles with en-suite facilities are €51–60; half board, €50–59 per person, is compulsory during school holidays. The restaurant offers a single menu at €18. Gîtes and apartments are also available for hire. *Free house apéritif offered to our readers on presentation of this guide.*

Montclar

04140

@ 🏠 |◉| **Les Alisiers**

It's on the D207, the road to Seyne, on the way out of St-Jean-Montclar.
☎04.92.35.34.80
Closed *Tues and Wed (except school holidays); a week in June; mid-Nov to mid-Dec.*
Disabled access.

Nice, serviceable welcome – it can sometimes take a while to get served, but that at least gives you time to appreciate the quiet of the valley; there's a panoramic view over the region from the wide terrace. Genuine, tasty French cuisine features on the menus €12–23. The house next door is a chalet-style farm with a big lawn. It's open all year round and has six rooms with en-suite facilities for €35–40.

Mougins

06250

@ |◉| **Resto des Arts**

Rue du Maréchal-Foch.
☎04.93.75.60.03
Closed *Mon and Tues (lunchtime only in the summer); 30 Nov–30 Dec.* **Disabled access.**

An appealing, homely place in a town full of glitzy establishments catering for celebs and millionaires. The cooking is traditional and good: only the freshest ingredients are used by Denise to prepare dishes such as *daube provençale, stouffi* of lamb with polenta, calf's head with sauce *gribiche* and stuffed baby vegetables. Gregory, formerly hairstylist to the stars, now waits at table, having decided to settle in Mougins. He's easy-going and very relaxed. The €11 lunch menu is a steal and the other one costs only €17.

Moustiers-Sainte Marie

04360

@ 🍴 🏠 **Hôtel Le Clos des Iris**

Chemin de Quinson; it's at the foot of the village, 50m from the Bastide de Moustiers.
☎04.92.74.63.46 ☎04.92.74.63.58
🌐www.closdesiris.fr.fm
Closed *Tues evening (mid-Nov to mid-March); 1–26 Dec.* **Disabled access. Car park.**

A charming Provençal *mas*, with pink walls and violet shutters, surrounded by chestnuts, cherry and fig trees and lots of flower beds. It's magnificently managed by the friendly young female owner. Each room is different and decorated with a lot of care, with fresh flowers and lots of little extras; doubles with shower or bath/wc €60–65. Peace and tranquillity reign and it's ideal for a romantic weekend – but don't forget to book. *Two free breakfasts (for a minimum stay of three nights 15 Oct–15 March) offered to our readers on presentation of this guide.*

@ 🍴 🏠 **Hôtel de la Ferme Rose★★★**

Chemin Embourgues; it's at the foot of the town, on the road to Sainte-Croix-du-Verdon.
☎04.92.74.69.47 ☎04.92.74.60.76
🌐www.lafermerose.fm
Closed *early Jan to end March; mid-Nov to Christmas.* **Disabled access. TV. Car park.**

This is a gem of a place, a typical Provençal farmhouse deep in the country. You'd expect traditional rustic décor, but not a bit of it. The owner, a real fan of the 1950s and 1960s, has decorated the bar and the bedrooms with a jukebox, bistro tables, coat-stands and lots of bric-à-brac dating from that era. Even the kitchen, where they prepare breakfast, continues the theme. It could so easily look a bit tacky, but everything fits in perfectly. The rooms are really quiet and the ones on the ground floor have a pretty terrace; doubles €75–120 with shower/wc, or €130–150 with bath. The copious breakfast will definitely set you up for the day. *Free welcoming drink per person offered to our readers on presentation of this guide.*

Nice

06000

See map overleaf

@ 🏠 **Auberge de jeunesse**

Route forestière du Mont-Alban; from the train station, take the no. 17 bus to the "Sun Bus" station, then take no. 14 bus to the hostel in Mont-Boron. **Off map D3-1**
☎04.93.89.23.64 ☎04.92.04.03.10
🌐www.fuaj.org
Open *6.30am–noon and 5pm–midnight.*
Closed *early Oct to end Jan.*

Small Provençal house by the Mont-Boron forest with a fantastic view of Nice, with its port and the Baie des Anges. It is

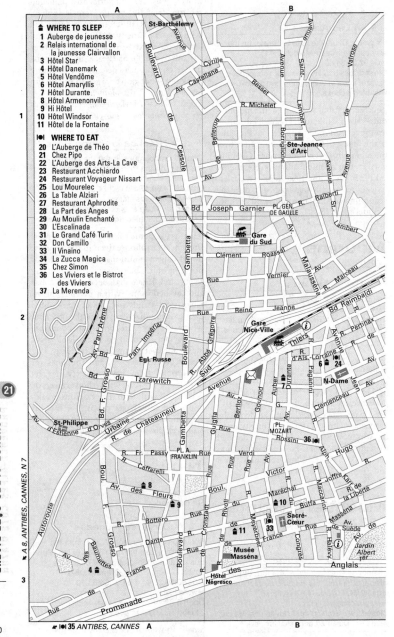

WHERE TO SLEEP
1 Auberge de jeunesse
2 Relais international de la jeunesse Clairvallon
3 Hôtel Star
4 Hôtel Danemark
5 Hôtel Vendôme
6 Hôtel Amaryllis
7 Hôtel Durante
8 Hôtel Armenonville
9 Hi Hôtel
10 Hôtel Windsor
11 Hôtel de la Fontaine

WHERE TO EAT
20 L'Auberge de Théo
21 Chez Pipo
22 L'Auberge des Arts-La Cave
23 Restaurant Acchiardo
24 Restaurant Voyageur Nissart
25 Lou Mourelec
26 La Table Alziari
27 Restaurant Aphrodite
28 La Part des Anges
29 Au Moulin Enchanté
30 L'Escalinada
31 Le Grand Café Turin
32 Don Camillo
33 Il Vinaino
34 La Zucca Magica
35 Chez Simon
36 Les Viviers et le Bistrot des Viviers
37 La Merenda

A 8, ANTIBES, CANNES, N 7

ANTIBES, CANNES   35

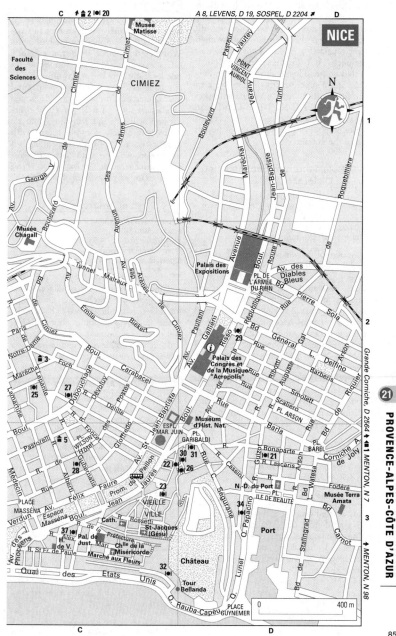

N

Musée Matisse

Faculté des Sciences

CIMIEZ

Musée Chagall

Tunnel - Malraux

Palais des Expositions

PL DE L'ARMÉE DU RHIN

Av. des Diables Bleus

🏛 3

27

25

Palais des Congrès et de la Musique "Acropolis"

29

Muséum d'Hist. Nat.

ESPL MAR. JUIN

PL. GARIBALDI

🏛 5

28

30 31

22 26

21

23

N.D. du Port

ILE DE BEAUTÉ

Musée Terra Amata

PLACE MASSÉNA

VIEILLE VILLE

Cath.
St-Jacques (Gésu)

34

Port

37

Pal. de Just.

Ch.le de la Miséricorde

Marché aux Fleurs

32

Château

Tour Bellanda

PLACE GUYNEMER

0   400 m

C   D

easy to understand why this hostel attracts travellers from all over the world with its friendly welcome and good atmosphere. Accommodation is in dormitories with six to eight beds (men and women sleep separately); €14.50 a night, breakfast included. FUAJ card is compulsory but it is sold on site. There's also a kitchen available, and a superb thirty-minute walk to the fort, with a view of Villefranche-sur-Mer harbour and Saint-Jean-Cap-Ferrat. Be warned that bookings are not accepted – the number of places available is posted up in the entrance.

⊛ 🛏 Relais International de la jeunesse Clairvallon

26 av. Scuderi; take bus no. 15 from the train station to the "Scuderi" stop. **Off map C1-2**
☏04.93.81.27.63
☏04.93.53.35.88
✉clajpaca@cote-dazur.com

A group of buildings set around an old middle-class house and surrounded by a superb park with a swimming pool in a quiet, residential neighbourhood on the outskirts of Cimiez. It's not far from the arenas (jazz festival, etc) and the Matisse and Chagall museums. Accommodation is €15 a night in a room with four, six or eight beds, including sheets and breakfast; half board €24.50–25.50, depending on the season. Menu at €9 served at lunch and dinner; in summer, meals can be taken in the park on the beautiful shady terrace. You can leave your luggage in the morning, before being warmly admitted to your room at 5pm (which is the time when they open).

⊛ 🛏 Hôtel Danemark*

3 av. des Baumettes. **Map A3-4**
☏04.93.44.12.04 ☏04.93.44.56.75
🖳www.hotel-danemark.com
Pay car park.

A quiet and discreet 1950s house, hidden in a residential neighbourhood of Nice. The rooms are simple, but tastefully decorated and clean, and you can take breakfast on the terrace. Doubles €40–51 with shower (toilets on the landing), €48–65 with shower/wc or bath. The clientele is madeup of regulars, so best to book ahead.

⊛ 🍴 🛏 Hôtel Star**

14 rue Biscarra. **Map C2-3**
☏04.93.85.19.03 ☏04.93.13.04.23

🖳www.hotel-star.com
Closed Nov. **TV.**

"The cheapest two-star hotel in Nice" is how the extremely welcoming and exuberant owner describes her establishment. Whether this is true or not, it certainly offers excellent value for money, and a fine location. Rue Biscarra is immediately attractive, as it's lined with low houses and bistro terraces. The rooms are decorated in classical style (apart from a few over-the-top bedheads and wall lamps) and are really comfortable. Double rooms with shower/wc are €48–60, depending on the season; €53–80 with bath. 10% discount on the room rate (in low season) offered to our readers on presentation of this guide.

⊛ 🍴 🛏 Hôtel Amaryllis

3 rue Alsace-Lorraine; in the area near the station. **Map B2-6**
☏04.93.88.20.24 ☏04.93.87.13.25
🖳www.hotelamaryllis.com
Open all year round. **TV.**

The rooms are plain, but they're comfortable and the windows are air-conditioned and double-glazed, so they're quiet. Doubles go for €53–67 with shower/wc or bath. Some rooms lead onto the quiet courtyard. The welcome is accommodating and friendly. 10% discount on the room rate offered to our readers on presentation of this guide.

⊛ 🍴 🛏 Hôtel Armenonville**

20 av. des Fleurs. **Map A3-8**
☏04.93.96.86.00 ☏04.93.44.66.53
🖳www.hotel-armenonville.com
Open all year round. **TV. Car park.**

A charming hotel (if you can ignore some of the buildings around it) with very reasonable prices for the city and very attentive service. Pretty early nineteenth-century villa with colonnades and stained glass windows, flanked by a flower garden. The décor in the rooms matches the spirit of the building, although a refurbishing process is gradually eliminating the outdated details. Doubles with shower/wc or bath are priced at €58–95. The most expensive ones are spacious, air-conditioned and overlook the garden. One free breakfast (for a minimum stay of two nights) offered to our readers on presentation of this guide.

⊛ 🛏 Hôtel Durante

16 av. Durante. **Map B2-7**
☏04.93.88.84.40 ☏04.93.87.77.76

Ⓦ www.hotel-durante.com
Car park.

This is set in a neighbourhood that is not the most obvious place to spend one's holidays, but it is a delightful building, hidden behind Italian-style shutters at the end of a private drive. It is decorated in warm colours and, although the rooms are small, they are impeccable and functional, as well as being pretty and quiet. Doubles go for €69–100 with shower/wc or bath, depending on the size and whether it has a terrace. The small, delightful courtyard has a few tables and is shaded by a few palm, orange and olive trees. An added bonus is free parking for the lucky ones who arrive early.

ⓦ 🕇 🏠 Hôtel Vendôme

26 rue Pastorelli. **Map C3-5**
☎04.93.62.00.77 🖷04.93.13.40.78
Ⓦ www.vendome-hotel-nice.com
Open all year round. **Pay car park.**

Impossible to miss this large, cosy hotel dating from the late nineteenth century, as it is a massive square shape. It has retained all its elegance (wrought-iron staircase, a big lounge with mouldings). Although the décor may hark back to another age, the fittings reflect modern standards of comfort. The attractive rooms are flooded with light and well equipped (air-conditioning, TV and bathrooms in most of them); they are painted a sober, relaxing blue. Double rooms are priced at €73–108 in low season and around €110–135 in high season. *One free breakfast per person per night and 10% discount on the room rate (Oct–March) offered to our readers on presentation of this guide.*

ⓦ 🏠 Hôtel Windsor***

11 rue Dalpozzo. **Map B3-10**
☎04.93.88.59.35 🖷04.93.88.94.57
Ⓦ www.hotelwindsornice.com
Restaurant closed Sun. **TV. Swimming pool. Pay car park.**

With its marvellous Oriental-looking foyer, its tropical garden planted with brilliantly coloured bougainvillea, palms and bamboos and its little swimming pool, this place is truly something special. Guests can use the sauna, Turkish baths and massage rooms, and there's a relaxation room decorated with plants and Thai statuettes. The owners are keen on contemporary art and each room has

been decorated by a different artist; doubles go for €75–105 with shower/wc, or €100–140 with bath. There's also a restaurant offering a set menu for €28.

ⓦ 🕇 🏠 Hôtel de la Fontaine***

49 rue de France. **Map B3-11**
☎04.93.88.30.38 🖷04.93.88.98.11
Ⓦ www.hotel-fontaine.com
Closed 8–13 Jan; **Disabled access. TV.**

Right in the centre of Nice, a short walk from the sea and the pedestrianized streets. Though it appears unremarkable from the outside, inside it's a different story. The good-looking rooms are clean and pleasant, and you can breakfast on the patio accompanied by the rushing fountain. You'll get a warm welcome from the friendly owner, who does everything to make sure you enjoy your stay. Double rooms with shower/wc €82–120; ask for one overlooking the courtyard as the rooms overlooking the road can be noisy. Top marks for the €8.50 buffet breakfast. *10% discount on the room rate (early Sept to end of April) offered to our readers on presentation of this guide.*

ⓦ 🕇 🏠 Hi Hôtel***

3 av. des Fleurs. **Map A3-9**
☎04.97.07.26.26 🖷04.97.07.26.27
Ⓦ www.hi-hotel.net
TV.

This is certainly the most singular of all the city's hotels. It was entirely conceived by the designer Matali Crasset, who used to work with Philippe Starck. Nine carefully worked-out concepts for forty-odd rooms which beggar description and are crying out to be experienced. However, you can get an idea from the examples of the plaited chestnut branches that divide the bathroom from the "Up and Down" room (one of the least expensive); the irresistible thrill of playing Robinson Crusoe in the "Indoor" room; the serenity of the immaculate "White and White", only disturbed by the discovery that what appears to be a canopied fourposter bed is in fact a bathtub – minimalist but colourful, intriguing, very modern and fun. Double rooms with shower/wc or bath and broadband Internet connection will set you back €180–390. There is also a rooftop pool in the form of a giant flower pot, a bar overhanging from a gondola that seems to be floating in air, a

㉑

PROVENCE-ALPES-CÔTE D'AZUR

853

quiet atmosphere and a slightly detached welcome (not unusual in this kind of place). The hotel breaks boundaries and is more an artistic experiment than luxury accommodation. *Free welcome drink of your choice offered to our readers on presentation of this guide.*

ⓔ |●| Chez Pipo

13 rue Bavastro; behind the port. **Map D3-21**
☏04.93.55.88.82
Closed *Mon (except July/Aug); last fortnight in Jan; last fortnight in Dec.*

Through the door, you glimpse the long wooden tables where customers sit side by side. They serve *socca*, the thin, flat cake made from chickpea flour which is a Nice speciality. Those in the know say that this place has the best *socca* in town; it's definitely worth trying, as is the *pissaladière* (onion tart), the courgette tart and the sweet Swiss chard pie. You won't spend much more than €9 on a full meal. It's a good idea to come early, otherwise you may have to wait for a table. Credit cards not accepted.

ⓔ 🎋 |●| Il Vinaino

33 rue de la Buffa. **Map B3-33**
☏04.93.87.94.25.
Closed *Sun; Mon lunchtime; a fortnight in Aug.*

An Italian restaurant run by Italians and numbering Italians among its customers – a good sign, from the outset. The side dish of Serrano ham and other tidbits that are spontaneously offered before ordering confirm the initial impression. The menu is short and the dishes are simple, but they are all good: Italian charcuterie, mixed salads, pasta. The weekday lunchtime menu costs €10, or reckon on €18 à la carte. The service is as delightful as the décor: large murals paying tribute to vegetables and painted wall tiles on the little counters that open onto the street and kitchen. *Free house digestif offered to our readers on presentation of this guide.*

ⓔ |●| Au Moulin Enchanté

1 rue Barberis. **Map D2-29**
☏04.93.55.33.14.
Closed *Sat lunch; Sun; mid-July to mid-Aug.*

Tasty, seasonal cooking at prices that make you wonder if you're really in Nice; lunchtime menu at €11.50, with dinner menus at €14 and €20. They also have an enticing wine list. A small, quiet terrace in front of a dining room that's not overly large either and seems like a Provençal bistro. The owner will explain his menus as if he was performing on a stage.

ⓔ 🎋 |●| Restaurant Voyageur Nissart

19 rue Alsace-Lorraine. **Map B2-24**
☏04.93.82.19.60
Closed *Mon; Aug.* **Open** *11.45am–2pm and 6.45–10pm.* **High chairs available.**

Good regional cuisine served in a rustic setting. Restaurants like this are rapidly vanishing. Three menus €12.40–19.90; there's one offering well-prepared Niçois dishes for €15.90. Specialities include *osso buco*, wild mushrooms in oil, ravioli, courgette tart, baby vegetables, peppers *à la provençale* and *soupe au pistou* (vegetable soup with pesto). Menus change daily, according to what's good at the market. *Free house apéritif (with the Niçois menu) offered to our readers on presentation of this guide.*

ⓔ |●| L'Auberge des Arts – La Cave

9 rue Pairolière; in the old Nice. **Map C3-22**
☏04.93.62.95.01
Closed *Sun; Mon.* **Disabled access. High chairs available.**

Lovely wine bistro where you choose your wine straight from the barrel, and can then take it away or drink on the premises with a quick bite. Better still, go downstairs to the glorious, vaulted, seventeenth-century dining room for a more formal meal. The menu exclusively lists bistro dishes; you'll pay €13 and €15 for lunch menus. In the evening it's à la carte only; expect to pay around €25 for a main course with dessert and wine. The waiter offers excellent advice about the wines. Good service, fair prices and great cooking all contribute to the success of this place.

ⓔ 🎋 |●| Restaurant Acchiardo

38 rue Droite; in the old Nice. **Map C3-23**
☏04.93.85.51.16
Closed *Sat; Sun; Aug.*

This very popular restaurant caters more for local people than for the tourist trade. It's in the old town, and the surroundings are very informal: the big tables are covered with red oilcloths and the atmosphere is cheery. The set menu costs €15, or reckon on around €18–25 à la carte. Dishes of the day are always good – tripe *à la niçoise*, *soupe au pistou* (vegetable soup with basil sauce), *daube*, ratatouille and ravioli with bolognaise sauce, pesto or Gorgonzola. Wine is served from the barrel. Cash only – no cheques or credit cards. *Free coffee offered to our readers on presentation of this guide.*

@ 옮 |O| Lou Mourelec

15 rue Biscarra. **Map C2-25**
☎04.93.80.80.11
Closed *Sun; Mon; 3 weeks in Aug; a weekend in Dec.* **Disabled access.**

Lou Mourelec is local dialect for "fine palate". The cuisine is rooted in local tradition. At lunchtime they serve only freshly cooked dishes of the day, all of which are listed on the blackboard – ravioli with meat sauce, sardines stuffed with Brousse cheese, *pissaladière* or octopus *à la niçoise* – and which cost around €16 each. Dinner dishes are more elaborate and there's an evening menu at €20. *Free house apéritif offered to our readers on presentation of this guide.*

@ 옮 |O| La Zucca Magica

4 bis quai Papacino. **Map D3-34**
☎04.93.56.25.27
Closed *Sun; Mon.*

A quirky, hugely popular place run by Marco, the vegetarian cousin of Luciano Pavarotti. The dining room is decorated with Halloween pumpkins and illuminated by a small forest of candles. There's no menu as such, and you simply eat what you're given – lasagne, red peppers stuffed with pasta, pumpkin and Gorgonzola tart and the like. The dining room is so dark that it is sometimes hard to see what's on your plate, but you can depend upon it being tasty and inventive, and everything is prepared from the freshest market produce. He uses a lot of chickpeas, lentils and beans, and employs seasonings that pay homage to his Roman background. A meal costs €17 at lunchtime and €27 for dinner. Children under 12 eat for free. Credit cards not accepted. *Free house apéritif or coffee offered to our readers on presentation of this guide.*

@ |O| 옮 Restaurant Aphrodite

10 bd. Dubouchage. **Map C2-27**
☎04.93.85.63.53

Closed *Sun; Mon.* **High chairs available.**

One of the finest restaurants in Nice. David Faure, who started out at the *Auberge des Arts*, has opened a stylish and warm place with a superb flower-filled terrace. The water playing in the fountain helps mask the street noise. Well-established cooking, as flavourful as it is creative, is available on the lunch menu (€19). There's a special "Nice regional menu" for €31, and a choice of other menus at €55–60. *Free house digestif offered to our readers on presentation of this guide.*

@ 옮 |O| L'Auberge de Théo

52 av. Cap-de-Croix; in the Simiez district. **Off map C1-20**
☎04.93.81.26.19
Closed *Mon; Sun out of season; 20 Aug–10 Sept.* **Open** *until 10.30pm.*

An inn with a delightful patio up in the hills of the Cimiez area. The dishes betray a strong Italian influence: fresh pasta with prawns, *tagliatta alla fiorentina*, deep-fried stuffed courgette flowers, chargrilled meat or fish and a choice of tasty pizzas so large that they hardly fit on the plates. Dishes vary each week according to what's good at the market; menus €19.50 (weekday lunchtimes), and €30.50. *Free house digestif offered to our readers on presentation of this guide.*

@ |O| Le Grand Café Turin

5 pl. Garibaldi. **Map D3-31**
☎04.93.62.29.52
Closed *second fortnight in Jan.* **Open** *10am–11pm.*

Le Grand Café Turin is a veritable institution in Nice, dating back over a century and specializing in irreproachably fresh seafood (the main attraction, as in itself the place is unremarkable). At any time of the day, you can enjoy oysters or a seafood platter comprising oysters, queen scallops, shrimps, whelks and sea urchins (in season). Both the interior dining rooms and the terrace are usually full (and noisy), but if you don't want to wait you can always try the annexe, *Le Petit Turin*. Reckon on around €20 for a meal à la carte. Cheques not accepted.

@ |O| 옮 L'Escalinada

22 rue Pairolière. **Map D3-30**
☎04.93.62.11.71.

More than 45 Niçois specialities are served here: stuffed suckling pig (*porchetta*), home-made ravioli and gnocchi, and even sliced sheep testicles. They serve a menu for €22, or you can choose dishes for €12–20. Customers eat at the foot of the steps in the old city. Credit cards not accepted. *Free Kir with portion of pissaladière offered to our readers on presentation of this guide.*

ⓔ |●| La Part des Anges

17 rue Gubernatis. **Map C3-28**
☏ 04.93.62.69.80
Closed *Sun; public holidays; first fortnight in Aug.* **Open** *10.30am–8pm (10pm Fri and Sat).*

A small bistro which draws local wine-lovers. There are only 20 seats but it's the ideal place to enjoy a dish of mushrooms or a *pot-au-feu* with a good glass of wine; à la carte you can expect to pay €22. The owner likes organic wines and he'll advise you which of the ones served by the glass will suit your mood and your meal. It's so popular that it's best to book.

ⓔ |●| La Table Alziari

4 rue François-Zanin. **Map D3-26**
☏ 04.93.80.34.03
Closed *Sun; Mon; 11–22 Jan; 9–20 Aug; 6–17 Dec.*

In a narrow, climbing street in old Nice, this restaurant has typical Côte d'Azur décor – yellow walls hung with pictures and a few tables outside. Set on each table is a bottle of Alziari olive oil, a family brand that's reputed for its quality. The short menu is scrawled up on the black-board; all dishes are freshly prepared and produce bought fresh from the market on the Cours Saleya. Flavourful local dishes: stuffed vegetables, deep-fried courgette flowers, stuffed sardines, cod *à la niçoise*. A complete meal, including wine, costs €25–30.

ⓔ |●| La Merenda

4 rue de la Terrasse. **Map C3-37**
Closed *Sat; Sun; public holidays; first fort-night in Aug.*

Merenda means "snack" in the local dia-lect, and they prove extremely popular. To such an extent that the tiny dining room (24 seats in all) is constantly packed. You should pass by first in order to book

(there's no telephone), or wait patiently, as there are two services. The queue on the street outside is an everyday sight. If you do manage to get a table, you will enjoy authentic, superbly executed, seasonal cooking, full of delicate flavours, created by Dominique Le Stanc, one of the major culinary figures in the region. No menu here, so reckon on around €27 à la carte. One day you might find Niçois tripe, the next stockfish, but the excellent stuffed sardines and the soup with *pistou* are per-manent features. Cheques and credit cards not accepted.

ⓔ |●| Chez Simon

275 rte. de Saint-Antoine-de-Ginestière; take av. de la Borlana then turn left down rte. de Saint-Antoine (follow the signs to the Archet hospital); it's at the foot of the Church of Saint-Antoine-de-Ginestière. **Off map A3-35**
☏ 04.93.86.51.62
Closed *Mon evening out of season.*

A village tavern in a ... village, even if it's been swallowed up by the agglomeration of Nice. It has been run by the same family for five generations and it doesn't seem to have changed since the time when – legend has it – Queen Victoria used to come here: terrace under the chestnut trees, large banquet hall, pétanque area. Tasty cooking, firmly rooted in the tra-ditions of Nice; reckon on €30–35 à la carte. They also offer a menu at €30 per person for a minimum of two people. Genuinely friendly service; booking is (highly) advisable.

ⓔ |●| Les Viviers et Le Bistrot des Viviers

22 rue Alphonse-Karr. **Map B3-36**
☏ 04.93.16.00.48.
Closed *Aug.* **Bistro closed** *Sun.* **Restaurant closed** *Sat lunch; Sun; Mon lunch.*

Two different rooms with two different atmospheres: convivial, nautical décor in the bistro (with wood panelling and glass paintings evoking the Roaring Twenties); the setting is more bourgeois and airy in the adjoining restaurant, but the food is equally irreproachable on either side. Some people claim that this is the best fish restaurant in Nice, and it could well be. In any case, the owners, Renaud and Marilène Geille, have put all their confi-dence in an extremely young chef, David Baqué, who has served his apprenticeship with Boyer in Reims and with Guérard.

This rising star won us over. Beautifully presented dishes with delicate flavours, like the house specialities of monkfish, Breton lobster and scallops, or the memorable raspberry soufflé. There is no mystery – the ingredients are supremely fresh and cooked with great precision – and the portions are extremely generous. In the bistro, the lunch menu costs €15, lunch and dinner menu in the restaurant at €30; expect to pay around €35–40 for a meal à la carte. Not that expensive, if you take into account the quality of the food and of the service (you will not be rushed).

Don Camillo

5 rue des Ponchettes; quai des États-Unis, turn left onto rue des Ponchettes. **Map C3-32**
☎04.93.85.67.95
Closed *Sun; Mon lunchtime.*

In an attempt to steer clear of the crowds while still remaining central, Stéphane Viano chose a quiet spot between the cours Saleya and the seafront to site his restaurant. The large dining room is attractively decorated in light colours, and the food is of high quality, using lots of local recipes and fresh fish: Gran Emma's *borsotti*, vegetable risotto with crispy bacon, monkfish steak cooked *à la plancha*, or rabbit *porchetta*. The lunch *formule* at €19 includes main course, dessert, coffee and wine, others €32–56 or €50 à la carte. Friendly, diligent service is guaranteed.

Villefranche-sur-Mer

06230 (7km E)

La Fiancée du Pirate**

8 bd. de la Corne-d'Or; towards the top of the town, on the N7.
☎04.93.76.67.40 ☎04.93.76.91.04
✉www.fianceedupirate.com
Disabled access. TV. Games available. Swimming pool. Car park.

This hotel is a relic from the 1950s, when the N7 was still a major European artery leading to Rome and beyond. Its nondescript façade is deceptive because inside there is a huge dining room (with exotic decoration) that extends onto a terrace with a pool and garden, and a dizzying view of the harbour. There's also a tearoom (open all the year round) that serves not only selected teas but also home-made cakes, coffees from all over the world and cold snacks in summer. Attractive,

refurbished double rooms with shower/wc or bath go for €50–100, depending on the season. Some of the rooms give directly onto the garden (although a couple also overlook the road); all bar one have a view of the sea. There's a dinner menu for €27 in summer. The young owner has managed to create the cheerful, relaxed atmosphere of a family house.

Restaurant Michel's

Place Amélie-Pollonnais; it's on the big square between the port and the old Villefranche.
☎04.93.76.73.24
Closed *Tues.*

This is the "in" place at the moment, and the atmosphere's pretty laid-back. The large terrace comes into its own on summer evenings. There are no set menus, but the à la carte menu is full of wonderful dishes – fish mixed grill, squid tagliatelli and seafood, mostly, prepared with seasonal produce. You'll pay about €32 for a meal à la carte.

La Mère Germaine

Quai Courbet; it's on the port.
☎04.93.01.71.39
Closed 15 Nov–24 Dec. **High chairs available.**

This restaurant is in a perfect situation on the port and is undoubtedly one of the best places between Nice and Monaco. It has a magnificent view of Villefranche's natural harbour, a lovely dining room, and a terrace. There's an army of smart waiters. Dishes are prepared using only the freshest ingredients and the fish and seafood are nothing less than wonderful: *bouillabaisse*, tuna marinated in coconut milk, fillets of sole cooked to perfection. Like everything else, the desserts are prepared in-house. Menu €37; à la carte, prices climb steeply – from €50. *Free coffee offered to our readers on presentation of this guide.*

Levens

06670 (20km N)

Le Mas Fleuri

19 quartier des Grands-Prés; around 2km from Levens, on the right when you reach the valley by the D19; around 200m after crossroads with the road from Saint-Martin-du-Var.
☎ and ☎04.93.79.70.35

Closed *Tues and Wed (early Oct to April, except for house guests).* **Disabled access. High chairs, baby changing table, baby bath and games available.**

Small inn on the side of a road, shaded by plane trees and bordered by a lawned garden. The ten or so rooms have been refurbished; they are simple but very clean and bright. Doubles €45; there are also some bigger ones for families. There is also an excellent chef in the kitchen offering dishes such as *millefeuille* of aubergines and *feuilleté* of langoustines: menus from €20; gastronomic menu €37. It's highly recommended for its warm welcome and fine cuisine. *Free house apéritif offered to our readers on presentation of this guide.*

Orange
84100

ⓒ ⅀ 🏠 Hôtel Le Glacier**

46 cours Aristide-Briand.
☎04.90.34.02.01 ℗04.90.51.13.80
ⓦwww.le-glacier.com
Closed *Sat and Sun (Jan–March); 18 Dec–31 Jan.* **TV. High chairs available. Car park.**

This comfortable hotel has been run by three generations of the Cunha family. All the rooms are decorated differently. Doubles with shower/wc or bath go for €48–70; breakfast €6. Musicians performing in the festival often stay here; it's doubtless the best value in town. There's free parking in the car park and and a lock-up garage for a charge. *10% discount on the room rate (except in July and Aug) offered to our readers on presentation of this guide.*

ⓒ ⅀ 🏠 Hôtel Arène***

Place de Langes; it's in the historic centre, near the town hall.
☎04.90.11.40.40 ℗04.90.11.40.45
ⓦwww.avignon-et-provence.com/hotelarene
Closed *8–30 Nov.* **TV. Pay car park.**

A quiet, delightful hotel in the pedestrianized area. The air-conditioned rooms are prettily decorated and cost €67–95 for a double with shower/wc or bath. A few of them have a terrace, where you can eat breakfast with Provençal pastries and jam made locally. *10% discount on the room rate (early Dec to end of March) offered to our readers on presentation of this guide.*

ⓒ |●| Le Forum

3 rue Mazeau.
☎04.90.34.01.09
Closed *Sat lunch (in winter); Mon; winter school holidays; 15 Aug–3 Sept.* **Disabled access.**

A really nice place, close to the theatre, with a pleasant yet small dining room (non-smoking). Cuisine is Provençal with gastronomic dishes that show off seasonal produce: black truffles in January, asparagus from March to May. A few classics are always on the menu: liver terrine with figs or scallops with creamed garlic. Menus €17–52 and a children's menu for €10. The wine list includes regional vintages at very fair prices and generally the establishment offers very competitive value for money. In season, it's advisable to book.

ⓒ |●| La Roselière

4 rue du Renoyer; it's to the right of the town hall.
☎04.90.34.50.42
Closed *Sun; Mon; Aug.* **Games available.**

The décor is a mish-mash and rather funky. If the weather's not good enough to eat outside, come inside and listen to the music, which ranges from Jacques Brel to Mahler. Fred changes the menu each week depending on the seasonal produce: regulars include pig's trotters, duck breast or Indonesian *nasi goreng istimewa*. Reckon on spending about €23 à la carte. The cellar is full of good, inexpensive wines. Credit cards not accepted.

Orcières
05170

ⓒ |●| Auberge-restaurant de Pont-Peyron

Pont-Peyron; below the station, on the right, before going up towards Orcières-Merlette.
☎04.92.55.75.20
Open *end June to early Sept.*

This farmhouse is set in the heart of the countryside and its only link with civilization is a suspension bridge. It is surrounded by animals who wander to and fro as they please. Inside the atmosphere is homely and relaxed, with a log fire when the weather demands. The owner, Jean-Louis, is a great sportsman. He was one of the organizers of the Croisière Blanche rally that crisscrosses the *département*. (The bridge was built for this event.) He will serve you delicacies typical of the valley: aubergine with Parmesan, home-made absinthe and chocolate *charlotte*, with menus at €15 and €20, or reckon on €22 à la carte. There is also a sunny terrace, a small wall specially designed so that children with aspirations to rock-climbing can practise and a variety of walking routes that start here. There are also plans to acquire a tracked vehicle which visitors will be able to use. All in all, this is an experience that's not to be missed. Credit cards are not accepted.

Peille
06440

⏚ 🏠 |●| 🍴 Auberge Le Belvédère

3 pl. Jean-Miol; it's on the edge of the village.
☏ 04.93.79.90.45 📠 04.93.91.93.47
Closed *Mon; Dec.* **Disabled access. High chairs and games available.**

Just five rooms, with a splendid view of the Esterel mountain and the village, in this old building which was once a school and later the town hall; doubles €40, with shower on the landing. There's a very welcoming dining room with bay windows overlooking the valley. Menus at €14.50 and €25; everything is fresh and tasty including nice local dishes like pesto soup, stockfish and gnocchi. *Free house digestif offered to our readers on presentation of this guide.*

Peillon
06440 (3km S)

⏚ 🏠 |●| Auberge de la Madone

Peillon-village.
☏ 04.93.79.91.17 📠 04.93.79.99.36
Closed *Wed; 7–31 Jan; 20 Oct–20 Dec.* **TV.**

If you want peace and quiet, this is the place to come. Comfortable rooms, completely refurbished in Provençal style, with balconies and an astonishing view of Peillon and the valley; doubles €95–195 (in high season). Half board is €140–170 per person, depending on the season. As for the food, the Millo family has been here for three generations staunchly defending an authentic Provençal cuisine based on supremely fresh ingredients. Their tradition is imbued with sunshine and they have succeeded in adding a few

magic touches of their own. The results are truly remarkable, and particularly enjoyable if you have lunch on the pretty terrace with its flowers, mimosas and centuries-old olive trees. Weekday lunchtime menu is priced at €32 (main course, dessert and wine); other menus €45–70. If you prefer a snack, you can always go to the Millo family's bistro in the village square (*La Table du Pourtaï*).

Pelvoux
05340

⏚ 🍴 🏠 |●| Le Saint-Antoine**

It's 25km southwest of Briançon. Follow the road towards Briançon for 16km, then turn right onto the D994 into the Vallouise valley and it's 11km on.
☏ 04.92.23.36.99 📠 04.92.23.45.20
🌐 www.hotel-st-antoine.com
Closed *Sun evening (out of season); 1 May–10 June; 30 Sept–15 Dec.* **High chairs and games available.**

The valley is on the edge of the Écrins national park and it's still wild. The hotel is a reliable, efficiently run establishment with a friendly atmosphere. Rooms are simple and clean and some have balconies overlooking the stream; doubles with basin €29–33, €37–46 with shower/wc or bath. Half board costs €39–43 per person. Honest, tasty traditional dishes – including the local "donkey's ears", ravioli, and duck breast with bilberries. Cheapest menu costs €14, with other menus at €17.50 and €23.50. *Free coffee (in the restaurant) or 10% discount on the room rate (March–April, June and Sept) or one day full board (for a stay of more than ten days) offered to our readers on presentation of this guide.*

Pontevès
83670

⏚ 🍴 🏠 |●| Le Rouge Gorge**

Quartier les Costs; take the D560 2km east of Barjols, go over the bridge and drive up the hill to the village.
☏ 04.94.77.03.97 📠 04.94.77.22.17
🌐 www.var-provence.com
Closed *Mon or Tues (out of season); Jan to end Feb.* **Disabled access (restaurant). TV. Swimming pool. Car park.**

Lively inn in a village that is typical of many between the Gorges du Verdon and the coast. The welcome is as warm as the climate. In the evening, you dine by the pool on good local dishes like pork terrine with foie gras, duck breast *paupiettes* with morels or scrambled eggs with truffles, with a choice of menus €19–32. Comfortable, unpretentious rooms with shower/wc or bath go for €51–58; ask for one overlooking the garden. Half board, compulsory in July and August, costs €50–54 per person. There are dozens of walks in the surrounding countryside. *Free house apéritif offered to our readers on presentation of this guide.*

Quinson

04500

@ ⊜ |●| ⅔ Relais Notre-Dame

It's near the Musée de la Préhistoire.
☎04.92.74.40.01 ⊕04.92.74.02.10
Restaurant closed *Mon evening and Tues (except July–Aug); mid-Oct to end Nov; 15 Dec–1 Feb.* **High chairs and games available. Swimming pool. Car park.**

The recent renovation of the fifteen rooms has freshened the whole place up and brought in a new clientele. Good, clean, refurbished doubles go for €35–38 with basin, depending on the season, and €47–56 with shower/wc or bath. Half board, requested in July and August, costs €46–50 per person. Menus, €14 (week-day lunchtime) and €15–38, list dishes such as tasty *pieds et paquets* (lamb's tripe and trotters), trout, local sausage, Valensole truffles, *aïoli*, ratatouille and home-made pastries. There's a nice terrace under the plane trees, along with a swimming pool, swing and small garden. Logis de France. *Free house apéritif offered to our readers on presentation of this guide.*

Saint-Laurent-du-Verdon

04500 (5km NE)

@ ⊜ |●| Le Moulin du Château***

Take the D11, then the D311; it's signposted in the village.
☎04.92.74.02.47 ⊕04.92.74.02.97
@imoch@club-internet.fr
Restaurant closed *lunchtime; Mon and Thurs evenings.* **Closed** *early Nov to early March.* **Disabled access. Car park.**

The Swiss owners of this hotel, set in a beautiful old house that once served as

the mill of the Saint-Laurent château, do everything to make their guests feel at home. It boasts an amazing reading room with the enormous original millstone, a terrace giving on to a large, elegant garden, and a few sophisticated and luxurious rooms. Such delights have their price, of course; double rooms, with shower/wc or bath, cost €74–102, depending on the season. This hotel is also distinguished, however, by its concern for the environment, and it is the only one in the Verdon region's natural park to be classified as "natural". The heating system runs on gas, and the cleaning products are ecologically sound. The restaurant uses fresh, seasonal produce, most of it organic. There is just one menu (€30).

Saint-Disdier

05250

@ ⅔ ⊜ |●| Auberge La Neyrette**

It's where the Saint-Étienne-en-Dévoluy road crosses the road to Veynes.
☎04.92.58.81.17 ⊕04.92.58.89.95
@www.laneyrette.com
Closed *13–30 April; 15 Oct–15 Dec.* **TV. High chairs and games available. Car park.**

Impeccable rooms in an old water mill standing in solitary splendour at the bottom of a little valley. There are only twelve rooms, and they fill quickly, so it's best to book. Doubles with shower/wc or bath go for €62. The restaurant is very good, offering menus €20–42: trout from the nearby lake, potato *tourtons* (rather like potato fritters) and hazelnut tart. *Free house apéritif offered to our readers on presentation of this guide.*

Saint-Jean-Cap-Ferrat

06230

@ ⅔ ⊜ Hôtel Le Clair Logis**

12 av. Centrale; it's in the centre of the penin-sula, on the corner of allée des Brises.
☎04.93.76.51.81 ⊕04.93.76.51.82
@www.hotel-clair-logis.fr
Closed *6–28 Jan; 12 Nov–15 Dec.* **Disabled access. TV. High chairs available. Car park.**

Situated in a quiet residential area, this haven of peace and tranquillity has an exotic garden and all eighteen rooms have a balcony or a little terrace. General de Gaulle came here to relax back in 1952. It's not cheap, though it is reasonable for the peninsula – a millionaire's haunt. Doubles with shower/wc or bath go for €90–180 depending on the season. Ideal for a romantic weekend on the Côte d'Azur – but you should reserve at least three weeks in advance. *10% discount on the room rate (1 Oct–31 March) offered to our readers on presentation of this guide.*

Saint-Martin-Vésubie
06450

⟨⟨ 🎿 🏠 |O| La Bonne Auberge**

Allée de Verdun; turn left as you leave Saint-Martin and head for Colmiane and Boreon.
☎04.93.03.20.49 ℗04.93.03.20.69
Closed *mid-Nov to mid-Feb*. **TV.**

This beautiful stone hotel is comfortable and well run. Well-maintained doubles go for €45–50 with shower/wc or bath; half board €42–46 per person. Try to avoid the rooms that look out onto the avenue – it gets particularly busy at the weekend. Menus, €18–25, list traditional, delicious food. There's a pleasant terrace, surrounded by a hedge. *Free house apéritif offered to our readers on presentation of this guide.*

Saint-Maurice
05800

⟨⟨ 🎿 🏠 |O| Hôtel-restaurant Le Val des Sources**

Les Barrengeards; before the village of Le Roux, turn right over the bridge then right again; it's on the left 300m on.
☎and ℗04.92.55.23.75
@le.val.des.sources@wanadoo.fr
Closed *1 Nov–1 April*. **High chairs and games available. Swimming pool. Car park.**

Comfortable hotel located in a wild valley offering simple doubles with good bedding for €51.50–73.50 with shower/wc or bath. The tasty food is nourishing and many of the dishes are local specialities: *oreilles d'âne* (a pastry case made in the shape of donkey's ears and filled with spinach and chard), ravioli with honey, *flozou* (potato tart with smoked bacon and shallots). Weekday menu €15 then

others €18–25 – it's best to book. Half board, which costs €47–60 per person, is compulsory in July and August. There are gîtes in the grounds and a covered, heated swimming pool. *Free house apéritif offered to our readers on presentation of this guide.*

Saint-Paul-de-Vence
06570

⟨⟨ 🏠 Auberge Le Hameau***

528 rte. de la Colle; 1km from the village on the D7.
☎04.93.32.80.24 ℗04.93.32.55.75
@www.le-hameau.com
Closed *mid-Nov to mid-Feb (except during Christmas school holiday)*. **TV. Swimming pool. Car park.**

Set deep in the countryside, this place has a superb view of the village of Saint-Paul. There's a pleasant terraced garden and a pool. Comfortable air-conditioned rooms with nice furniture go for €102–159 with shower/wc or bath, apartments cost €150. Breakfast is €12.50. Ask for a room in the main building; the annexe has less character.

Saint-Rémy-de-Provence
13210

⟨⟨ 🏠 🎿 Le Cheval Blanc**

6 av. Fauconnet.
☎04.90.92.09.28 ℗04.90.92.69.05
Closed *Nov–March*. **Disabled access. TV. Car park.**

Classic family hotel with rooms that are regularly renovated and prices that are reasonable for the area. Doubles with shower/wc are priced at €52, €60 with bath; one of the rooms is adapted for use by disabled guests. There's a terrace and a veranda. The private car park (nine places) is a considerable asset in the centre of Saint-Rémy. Dogs accepted without a charge.

⟨⟨ 🏠 Hôtel du Soleil**

35 av. Pasteur.
☎04.90.92.00.63 ℗04.90.92.61.07
@www.hotelsoleil.com
Closed *early Nov to early April*. **TV.**

Swimming pool. Car park.

The hotel is set around a large court-yard. The fifteen rooms are not big but well-equipped. Those with a bath are a bit bigger and have a terrace. Doubles €52–72 with shower/wc or bath. You'll be asked for a deposit with your reservation.

⟨⟨ 🏠 Hôtel l'Amandière**

Avenue Théodore-Aubanel; it's 700m from the town centre, in the direction of Noves.
☎04.90.92.41.00 ⓕ04.90.92.48.38
Closed end of Oct to end of March.
Disabled access. TV. Swimming pool. Car park.

A vibrant, appealing hotel just outside Saint-Rémy. Comfortable, spacious rooms €54 with shower/wc up to €64 with bath. With its wonderful breakfast, pretty garden, nice pool and warm welcome, this place is one of the best of its type.

⟨⟨ 🏠 |●| L'Hôtel des Ateliers de l'Image***

36 bd. Victor-Hugo; it's in the centre, coming from Les Baux.
☎04.90.92.51.50 ⓕ04.90.92.43.52
ⓦ www.hotelphoto.com
Restaurant closed Mon and Tues. **Disabled access. TV. Swimming pool. Car park.**

A "hotel concept" around photography. It's astonishingly tranquil, given its central location near the old town. Designer rooms with stylish photos all over the place go for €150–380, breakfast included. The bar has been set up in the old cinema. There are also two swimming pools, a big garden and a Franco-Japanese restaurant with a lovely sunny terrace. A meal à la carte will cost around €33.

⟨ |●| Restaurant La Gousse d'Ail

6 bd Marceau.
☎04.90.92.16.87
Closed first 3 Thurs of the month; 15 Jan–15 Feb; 15 –30 Nov. **Open** until 10pm.

Intimate atmosphere and food that offers value for money with a lunch menu at €15 and *menus-cartes* at €30 and €35, with different dishes each day. House specialities include *bouillabaisse* (Tues; by reservation), snails *à la provençale* and, for vegetarians, aubergines stuffed with veg and mozzarella. Lunch dishes generally revolve around fresh pasta and there's a great wine list. Jazz evenings are organized

on the last Thursday of each month, with a different band playing every other month. On fine days you can eat on the terrace.

⟨ |●| Sette Mezzo

34 bd. Mirabeau; go down the alleyway in front of the Florame perfume museum-boutique.
☎04.90.92.59.27
Closed Sun and Mon (out of season).

A hidden secret, greatly treasured by those in the know. On fine days you can eat on the terrace, in the shade of the chestnut trees in the place Moati. The food, a mixture of Provence and Italy, is fresh and satisfying, and it's served in a restful atmosphere, far from the hubbub of the town centre. The menu varies according to seasonal availability, and the whims of the chef, with a lunchtime menu at €15, and another at €29.

⟨⟨ |●| XA

24 bd. Mirabeau.
☎and ⓕ04.90.92.41.23
Closed Wed; end Oct to end March.

This place looks like a prettily decorated flat with its bistro chairs, mirrors and spotlights, not to mention its appealing terrace. There's only one menu for €24. The food is imaginative – parfait of aubergine or sardines Sicilian-style.

Graveson

13690 (9km NW)

⟨⟨ 🏠 Le Cadran Solaire**

5 rue du Cabaret-Neuf; take the D571 in the direction of Avignon and Eyragues, then the D29.
☎04.90.95.71.79 ⓕ04.90.90.55.04
ⓦ www.hotel-en-provence.com
Open Nov–March (by reservation only).
Disabled access. Car park.

An enchanting old posthouse in a quiet place. The rooms are comfortable and painted in contemporary colours; doubles €53–78 with shower/wc or bath. There's a shady garden and a terrace.

⟨⟨ 🏠 |●| Le Mas des Amandiers**

112 impasse des Amandiers; route d'Avignon.
☎04.90.95.81.76 ⓕ04.90.95.85.18
ⓦ www.hotel-des-amandiers.com
Closed Wed and Thurs lunchtimes; 15 Oct–15 March.

Disabled access. TV. High chairs and games available. Swimming pool. Pay car park.

This modern hotel offers attractive, reasonably priced rooms for €60 with bath, and there's a little restaurant where you can have dinner – menus €14, €18 and €32. Out of season, when they have more time, the owners might take you to the farmers' market with them or to visit the perfume museum; they know how to look after their guests. You may also wish to go on the botanical walk just around the hotel.

ⓒ 🌿 🏠 |●| Hôtel du Moulin d'Aure**

Quartier Cassoulen; it's just outside the village on the Tarascon road.
☏04.90.95.84.05 🖷04.90.95.73.84
🌐www.hotel-moulindaure.com
Restaurant closed 1 Oct–31 March.
TV. High chairs and games available. Swimming pool. Car park.

A haven of peace surrounded by vast grounds with pines and olive trees. The cicadas sing, the swimming pool awaits and the proprietress has a friendly smile. Comfortable, air-conditioned doubles cost €70–165. There's a holiday atmosphere in the restaurant; in summer you can eat grills, pasta and Italian specialities outside by the pool. There's a menu for €15 (weekday lunchtimes) and another for €35 in the evening, served to guests or by reservation. *Free coffee offered to our readers on presentation of this guide.*

Eygalières

13520 (10km SE)

ⓒ |●| Le Petit Bru

Avenue Jean-Jaurès; on the corner of the route D'Orgon.
☏04.90.90.60.34
Closed Thurs; Fri lunch; 15 Nov–20 Dec.

Formerly the *Bistrot d'Eygalières*, this is the trendiest restaurant in the area (with hefty prices to match); the single menu costs €30, including wine. The atmosphere is reminiscent of a family house in the foothills of the Alps. The expert chef, Wout Bru, was born in Bruges but has applied his prodigious technique, creativity and dynamism to Mediterranean cuisine, much to the delight of well-heeled locals.

Saint-Tropez

83990

ⓒ 🏠 |●| Hôtel Le Baron

23 rue de l'Aïoli.
☏04.94.97.06.57 🖷04.94.97.58.72
🌐www.hotel-le-baron.com
TV.

A small, typically Provençal hotel that offers peace and quiet (except in the peak hours of July-August), just two minutes from the port, at the foot of the citadel gardens. It offers around ten comfortable if slightly cramped rooms, complete with telephone and mini-bar, at reasonable prices, as well as a slightly more expensive suite for four people. Doubles with shower or bath cost €46–100, depending on the season. There is also a restaurant (specializing in Italian food) and a bar (specializing in beer). The owner was a Harley-Davidson fanatic in his youth, and anybody turning up on a motor bike will be given a specially warm welcome.

ⓒ 🏠 Lou Cagnard**

18 av. Paul-Roussel; it's a couple of minutes from the port and 250m from the place des Lices.
☏04.94.97.04.24
🌐www.hotel-loucagnard.com
Closed early Nov to end Dec. **TV. Car park.**

A large, typically Provençal house with nicely updated rooms for €46–55 with shower and €57–105 with shower/wc or bath, depending on the season. There's a pleasant terrace and flower garden, hearty breakfast and warm welcome. If you want a good night's sleep on summer nights you should reserve a room that looks onto the garden.

ⓒ |●| La Table du Marché

38 rue Clemenceau.
☏04.94.97.85.20
Closed 1 day a week (varies) out of season; around New Year (contact for exact information).

This restaurant, with its wine-coloured façade and bistro-style decor, lies a mere 50m from the market, so it's hardly surprising that its food is so fresh. Depending on the season, you'll be able to enjoy tomato pie, lobster *gratin*, chicken and macaroni cheese and any number of dishes served with the excellent home-made mashed potatoes. As for the desserts – chocolate lovers are in luck. The menus (€18 and €26, lunch and dinner) offer very good value for money; the cheapest offers three courses with a glass of wine, the other, two glasses of wine. À la carte, reckon on around €45.

◎ |●| Cantina

14 rue des Remparts; go up rue de la Mairie under the gateway and it's about 100m along on the right.
℡04.94.97.40.96
Closed *Nov– March.*

One of the few fashionable places in St-Tropez where the prices won't send a shiver down your spine. Out front there's a little mosaic-lined pond and a statue of the Virgin. They serve really exotic dishes indoors – Thai fish served on a banana leaf, noodles cooked in a wok, fajitas, sashimi, and so on. It's delicious, generously served and the place has real atmosphere. Lots of local people come here regularly in high and low season. You'll pay about €25–30 for a meal à la carte.

◎ 🎋 |●| L'Auberge des Maures

4 rue du Docteur-Bouttin; in an alleyway perpendicular to rue Allard.
℡04.94.97.01.50
Closed *mid-Nov to mid-Feb.* **Open** *evenings only.*

With its shady patio, bower of vines and field of lavender, this is an authentic Provençal restaurant in the heart of Saint-Tropez. The food on offer includes regional specialities (stuffed vegetables, courgette-flower *beignets*, marinated peppers, etc) but also a wide range of fish and barbecue dishes. Menu at €43, with a choice of ten starters, ten main courses and ten desserts; reckon on around €55 à la carte. *Free house apéritif offered to our readers on presentation of this guide.*

Ramatuelle
83350 (6km S)

◎ 🏠 |●| La Figuière***

Route de Tahiti; on the edge of Saint-Tropez.
℡04.94.97.18.21 ℡04.94.97.68.48
TV. Swimming pool. Car park.

This sophisticated hotel is actually closer to Saint-Tropez than the village of Ramatuelle, and it's only 500m from the Tahiti beach. Amongst its other assets are the typically Provençal architecture,

the vineyards and the swimming pool. The cool, comfortable double rooms cost €90–200, depending on the season. The cheapest are set in the main building, around the swimming pool, while the others have an unbeatable location opposite the vineyards. In both cases, they are equipped with air-conditioning, a safe, a mini-bar and a telephone. The service more than lives up to these classy surroundings.

◎ |●| Le Will

Route des Plages; around 3km from Ramatuelle.
℡04.94.79.81.45
Closed *Mon; 15 Oct to Palm Sunday.* **Open** *7–10.30pm.*

You're far from the madding crowds of tourists here; it is not by the beach or even in the village – it's right in the middle of a vineyard. It's a wonderful place to relax, in the shade of palm trees, and children love it as they can run around to their heart's content. The menu is not very extensive, but the fish and meat are good; single menu at €23, or reckon on just under €30 à la carte.

Saint-Véran
05350

◎ 🎋 🏠 |●| Les Chalets du Villard***

Quartier Le Villard.
℡04.92.45.82.08 ℡04.92.45.86.22
🌐www.leschaletsduvillard.fr
Closed *Tues lunchtime; 10 April–10 June; 20 Sept–20 Dec.* **TV. High chairs and games available.**

Exceptional place built entirely out of wood, with super-comfortable, spacious studios and two-roomed apartments with south-facing balconies. Each has a hi-fi, dishwasher and luxury bathroom, and some have whirlpool baths. There are even some studios adapted for people with allergies. Doubles with bath go for €55–135. The restaurant-grill *La Gratinée* is on the ground floor; menus are €19–29, children's menu €8 or €10, with dishes such as grilled meats and the house speciality, *queyraflette*. Facilities include tennis court, table football, table tennis and billiards. *10% discount on the room rate (Jan, June and Sept) offered to our readers on presentation of this guide.*

✆ ⌨ |●| La Maison d'Élisa

Le Raux; it's in lower Saint-Véran.
☎04.92.45.82.48
Closed *Easter to mid-June; 1 Sept–23 Dec.*
High chairs and games available.

Marie, Parisian by birth but a resident of Saint-Véran for two decades, is an artistic woman who has invested the place with her strong personality – there's more than a hint of 1968 in the air. The terrace has a superb view of the valley to the majestic peak of Roche Brune in the distance, and the dining room has splendid wooden floors. The place is stuffed with old photographs, hats, children's games and knick-knacks. The cuisine is creative, elegant and original: nettle soup, home-made tarts, spicy *fricassée* of veal and a chocolate *moelleux* dessert that melts in the mouth. It really doesn't matter that the service is slow. Meals are served only in the evening by reservation; you'll spend about €30 à la carte. She doesn't accept credit cards. *Free house digestif offered to our readers on presentation of this guide.*

Sainte-Maxime

83120

✆ ⌂ |●| ⌨ Hôtel-Restaurant-Montfleuri

3 av. Montfleuri; in a road at right angles with the avenue du Général-Leclerc.
☎04.94.55.75.10 ℗04.94.49.25.07
✉montfleuri.ste.maxime@wanadoo.fr
Closed *early Jan to mid-March; early Nov to Christmas.* **Restaurant open** *evenings only 7.30–9pm.* **TV. High chairs and cots available. Pay car park.**

From the outside this place looks like a deeply traditional seaside hotel. Inside, though, it's full of energy, run by a young couple who create a terrific atmosphere. All the rooms are different, and all are equally pleasant. Doubles with shower/wc €45–125, with bath €70–175 – the most expensive have a terrace and sea view. Good, family cooking served at tables set out around a Hollywoodesque swimming pool, with two menus at €20.50 and €25.50; expect to pay around €32 à la carte. A truly special place. *10% discount on the room rate (in low season) offered to our readers on presentation of this guide.*

✆ ⌨ ⌂ |●| Le Jas Neuf

112 av. du Débarquement; it's 2km from the Nartelle beach in the direction of the Gulf of Sainte-Maxime.
☎04.94.55.07.30 ℗04.94.49.09.71
✇www.hotel-jasneuf.com
Closed *Dec–Jan.* **TV. High chairs and games available. Swimming pool. Car park.**

A genuinely charming hotel run by a nice couple who go to great lengths to look after their guests. Very comfortable air-conditioned rooms, deftly decorated in Provençal style; doubles for €70–172. There's a wonderfully bright veranda and a smiling team. A tasty meal can be had for around €30. Life here is good, with the swimming pool and sun-loungers in the garden – miles from the turmoil and the crowds. *10% discount on the room rate (Sept–June) offered to our readers on presentation of this guide.*

✆ |●| Restaurant La Maison Bleue

24 bis rue Paul-Bert; it's in the pedestrianized area on the seafront.
☎04.94.96.51.92
Closed *Mon and Tues (Jan–March); Mon (in April); Wed (in Oct); Nov–Dec.* **High chairs available.**

A little house decorated in blue, ochre and yellow. The terrace, with its comfortable bench seats, is a lovely spot for a good meal: fish soup, fresh pasta and home-made gnocchi, pork with honey. There are two menus, one for €19 and another for €25. This is a very good place.

Issambres (Les)

83380 (4km NE)

✆ ⌂ |●| Le Provençal***

Take the N98 towards Saint-Raphaël.
☎04.94.55.32.33 ℗04.94.55.32.34
✇www.hotel.le.provencal.com
Closed *early Nov to early Feb.* **TV. High chairs and cots available. Car park.**

Just the place for an old-fashioned holiday, this charming hotel has a view over the gulf of Saint-Tropez and the beach. It's run by the Sauvan family, who are all smiles when you arrive – they are happy to advise you on what to do in the local area (watersports, golf, and so on). Their traditional cooking (menus €26–45) is superb, and you dine in the shade of the restaurant's terrace. Rooms with shower/wc or bath are priced at €59.30–108.

Saintes-Maries-de-la-Mer

13460

⟨ ⬆ Hôtel Méditérranée**

4 rue Frédéric-Mistral; it's in the middle of town near the arena.
☎04.90.97.82.09 ℗04.90.97.76.31
⊛www.mediterraneehotel.com
Closed *mid-Nov to mid-Feb.* **TV. High chairs available.**

A tiny hotel which is both clean and well-run. There are flowers and plants everywhere. Doubles €38.50–50 – some of them overlook the little courtyard. Individual garages for rent.

⟨ ⬆ ⅔ Hôtel de Cacharel

Route de Cacharel; 5km from the centre via the D85A.
☎04.90.97.95.44 ℗04.90.97.87.97
⊛www.hotel-cacharel.com
Disabled access. High chairs and games available. Swimming pool. Car park.

You arrive via a track full of potholes, thereby ensuring that you won't be accompanied by hordes of tourists. This old house, far from the road, is very peaceful, and its comfortable and well-converted rooms invite you to linger; doubles €105 with bath. Country platters (ham, sausage, goat's cheese) €17, are served until 8pm. The dining room has tables covered with old tiles and an impressive fireplace, along with a beautiful view of the Camargue and the lake; several of the bedrooms also offer stunning vistas. There's a swimming pool and horses are available. You should book well in advance. *Free house apéritif offered to our readers on presentation of this guide.*

⟨ ⅔ |●| Manade des Baumelles

Les cabanes de Cambon; take the route d'Aigües-Mortes.
☎04.90.97.84.37
Closed *in Jan.*

Lunchtime menu only (but you must book) at €30 all in, including an apéritif, wine and a tour of the estate, which all requires a good deal of time. You climb onto a cart to see the livestock and have a drink with the herdsmen in front of the restored stables, seated around a big table or, if the weather permits, on the terrace. Small Provençal starters (tomato pie, Arles sausage, *feuilleté à la bandade…*) are followed by a beef rib or a *feuilleté* of grey mullet *en papillote* and then copious desserts. And if a special event occurs in the herd (selection for a race or vaccination), you have the chance to witness it. Credit cards not accepted. *Free house apéritif offered to our readers on presentation of this guide.*

Salon-de-Provence

13300

⟨ ⅔ ⬆ Grand Hôtel de la Poste**

1 rue des Frères-Kennedy; it's at the end of the cours Carnot across from the Fontaine Moussue.
☎04.90.56.01.94 ℗04.90.56.20.77
⊛grandhotelprovence@wanadoo.fr
Closed *a week in Feb.* **TV.**

A good place to stay in the centre of town, with well-soundproofed rooms for €40–47 with shower/wc or bath; family rooms (sleeping four) €53. The new owners have completely refurbished the rooms and are extremely welcoming. *Eighth consecutive night free (early Nov to end March) as well as free breakfast per person offered to our readers on presentation of this guide.*

⟨ ⬆ ⅔ Hôtel Vendôme**

34 rue du Maréchal-Joffre.
☎04.90.56.01.96 ℗04.90.56.48.78
⊛www.ifrance.com/hotelvendome
TV.

The rooms in this hotel, decorated in intense Provençal colours, go for €40–53 with shower/wc or bath. All have huge, slightly retro bathrooms, and wonderful beds. Ask for one overlooking the cool, delightful patio. Professional welcome is given to guests. *10% discount on the room rate (1 Sept–31 March) offered to our readers on presentation of this guide.*

⟨ |●| La Salle à Manger

6 rue du Maréchal-Joffre; it's between the Fontaine Moussue and the Town Hall.
☎04.90.56.28.01
Closed *Sun; Mon.* **Disabled access. High chairs available.**

The Miège family took over this nineteenth-century residence and transformed it into a vibrant, lively place which is renowned for gourmet cuisine. It's a real pleasure to sit on the terrace under the chestnut trees or in the Rococo salons and enjoy the fine cuisine (foie gras, lamb in a pastry crust, and so on) at very reasonable prices. Weekday lunch menu €15 and another at €23 (starter and main course); reckon on paying €28 à la carte. They have a good selection of local wines on offer.

Pélisanne

13330 (4km E)

☺ |●| Le Moulin de Dodé

41 rue Georges Clemenceau; it's behind the church.
☎04.90.55.44.93
Closed Sun evening; Mon; Wed; last fortnight in July.

This converted seventeeth-century mill is now a good restaurant offering superb value for money. Dodé is the chef who, despite the air of simplicity, uses quality produce for his dishes and pays meticulous attention to flavourings. Weekday lunch *formule* costs €14.50 and menus €21–32. It has a crowd of local regulars who flood in – it's best to book on the weekend.

Sanary-sur-Mer

83110

☺ ⚒ |●| ⌂ Hôtel-restaurant de la Tour

24 quai du Général-de-Gaulle
☎04.94.74.10.10 ℻04.94.74.69.49
ⓦwww.sanary-hoteldelatour.com
Restaurant closed Tues; Wed. **Pay car park.**

This high building overlooking the port has an unusual neighbour – a medieval watchtower. After you've received an effusive welcome, the wide stairwell will lead you up to a comfortable, air-conditioned room, decorated in a classical, slightly bourgeois style. Doubles cost €54–80, depending on the season and degree of comfort. No. 25, on the corner giving onto the port, is particularly attractive – but be prepared for a certain amount of noise on the side facing the port (although this does not really detract from the superb location). The food on offer is also good – and, unsurprisingly, based on seafood; menus from €20 (lunchtime) to €44. *Free house apéritif offered to our readers on presentation of this guide.*

☺ ⚒ |●| L'En K

13 rue Louis-Blanc; in the centre, behind the town hall.
☎04.94.74.66.57
Closed Sun evening and Mon (except school holidays).

This restaurant, far from being a tourist trap, is a magnet for regular local customers in search of good, unpretentious food in a friendly, colourful setting. The cooking is original, with surprising touches; the knuckle of lamb with honey and rosemary is particularly recommended. The menu costs €25; reckon on €30 à la carte. This restaurant's success has snowballed to such an extent that it has opened an offshoot in the same street, designed for more limited budgets. *Free house liqueur offered to our readers on presentation of this guide.*

Sault

84390

☺ ⚒ |●| ⌂ Hostellerie du Val de Sault***

Ancien chemin d'Aurel; it's 2km from the centre of the village on the route de Saint-Trimit – follow the signs.
☎04.90.64.01.41 ℻04.90.64.12.74
ⓦwww.valdesault.com
Closed Nov to end March. **Restaurant closed** lunchtimes, out of season (except weekends and public holidays). **Disabled access. TV. Swimming pool. Car park.**

Buried in the countryside and dominated by Mont Ventoux, this little hotel complex is a haven of peace. Spacious, simply decorated wooden rooms all have a small sitting area and a terrace. Double rooms cost €167–302, October to May; half board is compulsory from June to September at €123–195 per person. There's a gym and a Jacuzzi in a lavender-scented room. In the kitchen, Yves is always improvising and changing his menus. There's one constant, however: the truffle menu (which the entire party has to order). Menus range in price from €34 to €63. *Free house apéritif offered to our readers on presentation of this guide.*

Seyne-les-Alpes

04140

☺ ⚒ |●| ⌂ Le Vieux Tilleul**

Les Auches; it's a ten-minute walk from the centre of the village.
☎04.92.35.00.04 ℻04.92.35.26.81
ⓦwww.vieux-tilleul.fr
Closed 15 Nov–26 Dec. **High chairs and games available. Swimming pool. Car park.**

Near-perfect hotel near the ski slopes in a sweet village in the Vallée de la Blanche. In summer you can lounge around in the shade of the huge trees in the grounds or by the pool. The rooms in the old farmhouse have been attractively and originally renovated; doubles €38 with basin, to €42–50 with shower/wc or bath. Honest cuisine with some mountain dishes and others from further afield: lamb haunch with cream, farm chicken with morels, cod with lemon zest, sheep's cheese salad, pork with Roquefort and the like. The weekday lunch menu starts at €14, with others €19–35. *10% discount on the room rate offered to our readers on presentation of this guide.*

Sisteron
04200

◎ 🎋 🏠 Hôtel du Rocher

It's at the foot of the town walls, 5 min from the centre of town, across the Durance and facing the bridge.
☎04.92.61.12.56 🖷04.92.62.65.59
🖳www.hotel.rocher.wanadoo.fr
Closed *Sun (except July/Aug); mid-Oct to March.* **High chairs, cots and games available.**

Although this place is right on the main road, which is busy during the day (especially in summer), it's quiet at night and the view of the citadel and the banks of the Durance below is fantastic – particularly from nos. 2 and 5. And the interior is far more attractive and lively than you might imagine from the outside. Doubles with basin go for €27, with shower/wc €35 and with bath €43. You have breakfast in the large dining room set with wooden tables. You'll be greeted with real warmth and a smile. It's best to book in summer. *10% discount on the room rate (except July–Aug) offered to our readers on presentation of this guide.*

◎ 🎋 🏠 |◉| Grand Hôtel du Cours***

Allée de Verdun.
☎04.92.61.04.51 🖷04.92.61.41.73
🄴hotelducours@wanadoo.fr
Closed *Nov–March.* **Restaurant closed** *Tues.* **TV. High chairs available. Pay car park.**

A chic hotel offering provincial atmosphere, courteous welcome and attentive service. The well-kept, spacious rooms are all very clean, but some are noisier than others – avoid those that look out onto the main road and plump instead for one with a view of the château or the cathedral. Doubles are priced at €56–78 with shower/wc or bath. The pleasant restaurant, with huge veranda and equally huge terrace, serves good local cuisine. *Free house apéritif or coffee offered to our readers on presentation of this guide.*

◎ |◉| Les Becs Fins

16 rue Saunerie; it's in the centre of the lower town, parallel to the tunnel.
☎04.92.61.12.04
Closed *Sun evening and Mon (except July/Aug); a week in June; a fortnight at end Nov to early Dec.* **High chairs available.**

A gourmet restaurant in a town that has a reputation for rearing excellent lamb. They're pretty serious about their cooking, but the atmosphere is relaxed, warm and friendly. The menus – €16 (weekday lunchtimes) and €22.50–51 – are well judged and in the best traditions of Provence.

Mison
04200 (11km NW)

◎ |◉| L'Iris de Suse

Mison-Village; take the N75, then turn left in the direction of Mison, following the signposts.
☎04.92.62.21.69
Open *daily.* **Disabled access.**

This little house on the edge of a pretty old village perched on a hill seems to be a painting come to life. There is an arbour in front of the small front door, which opens onto an extremely simple interior, with whitewashed walls, a few tables and some pictures on the wall – nothing more. This is not surprising when you consider that the owner works entirely alone, not only preparing the regional dishes (very ably) but also serving them. After the meal, he might even pull up a chair to your table to chat about economics or politics (and he doesn't mind if you disagree with him). The lunchtime menu (main course plus dessert) costs €14, and there are others at €18–25.20. It is advisable to book.

Tarascon
13150

◎ 🏠 Auberge de jeunesse

31 bd. Gambetta; 15 min on foot from the train station.
☎04.90.91.04.08 🖷04.90.91.54.17

On the outskirts of the old town, a youth hostel in an old Provençal house. It sleeps 55 people in small, basic but well-kept dormitories with eight to twelve beds, at €8.90 a night, breakfast €3.30. FUAJ card is compulsory but you can buy it on site. The red floor tiles and exposed beams in the dining room always delight foreign visitors. A kitchen is available, service is excellent and there's a pleasant family atmosphere.

ⓔ ⅔ ⌂ |●| **Hostellerie Saint-Michel**

Abbaye de Frigolet; it's 12km from the centre of town via the D970 and the D81.
☏04.90.90.52.70 ⓕ04.90.05.75.22
⊛www.frigolet.com
Car park.

A former abbey offering refurbished rooms with a variety of facilities; spacious doubles €45–55 with shower/wc or bath. Meals are served in an old refectory – it's got a fantastic entrance – or in the garden. Dishes on the menus (€12.50–22) include appetizing aïoli with rabbit and sautéed veal with honey and almonds. And you have to try the ice cream served with liqueur. *Free liqueur des Prémontrés offered to our readers on presentation of this guide.*

ⓔ ⅔ ⌂ **Hôtel de Provence**

7 bd. Victor-Hugo.
☏04.90.91.06.43 ⓕ04.90.43.58.13
ⓔhoteldeprovence@wanadoo.fr

Eleven spacious rooms in the former residence of the Marquis of Tarascon, which has been given a new lease of life by its new owners. Some rooms give onto the terrace; doubles are priced €53–58, with a suite at €84; gourmet breakfast €7. Possibility of brunch on Sunday, and a splendid afternoon tea is also served. More of a guesthouse than a traditional hotel, and you get a personalized welcome to match. *Free house apéritif offered to our readers on presentation of this guide.*

Thorenc
06750

ⓔ ⌂ |●| **Hôtel des Voyageurs★★**

Avenue Belvédère.
☏04.93.60.00.18 ⓕ04.93.60.03.51

Closed *Thurs out of season.* **TV. Car park.**

Twelve faultlessly clean rooms at €38–45. Half board, compulsory in season, costs €43–45 per person. The good restaurant offers a weekday menu at €14.50 and another at €24; they list dishes such as calf's head and sautéed rabbit *chasseur*. There's a pleasant terrace and garden with a view of the village.

Andon
06750 (4km SW)

ⓔ |●| **Le Christiana**

L'Audibergue; take the D5, then the D79.
☏04.93.60.45.41
Closed *Mon (except in summer and winter seasons); 1–27 Dec.* **Open** *lunchtime only.*

Set at the foot of the Audibergue ski runs, this restaurant sees a lot of regulars from Cannes. There's a menu at €20 or dish of the day for €11; you can help yourself to the five starters – country ham, fried garlic bread, *crudités*, terrines and calf's head – as often as you like, following them with tripe *à la niçoise*, roast lamb, wild boar or hare stew, cheese and dessert. Booking is essential at weekends and on public holidays.

Toudon
06830

ⓔ ⅔ |●| **La Capeline**

It's on the road to Roquestéron at Vescous.
☏04.93.08.58.06
Closed *Wed (March to end Oct); weekdays (early Nov to end Jan); Feb.* **Open** *lunchtime only.*

The old tram garage, formerly a coaching inn and local school, has been turned into a really nice restaurant. Cosy up to the fireplace out of season or take the air on the shaded veranda in summer; you get a lovely view of the valley below. Laurent Laugier, the chef, originates from Gilette but the dishes on the menus are specialities from the Vallée de l'Estéron. He ensures authenticity by getting his produce and supplies from local producers: *bavarois* with verbena, juicy chicken with ceps, *pissaladière*, ratatouille and so on. Market menus are served in the week priced at €20–23, a *menu terroir* is available at weekends for €25, and there's another menu at €26 served on public holidays. *Free coffee offered to our readers on presentation of this guide.*

㉑

Toulon

83000

◎ 🉐 🏠 Hôtel Molière*

12 rue Molière; it's in the pedestrianized area next to the theatre.
☎04.94.92.78.35 ℻04.94.62.85.82
Closed Jan. **TV.**

A very simple family hotel with unbeatable prices – an excellent place of its kind. The owners really know how to make you feel welcome and do their best to make sure you have a pleasant stay. Comfortable, clean, soundproofed doubles €24 with basin, up to €37 with shower/wc and TV. Nos. 18, 19 and 20 have a great view of the harbour. *10% discount on the room rate (for a two-night stay except in July/Aug) offered to our readers on presentation of this guide.*

◎ 🏠 🉐 Grand Hôtel Dauphiné**

10 rue Berthelot.
☎04.94.92.20.28 ℻04.94.62.16.69
🖰grandhoteldauphine.com
Disabled access. High chairs available. Pay car park.

Lots of regulars here, notably the opera singers and fans who attend performances at the Théâtre Municipal close by. The attractive and comfortable rooms all have hairdryer, mini-bar, air-conditioning and soundproofing; doubles with bath are good value for money at €54. Car parking is available 50m from the hotel. *10% discount on the room rate (except July/Aug) offered to our readers on presentation of this guide.*

◎ |●| 🉐 Le Confetti

40 rue Castillon; in the neighbourhood of Le Mourillon.
☎04.94.42.54.56
Closed Jan; end June. **Open** evenings 7.30–midnight (except Wed); lunchtime, by reservation only and for a minimum of five people. **Disabled access.**

In this tiny restaurant Madame does the cooking while her young son Bruno provides a charming service to the guests. It is worth visiting for both its friendly atmosphere and its regional, family cooking; the dishes change regularly but the Provençal *daube* with its trio of gnocchi, pasta and polenta always takes pride of place. Dishes €7; menus €10.50–13 with a choice of three starters, three main courses and three excellent desserts. It's advisable to book

as word has got around. Credit cards not accepted. *Free digestif offered to our readers on presentation of this guide.*

◎ |●| Les Enfants Gâtés

7 rue Corneille.
☎04.94.09.14.67
Open Mon–Fri (in summer); weekday lunchtimes and Sat evening (in low season).
Disabled access.

The décor is fresh and quietly contemporary – walls are given over to local artists – and there's a terrace, too. Olivier injects a personal touch into the highly flavoured dishes, adding a few ideas picked up on his travels to old family recipes from the Sète area. Dishes will cost you in the region of €15–25 à la carte.

◎ |●| 🉐 L'Eau à la Bouche

54 rue Muiron, Le Mourillon.
☎04.94.46.33.09
Open evenings only. **Closed** Sat; Sun; Mon; a week in Feb; Easter; 10 days at All Saints'; a week at Christmas.

This is a small unpretentious restaurant with an outdoor terrace that opens onto a little square in Le Mourillon, which is like a village inside the city. Everything here recalls the sea, which you can see gleaming in the distance – from the food to the dining room, lined with painted wood and adorned with nautical paintings and knick-knacks. It is run by a charming couple: he stays in the kitchen preparing dishes using only fresh local ingredients, such as calf's kidneys cooked in Banyuls wine (menu €28), while she waits at table with great diligence. *Free coffee offered to our readers on presentation of this guide.*

◎ |●| Le Jardin du Sommelier

20 allée Courbet; beside place d'Armes, behind the arsenal.
☎04.94.62.03.27
Closed Sat lunchtime; Sun.

The *sommelier* and chef who run the place believe that what's on your plate and what's in your glass are equally important. Their sunny restaurant is full of wonderful aromas and pretty colours; mouthwatering smells waft from the kitchens, where they prepare fabulous dishes. They offer a range of menus €32–39, or around €32 à la carte, and you can choose from a selection of about ten wines, served by the glass.

Tour-d'Aigues (La)

84240

⊚ ⚒ |◎| Auberge de la Tour

51 rue Antoine-de-Très; it's opposite the church.
☎04.90.07.34.64
Closed *Sat lunchtime; Sun evening and Mon (out of season); 15–28 Feb; 15–30 Nov.*

This restaurant has character, with its grey stone vaults and appealing shady terrace. Menus, €11 (weekday lunchtime) and €16–23, feature fish and traditional Provençal dishes like lamb tripe, meatballs *à la provençale*, kid *blanquette* and rabbit stuffed with *confit* of tomatoes. To sum up, we like this restaurant a lot. *Free house apéritif offered to our readers on presentation of this guide.*

Utelle

06450

⊚ ⚒ |◎| Aubergerie del Campo

Route d'Utelle.
☎04.93.03.13.12
Closed *a week in July.* **Open** *all year round; bookings preferred in the evenings.*

Just below the road climbing steeply up to Utelle, there's a lovingly restored shepherd's house dating from 1785. In the rustic dining room, with its handsome fireplace and olive-wood floors, you're served classic dishes like ravioli with duck and cep filling, king scallop *fricassée* with raspberry vinegar, trout braised with tarragon and splendid desserts. At lunchtime during the week, there's a *formule* for €15, and set menus go for €19.50–33. The beautiful terrace looks over the Gorges de la Vésubie and the atmosphere is very friendly. Credit cards not accepted. *Free digestif offered to our readers on presentation of this guide.*

Vaison-la-Romaine

84110

⊛ ⬙ ⚒ Hôtel Burrhus**

1 pl. Montfort; take the Bollène exit off the A7.
☎04.90.36.00.11 ☎04.90.36.39.05
🌐www.burrhus.com

Closed *15 Dec–20 Jan.* **TV. Pay car park.**

Attractive hotel, all ochre walls and wrought iron, with a billiard room. The bedrooms are distributed around a warren of corridors and they're all different – some are decorated in Provençal style, others are more basic. Doubles go for €47–69 with shower/wc or bath, breakfast €7. The owners are into contemporary art and hold regular exhibitions. We like this place a lot. *10% discount on the room rate from the second consecutive night (except July–Aug) offered to our readers on presentation of this guide.*

⊛ ⚒ ⬙ |◎| L'Hostellerie Le Beffroi***

Rue de l'Évêché; take the A7 in the direction of Bollène or Orange.
☎04.90.36.04.71 ☎04.90.36.24.78
🌐www.le-beffroi.com
Closed *end Jan to end March.* **Restaurant closed** *weekday lunchtimes; Tues; 1 Nov–1 April.* **TV. High chairs and games available. Swimming pool. Car park.**

Based in the upper town, this hotel is housed in two residences from the sixteenth and seventeenth centuries. All the ancient charm remains – old wood and stone, furniture in keeping – along with comforts of today; doubles with shower/wc or bath at €85–130, depending on the season. Great Provençal cooking with menus €27–41 and children's menu €12: salmon steak with sorrel, *feuilleté* of snails *à la provençale* – and a salad bar on the terrace and superb garden in summer. There's a great view of town from the swimming pool. *Free house apéritif offered to our readers on presentation of this guide.*

Valberg

06470

⊛ ⚒ ⬙ Hôtel Le Chastellan**

Rue Saint-Jean; it's behind the tourist office off the main square, up the road to the left.
☎04.93.02.57.41 ☎04.93.02.61.65
✉hotel-le-chastellan@wanadoo.fr
Closed *April; May.* **TV. High chairs available. Car park.**

This is a family-run hotel for families to stay in. It boasts 37 lovely rooms, a large, airy dining room and a games room for the children. Doubles with shower/wc or bath go for €60–70, and six family suites for €110; breakfast costs €8. All the rooms have shower/wc or bath and direct-dial telephone. This is the sort of hotel you want to come to in summer or winter. *10% discount on the room rate (except school holidays) offered to our readers on presentation of this guide.*

◎ ⅔ |●| Côté Jardin

It's behind the main square.
☎04.93.02.64.70
Closed *Nov.*

You rarely think of gourmet food when you think about ski resorts, but here's the exception to the rule. True, you can get *tartiflette, raclette* and fondue, but it would be a pity to opt for dishes that are more typical of Savoy than of Provence. The dishes on the menus (€14.50–30) taste good and the presentation is exceptional; expect to pay around €40 for a meal à la carte. The dining room faces the garden and the service is friendly. *Free coffee offered to our readers on presentation of this guide.*

Vence

06140

◎ 🏠 |●| ⅔ Auberge des Seigneurs**

Place Frêne; in the ramparts, on the outskirts of the old town.
☎04.93.58.04.24 ⊕04.93.24.08.01
Restaurant closed *Mon; Tues, Wed and Thurs lunchtimes; early Nov to mid-March.*

This beautiful fifteenth-century building is situated on the ramparts at the entrance to the old town. The rooms, which are more like suites, are named after painters; some have mountain views. Prices are more than reasonable – €70–85 with shower or bath. The restaurant offers sophisticated, imaginative cooking on menus €30–42. *Free digestif offered to our readers on presentation of this guide.*

◎ ⅔ |●| La Farigoule

15 av. Henri-Isnard.
☎04.93.58.01.27
Closed *Tues; Wed and Sat lunchtimes (in summer); Tues and Wed (in winter); Feb,*

autumn and Christmas school holidays.
Disabled access.

You come here as much for the atmosphere as the authentic Provençal cooking. The chef, who trained with the great Alain Ducasse in Juan-les-Pins, works with the best market produce, combining texture, colour and flavour. The veranda has been extended to accommodate more people, the little dining room is convivial, and there's a large terrace, which is very welcoming in summer. Menus start at €22 (lunchtime), with other menus €29–43 (the most expensive is a taster menu). *Free house apéritif offered to our readers on presentation of this guide.*

◎ |●| Le P'tit Provençal

4 pl. Clemenceau; in the heart of the old town.
☎04.93.58.50.64
Closed *Mon; Tues (lunchtime only in July/ Aug).* **High chairs available.**

A restaurant with a relaxed informal atmosphere in the centre of the old town. The food is extremely imaginative and typically Provençal. Dishes of the day are chalked up on the board at lunchtime and you'll pay around €30 for a meal; menus in the evening are priced €22 and €28. If you eat on the terrace you can admire the view of the lively, historic town.

Saint-Jeannet

06640 (8km NE)

◎ 🏠 ⅔ Hôtel l'Indicible*

Rue du Saumalier; take the D318.
☎04.92.11.01.08 ⊕04.92.11.02.06
⊛www.saint-jeannet.com
Closed *15 Jan–15 Feb.* **TV.**

A little hotel in the middle of the village run by Michel originally from Ghent in Belgium. Their hotel is in an old house which has been very attractively renovated and it provides rooms – €48–64 for a double with shower/wc or bath – with views over Le Baou, the hills and the sea in the distance. Snacks are served in the summer on the terrace. *Free coffee offered to our readers on presentation of this guide.*

PROVENCE-ALPES-CÔTE D'AZUR

Rhône-Alpes

Aix-les-Bains

73100

◎ ☎ |●| Auberge de jeunesse

Promenade du Sierroz; take town centre, bus
2 towards Grand Port, bus stop Camping.
℗04.79.88.32.88 ℱ04.79.61.14.05
ℯaix-les-bains@fuaj.org
Closed *from autumn school holiday to Feb
school holiday.* **Open** *6–10pm.* **Disabled
access. Car park.**

This youth hostel is relatively far from
the town centre but close to the "Lac du
Bourget" and only a few minutes away from
the port and the beaches. It's in a nice countryside area, which unfortunately is beginning to be surrounded by buildings. The
youth hostel has three floors; each bedroom
contains four beds and an en-suite bathroom. It costs €14 per person to stay the
night, breakfast included; you can hire sheets
and meals cost €8.75. FUAJ card is compulsory but you can buy it there. Reservations
recommended from May to Sept.

◎ ☎ |●| Hôtel Broisin*

10 ruelle du Revet.
℗04.79.35.06.15 ℱ04.79.88.10.10
Closed *22 Nov–15 March.* **TV.**

A little hotel in a quiet side street in the
centre of town, just a short walk from the
spa. It's a very typical spa town hotel with
the atmosphere of a family guesthouse;
many guests have been coming here for
years. The rooms have been freshened up
and prices are modest: depending on the
season, they go for €28–31 for a double
with basin, or €37–41 with shower/wc.
The restaurant doesn't merit a special visit;
it offers one menu at €11.

◎ ☎ |●| Hôtel-restaurant Les Platanes**

173 av. du Petit-Port; it's near the lake.
℗04.79.61.40.54 ℱ04.79.35.00.41
ⓦwww.savoiesport.com
Closed *Sun evening out of season; mid-Nov
to end Jan.* **TV. Car park.**

Set in a residential area near the lake,
this hotel has a lovely shaded terrace.
The firmly classic cuisine features many
Savoy specialities on menus ranging from
€19 to €44, and the chef also has a deft
touch with fish dishes. The décor in the
bedrooms has seen better days (some
rooms have just been refurbished), but the
facilities are good, and they're very quiet;
doubles with shower/wc go for €39–45.
They have live jazz on Friday and Saturday
nights.

◎ ⅋ ☎ |●| Hôtel-restaurant Le Manoir***

37 rue Georges-1er; it's behind the spa,
500m from town centre.
℗04.79.61.44.00 ℱ04.79.35.67.67
ⓦwww.hotel-lemanoir.com
Closed *normally a few weeks in Dec.* **TV.
High chairs available. Swimming pool. Pay
car park.**

The "*manoir*" is actually a series of outbuildings belonging to two Belle Époque
mansions. The cosy, well-equipped rooms
are decorated in a style that's in keeping
with the building. Doubles go for €79–149
with shower/wc or bath, depending on the
season. The sitting rooms are comfortable,
the garden pleasant, and the indoor swimming pool very 1930s Hollywood; there
are also a sauna, hammam, Jacuzzi and a
fitness room. Menus cost €25–49, and feature excellent regional cuisine and delicate

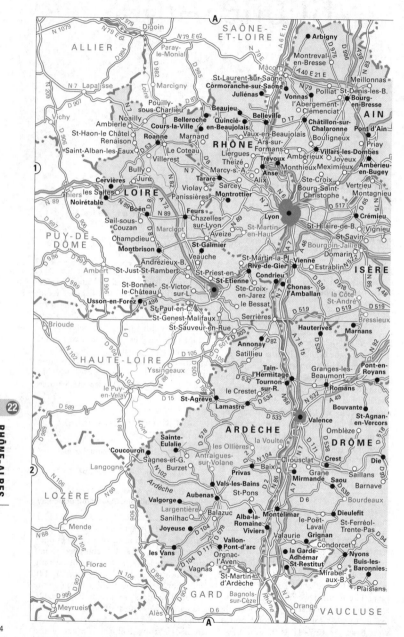

RHÔNE-ALPES

22

freshwater fish; there's also a good wine list. The young, relaxed staff create an easy-going atmosphere. *10% discount on the price of a room (1 Jan–30 April) offered to our readers on presentation of this guide.*

⊛ 🐾 |●| Restaurant L'Auberge du Pont Rouge

151 av. du Grand-Port; head towards the lake.
☎04.79.63.43.90
Closed *Mon evening; Tues; Wed; 21 Dec–9 Jan.*

A little out of the way (there are few good places to eat in the centre), this restaurant is always busy. You can dine on a simple veranda or in the gravel courtyard. The owners are friendly and the cooking is wonderful. The weekday lunch menu (at €14) and other menus (€23–30), include a combination of dishes from the south-west and fresh fish – which depends on what's landed from the lake. There are also specialities from Périgord. *Free house apéritif offered to our readers on presentation of this guide.*

Brison-Saint-Innocent
73100 (8km N)

⊛ 🐾 |●| Les Oliviers

212 rte. de Paris Brison-les-Oliviers; take the D991.
☎04.79.54.21.81
Closed *Tues (except July–Aug); mid-Jan to mid-Feb.* **Car park.**

This restaurant is set in a little hamlet by the side of Lake Bourget but is right by the road and not very far from the railway line. The owner uses the fish from the lake to create a seasonal menu full of spirit and good ideas, all at very reasonable prices: menus €16–45. *Free coffee offered to our readers on presentation of this guide.*

Alba-la-Romaine
07400

⊛ 🐾 |●| Restaurant La Petite Chaumière

Quartier de la Roche; it's signposted from the main square in Vieil Alba. Take the road at the bottom, it's 400m to the hamlet of La Roche.
☎04.45.52.43.50
Closed *Tues, Wed, Thurs (April–Sept); Mon–Fri (Oct and March); Sun evening to Fri evening (Nov–Feb); mid-Dec to mid-Jan.*

High chairs available.

The setting is very unusual and the welcome is delightful – it's one of our favourite places both for the cuisine and the surroundings. There are only a few tables inside, as most are on a lovely terrace overlooking an imposing tower of crumbling rocks. Traditional, old-fashioned, family cuisine – cream of carrot soup, sautéed lamb with spices and a real *crème caramel* – is served in handsome portions. Menus cost €11.50–15; there is a special evening menu when there is a concert at the Cavajazz. They don't have set specialities, though the savoury tart, cream of vegetable soup, lamb sautéed with spices and chocolate tart make a pretty regular appearance. Charge cards not accepted. Booking is advisable. *Free house apéritif offered to our readers on presentation of this guide.*

Saint-Pons
07580 (6km N)

⊛ 🏠 |●| Hostellerie Gourmande Mère Biquette***

Les Allignols; turn left off the N102 onto the D293, at Saint-Pons you should start to see signs for the inn, it's 4km further on.
☎04.75.36.72.61 ☎04.75.36.76.25
⊛www.logis-d-ardeche.com/merebriquette
Closed *Mon lunchtime; Wed lunchtime; mid-Nov to mid-Feb.* **TV. High chairs and games available. Swimming pool and tennis court. Car park.**

The natural setting for this old farmhouse is quite spectacular: the grounds are extensive and there are breathtaking views of the mountains and the valley. The country-style bedrooms are very handsome with lots of wood panelling, and they also include facilities such as mini-bar, hairdryer etc. Prices reflect the three-star quality, with doubles costing €55–78 with shower/wc or bath depending on comfort. There's a welcoming, refined restaurant serving good classics and a range of menus at €18–38: oxtail cooked in red wine, duck breast with honey and Calvados, local dishes. Logis de France.

Albertville
73200

⊛ 🐾 🏠 |●| Auberge Costaroche**

1 chemin Pierre-du-Roy; take the pont du Mirantin. It's near the medieval town of

Conflans and the château in Costaroche.
☎04.79.32.02.02 ⓕ04.79.31.37.59
ⓦwww.costaroche.fr.st
Restaurant closed Wed; 10 days in Jan; 10 days in Sept. **TV. Car park.**

A large, rather dull building in a residential area surrounded by a tree-filled garden. The owners give you a charming welcome, and the rooms have been discreetly renovated. Doubles with bath cost €39–49: ask for no. 17, 18, 27 or 28 which overlook the garden. The dining room is not very intimate but the cooking is decent: ravioli *Royans* with *gratin* of Tamié cheese (from the abbey), king prawns flambéed *à la provençal*, scallops *au noilly* (Vermouth), caramelized *pain perdu* (French toast). There's a weekday lunch menu for €12, with others €16–39. *10% discount on the price of a room (except weekends in winter) offered to our readers on presentation of this guide.*

Plancherine
73200 (8km W)

⌖ |●| Chalet des Trappeurs

Col de Tamié; from Albertville, follow the signs for Gilly-sur-Isère and then col de Tamié.
☎04.79.32.21.44
Closed Mon; generally a week at end June. **TV.**

The heliport and the faux antique statues are a little worrying, but inside things are different, and there's a large terrace. This characterful, attractive chalet is sturdily built of wood; huge logs burn in the hearth, hunting trophies line the walls and animal skins are draped on the benches. They serve Savoy specialities such as *tartiflette* and *fondue*, substantial omelettes and some remarkable local dishes: country-style fillet of lake whitefish, *civet* of piglet. The weekday lunch menu goes for €13 and other menus are €24–28. While you're in the area, buy some of the cheese made by the monks in the nearby abbey of Tamié.

Allevard
38580

⌖ 🏠 |●| Les Terrasses**

29 av. de Savoie; it's opposite the old train station.
☎04.76.45.84.42
ⓦwww.hotellesterrasses.com
Closed Wed; Sun evening; Easter school

holiday; Nov school holiday. **TV. High chairs and games available.**

A rather dull building from the outside, but it's been attractively renovated inside and decorated in shades of blue and white with posters of great artists' works on the walls. The corner bar in the veranda at the entrance is bright and the dining room is fresh and smart. There are good dishes on the menus – weekday menu at €13, with others up to €22 – including hot goat's cheese salad with honey, duck with gingerbread, fillets of lake whitefish with sesame and Chartreuse iced soufflé. Comfortable double rooms start at €32 (with wc on the landing), then €38–46 – nos. 8. 13 and 14 have a view over the garden. The owner will greet you very warmly to this special place. *Free house apéritif or coffee offered to our readers on presentation of this guide.*

Goncelin
38570 (10km SW)

⌖ |●| Restaurant Le Clos du Château

Take the D525 from Allevard.
☎04.76.71.72.04
Closed Sun and Mon evenings; Wed; a fortnight in Aug.

An extremely nice English couple runs this thirteenth-century house, in the mountains of Chartreuse and Belledonne. It's not easy to see it from the road because it's set in very extensive grounds. You dine in the shade of the hazels and ancient cedars with a view over the mountains in the summer, or in the restaurant, which has a French-style ceiling. Bag a table by the fire in winter. Suzie Glayser is in charge of the service while her husband, Laurent, who has worked at the Savoy and the Ritz in London, creates wonderful flavours in the kitchen. Specialities include crayfish ravioli in a creamy broth, and beef Wellington with foie gras. His *"menu du marché"* at €28.50 features expertly prepared fish and vegetables; other menus go up to €55.

Ferrière (La)
38580 (11km S)

⌖ 🏠 |●| Auberge Nemoz

Hameau La Martinette; take the D525 in the direction of Fond-de-France/Le Pleynet.
☎04.76.45.03.10
ⓦwww.nemoz.com
Closed early Nov to mid-Dec. **Restaurant**

open *every day in season (winter and summer); Wed–Sun and public holidays out of season.* **Car park.**

Tucked away in the heart of the forest, this stone chalet offers large, impressive rooms with rustic furniture and décor at €65–80, depending on the season, with breakfast included. A photo display in the entrance shows how the chalet was twice able to come back to life, phoenix-like, after fires. It is now far removed from the log cabin of old, because each time it has emerged bigger, prettier, more sophisticated (and more expensive). The owner is very chatty, and the atmosphere relaxed and friendly. In the restaurant, the log fire is always burning to serve *raclette* (€19.50), while full meals are served by candlelight, or on the attractive terrace in fine weather, with piano music in the background. The weekday lunchtime menu is €15, with others €22–28. The speciality is trout fished straight from the pond. It is essential to book in advance. *Free house apéritif (April–June and Sept–Oct) offered to our readers on presentation of this guide.*

Ambérieu-en-Bugey
01500

ⓒ |●| L'Amphitryon

91 rue Alexandre-Bérard; it's 200m from the town centre.
ⓣ04.74.38.26.51
Closed *Sun; Mon–Thurs evenings; 3 weeks in Aug; a week at Christmas.*

The welcome is effusive here, the service is efficient and the sophisticated food offers pleasant surprises. The meat and fish of the day are served with three elaborate accompaniments, such as carrot mousse, fresh mushrooms in creamy sauce and petit-pois and goat's cheese mousse. The salads are so substantial that they almost comprise a meal in themselves, while the terrines and other tasty starters are all home-made and the desserts are equally enticing. You can eat on the terrace on fine days. The weekday lunchtime menu costs €16, with others €23–28.

Meximieux
01800 (11km SW)

ⓒ ⚘ ⌂ |●| Hôtel-bar du Lion d'Or**

16 pl. Vaugelas; its on the central square.

ⓣ04.74.61.00.89 ⓕ04.74.61.43.80
Open *noon–3pm.* **TV. Pay car park.**

This hotel-bar was completely rebuilt after World War II. A German tank ploughed into it during the battle for the liberation of France that raged fiercely in this area. Double rooms cost €40; the large rooms, overlooking the quiet courtyard, have been recently refurbished. The ground-floor bar fills up with regulars but there will be space for you to have lunch; try the dish of the day for €7.50. This is a good little place to spend the night without breaking the bank. Exceptionally warm welcome. *Free house apéritif or coffee offered to our readers on presentation of this guide.*

ⓒ ⌂ Hôtel La Bérangère**

Route de Lyon.
ⓣ04.74.34.77.77 ⓕ04.74.34.70.27
ⓦwww.hotel-la-berangere.com
Disabled access. TV. Swimming pool. Car park.

This clean, modern and functional hotel is very well situated close to the beautiful medieval village of Pérouges. The rooms are comfortable and the service is friendly. Doubles with shower/wc cost €45, or €54.50 with bath. There is a bonus in summer: a swimming pool surrounded by lush vegetation.

ⓒ ⌂ |●| Hôtel-restaurant R. Jacquet***

Pont de Chazey, N84; take exit 7 to Pérouges-Meximieux from the N84.
ⓣ04.74.61.94.80 ⓕ04.74.61.92.07
ⓦwww.lamerejacquet.com
Restaurant closed *Sun evening; Sat lunchtime.* **Closed** *a week at end of Feb; third week in Aug; end Dec to mid-Jan.* **TV.**

You will be very well received in this sixteenth-century house turned hotel, run by the Jacquet family for several generations. Do not be put off by the proximity of the road; the rooms on the garden are very quiet, with lovely terraces overlooking the beautifully tended garden. Doubles cost €61–68. The restaurant also looks out onto this appealing setting through extensive bay windows; the food is more than capable of living up to these impressive surroundings. There's a weekday menu for €22, then others €34–45.

Bourg-Saint-Christophe

01800 (16km SW)

◎ ☎ |●| Auberge Chez Ginette*

Take the N84 to Pérouges, then take the D4.
℡04.74.61.01.49 ℻04.74.61.36.13
@auberge.chez.ginette@wanadoo.fr
Closed *Fri; Sat evening.* **TV. Car park.**

This hotel has earned a good reputation for the quality of its regional dishes and its warm, family atmosphere. Ginette receives her guests with obvious pleasure, while her son, Laurent, takes care of the equally generous cooking: fried frogs, royal carp with *Gamay du Bugey*, chicken in creamy sauce. Menus cost €23–34; double rooms with shower/wc go for €40–48. Logis de France.

Annecy

74000

See map overleaf

◎ ☎ Aléry Hôtel**

5 av. d'Aléry. **Map A2-1**
℡04.50.45.24.75. ℻04.50.51.26.90
@hotel.alery@wanadoo.fr
TV. Car park.

Characterful, traditional hotel in a good spot between the station and the old town. All the rooms are decorated in typical mountain style with pictures painted on wood, and they all have air-conditioning. Doubles go for €42–59 with shower/wc or bath, depending on the season. The owners welcome you charmingly, the facilities are perfect and you'll have a quiet night and a good breakfast.

◎ ☆ ☎ Hôtel du Nord**

24 rue Sommeiller; it's between the train station, the lake and the town centre. **Map A2-4**
℡04.50.45.08.78 ℻04.50.51.22.04
@www.annecy-hotel-du-nord.com
TV. Car park.

This hotel is in a great location. The place has a certain charm with its panelled reception and loggia on the first floor. The rooms – €46–59 with shower/wc or bath – are decorated in pastel colours, and have lovely bathrooms and air-conditioning; some look over old Annecy. The refurbished breakfast room with its parquet floor and modern furniture provides a pleasurable setting in which to start the

day. *10% discount on the room rate offered to our readers on presentation this guide.*

◎ ☆ ☎ |●| Hôtel Les Terrasses**

15 rue Louis Chaumontel; it's a 10-minute walk from the town centre. **Off map A1-5**
℡04.50.57.08.98 ℻04.50.57.05.28
@www.lac-annecy.com
Restaurant closed *Sat and Sun (except July–Aug); 12 Dec–9 Jan.* **Disabled access. High chairs available. Car park.**

A stunning old house, which has been transformed into a spruce, modern little hotel with a charming garden. The rooms are plain (white walls, pale wood furniture), quiet and comfortable, and cost €63–76 for a double with shower/wc or bath. Half board, compulsory from June to September, costs €44.50–56 per person. The area has little to offer; however the hotel is good value for money and the welcome excellent. There's a restaurant with menus at €11 and €15 – it's fine if you can't be bothered to go into town. *Free house apéritif offered to our readers on presentation of this guide.*

◎ ☆ ☎ Hôtel de Bonlieu***

5 rue de Bonlieu; it's beside the Palais de Justice. **Map B1-3**
℡04.50.45.17.16 ℻04.50.45.11.48
@www.annecybonlieuhotel.fr
Disabled access. TV. High chairs available. Pay car park.

A good, dependable little hotel with all mod cons near the lake and the old town, ideal if you're looking for peace and quiet. It's targeted more at young business execs than travellers, but you'll get a friendly welcome and prices are sensible: double rooms cost €72–80 with shower/wc or bath, depending on the season. There's a charge to use the car park at €6 per night from early May to the end of September. *10% discount on the room rate offered to our readers on presentation of this guide.*

◎ ☎ Hôtel du Palais de l'Isle***

13 rue Perrière; it's towards Chappuis and Semnoz. **Map B3-2**
℡04.50.45.86.87 ℻04.50.51.87.15
@www.hoteldupalaisdelisle.com
TV.

An imposing eighteenth-century residence, superbly located in narrow, winding old streets with the River Thiou running beneath. Doubles with bath

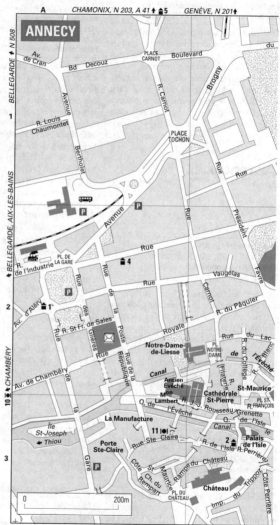

ANNECY

CHAMONIX, N 203, A 41 ↑ 🚢 5   GENÈVE, N 201 ↑

BELLEGARDE ↑ N 508

Av. de Cran

Bd   Decouz   PLACE CARNOT   Boulevard

Brogny

du

Avenue

R. Louis Chaumontet

Bertholet

R. Carnot

PLACE TOCHON

Rue

Rue

Président

1

BELLEGARDE, AIX-LES-BAINS

Avenue

P

P

Favre

R. de l'Industrie   PL. DE LA GARE

🚌 4

Rue

Rue

Vaugelas

Carnot

R. du Pâquier

Av. d'Aléry

Rue des Glières

Rue

Rue

Rue de la Poste

🚌 1

R. St Fr. de Sales

Royale

Rue   du   Lac

2

10 ↕ CHAMBÉRY

Notre-Dame-de-Liesse

Rue de la République

PL. NOTRE-DAME

R. du Collège

R. Filaterie

de

l'Évêché

R. Blanc

Av. de Chambéry

Canal

Ancien Évêché   Mⁿ Lambert

Cathédrale St-Pierre

St-Maurice

La Manufacture

Q. de   R. J.-J. Rousseau   l'Évêché

Grenette   de l'Isle

PL. ST-FRANÇOIS

Île St-Joseph   ← Thiou

11 |●|

Canal

2 🚌

Palais de l'Isle

3

Porte Ste-Claire

Rue Ste-Claire

R. de l'Isle   R. Perrière

Côte Ch. du Rempart

St Maurice

Rampe du Château

Château

Côte Perrière

Imp. du Tripoz

P

Gare

PL. DU CHÂTEAU

Château

0   200m

Basilique de la Visitation, Conserv. d'Art et d'Histoire ↘ Semnoz

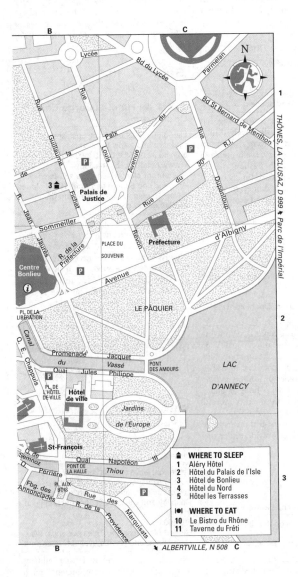

WHERE TO SLEEP
1 Aléry Hôtel
2 Hôtel du Palais de l'Isle
3 Hôtel de Bonlieu
4 Hôtel du Nord
5 Hôtel les Terrasses

WHERE TO EAT
10 Le Bistro du Rhône
11 Taverne du Fréti

cost €76–100; a few rooms overlook the palace, while others face the château and the old town. Soundproofing and air-conditioning are gradually being introduced. The modern rooms are superb, with furniture designed by Philippe Starck.

◉ 🛉 |◉| Le Bistro du Rhône

13 av. du Rhône; it's near the train station.
Off map A2-12
☏04.50.45.53.34
Closed *Mon and Tues evenings; Sat lunch-time; Sun; Aug.* **Disabled access.**

In a somewhat soulless area of the old town, this bistro has a really lovely dining room that is almost Provençal with its saffron yellow walls. Very well prepared and tasty dishes use the freshest market produce. There are weekday lunch menus at €11.30 and €12.80; dinner menus at €14.95 and €23. The relaxed atmosphere is underpinned by experienced service. *Free Kir offered to our readers on presentation of this guide.*

◉ |◉| Taverne du Fréti

12 rue Sainte-Claire; it's in the old town. **Map A3-11**
☏04.50.51.29.52
Closed *a fortnight in June.* **Open** *evenings 7–11.30pm; Sun lunchtime.*

The *Fréti* is one of the few places on this touristy street that still offers quality at reasonable prices. It's a cheese shop, and naturally enough they specialize in dishes that use it: sixteen types of fondue, *raclette*, *tartiflette* and potatoes with blue or goat's cheese. An à la carte meal costs around €15 to €20. There's a pretty dining room upstairs where you can eat if the weather's not good enough to sit outside under the arcade.

Sévrier
74320 (5km S)

◉ 🛉 |◉| Auberge du Bessard

525 rte. d'Albertville; it's on the N508.
☏04.50.52.40.45
Closed *20 Oct–20 March.* **Disabled access. Car park.**

If you dream of sitting on the banks of the lake with the water lapping at the terrace while you dine on fine fresh fish (whitebait, fillets of perch or char lake fish with sorrel), here's just the place.

It's something of a local institution and has been run by the same family for the last fifty years. There's a €15.60 weekday menu, another for €21 at the weekends and on public holidays, or you'll pay about €25 à la carte. The atmosphere is warm and friendly. *Free house liqueur offered to our readers on presentation of this guide.*

Saint-Jorioz
74410 (9km SE)

◉ 🛉 🏠 |◉| Hôtel-auberge de la Cochette**

Lieu-dit La Magne-à Saint-Eustache; go to St-Jorioz and follow the signs.
☏04.50.32.03.53 ☏04.50.32.02.70
⊛www.hotel-la-cochette.com
Restaurant closed *weekdays 15 March–30 April and end Sept to end April.* **Hotel closed** *1 Nov–15 March.* **High chairs and games available. Car park.**

Friendly country inn in a hamlet that offers a magnificent view over the lake of Annecy, 6km away as the crow flies. Nicely renovated rooms with lots of light wood cost €39–45 with shower/wc or bath, family rooms for three to four people go for €46–58. The food is delicious and traditional (breast of duck with honey, *feuilleté* of snails) with great menus at €17–28; you'll pay around €30 à la carte. The home-made bread and patisserie are scrumptious. *Free house liqueur or 10% discount on the room rate (except July–Aug) offered to our readers on presentation of this guide.*

Chapeiry
74540 (11km SW)

◉ 🛉 |◉| Auberge La Grange à Jules

Le Pelvoz; leave the A41 motorway at the Rumilly exit and take the N201 in the direction of Annecy. After Alby, turn left towards Chapeiry and you'll find it after the bridge on the right.
☏04.50.68.15.07
Closed *Mon, Tues and Thurs evenings; Wed.* **High chairs and games available. Car park.**

Though the façade isn't that alluring – more farm hangar than ancient grange – everything changes once you get inside. It's a cosily rustic place that feels miles away from the motorway. In summer, you can eat barbecues in the garden under the trees and among the flowers; in winter, the open fire takes the chill off the air. They create good, contemporary dishes using fresh ingredients with a range of menus (€22–35): potato tart with foie gras, chocolate *fondant*. Theme evenings are organized at weekends. *Free house liqueur offered to our readers on presentation of this guide.*

Gruffy
74540 (17.5km SW)

⏣ 🍴 🏠 |●| Aux Gorges du Chéran**

Pont de l'Abîme; take the N210 and 1km after Chaux turn onto the D5, once you've passed Gruffy, it's a further 1.5km.
☏04.50.52.51.13 ℗04.50.52.57.33
Closed *15 Nov–30 March.* **Restaurant closed** *Sun evening (except in July and Aug).* **TV. Car park.**

This peaceful chalet with a family atmosphere, surrounded by forest, practically clings to the cliff above the Chéran, opposite the bridge over the abyss. Spacious, comfortable, classically designed and refurbished rooms go for €42–54 with shower/wc or €58–64 with bath. Half board is preferred in summer, at a cost of €42–53 per person. The restaurant offers traditional and regional food with menus at €20–30 and a formule at €11. Specialities include beef fillet with morels and trout with almonds. *Free house apéritif offered to our readers on presentation of this guide.*

Semnoz (Le)
74320 (18km S)

⏣ 🏠 |●| 🍴 Chalet Hôtel Semnoz – Alpes 1704 metres**

Le Semnoz; take the D41.
☏04.50.01.23.17 ℗04.50.64.53.05
Closed *in May and Oct.* **Restaurant closed** *Sun evening and Mon out of season.* **Car park.**

A large late-nineteenth-century chalet, almost alone on Le Semnoz and with excellent views of the Alps. Since the 1950s it has been run by the family of the famous guide and ski champion Alfred Couttet (they will tell you his life story at the drop of a woolly hat) and they give their guests a very warm welcome. The rustic/mountain-style rooms are gradually being refurbished

and cost €32 for a double with washbasin, or €44–48 with shower/wc or bath. Classical, regional cuisine predominates on the menus, which range from €15 to €30. A word of advice: if you want the peak of Le Semnoz to yourself, or almost, avoid the high season. *Free house liqueur offered to our readers on presentation of this guide.*

Annonay
07100

⏣ 🍴 🏠 Hôtel du Midi**

17 pl. des Cordeliers; it's in the lower town.
☏04.75.33.23.77 ℗04.75.33.02.43
TV. Pay car park.

Set in a good location on a very lively square, this hotel is a sturdy building of remarkable dimensions, with wide corridors, large rooms (especially those overlooking the square) and thick, plush carpets. There are pictures and engravings of hot-air balloons all over the place – the Montgolfier brothers were born in Annonay. Doubles go for €32–48, depending on the level of comfort. *10% discount on the room rate (for a two-night stay 30 Sept–1 May) offered to our readers on presentation of this guide.*

⏣ |●| Restaurant Marc et Christine

29 av. Marc-Seguin; it's opposite the old station.
☏04.75.33.46.97
Closed *Sun evening; Mon; the Feb school holiday; mid-Aug to 1 Sept.* **Disabled access. High chairs available.**

The inventive cooking here is appreciated by an essentially local clientele. Christine gives her guests a warm welcome and ushers them into a sitting room decorated in peach tones; don't miss the mural painted on the wall illustrating the fable of the fox and the crow. Marc does the cooking, and prepares dishes that combine classic and local ingredients; the first menu is €18 (except Sun), with other menus €24–39. Menus change monthly and dishes may include crayfish and sweet onion soup or snails with pig's trotters. A large selection of wines is available and the owners clearly state the names of all their suppliers. In summer you can eat outside in the pleasant garden.

Satillieu

07290 (14km SW)

◎ ♫ ♞ |●| Hôtel-restaurant Chalet-Sapet**

Place de la Faurie; from Annonay, follow the signs first for the centre of town and then for Lalouvesc D578A.
℡04.75.34.95.42 ℻04.75.69.91.13
ⓦwww.chaletsapet.com
Closed 19 Dec–10 Jan. **TV. High chairs and baby changing facilities available. Swimming pool.**

This place, situated in the centre of the village, has an excellent reputation. The welcome is really nice and the cooking first-rate. One of the specialities is *crique ardéchoise,* made with grated potatoes sprinkled with garlic, onions and parsley; the frogs' legs with parsley, scallop *fricassée* and tripe are also good. Menus range from €14 to €23. The recently refurbished bedrooms are clean and comfortable; doubles with shower/wc or bath cost €41–45. There is also a family room available. Arrangements can be made for mountain biking or hiking, and there's an open-air pool. Logis de France. *Free house apéritif offered to our readers on presentation of this guide.*

Serrières

07340 (15km NE)

◎ ♫ ♞ |●| Hôtel-restaurant Schaeffer**.

It's on the N86.
℡04.75.34.00.07 ℻04.75.34.08.79
ⓦwww.hotel-schaeffer.com
Closed Sun evening; Mon; Tues and Sat lunchtime (July–Aug); Jan; autumn school holiday. **TV. High chairs available. Pay car park.**

A substantial house on the banks of the Rhône. It's a gourmet restaurant which uses the best seasonal produce; menus start at €22 (weekday lunchtimes), with others €33–85. Even the cheapest menu includes generous portions of food, beautifully prepared and presented, and all the little extras, such as appetizers and *petits fours,* normally reserved for the more expensive menus. The fine wine list includes a range of good Côtes-du-Rhônes and Hermitages but there are also some more modest bottles. Modern, functional, air-conditioned and soundproofed rooms go for €60 with bath; some have views of the river and the bridge. A high-quality place to stay, but one where you don't have to spend a fortune. Logis de France. *Free liqueur offered to our readers on presentation of this guide.*

Saint-Sauveur-en-Rue

42220 (25km SE)

◎ ♫ ♞ |●| Château de Bobigneux**

Bobigneux; take the N82 to Bourg-Argental, then take the D503 towards Le Puy for about 4km.
℡04.77.39.24.33 ℻04.77.39.25.74
ⓔchateau-de-bobigneux@wanadoo.fr
Closed Wed; from All Saint's Day to Easter. **High chairs and cots available. Car park.**

After eighteen years in Greenland the owners moved here and took over this sixteenth-century stone manor house, which is right next to a farm belonging to Madame's brother. They've created a delightful place to stay and prices are reasonable. The farm provides them with all the fresh produce they need, and Monsieur, who is a talented chef, creates great dishes. Try the oyster mushrooms in flaky pastry. There's a *"Campagnard"* menu served in the week for €12 and others at €16 and €23. The dining rooms have been pleasantly renovated, and the terrace and the garden are both lovely. On the first floor, six bright, spacious country-style rooms are reasonably priced at €36–42. Logis de France. *Free house apéritif offered to our readers on presentation of this guide.*

Anse

69480

◎ ♞ |●| Hôtel-restaurant Le Saint-Romain**

Route de Graves; it's signposted, 200m off the main road.
℡04.74.60.24.46 ℻04.74.60.24.46
ⓦwww.hotel-saint-romain.fr
Closed Sun evening (26 Nov–25 April). **TV. High chairs and games available. Car park.**

Traditional, classic hotel with honest cooking in the restaurant – terrine of foie gras with *confit* of pigeon, numerous ripe cheeses and home-made desserts. The dining room has sturdy beams and there's a pleasant terrace for summer, and the welcome is a little impersonal. Menus start at €19 (except Sun) up to €46. Rooms are sizeable and simple, with good beds; they cost €50 with bath/wc. Logis de France.

Marcy-sur-Anse

69480 (7km SW)

ⓐ |●| Le Télégraphe

Take the D79 for Lachassagne and turn left onto the D70.
☎04.74.60.24.73
Closed *Sun evening; Mon.* **High chairs available. Car park.**

You can order any of the menus with confidence – there's a weekday lunch menu at €12, with five others €19–43. In the cheapest menu, the house terrine and *andouillette* with mustard sauce are delicious, while the *croustille* of St Marcellin goat's cheese has a real tang. The pleasant terrace is well away from the road, so it's quiet, and the friendly atmosphere makes the experience all the more pleasurable.

Alix

69380 (10km SW)

ⓐ ⚲ |●| Le Vieux Moulin

Chemin du Vieux Moulin; take the D39 in the direction of Lachassagne, turn left for Marcy, and Alix is signposted to the right.
☎04.78.43.91.66 ☎04.78.47.98.46
Closed *Mon and Tues (except some public holidays and for group reservations); 17 Aug–16 Sept.* **Disabled access. Car park.**

This mill built of pale gold stone has been converted into a charming restaurant with three cosy dining rooms and a barn for families or large groups. Four menus ranging from €22 (not served on public holidays) up to €47 list good, reliable dishes: sea-trout with sorrel, guinea-fowl with morels, frogs' legs, monkfish with cream and curry sauce and leek *fondue*. Afterwards you can have a game of *boules (pétanques)* or relax on the terrace. *Free coffee offered to our readers on presentation of this guide.*

Arbigny

01190

ⓐ ⚑ Le Moulin de la Brevette**

From the north, take the Tournus exit off the A6, then the D933 for Cuisery and Sermayer; from the south, take the Macon-Nord exit,

towards Pont-de-Vaux, then Sermayer via the D933.
☎03.85.36.49.27 ☎03.85.30.66.91
🌐www.moulindelabrevette.com
Disabled access. Pay car park.

This old mill – minus its wheel – stands deep in the countryside. The bedrooms, in a converted farmhouse, are large, bright, comfortable and quiet. Fully equipped doubles start at €50; nos. 15–19 and 29–32 have the best views. It's also possible to rent flats. Friendly and welcoming, this is the perfect spot to get away from all the noise and bustle of the town.

Aubenas

07200

ⓐ ⚑ |●| Hôtel des Négociants*

Place de l'Hôtel-de-Ville; it's in the old part of town opposite the château.
☎04.75.35.18.74
Closed *Sun; a fortnight in March; a fortnight in Oct.* **TV.**

Good central location and cheap prices. The clean rooms, most with TV, have decent beds and cost €22–38 depending on facilities (wash basin, shower and wc). The cuisine in the restaurant isn't especially refined but it has a faithful band of regulars. There's a choice of menus ranging from €10 to €19.50.

ⓐ ⚲ ⚑ |●| Auberge des Pins

95 rte. de Vals.
☎04.75.35.29.36 ☎04.75.89.00.15
Closed *15 Sept–15 Oct.* **Restaurant closed** *Sat (Jan–Feb); Sun (except in Aug).* **TV. Car park.**

A charming, sprawling building in a pleasant setting with lots of pine trees. Some of the rooms are big, others rather small, but they're all clean and most have air-conditioning; doubles with shower/wc or bath/wc cost €35–50. Half board, compulsory during July and August, costs €60–70 per person. Try to get a room at the back as the hotel is on the main road and the traffic can be heavy. The restaurant serves dishes such as country pâté with chestnuts and onion marmalade, and Lyonnais specials. The weekday lunch menu costs €12, then others €17–21. There's a car park and a free lock-up for motorbikes. *Free house apéritif offered to our readers on presentation of this guide.*

⚽ 🏠 |○| La Pinède**

Route du camping Les Pins; it's on the road
to Lentillère, the D235, 1.5km from the town
centre.
☎04.75.35.25.88 ⓕ04.75.93.06.42
ⓦwww.la-pinede.fr
Closed *Fri lunchtimes and Sat evenings from
mid-Oct to March (except school holidays);
1 Dec–31 Jan.* **TV. High chairs available.
Swimming pool. Car park.**

A traditional, welcoming holiday hotel
in a very peaceful location – it's probably best to book in summer. Pleasant
doubles in the main building and the
annexe go for €48–50 with shower/wc
or bath; half board, compulsory in July
and August, costs €47–48 per person. The
restaurant offers decent value for money,
with menus €17–29. Regional specialities
include mixed salad with melted cheese,
pike-perch *au Saint-Joseph* and flan; good
breakfast, too. There's a swimming pool
with a panoramic view.

⚽ |○| Restaurant Le Fournil

34 rue du 4-Septembre.
☎04.75.93.58.68
Closed *Sun; Mon; the Feb, autumn and
Christmas school holidays; last week in June
and first week in July.* **Disabled access.**

This handsome fifteenth-century building
with its patio and vaults is the ideal setting to try the exquisite dishes prepared
by Michel Leynaud. His establishment is
stylish, from the welcome to the gourmet
food such as curried medallions of monkfish; the desserts are superb. Menus are
reasonably priced at €18–33.

Sanilhac
07110 (25km SW)

⚽ 🍴 🏠 |○| Auberge de la Tour de Brison**

Take the D104, then the D103 in the direc-
tion of Largentière, then follow the road to
Montréal.
☎04.75.39.29.00 ⓕ04.75.39.19.56
ⓦwww.benilbrison.com
Closed *Tues evening and Wed (except
July–Aug); Nov–March.* **Disabled access.
TV. High chairs and games available.
Swimming pool. Car park.**

This pleasant hotel, run by a nice couple,
has twelve air-conditioned rooms, some
with whirlpool bath and (on a clear day) a
view of the Alps. Doubles cost €47–65 with
shower/wc or bath; half board, compulsory

in July and August, costs €54 per person.
The menu, at €25, is very generously
served. Dishes include chicken liver mousse
with chestnuts, traditional *caillette* and duck
breast cooked in port. There are tennis
courts and a swimming pool on the spot
and lots of other activities in the area. Logis
de France. *Free house apéritif or coffee offered to
our readers on presentation of this guide.*

Autrans
38880

⚽ 🏠 |○| Hôtel de la Poste***

Place de l'Église.
☎04.76.95.31.03 ⓕ04.76.95.30.17
ⓦwww.hotel-barnier.com
Closed *Sun evening and Mon out of season;
20 April–7 May; 20 Oct–1 Dec.* **TV. High
chairs available. Swimming pool. Car park.**

A local institution that's been run by the
same family since 1937. The thirty rooms
all have good facilities; some have sitting
rooms and balconies looking out over
the front. Three categories of doubles and
twin rooms go for €54–77, according to
the level of comfort and season. We prefer
the first category – they are not so big but
the decoration is more subtle. There are
splendid sporting facilities – take a look at
the superb covered swimming pool (open
all year) with its exotic décor, which you
reach via a private underground passageway. There's also a Jacuzzi, a fitness room
and a sauna (fee applies). Good cuisine
with a range of menus on offer at €18–45.
There's a nice terrace and garden. Logis
de France.

Méaudre
38112 (6km S)

⚽ 🍴 🏠 |○| Le Pertuzon**

Avenue du Vercors; take the D106 in the
direction of Villars-de-Lans.
☎04.76.95.21.17 ⓕ04.76.95.26.00
ⓦwww.perso.club-internet.fr/locana/
Closed *Sun evening (except in Feb, July and
Aug); Tues evening; Wed; a week in June; a
week early Nov; 1–20 Dec.* **TV. High chairs
available. Car park.**

An establishment with a smart, warm
dining room, cuisine of excellent reputation and nine pleasant rooms – nos. 104,
105 and 210 are best as they have a garden
view. Doubles with washbasin go for €40,
or €45 with shower/wc. The first menu

is a weekday lunch menu at €18 (€13 out of season), then other menus €25–52, including a regional menu which varies according to the seasons; typically it might include a salad Vercors, *Royans* ravioli, rabbit with Clairette de Die, and fruit *clafoutis*. The chef worked in Réunion and Egypt after qualifying from hotel school then came to Vercors. There's a nice garden and terrace in summer. *10% discount on the room rate in Oct, Nov and April (except during festivals) or free coffee offered to our readers on presentation of this guide.*

Beaufort-sur-Doron
73270

@ 🍴 🏠 |O| Hôtel-restaurant Le Grand Mont**

Place de l'Église; take the Albert-Beaufort road.
☎04.79.38.33.36 ℻04.79.38.39.07
Closed *Fri out of season (excluding school holidays); 25 April–8 May; Oct; first week in Nov.* **TV. High chairs available.**

An old house, with a spotless exterior, on the outskirts of the ancient village. The refurbished rooms are comfortable; doubles with shower/wc cost €49–65. In the restaurant, which is a traditional bistro with an old-style dining room, they serve primarily regional dishes on menus for €18–28: *diots* with *crozets* (local vegetable and pork sausages cooked in white wine and served with square-shaped noodles), omelette with Beaufort cheese, fish terrine or rabbit terrine. Logis de France. *10% discount on the room rate (in Nov and the first fortnight of April) offered to our readers on presentation of this guide.*

Beaujeu
69430

@ 🍴 🏠 |O| Hôtel-restaurant Anne de Beaujeu**

28 rue de la République.
☎04.74.04.87.58 ℻04.74.69.22.13
Closed *Sun evening; Mon; Tues lunchtime; 12 days in Aug; 20 Dec–20 Jan.* **TV. Car park.**

Though the hotel is named after the daughter of Louis XI (who lived in the late fifteenth century), the building is not of that era. It has a garden, a plush foyer and an impressive dining room. Doubles go for €52–63 with shower/wc or bath, some are quite big and can sleep three (supplement payable). They serve classic dishes and honest cooking on a range of menus costing €19–49, but you may find the bill a bit steep. They also have a fine wine list. *Free coffee and wine tasting offered to our readers on presentation of this guide.*

Belleroche
42670

@ 🍴 |O| Auberge "Le Bel' Roche"

It's in the centre of the village, opposite the post office, beside the church.
☎04.74.03.68.63
Closed *Mon and Tues evenings; Wed.*

An attractive setting in the heart of a sleepy village for excellent food served with a warm smile: rabbit with broad beans and lemon *confit*, ox cheek *parmentier*. They offer two menus of the day for €11 and €12, then other menus €15–25. You can eat on a small terrace bedecked with flowers on fine days or in the dining room decorated in warm colours. *Free coffee offered to our readers on presentation of this guide.*

Belleville
69220

@ 🍴 |O| Le Buffet de la Gare

Place de la Gare; it's near the train station.
☎04.74.66.07.36
Closed *evenings (except for reservations); weekends; 1–25 Aug; a week at Christmas.* **Car park.**

It's sometimes said that French train stations and their surroundings aren't as appealing as they once were. This restaurant is an exception: a cute little house full of flowers and plants, it's decorated with old posters, Art Deco light fixtures and quirky old mirrors. Hélène Fessy, the owner, always has a smile and a kind word for her customers, and her husband supplies the wine. The dish of the day costs €11.50, with menus at €13.50 and €17. Dishes chalked up on the board might include *tapenade*, house terrine, leeks vinaigrette, or stuffed tomatoes and courgettes, cheese and dessert. During the grape harvest, the place is still pretty busy at one o'clock in the morning. *Free house apéritif offered to our readers on presentation of this guide.*

Vaux-en-Beaujolais

69460 (15km SW)

☙ 𝔄 ᝰ I●I Auberge de Clochemerle**

Rue Gabriel-Chevallier; take the D43 in the direction of Odenas, and at Saint-Étienne-des-Oullières, turn left in the direction of Vaux.
☎04.74.03.20.16 🖷04.74.03.28.48
🌐www.georgeslegarde.com
Closed *Tues; Wed; 27 July–14 Aug.* **Disabled access. TV.**

All the rooms in this village inn – €43–51 with shower/wc or bath – have been freshly refurbished, though they have kept their charm because of the period furniture. The restaurant serves excellent food, which is in evidence on all the menus, and the prices are justified: menus range from €20 to €42. The more expensive ones feature more gourmet dishes but they all offer good value for money. It's one of the best restaurants in the area. *Free house apéritif offered to our readers on presentation of this guide.*

Liergues

69400 (24km SW)

☙ 𝔄 I●I Auberge de Liergues

Take the D35 in the direction of Tarare.
☎04.74.68.07.02
Closed *Tues evening; Wed; Sun evening; 13–30 Aug.*

The owner likes to have a good laugh and will practically insist on your having a glass of Beaujolais as soon as you arrive – and it's hard to resist in a place like this, where there are more local winegrowers about than tourists. There's a lunchtime menu, which costs €11 and includes terrine, braised ham, cheese and dessert, and another lunch menu for €13; other menus are €19–24. There are lots of specialities from Lyon and seasonal dishes like game. On the first floor, you can eat in the bistro with it's pink table cloths and wooden tables. *Free house apéritif offered to our readers on presentation of this guide.*

Boën

42130

☙ 𝔄 I●I Le Cuvage

La Goutte des Bois; it's 1km out of Boën in the direction of Leigneux, on a narrow road overlooking the D8.

☎04.77.24.15.08
Closed *Mon; Tues.* **High chairs available.**

Whether you eat on the veranda or the terrace, you'll feast your eyes on the superb panoramic view. The menus, ranging from €13.90 to €19.90, are built for big appetites and list charcuterie, house terrine, house foie gras, meats grilled over the embers and spit-roast suckling pig. On Saturday evenings they hold live burlesque and comedy shows, with menus at €15.90 and €20.90. *Free house liqueur offered to our readers on presentation of this guide.*

Sail-sous-Couzan

42890 (6km SW)

☙ 𝔄 ᝰ I●I Les Sires de Semur*

Les Promenades; take the N89.
☎04.77.24.52.40 🖷04.77.24.57.14
✉henri1983@aol.com
Closed *Fri evening; Sat lunchtime; Sun evening.* **TV. Disabled access. High chairs available.**

Situated on a village square dominated by the ruins of a medieval castle, this hotel is run by a very nice Burgundian man and his wife. The cooking is absolutely authentic but prepared by a chef who is always on the lookout for new ideas; there's a menu at €10.50 (weekday lunchtimes) then €16–37. One inspiration is ancient cookery – try his guinea-fowl in flaky pastry with a sauce from a recipe by Apicius, the Roman gourmet. The wine cellar is well stocked. The hotel is a decent one-star with seven rooms (€24–34), three of which have shower and wc on the landing. You'll enjoy the homely atmosphere. *Free house apéritif offered to our readers on presentation of this guide.*

Bonneval-sur-Arc

73480

☙ 𝔄 ᝰ I●I Hôtel La Bergerie**

It's 100m from the tourist office and the slopes.
☎04.79.05.94.97 🖷04.79.05.93.24
Closed *May; 1 Oct–20 Dec.* **High chairs and games available. Car park.**

A startling concrete block of a building hidden amongst the trees some distance from the rest of the village. The owners are friendly and offer excellent value for money. Classic rooms, most of which have south-facing balconies with views of the Evettes mountains, cost €50–54 with shower/wc or bath. Half board, which costs around €52–57 per person, is requested in winter and between 10 July and 20 August. Local dishes feature prominently on the menus, €12–22. *Free house apéritif offered to our readers on presentation of this guide.*

Bourg-en-Bresse

01000

⚇ ♒ ♠ |●| Hôtel-restaurant du Mail**

46 av. du Mail; from the centre of town, follow the signs for Villefranche-sur-Saône on the D936.
☏04.74.21.00.26 ⊕04.74.21.00.26
Closed *Sun evening; Mon; 18 July–9 Aug; 22 Dec–8 Jan.* **TV. High chairs available. Car park.**

The rather smart restaurant is popular with the locals, who flock here for Sunday lunch. Set menus at €19–52 list traditional local cooking such as frogs' legs sautéed with herbs, salad of artichokes and scallops, roast chicken of Bresse with tarragon and morels, and there's an impressive dessert trolley. The clean comfortable rooms are decorated in contemporary style, and you'll appreciate the air-conditioning in summer – some have been refurbished. Good-value doubles go for €44 with shower/wc and up to €55 with bath/wc. It's essential to book. Logis de France. *Free coffee offered to our readers on presentation of this guide.*

⚇ ♠ Le Logis de Brou**

132 bd. de Brou; it's just before the monastery, on the right.
☏04.74.22.11.55
⊛www.logisdebrou.com
TV. High chairs available. Pay car park.

A bleak 1960s building that's hardly brightened up by its blue balconies. But inside it's a comfortable, attractive hotel offering bright, clean, soundproofed rooms in soft colours. Doubles are good value for money at €55 with shower/wc, or €67 with bath.

⚇ ♠ Hôtel de France***

19 pl. Bernard; in the heart of the town.
☏04.74.23.30.24 ⊕04.74.23.69.90

⊛www.grand-hoteldefrance.com
TV. Pay car park.

Mid-nineteenth-century hotel in the centre of town, in a charming little square with a village atmosphere. The entrance is very grand, and you almost hesitate to walk on the beautiful mosaic floors. Modern facilities, attentive staff and a warm décor which has retained the hotel's character. Stylish and comfortable double rooms with shower/wc or bath go for €86 in low season and €89 in high season – it's a good idea to reserve. The hotel is connected to the next-door restaurant *Chez Blanc*, which is very handy.

⚇ |●| Chez Blanc

Place Bernard; it's on the main square.
☏04.74.45.29.11
High chairs available. Car park.

Like all the "*Blanc*" establishments attached to the great chef, the cooking here is refined, tasty, unusual and handsomely served. Lots of dishes feature local sautéed frogs' legs, pike with crayfish tails, kidneys *à la mâconnaise,* asparagus tips with poached egg and white wine, orange gâteau and sorbets. There's a menu of the day for €17 (€19 in the evening), with others €27–40; à la carte you'll pay around €35. The swift service comes with a smile and the modern decoration is light and fresh. The dining room is large but it's still a good idea to book.

⚇ |●| Restaurant Les 4 Saisons

6 rue de la République.
☏04.74.22.01.86
Closed *Sat lunchtime; Sun; Mon.*

There is a nautical air in this restaurant, as its yellow walls are adorned with photos of lighthouses and the tables are covered with navy blue tablecloths. In the kitchen, the talented chef adds judicious inventive twists to traditional dishes: free-range chicken with cream of Comté and Jura *vin jaune* (similar to sherry), cold cream of haricot beans with *dariole* of frog and argan oil. The desserts are no less striking, with their combination of spices, fruit and even vegetables: a trio of *crémes brûlées* (flavoured with saffron, lavender and balsamic vinegar); lemon tart with fresh ginger, saffron *coulis,* tomato sorbet, and the exquisite coconut ice cream with sliced fennel and pepper *confit* in olive oil. Such tasty, original cooking is available at remarkably low prices: weekday menus are at €17, and there are others at €25–47.

◎ 🍴 |●| La Brasserie du Français

7 av. Alsace-Lorraine; it's near the tourist office.
☎04.74.22.55.14
Closed Sat evening; Sun; 1 May; the first 3 weeks in Aug; a week between Christmas and New Year. **Disabled access. High chairs available.**

This splendid Second Empire dining room attracts a clientele of lawyers, journalists and Bourg notables. The ceiling mouldings and bevelled mirrors are lovely, and the service is as classy as the cooking. Menus (€22–49) feature excellent, honest regional cuisine and traditional brasserie dishes (dish of the day at €11): Bresse chicken or beef fillets with morels, Provençal scallops, marinated salmon. You'll pay around €45 à la carte. You can dine on the terrace in summer and the waiters are smartly dressed. *Free house apéritif offered to our readers on presentation of this guide.*

Saint-Denis-lès-Bourg
01000 (5km W)

◎ 🏠 |●| Hôtel-restaurant du Lac*

1981 rte. de Trévoux; it's between Saint-Denis and Corgenon.
☎04.74.24.24.73
Restaurant closed Wed; 16 Aug–10 Sept. **Hotel closed** 1 Nov–1 April. **Car park.**

A roomy family house on the edge of the lake, set back from the road. Rooms are clean and modern with doubles for €26–33 depending on facilities; breakfast (€5) is served in the downstairs restaurant. Various menus, ranging from €11 to €33, are bursting with the flavours of the region: *croustillant* of Bresse blue cheese, frogs' legs, chicken with cream, and home-made desserts. There's a little bar, a wide terrace, a lake and a field behind that's full of animals. It's ideal for families because the whole atmosphere is easy-going and unfussy. Charge cards not accepted.

Polliat
01310 (10km NW)

◎ 🏠 🛏 |●| Hôtel-restaurant de la Place**

51 pl. de la Mairie; take the N79.
☎04.74.30.40.19 ☎04.74.30.42.34

Closed *Sun evening; Mon; first fortnight in Jan; first fortnight in July.* **TV.**

This smart, brightly coloured little hotel with eight rooms is set on the village square, with an attractive terrace to the rear. The recently renovated rooms are comfortable and spotless: doubles cost €30–48.50. In the restaurant, the service is as excellent as the regional dishes on offer with menus €15.50–52. Logis de France.

Meillonnas
01370 (15km NE)

◎ 🍴 |●| Auberge au Vieux Meillonnas

Take the N83 in the direction of Lons-le-Saunier, then the D52 to Meillonnas.
☎04.74.51.34.46
Closed *Tues evening; Wed; Sun evening (except in summer); a week during Feb school holiday; last week of summer school holiday; autumn school holiday.* **Open** *noon–1.30pm and 7–8.30pm.* **Disabled access. High chairs and games available.**

This little village inn, a rustic stone house, is typical of this peaceful part of the world. It's worth making the trip for the chef's cooking. Nathalie will welcome you warmly and Frédéric takes charge in the kitchen, preparing dishes such as Bresse chicken with cream and mushrooms, frogs' legs with parsley, Provençal-style breast of pork, fillet of pike-perch, and roast pears with spices. The €10.40 menu is served at lunch on weekdays, and there are five other menus €15–34. In fine weather you can eat in the delightful garden with its weeping willows, pine trees and banana plants. *Free coffee offered to our readers on presentation of this guide.*

Montrevel-en-Bresse
01340 (19km NW)

◎ 🏠 |●| Hôtel Le Pillebois***

Take the D975 and it's 1.5km from Montrevel.
☎04.74.25.48.44 ☎04.74.25.48.79
www.hotellepillebois.com
Closed *3 weeks in Nov.* **Restaurant closed** *Sat lunchtime; Sun evening; Mon.* **TV. Swimming pool. Car park.**

This modern, very comfortable hotel offers bright, spacious rooms. Doubles cost €62–66; the rooms overlooking the car park are the quietest. Its restaurant, *L'Aventure*, lies alongside the swimming pool, so you can eat in a lush setting with your toes virtually in the water. The tasty, varied food is presented in thematic menus that are all equally accomplished: "market", seafood, local and gourmet. There is a weekday menu at €16.50, and others at €27–45. Logis de France.

Bourget-du-Lac (Le)
73370

⟪ 🏠 |●| Hôtel-restaurant Atmosphères**

618 rte. des Tournelles; it's 2.5km from Bourget, on the D42 in the direction of Les Catons.
☎04.79.25.01.29 ℗04.79.25.26.19
Closed *Tues; Wed (lunchtime only in July and Aug); end Feb; All Saints' Day.* **TV. Car park.**

This peaceful hotel stands in the heart of the countryside at the foot of the Dent du Chat Mountain. Doubles go for €47 with shower/wc; some rooms have a splendid view of the Bourget Lake which so inspired Lamartine, one of France's greatest poets. Food is contemporary and full of ideas and flavours, with menus at €17 (not served Sun) and €29–52.

⟪ 🎋 🏠 |●| Hôtel-restaurant du Lac

Boulevard du Lac.
☎04.79.25.00.10
Closed *Tues evening; Wed; 1 Dec–1 March.* **High chairs available. Car park.**

Open since 1900, and something of an institution. The dining room is very classic, and the food is nicely prepared. The menus for the most part concentrate on fish; in summer, you can sit on the flower-filled terrace and watch the comings and goings at the lakeshore. There are set menus at €22 (except Sun lunchtime and on public holidays) and €29–52. If you want to spend the night, they have ten modern studios, all with balcony. *Free coffee offered to our readers on presentation of this guide.*

Viviers-du-Lac
73420 (3km E)

⟪ |●| Restaurant La Maison des Pêcheurs

611 Les Rives du Lac; follow the lakeshore in the direction of Aix-les-Bains.

☎04.79.54.41.29
Closed *Mon evening; Tues; Wed; Jan.*

If you wander into the garden of this waterside restaurant, you'll see all the fishing boats that have been hauled out of the water to dry. In the bar, fishermen compare the size of their catch over a drink. And fish dishes are the mainstay of the kitchen's reputation: fillets of perch, fried freshwater fish, trout cooked in all kinds of ways and frogs' legs. There's a weekday lunch menu for €11.50, another weekday menu at €17.50, with others €20.50–36.

Bourg-Saint-Maurice
73700

⟪ 🎋 🏠 |●| Hôtel-restaurant La Petite Auberge*

Le Reverset; it's 1km from the centre of town on the N90 in the direction of Moûtiers. It's on a small road off to the right and is signposted.
☎04.79.07.05.86 ℗04.79.07.26.51
✉hotel.lapetiteauberge@wanadoo.fr
Closed *May; Oct; Nov.* **Restaurant closed** *Sun evening and Mon; May.* **High chairs and games available. Car park.**

This quiet little inn is away from the main road. Unpretentious if rather old-fashioned rooms go for €36 with shower and €40–45 with shower/wc or bath. A programme of refurbishment is planned. The restaurant (☎ 04.79.07.37.11), separate from the hotel, offers simple, pleasant food of consistent quality with a set weekday menu at €13, and others €18–22. You can eat in the low-ceilinged dining room in winter, or the tree-shaded terrace in summer. The service is fast and friendly. *10% discount on the room rate (except July–Aug) offered to our readers on presentation of this guide.*

⟪ 🏠 Hôtel Atlantic***

69 rte. d'Hauteville; it's 2km from the centre of town. Take the N90 in the direction of Moûtiers, then turn left onto the small road to Hauteville.
☎04.79.07.01.70 ℗04.70.07.51.55
🌐www.hotel-atlantic.com
Disabled access. TV. Pay car park.

This is a fairly recent stone building, but it's hard to believe that it hasn't been here forever. It's a chic little place, out near the countryside, and you receive a genuinely warm welcome. It is spacious and bright throughout, from the reception area to the rooms – wood and stone are very much in evidence, and there's a sauna. Doubles with shower/wc cost €40, or €60–70 with bath; some rooms, at €80, come with balconies and rooms with a terrace go for €130.

Séez
73700 (3km E)

◎ ♠ Auberge de jeunesse-La Verdache

It's 4km after Séez, in the direction of Tignes; turn down the little road to the right opposite Longefoy.
℡04.79.41.01.93 ⓕ04.79.41.03.36
ⓔseez-les-arcs@fuaj.org
Closed *fortnight in early May; 20 Sept–20 Dec (except for groups).* **Disabled access. Car park.**

Small group of buildings in the heart of the countryside, on the edge of the forest and on the banks of the River Isère. A very practical setting for organizing a sporting holiday: skiing, surfing, kayaking, rafting, hydrospeed, canyoning, hanggliding, mountain biking, hiking, etc. The pleasant bedrooms (with two to six beds) are brand new, or almost so in some cases. In summer, the price of a stopover, including breakfast, is €13.20; for more than three days, you must pay for half board at €21.80 per day. FUAJ card is compulsory but you can buy it there.

◎ ♣ ♠ |◑| Relais des Villards**

Villard-Dessus; it's 4km from the centre – take the N90 that goes up to the Petit-Saint-Bernard pass.
℡04.79.41.00.66 ⓕ04.79.41.08.13
ⓦwww.relais-des-villards.com
Closed *May; 1 Oct–20 Dec.* **Restaurant closed** *lunchtimes in winter.* **TV. Car park.**

You're just 20km from Italy here, and this typical chalet provides the last stop before the border for many travellers. Ten pleasant, attractive rooms with shower/wc are €42.70–64.60 depending on the season and facilities. You'll get a warm welcome and service with a smile. Cooking is traditional with a few Savoy specialities on the menus which cost €12–18.50. Logis de France. *Free house apéritif offered to our readers on presentation of this guide.*

Buis-les-Baronnies
26170

◎ ♣ ♠ Les Arcades – Le Lion d'Or**

Place du Marché.
℡04.75.28.11.31 ⓕ04.75.28.12.07
ⓦwww.hotelarcades.fr
Closed *Dec–Feb.* **TV. Swimming pool. Car park.**

Well-located hotel with a family atmosphere in the centre of town on a ravishing arcaded square. The furnishings in the hall are higgledy-piggledy but the rooms are smart with modern bathrooms and good beds. Doubles go for €42–60 with shower/wc or bath, depending on the comfort and the season. In summer, they open the garden to guests. It's best to reserve and to arrive before 9pm. *Free fruit juice or soft drink offered to our readers on presentation of this guide.*

◎ ♠ Escapade Cloître des Dominicains

Rue de la Cour-du-Roi-Dauphin; it's in the town centre.
℡04.75.28.06.77 ⓕ04.75.28.13.20
ⓦwww.escapade.vacances.com
Closed *Dec–March.* **Reception open** *9am–noon and 4–8pm.*

Housed in a sixteenth-century Dominican convent in the centre of town, this is a good option if you want to be centrally located without paying a fortune. It's very well run. Ask for a room looking out onto the cloisters; doubles with shower/wc for €52 (the rates go down the longer you stay). Apartments for two to five people can be rented by the week and come with small kitchens, mezzanines and showers. Bikes can be parked in the courtyard.

◎ |◑| La Fourchette

Les Arcades, place du Marché.
℡04.75.28.03.31
ⓔfourchette@faxvia.net
Closed *Sun evening; Mon (Mon lunchtime in season); Oct.* **High chairs available.**

The chef started here more than twenty years ago, and still approaches his work with the same serious professionalism, offering delicious regional cuisine and a smiling, friendly welcome. There's a pleasant dining room hung with watercolours. The specialities include *Royans* ravioli *au gratin*, lamb shank with herbs, *croust-ade* with morels and very tender meat. If you're lucky enough to find crayfish with cream and tarragon sauce on the menu, don't think twice about ordering it. Menus go for €14 weekday lunchtimes, then €23 and €35. They offer a good selection of local wines at honest prices: €6.50 and €9.

◉ ◉ Le Grill du Four à Pain

24 av. Boissis d'Anglas; coming into town, it's between the petrol station and the *Cocinelle* supermarket.
☎04.75.28.10.34
Closed *Mon and Tues out of season; Mon and Tues lunchtimes (in July/Aug).* **Disabled access. Car park.**

A nice little restaurant where the service is pleasant and the sophisticated food is good and inexpensive. The weekday lunch *formule* at €15 offers a main course plus a dessert; other menus are €20–45. Specialities include foie gras, and *cassolette* of scallops with pastis. The wines are very reasonably priced; the Coteaux-des-Baronnies starts at €7.50. There's a shaded terrace in the garden and reservations are essential.

Plaisians
26170 (8.5km SE)

◉ ◉ Auberge de la Clue

Take the D72 then the D526.
☎04.75.28.01.17
Closed *Mon–Fri and Sun evening (Nov–March); Mon (April to end Sept); second fortnight in Oct.* **Disabled access. High chairs available. Car park.**

Hordes of gourmets stream up the mountain to this place, especially at the weekend. The restaurant serves hefty portions of good, cheap food concocted by two brothers. Their mother, who's got a terrific laugh and a great line in conversation, looks after the dining room. She'll set a terrine on your table for you to help yourself until your meal arrives, then you have the choice between rabbit with olive paste, a delicious haggis-like preparation of baked pork and vegetables with herbs, pig's trotters, small apricot spelt pastry and lamb's sweetbreads. Menus are at €23 and €29. For dessert, try the quince sorbet with quince liqueur – it's out of this world. You can see Mont Ventoux from the window and there's a nice terrace surrounded by greenery. Credit cards not accepted.

Cervières
42440

◉ ◉ Les Trois Compères

Le bourg; it's between Noirétable and Les Salles, on the D24.
☎04.77.24.92.18

At the foot of the very beautiful village of Cervières, you can eat delicious food in the convivial, rustic dining room or on the flowery terrace with its unbeatable view of the Forez mountains. The owner enthusiastically concocts a different menu every day according to his mood and the seasonal ingredients to hand. He has great respect for culinary tradition and offers a number of very old recipes, such as gratin of frogs. The menu costs around €25 (there is no fixed price, because it varies according to the dishes and the ingredients used). His specialities include duck *magret* with myrtles and chestnuts, as well as game and even fish. Before settling down here three years ago, the owner had travelled widely: allow yourself to be surprised by his cooking – you will not be disappointed.

Chambéry
73000

◉ ♨ ♔ ◉ Hôtel Le Revard**

41 av. de la Boisse; it's opposite the train station.
☎04.79.62.04.64 ☎04.79.96.37.26
ⓦwww.ifrance.com/hotel-le-revard
Closed *weekends in June and Sept–Dec; other times, Sat and Sun evenings; May (except for group reservations).* **Disabled access. TV. High chairs available. Pay car park.**

Very welcoming staff greet you in reception. The rooms are rather cold and functional – like you'd find in a chain – but some, happily, look onto the pretty garden. Doubles with shower/wc cost €44–60, or €49–64 with bath; half board is requested Friday evening in February at a cost of €45–52 per person. The restaurant serves traditional and regional dishes with menus at €12–28. Logis de France. *10% discount on the room rate (except Fri during Feb) offered to our readers on presentation of this guide.*

ⓦ ⌂ |●| Hôtel-restaurant Savoyard**

35 pl. Monge; it's on the square next to the carré Curial.
☎04.79.33.36.55 ⓕ04.79.85.25.70
ⓔsavoyard@noos.fr
Closed Sun (except public holidays). **TV. Car park.**

This is a big, friendly establishment with ten or so soundproofed rooms with geranium-filled window boxes. Fully renovated, doubles with shower/wc go for €45; half board is requested from mid-July to the end of August, and costs €41 per person. The owner is descended from a long line of restaurateurs. Menus, ranging from €13 to €24, feature Savoy specialties, lake fish and regional dishes. Logis de France.

ⓦ ⅍ ⌂ |●| City Hôtel**

9 rue Denfert-Rochereau; it's between carré Curial and Saint-François cathedral.
☎04.79.85.76.79 ⓕ04.79.85.86.11
ⓦwww.acom.fr/cityhotel
Disabled access. TV. Pay car park.

The air-conditioned hotel is right in the centre of town, so the rooms overlooking the street are noisy. Even though the street has been pedestrianized the bars get lively, especially on Friday and Saturday nights, but the hotel is as quiet as can be at the back. The rooms are functional and decorated in a very contemporary style – which is a bit of a surprise in an eighteenth-century building. You'll get a friendly welcome and prices are decent: doubles go for €50 with shower or shower/wc and €56 with bath; some have just been refurbished. One free breakfast per room offered to our readers on presentation of this guide.

ⓦ ⅍ |●| L'Hypoténuse

141 carré Curial.
☎04.79.85.80.15
Closed Sun; Mon; public holidays; a week at Easter; last week in July and first 3 weeks in Aug. **Disabled access.**

Lovely dining room in an old building; the modern, tasteful décor is a successful contrast and makes a good backdrop for regular exhibitions. The cooking is sophisticated and flavourful – lake whitefish with chanterel mushrooms – and the menus offer good value: weekday lunch menu at €16.50, with others €21–42. In the

summer, they open up the small terrace on a huge courtyard. Free Kir offered to our readers on presentation of this guide.

ⓦ ⅍ |●| Restaurant La Vanoise

44 av. Pierre-Lanfrey; it's near the main post office.
☎04.79.69.02.78
Closed Sun evening and Mon (except May–Sept); 17 Aug–6 Sept.

The décor is bright, young and modern and the restaurant has a clientele of loyal regulars. In contrast, the cooking is traditional, but it does display brilliant, inventive touches, and dishes change regularly. The chef likes to cook all kinds of fish. Ask for your preferred cooking method: steamed, cooked in an aromatic stock, floured or fried. Dishes include bouillabaisse of sea fish, char lakefish with olive oil, red mullet grilled à la plancha, scallops with truffles. Carnivores should not be put off as they are also catered for. Menus start at €23 (not Sun), then €28 and €38; reckon on paying about €42 à la carte. The wine list is huge, including both prestigious Burgundies and little-known Savoy wines. It's best to book. Free coffee offered to our readers on presentation of this guide.

Chamonix
74400

ⓦ ⅍ ⌂ La Boule de Neige*

362 rue Joseph-Vallot; first right off place du Mont-Blanc, 200m down this road.
☎04.50.53.04.48 ⓕ04.50.55.91.09
ⓦwww.hotel-la-boule-de-neige.fr
Closed 15 Nov–15 Dec. **Car park.**

Small family hotel with the ambience, and the young international clientele, of a guesthouse; it's a very relaxed place. Rooms aren't luxurious, but they're comfy and recently renovated; doubles with shower/wc €57–62, depending on the season; nos. 3 and 4 have south-facing terraces. You can help yourself to as much breakfast as you like from the buffet, and there are hearty breakfast dishes à la carte. Free coffee offered to our readers on presentation of this guide.

ⓦ ⌂ Hôtel des Lacs**

992 rte. des Gaillands; take the route des Gaillands, which continues from the rue du

Docteur-Paccard and the avenue Ravanel-le-Rouge, the main streets in the town centre. It's at the foot of a rock used by climbers and right opposite Mont Blanc.
℗04.50.53.02.08 ℗04.50.53.66.64
Closed 15 April–15 June; 1 Oct–15 Dec. **High chairs available. Car park.**

This hotel, which faces Mont Blanc and is five minutes from the centre, is an old house with an old-fashioned bar. It's a different story in the rooms, however: they have been completely refurbished and are tasteful, functional and good value for money. Doubles cost €50–52 with shower or bath depending on the season; some even have a balcony and a view of the mountain. A polite and friendly welcome is guaranteed.

(((🏃 🏠 Hôtel du Faucigny**

118 pl. de l'Église; it's opposite the tourist office, in the centre.
℗04.50.53.01.17 ℗04.50.53.73.23
ⓦwww.hotel.faucigny-chamonix.com
Closed Nov. **TV. High chairs available. Car park.**

A little hotel with a homely atmosphere in a quiet street currently undergoing renovations. It's a family-run place with refurbished and comfortable rooms with perfectly adequate facilities; some with a view of Mont Blanc. Doubles cost €65–69 with shower/wc, depending on the season. There's a small, interior courtyard and a garden. *5% discount on the room rate offered to our readers on presentation of this guide.*

(((🏠 |●| Hôtel La Savoyarde***

28 rue des Moussoux; it's beside the Brévent cable-car station.
℗04.50.53.00.77 ℗04.50.55.86.82
ⓦwww.lasavoyarde.com
Restaurant closed Tues and Thurs lunchtimes; end May to early June; mid-Nov to mid-Dec. **Disabled access. TV. Car park.**

A peaceful, flower-filled chalet facing Mont Blanc. It's a nineteenth-century building, renovated throughout but with plenty of original features: parquet, tiling, woodwork, fireplaces. The rooms are contemporary, with little touches of mountain style, and their facilities and comfort levels justify the prices: doubles cost €94–137 depending on the season. Half board, requested during school holidays, costs €60–82 per person. Menus, at €16 and €31, offer good-value local dishes. À la carte, try the fillet of lake whitefish with hazelnuts.

((|●| Le Panier des Quatre Saisons

24 galerie Blanc-Neige; take Rue Paccard, then Galerie (first floor).
℗04.50.53.98.77
Closed Wed; Thurs lunchtime; 25 May–16 June; 15 Nov–5 Dec. **Disabled access. High chairs available.**

A flight of stairs off la rue Paccard leads to this small, charming restaurant (very "back to nature") offering excellent cooking. For freshness and inventiveness it's unmatched by any of the touristy places – and it's good value for money with menus priced at €21.50–38. The friendly, personal welcome is refreshing in a town where so many restaurants herd you in and out as fast as possible.

Argentière
74400 (7km NE)

((🏃 |●| La Crèmerie du Glacier

766 rte. de la Glacière; take the dirt road after the Lognan cable car (it's signposted).
℗04.50.54.07.52
Closed Tues evening and Wed in winter (except school holidays); Oct to end Dec. **Open** noon–3pm and 7–10pm in summer; all day in winter. **Car park.**

A newly built chalet, way out in the forest, where you can eat well from noon to 10pm. Dishes include simple omelettes with big salads, fondue with ceps and morels in pastry. For a truly regional treat, and if you reserve in advance, you can try *farcon* with salad and dessert. There's a lunch menu at €10, with others up to €23; expect to pay €20 à la carte. *Free house apéritif offered to our readers on presentation of this guide.*

Houches (Les)
74310 (8km SW)

((🏃 🏠 Auberge Le Montagny**

Lieu-dit Le Pont; as you come into the village from Chamonix, it's 450m further along on the left (it's easy to miss the sign).
℗04.50.54.57.37 ℗04.50.54.52.97
ⓦwww.perso.wanadoo.fr/hotel.montagny
Closed May; 1 Nov–15 Dec. **TV. Car park.**

This farm was built in 1876 in the centre of a tranquil mountain hamlet. You'd hardly realize that now because of all the changes that have been made, but it still has a cosy charm and the wood panelling hasn't been tampered with. The rooms are

RHÔNE-ALPES

huge and pretty, and all have superb, bright bathrooms; doubles are €74. The ski slopes are nearby and the welcome is friendly and attentive. *10% discount on the room rate (out of school holidays) offered to our readers on presentation of this guide.*

Chamousset

73390

@ 🎿 🏠 |O| Hôtel-restaurant Christin**

La Lilette; take the N90 from Albertville in the direction of Chambéry, and when you reach Pont-Royal, follow the signs for Chamousset.
℡04.79.36.42.06 ℻04.79.36.45.43
Closed Sun evening; Mon; a week in early Jan; a week in early May; a fortnight end Sept. **TV. Car park.**

A perfect country inn on a tiny square shaded by chestnut trees. You can hear a little brook flowing somewhere nearby, but you can't see it through the thick vegetation. The pleasant dining room has huge bay windows. The classic cuisine uses excellent ingredients and, given the huge portions, proves good value. There's a weekday lunchtime menu at €14, with others €19–32. The rooms are in the annexe and, though somewhat lacking in charm, they're spacious and comfortable; doubles go for €39–50 with shower/wc or bath. If you're a light sleeper, the trains going by at night may disturb you. Logis de France. *Free house apéritif offered to our readers on presentation of this guide.*

Champagny-en-Vanoise

73350

@ 🎿 🏠 |O| Les Chalets du Bouquetin****

Le Planay; head in the direction of Champagny-le-Haut.
℡04.79.55.01.13 ℻04.79.55.04.76
🌐www.bouquetin.com
Closed 15 Sept–17 Dec. **Restaurant closed** Mon and Sat lunchtimes (Sat lunchtime only in summer); Sun. **Disabled access. TV. High chairs and cots available. Car park.**

This restaurant is hidden away in a small house, decorated in a typical local style with lots of wood and stone. The menus – €18–30 – change every day and list good, wholesome local dishes; you can eat à la carte for

around €30. Specialities include *raclette*, meat cooked on a hot stone, fondue, *pela* (potatoes, onions and Reblochon cheese) and *croûte savoyarde* (ham on a base of flaky pastry with cheese sauce). On the other side of the (small) street large chalets hold various types of accommodation: rooms and flats for two to twenty people. Doubles with bath go for €60–70, and you can rent by the week. *Free house apéritif offered to our readers on presentation of this guide.*

Châtel

74390

@ 🎿 🏠 |O| Hôtel-restaurant Les Fougères**

Route du Petit-Châtel.
℡04.50.73.21.06 ℻04.50.73.38.34
Closed 20 April–10 July; 1 Sept–20 Dec. **Restaurant open** evenings 7–8.30pm; in winter for hotel guests only. **TV. High chairs and games available. Garage and car park (free in summer).**

This authentic old farm has been restored without losing its original style. It's a cheerful establishment run by a dynamic young couple. In summer it's a perfect place to unwind for a bit, while in winter everyone gets to know each other over fondue. The restaurant's not open in summer, though a good buffet breakfast is served. Well-equipped, renovated double rooms (some with a terrace) with shower/wc go for €41–58, breakfast included; in winter, half board is compulsory at €48–58 per person and there's a weekly charge of €30 for the garage and €15 for the car park. In summer, guests have use of a small kitchen. *10% discount on the room rate (in summer) offered to our readers on presentation of this guide.*

@ 🏠 |O| 🎿 Hôtel-restaurant La Perdrix Blanche**

Pré-de-la-Joux; it's 2.5km from the centre in the direction of le Linga, at the bottom of the cable lifts.
℡04.50.73.22.76 ℻04.50.73.35.21
🌐www.laperdrixblanche.com
Closed 1 May–15 June; 15 Sept–1 Dec. **TV. High chairs and games available. Car park.**

This delightful chalet stands among the fir trees. Rooms are simple and cosy, and some have a balcony. Doubles go for €52–75 with shower/wc or bath; half board, requested in winter, costs €40–65 per person. The typical local cooking – *tartiflette, raclette, berthoud* (marinated cheese baked in the oven) and fondue – is just the thing after a day's skiing or hiking, and the menus, €13–22, satisfy even the biggest of appetites. Logis de France. *Free house apéritif offered to our readers on presentation of this guide.*

⑨ 🎿 |●| Restaurant L'Abreuvoir-Chez Ginette**

Hameau de Vonnes; head for Switzerland and you'll find the restaurant 1km out of town, very near Lac de Vonnes.
☎04.50.73.24.89
Car park.

Berthoud de la vallée d'Abondance, the local speciality, is prepared very well at this authentic, country place. It's an absolutely delicious dish in which cheese is diced and marinated in white wine vinegar, Madeira and garlic before being put into the oven. They do other Savoy specialities with a range of menus for €13–40, and on holiday nights Louky gets his accordion out and everyone has a great time. From the garden, you get a great view of the mountain and the lake, which is lit up at night. *Free house apéritif offered to our readers on presentation of this guide.*

⑨ 🎿 |●| Restaurant La Bonne Ménagère

It's one street north of the tourist office.
☎04.50.73.24.45
Closed *lunchtimes in summer; Sun lunchtime only the rest of the year; end May to early June; mid-Sept to mid-Dec.*

You'll get a delightful welcome here. The two dining rooms, decorated with old enamel plaques and little bunches of dried flowers, are popular with the local ski crowd. They serve starters such as charcuterie and main dishes like *berthoud*, fondue, *croûte aux champignons* (mushrooms on a layer of flaky pastry covered with cheese and then grilled), and *tartiflette*. The prices are fair; you'll pay around €20–22 à la carte. Credit cards not accepted. *Free house apéritif offered to our readers on presentation of this guide.*

Chapelle d'Abondance (La)
74360 (5km NW)

⑨ 🎿 🏠 |●| L'Ensoleillé**

Rue Principale.
☎04.50.73.50.42 ☎04.50.73.52.96
🌐www.hotel-ensoleille.com

Closed *Tues (restaurant); early April to end May; mid-Sept to end Dec.* **TV. Swimming pool. High chairs and games available. Car park.**

The hotel, in a huge family house, thoroughly deserves its good reputation. Most rooms have been renovated and have rustic, wooden furniture. Doubles with shower/wc or bath go for €60–80; half board, from €50 up to €80 per person, is requested during the February and Christmas school holidays. There's a heated swimming pool, sauna, hammam and Jacuzzi. Madame and her husband look after the dining room and the guests, one son runs the bar and the *Carnotzet* (where the fondue lovers gather) and the other son is the chef. He uses only the finest ingredients; there's a weekday lunch menu at €19, with others from €21 up to €50. *10% discount on the room rate (room only and not half board rate) offered to our readers on presentation of this guide.*

⑨ 🎿 🏠 |●| Les Gentianettes**

Route de Chevennes.
☎04.50.73.56.46 ☎04.50.73.56.39
🌐www.gentianettes.fr
Closed *Easter Mon to Ascension; 20 Sept–20 Dec.* **Open** *noon-1.30/2pm.* **Disabled access. TV. High chairs and games available. Swimming pool. Car park.**

This hotel is in the centre of the village, away from the noisy road and just footsteps from the cross-country ski trails. There are thirty bright, comfortable rooms costing €75–125 with shower/wc or bath, depending on the season; half board is priced at €66–91 per person. The restaurant, decorated like a mountain chalet, serves sophisticated cuisine that's unusually inventive for the region with a range of menus for €19–55. Facilities include a pretty little indoor swimming pool, Jaccuzi, steam bath and sauna. *Free house apéritif or coffee offered to our readers on presentation of this guide.*

Châtillon-en-Diois
26410

⑨ 🎿 🏠 |●| Hôtel-restaurant du Dauphiné

Place Pierre Dévoluy; it's opposite the tourist office.
☎04.75.21.13.13
📧hoteldudauphine@wanadoo.fr

Closed *autumn and Christmas school holidays.* **Restaurant closed** *Tues and Sun evenings and Wed (Sept–June).* **TV. High chairs available.**

An old hotel-café-restaurant right in the heart of the village. Its eight rooms – €39–53 with shower/wc – are nicely old-fashioned but painted in fresh colours; the old furniture adds lots of charm and the floorboards creak. Room 5 has an iron bedstead and the bathroom is discreetly hidden in an alcove. There's a shaded terrace overlooking the road and an attractively decorated dining room with an old mirror, bistro tables and friezes on the walls. The changing seasons and the whims of the chef are reflected in the frequent changes in the menus: fresh goat's cheese with pesto and pickled tomatoes, *confit* of leg of lamb with spices, *aiguillette* of guinea-fowl with blackcurrants. The €13.50 *menu du jour* and the *menu terroir* are at €23 and both include a glass of wine; you'll pay around €26 for a menu à la carte. The village children are to be envied as the restaurant also prepares the meals for the village school. Even if you're not eating you should try the home-made plant syrups – thyme, sage and lime – and the unusual *"café du barman"*. *Free house apéritif or 10% discount on the room rate (Dec–Feb) offered to our readers on presentation of this guide.*

Châtillon-sur-Chalaronne

01400

««» 🎋 🏠 |●| La Tour – Cocooning et Gastronomie***

Place de la République; it's opposite the fairground.
☎04.74.55.05.12 ☎04.74.55.09.19
🌐www.hotel-latour.com
Closed *Sun evening; Wed.* **Disabled access. TV. High chairs and cots available. Pay car park.**

"Opening your house is like opening your heart". That's the promise made by this hotel in the heart of an enchanting medieval village, and the expansive, youthful service manages to live up to these expectations. There is the added benefit of an impressive fourteenth-century building complete with half-timbering, exposed stone, a redbrick, pepper-

box tower and a pretty riverside garden. This has been the setting for a hotel for almost a century, but it was stunningly restored a few years ago, with a delightfully aged look and varied décor: a snug reception lounge, a purple dining room with zebra-skin chairs, an Italian-style terrace upstairs. The spacious, colourful bedrooms have also been decorated with great attention to detail. Some 300m away, an annexe (the *Clos de la Tour*) has recently been opened in a beautiful eighteenth-century building; its fifteen (more expensive) rooms succeed in combining an old-fashioned atmosphere with modern design: bathtub in the centre of the room, four-poster beds and eiderdowns; double rooms with shower/wc or bath are priced at €89–145. The restaurant offers skilful reinterpretations of traditional dishes: large morels stuffed with vegetable ravioli, Bresse poultry stuffed with foie gras, marinated scallops and langoustine risotto. The cheapest menu goes for €18 (except Fri evening and weekends), with others €23–58. There is also a floral decoration/interior design shop in the entrance to the hotel. Logis de France. *Welcoming drink offered to our readers (with dessert) on presentation of this guide.*

Abergement-Clémenciat (L')

01400 (6km NW)

««» |●| Restaurant Le Saint-Lazare

Take the D2.
☎04.74.24.00.23
Closed *Wed; Thurs; Sun evening; Feb school holiday; second fortnight in July.* **Disabled access. High chairs available.**

This is one of the best tables in the region and the setting in a large, bright dining room is ideal. The service is attentive and the dishes are inventive and delicate, with a good number of imaginative fish dishes: pike-perch in season, sardines stuffed with minced chard. Also on offer are dishes using local, farm-raised chickens and meat. For dessert, try the pear *orientale*. The weekday menu at €28, as well as the other menus, €32–70, are good value for money. The wines are selected from local growers but there are also some from further afield.

Chonas l'Amballan

38121

◉ ☎ |●| Domaine de Clairefontaine**

Chemin des Fontanettes; take the N7. It's 8km south of Vienne.
℡04.74.58.81.52 ℻04.74.58.80.93
🌐www.domaine-de-clairefontaine.fr
Closed Mon; Tues; third week in Aug; 15 Dec–16 Jan. **TV. Car park.**

A mansion in a magnificent estate that is more than three hundred years old. The very spacious rooms in the Domaine are furnished with taste. There are plans to update them so hurry to make the most of the prices before they go up: doubles cost from €43 in the Domaine, and from €110 in the Jardins de Clairefontaine. There are two breakfast options at €11 and €20. The cuisine is very stylish and prepared by Philippe Girardon (voted the best trainee chef in France), but the menus are in the upper price bracket – €44–95. You'll receive the professional welcome you should expect in such a place but the prices are out of reach. Tennis courts and *boules* are available to guests.

Clusaz (La)

74220

◉ 🎿 ☎ |●| Les Airelles**

Place de l'Église; it's on the church square.
℡04.50.02.40.51 ℻04.50.32.35.33
🌐www.clusaz.com
Closed Tues; Sun evening (May–June, Sept–Oct); 17 Nov–13 Dec. **TV. High chairs available. Car park (free in summer).**

A dream of a hotel in the centre of the village. It's been carefully renovated and offers bright, colourful doubles with shower/wc or bath at €53–60. Half board, €51–89 per person, is compulsory during the winter school holidays. Guests have use of the Jacuzzi, sauna and swimming pool in the hotel *Les Sapins*, a bit further up, which belongs to relatives. Genuine, simple welcome, just like the food. The menus, costing €20–28, list all the regional specialities. Logis de France. *Free house apéritif offered to our readers on presentation of this guide.*

Manigod

74230 (12km SW)

◉ 🎿 ☎ |●| Hôtel-restaurant de la Vieille Ferme**

Col de Merdassier; from Thônes, take the D909 then the D16 towards Manigod, go through La Croix-Fry and head for the resort of L'Étale.
℡04.50.02.41.49 ℻04.50.32.65.53
Closed Wed (except school holidays); 15 April–15 June; 30 Oct–20 Dec. **TV. High chairs and games available. Car park.**

An archetypal Alpine chalet at the foot of the Étale ski slopes. They have a mere six small but modern rooms, at €50 with shower/wc or bath; half board, compulsory during the Feb and Christmas school holidays, costs €46–51. In the restaurant, the food is as typical and authentic as the place itself – try the *farcement, pela* and *escalope savoyarde*. There's a lunchtime menu at €10, with others €14–25; *Free coffee offered to our readers on presentation of this guide.*

Combloux

74920

◉ 🎿 ☎ |●| Les Granits**

1409 rte. de Sallanches; it's 1.5km from the centre on the Sallanches road.
℡04.50.58.64.46 ℻04.50.58.61.63
🌐www.lesgranits.com
Closed lunchtimes in summer (restaurant); early April to mid-June; mid-Sept to Christmas. **Disabled access. TV. High chairs and games available. Car park.**

Nice family hotel that's been going since the 1940s. Plain but clean double rooms go for €49–60, depending on the degree of comfort; some have a view of Mont Blanc. Half board, compulsory during the Feb and Christmas school holidays, costs €46.50–51.50 per person. It's quite close to a road – not a very busy one, but if you want to ensure a quiet night, ask for a room in the annexe or at the rear. In the attractive dining room you can choose from menus at €15 and €17. Typical Savoy dishes are served: *raclette, diots, crozets, tartiflette* and fondue. *Free coffee offered to our readers on presentation of this guide.*

◉ 🎿 ☎ |●| Hôtel-restaurant Le Coin Savoyard**

300 rte. de la Cry; it's opposite the church.

☎04.50.58.60.27 📠04.50.58.64.44
🌐www.coin-savoyard.com
Closed *Mon out of season; 15 April to early June; 15 Sept–8 Dec.* **TV. Swimming pool. Car park.**

Lots of people come to this prettily modernized nineteenth-century farm building year after year, so it's best to book well in advance. The ten rooms are absolutely delightful (even more so since their recent refurbishment). Doubles with bath cost €80–120, and half board is available at €60–90 per person. You can have a drink or something light for dinner – they do a good fondue with ceps – in a traditional, cosy Savoy setting. There are no set menus, so expect to pay around €25-30 à la carte, with drinks on top. There's a sunny terrace facing Mont Blanc and the pool is great in summer. *Free house apéritif offered to our readers on presentation of this guide.*

Praz-sur-Arly
74120 (13km SW)

ⓦ 🌴 🏠 |●| La Griyotire★★★

Route de la Tonnaz; take the N212.
☎04.50.21.86.36 📠04.50.21.86.34
🌐www.griyotire.com
Closed *Easter to mid-June; mid-Sept to Christmas school holiday.* **Restaurant closed lunchtime. TV. High chairs and games available. Swimming pool. Car park.**

A dream of an Alpine chalet in the middle of a family resort not far from Megève, set well away from the main road that runs through the middle of the village. The rooms have been decorated with exquisite taste and each one is different. There's lots of wood everywhere and the feather beds are gloriously soft. Doubles with shower/wc or bath start from €85 up to €130 for a suite; half board, compulsory during the Feb and Christmas school holidays, is €75–97 per person. You get a charming welcome and a family atmosphere – there's even a games room for the children. The food on offer includes *pela, escalope savoyarde* and, on winter evenings, fondue and *raclette*; the set menu is at €27. There's a lovely garden, a sauna, a hammam and a massage room, and the swimming pool is open in summer. *Free house apéritif offered to our readers on presentation of this guide.*

Condrieu
69420

ⓦ 🌴 🏠 |●| Hôtel-restaurant La Réclusière★★

14 rte. Nationale; on the N86.
☎04.74.56.67.27 📠04.74.56.80.05
Closed *Tues; Feb school holiday.* **Disabled access. TV. Car park.**

Talented chef Martin Fleischmann has enlarged this restaurant, divided into three dining rooms, each decorated in a different style; he has also added some comfortable bedrooms. Doubles with shower/wc or bath cost €51–74. In the restaurant, the menus – €12 at weekday lunchtimes, then €18–44 – change seasonally, but may list such dishes as minestrone with shellfish and saffron, duck breast with apples fried with smoked bacon and spiced *jus* and Armagnac ice cream. Good wine list and attentive service. *Free house apéritif offered to our readers on presentation of this guide.*

Contamines-Montjoie (Les)
74170

ⓦ 🌴 🏠 |●| Le Mont-Joly★

La Chapelle, 2564 rte. du Plan du Moulin.
☎04.50.47.00.17 📠04.50.47.91.40
🌐www.montjoly.com
Closed *Oct–Nov; spring.* **High chairs and cots available. Car park.**

This pretty gingerbread hotel on the outskirts of town, recently taken over by a young couple, is friendly and quiet. It offers simple, freshly decorated rooms and a few chalets next to the main building. Depending on the season, doubles cost €33–39 with basin, €43–48 with shower, and €46–52 with shower/wc. Two of the rooms are large enough to sleep a whole family. The menu is at €15. There's a nice terrace surrounded by trees with a view of the mountains. *Free house apéritif offered to our readers on presentation of this guide.*

ⓦ 🌴 🏠 La Clef des Champs★

Route de la Frasse; it's above the village, in the street opposite the tourist office.
☎04.50.47.06.09 📠04.50.47.09.49
✉daniel.mattel@wanadoo.fr

Closed *20 April–20 June; 8 Sept–20 Dec.*
High chairs and cots available. Car park.

An old restored farmhouse set on the slopes in the resort. Reservations are essential during the winter and summer seasons, when half board is compulsory and costs €36–39.10 per person. At other times, doubles with shower/wc go for €41.40; nos. 2, 3, 4 and 9 have balconies with views over the valley. They offer special rates for children under eight. The restaurant is open to residents only. *Free house apéritif offered to our readers on presentation of this guide.*

⍟ 🏠 |●| Hôtel-restaurant Le Gai Soleil**

288 chemin des Loyers; it's above the church.
☎04.50.47.02.94 📠04.50.47.18.43
🌐www.gaisoleil.com
Closed *mid-April to mid-June; mid-Sept to mid-Dec.* **Car park.**

Set in an old wooden farmhouse, built in 1823, this is a beautifully decorated hotel that's maintained with great care. You'll get a tremendous welcome. Handsome rooms, all with shower/wc or bath and some with a mezzanine floor capable of sleeping parents and children alike, go for €51–70 depending on the season. Half board, at €48–61, is compulsory during the school holidays. In the restaurant, there are menus at €18 and €25. Logis de France.

Contrevoz

01300

⍟ 🌴 |●| L'Auberge de Contrevoz – La Plumardière

Take the D32 in the direction of Ordonnaz.
☎04.79.81.82.54
Closed *Sun evening in winter; Mon; 24 Dec–30 Jan.*

A charming inn in a countryside village. This huge farmhouse has retained some of its original features, including the big fireplace and an enormous pair of blacksmith's bellows. There's a wonderful garden full of fruit trees where you can eat in good weather. Regional cuisine with an original twist is featured on the €15.50 weekday lunch menu: country salad, roast chicken with thyme and potatoes *dauphinoise*. However, the cooking is so good that you might be tempted by the costlier menus at €23–38. Try the foie gras, the home-smoked salmon and duck fillets. Menus change regularly. *Free coffee offered to our readers on presentation of this guide.*

Ceyzérieu

01350 (11km NE)

⍟ 🏠 |●| Relais du Marais

Take the D904 to Viripu-le-Grand, then the D105; it's on the village square, opposite the church.
☎04.79.87.01.61
Restaurant closed *Sun evening; Mon.* **TV. Swimming pool. Car park.**

This hotel-bar-restaurant offers clean, bright but soberly decorated rooms; the ones to the rear have terraces with a wonderful view of the garden and the mountains beyond. Double rooms with shower/wc cost €37–41. The restaurant offers quick meals (lunchtime menu €11, then others €17–25), but it is tempting to linger around the large pool, complemented by a children's paddling pool, and enjoy the youthful atmosphere. You are sure to receive a warm welcome here, and will soon feel at home.

Belmont-Luthézieu

01260 (14km NE)

⍟ 🏠 |●| Au Vieux Tilleul

Take the D904 to Virieu-le-Grand, then the D8.
☎04.79.87.64.51 📠04.79.87.54.50
TV.

This hotel-restaurant lost in the tranquillity of the Haut-Bugey is a pleasant surprise, ideal for a stopover or romantic weekend. The owner has anticipated the latter eventuality, because apart from the usual menus (€17–38), he offers a "*tête-à-tête*" dinner for two at €125. Everything here is good value and meticulously executed – not only the food and service, but also the decoration. Blue and yellow are the dominant colours, and the rooms are decorated with exquisite taste (some even have a designer-style bathroom inside the room itself). Doubles cost €39–46.

22

RHÔNE-ALPES

Cormoranche-sur-Saône

01290

@ 𝓐 ☎ |●| Hôtel-restaurant Chez la Mère Martinet

Take the N6 in the direction of Villefranche as far as Crêches-sur-Saône and then the D51; alternatively, take the D51 from Saint-Laurent-sur-Saône. It's in the village.
☎03.85.36.20.40 ℻03.85.31.77.19
Closed *Mon and Tues evenings; Wed; Feb.*
TV. Car park.

A nice little village inn where you'll receive a very warm welcome. Menus, ranging from €14 (not Sun) up to €47, change every two months, but always list delicious local cuisine: chicken breast with cream, fresh frogs' legs with parsley and garlic, Charolais beef steak with Bresse blue cheese sauce, hot sausage, home-made pastries. In fine weather you can sit out on the little terrace in the garden. There are a few double rooms with bath; they go for €45. *Free house apéritif offered to our readers on presentation of this guide.*

Saint-Laurent-sur-Saône

01750 (8km N)

@ |●| Le Saint-Laurent

1 quai Bouchacourt; take the D51. It's on the quay near the old bridge.
☎03.85.39.29.19
Disabled access. High chairs available.

This is another restaurant in the extending empire of the great chef Georges Blanc. You get the usual efficiency, kindness, originality and skill, as evidenced in inspiring dishes such as Bresse chicken with cream and *vin jaune* (white wine from Jura), Burgundy snails ravioli, large spicy prawns, and caramelized apple. There's also a weekday lunch menu at €17, with others starting from €19 up to €40. There's also a fine list of wines. The decoration is simple with a few old ornaments dotted elegantly around the dining room; black-and-white photographs and old adverts cover the walls. You won't be disappointed – unless you forget to book, that is.

Corps

38970

@ 𝓐 ☎ |●| Hôtel de la Poste**

Place de la Mairie; take the N85.
☎04.76.30.00.03 ℻04.76.30.02.73
@www.hotel-restaurant-delas.com
Closed *3 Jan–15 Feb.* **Disabled access. TV. High chairs available. Car park.**

This hotel, in the centre of the village on the "route Napoléon", is one of the best-known places in the region. The heavy, fussy, old-fashioned interior décor may not be to all tastes, but the rooms, all different, are comfortable. Depending on the facilities, they cost €38.50–70; nos. 1, 2, 5, 7, 8, 12 and 15 are equipped with a Jacuzzi (no. 7 also has a beautiful terrace-mezzanine overlooking the rear). The cooking has a well-established reputation. Menus cost €19.50–38, but go for à la carte, as you will have an enormous choice: queen scallops with morels, joint of lamb cooked on a spit, wild boar stew, calf's sweetbreads with cream, trout braised with crayfish, wild duck *grand-mère*. There's a fight for tables on the terrace in good weather, even though the road goes past right in front. Free access to the swimming pool of the Chateau des Herbeys, 15km away on the Gap road. Logis de France. *Free coffee or house liqueur offered to our readers on presentation of this guide.*

Coucouron

07470

@ ☎ |●| Hôtel-restaurant Au Carrefour des Lacs**

☎04.66.46.12.70 ℻04.66.46.16.42
Closed *Dec–Feb.* **TV. Car park.**

An attractive mountain inn near a lake in the middle of the Ardèche plateau. Clean double rooms cost €30–44 depending on the level of comfort. The handsome dining room offers good food prepared from fresh ingredients, including fine charcuterie, delicious local cheeses and home-made desserts. Set menus are €12 (weekday lunchtimes) and €14–24.

Cours-la-Ville

69470

ⓒ 🎿 ☎ |O| Hôtel Le Pavillon**

Col du Pavillon; it's 3km from Cours-la-Ville on the D64 heading in the direction of Écharmeaux.
℡04.74.89.83.55 ℗04.74.64.70.26
ⓦwww.hotel-pavillon.com
Closed *Fri and Sun evenings, Sat (Oct–end of April); Fri (except July–Aug) and Sun evening (May–Oct); Feb.* **Disabled access. TV. High chairs available. Car park.**

This hotel, surrounded by fir trees, stands absolutely alone at an altitude of 755m, 10 km from a lake. It is therefore an ideal base for hikes and bike rides. The modern, comfortable rooms with Internet access go for €53–55 with shower/wc or bath, and the ground-floor ones have a private terrace and a view over the small animal park. Breakfast is at €7.50. The pleasant restaurant offers a weekday menu at €22, with others going up to €41. Dishes include quail terrine with morels and *brioche*, fillet of Charolais beef, foie gras, halibut *cassolette*. On weekdays, copious platters (€18 with dessert) are perfect for a quick meal. Logis de France. *Free jar of home-made jam offered to our readers on presentation of this guide.*

Marnand

69240 (10km S)

ⓒ 🎿 ☎ |O| Hôtel-restaurant La Terrasse**

From Thizy, turn left in the town centre in the direction of Marnand.
℡04.74.64.19.22 ℗04.74.64.25.95
ⓦwww.laterrasse-marnand.com
Closed *Sun evening; Mon (hotel open in the evening); Feb and Nov school holidays.* **Disabled access. TV. High chairs and children's playroom available. Car park.**

Occupying a converted industrial building, this well-designed hotel looks great, and it's in a good location with lovely views over the Beaujolais hills from each room. Brightly decorated doubles with bath go for €49. The restaurant is just as attractive, with traditional dishes like Charolais fillet and fresh fruit ice cream with chocolate sauce. Menus cost €12.50 (weekdays only), then €19–60. Easy-going welcome. *Free house liqueur offered to our readers on presentation of this guide.*

Crémieu

38460

ⓒ 🎿 ☎ |O| L'Auberge de la Chaite**

Cours Baron-Raverat.
℡04.74.90.76.63 ℗04.74.90.88.08
Closed *Sun evening; Mon; Tues lunchtime; Easter school holiday; 20 Dec–12 Jan.* **TV. High chairs available. Car park.**

A beautiful setting in a medieval village with ruined fortifications. Double rooms cost €40 with shower, €44 with shower/wc, or €48 with bath; those overlooking the garden (nos. 1, 2, 7 and 8) have had a lovely make-over. You'll be treated like a king in the restaurant or on the terrace. There are menus at €15 (not Sunday), €19.50 and €33: typical dishes include roast pigeon with garlic or roast duck with peaches, and vanilla *blancmange*. Logis de France. *10% discount on the room rate (except July, Aug and Sept) offered to our readers on presentation of this guide.*

ⓒ 🎿 |O| Les Castors

41 rue Porcherie.
℡04.74.90.02.49
Closed *Thurs and Sun evenings; Mon; a week in March; a week in June; a fortnight end Sept; a week at Christmas.* **Disabled access. High chairs available.**

One of those places that doesn't look like much outside, but the pleasant dining room offers the best food in town. Good, tasty dishes: ostrich fillet with green peppercorns, fresh pan-fried foie gras, veal chops with morels, and excellent savoury and sweet crêpes. The weekday lunchtime menu costs €10, with others €18–41; the €18 menu changes monthly. *Free coffee offered to our readers on presentation of this guide.*

Saint-Hilaire-de-Brens

38460 (6km SE)

ⓒ 🎿 |O| Au Bois Joli

La Gare; coming from Crémieu, it's at the junction of the Morestel and Bourgoin-Jallieu roads.
℡04.74.92.81.82
Closed *evenings; Mon; mid-Aug to mid-Sept.* **High chairs and games available. Car park.**

This renowned restaurant has been run for generations by the Vistalli family. It has two large dining rooms, decorated with cowbells, that can accommodate about a hundred people. Try gâteau of chicken livers with crayfish sauce, Provençal-style frog's legs, pike-perch fillet with sorrel or game including wild boar in season. The €11.50 lunch menu (not Sun) includes cheese and dessert, and there are others going up to €27. Also on offer are delicious, inexpensive wines such as Bugey and Savoie. *Free coffee offered to our readers on presentation of this guide.*

Vertrieu
38390 (21km N)

⊚ |●| Le Delphilion

Take the D65; it's in the village.
☎04.74.90.10.19

It is worth phoning beforehand to make sure that this restaurant is open out of season and, above all, to check that it's not already fullly booked, as its lovely, peaceful garden alongside the Rhône is extremely popular with local gourmets. The food is painstakingly prepared and executed: rabbit terrine in jelly, cod in a walnut crust, pike-perch with red wine, hock of veal with ceps, gâteaux (walnut or Chartreux), poached pear and *chaud-froid* of spiced bread. All the menus are superb from start to finish, and made even more remarkable by the extremely accessible prices: the weekday lunchtime menu costs €16 (including wine), then there are four more from €19.50 to €35. The wines are also good value for money, particularly the small selection of somewhat rare local vintages, such as that of the Pay des Balmes Dauphinoises.

Crest
26400

⊚ ⅍ 🏠 |●| Le Kléber*

6 rue Aristide-Dumont; it's in the centre of town by the town hall.
☎04.75.25.11.69 ☎04.75.76.82.82
Closed *Sun evening; Mon; Tues lunchtime; a fortnight early Jan; a fortnight end Aug.* **TV. Pay car park.**

This smart-looking little restaurant is decorated in ochre colours. It's known for its gourmet food and specializes in fish and regional dishes. The famous gastronomic chef, Maurice Pellier, takes the orders.

There's a weekday menu at €18, with others up to €43; menus may include ceps salad with slivers of duck, lobster stew with a verbena infusion, and *aiguillette* of beef with *bordelaise* sauce. A few prettily decorated rooms (one recently refurbished with good taste) are available at affordable prices: doubles cost €32–55, depending on the comfort. This is the most attractive place in town. *Free house apéritif offered to our readers on presentation of this guide.*

⊚ ⅍ |●| La Tartine

10 rue Peysson; it's near the church of Saint-Sauveur.
☎04.75.25.11.53
Closed *Sun and Sat lunchtimes (July–Aug); Mon, Wed evening, Sat lunchtime and Sun out of season; Feb school holiday; a fortnight end June to early July; Nov school holidays.* **High chairs and games available. Children's playroom.**

The restaurant occupies the whole of the first floor of a very old house that is typical of the ones you find in old Crest. There's a piano in the large, lofty dining room – this place is popular with musicians – and your visit may well coincide with an impromptu jazz jam. Véronique, the owner, makes imaginative snacks, offers a dish of the day, various grilled dishes and simple local specialities such as ravioli and *défarde* (based on tripe and sheep's feet). There's a "*menu du jour*" at €10, with others €12–23. It's very busy at lunchtime and at the weekend so it's advisable to book. *Free coffee offered to our readers on presentation of this guide.*

Grane
26400 (8km W)

⊚ ⅍ 🏠 |●| Restaurant Giffon**

Place de l'Église; on the D104.
☎04.75.62.60.64 ☎04.75.62.70.11
🖰www.hotelrestaurant-giffon.com
Closed *Mon and Tues.* **TV. High chairs available.**

There are only seven simple rooms here, with one above the restaurant large enough to sleep a whole family; doubles go for €44–51. The food explains why the chef has made the restaurant such a local favourite: foie gras with honeyed pears and pink peppercorns, *noisette* of lamb with truffle medallions cooked in their juices, char with truffle butter and morels. Desserts are excellent and there's a good wine list. Menus start from €22 (not served Sat evening or Sun lunch) and go up to €56. Impeccable welcome and service. *Free coffee or 5% discount on the room rate offered to our readers on presentation of this guide.*

Saillans
26340 (16km E)

⊛ ♈ |●| La Pantoufle Rieuse

43 Grande-Rue; take the D93, along the River Drôme.
☎04.75.21.59.60
Closed *Tues in summer; Mon–Fri lunchtimes out of season; 15 Nov–15 Jan.* **Games available.**

A charming restaurant in a pretty village. The owner brings flavours from distant lands to her cuisine: there's a nice "*formule assiette découverte*" providing a dish from a different place every two days (every week out of season), and a monthly "*assiette du monde*" – a culinary journey overseas to destinations such as China, Portugal and Armenia. The dishes are tasty and often surprising and are always prepared with fresh ingredients. Menus are €12.50–14.50, with a meal à la carte costing around €19. Out of season, the opening hours are not always respected. *Free coffee offered to our readers on presentation of this guide.*

Omblèze
26400 (29.5km NE)

⊛ ♈ ♔ |●| Auberge du Moulin de la Pipe

From Crest follow the road to Die, at Mirabel et Blacons, turn onto the D70 as far as Plan-de-Baix, then take the D578 for a further 5km.
☎04.75.76.42.05 ☎04.75.76.42.60
ⓦwww.moulindelapipe.com
Closed *mid-Nov to Feb school holiday.* **Restaurant closed** *Tues and Wed out of season.* **Disabled access. High chairs and games available. Car park.**

The owner will take great delight in telling the story of this old restored mill that lies at the far end of a valley with views of the gorges, a river and the waterfalls. It attracts outdoorsy people of all ages who come to Omblèze for the climbing school, flying trapeze and circus courses and the rock, blues and reggae concerts. The various *formules* include dishes such as foie gras ravioli, *caillette* with onion

preserve, *dauphinoise* potatoes *au gratin* and chocolate *fondant* with lavender. Home-made bread and attractive dishes are on offer all day, along with draught beer, in the dining room or on the terrace. There's a weekday lunch menu at €14.50, and others up to €25, including one vegetarian menu. A few double rooms are available for €47.50–55, depending on the season, as well as three cottages for groups and three furnished, fully equipped apartments. *10% discount on the room rate (except in summer) offered to our readers on presentation of this guide.*

Die
26150

⊛ ♈ ♔ Hôtel des Alpes**

87 rue Camille-Buffardel.
☎04.75.22.15.83 ☎04.75.22.09.39
ⓦwww.hotelalpes.fr
Open *daily all year round.* **Disabled access. TV. High chairs and cots available. Pay car park.**

The wide staircase is all that remains from this former fourteenth-century coaching inn. Nonetheless the hotel offers 24 comfortable rooms with good facilities – the second-floor ones have a splendid view of the Glandasse mountains and are very quiet. Doubles cost €42–47, and some large family rooms are also available. Some people might find that the pink everywhere in the house is too much, though, and Madame's passion for jigsaw puzzles adds to the kitsch. That said, the welcome is pleasant and it's a good base for exploring the town and the countryside. Logis de France. *Free breakfast per room (1 Nov–30 April) offered to our readers on presentation of this guide.*

⊛ |●| Restaurant des Batets

Quartier des Batets; it's 3km from the centre of town. On leaving the town, in the direction of Crest, take the D518 towards Chamaloc-col de Rousset for 2km.
☎04.75.22.11.45
Closed *Sun evening; Wed; 15–30 Oct.* **Games available. Car park.**

If you're footsore and weary from walking in the Vercors, this old farmhouse (a converted seventeenth-century sheep pen) with its arched dining room and terrace will come as a welcome sight. Try the guinea-fowl with thyme, trout fillets or the boned quail with juniper and a glass of local wine like a Châtillon-Champassias from Cornillon. There's an all-in, organic set lunch for €17, and other menus €21–38, including a vegetarian menu, as well as an impressive wine list. It can get very busy.

Barnave

26310 (13km S)

◉ 🏄 ♨ |◉| L'Aubergerie

Grande-Rue.
☎04.75.21.82.13 ⓕ04.75.21.84.31
ⓔlaubergerie@wanadoo.fr
Restaurant closed *Tues in season; Mon–Fri in winter.* **High chairs and games available. TV.**

You know you're here when you see the sheep sign. The large dining room occupies a converted stable, and upstairs there's an informal café where villagers come to play cards. They serve dishes such as small, warm *caillettes* with salad, guinea-fowl with oyster mushrooms and rabbit in Clairette de Die, a local sparkling wine. Menus €13–20. The oldest house in the village has been converted to provide five tasteful, simply decorated rooms (€32 with shower/wc or bath), two of which are equipped with kitchens and can be rented for a weekend or whole week. *Free house apéritif offered to our readers on presentation of this guide.*

Dieulefit

26220

◉ 🏄 |◉| Auberge Les Brises

Route de Nyons; it's 1.5km from the centre of town.
☎04.75.46.41.49
Closed *Tues; Mon evening and Wed out of season; 15 Jan–15 March; a week in November.*

This restaurant has quickly made a name for itself for its good food and friendly reception. Chef Didier and his wife Marie-Anne have created a little corner of their native Brittany in the Drôme, though they've swapped the flavours of the Atlantic for local ones – try the duck ham salad or the egg custard with Picodon cheese. Very appealing menus, such as the weekday lunch *menu express* at €13, and others €19–34, list dishes such as snail

profiteroles with garlic butter, *croustillant* of whiting stuffed with garlic, fish *blanquette* with morels and many home-made desserts including a *crème brûlée* with thyme. Eat on the shady terrace in summer or in the rustic dining room. *Free house apéritif offered to our readers on presentation of this guide.*

Poët-Laval (Le)

26160 (6km W)

◉ 🏄 ♨ |◉| Les Hospitaliers***

It's halfway between La Bégude and Dieulefit.
☎04.75.46.22.32 ⓕ04.75.56.49.99
ⓦwww.hotel-les-hospitaliers.com
Restaurant closed *Mon and Tues (except for hotel guests) out of season; 1 Jan–15 March; 9 Nov–31 Dec.* **Open** *daily July to mid-Sept.* **TV. High chairs available. Swimming pool.**

The hotel looks down over one of the loveliest villages in the Drôme; it's an idyllic place for a romantic weekend. There are some twenty rooms at €65-115, prices depending on the season and facilities; almost all have recently been refurbished. The salon and dining room are superb with pale wood, ancient beams and cosy furnishings; it seems to come from another era. The terrace looks over marvellous countryside and is a great place for dinner as the sun goes down. It's advisable to stick to the menus (€27–53), because à la carte can be pricey.

Divonne-les-Bains

01220

◉ ♨ |◉| Hôtel-restaurant Le Nid

388 rue Fontaine; it's behind the casino.
☎04.50.20.03.61
ⓔhotel-lenid@wanadoo.fr
TV.

This pretty hotel, right in the town centre, offers nine bright, spotless, comfortable and totally refurbished rooms in pastel yellows, blues and greens, with the added bonus of a flowery garden to the rear and an enchanting, cheerful owner. The rooms cost €30 with a washbasin and €43–50 with shower/wc. In the restaurant, the menu costs €13, and there's a dinner tray for €6 comprising soup, yoghurt, and a piece of fruit and bread.

@ ♠ |●| **La Terrasse Fleurie****

315 rue Fontaine; it's just behind the casino.
℡04.50.20.06.32 🖷04.50.20.40.34
Restaurant open to hotel guests only.
Closed early Oct to mid-March. **TV.**

A very quiet and aptly named hotel with a flowery terrace and balcony. It's remarkably peaceful, despite being so close to the centre of town. The modern rooms have some charm; doubles with shower/wc or bath cost €56–58. There is a possibility of half board (for a stay of seven days or more) or full board (for three weeks). The restaurant offers simple, inexpensive home cooking on menus at €12 and €15. Excellent value for Divonne.

Évian

74500

@ 🍴 ♠ **Hôtel Continental****

65 rue Nationale.
℡04.50.75.37.54 🖷04.50.75.31.11
🌐www.hcontinentalevian.com
Closed Jan. **TV.**

The owners of this hotel, who spend a lot of time in the USA, have made it lively and welcoming. Each room has character and the atmosphere is genuinely friendly. Great prices considering the charm of the place and the size of the rooms: doubles go for €45–65 with shower/wc or bath, depending on the season. *10% discount on room rate (except July–Aug and bank holiday weekends) offered to our readers on presentation of this guide.*

Publier

74500 (3.5km W)

@ 🍴 ♠ |●| **Hôtel Le Chablais – Restaurant L'Eau à la Bouche****

Rue du Chablais; it's on the D11.
℡04.50.75.28.06 🖷04.50.74.67.32
🌐www.hotel-chablais.com
Closed Mon; Sun evening; 21–28 Dec. **TV.**
High chairs available. Car park.

Classic family hotel. Rooms vary in comfort, although some have been refurbished in a contemporary, somewhat formalist style; a good half of them have a superb view of the lake. Doubles go for €60–75 with shower/wc or bath. The dining room, where you eat traditional cuisine, also has a good view. There's a

brasserie lunchtime menu at €16, and restaurant menus for €16–38. *Free house apéritif or 10% discount on the room rate (except July–Aug) offered to our readers on presentation of this guide.*

Thollon-les-Memises

74500 (10km E)

@ 🍴 ♠ |●| **Hôtel Bon Séjour****

Le Nouy; take the D24.
℡04.50.70.92.65 🖷04.50.70.95.72
🌐www.bon-sejour.com
Closed 28 Oct–20 Dec. **Open** noon–1.15pm and 7–8.30pm. **TV. High chairs and games available. Table tennis and tennis court. Car park.**

This is a family hotel where everyone helps out. The younger Duponts are refurbishing the bedrooms one by one; doubles with shower/wc or bath cost €46–54. The good, tasty mountain cuisine in the restaurant is prepared with care and served generously. Prices are attractive, too, with menus at €15 (not Sun) and €16–25. There's a terrace and a garden. Logis de France. *Free house apéritif offered to our readers (on half board or full board only) on presentation of this guide.*

Evosges

01230

@ ♠ |●| **L'Auberge Campagnarde****

It's around 20km from Ambérieu-en-Bugey and almost 10km from Saint-Rambert.
℡04.74.38.55.55 🖷04.74.38.55.62
📧auberge-campagnarde@wanadoo.fr
Closed Tues evening and Wed (open with booking 15 May–15 Sept); Jan; first week of Sept; second fortnight of Nov. **TV. High chairs and games available. Swimming pool. Car park.**

The winding road up is gorgeous, threading through steep vineyards and past huge white rocks that erupt from the bushes. The inn is like a holiday complex offering games for the children and mini-golf. Most rooms have been renovated and they're comfortable and quiet, costing €40 with shower/wc, or €50 with bath. Be sure to reserve from mid-May to mid-Sept. In the cosy dining room you can enjoy dishes made with top-quality produce: guinea-fowl *fricassée* with balsamic vinegar, snail stew, rabbit stuffed with mushrooms, chicken *suprême* and hazelnut tart. Menus start from €21 for a weekday lunch, up to €48. The cuisine is full of flavour and some of the dishes are very subtle. It is advisable to book. Logis de France.

Pezières-Resinand (Les)

01110 (6km NW)

@ 🎋 |●| Le Boomerang

Take the N504 to Saint-Rambert and then turn left onto the D34; it's signposted from the village of Oncieu.
☎04.74.38.58.60
Closed *Sun evening; Mon; whenever the boss goes shopping in Australia; 16 Sept–22 Oct.*

Just one of a few scattered houses huddled in one of Bugey's superb isolated valleys, this unusual inn is owned by Brent Perkins, originally from Adelaide, who settled here with his kangaroo after marrying a French woman. You'll get a genuine barbie – even a vegetarian one – along with steak and British and Australian sauces, ostrich fillets and roast emu with bush herbs. Menus range from €15 to €29. The wine list is divided between Australia and Bugey. They open a tearoom in the afternoon, with a selection of English and Australian teas and pastries; there is also a small shop with Aboriginal T-shirts, spices and produce from the Australian bush. It's advisable to phone beforehand in season. Credit cards not accepted. *Free liqueur offered to our readers on presentation of this guide.*

Feurs

42110

@ |●| Chalet de la Boule d'Or

42 rte. de Lyon; it's near the Feurs east exit.
☎04.77.26.20.68
Closed *Sun evening; Mon; Wed evening; a fortnight in Jan; 3 weeks in Aug.* **Disabled access.**

A gourmet restaurant that's not too expensive on weekdays. The staff are attentive without being intrusive, the food is delicate and the wines have been carefully selected (though prices are quite high). All the dishes are good: snail casserole with herb butter *en croûte*, baked monkfish with cloves of garlic, sliced

veal kidneys with Meaux mustard and a superb dessert trolley. The appetizers are full of subtle flavours and the desserts are out of this world. In fine weather, eat outside in the yard by the chestnut tree. There's a wide choice of menus, with the cheapest at €17 (except Sat evening and Sun), and others €27–55.

Panissières

42360 (12km NE)

@ 🏠 |●| Hôtel-restaurant de la Poste**

15 rue J-B Guerpillon; take the D89 then the D60 in the direction of Tarare.
☎04.77.28.64.00 ☎04.77.28.69.94
✉mireille.collas@worldonline.fr
Restaurant closed *Fri; Sat lunchtime.* **TV.**

A popular hotel in a restored old house. The rooms are simple but good value, with doubles going for €34. There are superb views over the Forez mountains, and the elegant dining room serves decent, good cooking. Specialities include foie gras, house rabbit terrine, and hot sausage salad. The weekday lunchtime menus are at €9 and €11, others €10.50–24.50.

Flumet

73590

@ 🎋 🏠 Hostellerie Le Parc des Cèdres***

☎04.79.31.72.37 ☎04.79.31.61.66
Closed *Jan; late March to mid-June; mid-Sept to mid-Dec.* **TV. Games available. Car park.**

The family who have run this establishment for more than a century belong to the old school of hotel-keeping. The building is surrounded by substantial grounds planted with cedar trees, there are club chairs in the sitting room and a snooker table in the bar. Some of the rooms were redecorated in the 1970s while others are more traditionally rustic. Doubles cost €45–60 with shower/wc or bath, depending on the season; some have a terrace (nos. 14 and 15) or a balcony (no. 8 or no. 23). In the restaurant, good-quality produce makes for good cooking. The terrace under the cedar trees is wonderful in summer. *10% discount on the room rate offered to our readers on presentation of this guide.*

Notre-Dame-de-Bellecombe

73590 (5km S)

☜ |●| La Ferme de Victorine

Le Planay; take the N218 in the direction of Les Saisies and 3km before Notre-Dame-de-Bellecombe, take the left towards Le Planay.
☏04.79.31.63.46
Closed *Sun evening and Mon (April to mid-June); mid-June to early July; mid-Nov to mid-Dec.* **Disabled access.**

The dining room has a huge fireplace for cold winter days and, in the summer, they open a bright, sunny terrace with a great view of the mountain. Menus (€19 at lunchtime in the week and €28–37) list nicely prepared traditional Savoy dishes. Good Savoy wines also available.

Saisies (Les)

73620 (14km SE)

☜ 🏠 |●| Le Météor*

1440 rte. de Bisanne; it's 2km from the ski slopes. Follow the signs to the Village Vacances.
☏04.79.38.90.79 ☏04.79.38.97.00
✉le.meteor@wanadoo.fr
Closed *May–June; early Sept to end Nov.* **TV. High chairs available. Car park.**

This typical, wooden chalet built in a mountain meadow is quietly set apart from the ski resort but just 100m from the slopes. The rooms, nothing special but perfectly acceptable, cost €43 with shower/wc; in winter half board is compulsory and costs €43–51 per person. There's a lunch menu at €13, with others €20–25. They serve Savoy specialities such as fondue, *raclette* and *tartiflette*.

☜ 🎋 |●| Restaurant Le Chaudron

Take the D218; it's beside the police station.
☏04.79.38.92.76
Closed *1 May–1 July; 30 Sept–15 Dec.*
Games available.

Though the decoration at this friendly restaurant is typical of hundreds of places in the mountains, the food is good. The regional dishes are amply served and fortifying after a day's skiing: *diots*, fondue, *potence*, *reblochonnade*, fillets of lake whitefish (a type of salmon), and beef topped with cheese. Menus start at €21, or reckon on around €25 à la carte. There's a nice terrace where you can get a good view of the pistes. *Free house liqueur offered to our readers on presentation of this guide.*

Garde-Adhémar (La)

26700

☜ 🏠 |●| Logis de l'Escalin***

Quartier Les Martines, rte. de Donzère; via the A7, take the Montélimar-Sud or Bollène exit. It's 1.5km along the road to Donzère.
☏04.75.04.41.32 ☏04.75.04.40.05
✉www.lescalin.com
Closed *Sun evening; Mon.* **TV. Car park.**

A little hotel on the side of a hill overlooking the Rhône Valley. The motorway is a couple of kilometres away as the crow flies, but seems much, much further. The hotel, a handsome building in local style painted white with blue shutters, provides fifteen fresh, refurbished rooms in the main building, and seven more in a newer annexe; doubles go for €60–80, depending on the comfort and the season. In the restaurant, dishes include hot *escalopine* of foie gras, pan-fried red mullet, garlic braised ham and veal with cream and tarragon sauce. Menus are €21-69. There's a fine selection of wines, with several vintages from Côtes-du-Rhône and Tricastin, as well as a pleasant shady garden in which to sample them.

Gex

01170

☜ 🎋 🏠 Hôtel du Parc**

58 passage de la Curonne; it's in the heart of the town, on the road from Divonne-les-Bains.
☏04.50.41.50.18 ☏04.50.42.37.29
✉hotel.parc@wanadoo.fr
Closed *Sun; 2–25 Jan; 1–15 Sept.* **TV. Car park.**

This traditional, characterful hotel has been run by the same family for over seventy years. The park it's named after is across the road and the hotel itself has a huge, prize-winning garden full of geraniums, roses, begonias and all sorts of colourful flowers. Rooms go for €56–68 with shower/wc or bath; on a clear day you can see Mont Blanc from no.19. Book in advance. Logis de France. *10% discount on the room rate offered to our readers on presentation of this guide.*

RHÔNE-ALPES

Segny

01170 (6km SE)

⊚ ⅍ ♨ La Bonne Auberge**

240 rue du Vieux-Bourg; take the N5. It's in the centre of the village.
☎04.50.41.60.42 ℗04.50.41.71.79
Closed 20 Dec–30 March.
TV. Car park.

An authentic country inn hidden from the road by the trees in the garden. Attractive, well-maintained rooms cost €40–50 with shower/wc or bath – good value for a hotel near Gex. There's no restaurant (although there are places to eat in the village). They do serve breakfast, though, complete with home-made jams. Warm welcome and family atmosphere. *10% discount on the room rate offered to our readers on presentation of this guide.*

Crozet

01170 (8km SW)

⊚ ♨ |●| Bois Joly**

Route de la Télécabine; take the D984 in the direction of Bellegarde and turn right onto the D89 as far as Crozet; it's 500m from the cable car.
☎04.50.41.01.96 ℗04.50.42.48.47
Closed Fri. **TV. Disabled access. High chairs and games available. Swimming pool. Car park.**

This is a big establishment on the lower slopes of the Jura that was totally refurbished in 2001. There is a splendid view of the Alps from the terrace, where you can eat in fine weather. The rooms have good facilities – some of them with balconies – and are reasonably priced for the area: €46 with shower/wc or bath. The restaurant provides generous portions of regional dishes such as frogs' legs, duck breast with green peppers or sea perch. Menus range from €12 to €26.10.

Grand-Bornand (Le)

74450

⊚ ⅍ ♨ |●| Hôtel-restaurant Les Glaïeuls**

It's at the foot of the slopes, from where the cable cars start.
☎04.50.02.20.23 ℗04.50.02.25.00
ⓦwww.hotel-lesglaieuls.com

Closed mid-April to mid-June; mid-Sept to 20 Dec. **TV. Car park.**

A very well-run hotel. Though the façade is pretty ordinary, in summer the flowers at every window and on the terrace make it look lovely. It's a very traditional place, with cosy sitting rooms and classic décor. The owners are polite and friendly. Rooms have good facilities and cost €28.40–86 with shower/wc or bath. Good classic cooking in the restaurant with menus from €13.70 (weekday lunchtimes) to €30; you'll pay around €29 à la carte. There's a sunny terrace. Logis de France.

⊚ ♨ Hôtel les Cimes***

Le Chinaillon.
☎04.50.27.00.38 ℗04.50.27.08.46
ⓦwww.hotel-les-cimes.com
Closed 30 April–20 June; 1 Sept–1 Dec. **TV. Car park.**

A stone's throw from the old village of Chinaillon and 100m from the pistes, this is a traveller's dream come true. The couple who run the place have converted an ordinary establishment above a chic boutique into a friendly inn which is full of the fragrance of wood and polish. Bedrooms are wonderfully quiet, with comfortable feather beds. Doubles cost €84–155 with shower/wc or with bath, depending on the season; the price includes a superb breakfast, and half board can be arranged with a restaurant nearby. The owners look after their guests very well.

⊚ ⅍ |●| La Ferme de Lormay

Vallée du Bouchet; it's 7km from the village, in the direction of the col des Annes – turn right when you get to the little chapel.
☎04.50.02.24.29
Closed Tues; weekday lunchtimes in winter; 20 April–20 June; 8 Sept–20 Dec. **Car park.**

Lovely restaurant in an old farm building. In summer, when they serve food on the terrace, try the chicken with crayfish, the trout or the house *quenelles*. When the weather gets cold the tables are put close together round the fireplace, and there is more charcuterie and pork on offer – the roast pork and bacon soup are both delicious, as are the tarts and the *clafoutis*. It's cooking you want to linger over. No menu here; reckon on €30–40 à la carte. Credit cards not accepted. *Free house apéritif offered to our readers on presentation of this guide.*

Grenoble

38000

See map overleaf

⊛ 🛍 Hôtel de l'Europe**

22 pl. Grenette; follow the signs to the Lafayette car park. It's in the pedestrian precinct. **Map C3-1**
℡ 04.76.46.16.94 ℻ 04.76.43.13.65
🖳 www.hoteleurope.fr
TV.

This hotel is in a lively pedestrianized area right in the centre of Grenoble, but the rooms – some 50 of them – are well-soundproofed and noise isn't a problem. It's a comfortable place, the welcome is genuine and the prices are unusually modest for the town: doubles cost €36 with washbasin and €75 with shower or bath/wc. Rooms are all regularly renovated. There's also a gym and a sauna. Rather disappointing breakfast.

⊛ 🍴 🛍 Hôtel des Patinoires**

12 rue Marie-Chamoux; it's 500m south of the Palais des Sports, via avenue Jeanne-d'Arc and 10 min from town centre. **Off map D3-2**
℡ 04.76.44.43.65 ℻ 04.76.44.44.77
🖳 www.hotel-patinoire.com
Closed Aug. **TV. Car park.**

One of the best hotels in town, and good value for money. The owners are genial, attentive, and there's a warm atmosphere and décor. It's superbly maintained and extremely quiet. Rooms cost €47 with shower/wc and €52 with bath. *One free breakfast per room offered to our readers on presentation of this guide.*

⊛ 🛍 Splendid Hôtel**

22 rue Thiers; follow the "Centre" signs, then take the cours Jean-Jaurès or the cours Berriat. **Map B3-3**
℡ 04.76.46.33.12 ℻ 04.76.46.35.24
🖳 www.splendid-hotel.com
Disabled access. TV. Pay car park.

The rooms in this small two-star hotel offer facilities usually only found in much bigger establishments: hair dryer, room service, Internet connection (for free) and, in some cases, air-conditioning and a hydromassage shower. The decoration was undertaken by artists, who have depicted famous children's figures on the walls (although some rooms have a more restrained, classical look). Double rooms

cost €63–79. Special mention should be given to breakfast: the basic offer (€5.90) can be supplemented, at a very reasonable price, by extras such as fresh orange juice, ham, eggs, etc. This imaginative charm is complemented by the warm welcome given to the guests.

⊛ 🍴 🍽 Café de la Table Ronde

7 pl. Saint-André. **Map C2-17**
℡ 04.76.44.51.41
Closed first week in Jan.

Located about as centrally as you can get, this café is an institution in Grenoble. Established in 1739, it's the second oldest café in France after *Le Procope* in Paris, and tradition, hospitality and conviviality are its watchwords. The terrace is a great vantage point from which to watch the world go by on the square, and the décor in the dining room is splendid. There are lots of good dishes: ravioli, *andouillette*, grilled beef, *diot* with shallots and *gratin dauphinois*, calf's head *à l'ancienne* and so on. The weekday lunch menu is at €10, with others at €21 and €29. Affordable wines include a Gamay de Savoie; some are served by the glass or jug. "Le Grenier" cabaret takes place on the first floor (Wed–Sat). *Free house apéritif offered to our readers on presentation of this guide.*

⊛ 🍴 🍽 La Frise

150 cours Berriat; it's by the Berriat tram stop. **Off map A3-11**
℡ 04.76.96.58.22
Closed evenings; Sat; Sun; Aug.

Near the Magasin, the contemporary art centre, this place has a bright, colourful interior with pictures by local artists on the walls. Tasty dishes are at €9; the set lunch for €12 includes a main course, dessert and coffee, and you'll pay a maximum of €14 for a meal à la carte. Dishes are prepared using fresh ingredients and served in big portions, and the delicious desserts are home-made. *Free Pot Lyonnais (wine) offered to our readers on presentation of this guide.*

⊛ 🍽 Le Coup de Torchon

8 rue Dominique-Villars. **Map D3-12**
℡ 04.76.63.20.58
Closed Sun; Mon.

This spruce restaurant is our latest discovery in Grenoble. The ingredients are extremely fresh, coming as they do from

RHÔNE-ALPES

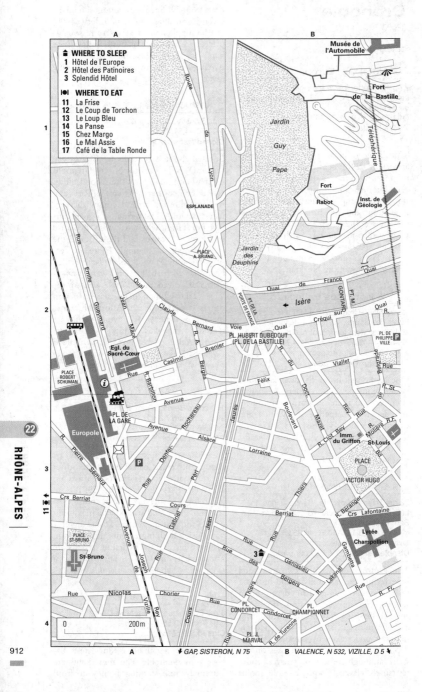

WHERE TO SLEEP
1 Hôtel de l'Europe
2 Hôtel des Patinoires
3 Splendid Hôtel

WHERE TO EAT
11 La Frise
12 Le Coup de Torchon
13 Le Loup Bleu
14 La Panse
15 Chez Margo
16 Le Mal Assis
17 Café de la Table Ronde

Musée de l'Automobile

Fort de la Bastille

Jardin Guy Pape

Fort Rabot

Inst. de Géologie

ESPLANADE

Téléphérique

PLACE A. BRIAND

Jardin des Dauphins

Isère

Quai de France

GONTARD

PT. DE LA PORTE DE FRANCE

PT. M.

Quai

Créqui

PL. DE PHILIPPE VILLE

Voie

Quai

PL. HUBERT DUBEDOUT (PL. DE LA BASTILLE)

Claude Bernard

R. A. Brenier

Viallet

R. St

Egl. du Sacré-Cœur

Casimir

Bergès

Félix

Dott.

Mazal

Rey

R. Molière

R.F.

PLACE ROBERT SCHUMAN

Rue

R. Barbillon

Avenue

Rochereau

Jaurès

Boulevard

R. Clot Bey

Imm. du Griffon

St-Louis

PL. DE LA GARE

Avenue

Alsace

Lorraine

PLACE VICTOR HUGO

Europole

Derrer

Petit

Thiers

R. Béranger

Crs Berriat

Cours

Berriat

Crs Lafontaine

PLACE ST-BRUNO

Gabriel Péri

Rue

Rue des

3

Génissieu

Lycée Champollion

Gambetta

St-Bruno

Rue

Nicolas

Chorier

Rue

Thiers

Bergers

Lakanal

R. Fr.

Rue

Joseph

Vieille

Rey

Cours

Rue

PL. CONDORCET

Condorcet

PL. CHAMPIONNET

R. de Turenne

0   200m

PL. J. MARVAL

22

RHÔNE-ALPES

11

A ⬇ GAP, SISTERON, N 75   B VALENCE, N 532, VIZILLE, D 5 ⬇

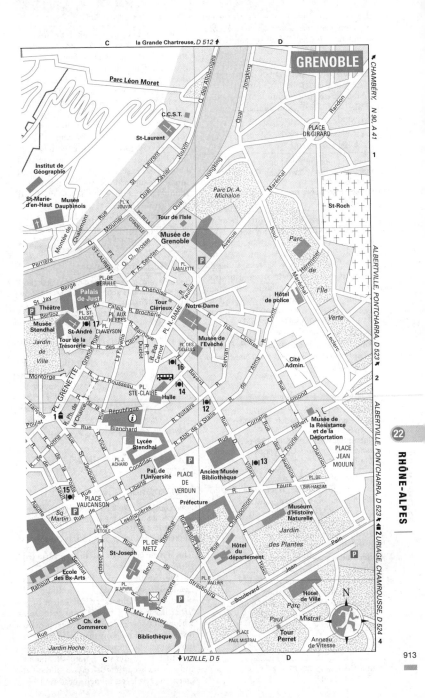

la Grande Chartreuse, *D 512* ↑

GRENOBLE

Parc Léon Moret

C.C.S.T.

St-Laurent

PLACE DR GIRARD

Institut de Géographie

Parc Dr. A. Michalon

St-Roch

St-Marie-d'en-Haut

Musée Dauphinois

PL X JOUVIN

Tour de l'Isle

Musée de Grenoble

PL DE BÉRULLE

R. Chenoise

Parc

Palais de Just.

Théâtre Berlioz

Palais

PL ST-ANDRÉ

PL AUX HERBES

Tour Clérieux

Notre-Dame

Hôtel de police

l'Île

Musée Stendhal

St-André

PL CLAVEYSON

Musée de l'Évêché

Verte

Jardin de Ville

Tour de la Trésorerie

PL DES TILLEULS

Cité Admin.

Montorge

16

PL. STE-CLAIRE

Halle

14

12

1

République

Blanchard

Musée de la Résistance et de la Déportation

PLACE JEAN MOULIN

Lycée Stendhal

PL. J. ACHARD

PL DE BIR-HAKEIM

13

PLACE DE VERDUN

Ancien Musée Bibliothèque

15

Pal. de l'Université

PLACE VAUCANSON

Préfecture

Muséum d'Histoire Naturelle

Sq. Martin

PL DE L'ÉTOILE

PL. DE METZ

St-Joseph

Hôtel du département

Jardin des Plantes

Ecole des Bx-Arts

PL D'APVRIL

PL. F. VALLIER

Ch. de Commerce

Bd. Mar. Lyautey

Hôtel de Ville

Parc

Jardin Hoche

Bibliothèque

PLACE PAUL MISTRAL

Paul Mistral

Tour Perret

Anneau de Vitesse

N

↓ VIZILLE, D 5

the city's top suppliers – in fact, some of them even eat here, which is recommendation in itself. When we ate here, we were treated to an impeccable three-meat terrine, a small quail, roasted to perfection and served with ravioli and a superb wine sauce, and, to finish, raspberries with Chiboust cream. Lunchtime menus are at €12.50 and €15, and dinner menus at €16 and €22.

@ 🎿 |◐| La Panse

7 rue de la Paix; it's near place de Verdun, reached via rue Voltaire. **Map C2-14**
☏04.76.54.09.54
Closed Sun; public holidays; mid-July to mid-Aug.

The minimalist décor at this place will be a bit too fashionable for some tastes, though it's brightened up by colourful pictures. The welcome's a bit cool, too. But the cooking is reliable and highly distinctive with a touch of sophistication. Dishes change all the time, but might include herring pâté with whisky, hot oysters or quail with foie gras. Menus are €13 weekday lunchtimes and €15–27 in the evening. There's a wide range of wines. Relaxed atmosphere. *Free house apéritif offered to our readers on presentation of this guide.*

@ 🎿 |◐| Le Loup Bleu

7 rue Dominique-Villars; it's behind the préfecture on place de Verdun. **Map D3-13**
☏04.76.51.22.70
Closed Sat lunchtime; Sun; Mon evening; public holidays; Aug. **Open** noon and evening until 10.15pm.

This unobtrusive restaurant, with the old shutters still in place, is quiet and atmospheric, and the cooking and the service are both first-rate. Dishes on the €13 lunch menu change with the seasons, but if you want a slightly more refined meal, go for the menus at €20 and €33, which offer traditional dishes and excellent meat and fish. Some are worth a mention: sea bass with walnut wine, pork *filet mignon* roasted with acacia honey, duck breast stuffed with foie gras, scallops with roasted ceps. *Free house apéritif offered to our readers on presentation of this guide.*

@ 🎿 |◐| Chez Margo

5 rue Millet. **Map C3-15**
☏04.76.46.27.87

Closed Sat lunchtime; Sun.

This restaurant, in a quiet little street, is often busy. Even on weekday evenings there's a reliable stream of regulars who drop in. The dining room is split-level, decorated in a smart-rustic style and the atmosphere is very informal. The cooking is traditional, prepared with care and the regional dishes are quite substantial. There's a €14 lunch menu, and others at €16.50–30. You get lots of choice: house foie gras, *fricassée* of scampi with ravioli, sliced veal sweetbreads with ginger and lime, *caillette* served on a potato cake, monkfish medallions with wild mushrooms, *confit* of duck thigh, *fondant* of two chocolates. Dishes of the day use fresh market produce. There's a short but good wine list. *Free house apéritif offered to our readers on presentation of this guide.*

@ 🎿 |◐| Le Mal Assis

9 rue Bayard; it's next to the cathedral, in an area abounding in antique shops. **Map C2-16**
☏04.76.54.75.93
Closed lunchtime; Mon; Sun; public holidays; 14 July–20 Aug.

This place, a local favourite, has wood panelling and a fireplace and charming service. Dishes include duckling in peaches and sweet spices, saddle of rabbit with tomatoes, fillet of bass in grapefruit butter sauce. There's a menu for €24. Credit cards not accepted. *Free house apéritif offered to our readers on presentation of this guide.*

Fontanil-Cornillon

38120 (7km N)

@ |◐| Au Taille-Bavette

2 av. Lousiane; take the N75, towards Voreppe. It's next to the *Hôtel Kyriad.*
☏04.76.75.47.70
Closed Tues evening; Sat evening; Sun.

This favourite haunt of unreconstructed carnivores, tucked away at the far end of the Abattoirs industrial estate, does not look very exciting from outside, and might even be considered downright ugly. What has it got going for it, in that case? The businesspeople and sales agents who flock here will tell you that it's ideal for a blowout (with a hearty steak, for example) and that it's better to ignore the menu and choose from the varied cuts of tender, succulent, parsleyed French meat available à la carte. Reckon on paying between €20 and €30, depending on your appetite.

Uriage-les-Bains
38410 (10km SE)

@ 2A 🏠 |●| Auberge du Vernon

Les Davids, 1274 rte. du Vernon; follow the signs for Chamrousse via col du Luitel, then follow the signs to the left after the Vizille roundabout.
℡04.76.89.10.56
Closed Sun evening; 25 Sept–1 April. **Car park.**

This country inn looks like something from a fairy story; it's a little farm with a pond, a huge tree, flowers all over the place and a phenomenal view of the mountains. The Girouds, who have run the place for thirty years, serve good home cooking in generous portions – this is real country food – including charcuterie and omelette paysanne, and veal sweetbreads with ceps to order. You'll pay €15 for the weekday lunch menu, with others from €21. If you want to stay here, six small but pretty doubles go for €36–50, depending on the degree of comfort, and half board is also available at €35–45 per person. Peace and quiet are guaranteed. *Free coffee offered to our readers on presentation of this guide.*

@ 🏠 |●| Les Mésanges**

Route des Mésanges, le Vachez; 1km along the Saint-Martin-d'Uriage road, turn right onto the Bouloud road.
℡04.76.89.70.69 ℡04.76.89.56.97
🖳www.hotel-les-mesanges.com
Closed 20 Oct–31 Jan. **Restaurant closed** *(except to hotel guests) Sun evening, Mon and Tues (Feb–April); Mon lunchtime and Tues (1 May–20 Oct).*
Disabled access. TV. High chairs and games available. Swimming pool. Car park.

The Prince family, who have owned this place since 1946, have established a solid reputation. All the rooms have been refurbished; the loveliest ones have big balconies from which you can see down the valley as far as Vizille, while the smaller ones look across the fields. Doubles cost €54–66 with shower/wc or bath. In the restaurant, specialities include veal with morels, saddle of pigeon with caramelized spices, strawberry soup, pig's trotters, duo of lamb with garlic *confit* and iced *pavé* with Chartreuse. It's all very rich in flavours and calories. Menus range from €22 to €50. Logis de France.

Sappey-en-Chartreuse (Le)
38700 (15km N)

@ 2A |●| Relais Fort Saint-Eynaud

Fort Saint-Eynard; it's just before Le Sappey (coming from Grenoble), on the right, on the D512.
℡04.76.85.25.24
Closed 1 Nov–1 May. **Open** Thurs–Sun (May, June, Sept–Oct); daily, except Sun evening and Mon (July–Aug). **Disabled access. High chairs available.**

The restaurant is on the Saint-Eynard summit at an altitude of 1340m. The belvedere is incorporated into the cliff face with an impressive view over Grenoble and the Grésilvaudan valley. There are two vaulted dining rooms with rough-hewn stone walls softened by a selection of pictures and wooden bistro tables swathed in tablecloths. Simple, uncomplicated fare: sandwiches, crêpes and cakes all at modest prices. The €11 menu lists a plate of charcuterie, omelette with chives, salad and dessert; there's another menu for €14 which includes *gratin dauphinois*, a home-made speciality. The Grenoblois swarm here for dinner in summer, when they put tables outside, so consider booking. It's also a bar. *Free house apéritif offered to our readers on presentation of this guide.*

Sarcenas
38700 (15km N)

@ 🏠 |●| L'Auberge de Sarcenas

Route du Col-de-Porte; take the D57.
℡04.76.88.81.11
🖳www.aubergedesarcenas.com
Closed Wed out of season and generally the whole week in slack periods.

The story of this building starts in the early eighteenth century, when work began on the construction of a château, but this was never finished and ended up a ruin. It then became, successively, a farm, a staging post and, in 1937, a hotel-*buvette* (some old signs remain from this period). The latter closed many years ago, but only recently it was valiantly taken over by a delightful young couple who have renovated the building from top to bottom to create a small hotel in a classical mould (apart from the small pet pigs wandering around the garden). The rooms are simple but pretty, while the dining room is strikingly attractive. The crowning glory, however, is the terrace, with its panoramic view of the whole valley. Double rooms cost €50 with shower/wc (although there are also a few at €35 with just a washbasin). The restaurant offers tasty food in copious portions on menus at €20–29: *gratin de crozets*, charcuterie, fondues and enormous grilled spareribs of pork.

Saint-Hugues-de-Chartreuse

38380 (27km N)

◎ 🎋 |◎| La Cabine

Take the D512 in the direction of Saint-Pierre-de-Chartreuse; it's next to the church-Museum of Contemporary Sacred Art.
☎04.76.88.67.19
Closed *Nov.* **Open** *daily during summer and winter holidays; weekends only the rest of the year.* **Disabled access. High chairs available.**

The restaurant is in a converted school. There's a nice combination of white wood and rough-hewn stone, with sculptures, tools, domestic implements and dried flowers to decorate the place. The pleasant terrace overlooks the forest and the beginning of the cross-country ski trails. Dishes include *tartiflette* (to order an hour in advance), fondues, lots of salads, savoury tarts, omelettes, crêpes and ice creams. Menus, €9.90–15, are served until 9.30pm. They have live music in the evening – jazz, blues and French songs. Credit cards not accepted. *Free house apéritif offered to our readers on presentation of this guide.*

Grignan

26230

◎ 🎋 🏠 Le Clair de la Plume***

Place du Mai.
☎04.75.91.81.30 ℗04.75.91.81.31
◎www.chateauxhotels.com/clairplume
Open *daily, all year.* **TV. High chairs available. Car park.**

Well situated in the old town across from one of the most beautiful washhouses in the Midi, this is a very elegant eighteenth-century house with a serene atmosphere and a small, relaxing garden. The whole

place emanates good taste, comfort and refinement. All the rooms (€90–105,with bath) are different, but each one is air-conditioned.You have breakfast (€10), including home-made jam, in the old kitchen, which is full of original character. Urbane, polite welcome. *10% discount on the room rate, Sun evening to Thurs, Nov–March (except during school holidays) offered to our readers on presentation of this guide.*

Valaurie

26230 (10km W)

◎ 🎋 🏠 |◎| Domaine Les Méjeonnes***

Take the D541.
☎04.75.98.60.60 ℗04.75.98.63.44
◎www.mejeonnes.com
Disabled access. TV. High chairs available. Swimming pool. Car park.

If you want to see this old farmhouse at its best, arrive in the mellow glow of late afternoon or in the evening when the floodlights illuminate the vines and the old stones. Lovely, spacious, comfortable rooms go for €64 for a double with shower/wc or bath. Menus at €20–30 list good, appetizing food. Service is a bit slow, but who's in a hurry?You'll get a courteous welcome – and the swimming pool is superb. *Free house apéritif offered to our readers on presentation of this guide.*

Hauterives

26390

◎ 🏠 |◎| Le Relais**

Place du Général-de-Miribel.
☎04.75.68.81.12 ℗04.75.68.92.42
Closed *Sun evening and Mon out of season; mid-Jan to end Feb.* **Restaurant closed** *Mon in summer.* **TV. High chairs available. Car park.**

The thick, sturdy walls of this handsome nineteenth-century building are lined with photos and engravings by Ferdinand Cheval – a local postman who constructed an extraordinary sculpture from stones he collected on his rounds. The large, refurbished, rustic bedrooms cost €30–40 with washbasin or shower, €50 with shower/wc, and the restaurant offers regional menus at €14–30.50. Lots of passing customers. Best to book. Logis de France.

Joyeuse

07260

@ 🦌 🛏 |O| **Hôtel de l'Europe****

☎04.75.39.51.26 ℗04.75.39.59.00
ⓦwww.ardeche-hotel.net
Open *all year.* **Disabled access. TV. High
chairs and games available. Swimming
pool** *May–Sept.* **Car park.**

You get fair value for a place that's on
the way to the gorges of the Ardèche and
the Cévennes. The large, refurbished and
standardized bedrooms go for €36–46,
depending on the season and degree of
comfort. They serve tasty, simple dishes
such as omelettes with ceps, quail cooked
in typical local style, chestnut cream caramel, and pizzas of impressive size. Menus
range from €11 to €17. The large heated
indoor pool has a great view over the
Cévennes; there's also a *boules* area. *10%
discount on the room rate (out of season) offered
to our readers on presentation of this guide.*

@ |O| **Restaurant Valentina**

Place de la Peyre; it's in the town.
☎04.75.39.90.65
Closed *Mon; mid-Sept to end March.*

This is the only restaurant in the old town,
and since it's well away from traffic, the
terrace overlooking the nice little square
is a pleasant place to sit. The owners are
a nice Italian couple who are keen travellers – there's a Lambretta they brought
back from Italy. Authentic Italian cooking is on offer: charcuterie, antipasti, *osso
buco*, pasta with pine nuts, tortellini with
ceps, tagliatelli with smoked salmon and
vodka sauce, also meat dishes. The home-
made desserts are seriously good. You'll
pay around €8.50 for a main course or
€22 for a menu. Good Italian wines.

Balazuc

07120 (11km NE)

@ 🦌 |O| **La Granja Delh
Gourmandas**

It's in the village, 50m from the church; take
the D104 to Uzer, then the D294.
☎04.75.37.74.26
Open *daily mid-June to end Aug (bookings
only for weekends from May to mid-June).*
**Disabled access. High chairs and games
available.**

This is a restaurant that stands out from
the crowd. There's no dining room, just

a few tables set in the open air and
under a little porch. The food is not only
guaranteed to be fresh (there's no freezer
here), it is also organically grown. They
serve fine, original salads, generous but
light, made from local produce, including
seasonal fruit for around €9.50; menus
are at €10 and €21. The desserts and
ice creams are also home-made and are
equally delicious. Sometimes there are
storytelling evenings (you can choose the
story you want from a menu) or magic
shows guaranteed to delight children; you
might even run into a fortune teller. A
really inviting place.

Juliénas

69840

@ 🦌 🛏 |O| **Chez la Rose****

It's in the centre.
☎04.74.04.41.20 ℗04.74.04.49.29
ⓦwww.chez-la-rose.fr
Restaurant closed *Mon; Tues, Thurs and Fri
lunchtimes (except on public holidays); 10–26
Dec; Feb school holiday.* **TV. High chairs
available. Car park.**

With its elegant façade, this building
has the look of an old posthouse. The
main building houses comfortable, rustic
bedrooms while those across the road are
genuine suites with a sitting room – one
even has a private garden. Doubles with
shower/wc or bath cost €42–60; suites
go for €68–100. The magnificent dining
room is a perfect setting for famously
tasty regional cooking produced by a
seriously good chef: terrine of pressed
duck breast, foie gras, *coq au vin* and lobster stew. Menus range from €26 to €48.
They also prepare dishes for takeaway and
they are open for light meals Monday to
Friday (11am–6pm) in season. 20% discount on the room rate is offered if you
dine in the restaurant. Logis de France.
*Free coffee offered to our readers on presenta-
tion of this guide.*

Laffrey

38220

@ 🦌 🛏 |O| **La Pacodière**

Route du Lac; it's on the N85, around 10km
from Vizille, it's the first house on the left, set
back from the route du Lac.
☎04.76.73.16.22 ℗04.38.72.92.20

RHÔNE-ALPES

Closed *Mon–Thurs evenings (early Oct to late April); Jan.* **Disabled access. High chairs and games available. Car park.**

Three thoughtfully decorated doubles with bath or shower go for €53; the one at the back is particularly pretty. There's a reading room in the roof space. The dining room is also pleasant, its tables laid with checked cloths, and in summer you can eat on the terrace that leads to the lawn. Good, classic cuisine includes dishes like trout and pike pâté with morels, chicken with duck foie gras, and pike-perch with crayfish *coulis*. Menus are €21–36. *Free house apéritif offered to our readers on presentation of this guide.*

Lamastre
07270

@ 🏠 |●| **Hôtel du Midi – Restaurant Barattéro**

☎04.75.06.41.50 ℗04.75.06.49.75
Closed *Mon; Fri and Sun evenings; end Dec to mid-Feb.* **TV. Car park.**

A gourmet restaurant that has enjoyed a good reputation for several decades. The dining room is classy and cosy. You get the measure of the cooking from the cheapest menu at €32, though the pricier ones – €34–76 – include dishes with more unusual and luxurious ingredients: Bresse chicken cooked in a bladder, a divine iced chestnut soufflé. The service is meticulous and old-style French: you feel rather as if you have to sit straight at your table and not clatter your cutlery. Rooms in the hotel are equally cosy and perfectly maintained; doubles cost €78–95 with shower/wc or bath.

Crestet (Le)
07270 (8km NE)

@ 🎋 🏠 |●| **La Terrasse★★**

Take the D534 in the direction of Tournon; Crestet is on the left.
☎04.75.06.24.44 ℗04.75.06.23.25
Closed *Sat in winter; Jan.* **Disabled access. TV. Swimming pool. Car park.**

There's an air of serenity in this classic establishment – you get the feeling that the people here really know how to live. Acceptable rooms cost from €35 to €39. In the restaurant, they list a good selection of regional dishes; it's worth trying the

Picodon, the local goat's cheese, which has a slightly piquant flavour. The dining room has a lovely view of the Doux valley and, in summer, when the swimming pool area is ablaze with flowers, a rampant vine provides shade for the terrace. Menus are €11 and €17–23. Logis de France. *Free house apéritif offered to our readers on presentation of this guide.*

Lanslebourg
73480

@ 🏠 |●| **Hôtel de la Vieille Poste★★**

Grande-Rue.
☎04.79.05.93.47 ℗04.79.05.86.85
🖳www.lavieilleposte.com
Closed *mid-April to mid-June; 26 Sept–26 Dec.* **TV. High chairs and games available.**

This fine hotel in the middle of the biggest ski station in Maurienne has been run by the same owners for a good thirty years. Guests are so warmly welcomed that they are made to feel part of the family. The rooms have recently been refurbished in a fairly neutral modern style and are quite comfortable; most have a balcony. Doubles with shower/wc or bath cost around €45–50. The restaurant serves simple but satisfying local fare on menus at €13–25. All in all, it offers remarkable value for money for this region, so it's easy to see why so many customers keep on coming back. Logis de France.

Lhuis
01680

@ 🏠 |●| **Bar-hôtel-restaurant de La Tour**

It's 20km from Belley, going west on the D41.
☎04.74.39.81.67
Closed *Tues evening; Wed; end Aug.*

This small five-room hotel, with its convivial bar and terrace shaded by linden trees, stands opposite the delightful village church. There's a series of delicious themed menus for €18–25: "fisherman's" (sea bream with saffron); "country" (rabbit with mustard seed) and "farmyard" (poultry). The atmosphere is relaxed, the service cheerful and friendly. There are two double rooms with their own shower/wc at €31, including breakfast; the others share a bathroom on the landing.

Montagnieu

01470 (9km NW)

◎ 🏛 |◎| Hôtel-restaurant Rolland**

Les Granges-de-Montagnieu; take the D79.
℡04.74.36.73.45 ℗04.74.36.70.98
Closed *Fri evening; Sun evening; mid-Sept
to mid-Oct.* **Disabled access. TV. Games
available. Car park.**

The rooms here have all been tastefully refurbished in restrained but pretty
pale colours, with simple, elegant brand-
new furniture. Everything is immaculately
clean and the service is attentive. The
double rooms (€46) share a shower/wc
on the landing. The weekday menus cost
€11–15, with others at €20–34. Logis
de France.

Lyon

69000

See map overleaf

1st arrondissement

◎ 𝒳 🏛 Hôtel Saint-Vincent**

9 rue Pareille; M° Hôtel-de-Ville. **Map B1-1**
℡04.78.27.22.56 ℗04.78.30.92.87
🌐www.hotel-saintvincent.com
TV.

This hotel is freshly redecorated and definitely not lacking in character – all the
rooms have parquet floors and some boast
beautiful fireplaces. The hotel is made up
of four different buildings with internal
courtyards; you reach the rooms through
a maze of corridors. Doubles cost €47
with shower/wc or bath; there are also a
few triples at €60. An excellent welcome
is guaranteed.

◎ 🏛 Hôtel de Paris***

16 rue de la Platière; M° Hôtel-de-Ville. **Map
C2-6**
℡04.78.28.00.95 ℗04.78.39.57.64
🌐www.hoteldeparis-lyon.com
TV.

Very lovely hotel with a nineteenth-century frontage. Note the superb ink fresco
in the entrance, created by a Japanese
artist. A grand, serpentine staircase leads to
the upper floors, where each of the thirty
rooms is decorated in a different style. The
furniture is antique, with Voltaire armchairs or Art Nouveau wardrobes. Doubles
go for €53–68 with shower/wc or bath;

breakfast is available at €6.50. An unusual,
appealing place right in the heart of the
town centre, with a reception open all
night long.

◎ 𝒳 |◎| Alyssaar

29 rue du Bât-d'Argent; M° Hôtel-de-Ville.
Map D2-43
℡04.78.29.57.66
Closed *Sun; Mon; first three weeks in Aug.*
Open *evenings only.*

Alyssaar is a Syrian whose genuine kindness makes his customers feel special. He
will happily explain the various specialities
served on the "*assiette du Calife*", a selection of Syrian delicacies, and in which
order you should eat them. The beef
with cherries or mint is amazing, as is
the lamb kebab with aubergines and the
chicken sautéed in sesame cream. And the
"Thousand-and-one-nights" dessert is a
revelation. Menus cost €12–19; you'll pay
around €20 à la carte. Credit cards not
accepted. *Free house liqueur offered to our
readers on presentation of this guide.*

◎ |◎| Restaurant Chez Georges
– Au P'tit Bouchon

8 rue du Garet; M° Hôtel-de-Ville or Louis-
Pradel. **Map D1-20**
℡04.78.28.30.46
Closed *Sat; Sun; Aug.*

Set this down alongside an old Paris bistro
and you wouldn't be able to tell them
apart – it's got the checked tablecloths,
the imitation leather benches, the mirror-
lined walls and the original, zinc-topped
bar. The attentive but unobtrusive owner
serves at table while his wife is busy in the
handkerchief-sized kitchen. Well-balanced
Lyonnais menus list sausage with lentils,
andouillette in mustard sauce (pork sausage),
pike *quenelles*, tripe *au gratin*, an astonishingly good Saint-Marcellin (a mild cheese
from the Dauphiné) and a great upside-
down apple tart. Set menus are €15.50 at
lunchtimes, otherwise €20.50; expect to
pay around €25 à la carte.

◎ 𝒳 |◎| L'Étage

4 pl. des Terreaux; M° Hôtel-de-Ville. **Map
C1-44**
℡04.78.28.19.59
Closed *Sun; Mon; public holidays; 27 July–
27 Aug; a week in winter.*

Push open the door and you find yourself
in a wood-panelled salon draped in red.

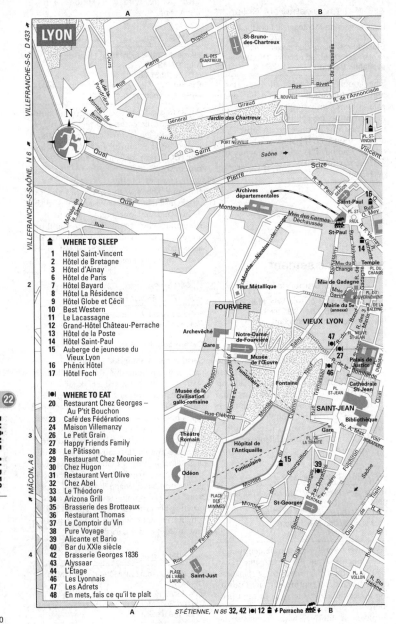

LYON

⌂ WHERE TO SLEEP

1 Hôtel Saint-Vincent
2 Hôtel de Bretagne
3 Hôtel d'Ainay
6 Hôtel de Paris
7 Hôtel Bayard
8 Hôtel La Résidence
9 Hôtel Globe et Cécil
10 Best Western
11 Le Lacassagne
12 Grand-Hôtel Château-Perrache
13 Hôtel de la Poste
14 Hôtel Saint-Paul
15 Auberge de jeunesse du
   Vieux Lyon
16 Phénix Hôtel
17 Hôtel Foch

|●| WHERE TO EAT

20 Restaurant Chez Georges –
   Au P'tit Bouchon
23 Café des Fédérations
24 Maison Villemanzy
26 Le Petit Grain
27 Happy Friends Family
28 Le Pâtisson
29 Restaurant Chez Mounier
30 Chez Hugon
31 Restaurant Vert Olive
32 Chez Abel
33 Le Théodore
34 Arizona Grill
35 Brasserie des Brotteaux
36 Restaurant Thomas
37 Le Comptoir du Vin
38 Pure Voyage
39 Alicante et Bario
40 Bar du XXIe siècle
42 Brasserie Georges 1836
43 Alyssaar
44 L'Étage
46 Les Lyonnais
47 Les Adrets
48 En mets, fais ce qu'il te plaît

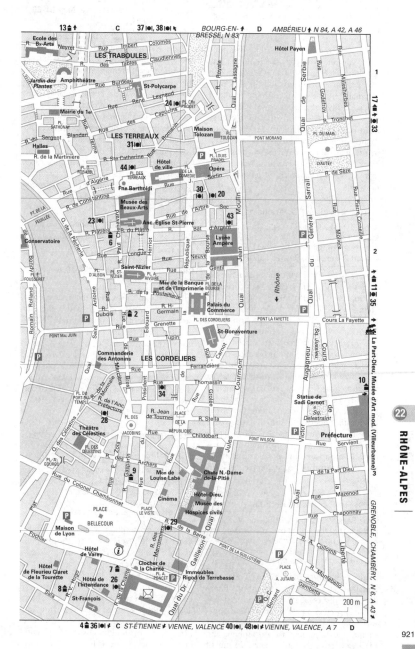

From the tables by the windows you get a good view of the fountain. The cooking is elegant, fine and precise, and though the dishes change frequently the quality remains the same: *marbré* of chicken with pickled onions and apple chutney, roast salmon with paprika, semolina and hazelnut oil, Saint-Marcellin goat's cheese, foie gras in a Beaujolais jelly, figs in milk marmalade, lightly cooked freshed scallops. There's a dish of the day at €11 (not Sat), with menus €18–26; if you want a change from Lyonnais dishes, there's a lobster menu for €51 (you must order two days in advance). Lots of regulars, so you should book at least a few days in advance. *Free coffee offered to our readers on presentation of this guide.*

☺ |●| Café des Fédérations

8 rue du Major-Martin; M° Hôtel-de-Ville.
Map C2-23
☎04.78.28.26.00
Closed Sat evening; Sun; 25 July–25 Aug.

Scenes from the classic Tavernier movie, *L'Horloger de Saint-Paul*, were filmed in this local institution – and it hasn't changed a bit. It is a great Lyonnais *bouchon* (the name given to the city's popular brasserie-restaurants) and the perfect place to taste really good Lyonnais cuisine. The dishes are traditional: *gras-double* (marinated for two days in white wine and mustard), *tablier de sapeur* (ox tripe egged, crumbed and grilled), calf's head *ravigote*. Splendid hors d'œuvres include charcuterie, bowls of lentils, beetroot, brawn and calf's feet, mixed seasonal salads and sausage cooked in red wine. The lunch menu is at €20; the more copious evening menu at €23 has more choice. Service is swift and friendly.

☺ |●| Restaurant Vert Olive

9 rue Saint-Polycarpe; M° Hôtel-de-Ville; it's at the foot of the slopes of Croix-Rousse, behind the place des Terreaux. **Map C1-31**
☎04.78.28.15.31
Closed Sun; Mon–Wed evenings.

Both the food and the welcome are equally generous and delightful. There are good dishes of the day at around €9, lovingly prepared poultry dishes and copious, tasty and colourful salads; The dinner menu is €21. Convivial atmosphere and moderate bills. Attentive service. One of our favourites.

☺ 👤 |●| Chez Hugon

12 rue Pizay; M° Hôtel-de-Ville. **Map D1-30**
☎04.78.28.10.94
Closed Sat; Sun; Aug.

As you wander around the town hall area, you'll find this authentic Lyonnais *bouchon* in a little alley. It's remained unchanged over the years. The dining room has only a few tables, covered with checked tablecloths, where you can eat excellent Lyon specialities: veal stew, white pudding with apples, *tablier de sapeur* (ox tripe egged, crumbed and grilled), and *gâteau de foies de volaille* (chicken livers mixed with foie gras, eggs and cream). Menus are at €22 and €32; à la carte, reckon on paying €25. There's a nice atmosphere, with lots of locals. *Free coffee offered to our readers on presentation of this guide.*

☺ |●| Maison Villemanzy

25 montée Saint-Sébastien; M° Croix-Pâquet.
Map C1-24
☎04.72.98.21.21
Closed Sun; Mon lunchtime; 2–16 Jan. **High chairs available.**

This unspoilt house, once the residence of a doctor-colonel, sits high above the city on the slopes of La Croix-Rousse. There's a magnificent terrace from where you can survey the town – the view's very popular, so it's best to book. Guillaume Mouchel, in charge in the kitchens, was a pupil of Jean-Paul Lacombe, one of Lyon's great chefs. To eat lightly, go for the dish of the day plus green salad for €11; otherwise, choose the menu at €22.50.

2nd arrondissement

☺ 👤 🏠 Hôtel d'Ainay*

14 rue des Remparts-d'Ainay; M° Ampère-Victor-Hugo. **Off map C4-3**
☎04.78.42.43.42 ☎04.72.77.51.90
✉hotel-ainay@wanadoo.fr
TV. Cots available. Pay car park.

If you're on a budget, this very simple hotel will suit you down to the ground; it's in a quiet, rather delightful pedestrianized neighbourhood not far from the magnificent basilica. The friendly young couple who run it put a good deal of effort into creating a restful atmosphere. The rooms have good double glazing and look onto the road, the courtyard or the place Ampère. Doubles cost €31–37 with basin or shower, or €40 and €43 with shower/wc or bath. *One free breakfast per room offered to our readers on presentation of this guide.*

≪ ⅔ ☗ Hôtel de Bretagne*

10 rue Dubois; M° Cordeliers; it's halfway between the Saône and the place des Cordeliers. **Map C2-2**
☏04.78.37.79.33 ℻04.72.77.99.92
☒www.hoteldebretagne-lyon.com
TV.

In a quiet little street in the heart of town. The thirty rooms are clean, smart and soundproofed – particularly handy for the ones overlooking the street, which are big and bright. Those over the courtyard are very gloomy. Doubles with shower/wc cost €48.50, and there are also rooms that sleep three or four. *10% discount on the room rate offered to our readers on presentation of this guide.*

≪ ☗ Hôtel La Résidence***

18 rue Victor-Hugo; M° Bellecour or Ampère-Victor-Hugo. **Map C4-8**
☏04.78.42.63.28 ℻04.78.42.85.76
☒www.resitel.com
Disabled access. TV.

Halfway between Perrache and Bellecour in a lively pedestrianized street with lots of shops. They practise old-style hotel-keeping here and it's one of the cheapest three-stars in town. The rooms have all had a makeover and are cosy and air-conditioned – they're €68 with shower/wc or bath.

≪ ☗ Hôtel Bayard**

23 pl. Bellecour; M° Bellecour; it's in Lyon's biggest square, near the main post office. **Map C4-7**
☏04.78.37.39.64 ℻04.72.40.95.51
☒www.hotelbayard.com
TV. High chairs and cots available. Pay car park.

There are only fifteen rooms in this hotel, and the place has a lot of regulars, so it's a good idea to book. No two rooms are alike. Some have lots of personality: no. 2, in particular, has a four-poster bed, polished parquet floor and a great view of the place Bellecour; nos. 5 and 8 both have an enormous bathroom; no. 15, which overlooks the courtyard, can sleep four. Doubles range from €70.10 to €110.10, depending on the season and degree of comfort; breakfast is included, and is served in a quiet area with a rural

feel. Follow the signs up the stairs to the reception on the first floor.

≪ ☗ |●| Grand Hôtel Château-Perrache*****

12 cours Verdun-Rambaud; M° Perrache; it's just behind Perrache station. **Off map B4-12**
☏04.72.77.15.00 ℻04.78.37.06.56
☒www.accorhotels.com
Closed *Sat lunch; Christmas.* **Disabled access. TV. Pay car park.**

Formerly the *Terminus hotel* built in 1906 by the PLC company. It's an edifice on a monumental scale; the entrance, protected by a wrought iron canopy, is said to be the only genuine example of Art Nouveau in Lyon. Devanne and Curieux were the architects and their style is picked up throughout the beautiful interior; cornices are decorated by sculptured, floral friezes and, exceptionally, the iron-work, window panes and furniture have been carefully preserved. The Majorelle panels turn the restaurant into a place of beauty, too, with its fine paintings and sculptures. Spacious and bright double rooms go from €109, with upper rooms at €142–157. It's a quiet place, ideally located near the station and a good walk to place Bellecour.

≪ ⅔ ☗ Hôtel Globe et Cécil***

21 rue Gasparin; M° Bellecour. **Map C3-9**
☏04.78.42.58.95 ℻04.72.41.99.06
☒www.globeetcecilhotel.com
TV.

A top-notch three-star in the city centre. Each room has been decorated in a style appropriate to its size and has its own character – some have handsome marble fireplaces, balconies and air-conditioning. The rooms that overlook the street are brighter than the others. The service can't be faulted, and it comes with a smile. Doubles cost €150 with shower/wc or bath, including an excellent breakfast. Dogs are accepted at €8 per day. *10% discount on the room rate offered to our readers on presentation of this guide.*

≪ |●| Restaurant Chez Mounier

3 rue des Marronniers; M° Bellecour. **Map C3-29**
☏04.78.37.79.26
Closed *Sun evening; Mon; first week in Jan; the week of the 8 May; second fortnight in Aug; first week in Sept.*

Lyon is famous for its puppets; the one in

22

this restaurant window, smiling at passers-by and inviting them in, is the comic character Guignol. This is the most authentic of the *bouchons* in this touristy street, with two bare little dining rooms. There's a good atmosphere created by Christine Moinier, and the regional cooking has character: *gnafrons* (little sausages), *tablier de sapeur* (ox tripe egged, crumbed and grilled). For the €7.40 weekday lunchtime menu you get the dish of the day plus cheese or dessert; this goes up to €10 at night. There are also two other menus for €14 and €16. Credit cards not accepted.

ⓔ 🍴 |●| Le Petit Grain

19 rue de la Charité; M° Ampère or Bellecour; it's opposite the Textiles Museum and the Museum of Decorative Arts. **Map C4-26**
ⓣ04.72.41.77.85
Closed Sun; 15–30 Aug. **Open** 10am–6pm (4pm on Mon).

A simple little snack bar in an old milliner's shop near rue Auguste-Comte, the street with all the antique shops. It's prettily decorated with a scattering of objects picked up from street markets by the cheerful Vietnamese owner. You can have a substantial *bo bun* (stir-fried beef or chicken with rice noodles and lots of herbs), Saigon pancakes, chicken with ginger, and a host of fresh salads. Terrific tarts, too: pear and chocolate or apple. Menus are from €7.50 (one course only) and there's a dish of the day at €10.50. *Free apéritif offered to our readers on presentation of this guide.*

ⓔ |●| Arizona Grill

8 rue Ferrandière; M° Cordeliers **Map C3-34**
ⓣ04.78.42.35.02
Closed Sun; Mon; Aug; a week at New Year.

This place, by rescuing the American speciality from the indignities it has suffered for so long, proves that a hamburger does not have to be a rubbery lump of minced meat shoved between two pieces of cardboard passing as bread. Here a hamburger is served on a plate: 200 or 300g of excellent, fresh beef, minced and fried, then served with chunky fries. There's a lunchtime menu at €10, then others at €16 and €19; reckon on €20 à la carte. This restaurant thumbs its nose at all the fast-food joints and meat factories that infest tourist centres. It's a friendly place, ideally suited to families.

ⓔ 🍴 |●| Le Pâtisson

17 rue du Port-du-Temple; M° Bellecour. **Map C3-28**
ⓣ04.72.41.81.71
ⓦwww.lepatisson.com
Closed Fri evening; Sat (open Sat evening Oct–March); Sun; a week around 15 Aug.
High chairs available.

Yves Perrin, owner of one of the few organic and vegetarian restaurants in the city, has been a finalist in two prestigious culinary competitions – his diplomas are proudly displayed on the walls. Try *seitan escalope* with mustard, medallions of tofu with a *julienne* of saffron-flavoured vegetables or the millet and Provençal-style aubergine. Menus are at €11.20 and €12.70 at lunchtime, and €15.70 and €18.70 in the evening. It's a pity the décor is so gloomy. No smoking. *Free house apéritif offered to our readers on presentation of this guide.*

ⓔ |●| Restaurant Thomas

6 rue Laurencin; M° Ampère. **Off map C4-36**
ⓣ04.72.56.04.76
Closed Sun; Mon; 1–15 May; 1–21 Aug.

The young chef here really appreciates his extremely fresh ingredients, bringing out their flavour and seasoning them with precision, without drowning them in any fancy excesses. From the starters to the desserts, the results are exquisite. The lunch menu is at €15, and the dinner menu at €29; for these prices, the quality is remarkable. The wines seem to have been chosen with as much care as the dishes. Impeccable, friendly service. The setting is also worthy of note – it's discreet, tasteful and is equipped with air-conditioning.

ⓔ |●| Chez Abel

25 rue Guynemer; M° Ampère; from the Ainay Abbey, go straight ahead. It's on the left, after the archway. **Off map B4-32**
ⓣ04.78.37.46.18
Closed Sat; Sun; Aug; a week between Christmas and New Year.

This place, just a stone's throw from the Saône and 200m from the basilica, has very old wainscoting and a creaky parquet floor. It looks like a folk museum, full of oddments, hefty wooden tables and a beer pump from 1925. House specialities include grilled pig's trotters, house terrine, chicken with rice, tripe and *quenelles* of pike. The lunch menu is at €16, with others €23 and €30. There's a terrace, seating twenty, overlooking rue Bourgelade.

◎ 🍴 |◉| Brasserie Georges 1836

30 cours de Verdun; it's by Perrache station. **Off map B4-42**
℡04.72.56.54.54
Open *11.30am–11.15pm (open till 12.15am Fri and Sat)*. **High chairs and games available. Disabled access.**

This cosmopolitan Art Deco brasserie, which has been open since 1836, is a barn of a place – it seats 1000 diners served by a staff of 200. The cuisine is in the same grand tradition: sausage in brioche, *quenelle* of pike and, inevitably, *choucroute*. Menus start from €18.50 and go up to €24; ham with mashed potatoes is served free to children under three. They serve good beer and the atmosphere is cheery, with a lively jazz evening on Saturday. There is also a new "micro-brasserie", which serves beer brewed on the premises. *Free house apéritif offered to our readers on presentation of this guide.*

3rd arrondissement

◎ 🍴 🏠 Le Lacassagne***

245 av. Lacassagne; M° Grange-Blanche, then a 10 min walk; near the hospitals and the town of Bron; bus # 28. **Off map D2-11**
℡04.78.54.09.12 ℻04.72.36.99.23
🌐www.hotel-lacassagne.fr
TV. High chairs and cots available. Pay car park.

You'll need a car to get to this pleasant, unpretentious hotel on the edge of town. It has big rooms; some overlook a garden. Nice welcome and reasonable prices: doubles cost €47–62 with shower/wc or bath. Light meals are provided on request – salad, *croque-monsieur*, cream cheese and so on – for €11–13. *10% discount on the room rate offered to our readers on presentation of this guide.*

◎ 🏠 🍴 Best Western** Créqui Lyon Part-Dieu

37 rue de Bonnel; M° Guichard; to reach the city centre (ie the peninsula), cross the Wilson Bridge and then walk for 10 min. **Off map D3-10**
℡04.78.60.20.47 ℻04.78.62.21.12
Disabled access. TV. Pay car park.

This spruce hotel near the law courts has recently almost doubled the number of rooms from 28 to 49. They have all been refurbished and are comfortable, with cheerful décor, air-conditioning and soundproofing; they cost €65–135 with bath. Smiling, professional staff. *10% discount on the room rate at the weekend and in school holidays (except during trade fairs) offered to our readers on presentation of this guide.*

4th arrondissement

◎ 🏠 Hôtel de la Poste

1 rue Victor Fort; M° Croix-Rousse. **Off map C1-13**
℡ and ℻04.78.28.62.67

One of the least expensive hotels in town, located in the heart of the marvellous Croix-Rousse neighbourhood. It's housed in a working-class block of flats and though the building doesn't exactly ooze charm, it's very well maintained. The lovely proprietress has a friendly smile for everybody, but reserves half of her twenty rooms for her regulars. Rooms cost €19–27 with basin and €35 with shower.

◎ |◉| Le Comptoir du Vin

2 rue de Belfort; M° Croix-Rousse. **Off map C1-37**
℡04.78.39.89.95
Closed *Sat evening; Sun; 10-20 Aug.*

This little bar-restaurant is surely the lifeblood of the Croix-Rousse neighbourhood, light years away from the conceptual eateries and marketing campaigns that are now all the rage. Here there's an old-style bistro atmosphere with jovial owners and copious, unpretentious home cooking. The meat is particularly good, whether fried or served with sauce. Dishes cost €7–10. The wines are at very reasonable prices that go down well with the regulars who pack the place and fill it with laughter. As they say in Lyon, "it's better to get hot from eating than cold from working". Credit cards not accepted.

◎ 🍴 |◉| Pure Voyage

8 rue Pailleron; M° Hénon. **Off map C1-38**
℡04.72.07.75.79
Closed *lunchtime; Sun; Aug.* **Disabled access.**

A laid-back place tucked behind the Croix-Rousse theatre: laid-back décor, laid-back music, laid-back comfort (you get the idea). The food and service, however, are much better than in most restaurants of this type. The menu is made up of dishes from overseas, such as Creole-style stuffed shellfish with rum and lime and lamb *confit* rubbed with *raz el-hanout* and served in a reduction of sherry. The presentation is meticulous and the prices are extremely reasonable: lunchtime menu at €18; at night reckon on €40–50 à la carte for a full meal with drinks. *Free house apéritif offered to our readers on presentation of this guide.*

5th arrondissement

ⓔ ᛝ Auberge de Jeunesse du Vieux Lyon

41–45 montée du Chemin-Neuf; Mº Saint-Jean, then a 5 min climb; from La Part-Dieu station take # 28 bus; from Perrache take # 31 bus; from place Saint-Jean take the funicular to Minimes station. **Map B3-15**
☎04.78.15.05.50 ℻04.78.15.05.51
ⓦwww.hostelbooking.com
New arrivals *7am–noon and 2pm–1am, but the hostel is open round the clock.* **Disabled access.**

To enjoy the most extraordinary view that the city has to offer, you have two choices: check into *La Villa Florentine*, a four-star luxury hotel, or rush to this youth hostel and save yourself at least €150 a night. It opened in 1998 in this renovated building looking down on the city, a mere five minutes from the Renaissance neighbourhood of old Lyon. There are 180 beds in all (two to six per room, most with a toilet) at €12.70 a night, including tax and breakfast; sheets can be hired for €2.70. Obviously, a FUAJ card is compulsory: €10.70 and €15.50, for visitors aged under or over 26, respectively. Bar, garage for bikes, laundry, Internet connection (€6.85 per hour) and even a tiered garden, literally dug into the hillside. There's no cafeteria, but a kitchen is available for residents. All the mod cons with a genuinely friendly welcome and atmosphere; to top it all, there are a host of activities that make it a really vibrant place; exhibitions of photos, jazz and classical concerts. And then there's that view.

ⓔ ᛝ Hôtel St Paul**

6 rue de la Lainerie; Mº Vieux Lyon; take bus # 1 from La Part-Dieu station. **Map B2-14**
☎04.78.28.13.29 ℻04.72.00.97.27
ⓦwww.hotelstpaul.fr
Closed *Wed (except July–Aug); 11 Nov–11 Feb.* **TV. Internet available. Pay car park.**

The only two-star in Vieux Lyon, close to the spot where Bertrand Tavernier

made his film *L'Horloger de Saint Paul*. Its twenty rooms are spread across a group of Renaissance buildings; doubles with shower cost €42, shower/wc or bath €45–59. All of the rooms are sound-proofed. The staff do everything they can to make you feel very welcome, and can provide information about what's on in town.

ⓔ ᛝ ᛝ Phénix Hôtel***

7 quai de Bondy; Mº Hôtel-de-Ville; it's in the Saint-Paul neighbourhood, next to the station of the same name. **Map B2-16**
☎04.78.28.24.24 ℻04.78.28.62.86
ⓦwww.hotel-le-phenix.fr
Disabled access. TV. Pay car park.

The hotel, in a splendid seventeenth-century building, offers big, tastefully decorated rooms that have been expertly soundproofed and equipped with air-conditioning. It's also the only hotel in town to offer a view of the Saône. Rooms are beautifully appointed and impeccably maintained; doubles go for €147–162, with breakfast at €11.50. Very professional welcome and an international clientele. They host real jazz evenings every second Thursday from Sept to May. This hotel participates in the "Good Weekend in Lyon" programme. *Free house apéritif offered to our readers on presentation of this guide.*

ⓔ |●| Les Lyonnais

1 rue Tramassac; Mº Vieux-Lyon. **Map B3-46**
☎04.78.37.64.82
Closed *Sun evening; Mon; one week in early Jan; 1–15 Aug.* **Disabled access.**

An imitation Lyon *bouchon*, since it opened ten years ago, this friendly place has drawn regular crowds for its efficient service, good food and affordable prices. The weekday set lunch is at €11; in the evening, menus cost €19, including a "*menu du marché*" which changes with the seasons and a "*menu Lyonnais*". Dishes include *tabliers de sapeur*, hot sausages, and calf's head with sauce *gribiche*.

ⓔ |●| Les Adrets

30 rue du Bœuf; Mº Vieux-Lyon. **Map B2-47**
☎04.78.38.24.30
Closed *Sat; Sun; Aug.* **Disabled access. High chairs available.**

This typically Lyonnais place isn't at the forefront of fashion but it's always full of people. The lunch menu (€13) is brilliant:

excellent dishes including as good a fish soup as you'll eat in Marseille, scallop and prawn salad, grilled ravioli, pressed herrings with Jerusalem artichokes, marinated salmon and *croustillant* of pike-perch fillet with spiced bread. It's perfectly accompanied by a jug of wine, which, like the coffee, is included in the price. Other menus are €19–38.

⊛ |●| Happy Friends Family

29 rue du Boeuf; M° Vieux-Lyon. **Map B2/3-27**
℡04.72.40.91.47
Closed *Mon; 15–30 Aug*. **Open** *evenings only (7.30–10pm); Sun lunchtime by booking only*. **Disabled access.**

Lots of delicate and unusual ingredients used in inventive combinations here: *millefeuille* of lamb cutlets in a spice crust, pan-fried Jerusalem artichokes with grapes, cream of chestnut-pumpkin soup scented with cardamom, mushrooms stuffed with snails and Saint-Marcellin cheese *gratin*. Menus cost €21–30; you'll spend around €50 à la carte if you include a bottle of wine such as a Pécharmant. It's best to book.

⊛ |●| Alicante el Bario

16 rue Saint-Georges; M° Vieux-Lyon. **Map B3-39**
℡04.78.37.99.11
Closed *lunchtime; Sun; Mon; 3 weeks in July-Aug*.

Tapas are often considered mere titbits and it has to be admitted that they are rarely very good. Here, however, they are delicious and it is easy to make up a full meal with them. Other options include grilled fish or Valencia-style paella (the house speciality). Reckon on €25 à la carte; the menus (€25 and €30) are only available for groups. You will find a warm welcome, attentive service and gaudy décor worthy of an Almodovar film (often enhanced by a soundtrack of flamenco music).

6th arrondissement

⊛ ♜ Hôtel Foch***

59 av. Foch; M° Foch; it's in the centre of the 6ᵉ arrondissement, 5 min walking distance to the peninsula. **Off map D1-17**
℡04.78.89.14.01 ℻04.78.93.71.69
⊛www.hotel-foch.fr
Disabled access. TV. Pay car park.

A charming, discreet hotel on the second floor of an old building. The reception has a salon with leather sofas, and there's carpet on the breakfast room floor. It's a quiet place with spacious, well-appointed rooms, and it feels luxurious but not ostentatious. Doubles go for €70–85 with shower/wc or bath, depending on the season. Friendly, personal welcome. This hotel participates in the "Good Weekend in Lyon" programme.

⊛ 𝒜 |●| Brasserie des Brotteaux

1 pl. Jules Ferry; M° Brotteaux. **Off map D2-35**
℡04.72.74.03.98
Closed *Sun*. **Café open** *from 7.30am.* **Restaurant open** *11.30am–2.30pm and 7.30–10pm.* **High chairs available.**

A marvellous place that's remained unchanged since 1913. There's a large dining room seating ninety, with another sixty places on the terrace opposite the old Les Brotteaux station. The décor involves etched mirrors, colourful ceramics and draped red curtains – a theatrical setting in direct contrast with the simple, serious cooking. Laurent Morel worked with the famed chef Point, and Emmanuel Faucon, the boss, is a straight-talking Lyonnais. Dishes are handsomely served but also originally presented: *émincé* of beef with Saint Marcellin sauce, pressed foie gras with apples caramelized in cider. Everything is made in house. It's very good value, and a must for both the cuisine and the setting. Menus are €16–27; there are various platters for €15–16: "fisherman's", "Italian" or "brasserie". *Free house apéritif offered to our readers on presentation of this guide.*

⊛ 𝒜 |●| Le Théodore

34 cours Franklin-Roosevelt; M° Foch. **Off map D1-33**
℡04.78.24.08.52
Closed *Sun; public holidays; the week including 15 Aug*. **Bar open** *8am–midnight*. **Restaurant open** *noon–2pm and 7–10.30pm (7–11pm Fri and Sat)*. **Disabled access. High chairs available.**

The terrace of this lovely establishment is great in summer. Quality produce goes into making refined dishes that are colourful and full of flavour: home-made duck pâté *en croûte*, ravioli stuffed with morels, calves' kidneys. The dish of the day is at €11, and there's a set lunch at €18.50 (or €16.50 without either starter or dessert); other menus are at €20.50–42. The nice wine list lets you try a variety of lesser known reds or whites from the Rhône

RHÔNE-ALPES

valley; the Saint-Perray made from the Viognier grape is ideal with the fresh pike fish balls. *Free house apéritif offered to our readers on presentation of this guide.*

7th arrondissement

ⓒ 🐉 |●| Bar du XXIe siècle

3 av. Berthelot; M° Jean-Macé. **Off map D4-40**
☎04.78.72.00.66
Closed *Sun; 3 weeks in Aug.* **Open** *lunchtime only; bar open until 5pm.*

After an overwhelming visit to the Museum of the Resistance and Deportation, this little bistro is an ideal place to recover your spirits and strength. Annick and Élisabeth extend the same warm welcome to both newcomers and regulars. The delicious home cooking is of the type that is hard to find these days (everything is home-made, even the desserts); examples include lentil salad, veal *marengo*, and *blanquette*. The menu of the day costs €12.50, with starter, main course and dessert. *Free house apéritif offered to our readers on presentation of this guide.*

ⓒ |●| En mets, fais ce qu'il te plaît

43 rue Chevreul; M° Jean-Macé. **Off map D4-48**
☎04.78.72.46.58
Closed *Sat; Sun; Aug.*

A really good restaurant with two dining rooms; you can see into the kitchen from the first one, which has a bar, while the second has metal grilles at the windows and tables lit by modern, colourful lamps. It's a relaxing place, with easy-going, attentive service. The menu changes every three weeks but typical offerings include fresh vegetables with olive oil, good succulent duck, fresh sea trout served on a bed of spinach and excellent seafood. The produce and ingredients are the freshest, and the attention paid to precise cooking is impressive. There's a weekday lunch menu at €23, and menu "*dégustation*" in the evening for €48; expect to pay around €40 à la carte. A selection of good wines are served by the glass.

Aveize
69610 (26km W)

ⓒ 🐉 🛏 |●| Hôtel-restaurant Rivollier

Take the D11.
☎04.74.26.01.08 ☎04.74.26.01.90

Closed *Sun evening; Mon.* **Disabled access. TV.**

It's a wonder how a place this size can survive in such a small village. But once you've experienced the sheer professionalism, first-class welcome and service, and eaten a superb meal in the pleasant airy dining room, you'll be less surprised. They offer delectable menus at €11 (weekdays) and €16–26, along with a wide selection of dishes of the day such as salmon with dill, terrine of duck with prunes, pike soufflé with shrimps, *soufflé glacé au Grand Marnier*. If you're stuck for accommodation, they also have eight very basic rooms at €34 with shower/wc. *Free coffee offered to our readers on presentation of this guide.*

Marnans
38980

ⓒ 🛏 |●| L'Auberge du Prieur

2 pl. du Prieuré; take the D51 then the D20 in the direction of Le Roybon, near the Forêt de Chambaran.
☎04.76.36.28.71
Closed *Mon, Tues and Sun evenings (July–Aug); Tues and Wed the rest of the year.* **TV. High chairs available.**

A young couple run this place; Cécile does the cooking and her nice husband handles the service. The cooking style is an eclectic mix, using more than a few medieval recipes. Everything is home-made (except the cheese and ice cream) and the menus change every couple of months. Menus are €15.50 (not served Sunday lunch or public holidays) and €20.50–32 (the latter needs to be ordered in advance). There's also a medieval menu which includes such things as Saint-Marcellin terrine with beetroot in walnut oil, mustard duck stew, and cheese. The terrace overlooks the superb, twelfth-century, Romanesque church. It's best to book.

Mens
38710

ⓒ 🐉 🛏 Auberge de Mens***

Place du Breuil; it's right in the town centre.
☎04.76.34.81.00 ☎04.76.34.80.90
ⓔaubergedemens.free.fr
Disabled access. TV. High chairs and games available. Car park.

This huge, skilfully renovated house offers comfortable rooms at €45 for a double with shower/wc or bath. The new décor is fresh and colourful and there's a lovely garden where you can relax on quiet evenings, as well as a fireplace in winter. Food is also served. *Free house apéritif offered to our readers on presentation of this guide.*

☺ |●| Café des Arts

Boulevard Édouard-Arnaud (Centre)
☎04.76.34.68.16
Closed *evenings and Wed out of season (except for prior reservations); Sun evening in season.* **TV.**

This charming place is the most famous café in the Trièves and it's listed as a historic monument. In 1896, Gustave Riquet, a painter from Picardy, decorated the ceilings and walls with beautiful allegorical frescoes and views of the countryside. The self-taught chef-owner prepares superb dishes that vary according to what's good at market. The choice is limited, but you can be sure that whatever is on offer will be inspired. Try the house terrine of foie gras and the fresh fish if they're available. There's a lunctime menu at €11.50, then others €14–17.

Chichilianne
38930 (16km SW)

☺ 🎋 🏠 |●| Au Gai Soleil du Mont-Aiguille**

La Richardière; take the N75 then the D7, then walk from the foot of Mont Aiguille.
☎04.76.34.41.71 ℻04.76.34.40.63
🖥www.hotelgaisoleil.com
Closed *25 Oct–20 Dec.* **TV. High chairs and games available.**

Surrounded by a fantastic ring of mountains (ideal hiking country in both summer and winter), this hotel is at the foot of Mont Aiguille among the woods, copses and wheat fields. The house, built in 1720, has its original stone staircase, and there's been a hotel here for fifty years. The owner is warm-hearted and welcoming. The 25 well-kept rooms are very reasonably priced at €37–49.50, depending on the degree of comfort. Good classic dishes are served in the restaurant: foie gras, house terrine, country-style tart, chicken liver soufflé, and pork stew. Menus are at €13 (not Sun), then €19–32; cheaply priced wines. It's lively in high season. *10% discount on the room rate (Jan–March) offered to our readers on presentation of this guide.*

Mijoux
01410

☺ 🏠 |●| Les Egravines**

Route de la Bussole; it's on the way out of Mijoux, going towards the Col de la Faucille.
☎04.50.41.30.65 ℻04.50.41.07.93
Car park.

This hotel appealed to us for its warm welcome, its atmosphere of a large modern chalet and, above all, the stunning view from its enormous terrace. Its location at the foot of the ski runs and the start of the hiking trail makes it very popular, so it is advisable to book. Double rooms cost €45–79. In the restaurant, there is a winter menu at €17; in summer you have to eat à la carte – there are salads at €10 and grilled dishes at €13. Logis de France.

Mirmande
26270

☺ 🎋 |●| Restaurant Margot

It's near the post office, in the lower part of the village.
☎04.75.63.08.05
Closed *Tues (early Oct–late April); Jan–Feb.* **High chairs available.**

This restaurant, like the village, is a mixture of stylishness and rustic simplicity. It's a place for people who love old-style cooking. In summer you can go inside to cool off in the tastefully decorated dining room with an old wooden table, or sit out on a bench on the terrace in the shade of the climbing vines. There's a weekday lunch menu at €14 and others up to €25. You get a good choice of regional specialities but dishes constantly change: *pot-au-feu* of guinea-fowl, lamb with honey and spices, chocolate *fondant*. Sometimes they host jazz evenings on Thursdays. *Free house apéritif offered to our readers on presentation of this guide.*

Cliousclat
26270 (2km N)

☺ 🏠 |●| La Treille Muscate**

It's on the D57.
☎04.75.63.13.10 ℻04.75.63.10.79
🖥www.latreillemuscate.com
Closed *Wed; 5 Dec–12 Feb.* **Disabled access. TV. Car park.**

A large, pretty house with green shutters

and walls half-covered in ivy. Inside, the rooms have a sophisticated charm and some have a terrace with a view over the countryside; they cost €55–115. There's a lovely enclosed garden and the dining room is bright and roomy with a corner fireplace and a few stylish tables. The cuisine, which uses local produce, is typical of this sunny region: pig's cheeks with lemon and ginger, pressed chicken in a *pot-au-feu* with mustard, haddock pie on a bed of sauerkraut *confit*, *aïoli* fish *tajine*. The weekday lunch menu, at €15, offers great value; there's another menu at €26.

Modane

73500

@ 🌣 🛏 |●| Hôtel-restaurant Le Perce-Neige**

14 av. Jean-Jaurès; it's opposite the station. Take the A43 exit 30.
📞 04.79.05.00.50 📠 04.79.05.12.92
📧 auperceneige@wanadoo.fr
Closed *Sun (24 April–19 June and 16 Sept–18 Dec); 1–19 May; 22 Oct–5 Nov.* **Disabled access. TV. High chairs available.**

This is an ideal place for an overnight stop in a town that is not sufficiently appealing for a longer stay. The rooms are simple; doubles go for €44 with shower/wc and €57 with bath. They're all well soundproofed, which is just as well since the hotel is on the road and opposite the railway track. The nicest rooms are at the back, overlooking the river. Traditional local cooking is listed on menus ranging from €14.50 to €20. Logis de France. *10% discount on the room rate (20 May–20 June) offered to our readers on presentation of this guide.*

Montbrison

42600

@ 🛏 |●| Le Gil de France**

18 bis boulevard Lachèze; it's just beyond the centre.
📞 04.77.58.06.16 📠 04.77.58.73.78
📧 gil-de-france@wanadoo.fr
Restaurant closed *Fri and Sun evenings (1 Oct–1 June).* **Disabled access. TV. High chairs available. Car park.**

A modern hotel on the outskirts of town, situated in front of a big park.

The rooms are bright and fresh with modern facilities and go for €46 with shower/wc or bath. Menus are at €11 for a weekday lunch, and €15.50–27.50. Good welcome.

Champdieu

42600 (5km NW)

@ 🌣 |●| Hostellerie du Prieuré

Route de Boën; it's on the D8, away from the centre.
📞 04.77.58.31.21
Closed *Wed; early Aug; a week in winter; open Tues and Thurs evenings by reservation only.* **Disabled access. High chairs available.**

A nice place, on the border of the *département*, that is run by a chef who's absolutely expert at traditional cooking techniques. He offers a simple weekday lunch menu for €10 (including a drink) and more complex choices on the other menus at €16.50–24. Specialities include frogs' legs. *Free coffee offered to our readers on presentation of this guide.*

Montélimar

26200

@ 🛏 Hôtel Pierre**

7 pl. des Clercs; it's near the church of Sainte-Croix in the old town.
📞 04.75.01.33.16
TV.

This prettily renovated sixteenth-century town house on a small square is delightful. Its porch, candelabra-studded corridor, paved courtyard, ivy-covered terrace and dressed stone staircase create a striking atmosphere. The twelve rooms – €27 with basin, €41 with bath – are fairly ordinary compared to the rest of the place, though some have been refurbished. The best is no. 2, which has a balcony swamped in Virginia creeper. Breakfast is not included in the price of the rooms. There's space to park bikes.

@ 🌣 🛏 Hôtel du Parc**

27 bd. Charles-de-Gaulle.
📞 04.75.01.00.73 📠 04.75.51.27.93
🌐 www.hotelduparc-montelimar.com
TV. Cots available. Pay car park.

Classic hotel, opposite the park, modernized and well-situated, near the town centre. Bright, comfortable rooms with double glazing cost €44–60 with shower/wc or bath; choose the rooms at the back which are very quiet. The owners keep it spotless and welcome you most civilly. *Fresh orange juice offered at breakfast to our readers on presentation of this guide.*

⊛ 🔔 Sphinx Hôtel**

Les Allées Provençales, 19 bd. Marre-Desmarais.
☎04.75.01.86.64 ⊕04.75.52.34.21
ⓦwww.sphinx-hotel.fr
Closed *Christmas to mid-Jan.* **TV. Pay car park.**

Exceedingly well-located away from the traffic noise, this is a lovely seventeenth-century private mansion with an ivy-swathed exterior and wood panelling and antique furniture inside. The salon has a tranquil atmosphere. The rooms are adorable and have good facilities and comfort; doubles cost €50–63 with shower/wc or bath, depending on the season. When it's sunny, breakfast is served on the terrace. You get an appropriately stylish welcome.

⊛ 🍴 Le Chalet du Parc

Les Allées Provençales, Boulevard Marre-Desmarais; it's behind the bandstand and the tourist office.
☎04.75.51.16.42
Closed *Mon; Tues; a fortnight in Feb; a fortnight end Sept.* **Disabled access.**

A dynamic young couple took over this place with the express aim of turning it into a top-class gourmet restaurant. And the cooking is indeed inspired, produced by a chef who's bursting with ideas and enthusiasm. He puts together remarkable combinations of flavours and uses only fresh produce: *aiguillettes* of duck with lemon and ginger, *pressé* of home-made foie gras, scallop salad with saffron-flavoured olive oil and luscious *dôme de chocolat* with iced vanilla. Menus are at €18 and €26. The downstairs dining room is still a little bare but they've put all the effort into what really counts – the cooking. On nice days, you can sit on the terrace overlooking the park. The sort of place you would like to come across more often. *Free coffee offered to our readers on presentation of this guide.*

Montrottier

69770

⊛ 🍴 🔔 🍴 L'Auberge des Blés d'Or**

La Curtillat, route de Saint-Julien-sur-Bibost. Take the N89, then the D7; after Saint-Bel, head for Bibost, then take the D246 and keep going for 2km before reaching Montrottier.
☎ and ⊕04.74.70.13.56
Closed *evenings (except by reservation); Tues.* **Disabled access. TV. Car park.**

It's best to book in season to be sure of a room or a table; out of season, check that they're serving meals. This country inn, which stands alone among the fields and is surrounded by flowers, has been superbly restored. Double rooms with shower/wc cost €58; boasting all mod cons (as well as total silence), they are in an annexe and look over the valley. Half board is also available at €48 per person. The lovely, rustic dining room has a creaking parquet floor and vast beams. The cuisine is flavoursome with a regional slant: menus are at €16 (weekdays) and €22. You can sit on your terrace watching the sun go down behind the hills, with the church of Montrottier illuminated in the distance. *Free house apéritif offered to our readers on presentation of this guide.*

Morzine

74110

⊛ 🍴 🔔 🍴 Hôtel Les Lans***

Village des Prodains; it's 300m from the ski-lift going up to Avoriaz.
☎04.50.79.00.90 ⊕04.50.79.15.22
ⓦwww.leslans.com
Closed *spring and autumn.* **Open** *evenings 7–8pm.* **TV. Car park.**

Monsieur used to be a ski instructor, Madame's mad about local history and culture – today, along with their two daughters, they put life into this huge newly built chalet. The prices are unbeatable considering what you get. Half board is compulsory, costing €42–70 per person, depending on the season. Monsieur Mallurez happily takes care of the cooking but escapes from the kitchen once a week to take people on wildlife discovery trips, while Madame conducts guided tours. During the high season, they give priority to long-stay bookings. *10% discount on the room rate (after 4 nights) offered to our readers on presentation of this guide.*

☕ 🛏 |●| Les Prodains**

Village des Prodains; it's at the foot of the Avoriaz ski-lift.
☎04.50.79.25.26 📠04.50.75.76.17
✉hotellesprodains@aol.com
Closed 21 April–25 June; 10 Sept–7 Dec. **TV. Swimming pool. Car park.**

You'll get a very warm welcome at this friendly family establishment at the foot of the ski runs. The chalet has pretty rooms, which are gradually being renovated; some have balconies with a fantastic view of the slopes. Doubles with shower/wc or bath are from €48 in summer, and €62 in winter. The huge terrace gets swamped by skiers as soon as the sun comes out. Menus range from €18.50 to €23; although you can certainly get a tasty *tartiflette*, the inventive cooking is not limited to mountain dishes. There's a swimming pool with a solarium and sauna in summer, which is also when the boss offers trips to a nearby mountain cabin where he serves tasty mountain dishes.

☕ 🎋 |●| Restaurant La Grangette

It's opposite the Nyon cable car.
☎04.50.79.05.76
Closed Mon evening; 20 April–1 June; 25 Sept–25 Oct; 15 Nov–15 Dec.

A little family business at the foot of the ski slopes where you can enjoy a tasty meal in a friendly atmosphere. The €13.50 weekday lunch menu provides a starter, main course and dessert; other menus cost €18.50–34. The house speciality is frogs' legs in cream sauce, but they also serve excellent snails and foie gras. Lots of walking trails start (and finish) here. *Free house apéritif offered to our readers on presentation of this guide.*

☕ 🎋 |●| La Chamade

Centre; it's near the tourist office.
☎04.50.79.13.91
Closed Tues and Wed out of season; May; mid-Nov to mid-Dec.

This is a local institution. First impressions might lead you to dismiss it as touristy and kitsch, offering little but salads and pizzas. Venture in, however, to experience delicious local specialities prepared by the young chef. He adores pork in all its guises, and offers, among other things, pâté

of pig's head, *atriaux* (a type of patty) and mountain suckling pig with apple fritters. There's one menu at €42, or expect to pay €30 à la carte. *Free house liqueur offered to our readers on presentation of this guide.*

Montriond
74110 (6km NW)

☕ |●| 🎋 Auberge La Chalande

Lieu-dit Ardent.
☎04.50.79.19.69
Closed Mon; 20 April–30 June; 15 Sept–15 Dec. **High chairs available.**

This old chalet feels like it's way out in a lost mountain hamlet – though it's actually at the foot of the ski lifts going up to Avoriaz. It used to belong to the owner's mother, and he hasn't changed the warm, rustic surroundings a bit. He turns out delicious dishes, whether you choose from the menus (€25–36), or go à la carte: cheese *croûte*, braised sausage with leeks and potato fritters. Reservation is essential. *Free house liqueur or coffee offered to our readers on presentation of this guide.*

Nantua
01130

☕ 🛏 |●| Hôtel-restaurant L'Embarcadère**

13 av. du Lac.
☎04.74.75.22.88 📠04.74.75.22.25
✉hotelembarcadere@wanadoo.fr
Closed 20 Dec–5 Jan. **TV. Games available.**

This hotel is particularly distinguished by its location on the edge of Lake Nantua. The totally refurbished rooms (€50–65, depending on the view – mountains, lake, etc) are bright, functional and comfortable, with air-conditioning and Internet connection. The weekday menu is priced at €22, and the others at €29.50–55. Logis de France.

☕ |●| Restaurant Belle Rive

23 rte. de la Cluse; take the N84 from La Cluse and it's just before you get to Nantua.
☎04.74.75.16.60
Closed Tues and Thurs evenings; Wed in winter. **Open** all day, every day in summer. **Car park.**

This place, right by the lake, is popular with families having big get-togethers and local workers coming for lunch. You'll need to book or get there early if you want a table on the pleasant veranda overlooking the lake. The €11 lunch menu is pretty decent, and there are others at €15–31. They specialize in the famous *quenelles de Nantua* (meatballs served with a crayfish butter sauce); you have to wait a full fifteen minutes for them, but they're freshly cooked and well worth it. They also offer house foie gras, house smoked salmon, terrines and so on. Efficient service.

Charix

01130 (10km NE)

◎ ☎ |O| Auberge du Lac Genin

Take the N84 in the direction of Bellegarde, then turn left at Le Martinet on to the D95 (follow the signs).
℡ 04.74.75.52.50 ℻ 04.74.75.51.15
✆ www.lacgenin.com
Closed Sun evening; Mon; 15 Oct–1 Dec. **TV. High chairs and games available. Car park.**

The magnificent lake and the setting in the beautiful dark Jura forests make the trip up here worthwhile. In summer, it's a paradise for fishermen and walkers, but be sure to have the right equipment and chains on your car tyres in winter – the weather can be very severe. Unsurprisingly, the best rooms have windows onto the lake. They aren't exactly luxurious, but prices aren't high: €20 with basin, €31 with shower/wc and €40 with bath. In the restaurant, the €11.50 menu is pretty ordinary, but there are three others up to €19 listing mountain ham, meats grilled on the open fire, wine sausage and veal cutlet with mustard. It's substantial rather than gourmet cooking and there's a real family atmosphere. In summer the place gets very full. Nice welcome. Logis de France.

Lalleyriat

01130 (12km E)

◎ ☆ |O| Les Gentianes

Take the N84 in the direction of Bellegarde as far as Neyrolles and then the D55.
℡ 04.74.75.31.80
Closed Mon; Tues; Sun evening; 6–31 Jan.
Disabled access. High chairs and games available.

An adorable village inn that has just obtained first prize in the Ain *département* competition for restaurant with the best floral displays. The menu is varied and

the cuisine inventive: *escalope* of foie gras with grapes, scallops *feuilleté* with shallot cream, pike-perch fillet with *vin jaune* sauce. Prices are fair: menus cost from €24 (weekdays) to €49; reckon on €30 à la carte. You can eat on the terrace in fine weather. Charming and friendly welcome. *Free house apéritif offered to our readers on presentation of this guide.*

Lancrans

01200 (17km SE)

◎ ☆ ☎ |O| Le Sorgia**

Grande-Rue; take the N84 then the D991 to Lélex and Mijoux.
℡ 04.50.48.15.81 ℻ 04.50.48.44.72
Closed Mon; Sat lunchtime; Sun evening; 1–5 Jan; 20 Aug–15 Sept; 20–31 Dec. **TV. High chairs and games available. Car park.**

An old village bar-restaurant named after the mountain in front of it. Over the last century it has grown to become a hotel-restaurant with a balcony and veranda overlooking the valley. The rooms are comfortable and pleasant and filled with period furniture. Doubles go for €46 with shower/wc and €50 with bath. They serve simple, local dishes in generous portions: lake whitefish (freshwater salmon) cooked in Savoy wine, pan-fried scallops with oyster mushrooms, snails and baby mushrooms in flaky pastry. The weekday menu is at €14, with others €23 and €29. Pleasant welcome. Logis de France. *Free house apéritif offered to our readers on presentation of this guide.*

Noirétable

42440

◎ ☆ ☎ |O| Hôtel-restaurant Au Rendez-vous des Chasseurs**

Route de l'Hermitage; it's 1km from the centre of the village on the D53 (in the direction of Vollore-Montagne).
℡ 04.77.24.72.51 ℻ 04.77.24.93.40
Closed Sun evening and Mon out of season; Sun (Jan–Feb); 22 Feb–3 March; 12 Sept–6 Oct. **TV. Car park.**

Though the thundering motorway is just 6km away, all you can see from the dining room of this hotel are the Forez mountains. The inn has fourteen rooms costing €26 with basin and €38 with shower/wc or bath. The cheapest menu in the week is at €10.50; the others are at €18–33. All the scents and flavours of Forez can be found in the dishes here, which might include home-made charcuterie, grilled trout, *parfait* of chicken liver with bilberries, pigeon *pot-au-feu*, chicken legs stuffed with Fourme cheese and game in season. Logis de France. *Free coffee offered to our readers on presentation of this guide.*

Salles (Les)
42440 (5km NE)

✆ ⚥ ⌂ |●| Domaine de la Plagnette

Via the A72-E70 motorway, take the Noirétable exit then go in the direction of Saint-Julien-la-Vêtre; after the village of Chaumette, turn left in the direction of La Plagnette; via the N89 from Boën, turn right towards Les Salles in Saint-Jules-la-Vêtre; after Le Verdier, turn right in the direction of La Plagnette.
☎04.77.97.74.10 ℻04.77.97.74.11
✉domaine@plagnette.com
Closed *Wed (but phone first in July–Aug);* Jan. **Disabled access. TV. High chairs and games available. Car park.**

This establishment is distinguished by the comfort of its high-quality accommodation, the beauty of its unspoilt natural surroundings, its convivial service and its peaceful atmosphere. You will be warmly welcomed into the old, restored farmhouse, near a large lake replete with fish and surrounded by a wood. Apart from the seven spacious, well-equipped rooms, there are also two self-catering cottages ideal for families (they sleep eight people). Double rooms go for €44. The restaurant is a more recent addition that adjoins the farm and offers simple, regional food at reasonable prices. Dishes include *fourmiflette* (*tartiflette* with Fourme cheese) and *pannequets* with Fourme from Montbrison. There's a weekday menu at €10, then others €13.50–20. *Free coffee offered to our readers on presentation of this guide.*

Juré
42430 (20km NE)

✆ ⚥ |●| Auberge Le Moulin

Take the D53 and turn right onto the D86 before you get to Saint-Just-en-Chevalet.
☎04.77.62.55.24
Closed *mid Nov–early March.* **Open** *Sat, Sun and public holidays March–Nov from*

11.30am–8.30pm; Tues–Sun July–Aug.
Disabled access. High chairs available.

This little inn in an old mill has an idyllic setting. Its electricity is supplied by the stream running underneath, and apparently, the Lumière brothers made their first moving pictures here. The country menus, €11–18, are delicious, and offer excellent home-made terrines cooked in a wood-fuelled oven, rissoles, charcuteries, omelettes, free-range poultry, and home-made pastries. Very affordable wines. It's a shame it's not open more. Credit cards not accepted. *Free glass of cider offered to our readers on presentation of this guide.*

Nyons
26110

✆ ⌂ |●| La Picholine***

Promenade de la Perrière; it's on the hilltop as you come into the town.
☎04.75.26.06.21 ℻04.75.26.40.72
⊕www.picholine26.com
Closed *Feb; end Oct to mid-Nov.* **Restaurant closed** *Mon and Tues (Oct–April); Mon only (May–Sept).* **TV. Swimming pool. Car park.**

The décor in the foyer and the restaurant is a bit chichi, but the owners make a real fuss of their guests. Big, light and pleasant rooms go for €54–72; ask for a room that has a breathtaking view looking south to the valley and the garden or to the swimming pool. Half board, €53–66 per person, is compulsory during July and August. Decent food – the menus (€22.50–39) offer extremely satisfying regional dishes. The swimming pool is surrounded by olive trees. Logis de France.

✆ |●| Le Petit Caveau

9 rue Victor Hugo; it's in the street at right angles to the Pavillon du Tourisme.
☎04.75.26.20.21
Closed *Sun evening; Mon.*

Good wine, experienced chef and excellent cuisine – you get the best of both worlds at reasonable prices. An ingenious set lunch menu allows you to try different wines depending on your mood, as well as the roast saddle of rabbit with hazelnuts, roast lamb, *confit* of lamb chops, sweetbread and kidney kebabs or red pepper risotto. The lunch menu is at €18 (not Sun or public holidays), with others €29–45.

Condorcet

26110 (7km NE)

⬡ |●| La Charrette Bleue

Route de Gap; it's 7km from Nyons, on the D94 in the direction of Gap.
☎04.75.27.72.33
Closed Tues, Wed and Sun evenings (Oct–March); Wed (July–Aug); mid-Dec to end Jan.

Word of mouth is always the best publicity – just follow the trail and you'll get here. Very professional, honest cooking combines tradition with an individual twist. Fresh herbs from the hills and the heath are deliciously combined. Great dishes include *fricassée* of chicken in *bouillabaisse* with *rouille* and garlic *croûtons*, roast lamb in a garlic crust and homemade terrine of duck *confit*. Menus range in price from €18 (weekday lunchtimes) to €38 (this one includes foie gras). There are lots of Côtes-du-Rhône wines on the list; glasses of wine cost from €2.70, bottles at €9.50. The dining room is prettily arranged and there's a terrace for sunny days – the best tables are under the olive trees. Delectable cuisine, warm welcome and efficient service.

Mirabel-aux-Baronnies

26110 (7km SW)

⬡ ⚵ |●| La Coloquinte

Avenue de la Résistance; take the D538 in the direction of Vaison-la-Romaine.
☎04.75.27.19.89
Closed Mon and Wed out of season; Christmas to early Jan. **Disabled access. High chairs available.**

When the sun's out it's nice to sit on the lovely shaded patio; otherwise you dine in the colourful dining room with hefty beams and well-spaced tables. The food is good and only fresh seasonal produce is used. Menus range from €20 to €35; à la carte, reckon on €35. The colourful dishes are full of flavour, very carefully prepared and seasoned – the fish is cooked to perfection, and the terrines are great, too. To finish, they offer a fine choice of perfectly ripe cheeses and various desserts. The wine list includes a good selection of Côtes-du-Rhones. *Free Myròs offered to our readers on presentation of this guide.*

Saint-Ferréol-Trente-Pas

26110 (10km NE)

⬡ ⬆ |●| Auberge de Trente Pas

It's in the village; from Nyons, take the D94, then the D70 in the direction of Bourdeaux.
☎ and ☎04.75.27.71.39
🖥www.guideweb.com/provence/hotel/trente-pas
Closed mid-Oct to mid-March. **Restaurant closed** lunchtimes; open evenings by reservation only. **Reading area for children.**

The village is typical of those found in the mountains of the Drôme. This straightforward establishment has very simple, clean rooms and family cuisine prepared with soul. You're served in the convivial dining room. There's just one menu at €15; a bottle of frisky local Syrah costs €11.50. Véronique makes you feel welcome; she's enjoying her country retreat after years in polluted Paris. Rooms start at €34 with basin or shower (wc on the landing) and rise to €42 with shower/wc. There is a possibility of half board, and cottages are also available for €13 per person. Credit cards not accepted.

Ornon

38520

⬡ ⚵ |●| Restaurant Le Potiron

La Palud; take the D526 in the direction of La Mure.
☎04.76.80.63.27
Closed Thurs evening out of season; 1 Nov to mid-March. **Disabled access. Car park.**

You'll find this restaurant on a bend in the road; it has a warm décor and is always pretty busy. Good snacks are served all day – *casse-croûte campagnard*, ham, bacon omelette, fresh cream cheese, soup, salad, terrine. The omelette soufflé with crayfish tails is recommended. Menus are €16.50–26.50 and around €35 à la carte. The cheap menu is recommended for a plate of ham or other meat served with vegetables prepared in Dany's own special way – in the form of a celery flan – or as courgette fritters with coriander. For dessert, the violet *crème brûlée* is a revelation. *Free house apéritif offered to our readers on presentation of this guide.*

Oyonnax

01100

@ 🎿 ♨ |●| Hôtel-restaurant Buffard**

Place de l'Église; it's near the train station.
☎04.74.77.86.01 ⊕04.74.73.77.68
🕸www.hotelbuffard.com
Closed last week in July; first fortnight in Aug. **Restaurant closed** Fri and Sun evenings; Sat. **TV. High chairs available. Car park.**

This hotel-restaurant has maintained its excellent reputation for more than a hundred years – it celebrated its centenary in 1998. Double rooms with period furniture cost €30–58, depending on the comfort and the season. In the restaurant they serve rich home cooking in generous portions on menus from €12 to €30. Specialities include *quenelles Nantua*, *gratin* of crayfish tails, chicken *fricassée* with *vin jaune*, *délice* of duck liver, *escalope franc-comtoise*. Logis de France. *Free house liqueur offered to our readers on presentation of this guide.*

@ ♨ Nouvel Hôtel**

31 rue René-Nicod; it's 150m from the train station, 5 min from the town centre on foot.
☎04.74.77.28.11 ⊕04.74.77.03.71
🕸www.nouvel-hotel.fr
TV. Pay car park.

This hotel lives up to its name, as it has recently been renovated, achieving a charm in the reception that perfectly matches the friendly welcome. The refurbished rooms are good value: doubles cost €35–42, depending on the facilities. It's the little things they do that make all the difference: you can have breakfast brought to your room for no extra charge.

Peisey-Nancroix

73210

@ 🎿 |●| Restaurant Chez Félix

Plan-Peisey; it's between Les Mélèzes and Val Landry.
☎04.79.07.92.41
Closed Mon in winter; mid-April to mid-Dec. **Car park.**

This nineteenth-century Alpine chalet – with a lovely annexe in summer – is situated on the edge of the Vanoise park.

This place serves crêpes and regional specialities including *diots* with polenta, *berthoud*, *tartiflette* and so on. The dish of the day costs around €9.60, and the *"menu campagnard"* €13.50; you'll spend about €13 à la carte if you opt for crêpes, or around €25 for a Savoyard meal. *Free coffee offered to our readers on presentation of this guide.*

Pont-d'Ain

01160

@ |●| Restaurant-bar Le Terminus

71 rue Saint-Exupéry; take exit 9 off the A42, then take the N75 in the direction of Bourg-en-Bresse. It's on the edge of the town, opposite the train station.
☎04.74.39.07.17
Closed Sun evening; Mon; evenings before public holidays. **Car park.**

This restaurant has two pretty little dining rooms and a terrace for warm weather. The real effort goes into the cooking rather than the décor; you get generous portions of regional food at decent prices. Try the Bresse chicken with cream, the parsleyed veal kidneys or the frogs' legs. Menus start at €11.50, with others €13–22. Friendly welcome and efficient service.

Priay

01160 (7km SW)

@ |●| La Mère Bourgeois

Rue de la Côtière; take exit no. 8 (to Ambérien-en-Bugey) from the A42 motorway.
☎04.74.35.61.81
Closed Wed; Thurs; first week in June; 16 Aug–6 Sept; during Christmas school holiday.

La Mère Bourgeois won three Michelin stars for this restaurant back in 1933; nowadays, the high standards are maintained by the chef Hervé Rodriguez, although in a very different setting – completely renovated, youthful, breezy and sophisticated. The cooking has evolved along similar lines, resulting in subtle, daring combinations of flavours. The highly original dishes, served in generous portions, reflect the seasonal availability of their ingredients, as well as the inexhaustible curiosity and imagination of their creator. Accordingly, the offer ranges from the market menu at €23 to the "Indiana" menu at €69, made up of four dishes with inspiration from all over the world, plus a dessert. In fine weather, the influence of southern climes is even more apparent if you eat in the colourful, closed courtyard bedecked with flowers. A warm welcome is guaranteed (even if you turn up just before closing time on a public holiday).

Pont-en-Royans
38680

◎ ☎ |◎| Hôtel-restaurant du Musée de l'Eau**

Place du Breuil.
☎04.76.36.15.53 ℗04.76.36.97.32
✉www.hotel-musee-eau.com
Open every day throughout the year
(museum closed Mon except during school holidays). **TV.**

This is the type of hotel that Pont-en-Royans was long lacking, although its 31 rooms do not go very far in an area stretched by a voracious demand for accommodation. It is set in an enormous cultural complex, skilfully converted from an old factory nestling under the sloping banks of the Bourne. The rooms, which vary in size, are decorated in a modern style, with an emphasis on functionality, and enjoy magnificent views of either the rooftops of the old town or the river; doubles cost €39–52, according to the season and degree of comfort. The place really comes into its own, however, in the restaurant. It is an official showcase for both the *département* and the Natural Park, hence the tasty farm produce labelled "Vercors" (trout, walnut ravioli, charcuterie, cheese). Menus range from €15 to €35. The combination of state-of-the-art design and rural tradition is totally convincing, and only enhanced by the friendly, attentive service. The dining room is a little cold, but there is a stunning terrace with panoramic views, refreshed in summer by a light spray courtesy of the nearby Water Museum.

Privas
07000

◎ ⅍ ☎ |◎| Hôtel la Chaumette Porte des Suds***

Avenue du Vanel; it's 10 min from the centre on foot.
☎04.75.64.30.66 ℗04.75.64.88.25
✉www.hotelchaumette.fr

Closed Sat lunch. **Disabled access. TV. High chairs and games available. Swimming pool. Car park.**

This hotel dates from the 1970s but it has managed to take on a new lease of life. The comfortable rooms, complete with air-conditioning, are decorated in the warm colours of the South, just like the restaurant. Double rooms go for €59–82, depending on the degree of comfort. The cooking is original and seasonal, drawing on local produce. The weekday lunchtime menu is at €16.50; others go up to €43. There's a good breakfast and fine wine list. The atmosphere is more than charming, for this hotel exudes a serenity all its own. Logis de France. *Free house apéritif offered to our readers on presentation of this guide.*

◎ ⅍ |◎| Le Gourmandin

Cours de l'Esplanade; it's on the corner of rue Pierre-Fillat.
☎04.75.64.51.52
Closed Sun evening; Mon. **Disabled access. High chairs available.**

This is the best place to eat in Privas – you could genuinely call it a fine table. Philippe Bourjas has a way of modernizing local dishes and refining old recipes with delicate and creative adjustments. And he doesn't stint on the portions, generously served. There's a weekday lunchtime *formule* at €11.50, as well as four other menus at €15–36.50. The setting is sober, the service conscientious and pleasant but without fuss. There's a good wine list. Good value for money. *Free coffee offered to our readers on presentation of this guide.*

Baix
07210 (24km E)

◎ ☎ |◎| L'Auberge des 4 Vents**

Route de Chomérac; take the D2, then turn right on the N86, 3km from Baix.
☎ and ℗04.75.85.84.49
Closed Sat lunchtime and Sun evening out of season; 3 weeks in Jan. **Disabled access. TV. Car park.**

There's a soothing atmosphere in the large and light but soberly decorated dining room with an unusual pyramidal ceiling. Good, local dishes are listed on the "*menu du jour*" at €11 and on the others at €17–36. The wines are fairly priced, too.

The smart, quiet rooms in the annexe cost €28–40 depending on facilities; they're all clean and modern.

Quincié-en-Beaujolais
69430

@ |●| Restaurant Au Raisin Beaujolais

Saint-Vincent; take the D37 from Beaujeu in the direction of Saint-Vincent. It's on the right about 4km along the road.
☎04.74.04.32.79
Closed *evenings; Sat; first three weeks in Aug; last week in Dec.* **Disabled access. High chairs available.**

The food at this unpretentious bistro is just what you need to soak up all those wine tastings. The chatty proprietor looks after the dining room while his wife runs the kitchen, preparing the tasty, slowly cooked dishes. There's a weekday menu at €11.40, then three others going up to €22.10. Dishes include Beaujolais salad, terrine, *andouillette* with white wine and fromage blanc. Frogs' legs are available if ordered. When it comes to the wine, you have a huge choice of Beaujolais *appellations*. There's an enclosed, air-conditioned terrace, which is great in summer.

@ ⚶ |●| Auberge du Pont des Samsons

Le-Pont-des-Samsons; take the D37 in the direction of Beaujeu.
☎04.74.04.32.09
Closed *Wed evening; Thurs; 2–12 Jan.* **Car park.**

The crossroads is hardly an ideal location, and the restaurant doesn't look much from the outside, but the décor is nice and it's spotlessly clean. Better still, the excellent dishes are served in huge portions: Provençal-style frogs' legs, foie gras, crispy snail salad, lemon sole with almonds, duck breast with red fruits, brioche with morel sauce, steak with green peppercorns. There's a menu served every day except public holidays at €17, with others at €23 and €28; expect to pay around €30 à la carte. Attentive service from start to finish. *Free coffee offered to our readers on presentation of this guide.*

Rive-de-Gier
42800

@ ⚶ |●| Restaurant Georges Paquet

Combeplaine; take exit 11 off the A47.
☎04.77.75.02.18
Closed *Tues (except public holidays); Sun–Fri evenings; a week in Feb; 20 July–20 Aug.* **Disabled access. Car park.**

Set in a desolate area of factories and industrial wasteland between the motorway and the main road, this restaurant serves good food. It's got a hushed atmosphere and is decorated in bright, warm colours. The speciality is seafood and there are all sorts of fish served with tasty sauces. The weekday menu, at €15, offers a choice of three starters and three main courses followed by cheese or dessert; other menus at €24–42. Gourmets can also go to the *Hostellerie de la Renaissance* (41-rue Marrel, ☎04.77.75.04.31), the top restaurant in Rive-de-Gier. *Free coffee offered to our readers on presentation of this guide.*

Saint-Martin-la-Plaine
42800 (7km NW)

@ |●| Le Flamant Rose

Take the D37, and follow the signs to the Parc Zoologique; it's just opposite.
☎04.77.75.91.13
Closed *Sun–Thurs evenings; 1–15 Aug.* **Disabled access. High chairs available.**

The beautiful terrace is the only lovely thing about this big building, which stands in front of a stretch of water opposite the zoo. Inside, however, the two dining rooms get lots of light. The weekday lunch menu is at €10, and there are others €18–38. The chef takes some risks, successfully combining sweet and savoury flavours.

Sainte-Croix-en-Jarez
42800 (10km SE)

@ ⚶ 🏠 |●| Le Prieuré*

Take the D30, towards Sainte-Croix-en-Jarez.
☎04.77.20.20.09 ☎04.77.20.20.80
Closed *Mon; 2 Jan–28 Feb.*

The road leading up to this delightful and beautiful place runs along the Couzon and past the dam. Here you get bed and board in the former guest quarters of a thirteenth-century monastery – most of it dismantled during the Revolution, when its stones were used to build the village. The four rooms, €54 with bath, are simple but well equipped and wonderfully quiet. The restaurant has a beamed ceiling; here you eat unpretentious, traditional cuisine and regional dishes including home-made terrines, chicken stuffed with morels, minced tripe *au gratin*, charcuterie and fresh cheeses. There's a weekday menu for €17, and others €24–40. The ground-floor bar has a lovely vaulted ceiling and in summer there's a terrace on the village square – you'll appreciate the freshness of the air up here. Logis de France. *Free coffee offered to our readers on presentation of this guide.*

Roanne

42300

◎ 🏠 Hôtel de la Grenette

12 pl. Maréchal-de Lattre-de-Tassigny; it's by Roanne Castle and Saint-Étienne Church.
℡04.77.71.25.59 ℻04.77.71.29.69
Closed *Christmas.* **TV. Pay car park.**

A little hotel taken over by a lovely lady who passionately believes that this type of family establishment has a place in a town centre. Rooms are basic but well maintained; they cost €39 with shower, or €43 with shower/wc. The reception is shut on Friday, Saturday and Sunday, so you'll need to phone in advance.

◎ 🏠 Hôtel Terminus**

15 cours de la République, place de la Gare; it's opposite the train station.
℡04.77.71.79.69 ℻04.77.72.90.26
🌐www.hotel-terminus-roanne.com
Closed *last week in Dec* **TV. High chairs available. Pay car park.**

A good hotel of its kind, and well-located. It has about fifty rooms with bath (€40.50–46); they're pretty standard, but most of the bathrooms have been refurbished. Ask for a room overlooking the courtyard, where it's quieter. The terrace is nice in summer. Friendly welcome.

◎ 🏠 Grand Hôtel***

18 cours de la République; it's in the town centre, opposite the train station.
℡04.77.71.48.82 ℻04.77.70.42.40
🌐www.grand-hotel.fr

Closed *first 3 weeks in Aug; 2 weeks after Christmas.* **TV. Pay car park.**

This hotel could easily be like so many other practical but rather sad station hotels, but in fact it is one of the most appealing in the whole region, with an unusually well-decorated reception and meticulously maintained rooms, all of them different. Double rooms go for €63–82. It thoroughly deserves its three stars.

◎ ◐ Le Central

20 cours de la République; it's opposite the train station.
℡04.77.67.72.72
Closed *Sun; Mon; first 3 weeks in Aug.* **Disabled access.**

The Troisgros family – the nationally and internationally renowned chefs – have opened up this bistro as a less expensive complement to their gourmet flagship, *Troisgros*, in the halls of an old hotel. Rigged up to look like an old-fashioned shop, it displays up-market grocery produce on shelves on the walls, along with old black-and-white photographs of wine-producers, cheesemakers, farmers, etc. The kitchen, partly opening onto the dining room, turns out simple but inventive and sophisticated dishes, worthy of the *Troisgros* trademark. There are weekday lunchtime menus at €18 and €23, and a dinner menu at €26. The service is of a similarly high standard.

◎ 🍴 ◐ L'Aventure

24 rue Pierre-Despierre. It's on the edge of Roanne, coming from Coteau.
℡04.77.68.01.15
Closed *Sun; Mon; a fortnight in Jan; first fortnight in Aug.*

Jean-Luc Trambouze is a young chef from Roanne who's on the way up. You'll find his restaurant in a small street near the Loire. The frontage is bistro-blue but inside there's a cosy dining room decorated in pale colours. The kitchen opens out into the dining room – not to be showy but to add to the friendly atmosphere. The chef's dishes are full of imagination and fresh ideas. There are no particular specialities: it's the dynamism of the cooking and the audaciousness of the seasonings that make the dishes so distinctive. There's an excellent lunch menu for €20, which includes wine, as well as four other menus at €22–40. Affordable wine list. *Free coffee offered to our readers on presentation of this guide.*

Coteau (Le)
42120 (1km SE)

⊚ |●| L'Auberge Costelloise

2 av. de la Libération; it's on the banks of the Loire, near the bridge going from Roanne to Coteau.
☎04.77.68.12.71
Closed *Sun; Mon; first week in May; 7 Aug–6 Sept; 26 Dec to early Jan.*

A cosy atmosphere and discreet but attentive service set the tone for the high-quality cooking of Christophe Souchon: gâteau of *foies blonds* with lobster *coulis*, fried foie gras with beetroot and walnut *coulis*. Menus are at €16 for a weekday lunch, €26 and €36 for a weekday lunch and dinner with wine, with others €38–64. A real haven for gourmets.

Villerest
42300 (5km S)

⊚ ♙ Hôtel du Domaine de Champlong**

From Roanne, go in the direction of Clermont-Ferrand straight on to the suburbs of Clermont, ignoring the signs to Villerest centre, then take the first left after the sign for "The Cabaret de l'âne"; from the A72, take the Saint-Germain-Laval exit at 24km in the direction of Roanne.
☎04.77.69.78.78 ☎04.77.69.35.45
ⓦwww.hotel-champlong.com
Closed *Feb.* **TV. Swimming pool. Car park.**

This hotel boasts a remarkable location in the countryside, just a few minutes from Roanne but also within easy distance of a boating centre, a golf course, a gourmet restaurant, four tennis courts and a riding club. So, although the rooms are comfortable and have their own terrace or balcony and the service is excellent, this establishment can also be recommended for its peaceful setting and the host of activities on offer nearby. Double rooms cost €59–79.

⊚ |●| Château de Champlong

100 chemin de la Chapelle; from Roanne, go in the direction of Clermont-Ferrand straight on to the suburbs of Clermont, ignoring the signs to Villerest centre, then take the first left after the sign for "The Cabaret de l'âne".

☎04.77.69.69.69
Closed *Mon; Tues; Sun evening; 3 weeks in Feb; 3 weeks in Nov.*

This fourteenth-century château provides an unbeatable setting for the delicious seasonal dishes prepared by Olivier Boizet. Customers savour his regional cuisine amid the splendour of a dining room adorned with seventeenth-century paintings. The cheapest menu goes for €21 (weekdays), with others €28–60. You will leave this wonderful place with only one thought in mind: to come back soon.

Renaison
42370 (12km W)

⊚ ♙ |●| Hôtel-restaurant Central**

8 rue du 10-Août-1944; it's in the centre of the village, on the main square.
☎04.77.64.25.39 ☎04.77.62.13.09
Closed *Wed; Feb school holiday.* **TV. Pay car park.**

A small hotel with nine comfortable rooms; doubles with shower or shower/wc cost €30–46. Its restaurant offers regional menus from €20 to €30. Very good service. Logis de France.

Saint-Alban-les-Eaux
42370 (12km SW)

⊚ |●| Le Petit Prince

Take the D31; it's in the village.
☎04.77.65.87.13
Closed *Mon; Tues in winter; a fortnight in Feb; last week in Aug; 3 weeks in Oct.*

Here, the menu regales you with a brief history of the restaurant, whose origins go back to a family inn in 1534. It is now one of the top restaurants in the vicinity, thanks to the delicious, creative cooking of its chef, Christophe Arnaud, particularly distinguished by his Provençal-style *fricassée* of fresh frogs and complemented by a selection of local wines and exquisite Saint-Alban water. The home-made desserts are equally impressive. There is a weekday menu at €22, then others at €26–45; their contents vary with the seasons. There are two dining rooms – one small and cosy, the other bigger and more impersonal – but the best place to eat, weather permitting, is the large, rustic terrace.

Saint-Haon-le-Châtel

42370 (12km W)

@ 🎋 |●| Au Natur'elles

It's in the centre of the village, opposite the Town Hall.
☎04.77.62.12.01
Closed *Mon and Wed in winter; Mon and Tues in summer; a week in early Jan; a week during Feb school holiday; a week at Easter.* **Disabled access.**

A delightful country bistro with a warm, family atmosphere in the pretty village of Saint-Haon-le-Châtel. The cooking is simple but tasty and very reasonably priced: the weekday lunchtime menu is €12, with others €18–24. The rustic dining room is attractively decorated, right up to the ceiling, which is embellished by pitchforks and hessian sacks. *Free coffee offered to our readers on presentation of this guide.*

Pouilly-sous-Charlieu

42720 (14km N)

@ |●| Auberge du Château de Tigny

Take the D487, at the village's exit between Pouilly-sous-Charlieu and Charlieu.
☎04.77.60.09.55
Closed *Mon, Tues, Wed and Thurs evenings (5 Oct–5 May); 1–15 Jan; 15 Sept–7 Oct; 25–30 Dec.*

This is undoubtedly a favourite spot in the Roanne region. Jacques Rivière, a sometime market gardener who supplied the region's top restaurants, gave it all up to restore a magnificent little manor house and turn it into this delightful inn. The menus are exceptional, both for the wide choice offered and for the freshness of the innovative cooking, especially the fish. It's also the best value for money in the region: the weekday lunch menu costs €18 and gourmet menus are €25–36. When the weather's nice, you can dine on the pleasant terrace or in the cool interior. There's also an exhibition of enchanting painted porcelain. The river and lake add to the wonderful setting.

Noailly

42640 (15km NW)

@ ♜ |●| Château de La Motte★★★

La Motte; take the N7 to Saint-Germain-Lespinasse, then the D4 in the direction of Charlieu; it's between Noailly and La Benisson-Dieu.
☎04.77.66.64.60 ☎04.77.66.68.10
🖥www.chateaudelamotte.fr.st
TV. Car park. Swimming pool.

This romantic château may be beyond the price range of modest travellers, but if you want to go on a spree this is a good enough place to do it, due to the charm of its tastefully furnished and extremely comfortable rooms (each named after a famous writer), its eighteenth-century salon, its park with paths running through the trees and its evocative pond complete with a pergola. Double rooms go for €69–98, according to the degree of comfort. You can have a communal dinner shared with the owner at €23, including wine and coffee. The cuisine is based on fresh, local products.

Ambierle

42820 (18km NW)

@ |●| Le Prieuré

It's in the centre of the village.
☎04.77.65.63.24
Closed *Tues and Sun evenings; Wed; 3 weeks in Jan–Feb; a fortnight in Sept.* **Disabled access.**

In this well-known restaurant, pride of place goes to the fresh, local ingredients: vegetables, ducks, crayfish, etc. They are supplied by producers from the region and then treated with daring and talent by the chef, who creates surprising but delicious blends of cheese, fruit and vegetables. Dishes include fresh goat's cheese with walnut oil and leek *confit*, and Fourme cheese with baked pear on a bed of Guaranjá chocolate. He is also extremely skilful in his addition of spices and herbs to meat and fish: *magret de canard* Pacaudois with spiced honey, grilled bass with herb butter and hyssop. There's a weekday lunchtime menu at €20, with others €24–47. During July and August there is a market in the village every Friday from 5 to 9pm; to coincide with this, the chef offers a special menu featuring the products he buys there.

Bully

42260 (20km S)

@ |●| Port de Bully

Pont de Presle; it's between Saint-Polgues and Cordelle, on the D45.

☎04.77.65.23.36
Closed *Mon and Wed (Sept–Easter); Feb.*
Games available.

Irène and Stéphane Mouterot had the idea of establishing this charming bar-restaurant above the harbour of Port de Bully. The terrace offers a wonderful view of the hundred-odd boats that are anchored in this curve on the Villerest Lake. You can come and revel in the beauty of the place over a drink or a reasonably priced meal: weekday lunchtime menu at €10, with weekend menus at €13 and €22. One of the main culinary attractions is "Irène's mystery frogs" (served at weekends or weekday dinners, by prior booking) – the recipe is a closely guarded secret.

Romans-sur-Isère

26100

⬇ 🏠 Hôtel Magdeleine

31 av. Pierre Sémard; the road runs at right angles to the station.
☎04.75.02.33.53 ☎04.75.72.78.38
🌐www.magdeleinehotel.fr.st
Closed *Sun (except by reservation).* **TV. Cots available. Pay car park.**

A strategically placed hotel right near the station, the historic centre and the factory warehouses. The owner originates from the Vosges and he runs the place expertly. He does everything himself – reception, cleaning, breakfasts and even the ironing. The fifteen pleasant rooms are being renovated one by one; they're quite big and have new bedding and efficient double-glazing. Doubles with shower/wc or bath cost €39. It's spotlessly clean and you get a genuinely warm welcome.

⬇ 🍴 🏠 |●| Hôtel des Balmes**

Hameau des Balmes; it's about 4km from the centre. Take the D532, the Tain road for 2km, then turn right in the direction of Les Balmes.
☎04.75.02.29.52 ☎04.75.02.75.47
🌐www.hoteldesbalmes.com
Closed *Sun evening out of season; first week in Jan.* **Restaurant closed** *Mon lunchtime.* **TV. High chairs available. Swimming pool. Car park.**

This hotel, in a sleepy little village, has twelve pretty rooms with bath and balcony for €44–50. In the restaurant, *Au Tahiti*, the owners have created an exotic décor

with glass beads and shells. The cooking is strictly regional French – Drôme guinea-fowl, lamb from the Préalpes – and menus are affordable at €13–24.50. Bikers are welcome to use the garage. Logis de France. *Free fruit juice or soft drink offered to our readers on presentation of this guide.*

⬇ 🍴 |●| Restaurant La Cassolette

16 rue Rebatte; it's in a pedestrianized street near the Jacquemart Tower.
☎04.75.02.55.71
Closed *Sun; Mon; end July to mid-Aug.*

An intimate restaurant in a charming, thirteenth-century building, where the three dining rooms have vaulted ceilings. There's a range of menus from €13 to €35, listing such dishes as mullet with peppers, scallop ravioli and duck in Côtes-du-Rhône. The dish of the day is €8. Extensive wine list. *Free coffee offered to our readers on presentation of this guide.*

⬇ 🍴 |●| Le Café des Arts

49 cours Pierre-Didier.
☎04.75.02.77.23
Closed *Sat lunchtime; Sun.* **Disabled access.**

The round dining room is encircled by a veranda. It's a bit smart but not formal because it's softened by lots of green plants and you can watch the chefs behind the glass. The dishes are substantial, with plenty of of fresh fish – try tuna and salmon *tartare*, baked sea bream with dill sauce, or pan-fried king prawns on a bed of red peppers. Local dishes figure on the menus too, and carnivores are well catered for: duck breast with orange, foie gras, steak *tartare*. Set lunches go for €14–25 and the dish of the day is €10; wine is available by the glass. The staff are efficient and friendly; the owner will extend a businesslike welcome. They open the terrace under the plane trees when the sun shines; it's cut off from the road (which can be noisy in the daytime) by a thick green hedge. *Free coffee offered to our readers on presentation of this guide.*

Granges-lès-Beaumont

26600 (7km W)

⬇ 🍴 🏠 |●| Les Vieilles Granges**

It's 6km from Romans. Take the D53 Tain road, then turn left at the sign, opposite the "lycée horticole".

☎04.75.71.50.43 🖶04.75.71.59.79
🌐www.vieilles-granges.com
Closed *Sun evening; Mon; Tues lunchtime.*
**Disabled access. TV. High chairs available.
Car park.**

This collection of old buildings overlooking the Isère, surrounded by mature fruit trees, has been renovated and turned into a romantic hotel-restaurant with a terrace shaded by lime trees. Comfortable double rooms go for €39–60 with shower/wc or bath – the more expensive ones have a river view. In the dining room you can eat tasty food, such as ravioli, fillet of ostrich and *caillette* (pork and vegetable faggots); menus are at €17–29. *Free house apéritif offered to our readers on presentation of this guide.*

Saint-Agnan-en-Vercors

26420

≪ 🎋 🏠 🍴 **Auberge Le Collet**

It's on the D518, 1km outside La Chapelle-en-Vercors.
☎04.75.48.13.18 🖶04.75.48.13.25
✉aubergelecollet@club-internet.fr
Closed *a week in June; a week in Nov; a week in early Dec.* **Restaurant closed** *Sun evening; Mon and Tues (except during school holidays).* **High chairs and games available.**

This substantial mountain house is in the heart of the Vercors and provides an ideal spot for a well-earned rest. The owner's son, Guillaume, also offers his service as an instructor and takes you fishing or for walks on the region's plateau. The traditionally decorated dining room is lovely with sturdy wooden beams, wooden floors and rough-cast on the walls ornamented by old photos. The warming log fire chases away the winter chill. Meals are simple, filling, economic and most welcome. The weekday lunch menu, at €13 for a starter, main course, cheese or dessert, is excellent value; they offer Landes specialities on other menus at €16–27. The owners spent some time in the southwest and brought back a batch of good recipes: *confits*, foie gras, *garbure,* Salard potatoes and so on. It makes a nice change from local mountain food. The six simple but well-arranged rooms are meticulously maintained; doubles go for €40 with shower/wc. The welcome is genuinely warm. *Free house apéritif offered to our readers on presentation of this guide.*

Saint-Agrève

07320

≪ 🏠 🍴 **Domaine de Rilhac★★★**

Lieu-dit Rilhac; from Saint-Agrève, follow the road to Le Cheylard for about 1km; take the D21 fork off the D120 and follow the signs.
☎04.75.30.20.20 🖶04.75.30.20.00
🌐www.domaine-de-rilhac.com
Closed *Tues evening; Wed; Thurs lunchtime; 20 Dec to early March.* **Disabled access. TV. Games available. Car park.**

A sixteenth-century farm that has been tastefully restored and converted into a delightful hotel-restaurant. It's a luxury place at affordable prices, set deep in the countryside in a stunning spot facing mounts Mézenc and Gerbier. It has a dressed-stone façade, blue shutters and finely engraved wrought ironwork inside, which goes well with the ochre plaster and the exposed beams. There are six double rooms at €80–110, depending on the comfort and the season; breakfast (€14) is served until 10.30am. Half board is compulsory in July and August at a cost of €97–118 per person. There's a weekday lunch menu at €23 and others €36–68. The à la carte menu changes with the seasons; specialities include trout salad, *carpaccio* of beef and iced nougat with *marrons glacés.*

Saint-Auban-sur-l'Ouvèze

26170

≪ 🏠 🍴 **Auberge de la Clavelière**

It's in the main street of the village, on the D546, halfway between Buis-les-Baronnies and Séderon.
☎ and 🖶04.75.28.61.07
🌐www.guideweb.com/provence/hotel/claveliere
Closed *Sat lunchtime; may be closed in winter (but call to check); a week in June; a fortnight in Sept; a fortnight at Christmas.* **Swimming pool. Car park.**

Charming village way off the beaten track. In its centre stands this simple, warm and welcoming hotel in a solid stone house, where comfortable double rooms go for €45. The cooking offers stalwart family-style and regional dishes. Regular customers head here on weekday lunchtimes to make the most of the €12 menu. The menus at €20 and €25 are more elaborate: sardines *escabèche, croustil-*

RHÔNE-ALPES

lant of duck breast, Provençal-style salad of king prawns, and honey and lavender flan.

Saint-Didier-de-la-Tour
38110

⊚ 🏕 |●| Aux Berges du Lac

58 rte. du Lac; take the N6. It's 1km from La Tour-du-Pin.
☎04.74.97.32.82
Closed *evenings during the week (Sept–May); Christmas school holiday.* **Disabled access. High chairs and games available.**

This place has got it right. You can have a nice meal and enjoy yourself in an atmosphere that's so good that you scarcely notice the occasional noise from passing trains. There's a huge bay window with a view of the lake and a terrace in summer. Menus are cheap at €8–27; among other things, the chef prepares excellent frogs' legs and fried fish. It's perfect for Sunday lunch; think about reserving. *Free Kir offered to our readers on presentation of this guide.*

Montferrat
38620 (15km SE)

⊚ |●| Auberge Féfette

Le Vernay; take the N6 to Les Abrets, then the N75; from Montferrat, take the route du Lac.
☎04.76.32.40.46
Closed *Mon evening; Tues; 20–30 April; 10–30 Oct.* **Car park.**

A nice little house way out in the countryside. It's a family affair run by the Groseilles; the son is the chef while his father runs the dining room. Good menus from €19.60 up to €28, with dishes that change with the seasons: *papillotte* of foie gras with raspberries, roast monkfish with sea salt, potted lamb with apricots, *fricassée* of lobster in Banyuls wine, *cassolette* of scallops, sole and ravioli. You'll pay around €38 for a meal à la carte. Dine on the terrace in good weather. It's best to book.

Vignieu
38890 (16km NW)

⊚ 🏠 |●| Château de Chapeau Cornu***

Take the N6 in the direction of La Tour-du-Pin, then turn left (D19) in the direction of Morestel; keep going for another 7km; Vignieu is on the left.

☎04.74.27.79.00 ⊕04.74.92.49.31
ⓦwww.chateau-chapeau-cornu.fr
Closed *Dec to end Jan.* **Restaurant closed** *Sun evening (except July–Aug).* **TV. High chairs and games available. Swimming pool. Car park.**

An unusual name for a fantastic place which occupies a thirteenth-century castle surrounded by a nine-acre wooded park. It's now a charming hotel-restaurant offering bright, comfortable double rooms furnished with antiques and contemporary art. Rooms for two to four people cost €67–79, with shower/wc or bath. Meals are served in the vaulted dining rooms or on the terrace; all dishes are prepared using local produce. The weekday lunch menu of the day, which includes wine and coffee, costs €22; other menus €30–57. Specialities include pan-fried foie gras served hot. Out of season they offer a special deal – one night, two meals including apéritif and wine and two breakfasts served in your room for €150–170.

Domarin
38300 (20km W)

⊚ 🏕 🏠 Hôtel des Dauphins

8 rue François Berrier; take the N6 or A43 to Bourgoin-Jallieu and keep going for another 0.5km near the Bourgoin train station and 500m from the centre. It's in a road to the left opposite the Total petrol station, after the Lyon roundabout.
☎04.74.93.00.58 ⊕04.74.28.27.39
ⓔhotel.desdauphins@wanadoo.fr
Disabled access. TV.

A very quiet place not far from the centre offering non-smoking rooms with all facilities (shower or bath, wc, telephone). They are set in the main building (some in the second-floor attic) and on the ground floor of an annexe, either looking on to the garden or, slightly less attractive, on the second floor. Doubles cost €35–41, depending on the degree of comfort; rooms 25 and 35 can sleep a third person. Buffet breakfast at €4.50. There's a terrace next to the lawn. Cordial service.

Saint-Savin
38300 (23km NW)

⊚ |●| Restaurant Le Demptézieu

Place du Château; go in the direction of Bourgoin-Jallieu, then take the D143 on the right.

☎04.74.28.90.49
Closed *Mon; Tues; first fortnight in Jan.* **Car park.**

Yves and Corinne Bello have turned this old village café into a wonderful gourmet restaurant. They'll give you a very natural welcome and unpretentious service with a smile. Dishes are elaborate and tuned to today's tastes: scallops, fondue of leeks, duck foie gras in Saint-Savin wine, lobster cannelloni with *espelette* peppers. The weekday lunch menu, at €11, includes a quarter-litre of wine and coffee; other menus €16–30. You're guaranteed a delicious meal, although it might take a while to reach your table.

Saint-Étienne

42000

◎ ☎ Continental Hôtel

10 rue François-Gillet; it's in the town centre, near the municipal tourist office and the Town Hall. Coming from Lyon, take rue de la Montat, then place Fourneyron and rue de la République, then turn left before place Dorian into rue François-Gillet.
☎04.77.32.58.43 ℗04.77.37.94.06
Closed *last fortnight in July.* **TV. Pay car park.**

You will receive a warm welcome in this colourful, recently refurbished family hotel. Its central location in a quiet street, its enclosed garage and accessible prices all add up to a place that we can highly recommend. Double rooms go for €29–39. Free wireless Internet connection.

◎ ☎ Hôtel Le Cheval Noir**

11 rue François-Gillet.
☎04.77.33.41.72 ℗04.77.37.79.19
Closed *Aug.* **TV. Pay car park.**

Spacious, pastel-tone rooms, slightly old-fashioned but clean. Prices are modest considering its central location: doubles go for €45.50 with shower/wc and €51.50 with bath.

◎ ☼ ☎ |●| Hôtel Terminus du Forez***

31 av. Denfert-Rochereau; it's opposite the Châteaucreux station, five minutes from the centre.
☎04.77.32.48.47 ℗04.77.34.03.30
ⓦwww.logisdefrance42.com

Closed *Mon and Sat lunchtimes; Sun; 1 July–29 Aug; 26–30 Dec.* **TV. Car park.**

Charming, classic three-star hotel, with stylish rooms with original paintings on the walls. Doubles cost €59 with shower/wc and €69 with bath. The rooms on the third floor have an Egyptian style, and if you walk down the stairs you can pick up a guide to the local tourist attractions in the region. On the ground floor, the restaurant *La Loco*, where they serve seasonal dishes, is more than satisfactory; menus range from €11 to €28. Excellent welcome. Logis de France. *10% discount on the room rate Fri–Sun (except during special events) offered to our readers on presentation of this guide.*

◎ ☼ ☎ |●| L'Albatros***

67 rue Saint-Simon; turn left after the arms factory, opposite the golf course.
☎04.77.41.41.00 ℗04.77.38.28.16
ⓦwww.albatros-hotel.com
Closed *6-16 Aug; 23 Dec–3 Jan.* **Restaurant closed** *Sat and Sun in winter.* **Disabled access. TV. Swimming pool. Car park.**

This *Best Western* offers all mod cons, and it's a nice place to enjoy peace and quiet, overlooking the golf course, in the upper part of the town. Modern, comfortable rooms go for €86–145; menus cost €17–27. *Free house apéritif offered to our readers on presentation of this guide.*

◎ |●| Le Cercle

15 pl. de l'Hôtel-de-Ville.
☎04.77.25.27.27
Closed *Sun evening; Mon; 4 weeks in Aug.*

This restaurant occupies part of the former premises of the Saint-Étienne bridge club, in a superb building opposite the town hall. The owners have kept the panelling and the gilding in one of the most beautiful rooms, which is pure Napoleon III in style. The restaurant attracts local worthies but prices are nevertheless very reasonable, with a weekday set lunch at €12 and more extensive lunchtime menus at €14–56. Decent food, pleasantly presented, and friendly service.

◎ |●| Cornes d'Aurochs!

18 rue Michel-Servet; it's 150m from the Town Hall.
☎04.77.32.27.27

Closed *Sat and Mon lunchtimes; Sun; 20 July–25 Aug.* **Car park by booking.**

A fun bistro offering Lyonnais cooking and traditional specials including *andouillette, tablier de sapeur*, a *"Gargantua"* platter (which gives you a bit of everything), steak *tartare*, fillet steak with ceps, duck *confit*, and Lucullus sweetbreads of veal with morels. The €13 lunch menu is a good deal, with others €18–35. The owner is jovial, and his wife smiling and welcoming.

⚐ |●| La Mandragore

15 rue des Martyrs-de-Vingré; it's in the town centre, between place Dorian and place Chavanelle.
☎04.77.38.50.70
Closed *Sun; Mon lunch; last fortnight in Dec; last fortnight in Aug.*

A newcomer in a street already enlivened by a number of restaurants. It has chic, sunny décor and offers extremely fresh food at very reasonable prices. The weekday lunchtime menu is €15; others are €30 and €42. On fine days you can eat on the terrace, under the large white parasols.

⚐ |●| Aux deux Cageots

3 pl. Grenette; it's in the town centre, near the place des Ursules.
☎04.77.32.89.85
Closed *Sat lunch; Sun; Mon.*

This is the most fashionable bar-restaurant in town, the place where would-be jet-setters come to be seen. There is always a party atmosphere and the attentive, jovial owner, Jacques Dargnat, makes sure that everybody has a good time. The food is equally exciting, with daringly original sweet-savoury mixtures and an excellent use of herbs and spices. There's a lunchtime menu for €16, then another at €31. The menu changes several times a month, which gives you a good excuse to come here more often. Booking highly advisable.

⚐ ⚑ |●| Chez Marco

2 pl. Chavanelle; it's near the fire station.
☎04.77.33.92.47
Closed *lunchtimes; Sun; Mon; Aug.* **Disabled access.**

A well-known restaurant where actors and sundry night-owls meet up. Photos of the regulars cover the walls of the cosy little dining room. When you've finished a

lovingly prepared meal you'll want to be told the recipe for the *diable au corps*, the explosive house cocktail – they actually set light to it. Menus range from €20 to €35. The posh cooking is the sort you get in a classic Lyonnais bistro: chicken with prawns, *tablier du sapeur*, cheese soufflé. Best to book. *Free coffee offered to our readers on presentation of this guide.*

⚐ |●| Nouvelle

30 rue St-Jean.
☎04.77.32.32.60
Closed *Sun; Mon; second and third week in Aug.*

The best place to eat in Saint-Étienne, right in the centre of town. It's got everything a gourmet restaurant should have: chic but subtle décor, professional staff and the kind of menu you dream about; it doesn't, however, charge the prices you might expect. There's a wide choice of menus at €28 (weekday lunch) and from €40 to €65. Portions are generous, and it's all very imaginative. It's best to book.

Saint-Priest-en-Jarez
42270 (2km N)

⚐ |●| Restaurant du Musée

Lieu-dit La Terrasse; follow the signs to the Museum of Modern Art.
☎04.77.59.24.52
Closed *Mon; Wed evening; Sun evening.* **Disabled access.**

Stéphane Laurier (who runs the *Nouvelle* restaurant in town) has taken over this restaurant inside the modern art museum. His cooking is very inventive, skilfully using spices and mixing unusual flavours – try the *croustillant* of fish, or the trout with grilled almonds. There are constantly changing lunch menus at €12 and €15, with other menus at €19–23; you'll spend about €27 à la carte. Excellent value for money and efficient service. There's a lovely terrace that opens in warm weather.

Saint-Genest-Malifaux
42660 (12km S)

⚐ ⚑ 🏠 |●| Auberge de Campagne La Diligence**

Le Château du Bois; take the N82 to Bicêtre, then the D501. It's 3km from the village and 2km from the col du Grand-Bois.

ⓣ04.77.39.04.99 ⓕ04.77.39.01.80
Closed Mon; Tues and Wed (except July–Aug); Jan. **Games available. Pay car park.**

This was originally a farmhouse belonging to the thirteenth-century castle, which is still inhabited. Now it's a really nice restaurant and is part of the agricultural college of Saint-Genest. The food is good and service pleasant, with a seasonal menu at €12 (except Sun), and others €18–24. On offer are flavoursome dishes such as free-range guinea-fowl with watercress, or *verveine parfait glacé* with crispy bitter chocolate. The handsome dining room has a fireplace and there's a terrace in the farm courtyard. You can sleep in a cottage (€12 per night, or half board €28 per person) or camp in the grounds for next to nothing. It's a horse farm, so you can go riding. It's advisable to book. *Free coffee offered to our readers on presentation of this guide.*

◎ ⚑ |●| **Restaurant Montmartin**

18 rue du Velay; take the N82, then the D501 to Plafony. It's in the town centre, 100m from the church, opposite the college.
ⓣ04.77.51.21.25
Closed evenings; Wed; Fri; mid-Jan to end Feb.

Located in one of the less attractive villages in this part of the world, this place was established after World War II by the grandmother of the present owners – they've kept the warm atmosphere and the creaking parquet. There's no nouvelle cuisine here; this is the place for generous portions of rich food including morels, frogs' legs and *quenelles*. The weekday menu is €12.50, and there are others at €19–29; specialities not on the menu can be ordered in advance. It's very popular with families for Sunday lunch. Credit cards not accepted. *Free coffee offered to our readers on presentation of this guide.*

Saint-Victor-sur-Loire

42230 (15km W)

◎ |●| **Le Croque Cerise**

Base Nautique de Saint-Victor; take the D3A.
ⓣ04.77.90.07.54
Closed Sun and Wed evenings; Mon; Jan. **Disabled access.**

The big building is not particularly elegant, but the dining rooms with their large windows and the terrace by the harbour are really pleasant. The dishes are attentively prepared and simple, such as whitebait, but there are also inventive offerings like seafood *cassoulet*, and *magret de canard* with blackcurrant. The weekday lunch menu, at €13, includes a main course, dessert and coffee; other menus are €18–28. The food, service and welcome are spot-on.

Bessat (Le)

42660 (18km SE)

◎ ⚑ 🛏 |●| **Auberge de la Jasserie**

La Jasserie; it's 6km after Le Bessat, at 1310m of altitude – follow the signs from the village.
ⓣ04.77.20.40.16 ⓕ04.77.20.45.43
ⓔmassonseverine@wanadoo.fr
Closed Wed in winter (except during school holidays). **Disabled access. High chairs available. Car park.**

This old farmhouse, with its little bell tower, is a bit of an institution. It's one of those simple country inns that hasn't changed for generations, where you sit at wooden tables and chairs in a huge old dining room. It's at the bottom of the ski runs so it's an ideal place to warm up over a hot chocolate and a slice of bilberry tart. The only drawback is that it's rather crowded and noisy at the weekend. Menus are at €10 (except Sun lunchtime), and €12–30. You can also stay here for €11 a night, breakfast included, sleeping in bunk beds in a rather spartan dormitory with little privacy – but to do this, you have to have dinner here beforehand. *Free house apéritif offered to our readers on presentation of this guide.*

◎ ⚑ 🛏 |●| **Hôtel La Fondue – Restaurant Chez le Père Charles***

Grande-Rue; take the D8. It's in the centre of the village.
ⓣ04.77.20.40.09 ⓕ04.77.20.45.20
ⓦwww.pere-charles.com
Closed Sun evening; Mon lunchtime; mid-Nov to mid-March. **Disabled access. TV.**

A good restaurant way up at 1170m in the middle of the Pilat regional park, where the people of Lyon and Saint-Étienne come to get a bit of fresh air. Splendid gourmet dishes include goose foie gras, *tournedos* with paprika cream or the home speciality: trout stuffed with ceps. The dish of the day is at €10, and there are several menus at €14–48. Doubles cost €45–60 with shower/wc or bath. The bathrooms are big but the rooms with shower have a rather strange arrangement – a revolving cupboard which hides the toilet and the shower. *Free coffee, fruit juice or soft drink offered to our readers on presentation of this guide.*

Saint-Just-Saint-Rambert

42170 (19km NW)

ⓒ 🍴 🍽️ Restaurant du Rempart

2 rue de la Loire; going in the direction of St-Genest-Lerpt, take the west turning off the D8.
☎04.77.52.13.19
Closed *Sun and Wed evenings; Mon; a week during Feb school holiday; 3 weeks in Aug.*

A couple of rustic dining rooms up on the first floor of a very old house built into the town walls. There's a gifted, inventive chef at work with excellent lamb and fish dishes such as sea bream pan-fried on the skin with green beans or the *bouillabaisse* with thyme. The weekday lunchtime menu, which includes wine and coffee, is at €11; other menus €15.50–32.50. In summer, meals are served on the flowery terrace at the foot of the town walls. Smiling, pleasant service. *Free coffee offered to our readers on presentation of this guide.*

Saint-Galmier

42330

ⓒ 🍴 🏠 🍽️ La Charpinière***

Lieu-dit la Charpinière; take the D12. It's on the edge of Saint-Galmier.
☎04.77.52.75.00 📠04.77.54.18.79
🌐www.lacharpiniere.com
Disabled access. TV. High chairs and games available. Swimming pool. Car park.

A splendid establishment in substantial grounds that guarantee peace and quiet. Pleasant and functional rooms go for €90–103. They have a range of facilities including a health and fitness centre, tennis courts and a swimming pool. The restaurant is in a conservatory and offers high-quality cooking that's both original

and refined. Try the fried fillet of red mullet, crispy Parma ham or *millefeuille* with grilled aubergines. There's a weekday menu at €13, with other menus €23–45. Particularly attentive service. *Free house apéritif offered to our readers on presentation of this guide.*

ⓒ 🍽️ Le Bougainvillier

Pré-Château; it's signposted from the Badoit spring on the banks of the Coise.
☎04.77.54.03.31
Closed *Sun and Wed evenings; Mon; Feb school holiday; Aug.* **Disabled access. High chairs available.**

A pretty building swathed in Virginia creeper in the rather stylish little town that is the source of Badoit mineral water. In the evening, the local inhabitants form a queue to collect their free fizzy water. The restaurant has three dining rooms, one of them a veranda overlooking a walled garden by the water's edge. Gérard Charbonnier is one of the most interesting young chefs in the area. He spent two years in Gagnaire's well-known restaurant, where he was encouraged to be creative. His fish dishes are delicate and skilfully prepared. Menus start from €25 (except Sat evening and Sun) and go up to €52. Charming, low-key welcome.

Veauche

42340 (6km S)

ⓒ 🏠 🍽️ Hôtel-restaurant de la Gare

55 av. H.-Planchet; take the D12. It's next to the train station and a huge factory.
☎04.77.54.60.10 📠04.77.06.00.13
Closed *3.30–6pm; Fri, Sat and Sun evenings; the week of 15 Aug.* **Disabled access. High chairs available. Car park.**

A reliable neighbourhood restaurant providing good food at sensible prices. There's a weekday menu at €9.50, and others at €13–40. The menus list fine, delicately prepared dishes: home-made foie gras, terrine and fish dishes. Pleasant, conventional décor and a warm friendly welcome. The hotel has ten basic rooms for €27 with shower/wc. A place to bear in mind if you're stuck for somewhere to stay – in general circumstances, however, the view of the station and the factory is probably not quite what you're looking for. Good welcome.

Andrezieux-Bouthéon

42160 (8km SW)

@ 🖈 🏠 |●| Les Iris***

32 av. Jean-Martouret; from the motorway,
take the exit to Andrezieux-centre, follow
directions first to the town centre then to the
train station.
☎04.77.36.09.09 ℻04.77.36.09.00
Closed 1–20 Jan; a week in Aug. **Restaurant
closed** Mon; Sat lunch; Sun evening. **Hotel
open** daily. **TV. Car park. Swimming pool.**

This handsome residence, which you reach
by ascending two elegant flights of steps,
stands on the outskirts of a rather industrial
town near Saint-Étienne airport. The ten
functional but pleasant and redecorated
bedrooms, named after flowers, are in the
annexe. They overlook the swimming pool
and the garden with its gigantic cedar
trees, and cost €69–80 with bath. The
restaurant serves sophisticated food and
has sophisticated décor to match. Flowers
and fresh herbs blend beautifully with
fish, meat and vegetables to produce delicious and refined cooking that surprises.
Menus, which change weekly, go from €23
(except Sun) to €62. *Free coffee offered to our
readers on presentation of this guide.*

Chazelles-sur-Lyon

42140 (10km NE)

@ 🖈 🏠 |●| Château Blanchard**

36 rte. de Saint-Galmier; it's 50m from the
Hat Museum.
☎04.77.54.28.88 ℻04.77.54.36.03
Closed Sun evening; Mon; 10–25 Aug.
**Disabled access. TV. High chairs and
games available. Car park.**

This so-called castle, in France's millinery
capital, is actually a 1930s folly that was
once the home of a hat-maker. It lay
neglected for forty years but has since
been restored to its original splendour.
The garish frontage is decorated with
friezes, while inside the décor is a glorious
confusion of neo-greco-classical-kitsch.
Very well-equipped doubles go from €58
with bath; no. 6 has its original décor. Half
board is also available at €60 per person.
The restaurant fits into its surroundings
very nicely. You'll get a warm welcome
and classic, well-presented menus at €19–
35. They specialize in fresh fish and subtle
desserts. You can dine on the terrace. Logis
de France. *Free house liqueur offered to our
readers on presentation of this guide.*

Saint-Jean-de-Maurienne

73300

@ 🖈 🏠 |●| Hôtel-restaurant du Nord**

Place du Champ-de-Foire.
☎04.79.64.02.08 ℻04.79.59.91.31
🖥www.hoteldunord.net
Closed Sun evening (except Feb and July–
Aug); Mon lunchtime; Easter school holiday;
Nov school holiday. **Disabled access. TV.
High chairs available. Car park.**

A former coaching inn with a little tower.
The restaurant, which has a vaulted ceiling and stonewalls, is in the old stables.
It's the best place to eat in town; the
cooking is well judged, and although it's
classic the chef has some original ideas.
There's a €15 menu (not served Sun and
public holidays), with others €20–40.
The rooms are spacious and offer good
value for money: doubles cost €45 with
shower/wc. There's a garage available for
bikes and motorbikes. *10% discount on
the room rate (except July–Aug) or free house
apéritif offered to our readers on presentation
of this guide.*

Saint-Martin-de-Belleville

73440

@ 🖈 🏠 |●| La Bouitte

Quartier Saint-Marcel; take the D117 towards
Les Ménuires (about 2km).
☎04.79.08.96.77 ℻04.79.08.96.03
🖥www.la-bouitte.com
Closed early May to early July; early Oct to
mid-Dec. **TV. Disabled access. High chairs
available. Pay car park.**

Old stone and wood chalet that combines
tradition with elegance. Without doubt,
this is the best restaurant in the valley. It
offers local cooking with a finesse that
belies its apparent simplicity; the speciality
is *escalope* of foie gras on a corn pancake
with honey sauce. Save room for the marvellous desserts. The menus, at €42–125,
are a little pricey, but well worth it for the
wonderful food. To prolong your pleasure,
they have a few charming rooms, decorated in mountain style; doubles with bath
go for €170–196, breakfast included. *Free
house apéritif offered to our readers on presentation of this guide.*

22

RHÔNE-ALPES

Saint-Paul-lès-Monestier

38650

@ 🎿 🏠 |O| Au Sans Souci**

At Monestier-de-Clermont; it's about 35km south of Grenoble via the N75 (in the direction of Sisteron); once in Monestier-de-Clermont, take the D8 Gresse-en-Vercors road.
℡04.76.34.03.60 ℻04.76.34.17.38
ⓦperso.wanadoo.fr/au-sans-souci
Closed *Sun evening and Mon (except July–Aug); 20 Dec–30 Jan.* **TV. High chairs available. Swimming pool. Car park.**

This family-run hotel, surrounded by greenery at the foot of the Vercors regional park, has been running smoothly for four generations. It's a pleasure to be here, and you'll feel even better after a meal in the welcoming restaurant. They offer menus from €18 (except Sun) to €30. Excellent specialities include morels stuffed with foie gras, crayfish risotto and nougat with honey. If you want to stay here, double rooms go for €60 with shower/wc or bath. You can play bowls, tennis or pool. Logis de France. Booking is highly advisable. *Free coffee offered to our readers on presentation of this guide.*

Saint-Restitut

26130

@ 🎿 |O| Restaurant Les Buisses

Route de Juze-la-Rousee; take the D59, then the D218.
℡04.75.04.96.50
Closed *Mon, Sat lunchtime and Sun evening in winter; Sat, Mon and Tues lunchtimes in summer; a fortnight mid-March.* **Disabled access.**

A beautiful country house way out in the forest with a Provençal garden. In summer the crickets sing, and you sit out on the terrace to enjoy robustly flavoured cooking from the south. There's also a spacious, newly decorated dining room with a working fireplace. You can lunch à la carte for around €18 (choosing from a selection of six enticing starters and main courses), otherwise there is a menu at €25, cheese and desserts included. Specialities include lamb fondue, *assiette des Buisses* (a platter of aubergine, peppers, pickled tomatoes and courgettes drizzled with local olive oil), and deep-fried courgette flowers.

Remarkable wine list, with an emphasis on regional vintages. Lovely welcome and a nice relaxed atmosphere. *Free house apéritif offered to our readers on presentation of this guide.*

Sainte-Eulalie

07510

@ 🎿 🏠 |O| Hôtel du Nord**

It's opposite the church.
℡04.75.38.80.09 ℻04.75.38.85.50
ⓦwww.ardeche-tourisme.com/hotel-du-nord
Closed *Tues evening and Wed (except July–Aug); 11 Nov to early March.* **Disabled access. TV. Car park.**

Two sitting rooms, one with a veranda; both have magnificent views over the Loire plain. Double rooms cost €44–52 with shower/wc or bath. Menus (€17–33) list interesting specialities such as duck thigh *confit* with bilberry sauce, trout soufflé with *beurre blanc* and pork *estouffade* in Ardèche wine. For dessert you absolutely must try the *crème brûlée* with bilberries and raspberries. This place is a magnet for fans of fly-fishing – the chef is smitten by the sport. Logis de France. *Free house apéritif offered to our readers on presentation of this guide.*

Sagnes et Goudoulet

07450 (8km SE)

@ 🎿 🏠 |O| Hostellerie Chaneac**

It's in the edge of the village, on the Burzet road.
℡04.75.38.80.88 ℻04.75.38.80.54
ⓦwww.ardeche-tourisme.com
Closed *last week in Aug.* **Restaurant open** *weekends; evenings only in July–Aug; otherwise groups only, with prior reservation.* **Disabled access. High chairs available. Car park.**

Instead of leaving the country for the town, the young chef decided to stay and take over the family business – he's the fourth generation to run the place. The climate is harsh and the winters are long which doesn't make things easy, so business is seasonal – sometimes when the snow is deep, it's hard even to get deliveries up here. Inside the thick walls, the rooms are comfortable and the walls are built of stone and wood. Doubles go for €40-42; half board is compulsory in July and August at €38–40 per person. The chef uses carefully selected local produce and he makes the charcuterie and bread himself, as well as the terrines of wild plants and local trout. Menus are at €17 and €25. Credit cards not accepted. *Free house apéritif or liqueur offered to our readers on presentation of this guide.*

Sallanches
74700

⊚ 🏠 |●| Auberge de l'Orangerie**

3 carrefour de la Charlotte; it's 3km east of the city centre on the D13 in the direction of Passy.
☎04.50.58.49.16 🖷04.50.58.54.63
🌐perso.wanadoo.fr/auberge-orangerie
Closed 5–27 Jan; 2–24 June. **Restaurant closed** Mon; Tues, Wed and Thurs lunchtimes; Sun evening. **TV. High chairs and games available. Car park.**

Though the hotel is right on a roundabout, its rooms are well soundproofed. The décor is basic but it does have a little something, and most of all it's very comfortable. Prices are very fair for the region: doubles with shower/wc or bath cost €40–55. The dining room is a random mixture of rustic and kitsch, but the cuisine has a clear, contemporary identity. The chef works with delicacy and cares for every detail. Expect to pay €31–46 à la carte.

Samoëns
74340

⊚ 🏕 🏠 |●| Le Moulin du Bathieu**

Vercland: take the D4 in the direction of Morillon, then turn left to Samoëns 1600.
☎04.50.34.48.07 🖷04.50.34.43.25
🌐www.bathieu.com
Closed June; 4 Nov–20 Dec. **TV. Car park.**

Traditional house in the heart of the countryside. The only thing to break the silence here is the babbling brook that used to turn the millwheel. The bedrooms, with their wood-clad walls, have a warm, soothing feel. Several of them are split-level, making them ideal for families. Doubles with shower/wc or bath cost €55–120, depending on the comfort. You have to book to eat in the restaurant. Menus range from €23 to €30, and feature Savoyard specialities. *Free coffee offered to our readers on presentation of this guide.*

⊚ |●| La Fandolieuse – La Cour

☎04.50.34.98.28
Closed Sun (except during school holidays); May–June; Sept–Nov. **Open** noon–2pm and 6–11pm.

In the fifteenth century, the people of this valley spoke a poetic, sing-song dialect called Mourmé; *fandolieuse* is their word for "dancer". This pleasant little crêperie, in a sixteenth-century house with wainscoted walls, has given all its crêpes a Mourmé name: *Tapotu* means drum, *violurin* means musician, *crépioti* describes the crackling ice and *souffluche,* the biting wind. They also do fondues and a very substantial soup made with bread, Tomme cheese and onions – it's a local speciality, traditionally eaten on the feast of Saint Christopher. À la carte only; expect to pay around €15.

Saou
26400

⊚ |●| L'Oiseau sur Sa Branche

La Placette.
☎04.75.76.02.03
Closed Mon and Tues out of season; Dec and Jan. **Disabled access.**

Converted by a restaurateur-poet who settled here after years of travelling, this red and yellow bistro has an old packing case and a map of the world in the hall. Dishes are an array of colours and flavours, and your choice arrives at the table labelled with its name. You can have the dish of the day at €9.50, otherwise there's a weekday lunchtime "*menu du bistro*" at €16, and other menus at €21–26. Not surprisingly, it attracts a lot of regular customers. To cap it all, there's a lovely terrace in the shade of the plane trees, which is great for breakfast in fine weather or very romantic in the moonlight.

Sutrieu
01260

⊚ 🏠 |●| Auberge du Col de la Lèbe*

Charancin; it's 6km from Champagne-en-Valromey, 8km from Hauteville.
☎04.79.87.64.54 🖷04.79.87.54.26
Restaurant closed Mon and Tues (restaurant closed Mon evening and Tues in July–Aug);

RHÔNE-ALPES

mid-Nov to mid-April; 20–30 June. **TV. High chairs available. Swimming pool. Car park.**

Right out in the country, on the way up to the pass, this restaurant has a cosy dining room with lots of wood and houseplants. The service is stylish but not in the least pretentious, and the sophisticated cooking includes duo of foie gras, free-range chicken with morels, *empereur* with sesame seeds. They also do grills over the coals. Menus range from €11 to €28. The rooms are fairly modest but their old-fashioned air gives them a degree of style and you're guaranteed lots of peace and quiet; doubles cost €42–44. You get a wonderful view of the Valromey valley from the swimming pool.

Tain l'Hermitage
26600

@ ☎ **Hôtel Les 2 Coteaux****

18 rue Joseph Péala; take the N7; it's on the bank of the Rhône by the pedestrian bridge.
☏04.75.08.33.01 ☏04.75.08.44.20
Closed *Sun evening mid-Nov to end Jan.* **TV. High chairs available. Pay car park.**

A family hotel in a superb location on the banks of the Rhône just by a bridge to the Ardèche. The rooms have mostly been refurbished; the west-facing ones have a magnificent view of the river and the Château de Tournon – one room (no. 5) even has a small terrace. That said, those at the back also have a lovely view, this time over the Hermitage hills. Doubles with hand basin or shower cost €35–38, with shower/wc or bath €46–60. The breakfast terrace also has a gorgeous view of the Rhône flowing by.

@ 🎄 |O| **Des Terrasses du Rhône-au-Sommelier**

13 rue Joseph Péala.
☏04.75.08.40.56
Open *11am–3pm and 6pm–midnight.* **Closed** *Sun; Mon.*

An ideal place if you're after a tasty snack and a glass of good wine, serving excellent sandwiches with a wide variety of fillings. Fabien Louis is a trained *sommelier*, so the honest wines are carefully chosen. There's a sandwich menu at €10 (lunch and dinner) including two glasses of wine, or go for the charcuterie platter and a glass

of Saint-Joseph for €7. On a summer's evening, the *bonhomie* spills out onto the road. They organize walks through the vineyards. *One glass of wine chosen by the sommelier offered to our readers on presentation of this guide.*

Tarare
69170

@ 🎄 |O| **Restaurant Jean Brouilly**

3 ter, rue de Paris. Take the N7 exit in the direction of Roanne
☏04.74.63.24.56
Closed *Sun; Mon; Feb school holiday; 8–31 Aug.* **Car park.**

The Brouillys have been running things here for more than twenty years. The house, built by an industrialist, is pretty typical of the region and has beautiful grounds. Jean Brouilly is a considerable chef and a welcoming man. Whether you choose the duck supreme with spices, langoustines *en escabèche* with a salad of flowers or, in season, the kid with its giblets garnished with mustard seeds, you'll appreciate his skilful handling of fresh produce and delicate balancing of flavours. He combines herbs, spices and wild produce to most original effect. Menus are at €32–65; expect to pay around €50 à la carte. On warm days you can eat on the veranda and admire the grounds. *A free glass of Beaujolais offered to our readers on presentation of this guide.*

Violay
42780 (11km SW)

@ 🎄 ☎ |O| **Hôtel-restaurant Perrier****

Place de l'Église; from Feurs, head for Balbigny then take the D1 in the direction of Tarare.
☏04.74.63.91.01 ☏04.74.63.91.77
Closed *Fri evening (Nov–June).* **TV. High chairs and games available. Car park.**

Jean-Luc Clot and his wife will make you feel very welcome when you arrive. The village is a popular centre for cross-country skiing and there's a pretty church over the road from the hotel. It's well run and prices are affordable: €30 for a double with basin or shower, or €37–42 with shower/wc or bath. Much of the cooking in the restaurant is inspired by the cuisine of southwest France. Prices are reasonable: menus cost €10.60–36, among them a *"menu terroir"* which includes wine and coffee. Try the home-made terrine with almonds, the scallops *à la normande* or the shark steak. Logis de France. *Free house apéritif offered to our readers on presentation of this guide.*

Sarcey
69490 (13km E)

Le Chatard**

1 allée du Mas; take the N7 in the direction of Lyon, turn left onto the D118; it's 10km from there.
☎04.74.26.85.85 ℻04.74.26.89.99
www.le-chatard.com
Closed *first three weeks in Jan.* **Restaurant closed** *Mon; Tues; Sun evening.* **Disabled access. TV. High chairs and games available. Swimming pool. Car park.**

A reliable, peaceful hotel-restaurant with a nice swimming pool. The restaurant attracts businesspeople and local families because of the prices and the top-quality traditional cuisine. Menus start from €16 for a weekday lunch and go up to €40. Try the duck foie gras or the smoked salmon. The rooms don't have huge charm but they do have all the mod cons. Doubles go for €59 with shower/wc or bath; half board available for a stay of three nights or more at €47 per person. Logis de France. *10% discount on the room rate (20 Jan–30 April) offered to our readers on presentation of this guide.*

Thonon-les-Bains
74200

Restaurant Le Victoria

5 pl. des Arts.
☎04.50.71.02.82
Closed *between Christmas and New Year's Day.* **High chairs available.**

The lovely Belle Époque glass frontage is overrun by greenery, which makes the dining room pleasantly private. They serve good, traditional cooking using fine ingredients, and prepare tasty dishes of both freshwater and sea fish – try the sea bass in a salt crust. In summer they offer huge crispy salads. Menus are at €13.50 (not Sun), €15 and €20. *Free house apéritif or coffee offered to our readers on presentation of this guide.*

Margencel
74200 (6km SW)

Hôtel-restaurant Les Cygnes**

Port de Séchex; take the N5; when you get to Margencel, head for the port of Séchex on the D33.
☎04.50.72.63.10 ℻04.50.72.68.22
www.restaurant-les-cygnes.fr
Closed *Wed out of season; mid-Nov to early Feb.* **TV. High chairs, baby-changing tables and cots available. Car park.**

Known simply as *Chez Jules*, this is a local institution in a small port by the side of Lake Geneva that's been going since the 1930s. The restaurant is famous for fresh fish – try the soup of freshwater fish, fillets of perch or lake whitefish (a type of salmon) *à l'ancienne*. Menus cost €20–33. A terrace has recently been added. The rooms are delightful and some have a lake view: doubles with shower/wc go for €50–51.50, depending on the season. Logis de France. *10% discount on the room rate offered to our readers on presentation of this guide.*

Armoy
74200 (6.5km SE)

Hôtel-restaurant Le Chalet**

L'Ermitage; it's on the D26.
☎04.50.71.08.11 ℻04.50.71.33.88
www.hotel-le-chalet.com
Closed *Dec; Jan.* **Restaurant closed** *lunchtimes; out of season (except by reservation).* **TV. Car park. Swimming pool.**

This building, which does indeed resemble a Swiss chalet, stands at the top of a wooded slope high above the village and Lake Geneva. You get lots of peace and quiet and a superb view from most of the rooms, some of which have their own terrace. If you're here in summer, ask to sleep in one of the wooden chalets around the swimming pool; two of them have recently been joined together to form a bungalow for four to six people. Doubles cost around €30 with basin, or €41–46 with shower/wc or bath, depending on the season. The cuisine is carefully prepared: home-made charcuterie, salmon with tarragon; menus are at €15–24. There's a big garden and a fine view of the lake. *Free house apéritif offered to our readers on presentation of this guide.*

Yvoire

74140 (17km W)

⊛ 沝 |●| Le Bateau Ivre

Grande Rue; take the N5 towards Sciez, then
the D25.
☎04.50.72.81.84
Closed *Wed and Thurs out of season; Jan;
first week in Feb.* **Open** *daily (mid-June to
mid-Sept).*

A fresh little dining room in an old house
in this charming (touristy) village. The
young chef works equally enthusiastically on fish dishes or desserts, and you'll
get smiling service even when the place
is full. The cheapest menu is at €15.50
(except Sat evening and Sun lunchtime),
with others €15.90–23.50. It's a genuinely
lovely place. *Free house apéritif offered to our
readers on presentation of this guide.*

Tournon-sur-Rhône

07300

⊛ 沝 🛏 |●| Hôtel Azalées**

6 av. de la Gare; it's at the start of the
Vivarais railway.
☎04.75.08.05.23 ☎04.75.08.18.27
🖳www.hotel-azalees.com
Closed *Sun evening (15 Oct–15 March);
23 Dec–5 Jan.* **Disabled access. TV. High
chairs available. Car park.**

You can sit on the terrace and watch the
steam train puffing its way through Haut-
Vivarais en route to Lamastre. Comfortable,
modern doubles go for €45 with shower/
wc or bath. Menus, €16.50–30, list mainly
regional cooking with a good goat's cheese
flan, tasty pork cheek and, for dessert, iced
chestnut soufflé. Logis de France. *10%
discount on the room rate offered to our readers
on presentation of this guide.*

⊛ 沝 |●| Restaurant L'Estragon

6 pl. Saint-Julien; it's opposite the church.
☎04.75.08.87.66
Closed *Wed (except in summer); mid-Feb to
mid-March.*

In a great location, in the middle of
a pedestrianized area very close to the
Rhône, this place offers good, simple food
at reasonable prices: menus €11–17.50.
There's a "*pierre chaude*" (hot stone) menu,
comprising a salad, veal or steak, cheese
and dessert. The salads are huge and the

pike-perch with red wine and pickled
shallots is very tasty. Efficient, attentive
service. *Free house apéritif offered to our readers on presentation of this guide.*

⊛ 沝 |●| Restaurant Aux Sablettes

187 rte. de Lamastre; go 3km along the
Lamastre road, turn left, and it's opposite the
Camping des Acacias.
☎04.75.08.44.34
Closed *Tues evening and Wed (except July–
Aug); a fortnight in winter.* **Car park.**

This restaurant and bar, which specializes in beer, is a bit out of the way,
but it's popular with young locals and
people from the nearby campsite. The
décor doesn't have particular character, but
the menu lists a few original specialities:
two-cheese fondue, meats and even desserts like mousses and tarts cooked with
beer. Teetotallers will be well satisfied with
the grills, the ravioli, a delicious regional
speciality or any of the pizzas baked in a
wood-fired oven. Menus range from €11
to €23. *Free coffee offered to our readers on
presentation of this guide.*

Trévoux

01600

⊛ 沝 🛏 |●| Hôtel des Voyageurs**

28 rue du Palais; it's near the Parliament
building.
☎04.74.00.12.34 ☎04.74.00.64.24
Closed *from Christmas to New Year.*
Restaurant closed *Sun evening* **TV.**

This is the only hotel in town but it
doesn't rest on its laurels and the service
is friendly and attentive. It's been nicely
and cleanly decorated; doubles go for €32
with shower/wc or bath. There's a bar-restaurant on the ground floor that provides
simple, home cooking. The weekday menu
at €11 includes a buffet of hors d'oeuvre,
dish of the day, dessert, wine and coffee.
*Free house apéritif offered to our readers on
presentation of this guide.*

⊛ |●| Chez Bruno

8 Grande-Rue; it's opposite the church.
☎04.74.00.20.75
Closed *Sun; Tues and Thurs evenings; 10
days at Easter; a fortnight in Aug; 10 days at
Christmas.* **Disabled access.**

On the face of things this is an ordinary-
looking place but it has a lot going for it: a

lovely smiling welcome, air-conditioning, tasty dishes with menus that change all the time and lots of quick meals for not much money. Specialities are not necessarily local – *bouillabaisse* Sétoise and *fondue Savoyarde* – but they're all full of flavour. There's a huge buffet table with starters, main courses and home-made desserts. The buffet lunch costs €15, otherwise there's a weekday lunch menu at €10; other menus are €16–20. The plates and serving dishes are made by Bruno's father-in-law, and the décor is bright with lots of paintings by Bruno's wife. It's simple, efficient and a real pleasure.

Usson-en-Forez
42550

ⓐ 🏕 🛖 |●| Hôtel Rival*

Rue Centrale.
℡04.77.50.63.65 ⓕ04.77.50.67.62
ⓔhotelrival@msn.com
Closed Mon (Oct–June); last week in June; 12 Nov–11 Dec. **TV. High chairs and games available. Car park.**

A typical family hotel in a little mountain village up in the Forez. The restaurant serves large portions of traditional dishes, with a weekday menu for €12 and others €20–38. Try the *forézienne* salad and the Fourme fondue. You can eat in the dining room with its huge fireplace, or, on good days, on the terrace. The rooms are clean and affordable, if lacking in character; doubles go for €24 with basin and €40 with shower/wc or bath. Two cottages have recently been opened. Very friendly proprietress. Logis de France. *10% discount on the room rate (except July–Aug) offered to our readers on presentation of this guide.*

Saint-Bonnet-le-Château
42380 (14km NE)

ⓐ 🏕 |●| Le Befranc**

7 rte. d'Audel; it's on the edge of town, just before the exit of Usson-en-Forez, take the small road, down on your left by the petrol station.
℡04.77.50.54.54 ⓕ04.77.50.73.17
Closed Sun evening and Mon out of season; Feb. **Disabled access. TV. Car park.**

This beautiful town with a medieval centre is the capital of *pétanque*. The hotel is a short distance from the centre and offers spruce

rooms that have been attractively decorated. Doubles (€38) are comfortable, simple but clean. Regional dishes are the order of the day in the restaurant and menus are priced at €12.50 for a weekday lunch, and €16.50–33. Try the rabbit with fig *compote*. Logis de France.

ⓐ 🏕 |●| La Calèche

2 rue du Commandant-Marey.
℡04.77.50.15.58
Closed Tue evening; Wed; Sun evening; Feb school holiday; first week in July; last week in Nov. **Disabled access. High chairs available.**

A mansion house where you will be received with a smile before you relish the owner's cooking. The variety and originality of the dishes and the quality of their ingredients have earned this restaurant a solid reputation, so it's advisable to book. Menus cost €15.50–40 and à la carte is also available. You need to book in advance a special "all-lobster" or "discovery" (foie gras, John Dory and pigeon) menu at €36. *Free liqueur on the house offered to our readers on presentation of this guide.*

Valence
26000

ⓐ 🏕 🏠 Hôtel Continental**

29 av. Pierre-Sémard.
℡04.75.44.01.38 ⓕ04.75.44.03.90

Don't be misled by the impersonal and cramped look of this hotel; it has large rooms and a retro charm. All the rooms are different, but nearly all of them have been refurbished in a simple, pleasant way. Some have lovely furniture and large bathrooms, particularly nos. 104 and 206. Doubles with shower and/wc or bath cost €33–39. Not bad for a two-star hotel, but you will have to hurry to sample it, as the owners are planning to retire at the end of the year. *One breakfast per room (Oct to end of April) offered to our readers on presentation of this guide.*

ⓐ 🏕 🏠 Hôtel de l'Europe**

15 av. Félix-Faure; it's in the town centre, opposite the place Leclerc.
℡04.75.82.62.65 ⓕ04.75.82.62.66
Closed Sun 2–6pm. **TV. Pay car park.**

A conveniently located hotel with reasonably priced air-conditioned rooms.

The hotel has been tastefully refurbished and the double-glazing is very effective at keeping out the noise from the street below. Doubles go for €41–52 with shower/wc or bath. Special break at €54. Good service. *One breakfast per room per night (in low season) offered to our readers on presentation of this guide.*

◎ ⅍ |◎| Le Bistrot des Clercs

48 Grande-Rue.
☎04.75.55.55.15
Closed *Sun evening.* **Open** *noon–2.30pm and 7–11pm (midnight Fri and Sat).* **Disabled access.**

A great bistro offering solid regional dishes prepared with creativity. Chabran, one of the best chefs of the region, offers honest cuisine that's tasty and generously served; menus are at €16 and €25. The wine list is very well balanced, offering a number of good quality vintages. *Free coffee offered to our readers on presentation of this guide.*

◎ |◎| Restaurant One Two...Tea

37 Grande-Rue.
☎04.75.55.96.31
Closed *Sun; public holidays; a fortnight mid-Aug.* **Disabled access.**

The interior is a combination of brick and wood, there are pictures on the walls and vases full of flowers – all to create a "British look". It's crammed at lunchtime and for dinner, though an upstairs room and a small terrace take the overflow in summer. You'll get a substantial meal for a modest €18, or €9 for a dish of the day. Dishes include chicken liver gâteau, *caillette* (a sort of haggis) with shallots and wine sauce, ravioli with cream and absinthe sauce, salmon fillet with anchovy butter and huge salads. Good value for money and the staff are welcoming.

◎ ⅍ |◎| Restaurant L'Épicerie

18 pl. Saint-Jean; it's next to Saint-Jean church.
☎04.75.42.74.46
Closed *Sat lunchtime; Sun; public holidays; Aug; Christmas to early Jan.* **Disabled access.**

It's some time since the grocer's shop closed, but the restaurant that took over the premises continues to flourish. Good, regional dishes are on offer: cream of lentil soup with diced foie gras, home-made crab-and-olive ravioli, red mullet

with aubergine caviar and *coulis* of velvet swimming crab, and diced roast lamb with Pavot blue cheese and Syrah wine sauce. Menus range from €23 to €58. When the weather's nice, you can sit on the terrace on a little square opposite an old covered market and be at peace with the world. *Free coffee offered to our readers on presentation of this guide.*

◎ |◎| Auberge du Pin

285 bis av. Victor Hugo; take the A7, then the Valence Sud exit to the town centre.
☎04.75.44.53.86
Open *daily all year.* **Disabled access.**

The *Maison Pic* is a four-star establishment with a Relais & Châteaux sign and prices to match; this next door *Auberge* is much more affordable, but all its delicious dishes come from its more up-market neighbour's kitchen. There's a *menu-carte* at €30, a starter plus main course package at €27 or a main course with dessert package at €25. The dishes change very frequently but the emphasis is always on rustic, aromatic local flavours. The bright yellow dining room is small, so you ought to reserve in autumn and winter when the terrace isn't open.

Valgorge
07110

◎ ⅍ 🏠 |◎| Hôtel Le Tanargue**

☎04.75.88.98.98 ☎04.75.88.96.09
⊛www.hotel-le-tanargue.com
Closed *Sun evening and Mon (early Oct to end Dec, except during Nov school holiday); Tues (mid-Nov to end Dec); evenings (25 Dec to mid-March).* **TV. Disabled access. High chairs and games available. Car park.**

Huddling at an altitude of 500m at the foot of the Tanargue massif on the edge of the Ardèche, this cosy hotel offers large pretty doubles for €41–55 with shower/wc or bath/wc. Ask for one with a view of the valley. There's a weekday lunch menu for €11.50 (starter, main course, dessert and coffee) then others at €14–28. Specialities include baked fillet of bass with *confit* of onions and poultry gravy, and beef fillet with Auvergne blue cheese. Portions are generous and particular care is paid to preparing the vegetable dishes. Wine is served by the glass. The dining room is vast, attractive, and decorated with attention to detail. Logis de France. *10% discount on the room rate (except July–Aug) offered to our readers on presentation of this guide.*

Valloire

73450

☕ 🏠 |◉| Hôtel Christiania**

☎04.79.59.00.57 📠04.79.59.00.06
🌐www.christiania-hotel.com
Closed *21 April–15 June; 15 Sept–10 Dec.*
TV. High chairs available. Pay car park.

Everyone in Valloire seems to drop in for a drink at the lively bar at some point during the day. They're all sports fans and express forthright views on stories in *L'Équipe*, the French daily sports paper. There's a relaxed, friendly, family atmosphere. The rooms are stylish with good facilities, and cost €49–63 with shower/wc or bath; a new suite with two bedrooms has recently been added. Half board, compulsory in winter, costs €55–70 per person. The big dining room next to the bar offers home cooking and great traditional dishes. Menus range from €16 to €30. Logis de France.

**☕ 🍴 🏠 |◉| Hôtel La Setaz
– Restaurant Le Gastilleur*****

Rue de la Vallée d'Or
☎04.79.59.01.03 📠04.79.59.00.63
🌐www.la-setaz.com
Closed *Mon lunchtime in summer; 20 April to early June; 20 Sept–20 Dec.* **TV. High chairs and games available. Swimming pool. Car park.**

Despite its unprepossessing exterior, this is a very classy place. The chef prepares the kind of dishes that take his French customers back to their childhood and adapts them to suit modern tastes. You will find some of his specialities on the menus at €20 (weekday menu) and €27–37. Service is flawless and you'll get a pleasant welcome. In summer they open the heated swimming pool and often have barbecues in the peaceful garden. The hotel rooms are starkly contemporary, but they face due south and some have balconies or terraces. Doubles with shower/wc or bath cost €55–90, depending on the season. Half board is compulsory in winter and costs €55–63 per person. *Free coffee offered to our readers on presentation of this guide.*

☕ |◉| L'Asile des Fondues

Rue des Grandes Alpes; it's near the church

and the tourist office.
☎04.79.59.04.71
Closed *1 May–26 June; 1 Sept–18 Dec.*

The restaurant has a charming country dining room with lots of style. The welcome you get is so lovely that you'll be tempted to come back time and time again – if you can cope with the touristy bits, that is. They offer hearty specialities like fondue, *raclette* (to order) and *diot*, the local pork and vegetable sausages in white wine. You can eat for €19–27 à la carte.

Vallon-Pont-d'Arc

07150

☕ 🍴 🏠 Hôtel des Sites**

In Salavas, very close to Vallon; follow the road to Salavas-Barjac; it's 500m after the bridge, on the left.
☎04.75.88.00.85 📠04.75.88.44.60
High chairs available.

This hotel, recently taken over by a friendly young couple, has rapidly gained a new lease of life. The refurbished rooms are attractive, with sponge-painted walls, individualized friezes and tasteful furniture. They offer good value for money at €35–47 for a double, depending on the season and degree of comfort; the most expensive ones have a terrace. Ask for a room overlooking the countryside rather than the street. A restaurant is available to the guests of this spruce, inviting hotel. *Free house apéritif offered to our readers on presentation of this guide.*

☕ 🏠 Hôtel Clos des Bruyères

Route des Gorges; it's just on the outskirts of Vallon, 100m from the roundabout, on the left, going towards Saint-Montan.
☎04.75.37.18.85 📠04.75.37.14.89
🌐www.closdesbruyeres.com
Closed *Tues; Wed lunchtime (except July and Aug); early Oct to end of March.* **Disabled access. Car park. Swimming pool.**

A modern-looking, standardized type of building by the side of the road, this hotel offers good facilities. Behind it there are nice green spaces with trees. Though the rooms are functional they have a touch of individuality. Doubles, depending on the facilities and the season, cost €46–57. Some have a view of the garden and the four swimming pools; avoid those that overlook the route des Gorges.

ⓒ |●| Restaurant Le Chelsea

Boulevard Peschère-Alizon; it's on the main street.
℡04.75.88.01.40
Closed *Oct–April.*

An Ardèche version of a trendy young restaurant. The little dining room, which leads out onto the garden, is decorated with pictures of cartoon characters. Salads (€7–10) are the Chelsea's thing, but they've added a few cooked dishes to their repertoire: Camembert salad with raspberries, duck breast with honey and mint, *croustillant* of salmon with curry. There's a menu at €20. A reliable place.

Vagnas
07150 (11km SW)

ⓒ ⌖ ▥ La Bastide d'Iris

It's 300m after Vagnas, on the right, going in the direction of Barjac.
℡04.75.88.44.77 ℻04.75.38.61.29
ⓦwww.labastidediris.com
Closed *Jan.* **Disabled access. TV. Swimming pool. Car park.**

Elegance, calm, space and serenity: these are the watchwords in this recently opened hotel with a hint of Provence about it. The attractively coloured rooms (yellow, ochre, mauve, green, etc) all have their own distinctive décor and atmosphere, which the cordial owner will not hesitate to modify whenever he receives a flash of inspiration. Double rooms cost €62–84, according to the season and the degree of comfort. You can have breakfast or admire the sunsets on the attractive terrace overlooking the vineyards. *5% discount on the room rate (except July–Aug) offered to our readers on presentation of this guide.*

Saint-Martin-d'Ardèche
07700 (22km SE)

ⓒ ⌖ ▥ |●| Hôtel-restaurant Le Bellevue**

Quai de l'Ardèche; take the D290 in the direction of Pont-Saint-Esprit.
℡04.75.04.66.72. ℻04.75.04.61.37
ⓦwww.hotel-bellevue-restaurant.com
Closed *15 Oct–1 April.* **TV. High chairs available. Swimming pool. Car park.**

The Bellevue has an elevated dining room and the terrace overlooks the port. The atmosphere is easy-going and they serve Ardèche specialities without frills – terrine,

various fish dishes, *caillette* with boiled potatoes and *crème caramel.* It's a nice, popular place. Menus range from €17 to €24. The rooms have been refurbished and are of superior quality, clean, with warm colours and air-conditioning; doubles cost €43 with shower/wc. Logis de France. *Free house apéritif offered to our readers on presentation of this guide.*

Orgnac-l'Aven
07150 (23km SE)

ⓒ ⌖ ▥ |●| Hôtel de l'Aven***

Place de la Mairie; take the D579 then the D217.
℡04.75.38.61.80 ℻04.75.38.66.39
ⓦwww.aven-sarrazin.com
Restaurant closed *Mon (except in season); Feb.* **Closed** *mid-Nov to Easter.* **TV. High chairs available. Car park.**

The attentive owner welcomes you to his simple establishment. The corridors and rooms smell fresh; some of the rooms are colourful, those facing south have balconies. Doubles with shower/wc or bath cost €44–47; half board is worth considering. The straightforward and unaffected regional cooking is served in a rustic-style dining room or on the terrace. Menus are €17–26. Logis de France. *10% discount on the room rate (in low season) offered to our readers on presentation of this guide.*

Valmorel
73260

ⓒ ▥ |●| Chalet du Crey**

Les Avanchers, hameau du Crey; take the D95; it's around 10km to the southeast of Moûtiers, below the ski resort.
℡04.79.09.87.00 ℻04.79.09.89.51
ⓦwww.chalet-du-crey.com
Closed *20 April–31 May; 30 Sept–20 Dec.* **Disabled access. TV. High chairs available. Swimming pool. Car park.**

A classic family-run chalet in an authentic mountain hamlet. Everyone knows how to give you a warm welcome. Rooms are well appointed; doubles with shower/wc or bath cost €38–45 in summer. Half board, compulsory during the February school holiday, costs €39–53 per person per night. There are family rooms for four to five people, available too. In the restaurant, menus, which list mountain dishes, cost €12 and €18. À la carte, you

can choose from a range of Savoy specialities, and you'll spend about €30. The vast
swimming pool, open in summer, is rather
unusual – it's inflatable.

☺ ⅍ |O| Restaurant Le Ski Roc

Le Bourg-Morel; it's in a pedestrianized street
off the main street.
☎04.79.09.83.17
Closed *25 April–20 June; 5 Sept–15 Dec.*
Open *until midnight.* **High chairs available.**

This is the place to eat in Valmorel. The
wine bar is decorated in a discreetly baroque
style, and they dish up good food, with
mountain specialities and some modern
choices. Take a nice glass of local wine with
a toasted sandwich. There are menus for
€14 (lunchtime only) and €23. Covered
and heated terrace. *Free house liqueur offered
to our readers on presentation of this guide.*

Léchère (La)
73260 (12km N)

☺ ⅍ |O| Restaurant La Vieille
Forge

Bellecombe; take the D95 and the D97 in the
direction of Albertville.
☎04.79.24.17.97
Closed *Tues (except July–Aug); Feb.* **Open**
*7.30pm–midnight (until 4am Fri–Sat); in
summer open every lunchtime and evening
until 4am.* **Disabled access. Games available. Car park.**

You won't find the usual stultified spa
town atmosphere in this restaurant. It used
to be a blacksmith's, and the décor features some of the old smithy equipment.
Tasty, traditional cooking, Savoy specialities, meat dishes in sauce, mushrooms and
duck breast are listed on the set menus at
€10.50–40; some of these include wine.
You'll pay around €18 for a menu à
la carte. There's live music every Friday
and they're open very late – until 4am
in summer. *Free house apéritif, coffee, house
liqueur, fruit juice or soft drink offered to our
readers on presentation of this guide.*

Vals-les-Bains
07600

☺ 🛏 |O| Hôtel Saint-Jean**

112 bis, rue Jean-Jaurès; it's right in the town
centre, slightly set back from the road, on the
banks of the River Voltour.

☎04.75.37.42.50 ☎04.75.37.54.77
🌐www.guideweb.com/ardeche/hotel/saint-jean
Closed *Nov to mid-April.* **TV. Car park.**

A tall nineteenth-century building with a
slightly sad exterior but an exuberant welcome and comfortable rooms. They have
all been renovated and are lovely, though
some of them are quite small. Doubles
cost €49–60 with shower/wc or bath/wc.
There's a big dining room with wide bay
windows offering menus for €14.90–25.
It's a classic-style place that offers peace
and quiet. Nice welcome.

☺ ⅍ 🛏 |O| Grand Hôtel de Lyon***

11 av. Paul-Ribeyre.
☎04.75.37.43.70 ☎04.75.37.59.11
🌐www.sud.ardeche.com/tourism/ohi
Closed *Oct to end April.* **Disabled access.
TV. High chairs available. Swimming pool.**

A solid, serious hotel built at the beginning of
the twentieth century, it's a place that won't
let you down. The rooms are big, painted
in pastel shades and well maintained. The
bedding is cosy and smells of roses. Doubles
cost €55–82, and half board is also available.
The swimming pool has a wave machine
and a waterfall, plus it's heated. There's a
TV room, a billiards room and a pretty little
dining room serving honest, fortifying dishes
of quality food. Menus are at €15 (weekday
lunchtime) and then €20–40. Free covered
garage for motorbikes. Logis de France. *Free
house apéritif offered at the restaurant to our readers on presentation of this guide.*

☺ 🛏 |O| Hôtel-restaurant Le
Vivarais

5 rue Claude Expilly.
☎04.75.94.65.85 ☎04.75.37.65.47
Closed *Feb.* **TV. Swimming pool. Car park.**

Easy to find, this is the most beautiful
building in town and it's painted pink.
Since 1930, they have been perfecting the
art of providing good beds and good food
for their guests. The décor is Art Deco,
from the wallpaper and the colours to
the furniture and even some of the baths.
Doubles go for €78–98 (including breakfast), with shower/wc or bath. The standard at table is just as high and Madame
is a wonderful advocate for her region's
cuisine. Menus range from €35 to €58.

☺ |O| Restaurant Chez Mireille

3 rue Jean-Jaurès; it's at the end of the main
road, next to the Town Hall.

☎04.75.37.49.06
Closed *Tues and Wed evenings out of season; a week in early Nov.* **High chairs available.**

Chez Mireille is run by Colette, whose cooking is highly recommended. Everything is prepared in her kitchen – it may seem odd to have to say this, but it's not always the case in other establishments. The filling *menu ardéchois* has two starters, and is simply superb. While the cooking is certainly respectful of tradition, there's something individual about it, too. Menus cost €10–28.

Vans (Les)
07140

⊛ ⅍ ☎ |●| Hôtel Les Cévennes
Place Ollier; it's in the main square.
☎04.75.37.23.09
Closed *Sun evening and Mon; first fortnight in May; first fortnight in Oct.* **Car park.**

From the minute you walk in, you're aware of a very special atmosphere – a sort of gentle madness that's infected the place for nigh-on forty years, tempered with the straight talking of the *patronne* Marie-Renée. The highly individual décor is a real jumble, with flowers, paintings, photos and old documents all jostling for space. The restaurant serves generous portions of crêpes from the Cévennes, *coq au vin*, and many regional dishes. There are set menus at €17–30. It is undoubtedly better-known for its cooking than as a hotel, but its double rooms with basin go for €25, with shower and wc on the landing. Half board is compulsory in summer at €32 per person. *Free coffee offered to our readers on presentation of this guide.*

⊛ ⅍ ☎ Hôtel Le Mas de l'Espaïre**
Bois de Païolive; it's 5km from Les Vans, in the direction of the bois de Païolive.
☎04.75.94.95.01 ☎04.75.37.21.00
⊛www.hotel-espaire.fr
Closed *mid-Nov to mid-March.* **Disabled access. TV. Swimming pool. Car park.**

There's a sense of calm in this sturdy, imposing building in a splendid setting, and you're put at your ease by the excellent welcome. All the facilities you need for a good stay are here: lots of space inside and out, a swimming pool and even cicadas chirruping in the background.

Doubles go for €65–82, depending on the size and the season. You can go on wonderful walks through the magical Païolive forest, which adjoins the property. *Free house apéritif offered to our readers on presentation of this guide.*

⊛ ⅍ |●| La Rose des Vans
11 rue des Bourgades.
☎04.75.37.38.05
Closed *Wed lunchtime in season; Tues evening and Wed out of season; Jan–March.* **Open** *Fri and Sat in autumn and in winter.*

This is a pleasant restaurant that pays tribute to local produce while also adding a few Oriental touches. There are menus for €12.50–15, and platters at €12-13. The dining room may be a bit spartan, but there's a little courtyard hidden in the back that more than makes up for it – not to mention the striking toilets, where the owners have really splashed out. *Free house apéritif offered to our readers on presentation of this guide.*

⊛ |●| Restaurant Le Grangousier
Rue Courte; it's opposite the church.
☎04.75.94.90.86
Closed *Wed (July–Aug); Tues out of season; 1 Jan–14 Feb; 1–15 Dec.* **High chairs available.**

This stylish restaurant serves daily menus and gourmet menus that will delight even the most ardent foodie. The cooking is imaginative – salad of pan-fried foie gras with chestnuts and *vacherin* with chestnuts. The dining room, with its vaulted ceiling and dressed stone walls, is the perfect setting for these wonderful delicacies and although the place is smart, prices are fair, with menus costing €18–52. The dish of the day changes daily. The wine list includes a number of very affordable local vintages.

Venosc
38520

⊛ ☎ |●| Hôtel-restaurant Les Amis de la Montagne*
Le Courtil; towards Grenoble, take N91 in the direction of Briançon; in Les Clapiers, take the D530; or take the cable car from Les Deux-Alpes.
☎04.76.11.10.00 ☎04.76.80.20.56
⊛www.hotel-venosc-deux-alpes.com
Closed *lunchtime in winter except weekends;*

*in summer, closed only Mon lunch; 15 April–
20 June; 8 Sept–20 Dec.* **TV. High chairs
available. Swimming pool.**

What the Durdan clan don't know about
Venosc, a little mountain village 1000m up,
isn't worth knowing. They run hotels, cottages, restaurants, shops and boutiques, give
skiing lessons and rent out rooms. Most of
their efforts, however, are focused on this
hotel, which is a sheer delight if you're after
peace and quiet. Rooms go for €55–86
(depending on the degree of comfort and
the season) with shower/wc or bath, some
with balconies; half board costs €50–68
per person. Copious breakfast. You dine
in the grillroom, which has lots of atmosphere. Menus, from €17, list regional food:
the speciality is *grenaillade* (potatoes with
Saint-Marcellin, a mild goat's cheese) but
you'll also find *tartiflette*, trout with walnuts,
fondues and *raclette*. The desserts look good
and taste even better. The hotel has a pool,
a Turkish bath and a sauna.

Vienne

38200

◎ 🏠 **Hôtel de La Poste****

47 cours Romestang
☎04.74.85.02.04 ℻04.74.85.16.17
TV.

This hotel has been totally renovated but
has managed to preserve its old-fashioned
charm. Its 36 rooms are undoubtedly
the finest in the town centre (the only
ones, in fact, apart from the chain hotel
by the station), so the fact that this hotel
dating back over a century has reopened
is very good news for the town. The
extremely comfortable double rooms cost
€50 (with shower) and €55 (with bath).
Unfortunately, the service can be erratic.

◎ |●| **Restaurant L'Estancot**

4 rue de la Table-Ronde.
☎04.74.85.12.09
Closed *Sun; Mon; public holidays; first
fortnight in Sept; Christmas to mid-Jan.*
Disabled access.

Situated in a quiet side street in the
old town near the Saint-André-le-Bas
church, *L'Estancot* has a pretty façade with
window boxes laden with flowers and a
long, beautiful dining room. Menus are
at €12.50 (weekday lunchtimes), €16
and €24. The house specialities are *criques*

(made with potatoes, chopped parsley
and eggs – only served evenings and Sat
lunch), and *paillassons* (plain potatoes)
accompanied by all sorts of delicious
things. Other delights include sea-urchin
flan with shellfish sauce, calves kidneys
with walnut wine and pears poached in
vanilla with caramel sauce. Super-fast
service. It is essential to book.

Estrablin
38780 (8km E)

◎ 🎿 🏠 **La Gabetière*****

Take the D502; it's on the left after the crossroads leading to Estrablin.
☎04.74.58.01.31 ℻04.74.58.08.98
Closed *1–10 Jan.* **TV. High chairs and
games available. Swimming pool. Car
park.**

You'll want to hide away forever in this
lovely, luxurious sixteenth-century stone
manor house – especially if you get a room
with a view of the grounds. The décor
is exquisitely tasteful and the welcome
is simple, warm and attentive. Rooms
cost €51–62 with bath, depending on
the season; a flat in the tower sleeps four.
There's a welcoming bar-cum-TV room,
a swimming pool and tables in the garden
where you can have your picnic. This
really is an unusually lovely place and the
charming *patronne* will give you all sorts of
information about what to see. *Free house
apéritif, fruit juice or soft drink offered to our
readers on presentation of this guide.*

Villard-de-Lans

38250

◎ 🏠 **Villa Primerose****

147 av. des Bains; it's 800m from the town
centre.
☎04.76.95.13.17 ℻04.76.95.19.07
🌐www.hotel-villa-primerose.com
Closed *1–30 April; 1 Oct–20 Dec.* **High
chairs available. Car park.**

Here's a place where they really make
you feel welcome. The quiet rooms in
this beautiful building look out onto the
Gerbier mountain range. You'll pay €25–
34 for a double with basin, or €40–45
with shower/wc; they have two communicating rooms, ideal for families. There's
no restaurant, but the owner lets residents
use the kitchens to cook meals that they
can eat in the dining room. The breakfast,

at €4.50, must be booked in advance; it's served as a buffet in the high season.

⌚ 🕭 🏠 |◉| À la Ferme du Bois Barbu**

It's 3km from the centre, going in the direction of Bois-Barbu.
☎04.76.95.13.09 🖷04.76.94.10.65
🖳www.fermeboisbarbu.com
Closed first week of Easter school holiday; third week in June; 15 Nov–7 Dec.
Restaurant closed Wed; Sun evening. **TV.**
High chairs and games available. Car park.

A real mountain inn on the edge of a forest and next to a not very busy road. You can sit on the lovely terrace or relax in a nice comfy armchair while Nadine, your hostess, plays the piano. The eight small rooms go for €52 (less out of season) with shower/wc; they've all been recently renovated. Half board is compulsory in high season at €50 per person. This place is ideal for cross-country skiers, since the trails are just nearby, as well as for hikers and mountain bikers. Menus, €16–28, list delicious local dishes that change according to the seasons: terrine of Bleu du Vercors cheese and hazelnuts, trout *rillettes*, bacon and oyster mushrooms in flaky pastry, local pork with onion marmalade and hazelnut *confit*, semi-cooked foie gras with wine, veal stuffed with nuts. It is advisable to book. *10% discount on the room rate (out of season) offered to our readers on presentation of this guide.*

⌚ 🏠 Les Bruyères**

31 rue Victor-Hugo.
☎04.76.95.11.83 🖷04.76.95.58.76
Open mid-Dec to early April; mid-April to mid-Oct. **TV.**

This hotel in the town centre was in dire need of an overhaul, and that is exactly what it has received; the new owners have even managed to endow it with a prestige that it never had before. The new mountain-style décor, based on pale wood, is warm and inviting, while the eighteen totally refurbished (and no-smoking) rooms are extremely comfortable and cost €56 for a double. Add to all that enchanting service and a superb breakfast buffet, and the recipe for success is complete. Logis de France.

⌚ ⌚ 🏠 Le Dauphin**

220 av. du Général-de-Gaulle; it's opposite the tourist office, set back a little from the square.

☎04.76.95.95.25 🖷04.76.95.56.33
🖳www.hotel-le-dauphin-vercors.com
Closed 15–30 April; 1–10 Oct. **TV.**

This is a friendly, efficiently run hotel with a family atmosphere that appeals to young and old alike. The rooms, which have recently been refurbished, are quiet and attractive – some of them enjoy a view of the fir trees. Doubles with shower or bath cost €58–64, depending on the season. *8% discount on the room rate after two consecutive nights (except during August and the winter holidays) offered to our readers on presentation of this guide.*

⌚ |◉| Les Alpages

67 rue de la République.
☎04.76.95.91.56
Closed Tues; Wed; during Easter school holiday; a fortnight from end June to mid-July; a fortnight in Oct; a week at Christmas.

This is a new restaurant, distinguished by the quality of both its service and food. The young owners are particularly keen on promoting local produce and recipes on the menus (€12–16), and so offer ravioli in a number of combinations, as well as different types of fondues and *raclettes*, and the famous local speciality of *vercouline*, a local variant of *raclette* prepared with Sassenage blue cheese.

⌚ ⌚ |◉| Malaterre

Lieu-dit Malaterre; from Villard, take the D215C, shortly after Bois-Barbu turn onto the forest road and follow the signs to Malaterre.
☎04.76.95.04.34
Open daily noon–6pm (July–Aug and mid-Dec to end of March); Fri evening (July–Aug); Sun only (Sept–Oct and April–June).

An excellent restaurant in an old wooden house in the forest. The building dates from the 1900s; there's no electricity and water is still brought up by tanker. Lydia and Bernard, who run a farm nearby, decided to revive this place by providing good food and drink for cross-country skiers and walkers – in winter, it can only be reached with snowshoes or skis. There's a fantastic variety of foresters' implements ornamenting the walls, and the atmosphere is genuinely warm. When the weather's fine it's wonderful to sit out on the terrace, and when it's cold you can warm your hands around a bowl of good vegetable soup and munch on home-made bread baked in the wood-fired oven. Menus, €12.50 and €18, list genuine regional cuisine which relies on fresh produce from the farm; try the Vercors platter, ravioli de Royans, *caillette*, blue Vercors cheese, mushroom omelette, charcuterie, *gratiné* of ravioli with oyster mushrooms and ceps or fillet of smoked trout. And leave space for pudding: there's home-made spice cake with honey and *tarte tatin*. To drink, you can choose between the local *rataplane* (sold by the litre), cider and local apple juice. On Friday evenings in summer, your hosts recount the legends of the Vercors around the fire. Credit cards not accepted. *Free house liqueur offered to our readers on presentation of this guide.*

Corrençon-en-Vercors

38250 (6km S)

ⓒ ♠ |●| Le Caribou

Le Clos de la Balme. Take the D215C; it's 2km after the golf course, practically at the foot of the ski runs.
☎04.76.95.82.82 ⊕04.76.95.83.17
ⓦwww.caribou-vercors.com
Closed *1 Oct–1 Dec; 1 March–5 May.* **High chairs and games available. Swimming pool. Car park.**

The rooms are painted in yellow, green or red and all have en-suite bathrooms and telephone. Costing €45, they can sleep two to three people (or even more in some cases). The restaurant has a lovely wooden floor and is decorated with souvenirs from Africa and Indonesia. Menus, which change frequently, range in price from €10 (lunchtime) to €26. The owners are lovely and they create a good-humoured atmosphere. There's lots to do: swimming pool, sauna, kids' games, ping-pong, painting class, and even a cabaret at apéritif time, as well as the "Festival from one Sunday to another", which takes place in the first week in August (ⓦwww.festival-dimanche.com). It's great for young families.

ⓒ ⅍ ♠ |●| Hôtel du Golf – Restaurant du Blois Fleuri***

It's on the D215C between the golf course and the centre of the village.
☎04.76.95.84.84 ⊕04.76.95.82.85
ⓦwww.planete-vercors.com/hotel-du-golf
Closed *Mon–Fri lunchtimes; April; 1 Nov–20 Dec.* **TV. High chairs and games available. Swimming pool. Car park.**

This old farmhouse was restored by the present owners' grandparents and they've recently had it renovated. There's nothing to match it in the luxury category in town. It offers a dozen rooms, some with a balcony and some sleeping up to five (reckon on €15 for each extra person). They're individually decorated and cosy with the bathroom and separate wc off the spacious entrance hall; wood panelling and dried flowers complete the picture. And those added extras are provided – mini-bar and dressing gowns. You'll pay €100–125 for a double room with bath, depending on the season. The restaurant opens up onto the terrace in good weather. Menus are €30–40. In the grounds there's a heated swimming pool and sauna. *One free breakfast per room offered to our readers on presentation of this guide.*

Rencurel

38680 (15km NW)

ⓒ ⅍ ♠ |●| Hôtel le Marronnier**

Take the D531 for 12km, then turn right on to the D35.
☎04.76.38.97.68 ⊕04.76.38.98.99
ⓦwww.hotellemarronnier.com
Closed *1 Nov–20 Dec; in winter, open only after prior reservation.* **Disabled access. TV. High chairs available. Swimming pool.**

A typical Vercors house belonging to a Dutch couple. All the rooms, which are located either in the main building or in the more sombre annexe, have en-suite bathrooms; nos. 1 and 2 have large terraces overlooking the solar-heated swimming pool. The bedding is high quality, though the doubles have single mattresses with individual duvets. Doubles cost €46–50, depending on the season. There's also a sauna, and a sitting room with a fireplace, library and TV. The cuisine is typical of the region, with a touch of the Mediterranean. There's a lunch menu at €17.50, with another at €21.50. *Free house apéritif or coffee offered to our readers on presentation of this guide.*

Villars-les-Dombes

01330

ⓒ |●| Restaurant L'Écu de France

105 rue du Commerce; it's on the main street, near to the church.
☎04.74.98.01.79

A traditional restaurant serving regional dishes – lots of Bresse chicken but also parsleyed frogs' legs and duck breast. It's an affordable place to eat in this somewhat touristy town: the weekday lunchtime menu is at €18.50, with others going up to €36. Old photographs of the town hang on the wall.

Bouligneux

01130 (4km NW)

@ 🏂 |●| Le Thou

Take the D2, the Chatillon-sur-Chalaronne road.
☏04.74.98.15.25
Closed *Mon; Tues; 2–23 Feb; 1–14 Oct.*
Disabled access.

An appealing restaurant in a village with a mere twenty inhabitants. The dining room walls are hung with a variety of pictures, and there's a mature garden with a terrace. The chef's speciality is carp served in many delicious guises: salad of smoked carp and quail's eggs, flaky pastry with carp and lobster *bisque*. The cheeses and the desserts are perfect and the wine list is splendid. It's a good idea to reserve, especially in summer. Menus cost €27–49, or expect to pay around €46 à la carte, including wine. *Free coffee offered to our readers on presentation of this guide.*

Joyeux

01800 (8km SE)

@ |●| La Bicyclette Bleue

Take the D904 for 7km and then turn right.
☏04.74.98.21.48
Closed *Tues evening and Wed (except July–Aug); mid-Dec to mid-Jan.* **Disabled access. High chairs and games available.**

An isolated country restaurant in a renovated farmhouse. It's fresh and friendly and efficiently run by a family and their donkey d'Artagnan. It's a lovely place to have lunch – fine in the dining room but even better under the awning. There are lots of unpretentious local dishes, which are attentively prepared and thoughtfully cooked: farmhouse chicken with cream sauce, carp fillet with sorrel, fresh frogs' legs. The lunch menu is €10, with other menus €18–33. Try the house cocktail made with sparkling Bugey wine. You can

rent a bike and take off through the countryside. Kids, especially, will love it.

Monthieux

01390 (9km SW)

@ 🏠 |●| Hôtel et Golf du Gouverneur-Restaurant Le Club House***

Château du Breuil; take the D904 as far as Lapeyrouse, then the D6 towards Lyon.
☏04.72.26.42.00 ☏04.72.26.42.20
🌐www.bestwestern.com/fr
Disabled access. TV. Swimming pool. Car park.

Golf lovers are in their element here. The 500-acre grounds, complete with ponds, rivers, immaculately tended lawns and three golf courses, provide the setting for the 53-room hotel (on the site of an old staging post), a swimming pool, a gourmet restaurant and, above all, the cheaper Club House, where golfers can recall the trials and tribulations of their rounds, eating on the terrace or in the park if weather permits. The gourmet restaurant is often closed at lunch, so phone first; it offers a menu at €32, while the Club House (open for lunch only) has a dish of the day at €10.50 and set menus at €13 and €16. In the hotel, double rooms cost €85–100, depending on the season.

Ambérieux-en-Dombes

01330 (11km W)

@ 🏂 🏠 |●| Auberge des Bichonnières**

Take the D904 at the edge of town off the road to Ars.
☏04.74.00.82.07 ☏04.74.00.89.61
🌐www.aubergedesbichonnieres.com
Closed *Mon and Tues lunchtimes in season; Sun evening, Mon and Tues lunchtimes (Oct–June); 15 Dec–15 Jan.* **TV. High chairs available. Car park.**

A very pleasant family hotel-restaurant in a lovely farm. There are pleasant, recently refurbished cosy rooms with beams, costing €50–60 with shower/wc or bath. The dining room is decorated in woody tones and there's a patio that's festooned with flowers in summer. Genuine gourmet cuisine is generously and elegantly served; classic dishes include frog casserole, chicken-liver gateau with crayfish tails, chicken *en cocotte* with cream and *gratin d'andouillette* with fried potatoes and onions. The express set weekday lunch, comprising a dish of the day and dessert, costs €15, and there are others at €24–€34, which change with the seasons. *Free house apéritif offered to our readers on presentation of this guide.*

Sainte-Croix
01120 (14km SE)

⟪ 🏠 |O| Chez Nous**

Take the D2 towards Montluel until the junction with the D61, with signposts to the village.
☎04.78.06.60.60 📠04.78.06.63.26
Closed *Sun evening, Mon and Tues (1 Oct–31 March)*. **Disabled access. High chairs available. Car park.**

Set well back from the road in the countryside, this comfortable establishment offers very quiet, comfortable rooms in a modern annexe; doubles cost €47. Though you can get traditional cuisine, they also list interesting variations on the regional theme. Specialities include fresh frogs' legs, free-range poultry with morels and cream, home-made duck foie gras and sea fish. Menus start at €20 (weekdays), with others at €25–46. Logis de France.

Ars-sur-Formans
01480 (19km W)

⟪ 🎿 🏠 |O| Hôtel-Restaurant La Bonne Étoile

Rue J.-M.-Vianney; take the D904, opposite the main car park.
☎04.74.00.77.38 📠04.74.08.10.18
Closed *Mon evening; Tues; Jan*. **TV**.

This village is where the relics of Saint Curé are to be found and it attracts many pilgrims. When the Pope visited, he had a meal in this very restaurant – the plate he used is hung up outside the door. It's a welcoming establishment, and the clean rooms smell delicious. Doubles cost €40 with shower/wc. The owner collects all sorts of knick-knacks – dolls and coffee pots in particular. The dishes are simple and unpretentious – mussel soup, pike-perch with vanilla, chicken with *vin jaune* – with menus from €12 (weekdays) up to €28. Reserve in advance, especially in the pilgrimage season. *10% discount on the room rate offered to our readers on presentation of this guide.*

Viviers
07220

⟪ |O| Restaurant de l'Horloge

Faubourg le Cire; it's on the N86, on the left going south.
☎04.75.52.62.43
Closed *Sun evening; Mon; 20 Dec–20 Jan*. **Disabled access.**

When you see the neon signs, it's hard to believe what awaits inside. The dining room is vast and decorated by huge murals from the nineteenth century, painted by passing artists. The robust, tasty Ardèche cooking is prepared using fresh market produce. You eat well and cheaply: the dish of the day, served at lunch and dinner, is €7, while three menus range from €10 (a bargain) up to €19.

Vonnas
01540

⟪ |O| L'Ancienne Auberge

Place du Marché.
☎04.74.50.90.50
Closed *Jan*. **Disabled access. High chairs available.**

Vonnas is the home town of star chef Georges Blanc – his own restaurant is across the road from this old inn, still run by his family. It's full of old family photographs and collections of bottles, and is opposite a romantic little wooden bridge over the Veyle. In summer you can enjoy the terrace and patio at the back. The service is polite, efficient and swift. You start with an appetizer and delicious cocktail, setting you up for your meal and the local regional wines. The recipes and produce come from the region: chicken liver and morels in pastry and sautéed frogs' legs "comme en Dombes", for example. And the prices are reasonable: the weekday lunchtime menu costs €18 and the others, at €27–40, are simply amazing value. It's a tad over-commercialized – lots of "Blanc" produce on sale – but it's still superb.

22

French food glossary

Basic terms

l'addition	bill/check	lait	milk
beurre	butter	moutarde	mustard
bio or biologique	organic	œuf	egg
bouteille	bottle	offert	free
chauffé	heated	pain	bread
couteau	knife	pimenté	spicy
cru	raw	plat	main course
cuillère	spoon	poivre	pepper
cuit	cooked	salé	salted/savoury
emballé	wrapped	sel	salt
à emporter	takeaway	sucre	sugar
formule	lunchtime set menu	sucré	sweet
fourchette	fork	table	table
fumé	smoked	verre	glass
huile	oil	vinaigre	vinegar

Snacks

un sandwich/une baguette	a sandwich		salad, tuna, anchovies and olive oil
au jambon	with ham		
au fromage	with cheese	panini	toasted Italian sandwich
au saucisson	with sausage		
à l'ail	with garlic	tartine	buttered bread or open sandwich
au poivre	with pepper		
au pâté (de campagne)	with pâté (country-style)	œufs	eggs
croque-monsieur	grilled cheese and ham sandwich	au plat	fried
		à la coque	boiled
croque-madame	grilled cheese and bacon, sausage, chicken or egg sandwich	durs	hard-boiled
		brouillés	scrambled
		omelette	omelette
		nature	plain
pain bagnat	bread roll with egg, olives,	aux fines herbes	with herbs
		au fromage	with cheese

Pasta (pâtes), pancakes (crêpes) and flans (tartes)

nouilles	noodles	raviolis	pasta parcels of meat or chard – a
pâtes fraîches	fresh pasta		

	Provençal, not Italian invention	pissaladière	tart of fried onions with anchovies and black olives
crêpe au sucre/aux œufs	pancake with sugar/ eggs	tarte flambée	thin pizza-like pastry topped with onion, cream and bacon or other combinations
galette	buckwheat pancake		
socca	thin chickpea flour pancake		
panisse	thick chickpea flour pancake		

Soups (soupes)

baudroie	fish soup with vegetables, garlic and herbs	potage	thick vegetable soup
bisque	shellfish soup	potée auvergnate	cabbage and meat soup
bouillabaisse	soup with five fish	rouille	red pepper, garlic and saffron mayonnaise served with fish soup
bouillon	broth or stock		
bourride	thick fish soup		
consommé	clear soup	soupe à l'oignon	onion soup with rich cheese topping
garbure	potato, cabbage and meat soup		
pistou	parmesan, basil and garlic paste added to soup	velouté	thick soup, usually fish or poultry

Starters (hors d'œuvres)

assiette anglaise	plate of cold meats	crudités	raw vegetables with dressings
assiette composée	mixed salad plate, usually cold meat and vegetables	hors d'œuvres	combination of the above plus smoked or marinated fish

Fish (poisson), seafood (fruits de mer) and shellfish (crustaces or coquillages)

aiglefin	small haddock or fresh cod	congre	conger eel
		coques	cockles
anchois	anchovies	coquilles St-Jacques	scallops
anguilles	eels		
barbue	brill	crabe	crab
baudroie	monkfish or anglerfish	crevettes grises	shrimp
bigourneau	periwinkle	crevettes roses	prawns
brème	bream	daurade	sea bream
bulot	whelk	éperlan	smelt or whitebait
cabillaud	cod	escargots	snails
calmar	squid	favou(ille)	tiny crab
carrelet	plaice	flétan	halibut
claire	type of oyster	friture	assorted fried fish
colin	hake	gambas	king prawns

hareng	herring	oursin	sea urchin
homard	lobster	palourdes	clams
huîtres	oysters	poissons de roche	fish from shoreline rocks
langouste	spiny lobster		
langoustines	saltwater crayfish (scampi)	praires	small clams
		raie	skate
limande	lemon sole	rouget	red mullet
lotte de mer	monkfish	saumon	salmon
loup de mer	sea bass	sole	sole
maquereau	mackerel	thon	tuna
merlan	whiting	truite	trout
moules (marinières)	mussels (with shallots in white wine sauce)	turbot	turbot
		violet	sea squirt

Fish dishes and terms

aïoli	garlic mayonnaise served with salt cod and other fish	grillé	grilled
		hollandaise	butter and vinegar sauce
anchoïade	anchovy paste or sauce	à la meunière	in a butter, lemon and parsley sauce
arête	fish bone	mousse/mousseline	mousse
assiette de pêcheur	assorted fish	pané	breaded
beignet	fritter	poutargue	mullet roe paste
darne	fillet or steak	raïto	red wine, olive, caper, garlic and shallot sauce
la douzaine	a dozen		
frit	fried		
friture	deep-fried small fish	quenelles	light dumplings
fumé	smoked	thermidor	lobster grilled in its shell with cream sauce
fumet	fish stock		
gigot de mer	large fish baked whole		

Meat (*viande*) and poultry (*volaille*)

agneau (de pré-salé)	lamb (grazed on salt marshes)	coquelet	cockerel
		dinde/dindon	turkey
andouille/ andouillette	tripe sausage	entrecôte	rib steak
		faux filet	sirloin steak
bavette	French cut of beef equivalent to flank	foie	liver
		foie gras	(duck/goose) liver
bifteck	steak	gibier	game
bœuf	beef	gigot (d'agneau)	leg (of lamb)
boudin blanc	sausage of white meats	grenouilles (cuisses de)	frogs (legs)
boudin noir	black pudding	grillade	grilled meat
caille	quail	hâchis	chopped meat or mince hamburger
canard	duck		
caneton	duckling	langue	tongue
contrefilet	sirloin roast	lapin/lapereau	rabbit/young rabbit

lard/lardons	bacon/diced bacon	poussin	baby chicken
lièvre	hare	ris	sweetbreads
merguez	spicy, red sausage	rognons	kidneys
mouton	mutton	rognons blancs	testicles
museau de veau	calf's muzzle	sanglier	wild boar
oie	goose	steak	steak
onglet	French cut of beef steak that makes a prime steak	tête de veau	calf's head (in jelly)
		tournedos	thick slices of fillet
		tripes	tripe
os	bone	tripoux	mutton tripe
poitrine	breast	veau	veal
porc	pork	venaison	venison
poulet	chicken	volailles	poultry

Meat and poultry dishes and terms

aïado	roast shoulder of lamb stuffed with garlic and other ingredients	choucroute	pickled cabbage with peppercorns, sausages, bacon and salami
aiguillette	long, thin slice (eg of meat or poultry)	civet	game stew
aile	wing	confit	meat preserve
au feu de bois	cooked over wood fire	côte	chop, cutlet or rib
au four	baked	cou	neck
baeckeoffe	Alsatian hotpot of pork, mutton and beef baked with potato layers	coq au vin	chicken slow-cooked with wine, onions and mushrooms
		cuisse	thigh or leg
blanquette, daube, estouffade, hochepôt, navarin, ragoût	types of stew	émincé	thin slivers (eg of pork)
		épaule	shoulder
		en croûte	in pastry
		farci	stuffed
blanquette de veau	veal in cream and mushroom sauce	garni	with vegetables
		gésier	gizzard
bœuf bourguignon	beef stew with Burgundy, onions and mushrooms	grillade	grilled meat
		grillé	grilled
		hâchis	chopped meat or mince hamburger
canard à l'orange	roast duck with an orange and wine sauce	magret de canard	duck breast
		marmite	casserole
canard pâté de périgourdin foie gras	roast duck with prunes and truffles	médaillon	round piece
		mijoté	stewed
carré	best end of neck, chop or cutlet	pavé	thick slice (of eg beef)
		pieds et paques	mutton or pork tripe and trotters
cassolette	dish served in a small casserole		
		poêlé	pan-fried
cassoulet	casserole of beans, sausages and duck/goose	poulet de Bresse	chicken from Bresse (the best)

pounti	a mixture of bacon and Swiss chard	steak tartare	raw chopped beef, topped with a raw egg yolk
râble	saddle	tagine	North African casserole
rôti	roast	tournedos rossini	beef fillet with foie gras and truffles
sauté	lightly fried in butter		
steak au poivre (vert/rouge)	steak in a black (green/red) peppercorn sauce	viennoise	fried in egg and breadcrumbs

Terms for steaks

bleu	almost raw	bien cuit	well done
saignant	rare	très bien cuit	very well done
à point	medium rare	brochette	kebab

Garnishes and sauces

américaine	white wine, cognac and tomato		braised lettuce
		chasseur	white wine, mushrooms and shallots
arlésienne au porto	with tomatoes, onions, aubergines, potatoes and rice in port	châtelaine	with artichoke hearts and chestnut purée
auvergnat	with cabbage, sausage and bacon	diable	strong mustard seasoning
béarnaise	sauce of egg yolks, white wine, shallots and vinegar	forestière	with bacon and mushroom
beurre blanc	sauce of white wine and shallots, with butter	fricassée	rich, creamy sauce
		mornay	cheese sauce
		pays d'auge	cream and cider
bonne femme	with mushroom, bacon, potato and onions	périgourdine	with foie gras and possibly truffles
bordelaise	in a red wine, shallot and bone-marrow sauce	piquante	gherkins or capers, vinegar and shallots
		provençale	tomatoes, garlic, olive oil and herbs
boulangère	baked with potatoes and onions	savoyarde	with Gruyère cheese
bourgeoise	with carrots, onions, bacon, celery and	véronique	grapes, wine and cream

Vegetables (légumes), herbs (herbes) and spices (épices)

ail	garlic	blette/bette	Swiss chard
anis	aniseed	cannelle	cinnamon
artichaut	artichoke	capre	caper
asperge	asparagus	cardon	cardoon, related to artichoke
avocat	avocado		
basilic	basil	carotte	carrot
betterave	beetroot	céleri	celery

champignons, cèpes, ceps, girolles, chanterelles, pleurotes	mushrooms
chou (rouge)	(red) cabbage
choufleur	cauliflower
concombre	cucumber
cornichon	gherkin
echalotes	shallots
endive	chicory
épinard	spinach
estragon	tarragon
fenouil	fennel
férigoule	thyme (in Provençal)
fèves	broad beans
flageolets	flageolet beans
gingembre	ginger
haricots	haricot beans
verts	string beans
rouges	kidney beans
beurres	yellow snap beans
laurier	bay leaf
lentilles	lentils
maïs	maize (corn)

menthe	mint
moutarde	mustard
oignon	onion
panais	parsnip
pélandron	type of string bean
persil	parsley
petits pois	peas
piment rouge/vert	red/green chilli pepper
pois chiche	chickpeas
pois mange-tout	snow peas
pignons	pine nuts
poireau	leek
poivron (vert, rouge)	sweet pepper (green, red)
pommes de terre	potatoes
primeurs	spring vegetables
radis	radish
riz	rice
safran	saffron
salade verte	green salad
sarrasin	buckwheat
tomate	tomato
truffes	truffles

Vegetable and cheese dishes and terms

aligot	puréed potato with Cantal cheese
allumettes	very thin chips
à l'anglaise	boiled
beignet	fritter
duxelles	fried mushrooms and shallots with cream
farci	stuffed
feuille	leaf
fines herbes	mixture of tarragon, parsley and chives
gratiné	browned with cheese or butter
à la grecque	cooked in oil and lemon
jardinière	with mixed diced vegetables
mousseline	mashed potato with cream and eggs

à la parisienne	sautéed potatoes, with white wine and shallot sauce
parmentier	with potatoes
petits farcis	stuffed tomatoes, aubergines, courgettes and peppers
raclette	grilled cheese with vegetables
râpée	grated or shredded
sauté	lightly fried in butter
truffade	potato cake with Cantal cheese
à la vapeur	steamed
en verdure	garnished with green vegetables

Fruit (fruit) and nuts (noix)

French	English	French	English
abricot	apricot	mangue	mango
acajou	cashew nut	marron	chestnut
amande	almond	melon	melon
ananas	pineapple	mirabelle	small yellow plum
banane	banana	myrtille	bilberry
brugnon, nectarine	nectarine	noisette	hazelnut
cacahouète	peanut	noix	walnuts; nuts
cassis	blackcurrant	orange	orange
cérise	cherry	pamplemousse	grapefruit
citron	lemon	pastèque	watermelon
citron vert	lime	pêche	peach
datte	date	pistache	pistachio
figue	fig	poire	pear
fraise (de bois)	strawberry (wild)	pomme	apple
framboise	raspberry	prune	plum
fruit de la passion	passion fruit	pruneau	prune
grenade	pomegranate	raisin	grape
groseille	redcurrant	reine-claude	greengage

Fruit dishes and terms

agrumes	citrus fruits
beignet	fritter
compôte	stewed fruit
coulis	sauce of puréed fruit
crème de marrons	chestnut purée
flambé	set aflame in alcohol
fougasse	bread flavoured with orange-flower water or almonds (can be savoury)
frappé	iced

Desserts (desserts or entremets) and pastries (pâtisserie)

bombe	moulded ice-cream dessert
brioche	sweet, high yeast breakfast roll
calisson	almond sweet
charlotte	custard and fruit in lining of almond fingers
chichi	doughnut shaped in a stick
clafoutis	heavy custard and fruit tart
crème Chantilly	vanilla-flavoured and sweetened whipped cream
crème fraîche	sour cream
crème pâtissière	thick, eggy pastry-filling
crêpe suzette	thin pancake with orange juice and liqueur
fromage blanc	cream cheese
gaufre	waffle
glace	ice cream
Île flottante/œufs à la neige	whipped egg-white floating on custard
macaron	macaroon
madeleine	small sponge cake
marrons Mont Blanc	chestnut purée and cream on a rum-soaked sponge cake
mousse au chocolat	chocolate mousse

omelette norvégienne	baked alaska
palmier	caramelized puff pastry
parfait	frozen mousse, sometimes ice cream
petit-suisse	a smooth mixture of cream and curds
petits fours	bite-sized cakes/ pastries
poires belle hélène	pears and ice cream in chocolate sauce
tarte tatin	upside-down apple tart
tarte tropezienne	sponge cake filled with custard cream topped with nuts
tiramisu	mascarpone cheese, chocolate and cream
yaourt/yogourt	yoghurt

Travel store

Rough Guides travel...

UK & Ireland
Britain
Devon & Cornwall
Dublin DIRECTIONS
Edinburgh DIRECTIONS
England
Ireland
Lake District
London
London DIRECTIONS
London Mini Guide
Scotland
Scottish Highlands & Islands
Wales

Europe
Algarve DIRECTIONS
Amsterdam
Amsterdam DIRECTIONS
Andalucía
Athens DIRECTIONS
Austria
Baltic States
Barcelona
Barcelona DIRECTIONS
Belgium & Luxembourg
Berlin
Brittany & Normandy
Bruges DIRECTIONS
Brussels
Budapest
Bulgaria
Copenhagen
Corfu
Corsica
Costa Brava DIRECTIONS
Crete
Croatia
Cyprus
Czech & Slovak Republics
Dodecanese & East Aegean
Dordogne & The Lot
Europe
Florence & Siena
Florence DIRECTIONS
France

French Hotels & Restos
Germany
Greece
Greek Islands
Hungary
Ibiza & Formentera DIRECTIONS
Iceland
Ionian Islands
Italy
Italian Lakes
Languedoc & Roussillon
Lisbon
Lisbon DIRECTIONS
The Loire
Madeira DIRECTIONS
Madrid DIRECTIONS
Mallorca & Menorca
Mallorca DIRECTIONS
Malta & Gozo DIRECTIONS
Menorca
Moscow
Netherlands
Norway
Paris
Paris DIRECTIONS
Paris Mini Guide
Poland
Portugal
Prague
Prague DIRECTIONS
Provence & the Côte d'Azur
Pyrenees
Romania
Rome
Rome DIRECTIONS
Sardinia
Scandinavia
Sicily
Slovenia
Spain
St Petersburg
Sweden
Switzerland
Tenerife & La Gomera DIRECTIONS
Turkey
Tuscany & Umbria

Venice & The Veneto
Venice DIRECTIONS
Vienna

Asia
Bali & Lombok
Bangkok
Beijing
Cambodia
China
Goa
Hong Kong & Macau
India
Indonesia
Japan
Laos
Malaysia, Singapore & Brunei
Nepal
The Philippines
Singapore
South India
Southeast Asia
Sri Lanka
Taiwan
Thailand
Thailand's Beaches & Islands
Tokyo
Vietnam

Australasia
Australia
Melbourne
New Zealand
Sydney

North America
Alaska
Boston
California
Canada
Chicago
Florida
Grand Canyon
Hawaii
Honolulu
Las Vegas DIRECTIONS
Los Angeles
Maui DIRECTIONS

Miami & South Florida
Montréal
New England
New Orleans DIRECTIONS
New York City
New York City DIRECTIONS
New York City Mini Guide
Orlando & Walt Disney World DIRECTIONS
Pacific Northwest
Rocky Mountains
San Francisco
San Francisco DIRECTIONS
Seattle
Southwest USA
Toronto
USA
Vancouver
Washington DC
Washington DC DIRECTIONS
Yosemite

Caribbean & Latin America
Antigua & Barbuda DIRECTIONS
Argentina
Bahamas
Barbados DIRECTIONS
Belize
Bolivia
Brazil
Cancùn & Cozumel DIRECTIONS
Caribbean
Central America
Chile
Costa Rica
Cuba
Dominican Republic
Dominican Republic DIRECTIONS
Ecuador
Guatemala
Jamaica

TRAVEL STORE

...music & reference

Mexico
Peru
St Lucia
South America
Trinidad & Tobago
Yúcatan

Africa & Middle East
Cape Town & the
  Garden Route
Egypt
The Gambia
Jordan
Kenya
Marrakesh
  DIRECTIONS
Morocco
South Africa, Lesotho
  & Swaziland
Syria
Tanzania
Tunisia
West Africa
Zanzibar

Travel Theme guides
First-Time Around the
  World
First-Time Asia
First-Time Europe
First-Time Latin
  America
Travel Online
Travel Health
Travel Survival
Walks in London & SE
  England
Women Travel

Maps
Algarve
Amsterdam
Andalucia & Costa
  del Sol
Argentina
Athens
Australia
Baja California
Barcelona
Berlin
Boston

Brittany
Brussels
California
Chicago
Corsica
Costa Rica & Panama
Crete
Croatia
Cuba
Cyprus
Czech Republic
Dominican Republic
Dubai & UAE
Dublin
Egypt
Florence & Siena
Florida
France
Frankfurt
Germany
Greece
Guatemala & Belize
Hong Kong
Iceland
Ireland
Kenya
Lisbon
London
Los Angeles
Madrid
Mallorca
Marrakesh
Mexico
Miami & Key West
Morocco
New England
New York City
New Zealand
Northern Spain
Paris
Peru
Portugal
Prague
Rome
San Francisco
Sicily
South Africa
South India
Sri Lanka
Tenerife
Thailand

Toronto
Trinidad & Tobago
Tuscany
Venice
Washington DC
Yucatán Peninsula

Dictionary Phrasebooks
Croatian
Czech
Dutch
Egyptian Arabic
European Languages
  (Czech, French,
  German, Greek,
  Italian, Portuguese,
  Spanish)
French
German
Greek
Hindi & Urdu
Hungarian
Indonesian
Italian
Japanese
Latin American
  Spanish
Mandarin Chinese
Mexican Spanish
Polish
Portuguese
Russian
Spanish
Swahili
Thai
Turkish
Vietnamese

Music Guides
The Beatles
Bob Dylan
Cult Pop
Classical Music
Elvis
Frank Sinatra
Heavy Metal
Hip-Hop
Jazz
Opera
Reggae

Rock
World Music (2 vols)

Reference Guides
Babies
Books for Teenagers
Children's Books, 0–5
Children's Books, 5–11
Comedy Movies
Conspiracy Theories
Cult Fiction
Cult Football
Cult Movies
Cult TV
The Da Vinci Code
Ethical Shopping
Gangster Movies
Horror Movies
iPods, iTunes & Music
  Online
The Internet
James Bond
Kids' Movies
Lord of the Rings
Macs & OS X
Muhammad Ali
Music Playlists
PCs and Windows
Poker
Pregnancy & Birth
Sci–Fi Movies
Shakespeare
Superheroes

Unexplained
  Phenomena
The Universe
Weather
Website Directory

Football
Arsenal 11s
Celtic 11s
Chelsea 11s
Liverpool 11s
Newcastle 11s
Rangers 11s
Tottenham 11s
Man United 11s

TRAVEL STORE

ROUGH GUIDES

not just travel

THE ROUGH GUIDE TO

Superheroes

THE COMICS ✳ THE COSTUMES ✳ THE CREATORS ✳ THE CATCHPHRASES

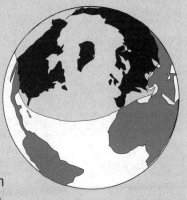

Small print and

Index

A Rough Guide to Rough Guides

In the summer of 1981, Mark Ellingham, a recent graduate from Bristol University, was travelling round Greece and couldn't find a guidebook that really met his needs. On the one hand there were the student guides, insistent on saving every last cent, and on the other the heavyweight cultural tomes whose authors seemed to have spent more time in a research library than lounging away the afternoon at a taverna or on the beach.

In a bid to avoid getting a job, Mark and a small group of writers set about creating their own guidebook. It was a guide to Greece that aimed to combine a journalistic approach to description with a thoroughly practical approach to travellers' needs – a guide that would incorporate culture, history and contemporary insights with a critical edge, together with up-to-date, value-for-money listings. Back in London, Mark and the team finished their Rough Guide, as they called it, and talked Routledge into publishing the book.

That first *Rough Guide to Greece*, published in 1982, was a student scheme that became a publishing phenomenon. The immediate success of the book – with numerous reprints and a Thomas Cook prize shortlisting – spawned a series that rapidly covered dozens of destinations. Rough Guides had a ready market among low-budget backpackers, but soon also acquired a much broader and older readership that relished Rough Guides' wit and inquisitiveness as much as their enthusiastic, critical approach. Everyone wants value for money, but not at any price.

Rough Guides soon began supplementing the "rougher" information about hostels and low-budget listings with the kind of detail on restaurants and quality hotels that independent-minded visitors on any budget might expect, whether on business in New York or trekking in Thailand.

These days the guides – distributed worldwide by the Penguin Group – offer recommendations from shoestring to luxury and cover more than 200 destinations around the globe, including almost every country in the Americas and Europe, more than half of Africa and most of Asia and Australasia. Our ever-growing team of authors and photographers is spread all over the world, particularly in Europe, the USA and Australia.

In 1994, we published the *Rough Guide to World Music* and *Rough Guide to Classical Music*; and a year later the *Rough Guide to the Internet*. All three books have become benchmark titles in their fields – which encouraged us to expand into other areas of publishing, mainly around popular culture. Rough Guides now publish:

- Travel guides to more than 200 worldwide destinations
- Dictionary phrasebooks to 22 major languages
- History guides ranging from Ireland to Islam
- Maps printed on rip-proof and waterproof Polyart™ paper
- Music guides running the gamut from Opera to Elvis
- Restaurant guides to London, New York and San Francisco
- Reference books on topics as diverse as the Weather and Shakespeare
- Sports guides from Formula 1 to Man Utd
- Pop culture books from *Lord of the Rings* to Cult TV
- World Music CDs in association with World Music Network

Visit **www.roughguides.com** to see our latest publications.

SMALL PRINT

Rough Guide credits

Layout: Ajay Verma
Cartography: Katie Lloyd-Jones
Picture editor: Harriet Mills
Production: Julia Bovis
Proofreader: Wendy Smith
Cover design: Chloë Roberts
Editorial: London Kate Berens, Claire Saunders, Geoff Howard, Ruth Blackmore, Polly Thomas, Richard Lim, Clifton Wilkinson, Alison Murchie, Sally Schafer, Karoline Densley, Andy Turner, Ella O'Donnell, Keith Drew, Edward Aves, Nikki Birrell, Helen Marsden, Alice Park, Sarah Eno, Joe Staines, Duncan Clark, Peter Buckley, Matthew Milton; **New York** Andrew Rosenberg, Richard Koss, Steven Horak, AnneLise Sorensen, Amy Hegarty, Hunter Slaton, April Isaacs
Design & Pictures: London Simon Bracken, Dan May, Diana Jarvis, Mark Thomas, Jj Luck; **Delhi** Madhulita Mohapatra, Umesh Aggarwal, Jessica Subramanian, Amit Verma, Ankur Guha
Production: Sophie Hewat, Katherine Owers
Cartography: London Maxine Repath,

Ed Wright; **Delhi** Manish Chandra, Rajesh Chhibber, Jai Prakash Mishra, Ashutosh Bharti, Rajesh Mishra, Animesh Pathak, Jasbir Sandhu, Karobi Gogoi
Online: New York Jennifer Gold, Suzanne Welles, Kristin Mingrone; **Delhi** Manik Chauhan, Narender Kumar, Manish Shekhar Jha, Rakesh Kumar, Lalit K. Sharma, Chhandita Chakravarty
Marketing & Publicity: London Richard Trillo, Niki Hanmer, David Wearn, Demelza Dallow, Louise Maher; **New York** Geoff Colquitt, Megan Kennedy, Katy Ball; **Delhi** Reem Khokhar
Custom publishing and foreign rights: Philippa Hopkins
Manager India: Punita Singh
Series editor: Mark Ellingham
Reference Director: Andrew Lockett
PA to Managing and Publishing Directors: Megan McIntyre
Publishing Director: Martin Dunford
Managing Director: Kevin Fitzgerald

Publishing information

This edition published 2005 by **Rough Guides Ltd**,
80 Strand, London WC2R 0RL
345 Hudson St, 4th Floor,
New York, NY 10014, USA
14 Local Shopping Centre,
Panchsheel Park,
New Delhi 110017, India
Distributed by the Penguin Group
Penguin Books Ltd,
80 Strand, London WC2R 0RL
Penguin Putnam, Inc.
375 Hudson Street, NY 10014, USA
Penguin Group (Australia)
250 Camberwell Road, Camberwell,
Victoria 3124, Australia
Penguin Books Canada Ltd,
10 Alcorn Avenue, Toronto, Ontario,
Canada M4V 1E4
Penguin Group (New Zealand)
Cnr Rosedale and Airborne Roads,
Albany, Auckland, New Zealand

Typeset in Bembo and Helvetica to an original design by Henry Iles.
Printed in Italy by LegoPrint S.p.A
1008pp includes index
A catalogue record for this book is available from the British Library
ISBN-13: 978-1-84353-557-7
ISBN-10: 1-84353-557-2
The publishers and authors have done their best to ensure the accuracy and currency of all the information in **The Rough Guide to French Hotels & Restaurants**, however they can accept no responsibility for any loss, injury, or inconvenience sustained by any traveller as a result of information or advice contained in the guide.

1   3   5   7   9   8   6   4   2

SMALL PRINT

Help us update

We've gone to a lot of effort to ensure that this edition of **The Rough Guide to French Hotels & Restaurants** is accurate and up to date. However, things change – places get "discovered", opening hours are notoriously fickle, restaurants and hotels raise prices or lower standards. If you feel we've got it wrong or left something out, we'd like to know, and if you can remember the address, the price, the time, the phone number, so much the better.

We'll credit all contributions, and send a copy of the next edition (or any other Rough Guide if you prefer) for the best letters. Everyone who writes to us and isn't already a subscriber will receive a copy of our full-colour thrice-yearly newsletter. Please mark letters: **"Rough Guide to French Hotels & Restaurants Update"** and send to: Rough Guides, 80 Strand, London WC2R 0RL, or Rough Guides, 4th Floor, 345 Hudson St, New York, NY 10014. Or send an email to **mail@roughguides.com**

Have your questions answered and tell others about your trip at **www.roughguides.atinfopop.com**

Readers' letters

Thanks to all the readers who have taken the time to write in with comments and suggestions (and apologies if we've inadvertently omitted or misspelt anyone's name):

Sara James, Keith Clark, Peter Trueman, Irene Leithhead, John Naylor, John Fletcher.

Photo credits

Cover

Main front: Hotel & restaurant of Chateau Eze, village of Eze © Corbis
Small front top picture: Macaroons © Corbis
Small front lower picture: waiter, Paris © Alamy
Back top picture: Honfleur, Normandie © Alamy
Back lower picture: Chambres d'Hôtes sign © Alamy

Title page

p.1 Tree-lined road, Provence © Robert Harding Picture Library/Alamy

Full page

p.2 Kir apéritif and poppies, France © Kathryn Kleinman/FoodPix Getty Images

Introduction

p.6 Window, Hôtel-restaurant Cuq en Terrasses, Cuq-Toulza © Jacphot/Hôtel-restaurant Cuq en Terrasses/ www.cuqenterrasses.com
p.7 Hôtel Charembeau swimming pool © Hôtel Charembeau/www.charembeau.com
p.8 Hôtel-restaurant Lameloise entrance © Eliophot Preschesmisky BR/Hôtel-restaurant Lameloise/www.lameloise.fr
p.9 Hostellerie Le Vert sitting room © Hostellerie Le Vert/www.hotellevert.com
p.10 Salade de chèvre chaud © Benjamin F Fink Jr/FoodPix Getty Images
p.11 Breakfast in the garden at Hôtel-restaurant Cuq en Terrasses © Jacphot/Hôtel-restaurant Cuq en Terrasses/www.cuqenterrasses.com
p.12 Hôtel Anne d'Anjou courtyard © Hôtel Anne d'Anjou/www.hotel-anneanjou.com

15 Rough Guide Favourites

p.13 Hôtel Arraya © Hôtel Arraya/www.arraya .com
p.13 Hôtel-restaurant l'Océan © Hôtel-restaurant l'Océan/www.re-hotel-ocean.com
p.14 L'Auberge Campagnarde © Auberge Campagnarde
p.14 Les Lions de Beauclerc © Les Lions de Beauclerc/www.leslionsdebeauclerc.free.fr
p.14 Hot air ballooning near Domaine de la Rhue © Domaine de la Rhue/www.domainedelarhue .com
p.14 Hôtel des Voyageurs © Hôtel des Voyageurs/www.hoteldesvoyageursparis.com
p.14 Hôtel Charembeau © Hôtel Charembeau/ www.charembeau.com
p.15 Louis-Bernard Puech, Hôtel-restaurant Beausejour au Calvinet/www.cantal -restaurant-puech.com
p.15 Hôtel de Londres © Hôtel de Londres/www .lelondres.com
p.15 Hôtel-Restaurant Les Lacs d'Halco © Hôtel-restaurant Les Lacs d'Halco
p.15 Hôtel-restaurant Anne de Bretagne © Hôtel-restaurant Anne de Bretagne/www .annedebretagne.com
p.16 Chateau de Fourcès © Chateau de Fourcès/ www.chateau-fources.com
p.16 Hôtel-restaurant Les Chalets du Villard © Hôtel-restaurant Les Chalets du Villard/www .leschaletsduvillard.fr
p.16 Bernard Rambaud, Le Pressoir © Le Pressoir/www.le-pressoir-st-ave.com
p.16 Wines from the Auberge du Vieux Vigneron vineyards © Auberge du Vieux Vigneron/www .aubergeduvieuxvigneron.com

Index

Map entries are in colour.

INDEX

INDEX

1005

T

U

V

W

X

Y

Z